RAND McNALLY

ZIP CODE FINDER

Reproducing or recording maps, tables, text listings, or any other material which appears in this publication by photocopying, electronic storage or retrieval, or by any other means, is prohibited.

The information in the *Zip Code Finder* was collected directly from the Rand McNally *1994 Commercial Atlas & Marketing Guide* and other Rand McNally products.

Hospital names and zip codes printed by permission of the American Hospital Association (Source: *AHA Guide to the Health Care Field,* published by the American Hospital Association, copyright 1992).

The *Rand McNally Zip Code Finder* and its contents are not affiliated with the U.S. Postal Service.

Rand McNally Zip Code Finder
Table of Contents

INTRODUCTION

BASIC LISTINGS AND
3-DIGIT ZIP CODE MAPS

State	3-Digit Map	Listings	State	3-Digit Map	Listings
Staten Island		387	Memphis		525
North Carolina	392-393	391	Nashville		526
Charlotte		395	Texas	534-535	536
North Dakota	408-409	410	Dallas		540
Ohio	414-415	413	Fort Worth		543
Cincinnati		418	Houston		546
Cleveland		419	San Antonio		555
Columbus		419	Utah	562-563	561
Oklahoma	440-441	442	Vermont	566-567	568
Oklahoma City		445	Virginia	572-573	574
Oregon	448-449	450	Norfolk		585
Pennsylvania	456-457	455	Washington	592-593	594
Philadelphia		483	Seattle		599
Pittsburgh		485	West Virginia	602-603	604
Rhode Island	92-93	498	Wisconsin	616-617	615
South Carolina	500-501	502	Milwaukee		624
South Dakota	510-511	509	Wyoming	632-633	631
Tennessee	514-515	516			

MAJOR CITIES WITH
5-DIGIT ZIP CODE MAPS

City	5-Digit Map	City	5-Digit Map
Atlanta, GA	126	Minneapolis, MN	297
Boston, MA	265	New York, NY	380, 381
Chicago, IL	152	Philadelphia, PA	484
Dallas, TX	541	San Francisco, CA	80
Detroit, MI	279	St. Paul, MN	300
Kansas City, KS	206	Washington, DC	103
Los Angeles, CA	73		

INTRODUCTION

The Rand McNally *Zip Code Finder* is a complete and convenient reference containing zip code listings for more than 120,000 places in the United States. Arranged alphabetically by state, these listings enable you to quickly and easily find zip codes. The *Zip Code Finder's* listings are visually enhanced by a detailed 3-digit zip code map for each state. These maps show the location of towns and cities within Zip Code Sectional Areas.

Listings for 50 major U.S. cities include zip codes for selected hospitals, military installations, hotels/motels, colleges, universities and financial institutions. The Washington, D.C. listing additionally includes zip codes for government offices.

Included in the listings is a telephone number for each multiple zip code city. By using this number, you can readily determine which of the city's zip codes you need. Listings for cities with only two zip codes, one of which is for the delivery **area** and the other for **post office boxes**, do not include telephone numbers. Instead, footnotes designate which zip code is for the delivery area (*), and which zip code is for post office boxes (†). Five-digit zip code maps display zip code boundaries for each of thirteen multiple zip code cities.

The Rand McNally *Zip Code Finder* saves you time and money. Information provided on postal rates and regulations, plus the locations of post office division offices, helps you to mail economically and efficiently. Convenient listings of toll-free numbers for car rentals, airline reservations and hotel/motel accommodations place these services at your fingertips. In addition, telephone area code lists provide a helpful and economical reference when placing long-distance calls.

THE MEANING OF YOUR ZIP CODE

Zip codes, set up to improve mail distribution, define areas within the U.S.

The country is divided into ten geographic regions that consist of three or more states. Each of these regions is assigned a number 0-9. This number is the first digit of your zip code.

Within the ten geographic regions, states are further divided into smaller geographic units. The second and third digits of your zip code identify these units.

Together, the first three digits of your zip code identify either a particular Sectional Center or Multi-Coded City. Sectional Centers and Multi-Coded Cities have similar postal functions. A Sectional Center, usually the natural center of local transportation, is a large post office serving smaller surrounding post offices. The Multi-Coded City is a main city post office which serves its stations and branches within the city's neighborhoods.

The final two digits of your zip code identify the post offices served by the Sectional Center or branches and stations served by the city post office.

The example below further illustrates the meaning of a 5-digit zip code:

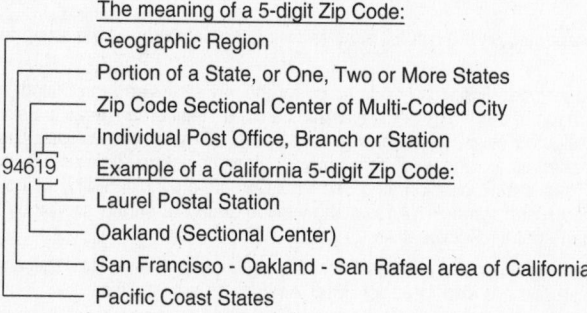

The meaning of a 5-digit Zip Code:
- Geographic Region
- Portion of a State, or One, Two or More States
- Zip Code Sectional Center of Multi-Coded City
- Individual Post Office, Branch or Station

94619 Example of a California 5-digit Zip Code:
- Laurel Postal Station
- Oakland (Sectional Center)
- San Francisco - Oakland - San Rafael area of California
- Pacific Coast States

USING THE ZIP CODE FINDER

Using the Rand McNally *Zip Code Finder* is easy. If you have the name of a city or town, but don't know its zip code, check the basic listings.

The basic listings are organized by state. Cities and towns are arranged alphabetically within each state.

Since it is not uncommon for the name of a city or town to occur more than once within a state, the *Zip Code Finder* differentiates between such cities or towns in several ways. First, if a city or town has the same name as another city or town, but is located in a different county, the *Zip Code Finder* will list the county in which the city or town is located. The county will be listed in parenthesis following the name of the city or town for all places that have a name which is identical to the name of another place within the same state. For example:

Altamont (Effingham County)..	62411
Altamont (Madison County)	62035

In most cases, listing the county in which a city or town is located will differentiate between places with the same name. However, since the *Zip Code Finder* also lists townships and "towns,"* places that are "part of" other places, places that are defined by the Bureau of the Census, and several other types of localities, additional differentiation may be shown in parenthesis following the name of the place. For example:

Ashford	06278
Ashford (Town)..................	06250

In this case, the first listing refers to a single community that has the same name as the larger civil division which contains it and several other communities or places as well. The zip code for the larger civil division is shown in the second listing.

For places with more than one zip code, the *Zip Code Finder* provides the *range* of zip codes as shown below:

Belleville   62220-25
For specific Belleville Zip Codes
call (618) 233-0391, or
your local postmaster.

In this example, the hyphenated numbers indicate the zip code range for Belleville. To obtain the zip code for a specific address within this multi-coded city, telephone the number shown. (Listings for cities with only two zip codes, one for the delivery **area** and one for **post office boxes**, include footnotes that designate the nature of the zip code, * and † respectively.)

In addition to the telephone number for zip code information, a 5-digit zip code map is provided for each of the following cities:

- Atlanta, GA
- Boston, MA
- Chicago, IL
- Dallas, TX
- Detroit, MI
- Kansas City, KS
- Los Angeles, CA
- Minneapolis, MN
- New York, NY
- Philadelphia, PA
- San Francisco, CA
- St. Paul, MN
- Washington, D.C.

The 5-digit zip code map appears on the first full page following the beginning of the listing for each city shown above.

The *Zip Code Finder* also includes 3-digit zip code maps for the fifty states and the District of Columbia. More detailed maps of the 3-digit Sectional Areas around major urban areas are also provided. In addition to selected cities, towns and military bases, all state capitals, counties, county seats and Sectional Areas are shown on these maps. These maps provide a population key based on the 1980 Census of Population, and Sectional Centers are indicated by a circle around their respective population symbols. (Arrows show that a Sectional Area is served by a Sectional Center located in another Sectional Area.)

Zip Codes for selected hospitals, military installations, hotels, motels, banks, savings and loans, colleges, and universities are also listed for 50 of America's Largest Cities.

* In certain states, the civil divisions know as "townships" or "towns" have significant local importance. These civil divisions frequently include several distinct communities or places, and one of these places may bear the same name as the civil division. In the *Zip Code Finder*, "townships" are included in the listings for Illinois, Indiana, Michigan, Ohio, New Jersey and Pennsylvania, and "towns" are included for Connecticut, Maine, Massachusetts, New Hampshire, New York, Rhode Island, Vermont and Wisconsin.

STANDARD ABBREVIATIONS FOR ADDRESSES

Listed below are two-letter state abbreviations which can be used in addressing mail.

Two-Letter State Abbreviations

Alabama AL	Kentucky KY	North Dakota ND
Alaska AK	Louisiana LA	Ohio OH
Arizona AZ	Maine ME	Oklahoma OK
Arkansas AR	Maryland MD	Oregon OR
California CA	Massachusetts MA	Pennsylvania PA
Colorado CO	Michigan MI	Rhode Island RI
Connecticut CT	Minnesota MN	South Carolina SC
Delaware DE	Mississippi MS	South Dakota SD
District of Columbia DC	Missouri MO	Tennessee TN
Florida FL	Montana MT	Texas TX
Georgia GA	Nebraska NE	Utah UT
Hawaii HI	Nevada NV	Vermont VT
Idaho ID	New Hampshire NH	Virginia VA
Illinois IL	New Jersey NJ	Washington WA
Indiana IN	New Mexico NM	West Virginia WV
Iowa IA	New York NY	Wisconsin WI
Kansas KS	North Carolina NC	Wyoming WY

SELECTED TOLL - FREE RESERVATION NUMBERS

To save you time and facilitate your reservations needs, the following toll-free reservation numbers are provided for selected lodging accommodations, car rental services and major airlines. (All numbers listed were effective at time of publication.)

AIRLINES

American
800-433-7300

Continental
800-525-0280

Delta
800-221-1212

Northwest
800-225-2525

TWA
800-221-2000

United
800-241-6522

U.S. Air
800-428-4322

HOTEL/MOTELS

Best Western
International, Inc.
800-528-1234

Days Inn
800-325-2525

Embassy Suites
800-EMBASSY

Fairmont Hotels
800-527-4727

Guest Quarters
800-424-2900

Harley Hotels
800-321-2323

Helmsley Hotels
800-221-4982

Holiday Inns
800-HOLIDAY

Howard Johnson's
Motor Lodges
800-654-2000

Hyatt Hotels Corp
800-228-9000

Marriott
800-228-9290

Omni/Supranational
Hotels
800-843-6664

Preferred Hotels
800-323-7500

Quality Inns
800-228-5151

Radisson Hotels Int'l
800-333-3333

Ramada Inns, Inc.
800-228-2828

Regent International
Hotels
800-545-4000

Sheraton Hotels
& Motor Inns
800-325-3535

Stouffer Hotels & Resorts
800-HOTELS-1

Westin Hotels
800-228-3000

CAR RENTAL COMPANIES

Agency Rent-A-Car
800-321-1972
800-362-1794 (Ohio only)

Alamo Rent-A-Car
800-327-9633

Allstate Rent-A-Car
800-634-6186 (except NV)

American International
Rent-A-Car
800-782-0511

Avis Reservations Center
800-331-1212 (Domestic)
800-331-1084 (International)

Budget Rent-A-Car
800-527-0700

Enterprise Rent-A-Car
800-325-8007

Hertz Corporation
800-654-3131

National Car Rental
800-328-4567

Payless Car Rental
800-PAYLESS

Sears Rent-A-Car
800-527-0770

Thrifty Rent-A-Car
800-367-2277

Value Rent-A-Car
800-327-2501

TELEPHONE AREA CODE AND TIME ZONE INFORMATION

The following tables list telephone area codes used in the United States. The first table is arranged in alphabetical order by state. The second table lists telephone area codes in numerical order.

The United States (including Alaska and Hawaii) is divided longitudinally into six time zones. If you were traveling from east to west, you would pass through the time zones in the following order: Eastern Standard Time (EST), Central Standard Time (CST), Mountain Standard Time (MST), Pacific Standard Time (PST), Alaska Time (AK), and Hawaii Time (HI).

Each time you enter a new time zone, it becomes one hour earlier. When it is 5 p.m. Eastern Standard Time (EST), it is 4 p.m. Central Standard Time (CST), 3 p.m. Mountain Standard Time (MST), etc. For your convenience, the appropriate time zone is listed in parentheses after each area code below. The map on pages 12 and 13 details the time zone boundaries.

Aphabetical List of Telephone Area Codes

Alabama	205
Montgomery (CST)	205
Alaska (AK-HI)	907
Juneau (AK)	907
Arizona (MST)	602
Phoenix (MST)	602
Arkansas	501
Little Rock (CST)	501
California	
Anaheim (PST)	714
Bakersfield (PST)	805
Eureka (PST)	707
Fresno (PST)	209
Long Beach (PST)	310
Los Angeles (PST)	213
Oakland (PST)	510
Pasadena (PST)	818
Riverside (PST)	909
Sacramento (PST)	916
San Diego (PST)	619
San Francisco (PST)	415
San Jose (PST)	408
Colorado	
Colorado Springs (MST)	719
Denver (MST)	303
Connecticut	203
Hartford (EST)	203
Delaware	302
Dover (EST)	302
District of Columbia	202
Washington (EST)	202
Florida (CST,EST)	
Jacksonville (EST)	904
Miami (EST)	305
Orlando (EST)	407
St. Petersburg (EST)	813
Tallahassee (EST)	904
Georgia	
Atlanta (EST)	404
Columbus (EST)	706
Savannah (EST)	912
Hawaii (HI)	808
Honolulu (AK-HI)	808
Idaho (MST,PST)	208
Boise (MST)	208
Illinois	

Chicago (CST)	312
Aurora (CST)	708
Peoria (CST)	309
Rockford (CST)	815
Springfield (CST)	217
West Frankfort (CST)	618
Indiana (CST,EST)	
Evansville (EST)	812
Indianapolis (EST)	317
South Bend (EST)	219
Iowa	
Council Bluffs (CST)	712
Des Moines (CST)	515
Dubuque (CST)	319
Kansas (CST,MST)	
Topeka (CST)	913
Wichita (CST)	316
Kentucky (CST,EST)	
Covington (EST)	606
Frankfort (EST)	502
Louisville (EST)	502
Louisiana	
Baton Rouge (CST)	504
New Orleans (CST)	504
Shreveport (CST)	318
Maine	207
Augusta (EST)	207
Maryland	
Annapolis (EST)	410
Rockville	301
Massachusetts	
Boston (EST)	617
Lowell (EST)	508
Springfield (EST)	413
Michigan (CST,EST)	
Detroit (EST)	313
Escanaba (EST)	906
Grand Rapids (EST)	616
Lansing (EST)	517
Warren (EST)	810
Minnesota	
Duluth (CST)	218
Minneapolis (CST)	612
Rochester (CST)	507
St. Paul (CST)	612
Mississippi	601

TELEPHONE AREA CODE AND TIME ZONE INFORMATION, CONT'D.

Aphabetical List of Telephone Area Codes, continued

Jackson (CST)	601	Salem (PST)	503	
Missouri		Pennsylvania		
Jefferson City (CST)	314	Allentown (EST)	610	
Kansas City (CST)	816	Erie (EST)	814	
St. Louis (CST)	314	Harrisburg (EST)	717	
Springfield (CST)	417	Philadelphia (EST)	215	
Montana	406	Pittsburgh (EST)	412	
Helena (MST)	406	Rhode Island	401	
Nebraska (CST,MST)		Providence (EST)	401	
Lincoln (CST)	402	South Carolina	803	
North Platte (CST)	308	Columbia (EST)	803	
Omaha (CST)	402	South Dakota (CST,MST)	605	
Nevada	702	Pierre (CST)	605	
Carson City (PST)	702	Tennessee (CST,EST)		
New Hampshire	603	Memphis (CST)	901	
Concord (EST)	603	Nashville (CST)	615	
New Jersey		Texas (CST,MST)		
Elizabeth (EST)	908	Abilene (CST)	915	
Newark (EST)	201	Amarillo (CST)	806	
Trenton (EST)	609	Austin (CST)	512	
New Mexico	505	Beaumont (CST)	409	
Santa Fe (MST)	505	Dallas (CST)	214	
New York		Fort Worth (CST)	817	
Albany (EST)	518	Houston (CST)	713	
Binghamton (EST)	607	San Antonio (CST)	210	
Buffalo (EST)	716	Tyler (CST)	903	
Hempstead (EST)	516	Utah	801	
New York (EST)	212	Salt Lake City (MST)	801	
New York (EST)	718	Vermont	802	
New York (EST)	917	Montpelier (EST)	802	
North Carolina		Virginia		
Charlotte (EST)	704	Richmond (EST)	804	
Greensboro (EST)	910	Roanoke (EST)	703	
Raleigh (EST)	919	Washington		
North Dakota (CST,MST)	701	Olympia (PST)	206	
Bismark (CST)	701	Seattle (PST)	206	
Ohio		Spokane (PST)	509	
Cincinnati (EST)	513	West Virginia		
Cleveland (EST)	216	Charleston (EST)	304	
Columbus (EST)	614	Wisconsin		
Toledo (EST)	419	Eau Claire (CST)	715	
Oklahoma		Madison (CST)	608	
Oklahoma City (CST)	405	Milwaukee (CST)	414	
Tulsa (CST)	918	Wyoming	307	
Oregon (MST,PST)	503	Cheyenne (MST)	307	

Numerical List of Telephone Area Codes

Area Code...	Location (Time Zone)	Area Code...	Location (Time Zone)
201	New Jersey (EST)	212	New York (EST)
202	District of Columbia (EST)	213	California (PST)
203	Connecticut (EST)	214	Texas (CST)
205	Alabama (CST)	215	Pennsylvania (EST)
206	Washington (PST)	216	Ohio (EST)
207	Maine (EST)	217	Illinois (CST)
208	Idaho (MST,PST)	218	Minnesota (CST)
210	Texas (CST)	219	Indiana (CST,EST)

TELEPHONE AREA CODE AND TIME ZONE INFORMATION, CONT'D.

Numerical List of Telephone Area Codes, continued

Area Code...	Location (Time Zone)	Area Code...	Location (Time Zone)
301......	Maryland (EST)	609......	New Jersey (EST)
302......	Delaware (EST)	610......	Pennsylvania (EST)
303......	Colorado (MST)	612......	Minnesota (CST)
304......	West Virginia (EST)	614......	Ohio (EST)
305......	Florida (EST)	615......	Tennessee (CST,EST)
307......	Wyoming (MST)	616......	Michigan (EST)
308......	Nebraska (CST,MST)	617......	Massachusetts (EST)
309......	Illinois (CST)	618......	Illinois (CST)
310......	California (PST)	619......	California (PST)
312......	Illinois (CST)	701......	North Dakota (CST,MST)
313......	Michigan (EST)	702......	Nevada (PST)
314......	Missouri (CST)	703......	Virginia (EST)
315......	New York (EST)	706......	Georgia (EST)
316......	Kansas (CST,MST)	707......	California (PST)
317......	Indiana (EST)	708......	Illinois (CST)
318......	Louisiana (CST)	712......	Iowa (CST)
319......	Iowa (CST)	713......	Texas (CST)
401......	Rhode Island (EST)	714......	California (PST)
402......	Nebraska (CST,MST)	715......	Wisconsin (CST)
404......	Georgia (EST)	716......	New York (EST)
405......	Oklahoma (CST)	717......	Pennsylvania (EST)
406......	Montana (MST)	718......	New York (EST)
407......	Florida (EST)	719......	Colorado (MST)
408......	California (PST)	800......	Inward Watts
409......	Texas (CST)	801......	Utah (MST)
410......	Maryland (EST)	802......	Vermont (EST)
412......	Pennsylvania (EST)	803......	South Carolina (EST)
413......	Massachusetts (EST)	804......	Virginia (EST)
414......	Wisconsin (CST)	805......	California (PST)
415......	California (PST)	806......	Texas (CST)
417......	Missouri (CST)	808......	Hawaii (AK-HI)
419......	Ohio (EST)	810......	Michigan (EST)
501......	Arkansas (CST)	812......	Indiana (CST,EST)
502......	Kentucky (CST,EST)	813......	Florida (EST)
503......	Oregon (MST,PST)	814......	Pennsylvania (EST)
504......	Louisiana (CST)	815......	Illinois (CST)
505......	New Mexico (MST)	816......	Missouri (CST)
507......	Minnesota (CST)	817......	Texas (CST)
508......	Massachusetts (EST)	818......	California (PST)
509......	Washington (PST)	901......	Tennessee (CST)
510......	California (PST)	903......	Texas (CST)
512......	Texas (CST)	904......	Florida (CST,EST)
513......	Ohio (EST)	906......	Michigan (CST,EST)
515......	Iowa (CST)	907......	Alaska (AK-HI)
516......	New York (EST)	909......	California (PST)
517......	Michigan (EST)	910......	North Carolina (EST)
518......	New York (EST)	912......	Georgia (EST)
601......	Mississippi (CST)	913......	Kansas (CST,MST)
602......	Arizona (MST)	914......	New York (EST)
603......	New Hampshire (EST)	915......	Texas (CST,MST)
605......	South Dakota (CST,MST)	917......	New York (EST)
606......	Kentucky (EST)	918......	Oklahoma (CST)
607......	New York (EST)	919......	North Carolina (EST)
608......	Wisconsin (CST)		

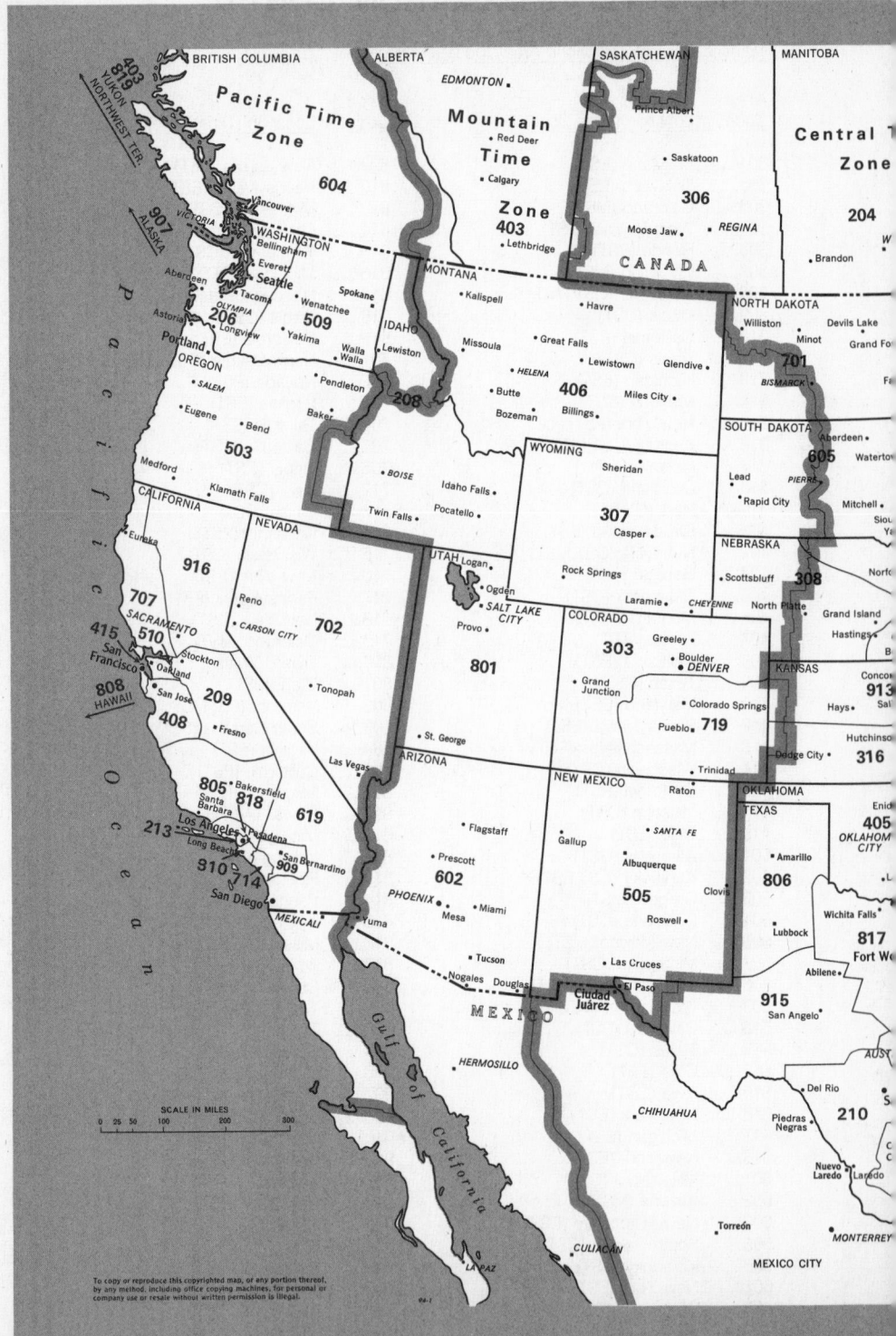

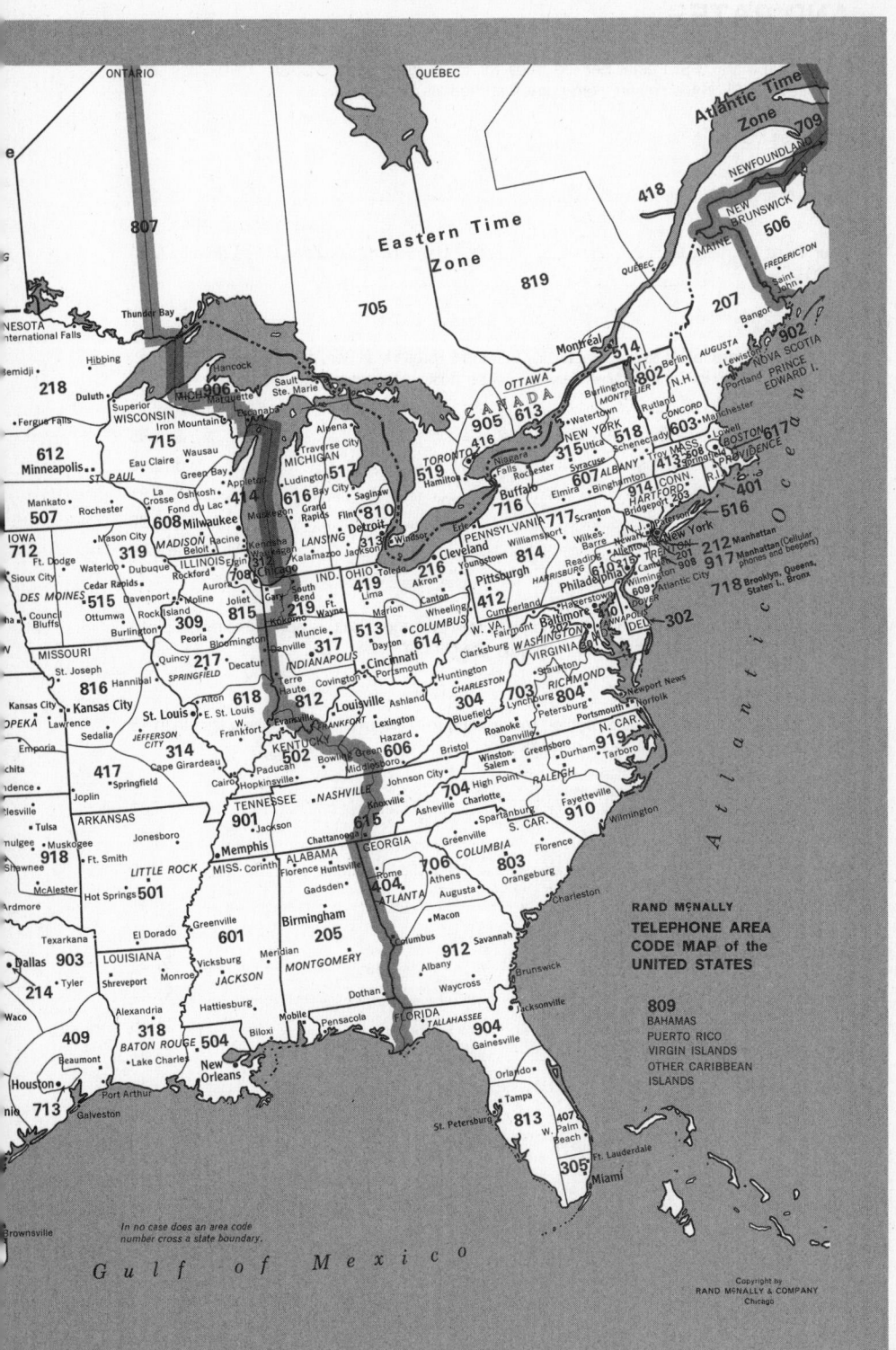

RAND McNALLY

TELEPHONE AREA CODE MAP of the UNITED STATES

809
BAHAMAS
PUERTO RICO
VIRGIN ISLANDS
OTHER CARIBBEAN
ISLANDS

In no case does an area code number cross a state boundary.

DOMESTIC POSTAL REGULATIONS AND RATES

Listed below are U.S. Postal Service rates for First-Class, Second-Class, Third-Class, and Express Mail. (All rates shown were current at the time of publication.)

First-Class Mail
Letters

11 oz. or less .... first oz. 29¢

each additional oz. 23¢

Over 11 oz. .... Use First Class Zone Rates (Priority Mail)

Post Cards .... 19¢

Express Mail
Packages that are taken to a postal facility offering Express Mail Service, and addressed to an area which also has Express Mail Service, will be delivered next day to the addressee.

½ lb. or less $9.95

Over 1 lb. and up to 2 lbs. $13.95

Over 2 lbs. and up to 3 lbs. $15.95

Over 3 lbs. and up to 4 lbs. $17.95

Over 4 lbs. and up to 5 lbs. $19.95

6 lbs. up to 70 lbs. .... Consult Postmaster

Second-Class Mail
Newspapers and periodicals with second-class mail privileges. Rate is applicable single piece third- or fourth-class rate for copies mailed by the general public.

Third-Class Mail
Circulars, books, catalogs, other printed matter, and merchandise, etc. weighing less than 16 oz. Over 16 oz., mail at the fourth-class rate.

Single Piece Rate

0 to 1 oz. .... 29¢

Over 1 to 2 ozs. .... 52¢

Over 2 to 3 ozs. .... 75¢

Over 3 to 4 ozs. .... 98¢

Over 4 to 6 ozs. $1.21

Over 6 to 8 ozs. $1.33

Over 8 to 10 ozs. $1.44

Over 10 to 12 ozs. $1.56

Over 12 to 14 ozs. $1.67

Over 14 but less than 16 ozs. $1.79

SMALL PARCEL RATES

Ground service rates for packages of 1 to 20 pounds are shown for the U.S. Postal Service, United Parcel Service (UPS), and Roadway Package System (RPS). Air freight rates for packages of 1 to 5 pounds and express letters, are also shown for selected air freight companies. (All rates shown were current at the time publication.)

In order to use the ground zone rate charts presented below for the U.S. Postal Service, United Parcel Service (UPS), and Roadway Package System (RPS), you will need to contact the carrier of your choice and request the zone chart that applies to your specific geographic location. This chart will enable you to determine the zone which corresponds to the destination of your parcel. Contact your local post office or UPS office; RPS may be contacted by calling the toll-free number which appears beneath the RPS Ground Zones Chart.

GROUND SERVICE RATES

United States Post Office Parcel Post Rates

First-Class Zone Rates (Priority Mail): All first-class mail weighing over 12 oz. Maximum weight is 70 lbs., size is limited to 108 inches in combined length and girth.

Weight over 12 oz. and not exceeding	Zones					
	Local 1, 2 & 3	4	5	6	7	8
1 #	$ 2.90	$ 2.90	$ 2.90	$ 2.90	$ 2.90	$ 2.90
2 #	2.90	2.90	2.90	2.90	2.90	2.90
3 #	4.10	4.10	4.10	4.10	4.10	4.10
4 #	4.65	4.65	4.65	4.65	4.65	4.65
5 #	5.45	5.45	5.45	5.45	5.45	5.45
6 #	5.55	5.75	6.10	6.85	7.65	8.60
7 #	5.70	6.10	6.70	7.55	8.50	9.65
8 #	5.90	6.50	7.30	8.30	9.40	10.70
9 #	6.10	7.00	7.95	9.05	10.25	11.75
10 #	6.35	7.55	8.55	9.80	11.15	12.80
11 #	6.75	8.05	9.20	10.55	12.05	13.80
12 #	7.15	8.55	9.80	11.30	12.90	14.85
13 #	7.50	9.10	10.40	12.05	13.80	15.90
14 #	7.90	9.60	11.05	12.80	14.65	16.95
15 #	8.30	10.10	11.65	13.55	15.55	18.00
16 #	8.70	10.65	12.30	14.30	16.45	19.05
17 #	9.10	11.15	12.90	15.05	17.30	20.10
18 #	9.50	11.65	13.55	15.80	18.20	21.10
19 #	9.90	12.20	14.15	16.50	19.05	22.15
20 #	10.30	12.70	14.75	17.25	19.95	23.20

For additional rate information, call your local Post Office.

SMALL PARCEL RATES, CONT'D.

United Parcel Service (UPS) (Commercial deliveries only.)

Ground Zones

Weight not to exceed	2	3	4	5	6	7	8
1 #	$ 2.28	$ 2.43	$ 2.66	$ 2.74	$ 2.83	$ 2.91	$ 2.97
2 #	2.30	2.46	2.93	3.03	3.24	3.34	3.58
3 #	2.40	2.63	3.12	3.27	3.53	3.63	3.95
4 #	2.50	2.78	3.24	3.43	3.66	3.85	4.23
5 #	2.61	2.90	3.31	3.51	3.83	4.03	4.44
6 #	2.72	2.98	3.37	3.58	3.99	4.21	4.58
7 #	2.83	3.05	3.43	3.63	4.11	4.40	4.80
8 #	2.94	3.11	3.49	3.70	4.24	4.62	5.16
9 #	3.04	3.19	3.54	3.79	4.38	4.89	5.57
10 #	3.14	3.28	3.60	3.91	4.55	5.22	5.98
11 #	3.23	3.38	3.69	4.10	4.79	5.55	6.41
12 #	3.32	3.49	3.80	4.29	5.06	5.90	6.83
13 #	3.39	3.61	3.91	4.50	5.34	6.29	7.28
14 #	3.46	3.74	4.06	4.72	5.63	6.65	7.74
15 #	3.54	3.89	4.22	4.95	5.92	7.03	8.19
16 #	3.61	4.05	4.38	5.18	6.24	7.41	8.63
17 #	3.69	4.20	4.55	5.39	6.53	7.78	9.08
18 #	3.75	4.34	4.71	5.61	6.83	8.16	9.53
19 #	3.85	4.44	4.88	5.81	7.15	8.53	9.98
20 #	3.99	4.60	5.06	6.05	7.44	8.89	10.43

For additional rate information, contact your local United Parcel Service office.

Roadway Package System (RPS) (Commercial deliveries only.)

Ground Zones

Weight not to exceed	2	3	4	5	6	7	8
1 #	$ 2.28	$ 2.43	$ 2.66	$ 2.74	$ 2.83	$ 2.91	$ 2.97
2 #	2.30	2.46	2.93	3.03	3.24	3.34	3.58
3 #	2.40	2.63	3.12	3.27	3.53	3.63	3.95
4 #	2.50	2.78	3.24	3.43	3.66	3.85	4.23
5 #	2.61	2.90	3.31	3.51	3.83	4.03	4.44
6 #	2.72	2.98	3.37	3.58	3.99	4.21	4.58
7 #	2.83	3.05	3.43	3.63	4.11	4.40	4.80
8 #	2.94	3.11	3.49	3.70	4.24	4.62	5.16
9 #	3.04	3.19	3.54	3.79	4.38	4.89	5.57
10 #	3.14	3.28	3.60	3.91	4.55	5.22	5.98
11 #	3.23	3.38	3.69	4.10	4.79	5.55	6.41
12 #	3.32	3.49	3.80	4.29	5.06	5.90	6.83
13 #	3.39	3.61	3.91	4.50	5.39	6.29	7.28
14 #	3.46	3.74	4.06	4.72	5.63	6.65	7.74
15 #	3.54	3.89	4.22	4.95	5.92	7.03	8.19
16 #	3.61	4.05	4.38	5.18	6.24	7.41	8.63
17 #	3.69	4.20	4.55	5.39	6.53	7.78	9.08
18 #	3.75	4.34	4.71	5.61	6.83	8.16	9.53
19 #	3.85	4.44	4.88	5.81	7.15	8.53	9.98
20 #	3.99	4.60	5.06	6.05	7.44	8.89	10.43

For additional rate information, call 1-800-ROADPAK.

SMALL PARCEL RATES, CONT'D.

AIR FREIGHT RATES FOR SELECTED PRIVATE CARRIERS

With the exception of UPS, most private carriers offer a variety of services, including overnight and second-day delivery. Most provide free envelopes and shipping containers and offer discounts for drop-off by the sender.

All of the private carriers listed provide pick-up as well as delivery. Most have drop-off boxes available in convenient locations. Next-day air and second-day air delivery times vary by carrier.

For your convenience in obtaining additional information on rates for heavier shipments, multiple shipments and frequent shipper discounts, toll-free numbers have been included in the rate tables. (All rates shown were current at the time of publication. Rates are subject to change without notice.)

United Parcel Service (UPS)

Next-Day Air Letter

$10.50 (Continental U.S.)

2nd-Day Air Letter

$5.50 (Continental U.S.)

Next-Day Air Package

Lbs.	Continental U.S.	AK & HI
1	$14.75	$19.75
2	15.25	20.50
3	17.25	22.50
4	18.50	24.00
5	20.00	25.50

2nd-Day Air Package

Lbs.	Continental U.S.	AK & HI
1	$ 5.75	$ 9.75
2	6.50	11.00
3	7.25	12.25
4	7.75	13.50
5	8.50	14.75

Federal Express (1-800-238-5355)

Priority
Overnight Letter

$15.50 (up to 8 oz.)

Standard
Overnight Letter

$11.50 (up to 8 oz.)

Priority Overnight Service (Pkg. delivery by 10:30 AM)		Standard Overnight Service (Pkg. delivery by 3:00 PM)		Economy Service (Pkg. delivery by 4:30 PM on 2nd day)	
Lbs.	Price *	Lbs.	Price *	Lbs.	Price *
1	$22.50	1	$15.50	1	$13.00
2	24.25	2	16.50	2	14.00
3	27.00	3	17.50	3	15.00
4	29.75	4	18.50	4	16.00
5	32.50	5	19.50	5	17.00

SMALL PARCEL RATES, CONT'D.

Airborne (General office, 1-800-426-2323; Washington state, 1-800-562-2227)

Overnight Letter
(Delivery by 12:00 PM)

$14.00 * (up to 8 oz.)

Select Delivery Service
(Delivery by 3:00 PM)

$8.00 * (up to 8 oz.)

(The above rates are for Non-Discounted service.)

"Express One" Service
(Next day, door-to-door pkg. delivery)

Lbs.	Price *
2	$25.00
3	30.00
4	36.00
5	38.00

Emery (1-800-HI-EMERY)
For specific rate information, call Emery's toll-free telephone number, listed above.

Burlington Air Express (1-800-CALL-BAX)
For specific rate information, call Burlington's toll-free telephone number, listed above.

Contact the toll-free "800" telephone numbers for further information.

* Prices not applicable for shipments from Continental U.S. to or between Alaska and Hawaii.

U.S. POSTAL SERVICE FIELD DIVISION OFFICES

The following is a list of Marketing and Communications Directors for each of the Postal Services 71 divisions. In the event that you have questions about mailing procedures, rates or regulations, contact the appropriate divisional office. The listings below were current as of September, 1992 and are subject to change.

NORTHEAST REGION

Albany, NY Division
Director, Marketing & Communications
  Barry D. Brennan (518) 452-2472

Boston, MA Division
Director, Marketing & Communications
  Lois A. Murphy (617) 654-5700

Brooklyn-Queens, NY Division
Director, Marketing & Communications
  Betty A. Rowe (718) 321-5139

Caribbean Division
Director, Marketing & Communications
  Roberto Perez de Leon (809) 767-2260

Hartford, CT Division
Director, Marketing & Communications
  Bruce D. Parmiter (203) 524-6077

Manchester, NH Division
Director, Marketing & Communications
  Paul F. Beaver (603) 644-4195

Newark, NJ Division
Director, Marketing & Communications
  Sidney McAbee (201) 669-0770

New Brunswick, NJ Division
Director, Marketing & Communications
  Joseph J. Freitas, Jr. (908) 819-3602

New York, NY Division
Director, Marketing & Communications
  John L. Ghisoni (212) 330-3070

Providence, RI Division
Director, Marketing & Communications
  Spiro T. Kyriakakis (401) 276-6959

Springfield, MA Division
Acting Director, Marketing & Communications
  John F. Basile (413) 731-0504

Westchester, NY Division
Director, Marketing & Communications
  Teresa B. Whalen (914) 345-1238

Western New York
Director, Marketing & Communications
  Nicholas A. Fabozzi (716) 846-2505

EASTERN REGION

Baltimore, MD Division
Acting Director, Marketing & Communications
  Joseph H. Raia (410) 347-4516

Charleston, WV Division
Director, Marketing & Communications
  Carolyn B. Drury (304) 340-4235

Cincinnati, OH Division
Director, Marketing & Communications
  Kathleen Boehm (513) 684-5489

Cleveland, OH Division
Director, Marketing & Communications
  Edmonia K. Page (216) 443-4076

Columbia, SC Division
Director, Marketing & Communications
  Hugh Hampton (803) 731-5900

Columbus, OH Division
Director, Marketing & Communications
  Edlen G. Johnson (614) 469-4412

Greensboro, NC Division
Acting Director, Marketing & Communications
  Stephen F. Ashworth (919) 668-1208

Harrisburg, PA Division
Director, Marketing & Communications
  Robert Chapman (717) 257-4803

Louisville, KY Division
Director, Marketing & Communications
  Dennis W. Patti (502) 454-1784

Philadelphia, PA Division
Director, Marketing & Communications
  Richard F. Nye (215) 895-8810

Pittsburgh, PA Division
Director, Marketing & Communications
  Sarah E. Howard (412) 359-7851

Richmond, VA Division
Director, Marketing & Communications
  Gail Sonnenberg (804) 775-6137

South Jersey Division
Director, Marketing & Communications
  Michael E. Kurtzman (609) 933-4245

Southern MD Division
Acting Director, Marketing & Communications
  Judy Walker (301) 499-7561

SOUTHERN REGION

Atlanta, GA Division
Director, Marketing & Communications
  Donald R. Warner (404) 765-7254

Birmingham, AL Division
Director, Marketing & Communications
  Margie M. Cather (205) 521-0416

Dallas, TX Division
Director, Marketing & Communications
  Gerald R. Carr (214) 393-6767

Houston, TX Division
Director, Marketing & Communications
  Richard M. Sanchez (713) 226-3713

Jackson, MS Division
Director, Marketing & Communications
  Robert Rankin (601) 968-0501

Jacksonville, FL Division
Director, Marketing & Communications
  Cheryl D. Pawlowski (904) 359-2929

Little Rock, AR Division
Director, Marketing & Communications
  Roxie Brown (501) 371-0301

Memphis, TN Division
Director, Marketing & Communications
  John V. Rountree (901) 521-2182

Miami, FL Division
Director, Marketing & Communications
  Marjorie M. Brown (305) 470-0232

Nashville, TN Division
Director, Marketing & Communications
  K. M. Loggins (615) 885-9113

New Orleans, LA Division
Director, Marketing & Communications
  Anthony J. Brescia (504) 589-1121

Oklahoma City, OK Division
Director, Marketing & Communications
  Susan M. Plonkey (405) 278-6111

San Antonio, TX Division
Director, Marketing & Communications
  Richard W. Stephens (512) 657-8500

Tampa, FL Division
Director, Marketing & Communications
  Virginia Ramos (813) 877-0825

CENTRAL REGION

Chicago, IL Division
Director, Marketing & Communications
  Jimmy Mason (312) 765-3034

Denver, CO Division
Director, Marketing & Communications
  Marilyn Terrell (303) 297-6178

Des Moines, IA Division
Director, Marketing & Communications
  Samuel C. Gonzalez (515) 283-7593

Detroit, MI Division
Acting Director, Marketing &
Communications
  Richard Gentry (313) 226-8634

Grand Rapids, MI Division
Director, Marketing & Communications
  Earl S. Douglas (616) 776-6156

Indianapolis, IN Division
Director, Marketing & Communications
  Bernard A. Dargo (317) 464-6452

Kansas City, MO Division
Director, Marketing & Communications
  Nathan W. Henderson (816) 374-9170

Milwaukee, WI Division
Director, Marketing & Communications
  William Matheson (414) 287-2546

North Suburban, IL Division
Director, Marketing & Communications
  Wayne J. Gardner (708) 260-5523

Omaha, NE Division
Director, Marketing & Communications
  Richard S. Shaver (402) 348-2550

St. Louis, MO Division
Director, Marketing & Communications
  Robert W. Roberts (314) 436-4505

South Suburban, IL Division
Director, Marketing & Communications
  Betty M. Jones (708) 563-5564

Twin Cities Division
Director, Marketing & Communications
  John J. Kelliher (612) 349-4992

Wichita, KS Division
Director, Marketing & Communications
  Richard L. Carney (316) 946-4615

WESTERN REGION

Anchorage, AK Division
Director, Marketing & Communications
W. Mike Barfield (907) 261-5418

Honolulu, HI Division
Director, Marketing & Communications
Hal F. Lee (808) 423-3718

Long Beach, CA Division
Director, Marketing & Communications
Rufus F. Porter (310) 983-3002

Los Angeles, CA Division
Director, Marketing & Communications
Armando Dominguez (213) 586-1475

Oakland, CA Division
Director, Marketing & Communications
Linda A. Deaktor (510) 874-8293

Phoenix, AZ Division
Director, Marketing & Communications
Ronald C. Abalos (602) 225-3100

Portland, OR Division
Director, Marketing & Communications
Barbara Van Arsdall (503) 294-2305

Sacramento, CA Division
Director, Marketing & Communications
E. Jackson Bryant (916) 923-3141

Salt Lake City, UT Division
Director, Marketing & Communications
Margaret L. Parsons (801) 974-2304

San Diego, CA Division
Director, Marketing & Communications
Gerald Vega (619) 221-3326

San Francisco, CA Division
Director, Marketing & Communications
Ruth E. Brooks (415) 550-5276

San Jose, CA Division
Acting Director, Marketing &
Communications
John DiPeri (408) 723-6100

Santa Ana, CA Division
Director, Marketing & Communications
Michael F. Flores (714) 662-6223

Seattle, WA Division
Director, Marketing & Communications
Peter A. Craft (206) 285-1335

Tucson, AZ Division
Director, Marketing & Communications
Polo J. Martinez, Jr. (602) 325-9815

Van Nuys, CA Division
Director, Marketing & Communications
Elizabeth A. Hanson (818) 908-6960

	ZIP
Abanda	36274
Abbeville	36310
Abel	36258
Abercrombie	35042
Aberfoil	36089
Abernant	35440
Abernathy	36264
Acipcoville (Part of Birmingham)	35207
Ackerville	36768
Acmar	35094
Active	36793
Ada	36069
Adamsburg	35967
Adamsville	35005
Addison	35540
Adger	35006
Adler	36779
Ai	36264
Aimwell	36782
Airport Highlands (Part of Birmingham)	35206
Akron	35441
Alabama City (Part of Gadsden)	35904
Alabama Fork	35611
Alabama Port	36523
Alabama Shores	35660
Alabaster	35007
	35144
For specific Alabaster Zip Codes call (205) 663-3971, or your local postmaster.	
Alaga	36343
Alberta	36720
Alberta City (Part of Tuscaloosa)	35401
Alberton	36453
Albertville	35950
Alder Springs	35950
Aldrich	35115
Aldridge	35580
Aldridge Grove	35650
Alexander City	35010
Alexandria	36250
Alexis	35960
Aliceville	35442
Allen	36419
Allens Crossroads	35175
Allenton	36768
Allenton Station	36768
Allenville (Hale County)	36738
Allenville (Marengo County)	36738
Allgood	35013
Allsboro	35616
Allsop	36272
Alma	36501
Almeria	36089
Almond	36276
Alpine (DeKalb County)	35984
Alpine (Talladega County)	35014
Altadena Valley	35243
Alton	35015
Altoona	35952
America	35580
Andalusia	36420
Anderson (Etowah County)	35901
Anderson (Lauderdale County)	35610
Andrews Chapel	35619
Angel	36265
Annemanie	36721
Anniston	36201-06
For specific Anniston Zip Codes call (205) 236-6355, or your local postmaster.	
Anniston Army Depot	36201
Ansley	36081
Antioch (Calhoun County)	36253
Antioch (Covington County)	36420
Antioch (Pike County)	36081
Appleton	36426
Aqua Vista	35645
Aquilla	36558
Arab	35016
Ararat	36921
Arbacoochee	36264
Arbor Acres (Part of Huntsville)	35810
Ardell	35053
Ardilla (Part of Dothan)	36301
Ardmore	35739
Ardmore Highway (Part of Huntsville)	35805
Argo	35173
Argo Heights	35550
Arguta	36360
Ariton	36311
Arkadelphia	35033
Arkwright (Part of Vincent)	35178
Arley	35541
Arlington	36722

	ZIP
Armstead	35121
Armstrong	36089
Arona	35957
Arrowhead	36109
Arrowwood (Part of Tuscaloosa)	35405
Asberry	36272
Asbury (Dale County)	36360
Asbury (Marshall County)	35950
Ashbank	35578
Ashby	35035
Ashford	36312
Ashland (Clay County)	36251
Ashland (Madison County)	35811
Ashridge	35565
Ashville	35953
Aspel	35768
Athens	35611
Atkinson	36784
Atmore	36502-04
For specific Atmore Zip Codes call (205) 368-2871, or your local postmaster.	
Attalla	35954
Atwood	35571
Auburn	36830-49
For specific Auburn Zip Codes call (205) 821-3754, or your local postmaster.	
Augustin	36701
Aurora	35957
Aurora Springs	35616
Austinville (Part of Decatur)	35601
Autaugaville	36003
Avalon Park (Part of Hueytown)	35020
Avant	36033
Avery (Part of Stevenson)	35772
Avoca	35653
Avon	36312
Avondale (Part of Birmingham)	35222
Avondale Mill (Part of Alexander City)	35010
Avondale Village (Part of Pell City)	35125
Avon Park (Part of Birmingham)	35234
Awin	36768
Axis	36505
Ayres	35126
Babbie	36420
Bacon Level	36274
Bagley	35062
Bailey Springs	35645
Baileyton	35019
Baileytown	35019
Baker Hill	36004
Bald Hill	36375
Baldwin Farms	36083
Balkum	36345
Ballplay	35903
Bangor	35079
Bankhead (DeKalb County)	35984
Bankhead (Walker County)	35580
Banks	36005
Bankston	35542
Barachias (Part of Montgomery)	36064
Barber	36312
Barfield	36266
Barlow	36558
Barlow Bend	36545
Barnes	36311
Barnesville	35570
Barnett Chapel	35572
Barnett Crossroads	36426
Barney	35550
Barnisdale Forest (Part of Birmingham)	35215
Barnwell	36532
Barrytown	36908
Barton	35616
Basham	35640
Bashi	36784
Basin	36323
Bass	35772
Bassetts Creek	36585
Batesville	36053
Battelle	35989
Battens Crossroads	36316
Battleground	35179
Battles Wharf	36532
Bay Minette	36507
Bayou La Batre	36509
Bay Shore Junction (Part of Prichard)	36610
Bayside (Part of Decatur)	35603
Bay Springs	35960
Bayview	35005
Bazemore	35559

	ZIP
Beachwood Park (Part of Birmingham)	35212
Beamon	36360
Bean Rock	35175
Bear Creek	35543
Bear Point	36561
Beasons Mill	36264
Beatrice	36425
Beaty Crossroads (Part of Ider)	35981
Beauregard	36801
Beaverton	35544
Beaver Town	35442
Beck	36420
Beehive	36865
Bel Air (Jefferson County)	35210
Bel Air (Mobile County)	36616
Bel Air Mall (Part of Mobile)	36616
Belforest	36526
Belgreen	35653
Belk	35545
Bellamy	36901
Bellefontaine	36567
Bellefonte	35752
Bellefountaine	36582
Bellemeade	35630
Belle Mina	35615
Belleville	36401
Bellevue (Part of Gadsden)	35901
Bell Springs	35622
Bellview	36726
Bellwood (Geneva County)	36313
Bellwood (Jefferson County)	35064
Belmont	35470
Beloit	36759
Beltline (Part of Decatur)	35601
Belview Heights (Part of Tuscumbia)	35674
Bemiston (Part of Talladega)	35160
Bendale (Part of Birmingham)	35217
Benevola	35466
Benoit	35550
Bentley Hills (Part of Mountain Brook)	35216
Benton	36785
Ben Vines Gap (Part of Maytown)	35118
Berkley	35748
Berlin	35055
Bermuda (Conecuh County)	36401
Bermuda (Monroe County)	36460
Berney Points (Part of Birmingham)	35211
Berry	35546
Bertha	36353
Bessemer	35020-23
For specific Bessemer Zip Codes call (205) 428-9163, or your local postmaster.	
Bessemer Gardens (Part of Hueytown)	35020
Bessemer Homestead (Part of Bessemer)	35020
Bessie	35062
Bessie Junction	35062
Bethany	35452
Bethel (Barbour County)	36311
Bethel (Limestone County)	35620
Bethel (Cullman County)	35057
Bethlehem	36046
Beulah (Covington County)	36467
Beulah (Greene County)	35469
Beulah (Lee County)	36854
Beverly Station (Part of Birmingham)	35211
Bexar	35570
Bibbville	35188
Biddle Crossroads (Part of Henagar)	35978
Bigbee	36510
Big Creek	36301
Big Oak	35645
Big Springs	35188
Billingsley	36006
Billy Goat Hill	35960
Birdine	36740
Birdsong	35055
Birmingham	35201-61
For specific Birmingham Zip Codes call (205) 521-0451, or your local postmaster.	
Birmingham Green (Part of Birmingham)	35237
Birwat (Part of Tarrant)	35217
Bishop	35616
Biven	35214
Black	36314
Blackankle	35768
Black Creek	35207
Black Diamond	35023
Black Rock	36042

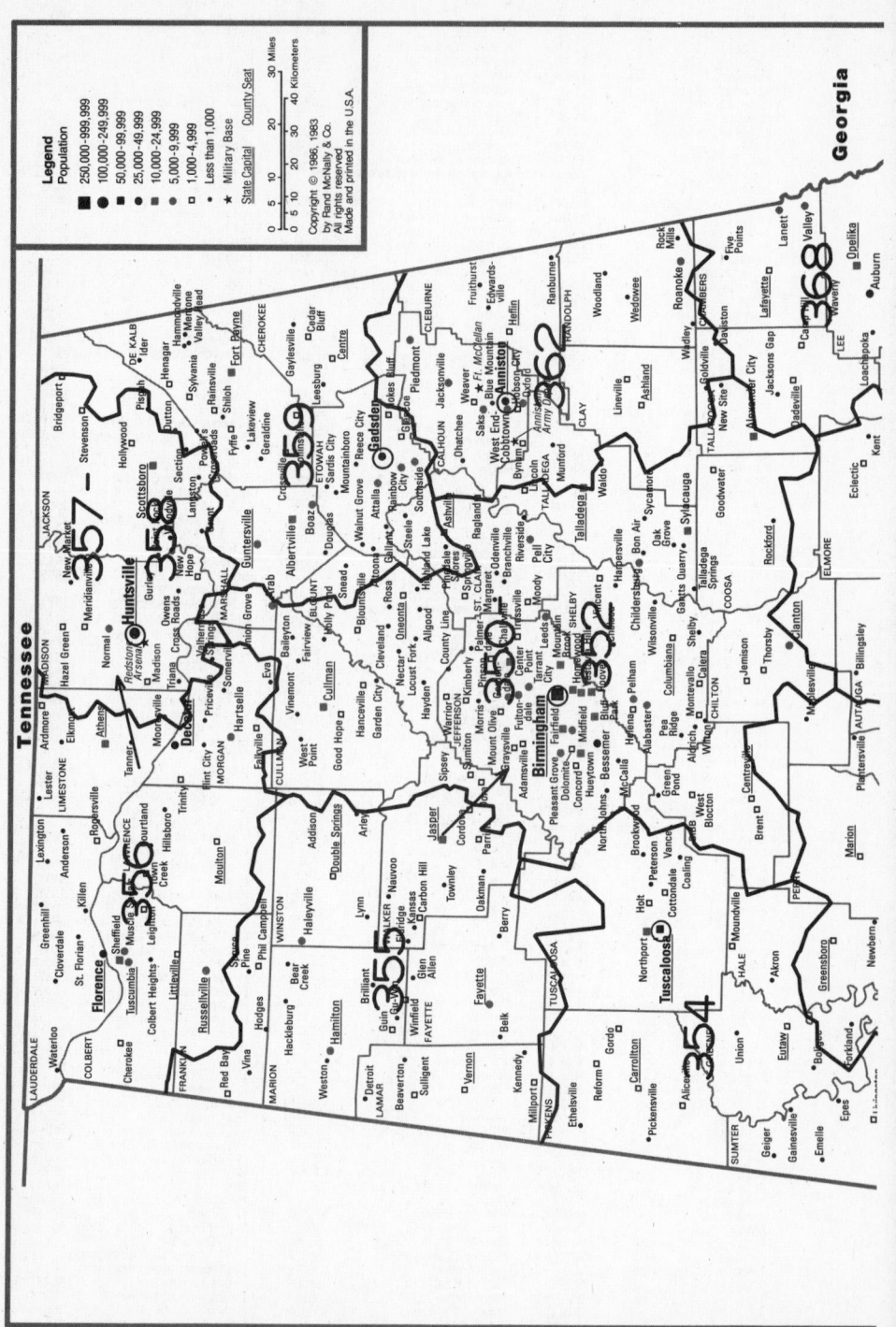

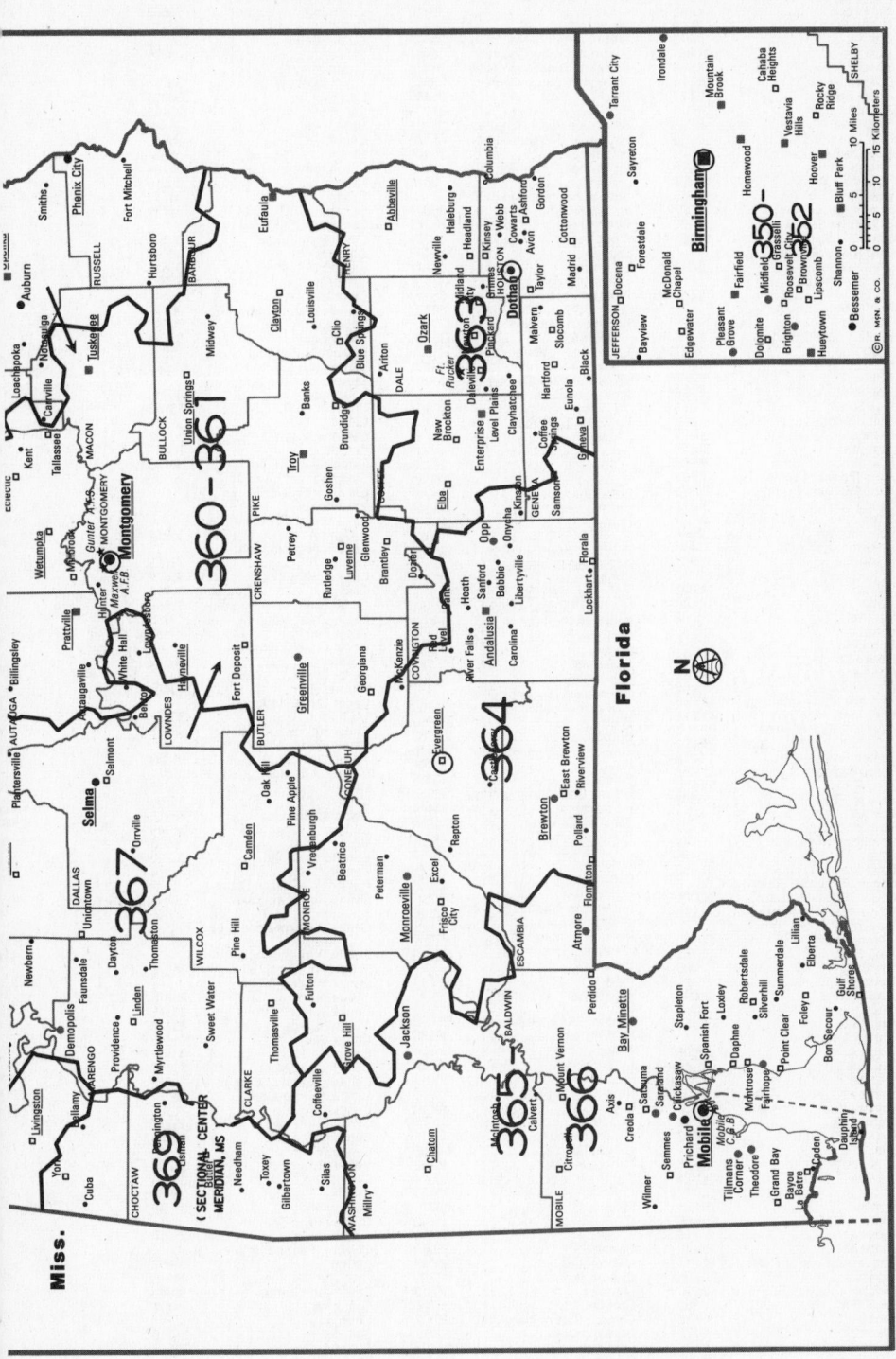

	ZIP
Blacksher	36507
Blackwood	36345
Bladon Springs	36919
Blanche	35973
Blanton	36854
Bleecker	36874
Blossburg	35073
Blount Springs	35079
Blountsville	35031
Blow Gourd	35049
Blue Creek	35023
Blue Creek Junction (Part of Bessemer)	35020
Blue Mountain	36201
Blue Pond	35959
Blue Ridge	36092
Blue Ridge Estates	35226
Blues Old Stand	36061
Blue Spring (Part of Huntsville)	35810
Blue Springs (Barbour County)	36017
Blue Springs (Blount County)	35031
Blue Springs (Covington County)	36467
Blue Springs Garden	35811
Bluff	35555
Bluff Park	35226
Bluff Spring	36251
Bluff Springs	36323
Blufftton	30138
Boar Tush	35565
Boaz	35957
Bobo (Fayette County)	35594
Bobo (Madison County)	35773
Boiling Springs	36271
Boldo	35501
Boley Springs	35546
Boligee	35443
Bolinger	36903
Bolivar	35740
Bolling	36033
Bomar	35960
Bon Air	35032
Bonita	36749
Bonneville	35611
Bonnie Doone	35611
Bon Secour	36511
Booth	36008
Boot Hill	36048
Boothtown	36521
Boozer Heights (Part of Oxford)	36201
Borden Springs	36262
Borden Wheeler Springs	36262
Borom	36860
Boston (Part of Brilliant)	35548
Boswell	36081
Bowles	36401
Bowmans Crossroads	35444
Boyd	35470
Boyd Crossing	35490
Boykin (Escambia County)	36426
Boykin (Wilcox County)	36723
Boyles (Part of Birmingham)	35217
Boylston (Part of Montgomery)	36110
Boys Ranch	36761
Bradford	35089
Bradley	36420
Bradleyton	36041
Braggs	36761
Branchville	35120
Brandontown (Part of Huntsville)	35805
Brannon Springs	36271
Brannon Stand	36301
Brantley (Crenshaw County)	36009
Brantley (Dallas County)	36703
Brantleyville	35114
Bremen	35033
Brent	35034
Brewersville	35470
Brewton	36426*
	36427†
Briar Hill	36035
Brick	35660
Bridgeport	35740
Bridgeville	35442
Bridlewood Forest Estates	35215
Brierfield	35035
Brighton	35020
Bright Star	35980
Brilliant	35548
Brisco Store	35772
Broadmoor (Part of Bessemer)	35020
Bromley	36507
Brompton	35094
Brookhurst (Jefferson County)	35215

	ZIP
Brookhurst (Madison County)	35810
Brookland	36453
Brookley (Part of Mobile)	36605
Brooklyn (Coffee County)	36467
Brooklyn (Conecuh County)	36429
Brooklyn (Cullman County)	35083
Brooks	36456
Brookside	35036
Brooksville (Blount County)	35031
Brooksville (Morgan County)	35670
Brookwood	35444
Brookwood Forest (Part of Athens)	35611
Brookwood Village (Part of Homewood)	35209
Broomtown	35973
Broughton	36274
Browns	36759
Brownsboro	35741
Browns Corner	35773
Browns Crossroad	36310
Browns Crossroads	36360
Browntown (Jackson County)	35978
Brown Town (Mobile County)	39451
Brownville (Clay County)	35072
Brownville (Conecuh County)	36401
Brownville (Jefferson County)	35211
Brownville (Tuscaloosa County)	35476
Bruceville	36089
Brundidge	36010
Brunnet Heights	35217
Brushy Pond	35033
Bryant	35958
Bryant's Lower Landing	36579
Bryce Hospital (Part of Tuscaloosa)	35401
Buchanan Peninsula	35616
Buckhorn (Madison County)	35761
Buckhorn (Pike County)	36081
Buck Island Shores	35976
Bucks	36512
Bucksnort	35747
Buena Vista	36425
Buena Vista Highlands (Part of Homewood)	35209
Buffalo	36862
Buggs Chapel	35763
Buhl	35446
Bull City	35468
Bullock	36009
Bullock Correctional Facility	36089
Burchfield	35444
Burgreen Corners	35758
Burks Gardens (Part of Tuscaloosa)	35401
Burkville	36752
Burl	36753
Burlington	36078
Burningtree Estates (Part of Decatur)	35603
Burningtree Mountain	35603
Burns	36272
Burnsville	36703
Burnt Corn	36431
Burntout	35593
Burnwell	35038
Burstall (Part of Bessemer)	35020
Bushy Creek	36033
Butler	36904
Butler Springs	36030
Buttston	36853
Buyck	36080
Bynum	36253
Caddo	35673
Caffee Junction	35111
Cahaba	36767
Cahaba Heights	35243
Cahaba Hills (Part of Leeds)	35094
Cahaba River Estates	35020
Calcis	35178
Caldwell	35146
Caledonia	36753
Calera	35040
Calhoun	36047
Calumet	35580
Calvert	36513
Camden	36726
Camelot (Part of Huntsville)	35803
Cameronsville	35772
Campbell	36727
Campbells Crossroads	36266
Campbellville	35063
Camp Hill	36850
Camp Oliver	35130
Canoe	36502

	ZIP
Cantebury Heights (Part of Mobile)	36609
Cantelous Spur	36113
Canton Bend	36726
Capell	36726
Capitol Heights (Part of Montgomery)	36107
Capps	36353
Capshaw	35742
Carbon Hill	35549
Cardiff	35041
Carlisle	35957
Carlowville	36761
Carlton	36515
Carns	35746
Carolina	36420
Carolyn (Part of Montgomery)	36106
Carpenter	36507
Carriger	35611
Carr Mill	36251
Carrollton	35447
Carrville (Part of Tallassee)	36078
Carson	36548
Carter Grove	35750
Cartersville	35967
Cartwright	35620
Carver Court (Part of Tuskegee)	36088
Casemore	36742
Casey	36701
Castleberry	36432
Catalpa	36081
Catherine	36728
Catoma	36108
Cavalry Hill (Part of Huntsville)	35805
Cave Spring (Etowah County)	35954
Cave Spring (Madison County)	35763
Cave Springs	35674
Cecil	36013
Cedar Bluff	35959
Cedar Cove	35453
Cedar Fork	36482
Cedar Grove (Baldwin County)	36542
Cedar Grove (Covington County)	36420
Cedar Grove (Jackson County)	35772
Cedar Hill (Fayette County)	35555
Cedar Hill (Limestone County)	35739
Cedar Hill Estates	35674
Cedar Plains	35622
Cedar Point	35760
Cedar Springs	36265
Cedrum	35549
Center	35565
Centercrest	35215
Centergrove	35670
Center Hill (Cullman County)	35077
Center Hill (Lauderdale County)	35648
Center Hill (Limestone County)	35773
Center Point (Clarke County)	36524
Center Point (Jefferson County)	35215
Center Point Gardens	35215
Center Springs	35172
Center Star	35645
Centerville	36401
Centerwood Estates	35215
Central (Cullman County)	35055
Central (Elmore County)	36024
Central City	36330
Central Crossroads	35978
Central Heights	35633
Central Highlands (Part of Birmingham)	35206
Central Mills	36773
Centre	35960
Centreville	35042
Century Plaza (Part of Birmingham)	35210
Ceramic (Part of Phenix City)	36867
Chalkville	35215
Chalybeate Springs	35643
Champion	35121
Chance	36751
Chancellor	36316
Chandler Springs	35160
Chapel Hill (Chambers County)	36862
Chapel Hill (Jefferson County)	35216
Chapman	36015

	ZIP
Chapman Heights (Part of Huntsville)	35810
Chase	35811
Chastang	36560
Chatom	36518
Chelsea (Madison County)	35801
Chelsea (Shelby County)	35043
Cherokee	35616
Cherokee Bluffs	36078
Cherokee Forest (Part of Mountain Brook)	35223
Cherry Grove	35611
Chesson	36029
Chesterfield	30731
Chestnut	36425
Chestnut Grove	36010
Chetopa	35139
Chickasaw	36611
Chigger Hill	35971
Childersburg	35044
Chilton	36451
China	36401
China Grove	36081
Chinneby	36268
Chisholm (Part of Montgomery)	36110
Choccolocco	36254
Choctaw Bluff	36545
Choctaw City	36904
Choctow Corner (Part of Thomasville)	36784
Chosea Springs	36201
Christiana	36258
Chrysler	36550
Chulafinnee	36264
Chunchula	36521
Circlewood (Part of Tuscaloosa)	35405
Citronelle	36522
Claiborne	36470
Clairmont Springs	35160
Clanton	35045
Clarksville	36524
Claud	36024
Clay	35048
Clay City	36532
Clayhatchee	36322
Clayhill	36784
Claysville	35976
Clayton	36016
Clear Springs	35121
Clearview (Covington County)	36028
Clearview (Crenshaw County)	36041
Cleveland (Blount County)	35049
Cleveland (Fayette County)	35542
Cleveland Crossroads	35072
Cliff Haven (Part of Sheffield)	35660
Clift Acres	35758
Clinton	35448
Clintonville	36351
Clio	36017
Clisby Park (Part of Montgomery)	36104
Clopton	36317
Cloverdale (Jefferson County)	35215
Cloverdale (Lauderdale County)	35617
Cloverdale (Mobile County)	36541
Cloverdale (Montgomery County)	36105
Cloverdale (Tuscaloosa County)	35401
Cloverdale Heights	35630
Cloverland (Part of Montgomery)	36105
Clowers Crossroads	36010
Clubview Heights (Part of Gadsden)	35901
Coal Bluff	36769
Coalburg	35068
Coal City	35131
Coal Fire	35481
Coaling	35449
Coalmont	35114
Coal Valley	35579
Coatopa	35470
Cobb City (Part of Glencoe)	35905
Cobbs Ford	36025
Cobb Town	36201
Cochrane	35442
Coden	36523
Cody	35555
Coffee Junction	35111
Coffee Springs	36318
Coffeeville	36524
Cohasset	36474
Coker	35452
Colbert Heights	35674

	ZIP
Cold Springs (Cullman County)	35033
Cold Springs (Elmore County)	36022
Coldwater (Calhoun County)	36260
Coldwater (Cleburne County)	36262
Cole Spring	35622
Collbran	35967
Collins Chapel	35045
Collinsville	35961
Collirene	36785
Coloma	35960
Colonial Gardens	35759
Colonial Heights (Part of Tuscumbia)	35674
Colony (Cullman County)	35077
Colony (Tuscaloosa County)	35476
Columbia	36319
Columbiana	35051
Columbus City	35976
Colwell	35905
Comer	36053
Concord (Blount County)	35049
Concord (Fayette County)	35555
Concord (Jefferson County)	35023
Congo	35959
Conifer	36078
Consul	36728
Cook Springs	35052
Cool Springs	35953
Coon Creek	35063
Coopers	35045
Coosa Court (Part of Childersburg)	35044
Coosada	36020
Coosa River	36022
Copeland	36558
Copeland Bridge	35961
Copper Springs	35120
Coppinville (Part of Enterprise)	36330
Corcoran (Part of Troy)	36081
Cordova	35550
Corinth (Bullock County)	36081
Corinth (Cullman County)	35179
Corinth (Randolph County)	36278
Corner	35180
Cornhouse	36274
Cornwall Furnace	35959
Corona	35579
Cortelyou	36585
Cotaco	35670
Cottage Grove	35089
Cottage Hill (Jefferson County)	35127
Cottage Hill (Mobile County)	36609
Cottondale	35453
Cottonton	36851
Cottontown	35646
Cotton Valley	36083
Cottonville	35747
Cottonwood	36320
Country Club Acres (Part of Athens)	35611
Country Club Estates (Madison County)	35201
Country Club Estates (Mobile County)	36608
Country Club Village (Part of Mobile)	36608
Country Estates (Jefferson County)	35215
Country Estates (Madison County)	36108
County Line (Blount County)	35172
County Line (Pike County)	36034
County Line (Covington County)	36453
Courtland	35618
Covin	35555
Cowarts	36321
Cox Beach (Part of Satsuma)	36572
Coxey	35611
Coy	36435
Cragford	36255
Crane Hill	35053
Crawford (Mobile County)	36608
Crawford (Russell County)	36867
Creek Stand	36089
Creeltown	35063
Creola	36525
Crescent Heights (Part of Lipscomb)	35020
Crestline (Part of Mountain Brook)	35213
Crestline Gardens (Part of Birmingham)	35210
Crestline Heights (Part of Mountain Brook)	35213

	ZIP
Crestline Park (Part of Birmingham)	35213
Crestview (Part of Mobile)	36609
Crestview Gardens (Part of Pell City)	35125
Crestwood (Part of Huntsville)	35807
Creswell	35078
Crews	35586
Crichton (Part of Mobile)	36607* 36670†
Crockett Junction	35118
Cromwell	36906
Crooked Oak	35674
Cropwell (Part of Pell City)	35054
Crosby	36343
Cross Key	35620
Crossroads (Baldwin County)	36507
Cross Roads (Clarke County)	36570
Crossroads (Marshall County)	35976
Crosston	35126
Crossville (DeKalb County)	35962
Crossville (Lamar County)	35592
Crudup (Part of Reece City)	35954
Crumley Chapel	35214
Cuba	36907
Cullman	35055* 35056†
Cullomburg	36919
Cunningham (Clarke County)	36727
Cunningham (Pickens County)	35442
Curry (Talladega County)	36268
Curry (Walker County)	35501
Currytown	36350
Curtis	36323
Curtiston (Part of Attalla)	35954
Cusseta	36852
Cypress	35474
Cyril	36912
Dadeville	36853
Daisy City	35214
Daleville	36322
Dallas (Blount County)	35172
Dallas (Madison County)	35801
Damascus (Coffee County)	36323
Damascus (Escambia County)	36426
Dancy	35442
Dancy Quarter (Part of Decatur)	35603
Danley	36323
Danville	35619
Danway	36801
Daphne	36526
Dargin	35040
Darlington	36726
Darwin Downs (Part of Huntsville)	35801
Dauphin Island	36528
Davis Hills (Part of Huntsville)	35805
Daviston	36256
Davisville	36083
Dawes	36601
Dawson	35963
Dawsons Mill	36749
Dayton	36731
De Armanville	36257
Deason Hill	35550
Deatsville	36022
Deavertown	35049
Decatur	35601-09
For specific Decatur Zip Codes call (205) 355-1211, or your local postmaster.	
Deer Park	36529
DeFoor	35565
Delchamps	36523
Delmar	35551
Delta	36258
Demopolis	36732
Dempsey	35653
Deposit	35761
Detroit	35552
Devenport	36047
Dexter	36092
Diamond	35976
Dickert	36276
Dickinson	36436
Dillard	36360
Dilworth	35063
Dime	35581
Dixiana	35126
Dixie	36420
Dixieland	36867
Dixie Springs	35579
Dixon Corner	36544

* **Area Zip Code** † **Post Office Boxes**

	ZIP		ZIP		ZIP
Dixons Mills	36736	Eddy (Part of Arab)	35016	Fairview (Cullman County)	35055
Dixonville	36426	Eden (Part of Pell City)	35125	Fairview (DeKalb County)	35963
Docena	36060	Edgefield (Barbour County)	36016	Fairview (Jefferson County)	35208
Dock	36037	Edgefield (Jackson County)	35772	Fairview (Limestone County)	35611
Dogtown	35549	Edgemont (Part of		Fairview (Marion County)	35564
Dolcito (Part of Tarrant)	35217	Homewood)	35209	Fairview (Mobile County)	36587
Doliska (Part of Dora)	35130	Edgemont Park (Part of		Fairview (Morgan County)	35601
Dolomite	35061	Homewood)	35209	Fairview (St. Clair County)	35131
Dolonah	35023	Edgewater	35224	Fairview (Winston County)	35540
Dora	35062	Edmonton Heights (Part of		Fairview West	35077
Doster	36311	Huntsville)	35810	Falkville	35622
Dothan	36301-04	Edna	36922	Fannie	36441
For specific Dothan Zip Codes call		Edwardsville	36261	Farill	35959
(205) 794-8567, or your local		Edwin	36317	Farley (Part of Huntsville)	35802
postmaster.		Egypt	35952	Farmersville	36761
Double Bridges (Henry		Eight Mile (Part of Prichard)	36613*	Farmville	36801
County)	36310		36663†	Fatama	36726
Double Bridges (Marshall		Elamville	36311	Faunsdale	36738
County)	35957	Elba	36323	Fayette	35555
Doublehead	36862	Elberta	36530	Fayetteville	35150
Double Springs	35553	Eldridge	35554	Federal Prison Camp	36112
Douglas (DeKalb County)	35967	Elgin	35652	Fergusons Cross Roads	35972
Douglas (Marshall County)	35964	Eliska	36480	Fernbank	35576
Douglasville (Part of		Elkmont	35620	Fernland	36541
Birmingham)	35207	Elkwood	38449	Fernwood Estates	35215
Downing	36052	Ellards	35034	Fieldstown (Part of	
Downs	36039	Elliotsville (Part of Alabaster)	35007	Gardendale)	35071
Downtown (Part of		Ellisville (Baldwin County)	36551	Fig Tree	36749
Huntsville)	35801	Ellisville (Cherokee County)	35960	Finchburg	36444
Downtown (Part of		Elmore	36025	Finley Crossing	36784
Montgomery)	36104	Elmore Correctional Facility	36025	Fisher Crossroads (Part of	
Downtown (Part of		Elrod	35458	Fort Payne)	35967
Tuscaloosa)	35401	Elsanor	36567	Fishhead	36258
Dozier	36028	Elsmeade (Part of		Fish Pond	35643
Draper Correctional Center	36025	Montgomery)	36116	Fish River	36555
Drewry	36460	Elting (Part of Florence)	35630	Fisk	35750
Drummond	35063	Elyton (Part of Birmingham)	35204	Fitzpatrick	36029
Dry Forks	36726	Emelle	35459	Five Points (Blount County)	35049
Dry Valley	35096	Emerald Shores	35630	Five Points (Chambers	
Dublin	36069	Empire	35063	County)	36855
Duck Nest Springs	36268	Englewood	35405	Five Points (Cleburne	
Ducksprings	35954	English Village (Jefferson		County)	36264
Dudley	35490	County)	35223	Five Points (Dale County)	36352
Dudleyville	36850	English Village (Madison		Five Points (Dallas County)	36767
Duke	36279	County)	35802	Five Points (Elmore County)	36025
Dulin	35594	Enon (Bullock County)	36053	Five Points (Houston	
Duncan Crossroads	35771	Enon (Cullman County)	35179	County)	36320
Duncanville	35456	Enon (Houston County)	36376	Five Points (Lawrence	
Dundee	36344	Enon (Pike County)	36005	County)	35619
Dunn	36081	Ensley (Part of Birmingham)	35218	Five Points (Madison	
Dunns	36420	Enterprise (Coffee and Dale		County)	35773
Dupree	36312	County)	36330*	Five Points (Marshall	
Dutton	35744		36331†	County)	35755
Duval (Part of Opp)	36467	Enterprise (Chilton County)	36091	Five Points (Walker County)	35501
Dyas	36507	Eoda	36420	Five Points East (Part of	
Dyers Crossroads	35055	Eoline	35042	Irondale)	35210
Eady City (Part of Valley)	36854	Epes	35460	Five Points West Shopping	
Eagle	35540	Equality	36026	City (Part of Birmingham)	35208
Earlytown	36453	Erin	36266	Flat Creek	35130
Eastaboga	36260	Escambia Correctional		Flat Rock (Clay County)	36266
East Birmingham (Part of		Center	36503	Flat Rock (Jackson County)	35966
Birmingham)	35204	Escatawpa	36584	Flat Top	35062
East Boyles (Part of		Estelle	36726	Flatwood (Montgomery	
Birmingham)	35217	Estes Crossroads	36272	County)	36110
East Brewton	36426	Estillfork	35745	Flatwood (Walker County)	35549
Eastbrook (Part of		Ethel	36081	Flatwood (Wilcox County)	36728
Montgomery)	36109	Ethelsville	35461	Fleetwood	35453
East Brookwood	35444	Euclid Estates (Part of		Fleming Meadows (Part of	
Eastdale (Part of		Mountain Brook)	35217	Huntsville)	35802
Montgomery)	36117	Eufaula	36027*	Flemington Heights (Part of	
Eastdale Mall (Part of			36072†	Huntsville)	35802
Montgomery)	36109	Eulaton	36201	Fleta	36043
Eastern Valley	35020	Eunola	36340	Flint City (Part of Decatur)	35601
East Gadsden (Part of		Eureka	35772	Flomaton	36441
Gadsden)	35903	Eutaw	35462	Florala	36442
East Hampton (Part of		Eva	35621	Floral Crest	35774
Athens)	35611	Evansboro	36913	Florence	35630-33
East Haven	35215	Evansville	35441	For specific Florence Zip Codes	
East Irondale (Part of		Evergreen (Autauga County)	36006	call (205) 764-6961, or your local	
Irondale)	35210	Evergreen (Conecuh		postmaster.	
East Killen (Part of Killen)	35645	County)	36401	Florette	35670
East Lake (Part of		Ewell	36360	Flower Hill	35643
Birmingham)	35206	Excel	36439	Floyd	36024
East Point	35055	Exmoor	36782	Foley	36535*
East Side (Part of		Fabius	35966		36536†
Tuscaloosa)	35404	Fackler	35746	Ford City	35660
East Tallassee (Part of		Fadette	36375	Forest	35461
Tallassee)	36023	Fairdale	35042	Forest Brook Estates	35226
East Thomas (Part of		Fairfax (Part of Valley)	36854	Forestdale	35214
Birmingham)	35204	Fairfield (Covington County)	36420	Forester	36067
Eastwood (Blount County)	35121	Fairfield (Jefferson County)	35064	Forester Chapel	36276
Eastwood (Jefferson		Fairfield (Lawrence County)	35650	Forest Hill (Part of Mobile)	36608
County)	35224	Fairfield Highlands (Part of		Forest Hills (Calhoun	
Eastwood Mall (Part of		Midfield)	35064	County)	36201
Birmingham)	35234	Fairford	36553	Forest Hills (Jefferson	
Ebenezer	35179	Fairhope	36532*	County)	35064
Echo	36350		36533†	Forest Hills (Lauderdale	
Echola	35457	Fairmont	35611	County)	35630
Echols Crossroads	35670	Fairoaks	35477	Forest Hills (Talladega	
Echols Hills (Part of		Fairview (Chilton County)	35045	County)	35044
Huntsville)	35801	Fairview (Coffee County)	35323	Forest Home	36030
Eclectic	36024	Fairview (Conecuh County)	36401		

* Area Zip Code   † Post Office Boxes

* Area Zip Code   † Post Office Boxes

Place	ZIP
Henagar	35978
Henderson	36035
Hendrick Mill	35121
Hendrix	35121
Henryville	35976
Henson Springs	35544
Herbert	36401
Heron Bay	36523
Hester Heights (Part of Russellville)	35653
Hickory	35442
Hickory Flat	36274
Hickory Grove	35650
Hickory Hills (Lauderdale County)	35630
Hickory Hills (Morgan County)	35603
Hideaway Hills	35645
Higdon	35979
High Bluff	36344
Highland (Part of Lineville)	36266
Highland Home	36041
Highland Lake	35121
Highland Park (Part of Montgomery)	35107
Highmound	35980
High Point (DeKalb County)	35989
High Point (Marshall County)	35950
High Ridge	36089
Hightogy	35592
Hightower	36263
Hillandale (Part of Huntsville)	35805
Hillard	35587
Hillman	35020
Hillman Gardens	35020
Hillman Park	35020
Hillsboro (Lawrence County)	35643
Hillsboro (Madison County)	35761
Hillsdale (Part of Jasper)	35501
Hilltop (Part of Bessemer)	35020
Hillview	35214
Hinton	39355
Hirsch	36871
Hissop	35089
Hobbs Island	35803
Hobgood	35674
Hoboken (Barbour County)	36027
Hoboken (Marengo County)	36782
Hobson	36518
Hobson City	36201
Hodge	35744
Hodges	35571
Hodges Store	35619
Hodgesville	36301
Hodgewood	36921
Hogglesville	35474
Hog Jaw	35016
Hokes Bluff	35903
Holiday Homes (Part of Huntsville)	35807
Holiday Park Estates	35215
Holland Gin	35620
Holley Crossroads	36272
Hollins	35082
Hollis Crossroads	36264
Holly Grove	35587
Holly Pond	35083
Holly Springs	35146
Hollytree	35751
Hollywood (Jackson County)	35752
Hollywood (Jefferson County)	35209
Holman	36503
Holman Prison	36502
Holt	35404
Holt Junction (Part of Tuscaloosa)	35401
Holtville	36022
Holy Trinity	36859
Homewood	35209
Honoraville	36042
Hoods Crossroads	35121
Hoover (Jefferson County)	35216
Hoover (Madison County)	35749
Hope Hull	36043
Hopewell (Cherokee County)	35959
Hopewell (Cleburne County)	36264
Hopewell (DeKalb County)	35950
Hopewell (Jefferson County)	35020
Hoppes	35535
Hornady	36039
Horn Hill	36467
Horton	35980
Hortons Mill	35121
Houston	35572
Howard	35549
Howells Cross Roads	35960
Howelton	35952
Howton	35453
Hubbertville (Part of Glen Allen)	35555
Hudson Gardens (Part of Lipscomb)	35020
Hudson Settlement	35501
Hueytown	35023
Hueytown Crest (Part of Hueytown)	35020
Huffman (Part of Birmingham)	35215
Huffman Gardens (Part of Birmingham)	35215
Hugo	36783
Huguley	36854
Hulaco	35087
Hull (Part of Sumiton)	35063
Humpton	35776
Hunter (Part of Montgomery)	36108
Huntsville	35801-24
For specific Huntsville Zip Codes call (205) 461-6602, or your local postmaster.	
Huntsville Park (Part of Huntsville)	35807
Hurricane	36507
Hurtsboro	36860
Hustleville	35950
Hustontown	35645
Huxford	36543
Hyatt	35980
Hybart	36444
Hytop	35768
Idaho	36251
Ider	35981
Independence	36067
Indian Creek	36061
Indian Hill (Part of Childersburg)	35044
Indian Hills	35244
Indian Springs (Lauderdale County)	35630
Indian Springs (Mobile County)	36613
Indian Valley	35244
Industrial City (Part of Hueytown)	35023
Industry	36033
Inglenook (Part of Birmingham)	35217
Ingram	35474
Inland	35121
Inmanfield	35540
Ino	36453
Institute	36778
Interburan Heights (Part of Fairfield)	35064
Inverness (Bullock County)	36089
Inverness (Shelby County)	35242
Ironaton	36268
Iron City	36201
Irondale	35210
Irvington	35544
Isabella	36750
Isbell	35653
Ishkooda (Part of Birmingham)	35211
Isney	36919
Ivalee	35954
Ivanhoe (Part of Birmingham)	35222
Jachin	36910
Jack	36346
Jackson (Choctaw County)	36921
Jackson (Clarke County)	36545
Jackson Heights (Part of Mobile)	36609
Jackson Oak	36526
Jacksons Gap	36861
Jacksonville	36265
Jack Springs	36502
Jagger	35578
Jamestown	35973
Jamesville	36879
Jarrett (Part of Valley)	36854
Jasper	35501*
	35502†
Java	36010
Jay Villa	36401
Jeddo	36480
Jeff	35806
Jefferson	36745
Jefferson Hills (Part of Birmingham)	35217
Jefferson Park	35210
Jemison	35085
Jena	35480
Jenifer	36268
Jericho	36756
Jernigan	36851
Jerusalem Heights	35405
Joe Wheeler Dam	35672
Johnsons Crossing	35077
Johnsonville	36401
Jones	36749
Jonesboro (Baldwin County)	36526
Jonesboro (Franklin County)	35653
Jonesboro (Jefferson County)	35020
Jones Chapel	35057
Jones Crossroads	35611
Jones Valley (Part of Birmingham)	35211
Jones Valley Estates (Part of Huntsville)	35802
Joppa	35087
Joquin	36035
Jordan (Elmore County)	36092
Jordan (Washington County)	36518
Jordans Mill	35593
Josephine	36530
Joseph Springs	36201
Josie	36005
Julia Tutwiler Prison for Women	36092
Kahatchie	35044
Kansas	35573
Kaolin (Part of Phenix City)	36867
Kaulton (Part of Tuscaloosa)	35401
Keego	36426
Keener	35954
Kellerman	35468
Kelly	36322
Kelly Springs (Part of Dothan)	36301
Kellyton	35089
Kendale Gardens	35630
Kennedy	35574
Kent (Elmore County)	36045
Kent (Pike County)	36035
Kenwood	35226
Ketona (Part of Tarrant)	35217
Key	35960
Keyno	35089
Keys Mill	35761
Keystone (Part of Pelham)	35007
Keyton	36330
Kilby (Part of Montgomery)	36114
Kilby Corrections Facility	36109
Kilgore	35062
Killen	35645
Killough Springs (Part of Birmingham)	35235
Kilpatrick	35950
Kimberly	35091
Kimbrel	35111
Kimbrough	36769
Kincheon	35045
Kings Landing (Baldwin County)	36567
Kings Landing (Dallas County)	36775
Kingston (Part of Birmingham)	35234
Kingsway Terrace (Part of Birmingham)	35206
Kingtown	35652
Kingville	35574
Kinsey	36301
Kinston	36453
Kinterbish	36907
Kirbytown	35755
Kirk	35466
Kirkland	36426
Kirklands Crossroads	36345
Kirks Grove	35960
Klein	35078
Klondike	35580
Knightens Crossroads	36272
Knoxville	35469
Koenton	36558
Kowaliga Beach	35010
Krafton (Part of Prichard)	36610
Kyles	35746
Kymulga	35014
Laceys Chapel	35020
Laceys Spring	35754
Lacon	35622
Ladiga	36272
Ladonia (Russell County)	36867
Lafayette	36862
Lagoon Park (Part of Montgomery)	36117
Lake Coves	35630
Lake Drive Estates (Part of Homewood)	35209
Lake Forest	36526
Lake Purdy	35242
Lakeside Acres	35645
Lakeside Highlands (Part of Florence)	35630
Lakeview (DeKalb County)	35971
Lakeview (Marshall County)	35976

* Area Zip Code   † Post Office Boxes

Name	ZIP
Lakeview Highlands (Part of Muscle Shoals)	35660
Lakewood (Jefferson County) ...	35234
Lakewood (Limestone County) ...	35611
Lakewood (Madison County) ...	35810
Lakewood Estates (Part of Bessemer)	35020
Lamison	36728
Land	36904
Landersville	35650
Lands Crossroads (Part of Rainsville)	35986
Lane Springs	35616
Lanett	36863
Langdale (Part of Valley) ..	36854
Langston.................	35755
Langtown	35650
Laniers	35014
Lapine (Crenshaw County)	36041
Lapine (Montgomery County) ...	36046
La Place	36075
Larkinsville	35768
Larkwood	35215
Lasca	36784
Latham	36579
Lathamville	35962
Lattiwood	35950
Lauderdale Beach	35630
Laurendine	36582
Lavaca	36911
Lawley	36793
Lawrence	35959
Lawrence Cove	35621
Lawrence Mill	35555
Lawrenceville	36310
Leatherwood	36201
Lebanon (Cleburne County)	36269
Lebanon (DeKalb County) ...	35961
Lecta	36264
Leeds	35094
Leeds Mineral Well (Part of Leeds)	35094
Leesburg	35983
Leesdale (Part of Falkville) .	35622
Leggtown	35620
Le Grand	36105
Leighton	35646
Lenlock (Part of Anniston) .	36201
Lenox...................	36454
Leon....................	36028
Leroy	36548
Leslie	36790
Lester	35647
Letcher	35776
Letchers	36201
Letohatchee	36047
Level Plains	36322
Levelroad	36276
Levert...................	36779
Lewis	36350
Lewisburg (Part of Birmingham)	35207
Lewiston	35462
Lexington	35648
Liberty (Blount County)	35031
Liberty (Butler County)	36037
Liberty (DeKalb County) ...	35957
Liberty City	36866
Liberty Highlands	35210
Liberty Hill (Franklin County)	35581
Liberty Hill (Jackson County) ...	35966
Libertyville	36420
Lightwood	36022
Ligon Springs	35653
Lillian	36549
Lily Flag (Part of Huntsville)	35802
Lime	36274
Lime Kiln	35616
Limestone	36460
Lim Rock	35776
Lincoln (Madison County) ..	35810
Lincoln (Talladega County) .	35096
Lincoya Estates (Part of Vestavia Hills)	35216
Lindbergh	35073
Linden	36748
Lineville	36266
Linwood	36081
Lipscomb	35020
Lisman	36912
Little Oak	36081
Little River (Baldwin County)	36550
Little River (Cherokee County) ...	35959
Little Rock	36502
Little Shawmut	36863
Little Texas..............	36083
Littleton (Etowah County) ..	35954
Littleton (Jefferson County)	35073
Littleville (Colbert County) .	35653
Littleville (Winston County)	35565
Live Oak Landing	36507
Livingston	35470
Loachapoka.............	36865
Loango	36474
Locke Crossroads	35620
Lockhart	36455
Lock Six	35645
Lock Three	35652
Locust Fork	35097
Loflin	36851
Logan	35098
Logton..................	36081
Lola City	35173
Lomax	35045
London (Conecuh County) .	36432
London (Montgomery County) ...	36064
Long Island	35958
Longleaf Estates (Part of Decatur)	35603
Longview (Cullman County)	35179
Longview (Shelby County) .	35137
Longwood (Part of Huntsville)	35801
Loop (Cherokee County)...	35959
Loop (Mobile County).....	36606
Loree	36401
Lott	36613
Lottie	36502
Louisville	36048
Love Hill	36312
Lovelace Crossroads	35630
Loveless	35967
Loveless Park	35020
Lovick	35173
Lower Peach Tree	36751
Lowery..................	36453
Lowerytown	35184
Low Gap	35120
Lowndesboro	36752
Lowry Mill	36346
Loxley	36551
Loxley Heights	36551
Lucille	35184
Lugo	36027
Lumbull	35543
Luttrell	35971
Luverne	36049
Lydia	35967
Lyeffion	36401
Lynn	35575
Lynn Crossing............	35073
Lynndale (Part of Montgomery)...........	36105
Lynn Haven (Part of Tuscaloosa)...........	35404
Lynns Park	35550
Lytle	36477
Mabson	36360
McCalla	35111
McClure Town...........	36081
McCollum	35501
McCord Crossroads	35960
McCulley Hill	35184
McCullough	36502
McDonald Chapel	35224
McDowell	35470
Macedonia (Cleburne County) ...	36273
Macedonia (Jackson County) ...	35771
Macedonia (Montgomery County) ...	36036
Macedonia (Walker County)	35501
McElderry	36268
McFarland Mall (Part of Tuscaloosa)...........	35405
McGhees Bend	35960
McGinty (Part of Valley) ...	36854
McIntosh	36553
McKenzie	36456
McKestes	35963
McKinley	36728
McLarty.................	35980
McLendon	36851
McMullen	35442
Macon	36271
McQueen	36066
McShan	35471
McVay	36451
McVille	35950
McWilliams	36753
Madison	35758
Madison Crossroads.......	35772
Madison Square Mall (Part of Huntsville)	35806
Madrid	36320
Magazine (Part of Mobile) .	36610
Magnolia	36754
Magnolia Beach (Part of Fairhope)	36532
Magnolia Springs	36555
Magnolia Terminal	36722
Majestic	35116
Malbis	36526
Malcolm.................	36556
Mall, The (Part of Huntsville)	35801
Malone..................	36276
Malta	36502
Malvern	36349
Mamie	36052
Manack	36752
Manchester	35501
Manila	36586
Manley Crossroads	35758
Manningham	36037
Mansion View	35630
Mantua	35462
Maple Hill	38449
Maplesville	36750
Maplewood (Jefferson County) ...	35094
Maplewood (Madison County) ...	35758
Marble City Heights (Part of Sylacauga)	35150
Marble Valley	35150
Marbury	36051
Marcoot	36862
Margaret	35112
Margerum	35616
Marietta	35579
Marion	36756
Marion Junction	36759
Markeeta	35094
Marl....................	36477
Marley Mill	36360
Marlow..................	36580
Mars Hill (Part of Florence)	35630
Martins (Part of Birmingham)	35208
Martintown	35752
Martinville	36502
Martling	35950
Marvel	35115
Marvyn	36801
Marylee	35501
Maryville	35954
Massey	35619
Masterson Mill	35650
Mathews	36052
Mattawana	35121
Maud	35616
Maxine	35130
Maxwell	35401
Maxwellborn	36272
Maxwell Heights (Part of Montgomery)	36113
Mayes Crossroads	35903
Mayfair (Jefferson County)	35209
Mayfair (Madison County) .	35801
Maylene (Part of Alabaster)	35007
Maynards Cove	35768
Maysville	35748
Maytown	35118
Meadowbrook	35242
Meadow Crossroads	36874
Meadow Hills (Part of Huntsville)	35810
Mechanicsville	36874
Media	35062
Meeksville...............	36081
Megargel	36457
Mehama	35653
Mellow Valley	36255
Melrose (Conecuh County)	36401
Melrose (Pickens County) .	35471
Melton	36776
Meltonsville	35755
Melville	35541
Melvin	36913
Memphis	39341
Mentone	35984
Mercury	35811
Meridianville	35759
Merry	36064
Mertz (Part of Mobile)......	36606
Mexboro	36445
Mexia	36458
Mexia Crossing	36458
Micaville	36264
Middle Brooks Cross Roads	36879
Middleton	36271
Midfield	35228
Midland City.............	36350
Midtown (Part of Mobile)...	36640
Midway (Bullock County) ..	36053
Midway (Butler County) ...	36042
Midway (Chilton County) ...	36051

	ZIP
Midway (Clay County)	35072
Midway (Lawrence County)	35650
Midway (Monroe County)	36768
Miflin	36530
Mignon	35150
Miles (Part of Fairfield)	35064
Millbrook	36054
Miller	36748
Millers Ferry	36760
Millertown	36613
Millerville	36267
Milport	35576
Milry	36558
Mills Quarter's	36535
Milltown	36862
Mill Village (Part of Guntersville)	35976
Milstead	36075
Milton	36749
Mineral Springs	35085
Minooka	35040
Minor	35224
Minor Terrace (Part of Childersburg)	35044
Minter	36761
Minvale (Part of Fort Payne)	35967
Mitchell	36029
Mitchell Town	35645
Mobile	36601-95
For specific Mobile Zip Codes call (205) 694-5917, or your local postmaster.	
Mobile Festival Centre (Part of Mobile)	36609
Mobile Junction	35023
Moffett	36587
Mollie	36906
Molloy	35586
Mon Louis	36523
Monroeville	36460*
	36461†
Monrovia	35806
Montague	35740
Monterey	36030
Monterey Heights	36877
Monte-Sano (Part of Birmingham)	35228
Montevallo	35115
Monte Vista (Part of Gadsden)	35901
Montgomery	36101-99
For specific Montgomery Zip Codes call (205) 244-7500, or your local postmaster.	
Montgomery Mall (Part of Montgomery)	36116
Monticello	36005
Montrose	36559
Moody	35094
Moorefield	36862
Moores Bridge	35476
Moores Crossroad	35971
Moores Crossroads	36274
Moores Mill	35811
Mooresville	35649
Moreland	35572
Morgan (Part of Bessemer)	35020
Morgan City	35175
Moriah	35136
Morningside	35215
Morris	35116
Morvin	36762
Moshat	35960
Mosses	36040
Mossy Grove	36081
Mostellers	35143
Motley	36276
Moulton	35650
Moulton Heights (Part of Decatur)	35601
Moundville	35474
Mountainboro	35957
Mountain Brook (Jefferson County)	35223
Mountain Brook (Madison County)	35801
Mountain Brook Village (Part of Mountain Brook)	35223
Mountain Chest (Part of Guntersville)	35976
Mountain Creek	36051
Mountain Grove	35031
Mountain Home	35673
Mountain Park (Part of Birmingham)	35217
Mountain View (Part of Guntersville)	35976
Mountain Woods (Part of Vestavia Hills)	35216
Mountain Woods Park (Part of Vestavia Hills)	35216
Mount Andrew	36053

	ZIP
Mount Carmel (Jackson County)	35740
Mount Carmel (Marshall County)	35976
Mount Carmel (Montgomery County)	36046
Mount Hebron (Greene County)	35443
Mount Hebron (Marshall County)	35957
Mount Hester	35616
Mount Hope	35651
Mount Ida	36009
Mount Jefferson	36801
Mount Meigs	36057
Mount Nebo	36785
Mount Olive (Coosa County)	35072
Mount Olive (Jefferson County)	35117
Mount Pleasant (Coffee County)	36330
Mount Pleasant (Monroe County)	36480
Mount Rozell	35647
Mount Sinai	36113
Mount Star	35653
Mount Sterling	36904
Mount Union	36401
Mount Vernon (Cullman County)	35179
Mount Vernon (DeKalb County)	35967
Mount Vernon (Fayette County)	35555
Mount Vernon (Mobile County)	36560
Mount Willing	36032
Mount Zion	36069
Muck City	35650
Mud Creek (Jackson County)	35752
Mud Creek (Jefferson County)	35006
Mulga	35118
Mulga Mine	35118
Munford	36268
Murphy	35677
Murrays Chapel	35146
Muscadine	36269
Muscadine Junction	36269
Muscle Shoals	35661
Muscoda	35020
Mynot	35616
Myrick Chapel	36022
Myrtlewood	36763
Nadawah	36726
Naftel	36046
Nanafalia	36764
Nances Creek	36272
Napier Field	36301
Napoleon	36280
Nat	35776
Natchez	36425
Nathan (Part of Arley)	35541
Natural Bridge	35577
Nauvoo	35578
Navco (Part of Mobile)	36605
Nebo	35758
Nectar	35049
Needham	36915
Needmore (Marshall County)	35957
Needmore (Pike County)	36081
Needmore (Winston County)	35565
Neel	35640
Neenah	36726
Nellie	36726
Neshota (Part of Mobile)	36605
Nesmith (Cullman County)	35057
Ne Smith (Lawrence County)	35672
Nettleboro	36436
Newbern	36765
Newberry Crossroads	35960
New Brashier Chapel	35950
New Brockton	36351
Newburg	35653
New Castle	35119
New Center	35640
New Dora (Part of Dora)	35062
Newell	36270
New Georgia	35540
New Haven	35758
New Hill (Part of Lipscomb)	35020
New Home	35978
New Hope (Coffee County)	36010
New Hope (Cullman County)	35083
New Hope (Jackson County)	35768

	ZIP
New Hope (Madison County)	35760
New Hope (Shelby County)	35243
New Hopewell	36264
New Lexington	35546
New London	35054
New Market	35761
New Moon	35973
New Prospect (Autauga County)	36051
New Prospect (Hale County)	35441
New Sharon	35750
New Site	35010
Newsome (Part of Rainsville)	35986
Newton (Dale County)	36352
Newton (Houston County)	36301
Newtonville	35555
Newtown (Franklin County)	35653
New Town (Jackson County)	35772
Newville	36353
Nichburg	36475
Nicholsville	36784
Nitrate City	35660
Nixburg	36026
Nix Mill	35581
Nixons Chapel	35980
Noah	35960
Nokomis	36502
Nolandale (Part of Madison)	35758
Nolan Hills (Part of Madison)	35758
Normal (Part of Huntsville)	35762
Normandale Shopping Center (Part of Montgomery)	36111
North Arab (Part of Arab)	35016
North Athens (Part of Athens)	35611
North Birmingham (Part of Birmingham)	35207
North Courtland	35618
North Daye Hill	35749
North Elmore	36025
North Florence (Part of Florence)	35630
North Highlands (Part of Hueytown)	35020
North Johns	35006
North Mobile (Part of Chickasaw)	36611
Northport	35476
Northside (Part of Dothan)	36304
Northside Acres	35806
Northside Mall (Part of Dothan)	36303
North Smithfield Estates ...	35214
North Smithfield Manor (Part of Birmingham)	35207
North Vinemont	35179
North Walter	35055
Northwood Hills (Part of Florence)	35630
Norton	35803
Norwood (Part of Birmingham)	35234
Notasulga	36866
Nottingham	35014
Nuckols	36856
Nymph	36401
Oak	36535
Oak Bowery	36862
Oak Crossing (Part of Leeds)	35094
Oakdale	35611
Oakdale Acres	35611
Oak Grove (Autauga County)	36067
Oak Grove (Mobile County)	36613
Oak Grove (Talladega County)	35150
Oak Grove (Chilton County)	35085
Oak Grove (Franklin County)	35653
Oak Grove (Jefferson County)	35006
Oak Grove (Limestone County)	35739
Oak Hill (DeKalb County)	35962
Oak Hill (Wilcox County) ...	36766
Oakhurst (Part of Birmingham)	35207
Oakland	35630
Oakleigh Estates (Part of Gadsden)	35901
Oak Level	36262
Oakman	35579
Oakmulgee	36793
Oak Ridge (Morgan County)	35640

	ZIP
Oak Ridge (St. Clair County)	35125
Oak Ridge Park (Part of Birmingham)	35212
Oakville (Jefferson County)	35206
Oakville (Lawrence County)	35619
Oakwood (Part of Bessemer)	35020
Oakwood College	35896
Oakworth (Part of Decatur)	35601
Oaky Grove	36353
Oaky Streak	36037
Octagon	36748
Odena	35150
Oden Ridge	35621
Odenville	35120
Odom	36456
Ofelia	36266
Ohatchee	36271
Old Bethel	35646
Old Burleson	35593
Old Davistown	36201
Old Fabius	35966
Oldfield (Part of Sylacauga)	35150
Old Jonesboro	35215
Old Kingston	36067
Old Maylene (Part of Alabaster)	35114
Old Monrovia	35806
Old Nauvoo	35653
Old Samuel	36908
Old Spring Hill	36742
Old Texas	36768
Old Town (Conecuh County)	36401
Old Town (Dallas County)	36785
Oleander	35175
Oliver	35652
Ollie	36460
Olney	35442
Olustee	36081
Omaha	36274
O'Neal	35611
Oneonta	35121
Onycha	36467
Opelika	36801-03
For specific Opelika Zip Codes call (205) 745-3561, or your local postmaster.	
Opine (Clarke County)	36784
Opine (Covington County)	36467
Opp	36467
Orange Beach	36561
Orchard (Part of Mobile)	36618
Ord (Part of Gadsden)	35901
Orion	36081
Orrville (Dallas County)	36767
Orrville (Limestone County)	35671
Osanippa	36854
Osborn	36779
Oswichee	36856
Our Town	35010
Overbrook	35150
Overlook (Part of Mobile)	36608
Overton	35210
Owassa	36401
Owens Cross Roads	35763
Owenton (Part of Birmingham)	35204
Oxford	36203
Oxford Lake (Part of Oxford)	36201
Oxmoor	35211
Oyster Bay	36535
Ozark	36360*
	36361†
Painter	35962
Paint Rock	35764
Palestine	36262
Palmerdale	35123
Palmers Crossroads	36480
Palmetto	35481
Palmetto Beach	36542
Palos	35130
Panola (Crenshaw County)	36046
Panola (Sumter County)	35477
Pansey	36370
Paran	36274
Park City	35526
Parkdale	35072
Park Hill (Part of Pell City)	35125
Parkland (Part of Jasper)	35501
Parkway City (Part of Huntsville)	35801
Parkway Estates (Part of Huntsville)	35802
Parkwood	35020
Parrish	35580
Partridge Crossroads	35180
Patsburg	36049
Patton	35579

	ZIP
Patton Chapel (Part of Hoover)	35216
Paul	36469
Pauls Hill	35020
Pawnee	35217
Peacock	36451
Pea Ridge (Escambia County)	36426
Pea Ridge (Fayette County)	35546
Pea Ridge (Madison County)	35801
Pea Ridge (Marion County)	35563
Pea Ridge (Shelby County)	35115
Pearson	35456
Pebble	35565
Peeks Corner	35961
Peeks Hill	36271
Peets Corner	35611
Pelham	35124
Pelham Heights (Part of Anniston)	36201
Pell City	35125
Penfield Heights (Part of Birmingham)	35217
Penn	35619
Pennington	36916
Pennsylvania (Part of Satsuma)	36572
Penton	36862
Pentonville	35136
Pepperell (Part of Opelika)	36801
Perdido	36562
Perdido Beach	36530
Perdue Hill	36470
Perote	36061
Perry Chapel	36586
Perry Store	36453
Perryville	36701
Peterman	36471
Peterson	35478
Petersville	35633
Petrey	36062
Petronia	36785
Pettusville	35620
Peytonia Points	35660
Phalin	35456
Phelan	35055
Phenix City	36867-69
For specific Phenix City Zip Codes call (205) 298-7871, or your local postmaster.	
Phil Campbell	35581
Phillips Estates (Part of Bessemer)	35020
Phillipsville	36507
Phoenixville (Part of Birmingham)	35221
Pickensville	35447
Pickering	36758
Piedmont (Calhoun County)	36272
Piedmont (Madison County)	35801
Piedmont Springs	36272
Pierce	36587
Pigeon Creek	36037
Pike Road	36064
Pikeville	35768
Pilgrims Rest (Part of Southside)	35901
Pinckard	36371
Pinder Hill	35772
Pine Apple	36768
Pine Beach	36542
Pinebelt	36767
Pine Dale (Limestone County)	35739
Pinedale (Montgomery County)	36106
Pinedale Acres (Lauderdale County)	35645
Pinedale Acres (Limestone County)	35611
Pinedale Shores	35953
Pine Flat	36022
Pine Grove (Baldwin County)	36507
Pine Grove (Bullock County)	36053
Pine Grove (Cherokee County)	35960
Pine Grove (Lee County)	36801
Pine Grove (Tallapoosa County)	36850
Pine Hill (Randolph County)	36263
Pine Hill (Wilcox County)	36769
Pine Level (Autauga County)	36022
Pine Level (Coffee County)	36323
Pine Level (Montgomery County)	36065
Pine Mountain	35133
Pine Orchard	36471
Pine Ridge	35967
Pineview (Part of Irondale)	35210

	ZIP
Pinewood Terrace (Part of Childersburg)	35044
Piney	35960
Piney Bend	35593
Piney Chapel	35611
Piney Grove (Lawrence County)	35619
Piney Grove (Marion County)	35548
Piney Woods	36262
Pinkeyville	35072
Pinkney City	35214
Pinnell	36850
Pinson	35126
Pinson-Clay-Chalkville	35215
Pintlalla	36043
Pisgah (Jackson County)	35765
Pisgah (Limestone County)	35773
Pisgah (Montgomery County)	36036
Pittsview	36871
Plainview (Cleburne County)	36264
Plainview (DeKalb County)	35986
Plant City	36863
Plantersville (Dallas County)	36758
Plantersville (Talladega County)	35014
Plateau (Part of Prichard)	36610
Plaza De Malaga (Part of Mobile)	36685
Pleasant Acres	35811
Pleasant Gap	36272
Pleasant Grove (Chilton County)	35085
Pleasant Grove (Jackson County)	35772
Pleasant Grove (Jefferson County)	35127
Pleasant Grove (Marshall County)	35950
Pleasant Hill (Barbour County)	36027
Pleasant Hill (Choctaw County)	36908
Pleasant Hill (Dallas County)	36701
Pleasant Hill (Escambia County)	36502
Pleasant Hill (Franklin County)	35585
Pleasant Hill (Jefferson County)	35020
Pleasant Home	36420
Pleasant Plains	36312
Pleasant Ridge (Franklin County)	35653
Pleasant Ridge (Greene County)	35462
Pleasant Ridge (Pike County)	36034
Pleasant Site	35582
Pletcher	36750
Plevna	35761
Poarch	36502
Poarch Creek Indian Reservation	36502
Pocahontas	35549
Pogo	35582
Point Clear	36564
Polk	36785
Pollard	36441
Pollards Bend	35983
Ponderosa Estates	36575
Ponders	36853
Pondville	35034
Pool	35619
Pooles Crossroads	36274
Pools Crossroads	35045
Pope	36769
Poplarridge	35760
Poplar Springs (Marshall County)	35950
Poplar Springs (Winston County)	35578
Port Birmingham	35118
Porter	35005
Portersville	35961
Posey Mill	35565
Poseys Crossroads	36067
Postoak	36089
Potash	36274
Potter	36701
Powderly (Part of Birmingham)	35211
Powderly Hills (Part of Birmingham)	35211
Powell	35971
Powers	35474
Powhatan	35118
Powledge	36874
Praco	35130
Prairie	36771
Prairieville	36742

	ZIP
Pratt City (Part of Birmingham)	35214
Prattmont (Part of Prattville)	36067
Pratts	36016
Prattville	36066-67
For specific Prattville Zip Codes call (205) 365-6467, or your local postmaster.	
Prescott	35125
Preston	35768
Prestwick	36548
Priceville	35601
Prichard	36610
Pride	35674
Primitive Ridge	35184
Princeton	35766
Pronto	36081
Prospect	35578
Providence (Butler County)	36033
Providence (Cullman County)	35179
Providence (Marengo County)	36742
Providence (Walker County)	35579
Prudence	36871
Pruitton	35630
Pulaski Pike (Part of Huntsville)	35810
Pulltight	35548
Pumpkin Center (DeKalb County)	35967
Pumpkin Center (Morgan County)	35619
Pumpkin Center (Walker County)	35130
Pushmataha	36912
Putnam	36784
Pyriton	36266
Queenstown	35173
Quintard Mall (Part of Oxford)	36201
Quinton	35130
Quintown	35130
Rabb	36401
Rabbittown (Calhoun County)	36272
Rabbit Town (Marshall County)	35950
Rabbittown (Winston County)	35565
Rabun	36507
Ragland	35131
Raimund	35020
Rainbow	35758
Rainbow City	35906
Rainbow Mountain Heights (Madison County)	35758
Rainsville	35986
Ralph	35480
Ramer	36069
Ranburne	36273
Randolph	36792
Range	36473
Rash	35772
Rayburn (Part of Guntersville)	35976
Read's Mill	36279
Red Bank	35672
Red Bay	35582
Reddock Springs	36037
Red Eagle Honor Farm	36101
Red Hill (Blount County)	35063
Red Hill (Elmore County)	36078
Red Hill (Marshall County)	35976
Redland Heights (Part of Valley)	36854
Red Level	36474
Redmont Park (Part of Mountain Brook)	35213
Red Ore	35020
Red Rock	35674
Red Rock Junction	35616
Redstone Arsenal (census designated place)	35898
Redstone Arsenal	35809
Redtown	36502
Reece City	35954
Reedtown (Part of Russellville)	35653
Reeltown	36078
Reform	35481
Regency (Part of Florence)	35630
Regent Forest	35226
Rehobeth	36301
Rehoboth	36720
Reid	35611
Remlap	35133
Renfroe	35160
Reno	35111
Repton	36475
Republic	35214
Rhoades	36453

	ZIP
Rhodesville	35630
Rice	35201
Richmond	36761
Richmond Hills (Part of Tuscumbia)	35674
Rideout Village (Part of Huntsville)	35806
Riderwood	36904
Ridgecrest	36105
Ridgeville (Butler County)	36030
Ridgeville (Etowah County)	35954
Ringgold	35973
Ripley	35611
Riverbend	35184
Riverdale (Part of Mentone)	35984
River Falls	36476
Rivermont (Colbert County)	35660
Rivermont (Lauderdale County)	35630
River Park	36532
Riverside (Blount County)	35031
Riverside (St. Clair County)	35135
Riverton	35616
River View (Chambers County)	36854
Riverview (Chambers County)	36854
Riverview (Escambia County)	36426
Riverview (Tuscaloosa County)	35401
Riverwood (Part of Tuscaloosa)	35406
Roanoke	36274
Roanoke Junction (Part of Opelika)	36801
Roba	36089
Robbins Crossroads	35062
Roberta	35040
Roberts	36420
Robertsdale	36567
Robinsons	36752
Robinson Springs	36025
Robinsonville	36502
Robinwood	35217
Rock City (Jackson County)	35771
Rock City (Marion County)	35594
Rockdale	35020
Rocket	35808
Rockford	35136
Rock Hill	36426
Rock House	35771
Rockledge	35954
Rock Mills	36274
Rock Run	36272
Rock Spring (Part of Glencoe)	35905
Rock Spring Quarry (Part of Glencoe)	35905
Rock Springs (Blount County)	35031
Rock Springs (Choctaw County)	36904
Rock Stand	36274
Rockville	36545
Rockwest	36726
Rockwood	35653
Rocky Head	36311
Rocky Hill	35672
Rocky Hollow	35550
Rocky Ridge	35243
Rodentown	35957
Roebuck (Part of Birmingham)	35206
Roebuck Crest Estates (Part of Birmingham)	35215
Roebuck Forest (Part of Birmingham)	35235
Roebuck Gardens (Part of Birmingham)	35235
Roebuck Park (Part of Birmingham)	35215
Roebuck Plaza	35235
Roebuck Springs (Part of Birmingham)	35206
Roebuck Terrace (Part of Birmingham)	35206
Roeton	36010
Rogersville	35652
Rolling Hills (Part of Decatur)	35603
Rollins	36022
Romar Beach	36561
Rome	36420
Romulus	35446
Roper	35173
Rosa	35121
Rosalie	35765
Roseboro	37328
Rosebud	36766
Rosedale (Part of Homewood)	35209

	ZIP
Rose Hill (Covington County)	36028
Rose Hill (Jefferson County)	35210
Rosemont (Part of Birmingham)	35221
Rose Park (Part of Florence)	35630
Rosinton	36567
Rossland City	35555
Round Hill	36784
Round Mountain	35959
Rowells Crossroad	36879
Roxana	36879
Royal	35031
Ruffner (Part of Irondale)	35210
Russell Heights (Part of Leeds)	35094
Russell Mill (Part of Alexander City)	35010
Russell Village (Part of Decatur)	35603
Russellville	35653
Rutan	36518
Ruth	35016
Rutherford	36860
Rutledge	36071
Rutledge Heights (Jefferson County)	35064
Rutledge Heights (Madison County)	35816
Ryan	35115
Ryan Crossroads	35087
Ryland	35767
Saco	36081
Safford	36773
Saginaw	35137
Sahama Village (Part of Tuscaloosa)	35401
St. Bernard	35055
St. Clair	36752
St. Clair Correctional Facility	35120
St. Clair Springs	35146
St. Elmo	36568
St. Florian	35630
Saints Crossroads	35653
St. Stephens	36569
Saks	36201
Salem (Dallas County)	36767
Salem (Fayette County)	35546
Salem (Lee County)	36874
Salem (Limestone County)	35620
Salitpa	36570
Samantha	35482
Samford University (Part of Homewood)	35229
Samson	36477
Samuels Chapel	35952
Sandfield	36081
Sandfort	36875
Sandhurst Park (Part of Huntsville)	35802
Sand Rock	35961
Sandtown	35546
Sandusky (Part of Birmingham)	35214
Sandy Creek	36850
Sandy Ridge	36047
Sanford	36420
Sanie	35120
San Souci Beach (Part of Bayou La Batre)	36509
Santuck	36092
Sapps	35447
Saragossa	35578
Saraland	36571
Saratoga (Part of Albertville)	35950
Sardine	36441
Sardis (Bullock County)	36089
Sardis (Dallas County)	36775
Sardis (Walker County)	35550
Sardis City	35957
Sardis Springs	35611
Satsuma	36572
Saucer	36030
Saville	36041
Sawyerville	36776
Sayre	35139
Scant City	35016
Scarce Grease	35647
Scenic Heights (Part of Gadsden)	35901
Schenks	36279
Schmits Mill	35096
Schuster Springs	36768
Scotland	36471
Scotrock (Part of Alabaster)	35007
Scott City	35094
Scottland	36089
Scottsboro	35768
Scranage	36502
Scranton	36313
Scyrene	36436

	ZIP
Seaboard	36522
Seacliff (Part of Fairhope)	36532
Seale	36875
Sealy Springs (Part of Cottonwood)	36320
Searight	36028
Searles	35444
Section	35771
Segco	35580
Selbrook	36108
Selfville	35133
Sellers	36046
Sellersville	36318
Selma	36701-03

For specific Selma Zip Codes call (205) 874-4678, or your local postmaster.

	ZIP
Selma Mall (Part of Selma)	36703
Selmont	36703
Selmont-West Selmont	36703
Seman	36024
Seminole	36567
Semmes	36575
Service	36919
Seven Hills	36601
Seymour Bluff	36542
Shacklesville	36033
Shades Crest Estates	35226
Shady Grove (Clay County)	35072
Shady Grove (Coffee County)	36323
Shady Grove (Franklin County)	35581
Shady Grove (Pike County)	36035
Shady Lane (Part of Huntsville)	35810
Shanghai	35611
Shannon	35142
Shawmut (Part of Valley)	36854
Shawnee	36726
Sheffield	35660-62

For specific Sheffield Zip Codes call (205) 383-0252, or your local postmaster.

	ZIP
Shelby	35143
Shellhorn	36081
Sherman Heights (Part of Anniston)	36201
Sherwood Forest (Part of Florence)	35630
Sherwood Park (Part of Huntsville)	35206
Shiloh (DeKalb County)	35967
Shiloh (Marengo County)	36754
Shiloh (Pike County)	36005
Shinebone	36266
Shingle	35581
Shoals Acres	35645
Shopton	36029
Short Creek	35118
Shorter	36075
Shorterville	36373
Shortleaf (Part of Demopolis)	36732
Shottsville	35570
Shreve	36456
Sico	35150
Siddonsville	36738
Sigma	36319
Sikesville	36276
Silas	36919
Siloam	36907
Siluria (Part of Alabaster)	35144
Silver Cross	36919
Silverhill	36576
Silver Run	36268
Simcoe	35055
Simmons Crossroads	36879
Simmsville	35043
Sims Chapel	36553
Simsville	36089
Sipsey	35584
Six Mile	35035
Six Way	35603
Skaggs Corner (Part of Ider)	35978
Skeggs Crossroads	35072
Skinem	35750
Skinnerton	36401
Skipperville	36374
Skirum	35963
Skyland (Part of Tuscaloosa)	35407
Skyline	35768
Skyline Acres	35758
Skyline Estates	35226
Sky Ranch	35226
Skyview (Part of Bessemer)	35020
Slackland	35901
Slocomb	36375
Smithfield (Part of Birmingham)	35204
Smith Hill	35184

	ZIP
Smith Institute	35957
Smiths	36877
Smiths Crossroads (Part of Glencoe)	35903
Smithson	35020
Smithsonia	35630
Smoke Rise	35133
Smut Eye	36061
Smyer	36727
Smyrna	36301
Snead	35952
Snoddy	35462
Snowdoun	36105
Snow Hill	36778
Snowtown	35062
Socapatoy	35089
Society Hill	36801
Soleo	35072
Somerville	35670
South (Covington County)	36474
South (Montgomery County)	36116
South Calera (Part of Calera)	35040
South Gadsden (Part of Gadsden)	35901
South Gate Mall (Part of Muscle Shoals)	35660
South Guntersville (Part of Guntersville)	35976
South Haleyville (Part of Haleyville)	35565
South Highlands (Part of Birmingham)	35205
South Lowell	35501
Southmont (Part of Montgomery)	36105
South Orchard	36582
South Park Estates (Part of Huntsville)	35802
South Sheffield (Part of Tuscumbia)	35674
Southside	35901
	35903

For specific Southside Zip Codes call (205) 547-6391, or your local postmaster.

	ZIP
Southtown (Part of Guntersville)	35976
Southwood (Part of Homewood)	35209
Souwilpa	36919
Spanish Fort	36527
Speake	35619
Speed	36026
Speeds Water Mill	35466
Speigener	36022
Spivey's	36535
Sprague	36069
Springbrook (Part of Tuscaloosa)	35405
Springdale (Part of Tarrant)	35217
Springdale Mall (Part of Mobile)	36606
Springfield (Clarke County)	36784
Springfield (Lauderdale County)	35652
Springfield (Randolph County)	36274
Spring Garden	36275
Spring Hill (Barbour County)	36053
Spring Hill (Mobile County)	36608
Spring Hill (Pike County)	36081
Spring Hill (Walker County)	35549
Spring Valley (Colbert County)	35674
Spring Valley (Montgomery County)	36116
Springville	35146
Springville Lake Estates	35146
Sprott	36779
Spruce Pine	35585
Standard	35580
Standing Rock	36855
Stanley	36420
Stansel	35481
Stanton	36790
Stapleton	36578
Star	35576
State Line	36320
Statesville	36703
Steele	35987
Steele Crossing	37328
Steelwood	36551
Steenson Hollow (Part of Muscle Shoals)	35660
Steiner (Part of Montgomery)	36111
Sterrett	35147
Stevenson	35772
Stewart	35441
Stewartsville	35150
Stills Cross Road	36081

	ZIP
Stockdale	36268
Stockton	36579
Stokeley (Part of Andalusia)	36420
Stokes	35456
Stones	36054
Stoney Point	36022
Stotesville	35184
Stough	35555
Straight Mountain	35121
Strata	36046
Strawberry	35016
Stroud	36855
Studdards Crossroads	35549
Sturkie	36862
Suggsville	36482
Sulligent	35586
Sulphur Springs (Blount County)	35079
Sulphur Springs (DeKalb County)	30738
Sulphur Springs (Jackson County)	35966
Sulphur Springs (Madison County)	35761
Sumiton	35148
Summerdale	36580
Summerfield	36701
Summit	35031
Summit Farm	35023
Sumterville	35460
Sunflower	36581
Sunny Cove	36582
Sunny South	36769
Sunset Cove (Part of Huntsville)	35802
Sunset Mill Village (Part of Selma)	36701
Sunset Shores	36535
Sun Valley	35215
Surginer	36754
Susan Moore	35952
Suspension	36089
Suttle	36701
Swaim	35764
Swancott	35758
Swearengin	35768
Sweet Water	36782
Sycamore	35149
Sylacauga	35150
Sylvan Grove	36350
Sylvania	35988
Sylvan Springs	35118
Tabernacle (Coffee County)	36351
Tabernacle (Houston County)	36301
Tabor	35901
Taft	35973
Taits Gap	35121
Talladega	35160
Talladega Springs	35150
Tallahatta Springs	36784
Tallapoosa City (Part of Tallassee)	36078
Tallassee	36078
Tallaweka (Part of Tallassee)	36078
Talucah	35775
Tanner	35671
Tanner Crossroads	35671
Tanner Heights (Part of Hartselle)	35640
Tanner Williams	36587
Tanyard (Bullock County)	36061
Tanyard (St. Clair County)	35125
Tarentum	36010
Tarpley (Part of Birmingham)	35211
Tarrant	35217
Tarrant Heights	35217
Tasso	36767
Tattiersville	36524
Taylor	36301
Taylors Crossroads	36274
Taylorville	35405
Teals Crossroads	36311
Teasleys Mill	36052
Tecumseh	30138
Teddy	36426
Tenant	36274
Ten Broeck (Part of Lakeview)	35971
Tennala	35960
Tennille	36010
Tensaw	36579
Terese (Part of Eufaula)	36027
Terry Heights (Part of Huntsville)	35805
Texasville	36016
Thach	35501
Tharptown	35653
Thatch	35620

	ZIP		ZIP		ZIP
The Cedars (Part of Florence)	35630	Union Grove (Jefferson County)	35005	Wall Street	35758
The Highlands (Etowah County)	35901	Union Grove (Marshall County)	35175	Walnut Grove	35990
The Highlands (Madison County)	35810	Union Hill (Cleburne County)	36273	Walnut Hill	36853
Theodore	36582*	Union Hill (Limestone County)	35610	Walnut Park (Part of Gadsden)	35904
	36590†	Union Hill (Morgan County)	35622	Walter	35077
The Ridge	36460	Union Springs	36089	Wannville	35752
Thomas (Autauga County)	36067	Uniontown	36786	Ward	36922
Thomas (Jefferson County)	35214	Unity (Autauga County)	36006	Ware	36078
Thomas Acres (Part of Bessemer)	35020	Unity (Coosa County)	35183	Warrenton	35976
Thomas F. Station Correctional Center	36025	Unity (Tuscaloosa County)	35401	Warrior	35180
Thomas Hill (Part of Sylacauga)	35150	Universal Heights	35404	Warriorstand	36089
Thomaston	36783	University (Part of Tuscaloosa)	35486	Warsaw	35477
Thomasville	36784	University Mall (Part of Tuscaloosa)	35401	Waterford (Part of Newton)	36352
Thompson	36089	University of Montevallo (Part of Montevallo)	35115	Waterloo	35677
Thorn Hill	35565	University of South Alabama (Part of Mobile)	36608	Water Valley	36908
Thornton	36853	Upper Coalburg	35068	Watson (Cherokee County)	35973
Thorntontown	35652	Upper Green Hill	35630	Watson (Jefferson County)	35181
Thorsby	35171	Upshaw	35540	Watsonville	36753
Three Notch	36053	Uriah	36480	Watts Mill	36266
Threet	35617	Valdosta (Part of Tuscumbia)	35674	Wattsville	35182
Thurston	36340	Valhermoso Springs	35775	Waugh	36109
Tibbie	36583	Vallegrande	36703	Waverly	36879
Tilden	36761	Valley	36854*	Wawbeek	36502
Till	36033		36872†	Wayne	36782
Tiller Crossroads	36850	Valley Creek	35020	Wayside	35594
Tillery Crossroads	36854	Valley Creek Junction	36758	Weatherly Heights (Part of Huntsville)	35802
Tillmans Corner	36619	Valley Head	35989	Weaver	36277
Tinela	36481	Valley View	35640	Webb	36376
Titus	36080	Vance	35490	Webb Addition (Part of Scottsboro)	35768
Toadvine	35020	Vanderbilt (Part of Birmingham)	35204	Webster Chapel	35903
Toddtown	36451	Vandiver	35176	Wedgewood	36108
Tompkinsville	36916	Vangale	36782	Wedgworth	36776
Toney	35773	Vaughn	36579	Wedowee	36278
Toonersville	35652	Vaughn Corners	35758	Weed Crossroad	36009
Toulminville (Part of Mobile)	36610	Verbena	36091	Weeden Heights (Part of Florence)	35630
Town Creek	35672	Verlie (Part of Alabaster)	35007	Weeks	36453
Townley	35587	Vernledge	36049	Wegra	35130
Toxey	36921	Vernon	35592	Wehadkee	36274
Trade	35053	Vernontown	35184	Wellington	36279
Trafford	35172	Vestavia Hills	35216	Welti	35055
Travis Bridge	36401	Vestavia Hills Centre (Part of Vestavia Hills)	35216	Wende	36860
Tredegar	36265	Vesthaven (Part of Vestavia Hills)	35216	Wenonah (Part of Birmingham)	35211
Trenton	35774	Veterans Hospital (Part of Tuscaloosa)	35401	Weogufka	35183
Triana	35758	Veto	35620	Weoka	36092
Trickem	36785	Vick (Part of Centreville)	35042	Wessington	35040
Trimble	35057	Victoria	36323	West (Part of Huntsville)	35805
Trinity	35673	Vida	36067	West Alexandria	36250
Trotwood Park (Part of Birmingham)	35206	Vidette	36049	West Bend	36524
Troy	36081	Vienna	35442	West Blocton	35184
Trussville	35173	Viewpoint	35963	West End (Calhoun County)	36201
Tuckabatchie	36078	Vigo	36272	West End (Jefferson County)	35211
Tuckahoe Heights (Part of Gadsden)	35901	Village Creek (Part of Birmingham)	35207	West End (Montgomery County)	36104
Tucker Crossroads	35959	Village Springs	35126	West End-Cobbtown	36201
Tumbleton	36345	Villula	36871	West Ensley	35224
Tunnel Springs	36471	Vina	35593	Western Hills (Part of Mobile)	36618
Tupelo	35768	Vincent	35178	Western Hills Estates	35749
Turkestan	36753	Vinegar Bend	36584	Western Hills Mall (Part of Fairfield)	35064
Turkey Branch	36555	Vine Hill	36758	West Greene	35491
Turkeytown	35901	Vineland	36784	West Highlands (Part of Hueytown)	35023
Turner Crossroads	36351	Vineland Park (Part of Hueytown)	35020	West Huntsville (Part of Huntsville)	35807
Tuscaloosa	35401-07	Vinemont	35179	West Jefferson	35130
	35485-87	Vinesville (Part of Birmingham)	35208	West Lake Highlands (Part of Bessemer)	35020
For specific Tuscaloosa Zip Codes call (205) 553-6415, or your local postmaster.		Virginia	35020	Westlake Mall (Part of Bessemer)	35020
Tuscumbia	35674	Virginia Shores	35660	Westlawn (Part of Huntsville)	35807
Tuskegee	36083	Vocation	36480	West Monroeville (Part of Monroeville)	36460
Tuskegee Institute	36087†	Volanta (Part of Fairhope)	36532	Weston (Part of Hamilton)	35570
	36088*	Vredenburgh	36481	Westover	35185
Twilley Town	35130	Vulcan City (Part of Birmingham)	35207	West Point	35057
Twin	35563	Waco	35653	West Pratt (Part of Dora)	35062
Twin Oaks (Part of Montgomery)	36123	Wacoochee Valley	36874	West Sayre	35062
Twinsprings	36027	Wadley	36276	West Selmont	36703
Tyler	36785	Wadsworth	36022	West Side (Jefferson County)	35020
Tyler Crossroads	36048	Wagar	36585	West Side (Montgomery County)	36108
Tyson	36043	Wagarville	36585	West Wellington	36279
Tysonville	36075	Wahouma (Part of Birmingham)	35206	Westwood	35005
Uchee	36858	Walco (Part of Sylacauga)	35150	Wetumpka	36092
Underwood (Lauderdale County)	35630	Waldo	35160	Whatley	36482
Underwood (Shelby County)	35115	Walker Chapel (Part of Fultondale)	35068	Wheat	35053
Underwood Crossroads	35646	Walkers Corner	35055	Wheeler	35618
Underwood-Petersville	35630	Walker Springs	36586	Wheelerville (Part of Mobile)	36608
Union (Etowah County)	35957	Walkerton (Part of Pell City)	35125	Whistler (Part of Mobile)	36612
Union (Greene County)	35462	Wallace	36426	White City (Autauga County)	36051
Union (Henry County)	36310	Walley	36584	White City (Cullman County)	35077
Union (Morgan County)	35670	Wallsboro	36092	White Hall	36040
Union (Tallapoosa County)	36853				
Union Academy	36330				
Union Grove (Chilton County)	35085				
Union Grove (Cullman County)	35083				

* Area Zip Code   † Post Office Boxes

	ZIP
Whitehead	35652
Whitehouse	35565
Whitehouse Forks	36507
Whiteoak (Colbert County)	35646
White Oak (Henry County)	36310
Whiteoak (Marshall County)	35950
White Plains (Calhoun County)	36201
White Plains (Chambers County)	36862
Whites Bluff	36767
Whitesboro	35957
Whitesburg Estates (Part of Huntsville)	35802
Whites Chapel (Part of Moody)	35173
Whites Gap	36265
Whitesville	35957
Whitfield	36925
Whitney (Part of Ashville)	35953
Whiton	35962
Whorton	35960
Wicksburg	36352
Wiggins (Part of Babbie)	36420
Wigginsville	35611
Wiginton	35564
Wilburn	35033
Wiley (Montgomery County)	36105
Wiley (Tuscaloosa County)	35501
Wilkes (Part of Midfield)	35064
Wilkinstown	36081
Williamstown	35580
Willowbrook (Part of Huntsville)	35802
Willow Springs	36092
Wills Crossroads	36310
Wills Valley	35967
Wilmer	36587

	ZIP
Wilson Lake Shores	35660
Wilson Quarters	36303
Wilsonville	35186
Wilton	35187
Wimberly	36921
Winburn	35094
Windham Springs	35546
Windsor Highlands (Part of Homewood)	35209
Winfield	35594
Wing	36483
Wingard	36035
Winn	36545
Winninger	35776
Winslow	36003
Winterboro	35014
Winton	35670
Wolf Creek	35125
Wolf Springs	35672
Womack Hill	36908
Woodaire Estates	35215
Woodbluff	36727
Wooddale	35244
Woodford	35470
Woodland (Macon County)	36866
Woodland (Randolph County)	36280
Woodland Forest	35405
Woodland Lake	35111
Woodlawn (Part of Birmingham)	35212
Woodlawn Heights (Franklin County)	35653
Woodlawn Heights (Jefferson County)	35212
Woodley Park (Part of Montgomery)	36116

	ZIP
Woodmeadow (Part of Hoover)	35226
Woodmont (Part of Hueytown)	35020
Woodstock	35188
Woodstock Junction	35188
Woodville	35776
Woodward	35020
Woolfolk	36268
Wren	35650
Wright	35677
Wright Crossroads	36830
Wyatt	35130
Wylam (Part of Birmingham)	35224
Wynnville	35952
Yantley	36912
Yarbo	36558
Yelling Settlement	36526
Yellow Bluff	36769
Yellow Creek Falls	35959
Yellowleaf	35186
Yellow Pine	36539
Yerkwood	35062
York	36925
Youngblood	36081
Youngs Chapel	35903
Yucca	35966
Yupon	36555
Zimco	36451
Zion (Montgomery County)	36047
Zion (Pickens County)	35466
Zion City (Part of Birmingham)	35207
Zion Heights (Part of Birmingham)	35207
Zip City	35630
Zoar	36323

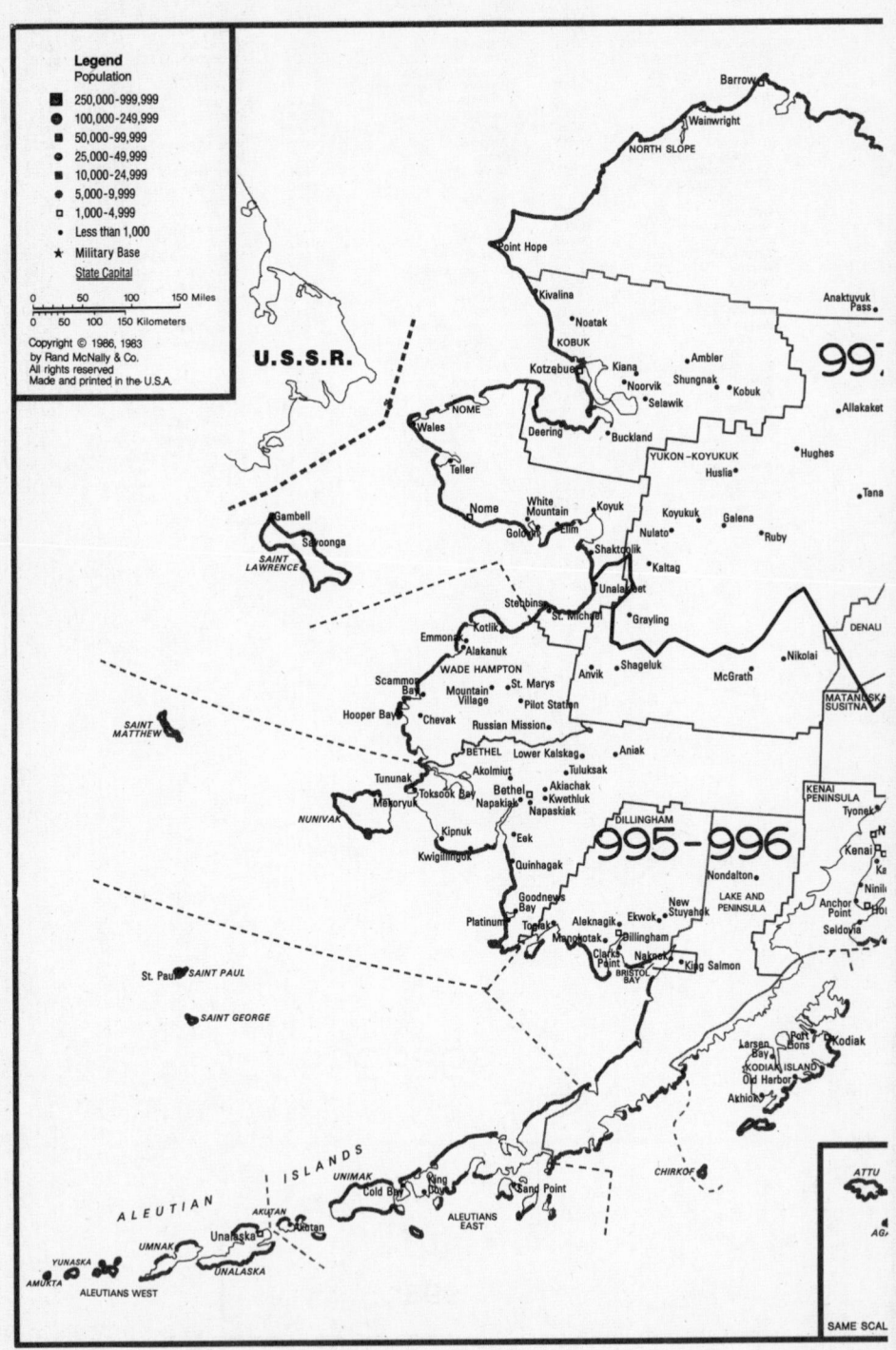

Legend
Population
■ 250,000-999,999
● 100,000-249,999
■ 50,000-99,999
● 25,000-49,999
■ 10,000-24,999
● 5,000-9,999
□ 1,000-4,999
• Less than 1,000
★ Military Base
State Capital

0   50   100   150 Miles
0   50   100   150 Kilometers

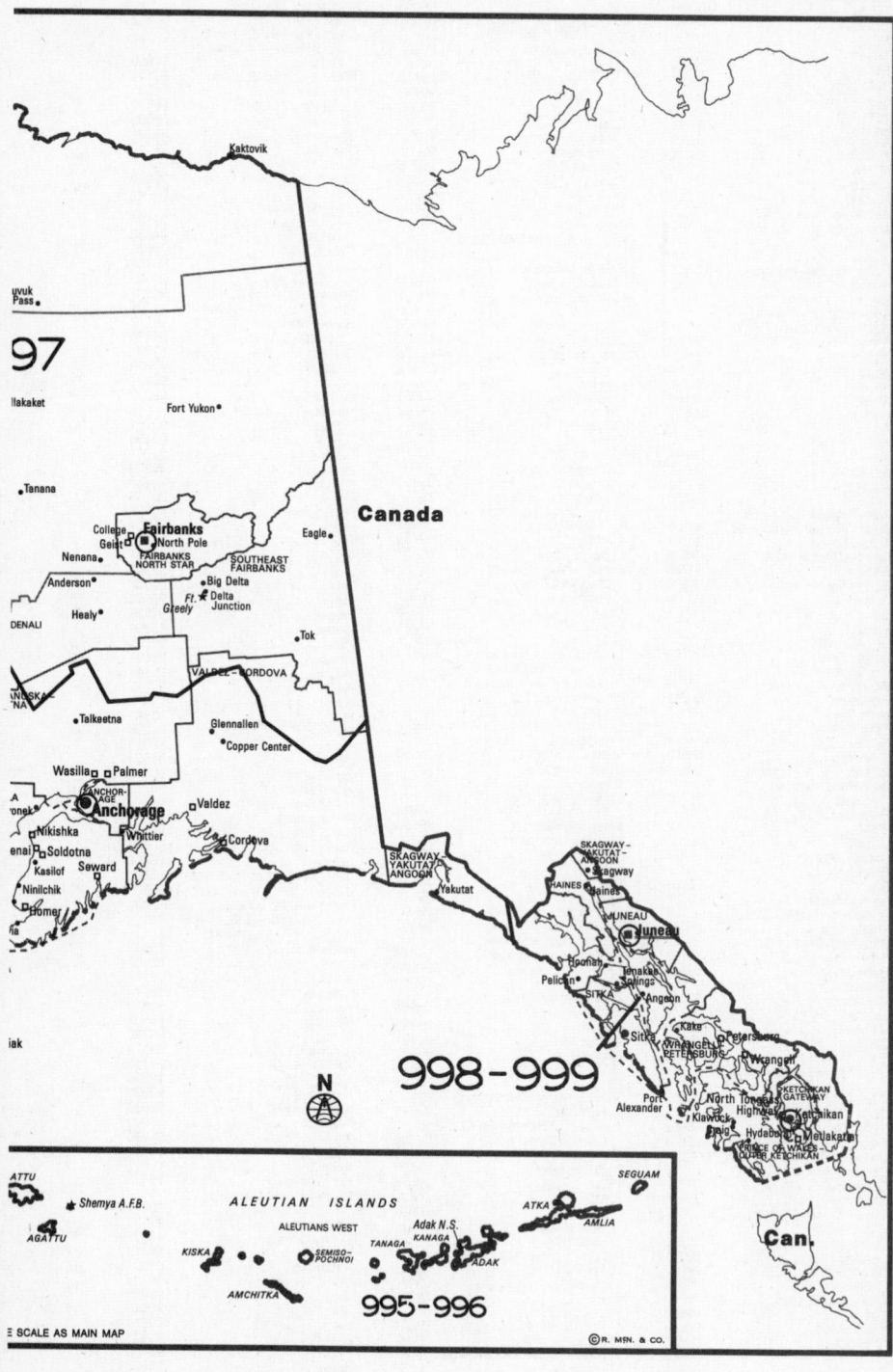

Kaktovik

uvuk
Pass

97

Ilakaket

Fort Yukon

Tanana

College
Geist
Fairbanks
North Pole
FAIRBANKS
NORTH STAR

Canada

Eagle

SOUTHEAST
FAIRBANKS

Nenana

Anderson

Big Delta
Ft.
Greely
Delta
Junction

DENALI

Healy

Tok

NSKA-
NA

Talkeetna

VALDEZ-CORDOVA

Glennallen

Copper Center

Wasilla
Palmer

onet

ANCHOR-
AGE
Anchorage

Valdez

Nikishka

Whittier

Cordova

SKAGWAY-
YAKUTAT-
ANGOON

SKAGWAY-
YAKUTAT-
ANGOON

enai
Soldotna

Kasilof

Seward

Yakutat

Skagway

HAINES
Haines

Ninilchik

Homer

JUNEAU

Juneau

na

Hoonah

Pelican

Tenakee
Springs

iak

SITKA

Angoon

998-999

Kake

Sitka

WRANGELL-
PETERSBURG

Petersburg

Wrangell

KETCHIKAN
GATEWAY

Port
Alexander

North Tongass
Highway
Klawock
Craig

Ketchikan

Hydaburg

Metlakatla

PRINCE OF WALES-
OUTER KETCHIKAN

N

ATTU

Shemya A.F.B.

ALEUTIAN ISLANDS

SEGUAM

AGATTU

ALEUTIANS WEST

Adak N.S.
KANAGA

ATKA

AMLIA

KISKA

SEMISO-
POCHNOI

TANAGA

ADAK

Can.

AMCHITKA

995-996

E SCALE AS MAIN MAP

©R. M?N. & CO.

	ZIP		ZIP		ZIP
Adak Naval Air Station	99502	Chisana	99780	Fox	99701
Adak Station	99502	Chistochina	99586	Fox River	99603
Akhiok	99615	Chitina	99566	Freshwater Bay (Sitka	
Akiachak	99551	Chuathbaluk	99557	Borough)	99803
Akiak	99552	Chugiak (Part of		Freshwater Bay (Skagway-	
Akutan	99553	Anchorage)	99567	Hoonah-Angoon Census	
Alakanuk	99554	Circle	99733	Division)	99829
Alatna (Part of Allakaket)	99720	Circle Hot Springs Station	99730	Fritz Cove (Part of Juneau)	99801
Alcan	99764	Clam Gulch	99568	Fritz Creek	99603
Aleknagik	99555	Clark's Point	99569	Funter Bay	99850
Alexander	99695	Clear	99704	Gakona	99586
Alitak	99697	Clearwater Ranch	99737	Galena	99741
Allakaket	99720	C!over Pass	99901	Gambell	99742
Ambler	99786	Coffman Cove	99918	Game Creek	99829
Amchitka	99501	Cohoe	99610	Ganes Creek	99675
Amook	99697	Cold Bay	99571	Geist	99701
Anaktuvuk Pass	99721	Coldfoot	99701	Girdwood (Part of	
Anchorage	99501-04	College	99708	Anchorage)	99587
	99507-24	College (census designated		Glennallen	99588
	99599	place)	99701	Gold Creek	99695
For specific Anchorage Zip Codes		College Village (Part of		Golovin	99762
call (907) 564-2842, or your local		Anchorage)	99504	Goodnews Bay	99589
postmaster.		Collegiate Park	99701	Goodnews Mining Camp	99651
Anchorage 5th Avenue		Colorado	99695	Graehl (Part of Fairbanks)	99701
Shopping Center (Part of		Cooper Landing	99572	Granite Mountain	99762
Anchorage)	99501	Copper Center	99573	Grayling	99590
Anchor Point	99556	Copperville	99573	Gulkana	99695
Anderson	99744	Cordova	99574	Gustavus	99826
Angoon	99820	Cosna	99756	Haines	99827
Aniak	99557	Cottonwood	99654	Halibut Cove	99603
Annette	99926	Council	99762	Hamilton Acres (Part of	
Anvik	99558	Covenant Life	99827	Fairbanks)	99701
Arctic Village	99722	Craig	99921	Happy Valley	99556
Atka	99547	Crooked Creek	99575	Harding Lake	99701
Atmautluak	99559	Crown Point	99631	Hawk Inlet	99850
Atqasuk	99791	Cube Cove	99850	Haycock	99753
Attu	99502	Deadhorse	99734	Healy	99743
Auke Bay (Part of Juneau)	99821	Debarr Shopping Center		Healy Lake	99737
Aurora (Part of Fairbanks)	99701	(Part of Anchorage)	99504	Herring Cove	99901
Aurora Lodge	99701	Deering	99736	Hobart Bay	99850
Baranof (Part of Sitka)	99835	Delta Junction	99737	Hogatza	99701
Barrow	99723	Denali National Park	99755	Hollis	99901
Bartlett Cove	99826	Derby Tract (Part of		Holy Cross	99602
Beaver	99724	Fairbanks)	99701	Homer	99603
Bell Island Hot Springs	99901	Dillingham	99576	Hoonah	99829
Beluga	99695	Dora Bay	99901	Hooper Bay	99604
Bethel	99559	Dot Lake	99737	Hope	99605
Bettles Field	99726	Douglas (Part of Juneau)	99824	Houston	99694
Big Delta	99737	Downtown (Post Office)		Hughes	99745
Big Horn	99701	(Part of Anchorage)	99510	Huslia	99746
Big Lake	99652	Downtown (Part of		Hydaburg	99922
Birch Creek	99740	Fairbanks)	99707	Hyder	99923
Birch Estates	99701	Driftwood Bay	99695	Icy Bay	99695
Birchwood (Part of		Dry Creek	99737	Igiugig	99613
Anchorage)	99567	Duncan Canal	99833	Iliamna	99606
Bird (Part of Anchorage)	99540	Dutch Harbor	99692	Indian (Part of Anchorage)	99540
Bjerremark (Part of		Eagle	99738	Indian River	99720
Fairbanks)	99701	Eagle River (Part of		Island Homes (Part of	
Black Sand	99689	Anchorage)	99577	Fairbanks)	99701
Bluff	99762	Eagle Village	99738	Ivanof Bay	99695
Border	99780	Eastchester (Part of		Jakolof Bay	99695
Boswell Bay	99574	Anchorage)	99520	Jennie M.	99701
Boundary	99780	Edna Bay	99901	Johnston (Part of Fairbanks)	99701
Boyd	99701	Eek	99578	Juneau	99801-11
Brevig Mission	99785	Egegik	99579	For specific Juneau Zip Codes call	
Broadmoor Acres	99701	Eielson Air Force Base	99702	(907) 586-7138, or your local	
Brooks Lodge	99613	Eklutna (Part of Anchorage)	99567	postmaster.	
Browerville (Part of Barrow)	99723	Eklutna Housing Project		Kachemak	99603
Buckland	99727	(Part of Anchorage)	99645	Kake	99830
Butte	99645	Ekuk	99695	Kako	99657
Campbell (Part of		Ekwok	99580	Kaktovik	99747
Anchorage)	99517	Elfin Cove	99825	Kalifonsky	99610
Candle	99752	Elim	99739	Kalskag	99607
Cantwell	99729	Ellamar	99695	Kaltag	99748
Cape Lisburne	99766	Emmonak	99581	Kanakanak	99576
Cape Newenham	99576	English Bay	99603	Kantishna	99755
Cape Newenham Air Force		Eska	99674	Karluk	99608
Station	99576	Ester	99725	Kasaan	99901
Cape Pole	99901	Eureka (Matanuska-Susitna		Kashegelok	99668
Cape Romanzof Air Force		Borough)	99645	Kasigluk	99609
Station	99559	Eureka (Yukon-Koyukuk		Kasilof	99610
Cape Yakataga	99695	Census Division)	99756	Kasitsna Bay	99695
Carlanna (Part of Ketchikan)	99901	Evansville	99726	Kenai	99611
Central	99730	Excursion Inlet	99850	Kenai Lake	99572
Chalkyitsik	99788	Eyak	99574	Kenai Packers Cannery	
Chandalar	99701	Fairbanks	99706-12	(Part of Kenai)	99611
Charcoal Point (Part of		For specific Fairbanks Zip Codes		Kennicott	99588
Ketchikan)	99901	call (907) 474-0722, or your local		Kenny Cove	99695
Chase	99676	postmaster.		Kenny Lake	99573
Chatanika	99712	False Pass	99583	Ketchikan	99901
Chatham (Part of Sitka)	99803	Farewell	99627	Kiana	99749
Chefornak	99561	Ferry	99743	King Cove	99612
Chena Hot Springs	99701	Fire Lake (Part of		King Salmon	99613
Chenega	99693	Anchorage)	99577	Kipnuk	99614
Chernofski	99685	Fishhook Junction	99645	Kitoi Bay	99697
Chevak	99563	Flat	99584	Kivalina	99750
Chickaloon	99674	Fort Greely	99737	Klawock	99925
Chicken	99732	Fort Wainwright	99703	Klukwan	99827
Chignik	99564	Fortymile Roadhouse	99737	Knik	99654
Chignik Lagoon	99565	Fort Yukon	99740	Knudson Cove	99901
Chignik Lake	99548	Four Corners	99645	Kobuk	99751
Chiniak	99615				

	ZIP		ZIP		ZIP
Kodiak	99615-19	Nenana Native Village (Part		Russian Jack (Part of	
For specific Kodiak Zip Codes call		of Nenana)	99760	Anchorage)	99508
(907) 486-4721, or your local		Newhalen	99606	Russian Mission	99657
postmaster.		New Stuyahok	99636	St. George Island	99591
Kodiak Station	99615	Newtok	99559	St. John Harbor	99929
Kokhanok	99606	Nightmute	99690	St. Marys	99658
Kokrines	99668	Nikiski	99635	St. Marys Mission (Part of	
Koliganek	99576	Nikolaevsk	99556	St. Marys)	99658
Kongiganak	99559	Nikolai	99691	St. Michael	99659
Kotlik	99620	Nikolski	99638	St. Paul Island	99660
Kotzebue	99752	Ninilchik	99639	Salamatof	99611
Koyuk	99753	Noatak	99761	Salcha	99714
Koyukuk	99754	Nome	99762	Salmon Creek (Part of	
Kupreanof	99833	Nondalton	99640	Juneau)	99801
Kustatan	99682	Noorvik	99763	Sand Lake (Part of	
Kwethluk	99621	North Douglas (Part of		Anchorage)	99522
Kwigillingok	99622	Juneau)	99801	Sand Point	99661
Labouchere Bay	99927	North Pole	99705	Savoonga	99769
Lake Minchumina	99757	Northway	99764	Saxman	99901
Lake Nancy	99688	Northway Junction	99764	Saxman East (Part of	
Lakloey Hill	99701	Northway Village	99764	Saxman)	99901
Larsen Bay	99624	Nuiqsut	99789	Scammon Bay	99662
Lawing	99664	Nulato	99765	Scow Bay	99833
Lazy Mountain	99645	Nunaka Valley (Part of		Seal Bay	99697
Lemeta (Part of Fairbanks)	99701	Anchorage)	99504	Selawik	99770
Lemon Creek (Part of		Nunapitchuk	99641	Seldovia	99663
Juneau)	99801	Nyac	99557	Seward	99664
Lena Cove (Part of Juneau)	99801	Okagamute	99607	Shageluk	99665
Levelock	99625	Old Andreafski	99658	Shaktoolik	99771
Liberty	99738	Old Harbor	99643	Shanley (Part of Fairbanks)	99701
Lignite	99743	Olnes	99701	Sheldon Point	99666
Lime Village	99627	Olsonville	99576	Shemya Air Force Base	99501
Little Diomede	99762	Oscarville	99559	Shemya Station	99501
Little Port Walter	99835	Ouzinkie	99644	Shishmaref	99772
Livengood	99701	Palmer	99645	Shungnak	99773
Long	99768	Paradise Hill	99602	Sitka	99835
Long Island (Matanuska-		Parks	99697	Situk	99689
Susitna Borough)	99654	Paxson	99737	Skagway	99840
Long Island (Prince of		Pederson Point	99633	Skwentna	99667
Wales-Outer Ketchikan		Pedro Bay	99647	Slana	99586
Census Division)	99922	Pelican	99832	Slaterville (Part of Fairbanks)	99701
Lost River (Nome Census		Peninsula Point	99901	Sleetmute	99668
Division)	99762	Pennock Island	99901	Snowball	99701
Lost River (Yakutat		Perryville	99648	Snug Harbor	99572
Borough)	99689	Petersburg	99833	Soldotna	99669
Lower Kalskag	99626	Peters Creek (Part of		Solomon	99790
Lower Mendenhall Valley		Anchorage)	99567	Sourdough	99586
(Part of Juneau)	99801	Pilot Point	99649	South (Part of Anchorage)	99511
Lutak	99827	Pilot Station	99650	South Bjerremark	99701
McCarthy	99695	Pitkas Point	99658	South Naknek	99670
McGrath	99627	Pittman	99654	Spenard (Part of	
Mack	99701	Platinum	99651	Anchorage)	99509
McKinley Acres	99701	Pleasant Valley	99701	Sprucewood	99701
Main Office (Part of		Point Baker	99927	Squaw Harbor	99661
Anchorage)	99502	Point Barrow DEW Station	99723	Stebbins	99671
Manley Hot Springs	99756	Point Higgins	99901	Steele Creek	99738
Manokotak	99628	Point Hope	99766	Steese	99710
Mansfield Village	99760	Point Lay	99759	Sterling	99672
Marshall	99585	Point Whiteshed	99574	Stevens Village	99774
Marvel Creek	99557	Polk Inlet	99922	Stony River	99557
Mary's Igloo	99778	Poorman	99645	Strelna	99566
Matanuska	99645	Portage (Part of Anchorage)	99587	Summit	99729
May Creek	99695	Portage Creek	99695	Summit Lodge	99586
Meade River	99791	Port Alexander	99836	Sunnyside	99832
Meadow Lakes	99654	Port Alice	99836	Sunshine	99695
Medfra	99627	Port Alsworth	99653	Suntrana	99743
Meekins Roadhouse	99645	Port Armstrong	99836	Sutton	99674
Meier	99737	Port Ashton	99695	Takotna	99675
Mekoryuk	99630	Port Bailey	99697	Talkeetna	99676
Mendeltna	99588	Port Clarence	99790	Tanacross	99776
Mendeltna Lodge	99645	Port Graham	99603	Tanana	99777
Mendenhall (Part of Juneau)	99803	Port Heiden	99549	Tatalina	99627
Mendenhall Flats (Part of		Port Lions	99550	Tatitlek	99677
Juneau)	99801	Portlock	99663	Tee Harbor (Part of Juneau)	99801
Mentasta Lake	99780	Port Moller	99571	Telida	99695
Metlakatla	99926	Port Protection	99901	Teller	99778
Meyers Chuck	99903	Port Walter	99835	Tenakee Springs	99841
Midtown (Part of		Port Williams	99697	Terror Bay	99697
Anchorage)	99503	Potter (Part of Anchorage)	99501	Tetlin	99779
Minto	99758	Primrose	99631	Thane (Part of Juneau)	99801
Montana	99688	Prudhoe Bay	99734	Thorne Bay	99919
Moose Creek	99701	Quartz Creek	99572	Tiekel	99686
Moose Pass	99631	Queen	99576	Tin City	99783
Moser Bay	99697	Quinhagak	99655	Togiak	99678
Mosquito Lake	99827	Rainbow (Part of		Tok	99780
Mountain Point	99901	Anchorage)	99501	Tokeen	99901
Mountain View (Part of		Rampart	99767	Toksook Bay	99637
Anchorage)	99508	Red Devil	99656	Tonsina	99573
Mountain Village	99632	Red Mountain	99603	Totem Bight	99901
Mount Edgecumbe (Part of		Red Salmon	99633	Totem Park	99701
Sitka)	99835	Rego	99701	Trapper Creek	99683
Mud Bay	99901	Ridgeway	99669	Tuluksak	99679
Muldoon (Part of		Rodman (Part of Sitka)	99835	Tuntutuliak	99680
Anchorage)	99504	Rogers Park (Part of		Tununak	99681
Nabesna	99586	Anchorage)	99508	Turnagain (Part of	
Naknek	99633	Rowan Bay (Skagway-		Anchorage)	99517
Napaimute	99557	Hoonah-Angoon Census		Turnagain by-the-Sea (Part	
Napakiak	99634	Division)	99835	of Anchorage)	99517
Napaskiak	99559	Rowan Bay (Wrangell-		Turnagain Heights (Part of	
Naukati Bay	99925	Petersburg Census		Anchorage)	99517
Nelson Lagoon	99571	Division)	99836	Twin Hills	99576
Nenana	99760	Ruby	99768	Two Rivers	99716

	ZIP		ZIP		ZIP
Tyonek	99682	View Cove	99901	White Mountain	99784
Uganik	99697	Wainwright	99782	Whites Crossing	99688
Ugashik	99613	Wales	99783	Whitestone Logging Camp	99829
Umiat	99701	Ward Cove	99928	Whitney (Part of Anchorage)	99501
Unalakleet	99684	Wasilla	99687	Whittier	99693
Unalaska	99685		99654	Wilcox	99701
Ungalik	99684	For specific Wasilla Zip Codes call (907) 376-5327, or your local postmaster.		Wilcox Estates	99701
University Center (Part of Anchorage)	99503			Wild Lake	99726
University Park	99701	Waterfall	99901	Willow	99688
Upper Mendenhall Valley (Part of Juneau)	99801	West Fairwest	99701	Wiseman	99790
Upper Nickeyville (Part of Ketchikan)	99901	Westgate (Part of Fairbanks)	99701	Womens Bay	99615
U.S. Coast Guard Station	99619	West Juneau (Part of Juneau)	99801	Woodland Park (Part of Anchorage)	99517
Usibelli	99743	West Point	99697	Wood River	99576
Valdez	99686	Westwood	99701	Wrangell	99929
Vank Island	99929	Whale Pass	99901	Yakutat	99689
Venetie	99781			Yankee Creek	99675
				Zachar Bay	99697

	ZIP
Adamana	86025
Adamsville	85232
Agua Caliente	85333
Agua Linda	85640
Aguila	85320
Ahwatukee (Part of Phoenix)	85044-45
	85048
	85076
For specific Ahwatukee Zip Codes call (602) 407-2024, or your local postmaster.	
Airpark (Part of Scottsdale)	85260
Ajo	85321
Akchin (Pima County)	85634
Ak-Chin (Pinal County)	85239
Alamo Crossing	85357
Alchesay Flat	85941
Ali Chuk	85634
Ali Molina	85634
Allentown	86506
Alpine	85920
Amado	85645
Anegam	85634
Apache	88056
Apache Flats	85613
Apache Grove	85534
Apache Ho (Part of Apache Junction)	85220
Apache Junction	85217-20
	85278
For specific Apache Junction Zip Codes call (602) 982-2121, or your local postmaster.	
Apache Wells	85215
Arcadia (Part of Phoenix)	85018
	85060
For specific Arcadia Zip Codes call (602) 407-2025, or your local postmaster.	
Arcosanti	86333
Arivaca	85601
Arizola	85222
Arizona City	85223
Arizona Shores	85344
Arizona State Prison Complex-Douglas	85607
Arizona State Prison Complex-Perryville	85338
Arizona State Prison Complex-Tucson	85706
Arizona State Prison Complex-Florence	85232
Arizona State Prison-Safford	85546
Arlington	85322
Artesa	85634
Artesia	85546
Ash Fork	86320
Avondale	85323
Avra Valley	85653
Aztec	85333
Baby Rock	86633
Bacobi	86030
Bagdad	86321
Bakerville (Part of Bisbee)	85603
Bapchule	85221
Bayless Shopping Center (Part of Apache Junction)	85220
Beardsley	85373
Beautys Estates	85621
Beaver Dam	86432
Bella Vista Estates (Part of Sierra Vista)	85635
Bellemont	86015
Ben Franklin (Part of Phoenix)	85080
Benson	85602
Beyerleville	85621
Big Park	86335
Biltmore Fashion Park (Part of Phoenix)	85016
Bisbee	85603
Bisbee Junction	85603
Bitahochee	86031
Bitter Springs	86036
Black Canyon City	85324
Black Hills (Part of Clarkdale)	86324
Blackwater	85228
Blue	85922
Blue Gap	86520
Bluewater	85344
Bonita	85643
Bouse	85325
Bowie	85605
Boys Ranch	85242
Braemer (Part of Peoria)	85345
Branding Iron	85701
Brenda	85348
Bridge Canyon Country Estates	86337
Bridgeport	86326

	ZIP
Briggs Townsite (Part of Bisbee)	85603
Buckeye	85326
Buckhorn	85205
Buena Vista	85546
Bullhead City	86426
	86429-30
For specific Bullhead City Zip Codes call (602) 754-3717, or your local postmaster.	
Bumble Bee	86333
Burnt Water	86512
Bushman Acres	86047
Bylas	85530
Cactus (Part of Phoenix)	85032
	85046
For specific Cactus Zip Codes call (602) 407-2026, or your local postmaster.	
Cactus Flat	85546
Cactus Forest	85232
Calva	85530
Camelview Plaza (Part of Scottsdale)	85251
Cameron	86020
Camp Creek	85331
Camp Verde	86322
Camp Verde Indian Reservation	86322
Cane Beds	86022
Canelo	85611
Canyon (Part of Mesa)	85204
Canyon Day	85941
Capitol (Part of Phoenix)	85005
	85009
For specific Capitol Zip Codes call (602) 484-9014, or your local postmaster.	
Carefree	85377
Carmen	85640
Carrizo	85901
Casa Blanca	85221
Casa Grande	85222
	85230
For specific Casa Grande Zip Codes call (602) 836-7221, or your local postmaster.	
Casas Adobes	85704
Cascabel	85602
Cashion	85329
Castle Hot Springs	85342
Castle Rock Shores	85344
Catalina	85738
Catalina Foothills	85718
Cave Creek	85331
Cedar Creek	85941
Cedar Ridge	86020
Centerville (Part of Clarkdale)	86324
Central	85531
Central Heights	85501
Central Heights-Midland City	85532
Chambers	86502
Chandler	85224-26
	85244
	85248-49
For specific Chandler Zip Codes call (602) 963-6643, or your local postmaster.	
Chandler Heights	85227
Chaparral (Part of Chandler)	85224
Cherry	86327
Chevelon	86001
Chiawuli Tak	85634
Chilchinbito	86033
Childs	85321
Chinle	86503
Chino Valley	86323
Chloride	86431
Choulic	85634
Christmas	85292
Chris-Town Center (Part of Phoenix)	85015
Chuichu	85222
Cibecue	85911
Cibola	85328
Cienega Springs	85344
Circle City	85342
Citrus Gardens	85201
Clarkdale	86324
Claypool	85532
Clay Springs	85923
Cleator	86333
Clifton	85533
Coal Mine Mesa	86045
Cobblestone Village (Part of Peoria)	85381
Cochise	85606
Cocopah Indian Reservation	85350
College (Part of Tucson)	85722
Colorado City	86021

	ZIP
Colorado River Indian Reservation	85344
Comobabi	85634
Concho	85924
Congress	85332
Continental	85640
Coolidge	85228
Coolidge Dam	85542
Co-op Village	85339
Copper Mine	86040
Copper Queen (Part of Bisbee)	85603
Cordes Lakes	86333
Cork	85536
Cornfields	86505
Cornville	86325
Coronada Foothills Estates	85718
Corona de Tucson	85726
Coronado (Part of Tucson)	85711*
	85732†
Coronado Unit	86047
Cortaro	85652
Cottonwood	86326
Cottonwood Station	86503
Cottonwood-Verde Village	86326
Country Life	85201
Cove	87420
Covered Wells	85634
Cowlic	85634
Cow Springs	86044
Crane	85364
Crestview (Part of Bisbee)	85603
Cross Canyon	86511
Crown King	86343
Cuckelbur	85222
Cutter	85501
Dam View	85344
Date	85332
Dateland	85333
Davis Dam	86430
Davis-Monthan Air Force Base	85702
Deer Valley (Part of Phoenix)	85023
Del Rio	86323
Dennehotso	86535
Desert (Part of Mesa)	85206*
	85216†
Desert Carmel	85222
Desert Harbor (Part of Peoria)	85381
Desert Hills (Mohave County)	86403
Desert Hills (Pima County)	85718
Desert Sands	85208
Desert View	86023
Dewey	86327
Dewey-Humboldt	86329
Diamond Valley	86301
Dilkon	86047
Discovery at the Orchard (Part of Peoria)	85381
Dobson (Part of Mesa)	85202*
	85274†
Dolan Springs	86441
Dome	85365
Don Luis (Part of Bisbee)	85603
Dos Cabezas	85643
Double Adobe	85617
Douglas	85607-08
	85655
For specific Douglas Zip Codes call (602) 364-3631, or your local postmaster.	
Downtown (Part of Flagstaff)	86001
Downtown (Part of Kingman)	86402
Downtown (Part of Phoenix)	85003
Downtown (Part of Tempe)	85281
Downtown (Part of Tucson)	85701*
	85702†
Dragoon	85609
Drake	86334
Dreamland Villa	85205
Drexel Heights	85706
Dudleyville	85292
Duncan	85534
Dysart	85345
Eagar	85925
Eagle Creek	85533
East Flagstaff (Part of Flagstaff)	86001
East Fork	85941
East Plantsite (Part of Clifton)	85540
Eden	85535
Ehrenberg	85334
El Con Regional Shopping Center (Part of Tucson)	85716
Eleven Mile Corner	85222
Elfrida	85610

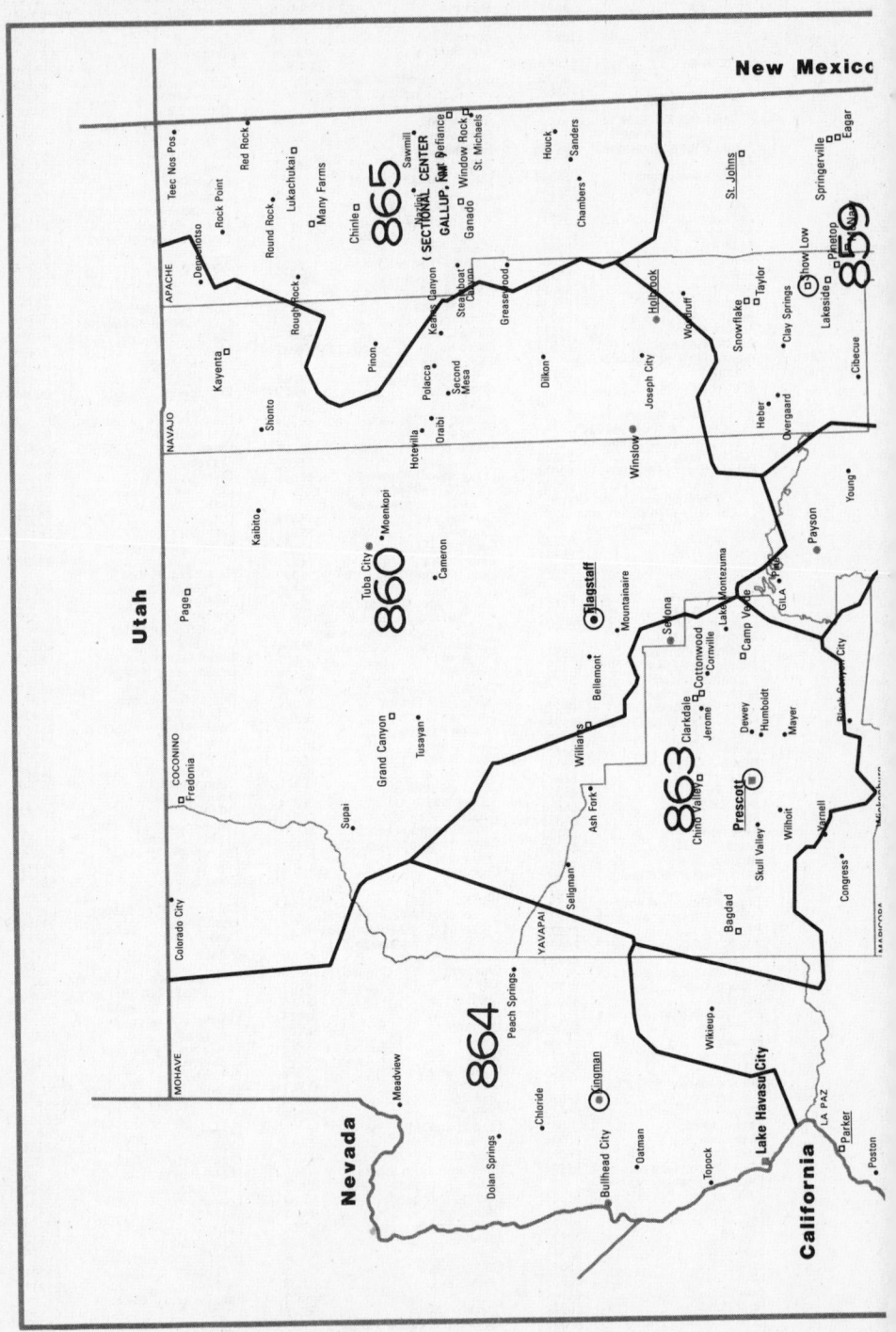

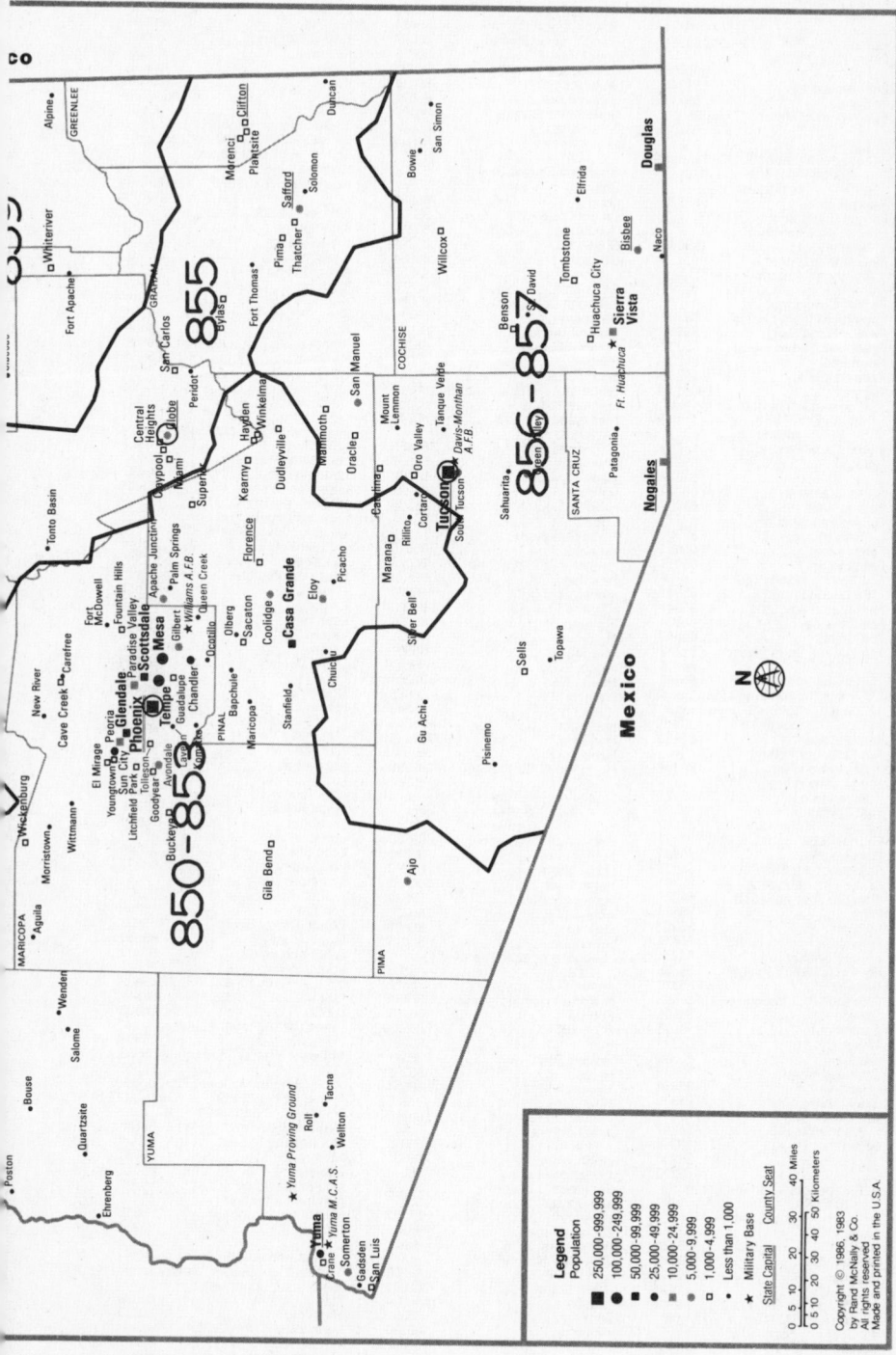

ZIP

Elgin	85611
El Mirage	85335
El Mirage (mobile home park)	85201
Eloy	85231
El Pueblecito (Part of Yuma)	85364
Emery Park (Part of Tucson)	85706
Empire Landing	85344
Fairbank	85621
Falcon (Part of Mesa)	85205
	85207
	85215

For specific Falcon Zip Codes call (602) 834-5118, or your local postmaster.

Falcon Estates	85203
Federal Correctional Institution (Graham County)	85546
Federal Correctional Institution (Maricopa County)	85027
Federal Correctional Institution (Pima County)	85706
Federal Prison Camp	85546
Fiesta Mall (Part of Mesa)	85202
Fiesta Park	85201
Fishers Landing	85365
Flagstaff	86001-04

For specific Flagstaff Zip Codes call (602) 527-2440, or your local postmaster.

Flecha Caida Estates	85718
Florence	85232*
	85279†
Florence Junction	85219
Flowing Wells	85705
Forbing Park (Part of Prescott)	86301
Forest Lakes	85931
Fort Apache	85926
Fort Apache Indian Reservation	85941
Fort Apache Junction	85941
Fort Defiance	86504
Fort Grant	85643
Fort Lowell (Part of Tucson)	85712
	85715
	85749

For specific Fort Lowell Zip Codes call (602) 721-8503, or your local postmaster.

Fort McDowell	85257
Fort McDowell Indian Reservation	85264
Fort Mohave Indian Reservation	86427
Fort Thomas	85536
Fortuna Foothills	85356
Fountain East	85201
Fountain Hills	85269
Fountain of the Sun	85208
Foxfire (Part of Peoria)	85381
Foxwood (Part of Peoria)	85381
Franklin	85534
Fredonia	86022
Fresnal Canyon	85634
Friendly Corners	85231
Fry (Part of Sierra Vista)	85635
Gadsden	85336
Galena (Part of Bisbee)	85603
Ganado	86505
Geronimo	85536
Gibson	85321
Gila Bend	85337
Gila Bend Indian Reservation	85634
Gila Crossing	85339
Gila River Indian Reservation	85247
Gilbert	85233-34
	85296
	85299

For specific Gilbert Zip Codes call (602) 892-0010, or your local postmaster.

Gisela	85541
Gladden	85320
Gleeson	85610
Glendale	85301-08
	85310-18

For specific Glendale Zip Codes call (602) 842-0099, or your local postmaster.

Glen Ilah	85362
Globe	85501*
	85502†
Golden Valley	86413
Goldfield	85219
Goodyear	85338

ZIP

Goodyear Farms (Part of Litchfield Park)	85340
Graham	85552
Grand Canyon	86023
Grand Canyon Caverns	86434
Grand Canyon Estates	86023
Grand View	86301
Grasshopper Junction	86401
Gray Mountain	86016
Greasewood	86505
Greasewood Springs	86507
Greaterville	85637
Green Valley	85614*
	85622†
Greenway (Part of Glendale)	85306
Greer	85927
Gripe	85546
Groom Creek	86303
Guadalupe	85283
Gunsight	85321
Gu Oidak	85634
Guthrie	85533
Gu Vo	85634
Hacienda De Valencia	85201
Hackberry	86411
Haivana Nakya	85634
Hamilton Corner	85248
Hano	86042
Happy Jack	86024
Harcuvar	85348
Harmony Villa	85201
Hassayampa	85343
Havasupai Indian Reservation	86435
Hawkins	85332
Hawley Lake	85930
Hayden	85235
Hayden Junction	85235
Heber	85928
Heber-Overgaard	85928
Hereford	85615
Hermits Rest	86023
Hickiwan	85634
Hidden Springs	86020
Highland Park	85603
Highland Pines	86301
Higley	85236
Hillside	86301
Hilltop	85632
Ho-Kay-Gan	86301
Holbrook	86025
Holiday	85344
Hollywood	85546
Hon Dah	85935
Hope	85348
Hopi (Part of Scottsdale)	85258
	85261

For specific Hopi Zip Codes call (602) 998-9444, or your local postmaster.

Hopi Indian Reservation	86039
Horn	85333
Horse Mesa	85290
Horse Thief	86333
Hotason Vo	85634
Hotevilla	86030
Houck	86506
Huachuca City	85616
Huachuca Terrace (Part of Bisbee)	85603
Hualapai	86412
Hualapai Indian Reservation	86434
Hubbell	86505
Humboldt	86329
Hunt	85924
Hunters Point	86511
Hyder	85333
Immanuel Mission	86514
Indian Gardens	86336
Indian Ridge Estates	85715
Indian School (Part of Phoenix)	85014
Indian Wells	86031
Inscription House	86044
Inspiration	85532
Iron Springs	86330
Jackrabbit	85222
Jackson Acres	86301
Jacob Lake	86022
Jade Park North (Part of Phoenix)	85308
	85541
Jakes Corner	86034
Jeddito	86331
Jerome	86331
Johnson	85609
Joseph City	86032
Juniper Heights	86301
Kachina Village	86001
Kaibab	86022
Kaibab Indian Reservation	86022
Kaibito	86053

ZIP

Kaihon Kug	85634
Kaka	85321
Kansas Settlement	85643
Katherine	86430
Kayenta	86033
Keams Canyon	86034
Kearny	85237
Kelvin	85237
Kerwo	85634
Kingman	86401-02
	86413

For specific Kingman Zip Codes call (602) 753-2480, or your local postmaster.

Kinlichee	86505
Kino (Part of Tucson)	85703†
	85705*
Kino Hills	85621
Kino Springs	85621
Kinsley Ranch	85640
Kirkland	86332
Kirkland Junction	86332
Klagetoh	86505
Klondyke	85643
Kofa (Part of Yuma)	85364
Kohatk	85634
Komatke	85339
Ko Vaya	85634
Kykotsmovi	86039
Lake Havasu City	86403-06

For specific Lake Havasu City Zip Codes call (602) 855-2361, or your local postmaster.

Lake Mead City	86444
Lake Mead Rancheros	86401
Lake Mohave	86430
Lake Montezuma	86342
Lakeside (La Paz County)	85344
Lakeside (Navajo County)	85929
Lamplighter Village (Part of Clarkdale)	86324
La Palma	85222
Las Ligas (Part of Avondale)	85323
Laveen	85339
Lees Ferry	86036
Leisure World	85206
Leupp	86035
Leupp Corner	86047
Liberty	85326
Ligurta	85356
Lincon	85634
Litchfield Greens (Part of Litchfield Park)	85340
Litchfield Park	85340
Little Acres	85501
Littlefield	86432
Little Tucson	85634
Lizard Acres	85373
Lochiel	85624
Loma Linda	85619
Lone Star	85546
Long Valley	86001
Los Arcos Mall (Part of Scottsdale)	85257
Los Gatos	85255
Lowell (Part of Bisbee)	85603
Lower Miami	85539
Low Mountain	86503
Lukachukai	86507
Luke Air Force Base	85309
Lukeville	85341
Lupton	86508
Lynx Estates (Part of Prescott Valley)	86301
McDowell (Part of Phoenix)	85008
	85010

For specific McDowell Zip Codes call (602) 275-1997, or your local postmaster.

McGees Settlement	85736
McGuireville	86335
McNary	85930
McNeal	85617
Madera Canyon	85706
Mammoth	85618
Many Farms	86538
Marana	85238
	85653

For specific Marana Zip Codes call (602) 682-3561, or your local postmaster.

Marble Canyon	86036
Maricopa	85239
Maricopa (AK-Chin) Indian Reservation	85247
Maricopa Village	85339
Marine Corps Air Station	85369
Mariposa Manor	85621
Martinez Lake	85365
Maryvale (Part of Phoenix)	85031

	ZIP
....	85063

For specific Maryvale Zip Codes call (602) 247-7664, or your local postmaster.

	ZIP
Mayer	86333
Meadow Brook (Part of Yuma)	85364
Meadview	86444
Mennonite Mission	86505
Mesa	85201-16
....	85274-77

For specific Mesa Zip Codes call (602) 969-9171, or your local postmaster.

	ZIP
Mesa Del Oro	85219
Mescal	85602
Metrocenter (Part of Phoenix)	85021
Mexican Town	85321
Mexican Water	86514
Miami	85539
Miami Gardens	85539
Middle Verde (Part of Camp Verde)	86322
Midland City	85501
Miller Valley (Part of Prescott)	86301
Miracle Valley	85615
Miramonte Acres (Part of Bisbee)	85603
Mishongnovi	86043
Mission	85706
....	85714
....	85734

For specific Mission Zip Codes call (602) 746-3695, or your local postmaster.

	ZIP
Mobile	85239
Moccasin	86022
Moenave	86045
Moenkopi	86045
Mohave Valley	86440
Morenci	85540
Mormon Lake	86038
Morristown	85342
Mountainaire	86001
Mountain View (Cochise County)	85603
Mountain View (Maricopa County)	85213*
	85275†
Mountain View (Pima County)	85752
Mount Elden (Part of Flagstaff)	86001
Mount Lemmon	85619
Munds Park	86017
Na-Ah-Tee Canyon	86025
Naco	85620
Northern Arizona University (Part of Flagstaff)	86011
Navajo	86509
Navajo Depot Activity	86015
Navajo Indian Reservation	86515
Navajo Mountain Trading Post	86044
Navajo Spring	86036
Navajo Station	86505
Nazlini	86540
Nelson	86434
New Hope	85201
New Kingman-Butler	86401
New Oraibi	86039
New River	85027
New Tucson (Part of Tucson)	85714
Nicksville	85615
Nogales	85621
....	85628
....	85662

For specific Nogales Zip Codes call (602) 287-9246, or your local postmaster.

	ZIP
Nogales West	85621
Nolia	85634
Normal Junction (Part of Tempe)	85281
Northeast (Part of Phoenix)	85016*
....	85064†
Northern Hills	85704
North Komelik	85634
Northridge Park	86314
North Rim	86052
Northwest (Part of Phoenix)	85017
....	85061

For specific Northwest Zip Codes call (602) 249-6344, or your local postmaster.

	ZIP
Nortons Corner	85225
Nutrioso	85932
Oak Creek	86341
Oak Knoll Village	86301

	ZIP
Oak Springs	86511
Oasis Park (Part of Apache Junction)	85220
Oatman	86433
Ocotillo	85248
Octave	85332
Olberg	85247
Old Columbine	85546
Old Oraibi	86039
Oracle	85623
Oracle Foot Hill Estates ...	85704
Oracle Junction	85738
Orange Grove Estates	85704
Oro Valley	85737
Osborn (Part of Phoenix) ..	85013
....	85067

For specific Osborn Zip Codes call (602) 235-9118, or your local postmaster.

	ZIP
Overgaard	85933
Page	86040
Page Springs	86325
Palm Springs (Part of Apache Junction)	85219
Palominas	85615
Palo Verde	85343
Pan Tak	85634
Papago (Part of Scottsdale)	85257
Papago Indian Reservation	85634
Paradise	85632
Paradise Valley	85253
Paradise Valley Mall (Part of Phoenix)	85032
Park Central Mall (Part of Phoenix)	85013
Parker	85344
Parker Creek	85501
Parker Strip	85344
Park Mall (Part of Tucson)	85711
Parks	86018
Pascua Yaqui Indian Reservation	85746
Patagonia	85624
Paulden	86334
Paul Spur	85607
Payson	85541*
	85547††
Peach Springs	86434
Pearce	85625
Peeples Valley	86332
Peoria	85345
....	85380-82

For specific Peoria Zip Codes call (602) 979-1841, or your local postmaster.

	ZIP
Peoria	85345
Peralta Estates	85219
Peridot	85542
Perkinsville	86323
Perryville	85326
Petrified Forest National Park	86028

Phoenix 85001-86

For specific Phoenix Zip Codes call (602) 407-2049, or your local postmaster.

COLLEGES & UNIVERSITIES

	ZIP
DeVry Institute of Technology-Phoenix	85021
University of Phoenix	85072

FINANCIAL INSTITUTIONS

	ZIP
Bank of America, Arizona	85003
Chase Bank of Arizona	85012
Citibank (Arizona)	85012
First Interstate Bank of Arizona, N.A.	85003
The Valley National Bank of Arizona	85004

HOSPITALS

	ZIP
Arizona State Hospital	85008
Carl T. Hayden Veterans Affairs Medical Center ...	85012
Good Samaritan Hospital Medical Center	85006
Healthwest Regional Medical Center	85016
John C. Lincoln Hospital and Health Center	85020
Maricopa Medical Center	85008
St. Joseph's Hospital and Medical Center	85013

HOTELS/MOTELS

	ZIP
Arizona Biltmore	85016
Embassy Suites Hotel	85016
Embassy Suites Camelhead	85008
Doubletree Suites Hotel	85008

	ZIP
Holiday Inn-Corporate Center	85029
Hyatt Regency Phoenix at Civic Plaza	85004
The Pointe Hilton Resort at Squaw Peak	85020
Ramada Inn Metrocenter ...	85029
Sheraton Greenway Inn	85023

MILITARY INSTALLATIONS

	ZIP
Arizona Air National Guard, FB6021, Sky Harbor International Airport	85034
Pia Oik	85634
Picacho	85241
Picture Rocks	85653
Pima	85543
Pine	85544
Pinedale	85934
Pine Lake	86401
Pine Springs	86506
Pinetop (Part of Pinetop-Lakeside)	85935
Pinetop-Lakeside	85935
Pinnacle Peak Village	85255
Pinon	86510
Pioneer (Part of Mesa)	85210
Pirtleville	85626
Pisinemo	85634
Plantsite	85540
Plaza Del Rio (Part of Peoria)	85381
Polacca	86042
Poland Junction	86333
Pomerene	85627
Ponderosa Park	86301
Portal	85632
Porter Creek Estates	85929
Porter Mountain Estates ...	85929
Poston	85371
Prescott .... * ...	86301-04
....	86313

For specific Prescott Zip Codes call (602) 778-1890, or your local postmaster.

	ZIP
Prescott Valley	86312†
	86314*
Presidential Estates	85616
Pumpkin Center	85553
Quartzsite	85346*
	85359†
Queen Creek	85242
Queen Valley	85219
Querino	86506
Rainbow Valley	85326
Ranch del Sol	85296
Rancho del Rio	85344
Randolph	85222
Reata Pass	85251
Redington	85602
Red Lake	86046
Red Mesa	86514
Red Rock (Apache County)	87420
Red Rock (Pinal County) ...	85245
Red Valley	86544
Rillito	85654
Rimrock	86335
Rincon (Part of Tucson) ...	85710*
	85731†
Rio Rico	85621
	85648

For specific Rio Rico Zip Codes call (602) 281-7223, or your local postmaster.

	ZIP
Rio Rico East	85621
Rio Salado (Part of Phoenix)	85074
Rio Verde	85263
Riverside Stage Stop	85237
Riverside Terrace	85704
Riviera (Part of Bullhead City)	86439
....	86442

For specific Riviera Zip Codes call (602) 758-5711, or your local postmaster.

	ZIP
Rock Point	86545
Rock Springs	85026
Roll	85347
Roosevelt	85545
Roosevelt Estates	85545
Roosevelt Resort	85545
Rough Rock	86503
Round Rock	86547
Royal Estates	85621
Rye	85541
Sacate	85221
Sacaton	85247
Sacaton Flats	85247
Sacred Mountain	86001
Safford	85546*
	85548†

	ZIP
Saginaw (Part of Bisbee)...	85603
Sahuarita	85629
Sahuarita Heights	85629
St. David	85630
St. Johns	85936
St. Michaels	86511
Salado	85936
Salina	86503
Salome	85348
Salt River Indian Reservation	85256
Salt River Powder District Camp	85545
San Carlos	85550
San Carlos Indian Reservation	85550
Sanchez	85546
Sanders	86512
Sand Springs	86039
San Jose (Cochise County)	85603
San Jose (Graham County)	85546
San Lucy Village	85337
San Luis (Pima County)	85634
San Luis (Yuma County)...	85349
San Manuel	85631
San Miguel	85634
San Pedro	85634
San Rafael Terrace (Part of Bisbee)	85603
San Simon	85632
Santa Cruz	85339
Santa Maria (Maricopa County)	85009
Santa Maria (Yavapai County)	85332
Santan	85247
Santa Rita	85640
Santa Rosa	85634
San Xavier	85746
San Xavier Indian Reservation	85634
Sasabe	85633
Sawmill	86549
Schuchk	85634
Schuchuli	85634
Scottsdale	85250-52
	85254-62
	85264-67
	85271

For specific Scottsdale Zip Codes call (602) 949-7100, or your local postmaster.

	ZIP
Scottsdale Fashion Square (Part of Scottsdale)	85251
Scottsdale Galleria (Part of Scottsdale)	85251
Second Mesa	86043
Sedona	86336
	86339-41
	86351

For specific Sedona Zip Codes call (602) 282-3511, or your local postmaster.

	ZIP
Seligman	86337
Sells	85634
Sentinel	85333
Shaw Butte (Part of Phoenix)	85071
Sheldon	85534
Sherwood (Part of Mesa)	85204*
	85214†
Shipolovi	86043
Shongopovi	86043
Shonto	86054
Shopishk	85634
Show Low	85901
Shumway	85901
Sichomovi	86042
Sierra Adobe (Part of Phoenix)	85023-24
	85027

For specific Sierra Adobe Zip Codes call (602) 492-0292, or your local postmaster.

	ZIP
Sierra Bonita	85643
Sierra Vista	85635-36
	85670-71

For specific Sierra Vista Zip Codes call (602) 458-2540, or your local postmaster.

	ZIP
Sierra Vista Southeast	85615
Sil Nakaya	85634
Silverbell (Part of Tucson)	85745
	85754

For specific Silverbell Zip Codes call (602) 622-5210, or your local postmaster.

	ZIP
Site Six (Part of Lake Havasu City)	86403
Skull Valley	86338
Skyline Bel Aire Estates....	85718
Skyway Village	85205

	ZIP
Smoke Signal	86503
Snowflake	85937
Solomon	85551
Somerton	85350
Sonoita	85637
Sonora Town	85233
South Bisbee	85603
South Central (Part of Phoenix)	85040
	85066

For specific South Central Zip Codes call (602) 268-1162, or your local postmaster.

	ZIP
Southgate Mall (Part of Yuma)	85364
South Komelik	85634
South Santan	85247
South Tucson	85713*
	85725†
Springerville	85938
Spring Valley	86333
Stanfield	85272
Stanton	85332
Stargo	85540
Star Valley	85541
Steamboat Canyon	86505
Stoneman Lake	86024
Strawberry	85544
Sun (Part of Tucson)	85717†
	85719*
	85733†

For specific Sun Zip Codes call (602) 881-1096, or your local postmaster.

	ZIP
Sun City	85351
	85372-73

For specific Sun City Zip Codes call (602) 974-3623, or your local postmaster.

	ZIP
Sun City West	85375
Sunflower	85201
Sunizona	85625
Sun Lakes	85248
Sunnyslope (Part of Phoenix)	85020
	85068

For specific Sunnyslope Zip Codes call (602) 870-3947, or your local postmaster.

	ZIP
Sunrise	86047
Sunrise Springs	86505
Sunset	85643
Sunset Acres	85603
Sunshine Acres (Part of Mesa)	85201
Sunsites	85625
Suntown (Part of Peoria)...	85345
Sun Valley	86029
Supai	86435
Superior	85273
Superstition Estates (Part of Apache Junction)	85220
Superstition Springs Center (Part of Mesa)	85206
Supi Oidak	85634
Surprise	85374
Sweetwater (Apache County)	87401
Sweetwater (Maricopa County)	85326
Sweetwater (Pinal County)	85221
Swift Trail Junction	85546
Tacna	85352
Tapco	86324
Tat Momoli	85634
Tatria Toak	85634
Taylor	85939
Teec Nos Pos	86514
Tees To	86047
Tempe	85280-85

For specific Tempe Zip Codes call (602) 220-0258, or your local postmaster.

	ZIP
Temple Bar Marina	86443
Tes Nez Iah	86033
Thatcher	85552
Theba	85337
The Gap	86020
Thomas Mall (Part of Phoenix)	85018
Three Points	85714
Three Way	85534
Tintown (Part of Bisbee)...	85603
Tolani	86047
Tolleson	85353
Toltec (Part of Eloy)	85231
Tombstone	85638
Tonalea	86044
Tonopah	85354
Tonto Basin	85553
Topawa	85639
Topock	86436

	ZIP
Toreva	86043
Tortilla Flat	85290
Totopitk	85634
Tovrea (Part of Phoenix) ...	85034
Tower Plaza Mall (Part of Phoenix)	85018
Toyei	86505
Tremaine	85225
Tri-City Mall (Part of Mesa)	85201
Truxton	86434
Tsaile	86556
Tubac	85646
Tuba City	86045
Tucson	85701-54

For specific Tucson Zip Codes call (602) 620-5142, or your local postmaster.

	ZIP
Tucson Country Club Estates	85715
Tucson Estates	85715
Tucson National Estates ...	85704
Tumacacori	85640
Turkey Flat	85546
Tusayan	86023
Tusconita	85706
Twin Arrows (Part of Flagstaff)	86001
Twin Buttes	85629
Twin Knolls	85207
Two Story	86511
University of Arizona (Part of Tucson)	85717
Upper Greasewood Trading Post	86507
Upper Wheatfields	86556
Utting	85348
Vahki	85221
Vail	85641
Vaiva Vo	85634
Valencia	85326
Valencia West	85746
Valentine	86437
Valley Farms	85291
Valley West Mall (Part of Glendale)	85301
Vamori	85634
Vandenberg Village	85708
Vaya Chin	85634
Velda Rose Estates	85205
Velda Rose Gardens	85201
Ventana	85634
Ventana Lakes (Part of Peoria)	85382
Venture Out	85201
Vernon	85940
Vicksburg	85348
Village Meadows (Part of Sierra Vista)	85635
Waddell	85355
Wagoner	86332
Wahak Hotrontk	85634
Wahweap	86040
Walker	86301
Walnut Grove	86332
Walpi	86042
Warren (Part of Bisbee)....	85603
Washington (Part of Phoenix)	85021
	85051
	85069

For specific Washington Zip Codes call (602) 249-0028, or your local postmaster.

	ZIP
Washington Camp	85624
Wellton	85356
Wenden	85357
Westbrook Village (Part of Peoria)	85382
West Chandler (Part of Chandler)	85224
Westfield (Part of Peoria)	85345
Westgate	85611
Westgreen Estates (Part of Peoria)	85345
West Plaza Shopping Center (Part of Phoenix)	85017
Westridge (Part of Phoenix)	85033
	85075

For specific Westridge Zip Codes call (602) 873-1231, or your local postmaster.

	ZIP
Westridge Mall (Part of Phoenix)	85033
West Sedona (Part of Sedona)	86340
Westward Quest	85201
Wheatfields	86515
Whetstone	85613
Whipple (Part of Prescott)	86313
Whippoorwill	86503
Whispering Hills (Part of Sierra Vista)	85635

	ZIP		ZIP		ZIP
White Clay	86504	Willcox	85643	Woodsprings	86505
White Cone	86025	Williams	86046	Yarnell	85362
White Mountain Lake	85912	Williams Air Force Base	85240	Yava	86301
Whiteriver (Navajo County)	85941	Willow Beach	86445	Yavapai Indian Reservation	86301
White Tanks	85326	Willow Canyon	85619	York	85534
Why	85321	Willow Valley Estates	86440	Young	85554
Wickenburg	85358	Window Rock	86515	Youngtown	85363
	85390	Winkelman	85292	Yucca	86438
For specific Wickenburg Zip Codes call (602) 684-2138, or your local postmaster.		Winona	86001	Yuma	85364-69
		Winslow	86047	For specific Yuma Zip Codes call (602) 783-2124, or your local postmaster.	
Wide Ruin	86502	Winwood	85603		
Wikieup	85360	Wittmann	85361	Yuma Proving Ground	85365
Wilhoit	86332	Wood Hills	85616		
		Woodruff	85942		

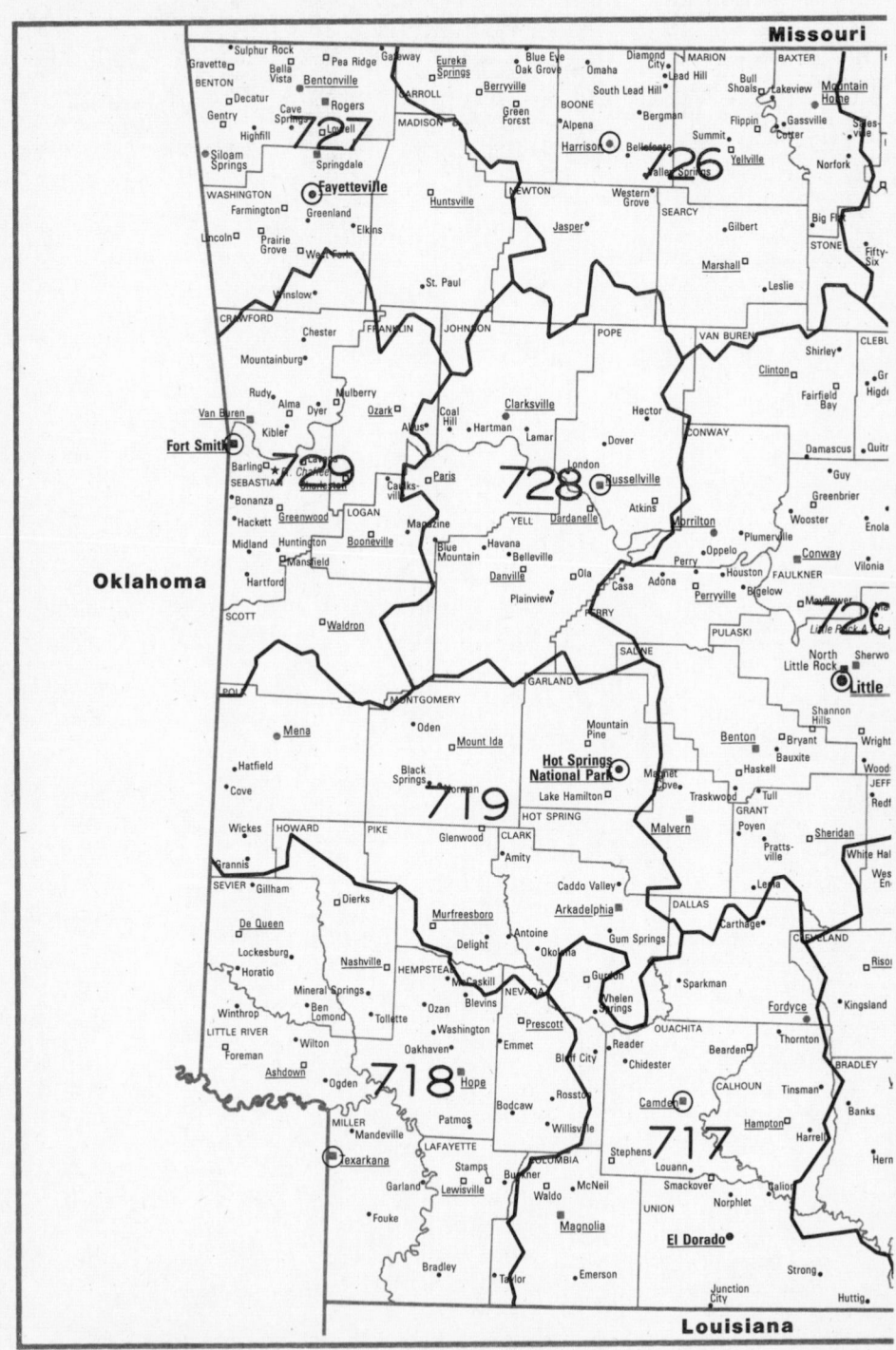

	ZIP		ZIP		ZIP
Abbott	72944	Bates	72924	Blytheville	72315-19
Aberdeen	72134	Batesville	72501*	For specific Blytheville Zip Codes	
Acorn	71953		72503†	call (501) 763-3690, or your local	
Ada	72001	Battlefield	71801	postmaster.	
Adkins Lake	71601	Baucum	72117	Board Camp	71932
Adona	72001	Bauxite	72011	Bodcaw	71858
Agnos	72513	Baxter	71638	Bogg Springs	71944
Alabam	72740	Bay	72411	Bolding	71747
Albert Pike (Part of Hot		Bayou Meto (Arkansas		Boles	72926
Springs)	71913	County)	72160	Bonanza	72916
Albion	72143	Bayou Meto (Lonoke		Bondsville	72354
Alco	72610	County)	72086	Bonnerdale	71933
Alexander (Greene County)	72450	Bay Village	72324	Bono (Craighead County)	72416
Alexander (Pulaski County)	72002	Bear Creek Springs	72601	Bono (Faulkner County)	72058
Algoa	72112	Bearden	71720	Booker	72117
Alicia	72410	Beaver	72613	Booneville	72927
Alix	72820	Beaver Shores	72756	Booster	72645
Allbrook	71851	Beck	72348	Boothe	72927
Alleene	71820	Becton	72036	Boston	72752
Allison	72560	Beebe	72012	Boswell	72516
Aliport	72046	Bee Branch	72013	Botkinburg	72031
Alma	72921	Beech Grove (Dallas		Boughton	71857
Almond	72550	County)	71742	Bowen	71940
Almyra	72003	Beech Grove (Greene		Bowman	72437
Alpena	72611	County)	72412	Boxley	72740
Alpine	71920	Beedeville	72014	Boyd	71837
Alread	72031	Beirne	71721	Boydell	71658
Altheimer	72004	Bellaire	71638	Boyd Hill	71845
Alto	72354	Bella Vista	72714	Boydsville	72461
Altus	72821	Bellefonte	72601	Boynton	72438
Aly	72857	Belle Meade	72348	Bradford	72020
Amagon	72005	Belleville	72824	Bradley	71826
Amanca	72376	Bells Chapel	72823	Brady (Part of Little Rock)	72205
Amboy (Part of North Little		Bellville	71846	Bragg City	71726
Rock)	72118	Belton	71852	Brakebill	72478
Amity	71921	Ben	72530	Branch	72928
Amy	71701	Ben Gay	72466	Brasfield	72017
Andy	72376	Ben Hur	72856	Bredlow Corner	72046
Annieville	72434	Ben Lomond	71823	Brentwood	72959
Antioch (Perry County)	72070	Benton	72015	Brewer	72044
Antioch (White County)	72012		72018	Brickeys	72320
Antoine	71922	For specific Benton Zip Codes call		Briggsville	72828
Aplin	72126	(501) 778-2920, or your local		Brighton	72450
Appleton	72822	postmaster.		Bright Star	71834
Apt	72401			Brightwater	72756
Arbor Grove	72433	Bentonville	72712	Brinkley	72021
Ard	72834	Benton Work Release and		Brister	71740
Arden	71822	Pre Release Center	72015	Brockett	72455
Arkadelphia	71923	Bergman	72615	Brockwell	72517
Arkana	71826	Berryville	72616	Brookland	72417
Arkansas City	71630	Beryl	72032	Brown's Crossing	71640
Arkinda	71836	Best	72756	Brown Springs	72104
Arkola	72940	Bethany	71833	Brownstown	71846
Arlberg	72031	Bethel	72450	Brownsville	72067
Armorel	72310	Bethel Heights	72764	Bruins	72348
Armstrong	72482	Bethesda	72501	Brumley	72032
Armstrong Springs	72143	Beulah	72017	Brummitt	72160
Artesian	71744	Bevis Corners	72142	Bruno	72618
Artist Point	72946	Bexar	72515	Brush Creek	72084
Ashdown	71822	Bidville	72959	Bryant	72022
Asher (Madison County)	72727	Bigelow	72016		72089
Asher (Pulaski County)	72204	Big Flat	72617	For specific Bryant Zip Codes call	
Ash Flat	72513	Big Fork	71953	(501) 847-2226, or your local	
Athelstan	72370	Biggers	72413	postmaster.	
Athens	71971	Big Lake	72442	Bryant Addition	72857
Atkins	72823	Big Springs	72657	Buckeye	72438
Atlanta	71740	Billingsley's Corner	71866	Buckner	71827
Attica	72455	Billstown	71958	Buck Range	71851
Aubrey	72311	Bingen	71852	Buckville	71956
Augsburg	72847	Birdell	72455	Buena Vista	71764
Augusta	72006	Birdeye	72314	Buffalo City	72653
Aurelle	71765	Birdsong	72386	Buie	72129
Aurora	72740	Birdtown	72157	Bullfrog Valley	72837
Austin (Conway County)	72031	Birta	72853	Bull Shoals	72619
Austin (Lonoke County)	72007	Biscoe	72017	Bunney	72414
Auvergne	72112	Bismarck	71929	Burdette	72321
Avilla	72002	Blackburn	72959	Burg	71833
Avoca	72711	Blackfish	72346	Burlington	72662
Avon	71832	Black Fork	71953	Burnville	72936
Back Gate	71639	Black Oak (Craighead		Buroak	72650
Baker	72482	County)	72414	Burtsell	71962
Balch	72009	Black Oak (Poinsett County)	72386	Busch	72632
Bald Knob	72010	Black Rock	72415	Bussey	71860
Baldwin (Part of Fayetteville)	72701	Black Springs	71960	Butlerville	72176
Ballard	72513	Blackton	72069	Butterfield	72104
Band Mill	72517	Blackville (Conway County)	72823	Byron	72576
Banks	71631	Blackville (Jackson County)	72112	Cabanol	72616
Banner	72523	Blakely	71931	Cabot	72023
Barber	72927	Blakemore	72046	Caddo Gap	71935
Barcelona	72955	Blevins	71825	Caddo Valley	71923
Bard	72450	Bloomer	72933	Cain	72946
Bardstown	72350	Bloomfield	72734	Calamine	72466
Barfield	72315	Blossom	72392	Caldwell	72322
Barling	72923	Blue Ball	72833	Cale	71828
Barney	72047	Blue Eye	65601	Caledonia	71749
Barton	72312	Blue Hill	72118	Calhoun	71753
Barton Eddins	72312	Blue Mountain	72826	Calico Rock	72519
Bashe (Part of Fort Smith)	72901	Blue Springs	71909	Calion	71724
Bass	72655	Blue Springs Village	72764	Calmer	71665
Bassett	72313	Bluff City	71722	Calumet	72315
Batavia	72601	Bluffton	72827	Camark	71701
Batchelor	72366			Camden	71701

	ZIP		ZIP		ZIP
Cammack Village	72207	Cherokee Village-Hidden		Crossroads (Prairie County)	72040
Camp	72520	Valley	72525	Crows	72015
Campbell Station	72473	Cherry Hill (Perry County)	72126	Crumpler	72644
Camp Joseph T. Robinson	72205	Cherry Hill (Polk County)	71953	Crumrod	72328
Canaan	72650	Cherry Valley	72324	Crystal Hill	72118
Canal Gardens	72348	Chester	72934	Crystal Springs	71968
Cane Creek	72150	Chickalah	72834	Crystal Springs Landing	71968
Canehill	72717	Chicot Junction	71640	Cullendale (Part of Camden)	71701
Caney (Faulkner County)	72032	Chidester	71726	Culpeper	72031
Caney (Hot Spring County)	71929	Childress	72447	Cumi	72544
Caney Valley	71921	Chimes	72645	Cummins Unit	71644
Canfield	71845	Chismville	72943	Curtis	71728
Cantwell	72422	Choctaw	72028	Cushman	72526
Capps	72601	Choctaw Acres	72031	Cypert	72366
Capps City	71069	Christy Acres	72015	Cypress Valley	72156
Caraway	72419	Chula	72857	Dabney	72110
Carbon City	72855	Cincinnati	72769	Daisy	71950
Carden Bottoms	72834	Clarendon	72029	Dalark	71923
Careyville	71765	Clarkedale	72325	Dallas	71953
Carlile Highland	72653	Clarkridge	72623	Dalton	72455
Carlisle	72024	Clarks Corner	72394	Damascus	72039
Carmel	71671	Clarksville	72830	Danville	72833
Carmi	72438	Clay	72143	Dardanelle	72834
Carolan	72927	Clear Lake (Grant County)	72150	Datto	72424
Carpenter	71642	Clear Lake (Mississippi		Davis Creek	72129
Carpenter Addition	71655	County)	72315	Dawn Hill Country Club	72761
Carroll's Corner	72442	Clear Point	72756	Dayton	72940
Carrollton	72611	Clear Spring	71962	DeAnn	71801
Carryville	72454	Cleveland	72030	Deans Market	72921
Carson	72370	Clifty	72756	Dean Springs	72921
Carter Cove Use Area	72857	Clinton	72031	Decatur	72722
Carthage	71725	Clover Bend	72433	Deckerville	72386
Casa	72025	Clow	71855	Deep Elm	71653
Cash	72421	Clyde	72717	Deer	72628
Cass	72949	Coaldale	74937	Deerfield	72328
Casscoe	72026	Coal Hill	72832	Delaney	72727
Catalpa	72854	Coffeeville	72020	Delaplaine	72425
Catcher	72956	Coffman (Greene County)	72450	Delaware	72835
Catholic Point	72027	Coffman (Lawrence County)	72433	Delfore	72438
Cathy Lake	72396	Coldwater	72373	Delight	71940
Cato	72114	Coleman	71655	Dell	72426
Catron	72367	Colfax	72653	De Luce	72042
Caulksville	72951	College City	72476	Denmark	72020
Cauthron (Logan County)	72927	Collegehill	71752	Dennard	72629
Cauthron (Scott County)	72958	College Station	72053	Denning	72821
Cavanaugh (Part of Fort		Collegeville	72002	Denton	72458
Smith)	72901	Collins	71634	Denver	72638
Cave City	72521	Colt	72326	Denwood	72386
Cave Creek	72501	Columbus	71831	De Queen	71832
Cave Springs	72718	Combs	72721	Dermott	71638
Cecil	72930	Cominto	71655	De Roche	71929
Cedar Creek	72950	Compton	72624	Des Arc	72040
Cedar Grove	72534	Concord	72523	Desha	72527
Cedarville	72932	Congo	72015	Detonti	72011
Center	72542	Connells Point	72366	De Valls Bluff	72041
Center Hill (Greene County)	72450	Conway	72032*	Dewey (Chicot County)	71638
Center Hill (White County)	72033		72033†	Dewey (White County)	72121
Center Point (Clark County)	71743	Copper Mine	72756	De Witt	72042
Center Point (Hempstead		Cord	72524	Dialion	71665
County)	71801	Corinth	72824	Diamond Bay	72531
Center Point (Howard		Corley	72855	Diamond City	72630
County)	71852	Cornerstone	72004	Diamondhead	71913
Center Point (Prairie		Cornerville	71667	Dian (Part of Prescott)	71857
County)	72064	Corning	72422	Diaz	72043
Center Ridge (Clark County)	71921	Cotter	72626	Dickey Heights	72768
Center Ridge (Cleburne		Cotterneck	71742	Dicus	72476
County)	72543	Cottonbelt	71720	Dierks	71833
Center Ridge (Conway		Cotton Plant	72036	Dillen	72854
County)	72027	Cottonshed	71851	Dixie (Craighead County)	72437
Centerton	72719	Cottonwood Corner		Dixie (Pulaski County)	72114
Center Valley	72801	(Craighead County)	72447	Dixie (Woodruff County)	72006
Centerville (Faulkner		Cottonwood Corner		Dixieland Mall (Part of	
County)	72058	(Mississippi County)	72370	Rogers)	72756
Centerville (Hempstead		Council	72320	Doddridge	71834
County)	71835	Cove	71937	Dogpatch	72648
Centerville (Yell County)	72829	Cowell	72856	Dogtown	71832
Central (Clark County)	71923	Cowlingsville	71846	Dogwood (Part of	
Central (Cross County)	72396	Coy	72037	Blytheville)	72315
Central (Hot Spring County)	72104	Cozahome	72639	Dogwood Acres	71957
Central (Sevier County)	71842	Crabapple Point	71724	Dollarway (Part of Pine	
Central Baptist College (Part		Crabtree	72031	Bluff)	71602
of Conway)	72032	Cravens	72949	Dolph	72528
Central City (Garland		Crawfordsville	72327	Donaldson	71941
County)	71913	Creigh	72366	Dongola	72650
Central City (Sebastian		Crigler	71667	Doniphan	72143
County)	72941	Crockett	72454	Dora	72956
Central Mall (Part of Fort		Crocketts Bluff	72038	Double Bridges	72358
Smith)	72903	Crosses	72701	Douglas	71643
Cerrogordo	71866	Crossett	71635	Douglas Corner	72205
Chambersville	71766	Crossroads (Cleburne		Dover	72837
Chapel Hill	71832	County)	72131	Dowdy	72524
Charleston	72933	Cross Roads (Hot Spring		Drakes Creek	72740
Charlotte	72522	County)	71933	Drasco	72530
Chasewood Landing	71969	Crossroads (Izard County)	72566	Driggs	72943
Chatfield	72348	Crossroads (Jackson		Dripping Springs	72955
Chelford	72386	County)	72112	Driver	72329
Cherokee City	72734	Cross Roads (Little River		Dryden	72401
Cherokee Village	72525	County)	71866	Dryfork	72740
	72529	Cross Roads (Logan		Dublin	72863
For specific Cherokee Village Zip		County)	72863	Duff	72675
Codes call (501) 257-2662, or		Cross Roads (Madison		Dumas	71639
your local postmaster.		County)	72738	Durham	72727

* Area Zip Code   **† Post Office Boxes**

	ZIP
Dutch Mills	72744
Dutton	72760
Dyer	72935
Dyess	72330
Eagle Mills	71720
Eagle Point	72531
Eagleton	71953
Earle	72331
East Black Oak	72386
East Camden	71701
East End	72065
Eastview	72351
Eaton	72458
Ebenezer	71764
Ebony	72364
Echo	72927
Economy	72823
Eden Isle	72543
Edgemont	72044
Edmondson	72332
Eglantine	72153
Egypt	72427
Elaine	72333
El Dorado	71730*
	71731†
Elevenpoint	72455
Elgin	72112
Elizabeth	72531
Elkins	72727
Elk Ranch	72632
Elliott	71701
Ellison	72152
Elm Springs	72728
Elm Store	65778
Elmwood	72601
Elnora	72455
El Paso	72045
Emerson	71740
Emmet	71835
Empire	71661
Enders	72131
Engelberg	72455
England	72046
English	72004
Enola	72047
Enterprise	72901
Eros	72633
Erwin	72112
Ethel	72048
Etna	72949
Etowah	72428
Euclid Heights (Part of Hot Springs)	71901
Eudora	71640
Eula	72675
Eureka Springs	72632
Evansville	72729
Evening Shade (Hempstead County)	71801
Evening Shade (Scott County)	72958
Evening Shade (Sharp County)	72532
Evening Star	72422
Everton	72633
Excelsior	72936
Fairbanks	72131
Fairfield (Part of Little Rock)	72209
Fairfield Bay	72088
Fairmont	72160
Fair Oaks	72397
Fairview (Chicot County)	71653
Fairview (Lonoke County)	72086
Fairview (Marion County)	72650
Fairview (Ouachita County)	71701
Fairview (Sevier County)	71841
Fairwood	71913
Falcon	71827
Falls Chapel	71846
Fallsville	72854
Fancy Hill	71935
Fannie	71970
Farelly Lake	72160
Fargo	72021
Farmington	72730
Farmville	71671
Farville	72417
Fayetteville	72701-03
For specific Fayetteville Zip Codes call (501) 442-8286, or your local postmaster.	
Felsenthal	71747
Felton	72360
Fender	72476
Fendley	71921
Fenter	72167
Ferguson	72328
Ferguson Crossroads	71837
Fern	72946
Ferndale	72208
Fifty-Six	72533
Figure Five	72956

	ZIP
Finch	72450
Fisher (Craighead County)	72421
Fisher (Poinsett County)	72429
Fitzgerald (Part of Diaz)	72112
Fitzgerald Crossing	72396
Fitzhugh	72006
Fivemile	72530
Flag	72645
Flat Rock	72847
Flint Springs	72583
Flippin	72634
Floodway	72442
Floral	72534
Florence	71655
Floyd	72143
Fomby	71822
Fontaine	72416
Fordyce	71742
Foreman	71836
Forest Grove (Columbia County)	71740
Forest Grove (Lafayette County)	71861
Forest Park (Part of Little Rock)	72207
Formosa	72031
Forrest City	72335
Fort Chaffee	72905
Fort Douglas	72854
Fort Lynn	71837
Fort Smith	72901-17
For specific Fort Smith Zip Codes call (501) 484-6370, or your local postmaster.	
Fortune	72373
Forty Four	72585
Forum	72740
Fouke	71837
Fountain Hill	71642
Fountain Lake	71901
Fourche	72016
Fourche Junction	72857
Fourche Valley	72827
Fourmile Hill	72143
Fox	72051
Francis	72601
Franklin	72536
Free Hope	71753
Frenchmans Bayou	72338
Frenchport	71701
Fresno	71643
Friendship (Cleveland County)	71665
Friendship (Columbia County)	71860
Friendship (Hot Spring County)	71942
Friley	72752
Fritz	72461
Fryatt	72554
Frys Mill	72386
Fulton	71838
Furlow	72086
Gaines Landing	71653
Gainesville	72450
Gainsboro	72501
Gaither	72601
Galla Rock	72823
Gallatin	72761
Galloway	72117
Gamaliel	72537
Gammon	72364
Gardner	71765
Garfield	72732
Garland City	71839
Garland Springs	72111
Garner	72052
Garner's Farm	71742
Garnett	71667
Garret Grove	72368
Garrett	72846
Garrett Bridge	71639
Gassville	72635
Gateway	72733
Gaylor	72657
Geneva	71832
Genoa	71840
Gentry	72734
George Creek	72687
Georgetown (Madison County)	72773
Georgetown (Pope County)	72847
Georgetown (White County)	72143
Gepp	72538
Geridge	72046
Gethsemane	72004
Gibbs	71969
Gibson (Craighead County)	72401
Gibson (Pulaski County)	72120
Gieseck	72373
Gifford	72104
Gilbert	72636

	ZIP
Gilchrist	72358
Giles Spur	72476
Gilkey	72853
Gillett	72055
Gillham	71841
Gilmore	72339
Gin City	71826
Gladden	72331
Gleason	72032
Glemore	72801
Glencoe	72539
Glendale	71667
Glen Rose	72104
Glenview (Part of North Little Rock)	72117
Glenwood	71943
Gobblers Point	72080
Gobell	72366
Gold Creek	72032
Golden City	72927
Golden Lake	72395
Gold Lake Estates	72032
Goobertown	72417
Good Hope	71726
Goodwin	72340
Goose Camp	72840
Goshen	72735
Gosnell	72319
Gould	71643
Gourd	71639
Gourd Neck	72101
Grady	71644
Grand Glaise	72020
Grandview	72601
Grange	72521
Grannis	71944
Grapevine	72057
Graphic	72921
Grassy Lake Bottom	72331
Gravel Hill (Van Buren County)	72030
Gravel Hill (White County)	72136
Gravelly	72838
Gravelridge (Bradley County)	71631
Gravel Ridge (Pulaski County)	72076
Graves Chapel	71846
Gravesville	72039
Gravette	72736
Gray Rock	72855
Grays	72101
Grayson	72927
Greasy Corner	72346
Green Acres	72756
Greenbrier	72058
Greene High	72450
Greenfield	72432
Green Forest	72638
Green Hill	71675
Greenland	72737
Green Tree	72031
Greenway	72430
Greenwich Village	75502
Greenwood (Franklin County)	72949
Greenwood (Sebastian County)	72936
Greers Ferry	72067
Gregory	72059
Grider	72370
Griffith Spring	71667
Griffithtown	71923
Griffithville	72060
Grubbs	72431
Guernsey	71801
Guion	72540
Gum Corner	71640
Gum Log	72801
Gum Springs (Clark County)	71923
Gum Springs (Newton County)	72641
Gurdon	71743
Guy	72061
Hackett	72937
Hagarville	72839
Half Moon	72315
Halley	71638
Halley Junction	71638
Halliday	72443
Hamburg	71646
Hamil	72460
Hamilton	72024
Hampton	71744
Hampton's Landing	72041
Hancock	72419
Hanna	71640
Hannaberry	72160
Hanover	72560
Happy	72143
Happy Bend	72823
Happy Corners	72438

* Area Zip Code   † Post Office Boxes

Place	ZIP	Place	ZIP	Place	ZIP
Hardin	71602	Holman	72846	Jerusalem	72080
Hardy	72542	Holub	72360	Jessieville	71949
Hargrave Corner	72461	Homan	75502	Jesup	72466
Harlow	71766	Homewood	72025	Joan	71923
Harmon (Boone County)	72601	Hon	72958	Johnson	72741
Harmon (Washington		Hooker	72450	Johnson Addition	72411
County)	72701	Hope	71801	Johnstown	72112
Harmontown	72501	Hopeville	71766	Johnsville	71647
Harmony (Columbia County)	71753	Hopewell (Cleburne County)	72137	Joiner	72350
Harmony (Johnson County)	72830	Hopewell (Greene County)	72443	Jolliff Store	72442
Harmony (Madison County)	72740	Hopewell (Lawrence		Jonesboro	72401-03
Harmony (White County)	72143	County)	72433	For specific Jonesboro Zip Codes	
Harmony Grove	71701	Hopper	71935	call (501) 972-8400, or your local	
Harness	72645	Horatio	71842	postmaster.	
Harp	72104	Horseshoe	72112	Jones Mills	72105
Harrell	71745	Horseshoe Bend	72512	Jonesville	71837
Harriet	72639	Horseshoe Lake (Crittenden		Jonquil	72346
Harrisburg	72432	County)	72348	Joplin	71957
Harrison	72601*	Horseshoe Lake (Woodruff		Jordan	72519
	72602†	County)	72006	Joy	72143
Hartford	72938	Horton	72326	Joyce City	71762
Hartman	72840	Hot Springs Mall (Part of		Joyland Park	72927
Hartwell	72740	Hot Springs National		Judd Hill	72472
Harvey	72841	Park)	71901	Judsonia	72081
Haskell	72015	Hot Springs National Park	71901-14	Julius	72327
Hasty	72640		71951	Jumbo	72556
Hatchie Coon	72472	For specific Hot Springs National		Junction City	71749
Hatfield	71945	Park Zip Codes call		Kansas	71772
Hattieville	72063	(501) 623-7704,		Kearney	72132
Hatton	71946	or your local postmaster.		Kedron	71665
Havana	72842	Hot Springs Village	71909	Keiser	72351
Hayley	72040	Hot Springs Village (census		Kellum	71832
Haynes	72341	designated place)	71901	Kelso	71674
Hazen	72064	Houston	72070	Kenova	71762
Heafer	72331	Howell	72071	Kensett	72082
Healing Springs	72712	Hoxie	72433	Kent	71701
Heart	72539	Hudspeth	71638	Kentucky	72015
Heber Springs	72543	Huff	72501	Kenwood	72823
Hebron	71660	Huffman	72315	Keo	72083
Hector	72843	Hughes	72348	Kerlin	71753
Helena	72342	Hulbert (Part of West		Kerr	72142
Helena Crossing (Part of		Memphis)	72301	Kibler	72956
Helena)	72342	Humnoke	72072	Kimberley	71958
Helena Junction	72342	Humphrey	72073	Kindall	72374
Hempwallace	71964	Hunt	72844	King	71841
Henderson	72544	Hunter	72074	Kingsland	71652
Henderson College (Part of		Huntington	72940	Kingston (Madison County)	72742
Arkadelphia)	71923	Huntsville	72740	Kingston (Yell County)	72853
Hendrix College (Part of		Hurricane Grove	71957	Kingswood Estates	72653
Conway)	72032	Hutchinson	72534	Kingtown	72366
Hensley	72065	Huttig	71747	Kirby	71950
Herbine	71665	Hydrick	72324	Kirkland	71751
Hergett	72401	Ida	72546	Knob	72436
Heritage Estates	72653	Imboden	72434	Knobel	72435
Herman	72401	Immanuel	72003	Knoxville	72845
Hermitage (Bradley County)	71647	Index	75502	Koch Ridge	72031
Hermitage (Pulaski County)	72206	Indian Bay	72069	Lacey	71655
Herndon	72401	Indiandale (Part of Hot		Laconia	72379
Hervey	75502	Springs)	71901	LaCrosse	72584
Heth	72346	Indianhead Lake Estates		Ladd	71601
Hickeytown	72847	(Part of North Little Rock)	72116	Ladelle	71655
Hickman	72315	Indian Meadows	65733	Lafe	72436
Hickoria	72422	Indian Springs	72002	Lafferty	72561
Hickory Creek	72745	Industrial (Part of Little		La Grange	72352
Hickory Flat	72121	Rock)	72209	Lake Bull Shoales Estates	72687
Hickory Hill	72110	Ingalls	71647	Lake Catherine	71901
Hickory Plains	72066	Ingleside	72112	Lake City	72437
Hickory Ridge	72347	Ingram	72478	Lake Dick	72004
Hickory Valley	72521	Ink	71953	Lake Elmdale	72764
Hicks	72366	Ione	72927	Lake Francis	72761
Hicks Station	72394	Iron Springs	72206	Lake Hamilton	71913
Hicksville	72366	Island Town	72112	Lake Poinsett	72432
Hidden Valley	72542	Iuka	72519	Lakeport	71653
Higden	72067	Ivan	71748	Lakeside (Garland County)	71901
Higgins (Part of Little Rock)	72206	Ivesville	72207	Lakeside (Ouachita County)	71701
Higginson	72068	Ivy	71725	Lakeside Country Club	72065
Highfill	72734	Jabb	72046	Lakeside Terrace	72653
Highland	72542	Jackson Heights (Part of		Lakeview (Baxter County)	72642
Highland Estates	72745	Jacksonville)	72076	Lakeview (Conway County)	72110
Hill Creek	72127	Jacksonport	72075	Lake View (Craighead	
Hillcrest (Johnson County)	72830	Jacksonville	72076*	County)	72437
Hillcrest (Pulaski County)	72205		72078†	Lake View (Phillips County)	72342
Hilleman	72101	Jamestown (Independence		Lakeview Estates	71970
Hilltop	72482	County)	72501	Lake Village	71653
Hilo	71647	Jamestown (Johnson		Lakeway	72687
Hindsville	72738	County)	72830	Lakewood (Jefferson	
Hiram	72179	Japton	72740	County)	72004
Hiwasse	72739	Jarrett	72444	Lakewood (Pulaski County)	72116
Hobbs Spur	72952	Jasmine	72060	Lakewood Estates	75501
Holiday Hills	72531	Jasper	72641	Lamar	72846
Holiday Island	72632	Jefferson	72079	Lamartine	71770
Holland	72173	Jefferson Square (Part of		Lambert	71929
Hollis	72857	Pine Bluff)	71601	Lambrook	72353
Holly Grove	72069	Jeffersonville	72360	Landers	72472
Holly Hills	72501	Jeffrey	72118	Landis	72650
Holly Island	72461	Jennette	72327	Laneburg	71844
Holly Ridge	71640	Jennie	71649	Langford	72004
Holly Springs (Dallas		Jenny Lind	72916	Langley	71952
County)	71763	Jenson	72937	Lanieve	72416
Holly Springs (White		Jericho	72327	Lansing	72327
County)	72143	Jerome	71650	Lanty	72063
Hollywood	71923	Jersey	71651	Lapile	71765

* **Area Zip Code**   † **Post Office Boxes**

	ZIP		ZIP		ZIP
La Plaza Acres	72143	McDonald	72373	Midway (White County)	72568
Larkin	72584	McDougal	72441	Midway Corner	72376
Larue	72756	Macedonia (Columbia		Milford	71846
Latour	72355	County)	71753	Mill Creek (Pope County)	72801
Lauratown	72433	Macedonia (Conway		Mill Creek (Sebastian	
Lavaca	72941	County)	72063	County)	72901
Lawson	71750	McElroy	72396	Mill Creek Estates	72687
Lazy Acres	65733	McEntre	72476	Milligan Ridge	72442
Leachville	72438	Macey	72447	Milltown	72936
Lead Hill	72644	McFadden	72347	Milo	71646
Lebanon	71846	McGehee	71654	Mimosa Circle	72513
Lee Creek	72934	McGintytown	72058	Mineral	71841
Lehi	72364	McGregor	72036	Mineral Springs	71851
Leitner (Part of Pine Bluff)	71601	McHue	72501	Minorca	72444
Leola	72084	McJester	72121	Minturn	72445
Leonard	72461	McKamie	71860	Mist	71646
Lepanto	72354	Macks	72112	Mitchell	72583
Leslie	72645	McMilan Corner	71653	Mitchellville	71639
Lester	72437	McNab	71838	Mixon	72927
Letona	72085	McNeil	71752	Moark	72422
Levy (Part of North Little		McNutt	72476	Mohawk	71740
Rock)	72118	Macon	72076	Moko	72557
Lewisville	71845	Macon Lake	71653	Monarch	72687
Lexa	72355	McRae	72102	Monette	72447
Lexington	72031	Madding	72004	Monkey Run	72635
Liberty	72835	Madison	72359	Monnie Springs	72135
Liberty Hall	72834	Magazine	72943	Monroe	72108
Liberty Valley	72010	Magic Springs	72650	Montana	72840
Lick Mountain	72027	Magness	72553	Monte Ne Shores	72756
Light	72439	Magnet Cove	72104	Monterey	72373
Limedale	72501	Magnolia	71753	Monticello	71655
Limestone	72628	Main Street (Part of North		Montongo	71655
Lincoln	72744	Little Rock)	72119	Montreal	72940
Linder	72058	Mallet Town	72157	Montrose	71658
Lisbon	71730	Mallory Spur	72348	Moore	72856
Little Bay	71766	Malvern	72104	Moore Camp	71822
Little Flock	72756	Mammoth Spring	72554	Moorefield	72501
Little Garnett	71667	Mandalay	72442	Moreland	72801
Little Italy	72016	Mandeville	75501	Morgan	72118
Little Red	72121	Manfred	71935	Morganton	72013
Little River	72442	Mangrum	72414	Morning Star (Garland	
Little River Country Club	71866	Manila	72442	County)	71901
Little Rock	72201-31	Manning	71763	Morning Star (Searcy	
	72295	Mansfield	72944	County)	72650
For specific Little Rock Zip Codes		Many Island	72554	Morning Sun	72143
call (501) 375-8148, or your local		Maple	72616	Moro	72368
postmaster.		Maple Corner	72374	Morobay	71651
Little Rock Air Force Base	72099	Maple Grove	72472	Morrilton	72110
Locke	72946	Maple Springs	72571	Morris	71828
Lockesburg	71846	Marble	72740	Morrison Bluff	72863
Locust Bayou	71701	Marcella	72555	Morriston	72576
Locust Grove	72550	Marche	72118	Morrow	72749
Lodge Corner	72160	Marc Lyn Estates	72687	Morton	72101
Lodi	71943	Marianna	72360	Mosby	72328
Logan	72761	Marie	72395	Moscow	71659
Lollie	72106	Marion	72364	Mosley	72834
London	72847	Marked Tree	72365	Mossville	72641
Lonelm	72947	Marmaduke	72443	Mounds (Crittenden County)	72376
Lone Pine	72650	Marsden	71647	Mounds (Greene County)	72461
Lono	72084	Marsena	72650	Mountainburg	72946
Lonoke	72086	Marshall	72650	Mountain Crest	72727
Lonsdale	72087	Mars Hill	71860	Mountain Fork	71953
Lookout (Benton County)	72756	Martindale	72204	Mountain Harbor	71957
Lookout (Monroe County)	72134	Martinville	72204	Mountain Home	72653
Lorado	72401	Marvell	72366	Mountain Pine	71956
Lorine	72455	Marvinville	72842	Mountain Springs	72023
Lost Bridge Village	72732	Marysville	71753	Mountain Top	72949
Lost Cane	72442	Mason Valley	72712	Mountain Valley	71901
Lost Corner	72080	Masonville	71654	Mountain View	72560
Louann	71751	Massard (Part of Fort Smith)	72901	Mount Elba	71660
Louise	72376	Maumee	72675	Mount Elba Edition	71665
Lowell	72745	Maumelle	72113	Mount Gayler	72959
Lower Boydsville	72461	Maxville	72521	Mount George	72833
Lower Poplar Ridge	72414	Mayfield	72703	Mount Hersey	72685
Lower White Oak Lake	71726	Mayflower	72106	Mount Holly	71758
Low Gap	72641	Maynard	72444	Mount Ida	71957
Luber	72560	Maysville	72747	Mount Judea	72655
Lucas	72927	Mazarn	71933	Mount Moriah	71958
Ludwig	72830	Meadow Cliff	72335	Mount Olive (Bradley	
Lumber	71770	Meeks Settlement	71962	County)	71647
Luna	71653	Melbourne	72556	Mount Olive (Conway	
Lundell	72367	Mellwood	72367	County)	72127
Lunenburg	72556	Melrose	72550	Mount Olive (Izard County)	72556
Lunsford	72437	Mena	71953	Mount Olive (Washington	
Lurton	72856	Menifee	72107	County)	72727
Lutherville	72846	Meridian	71635	Mount Pisgah	72143
Luxora	72358	Meroney	71643	Mount Pleasant (Izard	
Lynch (Part of North Little		Merrivale (Part of Little		County)	72561
Rock)	72117	Rock)	72209	Mount Pleasant (Miller	
Lynn	72440	Mesa	72041	County)	75502
Mabelvale (Part of Little		Metalton	72601	Mount Sherman	72641
Rock)	72103	Middlebrook	72444	Mount Tabor	71956
McAlmont	72117	Middleton	72027	Mount Vernon (Faulkner	
McArthur	71654	Midland	72945	County)	72111
McBrides	65733	Midland (Part of Ft. Smith)	72904	Mount Vernon (Johnson	
McCain Mall (Part of North		Midway (Baxter County)	72651	County)	72840
Little Rock)	72116	Midway (Hot Spring County)	71941	Mozart	72051
McCaskill	71847	Midway (Howard County)	71852	Muddyfork	71852
McClelland	72006	Midway (Jackson County)	72479	Mulberry	72947
McCormick	72472	Midway (Lafayette County)	71845	Mull	72687
McCreanor	72024	Midway (Logan County)	72865	Murfreesboro	71958
McCrory	72101	Midway (Nevada County)	71857	Murphys Corner	72112

* Area Zip Code   **† Post Office Boxes**

	ZIP		ZIP		ZIP
Mustin Lake	71701	Oaklawn (Part of Hot		Pea Ridge (Benton County)	72751
Myron	72513	Springs)	71901	Pea Ridge (Desha County)	71674
Nady	72166	Oak Park (Part of Pine Bluff)	71603	Pearson	72131
Nail	72628	Oark	72852	Pecan Point	72350
Nance	72087	Oden	71961	Peel	72668
Nashville	71852	O'Donnell Bend	72358	Pelsor	72856
Nathan	71852	Ogden	71853	Pencil Bluff	71965
Natural Dam	72948	Ogemaw	71764	Pendleton	71639
Natural Steps	72135	Oil Trough	72564	Penjur	72348
Naylor	72173	O'Kean	72449	Pennington	72005
Neal Springs	71842	Okolona	71962	Pennys	71846
Nebo	71667	Ola	72853	Penrose	72101
Needham	72437	Old Alabam	72740	Peppers Landing	72041
Needmore	72958	Old Austin	72007	Perla	72104
Nella	71953	Old Grand Glaise	72020	Perry	72125
Nelsonville	72466	Old Hickory	72063	Perrytown	71801
Nettleton (Part of		Old Jenny Lind	72901	Perryville	72126
Jonesboro)	72401	Old Joe	72658	Peter Pender	72933
Neuhardt	72376	Old Town	72389	Peter Rock Acres	72031
Newark	72562	Old Union	71730	Pettigrew	72752
New Augusta (Part of		Old Weona	72472	Pettus	72086
Augusta)	72006	Olio	72958	Pettyville	72442
New Blaine	72851	Oliver	72958	Pfeiffer	72501
Newburg	72556	Olmstead	72116	Philadelphia	72401
New Dixie	72016	Olvey	72601	Philander Smith College	
New Edinburg	71660	Olyphant	72020	(Part of Little Rock)	72202
Newell	71730	Oma	71964	Phillips Bayou	72360
New Gascony	72004	Omaha	72662	Phoenix Village (Part of Fort	
New Hope (Dallas County)	71763	Omega (Carroll County)	72616	Smith)	72901
New Hope (Drew County)	71655	Omega (Yell County)	72834	Pickens (Desha County)	71662
New Hope (Hempstead		Onda	72774	Pickens (White County)	72143
County)	71801	One Horse Store	72160	Pickering	71730
New Hope (Independence		Oneida	72369	Piercetown	72641
County)	72501	Onia	72663	Piggott	72454
Newhope (Pike County)	71959	Onyx	72857	Pike City	71958
New Hope (Pope County)	72801	Opal (Polk County)	71953	Pilgrims Rest	72764
New London	71765	Opal (White County)	72012	Pindall	72669
Newnata	72657	Oppelo	72110	Pine Bluff	71601-13
Newport	72112	Optimus	72519	For specific Pine Bluff Zip Codes	
New Spadra	72830	Orion	72132	call (501) 536-3535, or your local	
New Summit (Part of		Orlando	71660	postmaster.	
Benton)	72011	Osage	72638	Pine Bluff Arsenal	71602
New Town (Crawford		Osage Mills	72712	Pine Bluff Southeast (Part of	
County)	72921	Osage Village	72531	Pine Bluff)	71601
Newtown (Jefferson		Osceola	72370	Pine City	72069
County)	72004	Ott	65626	Pine Grove	71763
Nimmo	72143	Otto	72173	Pine Grove Valley	72944
Nimmons	72461	Otwell	72401	Pine Ridge	71966
Nimrod	72126	Ouachita	71763	Pine Tree	72326
Nine Elms	72761	Ouachita College (Part of		Pineville	72566
Noble Lake	71601	Arkadelphia)	71923	Piney (Garland County)	71913
Nodena	72395	Overcup (Conway County)	72110	Piney (Johnson County)	72847
Noland	72455	Overcup (Woodruff County)	72101	Piney Grove	71845
Norfolk Lake Estates	72544	Owensville	72087	Pinnacle	72135
Norfork	72658	Oxford	72565	Pisgah (Pike County)	71940
Norfork Village	72658	Oxley	72645	Pisgah (Yell County)	72834
Norman	71960	Ozan	71855	Pitman	72444
Norphlet	71759	Ozark	72949	Pitts	72421
Norristown (Part of		Ozark Acres (Baxter		Plainfield	71740
Russellville)	72801	County)	72635	Plainview (White County)	72081
North Bingen	71852	Ozark Acres (Sharp County)	72482	Plainview (Yell County)	72857
North Cedar (Part of Pine		Ozark Lithia	71901	Plant	72031
Bluff)	71601	Ozone	72854	Pleasant Grove (Craighead	
North Crossett	71635	Pace City	71751	County)	72401
North Dardanelle	72801	Palestine	72372	Pleasant Grove (Stone	
Northern Ohio	72365	Palmyra	71667	County)	72567
North Heights (Part of		Pangburn	72121	Pleasant Grove (Van Buren	
Texarkana)	75502	Pankey (Part of Little Rock)	72212	County)	72030
North Hughes	72348	Panther Forest	71653	Pleasant Hill (Crawford	
North Little Rock	72113-20	Paradise Landing	72106	County)	72947
For specific North Little Rock Zip		Paragould	72450-51	Pleasant Hill (Cross County)	72396
Codes call (501) 758-1707, or		For specific Paragould Zip Codes		Pleasant Hill (Garland	
your local postmaster.		call (501) 236-7636, or your local		County)	71901
Northpoint	72135	postmaster.		Pleasant Hill (Nevada	
Northwest Arkansas Mall		Paraloma	71846	County)	71857
(Part of Fayetteville)	72701	Paris	72855	Pleasant Plains	72568
Norvell (Part of Earle)	72331	Parkdale	71661	Pleasant Ridge	72632
Nuckles	72020	Parkers	72206	Pleasant Valley (Carroll	
Number Nine	72315	Parkers Chapel	71730	County)	72616
Nunley	71953	Parkers-Iron Springs	72206	Pleasant Valley (Faulkner	
Oak Bower	71929	Park Grove	72029	County)	72058
Oak Forest (Lee County)	72360	Park Hill (Part of North Little		Pleasant Valley (Izard	
Oak Forest (Pulaski County)	72201	Rock)	72116	County)	72519
Oak Grove (Carroll County)	72660	Parkin	72373	Pleasant Valley (Lafayette	
Oak Grove (Clark County)	71728	Park Place	72320	County)	71826
Oak Grove (Hot Spring		Park Plaza (Part of Little		Pleasant Valley (Perry	
County)	72104	Rock)	72205	County)	72016
Oak Grove (Little River		Parks	72950	Pleasant Valley (Pope	
County)	71822	Parma	72044	County)	72837
Oak Grove (Lonoke County)	72007	Parmenter Addition	72315	Pleasant View (Conway	
Oak Grove (Nevada		Parnell	72023	County)	72110
County)	71858	Paron	72122	Pleasant View (Franklin	
Oak Grove (Perry County)	72070	Parthenon	72666	County)	72949
Oak Grove (Pope County)	72801	Pastoria	72152	Pleasure Heights	72745
Oak Grove (Pulaski County)	72118	Patmos	71801	Plumerville	72127
Oak Grove (Sevier County)	71846	Patrick	72727	Plunketts	72017
Oak Grove (Washington		Patsville	71647	Pocahontas	72455
County)	72764	Patterson	72123	Point Cedar	71921
Oak Grove Heights	72450	Pawheen	72438	Pollard	72456
Oakhaven	71801	Payneway	72472	Ponca	72670
Oak Hill	71822	Peach Orchard	72453	Ponders	72476
Oakland	72661	Pearcy	71964	Pontoon	72025

* Area Zip Code   † Post Office Boxes

Place	ZIP	Place	ZIP	Place	ZIP
Poplar Grove	72374	Rocky Hill	72629	Shady Grove (Johnson County)	72830
Portia	72457	Rocky Mound (Hempstead County)	71801	Shady Grove (Mississippi County)	72442
Portland	71663	Rocky Mound (Miller County)	71837	Shady Grove (Nevada County)	71857
Posey	72392	Rodney	72519	Shady Grove (Poinsett County)	72472
Possum Grape	72020	Roe	72134	Shakertown	71923
Postelle	72366	Rogers	72756*	Shannon	72455
Post Oak	71658		72757†	Shannondale	72348
Potter	71953	Rogers Avenue (Part of Fort Smith)	72903	Shannon Hills	72103
Potter Junction	71953	Rohwer	71666	Shannonville	72331
Pottsville	72858	Roland	72135	Sharman	71860
Poughkeepsie	72569	Rolla	72104	Sharum	72455
Powhatan	72458	Romance	72136	Shaw	72015
Poyen	72128	Rondo (Lee County)	72355	Shearerville	72346
Prairie Creek	72756	Rondo (Miller County)	75502	Shelbyville	72521
Prairie Grove	72753	Rosa	72358	Shell Lake	72346
Prairie View	72863	Rosboro	71921	Sheppard	71838
Prattsville	72129	Rose Bud	72137	Sheridan	72150
Prescott	71857	Rose City (Part of North Little Rock)	72117	Sherrill	72152
Preston	72032	Rose Hill	71655	Sherwood	72120
Preston Ferry	72134	Roseland	72442	Sherwood Hills	72105
Price Place	65729	Rose Meadow (Part of Little Rock)	72206	Shiloh (Howard County)	71851
Prim	72130	Roseville	72949	Shiloh (Pope County)	72801
Princedale	72373	Rosie	72571	Shippen	72351
Princeton	71725	Ross	72846	Shirley	72153
Process City	71832	Rosston	71858	Shoffner	72112
Proctor	72376	Ross Van-Ness	71640	Shover Springs	71801
Promised Land (Mississippi County)	72315	Rotan	72370	Sidney	72577
Promised Land (Poinsett County)	72472	Round Pond	72378	Sidon	72137
Providence	72081	Rover	72860	Signal Hill	72560
Provo	71846	Rowell	71665	Siloam Springs	72761
Pruitt	72648	Roy	71852	Silver	71957
Pumpkin Bend	72101	Royal	71968	Silver Hill	72675
Pyatt	72672	Royal Oak	72103	Silver Ridge (Cleburne County)	72530
Quarry Heights	72826	Rubicon	72015	Silver Ridge (Sevier County)	71846
Quinn	71730	Ruddell Hill	72501	Sims	71969
Quitman	72131	Rudy	72952	Simsboro	72348
Raggio	72320	Rule	72638	Sitka	72482
Ragtown	72069	Rumley	72645	Skunkhollow	72032
Rainbow Island	72121	Rupert	72031	Slaytonville	72937
Ralph	72687	Rushing	72051	Slonikers Mill	72372
Rambo Riveria	72756	Russell	72139	Slovak	72160
Ramsey	71742	Russellville	72801*	Smackover	71762
Ramsey Hill	72501		72811†	Smale	72021
Ranger	72824	Rutherford	72501	Smearney	71647
Ratcliff	72951	Rye	71665	Smithdale	72373
Ratio	72333	Sacred Heart	72840	Smiths Corner	72368
Ravanna	75556	Saddle	72554	Smithville (Lawrence County)	72466
Ravenden	72459	Saffell	72572	Smithville (Miller County)	71834
Ravenden Springs	72460	Sage	72573	Snow	72687
Rawlison	72348	Saginaw	71941	Snowball	72650
Ray Lee Addition	72801	St. Charles	72140	Snow Hill	71751
Reader	71726	St. Francis	72464	Snow Lake	72379
Readland	71640	St. Joe	72675	Snyder	71658
Rea Valley	72634	St. Matthews	71752	Social Hill	72104
Rector	72461	St. Paul	72760	Solgohachia	72156
Redfield	72132	St. Vincent	72063	Sonora	72764
Redland	71857	Salado	72575	South Bend	72076
Red Leaf	71653	Salem (Fulton County)	72576	South Crossett (Part of Crossett)	71635
Red Onion	72447	Salem (Lee County)	72368	Southern Hills	72601
Red Springs	71743	Salem (Pike County)	71943	Southern State College (Part of Magnolia)	71753
Red Star	72752	Salem (Saline County)	72015	South Fort Smith (Part of Fort Smith)	72906
Red Wing	71832	Salesville	72653	South Jacksonville (Part of Jacksonville)	72076
Reed	71670	Saltillo	72032	Southland (Craighead County)	72437
Reedville	71639	Salus	72854	Southland (Phillips County)	72355
Relfs Bluff	71667	Sand Hill	72040	South Lead Hill	72644
Remmel	72112	Sandtown	72501	South Lewisville	71845
Rena	72956	Sandy Bend	71765	South Ozark	72949
Republican	72058	Sandyland	71762	South Sheridan	72150
Revel	72006	Sandy Ridge	72315	South Shore Park	72543
Rex	72031	Sans Souci	72370	South Side (Independence County)	72501
Reydell	72133	Sarassa	71644	South Side (Pulaski County)	72206
Reyno	72462	Saratoga	71859	Southside (Van Buren County)	72013
Rich	72021	Sardis	72011	Spadra	72830
Richardson	72004	Savoy	72703	Sparkman	71763
Richland View	72727	Schaal	71851	Spence Junction	72856
Richmond	71822	Schaberg	72946	Spirit Lake	71845
Richwood	72476	Schooley	71851	Springdale	72762-66
Richwoods	71923	Schug	72450	For specific Springdale Zip Codes call (501) 751-4441, or your local postmaster.	
Ridgeway	72601	Scotland	72141		
Rio Vista	72010	Scott	72142		
Risher	72421	Scottsville	72837	Springfield	72157
Rison	71665	Scott Valley	72360	Springhill (Faulkner County)	72058
Rivercliff Estates	72756	Scranton	72863	Spring Hill (Hempstead County)	71801
Riverdale	72941	Screeton	72064	Spring Lake Estates	72653
River Mountain	72835	Searcy	72143	Springtown	72767
Riverside	72101	Seaton	72046	Spring Valley (Independence County)	72501
Rivervale	72377	Seaton Dump	72046		
Riverview	72110	Sedgwick	72465		
Riverview Addition	72501	Sellers Store	72542		
Rixey (Part of North Little Rock)	72117	Selma	71670		
Robertsville	72063	Seyppel	72348		
Robinson	72761	Shady	71953		
Rob Roy	72004	Shady Grove (Faulkner County)	72058		
Rock Hill	71846	Shady Grove (Fulton County)	72583		
Rockport	72104				
Rock Springs	71675				
Rockwell (Garland County)	71901				
Rockwell (Garland County)	71913				
Rocky	71953				

	ZIP		ZIP		ZIP
Spring Valley (Pulaski County)	72210	Three Way	72370	Viola	72583
		Tichnor	72166	Violet Hill	72584
Spring Valley (Washington County)	72764	Tie Plant (Part of North Little Rock)	72117	Vista Shores	72732
Sprudel	71838	Tillar	71670	Wabash	72389
Stacy (Crittenden County)	72384	Tilly	72679	Wabbaseka	72175
Stacy (Poinsett County)	72472	Tilton	72347	Wakefield Village (Part of	
Stamps	71860	Timber Lake Manor	72531	Little Rock)	72201
Standard-Umsted	71762	Timber Lane	71833	Walcott	72474
Stanford	72450	Timbo	72680	Waldenburg	72475
Star City	71667	Tinsman	71767	Waldo	71770
State Capitol (Part of Little Rock)	72201	Toad Suck	72016	Waldron	72958
		Togo	72373	Walker (Columbia County)	71753
State Line (Columbia County)	71740	Tokio	71852	Walker (White County)	72143
		Toledo	71665	Walker's Corner	72142
State Line (Lafayette County)	71861	Tollette	71851	Walkers Creek	71861
		Tollville	72041	Walkerville	71740
State Services	72158	Toltec	72142	Wallace	71836
State University (Part of Jonesboro)	72467	Tomahawk	72675	Walnut	72854
		Tomato	72381	Walnut Corner (Greene County)	72416
Staves	71665	Tomberlin	72046		
Stelltown	71940	Toneyville (Part of Jacksonville)	72076	Walnut Corner (Phillips County)	72312
Stephens	71764			Walnut Grove (Clay County)	72435
Steprock	72159	Tongin	72320	Walnut Grove (Independence County)	72524
Stevens Creek	72010	Tontitown	72770		
Stevens Landing	72472	Trammellville	72461	Walnut Grove (Van Buren County)	72031
Stokes	72455	Traskwood	72167		
Stonewall	72450	Treasure Hills	72032	Walnut Grove (Washington County)	72730
Stony Point	72070	Treat	72854		
Story	71970	Trenton	72374	Walnut Grove (Yell County)	72842
Strangers Home	72410	Troy	71764	Walnut Hill	71826
Strawberry (Johnson County)	72846	Trumann	72472	Walnut Ridge	72476
		Tucker	72168	Walnut Springs	71842
Strawberry (Lawrence County)	72469	Tuckerman	72473	Walters	72438
		Tuckertown	72321	Waltreak	72833
Stringtown	71842	Tucker Unit	72168	Wampler Spur (Part of Pine Bluff)	71601
Strong	71765	Tulip	71725		
Stump City	72346	Tull	72015	Ward	72176
Sturkie	72578	Tully	72472	Wardell	72350
Stuttgart	72160	Tulot	72472	War Eagle	72756
Subiaco	72865	Tumbling Shoals	72581	Warm Springs	72478
Success	72470	Tupelo	72169	Warner	71701
Sugar Grove	72927	Turkey Scratch	72366	Warren	71671
Sugarloaf Lake	72937	Turner	72383	Washburn	72936
Sulphur City	72701	Turrell	72384	Washington	71862
Sulphur Rock	72579	Tuttle	72727	Washita	71957
Sulphur Springs (Benton County)	72768	Twentythree	72010	Watalula	72949
		Twin Lakes (Part of Little Rock)	72201	Waterloo	71858
Sulphur Springs (Jefferson County)	71603			Watkins Corner	72366
		Twin Springs	72205	Watson	71674
Sulphur Springs (Johnson County)	72830	Twist	72331	Watson Chapel (Part of Pine Bluff)	71601
		Tyro	71639		
Sulphur Springs (Yell County)	72834	Tyronza	72386	Wattensaw	72086
		Ulm	72170	Waveland	72867
Summers	72769	Umpire	71971	Waverly	72376
Summerville	71744	Union (Fulton County)	72576	Wayton	72628
Summit	72677	Union (Sevier County)	71832	Webb City	72949
Sumpter	71647	Union Hill	72020	Weber	72166
Sunnydale	72081	Uniontown	72955	Wedington	72701
Sunny Hill (Part of Searcy)	72143	Unionville	71665	Wedington Woods	72701
Sunset (Crittenden County)	72364	Unity	71852	Weiner	72479
Sunset (Washington County)	72959	University Mall (Part of Little Rock)	72205	Welcome	71861
				Welcome Home	72650
Sunshine (Ashley County)	71661	University of Arkansas at Monticello (Part of Monticello)	71655	Weldon	72112
Sunshine (Garland County)	71968			Wellford	71640
Supply	72444			Weona	72472
Sutton	71835	University of Central Arkansas (Part of Conway)	72032	Wesley	72773
Swain	72628			Wesley Chapel	72110
Swan Lake	72004	Uno	72421	Wesson	71749
Sweden	72004	Upper White Oak Lake	71726	West (Part of Springdale)	72762
Sweethome (Montgomery County)	71957	Urbana	71768		72766
		Urbanette	72601	For specific West Zip Codes call (501) 750-3216, or your local postmaster.	
Sweet Home (Pulaski County)	72164	Ursula	72933		
		Vaden	71923		
Swifton	72471	Vail	72438	West Camden Heights (Part of Camden)	71701
Sycamore Bend	72348	Valley Gin	71837		
Sylamore	72556	Valley Springs	72682	West Crossett	71635
Sylvan Hills (Part of Sherwood)	72116	Valley View	72401	West End (Part of Pine Bluff)	71601
		Van	72042		
Sylvania	72176	Van Buren	72956	Western Grove	72685
Sylverino	75502	Vandervoort	71972	West Fork	72774
Tafton	72183	Vanndale	72387	West Gum Springs (Part of Gum Springs)	71923
Talley	71740	Varner Unit	71644		
Tall Trees	72322	Vaughn	72712	West Hartford	72938
Tamo	71644	Velvet Ridge	72010	West Helena	72390
Tanglewood	72756	Vendor	72683	West Line	74734
Tannenbaum	72530	Verona	72618	West Marche	72118
Tarry	71667	Vesta	72933	West Memphis	72301*
Tate	72927	Veterans Administration Facility (Part of North Little Rock)	72114		72303†
Tates Bluff	71726			West Pangburn	72121
Taylor	71861			West Point (Benton County)	72734
Tech (Part of Russellville)	72801	Vick	71647	West Point (White County)	72178
Tennessee	71655	Victoria	72370	West Ridge	72391
Texarkana	75502	Village	71769	Westville	72956
Thebes	71658	Vilonia	72173	Westwood (Part of Little Rock)	72201
Thida	72165	Vimy Ridge	72002		
Thompson Grove	72348	Vincent	72327	Wharton	72740
Thornburg	72126	Vine Prairie	72947	Wheatley	72392
Thorney	72727	Vineyard	72360	Wheeler	72775
Thornton	71766	Viney Grove	72753	Wheeling	72576
Three Brothers	72653	Vinity Corner	72143	Whelen Springs	71772
Three Creeks	71749			Whispering Springs	72067

* Area Zip Code   **† Post Office Boxes**

	ZIP		ZIP		ZIP
Whistleville	72442	Windamere (Part of Little		Woodrow	72130
Whitaker	72432	Rock)	72201	Woodson	72180
White	71635	Winesburg	72401	Wooster	72181
White Cliffs	71846	Winfield	72958	Worden	72010
White Hall (Drew County)	71655	Winfrey	72959	Wright	72182
White Hall (Jefferson		Wing	72860	Wrights Corner	72010
County)	71602	Winslow	72959	Wrightsville	72183
Whitehall (Lee County)	72320	Winston Terrace (Part of		Wrightsville Unit	72183
Whitehall (Poinsett County)	72432	Little Rock)	72201	Wycamp	72390
Whiteoak	72949	Winthrop	71866	Wye	72016
White Oak Bluff	71665	Wirth	72554	Wyman	72701
White Rock	72701	Wiseman	72587	Wynne	72396-97
Whitetown	71961	Witcherville	72940	For specific Wynne Zip Codes call	
Whiteville	72635	Witherspoon	71923	(501) 238-2131, or your local	
Whitmore	72394	Witter	72776	postmaster.	
Whitton	72386	Wittsburg	72396	Wyola	72959
Wickes	71973	Witts Springs	72686	Yale	72752
Wideman	72585	Wiville	72101	Yancopin	71674
Widener	72394	Wolf Bayou	72530	Yancy	71855
Wiederkehr Village	72821	Wonderview	72063	Yarbro	72315
Wilburn	72179	Woodberry	71744	Yardelle	72685
Wild Cherry	72576	Woodland	72830	Y City	72926
Wildwood	72346	Woodland Corner	72315	Yellow Bayou	71653
Williamson	71842	Woodland Heights (Part of		Yellville	72687
Williford	72482	Little Rock)	72201	Yocana	71953
Willisville	71864	Woodland Hills (Fulton		Yoestown	72921
Willow	72084	County)	72542	Yorktown	71678
Wilmar	71675	Woodland Hills (Saline		Zachery	72366
Wilmot	71676	County)	72002	Zent	72021
Wilson (Mississippi County)	72395	Woodlawn (Cleveland		Zinc	72601
Wilson (Pope County)	72823	County)	71665	Zion	72556
Wilton	71865	Woodlawn (Lonoke County)	72007	Zion Hill	72110
Winchester	71677				

	ZIP		ZIP		ZIP
'A' (Postal Station) (Part of			91737		92513
San Francisco)	94115	For specific Alta Loma Zip Codes		For specific Arlington Zip Codes	
Aberdeen	93526	call (714) 987-3100, or your local		call (714) 788-4600, or your local	
Acacia Acres	93291	postmaster.		postmaster.	
Academy	93611	Alta Sierra (Kern County)	93285	Arlington Heights Estate	95934
Acampo	95220	Alta Sierra (Nevada County)	95949	Arlynda Corners	95536
Actis Gardens	93501	Altaville (Part of Angels		Armistead	93527
Acton	93510	Camp)	95221	Armona	93202
Adams Springs	95426	Alta Vista	93514	Army Point	94510
Adelaida	93446	Alto (Part of Mill Valley)	94941	Army Terminal (Part of	
Adelanto	92301	Alton	95540	Oakland)	94626
Adin	96006	Alturas	96101	Arnold	95223
Adobe Corners	92392	Alvarado (Part of Union		Arnold Heights	92508
Aerial Acres	93523	City)	94587	Aromas	95004
Aetna Springs	94567	Alviso (Part of San Jose)	95002	Arrowbear Lake	92382
Afton	95920	Amador City	95601	Arrowhead Highlands	92325
Agate Bay	96140	Amarillo Beach	90265	Arroyo Grande	93420*
Ager	96064	Ambassador (Part of Los			93521†
Agnew (Part of Santa Clara)	95054	Angeles)	90005	Arroyo Vista (Part of Dublin)	94566
	95056	Ambler Park	93901	Artesia	90701-03
For specific Agnew Zip Codes call		Amboy	92304	For specific Artesia Zip Codes call	
(408) 452-4300, or your local		Ambrose	94565	(213) 860-6694, or your local	
postmaster.		American Canyon	94589	postmaster.	
Agoura Hills	91301*	American House	95981	Artois	95913
	91376†	Amphibious Base	92155	Arvin	93203
Agua Caliente	95476			Arvin (labor camp)	93308
Agua Caliente Indian		**Anaheim**	92801-25	Ash Creek	96057
Reservation	92262	For specific Anaheim Zip Codes		Ashland	94541
Agua Dulce	91350	call (714) 520-2600, or your local		Asian Village (Part of	
Aguanga	92536	postmaster.		Westminster)	92683
Ahwahnee	93601			Asilomar (Part of Pacific	
Airbase (Part of Santa		*FINANCIAL INSTITUTIONS*		Grove)	93950
Maria)	93454			Aspendell	93514
Airport (Part of Oakland)	94614	United California Savings		Asti	95425
Alabama Hills	93545	Bank	92805	Atascadero	93422*
Alameda	94501-02				93423†
For specific Alameda Zip Codes		*HOTELS/MOTELS*		Athens	90047
call (510) 748-5366, or your local				Atherton	94027
postmaster.		Anaheim Hilton & Towers	92802	Athlone	95333
Alamo	94507	Sheraton-Anaheim Hotel	92802	Atlanta	95366
Alamo Oaks (Part of				Atwater	95301
Danville)	94526	Anaheim Hills (Part of		Atwood (Part of Placentia)	92601
Alamorio	92227	Anaheim)	92808	Auberry	93602
Albany	94706	Anaheim Plaza (Part of		Auburn	95602-04
Alberhill	92530	Anaheim)	92801	For specific Auburn Zip Codes call	
Albion	95410	Ana Verde (Part of		(916) 885-7944, or your local	
Albrae (Part of Fremont)	94538	Palmdale)	93551	postmaster.	
Alcatraz (Part of San		Anchor Bay	95445	August	95201
Francisco)	94123	Anderson	96007	Avalon	90704
Alderbrook Tract (Part of		Anderson Springs	95461	Avalon Village (Part of	
Cupertino)	95014	Andrew Jackson (Part of		Carson)	90745
Aldercroft Heights	95030	San Diego)	92115	Avenal	93204
Alderpoint	95511	Angels Camp	95222	Avery	95224
Alder Springs	93602	Angelus Oaks	92305	Avila Beach	93424
Alessandro (Part of		Angiola	93212	Avocado Heights	91746
Riverside)	92508	Angora Highlands	96150	Azusa	91702
Alexander Valley	95441	Angwin	94508	'B' (Postal Station) (Part of	
Alhambra	91801-99	Annapolis	95412	San Francisco)	94126
For specific Alhambra Zip Codes		Annex III (Part of Los		Baden (Part of South San	
call (818) 289-9101, or your local		Angeles)	91405	Francisco)	94080
postmaster.		Antelope	95678	Badger	93603
Alhambra Valley	94553	Antelope Acres	93534	Bailey (Part of Whittier)	90601
Alisal (Part of Salinas)	93905	Antelope Valley Mall (Part of		Baker	92309
Aliso Viejo	92656	Palmdale)	93550	Baker Ranch	95631
Alleghany	95910	Antioch	94509*	Bakersfield	93301-89
Allendale	95688		94531†	For specific Bakersfield Zip Codes	
Allensworth	93219	Antonio	93437	call (805) 861-4346, or your local	
Alliance (Part of Arcata)	95521	Anza	92539	postmaster.	
Allied Gardens (Part of San		Applegate	95703	Bakersfield East (Part of	
Diego)	92120	Apple Valley	92307-08	Bakersfield)	93305
Almaden Plaza (Part of San		For specific Apple Valley Zip		Bakersfield Plaza (Part of	
Jose)	95118	Codes call (619) 247-7819, or		Bakersfield)	93308
Almaden Valley (Part of San		your local postmaster.		Bakersfield South (Part of	
Jose)	95120	Aptos	95001†	Bakersfield)	93304
Almanor (Plumas County)	95923		95003*	Balance Rock	93260
Almanor (Plumas County)	96020	Aptos Hills-Larkin Valley	95003	Balboa (Part of Newport	
Almonte	94941	Arbolada (Part of Ojai)	93023	Beach)	92661
Alondra	90249	Arbuckle	95912	Balboa Bay Shores (Part of	
Alpaugh	93201	Arcade (Los Angeles		Newport Beach)	92663
Alpine	91901*	County)	90052	Balboa Island (Part of	
	91903†	Arcade (Sacramento		Newport Beach)	92662
Alpine Forest	93561	County)	95821	Balch Camp	93602
Alpine Heights	91901	Arcadia	91006-07	Balderson Station	95634
Alpine Meadows	96146		91066	Baldwin Hills Regional	
Alpine Village (Riverside			91077	Shopping Mall (Part of	
County)	92262	For specific Arcadia Zip Codes		Los Angeles)	90067
Alpine Village (Tulare		call (818) 446-4678, or your local		Baldwin Lake	92314
County)	93265	postmaster.		Baldwin Park	91706
Alta	95701	Arcata	95521	Baldy Mesa	92371
Altadena	91001-03	Arch Beach Heights (Part of		Ballarat	93562
For specific Altadena Zip Codes		Laguna Beach)	92651	Ballard	93463
call (818) 794-1147, or your local		Arden	95825	Ballico	95303
postmaster.		Arden-Arcade	95821	Ballou (Part of Ontario)	91761
Alta Heights (Part of Napa)	94559	Arden Fair Mall (Part of		Balls Ferry	96007
Alta Hill	95945	Sacramento)	95815	Baltimore Park (Part of	
Al Tahoe (Part of South		Arden Town	95825	Larkspur)	94939
Lake Tahoe)	96151	Ardmore (Part of South		Bandini (Part of Commerce)	90040
Alta Loma (Part of Rancho		Gate)	90280	Bangor	95914
Cucamonga)	91701	Arena	95301	Bankhead Springs	91934
		Argus	93562	Banner	92036
		Arleta (Part of Los Angeles)	91331	Banning	92220
		Arlington (Part of Riverside)	92503	Banta	95304

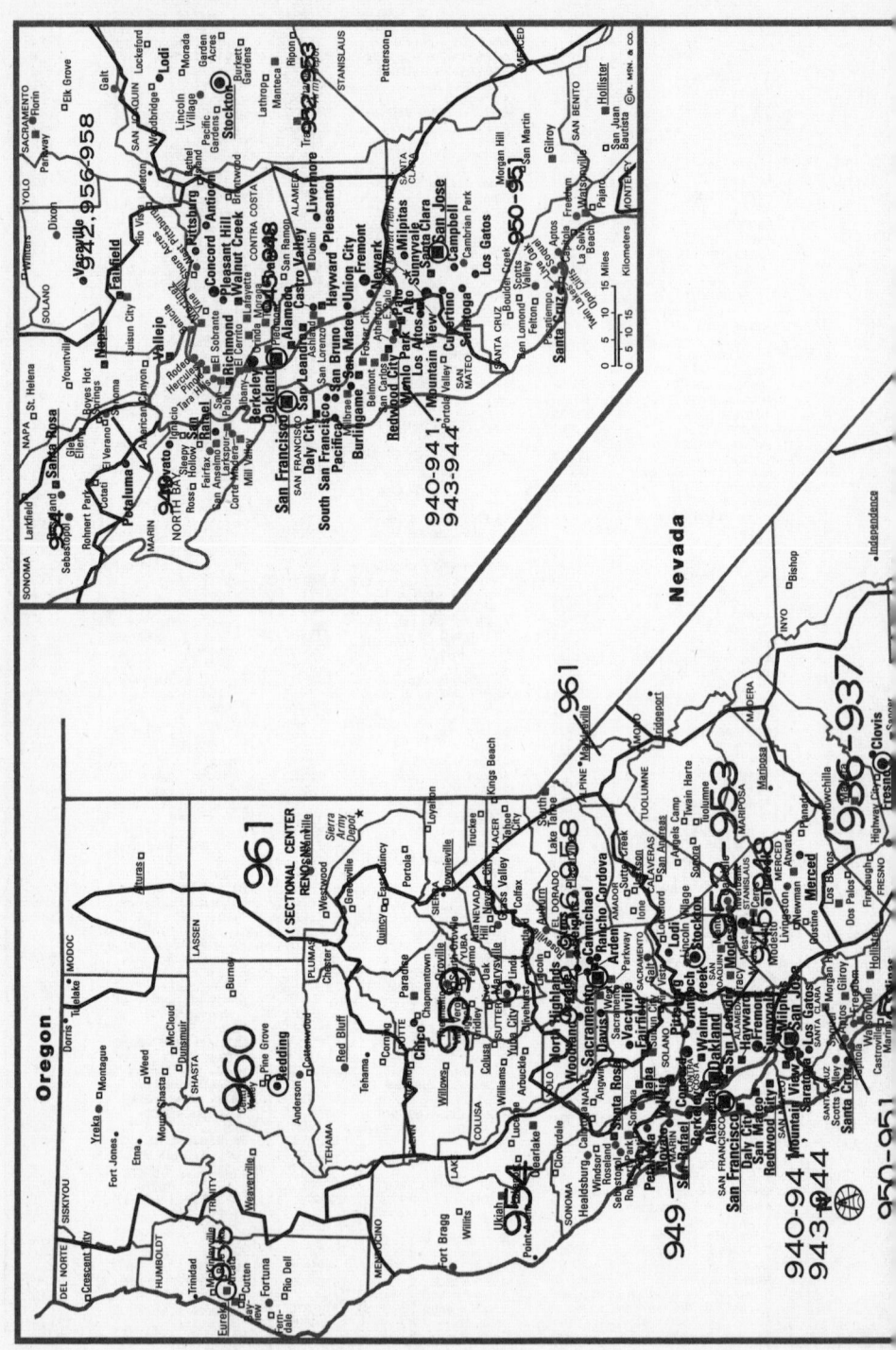

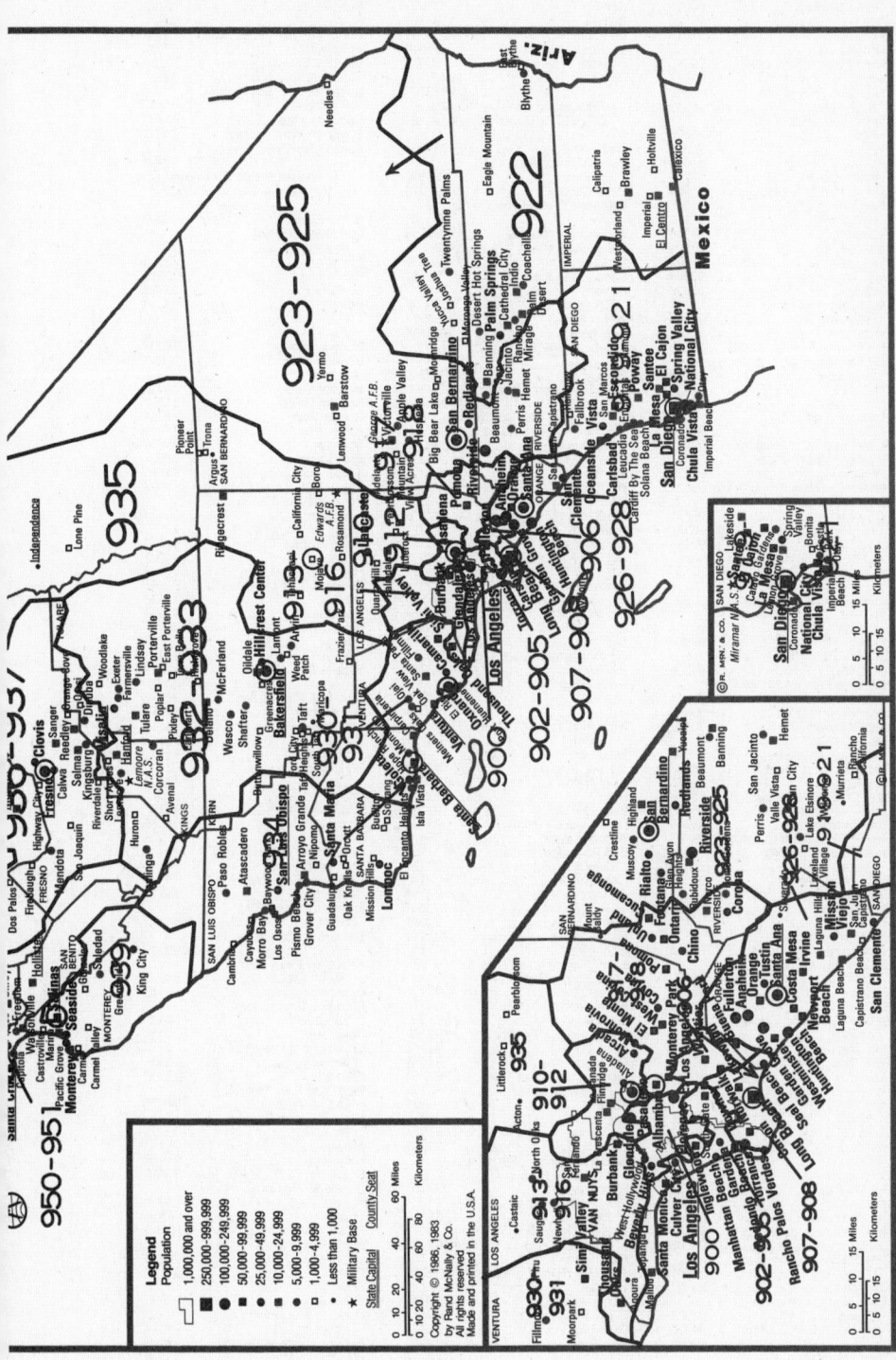

	ZIP
Barber City (Part of Westminster)	92683
Bard	92222
Bardsdale	93015
Barona	92040
Barona Indian Reservation	92040
Barrett	91917
Barrington (Part of Los Angeles)	90049
Barron Park (Part of Palo Alto)	94306
Barstow	92311*
	92312†
Barstow Colony	93705
Barton (Part of Fresno)	93702
Base Line (Part of San Bernardino)	92410
Bassett	91746
Bassetts	96125
Bass Lake	93604
Bass Lake Height	93644
Batavia	95620
Baumberg (Part of Hayward)	94545
Baxter	95701
Bay (Part of Big Bear Lake)	92315
Bay Fair Mall (Part of San Leandro)	94578
Bayliss	95943
Bayo Vista	94572
Bay Park (Part of San Diego)	92110
Bayshore (Part of Brisbane)	94005
Bayshore Mall (Part of Eureka)	95501
Bayside (Humboldt County)	95524
Bayside (Santa Clara County)	95131
	95134
	95164
For specific Bayside Zip Codes call (707) 822-1683, or your local postmaster.	
Bayview (Humboldt County)	95503
Bay View (San Francisco County)	94124
Bayview-Montalvin	94806
Bayview Park (Contra Costa County)	94806
Bay View Park (Monterey County)	93955
Baywood-Los Osos	93402
Baywood Park	93402
Beach Center (Part of Huntington Beach)	92648
Beale Air Force Base	95903
Bear Creek	95340
Bear Creek Estates	95006
Bear River Lake	95666
Bear River Pines	95945
Bear Valley (Alpine County)	95223
Bear Valley (Mariposa County)	95338
Bear Valley Springs	93561
Beaumont	92223
Beckwourth	96129
Bee Rock	93426
Bel Air (Part of Los Angeles)	90024
Bel Aire Estates (Part of Tiburon)	94920
Belden	95915
Bell	90201
Bella Vista (Contra Costa County)	94565
Bella Vista (Kern County)	93283
Bella Vista (Los Angeles County)	90022
Bella Vista (Shasta County)	96008
Belle Haven (Part of Menlo Park)	94025
Belleview	95370
Bellflower	90706*
	90707†
Bell Gardens	90201
Bell Mountain	92392
Belltown	92509
Bel Marin Keys	94947
Belmont	94002*
	94003†
Belmont Shore (Part of Long Beach)	90803
Belridge Farms	93251
Belvedere (Los Angeles County)	90022
Belvedere (Marin County)	94920
Belvedere Gardens	90022
Belvedere-Tiburon (Part of Belvedere)	94920
Belvernon Gardens (Part of Tiburon)	94920
Benbow	95542

	ZIP
Bend	96080
Ben Hur	93653
Benicia	94510
Ben Lomond	95005
Benton	93512
Berenda	93637
Berkeley	94701-05
	94707-20
For specific Berkeley Zip Codes call (415) 649-3100, or your local postmaster.	
Bermuda Dunes	92201
Bernal (Part of San Francisco)	94110
Berry Creek	95916
Berryessa (Part of San Jose)	95132
Berryessa Highlands	94558
Berryessa Park	94558
Berteleda	95531
Bertsch Terrace	95531
Bethany Park (Part of Scotts Valley)	95066
Bethel Island	94511
Betteravia	93454
Beverly Center (Part of Los Angeles)	90048
Beverly Hills	90209-13
For specific Beverly Hills Zip Codes call (213) 247-3400, or your local postmaster.	
Bicentennial (Part of Los Angeles)	90048
Bieber	96009
Big Bar	96010
Big Basin	95006
Big Bear City	92314
Big Bear Lake	92315
Big Bend	96011
Big Chief	96161
Big Creek	93605
Big Eddy Estates	96028
Biggs	95917
Big Lagoon Park	95570
Big Meadows	95223
Big Oak Flat	95305
Big Pine	93513
Big Pine Indian Reservation	93513
Big River	92242
Big Springs	96064
Big Sur	93920
Big Trees	95018
Bijou (Part of South Lake Tahoe)	96156
Bijou Park (Part of South Lake Tahoe)	96156
Binghamton	95620
Biola	93606
Birch Hill	92060
Birch Meadow Acres	95945
Birdcage Walk	95610
Bird Rock (Part of San Diego)	92037
Birds Landing	94512
Bishop	93514*
	93515†
Bishop Acres	93263
Bishop Indian Reservation	93514
Bitterwater	93930
Bixby (Part of Long Beach)	90807
Bixby Knolls (Part of Long Beach)	90807
Black Bear	96031
Blackhawk	94506
Black Meadow Landing	92267
Black Point	94947
Blackrock	93526
Blackstone (Part of Fresno)	93710
Blackwells Corner	93249
Blairsden	96103
Blanco	93901
Blocksburg	95514
Bloomfield	94952
Bloomfield Acres (Part of Arcata)	95521
Bloomington	92316
Blossom Hill (Part of San Jose)	95123
Blossom Valley (Part of Mountain View)	94040
Blue Canon	95715
Blue Hills (Part of Saratoga)	95070
Blue Jay	92317
Blue Lake	95525
Blue Lakes	95493
Bluewater	92242
Bluff Creek	95546
Blythe	92225-26
For specific Blythe Zip Codes call (619) 922-6157, or your local postmaster.	
Bodega	94922

	ZIP
Bodega Bay	94923
Bodfish	93205
Bolinas	94924
Bolsa (Part of Westminster)	92683
Bolsa Knolls	93906
Bombay Beach	92257
Bonadelle Ranchos	93637
Bonadelle Ranchos-Madera Ranchos	93637
Bonds Corner	92250
Bonita (Madera County)	93637
Bonita (San Diego County)	91902
	91908
For specific Bonita Zip Codes call (619) 475-4324, or your local postmaster.	
Bonny Doon	95060
Bonnyview (Part of Redding)	96001
Bonsall	92003
Boonville	95415
Bootjack	95338
Boron	93516*
	93596†
Borosolvay	93562
Borrego Springs	92004
Borrego Wells	92004
Bostonia	92021
Boulder Creek	95006
Boulder Oaks	91962
Boulder Park	91934
Boulevard	91905
Bowman	95604
Box Springs	92507
Boyes Hot Springs	95416
Boyle (Part of Los Angeles)	90033
Boyle Heights (Part of Los Angeles)	90033
Boys Republic (Part of Chino Hills)	91710
Brackney	95005
Bradbury	91010
Bradford (Part of Hayward)	94541
Bradley	93426
Brandeis	93064
Branscomb	95417
Brawley	92227
Bray	96058
Brea	92621*
	92622†
Brea Mall (Part of Brea)	92621
Brentwood	94513
Briceburg	95345
Briceland	95542
Bridgehead	94509
Bridgeport (Mariposa County)	95338
Bridgeport (Mono County)	93517
Bridgeport (Nevada County)	95977
Bridgeville	95526
Brisbane	94005
Bristol (Part of Santa Ana)	92703
Broadmoor	94015
Broadway (Sacramento County)	95818
Broadway (San Mateo County)	94010
Broadway Manchester (Part of Los Angeles)	90003
Broadway Plaza (Part of Walnut Creek)	94596
Brockway	96143
Broderick (Part of West Sacramento)	95605
Brookdale	95007
Brookhurst Center (Part of Anaheim)	92804
Brooks	95606
Brookside Park (Part of Portola Valley)	94028
Browns Corner (Part of Woodland)	95695
Browns Valley	95918
Brownsville	95919
Bruceville	95758
Brundage (Part of Bakersfield)	93307
Brush Creek	95916
Bryant (Part of Long Beach)	90805
Bryn Mawr (Part of Loma Linda)	92318
Bryson	93426
Bryte (Part of West Sacramento)	95605
Buckeye (El Dorado County)	95634
Buckeye (Shasta County)	96003
Buckhorn Lodge	95666
Buckingham Park	95451
Buck Meadows	95321
Bucks Bar	95667
Bucks Lake	95971

	ZIP
Bucks Lake Lodge	95971
Bucktail	96052
Buellton	93427
Buena (Part of Vista)	92083
Buena Park	90620-24
For specific Buena Park Zip Codes call (714) 523-1960, or your local postmaster.	
Buena Park Mall (Part of Buena Park)	90620
Buenaventura Plaza (Part of Ventura)	93003
Buena Vista (Amador County)	95640
Buena Vista (Sonoma County)	95476
Buffalo Hill	95634
Buhach	95340
Bummerville	95255
Burbank....................	91501-10
For specific Burbank Zip Codes call (818) 846-3155, or your local postmaster.	
Burkett Acres (Part of Stockton)	95215
Burkett Gardens	95205
Burlingame	94010-12
For specific Burlingame Zip Codes call (415) 342-7694, or your local postmaster.	
Burlingame Hills (Part of Burlingame)	94010
Burney	96013
Burnt Ranch................	95527
Burrel	93607
Burrough	93667
Burson	95225
Butano Canyon.............	94060
Butte City	95920
Butte Creek	95928
Butte Meadows	95942
Buttonwillow	93206
Byron	94514
'C' (Postal Station) (Part of San Francisco)	94140
Cabazon	92230
Cabazon Indian Reservation	92201
Cabin Cove	93271
Cabrillo (Part of Long Beach)	90810
Cabrillo Estates............	93402
Cache Creek	93501
Cachuma Village	93101
Cadiz	92319
Cahuilla	92539
Cahuilla Estates	92539
Cahuilla Hills	92260
Cahuilla Indian Reservation	92543
Cairns Corner	93247
Cajon Junction	92403
Calabasas	91302*
	91372†
Calabasas Highlands	91302
Calabasas Park	91302
Calaveras (Part of Stockton)	95207*
	95267†
Calaveras Yacht and Country Club Estates....	95204
Calaveritas	95249
Calavo Gardens	91941
Calexico	92231*
	92232†
Calexico Lodge	91905
Calico	92398
Cal-Ida	95922
Caliente	93518
California City	93504†
	93505*
California Correctional Institution (Kern County)	93561
California Correctional Center (Lassen County)	96130
California Hot Springs......	93207
California Medical Facility	95688
California Polytechnic State University-San Luis Obispo	93407
California Rehabilitation Center (Part of Norco)...	91760
California State Prison-Amador	95640
California Valley	93453
Calimesa	92320
Calipatria	92233
Calistoga..................	94515
Calla......................	95336
Callahan	96014
Calpella	95418
Calpine	96124
Calville	95521
Calwa (Part of Fresno)	93725
Camanche Lake............	95640

	ZIP
Camarillo	93010-12
For specific Camarillo Zip Codes call (805) 482-8894, or your local postmaster.	
Camarillo Heights (Part of Camarillo)	93010
Cambria	93428
Cambrian Park	95124
Camden	93242
Camellia (Part of Sacramento)	95819
Cameo Acres (Part of Danville)	94526
Cameron Corners	91906
Cameron Creek Colony	93223
Cameron Park..............	95682
Camino	95709
Camino Heights	95709
Campbell	95008-09
	95011
For specific Campbell Zip Codes call (408) 378-2153, or your local postmaster.	
Campbell Hot Springs	96126
Camp Connell	95223
Camp Evers (Part of Scotts Valley)	95066
Camp Meeker	95419
Camp Nelson	93208
Campo	91906
Campo Indian Reservation	91906
Campo Seco	95226
Camp Pendleton	92055
Camp Pendleton Marine Corps Base	92055
Camp Pendleton North	92055
Camp Pendleton South	92055
Camp Richardson	96150
Camp Sierra...............	93664
Camp St. Michael	95585
Camp Ten	95634
Camptonville	95922
Camp Wishon	93265
Camulos	93040
Canby	96015
Canebrake	93255
Canoga Annex (Part of Los Angeles)	91304
Canoga Park	91303-09
For specific Canoga Park Zip Codes call (818) 340-7525, or your local postmaster.	
Cantil	93519
Cantua Creek	93608
Canyon	94516
Canyon Acres (Part of Laguna Beach)	92651
Canyon Country (Part of Santa Clarita)	91351*
	91386†
Canyon Crest (Part of Riverside)	92507*
	92517†
Canyon Crest Heights (Part of Riverside)	92507
Canyondam	95923
Canyon Lake	92587
Capay (Glenn County)	95963
Capay (Yolo County)	95607
Capetown..................	95536
Capistrano Beach (Part of Dana Point)	92624
Capistrano Highlands (Part of Laguna Hills)	92653
Capital Hill (Part of Paso Robles)	93446
Capitola	95010
Capitol Square (Part of San Jose)	95133
Carbona	95376
Carbon Beach.............	90265
Carbon Canyon (Part of Chino Hills)	91710
Cardiff By The Sea (Part of Encinitas)	92007
Cardwell (Part of Fresno)	93704
Caribou	95915
Carlotta	95528
Carlsbad	92008-09
	92018
For specific Carlsbad Zip Codes call (619) 729-2456, or your local postmaster.	
Carlton Hills (Part of Santee)	92071
Carmel	93921-23
For specific Carmel Zip Codes call (408) 625-4411, or your local postmaster.	
Carmel By The Sea (Part of Carmel)	93921
Carmel Highlands	93923
Carmel Hills	93923

	ZIP
Carmel Point	93923
Carmel Valley	93924
Carmel Woods	93923
Carmenita (Part of Santa Fe Springs)	90670
Carmet.....................	94923
Carmichael	95608*
	95609†
Carnelian Bay	96140
Carpinteria	93013*
	93014†
Carquinez Heights (Part of Vallejo)	94590
Carriage Hills	91977
Carrick Addition	96094
Carson.....................	90745-47
	90749
For specific Carson Zip Codes call (310) 549-2800, or your local postmaster.	
Carson Heights Mesa......	93550
Carson Hill	95222
Carson Mall (Part of Carson)...................	90746
Cartago	93549
Caruthers	93609
Carvin Creek Homesites ...	96126
Casa Blanca (Part of Riverside)	92504
Casa Conejo	91359
Casa Correo (Part of Concord)	94521
Casa de Oro	91977
Casa de Oro-Mount Helix	91977
Cascadel Woods	93643
Casitas Springs	93001
Casmalia	93429
Caspar....................	95420
Cassel	96016
Castaic	91310†
	91384*
Castella	96017
Castellammare (Part of Los Angeles)	90272
Castle Air Force Base	95342
Castle Garden	95301
Castle Park (Part of Chula Vista)	91911
Castle Rock Springs	95461
Castlewood	94588
Castro City (Part of Mountain View)	94042
Castro Valley	94546
	94552
For specific Castro Valley Zip Codes call (510) 581-0191, or your local postmaster.	
Castroville	95012
Catalina (Part of Pasadena)	91116
Cathedral City	92234*
	92235†
Catheys Valley	95306
Cawelo	93308
Cayucos	93430
Cazadero	95421
Cecilville	96031
Cedar (Part of Lancaster)	93534*
	93584†
Cedarbrook	93641
Cedar Crest	93605
Cedar Flat	96140
Cedar Glen	92321
Cedar Grove (El Dorado County)...................	95709
Cedar Grove (Fresno County)...................	93633
Cedarpines Park...........	92322
Cedar Ridge (Nevada County)...................	95924
Cedar Ridge (Tuolumne County)...................	95370
Cedar Slope	93265
Cedar Stock	96052
Cedar Valley	93644
Cedarville	96104
Centerpoint Mall (Part of Oxnard)...................	93033
Centerville (Alameda County)...................	94536
Centerville (Fresno County)	93657
Central City Mall (Part of San Bernardino)	92401
Central Valley	96019
Centre	95860
Century City (Part of Los Angeles)	90067
Century City Shopping Center (Part of Los Angeles)	90067
Ceres	95307
Cerritos	90703

* Area Zip Code   **† Post Office Boxes**

	ZIP
Cerro Villa Heights (Part of Villa Park)	92667
Chalfant	93514
Challenge	95925
Challenge-Brownsville	95925
Chambless	92319
Champagne Fountain (Part of Saratoga)	95070
Channel Islands	93030
Chapmantown (Part of Chico)	95926
Chapman Woods	91107
Chappo	92055
Charter Oak	91724
Chatsworth	91311-13
For specific Chatsworth Zip Codes call (818) 341-9551, or your local postmaster.	
Chatsworth Lake Manor	91311
Chawanakee	93602
Cheeseville	96037
Chemehuevi Indian Reservation	92363
Chemeketa Park	95030
Cherokee (Butte County)	95965
Cherokee (Nevada County)	95959
Cherokee Strip	93263
Cherry Creek Acres	95949
Cherryland	94541
Cherry Valley	92223
Chester	96020
Chestnut (Part of South San Francisco)	94080
Chicago Park	95712
Chico	95926-28
For specific Chico Zip Codes call (916) 343-5531, or your local postmaster.	
Chilcoot	96105
Childs Meadows	96061
Chili Bar	95667
China (Part of San Francisco)	94108
China Camp	94901
China Lake (Part of Ridgecrest)	93555
China Lake Naval Weapons Center	93555
Chinatown (Part of San Francisco)	94108
Chinese Camp	95309
Chino	91708-10
For specific Chino Zip Codes call (714) 627-3631, or your local postmaster.	
Chino Hills	91708
Chinowths Corner (Part of Visalia)	93277
Chinquapin	95389
Chiquita Lake	95634
Chiriaco Summit	92201
Cholame	93431
Chowchilla	93610
Christian Valley	95602
Christofferson	93610
Chrome	95963
Chualar	93925
Chuckwalla Valley State Prison	92225
Chula Vista	91909-15
For specific Chula Vista Zip Codes call (619) 422-9221, or your local postmaster.	
Chula Vista Shopping Center (Part of Chula Vista)	91910
Cima	92323
Circle Oaks	94558
Cisco	95728
Citrus	91702
Citrus Heights	95610-11
	95621
For specific Citrus Heights Zip Codes call (916) 725-2060, or your local postmaster.	
City Hall (Part of San Francisco)	94102
City Heights (Part of San Diego)	92105
City of Industry	91714-16
For specific City of Industry Zip Codes call (818) 855-6699, or your local postmaster.	
City Shopping Center, The (Part of Orange)	92668
City Terrace	90063
Civic Center (Part of Fresno)	93721
Civic Center (Part of La Habra)	90633
Civic Center (Part of Los Angeles)	91401

	ZIP
Civic Center (Part of San Rafael)	94903
Civic Center (Part of Santa Ana)	92701
Civic Center Annex (Part of Oakland)	94612
Clairemont (Part of San Diego)	92117
Clam Beach	95521
Claremont	91711
Clarksburg	95612
Clarksville	95682
Clay	95638
Clayton	94517
Clear Creek (Lassen County)	96137
Clear Creek (Siskiyou County)	96039
Clearlake	95422
Clearlake Oaks	95423
Clearlake Park (Part of Clearlake)	95424
Clearlake Riviera	95451
Clements	95227
Cleone	95437
Cliff Haven (Part of Newport Beach)	92663
Clifton	90277
Clingans Junction	93675
Clinter (Part of Fresno)	93703
Clinton	95642
Clio	96106
Clipper Gap	95603
Clipper Mills	95930
Cloverdale (Shasta County)	96007
Cloverdale (Sonoma County)	95425
Clovis	93611-13
For specific Clovis Zip Codes call (209) 299-3118, or your local postmaster.	
Clyde	94520
Coachella	92236
Coalinga	93210
Coarsegold	93614
Coarsegold Creek Ranch	93614
Coarsegold Highlands	93614
Cobb	95426
Cockatoo Grove (Part of Chula Vista)	91910
Coddington Center (Part of Santa Rosa)	95401
Coddingtown (Part of Santa Rosa)	95406
Codora	95970
Coffee Creek	96091
Cohasset	95926
Coit	93640
Cold Fork	96080
Cole (Part of West Hollywood)	90046
Coleville	96107
Colfax	95713
College City	95931
College Grove Center	92115
College Heights (Kern County)	93305
College Heights (San Bernardino County)	91786
College Heights (Santa Cruz County)	95003
College Park (Part of Thousand Oaks)	91360
College Plaza (Part of Oceanside)	92056
Collegeville	95206
Collier (Part of Los Angeles)	91307
Collierville	95220
Collinsville	94585
Colma	94014
Coloma	95613
Colonial (Part of Sacramento)	95820
Colonial Juarez (Part of Fountain Valley)	92708
Colony	92363
Colorado	90404-05
	90411
For specific Colorado Zip Codes call (310) 576-2610, or your local postmaster.	
Colorado River Indian Reservation	85344
Colton	92324
Columbia	95310
Columbus (Part of Bakersfield)	93306
Colusa	95932
Commerce	90040
Commonwealth (Part of Fullerton)	92632

	ZIP
Community Center (Part of Simi Valley)	93065
Comptche	95427
Compton	90220-24
For specific Compton Zip Codes call (213) 638-0394, or your local postmaster.	
Concepcion	93436
Concord	94518-22
	94524
	94527
	94529
For specific Concord Zip Codes call (415) 687-1500, or your local postmaster.	
Concord Naval Weapons Station	94520
Concow	95969
Conejo	93662
Conejo Valley (Part of Thousand Oaks)	91360
Confidence	95383
Convict Lake	93514
Cool	95614
Copco	96064
Copper Cove	95228
Copperopolis	95228
Copsey Creek	95457
Corbin Village (Part of Los Angeles)	91364
Corcoran	93212
Cordelia	94585
Corning	96021
Corona	91718-20
For specific Corona Zip Codes call (714) 737-0451, or your local postmaster.	
Corona Del Mar (Part of Newport Beach)	92625
Coronado	92118*
	92178†
Coronado Naval Amphibious Base	92155
Corona Mall (Part of Corona)	91720
Coronita	91720
Corral Beach	90265
Corralitos	95076
Correctional Training Facility	93960
Corte Madera	94925
	94976
For specific Corte Madera Zip Codes call (415) 924-4463, or your local postmaster.	
Coso Junction	93549
Costa Mesa	92626-28
For specific Costa Mesa Zip Codes call (714) 546-5330, or your local postmaster.	
Cosumnes	95683
Cotati	94931
Coto De Caza	92691
Cottage Springs	95223
Cotton Center	93257
Cottonwood	96022
Coulterville	95311
Country Club	95204
Country Club Acres	93644
Country Club Centre	95825
Country Club Estates	93401
Country Club Plaza	95825
Country Modern	93501
County East Mall (Part of Antioch)	94509
Court (Part of Martinez)	94553
Courtland	95615
Covelo	95428
Covina	91722-24
For specific Covina Zip Codes call (818) 966-8391, or your local postmaster.	
Covington Mill	96052
Cowan Heights	92705
Cowell (Part of Concord)	94518
Coy Flat	93208
Coyote (Part of San Jose)	95013
Craf	92359
Crafton	92359
Crenshaw (Part of Los Angeles)	90008
Crenshaw-Imperial (Part of Inglewood)	90303
Crescent City	95531
Crescent City North	95531
Crescent Mills	95934
Cressey	95312
Crest	92021
Crestline	92325
Crestmore	92316
Crestmore Heights	92509
Creston	93432
Crest Park	92326

* Area Zip Code   † Post Office Boxes

	ZIP		ZIP		ZIP
Crestview Village	95608	Del Monte Heights (Part of		Downtown (Part of Sonora)	95370
Crockett	94525	Seaside)	93955	Downtown Plaza (Part of	
Cromberg	96103	Del Monte Park (Part of		Sacramento)	95814
Crossroads (Part of Santa		Pacific Grove)	93950	Doyle (Lassen County)	96109
Rosa)	95401	Del Monte Shopping Center		Doyle (Tulare County)	93258
Crossroads Plaza (Part of		(Part of Monterey)	93940	Drakesbad	96020
Pico Rivera)	90661	Del Paso Heights (Part of		Dryden Flight Research	
Crowley Lake (Part of		Sacramento)	95838	Center	93523
Mammoth Lakes)	93546	Del Rey	93616	Drytown	95699
Crown Point (Part of San		Del Rey Oaks	93940	Duarte	91009†
Diego)	92109	Del Rio Woods	95448		91010*
Crows Landing	95313	Del Rosa (Part of San		Dublin	94568
Crutcher (Part of		Bernardino)	92404	Ducor	93218
Paramount)	90723	Del Sur (Part of Lancaster)	93536	Dulzura	91917
Crystal Court (Part of Costa		Delta (Part of Stockton)	95202	Duncans Mills	95430
Mesa)	92626	De Luz	92028	Dunlap	93621
Crystal Cove	92651	Del Valle (Part of Los		Dunlap Acres (Part of	
Cucamonga	91729-30	Angeles)	90015	Yucaipa)	92399
	91739	Delways	95695	Dunmovin	93549
For specific Cucamonga Zip		Democrat Hot Springs	93301	Dunneville Corners	95023
Codes call (714) 987-4641, or		Denair	95316	Dunnigan	95937
your local postmaster.		Denny	95527	Dunsmuir	96025
Cudahy	90201	Denverton	94585	Durham	95938
Cuesta-by-the-Sea	93402	Derby Acres	93224	Dustin Acres	93268
Culver City	90230-33	Descanso	91916	Dutch Flat	95714
For specific Culver City Zip Codes		Desert	92364	'E' (Postal Station) (Part of	
call (213) 391-6374, or your local		Desert Beach	92254	San Francisco)	94107
postmaster.		Desert Center	92239	Eagle Lake Resort	96130
Cummings	95454	Desert Hot Springs	92240-41	Eagle Mountain	92239
Cunningham	95472	For specific Desert Hot Springs		Eagle Rock (Part of Los	
Cupertino	95014-16	Zip Codes call (619) 329-6933, or		Angeles)	90041
For specific Cupertino Zip Codes		your local postmaster.		Eagle Rock Plaza (Part of	
call (408) 252-6798, or your local		Desert Lake	93516	Los Angeles)	90041
postmaster.		Desert Shores	92274	Eagle Tree	95690
Curry Village	95389	Desert View Highlands	93550	Eagleville	96110
Curtiss Heights (Part of		Des Moines (Part of La		Earlimart	93219
Arcata)	95521	Habra)	90631	Earp	92242
Curtner (Part of Fremont)	94539	Deuel Vocational Institution	95376	East (Part of Downey)	90239
Cutler	93615	Devils Den	93204	East Anaheim Shopping	
Cutten	95534	Devore	92407	Center (Part of Anaheim)	92806
Cuyama	93214	Devore Heights	92407	East Applegate	95703
Cypress	90630	Diablo	94528	East Bakersfield (Part of	
Cypress South (Part of		Diamond (Part of Santa		Bakersfield)	93305
Cypress)	90630	Ana)	92704	East Baldy Mesa	92371
Daggett	92327	Diamond Bar	91765	East Bluff (Part of Newport	
Dairyland	93610	Diamond Heights (Part of		Beach)	92660
Dairyville	96080	San Francisco)	94131	East Blythe	92225
Dales	96080	Diamond Springs	95619	East Compton	90221
Daly City	94014-17	Diamond Springs Heights	95619	East Foothills	95127
For specific Daly City Zip Codes		Di Giorgio	93217	East Fresno (Part of Fresno)	93727
call (415) 756-2303, or your local		Dillon Beach	94929	Eastgate (Part of Beverly	
postmaster.		Dimond (Part of Oakland)	94602	Hills)	90211
Dana	96028	Dinkey Creek	93664	East Gridley	95948
Dana Point	92629	Dinsmore	95526	East Guernewood	95446
Danby	92332	Dinuba	93618	East Hemet	92544
Danville	94506	Discovery Bay	94513	East Highlands	92346
	94526	Disneyland (Part of		East Irvine (Part of Irvine)	92650
For specific Danville Zip Codes		Anaheim)	92802	East La Mirada	90638
call (510) 736-5044, or your local		Dixieland	92273	Eastland Shopping Center	
postmaster.		Dixon	95620	(Part of West Covina)	91791
Daphnedale Park	96101	Dixon Lane-Meadow Creek	93514	East Linda	95901
Dardanelle	95314	Dobbins	95935	East Long Beach (Part of	
Darrah	95338	Dockweiler (Part of Los		Long Beach)	90804
Darwin	93522	Angeles)	90007	East Los Angeles	90022
Daulton	93637	Dogtown (Calaveras		East Lynwood (Part of	
Davenport	95017	County)	95249	Lynwood)	90262
Davis	95616*	Dogtown (Marin County)	94924	Eastmont (Part of Oakland)	94605
	95617†	Doheny Park	92624	Eastmont Mall (Part of	
Davis Creek	96108	Dollar Point	96145	Oakland)	94605
Day	96056	Dollar Ranch (Part of		East Nicolaus	95622
Dayton	95928	Walnut Creek)	94595	Easton	93706
Day Valley	95076	Dolomite	93545	East Palo Alto (San Mateo	
Deane Brothers	91350	Dominguez (Part of Carson)	90810	County)	94303
Dearborn Park	94060	Donlon (Part of Oxnard)	93030	East Palo Alto (Santa Clara	
Death Valley	92328	Donner	96162	County)	94303
Death Valley Junction	92328	Donner Lake	96161	East Pasadena	91107*
Decoto (Part of Union City)	94587	Don Pedro Camp	95329		91117†
Deep Springs	89010	Dorrington	95223	East Porterville	93257
Deer Creek	96061	Dorris	96023	East Quincy	95971
Deer Lick Springs	96076	Dos Palos	93620	East Richmond Heights	94805
Deer Park (Napa County)	94576	Dos Rios	95429	Eastridge (Part of San Jose)	95122*
Deer Park (Santa Cruz		Douglas City	96024		95173†
County)	95003	Douglas Flat	95229	East San Diego (Part of San	
Del Aire	90250	Downey	90239-42	Diego)	92105
Del Amo (Part of Torrance)	90503	For specific Downey Zip Codes		East San Gabriel	91775
Del Amo Fashion Center		call (213) 923-5465, or your local		East San Pedro (Part of Los	
(Part of Torrance)	90503	postmaster.		Angeles)	90731
Delano	93215*	Downieville	95936	East Santa Cruz (Part of	
	93216†	Downtown (Part of		Santa Cruz)	95060
Del Dios	92029	Bakersfield)	93303	Eastside Acres	93622
Delevan	95988	Downtown (Part of		Eastside Ranch	93622
Delft Colony	93618	Burbank)	91502	East Sonora	95370
Delhi	95315	Downtown (Part of		East Stockton (Part of	
Delkern	93307	Manhattan Beach)	90266	Stockton)	95205
Delleker	96122	Downtown (Part of Ontario)	91761		95215
Del Loma	96010	Downtown (Part of		For specific East Stockton Zip	
Del Mar (San Diego County)	92014	Riverside)	92501*	Codes call (209) 466-9334, or	
Del Mar (Santa Cruz			92502†	your local postmaster.	
County)	95060	Downtown (Part of San		East Tustin	92705
Del Mesa	94904	Bernardino)	92401	East Vallejo (Part of Vallejo)	94590
Del Monte Forest	93953	Downtown (Part of San		East Ventura (Part of	
		Diego)	92101	Ventura)	93003

	ZIP
Eastview (Part of Rancho Palos Verdes)	90734
Echo Lake	95721
Echo Park (Part of Los Angeles)	90026
Edendale (Part of Los Angeles)	90026
Edgemar (Part of Pacifica)	94044
Edgemont (Part of Moreno Valley)	92508
Edgemont Acres	93523
Edgewater Estates	91977
Edgewood	96094
Edison	93220
Edmundson Acres	93203
Edwards	93523*
	03524†
Edwards Air Force Base	93523
Edwards Estates	93523
Edwards Palisades	93523
Eel Rock	95554
Eight Mile House	95709
El Bonita	95446
El Cajon	92019-22
For specific El Cajon Zip Codes call (619) 442-0727, or your local postmaster.	
El Camino	96035
El Camino North Shopping Center (Part of Oceanside)	92054
El Casco Lake	92373
El Centro	92243*
	92244†
El Cerrito (Contra Costa County)	94530
El Cerrito (Riverside County)	91720
El Cerrito Plaza (Part of El Cerrito)	94530
Elders Corner	95603
Elderwood	93286
El Dorado	95623
El Dorado Hills	95762
Eldridge	95431
El Encanto Heights	93117
El Granada	94018
Elizabeth Lake	93551
Elk	95432
Elk Creek	95939
Elk Grove	95624
	95758-59
For specific Elk Grove Zip Codes call (916) 685-5700, or your local postmaster.	
Elkhorn	95012
Elk River	95503
Elk River Corners	95503
Ellwood	93118
El Macero (Part of Davis)	95618
Elmhurst (Part of Oakland)	94603
Elmira	95625
El Mirador	93247
El Mirage	92301
El Modena (Part of Orange)	92667
El Monte	91731-34
For specific El Monte Zip Codes call (818) 443-8995, or your local postmaster.	
El Monte (Part of Concord)	94521
El Monte Park	92040
Elm View	93609
Elmwood (Part of Berkeley)	94705
El Nido	95317
El Portal	95318
El Porto Beach (Part of Manhattan Beach)	90266
El Pueblo	94565
El Rio	93030
El Rio Villa	95694
El Segundo	90245
El Sereno (Part of Los Angeles)	90026
El Sobrante	94803
	94820
For specific El Sobrante Zip Codes call (510) 262-1960, or your local postmaster.	
El Sueno	93110
El Toro	92610
	92630
For specific El Toro Zip Codes call (714) 837-1220, or your local postmaster.	
El Toro Marine Corps Air Station	92709
El Toro Station	92709
El Verano	95433
Elverta	95626
El Viejo	95353†
	95354*
Emandal	95490
Emerald Bay	92651

	ZIP
Emerald Lake Hills	94062
Emeryville	94608*
	94662†
Emigrant Gap	95715
Empire	95319
Encanto (Part of San Diego)	92114
Encinal (Part of Sunnyvale)	94087
	94090
For specific Encinal Zip Codes call (408) 245-0617, or your local postmaster.	
Encinitas	92023-24
For specific Encinitas Zip Codes call (619) 753-6446, or your local postmaster.	
Encino (Part of Los Angeles)	91316
	91416
	91426
	91436
For specific Encino Zip Codes call (818) 908-6919, or your local postmaster.	
Enterprise (Part of Redding)	96001
Erwin Lake	92386
Escalle (Part of Larkspur)	94939
Escalon	95320
Escondido	92025-27
	92029-30
	92046
For specific Escondido Zip Codes call (619) 745-1912, or your local postmaster.	
Escondido Junction (Part of Oceanside)	92054
Escondido Village Mall (Part of Escondido)	92027
Esparto	95627
Esplanade, The	93030
Essex	92332
Estrella	93451
Estudillo (Part of San Leandro)	94577
Etiwanda (Part of Rancho Cucamonga)	91739
Etna	96027
Ettersburg	95542
Eucalyptus Hills	92040
Eugene	95230
Eureka	95501-03
For specific Eureka Zip Codes call (707) 442-1768, or your local postmaster.	
Exeter	93221
'F' (Postal Station) (Part of San Francisco)	94112
Fairfax (Kern County)	93307
Fairfax (Marin County)	94930
	94978
For specific Fairfax Zip Codes call (415) 453-3146, or your local postmaster.	
Fairfield	94533
Fairhaven	95564
Fairmead	93610
Fairmont	93534
Fairmont Hospital	94578
Fairmont Terrace	94577
Fairmount (Part of El Cerrito)	94530
Fair Oaks (Sacramento County)	95628
Fair Oaks (San Joaquin County)	95205
Fairview (Alameda County)	94542
Fairview (Trinity County)	96052
Fairview (Tulare County)	93238
Fairway Park (Part of Hayward)	94544
Falk	95503
Fallbrook	92028
	92088
For specific Fallbrook Zip Codes call (619) 726-7880, or your local postmaster.	
Fallbrook Junction	92055
Fallbrook Mall (Part of Los Angeles)	91307
Fallen Leaf	96151
Falling Springs	91702
Fallon	94971
Fall River Mills	96028
Fallsvale	92339
Famoso	93250
Fancher	93727
Farmers Market (Part of Los Angeles)	90036
Farmersville	93223
Farmington	95230
Fashion Valley Center (Part of San Diego)	92108
Fawnskin	92333

	ZIP
Fay Creek	93283
Feather Falls	95940
Feather River	96020
Feather River Inn	96103
Feather River Park	96103
Federal (Part of Anaheim)	92805
Federal (Part of Covina)	91723
Federal (Part of Los Angeles)	90012
Federal Building (Part of Oxnard)	93030
Federal Building (Part of San Francisco)	94102
Federal Correctional Institution	94568
Federal Prison Camp	93516
Federal Terrace (Part of Vallejo)	94590
Fellows	93224
Felterwood	95531
Felton (census designated place)	95041
Felton	95018
Felton Grove	95018
Fernbridge	95540
Fernbrook	92065
Ferndale	95536
Fern Valley	92549
Fernwood	90290
Fetters Hot Springs	95476
Fetters Hot Springs-Agua Caliente	95476
Fickle Hill	95521
Fiddletown	95629
Fieldbrook	95521
Fields Landing	95537
Fig Garden (Part of Fresno)	93704
Fig Garden Village (Part of Fresno)	93704
Figueroa (Part of Los Angeles)	91001
Fillmore	93015*
	93016†
Fine Gold	93643
Finley	95435
Firebaugh	93622
Fire Mountain	96061
Firestone (Part of South Gate)	90280
Firestone Park	90001
First Street (Part of Oceanside)	92049
	92054
For specific First Street Zip Codes call (619) 722-6420, or your local postmaster.	
Fish Camp	93623
Fish Springs	93513
Fisk (Part of San Francisco)	94122
Fitchburg (Part of Oakland)	94621
Five Brooks	94950
Five Mile Terrace	95667
Five Points (Fresno County)	93624
Five Points (San Diego County)	92110
Flamingo Heights	92284
Flinn Springs	92021
Flintridge (Part of La Canada Flintridge)	91011
Florence	90001
Florence-Graham	90001
Florin	95828
Florin Mall (Part of Sacramento)	95823
Floriston	96111
Flosden Acres (Part of Vallejo)	94590
Flournoy	96029
Flower Village	93305
Fly in Acres	95223
Folsom	95630
Folsom Junction (Part of Folsom)	95630
Fontana	92334-37
For specific Fontana Zip Codes call (714) 822-8039, or your local postmaster.	
Foothill Farms	95841
Forbestown	95941
Ford City	93268
Forest	95910
Foresta	95389
Forest Falls	92339
Forest Glen	96041
Foresthill	95631
Forest Home (Amador County)	95669
Forest Home (San Bernardino County)	92339
Forest Knolls	94933
Forest Lake	95426
Forest Park	95006

	ZIP
Forest Ranch	95942
Forest Springs (Nevada County)	95949
Forest Springs (Santa Cruz County)	95006
Forestville	95436
Forks of Salmon	96031
Forrest Park	91350
Fort Baker	94965
Fort Barry	94965
Fort Bidwell	96112
Fort Bidwell Indian Reservation	96112
Fort Bragg	95437
Fort Cronkhite	94965
Fort Dick	95538
Fort Goff	96086
Fort Hunter Liggett	93928
Fort Independence Indian Reservation	93526
Fort Irwin	92310
Fort Jones	96032
Fort Mason (Part of San Francisco)	94123
Fort McArthur (Part of Los Angeles)	90731
Fort Miley (Part of San Francisco)	94121
Fort Mohave Indian Reservation	92363
Fort Ord	93941
Fort Ord Village (Part of Seaside)	93941
Fort Seward	95511
Fort Sutter (Part of Sacramento)	95816
Fortuna	95540
Fort Yuma	85364
Fort Yuma Indian Reservation	92283
Foster City	94404
Fountainhead Springs	93257
Fountain Valley	92708*
	92728†
Four Corners (Kramer Junction)	93516
Four Corners (Part of Twentynine Palms)	92277
Four Corners (Madera County)	93637
Fouts Springs	95979
Fowler	93625
Fox Creek	95528
Fox Hills (Part of Culver City)	90233
Fox Hills Mall (Part of Culver City)	90230
Foy (Part of Los Angeles)	90017
Franciscan Park (Part of Daly City)	94014
Franklin	95758
Frazier Park	93222†
	93225*
Fredericksburg	96120
Freedom	95019
Freeman Junction	93527
Freestone	95472
Fremont	94536-39
	94555
For specific Fremont Zip Codes call (415) 792-8654, or your local postmaster.	
Fremont Hub Shopping Center (Part of Fremont)	94538
French Camp	95231
French Corral	95960
French Gulch	96033
Fresh Pond	95726
Freshwater	95503
Freshwater Corners	95503
Fresno	93650
	93701-94
For specific Fresno Zip Codes call (209) 487-7700, or your local postmaster.	
Fresno Fashion Fair (Part of Fresno)	93710
Friant	93626
Friendly Hills	92252
Fruitland	95554
Fruitridge	95820
Fruitvale (Alameda County)	94601
Fruitvale (Kern County)	93308
Fruto	95988
Fullerton	92631-35
For specific Fullerton Zip Codes call (714) 525-3893, or your local postmaster.	
Fulton	95439
'G' (Postal Station) (Part of San Francisco)	94114

	ZIP
Gabilan (Part of Salinas)	93906
Gabilan Acres	93906
Galleria at South Bay, The (Part of Redondo Beach)	90278
Galleria at Tyler (Part of Riverside)	92503
Gallinas	94903
Galt	95632
Garberville	95542
Gardena	90247-49
For specific Gardena Zip Codes call (213) 327-9114, or your local postmaster.	
Garden Acres	95205
Garden Farms	93422
Garden Gate Village (Part of Cupertino)	95014
Garden Grove	92640-45
For specific Garden Grove Zip Codes call (714) 537-1331, or your local postmaster.	
Garden Valley	95633
Garden Village (Part of Daly City)	94015
Garey	93454
Garfield	93205
Garlock	93554
Gasoline Alley	95603
Gas Point	96022
Gasquet	95543
Gateway (Los Angeles County)	90232
Gateway (Nevada County)	96161
Gaviota	93117
Gazelle	96034
Geary (Part of San Francisco)	94121
Gene	92267
Genesee	95983
Genesee Plaza (Part of San Diego)	92111
George AFB (census designated place)	92392
George Air Force Base	92394
Georgetown	95634
George Washington (Part of San Diego)	92103
Gerber	96035
Gerber-Las Flores	96035
Geyserville	95441
Gilman Hot Springs	92583
Gilroy	95020*
	95021†
Glamis	92227
Glassell (Part of Los Angeles)	90065
Glen Arbor	95005
Glen Avon	92509
Glenbrook (Lake County)	95461
Glenbrook (Nevada County)	95945
Glenburn	96028
Glencoe	95232
Glencove (Part of Vallejo)	94590
Glendale (Los Angeles County)	91201-26
For specific Glendale Zip Codes call (818) 502-3202, or your local postmaster.	
Glendale (Humbolt County)	95521
Glendale Galleria (Part of Glendale)	91210
Glendora	91740-41
For specific Glendora Zip Codes call (818) 335-6957, or your local postmaster.	
Glen Ellen	95442
Glenhaven	95443
Glen Martin	92305
Glenn	95943
Glennville	93226
Glenoaks (Part of Burbank)	91504
Glenshire-Devonshire	96161
Glenview (Los Angeles County)	90290
Glenview (San Diego County)	92021
Glenwood	95066
Glorietta (Part of Orinda)	94563
Goffs	92332
Golden Hill (Part of San Diego)	92102
Golden Hills (Calaveras County)	95249
Golden Hills (Kern County)	93561
Gold Flat	95959
Gold Gulch	95018
Gold Hill	95667
Gold River	95670
Gold Run	95717
Goleta	93117
Gonzales	93926

	ZIP
Goodyears Bar	95944
Gorda	93920
Gordon Valley	94585
Gorman	93243
Goshen	93227
Government Island (Part of Alameda)	94501
Graeagle	96103
Graham	90002
Granada Hills (Part of Los Angeles)	91344
Grand Central (Part of Glendale)	91201*
	91221†
Grand Lake (Part of Oakland)	94610
Grand Terrace	92324
Grandview	92311
Grangeville	93230
Granite Bay	95746
Granite Hill (Part of Grass Valley)	95945
Granite Hills	92019
Graniteville	95959
Grantville (Part of San Diego)	92120
Grapevine	93243
Grass Valley	95945
	95949
For specific Grass Valley Zip Codes call (916) 273-7233, or your local postmaster.	
Graton	95444
Grayson	95363
Greeley	93307
Greeley Hill	95311
Green (Part of Los Angeles)	90037
Greenacres	93308
Greenbrae	94904
Greenbrook (Part of Danville)	94526
Greenfield	93927
Greenmead (Part of Los Angeles)	90059
Green Meadows (Part of Davis)	95616
Greenspot	92359
Green Valley	91350
Green Valley Estates	94585
Green Valley Lake	92341
Greenview	96037
Greenview Acres (Part of Arcata)	95521
Greenville	95947
Greenwich Village (Part of Thousand Oaks)	91360
Greenwood	95635
Grenada	96038
Gridley	95948
Griffith (Part of Los Angeles)	90039
Grimes	95950
Grizzly Flats	95636
Grossmont (Part of La Mesa)	91942
Groveland	95321
Groveland-Big Oak Flat	95321
Grover Beach	93433*
	93483†
Guadalupe	93434
Gualala	95445
Guasti (Part of Ontario)	91743
Guatay	91931
Guerneville	95446
Guernewood Park	95446
Guernsey	93230
Guinda	95637
Gustine	95322
Hacienda	95436
Hacienda Heights	91745
Haiwee	93549
Halcyon	93420
Hales Grove	95585
Half Moon Bay	94019
Hall (Part of Union City)	94587
Halloran Springs	92364
Halls Corner	93245
Hallwood	95901
Hamburg	96045
Hamilton (Part of Palo Alto)	94301
Hamilton City	95951
Hammer Ranch (Part of Stockton)	95209
	95919
For specific Hammer Ranch Zip Codes call (209) 957-7972, or your local postmaster.	
Hammil	93514
Hammonton	95901
Hancock (Part of Los Angeles)	90044

	ZIP
Hanford	93230-32
For specific Hanford Zip Codes call (209) 582-2507, or your local postmaster.	
Happy Camp	96039
Harbin Springs	95461
Harbin Springs Annex	95461
Harbison Canyon	92020
Harbor City (Part of Los Angeles)	90710
Harbor Island (Part of Newport Beach)	92660
Harbor Side (Part of Chula Vista)	91911
Hardman Center (Part of Riverside)	92504
Hardwick	93230
Harlem Springs (Part of Highland)	92346
Harmony	93435
Harmony Grove	92029
Harris	95542
Harrison Park	92036
Hartland	93603
Harvard	92398
Haskell Creek Homesites	96124
Haskins Resort	95971
Hat Creek	96040
Hathaway Pines	95233
Hatton Fields	93923
Havasu Lake	92363
Havilah	93518
Hawaiian Gardens	90716
Hawkins Bar	95563
Hawkinsville	96097
Hawthorne	90250*
	90251†
Hayfork	96041
Hayward	94540-45
	94557
For specific Hayward Zip Codes call (415) 783-2400, or your local postmaster.	
Hayward Highlands (Part of Hayward)	94542
Hazard	90063
Healdsburg	95448
Heather Glen	95703
Heber	92249
Helena	96048
Helendale	92342
Helm	93627
Hemet	92543-46
For specific Hemet Zip Codes call (714) 658-3263, or your local postmaster.	
Henderson (Part of Porterville)	93258
Henderson Center (Part of Eureka)	95501
Henderson Village	95240
Henley	96044
Henleyville	96021
Herald	95638
Hercules	94547
Heritage Ranch	93446
Herlong	96113
Hermosa Beach	90254
Hernandez	95023
Herndon (Part of Fresno)	93711
Hesperia	92340
	92345
For specific Hesperia Zip Codes call (619) 244-2267, or your local postmaster.	
Heyer	94546
Hickman	95323
Hidden Hills	91302
Hidden Lake Estate	93637
Hidden Lakes Estates	93626
Hidden Meadows	92025
Hidden Valley	95560
Hidden Valley Lake	95457
Highgrove	92507
Highland	92346
Highland Park (Kern County)	93308
Highland Park (Los Angeles County)	90042
Highlands	94402
Highway City (Part of Fresno)	93706
Highway Highlands (Part of Glendale)	91214
Hilarita (Part of Tiburon)	94920
Hildreth	93645
Hillcrest (Los Angeles County)	90301
Hillcrest (San Diego County)	92103
Hillcrest Center (Part of Bakersfield)	93306
Hillcrest Park	94590

	ZIP
Hillsborough	94010
Hillsdale (Part of San Mateo)	94403
Hillsdale Shopping Center (Part of San Mateo)	94403
Hills Flat (Part of Grass Valley)	95945
Hilltop (Contra Costa County)	94806
Hilltop (Kern County)	93307
Hillview (Part of San Jose)	95121
Hilmar	95324
Hilt	96044
Hilton	95436
Hinkley	92347
Hiouchi Valley	95531
Hirschdale	96161
Hi Vista	93535
Hoaglin	95595
Hobart (Part of Vernon)	90058
Hobart Mills	96161
Hobergs	95426
Hodge	92311
Holiday (Part of Anaheim)	92802
Holiday Lake (Part of Morgan Hill)	95037
Hollister	95023*
	95024†
Hollydale (Los Angeles County)	90280
Hollydale (Sonoma County)	95436
Hollywood (Part of Los Angeles)	90028
Hollywood Beach	93035
Hollywood by the Sea	93035
Hollywood Riviera (Part of Torrance)	90277
Holmes	95569
Holt	95234
Holtville	92250
Holy City	95044
Home Garden	93239
Home Gardens	91720
Homeland	92548
Homestead (Kern County)	93527
Homestead (Riverside County)	92539
Homestead (San Joaquin County)	95206
Homestead Valley	94941
Homewood	96141
Honby	91350
Honcut	95965
Honeydew	95545
Hood	95639
Hooker	96022
Hookston (Part of Pleasant Hill)	94523
Hoopa	95546
Hoopa Valley Indian Reservation	95546
Hope Ranch	93105
Hopeton	95369
Hope Valley	96120
Hopland	95449
Hornbrook	96044
Hornitos	95325
Horse Creek	96045
Horseshoe Bar	95650
Horton Plaza (Part of San Diego)	92101
Howard Landing	95690
Howest (Part of Burlingame)	94010
Hub City (Part of Compton)	90220
Hudson	95355-57
For specific Hudson Zip Codes call (209) 551-9444, or your local postmaster.	
Hughes (Part of Fresno)	93705
Hughson	95326
Humboldt Bay CGAS	95521
Humboldt Hill	95537
Hume	93628
Humphreys Station	93611
Hunters Valley	95325
Huntington (Part of Huntington Beach)	92646
Huntington Beach	92605
	92615
	92646-49
For specific Huntington Beach Zip Codes call (714) 847-5665, or your local postmaster.	
Huntington Center (Part of Huntington Beach)	92647
Huntington Harbor (Part of Huntington Beach)	92649
Huntington Lake	93629
Huntington Park	90255
Huron	93234
Hyampom	96046

	ZIP
Hyde Park (Part of Los Angeles)	90043
Hydesville	95547
Idlewild	93260
Idria	95023
Idyllwild	92549
Idyllwild-Pine Cove	92549
Ignacio	94947
Igo	96047
Imola	94558
Imperial	92251
Imperial Beach	91932-33
For specific Imperial Beach Zip Codes call (619) 423-4545, or your local postmaster.	
Imperial Crest (Part of Norwalk)	90650
Incline	95318
Independence	93526
Indian Beach	95443
Indian Falls	95934
Indian Hill Mall (Part of Pomona)	91767
Indian Lakes Estates	93614
Indian Mission	93602
Indianola	95503
Indian Springs	93644
Indian Wells (Kern County)	93527
Indian Wells (Riverside County)	92210
Indio	92201-03
For specific Indio Zip Codes call (619) 347-3442, or your local postmaster.	
Industrial (Part of Santa Ana)	92705
Inglenook	95437
Ingleside (Part of San Francisco)	94112
Inglewood	90301-12
For specific Inglewood Zip Codes call (213) 301-1230, or your local postmaster.	
Ingot	96008
Inland Center (Part of San Bernardino)	92408
Inskip	95978
Interlaken	95076
Inverness	94937
Inverness Park	94956
Inwood	96088
Inyokern	93527
Ione	95640
Iowa Hill	95713
Irish Beach	95459
Iron Mountain	92242
Irvine	92709-10
	92713-20
For specific Irvine Zip Codes call (714) 474-0407, or your local postmaster.	
Irvington (Part of Fremont)	94538
Irwin	95324
Irwindale	91706
Irwin Estates	92311
Island Mountain	95542
Isla Vista	93117
Isleton	95641
Ivanhoe	93235
Ivanpah	92364
'J' (Postal Station) (Part of San Francisco)	94117
Jacinto Grange	95943
Jackie Robinson	91103-04
For specific Jackie Robinson Zip Codes call (818) 304-7134, or your local postmaster.	
Jackson	95642
Jackson Gate (Part of Jackson)	95642
Jacumba	91934
Jalama	93436
Jamesburg	93924
Jamestown	95327
Jamul	91935
Janesville	96114
Japan Center (Part of San Francisco)	94115
Jarbo	95965
Jelly	96080
Jenner	95450
Jenny Lind	95252
Jesmond Dene	92026
Jimtown	95448
Johannesburg	93528
John Adams (Part of San Diego)	92116
Johnsondale	93238
Johnson Park	96013
Johnstonville	96130
Johnstown	92021
Johnsville	96103

* Area Zip Code   † Post Office Boxes

	ZIP		ZIP		ZIP
Jolon	93928		92677	Land Park (Part of	
Jonesville	95942	For specific Laguna Beach Zip		Sacramento)	95822
Joshua Hills (Part of		Codes call (714) 494-4122, or		Landscape (Part of	
Palmdale)	93550	your local postmaster.		Berkeley)	94707
Joshua Tree	92252	Laguna Creek	95758	Lansdale (Part of San	
Julian	92036	Laguna Hills	92653*	Anselmo)	94960
Junction City	96048		92654†	La Palma	90623
June Lake	93529	Laguna Hills Mall (Part of		La Panza	93432
June Lake Junction	93529	Laguna Hills)	92653	La Patera	93117
Juniper Hills	93543	Laguna Lake (Part of San		La Porte	95981
Juniper Lake Resort	96020	Luis Obispo)	93405	La Puente	91744-49
Juniper Springs	92548	Laguna Niguel	92677	For specific La Puente Zip Codes	
Jurupa	92509	Lagunitas	94938	call (818) 968-9311, or your local	
Kaiser Center (Part of		Lagunitas-Forest Knolls	94933	postmaster.	
Oakland)	94612	La Habra	90631-33	La Quinta	92253
Kaiser Eagle Mountain	92239	For specific La Habra Zip Codes		Larabee	95569
Kaweah	93237	call (714) 992-5620, or your local		La Riviera	95826
Keddie	95971	postmaster.		Larkfield	95401
Keeler	93530	La Habra Fashion Square		Larkfield-Wikiup	95403
Keene	93531	(Part of La Habra)	90631	Larkspur	94939
Kelly	96020	La Habra Heights	90631		94977
Kelsey	95643	La Honda	94020	For specific Larkspur Zip Codes	
Kelseyville	95451	Lairport (Part of El		call (415) 924-4792, or your local	
Kelso	92309	Segundo)	90245	postmaster.	
Kennedy Meadow	95370	La Jolla (Part of San Diego)	92037-39	Larson Tract	93240
Kennedy Ranch	95449		92092-93	Larwin Plaza (Part of	
Kensington	94707	For specific La Jolla Zip Codes		Vallejo)	94590
Kensington Park (Part of		call (619) 454-7139, or your local		Las Cruces	93117
San Diego)	92116	postmaster.		La Selva Beach	95076
Kentfield	94904	La Jolla (Part of Placentia)	92670	Las Flores (Los Angeles	
Kentwood-In-The Pines	92036	La Jolla Indian Reservation	92025	County)	90265
Kent Woodlands	94904	Lake Alpine	95223	Las Flores (Tehama County)	96035
Kenwood	95452	Lake Arrowhead	92352	La Sierra (Part of Riverside)	92505*
Keough Hot Springs	93514	Lake Arrowhead (census			92515†
Kerman	93630	designated place)	92317	La Sierra Heights (Part of	
Kern City (Part of		Lake Christopher (Part of		Riverside)	92505
Bakersfield)	93309	South Lake Tahoe)	96150	Las Lomas	95076
Kern Homes	93308	Lake City	96115	Las Posas Estates	93010
Kernvale	93240	Lake Earl	95531	Lathrop	95330
Kernville	93238	Lake Elsinore	92530-32	La Tijera (Part of Los	
Keswick	96001	For specific Lake Elsinore Zip		Angeles)	90043
Kettleman City	93239	Codes call (714) 674-3720, or		Laton	93242
Kevet (Part of Santa Paula)	93060	your local postmaster.		Latrobe	95682
Keyes	95328	Lake Forest	96145	Laurel (Part of Oakland)	94619
Kilkare Woods	94586	Lakehead	96051	Laurel Canyon (Part of Los	
King (Part of Santa Ana)	92706	Lake Henshaw	92070	Angeles)	91605
King City	93930	Lake Hills Estates	95762	Laurel Plaza (Part of Los	
King Island	95219	Lake Hughes	93532	Angeles)	91606
King Salmon	95503	Lake Isabella	93240	Laurelwood (Part of Los	
Kings Beach	96143	Lake Kirkwood	95646	Angeles)	91604
Kingsburg	93631	Lakeland Village	92530	La Verne	91750
Kings Mall (Part of Hanford)	93230	Lake Los Angeles	93550	La Vina	93637
Kingvale	95728	Lake Madera Country		Lawndale (Los Angeles	
Kirkville	95645	Estates	93637	County)	90260-61
Kirkwood (Alpine County)	95646	Lake Marie Estates	93455	For specific Lawndale Zip Codes	
Kirkwood (Tehama County)	96021	Lake Mary	93546	call (213) 679-0121, or your local	
Kit Carson	95644	Lake Morena Village	91906	postmaster.	
Klamath	95548	Lake Murray (Part of San		Lawndale (Sonoma County)	95452
Klamath Glen	95548	Diego)	92119	Lawrence (Part of Danville)	94506
Klamath River	96050	Lake Nacimiento	93446	Laws	93514
Klinefelter	92363	Lake Of The Pines	95603	Layman	96103
Kneeland	95549	Lake of the Woods	93225	Laytonville	95454
Knightsen	94548	Lake Pillsbury Homesites	95469	Lazy Acre	93311
Knights Ferry	95361	Lake Pillsbury Resort	95469	Lebec	93243
Knights Landing	95645	Lakeport	95453	Lee	96020
Knob	96076	Lake San Marcos	92069	Lee Vining	93541
Knotts Berry Farm (Part of		Lakeshore	93634	Leggett	95585
Buena Park)	90620	Lakeshore Lodge	95971	Le Grand	95333
Knowles	93653	Lakeside	92040	Leisure Acres	93643
Konocti	95451	Lakeside Farms	92040	Leisure Town (Part of	
Kono Tayee	95443	Lake Tamarisk	92239	Vacaville)	95687
Korbel	95550	Lakeview (Kern County)	93307	Leisure World (Part of Seal	
Krug (Part of St. Helena)	94574	Lakeview (Riverside County)	92567	Beach)	90740
Kyburz	95720	Lakeview (San Diego		Leliter	93527
La Barr Meadows	95949	County)	92040	Lemoncove	93244
La Canada (Part of La		Lakeville	94954	Lemon Grove	91945-46
Canada Flintridge)	91011	Lake Williams Estates	92386	For specific Lemon Grove Zip	
La Canada Flintridge	91011*	Lakewood	90711-15	Codes call (619) 466-3263, or	
	91012†	For specific Lakewood Zip Codes		your local postmaster.	
La Costa (Los Angeles		call (213) 866-1741, or your local		Lemon Heights	92705
County)	90265	postmaster.		Lemoore	93245
La Costa (San Diego		Lakewood Center Mall (Part		Lemoore Naval Air Station	93245
County)	92008	of Lakewood)	90712	Lennox	90304
La Costa Beach	90265	La Loma (Part of Modesto)	95354	Lenwood	92311
La Crescenta	91214*	Lamanda Park (Part of		Leona Valley	93551
	91224†	Pasadena)	91107	Leucadia (Part of Encinitas)	92024
La Crescenta-Montrose	91214	La Mesa	91941-44	Lewiston	96052
La Cresta (Kern County)	93305	For specific La Mesa Zip Codes		Lexington Hills	95044
La Cresta (San Diego		call (619) 466-3283, or your local		Liberty Acres	90250
County)	92020	postmaster.		Liberty Farms	95620
La Cumbre Plaza (Part of		La Mirada	90637*	Libfarm	95620
Santa Barbara)	93105		90638†	Lido Isle (Part of Newport	
Ladera	94028	La Mirada Mall (Part of La		Beach)	92663
Ladera Heights	90045	Mirada)	90638	Likely	96116
Lafayette	94549	Lamont	93241	Lily Valley	95255
La Grange	95329	Lanare	93656	Limco	93060
Laguna	95758	Lancaster	93534-39	Lincoln	95648
Laguna Beach	92607		93584-86	Lincoln Acres	91947
	92651-52	For specific Lancaster Zip Codes		Lincoln Heights (Part of Los	
		call (805) 948-1691, or your local		Angeles)	90031
		postmaster.		Lincoln Village (Los Angeles	
		Landers	92285	County)	90810

	ZIP
Lincoln Village (San Joaquin County)	95207
Linda	95901
Linda Vista (Los Angeles County)	91103
Linda Vista (San Diego County)	92111
Linda Vista (Santa Clara County)	95127
Lind Cove	93221
Linden	95236
Linden Avenue (Part of South San Francisco)	94080
Lindenwood (Part of Menlo Park)	94027
Lindsay	93247
Lingard	95333
Linnell	93292
Linns Valley	93226
Litchfield	96117
Little Lake	93542
Little Norway	95721
Little Reed Heights (Part of Tiburon)	94920
Littleriver	95456
Littlerock	93543
Little Saigon (Part of Westminster)	92683
Little Shasta	96064
Little Valley	96053
Live Oak (Santa Cruz County)	95062
Live Oak (Sutter County)	95953
Live Oak Acres (Tehama County)	96080
Live Oak Acres (Ventura County)	93022
Live Oak Canyon	91750
Live Oak Springs	91905
Livermore	94550*
	94551†
Livingston	95334
Llano	93544
Lobitos	94019
Lobo (Part of Stanton)	90680
Loch Lomond	95426
Locke	95690
Lockeford	95237
Lockhart	92347
Lockwood	93932
Lodgepole	93262
Lodi	95240-42
For specific Lodi Zip Codes call (209) 369-9545, or your local postmaster.	
Lodoga	95979
Logan Heights (Part of San Diego)	92113
Loleta	95551
Loma (Part of Long Beach)	90814
Loma Linda	92354
Loma Mar	94021
Loma Portal (Part of San Diego)	92110
Loma Rica	95901
Lomas Santa Fe (Part of Solana Beach)	92075
Loma Verda (Part of Novato)	94949
Lomita	90717
Lomita Park (Part of San Bruno)	94066
Lompico	95018
Lompoc	93436-38
For specific Lompoc Zip Codes call (805) 736-4561, or your local postmaster.	
London	93618
Lone Pine	93545
Lone Pine Indian Reservation	93545
Long Barn	95335
Long Beach	90801-53
For specific Long Beach Zip Codes call (310) 494-2371, or your local postmaster.	

COLLEGES & UNIVERSITIES

	ZIP
California State University-Long Beach	90840

FINANCIAL INSTITUTIONS

	ZIP
Farmers & Merchants Bank of Long Beach	90802
Harbor Bank	90802
National Bank of Long Beach	90807

HOSPITALS

	ZIP
Long Beach Community Hospital	90804
Long Beach Memorial Medical Center	90806
St. Mary Medical Center	90801
Veterans Affairs Medical Center	90822

HOTELS/MOTELS

	ZIP
Hyatt Regency Long Beach	90802
Hotel Queen Mary	90802
Ramada Inn - Long Beach	90804

MILITARY INSTALLATIONS

	ZIP
Long Beach Naval Shipyard	90810
Naval Regional Contracting Center Detachment	90822
Supervisor of Shipbuilding, Conversion and Repair, Long Beach	90822

	ZIP
Long Beach Plaza (Part of Long Beach)	90802
Longvale	95490
Lonoak	93930
Lonoke (Part of Gilroy)	95020
Lookout	96054
Lookout Ranchettes	96054
Loomis	95650
Loomis Corners	96003
Loraine	93518
Loree Estates	95014
Los Alamitos	90720*
	90721†
Los Alamitos Naval Air Station	90720
Los Alamos	93440
Los Altos	94022-24
For specific Los Altos Zip Codes call (415) 948-6000, or your local postmaster.	
Los Altos Hills	94022
Los Altos Shopping Center (Part of Long Beach)	90815
Los Amigos (Part of Downey)	90240
Los Angeles	90001-45
	90047-68
	90070-99
	90101
For specific Los Angeles Zip Codes call (213) 586-1737, or your local postmaster.	

COLLEGES & UNIVERSITIES

	ZIP
California State University-Los Angeles	90032
Loyola Marymount University	90045
Mount Saint Mary's College	90049
Northrop University	90301
Occidental College	90041
University of California-Los Angeles	90024
University of Southern California	90089

FINANCIAL INSTITUTIONS

	ZIP
American International Bank	90017
The Bank of California, National Association	90071
Bankers Trust Company of California, N.A.	90071
California Commerce Bank	90017
California Federal Bank	90036
California Korea Bank	90010
Canadian Imperial Bank of Commerce	90071
Capital Bank of California	90067
Cathay Bank	90012
Century Bank	90010
Dai-Ichi Kangyo Bank of California	90013
East-West Federal Bank, F.S.B.	90012
Family Savings Bank	90016
Far East National Bank	90012
1st Business Bank	90071
First Interstate Bank, Ltd.	90017
First Interstate Bank of California	90017
First Los Angeles Bank	90067
First Public Savings Bank	90012
Founders National Bank of Los Angeles	90008
General Bank	90012
Guardian Bank	90017
Hancock Savings Bank	90004
Hanmi Bank	90010
Highland Federal Bank	90041
Home Savings of America, F.A.	90010
Manufacturers Bank	90071
Marathon National Bank	90064
Mercantile National Bank	90067
Metrobank	90024
Standard Savings Bank	90012
Sterling Bank	90010
Tokai Bank of California	90014
Union Bank	90071
Western Bank	90024

HOSPITALS

	ZIP
California Medical Center-Los Angeles	90015
Cedars-Sinai Medical Center	90048
Childrens Hospital of Los Angeles	90027
Hospital of the Good Samaritan	90017
Kaiser Foundation Hospital	90027
LAC-King-Drew Medical Center	90059
LAC-University of Southern California Medical Center	90033
St. Vincent Medical Center	90057
University of California Los Angeles Medical Center	90024
Veterans Affairs Medical Center-West Los Angeles	90073

HOTELS/MOTELS

	ZIP
The Biltmore Hotel	90071
Holiday Inn-Downtown	90017
Hyatt Regency Los Angeles-at Broadway Place	90017
Los Angeles Hilton & Towers	90017
The New Otani Hotel & Garden	90012
Sheraton Grande	90071
University Hilton-Los Angeles	90007
The Westin Bonaventure	90071

MILITARY INSTALLATIONS

	ZIP
Los Angeles Air Force Station	90009
Military Airlift Command	90045
United States Army Engineer District, Los Angeles	90053

	ZIP
Los Banos	93635
Los Berros	93420
Los Cerritos Center (Part of Cerritos)	90701
Los Coyotes Indian Reservation	92086
Los Deltos	93622
Los Feliz (Part of Los Angeles)	90027
Los Gatos	95030-32
For specific Los Gatos Zip Codes call (408) 354-6666, or your local postmaster.	
Los Molinos	96055
Los Nietos	90606
Los Olivos	93441
Los Osos	93402*
	93412†
Los Ranchitos	94903
Los Serranos	91709
Lost Hills	93249
Lost Lake	92225
Los Trancos Woods	94028
Los Tules	92086
Lotus	95651
Lovelock	95954
Lower Echo Lake	95721
Lower Lake	95457
Lowrey	96080
Loyalton	96118
Loyola	94024
Lucas Valley	94903
Lucas Valley-Marinwood	94903
Lucerne	95458
Lucerne Valley	92356
Lucia	93920
Ludlow	92338
Lugo (Part of Los Angeles)	90023
Lugonia (Part of Redlands)	92375
Lunada Bay (Part of Palos Verdes Estates)	90274
Lundy	93541
Lushmeadows Mountain Estates	95338
Luther Burbank (Part of Santa Rosa)	95402
Lyman Springs	96075
Lynwood	90262
Lynwood Gardens (Part of Lynwood)	90262

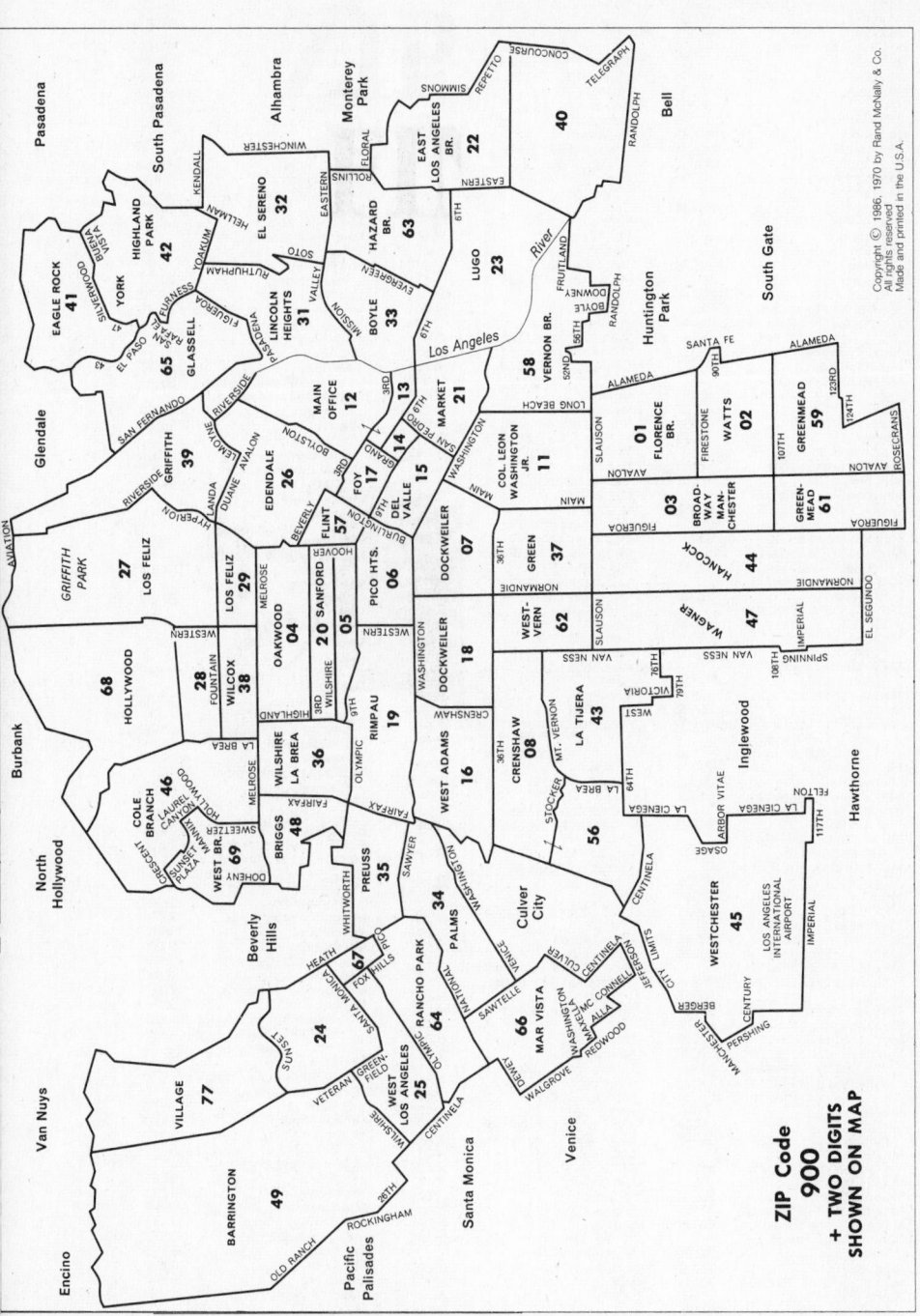

ZIP Code
900
+ TWO DIGITS
SHOWN ON MAP

ZIP | ZIP | ZIP

	ZIP
Lytle Creek	92358
Lytton	95448
McArthur	96056
McCann	95569
McClellan Air Force Base	95652
McCloud	96057
Macdoel	96058
McFarland	93250
McHie	96080
McIntyre Park	92225
McKeon	95631
McKinleyville	95521
McKittrick	93251
McKnight Acres	94590
Mc Laren (Part of San Francisco)	94134
Maclay (Part of San Fernando)	91340
McMillan Manor (Part of Oxnard)	93030
Madeline	96119
Madera	93637-39
For specific Madera Zip Codes call (209) 673-9288, or your local postmaster.	
Madera (Railroad Station)	93637
Madera Acres	93637
Madera Country Club Estates	93637
Madera Highlands	93637
Madera Ranchos	93637
Madison	95653
Madonna Road Plaza (Part of San Luis Obispo)	93405
Mad River	95552
Madrone (Part of Morgan Hill)	95037
Magalia	95954
Magnolia (Imperial County)	92227
Magnolia (Santa Barbara County)	93111
Magnolia Avenue (Part of Riverside)	92506
Magnolia Center (Part of Riverside)	92506
Magnolia Park (Part of Burbank)	91505
MainPlace/Santa Ana (Part of Santa Ana)	92701
Malaga	93725
Malibu	90263-65
For specific Malibu Zip Codes call (310)456-2018, or your local postmaster.	
Malibu Beach	90265
Malibu Bowl	90265
Malibu Canyon Homes	91302
Mall at Northgate, The (Part of San Rafael)	94903
Mall at Weberstown, The (Part of Stockton)	95207
Mall of Orange, The (Part of Orange)	92665
Mammoth Lakes	93546
Manchester	95459
Manchester Center (Part of Fresno)	93726
Manhattan Beach	90266
Manhattan Village (Part of Manhattan Beach)	90266
Manila	95521
Manka's Corners	94585
Manlove	95826
Manor (Part of Fairfax)	94930
Manteca	95336-37
For specific Manteca Zip Codes call (209) 823-3232, or your local postmaster.	
Manton	96059
Manzana	95444
Manzanita	95948
Manzanita Indian Reservation	91905
Maple Creek	95550
Maravilla Park	90022
Marcelina (Part of Torrance)	90501
March Air Force Base	92518
Marcus Foster (Part of Oakland)	94624
Maricopa	93252
Marina (Monterey County)	93933
Marina (Part of San Francisco)	94123
	94147
For specific Marina Zip Codes call (408) 384-9313, or your local postmaster.	
Marina Del Rey	90292*
	90295†
Marin City	94965
Marin Country Club Estates (Part of Novato)	94949

	ZIP
Marine Corps Air Station (H)	92709
Marine Corps Logistics Support Base, Pacific	92311
Marine Corps Supply Center, West Yermo Area	92398
Mariner (Part of Seal Beach)	90740
Marinwood	94903
Mariposa	95338
Market (Part of Los Angeles)	90021
Markleeville	96120
Marloma (Part of Rolling Hills Estates)	90274
Marne (Part of City of Industry)	91743
Marshall	94940
Marshall Station	93611
Martell	95654
Martinez	94553
Martins Beach	94019
Mar Vista (Part of Los Angeles)	90066
Marysville	95901
Massack	95971
Mather Air Force Base	95655
Mather Heights	95655
Maxwell	95955
Mayflower Village	91016
Maywood	90270
Meadowbrook	92570
Meadowbrook Woods	92326
Meadow Lake Park	96161
Meadow Lakes	93602
Meadowsweet (Part of Corte Madera)	94925
Meadow Valley	95956
Meadow Vista	95722
Mead Valley	92570
Mecca	92254
Media City Center (Part of Burbank)	91505
Medicine Lake Lodge	96134
Meeks Bay	96142
Meiners Oaks	93023
Melody Oaks	95642
Meloland	92243
Melvin (Part of Clovis)	93611
Mendocino	95460
Mendota	93640
Menifee	92584
Menlo Park	94025-29
For specific Menlo Park Zip Codes call (415) 323-0038, or your local postmaster.	
Mentone	92359
Merced	95340-44
	95348
For specific Merced Zip Codes call (209) 723-1063, or your local postmaster.	
Merced Falls	95369
Merced Mall (Part of Merced)	95348
Meridian	95957
Mesa Center (Part of Costa Mesa)	92627
Mesa Grande	92070
Mesa Verde	92225
Metro (Part of Sacramento)	95814
Metropolitan (Humboldt County)	95540
Metropolitan (Los Angeles County)	90014
Mettler	93301
Mexican Colony	93263
Meyers (Part of South Lake Tahoe)	96158
Michigan Bluff	95631
Michillinda	91107
Mid City (Part of Stockton)	95202
Midco (Part of Santa Maria)	93454
Middlefield Road	94061
Middle River	95234
Middletown	95461
Midpines	95345
Midtown (Part of Chico)	95926
Midway	96088
Midway City	92655
Mikon (Part of West Sacramento)	95605
Milford	96121
Millbrae	94030*
	94031†
Millbrae Meadows (Part of Millbrae)	94030
Mill City	93546
Mill Creek	96061
Mill Creek Park	92359
Millers Corners	93637
Mills College (Part of Oakland)	94613
Mill Valley	94941*

	ZIP
	94942†
Millville	96062
Milo	93265
Milpas (Part of Santa Barbara)	93103
Milpitas	95035*
	95036†
Milton	95230
Mineral	96063
Mineral King	93271
Minkler	93657
Mint Canyon (Part of Santa Clarita)	91350
Mirabel Heights	95436
Mirabel Park	95436
Miracle Hot Springs	93301
Miracle Manor	93501
Miracle Mile (Part of Los Angeles)	90036
Miraleste (Part of Rancho Palos Verdes)	90274
Mira Loma	91752
Miramar (San Diego County)	92145
Miramar (San Mateo County)	94018
Mira Mesa (Part of San Diego)	92126
Miramonte (Fresno County)	93641
Mira Monte (Ventura County)	93023
Miranda	95553
Mira Vista (Part of Richmond)	94805
Mission (San Francisco County)	94110
Mission (San Luis Obispo County)	93406
Mission (Santa Clara County)	95051
Mission Annex (Part of San Francisco)	94103
Mission Beach (Part of San Diego)	92109
Mission City Annex (Part of Los Angeles)	91345
Mission Highlands	95476
Mission Hills (Los Angeles County)	91345
Mission Hills (San Diego County)	92103
Mission Hills (Santa Barbara County)	93436
Mission Rafael (Part of San Rafael)	94901
Mission San Jose (Part of Fremont)	94539
Mission Valley Center (Part of San Diego)	92108
Mission Viejo	92690-92
For specific Mission Viejo Zip Codes call (714) 364-5020, or your local postmaster.	
Mission Viejo Mall (Part of Mission Viejo)	92691
Missouri Triangle	93251
Mitchell Mill	95257
Mitchells Corner	93203
Mi-Wuk Village	95346
Moccasin	95347
Mococo (Part of Martinez)	94553
Modesto	95350-57
For specific Modesto Zip Codes call (209) 523-8326, or your local postmaster.	
Modjeska	92667
Modoc Recreational Estates	96101
Moffett Field Naval Air Station	94035
Mohave Manor	92311
Mojave	93501*
	93502†
Mojave Heights (Part of Victorville)	92392
Mojave Knolls	93501
Mokelumne Hill	95245
Monarch Bay (Part of Laguna Niguel)	92677
Monmouth	93725
Mono Hot Springs	93642
Mono Lake	93541
Mono Village	93517
Mono Vista	95372
Monrovia	91016*
	91017†
Monson	93618
Montague	96064
Montair (Part of Danville)	94526
Montalvin Manor	94806
Montalvo (Part of Ventura)	93003*
	93005†
Montara	94037

	ZIP
Monta Vista (Part of	
Cupertino)	95014
Montclair	91763
Montclair Plaza (Part of	
Montclair)	91763
Montebello	90640
Montebello Gardens (Part of	
Pico Rivera)	90660
Montebello Town Center	
(Part of Montebello)	90640
Montecito	93108
Monte Nido	91302
Monterey	93940
	93942-44
For specific Monterey Zip Codes	
call (408) 372-5803, or your local	
postmaster.	
Monterey Park	91754-55
For specific Monterey Park Zip	
Codes call (818) 288-4422, or	
your local postmaster.	
Monte Rio	95462
Monte Rosa	95446
Montesano	95446
Monte Sereno	95030
Monte Toyon	95003
Montgomery Creek	96065
Montgomery Village (Part of	
Santa Rosa)	95405
Montrose	91020*
	91021†
Moody (Part of Cypress)	90630
Moonridge (Part of Big Bear	
Lake)	92315
Moonstone	95570
Moorpark	93020*
	93021†
Moorpark Home Acres	93021
Morada	95212
Moraga	94556
Morena	92040
Moreno	92554-55
For specific Moreno Zip Codes	
call (714) 656-2590, or your local	
postmaster.	
Moreno Valley	92552-57
For specific Moreno Valley Zip	
Codes call (714) 656-2590, or	
your local postmaster.	
Moreno Valley Mall at	
Towngate (Part of	
Moreno Valley)	92508
Morgan Hill	95037*
	95038†
Mormon Bar	95338
Morningside Park (Part of	
Inglewood)	90305
Morongo Indian Reservation	92220
Morongo Valley	92256
Morro Bay	93442*
	93443†
Morro Palisades	93402
Moss Beach	94038
Mossdale	95330
Moss Landing	95039
Mountain Center	92561
Mountain Gate	96003
Mountain House (Alameda	
County)	95376
Mountain House (Butte	
County)	95916
Mountain Meadow	96091
Mountain Mesa	93240
Mountain Pass	92366
Mountain Ranch (Calaveras	
County)	95246
Mountain Ranch (Madera	
County)	93638
Mountain Rest	93664
Mountain Spring	91934
Mountain View (Kern	
County)	93307
Mountain View (Santa Clara	
County)	94039-43
For specific Mountain View Zip	
Codes call (415) 967-5721, or	
your local postmaster.	
Mountain View Acres	92392
Mount Aukum	95656
Mount Baldy	91759
Mount Bullion	95338
Mount Eden (Part of	
Hayward)	94557
Mount Hamilton	95140
Mount Hannah Lodge	95451
Mount Hebron	96058
Mount Helix	91941
Mount Hermon	95041
Mount Laguna	91948
Mount Shasta	96067
Mount Signal	92231
Mount View	94553

	ZIP
Mount Whitney	93545
Mount Wilson	91023
Mt. Roberta	95066
Mugginsville	96032
Muir (Part of Willits)	95490
Muir Beach	94965
Muir Woods	94941
Murietta	93640
Murphys	95247
Murray Park (Part of	
Larkspur)	94939
Murrieta	92562-64
For specific Murrieta Zip Codes	
call (714) 677-5927, or your local	
postmaster.	
Murrieta Hot Springs	92563
Muscoy	92405
Myers Flat	95554
Myrtletown	95501
Nadeau	90001
Napa	94558-59
For specific Napa Zip Codes call	
(707) 255-1791, or your local	
postmaster.	
Napa Junction	94590
Naples (Part of Long	
Beach)	90803
Nashville	95623
National City	91950-51
For specific National City Zip	
Codes call (619) 477-3173, or	
your local postmaster.	
Navajo (Part of San Diego)	92119
Naval Air Facility	92243
Naval Air Station (Alameda	
County)	94625
Naval Air Station (Kings	
County)	93245
Naval Base (Part of Port	
Hueneme)	93043
Naval Regional Medical	
Center	92055
Naval Weapons Station	
(Contra Costa County)	94520
Naval Weapons Station	
(Orange County)	90740
Navarro	95463
Navelencia	93654
Nebo	92311
Nebo Center	92311
Needles	92363
Nelson	95958
Nestor (Part of San Diego)	92053
Nevada City	95959
New Almaden	95042
Newark	94560
New Auberry	93602
Newberry Springs	92365
Newburg	95540
Newbury Park	91319†
	91320*
Newcastle	95658
New Cuyama	93254
Newell	96134
Newhall	91321-22
	91382-83
For specific Newhall Zip Codes	
call (805) 259-4897, or your local	
postmaster.	
Newhall Ranch (Part of	
Santa Clarita)	91350
New Helvetia (Part of	
Sacramento)	95815
Newman	95360
New Monterey (Part of	
Monterey)	93940
New Park Mall (Part of	
Newark)	94560
New Pine Creek	97635
Newport Beach	92657-63
For specific Newport Beach Zip	
Codes call (714) 640-8720, or	
your local postmaster.	
Newport Center Fashion	
Island (Part of Newport	
Beach)	92660
Newport Heights (Part of	
Newport Beach)	92663
Newport Island (Part of	
Newport Beach)	92663
Newtown (El Dorado	
County)	95667
Newtown (Nevada County)	95959
Newville	95963
Nicasio	94946
Nice	95464
Nichols	94565
Nicolaus	95659
Nigger Hill	95667
Nightingale	92561

	ZIP
Niguel Terrace (Part of	
Laguna Niguel)	92677
Niland	92257
Niles (Part of Fremont)	94536
Niles Junction (Part of	
Fremont)	94536
Nimshew	95954
Nipinnawassee	93601
Nipomo	93444
Nipton	92364
Nob Hill (Part of San	
Francisco)	94108
Noe Valley (Part of San	
Francisco)	94114
No Mirage	92259
Norco	91760
Nord	95926
Norden	95724
Normal Heights (Part of San	
Diego)	92116
North (Part of Los Angeles)	91342
North Auburn	95603
North Beach (Part of San	
Francisco)	94133
North Belridge	93429
North Berkeley (Part of	
Berkeley)	94709
North Bloomfield	95959
North Clairemont (Part of	
San Diego)	92117
North Columbia	95959
North County Fair (Part of	
Escondido)	92025
Northcrest (Part of Crescent	
City)	95531
North Downey (Part of	
Downey)	90240
Northeast Modesto (Part of	
Modesto)	95355
North Edwards	93523
North El Monte	91006
North Elsinore (Part of Lake	
Elsinore)	92530
Northern California	
Women's Facility	95213
North Fair Oaks	94025
North Fork	93643
North Gardena	90247
North Glendale (Part of	
Glendale)	91202*
	91222†
North Highlands	95660
North Hollywood	91601-03
	91605-07
	91609
	91615-17
For specific North Hollywood Zip	
Codes call (818) 503-0695, or	
your local postmaster.	
North Inglewood (Part of	
Inglewood)	90302
North Island Naval Air	
Station	92135
North Lakeport	95453
North Loma Linda (Part of	
Loma Linda)	92354
North Long Beach (Part of	
Long Beach)	90805
North Modesto (Part of	
Modesto)	95356
North Oakland (Part of	
Oakland)	94609
North Oaks	91350
North Palm Springs	92258
North Park (Part of San	
Diego)	92104
North Redondo Beach (Part	
of Redondo Beach)	90278
North Richmond	94804
Northridge	91324-28
For specific Northridge Zip Codes	
call (818) 349-4475, or your local	
postmaster.	
Northridge Center (Part of	
Salinas)	93906
Northridge Fashion Center	
(Part of Los Angeles)	91324
North Sacramento (Part of	
Sacramento)	95815
North San Juan	95960
North Shore	92254
North Torrance (Part of	
Torrance)	90504
North Valley Plaza (Part of	
Chico)	95926
North Whittier	91746
North Whittier Heights	91745
Norwalk	90650-52
For specific Norwalk Zip Codes	
call (213) 868-3247, or your local	
postmaster.	

* Area Zip Code   † Post Office Boxes

	ZIP
Norwalk Manor (Part of Norwalk)	90650
Novato	94945
	94947-49

For specific Novato Zip Codes call (415) 897-3171, or your local postmaster.

	ZIP
Noyo	95437
Nubieber	96068
Nuevo	92567
Nummi (Part of Fremont)	94538
Nut Tree (Part of Vacaville)	95696
Nyland Acres	93030
Oak Bottom	96095
Oakdale	95361
Oak Glen (Part of Yucaipa)	92399
Oak Grove (Butte County)	95966
Oak Grove (San Diego County)	92536
Oakhills	93907
Oakhurst	93644
Oak Knoll Hills (Part of Cupertino)	95014
Oak Knolls	93455
Oakland	94601-07
	94609-10
	94612-19
	94621-61

For specific Oakland Zip Codes call (415) 874-8200, or your local postmaster.

	ZIP
Oakley	94561
Oakmont (Part of Santa Rosa)	95409
Oak Park (Sacramento County)	95817
Oak Park (San Luis Obispo County)	93446
Oak Park (Ventura County)	91301
Oak Park Estates	95249
Oakridge (Part of Stockton)	95207
Oakridge Mall (Part of San Jose)	95123
Oak Run	96069
Oaks (Part of Arroyo Grande)	93420
Oaks, The (Part of Thousand Oaks)	91360
Oak Shores	93426
Oak View	93022
Oakville	94562
Oakwood (Part of Los Angeles)	90004
Oasis	89010
O'Brien	96070
Occidental (Sonoma County)	95465
Ocean Beach (Part of San Diego)	92107
Oceano	93445
Ocean Park (Part of Santa Monica)	90405
	90409

For specific Ocean Park Zip Codes call (310) 576-2670, or your local postmaster.

	ZIP
Oceanside	92049-52
	92054-58

For specific Oceanside Zip Codes call (619) 433-8711, or your local postmaster.

	ZIP
Ocean View (Orange County)	92647
Ocean View (San Francisco County)	94112
Ocean View (Sonoma County)	94923
Ockenden	93664
Ocotillo	92259
Ocotillo Wells	92004
Odd Fellows Park	95446
Oildale	93308
Ojai	93023*
	93024†
Olancha	93549
Old Fort Jim	95667
Old Gilroy	95020
Old Hopland	95449
Old Mammoth (Part of Mammoth Lakes)	93546
Old River	93309
Old San Diego (Part of San Diego)	92110
Old Station	96071
Old Town	93643
Old Towne (Part of Tehachapi)	93561
Oleander	93725
Olema	94950
Oleum	94572
Olinda (Orange County)	92621
Olinda (Shasta County)	96007

	ZIP
Olive (Part of Orange)	92665
Olivehurst	95961
Olivenhain (Part of Encinitas)	92024
Olympia	95018
Olympic (Part of Beverly Hills)	90212
Olympic Valley	96146
Omo Ranch	95684
O'Neals	93645
One Hundred Palms	92274
Ono	96047
Ontario	91761-62
	91764
	91758
	91798

For specific Ontario Zip Codes call (714) 983-1873, or your local postmaster.

	ZIP
Ontario Mail Facility (Part of Ontario)	91761
Onyx	93255
Opal Cliffs	95062
Ophir	95603
Orange	92613
	92664-69

For specific Orange Zip Codes call (714) 997-1255, or your local postmaster.

	ZIP
Orange Center (Part of Riverside)	92501
Orange Cove	93646
Orangefair Mall (Part of Fullerton)	92632
Orange Glen (Part of Escondido)	92027
Orange Heights (Part of Upland)	91786
Orangehurst (Part of Fullerton)	92633
Orange Park Acres	92669
Orangevale	95662
Orangewood (Part of Pasadena)	91115
Orcutt	93455*
	93457†
Ord	93941
Ordbend	95943
Oregon City	95965
Oregon House	95962
Orick	95555
Orinda	94563
Orinda Village (Part of Orinda)	94563
Orland	95963
Orleans	95556
Ormand	92509
Oro Fino	96032
Oro Grande	92368
Oro Loma	93622
Orosi	93647
Oroville	95965-66

For specific Oroville Zip Codes call (916) 533-4515, or your local postmaster.

	ZIP
Oroville East	95965
Osbourne (Part of Los Angeles)	90028
Otay (Part of Chula Vista)	91911
Otay Mesa (Part of Chula Vista)	92154
Otterbein	91748
Outingdale	95684
Oval (Part of Visalia)	93291
Oxnard	93030-35

For specific Oxnard Zip Codes call (805) 485-6722, or your local postmaster.

	ZIP
Oxnard Beach	93035
Pabrico (Part of Union City)	94587
Pachappa	92506
Pacheco	94553
Pacific (Part of Long Beach)	90806
Pacifica	94044*
	94045†
Pacific Beach (Part of San Diego)	92109
Pacific Gardens	95204
Pacific Grove	93950
Pacific Grove Acres (Part of Pacific Grove)	93950
Pacific House	95726
Pacific Manor (Humboldt County)	95521
Pacific Manor (San Mateo County)	94044
Pacific Missile Test Center-Point Mugu	93042
Pacific Palisades (Part of Los Angeles)	90272
Pacific Shores	95531
Pacific Valley	93920

	ZIP
Pacoima	91331-34

For specific Pacoima Zip Codes call (818) 896-7491, or your local postmaster.

	ZIP
Paddison Square (Part of Norwalk)	90652
Paicines	95043
Paintersville	95615
Pajaro	95076
Pala	92059
Pala Indian Reservation	92059
Pala Mesa Village	92028
Palermo	95968
Palm City (Part of Palm Desert)	92211
Palmdale	93550-52
	93590-91

For specific Palmdale Zip Codes call (805) 947-4134, or your local postmaster.

	ZIP
Palmdale East	93550
	93552
	93591

For specific Palmdale East Zip Codes call (805) 947-4134, or your local postmaster.

	ZIP
Palm Desert	92211
	92255
	92260-61

For specific Palm Desert Zip Codes call (619) 568-5803, or your local postmaster.

	ZIP
Palm Desert Country	92211
Palm Desert Town Center (Part of Palm Desert)	92260
Palmer Creek	95540
Palms (Part of Los Angeles)	90034
Palm Springs	92262-64

For specific Palm Springs Zip Codes call (619) 325-9631, or your local postmaster.

	ZIP
Palm Springs Mall (Part of Palm Springs)	92262
Palo Alto	94301-09

For specific Palo Alto Zip Codes call (415) 321-4310, or your local postmaster.

	ZIP
Palo Cedro	96073
Paloma	95252
Palomar Mountain	92060
Palomar Park	94062
Palos Verdes Estates	90274
Palos Verdes Peninsula (Part of Rolling Hills Estates)	90274
Palo Verde	92266
Palo Vista (Part of Vista)	92083
Panoche	95043
Panorama Heights (Orange County)	92705
Panorama Heights (Tulare County)	93260
Panorama Mall (Part of Los Angeles)	91402
Pappas	93640
Paradise (Butte County)	95967†
	95969*
Paradise (Stanislaus County)	95351
	95358

For specific Paradise Zip Codes call (209) 523-8326, or your local postmaster.

	ZIP
Paradise Cay (Part of Tiburon)	94920
Paradise Estates	93514
Paradise Hills (Part of San Diego)	92139
Paradise Park	95060
Paraiso Springs	93960
Paramount	90723
Parchers Camp	93514
Park (Part of Berkeley)	94702
Park Central (Part of Alameda)	94501
Parker Dam	92267
Parkfield	93451
Parkmoor (Part of San Jose)	95128
Parksdale	93637
Parkside (Part of San Francisco)	94116
Park Siding (Part of Petaluma)	94952
Park Village	92328
Parkway	95823
Parkway Plaza (Part of El Cajon)	92020
Parkway-South Sacramento	95823
Parkwood	93637
Parlier	93648

* Area Zip Code **† Post Office Boxes**

ZIP		ZIP		ZIP

Pasadena 91101-18
For specific Pasadena Zip Codes
call (818) 304-7183, or your local
postmaster.
Pasatiempo 95060
Paskenta 96074
Paso Robles 93446*
.... 93447†
Patata (Part of South Gate) 90280
Patrick Creek 95543
Patricks Point 95570
Patterson (Stanislaus
County) 95363
Patterson (Tulare County) 93291
Patton 92369
Patton Village 96113
Pauma Indian Reservation 92061
Pauma Valley 92061
Paxton 95971
Paynes Creek 96075
Paynesville 96120
Peanut 96041
Pearblossom 93553
Peardale 95945
Pearland (Part of Palmdale) 93550
Pearsonville 93527
Pebble Beach 93953
Pechanga Indian
Reservation 92590
Pecwan 95546
Pedley 92509
Pedro Valley (Part of
Pacifica) 94044
Pelican Bay State Prison ... 95531
Peninsula Center (Part of
Rolling Hills Estates) 90274
Peninsula Village 96137
Penngrove 94951
Pennington 95953
Penn Valley 95946
Penryn 95663
Pentz 95965
Pepperwood 95565
Peralta Hills 92667
Perkins 95826
Perris 92570-72
For specific Perris Zip Codes call
(714) 657-2396, or your local
postmaster.
Perry (Part of Whittier) 90603
Pescadero 94060
Petaluma 94952-55
.... 94975
.... 94999
For specific Petaluma Zip Codes
call (707) 762-0051, or your local
postmaster.
Peters 95236
Petrolia 95558
Phelan 92329
.... 92371
For specific Phelan Zip Codes call
(619) 868-6307, or your local
postmaster.
Phillipsville 95559
Philo 95466
Phoenix Lake-Cedar Ridge 95370
Phoenix Lake Country Club
Estates 95370
Pico (Part of Pico Rivera) 90660
Pico Heights (Part of Los
Angeles) 90006
Pico Rivera 90660-62
For specific Pico Rivera Zip Codes
call (213) 942-7008, or your local
postmaster.
Piedmont 94611
.... 94620
For specific Piedmont Zip Codes
call (510) 251-3130, or your local
postmaster.
Piedra 93649
Pierce Lake Estates 93644
Piercy 95587
Pierpoint Springs 93208
Pike 95960
Pilot Hill 95664
Pine Cove (Riverside
County) 92549
Pine Cove (Trinity County) 96052
Pinecrest 95364
Pinedale (Part of Fresno)... 93650
Pine Flat (Fresno County) 93649
Pine Flat (Tulare County)... 93207
Pine Grove (Amador
County) 95665
Pine Grove (Lake County) 95426
Pine Grove (Mendocino
County) 95437
Pine Grove (Shasta County) 96079
Pine Hills (Humboldt
County) 95503

Pine Hills (San Diego
County) 92036
Pinehurst 93641
Pine Mountain Club 93222
Pine Mountain Lake 95321
Pineridge 93602
Pine Valley 91962
Pinnacles 95043
Pinole 94564
Pinon Hills 92372
Pinon Pines Estates 93225
Pinyon Crest 92262
Pinyon Pines 92561
Pioneer 95666
Pioneer Point 93562
Pioneertown 92268
Piru 93040
Pismo Beach .... 93448†
.... 93449*
Pittsburg 94565
Pittville 96056
Pixley 93256
Placentia 92670
Placerville 95667
Plainsburg 95333
Plainview 93267
Planada 95365
Planehaven 95652
Plantation 95421
Plaster City 92243
Platina 96076
Playa (Part of Laguna
Beach) 92652
Playa Del Rey (Part of Los
Angeles) 90293*
.... 90296†
Playa Vista (Part of Los
Angeles) 90094
Playmor (Part of Chula
Vista) 91911
Plaza (Los Angeles County) 91102
Plaza (Orange County)..... 92666
Plaza (Santa Clara County) 94086
Plaza Camino Real (Part of
Carlsbad) 92008
Plaza Center (Part of
Ontario) 91762
Plaza Pasadena (Part of
Pasadena) 91101
Pleasant Grove 95668
Pleasant Hill 94523
Pleasanton 94566
.... 94588
For specific Pleasanton Zip Codes
call (510) 846-5631, or your local
postmaster.
Pleasant Valley 95667
Pleasant View 93260
Plymouth 95669
Poinsettia Tract 94565
Point Arena 95468
Point Dume 90265
Point Loma (Part of San
Diego) 92106
Point Pleasant 95758
Point Reyes Station 94956
Point Richmond (Part of
Richmond) 94807
Poker Flat 95228
Pollock Pines 95726
Pomona 91766-69
For specific Pomona Zip Codes
call (714) 623-4476, or your local
postmaster.
Pond 93280
Ponderosa Sky Ranch 96075
Pondosa 96057
Pope Valley 94567
Poplar 93258
Port Chicago 94520
Port Costa 94569
Porter Ranch (Part of Los
Angeles) 91326
Porterville 93257*
.... 93258†
Porterville Development
Center 93257
Porterville West (Part of
Porterville) 93257
Port Hueneme 93041*
.... 93044††
Port Kenyon 95536
Portola 96122
Portola Hills 92691
Portola Valley 94028
Port San Luis 93424
Portuguese Bend (Part of
Rancho Palos Verdes) ... 90274
Posey 93260
Poso Park 93260

Postal Avenue (Part of
Moreno Valley) 92556-57
For specific Postal Avenue Zip
Codes call (714) 242-6459, or
your local postmaster.
Post Office Annex (Part of
Burlingame) 94010
Potrero (San Diego County) 91963
Potrero (San Francisco
County) 94110
Potter Valley 95469
Poway 92064*
.... 92074†
Power Tract 93283
Pozo 93453
Prather 93651
Prattville 95923
Presidential Heights (Part of
San Clemente) 92672
Preston Heights (Part of
Arcata) 95521
Preuss (Part of Los
Angeles) 90035
Priest Valley 93210
Princeton (Colusa County) 95970
Princeton (San Mateo
County) 94019
Proberta 96078
Project City 96079
Promenade Mall (Part of
Los Angeles)............. 91367
Prosser Lakeview Estates 96161
Prunedale 93907
Pudding Creek 95437
Puente Junction (Part of
City of Industry) 91744
Puerco Beach 90265
Pulga 95965
Pumpkin Center 93309
Putah Creek Park 94558
Quail Valley 92587
Quaking Aspen 93265
Quartz Hill 93536
Quincy 95971
Quincy-East Quincy 95971
Quintette 95634
Quito (Part of Saratoga).... 95070
Rackerby 95972
Radec 92543
Rafael Village (Part of
Novato) 94949
Rail Road Flat 95248
Rainbow 92028
Raisin 93652
Ralph 95370
Ramirez (Part of Los
Angeles) 90037
Ramona 92065
Ramona Acres 93432
Ramona Woods 95006
Ramos Village 95336
Rancheria 95449
Ranch House 92055
Ranchita 92066
Rancho Bernardo (Part of
San Diego) 92128
Rancho Buena 96022
Rancho California (Part of
Temecula) 92590
Rancho Cordova 95670
.... 95741-42
For specific Rancho Cordova Zip
Codes call (916) 635-9876, or
your local postmaster.
Rancho Cucamonga 91729-30
.... 91739
For specific Rancho Cucamonga
Zip Codes call (714) 987-4641, or
your local postmaster.
Rancho Del Mar 94590
Rancho Del Rey (Part of
Chula Vista) 91909
.... 91911
For specific Rancho Del Rey Zip
Codes call (619) 422-9221, or
your local postmaster.
Rancho Mirage 92270
Rancho Murieta
(Sacramento County) 95683
Rancho Palos Verdes 90274
Rancho Park (Part of Los
Angeles) 90064
Rancho Penasquitos (Part
of San Diego) 92129
Rancho Rinconada 95014
Rancho San Diego 91941
Rancho Santa Fe 92067
Rancho Santa Margarita ... 92688
Randall Island 95615
Randolph 96126
Randsburg 93554
Ravendale 96123

* **Area Zip Code** † **Post Office Boxes**

	ZIP		ZIP		ZIP
Ravenswood (Part of East		River Road (Part of		Rowland (Part of City of	
Palo Alto)	94303	Modesto)	95351	Industry)	91743
Rawhide	95370	Riverroad Estates	93637	Rowland Heights	91748
Rawson	96080	Riverside	92501-17	Rubidoux	92509
Raymond	93653		92519	Rucker	95020

Ravenswood (Part of East Palo Alto) 94303
Rawhide 95370
Rawson 96080
Raymond 93653
Raynor Park (Part of
  Sunnyvale) 94087
Red Bank 96080
Red Bluff 96080
Redcrest 95569
Redding 96001-03
  96049
  96099
  For specific Redding Zip Codes
  call (916) 223-7502, or your local
  postmaster.
Red Hill 92705
Redlands 92373-75
  For specific Redlands Zip Codes
  call (714) 793-2171, or your local
  postmaster.
Red Mountain 93558
Redondo Beach 90277-78
  For specific Redondo Beach Zip
  Codes call (213) 376-2472, or
  your local postmaster.
Reds Meadow 93546
Red Top 95340
Redway 95560
Redwood City 94059
  94061-65
  For specific Redwood City Zip
  Codes call (415) 368-4181, or
  your local postmaster.
Redwood Estates 95044
Redwood Grove 95006
Redwood Lodge 95437
Redwood Retreat 95020
Redwood Terrace 94020
Redwood Valley 95470
Reedley 93654
Relief 95959
Represa 95630
Requa 95548
Rescue 95672
Reseda 91335-37
  For specific Reseda Zip Codes
  call (818) 342-6111, or your local
  postmaster.
Rheem (Part of San Pablo) 94801
Rheem Valley (Part of
  Moraga) 94570
Rialto 92376*
  .... 92377†
Rice 92280
Richardson Springs 95973
Richfield 96021
Richgrove 93261
Richmond 94801-02
  94804-05
  94807-08
  For specific Richmond Zip Codes
  call (415) 232-9709, or your local
  postmaster.
Richmond (Part of San
  Francisco) 94118
Richvale 95974
Ridgecrest 93555*
  .... 93556†
Rimcrest (Part of Palm
  Springs) 92264
Rimforest 92378
Rimpau (Part of Los
  Angeles) 90019
Rimrock 92268
Rincon 92061
Rincon Center (Part of San
  Francisco) 94119
Rincon Indian Reservation 92025
Rincon Valley (Part of Santa
  Rosa) 95409
Rio Bonito 95917
Rio Bravo 93306
Rio Dell (Humboldt County) 95562
Rio Dell (Sonoma County) 95436
Rio del Mar 95003
Rio Linda 95673
Rio Nido 95471
Rio Oso 95674
Rio Vista 94571
Ripley 92272
Ripon 95366
Ripperdan 93637
Rivera (Part of Pico Rivera) 90660
Riverbank 95367
Riverbank Army Ammunition
  Plant 95367
Riverdale 93656
River Kern 93238
River Oaks 95045
River Pines 95675

River Road (Part of
  Modesto) 95351
Riverroad Estates 93637
Riverside 92501-17
  92519
  For specific Riverside Zip Codes
  call (714) 276-6686, or your local
  postmaster.
Riverside (Part of Newport
  Beach) .... 92659†
  .... 92663*
Riverside Grove 95006
Riverside Park 95528
Riverside Plaza (Part of
  Riverside) 92506
Riverview 92040
Riverview Farms 92040
Riviera Cliff 95204
Roads End 93238
Robbins 95676
Robertsville (Part of San
  Jose) 95118
Robinsons Corner 95965
Robles Del Rio 93924
Rob Roy Junction 95003
Rockaway Beach (Part of
  Pacifica) 94044
Rock Creek 95965
Rock Crest 95980
Rock Haven 93664
Rocking Horse Ranchos
  (Part of Rancho Palos
  Verdes) 90731
Rocklin 95677
  95765
  For specific Rocklin Zip Codes
  call (916) 624-2400, or your local
  postmaster.
Rockport 95488
Rockridge (Part of Oakland) 94618
Rockville 94585
Rodeo 94572
Rodgers Flat 95980
Rogina Heights 95482
Rohnert Park 94927*
  .... 94928†
Rohnerville 95540
Rolinda 93706
Rolling Hills (Los Angeles
  County) 90274
Rolling Hills (Madera
  County) 93637
Rolling Hills (Riverside
  County) 92539
Rolling Hills Estates (Los
  Angeles County) 90274
Rolling Hills Estates (San
  Luis Obispo County) ... 93401
Rolling Hills Plaza (Part of
  Torrance) 90505
Rolling Hills Riviera (Part of
  Rancho Palos Verdes) .. 90731
Rollingwood 94806
Romie Lane (Part of
  Salinas) 93901
Romoland 92585
Roosevelt Corner 93534
Roosevelt Terrace 94590
Rosamond 93560
Rose Bowl (Part of
  Pasadena) 91103
Rosedale 93308
Roseland 95407
Rosemead 91770
Rosemead Square (Part of
  Rosemead) 91770
Rosemont (Sacramento
  County) 95826
Rosemont (San Diego
  County) 92065
Roseville 95661
  95678
  95747
  For specific Roseville Zip Codes
  call (916) 782-1203, or your local
  postmaster.
Rosewood (Part of Eureka) 95503
Ross 94957
Ross Corner 92222
Rossmoor 90720
Rossmoor Business Center
  (Part of Seal Beach) ... 90740
Rossmoor Highlands (Part
  of Los Alamitos) 90720
Rough And Ready 95975
Round Hill Country Club . 94507
Round Mountain 96084
Round Valley 93514
Round Valley Indian
  Reservation 95428
Rovana 93514

Rowland (Part of City of
  Industry) 91743
Rowland Heights 91748
Rubidoux 92509
Rucker 95020
Rumsey 95679
Running Springs 92382
Rupert 95901
Russell (Part of Hayward) . 94541
Russian River Terrace ... 95436
Ruth 95526
Rutherford 94573
Ryde 95680
Sabre City 95678
Sacramento 94203-99
  95801-66
  For specific Sacramento Zip
  Codes call (916) 921-0280, or
  your local postmaster.
Sacramento Area Mail
  Processing Center 95798-99
  For specific Sacramento Area Mail
  Processing Center Zip Codes call
  (916) 373-8100, or your local
  postmaster.
Sacramento South 95820
Sage 92544
Sage Valley 96113
St. Bernard 96061
St. Francis Heights (Part of
  Daly City) 94015
St. Helena 94574
St. James Park (Part of San
  Jose) 95113
St. Johns 93286
St. Marys College (Part of
  Moraga) 94575
St. Matthew (Part of San
  Mateo) 94401
  94405
  For specific St. Matthew Zip
  Codes call (415) 343-5618, or
  your local postmaster.
Salida 95368
Salinas 93901-15
  For specific Salinas Zip Codes call
  (408) 422-8687, or your local
  postmaster.
Salinas Resort 95451
Salmon Creek 94923
Salton City 92275
Salton Sea Beach 92274
Saltus 92304
Salvador (Part of Napa) .. 94558
Salyer 95563
Samoa 95564
San Andreas 95249
San Anselmo 94960
  94979
  For specific San Anselmo Zip
  Codes call (415) 453-0830, or
  your local postmaster.
San Antonio Heights 91784
San Antonio Shopping
  Center (Part of Mountain
  View) 94040
San Ardo 93450
San Benito 95043
San Bernardino 92401-27
  For specific San Bernardino Zip
  Codes call (714) 884-3626, or
  your local postmaster.
San Bruno 94066*
  .... 94067†
San Carlos 94070*
  .... 94071†
San Carlos (Part of San
  Diego) 92119
San Clemente 92672-74
  For specific San Clemente Zip
  Codes call (714) 492-3494, or
  your local postmaster.
Sand City 93955
Sand Hill 94561

San Diego 92101-17
  92119-42
  92145-72
  92174-77
  92182-98
  For specific San Diego Zip Codes
  call (619) 627-0915, or your local
  postmaster.

COLLEGES & UNIVERSITIES

National University 92108
Point Loma Nazarene
  College 92106
San Diego State University 92182
United States International
  University 92131
University of San Diego ... 92110

	ZIP
FINANCIAL INSTITUTIONS	
The Bank of Rancho	
Bernardo	92128
The Bank of San Diego	92101
First National Bank	92101
Flagship Federal Savings	
Bank	92122
Girard Savings Bank	92122
International Savings Bank	92108
Peninsula Bank of San	
Diego....................	92106
San Diego National Bank	92101
San Diego Trust & Savings	
Bank	92101
HOSPITALS	
Kaiser Foundation Hospital	92120
Mercy Hospital and Medical	
Center	92103
Naval Hospital	92134
Sharp Cabrillo Hospital.....	92110
Sharp Memorial Hospital ...	92123
University of California San	
Diego Medical Center ...	92103
Veterans Affairs Medical	
Center	92161
HOTELS/MOTELS	
Bahia Hotel.................	92109
Best Western Seven Seas	92108
Catamaran Resort Hotel ...	92109
Dana Inn & Marina	92109
Hyatt Islandia	92109
Park Manor Suites Hotel ...	92103
Ramada Inn	92108
San Diego Hilton Beach &	
Tennis Resort	92109
Sheraton Harbor Island	
Hotel	92101
The Westgate Hotel	92101
MILITARY INSTALLATIONS	
Coast Guard Air Station,	
San Diego	92101
Marine Corps Recruiting	
Depot, San Diego	92140
Naval Air Station, Miramar	92145
Naval Air Station, North	
Island	92135
Naval Hospital, San Diego	92134
Naval Command Control	
and Ocean Surveillance	
Center	92132
Naval Supply Center, Fuel	
Department, Point Lom	
Annex	92132
Naval Supply Center, San	
Diego...................	92136
Naval Training Center, San	
Diego...................	92133
San Diego International	
Airport, Military	92101
Supervisor of Shipbuilding,	
Conversion and Repair,	
San Diego	92163
San Diego Country Estates	92065
San Dimas	91773
Sandy Korner	92274
San Felipe	95023
San Fernando	91340-46
....	91392-95
For specific San Fernando Zip	
Codes call (818) 365-0683, or	
your local postmaster.	
Sanford (Part of Los	
Angeles)	90005
San Francisco	94101-88
For specific San Francisco Zip	
Codes call (415) 550-6500, or	
your local postmaster.	
COLLEGES & UNIVERSITIES	
Golden Gate University	94105
San Francisco State	
University	94132
University of California-	
Hastings College of Law	94102
University of California-San	
Francisco	94143
University of San Francisco	94117
FINANCIAL INSTITUTIONS	
Bank of America National	
Trust & Savings	
Association	94104
The Bank of California,	
National Association	94104
Bank of Canton of	
California	94111

	ZIP
Bank of San Francisco	94111
Bank of the Orient........	94104
Bank of the West..........	94104
California Savings & Loan,	
A Federal Association ...	94102
Continental Savings of	
America	94104
East-West Federal Bank ...	94111
Home Federal Savings	
Association	94108
Home Savings of America	94121
Pacific Bank, National	
Association	94104
Redwood Bank............	94111
Sanwa Bank California	94111
The Sumitomo Bank of	
California	94104
Union Bank	94104
United Savings Bank, F.S.B.	94102
Wells Fargo Bank, N.A.	94104
HOSPITALS	
Kaiser Foundation Hospital	94115
Laguna Honda Hospital and	
Rehabilitation Center	94116
Letterman U.S. Army	
Hospital.................	94129
Mount Zion Medical Center	
of University of California	
- San Francisco	94115
San Francisco General	
Hospital Medical Center	94110
St. Francis Memorial	
Hospital.................	94109
St. Mary's Hospital and	
Medical Center..........	94117
University of California, San	
Francisco Medical Center	94143
Veterans Affairs Medical	
Center	94121
HOTELS/MOTELS	
Best Western Americania	94103
Grand Hyatt San Francisco	94108
The Mark Hopkins Inter-	
Continental	94108
Miyako Hotel	94115
Parc 55 Hotel	94102
San Francisco Hilton.......	94102
San Francisco Marriott	
Fisherman's Wharf	94133
Sir Francis Drake Hotel ...	94102
Stouffer Stanford Court	
Hotel	94108
MILITARY INSTALLATIONS	
Coast Guard Air Station,	
San Francisco	94501
Letterman Army Medical	
Center	94129
Naval Station, Treasure	
Island	94130
Presidio of San Francisco	94129
United States Army	
Engineer District, San	
Francisco	
....	94105
San Francisco Recreation	
Camp	95655
San Gabriel	91775-78
For specific San Gabriel Zip	
Codes call (818) 287-9661, or	
your local postmaster.	
Sanger....................	93657
San Geronimo.............	94963
San Gregorio	94074
San Jacinto	92581-83
For specific San Jacinto Zip	
Codes call (714) 654-7922, or	
your local postmaster.	
San Joaquin..............	93660
San Joaquin River Club	95385
San Jose	95101-96
For specific San Jose Zip Codes	
call (408) 452-4300, or your local	
postmaster.	
San Jose Recreation Camp	95321
San Juan Bautista	95045
San Juan Capistrano	92675
....	92679
....	92693
For specific San Juan Capistrano	
Zip Codes call (714) 364-5020, or	
your local postmaster.	
San Juan Plaza (Part of San	
Juan Capistrano)	92675
San Lawrence Terrace	93451
San Leandro	94577-79
For specific San Leandro Zip	
Codes call (415) 483-0550, or	
your local postmaster.	

	ZIP
San Lorenzo	94580
San Lorenzo Park	95006
San Lorenzo Woods.......	95006
San Lucas	93954
San Luis Obispo	93401-12
For specific San Luis Obispo Zip	
Codes call (805) 543-1882, or	
your local postmaster.	
San Luis Rey (Part of	
Oceanside)	92068
San Luis Rey Heights......	92028
San Marcos	92069*
	92079†
San Marin (Part of Novato)	94945
San Marino	91108*
	91118†
San Martin	95046
San Mateo	94401-10
For specific San Mateo Zip Codes	
call (415) 349-2301, or your local	
postmaster.	
San Mateo Fashion Island	
(Part of San Mateo)	94404
San Miguel	93451
San Onofre...............	92672
San Pablo................	94806
San Pasqual Indian	
Reservation	92082
San Pedro	90731-34
For specific San Pedro Zip Codes	
call (213) 831-3246, or your local	
postmaster.	
San Quentin...............	94964
San Rafael	94901-15
For specific San Rafael Zip Codes	
call (415) 459-0944, or your local	
postmaster.	
San Ramon	94583
San Ramon Village (Part of	
Dublin).................	94568
San Roque (Part of Santa	
Barbara)	93105
San Simeon	93452
San Simeon Acres.........	93452
Santa Ana	92701-07
....	92711-12
	92799
For specific Santa Ana Zip Codes	
call (714) 662-6445, or your local	
postmaster.	
Santa Ana Heights	92701
Santa Ana Marine Corps Air	
Facility..................	92709
Santa Anita Fashion Park	
(Part of Arcadia)	91007
Santa Barbara	93101-90
For specific Santa Barbara Zip	
Codes call (805) 564-2266, or	
your local postmaster.	
Santa Clara	95050-56
For specific Santa Clara Zip	
Codes call (408) 452-4300, or	
your local postmaster.	
Santa Clarita	91321-22
....	91350-51
....	91354-55
	91380
....	91382-83
	91385-86
For specific Santa Clarita Zip	
Codes call (805) 254-1684, or	
your local postmaster.	
Santa Clarita	91321-22
For specific Santa Clarita Zip	
Codes call (805) 254-1684, or	
your local postmaster.	
Santa Clarita	91354-55
For specific Santa Clarita Zip	
Codes call (805) 254-1684, or	
your local postmaster.	
Santa Cruz	95060-65
For specific Santa Cruz Zip Codes	
call (408) 426-5200, or your local	
postmaster.	
Santa Cruz Gardens	95062
Santa Fe Plaza	90605
Santa Fe Springs	90670*
....	90671†
Santa Margarita	93453
Santa Maria	93454-57
For specific Santa Maria Zip	
Codes call (805) 922-1911, or	
your local postmaster.	
Santa Maria Town Center	
(Part of Santa Maria)	93454
Santa Monica	90401-11
For specific Santa Monica Zip	
Codes call (213) 576-2626, or	
your local postmaster.	
Santa Monica Canyon (Part	
of Los Angeles)	90402

* Area Zip Code   † Post Office Boxes

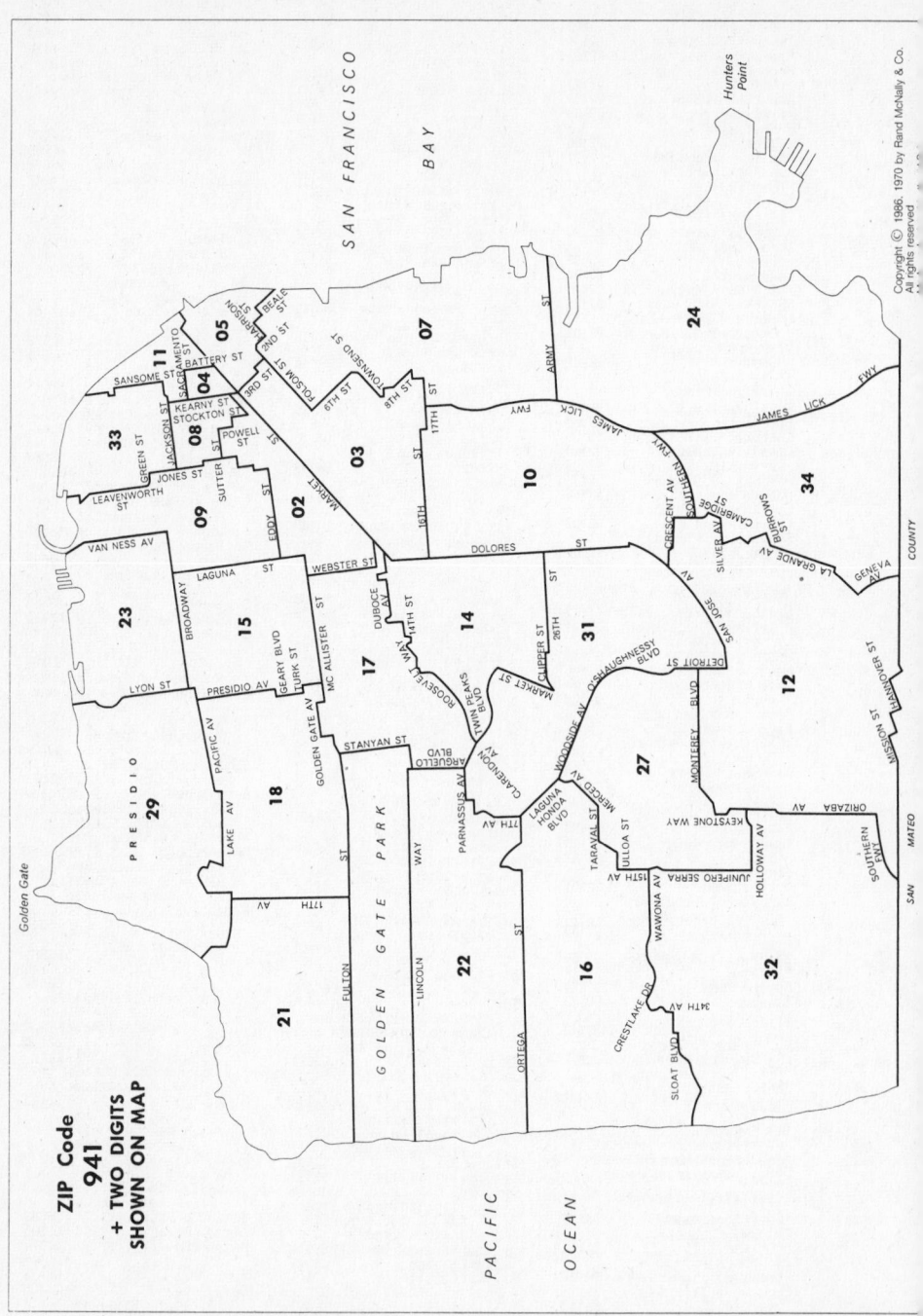

ZIP Code
941
+ TWO DIGITS
SHOWN ON MAP

	ZIP
Santa Monica Place (Part of Santa Monica)	90401
Santa Nella	95322
Santa Paula	93060*
	93061†
Santa Rita (Monterey County)	93906
Santa Rita (Santa Barbara County)	93436
Santa Rita Park	93661
Santa Rosa	95401-09
For specific Santa Rosa Zip Codes call (707) 528-8763, or your local postmaster.	
Santa Rosa Indian Reservation (Kings County)	93245
Santa Rosa Indian Reservation (Riverside County)	92543
Santa Rosa Island Air Force Station	93041
Santa Rosa Plaza (Part of Santa Rosa)	95401
Santa Susana (Part of Simi Valley)	93063
Santa Venetia	94901
Santa Western (Part of Los Angeles)	90072
Santa Ynez	93460
Santa Ysabel	92070
Santa Ysabel Indian Reservation	92070
Santee	92071*
	92072†
San Ysidro (Part of San Diego)	92143†
	92173*
Saranap	94595
Saratoga	95070*
	95071†
Saratoga Springs	95493
Sather Gate (Part of Berkeley)	94704
Saticoy (Part of Ventura)	93004*
	93007†
Sattley	96124
Saugus (Part of Santa Clarita)	91350
Sausalito	94965*
	94966†
Saviers (Part of Oxnard)	93033
Sawyers Bar	96027
Scenic Brook Estates	95370
Scenic Center (Part of Modesto)	95355
Scheideck	93252
Schellville	95476
Scotia	95565
Scotland	92358
Scott Bar	96085
Scotts Valley	95066*
	95067†
Seacliff	95003
Seahaven	94937
Seal Beach	90740
Seal Beach Naval Weapons Station	90740
Seal Cove	94038
Searles Valley	93562
Seaside	93955
Sebastiani (Part of Sonoma)	95476
Sebastopol (Nevada County)	95960
Sebastopol (Sonoma County)	95472*
	95473†
Sedco Hills	92530
Seeley	92273
Seiad Valley	96086
Selby	94525
Selma	93662
Seneca	95923
Sepulveda (Part of Los Angeles)	91343
Sequoia Crest	93265
Sequoia Mall (Part of Visalia)	93277
Sequoia National Park	93262
Serena Park	93013
Serene Lakes	95728
Serra (Part of Dana Point)	92624
Serra Mesa (Part of San Diego)	92123
Serramonte (Part of Daly City)	94015
Serramonte Center (Part of Daly City)	94015
Sespe	93015
Seven Oaks	92305
Seven Pines	93526
Seville	93291

	ZIP
Shadow Hills	95461
Shady Glen	95713
Shafter	93263
Shandon	93461
Sharon Heights (Part of Menlo Park)	94025
Sharpe Army Depot	95331
Sharp Park (Part of Pacifica)	94044
Shasta	96087
Shasta Forest Village	96088
Shaver Lake	93664
Shaver Lake Heights	93664
Shaver Lake Point	93664
Shaw City (Part of Fresno)	93704
Sheepranch	95250
Sheldon	95624
Shell Beach (Part of Pismo Beach)	93449
Shelter Cove (Humboldt County)	95589
Shelter Cove (San Mateo County)	94044
Sheridan	95681
Sherman Oaks (Part of Los Angeles)	91403
	91413
	91423
For specific Sherman Oaks Zip Codes call (818) 908-6912, or your local postmaster.	
Sherman Oaks Galleria (Part of Los Angeles)	91403
Sherwood (Part of Salinas)	93906
Sherwood Forest	94803
Sherwood Mall (Part of Stockton)	95207
Shingle Springs	95682
Shingletown	96088
Shinn (Part of Fremont)	94536
Shively	95555
Shore Acres	94565
Short Acres (Part of Hanford)	93230
Shoshone	92384
Sierra (Part of Fresno)	93703
Sierra Army Depot	96113
Sierra Brooks	96118
Sierra Cedars	93664
Sierra City	96125
Sierra Conservation Center	95327
Sierra Heights	93247
Sierra Lake Estates	93664
Sierra Madre	91024*
	91025†
Sierra Pines	89439
Sierra Sky Park (Part of Fresno)	93722
Sierra Village No. 1	95346
Sierraville	96126
Signal Hill	90806
Silverado	92676
Silver City	93271
Silver Fork	95720
Silver Lake	95666
Silver Strand	93035
Simi Valley	93062-63
	93065
	93093
For specific Simi Valley Zip Codes call (805) 526-1331, or your local postmaster.	
Simmler	93453
Simms (Marin County)	94901
Simms (San Joaquin County)	95366
Sisquoc	93454
Sites	95979
Skaggs Island	95476
Skyforest	92385
Skyhigh	95223
Skyline East	92311
Skyline North	92311
Sky Londa (Part of Woodside)	94062
Sky Valley	92241
Sleepy Hollow (Marin County)	94960
Sleepy Hollow (San Bernardino County)	91710
Slide Inn	95335
Sloat	96103
Sloughhouse	95683
Smartville	95977
Smiley Heights (Part of Redlands)	92373
Smiley Park	92382
Smithflat	95667
Smith River	95567
Smoke Tree (Part of Palm Springs)	92262
Snelling	95369
Snow Creek	92282

	ZIP
Snowline	95709
Soboba Hot Springs	92583
Soboba Indian Reservation	92583
Soda Bay	95451
Soda Springs	95728
Solana Beach	92075
Solano Mall (Part of Fairfield)	94533
Soledad	93960
Solemint (Part of Santa Clarita)	91350
Solvang	93463*
	93464†
Somerset	95684
Somesbar	95568
Somis	93066
Sonoma	95476
Sonoma Vista	95476
Sonora	95370
Sonora Junction	93517
Soquel	95073
Sorensen (Part of Hayward)	94544
Sorensens	96120
Soto (Part of Huntington Park)	90255
Soulsbyville	95372
South Alhambra (Part of Alhambra)	91803
South Belridge	93251
South Berkeley (Part of Berkeley)	94703
South Coast Plaza (Part of Costa Mesa)	92626
South Corona (Part of Corona)	91718
South Dos Palos	93665
South Downey (Part of Downey)	90242
Southeastern (Part of San Diego)	92113
South El Monte	91733
South Fontana (Part of Fontana)	92337
South Fork (Humboldt County)	95569
South Fork (Madera County)	93643
South Fork (Mariposa County)	95318
South Gardena (Part of Gardena)	90247
South Gate	90280
South Hills (Part of West Covina)	91791
South Laguna (Part of Laguna Beach)	92677
South Lake	93240
South Lake Tahoe	96150-58
For specific South Lake Tahoe Zip Codes call (916) 544-2208, or your local postmaster.	
Southland Shopping Center (Part of Hayward)	94545
South Leggett	95585
South Los Angeles (Part of Los Angeles)	90061
South Main (Part of Santa Ana)	92707
South Modesto (Part of Modesto)	95350
South Oroville	95965
South Pasadena	91030*
	91031†
Southport (Part of West Sacramento)	95691
South San Francisco	94080-83
For specific South San Francisco Zip Codes call (415) 588-2855, or your local postmaster.	
South San Gabriel	91770
South San Jose Hills	91744
South San Leandro (Part of San Leandro)	94578
South Santa Rosa	95401
South Shafter	93263
South Shore Shopping Center (Part of Alameda)	94501
South Taft	93268
South Whittier	90605
South Whittier Heights	90605
South Yuba City	95991
Spanish Flat (El Dorado County)	95633
Spanish Flat (Napa County)	94558
Spanish Hills	91720
Spanish Ranch	95956
Spaulding	96130
Spicer City	93206
Spreckels	93962
Spring Creek Tract	96158
Springfield	95370
Spring Garden	95971

* Area Zip Code   ***† Post Office Boxes***

	ZIP
Spring Hill (Part of Grass Valley)	95945
Springstowne (Part of Vallejo)	94591
Spring Valley	91976-79
For specific Spring Valley Zip Codes call (619) 670-9815, or your local postmaster.	
Spring Valley Lake (Part of Apple Valley)	92392
Springville	93265
Spruce Point	95503
Spurgeon (Part of Santa Ana)	92701
Squaw Valley	93675
Squirrel Mountain Valley	93240
Stadium (Part of Anaheim)	92825
Stafford	95565
Stallion Springs	93561
Stamoules	93640
Standard	95373
Standish	96128
Stanford	94305
Stanford Shopping Center (Part of Palo Alto)	94304
Stanton	90680
Starlight	93514
Starlite Pines	96088
State Capitol (Part of Sacramento)	95814
Stateline (Part of South Lake Tahoe)	96157
State Street (Part of Huntington Park)	90255
Steele Park	94558
Steinbeck (Part of Salinas)	93901
Stent	95370
Stephens (Part of Santa Fe Springs)	90670
Sterling Park (Part of Daly City)	94017
Stevinson	95374
Stewarts Point	95480
Stewart Springs	96094
Stine Station (Part of Bakersfield)	93309
Stinson Beach	94970
Stirling City	95978
Stockdale (Part of Bakersfield)	93309
Stockton	95201-19
	95267-69
For specific Stockton Zip Codes call (209) 983-6317, or your local postmaster.	
Stonegate (Part of Portola Valley)	94028
Stonehurst (Part of Oakland)	94603
Stone Lagoon	95570
Stoneman (Part of Alhambra)	91801
Stonestown (Part of San Francisco)	94132
Stonewood Shopping Center (Part of Downey)	90241
Stonyford	95979
Storrie	95980
Stovepipe Wells	92328
Stratford	93266
Strathmore	93267
Strawberry (El Dorado County)	95720
Strawberry (Marin County)	94941
Strawberry (Tuolumne County)	95375
Strawberry Valley	95981
Stuart	92054
Studebaker (Part of Norwalk)	90650
Studio City (Part of Los Angeles)	91604*
	91614†
Suburban Acres	96080
Sugarloaf	92386
Sugarloaf Mountain Park	93260
Sugar Pine (Madera County)	93644
Sugar Pine (Tuolumne County)	95383
Suisun City	94585
Sulphur Springs	93060
Sultana	93666
Summer Home	95336
Summerhome Park	95436
Summerland	93067
Summit	92345
Summit City	96089
Sumner Hill	93637
Sun City	92585-87
For specific Sun City Zip Codes call (714) 679-1737, or your local postmaster.	

	ZIP
Sunfair	92252
Sunkist (Part of Anaheim)	92806
Sunland	91040*
	91041†
Sunny Brae (Part of Arcata)	95521
Sunnybrook	95640
Sunny Hills (Part of Fullerton)	92632
Sunnymead (Part of Moreno Valley)	92553
Sunnyside (Fresno County)	93727
Sunnyside (Placer County)	96145
Sunnyside (San Diego County)	91902
Sunnyside-Tahoe City	96145
Sunnyslope (Butte County)	95914
Sunnyslope (Riverside County)	92509
Sunnyvale	94086-91
For specific Sunnyvale Zip Codes call (408) 732-0121, or your local postmaster.	
Sunnyvale Town Center (Part of Sunnyvale)	94086
Sunny Vista (Part of Chula Vista)	91910
Sunol	94586
Sunrise Mall	95610
Sunrise Vista	95541
Sunset (Humboldt County)	95521
Sunset (Part of San Francisco)	94122
	94172
For specific Sunset Zip Codes call (415) 759-1707, or your local postmaster.	
Sunset Beach (Orange County)	90742
Sunset Beach (Santa Cruz County)	95076
Sunset Cliffs (Part of San Diego)	92107
Sunset Hills	91745
Sunset Terrace	93402
Sunset Tract	93022
Sunset View	95945
Sunset Whitney Ranch (Part of Rocklin)	95677
Sunshine Homes	91350
Sunshine Summit	92536
Sun Valley	91352*
	91353†
Sunvalley (Part of Concord)	94520
Sun Village (Part of Palmdale)	93550
Surf	93436
Surfside (Part of Seal Beach)	90743
Susana Knolls (Part of Simi Valley)	93063
Susanville	96130
Sutter	95982
Sutter Creek	95685
Sutter Hill	95685
Sutter Island	95615
Sutter Street (Part of San Francisco)	94104
Swall Meadows	93514
Swanton	95017
Sweet Brier	96017
Sweetwater	95451
Sycamore (Colusa County)	95957
Sycamore (Contra Costa County)	94526
Sylmar (Part of Los Angeles)	91345
Sylvia Park	90290
Table Bluff	95551
Taft	93268
Taft Heights	93268
Tahoe City	96145
Tahoe Keys (Part of South Lake Tahoe)	96154
Tahoe Paradise (Part of South Lake Tahoe)	96155
Tahoe Pines	96141
Tahoe Valley (Part of South Lake Tahoe)	96158
Tahoe Vista	96148
Tahoma	96142
Talica (Part of Oceanside)	92054
Talmage	95481
Tamal	94974
Tamalpais-Homestead Valley	94941
Tamalpais Valley	94941
Tamarack	95223
Tanforan (Part of South San Francisco)	94080
Tanforan Park (Part of San Bruno)	94066
Tangair	93437

	ZIP
Tanglewood	95018
Tara Hills	94564
Tarpey (Part of Fresno)	93727
Tarzana	91356*
	91357†
Tassajara Hot Springs	93924
Taurusa	93291
Taylorsville	95983
Tecate	91980
Tecnor	96058
Tecopa	92389
Tecopa Hot Springs	92389
Tehachapi	93561
	93581-82
For specific Tehachapi Zip Codes call (805) 822-3276, or your local postmaster.	
Tehama	96090
Temecula	92589-93
For specific Temecula Zip Codes call (909) 699-1121, or your local postmaster.	
Temelec	95476
Temple City	91780
Templeton	93465
Tennant	96058
Tent City (Part of Coronado)	92118
Terminal Annex (Part of Los Angeles)	90054
Terminous	95240
Termo	96132
Terra Bella	93270
Terra Linda (Part of San Rafael)	94901
Textile (Part of Los Angeles)	90015
The Falls	93604
The Forks (Madera County)	93604
The Forks (Mendocino County)	95482
The Geysers	95425
The Hermitage	95585
The Oaks	95945
The Pines	93604
Thermal	92274
Thermalito	95965
The Sea Ranch	95497
Thomas Mountain	92561
Thornton	95686
Thousand Oaks	91358-62
For specific Thousand Oaks Zip Codes call (805) 497-8661, or your local postmaster.	
Thousand Palms	92276
Three Arch Bay (Part of Dana Point)	92677
Three Point	93532
Three Rivers	93271
Three Rocks	93608
Tiburon	94920
Tierra Buena	95991
Tierra del Sol	91905
Tionesta	96134
Tipton	93272
Tivy Valley	93657
Tobin	95965
Tocaloma	94950
Todd Valley	95631
Todos Santos (Part of Concord)	94522
Tollhouse	93667
Toluca Lake (Part of Los Angeles)	91610
Tomales	94971
Toms Place	93514
Tonyville	93247
Tooleville	93221
Topanga	90290
Topanga Beach	90265
Topanga Oaks	90290
Topanga Park	90290
Topanga Plaza (Part of Los Angeles)	91303
Topaz	96133
Top of the World (Part of Laguna Beach)	92651
Tormey	94525
Torrance	90501-10
For specific Torrance Zip Codes call (213) 328-9363, or your local postmaster.	
Torres-Martinez Indian Reservation	92274
Torrey Pines Homes (Part of San Diego)	92037
Tower (Part of Fresno)	93728
Town and Country (Riverside County)	92553
Town and Country (Sacramento County)	95821

	ZIP
Town Center (Los Angeles County)	93550
Town Center (Tulare County)	93291
Town Center Corte Madera (Part of Corte Madera)	94925
Trabuco Canyon	92678
Trabuco Highlands	92691
Tracy	95376-78
For specific Tracy Zip Codes call (209) 835-4774, or your local postmaster.	
Trade Center (Part of Long Beach)	90831*
	90832†
Tranquillity	93668
Traver	93673
Tres Pinos	95075
Trevarno (Part of Livermore)	94550
Trigo	93637
Trimmer	93657
Trinidad	95570
Trinity Alps	96052
Trinity Center	96091
Trinity Village	95527
Triple R Estates	93257
Trona	93562*
	93592†
Tropico (Part of Glendale)	91204-05
	91208
For specific Tropico Zip Codes call (818) 502-3251, or your local postmaster.	
Tropico (Kern County)	93560
Trowbridge	95659
Truckee	96160-62
Tujunga	91042*
	91043†
Tulare	93274*
	93275†
Tulelake	96134
Tule River Indian Reservation	93257
Tunitas	94019
Tuolumne	95379
Tuolumne Meadows	95389
Tupman	93276
Turlock	95380-82
For specific Turlock Zip Codes call (209) 632-3801, or your local postmaster.	
Turner	95336
Tustin	92680*
	92681†
Tustin Foothills	92680
Tuttle	95340
Tuttletown	95370
Tuxedo Country Club Estates	95204
Tuxedo Park (Part of Stockton)	95204
T.V. Bell (Part of Merced)	95340
Twain	95984
Twain Harte	95383
Twentynine Palms	92277-78
For specific Twentynine Palms Zip Codes call (619) 367-3501, or your local postmaster.	
Twentynine Palms Base	92278
Twentynine Palms Marine Corps Base	92278
Twentytwo Mile House	93637
Twin Bridges	95735
Twin Creeks	95120
Twin Lakes (Lake County)	95457
Twin Lakes (Mono County)	93517
Twin Lakes (Santa Cruz County)	95060
Twin Oaks	92069
Twin Peaks	92391
Two Rock Coast Guard Station	94952
Tyler Mall (Part of Riverside)	92503
Ukiah	95482
Ulmar (Part of Livermore)	94550
Union (Part of Napa)	94558
Union City	94587
Union Hill	95945
Universal City (Part of Los Angeles)	91608
University (Orange County)	92716
University (Santa Barbara County)	93107
University City (Part of San Diego)	92122
University of California-Davis	95616
University of Santa Clara (Part of Santa Clara)	95050
University Towne Centre (Part of San Diego)	92122
Upland	91785†
	91786*

	ZIP
Upper Lake	95485
Uptown (Part of San Bernardino)	92405
Vaca (Part of Vacaville)	95687
Vacation	95446
Vacaville	95687-88
	95696
For specific Vacaville Zip Codes call (707) 448-2030, or your local postmaster.	
Valencia	91354-55
	91385
For specific Valencia Zip Codes call (805) 254-1684, or your local postmaster.	
Valinda	91744
Valla (Part of Santa Fe Springs)	90670
Vallco Fashion Park (Part of Cupertino)	95014
Vallecito	95251
Vallecitos Town Center (Part of San Marcos)	92069
Vallejo	94589-92
For specific Vallejo Zip Codes call (707) 642-4441, or your local postmaster.	
Vallemar (Part of Pacifica)	94044
Valle Vista (Alameda County)	94541
Valle Vista (Riverside County)	92544
Valley Acres	93268
Valley Center	92082
Valley Estates	93283
Valley Fair (Part of San Jose)	95128
Valley Ford	94972
Valley Home	95384
Valley Lake Ranchos	93637
Valley of Enchantment	92325
Valley of the Moon	92325
Valley Plaza (Imperial County)	92243
Valley Plaza (Kern County)	93304
Valley Plaza (Los Angeles County)	91606
Valley Springs	95252
Valley View Park	92325
Valley Village (Part of Los Angeles)	91607
Valona	94525
Val Verde Park	91350
Valyermo	93563
Vandenberg Air Force Base	93437
Vandenberg Village	93436
Van Nuys	91401-02
	91404-12
For specific Van Nuys Zip Codes call (818) 908-6608, or your local postmaster.	
Vanowen (Part of Los Angeles)	91405
Vasona (Part of Los Gatos)	95030
Venice (Part of Los Angeles)	90291*
	90294†
Ventucopa	93252
Ventu Park (Part of Thousand Oaks)	91320
Ventura	93001-09
For specific Ventura Zip Codes call (805) 643-5457, or your local postmaster.	
Verdemont	92402
Verdi	89439
Verdugo City (Part of Glendale)	91046
Verdugo Viejo	91206-08
	91226
For specific Verdugo Viejo Zip Codes call (213) 586-1467, or your local postmaster.	
Vernalis	95385
Vernon	90058
Vernon Landing	95659
Verona	95659
Veteran Heights	94508
Veterans Administration	90073
Veterans Bureau Hospital (Part of Palo Alto)	94304
Veterans Home (Part of Yountville)	94599
Veterans Hospital (Part of Los Angeles)	91343
Victor	95253
Victoria Court (Part of Santa Barbara)	93101
Victoria Park (Part of Carson)	90746

	ZIP
Victorville	92392-94
For specific Victorville Zip Codes call (619) 245-7723, or your local postmaster.	
Victory Center (Part of Los Angeles)	91606
Vidal	92280
Vidal Junction	92280
Viejas Indian Reservation	91901
View Park	90043
View Park-Windsor Hills	90043
Viking (Part of Long Beach)	90808
Village (Los Angeles County)	90024
Village (Santa Clara County)	95071
Villa Grande	95486
Villa Park	92667
Villa Verona	95965
Vina	96092
Vincent	91722
Vineburg	95487
Vine Hill	94553
Vintage Faire Mall (Part of Modesto)	95356
Vinton	96135
Vinvale (Part of South Gate)	90280
Viola	96088
Virginia Colony	93021
Virner	95634
Visalia	93277-79
	93291-92
For specific Visalia Zip Codes call (209) 732-8073, or your local postmaster.	
Visalia Mall (Part of Visalia)	93277
Visitacion (Part of San Francisco)	94134
Vista	92083-85
For specific Vista Zip Codes call (619) 726-0772, or your local postmaster.	
Vista Del Mar (Part of San Clemente)	92672
Vista del Morro	93402
Vista Grande	93637
Vista La Mesa (Part of La Mesa)	91941
Vista Park	93307
Volcano	95689
Volcanoville	95634
Volta	93635
Vorden	95690
Waddington	95536
Wagner (Part of Los Angeles)	90047
Wagy Flats	93240
Walerga	95660
Walker (Los Angeles County)	90201
Walker (Mono County)	96107
Walker Landing	95690
Wallace	95254
Walnut	91788†
	91789*
Walnut Creek	94593-98
For specific Walnut Creek Zip Codes call (415) 935-1842, or your local postmaster.	
Walnut Creek West	94596
Walnut Grove	95690
Walnut Heights	94596
Walnut Park	90255
Walteria (Part of Torrance)	90505
Warm Springs (Part of Fremont)	94539
Warner Ranch (Part of Moreno Valley)	92553
Warner Springs	92086
Wasco	93280
Washington (Part of Los Angeles)	90011
Washington (Part of Pasadena)	91114
Washington (Nevada County)	95986
Washington Manor (Part of San Leandro)	94579
Waterford	95386
Waterloo	95215
Waterman Gardens (Part of San Bernardino)	92410
Watson (Part of Carson)	90745
Watsonville	95076*
	95077†
Watsonville Junction	95076
Watts (Part of Los Angeles)	90002
Watts Valley	93667
Waukena	93282
Waverly Heights (Part of Thousand Oaks)	91360
Wawona	95389
Weaverville	96093

* Area Zip Code   † Post Office Boxes

ZIP

	ZIP
Acres Green	80124
Adams	80022
Adams City (Part of Commerce City)	80022
Agate	80101
Aguilar	81020
Airport Mail Facility (Part of Denver)	80207
Akron	80720
Alameda (Part of Lakewood)	80215
Alamosa	81101*
	81102†
Alamosa East	81101
Alcott (Part of Denver)	80212
Alder	81155
Allenspark	80510
Allison	81137
Alma	80420
Almont	81210
Alpine (Chaffee County)	81236
Alpine (Rio Grande County)	81154
Altura (Part of Aurora)	80011
Altura Annex (Part of Aurora)	80011
Alvin	80758
American City	80427
Ames	81426
Amherst	80721
Andersonville (Part of Fort Collins)	80521
Angel Acres	80433
Antlers	81650
Anton	80801
Antonito	81120
Apache City	81089
Apex	80427
Appleton	81501
Applewood	80401
Applewood Village (Part of Wheat Ridge)	80033
Arabian Acres	80816
Arapahoe	80802
Arapahoe East (Part of Greenwood Village)	80112
Arboles	81121
Aristocrat Ranchettes	80621
Arlington	81021
Aroya	80862
Arriba	80804
Arriola	81323
Arvada	80001-06

For specific Arvada Zip Codes call (303) 421-2200, or your local postmaster.

	ZIP
Aspen	81611-12

For specific Aspen Zip Codes call (303) 925-7523, or your local postmaster.

	ZIP
Aspen (Part of Fort Collins)	80527
Aspen-Gerbaz	81611
Aspen Park	80433
Association Camp	80511
Atwood	80722
Ault	80610
Aurora	80010-19
	80040-47

For specific Aurora Zip Codes call (303) 364-9215, or your local postmaster.

	ZIP
Aurora Mall (Part of Aurora)	80012
Austin (Part of Orchard City)	81410
Avon	81620
Avondale	81022
Bailey	80421
Bakersville	80476
Baldwin	81230
Balltown	81228
Barnesville	80624
Barr	80601
Bartlett	81090
Barton	81041
Basalt	81621
Battlement Mesa	81636
Baxterville	81132
Bayfield	81122
Beacon Hill	80860
Bear Valley (Part of Denver)	80227
	80232
	80235-36

For specific Bear Valley Zip Codes call (303) 986-6808, or your local postmaster.

	ZIP
Bear Valley Shopping Center (Part of Denver)	80227
Beaver Ridge	80440
Bedrock	81411
Beecher Island	80758
Belle Plain (Part of Pueblo)	81001
Bellvue	80512
Belmar (Part of Lakewood)	80226

	ZIP
Belmont (Part of Pueblo)	81001
Bendemeer Valley	80439
Bennett	80102
Bergen Park	80439
Berthoud (Larimer County)	80513
Berthoud (Weld County)	80513
Berthoud Falls	80438
Berthoud Pass	80452
Bethune	80805
Beulah	81023
Beverly Hills	80104
Big Bend	81092
Big Elk Meadows	80540
Black Forest	80908
Black Hawk	80422
Blanca	81123
Blende	81006
Blue Mountain	81610
Blue Mountain Estates	80401
Blue Ridge	80424
Blue River	80424
Blue Valley	80452
Bonanza	81155
Boncarbo	81024
Bond	80423
Bondad	81301
Boone	81025
Boulder	80301-08

For specific Boulder Zip Codes call (303) 938-1100, or your local postmaster.

	ZIP
Boulder Heights	80302
Bountiful	81140
Bovina	80818
Bowie	81428
Bow Mar	80120
Boxelder Estates	80521
Boyero	80806
Bracewell	80631
Brandon	81026
Branson	81027
Breckenridge	80424
Breen	81326
Brewster	81226
Briargate (Part of Colorado Springs)	80918
Brigadoon Glen	80501
Briggsdale	80611
Brighton	80601
Bristol	81028
Broadmoor (Part of Colorado Springs)	80906
Broadway Estates	80120
Broken Arrow Acres	80433
Brook Forest	80439
Brook Forest Estates	80439
Brookridge	80120
Brookside	81212
Brookvale	80439
Broomfield	80020-21
	80038

For specific Broomfield Zip Codes call (303) 466-1711, or your local postmaster.

	ZIP
Brownlee	80480
Brownsville	80026
Brush	80723
Buckeye	80549
Buckingham (Part of Fort Collins)	80521
Buckingham Plaza (Part of Aurora)	80012
Buckingham Square (Part of Aurora)	80012
Buda	80513
Buena Vista	81211
Buena Vista Correctional Facility	81211
Buffalo Creek	80425
Buford	81641
Burland Ranchettes	80470
Burlington	80807
Burns	80426
Byers	80103
Caddoa	81044
Cadet	80841
Cahone	81320
Calhan	80808
California Oil Camp	81648
Camp Bird	81427
Camp George West	80401
Campion	80537
Campo	81029
Canfield	80026
Canon	81120
Canon City	81212-15

For specific Canon City Zip Codes call (719) 275-6877, or your local postmaster.

	ZIP
Capitol Hill (Part of Denver)	80218
Capulin	81124
Carbondale	81623

	ZIP
Cardiff	81601
Carr	80612
Cascade	80809
Cascade-Chipita Park	80809
Castle Rock	80104
Castlewood	80120
Cattle Creek	81623
Cedar	81431
Cedar Cove	80537
Cedaredge	81413
Center	81125
Central City	80427
Chaddsford (Part of Aurora)	80014
Chama	81126
Chambers Square (Part of Aurora)	80011
Chapel Hills	80907
Chatfield Estates	80123
Chautauqua (Part of Boulder)	80302
Cheraw	81030
Cherry Creek (Part of Denver)	80206
Cherry Creek Shopping Center (Part of Denver)	80206
Cherry Hills Crest	80120
Cherry Hills Manor	80120
Cherry Hills Village	80110
Cherry Knolls	80120
Cherry Park	80110
Cherry Valley	80116
Cherrywood Village	80120
Cheyenne Canon (Part of Colorado Springs)	80907
Cheyenne Wells	80810
Chimney Rock	81127
Chipita Park	80809
Chivington	81036
Chromo	81128
Chula Vista	80401
Cimarron	81220
Cimarron Hills	80906
Cinderella City (Part of Englewood)	80110
Citadel, The (Part of Colorado Springs)	80909
Clark	80428
Clifton	81520
Climax	80429
Coal Creek	81221
Coaldale	81222
Coalmont	80430
Cokedale	81032
Collbran	81624
College Heights (Part of Durango)	81301
Colona	81401
Colorado City (El Paso County)	80904
Colorado City (Pueblo County)	81019
Colorado Mountain Estates	80816
Colorado Sierra	80401
Colorado Springs	80901-98

For specific Colorado Springs Zip Codes call (719) 570-5377, or your local postmaster.

	ZIP
Colorado Technical College	80907
Columbine (census designated place)	80123
Columbine (Jefferson and Arapahoe Counties)	80120
Columbine (Routt County)	80428
Columbine Hills	80120
Columbine Knolls	80120
Columbine Knolls South	80123
Columbine Manor	80120
Columbine Valley	80123
Commerce City	80022*
	80037†
Como	80432
Conejos	81129
Conifer	80433
Conifer Mountain	80433
Conifer Park	80433
Cope	80812
Copper Mountain	80443
Copper Spur	80423
Cornish	80611
Coronado	80229
Cortez	81321
Cory (Part of Orchard City)	81414
Cotopaxi	81223
Country Acres	80534
Country Club Estates	80521
Country Club Park	80303
Cowdrey	80434
Cragmor (Part of Colorado Springs)	80907
Craig	81625*
	81626†
Craig South Highlands	81625

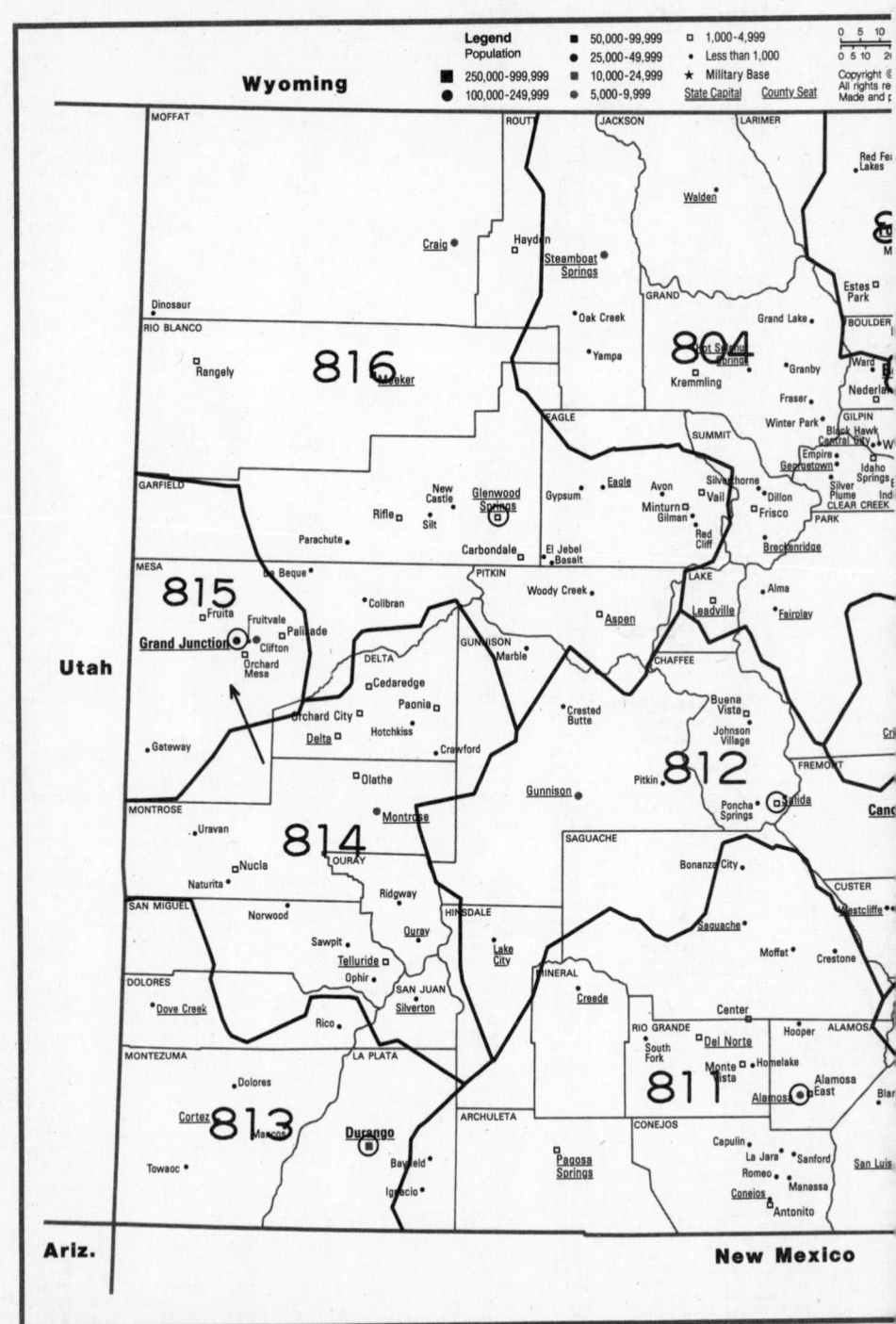

Legend
Population
■ 250,000-999,999
● 100,000-249,999
■ 50,000-99,999
● 25,000-49,999
● 10,000-24,999
● 5,000-9,999
□ 1,000-4,999
· Less than 1,000
★ Military Base
☆ State Capital   County Seat

Wyoming

Utah

Ariz.

New Mexico

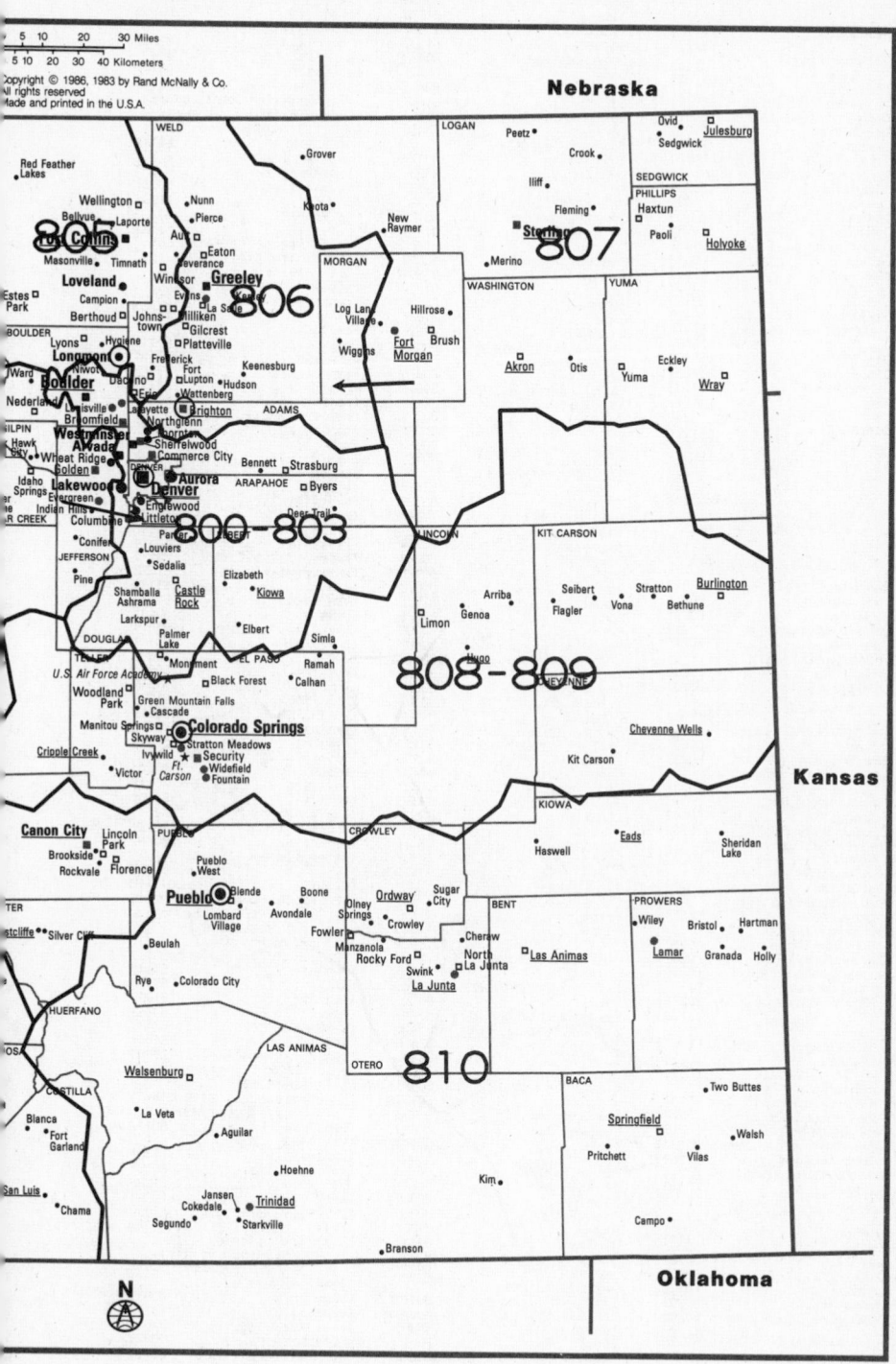

	ZIP
Crawford	81415
Creede	81130
Crescent	80401
Crested Butte	81224*
	81225†
Crestmoor (Part of Glendale)	80222
Crestone	81131
Crestwoods	80424
Crews	80911
Cripple Creek	80813
Crisman	80302
Crook	80726
Crossroads Mall (Part of Boulder)	80301
Crowley	81033
Crystola	81055
Cuchara	81069
Cuerna Verde	81069
Dacono	80514
Dailey	80728
De Beque	81630
Deckers	80135
Deepcreek	80428
Deer Creek Valley Ranchos	80470
Deer Park	80467
Deer Trail	80105
Delhi	81059
Del Norte	81132
Delta	81416
Denver	80201-14
	80216-25
	80227
	80229
	80231
	80233-95

For specific Denver Zip Codes call (303) 297-6000, or your local postmaster.

COLLEGES & UNIVERSITIES

Metropolitan State College of Denver	80217
Regis University	80221
University of Colorado at Denver	80217
University of Colorado Health Sciences Center	80262
University of Denver	80208

FINANCIAL INSTITUTIONS

The Bank of Cherry Creek, N.A.	80206
Bank One-Denver	80202
Bank Western, Federal Savings Bank	80202
Central Bank, National Association	80202
Colorado National Bank	80202
Colorado State Bank of Denver	80202
First Federal Savings Bank of Colorado	80202
First Interstate Bank of Denver, N.A.	80270
First National Bank of Southeast Denver	80210
Guaranty Bank & Trust Co.	80202
Mountain States Bank	80218
Norwest Bank-Denver, National Association	80274

HOSPITALS

Denver Health and Hospitals	80204
Porter Memorial Hospital	80210
Presbyterian-St. Luke's Medical Center	80203
Rose Medical Center	80220
Saint Joseph Hospital	80218
St. Anthony Hospital Central	80204
University Hospital	80262
Veterans Affairs Medical Center	80220

HOTELS/MOTELS

The Brown Palace Hotel	80202
Embassy Suites-Downtown	80202
Marriot City Center-Denver	80202
Oxford Hotel	80202
Radisson Hotel Denver	80202
Warwick Hotel	80203
Westin Hotel, Tabor Center	80202

MILITARY INSTALLATIONS

Defense Finance and Accounting Service	80297
Denver Merchandise Mart	80216
Derby	80022
Derby Junction	80426

	ZIP
Devine	81001
Dillon	80435
Dinosaur	81610
Divide	80814
Dolores	81323
Dome Rock	80433
Dorey Lakes	80401
Dory Hill	80401
Dotsero	81637
Dove Creek	81324
Downieville	80436
Downtown (Part of Englewood)	80110
Doyleville	81239
Drake	80515
Drakes (Part of Fort Collins)	80521
Dream House Acres	80120
Dry Creek Basin	81431
Dumont	80436
Dupont	80024
Durango	81301*
	81302†
Eads	81036
Eagle	81631
Eagle-Vail	81620
Eastlake (Adams County)	80614
Eastlake (Pueblo County)	81004
East Portal	80474
Eastridge (Part of Aurora)	80014
Eastridge South (Part of Aurora)	80014
East Weston	81091
Eaton	80615
Echo Lake	80452
Eckert (Part of Orchard City)	81418
Eckley	80727
Edgemont (Part of Lakewood)	80401
Edgewater	80214
Edison	80864
Edith	81128
Edler	81073
Edwards	81632
Egnar	81325
Elbert	80106
Eldora	80466
Eldorado Springs	80025
Elephant Park	80439
Eleven Mile Village	80827
Elizabeth	80107
El Jebel	81628
Elk Creek Acres	80470
Elk Creek Highlands	80470
Elkdale	80478
Elkhorn Acres	80470
Elk Springs	81633
Elkton	80860
Ellicott	80808
El Moro	81082
El Rancho	80401
El Vado	80302
Elwell	80534
Emma (Eagle County)	81623
Emma (Pitkin County)	81623
Empire	80438
Englewood	80110-12
	80150-56

For specific Englewood Zip Codes call (303) 761-0474, or your local postmaster.

Erie	80516
Erie Air Park (Part of Erie)	80516
Escalante Forks	81416
Estes Park	80517
Estrella	81101
Evans	80620
Evanston	80530
Evergreen	80439
Ever Green Hills	80439
Evergreen West	80439
Fairplay	80440
Fairview	81069
Fairview Estates	80123
Fairway Estates	80521
Falcon	80908
Falcon Estates	80908
Falfa	81301
Fall Creek	81430
Farisita	81040
Farmers	80631
Federal Correctional Institution	80110
Federal Heights	80221
Fenders	80465
Ferncliff	80510
Firestone	80520
First View	80810
Flagler	80815
Fleming	80728
Flintwood Hills	80116
Florence	81226

	ZIP
Florissant	80816
Florissant Heights	80816
Fondis	80106
Foothills Fashion Mall (Part of Fort Collins)	80525
Forest Hills	80401
Fort Carson	80913
Fort Collins	80521-27

For specific Fort Collins Zip Codes call (303) 482-2837, or your local postmaster.

Fort Garland	81133
Fort Logan (Part of Sheridan)	80236
Fort Lupton	80621
Fort Lyon	81038
Fort Morgan	80701
	80705

For specific Fort Morgan Zip Codes call (303) 867-7111, or your local postmaster.

Fountain	80817
Fountain Valley School	80911
Fowler	81039
Fox Creek	81120
Foxton	80433
Franktown	80116
Fraser	80442
Frederick	80530
Friendship Ranch	80470
Friendship Ranch Estates	80470
Frisco	80443
Fruita	81521
Fruitvale	81504
Galeton	80622
Garcia	81134
Garden City	80631
Gardner	81040
Garfield	81227
Gateway (Arapahoe County)	80014
Gateway (Douglas County)	80126
Gateway (Mesa County)	81522
Gato	81147
Gem Village	81122
Genesee	80401
Genoa	80818
Georgetown	80444
Gilcrest	80623
Gill	80624
Gilman	81645
Glade Park	81523
Glen Comfort	80515
Glendale	80222
Glendevey	82063
Gleneagle	80132
Glenelk	80470
Glen Haven	80532
Glen Isle	80421
Glen Park (Part of Palmer Lake)	80133
Glentivar	80440
Glenwood Springs	81601*
	81602†
Golden	80401-03

For specific Golden Zip Codes call (303) 278-8537, or your local postmaster.

Golden Acres (Part of Longmont)	80501
Goldfield	80860
Gold Hill	80302
Goodnight	81005
Goodrich	80653
Gould	80480
Granada	81041
Granby	80446
Grand Junction	81501-06

For specific Grand Junction Zip Codes call (303) 244-3400, or your local postmaster.

Grand Lake	80447
Grand Mesa	81413
Grandview	81301
Grandview Estates	80134
Granite	81228
Grant	80448
Gray's Mary Greenwood	81069
Greeley	80631-34

For specific Greeley Zip Codes call (303) 353-0398, or your local postmaster.

Greeley Mall (Part of Greeley)	80631
Greenland	80118
Green Mountain (Part of Lakewood)	80228
Green Mountain Camp	80459
Green Mountain Estates (Part of Lakewood)	80228
Green Mountain Falls	80819
Green Mountain Village (Part of Lakewood)	80228

* **Area Zip Code** † **Post Office Boxes**

	ZIP
Mountain View (Larimer County)	80521
Mountain View Acres	81101
Mountain View Lakes	80470
Mount Crested Butte	81225
Mount Massive Lakes	80461
Mount Princeton Hot Springs	81236
Mount Vernon Club Place	80401
Mutual	81089
Nast	81642
Nathrop	81236
Naturita	81422
Nederland	80466
Nevadaville	80427
New Castle	81647
New Raymer	80742
Nighthawk	80135
Nine Mile Corner	80026
Niwot	80544
Nob Hill	80122
North Avondale	81022
North Boulder (Part of Boulder)	80302
North Cherry Creek Valley	80231
North Delta	81416
North End (Part of Colorado Springs)	80907
Northglenn	80233
Northglenn Mall (Part of Northglenn)	80233
North La Junta (Part of La Junta)	81050
North Pecos	80221
North Pole	80809
North Valley Shopping Center (Part of Thornton)	80229
North Washington Heights	80229
North Yard (Part of Denver)	80221
Norwood	81423
Nucla	81424
Numa	81063
Nunn	80648
Nutria	81147
Oak Creek	80467
Oak Grove	81401
Oehlmann Park	80433
Ohio	81237
Olathe	81425
Olney Springs	81062
Olympus Heights	80515
Ophir	81426
Orchard	80649
Orchard City	81410
Orchard Mesa	81501
Ordway	81063
Ormandale	81005
Ortiz	81120
Otis	80743
Ouray	81427
Ovid	80744
Oxford	81137
Pactolus	80401
Padroni	80745
Pagosa	81147
Pagosa Springs	81147
Paisaje	81120
Palisade	81526
Palmer Lake	80133
Palos Verdes	80123
Palos Verdes East	80110
Pandora	81435
Paoli	80746
Paonia	81428
Parachute	81635
Paradox	81429
Paragon Estates	80303
Park Center	81212
Park City	80420
Parker	80134
Park Hill (Part of Denver)	80207
Park Vista Estates	80908
Parlin	81239
Parshall	80468
Peaceful Valley	80540
Peagreen	81416
Peak Seven West	80424
Peckham	80645
Peetz	80747
Penitentiary (Part of Canon City)	81212
Penrose	81240
Peyton	80831
Pheasant Run (Part of Aurora)	80015
Phippsburg	80469
Pierce	80650
Pine	80470
Pinebrook Hills	80302
Pinecliffe	80471
Pine Crest (Part of Palmer Lake)	80133

	ZIP
Pine Hills	80132
Pine Nook	80135
Pine Park Estates	80465
Pinewood Springs	80540
Pinnacle Park	80631
Pinon	81008
Pinon Acres	81301
Pinon Canyon	81082
Pitkin	81241
Placerville	81430
Plateau City	81624
Platner	80743
Platoro	81144
Platteville	80651
Plaza	81132
Pleasant View (Jefferson County)	80401
Pleasant View (Montezuma County)	81331
Poncha Springs	81242
Ponderosa	80424
Ponderosa Hills	80134
Ponderosa Park	80107
Poudre Park	80521
Powderhorn	81243
Powder Wash	82901
Pritchett	81064
Proctor	80736
Prospect Heights	81212
Prospect Valley	80643
Prowers	81052
Pryor	81065
Pueblo	81001-06
For specific Pueblo Zip Codes call (719) 544-0132, or your local postmaster.	
Pueblo Army Depot	81001
Pueblo Dam	81003
Pueblo Mall (Part of Pueblo)	81008
Pueblo West	81007
Punkin Center	80821
Quincy (Part of Aurora)	80015
Radium	80423
Ragged Mountain	81434
Rainbow Valley	80814
Ramah	80832
Rand	80473
Rangely	81648
Rangeview Estates (Boulder County)	80501
Range View Estates (Weld County)	80631
Rattlesnake Buttes	81089
Raymond	80540
Read	81416
Red Cliff	81649
Red Feather Lakes	80545
Redlands	81503
Redmesa	81326
Red Rock Ranch	80132
Redstone	81623
Redvale	81431
Red Wing	81066
Rembrandt Place	80121
Rezago	81082
Richfield	81140
Rico	81332
Ridgeview Hills	80122
Ridgway	81432
Rifle	81650
Rinn	80501
Rio Blanco	81650
Riverside	80540
Roberta	81050
Rockvale	81244
Rocky Ford	81067
Rocky Mountain Arsenal	80022
Rogers Mesa	81419
Roggen	80652
Roland Valley	80470
Rollinsville	80474
Romeo	81148
Rosedale (Part of Garden City)	80631
Rosita	81252
Roswell (Part of Colorado Springs)	80907
Rowena	80455
Roxborough Park	80125
Royal Gorge	81246
Royal Ranch	80470
Ruedi	81621
Rulison	81635
Rush	80833
Russell Gulch	80427
Rustic	80512
Rye	81069
Rye Ranchettes	81069
Sable (Part of Aurora)	80011
Saguache	81149
Saint Charles Mesa	81006
St. Elmo	81236

	ZIP
St. Petersburg	80728
Salida	81201
Salina	80302
Salt Creek (Part of Pueblo)	81006
San Acacio	81151
San Antonio	81120
Sand Creek (Part of Commerce City)	80022
Sandown (Part of Denver)	80216
Sanford	81151
Sangre De Cristo Ranches	81133
San Isabel	81069
San Juan	81070
San Luis	81152
San Pablo	81153
San Pedro	81153
Santa Fe (Denver County)	80204
Santa Fe (Pueblo County)	81003
Sapinero	81247
Sarcillo	81082
Sarcillo Canon	81091
Sargents	81248
Sargents School	81144
Sawpit	81430
Security	80911
Security-Widefield	80911
Sedalia	80135
Sedgwick	80749
Segundo	81070
Seibert	80834
Semper	80021
Severance	80546
Shadow Mountain	80447
Shadows North	80424
Shaffers Crossing	80433
Shamballa Ashrama	80135
Shauano Vista	81201
Shaw Heights	80030
Shaw Heights Mesa	80030
Shawnee	80475
Sheridan	80110
Sheridan Lake	81071
Sherrelwood	80221
Sherrelwood Estates	80221
Silt	81652
Silver Cliff	81252
Silver Creek	80446
Silver Heights	80104
Silver Plume	80476
Silver Shekel	80424
Silver Springs	80470
Silver Spruce	80301
Silverthorne	80498
Silverton	81433
Simla	80835
Singleton	80475
Skyland Village (Part of Westminster)	80030
Skyline	80222
Sky Village	80465
Skyway (El Paso County)	80906
Skyway (Mesa County)	81643
Skyway Estates (Part of Colorado Springs)	80906
Skyway Park (Part of Colorado Springs)	80906
Slater	81653
Slick Rock	81333
Smeltertown	81201
Smoky Hill (Part of Aurora)	80015
Snowmass	81654
Snowmass Village	81615
Snow Mountain Ranch	80446
Snyder	80750
Somerset	81434
South Boulder (Part of Boulder)	80303
South Canon (Part of Canon City)	81212
South Denver (Part of Denver)	80209
Southern Ute Indian Reservation	81137
South Fork	81154
Southglenn	80122
South Park City (Part of Fairplay)	80440
South Platte	80433
South Roggen	80652
Southwind	80120
Southwood	80120
Spanish Colony	80631
Spanish Village	80644
Spar City	81130
Sparks	82901
Sphinx Park	80470
Spivak (Part of Lakewood)	80214
Springfield	81073
Spring Valley	80814
Sprucedale	80439
Squaw Point	81324
Stanley Park	80439

	ZIP
Starkville	81074
Steamboat 1981	80477
Steamboat Plaza (Part of Steamboat Springs)	80488
Steamboat Springs	80477
	80487-88
For specific Steamboat Springs Zip Codes call (303) 879-3556, or your local postmaster.	
Steamboat Village (Part of Steamboat Springs)	80487
Sterling	80751
Stockyards (Part of Denver)	80216
Stoneham	80754
Stoner	81323
Stonewall	81091
Stonington	81090
Strasburg	80136
Stratmoor	80906
Stratmoor Hills	80906
Stratton	80836
Stratton Meadows (Part of Colorado Springs)	80906
Stratton Park (Part of Colorado Springs)	80907
Stringtown	80461
Sugar City	81076
Sugarloaf	80302
Summit Cove	80435
Summitville	81132
Sunbeam	81640
Sunnyside (Boulder County)	80466
Sunnyside (La Plata County)	81301
Sunnyslopes	80020
Sunset (Part of Pueblo)	81005
Sunshine	80302
Superior	80027
Surrey Ridge	80104
Sutank	81623
Swallows	81003
Swede Corners	81149
Sweetwater	81637
Swink	81077
Swissvale	81201
Switzerland Village	80470
Tabernash	80478
Tallahassee School	81212
Tamarron	81301
Tanglewood Acres	81252
Tarryall	80827
Taylor Park	81210
Telluride	81435
Templeton (Part of Colorado Springs)	80936
Ten Mile Vista	80424
Tennyson Heights (Part of Fort Collins)	80521
Terminal Annex (Part of Denver)	80217
Texas Creek	81223
Thatcher	81059
The Meadows	80127
The Mesa	80904
The Pinery	80134
The Shadows	80424
The Springs	80906
Thomasville	81642
Thornton	80229
Thurman	80801
Tiffany	81137
Timbers (Part of Aurora)	80014
Timnath	80547
Timpas	81050
Tincup	81210
Tiny Town	80465
Tolland	80474
Toltec	81089
Toponas	80479

	ZIP
Tordal Estates	80424
Torres (Las Animas County)	81091
Torres (Rio Grande County)	81144
Towaoc	81334
Towner	81071
Tranquil Acres	80863
Trimble	81301
Trinchera	81081
Trinidad	81082
Troutdale	80439
Trout Haven	80814
Trout Lake	81426
Truckton	80864
Trujillo	81147
Trumbull	80135
Twin Forks	80454
Twin Lakes	81251
Twin Rock	80816
Twin Spruce	80401
Two Buttes	81084
Tyrone	81059
Unaweep	81527
Uncompahgre	81401
Union	80750
Union Stockyards (Part of Denver)	80216
University Hills Mall (Part of Denver)	80222
University Park (Part of Denver)	80210
	80250
For specific University Park Zip Codes call (714) 997-1255, or your local postmaster.	
Uravan	81422
U.S. Air Force Academy	80840*
	80841†
Ute Heights	81201
Ute Mountain Indian Reservation	81334
Utleyville	81064
Vail	81657*
	81658†
Vallecito	81122
Valley Hi Mountain Estates	80816
Valley of Blue	80424
Vancorum	81422
Velasquez Plaza	81091
Vernon	80755
Victor	80860
Viejo San Acacio	81151
Vigil	81091
Vilas	81087
Village East (Part of Aurora)	80012
Villa Grove	81155
Villa Italia Center (Part of Lakewood)	80226
Villegreen	81049
Vineland	81001
Virginia Dale	80548
Vista Grande (Part of Colorado Springs)	80918
Vista Verde	80120
Vollmar	80621
Vona	80861
Vroman	81067
Waconda Hills	80132
Wagner Manor	80302
Wagon Wheel Gap	81154
Wahatoya	81055
Wah Keeney Park	80439
Wahketa Village	80701
Walden	80480
Wallace Village	80021
Walnut Hills	80112
Walsenburg	81089
Walsh	81090

	ZIP
Waltonia	80515
Wamblee Park	80433
Wamblee Valley	80433
Wandcrest Park	80470
Ward	80481
Waterton	80125
Watkins	80137
Wattenberg	80621
Waverly	81101
Welby	80229
Weldona	80653
Wellington	80549
Wellshire (Part of Denver)	80222
Wellsville	81201
West (Part of Greeley)	80634
Westcliffe	81252
West End (Part of Colorado Springs)	80904
Western Hills	80221
West Farm	81052
Westland Center (Part of Lakewood)	80215
Westminster	80030-31
	80035-36
For specific Westminster Zip Codes call (303) 429-0340, or your local postmaster.	
Westminster East	80221
Westminster Mall (Part of Westminster)	80030
Weston	81091
Westridge	80634
West Vail (Part of Vail)	81657
Westwood (Part of Denver)	80219
Westwood Lake	80863
Wetmore	81253
Wheat Ridge	80033*
	80034†
Wheeler	80401
White Pine	81248
Whitewater	81527
Widefield	80911
Wiggins	80654
Wild Horse (Cheyenne County)	80862
Wild Horse (Pueblo County)	81001
Wiley	81092
Willard	80741
Williamsburg (Fremont County)	81226
Williamsburg (Jefferson County)	80127
Willowbrook	80465
Willow Creek	80110
Willow Gulch	81423
Wilson Lake Estates	80816
Windsor	80550
Windsor Gardens (Part of Denver)	80231
Winter Park	80482
Wolcott	81655
Wondervu	80401
Woodglen (Part of Thornton)	80229
Woodland Acres	81069
Woodland Park	80863*
	80866†
Woodmar Village	80123
Woodmoor	80908
Woodrow	80757
Woody Creek	81656
Wray	80758
Yampa	80483
Yellow Jacket	81335
Yoder	80864
Yorkborough (Part of Thornton)	80229
Yuma	80759

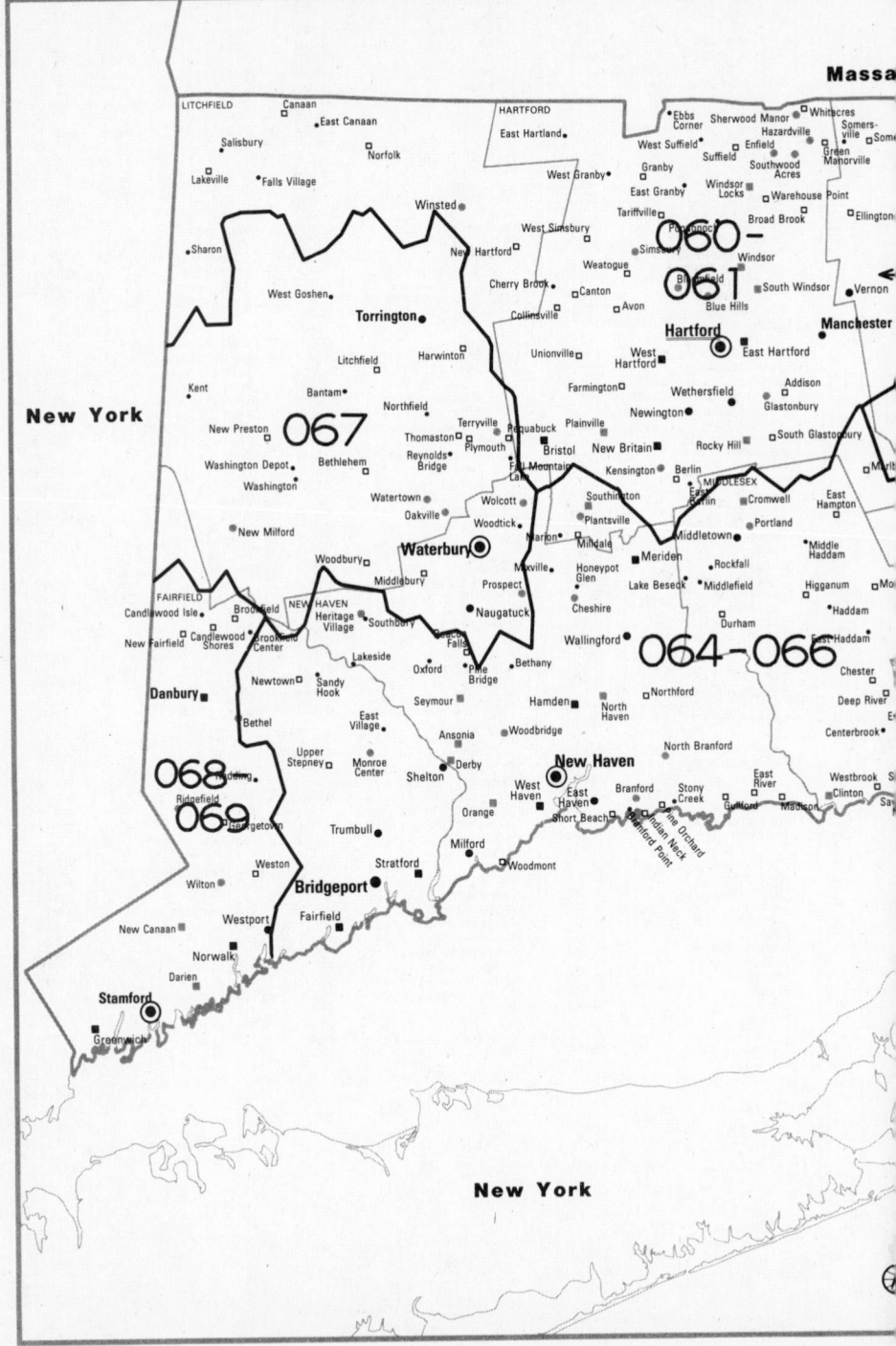

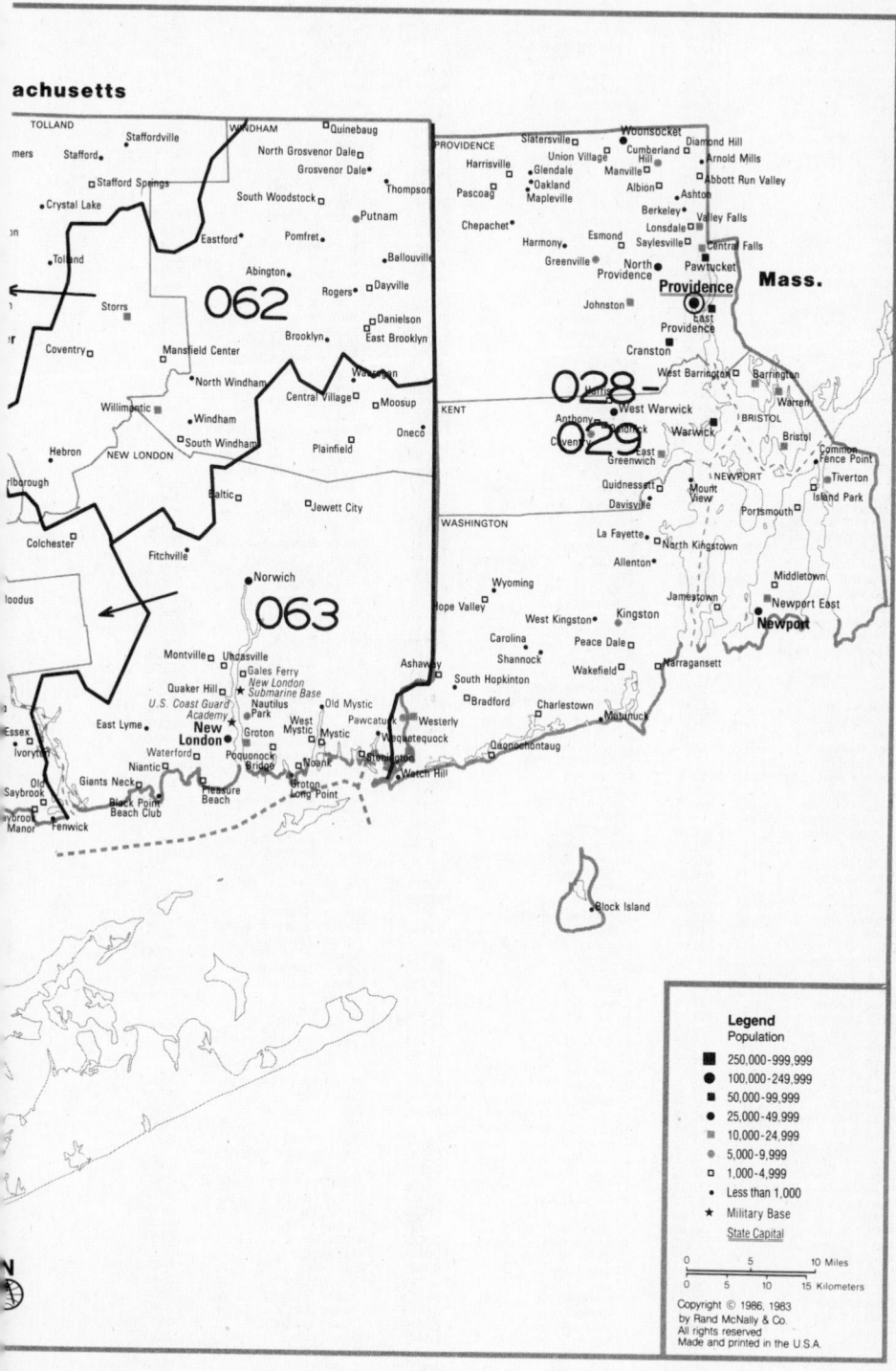

achusetts

TOLLAND
Staffordville
Stafford
mers
Stafford Springs
Crystal Lake
Tolland
Storrs
Coventry
Mansfield Center
NEW LONDON
Hebron
rlborough
Colchester
loodus
Essex
Ivoryton
Old Saybrook
aybrook
Manor
Fenwick

WINDHAM
Quinebaug
North Grosvenor Dale
Grosvenor Dale
Thompson
South Woodstock
Putnam
Eastford
Pomfret
Ballouville
Abington
Dayville
Rogers
Danielson
Brooklyn
East Brooklyn
North Windham
Wauregan
Central Village
Moosup
Windham
Oneco
South Windham
Plainfield
Jewett City
Baltic
Fitchville
Norwich
Uncasville
Montville
Gales Ferry
New London
Submarine Base
Quaker Hill
Nautilus
Park
Old Mystic
U.S. Coast Guard
Academy
West
Pawcatuck
East Lyme
New
Groton
Mystic
Mystic
London
Weequetequock
Waterford
Poquonock
Noank
Niantic
Bridge
Giants Neck
Groton
Long Point
Pleasure
Black Point
Beach
Beach Club
Watch Hill

062

063

PROVIDENCE
Slatersville
Woonsocket
Diamond Hill
Cumberland
Arnold Mills
Harrisville
Union Village
Hill
Glendale
Manville
Abbott Run Valley
Pascoag
Oakland
Albion
Ashton
Mapleville
Berkeley
Valley Falls
Chepachet
Lonsdale
Harmony
Esmond
Saylesville
Central Falls
Greenville
North
Pawtucket
Providence
Johnston
Providence
East
Providence
Cranston
West Barrington
Barrington
028—
West Warwick
Warren
029
Anthony
Warwick
BRISTOL
Coventry
Bristol
East
Common
Greenwich
Fence Point
NEWPORT
Tiverton
Quidnessett
Mount
Island Park
Davisville
View
Portsmouth
La Fayette
WASHINGTON
North Kingstown
Allenton
Middletown
Wyoming
Jamestown
Newport East
Hope Valley
Kingston
Newport
West Kingston
Peace Dale
Carolina
Shannock
Wakefield
South Hopkinton
Narragansett
Ashaway
Bradford
Charlestown
Westerly
Matunuck
Quonochontaug
Stonington

Mass.

Providence

KENT

Block Island

Place	ZIP	Place	ZIP	Place	ZIP
Abington	06230	Brendan Heights	06078	Church Hill	06794
Addison	06033	Bretton Heights (Part of		Churchwood	06357
Agua Vista (Part of		Middletown)	06457	Clam Island	06405
Danbury)	06810	Bridgeport	06601-10	Clarks Corner	06256
Aljen Heights	06339	For specific Bridgeport Zip Codes		Clarks Falls	06359
Allerton Farms (Part of		call (203) 332-5337, or your local		Clarksville	02891
Naugatuck)	06770	postmaster.		Clearview Heights	06076
Allingtown (Part of West		Bridgeport (Town)	06604	Clinton (Town)	06413
Haven)	06516	Bridgewater	06752	Clinton	06413
Almyville	06354	Bridgewater (Town)	06752	Clinton Beach	06413
Alpine	06810	Brighton Beach	06371	Clintonville	06473
Amenia Union	06069	Bristol	06010*	Cobalt	06414
Amesville	06031		06011†	Codfish Hill	06801
Amity (Part of New Haven)	06524	Bristol Terrace (Part of		Colburn Hill	06076
Amston	06231	Naugatuck)	06770	Colchester	06415
Andover	06232	Broad Brook	06016	Colchester (Town)	06415
Andover (Town)	06232	Bromica	06757	Colebrook	06021
Ansonia	06401	Brookfield	06804	Colebrook (Town)	06021
Ansonia (Town)	06401	Brookfield (Town)	06804	Collinsville	06022
Ashford	06278	Brookfield Center	06804	Colonial Manor	06360
Ashford (Town)	06250	Brooklyn	06234	Columbia	06237
Ashford Lake	06250	Brooklyn (Town)	06234	Columbia (Town)	06237
Aspetuck	06880	Brook Valley (Part of		Compo Beach	06880
Attawan Beach	06357	Naugatuck)	06770	Compo Hill	06880
Attawaugan	06241	Bruce Park	06830	Conantville	06226
Atwoodville	06250	Brush Island	06820	Congamond Lakes	06093
Avery Heights	06776	Buckingham	06033	Connecticut Correctional	
Avery Hill	06339	Buckland	06040	Center (New Haven	
Avon	06001	Bucks Corners	06073	County)	06410
Avon (Town)	06001	Bulls Bridge	06785	Connecticut Correctional	
Baileyville	06455	Bunker Hill (Part of		Institution (Hartford	
Bakersville	06057	Waterbury)	06708	County)	06082
Ballouville	06233	Burlington	06013	Connecticut Correctional	
Ball Pond	06812	Burlington (Town)	06085	Institution (Tolland	
Baltic	06330	Burnside	06108	County)	06071
Banksville	06830	Burr Hill	06419	Connecticut Post Mall (Part	
Bantam	06750	Burrville (Part of Torrington)	06790	of Milford)	06460
Barkhamsted (Town)	06063	Burwells Beach (Part of		Conning Towers	06340
Barnum (Part of Bridgeport)	06605	Milford)	06460	Conning Towers-Nautilus	
Barry Square (Part of		Byram	06830	Park	06340
Hartford)	06134	Camp Bethel	06438	Copaco Shopping Center	06002
Bartlett Corners	06375	Camptown (Part of Derby)	06418	Cornwall	06753
Bayview (Part of Milford)	06460	Canaan	06018	Cornwall (Town)	06753
Beacon Falls	06403	Canaan (Town)	06031	Cornwall Bridge	06754
Beacon Falls (Town)	06403	Candleset Cove	06776	Cornwall Center	06796
Beardsley (Part of		Candlewood Hill	06441	Cornwall Hollow	06031
Bridgeport)	06606	Candlewood Hills	06810	Cos Cob	06807
Beaverbrook (Part of		Candlewood Isle	06812	Cottage Grove	06002
Danbury)	06810	Candlewood Knolls	06810	Coventry	06238
Beckettville (Part of		Candlewood Lake Club	06804	Coventry (Town)	06238
Danbury)	06810	Candlewood Lake Estates	06784	Cranbury (Part of Norwalk)	06851
Bedlam Corner	06256	Candlewood Orchards	06804	Cranska Village	06354
Bel Aire Estates	06355	Candlewood Point	06776	Crescent Beach	06357
Belden (Part of Norwalk)	06850	Candlewood Shores	06804	Cromwell (Town)	06416
Belle Haven	06830	Candlewood Springs	06776	Cromwell	06416
Bell Island (Part of Norwalk)	06853	Candlewood Trails	06776	Cromwell Hills	06416
Belltown (Part of Stamford)	06906	Cannondale	06897	Crystal Lake	06029
Berkshire	06482	Canterbury	06331	Daleville	06279
Berkshire Estates	06488	Canterbury (Town)	06331	Damascus	06405
Berkshire Shopping Center		Canton	06019	Danbury	06810-11
(Part of Danbury)	06810	Canton (Town)	06019		06813
Berlin	06037	Canton Center	06020	For specific Danbury Zip Codes	
Berlin (Town)	06037	Carl Robinson Correctional		call (203) 748-1230, or your local	
Beseck Lake	06455	Institution	06082	postmaster.	
Bethany	06524	Carmel Hill	06751	Danbury Fair Mall (Part of	
Bethany (Town)	06524	Castle Hill	02891	Danbury)	06810
Bethel (Town)	06801	Cedar Beach (Part of		Danbury Quarter	06098
Bethel	06801	Milford)	06460	Danbury Shopping Center	
Bethlehem	06751	Cedar Heights (Part of		(Part of Danbury)	06810
Bethlehem (Town)	06751	Danbury)	06810	Danielson	06239
Birch Groves	06776	Cedarhurst	06482	Darien (Town)	06820
Birch Hill	06757	Cedar Knolls	06776	Darien	06820
Birch Meadow	06479	Cedar Lake (Part of Bristol)	06010	Dayville	06241
Birch Mountain	06040	Cedar Land	06488	Deep River	06417
Birchwood	06095	Center	06611		06419
Birdland	06082	Centerbrook	06409	For specific Deep River Zip Codes	
Bishop	06374	Center Groton	06340	call (203) 526-5970, or your local	
Bishops Corner	06137	Center Hill	06057	postmaster.	
Bissell	06074	Centerville	06518	Deep River (Town)	06417
Black Point	06357	Centerville-Mount Carmel	06518	Deer Island	06758
Black Point Beach Club	06357	Central (Part of Hartford)	06103	Deer Run Shores	06784
Bloomfield	06002	Central Commons (Part of		Derby	06418
Bloomfield (Town)	06002	Bridgeport)	06607	Derby (Town)	06418
Blue Hills (Bloomfield Twp.)	06002	Central Manchester	06040	Derby Junction (Part of	
Blue Hills (Hartford Twp.)	06132	Central Village	06332	Derby)	06418
Boardman Manor	06776	Chaffeeville	06268	Derby Neck (Part of Derby)	06418
Boardmans Bridge	06776	Chalkers Beach	06475	Devil's Backbone	06751
Bolton	06043	Chaplin	06235	Devon (Part of Milford)	06460
Bolton (Town)	06043	Chaplin (Town)	06235	Diamond Lake	06033
Bolton Center	06040	Chapman Beach	06498	Dibble Hill	06796
Bonny Brook	06776	Charcoal Ridge	06812	Dickerman's Corner	06479
Borough (Part of Groton)	06340	Cherry Brook	06020	Doanville	06384
Botsford	06404	Cherry Hill	06796	Dodgingtown	06470
Boulder Lake	06413	Cherrywood	06479	Dolphin Gardens	06340
Bozrah (Town)	06334	Cheshire	06410	Double Beach	06405
Bozrah	06334	Cheshire (Town)	06410	Dowd's Corner	06019
Branchville	06829	Chester	06412	Downersville	02891
Brandy Hill	06277	Chester (Town)	06412	Drakeville (Part of	
Branford	06405	Chickahominy	06830	Torrington)	06790
Branford (Town)	06405	Chippens Hill (Part of		Durham	06422
Branford Hills	06405	Bristol)	06010	Durham (Town)	06422
Branhaven Shopping Center	06405	Christy Hill Estates	06335	Durham Center	06422

***** Area Zip Code   † Post Office Boxes

	ZIP
Eagleville	06268
East Berlin	06023
East Bristol (Part of Bristol)	06010
East Brooklyn	06239
East Canaan	06024
East Cornwall	06759
East Derby (Part of Derby)	06418
East End (Part of Waterbury)	06705
Eastern Point (Part of Groton)	06340
East Farmington Heights	06032
East Farms (Part of Waterbury)	06705
Eastford	06242
Eastford (Town)	06242
East Glastonbury	06025
East Granby	06026
East Granby (Town)	06026
East Great Plain (Part of Norwich)	06360
East Haddam	06423
East Haddam (Town)	06423
East Haddam Landing	06423
East Hampton	06424
East Hampton (Town)	06424
East Hampton Center	06424
East Hartford (Town)	06108
East Hartford	06108
	06118
	06128
	06138
For specific East Hartford Zip Codes call (203) 528-6529, or your local postmaster.	
East Hartland	06027
East Haven (Town)	06512
East Haven	06512
East Hill	06019
East Killingly	06243
East Litchfield	06759
East Lyme	06333
East Lyme (Town)	06333
East Morris	06763
East Mountain (Part of Waterbury)	06706
East New London (Part of New London)	06320
East Norwalk (Part of Norwalk)	06601
Easton	06612
Easton (Town)	06612
East Plymouth	06786
East Port Chester	06830
East Putnam	06260
East River	06443
East Thompson	06277
East Village	06468
East Wallingford	06492
East Willington	06279
East Windsor (Town)	06016
East Windsor	06088
East Windsor Hill	06028
East Woodstock	06244
Ebbs Corner	06093
Edgewood (Hartford County)	06010
Edgewood (Tolland County)	06076
Ekonk	06354
Ekonk Hill	06384
Ellington	06029
Ellington (Town)	06029
Elliot	06259
Ellsworth	06069
Elm Hill	06111
Elmville	06241
Elmwood	06133
Elys Ferry	06371
Enders Island	06378
Enfield	06082*
	06083†
Enfield Square	06082
Enfield Street	06082
Essex	06426
Essex (Town)	06426
Ethel Acres	06351
Ettadore Park (Part of Milford)	06460
Fabyan	06255
Fairfield	06430-32
For specific Fairfield Zip Codes call (203) 255-4591, or your local postmaster.	
Fairfield Hills Hospital	06470
Fairground (Part of Norwich)	06360
Fair Haven (Part of New Haven)	06513
Fair Lawn (Part of Waterbury)	06705
Fairmount (Part of Waterbury)	06706
Fairy Lake	06370

	ZIP
Fall Mountain (Part of Bristol)	06010
Fall Mountain Lake	06786
Falls Switch (Part of Norwich)	06360
Falls Village	06031
Farmington	06032
	06034
For specific Farmington Zip Codes call (203) 677-9147, or your local postmaster.	
Farmington (Town)	06032
Far View Beach (Part of Milford)	06460
Federal (Part of New Haven)	06510
Federal Correctional Institution	06810
Fenwick	06475
Fenwood	06475
Ferris Estates	06776
Ferry Point	06475
Ferry View Heights	06335
Field Crest Estates	06355
Firetown	06070
Five City Plaza Shopping Center	06032
Five Points (Fairfield County)	06896
Five Points (Hartford County)	06035
Flanders	06757
Flax Hill (Part of Norwalk)	06850
Floral Park	06475
Floydville	06035
Forbes Village	06108
Forest Glen	06475
Forest Heights (Part of Milford)	06460
Forest Hills	06489
Forest Park	06248
Forestville (Part of Bristol)	06010
Fort Hill	06776
Fort Trumbull Beach (Part of Milford)	06460
Fox Den	06001
Foxon	06512
Franklin	06254
Franklin (Town)	06254
Franklin Square (Part of Norwich)	06360
Furnace Hollow	06076
Gales Ferry	06335
Gallows Hill	06896
Gaylordsville	06755
Georgetown (Fairfield County)	06829
Georgetown (Hartford County)	06479
Germantown (Part of Danbury)	06810
Giants Neck	06357
Giants Neck Heights	06357
Gildersleeve	06480
Gilead	06248
Gilman	06336
Glasgo	06337
Glastonbury	06033
Glastonbury (Town)	06033
Glen	06896
Glenbrook (Part of Stamford)	06906
Glenville	06830
Golden Spur	06385
Good Hill (Kent Twp.)	06757
Good Hill (Woodbury Twp.)	06798
Good Hill (New Haven County)	06478
Goodrich Heights	06416
Goodsell Point	06405
Goshen	06756
Goshen (Town)	06756
Goshen	06385
Goshen Hills	06249
Governor's Hill	06478
Granby	06035
Granby (Town)	06035
Granite Bay	06405
Grappaville	06750
Grassy Hill (Litchfield County)	06798
Grassy Hill (New London County)	06371
Grassy Plain	06801
Great Hammock	06475
Great Harbor	06437
Great Meadows	06810
Greenfield Hill	06430
Greenhaven Shores	02891
Green Manorville	06082
Greens Farms	06436
Greenville (Part of Norwich)	06360

	ZIP
Greenwich	06830-36
For specific Greenwich Zip Codes call (203) 869-3737, or your local postmaster.	
Greystone	06786
Griswold (Town)	06351
Griswoldville	06109
Grosvenor Dale	06246
Groton	06340
Groton (Town)	06340
Groton Heights (Part of Groton)	06340
Groton Lake Shores	06357
Groton Long Point	06340
Grove Beach	06413
Gugliotti	06479
Guilford	06437
Guilford (Town)	06437
Guilford Lake	06437
Gurleyville	06268
Haddam	06438
Haddam (Town)	06438
Haddam Neck	06424
Hadlyme	06439
Hale Court	06880
Hallville	06365
Hamburg	06371
Hamden (Town)	06514
Hamden	06514
	06517-18
For specific Hamden Zip Codes call (203) 782-7114, or your local postmaster.	
Hamden Plaza	06514
Hampton	06247
Hampton (Town)	06247
Hank Hills	06268
Hanover	06350
Happyland	06365
Harborview (Fairfield County)	06853
Harbor View (Middlesex County)	06413
Harrisons	06375
Harrisville	06281
Hartford	06101-06
	06112-15
	06120-26
	06132
	06134
	06140-99
For specific Hartford Zip Codes call (203) 524-6004, or your local postmaster.	
Hartford (Town)	06101
Hartland (Town)	06027
Harwinton	06791
Harwinton (Town)	06790
Hawks Nest Beach	06371
Hawleyville	06440
Hawthorne Terrace (Part of Danbury)	06810
Hayden	06095
Hayestown (Part of Danbury)	06810
Hazardville	06082
Headquarters	06759
Hebron	06248
Hebron (Town)	06248
Heritage Village	06488
Hidden Lake	06441
Higganum	06441
Highland Park	06040
Hi-Ho Center (Part of Bridgeport)	06604
Hillside (Part of Bridgeport)	06610
Hitchcock Lake	06716
Holiday Homes (Part of Colchester)	06415
Hollywyle Park	06810
Holy Apostles College	06416
Honeypot Glen	06410
Hopeville (New Haven County)	06706
Hopeville (New London County)	06351
Horton Hill (Part of Naugatuck)	06770
Hotchkissville	06798
Huckleberry Hill	06001
Hungary Hill	06377
Huntington (Part of Shelton)	06484
Hydeville	06075
I-91 Exit 8 Mall (Part of New Haven)	06515
Indian Cove	06437
Indian Neck	06405
Ivoryton	06442
Jericho Hill	06371
Jewett City	06351
Jordan Village	06385
Kelseytown	06413

	ZIP
Kensington	06037
Kent	06757
Kent (Town)	06757
Kent Furnace	06757
Kenyonville	06282
Kilby (Part of New Haven)	06519
Killingly (Town)	06239
Killingly Center	06241
Killingworth	06419
Killingworth (Town)	06419
Kings Corner	06088
Knollcrest	06810
Knollwood	06475
Lake Bashan	06423
Lake Beseck	06455
Lake Bungee	06282
Lake Garda	06013
Lake Hayward	06415
Lake Plymouth	06782
Lake Pocotopaug	06424
Lakeside (Litchfield County)	06758
Lakeside (New Haven County)	06488
Lakeview Terrace	06076
Lakeville	06039
Lakewood (Part of Waterbury)	06704
Lattins Landing (Part of Danbury)	06810
Laurel (Part of Middletown)	06457
Laurel Beach (Part of Milford)	06460
Laurel Hill (Part of Norwich)	06360
Laysville	06371
Lebanon	06249
Lebanon (Town)	06249
Ledyard	06339
Ledyard (Town)	06339
Leesville	06469
Leetes Island	06437
Leffingwell	06360
Liberty Hill	06249
Lime Rock	06039
Lisbon	06351
Lisbon (Town)	06351
Litchfield	06759
Litchfield (Town)	06759
Little Boston	06875
Little City	06441
Long Hill (Fairfield County)	06611
Long Hill (Middlesex County)	06457
Long Hill (New Haven County)	06704
Long Hill (New London County)	06340
Long Ridge (Part of Stamford)	06901
Lordship	06497
Lords Point	06378
Lydallville	06040
Lyme	06371
Lyme (Town)	06371
Lyons Plains	06880
Macedonia	06757
Madison	06443
Madison (Town)	06443
Manchester (Town)	06040
Manchester	06040
	06045

For specific Manchester Zip Codes call (203) 643-2735, or your local postmaster.

	ZIP
Manchester Green	06040
Mansfield (Town)	06250
Mansfield Center	06250
Mansfield City	06268
Mansfield Depot	06251
Mansfield Four Corners	06268
Mansfield Hollow	06250
Maple Hill	06111
Maplewood (Part of Derby)	06418
Marble Dale	06777
Margerie Manor (Part of Danbury)	06810
Marion	06444
Marlborough	06447
Marlborough (Town)	06447
Maromas (Part of Middletown)	06457
Mashantucket Pequot Indian Reservation	06339
Mashapaug	06076
Mason Island	06355
Massapeag	06382
Mayberry Village	06108
Mechanicsville	06277
Melrose	06049
Melville Village	06430
Meriden	06450
Meriden (Town)	06450

	ZIP
Meriden Square (Part of Meriden)	06451
Merrow	06251
Mianus	06807
Middle Beach	06443
Middlebury	06762
Middlebury (Town)	06762
Middlefield	06455
Middlefield (Town)	06455
Middle Haddam	06456
Middletown	06457
Middletown (Town)	06460
Midway	06340
Milbrook	06830
Milford	06460
Milford (Town)	06460
Milford Lawns (Part of Milford)	06460
Millbrook	06518
Milldale	06467
Millington	06423
Mill Plain (Part of Danbury)	06810
Millville (Part of Naugatuck)	06770
Milton	06759
Mixville	06410
Mohegan	06382
Momauguin	06512
Monroe	06468
Monroe (Town)	06468
Monroe Center	06468
Montowese	06473
Montville	06353
Montville (Town)	06353
Montville Manor	06370
Moodus	06469
Moosup	06354
Morningside (Part of Milford)	06460
Morris	06763
Morris (Town)	06763
Morris Cove	06512
Mount Carmel	06518
Mount Hope	06250
Murphy Road Annex (Part of Hartford)	06114
Murray	06430
Myrtle Beach (Part of Milford)	06460
Mystic	06355
Naugatuck	06770
Naugatuck (Town)	06770
Naugatuck Gardens (Part of Milford)	06460
Naugatuck Valley Mall (Part of Waterbury)	06705
Nautilus Park	06340
Nepaug	06057
Newberry Corner (Part of Torrington)	06790
New Britain	06050-53

For specific New Britain Zip Codes call (203) 223-3681, or your local postmaster.

	ZIP
New Canaan (Town)	06840
New Canaan	06840
Newent	06351
New Fairfield	06812
New Fairfield (Town)	06810
Newfield	06607
Newfield Heights (Part of Middletown)	06457
Newhallville (Part of New Haven)	06511
New Hartford	06057
New Hartford (Town)	06057
New Haven	06501-11
	06513
	06515
	06519-21
	06530-36

For specific New Haven Zip Codes call (203) 782-7203, or your local postmaster.

	ZIP
Newington (Town)	06131
Newington	06111*
	06131†
Newington Junction	06111
New London	06320
New London (Town)	06320
New London Submarine Base	06349
New Milford	06776
New Milford (Town)	06776
New Preston	06777
New Preston-Marble Dale	06777
Newtown	06470
Newtown (Town)	06470
New Village	06374
Niantic	06357
Nichols	06611
Noank	06340
Noble (Part of Bridgeport)	06608
Norfolk	06058

	ZIP
Norfolk (Town)	06058
Noroton	06820
Noroton Heights	06820
North Ashford	06282
North Bloomfield	06002
North Branford	06471
North Branford (Town)	06471
North Bridgeport (Part of Bridgeport)	06601
North Canaan (Town)	06018
North Canton	06059
North Cornwall	06796
North End (Part of Waterbury)	06704
North Farms	06471
Northfield	06778
Northford	06472
North Franklin	06254
North Glenwood	06335
North Granby (Hartford County)	06060
North Grosvenor Dale	06255
North Guilford	06437
North Haven (Town)	06473
North Haven	06473
North Kent	06757
North Madison	06443
North Mianus	06807
North Plain	06423
North Sterling	06377
North Stonington	06359
North Stonington (Town)	06359
North Thompsonville	06082
Northville	06776
North Westchester	06474
North Wilton	06897
North Windham	06256
Norwalk	06850-56

For specific Norwalk Zip Codes call (203) 838-4881, or your local postmaster.

	ZIP
Norwich	06360
Norwich (Town)	06360
Norwich Hospital	06365
Norwichtown (Part of Norwich)	06360
Nut Plains	06437
Oakdale	06370
Oakdale Heights	06370
Oakdale Manor	06488
Oakland Gardens	06032
Oakville	06779
Oakwood Acres	06812
Occum (Part of Norwich)	06360
Old Greenwich	06870
Old Lyme	06371
Old Lyme (Town)	06371
Old Lyme Shores	06371
Old Mystic	06372
Old Saybrook	06475
Old Saybrook (Town)	06475
Old Saybrook Shopping Center	06475
Old State House (Part of Hartford)	06123
Oneco	06373
Orange (Town)	06477
Orange	06477
Orcutts	06076
Oronoke (Part of Waterbury)	06708
Oronoque	06497
Oswegatchie	06385
Overlook (Part of Waterbury)	06710
Owenoke	06880
Oxford	06478
Oxford (Town)	06478
Ox Hill (Part of Norwich)	06360
Oxoboxo Lake	06370
Pachaug	06351
Palestine	06470
Palmertown	06353
Paradise Green	06497
Parcel Post (Part of Milford)	06460
Parkville (Part of Hartford)	06106
Pavilion at Buckland Hills, The	06040
Pawcatuck	06379
Pemberwick	06830
Pequabuck	06781
Perkins Corner	06226
Phoenixville	06235
Pine Bridge	06403
Pine Grove (Litchfield County)	06031
Pine Grove (New London County)	06357
Pine Meadow	06061
Pine Orchard	06405
Pine Rock Park (Part of Shelton)	06484
Plainfield	06374

	ZIP		ZIP		ZIP
Plainfield (Town)	06374		06478	Taft Station (Part of	
Plainville (Town)	06062	For specific Seymour Zip Codes		Norwich)	06360
Plainville	06062	call (203) 888-3830, or your local		Taftville (Part of Norwich)	06380
Plantsville	06479	postmaster.		Talcott Village	06032
Platts Mills (Part of		Shady Rest	06482	Talcottville	06066
Waterbury)	06706	Shailerville	06438	Talmadge Hill	06840
Plaza (Part of Waterbury)	06704	Sharon	06069	Tariffville	06081
Pleasant Acres (Part of		Sharon (Town)	06069	Terminal (Part of New	
Danbury)	06810	Sharon Valley	06069	Haven)	06511
Pleasant Valley	06063	Shelton	06484	Terryville	06786
Pleasure Beach	06385	Shelton (Town)	06484	Thamesville (Part of	
Plymouth	06782	Sherman	06784	Norwich)	06360
Plymouth (Town)	06782	Sherman (Town)	06784	Thomaston	06787
Point Beach (Part of Milford)	06460	Sherman Corner	06256	Thomaston (Town)	06787
Point O'Woods	06376	Sherwood Manor	06082	Thompson	06277
Pomfret	06258	Shippan Point (Part of		Thompson (Town)	06277
Pomfret (Town)	06258	Stamford)	06902	Titicus	06877
Pomfret Center	06259	Short Beach	06405	Tokeneke	06820
Pomfret Landing	06259	Silver Beach (Part of		Tolland	06084
Pond Point (Part of Milford)	06460	Milford)	06460	Tolland (Town)	06084
Ponset	06441	Silver Lane	06138	Torringford (Part of	
Pootatuck Park	06482	Simsbury	06070	Torrington)	06790
Poquetanuck	06365	Simsbury (Town)	06070	Torrington (Town)	06790
Poquonock	06064	Skiff Mountain	06757	Torrington	06790
Poquonock Bridge	06340	Somers	06071	Town Hill	06057
Portland (Town)	06480	Somers (Town)	06071	Town Plot Hill (Part of	
Portland	06480	Somersville	06072	Waterbury)	06708
Presidential	06082	Sound View	06371	Trails Corner	06340
Preston	06365	South Britain	06487	Trumbull (Town)	06612
Preston (Town)	06365	Southbury	06488	Trumbull	06611
Prospect (Town)	06712	Southbury (Town)	06488	Trumbull Shopping Center	06611
Prospect	06712	South Canaan	06031	Trumbull Shopping Park	06611
Prospect Beach (Part of		South Coventry	06238	Turn of River (Part of	
West Haven)	05516	South Ellsworth	06069	Stamford)	06901
Puddle Town	06022	South End (Fairfield County)	06902	Turnpike	06066
Putnam	06260	South End (New Haven		Twin Lakes	06079
Putnam (Town)	06260	County)	06512	Tyler Lake Heights	06756
Putnam Heights	06260	South Farms (Part of		Uncasville	06382
Putney	06497	Middletown)	06457	Uncasville-Oxoboro Valley	06382
Quaddick	06277	South Glastonbury	06073	Union	06076
Quaker Farms	06478	South Glenwoods	06335	Union (Town)	06076
Quaker Hill	06375	Southington	06489	Union City (Part of	
Quarryville	06040	Southington (Town)	06489	Naugatuck)	06770
Quebec	06239	South Kent	06785	Unionville	06085
Quinebaug	06262	South Killingly	06239	Unity Plaza (Part of	
Quinnipiac	06492	South Lyme	06376	Hartford)	06140
Rawson	06247	South Manchester	06040	Upper Stepney	06468
Redding (Town)	06875	South Meriden (Part of		Vernon (Town)	06066
Redding	06875	Meriden)	06451	Vernon	06066
Redding Ridge	06876	South Norfolk	06058	Vernon Center	06066
Reynolds Bridge	06787	South Norwalk (Part of		Versailles	06383
Ridgebury	06877	Norwalk)	06854	Versailles Station	06383
Ridgefield	06877	Southport	06490	Village Hill	06249
Ridgefield (Town)	06877	South Wethersfield	06109	Voluntown (Town)	06384
Ridgeway (Part of Stamford)	06905	South Willington	06265	Voluntown	06384
Ridgewood	06413	South Windham	06266	Wailacks Point (Part of	
Ridgewood Park	06385	South Windsor	06074	Stamford)	06902
Rising Corner	06093	South Windsor (Town)	06074	Wallingford (Town)	06492
Rivercliff (Part of Milford)	06460	Southwood Acres	06082	Wallingford	06492
River Glen	06032	South Woodstock	06267	Wallingford Center	06492
Riverside (Greenwich Twp.)	06878	Sport Hill	06612	Walnut Beach (Part of	
Riverside (Newtown Twp.)	06482	Sprague (Town)	06330	Milford)	06460
Riverside (Hartford County)	06022	Springdale (Part of		Walnut Hill	06333
Riverside (New Haven		Stamford)	06907	Walnut Tree Hill	06482
County)	06478	Spring Hill	06268	Wamphassuc Point	06378
Riversville	06830	Spring Lake Village	06489	Wapping	06074
Riverton	06065	Stafford	06075	Warren	06754
Robertsville	06065	Stafford (Town)	06075	Warren (Town)	06753
Rockfall	06481	Stafford Springs	06076	Warrenville	06278
Rock Ridge	06830	Staffordville	06077	Washington (Town)	06793
Rocky Hill (Town)	06067	Stamford	06901-12	Washington Depot	06793-94
Rocky Hill	06067	For specific Stamford Zip		For specific Washington Depot Zip	
Rogers	06263	Codes call (203) 326-2158, or your local		Codes call (203) 868-7474, or	
Round Hill	06830	postmaster.		your local postmaster.	
Rowayton (Part of Norwalk)	06853	Stamford Town Center (Part		Washington Green	06793
Roxbury	06783	of Stamford)	06901	Washington Hill	06059
Roxbury (Town)	06783	Stanwich	06830	Washington Square (Part of	
Roxbury Falls	06783	State Line	06076	Norwich)	06360
Sachem Head	06437	Station A (Part of Hartford)	06126	Waterbury	06701-10
Salem	06420	Sterling	06377		06720-26
Salem (Town)	06420	Sterling (Town)	06377	For specific Waterbury Zip Codes	
Salisbury	06068	Sterling Hill	06354	call (203) 574-6553, or your local	
Salisbury (Town)	06068	Stetson Corner	06234	postmaster.	
Samp Mortar	06430	Stevenson	06491	Waterbury (Town)	06701
Sandy Beach	06758	Stonington	06378	Waterbury Plaza Shopping	
Sandy Hook	06482	Stonington (Town)	06378	Center (Part of	
Sanfordtown	06896	Stony Corners	06001	Waterbury)	06704
Saugatuck	06880	Stony Creek	06405	Waterford	06385
Saugatuck Shores	06880	Storrs	06268	Waterford (Town)	06385
Saunders Point	06357	Straitsville (Part of		Waterside (Part of	
Savin Rock (Part of West		Naugatuck)	06770	Stamford)	06901
Haven)	06516	Stratfield	06432	Watertown	06795
Saybrook Manor	06475	Stratford (Town)	06497	Watertown (Town)	06795
Saybrook Point	06475	Stratford	06497	Waterville (Part of	
Scantic	06088	Stratmore Farms	06492	Waterbury)	06704
Scitico	06082	Suburban Enfield Mall	06082	Wauregan	06387
Scotland	06264	Suffield	06078	Wauwecus Hill (Part of	
Scotland (Town)	06264	Suffield (Town)	06078	Norwich)	06360
Seaview Beach	06443	Summer Hill	06492	Weatogue	06089
Secret Lake	06001	Sunrise Hill	06525	Webster Square Shopping	
Seymour (Town)	06483	Taconic	06079	Center	06037
Seymour	06483			Weekeempee	06798

	ZIP		ZIP		ZIP
Welles Village	06033	Weston	06883	Williams Crossing	06249
Wells Quarter Village	06109	Weston (Town)	06880	Willimantic	06226
Wequetequock	02891	Westport	06880*	Willington (Town)	06279
Wesleyan (Part of			06881†	Willington Hill	06279
Middletown)	06457	West Putnam Avenue	06830	Willow Point	06388
West Ashford	06250	West Redding	06896	Wilsonville	06255
West Avon	06001	West Shore (Part of West		Wilton	06897
West Bantam	06750	Haven)	06516	Wilton (Town)	06897
Westbrook	06498	West Side (Part of Norwich)	06360	Winchester (Town)	06094
Westbrook (Town)	06498	West Side Hill (Part of		Winchester Center	06094
Westchester	06415	Waterbury)	06708	Windham	06280
West Cornwall	06796	West Simsbury	06092	Windham (Town)	06280
West End (Part of Bristol)	06010	West Stafford	06076	Winding Lanes	06001
Westfarms	06032	West Suffield	06093	Windsor	06095
West Farms Village (Part of		West Thompson	06255	Windsor (Town)	06095
New Britain)	06050	West Torrington (Part of		Windsor Locks (Town)	06096
Westfield (Part of		Torrington)	06790	Windsor Locks	06096
Middletown)	06457	Westview Acres	06478	Windsorville	06016
Westford	06076	Westville (Part of New		Winnipauk (Part of Norwalk)	06851
West Goshen	06756	Haven)	06515	Winsted	06098
West Granby	06090	West Wauregan	06387	Winthrop	06417
West Hartford (Town)	06107	West Willington	06279	Wolcott	06716
West Hartford	06107	Westwood Park (Part of		Wolcott (Town)	06716
	06110	Norwich)	06360	Woodbridge (Town)	06525
	06117	West Woods	06069	Woodbridge	06525
	06119	West Woodstock	06281	Woodbury	06798
	06127	Wethersfield (Town)	06129	Woodbury (Town)	06798
	06133	Wethersfield	06109*	Woodlake	06798
	06137		06129†	Woodmont	06460
For specific West Hartford Zip		Wethersfield Shopping		Woodstock	06281
Codes call (203) 231-2871, or		Center	06109	Woodstock (Town)	06281
your local postmaster.		Wheeler Farms (Part of		Woodstock Valley	06282
West Hartland	06091	Milford)	06460	Woodtick	06716
West Haven	06516	Whigville	06013	Woodville	06777
West Haven (Town)	06516	Whipstick	06877	Yale (Part of New Haven)	06520
West Lakes	06437	Whitacres	06082	Yalesville	06492
West Mystic	06388	White Sands Beach	06371	Yantic (Part of Norwich)	06389
West Norfolk	06058	Whitneyville	06517	Zoar	06482
West Norwalk (Part of		Wildermere Beach (Part of			
Norwalk)	06851	Milford)	06460		

Place	ZIP
Adams Crossroads	19950
Adamsville	19950
Afton	19810
Alapocas	19803
Albertson Park	19808
Analine Village	19703
Andrewville	19950
Anglesey	19807
Angola	19958
Angola Beach	19951
Angola by the Bay	19958
Anne Acres	19971
Arden	19803
Ardencroft	19810
Ardentown	19810
Argos Corner	19963
Arundel	19808
Ashbourne Hills	19703
Ashland	19807
Ashley	19804
Atlanta	19933
Atlanta Estates	19973
Augustine Beach	19731
Avalon	19808
Bacon	19940
Bakers Choice	19946
Baldton (Part of New Castle)	19720
Bayard	19945
Bay Berry Dunes	19930
Bay View Beach	19709
Bay View Park	19930
Bayville	19975
Bay Vista	19971
Bear	19701
Beaver Brook Apartments	19720
Beaverdam Heights	19973
Bellefonte	19809
Bellemoor	19804
Bellevue	19809
Belltown	19958
Belmont Hall	19977
Belvedere	19804
Bestfield	19804
Bethany Beach	19930
Bethany Dunes	19930
Bethany Village	19930
Bethel	19931
Big Mills Bridge	19956
Big Oak Corners	19977
Big Pine	19950
Big Stone Beach	19963
Binns Village (Part of Newark)	19711
Birchwood Park	19711
Blackbird	19734
Blackiston	19938
Blackwater Village	19939
Blades	19973
Blue Hen Mall (Part of Dover)	19901
Blue Rock Manor	19803
Bowers	19946
Bowers Beach	19946
Boxwood	19804
Brack-Ex	19805
Brandywine	19810
Brandywine Estates	19703
Brandywine Springs Manor	19808
Brandywood	19810
Breezewood (Kent County)	19943
Breezewood (New Castle County)	19713
Brenford	19977
Briar Park	19901
Bridgeville	19933
Broadacres	19973
Broad Creek	19956
Broadkill Beach	19968
Brookbend	19713
Brookdale Heights	19934
Brookhaven	19711
Brookland Terrace	19805
Brookside	19713
Brookview Apartments	19703
Brownsville	19952
Bull Pine Corners	19947
Bunting	19975
Buttonwood (Part of New Castle)	19720
Camden	19934
Camden-Wyoming (Part of Wyoming)	19934
Cannon	19933
Canterbury	19943
Capitol Green (Part of Dover)	19901
Capitol Park	19901
Cardiff	19810
Carlisle Village	19901
Carrcroft	19803
Carrcroft Crest	19803

Place	ZIP
Carter	19901
Castle Hills	19720
Catalina Gardens (Part of Newark)	19711
Cave Colony	19968
Cedar Beach	19963
Cedarbrook Acres	19977
Cedar Heights	19804
Centerville	19807
Chalfonte	19810
Channin	19803
Chapel Hill	19711
Chatham	19810
Chelsea Estates	19720
Cherokee Woods	19713
Chestnut Hill Estates	19713
Chestnut Knoll	19963
Cheswold	19936
Christiana	19702
Christiana Acres	19720
Clarksville	19970
Claymont	19703
Clayton	19938
Clearfield	19703
Cleland Heights	19805
Clifton Park Manor	19802
Cocked Hat	19933
College Park (Part of Newark)	19711
Collins Park	19720
Colmar Manor	19977
Colonial Heights	19805
Colonial Park	19805
Columbia	19940
Concord	19973
Concord Mall	19803
Concord Manor	19803
Cool Spring	19968
Cooper Farm	19808
Cottonpatch Hill	19930
Country Club Estates	19963
Coventry	19720
Coverdale Crossroads	19933
Covered Bridge Farms	19711
Covey Creek	19958
Cragmere	19809
Cragmere Woods	19809
Craigs Mill	19973
Cranston Heights	19808
Crossgates (Part of Dover)	19901
Cross Keys	19966
Dagsboro	19939
Darley Woods	19810
Dartmouth Woods	19810
Deerhurst	19803
Delaplane Manor	19711
Delaware City	19706
Delaware Correctional Center	19977
Delaware Heights	19807
Del Haven Estates	19962
Delmar	19940
Del Park Manor	19808
Devon	19810
Devonshire	19810
Dewey Beach	19971
Diamond Acres	19939
Dobbinsville (Part of New Castle)	19720
Dover	19901-03
For specific Dover Zip Codes call (302) 734-5821, or your local postmaster.	
Dover AFB Housing Annex	19901
Dover Base Housing	19901
Doverbrook Gardens	19901
Dover Mall (Part of Dover)	19901
Downs Chapel	19938
Drummond North	19711
Dublin Hill	19933
Dunleith	19801
Dunlinden Acres	19808
Dupont Manor	19901
Du Ross Heights	19720
Dutch Acres	19958
Eastman Heights	19963
Eastover Hills (Part of Dover)	19901
Eberton	19901
Eden Park	19720
Edge Hill (Part of Dover)	19901
Edgehill Acres (Part of Dover)	19901
Edgemoor (New Castle County)	19809
Edgemoor (New Castle County)	19802
Edgemoor Gardens	19802
Edgemoor Terrace	19802
Edgewater Acres	19975
Edgewood Hills	19802
Edwardsville	19943

Place	ZIP
Ellendale	19941
Elmhurst	19804
Elsmere	19805
Elsmere Junction (Part of Elsmere)	19805
English Village	19711
Evergreen Acres	19963
Fairfax	19803
Fairfield Farms	19901
Fairmount	19951
Fairwinds	19701
Farmington	19942
Faulkland	19808
Faulkland Heights	19808
Faulkwoods	19808
Federal (Part of Newark)	19711
Felton	19943
Felton Heights	19943
Felton Manor	19943
Fenwick Island	19944
Fieldsboro	19734
Fireside Park	19713
Flemings Corner	19952
Flemings Landing	19734
Forest Brook Glen	19804
Forest Hills Park	19803
Four Seasons	19702
Foxhall Courtside	19901
Fox Hollow	19958
Frankford	19945
Frederica	19946
Galewood	19803
Garfield Park	19720
Gateway Farms	19707
Georgetown	19947
Ginns Corner	19734
Glasgow	19711
Glasgow Court	19702
Glasgow Pines	19702
Glen Berne Estates	19804
Glendale	19711
Glenville	19804
Goldey Beacom College	19808
Gordon Heights	19802
Gordy Estates	19804
Granogue	19807
Gravel Hill	19947
Graylyn Crest	19803
Green Acres	19803
Green Bank	19808
Greenbriar	19720
Greenshire	19703
Greentree	19703
Greenview	19901
Greenville (Kent County)	19952
Greenville (New Castle County)	19807
Greenville Place	19807
Greenwood	19950
Gulls Nest	19930
Gumboro	19945
Guyencourt	19807
Gwinhurst	19809
Hall Estates	19963
Hamilton Park	19720
Hanbys Corner	19810
Harbeson	19951
Hardscrabble	19973
Harmony Hills	19711
Harrington	19952
Hartly	19953
Hayden Park	19804
Hearns Crossroads	19956
Hearns Mill	19973
Heather Woods	19702
Henlopen Acres	19971
Henry Clay	19807
Hickman	21629
Hickory Hill	19966
Hickory Ridge	19977
Highland Acres (Kent County)	19901
Highland Acres (Sussex County)	19958
Highland West	19808
High Point Park	19946
Hillcrest	19809
Hillside Acres	19943
Hillside Heights	19711
Hilltop Manor	19809
Hitchens Crossroads	19956
Hockessin	19707
Holiday Acres	19939
Hollandsville	19943
Holletts Corners	19938
Holloway Terrace	19720
Holly Oak (New Castle County)	19809
Holly Oak (Sussex County)	19973
Holly Oak Terrace	19809
Hollyville	19951
Houston	19954

	ZIP		ZIP		ZIP
Huntley	19901	*For specific Newark Zip Codes call (302) 737-5770, or your local postmaster.*		Rose Gate	19720
Hyde Park	19808			Rose Hill	19720
Idella	19804			Rose Hill Gardens	19720
Indian Beach	19971			Roselle	19805
Indian Field	19810	New Castle	19720	Roseville Park	19711
Indian River Acres	19939	New Castle Manor (Part of New Castle)	19720	Roxana	19945
Iron Hill Apartments	19702	Newkirk Estates	19711	Rutherford	19711
Ivy Ridge	19720	Newport	19804	St. Georges	19733
Jefferson Farms	19720	Newport Heights	19804	Sandtown	19943
Jimtown	19958	Northcrest	19810	Sandy Brae	19958
Johnson	19975	North Hills	19809	Scottfield	19711
Johnstown	19950	North Ridge	19703	Scotts Corner	19933
Jones Crossroads	19956	North Seaford Heights	19973	Seabreeze	19971
Keen-Wik	19975	Northshire	19810	Sea Del Estates	19930
Kenilworth	19703	North Shores (Kent County)	19963	Seaford	19973
Kenmore Park	19973	North Shores (mail Milton)	19968	Seaford Heights	19973
Kent Acres	19901	North Shores (mail Rehoboth Beach)	19971	Sedgley Farms	19807
Kenton	19955	North Shores (mail Seaford)	19973	Seeneytown	19938
Kiamensi	19804	North Star	19711	Selbyville	19975
Kirkwood	19708	Northwest Dover Heights (Part of Dover)	19901	Shady Lane	19901
Kitts Hummock	19901	Northwood	19803	Shaft Ox Corner	19966
Klair Estates	19808	Oak Forest Estates	19953	Sharpley	19803
Kynlyn Apartments	19809	Oak Grove (Kent County)	19901	Shawnee Acres	19963
Lake Pines	19956	Oak Grove (New Castle County)	19805	Shawtown (Part of New Castle)	19720
Lamatan	19711	Oak Grove (Sussex County)	19973	Shell Bridge	19956
Lancashire	19810	Oak Hill	19805	Shellburne	19803
Lancaster Court	19805	Oak Lane Manor	19803	Sherwood (Part of Dover)	19901
Lancaster Village	19805	Oakley	19941	Sherwood Acres	19945
Laurel	19956	Oakmont	19720	Sherwood Park	19808
Lebanon	19901	Oak Orchard	19966	Shipley Heights	19803
Leedom Estates	19720	Ocean View	19970	Shortly	19947
Leipsic	19901	Ocean Village	19930	Silverbrook	19805
Lewes	19958	Odessa	19730	Silver Lake Shores	19971
Lewes Beach (Part of Lewes)	19958	Ogletown	19711	Silverside Heights	19809
Liftwood	19803	Old Furnace	19947	Silview	19804
Limestone Acres	19808	Omar	19945	Simonds Gardens	19720
Limestone Gardens	19808	Orchard Acres	19943	Slaughter Beach	19963
Lincoln	19960	Overview Gardens	19720	Smyrna	19977
Lindenmere	19809	Owens	19950	Smyrna Landing (Part of Smyrna)	19977
Little Creek	19961	Owls Nest Estates	19807	Snug Harbor	19973
Little Heaven	19946	Palm Springs Manor	19711	South Bethany	19930
Llangollen Estates	19720	Paris Villa	19962	South Bowers	19963
London Village	19962	Pembrey	19803	South Dover Acres (Part of Dover)	19901
Long Neck	19966	Penarth	19803	Spruance City	19977
Longview Farms	19810	Penn Acres	19720	Stanton	19804
Lowe	19956	Pennrock	19809	Star Hill	19901
Lowes Crossroads	19966	Penny Hill	19809	Staytonville	19952
Lumbrook (Part of Newark)	19711	Pepper	19956	Stockdale	19703
Lynch Heights	19963	Pepperbox	19956	Stockley	19947
Lyndalia	19804	Perry Park	19810	Stockton	19720
Lynnfield	19803	Perth	19803	Stoneybrook Apartments	19703
McClellandville	19711	Petersburg	19979	Stratford	19720
McDaniel Heights	19803	Pickering Beach	19901	Summit Bridge	19709
Magnolia	19962	Pine Creek	19711	Surrey Park	19803
Manor	19720	Pinetown	19958	Sussex Correctional Institution	19947
Manor Park	19720	Pine Tree Corners	19734	Sussex Shores	19930
Manor Park Apartments	19720	Piney Grove	19947	Swain Acres	19947
Maplecrest	19808	Pleasant Hill	19804	Swann Keys	19975
Marabou Meadows	19702	Pleasanton Acres	19901	Swanwyck	19720
Marshallton	19808	Pleasantville	19720	Swanwyck Estates	19720
Marvels Crossroads	19952	Plymouth	19943	Swanwyck Gardens	19720
Marydel	19964	Polly Drummond	19711	Sycamore	19956
Mastens Corner	19943	Polly Drummond Hill	19711	Sycamore Gardens	19711
Mayfair (Part of Dover)	19901	Porter	19701	Talleyville	19803
Mayfield	19803	Port Mahon	19901	Tanglewood	19713
Mayview Manor	19720	Port Penn	19731	Tarleton	19803
Meadowbrook	19804	Portsville	19956	Taylor Estates	19901
Meadowbrook Acres	19962	Primehook Beach	19963	Taylors Bridge	19734
Meadowood	19711	Quakertown	19958	The Beeches (Part of Dover)	19901
Mechanicsville	19711	Radnor Green	19703	The Cedars	19808
Meeting House Hill	19711	Radnor Woods	19703	The Island	19973
Melody Meadows	19702	Rambleton Acres	19720	The Timbers	19803
Middleford	19973	Ramblewood	19810	Thomas Landing	19734
Middlesex Beach	19930	Redden	19947	Thompsonville	19963
Middletown	19709	Redden Crossroads	19947	Tidbury Manor	19901
Midvale	19720	Red Lion	19701	Todd Estates	19713
Midway	19971	Reeves Crossing	19943	Towne Point (Part of Dover)	19901
Milford	19963	Rehoboth Beach	19971	Townsend	19734
Milford Cross Roads	19711	Reliance	19973	Tuxedo Park	19804
Millpond Acres	19958	Richardson Park	19805	Twin Eagle Farms	19938
Millsboro	19966	Rising Sun	19934	Tybrook	19808
Millville	19970	Rising Sun-Lebanon	19901	Union Street (Part of Wilmington)	19805
Milton	19968	Riverdale	19966	Valley Run	19810
Minquadale	19720	Riverside Gardens	19703	Van Dyke Village (Part of New Castle)	19720
Mispillion Light	19963	Riverview (Kent County)	19962	Varlano	19702
Mission	19966	Riverview (Sussex County)	19966	Vernon	19952
Montchanin	19710	Robscott Manor	19713	Village of Drummond Hill	19711
Monterey Farms	19720	Rockland	19732	Village of Garrisons Lake	19977
Morris Estates (Part of Dover)	19901	Rodney Square (Part of Wilmington)	19801	Village of Windhover	19702
Mount Cuba	19807	Rodney Village	19901	Villa Monterey	19809
Mount Pleasant	19709	Rodric Village	19901	Viola	19979
Naamans Gardens	19810	Rogers Haven	19970	Voshells Cove	19901
Naamans Manor	19810	Rogers Manor (Part of New Castle)	19720	Ward	19940
Naamans Trailer Park	19703	Rolling Hills	19804	Warwick	19966
Nanticoke Acres	19973	Rolling Park	19703	Washington Heights	19971
Nassau	19969	Rosedale Beach	19966		
Newark	19711-15				

* Area Zip Code † Post Office Boxes

	ZIP
Washington Park (Part of New Castle)	19720
Webb Manor	19963
Webster Farms	19803
Wedgewood Acres	19720
Weisman Acres	19963
Wellington Woods	19702
Welshire	19803
West Beach	19939
Westfield	19804
West Haven	19807
West Meadow	19711
Westover Hills	19807
West Park	19807
Westview	19804
Westwood Manor	19810
Whaleys Corners	19956
Whaleys Crossroads	19956
Whiteleysburg	19943
White Oak Farms (Part of Dover)	19901
Whitesville	19940

	ZIP
Widener University / Delaware Campus	19803
Williamsville (Kent County)	19954
Williamsville (Sussex County)	19975
Willow Grove	19934
Willow Run	19805
Wilmington	19801-99
For specific Wilmington Zip Codes call (302) 323-3783, or your local postmaster.	
Wilmington College	19720
Wilmington Manor	19720
Wilmington Manor Gardens	19720
Wilmont	19810
Windermer	19804
Windsor Hills	19803
Windy Bush	19810
Windy Hills	19711
Winterthur	19735
Woodbine	19803
Woodbrook (Kent County)	19901

	ZIP
Woodbrook (New Castle County)	19803
Woodcrest (Kent County)	19901
Woodcrest (New Castle County)	19804
Wooddale	19807
Woodenhawk	19950
Woodland (New Castle County)	19805
Woodland (Sussex County)	19973
Woodland Beach	19977
Woodshade	19702
Woods Haven	19963
Woodside	19980
Woodside East	19980
Woodside Hills	19809
Woods Manor	19901
Workmans Corners	19947
Wyoming	19934
York Beach (Part of South Bethany)	19930
Yorklyn	19736

* Area Zip Code **† Post Office Boxes**

	ZIP
Anacostia (Part of Washington)	20020
Barnaby Terrace (Part of Washington)	20032
Benjamin Franklin (Part of Washington)	20004
Benning (Part of Washington)	20019
Blue Plains (Part of Washington)	20032
Bolling Air Force Base (Part of Washington)	20332
Brightwood (Part of Washington)	20011
Brightwood Park (Part of Washington)	20011
Brookland (Part of Washington)	20017
Calvert (Part of Washington)	20007
Cardinal (Part of Washington)	20017
Central (Part of Washington)	20005
Chillum (Part of Washington)	20011
Cleveland Park (Part of Washington)	20008
Colonial Village (Part of Washington)	20012
Columbia Heights (Part of Washington)	20009
Congress Heights (Part of Washington)	20032
Congress Park (Part of Washington)	20032
Customs House (Part of Washington)	20018
Douglas Dwellings (Part of Washington)	20020
Eagle (Part of Washington)	20016
Eckington (Part of Washington)	20002
Fairfax Village (Part of Washington)	20020
Farragut (Part of Washington)	20036
Fort Davis (Part of Washington)	20020
Fort Lincoln (Part of Washington)	20018
Fort McNair (Part of Washington)	20319
Friendship (Part of Washington)	20016
F Street (Part of Washington)	20004
Garfield Heights (Part of Washington)	20020
Georgetown (Part of Washington)	20007
Glover Park (Part of Washington)	20007
Good Hope (Part of Washington)	20020
Hillcrest (Part of Washington)	20020
Hoya (Part of Washington)	20007
Kalorama (Part of Washington)	20009
Kendall Green (Part of Washington)	20002
Knox Hill Dwellings (Part of Washington)	20020
Lamond (Part of Washington)	20011
Le Droit Park (Part of Washington)	20001
L'Enfant Plaza (Part of Washington)	20024
Les Champs (Part of Washington)	20037
McLean Gardens (Part of Washington)	20016
Manor Park (Part of Washington)	20011
Martin Luther King, Jr. (Part of Washington)	20043
Mid City (Part of Washington)	20005
Mount Pleasant (Part of Washington)	20010
Naval Research Laboratory (Part of Washington)	20375
Naylor Gardens (Part of Washington)	20020
Northeast (Part of Washington)	20002
Northwest (Part of Washington)	20015
Palisades (Part of Washington)	20016
Park View (Part of Washington)	20010

	ZIP
Petworth (Part of Washington)	20011
Philatelic Sales Division (Part of Washington)	20265
Randle (Part of Washington)	20020
Saint Elizabeth (Part of Washington)	20032
Shepherd (Part of Washington)	20032
Southeast (Part of Washington)	20003
Southwest (Part of Washington)	20024
Spring Valley (Part of Washington)	20016
State Department (Part of Washington)	20520
Techworld (Part of Washington)	20091
Temple Heights (Part of Washington)	20009
Tenleytown (Part of Washington)	20016
Terra Cotta (Part of Washington)	20011
The Palisades (Part of Washington)	20016
T Street (Part of Washington)	20009
Twentieth Street (Part of Washington)	20036
Twining (Part of Washington)	20020
U.S. Naval Station (Part of Washington)	20374
Walter Reed (Part of Washington)	20012
Washington	20001-99
	20101-99
	20201-99
	20301-72
	20501-99

For specific Washington Zip Codes call (202) 682-9595, or your local postmaster.

COLLEGES & UNIVERSITIES

	ZIP
American University	20016
Catholic University of America	20064
Gallaudet University	20002
George Washington University	20052
Georgetown University	20057
Howard University	20059
University of the District of Columbia	20008

FINANCIAL INSTITUTIONS

	ZIP
American Security Bank, N.A.	20013
Citizen's Bank of Washington, National Association	20005
Columbia First Bank, F.S.B.	20005
Crestar Bank, N.A.	20005
Dominion Bank of Washington, National Association	20005
First American Bank, N.A.	20005
Home Federal Savings Bank	20015
Independence Federal Savings Bank	20036
Industrial Bank of Washington	20011
NationsBank of D.C., N.A.	20006
Oba Federal Savings & Loan Association	20004
Riggs National Bank of Washington, D.C.	20005
Signet Bank, N.A.	20036
Washington Federal Savings Bank	20016

GOVERNMENT OFFICES

	ZIP
ACTION	20525
Administrative Committee of the Federal Register	20408
Administrative Conference of the United States	20037
Administrative Office of the United States Courts	20544
Advisory Commission on Intergovernmental Relations	20575
Advisory Council on Historic Preservation	20004
African Development Foundation	20005

	ZIP
Agency for International Development	20523
American Battle Monuments Commission	20314
Appalachian Regional Commission	20235
Architect of the Capitol	20515
Architectural and Transportation Barriers Compliance Board	20004
Board for International Broadcasting	20036
Bureau of Alcohol, Tobacco and Firearms	22043
Bureau of Engraving and Printing	20228
Bureau of Prisons	20534
Central Intelligence Agency	20505
Citizens' Stamp Advisory Committee	20260
Commission of Fine Arts	20001
Commission on Civil Rights	20425
Committee for the Implementation of Textile Agreements	20230
Committee on Foreign Investment in the United States	20220
Commodity Futures Trading Commission	20581
Congressional Budget Office	20515
Consumer Product Safety Commission	20207
Coordinating Council on Juvenile Justice and Delinquency Prevention	20531
Council of Economic Advisors	20500
Council on Environmental Quality	20503
Defense Intelligence Agency	20340
Defense Investigative Service	20324
Defense Legal Services Agency	20301
Defense Mapping Agency	22031
Defense Nuclear Agency	20305
Defense Security Assistance Agency	20301
Delaware River Basin Commission	20240
Department of Agriculture	20250
Department of Commerce	20230
Department of Defense	20301
Department of Education	20202
Department of Energy	20585
Department of Health and Human Services	20201
Department of Housing and Urban Development	20410
Department of Justice	20530
Department of Labor	20210
Department of State	20520
Department of the Air Force	20330
Department of the Army	20310
Department of the Interior	20240
Department of the Navy	20350
Department of the Treasury	20220
Department of Transportation	20590
Department of Veterans Affairs	20420
Development Coordination Committee	20523
Drug Enforcement Administration	20537
Endangered Species Committee	20240
Environmental Protection Agency	20460
Equal Employment Opportunity Commission	20507
Export Administration Review Board	20230
Export-Import Bank of the United States	20571
Federal Aviation Administration	20591
Federal Bureau of Investigation	20535
Federal Communications Commission	20554
Federal Deposit Insurance Corporation	20429
Federal Election Commission	20463
Federal Emergency Management Agency	20472
Federal Financial Institutions Examination Council	20037

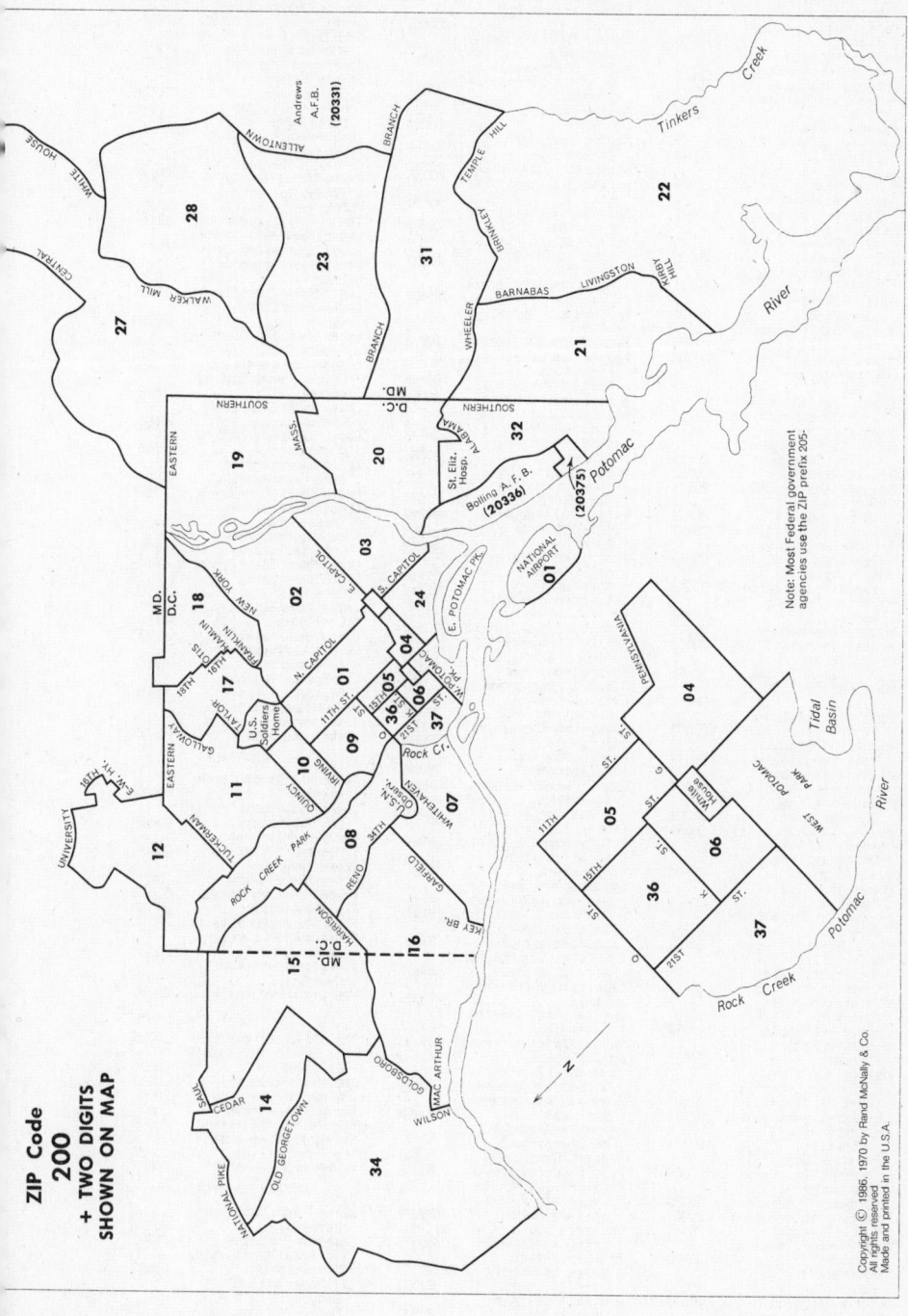

ZIP Code
200
+ TWO DIGITS
SHOWN ON MAP

Note: Most Federal government agencies use the ZIP prefix 205-

	ZIP		ZIP		ZIP
Naval Research Laboratory	20375	Washington Square (Part of		Woodley Park (Part of	
Naval Security Station	20390	Washington)	20036	Washington)	20008
United States Property and		Watergate (Part of		Woodley Road (Part of	
Fiscal Office, Washington		Washington)	20037	Washington)	20008
D.C.	20315	Wesley Heights (Part of		Woodridge (Part of	
Walter Reed Medical Center	20307	Washington)	20016	Washington)	20018
		West End (Part of			
Washington Highlands (Part		Washington)	20037		
of Washington)..........	20032				

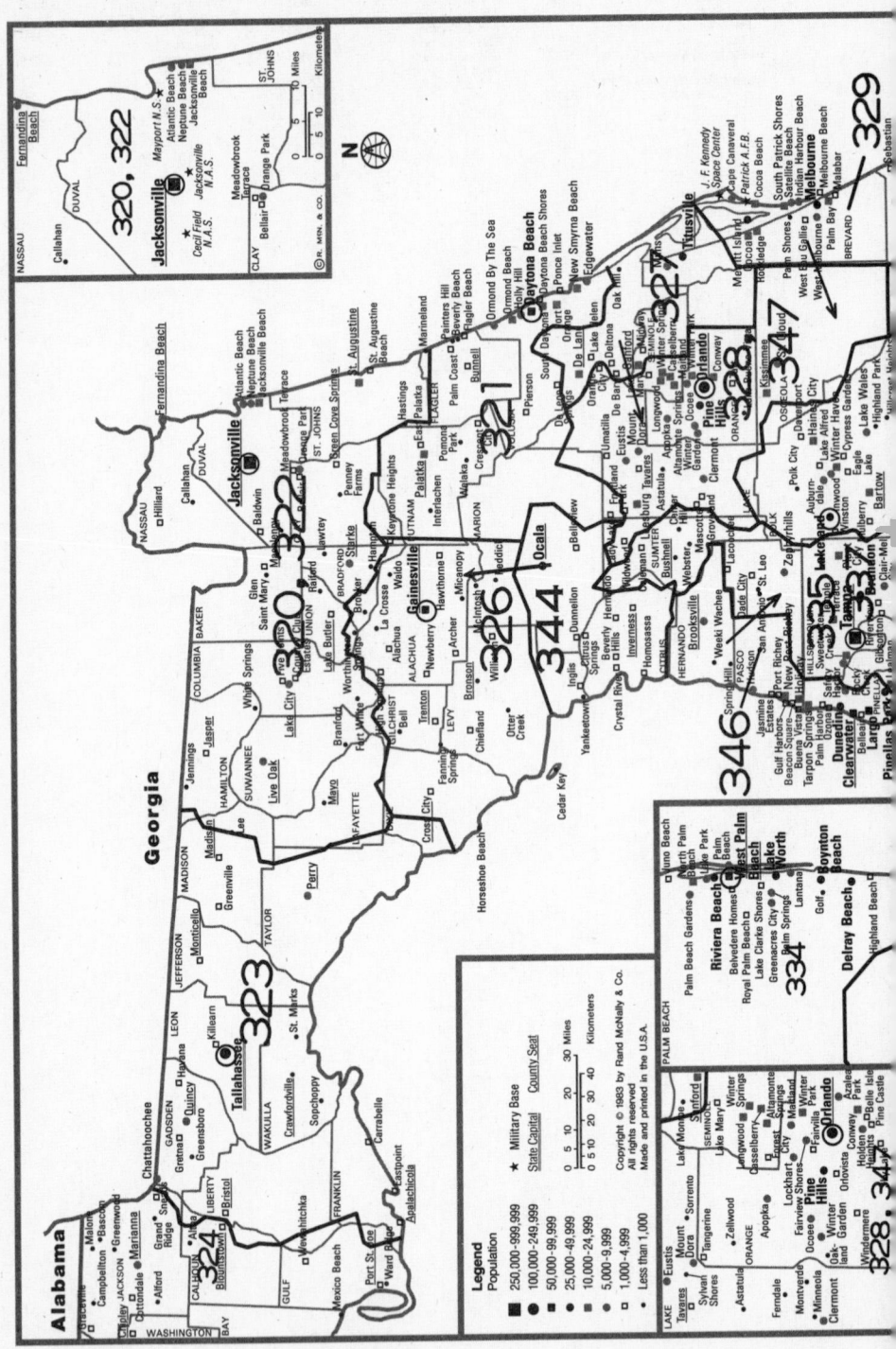

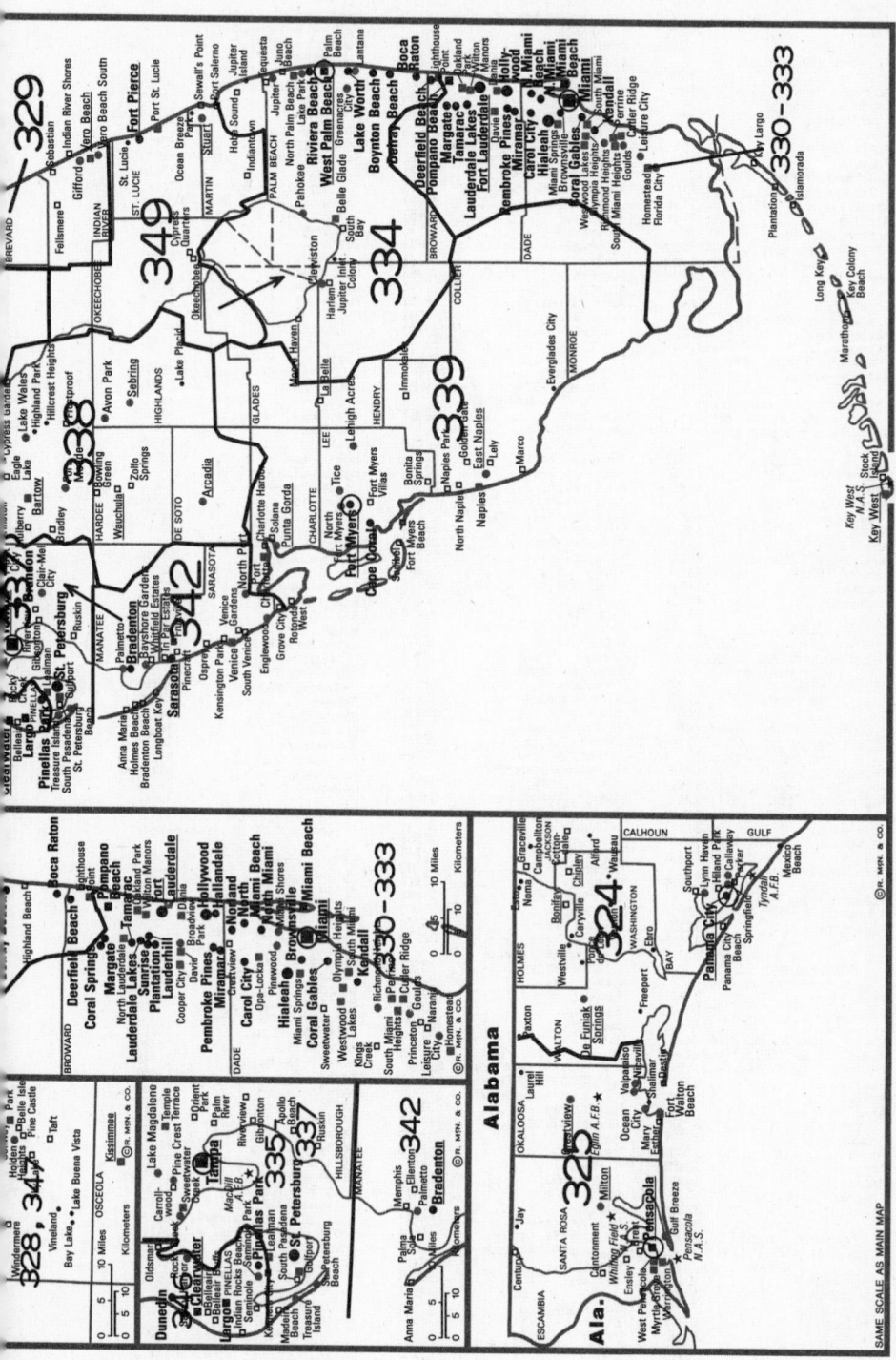

	ZIP
A (Part of Palm Beach)	33480
Aberdeen	33437
Abe Springs	32424
Acline	33950
Adams Beach	32347
Adamsville (Hillsborough County)	33534
Adamsville (Sumter County)	34785
Airport Siding (Part of Jacksonville)	32229
Alachua	32615
Aladdin City	33187
Alamana	32168
Alderman Park (Part of Jacksonville)	32211
Alford	32420
Allandale	32119
Allanton	32404
Allapattah (Part of Miami)	33142*
	33242†
Allentown	32570
Alliance	32446
Alligator Point	32327
Aloma (Part of Winter Park)	32792
Alpine Heights	32433
Altamonte Mall (Part of Altamonte Springs)	32701
Altamonte Springs	32701
	32714-16
For specific Altamonte Springs Zip Codes call (407) 682-3977, or your local postmaster.	
Altha	32421
Alton	32066
Altoona	32702
Alturas	33820
Alumni Village (Part of Tallahassee)	32310
Alva	33920
Amelia City	32034
Amelia Island Plantation	32034
American Beach	32034
Anclote	34691
Andalusia	32110
Andover	33169
	33179
For specific Andover Zip Codes call (305) 470-0327, or your local postmaster.	
Andover Golf Estates	33169
Andover Lake Estates	33169
	33179
For specific Andover Lake Estates Zip Codes call (305) 470-0327, or your local postmaster.	
Andrews	32046
Angel City	32952
Angler Park	33037
Angus Valley	33544
Anna Maria	34216
Anthony,	32617
Antioch	33565
Apalachee Correctional Institution	32324
Apalachee Ridge (Part of Tallahassee)	32301
Apalachicola	32320
	32329
For specific Apalachicola Zip Codes call (904) 653-9554, or your local postmaster.	
Apollo Beach	33572
Apopka	32703-04
	32712
For specific Apopka Zip Codes call (407) 886-2951, or your local postmaster.	
Aquarina	32951
Araquey	32095
Arbor Hills (Part of Tallahassee)	32308
Arcadia	33821
Archer	32618
Argyle	32422
Aripeka	34679
Arlington (Part of Jacksonville)	32211
	32239
For specific Arlington Zip Codes call (904) 744-5222, or your local postmaster.	
Arlington Hills (Part of Jacksonville)	32211
Arlingwood (Part of Jacksonville)	32211
Armstrong	32033
Arran	32327
Arredondo	32608
Asbury Lake	32043
Ashton	34771
Ashville	32331
Astatula	34705

	ZIP
Astor	32102
Astor Park	32102
Astronaut Trail (Part of Titusville)	32782
Athena	32347
Atlantic Beach	32233
Atlantic Boulevard (Part of Coral Springs)	33071
	33077
For specific Atlantic Boulevard Zip Codes call (305) 346-9446, or your local postmaster.	
Atlantic Boulevard Estates (Part of Jacksonville)	32225
Atlantic Heights (Part of Miami Beach)	33139
Atlantis	33462
Auburn	32536
Auburndale	33823
Aucilla	32344
Audubon	32952
Aurantia	32754
Autumn Woods	34683
Avalon Beach	32583
Aventura	33160
	33180
For specific Aventura Zip Codes call (305) 567-5179, or your local postmaster.	
Aventura Mall	33180
Avenues, The (Part of Jacksonville)	32216
Avondale (Part of Jacksonville)	32205
Avon Park	33825
Avon Park Air Force Base	33825
Avon Park Correctional Institution	33825
Avon Park Estates	33825
Avon Park Lakes	33825
Azalea Park	32807
Babson Park	33827
Bagdad	32530
Bahia Oaks	34474
Bahia Shores (Part of St. Petersburg Beach)	33706
Baker	32531
Baker Correctional Institution	32072
Baker Settlement	32464
Bakersville	32092
Bal-Alex Estates	32561
Baldwin	32234
Bal Harbour	33154
Bal Harbour Shops (Part of Bal Harbour)	33154
Ballantine Manor	34243
Ballast Point (Part of Tampa)	33611
Balm	33503
Bamboo	34748
Barberville	32105
Bardin	32177
Bardmoor	34641
Bare Beach	33440
Barefoot Bay	32976
Barrineau Park	32533
Barry University (Part of Miami Shores)	33161
Barth	32533
Bartow	33830
Bascom	32423
Basinger	34972
Baskin	34644
	34648
For specific Baskin Zip Codes call (813) 584-2191, or your local postmaster.	
Bassville Park	34788
Basswood Estates	34972
Baum	32308
Bay Acres	34229
Bayard (Part of Jacksonville)	32258
Bay Crest Park	33615
Bay Grove	32439
Bay Harbor Islands	33154
Bayhead (Bay County)	32466
Bay Head (Pasco County)	33525
Bay Hill	32819
Bay Lake	34736
Bayonet Point	34667
Bayou George	32405
Bay Pines	33504
Bay Point (Bay County)	32411
Bay Point (Dade County)	33137
Bayport	34607
Bayridge	32703
Bayshore	33917
Bayshore Gardens	34207
Bayshore Manor	33917

	ZIP
Bay Springs	32568
Bayview	32401
Bay Vista (Dade County)	33181
Bay Vista (Pinellas County)	33712
Bayway (Part of St. Petersburg)	33715
Baywood	32140
Baywood Village	34683
Beach	32963*
	32964†
Beach Haven	32507
Beach Highlands	32459
Beach Park (Part of Tampa)	33609
	33629
For specific Beach Park Zip Codes call (813) 286-7599, or your local postmaster.	
Beachville	32071
Beachwood (Part of Jacksonville)	32246
Beacon Beach	32403
Beacon Groves	34683
Beacon Hill	32456
Beacon Hills (Part of Jacksonville)	32225
Beacon Lakes	34691
Beacon Light (Part of Lighthouse Point)	33064
Beacon Square	34691
Bealsville	33567
Bean City	33440
Bear Creek	32401
Bear Lake	32703
Bearss Plaza	33612
Beauclere Gardens (Part of Jacksonville)	32257
Beaver Creek	32531
Becker	32097
Beckhamtown	32640
Beeghly Heights (Part of Jacksonville)	32218
Bee Ridge	34233
Bel-Air (Part of Sanford)	32771
Belair Beach	32408
Bell	32619
Bellair	32073
Bellair-Meadowbrook Terrace	32073
Bellair Plaza (Part of Daytona Beach)	32118
Belleair	34616
Belleair Beach	34635
Belleair Bluffs	34640
Belleair Shore	34635
Belle Glade	33430
Belle Glade Camp	33430
Belle Isle	32809
Belleview	34420-21
For specific Belleview Zip Codes call (904) 245-8777, or your local postmaster.	
Belleview Heights	34420
Bellview	32506
	32526
For specific Bellview Zip Codes call (904) 944-5357, or your local postmaster.	
Bellwood	32780
Belvedere Homes	33409
Benbow	33440
Bennett	32466
Bent Tree Village	34241
Ben White Raceway (Part of Orlando)	32810
Beresford	32720
Berkshire Estates	34241
Berry	33868
Berrydale	32565
Bertha	32792
Bethany	34251
Bethel	32327
Bethlehem	32425
Bethune Beach	32169
Betmar Acres	33541
Betton Hills (Part of Tallahassee)	32312
Beulah (Escambia County)	32526
Beulah (Orange County)	34787
Beverly Beach	32136
Beverly Hills	34464-65
For specific Beverly Hills Zip Codes call (904) 746-3076, or your local postmaster.	
Beverly Hills (Part of Jacksonville)	32208
Beverly Terrace	34234
Bevilles Corner	33513
Big Bayou (Part of St. Petersburg)	33705*
	33739†
Big Coppitt Key	33040

	ZIP
Big Cypress Seminole Indian Reservation	33440
Big Pine Key	33043
Big Scrub	32179
Biltmore (Part of Jacksonville)	32205
Biltmore Beach	32408
Bird Key (Part of Sarasota)	34236
Biscayne Gardens	33162
	33169
For specific Biscayne Gardens Zip Codes call (305) 470-0327, or your local postmaster.	
Biscayne One (Part of Miami)	33111†
	33131*
Biscayne Park	33161
Biscayne Plaza Shopping Center (Part of Miami)	33138
Biscayne St. Thomas College	33054
Bithlo	32807
Black Creek	32439
Black Jacks	32680
Blackman	32531
Black Rock	32097
Bland	32615
Blanton	33525
Blichton	34482
Bloomingdale	33594
Blountstown	32424
Bloxham	32310
Blue Gulf Beach	32459
Blue Lake	32720
Blue Mountain Beach	32459
Blue Springs	34797
Bluff Springs	32535
Boardman	32633
Boca Del Mar	33433
Boca Grande	33921
Boca Pointe	33433
Boca Raton	33427-29
	33431-34
	33481
	33486-87
	33496-98
For specific Boca Raton Zip Codes call (407) 994-2700, or your local postmaster.	
Boca West	33434
Bogia	32568
Bokeelia	33922
Bonaventure	33326
Bonifay	32425
Bonita Beach	33923
Bonita Shores	33923
Bonita Springs	33923*
	33959†
Bonnie Loch	33064
Bookertown	32771
Bostwick	32007
Boulougne	32046
Bowden (Part of Jacksonville)	32216
Bowling Green	33834
Boyd	32347
Boyette	33547
Boynton Beach	33424-26
	33435-37
For specific Boynton Beach Zip Codes call (407) 738-5220, or your local postmaster.	
Boynton Beach Mall (Part of Boynton Beach)	33426
Boys Ranch	32060
Braden Castle (Part of Bradenton)	34208
Braden River	34201-03
	34208
For specific Braden River Zip Codes call (813) 758-6797, or your local postmaster.	
Bradenton	34201-10
	34280-82
For specific Bradenton Zip Codes call (813) 746-4195, or your local postmaster.	
Bradenton Beach	34217
Bradfordville	32312
Bradley	33835
Bradshaw Acres	34711
Brandon	33509-11
For specific Brandon Zip Codes call (813) 689-1616, or your local postmaster.	
Branford	32008
Brannonville	32401
Bratt	32535
Brent	32503

	ZIP
	32505
For specific Brent Zip Codes call (904) 433-0065, or your local postmaster.	
Brentwood (Duval County)	32206
Brentwood (Sarasota County)	34232
Bright (Part of Hialeah)	33013
Brighton	34972
Brighton Seminole Indian Reservation	33471
Briny Breezes	33435
Bristol	32321
Britton Plaza (Part of Tampa)	33611
Broadview Park	33317
Broadview-Pompano Park	33068
Broadwater (Part of St. Petersburg)	33711
Brock Crossroad	32463
Bronson	32621
Brooker	32622
Brooklyn (Part of Jacksonville)	32204
Brookridge	34613
Brooksville	34601-05
	34609-14
For specific Brooksville Zip Codes call (904) 799-4441, or your local postmaster.	
Browardale	33311
Broward Correctional Institution	33024
Broward Mall (Part of Plantation)	33388
Brownsdale	32565
Brownsville (Dade County)	33142
Brownsville (Escambia County)	32505
Browntown	32440
Brownville	33821
Bruce	32455
Bruceville	34488
Bryant	33439
Bryceville	32009
Brynwood	33912
Buccaneer Estates	33054
Buchanan	33890
Buckhead Ridge	34974
Buckhorn	32358
Buckingham	33905
Buckingham West	32601
Buena Ventura Lakes	34743
Buena Vista (Dade County)	33137
Buena Vista (Jackson County)	32460
Buena Vista (Orange County)	32830
Buena Vista (Pasco County)	34691
Buffalo	32189
Bunche Park	33054
Bunker (DeSoto County)	33821
Bunker (Walton County)	32459
Bunnell	32110
Burbank	32134
Burnett's Lake (Part of Alachua)	32615
Bushnell	33513
Butler Beach	32084
Byrneville	32535
Calhoun Correctional Institution	32424
Callahan	32011
Callaway	32404
Camellia Gardens	32809
Camelot Park (Part of Tallahassee)	32301
Cameron City	32771
Campbell	34746
Campbellton	32426
Camps Mine	34601
Campton	32567
Campville	32640
Canaan	32771
Canal Point	33438
Candler	32111
Cannon Town	32531
Canoe Creek	34990
Cantonment	32533
Cape Canaveral	32920
Cape Coral	33904
	33909-10
	33914-15
	33990-91
For specific Cape Coral Zip Codes call (813) 772-5515, or your local postmaster.	
Cape Coral Central (Part of Cape Coral)	33915
Cape Haze	33946
Capital Hills (Part of Tallahassee)	32308

	ZIP
Capitola	32311
Capps	32336
Capri Isle (Part of Treasure Island)	33706
Captiva	33924
Carleton	32640
Carl Fisher (Part of Miami Beach)	33139
Carlson	33538
Carlton Village	32159
Carol City	33055-56
For specific Carol City Zip Codes call (305) 620-0390, or your local postmaster.	
Carr	32421
Carrabelle	32322
Carrabelle Beach	32322
Carraway	32177
Carrollwood	33618*
	33688†
Carrollwood Village	33618
	33624
For specific Carrollwood Village Zip Codes call (813) 961-2962, or your local postmaster.	
Carters Corner	33823
Carver (Part of Jacksonville)	32209
Carver Manor (Part of Jacksonville)	32209
Carver Ranches	33023
Caryville	32427
Casa Bianco	32344
Casey Key	34275
Cason Inglis Acres	34449
Cassadaga	32706
Casselberry	32707-08
	32718-19
	32730
For specific Casselberry Zip Codes call (407) 339-5919, or your local postmaster.	
Cassia	32726
Causeway Isles (Part of St. Petersburg)	33707
Cedar Creek	34488
Cedar Grove	32401
	32405
For specific Cedar Grove Zip Codes call (904) 747-4840, or your local postmaster.	
Cedar Hammock	34207
Cedar Hills (Part of Jacksonville)	32210
Cedar Hills Estates (Part of Jacksonville)	32210
Cedar Key	32625
Cedar Lake Estates	34428
Cedar Point (Part of Jacksonville)	32226
Cedar Shores (Part of Ocala)	34471
Center Hill	33514
Centerville (Part of Tallahassee)	32308
	32312
For specific Centerville Zip Codes call (904) 385-0824, or your local postmaster.	
Central Florida Reception Center	32862
Central Plaza (Part of St. Petersburg)	33713
Central Shopping Plaza (Part of Miami)	33126
Century	32535
Century Village	33409
Cerrogordo	32464
Chain O'Lakes	32767
Chaires	32311
Charlotte Beach	33927
Charlotte Harbor	33980
Charlotte Park	33950
Chaseville (Part of Jacksonville)	32211
Chason	32421
Chassahowitzka	34447
Chatmar	34432
Chattahoochee	32324
Cherry Lake (Madison County)	32340
Cherry Lake (Sumter County)	32159
Chester	32097
Chestnut Hill Ranches	34482
Chiefland	32626
Chipley	32428
Chipola	32421
Chipola Terrace	32446
Choctaw	32459
Choctaw Beach	32439
Chokoloskee	33925
Christina	33813

	ZIP
Christmas	32709
Chuluota	32766
Chumuckla	32571
Cinco Bayou	32548
Cisky Park	34748
Citra	32113
Citronelle	34433
Citrus (Part of Inverness)	34450
Citrus Center	33471
Citrus Park	33624
Citrus Springs	34433
City of Sunrise	33313
	33323-24
	33338
	33345
	33351

For specific City of Sunrise Zip Codes call (305) 748-8675, or your local postmaster.

	ZIP
Clair-Mel City	33619
Clarcona	32710
Clark	32643
Clarksville	32430
Clear Springs (Okaloosa County)	32567
Clear Springs (Walton County)	32567
Clearwater	34615-30

For specific Clearwater Zip Codes call (813) 441-4511, or your local postmaster.

	ZIP
Clearwater Beach (Part of Clearwater)	34630
Clearwater Coast Guard Air Station	34622
Clearwater Mall (Part of Clearwater)	34624
Clermont	34711*
	34712†
Cleveland	33982
Cleveland Street (Part of Clearwater)	34615
Clewiston	33440
Clifton (Part of Jacksonville)	32211
Clinton Heights	33525
Cloud Lake	33406
Cluster Springs	32433
Coastland Center (Part of Naples)	33940
Cobbtown	32565
Cocoa	32922-27

For specific Cocoa Zip Codes call (407) 636-6565, or your local postmaster.

	ZIP
Cocoa Beach	32931*
	32932†
Cocoa West	32922
Coconut	33923
Coconut Creek	33063
	33066
	33073

For specific Coconut Creek Zip Codes call (305) 974-6080, or your local postmaster.

	ZIP
Coconut Grove (Part of Miami)	33133*
	33233†
Cody	32344
Colee (Part of Fort Lauderdale)	33301*
	33303†
Coleman	33521
College Park (Duval County)	32209
College Park (Marion County)	34474
College Park (Orange County)	32804
College Point	32444
Collier City (Part of Pompano Beach)	33069
Collier Manor-Cresthaven	33064
Colonial Gables	34232
Colonial Hills	34652
Colonial Manor (Part of Jacksonville)	32207
Colonial Plaza (Part of Orlando)	32803
Colonialtown (Part of Orlando)	32803
Columbia	32055
Combee Settlement	33805
Compass Lake	32420
Compass Lake Hills	32420
Conch Key	33050
Concord	32333
Concord Shopping Plaza	33165
Conner	34488
Connersville	33830
Conway	32806

	ZIP
	32812

For specific Conway Zip Codes call (407) 240-9496, or your local postmaster.

	ZIP
Cooks Hammock	32066
Cooper City	33328
Copeland	33926
Copeland Settlement	32609
Coquina Key (Part of St. Petersburg)	33705
Cora	32565
Coral Cove	34231
Coral Gables	33114
	33134
	33146

For specific Coral Gables Zip Codes call (305) 445-8842, or your local postmaster.

	ZIP
Coral Gardens	34997
Coral Ridge Shopping Plaza (Part of Fort Lauderdale)	33306*
	33339†
Coral Springs	33065
	33067
	33075-76

For specific Coral Springs Zip Codes call (305) 752-7640, or your local postmaster.

	ZIP
Coral Square (Part of Coral Springs)	33071
Coral Terrace	33144
	33156

For specific Coral Terrace Zip Codes call (305) 470-0327, or your local postmaster.

	ZIP
Coral Way Village	33155
Coralwood Mall (Part of Cape Coral)	33904
Cordova (Part of Pensacola)	32503
Cordova Lakes (Part of Bradenton)	34209
Cordova Mall (Part of Pensacola)	32504
Corkscrew	33934
Corley Island	34748
Cornwell	33857
Coronet	33566
Corry Station Naval Training Center	32511
Cortez	34215
Cortez Road (Part of Bradenton)	34210
Cottage Hill	32533
Cottondale	32431
Cotton Plant	34474
Country Club	33015
Country Club Acres	33484
Country Club Estates (Columbia County)	32055
Country Club Estates (Polk County)	33805
Country Club Manor (Part of Sanford)	32771
Country Club Trail	33436-37

For specific Country Club Trail Zip Codes call (407) 732-6689, or your local postmaster.

	ZIP
Countryside (Marion County)	34481
Countryside (Pinellas County)	34621
Countryside Mall (Part of Clearwater)	34621
Countryway	33635
Courtenay	32952
Cove (Part of Panama City)	32401
Cox	32424
Coytown (Part of Orlando)	32803
Crackertown (Part of Inglis)	34449
Crandall	32097
Crawford	32009
Crawfordville	32326†
	32327*
Crescent Beach (Sarasota County)	34242
Crescent Beach (St. Johns County)	32086
Crescent City	32112
Crescent Shores Heights	32157
Crestview	32536
Crewsville	33890
Crooked Lake Park	33853
Croom-A-Coochee	33597
Cross City	32628
Cross City Correctional Institution	32628
Cross County Mall	33409
Cross Creek	32640
Crossroads	33709-10

	ZIP
	33743

For specific Crossroads Zip Codes call (813) 343-1277, or your local postmaster.

	ZIP
Crows Bluff	32720
Crystal Beach	34681
Crystal Lake (Polk County)	33801*
	33803†
Crystal Lake (Washington County)	32409
Crystal River	34423
	34428-29

For specific Crystal River Zip Codes call (904) 795-2030, or your local postmaster.

	ZIP
Crystal Springs	33524
Cudjoe	33042
Cudjoe Key	33044
Cunningham Acres	33541
Curlew	34683
Curtis Mill	32358
Cutler	33157-58

For specific Cutler Zip Codes call (305) 233-6859, or your local postmaster.

	ZIP
Cutler Ridge	33157
	33189-90

For specific Cutler Ridge Zip Codes call (305) 233-6859, or your local postmaster.

	ZIP
Cutler Ridge Mall	33189
Cypress (Broward County)	33060
Cypress (Jackson County)	32432
Cypress Creek	33850
Cypress Gardens	33884
Cypress Lake	33919
Cypress Lake Estates	33919
Cypress Lakes	33417
Cypress Point	32131
Cypress Quarters	34972
Cypress Trace	33907
Dade City	33525*
	33526†
Dade City North	33525
Dade Correctional Institution	33034
Dadeland Mall	33156
Dalkeith	32465
Dallas	34491
Dames Point (Part of Jacksonville)	32226
Dania	33004
Danks Corner	34491
Darby	33525
Darlington	32464
Davenport	33837
Davie	33312
	33314
	33325-26
	33328-32

For specific Davie Zip Codes call (305) 474-2557, or your local postmaster.

	ZIP
Davis Islands (Part of Tampa)	33606
Day	32013
Daytona Beach	32114-29
	32198

For specific Daytona Beach Zip Codes call (904) 274-3500, or your local postmaster.

	ZIP
Daytona Beach Shores	32116
Daytona Highbridge Estates	32114
Daytona Mall (Part of Daytona Beach)	32114
Daytona Park Estates	32720
De Bary	32713
Deerfield Beach	33441-43

For specific Deerfield Beach Zip Codes call (305) 427-3600, or your local postmaster.

	ZIP
Deerfield Lakes	32011
Deerfield Mall (Part of Deerfield Beach)	33442
Deerland	32536
Deer Park	32901
Deer Point	32405
Deerwood (Part of Jacksonville)	32256
De Funiak Springs	32433
Dekle Beach	32347
De Land	32720-24

For specific De Land Zip Codes call (904) 734-7600, or your local postmaster.

	ZIP
De Land Highlands	32720
De Land Southwest	32720
De Leon Springs	32130
Delespine	32927
Dellwood (Jackson County)	32442
Dellwood (Leon County)	32303
Delray Beach	33444-47

* Area Zip Code   † Post Office Boxes

* Area Zip Code   † Post Office Boxes

	ZIP
	33128-32
	33136

For specific Flagler Zip Codes call (305) 294-2557, or your local postmaster.

	ZIP
Flagler (Monroe County) ...	33040
	33045

For specific Flagler Zip Codes call (305) 371-2911, or your local postmaster.

	ZIP
Flagler Beach	32136
Flagler Estates	32145
Flagler-Tamiami (Part of Miami).....................	33126
	33144

For specific Flagler-Tamiami Zip Codes call (305) 261-5102, or your local postmaster.

	ZIP
Flamingo	33034
Flamingo Bay	33956
Flamingo Plaza (Part of Hialeah)..................	33010
Flemington	32686
Fletcher	33612*
	33695†
Florahome	32140
Floral Bluff (Part of Jacksonville)	32211
Floral City	34436
Floral Park	33462
Florence Lake	33881
Florence Villa (Part of Winter Haven)..........	33881
	33885

For specific Florence Villa Zip Codes call (813) 293-8423, or your local postmaster.

	ZIP
Florida City	33034
Florida Correctional Institution	32663
Florida Gardens	33460
Florida International University	33199
Floridana Beach	32951
Florida Ridge	32962
Florida State Prison	32091
Florida State University (Part of Tallahassee)..........	32313
Florosa	32569
Flowersville	32567
Fluffy Landing	32439
Footman	32952
Forest City	32714
Forest Heights (Part of Tallahassee)	32303
Forest Hills (Hillsborough County).................	33612
	33682

For specific Forest Hills Zip Codes call (813) 935-8054, or your local postmaster.

	ZIP
Forest Hills (Lake County)	32720
Forest Hills (Pasco County)	34690
Forest Hills (Volusia County)	32174
Forest Island Park	33908
Forest Lakes (Pinellas County)	34677
Forest Lakes (Sarasota County)	34232
Forest Lakes Park	32179
Forest Ridge Village (Part of Fernandina Beach)	32034
Formosa (Part of Orlando)	32804
Fort Basinger.............	34972
Fort Caroline Club Estates (Part of Jacksonville)	32211
Fort Drum	34972
Fort George Island (Part of Jacksonville)............	32226
Fort Green	33834
Fort Green Springs	33834
Fort King Acres	33541
Fort Lauderdale	33301-94

For specific Fort Lauderdale Zip Codes call (305) 527-2074, or your local postmaster.

COLLEGES & UNIVERSITIES

	ZIP
Nova University............	33314

FINANCIAL INSTITUTIONS

	ZIP
NationsBank of Florida, N.A.	33301
Sun Bank/South Florida, N.A.	33301

HOSPITALS

	ZIP
Broward General Medical Center..................	33316
Florida Medical Center Hospital.................	33313
Holy Cross Hospital	33308

	ZIP
North Ridge Medical Center	33334

HOTELS/MOTELS

	ZIP
Best Western Oceanside Inn	33316
Best Western Marina Inn & Yacht Harbor	33316
Days Inn Fort Lauderdale	33312
Crown Sterling Suites	33309
Crown Sterling Suites	33316
Holiday Inn Coral Springs	33065
Holiday Inn Lauderdale-by-the-Sea	33308
Holiday Inn Ft.Lauderdale North	33309
Holiday Inn Ft.Lauderdale West	33319
Howard Johnson's	33315
Howard Johnson's Resort Hotel & Villas	33308
Howard Johnson's North	33308
Howard Johnson's Oceans Edge Resort	33304
TravelLodge-Oceanfront ...	33304

MILITARY INSTALLATIONS

	ZIP
Naval Surface Warfare Center, Fort Lauderdale	33315
Fort Lonesome	33547
Fort McCoy	32134
Fort Meade	33841
Fort Myers	33901-03
	33905-08
	33911-13
	33916-19

For specific Fort Myers Zip Codes call (813) 334-2116, or your local postmaster.

	ZIP
Fort Myers Beach	33931-32

For specific Fort Myers Beach Zip Codes call (813) 463-9151, or your local postmaster.

	ZIP
Fort Myers Shores	33905
Fort Myers Villas..........	33912
Fort Ogden	33842
Fort Pierce	34945-51
	34954
	34979-82

For specific Fort Pierce Zip Codes call (407) 461-2460, or your local postmaster.

	ZIP
Fort Pierce Beach (Part of Fort Pierce)	34949
Fort Pierce North	34946-47

For specific Fort Pierce North Zip Codes call (407) 461-8014, or your local postmaster.

	ZIP
Fort Pierce Shores	34949
Fort Pierce South	34981-82

For specific Fort Pierce South Zip Codes call (407) 461-2460, or your local postmaster.

	ZIP
Fort Taylor (Part of Key West)	33040
Fort Union	32060
Fort Walton Beach	32547-49

For specific Fort Walton Beach Zip Codes call (904) 243-2311, or your local postmaster.

	ZIP
Fort White	32038
Forty Ninth Street (Part of Gulfport)................	33707
Fountain	32438
Four Mile Village	32459
Fowler Bluff	32626
Foxcroft (Part of Tallahassee)	32308
Fox Town	33809
Francis....................	32177
Franklin Park	33916
Franklintown..............	32034
Freeport..................	32439
Frink	32430
Frontenac	32927
Frostproof................	33843
Fruit Cove	32259
Fruitland	32112
Fruitland Park	34731
Fruitville	34232
Fuller Heights	33860
Fussels Corner	33823
Gainesville	32601-14

For specific Gainesville Zip Codes call (904) 377-1912, or your local postmaster.

	ZIP
Gainesville Mall (Part of Gainesville)	32601
Galleria at Fort Lauderdale, The (Part of Fort Lauderdale)	33304

	ZIP
Galliver	32564
Galloway..................	33809
Galt City	32583
Galt Ocean Mile (Part of Fort Lauderdale)	33308
Gandy	33702
Garden City (Duval County)	32218
Garden City (Okaloosa County).................	32536
Garden Grove Estates	34609
Gardens, The (Part of Palm Beach Gardens)	33410
Gardenville	33534
Gardner...................	33890
Gaskin	32433
Gateway (Part of Fort Lauderdale)..............	33338
Gateway Center (Part of Jacksonville)............	32206
Gateway Mall (Part of St. Petersburg).............	33702*
	33742†
Gator Creek Estates	34241
Geneva	32732
Georgetown (Madison County).................	32340
Georgetown (Putnam County).................	32139
Georgiana	32952
Gibson	32333
Gibsonia	33809
Gibsonton	33534
Gifford	32960-61
	32967

For specific Gifford Zip Codes call (407) 567-5206, or your local postmaster.

	ZIP
Gilberts Mill	32428
Gillette	34221
Gilmore (Part of Jacksonville)	32211
Gladeview.................	33147
	33150

For specific Gladeview Zip Codes call (305) 836-9710, or your local postmaster.

	ZIP
Glencoe...................	32168
Glendale (Leon County)....	32303
Glendale (Walton County)	32433
Glen Oaks (Part of Sarasota)	34232
Glen Ridge................	33406
Glen Saint Mary	32040
Glenvar Heights	33143
	33155

For specific Glenvar Heights Zip Codes call (305) 661-8101, or your local postmaster.

	ZIP
Glenwood (Nassau County)	32097
Glenwood (Volusia County)	32722
Glory	32351
Glynlea Park (Part of Jacksonville)	32216
Golden Beach	33160
Golden Gate (Collier County).................	33999
Golden Gate (Martin County).................	34997
Golden Gate Estates	33964
	33999

For specific Golden Gate Estates Zip Codes call (813) 455-5425, or your local postmaster.

	ZIP
Golden Glades	33055
Golden Hills	34482
Golden Isles (Part of Hallandale)	33009
Golden Lakes	33411
Goldenrod	32733
Golden Shores	33160
Golfview	33406
Golfview Park	33853
Gomez	33455
Gonzalez..................	32560
Goodbys (Part of Jacksonville)	32257
Good Hope	32531
Goodland	33933
Gopher Ridge	32145
Gordon	32433
Gordon Chapel	32640
Gordonville	33830
Gotha	34734
Goulding	32501
Goulds....................	33170
Governor's Square Mall (Part of Tallahassee)	32301
Graceville	32440
Graham	32042
Grahamsville	34488
Grand Crossing (Part of Jacksonville)............	32209

	ZIP
Grandin	32138
Grand Island	32735
Grand Park (Part of Jacksonville)	32209
Grand Ridge	32442
Grandview	32131
Grangers Mill	32055
Grant	32949
Grassy Key	33050
Gratigny (Part of North Miami)	33168
Grayton Beach	32459
Greater Northdale	33624
Greenacres	33463
Greenbriar	32771
Green Cove Springs	32043
Greenhead	32428
Green Hills	32438
Greenland (Part of Jacksonville)	32256
	32258
For specific Greenland Zip Codes call (904) 642-2066, or your local postmaster.	
Greensboro	32330
Greenville	32331
Greenwood (Jackson County)	32443
Greenwood (Santa Rosa County)	32565
Grenelefe	33844
Gretna	32332
Griffin	33801
Gross	32097
Grove City	34224
Groveland	34736
Grove Park (Alachua County)	32640
Grove Park (Duval County)	32216
Grove Park (Polk County)	33801
Gulf Beach	32507
Gulf Beach Heights	32507
Gulf Breeze	32561-62
	32566
For specific Gulf Breeze Zip Codes call (904) 932-2662, or your local postmaster.	
Gulf City	33570
Gulf Gate East	34231
	34276
For specific Gulf Gate East Zip Codes call (813) 924-8116, or your local postmaster.	
Gulf Gate Estates	34231
Gulf Gate Mall	34231
Gulf Hammock	32639
Gulf Harbors	34652
Gulf Pines	32459
Gulfport	33707*
	33737†
Gulf Resort Beach (Part of Panama City Beach)	32407
Gulf Stream	33483
Hague	32601
Haines City	33844*
	33845†
Hainesworth	32615
Hallandale	33008†
	33009*
Hamilton (Part of Pompano Beach)	33072
Hammock	32137
Hammocks	33196
Hampton	32044
Hamptons at Boca Raton	33434
Hanson	32340
Harbinwood Estates	32303
Harbor Bluffs	34640
Harbor Oaks	32127
Harbor Shores	34748
Harbor View (Charlotte County)	33980
Harborview (Duval County)	32209
Harbour Heights	33983
Hardaway	32324
Hardeetown (Part of Chiefland)	32626
Hardin Heights	32324
Harlem	33440
Harmony Heights	34946
Harold	32563
Harshaw (Part of St. Petersburg)	33713
Hastings	32145
Hatchbend	32008
Havana	32333
Haverhill	33413
	33417
For specific Haverhill Zip Codes call (407) 697-2040, or your local postmaster.	

	ZIP
Hawthorne (Alachua County)	32640
Hawthorne (Lake County)	34748
Heathrow	32746
Hedges	32097
Heilbronn	32091
Henderson Creek	33961
Hendry Correctional Institution	33934
Heritage Estates	32960
Hernando	34442
Hernando Beach	34607
Hernando City Heights	34442
Hernando Ridge	33525
Herndon (Part of Orlando)	32803
Hero	32097
Hesperides	33853
Hialeah	33010-17
For specific Hialeah Zip Codes call (305) 888-6491, or your local postmaster.	
Hialeah Gardens	33016
Hialeah Lakes (Part of Hialeah)	33014
Hiawasee	32818
Hibernia	32043
Hibiscus	32757
Hickory Hill	32464
Hidden Lake Villas (Part of Sanford)	32773
Hidden Oaks	33173
Hidden River	34240
Highland	32058
Highland Beach	33487
Highland City	33846
Highland Lakes	34684
Highland Park (Franklin County)	32320
Highland Park (Polk County)	33853
Highland Park (Seminole County)	32771
Highlands (Part of Jacksonville)	32218
Highlands Lakes	33825
Highlands Park Estates	33852
Highland View	32456
High Point (Hernando County)	34613
High Point (Palm Beach County)	33484
Highpoint (Pinellas County)	34620
High Springs	32643
Highway Park	33852
Hiland Park (Bay County)	32405
Hildreth	32008
Hillcrest Heights	33827
Hilldale (Part of Tampa)	33614*
	33684†
Hilliard	32046
Hill N Dale	34602
Hillsboro Beach	33062*
	33072†
Hillsborough Correctional Institution	33569
Hinson	32333
Hinson Crossroads	32427
Hobe Sound	33455*
	33475†
Hog Valley	32134
Holden Heights	32805
	32839
For specific Holden Heights Zip Codes call (407) 843-6400, or your local postmaster.	
Holder	34445
Holiday	34690-91
For specific Holiday Zip Codes call (813) 942-3621, or your local postmaster.	
Holiday Harbor (Part of Jacksonville)	32224
Holiday Heights	32037
Holiday Manor	33844
Holland Crossroads	32425
Holley	32561
Holliday Hill (Part of Jacksonville)	32216
Hollister	32147
Holly Ford (Part of Jacksonville)	32218
Holly Hill	32117
Holly Hills (Part of Tallahassee)	32303
Holly Point (Part of Orange Park)	32073
Hollywood	33019-29
	33081
	33083-84
For specific Hollywood Zip Codes call (305) 527-2074, or your local postmaster.	
Hollywood Beach	32413

	ZIP
Hollywood Beach Gardens (Part of Hollywood)	33021
Hollywood Fashion Center (Part of Hollywood)	33023
Hollywood Hills (Part of Hollywood)	33021*
	33081†
Hollywood Mall (Part of Hollywood)	33021
Hollywood Seminole Indian Reservation	33024
Holmes Beach	34218
Holmes Correctional Institution	32425
Holmes Valley	32462
Holopaw	32901
Holt	32564
Homeland	33847
Homestead	33030-35
	33039
	33090-92
For specific Homestead Zip Codes call (305) 247-2641, or your local postmaster.	
Homestead Air Force Base	33039
Homestead Ridge	32308
Homosassa	34446
	34448
	34487
For specific Homosassa Zip Codes call (904) 628-2396, or your local postmaster.	
Homosassa Springs	34447
Honeyville	32465
Hooker Point (Hendry County)	33440
Hooker Point (Hillsborough County)	33605
Hopewell (Hillsborough County)	33566
Hopewell (Madison County)	32340
Horseshoe Beach	32648
Hosford	32334
Houston	32060
Howard	33176
Howard Creek	32465
Howey-in-the-Hills	34737
Hudson	34667
Hull	33821
Hunt Club	32703
Huntington	32112
Huntington Estates	32303
Huntington Woods (Part of Tallahassee)	32303
Hurlburt Field	32544
Hutchinson Island South	34949
Hyde Grove (Part of Jacksonville)	32210
Hyde Park (Duval County)	32210
Hyde Park (Hillsborough County)	33606
	33609
For specific Hyde Park Zip Codes call (813) 253-3140, or your local postmaster.	
Hyde Park (Wakulla County)	32327
Hypoluxo	33462
Iddo	32331
Immokalee	33934
Imperial Lakes	33860
Imperial Point	34644
Indialantic	32903
Indian Bluff	32466
Indian Bluff Island	34683
Indian Creek	33154
Indian Harbour Beach	32937
Indian Head Acres (Part of Tallahassee)	32301
Indian Hills (Part of Cocoa)	32922
Indian Lake Estates	33855
Indian Mound Village	32771
Indianola	32952
Indian Pass	32456
Indian River City (Part of Titusville)	32780
Indian River Correctional Institution	32968
Indian River Estates	34982
Indian River Shores	32963
Indian Rocks Beach	34635
Indian Shores	34635
Indiantown	34956
Indian Wells	34746
Indrio	34946
Inglis	34449
Inlet Beach	32413
Innerarity Point	32507
Innisbrook	34684
Interbay (Part of Tampa)	33611*
	33681†
Intercession City	33848
Interlachen	32148

* **Area Zip Code**   † **Post Office Boxes**

ZIP

Inverness 34450-53
For specific Inverness Zip Codes
call (904) 726-2757, or your local
postmaster.
Inverrary (Part of Lauderhill) 33319
Inwood (Jackson County) 32460
Inwood (Polk County) 33881
Iona 33908
Irvine 32686
Islamorada 33036
Island Estates (Part of
Clearwater) 34630
Island Grove 32654
Islandia 33131
Isleboro (Part of New
Smyrna Beach) 32168
Isle of Palms (Duval County) 32250
Isle of Palms (Pinellas
County) 33706
Isle Of Palms South (Part of
Jacksonville) 32250
Isles of Capri 33962
Isleworth 34786
Istachatta 34636
Istokpoga Shores 33857
Ivan 32327
Ives Estates 33162
Izagora 32427
Jacksonville 32201-76
For specific Jacksonville Zip
Codes call (904) 355-7311, or
your local postmaster.
Jacksonville Air Transfer
Office (Part of
Jacksonville) 32229
Jacksonville Beach .... 32240†
                          32250*
Jacksonville Heights (Part of
Jacksonville) 32210
Jacob City 32431
Jamaica Bay 33912
Jan Phyl Village 33880
Jarrott 32344
Jasmine Estates 34668
Jasper 32052
Jay 32565
Jena 32359
Jennings 32053
Jensen Beach 34957*
                          34958†
Jerome 33926
Jessamine 33525
John's Lake 34787
Johnson 32640
Johnson's Corner 32767
Jonathan's Landing 33477
Jonesville 32669
Judson 32693
Julington Forest (Part of
Jacksonville) 32258
June Park 32901
Jungle (Part of St.
Petersburg) 33710
Juniper 32330
Juno Beach 33408
Jupiter 33458
                          33468-69
                          33477-78
For specific Jupiter Zip Codes call
(407) 746-3620, or your local
postmaster.
Jupiter Inlet Beach Colony 33469
Jupiter Island 33455
Kathleen 33849
Keaton Beach 32347
Kenansville 34739
Kendale Lakes 33175
                          33183
For specific Kendale Lakes Zip
Codes call (305) 235-7511, or
your local postmaster.
Kendale Lakes Mall 33183
Kendall 33156
                          33173
                          33176
                          33256
For specific Kendall Zip Codes
call (305) 235-7511, or your local
postmaster.
Kendall Green 33064
Kendall Lakes West 33193
Kendall Town & Country ... 33183
Kendrick 34475
Kennedy Space Center 32815
Kenneth City 33709
Kensington Park 34235
Kerr City 32134
Keuka 32148
Key Biscayne 33149
Key Colony Beach 33051
Key Largo 33037
Key Largo Park 33037

ZIP

Key Largo Village 33037
Keystone Heights 32656
Keystone Islands (Part of
North Miami) 33181
Keysville 33547
Key West 33040-41
                          33045
For specific Key West Zip Codes
call (305) 294-2557, or your local
postmaster.
Key West Naval Air Station 33040
Killarney 34740
Killearn Acres 32308
Killearn Estates (Part of
Tallahassee) 32308
Killearn Lakes 32312
Kinard 32449
Kincaid Hills 32601
Kings Bay 33158
Kings Ferry 32046
Kingsley Lake 32091
Kingsley Village 32091
Kings Point 33484
Kings Road (Part of
Jacksonville) 32254
Kingswood Manor 32804
Kissimmee 34741-47
                          34758-59
For specific Kissimmee Zip Codes
call (407) 846-3121, or your local
postmaster.
Kissimmee Park 34772
Knights 33565
Korona 32110
Kossuthville 33823
Kynesville 32431
La Belle 33935
Lackawana Estates 32640
Lacoochee 33537
La Crosse 32658
Lady Lake 32158-59
La Gorce Island (Part of
Miami Beach) 33141
La Grange 32796
Laguna Beach 32413
Lake Alfred 33850
Lake Ashby Shores 32168
Lake Bird 32347
Lake Brantley 32750
Lakebreeze 32303
Lake Bryant 32179
Lake Buena Vista 32830
Lake Butler 32054
Lake Cain Hills 32805
Lake Charm (Part of
Oviedo) 32765
Lake City 32055*
                          32056†
Lake Clarke Shores 33406
Lake Como 32157
Lake Correctional Institution 34711
Lake Crescent Estates 32112
Lake Forest (Broward
County) 33023
Lake Forest (Duval County) 32208
Lake Forest Hills (Part of
Jacksonville) 32208
Lake Frances (Part of
Tavares) 32778
Lake Garfield 33830
Lake Geneva 32160
Lake Hamilton 33851
Lake Harbor 33459
Lake Harris Shores 32778
Lake Haven Estates 33872
Lake Helen 32744
Lake Jem 32745
Lake Joanna 32726
Lake Josephine 33872
Lake Kathryn Heights 32720
Lakeland 33801-13
For specific Lakeland Zip Codes
call (813) 683-6245, or your local
postmaster.
Lakeland Highlands 33813
Lakeland Mall (Part of
Lakeland) 33801
Lakeland Square (Part of
Lakeland) 33809
Lake Letta 33825
Lake Lindsey 34601
Lake Lorraine 32579
Lake Lotela 33825
Lake Lucerne 33055-56
                          33169
For specific Lake Lucerne Zip
Codes call (305) 470-0327, or
your local postmaster.
Lake Lucina (Part of
Jacksonville) 32211
Lake Mack Park 32720

ZIP

Lake Magdalene 33612-13
For specific Lake Magdalene Zip
Codes call (813) 877-0746, or
your local postmaster.
Lake Marian Highlands 34739
Lake Mary 32746*
                          32795†
Lake Mendelin Estates 32703
Lake Miona Heights 34785
Lake Monroe 32747
Lakemont 33825
Lake Mystic 32321
Lake of the Hills 33853
Lake Panasoffkee 33538
Lake Park 33403
Lake Pasadena Heights 33525
Lake Placid 33852
Lakeport 33471
Lake Sarasota 34241
Lake Saunders 32757
Lakes by the Bay 33157
                          33189-90
For specific Lakes by the Bay Zip
Codes call (305) 233-6859, or
your local postmaster.
Lake Shore (Part of
Jacksonville) 32210*
                          32238†
Lakeside 32073
Lakeside Green 33417
Lakeside Hills 32140
Lakes Mall (Part of
Lauderdale Lakes) 33319
Lake St. George 34684
Lake Wales 33853
                          33859
                          33867
For specific Lake Wales Zip
Codes call (813) 676-2531, or
your local postmaster.
Lake Weir 32179
Lake Winnott 32640
Lakewood (Duval County) 32207
Lakewood (Walton County) 32433
Lakewood Heights (Part of
Tallahassee) 32311
Lakewood Park 34951
Lakewood Village 32303
Lake Worth 33460-67
For specific Lake Worth Zip
Codes call (407) 964-1102, or
your local postmaster.
Lamont 32336
Lamplighter (Part of
Gainesville) 32609
Lam Smith Crossroads 32425
Lanark Village 32323
Land O'Lakes 34639
Lane (Part of Jacksonville) 32254
Lantana 33462*
                          33465†
Lantana Homes 33463
Largo 34640-49
For specific Largo Zip Codes call
(813) 584-2191, or your local
postmaster.
Largo Mall (Part of Largo) 34641
Larkin Fish Camp 32321
Lauderdale-by-the-Sea 33308
Lauderdale Lakes 33309
                          33311
                          33313
                          33319
For specific Lauderdale Lakes Zip
Codes call (305) 527-2077, or
your local postmaster.
Lauderhill 33313
                          33319
                          33351
For specific Lauderhill Zip Codes
call (305) 587-2450, or your local
postmaster.
Lauderhill Mall (Part of
Lauderhill) 33313
Laurel 34272
Laurel Grove (Part of
Orange Park) 32073
Laurel Hill 32567
Laurel Park (Escambia
County) 32505
Laurel Park (Orange
County) 32809
Lawtey 32058
Lazy Lagoon 33982
Lazy Lake 33305
Lealman 33714
Lebanon 34431
Lecanto 34460-61
                          34464-65
For specific Lecanto Zip Codes
call (904) 746-2424, or your local
postmaster.

---

* **Area Zip Code**   † **Post Office Boxes**

	ZIP
Lee	32059
Lee Cypress	33926
Leesburg	34748-49
	34788-89
For specific Leesburg Zip Codes call (904) 787-3679, or your local postmaster.	
Lehigh (Part of Tallahassee)	32301
Lehigh Acres	33936
	33970-71
For specific Lehigh Acres Zip Codes call (813) 369-2159, or your local postmaster.	
Leisure City	33033
Leisure Lakes	33852
Lely	33961
Lemon Bluff	32764
Lemon City (Part of Miami)	33127
	33137
For specific Lemon City Zip Codes call (305) 576-0404, or your local postmaster.	
Lemon Grove	33873
Leon (Part of Tallahassee)	32303*
	32315†
Leonards	32424
Leonia	32464
Leonton	32344
Lessie	32046
Liberty	32433
Liberty City (Part of Miami)	33142
Liberty Square (Part of Miami)	33147
Lido Key (Part of Sarasota)	34239
Lighthouse Point (Broward County)	33064*
	33074†
Lighthouse Point (Martin County)	34994
Lily	33865
Limestone (Hardee County)	33865
Limestone (Jefferson County)	32344
Limona	33510
Lincoln City	32091
Lincoln Estates (Part of Gainesville)	32601
Lincoln Road Mall (Part of Miami Beach)	33139
Linden	33597
Lindgren Acres	33186
Lisbon	34788
Lithia	33547
Little Acres	34736
Little Gasparilla	33946
Little Havana (Part of Miami)	33125
Little Hollywood	32976
Little Lake City	32619
Little River (Part of Miami)	33138*
	33238†
Little River Springs	32071
Little Torch Key	33042
Live Oak (Suwannee County)	32060
Live Oak (Washington County)	32462
Live Oak Island	32327
Lloyd	32337
Lochloosa	32662
Lochmoor	33903
Lochmoor Waterway Estates	33903
Lock Arbor (Part of Sanford)	32773
Lockhart	32810
Londonderry (Part of Orlando)	32808
Longboat Key	34228
Long Key	33001
Longwood (Okaloosa County)	32579
Longwood (Seminole County)	32750
	32752
	32779
	32791
For specific Longwood Zip Codes call (407) 682-7559, or your local postmaster.	
Lorida	33857
Lotus	32952
Loughman	33858
Lovedale	32423
Lovett	32331
Lovewood	32431
Lowell	32663
Lower Clay Landing	32626
Lower Grand Lagoon	32401
Lower Matecumbe Key	33036
Loxahatchee	33470
Lucerne Avenue (Part of Lake Worth)	33460

	ZIP
Lucerne Park (Part of Winter Haven)	33881
Ludlam (Part of Miami)	33155*
	33255†
Lullwater Beach (Part of Panama City Beach)	32407
Lulu	32061
Lumberton	33540
Lundy	32177
Luraville	32060
Lutz	33549
Lynne	34488
Lynn Haven	32444
Mabel	33514
Mabry Manor (Part of Tallahassee)	32310
McAlpin	32062
Macclenny	32063
Macclenny II	32063
MacDill Air Force Base	33608†
	33621*
McDavid	32568
Macedonia	32424
McGregor	33919
McIntosh	32664
McKinnon	32568
McLellen	32570
McMeekin	32640
Madeira Beach	33708*
	33738†
Madison	32340*
	32341†
Magnolia Beach	32408
Magnolia Gardens (Part of Jacksonville)	32209
Magnolia Springs	32043
Mainland (Part of Ormond Beach)	32174
Mainlands Center (Part of Pinellas Park)	34666
Maitland	32751
	32794
For specific Maitland Zip Codes call (407) 647-5505, or your local postmaster.	
Malabar	32950
Malone	32445
Manalapan	33462
Manasota	34260
Manasota Key	34223
Manatee (Part of Bradenton)	34208
Mandarin (Part of Jacksonville)	32223*
	32241†
Mango	33550
Mango (census designated place)	33584
Mango Hills	33584
Mangonia Park	33407
Marathon	33050
Marathon Shores	33052
Maravilla (Part of Fort Pierce)	34982
Marco	33937
	33969
For specific Marco Zip Codes call (813) 394-3621, or your local postmaster.	
Margate	33063
	33066
	33068
For specific Margate Zip Codes call (305) 974-6080, or your local postmaster.	
Marianna	32446-47
For specific Marianna Zip Codes call (904) 482-4951, or your local postmaster.	
Marietta (Part of Jacksonville)	32220
Marineland	32086
Mariner Mall	32505
Mariner Sands	34997
Marion Correctional Institution	32663
Marion Oaks	34473
Market Square Mall (Part of Jacksonville)	32207
Martel	34475
Martin	32617
Martin Correctional Institution and Work Camp	34956
Martin Downs	34990
Mary Esther	32569
Masaryktown	34609
Mascotte	34753
Matlacha	33909
Maxcy Quarters	33843
Maximo Moorings (Part of St. Petersburg)	33711

	ZIP
Maxville (Part of Jacksonville)	32234
Mayfair in the Grove (Part of Miami)	33133
Mayo	32066
Mayo Correctional Institution	32066
Mayo Junction	32066
Mayport (Part of Jacksonville)	32233*
	32267†
Mayport Naval Station	32227*
	32228†
Meadowbrook	32808
Meadowbrook Terrace	32073
Meadowlawn (Part of St. Petersburg)	33702
Meadowlea on the River	32713
Meadow Wood	32824
Mecca	32771
Medart	32327
Medley	33178
Medulla	33811
Melbourne	32901-02
	32904-10
	32934-36
	32940-41
For specific Melbourne Zip Codes call (407) 254-3433, or your local postmaster.	
Melbourne Beach	32951
Melbourne Shores	32951
Melbourne Square (Part of Melbourne)	32904
Melbourne Village	32904
Melody Hills (Part of Tallahassee)	32308
Melrose	32666
Melrose Park (Broward County)	33312
Melrose Park (Columbia County)	32055
Memphis	34221
Memphis Heights	34221
Merritt Island	32952*
	32954†
Merritt Square	32952
Metro Mall (Part of Fort Myers)	33916
Mexico Beach	32410
Miami	33101-99
	33201-99
For specific Miami Zip Codes call (305) 470-0327, or your postmaster.	

COLLEGES & UNIVERSITIES

Barry University	33161

FINANCIAL INSTITUTIONS

American Savings of Florida, F.S.B.	33169
Barnett Bank of South Florida, N.A.	33131
Capital Bank	33131
Chase Federal Bank	33156
Citizens Federal Bank	33131
City National Bank of Florida	33130
Coconut Grove Bank	33133
Continental National Bank of Miami	33135
Coral Gables Federal Savings & Loan Association	33156
County National Bank of South Florida	33137
Dadeland Bank	33156
Eagle National Bank of Miami	33132
Intercontinental Bank	33131
Northern Trust Bank of Florida, N.A.	33131
Ocean Bank	33126
Pacific National Bank	33131
Republic National Bank of Miami	33126
SafraBank, N.A.	33132
Sun Bank/Miami, N.A.	33131
Terrabank, N.A.	33145
Totalbank	33145
United National Bank	33130

HOSPITALS

Aventura Hospital & Medical Center	33175
Baptist Hospital of Miami	33176
Cedars Medical Center	33136
Golden Glades Regional Medical Center	33169
Jackson Memorial Hospital	33136
Mercy Hospital	33133

* Area Zip Code   **† Post Office Boxes**

	ZIP
North Shore Medical Center	33150
South Miami Hospital	33143
Veterans Affairs Medical Center	33125

HOTELS/MOTELS

	ZIP
Hyatt Regency Miami, Center at Riverwalk	33131
Miami Airport Hilton & Marina	33126
Radisson Mart Plaza Hotel	33126

MILITARY INSTALLATIONS

	ZIP
7th Coast Guard District, Miami	33131
Miami Beach	33109
	33119
	33139-41
For specific Miami Beach Zip Codes call (305) 672-8793, or your local postmaster.	
Miami Coast Guard Station	33054
Miami Gardens	33023
Miami Gardens-Utopia-Carver	33023
Miami Lakes	33014
Miami Shores	33138*
	33153†
Miami Springs	33166*
	33266†
Micanopy	32667
Micco (Brevard County)	32958
Micco (Brevard County)	32976
Miccosukee	32309
Miccosukee Hills (Part of Tallahassee)	32308
Miccosukee Indian Reservation	33440
Middle (Part of Lake Mary)	32799
Middleburg	32050
	32068
For specific Middleburg Zip Codes call (904) 282-5721, or your local postmaster.	
Mid Florida Lakes	34788
Mid Town Plaza (Part of Sarasota)	34239
Midway (Broward County)	33322
Midway (Gadsden County)	32343
Midway (Hillsborough County)	33565
Midway (Seminole County)	32771
Millcreek	32092
Millers Ferry	32462
Milligan	32537
Millview	32506
Millville (Part of Panama City)	32401
Milton	32570-72
	33583
For specific Milton Zip Codes call (904) 623-3807, or your local postmaster.	
Mi-Lu Estates	32159
Mims	32754
Mineral Springs	32565
Minneola	34755
Miracle City Mall (Part of Titusville)	32780
Miracle Mile (Part of Fort Myers)	33901
Miramar	33023
	33025
	33027
	33029
For specific Miramar Zip Codes call (305) 436-7200, or your local postmaster.	
Miramar Beach	32541
Miramar Terrace (Part of Jacksonville)	32207
Mission Bay	33428
Mission City	32168
Mission Hills (Part of Clearwater)	34619
Mobile Gardens	34224
Moffitt	33890
Molino	32577
Molino Crossroads	32533
Monroes Corner	34491
Montbrook	32696
Montclair	34748
Monteocha	32609
Monterey (Part of Jacksonville)	32211
Monticello	32344-45
Montverde	34756
Monument Lakes (Part of Jacksonville)	32225
Moon Lake Estates	34654
Moore Haven	33471

	ZIP
Moreland Park	34785
Morningside (Part of Miami)	33137
Morningside Park	32809
Morrison Bluff	32102
Morriston	32668
Morse Shores	33905
Mosley Hall	32331
Moss Bluff	32179
Moss Town	33537
Mossy Head	32434
Moultrie	32086
Mountain Park	34601
Mount Carmel	32565
Mount Dora	32757
Mount Pleasant	32352
Mount Plymouth	32776
Mount Royal	32193
Mulberry	33860
Munson	32570
Murat Hills (Part of Tallahassee)	32304
Murdock	33938
Murray Hill (Part of Jacksonville)	32205
	32236
	32254
For specific Murray Hill Zip Codes call (904) 781-2651, or your local postmaster.	
Myakka City	34251
Myakka Head	33865
Myakka Valley Ranchos	34241
Myrtis	32055
Myrtle Grove	32506*
	32516†
Nalcrest	33856
Naples	33939-42
	33961-64
For specific Naples Zip Codes call (813) 262-5411, or your local postmaster.	
Naples Manor	33961
Naples Park	33963
Naranja	33032-33
For specific Naranja Zip Codes call (305) 247-2641, or your local postmaster.	
Narcoossee	34771
Nash	32336
Nashua	32189
Nassau Village	32011
Nassau Village-Ratliff	32011
Nassauville	32034
National Gardens	32174
Naval Air Station	32508
Naval Coastal Systems Lab	32407
Navarre	32566
Navy Point	32507
Neptune Beach	32233
Neptune Shores	34744
New Berlin (Part of Jacksonville)	32226
Newberry	32669
Newburn	32060
New Eden	34771
New Harmony	32433
New Hope (Holmes County)	32464
New Hope (Washington County)	32462
Newmans Lake Homesites	32601
Newport (Monroe County)	33037
Newport (Wakulla County)	32327
New Port Richey	34652-56
For specific New Port Richey Zip Codes call (813) 849-4333, or your local postmaster.	
New Port Richey East	34653
New River (Part of Fort Lauderdale)	33302†
	33312*
New River Correctional Institution	32083
New Smyrna Beach	32168-70
For specific New Smyrna Beach Zip Codes call (904) 427-1377, or your local postmaster.	
New Zion	33865
Niceville	32578*
	32588†
Nichols	33863
Nobles (Part of Pensacola)	32504
	32514
For specific Nobles Zip Codes call (904) 434-9137, or your local postmaster.	
Nobleton	34661
Nocatee	33864
Nokomis	34274*
	34275†
Noma	32452
Norland	33169*
	33269†

	ZIP
Normandy (Dade County)	33141
Normandy (Duval County)	32205
Normandy Mall (Part of Jacksonville)	32254
Normandy Manor (Part of Jacksonville)	32221
Normandy Village (Part of Jacksonville)	32210
North Andrews Gardens	33309
	33334
For specific North Andrews Gardens Zip Codes call (305) 568-1323, or your local postmaster.	
North Babcock (Part of Melbourne)	32901
North Bay Village	33141
North Beach	32095
North Brooksville	34601
Northcliffe	32561
Northcrest	32703
Northdale	33624
North De Land	32720
Northeast Florida State Hospital	32063
North Florida Reception Center	32054
North Fort Myers	33903
	33917
For specific North Fort Myers Zip Codes call (813) 995-4318, or your local postmaster.	
North Jacksonville (Part of Jacksonville)	32218
	32226
For specific North Jacksonville Zip Codes call (904) 355-7311, or your local postmaster.	
North Key Largo	33037
North La Belle	33935
North Lauderdale	33068
North Meadowbrook Terrace	32073
North Miami	33161
	33168
	33261
For specific North Miami Zip Codes call (305) 470-0327, or your local postmaster.	
North Miami Beach	33160
	33162
	33179
	33181
For specific North Miami Beach Zip Codes call (305) 944-5339, or your local postmaster.	
North Naples	33963
North Oak Hill (Part of Jacksonville)	32210
North Palm Beach	33408
North Port	34287
North Redington Beach	33708
North River Shores	34994
North Sarasota	34234
North Shore (Part of Jacksonville)	32208
North Side (Part of Panama City)	32406
Northside Shopping Center	33147
Northwood (Part of West Palm Beach)	33407
Northwood Mall (Part of Tallahassee)	32303
Northwood Pines (Part of Gainesville)	32605
Northwood Plaza (Part of Clearwater)	34621
Norwood (Part of Jacksonville)	32208
Nubbin Ridge	32531
Nutall Rise	32336
Oak	34479
Oakbrook (Part of Ocala)	34470
Oak Crest (Alachua County)	32640
Oakcrest (Marion County)	34479
Oakdale	32446
Oak Forest	34436
Oak Grove (Escambia County)	32568
Oak Grove (Gadsden County)	32324
Oak Grove (Gulf County)	32456
Oak Grove (Hardee County)	33873
Oak Grove (Lake County)	32159
Oak Grove (Okaloosa County)	32531
Oak Grove (Sumter County)	33597
Oak Harbor (Part of Jacksonville)	32233
Oak Haven (Part of Jacksonville)	32211
Oak Hill	32759

* Area Zip Code   *† Post Office Boxes*

	ZIP		ZIP		ZIP

	ZIP
Paradise Heights	32703
Paradise Island (Part of Treasure Island)	33706
Paradise Palms (Part of Boca Raton)	33486
Paradise Park	34946
Paradise Point (Part of Crystal River)	34429
Park Avenue (Part of Tallahassee)	32302
Parker	32404
Parkland	33060
Parkside (Part of Tallahassee)	32303
Parmalee	34251
Parramore	32423
Parrish	34219
Pasadena Shores	33525
Pass-a-Grille Beach (Part of St. Petersburg Beach)	33706*
	33741†
Patersonville	32131
Patrick Air Force Base	32925
Paxton	32538
Peaceful Acres	34431
Peace River Shores	33982
Peach Orchard	32618
Pecan Park (Part of Jacksonville)	32218
Pedro	34491
Pelican Bay	33940
Pelican Lake	33491
Pembroke Park	33009
	33023

For specific Pembroke Park Zip Codes call (305) 457-8456, or your local postmaster.

Pembroke Pines	33019-20
	33022-29
	33084

For specific Pembroke Pines Zip Codes call (305) 432-8331, or your local postmaster.

Peniel	32177
Peninsula (Hillsborough County)	33609*
	33679†
Peninsula (Volusia County)	32118
Penney Farms	32079
Pennsuco	33010
Pensacola	32501-26
	32534
	32573-76
	32581-82
	32589-98

For specific Pensacola Zip Codes call (904) 434-9184, or your local postmaster.

Pensacola Beach	32561
Pensacola Heights (Part of Pensacola)	32503
Pensacola Naval Air Station	32508
Peppertree Bay	34231
Perdido Bay	32507
Perrine	33157*
	33257†
Perry	32347
Pettis Springs	32331
Pheasant Walk	33487
Phillip Gardens	34231
Pickettville (Part of Jacksonville)	32205
Picnic	33547
Picolata	32092
Piedmont (Leon County)	32312
Piedmont (Orange County)	32703
Pierce	33860
Pierson	32180
Pine Castle	32809
	32839

For specific Pine Castle Zip Codes call (407) 855-3010, or your local postmaster.

Pinecraft	34239*
	34278†
Pinecrest	33547
Pineda	32935
Pine Dale	33860
Pine Forest	32506
Pine Grove (Osceola County)	34771
Pine Grove (Suwannee County)	32060
Pine Hill Estates	32601
Pine Hills (Lake County)	32726
Pine Hills (Orange County)	32808
	32818

For specific Pine Hills Zip Codes call (407) 293-3274, or your local postmaster.

Pine Hills Center	32808

	ZIP
Pine Island (Calhoun County)	32424
Pine Island (Hernando County)	34607
Pine Island Center	33945
Pine Island Ridge (Broward County)	33324
Pine Island Ridge (Lee County)	33922
Pine Island Ridge Plaza (Part of Davie)	33324
Pine Lakes	32726
Pineland	33945
Pineland Gardens (Part of Jacksonville)	32216
Pine Level	33821
Pinellas Park	34664-66

For specific Pinellas Park Zip Codes call (813) 546-0007, or your local postmaster.

Pinellas Square (Part of Pinellas Park)	34665
Pine Log	32437
Pine Manor	33907
Pineola	34436
Pine Ridge	33940
Pine Ridge Country Estates	34465
Pine Run	34481
Pine Shores	34231
Pinesville	32618
Pinetta	32350
Pineville	32568
Pinewood	33168
Pinewood Park	33147
	33150

For specific Pinewood Park Zip Codes call (305) 836-9710, or your local postmaster.

Pinland	32347
Pipers Landing	34990
Pirate Harbor	33955
Pirates Wood	32097
Pittman (Holmes County)	32427
Pittman (Lake County)	32702
Placida	33946-47

For specific Placida Zip Codes call (813) 697-1511, or your local postmaster.

Placid Lakes	33852
Plantation (Broward County)	33313
	33317-18
	33322-24

For specific Plantation Zip Codes call (305) 587-2450, or your local postmaster.

Plantation (Monroe County)	33036
Plantation (Sarasota County)	34293
Plant City	33564-67

For specific Plant City Zip Codes call (813) 752-4111, or your local postmaster.

Playland Estates (Part of Hollywood)	33021
Playland Isles	33312
Pleasant Grove (Escambia County)	32507
Pleasant Grove (Hillsborough County)	33530
Pleasant Grove (Walton County)	32567
Pleasant Ridge	32433
Plummer (Part of Jacksonville)	32219
Plymouth	32768
Poinciana	33467
Poinciana Park	32962
Poinciana Place	34758-59
Poinciana Village	33942
Point Baker	32570
Point Brittany (Part of St. Petersburg)	33715
Point O' Rocks	34242
Point Washington	32454
Polk City	33868
Polk Correctional Institution	33868
Polly Town (Part of Jacksonville)	32218
Pomona Park	32181
Pompano Beach	33060-69
	33071-74

Call your local postmaster.

Pompano Beach Highlands	33064
Pompano Park	33319
Pompano Square (Part of Pompano Beach)	33062
Ponce (Part of Coral Gables)	33134
Ponce de Leon	32455
Ponce Inlet	32127
Ponte Vedra	32082
Ponte Vedra Beach	32004†
	32082*

	ZIP
Poplar Head	32425
Port Charlotte	33948-49
	33952-54
	33980-81

For specific Port Charlotte Zip Codes call (813) 625-6011, or your local postmaster.

Port Charlotte Town Center	33948
Port Everglades (Part of Fort Lauderdale)	33316
Port Hatchineha	33844
Port La Belle	33935
Portland	32439
Port Malabar (Part of Palm Bay)	32905
Port Mayaca	33438
Port Orange	32129
Port Richey	34667-74

For specific Port Richey Zip Codes call (813) 849-1233, or your local postmaster.

Port Salerno	34992
Port Sewall	34996
Port St. Joe	32456
Port St. John	32927
Port St. Lucie	34952-53
	34983-88

For specific Port St. Lucie Zip Codes call (407) 878-7088, or your local postmaster.

Port St. Lucie-River Park	34983
Port Tampa City (Part of Tampa)	33616
Pottsburg (Part of Jacksonville)	32216
	32245-46

For specific Pottsburg Zip Codes call (904) 647-2066, or your local postmaster.

Powell	34609
Pretty Bayou	32401
Princeton	33032*
	33092†
Produce (Part of Tampa)	33610*
	33680†
Progress Village	33619
Prospect	33309
Prosperity	32464
Providence (Polk County)	33809
Providence (Union County)	32054
Pumpkin Center	34797
Punta Gorda	33950-51
	33955
	33982-83

For specific Punta Gorda Zip Codes call (813) 639-3395, or your local postmaster.

Punta Gorda Isles (Part of Punta Gorda)	33950
Punta Rassa	33908
Putnam Hall	32185
Quail Heights	33157
	33170
	33187
	33189-90
	33197

For specific Quail Heights Zip Codes call (305) 233-6859, or your local postmaster.

Queens Cove	34947
Quincy	32351
	32353

For specific Quincy Zip Codes call (904) 627-8490, or your local postmaster.

Raccoon Key	33040
Raiford	32083
Rainbow Lakes (Marion County)	34431
Rainbow Lakes (Palm Beach County)	33437
Rainbow Springs	34432
Raleigh	32696
Ramblewood (Part of Sanford)	32773
Ramrod Key	33042
Ratliff	32011
Ravenna Park	32771
Recruit Training Command	32893
Red Bay	32455
Reddick	32686
Red Head	32437
Redington Beach	33708
Redington Shores	33708
Redland	33031
Red Level	34428
Regal Oaks	34744
Regal Park	34475
Regency (Part of Jacksonville)	32211
Regency Park (Part of Jacksonville)	32225

	ZIP
Regency Square (Part of Jacksonville)	32225
Resota Beach	32409
Rex	32640
Ribault Manor (Part of Jacksonville)	32208
Rice Creek	32177
Rich Bay	32333
Richey Lakes	34653
Richland	33540
Richloam	33597
Richmond Heights	33176
Richter Crossroads	32440
Ridge Harbor	33982
Ridge Manor	33525
Ridgeway	33903
Ridgewood	32065
Ridgewood Estates	34232
Ridge Wood Heights	34231
Rio	34957
Riomar (Part of Vero Beach)	32963
Riverdale (Hernando County)	33525
Riverdale (St. Johns County)	32095
River Forest (Part of Jacksonville)	32211
Riverhaven Village	34447
River Isles (Part of Bradenton)	34208
Riverland	33312
River Park	34983
River Retreats	34431
Riverside (Dade County)	33135
Riverside (Duval County)	32204
River Trails	33917
Riverview (Duval County)	32208
Riverview (Hillsborough County)	33569
Riviera Beach	33404*
	33419†
Robin Hill	32701
Robinson Heights	32667
Robinwood	32808
	32818
For specific Robinwood Zip Codes call (407) 293-3274, or your local postmaster.	
Rochelle	32601
Rock Bluff	32321
Rockdale	33157
Rock Harbor	33037
Rock Hill (Okaloosa County)	32531
Rock Hill (Walton County)	32433
Rock Hill (Washington County)	32428
Rockledge	32955*
	32956†
Rocksprings (Marion County)	34431
Rock Springs (Orange County)	32703
Rocky Creek	33615
Rocky Point	32608
Roeville	32583
Ro-Len Lake Gardens (Part of Hallandale)	33009
Rolling Acres	34602
Rolling Hills (Duval County)	32221
Rolling Hills (Marion County)	34474
Rolling Hills (Polk County)	33860
Rolling Ranches	34431
Romeo	34432
Roosevelt Mall (Part of Jacksonville)	32210
Rosedale	32324
Roseland	32957
Rosewood	32625
Rotonda	33946
Rotonda West	33946
Round Lake	32420
Royal	34785
Royal Gardens Estates	34209
Royal Palm Beach	33411
Royal Palm Village	33908
Royals Cross Roads	32464
Royal Terrace (Part of Jacksonville)	32209
Rubonia	34221
Runnymeade	32303
Ruskin	33570-71
	33573
For specific Ruskin Zip Codes call (813) 645-1820, or your local postmaster.	
Russell	32043
Rutland	33538
Sabal Palm Estates	33068
Saddlebunch Keys	33040
Saddle Creek	34241
Safety Harbor	34695

	ZIP
St. Andrews (Part of Panama City)	32401
St. Armands (Part of Sarasota)	34236
St. Augustine	32084-86
	32092
	32095
For specific St. Augustine Zip Codes call (904) 829-8716, or your local postmaster.	
St. Augustine Beach	32086
St. Augustine Shores	32086
St. Augustine South	32086
St. Catherine	33513
St. Cloud	34769-73
For specific St. Cloud Zip Codes call (407) 892-3779, or your local postmaster.	
St. George Island	32328
Saint James	32358
St. James City	33956
Saint Joe Beach	32456
St. Johns Park (Duval County)	32210
St. Johns Park (Flagler County)	32110
St. Johns River Estates (Putnam County)	32189
Saint Johns River Estates (Seminole County)	32771
Saint Josephs	32771
St. Leo	33574
St. Lucie	34946
St. Marks	32355
St. Nicholas (Part of Jacksonville)	32207
St. Petersburg	33701-84
For specific St. Petersburg Zip Codes call (813) 323-6516, or your local postmaster.	
St. Petersburg Beach	33706
	33715
	33736
For specific St. Petersburg Beach Zip Codes call (813) 367-2261, or your local postmaster.	
St. Teresa	32358
Saint Vincent de Paul Regional Seminary	33436
Salem	32356
Salt Springs	32134
Samoset	34208
Sample Square (Part of Pompano Beach)	33064
Sampson City	32091
Samsula	32168
Samsula-Spruce Creek	32168
San Antonio	33576
San Blas	32456
San Carlos Park	33912
Sandalfoot Cove	33428
Sandalwood (Part of Jacksonville)	32246
Sand Cut	33438
Sanderson	32087
Sandestin	32541
Sand Lake (Part of Orlando)	32819
	32821
	32836-37
For specific Sand Lake Zip Codes call (407) 351-9037, or your local postmaster.	
Sandlefoot Cove	33428
	33433
For specific Sandlefoot Cove Zip Codes call (407) 479-0650, or your local postmaster.	
Sandy	34251
Sandy Point	32008
Sanford	32771-73
For specific Sanford Zip Codes call (407) 322-2892, or your local postmaster.	
Sanibel	33957
San Jose (Part of Jacksonville)	32217
San Marco (Part of Jacksonville)	32207
San Mateo (Duval County)	32218
San Mateo (Putnam County)	32187
San Souci (Part of Jacksonville)	32216
San Souci Estates (Part of North Miami)	33181
San Souci Lakes	33917
Sans Souci	33982
Santa Fe	32616
Santa Monica	32413
Santa Rosa Beach	32459
Santa Rosa Mall (Part of Mary Esther)	32569
Santos	34474

	ZIP
Sarabay Acres	34229
Sarasota	34230-43
	34276-78
For specific Sarasota Zip Codes call (813) 952-9720, or your local postmaster.	
Sarasota Heights (Part of Sarasota)	34239
Sarasota Main Plaza (Part of Sarasota)	34236
Sarasota Springs	34232
Sarasota Square	34238
Saratoga	32189
Sarno Plaza (Part of Melbourne)	32935
Sasafrass Acres	32038
Satellite Beach	32937
Satsuma	32189
Saufley Field	32509
Sawdust	32351
Sawgrass	32082
Sawgrass Mills (Part of City of Sunrise)	33323
Scenic Heights (Part of Tallahassee)	32303
Scotland	32333
Scott Lake	33056
Scotts Ferry	32424
Scottsmoor	32775
Seaglades	32507
Seagrove Beach	32459
Sea Ranch Lakes	33062
Searstown Mall (Part of Titusville)	32780
Seascape	32541
Seaside	32459
Sebastian	32958
	32976-78
For specific Sebastian Zip Codes call (407) 589-4397, or your local postmaster.	
Sebastian Highlands (Part of Sebastian)	32958
Sebring	33870-72
For specific Sebring Zip Codes call (813) 382-1151, or your local postmaster.	
Sebring Country Estates	33870
Sebring Hills	33872
Sebring Hills South	33870
Sebring Ridge	33870
Sebring Shores	33870
Seffner	33584
Seminole (Okaloosa County)	32578
Seminole (Pinellas County)	34642
Seminole Heights (Part of Tampa)	33603*
	33673†
Seminole Mall (Part of Seminole)	34642
Seminole Manor (Leon County)	32310
Seminole Manor (Palm Beach County)	33460
Seminole Park	34647
Seminole Plaza (Part of Casselberry)	32707
Seven Springs	34655
Seville	32190
Sewall's Point	34996
Shadeville	32327
Shadow Run	33569
Shady	34474
Shady Grove (Jackson County)	32442
Shady Grove (Taylor County)	32357
Shalimar	32579
Shamrock	32628
Shangri La	33584
Shannon Forest (Part of Tallahassee)	32308
Shannon Woods	32607
Sharpes	32959
Shawnee	33440
Shell Point	32327
Shenandoah (Part of Miami)	33145*
	33245†
Sherman	34974
Sherwood Forest (Duval County)	32208
Sherwood Forest (Osceola County)	34746
Sherwood Park (Part of Delray Beach)	33445
Shockley Heights	32702
Shockley Hills	32702
Shore Acres (Part of St. Petersburg)	33705
Siesta Key	34242
Siesta Lago	34746
Silver Beach Heights	32784

* Area Zip Code   **† Post Office Boxes**

	ZIP
Silver Lake	34788
Silver Sands (Part of Panama City Beach)	32407
Silver Springs (Marion County)	34488-89
For specific Silver Springs Zip Codes call (904) 687-4480, or your local postmaster.	
Silver Springs (Okaloosa County)	32536
Silver Springs Shores	34472
Simmons Point	32346
Singer Island (Part of Riviera Beach)	33404
Sink Creek	32446
Sirmans	32331
Skycrest (Part of Clearwater)	34615
Sky Lake	32809
Skylake Mall	33162
Skyland Meadows	34442
Skyline Hills (Part of Lady Lake)	32159
Slavia	32765
Slones Ridge	34736
Snapper Creek	33116
	33176
	33186
	33196
For specific Snapper Creek Zip Codes call (305) 274-9050, or your local postmaster.	
Sneads	32460
Snell Isle (Part of St. Petersburg)	33705
Snow Hill	32765
Socrum	33809
Solana	33950
Sopchoppy	32358
Sorrento	32776
Sorrento Shores	34229
Sorrento Shores South	34275
South Apopka	32703
South Bay	33493
South Beach (Dade County)	33139
South Beach (Indian River County)	32963
Southboro (Part of West Palm Beach)	33405
South Bradenton	34205
South Brooksville	34601
South Clermont	34711
South Clinton Heights	33525
South Daytona	32121
Southeast Arcadia	33821
South Florida Mail Processing Center (Part of Pembroke Pines)	33082
Southgate	34239*
	34277†
South Gate Plaza (Part of Sarasota)	34239
South Gate Ridge	34233
South Jacksonville (Part of Jacksonville)	32207*
	32247†
South Merritt Estates	32952
South Miami	33143
	33155
	33243
For specific South Miami Zip Codes call (305) 661-1734, or your local postmaster.	
South Miami Heights	33157
South Mulberry	33860
South Palm Beach	33480
South Pasadena	33707
South Patrick Shores	32937
South Pine Lakes	32726
South Ponte Vedra Beach	32082
Southport (Bay County)	32409
South Port (Osceola County)	34746
South Punta Gorda Heights	33955
South Sarasota	34231
Southside (Part of Ft. Lauderdale)	33335
Southside (Part of Lakeland)	33807
	33811
	33813
For specific Southside Zip Codes call (305) 761-1194, or your local postmaster.	
Southside Estates (Part of Jacksonville)	32216
South Trail	34231
South Venice	34293
South Weeki Wachee	34606
Southwood	32809
Sparr	32192
Spring Creek	32327
Springfield (Bay County)	32401

	ZIP
Springfield (Duval County)	32206
Spring Glen (Part of Jacksonville)	32207
Springhead	33566
Spring Hill	34606-08
For specific Spring Hill Zip Codes call (904) 683-3634, or your local postmaster.	
Springhill	32071
Spring Lake (Hernando County)	34602
Spring Lake (Highlands County)	33870
Spring Oaks (Part of Altamonte Springs)	32714
Springside	32177
Springs Plaza (Part of Longwood)	32779
Spruce Creek	32119
Spuds	32033
Starke	32091
State Capitol (Part of Tallahassee)	32399
State Line	32426
Station A (Part of Daytona Beach)	32122
Station F (Part of Jacksonville)	32206
Steinhatchee	32359
Stetson University (Part of De Land)	32720
Stock Island	33040
Stuart	34994-97
For specific Stuart Zip Codes call (407) 287-2171, or your local postmaster.	
Stucky Still	34736
Sugar Loaf Shores	33044
Sugar Mill (Hillsborough County)	33624
Sugar Mill (Volusia County)	32168
Sugarmill Woods	34446
Sulphur Springs (Part of Tampa)	33604*
	33674†
Sumatra	32335
Summerbrooke (Part of Tallahassee)	32312
Summerfield (Marion County)	34491-92
For specific Summerfield Zip Codes call (904) 245-2784, or your local postmaster.	
Summerfield (Hillsborough County)	33569
Summer Haven	32086
Summerland Key	33042
Summer Place	32960
Summerport Beach	34786
Sumner	32625
Sumter Correctional Institution	33513
Sumterville	33585
Sun City	33586
Sun City Center	33571
	33573
For specific Sun City Center Zip Codes call (813) 645-5884, or your local postmaster.	
Suncoast Estates	33917
Sun Haven	34231
Suniland	33156
Sunlake	32735
Sunland Estates	32771
Sunland Gardens	34947
Sunniland (Collier County)	33934
Sunniland (Dade County)	33156
Sun 'n Lake Acres	33852
Sun 'n Lake Estates	33852
Sun 'n Lakes	33870
Sunny Breeze Harbour	33821
Sunny Hills	32428
Sunny Isles	33160
Sunnyland	34233
Sunnyside (Bay County)	32461
Sunnyside (Lake County)	34748
Sun Ray Homes	33843
Sunrise (Part of Fort Lauderdale)	33304
Sunset	33183
	33283
For specific Sunset Zip Codes call (305) 596-9156, or your local postmaster.	
Sunset Harbor	34491
Sunset Islands (Part of Miami Beach)	33140
Sunshine Mall (Part of Clearwater)	34616
Suntree	32940
Sun Valley	34337
Surf	32346

	ZIP
Surfside	33154
Suwannee	32692
Suwannee Gardens	32680
Suwannee River Park Estates	32060
Suwannee Springs	32060
Suwannee Valley	32055
Svea	32567
Sweet Gum Head	32464
Sweetwater (Dade County)	33172
	33174
For specific Sweetwater Zip Codes call (305) 477-6708, or your local postmaster.	
Sweetwater (Liberty County)	32321
Sweetwater Creek	33615
Sweetwater Oaks	32750
Switzerland	32043
Sycamore	32351
Sydney	33587
Sylvania	32462
Sylvan Shores (Highlands County)	33852
Sylvan Shores (Lake County)	32757
Taft	32824
Talisman Estates	33525
Tallahassee	32301-04
	32306-08
	32310-17
	32399
For specific Tallahassee Zip Codes call (904) 877-4189, or your local postmaster.	
Tallahassee Mall (Part of Tallahassee)	32303
Tallevast	34270
Talleyrand (Part of Jacksonville)	32206
Tamarac	33319-21
For specific Tamarac Zip Codes call (305) 722-6080, or your local postmaster.	
Tamiami (Dade County)	33175
	33182
	33184
For specific Tamiami Zip Codes call (305) 261-5102, or your local postmaster.	
Tamiami (P.O. Station)	33144

Tampa 33601-97
For specific Tampa Zip Codes call (813) 877-0717, or your local postmaster.

COLLEGES & UNIVERSITIES

Tampa College	33614
University of South Florida	33620
University of Tampa	33606

FINANCIAL INSTITUTIONS

Bank of Tampa, The	33603
Barnett Bank of Tampa, N.A.	33602
Bay Financial Savings Bank	33615
Central Bank of Tampa	33609
First Florida Bank, National Association	33602
NationsBank of Florida, N.A.	33602
Sun Bank of Tampa Bay	33602

HOSPITALS

James A. Haley Veterans Hospitals	33612
St. Joseph's Hospital	33601
Tampa General Hospital	33601
University Community Hospital	33613

HOTELS/MOTELS

Days Inn Conference Center	33602
Embassy Suites Tampa Airport	33609
Marriott, Tampa Airport	33607
Marriot Westshore Hotel	33607
Tampa Airport Hilton at Metrocenter	33607

MILITARY INSTALLATIONS

MacDill Air Force Base	33608
Marine Corps Reserve Training Center, Tampa	33611
Tampa Bay Center (Part of Tampa)	33607
Tangelo Park	32819
Tangerine	32777
Tang-O-Mar Beach	32541
Tarpon Lake Village	34685

* Area Zip Code   † Post Office Boxes

	ZIP
Tarpon Springs	34688-89
For specific Tarpon Springs Zip Codes call (813) 937-5741, or your local postmaster.	
Tarpon Woods	34685
Tarrytown	33597
Tavares	32778
Tavernier	33070
Taylor	32087
Taylor Creek	34974
Tee and Green Estates	33982
Telogia	32360
Temple Terrace	33617*
	33687†
Tenille	32356
Tequesta	33469
Terra Ceia	34250
The Forest	33908
The Fountains	33467
The Hamptons	33434
The Landings (Lee County)	33919
The Landings (Sarasota County)	34231
The Meadows (Clay County)	32065
The Meadows (Lake County)	32702
The Meadows (Sarasota County)	34235
Theressa	32091
The Vineyards	33999
Thomas City	32344
Thompson Estates	32778
Thonotosassa	33592
Three Rivers	32322
Three Rivers Estates	32038
Tice	33905
Tierra Verde	33715
Tiger Point	32561
Tildenville	34787
Timberline Estates	34461
Timber Pines	34606
Timberwood Estates	34785
Tisonia (Part of Jacksonville)	32218
Titusville	32780-83
	32796
For specific Titusville Zip Codes call (407) 267-4826, or your local postmaster.	
Tocoi	32033
Tommytown (Part of Dade City)	33525
Tomoka Estates	32174
Torchlite	34711
Torrey	33834
Town and Country Plaza	32505
Town and River Estates	33919
Town Center At Boca Raton (Part of Boca Raton)	33431
Towne Mall (Part of Plantation)	33317
Town 'n' Country (census designated place)	33614-15
	33634
For specific Town 'n' Country Zip Codes call (813) 876-9147, or your local postmaster.	
Town 'n' Country	33615*
	33685†
Town Park Estates	33165
	33174
For specific Town Park Estates Zip Codes call (305) 226-7522, or your local postmaster.	
Trailer Estates	34281
Trailer Haven (Part of Melbourne)	32901
Trapnell	33567
Treasure Island (Dade County)	33141
Treasure Island (Lake County)	34788
Treasure Island (Pinellas County)	33706
Trenton	32693
Triangle Acres	32757
Trilby	33593
Tri Par Estates	34234
Tropic	32952*
	32965†
Tropical Acres	33569
Tropical Farms	34990
Tropical Gulf Acres	33955
Tropical Shores Manor	32778
Tropic Palms (Part of Delray Beach)	33444
Tropic Vista	33469
Truckland	33908
Turkey Creek	33567
Turner River	33943

	ZIP
Turquoise Beach	32459
Tuscanooga	34736
Tuskawilla (Part of Winter Springs)	32708
Twin City Mall (Part of North Palm Beach)	33408
Two Egg	32423
Tyndall Air Force Base	32403
Tyrone Square (Part of St. Petersburg)	33710
Uleta	33164
Umatilla	32784
Union Correctional Institution	32083
Union Park	32817
	32825
For specific Union Park Zip Codes call (407) 282-1421, or your local postmaster.	
University (Part of Gainesville)	32603*
	32604†
University Mall (Broward County)	33024
University Mall (Escambia County)	32504
University Of Miami (Part of Coral Gables)	33124
University of South Florida	33620
University of Tampa (Part of Tampa)	33606
University of West Florida	32514
University Park (Duval County)	32211
University Park (Orange County)	32817
University Plaza	33612
University Square	33612
University West	33612-13
For specific University West Zip Codes call (813) 935-8054, or your local postmaster.	
Upper Grand Lagoon	32407*
	32411†
USAF Hospital	32542
Useppa Island	33924
Valdez	32713
Valkaria	32905
Valparaiso	32580
Valrico	33594
Vamo	34231
Venetia (Part of Jacksonville)	32210
Venetian Islands (Part of Miami Beach)	33139
Venetian Isles (Pinellas County)	33705
Venetian Isles (Santa Rosa County)	32561
Venetia Terrace (Part of Jacksonville)	32244
Venice	34284-93
For specific Venice Zip Codes call (813) 485-9858, or your local postmaster.	
Venice Acres	34292
Venice East	34293
Venice Gardens	34293
Venus	33960
Verdie	32009
Vermont Heights	32033
Verna	34251
Vernon	32462
Vero Beach	32960-68
For specific Vero Beach Zip Codes call (407) 567-5206, or your local postmaster.	
Vero Beach Highlands	32962
Vero Beach South	32960
	32962
	32966
	32968
For specific Vero Beach South Zip Codes call (407) 567-5206, or your local postmaster.	
Vero Lake Estates	32967
Vero Shores	32962
Vicksburg	32401
Vilano Beach	32095
Vilas	32334
Village (Part of Deerfield Beach)	33442
Village Green (Brevard County)	32955
Village Green (Manatee County)	34209
Village of Golf	33436
Village of Pine Run	32174
Villages of Oriole	33446
Villas	33912
Villa Sabine	32561
Villa Tasso	32578

	ZIP
Vina del Mar (Part of St. Petersburg Beach)	33706
Virginia Gardens	33166
Volusia	32102
Volusia Mall (Part of Daytona Beach)	32114
Wabasso	32970
Wacahoota	32667
Waccasassa Lake	32693
Wacissa	32361
Wadesboro	32308
Wahneta	33880
Wahoo	33513
Wakulla	32327
Wakulla Gardens	32327
Wakulla Springs	32305
Waldo	32694
Wallace	32571
Walnut Hill	32568
Walsingham	34644
Walton	34957
Wannee	32619
Ward Ridge	32456
Warm Mineral Springs	34287
Warrington	32507
Washington Lake Estates (Part of Jacksonville)	32218
Washington Park	33311
Washington Shores (Part of Orlando)	32805
Waters Lake	32693
Watertown	32055
Waterway Estates	33903
Wauchula	33873
Wauchula Hills	33873
Waukeenah	32344
Wausau	32463
Waverly	33877
Waverly Hills (Part of Tallahassee)	32312
Weathersfield	32714
Webster	33597
Weeki Wachee	34606
Weeki Wachee Acres	34606
Weeki Wachee Gardens	34607
Weirsdale	32195
Wekiva Springs	32750
Wekiwa Acres	32703
Welaka	32193
Welcome	33547
Wellborn	32094
Wellington	33414
Wesconnett (Part of Jacksonville)	32244
Wesley Chapel	33543-44
For specific Wesley Chapel Zip Codes call (813) 782-2013, or your local postmaster.	
Wesley Manor	32223
West Atlantic (Part of Coral Springs)	33071*
	33077†
West Bay	32413
West Bradenton	34209
Westchester	33144
	33155
	33165
	33174
For specific Westchester Zip Codes call (305) 445-8841, or your local postmaster.	
West Dade	33196
West De Land	32720
West End (Broward County)	33326
West End (Calhoun County)	32424
West End (Jackson County)	32446
Western Acres	33903
West Farm	32340
West Frostproof	33843
Westgate (Manatee County)	34205
Westgate (Palm Beach County)	33409
Westgate-Belvedere Homes	33409
West Holly Hill	32117
West Hollywood (Part of Pembroke Pines)	33023*
	33083†
West Jacksonville (Part of Jacksonville)	32205
West Kendall	33296
Westland Mall (Part of Hialeah)	33012
West Lantana (Part of Lantana)	33462
West Little River	33147
	33150
For specific West Little River Zip Codes call (305) 754-2524, or your local postmaster.	
West Melbourne	32904
West Miami	33144

* Area Zip Code   † Post Office Boxes

	ZIP
....	33155
For specific West Miami Zip Codes call (305) 385-1366, or your local postmaster.	
Weston	33326
West Palm Beach	33401-07
....	33409-20
For specific West Palm Beach Zip Codes call (407) 697-1933, or your local postmaster.	
West Palmetto Park (Part of Boca Raton)	33427
....	33486
For specific West Palmetto Park Zip Codes call (407) 844-7277, or your local postmaster.	
West Panama City Beach (Part of Panama City Beach)	32413
West Park	33614
West Pensacola	32505
Westridge	33433
West Samoset	34208
West Scenic Park	33853
West Shore Plaza (Part of Tampa)	33609
West Tampa (Part of Tampa)	33607*
....	33677†
Westview	33168
Westville	32464
Westwood (Duval County)	32244
Westwood (Orange County)	32808
Westwood Acres	34474
Westwood Lakes	33165
Wewahitchka	32465
Whiskey Creek	33919
Whispering Pines (Madison County).................	32340
Whispering Pines (Okeechobee County) ..	34972
Whispering Pines (Putnam County).................	32139
Whisper Walk	33496
White City (Gulf County) ...	32465
White City (St. Lucie County).................	34981
Whitehouse (Part of Jacksonville)	32220
White Springs (Hamilton County).................	32096
White Springs (Liberty County).................	32321
Whitfield	34243
Whitfield Estates...........	34243
Whiting Field	32570

	ZIP
Whitney	34748
Whitney Beach (Part of Longboat Key)	34228
Wilbur-By-The-Sea	32127
Wilcox	32693
Wildwood	34785
Williamsburg	32821*
....	32823†
Williams Point	32959
Willis Landing	32465
Williston	32696
Williston Highlands	32696
Willow Oak	33860
Wilson Corner	33597
Wilson Neck	32097
Wilton Manors	33305-06
....	33311
....	33334
For specific Wilton Manors Zip Codes call (305) 527-2077, or your local postmaster.	
Wimauma	33598
Windermere	34786
Winding Lakes	33428
Windsor	32601
Winfield	32055
Winston (census designated place)	33801
....	33803
For specific Winston Zip Codes call (813) 688-5572, or your local postmaster.	
Winston	33803
Winter Beach.............	32971
Winter Garden............	34777†
....	34787*
Winter Haven	33880-85
For specific Winter Haven Zip Codes call (813) 294-4157, or your local postmaster.	
Winter Haven Mall (Part of Winter Haven)..........	33880
Winter Park	32789-90
....	32792-93
For specific Winter Park Zip Codes call (407) 647-3621, or your local postmaster.	
Winter Park Estates........	32792
Winter Park Mall (Part of Winter Park)	32789
Winter Springs	32708*
....	32719†
Wiscon	34609
Woodland (Part of Boca Raton)	33431*

	ZIP
....	33481†
Woodland Drives (Part of Tallahassee)	32301
Woodlawn (Bay County) ...	32407
Woodlawn (Pinellas County)	33704
Woodlawn (St. Johns County).................	32095
Woodlawn Beach	32561
Wood Memorial Hospital ...	33821
Woodmont (Part of Tamarac)	33321
Woods	32321
Woods and Lakes	32179
Woodville	32362
Woodward Avenue (Part of Tallahassee)	32304*
....	32316†
Worthington Springs	32697
Wright	32547
Wulfert (Part of Sanibel)....	33957
Wynnehaven Beach	32569
Wynwood (Dade County)	33127
Wynwood (Seminole County).................	32771
Yacht Club Colony	33917
Yalaha	34797
Yankeetown	34498
Ybor City (Part of Tampa)	33605*
....	33675†
Yeehaw Junction	34972
Yellow Pine	32340
Yelvington................	32131
York	34474
Youmans	33566
Youngstown	32466
Yukon (Part of Jacksonville)	32244
Yulee	32097
Yulee Heights	32097
Yulee Woods	32097
Zellwood	32798
Zephyrhills	33539-44
For specific Zephyrhills Zip Codes call (813) 782-2013, or your local postmaster.	
Zephyrhills Correctional Institution	33539
Zephyrhills North	33540
Zephyrhills South	33540-41
For specific Zephyrhills South Zip Codes call (813) 782-2013, or your local postmaster.	
Zephyrhills West............	33541
Zolfo Springs	33890
Zuber	34475

	ZIP
Aaron	30450
Abac	31794
Abba	31750
Abbeville	31001
Abbott	30207
Abbottsford	30240
Aberdeen (Part of Peachtree City)	30269
Acree	31791
Acworth	30101*
	30102†
	30103
Adairsville	30103
Adams Park (Fulton County)	30311
Adams Park (Twiggs County)	31020
Adamsville (Part of Atlanta)	30331
Adasburg	30673
Adel	31620
Adgateville	31038
Adrian	31002
Agnes	30817
Agnes Scott College (Part of Decatur)	30030
Agricola	30820
Ailey	30410
Air Line	30516
Airport Mail Facility (Part of Atlanta)	30320
Akin	30415
Alamo	30411
Alapaha	31622
Albany	31701-07
For specific Albany Zip Codes call (404) 883-7600, or your local postmaster.	
Albion Acres	30906
Alcovy	30209
Alcovy Shores	31064
Aldora	30204
Alexander	30456
Alfords	31791
Aline	30420
Allendale (Gwinnett County)	30245
Allendale (Muscogee County)	31909
Allenhurst	31301
Allentown	31003
Allenville	31639
Allenwood	31061
Allie	30222
Alma	31510
Almon	30209
Almond Park (Part of Atlanta)	30318
Alpharetta	30201-02
	30239
For specific Alpharetta Zip Codes call (404) 475-7235, or your local postmaster.	
Alpine	30731
Alps Road (Part of Athens)	30604
Alston	30412
Altamaha	30453
Alta Vista (Part of Columbus)	31907
Altman	30467
Alto	30510
Alto Park	30165
Alvaton	30218
Amboy	31714
Ambrose	31512
Americus	31709
Amity	30817
Amos Mill	35967
Amsterdam	31734
Anderson City	31744
Andersonville	31711
Andrew Wood (Part of Columbus)	31903
Anguilla	31525
Ansley	30828
Ansley Estates	30274
Anthony Terrace (Part of Macon)	31206
Antioch (Polk County)	30125
Antioch (Troup County)	30240
Aonia	30673
Apalachee	30650
Apple Valley	30529
Appling	30802
Arabi	31712
Aragon	30104
Aragon Park	30901
Arcade	30549
Arch City	30701
Arco	31520
Arcola	30415
Ardick	31331
Ardmore	31329
Ardsley Park (Part of Savannah)	31405
Argyle	31623

	ZIP
Arkwright	31204
Arlington	31713
Arlington Park (Part of Macon)	31204
Armstrong State College	31406
Armuchee	30105
Arnco Mills	30263
Arnoldsville	30619
Arp	31783
Arrowhead Village	30236
Ascalon	30738
Ashburn	31714
Ashford Park	30319
Ashintilly	31331
Ashland	30521
Athens	30601-13
For specific Athens Zip Codes call (404) 613-2195, or your local postmaster.	
Atkinson	31543
Atlanta	30301-94
	31119-56
For specific Atlanta Zip Codes call (404) 765-7261, or your local postmaster.	

COLLEGES & UNIVERSITIES

	ZIP
Clark Atlanta University	30314
Emory University	30322
Georgia Institute of Technology	30332
Georgia State University	30303
Morris Brown College	30314
Oglethorpe University	30319
Spelman College	30314

FINANCIAL INSTITUTIONS

	ZIP
Bank South, National Association	30303
Citizens Trust Bank	30303
First Union National Bank of Georgia	30303
Georgia Federal Bank, F.S.B.	30303
The Prudential Bank and Trust Company	30328
Southern Federal Savings Association of Georgia	30308
SouthTrust Bank of Georgia, N.A.	30303
Trust Company Bank	30303
Wachovia Bank of Georgia, National Association	30303

HOSPITALS

	ZIP
Crawford Long Hospital of Emory University	30365
Emory University Hospital	30322
Georgia Baptist Medical Center	30312
Grady Memorial Hospital	30335
HCA West Paces Ferry Hospital	30327
Northside Hospital	30342
Piedmont Hospital	30309
Saint Joseph's Hospital of Atlanta	30342

HOTELS/MOTELS

	ZIP
The Atlanta Hilton & Towers	30303
Holiday Inn Buckhead	30026
Lanier Plaza Hotel & CC	30324
Marriott Perimeter Center	30346
Omni Hotel at CNN Center	30335
Ramada Hotel & Conference Center	30338
The Ritz-Carlton Atlanta	30303
Sheraton Inn Atlanta Airport	30344
Westin Peachtree Plaza	30303

MILITARY INSTALLATIONS

	ZIP
United States Army Engineer Division, South Atlantic Division	30335
United States Property and Fiscal Office for Georgia	30316
Atlanta Naval Air Station	30060
Attapulgus	31715
Attapulgus Station	31715
Attica	30607
Auburn	30203
Audubon	30735
Augusta	30901-19
For specific Augusta Zip Codes call (404) 724-7436, or your local postmaster.	
Aumond Heights	30909
Aumond Place	30909
Auraria	30534
Austell	30001

	ZIP
Autreyville	31768
Autumn Forest	30236
Avallon	30328
Avalon (Chatham County)	31419
Avalon (Stephens County)	30557
Avans	30752
Avants	30411
Avera	30803
Avert Acres	31705
Avery	30115
Avondale (Bibb County)	31206
Avondale (McDuffie County)	30814
Avondale (Muscogee County)	31903
Avondale Estates	30002
Avondale Heights (Part of Columbus)	31903
Avondale Park (Part of Savannah)	31404
Axson	31624
Ayersville	30577
Azalea Park (Part of Macon)	31204
Babcock	31737
Bachlott	31553
Baconton	31716
Bainbridge	31717
Bairdstown	30669
Baker Village (Part of Columbus)	31903
Baldwin	30511
Baldwin Park (Part of Savannah)	31401
Baldwinville	31812
Ball Ground (Cherokee County)	30107
Ball Ground (Murray County)	30705
Baltimore (Part of Washington)	30673
Banning	30185
Bannockburn	31639
Barksdale	31082
Barnesville	30204
Barnett	30821
Barnett Shoals	30605
Barney	31625
Barneyville	31647
Barnhill	30457
Barnsley	30145
Barrett Parkway (Part of Kennesaw)	30144
Barretts	31602
Barrettsville	30534
Barrow Heights	30680
Bartletts Ferry	31808
Barton Village	30906
Bartonwoods	30307
Bartow	30413
Barwick	31720
Bascom	30467
Bass Crossroads	30230
Batesville	30523
Bath	30805
Battery Point	31404
Battle Forest (Part of Decatur)	30034
Baughs Crossroads	31833
Baxley	31513
Bay	31756
Bay Branch	30467
Bayview	31316
Beach	31554
Beachton	31792
Beacon Heights	30650
Beallwood (Part of Columbus)	31904
Beaulieu	31406
Beaumount	30736
Beaverdale	30721
Bedingfield (Part of Macon)	31206
Beechwood Shopping Center (Part of Athens)	30606
Belair	30907
Belair Hills Estates	30909
Belfast	31324
Beliemeade	30906
Bellton (Part of Lula)	30554
Bellville	30414
Bellville Bluff	31331
Belmont (DeKalb County)	30086
Belmont (Hall County)	30507
Belmont Hills Shopping Center (Part of Smyrna)	30080
Belvedere	30032
Belvedere Park	30032
Belvedere Plaza	30032
Belvins Acres	30736
Bemiss	31602
Benedict	30125
Benevolence	31740
Ben Hill (Part of Atlanta)	30331

* Area Zip Code   † Post Office Boxes

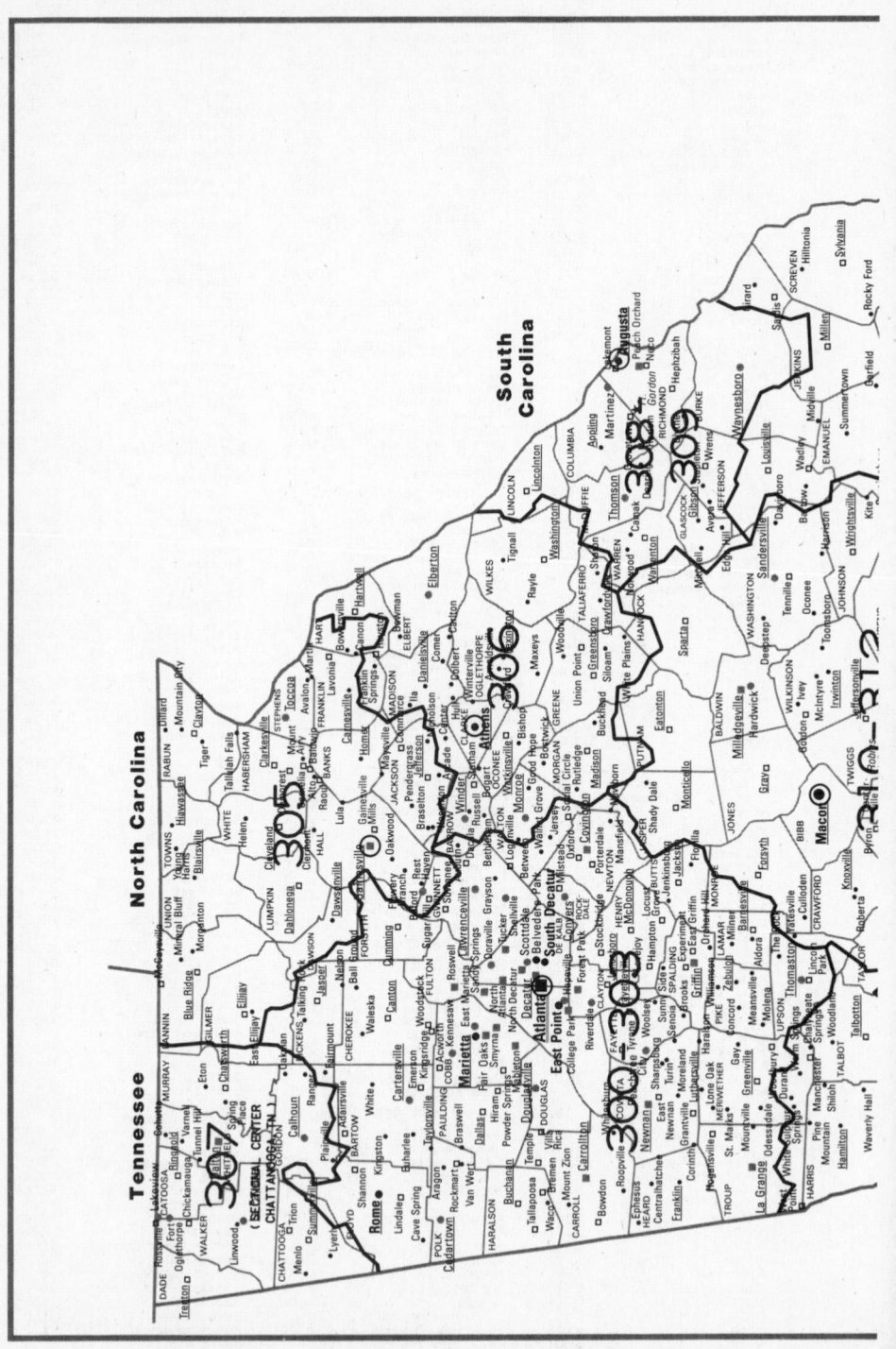

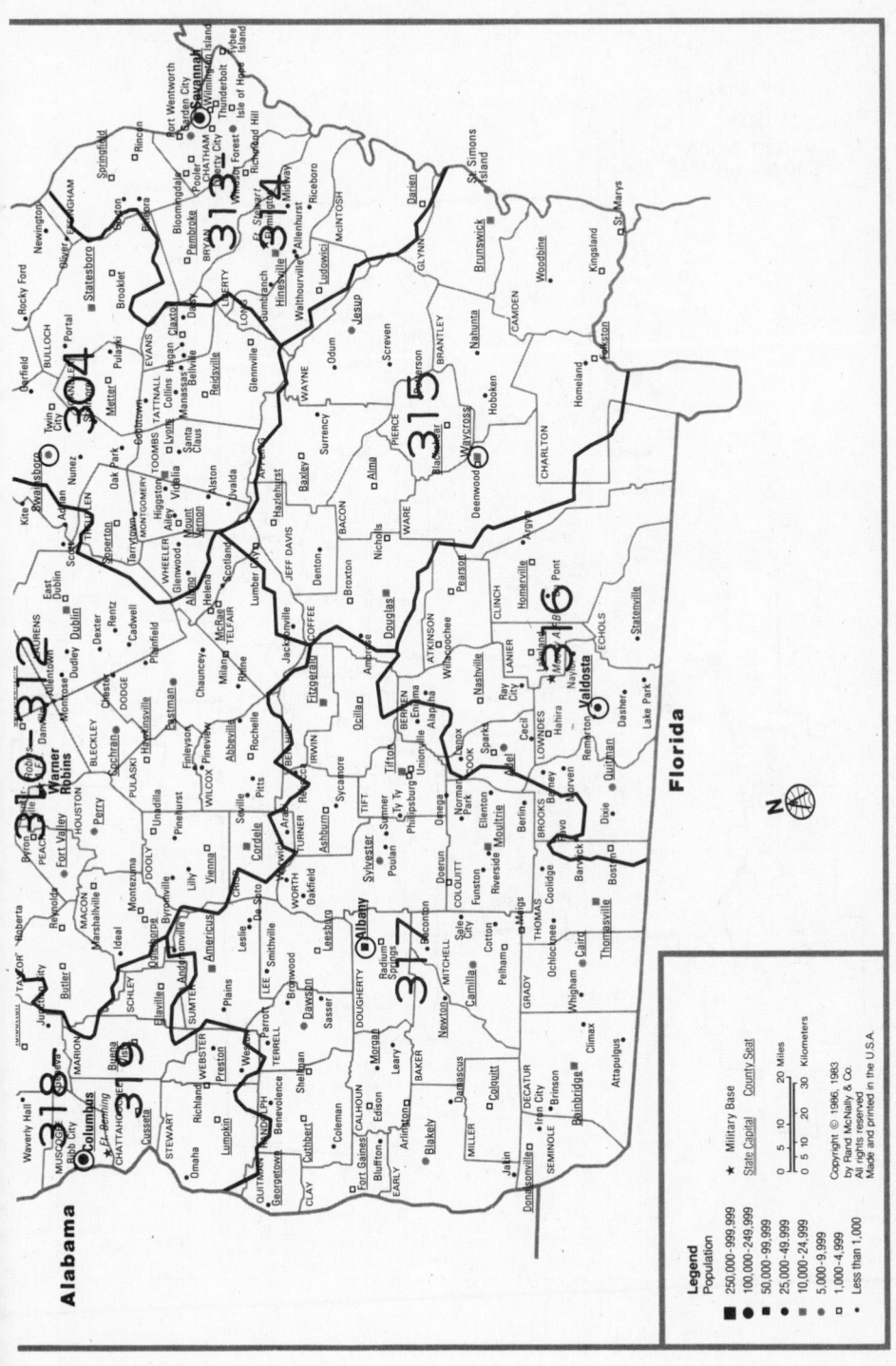

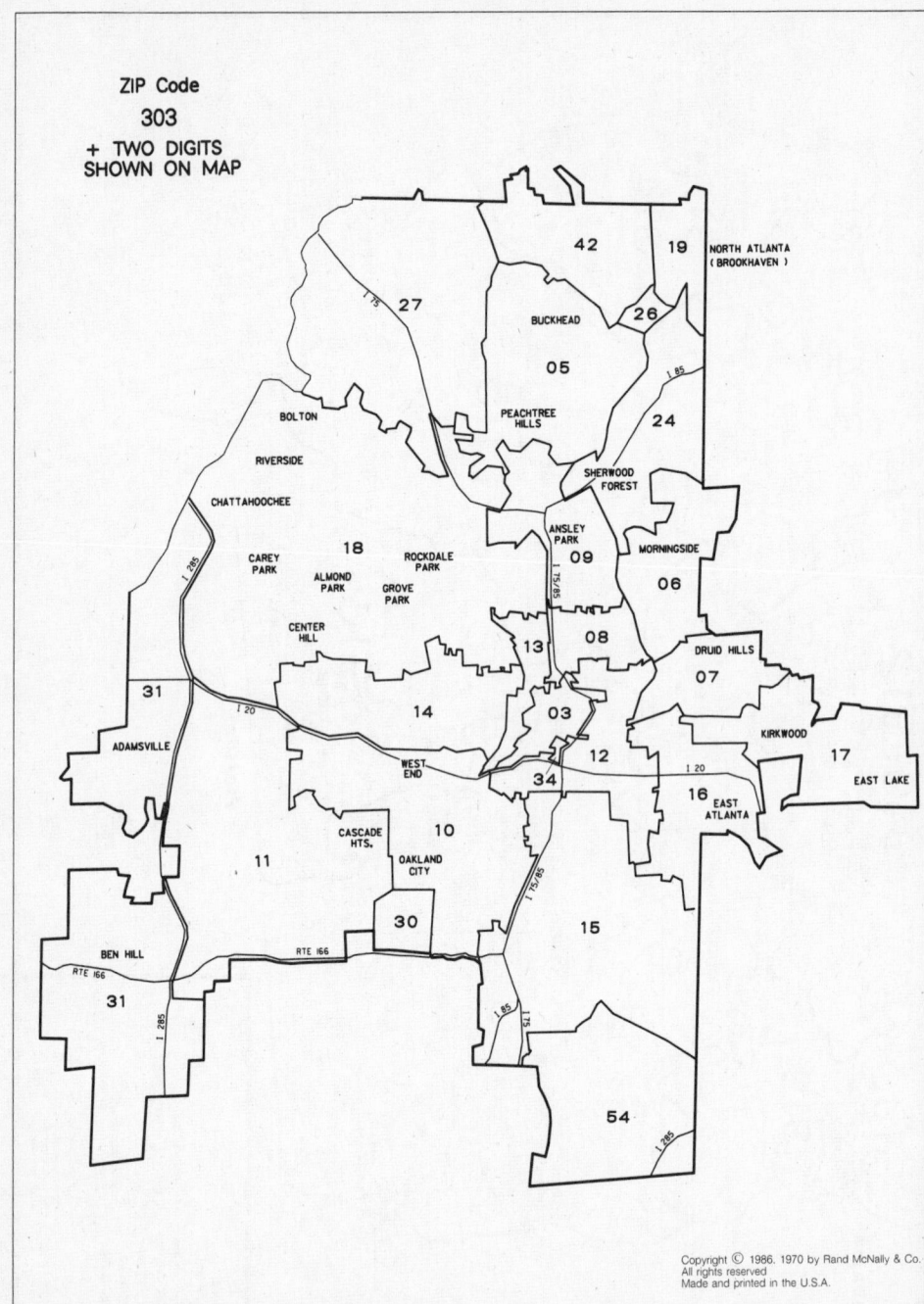

ZIP Code
303
+ TWO DIGITS
SHOWN ON MAP

42

19   NORTH ATLANTA
     (BROOKHAVEN)

27   BUCKHEAD   26

     05

PEACHTREE
HILLS   24

BOLTON

RIVERSIDE   SHERWOOD
                FOREST

CHATTAHOOCHEE

              ANSLEY
              PARK
18   09   MORNINGSIDE
CAREY   ROCKDALE
PARK   PARK   06
    ALMOND
    PARK GROVE
         PARK

CENTER   DRUID HILLS
HILL   13   08   07

31   03   KIRKWOOD
         14   17
ADAMSVILLE   EAST LAKE
         WEST   12
         END   34   16   EAST
                           ATLANTA
    CASCADE 10
    HTS.
         OAKLAND
    11   CITY

         30   15

BEN HILL
         RTE 166
31

              54

	ZIP
....	31131
For specific Ben Hill Zip Codes call (912) 423-7929, or your local postmaster.	
Benning Hills (Part of Columbus)	31903
Bentley Place	30741
Benton	30165
Bent Tree	30143
Berckman Hills	30909
Berckman Village	30909
Berkeley Lake	30136
Berkshire Woods (Part of Savannah)	31419
Berlin	31722
Berner	31029
Berryton	30747
Berzelia	30814
Bethany	31762
Bethel (Jasper County)	31064
Bethel (Randolph County)	31740
Bethesda (Chatham County)	31406
Bethesda (Greene County)	30669
Bethesda (Gwinnett County)	30245
Bethlehem	30620
Between	30655
Beulah (Hancock County)	31087
Beulah (Lincoln County)	30668
Beulah (Paulding County)	30153
Beulah Heights (Part of Atlanta)	30312
Beverly Hills	30741
Bexton	30259
Bibb City	31904
Bibb Mills	31029
Bickley	31554
Big Canoe	30143
Big Creek	30131
Big Springs	30240
Billarp	30187
Bingville (Part of Savannah)	31405
Birdie	30223
Birmingham	30201
Bishop	30621
Blackjack	30276
Blackshear	31516
Blackshear Place	30507
Blacksville	30253
Blackville	30457
Blackwells	30066
Blackwood	30701
Blaine	30175
Blairsville	30512
Blair Village (Part of Atlanta)	30354
Blakely	31723
Blandford	31326
Bland Villa	31015
Blandy (Part of Milledgeville)	31061
Blitchton	31308
Bloomfield Gardens (Part of Macon)	31206
Bloomingdale	31302
Blount	31029
Blowing Springs	30725
Blue Ridge	30513
Blue Spring	30736
Blue Springs (Dougherty County)	31707
Blue Springs (Screven County)	30446
Bluffton	31724
Blun	30401
Blundale	30401
Blythe	30805
Bogart	30622
Bold Spring	30655
Bolingbroke	31004
Bolton (Part of Atlanta)	30318
Bona Bella	31406
Bonair	30907
Bonaire	31005
Bonanza	30236
Bond	30633
Boneville	30806
Booker Washington Heights (Part of Columbus)	31909
Boozeville	30147
Boston	31626
Bostwick	30623
Bowden Hills (Part of Macon)	31201
Bowdon	30108
Bowdon Junction	30109
Bowens Mill	31750
Bowersville	30516
Bowman	30624
Box Spring	31801
Boyd Highlands	30736
Boydville	30577
Boykin	31737
Boynton	30736
Boys Estate	31523

	ZIP
Bradley	31032
Branchville	31730
Brantley	31803
Braselton	30517
Braswell	30153
Bremen	30110
Brent	31029
Brentwood (Dougherty County)	31707
Brentwood (Wayne County)	31555
Brest	31716
Brewton	31021
Briarcliff (Part of Atlanta)	30329
Briarwood (Chatham County)	31408
Briarwood (Columbia County)	30907
Briarwood (Fulton County)	30344
Briarwood (Rockdale County)	30207
Briar Wood Estates	30068
Brick Store	30279
Bridgeboro	31705
Bridgeman Heights	31201
Brighton	31794
Brighton Woods (Part of Pooler)	31322
Brinson	31725
Brisbon	31324
Bristol	31518
Bristol Forest (Part of Macon)	31201
Bristol Woods	30208
Broad	30668
Broadhurst	31545
Broadview (Part of Atlanta)	30324
Brockton	30549
Bronco	30728
Bronwood	31726
Brookfield	31727
Brookfield West	30907
Brookhaven (Bibb County)	31206
Brookhaven (Muscogee County)	31906
Brooklet	30415
Brooklyn	31825
Brooks	30205
Brookstone (Cobb County)	30101
Brookstone (Muscogee County)	31904
Brookstore Place	30342
Brooksville	31740
Brookton	30506
Brookvale Estates	30736
Brookview	31406
Brookwood (Forsyth County)	30202
Brookwood (Laurens County)	31021
Brookwood (Richmond County)	30909
Browndale	31036
Browns (Baldwin County)	31061
Browns (Dade County)	30752
Brownsville	30133
Browntown	31543
Brownwood	30650
Broxton	31519
Brunswick	31520-21 31523-25
For specific Brunswick Zip Codes call (912) 265-6186, or your local postmaster.	
Brynwood	30909
Buchanan	30113
Buckhead (Fulton County)	30339
Buckhead (Morgan County)	30625
Bucktown	30108
Budapest	30176
Buena Vista	31803
Buffington	30114
Buford	30518
Bullard	31020
Bulloch Crossroads	31816
Bumphead	31806
Bunker Hill	30512
Burning Bush	30736
Burnside	31406
Burnside Island	31406
Burroughs	31405
Burwell	30117
Bushnell	31533
Butler (Dougherty County)	31705
Butler (Taylor County)	31006
Butler Manor	30905
Butts	30442
Byers Crossroads	30185
Byne Crossroads	31763
Byromville	31007
Byron	31008
Cabaniss	31029
Cadley	30821

	ZIP
Cadwell	31009
Cagle	30143
Cairo	31728
Caleb	30058
Calhoun	30701-03
For specific Calhoun Zip Codes call (706) 629-3053, or your local postmaster.	
Callaway	30660
Calvary	31729
Camak	30807
Camellia Terrace (Part of Savannah)	31404
Camelot (Clarke County)	30606
Camelot (Clayton County)	30236
Cameron	30467
Camilla	31730
Campania	30814
Campbellton	30213
Campton	30655
Campus (Part of Athens)	30605
Canal Lake	30512
Candler	30507
Candler-McAfee	30032
Cannon Crossing	30742
Cannon Gate	30907
Cannonville	30240
Canon	30520
Canoochee	30471
Canton	30114-15
Canton Plaza (Part of Marietta)	30066
Capel	31728
Capitol Hill (Part of Atlanta)	30334
Captola	30467
Carbondale	30721
Carey Park (Part of Atlanta)	30318
Carl	30203
Carlton	30627
Carmichael Crossroads	30115
Carnegie	31740
Carnes Creek	30577
Carnesville	30521
Carnigan	31319
Carns Mill	30175
Caroline Park (Part of Columbus)	31904
Carrollton	30116-18
For specific Carrollton Zip Codes call (404) 834-4491, or your local postmaster.	
Carrs	31087
Carsonville	31006
Cartecay	30540
Carter Acres (Part of Columbus)	31903
Carters	30705
Carters Grove	30660
Cartersville	30120
Carver Heights (Part of Columbus)	31906
Carver Village (Part of Savannah)	31401
Cary	31014
Cascade Heights (Part of Atlanta)	30311
Cascade Hills (Part of Columbus)	31904
Cash	30701
Cassandra	30707
Cassville	30123
Castle Park (Part of Valdosta)	31604
Castlewood (Part of Columbus)	31907
Cataula	31804
Catlett	30728
Cave Spring	30124
Cecil	31627
Cedar Creek	30274
Cedar Creek Park	30605
Cedar Crossing	30436
Cedar Grove (Chatham County)	31419
Cedar Grove (DeKalb County)	30027
Cedar Grove (Fulton County)	30213
Cedar Grove (Laurens County)	31021
Cedar Grove (Walker County)	30707
Cedar Hammock	31406
Cedar Hills (Part of Columbus)	31907
Cedar Point	31332
Cedar Springs	31732
Cedartown	30125
Celeste	30673
Cenchat	30707
Centennial	30663

* Area Zip Code   † Post Office Boxes

	ZIP
Center (Bartow County)	30120
Center (Jackson County)	30601
Center (Toombs County)	30474
Center Hill (Colquitt County)	31768
Center Hill (Fulton County)	30318
Center Point	30179
Centerpost	30728
Centerville (Elbert County)	30635
Centerville (Gwinnett County)	30058
Centerville (Houston County)	31028
Centerville (Talbot County)	31812
Central City (Part of Atlanta)	30303
Central City Retail (Part of Atlanta)	30302
Centralhatchee	30217
Central Junction (Part of Garden City)	31408
Century	31763
Chalybeate Springs	31816
Chamberlain	30728
Chamblee	30341
Chambliss	31709
Chapel Hill	30134
Chappel	30257
Charing	31058
Charles (Stewart County)	31815
Charles (Toombs County)	30474
Charleston South	30906
Charlotteville	30473
Charter Oaks (Part of Columbus)	31909
Chaservile	31647
Chastain	31738
Chatham City (Part of Garden City)	31408
Chatham Villa (Part of Garden City)	31408
Chatsworth	30705
Chattahoochee (Part of Atlanta)	30318
Chattahoochee Plantation	30067
Chattanooga Valley	30725
Chatterton	31554
Chattoogaville	30730
Chauncey	31011
Checkero	30525
Chelsea	30731
Chennault	30668
Cherokee (Part of Macon)	31204
Cherokee Forest	30188
Cherrylog	30522
Cheshire Bridge (Part of Atlanta)	30324
Chestatee	30130
Chester	31012
Chestnutflat	30728
Chestnut Mountain	30502
Chickamauga	30707
Chickasawhatchee	31742
Chicopee	30507
China Hill	31077
Chippewa Terrace (Part of Savannah)	31406
Choestoe	30512
Chubbtown	30124
Chula	31733
Cinderella Hills	30736
Cisco	30708
Civic Center (Part of Atlanta)	30308
Clarkdale	30020
Clarke Dale	30605
Clarkesville	30523
Clarksboro	30607
Clarkston	30021
Clarkview (Part of Macon)	31204
Claxton	30417
Clayfields	31054
Clayton	30525
Clearview (Part of Savannah)	31401
Clem	30116
Clermont	30527
Cleveland	30528
Cliftondale	30337
Climax	31734
Clinchfield	31013
Clinton	31032
Cloudland	30731
Cloverdale	30738
Clubview Heights (Part of Columbus)	31906
Clyattville	31601
Clyo	31303
Coal Mountain	30130
Coastal Correctional Institution	31408
Cobb	31735
Cobb Centre Mall (Part of Smyrna)	30080

	ZIP
Cobbtown	30420
Cochran	31014
Coffee	31551
Coffee Bluff Plantation (Part of Savannah)	31419
Cogdell	31634
Cohutta	30710
Cohutta Springs	30711
Colbert	30628
Cole City	30752
Coleman	31736
Colemans Lake	30441
Colesburg	31569
College (Part of Fort Valley)	31030
College Heights (Dougherty County)	31705
College Heights (Muscogee County)	31906
College Park	30337
Collins	30421
Collinsville	30058
Colomokee	31723
Colonial Oaks (Part of Savannah)	31419
Colonial Place	31705
Colonial Village (Part of Savannah)	31406
Colony Park	30909
Colquitt	31737
Columbia Heights	30907
Columbus	31901-09
For specific Columbus Zip Codes call (404) 563-0100, or your local postmaster.	
Columbus Heights (Part of Macon)	31204
Columbus Square (Part of Columbus)	31906
Colwell	30541
Comer	30629
Commerce	30529
Concord (Jasper County)	31064
Concord (Pike County)	30206
Concord (Schley County)	31806
Concord (Sumter County)	31709
Coney	31015
Conley	30027
Constitution	30316
Conyers	30207-08
For specific Conyers Zip Codes call (404) 483-8378, or your local postmaster.	
Cooksville	30230
Cooktown	31737
Coolidge	31738
Cool Spring	31771
Cooper Creek Park (Part of Columbus)	31907
Cooper Heights	30707
Coopers	31031
Coosa	30165
Copeland	31077
Cordele	31015
Corinth	30230
Cornelia	30531
Cotton	31739
Cotton Hill	31767
Council	31631
Country Club Estates	31520
Country Club Hills (Part of Augusta)	30904
Country Park	30906
Country Place	30809
Country Side (Part of Savannah)	31406
County Line (Barrow County)	30680
County Line (DeKalb County)	30032
Court Square (Part of Dublin)	31021
Covena	30401
Coverdale	31714
Covington	30209
Covington Mills (Part of Covington)	30209
Cox	31331
Coxs Crossing	30321
Crabapple	30201
Crandall	30711
Craneeater	30701
Cravey	31060
Crawford	30630
Crawfordville	30631
Crescent	31304
Crest	30286
Cresthill	31406
Crest Hill Gardens (Part of Savannah)	31406
Crestview	31713
Crestwell Heights	31204
Crosland	31771

	ZIP
Cross Keys (Part of Macon)	31201
Crossroads (Hart County)	30516
Crossroads (Liberty County)	31323
Crossroads at Stewart Lakewood, The (Part of Atlanta)	30315
Cruse	30245
Crystal Springs (Bibb County)	31201
Crystal Springs (Floyd County)	30105
Crystal Valley (Part of Columbus)	31907
Culloden	31016
Culverton	31087
Cumberland	30339
Cumming	30130*
	30131†
Curryville	30701
Curtis	30513
Cusseta	31805
Custer Terrace (Part of Columbus)	31905
Cuthbert	31740
Cypress Mills	31520
Dacula	30211
Daffin Heights (Part of Savannah)	31404
Dahlonega	30533
Daisy	30423
Dakota	31714
Dallas	30132
Dallas Heights	30906
Dallondale	30741
Dalton	30719-22
For specific Dalton Zip Codes call (404) 278-7450, or your local postmaster.	
Damascus (Early County)	31741
Damascus (Gordon County)	30701
Dames Ferry	31046
Danburg	30668
Daniel	31324
Daniel Springs	30669
Danielsville	30633
Danville	31017
Darien	31305
Dasher	31601
Davisboro	31018
Davis Crossroads	30707
Dawesville	31792
Dawnville	30721
Dawson	31742
Dawsonville	30534
Days Crossroads	31751
Dearing	30808
Decatur	30030-37
	30089
For specific Decatur Zip Codes call (404) 378-8857, or your local postmaster.	
Deenwood	31503
Deepstep	31082
Deer Run	30208
Deerwood Forest	30906
Deerwood Park	30032
Delhi	30668
Dellwood	30401
DeLowe (Part of East Point)	30344
Demorest	30535
Denmark	30415
Dennis	31024
Denton	31532
Denver	30217
Deptford (Part of Savannah)	31404
De Soto	31743
De Soto Park	30161
Desser	31745
Devereux	31087
Dewberry	30741
Dewy Rose	30634
Dexter	31019
Dial	30513
Dialtown	30267
Diamond Hill	30628
Dickey	31746
Digbey	30205
Dillard	30537
Dillon	31792
Dinglewood (Part of Columbus)	31906
Dixie (Brooks County)	31629
Dixie (Newton County)	30209
Dixie Heights (Part of Albany)	31705
Dixie Union	31503
Dobbins Air Force Base ...	30060
Dock Junction	31520
Doctortown	31545
Doerun	31744
Doles	31791
Donald	31316

* Area Zip Code   † Post Office Boxes

	ZIP
Donalsonville	31745
Donegal	30458
Donovan	31096
Doogan	30708
Dooling	31063
Doraville	30340
Dorchester (Liberty County)	31320
Dorchester (Richmond County)	30909
Dot	30108
Double Branches	30817
Doublegate	31707
Double Run	31072
Dougherty	30534
Douglas	31533
Douglasville	30133-35
For specific Douglasville Zip Codes call (404) 765-7261, or your local postmaster.	
Dove Creek	30635
Dover	30424
Doverel	31742
Downs	31018
Downtown (Part of Atlanta)	30301
Downtown (Part of Columbus)	31901
Doyle	31803
Drakes Still	31745
Draketown	30179
Dranesville	31803
Drayton	31092
Dresden	30263
Drew	30130
Druid Hills	30333
Dry Branch (Jenkins County)	30822
Dry Branch (Twiggs County)	31020
Dry Pond	30529
Dublin	31021*
	31040†
Dubois	31014
Ducktown	30130
Dudley	31022
Due West	30064
Duffee	31730
Dugdown	30113
Duluth	30136
Dumas	31824
Dunaire	30032
Duncan Park	37412
Dunwoody	30338
Du Pont	31630
Durand	31830
Dutch Island	31406
Eagle Cliff	30725
Eagle Grove	30520
Eason	31792
East Albany (Part of Albany)	31701
Eastanollee	30538
East Armuchee	30728
East Athens	30683
East Atlanta (Part of Atlanta)	30316
East Boundary	30901
East Boynton	30736
East Columbus	31907
East Dublin	31021
East Edgewood (Part of Columbus)	31907
East Elijay	30539
East Griffin	30223
East Highlands (Part of Columbus)	31901
East Juliette	31046
East Lake (Part of Decatur)	30030
Eastman	31023
East Marietta	30062
East Meadow	30605
East Newnan	30263
East Point	30344
East Savannah (Part of Savannah)	31404
East Side (Part of Dalton)	30719
East Town (Part of Albany)	31705
East Trion (Part of Trion)	30753
Eastview	30901
Eastville	30621
Eastwood	30316
Eastwood (Part of Atlanta)	30317
Eatonton	31024
Ebenezer	30279
Echeconnee	31008
Echota	30701
Eden	31307
Edge Hill	30810
Edgemoor East	30236
Edgemoor West	30236
Edgewater (Part of Savannah)	31406
Edgewater Park (Part of Savannah)	31406

	ZIP
Edgewood (Columbia County)	30907
Edgewood (Muscogee County)	31907
Edison	31746
Edith	31631
Ednaville	30517
Egypt	31329
Elberta	31093
Elberton	30635
Elder	30677
Eldora	31308
Eldorado	31794
Eldorendo	31737
Eleanor Village	31705
Elim	31316
Elizabeth (Part of Marietta)	30060
Elko	31025
Ellabell	31308
Ella Gap	30540
Ellaville	31806
Ellenton	31747
Ellenwood	30049
Ellerslie	31807
Ellijay	30540
Elliotts Bluff	31558
Ellwood	30805
Elmodel	31770
Elza	30453
Embry Hills	30341
Emerson	30137
Emerson Park	31503
Emit	30458
Emma	30534
Emmalane	30442
Emory University	30322
Empire	31014
Englewood (Part of Columbus)	31907
Enigma	31749
Enon Grove	30217
Enterprise	30627
Ephesus	30217
Epworth	30541
Epworth Acres	31522
Eric	30411
Esom Hill	30138
Etna	30125
Eton	30724
Euharlee	30120
Eulonia	31331
Evans	30809
Evansville	30240
Everett	31525
Everett Springs	30105
Evergreen	31707
Excelsior	30439
Executive Park	30347
Experiment (census designated place)	30223
Experiment	30212
Faceville	31717
Fairburn	30213
Fairchild	31745
Fairfax	31552
Fairfield (Part of Savannah)	31404
Fairlawn Acres (Part of Fort Oglethorpe)	30741
Fairmount	30139
Fair Oaks	30060
Fairplay (Douglas County)	30187
Fairplay (Morgan County)	30663
Fairview (Franklin County)	30553
Fairview (Habersham County)	30535
Fairview (Jackson County)	30567
Fairview (Walker County)	30741
Fairway Oaks (Part of Savannah)	31406
Fairway Village	30906
Fancy Hall	31324
Fantasy Hills	30725
Fargo	31631
Farmdale	30467
Farmers High	30117
Farmington	30638
Farmville	30701
Farrar	31085
Fashion	30705
Faulkner	30107
Fayetteville	30214
Federal Reserve (Part of Atlanta)	30303
Federal Station (Part of Albany)	31702
Fellwood Homes (Part of Savannah)	31401
Felton	30140
Fernwood (Part of Savannah)	31404
Ficklin	30673
Ficklings Mill	31006

	ZIP
Fidele	30735
Fife	30213
Fincherville	30233
Findlay	31070
Finleyson	31071
Fish Creek	30125
Fitzgerald	31750
Fitzgerald Cotton Mill	31750
Fitzpatrick	31044
Five Forks (Gwinnett County)	30245
Five Forks (Thomas County)	31626
Fivemile Still	31634
Five Points (Fulton County)	30303
Five Points (Lowndes County)	31601
Five Points (Macon County)	31063
Five Points (Marion County)	31803
Five Points (Randolph County)	31786
Five Points (Taylor County)	31006
Five Points (Treutlen County)	30457
Five Springs	30721
Flat Rock (Muscogee County)	31907
Flat Rock (Putnam County)	31024
Flat Shoals	30516
Fleetwood (Part of Savannah)	31404
Fleming	31309
Fleming Heights	30906
Flemington	31313
Flint	31716
Flint Hill	31826
Flint River	31711
Flint River Estates	30236
Flintside	31735
Flintstone	30725
Flintwood	30274
Flippen	30253
Floral Hill	30668
Florence	31821
Flovilla	30216
Flowery Branch	30542
Floyd	30059
Floyd Springs	30105
Folkston	31537
Folsom	30103
Forest Estates	30909
Forest Hills (Muscogee County)	31907
Forest Hills (Richmond County)	30909
Forest Lake (Part of Macon)	31210
Forest Park (Clayton County)	30050*
	30051†
Forest Park (Dougherty County)	31701
Forest Park (Richmond County)	30904
Forest River Farms (Part of Savannah)	31406
Forrest Hills (Part of Savannah)	31404
Forsyth	31029
Fort Benning	31905
Fort Benning South	31905
Fort Gaines	31751
Fort Gillem	30050
Fort Gordon	30905
Fort Lamar	30633
Fort McAllister	31324
Fort Oglethorpe	30742
Fort Screven (Part of Tybee Island)	31328
Fortson (Part of Columbus)	31808
Fortsonia	30635
Fort Stewart (census designated place)	31313
Fort Stewart	31314
Fort Valley	31030
Foster Hills	30736
Fosters Mills	30161
Four Points (Part of Albany)	31705
Four Seasons	30207
Fowlstown	31752
Fox (Part of Rome)	30161
Foxboro	31602
Frances Hollow	30207
Franklin	30217
Franklin Springs	30639
Franklinton	31020
Frazier	31014
Free Home	30115
Friendship (Polk County)	30125
Friendship (Sumter County)	31709
Frolona	30217
Fruitland	31630
Fry	30555
Fullwood Springs	30125

	ZIP		ZIP		ZIP
Funston	31753	Grandview	30143	Harris City	30222
Furniture City	30001	Grange	30434	Harrison	31035
Gabbettville	30240	Granite Hill	31087	Harrisonville	30230
Gaddistown	30572	Grantville	30220	Harrock Hall	31406
Gaillard	31078	Gratis	30655	Hartford	31036
Gaines Community	30605	Graves	31742	Harts	30810
Gaines School	30605	Gray	31032	Hartsfield	31756
Gainesville	30501-07	Gray Hill	31833	Hartwell	30643
For specific Gainesville Zip Codes call (404) 532-3138, or your local postmaster.		Graymont (Part of Twin City)	30471	Harvest	30523
				Haskins Crossing	31022
		Grays	31404	Hassier Mill	30740
Gainesville Mills	30501	Grayson	30221	Hatcher	31754
Galloway	30513	Graysville	30726	Hatcher's Store	30830
Garden Acres Estates (Part of Pooler)	31322	Great Southwest Industrial Park (Part of Atlanta)	30336	Hatley	31015
				Hawkinsville	31036
Garden City	31408	Green Acres (Catoosa County)	30741	Haylow	31630
Garden Lakes	30165			Hayneville	31036
Garden Valley	31041	Green Acres (Chatham County)	31404	Hayston	30255
Gardi	31545			Hazlehurst	31539
Gardner (Part of Oconee)	31067	Green Acres (Clarke County)	30605	Head River	30731
Garfield	30425			Heardville	30130
Garland	30533	Green Acres Estate (Part of Dublin)	31021	Hebardville	31503
Garnersville	31767			Helen	30545
Garretta	31021	Greenbriar (Part of Atlanta)	30331	Helena	31037
Gasco (Part of Atlanta)	30301	Green Island Hills (Part of Columbus)	31904	Hemp	30560
Gates City (Part of Atlanta)	30312			Henderson	31025
Gateway (Part of Thomasville)	31792	Greenough	31716	Hentown	31723
		Greensboro	30642	Hephzibah	30815
Gay	30218	Greens Cut	30906	Herndon	30441
Geneva	31810	Greenville	30222	Herod	31742
Gentian (Part of Columbus)	31907	Greenway (Emanuel County)	30441	Hiawassee	30546
Georgetown (Chatham County)	31405			Hickory Bluff	31565
		Greenway (Fulton County)	30075	Hickory Flat (Banks County)	30554
Georgetown (Quitman County)	31754	Greenwood (Henry County)	30253	Hickory Flat (Cherokee County)	30115
		Greenwood (Mitchell County)	31730		
Georgetown Estates	30906			Hickory Level	30116
Georgia Diagnostic and Classification	30233	Greenwood (Lanier County)	31649	Hickory Ridge (Part of Macon)	31204
		Greenwood Forest	31649		
Georgia Pacific Sru (Part of Atlanta)	30303	Gregorys Mill	30711	Hickox	31553
		Gresham Park	30316	Hicks Circle	30207
Georgia Southern (Part of Statesboro)	30458	Gresham Road (Part of Marietta)	30067	Hidden Acres	30207
				Hidden Lake (Part of Savannah)	31419
Georgia Southwestern College (Part of Americus)	31709	Greshamville	30650		
		Gresston	31023	Higdon	30541
		Griffin	30223*	Higgston	30410
Georgia State Prison	30453		30224†	Highfalls	30233
Georgia Training and Development Center	30518	Grimball Park	31406	Highgate	30909
		Griswoldville	31201	Highland Circle (Part of Macon)	31211
Georgia University (Part of Athens)	30612	Grizzletown	30101		
		Grooverville	31626	Highland Heights	31709
Germany	30525	Grovania	31036	Highland Mills	30223
Gibson	30810	Groveland (Bryan County)	31321	Highland Park (Part of Savannah)	31406
Gill	30668	Groveland (Chatham County)	31405		
Gillis Springs	30457			Highland Pines (Part of Columbus)	31909
Gillsville	30543	Grove Park (Chatham County)	31406		
Girard	30426			High Point (Newton County)	30209
Gladesville	31064	Grove Park (Fulton County)	30318	High Point (Walker County)	30707
Gladys	31622	Grove Point	31405	High Shoals	30645
Glasgow	31626	Grovetown	30813	Hightower	30130
Gleason Heights (Part of Pooler)	31322	Gumbranch	31313	Hill City	30735
		Gumlog (Towns County)	30582	Hillcrest	30240
Glencliff	30286	Gum Log (Union County)	30512	Hillcrest Heights (Part of Macon)	31204
Glen Haven	30032	Gumlong	30553		
Glenloch	30217	Guysie	31510	Hillman	30631
Glenloch Village (Part of Peachtree City)	30269	Guyton	31312	Hillsboro	31038
		Habersham	30544	Hillsdale	31794
Glenmore	31503	Haddock	31033	Hillside (Part of La Grange)	30240
Glenn	30217	Hagan	30429	Hilltonia	30467
Glenn Hills	30906	Haggards Crossroads	30633	Hilton	31723
Glennville	30427	Hahira	31632	Hilton Heights (Part of Columbus)	31906
Glenridge (Part of Atlanta)	30342	Halcyondale	30467		
Glenwood (Floyd County)	30165	Hale Gap	30752	Hinesville	31313-14
Glenwood (Wheeler County)	30428	Halfmoon Landing	31320	For specific Hinesville Zip Codes call (912) 876-3978, or your local postmaster.	
Glenwood Hills	30032	Halls	30145		
Glory	31622	Halls Crossing	31018		
Gloster	30245	Hallwood	31024	Hinkles	30738
Glynn Haven	31522	Halycon Bluff	31401	Hinsonton	31765
Goat Town	31082	Hamilton	31811	Hinton	30143
Gobblers Hill	31805	Hammett	31078	Hiram	30141
Gober	30107	Hampton	30228	Hi Roc Shores	30207
Godfrey	30650	Handy	30263	Hobby	31714
Godwinsville	31023	Haney	30124	Hoboken	31542
Goggins	30204	Hannah	30187	Hogansville	30230
Golden Isle	31410	Hannahs Mill	30286	Hoggard Mill	31770
Goldmine	30520	Hannatown	31717	Hog Hammock	31327
Goldsboro	31014	Hansell	31765	Holbrook	30130
Goldson	31006	Hapeville	30354	Holcomb Bridge (Part of Roswell)	30076
Goodes	30268	Haralson	30229		
Good Hope	30641	Harbins	30620	Holland	30730
Goolsby	31064	Harbor Creek	31410	Hollingsworth	30510
Gordon	31031	Hard Cash	30634	Hollis	31778
Gordon Springs	30740	Hardwick	31034	Hollonville	30292
Gordonston (Part of Savannah)	31404	Hardwicke	31324	Holly Hills (Part of Columbus)	31906
		Harlem	30814		
Gordy	31791	Harmony	31024	Holly Springs (Cherokee County)	30142
Gore	30747	Harmony Church	31905		
Goss	30635	Harp	30214	Holly Springs (Jackson County)	30558
Gough	30811	Harper Mill (Part of Lake City)	30260		
Graball	30668			Hollywood	30523
Gracewood	30812	Harrietts Bluff	31569	Holt	31798
Grady	30153	Harrington	31522	Homeland	31537
Graham	31513	Harrisburg	30747	Homer	30547

	ZIP
Homerville	31634
Honey Creek	30208
Hooker	30752
Hopeful	31730
Hopeulikit	30458
Hopewell (Cherokee County)	30115
Hopewell (Harris County)	31822
Horns	31078
Hornsby	30901
Horseleg Estates	30165
Hortense	31543
Hoschton	30548
Houston Avenue (Part of Macon)	31206
Houston Lake	31047
Houston Mall (Part of Warner Robins)	31093
Howard	31039
Howell	31636
Howell Mill (Part of Atlanta)	30325
Howells Transfer (Part of Atlanta)	30301
Howell Tower (Part of Atlanta)	30318
Huber	31201
Hubert	30415
Huffer	31533
Hughland	30438
Hulett	30116
Hull	30646
Hunter	30467
Hunters Point (Part of Columbus)	31909
Huntington	31709
Hunts Corner	30701
Hurst	30560
Hutchins	30630
Ideal	31041
Ila	30647
Imlac	30293
Imperial	31024
Inaha	31790
Indian Hills	30236
Indianola	31602
Indian Springs (Butts County)	30216
Indian Springs (Catoosa County)	30736
Industrial (Part of Atlanta)	30336
Industrial City	30705
Ingleside (Part of Macon)	31204
Inman	30232
Iron City	31759
Irondale	30236
Irwins Crossroads	31089
Irwinton	31042
Irwinville	31760
Isabella	31791
Islandwood	31410
Isle of Hope	31406
Isle of Hope-Dutch Island	31406
Ivey	31031
Ivy Log	30512
Jackson	30233
Jacksons Crossroads	30668
Jacksons Store	30668
Jacksonville (Telfair County)	31544
Jacksonville (Towns County)	30582
Jake	30182
Jakin	31761
Jamaica Estates	30907
James	31032
Jamestown	31503
Jarrell	31006
Jasper	30143
Jay Bird Springs	31011
Jefferson	30549
Jeffersonville	31044
Jekyll Island	31527
Jenkinsburg	30234
Jersey	30235
Jerusalem (Camden County)	31568
Jerusalem (Pickens County)	30143
Jesup	31545
Jewell	31045
Jewtown	31522
Jinks	31717
Johnson Corner	30436
Johnson Crossroads	31822
Johnstonville	30204
Jolly	30292
Jones	31323
Jones Acres	31201
Jonesboro	30236*
	30237†
Jones Creek	30512
Jones Crossroads	31822
Jonesville	30108
Jordan	30411

	ZIP
Jordan City (Part of Columbus)	31904
Jot Em Down Store	31516
Joy Lake	30260
Juliette	31046
Junction City	31812
Juniper	31801
Juno	30534
Kansas	30182
Kathleen	31047
Keith	30755
Keithsburg	30114
Keller	31324
Kelley Hill	31905
Kelleytown	30253
Kelly	31085
Kemp	30401
Kenilworth	30909
Kennesaw	30144
Kensington	30707
Kensington Park (Part of Savannah)	31405
Kenwood (Fayette County)	30214
Kenwood (Muscogee County)	31909
Keysville	30816
Kibbee	30474
Kiker	30540
Kildare	30446
Killarney	31761
Kimbrough	31825
Kinderlou	31601
Kings	30209
Kings Bay	31547
Kings Bay Base	31547
Kingsboro	31811
Kingsland	31547
Kingsridge	30188
Kingston (Bartow County)	30145
Kingston (Muscogee County)	31904
Kingston (Richmond County)	30909
Kings Wood (Chatham County)	31401
Kingswood (Clarke County)	30606
Kings Wood (Richmond County)	30904
Kirkland (Atkinson County)	31642
Kirkland (Jeff Davis County)	31539
Kirkwood (Colquitt County)	31768
Kirkwood (Muscogee County)	31904
Kite	31049
Klondike (DeKalb County)	30058
Klondike (Houston County)	31036
Knott	30240
Knoxville	31050
Kramer	31001
La Crosse	31806
La Fayette	30728
Lafayette Plaza (Part of Albany)	31707
La Grange	30240*
	30241†
Lake	30125
Lake Arrowhead	30183
Lake Capri Estates	30058
Lake Cindy	30228
Lake City	30260
Lake Creek	30125
Lake Hills	30263
Lake Howard	30728
Lake Jodeco	30236
Lakeland	31635
Lake Lanier Islands	30518
Lake Lucerne	30247
Lakemont (Rabun County)	30552
Lakemont (Richmond County)	30901
Lake Park	31636
Lakeshore Estates (Part of Gainesville)	30501
Lakeshore Mall (Part of Gainesville)	30501
Lakeside Hills (Part of Macon)	31201
Lakeside Park	31406
Lake Talmadge	30228
Lake Tara	30236
Lakeview (Bleckley County)	31014
Lakeview (Catoosa County)	30741
Lakeview (Peach County)	31030
Lakeview Estates	30207
Lakewood (Clarke County)	30605
Lakewood (Fulton County)	30315
Lakewood Heights (Part of Atlanta)	30315
Lamar	31709
Lamara Heights (Part of Savannah)	31405

	ZIP
Lamarville (Part of Savannah)	31405
Landrum	30534
Lanier	31321
Laroche Park (Part of Savannah)	31404
Lashley	31005
Lathemtown	30115
Laurel Hills (Part of Columbus)	31904
Lavender	30165
La Vista	30329
Lavonia	30553
Lawrenceville	30243-46
For specific Lawrenceville Zip Codes call (404) 963-7118, or your local postmaster.	
Lax	31774
Leaf	30528
Leafmore	30033
Leah	30802
Leary	31762
Leathersville	30817
Lebanon	30146
Lee (Part of Lake City)	30260
Lee Correctional Institution	31763
Leefield	30415
Lee Pope	31030
Leesburg	31763
Lees Crossing (Part of La Grange)	30240
Lees Mill	30214
Leland	30059
Leliaton	31650
Lena	30101
Lenox	31637
Lenox Square (Part of Atlanta)	30326
Leslie	31764
Lewis	30467
Lewis Corner	30701
Lewiston	30809
Lexington	30648
Lexsy	30401
Liberty	30678
Liberty City (Part of Savannah)	31405
Liberty Hill	30257
Lifsey	30295
Lilburn	39226†
	30247*
Lilly	31051
Lillypond	30701
Limestone	31014
Lincoln Hills (Part of Columbus)	31909
Lincoln Park	30286
Lincolnton	30817
Lindale	30147
Lindbergh Plaza (Part of Atlanta)	30324
Lindsey Creek (Part of Columbus)	31907
Lindsley Park (Part of Macon)	31206
Linesville	30631
Linton	31087
Linwood	30728
Lions Gate	30327
Listonia	31015
Lithia Springs	30057
Lithonia	30038
	30058
For specific Lithonia Zip Codes call (404) 482-6554, or your local postmaster.	
Little Five Points (Part of Atlanta)	30307
Little Hope	31745
Little Miami	31601
Livingston	30161
Lizella	31052
Loco	30817
Locust Grove	30248
Loftin	31816
Loganville	30249
Lollie	31021
Lone Oak	30230
Long Cane	30240
Lookout Mountain	30750
Lorane	31201
Lorenzo	31329
Lorwood (Part of Savannah)	31406
Lost Mountain	30073
Lothair	30457
Lotts	31519
Louise	30230
Louisville	30434
Louvale	31814
Lovejoy	30250
Lovett	31021
Loving	30560

	ZIP
Lowell	30116
Lowndes Correctional Institution	31602
Lowry	30214
Lucile	31723
Lucius	30522
Ludowici	31316
Ludville	30175
Luella	30248
Lula	30554
Lulaton	31553
Lumber City	31549
Lumpkin	31815
Lundberg	30673
Luthersville	30251
Luvdale	31701
Luxomni	30247
Lyerly	30730
Lyn Hills (Part of Columbus)	31909
Lynhurst	31406
Lynmore Estates (Part of Macon)	31206
Lynn	31717
Lynnwood	30741
Lyons	30436
Lytle	30707
McAfee	30032
McBean	30906
Mableton	30059
McCaysville	30555
McCollum	30263
McDaniels	30701
McDonald Acres	30741
McDonough	30253
Macedonia (Cherokee County)	30115
Macedonia (Towns County)	30546
McElroys Mill	30249
McGregor	30410
Machen	31064
McIntosh	31320
McIntosh Mill Village	30263
McIntyre	31054
McKinnon	31545
Macland	30073
Macon	31201-12
For specific Macon Zip Codes call (912) 741-8400, or your local postmaster.	
Macon Correctional Center	31201
Macon Mall (Part of Macon)	31206
McPherson	30132
McRae	31055
McWhorter	30134
Madison	30650
Madola	30541
Madras	30263
Madray Springs	31545
Magby Gap	30752
Magnet	30208
Magnolia (Chatham County)	31406
Magnolia (Fulton County)	30318
Magruder	30441
Mallorysville	30668
Manassas	30438
Manchester	31816
Manningtown	31545
Manor	31550
Mansfield	30255
Manta	31805
Marblehill	30148
Maretts	30553
Maridale Estates (Part of Columbus)	31904
Marietta	30007
	30060-68
	30090
For specific Marietta Zip Codes call (404) 424-0140, or your local postmaster.	
Marietta Campground	30062
Marine Corps Logistics Base	31704
Marion	31020
Marketplace at North DeKalb (Part of Decatur)	30033
Marlborough	30236
Marlow	31312
Marshallville	31057
Mars Hill	30101
Martech (Part of Atlanta)	30324
Martin	30557
Martinez	30907
Massee	31620
Matt	30130
Matthews	30818
Mattox	31537
Mauk	31058
Maura Estates	30906
Maxeys	30671
Maxim	30817
Maxwell	31085

	ZIP
Mayday	31636
Mayfair (Part of Savannah)	31406
Mayfield	31087
Mayhaw	31723
Maysville	30558
Meadowbrook (Part of Macon)	31204
Meadow Grove	30906
Meansville	30256
Mechanicsville	30340
Meeks	31049
Meigs	31765
Meinhard (Part of Port Wentworth)	31407
Meldrim	31318
Melrose	31636
Mendes	30427
Menlo	30731
Mercer University (Part of Macon)	31204
Meridian	31319
Merrillville	31738
Mershon	31551
Mesena	30819
Metasville	30673
Metcalf	31792
Metter	30439
Mica	30107
Middleton	30635
Midland (Part of Columbus)	31820
Midtown (Part of Atlanta)	30309
Midville	30441
Midway (Catoosa County)	30741
Midway (Clinch County)	31634
Midway (Liberty County)	31320
Midway (Tattnall County)	30427
Midway-Hardwick	31061
Milan	31060
Miles Park	30906
Milford	31762
Mill Creek	30740
Mill Creek Estates	30506
Milledgeville	31061
Millen	30442
Millers Mill	30281
Millhaven	30467
Millwood	31552
Milner	30257
Milstead	30207
Mineola	31602
Mineral Bluff	30559
Minish	30646
Minnesota	31744
Mission Ridge (Part of Rossville)	30741
Mitchell (Dodge County)	31023
Mitchell (Glascock County)	30820
Mize	30577
Mizell	31006
Mock Road (Part of Albany)	31705
Modoc	30401
Molena	30258
Moncrief	32301
Moniac	31646
Monroe	30655
Montclair	30907
Monteith (Part of Port Wentworth)	31407
Montevideo	30635
Montezuma	31063
Montgomery	31406
Montgomery Correctional Institution	30445
Monticello (Jasper County)	31064
Monticello (Richmond County)	30906
Montreal	30033
Montrose	31065
Moody Air Force Base	31601
Moody Field	31601
Moons	30725
Moores	31021
Mora	31650
Moreland	30259
Morgan (Calhoun County)	31766
Morgan (Haralson County)	30110
Morganton	30560
Morganville	30757
Morningside (Fulton County)	30324
Morningside (Muscogee County)	31909
Morningside Hills	30501
Morris	31767
Morris Brown (Part of Atlanta)	30314
Morris Estates	30736
Morris Siding (Part of Atlanta)	30301
Morrow	30260
Mortons	31405
Morven	31638

	ZIP
Mossy Creek	30528
Moultrie	31768*
	31776†
Mountainbrook (Part of Pine Mountain)	31822
Mountain City	30562
Mountain Hill	31811
Mountain Park (Fulton County)	30075
Mountain Park (Gwinnett County)	30087
Mountaintown	30540
Mountain View (Clayton County)	30321
Mountain View (Walker County)	30741
Mount Airy	30563
Mount Berry	30149
Mount Bethel	30060
Mount Carmel	30728
Mount Olivet	30643
Mount Pleasant (Banks County)	30547
Mount Pleasant (Wayne County)	31543
Mount Vernon (Montgomery County)	30445
Mount Vernon (Walton County)	30655
Mount Vernon (Whitfield County)	30740
Mountville	30261
Mount Zion	30150
Moxley	30477
Mulberry	30680
Mulberry Grove	31804
Mulberry Heights (Part of Albany)	31705
Mulberry Street (Part of Macon)	31201
Munnerlyn	30830
Murphy	31738
Murray Hills	30909
Murrays Crossroads	31806
Murrayville	30564
Musella	31066
Myrtle Grove	31324
Mystic	31769
Nahunta	31553
Nails Creek	30521
Nance Springs	30721
Nankipooh (Part of Columbus)	31909
Naomi	30728
Nashville	31639
National Hills	30904
Naylor	31641
Neal	30206
Nebo	30132
Needmore	31631
Neese	30646
Nelson	30151
Nevils	31321
Newark	31792
Newborn	30262
New Branch	30436
New Elm	31768
New England	30752
New Era	31709
New Georgia	30132
New Holland	30501
New Home	30752
New Hope (Gilmer County)	30540
New Hope (Gwinnett County)	30245
New Hope (Lincoln County)	30817
New Hope (Paulding County)	30132
Newington	30446
Newnan	30263-65
For specific Newnan Zip Codes call (404) 253-2725, or your local postmaster.	
New Point	31780
New Salem	30547
Newton	31770
Newtown (Fulton County)	30202
New Town (Gordon County)	30701
New Town (Wilkes County)	30673
New York (Part of Aragon)	30153
Neyami	31763
Nicholasville	31713
Nicholls	31554
Nicholson	30565
Nickelsville	30701
Nicklesville	31042
Nickleville	31797
Nickville	30634
Noah's Station	30818
Noble	30728
Noonday	30066

	ZIP
Norcross	30091-93
For specific Norcross Zip Codes call (404) 448-2241, or your local postmaster.	
Norcross	30071
Norman	30668
Norman Park	31771
Normantown	30474
Norris	30828
Norristown	30447
North Atlanta	30319
North Canton	30114
North Decatur	30033
North Druid Hills (DeKalb County)	30033
North Dublin (Part of Dublin)	31021
North Elberton	30635
Northgate (Part of Columbus)	31907
North Highland (Part of Atlanta)	30306
North Highlands (Part of Columbus)	31904
North High Shoals	30645
Northlake	30345
Northridge	30350*
	31150†
North Roswell (Part of Roswell)	30075
North Side (Fulton County)	30305
Northside (Houston County)	31093
North West Point	31833
Norton Acres	30906
Norwood	30821
Note	31024
Nuberg	30634
Nunez	30448
Oakdale (Chatham County)	31405
Oakdale (Cobb County)	30080
Oakfield	31772
Oak Forest (Chatham County)	31404
Oak Forest (Clayton County)	30236
Oak Grove (Carroll County)	30117
Oak Grove (Cherokee County)	30102
Oak Grove (DeKalb County)	30033
Oak Grove (Troup County)	31822
Oakhaven	31707
Oak Hill (Gilmer County)	30540
Oak Hill (Newton County)	30209
Oakhurst (Part of Savannah)	31406
Oakland	30218
Oakland City (Part of Atlanta)	30301
Oakland Heights	30120
Oakland Park (Chatham County)	31404
Oakland Park (Muscogee County)	31903
Oaklawn	30263
Oakleaf Plantation	30067
Oakman	30732
Oak Mountain	31826
Oak Park	30401
Oakwood	30566
Oasis	30513
Oatland Island	31410
Ocee	30202
Ochillee	31905
Ochlocknee	31773
Ochwalkee	30428
Ocilla	31774
Oconee	31067
Oconee Heights	30607
Odessadale	30222
Odum	31555
Offerman	31556
Ogeechee	30467
Ogeechee Farms	31405
Ogeechee Road	31405
Ogeecheeton (Part of Savannah)	31401
Oglethorpe (Chatham County)	31406
Oglethorpe (Macon County)	31068
Oglethorpe Mall (Part of Savannah)	31406
Oglethorpe Park (Part of Savannah)	31406
Oglethorpe University	30319
Ogletree Woods (Part of Columbus)	31909
Ohoopee	30436
Okefenokee	31503
Ola	30253
Old Damascus	31741
Old National (Part of Atlanta)	30349
Old South	30236
Olive Branch	31827

	ZIP
Oliver	30449
Olney	31308
Omaha	31821
Omega	31775
Oostanaula	30701
Ophir	30107
Orange	30115
Orchard Hill	30266
Orchard Hills	30741
Orianna (Laurens County)	31002
Orianna (Treutlen County)	30457
Orland	30457
Ormewood (Part of Atlanta)	30312
Oscarville	30506
Osierfield	31750
Other	30132
Ottawa Estates (Part of Bloomingdale)	31302
Owen	31516
Owensboro	31079
Owltown	30512
Oxford	30267
Pace	30209
Pachitta	31740
Padena	30560
Palalto	31064
Palmetto (Fulton County)	30268
Palmetto (Oglethorpe County)	30627
Palmyra	31763
Pancras	31061
Panhandle	31076
Pannell	30655
Panola	30058
Pantertown	30559
Panthersville	30032
Paoli	30629
Paradise Park (Chatham County)	31406
Paradise Park (Wayne County)	31545
Paradise Valley	30607
Parhams	30521
Parkchester (Part of Columbus)	31906
Park City (Part of Fort Oglethorpe)	30741
Parkers	30467
Parkersburg	31406
Parkerville	31744
Park Hill (Part of Gainesville)	30501
Parkwood (Part of Savannah)	31404
Parrott	31777
Pateville	31015
Patillo	30233
Patten	31626
Patterson	31557
Pavo	31778
Payne (Bibb County)	31201
Payne (Cherokee County)	30102
Peach Orchard	30906
Peachtree Center (Part of Atlanta)	30343
Peachtree City	30269
Peachtree Hills (Part of Atlanta)	30305
Peachtree Mall (Part of Columbus)	31909
Pearly	31021
Pearson	31642
Pebble City	31784
Pedenville	30206
Pelham	31779
Pembroke	31321
Pendergrass	30567
Pendley Hills	30032
Penfield	30669
Penia	31015
Pennick	31525
Pennington	30650
Pennville	30747
Peoples Still	31797
Pepperton (Part of Jackson)	30233
Perkins	30822
Perry	31069
Persimmon	30525
Petross	30474
Phelps	30720
Phillips	30907
Phillipsburg	31794
Philomath	30660
Phinizy	30802
Phipps Plaza (Part of Atlanta)	30326
Phoenix	31024
Pickard	30286
Piedmont (Jasper County)	31064
Piedmont (Lamar County)	30204
Pierceville	37317
Pineboro	31768
Pine Chapel	30701

	ZIP
Pine Gardens (Part of Savannah)	31404
Pine Grove	31513
Pine Harbor	31331
Pine Hill (Part of Columbus)	31903
Pinehurst (Dooly County)	31070
Pinehurst (Henry County)	30281
Pine Lake	30072
Pineland	31631
Pine Log	30171
Pine Mountain (DeKalb County)	30058
Pine Mountain (Harris County)	31822
Pine Mountain (Rabun County)	29664
Pine Mountain Valley	31823
Pineora	31312
Pine Park	31728
Pine Valley (Cook County)	31620
Pine Valley (Richmond County)	30904
Pineview	31071
Pinewood Shores	30207
Piney Bluff	31565
Piney Grove	31808
Pin Point	31406
Pinson	30161
Pio Nono (Part of Macon)	31206
Pirkle Woods	30130
Pitts	31072
Pittsburg	30084
Plainfield	31073
Plains	31780
Plainview (Franklin County)	30521
Plainview (Whitfield County)	30720
Plainville	30733
Planter	30646
Pleasant Hill (Fulton County)	30337
Pleasant Hill (Gwinnett County)	30136
Pleasant Hill (Talbot County)	31836
Pleasant Hill (Terrell County)	31742
Pleasant Valley (Bartow County)	30103
Pleasant Valley (Dooly County)	31092
Pocataligo	30633
Pointe South	30236
Point Peter	30627
Pollards Corner	30802
Pomona	30223
Pond Spring	30707
Pooler	31322
Pope City	31079
Popes Ferry	31046
Poplar Springs (Haralson County)	30113
Poplar Springs (Oconee County)	30677
Portal	30450
Porter	31014
Porterdale	30270
Porter Springs	30533
Portland	30104
Port Royal	31324
Port Wentworth	31407
Port Wentworth Junction (Part of Port Wentworth)	31407
Postell	31201
Potterville	31076
Poulan	31781
Powder Springs	30073
Powell Place	31701
Powelton	31087
Powers Lake	30327
Powersville	31008
Prather	30673
Prattsburg	31827
Presley	30546
Preston	31824
Pretoria	31701
Price	30506
Pridgen	31519
Primrose	30222
Princeton (Part of Athens)	30601
Pringle	31096
Prior	30125
Pritchetts	31744
Privette Heights	30060
Prospect	31064
Pulaski	30451
Pumpkin Center	30814
Putnam	31803
Putney	31782
Pyles Marsh	31525
Pyne	30240
Queensland	31750
Quitman	31643
Rabbit Hill	31324
Rabun Gap	30568
Race Pond	31537

	ZIP
Radium Springs	31702
Raines	31015
Raleigh	30293
Ramhurst	30705
Randall	31815
Ranger	30734
Raoul	30510
Raulerson (Brantley County)	31557
Raulerson (Pierce County)	31557
Ravenwood	30907
Raybon	31553
Ray City	31645
Rayle	30660
Raymond	30265
Raytown	30631
Rebecca	31783
Rebie	31012
Recovery	32324
Redan (DeKalb County)	30074
Redbud	30701
Red Clay	30710
Red Hill (Franklin County)	30521
Red Hill (Stewart County)	31825
Red Lane	30501
Red Oak	30272
Red Rock (Paulding County)	30101
Red Rock (Worth County)	31791
Red Stone	30549
Red Store Crossroads	31770
Reed Creek	30643
Reese	30828
Reeves	30701
Regency Mall (Part of Augusta)	30904
Register	30452
Rehoboth	30033
Reidsboro	30292
Reidsville	30453
Reka	31321
Relay	30125
Remerton	31601
Renfroe	31805
Reno	31728
Rentz	31075
Reo	30740
Resaca	30735
Resseaus Crossroads	31024
Rest Haven	30518
Retreat	31323
Rex	30273
Reynolds	31076
Reynoldsville	31745
Rhine	31077
Riceboro	31323
Richfield (Part of Savannah)	31405
Richland	31825
Richmond Hill	31324
Richwood	31092
Rico	30268
Riddleville	31018
Ridgefield Heights (Part of Columbus)	31907
Ridgeville	31331
Ridgewood	30909
Rincon	31326
Ringgold	30736
Rio	30223
Rio Vista (Chatham County)	31406
Rio Vista (Dougherty County)	31705
Rising Fawn	30738
Riverdale	30274
	30296
For specific Riverdale Zip Codes call (404) 997-5566, or your local postmaster.	
Riverland Terrace (Part of Columbus)	31903
River Oaks	31410
River Road	31707
Rivers End (Part of Savannah)	31406
Riverside (Bibb County)	31204
Riverside (Colquitt County)	31768
Riverside (Floyd County)	30161
Riverside (Fulton County)	30318
Rivertown	30213
Riverturn	31745
Riverview (Part of Macon)	31204
Rivoli (Part of Macon)	31210
Roanoke Acres	31750
Roberta	31078
Robertstown	30545
Robertsville	30707
Robins AFB	31098
Robins Air Force Base	31098
Robinson	30669
Rochelle	31079
Rock Branch	30635
Rock Chapel	30058
Rockdale (Part of Atlanta)	30318

	ZIP
Rock Hill	31723
Rockingham	31510
Rockledge	30454
Rockmart	30153
Rock Spring	30739
Rockville	31024
Rocky Creek	30701
Rocky Face	30740
Rocky Ford	30455
Rocky Mount	30251
Rocky Plains	30209
Roddy	31014
Rogers	30529
Rogers Correctional Institution	30453
Rolling Green	30207
Rolling Meadows	30905
Rome	30161-65
For specific Rome Zip Codes call (404) 232-1073, or your local postmaster.	
Roopville	30170
Roosterville	30170
Roper	31539
Ropers Crossroads	30809
Roscoe	30263
Rosebud	30249
Rosedale	30701
Rose Dhu	31406
Rose Hill (Chatham County)	31406
Rose Hill (Pike County)	30256
Rose Hill Heights (Part of Columbus)	31904
Rosemont	30802
Rosemont Park	30161
Rosier	30434
Rossignol Hill (Part of Garden City)	31408
Rossville	30741
Roswell	30075-77
For specific Roswell Zip Codes call (404) 993-6778, or your local postmaster.	
Round Oak	31038
Roundtop	30540
Rover	30292
Rowena	31713
Roxanna	30132
Royston	30662
Ruckersville	30635
Rudden	31024
Rupert	31081
Russell	30680
Russellville	31016
Rutledge	30663
Rydal	30171
Ryo	30139
Saginaw	31554
St. Charles	30259
St. Clair	30816
St. George	31646
St. Marks	30230
St. Marys	31558
St. Marys Hills (Part of Columbus)	31906
St. Simons Island	31522
Sale City	31784
Salem Arms	30906
Sanborn	31705
Sandalwood	31701
Sand Bed	31047
Sandersville	31082
Sandfly	31406
Sand Hill (Brooks County)	31778
Sand Hill (Carroll County)	30180
Sand Hill (Muscogee County)	31905
Sand Hills	30904
Sandtown	30673
Sandy Cross (Franklin County)	30662
Sandy Cross (Oglethorpe County)	30627
Sandy Plains	30075
Sandy Springs	30328
Sanford (Madison County)	30646
Sanford (Stewart County)	31815
Sangrena Woods (Part of Pooler)	31322
Santa Claus	30436
Sapelo Island	31327
Sapp	31014
Sardis	30456
Sargent	30275
Sasser	31785
Satolah	30525
Sautee-Nacoochee	30571
Savannah	31401-99
For specific Savannah Zip Codes call (912) 236-7851, or your local postmaster.	

	ZIP
Savannah Gardens (Part of Savannah)	31404
Sawdust	30814
Sawhatchee	31723
Scarboro	30442
Scarbrough Cross Roads	30049
Scarlet	31569
Schatulga (Part of Columbus)	31820
Schlatterville	31501
Schley	31768
Scotland	31083
Scott	31002
Scottdale	30079
Scottsboro	31061
Screven	31560
Screven Fork	31320
Screvens Point	31410
Seabrook	31320
Seagraves	30646
Sea Island	31561
Sea Palms	31522
Sells	30548
Seney	31004
Senoia	30276
Sessoms	31554
Seville	31084
Shady Dale	31085
Shake Rag	30174
Shannon	30172
Sharon	30664
Sharon Park (Part of Garden City)	31408
Sharpe	30728
Sharphagen	31745
Sharpsburg	30277
Sharps Spur	30410
Sharp Top	30114
Shawnee	31329
Sheffield	30909
Shell Bluff	30830
Shellman	31786
Shellman Bluff	31331
Shelly	31778
Shenandoah	30265
Sheppards	30467
Sherwood (Clayton County)	30236
Sherwood (Richmond County)	30904
Sherwood Forest (Bibb County)	31206
Sherwood Forest (Coweta County)	30263
Sherwood Forest (DeKalb County)	30032
Sherwood Forest (Floyd County)	30161
Shields Crossroads	30707
Shiloh (Harris County)	31826
Shiloh (Lowndes County)	31634
Shiloh (Madison County)	30633
Shiloh (Sumter County)	31709
Shingler	31781
Shirley Hills (Part of Macon)	31211
Shirley Park (Part of Savannah)	31404
Shoal Creek	30553
Shoals	30820
Shurlington (Part of Macon)	31211
Sigsbee	31744
Silco	31537
Silica Hills	31705
Silk Hope	31401
Silk Mills	30635
Siloam	30665
Silver City	30506
Silver Creek	30173
Silver Crest	30906
Silver Pines	31206
Simpson	30217
Six Mile	30165
Skidaway Island	31411
Skipperton	31206
Skyland	30319
Skyland Terrace (Part of Savannah)	31401
Sky Valley	30525
Smarr	31086
Smiths Crossroads (Harris County)	31823
Smiths Crossroads (Troup County)	30240
Smithsonia	30628
Smithville	31787
Smyrna	30080-82
For specific Smyrna Zip Codes call (404) 436-5246, or your local postmaster.	
Snake Nation	30513
Snapfinger	30058
Snapping Shoals	30209
Snead	30809

	ZIP		ZIP		ZIP
Snellville	30278	Stonewall (Part of Union		Thunderbolt	31404
Snipesville	31532	City)	30349	Thurmock	30567
Snow Spring	31091	Stoney Point	30170	Thurston	30642
Snug Harbor Estates	30504	Stovall (Habersham County)	30531	Thyatira	30549
Soapstick	30701	Stovall (Meriwether County)	30222	Ticknor	31744
Social Circle	30279	Stratford (Part of Atlanta)	30311	Tifton	31793†
Sofkee	31206	Strouds	31016		31794*
Somerset Park (Part of		Stuckey	30428	Tiger	30576
Savannah)	31419	Subligna	30747	Tignall	30668
Sonoraville	30701	Suches	30572	Tilton	30720
Soperton	30457	Sudie	30132	Timothy Estates	30606
South Augusta	30901	Sugar Hill (Gwinnett County)	30518	Tippettville	31092
South Base (Part of Warner		Sugar Hill (Hall County)	30507	Tison	30427
Robins)	31098	Sugartown	30755	Titus	30546
South Cobb	30001	Sugar Valley	30746	Toccoa	30577
Southdale	30906	Sulphur Springs	30738	Toccoa Falls	30598
South Decatur	30034	Sulphur Springs Station	35967	Toco Hills	30329
South DeKalb Mall	30034	Sumach	30705	Toledo	31646
Southern Tech (Part of		Summertown	30466	Tom	31049
Marietta)	30062	Summerville	30747	Toms Creek	30557
Southgate Villa	30906	Summit (Part of Twin City)	30471	Toney Valley (Part of	
South Glen	30236	Sumner	31789	Decatur)	30032
Southlake Mall (Part of		Sumter	31709	Toomsboro	31090
Morrow)	30260	Sunbury	31320	Topeka Junction	30285
Southland	30906	Sunny Acres	31701	Town and Country	30815
South Macon (Part of		Sunnydale Acres (Part of		Town and Country Acres	31707
Macon)	31206	Macon)	31201	Town and Country	
South Moultrie (Part of		Sunny Side (Spalding		Shopping Center (Part of	
Moultrie)	31768	County)	30284	Marietta)	30060
South Nellieville	30901	Sunnyside (Ware County)	31501	Towns	31055
South Newport	31323	Sunset	31768	Townsend	31331
Southover (Part of		Sunset Heights (Part of		Traders Hill	31537
Savannah)	31405	Gainesville)	30501	Tranquilla Woods (Part of	
South Pooler	31322	Sunset Park (Part of		Savannah)	31419
Southside (Part of		Savannah)	31404	Trans	30728
Savannah)	31419	Sunset Village	30286	Travisville	31634
Spalding	31063	Sunshine Acres (Part of		Tremont (Crisp County)	31015
Spanish Trace	30906	Columbus)	31909	Tremont (Richmond County)	30907
Spann	31096	Sunsweet	31794	Tremont Park (Part of	
Sparks	31647	Surrency	31563	Savannah)	31405
Sparta	31087	Sutalee	30184	Trenton	30752
Spence	31779	Suttles Mill	30728	Trice	30286
Spencer Hills	30741	Suttons Corner	31724	Trickum	30755
Split Silk	30249	Suwanee	30174	Trimble	30230
Spout Spring Crossroads	30542	Swainsboro	30401	Trion	30753
Spring Bluff	31565	Swan Lake	30281	Troutman	31740
Springfield	31329	Swords	30625	Trudie	31557
Spring Hill (Chatham		Sybert	30817	Tucker	30084*
County)	31404	Sycamore	31790		30085†
Spring Hill (Wheeler County)	30411	Sylvan Hills (Part of Atlanta)	30310	Tugaloo (Part of Tallulah	
Spring Lake (Part of		Sylvania	30467	Falls)	30573
Columbus)	31909	Sylvester	31791	Tulakes (Part of Columbus)	31904
Spring Place	30705	Tails Creek	30540	Tunnel Hill	30755
Springvale (Randolph		Talahi Island	31410	Turin	30289
County)	31767	Talbotton	31827	Turner City (Part of Albany)	31705
Springvale (sta.) (Randolph		Talking Rock	30175	Turners Rock	31406
County)	31767	Tallapoosa	30176	Turnerville	30580
Spring Valley (Part of		Tallulah Falls	30573	Tusculum	31329
Columbus)	31909	Tallulah Lodge	30573	Tuxedo (Part of Atlanta)	30342
Springview Acres (Part of		Talmo	30575	Twin City	30471
Gainesville)	30501	Talona	30175	Twin Lakes	31636
Staley Heights (Part of		Tanglewood (Clarke		Tybee Island	31328
Savannah)	31405	County)	30606	Tyler	31064
Stanleys Store	30436	Tanglewood (Richmond		Tyrone (Fayette County)	30290
Stanton Woods	30208	County)	30909	Tyrone (Wilkes County)	30673
Stapleton	30823	Tarboro	31568	Ty Ty	31795
Stark	30233	Tarrytown	30470	Tyus	30108
Starr	30207	Tarver	31631	Unadilla	31091
Starrs Mill	30214	Tarversville	31020	Union (Marion County)	31803
Starrsville	30209	Tate	30177	Union (Paulding County)	30179
State College	31404	Tate City	30525	Union (Quitman County)	31767
Statenville	31648	Tatumsville (Part of		Union (Stewart County)	31821
State Sanitarium	31061	Savannah)	31405	Unionburg	31794
Statesboro	30458*	Tax	31826	Union City	30291
	30460†	Taylorsville	30178	Union Hill	30201
Statham	30666	Tazewell	31803	Union Point	30669
Staunton	31637	Teloga	30747	Unionville (Bibb County)	31204
Steadham Store	31717	Temperance	31077	Unionville (Tift County)	31794
Steadman	30176	Temple	30179	Unity	30521
Steam Mill	31745	Temple Grove	30711	University Heights	30605
Steffen Wood Estates (Part		Tennga	30751	Upatoi (Part of Columbus)	31829
of Pooler)	31322	Tennille	31089	Upton	31533
Stellaville	30833	Terrace Manor	30906	Uptonville	31537
Stephens	30667	Terrell	31789	Uvalda	30473
Stephensville	30752	Texas	30217	Vada	31734
Sterling	31525	Thalmann	31525	Valdosta	31601-04
Stevens Pottery	31031	The Hill (Part of Augusta)	30904	For specific Valdosta Zip Codes	
Stewart	30209	The Landings	31411	call (912) 242-8201, or your local	
Stewart Town	30752	The Rock	30285	postmaster.	
Stilesboro	30120	Thomasboro	30455	Valley Forge	30906
Stillmore	30464	Thomaston	30286	Valley View	30725
Stillwell	31329	Thomasville (Fulton County)	30315	Valona	31332
Stilson	30415	Thomasville (Thomas		Vanceville	31794
Stockbridge	30281	County)	31792*	Vandiver Heights	30066
Stockton	31649		31799†	Vanna	30662
Stockwood	30188	Thomas Woods	30906	Vans Valley	30161
Stone Mountain	30083	Thompson	31601	Van Wert	30153
	30086-88	Thompsonville	30738	Varnell	30756
For specific Stone Mountain Zip		Thomson	30824	Vaughn	30223
Codes call (404) 469-4544, or		Thornhedge	30274	Veal	30108
your local postmaster.		Thornton Estates	30236	Veazey	30642
		Thrift	30442	Vega	30256

	ZIP		ZIP		ZIP
Veribest	30627	Welcome	30263	Winder	30680
Vernonburg	31406	Welcome Hill	30753	Windermere	30904
Vernon View	31406	Wenona	31015	Windsor	30249
Vesta	30627	Weracoba Heights (Part of		Windsor Estates	30263
Veterans Hospital (Part of		Columbus)	31906	Windsor Forest (Chatham	
Augusta)	30909	Wesley (Emanuel County)	30401	County)	31419
Victoria	30188	Wesley (Taylor County)	31812	Windsor Forest (Richmond	
Victory	30108	Wesleyan College (Part of		County)	30904
Victory Heights (Part of		Macon)	31201	Windsor Park (Lowndes	
Savannah)	31404	Wesleyan Estates	31204	County)	31601
Vidalia	30474	Wesleyan Woods (Part of		Windsor Park (Muscogee	
Vidette	30434	Macon)	31210	County)	31909
Vienna	31092	West Augusta	30901	Windward (Part of	
View	30531	West Bainbridge (Part of		Savannah)	31419
Villanow	30728	Bainbridge)	31717	Windy Ridge	30559
Villa Rica	30180	West Brow	30738	Winfield	30824
Vineland	30909	West Crossing	30176	Winokur	31537
Vineville (Part of Macon)	31204	West Dublin (Part of Dublin)	31021	Winona Park	31503
Vinings	30339	West End (Floyd County)	30165	Winship Gardens (Part of	
Vinson Village (Part of		West End (Fulton County)	30310	Macon)	31204
Macon)	31206	Westgate (Part of Albany)	31707	Winston	30187
Vista-Grove	30033	Westgate Mall (Part of		Winterville	30683
Vulcan	30738	Macon)	31206	Withers	31630
Waco	30182	Westgate Park	30607	Woodbine	31569
Wadley	30477	West Georgia College (Part		Woodbury	30293
Wagon Wheel	31647	of Carrollton)	30118	Woodcliff	30467
Wahoo	30533	West Green	31567	Woodgate	30909
Walden	31206	Westhampton	30907	Woodlake	30906
Waleska	30183	West Hills	30907	Woodlake Landing	30274
Walker Correctional		Westmont	30907	Woodland	31836
Institution	30739	Westoak	30062	Woodland Hills (Laurens	
Walker Park	30655	Weston	31832	County)	31021
Walkersville	31516	West Point	31833	Woodland Hills (Walker	
Wallace	31036	West Rome (Part of Rome)	30164	County)	30741
Wallaceville	30707	West Savannah (Part of		Woodlawn (Part of	
Walls Crossing	31806	Savannah)	31401	Savannah)	31406
Walnut Grove (Walker		Westside (Catoosa County)	30741	Woodlawn Estates (Part of	
County)	30728	Westside (Hall County)	30501	Columbus)	31907
Walnut Grove (Walton		West Valdosta	31601	Woodlawn Terrace (Part of	
County)	30209	West Vidalia (Part of Vidalia)	30474	Garden City)	31406
Walnut Square (Part of		Westwick	30909	Woodridge Estates	31410
Dalton)	30720	Westwood	31750	Woods Grove	30582
Walthourville	31333	Wexwood	30274	Wood Station	30736
Ware Correctional Institution	31503	Wheat Hill (Part of Garden		Woodstock	30188
Waresboro	31564	City)	31408	Woodville (Chatham	
Wares Crossroads	30240	Wheeler Heights	31201	County)	31401
Waresville	30217	Whigham	31797	Woodville (Greene County)	30669
Waring	30720	Whistleville	30680	Woolsey	30214
Warm Springs	31830	Whitaker	31543	Wooster	30218
Warner Robins	31088	White	30184	Wormsloe	31406
	31093	White Bluff (Part of		Worth	31714
	31095	Savannah)	31406	Worthville	30233
	31098-99	White City	30187	Wray	31798
For specific Warner Robins Zip		White Hall	30605	Wrens	30833
Codes call (912) 922-3121, or		Whitehouse	30253	Wright Landing	30236
your local postmaster.		Whitemarsh Island	31404	Wright Square (Part of	
Warren Terrace	30741	White Oak	31568	Savannah)	31401
Warrenton	30828	White Plains	30678	Wrightsville	31096
Warsaw	30202	Whitesburg	30185	Wymberly	31406
Warthen	31094	Whitestone	30175	Wynngate	30907
Warwick	31796	White Sulphur Springs	31822	Wynnton (Part of	
Washington	30673	Whitesville	31833	Columbus)	31906
Waterloo	31733	Whitworth	30553	Yahoola	30533
Waterport	30249	Wilbanks Store	30711	Yates	30263
Waters	30467	Wildwood	30757	Yatesville	31097
Watkinsville	30677	Wiley	30581	Yellow Bluff Fishing Village	31320
Waverly (Camden County)	31565	Willacoochee	31650	Yeomans	31742
Waverly (Richmond County)	30909	Willard	31024	Yonah	30510
Waverly Hall	31831	Williamsburg Manor (Part of		Yonkers	31014
Waverly Heights (Part of		Savannah)	31419	Yorktown (Part of	
Macon)	31206	Williamson	30292	Columbus)	31907
Waverly Park	30741	Williams Plaza (Part of		Yorkville	30132
Wax	30104	Warner Robins)	31093	Youngcane	30512
Wayback	31746	Wilmington Island	31410	Young Harris	30582
Waycross	31501-03	Wilmington Park	31410	Youngs	30125
For specific Waycross Zip Codes		Wilshire (Part of Savannah)	31419	Youngstown	30512
call (912) 283-2822, or your local		Wilshire Estates (Part of		Youth	30249
postmaster.		Savannah)	31419	Zaidee	30457
Wayne Correctional		Wilsons Church	30558	Zebina	30833
Institution	31555	Wilsonville	31554	Zebulon	30295
Waynesboro	30830	Wimberly on the Marsh	31406	Zeigler	30467
Waynesville	31566	Wimbish Wood (Part of		Zenith	31078
Wayside	31032	Macon)	31210	Zetella	30223
Webb	30201	Winchester	31057	Zetto	31751
Weber	31639	Winchester Hills	30207	Zingara	30207

	ZIP
Ahualoa	96727
Ahuimanu	96744
Aiea	96701
Aiea Heights	96701
Aiea Shopping Center	96701
Aikahi	96734
Aina Haina (Part of Honolulu)	96821
	96824

For specific Aina Haina Zip Codes call (808) 373-2555, or your local postmaster.

Akasaki Camp	96774
Alabama Village	96784
Alewa Heights (Part of Honolulu)	96819
Aliamanu	96818
Amaulu Camps	96720
Anahola	96703
Andrade Camp	96783
Barbers Point Housing	96862
Barbers Point Naval Air Station	96762
Brigham Young University-Hawaii	96762
Camp 106	96727
Camp H.M. Smith Marine Corps Base	96861
Captain Cook	96704
Chinatown (Part of Honolulu)	96817
Chin Chuck	96710
Coconut Grove	96734
Coral Gardens	96744
Crestview	96797
Downtown (Part of Hilo)	96720
Downtown (Part of Honolulu)	96813
Downtown (Maui County)	96767
Dowsett Highlands (Part of Honolulu)	96817
Eight and One-half Mile Camp	96749
Eightmile Camp	96749
Eleele	96705
Elevenmile Homestead	96760
Ewa	96706
Ewa Beach	96706-07

For specific Ewa Beach Zip Codes call (808) 689-5033, or your local postmaster.

Ewa Gentry	96706
Fernandez Village	96706
Ford Island	96818
Fort Shafter	96819
Foster Village	96818
Glenwood	96771
Haaheo	96720
Haena	96714
Haiku	96708
Haiku-Pauwela	96708
Haina	96727
Hakalau	96710
Halaula	96755
Halawa (Hawaii County)	96755
Halawa (Honolulu County)	96701
Halawa (Maui County)	96748
Halawa Heights	96701
Halawa Hills	96701
Haleiwa	96712
Halepalaoa Landing	96763
Haliimaile	96768
Hamoa	96713
Hana	96713
Hanalei	96714
Hanamaulu	96715
Hanapepe	96716
Hanapepe Heights	96716
Haou	96713
Happy Valley	96793
Hauula	96717
Hawaiian Beaches	96778
Hawaiian Ocean View	96704
Hawaiian Paradise Park	96778
Hawaiian Village (Part of Honolulu)	96813
Hawaii Kai (Part of Honolulu)	96825
Hawaii National Park	96718
Hawaii State Hospital	96744
Hawi	96719
Heeia	96744
Hickam Air Force Base	96818
Hickam Housing	96818
Highway Village	96728
Hilo	96720*
	96721†
Hoaeae	96797
Hokamahoo House Lot	96764
Holualoa	96725
Honalo	96750
Honaunau	96726

	ZIP
Honaunau-Napoopoo	96726
Honohina	96710
Honokaa	96727
Honokahua	96761
Honokai Hale	96707
Honokohau	96725
Honokowai	96761
Honolulu	96801-39

For specific Honolulu Zip Codes call (808) 423-3990, or your local postmaster.

COLLEGES & UNIVERSITIES

Chaminade University of Honolulu	96816
Hawaii Pacific College	96813
University of Hawaii at Manoa	96822

FINANCIAL INSTITUTIONS

American Savings Bank, F.S.B.	96813
Bank of Hawaii	96813
Central Pacific Bank	96813
City Bank	96813
First Federal Savings & Loan Association of America	96813
First Hawaiian Bank	96813
Hawaii National Bank	96817
International Savings & Loan Association, Ltd.	96813
Liberty Bank	96817
Pioneer Federal Savings Bank	96813
Territorial Savings & Loan Association	96813

HOSPITALS

Kuakini Medical Center	96817
Queen's Medical Center	96813
Tripler Army Medical Center	96859

HOTELS/MOTELS

Ambassador Hotel of Waikiki	96815
Outrigger Waikiki Tower	96815
The Breakers	96815
Colony Surf Hotel	96815
Coral Reef Hotel-Aston	96815
Halekulani Hotel	96815
Hawaiian Monarch	96815
Hawaiian Regent	96815
Hawaiian Waikiki Beach Hotel	96815
Hawaiiana Hotel	96815
Hilton Hawaiian Village	96815
Holiday Inn-Honolulu Airport	96819
Hyatt Regency Waikiki	96815
Ilikai, The	96815
Ilima Hotel	96815
Kahala Hilton	96816
Miramar at Waikiki	96815
New Otani Kaimana Beach Hotel	96815
Outrigger Coral Seas	96815
Outrigger East	96815
Outrigger Malia	96815
Outrigger Prince Kuhio	96815
Outrigger Surf	96815
Outrigger Waikiki	96815
Outrigger West	96815
Pacific Beach Hotel	96815
Pagoda Hotel	96814
Park Shore Hotel	96815
Royal Hawaiian Hotel	96815
Sheraton Princess Kaiulani Hotel	96815
Sheraton-Waikiki	96815
Waikiki Beachcomber	96815
Waikikian On The Beach-Aston	96815
Honomakau	96755
Honomu	96728
Honouliuli	96706
Honuapo	96772
Hookena	96704
Hoolehua	96729
Hoopuloa	96726
Huehue	96725
Huelo	96708
Iroquois Point	96706
Iwasaki Camp	96760
Iwilei (Part of Honolulu)	96817
Kaawa	96730
Kaahumanu Center	96732
Kaalaea	96744
Kaalawai	96821
Kaanapali	96761
Kaapahu	96776

	ZIP
Kaapoko Homesteads	96781
Kaauhuhu Homesteads	96719
Kaawanui Village	96769
Kahakuloa	96793
Kahala Mall	96816
Kahaluu (Hawaii County)	96725
Kahaluu (Honolulu County)	96744
Kahaluu-Keauhou	96725
Kahana (Honolulu County)	96717
Kahana (Maui County)	96761
Kahei Homesteads	96719
Kahua	96755
Kahuku (Hawaii County)	96772
Kahuku (Honolulu County)	96731
Kahului	96732*
	96733†
Kaiaakea	96773
Kaieie Homesteads	96781
Kailua (Honolulu County)	96734
Kailua (Maui County)	96708
Kailua Kona	96739-40
	96745

For specific Kailua Kona Zip Codes call (808) 329-1927, or your local postmaster.

Kai Malino	96704
Kaimu	96778
Kaimuki (Part of Honolulu)	96816
Kainaliu	96750
Kainalu	96748
Kaiwiki	96720
Kalae	96757
Kalaheo	96741
Kalamaula	96748
Kalaoa	96740
Kalaoa Homesteads	96725
Kalapana	96778
Kalauao	96701
Kalaupapa	96742
Kalepolepo	96753
Kalihi (Part of Honolulu)	96819
Kalihi Kai (Part of Honolulu)	96818
Kalihi Shopping Center (Part of Honolulu)	96819
Kalihiwai	96754
Kaluaaha	96748
Kamaili	96778
Kamalo	96748
Kamehameha Heights (Part of Honolulu)	96819
Kamiloloa	96748
Kamooloa	96791
Kamuela	96743
Kaneohe	96744
Kaneohe Station	96863
Kaniahiku Village	96778
Kapaa	96746
Kapaau	96755
Kapahulu (Part of Honolulu)	96815
Kapaia	96766
Kapaka	96747
Kapalama (Part of Honolulu)	96817
Kapalua	96761
Kapehu	96780
Kapoho	96778
Kapulena	96727
Kaumakani	96747
Kaumalapau	96763
Kaumana	96720
Kaunakakai	96748
Kaupakalua	96708
Kaupo	96713
Kawaihae	96743
Kawaihua	96746
Kawailoa	96712
Kawailoa Beach	96712
Kawainui	96783
Kawela (Honolulu County)	96731
Kawela (Maui County)	96748
Keaau	96749
Keaau Camp	96749
Keaau Ranch	96749
Kealakehe Homesteads	96740
Kealakekua	96750
Kealia	96751
Keanae	96708
Keauhou	96740
Keaukaha	96720
Keawakapu	96753
Keehia	96774
Keei	96726
Kehena	96778
Kekaha	96752
Kelawea	96761
Keokea (Hawaii County)	96704
Keokea (Maui County)	96790
Keolu Hills	96734
Kihei	96753
Kilauea	96754
Kilauea Military Camp	96718
Kilauea Settlement	96785

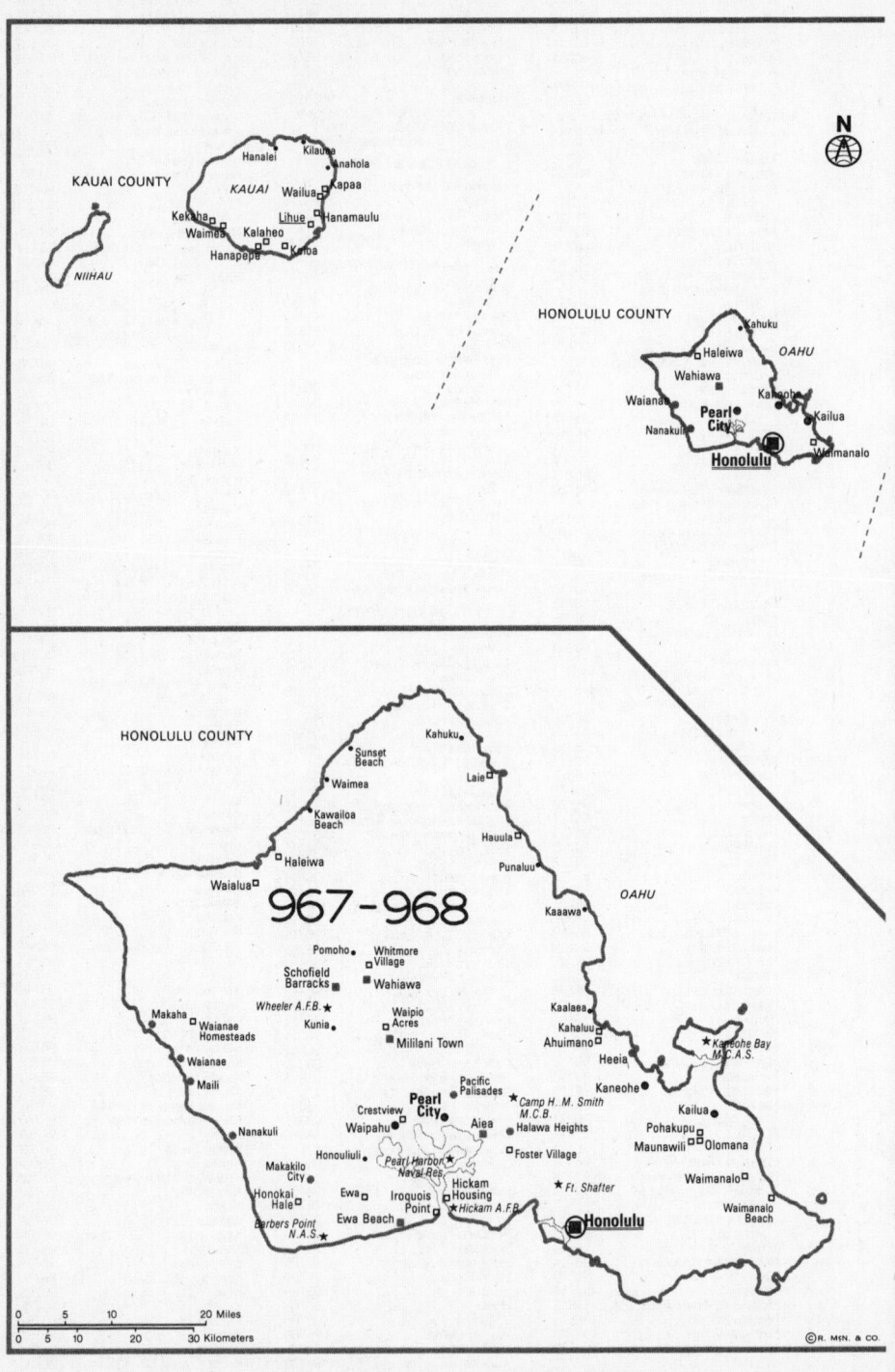

N

KAUAI COUNTY

KAUAI

NIIHAU

Hanalei
Kilauea
Anahola
Wailua
Kapaa
Kekaha
Lihue
Hanamaulu
Waimea
Kalaheo
Hanapepe
Koloa

HONOLULU COUNTY

OAHU

Kahuku
Haleiwa
Wahiawa
Kaneohe
Waianae
Kailua
Pearl City
Nanakuli
Honolulu
Waimanalo

HONOLULU COUNTY

OAHU

967-968

Kahuku
Sunset Beach
Laie
Waimea
Kawailoa Beach
Hauula
Haleiwa
Punaluu
Waialua
Kaaawa
Pomoho
Whitmore Village
Schofield Barracks
Wahiawa
Makaha
Kaalaea
Wheeler A.F.B. ★
Kahaluu
Waianae Homesteads
Kunia
Waipio Acres
Ahuimano
Waianae
Mililani Town
Heeia
Maili
Kaneohe Bay M.C.A.S.
Nanakuli
Pacific Palisades
Kaneohe
Crestview
Pearl City
Camp H. M. Smith M.C.B.
Kailua
Waipahu
Aiea
Halawa Heights
Pohakupu
Honouliuli
Foster Village
Maunawili
Olomana
Makakilo City
Pearl Harbor Naval Res.
Honokai Hale
Ewa
Hickam Housing
Ft. Shafter
Waimanalo
Iroquois Point
Barbers Point N.A.S. ★
Ewa Beach
Hickam A.F.B.
Waimanalo Beach
Honolulu

0   5   10   20 Miles
0   5   10   20   30 Kilometers

©R. MtN. & CO.

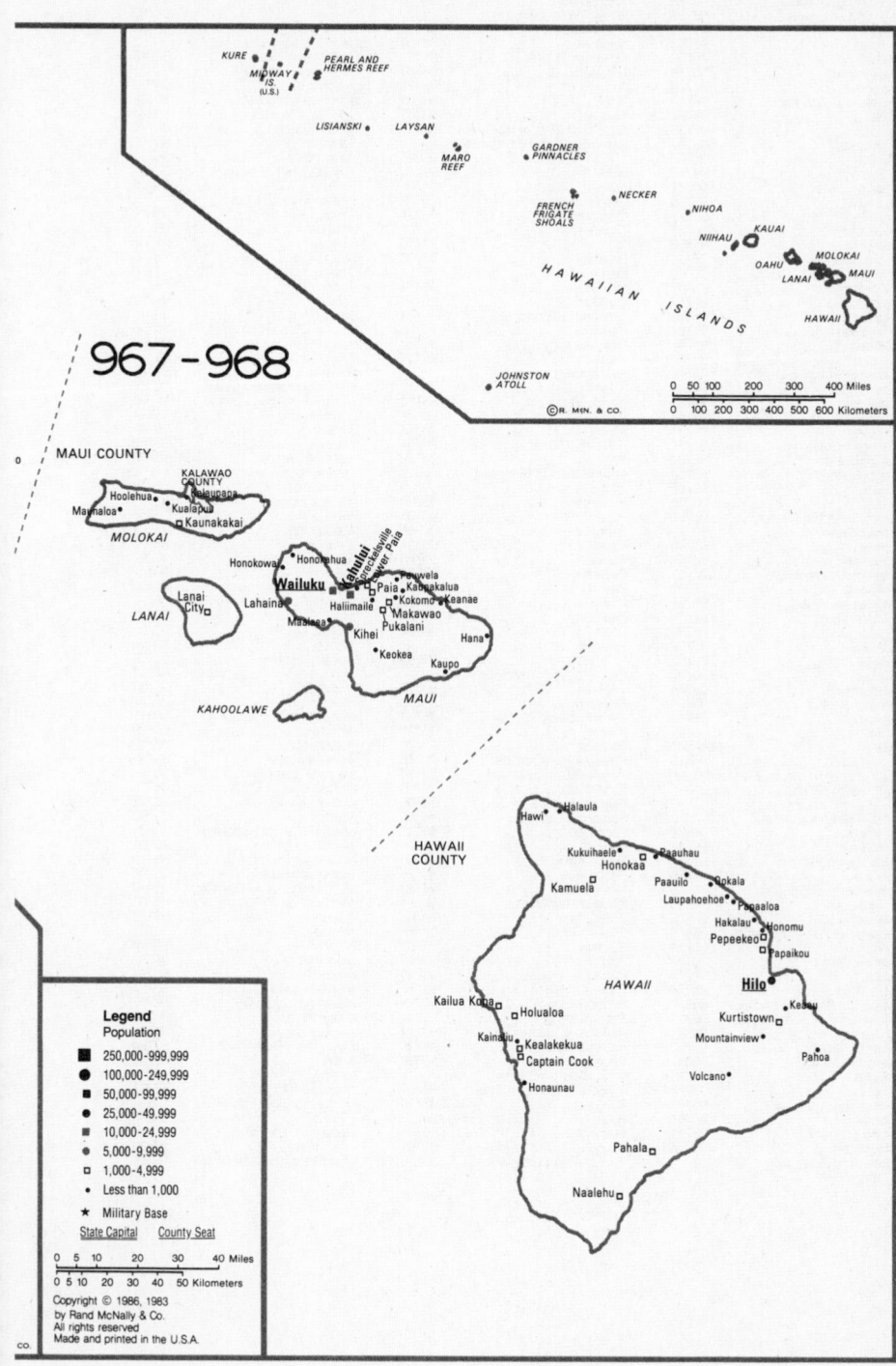

967-968

KURE •
MIDWAY
IS.
(U.S.)
PEARL AND
HERMES REEF

LISIANSKI •   • LAYSAN

MARO
REEF •

GARDNER
PINNACLES

• NECKER

FRENCH
FRIGATE
SHOALS

• NIHOA

NIIHAU   KAUAI

OAHU   MOLOKAI
LANAI   MAUI

H A W A I I A N   I S L A N D S

HAWAII

JOHNSTON
ATOLL •

©R. M°N. & CO.

| 0 | 50 | 100 | 200 | 300 | 400 Miles |
| 0 | 100 | 200 | 300 | 400 | 500 | 600 Kilometers |

MAUI COUNTY

KALAWAO
COUNTY

Hoolehua •   • Kalaupapa
Maunaloa •   • Kualapuu
□ Kaunakakai

MOLOKAI

Honokowai •   • Honokohua

Waikapu

Wailuku   Kahului
                 Puuneene • Paia
Lahaina   Haliimaile
Lanai   Paia
City □   Puuwela
                 • Kaonakalua
LANAI   Maalaea   • Kokomo • Keanae
                 • Makawao
                 Pukalani   Hana •
                 Kihei
                 • Keokea
                                   Kaupo •

KAHOOLAWE   MAUI

HAWAII
COUNTY

Hawi •   Halaula
                Kukuihaele • Paauhau
                Honokaa □
Kamuela •   Paauilo • Ookala
                Laupahoehoe • Papaaloa
                Hakalau • • Honomu
                Pepeekeo • Papaikou

HAWAII   Hilo

Kailua Kona □
        • Holualoa   Kurtistown □ • Keaau
Kainaliu •   Mountainview •
   • Kealakekua   Pahoa •
   □ Captain Cook
   • Honaunau   Volcano •

                Pahala □

        Naalehu □

Legend
Population
■ 250,000-999,999
● 100,000-249,999
● 50,000-99,999
● 25,000-49,999
■ 10,000-24,999
● 5,000-9,999
□ 1,000-4,999
• Less than 1,000
★ Military Base
State Capital   County Seat

| 0 | 5 | 10 | 20 | 30 | 40 Miles |
| 0 | 5 | 10 | 20 | 30 | 40 | 50 Kilometers |

Place	ZIP
Kipahulu	96713
Kipu (Kauai County)	96766
Kipu (Maui County)	96757
Koali	96713
Koele	96763
Kokee	96752
Kokohahi	96744
Kokomo	96708
Kolekole Beach Park	96710
Kolo	96704
Koloa	96756
Kualapuu	96757
Kualoa	96730
Kuhio Village	96743
Kuhua	96761
Kukaiau	96776
Kukui	96771
Kukuihaele	96727
Kukuiula	96756
Kukui Village	96774
Kula	96790
Kumukumu	96703
Kunia	96759
Kupolo	96766
Kurtistown	96760
Lahaina	96761*
	96767†
Lahaina Shopping Center	96761
Laie	96762
Lalakoa	96763
Lanai City	96763
Lanikai	96734
Lanikai Heights	96734
Laupahoehoe	96764
Laupahoehoe Point	96764
Lawai	96765
Lihue	96766
Lihue Shopping Center	96766
Lower Paia	96779
Lower Village	96706
Lualualei	96792
Lualualei Homesteads	96792
Maalaea	96793
McGerrow Village	96784
McGrew Point	96701
Maili	96792
Makaha	96792
Makaha Valley	96792
Makakilo City	96706
Makapala	96755
Makawao	96768
Makaweli	96769
Makena	96753
Makiki	96822-23
	96826

For specific Makiki Zip Codes call (808) 536-9903, or your local postmaster.

Place	ZIP
Makiki Heights (Part of Honolulu)	96822
Mana	96752
Mark Twain Estates	96772
Maulua	96780
Maunalani Heights (Part of Honolulu)	96816
Maunaloa	96770
Maunalua (Part of Honolulu)	96816
Maunawili	96734
Mililani Town	96789
Milolii	96726
Milo Village	96774
Moanalua (Part of Honolulu)	96819
Moiliili (Part of Honolulu)	96814
Mokuleia	96791
Momilani Estates	96782
Mountain View	96771
Muolea	96713
Naalehu	96772
Nanakuli	96792
Napili	96761
Napili-Honokowai	96761
Napoopoo	96704
Naval Communication Station	96786
Navy Cantonment (Part of Honolulu)	96818
Navy Terminal (Part of Honolulu)	96818
Nawiliwili	96766
Newtown Estates	96701
Nine Miles	96749
Ninole	96773
Niulii	96755
Niumalu	96766
Niu Valley (Part of Honolulu)	96821
Niu Valley Shopping Center (Part of Honolulu)	96821
Niu Village	96774
Numila	96705
Olinda	96768
Olomana	96734
Olowalu	96761
Omao	96756
Omapio	96790
Onomea	96781
Ookala	96774
Opihikao	96778
Orpheum Village	96779
Paauhau	96775
Paauhau Mauka	96727
Paauilo	96776
Pacific Heights (Part of Honolulu)	96817
Pacific Palisades	96782
Pahala	96777
Pahoa	96778
Pahoehoe	96704
Paia	96779
Palama (Part of Honolulu)	96817
Palani Junction	96725
Panaewa	96720
Papa	96704
Papaaloa	96780
Papaikou	96781
Paukaa	96720
Paukukalo	96793
Paumalu	96712
Pauwela	96708
Pearl City	96782
Pearl City Heights	96782
Pearl Harbor Naval Reservation	96860
Pearl Harbor Naval Supply Center	96860
Pepeekeo	96783
Pepeekeo Mill	96783
Pihana	96793
Piihonua	96720
Pohakea Homesteads	96776
Pohakupu	96734
Pohoiki	96778
Poipu	96756
Pomoho	96786
Port Allen	96705
Portlock	96825
Prince Kuhio Plaza	96720
Princeville	96722
Puako	96743
Pualaea Homestead	96764
Pua Loke	96766
Puhi	96766
Pukalani	96788
Pukoo	96748
Pulehu	96790
Punaluu (Hawaii County)	96777
Punaluu (Honolulu County)	96717
Puohala Village	96744
Pupukea	96712
Puuanahulu	96725
Puueo	96720
Pu'uhonua o Honaunau National Historical Park	96726
Puu Hue	96719
Puuiki	96713
Ruunene	96784
Puunoa	96761
Puunui (Part of Honolulu)	96819
Puuohala	96793
Puu Waawaa	96740
Puuwai	96769
Renton Village	96706
Royal Hawaiian (Part of Honolulu)	96815
St. Louis Heights (Part of Honolulu)	96816
Schofield Barracks	96786
Spanish Village B	96784
Spreckelsville	96779
Submarine Base	96818
Sunset Beach	96712
Tantalus (Part of Honolulu)	96822
Tenney	96706
Timber Town (Part of Honolulu)	96826
Ualapue	96748
Ulumalu	96708
Ulupalakua	96790
Umikoa	96776
Union Mill	96719
University	96822
Upolu Point	96719
Varona Village	96706
Village Park	96797
Village Seven	96705
Volcano	96785
Wahiawa (Honolulu County)	96786
Wahiawa (Kauai County)	96705
Waiahole	96744
Waiaka	96743
Waiakea	96720
Waiakea Camps	96720
Waialae-Kahala (Part of Honolulu)	96816
Waialua (Honolulu County)	96791
Waialua (Maui County)	96748
Waialua Mill	96791
Waianae	96792
Waianae Homesteads	96792
Waiau	96782
Waiau View Estates	96782
Waiawa Correctional Facility	96782
Waiehu	96793
Waiehu Village	96793
Waihee	96793
Waihee-Waiehue	96793
Waikane	96744
Waikapu	96793
Waikele	96797
Waikiki (Part of Honolulu)	96815
Waikoloa	96738
Wailea	96710
Wailea-Makena	96753
Wailua (Kauai County)	96746
Wailua (Maui County)	96708
Wailua Homesteads	96746
Wailuku	96793
Wailupe (Part of Honolulu)	96821
Waimalu	96701
Waimanalo	96795
Waimanalo Beach	96795
Waimea (Honolulu County)	96712
Waimea (Kauai County)	96796
Wainaku	96720
Wainee	96761
Wainiha	96714
Waiohinu	96772
Waipahu	96797
Waipio (Hawaii County)	96727
Waipio (Honolulu County)	96797
Waipio Acres	96786
Waipouli	96746
Waipunalei Homesteads	96764
Wharf	96761
Wheeler Air Force Base	96854
Whitmore Village	96786
Wilhelmina Rise (Part of Honolulu)	96816
Woodlawn (Part of Honolulu)	96822
Wood Valley Homesteads	96777

* Area Zip Code   † Post Office Boxes

	ZIP		ZIP		ZIP
Aberdeen	83210	Carlin Bay	83833	Eagle (Shoshone County)	83874
Acequia	83350	Carmen	83462	Eagle Rock (Part of Idaho	
Ahsahka	83520	Cascade	83611	Falls)	83402
Alameda (Part of Pocatello)	83201	Castleford	83321	Easley Hot Springs	83340
Albion	83311	Cataldo	83810	East Hope	83836
Aldape Heights (Part of		Cathedral Pines	83340	East Kamiah	83536
Boise)	83701	Cavendish	83537	East Lewiston (Part of	
Algoma	83860	Central	83217	Lewiston)	83501
Almo	83312	Central Cove	83676	Eastport	83826
Alpha	83611	Challis	83226	Eaton	83672
Alton	83454	Chapin	83455	Echo Beach	83858
American Falls	83211	Chatcolet	83851	Eddiville	83814
Ammon	83404	Cherry Creek	83252	Eden	83325
Anderson Dam	83647	Cherry Lane (Part of Boise)	83705	Edgemere	83856
Annis	83442	Chester	83421	Edmonds	83440
Apple Valley	83660	Chesterfield	83217	Egin	83445
Arbon	83212	Chilco	83801	Elba	83326
Arbon Valley	83203	Chubbuck	83202	Elk City	83525
Archer	83440	Churchill	83318	Elk River	83827
Arco	83213	Clagstone	83856	Ellis	83235
Argora	83423	Clark Fork	83811	Elmira	83862
Arimo	83214	Clarkia	83812	Emida	83861
Artesian City	83344	Clawson	83452	Emmett	83617
Ashton	83420	Clayton	83227	Enaville	83839
Athol	83801	Clearwater	83539	Enkraft	83350
Atlanta	83601	Clementsville	83436	Enrose	83605
Atomic City	83215	Cleveland	83263	Evergreen	83654
Avery	83802	Cliffs	97910	Excelsior Beach	83858
Avon	83823	Clifton	83228	Fairfield	83327
Baker	83467	Clover	83316	Fairview (Franklin County)	83263
Bancroft	83217	Coats	83350	Fairview (Twin Falls County)	83316
Banida	83263	Cobalt	83229	Fall Creek (Elmore County)	83647
Banks	83602	Cocolalla	83813	Fall Creek (Idaho County)	83530
Bannock (Part of Pocatello)	83204	Coeur d'Alene	83814-16	Falls City	83338
Basalt	83218	For specific Coeur d'Alene Zip		Featherville	83647
Basin	83346	Codes call (208) 773-4922, or		Felt	83424
Bates	83422	your local postmaster.		Fenn	83531
Bayview	83803	Coeur d'Alene Indian		Ferdinand	83526
Beachs Corner	83401	Reservation	83851	Fernan Lake Village	83814
Bear	83612	Colburn	83865	Fernwood	83830
Bellevue	83313	Cole Village (Part of Boise)	83704	Filer	83328
Belmont	83801	Collister (Part of Boise)	83703	Firth	83236
Bench	83241	Coltman	83401	Fish Haven	83287
Benewah	83861	Columbus Park (Part of		Florence	83542
Bennington	83254	Boise)	83705	Fort Hall (Bannock County)	83203
Berger	83301	Conda	83230	Fort Hall (Bingham County)	83203
Bern	83220	Conkling Park	83876	Fort Hall Indian Reservation	83203
Big Creek	83677	Conner	83442	Fox Creek	83455
Big Little Acres	83338	Coolin	83821	Franklin (Ada County)	83704
Big Springs (Part of Island		Cooperville	83554	Franklin (Franklin County)	83237
Park)	83433	Corral	83322	Franklin Park (Part of Boise)	83704
Blackfoot	83221	Cotterel	83323	Fraser	83544
Black Lake	83861	Cottonwood	83522	Freedom	83120
Blackrock	83245	Council	83612	Frisco	83873
Blaine	83843	Country Club Mall (Part of		Fruitland	83619
Blanchard	83804	Idaho Falls)	83401	Fruitvale	83620
Bliss	83314	Country Club Manor (Part of		Galena	83340
Bloomington	83223	Boise)	83705	Gannett	83313
Boise	83701-88	Country Club Terrace (Part		Gardena	83629
For specific Boise Zip Codes call		of Boise)	83705	Garden City	83704
(208) 383-4211, or your local		Craigmont	83523	Garden Valley	83622
postmaster.		Crescent	83537	Garfield	83442
Boise Airport (Part of Boise)	83715	Crouch	83622	Garwood	83835
Boise Town Square (Part of		Crystal	83672	Gem	83873
Boise)	83701	Culdesac	83524	Genesee	83832
Boles	83522	Culver	83865	Geneva	83238
Bone	83427	Cuprum	83612	Georgetown	83239
Bonners Ferry	83805	Curry	83328	Gibbonsville	83463
Borah (Part of Boise)	83702	Dalton Gardens	83814	Gibson	83221
Bovill	83806	Daniels	83252	Gibson City (Part of	
Bowmont	83686	Darlington	83255	Pinehurst)	83850
Box Canyon (Part of Island		David Taylor Research		Gifford	83541
Park)	83429	Center, Acoustic		Glendale	83263
Bradley (Part of Kellogg)	83837	Research Detachment	83803	Glengary	83864
Bridge	83342	Davis Acres (Part of Garden		Glenns Ferry	83623
Bruneau	83604	City)	83704	Glenwood (Clearwater	
Bruneau Valley	83604	Dayton	83232	County)	83544
Buhl	83316	Deary	83823	Glenwood (Idaho County)	83536
Buist	83243	Declo	83323	Golden	83530
Bunn	83873	Deep Creek (Oneida		Gooding	83330
Burgdorf	83638	County)	83252	Goodrich	83612
Burke	83873	Deep Creek (Twin Falls		Goshen	83274
Burley	83318	County)	83316	Grace	83241
Burmah	83349	Delta	83873	Grand Teton Mall (Part of	
Burton	83440	Dent	83544	Idaho Falls)	83401
Butler Bay	83861	Denton (Part of Boise)	83704	Grandview (Bingham	
Butte City	83213	Denver	83530	County)	83210
Cabinet	83811	Desmet	83824	Grand View (Owyhee	
Cache	83452	Dietrich	83324	County)	83624
Calder	83808	Dingle	83233	Grangemont	83544
Caldwell	83605*	Dixie	83525	Grangeville	83530
	83606†	Doles	83605	Granite	83801
Caldwell Labor Camp	83605	Donnelly	83615	Grant	83442
Cambridge (Bannock		Dover	83825	Grasmere	83604
County)	83234	Downey	83234	Gray	83285
Cambridge (Washington		Driggs	83422	Greencreek	83533
County)	83610	Drummond	83420	Greenleaf	83626
Cameron	83537	Dubois	83423	Greenwood	83335
Cardiff	83546	Duck Valley Indian		Greer	83544
Care-Free Estates	83318	Reservation	89832	Gross	83657
Carey	83320	Dudley	83810	Groveland	83221
Careywood	83809	Eagle (Ada County)	83616	Gwenford	83252

* Area Zip Code   † Post Office Boxes

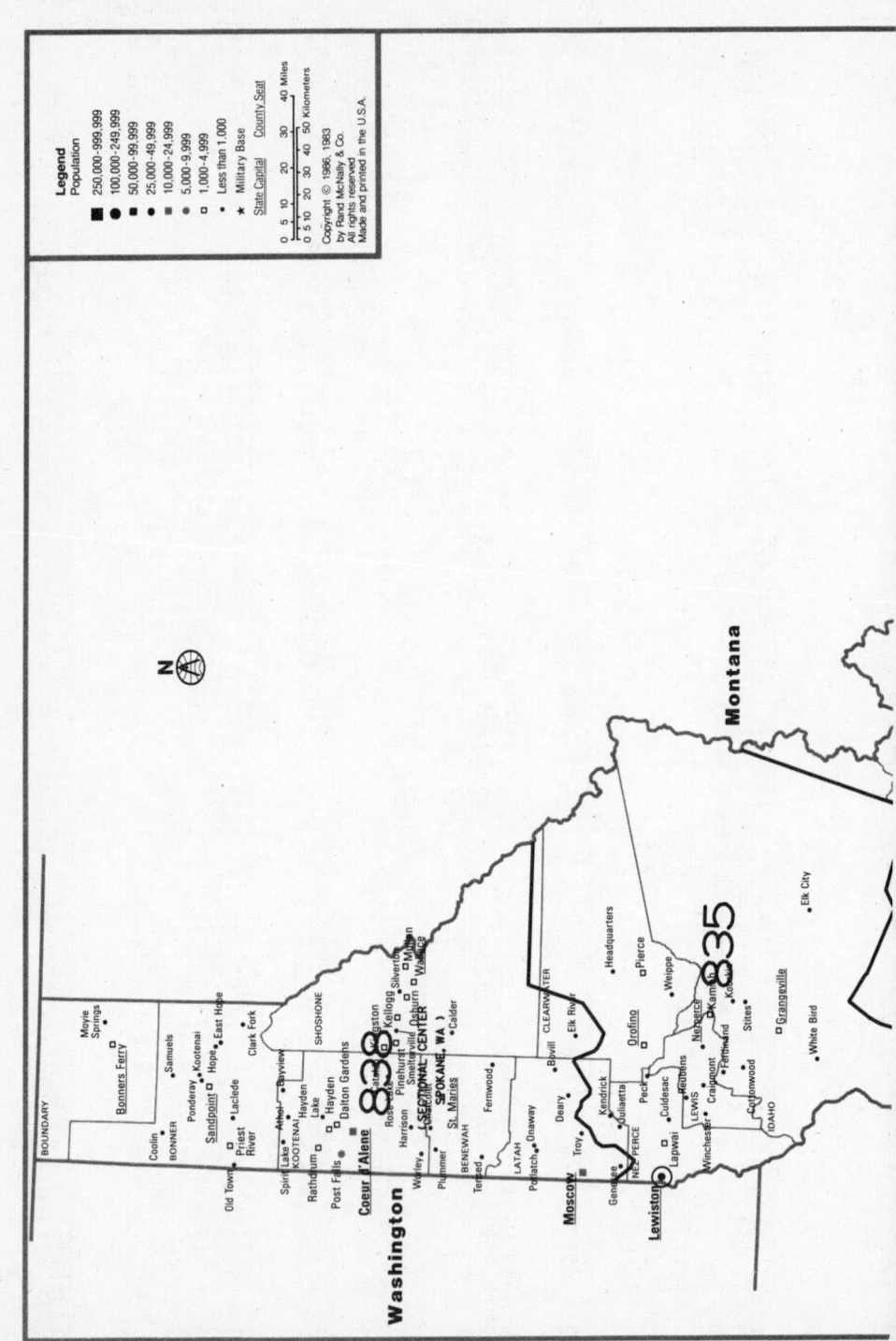

Legend
Population
■ 250,000-999,999
● 100,000-249,999
▪ 50,000-99,999
▫ 25,000-49,999
• 10,000-24,999
• 5,000-9,999
▫ 1,000-4,999
• Less than 1,000
★ Military Base
State Capital   County Seat

0 5 10 20 30 40 Miles
0 5 10 20 30 40 50 Kilometers

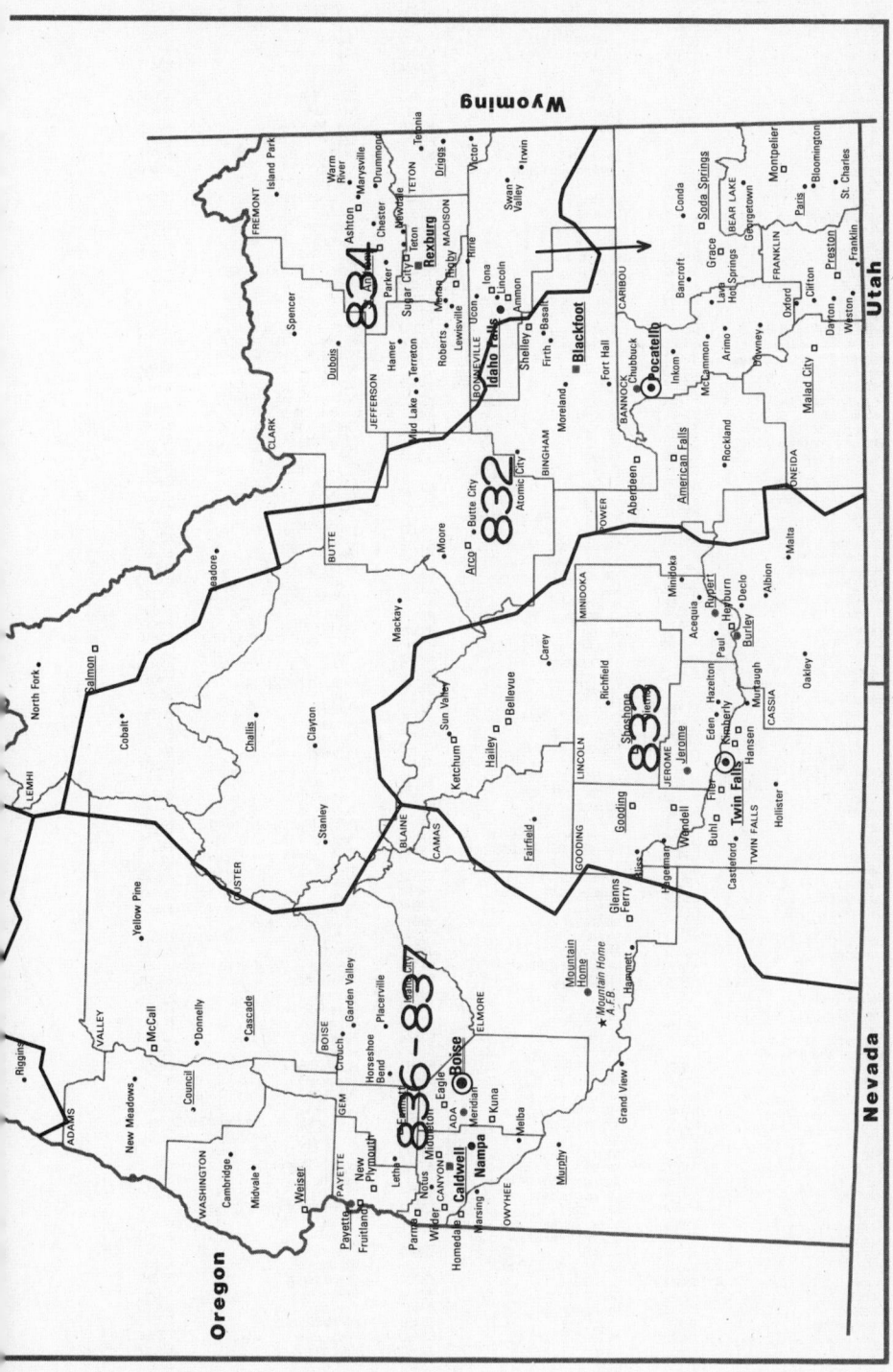

* Area Zip Code   † Post Office Boxes

	ZIP
Red River Hot Springs	83525
Reno	83423
Reubens	83548
Rexburg	83440
Reynolds	83650
Richfield	83349
Riddle	83604
Rigby	83442
Riggins	83549
Ririe	83443
Riverdale	83263
Riverside (Bingham County)	83221
Riverside (Canyon County)	83605
Riverside (Clearwater County)	83544
Roberts	83444
Robin	83214
Rock Creek	83334
Rockford	83221
Rockford Bay	83814
Rockland	83271
Rocky Bar	83647
Rocky Point (Benewah County)	83851
Rocky Point (Bonner County)	83821
Rogerson	83302
Rose	83221
Roseberry	83615
Rose Lake	83810
Roseworth	83321
Roswell	83660
Roy	83271
Rupert	83350
Sagle	83860
St. Anthony	83445
St. Charles	83272
St. Joe	83861
St. John	83252
St. Leon	83401
St. Maries	83861
Salem	83440
Salmon	83467
Samaria	83252
Samuels	83862
Sanders	83870
Sandpoint	83864
Sandy Shores Addition	83821
Santa	83866
Selle	83864
Setters	83876
Sharon	83260
Shelley	83274
Shelton	83401
Sherwood Beach	83821
Shoshone	83352
Shoup	83469
Silver City	83650
Silver Creek Plunge	83602
Silver Sands Beach	83858
Silverton	83867
Skyline (Part of Idaho Falls)	83402
Slate Creek	83554
Slickpoo	83524

	ZIP
Small	83423
Smelter Heights (Part of Kellogg)	83837
Smelterville	83868
Smiths Ferry	83611
Soda Springs	83276
Soldier	83327
Soldiers Home (Part of Boise)	83704
South Boise (Part of Boise)	83706
South Gate Plaza (Part of Lewiston)	83501
South Park (Part of Pocatello)	83204
Southside (Part of Boise)	83706
Southwick	83537
Spalding	83551
Spencer	83446
Spirit Lake	83869
Springdale	83318
Springfield	83277
Squirrel	83420
Standrod	83342
Stanley	83278
Star	83669
Starkey	83620
Starrhs Ferry	83318
State Line	83854
Sterling	83210
Stites	83552
Stoddard	83686
Stone	83252
Sugar City	83448
Sunbeam	83278
Sunnydell	83440
Sunnyside	83864
Sunnyslope	83605
Sun Valley	83353-54
For specific Sun Valley Zip Codes call (208) 622-5265, or your local postmaster.	
Swan Falls	83634
Swanlake	83281
Swan Valley	83449
Sweet	83670
Sweetwater	83540
Syringa	83539
Taber	83221
Talache	83860
Tamarack	83612
Taylor	83401
Teakean	83541
Tendoy	83468
Tenmile	83642
Tensed	83870
Terreton	83450
Teton	83451
Tetonia	83452
Thatcher	83283
Thomas	83221
Thomas Junction	83221
Thornton	83440
Three Creek	83301
Topaz	83246

	ZIP
Transfer (Part of Lewiston)	83501
Treasureton	83263
Trestle Creek	83836
Triumph	83333
Troy	83871
Turner Bay	83833
Tuttle	83314
Twin Falls	83301*
	83303†
Twin Groves	83445
Twin Lakes	83858
Twinlow	83858
Tyhee	83201
Ucon	83454
Unity	83318
University (Part of Moscow)	83843
Ustick	83704
Valley View Heights (Part of Lewiston)	83501
Victor	83455
View	83318
Viola	83872
Virginia	83234
Waha	83501
Wallace	83873
Wapello	83221
Wardboro	83254
Wardner	83837
Warm Lake	83611
Warm River	83420
Warren	83671
Washoe	83661
Wayan	83276
Webb	83540
Weippe	83553
Weiser	83672
Weitz	83605
Wendell	83355
Westgate Acres (Part of Boise)	83704
Westlake	83526
Westmond	83860
Westmoreland (Part of Boise)	83704
West Mountain	83611
Weston	83286
Whiskeyjack	83864
White Bird	83554
Whitney (Ada County)	83705
Whitney (Franklin County)	83263
Wilder	83676
Wilford	83445
Winchester	83555
Winder	83263
Winona	83539
Wolf Lodge	83814
Wolverine	83236
Woodland	83536
Woodland Park	83873
Woodruff	83252
Woodville	83274
Worley	83876
Yellow Pine	83677

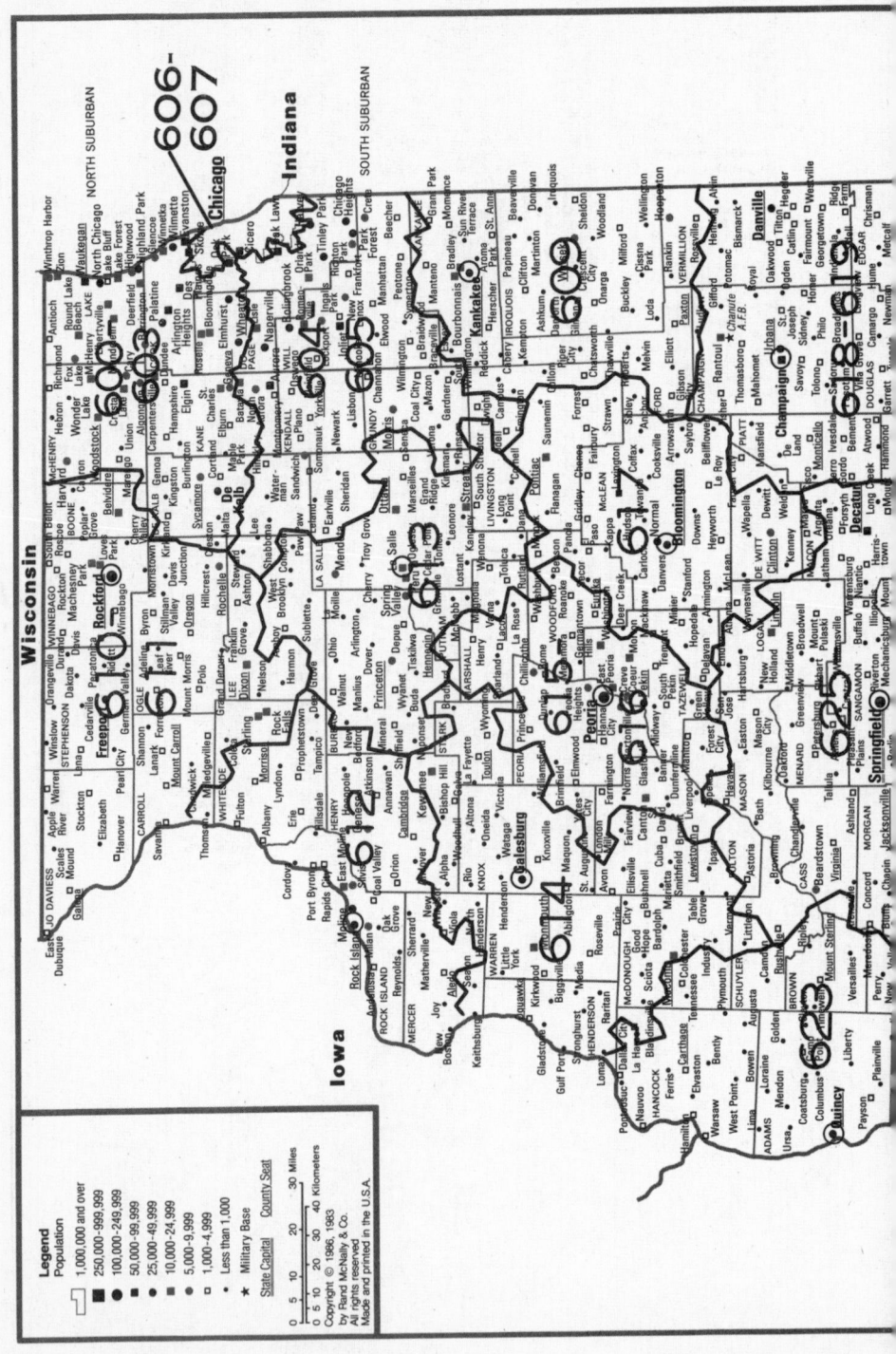

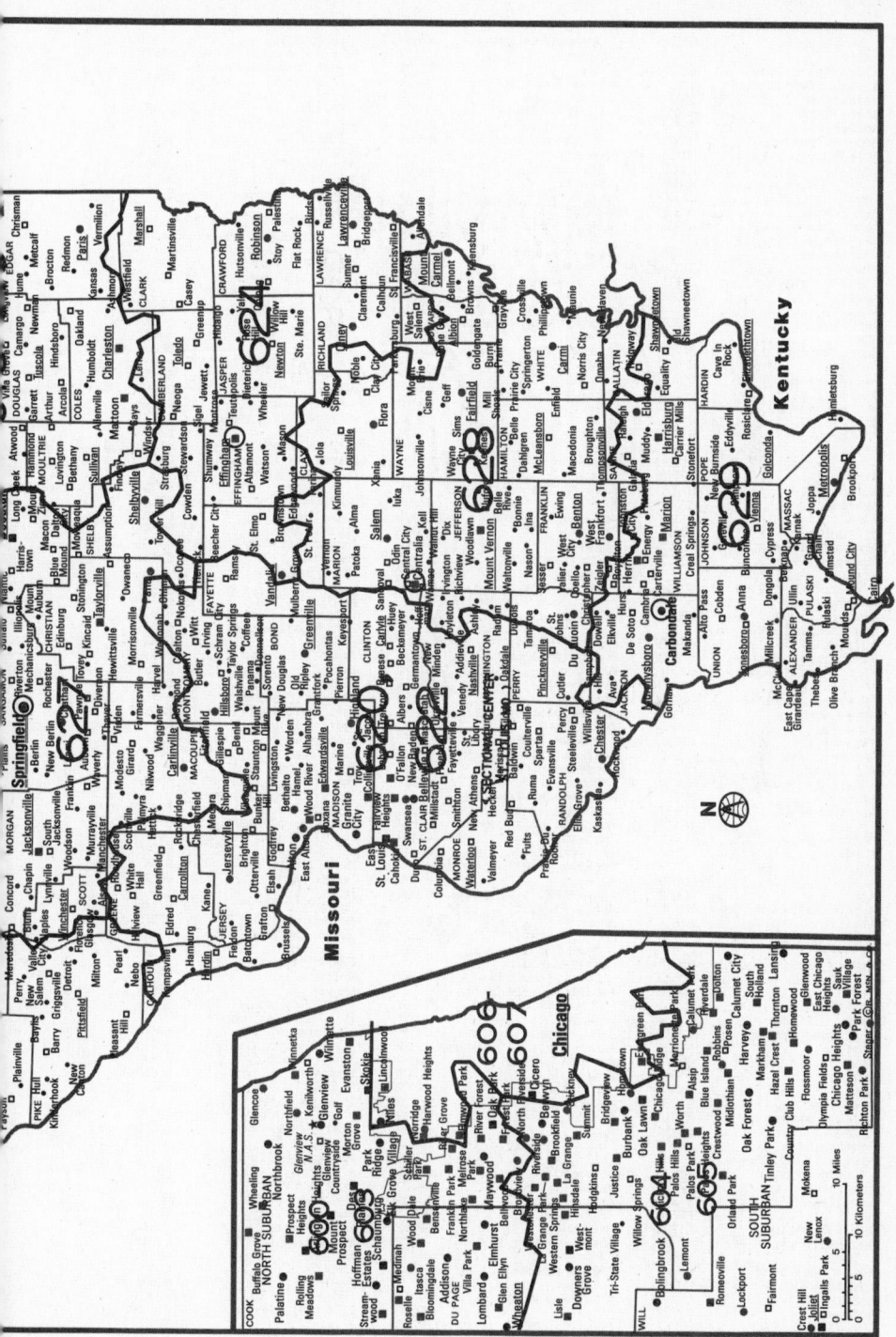

Name	ZIP	Name	ZIP	Name	ZIP
Abingdon	61410	Andres	60468	Atwood	61913
Abington (Township)	61476	Andrew	62707	Atwood Heights (Part of	
Acacia Acres	60525	Anna	62906	Alsip)	60658
Acme Station (Part of		Anna Mental Health and		Auburn (Clark County)	
Bartonville)	61607	Developmental Center	62906	(Township)	62441
Adair	61411	Annapolis	62413	Auburn (Sangamon County)	62615
Adams (Adams County)	62347	Annawan	61234	Auburn (Sangamon County)	
Adams (La Salle County)		Annawan (Township)	61234	(Township)	62615
(Township)	60531	Antioch	60002	Auburn Park (Part of	
Adams Corner	62410	Antioch (Township)	60002	Chicago)	60620
Addieville	62214	Appanoose (Township)	62354	Auburn Woods (Part of	
Addison (Township)	60101	Apple Canyon Lake	61001	Palatine)	60067
Addison	60101	Applegate (Part of		Audubon (Township)	62075
Adeline	61047	Schaumburg)	60194	Augsburg	62885
Aden	62895	Apple River	61001	Augusta	62311
Adrian	62310	Apple River (Township)	61001	Augusta (Township)	62311
Aero Estates	60564	Appleton	61428	Aurora	60504-07
Aetna (Coles County)	61938	Appletree (Part of Country		For specific Aurora Zip Codes call	
Aetna (Logan County)		Club Hills)	60477	(708) 897-2221, or your local	
(Township)	61749	Apple Valley (Part of		postmaster.	
Afolkey	61018	Glenview)	60025	Aurora (Township)	60505
Afton (Township)	60115	Appoloosa West	60119	Austin (Cook County)	60644
Agnew	61081	Aptakisic	60069	Austin (Macon County)	
Airport	61074	Arboretum East	60137	(Township)	62573
Airport Heights	61607	Arboretum Villages (Part of		Austin View	60463
Akin	62805	Lisle)	60532	Aux Sable (Township)	60447
Akron (Township)	61559	Arboretum West	60137	Ava	62907
Alan Dale	62035	Arbor Trails (Part of Park		Avalon Park (Part of	
Alba (Township)	61235	Forest)	60466	Chicago)	60619
Albany	61230	Arbury Hills	60448	Avena	62458
Albany (Township)	61230	Arcadia	62650	Avena (Township)	62458
Albers	62215	Archer	62707	Avery Hill	62223
Albion	62806	Archie	61876	Aviston	62216
Alden	60001	Arcola	61910	Avoca (Township)	61739
Alden (Township)	60001	Arcola (Township)	61910	Avon (Fulton County)	61415
Aldridge	62998	Arenzville	62611	Avon (Lake County)	
Aledo	61231	Arenzville (Township)	62611	(Township)	60030
Alexander	62601	Argenta	62501	Avondale (Part of Chicago)	60641
Alexis	61412	Argo (Part of Summit)	60501	Ayers (Township)	61816
Algonquin	60102	Argo Fay	61053	Babcock	61244
Algonquin (Township)	60102	Argyle	61011	Babson (Part of St. Charles)	60174
Algonquin Shores	60102	Arispie (Township)	61368	Babylon	61415
Algonquin Trails (Part of		Arlington	61312	Baden Baden (Part of	
Mount Prospect)	60056	Arlington Heights	60004-06	Pierron)	62273
Alhambra	62001	For specific Arlington Heights Zip		Bader	62624
Alhambra (Township)	62001	Codes call (708) 253-7456, or		Baileyville	61007
Allen (La Salle County)		your local postmaster.		Bainbridge (Township)	62639
(Township)	60470	Arlington Ridge (Part of		Baker	60531
Allen (Mason County)	62682	Arlington Heights)	60004	Baker Lake	60010
Allen (Whiteside County)	61071	Armington	61721	Bakerville	62864
Allendale	62410	Armstrong	61812	Balcom	62906
Allen Grove (Township)	62682	Arnold	62650	Bald Bluff (Township)	61476
Allens Corners	60140	Aroma (Township)	60901	Bald Hill (Township)	62883
Allentown	61568	Aroma Park	60910	Baldwin	62217
Allenville	61951	Aroma Park Northwest	60901	Baldwin Beach	62644
Allerton	61810	Arrington (Township)	62886	Bales Lake	60948
Allin (Township)	61774	Arrowhead (DuPage		Ball (Township)	62629
Allison (Township)	62439	County)	60187	Ballou	60481
Alma	62807	Arrowhead (Kankakee		Banner (Effingham County)	
Alma (Township)	62807	County)	60914	(Township)	62461
Almora	62123	Arrowhead (McDonough		Banner (Fulton County)	61520
Almora Heights	60123	County)	61455	Banner (Fulton County)	
Alorton	62207	Arrowhead Hills	60543	(Township)	61520
Alpha	61413	Arrowsmith (Township)	61772	Bannister	62881
Alsey	62610	Arrowsmith	61722	Bannockburn	60015
Alsip	60658	Arrow Wood	62035	Barclay	62561
Alsip Woods (Part of Alsip)	60658	Artesia (Township)	60918	Bardolph	61416
Alta	61614	Arthur	61911	Bargerville	62960
Altamont (Effingham		Asbury (Township)	62871	Barnett (De Witt County)	
County)	62411	Ashburn (Part of Chicago)	60652	(Township)	61727
Altamont (Madison County)	62035	Ash Grove (Iroquois		Barnett (Montgomery	
Alto (Township)	60553	County) (Township)	60953	County)	62056
Alton	62002	Ash Grove (Shelby County)		Barnhill	62809
Alton (Township)	62002	(Township)	61957	Barnhill (Township)	62809
Altona	61414	Ashkum	60911	Barr (Macoupin County)	
Alton Square (Part of Alton)	62002	Ashkum (Township)	60911	(Township)	62674
Alto Pass	62905	Ashland	62612	Barr (Sangamon County)	62613
Altorf	60914	Ashland (Township)	62612	Barren (Township)	62812
Alvin	61811	Ashley	62808	Barrington	60010*
Alworth	61088	Ashley (Township)	62808		60011†
Amboy	61310	Ashmore	61912	Barrington Center (Part of	
Amboy (Township)	61310	Ashmore (Township)	61912	Barrington Hills)	60010
Amenia	61856	Ashton	61006	Barrington Highlands	60010
America	62996	Ashton (Township)	61006	Barrington Hills	60010
Americana Village (Part of		Assumption	62510	Barrington Square (Part of	
Glendale Heights)	60139	Assumption (Township)	62510	Hoffman Estates)	60195
Ames	62277	Astoria	61501	Barrington Woods	60074
Amity (Township)	61319	Astoria (Township)	61501	Barrow	62082
Anchor	61720	Athens	62613	Barry	62312
Anchor (Township)	61720	Athensville	62082	Barry (Township)	62312
Anchorage (Part of		Athensville (Township)	62082	Barstow	61236
Glenview)	60026	Atkinson	61235	Bartelso	62218
Ancient Tree (Part of		Atkinson (Township)	61235	Bartlett	60103
Northbrook)	60062	Atlanta	61723	Bartonville	61607
Ancona	61311	Atlanta (Township)	61723	Basco	62313
Andalusia	61232	Atlas	62370	Base (Part of Rantoul)	61866
Andalusia (Township)	61232	Atlas (Township)	62370	Batavia	60510
Anderman Acres	60544	Atlee Ogles	62223	Batavia (Township)	60510
Anderson (Township)	62441	Atrium (Part of Elmhurst)	60126	Batavia Highlands (Part of	
Anderson Lake	61501	Atterbury	62675	Batavia)	60510
Andover	61233	Attila	62974	Batchtown	62006
Andover (Township)	61233	Atwater	62511	Bates	62670

	ZIP
Braidwood	60408
Brainerd (Part of Chicago)	60620
Branding	62013
Brandywine	60181
Branigar Estates	60007
Breckenridge	62563
Breeds	61520
Breese	62230
Breese (Township)	62230
Bremen (Cook County) (Township)	60426
Bremen (Randolph County)	62233
Brementowne Mall (Part of Tinley Park)	60477
Brenton (Township)	60959
Brentwood (Part of Des Plaines)	60016
Brentwood Estates	60074
Brereton	61520
Brettwood (Part of Decatur)	62526
Briar Bluff	61240
Briarbrook Village (Part of Wheaton)	60187
Briarcliffe (Part of Wheaton)	60187
Briarcliffe Knolls (Part of Wheaton)	60187
Briarcliff Estates (Part of Bourbonnais)	60914
Briarwick	61938
Briarwood	61107
Briarwoods Estates (Part of Deerfield)	60015
Briarwood Trace	62901
Brickman Manor (Part of Mount Prospect)	60056
Brickyard, The (Part of Chicago)	60635
Bridgelane	61265
Bridgeport	62417
Bridgeport (Township)	62417
Bridgeview	60455
Bridgeway Addition (Part of Moline)	61265
Bridle Creek Estates	60175
Brierwood	60175
Bright Oaks (Part of Cary)	60013
Brighton	62012
Brighton (Township)	62012
Brighton Park (Part of Chicago)	60632
Brimfield	61517
Brimfield (Township)	61517
Brisbane	60451
Bristol	60512
Bristol (Township)	60512
Bristol Lake	60560
Bristol Ridge	60560
Broadlands	61816
Broadmoor	61421
Broadview	60153
Broadway (Part of Rockford)	61106
Broadwell	62634
Broadwell (Township)	62634
Brocton	61917
Brooke Estates (Part of Highland Park)	60035
Brookeridge	60515
Brookfield (Cook County)	60513
Brookfield (La Salle County) (Township)	60470
Brook Forest (Part of Oak Brook)	60521
Brookforest North	60435
Brookhaven	61277
Brookhaven Manor (Part of Darien)	60561
Brookhill	60048
Brooklyn (Schuyler County)	62367
Brooklyn (Schuyler County) (Township)	62367
Brooklyn (Lee County) (Township)	61318
Brookport	62910
Brooks	62040
Brookside (Clinton County) (Township)	62801
Brookside (Kane County)	60175
Brooks Isle	61061
Brookview	61614
Brookville	61064
Brookville (Township)	61064
Brookwood (Part of Prospect Heights)	60070
Brookwood (Part of Rolling Meadows)	60008
Brookwood (Kane County)	60174
Brookwood Estates (Part of Wood Dale)	60191
Brothers	61858
Broughton (Hamilton County)	62817

	ZIP
Broughton (Livingston County) (Township)	60934
Brouilletts Creek (Township)	61924
Brown (Township)	61845
Brownfield	62938
Browning (Franklin County) (Township)	62812
Browning (Schuyler County)	62624
Browning (Schuyler County) (Township)	62624
Browns	62818
Brownstown	62418
Brownsville	62821
Brownwood	61747
Brubaker	62807
Bruce (La Salle County) (Township)	61364
Bruce (Moultrie County)	61951
Brunning	60441
Brunswick	62534
Brushy (Township)	62935
Brushy Mound (Township)	62033
Brussels	62013
Bryant	61519
Bryce	60953
Bryn Mawr (Part of Chicago)	60649
Buck (Township)	61944
Buckeye (Township)	61013
Buckhart (Christian County) (Township)	62531
Buckhart (Sangamon County)	62545
Buckheart (Township)	61563
Buckhorn	62353
Buckhorn (Township)	62375
Buckingham	60917
Buckley	60918
Buckner	62819
Bucks	61745
Buda	61314
Budd	61313
Buena Vista (Saline County)	62946
Buena Vista (Schuyler County) (Township)	62681
Buena Vista (Stephenson County)	61032
Buffalo (Ogle County) (Township)	61064
Buffalo (Sangamon County)	62515
Buffalo Grove (Cook County)	60089
Buffalo Grove (Ogle County)	61064
Buffalo Hart	62515
Buffalo Hart (Township)	62515
Buffalo Prairie	61237
Buffalo Prairie (Township)	61237
Bull Creek	60048
Bullock Addition	61241
Bull Valley	60098
Bulpitt	62517
Buncombe	62912
Bungay	62887
Bunker Hill	62014
Bunker Hill (Township)	62014
Bunkum (Part of Fairview Heights)	62208
Bunsenville	61846
Burbank	60459
Burches	60914
Bureau	61315
Bureau (Township)	61379
Burgess (Bond County) (Township)	62275
Burgess (Mercer County)	61231
Burksville	62298
Burlington	60109
Burlington (Township)	60109
Burnham	60633
Burnham Mill (Part of Elgin)	60123
Burns (Township)	61443
Burnside (Cook County)	60617
Burnside (Hancock County)	62318
Burnside's Lakewood (Part of Richton Park)	60466
Burnt Prairie	62820
Burnt Prairie (Township)	62821
Burritt (Township)	61088
Burr Oak (Part of Blue Island)	60406
Burr Oaks (Part of Joliet)	60435
Burrowsville	61929
Burr Ridge	60521
Burt	61721
Burton	62301
Burton (Adams County) (Township)	62301
Burton (McHenry County) (Township)	60081
Burtons Bridge	60050
Burtonview	62656

	ZIP
Bush (Jackson County)	62901
Bush (Williamson County)	62924
Bushnell	61422
Bushnell (Township)	61422
Bushton	61920
Butler (Montgomery County)	62015
Butler (Vermilion County) (Township)	60960
Butler Grove (Township)	62015
Butterfield	60148
Butterfield West	60137
Button (Township)	60960
Buysse Addition	61240
Buzzville	62644
Byron	61010
Byron (Township)	61010
Byron Hills (Ogle County)	61010
Byron Hills (Rock Island County)	61275
Cabery	60919
Cable	61281
Cache	62913
Cadiz	62931
Cadwell	61911
Cahokia (Macoupin County) (Township)	62023
Cahokia (St. Clair County)	62206
Cairo	62914
Caledonia	61011
Caledonia (Township)	61011
Calhoun	62419
Calumet (Township)	60406
Calumet (Part of East Hazel Crest)	60429
Calumet City	60409
Calumet Harbor (Part of Chicago)	60633
Calumet Park	60643
Calvin	62827
Camargo	61919
Camargo (Township)	61919
Cambria	62915
Cambridge	61238
Cambridge (Township)	61238
Cambridge (Part of Libertyville)	60048
Camden	62319
Camden (Township)	62319
Camelot	62401
Cameo Terrace (Part of Wheeling)	60090
Cameron	61423
Campbell Hill	62916
Campbells Island	61244
Camp Epworth	61038
Camp Ground	62864
Camp Grove	61424
Camp Logan	60099
Camp Point	62320
Camp Point (Township)	62320
Campton (Township)	60183
Campus	60920
Campus Walk (Part of Elgin)	60120
Camridge West (Part of Mundelein)	60060
Candlewood Estates	61853
Canoe Creek (Township)	61257
Canteen (Township)	62204
Canterbury Lane (Part of Glenview)	60025
Canterbury Shopping Center (Part of Markham)	60426
Canton	61520
Canton (Township)	61520
Cantrall	62625
Capital (Township)	62707
Capitol (Part of Springfield)	62701
Capri Gardens	60074
Capri Village	60074
Capron	61012
Carbon (Part of O'Fallon)	62269
Carbon Cliff	61239
Carbondale	62901-03
For specific Carbondale Zip Codes call (618) 457-3800, or your local postmaster.	
Carbon Hill	60416
Cardiff	60420
Carlinville (Township)	62626
Carlinville	62626
Carlock	61725
Carlsburg	62069
Carlyle	62231
Carlyle (Township)	62231
Carlysle (Part of Schaumburg)	60194
Carman	61425
Carman (Township)	61425
Carmi	62821
Carmi (Township)	62821
Carol Stream	60188

	ZIP
....	60197-99

For specific Carol Stream Zip
Codes call (708) 260-5137, or
your local postmaster.

	ZIP
Carpenter	62025
Carpentersville	60110
Carriage Creek (Part of Richton Park)	60466
Carriage Park	60543
Carriage Way Court	60074
Carrier Mills	62917
Carriers Mills (Township) ...	62917
Carrigan (Clinton County)	62231
Carrigan (Marion County) (Township)	62875
Carroll (Township)	61870
Carroll Addition (Champaign County)	61801
Carroll Addition (Ford County)	60936
Carrollton	62016
Carrollton (Township)	62016
Carrollwood (Part of Wood River)	62095
Carson (Township)	62080
Carterville	62918
Carthage	62321
Carthage (Township)	62321
Carthage Lake	61425
Cartter	62853
Cartwright (Township)	62677
Cary	60013
Casey	62420
Casey (Township)	62420
Caseyville	62232
Caseyville (Township)......	62232
Casner (Jefferson County) (Township)	62898
Casner (Macon County) ...	62552
Cass (Township)	61477
Castellean Lower	61021
Castellean Upper	61021
Castleton	61426
Catatoga 2	60123
Catatoga	60123
Catlin	61817
Catlin (Township)	61817
Cave (Township)	62890
Cave In Rock	62919
Cayuga	61764
Cazenovia	61545
Cazenovia (Township)	61545
Cedar (Township)	61410
Cedar Glen	60543
Cedar Grove	62959
Cedar Island	60020
Cedar Meadows...........	62269
Cedar Park	62040
Cedar Point	61316
Cedar Run (Part of Wheeling)	60090
Cedarville	61013
Centaur Estate	61008
Center Hill	61053
Centerville (Calhoun County)	62036
Centerville (Knox County)	61485
Centerville (Macoupin County)	62685
Centerville (Piatt County)...	61854
Centerville (White County)	62821
Central (Township)	62246
Central City (Grundy County)	60407
Central City (Marion County)	62801
Centralia	62801
Centralia (Township)	62801
Central Park	61832
Central Street (Part of Evanston)	60201
Centre, The (Part of Park Forest)	60466
Centreville (Township)	62207
Centreville.................	62207
Century Oaks (Part of Elgin)	60123
Century Oaks West (Part of Elgin)	60123
Cerro Gordo	61818
Cerro Gordo (Township) ...	61818
Chadwick	61014
Chalfin Bridge	62244
Chalmers (Township)	61455
Chambersburg	62323
Chambersburg (Township)	62323
Chambord (Part of Oak Brook)	60521
Champaign	61820-26

For specific Champaign Zip
Codes call (217) 373-6000, or
your local postmaster.

	ZIP
Champaign City (Township)	61820
Champlin...................	61739

	ZIP
Chana	61015
Chandlerville	62627
Chandlerville (Township) ...	62627
Channahon (Township)	60410
Channahon.................	60410
Channel Lake	60002
Chantily (Part of Highland Park)	60035
Chapin....................	62628
Chapman..................	62032
Charleston	61920
Charleston (Township)	61920
Charlestowne Mall (Part of St. Charles)	60174
Charlotte	60921
Charlotte (Township)	60921
Charlotte Hills	62274
Charter Grove	60178
Chasco	62923
Chateau Terrace	62221
Chatham (Cook County) ...	60619
Chatham (Sangamon County)	62629
Chatham (Sangamon County) (Township)	62629
Chatham Manor (Part of Buffalo Grove)	60089
Chatsworth	60921
Chatsworth (Township)	60921
Chatton	62346
Chauncey	62466
Chautauqua	62028
Chautauqua Park (Mason County)	62644
Chautauqua Park (Menard County)	62675
Chebanse.................	60922
Chebanse (Township)	60927
Checkrow	61415
Chelsea Cove (Part of Wheeling)	60090
Cheltenham (Part of Chicago)	60649
Chemung	60033
Chemung (Township)	60033
Cheneys Grove (Township)	61770
Cheneyville	60942
Chenoa	61726
Chenoa (Township)	61726
Chenot Place	62221
Cherry	61317
Cherry Grove-Shannon (Township)	61046
Cherry Hill	60431
Cherry Hills (Champaign County)	61821
Cherry Hills (Kane County)	60506
Cherry Point	61924
Cherryvale Mall (Part of Cherry Valley)	61016
Cherry Valley (Township) ...	61016
Cherry Valley	61016
Cherrywood (Christian County)	62568
Cherrywood (Will County)	60440
Chester (Logan County) (Township)	62656
Chester (Randolph County)	62233
Chesterfield (Cook County)	60619
Chesterfield (Macoupin County)	62630
Chesterfield (Macoupin County) (Township)	62630
Chesterville...............	61911
Chestline..................	62314
Chestnut (Knox County) (Township)	61544
Chestnut (Logan County)	62518
Chestnut Street (Part of Chicago)...............	60610

Chicago 60601-41
.... 60643-49
.... 60667-99
.... 60701
.... 60799

For specific Chicago Zip Codes
call (312) 765-3585, or your local
postmaster.

COLLEGES & UNIVERSITIES

	ZIP
Chicago State University ...	60628
Columbia College	'60605
De Paul University	60604
DeVry Institute of Technology-Chicago.....	60618
Illinois Institute of Technology	60616
John Marshall Law School	60604
Keller Graduate School of Management............	60606

	ZIP
Loyola University of Chicago	60611
Moody Bible Institute	60610
Mundelein College	60660
North Park College & Theological Seminary	60625
Northeastern Illinois University	60625
Roosevelt University	60605
Rush University	60612
Saint Xavier College	60655
School of Art Institute of Chicago	60603
University of Chicago	60637
University of Illinois at Chicago	60680

FINANCIAL INSTITUTIONS

	ZIP
Amalgamated Bank of Chicago	60603
American National Bank and Trust Company of Chicago	60690
Associated Bank Chicago	60601
Avondale Federal Savings Bank	60602
Bank of Commerce & Industry................	60631
Bell Federal Savings & Loan Association	60603
Belmont National Bank of Chicago	60657
Beverly Bank	60643
Boulevard Bank, N.A.	60611
Calumet Federal Savings & Loan	60617
Central Federal Savings & Loan Association of Chicago	60657
Chesterfield Federal Savings & Loan Association	60643
Chicago City Bank & Trust Company	60621
The Chicago-Tokyo Bank	60602
Cole Taylor Bank	60607
Colonial Bank	60634
Columbia National Bank of Chicago	60656
Commercial National Bank of Chicago	60625
Continental Bank, National Association	60697
Cosmopolitan Bank and Trust	60610
Cragin Federal Bank for Savings.................	60639
Damen Federal Bank for Savings.................	60609
Devon Bank...............	60645
Drexel National Bank	60616
Fidelity Federal Savings Bank	60641
The First Commercial Bank	60626
First Cook Community Bank	60659
First Federal Savings of Hegewisch	60633
First National Bank of Chicago	60670
First National Bank of Evergreen Park	60638
First National Bank of Lincolnwood	60659
First Security Federal Savings Bank	60622
First State Bank of Chicago	60656
Harris Trust and Savings Bank	60603
Heritage Pullman Bank & Trust Company	60628
Hoyne Savings Bank	60630
Hyde Park Bank & Trust Company	60615
Independence Bank of Chicago	60619
Irving Federal Bank for Savings.................	60618
Jefferson State Bank	60630
Lake Shore National Bank	60611
Lakeside Bank	60604
LaSalle Bank-Lake View ...	60657
LaSalle National Bank......	60603
LaSalle Northwest National Bank	60641
Liberty Federal Savings Bank	60659
Liberty Bank for Savings...	60647
Lincoln National Bank......	60613
Lincoln Park Federal Savings & Loan Association	60613

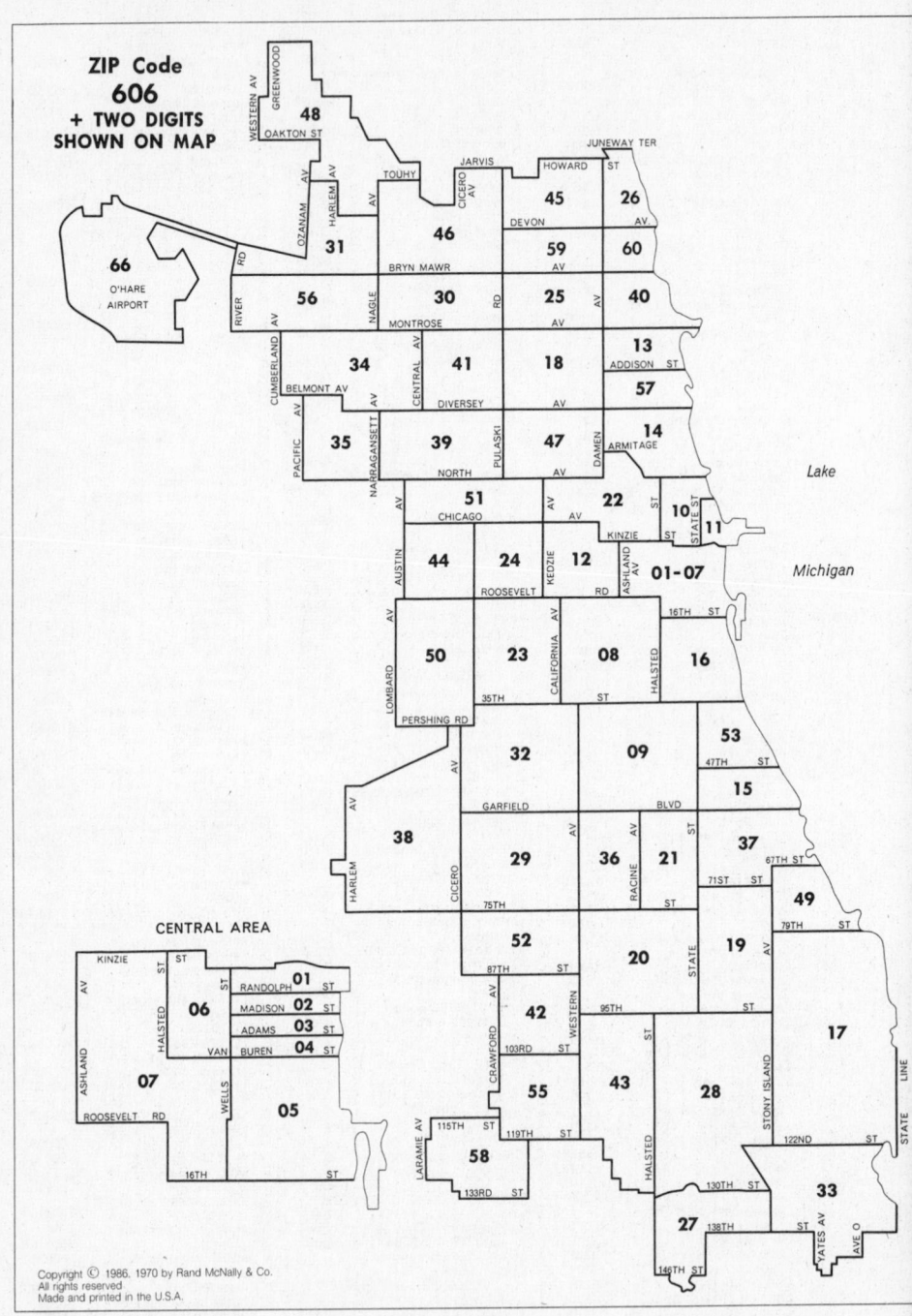

ZIP Code
606
**+ TWO DIGITS
SHOWN ON MAP**

66
O'HARE
AIRPORT

Lake

Michigan

CENTRAL AREA

ZIP | ZIP | ZIP

Place	ZIP
Dee Road (Part of Park Ridge)	60068
Deer Park (La Salle County) (Township)	61348
Deer Park (Lake County)	60010
Deer Plain	62013
Deer Run	60175
Deerwood Estates	62471
Degognia (Township)	62950
De Kalb	60115
De Kalb (Township)	60115
Delafield	62859
De Land	61839
Delavan	61734
Delavan (Township)	61734
Del-Bar	61520
Delhi	62052
Dellwood Highlands	60441
Del Mar Woods	60015
DeLong	61436
Del Rey	60968
Delwood	62946
Dement (Township)	61068
Denison (Township)	62460
Denmark	62238
Denning (Township)	62896
Dennison	62423
Denny	62832
Denver (Hancock County)	62321
Denver (Richland County) (Township)	62868
Depue	61322
Derby (Ford County)	60936
Derby (Saline County)	62947
Derinda (Township)	61028
Derinda Center	61028
Derry (Township)	62312
Deselm	60950
De Soto	62924
De Soto (Township)	62924
Des Plaines	60016-19
For specific Des Plaines Zip Codes call (708) 827-5591, or your local postmaster.	
Des Plaines Manor (Part of Des Plaines)	60016
Des Plaines Terrace (Part of Des Plaines)	60016
Detroit	62332
Detroit (Township)	62332
Devereux Heights (Part of Springfield)	62707
Devonshire (Part of Des Plaines)	60018
Dewey	61840
Dewitt	61735
De Witt (Township)	61735
Dewmaine	62918
Dexter	62411
Diamond	60416
Diamond City	62859
Diamond Lake	60060
Diamond Town	62274
Dieterich	62424
Dillon	61568
Dillon (Township)	61568
Dillsburg	61866
Dimmick (Township)	61301
Diona	62428
Disco	61450
Diswood	62988
Divernon	62530
Divernon (Township)	62530
Divide	62889
Division Street (Part of Chicago)	60651
Dix (Ford County) (Township)	60933
Dix (Jefferson County)	62830
Dixmoor	60406
Dixon	61021
Dixon (Township)	61021
Dixon Springs	62943
Dobbins Downs	61801
Dodds (Township)	62864
Doddsville	61452
Dollville	62571
Dolson (Township)	61944
Dolton	60419
Dongola	62926
Donnellson	62019
Donovan	60931
Dora (Township)	61925
Dorans	61938
Dorchester	62033
Dorchester (Township)	62009
Dorr (Township)	60098
Dorris Park (Part of Harrisburg)	62946
Dorsey	62021
Douglas (Clark County) (Township)	62441

Place	ZIP
Douglas (Effingham County) (Township)	62401
Douglas (Iroquois County) (Township)	60938
Douglas (Knox County)	61572
Douglas (St. Clair County)	62243
Douglas Park	61081
Dover	61323
Dover (Township)	61356
Dow	62022
Dowell	62927
Downers Fairview (Part of Downers Grove)	60515
Downers Grove	60515-17
For specific Downers Grove Zip Codes call (312) 969-2001, or your local postmaster.	
Downers Grove (Township)	60559
Downers Grove Estates	60515
Downey (Part of North Chicago)	60064
Downs	61736
Downs (Township)	61736
Downtown (Part of Bloomington)	61701
Downtown (Part of Carbondale)	62901
Downtown (Part of Des Plaines)	60016
Downtown (Part of Glen Ellyn)	60137
Downtown (Part of La Salle)	61301
Downtown (Part of Northbrook)	60062
Downtown (Part of Quincy)	62301
Downtown (Part of Rockford)	61101
Downtown (Part of Springfield)	62701
Drake	62092
Dresden Acres	60450
Drexel (Part of Cicero)	60650
Drivers	62898
Druce Lake	60046
Drummer (Township)	60936
Drury (Township)	52761
Dry Grove (Township)	61732
Dry Point (Township)	62422
Dubois	62831
Du Bois (Township)	62831
Duck Lake Woods	60041
Dudley	61944
Dudleyville	62246
Duncan (Mercer County) (Township)	61231
Duncan (Stark County)	61559
Duncans Mills	61542
Duncanville	62454
Dundas	62425
Dundee	60118
Dundee (Township)	60118
Dunfermline	61524
Dunham (Township)	60033
Dunhurst (Part of Wheeling)	60090
Dunkel	62557
Dunlap	61525
Dunlap Lake (Part of Edwardsville)	62025
Dunleith (Township)	61025
Dunn	61951
Dunning (Part of Chicago)	60634
Du Page (Township)	60441
Dupo	62239
Du Quoin	62832
Durand	61024
Durand (Township)	61024
Durham	62330
Durham (Township)	62330
Durley Camp	62025
Dutch Creek Woodlands	60050
Dutch Hollow (Part of Belleville)	62221
Duvall	62565
Dwight	60420
Dwight (Township)	60420
Dwight Correctional Center	60420
Dykersburg	62987
Eagarville	62023
Eagle (Township)	61364
Eagle Creek (Township)	62934
Eagle Heights	60123
Eagle Lake	60401
Eagle Park	62060
Eagle Point (Township)	61064
Eagle Point Bay	62939
Earl (Township)	60518
Earl Estates	60554
Earlville	60518
East Alton	62024
East Bend (Township)	61840
East Brooklyn	60474
East Cape Girardeau	62957

Place	ZIP
East Carondelet	62240
East Clinton	61252
East Dubuque	61025
East Dundee	60118
East Eldorado (Township)	62930
Eastern (Township)	62812
East Fork (Clinton County) (Township)	62283
East Fork (Montgomery County) (Township)	62017
East Fulton	61252
East Galena (Township)	61036
East Galesburg	61430
Eastgate	62881
East Gillespie	62033
East Grove (Township)	61349
East Hannibal	62343
East Hardin	62031
East Hazel Crest	60429
East Keokuk (Part of Hamilton)	62341
Eastland Mall (Part of Bloomington)	61701
East Lincoln (Township)	62656
East Loon Lake	60002
East Lynn	60932
East Meadowbrook	62067
East Meadowview (Part of Bradley)	60915
East Moline	61244
East Nelson (Township)	61951
East Newbern	62022
East Oakland (Township)	61943
Easton	62633
East Peoria	61611
East River	60964
East Rockford (Part of Rockford)	61110
East Side (Cook County)	60617
East Side (Kankakee County)	60954
East St. Louis	62201-08
For specific East St. Louis Zip Codes call (618) 875-0200, or your local postmaster.	
East Wenona	61377
Eastwood Manor	60050
Eaton	62454
Eberle	62424
Echo Lake	60047
Eckard	62644
Eddyville	62928
Edelstein	61526
Eden (La Salle County) (Township)	61370
Eden (Peoria County)	61536
Eden (Randolph County)	62286
Eden Park	62933
Edford (Township)	61254
Edgar	61924
Edgar (Township)	60118
Edgebrook (Cook County)	60646
Edgebrook (DeKalb County)	60178
Edgemont (Part of East St. Louis)	62203
Edgewater Beach	62231
Edgewood (Champaign County)	61801
Edgewood (Effingham County)	62426
Edgewood (Woodford County)	61530
Edgewood Heights	61008
Edgington	61284
Edgington (Township)	61284
Edinburg	62531
Edison Park (Part of Chicago)	60631
Edison Square (Part of Waukegan)	60085
Edwards	61528
Edwardsville	62025
Edwardsville (Township)	62025
Edwardsville Junction (Part of Edwardsville)	62025
Effingham	62401
Effner	60966
Egan	61047
Egyptian Hills	62922
Egyptian Shores	62922
Eight Mile Prairie	62918
Eighty-Seventh Street (Part of Chicago)	60619
Eighty-Third Street (Part of Chicago)	60617
Eiker Addition	61448
Eileen (Part of Coal City)	60416
Ela (Township)	60047
Elam Lake	61951
Elba (Gallatin County)	62871
Elba (Knox County) (Township)	61489

	ZIP		ZIP		ZIP
Flowerfield Acres (Part of Lombard)	60148	Frankfort (Will County)	60423	Gays	61928
Floyd (Township)	61423	Frankfort (Will County) (Township)	60423	Geff	62842
Fondulac (Tazewell County) (Township)	61611	Frankfort Heights (Part of West Frankfort)	62840	Genesee (Township)	61270
Fon-Du-Lac (Will County)	60544	Frankfort Square	60423	Geneseo	61254
Foosland	61845	Franklin (DeKalb County)		Geneseo (Township)	61254
Ford City Shopping Center (Part of Chicago)	60652	(Township)	60146	Geneseo Hills	61254
Fordham (Part of Chicago)	60619	Franklin (Morgan County)	62638	Geneva	60134
Ford Heights	60411	Franklin Grove	61031	Geneva (Township)	60134
Forest Acres	62201	Franklin Park	60131	Genoa	60135
Forest City	61532	Franklin Square	60423	Genoa (Township)	60135
Forest City (Township)	61532	Franklinville	60098	Gent City	62959
Forest Estates	60067	Frederick	62639	Gentry Acres	62918
Forest Gardens	60084	Frederick (Township)	62639	Georgetown (Township)	61846
Forest Glen (Part of Chicago)	60630	Freeburg	62243	Georgetown (Carroll County)	61046
Foresthaven	60045	Freeburg (Township)	62243	Georgetown (McDonough County)	61455
Forest Heights (Part of Chicago Heights)	60411	Freedom (Carroll County) (Township)	61046	Georgetown (Vermilion County)	61846
Forest Hill (Part of Chicago)	60652	Freedom (La Salle County) (Township)	61350	Gerald	61812
Forest Hills Estates	62471	Freeman Spur	62841	Gerlaw	61435
Forest Homes	62018	Freeport	61032	German (Township)	62421
Forest Lake	60047	Freeport (Township)	61032	Germantown	62245
Forest Manor	60441	Fremont (Morgan County)	60060	Germantown (Township)	62245
Forest Park	60130	Fremont Center	60060	Germantown	61548
Forest River	60056	Fremont Junction (Part of Hanover Park)	60103	Germantown Hills	61548
Forest View	60402	Frenchman's Cove (Part of Arlington Heights)	60004	German Valley	61039
Forest View Hills (Part of Oak Forest)	60452	French Village (Part of Fairview Heights)	62208	Germanville (Township)	60921
Forman	62908	Frentress Lake	61025	Gibson City	60936
Forrest	61741	Friends Creek (Township)	62501	Gibsonia	62954
Forrest (Township)	61741	Friendsville	62863	Gifford	61847
Forrestal Village (Part of North Chicago)	60088	Frisco	62836	Gila	62445
Forreston	61030	Frog City	62913	Gilberts	60136
Forreston (Township)	61030	Frogtown (Clinton County)	62231	Gilchrist	61486
Forsyth	62535	Frogtown (Washington County)	62271	Gilead	62006
Fort Dearborn	60610-11	Frontenac	60563	Gillespie	62033
For specific Fort Dearborn Zip Codes call (312) 644-7603, or your local postmaster.		Frontenac Place	62035	Gillespie (Township)	62033
		Frost	62901	Gillespie Lakes	62033
Fort Gage	62241	Fruit	62025	Gillum	61701
Fort Russell (Township)	62010	Fruitland	61265	Gilman	60938
Forty-Seventh Street (Cook County)	60615	Fry's Wheatland View	60565	Gilmer (Township)	62328
Foss Acres (Part of Waukegan)	60088	Fulton	61252	Gilmore	62443
Foster (Madison County) (Township)	62002	Fulton (Township)	61252	Gilmore Lake	62236
Foster (Marion County) (Township)	62807	Fults	62244	Gilson	61436
Fosterburg	62002	Funkhouser	62401	Ginger Creek (Part of Oak Brook)	60521
Foster Pond	62298	Funks Grove	61754	Ginger Hill (Part of Milan)	61264
Fountain	62295	Funks Grove (Township)	61754	Girard	62640
Fountain Bluff (Township)	62950	Future City	62914	Girard (Township)	62640
Fountain Creek	60942	Fyre Lake	61281	Givins (Part of Chicago)	60620
Fountain Creek (Township)	60942	Gages Lake	60030	Gladstone	61437
Fountain Gap	62236	Galatia	62935	Gladstone (Township)	61437
Fountain Green	62321	Galatia (Township)	62935	Gladstone Commons (Part of Mount Prospect)	60056
Fountain Green (Township)	62321	Gale	62990	Gladstone Park (Part of Chicago)	60630
Four Lakes	60532	Galena	61036	Glasford	61533
Four Mile (Township)	62895	Galena Oaks	61028	Glasgow	62694
Fowler	62338	Galesburg	61401*	Glass Works (Part of Alton)	62002
Fox (Jasper County) (Township)	62448		61402†	Glen (Part of Glen Carbon)	62034
Fox (Kendall County)	60560	Galesburg City (Township)	61401	Glen Acres (Part of Rosemont)	60018
Fox (Kendall County) (Township)	60560	Galesville	61854	Glenarm	62536
Fox Chase (Part of St. Charles)	60174	Gallagher	62450	Glen Arms	60041
Foxcroft	60137	Galnipper Place	62047	Glenavon	61724
Foxfield	60175	Galt	61037	Glenayre (Part of Glenview)	60025
Fox Lake	60020	Galton	61910	Glenayre Gardens (Part of Glenview)	60025
Fox Lake Hills	60046	Galva	61434	Glenbard South	60532
Fox Lake Vista	60081	Galva (Township)	61434	Glenbrook Countryside	60062
Fox Lawn	60560	Ganeer (Township)	60954	Glenburn	61858
Fox Point (Part of Barrington)	60010	Ganntown	62943	Glen Carbon	62034
Fox Ridge (Part of South Elgin)	60177	Garber	60936	Glencoe	60022
Fox River Bluffs 2	60118	Gardena (Part of East Peoria)	61611	Glendale (Pope County)	62985
Fox River Estates	60174	Garden Heights	62946	Glendale (Rock Island County)	61282
Fox River Gardens	60560	Garden Hill (Township)	62899	Glendale Gardens (Part of Wood River)	62024
Fox River Grove	60021	Garden Hills (Part of Champaign)	61821	Glendale Heights	60139
Fox River Heights	60174	Garden Homes	60655	Glen Ellyn	60137*
Fox River Valley Gardens	60010	Garden of Eden	60954		60138†
Fox Valley Center (Part of Aurora)	60505	Garden Plain	61252	Glen Ellyn Countryside	60137
Fox Valley East (Part of Aurora)	60505	Garden Plain (Township)	61252	Glen Ellyn Woods	60137
Fox Valley Mail Processing Center	60598-99	Garden Prairie	61038	Glengarry (Part of Geneva)	60134
For specific Fox Valley Mail Processing Center Zip Codes call (708) 897-2221, or your local postmaster.		Garden Quarter (Part of Elgin)	60123	Glen Hill (Part of Glendale Heights)	60139
		Gardner (Grundy County)	60424	Glenn	62280
		Gardner (Sangamon County) (Township)	62677	Glennshire (Part of Lake Zurich)	60047
Fox Valley Villages (Part of Aurora)	60505	Gards Point	62863	Glen Oak	60137
Frankfort (Franklin County) (Township)	62896	Garfield (Grundy County) (Township)	60424	Glen Park	60551
		Garfield (La Salle County)	61377	Glen Ridge (Part of Matteson)	60443
		Garfield Park (Part of Chicago)	60624	Glenshire (Part of Glenview)	60025
		Garland	61917	Glenview (Cook County)	60025
		Garrett	61913	Glen View (St. Clair County)	62269
		Garrett (Township)	61913	Glenview Countryside	60025
		Gary Gardens	60188	Glenview Estates	60025
		Gas Light Village	60450	Glenview Naval Air Station	60026
		Gateway Yard (Part of East St. Louis)	62207	Glenview Terrace (Part of Glenview)	60025
				Glenview Woodlands	60025

	ZIP
Glenwood	60425
Glenwood Estates (Part of Glenwood)	60425
Glenwood Plaza (Part of Glenwood)	60425
Godfrey	62035
Godfrey (Township)	62035
Godley	60407
Golconda	62938
Gold (Township)	61344
Golden	62339
Golden Acres	60025
Golden Eagle	62036
Golden Gardens (Part of Centreville)	62206
Goldengate	62843
Golden Highridge (Part of Des Plaines)	60016
Golden Lilly	62914
Golden Manor (Part of Des Plaines)	60016
Gold Hill (Township)	62984
Golena Knolls	61523
Golf	60029
Golf Mill Shopping Center (Part of Niles)	60714
Golfview Hills	60521
Goode (Township)	62884
Goodenow	60401
Goodfarm (Township)	60424
Goodfield	61742
Good Hope	61438
Goodings Grove	60441
Goodrich	60913
Goodwine	60939
Goofy Ridge	61567
Goose Creek (Township)	61839
Goose Lake (Township)	60444
Gordons	62454
Goreville	62939
Gorham	62940
Goshen (Township)	61483
Gossett	62869
Grafton (Jersey County)	62037
Grafton (McHenry County) (Township)	60142
Graham Correctional Center	62049
Grand Chain	62941
Grand Crossing (Part of Chicago)	60619
Grand Detour	61021
Grand Detour (Township)	61021
Grand Prairie (Township)	62898
Grand Rapids (Township)	61325
Grand Ridge	61325
Grand Tower	62942
Grand Tower (Township)	62942
Grandview (Carroll County)	61285
Grandview (Edgar County)	61944
Grandview (Edgar County) (Township)	61944
Grandview (Sangamon County)	62707
Grandview (Woodford County)	61611
Grandville (Township)	62481
Grandwood Park	60031
Grange	61872
Granite City	62040
Granite City (Township)	62040
Grant (Lake County) (Township)	60041
Grant (Vermilion County) (Township)	60942
Grantfork	62249
Grant Park	60940
Grantsburg	62943
Granville	61326
Granville (Township)	61326
Grape Creek	61832
Grass Lake	60002
Gray (Township)	62844
Grayland (Part of Chicago)	60641
Graymont	61743
Graymoor (Part of Olympia Fields)	60461
Grayslake	60030
Grays Siding	61858
Grayville	62844
Green Acres (McDonough County)	61455
Green Acres (Sangamon County)	62707
Greenbriar (Part of New Lenox)	60451
Greenbriar Addition	62918
Greenbrook Country (Part of Hanover Park)	60103
Greenbush	61415
Greenbush (Township)	61415
Greene (Mercer County) (Township)	61486

	ZIP
Greene (Woodford County) (Township)	61516
Greenfield (Greene County)	62044
Greenfield (Grundy County) (Township)	60474
Green Garden (Township)	60423
Greenleaf Hills	61842
Green Meadows (Cook County)	60103
Green Meadows (Kane County)	60510
Green Oak	61356
Green Oaks	60048
Greenpond	62361
Green River	61241
Green Rock	61241
Greentree (Part of Libertyville)	60048
Greenup	62428
Greenup (Township)	62428
Green Valley (DuPage County)	60148
Green Valley (Tazewell County)	61534
Greenview	62642
Greenville (Bond County)	62246
Greenville (Bureau County) (Township)	61376
Greenwich	60901
Greenwood (Christian County) (Township)	62546
Greenwood (McHenry County)	60098
Greenwood (McHenry County) (Township)	60098
Greenwood Acres	61840
Greenwood Meadows	62035
Greer	60973
Gresham (Part of Chicago)	60620
Gridley	61744
Gridley (Township)	61744
Grigg	62278
Griggsville	62340
Griggsville (Township)	62340
Grimes Addition	61081
Grimsby	62940
Grinnell	62908
Grisham (Township)	62077
Griswold	60929
Gromers Woods	60120
Gross	62931
Grove (Township)	62448
Grove, The (Part of Downers Grove)	60517
Grove City	62531
Groveland (La Salle County) (Township)	61358
Groveland (Tazewell County)	61535
Groveland (Tazewell County) (Township)	61535
Grover (Township)	62837
Grupe	62401
Guilford	61036
Guilford (Township)	61028
Gulf Port	52601
Gurnee	60031
Gurnee Mills (Part of Gurnee)	60031
Guthrie	60936
Hadley	62312
Hadley (Township)	62312
Haegers Bend	60102
Hafer	62918
Hagaman	62630
Hagarstown	62247
Hagener (Township)	62618
Hahnaman	61243
Hahnaman (Township)	61283
Haines (Township)	62853
Hainesville	60030
Haldane	61030
Hale (Township)	61462
Half Day	60069
Hall (Township)	61362
Hallidayboro	62932
Hallock (Iroquois County)	60973
Hallock (Peoria County) (Township)	61526
Hallville	61727
Halsey Village (Part of Waukegan)	60088
Halsted Street (Part of Chicago)	60608
Hamburg (Bond County)	62262
Hamburg (Calhoun County)	62045
Hamel	62046
Hamel (Township)	62046
Hamilton (Hancock County)	62341
Hamilton (Lee County) (Township)	61349
Hamlet	61231

	ZIP
Hamletsburg	62944
Hammond	61929
Hampshire	60140
Hampshire (Township)	60140
Hampshire Manor (Part of Hampshire)	60140
Hampton	61256
Hampton (Township)	61256
Hampton Court (Part of Country Club Hills)	60477
Hancock (Township)	62321
Hanna (Township)	61254
Hanna City	61536
Hanover (Township)	61041
Hanover (Cook County) (Township)	60103
Hanover (Jo Daviess County)	61041
Hannon (Jo Daviess County) (Part of Taylorville)	62568
Hanover Highlands (Part of Hanover Park)	60103
Hanover Park	60103
Hanover Park-Ontarioville (Part of Hanover Park)	60103
Hanover Square (Part of Hanover Park)	60103
Hanson	62080
Hanson Park (Part of Chicago)	60639
Happy Hills	60175
Happy Hollow Lake	61428
Harbor Dell	62035
Harbor Estates	60010
Harco	62945
Hardin (Calhoun County)	62047
Hardin (Pike County) (Township)	62355
Harding	60518
Hardinville	62449
Harlem (Stephenson County) (Township)	61032
Harlem (Winnebago County)	61111
Harlem (Winnebago County) (Township)	61111
Harlem Avenue (Part of Berwyn)	60402
Harlem-Irving Plaza (Part of Chicago)	60634
Harmon	61042
Harmon (Township)	61042
Harmony (Hancock County) (Township)	62321
Harmony (Jefferson County)	62864
Harmony (McHenry County)	60140
Harmony Village (Part of Wheeling)	60090
Harp (Township)	61727
Harper	61030
Harpster	61845
Harris (Fulton County) (Township)	61459
Harris (Piatt County)	61842
Harrisburg	62946
Harrisburg (Township)	62946
Harrison (Jackson County)	62966
Harrison (Winnebago County)	61072
Harrison (Winnebago County) (Township)	61072
Harrisonville (Grundy County)	60416
Harrisonville (Monroe County)	62295
Harristown	62537
Harristown (Township)	62537
Harter (Township)	62839
Hartford	62048
Hartland	60098
Hartland (Township)	60098
Hartsburg	62643
Harvard	60033
Harvard Hills	61571
Harvel	62538
Harvel (Township)	62538
Harvey	60426
Harwood (Township)	61847
Harwood Heights	60656
Hastings	61810
Hatcher Woods	60450
Havana	62644
Havana (Township)	62644
Haw Creek (Township)	61458
Hawthorn Center (Part of Vernon Hills)	60060
Hawthorne (Part of Chicago) (Cook County)	60623
Hawthorne (Part of Cicero) (Cook County)	60650
Hawthorne (White County) (Township)	62821

	ZIP		ZIP		ZIP
Hawthorn Woods	60047	High Point (Part of Hoffman		Hookdale	62284
Hawthrone Hills	62864	Estates)	60195	Hoopeston	60942
Hayes	61953	Highview Estates	60514	Hooppole	61258
Hayford (Part of Chicago)	60652	Highway Village (Part of		Hoosier (Township)	62858
Haymarket (Part of		East Peoria)	61611	Hope (La Salle County)	
Chicago)	60606	Highwood (Lake County)	60040	(Township)	61334
Haypress	62027	Highwood (St. Clair County)	62221	Hope (Vermilion County)	61812
Hazel Crest	60429	Highwood Terrace (Part of		Hopedale	61747
Hazelcrest Highlands (Part		Belleville)	62221	Hopedale (Township)	61747
of Hazel Crest)	60429	Hilcrest	62089	Hopewell	61565
Hazel Dell	62428	Hildreth	61876	Hopewell (Township)	61540
Hazelgreen (Part of Alsip)	60482	Hill Correctional Center	61401	Hop Hollow	62035
Hazelhurst	61064	Hillcrest (Calhoun County)	62045	Hopkins (Township)	61081
Hazelwood	61254	Hillcrest (Christian County)	62568	Hopkins Park	60944
Hazelwood Heights	61254	Hillcrest (Cook County)	60439	Hopper	61480
Hazelwood West	61254	Hillcrest (Douglas County)	61953	Horace	61924
Headyville	62424	Hillcrest (Henry County)	61254	Horatio Gardens	60069
Healy (Part of Chicago)	60639	Hillcrest (Ogle County)	61068	Hord	62858
Heapsville	61425	Hilldale Villages (Part of		Hornsby	62056
Heartville	62401	Hoffman Estates)	60195	Horseshoe	62934
Heathercrest (Part of		Hillerman	62941	Houston (Adams County)	
Northbrook)	60062	Hillery	61832	(Township)	62339
Heatherfield	60450	Hillsboro	62049	Houston (Randolph County)	62286
Heatherlea	60074	Hillsboro (Township)	62049	Howardton	62942
Heathsville	62427	Hillsdale	61257	Howe (Part of Depue)	61322
Hebron	60034	Hillside (Cook County)	60162	Howe Terrace	60010
Hebron (Township)	60034	Hillside (Kankakee County)	60901	Hoyleton	62803
Hecker	62248	Hillside Manor	60901	Hoyleton (Township)	62803
Hegeler	61832	Hill Top	62675	Hubbard Woods (Cook	
Hegewisch (Part of		Hillview	62050	County)	60093
Chicago)	60633	Hillyard (Township)	62676	Hubbard Woods (Marion	
Helena	62466	Himrod	61883	County)	62801
Helmar	60541	Hinckley	60520	Hubly	62642
Helvetia (Township)	62249	Hindsboro	61930	Hudgens	62959
Heman	62573	Hinsdale	60521-22	Hudson	61748
Henderson	61439	For specific Hinsdale Zip Codes		Hudson (Township)	61748
Henderson (Township)	61439	call (708) 323-1490, or your local		Huegely	62803
Henderson	62033	postmaster.		Huey	62252
Henderson Grove	61401	Hinswood (Part of Darien)	60561	Hugh's Addition	62684
Hendryx Manor	61614	Hire (Township)	62326	Hugo	61953
Hennepin	61327	Hitt	61051	Hull	62343
Hennepin (Township)	61327	Hittle (Township)	61721	Humboldt	61931
Henning	61848	Hodgetown	62865	Humboldt (Township)	61931
Henry	61537	Hodgkins	60525	Hume (Edgar County)	61932
Henry (Township)	61537	Hoffman	62250	Hume (Whiteside County)	
Hensley (Township)	61820	Hoffman Estates	60194-95	(Township)	61071
Henton	62565	For specific Hoffman Estates Zip		Humm Wye	62938
Herald	62845	Codes call (708) 885-6510, or		Humrick	61870
Heralds Prairie (Township)	62869	your local postmaster.		Hunt City	62480
Herbert	60145	Hoffmann Edition	60924	Hunt City (Township)	62480
Herborn	62465	Holbrook	60411	Hunter (Boone County)	61011
Heritage (Part of Moline)	61265	Holcomb	61043	Hunter (Edgar County)	61944
Heritage Estates (Part of		Holden	62832	Hunter (Edgar County)	
Bourbonnais)	60914	Holder	61736	(Township)	61944
Hermon	61458	Holiday Hills	60050	Hunter Trail (Part of Oak	
Hermosa (Part of Chicago)	60639	Holiday Shores	62025	Brook)	60521
Herod	62947	Holland	62414	Huntington (Part of	
Herrick	62431	Holland (Township)	62414	Naperville)	60540
Herrick (Township)	62431	Hollandia	62221	Huntington Commons (Part	
Herrin	62948	Hollenback	60450	of Mount Prospect)	60056
Herscher	60941	Hollendale (Part of South		Huntington Park (Part of	
Hersman	62353	Holland)	60473	Elgin)	60120
Hervey City	62549	Holliday	62414	Huntinton Park	62035
Hettick	62649	Hollis (Township)	61607	Huntley	60142
Hewittville	62568	Hollowayville	61356	Huntsville	62344
Heyworth	61745	Hollydale (Part of		Huntsville (Township)	62344
Hickory (Township)	62624	Homewood)	60430	Hurlbut (Township)	62634
Hickory Falls	60097	Hollywood (Part of		Hurricane (Township)	62080
Hickory Grove	62301	Brookfield)	60513	Hurst	62949
Hickory Hill (Township)	62895	Hollywood Heights	62232	Hutchins Park	61103
Hickory Hills (Cook County)	60457	Hollywood Ridge (Part of		Hutsonville	62433
Hickory Hills (Piatt County)	61884	Wheeling)	60090	Hutsonville (Township)	62433
Hickory Hollow	60118	Holmes Center	61523	Hutton	61920
Hickory Point (Macon		Homberg	62938	Hutton (Township)	61920
County) (Township)	62526	Home Gardens (Part of		Hyde Park (Part of Chicago)	60615
Hickory Point (Shelby		Danville)	61832		60653
County)	62565	Homer (Champaign County)	61849	For specific Hyde Park Zip Codes
Hickoryville	63673	Homer (Will County)		call (312) 924-9221, or your local
Hicks	62947	(Township)	60441	postmaster.
Hidalgo	62432	Homerican Villas (Part of		Idaville Corner	60924
Hidden Creek	60074	Des Plaines)	60016	Ideal	61285
Hidden Hills	61455	Homestead (Part of		Idlewild	60030
Higginsville	61865	O'Fallon)	62269	Idlewood	62864
High Knob	60187	Hometown	60456	Iliana	47982
High Lake	60185	Homewood (Cook County)	60430	Illiana Heights	60954
Highland (Grundy County)		Homewood (Rock Island		Illini (Township)	62573
(Township)	60437	County)	61265	Illinois Center (Part of	
Highland (Madison County)	62249	Homewood Acres	60430	Marion)	62959
Highlander	62901	Homewood Shores (Part of		Illinois City	61259
Highland Haven	60123	Homewood)	60430	Illinois River Correctional	
Highland Hills	60148	Homewood Terrace (Part of		Center	61520
Highland Lake	60030	Homewood)	60430	Illinois Veterans Home (Part	
Highland Park (Lake		Honegger	61741	of Quincy)	62301
County)	60035	Honey Bend	62056	Iliopolis	62539
Highland Park (Marion		Honey Creek (Adams		Iliopolis (Township)	62539
County)	62881	County) (Township)	62325	Imbs	62240
Highlands (Cook County)	60411	Honey Creek (Crawford		Imperial	60048
Highlands (DuPage County)	60521	County) (Township)	62427	Ina	62846
Highlands-Clarks	60543	Honey Creek (Ogle County)	61015	Independence (Pike County)	62363
Highland Shores	60097	Honey Point (Township)	62056	Independence (Saline	
Highlawn (Part of Riverdale)	60627	Hononegah Heights	61073	County) (Township)	62946
High Meadows	61607	Hoodville	62859	Indian Creek (Lake County)	60060

	ZIP		ZIP		ZIP
Indian Creek (White County)		Jenkins	61727	Kewanee	61443
(Township)	62869	Jerome	62707	Kewanee (Township)	61443
Indian Grove (Township)	61739	Jersey (Township)	62052	Keyesport	62253
Indian Head Park	60525	Jerseyville	62052	Keyesport Landing	62253
Indian Hill (Cook County)	60093	Jewett	62436	Key West (Part of Niles)	60016
Indian Hill (DuPage County)	60563	Jimtown	61872	Kickapoo	61528
Indian Hills (Cook County)	60411	Johannisburg	62214	Kickapoo (Township)	61528
Indian Hills (Jo Daviess		Johannisburg (Township)	62214	Kidd	62277
County)	61025	Johnsburg	60050	Kidley	61924
Indian Oaks (Kankakee		Johnson (Christian County)		Kilbourne	62655
County)	60914	(Township)	62568	Kilbourne (Township)	62655
Indian Oaks (Will County)	60440	Johnson (Clark County)		Kildeer	60047
Indianola	61850	(Township)	62420	Kimberly Heights	60477
Indian Point (Knox County)		Johnsonville	62850	Kincaid	62540
(Township)	61410	Johnston City	62951	Kinderhook	62345
Indian Point (Lake County)	60002	Johnstown	62440	Kinderhook (Township)	62345
Indian Point (Menard		Joliet	60431-36	King (Township)	62546
County)	62613	For specific Joliet Zip Codes call		Kingdom	61021
Indian Prairie (Township)	62823	(815) 741-7813, or your local		Kingman	62463
Indian Ridge (McHenry		postmaster.		Kings	61045
County)	60097	Jonathan Creek (Township)	61911	Kings Cove (Part of	
Indian Ridge (Piatt County)	61884	Jones (Coles County)	61938	Deerfield)	60015
Indiantown (Township)	61421	Jones (Cook County)	60452	Kings Island (Part of Fox	
Indian Trail Estates	60015	Jonesboro	62952	Lake)	60020
Industrial Park	62864	Jones Ridge	62280	Kings Park (Part of	
Industry	61440	Jonesville	61348	Bolingbrook)	60440
Industry (Township)	61440	Joppa	62953	Kingston (Adams County)	62312
Ingalls Park	60431	Jordan (Township)	61081	Kingston (DeKalb County)	60145
Ingalton	60185	Joshua (Township)	61432	Kingston (Dekalb County)	
Ingleside (Lake County)	60041	Joslin	61257	(Township)	60145
Ingleside Shores	60041	Joy	61260	Kingston Mines	61539
Ingraham	62434	Joywood Farms Estates	62028	Kingswood	60175
Ingram Hill	62946	Jubilee (Township)	61559	Kinkaid (Township)	62907
International Village (Cook		Junction	62954	Kinmundy	62854
County)	60194	Junction City	62882	Kinmundy (Township)	62854
International Village (DuPage		Justice	60458	Kinsman	60437
County)	60148	Kampsville	62053	Kirkland	60146
International Village (Will		Kane	62054	Kirksville	61951
County)	60440	Kane (Township)	62054	Kirkwood	61447
Inverness	60067	Kaneville	60144	Kishwaukee Glen	61109
Inverness on the Ponds		Kaneville (Township)	60144	Klein Acres (Part of	
(Part of Inverness)	60067	Kangley	61364	Rantoul)	61866
Iola	62847	Kankakee	60901	Klendworth Addition	61250
Ipava	61441	Kankakee (Township)	60901	Klondike (Alexander	
Irene	61016	Kankakee Valley	60964	County)	62914
Irishtown (Township)	62253	Kansas (Edgar County)	61933	Klondike (Lake County)	60002
Irondale (Part of Chicago)	60617	Kansas (Edgar County)		Klondyke	62466
Iroquois	60945	(Township)	61933	Knapp's Noll	61072
Iroquois (Township)	60928	Kansas (Woodford County)		Knight Prairie (Township)	62859
Irving	62051	(Township)	61725	Knollcrest (Part of Hazel	
Irving (Township)	62051	Kappa	61738	Crest)	60429
Irving Park (Part of Chicago)	60641	Karbers Ridge	62955	Knollwood (Christian	
Irvington	62848	Karnak	62956	County)	62568
Irvington (Township)	62848	Kasbeer	61328	Knollwood (Lake County)	60044
Irwin	60901	Kaskaskia (Fayette County)		Knollwood (Part of Lake	
Isabel (Edgar County)	61943	(Township)	62892	Zurich)	60047
Isabel (Fulton County)		Kaskaskia (Randolph		Knollwood (Sangamon	
(Township)	61542	County)	63673	County)	62684
Island Grove (Jasper		Kaskaskia Heights	62217	Knottingham (Part of	
County)	62467	Kaskaskia River	62231	Downers Grove)	60515
Island Grove (Sangamon		Kaufman	62001	Knox (Township)	61448
County) (Township)	62677	Kedron	62934	Knoxville	61448
Island Lake	60042	Kedzie (Part of Chicago)	60623	Kortcamp (Part of Schram	
Itasca	60143	Kedzie Grace (Part of		City)	62049
Itasca Ranchettes	60143	Chicago)	60618	Kraft Addition	62812
Iuka	62849	Keene (Township)	62349	Kriegh Addition	61448
Iuka (Township)	62849	Keenes	62851	Kristal Lake Ranch	61032
Ivanhoe (Cook County)	60627	Keeneyville	60172	Kuhn	62025
Ivanhoe (Lake County)	60060	Keensburg	62852	La Clede	62426
Ivanhoe (Will County)	60440	Keith (Township)	62878	La Clede (Township)	62426
Ivanhoe Estates	61801	Keithsburg	61442	Lacon	61540
Ivesdale	61851	Keithsburg (Township)	61442	Lacon (Township)	61540
Ivy Glen (Part of Aurora)	60506	Kell	62853	La Crosse	61450
Ivy Heights (Part of Wood		Kellart Lake	60924	Ladd	61329
River)	62024	Kellerville	62324	Laenna (Township)	62548
Jackson (Effingham County)		Kelleyville (Part of Westville)	61883	Lafayette (Coles County)	
(Township)	62401	Kelly (Township)	61412	(Township)	61938
Jackson (Will County)		Kemp	61910	Lafayette (Ogle County)	
(Township)	60421	Kemper	62063	(Township)	61006
Jackson Park (Part of		Kempton	60946	Lafayette (Randolph	
Chicago)	60637	Kendall (Township)	60560	County)	63673
Jacksonville	62650*	Kendall Hills	62024	La Fayette (Stark County)	61449
	62651†	Keneddy	61080	La Fontaine (Part of	
Jacksonville Correctional		Kenilwicke	60067	Glenview)	60025
Center	62650	Kenilworth	60043	Lafox	60147
Jacob	62950	Kenney	61749	Lagrange (Bond County)	
Jalapa	62054	Ken Rock	61109	(Township)	62019
Jamaica	61841	Kensington (Part of		La Grange (Brown County)	62378
Jamaica (Township)	61841	Chicago)	60628	La Grange (Cook County)	60525
Jamesburg	61865	Kensington Junction (Part		La Grange Highlands	60525
Jamestown (Clinton County)	62275	of Chicago)	60628	La Grange Park	60525
Jamestown (Perry County)	62238	Kent	61044	La Grange Road (Part of La	
Janesville	62435	Kent (Township)	61044	Grange)	60525
Jarvis (Township)	62294	Kenton (Part of Chicago)	60644	Laguna Woods	60462
Jasper (Township)	62837	Kentucky	61944	La Harpe	61450
Jefferson (Cook County)	60630	Kenwood (Champaign		La Harpe (Township)	61450
Jefferson (Stephenson		County)	61821	La Hogue	60938
County)	61062	Kenwood (Cook County)	60615	Lake	62283
Jefferson Square Mall (Part		Keptown	62411	Lake (Township)	62801
of Joliet)	60436	Kernan	61364	Lake Barrington	60010
Jeffries	62951	Kerr (Township)	61847	Lake Bluff	60044
Jeiseyville	62568	Kerton (Township)	62644	Lake Boulevard Addition	61832

	ZIP		ZIP		ZIP
Lake Bracken	61401	Lamplighter (Part of		Liberty Park	60559
Lake Briarwood	60004	Towanda)	61776	Libertyville	60048
Lake Camelot	61547	Lanark	61046		60092
Lake Carlinville	62626	Lancaster (Stephenson		For specific Libertyville Zip Codes	
Lake Catherine	60002	County) (Township)	61032	call (708) 362-2266, or your local	
Lake Centralia	62801	Lancaster (Wabash County)	62855	postmaster.	
Lake Charleston	61920	Landers (Part of Chicago)	60652	Libertyville (Township)	60048
Lake Charlotte	60174	Landes	62466	Lick	62629
Lake City	61937	Landings, The (Part of		Lick Creek	62912
Lakecrest (Montgomery		Lansing)	60438	Licking (Township)	62449
County)	62049	Lane	61750	Lidice (Part of Crest Hill)	60435
Lake Crest (Williamson		Lanesville	62515	Lightsville	61047
County)	62922	Lanesville (Township)	62515	Lilac Circle Homes (Part of	
Lake Estates	62959	Langleyville	62568	Lombard)	60148
Lake Forest	60045	Lansing	60438	Lilly	61755
Lake Forest Estates (Part of		Laona (Township)	61024	Lily Cache	60544
Belleville)	62221	La Place	61936	Lily Cache Acres	60544
Lake Fork	62541	La Prairie (Adams County)	62346	Lily Lake	60151
Lake Fork (Township)	62548	La Prairie (Marshall County)		Lilymoor	60050
Lake Holiday	60548	(Township)	61523	Lima	62348
Lakehurst Shopping Center		La Prairie Center	61565	Lima (Township)	62348
(Part of Waukegan)	60085	Larchland	61462	Limerick	61349
Lake in the Hills	60102	Larkdale (Lake County)	60084	Limestone (Kankakee	
Lake in the Woods	60515	Larkdale (Macon County)	62521	County) (Township)	60901
Lake Iroquois	60948	Larkinsburg (Township)	62426	Limestone (Peoria County)	
Lake Ka-Ho	62069	La Rose	61541	(Township)	61604
Lake Killarney	60013	La Salle	61301	Limestone (Peoria County)	61607
Lake Lancelot	61547	La Salle (Township)	61301	Lincoln (Logan County)	62656
Lakeland Hills (Jackson		Latham	62543	Lincoln (Ogle County)	
County)	62901	Latona	62479	(Township)	61064
Lakeland Hills (St. Clair		Laura	61451	Lincoln Addition (Part of	
County)	62221	La Vergne (Part of Berwyn)	60402	Wood River)	62095
Lakeland Park (Part of		Lawndale (Logan County)	61751	Lincoln Correctional Center	62656
McHenry)	60050	Lawndale (McLean County)		Lincoln Developmental	
Lake Lawrence	47591	(Township)	61728	Center	62656
Lake Louise	61010	Lawn Ridge	61526	Lincoln Estates	60423
Lake Lynwood (Cook		Lawrence (Lawrence		Lincoln Gardens (Part of	
County)	60411	County) (Township)	62439	Alton)	62002
Lake Lynwood (Henry		Lawrence (McHenry		Lincoln Highway (Part of	
County)	61262	County)	60033	Olympia Fields)	60461
Lake Mantero	60950	Lawrenceville	62439	Lincoln Hills	60137
Lake Marie	60002	Layton	62681	Lincoln Mall (Part of	
Lake Marion	60110	Leaf River	61047	Matteson)	60443
Lake Mattoon	62447	Leaf River (Township)	61047	Lincoln Park (Part of	
Lakemoor	60050	Leaverton Park	62451	Chicago)	60614
Lake Oakland	61943	Lebanon	62254		60657
Lake of the Winds (Part of		Lebanon (Township)	62254	For specific Lincoln Park Zip	
Wheeling)	60090	Leclaire (Part of		Codes call (312) 525-5959, or	
Lake of the Woods		Edwardsville)	62025	your local postmaster.	
(Champaign County)	61820	Ledford	62946	Lincolnshire (Lake County)	60069
Lake of the Woods (Peoria		Lee (Brown County)		Lincolnshire (Will County)	60417
County)	61525	(Township)	62375	Lincolnshire Fields	61821
Lake Pana	62557	Lee (Fulton County)		Lincolnwood	60645
Lake Park	61821	(Township)	61470		60659
Lake Park Estates	60067	Lee (Lee County)	60530	For specific Lincolnwood Zip	
Lake Park Forest	60067	Lee Center	61331	Codes call (312)463-1210, or your	
Lake Petersburg	62675	Lee Center (Township)	61331	local postmaster.	
Lake Piasa	62012	Leech (Township)	62833	Lincolnwood Hills	60451
Lake Ranier	62626	Leeds	61377	Lincolnwood Town Center	
Lake Sara	62401	Leef (Township)	62249	(Part of Lincolnwood)	60645
Lakeshore Acres	62231	Leepertown (Township)	61315	Lindenhurst	60046
Lakeside Knolls	62049	Leesburg	61501	Lindenhurst Estates (Part of	
Lakeside Villas (Part of		Leesville	60964	Lindenhurst)	60046
Wheeling)	60090	Lehigh	60901	Lindenwood	61049
Lake Summerset	61019	Leisure Lea	60543	Linder (Township)	62016
Lake Tacoma	62901	Leisure Village (Part of Fox		Linn (Wabash County)	62410
Lake Tara Estates	60118	Lake)	60020	Linn (Woodford County)	
Lake Thunderbird	61560	Leland	60531	(Township)	61570
Lakeview (Part of Chicago)	60613	Leland Grove	62707	Linrose Heights	62216
Lakeview Acres	62234	Leland Lake	62650	Lintner	61929
Lakeview Estate	62881	Lemont	60439	Lioncrest (Part of Richton	
Lakeview Estates (Jefferson		Lemont (Township)	60439	Park)	60466
County)	62864	Le Moyne (Part of Chicago)	60638	Lis	62448
Lake View Estates		Lena	61048	Lisbon	60541
(Williamson County)	62958	Lenox (Township)	61462	Lisbon (Township)	60541
Lakeview Heights (Part of		Lenzburg	62255	Lisbon Center	60541
Fairfield)	62837	Lenzburg (Township)	62257	Lisle	60532
Lake Villa	60046	Leonard	60938	Lisle (Township)	60532
Lake Villa (Township)	60046	Leon Corners	61277	Litchfield (Kankakee	
Lake Wildwood	61336	Leonore	61332	County)	60954
Lake Williamson	62626	L'Erable	60927	Litchfield (Montgomery	
Lakewood (Cook County)	60466	Lerna	62440	County)	62056
Lakewood (DuPage County)	60185	Le Roy (Boone County)		Literberry	62660
Lakewood (Madison		(Township)	61012	Little America	61542
County)	62035	Le Roy (McLean County)	61752	Little Indian	62691
Lakewood (McHenry		Levan (Township)	62966	Little Mackinaw (Township)	61759
County)	60014	Levee (Township)	62343	Little Rock	60545
Lakewood (Shelby County)	62438	Leverett	61821	Little Rock (Township)	60545
Lakewood (Shelby County)		Lewistown	61542	Little Swan Lake	61415
(Township)	62438	Lewistown (Township)	61542	Littleton	61452
Lakewood Park	62901	Lewood	60544	Littleton (Township)	61452
Lakewood Shores	60481	Lexington	61753	Little York	61453
Lakewood Village (Part of		Lexington (Township)	61753	Lively Grove	62268
Carpentersville)	60110	Leyden (Township)	60131	Lively Grove (Township)	62268
Lake Zurich	60047	Liberty	62347	Liverpool	61543
Lamard (Township)	62842	Liberty (Township)	62347	Liverpool (Township)	61543
Lamb	62919	Liberty (Effingham County)		Livingston (Clark County)	62441
Lambert	60439	(Township)	62414	Livingston (Madison	
La Moille	61330	Liberty (Saline County)	62946	County)	62058
La Moille (Township)	61349	Liberty Acres	60048	Loami	62661
Lamoine (Township)	61415	Liberty Lake (Part of		Loami (Township)	62661
Lamotte (Township)	62451	Libertyville)	60048		

	ZIP
Loch Lomond (Part of Mundelein)	60060
Lockhaven	62035
Lockport	60441
	60446
For specific Lockport Zip Codes call (815) 838-9104, or your local postmaster.	
Lockport (Township)	60441
Locust (Township)	62555
Loda	60948
Loda (Township)	60948
Lodemia	61739
Lodge	61856
Logan (Edgar County)	61924
Logan (Franklin County)	62856
Logan (Peoria County) (Township)	61536
Logan Correctional Center	62656
Logan Square (Part of Chicago)	60647
Log Cabin Camp	60954
Lomax	61454
Lomax (Township)	61454
Lombard	60148
Lombardville	61421
London Mills	61544
Lone Grove (Township)	62880
Lone Tree	61368
Long Branch (Mason County)	62644
Long Branch (Saline County) (Township)	62935
Long Creek	62521
Long Creek (Township)	62521
Long Grove	60047
Long Lake	60041
Long Meadow (Part of Downers Grove)	60515
Long Point	61333
Long Point (Township)	61333
Longshadow	60175
Longview	61852
Longwood Farms (Part of Chicago Heights)	60411
Longwood Manor	60563
Loogootee	62857
Looking Glass (Township)	62265
Lookout Point	60097
Loon Lake	60002
Loop (Part of Chicago)	60601-05
For specific Loop Zip Codes call (312) 427-4225, or your local postmaster.	
Loraine (Adams County)	62349
Loraine (Henry County) (Township)	61277
Loran	61062
Loran (Township)	61062
Lords' Park Manor (Part of Elgin)	60120
Lorenzo	60481
Loretto	60460
Lorraine Park (Part of Wheaton)	60187
Lostant	61334
Lost Lake	61070
Lost Nation	61021
Lotus	61845
Lotus Woods	60081
Lou Del	62298
Loudon (Township)	62414
Louis Joliet Mall (Part of Joliet)	60435
Louisville	62858
Louisville (Township)	62858
Love (Township)	61870
Lovejoy (Iroquois County) (Township)	60973
Lovejoy (St. Clair County)	62059
Loves Park	61111
	61130-32
For specific Loves Park Zip Codes call (815) 877-7071, or your local postmaster.	
Lovington	61937
Lovington (Township)	61937
Lowder	62662
Lowe (Township)	61911
Lowell	61370
Lowpoint	61545
Loxa	61938
Lucas (Township)	62424
Ludlow	60949
Ludlow (Township)	60949
Lukin (Township)	62417
Lumaghi Heights	62234
Luther	62664
Lyman (Township)	60962
Lynchburg (Township)	62617
Lyndon	61261
Lyndon (Township)	61261

	ZIP
Lynn (Henry County) (Township)	61262
Lynn (Knox County) (Township)	61414
Lynn Center	61262
Lynn Gardens	60901
Lynnville (Morgan County)	62650
Lynnville (Ogle County) (Township)	61049
Lynnwood (Cook County)	60411
Lynnwood (Kendall County)	60543
Lynnwood (La Salle County)	61354
Lynwood	60411
Lyons	60534
Lyons (Township)	60525
Lyons (Part of Belgium)	61883
McCall	62321
McClellan (Township)	62894
McClure	62957
McClusky	62052
McConnell	61050
McCook	60525
McCormick	62987
McCullom Lake	60050
McCully	61764
McDowell	61764
Macedonia	62860
McGirr	60556
McHenry	60050*
	60051†
McHenry Shores (Part of McHenry)	60050
Machesney Park	61115
Machesney Park Mall (Part of Machesney Park)	61115
MacIntoch	61364
McIntosh	60123
McKee (Township)	62347
McKeen	62441
McKendree (Township)	61832
Mackinaw (Township)	61755
Mackinaw	61755
Mackler Heights (Part of Chicago Heights)	60411
McLean	61754
McLeansboro	62859
McLeansboro (Township)	62859
McNabb	61335
Macomb (McDonough County)	61455
Macomb (McDonough County) (Township)	61438
Macomb City (Township)	61455
Macon (Bureau County) (Township)	61314
Macon (Macon County)	62544
Macoupin	62676
McQueen	60185
McVey	62640
Madison (Madison County)	62060
Madison (Richland County) (Township)	62450
Madonnaville	62298
Maeystown (Monroe County)	62256
Magnet	61938
Magnolia	61336
Magnolia (Township)	61336
Mahomet	61853
Mahomet (Township)	61853
Maine (Cook County) (Township)	60016
Maine (Grundy County) (Township)	60444
Main Post Office (Part of Chicago)	60607
Main Street (Part of Evanston)	60202
Makanda	62958
Makanda (Township)	62958
Malden	61337
Malibu Village	62901
Mallard West (Part of Schaumburg)	60194
Malone (Township)	61534
Malta	60150
Malta (Township)	60150
Malvern	61270
Manchester (Boone County) (Township)	61011
Manchester (Scott County)	62663
Manhattan	60442
Manhattan (Township)	60442
Manito	61546
Manito (Township)	61546
Manlius (Bureau County)	61338
Manlius (Bureau County) (Township)	61338
Manlius (LaSalle County) (Township)	61360
Mannheim (Part of Franklin Park)	60131

	ZIP
Mannon	61272
Mansfield	61854
Manteno	60950
Manteno (Township)	60950
Manville	61319
Maplebrook (Part of Naperville)	60565
Maple Grove	62476
Maple Lane	61081
Maple Park	60151
Maple Point	62428
Maples Mill	61542
Mapleton	61547
Maplewood (Cook County)	60647
Maplewood (St. Clair County)	62206
Maplewood Estates	61520
Maquon	61458
Maquon (Township)	61458
Marblehead	62301
Marcelline	62376
Marcoe	62864
Mardell Manor	61607
Marengo	60152
Marengo (Township)	60152
Marietta	61459
Marigold	62242
Marina Terrace	60543
Marina Village	60543
Marine	62061
Marine (Township)	62061
Marion (Lee County) (Township)	61310
Marion (Ogle County) (Township)	61015
Marion (Williamson County)	62959
Marion Circle	60554
Marion Country Club	62959
Marion Hills (Part of Darien)	60561
Marissa	62257
Marissa (Township)	62257
Mark	61340
Market Place (Part of Champaign)	61820
Markham (Cook County)	60426
Markham (Morgan County)	62628
Markham City (Part of Bluford)	62814
Marley (Edgar County)	61944
Marley (Will County)	60448
Marlow	62872
Marnico Village	62650
Maroa	61756
Maroa (Township)	61756
Marquette Heights	61554
Marrowbone (Township)	61914
Mars (Part of Chicago)	60639
Marseilles	61341
Marshall	62441
Marshall (Township)	62441
Marston	61279
Martin (Crawford County) (Township)	62454
Martin (McLean County) (Township)	61728
Martinsburg	62363
Martinsburg (Township)	62363
Martinsville	62442
Martinsville (Township)	62442
Martinton	60951
Martinton (Township)	60951
Mary Crest (Part of Country Club Hills)	60477
Marydale	62231
Marydale Manor (Part of Dolton)	60419
Maryland	61064
Maryland (Township)	61007
Mary Meadows	60175
Maryville	62062
Mascoutah	62258
Mascoutah (Township)	62258
Mason	62443
Mason (Township)	62443
Mason City (Township)	62664
Mason City	62664
Massbach	61028
Massilon (Township)	62883
Matanzas Beach	62644
Matherville	61263
Matteson	60443
Mattoon	61938
Mattoon (Township)	61938
Maud	62863
Maunie	62861
Maxwell (Township)	62661
May (Christian County) (Township)	62567
May (Lee County) (Township)	61367
Mayberry (Township)	62817
Mayfair (Cook County)	60630

	ZIP		ZIP		ZIP
Mayfair (Tazewell County)	61550	Middleport (Township)	60970	Montgomery (Crawford County) (Township)	62427
Mayfield (Township)	60178	Middlesworth	62565	Montgomery (Kane County)	60538
Maynard Lake	61821	Middletown	62666	Montgomery (Woodford County) (Township)	61733
Mays	61944	Midland City	61727	Monticello	61856
Maysville	62340	Midland Hills	62958	Monticello (Township)	61856
Maytown	61310	Midlothian	60445	Montmorency (Township)	61071
Mayview	61801	Midway (Madison County)	62067	Montrose	62445
Maywood	60153	Midway (Massac County)	62960	Moon Lake Village (Part of Hoffman Estates)	60195
Mazon	60444	Midway (Tazewell County)	61554	Moonshine	62442
Mazon (Township)	60444	Midway (Vermilion County)	61883	Moores Prairie (Township)	62810
Meacham (Township)	62854	Midwest (Part of Chicago)	60612	Mooseheart	60539
Meadowbrook (Madison County)	62010	Midwest Club (Part of Oak Brook)	60521	Moraine Valley Facility (Part of Bridgeview)	60455
Meadowbrook (McDonough County)	61455	Milam (Township)	62544	Morea	62451
Meadowbrook East (Part of Wheeling)	60090	Milan (DeKalb County) (Township)	60550	Morehaven	61073
Meadowbrook West (Part of Wheeling)	60090	Milan (Rock Island County)	61264	Morgan (Township)	61943
Meadowdale (Part of Carpentersville)	60110	Mildred	62707	Morgan Park (Part of Chicago)	60643
Meadowdale Shopping Center (Part of Carpentersville)	60110	Miles Station	62012	Morgan's Gate	60067
Meadow Heights (Part of Collinsville)	62234	Milford	60953	Moriah	62420
Meadow Knolls (Part of Schaumburg)	60194	Milford (Township)	60953	Moro	62067
Meadowlake	61821	Milks Grove (Township)	60941	Moro (Township)	62067
Meadows	61726	Millbrook (Kendall County)	60536	Morris	60450
Meadowview (Kane County)	60175	Millbrook (Peoria County) (Township)	61451	Morris (Township)	60450
Meadowview (Kankakee County)	60901	Millburn	60046	Morris Hills (Part of Collinsville)	62234
Mechanicsburg	62545	Millcreek	62961	Morrison	61270
Mechanicsburg (Township)	62545	Milledgeville	61051	Morrisonville	62546
Medalist Park (Part of Palatine)	60067	Miller (Township)	61360	Morristown	61274
Media	61460	Miller Addition	61250	Morseville	61085
Media (Township)	61460	Miller City	62962	Morton	61550
Medina (Township)	61523	Miller Lake	62864	Morton (Township)	61550
Medinah	60157	Millersburg	61231	Morton Grove	60053
Medinah on the Lake (Part of Bloomingdale)	60108	Millersburg (Township)	61260	Morton Park (Part of Cicero)	60650
Medora	62063	Millersville	62557	Moser Highlands (Part of Naperville)	60540
Meeks	61846	Miller Woods	60411	Mosquito (Township)	62547
Meersman	61244	Millhurst	60545	Mossville	61552
Melrose (Township)	62478	Millington	60537	Mound (Effingham County) (Township)	62411
Melrose (Adams County) (Township)	62301	Mills (Township)	62246	Mound (McDonough County) (Township)	61455
Melrose (Clark County)	62478	Mill Shoals	62862	Mound City	62963
Melrose Park	60160-61	Mill Shoals (Township)	62862	Mounds	62964
....	60164	Mill Spring	62035	Mountain (Township)	62946
For specific Melrose Park Zip Codes call (708) 343-2150, or your local postmaster.		Millstadt	62260	Mountain Glen	62920
Melville (Part of Godfrey)	62035	Millstadt (Township)	62260	Mount Auburn	62547
Melvin	60952	Milmine	61855	Mount Auburn (Township)	62547
Menard	62259	Milo (Township)	61421	Mount Carbon	62966
Mendon	62351	Milo	61421	Mount Carmel	62863
Mendon (Township)	62351	Milton (DuPage County) (Township)	60187	Mount Carroll	61053
Mendota	61342	Milton (Pike County)	62352	Mount Carroll (Township)	61053
Mendota (Township)	61342	Mindale	62319	Mount Clair	62035
Menominee (Township)	61025	Mineral	61344	Mount Clare	62033
Menominee	61025	Mineral (Township)	61344	Mount Erie	62446
Meppen	62013	Mineral Springs	61081	Mount Erie (Township)	62446
Mercer (Township)	61231	Minier	61759	Mount Greenwood (Part of Chicago)	60655
Mercer Street (Part of Decatur)	62522	Minonk	61760		60658
Merchandise Mart (Part of Chicago)	60654	Minonk (Township)	61760	For specific Mount Greenwood Zip Codes call (312) 238-1477, or your local postmaster.	
Meredosia	62665	Minooka	60447		
Meriden	61342	Missal	61364	Mount Hope (Township)	61754
Meriden (Township)	61342	Mission (Township)	60551	Mount Joy	61723
Meridian (Township)	62283	Mission Hills	60062	Mount Morris	61054
Meridian Heights (Part of Mounds)	62964	Mississippi (Township)	62022	Mount Morris (Township)	61054
Mermet	62908	Missouri (Township)	62353	Mount Olive	62069
Merna	61758	Mitchell	62040	Mount Olive (Township)	62069
Merriam	62837	Mitchellsville	62917	Mount Palatine	61334
Merrimac	62295	Mitchie	62295	Mount Pleasant (Union County)	62912
Merrionette Park	60655	Mobet Meadows	61275	Mount Pleasant (Whiteside County) (Township)	61270
Merritt	62650	Mobile City	61401	Mount Prospect	60056
Merry Oaks	61244	Moccasin	62411	Mount Prospect Gardens (Part of Mount Prospect)	60056
Mesa Lake	62855	Moccasin (Township)	62411	Mount Prospect Plaza (Part of Mount Prospect)	60056
Metamora	61548	Mode	62444	Mount Pulaski	62548
Metamora (Township)	61548	Modena	61491	Mount Pulaski (Township)	62548
Metcalf	61940	Modesto	62667	Mount Sterling	62353
Metropolis	62960	Modoc	62261	Mount Sterling (Township)	62353
Mettawa	60048	Moecherville	60504	Mount Vernon	62864
Meyer (Adams County)	62379	Mohawk (Part of Bensenville)	60106	Mount Vernon (Township)	62864
Meyer (Kankakee County)	60901	Mokena	60448	Mount Zion	62549
Meyerbrook	60545	Moline	61265*	Mount Zion (Township)	62549
Meyers Bay (Part of Fox Lake)	60050		61266†	Moweaqua	62550
Michael	62065	Momence	60954	Moweaqua (Township)	62550
Middlebury (Part of Barrington Hills)	60010	Momence (Township)	60954	Mozier	62070
Middle Creek (Hancock County)	62321	Mona (Township)	60964	Mozier Landing	62045
Middlecreek (Kane County)	60175	Monee	60449	Mt. Vernon	61025
Middlefork (Township)	61865	Monee (Township)	60449	Muddy	62965
Middle Grove	61531	Money Creek (Township)	61753	Mulberry Grove	62262
		Monica	61559	Mulberry Grove (Township)	62262
		Monmouth	61462	Mulkeytown	62865
		Monmouth (Township)	61462	Muncie	61857
		Monroe (Township)	61052	Mundelein	60060
		Monroe Center	61052	Mundelein Ridge Estates (Part of Mundelein)	60060
		Monroe City	62298		
		Mont	62025		
		Montague Forest	60123		
		Mont Clare (Part of Chicago)	60639		
		Montebello (Township)	62341		
		Monterey	61520		
		Monterey Village (Part of University Park)	60466		
		Montezuma	62361		
		Montezuma (Township)	62361		

* Area Zip Code † Post Office Boxes

	ZIP
Munson (Township)	61238
Munster	61364
Murdock	61941
Murdock (Township)	61941
Murphy Acres	60435
Murphysboro	62966
Murphysboro (Township)	62966
Murrayville	62668
Myers Lake	62568
Mylith Park	60050
Myrtle	61047
Naausay (Township)	60560
Nachusa	61057
Nachusa (Township)	61057
Nameoki (Madison County) (Township)	62040
Nameoki (Madison County)	62040
Nantucket Cove (Part of Schaumburg)	60194
Naperville	60540
	60563-67

For specific Naperville Zip Codes call (708) 717-2662, or your local postmaster.

Naperville (Township)	60540
Naplate	61350
Naples	62665
Nashua (Township)	61061
Nashville	62263
Nashville (Township)	62263
Nason	62866
Natalie Estates (Part of Oak Forest)	60452
National Stock Yards	62071
Natrona	62682
Nauvoo	62354
Nauvoo (Township)	62354
Navajo Hills (Part of Palos Heights)	60463
Neadmore	62442
Nebo	62355
Nebraska (Township)	61740
Neelys	62621
Nekoma	61490
Nelson	61058
Nelson (Township)	61058
Neoga (Township)	62447
Neoga	62447
Neponset	61345
Neponset (Township)	61345
Nerska (Part of Chicago)	60632
Nettle Creek (Township)	60541
Neunert	62950
Nevada (Township)	60460
Nevins	61944
Newark	60541
New Athens	62264
New Athens (Township)	62264
New Baden	62265
New Bedford	61346
New Berlin	62670
New Berlin (Township)	62670
Newbern	62022
New Blossom Hill (Part of Cary)	60013
New Boston	61272
New Boston (Township)	61272
Newburg (Macon County)	62501
Newburg (Pike County) (Township)	62363
New Burnside	62967
Newby	61938
New Camp	62921
New Canton	62356
Newcastle	62987
New Century Town (Part of Vernon Hills)	60060
New City	62563
New Columbia	62943
Newcomb (Township)	61853
New Delhi	62052
New Dennison	62959
New Douglas	62074
New Douglas (Township)	62074
Newell (Township)	61832
New Hanover	62298
New Hartford	62363
New Haven	62867
New Haven (Township)	62867
New Hebron	62454
New Holland	62671
New La Grange	62378
New Lebanon	60140
New Lenox	60451
New Lenox (Township)	60451
New Liberty	62910
Newman	61942
Newman (Township)	61942
Newmansville	62612
Newmansville (Township)	62612
New Memphis (Clinton County)	62266

	ZIP
New Milford	61109
New Minden	62263
New Palatine	62297
New Philadelphia	61459
Newport (Lake County) (Township)	60083
Newport (Madison County)	62060
New Salem (McDonough County) (Township)	61482
New Salem (Pike County)	62357
New Salem (Pike County) (Township)	62357
Newton (Jasper County)	62448
Newton (Whiteside County) (Township)	61250
Newtown (Livingston County) (Township)	61311
Newtown (Vermilion County)	61858
New Trier (Township)	60093
New Virginia	62951
New Windsor	61465
Niantic	62551
Niantic (Township)	62551
N I F A (Northern Illinois Fair Association) (Part of North Aurora)	60542
Niles (Township)	60076
Niles	60714
Nilwood	62672
Nilwood (Township)	62640
Nineteenth Avenue (Part of Melrose Park)	60160
Niota	62358
Nippersink Terrace	60081
Nixon (Township)	61882
Nixon's Greenwood-Central	60025
Noble	62868
Noble (Township)	62868
Nokomis	62075
Nokomis (Township)	62075
Nolle Hill	62036
Nora	61059
Nora (Township)	61059
Nordic Acres	61008
Nordic Park	60143
Normal	61761
Normal (Township)	61761
Normal Junction (Part of Normal)	61761
Norman (Township)	60450
Normandale	61554
Normandy	61376
Normandy Heights	62864
Normandy Hill (Part of Northbrook)	60062
Normandy Villa (Part of Chicago Heights)	60411
Norpaul (Part of Franklin Park)	60131
Norridge	60656
Norris	61553
Norris City	62869
North (Part of Evanston)	60201
North Alton (Part of Alton)	62002
North Arm	61944
North Aurora	60542
North Barrington	60010
Northbelt Homesites (Part of Belleville)	62221
Northbrook	60062*
	60065†
Northbrook Court (Part of Northbrook)	60062
Northbrook Knolls (Part of Northbrook)	60062
Northbrook West	60062
North Chicago	60064
North Chillicothe (Part of Chillicothe)	61523
North Dixon (Part of Dixon)	61021
Northeast (Township)	62339
Northern (Township)	62860
Northern Heights	61010
Northern Hills	61032
Northern Illinois Fair Association (N I F A) (Part of Aurora)	60542
Northfield	60093
Northfield (Township)	60025
Northfield Woods	60025
North Fork (Township)	62979
Northgate (Part of Hanover Park)	60103
Northgate Shopping Center (Part of Aurora)	60506
North Glen Ellyn	60137
North Hampton	61523
North Harvey (Part of Harvey)	60426
North Henderson	61466
North Henderson (Township)	61466

	ZIP
North Hills	60060
Northlake	60164
North Lakewood	62881
Northland Mall (Part of Sterling)	61081
North Libertyville Estates	60048
North Litchfield (Township)	62056
Northmore	62035
Northmore Heights (Part of Effingham)	62401
North Mounds	62964
North Muddy (Township)	62479
North Okaw (Township)	61938
North Oregon	61061
North Otter (Township)	62690
North Palmyra (Township)	62667
North Park (Part of Machesney Park)	61115
North Park Mall (Part of Villa Park)	60181
North Pekin	61554
North Plato	60140
Northpoint Estates (Part of Bourbonnais)	60914
Northpoint Shopping Center (Part of Arlington Heights)	60004
North Prairie Acres	61953
North Riverside	60546
North Riverside Park Mall (Part of North Riverside)	60546
North Shoreland	62959
North Suburban Facility (Part of River Grove)	60199
Northtown (Part of Chicago)	60645
	60659

For specific Northtown Zip Codes call (312) 463-1210, or your local postmaster.

North Venice (Part of Venice)	62090
Northville (Township)	60551
Northwood	61801
Northwoods (DeKalb County)	60135
North Woods (DuPage County)	60185
Northwoods (St. Clair County)	62269
Northwoods Place (Part of East Alton)	62024
Northwoods Shopping Center (Part of Peoria)	61613
Norton (Township)	60917
Nortonville	62668
Norway	60551
Norwood (Mercer County)	61412
Norwood (Peoria County)	61604
Norwood Park (Cook County) (Township)	60656
Norwood Park (Cook County)	60631
Nottingham Park (Part of Bridgeview)	60638
Nottingham Woods	60119
Novak Park	60174
Nubbin Ridge	62835
Nunda (Township)	60012
Nutwood	62031
Oak	62947
Oak Bluff Estates	61038
Oak Brook (DuPage County)	60521
Oakbrook (Macoupin County)	62626
Oakbrook Center (Part of Oak Brook)	60521
Oakbrook Terrace	60181
Oakdale (Cook County)	60619
Oakdale (Washington County)	62268
Oakdale (Washington County) (Township)	62268
Oakdale Woods	60106
Oakford	62673
Oak Forest	60452
Oak Grove (Madison County)	62035
Oak Grove (Rock Island County)	61264
Oak Hill	61518
Oak Hills	62232
Oak Hills Estates	61008
Oak Knolls	60118
Oakland (Coles County)	61943
Oakland (Schuyler County) (Township)	62681
Oak Lawn	60453-59

For specific Oak Lawn Zip Codes call (708) 598-6305, or your local postmaster.

Oaklawn (Part of Danville)	61832
Oakley	62552

	ZIP
Oakley (Township)	62552
Oak Manor	60545
Oak Meadows	60185
Oak Park	60301-04
For specific Oak Park Zip Codes call (708) 848-7900, or your local postmaster.	
Oak Park (Township)	60302
Oak Ridge	61548
Oak Run	61428
Oak Spring Woods	60048
Oakwood (DuPage County)	60559
Oakwood (Henderson County)	61437
Oakwood (Peoria County)	61605
Oakwood (Vermilion County)	61858
Oakwood (Vermillion County) (Township)	61858
Oakwood Acres (Part of Geneseo)	61254
Oakwood Hills	60013
Oakwood Shores	60097
Obed	62510
Oblong	62449
Oblong (Township)	62449
Oconee	62553
Oconee (Township)	62553
Ocoya	61764
Odell	60460
Odell (Township)	60460
Odgen	62863
Odin	62870
Odin (Township)	62870
O'Fallon	62269
O'Fallon (Township)	62269
Ogden	61859
Ogden (Township)	61859
Ogden Park (Part of Chicago)	60636
Oglesby	61348
O'Hare Airport (Part of Chicago)	60666
Ohio	61349
Ohio (Township)	61349
Ohio Grove (Township)	61231
Ohlman	62076
Oil Center (Part of Centralia)	62801
Oilfield	62420
Okaw (Township)	62534
Okawville	62271
Okawville (Township)	62271
Oklahoma Addition	62451
Old Camp	62921
Old Du Quoin	62832
Oldenburg	62024
Olde Salem (Part of Hanover Park)	60103
Old Farm (Part of Naperville)	60563
Old Gilchrist	61231
Old Kane	62054
Old Marissa (Part of Marissa)	62257
Old Mill Creek	60083
Old Mill Grove (Part of Lake Zurich)	60047
Old Niota	62358
Old Orchard Shopping Center (Part of Skokie)	60077
Old Pearl	62361
Old Ripley	62275
Old Ripley (Township)	62275
Old Shawneetown	62984
Old Stonington	62567
Oldtown (McLean County) (Township)	61701
Oldtown (Saline County)	62987
Olena	61480
Olio (Township)	61530
Olive (Township)	62058
Olive Branch	62969
Oliver	62441
Olivet	61846
Olmsted	62970
Olney	62450
Olney (Township)	62450
Olympia Fields	60461
Olympia Gardens	60411
Olympic Terrace (Part of Naperville)	60540
Olympic Village (Part of Chicago Heights)	60411
Omaha	62871
Omaha (Township)	62871
Omega	62849
Omega (Township)	62849
Omphghent (Township)	62097
Onarga	60955
Onarga (Township)	60955
Oneco	61060
Oneco (Township)	61060

	ZIP
One Hundred Fourty-seventh Street (Part of Harvey)	60426
One Hundred Third Street (Part of Chicago)	60628
Oneida	61467
Ontario (Township)	61467
Ontario Street (Part of Chicago)	60611
Ontarioville	60103
Opdyke	62872
Opheim	61468
Ophir (Township)	61342
Oquawka	61469
Oquawka (Township)	61469
Ora (Township)	62971
Oran (Township)	62512
Orange (Clark County) (Township)	62442
Orange (Knox County) (Township)	61436
Orange Prairie	61614
Orangeville	61060
Oraville	62971
Orchard (Township)	62850
Orchard Acres	60014
Orchard Estates	60187
Orchard Heights	62450
Orchard Mines	61607
Orchard Place (Part of Des Plaines)	60018
Orchard Valley	60031
Orchardville	62899
Oreana	62554
Oregon	61061
Oregon (Township)	61061
Orel (Township)	62895
Orient	62874
Orion (Fulton County) (Township)	61520
Orion (Henry County)	61273
Orland (Township)	60462
Orland Hills	60462
Orland Hills (Westhaven)	60477
Orland Park	60462
Orland Park Place (Part of Orland Park)	60462
Orland Square (Part of Orland Park)	60462
Orleans	62601
Orleans Terrace (Part of Addison)	60101
Orvil (Township)	62635
Osage (Franklin County)	62983
Osage (La Salle County) (Township)	61377
Osbernville	62513
Osborn	61257
Osceola	61345
Osceola (Township)	61421
Osco	61274
Osco (Township)	61274
Oskaloosa	62899
Oskaloosa (Township)	62899
Osman	61843
Ospur	61727
Ossami Lake (Part of Morton)	61550
Oswego	60543
Oswego (Township)	60543
Otego (Township)	62418
Ottawa	61350
Ottawa (Township)	61350
Otter Creek (Jersey County) (Township)	62052
Otter Creek (La Salle County) (Township)	61364
Otterville	62037
Otto	60922
Otto (Township)	60922
Otto Mall (Part of Chicago Heights)	60411
Ottville	61362
Outter Creek	62031
Owaneco	62555
Owego (Township)	61764
Owen (Township)	61103
Oxford (Township)	61413
Oxville	62621
Ozark	62972
Pacesetter Park (Part of South Holland)	60473
Paderborn	62298
Padua	61737
Painesville	62948
Palatine	60067
	60074
	60078
	60094-95
For specific Palatine Zip Codes call (708) 590-8000, or your local postmaster.	

	ZIP
Palatine (Township)	60067
Palermo	61876
Palestine (Crawford County)	62451
Palestine (Woodford County) (Township)	61771
Palmer	62556
Palmyra	61021
Palmyra (Township)	61021
Palmyra (Macoupin County)	62674
Paloma	62359
Palos (Township)	60464
Palos Gardens	60463
Palos Heights	60463
Palos Hills	60465
Palos Park	60464
Palos Westgate (Part of Palos Heights)	60463
Palsgrove	61053
Pam Anne Estates	60025
Pana	62557
Pana (Township)	62557
Panama	62077
Pankeyville	62946
Panola	61738
Panola (Township)	61738
Panther Creek (Township)	62627
Papineau	60956
Papineau (Township)	60956
Paradise	61938
Paradise (Township)	61938
Paradise Acres	62918
Paris	61944
Paris (Township)	61944
Park City	60085
Parker (Clark County) (Township)	62474
Parker (Johnson County)	62922
Parkersburg	62452
Parkfield Terrace	62206
Park Forest	60466
Park Hills (Part of Effingham)	62401
Parkhome (Part of Cicero)	60650
Park Lane	60964
Park Manor (Part of Chicago)	60619
Park Meadows (Part of Rolling Meadows)	60008
Park Ridge	60068
Parkville	61872
Parkway (Part of North Riverside)	60546
Parkwood (Part of Elgin)	60120
Parkwood Village (Part of Elgin)	60120
Parnell	61842
Parrish	62890
Parrish Addition	62930
Partridge (Township)	61545
Partridge Hill (Part of Hoffman Estates)	60195
Passport	62868
Patoka	62875
Patoka (Township)	62875
Patterson	62078
Patterson (Township)	62078
Patterson Heights	62035
Patterson Springs	61919
Patton (Ford County) (Township)	60957
Patton (Wabash County)	62863
Pattonsburg	61369
Paulton	62959
Pavilion	60560
Pawnee	62558
Pawnee (Township)	62558
Paw Paw (DeKalb County) (Township)	60518
Paw Paw (Lee County)	61353
Paxton	60957
Paynes Point	61015
Payson	62360
Payson (Township)	62360
Peach Orchard (Township)	60952
Pea Ridge (Township)	62375
Pearl	62361
Pearl (Township)	62361
Pearl City	61062
Pebble Beach	60450
Pecan Grove	62031
Pecatonica	61063
Pecatonica (Township)	61063
Peerless	60544
Pekin	61554*
	61555†
Pekin Heights (Part of Pekin)	61554
Pekin Mall (Part of Pekin)	61554
Pella (Township)	60959
Pembroke (Township)	60964
Pendleton (Township)	62810
Penfield	61862

	ZIP		ZIP		ZIP
Penn (Shelby County) (Township)	62550	Pistakee Bay	60050	Poplar Grove (Boone County) (Township)	61065
Penn (Stark County) (Township)	61421	Pistakee Heights (Part of Fox Lake)	60050	Poplar Grove (Rock Island County)	61244
Pennsylvania (Township)	62664	Pistakee Highlands (McHenry County)	60050	Port Byron	61275
Penny Oaks (Part of Macomb)	61455	Pistakee Hills	60050	Port Byron (Township)	61275
Penrose	61081	Pistaqua Heights	60050	Port Jackson	62427
Peoria	61601-07	Pitchin	60924	Portland (Township)	61277
	61612-56	Pitman (Township)	62572	Portland	61277
For specific Peoria Zip Codes call (309) 671-8813, or your local postmaster.		Pittsburg (Fayette County)	62471	Port Ridge (Part of Lockport)	60441
		Pittsburg (Williamson County)	62974	Posen (Cook County)	60469
Peoria City (Township)	61601	Pittsfield	62363	Posen (Washington County)	62263
Peoria Heights	61614	Pittsfield (Township)	62363	Posey	62231
Peotone	60468	Pittwood	60970	Post Oak	62418
Peotone (Township)	60468	Pixley (Township)	62868	Potomac	61865
Pepper Tree	60067	Plainfield	60544	Pottawatawi Highlands (Part of Tinley Park)	60477
Pequot (Part of Coal City)	60416	Plainfield (Township)	60544	Pottstown	61614
Percy	62272	Plainfield Acres	60544	Powder Creek	62223
Perdueville	60957	Plainview	62676	Powder Mill Woods	62220
Perks	62973	Plainville	62365	Powellton	62358
Perry	62362	Plano	60545	Prairie (Crawford County) (Township)	62442
Perry (Township)	62362	Plato (Township)	60123	Prairie (Edgar County) (Township)	61924
Perryton (Township)	61279	Plato Center	60170		
Perryville	61016	Plattville	60560	Prairie (Hancock County) (Township)	62321
Persifer (Township)	61436	Playfield (Part of Crestwood)	60445	Prairie (Randolph County)	62278
Peru	61354	Plaza (Part of Belleville)	62223	Prairie (Shelby County) (Township)	62463
Peru (Township)	61354	Pleasant (Township)	61441	Prairie Center	61350
Peru Mall (Part of Peru)	61354	Pleasant Dale (Part of Burr Ridge)	62525	Prairie City	61470
Pesotum	61863	Pleasantdale Estates	60439	Prairie City (Township)	61470
Pesotum (Township)	61863	Pleasant Grove (Coles County) (Township)	62440	Prairie Court (Part of Oak Park)	60301
Peters (Part of Glen Carbon)	62034	Pleasant Grove (Johnson County)	62912	Prairie Creek (Township)	62635
Petersburg (Menard County)	62675	Pleasant Hill (DuPage County)	60188	Prairie Du Long (Township)	62243
Petersburg (St. Clair County)	62269	Pleasant Hill (Jackson County)	62901	Prairie du Pont	62240
Peters Creek	62931	Pleasant Hill (McLean County)	61753	Prairie Du Rocher	62277
Peterson Avenue (Part of Chicago)	60646	Pleasant Hill (Pike County)	62366	Prairie Estates	62675
Petite Lake	60002	Pleasant Hill (Pike County) (Township)	62366	Prairie Green (DuPage County)	60187
Petrolia	62417	Pleasant Hills	60172	Prairie Green (Iroquois County) (Township)	60942
Petty (Township)	62466	Pleasant Mound	62284	Prairie Grove	60050
Pharoah's Gardens	62932	Pleasant Mound (Township)	62284	Prairie Home	62550
Pheasant Creek (Part of Northbrook)	60062	Pleasant Plains	62677	Prairie Ridge (Part of Hoffman Estates)	60195
Pheasant Hollow	60187	Pleasant Ridge (Livingston County) (Township)	61741	Prairieton (Township)	62550
Pheasant Meadows	60401	Pleasant Ridge (Madison County)	62234	Prairietown	62097
Pheasant Ridge	60544			Prairie View	60069
Pheasant Ridge (Part of Mokena)	60448	Pleasant Run (Part of Wheeling)	60090	Prairieville	61021
Phelps	62240	Pleasant Vale (Township)	62356	Preemption	61276
Phenix (Township)	61254	Pleasant Valley (Township)	61085	Preemption (Township)	61276
Philadelphia	62612	Pleasant View (Macon County) (Township)	62513	Prentice	62612
Philadelphia (Township)	62612	Pleasant View (Schuyler County)	62681	Presswood Hills	62274
Phillippe (Part of Rolling Meadows)	60008	Plumfield	62896	Prestbury	60506
Phillips (Township)	62827	Plum Grove Countryside (Part of Rolling Meadows)	60008	Preston (Randolph County)	62242
Phillipstown	62827	Plum Grove Estates	60067	Preston (Richland County) (Township)	62450
Philo	61864	Plum Grove Hills (Part of Rolling Meadows)	60008	Preston Heights	60431
Philo (Township)	61864	Plum Grove Village (Part of Rolling Meadows)	60008	Prestwick	60423
Phinney	61801	Plum Grove Woods	60067	Prickett (Part of Edwardsville)	62025
Phoenix	60426	Plum Hill	62263	Princeton	61356
Piasa (Jersey County) (Township)	62012	Plum Hill (Township)	62214	Princeton (Township)	61356
Piasa (Macoupin County)	62079	Plum Hollow	61021	Princeville	61559
Piasa Hills	62035	Plymouth	62367	Princeville (Township)	61559
Picadilly Terrace	60514	Plymouth Farms (Part of Vernon Hills)	60060	Proctor	60936
Pickaway (Township)	61914	Poag	62025	Prophetstown	61277
Pierce (Township)	60151	Pocahontas	62275	Prophetstown (Township)	61277
Pierceburg	62449	Poe	62278	Prospect	61866
Pierron	62273	Point Pleasant (Township)	61473	Prospect Heights	60070
Pierson	61929	Point West (Part of Lombard)	60148	Prospect Meadows (Part of Mount Prospect)	60056
Piety Hill	61348	Polk (Township)	62626	Prospect Park (Part of Fairview Heights)	62208
Pigeon Grove (Township)	60924	Polo	61064	Providence	61368
Pike (Livingston County) (Township)	61726	Pomona	62975	Provincetown (Part of Country Club Hills)	60477
Pike (Pike County)	62370	Pomona (Township)	62975	Proving Ground	61074
Pilot (Kankakee County) (Township)	60941	Pond	62995	Proviso (Township)	60160
Pilot (Vermilion County) (Township)	61831	Pontiac	61764	Prudential Plaza (Part of Chicago)	60601
Pilot Grove (Township)	62318	Pontiac (Township)	61764	Pruett	62458
Pilot Knob (Township)	62263	Pontiac (Part of Fairview Heights)	62232	Pujol	63673
Pilsen (Part of Chicago)	60608	Pontiac Correctional Center	61764	Pulaski	62976
Pinckneyville	62274	Pontiac Station (Part of Fairview Heights)	62268	Pulleys Mill	62939
Pine Creek (Township)	61064	Pontoon Beach	62040	Pullman (Part of Chicago)	60628
Pinecrest	60435	Pontoosuc	62330	Pullman Junction (Part of Chicago)	60617
Pine Grove	60450	Pontoosuc (Township)	62330	Putman (Township)	61427
Pinelands	60174	Pope (Township)	62875	Putnam	61560
Pine Meadow (Part of Bolingbrook)	60440	Poplar City	62633	Quarry (Township)	62037
Pine Ridge	61254	Poplar Grove (Boone County)	61065	Quatoga	62035
Pine Rock (Township)	61015			Quincy	62301-06
Pingree Grove	60140			For specific Quincy Zip Codes call (217) 224-4950, or your local postmaster.	
Pinkstaff	62439				
Pin Oak (Township)	62025				
Pioneer Acres	61025				
Pioneer Terrace	60115			Quincy Mall (Part of Quincy)	62301
Piopolis	62859			Quiver (Township)	62644
Piper City	60959				
Pisgah	62650				

	ZIP		ZIP		ZIP
Quiver Beach	62644	Richland Grove (Township)	61281	Rob Roy Country Club (Part	
Raccoon (Township)	62801	Richmond	60071	of Prospect Heights)	60070
Racine Avenue (Part of		Richmond (Township)	60071	Roby	62545
Chicago)	60628	Richmond Estates (Part of		Rochelle	61068
Raddle	62950	Oak Forest)	60452	Rochester	62563
Radford	62550	Richton Hills (Part of		Rochester (Township)	62563
Radnor (Township)	61525	Richton Park)	60466	Rochester	62863
Radom	62876	Richton Park	60471	Rock	62938
Rainbow Hills	60174	Richview	62877	Rockbridge	62081
Rakers Addition	62216	Richview (Township)	62877	Rockbridge (Township)	62081
Raleigh	62977	Richwood (Township)	62031	Rock City	61070
Raleigh (Township)	62977	Richwoods (Crawford		Rock Creek (Adams	
Ramona Place	62035	County)	62451	County)	62301
Ramsey	62080	Richwoods (Peoria County)		Rock Creek (Hancock	
Ramsey (Township)	62080	(Township)	61614	County) (Township)	62321
Randhurst Shopping Center		Ricks (Township)	62546	Rock Creek (Hardin County)	62919
(Part of Mount Prospect)	60056	Ridge (Township)	62565	Rock Creek-Lima	
Randolph	61745	Ridgecrest	62450	(Township)	61046
Randolph (Township)	61745	Ridge Farm	61870	Rockdale	60436
Randolph Street (Part of		Ridgefield	60012	Rock Falls	61071
Chicago)	60601	Ridgeland (Township)	60968	Rockford	61101-10
Range	62864	Ridgemoor (Part of			61112-14
Rankin	60960	Willowbrook)	60521		61125-26
Ransom	60470	Ridge Prairie Heights (Part		For specific Rockford Zip Codes	
Ransom Ridge Estates (Part		of O'Fallon)	62269	call (815) 229-4811, or your local	
of Park Ridge)	60068	Ridgeville	60955	postmaster.	
Rantoul	61866	Ridgewood (Part of Western		Rockford (Township)	61101
Rantoul (Township)	61866	Springs)	60558	Rockgate Estates	62035
Rapatee	61544	Ridgewood East	60452	Rock Grove	61070
Rapids City	61278	Ridgewood West (Part of		Rock Grove (Township)	61070
Rardin	61920	Oak Forest)	60452	Rock Island	61201-04
Raritan	61471	Ridgway	62979	For specific Rock Island Zip	
Raritan (Township)	61471	Ridgway (Township)	62979	Codes call (309) 793-7200, or	
Rasmussen Addition	60936	Ridott	61067	your local postmaster.	
Raven	61924	Ridott (Township)	61067	Rock Island Arsenal	61299
Ravenswood (Part of		Rieuf's Meadows	61341	Rockport	62370
Chicago)	60625	Riffel	62858	Rock River Terrace	61010
Ravinia (Part of Highland		Riggston	62694	Rock Run (Township)	61019
Park)	60035	Riley (Township)	61038	Rockton	61072
Ravinia Park (Part of		Riley Center	60152	Rockton (Township)	61072
Highland Park)	60035	Rinard	62878	Rockvale (Township)	61061
Rawalts	61520	Ring Neck	60543	Rock Vale Heights	61010
Rawlins (Township)	61036	Ringwood	60072	Rockville (Township)	60950
Ray	62681	Rio	61472	Rockwell (Part of La Salle)	61301
Raymond (Champaign		Rio (Township)	61472	Rockwood	62280
County) (Township)	61852	Ripley	62353	Rocky Run (Township)	62373
Raymond (Montgomery		Ripley (Township)	62353	Rodden	61041
County)	62560	Rising Sun	62821	Rogers (Township)	60946
Raymond (Montgomery		Ritchason Addition	62896	Rogers Park (Part of	
County) (Township)	62560	Ritchie	60481	Chicago)	60626
Reader	62630	Riverair	62035		60660
Reading	61311	Rivercrest Center (Part of		For specific Rogers Park Zip	
Reading (Township)	61311	Crestwood)	60607	Codes call (312) 508-1200, or	
Rector (Township)	62930	Riverdale (Cook County)	60627	your local postmaster.	
Red Bud	62278	Riverdale (Winnebago		Rolling Acres (Champaign	
Reddick	60961	County)	61073	County)	61866
Redmon	61949	River Forest	60305	Rolling Acres (Peoria	
Red Oak	61032	River Forest (Township)	60305	County)	61614
Red Oak Terrace (Part of		River Glen	60010	Rolling Green	61938
Highland Park)	60035	River Grange Lakes	60175	Rolling Hills (Clinton County)	62293
Reed (Township)	60408	River Grove	60171	Rolling Hills (Piatt County)	61884
Reed City	61547	River Heights (Part of		Rolling Meadows (Cook	
Reeds Station	62924	Danville)	61832	County)	60008
Rees	62638	River Isle	60954	Rolling Meadows	
Reevesville	62943	River Oaks Center (Part of		(McDonough County)	61455
Regency Grove	60515	Calumet City)	60409	Rollo	60518
Regency Terrace (Part of		River Reach	61008	Rome (Jefferson County)	
Bloomingdale)	60108	River Ridge	60560	(Township)	62830
Reilly	60960	Riverside (Adams County)		Rome (Peoria County)	61562
Reily Lake	62241	(Township)	62301	Rome Heights	61523
Rellswood Hills	61008	Riverside (Cook County)	60546	Romeoville	60441
Renault	62279	Riverside (Cook County)		Romine (Township)	62849
Renchville	61523	(Township)	60546	Rondout	60044
Rend City	62812	Riverside Island (Part of Fox		Roodhouse	62082
Reno	62246	Lake)	60020	Roodhouse (Township)	62082
Rentchler	62221	Riverside Lawns	60546	Rooks Creek (Township)	61764
Reseda (Part of Palatine)	60067	Riverside Park	60050	Rooney Heights	60435
Resthaven	60481	Riverton	62561	Roosevelt Road (Part of	
Reynolds (Lee County)		Riverview (Carroll County)	61285	Chicago)	60607
(Township)	61006	Riverview (Lee County)	61021	Roots	62277
Reynolds (Rock Island		Riverview (Whiteside		Root Spring	60013
County)	61279	County)	61071	Ropers Landing	62938
Reynoldsburg	62991	Riverview Heights	60543	Rosamond	62083
Reynoldsville	62952	Riverwoods	60015	Rosamond (Township)	62083
Rice (Jo Daviess County)		Rivoli (Township)	61465	Roscoe	61073
(Township)	61036	Roaches	62898	Roscoe (Township)	61073
Rice (Perry County)	62274	Roachtown	62260	Rose (Township)	62565
Rice Lake	61401	Roanoke	61561	Rosebud	62938
Rich (Township)	60471	Roanoke (Township)	61561	Rosecrans	60083
Richards	60450	Robbins	60472	Rosedale	62031
Richardson	60151	Robbs	62985	Rosedale (Township)	62031
Richardson Estates	61801	Robein (Part of East Peoria)	61611	Rosefield (Township)	61529
Richfield	62365	Roberts (Ford County)	60962	Rose Hill (Cook County)	60640
Richfield (Township)	62365	Roberts (Marshall County)		Rose Hill (DuPage County)	60515
Richland (La Salle County)		(Township)	61375	Rose Hill (Jasper County)	62432
(Township)	61334	Roberts Park (Part of		Rose Lake (Part of Fairmont	
Richland (Marshall County)		Bridgeview)	60453	City)	62201
(Township)	61570	Robin Hill (Part of Joliet)	60435	Roseland (Part of Chicago)	60628
Richland (Sangamon		Robinson	62454	Rose Lawn (Part of	
County)	62677	Robinson (Township)	62454	Chicago)	60628
Richland (Shelby County)		Robinson Correctional		Roselle	60172
(Township)	62465	Center	62454	Rosemont (Cook County)	60018

* Area Zip Code   † Post Office Boxes

	ZIP		ZIP		ZIP
Summit-Argo (Part of Summit)	60501	Terre Haute (Township)	61454	Towanda (Township)	61776
Summit Heights	62089	Teutopolis	62467	Tower Hill	62571
Summum	61501	Teutopolis (Township)	62467	Tower Hill (Township)	62571
Sumner (Kankakee County) (Township)	60940	Texas (Township)	61727	Tower Lakes	60010
Sumner (Lawrence County)	62466	Texas City	62930	Town and Country	62901
Sumner (Warren County) (Township)	61453	Texico	62889	Towne Oaks	61535
Sumpter (Township)	62468	Thackeray	62859	Tradewinds	60115
Sunbeam	61231	Thawville	60968	Trago Lake	62839
Sunbury (Livingston County)	61313	Thayer	62689	Tremont (Madison County)	62035
Sunbury (Livingston County) (Township)	61313	Thebes	62990	Tremont (Tazewell County)	61568
Sunfield	62832	Thebes Junction (Part of Thebes)	62990	Tremont (Tazewell County) (Township)	61568
Sunny Acres (Champaign County)	61853	The Burg	61318	Trenton	62293
Sunny Acres (Kankakee County)	60950	The Clusters (Part of Bolingbrook)	60440	Trilla	62469
Sunny Crest	60430	The Covered Bridges (Part of Carol Stream)	60188	Trimble	62454
Sunnydale	61021	The Fairway of Country Lakes (Part of Naperville)	60563	Triple Lance Heights	62901
Sunny Hill	61273	The Greens of Woodgate (Part of Matteson)	60443	Tri-State Village	60521
Sunny Hill Estates	61273	The Grove Shopping Center (Part of Elk Grove Village)	60007	Triumph	61371
Sunny Hills Estates	60515	The Knolls	60175	Triumvera	60025
Sunnyland (Tazewell County)	61571	The Laurels (Part of Justice)	60458	Trivoli	61569
Sunny Land (Will County)	60435	The Ledges	61073	Trivoli (Township)	61569
Sunnyside (McHenry County)	60050	The Meadows	60532	Trout Valley (Part of Cary)	60013
Sunnyside (Williamson County)	62948	The Old Farm	61821	Trowbridge	62447
Sunnyside Acres	62531	Third Lake	60046	Troxel	60151
Sun Prairie Seed	61873	Thomas	61283	Troy (Madison County)	62294
Sun Ridge (Part of Hoffman Estates)	60195	Thomasboro	61878	Troy (Will County) (Township)	60435
Sunrise Ridge (Part of Romeoville)	60441	Thomas Eddition	61364	Troy Grove	61372
Sun River Terrace	60964	Thomasville	62533	Troy Grove (Township)	61372
Sunset Acres (Lake County)	60048	Thompson (Township)	61001	Tru Lock Acres	61455
Sunset Acres (Stephenson County)	61032	Thompson Addition	61241	Trumbull	62821
Sunset Harbor	62959	Thompsonville	62890	Truro (Township)	61489
Sunset Hills (Part of Roselle)	60172	Thomson	61285	Tullamore (Part of Mundelein)	60060
Sunset Lake	62640	Thornhill (Part of Carol Stream)	60187	Tunbridge (Township)	61749
Sunset Trailer Park (Part of Glenview)	60025	Thornton	60476	Tunnel Hill	62991
Sutter	62373	Thornton (Township)	60476	Turnberry	60014
Sutton	60010	Thornton Junction (Part of South Holland)	60473	Tuscola	61953
Sutton Point (Part of Northbrook)	60062	Thornwilde (Part of Warrenville)	60555	Tuscola (Township)	61953
Swan (Township)	61473	Thunderbird Lake	62012	Twelvemile Corner	61318
Swan Creek	61473	Tice	62675	Twenty-Second Street (Part of Chicago)	60616
Swansea	62221	Ticona	61370	Twenty-Seventh Street (Part of Chicago)	60616
Swanwick	62237	Tierra Grande (Part of Country Club Hills)	60477	Twenty-Third Street (Part of Chicago)	60616
Swedona	61262	Tilden	62292	Twigg (Township)	62829
Sweetwater	62642	Tilton	61833	Twilight Terrace	62221
Swiss Valley (Part of Crete)	60417	Timber (Township)	61533	Twin City (Part of Champaign)	61801
Swissville (Part of Dixon)	61021	Timberbrook	61254	Twin Creek Acres	61010
Swygert	61764	Timbercrest (Part of Schaumburg)	60194	Twin Lakes	62294
Sycamore	60178	Timber Lake (Carroll County)	61053	Twin Oaks (Part of Joliet)	60435
Sycamore (Township)	60178	Timber Lake (Lake County)	60010	Tyrone (Township)	62822
Sylvan Hill	60462	Timberlake Estate	62568	Udina	60123
Sylvan Lake	60060	Timberlake Estates	60521	Ulah	61238
Symerton	60481	Timberlake Village (Part of Mount Prospect)	60056	Ullin	62992
Symmes (Township)	61944	Timber Lane	61008	Union (Cumberland County) (Township)	62428
Table Grove	61482	Timberline	60435	Union (Effingham County) (Township)	62424
Tabor	61778	Timber Ridge (Cook County)	60457	Union (Fulton County) (Township)	61415
Taggert Woods	62626	Timber Ridge (DuPage County)	60190	Union (Livingston County) (Township)	60460
Talkington (Township)	62692	Timber Terrace	60115	Union (Logan County)	62635
Tall Trees (Part of Glenview)	60025	Timber Trails (Part of Oak Brook)	60521	Union (McHenry County)	60180
Talluia	62688	Timber View	61801	Union Center	62428
Tamalco	62253	Timberview	61853	Union Grove	61270
Tamalco (Township)	62253	Time	62363	Union Grove (Township)	61270
Tamarac (Part of Flossmoor)	60422	Timewell	62375	Union Hill (Kankakee County)	60969
Tamaroa	62888	Timothy	62428	Union Hill (St. Clair County)	62232
Tamms	62988	Tinley Park	60477	Union Stock Yards (Part of Chicago)	60609
Tampico	61283	Tinley Terrace (Part of Tinley Park)	60477	Uniontown	61572
Tampico (Township)	61283	Tioga	62351	Unionville (Massac County)	62910
Tanbark (Part of Tinley Park)	60477	Tipton	62298	Unionville (Vermilion County)	61883
Tanglewood (Part of Hanover Park)	60103	Tiskilwa	61368	Unionville (Whiteside County)	61270
Tate (Township)	62935	Todds Mill	62263	Unity (Alexander County)	62993
Tatumville	62988	Todds Point	61914	Unity (Piatt County) (Township)	61913
Taylor (Township)	61021	Todds Point (Township)	61914	University (Part of Urbana)	61801
Taylor Ridge	61284	Toledo	62468	University Heights (Part of Charleston)	61920
Taylor Springs	62089	Tolono	61880	University Mall (Part of Carbondale)	62901
Taylorville	62568	Tolono (Township)	61880	University Park	60466
Taylorville (Township)	62568	Toluca	61369	Upper Alton (Part of Alton)	62002
Taylorville Correctional Center	62568	Tomahawk Bluff	61301	Uptown (Part of Chicago)	60640
Techny	60082	Tompkins (Township)	61447	Urbain	62822
Teheran	62664	Toms Prairie	62837	Urban (Part of Taylorville)	62568
Temple Hill	62938	Tonica	61370	Urbana	61801
Tenerelli	60511	Tonti	62881	Urbana (Township)	61801
Tennessee	62374	Tonti (Township)	62881	Urbandale	62914
Tennessee (Township)	62374	Topeka	61567	Ursa	62376
Terminal Junction (Part of Rock Island)	61201	Toronto	62707	Ursa (Township)	62376
Terra Cotta	60014	Toulon	61483	Ustick (Township)	61270
Terre Haute	61454	Toulon (Township)	61483	Utica	61373
		Tovey	62570	Utica (Township)	61373
		Towanda	61776	Vale Vue Acres	62650

	ZIP		ZIP		ZIP
Valier	62891	Wade (Clinton County)		Waynesville (Township)	61778
Valley (Township)	61491	(Township)	62231	Weathersfield (Part of	
Valley City	62340	Wade (Jasper County)		Schaumburg)	60194
Valley Lo (Part of Glenview)	60025	(Township)	62448	Weaver	62423
Valley View (DeKalb		Wadsworth	60083	Webber (Township)	62814
County)	60145	Waggoner	62572	Webster	62321
Valley View (DuPage		Wakefield	62448	Webster Park (Part of	
County)	60137	Waldo (Township)	61744	Spring Valley)	61362
Valley View (Kane County)	60174	Walker (Township)	62373	Wedgewood Estates	62293
Valley View (Tazewell		Walkerville	62050	Wedron	60557
County)	61611	Walkerville (Township)	62050	Weedman	61842
Valmeyer	62295	Wall (Township)	60948	Wee-Ma-Tuk Hills	61427
Van Burensburg	62032	Wallace (Township)	61350	Weldon	61882
Van Buren Street (Part of		Wallingford	60442	Welge	62288
Chicago)	60601	Walnut	61376	Weller (Township)	61238
Vance (Township)	61841	Walnut (Township)	61376	Wellington	60973
Vandalia	62471	Walnut Grove (Knox		Wellington Heights	60435
Vandalia (Township)	62471	County) (Township)	61414	Wells	62871
Vandalia Correctional		Walnut Grove (McDonough		Wendelin	62448
Center	62471	County)	61470	Wenona	61377
Van Orin	61374	Walnut Grove (McDonough		Wenonah	62075
Varna	61375	County) (Township)	61438	Wentworth Avenue (Part of	
Velma	62568	Walnut Hill	62893	Calumet City)	60409
Venedy	62214	Walnut Park	62231	Wesley (Tazewell County)	61611
Venedy (Township)	62214	Walnut Prairie	62477	Wesley (Will County)	
Venetian Village	60046	Walpole	62817	(Township)	60481
Venice	62090	Walsh	62297	West (Effingham County)	
Venice (Township)	62090	Walshville	62091	(Township)	62458
Venice Crossing (Part of		Walshville (Township)	62091	West (McLean County)	
Venice)	62090	Waltham	61373	(Township)	61722
Vera	62080	Waltham (Township)	61373	Westaway	60504
Vergennes	62994	Walton	61021	Westbrook	61853
Vergennes (Township)	62994	Waltonville	62894	Westbrook Estates (Part of	
Vermilion (Edgar County)	61955	Wamac	62801	O'Fallon)	62269
Vermilion (La Salle County)		Wanda	62025	West Brooklyn	61378
(Township)	61370	Wanlock	61231	West Brook Village (Part of	
Vermilion Grove	61870	Wapella	61777	Macomb)	61455
Vermilion Heights	61832	Wapella (Township)	61777	Westbury (Part of	
Vermilionville	61370	Wards Grove (Township)	61048	Bolingbrook)	60440
Vermillion Estates	61764	Ware	62952	Westchester	60154
Vermont	61484	Warner	61273	West Chicago	60185*
Vermont (Township)	61484	Warren (Jo Daviess County)	61087		60186†
Vernon (Lake County)		Warren (Jo Daviess County)		West City	62812
(Township)	60069	(Township)	61087	West Clinton Estates	62265
Vernon (Marion County)	62892	Warren (Lake County)		Westdale Gardens	60126
Vernon Hills	60061	(Township)	60031	West Deerfield (Township)	60015
Verona	60479	Warren G. Murray		West End	62890
Versailles	62378	Developmental Center	62801	Western (Township)	61273
Versailles (Township)	62378	Warrenhurst (Part of		Western Avenue (SOO	
Versailles-on-the-Lake (Part		Warrenville)	60555	Station)(Part of Chicago)	60612
of Schaumburg)	60194	Warren Park (Part of Cicero)	60650	Western Avenue (Burlington	
Veterans Administration		Warrensburg	62573	Northern Station)(Part of	
Medical Center	60064	Warrenville	60555	Chicago)	60608
Vets Row	61523	Warsaw	62379	Western Illinois Correctional	
Vevay Park	62420	Warsaw (Township)	62379	Center	62353
Vicic (Part of East Peoria)	61611	Wartburg	62298	Western Knolls	62707
Victor (Township)	60556	Wartrace	62943	Western Mound (Township)	62630
Victoria	61485	Wasco	60183	Western Springs	60558
Victoria (Township)	61485	Washburn	61570	Westervelt	62574
Vienna (Grundy County)		Washington (Carroll County)		Westfield (Part of Joliet)	60435
(Township)	60479	(Township)	61074	Westfield (Bureau County)	
Vienna (Johnson County)	62995	Washington (Tazewell		(Township)	61312
Village Crossing (Part of		County)	61571	Westfield (Clark County)	62474
Skokie)	60076	Washington (Tazewell		Westfield (Clark County)	
Village Mall (Part of Danville)	61832	County) (Township)	61571	(Township)	62474
Village Square	60515	Washington (Will County)		West Frankfort	62896
Villa Grove	61956	(Township)	60401	West Frankfort Lake	62896
Villa Grove Junction (Part of		Washington Heights (Part of		West Galena (Township)	61036
Villa Grove)	61956	Chicago)	60628	Westgate	62959
Villa Hills	62223	Washington Park	62204	West Glen (Part of Peoria)	61614
Villa Marie	62035	Washington Square Mall		West Glenview	60025
Villa Park	60181	(Part of Homewood)	60430	West Hallock	61526
Villa Ridge	62996	Wasson	62930	West Jersey	61483
Villas Salceda (Part of		Wataga	61488	West Jersey (Township)	61483
Northbrook)	60062	Waterford (DuPage County)	60521	West Kankakee (Part of	
Villa Verde (Part of Buffalo		Waterford (Fulton County)		Kankakee)	60901
Grove)	60090	(Township)	61542	West Lake (Crawford	
Villa West	60462	Waterloo	62298	County)	62454
Villa Westbrook (Part of		Waterman	60556	Westlake (DuPage County)	60139
Macomb)	61455	Water Tower Place (Part of		West Lake Forest (Part of	
Vincennes Trail	60954	Chicago)	60611	Lake Forest)	60045
Vinegar Hill (Township)	61036	Watertown (Part of East		West Liberty	62475
Viola (Lee County)		Moline)	61244	West Lincoln (Township)	62656
(Township)	61318	Watervalley	62920	West Meadowview (Part of	
Viola (Mercer County)	61486	Watseka	60970	Kankakee)	60901
Virden	62690	Watson	62473	West Miltmore	60046
Virden (Township)	62690	Watson (Township)	62473	Westmont	60559
Virgil	60182	Wauconda	60084	Westmore (Part of	
Virgil (Township)	60182	Wauconda (Township)	60084	Lombard)	60148
Virginia	62691	Waukegan	60079	Weston	61726
Virginia (Township)	62691		60085-87	West Peoria	61604
Volo	60073	For specific Waukegan Zip Codes		West Peoria (Township)	61604
Vonachen Knolls	61523	call (708) 662-6800, or your local		West Point (Hancock	
Von Glenn Acres	61010	postmaster.		County)	62380
Voorhies	61813	Wauponsee (Township)	60450	West Point (Morgan County)	62650
Vulcan (Part of East		Waverly	62692	West Point (Stephenson	
Carondelet)	62240	Waycinden Park	60016	County) (Township)	61048
Wabash (Township)	62441	Wayne (Township)	60185	Westport (Knox County)	61401
Wacker (Carroll County)	61053	Wayne	60184	Westport (Lawrence	
Wacker (Kendall County)	60560	Wayne Center	60185	County)	47591
Waddams (Township)	61050	Wayne City	62895	West Pullman (Part of	
Waddams Grove	61048	Waynesville	61778	Chicago)	60628

	ZIP
Westridge (Cook County)	60070
West Ridge (Douglas County)	61953
West Salem	62476
West Sandford	61944
West Twenty-Second St. (Part of Chicago)	60650
West Union	62477
Westville	61883
Westwood (Part of Addison)	60101
West York	62478
Wetaug	62926
Wethersfield (Township)	61277
Wetzel	61944
Wheatfield (Township)	62231
Wheatland (Bureau County) (Township)	61368
Wheatland (Fayette County) (Township)	62418
Wheatland (Will County) (Township)	60544
Wheaton	60187*
	60189†
Wheaton Center (Part of Wheaton)	60187
Wheeler	62479
Wheeling	60090
Wheeling (Township)	60090
Whiskey Corners	60071
Whiskey Creek	60185
Whispering Hills	60050
Whispering Oaks (Part of Lake Forest)	60045
Whitaker	60940
Whiteash	62959
White City	62069
White Cliffs	62035
Whitefield	61537
Whitefield (Township)	61537
Whitehall (Cook County)	60056
White Hall (Greene County)	62092
White Hall (Greene County) (Township)	62092
White Heath	61884
White Oak (Township)	61725
White Oaks	61021
White Oaks Bay	60097
White Oaks Mall (Part of Springfield)	62704
White Pigeon	61270
White Pines	60106
White Post	62093
White Rock (Lee County)	61021
White Rock (Ogle County)	61015
White Rock (Ogle County) (Township)	61045
Whites Addition	61244
Whitford Place	62035
Whitley (Township)	61928
Whitmore (Township)	62501
Whittington	62897
Wichert	60964
Wicker Park (Part of Chicago)	60622
Wickmore	62035
Wideview	60175
Wieisbrook	62918
W. I. Junction (Part of Chicago)	60621
Wilbern	61570
Wilberton (Township)	62885
Wilbur Heights	61821
Wilcox (Clay County)	62824
Wilcox (Hancock County) (Township)	62379
Wildrose	60174
Wildwood (Cook County)	60628
Wildwood (Kane County)	60504
Wildwood (Lake County)	60030
Wildwood (Lake County)	60081
Wildwood Addition (Part of Moline)	61265
Wildwood Valley	60123
Will (Township)	60468
Willard (Alexander County)	62962
Willard (St. Clair County)	62269
Willeys	62568
Williams (Township)	62693
Williamsburg	61937
Williamsfield	61489
Williamson	62088
Williams Park	60084
Williams Place	62035
Williamsville	62693
Willisville	62997
Willow	61085
Willoway (Part of Naperville)	60540
Willoway Manor (Part of Willowbrook)	60521
Willow Branch (Township)	61830
Willowbrook (DuPage County)	60521
Willowbrook (Kendall County)	60512
Willowbrook (Will County)	60417
Willow Brooke	61080
Willow Creek (Township)	60530
Willow Estates (DeKalb County)	60135
Willow Estates (Iroquois County)	60912
Willow Hill	62480
Willow Hill (Township)	62480
Willow's East (Part of Glenview)	60025
Willow Springs	60480
Willow Wood (Part of Palatine)	60067
Wilmette	60091
Wilmington	60481
Wilmington (Township)	60481
Wilshire Bluffs Estate	61008
Wilson (Township)	61777
Wilson Avenue (Part of Chicago)	60640
Wilson Heights	62234
Wilsonville	62093
Wilton (Township)	60442
Wilton Center	60442
Winchester	62694
Winden Oak	60119
Windham Manor (Part of Northbrook)	60062
Windings	60175
Windsor	61957
Windsor (Township)	61957
Windsor Estates West (Part of Mount Prospect)	60056
Windsor Park (Champaign County)	61801
Windsor Park (Cook County)	60649
Windsor Square (Part of Peoria)	61614
Wine Hill	62288
Winfield	60190
Winfield (Township)	60185
Wing	61741
Winkle	62237
Winnebago	61088
Winnebago (Township)	61088
Winneshiek	61032
Winnetka	60093
Winslow	61089
Winslow (Township)	61089
Winston Hills (Part of Woodridge)	60515
Winston Park (Part of Palatine)	60067
Winston Park Northwest (Part of Palatine)	60067
Winston Park South (Part of Country Club Hills)	60477
Winston Plaza Shopping Center (Part of Melrose Park)	60160
Winston Village (Part of Bolingbrook)	60440
Winston Woods (Part of Bolingbrook)	60440
Winterrowd	62424
Winthrop Harbor	60096
Wireton (Part of Blue Island)	60406
Witt	62094
Witt (Township)	62094
Woburn	62246
Wolf Lake	62998
Womac	62626
Wonder Lake	60097
Wonder View	60097
Wonder Woods	60097
Woodbine	61085
Woodbine (Township)	61085
Woodborough (Part of Homewood)	60430
Woodburn	62014
Woodbury	62445
Woodbury (Township)	62445
Wood Dale (DuPage County)	60191
Wooddale (Peoria County)	61607
Wooded Shores	60097
Woodfield (Part of Schaumburg)	60173
Woodford	61516
Woodford Heights	61548
Woodgate	60178
Wood Hill (Part of University Park)	60466
Woodhill Estates	61038
Woodhull	61490
Woodland (Carroll County) (Township)	61053
Woodland (Fulton County) (Township)	61501
Woodland (Iroquois County)	60974
Woodland (Kankakee County)	60954
Woodland Addition	61350
Woodland Heights (Part of Streamwood)	60103
Woodland Hills (Part of Batavia)	60510
Woodland Lake	61817
Woodland Shores	61021
Woodlawn (Cook County)	60637
Woodlawn (Jefferson County)	62898
Woodlawn Heights	61081
Woodmere (Part of Libertyville)	60048
Woodridge	60517
Wood River	62095
Wood River (Township)	62095
Woodruff (Part of Chicago)	60619
Woods Edge	61801
Woodside (Township)	62703
Woodside Estates (Part of Oak Brook)	60521
Woodson	62695
Woodstock (McHenry County)	60098
Woodstock (Schuyler County) (Township)	62681
Woodview Manor (Part of Prospect Heights)	60070
Woodville (Township)	62027
Woodworth	60953
Woody	62016
Woodyard (Edgar County)	61924
Woodyard (Fayette County)	62885
Wooster Lake	60041
Woosung	61091
Woosung (Township)	61091
Worden	62097
Worth (Cook County)	60482
Worth (Cook County) (Township)	60482
Worth (Woodford County) (Township)	61548
Wrights	62098
Wrights (Township)	62098
Wrights Corner	62414
Wyanet	61379
Wyanet (Township)	61379
Wynoose	62868
Wyoming (Lee County) (Township)	61353
Wyoming (Stark County)	61491
Wysox (Township)	61051
Wythe (Township)	62373
Xenia	62899
Xenia (Township)	62899
Yale	62481
Yankee Ridge	61801
Yantisville	62534
Yard Center (Part of Dolton)	60419
Yates (Township)	61726
Yates City	61572
Yatesville	62612
Yellowhead (Township)	60940
Yeoward Addition	61071
York (Carroll County) (Township)	61285
York (Clark County)	62477
York (Clark County) (Township)	62477
York (DuPage County) (Township)	60181
York Center	60148
Yorkfield	60126
Yorkshire Woods (Part of Oak Brook)	60521
Yorktown (Bureau County)	61283
Yorktown (Henry County) (Township)	61277
Yorktown Shopping Center (Part of Lombard)	60148
Yorkville	60560
Young America (Township)	61940
Young Hickory (Township)	61544
Youngstown	61473
Zanesville (Township)	62572
Zearing	61337
Zeigler	62999
Zenith	62899
Zif (Township)	62824
Zion (Carroll County)	61074
Zion (Lake County)	60099
Zion (Lake County) (Township)	60099
Zuma (Township)	61257
Zurich Heights (Part of Lake Zurich)	60047

* Area Zip Code   † Post Office Boxes

	ZIP
Abbey Dell	47469
Aberdeen	47040
Abington	47330
Abington (Township)	47330
Aboite	46783
Aboite (Township)	46804
Acme	47274
Acton (Part of Indianapolis)	46259
Adams (Allen County) (Township)	46774
Adams (Carroll County) (Township)	47960
Adams (Cass County) (Township)	46988
Adams (Decatur County)	47240
Adams (Decatur County) (Township)	47272
Adams (Hamilton County) (Township)	46069
Adams (Madison County) (Township)	46056
Adams (Morgan County)	46151
Adams (Morgan County) (Township)	46151
Adams (Parke County) (Township)	47872
Adams (Ripley County) (Township)	47041
Adams (Warren County) (Township)	47975
Adamsboro	46947
Adams Lake	46795
Adams Mill	46920
Addison (Township)	46176
Addmore (Part of Clarksville)	47129
Ade	47922
Advance	46102
Ainsworth	46342
Air Mail Field (Part of Indianapolis)	46241
Akron	46910
Alamo	47916
Albany	47320
Albion	46701
Albion (Township)	46701
Aldine	46366
Alert	47283
Alexandria	46001
Alfont	46040
Alford	47567
Alfordsville	47553
Algers	47567
Alida	46391
Allen (Miami County) (Township)	46951
Allen (Noble County) (Township)	46755
Allendale	47802
Allens Acres	46077
Allensville	47011
Allisonville (Part of Indianapolis)	46250
Allman	46158
Alma Lake	47834
Alpine	47331
Alquina	47331
Alta	47854
Alto	46902
Alton	47137
Altona	46738
Alvarado	46742
Amber Valley	47803
Ambia	47917
Amboy	46911
Americus	47905
Ames (Part of Crawfordsville)	47933
Amity	46131
Amo	46103
Anderson	46011-18
For specific Anderson Zip Codes call (317) 643-3356, or your local postmaster.	
Anderson (Township)	46016
Anderson (Perry County) (Township)	47586
Anderson (Rush County) (Township)	46156
Anderson (Warrick County) (Township)	47630
Andersonville	47024
Andrews	46702
Angola	46703
Annandale Estates	47448
Annapolis	47832
Anoka	46947
Ansley Acres	46804
Anthony	47302
Antioch	46041
Antiville	47371
Apache Acres	47805

	ZIP
Arba	47355
Arcadia	46030
Arcana	46952
Arcola	46704
Arctic Springs (Part of Jeffersonville)	47130
Arda	47567
Ardmore	46628
Argos	46501
Ari	46723
Ar'les Acres	46060
Arlington (Monroe County)	47401
Arlington (Rush County)	46104
Arlington Park	46815
Armiesburg	47862
Armstrong	47720
Armstrong (Township)	47720
Armuth Acres	47203
Arney	47431
Aroma	46031
Arrowhead Park	46580
Art	47834
Arthur	47598
Artic	46721
Ashboro	47840
Asherville	47834
Ash Grove	47920
Ashland (Henry County)	47362
Ashland (Morgan County) (Township)	46151
Ashley	46705
Athens	46912
Atherton	47874
Atkinsonville	47868
Atlanta	46031
Attica	47918
Atwood	46502
Aubbeenaubbee (Township)	46975
Auburn	46706
Auburn Junction	46706
Augusta (Marion County)	46268
Augusta (Pike County)	47598
Aultshire (Part of Muncie)	47302
Aurora	47001
Austin	47102
Avalon Hills (Part of Indianapolis)	46250
Avery	46041
Avilla	46710
Avoca	47420
Avon	46168
Avondale	46952
Ayr	46550
Ayrshire	47598
Azalia	47232
Babcock	46383
Bacon (Part of Indianapolis)	46220
Baileys Corner	47978
Bainbridge (Dubois County) (Township)	47546
Bainbridge (Putnam County)	46105
Baker (Township)	47433
Bakers Corners	46069
Bakertown	46701
Balbec	47369
Baldwin Heights (Part of Princeton)	47670
Bandon	47514
Banquo	46940
Banta	46106
Bar-Barry Heights (Part of West Lafayette)	47906
Barbee	46562
Bargersville	46106
Barkley (Township)	47978
Barnaby Acres	47201
Barnard	46172
Barr (Township)	47519
Barrick Corner	47841
Bartlettsville	47421
Bartley	47805
Barton (Township)	47613
Bartonia	47390
Bass Lake	46534
Batesville	47006
Bath	47010
Bath (Township)	47010
Battle Ground	47920
Baugh City	47610
Baugo (Township)	46514
Bayfield	46562
Beal	47591
Bean Blossom (Brown County)	46160
Bean Blossom (Monroe County) (Township)	47429
Bear Branch	47018
Bearcreek (Township)	47326
Beard	46041
Beardstown	46996
Bear Lake	46701
Beatrice	46341

	ZIP
Beattys Corner	46360
Beaver (Newton County) (Township)	47963
Beaver (Pulaski County) (Township)	46996
Beaver City	47922
Becks Grove	47235
Becks Mill	47167
Bedford	47421
Bedford Heights (Part of Bedford)	47421
Beecamp	47250
Beech Brook	46176
Beech Creek (Township)	47459
Beech Grove (Marion County)	46107
Beech Grove (Morgan County)	46151
Beechwood	47137
Bee Ridge	47834
Bell Center	47925
Bellefountain	47371
Belle Union	46120
Belleview	47250
Belleville	46118
Bellmore	47830
Bell Rohr Park	46538
Belmont (Brown County)	47448
Belmont (Henry County)	47362
Belshaw	46356
Ben Davis (Part of Indianapolis)	46241
Bengal	46131
Benham	47042
Bennetts	46901
Bennettsville	47143
Bennington	47011
Benton	46526
Benton (Township)	46526
Benton (Township)	47401
Bentonville	47322
Benwood	47834
Berlien	46703
Berne	46711
Berwick Manor (Part of Shelbyville)	46176
Bethany	46111
Bethel (Posey County) (Township)	47616
Bethel (Wayne County)	47341
Bethel Village	47201
Bethlehem (Township)	47104
Bethlehem (Cass County) (Township)	46988
Bethlehem (Clark County)	47104
Between-the-Lakes Park	46538
Beverly Shores	46301
Bicknell	47512
Big Creek (Township)	47929
Bigger (Township)	47265
Big Lake	46725
Big Springs	46069
Billingsville	47353
Billtown	47834
Billville	47834
Bippus	46713
Birdseye	47513
Birmingham	46951
Black (Township)	47620
Blackhawk (Allen County)	46805
Blackhawk (Vigo County)	47866
Blackhawk Beach	46383
Blackhawk Forest	46805
Blackiston Heights (Part of Clarksville)	47129
Blackiston Mill	47129
Blackiston Village (Part of Clarksville)	47129
Black Oak (Part of Gary)	46406
Blaine	47371
Blairsville	47638
Blanford	47831
Blocher	47138
Bloomfield (Greene County)	47424
Bloomfield (Lagrange County) (Township)	46761
Bloomfield (Spencer County)	47611
Bloomingdale	47832
Blooming Grove	47012
Blooming Grove (Township)	47012
Bloomingport	47355
Bloomington	47401-08
For specific Bloomington Zip Codes call (812) 334-4030, or your local postmaster.	
Blountsville	47354
Blue Creek (Adams County) (Township)	46772
Blue Creek (Franklin County) (Township)	47041
Blue Lake	46723

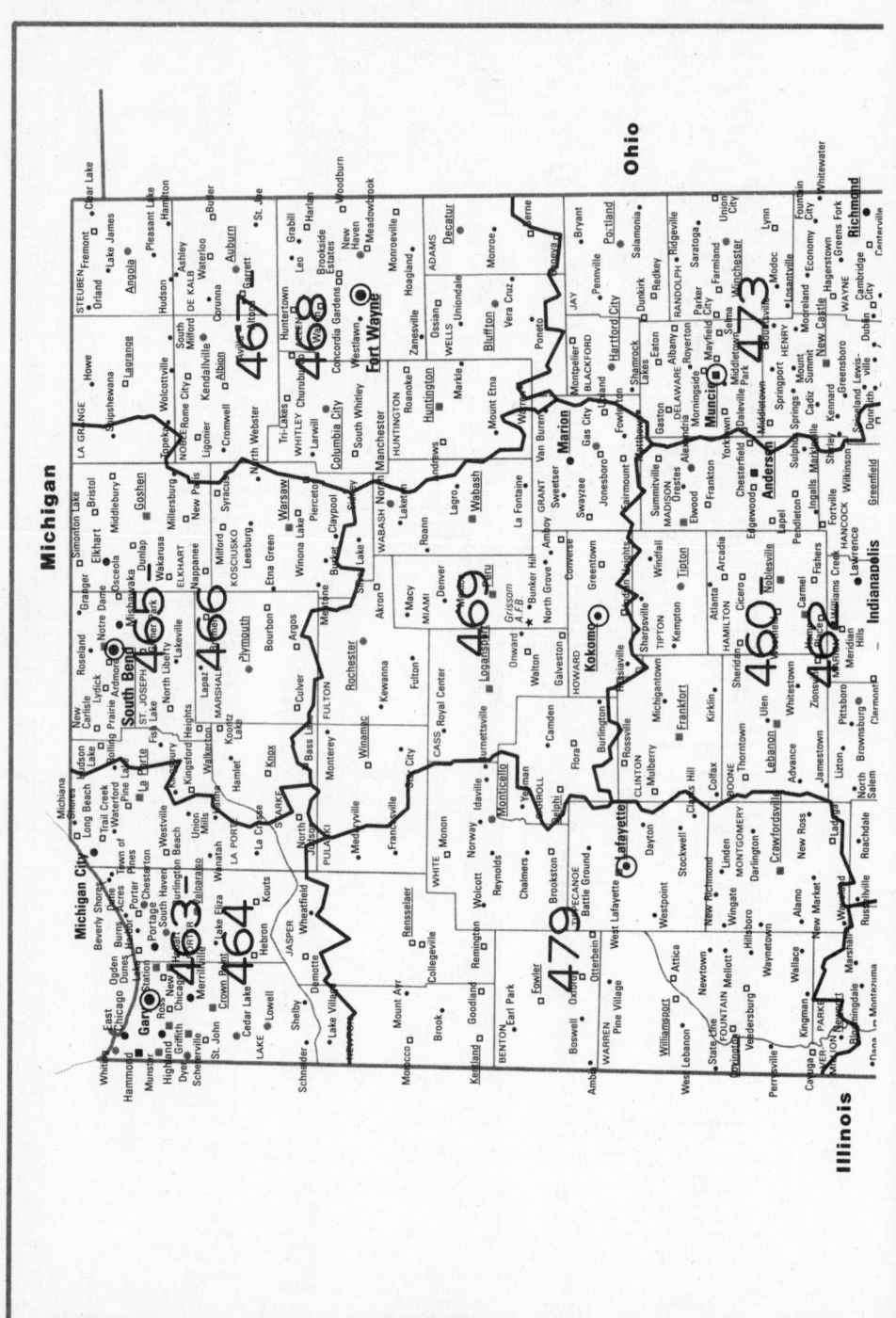

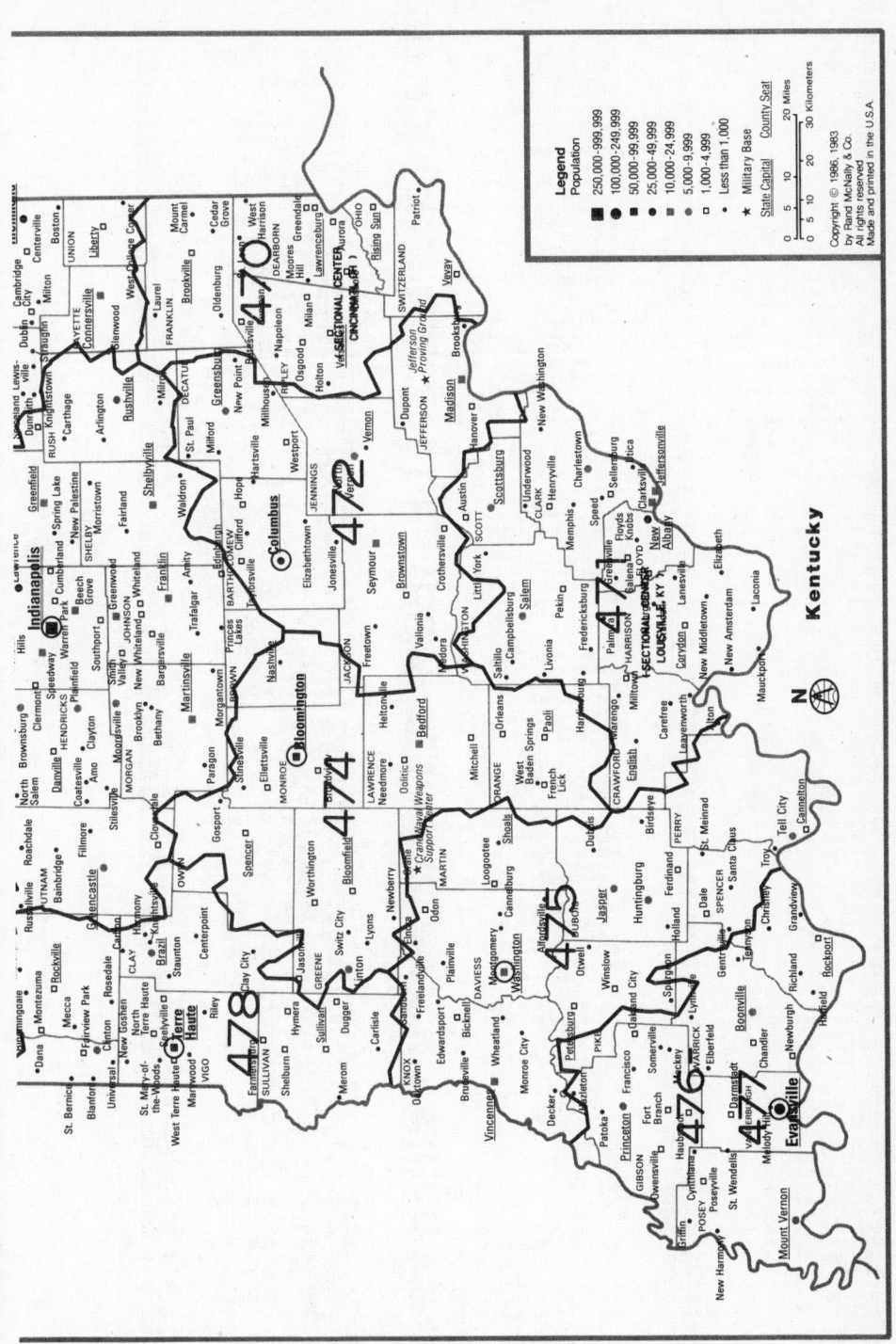

	ZIP
Blue Ridge	46176
Blue River (Hancock County) (Township)	46140
Blue River (Harrison County) (Township)	47115
Blue River (Henry County) (Township)	47360
Blue River (Johnson County) (Township)	46124
Bluff Point	47371
Bluffs	46151
Bluffton	46714
Bobtown	47274
Bogard (Township)	47568
Boggstown	46110
Bogle Corner	47438
Bolivar (Township)	47970
Bonnell	47022
Bonnenburger	47130
Bono	47446
Bono (Township)	47446
Boon (Township)	47601
Boone (Cass County) (Township)	46978
Boone (Crawford County) (Township)	47137
Boone (Dubois County) (Township)	47546
Boone (Harrison County) (Township)	47135
Boone (Madison County) (Township)	46036
Boone (Porter County) (Township)	46341
Boone Grove	46302
Boonville	47601
Borden	47106
Boston	47324
Boston (Township)	47324
Boswell	47921
Boundary	47371
Bourbon	46504
Bourbon (Township)	46504
Bowers	47940
Bowerstown	46750
Bowling Green	47833
Bowman	47567
Bowman Acres (Part of Greenfield)	46140
Boxley	46069
Boyleston	46057
Bracken	46750
Bradford	47107
Bradford Village (Part of Marion)	46952
Bradley	47611
Bramble	47553
Branchville	47514
Branchville Training Center	47586
Brandywine (Hancock County) (Township)	46140
Brandywine (Shelby County) (Township)	46126
Braytown	47043
Brazil	47834
Brazil (Township)	47834
Breezewood	46952
Breezewood Park	47302
Breezy Point	47960
Bremen	46506
Brems	46534
Brendan Wood (Part of Lebanon)	46052
Brendonwood (Part of Indianapolis)	46226
Brent Woods (Part of Shelbyville)	46176
Bretzville	47542
Brewersville	47265
Brewington Woods	47302
Briarwood	46157
Brice	47371
Brick Chapel	46135
Bridgeport (Part of Indianapolis)	46231
Bridgeton	47836
Brierwood Hills	46804
Bright	47025
Brighton	46746
Brightwood (Part of Indianapolis)	46218
Brimfield	46720
Brinckley	47340
Bringhurst	46913
Bristol	46507
Bristow	47515
Broadlands	47805
Broad Ripple (Part of Indianapolis)	46220
Broadview (Grant County)	46952
Broadview (Lawrence County)	47421

	ZIP
Broadview (Monroe County)	47401
Bromer	47452
Brook	47922
Brookfield	46126
Brook Haven	46952
Brook Knoll (Part of Bedford)	47421
Brooklyn	46111
Brookmoor	46158
Brooks	46060
Brooksburg	47250
Brookside Estates (Allen County)	46805
Brookside Estates (Vigo County)	47802
Brookston	47923
Brook Trails	46637
Brookville	47012
Brookville (Township)	47012
Brookville Heights	46163
Brookwood (Part of Warsaw)	46580
Broom Hill	47106
Brown (Hancock County) (Township)	47384
Brown (Hendricks County) (Township)	46112
Brown (Montgomery County) (Township)	47933
Brown (Morgan County) (Township)	46158
Brown (Ripley County) (Township)	47250
Brown (Washington County) (Township)	47108
Brownsburg	46112
Browns Crossing	46151
Brownstown (Township)	47220
Brownstown (Crawford County)	47118
Brownstown (Jackson County)	47220
Browns Valley	47933
Brownsville	47325
Brownsville (Township)	47325
Bruce Lake	46939
Bruceville	47516
Brummitt Acres	46304
Brunswick (Lake County)	46303
Brunswick (Lake County)	46406
Brushy Prairie	46761
Bryant	47326
Bryantsburg	47250
Bryantsville	47446
Buck Creek (Hancock County) (Township)	46140
Buck Creek (Tippecanoe County)	47924
Buckeye	46792
Buckskin	47647
Bucktown	47838
Bud	46131
Buddha	47421
Buena Vista	47024
Buffalo	47925
Buffaloville	47550
Buffington (Part of Gary)	46406
Bufkin	47620
Bugtown	47633
Bullocktown	47601
Bunker Hill (Fayette County)	47331
Bunker Hill (Knox County)	47591
Bunker Hill (Miami County)	46914
Bunker Hill (Washington County)	47167
Burdick	46304
Burglen Hills (Part of Tell City)	47586
Burket	46508
Burlington	46915
Burlington (Township)	46915
Burlington Beach	46383
Burnett	47805
Burnettsville	47926
Burney	47222
Burns City	47553
Burns Harbor	46304
Burnsville	47201
Burr Oak (Marshall County)	46511
Burr Oak (Noble County)	46701
Burrows	46916
Busseron	47561
Busseron (Township)	47561
Butler (De Kalb County)	46721
Butler (De Kalb County) (Township)	46763
Butler (Franklin County) (Township)	47006
Butler (Miami County) (Township)	46970
Butler Center	46738
Butlerville	47223

	ZIP
Byrneville	47122
Byron	46371
Caborn	47620
Cadiz	47362
Caesar Creek (Township)	47018
Cagle Mill	47868
Cain (Township)	47949
Cairo	47906
Cale	47581
California (Township)	46534
Calumet (Township)	46402
Calvertville	47424
Cambria	46041
Cambridge City	47327
Camby (Part of Indianapolis)	46113
Camden	46917
Cammack	47302
Campbell (Jennings County) (Township)	47023
Campbell (Warrick County) (Township)	47610
Campbellsburg	47108
Campbelltown	47598
Canaan	47224
Candleglo Village	46176
Candle Light Village (Part of Columbus)	47201
Cannelburg	47519
Cannelton	47520
Cannelton Heights (Part of Cannelton)	47520
Canton	47167
Carbon	47837
Carbondale	47993
Cardonia	47834
Carefree	47137
Carey (Part of Noblesville)	46060
Carlisle	47838
Carlos City	47355
Carmel	46032*
	46033†
Carp	47460
Carpenter (Township)	47977
Carpentersville	46172
Carr (Clark County) (Township)	47143
Carr (Jackson County) (Township)	47260
Carriage Estates (Bartholomew County)	47201
Carriage Estates (Hancock County)	46163
Carrollton	46913
Carrollton (Township)	46929
Carter (Township)	47523
Cartersburg	46114
Carthage	46115
Carwood	47106
Cascade Heights (Part of Bloomington)	47401
Cass (Clay County) (Township)	47868
Cass (Dubois County) (Township)	47541
Cass (Greene County) (Township)	47449
Cass (La Porte County) (Township)	46390
Cass (Ohio County) (Township)	47040
Cass (Pulaski County) (Township)	47957
Cass (Sullivan County)	47882
Cass (Sullivan County) (Township)	47882
Cass (White County) (Township)	47960
Cassville	46901
Castleton	46250
Castleton Square (Part of Castleton)	46250
Cataract	47460
Cates	47952
Catlin	47872
Cato	47598
Cavanaugh (Part of Gary)	46406
Cayuga	47928
Cedar Canyons	46825
Cedar Creek (Allen County) (Township)	46741
Cedar Creek (De Kalb County)	46738
Cedar Creek (Lake County) (Township)	46356
Cedar Grove	47016
Cedar Lake	46303
Cedar Point	47960
Cedar Shores	46741
Cedarville	46741
Celestine	47521
Cemar Estates	47805

* Area Zip Code   † Post Office Boxes

	ZIP
Cementville (Part of Jeffersonville)	47129
Centenary	47842
Centennial	47952
Center (Benton County) (Township)	47944
Center (Boone County) (Township)	46052
Center (Clinton County) (Township)	46041
Center (Dearborn County) (Township)	47001
Center (Delaware County) (Township)	47302
Center (Gibson County) (Township)	47649
Center (Grant County) (Township)	46952
Center (Greene County) (Township)	47424
Center (Hancock County) (Township)	46140
Center (Hendricks County) (Township)	46122
Center (Howard County)	46902
Center (Howard County) (Township)	46902
Center (Jay County)	47371
Center (Jennings County) (Township)	47265
Center (La Porte County) (Township)	46350
Center (Lake County) (Township)	46307
Center (Marion County) (Township)	46204
Center (Marshall County) (Township)	46563
Center (Martin County) (Township)	47553
Center (Porter County) (Township)	46383
Center (Posey County) (Township)	47620
Center (Ripley County) (Township)	47037
Center (Rush County) (Township)	46148
Center (Starke County) (Township)	46534
Center (Union County) (Township)	47353
Center (Vanderburgh County) (Township)	47710
Center (Warrick County)	47601
Center (Wayne County) (Township)	47330
Centerpoint	47840
Center Square	47043
Centerton	46151
Center Valley	46158
Centerville (Spencer County)	47611
Centerville (Wayne County)	47330
Central	47110
Central Barren	47161
Centre (Township)	46614
Century Consumer Mall (Part of Merrillville)	46410
Ceylon	46740
Chain O'Lakes	46628
Chalmers	47929
Chambersburg	47454
Champlin Meadows (Part of Martinsville)	46151
Chandler	47610
Chapel Bluff (Part of Columbus)	47201
Chapel Hill (Marion County)	46224
Chapelhill (Monroe County)	47436
Chapel Manor (Part of Merrillville)	46410
Charlemac Village (Part of Indianapolis)	46259
Charlestown	47111
Charlestown (Township)	47111
Charle Sumac Estates (Part of Indianapolis)	46259
Charlottesville	46117
Chase	47921
Chelsea	47138
Cherokee Terrace	47130
Cherry Grove	47933
Chester (Wabash County) (Township)	46962
Chester (Wayne County)	47374
Chester (Wells County) (Township)	46781
Chesterfield	46017
Chesterton (Hamilton County)	46280
Chesterton (Porter County)	46304

	ZIP
Chesterville	47032
Chestnut Hill (Part of Chesterton)	46304
Chestnut Ridge	47274
Chicago Avenue (Part of East Chicago)	46312
Chili	46926
China	47250
Chippewa (Part of South Bend)	46614
Chrisney	47611
Christiansburg	47201
Christmas Lake Village (Part of Santa Claus)	47579
Churubusco	46723
Cicero (Hamilton County)	46034
Cicero (Tipton County) (Township)	46031
Cicero Heights	46072
Cincinnati	47424
Circle Park	46742
Circleville	46173
Clare	46060
Clark (Johnson County) (Township)	46142
Clark (Montgomery County) (Township)	47954
Clark (Perry County) (Township)	47515
Clarksburg	47225
Clarks Hill	47930
Clarks Landing	46742
Clarksville (Clark County)	47129
Clarksville (Hamilton County)	46060
Clay (Bartholomew County) (Township)	47201
Clay (Carroll County) (Township)	46923
Clay (Cass County) (Township)	46947
Clay (Dearborn County) (Township)	47032
Clay (Decatur County) (Township)	47240
Clay (Hamilton County) (Township)	46032* 46033†
Clay (Hendricks County) (Township)	46121
Clay (Howard County) (Township)	46901
Clay (Kosciusko County) (Township)	46580
Clay (Lagrange County) (Township)	46761
Clay (Miami County) (Township)	46914
Clay (Morgan County) (Township)	46111
Clay (Owen County) (Township)	47460
Clay (Pike County) (Township)	47640
Clay (Spencer County) (Township)	47579
Clay (St. Joseph County) (Township)	46637
Clay (Wayne County) (Township)	47345
Clay City (Clay County)	47841
Clay City (Spencer County)	47550
Claypool	46510
Claysville	47108
Clayton	46118
Clear Creek (Huntington County) (Township)	46750
Clear Creek (Monroe County)	47426
Clear Creek (Monroe County) (Township)	47401
Clear Lake (Township)	46737
Clear Lake	46737
Clear Spring (Jackson County)	47220
Clearspring (Lagrange County) (Township)	46571
Clermont	46234
Clermont Heights	46112
Cleveland (Elkhart County) (Township)	46514
Cleveland (Hancock County)	46140
Cleveland (Whitley County) (Township)	46787
Clifford	47226
Clifty (Township)	47246
Clifty Village	47203
Clinton (Boone County) (Township)	46052
Clinton (Cass County) (Township)	46947

	ZIP
Clinton (Decatur County) (Township)	47240
Clinton (Elkhart County) (Township)	46526
Clinton (La Porte County) (Township)	46382
Clinton (Putnam County) (Township)	46135
Clinton (Vermillion County)	47842
Clinton (Vermillion County) (Township)	47842
Clinton Falls	46135
Cloud Crest Hills	47448
Cloverdale	46120
Cloverdale (Township)	46120
Cloverland	47834
Clover Village	46126
Clunette	46538
Clymers	46947
Coal Bluff	47874
Coal City	47427
Coal Creek (Fountain County)	47932
Coal Creek (Montgomery County) (Township)	47994
Coalmont	47845
Coatesville	46121
Cochran (Part of Aurora)	47001
Coe	47598
Coesse	46725
Coesse Corners	46725
Coffey	47448
Cofield Corner	47040
Colburn	47931
Colburn Acres	46536
Cold Springs (Dearborn County)	47032
Cold Springs (Steuben County)	46742
Colfax (Clinton County)	46035
Colfax (Newton County) (Township)	46349
Collamer	46787
College Corner (Jay County)	47371
College Corner (Union County)	45003
College Hill (Part of Logansport)	46947
College Mall (Part of Bloomington)	47401
College Meadows	46240
Collegeville	47978
Collett	47371
Collins	46725
Coloma	47872
Colonial Hills	47630
Colonial Park	47802
Colonial Village	46040
Columbia (Dubois County) (Township)	47527
Columbia (Fayette County)	47331
Columbia (Fayette County) (Township)	47331
Columbia (Gibson County) (Township)	47660
Columbia (Jennings County) (Township)	47265
Columbia (Whitley County) (Township)	46725
Columbia City	46725
Columbus	47201-03
For specific Columbus Zip Codes call (812) 378-2089, or your local postmaster.	
Commercial Place (Part of Greencastle)	46135
Commiskey	47227
Como	47371
Concord (De Kalb County)	46706
Concord (De Kalb County) (Township)	46785
Concord (Elkhart County) (Township)	46514
Concord (Tippecanoe County)	47905
Concordia Gardens (Part of Fort Wayne)	46825
Connersville	47331
Connersville (Township)	47331
Continental Camp	47616
Converse	46919
Cook (Part of Cedar Lake)	46303
Cool Spring (Township)	46360
Coolwood Acres	46383
Cope	46151
Coppess Corner	46772
Cordry Lake	46164
Corn Brook	47203
Cornettsville	47568
Correct	47042

	ZIP		ZIP		ZIP
Correctional Industrial Complex	46064	De Camp Gardens	46516	Dunlap	46514
Cortland	47228	Decatur (Adams County)	46733	Dunlapsville	47353
Corunna	46730	Decatur (Marion County) (Township)	46241	Dunn	47944
Cory	47846	Decker (Knox County)	47524	Dunnington	47944
Corydon	47112	Decker (Knox County)		Dunns Bridge	46380
Cosperville	46794	(Township)	47524	Dunreith	47337
Cottage Grove	47353	Deedsville	46921	Dupont	47231
Cotton (Township)	47011	Deep River	46342	Durbin	46060
Country Club Gardens	46804	Deer Creek (Carroll County)	46917	Dutch Town (Part of Garrett)	46738
Country Club Heights	46011	Deer Creek (Carroll County) (Township)	46923	Dyer	46311
Country Club Meadows (Part of Evansville)	47710	Deer Creek (Cass County) (Township)	46932	Eagle (Township)	46077
Countryside Estates	46805	Deer Creek (Miami County)		Eagle Creek (Township)	46341
Country Terrace	47302	(Township)	46959	Eagledale Plaza Shopping Center (Part of	
Country Village	47303	Deerfield (Bartholomew		Indianapolis)	46222
Courter	46970	County)	47201	Eagle Hollow	47250
Coveyville	47421	Deerfield (Randolph County)	47380	Eagletown	46074
Covington	47932	Deerfield (Vigo County)	47802	Eagle Village	46077
Covington Dells	46804	Deer Park	46310	Eaglewood Estates	46077
Covington Plaza (Part of Fort Wayne)	46804	Deers Mills	47989	Earle	47711
Cowan	47302	De Gonia	47601	Earlham (Part of Richmond)	47374
Coxville	47874	Delaware (Delaware County)		Earl Park	47942
Craig (Township)	47043	(Township)	47320	East Cedar Lake (Part of Cedar Lake)	46303
Craig Highlands	46060	Delaware (Hamilton County)		East Chicago	46312
Craigville	46731	(Township)	46060	East Clifford	47203
Crandall	47114	Delaware (Ripley County)	47037	East Columbus (Part of Columbus)	47201
Crane	47522	Delaware (Ripley County)		East Enterprise	47019
Crane Naval Depot	47522	(Township)	47037	Eastern Heights (Part of Bloomington)	47401
Crane Naval Weapons Support Center	47522	Delong	46922	Eastgate (Bartholomew County)	47201
Crawfordsville	47933	Delp	47905	Eastgate (Clark County)	47130
Cree Lake	46755	Delphi	46923	East Gate (Hancock County)	46040
Crest Manor (Part of South Bend)	46614	Deming	46034	Eastgate (Marion County)	46219
Crestmoor (Part of Shelbyville)	46176	Democrat (Township)	46920	Eastgate Consumer Mall (Part of Indianapolis)	46219
Creston	46356	Demotte	46310	East Glenn	47803
Crestview	46383	Denham	46925	Eastland Gardens (Part of Fort Wayne)	46816
Crestview Heights	46158	Denmark	47427	Eastland Mall (Part of Evansville)	47715
Crestwood (Part of Fort Wayne)	46804	Denver	46926	East Monticello	47960
Crete	47355	Depauw	47115	East Mount Carmel	47665
Crisman (Part of Portage)	46368	Deputy	47230	East Oolitic	47421
Critchfield	46142	Derby	47525	East Park (Part of Frankfort)	46041
Crocker (Part of Portage)	46383	Desoto	47302	Eastridge Manor	47203
Crompton Hill	47842	Devon Park (Part of Muncie)	47304	East Shelburn (Part of Shelburn)	47879
Cromwell	46732	Devonshire (Part of Lawrence)	46226	East Shoals (Part of Shoals)	47581
Crooked Lake	46703	Dewey (Township)	46348	East Union	46031
Cross Plains	47017	Diamond	47874	Eastwich (Part of Lafayette)	47901
Crothersville	47229	Diamond Lake	46794	Eaton	47338
Crown Center	46157	Diamond Valley (Part of Evansville)	47710	Echo Heights (Part of Muncie)	47302
Crown Colony	46816	Dick Johnson (Township)	47834	Eckerty	47116
Crown Point	46307	Dike (Part of Princeton)	47670	Economy	47339
Crows Nest	46208	Dillman	46792	Eddy	46795
Crumley Crossing	47336	Dillsboro	47018	Eden (Hancock County)	46140
Crump Estates (Part of Columbus)	47201	Diplomat Plaza (Part of Fort Wayne)	46806	Eden (Lagrange County) (Township)	46571
Crumstown	46554	Disko	46982	Edgerton	46797
Crystal	47527	Dixon	46773	Edgewater	46383
Cuba (Allen County)	46741	Doans	47424	Edgewood (Bartholomew County)	47201
Cuba (Bartholomew County)	46124	Dodd	47587	Edgewood (La Porte County)	46360
Cuba (Owen County)	47460	Dodds Bridge	47849	Edgewood (Lawrence County)	47421
Culver	46511	Dogwood	47135	Edgewood (Madison County)	46011
Culver Military Academy (Part of Culver)	46511	Dolan	47401	Edgewood (Marion County)	46227
Cumback	47501	Domestic	46714	Edgewood Park	46818
Cumberland	46229	Donaldson	46513	Edinburgh	46124
Cunot	46120	Dongola	47660	Edison Park (Part of South Bend)	46615
Curby	47118	Doolittle Mills	47118	Edna Mills	46065
Curry (Township)	47879	Door Village	46350	Edwardsport	47528
Curryville (Adams County)	46731	Dover (Boone County)	46052	Edwardsville	47150
Curryville (Sullivan County)	47879	Dover (Dearborn County)	47022	Eel (Township)	46947
Curtisville	46036	Dover Hill	47581	Eel River (Allen County) (Township)	46723
Cutler	46920	Dovers View	46072	Eel River (Hendricks County) (Township)	46165
Cuzco	47432	Dowden Acres	47802	Effner	60966
Cyclone	46041	Downtown (Part of Gary)	46402	Ege	46763
Cynthiana	47612	Downtown (Part of Kokomo)	46901	Ehrmandale	47805
Cypress	47712	Downtown (Part of Lafayette)	47902	Ekin	46031
Dabney	47023	Downtown (Part of Muncie)	47305	Elberfeld	47613
Daggett	47427	Dreamwold Heights	46637	El Dorado	46142
Daisy Hill	47106	Dresden	47453	Elizabeth	47117
Dale	47523	Dresser	47885	Elizabethtown	47232
Daleville	47334	Drexel Gardens (Part of Indianapolis)	46241	Elizaville	46052
Dallas (Township)	46702	Driftwood (Township)	47281	Elkhart	46514-17
Dalton	47346	Dublin	47335	For specific Elkhart Zip Codes call (219) 293-5502, or your local postmaster.	
Dalton (Township)	47346	Dubois	47527		
Dana	47847	Dubois Crossroads	47527		
Danville	46122	Duck Creek (Township)	46036	Elkhart (Elkhart County) (Township)	46526
Darlington	47940	Dudley (Township)	47387		
Darmstadt	47711	Dudleytown	47274		
Darrough Chapel	46901	Duff	47542		
Davis (Fountain County) (Township)	47918	Dugger	47848		
Davis (La Porte County)	46360	Dundee	46001		
Davis (Starke County) (Township)	46532	Dune Acres	46304		
Daylight	47711	Dune Acres Station (Part of Dune Acres)	46304		
Dayton	47941	Duneland Beach	46360		
Dayville	47630	Dunfee	46818		
Deacon	46994	Dunkirk (Cass County)	46947		
		Dunkirk (Jay County)	47336		

	ZIP		ZIP		ZIP
Elkhart (Noble County)		Ferdinand	47532	Franklin (Marion County)	
(Township)	46794	Ferdinand (Township)	47532	(Township)	46239
Elkinsville	47448	Ferguson Hill	47885	Franklin (Montgomery	
Ellettsville	47429	Fewell Rhoades	46151	County) (Township)	47940
Ellis	47848	Fiat	47326	Franklin (Owen County)	
Elliston	47424	Fickle	46041	(Township)	47431
Elmdale	47933	Fields	46158	Franklin (Pulaski County)	
Elmira (Township)	46761	Fifteenth Avenue (Part of		(Township)	46996
Elmore (Township)	47529	Gary)	46407	Franklin (Putnam County)	
Elmwood (Part of Peru)	46970	Fillmore	46128	(Township)	46172
Elnora	47529	Fincastle	46172	Franklin (Randolph County)	
Elrod	47018	Finley (Township)	47170	(Township)	47380
Elston	47905	Finly	46129	Franklin (Ripley County)	
Elwood	46036	Fishers	46038	(Township)	47031
Elwren	47401	Fishersburg	46051	Franklin (Washington	
Eminence	46125	Fisher's Woodland	46060	County) (Township)	47167
Emison	47530	Fish Lake (La Porte County)	46574	Franklin (Wayne County)	47346
Emma	46571	Fish Lake (Lagrange		Franklin (Wayne County)	
Emporia	46056	County)	46761	(Township)	47341
Enchanted Hills	46732	Five Points (Marion County)	46239	Franklin Hills (Part of Tell	
Englewood (Part of		Five Points (Morgan		City)	47586
Bedford)	47421	County)	46158	Frankton	46044
English	47118	Five Points (Whitley County)	46725	Fredericksburg	47120
English Lake	46366	Flat Rock (Bartholomew		Fredonia	47137
Enochsburg	47240	County) (Township)	47201	Freedom	47431
Enos	47963	Flat Rock (Shelby County)	47234	Freeland Park	47944
Enos Corners	47660	Flat Rock Park	47201	Freelandville	47535
Epsom	47568	Flat Rock Park North (Part		Freeman	47460
Epworth Forest	46555	of Columbus)	47201	Freeport	46161
Erie	46970	Fleming	47274	Freetown	47235
Erie (Township)	46970	Fletcher	46939	Fremont (Township)	46737
Ervin (Township)	46929	Flint	46703	Fremont	46737
Etna (Kosciusko County)		Flintwood (Part of		French (Adams County)	
(Township)	46524	Columbus)	47201	(Township)	46714
Etna (Whitley County)	46725	Flora (Carroll County)	46929	French (Ohio County)	47001
Etna Green	46524	Flora (Miami County)	46970	French Lake	47802
Etna-Troy (Township)	46764	Florence	47020	French Lick	47432
Eugene	47928	Florida (Madison County)	46011	French Lick (Township)	47432
Eugene (Township)	47928	Florida (Parke County)		Frenchtown	47115
Eureka	47635	(Township)	47874	Friendship	47021
Evanston	47531	Floyd (Township)	46121	Friendswood	46113
Evansville	47701-99	Floyds Knobs	47119	Fritchton	47591
For specific Evansville Zip Codes		Folsomville	47614	Fritz Corner	47585
call (812) 429-3400, or your local		Fontanet	47851	Fruitdale	46160
postmaster.		Foraker	46526	Fugit (Township)	47240
Evergreen Acres (Part of		Foresman	47922	Fulda	47536
Clarksville)	47129	Forest	46039	Fulton (Fountain County)	
Everroad Park East (Part of		Forest (Township)	46039	(Township)	47932
Columbus)	47203	Forest Hill	47240	Fulton (Fulton County)	46931
Everroad Park West (Part of		Forest Park (Part of		Furnace	47424
Columbus)	47203	Columbus)	47201	Furnessville	46304
Everton	47331	Forest Park Beach	46742	Gadsden	46052
Ewing (Part of Brownstown)	47220	Forest Park Heights	47401	Galena (Floyd County)	47119
Fair Acres (Part of Salem)	47167	Forest Park North (Part of		Galena (La Porte County)	
Fairbanks (Sullivan County)		Columbus)	47201	(Township)	46371
(Township)	47849	Forest Ridge (Allen County)	46804	Galveston	46932
Fairbanks (Sullivan County)	47849	Forest Ridge (Grant County)	46952	Gambill	47848
Fairfield (De Kalb County)		Forest Ridge Estates	46804	Gar Creek	46774
(Township)	46730	Forrest Hills	46036	Garden Acres (Boone	
Fairfield (Franklin County)		Fort Branch	47648	County)	46071
(Township)	47012	Fort Ritner	47430	Garden Acres (Monroe	
Fairfield (Tippecanoe		Fortville	46040	County)	47401
County) (Township)	47904	Fort Wayne	46801-99	Garden City	47201
Fairfield Center	46730	For specific Fort Wayne Zip		Garfield (Part of	
Fair Grounds (Part of		Codes call (219) 427-7311, or		Indianapolis)	46203
Indianapolis)	46205	your local postmaster.		Garrett	46738
Fairland	46126	Foster	47932	Gary	46401-11
Fairlawn (Part of Columbus)	47201	Fountain	47918	For specific Gary Zip Codes call	
Fairmount	46928	Fountain City	47341	(219) 886-8011, or your local	
Fairmount (Township)	46928	Fountain Park (Jasper		postmaster.	
Fair Oaks	47943	County)	47977	Gasburg	46158
Fairplay (Township)	47465	Fountain Park (Steuben		Gas City	46933
Fairview	47331	County)	46742	Gaston	47342
Fairview (Township)	47331	Fountain Square (Part of		Gatchel	47586
Fairview (Randolph County)	47373	Indianapolis)	46203	Gatesville	46164
Fairview (Switzerland		Fountaintown	46130	Gateway Shopping Center	
County)	47011	Fowler	47944	(Part of Richmond)	47374
Fairview Park	47842	Fowlerton	46930	Gatewood (Part of Muncie)	47304
Fairwood Hills (Part of		Foxglen	46060	Gaynorsville	47240
Indianapolis)	46256	Fox Hill	46113	Geetingsville	46041
Fall Creek (Hamilton		Fox Lake	46703	Gem	46140
County) (Township)	46064	Fox Ridge	46135	Geneva (Adams County)	46740
Fall Creek (Henry County)		Francesville	47946	Geneva (Jennings County)	
(Township)	47356	Francisco	47649	(Township)	47273
Fall Creek (Madison		Frankfort	46041	Geneva (Shelby County)	47234
County) (Township)	46011	Franklin (De Kalb County)		Gentryville	47537
Falmouth	46127	(Township)	46721	Georgetown (Allen County)	46741
Farlen	47562	Franklin (Floyd County)		Georgetown (Cass County)	46947
Farmers	47431	(Township)	47117	Georgetown (Floyd County)	47122
Farmersburg	47850	Franklin (Grant County)		Georgetown (Floyd County)	
Farmers Retreat	47018	(Township)	46952	(Township)	47122
Farmersville	47620	Franklin (Harrison County)		Georgetown (Randolph	
Farmland	47340	(Township)	47136	County)	47340
Farrabee	47167	Franklin (Hendricks County)		Georgetown (St. Joseph	
Farrville	46952	(Township)	46180	County)	46635
Fayette (Boone County)	46052	Franklin (Henry County)		Georgia	47446
Fayette (Vigo County)		(Township)	47352	Georgia Heights (Part of	
(Township)	47885	Franklin (Johnson County)	46131	Merrillville)	46410
Fayetteville	47421	Franklin (Johnson County)		Gerald	47520
Federal (Part of		(Township)	46131	German (Bartholomew	
Indianapolis)	46204	Franklin (Kosciusko County)		County) (Township)	47201
Fenn Haven	47586	(Township)	46910		

	ZIP
German (Marshall County) (Township)	46506
German (St. Joseph County) (Township)	46628
German (Vanderburgh County) (Township)	47712
Germantown	47272
Gessie	47974
Gibson (Township)	47170
Gifford	47978
Gilboa (Township)	47944
Gilead	46951
Gill (Township)	47861
Gillam (Township)	46392
Gilman	46001
Gilmer Park	46624
Gilmour	47438
Gingrich	47960
Gings	46173
Giro	47640
Glen Aire	47803
Glenbrook Square (Part of Fort Wayne)	46805
Glendale	47558
Glendale Center (Part of Indianapolis)	46220
Glendale Lake	46952
Glen Eden	46703
Glenhall	47992
Glenns Valley (Part of Indianapolis)	46217
Glen Park (Part of Gary)	46409
Glenview	47203
Glenwood	46133
Glenwood Acres	47620
Glenwood Park (Part of Fort Wayne)	46805
Glezen	47567
Gnaw Bone	47448
Goblesville	46750
Goff	46952
Golden Acres	46815
Golden Hill	47960
Golden Lake	46779
Goldsmith	46045
Golfview Estates	47130
Goodland	47948
Goose Lake	46725
Goshen (Elkhart County)	46526*
	46527†
Goshen (Scott County)	47170
Gospel Grove	47803
Gosport	47433
Gowdy	46173
Grabill	46741
Graceland Heights (Part of Hagerstown)	47346
Grafton	47620
Graham (Township)	47230
Graham Valley	47601
Graham Woods	46304
Grammer	47236
Grandview (Monroe County)	47401
Grandview (Spencer County)	47615
Grandview Lake	47201
Grandview Village	47150
Granger	46530
Grant (Benton County) (Township)	47944
Grant (De Kalb County) (Township)	46793
Grant (Greene County) (Township)	47465
Grant (Newton County) (Township)	47948
Grant City	47384
Grantsburg	47123
Granville	47338
Grass (Township)	47611
Grass Creek	46935
Grasselli (Part of East Chicago)	46312
Grassy Fork (Township)	47274
Gravel Beach	46747
Gravelton	46542
Grayford	47265
Graysville	47852
Green (Grant County) (Township)	46928
Green (Hancock County) (Township)	46040
Green (Madison County) (Township)	46048
Green (Marshall County) (Township)	46501
Green (Morgan County) (Township)	46151
Green (Noble County) (Township)	46763
Green (Randolph County) (Township)	47368

	ZIP
Green (Wayne County) (Township)	47393
Green Acres	46410
Greenbriar (Marion County)	46260
Greenbriar (Putnam County)	46135
Greenbrier	47601
Greencastle	46135
Greencastle (Township)	46135
Green Center	46701
Greendale (Allen County)	46805
Greendale (Dearborn County)	47025
Greene (Jay County) (Township)	47371
Greene (Parke County) (Township)	47989
Greene (St. Joseph County) (Township)	46614
Greenfield (Hancock County)	46140
Greenfield (Lagrange County) (Township)	46746
Greenfield (Orange County) (Township)	47118
Greenfield Estates	46952
Greenfield Mills	46746
Greenhill	47970
Greenleaf Manor (Part of Elkhart)	46514
Green Meadows (Shelby County)	46126
Green Meadows (Tippecanoe County)	47906
Greenoak	46975
Greensboro	47344
Greensboro (Township)	47344
Greensburg	47240
Greensfork (Randolph County) (Township)	47335
Greens Fork (Wayne County)	47345
Greentown	46936
Green Tree Mall (Part of Clarksville)	47129
Greenvalley	46060
Greenview	46815
Greenville (Floyd County)	47124
Greenville (Floyd County) (Township)	47124
Greenville (Wells County)	46781
Greenwood (Johnson County)	46142-43
For specific Greenwood Zip Codes call (317) 881-2323, or your local postmaster.	
Greenwood (Lagrange County)	46795
Greenwood Park Mall (Part of Greenwood)	46142
Greer (Township)	47613
Gregg (Township)	46157
Greybrook Lake	47868
Griffin	47616
Griffith	46319
Grissom Air Force Base (Miami County)	46971
Groomsville	46049
Groveland	46105
Grovertown	46531
Guilford (Dearborn County)	47022
Guilford (Hendricks County) (Township)	46168
Guion	47872
Gulivoire Park	46624
Gurley Corner	47038
Guthrie	47421
Guthrie (Township)	47467
Guy	46936
Gwynneville	46144
Hacienda Village	46805
Hackleman	46928
Haddon (Township)	47838
Hadley	46121
Hagerstown	47346
Halbert (Township)	47581
Haleysbury	47281
Hall (Dubois County) (Township)	47546
Hall (Morgan County)	46157
Halteman Village (Part of Muncie)	47304
Hamblen (Township)	46164
Hamburg (Clark County)	47172
Hamburg (Franklin County)	47036
Hamilton (Clinton County)	46058
Hamilton (Delaware County) (Township)	47302
Hamilton (Jackson County) (Township)	47274
Hamilton (Madison County)	46011
Hamilton (Steuben County)	46742

	ZIP
Hamilton (Sullivan County) (Township)	47882
Hamilton Park	47302
Hamilton Village	47303
Hamlet	46532
Hammond	46320-27
For specific Hammond Zip Codes call (219) 932-1519, or your local postmaster.	
Hammond (Township)	47615
Hamor Heights	47203
Hancock	47115
Handy	47401
Hanfield	46952
Hanging Grove (Township)	47978
Hangman Crossing	47274
Hanna	46340
Hanna (Township)	46340
Hanover	47243
Hanover (Township)	47243
Hanover (Lake County) (Township)	46303
Hanover (Shelby County) (Township)	46161
Hanover Beach	47243
Happy Hollow Heights (Part of West Lafayette)	47906
Harbison (Township)	47527
Harbor (Part of East Chicago)	46312
Hardinsburg (Dearborn County)	47025
Hardinsburg (Washington County)	47125
Hardscrabble	46051
Harlan	46743
Harmony (Clay County)	47853
Harmony (Posey County) (Township)	47631
Harmony (Union County) (Township)	47331
Harper	47283
Harris (Township)	46530
Harrisburg	47331
Harris City	47240
Harrison (Bartholomew County) (Township)	47201
Harrison (Blackford County) (Township)	47359
Harrison (Boone County) (Township)	46052
Harrison (Cass County) (Township)	46947
Harrison (Clay County) (Township)	47841
Harrison (Daviess County) (Township)	47501
Harrison (Dearborn County) (Township)	47060
Harrison (Delaware County) (Township)	47302
Harrison (Elkhart County) (Township)	46526
Harrison (Fayette County) (Township)	47331
Harrison (Harrison County) (Township)	47122
Harrison (Henry County) (Township)	47384
Harrison (Howard County) (Township)	46979
Harrison (Knox County) (Township)	47591
Harrison (Kosciusko County) (Township)	46502
Harrison (Miami County) (Township)	46911
Harrison (Morgan County) (Township)	46151
Harrison (Owen County) (Township)	47433
Harrison (Pulaski County) (Township)	46939
Harrison (Spencer County) (Township)	47532
Harrison (Union County) (Township)	47353
Harrison (Vigo County) (Township)	47807
Harrison (Wayne County) (Township)	47327
Harrison (Wells County) (Township)	46714
Harrison Hills (Part of Columbus)	47201
Harrison Lake	47201
Harristown	47167
Harrisville	47390
Harrodsburg	47434
Hart (Township)	47619
Hartford (Adams County) (Township)	46740

	ZIP
Hartford (Ohio County)....	47001
Hartford City	47348
Hartford Place (Part of	
Columbus)...............	47201
Hartleyville	47421
Hartsdale (Part of	
Schererville)...........	46375
Hartsville	47244
Harveysburg	47952
Hashtown	47424
Haskells..................	46390
Hastings	46542
Hatfield	47617
Haubstadt.................	47639
Haw Creek (Township)	47246
Hawthorne Hills...........	46307
Hayden	47245
Haymond	47006
Haysville	47546
Hazelrigg.................	46052
Hazelwood (Allen County)	46805
Hazelwood (Hendricks	
County)................	46118
Hazelwood (Shelby County)	46176
Hazleton	47640
Headlee..................	47960
Heath	47905
Heather Heights (Part of	
Columbus)..............	47201
Heather Hills (Part of	
Indianapolis)...........	46229
Heaton Lake	46514
Hebron	46341
Hedrick	47993
Heilman	47523
Helmcrest (Part of Fortville)	46040
Helmer...................	46744
Helmsburg	47435
Helt (Township)	47847
Heltonville	47436
Hemlock	46937
Hemlock Lakes.............	47952
Henderson	46173
Hendricks (Johnson	
County)................	46142
Hendricks (Shelby County)	
(Township)..............	46176
Hendricksville	47459
Henry (Fulton County)	
(Township).............	46910
Henry (Henry County)	
(Township).............	47362
Henryville	47126
Hensley (Township)........	46181
Herbst	46952
Heritage Lake	46128
Herr.....................	46052
Hessen Cassel	46806
Hesston..................	46350
Hessville (Part of	
Hammond)..............	46323
Heth (Township)...........	47110
Heusler	47712
Hibbard	46511
Hibernia	47111
Hibernia Mills.............	47933
Hickory Grove (Township)	47984
Hickory Hills..............	46952
Hidden Valley	47025
Hideaway Lake............	47952
Highbanks	46555
High Lake	46701
Highland (Franklin County)	
(Township).............	47012
Highland (Greene County)	
(Township).............	47424
Highland (Lake County)....	46322
Highland (Vanderburgh	
County)................	47710
Highland (Vermillion County)	47854
Highland (Vermillion County)	
(Township).............	47974
Highland Meadows	46952
Highland Village (Part of	
Bloomington)...........	47401
Highwoods (Part of	
Indianapolis)...........	46222
Hiker Trace (Part of	
Columbus)..............	47201
Hildebrand Village	46176
Hill and Dale (Part of	
Sellersburg)............	47172
Hillcrest (Bartholomew	
County)................	47201
Hillcrest (Harrison County)	47112
Hillcrest (Porter County)....	46383
Hillcrest Circle (Part of	
Bedford)...............	47421
Hillendale	47006
Hillham	47432
Hillisburg	46046
Hills And Dales	47383

	ZIP
Hillsboro (Fountain County)	47949
Hillsboro (Henry County) ...	47362
Hillsdale (Vanderburgh	
County)................	47711
Hillsdale (Vermillion County)	47854
Hillview Estates............	47201
Hindostan Falls	47581
Hindustan	47401
Hitchcock	47167
Hi-View (Part of South	
Bend).................	46624
Hoagland	46745
Hobart	46342
Hobart (Township)	46342
Hobbieville	47462
Hobbs	46047
Hoffman Lake	46580
Hogan (Township)	47001
Hogtown..................	47140
Holaday Hills and Dales....	46032
Holiday Lakes	46738
Holiday Park	46902
Holland	47541
Hollandsburg	47872
Hollybrook Lake	47433
Holly Hills	47802
Holton	47023
Home Corner	46952
Homecroft	46227
Home Place	46240
Homer	46146
Homestead (Part of	
Greendale).............	47025
Honey Creek (Henry	
County)................	47356
Honey Creek (Howard	
County) (Township)	46979
Honey Creek (Vigo County)	
(Township).............	47802
Honey Creek (White	
County) (Township)	47980
Honeyville	46571
Hoosier Acres (Part of	
Bloomington)...........	47401
Hoosier Highlands	47868
Hoosierville	47834
Hoover...................	46947
Hope	47246
Hopewell (De Kalb County)	46706
Hopewell (Johnson County)	46131
Horace...................	47240
Horton	46069
Houston..................	47235
Hovey	47620
Howard (Howard County)	
(Township)..............	46901
Howard (Parke County)	47985
Howard (Parke County)	
(Township)..............	47859
Howard (Washington	
County) (Township)	47167
Howe	46746
Howell (Part of Evansville)	47712
Howesville	47438
Hubbell	47427
Hubbells Corner	47041
Hudson (La Porte County)	
(Township)..............	46552
Hudson (Steuben County)	46747
Hudson Lake..............	46552
Hudsonville	47558
Huff (Township)	47615
Huffman	47588
Hull Addition	46072
Hunter (Part of Indianapolis)	46239
Huntersville (Part of	
Batesville).............	47006
Huntertown...............	46748
Huntingburg	47542
Huntington (Township)	46750
Huntington	46750
Huntsville (Madison County)	46064
Huntsville (Randolph	
County)................	47358
Huron....................	47437
Hyde Park	47302
Hymera	47855
Hyndsdale	46151
Idaho (Part of Terre Haute)	47802
Idaville	47950
Ijamsville	46962
Imperial Gardens	46815
Imperial Hills (Part of	
Greenwood)	46227
Independence	47918
Independence Hill (Part of	
Merrillville).............	46410
Indiana Army Ammunition	
Plant..................	47111
Indiana Beach	47960
Indiana Oaks	47172

	ZIP
Indianapolis...............	46201-90
For specific Indianapolis Zip	
Codes call (317) 464-6150, or	
your local postmaster.	

COLLEGES & UNIVERSITIES

Butler University	46208
Indiana University-Purdue	
University at Indianapolis	46202
Marian College	46222
University of Indianapolis...	46227

FINANCIAL INSTITUTIONS

Bank One, Indianapolis,	
N.A.	46277
First of America Bank-	
Indiana	46224
INB National Bank	46266
Merchants National Bank	
and Trust Company of	
Indianapolis	46255
Peoples Bank & Trust	
Company	46204
Railroadmen's Federal	
Savings & Loan	
Association	46204
Union Federal Savings Bank	
of Indianapolis	46204

HOSPITALS

Community Hospitals of	
Indianapolis	46219
Indiana University Medical	
Center.................	46202
Methodist Hospital of	
Indianapolis	46202
Richard L. Roudebush	
Veterans Affairs Medical	
Center	46202
St. Vincent Hospital and	
Health Care Center......	46032
William N. Wishard	
Memorial Hospital	46202

HOTELS/MOTELS

Adam's Mark Indianapolis	46241
Airport Hilton Inn	46241
The Canterbury Hotel	46225
Embassy Suites Hotel	46204
Holiday Inn-Southeast......	46203
Indianapolis Hilton	46204
Marriott Hotel.............	46219
Radisson Suite Hotel-	
Indianapolis	46240

MILITARY INSTALLATIONS

Naval Air Warfare Center	46219
United States Property and	
Fiscal Office for Indiana	46241
United States Property and	
Fiscal Office, Camp	
Atterbury	46241
Indianapolis Union Stock	
Yards (Part of	
Indianapolis)...........	46241
Indiana State Farm	46135
Indiana State Reformatory	46064
Indiana State University	
Evansville Campus	47712
Indian Creek (Lawrence	
County) (Township)	47421
Indian Creek (Monroe	
County) (Township)	47401
Indian Creek (Pulaski	
County) (Township)	46985
Indian Creek Settlement ...	47512
Indianhead Lake...........	46122
Indian Heights	46902
Indian Hills	47201
Indian Lake (De Kalb	
County)................	46730
Indian Lake (Marion County)	46226
Indianola	46795
Indian Springs	47581
Indian Village (Noble	
County)................	46732
Indian Village (St. Joseph	
County)................	46637
Industry (Part of Muncie)...	47302
Ingalls...................	46048
Inglefield (Part of	
Darmstadt).............	47618
Innisdale	46001
Inverness	46703
Inwood	46563
Iona.....................	47591
Ireland	47545
Ironton	47581
Iroquois (Township)........	47922
Irvington (Part of	
Indianapolis)...........	46219

	ZIP		ZIP		ZIP
Irvington Plaza Shopping Center (Part of Indianapolis)	46219	Jackson (Wells County) (Township)	46991	Johnson (Gibson County) (Township)	47639
Island Park (Kosciusko County)	46580	Jackson (White County) (Township)	47926	Johnson (Knox County) (Township)	47591
Island Park (Steuben County)	46742	Jacksonburg	47327	Johnson (La Porte County) (Township)	46574
Iva	47564	Jackson Hill	47879	Johnson (Lagrange County) (Township)	46796
Ivanhoe (Part of Indianapolis)	46219	Jackson Park	47302	Johnson (Ripley County) (Township)	47042
Ivy Hills (Part of Indianapolis)	46220	Jacksons	46072	Johnson (Scott County) (Township)	47230
Jackson (Allen County) (Township)	46773	Jacksonville	47842	Johnsonville	47993
Jackson (Bartholomew County) (Township)	47274	Jalapa	46952	Johnstown (Greene County)	47471
Jackson (Blackford County) (Township)	47348	Jamestown (Boone County)	46147	Johnstown (Knox County)	47512
Jackson (Boone County) (Township)	46147	Jamestown (Steuben County)	46737	Jolietville	46069
Jackson (Brown County) (Township)	47448	Jamestown (Stuben County) (Township)	46737	Jonesboro	46938
Jackson (Carroll County) (Township)	46917	Jasonville	47438	Jonestown	47842
Jackson (Cass County) (Township)	46932	Jasper	47546* 47547†	Jonesville	47247
Jackson (Clay County) (Township)	47834	Jay City	47326	Joppa	46158
Jackson (Clinton County) (Township)	46041	Jefferson (Adams County) (Township)	46711	Jordan (Jasper County) (Township)	47978
Jackson (De Kalb County) (Township)	46706	Jefferson (Allen County) (Township)	46773	Jordan (Owen County)	47868
Jackson (Dearborn County) (Township)	47041	Jefferson (Boone County) (Township)	46071	Jordan (Warren County) (Township)	47993
Jackson (Decatur County) (Township)	47283	Jefferson (Carroll County) (Township)	46923	Judah	47421
Jackson (Dubois County) (Township)	47542	Jefferson (Cass County) (Township)	46978	Judson (Howard County)	46901
Jackson (Elkhart County) (Township)	46553	Jefferson (Clinton County) (Township)	46041	Judson (Parke County)	47856
Jackson (Fayette County) (Township)	47331	Jefferson (Dubois County) (Township)	47513	Judyville	47993
Jackson (Fountain County) (Township)	47949	Jefferson (Elkhart County) (Township)	46526	Julietta (Part of Indianapolis)	46239
Jackson (Greene County) (Township)	47462	Jefferson (Grant County) (Township)	46989	Junction (Part of Peru)	46970
Jackson (Hamilton County) (Township)	47030	Jefferson (Greene County) (Township)	47471	Kalorama Park	46538
Jackson (Hancock County) (Township)	46140	Jefferson (Henry County) (Township)	47388	Kankakee (Jasper County) (Township)	46374
Jackson (Harrison County) (Township)	47161	Jefferson (Huntington County) (Township)	46792	Kankakee (La Porte County) (Township)	46371
Jackson (Howard County) (Township)	46936	Jefferson (Jay County) (Township)	47371	Karwick (Part of Michigan City)	46360
Jackson (Huntington County) (Township)	46783	Jefferson (Kosciusko County) (Township)	46550	Kasson	47712
Jackson (Jackson County) (Township)	47274	Jefferson (Miami County) (Township)	46970	Keener (Township)	46310
Jackson (Jay County) (Township)	47326	Jefferson (Morgan County) (Township)	46151	Kellerville	47527
Jackson (Kosciusko County) (Township)	46566	Jefferson (Newton County) (Township)	47951	Kelso (Township)	47022
Jackson (Madison County) (Township)	46011	Jefferson (Noble County) (Township)	46701	Kempton	46049
Jackson (Miami County) (Township)	46919	Jefferson (Owen County) (Township)	47427	Kendallville	46755
Jackson (Morgan County) (Township)	46160	Jefferson (Pike County) (Township)	47564	Kennard	47351
Jackson (Newton County) (Township)	47963	Jefferson (Pulaski County) (Township)	46996	Kent (Jefferson County)	47250
Jackson (Orange County) (Township)	47432	Jefferson (Putnam County) (Township)	46120	Kent (Warren County) (Township)	47982
Jackson (Owen County) (Township)	46120	Jefferson (Sullivan County) (Township)	47838	Kentland	47951
Jackson (Parke County) (Township)	47837	Jefferson (Switzerland County) (Township)	47043	Kentwood (Part of Frankfort)	46041
Jackson (Porter County) (Township)	46304	Jefferson (Tipton County) (Township)	46072	Kenwood	47885
Jackson (Putnam County) (Township)	46172	Jefferson (Washington County) (Township)	47108	Kersey	46310
Jackson (Randolph County) (Township)	47390	Jefferson (Wayne County) (Township)	47346	Kewanna	46939
Jackson (Ripley County) (Township)	47034	Jefferson (Wells County) (Township)	46777	Keyser (Township)	46738
Jackson (Rush County) (Township)	46115	Jefferson (Whitley County) (Township)	46725	Keystone	46759
Jackson (Shelby County) (Township)	46176	Jefferson Proving Ground	47250	Kilmore	46041
Jackson (Spencer County) (Township)	47537	Jeffersonville	47129-31	Kimmell	46760
Jackson (Starke County) (Township)	46534	For specific Jeffersonville Zip Codes call (812) 284-4834, or your local postmaster.		Kinder	46106
Jackson (Steuben County) (Township)	46703	Jennings (Crawford County) (Township)	47137	Kingman	47952
Jackson (Sullivan County) (Township)	47855	Jennings (Fayette County) (Township)	47331	Kingsbury	46345
Jackson (Tippecanoe County) (Township)	47901	Jennings (Owen County) (Township)	46120	Kingsford Heights	46346
Jackson (Washington County) (Township)	47165	Jennings (Scott County) (Township)	47102	Kingsland	46777
Jackson (Wayne County) (Township)	47327	Jericho	47848	Kingston	47240
		Jerome	46936	Kingswood Terra	47802
		Jessups	47874	Kirkland (Township)	46733
		Jewell Village	47201	Kirklin (Township)	46050
		Jimtown	46514	Kirklin (Township)	46050
		Jockey	47637	Kirkpatrick	47955
		Johnsburg	47542	Kirksville	47401
		Johnson (Clinton County) (Township)	46041	Kirkville	47649
		Johnson (Crawford County) (Township)	47116	Kitchell	47353
		Johnson (Gibson County)	47665	Klemmes Corner	47012
				Klondyke (Parke County)	47862
				Klondyke (Vermillion County)	47842
				Knapp Lake	46732
				Knight (Township)	47711
				Knighthood Grove	46176
				Knighthood Village	46176
				Knight Ridge	47401
				Knightstown	46148
				Knightstown Lake	46148
				Knightsville	47857
				Kniman	46392
				Knob Hill	47711
				Knox (Jay County) (Township)	47336
				Knox (Starke County)	46534
				Kokomo	46901-04
				For specific Kokomo Zip Codes call (317) 455-8300, or your local postmaster.	
				Koleen	47439
				Koontz Lake	46574
				Kossuth	47167
				Kouts	46347
				Kramer	47918
				Kreitsburg	46311
				Kriete Corners	47274
				Kurtz	47249
				Kyana	47575

	ZIP
Kyle	47001
Laconia	47135
La Crosse	46348
Ladoga	47954
Lafayette	47901-05
For specific Lafayette Zip Codes call (317) 448-9245, or your local postmaster.	
Lafayette (Allen County) (Township)	46783
Lafayette (Floyd County) (Township)	47119
Lafayette (Madison County) (Township)	46011
Lafayette (Owen County) (Township)	47460
Lafayette Square (Part of Indianapolis)	46254
La Fontaine	46940
Lagrange	46761
Lagro	46941
Lagro (Township)	46941
Lake (Allen County) (Township)	46818
Lake (Kosciusko County) (Township)	46982
Lake (Newton County) (Township)	46349
Lake Bodona	46158
Lake Bruce	46939
Lake Cicott	46942
Lakecrest (Part of Noblesville)	46060
Lake Dalecarlia	46356
Lake Dilldear	47018
Lake Edgewood	46151
Lake Eliza	46383
Lake Everett	46808
Lake Front (Part of Whiting)	46394
Lake Hart	46158
Lake Hills	46375
Lake Holiday	47933
Lake James	46703
Lakeland (Part of Michigan City)	46360
Lake Latonka	46511
Lake Lincoln	47552
Lake Manitou	46975
Lake Maxine	47456
Lake McCoy	47240
Lake Mohee	47348
Lake Noji	47802
Lake of the Woods	46506
Lake Park	46552
Lakeside	46795
Lakeside Park (Part of Warsaw)	46580
Lakes of the Four Seasons	46307
Lake Station	46405
Lake Sullivan	47882
Laketon	46943
Lakeview (Franklin County)	47024
Lakeview (Lagrange County)	46795
Lake View (Porter County)	46383
Lakeview Estates	47802
Lake Village	46349
Lakeville	46536
Lake Wood (Grant County)	46952
Lakewood (Vigo County)	47802
Lakewood (White County)	47960
Lakewood Hills (Part of Evansville)	47711
Lalumiere	46350
Lamar	47550
Lamb	47043
Lamb Lake	46181
Lamong	46069
Lamplighter	46060
Lancaster (Huntington County)	46750
Lancaster (Huntington County) (Township)	46750
Lancaster (Jefferson County)	47250
Lancaster (Jefferson County) (Township)	47250
Lancaster (Wells County) (Township)	46714
Lancaster Park	47401
Landess	46944
Lane (Township)	47637
Lanesville	47136
Lantana Estate (Part of Shelbyville)	46176
Lantern Park	47302
Laotto	46763
Lapaz	46537
La Paz Junction	46563
Lapel	46051
La Porte	46350
Larimer Hill	47885

	ZIP
Larwill	46764
Lasalle Square (Part of South Bend)	46601
Laud	46725
Laughery (Township)	47006
Lauramie (Township)	47930
Laurel	47024
Laurel (Township)	47024
Lawndale (Part of Evansville)	47715
Lawrence	46226
Lawrence (Township)	46226
Lawrenceburg	47025
Lawrenceburg (Township)	47025
Lawrenceport	47446
Lawrenceville	47041
Lawton	46996
Laynecrest (Part of Muncie)	47304
Leases Corner	46950
Leavenworth	47137
Lebanon	46052
Lee	47978
Leesburg	46538
Leesville	47421
Leininger Acres	46072
Leipsic	47452
Leisure	46036
Leiters Ford	46945
Lena	47834
Leo	46765
Leopold	47551
Leopold (Township)	47551
Leota	47170
Leroy	46355
Letts	47240
Letts Corner	47240
Lewis (Clay County) (Township)	47438
Lewis (Vigo County) (Township)	47858
Lewisburg	46970
Lewis Creek	47234
Lewisville (Henry County)	47352
Lewisville (Morgan County)	46120
Lexington (Carroll County)	46920
Lexington (Scott County)	47138
Lexington (Scott County) (Township)	47138
Liber	47371
Liberty (Carroll County) (Township)	46916
Liberty (Crawford County) (Township)	47140
Liberty (Delaware County) (Township)	47383
Liberty (Fulton County) (Township)	46931
Liberty (Grant County) (Township)	46952
Liberty (Hendricks County) (Township)	46118
Liberty (Henry County) (Township)	47362
Liberty (Howard County) (Township)	46901
Liberty (Parke County) (Township)	47985
Liberty (Porter County) (Township)	46383
Liberty (St. Joseph County) (Township)	46554
Liberty (Shelby County) (Township)	46182
Liberty (Tipton County) (Township)	46068
Liberty (Union County)	47353
Liberty (Union County) (Township)	47353
Liberty (Wabash County) (Township)	46940
Liberty (Warren County) (Township)	47918
Liberty (Wells County) (Township)	46766
Liberty (White County) (Township)	47925
Liberty Center	46766
Liberty Hills	46804
Liberty Mills	46946
Liberty Park	46307
Libertyville	47885
Licking (Township)	47348
Liggett	47885
Ligonier	46767
Lilly Dale	47586
Lima (Township)	46746
Limberlost Hills	47803
Limedale	46135
Lincoln (Cass County)	46994
Lincoln (Hendricks County) (Township)	46112
Lincoln (La Porte County) (Township)	46365

	ZIP
Lincoln (Newton County) (Township)	46310
Lincoln (St. Joseph County) (Township)	46574
Lincoln (White County) (Township)	47950
Lincoln City	47552
Lincoln Heights (Clark County)	47129
Lincoln Heights (Madison County)	46001
Lincoln Hills	46383
Lincoln Park (Part of Clarksville)	47129
Lincoln Village (Part of Merrillville)	46410
Lincolnville	46992
Linden	47955
Linden Park (Part of Muncie)	47303
Lindenwood (Part of Indianapolis)	46227
Linkville	46563
Linn Grove	46769
Linnsburg	47933
Linton (Greene County)	47441
Linton (Vigo County) (Township)	47802
Linwood (Madison County)	46001
Linwood (Marion County)	46201
Lippe	47620
Lisbon	46755
Little	47567
Little Acres	47274
Little Point	46180
Little Saint Louis	47115
Little York	47139
Liverpool (Part of Lake Station)	46408
Livonia	47108
Lizton	46149
Locke	46550
Locke (Township)	46550
Lockhart (Township)	47585
Lockport	47926
Lodi	47952
Logan	47060
Logan (Township)	47060
Logan (Fountain County) (Township)	47918
Logan (Pike County) (Township)	47567
Logansport	46947
Logansport State Hospital	46947
Lomax	46374
London	46126
London Heights	46126
Long Acres	46176
Long Beach	46360
Long Lake	46962
Long Lake Island	46383
Longview Beach	47130
Loogootee	47553
Lookout	47041
Loon Lake	46725
Lorane	46725
Loree	46914
Losantville	47354
Lost Creek (Township)	47803
Lost River (Township)	47432
Lottaville (Part of Merrillville)	46410
Lotus	47353
Lovett	47265
Lovett (Township)	47265
Lowell (Bartholomew County)	47201
Lowell (Lake County)	46356*
	46399†
Lower Sunset Park	47960
Loyal	46975
Luce (Township)	47617
Lucerne	46950
Ludwig Park (Part of Fort Wayne)	46825
Lukens Lake	46974
Luray	47386
Luther	46787
Lutheran Lake	47274
Lydick	46628
Lyford	47874
Lynhurst	46241
Lynn (Posey County) (Township)	47620
Lynn (Randolph County)	47355
Lynnville	47619
Lyons	47443
Lyonsville	47331
McBride Heights	47130
McCarthy Addition (Part of Alexandria)	46001
McCarty	46142
McClellan (Township)	47963

ZIP

Mc Col Place (Part of
  Salem)................... 47167
McCool (Part of Portage) 46368
McCordsville.............. 46055
McCoysburg.............. 47978
McCutchanville........... 47711
McDaniel................. 46151
Mace.................... 47933
Mac-Fair-Mar............ 46947
McGrawsville............ 46911
Mackey................. 47654
McKinley................ 47108
McKinley Town and Country
  Shopping Center (Part of
  Mishawaka)............ 46545
McNatts................ 47359
Macy.................. 46951
Madison (Allen County)
  (Township)............ 46773
Madison (Carroll County)
  (Township)............ 46923
Madison (Clinton County)
  (Township)............ 46058
Madison (Daviess County)
  (Township)............ 47562
Madison (Dubois County)
  (Township)............ 47546
Madison (Jay County)
  (Township)............ 45846
Madison (Jefferson County) 47250
Madison (Jefferson County)
  (Township)............ 47250
Madison (Montgomery
  County) (Township)..... 47933
Madison (Morgan County)
  (Township)............ 46158
Madison (Pike County)
  (Township)............ 47567
Madison (Putnam County)
  (Township)............ 46135
Madison (St. Joseph
  County) (Township)..... 46614
Madison (Tipton County)
  (Township)............ 46072
Madison (Washington
  County) (Township)..... 47108
Madison State Hospital.... 47250
Magley................. 46733
Magnet................. 47555
Mahalasville............ 46151
Mahon................. 46750
Majenica............... 46750
Malden................. 46383
Malott Park (Part of
  Indianapolis)........... 46205
Maltersville............. 47542
Manchester............. 47001
Manchester (Township).... 47001
Manhattan.............. 46135
Manilla................ 46150
Manor Woods........... 46804
Mansfield.............. 47872
Manson................ 46041
Manville............... 47250
Maplecrest Shopping
  Center (Part of Kokomo) 46902
Maple Lane............. 46635
Maples................ 46806
Mapleton (Part of
  Indianapolis)........... 46208
Maple Valley............ 46117
Maplewood (Hendricks
  County)............... 46122
Maplewood (Vigo County) 47885
Maplewood Park......... 46805
Marco.................. 47443
Marengo................ 47140
Mariah Hill............. 47556
Marietta............... 46176
Marineland Gardens...... 46567
Marion................. 46952-53
  For specific Marion Zip Codes call
  (317) 668-8191, or your local
  postmaster.
Marion (Allen County)
  (Township)............ 46745
Marion (Boone County)
  (Township)............ 46069
Marion (Decatur County)
  (Township)............ 47261
Marion (Dubois County)
  (Township)............ 47546
Marion (Hendricks County)
  (Township)............ 46122
Marion (Jasper County)
  (Township)............ 47978
Marion (Jennings County)
  (Township)............ 47270
Marion (Lawrence County)
  (Township)............ 47446
Marion (Owen County)
  (Township)............ 47455

ZIP

Marion (Pike County)
  (Township)............ 47590
Marion (Putnam County)
  (Township)............ 46128
Marion (Shelby County).... 46176
Marion (Shelby County)
  (Township)............ 46176
Marion Heights.......... 47885
Marion Manor (Part of
  Valparaiso)............ 46383
Markland............... 47020
Markland Mall (Part of
  Kokomo)............... 46902
Markle................. 46770
Markleville............. 46056
Marlin Hills............ 47401
Marquette Farm......... 47805
Marquette Mall (Part of
  Michigan City).......... 46360
Marrs (Township)........ 47620
Marrs Center........... 47620
Marshall (Lawrence County)
  (Township)............ 47421
Marshall (Parke County).... 47859
Marshfield.............. 47993
Mars Hill (Part of
  Indianapolis)........... 46241
Marshtown.............. 46939
Martin Heights (Part of
  Salem)................. 47167
Martinsburg............ 47165
Martinsville............ 46151
Martz.................. 47841
Maryland............... 47802
Marysville (Clark County).. 47141
Marysville (Pike County)... 47598
Marywood.............. 47802
Matlock Heights (Part of
  Bloomington).......... 47401
Matthews............... 46957
Mattix Corner........... 46041
Mauckport.............. 47142
Maumee (Township)....... 46797
Mauzy................. 46173
Max................... 46052
Maxinkuckee............ 46511
Maxville............... 47340
Maxwell (Hancock County).. 46154
Maxwell (Morgan County).. 46151
Mayfield (Part of Muncie).. 47302
Maynard (Part of Munster).. 46321
Mays.................. 46155
Maysville............... 47501
Maywood (Part of
  Indianapolis)........... 46241
M-Dee Acres............ 46550
Meadowbrook (Allen
  County)............... 46774
Meadowbrook (Tippecanoe
  County)............... 47901
Meadowood (Elkhart
  County)............... 46514
Meadowood (Marion
  County)............... 46224
Meadowood Estates....... 46036
Meadows (Part of Terre
  Haute)................ 47803
Meadows Shopping Center
  (Part of Indianapolis)..... 46205
Meadowview............ 46947
Mead Village (Part of
  Columbus)............. 47201
Mecca................. 47860
Mechanicsburg (Boone
  County)............... 46050
Mechanicsburg (Henry
  County)............... 47356
Medaryville............ 47957
Medford............... 47302
Medina (Township)....... 47970
Medora................ 47260
Meiks................. 46176
Mellott............... 47958
Melody Acres (Part of
  Warsaw).............. 46580
Melody Hill............. 47711
Meltzer................ 46176
Memphis............... 47143
Mentone............... 46539
Mentor................ 47513
Meridian Hills.......... 46260
Merom................ 47861
Merriam............... 46701
Merrillville............. 46410
Metamora (Township)...... 47030
Metamora.............. 47030
Metea................. 46950
Metz.................. 46703
Mexico................ 46958
Miami (Cass County)
  (Township)............ 46947
Miami (Miami County)...... 46959

ZIP

Miami Bend............. 46947
Miami Trails Addition....... 46614
Michaelsville............ 46952
Michiana Shores......... 49117
Michigan (Clinton County)
  (Township)............ 46057
Michigan (La Porte County)
  (Township)............ 46360
Michigan City........... 46360
Michigantown........... 46057
Mickleyville (Part of
  Indianapolis)........... 46241
Middle (Township)........ 46167
Middleboro............. 47374
Middlebury............. 46540
Middlebury (Township)..... 46540
Middlefork (Clinton County) 46041
Middlefork (Jefferson
  County)............... 47231
Middletown (Henry County) 47356
Middletown (Shelby County) 46182
Middletown Park......... 47302
Midland................ 47445
Midway (Elkhart County)... 46526
Midway (Jefferson County) 47250
Midway (Spencer County) 47601
Midwest (Part of Portage) 46368
Mier.................. 46919
Mifflin................. 47118
Milan (Allen County)
  (Township)............ 46797
Milan (Ripley County)...... 47031
Milan Center........... 46774
Milford (Decatur County).... 47240
Milford (Kosciusko County) 46542
Milford (Lagrange County)
  (Township)............ 46795
Milford Junction......... 46542
Mill (Township).......... 46933
Mill Creek (Fountain County)
  (Township)............ 47952
Mill Creek (Hamilton
  County)............... 46060
Mill Creek (La Porte County) 46365
Milledgeville............ 46052
Miller (Dearborn County)
  (Township)............ 47025
Miller (Lake County)....... 46403
Millersburg (Elkhart County) 46543
Millersburg (Hamilton
  County)............... 46030
Millersburg (Orange County) 47454
Millersburg (Warrick County) 47610
Millersville (Part of
  Lawrence)............. 46226
Mill Grove (Blackford
  County)............... 47348
Millgrove (Steuben County)
  (Township)............ 46776
Millhousen............. 47261
Milligan............... 47872
Milltown............... 47145
Millville............... 47362
Milners Corner.......... 46140
Milo.................. 46991
Milroy (Jasper County)
  (Township)............ 47978
Milroy (Rush County)...... 46156
Milton (Jefferson County)
  (Township)............ 47250
Milton (Ohio County)....... 47018
Milton (Wayne County)..... 47357
Mineral................ 47424
Mineral Springs......... 46538
Mishawaka............. 46544-46
  For specific Mishawaka Zip Codes
  call (219) 255-9691, or your local
  postmaster.
Mitchell............... 47446
Mitchellville (Part of
  Indianapolis)........... 46201
Mitcheltree (Township)..... 47581
Mixerville.............. 47010
Moberly............... 47115
Modesto............... 47401
Modoc................ 47358
Mohawk............... 46140
Mongo................ 46771
Monitor............... 47905
Monmouth............. 46733
Monon................ 47959
Monon (Township)....... 47959
Monoquet............. 46580
Monroe (Adams County)... 46772
Monroe (Adams County)
  (Township)............ 46711
Monroe (Allen County)
  (Township)............ 46773
Monroe (Carroll County)
  (Township)............ 46929
Monroe (Clark County)
  (Township)............ 47126

* **Area Zip Code**   † **Post Office Boxes**

	ZIP
Monroe (Delaware County) (Township)	47302
Monroe (Grant County) (Township)	46952
Monroe (Howard County) (Township)	46979
Monroe (Jefferson County) (Township)	47250
Monroe (Kosciusko County) (Township)	46580
Monroe (Madison County) (Township)	46001
Monroe (Morgan County) (Township)	46157
Monroe (Pike County) (Township)	47584
Monroe (Pulaski County) (Township)	46996
Monroe (Putnam County) (Township)	46135
Monroe (Randolph County) (Township)	47368
Monroe (Tippecanoe County)	47901
Monroe (Washington County) (Township)	47167
Monroe City	47557
Monroe Manor	46350
Monroeville	46773
Monrovia	46157
Montclair	46149
Monterey	46960
Monterey Village (Part of Noblesville)	46060
Montezuma	47862
Montgomery (Daviess County)	47558
Montgomery (Gibson County) (Township)	47665
Montgomery (Jennings County) (Township)	47230
Montgomery (Owen County) (Township)	47460
Monticello	47960
Montmorenci	47962
Montpelier	47359
Moonlight Bay	46779
Moonville	46001
Moore	46721
Moorefield (Marion County)	46222
Moorefield (Switzerland County)	47250
Mooreland	47360
Moores Hill	47032
Mooresville	46158
Moral (Township)	46126
Moran	46041
Morgan (Harrison County) (Township)	47164
Morgan (Owen County) (Township)	47868
Morgan (Porter County) (Township)	46383
Morgan Park (Part of Chesterton)	46304
Morgantown	46160
Morningside (Part of Muncie)	47302
Morocco	47963
Morris	47033
Morristown	46161
Morton	46135
Moscow	46156
Mott Station	47161
Mound (Township)	47932
Mounds Mall (Part of Anderson)	46013
Mount Auburn (Shelby County)	46124
Mount Auburn (Wayne County)	47327
Mount Ayr	47964
Mount Carmel (Franklin County)	47012
Mount Carmel (Washington County)	47108
Mount Comfort	46140
Mount Etna	46750
Mount Healthy	47201
Mount Meridian	46135
Mount Olympus	47640
Mount Pisgah	46761
Mount Pleasant (Delaware County)	47302
Mount Pleasant (Delaware County) (Township)	47396
Mount Pleasant (Johnson County)	46131
Mount Pleasant (Martin County)	47553
Mount Pleasant (Perry County)	47520

	ZIP
Mounts	47665
Mount Sinai	47032
Mount Sterling	47043
Mount Summit	47361
Mount Vernon	47620
Mount Zion	46792
Mud Center (Part of Evansville)	47712
Mudlavia Springs	47918
Mulberry	46058
Mull	47394
Muncie	47302-08
For specific Muncie Zip Codes call (317) 286-9600, or your local postmaster.	
Muncie Mall (Part of Muncie)	47303
Munster	46321
Muren	47598
Murray	46714
Nabb	47147
Napoleon	47034
Nappanee	46550
Nashville	47448
Navilleton	47119
Nead	46970
Nebraska	47262
Needham	46162
Needham (Township)	46126
Needmore (Brown County)	47448
Needmore (Lawrence County)	47421
Negangards Corner	47031
Nevada	46068
Nevada Mills	46703
Nevins (Township)	47851
New Albany	47150*
	47151†
New Alsace	47022
New Amsterdam	47110
Newark	47459
New Augusta (Part of Indianapolis)	46268
New Bellsville	47201
Newbern	47201
Newberry	47449
New Boston (Harrison County)	47117
New Boston (Spencer County)	47531
New Britton	46060
New Brunswick	46052
Newburgh	47629†
	47630*
New Burlington	47302
Newbury (Township)	46565
New Carlisle	46552
Newcastle (Fulton County) (Township)	46975
New Castle (Henry County)	47362
New Chicago	46342
New Columbus	46011
New Corydon	47326
New Durham (Township)	46350
New Elizabethtown	47274
New Elliott	46319
New Fairfield	47012
New Farmington	47274
New Frankfort	47110
New Garden (Township)	47374
New Goshen	47863
New Harmony	47631
New Haven	46774
New Hope	47601
Newland	47978
New Lebanon	47864
New Lisbon (Henry County)	47366
New Lisbon (Randolph County)	47390
New London	46979
New Marion	47023
New Market	47965
New Maysville	46172
New Middletown	47160
New Mount Pleasant	47371
New Palestine	46163
New Paris	46553
New Philadelphia	47167
New Pittsburg	47390
New Point	47263
Newport	47966
New Richmond	47967
New Ross	47968
New Salem	46173
New Salisbury	47161
New Santa Fe	46970
Newton (Township)	47978
Newtonville	47615
Newtown	47969
New Trenton	47035
Newville	46721
Newville (Township)	46721

	ZIP
New Washington	47162
New Waverly	46961
New Whiteland	46184
New Winchester	46122
Nibbyville	46507
Niles (Township)	47338
Nine Mile	46809
Nineveh	46164
Nineveh (Township)	46164
Nisbet	47639
Noble (Cass County) (Township)	46947
Noble (Jay County) (Township)	47371
Noble (La Porte County) (Township)	46382
Noble (Noble County) (Township)	46796
Noble (Rush County) (Township)	46173
Noble (Shelby County) (Township)	47234
Noble (Wabash County) (Township)	46992
Noblesville	46060
Noblesville (Township)	46060
Noblitt Falls (Part of Columbus)	47201
Nora (Part of Indianapolis)	46240
Nora Plaza (Part of Indianapolis)	46240
Norland Park	46706
Normal	46986
Norman	47264
Normanda	46072
Normandy Addition (Part of Muncie)	47302
Norristown	47234
North (Lake County) (Township)	46312
North (Marshall County) (Township)	46506
Northaven (Part of Jeffersonville)	47130
North Bend (Township)	46534
Northcliff	47201
North Columbus (Part of Columbus)	47201
Northcrest Shopping Center (Part of Fort Wayne)	46805
North Crows Nest	46208
North Delphi	46923
Northeast (Township)	47452
Northern Meadows	46077
Northfield	46077
Northfield Village (Part of Lebanon)	46052
North Gate	47201
North Grove	46911
North Harbor (Part of Noblesville)	46060
North Hayden	46356
North Judson	46366
North Liberty	46554
North Madison (Part of Madison)	47250
North Manchester	46962
North Oaks	46714
North Ogilville	47201
North Park (Bartholomew County)	47280
North Park (Vanderburgh County)	47710
North Park Mall (Part of Marion)	46952
North Ridge Village	46240
North Salem	46165
North Terre Haute	47805
North Vernon	47265
North Webster	46555
Northwest (Township)	47469
Northwood (Elkhart County)	46550
Northwood (Putnam County)	46135
Northwood (Vigo County)	47805
Northwood Hills	46033
North Wood Park	46383
Norton	47432
Nortonsburg	47201
Norway	47960
Norwood Addition (Part of Muncie)	47304
Notre Dame	46556
Nottingham	47359
Nottingham (Township)	47359
Nulltown	47331
Numa	47874
Nyesville	47872
Nyona Lake	46951
Oakcrest	47201
Oakdale (Part of Peru)	46970
Oakford	46965

	ZIP
Oak Forest	47012
Oak Grove (Benton County) (Township)	47971
Oak Grove (Starke County)	46511
Oak Grove (Vigo County)	47802
Oak Hill	47660
Oakland City	47660
Oaklandon (Part of Lawrence)	46226
Oaklawn Terrace (Part of Jeffersonville)	47130
Oak Park (Clark County)	47130
Oaktown	47561
Oakville	47367
Oakwood	46742
Oakwood Commons	46952
Oakwood Park	46567
Oakwood Shores	46742
Oatsville	47567
Ober	46534
Occident	46115
Ockley	46923
Odell	47918
Odon	47562
Ogden	46148
Ogden Dunes	46368
Ogilville	47201
Ohio (Bartholomew County) (Township)	47201
Ohio (Crawford County) (Township)	47137
Ohio (Spencer County) (Township)	47635
Ohio (Warrick County) (Township)	47610
Ohio Falls (Part of Clarksville)	47129
Oil (Township)	47576
Old Bargersville	46106
Old Bath	47012
Oldenburg	47036
Old Milan	47031
Old Otto	47162
Old Pekin (Part of Pekin)	47165
Old St. Louis	47246
Old Stone	47630
Old Tip Town	46570
Oldtown (Part of Lawrenceburg)	47025
Old Watson (Part of Jeffersonville)	47130
Olean	47042
Olive (Elkhart County) (Township)	46573
Olive (St. Joseph County) (Township)	46552
Oliver	47620
Olive Street (Part of South Bend)	46619
Omega	46030
Ontario	46746
Onward	46967
Oolitic	47451
Ora	46968
Orange	47331
Orange (Township)	47331
Orange (Noble County) (Township)	46755
Orange (Rush County) (Township)	46173
Orangeville	47452
Orangeville (Township)	47542
Orchard Heights Addition	46624
Orchard Park	46280
Oregon (Clark County) (Township)	47141
Oregon (Starke County) (Township)	46574
Oregon Heights (Part of Hobart)	46405
Orestes	46063
Oriole	47551
Orland	46776
Orleans	47452
Orleans (Township)	47452
Orleans Southwest	46902
Ormas	46725
Osborn Landing	46580
Osceola	46561
Osgood	47037
Osolo (Township)	46514
Ossian	46777
Oswego	46538
Otis	46367
Otisco	47163
Otsego (Township)	46742
Otterbein	47970
Otter Creek (Ripley County) (Township)	47023
Otter Creek (Vigo County) (Township)	47805
Otter Lake	46703

	ZIP
Otter Village	47023
Otto	47162
Otwell	47564
Owasco	46065
Owen (Clark County) (Township)	47111
Owen (Clinton County) (Township)	46041
Owen (Jackson County) (Township)	47220
Owen (Warrick County) (Township)	47614
Owensburg	47453
Owensville	47665
Oxford	47971
Packertown	46510
Paint Mill Lake	47802
Palestine (Franklin County)	47012
Palestine (Kosciusko County)	46539
Palmer	46307
Palmyra (Harrison County)	47164
Palmyra (Knox County) (Township)	47591
Paoli	47454
Paoli (Township)	47454
Papakeechie Lake	46567
Paradise	47630
Paradise Lakes	46511
Paragon	46166
Paris	47230
Paris Crossing	47270
Parish Grove (Township)	47944
Park	47424
Parker City	47368
Parkersburg	47954
Parkers Settlement	47638
Park Fletcher	46241-42
For specific Park Fletcher Zip Codes call (317) 464-6241, or your local postmaster.	
Park Forest Estates (Part of Columbus)	47201
Parkmor (Part of Elkhart)	46514
Park Ridge (Part of Bloomington)	47401
Parkside (Part of Columbus)	47201
Park View Heights (Part of Peru)	46970
Parkway Hills	46804
Parkwood	47129
Parr	47978
Pate	47040
Patoka (Crawford County) (Township)	47175
Patoka (Dubois County) (Township)	47542
Patoka (Gibson County)	47666
Patoka (Gibson County) (Township)	47670
Patoka (Pike County) (Township)	47598
Patricksburg	47455
Patriot	47038
Patronville	47635
Patton	47960
Patton Hill	47421
Patton Lake	46151
Paw Paw (Township)	46974
Paxton	47865
Paynesville	47243
Peabody	46725
Pearsontown	47140
Pecksburg	46118
Peerless	47421
Pekin	47165
Pelzer	47601
Pence	47973
Pendleton	46064
Penn (Jay County) (Township)	47369
Penn (Parke County) (Township)	47832
Penn (St. Joseph County) (Township)	46544
Penn Meadows	46544
Penn Park	46742
Penntown	47041
Pennville (Jay County)	47369
Pennville (Wayne County)	47327
Peoga	46181
Peoria (Franklin County)	45056
Peoria (Miami County)	46970
Peppertown	47030
Perkinsville	46011
Perry (Allen County) (Township)	46748
Perry (Boone County) (Township)	46052
Perry (Clay County) (Township)	47846

	ZIP
Perry (Clinton County) (Township)	46041
Perry (Delaware County) (Township)	47302
Perry (Lawrence County) (Township)	47462
Perry (Marion County) (Township)	46227
Perry (Martin County) (Township)	47553
Perry (Miami County) (Township)	46974
Perry (Monroe County) (Township)	47401
Perry (Noble County) (Township)	46767
Perry (Tippecanoe County) (Township)	47901
Perry (Vanderburgh County) (Township)	47712
Perry (Wayne County) (Township)	47339
Perry Crossing	47172
Perry Manor (Part of Indianapolis)	46227
Perrysburg	46951
Perrysville	47974
Pershing (Jackson County) (Township)	47235
Pershing (Wayne County)	47370
Perth	47837
Peru	46970
Peru (Township)	46970
Petersburg	47567
Peterson	46733
Peters Switch	47274
Petersville	47201
Petroleum	46778
Pettit	47905
Pheasant Run	46819
Philadelphia	46140
Philomath	47325
Phlox	46936
Pickard	46050
Pierce (Township)	47167
Pierceton	46562
Pierceville	47039
Pierre Moran (Part of Elkhart)	46514
Pierson (Township)	47802
Pigeon (Vanderburgh County) (Township)	47708
Pigeon (Warrick County) (Township)	47523
Pike (Boone County)	46052
Pike (Jay County) (Township)	47371
Pike (Marion County) (Township)	46254
Pike (Ohio County) (Township)	47011
Pike (Warren County) (Township)	47991
Pikes Peak	47201
Pikeville	47590
Pilot Knob	47145
Pimento	47866
Pine (Benton County) (Township)	47970
Pine (Porter County) (Township)	46360
Pine (Warren County) (Township)	47975
Pine Grove Estates	47006
Pine Lake	46350
Pine Valley	47454
Pine Village	47975
Pinhook (La Porte County)	46350
Pinhook (Lawrence County)	47421
Pinola	46350
Pipe Creek (Madison County) (Township)	46036
Pipe Creek (Miami County) (Township)	46914
Pittsboro	46167
Pittsburg	46923
Plain (Township)	46538
Plainfield	46168
Plainville	47568
Plano	46151
Plato	46761
Plattsburg	47281
Pleasant (Allen County) (Township)	46798
Pleasant (Grant County) (Township)	46952
Pleasant (Johnson County) (Township)	46131
Pleasant (La Porte County) (Township)	46350
Pleasant (Porter County) (Township)	46347

* Area Zip Code   † Post Office Boxes

	ZIP
Pleasant (Steuben County) (Township)	46703
Pleasant (Switzerland County)	47224
Pleasant (Switzerland County) (Township)	47224
Pleasant (Wabash County) (Township)	46962
Pleasant Gardens	46171
Pleasant Lake	46779
Pleasant Mills	46780
Pleasant Plain	46792
Pleasant Run (Township)	47436
Pleasant Valley	46544
Pleasant View	46126
Pleasant View Village	46124
Pleasantville	47838
Pleasure Valley	46182
Plevna	46901
Plummer	47424
Plum Tree	46792
Plymouth	46563
Poe	46819
Point (Township)	47620
Point Commerce	47471
Point Idalawn	47468
Point Isabel	46928
Poland	47868
Polk (Huntington County) (Township)	46750
Polk (Marshall County) (Township)	46574
Polk (Monroe County) (Township)	47436
Polk (Washington County) (Township)	47165
Poneto	46781
Pontiac	47837
Popcorn	47462
Portage	46368
Portage (Township)	46368
Portage (Township)	46601
Porter (Porter County)	46304
Porter (Porter County) (Township)	46383
Portersville	47546
Port Fulton (Part of Jeffersonville)	47130
Portland	47371
Portland Mills	46135
Posey (Clay County) (Township)	47834
Posey (Fayette County) (Township)	47331
Posey (Franklin County) (Township)	47024
Posey (Harrison County) (Township)	47117
Posey (Rush County) (Township)	46104
Posey (Switzerland County) (Township)	47038
Posey (Washington County) (Township)	47120
Poseyville	47633
Pottawattomie Park	46360
Pottersville	47460
Powers	47371
Prairie (Henry County) (Township)	47360
Prairie (Kosciusko County) (Township)	46580
Prairie (La Porte County) (Township)	46340
Prairie (Tipton County) (Township)	46049
Prairie (Warren County) (Township)	47921
Prairie (White County) (Township)	47923
Prairie City	47834
Prairie Creek	47869
Prairie Creek (Township)	47869
Prairieton	47870
Prairieton (Township)	47870
Prairie Village	47802
Prather	46151
Preble	46782
Preble (Township)	46733
Prescott	46176
Presidential Village	46803
Pretty Lake	46795
Prince Hall Plaza (Part of Marion)	46952
Princes Lakes	46164
Princeton (Gibson County)	47670
Princeton (White County) (Township)	47995
Progress	47302
Progress Acres	47805
Prospect	47469
Providence	46106

	ZIP
Publico (Part of New Albany)	47150
Puckett	46952
Pulaski	46996
Pumpkin Center	47170
Purcell	47591
Purdue University	47906
Purdue University North Central Campus	46391
Putnamville	46170
Pyrmont	46923
Quail Meadows Estates (Part of Batesville)	47006
Queensville	47265
Quercus Grove	47040
Quincy	47456
Raber	46725
Raccoon (Parke County) (Township)	47874
Raccoon (Putnam County)	46172
Radioville	47957
Radley	46938
Radnor	46923
Raglesville	47562
Ragsdale	47573
Railroad (Township)	46374
Rainbow (Part of Indianapolis)	46222
Rainsville	47918
Raleigh	46173
Ramsey	47166
Randolph (Ohio County) (Township)	47040
Randolph (Tippecanoe County) (Township)	47981
Raub	47976
Ravenswood (Part of Indianapolis)	46240
Ravinamy	47906
Ray (Franklin County) (Township)	47036
Ray (Morgan County) (Township)	46166
Ray (Steuben County)	46737
Raymond	47010
Rays Crossing	46176
Raysville	46148
Reception Diagnostic Center	46168
Red Bridge	46911
Red Bush	47630
Redding (Township)	47274
Reddington	47274
Redkey	47373
Redmond Park	46567
Reed Station	47302
Reelsville	46171
Reeve (Township)	47553
Rego	47125
Reiffsburg	46714
Remington	47977
Reno	46121
Rensselaer	47978
Reo	47635
Republican (Township)	47138
Reserve (Township)	47862
Retreat	47229
Rexville	47250
Reynolds	47980
Riceville	47513
Richey Park	47960
Rich Grove (Township)	46996
Richland (Benton County) (Township)	47942
Richland (De Kalb County) (Township)	46730
Richland (Fountain County) (Township)	47969
Richland (Fulton County) (Township)	46975
Richland (Grant County) (Township)	46952
Richland (Greene County) (Township)	47424
Richland (Jay County) (Township)	47373
Richland (Madison County) (Township)	46011
Richland (Miami County) (Township)	46970
Richland (Monroe County) (Township)	47429
Richland (Rush County) (Township)	46173
Richland (Rush County) (Township)	46173
Richland (Spencer County)	47634
Richland (Steuben County) (Township)	46703
Richland (Whitley County) (Township)	46764
Richmond	47374*
	47375†

	ZIP
Richmond Square (Part of Richmond)	47374
Richmond State Hospital	47374
Richvalley	46992
Riddle	47118
Ridgemede (Part of Bloomington)	47401
Ridgeport	47424
Ridgeview (Part of Peru)	46970
Ridgeview Heights	46806
Ridgeville	47380
Ridgeway	46809
Ridinger Lake	46562
Rigdon	46036
Riley	47871
Riley (Township)	47871
Rileysburg	47932
Riley Village (Part of Shelbyville)	46176
Ripley (Montgomery County) (Township)	47933
Ripley (Pulaski County)	46996
Ripley (Rush County) (Township)	46115
Rising Sun	47040
Risse (Part of Frankfort)	46041
Rivare	46733
River Falls Mall (Part of Clarksville)	47129
River Forest	46011
Riverhaven	46802
River Ridge	47111
Riverside	47129-30
For specific Riverside Zip Codes call (317) 762-3360, or your local postmaster.	
Riverside	47918
Riverton	47861
River Vale	47446
Riverview	47849
Riverview Acres	47201
Riverwood	46060
Riviera Plaza (Part of Fort Wayne)	46815
Roachdale	46172
Roann	46974
Roanoke	46783
Robb (Township)	47633
Robertsdale (Part of Hammond)	46394
Robinson (Township)	47638
Robinwood	47803
Roble Woods	46383
Rob Roy	47918
Rochester	46975
Rochester (Township)	46975
Rockcreek (Township)	46714
Rock Creek (Bartholomew County) (Township)	47232
Rock Creek (Carroll County) (Township)	46923
Rock Creek (Huntington County)	46750
Rock Creek (Huntington County) (Township)	46750
Rockdale	47060
Rockfield	46977
Rockford (Jackson County)	47274
Rockford (Wells County)	46714
Rock Island (Part of Indianapolis)	46268
Rock Lake	46910
Rocklane	46142
Rockport	47635
Rockville	47872
Rockville Training Center	47872
Rocky Fork Lake	47834
Rocky Ripple	46208
Roland	47469
Roll	47348
Rolling Acres	47601
Rolling Hill Estates (Part of Schererville)	46410
Rolling Hills (Allen County)	46804
Rolling Hills (Clark County)	47111
Rolling Hills (Grant County)	46952
Rolling Prairie	46371
Rolling Ridge (Part of Shelbyville)	46176
Rollins	47581
Rome	47574
Rome City	46784
Romney	47981
Romona	47460
Root (Township)	46733
Roseburg (Grant County)	46952
Roseburg (Union County)	47353
Rosedale	47874
Rosedale Hills (Part of Indianapolis)	46227
Rose Hill Gardens	47805

* Area Zip Code   † Post Office Boxes

	ZIP
Sparta (Dearborn County) (Township)	47032
Sparta (Noble County) (Township)	46760
Spartanburg	47355
Spearsville	46181
Speed	47172
Speedway	46224
Speedway Shopping Center (Part of Speedway)	46224
Speicher	46992
Spelterville	47805
Spencer (De Kalb County) (Township)	46788
Spencer (Harrison County) (Township)	47115
Spencer (Jennings County) (Township)	47265
Spencer (Owen County)	47460
Spencerville	46788
Spiceland	47385
Spiceland (Township)	47385
Spice Valley (Township)	47437
Spraytown	47274
Springersville	47325
Springfield (Allen County) (Township)	46743
Springfield (Franklin County) (Township)	45056
Springfield (La Porte County) (Township)	46360
Springfield (Lagrange County) (Township)	46771
Springfield (Posey County)	47620
Spring Grove	47374
Spring Grove Heights (Part of Spring Grove)	47374
Spring Hill	46208
Spring Hill Estates	47802
Spring Lake	46140
Springport	47386
Springtown	46122
Spring Valley Estates	47802
Springville (La Porte County)	46350
Springville (Lawrence County)	47462
Springwood	47805
Spurgeon	47584
Spurgeons Corner	47235
Stacer	47639
Stafford (De Kalb County) (Township)	46721
Stafford (Greene County) (Township)	47578
Stampers Creek (Township)	47454
Stanford	47463
Star City	46985
Stardust Village	46060
Starlight	47106
State Line (Vigo County)	47885
State Line (Warren County)	47982
Staunton	47881
Stavetown	47012
Stearleyville	47834
Steele (Township)	47501
Steen (Township)	47597
Steinbarger Lake	46784
Steinmeir Estates (Part of Indianapolis)	46250
Stendal	47585
Sterling (Crawford County) (Township)	47118
Sterling (Fountain County)	47987
Steuben (Steuben County) (Township)	46705
Steuben (Warren County) (Township)	47993
Steubenville	46705
Stevenson	47610
Stewart	47993
Stewartsville	47633
Stilesville	46180
Stillwell	46351
Stinesville	47464
Stockdale	46974
Stockton (Township)	47441
Stockwell	47983
Stone	47394
Stonebluff	47987
Stoneburner Landing	46580
Stonecrest	46952
Stonegate Square (Part of Newburgh)	47630
Stone Head	47448
Stones Crossing	46142
Stoney Creek (Henry County) (Township)	47360
Stoney Creek (Randolph County) (Township)	47368
Stonington	47446
Stony Creek (Township)	46051

	ZIP
Stony Lonesome	47201
Stony Ridge	46538
Story	47448
Straughn	47387
Strawtown	46060
Stringtown (Boone County)	46052
Stringtown (Hancock County)	46140
Stroh	46789
Sugar Creek (Boone County) (Township)	46071
Sugar Creek (Clinton County) (Township)	46050
Sugar Creek (Hancock County) (Township)	46163
Sugar Creek (Montgomery County) (Township)	46035
Sugar Creek (Parke County) (Township)	47859
Sugar Creek (Shelby County)	46126
Sugar Creek (Shelby County) (Township)	46110
Sugar Creek (Vigo County) (Township)	47885
Sugar Ridge (Township)	47840
Sullivan	47882
Sulphur	47174
Sulphur Springs	47388
Suman	46383
Sumava Resorts	46379
Summit Grove	47842
Summit Ridge (Part of Fort Wayne)	46805
Summitville	46070
Sundown Manor	46158
Sunman	47041
Sunnybrook Acres	46805
Sunnymeadow	46815
Sunnymede (Allen County)	46803
Sunnymede (Wabash County)	46992
Sunnymede Woods	46803
Sunny Slopes	47401
Sunset Acres	46514
Sunset Parkway (Part of Seymour)	47274
Sunset Village	47111
Sunshine Gardens (Part of Indianapolis)	46217
Sunview	46040
Surprise	47274
Sussex Woods (Part of Hobart)	46342
Swan	46763
Swan (Township)	46763
Swanington	47944
Swayzee	46986
Sweetser	46987
Sweetwater Lake	46164
Switz City	47465
Sycamore	46936
Sycamore Hills	46036
Sycamore Knolls	47802
Sycamore Park	47885
Sylvan Hills	46952
Sylvania	47832
Sylvan Manor	46383
Syndicate	47842
Syracuse	46567
Tab	47917
Tabertown (Part of Seelyville)	47878
Talbot	47984
Tall Timbers	46952
Talma	46975
Tampico	47220
Tangier	47985
Tanglewood (Part of New Haven)	46774
Taswell	47175
Taylor (Greene County) (Township)	47424
Taylor (Harrison County) (Township)	47117
Taylor (Howard County) (Township)	46901
Taylor (Owen County) (Township)	47460
Taylors	47905
Taylorsville	47280
Tecumseh	47885
Teegarden	46574
Tee Lake	46350
Tefft	46380
Tell City	47586
Temple	47118
Templeton	47986
Tennyson	47637
Terhune	46069
Terrace Bay	47960

	ZIP
Terrace Lake (Part of Columbus)	47201
Terre Haute	47801-08
For specific Terre Haute Zip Codes call (812) 231-9414, or your local postmaster.	
Tetersburg	46072
Texas (Part of Aurora)	47001
Thayer	46381
The Hamlet	47303
Thomas Lake	46135
Thomaston	46390
Thorncreek (Township)	46725
Thornhope	46985
Thorntown	46071
Thurman	46774
Tilden	46122
Tillman	46773
Timbercrest (Allen County)	46804
Timbercrest (Cass County)	46947
Timberhurst	46795
Tiosa	46975
Tippecanoe (Carroll County) (Township)	46923
Tippecanoe (Kosciusko County) (Township)	46555
Tippecanoe (Marshall County)	46570
Tippecanoe (Marshall County) (Township)	46570
Tippecanoe (Pulaski County) (Township)	46960
Tippecanoe (Tippecanoe County) (Township)	47906
Tippecanoe Mall (Part of Lafayette)	47905
Tipton (Cass County) (Township)	46994
Tipton (Tipton County)	46072
Tipton Park (Part of Columbus)	47201
Toad Hop	47885
Tobin (Township)	47574
Tobinsport	47587
Tocsin	46777
Toledo	46750
Tolleston (Part of Gary)	46404
Toll Gate Heights	46714
Tomahawk Village (Part of Indianapolis)	46224
Topeka	46571
Toto	46534
Townley	46773
Town of Pines	46360
Tracy	46532
Traders Point (Part of Indianapolis)	46278
Trafalgar	46181
Trail Creek	46360
Travisville	46714
Treaty	46992
Tremont	46304
Trenton	47348
Trevlac	47448
Trier Ridge Park	46806
Tri-Lakes	46725
Trilobi Hills (Part of Lawrence)	46226
Trinity	47326
Trinity Springs	47581
Troy (Township)	47588
Troy (De Kalb County) (Township)	46721
Troy (Fountain County) (Township)	47932
Troy (Perry County)	47588
Tudor	47201
Tulip	47424
Tunker	46787
Tunnel Hill	47118
Tunnelton	47467
Turkey Creek (Township)	46567
Turkey Creek Meadows (Part of Merrillville)	46410
Turkey Track	46151
Turman (Township)	47882
Turner	47834
Twelve Mile	46988
Twelve Points (Part of Terre Haute)	47804
Twin Branch (Part of Mishawaka)	46544
Twin Brooks (Part of Indianapolis)	46227
Twin Crest	47201
Twin Lakes	46563
Twin Oaks Lake	46160
Tyner	46572
Ulen	46052
Underwood	47177
Underwood Meadows	46036

---

* **Area Zip Code** † **Post Office Boxes**

	ZIP
Union (Adams County) (Township)	46733
Union (Benton County) (Township)	47944
Union (Boone County) (Township)	46069
Union (Clark County) (Township)	47143
Union (Clinton County) (Township)	46041
Union (Crawford County) (Township)	47123
Union (De Kalb County) (Township)	46706
Union (Delaware County) (Township)	47302
Union (Elkhart County) (Township)	46550
Union (Fulton County) (Township)	46939
Union (Gibson County) (Township)	47648
Union (Hendricks County) (Township)	46149
Union (Howard County) (Township)	46936
Union (Huntington County) (Township)	46750
Union (Jasper County) (Township)	47943
Union (Johnson County) (Township)	46106
Union (La Porte County) (Township)	46346
Union (Madison County) (Township)	46017
Union (Marshall County) (Township)	46511
Union (Miami County) (Township)	46921
Union (Montgomery County) (Township)	47933
Union (Ohio County) (Township)	47001
Union (Parke County) (Township)	47872
Union (Perry County) (Township)	47555
Union (Pike County)	47640
Union (Porter County) (Township)	46342
Union (Randolph County) (Township)	47355
Union (Rush County) (Township)	46173
Union (Shelby County) (Township)	46150
Union (St. Joseph County) (Township)	46536
Union (Tippecanoe County) (Township)	47901
Union (Union County) (Township)	45003
Union (Vanderburgh County) (Township)	47712
Union (Wells County) (Township)	46777
Union (White County) (Township)	47960
Union (Whitley County) (Township)	46725
Union City	47390
Uniondale	46791
Union Mills	46382
Unionport	47340
Uniontown (Jackson County)	47229
Uniontown (Perry County)	47515
Unionville (New Unionville)	47401
Unionville	47468
Universal	47884
University Heights (Delaware County)	47303
University Heights (Marion County)	46227
University Park Mall (Part of Mishawaka)	46545
Upland	46989
Upper Long Lake	46701
Upper Sunset Park	47960
Upton	47620
Urbana	46990
Urbandale	46902
Urmeyville	46131
Utah (Part of Aurora)	47001
Utica	47130
Utica (Township)	47130
Valeene	47125
Valentine	46761
Valley Acres	46952
Valley Brook (Marion County)	46229

	ZIP
Valley Brook (Wabash County)	46992
Valley City	47110
Valley Mills (Part of Indianapolis)	46241
Valley View Hills	46514
Vallonia	47281
Vallyd Acres	46816
Valparaiso	46383*
	46384†
Van (Part of Logansport)	46947
Vanada Camps	47630
Van Bibber Lake	46135
Van Buren (Brown County) (Township)	47448
Van Buren (Clay County) (Township)	47837
Van Buren (Daviess County) (Township)	47553
Van Buren (Fountain County) (Township)	47932
Van Buren (Grant County)	46991
Van Buren (Grant County) (Township)	46991
Van Buren (Kosciusko County) (Township)	46542
Van Buren (Lagrange County) (Township)	46540
Van Buren (Madison County) (Township)	46070
Van Buren (Monroe County) (Township)	47401
Van Buren (Pulaski County) (Township)	46985
Van Buren (Shelby County) (Township)	46176
	47401
Van Buren Park	47460
Vandalia	46996
Vanmeter Park	46996
Vawter Park	46567
Veale (Township)	47501
Veedersburg	47987
Velpen	47590
Vera Cruz	46714
Vermillion (Township)	47966
Vermillion Acres	47885
Vermont	46901
Verne	47591
Vernon (Hancock County) (Township)	46040
Vernon (Jackson County) (Township)	47229
Vernon (Jennings County) (Township)	47282
Vernon (Jennings County) (Township)	47282
Vernon (Wabash County)	46940
Vernon (Washington County) (Township)	47108
Versailles	47042
Veterans Administration Medical Center (Part of Marion)	46952
Vevay	47043
Vicksburg	47441
Victor	47401
Vienna	47170
Vienna (Township)	47170
Vigo (Township)	47512
Vilas	47460
Vincennes (Township)	47591
Vincennes	47591
Virgie	47978
Vistula	46507
Volga	47250
Wabash (Adams County) (Township)	46740
Wabash (Fountain County) (Township)	47932
Wabash (Gibson County) (Township)	47665
Wabash (Jay County) (Township)	47326
Wabash (Parke County) (Township)	47860
Wabash (Tippecanoe County) (Township)	47906
Wabash (Wabash County)	46992
Wabash Shores (Part of West Lafayette)	47906
Wabash Valley Correctional Institute	47838
Wadena	47944
Wadesville	47638
Wakarusa	46573
Wakefield Village	46755
Wakeland	46166
Wake Robin Fields	46304
Walden	46805
Waldron	46182
Waldron Lake	46794
Walesboro	47201
Walford Manor	47130

	ZIP
Walker (Jasper County) (Township)	47978
Walker (Rush County) (Township)	46146
Walker Park	46538
Walkerton	46574
Walkerville (Part of Shelbyville)	46176
Wallace	47988
Wallen	46806
Wall Lake	46776
Walnut	46501
Walnut (Marshall County) (Township)	46501
Walnut (Montgomery County) (Township)	47933
Walnut Gardens	47960
Walnut Grove	46030
Walnut Heights	47421
Walnut Ridge (Clark County)	47130
Walnut Ridge (Jennings County)	47265
Walton	46994
Waltz (Township)	46992
Wanamaker (Part of Indianapolis)	46239
Wanatah	46390
Ward (Township)	47380
Warren (Clinton County) (Township)	46039
Warren (Huntington County)	46792
Warren (Huntington County) (Township)	46713
Warren (Marion County) (Township)	46219
Warren (Putnam County) (Township)	46135
Warren (St. Joseph County) (Township)	46552
Warren (Warren County) (Township)	47918
Warren Park	46219
Warrenton	47639
Warrington	46186
Warsaw	46580*
	46581†
Washington (Adams County) (Township)	46733
Washington (Allen County) (Township)	46808
Washington (Blackford County) (Township)	47348
Washington (Boone County) (Township)	46071
Washington (Brown County) (Township)	47448
Washington (Carroll County) (Township)	46947
Washington (Cass County) (Township)	46994
Washington (Clark County) (Township)	47162
Washington (Clay County) (Township)	47833
Washington (Clinton County) (Township)	46041
Washington (Daviess County)	47501
Washington (Daviess County) (Township)	47501
Washington (Dearborn County) (Township)	47001
Washington (Decatur County) (Township)	47240
Washington (Delaware County) (Township)	47342
Washington (Elkhart County) (Township)	46507
Washington (Gibson County) (Township)	47640
Washington (Grant County) (Township)	46952
Washington (Greene County) (Township)	47443
Washington (Hamilton County) (Township)	46074
Washington (Harrison County) (Township)	47110
Washington (Hendricks County) (Township)	46122
Washington (Jackson County) (Township)	47274
Washington (Knox County) (Township)	47516
Washington (Kosciusko County) (Township)	46562
Washington (La Porte County) (Township)	46350
Washington (Marion County) (Township)	46220

	ZIP		ZIP		ZIP
Washington (Miami County) (Township)	46970	Waynesville	47201	White River (Hamilton County) (Township)	46031
Washington (Monroe County) (Township)	47401	Waynetown	47990	White River (Johnson County) (Township)	46142
Washington (Morgan County) (Township)	46151	Wea (Township)	47901	White River (Randolph County) (Township)	47394
Washington (Newton County) (Township)	47922	Webster (Harrison County) (Township)	47112	White River Bluffs (Part of Bedford)	47421
Washington (Noble County) (Township)	46760	Webster (Wayne County)	47392	Whites Crossing	47441
Washington (Owen County) (Township)	47460	Webster (Wayne County) (Township)	47392	Whitestown	46075
Washington (Parke County) (Township)	47859	Wegan	47220	Whitesville	47933
Washington (Pike County) (Township)	47567	Wehmeir	47201	Whitewater (Franklin County) (Township)	47060
Washington (Porter County) (Township)	46383	Weisburg	47041	Whitewater (Wayne County)	47374
Washington (Putnam County) (Township)	46171	Wellington Heights (Part of Shelbyville)	46176	Whitfield	47553
Washington (Randolph County) (Township)	47394	Wells	46970	Whiting	46394
Washington (Ripley County) (Township)	47031	Wellsboro	46382	Wickliffe	47116
Washington (Rush County) (Township)	46127	Wellsburg	46714	Widner (Township)	47561
Washington (Shelby County) (Township)	46176	West (Township)	46563	Wilbur	46151
Washington (Starke County) (Township)	46534	Westacres	47302	Wildcat (Township)	46076
Washington (Tippecanoe County) (Township)	47924	West Atherton	47874	Wilders	46348
Washington (Warren County) (Township)	47993	West Baden Springs	47469	Wildwood	46952
Washington (Washington County) (Township)	47167	West Brook Acres (Part of Batesville)	47006	Wildwood Lake	47454
Washington (Wayne County) (Township)	47357	West Brook Downs	47401	Wilfred	47879
Washington (Whitley County) (Township)	46725	Westchester (Jay County)	47371	Wilkinson	46186
Washington Center	46725	Westchester (Porter County) (Township)	46304	Williams (Adams County)	46733
Washington Place (Part of Indianapolis)	46219	West College Corner	45003	Williams (Lawrence County)	47470
Washington Square (Part of Indianapolis)	46229	West Creek (Township)	46356	Williamsburg	47393
Washington Square Mall (Part of Evansville)	47715	West Elwood	46036	Williams Creek	46240
Washington Trails (Part of Indianapolis)	46229	Western Acres (Part of Chesterton)	46304	Williamsport	47993
Waterford	46360	Western Hills (Part of Mount Vernon)	47620	Williamstown	47240
Waterford Mills	46526	Westfield	46074	Willisville	47567
Waterloo (De Kalb County)	46793	West Fork	47118	Willow Branch	46187
Waterloo (Fayette County)	47331	West Franklin	47620	Willowbrook Estates	46151
Waterloo (Fayette County) (Township)	47331	West Harrison	47060	Willow Creek (Part of Portage)	46368
Waterswolde	46825	West Haven	46580	Willow Valley	47581
Wathen Heights	47130	West Hill	46383	Wills (Township)	46371
Watson	47130	West Indianapolis (Part of Indianapolis)	46221	Wilmington (De Kalb County) (Township)	46721
Waugh	46075	West Lafayette	47906-07	Wilmington (Dearborn County)	47001
Wauhob Lake	46383		47996	Wilmot	46562
Waveland	47989	For specific West Lafayette Zip Codes call (317) 448-9245, or your local postmaster.		Wilshire (Part of Frankfort)	46041
Waverly	46151			Wilson (Clark County)	47106
Waverly Woods	46151	Westland	46140	Wilson (Porter County)	46368
Wawaka	46794	Westlawn	46804	Wilson (Shelby County)	46176
Wawpecong	46901	West Lebanon	47991	Wilson Lake	46725
Waymansville	47201	West Liberty	46936	Winamac	46996
Wayne (Allen County) (Township)	46806	West Middleton	46995	Winchester	47394
Wayne (Bartholomew County) (Township)	47201	Westmoor (Part of Fort Wayne)	46804	Windemere Lake	47885
Wayne (Fulton County) (Township)	46939	West Muncie (Part of Yorktown)	47396	Windfall	46076
Wayne (Hamilton County) (Township)	46060	West Newton (Part of Indianapolis)	46183	Windom	47581
Wayne (Henry County) (Township)	46148	West Noblesville (Part of Noblesville)	46060	Windsor	47368
Wayne (Huntington County) (Township)	46940	West Peru (Part of Peru)	46970	Windsor Village (Part of Indianapolis)	46219
Wayne (Jay County) (Township)	47371	West Petersburg (Part of Petersburg)	47567	Winfield	46307
Wayne (Kosciusko County) (Township)	46590	Westphalia	47596	Winfield (Township)	46307
Wayne (Marion County) (Township)	46241	West Point (Howard County)	46901	Wingate	47994
Wayne (Montgomery County) (Township)	47990	Westpoint (Tippecanoe County)	47992	Winona	46534
Wayne (Noble County) (Township)	46755	West Point (White County) (Township)	47980	Winona Lake	46590
Wayne (Owen County) (Township)	47433	Westport	47283	Winslow	47598
Wayne (Randolph County) (Township)	47390	Westport Addition	47302	Winthrop	47918
Wayne (Starke County) (Township)	46366	Westside (Part of Aurora)	47001	Wirt	47250
Wayne (Tippecanoe County) (Township)	47992	West Terre Haute	47885	Wirt Station	47250
Wayne (Wayne County) (Township)	47374	Westville	46391	Witmer Manor	46795
Wayne Center	46755	Westville Correctional Center	46391	Witts	47353
Waynedale (Part of Fort Wayne)	46809	West Wabash	47712	Wolcott	47995
Waynesburg	47244		47719-20	Wolcottville	46795
		For specific West Wabash Zip Codes call (219) 563-3258, or your local postmaster.		Wolff	46151
				Wolflake	46796
		Westwood	47362	Wonder Lake	47802
		Wey Lake	47834	Wood (Township)	47106
		Wheatfield	46392	Woodbridge (Part of Bloomington)	47407
		Wheatfield (Township)	46392	Woodburn	46797
		Wheatland	47597	Woodbury	46055
		Wheatonville	47613	Woodcrest	46151
		Wheeler	46393	Woodgate	47802
		Wheeling (Carroll County)	46929	Woodgate East	47802
		Wheeling (Delaware County)	47342	Woodland	46619
		Whiskey Run (Township)	47145	Woodland Heights	46952
		Whitaker	46166	Woodland Lake	46160
		Whitcomb	47012	Woodland Park (Delaware County)	47302
		Whitcomb Heights	47885	Woodland Park (Lagrange County)	46795
		White Cloud	47112	Woodland Trace (Part of Carmel)	46032
		Whitehall	47401	Woodlawn Heights	46011
		Whiteland	46184	Woodridge	47803
		Whiteoak	47598	Woodruff	46795
		White Post (Township)	47957	Woodruff Place (Part of Indianapolis)	46201
		White Ridge	46952	Woodville	46304
		White River (Gibson County) (Township)	47666	Woodville Hills	47401
				Wooster (Kosciusko County)	46562
				Wooster (Scott County)	47138
				Worth (Township)	46075
				Worthington	47471
				Wright (Township)	47441

	ZIP		ZIP		ZIP
Wrights Corners	47001	York (Noble County)		Youngstown Acres	47802
Wyatt	46595	(Township)	46701	Youngstown Meadows	47802
Wynnedale	46208	York (Steuben County)	46737	Youngstown Shopping	
Yankeetown	47630	York (Steuben County)		Center (Part of	
Yeddo	47952	(Township)	46703	Jeffersonville)	47130
Yellowbanks	46555	York (Switzerland County)		Yountsville	47933
Yellow Creek Lake	46510	(Township)	47020	Yule Estates (Part of	
Yeoman	47997	Yorktown	47396	Alexandria)	46001
Yockey	47446	Yorkville	47022	Zanesville	46799
Yoder	46798	Young	46158	Zelma	47264
York (Benton County)		Young America	46998	Zenas	47223
(Township)	47942	Youngs Corner	47012	Zionsville	46077
York (Dearborn County)		Youngs Creek	47454	Zoar	47585
(Township)	47022	Youngstown	47802	Zulu	46773
York (Elkhart County)					
(Township)	46507				

	ZIP
Abingdon	52533
Ackley	50601
Ackworth	50001
Adair	50002
Adaza	50050
Adel	50003
Afton	50830
Agency	52530
Ainsworth	52201
Akron	51001
Albert City	50510
Albia	52531
Albion	50005
Alburnett	52202
Alden	50006
Alexander	50420
Algona	50511
Alleman	50007
Allendorf	51330
Allerton	50008
Allison	50602
Alpha	52130
Alta	51002
Alta Vista	50603
Alton	51003
Altoona	50009
Alvord	51230
Amana	52203
Amber	52205
Amboy	50208
Ames	50010-14

For specific Ames Zip Codes call (515) 292-2098, or your local postmaster.

	ZIP
Anamosa	52205
Anderson	51652
Andover	52701
Andrew	52030
Anita	50020
Ankeny	50021
Anthon	51004
Aplington	50604
Arcadia	51430
Archer	51231
Aredale	50605
Argyle	52619
Arion	51520
Arispe	50831
Arlington	50606
Armstrong	50514
Arnolds Park	51331
Artesian	50677
Arthur	51431
Asbury	52002
Ashton	51232
Aspinwall	51432
Atalissa	52720
Athelstan	50836
Atkins	52206
Atlantic	50022
Attica	50138
Auburn	51433
Audubon	50025
Augusta	52658
Aurelia	51005
Aureola	50653
Aurora	50607
Austinville	50608
Avery	52531
Avoca	51521
Avon	50047
Avon Lake	50047
Ayrshire	50515
Badger	50516
Bagley	50026
Baldwin	52207
Balltown	52073
Bancroft	50517
Bangor	50258
Bankston	52045
Barnes City	50027
Barnum	50518
Barrett Superette	50164
Bartlett	51654
Bassett	50645
Batavia	52533
Battle Creek	51006
Baxter	50028
Bayard	50029
Beacon	52534
Beaconsfield	50030
Beaman	50609
Beaver	50031
Beaverdale (Part of Des Moines)	50310
Beaverdale Heights	52655
Beckwith	52556
Bedford	50833
Beebeetown	51546
Beech	50225
Bel Air Beach	50588
Belknap	52537

	ZIP
Belle Plaine	52208
Bellevue	52031
Belmond	50421
Beloit	51240
Bennett	52721
Benton	50835
Bentonsport	52565
Berkley	50220
Bernard	52032
Bertram	52401
Berwick	50032
Bethlehem	50238
Bettendorf	52722
Bevington	50033
Big Mound	52630
Big Rock	52725
Bingham	51601
Birmingham	52535
Bladensburg	52501
Blairsburg	50034
Blairstown	52209
Blakesburg	52536
Blanchard	51630
Blencoe	51523
Blockton	50836
Bloomfield	52537
Blue Grass	52726
Bluff Park (Part of Montrose)	52639
Bluffton	52101
Bode	50519
Bolan	50448
Bonair	52155
Bonaparte	52620
Bondurant	50035
Boone	50036
Booneville	50038
Botna	51454
Bouton	50039
Boxholm	50040
Boyd	50659
Boyden	51234
Boyer	51448
Braddyville	51631
Bradford	50041
Bradgate	50520
Brainard	52141
Brandon	52210
Brayton	50042
Brazil	52574
Breda	51436
Bremer	50677
Bridgewater	50837
Brighton	52540
Bristow	50611
Britt	50423
Bronson	51007
Brooklyn	52211
Brooks	50841
Brunsville	51008
Brushy	50532
Bryant	52727
Bryantsburg	50641
Buchanan	52772
Buckcreek	50674
Buckeye	50043
Buck Grove	51528
Buckingham	50612
Buffalo	52728
Buffalo Center	50424
Buffalo Heights	52728
Burchinal	50469
Burlington	52601
Burnside	50521
Burr Oak	52131
Burt	50522
Bussey	50044
Cairo	52738
Calamus	52729
Calhoun	51555
California Junction	51555
Callender	50523
Calmar	52132
Calumet	51009
Camanche	52730
Cambria	50060
Cambridge	50046
Camp Dodge	50111
Canby	50048
Canton	52309
Cantril	52542
Capital Square (Part of Des Moines)	50393
Capitol Heights	50317
Carbon	50839
Carl	50841
Carlisle	50047
Carmel	51247
Carnarvon	51450
Carnes	51003
Carney	50021
Carnforth	52347

	ZIP
Carpenter	50426
Carroll	51401
Carson	51525
Carter Lake	51510
Cartersville	50469
Cascade	52033
Casey	50048
Casino Beach	50588
Castalia	52133
Castana	51010
Cedar	52543
Cedar Bluff	52772
Cedar Falls	50613
Cedar Rapids	52401-10

For specific Cedar Rapids Zip Codes call (319) 399-2900, or your local postmaster.

	ZIP
Cedar Valley	52358
Cedar View	50616
Centerdale	52776
Center Grove (Part of Dubuque)	52003
Center Junction	52212
Center Point	52213
Centerville (Appanoose County)	52544
Centerville (Boone County)	50036
Central (Part of Davenport)	52801
Central City	52214
Central College (Part of Pella)	50219
Central Heights (Part of Mason City)	50401
Centralia	52068
Chapin	50427
Chariton	50049
Charles City	50616
Charleston	52619
Charlotte	52731
Charter Oak	51439
Chatsworth	51011
Chelsea	52215
Cherokee	51012
Chester	52134
Chickasaw	50645
Chillicothe	52548
Church	52151
Churchville	50211
Churdan	50050
Cincinnati	52549
Clare	50524
Clarence	52216
Clarinda	51632
Clarion	50525
Clarkdale	52544
Clarksville	50619
Clayton	52049
Clayton Center	52043
Clearfield	50840
Clear Lake	50428
Cleghorn	51014
Clemons	50051
Clermont	52135
Cleves	50601
Climbing Hill	51015
Clinton	52732-33

For specific Clinton Zip Codes call (319) 242-6214, or your local postmaster.

	ZIP
Clio	50052
Clive	50322
Cloverdale	51249
Cloverhills (Part of West Des Moines)	50265
Clutier	52217
Coalville	50501
Coburg	51566
Coggon	52218
Coin	51636
Colesburg	52035
Colfax	50054
College Springs	51637
College Square Mall (Part of Cedar Falls)	50613
Collins	50055
Colo	50056
Colonial Village (Part of West Des Moines)	50266
Columbia	50057
Columbus City	52737
Columbus Junction	52738
Colwell	50620
Commerce (Part of West Des Moines)	50265
Conesville	52739
Confidence	52569
Conger	50240
Conover	52132
Conrad	50621
Conroy	52220
Conway	50833
Cool	50125

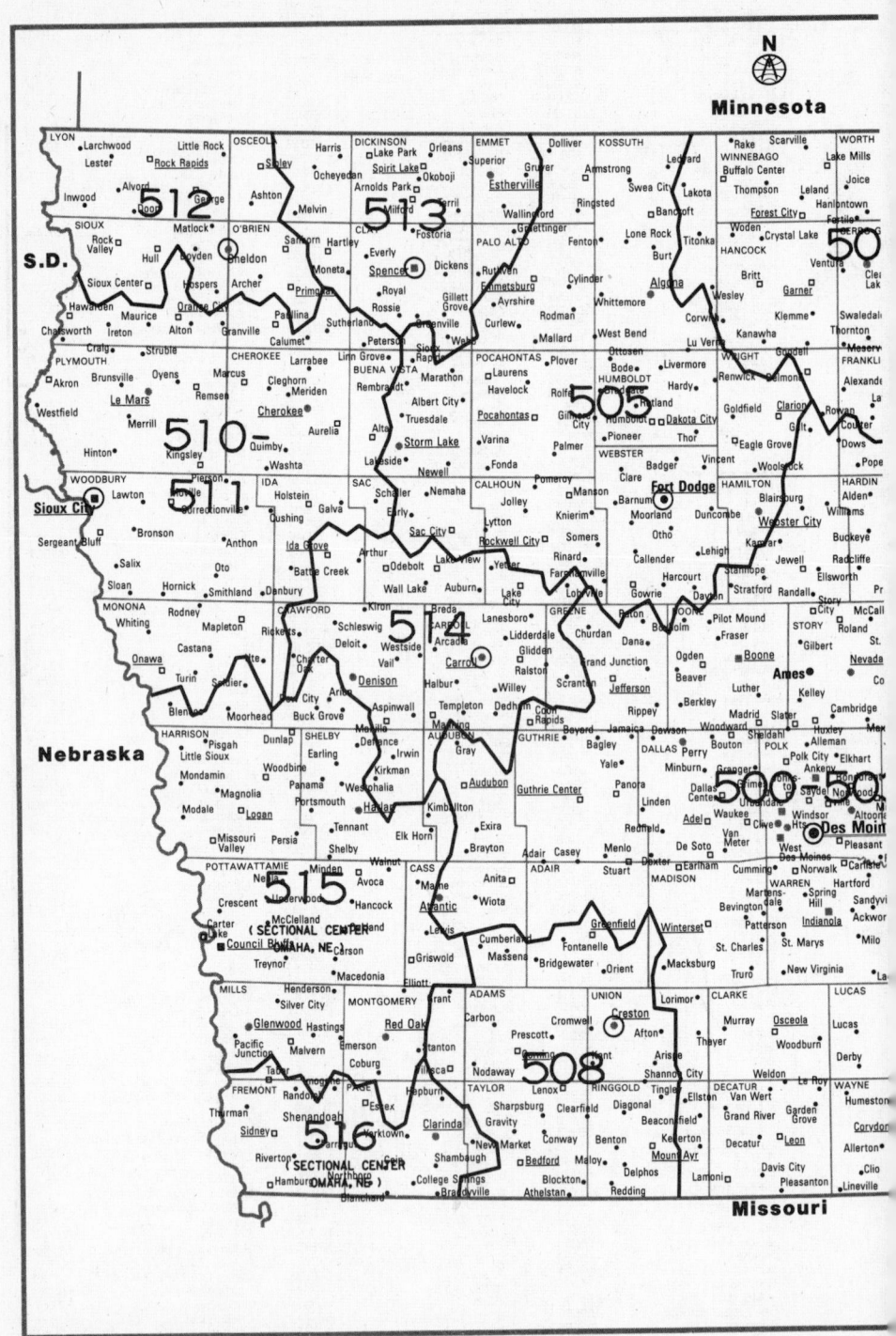

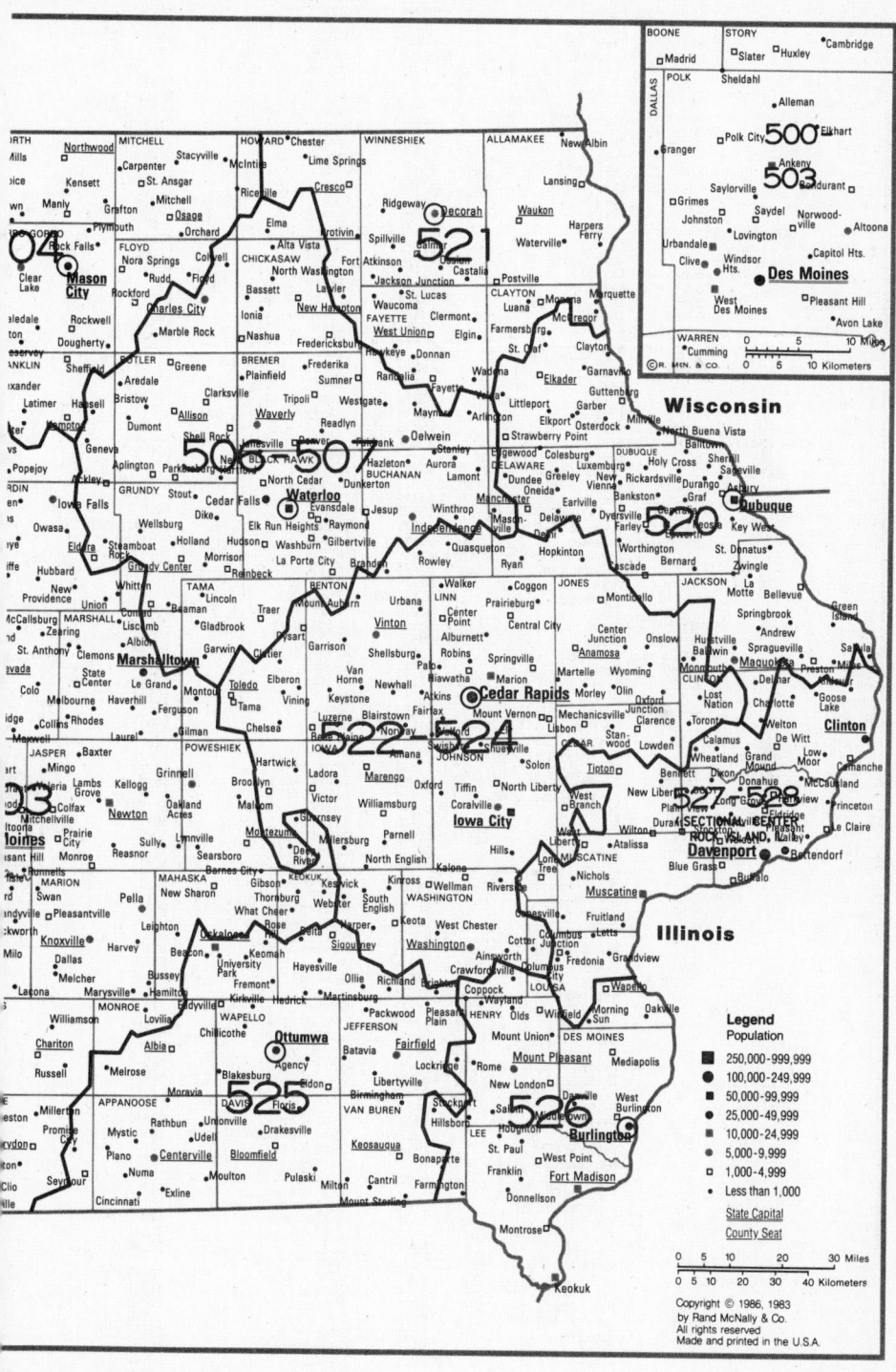

Legend
Population
- 250,000-999,999
- 100,000-249,999
- 50,000-99,999
- 25,000-49,999
- 10,000-24,999
- 5,000-9,999
- 1,000-4,999
- Less than 1,000

State Capital
County Seat

Copyright © 1986, 1983
by Rand McNally & Co.
All rights reserved
Made and printed in the U.S.A.

	ZIP
Coon Rapids	50058
Cooper	50059
Coppock	52654
Coralville	52241
Corley	51537
Cornelia	50525
Cornell	50585
Corning	50841
Correctionville	51016
Corwith	50430
Corydon	50060
Cosgrove	52322
Cotter	52738
Cottonville	52054
Coulter	50431
Council Bluffs	51501-03
	51593
For specific Council Bluffs Zip Codes call (712) 325-0630, or your local postmaster.	
Covington	52324
Craig	51017
Crandalls Lodge	51360
Cranston	52754
Crawfordsville	52621
Crescent	51526
Cresco	52136
Creston	50801
Crestwood (Part of Windsor Heights)	50311
Crocker	50226
Cromwell	50842
Crossroads Center (Part of Waterloo)	50703
Crossroads Mall (Part of Fort Dodge)	50501
Croton	52626
Crystal Lake	50432
Cumberland	50843
Cumming	50061
Curlew	50527
Cushing	51018
Cylinder	50528
Dahlonega	52501
Dakota City	50529
Dallas (Part of Melcher)	50062
Dallas Center	50063
Dana	50064
Danbury	51019
Danville	52623
Darbyville	52544
Davenport	52801-09
For specific Davenport Zip Codes call (319) 322-5991, or your local postmaster.	
Davis City	50065
Dawson	50066
Dayton	50530
Daytonville	52356
Dean	52572
Decatur	50067
Decorah	52101
Dedham	51440
Deep River	52222
Defiance	51527
Delaware	52036
Delhi	52223
Delmar	52037
Deloit	51441
Delphos	50844
Delta	52550
Denison	51442
Denmark	52624
Denver	50622
Depew	50528
Derby	50068
Des Moines	50301-95
For specific Des Moines Zip Codes call (515) 283-7500, or your local postmaster.	
De Soto	50069
Dewar	50623
Dewey	50853
De Witt	52742
Dexter	50070
Diagonal	50845
Dickens	51333
Dike	50624
Dillon	50158
Dinsdale	50669
Dixon	52745
Dodge Park (Part of Council Bluffs)	51501
Dodgeville	52650
Dolliver	50531
Donahue	52746
Donnan	52142
Donnellson	52625
Doon	51235
Dorchester	52140
Douds	52551
Dougherty	50433

	ZIP
Douglas	52175
Dow City	51528
Downey	52358
Dows	50071
Drakesville	52552
Dubuque	52001-04
For specific Dubuque Zip Codes call (319) 582-3674, or your local postmaster.	
Duck Creek Plaza (Part of Bettendorf)	52722
Dumont	50625
Dunbar	50158
Duncan	50423
Duncombe	50532
Dundee	52038
Dunkerton	50626
Dunlap	51529
Durango	52039
Durant	52747
Durham	50119
Dutchtown	52057
Dyersville	52040
Dysart	52224
Eagle Center	50701
Eagle Grove	50533
Eagle Point (Part of Dubuque)	52001
Earlham	50072
Earling	51530
Earlville	52041
Early	50535
East Amana	52203
East Des Moines (Part of Des Moines)	50309
East Fourteenth Street (Part of Des Moines)	50316
East Pleasant Plain	52540
Eddyville	52553
Edgewood	52042
Edgewood Park (Part of Bettendorf)	52722
Edna	51246
Egralharve	51360
Elberon	52225
Eldon	52554
Eldora	50627
Eldorado	52175
Eldridge	52748
Elgin	52141
Elkader	52043
Elkhart	50073
Elk Horn	51531
Elkport	52044
Elk Run Heights	50701
Elliott	51532
Ellston	50074
Ellsworth	50075
Elma	50628
Elon	52170
Elrick	52653
Elvira	52732
Elwood	52226
Ely	52227
Emeline	52207
Emerson	51533
Emery	50401
Emmetsburg	50536
Enterprise	50073
Epworth	52045
Essex	51638
Estherville	51334
Evans	52577
Evansdale	50707
Evanston	50532
Evergreen	52804
Everly	51338
Ewart	50171
Exira	50076
Exline	52555
Fairbank	50629
Fairfax	52228
Fairfield	52556
Fair Ground (Part of Dubuque)	52002
Fairmount Park (Part of Council Bluffs)	51503
Fairport	52761
Fairview	52205
Fanslers	50115
Farley	52046
Farlin	50077
Farmersburg	52047
Farmington	52626
Farnhamville	50538
Farragut	51639
Farrar	50161
Farson	52563
Faulkner	50601
Fayette	52142
Fenton	50539
Ferguson	50078

	ZIP
Fern	50665
Fernald	50201
Fertile	50434
Festina	52143
Fillmore	52033
Finchford	50647
First Street (Part of Cedar Rapids)	52407
Fiscus	50025
Five Points	52073
Flagler	50138
Florenceville	52136
Floris	52560
Floyd	50435
Folletts	52730
Fonda	50540
Fontanelle	50846
Forbush	52544
Forest City	50436
Fort Atkinson	52144
Fort Dodge	50501
Fort Dodge Junction (Part of Fort Dodge)	50501
Fort Madison	52627
Fostoria	51340
Four Corners	52635
Franklin	52625
Frankville	52162
Fraser	50036
Fredericksburg	50630
Frederika	50631
Fredonia	52738
Freeman	50401
Freeport	52101
Fremont	52561
Froelich	52047
Fruitland	52749
Fulton	52060
Galesburg	50232
Galland	52639
Galt	50101
Galva	51020
Gambrill	52756
Garber	52048
Garden City	50102
Garden Grove	50103
Gardiner	50039
Garnavillo	52049
Garner	50438
Garrison	52229
Garwin	50632
Gaza	51245
Geneva	50633
George	51237
Georgetown	52531
Germantown	51046
German Valley	50480
Germanville	52540
Giard	52157
Gibson	50104
Gifford	50259
Gilbert	50105
Gilbertville	50634
Gillett Grove	51341
Gilman	50106
Gilmore City	50541
Gladbrook	50635
Glasgow	52556
Glendale Acres	51503
Glendon	50164
Glenwood	51534
Glidden	51443
Goddard	50054
Goldfield	50542
Goodell	50439
Goose Lake	52750
Gowrie	50543
Grace Hill	52353
Graettinger	51342
Graf	52073
Grafton	50440
Grand (Part of Des Moines)	50309
Grand Junction	50107
Grand Mound	52751
Grand River	50108
Grandview	52752
Granger	50109
Granger Homesteads	50109
Granite	51241
Grant	50847
Grant Wood (Part of Bettendorf)	52722
Granville	51022
Gravity	50848
Gray	50110
Greeley	52050
Green Castle	50054
Greene	50636
Greenfield	50849
Greenfield Plaza	50315
Green Island	52064
Green Mountain	50637

	ZIP
Greenville	51343
Greenwood Acres	50021
Grimes	50111
Grinnell	50112
Griswold	51535
Grundy Center	50638
Gruver	51344
Guernsey	50172
Gunder	52162
Guss	50857
Guthrie Center	50115
Guttenberg	52052
Halbur	51444
Hale	52230
Hamburg	51640
Hamill	52625
Hamilton	50116
Hamlin	50117
Hampton	50441
Hancock	51536
Hanford	50401
Hanley	50240
Hanlontown	50444
Hanover	51002
Hansell	50640
Harcourt	50544
Hardy	50545
Harlan	51537
	51593

For specific Harlan Zip Codes call
(712) 755-5812, or your local
postmaster.

	ZIP
Harper	52231
Harpers Ferry	52146
Harris	51345
Harrisburg	52620
Hartford	50118
Hartley	51346
Hartwick	52232
Harvard	50008
Harvey	50119
Haskins	52201
Hastings	51540
Hauntown	52732
Havelock	50546
Haven	52339
Haverhill	50120
Hawarden	51023
Hawkeye	52147
Hawleyville	51632
Hawthorne	51566
Hayesville	52562
Hayfield	50438
Hazleton	50641
Hedrick	52563
Henderson	51541
Hepburn	51632
Herndon	50128
Herrold	50111
Hesper	52101
Hiawatha	52233
Hickman Road (Part of Urbandale)	50322
High	52203
Highland Center	52501
Highland Park (Part of Des Moines)	50333
Highlandville	52149
High Point	50103
Highview	50595
Hills	52235
Hillsboro	52630
Hinton	51024
Hiteman	52531
Hobarton	50511
Hocking	52531
Holbrook	52325
Holiday Lake	52211
Holland	50642
Holly Springs	51026
Holmes	50525
Holstein	51025
Holy Cross	52053
Homer	50595
Homestead	52236
Honey Creek	51542
Hopeville	50174
Hopkinton	52237
Hornick	51026
Horton	50677
Hospers	51238
Houghton	52631
Hubbard	50122
Hudson	50643
Hull	51239
Humboldt	50548
Humeston	50123
Huntington	51334
Hurstville	52060
Hutchins	50423
Huxley	50124
Iconium	52571

	ZIP
Ida Grove	51445
Imogene	51645
Independence	50644
Indian Creek (Part of Marion)	52302
Indianola	50125
Industry	50540
Inwood	51240
Ionia	50645
Iowa Army Ammunition Plant	52638
Iowa Center	50161
Iowa City	52240
	52242-46

For specific Iowa City Zip Codes
call (319) 354-1560, or your local
postmaster.

	ZIP
Iowa Falls	50126
Iowa State University (Part of Ames)	50011-13

For specific Iowa State University
Zip Codes call (515) 292-2098, or
your local postmaster.

	ZIP
Ira	50127
Ireton	51027
Ironhills	52060
Irving	52208
Irvington	50560
Irwin	51446
Ivy	50009
Jackson Junction	52150
Jacksonville	51537
Jamaica	50128
James	51108
Jamison	50210
Janesville	50647
Jefferson	50129
Jerico	50659
Jerome	52544
Jesup	50648
Jewell	50130
Joetown	52247
Johnston	50131
Johnston Station (Part of Johnston)	50131
Joice	50446
Jolley	50551
Jordan	50036
Julien	52003
Juniata	50588
Kalo	50569
Kalona	52247
Kamrar	50132
Kanawha	50447
Kellerton	50133
Kelley	50134
Kellogg	50135
Kendallville	52136
Kennedy Mall (Part of Dubuque)	52002
Kensett	50448
Kent	50850
Keokuk	52632
Keomah Village	52577
Keosauqua	52565
Keota	52248
Kesley	50649
Keswick	50136
Keystone	52249
Key West	52003
Kilbourn	52535
Killduff	50137
Kimballton	51543
Kingsley	51028
Kingston	52637
Kinross	52250
Kirkman	51447
Kirkville	52566
Kiron	51448
Klemme	50449
Klinger	50668
Knierim	50552
Knittel	50668
Knoke	50553
Knoxville	50138
Knoxville Estates	50138
Konigsmark	52401
Kossuth	52637
Koszta	52208
Lacelle	50213
Lacey	50207
Lacona	50139
Ladora	52251
La Fayette	52202
Lake Canyada	52804
Lake City	51449
Lake Mills	50450
Lake Park	51347
Lakeside	50588
Lake View	51450
Lakewood	50211
Lakota	50451

	ZIP
Lambs Grove	50208
Lamoille	50158
Lamoni	50140
Lamont	50650
La Motte	52054
Lanesboro	51451
Langdon	51301
Langworthy	52252
Lansing	52151
Lanyon	50544
La Porte City	50651
Larchwood	51241
Larrabee	51029
Latimer	50452
Laurel	50141
Laurens	50554
Lawler	52154
Lawn Hill	50206
Lawton	51030
Leando	52551
Lebanon (Sioux County)	51250
Lebanon (Van Buren County)	52565
Le Claire	52753
Ledyard	50556
Leeds (Part of Sioux City)	51108
Le Grand	50142
Lehigh	50557
Leighton	50143
Leland	50453
Le Mars	51031
Lenox	50851
Leon	50144
Le Roy	50123
Lester	51242
Letts	52754
Lewis	51544
Liberty	50210
Liberty Center	50145
Libertyville	52567
Lidderdale	51452
Lime City	52778
Lime Springs	52155
Linby	52580
Lincoln	50652
Lincoln Center	50841
Lindale Mall (Part of Cedar Rapids)	52402
Linden	50146
Lineville	50147
Linn Grove	51033
Linwood (Part of Buffalo)	52805
Lisbon	52253
Liscomb	50148
Little Cedar	50454
Littleport	52055
Little Rock	51243
Little Sioux	51545
Littleton	50648
Little Turkey	52154
Livermore	50558
Livingston	52549
Lockridge	52635
Logan	51546
Logansport	50036
Lohrville	51453
Lone Rock	50559
Lone Tree	52755
Long Grove	52756
Lorah	50022
Lorimor	50149
Lost Nation	52254
Lourdes	50628
Loveland	51555
Lovilia	50150
Lovington	50322
Lowden	52255
Lowell	52645
Low Moor	52757
Luana	52156
Lucas	50151
Lundstrom Heights	50021
Luther	50152
Luther Manor (Part of Bettendorf)	52722
Luton	51052
Lu Verne	50560
Luxemburg	52056
Luzerne	52257
Lyman	51535
Lynnville	50153
Lyons (Clinton County)	52732
Lyons (Linn County)	52302
Lytton	50561
McCallsburg	50154
McCausland	52758
McClelland	51548
Macedonia	51549
McGregor	52157
McIntire	50455
Macksburg	50155
McNally	51027

* Area Zip Code † Post Office Boxes

	ZIP		ZIP		ZIP
Macy	50601	Mona	50472	Numa	52575
Madison (Part of Council Bluffs)	51503	Mondamin	51557	Nyman	51566
Madrid	50156	Moneta	51346	Oakdale (Part of Coralville)	52319
Magnolia	51550	Monmouth	52309	Oakland	51560
Maine	52571	Monona	52159	Oakland Acres	50112
Malcom	50157	Monroe	50170	Oakland Mills	52641
Mallard	50562	Monteith	50115	Oakley	50049
Mall of the Bluffs (Part of Council Bluffs)	51503	Monterey	52537	Oakville	52646
Malone	52742	Montezuma	50171	Oakwood	50653
Maloy	50852	Montgomery	51360	Oasis	52358
Malvern	51551	Monti	52218	Ocheyedan	51354
Manawa (Part of Council Bluffs)	51501	Monticello	52310	Odebolt	51458
Manchester	52057	Montour	50173	Oelwein	50662
Manilla	51454	Montpelier	52759	Ogden	50212
Manly	50456	Montrose	52639	Okoboji	51355
Manning	51455	Mooar	52632	Old Balltown	52073
Manson	50563	Moorhead	51558	Olds	52647
Maple Heights	50616	Moorland	50566	Old Town	51351
Maple Hill	50514	Moran	50276	Olin	52320
Maple River	51401	Moravia	52571	Olivet	50143
Mapleton	51034	Morley	52312	Ollie	52576
Maquoketa	52060	Morningside (Part of Sioux City)	51106	Onawa	51040
Marathon	50565	Morning Sun	52640	Oneida	52057
Marble Rock	50653	Morrison	50657	Onslow	52321
Marcus	51035	Morse	52240	Ontario (Part of Ames)	50014
Marengo	52301	Morton Mills	50864	Oralabor	50021
Marietta	50158	Moscow	52760	Oran	50664
Marion	52302	Moulton	52572	Orange (Part of Waterloo)	50701
Mark	52537	Mount Auburn	52313	Orange City	51041
Marne	51552	Mount Ayr	50854	Orchard	50460
Marquette	52158	Mount Carmel	51401	Orient	50858
Marquisville	50313	Mount Etna	50841	Orilla	50061
Marsh	52659	Mount Joy	52804	Orleans	51360
Marshalltown	50158	Mount Pleasant	52641	Osage	50461
Marshalltown Mall (Part of Marshalltown)	50158	Mount Sterling	52573	Osborne	52043
Martelle	52305	Mount Union	52644	Osceola	50213
Martensdale	50160	Mount Vernon	52314	Osgood	50536
Martinsburg	52568	Mount Zion	52565	Oskaloosa	52577
Martinstown	52575	Moville	51039	Ossian	52161
Marysville	50116	Munterville	52536	Osterdock	52035
Mason City	50401*	Murphy	50677	Otho	50569
	50402†	Murray	50174	Otley	50214
Masonville	50654	Muscatine	52761	Oto	51044
Massena	50853	Muscatine Mall (Part of Muscatine)	52761	Otranto	50472
Massey	52003			Otter Creek	52079
Massillon	52255	Mystic	52574	Otterville	50644
Matlock	51244	Napier	50014	Ottosen	50570
Maurice	51036	Nashua	50658	Ottumwa	52501
Maxwell	50161	Nashville	52060	Ottumwa Junction (Part of Ottumwa)	52501
May City	51349	Nemaha	50567	Owasa	50126
Maynard	50655	Neola	51559	Oxford	52322
Maysville	52773	Nevada	50201	Oxford Junction	52323
Mechanicsville	52306	Nevinville	50801	Oxford Mills	52323
Mederville	52043	New Albin	52160	Oyens	51045
Mediapolis	52637	New Boston	52619	Pacific Junction	51561
Medora	50125	Newburg	50112	Packard	50619
Melbourne	50162	Newell	50568	Packwood	52580
Melcher	50163	New Era	52761	Painted Rocks	50214
Melrose	52569	Newhall	52315	Palmer	50571
Meltonville	50472	New Hampton	52659	Palm Grove	50501
Melvin	51350	New Hartford	50660	Palmyra	50047
Menlo	50164	New Haven	50461	Palo	52324
Meriden	51037	Newkirk	51238	Panama	51562
Merle Hay Mall (Part of Des Moines)	50310	New Liberty	52765	Panora	50216
Meroa	50461	New London	52645	Panorama Park	52722
Merrill	51038	New Market	51646	Paralta	52336
Meservey	50457	New Providence	50206	Paris (Davis County)	52552
Methodist Camp	51360	New Sharon	50207	Paris (Linn County)	52214
Meyer	50455	Newton	50208	Parkersburg	50665
Middle	52307	New Vienna	52065	Park Hills	50214
Middleburg	51041	New Virginia	50210	Park View	52748
Middletown	52638	Nichols	52766	Parnell	52325
Midlands Mall (Part of Council Bluffs)	51503	Noble	52641	Paton	50217
Midvale	50124	Nodaway	50857	Patterson	50218
Midway (Floyd County)	50616	Nora Springs	50458	Paullina	51046
Midway (Linn County)	52302	Nora Springs Junction (Part of Nora Springs)	50458	Payne	51640
Miles	52064	Northboro	51647	Pekin	52580
Milford	51351	North Branch	50002	Pella	50219
Miller	50438	North Buena Vista	52066	Peoria	50219
Millersburg	52308	North Central Correctional Facility	50579	Peosta	52068
Millerton	50165	North English	52316	Percival	51648
Milnerville	51062	North Grand Mall (Part of Ames)	50010	Perkins	51239
Millville	52052	North Liberty	52317	Perlee	52556
Milo	50166	Northpark Mall (Part of Davenport)	52806	Perry	50220
Milton	52570	North Side (Part of Sioux City)	51104	Pershing	50138
Minburn	50167	North Wall Lake (Part of Wall Lake)	51466	Persia	51563
Minden	51553	North Washington	50661	Peru	50222
Mineola	51554	Northwest (Linn County)	52405	Petersburg	52040
Mineral Ridge	50036	Northwest (Scott County)	52804	Peterson	51047
Minerva	50005	Northwood	50459	Petersville	52731
Mingo	50168	Norwalk	50211	Pierceville	52565
Missouri Valley	51555	Norway	52318	Pierson	51048
Mitchell	50461	Norwich	51601	Pilot Grove	52648
Mitchellville	50169	Norwood	50151	Pilot Mound	50223
Modale	51556	Norwoodville	50317	Pioneer	50541
Moingona	50036			Piper	50579
				Pisgah	51564
				Pittsburg	52565
				Pitzer	50072
				Plainfield	50666
				Plain View	52773

* Area Zip Code   **† Post Office Boxes**

	ZIP		ZIP		ZIP
Plano	52581	Roselle	51401	South Des Moines (Part of	
Plaza Hills (Part of Windsor		Ross	50025	Des Moines)	50315
Heights)	50311	Rossie	51357	South English	52335
Pleasantgrove	52645	Rossville	52159	Southern Hills Mall (Part of	
Pleasant Hill	50301	Rowan	50470	Sioux City)	51106
Pleasanton	50065	Rowley	52329	South Muscatine (Part of	
Pleasant Plain	52540	Royal	51357	Muscatine)	52761
Pleasant Prairie	52761	Rubio	52585	South Ottumwa (Part of	
Pleasant Valley	52767	Rudd	50471	Ottumwa)	52501
Pleasantville	50225	Runnells	50237	Southridge Mall (Part of Des	
Plover	50573	Russell	50238	Moines)	50315
Plymouth	50464	Ruthven	51358	Spaulding	50801
Pocahontas	50574	Rutland	50582	Spencer	51301
Polk City	50226	Ryan	52330	Sperry	52650
Pomeroy	50575	Sabula	52070	Spillville	52168
Popejoy	50227	Sac and Fox Indian		Spirit Lake	51360
Portland	50401	Reservation	52339	Spragueville	52074
Portsmouth	51565	Sac City	50583	Springbrook	52075
Postville	52162	Sageville	52001	Springdale	52358
Powersville	50636	St. Ansgar	50472	Spring Grove	52601
Prairieburg	52219	St. Anthony	50239	Spring Hill	50125
Prairie City	50228	St. Benedict	50511	Springville	52336
Prairie Grove	52655	St. Catherines	52003	Spruce Hills Village (Part of	
Prescott	50859	St. Charles	50240	Bettendorf)	52722
Preston	52069	St. Donatus	52071	Stacyville	50476
Primghar	51245	St. Joseph	50519	Stanhope	50246
Primrose	52625	St. Lucas	52166	Stanley	50671
Princeton	52768	St. Marys	50241	Stanton	51573
Prole	50229	St. Olaf	52072	Stanwood	52337
Promise City	52583	St. Paul	52657	Stanzel	50849
Prospect Hill (Part of		Salem	52649	State Center	50247
Burlington)	52601	Salina	52556	Steamboat Rock	50672
Protivin	52163	Salix	51052	Stennett	51566
Pulaski	52584	Sanborn	51248	Sterling	52070
Quarry	50158	Sand Springs	52237	Stiles	52537
Quasqueton	52326	Sandusky	52632	Stilson	50423
Quimby	51049	Sandyville	50001	Stockport	52651
Radcliffe	50230	Santiago	50169	Stockton	52769
Rake	50465	Saratoga	52155	Stone City	52205
Ralston	51459	Saude	52154	Storm Lake	50588
Randalia	52164	Savannah	52537	Story City	50248
Randall	50231	Sawyer	52627	Stout	50673
Randolph	51649	Saydel	50313	Strahan	51540
Rands	50579	Saylorville	50313	Stratford	50249
Rathbun	52544	Scarville	50473	Strawberry Point	52076
Raymar	50701	Schaller	51053	Stringtown	50851
Raymond	50667	Schleswig	51461	Struble	51057
Readlyn	50668	Schley	52136	Stuart	50250
Reasnor	50232	Sciola	50864	Suburban Heights	52556
Redding	50860	Scotch Grove	52331	Sully	50251
Redfield	50233	Scotch Ridge	50047	Sulphur Springs	50588
Red Line	51447	Scranton	51462	Summerset	50125
Red Oak	51566	Searsboro	50242	Summitville	52632
Red Rock Lakeview	50138	Sedan	52544	Sumner	50674
Reinbeck	50669	Selma	52588	Sunbury	52778
Rembrandt	50576	Seneca	51050	Sunshine	52544
Remsen	51050	Seney	51031	Superior	51363
Renwick	50577	Sergeant Bluff	51054	Sutherland	51058
Rhodes	50234	Sewal	50060	Sutliff	52253
Riceville	50466	Sexton	50483	Swaledale	50477
Richards	50579	Seymour	52590	Swan	50252
Richland	52585	Shaffton	52730	Swea City	50590
Richmond	52247	Shambaugh	51651	Swedesburg	52652
Rickardsville	52073	Shannon City	50861	Sweetland Center	52761
Ricketts	51460	Sharon Center	52240	Swisher	52338
Ridgeport	50036	Sharpsburg	50862	Tabor	51653
Ridgeway	52165	Shawondasse	52003	Taintor	50253
Rinard	50587	Sheffield	50475	Talleyrand	52248
Ringsted	50578	Shelby	51570	Tama	52339
Rippey	50235	Sheldahl	50243	Tara	50501
Rising Sun	50317	Sheldon	51201	Teeds Grove	52771
Ritter	51201	Shell Rock	50670	Templar Park	51360
Riverdale	52722	Shellsburg	52332	Templeton	51463
River Heights	52240	Shenandoah	51601†	Ten Mile	52727
River Junction	52755		51693*	Tennant	51574
Riverside (Washington		Sheridan	50157	Tenville	50864
County)	52327	Sherrill	52073	Tenville Junction	50864
Riverside (Woodbury		Sherwood	50579	Terril	51364
County)	51109	Shipley	50201	Thayer	50254
River Sioux	51545	Shueyville	52404	Thirty	52544
Riverton	51650	Siam	50833	Thompson	50478
Riverview Release Center	50208	Sibley	51249	Thor	50591
Roberts	50569	Sidney	51652	Thornburg	50255
Robertson	50601	Sigourney	52591	Thornton	50479
Robins	52328	Silver City	51571	Thorpe	52057
Robinson	52330	Sinclair	50665	Thurman	51654
Rochester	52772	Sioux Center	51250	Ticonic	51010
Rock Creek	50461	Sioux City	51101-11	Tiffin	52340
Rockdale (Part of Dubuque)	52003	For specific Sioux City Zip Codes		Timberland Heights (Part of	
Rock Falls	50467	call (712) 277-6411, or your local		Ames)	50014
Rockford	50468	postmaster.		Tingley	50863
Rock Rapids	51246	Sioux Rapids	50585	Tipton	52772
Rock Valley	51247	Six Mile	52732	Titonka	50480
Rockwell	50469	Slater	50244	Toddville	52341
Rockwell City	50579	Slifer	50543	Toeterville	50481
Rodman	50580	Sloan	51055	Toledo	52342
Rodney	51051	Smithland	51056	Toolesboro	52653
Roelyn	50566	Soldier	51572	Toronto	52343
Roland	50236	Solon	52333	Tracy	50256
Rolfe	50581	Somers	50586	Traer	50675
Rome	52642	South Amana	52334	Trenton	52641
Rose Hill	52586			Treynor	51575

	ZIP		ZIP		ZIP
Abbyville	67510	Belvue	66407	Castleton	67501
Abilene	67410	Bendena	66008	Catharine	67627
Ada	67414	Benedict	66714	Cato	66711
Adams	67128	Bennington	67422	Cave	67952
Admire	66830	Bentley	67016	Cawker City	67430
Agenda	66930	Benton	67017	Cedar (Johnson County)	66018
Aggieville Shopping Center		Bern	66408	Cedar (Smith County)	67628
(Part of Manhattan)	66502	Berryton	66409	Cedar Bluffs	67749
Agra	67621	Berwick	66534	Cedar Point	66843
Agricola	66871	Beulah	66743	Cedar Vale	67024
Akron	67156	Beverly	67423	Centerville	66014
Alamota	67839	Big Bow	67855	Centralia	66415
Albert	67511	Big Springs	66050	Centropolis	66067
Alden	67512	Bird City	67731	Chanute	66720
Alexander	67513	Birmingham	66436	Chapman	67431
Aliceville	66093	Bismarck Grove (Part of		Charleston	67853
Allen	66833	Lawrence)	66044	Chase	67524
Alma	66401	Bison	67520	Chautauqua	67334
Almena	67622	Black Wolf	67490	Cheney	67025
Altamont	67330	Blaine	66549	Cherokee	66724
Alta Vista	66834	Blair	66090	Cherryvale	67335
Alton	67623	Blakeman	67730	Chetopa	67336
Altoona	66710	Bloom	67865	Chicopee	66762
Americus	66835	Bloomington (Butler County)	67010	Child's Acres	67101
Ames	66901	Bloomington (Osborne		Chiles	66071
Amy	67850	County)	67473	Chisholm (Part of Wichita)	67217
Andale	67001	Blue Mound	66010	Cicero	67152
Andover	67002	Blue Rapids	66411	Cimarron	67835
Angelus	67738	Blue Valley (Part of		Circleville	66416
Angola	67337	Overland Park)	66213	Civic Center (Part of	
Anna	66701	Bluff City	67018	Kansas City)	66101
Anness	67106	Bogue	67625	Claflin	67525
Anson	67152	Boicourt	66075	Clare	66061
Antelope	66858	Bolton	67301	Claudell	67628
Anthony	67003	Bonita	66061	Clay Center	67432
Antioch	66083	Bonner Springs	66012	Clayton	67629
Antonino	67601	Bonnie Brae (Part of		Clearfield	66025
Arcadia	66711	Wichita)	67207	Clearview City	66019
Argentine (Part of Kansas		Bonnie Ridge	67401	Clearwater	67026
City)	66106	Boyle	66088	Clements	66843
Argonia	67004	Brainerd	67154	Clifton	66937
Arkansas City	67005	Brazilton	66743	Climax	67137
Arlington	67514	Bremen	66412	Clinton	66046
Arma	66712	Brenham	67059	Clonmel	67149
Armourdale (Part of Kansas		Brenner Heights (Part of		Clyde	66938
City)	66105	Kansas City)	66104	Coalvale	66711
Arnold	67515	Brewster	67732	Coats	67028
Arrington	66436	Bridgeport	67416	Codell	67630
Arthur Heights (Part of Bel		Bronson	66716	Coffeyville	67337
Aire)	67220	Brookhaven Estates	67230	Colby	67701
Arvonia	66523	Brookridge (Part of		Coldwater	67029
Asherville	67420	Overland Park)	66212	Collyer	67631
Ash Grove	67481		66282	Colony	66015
Ashland (Clark County)	67831	For specific Brookridge Zip Codes		Columbus	66725
Ashland (Riley County)	66502	call (913) 831-5302, or your local		Colwich	67030
Ashton	67051	postmaster.		Concordia	66901
Assaria	67416	Brookville	67425	Conway	67460
Atchison	66002	Brookwood Shopping		Conway Springs	67031
Atchison Mall (Part of		Center (Part of Topeka)	66614	Coolidge	67836
Atchison)	66002	Brownell	67521	Copeland	67837
Athol	66932	Browns Spur	67068	Corbin (Montgomery	
Atlanta	67008	Buckeye	67410	County)	67335
Attica	67009	Bucklin	67834	Corbin (Sumner County)	67032
Atwood	67730	Bucyrus	66013	Corinth Square Shopping	
Aubry	66085	Buffalo	66717	Center (Part of Prairie	
Auburn	66402	Buhler	67522	Village)	66208
Augusta	67010	Bunker Hill	67626	Corning	66417
Aulne	66861	Burden	67019	Corwin	67061
Aurora	67417	Burdett	67523	Cottonwood Falls	66845
Aurora Park (Part of Bel		Burdick	66838	Council Grove	66846
Aire)	67220	Burlingame	66413	Countryside	66222
Axtell	66403	Burlington	66839	County Acres (Part of	
Baileyville	66404	Burns	66840	Wichita)	67212
Bala	66531	Burr Oak	66936	Courtland	66939
Baldwin City	66006	Burrton	67020	Covert	67651
Bancroft	66428	Busby	67349	Cow Town (Part of Wichita)	67203
Barclay	66523	Bush City	66032	Coyville	66727
Barker (Part of Kansas City)	66104	Bushong	66833	Craig	66215
Barnard	67418	Bushton	67427	Crestline	66728
Barnes	66933	Buxton	66736	Croweburg	66756
Bartlett	67332	Byers	67021	Cruppers Corner	67501
Basehor	66007	Cairo	67035	Cuba	66940
Bassett	66749	Caldwell	67022	Cullen Village (Part of	
Bavaria	67401	Calista	67035	Topeka)	66619
Baxter Springs	66713	Callahan (Part of Wichita)	67209	Cullison	67124
Bayard	66039	Calvert	67622	Culver	67484
Bazaar	66845	Cambridge	67023	Cummings	66016
Bazine	67516	Camp Forsyth	66442	Cunningham	67035
Beagle	66064	Camp Funston	66442	Cunningham Highlands	
Beardsley	67730	Camp Naish	66111	(Part of Overland Park)	66204
Beattie	66406	Campus	67748	Curranville	66756
Beaumont	67012	Camp Whiteside	66442	Dalton	67152
Beaver	67525	Canada	66861	Damar	67632
Beeler	67518	Caney	67333	Danville	67036
Bel Aire	67220	Canton	67428	Dartmouth	67530
Bellaire	66952	Capaldo	66762	Dearing	67340
Belle Plaine	67013	Carbondale	66414	Deerfield	67838
Belleville	66935	Carlton	67429	De Graff	66840
Belmont	67068	Carlyle	66749	Delano (Part of Wichita)	67209
Beloit	67420	Carneiro	67425	Delavan	67449
Belpre	67519	Carona	66773	Delia	66418
Belvidere	67015	Cassoday	66842	Delphos	67436

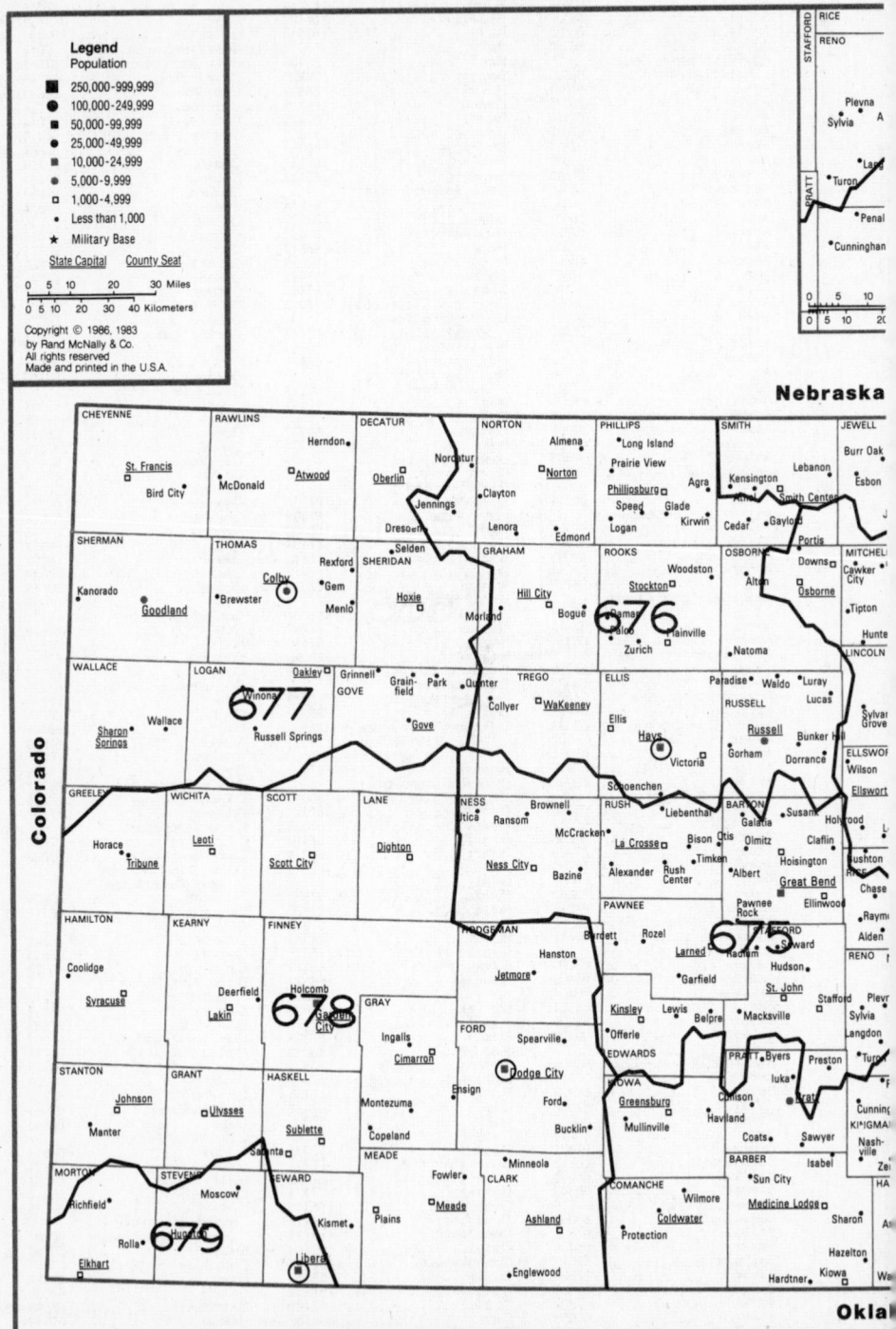

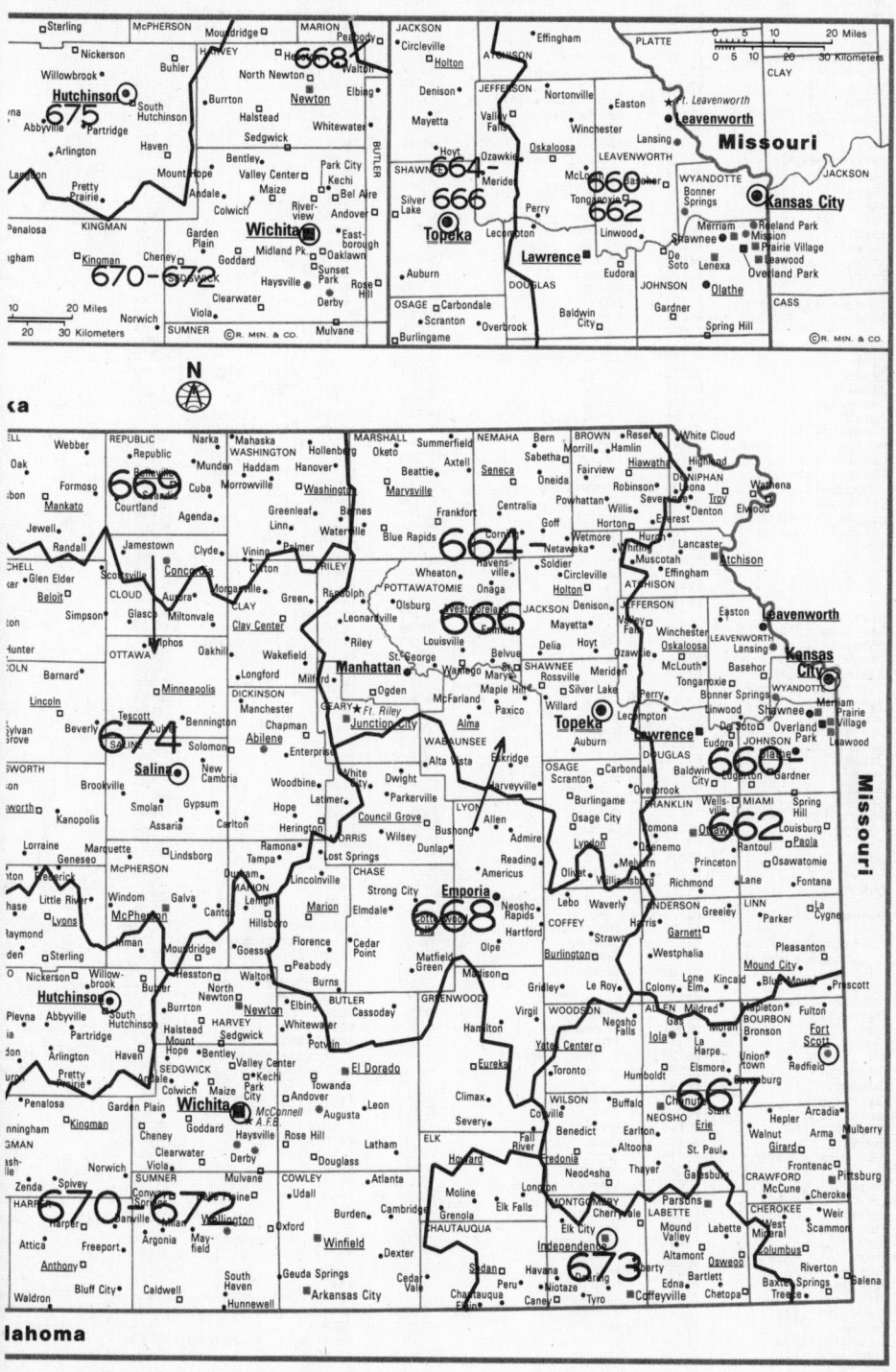

	ZIP
Denison	66419
Denmark	67455
Dennis	67341
Densmore	67645
Denton	66017
Denton-McWorter Addition	67101
Derby	67037
Dermot	67954
De Soto	66018
Detroit	67410
Devon	66701
Dexter	67038
Diamond Springs	66838
Dighton	67839
Dillwyn	67557
Dispatch	67430
Dodge City	67801
Doniphan	66002
Dorrance	67634
Douglass	67039
Dover	66420
Downs	67437
Downtown (Part of Wichita)	67202
Dresden	67635
Drury	67022
Dubuque	67634
Dundee	66521
Duluth	67530
Dunkirk	66762
Dunlap	66846
Duquoin	67058
Durham	67438
Dwight	66849
Earlton	66720
East Bank (Part of Iola)	66749
Eastborough	67206
East Forbes	66620
Eastgate Shopping Center (Part of Wichita)	67207
Easton	66020
Eastshore	66861
Edgerton	66021
Edmond	67636
Edna	67342
Edson	67733
Edwardsville	66113
Effingham	66023
Elbing	67041
El Dorado	67042
El Dorado Honor Camp	67042
Elgin	67361
Elk City	67344
Elk Falls	67345
Elkhart	67950
Ellinwood	67526
Ellis	67637
Ellsworth	67439
Elmdale	66850
Elmhurst (Part of Overland Park)	66204
Elmo	67451
Elmont	66618
Elsmore	66732
Elwood	66024
Elyria	67460
Emmeram	67671
Emmett	66422
Empire City (Part of Galena)	66739
Empire Junction (Part of Galena)	66739
Emporia	66801
Englevale	66756
Englewood	67840
Ensign	67841
Enterprise	67441
Erie	66733
Esbon	66941
Eskridge	66423
Eudora	66025
Eureka	67045
Eureka City Lake	67045
Everest	66424
Fairfax (Part of Kansas City)	66115
Fairmount	66048
Fairport	67665
Fairview	66425
Fairway	66205
Fall Leaf	66052
Fall River	67047
Falun	67442
Fanning	66087
Farlington	66734
Farlinville	66014
Farmington	66023
Faulkner	67336
Federal Penitentiary	66048
Fellsburg	67552
Fleming	66762
Floral	67156
Florence	66851
Flush	66535
Fontana	66026
Ford	67842
Forest Hills (Part of Wichita)	67206
Forest Lake (Part of Edwardsville)	66113
Formoso	66942
Fort Dodge	67843
Fort Leavenworth	66027
Fort Riley	66442
Fort Riley-Camp Whiteside	66442
Fort Riley North	66442
Fort Scott	66701
Fostoria (Osage County)	66413
Fostoria (Pottawatomie County)	66426
Four Corners	66537
Fowler	67844
Fox Town	66756
Frankfort	66427
Franklin	66735
Frederick	67444
Fredonia	66736
Freeport	67049
Friend	67871
Frontenac	66763
Fulton	66738
Furley	67147
Gage Center (Part of Topeka)	66604
Galatia	67565
Galena	66739
Galesburg	66740
Galva	67443
Garden City	67846
Garden Plain	67050
Gardner	66030
Gardner Lake	66030
Garfield	67529
Garland	66741
Garnett	66032
Gas	66742
Gaylord	67638
Gem	67734
Geneseo	67444
Geuda Springs	67051
Girard	66743
Glade	67639
Glasco	67445
Glendale	67425
Glen Elder	67446
Glen Park (Part of Kansas City)	66102
Glenville (Part of Wichita)	67217
Goddard	67052
Goessel	67053
Goff	66428
Golden Belt Spur (Part of Salina)	67401
Goodland	67735
Goodrich	66072
Gorham	67640
Gove	67736
Grainfield	67737
Granada	66550
Grand Summit	67023
Grandview (Part of Bonner Springs)	66012
Grandview Plaza	66441
Grantville	66429
Great Bend	67530
Greeley	66033
Green	67447
Greenbush	66743
Greenleaf	66943
Greensburg	67054
Greenwich	67055
Greenwich Heights	67207
Grenola	67346
Gretna	67661
Gridley	66852
Grigston	67871
Grinnell	67738
Gross	66711
Grove	66539
Groveland	67546
Gypsum	67448
Hackney	67156
Haddam	66944
Haggard	67835
Half Mound	66088
Halford	67701
Hallowell	66725
Halls Summit	66871
Halstead	67056
Hamilton	66853
Hamlin	66434
Hammond	66701
Hanover	66945
Hanston	67849
Hardtner	67057
Harlan	67641
Harper	67058
Harris	66032
Hartford	66854
Harveyville	66431
Haskell (Part of Lawrence)	66044
Havana	67347
Haven	67543
Havensville	66432
Haverhill	67010
Haviland	67059
Hays	67601
Haysville	67060
Hazelton	67061
Healy	67850
Hedville	67401
Heizer	67530
Hepler	66746
Herington	67449
Heritage Hills	66002
Herkimer	66508
Herndon	67739
Hesper	66025
Hessdale	66401
Hesston	67062
Hewins	67024
Hiattville	66701
Hiawatha	66434
Hickok	67880
Hickory Acres	66512
Hicrest (Part of Topeka)	66605
Hidden Lakes (Part of Wichita)	67212
Highland	66035
Highland Park (Part of Topeka)	66605
Hill City	67642
Hillcrest Shopping Center (Part of Lawrence)	66044
Hillsboro	67063
Hillsdale	66036
Hillside (Part of Wichita)	67208
Hitschmann	67525
Hoge	66086
Hoisington	67544
Holcomb	67851
Holland	67410
Hollenberg	66946
Holliday (Part of Shawnee)	66218
Holliday Square Shopping Center (Part of Topeka)	66611
Holton	66436
Holyrood	67450
Home	66438
Homewood	66095
Hope	67451
Hopewell	67557
Horace	67879
Horton	66439
Howard	67349
Hoxie	67740
Hoyt	66440
Hudson	67545
Hugoton	67951
Humboldt	66748
Hunnewell	67140
Hunter	67452
Huron	66041
Huscher	66901
Hutchinson	67501-04
For specific Hutchinson Zip Codes call (316) 662-1295, or your local postmaster.	
Hutchinson Mall (Part of Hutchinson)	67501
Idana	67432
Imes	66079
Independence	67301
Indian Creek (Part of Overland Park)	66207
Indian Ridge	66512
Indian Springs Shopping Center (Part of Kansas City)	66102
Indian Valley	66608
Indian Village	67337
Industry	67410
Ingalls	67853
Inman	67546
Iola	66749
Ionia	66949
Iowa Indian Reservation	66094
Iowa Point	66035
Isabel	67065
Iuka	67066
Jacobs Creek Landing	66854
Jamestown	66948
Jarbalo	66048
Jayhawk (Part of Lawrence)	66046
Jefferson	67301
Jennings	67643
Jetmore	67854
Jewell	66949
Johnson	67855
Junction City	66441

* Area Zip Code   † Post Office Boxes

	ZIP
Juniata	67423
Kackley	66948
Kalloch	67337
Kalvesta	67856
Kanona	67749
Kanopolis	67454
Kanorado	67741
Kansas City	66101-19

For specific Kansas City Zip Codes call (913) 573-2600, or your local postmaster.

COLLEGES & UNIVERSITIES

University of Kansas Medical Center	66103

FINANCIAL INSTITUTIONS

Brotherhood Bank and Trust	66101
Citizens Bank & Trust of Kansas City	66103
Home State Bank of Kansas City, Kansas	66101
Inter-State Federal Savings and Loan Association of Kansas City	66101
Security Bank of Kansas City	66101

HOSPITALS

Bethany Medical Center	66102
Providence Medical Center	66112
University of Kansas Hospital	66160

HOTELS/MOTELS

Best Western Flamingo Motel	66102
Best Western Inn	66103
Kansas State Penitentiary	66043
Kansas State University of Agriculture and Applied	66506
Keats	66502
Kechi	67067
Keene	66423
Kellogg	67156
Kelly	66538
Kendall	67857
Kennekuk	66439
Kenneth	66223
Kensington	66951
Kickapoo	66048
Kickapoo Indian Reservation	66439
Kimball	66733
Kimeo	66943
Kincaid	66039
Kingman	67068
Kingsdown	67858
Kinsley	67547
Kiowa	67070
Kipp	67401
Kirkwood	66762
Kiro	66539
Kirwin	67644
Kismet	67859
Labette	67356
La Crosse	67548
La Cygne	66040
Lafontaine	66736
La Harpe	66751
Lake Chaparral	66056
Lake City	67071
Lake Kahola	66846
Lake of the Forest (Part of Bonner Springs)	66012
Lake Quivira	66106
Lake Shore (Ellsworth County)	67454
Lake Shore (Jefferson County)	66070
Lakeshore (Shawnee County)	66605
Lakeside Acres Addition	67208
Lakeside Village	66070
Lakeview Heights	67230
Lake Wabaunsee	66401
Lakewood Hills	66070
Lakin	67860
Lamont	66855
Lancaster	66041
Lane	66042
Langdon	67583
Langley	67464
Lanham	68415
Lansing	66043
Larkinburg	66436
Larned	67550
Larned State Hospital	67550
Latham	67072
Latimer	67449
Lawrence	66044-47

	ZIP
	66049

For specific Lawrence Zip Codes call (913) 843-1681, or your local postmaster.

Lawton	66781
Leavenworth	66048
Leawood	66206
	66211

For specific Leawood Zip Codes call (913) 648-1163, or your local postmaster.

Lebanon	66952
Lebo	66856
Lecompton	66050
Lehigh	67073
Le Loup	66091
Lenape	66052
Lenexa	66210
	66214-15
	66219-20
	66227

For specific Lenexa Zip Codes call (913) 888-5234, or your local postmaster.

Lenexa Plaza (Part of Lenexa)	66215
Lenora	67645
Leon	67074
Leona	66532
Leonardville	66449
Leoti	67861
Leoville	67757
Le Roy	66857
Levant	67743
Lewis	67552
Liberal	67901-05

For specific Liberal Zip Codes call (316) 624-4031, or your local postmaster.

Liberty	67351
Liebenthal	67553
Lillis	66544
Lincoln	67455
Lincolnville	66858
Lindsborg	67456
Linn	66953
Linn Valley Lakes	66040
Linwood	66052
Little River	67457
Logan	67646
Lone Elm	66039
Lone Star	66046
Longford	67458
Long Island	67647
Longton	67352
Loretta	67520
Lorraine	67459
Lost Springs	66859
Louisburg	66053
Louisville	66450
Lovewell	66942
Lowell	66713
Lowemont	66020
Lucas	67648
Ludell	67744
Luray	67649
Lydia	67861
Lyndon	66451
Lyons	67554
McConnell Air Force Base	67221
McCracken	67556
McCune	66753
McDonald	67745
McFarland	66501
Mackie	66725
Macksville	67557
McLouth	66054
McPherson	67460
Madison	66860
Mahaska	66955
Maize	67101
Manchester	67463
Manhattan	66502
Mankato	66956
Manning	67871
Manter	67862
Maple City	67102
Maple Hill	66507
Mapleton	66754
Marienthal	67863
Marietta	66518
Marion	66861
Marion County Lake	66861
Marmaton	66701
Marquette	67464
Marysville	66508
Matfield Green	66862
Mayetta	66509
Mayfield	67103
Meade	67864
Mecca Acres	67230
Medicine Lodge	67104

	ZIP
Medina	66073
Medora	67502
Melrose	67336
Melvern	66510
Menlo	67753
Mentor	67465
Mercier	66439
Meriden	66512
Merriam	66202
Metcalf South Shopping Center (Part of Overland Park)	66212
Michigan	66528
Midland (Part of Wichita)	67216
Midland Park	67216
Midway (Kingman County)	67111
Midway (Rawlins County)	67739
Milan	67105
Milberger	67665
Mildred	66039
Milford	66514
Millbrook (Part of Wichita)	67212
Miller	66868
Milton	67106
Miltonvale	67466
Mingo	67701
Minneapolis	67467
Minneola	67865
Mission	66201†
	66205*
Mission Hills	66205
Mission Shopping Center (Part of Mission)	66222
Mission Woods	66205
Mitchell	67554
Modoc	67863
Moline	67353
Monmouth	66753
Monrovia	66023
Montana	67356
Montara	66619
Montezuma	67867
Monticello (Part of Shawnee)	66218
Mont Ida	66091
Montrose	66956
Monument	67747
Moran	66755
Moray	66087
Morehead	66776
Morganville	67468
Morland	67650
Morrill	66515
Morrowville	66958
Morse	66061
Moscow	67952
Mound City	66056
Moundridge	67107
Mound Valley	67354
Mount Hope	67108
Mount Vernon	67025
Mulberry	66756
Mullinville	67109
Mulvane	67110
Muncie (Part of Kansas City)	66111
Munden	66959
Munger (Part of Wichita)	67208
Munjor	67601
Murdock	67111
Muscotah	66058
Narka	66960
Nashville	67112
Natoma	67651
Navarre	67469
Neal	66863
Nekoma	67559
Neodesha	66757
Neosho Falls	66758
Neosho Rapids	66864
Ness City	67560
Netawaka	66516
Neuchatel	66521
Neutral	66725
New Albany	66759
New Almelo	67652
Newbury	66526
New Cambria	67470
New Lancaster	66040
Newman	66073
New Salem	67156
Newton	67114
Nickerson	67561
Nicodemus	67625
Niles	67480
Niotaze	67355
Norcatur	67653
Normandie Shopping Center (Part of Wichita)	67206
Northbranch	66936
Northern Hills	66608
North Newton	67117

* **Area Zip Code**   † **Post Office Boxes**

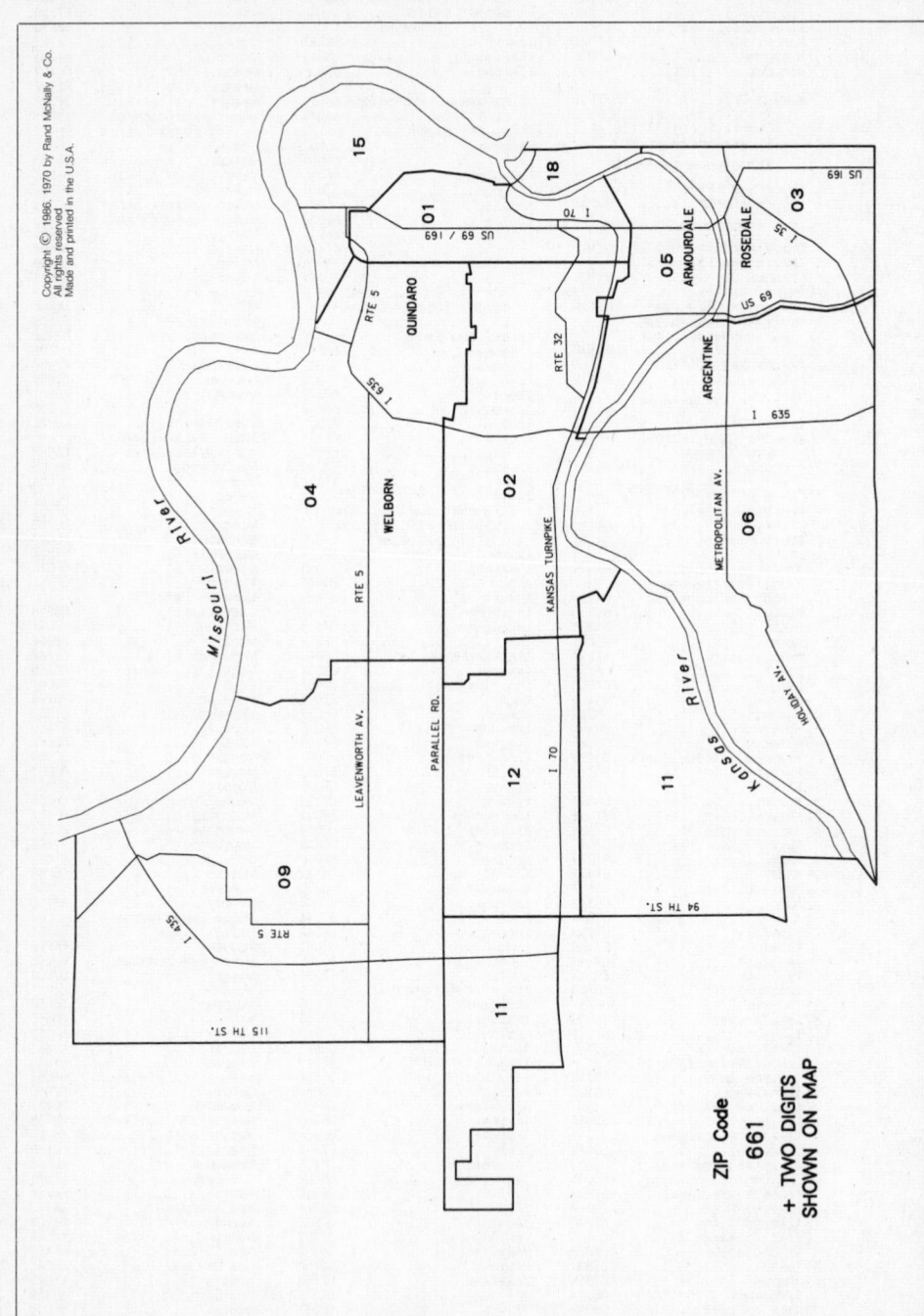

ZIP Code
661
+ TWO DIGITS
SHOWN ON MAP

	ZIP
North Osage City (Part of Osage City)	66523
North Topeka (Part of Topeka)	66608
North Wichita (Part of Wichita)	67204
Norton	67654
Nortonville	66060
Norway	66961
Norwich	67118
Oakhill	67472
Oakland (Part of Topeka)	66616
Oaklawn	67216
Oaklawn-Sunview	67216
Oakley	67748
Oak Park Mall (Part of Overland Park)	66214
Oak Valley	67352
Oberlin	67749
Ocheltree	66083
Odin	67562
Offerle	67563
Ogallah	67656
Ogden	66517
Oketo	66518
Olathe	66051
	66061-63
For specific Olathe Zip Codes call (913) 764-0375, or your local postmaster.	
Olathe East	66062-63
For specific Olathe East Zip Codes call (913) 782-3410, or your local postmaster.	
Olivet	66856
Olmitz	67564
Olpe	66865
Olsburg	66520
Onaga	66521
Oneida	66522
Opolis	66760
Orchard Park (Part of Parsons)	67357
Osage City	66523
Osawatomie	66064
Osborne	67473
Oskaloosa	66066
Ost	67108
Oswego	67356
Otego	66936
Otis	67565
Ottawa	66067
Ottumwa	66839
Overbrook	66524
Overland Park	66204
	66207
	66212-13
For specific Overland Park Zip Codes call (913) 831-5302, or your local postmaster.	
Oxford	67119
Ozawkie	66070
Packers (Part of Kansas City)	66105
Padonia	66434
Page City	67764
Palco	67657
Palmer	66962
Paola	66071
Paradise	67658
Park	67751
Park City	67219
Park East	67208
Parker	66072
Parkerville	66846
Parklane Shopping Center (Part of Wichita)	67218
Parsons	67357
Partridge	67566
Patterson	67020
Pauline (Part of Topeka)	66619
Pawnee Plaza Mall (Part of Wichita)	67211
Pawnee Rock	67567
Paxico	66526
Peabody	66866
Pearl	67431
Peck	67120
Peck Addition	66605
Penalosa	67035
Pence	67871
Pen Dennis	67874
Penokee	67659
Peoria	66067
Perry	66073
Perth	67152
Peru	67360
Petrolia	66720
Pfeifer	67660
Phillipsburg	67661
Pickrell Corner	67010
Piedmont	67122

	ZIP
Pierceville	67868
Pilsen	66861
Piper	66109
Piqua	66761
Pittsburg	66762-63
For specific Pittsburg Zip Codes call (316) 231-1500, or your local postmaster.	
Plains	67869
Plainville	67663
Pleasant Grove	66046
Pleasanton	66075
Plevna	67568
Plymell	67846
Plymouth	66801
Polk	66743
Pomona	66076
Portis	67474
Portland	67140
Potawatomi Indian Reservation	66439
Potter	66077
Potwin	67123
Powhattan	66527
Prairie View	67664
Prairie Village	66208
Prairie Village Shopping Center (Part of Prairie Village)	66208
Pratt	67124
Prescott	66767
Preston	67569
Pretty Prairie	67570
Princeton	66078
Prospect	67042
Prospect Park	67215
Protection	67127
Purcell	66041
Quenemo	66528
Quincy	66870
Quinter	67752
Radium	67550
Radley	66762
Rago	67128
Ramona	67475
Ranch Mart Shopping Center (Part of Leawood)	66206
Randall	66963
Randolph	66554
Ransom	67572
Rantoul	66079
Raymond	67573
Reading	66868
Reager	67654
Redel	66085
Redfield	66769
Redwing	67544
Reece	67045
Reno	66086
Republic	66964
Reserve	66434
Rexford	67753
Rice	66901
Richfield	67953
Richland	66409
Richmond	66080
Richter	66067
Riley	66531
Ringer (Part of Wichita)	67212
Ringo	66743
Riverdale	67152
Riverside (Part of Wichita)	67203
Riverton	66770
Riverview	67204
Robert L. Roberts (Part of Kansas City)	66104
Robinson	66532
Rock	67131
Rock Creek	66512
Rocky Ford	66502
Roeland Park	66203
Rolla	67954
Rolling Hills (Part of Wichita)	67212
Rome	67152
Roper	66714
Rosalia	67132
Rose	66783
Rosedale (Part of Kansas City)	66103
Rose Hill	67133
Roseland	66963
Rosewood (Part of Parsons)	67357
Rossville	66533
Roxbury	67476
Rozel	67574
Ruleton	67735
Rush Center	67575
Russell	67665
Russell Springs	67755
Sabetha	66534
Sac and Fox Indian Reservation	66434

	ZIP
Saffordville	66801
St. Benedict	66538
St. Francis	67756
St. George	66535
St. John	67576
St. Joseph	66938
St. Leo	67112
St. Mark	67030
St. Marys (Pottawatomie County)	66536
Saint Marys (Sedgwick County)	67050
St. Mary's College (Part of Leavenworth)	66048
St. Pats	66002
St. Paul	66771
St. Peter	67650
St. Theresa	67861
Salina	67401*
	67402†
Sand Spring	67410
Sanford	67550
Sarcoxie	66052
Satanta	67870
Saunders	67862
Savonburg	66772
Sawyer	67134
Saxman	67579
Scammon	66773
Scandia	66966
Schoenchen	67667
Schulte	67215
Scipio	66032
Scott City	67871
Scottsville	67420
Scranton	66537
Sedan	67361
Sedgwick	67135
Seguin	67740
Selden	67757
Selkirk	67861
Selma	66039
Seneca	66538
Severance	66087
Severy	67137
Seward	67577
Shady Bend	67455
Shady Brook	67449
Shallow Water	67871
Sharon	67138
Sharon Springs	67758
Sharpe	66871
Shaw	66733
Shawnee	66203
	66216-18
	66226
For specific Shawnee Zip Codes call (913) 831-5302, or your local postmaster.	
Shawnee Mission	66201-85
For specific Shawnee Mission Zip Codes call (913) 831-5302, or your local postmaster.	
Sherman	67356
Sherwin	66725
Sherwood Estates	66604
Shields	67874
Silverdale	67005
Silver Lake	66539
Simpson	67478
Sitka	67831
Skiddy	66872
Skidmore	66773
Smith Center	66967
Smolan	67479
Soldier	66540
Solomon	67480
Somerset	66071
South Dodge (Part of Dodge City)	67801
Southeast (Part of Wichita)	67218
Southgate Shopping Center (Part of Liberal)	67901
South Haven	67140
South Hoisington	67544
South Hutchinson	67505
South Mound	67357
South Radley	66762
South Seneca Gardens (Part of Wichita)	67217
Sparks	66035
Spearville	67876
Speed	67661
Spivey	67142
Springdale (Leavenworth County)	66020
Springdale (Sedgwick County)	67230
Spring Grove (Part of Galena)	66739
Spring Hill	66083
Stafford	67578

* Area Zip Code   † Post Office Boxes

	ZIP
Stanley	66221
	66223-24
For specific Stanley Zip Codes call (913) 897-2432, or your local postmaster.	
Stanton	66064
Stark	66775
State House (Part of Topeka)	66603
Sterling	67579
Stilwell	66085
Stippville	66725
Stockton	67669
Stony Point (Part of Kansas City)	66111
Strauss	66753
Strawn	66839
Strong City	66869
Studley	67759
Stull	66050
Stuttgart	67670
Sublette	67877
Suburban Heights (Part of Independence)	67301
Sugar Valley	66056
Summerfield	66541
Sun City	67143
Sunnydale	67147
Sunset Park (Part of Haysville)	67060
Suppesville	67106
Susank	67544
Sweetbriar Shopping Center (Part of Wichita)	67204
Sycamore	67363
Sylvan Grove	67481
Sylvia	67581
Syracuse	67878
Talmage	67482
Talmo	66935
Tampa	67483
Tanglewood Lake	66040
Tasco	67740
Tecumseh	66542
Terra Heights (Part of Topeka)	66609
Tescott	67484
Thayer	66776
The Dell (Part of Wichita)	67209
Thompsonville	66073
Timken	67582
Tipton	67485
Tonganoxie	66086
Topeka	66601-99
For specific Topeka Zip Codes call (913) 295-9100, or your local postmaster.	
Toronto	66777
Towanda	67144
Tower Grove (Part of Overland Park)	66204
Towne East Square (Part of Wichita)	67207
Towne West Square (Part of Wichita)	67209
Trading Post	66075
Traer	67749
Travel Air	67206
Treece	66778
Trego Center	67672
Tribune	67879
Trousdale	67059
Troy	66087
Turck	66725
Turkville	67663
Turner (Part of Kansas City)	66106
Turon	67583
Twin Lakes Shopping Center (Part of Wichita)	67203
Tyro	67364

	ZIP
Udall	67146
Ulysses	67880
Union Stock Yards (Part of Wichita)	67219
Uniontown	66779
University (Crawford County)	66762
University (Douglas County)	66044
Urbana	66720
Utica	67584
V.A. Hospital (Part of Topeka)	66622
Valeda	67337
Valencia	66604
Valley Center	67147
Valley Falls	66088
Varner	67068
Vassar	66543
Venango	67464
Verdi	67480
Vermillion	66544
Vernon	66783
Vesper	67455
Veterans Affairs Hospital (Part of Topeka)	66622
Victoria	67671
Vilas	66720
Village Square, The (Part of Dodge City)	67801
Vine Creek	67458
Vining	66937
Vinland	66006
Viola	67149
Virgil	66870
Vliets	66544
Voda	67631
Wabaunsee	66547
Waco	67120
Wagon Wheel Ranch	67010
Wagstaff	66071
Wakarusa	66546
WaKeeney	67672
Wakefield	67487
Waldo	67673
Waldron	67150
Walker	67674
Wallace	67761
Walnut	66780
Walton	67151
Wamego	66547
Washburn University (Part of Topeka)	66621
Washington	66968
Waterloo	67111
Waterville	66548
Wathena	66090
Watson	66542
Wauneta	67024
Waverly	66871
Wayne	66930
Wayside	67301
Wea	66013
Webber	66970
Webster	67669
Wego-Waco	67216
Weir	66781
Welborn (Part of Kansas City)	66104
Welda	66091
Wellington	67152
Wells	67488
Wellsford	67059
Wellsville	66092
Weskan	67762
Wesleyan (Part of Salina)	67401
Westboro (Part of Topeka)	66604
West Coffeyville	67337
Westfall	67455
Westlink Shopping Center (Part of Wichita)	67212

	ZIP
Westlink Village (Part of Wichita)	67212
West Mineral	66782
Westmoreland	66549
Westphalia	66093
Westport (Part of Wichita)	67217
West Ridge Mall (Part of Topeka)	66604
West Shore	66512
Westway Shopping Center (Part of Wichita)	67217
Westwood	66205
Westwood Hills	66205
Wetmore	66550
Wheaton	66551
Wheatridge Addition (Part of Wichita)	67212
Wheeler	67756
White Church (Part of Kansas City)	66109
White City	66872
White Cloud	66094
White Lakes Shopping Center (Part of Topeka)	66611
Whitewater	67154
Whiting	66552
Wichita	67201-20
	67223-78
For specific Wichita Zip Codes call (316) 946-4511, or your local postmaster.	
Wichita State University (Part of Wichita)	67208
Wilburton	67950
Wilder Junction	66018
Willard	66604
Williamsburg	66095
Williamstown	66073
Willis	66435
Willowbrook	67501
Willowdale	67142
Wilmore	67155
Wilmot	67131
Wilroads Gardens	67801
Wilsey	66873
Wilson	67490
Winchester	66097
Windom	67491
Windsor Park	67207
Windthorst	67876
Winfield	67156
Winfield State Hospital and Training Center	67156
Winifred	66427
Winona	67764
Winway (Part of Parsons)	67357
Wolcott (Part of Kansas City)	66109
Womer	66952
Wonsevu	66840
Woodbine	67492
Woodruff	67661
Woods	67951
Woodston	67675
Worden	66006
Wright	67882
Wyandotte West (Part of Kansas City)	66112
Xenia	66716
Yaggy	67501
Yale	66762
Yates Center	66783
Yocemento	67601
Yoder	67585
Zarah (Part of Shawnee)	66218
Zeandale	66502
Zenda	67159
Zenith	67578
Zook	67550
Zurich	67676

	ZIP		ZIP		ZIP
Aaron	42601	Arnold Ridge Estates (Part of Frankfort)	40601	Barterville	40311
Abbott	40006	Arrington Corner	42348	Barthell	42647
Abegall	41044	Artemus	40903	Barwick	41306
Aberdeen	42201	Arthurmable	41430	Bascom	41171
Absher	42728	Artville	40387	Bashford Manor Mall (Part of West Buechel)	40218
Access	41164	Arvel	40447	Baskett	42402
Acorn	42510	Ary	41712	Bass	42733
Acorn Village (Part of Henderson)	42420	Ashbyburg	42456	Bath	41836
Acton	42718	Ashcamp	41512	Battle	40040
Acup	41751	Asher	40803	Battle Run	41039
Adaburg	42347	Ashers Fork	40962	Battletown	40104
Adair	42348	Ashland	41101-05	Baughman	40906
Adairville	42202	For specific Ashland Zip Codes call (606) 327-2121, or your local postmaster.		Baughman Heights (Part of Danville)	40422
Adams	41230			Baxter (Harlan County)	40806
Adamson	41517			Baxter (Jefferson County)	40204
Add	41224	Ashland Park (Part of Lexington)	40502	Bayfork	42122
Addison	40143			Bayou	42081
Adeline	41129	Ashland Town Center (Part of Ashland)	41101	Bays	41310
Aden	41142			Bays Branch	41216
Adolphus	42120	Ashlock	42768	Bealers Knob	42371
Aetnaville	42368	Ashville	40291	Beals	42451
Aflex	41514	Askin	42343	Bear Branch	41714
Ages	40801	Atchison	42718	Beartown	41164
Ages-Brookside	40801	Athens (Part of Lexington)	40509	Bearville	41740
Air Mail Facility-Standiford Field (Amf-Sdf) (Part of Louisville)	40221		40515	Bear Wallow	42127
		For specific Athens Zip Codes call (606) 231-6700, or your local postmaster.		Beattyville	41311
Airport Gardens	41701			Beaumont	42124
Airview Estates	42701	Athertonville	42748	Beaumont Park (Part of Lexington)	40504
Akersville	42133	Athol	41307	Beauty	41203
Albany	42602	Atkinstown	40434	Beaver	41604
Alberta	40370	Atoka	40422	Beaver Bottom	41522
Alcalde	42501	Atwood	41063	Beaver Dam	42320
Alcorn	40447	Auburn	42206	Beaverlick	41094
Alexandria	41001	Audobon Acres (Part of Owensboro)	42301	Becknerville	40391
Algonquin Manor (Part of Louisville)	40211	Audubon Park	40213	Beckton	42141
Alhambra	41055	Augusta	41002	Beda	42347
Aliceton	40328	Ault	41164	Bedford	40006
Allais (Part of Hazard)	41701	Aurora	42048	Beech	41306
Allegre	42203	Austerlitz	40361	Beech Bottom	42539
Allen	41601	Austin	42123	Beechburg	41093
Allendale	42782	Auxier	41602	Beech Creek	42321
Allen Springs	42122	Avawam	41713	Beech Grove (Bullitt County)	40150
Allensville	42204	Avoca	42223		
Allock	41710	Avon (Part of Lexington)	40516	Beech Grove (Carter County)	41143
Almo	42020	Avondale (Part of Paducah)	42001		
Almo Heights	42020	Axtel	40143	Beech Grove (McLean County)	42322
Alonzo	42120	Azalea Hills	42420		
Alpha	42603	Bachelors Rest	41040	Beechland	42256
Alphoretta	41619	Backusburg	42054	Beechmont (Jefferson County)	40214
Alpine	42519	Bagdad	40003		
Alton	40342	Bailey Creek	40828	Beechmont (Muhlenberg County)	42323
Alton Station	40342	Baileys Switch	40906	Beechville	42129
Altro	41306	Bainbridge	42215	Beechwood	40359
Alumbaugh	40336	Baizetown	42349	Beechwood Village	40207
Alum Springs	40440	Baker Branch	41263	Beechy	41175
Alva	40863	Bakerton	42711	Beefhide	41537
Alvaton	42122	Bald Hill	41041	Beelerton	42041
Amandaville	42711	Baldrock	40741	Bee Lick	40419
Amba	41635	Baldwin	40475	Bee Spring	42207
Amburgey	41801	Ballard	40342	Beetle	41143
Ammie	40962	Ballardsville	40014	Bel-Air (Part of Winchester)	40391
Ammons	40170	Balltown (Nelson County)	40051	Belcher	41513
Amos	42153	Balltown (Whitley County)	40769	Belcourt	42456
Anchorage	40223	Balmoral (Part of Henderson)	42420	Belcraft	41858
	40245			Belfry	41514
For specific Anchorage Zip Codes call (502) 245-5791, or your local postmaster.		Baltimore	42066	Belknap	41342
		Bancroft (Jefferson County)	40222	Belknap Beach	40059
		Bancroft (Muhlenberg County)	42345	Bell City (Elliott County)	41171
Anco	41759	Bandana	42022	Bell City (Graves County)	42040
Andyville	40157	Bandy	42567	Bell County Forestry Camp	40977
Anna	42270	Bank Lick	41094	Bellefonte	41101
Anneta	42754	Banner	41603	Bellemeade	40222
Annville	40402	Baptist	41301	Bellepoint (Part of Frankfort)	40601
Ano	42510	Barbourmeade	40222	Belleview	41005
Ansel	42553	Barbourville	40906	Bellevue	41073
Anthoston	42420	Barcreek	40972	Bellewood	40207
Antioch	41003	Bardo	40831	Bell Farm	42647
Antioch Shores	42519	Bardstown	40004	Bells Run	42378
Anton	42431	Bardstown Junction	40165	Belltown	40033
Apex	42464	Bardwell	42023	Bellview (Part of Frankfort)	40601
Aqua Shores	40065	Barefoot	40311	Belmont (Bullitt County)	40150
Arat	42717	Bark Camp	40701	Belmont (Harrison County)	41031
Arch	42724	Barlow	42024	Belton	42324
Argillite	41121	Barnesburg	42501	Ben Bow	41230
Argo	41568	Barnetts Creek	41256	Bengal	42718
Argyle	42516	Barnrock	41219	Benham	40807
Arista	42718	Barnsley	42431	Benito	40849
Arjay	40902	Barnyard	40935	Bennettstown	42236
Arkansas	41649	Barrallton	40165	Benson	40601
Arkansas Creek	41649	Barren River	42101	Bent	42501
Arkle	40734	Barrier	42633	Benton	42025
Arlington (Carlisle County)	42021	Barr Street (Part of Lexington)	40501	Bentwoods	40601
Arlington (Madison County)	40475		40507	Berea	40403
Arlington Heights (Part of Frankfort)	40601		40584-96	Berea College (Part of Berea)	40404
Armstrong Hill	41164	For specific Barr Street Zip Codes call (606) 231-6747, or your local postmaster.		Berkley	42021
Arnett	41314			Berlin	41043
Arnold	42349			Bernice	40932

* Area Zip Code   † Post Office Boxes

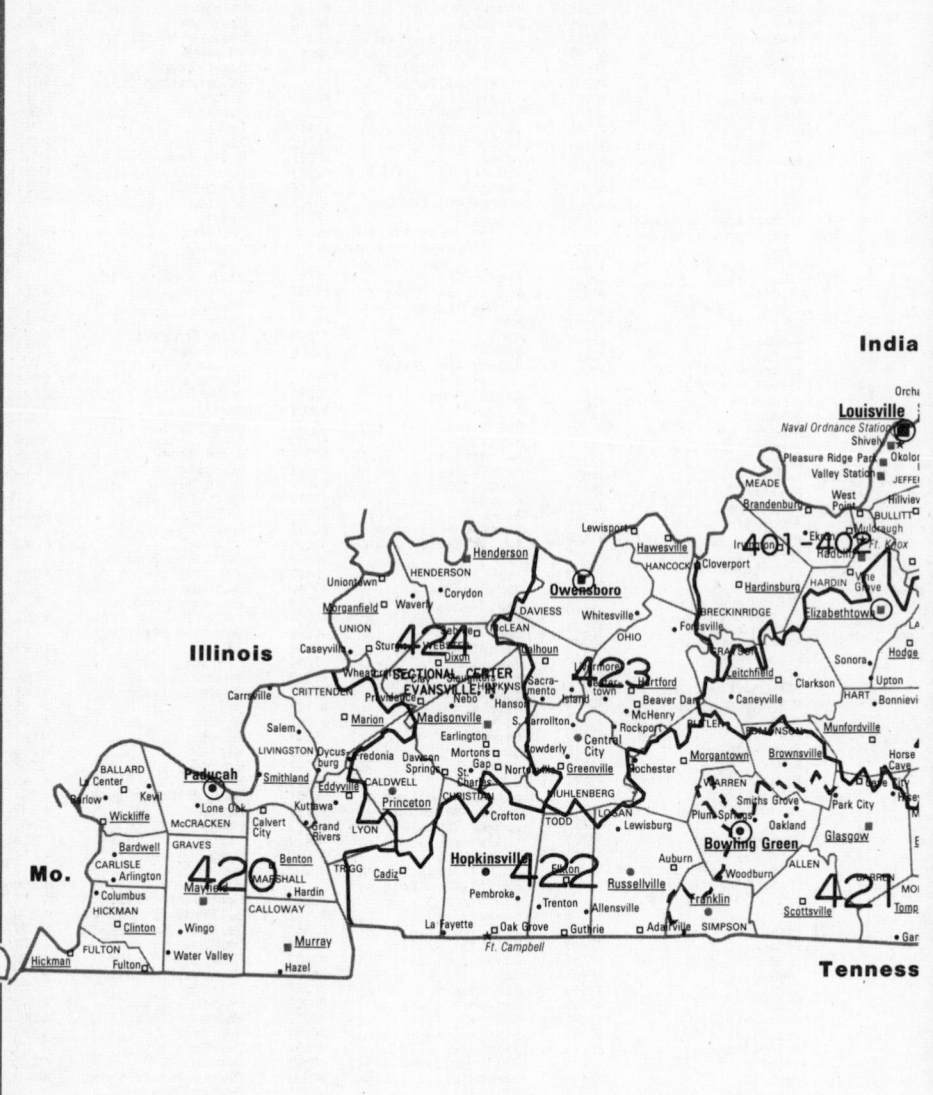

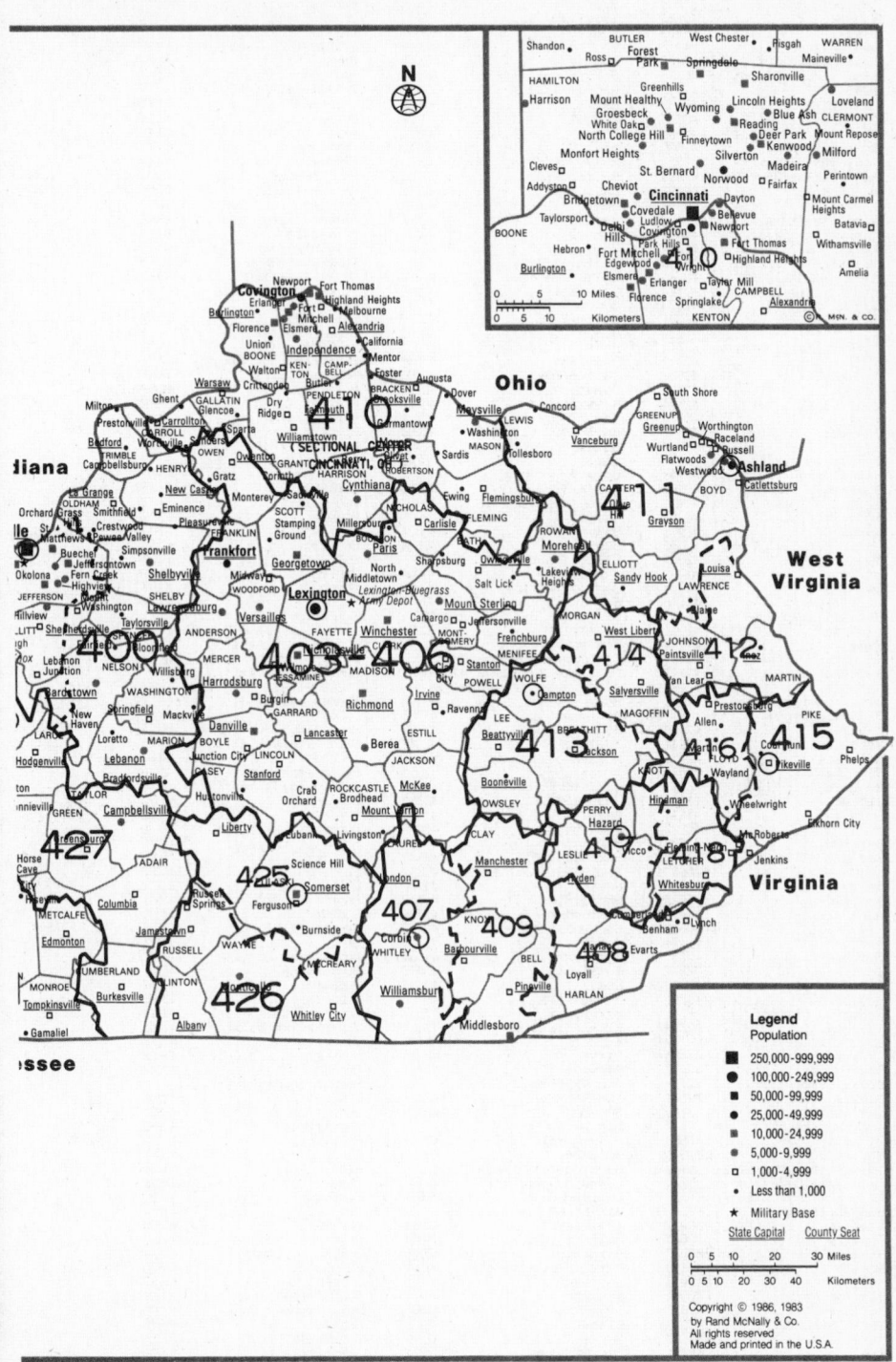

	ZIP
Bernstadt	40741
Berry	41003
Berrytown	40223
Bethanna	41465
Bethany	41313
Bethel (Bath County)	40306
Bethel (Jessamine County)	40356
Bethelridge	42516
Bethesda	42633
Bethlehem	40007
Betsey	42633
Betsy Layne	41605
Beulah (Hickman County)	42039
Beulah (Hopkins County)	42408
Beulah Heights	42607
Beverly	40913
Beverly Hills (Part of Danville)	40422
Bevier	42337
Bevinsville	41606
Bewleyville	40146
Biddle	40324
Big Bear Creek	42025
Big Bone	41091
Big Branch	41522
Big Clifty	42712
Big Creek	40914
Big Eddy	40601
Big Fork	41777
Biggs	41524
Bighill	40405
Big Laurel	40808
Big Rock	41777
Big Sandy Junction (Part of Catlettsburg)	41129
Big Spring	40106
Bigstone	41171
Big Woods	40387
Bimble	40915
Birdie	40342
Birdsville	42081
Birk City	42301
Birmingham	42044
Black Bottom	40828
Blackburn Correctional Complex	40511
Blackey	41804
Blackford	42403
Black Gnat	42718
Black Gold	42285
Blackjack (Simpson County)	42134
Black Jack (Simpson County)	42134
Black Mountain	40847
Black Rock	42754
Black Snake	40845
Blackwater	40741
Bladeston	41004
Blaine	41124
Blair	40823
Blairs Mills	41472
Blair Town	41501
Blanche	40902
Blanchet	41010
Blandville	42026
Blaze	41472
Bledsoe	40810
Blevins	41124
Blincoe	40037
Blood	42071
Bloomfield	40008
Bloomingdale	40391
Bloomington (Grayson County)	42754
Bloomington (Magoffin County)	41465
Bloss	40456
Blowing Spring	42743
Bluebank	41041
Blue Diamond	41719
Blue Grass (Part of Lexington)	40503
	40523-24
For specific Blue Grass Zip Codes call (606) 231-6740, or your local postmaster.	
Bluegrass Estates (Part of Danville)	40422
Blue Heron	42647
Bluehole	40962
Blue John	42519
Blue Level	42274
Blue Lick Springs	40311
Blue Moon	41655
Blue Ridge Manor	40223
Blue River	41607
Blue Spring	42211
Bluestone	40351
Blue Water Estates	42211
Bluff Boom	42743
Bluff City	42420
Board Tree	41528

	ZIP
Boatwright	42071
Boaz	42027
Bobs Creek	40815
Bobs Fork	41714
Bobtown	40403
Bohon	40330
Boiling Spring	42101
Boldman	41501
Boles	42167
Boltsfork	41168
Bolyn	41630
Bon	40769
Bon Air Hills	40601
Bonanza	41653
Bon Ayr	42160
Bond	40407
Bondurant	42050
Bondville	40372
Boneyville	40484
Bon Haven (Part of Winchester)	40391
Bonnie Brae	40065
Bonnieville	42713
Bonnyman	41719
Booker	40069
Boone	40403
Boone Aire	41042
Boone Heights	40906
Boonesboro	40475
Boonesborough	40475
Booneville	41314
Boons Camp	41204
Bordley	42404
Boreing	40740
Borowick Farms	40031
Boston (Butler County)	42268
Boston (Nelson County)	40107
Boston (Pendleton County)	41006
Botland	40004
Botto	40944
Bourbon Downs (Part of Bardstown)	40004
Bourbon Furnace	40360
Bourne	40444
Bow	42714
Bowen	40309
Bowling Green	42101-04
For specific Bowling Green Zip Codes call (502) 782-4202, or your local postmaster.	
Boyce	42122
Boyd	41003
Boyds Crossing	42782
Boydsville	42079
Boydtown	40324
Bracht	41030
Bracktown (Part of Lexington)	40510
Bradford	41043
Bradfordsville	40009
Bradley	41465
Bradshaw	40434
Brady (Part of Morehead)	40351
Brainard	41465
Bramlett	42743
Brandenburg	40108
Brandenburg Station	40108
Brandy	40351
Brandykeg	41653
Brassfield	40385
Braxton	40330
Breadens Creek	40927
Breckinridge	41031
Breckinridge Center	42437
Breeding	42715
Bremen	42325
Brentsville	40361
Brentwood (Part of Madisonville)	42431
Brewers	42025
Briartown (Part of Springfield)	40069
Briarwood	40222
Briarwood Manor (Part of Bowling Green)	42103
Bridgeport	40601
Bridge Street (Part of Paducah)	42003
Bridgeville	41004
Briensburg	42025
Brighton (Part of Lexington)	40505
Brightshade	40962
Brinegar	41164
Brinkley	41805
Bristow	42101
Britmart	42220
Broadbent Subdivision	42211
Broad Bottom	41501
Broad Fields	40207
Broad Ford	42726
Broadview Manor	40601
Broadway	42207

	ZIP
Broadwell	41031
Brodhead	40409
Broeck Pointe	40201
Bromley (Kenton County)	41016
Bromley (Owen County)	41086
Bromo	40456
Bronston	42518
Brookhaven (Part of Lexington)	40503
Brooklyn	42209
Brooks	40109
Brookside	40801
Brooksville	41004
Broughtentown	40419
Browder	42326
Browning	42274
Browning Corner	41040
Brownsboro	40014
Brownsboro Farm	40222
Brownsboro Village	40207
Browns Crossroads	42602
Browns Fork	41720
Browns Grove	42071
Browns Valley	42376
Brownsville (Edmonson County)	42210
Brownsville (Fulton County)	42050
Brownwood Manor	42303
Bruin	41125
Brushart	41144
Brush Grove	40040
Brutus	40972
Bryan	42629
Bryants Store	40921
Bryantsville	40410
Buchanan	41129
Buckettown	40475
Buckeye	40444
Buck Grove	40117
Buckhorn	41721
Buckingham	41636
Buckner	40010
Buechel	40218
	40228
For specific Buechel Zip Codes call (502) 454-1881, or your local postmaster.	
Buel	42327
Buena Vista (Garrard County)	40444
Buena Vista (Harrison County)	41031
Buena Vista (Lewis County)	41179
Buena Vista (Marshall County)	42044
Buffalo (Larue County)	42716
Buffalo (Trigg County)	42211
Buford	42376
Bug	42602
Bugtussle	42140
Bulan	41722
Bull Creek	41653
Bullittsville	41005
Burdick	42718
Burdine (Part of Jenkins)	41517
Burfield	42633
Burgin	40310
Burke	41171
Burkes Spring	40037
Burkesville	42717
Burkhart	41342
Burk Hollow	40769
Burkshire Terrace	40214
Burlington (Boone County)	41005
Burna	42028
Burnaugh	41129
Burnetta	42544
Burning Fork (Magoffin County)	41465
Burning Fork (Pike County)	41501
Burning Springs	40962
Burnside	42519
Burnwell	41518
Burr	40456
Burton	41612
Burtonville	41189
Bush	40724
Bushtown	40330
Buskirk (Morgan County)	41406
Buskirk (Pike County)	41544
Busseyville	41230
Busy	41723
Butler (Franklin County)	40601
Butler (Pendleton County)	41006
Butterfly	41719
Buttimer Hill (Part of Frankfort)	40601
Buttonsberry	42350
Bybee	40385
Bypro	41612
Cabell	42633
Cabot	42343

* Area Zip Code   † Post Office Boxes

Name	ZIP
Caddo	41040
Cadentown (Part of Lexington)	40505
Cadiz	42211
Cains Store	42544
Cairo	42420
Caldwell Manor (Part of Danville)	40422
Caleast	40475
Caledonia	42211
Calf Creek	41224
Calhoun	42327
California	41007
Calla	40336
Callaway	40977
Calloway	40456
Calvary	40033
Calvert City	42029
Calvin	40813
Camargo	40353
Cambridge	40220
Cambridge Shores	42044
Campbellsburg	40011
Campbellsville	42718-19
For specific Campbellsville Zip Codes call (502) 465-4251, or your local postmaster.	
Camp Dick Robinson	40444
Camp Dix	41127
Camp Grounds	40701
Camp Kennedy	40444
Camp Nelson (Jessamine County)	40444
Camp Nelson (Jessamine County)	40356
Camp Pleasant	40601
Camp Springs	41059
Camp Taylor (Part of Louisville)	40213
Campton	41301
Canada	41519
Canby	41010
Cane Creek	40741
Cane Valley	42720
Caney	41472
Caneyville	42721
Canmer	42722
Cannel City	41408
Cannon	40923
Cannonsburg	41102*
	41105†
Canoe	41339
Canton	42212
Canton Heights Estates	42211
Canyon Falls	41311
Capital Estates	40601
Capito	40965
Carbondale	42408
Carbon Glow	41832
Carcassonne	41804
Cardinal Hill	40004
Cardinal Hills (Part of Frankfort)	40601
Cardinal Valley (Part of Lexington)	40503
Cardwell	40330
Carlisle	40311
Carntown	41006
Carpenter	40906
Carr Creek	41847
Carrie	41725
Carrollton	41008
Carrsville	42081
Carter	41128
Carthage	41007
Cartwright	42602
Carver	41409
Cary	40977
Casey Creek	42728
Caseyville	42459
Cash	42784
Casky	42240
Catalpa	41129
Catawba	41040
Cat Creek	40380
Catlettsburg	41129
Causey	41777
Cave City	42127
Cavehill	42274
Cave Ridge	42129
Cave Spring	42265
Cawood	40815
Cayce	42041
Cecil	42001
Cecilia	42724
Cedar Bluff	42445
Cedar Brook	41031
Cedar Flats	42129
Cedar Grove	42220
Cedar Hill Heights	42518
Cedar Knoll Galleria (Part of Ashland)	41101
Cedar Run Creek	40601
Cedar Spring	42160
Cedar Springs	42164
Cedarville	40456
Center	42214
Centerfield	40014
Center Point	42167
Center Ridge	42071
Centertown	42328
Centerview	40145
Centerville	40324
Central Avenue (Part of Paducah)	42001
Central City	42330
Ceralvo	42369
Cerulean	42215
Chad	40823
Chalybeate	42171
Chambers	42348
Chance	42728
Chandlers Chapel	42206
Chandlerville	41257
Chapel Hill	42120
Chaplin	40012
Chapman	41230
Chappell	40816
Charleston	42408
Charleswood	40229
Charley	41230
Charters	41179
Chatham	41002
Chavies	41727
Chenault	40170
Chenoa	40977
Chenowee	41339
Cherokee (Jefferson County)	40205
	40225
For specific Cherokee Zip Codes call (606) 638-4840, or your local postmaster.	
Cherokee (Lawrence County)	41180
Cherry	42071
Cherrywood Village	40207
Chesnutburg	40962
Chestnut Gap	41314
Chestnut Grove	40065
Chevrolet	40831
Chevy Chase (Part of Lexington)	40502
Chicken Bristle	40484
Chilesburg (Part of Lexington)	40509
Chloe	41501
Choateville	40601
Christianburg	40065
Christine	42728
Christopher	41701
Church Hill	42240
Cinda	41728
Cinderella Estates	40229
Cisco	41410
Cisselville	40069
Clabber Bottom	40324
Clare	42134
Clarence	42567
Clark	40023
Clark Hill	41164
Clarksburg	41179
Clarkson	42726
Clark Street (Part of Paducah)	42001
Claryville (Campbell County)	41001
Claxton	42408
Clay	42404
Clay City	40312
Clayhole	41317
Clay Lick	40337
Claymour	42220
Claypool	42103
Claysville	41031
Clay Village	40065
Clear Creek Springs	40977
Clearfield	40313
Cleaton	42332
Clementsville	42539
Clemons	41719
Cleopatra	42327
Clermont	40110
Cliff (Part of Prestonsburg)	41653
Clifford	41230
Clifton	40383
Clifty	42216
Climax	40456
Clinton	42031
Clintonville	40361
Clio	40769
Closplint	40927
Clover Bottom	40447
Cloverdale (Part of Frankfort)	40601
Clover-Darby	40927
Cloverport	40111
Clovertown	40831
Cloyds Landing	42752
Clutts	40823
Coakley	42743
Coalgood	40818
Coal Run	41501
Coalton	41168
Cobb	42445
Cobhill	40415
Coburg	42743
Codyville (Part of Hardinsburg)	40143
Cofer	42129
Colby Hills	40391
Coldiron	40819
Cold Spring	41076
Cold Spring-Highland Heights (Part of Highland Heights)	41076
Coldstream	40202
Coldwater	42071
Coleman	41553
Colemansville	41003
Colesburg	40150
Coletown (Part of Lexington)	40515
Colfax	41049
College (Part of Berea)	40403
College Farm	41501
College Heights (Part of Bowling Green)	42101
College Hill	40385
College Park (Part of Frankfort)	40601
Collins	41501
Collista	41222
Colmar	40965
Colonial Terrace	40222
Colony (Part of Frankfort)	40601
Colson	41858
Columbia	42728
Columbus	42032
Colville	41031
Combs	41729
Comer	42327
Concord (Fleming County)	41041
Concord (Lewis County)	41131
Concord (McCracken County)	42001
Concord (Pendleton County)	41040
Concordia	40157
Conder	41514
Confederate	42038
Confederate Estates	40056
Confluence	41730
Congleton (Lee County)	41311
Congleton (McLean County)	42327
Conley	41411
Connersville	41031
Conoloway	42726
Consolation	40003
Constance	41009
Constantine	40114
Conway	40417
Cooktown	42123
Coolbrook	40601
Cool Springs	42320
Cooper	42633
Co-Operative	42647
Cooperstown	42276
Coopersville	42611
Copebranch	41339
Copland	41369
Copperfield	40223
Coral Hill	42141
Coral Ridge	40118
Corbin	40701*
	40702†
Cordell	41124
Cordia	41701
Cordova	41010
Corey	41142
Corinth (Grant County)	41010
Corinth (Logan County)	42276
Cork	42129
Corn Creek	40006
Corners	40146
Cornette	40729
Cornettsville	41731
Cornishville	40330
Corydon	42406
Costelow	42276
Cote	40828
Cottageville	41179
Cottle	41472
Cottonburg	40475
Country Club Estates	40475
Country Club Heights (Franklin County)	40601

* Area Zip Code   † Post Office Boxes

	ZIP		ZIP		ZIP
Country Club Heights (Mason County)	41056	Dal	40769	Dixville	40330
Country Lane Estates	40601	Dalesburg (Breathitt County)	41314	Dizney	40825
Country Manor	40065	Dalesburg (Fleming County)	41041	Dobson	41228
Countryside	40059	Dalton	42445	Dock	41653
Country Village	40014	Dan (Menifee County)	40387	Doddy	42164
Counts Crossroads	41164	Dan (Ohio County)	42349	Doe Creek	40336
Covedale	41179	Dana	41615	Doe Valley Estates	40108
Covington	41011-18	Danby	42276	Dogtown	42025
For specific Covington Zip Codes call (606) 261-4425, or your local postmaster.		Daniel Boone	42442	Dog Walk (Lincoln County)	40409
		Daniels Creek	41265	Dogwalk (Ohio County)	42766
		Danleytown	41144	Dogwood	42051
Cowan	41039	Dant	40037	Donaldson	42211
Cow Creek (Estill County)	40472	Danville	40422*	Donansburg	42743
Cowcreek (Owsley County)	41314		40423†	Donerail (Part of Lexington)	40511
Cox Bend	42519	Darfork	41701	Dongola	41858
Coxs Creek	40013	Darkmont	40828	Dorton	41520
Coxton	40831	Davella	41214	Dorton Branch	40977
Crab Orchard	40419	David	41616	Do Stop	42721
Cracker	41649	Davis	40370	Dot	42202
Crailhope	42214	Davisburg	40977	Douglas	41560
Craintown	41041	Davis Cross Roads	42268	Douglass Hills	40243
Crane Nest	40906	Davison Station	42361	Dover	41034
Cranks	40820	Davisport	41262	Downtown (Part of Louisville)	40201
Cranston	40351	Davistown (Garrard County)	40444		40203
Crawford	41719	Davistown (Woodford County)	40347	For specific Downtown Zip Codes call (502) 587-8546, or your local postmaster.	
Crayne	42033	Dawson Springs	42408		
Craynor	41614	Day	41858		
Creal	42764	Dayhoit	40824	Downtown (Warren County)	42101
Creekmore	42649	Daylight	42408	Doylesville	40475
Creekside	40222	Daysboro	41332	Dozier Heights	42431
Creekville	40962	Daysville	42276	Draffenville	42025
Creelsboro	42629	Dayton	41074	Draffin	41521
Crenshaw	40071	Deane	41812	Drake	42128
Crescent Hill (Part of Louisville)	40206	Deatsville	40013	Drakesboro	42337
Crescent Park	41017	Debord	41214	Draper (Part of Evarts)	40828
Crescent Springs	41017	Decker	42721	Drennon Springs	40011
Cressmont	41311	DeCoursey (Part of Taylor Mill)	41015	Dressen (Part of Harlan)	40831
Crest	42701	Decoy	41339	Dreyfus	40426
Crestmoor (Part of Bowling Green)	42101	Dee Acres	42366	Drift	41619
Creston	42539	Deep Springs (Part of Lexington)	40505	Dripping Spring	42171
Crestview	41076			Drip Rock	40336
Crestview Hills	41017	Deepwood (Part of Hopkinsville)	42240	Dr. Martin Luther King Jr. (Part of Louisville)	40211*
Crestview Hills Mall (Part of Crestview Hills)	41017	Deer Lick	42256		40251†
Crestwood (Fayette County)	40503	Defeated Creek	41833	Druid Hills	40207
Crestwood (Franklin County)	40601	Defiance	41760	Drum	42501
		Defoe	40017	Dry Creek	41862
Crestwood (Oldham County)	40014	Defries	42722	Dry Fork (Barren County)	42155
Creswell	42411	Dehart	41472	Dry Fork (Pike County)	41561
Crider	42445	Dekoven	42459	Dryhill	41749
Crittenden	41030	Delafield (Part of Bowling Green)	42101	Dry Ridge	41035
Crix	40313			Dublin	42039
Croakes	40069	Delaplain	40324	Dubre	42731
Crockett	41413	Delaware	42373	Duckers	40347
Crocus	42728	Delia	41097	Duckrun	40769
Crofton	42217	Delmer	42544	Duco	41465
Croley	42031	Delphia	41735	Duff	42754
Cromona	41810	Delta	42633	Duganville	40330
Cromwell	42333	Delville	40011	Dukedom	42085
Cropper	40057	Delvinta	41311	Dukes	42348
Crossgate	40222	Dema	41859	Dulaney	42445
Cross Keys	40065	Democrat	41858	Duluth	40403
Crossland	42049	De Mossville	41033	Dunbar	42219
Crown	41811	Demplytown	40014	Duncan (Casey County)	40442
Crowtown (Part of Princeton)	42445	Denney	42633	Duncan (Mercer County)	40330
Crummies	40815	Dennis	42276	Dundee	42338
Crutchfield	42041	Denniston	40316	Dunham (Part of Jenkins)	41537
Crystal	40420	Denton	41132	Dunlap	41524
Crystal Lake	40031	Denver	41215	Dunleary	41522
Cuba	42066	Depoy	42345	Dunmor	42339
Cubage	40856	Derby Hills	40383	Dunnville	42528
Cub Run	42729	Dermont	42303	Dunraven	41754
Culver	41211	Desda	42601	Durbin	41129
Culvertown	40051	Devon	41042	Durbintown	41003
Cumberland	40823	Devondale (Part of Graymoor-Devondale)	40222	Duval	40324
Cumberland City	42602			Dwale	41621
Cumberland College (Part of Williamsburg)	40769	Dewdrop	41171	Dwarf	41739
		Dewitt	40930	Dycusburg	42037
Cumberlane Estates (Part of Campbellsville)	42718	Dexter	42036	Dyer	40115
		Dexterville	42261	Dykes	42501
Cumminsville	41004	Diablock	41701	Eadsville	42633
Cundiff	42728	Diamond	42404	Eagle Creek	41098
Cunningham	42035	Dice	41736	Eagle Hill	41046
Cupio	40177	Dietz Acres	40121	Eagle Station	41083
Curdsville (Daviess County)	42334	Dillon	40865	Earlington	42410
Curdsville (Mercer County)	40330	Dimple	42261	East Bernstadt	40729
Curt	41339	Dingus	41417	Easterday	41008
Custer	40115	Dione	40823	Eastern	41622
Cutshin	41732	Dishman Springs	40906	East Fork	42129
Cutuno	41465	Disputanta	40456	East Hickman	40356
Cuzick	40475	Dix Fork	41564	East Jenkins (Part of Jenkins)	41537
Cyclone	42166	Dixie (Henderson County)	42406	Eastland	40004
Cynthiana	41031	Dixie (Kenton County)	41017	Eastland Park (Fayette County)	40505
Dabney	42501	Dixie Bend	42558		
Dabolt	40421	Dixie Manor Shopping Center	40258	Eastland Park (Warren County)	42104
Dahl	42501	Dixie Plantation (Part of Lexington)	40505	Eastland Shopping Center (Part of Lexington)	40505
Daisy	41733	Dixon	42409	East McDowell	41647
		Dix River Estates	40484	Easton	42343

	ZIP
East Pineville	40977
East Point	41216
East Union	40311
East View	42732
Eastwood	40018
Ebenezer (Mercer County)	40372
Ebenezer (Monroe County)	42167
Ebenezer (Muhlenberg County)	42337
Echo	42154
Echols	42320
Echo Point	42518
Echo Valley	40031
Eddyville	42038
Eddyville Shores	42038
Edenton	40475
Edgewater	41534
Edgewood (Franklin County)	40601
Edgewood (Jefferson County)	40213
Edgewood (Kenton County)	41017
Edgewood (Nelson County)	40004
Edmonton	42129
Edna	41419
Edwards	42256
Eglon	40447
Egypt	40430
Eighty Eight	42130
Ekron	40117
Elamton	41472
Elba	42327
Elcomb	40831
Eldridge	41149
Eli	42642
Elihu	42501
Elizabeth Station	40361
Elizabethtown	42701-02
For specific Elizabethtown Zip Codes call (502) 765-7230, or your local postmaster.	
Elizaville	41037
Elkatawa	41339
Elk Creek	40023
Elkfork	41421
Elk Horn	42733
Elkhorn City	41522
Elk Lake Shores	40359
Elkton	42220
Ella	42728
Ellington	42752
Elliottville	40317
Elisburg	40437
Eliston (Grant County)	41035
Eliston (Madison County)	40475
Ellisville	40311
Elmitch	42343
Ellwood	41538
Elmburg	40057
Elmer Davis Lake	40359
Elmrock	41640
Elmville	40601
Elna	41219
Elsie	41422
Elsinore	40601
Elsmere	41018
Elswick	41538
Elva	42082
Elys	40939
Emanuel	40734
Emerson	41135
Eminence	40019
Emlyn	40730
Emma	41653
Emmalena	41740
Empire	42442
Endicott	41626
End of Line	41667
Engle	41727
English	41008
Ennis	42337
Ensor	42366
Enterprise	41164
Eolia	40826
Epleys	42276
Epperson	42003
Epson	41465
Epworth	41189
Equality	42328
Eriline	40962
Erlanger	41018
Ermine	41815
Erose	40970
Essie	40827
Estesburg	40489
Estill	41627
Esto	42642
Ethridge	41095
Etna	42131
Etoile	42131
Etterwood	40324
Etty	41572
Eubank	42567

	ZIP
Eunice	42728
Evanston	41340
Evarts	40828
Eveleigh	42754
Ever	41465
Everett	42256
Evergreen	40601
Eversole	41314
Ewing	41039
Ewingford	40006
Ewington	40353
Exie	42743
Ezel	41425
Faber	40701
Fagan	40322
Fairbanks (Graves County)	42079
Fairbanks (Owen County)	40359
Fairdale (Jefferson County)	40118
Fairdealing	42025
Fairfield (Breckinridge County)	40144
Fairfield (Nelson County)	40020
Fairland	42602
Fairmeade	40207
Fairmont (Jefferson County)	40291
Fairmont (Webster County)	42404
Fairplay	42735
Fairview (Anderson County)	40342
Fairview (Boyd County)	41101
Fairview (Christian County)	42221
Fairview (Edmonson County)	42210
Fairview (Fleming County)	41039
Fairview (Kenton County)	41015
Fairview (Lyon County)	42038
Fairview (Whitley County)	40769
Fairview Heights (Part of Frankfort)	40601
Fairview Hill	41146
Fairway (Part of Lexington)	40502
Falcon	41426
Fall Rock	40932
Fallsburg	41230
Falls of Rough	40119
Falmouth	41040
Fancy Farm	42039
Fannin	41171
Fariston	40741
Farler	41774
Farmdale	40601
Farmers	40351
Farmers Mill	40831
Farmersville	42445
Farmington	42040
Farraday	41855
Farristown	40403
Faubush	42532
Faulconer	40422
Faxon	42071
Faye	41171
Fayette Mall (Part of Lexington)	40503
Faywood	40383
Fearisville	41179
Fearsville	42240
Feathersburg	42733
Federal Correctional Institution (Boyd County)	41102
Federal Correctional Institution (Fayette County)	40511
Fedscreek	41524
Feliciana	42085
Felty	40962
Fentress Lookout	40119
Fenwick (Part of Lexington)	40516
Ferguson (Logan County)	42276
Ferguson (Pulaski County)	42533
Ferguson Creek (Part of Pikeville)	41501
Fern Creek (Jefferson County)	40291
Ferndale	40977
Ferneaf	41034
Ferrells Creek	41513
Fiddle Bow	42408
Fielden	41177
Fillmore	41323
Fincastle	40222
Finchville	40022
Finley	42736
Finley Addition	42420
Finney	42141
Firebrick	41137
Firmantown	40383
Fisherville	40023
Fishtrap	41557
Fiskburg	41033
Fisty	41743
Fitch	41164
Fitchburg	40472
Five Forks	41230

	ZIP
Fivemile	41339
Fixer	41397
Flag Fork	40601
Flag Spring	41007
Flaherty	40175
Flat	41301
Flat Fork	41427
Flatgap	41219
Flat Lick	40935
Flat Rock (Caldwell County)	42411
Flat Rock (McCreary County)	42653
Flat Rock (Rockcastle County)	40460
Flat Rock (Simpson County)	42170
Flatwoods	41139
Fleming (Part of Fleming-Neon)	41840
Fleming-Neon	41840
Flemingsburg	41041
Flemingsburg Junction	41041
Flener	42261
Flingsville	41030
Flint Springs	42349
Flintville	41348
Flippin	42167
Floral	42348
Florence	41022†
	41042*
Florence Mall (Part of Florence)	41042
Florence Square (Part of Florence)	41042
Florress	41472
Flournoy	42437
Floyd	42567
Floydsburg	40014
Fogertown	40936
Folsom	41035
Folsomdale	42051
Fonde	40940
Fonthill	42642
Foraker	41465
Ford	40320
Fords Branch	41526
Fordsville	42343
Forest Grove	40391
Forest Hills (Jefferson County)	40299
Forest Hills (McCracken County)	42003
Forest Hills (Pike County)	41527
Forest Hills (Taylor County)	42718
Forks of Elkhorn	40601
Forkton	42167
Forrest Park (Part of Winchester)	40391
Fort Campbell	42223
Fort Campbell North	42223
Fort Knox	40121
Fort Mitchell	41017
Fort Spring (Part of Lexington)	40510
	40513
For specific Fort Spring Zip Codes call (606) 231-6700, or your local postmaster.	
Fort Thomas	41075
Fort Wright	41011
Foster	41043
Fount	40999
Fountain Run	42133
Fourmile	40939
Four Oaks	41040
Fourseam	41701
Fox	40336
Fox Chase	40165
Fox Creek	40342
Foxport	41093
Foxtown	40447
Frakes	40940
Frances	42064
Francisville	41048
Frankfort	40601-04
For specific Frankfort Zip Codes call (502) 223-3447, or your local postmaster.	
Franklin	42134-35
For specific Franklin Zip Codes call (502) 586-3522, or your local postmaster.	
Franklin Cross Roads	42724
Franklinton	40057
Frazer	42618
Fraziertown	40056
Fredericktown	40069
Fredonia	42411
Fredville	41465
Freeburn	41528
Freedom (Barren County)	42157
Freedom (Russell County)	42629
Free Union	42409

* Area Zip Code   † Post Office Boxes

Place	ZIP	Place	ZIP	Place	ZIP
Fremont	42003	Glenarm	40014	Greenville	42345
Frenchburg	40322	Glencoe	41046	Greenwood (McCreary	
Fresh Meadows	40824	Glendale	42740	County)	42634
Friendly Hills	40219	Glendale Junction	42740	Greenwood (Pendleton	
Frisby	42633	Glen Dean	40119	County)	41006
Fritz	41465	Glengary	40118	Greenwood (Warren	
Frogtown	40033	Glensboro	40342	County)	42104
Frogue	42714	Glens Fork	42741	Greenwood Mall (Part of	
Frontier Village (Part of		Glen Springs	41179	Bowling Green)	42104
Henderson)	42420	Glenview (Jefferson County)	40025	Gregory	42633
Frozen Creek	41339	Glenview (Shelby County)	40065	Gregoryville	41143
Fruit Hill	42217	Glenview Hills	40222	Gresham	42743
Fry	42743	Glenview Manor	40222	Grethel	41631
Fryer	42445	Glenville	42376	Grider	42717
Fuget	41266	Glenwood	41230	Griderville	42127
Fulgham	42031	Glo	41666	Griffin	42640
Fulton	42041	Globe	41164	Griffith	42301
Fultz	41143	Glomawr	41701	Griffytown	40243
Funston	42634	Goddard	41093	Grigsby	41722
Furnace	40472	Goering	42348	Grove Center	42437
Fusonia	41774	Goffs Corner	40391	Grundy	42501
Future City	42053	Goforth	41040	Guage	41339
Gabbard	41364	Goins	40763	Gubser Mill	41007
Gabe	42743	Goldbug	40769	Guerrant	41339
Gadberry	42735	Gold City	42134	Guffie	42327
Gaffey Heights	40121	Golden Ash	40831	Gullett	41465
Gage	42056	Golden Pond	42211	Gulnare	41501
Gainesville	42164	Golo	42054	Gulston	40830
Gainesway (Part of		Goochtown	42567	Gum Sulphur	40419
Lexington)	40502	Goodluck	42129	Gum Tree	42167
Gallup	41230	Goodnight	42127	Gunlock	41632
Galveston	41635	Goodwater	42501	Guston	40142
Gamaliel	42140	Goody	41514	Guthrie	42234
Gapcreek	42603	Goose Creek	40222	Guy	42101
Gap in Knob	40165	Goose Rock	40944	Gwinn Island	40422
Gapville	41433	Gordon	41819	Gypsy	41438
Gardenside (Part of		Gordon Ford	41472	Habit	42366
Lexington)	40504	Gordonsville	42276	Haddix	41331
	40533	Goshen	40026	Hadensville	42234
	40544	Gotts	42103	Hadley	42101
For specific Gardenside Zip		Grab	42743	Hager	41465
Codes call (606) 231-6744, or		Grace	40962	Hagerhill	41222
your local postmaster.		Gracey	42232	Hail	42501
Garden Springs (Part of		Gradyville	42742	Halcom	41171
Lexington)	40504	Graefenburg	40601	Haldeman	40329
Garden Village	41501	Graham	42344	Halfway	42150
Gardnersville	41033	Graham Hill	42420	Halifax	42164
Garfield	40140	Grahamville	42086	Hall (Jessamine County)	40356
Garlin	42728	Grahn	41142	Hall (Knott County)	41840
Garner (Boyd County)	41168	Gra-Mor	40004	Hallie	41821
Garner (Knott County)	41817	Grancer	42287	Halls Gap	40489
Garrard	40941	Grand Rivers	42045	Halls Store	42276
Garrett (Floyd County)	41630	Grandview (Part of		Halo	41606
Garrett (Meade County)	40117	Tompkinsville)	42167	Hamlin	42046
Garrettsburg	42236	Grandview Heights (Part of		Hammackville	42286
Garrison	41141	Frankfort)	40601	Hammond	41269
Garvin Ridge	41164	Grange City	41049	Hammonville	42757
Gascon	42129	Grangertown	42459	Hampton	42047
Gaskill (Part of Jenkins)	41537	Grants Lick	41001	Hampton Manor (Part of	
Gasper	42206	Grant Wood Hills	42420	Winchester)	40391
Gates	40351	Grapevine	42431	Handshoe	41640
Gatewood	42348	Grassy Creek	41332	Hanly	40356
Gatliff	40769	Grassy Lick	40353	Hannah	41124
Gatun	40806	Gratz	40327	Hansford	40456
Gausdale	40906	Gravel Switch	40328	Hanson	42413
Gaybourn	40383	Gray	40734	Happy	41746
Gays Creek	41745	Gray Hawk	40434	Happy Acre	42642
Geddes	42134	Graymoor (Part of		Happy Landing	40403
Geneva (Henderson		Graymoor-Devondale)	40222	Harbor Village	40324
County)	42406	Graymoor-Devondale	40222	Hardburly	41747
Geneva (Lincoln County)	40437	Grays Branch	41144	Hardin	42048
Gentrys Mill	42728	Grays Knob	40829	Hardinsburg	40143
Georgetown (Harlan		Grayson	41143	Hardin Springs	42783
County)	40843	Grayson Springs	42726	Hardmoney	42003
Georgetown (Scott County)	40324	Graysville	40146	Hardshell	41348
Germantown (Bracken		Greasy Creek	41562	Hardwick	42618
County)	41044	Great Crossing	40324	Hardy	41531
Germantown (Jefferson		Greear	41472	Hardyville	42746
County)	40217	Green	41164	Hare	40729
Gertrude	41004	Green Acres (Boyle County)	40422	Hargett	40336
Gesling	41128	Green Acres (Fayette		Harlan	40831
Gest	40057	County)	40511	Harlan Crossroads	42167
Gethsemane	40051	Greenbriar (Daviess County)	42303	Harlan Gas	40831
Ghent	41045	Greenbriar (Marion County)	40033	Harmony	40359
Gibbs	40906	Greenbriar (Oldham County)	40031	Harmony Lake Estates	40059
Gifford	41465	Greenbrier	40489	Harmony Village	40059
Gilbertsville	42044	Greencastle	42270	Harned	40144
Gillem Branch	41219	Greendale (Part of		Harold	41635
Gilley	41819	Lexington)	40511	Harper	41465
Gillmore	41301	Green Fields Estates	40391	Harreldsville	42256
Gilpin	42539	Green Grove	42714	Harrington Mill Estates	40065
Gilreath	42635	Green Hall	41328	Harris	41179
Gilstrap	42349	Green Hill (Jackson County)	40402	Harris Grove	42071
Gimlet	41164	Greenhill (Warren County)	42103	Harrisonville	40076
Girdler	40943	Green Hills	42728	Harrodsburg	40330
Girkin	42101	Greenland Park	40065	Harrods Creek	40027
Gishton	42325	Greenmount	40741	Harrods Hills (Part of	
Glasgow	42141-42	Green Road	40946	Lexington)	40513
For specific Glasgow Zip Codes		Greensburg	42743	Hart	40741
call (502) 651-8859, or your local		Green Spring	40222	Hartford	42347
postmaster.		Greenup	41144	Hartley	41572
Gleanings	40052	Greenview	41042	Harveyton	41719

* **Area Zip Code**　　† **Post Office Boxes**

	ZIP		ZIP		ZIP
Harvy	42025		40219	Humble	42642
Haskingsville	42743	For specific Highview Zip Codes		Hummel	40492
Hatcher	42718	call (502) 454-1650, or your local		Hunnewell	41121
Hatfield	41514	postmaster.		Hunt	40391
Hatton	40601	Highview (Ohio County)	42320	Hunter	41641
Hawesville	42348	Highway	42602	Hunter Hill	40258
Hawkeegan Point	40601	Hignite	40965	Hunters Hollow	40229
Hayes	41040	Hi Hat	41636	Hunters Trace	40216
Haynesville	42368	Hikes Point (Part of		Huntersville	42602
Hays	42171	Louisville)	40220*	Hunter Town	40383
Hays Crossing	40351		40250†	Hunting Creek (Part of	
Hayward	41173	Hilda	40351	Hopkinsville)	42240
Haywood	42141	Hillcrest	40475	Huntington Woods	40601
Hazard	41701*	Hillendale	41095	Huntsville	42251
	41702†	Hill-N-Dale	40065	Hurley	40447
Hazel	42049	Hill Ridge	40299	Hurricane Hills	40107
Hazel Green	41332	Hills and Dales	40222	Hurstbourne	40222
Hazel Patch	40729	Hillsboro	41049	Hurstbourne Acres	40220
Head of Grassy	41135	Hillsdale	42134	Hustonville	40437
Headquarters	40311	Hillside	42330	Hutch	40965
Hearin	42404	Hill Top (Fleming County)	41039	Hutchison	40361
Heath	42086	Hilltop (Grant County)	41097	Hyattsville	40444
Hebbardsville	42420	Hilltop (Logan County)	42202	Hyden	41749
Hebron	41048	Hill Top (McCreary County)	42647	Hydro	42171
Hebron Estates	40165	Hillview (Bullitt County)	40229	Iberia	42726
Hecla	42410	Hillview (Edmonson County)	42207	Ibex	41164
Hector	40962	Hima	40951	Ice	41858
Hedgeville	40444	Himyar	40906	Ida	42602
Heekin	41097	Hinda Heights (Part of		Ida May	41311
Heenon	41545	Lexington)	40502	Idle Hour (Part of Lexington)	40502
Heflin	42347	Hindman	41822	Idlewild	41005
Hegira	42717	Hinkle	40953	Ilsley	42408
Heidelberg	41333	Hinkleville	42056	Independence	41051
Heidrick	40949	Hinton	41010	Index (Part of West Liberty)	41472
Heiner	41722	Hinton Hills	40143	Indian Fields	40391
Helechawa	41332	Hippo	41653	Indian Hills (Carroll County)	41008
Helena	41055	Hiram	40823	Indian Hills (Christian	
Hellier	41534	Hisel	40447	County)	42240
Helton	40840	Hiseville	42152	Indian Hills (Franklin County)	40601
Hemp Ridge	40076	Hislope	42544	Indian Hills (Hardin County)	42701
Henderson	42420	Hitchins	41146	Indian Hills (Jefferson	
Hendricks	41465	Hite	41649	County)	40207
Hendron (McCracken		Hitesville	42437	Indian Hills (Russell County)	42642
County)	42001	Hobson	42718	Indian Hills (Scott County)	40324
Henrietta	41269	Hode	41267	Indian Hills (Warren County)	42103
Henry Clay (Fayette County)	40502	Hodgenville	42748	Indian Hills Cherokee	
	40522	Hogue	42553	Section	40207
For specific Henry Clay Zip Codes		Holbrook	41097	Indian Lake	42348
call (606) 231-6719, or your local		Holiday Hills (Part of		Indian Trail Square	40219
postmaster.		Lexington)	40504	Inez	41224
Henry Clay (Pike County)	41542	Holifield	42088	Ingle	42536
Henryville	40311	Holland	42153	Ingleside	42053
Henshaw	42437	Holliday	41474	Ingram	40955
Hensley (Breckinridge		Hollonville	41301	Insco	42276
County)	40146	Holloway Hills	42420	Insko	41443
Hensley (Clay County)	40962	Hollow Bill	42256	Inverness Estates (Part of	
Herbert	42368	Hollow Creek	40228	Frankfort)	40601
Herd	40435	Hollybush	41823	Iron Hill (Carter County)	41143
Heritage Village (Part of		Hollyhill	42635	Iron Hill (Lyon County)	42055
Campbellsville)	42718	Hollyvilla	40118	Ironville	41102
Hermitage Hills (Part of		Holmes Mill	40843	Ironworks Estates	40324
Lexington)	40505	Holt	42332	Iroquois (Part of Louisville)	40214
Hermon	42234	Holy Cross	40037		40209
Herndon	42236	Homer	42276	For specific Iroquois Zip Codes	
Herron Hill	41189	Homestead	40383	call (502) 368-8911, or your local	
Heselton	41179	Honaker	41639	postmaster.	
Hesler	40359	Honeybee	42634	Iroquois Heights	40214
Hestand	42151	Honey Fork	41513	Irvine	40336
Hi Acres (Part of Lexington)	40505	Honey Grove	42240	Irvington	40146
Hickman	42050	Honeysuckle Estates	40342	Irvins Store	42642
Hickory	42051	Hooktown	41031	Island	42350
Hickory Flat	42134	Hootentown	40391	Island City	41338
Hickory Grove (Cumberland		Hope	40334	Isom	41824
County)	42752	Hopeful Heights	41042	Isonville	41149
Hickory Grove (McCreary		Hopewell (Greenup County)	41163	Iuka	42045
County)	42638	Hopewell (Jefferson County)	40299	Ivel	41642
Hickory Hill	40222	Hopkinsville	42240-41	Ivis	41822
Hickory Hills (Part of		For specific Hopkinsville Zip		Ivor	41007
Frankfort)	40601	Codes call (502) 886-5259, or		Ivy Grove	40939
Hidalgo	42633	your local postmaster.		Ivyton	41444
Hide-A-Way Hills	40359	Hopson	42445	Jabez	42532
High Bridge	40390	Horntown	42642	Jackhorn	41825
High Falls	41301	Horse Branch	42349	Jackson	41339
Highgrove	40013	Horse Cave	42749	Jacksonville (Bourbon	
High Knob	40402	Horton	42320	County)	40361
Highland (Lincoln County)	40484	Hoskinston	40844	Jacksonville (Shelby	
Highland (Simpson County)	42134	Houston	41314	County)	40003
Highland Heights	41076	Houston Acres	40220	Jackstown	40311
Highland Park (Jefferson		Hovious Ridge	42728	Jacktown	40009
County)	40209	Howard Mills	40334	Jacobs	41150
Highland Park (Whitley		Howardstown	40028	Jamboree	41536
County)	40769	Howel	42262	Jamestown	42629
Highlands (Fayette County)	40511	Howe Valley	42724	Jarvis	40906
Highlands (Jefferson		Hubble	40444	Jason	41714
County)	40206	Hubbs	40921	Jasper Bend	42519
High Plains	40106	Huddy	41535	Jeff	41751
High Point	42086	Hudgins	42782	Jeffersontown	40269
Highsplint	40828	Hudson	40145		40299
Hightop	40741	Hueys Corners	41091		40229
Highview (Jefferson County)	40228	Hueysville	41640	For specific Jeffersontown Zip	
		Huff	42250	Codes call (502) 266-5844, or	
		Hulen	40845	your local postmaster.	

	ZIP		ZIP		ZIP
Jeffersonville	40337	Keysburg	42204	Leander	41228
Jeffrey	42157	Keyser Heights	41501	Leatha	41465
Jellico	40769	Kidder	42518	Leatherwood	41731
Jellico Creek	40769	Kidds Crossing	42611	Lebanon	40033
Jenkins	41537	Kidds Store	40437	Lebanon Junction	40150
Jenkinsville	40040	Kiddville	40353	Leburn	41831
Jenson	40977	Kildav	40828	Leckieville	41529
Jeptha	41472	Kilgore	41168	Lecta	42141
Jeremiah	41826	Kimbrell	40336	Ledbetter (Livingston	
Jericho (Henry County)	40068	Kimper	41539	County)	42058
Jericho (Larue County)	42748	Kinchloes Bluff	42330	Ledocio	41230
Jerico	42256	Kingbee	42516	Lee City	41342
Jessietown	40033	Kings Creek	41858	Leeco	41343
Jetson	42252	Kings Forest	40165	Leesburg	41031
Jett	40601	Kingsley	40205	Lees Lick	41031
Jetts Creek	41314	Kings Mountain	40442	LeGrande	42749
Jewell City	42456	Kingston (Fayette County)	40505	Leighton	40336
Jimtown (Fayette County)	40505	Kingston (Madison County)	40403	Leitchfield	42754-55
Jimtown (Washington		Kingswood	40144	For specific Leitchfield Zip Codes	
County)	40069	Kinniconick	41179	call (502) 259-3087, or your local	
Jinks	40336	Kino	42141	postmaster.	
Job	41224	Kirbyton	42023	Leitchfield Crossing (Part of	
Jock	42207	Kirk	41143	Munfordville)	42765
Johnetta	40460	Kirkmansville	42220	Lejunior	40849
Johns Creek	41265	Kirksey	42054	Lemon	42327
Johnsontown	40272	Kirksville	40475	Lenarue	40818
Johnsport (Part of		Kirkwood	40372	Lenore	40013
Campbellsville)	42718	Kirkwood Springs	42408	Lenox	41447
Johns Run	41143	Kite	41828	Lenoxburg	41040
Johnsville	41043	Kitts	40831	Leon	41143
Jonancy	41538	Knifley	42728	Lerose	41344
Jonesville (Grant County)	41052	Knob Lick	42154	Lesbas	40741
Jonesville (Hart County)	42757	Knottsville	42366	Leslie	42717
Joppa	42728	Knowlton	40380	Letcher	41832
Jordan	42050	Knoxfork	40906	Levee	40337
Josephine	40370	Knoxville	41097	Level Green	40456
Joy	42047	Kodak	41773	Levi	41314
Judio	42752	Kona	41829	Levias	42064
Judson	40444	Korea	40387	Lewisburg (Logan County)	42256
Judy	40334	Kragon	41339	Lewisburg (Mason County)	41056
Judyville	40311	Krypton	41754	Lewisport	42351
Julien	42232	Kuttawa	42055	Lexington	40501-96
Julip	40769	Kyrock	42285	For specific Lexington Zip Codes	
Jumbo	40484	Labascus	42539	call (606) 231-6700, or your local	
Junction City	40440	La Center	42056	postmaster.	
Juniper Hill (Part of		Lacey	41465	Lexington-Bluegrass Army	
Frankfort)	40601	Lacie	40075	Depot (Headquarters)	
Justell	41605	Lackey	41643	(Fayette County)	40511
Justice	42256	Lacon	42726	Lexington-Bluegrass Army	
Justiceville	41501	Laden	40865	Depot (Madison County)	40475
Kaler	42051	La Fayette	42254	Lexington Mall (Part of	
Kaliopi	41749	La Grange	40031	Lexington)	40502
Kansas	42069	Lair	41031	Liberty (Casey County)	42539
Karlus	42629	Lake	40741	Liberty (Webster County)	42409
Katharyn	40177	Lake Carnico	41039	Liberty (Whitley County)	40769
Kavanaugh	41129	Lake City	42045	Liberty Heights (Fayette	
Kayjay	40906	Lake Dreamland	40216	County)	40505
Keaton	41226	Lake Louisvilla	40014	Liberty Heights (Nicholas	
Keavy	40737	Lakeside Park	41017	County)	40311
Keefer	41010	Lakeview (Part of Fort		Liberty Road	41472
Keene	40339	Wright)	41011	Lick Branch	41472
Keeneland	40223	Lakeview Heights	40351	Lickburg	41465
Kehoe	41141	Lakeview-Mt. Tabor (Part of		Lick Creek	41540
Keith	40846	Lexington)	40502	Lick Fork	40313
Kelat	41003	Lakeview-Woodspoint (Part		Licking River	41472
Kellacey	41472	of Lexington)	40509	Lickskillet (Logan County)	42265
Kelly	42240	Lakeville	41465	Lickskillet (Meade County)	40175
Kellyville	42728	Lakeway Shore	42071	Lida	40741
Keltner	42761	Lakewood Acres (Part of		Liggett	40831
Ken Acres	40065	Lexington)	40502	Ligon	41604
Kenawood (Part of		Lamasco	42038	Liletown	42743
Lexington)	40505	Lamb	42155	Lily	40740
Kendall Springs	40360	Lambric	41340	Limaburg	41005
Kennianna	42046	Lamero	40341	Limestone	41164
Keno	42558	Lamont (McCracken		Limestone Springs	40165
Kensee	40769	County)	42053	Limeville	41175
Kenshores	42046	Lamont (Perry County)	41727	Lincoln	40962
Kentenia	40873	Lancaster	40444	Lincolnshire	40220
Kenton	41053	Lancelot Estates	40324	Lindseyville	42257
Kenton Hills (Part of		Lancer (Part of		Linefork	41833
Covington)	41011	Prestonsburg)	41653	Linton	42211
Kentontown	41064	Landsaw	41301	Linwood (Grayson County)	42726
Kenton Vale	41015	Langdon Place	40222	Linwood (Hart County)	42757
Kentucky Correctional		Langley	41645	Lionilli	41537
Institution for Women	40056	Langnau	40741	Lisletown	40391
Kentucky Dam Village	42044	Lanhamtown	42539	Lisman	42404
Kentucky Heights	41166	Lansdowne (Part of		Litsey	40069
Kentucky Mills (Part of		Lexington)	40502	Littcarr	41834
Jeffersontown)	40299	Larkslane	41817	Little	41339
Kentucky Oaks Mall (Part of		Latonia (Part of Covington)	41015	Little Barren	42743
Paducah)	42001	Latonia Lakes	41015	Little Bear Creek	42044
Kentucky State Reformatory	40032	Laura	41250	Little Creek	40902
Kenvir	40847	Laurel Creek	40962	Little Cypress	42029
Kenwood (Part of Louisville)	40214	Laurel Fork	40940	Little Dixie	41501
Kerby Knob	40441	Laurel Ridge	42259	Little Georgetown (Part of	
Kernie	41465	Lawhorn Hill	42539	Lexington)	40513
Kessinger	42765	Lawrenceburg	40342	Little Hickman	40356
Keswick	40769	Lawrenceville	41010	Little Mount	40071
Kettle	42752	Lawson	41339	Little Needmore	40422
Kettlecamp	41522	Lawton	41164	Little Rock	40311
Kettle Island	40958	Layman	40819	Little Sandy	41171
Kevil	42053	Leafdale	42748	Little Tar Springs	42348

	ZIP
Little Texas (Part of Lexington)	40513
Littleton	40962
Littrell	42752
Livermore	42352
Livia	42327
Livingston	40445
Lloyd	41156
Load	41144
Lockards Creek	40941
Lockport	40036
Lockwood Estates	40014
Locust	41008
Locust Grove (Clark County)	40391
Locust Grove (Pendleton County)	41040
Locust Hill	40144
Lodiburg	40146
Logana	40356
Logansport	42261
Logantown	40484
Log Lick	40391
Log Mountain	40977
Logville	41465
Lola	42059
Lombard	40380
London	40741-45

For specific London Zip Codes
call (606) 864-2251, or your local
postmaster.

	ZIP
Lone	41347
Lone Oak	42003
Lone Star	42713
Lone Way Acres	42718
Long Fork	41572
Longlick	40379
Long Ridge	40359
Long Run	40245
Long View	42701
Longview Estates	40422
Lookout	41542
Loradale (Part of Lexington)	40505
Loretto	40037
Lost Creek	41348
Lot	40769
Lothair (Part of Hazard)	41701
Lotus	40013
Louden	40769
Louellen	40828
Louisa	41230

Louisville 40201-99
For specific Louisville Zip Codes
call (502) 454-1650, or your local
postmaster.

COLLEGES & UNIVERSITIES

	ZIP
Spalding University	40203
University of Louisville	40292

FINANCIAL INSTITUTIONS

	ZIP
Citizens Fidelity Bank and Trust Company	40202
The Cumberland Federal Savings Bank	40202
First Kentucky Trust Company	40202
First National Bank of Louisville	40202
Great Financial Federal	40202
Liberty National Bank and Trust Company of Louisville	40202
Mid-America Bank of Louisville and Trust Company	40202
Republic Bank & Trust Company	40202
Stock Yards Bank & Trust Company	40206

HOSPITALS

	ZIP
Audubon Regional Medical Center	40217
Baptist Hospital East	40207
Jewish Hospital	40202
Methodist Evangelical Hospital	40202
Saints Mary and Elizabeth Hospital	40215
Suburban Medical Center	40207
University of Louisville Hospital	40202
Veterans Affairs Medical Center-Louisville	40206

HOTELS/MOTELS

	ZIP
The Brown-A.Camberley Hotel	40202
The Galt House Hotel	40202
Hyatt Regency Louisville	40202
Ramada Inn Brownsboro East	40207
Seelbach Hotel	40202

MILITARY INSTALLATIONS

	ZIP
Kentucky Air National Guard, FB6161 Standiford Field	40213
Naval Surface Warfare Center, Crane Division/Naval Ordnance Station, Louisville	40214
United States Army Engineer District, Louisville	40201

	ZIP
Lovelaceville	42060
Lovely	42131
Lowell	40461
Lower Kings Addition	41175
Lower Pompey	41501
Lowes	42061
Lowmansville	41232
Loyall	40854
Lucas	42156
Lucastown	41855
Lucky Fork	41364
Lucky Stop (Part of Jeffersonville)	40337
Ludlow	41016
Luner	40456
Lusby's Mill	40359
Luther Luckett Correctional Complex	40031
Luzerne	42345
Lykins	41465
Lynch	40855
Lyndale	40391
Lyndon	40222
	40241-42
	40252

For specific Lyndon Zip Codes
call (502) 425-4547, or your local
postmaster.

	ZIP
Lynn	41144
Lynn City	42372
Lynn Grove	42071
Lynnview	40213
Lynnville	42063
Lyons	40051
Lytten	41171
Mac	42718
McAfee	40330
McAndrews	41543
McBrayer	40342
McCarr	41544
McClure	41250
McCombs	41545
McCreary	40444
McDaniels	40152
McDowell	41647
Macedonia (Christian County)	42217
Macedonia (Jackson County)	40447
Maceo	42355
McGowan	42445
McHenry	42354
McKee	40447
McKinney	40448
McKinneysburg	41040
Mackville	40040
McQuady	40153
McRoberts	41835
McVeigh	41546
McVille	41005
McWhorter	40741
Madison Hills (Part of Richmond)	40475
Madisonville	42431
Madrid	42754
Magan	42343
Maggard	41465
Magnolia	42757
Magoffin	41465
Majestic	41547
Major	41314
Malaga	41301
Mallard Point	40324
Mallie	41836
Mall in St. Matthews, The (Part of St. Matthews)	40207
Malone	41451
Maloneton	41175
Mammoth Cave	42259
Manchester	40962
Mangum	42516
Manila	41238
Manitou	42436
Mannington	42217
Mannsville	42758
Manor Creek	40222

	ZIP
Man O' War Place (Part of Lexington)	40509
Manse	40461
Manton (Floyd County)	41649
Manton (Washington County)	40037
Maple Grove	42211
Maple Mount	42356
Maplesville	40741
Marcellus	40444
Marcum	40962
Marcus	41003
Maretburg	40456
Mariba	40345
Marion	42064
Mark	42501
Marksbury	40444
Marlowe	41858
Marrowbone	42759
Marshall (Marshall County)	42044
Marshall (Mason County)	41056
Marshallville	41452
Marshes Siding	42631
Martha	41159
Martin	41649
Martinsville	42159
Mary	41301
Mary Alice	40964
Marydell	40751
Maryhill Estates	40207
Mashfork	41465
Mason (Grant County)	41054
Mason (Magoffin County)	41465
Masonic Home (Part of Louisville)	40041
Masonville (Daviess County)	42376
Massac (McCracken County)	42001
Matanzas	42328
Matlock	42104
Matthew	41472
Mattingly	40111
Mattoon	42064
Mattoxtown (Part of Lexington)	40505
Maud	40069
Maulden	40486
Mavity	41129
Maxine	42776
Maxwell	42376
Mayfield	42066
Mayflower	41501
Mayking	41837
Maynard	42164
Mayo	40330
Mayo Village (Part of Pikeville)	41501
Mays Lick	41055
Maysville	41056
Maytown	41472
Maywood	40484
Mazie	41160
Meador	42164
Meadowbrook (Clark County)	40391
Meadowbrook (Shelby County)	40065
Meadowbrook Farm	40223
Meadow Creek	40759
Meadowrun	40065
Meadows (Fayette County)	40505
Meadows (Franklin County)	40601
Meadowthorpe (Part of Lexington)	40511
Meadow Vale	40222
Meadowview Estates	40220
Meads	41101
Meally	41234
Means	40346
Medora	40272
Meece	42501
Meeting Creek	42732
Melber	42069
Melbourne	41059
Meldrum	40965
Mell	42743
Melody Lake	40051
Melvin	41650
Memphis Junction	42101
Mentor	41007
Meredith	42754
Merewood (Part of Versailles)	40383
Meridian	41006
Merrick Place (Part of Lexington)	40502
Merrimac	40009
Merrittstown	42240
Merry Oaks	42171
Mershons	40729
Meshack	42167
Meta	41501

* Area Zip Code　　　† Post Office Boxes

	ZIP		ZIP		ZIP
Mexico	42064	Mortimer Station	42202	Nerinx	40049
Midas	41640	Mortons Gap	42440	Nero	41265
Middleburg	42541	Mortonsville	40383	Netty	41465
Middlesboro	40965	Moscow	42031	Nevada	40330
Middlesboro Mall (Part of		Moseleyville	42301	Nevelsville	42653
Middlesboro)	40965	Mossy Bottom	41501	Nevin	40342
Middleton	42134	Motley	42103	Nevisdale	40754
Middleton Heights (Part of		Mount Aerial	42128	New	40359
Shelbyville)	40065	Mountain Ash	40769	New Allen	41601
Middletown (Jefferson		Mountain Top	41164	Newburg	40213
County)	40243*	Mountain Valley	41385		40218-19
	40253†	Mount Auburn	41006	For specific Newburg Zip Codes
Middletown (Madison		Mount Carmel (Fleming		call (502) 454-1650, or your local
County)	40403	County)	41041	postmaster.
Midland (Bath County)	40371	Mount Carmel (Hopkins		Newby	40475
Midland (Muhlenberg		County)	42464	New Camp	41503
County)	42325	Mount Eden	40046	New Castle	40050
Midway (Calloway County)	42049	Mount Gilead (Green		New Columbus	41010
Midway (Crittenden County)	42064	County)	42743	Newcombe	41149
Midway (Meade County)	40142	Mount Gilead (Monroe		New Concord	42076
Midway (Woodford County)	40347	County)	42167	New Cypress (Hickman	
Milburn	42070	Mount Hermon	42157	County)	42031
Mildred	40447	Mount Lebanon	40356	New Cypress (Muhlenberg	
Milford	41061	Mount Olive (Casey County)	42539	County)	42345
Millard	41562	Mount Olive (Lee County)	41311	Newfound	40972
Mill Creek	41055	Mount Olivet	41064	Newfoundland	41171
Milledgeville	40437	Mount Pisgah	42633	Newgarden	40121
Miller (Fulton County)	42050	Mount Pleasant (Ohio		New Haven	40051
Miller (Nicholas County)	40311	County)	42333	New Hope	40052
Millersburg	40348	Mount Pleasant (Trimble		New Liberty	40355
Millers Creek	40472	County)	40006	Newman	42301
Millerstown	42726	Mount Salem	40437	New Market	40033
Million	40475	Mount Sherman	42764	Newport	41071-76
Mill Pond	40962	Mount Sterling	40353	For specific Newport Zip Codes
Millport	42372	Mount Tabor (Larue County)	42716	call (606) 291-5250, or your local
Mills	40970	Mount Tabor (Todd County)	42220	postmaster.
Millseat	41101	Mount Union	42120	Newport Shopping Center	
Mill Springs	42632	Mount Vernon (Rockcastle		(Part of Newport)	41071
Millstone	41838	County)	40456	New Providence	42049
Milltown (Adair County)	42761	Mount Vernon (Scott		New Roe	42120
Milltown (Nicholas County)	40350	County)	40324	New Salem	40437
Millville	40601	Mount Victor	42104	Newstead	42240
Millwood	42762	Mount Victory	42501	Newt	42743
Milner	40383	Mount Washington	40047	Newtown	40324
Milo	41262	Mount Zion (Allen County)	42164	New Zion (Jackson County)	40447
Milton	40045	Mount Zion (Pulaski County)	42553	New Zion (Scott County)	40324
Mirna	41457	Mount Zion (Grant County)	41035	Niagara	42420
Minerva	41062	Mousie	41839	Nicholasville	40340†
Minnie	41651	Moutardier	42754		40356*
Minor Lane Heights	40219	Mouthcard	41548	Nichols (Bullitt County)	40177
Minorsville	40379	Moxley	40363	Nichols (Hickman County)	42031
Mintonville	42539	Mozelle	40858	Nicholson (Kenton County)	41051
Miracle	40856	Mud Camp	42717	Nicholson (Trigg County)	42215
Mistletoe	41351	Muddy Ford	40324	Nickell	41332
Mitchell Hill (Part of		Mud Lick	42167	Nigh	41524
Madisonville)	42431	Muir (Part of Lexington)	40516	Nina	40444
Mitchellsburg	40452	Mulberry	40065	Nineteen	42320
Mize	41352	Muldraugh	40155	Ninevah	40342
Moberly	40475	Mulfordtown	42459	Nippa	41240
Mockingbird Valley	40207	Mullikin Junction	42028	Noble	41317
Moct	41385	Mullins	40456	Nobob	42166
Modoc	42714	Mummie	40486	No Creek	42347
Molus	40819	Munfordville	42765	Noctor	41357
Monford	42252	Murl	42633	Node	42214
Monica	41362	Murphyfork	41332	Noetown (Part of	
Monica Gardens	40065	Murphysville	41056	Middlesboro)	40965
Monitor	40006	Murray	42071	Nolansburg	40870
Monkeys Eyebrow	42056	Murray Hill	40222	Nolin	42776
Monroe	42746	Muses Mills	41065	Nolin Lake Estates	42726
Montclair (Fayette County)	40502	Music	41168	Nonesuch	40383
Montclair (Shelby County)	40067	Myers	40311	Nonnel	42337
Monterey	40359	Myra	41549	Nora	42602
Montgomery	42211	Mystic	40146	Norbourne Estates	40207
Montgomerys Mill	42743	Nada	40380	Norfleet	42544
Monticello	42633	Nancy	42544	Normal (Part of Ashland)	41101
Monticello Estates (Part of		Naomi	42544	Normandy	40071
Lexington)	40503	Napfor	41754	North Corbin	40701
Montpelier	42728	Naples	41102	Northfield	40222
Montrose (Part of		Napoleon	41046	North Irvine	40336
Lexington)	40516	Narrows	42358	North Middletown	40357
Montrose Park (Part of		Narvel	42602	Northpoint Training Center	40310
Frankfort)	40601	Nashtown	41189	Northtown	42749
Mooleyville	40143	Natlee	41010	Norton Branch	41168
Moon	41457	Natural Bridge	40376	Nortonville	42442
Moon Lake Estates	40324	Nazareth	40048	Norwood (Jefferson County)	40222
Moorefield	40350	Neafus	42766	Norwood (Pulaski County)	42553
Moore Hill	40701	Neave	41040	Nuckols	42352
Moores Creek	40402	Nebo (Hopkins County)	42441	Nugent Cross Roads	40383
Moores Ferry	40371	Nebo (Muhlenberg County)	42345	Nugym	40902
Mooresville	40069	Ned	41317	Number One	42633
Moorland	40223	Needmore (Boyle County)	40422	Oakbrook (Boone County)	41042
Moorman	42357	Needmore (Butler County)	42261	Oakdale (Breathitt County)	41339
Moranburg	41056	Needmore (Caldwell		Oakdale (Jefferson County)	40215
Morehead	40351	County)	42445	Oakdale (McCracken	
Moreland	40437	Nelse	41550	County)	42003
Morgan	41040	Nelson	42330	Oak Forest	42164
Morganfield	42437	Nelsonville	40107	Oak Grove (Christian	
Morgantown	42261	Neon (Part of Fleming-		County)	42262
Morning Glory	41031	Neon)	41840	Oak Grove (Ohio County)	42333
Morning View	41063	Neon Junction	41840	Oak Hill (Hopkins County)	42442
Morrill	40455	Neosheo	42134	Oak Hill (Pulaski County)	42501
Morris Fork	41314	Nepton	41039	Oakland	42159

	ZIP
Oakland Mills	40311
Oaklawn Estates	41222
Oak Level	42025
Oakley	40729
Oak Ridge (Edmonson County)	42207
Oak Ridge (Kenton County)	41051
Oaks (Bell County)	40856
Oaks (McCracken County)	42003
Oaks (Ohio County)	42343
Oakton	42031
Oakville	42263
Oakwood (Part of Lexington)	40511
O'Bannon	40223
Oddville	41031
Odessa	40360
Offutt	41237
Ogle	40962
Oil City	42141
Oil Springs	41238
Oil Valley	42633
Okolona	40219
	40229
	40259

For specific Okolona Zip Codes
call (502) 966-8049, or your local
postmaster.

	ZIP
Olaton	42361
Olcott	40977
Old Brownsboro Place	40222
Old Christianburg	40003
Old Flat Lick	40935
Oldham Acres	40059
Old Landing	41358
Old Olga	42629
Old Orchard	40447
Old Pine Grove	40391
Old Stephensburg	42781
Old Taylor Place	40026
Oldtown	41163
Old Volney	42265
Olga	42629
Olin	40447
Olive	42025
Olive Branch (Fleming County)	41041
Olive Branch (Shelby County)	40065
Olive Hill	41164
Ollie	42259
Olmstead	42265
Olney	42408
Olympia	40358
Olympia Springs	40358
Omaha	41843
Oneida	40972
Oneonta	41007
Ono	42642
Onton	42455
Open Gates (Part of Lexington)	40503
Ophir	41459
Orangeburg	41056
Orchard Grass Hills	40014
Ordinary	41171
Oregon	40372
Orkney	41647
Orlando	40460
Orr	41180
Ortiz	42455
Orville	40057
Osborn	41635
Oscaloosa	41858
Oscar	42056
Otia	42167
Ottawa	40409
Ottenheim	40489
Otter Pond	42445
Oven Fork	40861
Overlook (Part of Eddyville)	42038
Ovesen Heights	42748
Owensboro	42301-03

For specific Owensboro Zip
Codes call (502) 684-2301, or
your local postmaster.

	ZIP
Owensboro East (Part of Owensboro)	42303
Owensboro West (Part of Owensboro)	42301
Owenton	40359
Owingsville	40360
Owsley	41501
Oxford	40324
Oxmoor Center (Part of Louisville)	40222
Ozark	42728
Pactolus	41143
Paddock Place	40383

	ZIP
Paducah	42001-03

For specific Paducah Zip Codes
call (502) 444-7272, or your local
postmaster.

	ZIP
Paint Lick	40461
Paintsville	41240
Palestine	41091
Palma	42025
Palmer	40336
Panama	41472
Panco	40972
Panola	40385
Panorama Shores	42071
Panther	42376
Paragon Park (Part of Henderson)	42420
Paris	40361*
	40362†
Park City	42160
Parkers Lake	42634
Park Hills (Fayette County)	40502
Park Hills (Kenton County)	41011
Park Hills (Rowan County)	40351
Park Lake	41093
Parkland (Part of Louisville)	40211
Parksville	40464
Parkview Shores No. 1 (Allen County)	42164
Parkview Shores No. 2 (Allen County)	42164
Parkway Village	40207
Parmleysville	42640
Parnell	42633
Parrot	40465
Partridge	40862
Partridge Run (Part of Henderson)	42420
Pascal	42746
Patesville	42348
Pathfork	40863
Patrick	41230
Patsey	40380
Pauley (Part of Pikeville)	41501
Paw Paw	41551
Paxton	41385
Payne Gap	41537
Paynes Depot	40324
Payneville	40157
Payton	41332
Peabody	40914
Peach Grove	41006
Peach Orchard	41230
Peak	40324
Peaks Mill	40601
Pea Ridge (Scott County)	40379
Pea Ridge (Todd County)	42220
Pearl	40940
Pearman	42726
Peasticks	40360
Pebble	40360
Pebworth	41314
Peden Mill	42134
Peedee	42236
Pelfrey	40313
Pellville	42364
Pellyton	42728
Pembroke	42266
Pence	41313
Pendleton	40055
Penile	40272
Penny (Calloway County)	42071
Penny (Pike County)	41501
Pennyrile Mall (Part of Hopkinsville)	42240
Penrod	42365
Peonia	42726
Peoples	40467
Perry Park	40363
Perryville	40468
Persimmon Grove	41001
Persimon	42167
Petersburg	41080
Petersville	41179
Petra	41004
Petrie	42348
Petroleum	42120
Petros	42274
Pettit	42301
Pewee Valley	40056
Peytona	40065
Peyton Creek	41501
Peytonsburg	42768
Peytons Store	40437
Peytontown	40475
Phelps (Pike County)	41553
Phillipsburg	42736
Philpot	42366
Phyllis	41554
Pickett	42761
Pickway (Part of Lexington)	40503
Pierce	42743
Pig	42171

	ZIP
Pigeon	41501
Pigeonroost	40962
Pike View	42757
Pikeville	41501*
	41502†
Pilgrim	41250
Pilot Oak	42085
Pilot View	40391
Pinchem (Clark County)	40391
Pinchem (Todd County)	42234
Pinckard	40383
Pinckneyville	42078
Pine Bluffs	42046
Pine Grove (Clark County)	40391
Pine Grove (Laurel County)	40740
Pine Hill	40456
Pine Knob	42721
Pine Knot	42635
Pine Meadows (Part of Lexington)	40504
Pine Mountain	40810
Piner	41063
Pine Ridge	41360
Pine Top	41843
Pineville	40977
Piney Fork	42064
Piney Grove	42501
Pink	40356
Pinnacle	41358
Pinson	41543
Pinsonfork	41555
Pioneer	41005
Pioneer Village	40165
Pippa Passes	41844
Piqua	41064
Pisgah	40383
Piso	41501
Pitts	40472
Pittsburg	40755
Plainview (Part of Jeffersontown)	40224
Plank	40978
Plano	42104
Plantation	40222
Plato	42501
Pleasant Grove Hill	42240
Pleasant Hill (Butler County)	42273
Pleasant Hill (Mercer County)	40330
Pleasant Hill (Pendleton County)	41006
Pleasant Home	40359
Pleasant Ridge	42376
Pleasant Valley (Nicholas County)	41039
Pleasant Valley (Pike County)	41501
Pleasant View	40769
Pleasure Ridge Park	40258*
	40268†
Pleasureville (Fleming County)	41093
Pleasureville (Henry County)	40057
Plum	40361
Plummers Landing	41081
Plummers Mill	41093
Plum Springs	42101
Plumville	41056
Plymouth Village	40207
Poindexter	41031
Pointer	42544
Point Leavell	40444
Point Pleasant	42718
Polksville	40371
Polkville	42159
Polly	41858
Pomeroyton	40365
Pomp	41472
Ponderosa	42726
Pondsville	42171
Pongo	40456
Poole	42444
Poortown	40356
Pope	42128
Poplar	41128
Poplar Corner	40033
Poplar Flat	41189
Poplar Grove (Fleming County)	41041
Poplar Grove (McLean County)	42372
Poplar Grove (Owen County)	41046
Poplar Highlands	41169
Poplar Hills	40213
Poplar Plains	41041
Poplarville	42501
Porter	40370
Portland (Adair County)	42761
Portland (Jefferson County)	40212
Portland (Pendleton County)	41033
Port Royal	40058

	ZIP		ZIP		ZIP
Portsmouth	41339	Rella	40902	Roscoe	41171
Possum Trot	42029	Renaker	41003	Rose Crossroads	42629
Potters	41230	Render	42320	Rosefork	41301
Potters Fork	41537	Renfro Valley	40473	Rose Hill (Carter County)	41164
Pottsville (Graves County)	42051	Renfrow	42349	Rose Hill (Mercer County)	40330
Pottsville (Washington County)	40069	Repton	42064	Rose Terrace	40121
Powderly	42367	Revelo	42638	Rosetta	40146
Powells Creek	41501	Rex	42746	Roseville (Barren County)	42141
Powersburg	42633	Rexville	41332	Roseville (Hancock County)	42368
Powersville	41004	Reynolds Station	42368	Rosewood	42345
Prairie Village	40272	Reynoldsville	40374	Rosine	42370
Prater	41164	Rhea	40806	Ross	41059
Pratt	42455	Rheber	42528	Rossland	40734
Preachersville	40419	Rhoda	42210	Rosslyn	40380
Premium	41845	Rhodelia	40161	Rosspoint	40806
Prentiss	42320	Ribolt	41189	Rothwell	40322
Presidential	40004	Rice Station	40336	Roundhill (Edmonson County)	42275
Press	41339	Ricetown	41364	Round Hill (Madison County)	40475
Preston	40366	Riceville (Fulton County)	42041	Roundstone	40456
Preston Estates	41240	Riceville (Johnson County)	41258	Rouse (Part of Covington)	41014
Prestonia (Part of Louisville)	40213	Richardson	41230	Rousseau	41366
Prestonsburg	41653	Richardsville	42270	Routt	40299
Prestonville	41008	Richelieu	42206	Rowdy	41367
Price	41636	Richland	42431	Rowena	42629
Prices Mill	42134	Richlawn	40207	Rowland	40484
Pricetown (Casey County)	42539	Richmond	40475*	Rowletts	42772
Pricetown (Fayette County)	40509		40476†	Roxana	41848
Priceville	42765	Richmond Mall (Part of Richmond)	40475	Royalton	41464
Pride	42404	Rich Pond	42104	Royrader	40402
Primrose	41362	Richwood	41094	Royville	42642
Princess	41102	Ridgeview Estates (Part of Frankfort)	40601	Ruckerville	40391
Princeton	42445	Ridgeview Heights (Part of Independence)	41051	Ruddels Mills	40361
Printer	41655	Ridgeway	40849	Ruin	41171
Pritchardsville	42141	Riley	40328	Rumsey	42371
Privett	40486	Rileyville	40927	Rural	41514
Proctor	41311	Rineyville	40162	Rush	41168
Prospect	40059	Ringgold	42501	Russell	41169
Prosperity	42207	Ringos Mills	41049	Russell Heights (Part of Russell)	41169
Providence (Jessamine County)	40503	Rio Vista (Part of Loyall)	40854	Russell Springs	42642
Providence (Knox County)	40906	Risner	41649	Russellville	42276
Providence (Simpson County)	42134	Ritchie	41701	Ruth	42501
Providence (Trimble County)	40011	Ritner	42633	Rutherford	40927
Providence (Webster County)	42450	Rivals	40071	Rutland	41031
Provo	42267	River	41254	Ryan	41093
Pruden	37851	River Bluff	40059	Ryland	41015
Pryorsburg	42066	Riverfront (Part of Louisville)	40270	Ryland Heights	41015
Pryse	40471	River Oaks	42765	Sacramento	42372
Public	42501	River Park (Part of Lexington)	40502	Sadieville	40370
Pueblo	42633	River Ridge	40828	Sadler	42754
Pulaski	42567	Riverside	42270	St. Catharine	40061
Pumpkin Center	42445	Riverside Gardens	40216	St. Charles	42453
Puncheon	41828	Riverview	42003	St. Dennis (Jefferson County)	40216
Purdy	42728	Riverview Estates (Part of Harrodsburg)	40330	St. Elmo	42266
Putney	40865	Riverwood	40207	St. Francis	40062
Pyles	42058	Road Junction	41522	St. Helens	41368
Pyramid	41653	Roaring Spring	42211	St. John	42701
Quail	40409	Roark	40979	St. Johns	42001
Quality	42268	Robards	42452	St. Joseph (Daviess County)	42373
Quicksand	41363	Robinson	41031	St. Joseph (Marion County)	40060
Quincy	41166	Robinson Creek	41560	St. Mary	40063
Quinton	42518	Robinsville	40475	St. Matthews	40206-07
Rabbit Hash	41005	Robinswood	40207		40222
Rabbit Ridge	42441	Robinwood Estates (Part of Lexington)	40503		40257
Raccoon	41557	Rob Roy	42320	For specific St. Matthews Zip Codes call (502) 454-1650, or your local postmaster.	
Raceland	41169	Rochester	42273	St. Paul (Grayson County)	42754
Radcliff	40159†	Rockbridge	42167	St. Paul (Lewis County)	42170
	40160*	Rockcastle	42211	St. Regis Park	40220
Radcliff (Part of Lexington)	40505	Rockdale (Boyd County)	41102	St. Vincent	42437
Ragland	42053	Rockdale (Owen County)	40359	Saldee	41369
Railton	42171	Rockfield	42274	Salem (Livingston County)	42078
Randolph	42129	Rock Haven	40175	Salem (Russell County)	42642
Ransom	41531	Rockholds	40759	Salleeton	40033
Rapids	42134	Rockhouse	41561	Salmons	42134
Raven	41861	Rockland	42101	Saloma	42718
Ravenna	40472	Rockport	42369	Salt Gum	40935
Raymond	40176	Rock Springs	42406	Salt Lick	40371
Raywick	40060	Rockybranch	42640	Salt River (Part of Shepherdsville)	40165
Ready	42721	Rocky Hill (Barren County)	42141	Salt Well	40311
Rectorville	41056	Rocky Hill (Edmonson County)	42163	Salvisa	40372
Redbud	40828	Rodburn	40351	Salyersville	41465
Redbush	41219	Roederer Farm Center	40031	Sample	40143
Red Cross	42160	Roff	40178	Samuels	40013
Redfox	41847	Rogers	41365	Sandefur Crossing	42320
Red Hill (Allen County)	42164	Rogers Chapel	40380	Sanders	41083
Red Hill (Daviess County)	42376	Rogers Gap	40324	Sandgap	40481
Redhouse	40475	Rolling Acres (Part of Frankfort)	40601	Sand Hill (Estill County)	40336
Red Lick	42129	Rolling Fields	40207	Sand Hill (Harlan County)	40823
Red River	42202	Rolling Hills	40222	Sand Hill (Warren County)	42101
Redwine	41477	Rollington (Part of Pewee Valley)	40056	Sand Springs (Jackson County)	40447
Reed	42451	Rome	42301	Sand Springs (Rockcastle County)	40456
Reeds Crossing	40475	Romine	42718	Sandy	42325
Reedville	41143	Rookwood (Part of Lexington)	40505	Sandy Hook	41171
Reedyville	42275				
Regina	41559				
Region	42275				
Reidland	42003				
Reid Village	40353				
Relief	41472				

* Area Zip Code   † Post Office Boxes

	ZIP
Sano	42728
Sarah	41171
Saratoga	42445
Sardis	41056
Sassafras	41759
Sassafras Ridge	42050
Sasser	40741
Saul	40981
Savage	42602
Savage Branch	41129
Savoy	40769
Savoyard	42749
Sawyer	42643
Saxton	40769
Saylor	40840
Scale	42025
Scalf	40982
Schley	42202
Schochoh	42202
Schultztown	42320
Schweizer	42134
Science Hill	42553
Scottown	42320
Scottsburg	42445
Scotts Station	40065
Scottsville	42164
Scoville	41314
Scranton	40322
Scuddy	41760
Seatonville	40299
Seaville	40078
Sebastians Branch	41314
Sebree	42455
Seco	41849
Sedalia	42079
Segal	42210
Seitz	41466
Select	42333
Seminary	42602
Seminary Village (Part of Louisville)	40207
Semiway	42371
Seneca Gardens	40205
Senterville	41522
Se Ree	40164
Sergent	41858
Settle	42164
Settlers Point	40059
Seventy Six	42602
Sewell	41385
Sewellton	42629
Sextons Creek	40983
Seymour	42749
Shadeland (Part of Lexington)	40502
Shady Grove (Crittenden County)	42064
Shady Grove (McCracken County)	42003
Shady Grove (Metcalfe County)	42214
Shady Nook	41031
Shafter	42501
Sha Lawn Village	42718
Shannon	41055
Sharer	42235
Sharkey	40351
Sharon	41002
Sharondale	41514
Sharon Grove	42280
Sharpe	42025
Sharpsburg	40374
Sharpsville	40330
Shawhan	40361
Shawnee (Part of Louisville)	40212
Shawnee Estates (Part of Bowling Green)	42104
Shearer Valley	42633
Shelbiana	41562
Shelby (Part of Louisville)	40217
Shelby City (Part of Junction City)	40422
Shelby Gap	41563
Shelbyville	40065*
	40066†
Shepherdsville	40165
Shepola	42544
Sherburne	41041
Sheridan	42064
Sherman	41035
Sherwood Shores	42044
Shetland	40383
Shields	40849
Shiloh	42071
Shipley	42602
Shively	40216*
	40256†
Shopville	42554
Shore Acres	40601
Short Creek	42721
Short Town	40828
Shoulderblade	41339

	ZIP
Shreve	42343
Shrewsbury	42721
Sibert	40962
Sidell	40962
Sideview	40353
Sideway	41164
Sidney	41564
Siler (Knox County)	40701
Siler (Whitley County)	40763
Silerville	42649
Silica	41164
Siloam	41175
Silver City	42261
Silver Creek	40403
Silver Grove	41085
Silverhill	41467
Silver Lake Farm (Part of Frankfort)	40601
Simmons	42354
Simpson	41301
Simpsonville	40067
Sims Fork	40902
Sinai	40342
Sinking Fork	42240
Sirocco	40108
Sitka	41255
Sizerock	41762
Skillman	42348
Skinnersburg	40379
Skycrest (Part of Lexington)	40504
Skylight	40026
Skyline	41821
Slade	40376
Slat	42633
Slate Lick	40403
Slater	42087
Slate Valley	40360
Slaughters	42456
Slavans	42653
Slemp	41763
Slickford	42633
Slick Rock	42141
Sligo	40055
Sloans Valley	42555
Smilax	41764
Smile	40351
Smith	40815
Smithfield	40068
Smithland	42081
Smith Mills	42457
Smiths Creek	41164
Smiths Grove	42171
Smith Town	42647
Smithview	42721
Smithwood	42076
Smoky Valley	41164
Smyrna	40219
Snell	42501
Snow	42602
Snow Hill	40065
Soft Shell	41831
Soldier	41173
Somerset	42501-02
	42564
For specific Somerset Zip Codes call (606) 678-5712, or your local postmaster.	
Sonora	42776
Sorgho	42301
South	42754
South Buffalo	42716
South Campbellsville (Part of Campbellsville)	42718
South Carrollton	42374
Southdown	41815
South Elkhorn (Part of Lexington)	40503
Southern Hills (Part of Richmond)	40475
South Fork (Lincoln County)	40437
Southfork (Owsley County)	41314
Southgate	41071
South Higginsport	41002
South Highlands	42066
South Hill	42261
South Irvine	40336
Southland (Part of Lexington)	40503
South Marshall	42025
South Park	40118
South Park View	40219
Southport (Part of Lexington)	40503
South Portsmouth	41174
South Ripley	41034
South Shore	41175
South Shores	40065
South Union	42283
Southville	40065
South Wallins	40873
South Williamson	41503
Southwire	42348

	ZIP
Spa	42256
Spann	42633
Sparksville	42728
Sparta	41086
Spears	40502
Speck	42728
Speedwell	40475
Speight	41572
Spence (Part of Newport)	41071
Spencer	40353
Spider	41843
Spindletop	40324
Spiro	40456
Spottsville	42458
Spring Creek	40962
Springfield	40069
Spring Grove	42437
Springhill (Hickman County)	42031
Springhill (Nelson County)	40004
Springhill (Warren County)	42101
Spring Hill Estates	40601
Springlake	41015
Springlee	40207
Spring Lick	42779
Spring Mill	40228
Spring Station	40347
Spring Valley	40222
Sprout	40350
Spruce Pine	40874
Sprule	40906
Spurlington	42718
Spurlock	40972
Squib	42501
Squiresville	40359
Stab	42557
Stacy Fork	41472
Staffordsburg	41051
Staffordsville	41256
Stambaugh	41257
Stamping Ground	40379
Stanfill	40831
Stanford	40484
Stanley	42375
Stanton	40380
Stanville	41659
Stark	41164
Star Mills	42740
Stateland (Part of Richmond)	40475
State Line	42050
Static	42602
Station Camp	40336
Station No. 1 (Part of Tompkinsville)	42167
Stay	41364
Stearns (McCreary County)	42647
Steele	41566
Steff	42780
Stella (Calloway County)	42071
Stella (Magoffin County)	41465
Stephens	41177
Stephensburg	42781
Stephensport	40170
Stepstone	40360
Steubenville	42648
Stewart	40330
Stewartsville	41097
Stiles	40028
Stillwater	41301
Stinnett	40868
Stinnettsville	40146
Stinson	41143
Stockholm	42259
Stone	41567
Stonegate	40383
Stone Hedge Estates	40324
Stonestreet	40272
Stonewall (Bracken County)	41004
Stonewall (Scott County)	40370
Stonewall Estates (Fayette County)	40503
Stonewall Estates (Franklin County)	40601
Stoney Fork	40988
Stoney Point	41034
Stony Fork Junction (Part of Middlesboro)	40965
Stop	42633
Stopover	41568
Stormking	41701
Stovall	42160
Straight Creek	40977
Strait Creek	41132
Strathmoor Gardens	40205
Strathmoor Manor	40205
Strathmoor Village	40205
Straw	42259
Strawberry	42501
Stricklett	41179
Stringtown (Anderson County)	40342

Name	ZIP	Name	ZIP	Name	ZIP
Stringtown (Boone County)	41048	Teaberry	41660	Trisler	42343
Stringtown (Fleming County)	41049	Tedders	40906	Trosper	40995
Stringtown (Grant County)	41003	Teddy	42539	Troublesome	41712
Stringtown (Lawrence County)	41230	Teetersville	40831	Troy	40383
		Teges	40972	Tuckertown	42159
Stringtown (Madison County)	40475	Temperance	42134	Tuggleville	40845
		Temple Hill	42141	Tunnel Hill	42701
Stringtown (Magoffin County)	41465	Ten Broeck	40222	Turfland Mall (Part of Lexington)	40504
		Ten Spot	40828		
Stringtown (McLean County)	42372	Teresita	40359	Turkey	41314
		Terrapin	40330	Turkey Creek	41570
Stringtown (Mercer County)	40330	Terryville	41159	Turkey Foot	40370
Stringtown (Muhlenberg County)	42372	Texas	40069	Turkeytown	40419
		Texola	40471	Turners Station	40075
Strunk	42649	Thealka	41240	Turnersville	40484
Stubblefield	42088	The Colony (Fayette County)	40504	Turnertown (Butler County)	42268
Sturgeon	41314			Turnertown (Simpson County)	42134
Sturgis	42459	The Colony (Woodford County)	40383		
Sublett	41465			Tutor Key	41263
Sublimity City	40741	Thelma	41260	Tuttle	40741
Subtle	42129	The Moors	42044	Tway (Part of Harlan)	40831
Sudith	40371	The Ridge	41171	Twentysix	41472
Sugar Creek	41095	Thistleton Heights (Part of Frankfort)	40601	Twila	40873
Sugar Grove	42261			Twin Lakes	41091
Sugar Hill	42501	Thixton	40291	Twin Oaks (Part of Lexington)	40503
Sugartit	41042	Thomas	41626		
Sullivan	42460	Thompsonville	40069	Two Creeks	40601
Sulphur	40070	Thorn Hill (Franklin County)	40601	Tyewhoppety	42216
Sulphur Lick	42166	Thornhill (Jefferson County)	40222	Tyner	40486
Sulphur Springs	42358	Thornton	41855	Typo	41771
Sulphur Well (Jessamine County)	40356	Thorobred East Subdivision No. 2	42301	Tyrone	40342
				Ula	42501
Sulphur Well (Metcalfe County)	42129	Thousandsticks	41766	Ulvah	41731
		Threeforks (Martin County)	41261	Ulysses	41264
Summer Shade	42166	Three Forks (Warren County)	42159	Union	41091
Summersville	42782			Union City	40475
Summit (Boyd County)	41102	Threelinks	40456	Union Hall	40472
Summit (Hardin County)	42783	Three Mile	41144	Union Mills	40356
Summit Hills Heights (Part of Edgewood)	41017	Three Point	40815	Union Ridge	42365
		Three Springs (Hart County)	42746	Union Star	40171
Sumpter	42633	Three Springs (Warren County)	42104	Uniontown	42461
Sunfish	42284			University Estates	42701
Sunny Acres (Part of Taylor Mill)	41015	Thruston	42301	University Heights (Part of Hopkinsville)	42240
		Thurlow	42743		
Sunnybrook	42633	Tierra Linda (Part of Frankfort)	40601	Uno	42749
Sunny Corner	42348			Upchurch	42602
Sunnydale	42358	Tierra Linda III (Part of Frankfort)	40601	Upper Kings Addition	41175
Sunnyside	42101			Upper Tygart	41164
Sunrise	41031	Tilden	42409	Upton	42784
Sunset	41049	Tilford	42721	Urban	40962
Sunshine (Greenup County)	41175	Tiline	42083	Utica	42376
Sunshine (Harlan County)	40831	Tilton	41041	Utility	42348
Susie	42633	Timber Lake	42518	Uttingertown (Part of Lexington)	40516
Sussex Estates	40356	Timberwood Lake Shores	41010		
Suterville	40379	Tina	41740	Vada	41311
Sutherland	42376	Tinsley	40977	Valeria	41301
Sutton	41562	Tiny Town	42234	Valley Downs	40272
Suwanee	42055	Tiptop	41409	Valley Gardens	40258
Swallowfield	40601	Todds Point	40065	Valley Hill	40069
Swamp Branch	41258	Toddville	40444	Valley Oak	42501
Swampton	41465	Toler	41569	Valley Station	40258
Swanee Shores	41097	Toliver	41332		40272
Swan Lake	40906	Tollesboro	41189	For specific Valley Station Zip Codes call (502) 454-1650, or your local postmaster.	
Swanpond	40906	Tolliver Town	41810		
Sweeden	42285	Tolu	42084		
Sweeneyville	42718	Tomahawk	41262	Valley View (Bracken County)	41002
Sweet Owen	40359	Tompkinsville	42167		
Switzer	40601	Tonieville	42748	Valley View (Madison County)	40475
Sycamore	40223	Toonerville	41548		
Sycamore Estates	40383	Topmost	41862	Valley Village	40272
Sylvandell	41031	Topton	40741	Van	41858
Sylvania	40258	Torrent	41396	Vanarsdell	40330
Symbol	40729	Totz	40870	Vanceburg	41179
Symsonia	42082	Toulouse	41723	Vancleve	41385
Tabernacle	42220	Touristville	42633	Vanderburg	42409
Tablow	40330	Tousey	40119	Vandetta	42413
Tacky Town	40988	Town and Country (Daviess County)	42301	Vanhook	42501
Taffy	42347			Van Lear (Johnson County)	41265
Taft	41314	Town and Country (Logan County)	42276	Van Voorhis Manor	40121
Talbert	41377			Vanzant	40119
Talcum	41765	Towne Mall (Part of Elizabethtown)	42701	Varilla	40813
Tallega	41378			Varney	41571
Talmage	40330	Towne Square Mall (Part of Owensboro)	42301	Veech	40022
Tanbark	42752			Venters	41522
Tanglewood (Part of Frankfort)	40601	Tracy	42133	Verda	40828
		Trailwood Lakes	40003	Verna Hills	40391
Tanksley	40962	Tram	41663	Verne	40769
Tanner	42748	Trammel	42164	Vernon	42151
Tar Fork	40111	Trapp	40391	Verona	41092
Tar Hill	42754	Trappist	40051	Versailles	40383
Tarryon No 1	42055	Travellers Rest	41314	Vertrees	42785
Tates Creek Estates	40356	Treasure Island	40229	Vest	41772
Tateville	42558	Tremont	40873	Vester	42728
Tatham Springs	40078	Trent	41301	Vicco	41773
Tattersail Trails Estates	40701	Trenton	42286	Victory	40729
Tatumsville	42044	Tress Shop	42220	Village Center (Part of Harlan)	40831
Taulbee	41385	Tribbey	41722		
Taylor Mill	41015	Tribune	42064	Villa Hills	41016
Taylor Mines	42320	Tri City	42040	Vincent	41386
Taylorsport	41048	Trigg Furnace	42211	Vine Grove	40175
Taylors Store	42049	Trimble	42544	Vineyard	40356
Taylorsville	40071	Trinity	41179	Viola	42051

	ZIP
Viper	41774
Virden	40312
Virgie	41572
Visalia	41015
Volga	41266
Vortex	41301
Wabaco	41701
Wabash	42713
Wabd	40456
Waco	40385
Waddy	40076
Wadesboro	42048
Wagersville	40336
Wago	42602
Wait	42603
Wakefield	40071
Walden	40701
Waldo	41632
Wales	41572
Walker	40997
Walkertown (Part of Hazard)	41701
Wallaceton	40461
Wallingford	41093
Wallins Creek	40873
Wallonia	42211
Walltown	40489
Walnut Grove (Allen County)	42120
Walnut Grove (Caldwell County)	42411
Walnut Grove (Marshall County)	42025
Walnut Grove (Pulaski County)	42563
Walsh	41175
Waltersville	40312
Walton	41094
Waltz	40351
Wanamaker	42455
Waneta	40488
Warbranch	40874
Warco	41645
War Creek	41339
Warfield	41267
Warnock	41144
Warren	40906
Warsaw	41095
Washington (Part of Maysville)	41096
Wasioto	40977
Watauga	42602
Watch	40701
Waterford	40071
Watergap	41653
Waterloo	41005
Water Valley	42085
Waterview	42786
Watkinsville	40379
Watterson Park	40213
	40218

For specific Watterson Park Zip Codes call (502) 454-1650, or your local postmaster.

Watts	41348
Waverly	42462
Waverly Hills	40272
Wax	42726
Wayland	41666
Waynesburg	40489
Weaverton (Part of Henderson)	42420
Webbs	42743
Webbs Cross Roads	42642
Webbville	41180
Weberstown	42364
Webster	40176
Wedonia	41055
Weeksbury	41667
Weir	42345
Welborn	42501
Welchs Creek	42287
Welcome	42261
Weldon	40108
Wellhope	40456
Wellington (Jefferson County)	40205
Wellington (Menifee County)	40387
Wellington Place (Part of Bardstown)	40004
Wells	42330
Wellsburg	41043
Wells Landing	40422
Wendover	41775
Wentz	41731
Wesco	42431
Wesleyan Park (Part of Winchester)	40391
Wesleyville	41164
Westbend	40312
West Brook	42240
West Buechel	40218
West Clifty	42754

	ZIP
West Danville (Part of Danville)	40422
Western	42050
Western Kentucky Correctional Complex	42038
Western State Hospital	42240
West Fairview	41101
West Future City	42053
West Garrett	41630
Westgate (Part of Frankfort)	40601
West Irvine	40336
West Liberty	41472
West Louisville	42377
Weston	40311
West Paducah	42086
Westplains	42051
West Point	40177
Westport	40077
West Prestonsburg (Part of Prestonsburg)	41668
West Russell (Part of Flatwoods)	41169
West Somerset (Part of Somerset)	42564
West Van Lear	41268
Westview	40178
Westwood (Boyd County)	41101
Westwood (Jefferson County)	40222
Westwood Park (Part of Frankfort)	40601
Wheatcroft	42463
Wheatley	40389
Wheel	42061
Wheeler	40906
Wheelersburg	41465
Wheelwright	41669
Whick	41390
Whipps Millgate	40223
Whitaker (Floyd County)	41216
Whitaker (Letcher County)	41849
Whitco	41858
White City (Hopkins County)	42464
White City (Larue County)	42748
White Hall	40475
Whitehouse	41269
White Lily	42501
White Mills	42788
White Oak (Garrard County)	40444
White Oak (Morgan County)	41474
White Oak Junction	42647
White Plains (Allen County)	42164
White Plains (Hopkins County)	42464
Whitepost	41514
White Run	42349
Whitesburg	41858
White Sulphur (Caldwell County)	42411
White Sulphur (Scott County)	40324
Whitesville	42378
White Tower	41051
White Villa	41063
Whitewood	42743
Whitfield	40047
Whitley City	42653
Wiborg	42653
Wickliffe	42087
Wicks Well	42431
Widecreek	41391
Wilbur	41124
Wild Cat	40962
Wilder	41071
	41076

For specific Wilder Zip Codes call (606) 291-5250, or your local postmaster.

Wilderness Road	42259
Wildie	40492
Wildwood	40223
Wilhurst	41385
Willaila	40409
Willard	41181
Williams	41474
Williamsburg	40769
Williamsport	41271
Williamstown	41097
Willisburg	40078
Willow (Bracken County)	41004
Willow (Lee County)	41358
Willowcrest	40601
Willow Grove	41043
Willow Shade	42169
Willowtown	42718
Willow Tree	40472
Wilmore	40390
Wilson	42406
Wilsonville (Boyle County)	40422
Wilsonville (Spencer County)	40023
Wilstacy	41339

	ZIP
Wilton	40771
Winburn Estates (Part of Lexington)	40511
Winchester	40391*
	40392†
Wind Cave	40494
Winding Falls	40207
Windsor	42565
Windy	42655
Windy Hill	42349
Windy Hills	40207
Windyville	42210
Wingo	42088
Winifred	41219
Winlow Park	42064
Winston	40495
Winston Park (Part of Taylor Mill)	41015
Winwright	41501
Wiscoal	41759
Wisconsin	41759
Wisdom	42129
Wisemantown	40336
Wises Landing	40006
Wiswell	42071
Wittensville	41274
Witt Springs	40336
Wofford	40769
Wolf	41164
Wolf Coal	41339
Wolf Creek	40104
Wolfpit	41522
Wolverine	41339
Wonder	41626
Wonnie	41465
Woodbine	40771
Woodburn	42170
Woodbury	42288
Woodford Village (Part of Versailles)	40383
Woodlake	40601
Woodland Estates	41240
Woodland Hills	40243
Woodland Park (Part of Hazard)	41701
Woodlands (Part of Frankfort)	40601
Woodlawn (Campbell County)	41071
Woodlawn (McCracken County)	42003
Woodlawn (Nelson County)	40004
Woodlawn-Oakdale	42003
Woodlawn Park (Anderson County)	40342
Woodlawn Park (Jefferson County)	40207
Woodman	41568
Woods	41653
Woodsbend	41472
Woodson Bend	42518
Woodsonville	42765
Woodstock	42501
Woodville	42086
Wooleyville	42718
Woollum	40999
Wooton	41776
Worthington	41183
Worthington Hills	40223
Worthville	41098
Wray Gap	42633
Wrights	42718
Wrightsburg	42327
Wrigley	41477
Wurtland	41144
Wyett	41171
Wyman	42327
Yaden	40769
Yancey	40831
Yatesville	41230
Yeaddiss	41777
Yeager	41501
Yeaman	42361
Yellow Rock	41311
Yelvington	42355
Yerkes	41778
Yesse	42164
Yocum	41472
York	41175
Yosemite	42566
Younger Creek	42701
Youngs Creek	40701
Yuma	42733
Zachariah	41396
Zag	41472
Zandale (Part of Lexington)	40503
Zebulon	41501
Zelda	41129
Zion (Henderson County)	42420
Zion (Todd County)	42234
Zion Hill	40347
Zion Station	41035

* Area Zip Code   **† Post Office Boxes**

	ZIP		ZIP
Zoe	41397	Zula	42603
Zoneton (Part of Pioneer Village)	40165		

	ZIP
Abbeville	70510*
	70511†
Abby Plantation	70301
Aben	70346
Abington	71052
Abita Springs	70420
Acadia	70301
Acadia Academy	70535
Acme	71316
Acy	70774
Ada	71080
Addis	70710
Adeline	70544
Adner	71037
Advance (Part of Hodge)	71247
Afton	71282
Aimwell	71401
Airline Park	70003
Airview Terrace (Part of Alexandria)	71301
Ajax	71450
Akers	70421
Albania	70544
Albany	70711
Alberta	71016
Alco	71446
Alden Bridge	71006
Alexandria	71301-15
For specific Alexandria Zip Codes call (318) 484-4637, or your local postmaster.	
Alexandria Mall (Part of Alexandria)	71301
Alfalfa	71409
Alfords	70720
Alice B	70538
Alice C	70538
Allemand	70360
Allen	71469
Allendale	70767
Alliance	70037
Allon	70760
Alluvial City	70085
Aloha	71417
Aloysia	70788
Alsen	70807
Alto	71269
Alton	70458
Alvin Callender	70037
Ama	70031
Amelia	70340
Amite	70422
Anacoco	71403
Anandale	71301
Andrew	70548
Andrew Guillot Subdivision	70301
Angelina	70076
Angie	70426
Annadale	70788
Ansley	71270
Antioch (Claiborne Parish)	71040
Antioch (Lincoln Parish)	71275
Antonia	71467
Antonio	70767
Antrim	71064
Arabi	70032
Ararat	70601
Arbroth	70720
Arcadia	71001
Archibald	71218
Archie	71343
Arcola	70456
Ardoyne	70360
Argo	71343
Argyle	70360
Arizona	71040
Arklatex (Part of Mooringsport)	71060
Arlington	70808
Armistead	71019
Arnaudville	70512
Ashland (Natchitoches Parish)	71002
Ashland (Terrebonne Parish)	70360
Ashley	71282
Ashton	70538
Athens	71003
Atlanta	71404
Attakapas Landing	70390
Audubon (Part of Baton Rouge)	70806
Audubon Terrace	70808
Augusta (Iberville Parish)	70788
Augusta (Plaquemines Parish)	70037
Avalon	70392
Avandale	71366
Avery Island	70513
Avondale	70094
Aycock	71001
Azucena	71375
Bagdad	71417

	ZIP
Bains	70775
Baker	70704†
	70714*
Baldwin	70514
Ball	71405
Bancroft	70653
Bankers	70582
Banks	70807
Banks Springs	71418
Baptist	70403
Barataria	70036
Barber Spur	70586
Bardel	71269
Barnet Springs (Part of Ruston)	71270
Barron	71328
Barton	70346
Basile	70515
Baskin	71219
Baskinton	71219
Bastrop	71220*
	71221†
Batchelor	70715
Baton Rouge	70801-98
For specific Baton Rouge Zip Codes call (504) 381-0372, or your local postmaster.	
Batree	70090
Bawcornville	71291
Bayou Barbary	70754
Bayou Blue	70360
Bayou Cane	70359
Bayou Chicot	70586
Bayou Crab	70390
Bayou Current	71353
Bayou Gauche	70030
Bayou Goula	70716
Bayou Pigeon	70764
Bayou Sale	70538
Bayou Sorrel	70764
Baywood	70739
Beach Grove	71277
Beachview (Part of Kenner)	70065
Bear Creek	71008
Bear Skin	71266
Beaver	71463
Bee Bayou	71269
Beech Springs	71247
Beekman	71220
Beggs	71322
Bel	70658
Belah	71371
Belair	70040
Belair Cove	70586
Belcher	71004
Bell City	70630
Belle Amie	70345
Belle Chasse	70037
Belledeau	71341
Belle Place	70552
Belle Point	70084
Belle River	70339
Belle Rose	70341
Belle Terre (Assumption Parish)	70346
Belle Terre (Iberville Parish)	70764
Belleview	70570
Bellevue (Bossier Parish)	71037
Bellevue (Caldwell Parish)	71418
Bellfontaine	71815
Bell Helene	70734
Bellwood	71468
Belmont (Sabine Parish)	71406
Belmont (St. James Parish)	70743
Belmont (West Baton Rouge Parish)	70767
Benson	71419
Bentley	71407
Benton	71006
Bermuda	71456
Bernice	71222
Bertie	70390
Bertrandville (Assumption Parish)	70390
Bertrandville (Plaquemines Parish)	70040
Berwick	70342
Bethany	71007
Bienville	71008
Big Bend	71318
Big Branch	70445
Big Cane	71356
Big Creek	71219
Big Island	71328
Big Woods	70668
Billeaud	70518
Bissonnet	70003
Bivens	70653
Blackburn	71038
Black Hawk	71373
Blade	71342
Blanchard	71009

	ZIP
Blanche	71433
Blanks	70717
Blankston	71202
Blond	70433
Bluff Creek	70722
Bob Acres	70560
Bodcau	71037
Bodoc	71329
Bogalusa	70427-29
For specific Bogalusa Zip Codes call (504) 735-5921, or your local postmaster.	
Bohemia	70082
Bolden	71358
Boleyn	71450
Bolinger	71064
Bolivar	70444
Bonaire	70808
Bond	71463
Bonfouca	70458
Bonita	71223
Bon Marche Mall (Part of Baton Rouge)	70806
Bon Secour	70086
Book	71343
Boone's Corner	70065
Boothville	70038
Boothville-Venice	70038
Bordelonville	71320
Borgne Mouth	70092
Borodino	71355
Bosco	71202
Boscoville	70570
Bossier City	71111-13
	71171-72
For specific Bossier City Zip Codes call (318) 746-1481, or your local postmaster.	
Boston	70533
Boudreaux Canal	70344
Bourg	70343
Boutte	70039
Boyce	71409
Braithwaite	70040
Branch	70516
Breard (Part of Monroe)	71203
Breaux Bridge	70517
Breezy Hill	71467
Brewton's Mill	71031
Bridge City	70094
Brignac	70737
Bristol	70584
Brittany	70718
Broadmoor (Lafayette Parish)	70501
Broadmoor (Orleans Parish)	70125
Broadmoor (Terrebonne Parish)	70360
Broadview (Part of Baton Rouge)	70815
Brooks	70760
Brouillette	71351
Broussard	70518
Brown	71016
Brownell	71295
Brownfields	70811
Brown Heights	70714
Brownlee	71111
Brownsville-Bawcomville	71291
Brownville (Caldwell Parish)	71418
Brownville (Ouachita Parish)	71291
Brule	70372
Brule Guillot	70301
Bruly La Croix	70788
Bruly Saint Martin	70341
Brusle Saint Vincent	70390
Brusly	70719
Bryant (Part of New Iberia)	70560
Bryceland	71014
Buckeye	71328
Buckner	71269
Bueche	70720
Buhler	70663
Bull Run	70395
Bunkie	71322
Buras	70041
Buras-Triumph	70041
Burkplace	71016
Burr Ferry	71403
Burroughs	71418
Burrwood	70091
Burton Lane	70086
Bush	70431
Bushes	71295
Bywaters (Part of New Orleans)	70117
Caddo (Part of Oil City)	71061
Caddo Station	71082
Cade	70519
Cadeville	71238
Caernarvon	70040

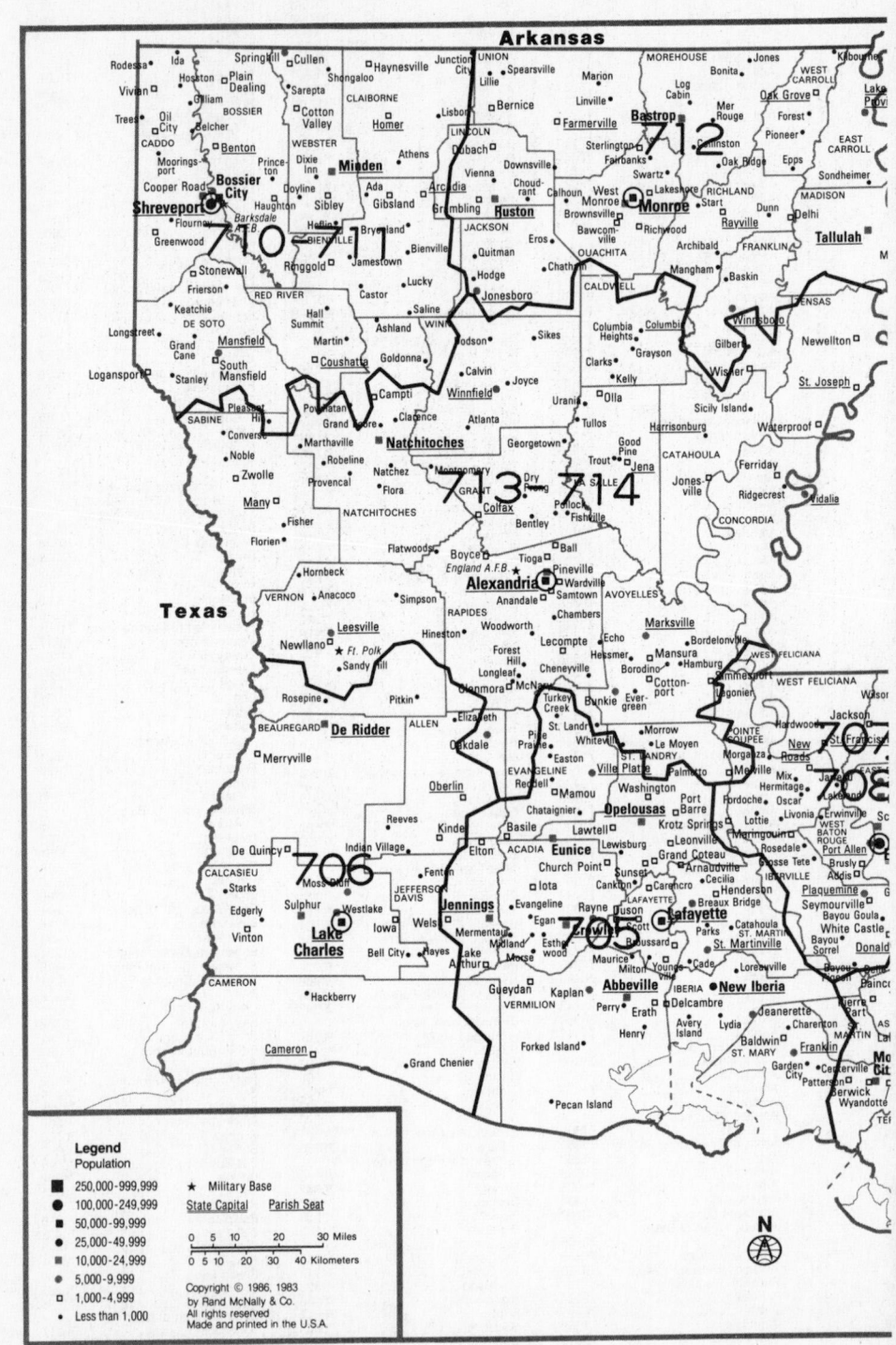

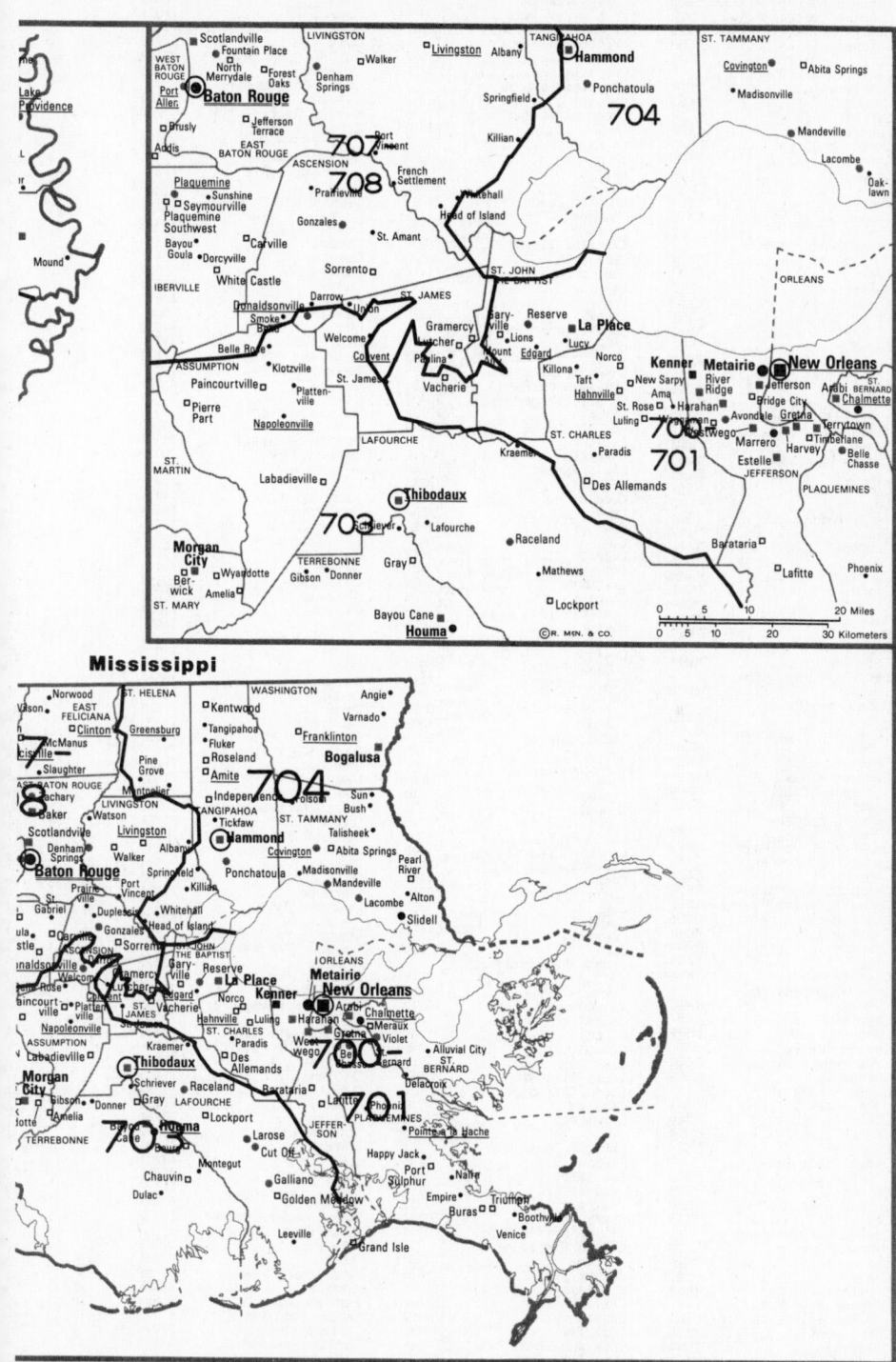

	ZIP
Caffery	70538
Calcasieu (Allen Parish)	71433
Calcasieu (Rapides Parish)	71433
Calhoun	71225
Calumet	70392
Calvin	71410
Camelia Gardens (Part of Alexandria)	71301
Cameron	70631
Camp Beauregard	71301
Camperdown	70538
Campti	71411
Cancienne	70390
Canebrake	71334
Caney	71446
Cankton	70584
Cannonburg	70788
Capitan	70592
Capitol (Part of Baton Rouge)	70804
Caplis	71111
Carencro	70520
Carlisle	70042
Carlton	71225
Carlyss	70663
Carmel	71052
Caroline	70552
Carrollton (Part of New Orleans)	70118
Carrollton Central Plaza (Part of New Orleans)	70118
Carrolwood	70068
Carterville	71064
Carthage Bluff Landing	70462
Cartwright	71227
Carville	70721
Caspiana	71115
Castle Village	71301
Castor	71016
Catahoula	70582
Catherine	70716
Cat Island	71418
Catuna	71052
Cavett	71004
Cecile	71105
Cecilia	70521
Cedar Crest	70816
Cedar Glen	70811
Cedar Grove (Assumption Parish)	70372
Cedar Grove (Caddo Parish)	71106
Cedar Grove (Plaquemines Parish)	70037
Cedarton	71227
Centenary (Part of Shreveport)	71104
Center Point	71323
Centerville (Evangeline Parish)	71367
Centerville (St. Mary Parish)	70522
Central (East Baton Rouge Parish)	70811
Central (St. James Parish)	70723
Central (Terrebonne Parish)	70360
Chacahoula	70395
Chackbay	70301
Chalmette	70043*
	70044†
Chalmette Vista	70043
Chamale Cove (Part of Slidell)	70460
Chamberlin	70767
Chambers	71346
Chandler Park (Part of Alexandria)	71301
Charenton	70523
Charles Park (Part of Alexandria)	71301
Charlotte	70560
Chase	71324
Chataignier	70524
Chateau Village (Part of Kenner)	70065
Chatham	71226
Chatman Town	70090
Chauvin	70344
Chef Menteur (Part of New Orleans)	70126
Cheneyville	71325
Cheniere	71291
Cherokee Court	70123
Cherokee Village (Part of Alexandria)	71301
Cherry Grove	70655
Chesbrough	70444
Chestnut	71070
Chickama	71346
Chickasaw	71263
Chinchuba	70448
Chipola	70441

	ZIP
Chitimacha Indian Reservation	70523
Chloe	70647
Choctaw (Iberville Parish)	70767
Choctaw (Lafourche Parish)	70301
Chopin	71412
Choudrant	71227
Choupique (Lafourche Parish)	70301
Choupique (St. Mary Parish)	70538
Chula	70372
Church Point	70525
Church Spur	70390
Cinclare	70767
Cindy Park	70075
Claiborne (Ouachita Parish)	71291
Claiborne (St. Tammany Parish)	70433
Claibourne Gardens	70094
Clare	71429
Clarence	71414
Clarks	71415
Clay	71270
Clayton	71326
Clayton Junction (Part of Clayton)	71326
Clearview Shopping Center	70002
Clearwater	71325
Clifton (Rapides Parish)	71455
Clifton (Washington Parish)	70438
Clinton	70722
Clio	70449
Clotilda	70394
Cloutierville	71416
Clovelly Farms	70345
Cocodrie	70344
Cocoville	71350
Coker	71052
Coleman	71282
Colfax	71417
Colgrade	71483
College (Part of Hammond)	70401
Collinsburg	71064
Collinston	71229
Colonial Heights	71109
Colquitt	71038
Columbia (Caldwell Parish)	71418
Columbia (St. John the Baptist Parish)	70049
Columbia Heights	71418
Como	71295
Concession	70037
Concord	71263
Constance Beach	70631
Consuella	71375
Contreras	70085
Convent	70723
Converse	71419
Conway	71260
Coon	70715
Cooper Road	71107
Coopers	71446
Copenhagen	71418
Cora	71444
Corbin (Part of Walker)	70785
Corey	71202
Corinth	71235
Cornerview	70737
Cornor	39669
Cortana Mall (Part of Baton Rouge)	70815
Coteau Holmes	70582
Coteau Rodaire	70512
Cotton Plant	71435
Cottonport	71327
Cotton Valley	71018
Couchwood	71018
Coulon Plantation	70301
Country Club Subdivision	70301
Coushatta	71019
Covington	70433*
	70434†
Covington Country Club Estates	70433
Cow Island	70510
Cravens	70656
Creedmoor	70085
Creole	70632
Crescent (Iberville Parish)	70764
Crescent (Terrebonne Parish)	70360
Creston	71020
Crew Lake	71269
Crews	71454
Crichton	71019
Cross-Road	71435
Crossroads (Lincoln Parish)	71235
Cross Roads (Red River Parish)	71019
Crowley	70526*
	70527†
Crown Point	70072

	ZIP
Crowville	71230
Crozier	70360
Cullen	71021
Curry	71483
Curtis	71112
Cut Off	70345
Cypremort	70538
Cypress (Natchitoches Parish)	71420
Cypress (Ouachita Parish)	71291
Cypress Gardens (St. Bernard Parish)	70075
Cypress Gardens (Terrebonne Parish)	70360
Cypress Island	70582
Daigleville (Part of Houma)	70360
Dalcour	70040
Danville	71008
D'Arbonne	71227
Darlington	70441
Darnell	71266
Darrow	70725
Daspit	70560
Davant	70046
Dean	71260
Dean Chapel	71291
De Broeck Landing	71106
Deerford	70791
Deer Park	71373
Dehlco	71269
Delacroix (St. Bernard Parish)	70085
Delacroix (St. Martin Parish)	70582
Del Bueno Park	70075
Delcambre	70528
Delhi	71232
Delta	71233
Delta Farms	70374
Denham Springs	70726*
	70727†
	70726
Dennis Mills	70449
Denson	70808
Dent Terrace	70633
De Quincy	70634
De Ridder	71416
Derry	70030
Des Allemands	71301
De Selle	71429
Dess	70047
Destrehan	70767
Devalls	71328
Deville	71220
Dewdrop	70083
Diamond	71107
Dixie	71280
Dixie Acres	71105
Dixie Gardens	71055
Dixie Inn	70748
Dixon Correctional Institute	71422
Dodson	70346
Donaldsonville	70352
Donner	70788
Dorcyville	71227
Douglas	71234
Downsville	70309
Downtown (Part of Alexandria)	70309
Downtown (Part of Monroe)	71201
Downtown (Part of Morgan City)	70380
Downtown (Part of Shreveport)	71101
Doyle (Part of Livingston)	70754
Doyline	71023
Drew (Calcasieu Parish)	70605
Drew (Ouachita Parish)	71291
Dry Creek	70637
Dry Prong	71423
Dubach	71235
Dubberly	71024
Duckroost	70774
Dufresne	70070
Dukedale	71006
Dulac	70353
Dunbarton	71334
Dunn	71232
Duplessis	70728
Dupont (Avoyelles Parish)	71329
Dupont (Pointe Coupee Parish)	70783
Duson	70529
Dutch Town	70734
Dykesville	71038
Easleyville	70441
Eastgate Plaza (Part of Shreveport)	71108
East Hammond (Part of Hammond)	70401
East Hodge	71247
East Louisiana State Hospital	70748
Easton	70586

	ZIP		ZIP		ZIP
East Point	71025	Forest	71242	Gouldsboro (Part of Gretna)	70053
East Side (Part of Lake Charles)	70601	Forest Glen	70445	Grambling	71245
Eastside Columbia	71418	Forest Hill	71430	Gramercy	70052
Eastwood	71037	Forest Oaks	70815	Grand Bayou	71052
Ebenezer	70526	Forest Park	71291	Grandbois	70343
Echo	71330	Forked Island	70510	Grand Caillou	70360
Eden	71371	Forksville	71225	Grand Cane	71032
Eden Isle	70458	Fort De Russy	71351	Grand Chenier	70643
Edgard	70049	Fort Jesup	71449	Grand Coteau	70541
Edgefield	71019	Fort Necessity	71243	Grand Ecore	71457
Edgerly	70668	Fort Polk	71459	Grand Isle	70358
Edna	70648	Fort Polk North	71459	Grand Lake	70605
Effie	71331	Fort Polk South	71459	Grand Point	70763
Egan	70531	Fosters (Part of Bossier City)	71111	Grand Prairie	70589
Elam	71378	Fosters Canal	70083	Grand River	70764
Elba	71353	Foules	71326	Grangeville	70422
Eliza	70764	Fourborge	70586	Grant	70644
Elizabeth	70638	Four Corners	70538	Gray	70359
Ellendale	70360	Four Forks (Caddo Parish)	71046	Gray Point	70586
Ellis	70526	Four Forks (Richland Parish)	71259	Grayson	71435
Ellsworth	70360	Fowler	71240	Green Acres (Concordia Parish)	71373
Elmer (Lafourche Parish)	70301	Francis Place	70075	Green Acres (East Baton Rouge Parish)	70811
Elmer (Rapides Parish)	71424	Franklin	70538	Green Acres (St. Charles Parish)	70030
Elmfield	70390	Franklinton	70438	Green Gables	71360
Elm Grove	71051	Fred	70791	Greenlaw	70444
Elm Hall	70390	Freetown (Assumption Parish)	70390	Green Lawn (Part of Kenner)	70065
Elm Hall Junction	70390	Freetown (St. Mary Parish)	70538	Green Lawn Terrace (Part of Kenner)	70065
Elm Park	70775	French Settlement	70733	Greensburg	70441
Elton	70532	Frenier	70068	Greenwell Springs	70739
Empire (Plaquemines Parish)	70050	Friendship	71008	Greenwood (Caddo Parish)	71033
Encalade	70083	Frierson	71027	Greenwood (St. Mary Parish)	70380
Energy (Part of Lafayette)	70598	Frisco	70755	Greenwood (Terrebonne Parish)	70356
England Air Force Base	71311	Frogmore	71334	Greenwood Park	71108
Englewood	71282	Frost	70754	Gretna	70053-54
English Turn	70040	Frost Town	71234		70056
Enola	70390	Fryeburg	71039	For specific Gretna Zip Codes call (504) 362-5610, or your local postmaster.	
Enon	70438	Fullerton	70642		
Enterprise (Catahoula Parish)	71425	Fulton	70657	Grosse Tete	70740
Enterprise (Iberia Parish)	70544	Funston	71049	Gueydan	70542
Eola	71322	Gaars Mill	71422	Gulf Outport (Part of New Orleans)	70146
Epps	71237	Gahagan	71019	Gullett	70422
Erath	70533	Galbraith	71447	Gum Ridge	71264
Eros	71238	Galion	71223	Gurley	70730
Erwinville	70729	Galliano	70354	Haaswood	70452
Essen Heights	70808	Galva	70421	Hackberry	70645
Estelle	70072	Galvez	70769	Hacketts Corner	70630
Esther	70510	Gandy Spur	71429	Hackley	70438
Estherwood	70534	Gansville	71422	Hagewood	71457
Ethel	70730	Garden City	70540	Hahnville	70057
Eunice	70535	Gardere	70810	Haile	71260
Eureka	71234	Gardner	71431	Haire	70548
Eva	71354	Garland	71322	Half Way (Assumption Parish)	70346
Evangeline	70537	Garyville	70051	Halfway (Red River Parish)	71019
Evans	70639	Gassoway	71254	Hall Summit	71034
Evelyn	71052	Gayles	71105	Hamburg	71339
Evergreen (Avoyelles Parish)	71333	Ged	70668	Hammet	71373
Evergreen (Webster Parish)	71055	Geismar	70734	Hammond	70401-04
Evergreen Fashion Square	70808	Gentilly (Part of New Orleans)	70122	For specific Hammond Zip Codes call (504) 345-6014, or your local postmaster.	
Extension	71239	Georgetown	71432		
Fairbanks	71240	Georgeville	70443	Hanna	71019
Fairlane	70360	Georgia	70390	Hanson City (Part of Kenner)	70062
Fairmont	71417	Getty Camp	70091	Happy Jack	70083
Fairview	71373	Gheens	70355	Harahan	70123
Farmer Spur (Part of Vienna)	71270	Gibbstown	70630	Hardwood	70775
Farmerville	71241	Gibsland	71028	Hargis	71454
Faubourg	70589	Gibson	70356	Hargrove	70633
Federal Correctional Institution	71463	Gilark	71055	Harlem (Plaquemines Parish)	70046
Felixville	70722	Gilbert	71336	Harlem (Vermilion Parish)	70510
Fellowship	71371	Gilleyville	71269	Harmon	71036
Fenris	70554	Gilliam	71029	Harrisonburg	71340
Fenton	70640	Gillis	70611	Harvey	70058*
Ferriday	71334	Girard	71269		70059†
Ferry Lake	71061	Glade	71343	Hathaway	70532
Fields	70653	Glencoe	70538	Haughton	71037
Fifth Ward	71351	Glen Dale	70049	Hawthorne	71446
Fillmore	71037	Glenmora	71433	Hayes	70646
Fisher	71426	Glenwild	70342	Haynesville	71038
Fishville	71467	Glenwood	70390	Hazelwood	70577
Fiske	71263	Gloria	70037	Head of Island	70449
Five Forks	71483	Gloster	71030	Hearn Island	71418
Flat Creek	71479	Glynn	70736	Hebert	71418
Flatwoods	71427	Godchaux	70394	Hecker	70647
Flora	71428	Godchaux Community	70068	Heflin	71039
Florence	70538	Gold Dust	71322	Helena	71366
Florien	71429	Golden Meadow	70357	Henderson	70517
Florissant	70085	Golden Star Plantation	70090	Henfer Park	70123
Flournoy	71109	Goldman	71375	Henry	70533
Floyd	71266	Goldonna	71031	Hermitage	70749
Fluker	70436	Goldridge	70788	Hessmer	71341
Foley (Allen Parish)	70655	Gonzales	70707†		
Foley (Assumption Parish)	70390		70737*		
Folsom	70437	Goodbee	70433		
Fondale	71201	Good Hope	70079		
Forbing	71106	Good Pine	71342		
Fordoche	70732	Goodwill	71263		
Foreman	70815	Goodwood	71353		
		Gordon	71038		
		Gorum	71434		
		Goudeau	71333		

* Area Zip Code   † Post Office Boxes

	ZIP		ZIP		ZIP
Hester	70743	Istrouma (Part of Baton		Lake Charles	70601-16
Hewes	70762	Rouge)	70805	For specific Lake Charles Zip	
Hickory (Avoyelles Parish)	71327	Ivan	71006	Codes call (318) 439-3631, or	
Hickory (St. Tammany		Jackson	70748	your local postmaster.	
Parish)	70452	Jackson Road	70748	Lake End	71019
Hickory Grove	71328	Jacoby	70753	Lake Forest (Part of New	
Hickory Valley	71473	Jamestown	71045	Orleans)	70187
Hicks	71446	Janie	71412	Lake Judge Perez	70083
Hico	71235	Jarreau	70749	Lakeland	70752
Higginbotham	70525	Jay	70374	Lake Providence	71254
Highland Acres	70123	Jeanerette	70544	Lakeshore	71201
Highland Park (Part of		Jean Lafitte	70067	Lakeside (Cameron Parish)	70542
Monroe)	71201	Jefferson (Jefferson Parish)	70121	Lakeside (Rapides Parish)	71360
Highland Park (Part of West		Jefferson (Lafayette Parish)	70501	Lakeside Shopping Center	70002
Monroe)	71291	Jefferson Island	70560	Lakeview (Caddo Parish)	71107
Highland Park (Terrebonne		Jefferson Terrace	70808	Lakeview (Natchitoches	
Parish)	70360	Jena	71342	Parish)	71456
Highland Park Heights	70808	Jennings	70546	Lakeview (Orleans Parish)	70124
Highland Road	70808	Jesuit Bend	70037	Lamar	71232
Highway Park (Part of		Jewella (Part of Shreveport)	71109	Lamourie	71346
Kenner)	70065	Jigger	71249	Lampman (Part of	
Hi-Land	70092	Johnson (St. John the		Abbeville)	70510
Hillaryville	70725	Baptist Parish)	71049	Landay Gautreaux	
Hillsdale	70422	Johnson (St. Mary Parish)	70538	Subdivision	70301
Hilltop	71268	Johnson Ridge	70301	Lapine	71291
Hilly	71235	Johnson's Bayou	70631	La Place	70068*
Hineston	71438	Johnson Street	70001		70069†
Hobart	70769	Jones	71250	Laran	71765
Hodge	71247	Jonesboro	71251	La Reusitte	70037
Hohen Solms	70788	Jonesburg	71269	Larose	70373
Holden	70744	Jones Park (Part of Kenner)	70065	La Rosen (Part of	
Holiday Park	70502	Jonesville	71343	Shreveport)	71118
Holloway	71328	Jordan Hill	71483	Larto	71343
Holly	71032	Joyce	71440	Latanier	71346
Holly Beach	70631	Junction	70653	Laurel Grove	70301
Hollybrook	71254	Junction City	71749	Laurel Hill	39669
Holly Grove	71378	Kadesh	71454	Laurel Lea	70808
Holly Ridge (Richland		Kahns	70767	Laurel Ridge	70788
Parish)	71269	Kaplan	70548	Laurel Valley Plantation	70301
Holly Ridge (Tensas Parish)	71375	Katy	70538	Lawhon	71045
Hollywood (Calcasieu		Keatchie	71046	Lawtell	70550
Parish)	70663	Kedron	70422	Lazy Acres	70360
Hollywood (Terrebonne		Keithville	71047	Leander	71438
Parish)	70360	Kelly	71441	Lebeau	71345
Hollywood (West Feliciana		Kellys	71270	Le Blanc	70651
Parish)	70775	Kendale	70062	Le Bleu	70601
Holmwood	70647	Kendrick's Ferry	71336	Lecompte	71346
Holum	71435	Kenilworth	70085	Lee Bayou	71326
Home Place	70083	Kenmore	70757	Lee Heights	71360
Homer	71040	Kennedy Heights	70094	Lees Creek	70427
Hopedale	70085	Kenner	70062-65	Lees Landing	70454
Hope Villa	70808	For specific Kenner Zip Codes call		Leesville	71446
Hornbeck	71439	(504) 469-1506, or your local			71496
Horse Bluff Landing	70462	postmaster.		For specific Leesville Zip Codes	
Hosston	71043	Kenner Junction (Part of		call (318) 239-2841, or your local	
Hotwells	71409	Kenner)	70062	postmaster.	
Houltonville	70447	Kentwood	70444	Leeville	70357
Houma	70360-64	Kickapoo	71030	Legonier	70753
For specific Houma Zip Codes call		Kilbourne	71253	Leighton	70301
(504) 868-3800, or your local		Killian	70462	Leland	71368
postmaster.		Killona	70066	Leleux	70560
Howard	71105	Kinder	70648	Lemannville	70346
Hubertville (Part of		King Hill	71019	Le Moyen	71356
Jeanerette)	70544	Kingston	71032	Lena	71447
Hudson	71422	Kingsville	71360	Leonville	70551
Hughes	71006	Kiroli Woods	71291	Leroy	70555
Humphreys	70356	Kisatchie	71468	Leton	71072
Hundley	70535	Kleinpeter	70808	Lettsworth	70753
Hunter	71052	Klondyke	70343	Levert	70582
Huron	70512	Klotzville	70341	Levins	71334
Hurricane	71003	Kolin	71360	Lewisburg (St. Landry	
Husser	70442	Kolter (Part of Keatchie)	71046	Parish)	70525
Hutton	71446	Koran	71037	Lewisburg (St. Tammany	
Hyde (Part of Simmesport)	71369	Kraemer	70371	Parish)	70448
Hymel	70090	Krotz Springs	70750	Lewiston	70444
Iberville	70776	Kurthwood	71443	Lewistown	70394
Ida	71044	Laark	71250	Liberty	71225
Idlewild (St. Mary Parish)	70392	Labadieville	70372	Liberty Hill	71008
Idlewild (Terrebonne Parish)	70364	Labarre	70751	Libuse	71348
Ikes	70634	Lacamp	71444	Liddieville	71295
Independence	70443	Lacassine	70650	Lillie	71256
Indian Bayou	70578	Lachute	71115	Linda Lee	70726
Indian Mound	70739	Lacombe	70445	Lindsay	70748
Indian Village (Allen Parish)	70648	Lacour	70715	Link	70516
Indian Village (Ouachita		Lafayette	70501-09	Linton	71006
Parish)	71225		70593-98	Linville	71260
Industrial (Part of		For specific Lafayette Zip Codes		Linwood	70514
Shreveport)	71107	call (318) 269-4800, or your local		Lions	70068
Ingleside	70390	postmaster.		Lisbon	71048
Innis	70747	Lafayette Square (Part of		Lismore	71343
Inniswold	70809	New Orleans)	70130	Litroe	71260
International Trade Mart		Lafayette Woods	70360	Little Caillou	70344
(Part of New Orleans)	70130	Lafitte	70067	Little Creek	71371
Intracoastal City	70510	Lafourche	70301	Little Prairie	70769
Iota	70543	Lagan	70086	Little Texas	70390
Iowa	70647	Lagonda	70380	Live Oak	70037
Irish Bend	70538	Lake	70769	Live Oak Hills	70433
Irma	71457	Lake Arthur	70549	Live Oak Manor	70094
Ironton	70083	Lake Bruin	71366	Liverpool	70441
Isabel	70427			Livingston	70754
Isle Labbe	70582			Livonia	70755
				Lobdell	70767

	ZIP		ZIP		ZIP
Lockhart	71277	Manifest	71343	Montrose	71457
Lockport	70374	Mansfield	71052	Montz	70068
Lockport Heights	70374	Mansura	71350	Mooringsport	71060
Locust Ridge	71366	Many	71449	Mora	71455
Logansport	71049	Maplewood (Part of		Morbihan	70560
Log Cabin	71220	Sulphur)	70663	Moreauville	71355
Logtown	71201	Marcel	70560	Moreland	71301
Lonepine	71367	Marco	71447	Morgan City	70380*
Lone Star (Iberville Parish)	70788	Maringouin	70757		70381†
Lone Star (St. Charles		Marion	71260	Morganza	70759
Parish)	70070	Marksville	71351	Morningside (Part of	
Longbridge (Avoyelles		Marrero	70072*	Shreveport)	71108
Parish)	71327		70073†	Morrisonville	70764
Long Bridge (Lafayette		Marsalis	71003	Morrow	71356
Parish)	70501	Mars Hill	71404	Morse	70559
Longlake	71418	Marthaville	71450	Morvant	70301
Longleaf	71448	Martin	71019	Morville	71373
Long Straw	71227	Martin Park (Part of		Moss Bluff	70611
Longstreet	71049	Alexandria)	71301	Moss Lake	70663
Longview	71295	Mason	71295	Mossville	70663
Longville	70652	Mathews	70375	Mot	71064
Longwood (Caddo Parish)	71060	Maurepas	70449	Mound	71282
Longwood (East Baton		Maurice	70555	Mount Airy	70076
Rouge Parish)	70780	Maxie	70526	Mount Carmel	71429
Loranger	70446	Mayfair (Part of Baton		Mount Hermon	70450
Loreauville	70552	Rouge)	70808	Mount Lebanon	71028
Lorelein	71336	Mayna	71343	Mount Moriah	71226
Lottie	70756	Meadowbrook	70056	Mount Olive	71268
Louisiana Army Ammunition		Meadow Park Heights	71108	Mount Sinai	71038
Plant	71102	Meaux	70510	Mount Union	71277
Louisiana Correctional and		Mechanicsville (Part of		Mount Zion (Lincoln Parish)	71235
Industrial School		Houma)	70360	Mount Zion (Winn Parish)	71454
(Beauregard Parish)	70633	Meeker	71346	Mowata	70535
Louisiana Correctional		Melder	71451	Mudville	71432
Institute for Women		Melrose	71452	Mulberry	70360
(Iberville Parish)	70776	Melville	71353	Myrtle Grove (Iberville	
Louisiana Tech (Part of		Meraux	70075	Parish)	70764
Ruston)	71272	Mermentau	70556	Myrtle Grove (Plaquemines	
Louisville (Part of Monroe)	71207	Mer Rouge	71261	Parish)	70083
Lower Bonne Idee	71264	Merrydale	70812	Naborton	71052
Lower Texas	70390	Merryville	70653	Nairn	70041
Loyds Bridge	71325	Messick	71019	Naomi	70037
Lozes	70560	Metairie	70001-11	Napoleonville	70390
Lucas	71105		70033	Napoleonville Junction (Part	
Lucky	71008		70055	of Thibodaux)	70301
Lucy	70049		70060	Naquin	70301
Ludington (Part of De		For specific Metairie Zip Codes		Natalbany	70451
Ridder)	70634	call (504) 831-7750, or your local		Natchez	71456
Ludvine	70374	postmaster.		Natchitoches	71457*
Lukeville	70719	Methvin	71019		71458†
Lula	71052	Michoud (Part of New		Neal Landing	70462
Luling	70070	Orleans)	70129	Nebo	71342
Luna	71291	Mid City (Part of New		Negreet	71460
Lunita	70661	Orleans)	70119	Nesser	70815
Lutcher	70071	Midland	70559	Newellton	71357
Lydia	70569	Midway (Bossier Parish)	71006	New Era	71354
Lyons Point	70526	Midway (La Salle Parish)	71342	Newhope	71266
MacArthur Village (Part of		Midway (Rapides Parish)	71430	New Iberia	70560*
Alexandria)	71301	Midway (St. Mary Parish)	70538		70562†
McBride	70360	Midway (Webster Parish)	71071	New Light (Richland Parish)	71259
McCall	70346	Milldale	70791	Newlight (Tensas Parish)	71357
McClendon	70438	Millerton	71038	New Llano	71461
McCrea	70715	Millerville (Acadia Parish)	70543		
McDade	71051	Millerville (East Baton Rouge		**New Orleans**	70101-90
McDonoghville (Part of		Parish)	70815	For specific New Orleans Zip	
Gretna)	70053	Millikin	71254	Codes call (504) 589-1111, or	
McGinty	71250	Milly Plantation	70764	your local postmaster.	
McIlhenny	70513	Milton	70558	*COLLEGES & UNIVERSITIES*	
McIntyre	71055	Mimosa Park	70070		
McKneeley	70732	Minden	71055-58	Dillard University	70122
McLeod	70374	For specific Minden Zip Codes		Louisiana State University	
McManus	70748	call (318) 377-1757, or your local		Medical Center	70112
McNary	71433	postmaster.		Loyola University	70118
McNeely	71417	Mineral Springs (Lincoln		New Orleans Baptist	
McNeese University (Part of		Parish)	71235	Theological Seminary	70126
Lake Charles)	70609	Mineral Springs (Ouachita		Southern University at New	
Madewood	70390	Parish)	71225	Orleans	70126
Madisonville	70447	Minerva	70360	Tulane University of	
Magda	71301	Minorca	71334	Louisiana	70118
Magnolia (Assumption		Mira	71059	University of New Orleans	70148
Parish)	70341	Mire	70578	Xavier University	70125
Magnolia (Livingston Parish)	70744	Mitchell	71419		
Magnolia (Natchitoches		Mittie	70654	*FINANCIAL INSTITUTIONS*	
Parish)	71456	Mix	70760	Alerion Bank, Inc.	70130
Magnolia (Plaquemines		Modeste	70376	Fidelity Homestead	
Parish)	70083	Moisant Airport (Part of		Association	70112
Magnolia (Terrebonne		Kenner)	70141	Fifth District Savings & Loan	
Parish)	70360	Moncla	71351	Association	70114
Magnolia (East Baton		Monette Ferry	71447	First National Bank of	
Rouge Parish)	70739	Monroe	71201-13	Commerce	70112
Magnolia Park	71417	For specific Monroe Zip Codes		Hibernia National Bank	70130
Magnolia Woods (Part of		call (318) 387-6161, or your local		Oak Tree Federal Savings	
Baton Rouge)	70808	postmaster.		Bank	70130
Maitland	71326	Montcalm	71275	Whitney National Bank	70130
Major (Part of New Roads)	70760	Montegut	70377		
Mallard Junction	70647	Monterey	71354	*HOSPITALS*	
Mamou	70554	Montgomery	71454	Ochsner Foundation	
Manchester	70647	Monticello (East Baton		Hospital	70121
Mandalay	70360	Rouge Parish)	70815	Southern Baptist Hospital	70115
Mandeville	70448*	Monticello (East Carroll		Touro Infirmary	70115
	70470†	Parish)	71254	Tulane University Hospital	
Mangham	71259	Montpelier	70422	and Clinics	70112

* **Area Zip Code**   † **Post Office Boxes**

	ZIP
Veterans Affairs Medical Center	70146

HOTELS/MOTELS

	ZIP
Holiday Inn Crowne Plaza	70130
Hotel Marie Antoinette	70130
Hotel Meridien New Orleans	70130
Hyatt Regency New Orleans at Superdome	70140
New Orleans Hilton Riverside and Towers	70140
Omni Royal Orleans	70140
Royal Sonesta Hotel	70140
Sheraton New Orleans Hotel	70130
The Westin Canal Place	70130

MILITARY INSTALLATIONS

	ZIP
Louisiana Air National Guard, FB6171, New Orleans Naval Air Station	70143
MTMC Gulf Outport	70146
Naval Support Activity	70142
Supervisor of Shipbuilding, Conversion and Repair, New Orleans	70142
United States Army Engineer District, New Orleans	70160
United States Property and Fiscal Office for Louisiana	70146
8th Coast Guard District, New Orleans	70130
8th Marine Corps District	70142
926th Fighter Group, New Orleans Naval Air Station (AFRES)	70143

	ZIP
New Roads	70760
New Rockdale	71052
New Safpy	70078
Newton	70601
New Verda	71404
Nibletts Bluff	70668
Nicholas	70560
Nicholls University (Part of Thibodaux)	70301
Nickel	71465
Ninock	71051
Noble	71462
Noles Landing	71073
Norah	70374
Norco	70079
Normandy Park	70094
Norris Springs	71368
Northeast Louisiana University (Part of Monroe)	71209
Northgate Mall (Part of Lafayette)	70501
North Hodge	71247
North Merrydale	70812
North Monroe	71201
North Plaquemine (Part of Plaquemine)	70764
North Shore	70458
North Shore Beach	70458
North Slidell (Part of Slidell)	70458
Northwestern (Part of Natchitoches)	71457
Norton Shop	71072
Norwood	70761
Notleyville	70512
Notnac	71357
Numa	70560
Nunez	70548
Oakdale	71463
Oak Forest	70356
Oak Grove (Ascension Parish)	70769
Oak Grove (Cameron Parish)	70643
Oak Grove (Grant Parish)	71417
Oak Grove (Lincoln Parish)	71275
Oak Grove (Sabine Parish)	71419
Oak Grove (West Carroll Parish)	71263
Oak Hills Place	70808
Oakland	71260
Oaklawn (St. Mary Parish)	70538
Oaklawn (St. Tammany Parish)	70445
Oakley	70390
Oak Manor	70815
Oaknolia	70777
Oak Ridge	71264
Oaks	71038
Oakshire Manor	70364
Oakville	70037
Oakwood Shopping Center (Part of Gretna)	70053
Oberlin	70655

	ZIP
Oil Center (Part of Lafayette)	70501
Oil City	71061
Okaloosa	71238
Old Athens	71003
Oldfield	70785
Old Jefferson	70816
Old Lafitte	70067
Old Shongaloo	71072
Olive Branch	70777
Oliver (Part of Hammond)	70401
Olivier	70560
Olla	71465
Ollie	70037
Omega	71276
Opelousas	70570*
	70571†
Orange Grove Plantation	70301
Oretta	70633
Oscar	70762
Ossun	70583
Ostrica	70041
Otis	71466
Ouachita City	71280
Oubre	70552
Oxford (De Soto Parish)	71052
Oxford (St. Mary Parish)	70538
Pace	71055
Packton	71483
Paincourtville	70391
Palmetto	71358
Palo Alto	70346
Panchoville	70532
Panola	71254
Paradis	70080
Paradise	71360
Paradise Manor	70123
Parhams	71343
Park Manor	70003
Parks	70582
Parkside Manor	70123
Park Vista (Part of Opelousas)	70570
Patoutville	70544
Patterson	70392
Paulina	70763
Pearl River	70452
Peason	71429
Pecan Grove	70094
Pecaniere	70512
Pecan Island	70548
Pecan Place	70764
Peck	71368
Pelican	71063
Perkins	70633
Perry	70575
Perryville	71220
Phoenix	70042
Pickering	71446
Pierre Bossier Mall (Part of Bossier City)	71112
Pierre Part	70339
Pierre Part Settlement	70339
Pilottown	70081
Pine	70438
Pine Coupee	71427
Pine Grove (Ouachita Parish)	71201
Pine Grove (St. Helena Parish)	70453
Pine Island	70532
Pine Oak Terrace (Part of Shreveport)	71108
Pine Prairie	70576
Pineville	71360*
	71361†
Pioneer	71266
Pitkin	70656
Pitreville	70525
Plain Dealing	71064
Plains	70791
Plainview	70427
Plaisance	70570
Plantation Acres (Part of Alexandria)	71301
Plaquemine	70764*
	70765†
Plaquemine Southwest (Part of Plaquemine)	70764
Plattenville	70393
Plaucheville	71362
Plaza in Lake Forest, The (Part of New Orleans)	70127
Pleasant Hill (Bienville Parish)	71028
Pleasant Hill (Sabine Parish)	71065
Pleasant Hills	70811
Pleasant Valley	71234
Plettenberg	70775
Point	71234
Point Au Chien	70377
Point Blue	70586

	ZIP
Pointe a la Hache	70082
Pointe Coupee	70760
Point Pleasant	71220
Poland	71301
Pollock	71467
Ponchatoula	70454
Ponchatoula Beach	70454
Pontchartrain Beach (Part of New Orleans)	70122
Poole	71051
Poplar Grove	70767
Portage	70512
Port Allen	70767
Port Barre	70577
Port Barrow (Part of Donaldsonville)	70346
Port Eads	70091
Porters Curve	70450
Porterville	71071
Port Fourchon	70357
Port Gardner	70791
Port Hickey	70791
Port Manchac	70421
Port of West Saint Mary	70538
Port Sulphur	70083
Port Vincent	70726
Potash	70083
Pot Cove	70586
Poufette	70560
Powhatan	71066
Poydras	70085
Prairie Ronde	70570
Prairieville	70769
Pratt	71028
Presque Isle	70363
Pride	70770
Prien	70605
Prien Lake Mall (Part of Lake Charles)	70601
Princeton	71067
Promised Land	70040
Prospect (Grant Parish)	71423
Prospect (St. Charles Parish)	70078
Provencal	71468
Providence	70062
Puckett	70791
Pumpkin Center	70403
Punkin Center	71247
Quaid	71343
Quimby	71282
Quitman	71268
Raceland	70394
Ragley	70657
Ramah	70757
Rambin	71063
Randolph	71256
Rapides	71409
Ratliff	70390
Rattan	71429
Rayne	70578
Rayville	71269
Readhimer	71070
Red Chute	71037
Reddell	70580
Red Gum	71334
Redland (Bossier Parish)	71064
Redland (Evangeline Parish)	70554
Red Oaks	70815
Reeves	70658
Reggio	70085
Reids	70656
Remy	70763
Reserve	70084
Rhinehart	71363
Rhymes	71269
Riceville	70542
Richard	70525
Richardson	70438
Richmond	71282
Richohoc	70538
Richwood	71201
Rideau Settlement	71358
Ridge	70578
Ridgecrest	71334
Ridgewood	70739
Rienzi Plantation	70301
Ringgold	71068
Rio	70427
Risinger Woods	71107
Riverlands	70068
River Ridge	70123
Riverton	71418
Riverwood	70433
Roanoke	70581
Robeline	71469
Robert	70455
Robson	71105
Rock	71447
Rock Hill	71423
Rocky Branch	71241
Rocky Mount	71064

	ZIP		ZIP		ZIP
Rodessa	71069	Sikes	71473	Summerville	71465
Rogers	71342	Sikes Ferry	71072	Sun	70463
Romeville	70723	Silverwood	70546	Sunnybrook	70814
Roosevelt	71276	Simmesport	71369	Sunny Hill	70438
Rosa	71345	Simms	71467	Sunrise	70767
Rosedale (Assumption		Simpson	71474	Sunset	70584
Parish)	70390	Simsboro	71275	Sunshine	70780
Rosedale (Iberville Parish)	70772	Singer	70660	Sun Spur	71232
Rosefield	71435	Siracusaville	70380	Supreme	70390
Roseland	70456	Slacks	70757	Susan Park (Part of Kenner)	70062
Rosepine	70659	Slagle	71475	Swampers	71295
Rougon	70773	Slaughter	70777	Swartz	71281
Rousseau	70394	Slidell	70458-61	Sweet Lake	70630
Roxana	71301	For specific Slidell Zip Codes call		Swords	70525
Roy	71016	(504) 643-5338, or your local		Taconey	71373
Ruby	71365	postmaster.		Taft	70057
Rum Center	71256	Sligo	71112	Talisheek	70464
Ruple	71038	Smithfield	70767	Talla Bena	71276
Rural Park	70123	Smith Ridge	70344	Tallulah	71282-84
Ruston	71270-73	Smoke Bend	70346	For specific Tallulah Zip Codes	
For specific Ruston Zip Codes call		Socola	70083	call (318) 574-0295, or your local	
(318) 255-3791, or your local		Soileau	70655	postmaster.	
postmaster.		Somerset	71357	Tangipahoa	70465
Ruth	70517	Sondheimer	71276	Tanglewood (East Baton	
Rynella	70560	Soniat	70788	Rouge Parish)	70811
Sadie	71260	Sorrell	70544	Tanglewood (Rapides	
Sadou	70529	Sorrento	70778	Parish)	71301
Sailes	71028	South Acres	70663	Tannehill	71422
St. Amant	70774	South Bend	70538	Tate Cove	70586
St. Benedict	70457	Southdown	70360	Taylor	71080
St. Bernard	70085	Southeast (Part of Baton		Taylor Hill	71447
St. Bernard Grove	70075	Rouge)	70808	Taylortown (Bossier Parish)	71051
St. Charles	70301	Southeast Louisiana		Taylortown (Union Parish)	71277
St. Clair	70040	Hospital	70448	Tchefuncte Estates	70433
St. Claude Heights	70032	Southern	70813	Temple	71474
St. Elmo	70725	Southfield (Part of		Tendal	71282
St. Francisville	70775	Shreveport)	71105	Terry	71263
St. Gabriel	70776	South Fort Trailer Park	71459	Terrytown	70053
St. Genevieve	71373	South Kenner	70094	Theriot	70397
St. Gertrude	70433	South Lafourche	70357	The Rock	71417
St. James	70086	South Mansfield	71052	Thibodaux	70301-10
St. Joe	70452	South Park (Caddo Parish)	71118	For specific Thibodaux Zip Codes	
St. John	70301	South Park (Rapides Parish)	71301	call (504) 447-3737, or your local	
St. Joseph	71366	South Park Mall (Part of		postmaster.	
St. Landry	71367	Shreveport)	71118	Thomas	70438
St. Martinville	70582	South Pass	70091	Thomastown	71282
St. Maurice	71471	Southport	70121	Thornwell	70549
St. Rosalie	70037	South Sherwood (Part of		Three Oaks	70032
St. Rose	70087	Baton Rouge)	70816	Three Rivers Heights	70433
St. Tammany	70445	Southside (Part of		Tickfaw	70466
St. Thomas	70390	Lafayette)	70503	Tidewater Camp	70091
Saline	71070	South Vacherie	70090	Tigerville	70049
Samstown	70788	Southwestern University		Timberlane	70053
Samtown	71301	(Part of Lafayette)	70504	Timber Trails	71360
Sandy Hill	71446	Spaulding	71441	Tioga	71477
Sardis (Sabine Parish)	71419	Spearsville	71277	Toca	70085
Sardis (Winn Parish)	71483	Spencer	71280	Toomey	70668
Sarepta	71071	Spillman	70748	Topsy	70601
Satsuma	70754	Splane Place (Part of West		Torbert	70781
Savoy	70535	Monroe)	71291	Toro	71429
Scarsdale	70040	Spokane	71334	Torras	70753
Schriever	70395	Springcreek	70444	Tower Park (Part of	
Scotlandville	70807	Springfield	70462	Leesville)	71446
Scott	70583	Spring Hill (Jackson Parish)	71251	Town and Country	71201
Searcy	71371	Springhill (Washington		Transylvania	71286
Sebastapol	70085	Parish)	70438	Trees	71082
Sellers	70079	Springhill (Webster Parish)	71075	Tremont	71227
Selma	71432	Spring Ridge (Caddo		Trenton	71052
Sentell	71107	Parish)	71047	Trinity (Catahoula Parish)	71343
Serena	71343	Spring Ridge (Sabine		Trinity (Iberville Parish)	70772
Seymourville	70764	Parish)	71065	Triumph	70041
Shadyside	70538	Springville (Livingston		Tropical Bend	70050
Shamrock	71469	Parish)	70754	Trout	71371
Sharon	71235	Springville (Red River		Truxno	71260
Sharon Hills	70811	Parish)	71019	Tullos	71479
Sharp	71447	Standard	71465	Tunica	70782
Shaw	71373	Stanley	71049	Turkey Creek	70585
Shelburn	71254	Star	70037	Turnerville (Part of	
Shelton	71220	Starhill	70748	Plaquemine)	70764
Shenandoah	70816	Staring (Part of Baton		Twin Oaks	71223
Sherburne	70750	Rouge)	70801	Uncle Sam	70792
Sheridan	70438	Starks	70661	Union	70723
Sherwood	71435	Start	71279	Union Church	71268
Shiloh (Tangipahoa Parish)	70422	State Line	70438	Union Hill (Rapides Parish)	71433
Shiloh (Union Parish)	71222	Stella	70040	Union Hill (Winn Parish)	71483
Shongaloo	71072	Stephensville	70380	Union Landing	70754
Shreve City Shopping		Sterlington	71280	Union Springs	71419
Center (Part of		Stevensdale	70815	Unionville	71235
Shreveport)	71105	Stevenson	71220	University (Part of Baton	
Shreveport	71101-10	Stonewall	71078	Rouge)	70803
	71115-66	Stoney Point	70438	Upland	71220
For specific Shreveport Zip Codes		Stonypoint	70739	Upstream	70123
call (318) 677-2334, or your local		Stumpf's Westside		Urania	71480
postmaster.		Shopping Center (Part of		Utility	71343
Shrewsbury	70121	Gretna)	70053	Vacherie	70090
Shuteston	70570	Sugarcreek	71001	Valmar	70075
Sibley (Lincoln Parish)	71227	Sugartown	70662	Valverda	70757
Sibley (Webster Parish)	71073	Sulphur	70663*	Vanceville	71111
Sicard (Part of Monroe)	71201		70664†	Varnado	70467
Sicily Island	71368	Summerfield	71079	Vatican	70520
Siegie	71291	Summer Grove (Part of		Vaughn	71220
Sieper	71472	Shreveport)	71118	Velma	70422

	ZIP		ZIP		ZIP
Venice	70091	Warsaw Landing	70462	Wildsville	71377
Ventress	70783	Washington	70589	Wildwood (Assumption	
Verda	71481	Waterloo	70783	Parish)	70390
Verdun	70754	Waterproof (Tensas Parish)	71375	Wildwood (East Baton	
Verdunville	70538	Waterproof (Terrebonne		Rouge Parish)	70808
Vernon	71270	Parish)	70360	Willhite	71234
Verret	70085	Watson	70786	Williams	71105
Veterans Administration		Waverly	71232	Williana	71423
Hospital (Part of		Waxia	70589	Willow Glen	71301
Shreveport)	71101	Weil	71301	Wills Point	70040
Vick	71331	Welcome	70086	Wilmer	70444
Vidalia	71373	Weldon	71222	Wilshire Park	71301
Vidrine	70586	Welsh	70591	Wilson	70789
Vienna	71270	Wemple	71052	Wilsona	71366
Vieux Carre (Part of New		Westdale	71105	Wilson Point	71301
Orleans)	70112	Western Kraft	71411	Wilton Subdivision	71107
Village East	70360	West Ferriday	71334	Winnfield	71483
Village St. George	70808	Westfield	70390	Winnsboro	71295
Ville Platte	70586	Westlake	70669	Wisner	71378
Vincent Landing	70663	Westminster	70809	Womack (Jackson Parish)	71226
Vincent Park	70075	West Monroe	71291-94	Womack (Red River Parish)	71068
Vinton	70668	For specific West Monroe Zip		Woodardville	71068
Violet	70092	Codes call (318) 387-8821, or		Woodhaven	70466
Vista Village Regional		your local postmaster.		Woodland	70083
Shopping Center (Part of		Weston	71251	Woodlawn (Assumption	
Opelousas)	70570	Westover	70767	Parish)	70390
Vivian	71082	West Pointe a la Hache	70083	Woodlawn (Jefferson Davis	
Vixen	71418	Westport	70656	Parish)	70647
Voorhies	71355	Westside (Rapides Parish)	71301	Woodlawn (Plaquemines	
Vowells Mill	71469	West Slidell (Part of Slidell)	70460	Parish)	70040
Wade Correctional Center	71038	Westwego	70094*	Woodlawn (Terrebonne	
Wadesboro	70454		70096†	Parish)	70360
Waggaman	70094	Weyanoke	70787	Woodside	71353
Wakefield	70784	Whatley Landing	71371	Woodville	71270
Waldheim	70433	Wheeling	71454	Woodworth	71485
Walker (Jackson Parish)	71251	White	70301	Wyandotte	70380
Walker (Livingston Parish)	70785	White Castle	70788	Wyatt	71251
Wallace	70049	Whitehall (La Salle Parish)	71342	Yellow Pine	71073
Wallace Ridge	71343	Whitehall (Livingston Parish)	70449	Youngsville	70592
Walls	70720	White Hall (St. James		Zachary	70791
Walters	71343	Parish)	70723	Zebedee	71269
Ward	71463	White Hills	70714	Zenoria	71371
Warden	71232	White Sulphur Springs	71371	Zion	71432
Wardview	71064	Whiteville	71322	Zion City (Part of Baton	
Wardville (Morehouse		Whittington	71301	Rouge)	70811
Parish)	71220	Wickland Terrace	70815	Zwolle	71486
Wardville (Rapides Parish)	71360	Wickliffe	70783	Zylks	71069
Warnerton	70438				

	ZIP
Abbot (Town)	04406
Abbotts Mill	04219
Abbot Village	04406
Acadia Terrace	04785
Acton	04001
Acton (Town)	04001
Addison	04606
Addison (Town)	04606
Admiralty Village	03904
Airport Mall (Part of Bangor)	04401
Albion	04910
Albion (Town)	04910
Alexander	04619
Alexander (Town)	04619
Alfred	04002
Alfred (Town)	04002
Alfred Mills	04002
Allagash (Town)	04774
Allagash	04774
Allens Mills	04938
Alna	04535
Alna (Town)	04535
Alna Center	04535
Alton (Town)	04468
Amherst	04605
Amherst (Town)	04605
Amity (Town)	04471
Andover	04216
Andover (Town)	04216
Anson	04911
Anson (Town)	04911
Appleton	04862
Appleton (Town)	04862
Argyle (Town)	04468
Aroostook Farm (Part of Presque Isle)	04769
Arrowsic (Town)	04530
Arundel (Town)	04046
Ashdale	04565
Ashland	04732
Ashland (Town)	04732
Ashville	04607
Athens	04912
Athens (Town)	04912
Atkinson (Town)	04426
Atkinson Corner	04426
Atkinson Mills	04426
Atlantic	04608
Auburn	04210-12
For specific Auburn Zip Codes call (207) 786-0604, or your local postmaster.	
Auburn Mall (Part of Auburn)	04210
Auburn Plains (Part of Auburn)	04210
Augusta	04330-38
For specific Augusta Zip Codes call (207) 622-6114, or your local postmaster.	
Aurora	04408
Aurora (Town)	04408
Avon (Town)	04966
Back Narrows	04537
Bailey Island	04003
Baileyville (Town)	04694
Baker Corner	04082
Balch Pond	03830
Bald Head	03907
Baldwin (Town)	04024
Bancroft	04497
Bancroft (Town)	04497
Bangor	04401*
	04402†
Bangor Mall (Part of Bangor)	04401
Bar Harbor	04609
Bar Harbor (Town)	04609
Baring	04619
Baring (Town)	04619
Bar Mills	04004
Barrett (Part of Caribou)	04736
Bartlett Mills	04043
Basin Mills	04473
Bass Harbor	04653
Batchelders Crossing	04350
Bath	04530
Bay Point	04548
Bayside (Hancock County)	04605
Bayside (Waldo County)	04915
Bayview (Part of Saco)	04072
Bayville	04536
Beals	04611
Beals (Town)	04611
Beans Corner	04225
Beaver Cove (Town)	04441
Beaver Dam	03901
Beddington (Town)	04622
Beech Ridge	03909
Belfast	04915
Belgrade	04917
Belgrade (Town)	04917
Belgrade Lakes	04918
Belmont (Town)	04915
Belmont Corner	04915
Benedicta	04733
Benton	04910
Benton (Town)	04910
Benton Falls	04901
Benton Station	04937
Bernard	04612
Berry Mills	04224
Berwick	03901
Berwick (Town)	03901
Bethel	04217
Bethel (Town)	04217
Biddeford	04005*
	04007†
Biddeford Pool (Part of Biddeford)	04006
Bingham	04920
Bingham (Town)	04920
Birch Harbor	04613
Birch Island	04011
Black Point	04074
Blackstrap	04105
Blackwell	04950
Blaine	04734
Blaine (Town)	04734
Blaisdell Corners	04027
Blake Corner	04250
Blanchard	04406
Blanchard (Town)	04406
Blue Hill	04614
Blue Hill (Town)	04614
Blue Hill Falls	04615
Blue Point	04074
Bolsters Mills	04040
Bonny Eagle	04093
Boothbay	04537
Boothbay (Town)	04537
Boothbay Harbor	04538
Boothbay Harbor (Town)	04538
Boothbay Park (Part of Saco)	04072
Bowdoin	04008
Bowdoin (Town)	04008
Bowdoinham	04008
Bowdoinham (Town)	04008
Bowerbank (Town)	04426
Bradford	04410
Bradford (Town)	04410
Bradford Center	04410
Bradley	04411
Bradley (Town)	04411
Bremen (Town)	04551
Brewer	04412
Bridgewater	04735
Bridgewater (Town)	04735
Bridgton	04009
Bridgton (Town)	04009
Brighton	04912
Brighton (Town)	04912
Bristol	04539
Bristol (Town)	04539
Brixham	03909
Broad Cove	04572
Brookhaven	04062
Brooklin	04616
Brooklin (Town)	04616
Brooks	04921
Brooks (Town)	04921
Brooksville (Town)	04617
Brooksville (Hancock County)	04617
Brookton	04413
Brown Corner (Aroostook County)	04750
Brown Corner (Waldo County)	04915
Brownfield (Town)	04010
Brownfield (Oxford County)	04010
Brownville	04414
Brownville (Town)	04414
Brownville Junction	04415
Brunswick	04011
Brunswick (Town)	04011
Brunswick Naval Air Station	04011
Brunswick Station	04011
Bryant Pond	04219
Buckfield	04220
Buckfield (Town)	04220
Bucks Harbor	04618
Bucksport	04416
Bucksport (Town)	04416
Bunganuc Landing	04011
Bunkers Harbor	04613
Burkettville	04574
Burlington	04417
Burlington (Town)	04417
Burnham	04922
Burnham (Town)	04922
Burnt Meadow Pond	04041
Bustins Island	04013
Buxton (Town)	04093
Buxton Center	04093
Byron	04275
Byron (Town)	04275
Calais	04619
Caldwel Corner	04281
Caldwell Corner	04281
Cambridge	04923
Cambridge (Town)	04923
Camden	04843
Camden (Town)	04843
Campbell (Part of Presque Isle)	04769
Camp Ellis (Part of Saco)	04072
Canaan	04924
Canaan (Town)	04924
Canton	04221
Canton (Town)	04221
Canton Point	04221
Cape Cottage	04107
Cape Elizabeth (Town)	04107
Cape Elizabeth	04107
Cape Neddick (York County)	03902
Cape Porpoise	04014
Capitol Island	04538
Caratunk	04925
Caratunk (Town)	04925
Cardville	04418
Caribou	04736
Caribou Road (Part of Presque Isle)	04769
Carmel	04419
Carmel (Town)	04419
Carrabassett	04947
Carrabassett Valley (Town)	04947
Carroll	04487
Carroll (Town)	04487
Carson	04786
Carthage	04224
Carthage (Town)	04224
Cary	04471
Cary (Town)	04471
Casco	04015
Casco (Town)	04015
Cash Corner (Part of South Portland)	04106
Castine	04421
Castine (Town)	04421
Castle Hill (Town)	04757
Caswell (Town)	04750
Cathance	04086
Cedar Grove	04342
Center Lebanon	04027
Center Lovell	04016
Center Minot	04258
Center Montville	04941
Center Vassalboro	04989
Centerville	04623
Centerville (Town)	04623
Central Aroostook (Town)	04760
Central Hancock (Town)	04640
Central Somerset (Town)	04920
Chamberlain	04541
Chapman	04757
Chapman (Town)	04757
Charleston	04422
Charleston (Town)	04422
Charleston Correctional Facility	04422
Charlotte (Town)	04666
Chases Pond	03909
Chebeague Island	04017
Chelsea	04330
Chelsea (Town)	04345
Cherryfield	04622
Cherryfield (Town)	04622
Chester	04458
Chester (Town)	04458
Chesterville	04938
Chesterville (Town)	04938
Chesuncook	04441
Chicopee	04038
China	04926
China (Town)	04926
Chisholm	04239
Christmas Cove	04568
Cider Hill	03909
City Point (Part of Belfast)	04915
Clapboard Island	04105
Clark Island	04859
Clarks Mill	04042
Clay Hill	03902
Clayton Lake	04737
Cliff Island (Part of Portland)	04019
Clifton	04428
Clifton (Town)	04428
Clinton	04927
Clinton (Town)	04927
Cobbs Bridge	04260
Coburn Gore	04936
Codyville (Town)	04490

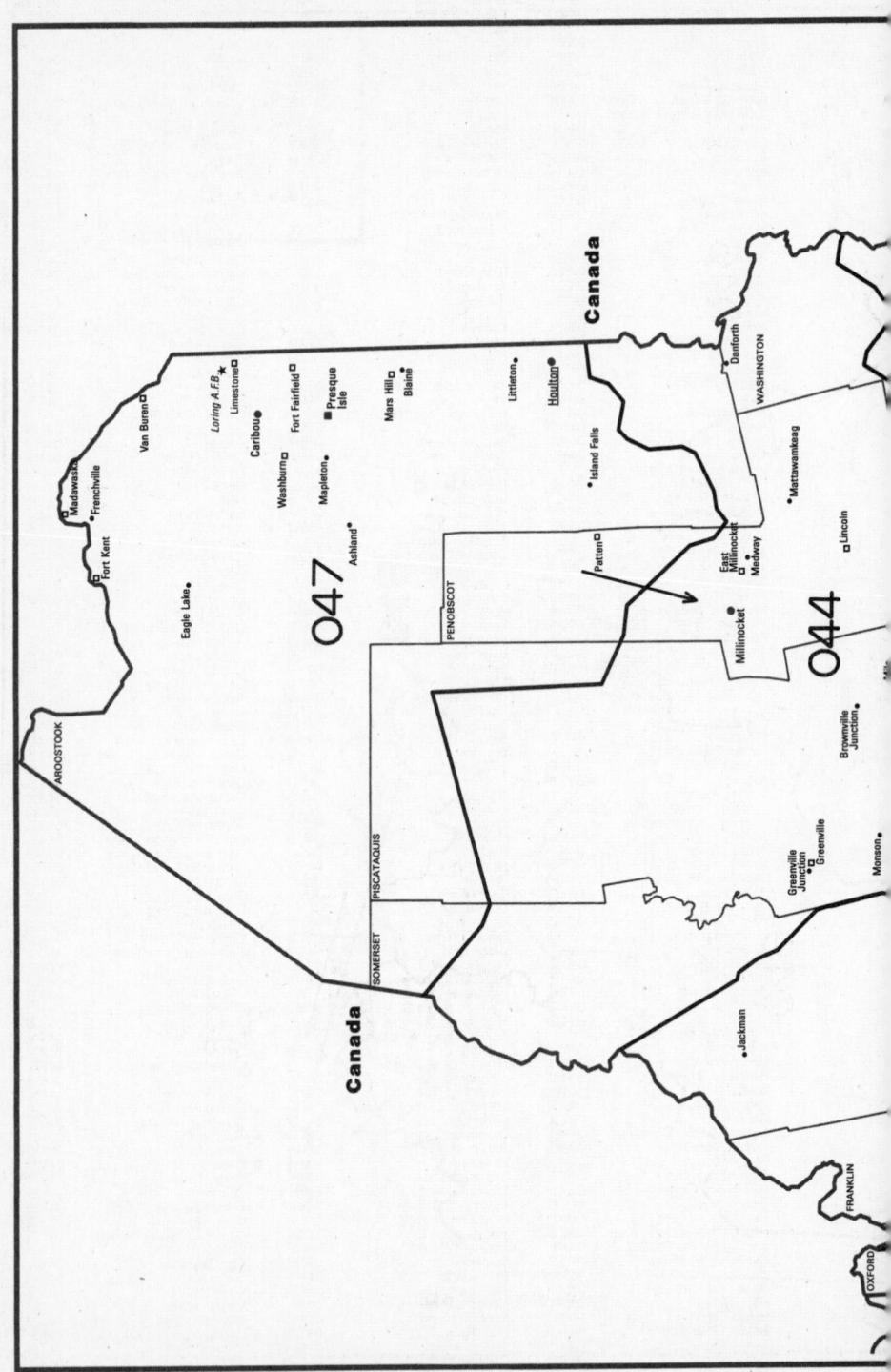

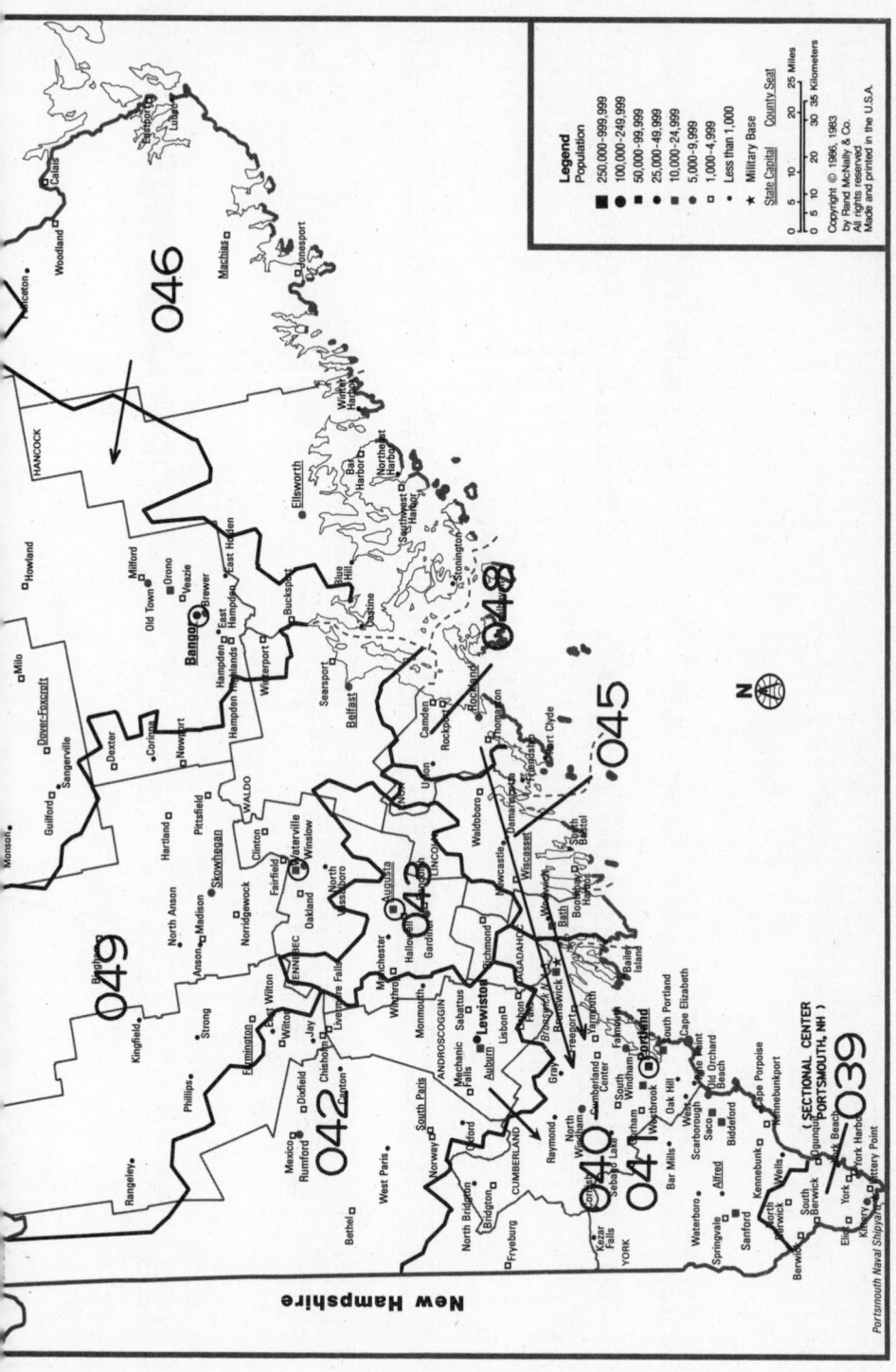

	ZIP		ZIP		ZIP
Colby	04736	Dog Island Corner (Part of		East Winthrop	04343
Colby College (Part of		Belfast)	04915	Eaton	04424
Waterville)	04901	Dogtown	04967	Eddington	04428
Coles Corner	04496	Dorman	04643	Eddington (Town)	04428
Columbia (Town)	04623	Douglas Hill	04024	Eden	04672
Columbia Falls	04623	Dover-Foxcroft	04426	Edes Falls	04055
Columbia Falls (Town)	04623	Dover-Foxcroft (Town)	04426	Edgecomb	04556
Concordville	03910	Dover South Mills	04426	Edgecomb (Town)	04556
Connor (Town)	04736	Downtown (Part of Portland)	04112	Edinburg (Town)	04448
Convene	04091	Drake Corner	04849	Edmunds	04628
Cooks Corner (Cumberland		Drakes Island	04090	Eggemoggin	04650
County)	04011	Dresden	04342	Egypt	04605
Cooks Corner (Waldo		Dresden (Town)	04342	Eliot	03903
County)	04987	Drew (Town)	04497	Eliot (Town)	03903
Cooks Mills	04015	Dryden	04225	Elizabeth Park	04106
Cooper (Town)	04638	Dry Mills	04039	Ellingswood Corner	04496
Coopers Corner	04046	Ducktrap	04849	Elliottsville (Town)	04464
Coopers Mills	04341	Dunkertown	04270	Ellis Pond	04275
Coplin (Town)	04982	Dunns Corner	04355	Ellsworth	04605
Corea	04624	Durgintown	04020	Ellsworth Falls (Part of	
Corinna	04928	Durham (Town)	04032	Ellsworth)	04605
Corinna (Town)	04928	Dyer Brook	04747	Embden (Town)	04958
Corinna Center	04928	Dyer Brook (Town)	04747	Emery Mills	04076
Corinth (Town)	04427	E (Town)	04758	Emerys Corner	04048
Cornish	04020	Eagle Island	04683	Empire	04258
Cornish (Town)	04020	Eagle Lake	04739	Enfield	04433
Cornville	04976	Eagle Lake (Town)	04739	Enfield (Town)	04433
Cornville (Town)	04976	East Andover	04226	English (Part of Presque	
Costigan	04423	East Auburn (Part of		Isle)	04769
Cote Corner	04750	Auburn)	04210	Estabrook Settlement	04471
Country Living	04073	East Baldwin	04024	Estcourt Station	04741
Cousins Island	04096	East Benton	04910	Estes Lake	04073
Coventry North	04048	East Bethel	04217	Etna	04434
Cranberry Isles	04625	East Blue Hill	04629	Etna (Town)	04434
Cranberry Isles (Town)	04625	East Boothbay	04544	Etna Center	04434
Crawford (Town)	04619	Eastbrook	04634	Eustis	04936
Crescent Lake	04015	Eastbrook (Town)	04634	Eustis (Town)	04936
Criehaven (Town)	04851	East Buckfield	04220	Exeter	04435
Crockett Corner	04069	East Central Franklin (Town)	04947	Exeter (Town)	04435
Crossman Corner	04252	East Central Penobscot		Exeter Center	04435
Crouseville	04738	(Town)	04417	Exeter Mills	04427
Crystal	04747	East Central Washington		Fairbanks	04938
Crystal (Town)	04747	(Town)	04628	Fairfield	04937
Cumberland (Town)	04021	East Corinth	04427	Fairfield (Town)	04937
Cumberland Center		East Denmark	04022	Fairfield Center	04937
(Cumberland County)	04021	East Dixfield	04227	Fairmount	04742
Cumberland Foreside	04110	East Dixmont	04932	Falmouth (Town)	04105
Cumberland Mills (Part of		East Dover	04426	Falmouth	04105
Westbrook)	04092	East Eddington	04428	Falmouth Foreside	04105
Cundys Harbor	04011	East Edgecomb	04556	Falmouth Shopping Center	04105
Curtis Corner	04263	East Exeter	04427	Farmingdale	04344
Cushing	04563	East Franklin	04634	Farmingdale (Town)	04344
Cushing (Town)	04563	East Friendship	04547	Farmington	04938
Cutler	04626	East Fryeburg	04010	Farmington (Town)	04938
Cutler (Town)	04626	East Hampden	04401	Farmington Falls	04940
Cutts Island	03905	East Hancock (Town)	04408	Farwells Corner	04988
Cyr (Town)	04785	East Harpswell	04011	Fayette	04349
Daigle	04743	East Hebron	04238	Fayette (Town)	04349
Dallas (Town)	04970	East Hiram	04041	Fayette Corner	04349
Damariscotta	04543	East Holden	04429	Felch Corner	04048
Damariscotta (Town)	04543	East Knox	04986	Ferry Beach (Part of Saco)	04072
Damariscotta Mills	04553	East Lamoine	04605	Fish Street	04037
Damariscotta-Newcastle	04543	East Lebanon	04027	Five Corners (Androscoggin	
Damascus	04419	East Limington	04049	County)	04256
Danforth	04424	East Livermore	04228	Five Corners (York County)	03906
Danforth (Town)	04424	East Lowell	04433	Five Islands	04548
Danville (Part of Auburn)	04223	East Machias	04630	Five Points (Part of	
Danville Corner (Part of		East Machias (Town)	04630	Biddeford)	04005
Auburn)	04210	East Madison	04976	Fletchers Landing	04605
Dark Harbor	04848	East Millinocket (Town)	04430	Forest City	04413
Davenport Cove	04424	East Millinocket	04430	Fort Fairfield	04742
Davis Island	04556	East Monmouth	04364	Fort Fairfield (Town)	04742
Days Ferry	04579	East Newport	04933	Fort Hill (Part of Biddeford)	04005
Dayton (Town)	04005	East New Portland	04961	Fort Kent	04743
Deblois	04622	East Northport	04915	Fort Kent (Town)	04743
Deblois (Town)	04622	Easton (Town)	04740	Fort Kent Mills	04744
Dedham	04429	Easton	04740	Fort Kent Village	04743
Dedham (Town)	04429	Easton Center	04740	Fortunes Rocks (Part of	
Deering (Part of Presque		East Orland	04431	Biddeford)	04005
Isle)	04769	East Orrington	04474	Fosters Corner	
Deer Isle	04627	East Otisfield	04270	(Cumberland County)	04062
Deer Isle (Town)	04627	East Palermo	04354	Fosters Corner (Waldo	
Delano Park	04106	East Parsonsfield	04028	County)	04921
Denmark	04022	East Peru	04290	Four Corners (Aroostook	
Denmark (Town)	04022	East Pittston	04345	County)	04750
Dennistown (Town)	04945	East Poland	04230	Four Corners (York County)	04043
Dennysville	04628	Eastport	04631	Frankfort	04438
Dennysville (Town)	04628	East Raymond	04071	Frankfort (Town)	04438
Derby	04463	East Sebago	04029	Franklin	04634
Detroit	04929	East Stoneham	04231	Franklin (Town)	04634
Detroit (Town)	04929	East Sullivan	04607	Freedom	04941
Dexter	04930	East Sumner	04220	Freedom (Town)	04941
Dexter (Town)	04930	East Surry	04605	Freeport	04032
Dickey	04774	East Thorndike	04986	Freeport (Town)	04032
Dickvale	04290	East Troy	04987	Frenchboro (Town)	04635
Dixfield	04224	East Union	04862	Frenchboro	04635
Dixfield (Town)	04224	East Vassalboro	04935	Frenchville	04745
Dixfield Center	04224	East Warren	04864	Frenchville (Frenchville	
Dixmont	04932	East Waterboro	04030	Town)	04745
Dixmont (Town)	04932	East Waterford	04088	Frenchville (Ashland Town)	04732
Dixmont Center	04932	East Wilton	04234	Friendship	04547
Dog Corner	04038	East Winn	04455	Friendship (Town)	04547

	ZIP
Frye	04275
Fryeburg	04037
Fryeburg (Town)	04037
Fryeburg Center	04037
Fryeburg Harbor	04037
Gardiner	04345
†...................................	04359
For specific Gardiner Zip Codes call (207) 582-6160, or your local postmaster.	
Garfield (Town)	04732
Garland	04939
Garland (Town)	04939
Georgetown	04548
Georgetown (Town)	04548
Gerrishville	04693
Gilbertville	04221
Gilead	04217
Gilead (Town)	04217
Glantz Corner	04062
Glenburn (Town)	04401
Glenburn Center	04401
Glen Cove	04846
Glendon	04572
Glenmere	04860
Glenwood (Town)	04497
Goodings (Part of Presque Isle)	04769
Good Will-Hinckley School	04944
Goodwins Mills	04005
Goose Rocks Beach	04046
Gorham	04038
Gorham (Town)	04038
Gotts Island	04653
Gould Landing	04401
Gouldsboro	04607
Gouldsboro (Town)	04607
Grand Beach	04064
Grand Isle	04746
Grand Isle (Town)	04746
Grand Lake Stream	04637
Grand Lake Stream (Town)	04637
Granite Hill (Part of Hallowell)	04347
Grass Corner	04750
Gray (Town)	04039
Gray	04039
Grays Corner	04676
Great Diamond Island (Part of Portland)	04109
Great Falls (Part of Auburn)	04210
Great Pond	04408
Great Pond (Town)	04408
Great Works (Part of Old Town)	04468
Greeley Landing	04426
Greenbush	04467
Greenbush (Town)	04467
Greene	04236
Greene (Town)	04236
Greenfield	04423
Greenfield (Town)	04423
Green Lake	04429
Greens Corner	04988
Greenville	04441
Greenville (Town)	04441
Greenville	04441
Greenville Junction	04442
Greenwood	04289
Greenwood (Town)	04289
Grimes Mill (Part of Caribou)	04736
Grindstone	04460
Grindstone Neck	04693
Grove	04638
Groveville	04038
Guerette	04783
Guilford	04443
Guilford (Town)	04443
Guillemette	04073
Guinea Corner (Part of Biddeford)	04005
Hackett Mills	04258
Halldale	04986
Hallowell	04347
Hall Quarry	04660
Hamlin	04785
Hamlin (Town)	04785
Hammond (Town)	04730
Hampden	04444
Hampden (Town)	04444
Hampden	04444
Hampden Highlands	04444
Hancock	04640
Hancock (Town)	04640
Hancock Point	04640
Hanover	04237
Hanover (Town)	04237
Harborside	04642
Hardings	04011
Harmon Beach	04075
Harmons Corner (Part of Auburn)	04210

	ZIP
Harmony	04942
Harmony (Town)	04942
Harpswell (Town)	04079
Harpswell Center	04079
Harrimans Point	04578
Harrington	04643
Harrington (Town)	04643
Harrison	04040
Harrison (Town)	04040
Hartford	04221
Hartford (Town)	04221
Hartland	04943
Hartland (Town)	04943
Hartsfords Point	04442
Harts Neck	04860
Hatch's Corner	04342
Haven	04616
Haynesville	04446
Haynesville (Town)	04446
Head of Tide (Part of Belfast)	04915
Head Tide	04535
Hebron	04238
Hebron (Town)	04238
Hebron Station	04238
Hendricks Harbor	04576
Hermon	04401
Hermon (Town)	04401
Hermon Center	04401
Heron Island	04568
Hersey (Town)	04765
Hibberts (Town)	04341
Higgins Beach	04074
Higginsville	04450
Highland (Knox County)	04864
Highland (Somerset County) (Town)	04961
Highland Lake (Part of Westbrook)	04092
Highland Lake Vista	04062
Highpine	04090
Hills Beach (Part of Biddeford)	04005
Hillside	04024
Hinckley	04944
Hiram	04041
Hiram (Town)	04041
Hodgdon	04730
Hodgdon (Town)	04730
Holden	04429
Holden (Town)	04429
Hollandville	04048
Hollis (Town)	04042
Hollis Center	04042
Holmes Mill (Part of Belfast)	04915
Hope	04847
Hope (Town)	04847
Houghton	04275
Houlton	04730
Houlton (Town)	04730
Howes Corner	04282
Howland	04448
Howland (Town)	04448
Hoyttown	04654
Hudson	04449
Hudson (Town)	04449
Hulls Cove	04644
Hunnewell Hill	04074
Hunts Corner	04217
Hutchins Corner	04942
Indian Island	04468
Indian Point	04660
Indian River	04606
Indian Township Indian Reservation	04668
Industrial (Part of Presque Isle)	04769
Industry (Town)	04938
Ingall's Hill	04009
Intervale	04260
Irish Settlement	04424
Island Falls	04747
Island Falls (Town)	04747
Isle au Haut	04645
Isle Au Haut (Town)	04645
Isle of Springs	04549
Islesboro	04848
Islesboro (Town)	04848
Islesford	04646
Jackman	04945
Jackman (Town)	04945
Jackson	04921
Jackson (Town)	04921
Jackson Corners	04921
Jacksonville	04630
Jay	04239
Jay (Town)	04239
Jefferson	04348
Jefferson (Town)	04348
Jemtland	04783
Jonesboro	04648
Jonesboro (Town)	04648

	ZIP
Jones Corner	04354
Jonesport	04649
Jonesport (Town)	04649
Kalers Corner	04572
Keegan	04785
Kelleyland	04694
Kendalls Corner (Part of Belfast)	04915
Kenduskeag	04450
Kenduskeag (Town)	04450
Kennebago Lake	04970
Kennebec	04654
Kennebunk	04043
Kennebunk (Town)	04043
Kennebunk Beach	04043
Kennebunk Landing	04043
Kennebunk Lower Village	04046
Kennebunkport	04046
Kennebunkport (Town)	04046
Kennedy Terrace	04785
Kents Hill	04349
Kezar Falls	04047
Kingfield	04947
Kingfield (Town)	04947
Kingman	04451
Kingman (Town)	04451
Kingsbury (Town)	04942
Kinney Shores (Part of Saco)	04072
Kittery	03904
Kittery (Town)	03904
Kittery Point	03905
Knights Landing	04414
Knightville (Part of South Portland)	04106
Knowles Corner	04780
Knox (Town)	04986
Knox Center	04986
Knox Corner	04986
Knox Station	04986
Kokadjo	04441
Lagrange	04453
Lagrange (Town)	04453
Lake Arrowhead Estates	04061
Lake City	04843
Lake Moxie	04985
Lake View (Town)	04463
Lakeville (Town)	04487
Lakewood	04976
Lambert Lake	04454
Lamoine (Town)	04605
Lamoine	04605
Lamoine Beach	04605
Lamoine Corner	04605
Larone	04937
Larrabee	04655
Lawry	04547
Lebanon (Town)	04027
Lee	04455
Lee (Town)	04455
Leeds (Town)	04263
Leeds	04263
Leeds Junction	04263
Levant	04456
Levant (Town)	04456
Lewiston	04240-43
For specific Lewiston Zip Codes call (207) 783-8551, or your local postmaster.	
Lewiston Junction (Part of Auburn)	04210
Lewiston Lower (Part of Lewiston)	04240
Lewiston Mall (Part of Lewiston)	04240
Lewiston Upper (Part of Lewiston)	04240
Libby Hill (Part of Gardiner)	04345
Liberty	04949
Liberty (Town)	04949
Lille	04749
Lily Bay	04441
Limerick	04048
Limerick (Town)	04048
Limerick Mills	04048
Limestone	04750-51
For specific Limestone Zip Codes call (207) 325-4838, or your local postmaster.	
Limington	04049
Limington (Town)	04049
Lincoln (Oxford County) (Town)	03579
Lincoln (Penobscot County)	04457
Lincoln (Penobscot County) (Town)	04457
Lincoln Center	04458
Lincoln Mills	04928
Lincolnville	04849
Lincolnville (Town)	04849
Lincolnville Center	04850

* Area Zip Code   † Post Office Boxes

* **Area Zip Code**   † **Post Office Boxes**

Place	ZIP	Place	ZIP	Place	ZIP
North Waterboro	04061	Pembroke (Town)	04666	Rangeley (Town)	04970
North Waterford	04267	Penley's Corner (Part of		Raymond	04071
North Wayne	04284	Auburn)	04210	Raymond (Town)	04071
Northwest Aroostook	04770	Penobscot	04476	Rayville	04270
Northwest Aroostook		Penobscot (Town)	04476	Razorville	04574
(Town)	04788	Penobscot Indian Island		Reach	04627
Northwest Bethel	04217	Reservation	04488	Readfield (Town)	04355
Northwest Hancock (Town)	04408	Perham	04766	Readfield	04355
Northwest Piscataquis		Perham (Town)	04766	Red Beach (Part of Calais)	04619
(Town)	04441	Perkins (Town)	04357	Redding	04292
Northwest Somerset (Town)	04945	Perry (Town)	04667	Reed (Town)	04497
North Whitefield	04353	Perry (Aroostook County)	04769	Reeds	04966
North Windsor	04361	Perry (Washington County)	04667	Richmond	04357
North Woodstock	04219	Perrys Corner	04048	Richmond (Town)	04357
North Yarmouth (Town)	04021	Peru	04290	Richmond Mill	04284
Norumbega	04617	Peru (Town)	04290	Richville	04075
Norway	04268	Peter Dana Point	04668	Ridlonville	04257
Norway (Town)	04268	Phair (Part of Presque Isle)	04769	Rileys	04239
Norway Center	04268	Phillips	04966	Ripley	04930
Norway Lake	04268	Phillips (Town)	04966	Ripley (Town)	04930
Number Four	04051	Phippsburg	04562	Ripley	04643
Oakfield	04763	Phippsburg (Town)	04562	Riverside	04330
Oakfield (Town)	04763	Pigeon Hill	04658	Riverview (Part of Presque	
Oak Hill (Androscoggin		Pike Corner	04415	Isle)	04769
County)	04273	Pine Cliff	04576	Robbinston	04671
Oak Hill (Cumberland		Pine Hill	03902	Robbinston (Town)	04671
County)	04074	Pine Park	04064	Robinhood	04530
Oakland	04963	Pine Point	04074	Robinson	04758
Oakland (Town)	04963	Pittsfield	04967	Robinson Corner	04240
Oak Point	04605	Pittsfield (Town)	04967	Robyville	04450
Oak Ridge (Part of		Pittston	04345	Rockland	04841
Biddeford)	04005	Pittston (Town)	04345	Rockport	04856
Oak Terrace	03904	Pittston Farm	04478	Rockport (Town)	04856
Ocean Park	04063	Plaisted	04767	Rockville	04841
Ocean Point	04544	Plantation Number Fourteen		Rockwood	04478
Oceanview Harbor	04074	(Town)	04628	Rogers Corners	04987
Oceanville	04681	Plantation Number Twenty-		Rome	04957
Ogontz	04478	one (Town)	04668	Rome (Town)	04957
Ogunquit	03907	Pleasant Beach	04858	Roque Bluffs	04654
Ogunquit (Town)	03907	Pleasantdale (Part of South		Roque Bluffs (Town)	04654
Olamon	04467	Portland)	04106	Ross Corner	04087
Olde Mill Brook	04074	Pleasant Hill (mail Portland)	04105	Round Pond	04564
Old Orchard Beach (Town)	04064	Pleasant Hill (mail Freeport)	04032	Roxbury	04275
Old Orchard Beach	04064	Pleasant Hill (mail		Roxbury (Town)	04275
Old Town	04468	Scarborough)	04074	Royal Corner (Part of	
Onawa	04443	Pleasant Lake	04619	Auburn)	04210
Oquossoc	04964	Pleasant Point	04563	Rumford	04276
Orffs Corner	04572	Pleasant Point Indian		Rumford (Town)	04276
Orient	04471	Reservation	04667	Rumford Center	04278
Orient (Town)	04471	Pleasant Pond	04925	Rumford Corner	04219
Orland	04472	Pleasant Ridge (Town)	04920	Rumford Junction (Part of	
Orland (Town)	04472	Pleasantville	04864	Auburn)	04210
Orono (Town)	04473	Plummer Island	04074	Rumford Point	04279
Orono	04473	Plymouth	04969	Sabattus	04280
Orrington	04474	Plymouth (Town)	04969	Sabattus (Town)	04280
Orrington (Town)	04474	Poland	04273	Sabbathday Lake	04274
Orrington Center	04474	Poland (Town)	04273	Saco	04072
Orrs Island	04066	Poland Spring	04274	St. Agatha	04772
Osborn (Town)	04605	Pond Cove	04107	St. Agatha (Town)	04772
Otis	04605	Poors Mills (Part of Belfast)	04915	St. Albans	04971
Otis (Town)	04605	Popham Beach	04562	St. Albans (Town)	04971
Otisfield	04270	Portage	04768	St. David	04773
Otisfield (Town)	04270	Portage Lake (Town)	04768	St. Francis	04774
Otter Creek	04665	Port Clyde	04855	St. Francis (Town)	04774
Owls Head	04854	Porter	04068	St. Francis College (Part of	
Owls Head (Town)	04854	Porter (Town)	04068	Biddeford)	04005
Oxbow	04764	Porterfield	04047	St. George	04857
Oxbow (Town)	04764	Porter Landing	04032	St. George (Town)	04857
Oxford	04270	Portland	04101-04	St. John	04743
Oxford (Town)	04270		04109	St. John (Town)	04743
Paine Corner	04281		04112	St. Josephs College	04062
Palermo	04354			Salem	04983
Palermo (Town)	04354	For specific Portland Zip Codes		Salmon Falls	04004
Palmyra	04965	call (207) 871-8411, or your local		Salsbury Cove	04672
Palmyra (Town)	04965	postmaster.		Sanderson Corners	04349
Paris	04271			Sandhill Corner	04341
Paris (Town)	04271	Portsmouth Naval Shipyard	03801	Sandy Beach	04401
Parker Head	04562	Pownal	04069	Sandy Creek	04009
Parkman	04443	Pownal (Town)	04069	Sandy Point	04972
Parkman (Town)	04443	Pownal Center	04069	Sandy River (Town)	04970
Parsonsfield	04048	Pratt Corner	04281	Sandy River Beach	04649
Parsonsfield (Town)	04028	Prentiss	04487	Sanford	04073
Passadumkeag	04475	Prentiss (Town)	04487	Sanford (Town)	04073
Passadumkeag (Town)	04475	Presque Isle	04769	Sangerville	04479
Passamaquoddy Indian		Prides Corner (Part of		Sangerville (Town)	04479
Township (Town)	04668	Westbrook)	04092	Sargentville	04673
Passamaquoddy Pleasant		Princeton	04668	Saunders (Part of Presque	
Point Indian Reservation		Princeton (Town)	04668	Isle)	04769
(Town)	04667	Promenade Mall (Part of		Scarboro Beach	04074
Patten	04765	Lewiston)	04240	Scarborough	04074
Patten (Town)	04765	Promised Land	04273	Scarborough (Town)	04074
Peabbles Cove	04107	Prospect	04981	Scituate	03909
Peaks Island (Part of		Prospect (Town)	04981	Scotland	03909
Portland)	04108	Prospect Ferry	04981	Scott (Part of Presque Isle)	04769
Pea Ridge	04458	Prospect Harbor	04669	Scribners Mill	04040
Pejepscot	04086	Prouts Neck	04074	Seabury	03909
Pelton Hill (Part of Augusta)	04330	Pulpit Harbor	04853	Seal Cove	04674
Pemaquid	04558	Pumpkin Valley	04009	Seal Harbor	04675
Pemaquid Beach	04554	Quimby	04770	Searsmont	04973
Pemaquid Harbor	04558	Quoddy Village (Part of		Searsmont (Town)	04973
Pemaquid Point	04554	Eastport)	04631	Searsport	04974
Pembroke	04666	Randolph (Town)	04346	Searsport (Town)	04974
		Randolph	04346		
		Rangeley	04970		

* Area Zip Code   † Post Office Boxes

	ZIP
Seawall	04656
Sebago (Town)	04029
Sebago Lake	04075
Sebasco	04565
Sebasco Estates	04565
Sebec	04481
Sebec (Town)	04481
Sebec Corners	04426
Sebec Lake	04482
Seboeis	04448
Seboeis (Town)	04448
Seboomook	04478
Seboomook Lake (Town)	04478
Sedgwick	04676
Sedgwick (Town)	04676
Shady Nook	03830
Shaker Village	04274
Shapleigh	04076
Shapleigh (Town)	04076
Shaw Mills	04075
Shawmut	04975
Sheepscot	04578
Sheridan	04775
Sherman	04776
Sherman (Town)	04776
Sherman Mills	04776
Shermans Corner	04949
Sherman Station	04777
Shin Pond	04765
Shirley (Town)	04485
Shirley Mills	04485
Sidney	04330
Sidney (Town)	04330
Silver Ridge	04776
Simonton Corners	04843
Simpson Corners	04932
Sinclair	04779
Skillings Corner	04210
Skowhegan	04976
Skowhegan (Town)	04976
Slab City (Oxford County)	04231
Slab City (Waldo County)	04849
Small Point	04567
Smithfield	04978
Smithfield (Town)	04978
Smithville	04680
Smyrna (Town)	04780
Smyrna Center	04780
Smyrna Mills	04780
Soldier Pond	04781
Solon	04979
Solon (Town)	04979
Somerville	04341
Somerville (Town)	04341
Sorrento	04677
Sorrento (Town)	04677
Sound	04660
South Acton	04027
South Addison	04606
South Andover	04216
South Arm	04216
South Aroostook (Town)	04730
South Bancroft	04424
South Berwick	03908
South Berwick (Town)	03908
South Blue Hill	04615
South Brewer (Part of Brewer)	04412
South Bridgton	04009
South Bristol	04568
South Bristol (Town)	04568
South Buxton	04038
South Casco	04077
South China	04358
South Corinth	04427
South Deer Isle	04681
South Dover	04426
South Durham	04032
Southeast Piscataquis (Town)	04463
South Eliot	03903
South Exeter	04928
South Franklin (Town)	04224
South Freeport	04078
South Gardiner (Part of Gardiner)	04359
South Gorham	04038
South Gouldsboro	04678
South Gray	04039
South Hancock	04605
South Harpswell	04079
South Hiram	04080
South Hollis	04042
South Hope	04862
South Jefferson	04553
South Lagrange	04453
South Lebanon	04027
South Levant	04456
South Lewiston (Part of Lewiston)	04240
South Liberty	04949
South Limington	04048

	ZIP
South Lincoln	04457
South Livermore	04254
South Lubec	04652
South Monmouth	04259
South Montville	04949
South Newcastle	04556
South Orland	04472
South Orrington	04474
South Oxford (Town)	04267
South Paris	04281
South Parsonsfield	04048
South Penobscot	04476
Southport	04576
Southport (Town)	04576
South Portland	04106*
	04116†
South Princeton	04668
South Rangeley	04964
South Rumford	04276
South Sanford	04073
South Side	03909
South Surry	04684
South Thomaston	04858
South Thomaston (Town)	04858
South Trescott	04652
South Union	04864
South Waldoboro	04572
South Warren	04864
South Waterford	04081
South West Bend	04252
Southwest Harbor	04679
Southwest Harbor (Town)	04679
Southwest Harbor Coast Guard Base	04679
South Windham	04082
South Windsor	04363
South Woodstock	04289
South Woodville	04458
Spears Corner	04345
Spragueville (Part of Presque Isle)	04769
Springfield	04487
Springfield (Town)	04487
Springvale	04083
Spruce Head	04859
Spruce Head Island	04859
Spruce Point	04538
Spruce Shores	04544
Squa Pan	04732
Square Lake (Town)	04743
Squirrel Island	04570
Stacyville	04782
Stacyville (Town)	04782
Standish	04084
Standish (Town)	04084
Starboard	04618
Starks	04911
Starks (Town)	04911
State Road	04769
Stebbins	04742
Steep Falls	04085
Stetson	04488
Stetson (Town)	04488
Steuben	04680
Steuben (Town)	04680
Stevens Corner	03830
Stevensville	04742
Stickney Corner	04574
Stillwater (Part of Old Town)	04489
Stockholm	04783
Stockholm (Town)	04783
Stockton Springs	04981
Stockton Springs (Town)	04981
Stoneham (Town)	04231
Stonington	04681
Stonington (Town)	04681
Stover Corner	04617
Stow	04058
Stow (Town)	04058
Stratton	04982
Stricklands	04263
Strong	04983
Strong (Town)	04983
Sullivan	04664
Sullivan (Town)	04664
Summerhaven (Part of Augusta)	04330
Sumner (Town)	04292
Sunset	04683
Sunshine	04627
Surfside	04064
Surry	04684
Surry (Town)	04684
Sutton Island	04662
Swans Island	04685
Swans Island (Town)	04685
Swanville	04915
Swanville (Town)	04915
Sweden (Aroostook County)	04762
Sweden (Oxford County) (Town)	04040
Tacoma	04350

	ZIP
Tainter Corner	04224
Tallwood	04355
Talmadge (Town)	04492
Tatnic	03906
Temple	04984
Temple (Town)	04984
Temple Heights	04915
Tenants Harbor	04860
The Forks (Town)	04985
The Kingdom	04941
The Ridge	04009
Thomaston	04861
Thomaston (Town)	04861
Thompson's Point	04055
Thorndike	04986
Thorndike (Town)	04986
Thorndike Center	04986
Thornton Heights (Part of South Portland)	04106
Todds Corner	04930
Topsfield	04490
Topsfield (Town)	04490
Topsham	04086
Topsham (Town)	04086
Tory Hill	04038
Town Farm Hill	04040
Town Hill	04609
Town House Corners	04046
Tracy Corners	04606
Trainor Corner	04345
Trap Corner	04289
Tremont (Town)	04653
Trenton	04605
Trenton (Town)	04605
Trevett	04571
Troutdale	04985
Troy	04987
Troy (Town)	04987
Troy Center	04987
Turbats Creek	04046
Turner	04282
Turner (Town)	04282
Turner Center	04283
Turnpike Mall (Part of Augusta)	04330
Twelve Corners	04254
Twombly (Town)	04417
Union	04862
Union (Town)	04862
Unionville	04622
Unity (Kennebec County) (Town)	04988
Unity (Waldo County) (Town)	04988
Unity (Waldo County) (Town)	04988
University Bookstore	04473
Upper Abbot	04406
Upper Frenchville	04784
Upper Gloucester	04260
Upton	04261
Upton (Town)	04261
Van Buren	04785
Van Buren (Town)	04785
Vanceboro	04491
Vanceboro (Town)	04491
Vassalboro	04989
Vassalborough (Town)	04989
Veazie (Town)	04401
Veazie	04401
Verona	04416
Verona (Town)	04416
Vienna	04360
Vienna (Town)	04360
Viking Village	04217
Vinalhaven	04863
Vinalhaven (Town)	04863
Wade (Town)	04786
Waite	04492
Waite (Town)	04492
Waites Landing	04105
Waldo	04915
Waldo (Town)	04915
Waldoboro	04572
Waldoboro (Town)	04572
Wales (Town)	04280
Wales Corner	04280
Walkers Mill	04217
Wallagrass	04781
Wallagrass (Town)	04781
Walnut Hill	04021
Walpole	04573
Waltham	04605
Waltham (Town)	04605
Wards Cove	04075
Wardtown	04032
Warren (Town)	04864
Warren (Knox County)	04864
Washburn	04786
Washburn (Town)	04786
Washburn Junction (Part of Presque Isle)	04769
Washington	04574

	ZIP		ZIP		ZIP
Washington (Town)	04574	West Fryeburg	04037	Willimantic (Town)	04443
Waterboro	04087	West Gardiner (Town)	04345	Wilson Corner (Part of	
Waterboro (Town)	04087	West Georgetown	04548	Ellsworth)	04605
Waterboro Center	04030	West Gorham	04038	Wilsons Mills	03579
Waterford	04088	West Gouldsboro	04607	Wilton	04294
Waterford (Town)	04088	West Gray	04039	Wilton (Town)	04294
Waterman Beach	04858	West Harpswell	04079	Windham (Town)	04062
Water Street (Part of		West Harrington	04643	Windham	04062
Augusta)	04330	West Hollis	04042	Windham Center	04062
Waterville	04901*	West Jonesport	04649	Windham Hill	04062
	04903†	West Kennebunk	04094	Windsor	04363
Waverly	04967	West Lebanon	04027	Windsor (Town)	04363
Wayne	04284	West Leeds	04263	Winkumpaugh Corners (Part	
Wayne (Town)	04284	West Levant	04456	of Ellsworth)	04605
Webster	04473	West Lovell	04051	Winn	04495
Webster (Town)	04487	West Lubec	04652	Winn (Town)	04495
Webster Corner	04250	Westmanland (Town)	04783	Winnecook	04922
Weeks Mills	04361	West Mills	04938	Winnegance	04530
Welchville	04270	West Minot	04288	Winslow	04901
Welcomes Corner (Part of		West Mount Vernon	04352	Winslow (Town)	04901
Auburn)	04210	West Newfield	04095	Winslows Mills	04572
Weld	04285	West Old Town (Part of Old		Winter Harbor	04693
Weld (Town)	04285	Town)	04468	Winter Harbor (Town)	04693
Wellington	04942	Weston	04424	Winterport	04496
Wellington (Town)	04942	Weston (Town)	04424	Winterport (Town)	04496
Wells	04090	West Paris	04289	Winterville	04788
Wells (Town)	04090	West Paris (Town)	04289	Winterville (Town)	04788
Wells Beach	04090	West Pembroke		Winthrop	04364
Wells Branch	04090	(Washington County)	04666	Winthrop (Town)	04364
Wesley	04686	West Penobscot	04476	Winthrop Center	04364
Wesley (Town)	04686	West Peru	04290	Wiscasset	04578
West Appleton	04949	Westpoint	04565	Wiscasset (Town)	04578
West Athens	04912	West Poland	04291	Wonsqueak Harbor	04613
West Auburn (Part of		Westport	04578	Woodfords (Part of	
Auburn)	04210	Westport (Town)	04578	Portland)	04103
West Baldwin	04091	West Princeton	04668	Woodland (Aroostook	
West Bath (Town)	04530	West Rockport	04865	County) (Town)	04736
West Bethel	04286	West Scarborough	04070	Woodland (Washington	
West Boothbay Harbor	04575	West Seboois	04462	County)	04694
West Bowdoin	04287	West Southport	04576	Woodmans Mills	04973
West Bridgton	04009	West Stonington	04681	Woodstock (Town)	04219
Westbrook	04092*	West Sullivan	04664	Woodville (Town)	04458
	04098†	West Sumner	04292	Woolwich	04579
West Brooklin	04616	West Surry	04605	Woolwich (Town)	04579
West Brooksville	04617	West Tremont	04690	Worthley Pond	04290
West Buxton	04093	West Trenton	04605	Wyman (Franklin County)	
West Central Franklin		West Waldoboro	04572	(Town)	04982
(Town)	04285	West Washington	04341	Wyman (Washington	
West Charleston	04422	West Winterport	04496	County)	04658
West Corinth	04427	Whitefield	04353	Wytopitlock	04497
West Cumberland	04021	Whitefield (Town)	04353	Yarmouth	04096
West Denmark	04010	White Rock	04038	Yarmouth (Town)	04096
West Durham	04069	Whites Corner	04260	York	03909
West Ellsworth (Part of		Whiting	04691	York (Town)	03909
Ellsworth)	04605	Whiting (Town)	04691	York Beach	03910
West End (Part of Portland)	04102	Whitney (Town)	04487	York Cliffs	03902
West Enfield	04493	Whitneyville	04692	York Harbor	03911
West Falmouth	04105	Whitneyville (Town)	04692	York Harbor (census	
West Farmington	04992	Wildes District	04046	designated place)	03909
Westfield	04787	Wildwood Park	04110	York Heights	03909
Westfield (Town)	04787	Wiley's Corner	04861	Youngs Corner (Part of	
West Forks	04985	Williamsburg	04414	Auburn)	04210
West Forks (Town)	04985	Willimantic	04443	Youngtown	04850
West Franklin	04634				

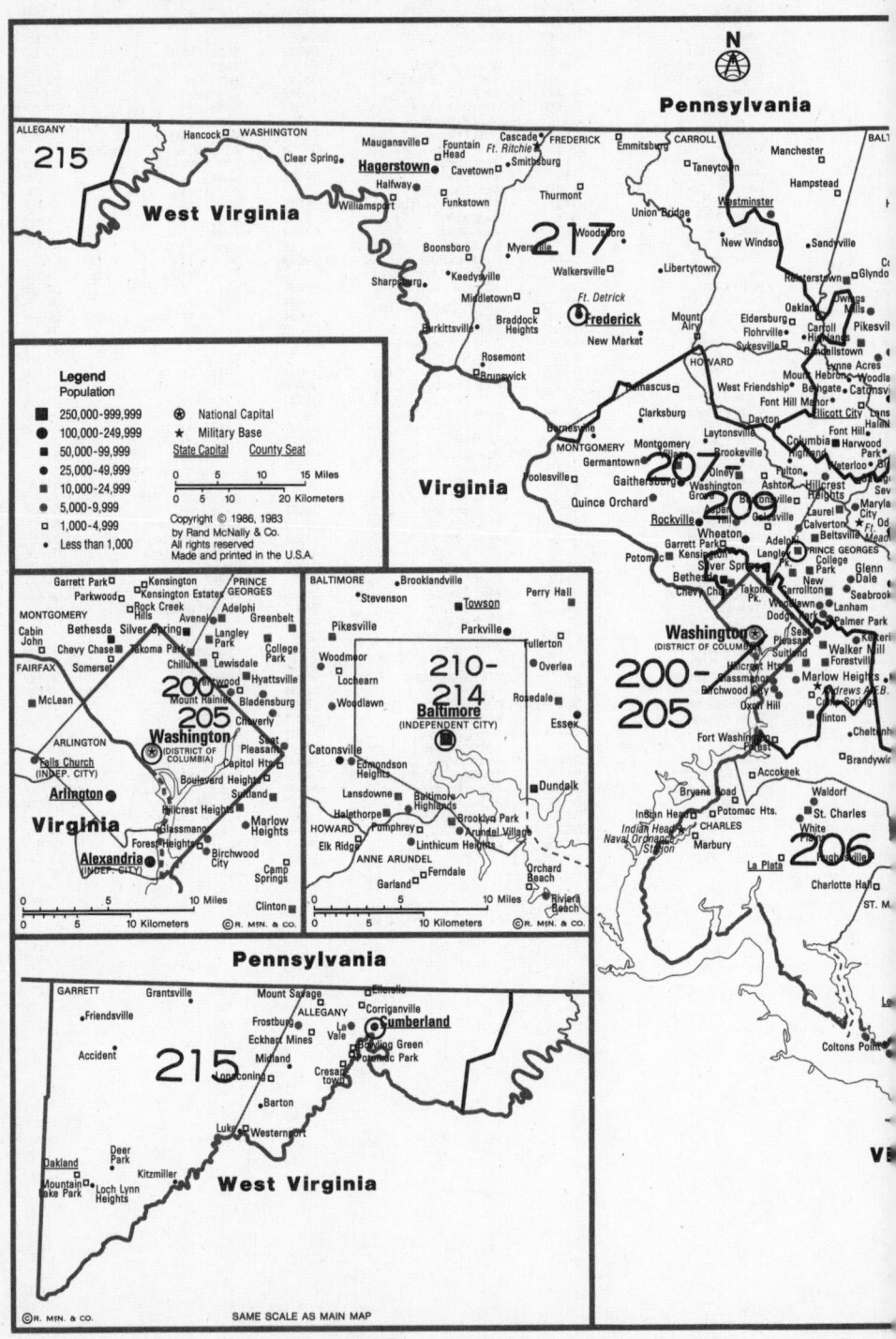

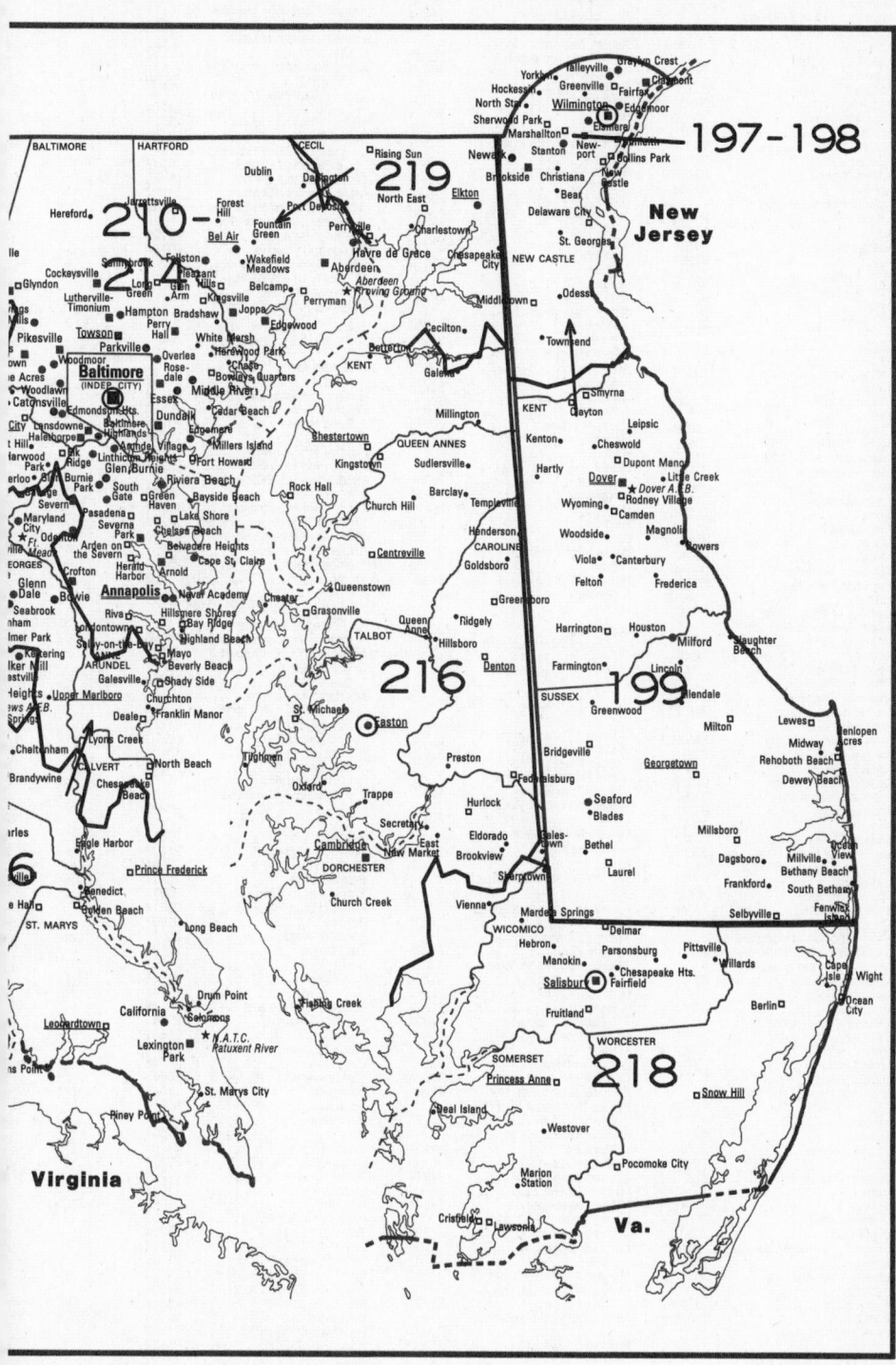

	ZIP
Abell	20606
Aberdeen	21001
Aberdeen Proving Ground (Harford County)	21005
Abingdon	21009
Academy Heights	21228
Academy Junction	21113
Accident	21520
Accokeek	20607
Accokeek Acres	20607
Accokeek Groves	20607
Acco Park	20607
Adamstown	21710
Adams Woods	20783
Adelina	20678
Adelphi (Prince George's County)	20783
Adelphi Hills	20783
Adelphi Manor	20783
Ady	21154
Aero Acres	21220
Aikin (Part of Perryville)	21903
Airey	21613
Albantown	21074
Albeth Heights	21163
Aldino	21001
Alesia	21107
Allanwood	20906
Allegany	21532
Allegany Grove	21502
Allen	21810
Allenford	21042
Allens Fresh	20632
Allenwood	21801
Allenwood Acres	20748
Allview	21045
Allview Estates	21046
Alpha	21104
Alpine Beach	21122
Altamont	21561
Alta Vista	20817
Alta Vista Gardens	20814
Alta Vista Terrace	20814
Amberly	21401
Amberly of Kings Court	21237
Amber Meadows (Part of Bowie)	20716
Amcelle	21502
Amcelle Acres	21502
American Cities	21044
American Corners	21632
Ammendale	20705
Anchorage (Part of Annapolis)	21403
Ancient Oak	20878
Ancient Oak North	20878
Andersontown	21629
Andover Estates	20692
Andrew Hills	20748
Andrews	21626
Andrews AFB	20331
Andrews Air Force Base	20331
Andrews Air Force Base Hospital	20331
Andrews Estates	20746
Andrews Manor	20746
Annapolis	21401-05

For specific Annapolis Zip Codes
call (301) 263-9292, or your local
postmaster.

	ZIP
Annapolis Junction	20701
Annapolis Rock	21797
Anneslie	21204
Antietam (Washington County)	21782
Apple Green	21754
Apple Grove	20744
Appleton Acres	21921
Appliance Park-East (Part of Baltimore)	21045
Appolds	21778
Aquasco	20608
Aragona Village	20744
Arbutus	21227
Arden-on-the-Severn	21032
Ardmore	20785
Ardwick	20785
Argonne Hills	20755
Argyle Park	20901
Arlington (Part of Baltimore)	21215
Armagh	21204
Arnold (Anne Arundel County)	21012
Arnold Heights	20746
Arnoldtown	21718
Arrowhead (Howard County)	21046
Arrow Head (Montgomery County)	20879
Arrowood	20817
Arundel Gardens	21225
Arundel Hills	21090

	ZIP
Arundel on the Bay	21403
Arundel Plaza	21146
Arundel View	21054
Arundel Village	21225
Asbury Methodist Home (Part of Gaithersburg)	20877
Ashburton	20817
Asher Glade	21531
Ashland	21030
Ashton	20861
Ashton Pond	20861
Ashton-Sandy Springs	20861
Asleigh	20817
Aspen Hill (Montgomery County)	20906
Aspen Hill Park	20853
Aspen Knolls	20853
Athol	21837
Atholton	21045
Atholton Manor	21045
Augusta	21758
Aurora Hills	21108
Auth Village	20746
Autrey Park (Part of Rockville)	20850
Autumn Hill	21043
Avalon Shores	20764
Avenue	20609
Avilton	21539
Avondale Grove	20782
Ayrlawn	20814
Back Bay Beach	20778
Back River Highlands	21221
Baden	20613
Bainbridge Naval Training Center	21904
Bakersville	21713
Bald Eagle	20613
Baldwin	21013
Baldwin Hill	21108
Baldwin Hills South	21032
Ballard	20735
Ballard Gardens	21220
Ballenger Creek	21701

	ZIP
Baltimore	21201-86

For specific Baltimore Zip Codes
call (410) 347-4430, or your local
postmaster.

COLLEGES & UNIVERSITIES

	ZIP
College of Notre Dame of Maryland	21210
Coppin State College	21216
Johns Hopkins University	21218
Loyola College	21210
Maryland Institute College of Art	21217
University of Maryland at Baltimore	21201

FINANCIAL INSTITUTIONS

	ZIP
American National Savings Association, F.A.	21201
Arundel Federal Savings Bank	21225
Atlantic Federal Savings Bank	21204
Baltimore County Savings Bank	21236
The Bank of Baltimore	21202
Bradford Federal Savings Bank	21212
Carrollton Bank	21201
Chase Bank of Maryland	21202
Citibank (Maryland), N.A.	21202
Fairfax Savings, a Federal Savings Bank	21202
First National Bank of Maryland, The	21201
Hamilton Federal Savings & Loan Association	21214
Harbor Federal Savings & Loan Association	21224
Leeds Federal Savings & Loan Association	21229
Loyola Federal Savings Bank	21201
Maryland National Bank	21202
Mercantile-Safe Deposit & Trust Company	21201
NationsBank of Maryland, N.A.	21201
Provident Bank of Maryland	21202
Rosedale Federal Savings & Loan Association	21206
Signet Bank/Maryland	21202
The First National Bank of Maryland	21201

HOSPITALS

	ZIP
Francis Scott Key Medical Center	21224
Franklin Square Hospital Center	21237
Good Samaritan Hospital of Maryland	21239
Greater Baltimore Medical Center	21204
Harbor Hospital Center	21225
Johns Hopkins Hospital	21287
Levindale Hebrew Geriatric Center and Hospital	21215
Liberty Medical Center	21215
Mercy Medical Center	21202
Sinai Hospital of Baltimore	21215
St. Agnes Hospital of The City of Baltimore	21229
St. Joseph Hospital	21204
Union Memorial Hospital	21218
University of Maryland Medical System	21201
Veterans Affairs Medical Center	21201

HOTELS/MOTELS

	ZIP
Baltimore Marriott Inner Harbor	21201
Baltimore Ramada Hotel	21244
Brookshire Inner Harbor Suite Hotel	21202
Cross Keys Inn	21210
Holiday Inn-Moravia	21206
Holiday Inn Inner-Harbor	21201
Hyatt Regency Baltimore Inner Harbor	21202
Omni Inner Harbor Hotel	21201
Sheraton Inner Harbor Hotel	21201
Sheraton Baltimore North	21204
Society Hill Hotel	21201
Tremont Hotel	21202
Tremont Plaza	21202

MILITARY INSTALLATIONS

	ZIP
Air Force Publications Distribution Center	21220
MTMC Baltimore Outport	21222
Coast Guard Yard, Curtis Bay	21226
Maryland Air National Guard, FB6191, Martin State Airport	21220
United States Army Engineer District, Baltimore	21203
United States Army Publications Distribution Center	21220

	ZIP
Baltimore Corner	21640
Baltimore Highlands	21227
Banks O'Dee	20664
Bannockburn	20814
Bannockburn Estates	20817
Bannockburn Heights	20817
Barclay	21607
Barefoot Acres	20619
Bar Harbor	21122
Bark Hill	21791
Barksdale	21921
Barnaby Manor	20744
Barnaby Run Estates	20745
Barnaby Village	20745
Bar Neck	21671
Barnes Corner	21917
Barnesville	20838
Barnesville (Sellman)	20842
Barrelville	21545
Barstow	20610
Bartholows	21771
Barton	21521
Bartonsville	21701
Battery Park	20814
Battle Grove	21222
Bayberry	21012
Bay City	21666
Bay Highlands	21403
Baynesville	21204
Bay Ridge	21403
Bayside Beach	21122
Bay View (Part of Baltimore)	21224
Bay View (Cecil County)	21901
Bay View Estates	21919
Beachville	20684
Beachwood Forest	21122
Beachwood Grove	21122
Beachwood on the Burley	21401
Beacon Heights	20737
Beacon Hill	21401
Beale Manor	21403
Beall Estates	20716

	ZIP
Beallsville	20839
Beantown	20601
Bear Creek Junction	21222
Beaufort Park	20759
Beauty Beach	21061
Beauvue	20650
Beaver Creek	21740
Beaver Dam	21851
Beaver Dam Estates	20785
Beaver Heights	20743
Beckleysville	21074
Bedford	20708
Bedfordshire	20854
Bel Air	21014-15
For specific Bel Air Zip Codes call (410) 838-6262, or your local postmaster.	
Bel Air (Allegany County)	21502
Belair (Prince George's County)	20715
Bel Air Acres (Charles County)	20601
Bel Air Acres (Harford County)	21014
Belair Buckingham (Part of Bowie)	20715
Belair Chapel Forge (Part of Bowie)	20715
Belair Foxhill (Part of Bowie)	20715
Belair Heather Hills (Part of Bowie)	20715
Belair Idlewild (Part of Bowie)	20715
Belair Kenilworth (Part of Bowie)	20715
Belair Longridge (Part of Bowie)	20715
Bel Air North	21050
Belair Overbrook (Part of Bowie)	20715
Belair Rockledge (Part of Bowie)	20715
Belair Shopping Center (Part of Bowie)	20715
Belair Somerset (Part of Bowie)	20715
Bel Air South	21015
Belair Tulip Grove (Part of Bowie)	20715
Belair White Hall (Part of Bowie)	20715
Belair Yorktown (Part of Bowie)	20715
Bel Alton	20611
Belcamp	21017
Belhaven	21122
Belleair Estates	20744
Belle Farm Estates	21208
Bellefonte	20735
Belle Grove	21766
Bellemead	20784
Belleview Estates	21146
Bellevue	21662
Bellevue Estates	20607
Bells Mill Village	20854
Belmar	21206
Bel Pre Estates	20906
Bel Pre Park	20906
Bel Pre Woods	20853
Beltsville	20704†
	20705*
Beltsville	20705
Beltsville Heights	20705
Beltway Plaza (Part of Greenbelt)	20770
Belvedere Heights	21012
Bembe Beach	21403
Benedict	20612
Benevola	21713
Bennsville	20603
Ben Oaks	21146
Benson	21018
Bentley Springs	21120
Bentons Pleasure	21619
Berkley	21034
Berkshire	20747
Berlin	21811
Berrett	21784
Berry	20603
Berrywood	21146
Berwyn (Part of College Park)	20740
Berwyn Heights	20740
Bestgate	21401
Bethany Manor	21042
Bethel (Carroll County)	21048
Bethel (Cecil County)	21915
Bethel (Frederick County)	21702
Bethel (Garrett County)	21550
Bethesda	20813-14
	20816-17
	20824

	ZIP
	20827
For specific Bethesda Zip Codes call (301) 652-7401, or your local postmaster.	
Bethgate	21043
Bethlehem	21609
Betterton	21610
Beulah	21643
Beverly Beach	21106
Beverly Farms	20854
Big Pines	20850
Big Pool	21711
Big Spring	21722
Bigwoods	21678
Billingsley Forest	20640
Birchwood City	20745
Birchwood Gardens	20708
Birdlawn	20744
Bird River Beach	21220
Birdsville	20776
Birmingham Estates	20705
Birmingham Terrace	20705
Bishop	21813
Bishops Head	21672
Bishopville	21813
Bitter Sweet	21403
Bittinger	21522
Bivalve	21814
Black Horse	21161
Blackrock Estates	20874
Blacks Corner	21157
Blackwater	21622
Bladensburg	20710
Bladenwoods (Part of Bladensburg)	20710
Blair	20910
Blenheim	21131
Bloomfield	21702
Blooming Rose Settlement	21531
Bloomington	21523
Bloomsbury	21228
Blossom Hills	21122
Blueball	21921
Blueberry Hills	20855
Blue Hill (Part of Hancock)	21750
Blue Mount	21111
Blue Mountain (Frederick County)	21788
Blue Mountain (Washington County)	21783
Blue Ridge Manor	20902
Blue Ridge View	21157
Blythedale	21903
Bolivar Heights	21769
Bolton	20601
Bond Mill Park	20707
Bonds	20607
Bon Haven	21401
Bonnie Acres	21043
Bonnie Brae	21784
Bonnie Brook	21613
Bonnie Knob (Part of Woodsboro)	21798
Bonnie Ridge	21209
Boonsboro	21713
Borden Shaft	21532
Boring	21020
Boulevard Heights	20743
Boulevard Park on the Magothy	21122
Bowens	20678
Bowie	20715-21
For specific Bowie Zip Codes call (301) 464-0707, or your local postmaster.	
Bowie State College	20715
Bowleys Quarters	21220
Bowling Green	21502
Bowlings Alley	20622
Boxhill North	21009
Boxiron	21829
Boxwood Village (Part of Greenbelt)	20770
Boyds	20841
Boyer Mill Heights	21774
Bozman	21612
Bradbury Heights	20743
Bradbury Park	20746
Braddock	21702
Braddock Estates (Part of Frostburg)	21532
Braddock Heights	21714
Bradley Farms	20854
Bradley Hills	20817
Bradley Hills Grove	20817
Bradley Woods	20817
Bradshaw	21021
Brady	21502
Braebrook Village	20770
Branchville (Part of College Park)	20740
Brandwine Farms	21047

	ZIP
Brandywine	20613
Brandywine Country	20772
Brandywine Heights	20613
Breathedsville	21740
Breezewood Farms	21163
Breezy Point	20732
Breezy Point Beach	21221
Brentwood	20722
Breton Beach	20650
Briarcrest Heights	21755
Briarwood (Charles County)	20601
Briarwood (Prince George's County)	20708
Briddletown	21811
Bridewell	20794
Bridgeport (Frederick County)	21787
Bridgetown (Washington County)	21742
Bridgetown	21636
Bright Oaks	21015
Brighton (Baltimore County)	21244
Brighton (Montgomery County)	20833
Brightview Woods	21108
Brightwood Acres	21740
Brinkleigh	21042
Brinkleigh Manor	21042
Brinkley Manor	20748
Brinklow	20862
Bristol	20711
Broad Creek	21160
Broadmoor	21030
Broad Run	21718
Broadview	20748
Broadview Acres	21701
Broadwater Estates	20744
Broadwater Point	20733
Broadwood Manor (Part of Rockville)	20851
Brock Bridge	20708
Brock Hall	20772
Brock Hall Estates	20772
Brock Hall Gardens	20772
Brock Hall Manor	20772
Brookdale	20815
Brookdale Heights	21801
Brooke-Jane Manor	20735
Brooke Manor	20745
Brookemanor Estates	20853
Brookeville	20833
Brook Hill	21702
Brooklandville	21093
Brooklyn (Part of Baltimore)	21225
Brooklyn-Curtis Bay	21225
Brooklyn Park	21225
Brookmead	20874
Brookmead North	20874
Brookmont	20816
Brookside Forest	20901
Brookside Manor	20782
Brookview	21659
Brookville Knolls	20833
Brookwood	20772
Brookwood Estates	20695
Broomes Island	20615
Browns Corner	21617
Brownsville (Queen Anne's County)	21617
Brownsville (Washington County)	21715
Browns Woods Villa	21401
Bruceville (Carroll County)	21757
Bruceville (Talbot County)	21673
Brunswick	21716
Bryans Road (Charles County)	20616
Bryantown (Charles County)	20617
Bryantown (Queen Anne's County)	21658
Bryant Square	21044
Bryant Woods	21044
Buckeystown	21717
Buckingham View	21157
Buck Lodge	20783
Bucktown	21613
Budds Creek	20659
Buena Vista	20678
Buffalo Run	21531
Burgundy Estates (Part of Rockville)	20851
Burgundy Knolls (Part of Rockville)	20850
Burgundy Village (Part of Rockville)	20850
Burkittsville	21718
Burning Tree Estates	20817
Burning Tree Manor	20817
Burns Corner (Part of Aberdeen)	21001
Burnt Mills	20901
Burnt Mills Hills	20901

* Area Zip Code   **† Post Office Boxes**

Place	ZIP	Place	ZIP	Place	ZIP
Burnt Mills Knolls	20901	Carrollwood	21220	Chesapeake Ranch Estates (Calvert County)	20657
Burnt Mills Manor	20901	Carrollwood Estate	21771	Chesapeake Terrace	21222
Burnt Mills Village	20901	Carsins Run	21001	Cheshaven	21919
Burrisville	21617	Carsondale	20706	Chester	21619
Burrsville	21629	Carter Hill (Part of Rockville)	20850	Chesterfield	21032
Burtner	21713	Carvel Beach	21226	Chesterfield Gardens	21122
Burtonsville	20866	Carver Heights	20653	Chester Harbor	21620
Bush	21009	Cascade	21719	Chester River Beach	21638
Bushs Corner	21132	Cashell Estates	20855	Chestertown	21620
Bushwood	20618	Casselman	21536	Chesterville	21651
Butler	21023	Castle Marina	21619	Chesterville Forest	21651
Butlertown	21678	Castleton	21034	Chestnut Grove (Frederick County)	21701
Buttercup Estates	21794	Catchpenny	21856	Chestnut Grove (Washington County)	21756
Buttonwood Beach	21919	Catoctin	21716	Chestnut Hill (Baltimore County)	21286
Byford Knolls	20895	Catoctin Furnace	21788	Chestnut Hill (Harford County)	21050
Bynum	21050	Catoctin View	21771	Chestnut Hill (Howard County)	21043
Bynum Ridge	21050	Catonsville	21228	Chestnut Hill Estates	21043
Byrdtown	21817	Catonsville Heights	21228	Chestnut Hills	20705
Cabin Creek	21643	Catonsville Manor	21207	Chestnut Ridge (Baltimore County)	21117
Cabin John	20818	Cavalier Country	20754	Chestnut Ridge (Prince George's County)	20737
Cabin John-Brookmont	20816	Cavetown	21720	Cheverly	20785
Cabin John Park	20818	Cayots	21915	Cheverly Manor	20785
Cactus Hill	20607	Cearfoss	21740	Chevy Chase	20815*
Cadillac Homes	21060	Cecilton	21913		20825†
California (St. Mary's County)	20619	Cedar Acres	21044	Chevy Chase Lake	20815
Callaway	20620	Cedar Beach	21221	Chevy Chase Manor	20815
Caltor Manor	20744	Cedar Grove	20876	Chevy Chase Section Five	20815
Calvary	21028	Cedar Grove Beach	21631	Chevy Chase Section Three	20815
Calvert (Part of Baltimore)	21202	Cedar Hall	21851	Chevy Chase Terrace	20815
Calvert (Cecil County)	21901	Cedar Haven	20608	Chevy Chase View	20895
Calvert Beach	20685	Cedar Heights	20743	Chevy Chase Village	20815
Calvert Beach-Long Beach	20685	Cedarhurst (Anne Arundel County)	20764	Chewsville	21721
Calvert Manor	20607	Cedarhurst (Carroll County)	21048	Chicamuxen	20640
Calverton	20705	Cedarhurst Acres	21830	Childs	21916
Cambria	21131	Cedarhurst-on-the-Bay	20764	Chillum	20783
Cambridge	21613	Cedar Lawn	21740	Chillum Estates	20783
Cambridge Estates	20735	Cedarmere	21117	Chillum Heights	20783
Camden (Part of Baltimore)	21201	Cedar Park (Part of Annapolis)	21401	Chillum Manor	20783
Camden (Wicomico County)	21810	Cedar Spring	21015	Chingville	20620
Camelback Village	20832	Cedartown	21863	Choptank	21655
Camelot (Harford County)	21015	Cedarville	20613	Christs Rock	21613
Camelot (Prince George's County)	20769	Centennial	21042	Church Creek	21622
Camotop	20854	Centennial Estates	21042	Church Hill (Frederick County)	21773
Campbell	21813	Center Court	20879	Church Hill (Queen Anne's County)	21623
Campbelltown	21813	Centerville	21754	Churchill Town Sector	20874
Camp Springs (Prince George's County)	20748	Centreville	21617	Churchton	20733
Camp Springs Forest	20748	Ceresville	21701	Churchville	21028
Campus Hills	21286	Chadwick Manor	21244	Cinnamon Ridge	20772
Canal	21904	Chalfone Manor	21228	Cissel Farms	20777
Candlewood Park	20855	Chalk Point	20778	Claggettsville	20872
Cannon Acres	21613	Champ	21853	Claiborne	21624
Canton (Part of Baltimore)	21224	Chance	21816	Claremont (Part of Baltimore)	21223
Cape Anne	20733	Chaney	20754	Clarksburg	20871
Cape Arthur	21146	Chaneyville	20736	Clarks Landing	20636
Cape Estate	21012	Chaneyville Farm Estates	20736	Clarksville	21029
Cape Isle of Wight	21842	Chapel	21601	Clarksville Ridge	21029
Cape Loch Haven	21037	Chapel Gate	21113	Clarysville	21532
Cape May Beach	21221	Chapel Hill	20744	Clayton Manor	21085
Cape St. Claire	21401	Chapel Hill Estates	20610	Clearfield	21157
Cape St. John	21401	Chapel Oaks	20743	Clear Spring	21722
Capital Estates	20695	Chapelview	21043	Clearview	21040
Capitol Heights	20731	Chaptico	20621	Clearview Manor	20745
	20743	Charles Manor	21047	Clearview Village	21122
	20791	Charlesmont	21222	Clearwater Beach	21226
For specific Capitol Heights Zip Codes call (301) 336-5650, or your local postmaster.		Charlestown (Allegany County)	21539	Clements	20624
Capitol Hills	21061	Charlestown (Cecil County)	21914	Clifford (Part of Baltimore)	21230
Capitol Plaza (Part of Landover Hills)	20784	Charlestown Manor Beach	21901	Cliffs City	21620
Capitol View Park	20910	Charlesville	21702	Clifton	21702
Capri Estate	21012	Charlotte Hall	20622	Clifton-East End (Part of Baltimore)	21213
Captains Hill	21842	Charlton	21722	Clifton on the Potomac	20664
Carderock Springs	20817	Charred Oak Estates	20817	Clifton Park	20901
Cardiff	21024	Chartley	21136	Clinton	20735
Carea	21161	Chartridge	21146	Clinton Acres	20613
Carleton East	20706	Chartwell	21146	Clinton Estates	20735
Carlos	21532	Chase	21027	Clinton Gardens	20735
Carlson Spring	20747	Chateau Valley	21042	Clinton Grove	20735
Carmichael	21658	Chatham	20783	Clinton Hills	20735
Carmody Hills	20743	Chattolanee	21117	Clinton Park	20735
Carmody Hills-Pepper Mill Village	20743	Chelsea Beach	21122	Clinton Vista	20735
Carney	21234	Chelsea Woods (Part of Greenbelt)	20770	Clinton Woods	20735
Carney Grove	21234	Cheltenham	20623	Clopper	20878
Carney Heights	21234	Cheltenham Forest	20735	Cloverfields	21666
Carole Highlands	20783	Chelten Park	20735	Clover Hill	21702
Carpenter Point	21903	Cherry Hill (Cecil County)	21921	Cloverlea	21106
Carroll (Part of Baltimore)	21229	Cherry Hill (Harford County)	21154	Cloverly	20904
Carroll County Trails	21048	Cherry Hill (mobile home park)	20705	Club of Stedwick	20879
Carroll Heights (Part of Hagerstown)	21740	Cherry Hill (Prince George's County)	20740	Clubside	20879
Carroll Highlands	21784	Cherrywalk	21830	Clydesdale Acres	21048
Carroll Island	21220	Chesaco Park	21237	Cobb Island	20625
Carroll Knolls	20910	Chesapeake Beach	20732		
Carroll Manor (Part of Takoma Park)	20912	Chesapeake City	21915		
Carrollton	21784	Chesapeake Estates	21666		
Carrollton Manor	21146	Chesapeake Heights	21801		
		Chesapeake Isle	21901		
		Chesapeake Landing	21620		

	ZIP
Cockeysville	21030-31
For specific Cockeysville Zip Codes call (410) 771-0780, or your local postmaster.	
Cohasset	20814
Cohill Estates	21750
Cokesburg	21851
Cokesbury	21904
Cold Spring Estates	20854
Coleman	21678
Colesville	20904-05
For specific Colesville Zip Codes call (301) 384-0656, or your local postmaster.	
Colesville Farm Estates	20904
Colesville Gardens	20904
Colesville Manor	20904
Colesville Park	20904
College (Part of Westminster)	21157
College Estates (Part of Frederick)	21701
College Gardens (Part of Rockville)	20850
College Heights Estates	20783
College Park	20740*
	20741†
College Park Woods (Part of College Park)	20740
College View	20902
Colmar Manor	20722
Colonial Acres (Cecil County)	21921
Colonial Acres (Harford County)	21014
Colonial Gardens	21228
Colonial Park (Baltimore County)	21207
Colonial Park (Washington County)	21740
Colonial Village	21208
Colony Heights	21502
Colony Ridge	21113
Colora	21917
Coltons Point	20626
Columbia	21044-46
For specific Columbia Zip Codes call (301) 381-0121, or your local postmaster.	
Columbia Beach	20764
Columbia Hills	21043
Columbia Park	20785
Compton	20627
Comus	20842
Concord	21632
Congressional Forest Estates	20817
Connecticut Avenue Estates	20902
Connecticut Avenue Hills	20902
Connecticut Avenue Park	20906
Connecticut Gardens	20902
Conowingo	21918
Conowingo Village	21034
Contee	20708
Cooksville	21723
Cooperstown	21023
Coopstown	21050
Copenhaver	20854
Copperville (Carroll County)	21787
Copperville (Talbot County)	21601
Coral Hills	20743
Corbett (Baltimore County)	21111
Corbett (Washington County)	21740
Cordova	21625
Cornersville	21613
Cornfield Harbor	20687
Corriganville	21524
Costen	21851
Cottage City	20722
Country Club Acres	21550
Country Club Estate	21060
Country Club Manor	21060
Country Club Park	21093
Country Club Village	20814
Country Place	20866
Country Road Estates	20754
Courthouse (Part of Rockville)	20850
Courtleigh	21133
Cove	21520
Coventry	21234
Cove Point	20657
Covers Corner	21776
Cowentown	21921
Coxby Estates	21037
Cox Creek Acres	21619
Crabtree	21561
Craigtown	21904
Cranberry	21157
Crapo	21626
Creagerstown	21788

	ZIP
Crellin	21550
Cremona	20659
Cresaptown	21502
Cresaptown-Bel Air	21502
Crescendo	21676
Cresthaven	20903
Crestleigh	21042
Crestview	20814
Crestview Manor	20735
Crestwood (Anne Arundel County)	21090
Crestwood (Wicomico County)	21801
Crestwood Acres	21040
Creswell	21015
Crisfield	21817
Crisp (Part of Baltimore)	21225
Criswood Manor	21029
Crocheron	21627
Crofton	21114
Cromwood	21234
Croom	20772
Crosby	21661
Crowder	21043
Crownsville	21032
Crownsville Hospital Center	21032
Croydon Park (Part of Rockville)	20850
Crumpton	21628
Crystal Beach	21919
Cub Hill	21234
Cuckhold Creek	20664
Cumberland	21501-05
For specific Cumberland Zip Codes call (301) 722-8190, or your local postmaster.	
Curtis Bay (Part of Baltimore)	21225
Cypress Creek	21146
Dailsville	21613
Daisy	21797
Dalton	21045
Damascus	20872
Dameron	20628
Dames Quarter	21820
Dam No. 4	21782
Daniel	21797
Daniels Park (Part of College Park)	20740
Danville	21557
Danwood	21801
Darcy Manor	20746
Dares Beach	20678
Dargan	21782
Darleigh Manor	21236
Darlington	21034
Darnestown	20874
Darryl Gardens	21162
Daugherty Town	21817
Davidsonville	21035
Dawson	26726
Dawsonville	20841
Day	21797
Daysville	21793
Dayton	21036
Deale	20751
Deale Beach	20751
Deal Island	21821
Deanwood Park	20743
Decatur Heights (Part of Bladensburg)	20710
Deep Creek	21012
Deep Creek Lake	21541
Deep Landing Estates	20639
Deerfield (Harford County)	21034
Deerfield (Montgomery County)	20817
Deerfield Run	20708
Deer Harbour	21801
Deer Park (Garrett County)	21550
Deer Park (Montgomery County)	20877
Deer Park (Prince George's County)	20748
Deer Park Estates	21048
Deer Park Heights	20748
Deers Head	21801
Defense Heights (Baltimore County)	21222
Defense Heights (Prince George's County)	20784
Delight	21117
Delmar	21875
Delmont	21144
Den Lee Acres	20735
Dennings	21776
Dennis Grove Apartments	20745
Denton	21629
Dentsville	20646
Derwood	20855
Detmold	21539
Detour	21757

	ZIP
Devonshire Forest	21093
Diamond Farms (Part of Gaithersburg)	20878
Dickerson	20842
Discovery-Spring Garden	21793
District Heights	20747*
	20753†
Dodge Park	20785
Dogwood Flats	21521
Dogwood Hills	21286
Dominion	21619
Doncaster	20640
Doncaster Village	21234
Donleigh	21046
Donnybrook	21204
Dorceytown	21771
Dorchester Estates	20735
Dorrs Corner	21108
Dorsey	21227
Dorseys Regard	20879
Doubs	21710
Dowell	20629
Downsville	21795
Drayden	20630
Dresden Green	20706
Drexel Woods	21228
Druid (Part of Baltimore)	21217
Drumcliff	20636
Drumeldra Hills	20904
Drum Point	20657
Drury	20711
Drybranch	21161
Dry Run	21722
Dublin	21034
Dufief	20878
Dulaney Village	21204
Dulls Corner	21401
Dumbarton	21208
Dumbarton Heights	21208
Dunbrook	21122
Dundalk	21222
Dundalk Shopping Center	21222
Dundalk-Sparrows Point	21222
Dundee Village	21220
Dunkirk	20754
Dunlaney Village	21093
Dunloggin	21042
Dunwood	21085
Dupont Heights	20746
Dynard	20621
Eagle Harbor	20608
Eakles Mills	21756
Earleigh Heights	21146
Earleville	21919
Earlton	21078
East Columbia Park	20785
Eastfield	21222
East Fort Foote Village	20744
East Meadow	20745
East New Market	21631
Easton	21601
Easton Point	21601
Eastover Knolls	20745
East Park Village	21061
Eastpines	20737
Eastpoint	21222
Eastpoint Mall	21224
Eastport (Part of Annapolis)	21403
East Riverdale (Prince George's County)	20737
East Springbrook	20904
Eastview (Carroll County)	21048
Eastview (Frederick County)	21702
Eastview Estates	21048
Eckhart Mines	21528
Eden	21822
Eder	21921
Edesville	21661
Edgemere	21221
Edgemont (Frederick County)	21702
Edgemont (Washington County)	21783
Edgemoor	20814
Edgewater	21037
Edgewater Beach	21037
Edgewater Village	21040
Edgewood (Frederick County)	21702
Edgewood (Harford County)	21040
Edgewood (Montgomery County)	20814
Edgewood Arsenal	21040
Edgewood Meadows	21040
Edmondson Ridge	21228
Edmonson Heights	21207
Edmonston	20781
Ednor	20905
Ednor Acres	20904
Elberon	20854
Elder Hill	21531
Eldersburg	21784

	ZIP
Eldorado	21659
Elioak	21044
Elk Mills	21920
Elkmore	21921
Elk Neck	21901
Elk Ranch Park	21921
Elkridge	21227
Elkton	21921*
	21922†
Elkton Heights (Part of Elkton)	21921
Elktonia	21401
Elkton Landing (Part of Elkton)	21921
Elkwood Estates	21921
Ellerslie	21529
Ellerton	21773
Ellicott City	21041-43
For specific Ellicott City Zip Codes call (410) 465-0440, or your local postmaster.	
Ellicott City (census designated place)	21043
Ellicott Mills (Baltimore County)	21228
Ellicott Mills (Howard County)	21043
Elliott	21869
Elmwood	21206
Elvaton Acres	21108
Elvatone Town	21061
Elwood	21643
Emmitsburg	21727
Emmorton	21009
Emory Grove (Baltimore County)	21071
Emory Grove (Montgomery County)	20877
Emory Hills	21048
Engles Mill	21520
Englewood	20785
English Manor	20853
English Village	20814
Enterprise Estates	20721
Enterprise Shopping Center	20706
Epping Forest	21401
Ernstville	21711
Essex	21221
Estonian Estates	20772
Etchison	20882
Eudowood	21204*
	21286†
Eutaw Forest	20603
Evanston	20747
Evergreen Estates	21146
Evergreen Hills	21048
Evergreen Overlook	20745
Evergreen Park	21221
Evergreen Valley Estates	21042
Evitts Creek	21502
Ewell	21824
Ewingville	21620
Fahrney Keedy Memorial Home	21713
Fairbank	21671
Fairfield (Part of Baltimore)	21226
Fairfield (Carroll County)	21157
Fairfield Knolls	20747
Fairgreen	20772
Fairgreen Acres	21740
Fair Haven	20754
Fairhaven on the Bay	20754
Fair Hill	21921
Fairidge	20879
Fairknoll	20905
Fairland	20904
Fairland Acres	20866
Fairland Heights	20904
Fairlee	21620
Fairmont	21014
Fairmount	21871
Fairmount Heights	20743
Fair Play	21733
Fairview (mobile home park)	20707
Fairview (Anne Arundel County)	21122
Fairview (Washington County)	21722
Fairview Estates	20904
Fairway	21015
Fairway Hills	20812
Fairway Island	20879
Fallsmont	21047
Fallston	21047
Family Estates	20743
Farmington (Cecil County)	21911
Farmington (Montgomery County)	20815
Farmsbrook	21702
Faulkner	20632
Faulkner Ridge	21044
Fawsett Farms	20854

	ZIP
Feagaville	21702
Federal Hill	21084
Federalsburg	21632
Felicity Cove	20764
Fellowship Forest	21204
Ferdinand Heights	21061
Ferndale	21061
Fernglen Manor	21061
Fernwood (Montgomery County)	20817
Fernwood (Prince George's County)	20737
Fernwood (mobile home park)	20743
Fiddlersburg	21740
Figgs Landing	21863
Finksburg	21048
Finzel	21532
Fishing Creek	21634
Fleishman Village	20746
Flickersville	21756
Flintstone	21530
Flohrville	21784
Florence	21797
Flower Valley	20853
Flower Valley Estates	20853
Fontana Village	21237
Font Hill	21042
Font Hill Manor	21042
Forest Estates	20910
Forest Glen	20910
Forest Greens	21001
Forest Heights	20745
Forest Hill	21050
Forest Knolls (Montgomery County)	20901
Forest Knolls (Prince George's County)	20744
Forest Lake	21050
Forest Lawn	21014
Forest Manor	20747
Forest Oaks	21784
Forest Park	20705
Forestville	20747
Forestville Estates	20747
Forge Acres	21128
Forge Heights	21128
Fork	21051
Forrest Hall	20659
Fort Foote Estates	20747
Fort Foote Village	20744
Fort George G. Meade	20755
Fort Howard	21052
Fort Meade	20755
Fort Ritchie	21719
Fort Sumner	20816
Fort Washington	20744*
	20749†
Fort Washington Estates	20744
Fort Washington Forest	20744
Foundry Siding (Part of Westernport)	21562
Fountaindale	21769
Fountain Green	21015
Fountain Green Heights	21015
Fountain Head	21742
Fountain Mills	21770
Fountain Rock (Part of Walkersville)	21793
Fountain Valley	21157
Four Locks	21722
Four Seasons Estates	21113
Four Winds	21204
Fowblesburg	21155
Fowlers Concord	20747
Fox Chapel	20876
Fox Chapel North	20876
Fox Chase	21061
Foxhall	20906
Foxhall Estates	21035
Fox Hills	20854
Fox Hills West	20854
Foxley Manor	21620
Fox Rest	20708
Fox Rest South	20708
Foxridge	21078
Fox Run Estates	20735
Foxville	21780
Franklin (Part of Baltimore)	21223
Franklin Manor Beach	20733
Franklin Manor on-the-Bay	20733
Franklin Park	20852
Franklin Square	20744
Franklinville (Baltimore County)	21087
Franklinville (Frederick County)	21788
Frederick	21701-05
For specific Frederick Zip Codes call (301) 662-2131, or your local postmaster.	
Frederick Junction	21701

	ZIP
Frederick Shopping Center (Part of Frederick)	21701
Frederick Towne Mall (Part of Frederick)	21702
Frederick Village	21228
Freedom Forest	21784
Freeland	21053
Free State Mall (Part of Bowie)	20715
Frenchtown (Part of Perryville)	21903
Friendly	20744
Friendly Farms	20744
Friends Creek	21727
Friendship (Anne Arundel County)	20758
Friendship (Frederick County)	21791
Friendship (Worcester County)	21811
Friendship Heights	20813
Friendship Park	21740
Friendsville	21531
Frizzelburg	21158
Frostburg	21532
Frostown	21769
Fruitland	21826
Fullerton	21236
Fulton	20759
Fulton Junction (Part of Baltimore)	21217
Funkstown	21734
Furnace Branch	21061
Gaither	21784
Gaithersburg	20877-79
	20882-86
	20898
For specific Gaithersburg Zip Codes call (301) 948-1894, or your local postmaster.	
Galena	21635
Galestown	19973
Galesville	20765
Gallant Green	20601
Gamber	21048
Gambrills	21054
Gannon	21562
Gapland	21736
Garfield	21783
Garland	21061
Garrett Forest	20906
Garrett Park	20896
Garrett Park Estates	20895
Garretts Mill	21758
Garrison	21055
Gatts Corner	21106
Gayfields	20906
George Island Landing	21864
Georgetown (Anne Arundel County)	20794
Georgetown (mail Chestertown)	21620
Georgetown (mail Georgetown)	21930
Georgetown Estates	20852
Georgetown Village	20812
Georgian Forest	20902
Germantown (Montgomery County)	20874-76
For specific Germantown Zip Codes call (301) 428-3839, or your local postmaster.	
Germantown (census designated place)	20874
Germantown (Worcester County)	21811
Germantown Estates	20874
Germantown Park	20874
Germantown View	20874
Gibson Island	21056
Gibson Manor	21015
Gilmore	21532
Gingerville Manor Estates	21037
Girdletree	21829
Gist	21784
Glade Towne (Part of Walkersville)	21793
Gladstone Acres	21034
Glassmanor	20745
Glazewood Manor (Part of Takoma Park)	20912
Glebe Heights	21037
Glenallen	20902
Glenarden	20706
Glen Arm	21057
Glen Brook	21042
Glenbrook Knolls	20814
Glenbrook Village	20814
Glen Burnie	21060-61
For specific Glen Burnie Zip Codes call (410) 766-8880, or your local postmaster.	

* **Area Zip Code**　　† **Post Office Boxes**

	ZIP		ZIP		ZIP
Glen Burnie	21061	Green Hill	21856	Harford Park	21234
Glen Burnie Mall	21061	Green Hill Acres	21742	Harford Square	21040
Glen Burnie Park	21061	Green Meadows (Charles		Harmans	21077
Glencoe (Baltimore County)	21152	County)	20640	Harmony (Caroline County)	21655
Glencoe (Kent County)	21645	Green Meadows (Prince		Harmony (Frederick County)	21769
Glen Cove	20816	George's County)	20782	Harmony Grove	21701
Glendale (Baltimore County)	21204	Greenmount (Part of		Harmony Hall	20744
Glendale (Wicomico		Hampstead)	21074	Harmony Hills	20906
County)	21801	Green Ridge (Allegany		Harness Woods	21403
Glen Echo	20812	County)	21766	Harney	21787
Glen Echo Heights	20816	Green Ridge (Baltimore		Harpers Choice	21044
Glenelg	21737	County)	21093	Harpers Corner	20659
Glen Ellen	21286	Greenridge (Harford		Harpers Mill	21108
Glen Elyn	21047	County)	21015	Harris Heights	21061
Glen Farms	21921	Greensboro	21639	Harrison Ferry	21643
Glen Gardens	21060	Greensburg	21783	Harrisonville	21133
Glen Hills	20850	Green Spring Hills	21085	Harrisville (Carroll County)	21771
Glen Isle	21401	Greentop Manor	21030	Harrisville (Cecil County)	21917
Glen Kyle	19711	Greentree (Anne Arundel		Harundale	21060
Glenmar (Baltimore County)	21220	County)	21061	Harundale Mall	21061
Glenmar (Howard County)	21043	Greentree (Montgomery		Harvest Hills	21047
Glen Mar Park	20814	County)	20879	Harwood (Anne Arundel	
Glen Mary Heights (Part of		Green Tree Manor	20817	County)	20776
Elkton)	21921	Greenvale Village	21783	Har-Wood (Howard County)	21227
Glenmont (Baltimore		Green Valley	21771	Harwood Estates	20748
County)	21239	Greenview Knolls	20653	Harwood Park	21227
Glenmont (Montgomery		Greenwich Forest	20814	Havenwood Hills	21783
County)	20902	Greenwood Acres	21401	Haverhill	21234
Glenmont Park	20906	Greenwood Farms	20777	Havre de Grace	21078
Glenmore	21061	Greenwood Forest	20706	Havre de Grace Heights	21078
Glen Morris	21136	Gregg Neck	21635	Hawbottom	21769
Glenn Dale	20769	Greystone Manor (Part of		Hawkeye	21631
Glenn Dale Heights	20769	Hagerstown)	21740	Hayes Landing	21811
Glenn Heights	21078	Grimesville	21053	Hazelhurst	21561
Glen Oaks	20854	Grosstown	20637	Hazelmoor	21919
Glenora Hills (Part of		Grove	21655	Head of the Creek	21856
Rockville)	20850	Grove Hill	21702	Hearn Bailey Farm	21801
Glen Park	20854	Guilford	20794	Heather Heights	21784
Glen Ridge	20784	Guilford Manor	21225	Heather Hill Apartments	20748
Glenside Park	21234	Gum Springs	20868	Hebbville	21244
Glenville	21034	Gum Springs Farm	20868	Hebron	21830
Glen Westover	19711	Gunners Lake Village	20874	Helen	20635
Glen Willows	20743	Gunpowder (Baltimore		Helen Estates	20635
Glenwood (Harford County)	21014	County)	21021	Henderson	21640
Glenwood (Howard County)	21738	Gunpowder (Harford		Henryton	21080
Glenwood Estates	21738	County)	21010	Herald Harbor	21032
Glenwood Park	20706	Gunpowder Estates	21128	Herald Square	21244
Glover Acres	21157	Gwenlee Estates	21738	Hereford	21111
Glymont	20640	Gwynn	21042	Heritage Farm	20854
Glyndon	21071	Gwynn Acres	21042	Heritage Harbor	21401
Goddard	20770	Gwynnbrook	21117	Heritage Hills	21061
Goddard Space Flight		Gwynn Oak (Part of		Heritage Walk	20852
Center	20770	Baltimore)	21207	Hermanville	20653
Golden Beach	20659		21244	Hermitage Park	20906
Golden Hill	21622	For specific Gwynn Oak Zip		Hernwood Heights	21133
Golden Ring	21237	Codes call (410) 944-9300, or		Herrington Manor	21550
Golden Ring Mall	21237	your local postmaster.		Hickman	21629
Goldsboro	21636	Hack Point	21919	Hickory	21014
Golf Club Shores	21811	Hacks Point Acre	21919	Hickory Hills (Part of Bel Air)	21014
Golts	21637	Hagerstown	21740-42	Hickory Ridge	21044
Good Acres	21740	For specific Hagerstown Zip		Hicksburg	21631
Good Hope	20905	Codes call (301) 797-8100, or		Hidden Point	21401
Goodwill	21851	your local postmaster.		High Bridge	20720
Gorman	26720	Halethorpe	21227	High Bridge Estates	20720
Gortner	21550	Halfway	21740	Highfield (Montgomery	
Goshen	20879	Halfway Manor	21740	County)	20879
Goshen Estates	20879	Hallett Heights	21863	Highfield (Washington	
Gotts	21032	Halley Estates	20695	County)	21719
Govans (Part of Baltimore)	21212	Halpine Village	20852	Highland (Frederick County)	21773
Governors Run	20676	Hambleton Estates	21140	Highland (Howard County)	20777
Graceham	21788	Hamilton (Part of Baltimore)	21214	Highland Beach	21403
Graceton	21160	Hamilton Park (Part of		Highland Park (Prince	
Grahamtown	21532	Hagerstown)	21740	George's County)	20743
Granby Woods	20855	Hamlet North	20855	Highland Park (Worcester	
Grand Bel Manor	20906	Hammondell Heights	21108	County)	21811
Grandview	21784	Hammond Park	20723	Highlands	20854
Granite	21163	Hampden (Part of		Highlands of Olney	20832
Grantsville	21536	Baltimore)	21211	Highland Stone	20854
Grasonville	21638	Hampshire Knolls	20783	Highlandtown (Part of	
Gratitude	21661	Hampstead	21074	Baltimore)	21224
Gray Haven	21222	Hampton (Baltimore County)	21286	High Point (Anne Arundel	
Gray Manor	21222	Hampton Gardens	21286	County)	21122
Gray Rock	21042	Hance Point	21901	High Point (Montgomery	
Grayton	20662	Hancock	21750	County)	20814
Greater Capitol Heights	20743	Hanesville	21678	Highpoint Heights	20705
Greater Upper Marlboro	20772	Hanover (Anne Arundel		High Point Manor	21050
Great Mills	20634	County)	21076	High Ridge	20723
Green Acres (Harford		Hanover (Howard County)	21076	High Ridge Park	20723
County)	21085	Hanson Valley View	20744	High View	21771
Green Acres (Montgomery		Hansonville	21701	High-View Estates (Carroll	
County)	20817	Harbor View (Anne Arundel		County)	21074
Greenbelt	20768†	County)	21037	Highview Estates (Howard	
	20770*	Harborview (Queen Anne's		County)	21042
Greenberry Hills	21740	County)	21619	Highview on the Bay	20779
Greenbriar	21713	Hardesty Estates	21035	Hillandale (Montgomery	
Greenbrier (Part of		Harewood	21220	County)	20903
Greenbelt)	20770	Harewood Park	21220	Hillandale Forest	20907
Greendale Estates	21047	Harford Estates	21050	Hillandale Heights	20903
Greenfield	20735	Harford Farms	21234	Hillcrest (Anne Arundel	
Greenfield Mills	21710	Harford Furnace	21015	County)	21225
Green Glade	21561	Harford Hills	21234	Hill Crest (Montgomery	
Green Haven	21122	Harford Mall (Part of Bel Air)	21014	County)	20912

* Area Zip Code   † Post Office Boxes

	ZIP
Hillcrest (Prince George's County)	20748
Hillcrest Estates	20748
Hillcrest Heights (Howard County)	20723
Hillcrest Heights (Prince George's County)	20748
Hillcrest Terrace	20748
Hillendale Shopping Center	21204
Hillmead	20817
Hillmeade	20769
Hillmeade Manor	20769
Hillsboro	21641
Hillsborough	20707
Hillside	21157
Hillsmere Estates	21403
Hillsmere Shores	21403
Hills Point	21613
Hill Top	20693
Hillwood Manor	20783
Hobbs	21629
Hoffman	21532
Holabird (Part of Baltimore)	21224
Holbrook	21133
Holiday Acres	21783
Holiday Beach	20732
Holiday Hills	21044
Holiday Park	20906
Holland Cliff Shores	20639
Holland Heights	21801
Hollaway Estates	20772
Hollinsworth Manor (Part of Elkton)	21921
Holly Beach	21221
Holly Gaf. Acres	20636
Holly Hall Terrace	21921
Holly Hill Harbor	21037
Holly Lake Estates	21801
Holly Spring	20747
Holly Tree	20601
Hollywood (Prince George's County)	20740
Hollywood (St. Mary's County)	20636
Hollywood Beach	21915
Hollywood Estates (Part of College Park)	20740
Hollywood Park	20904
Hollywood Shores	20636
Holmehurst	20720
Home Acres	20705
Homecrest	20906
Homestead Estates	20904
Homewood (Allegany County)	21502
Homewood (Montgomery County)	20895
Honga	21622
Hood College (Part of Frederick)	21701
Hoods Mill	21723
Hoopersville	21634
Hope Hill	21701
Hopewell	21817
Hopkins Mead	21029
Horizon Run	20877
Houcksville	21074
Howard Heights	21042
Howardville	21208
Hoyes	21531
Hudson	21613
Hughesville	20637
Hungerford Towne (Part of Rockville)	20852
Hunt Club Estates (Charles County)	20601
Hunt Club Estates (Howard County)	21227
Hunt Crest Estates	21286
Hunters Harbor	21122
Hunters Hill	21093
Hunters Ridge	20610
Huntersville	20659
Hunting Hills	20639
Hunting Lodge	21234
Hunting Park	21801
Huntington Terrace	20814
Huntingtown	20639
Huntsmoor	21227
Huntsville	20785
Hunt Valley	21030-31
For specific Hunt Valley Zip Codes call (410) 771-0780, or your local postmaster.	
Hunt Valley Mall	21030
Hurlock	21643
Hurry	20621
Hutton	21550
Huyett	21740
Hyattstown	20871

	ZIP
Hyattsville	20780-89
For specific Hyattsville Zip Codes call (301) 699-8905, or your local postmaster.	
Hyde Park (Baltimore County)	21221
Hyde Park (Wicomico County)	21801
Hydes	21082
Hynesboro	20706
Hynson	21632
Idlewild	20764
Idlewylde	21204
Ijamsville	21754
Ilchester	21043
Imperial Gardens	21133
Indian Creek Estates	20622
Indian Head	20640
Indian Head Manor	20616
Indian Head Naval Ordnance Station	20640
Indian Queen Estates	20744
Indian River Estates	20659
Indian Springs (Frederick County)	21702
Indian Springs (Washington County)	21711
Indiantown	21863
Ingleside	21644
Inverness	21222
Inverness Forest	20854
Inverness Woods	20854
Iron Hill	19711
Ironshire	21811
Ironsides	20643
Isabella Park	20783
Island Creek	20685
Island View Beach	21221
Issue	20645
Iverson Mall	20748
Ivy Hills	21043
Ivytown	21601
Jackson	21903
Jacksonville (Baltimore County)	21131
Jacksonville (Somerset County)	21817
Jacktown	21613
Jacobsville	21122
James	21613
Jarrettsville	21084
Jefferson	21755
Jefferson Heights (Prince George's County)	20743
Jefferson Heights (Washington County)	21740
Jennings	21536
Jersey Heights (Wicomico County)	21801
Jerusalem (Baltimore County)	21087
Jerusalem (Frederick County)	21773
Jerusalem (Montgomery County)	20837
Jessup	20794
Jesterville	21814
Jewell	20754
Johnsontown	21620
Johnsville (Carroll County)	21784
Johnsville (Frederick County)	21791
Jones	21146
Jonestown	21655
Joppa	21085
Joppa Heights	21234
Joppatowne	21085
Joppa View	21128
Josenhans Corner	21221
Joyce Acres	21012
Kalma Ridge	21032
Kalmia	21015
Kalmia Farms	21036
Kalten Acres	21158
Kastle Estates	20735
Kaywood Gardens (Part of Mount Rainier)	20712
Keedysville	21756
Keeler Glade	21531
Keifer	25434
Kemp Mill Estates	20902
Kemp Mill Farms	20902
Kempton	26292
Kemptown	21770
Ken Gar	20895
Kennedyville	21645
Kensington	20895
Kensington Estates	20895
Kensington Heights	20902
Kensington View	20895
Kent Island Estates	21666
Kentland	20785

	ZIP
Kentmore Park	21645
Kentmorr	21666
Kent Village	20785
Kenwood (Baltimore County)	21236
Kenwood (Montgomery County)	20815
Kenwood Beach	20676
Kerby Hills	20744
Kettering	20772
Kettering Estate Park	20772
Keymar	21757
Keysers Ridge	21536
Keystone Manor	20747
Keysville	21757
Kilbirnie Estates	21801
Kilbourn Estates	20748
Kilmarock	20912
Kimberly Gardens	20708
Kings Contrivance	21045
Kings County	21087
Kings Creek Estate	20772
Kingsford	20721
Kings Grove	21529
Kings Manor	20695
Kings Park	21233
Kings Ransom	21113
Kings Ridge	21234
Kingston	21871
Kingston Manor	20772
Kingstown	21620
Kingsville	21087
Kingwood Common	21244
Kirkham	21601
Kirkwood	20782
Kitzmiller	21538
Klej Grange	21851
Knettishall	21204
Knollview	21043
Knollwood (Baltimore County)	21204
Knollwood (Prince George's County)	20783
Knoxville	21758
Ladiesburg	21759
Lakeland (Anne Arundel County)	21146
Lakeland (Prince George's County)	20740
Lake Linganore	21701
Lake Normandy Estates	20854
Lake Roland	21209
Lake Shore	21122
Lakeside Manor	21801
Lakeside Park	21740
Lakeside Terrace	20817
Lakeside Vista	21085
Lakesville	21622
Lakeview (Howard County)	20723
Lakeview (Montgomery County)	20817
Lakewood	21801
Lakewood Estates (Calvert County)	20754
Lakewood Estates (Montgomery County)	20850
Lancaster	20603
Land-O-Lakes	20636
Landon Woods	20817
Landover (census designated page)	20784
Landover	20785
Landover Estates	20784
Landover Hills	20789
Landover Knolls	20785
Landover Park (Part of Cheverly)	20785
Lane Beach	20650
Langley Park (Prince George's County)	20783
Lanham	20706*
	20703†
Lanham Heights	20706
Lanham-Seabrook	20706
Lanham Woods	20706
Lansdowne	21227
Lansdowne-Baltimore Highlands	21227
Lantz	21780
Lapidum	21078
La Plata	20646
Lappans	21733
Larchmont Knolls	20895
Largo (Prince George's County)	20772
Largo/Kettering	20775
Largo Knolls	20772
Laurel	20707-09
	20723-26
For specific Laurel Zip Codes call (301) 498-1400, or your local postmaster.	

---

* Area Zip Code   † Post Office Boxes

	ZIP		ZIP		ZIP
Laurel Acres	21122	Longfellow	21043	Maplewood (Howard	
Laurel Brook	21047	Longfield Estates	20747	County)	21042
Laureldale	21234	Long Green	21092	Maplewood (Montgomery	
Laurel Grove	20659	Long Meadow (Carroll		County)	20814
Laurel Mall (Part of Laurel)	20708*	County)	21784	Maplewood (Prince	
	20726†	Long Meadow (Washington		George's County)	20744
Laurel Pines	20708	County)	21740	Marbury	20658
Laurel Shopping Center		Long Meadow Estates	20814	Mardela Springs	21837
(Part of Laurel)	20707*	Long Meadow Shopping		Margate	21060
	20726†	Center (Part of		Mariners	21817
Laurel Wood	20708	Hagerstown)	21740	Marion Station	21838
La Vale	21502	Long Meadow West	21208	Marley	21060
Lawndale Acres	21048	Long Point	21122	Marley Heights	21061
Lawsonia	21817	Long Reach	21045	Marley Station	21060
Layhill	20906	Longview Beach	20618	Marling Farms	21619
Layhill Gardens	20906	Longwood	20817	Marlow Heights	20748
Layhill Village	20906	Longwoods	21601	Marlton	20772
Laytonia	20877	Lord	21532	Marlywood	21286
Laytonsville	20879	Lord Calvert Estates	20736	Marriottsville	21104
Lees Woods	21014	Loreley	21162	Mars Estates	21221
Legion Avenue (Part of		Loretta Heights	21401	Marshall Hall	20616
Annapolis)	21401	Lothian	20711	Marshalls Corner	20646
Le Gore	21757	Louisville	21048	Marston	21776
Leisure World	20906	Lou Mar Estates	21009	Martin's Additions	20815
Leitersburg	21742	Love Point	21666	Martinsburg	20842
Leon	20711	Loveville	20656	Martins Woods (Part of New	
Leonardtown	20650	Lower Magothy Beach	21146	Carrollton)	20706
Leslie	21901	Lower Marlboro	20736	Marwood	21061
Level	21078	Loyola (Part of Baltimore)	21210	Marydel	21649
Lewis Corner	21811	Lucas Heights	21502	Maryland City	20724
Lewisdale	20783	Luke	21540	Maryland Correctional	
Lewis Heights	20783	Lusby	20657	Institution for Women	20794
Lewis Spring Manor	20735	Lusby Crossroads	21401	Maryland Correctional Pre-	
Lewistown (Frederick		Lute	20906	Release System	20794
County)	21701	Lutherville	21093	Maryland Line	21105
Lewistown (Talbot County)	21625	Lutherville-Timonium	21093*	Maryland Park	20743
Lexington Park	20653		21094†	Maryland Point	20662
Liberty Grove	21918	Lutz Hill	21237	Marymount	20814
Liberty Manor	21244	Luxmanor	20852	Maryvale (Part of Rockville)	20850
Libertytown (Frederick		Lynch	21646	Marywood	21014
County)	21762	Lynch Point	21222	Masons Beach	20751
Libertytown (Worcester		Lynnbrook (Anne Arundel		Mason Springs	20640
County)	21811	County)	21225	Massey	21650
Lime Kiln	21701	Lynnbrook (Charles County)	20601	Mattapex	21666
Linchester	21655	Lynne Acres	21244	Mattapony (Part of	
Lincoln Avenue	21740	Lyons Creek (Anne Arundel		Bladensburg)	20710
Lincoln Heights (Part of		County)	20711	Matthews	21601
Salisbury)	21801	Lyons Creek (Calvert		Maugansville	21767
Lincoln Manor	21102	County)	20754	Mayberry	21158
Lincoln Park (Part of		Lyons Homes	21222	Maydale	20868
Rockville)	20850	Mac Alpine	21042	Mayfield (Anne Arundel	
Lindamoor on the Severn	21401	McCahill Estates	20707	County)	21113
Linden	20907	McCanns Corner	21154	Mayfield (Howard County)	21043
Linden Chapel Hills	21036	McComas Beach	21550	Mayo	21106
Lineboro	21088	McCoole	26726	Mays Chapel	21093
Linganore-Bartonsville	21701	McDaniel	21647	Mays Chapel Village	21093
Linhigh	21236	Mc Daniel City	20603	Meadowbrook (Part of	
Linkwood	21835	Mac Donald Farms	20736	Bowie)	20715
Linsey Acres	20748	McDonogh	21208	Meadowbrook Estates	20876
Linsted on the Severn	21146	Mc Donogh Park	21133	Meadowcliff	21057
Linthicum	21090	Maceys Corner	21146	Meadowland	21093
Linthicum Heights	21090	McHenry	21541	Meadowood	20904
Linthicum Hills	21090	McKaig	21701	Meadowood of	
Linthicum Oaks	21090	McKay Beach	20650	Davidsonville	21035
Linwood (Carroll County)	21764	Mc Kendree	20879	Meadowvale Manor (Part of	
Linwood (Howard County)	21043	McKenney Hills	20910	Havre de Grace)	21078
Linwood Village	21122	McKinleyville	21661	Meadowview Park	21921
Lipins Corner	21122	McKinstrys Mill	21791	Mechanicsville	20659
Lisbon	21765	Maddox	20621	Medford	21776
Little Orleans	21766	Madison	21648	Melitota	21620
Little Washington	20747	Madonna	21084	Mellwood Hills	20772
Livingston Grove	20607	Madonna Manor	21084	Melody Acres	20622
Llandaff	21601	Magnolia	21101	Melrose	21102
Lloyds	21613	Magnolia Springs	20784	Melson	21875
Loartown	21532	Magothy Beach	21122	Merchants (Part of	
Lochearn	21207	Magothy Park Beach	21122	Baltimore)	21201
Loch Haven	21234	Mago Vista Beach	21012	Merrimack Park	20817
Loch Hill	21212	Magruder Landing	20613	Merritt Heights	21801
Loch Lynn Heights	21550	Main Street (Part of		Merrymount	21244
Loch Raven	21234	Salisbury)	21801	Michigan Park Hills	20782
Loch Raven Heights	21234	Malcolm	20601	Middleborough	21221
Loch Raven Village	21234	Mall in Columbia, The	21044	Middlebrook	20876
Locust Grove (Allegany		Malvern	21204	Middleburg	21757
County)	21502	Manchester	21102	Middlepoint	21773
Locust Grove (Kent County)	21645	Manchester Estates	20746	Middle River	21220
Locust Grove (Washington		Manhattan Woods	21146	Middlesex	21221
County)	21779	Manokin (Somerset County)	21836	Middlesex Shopping Center	21221
Locust Grove Beach	20732	Manokin (Wicomico County)	21801	Middleton Valley	20748
Locust Grove Station	21788	Manor	21111	Middletown (Baltimore	
Locust Hill Estates	20814	Manor Lake	20853	County)	21053
Locust Valley	21769	Manor Park	20853	Middletown (Frederick	
Lodgecliffe	21613	Manor View	21057	County)	21769
Lodge Forest	21222	Manor Woods	20853	Middletown Heights	21769
Lonaconing	21539	Maple Crest (Baltimore		Midland	21542
Londontown	21037	County)	21220	Midlothian	21543
Londontowne	21037	Maplecrest (Carroll County)	21157	Milford	21207
London Woods	20743	Maple Park	21801	Milford Mill	21244
Lone Oak	20814	Maple Plains	21801	Milford Park	21117
Long	21502	Mapleside (Part of		Milford Ridge	21244
Long Bar Harbor	21009	Cumberland)	21502	Millbrook (Part of Laurel)	20707
Long Beach	20685	Maple View	21157	Mill Creek South	20855
Long Corner	21771	Mapleville	21713	Mill Creek Towne	20707

Place	ZIP	Place	ZIP	Place	ZIP
Mill Creek Towne East	20855	Naval Air Facility	20390	Northwood Village	20901
Miller	21532	Naval Ordnance Station	20640	Norwood Corner	20906
Millers	21107	Naval Surface Warfare		Norwood Estates	20905
Millers Island	21219	Center	20903	Notch Cliff	21057
Millersville	21108	Naylor	20772	Nottingham	21237
Mill Green	21154	Neavitt	21652	Nottingham Woods	21236
Millington	21651	Needwood Estates	20855	Oak Acres	21701
Milison Plaza	20653	Neeld Estates	20639	Oak Court	21401
Mill Point	20621	Neelsville	20876	Oakcrest	20707
Mill Point Shores	20621	Neilwood	20852	Oakcrest Towers	20743
Millrace	21108	New Addition	21758	Oakdale	20853
Mill Run	21562	Newark	21841	Oak Estates	20622
Mills Choice	20879	New Birmingham Manor	20866	Oak Forest	21228
Millwood	20743	Newburg	20664	Oak Hollow	21122
Millwood Towne	20743	New Carrollton	20784	Oakhurst	20866
Mimosa Cove	20751	Newcomb	21653	Oakington	21078
Minefield	21154	New Germany	21536	Oakland (Baltimore County)	21053
Mitchell Manor	21550	New Hampshire Estates	20903	Oakland (Carroll County)	21784
Mitchellville (Prince		New Hampshire Gardens		Oakland (Garrett County)	21550
George's County)	20706	(Part of Takoma Park)	20912	Oakland (Prince George's	
Mitchellville (Prince		Newhope	20874	County)	20747
George's County)	20717	New London	21771	Oakland Acres	20622
Mondawmin/Metro Plaza		New Mark Commons (Part		Oakland Mills	21045
(Part of Baltimore)	21215	of Rockville)	20850	Oakland Park	21133
Monie	21853	New Market (Frederick		Oakland Terrace	20895
Monkton	21111	County)	21774	Oaklawn	20744
Monrovia	21770	New Market (St. Mary's		Oakleigh	21234
Montego (Part of Ocean		County)	20622	Oakleigh Forest	21146
City)	21842	New Market View	20771	Oakleigh Manor	21234
Montevideo (Anne Arundel		New Midway	21775	Oakley	20609
County)	21076	New Orchard Estates	20772	Oaklyn Manor	21085
Montevideo (Howard		Newport	20622	Oakmont	20814
County)	20794	Newport Hills	20895	Oak Orchard	20735
Montgomery Knolls	21043	Newton	21655	Oak Park (Baltimore	
Montgomery Square	20854	Newton Village	20781	County)	21227
Montgomery Village	20879	Newtown (Charles County)	20646	Oak Park (Garrett County)	21550
Montgomery White Oak	20904	Newtown (Kent County)	21678	Oak Ridge	21740
Montpelier	20708*	Newtown (Talbot County)	21625	Oak Springs	20868
	20709†	New Valley	21918	Oak Summit	21234
Montpelier Woods	20708	New Windsor	21776	Oak View	20903
Montrose	20852	Nikep	21546	Oakville (Somerset County)	21853
Monumental	21227	Nob Hill (Howard County)	21042	Oakville (St. Mary's County)	20659
Mooresfield	20759	Nob Hill (Montgomery		Oakwood	21918
Morantown	21532	County)	20903	Oakwood Knolls	20817
Morgan	21797	Nomira Heights (Part of		Ocean City	21842
Morgantown	20664	Elkton)	21921	Ocean City Harbor	21842
Morganza	20660	Norbeck	20906	Ocean Pines	21811
Morningside	20746	Normandy Heights	21043	Odenton	21113
Moscow	21521	Normans	21666	Odenton Gardens	21113
Mount Aetna	21740	Norris Corner	21009	Odenton Heights	21113
Mountain	21085	Norrisville	21161	Odenton Park	21113
Mountaindale	21788	Northampton (Baltimore		Odyssey	20736
Mountain Lake Park	21550	County)	21093	Oella	21228
Mountain View	21157	Northampton (Prince		Old Country Estates	21146
Mountain View Estates	20878	George's County)	20772	Olde Colonial Woods	20832
Mountain Wood	21122	North Barnaby	20745	Olde Fort Village	20744
Mount Airy	21771	North Beach	20714	Olde Towne Village (Part of	
Mount Briar	21756	North Beach Park	20714	)	20747
Mount Carmel	21122	North Bethesda	20814	Old Farm	20852
Mount Clare (Part of		North Branch	21502	Old Field (Dorchester	
Baltimore)	21223	North Brentwood	20722	County)	21622
Mount De Sales	21228	North Chevy Chase	20815	Oldfield (Frederick County)	21791
Mount Harmony	20736	North College Park (Part of		Old Field (Montgomery	
Mount Hebron	21042	College Park)	20740	County)	20854
Mount Hermon	21801	North Deale	20751	Old Fort Hills	20744
Mount Hope (Part of		North East	21901	Old Glory Beach	21060
Baltimore)	21215	Northeast Heights	21901	Old Salem Village	20904
Mount Lena	21713	North Englewood	20785	Old Severna Park	21146
Mount Olive	21771	Northern (Part of		Oldtown	21555
Mount Pleasant (Frederick		Hagerstown)	21740	Olive	21758
County)	21701	North Forestville	20747	Oliver Beach	21220
Mount Pleasant		North Fort Foote Village	20744	Olivet	20657
(Washington County)	21713	North Glade	21561	Olivet Hill	21637
Mount Pleasant (Wicomico		North Indian Head Estates	20616	Olney	20830†
County)	21874	North Junction (Part of			20832*
Mount Pleasant Beach	21122	Hagerstown)	21740	Olney	20832
Mount Rainier	20712	North Kensington	20902	Olney Mills	20832
Mount Saint Mary's College	21727	North Laurel (census		Olney Square	20832
Mount Savage	21545	designated place)	21784	Orangeville (Part of	
Mount Vernon	21853	North Laurel	20723	Baltimore)	21224
Mount Victoria	20661	North Laurel Park	20723	Oraville	20659
Mountview	21104	North Linthicum	21090	Orchard Beach	21226
Mountville	21701	North Ocean City (Part of		Orchard Hills (Baltimore	
Mount Washington (Part of		Ocean City)	21842	County)	21093
Baltimore)	21209	North Point	21222	Orchard Hills (Washington	
Mount Westley	21863	North Point Village	21222	County)	21742
Mount Zion	21649	North Potomac	20878	Oregon	21030
Mount Zoar	21918	North Potomac Vista	20745	Oriole	21853
Mousetown	21713	Northridge Manor	21740	Otter Point	21009
Muirkirk	20705	North Roblee Acres	20772	Overlea	21206
Mulberry Hills	21401	North Sherwood Forest	20904	Owen Brown	21045
Murray Hills	20745	Northshire	21222	Owings	20736
Myersdale (Part of		North Shore	21122	Owings Beach	20751
Hancock)	21750	North Springbrook	20904	Owings Mills (Baltimore	
Myersville	21773	North Wellham	21061	County)	21117
Nanjemoy	20662	Northwest Park		Owings Wood (Part of	
Nanticoke	21840	(Montgomery County)	20814	North Beach)	20714
Narrows	21638	Northwest Park		Oxford	21654
Narrows Park	21502	(Montgomery County)	20903	Oxon Hill	20745*
National Naval Medical		Northwood (Part of			20750†
Center	20814	Baltimore)	21239	Oxon Hill-Glassmanor	20745
Naval Academy	21402	Northwood Park	20901	Oxon Hill Village	20745

* Area Zip Code   † Post Office Boxes

Name	ZIP	Name	ZIP	Name	ZIP
Oxon Run Hills	20748	Pinesburg	21795	Presidential Park	20783
Oyster Harbor	21401	Pines on the Severn	21012	Presidential Towers	20783
Padonia	21030	Pinewiff Beach	21037	Presley Manor	20784
Pagetts Corner	20748	Pinewood Hill	20744	Preston	21655
Paint Branch Estates	20904	Piney Glen Farms	20854	Preston Manor	21009
Paint Branch Farm	20904	Piney Grove	21766	Price	21656
Palmer Park	20785	Piney Point	20674	Priceville	21152
Palmers Corner	20744	Pinto	21556	Prince Frederick	20678
Palmetto	21853	Pioneer City	21144	Princess Anne	21853
Paradise	21228	Piscataway	20607	Princeton	20746
Paradise Beach	21122	Piscataway Bay	20744	Principio Furnace	21903
Paramount	21740	Piscataway Estates	20744	Prophecy	20744
Paramount Manor	21740	Piscataway Hills	20744	Prospect Knolls	20720
Paris	*20736	Pisgah	20640	Prospect Walk	21044
Parkertown	21811	Pittsville	21850	Providence (Baltimore	
Parker Wharf	20685	Plainfield	21801	County)	21286
Park Hall (St. Mary's		Plane Number Four	21771	Providence (Cecil County)	21921
County)	20667	Pleasant Fields	20874	Public Landing	21863
Park Hall (Washington		Pleasant Grove (Baltimore		Pumphrey	21225
County)	21713	County)	21136	Puncheon Landing	21851
Parkhead	21711	Pleasant Grove (Frederick		Putnam	21050
Parkhurst Manor	21801	County)	21771	Putty Hill	21236
Parkland	20747	Pleasant Hill (Baltimore		Pylesville	21132
Parkland Apartments	20747	County)	21117	Quail Ridge	21227
Parkland Terrace	20746	Pleasant Hill (Cecil County)	21921	Quail Run	20879
Park Mills	21710	Pleasant Hills	21087	Quaint Acres	20904
Park Overlook	20855	Pleasant Ridge	21797	Quaker Neck Landing	21620
Parkridge	20878	Pleasant Springs	20613	Quantico	21856
Parkside	20814	Pleasant Valley (Allegany		Queen Anne	21657
Parkside Estates	20855	County)	21502	Queen Anne Colony	21666
Parkton	21120	Pleasant Valley (Carroll		Queens Chapel Manor (Part	
Parktowne	21234	County)	21158	of Hyattsville)	20782
Parkview	20735	Pleasant Valley (Washington		Queenstown (Prince	
Parkville	21234	County)	21783	George's County)	20712
Park West	21061	Pleasant View (Frederick		Queenstown (Queen Anne's	
Parkwood	20814	County)	21710	County)	21658
Parole	21401	Pleasant View (Howard		Queenswood	20772
Parsonsburg	21849	County)	21043	Quince Orchard	20878
Partridge Place	20879	Pleasantville	21061	Quincy Manor	20784
Pasadena	21122	Pleasant Walk	21773	Rabbit Town	21869
Patapsco	21048	Plumgar	20876	Radiant Valley	20784
Patterson (Part of Baltimore)	21231	Plum Point	20639	Ramblewood Village	20735
Patuxent	21113	Pocomoke City	21851	Ramgate	20744
Patuxent Beach	20619	Pointer Ridge (Part of		Rancleigh (Baltimore	
Patuxent Institution	20794	Bowie)	20716	County)	21209
Patuxent Manor	21035	Point Lookout	20687	Rancleigh (Part of	
Patuxent Naval Air Test		Point of Rocks	21777	Baltimore)	21209
Center	20670	Point of Rocks Estates	21777	Randalia	21915
Patuxent Palisades	20754	Point Pleasant	21060	Randallstown	21133
Patuxent Park	20653	Pomfret	20675	Randle Cliff Beach	20732
Patuxent River	20670	Pomona	21620	Randolph Farms	20852
Peach Orchard Heights	20866	Pomonkey	20640	Randolph Hills	20852
Peachwood	20905	Ponder Cove	21037	Random Heights	21157
Peacock Corners	21651	Pondsville	21783	Raspeburg (Part of	
Pearl	21701	Pooks Hill	20814	Baltimore)	21206
Pectonville	21711	Poole	21034	Rawlings	21557
Pendennis Mount	21401	Poolesville	20837	Rawlings Heights	21557
Peninsula General Hospital		Popes Creek	20664	Raynor Heights	21090
(Part of Salisbury)	21801	Poplar Grove	21154	Rayville	21120
Pen Mar	21719	Poplar Hill	20613	Red Coat Woods	20854
Pen-Mar Shopping Center	20747	Poplar Hill Estates	20735	Reddings Corner	21678
Penn Mary Junction (Part of		Poplar Knob	21788	Redford Estates	20744
Baltimore)	21224	Poplar Springs	21771	Red Hill	20658
Pepper Mill Village	20743	Port Covington (Part of		Redhouse	21550
Perry Hall (Baltimore		Baltimore)	21230	Redland	20855
County)	21128	Port Deposit	21904	Red Point	21901
Perry Hall Estates	21236	Porters Park	21221	Reeder Development (Part	
Perry Hall Manor	21128	Porterstown	21756	of Frederick)	21701
Perry Hall Shopping Center	21128	Port Herman	21915	Reese	21157
Perry Hall Village	21128	Port Republic	20676	Reese Manor	21048
Perryman	21130	Port Tobacco	20677	Regal Estates	20754
Perry Point	21902	Port Tobacco Riviera	20677	Regency Estates	20852
Perrys Corner	21638	Potomac (census		Regent Park	20854
Perry View	21128	designated place)	20851	Regent Square (Part of	
Perryville	21903	Potomac	20854	Rockville)	20850
Perrywood Estates	20866	Potomac Commons	20854	Rehobeth	21857
Perry Wright	20640	Potomac Falls Estates	20854	Reid	21740
Petersburg	21643	Potomac Green	20854	Reids Grove	21659
Petersville	21758	Potomac Heights (Charles		Reisterstown	21136
Pfeiffer Corners	21045	County)	20640	Reisterstown Road Plaza	
Pheasant Run	20708	Potomac Heights		(Part of Baltimore)	21215
Phoenix	21131	(Washington County)	21740	Relay	21227
Picketts Corner	21797	Potomac Hills	20854	Reliance	19973
Pike (Part of Rockville)	20852	Potomac Park	21502	Rest Haven	20751
Pikesville	21208	Potomac Ranch	20854	Revell	21012
Pilot Town	21918	Potomac Shores (Charles		Revere Park	21234
Pindell	20711	County)	20677	Reynolds	21521
Pine Cliff	21701	Potomac Shores (St. Mary's		Rhodesdale	21659
Pinecrest (Part of Takoma		County)	20650	Rhodes Point	21824
Park)	20912	Potomac View	20664	Riawakin Acres	21830
Pinedale	21128	Potomac View Estates	20854	Richards Oak	21917
Pinefield	20601	Potomac Village	20854	Ricmar	21801
Pine Grove	21801	Potomac Vista	20745	Riderwood	21139
Pine Grove Village	21122	Potomac Woods (Part of		Riderwood Hills	21139
Pine Hill Estates	20601	Rockville)	20854	Ridge	20680
Pinehurst Estates	20744	Pot Spring	21093	Ridge Lake	21042
Pinehurst on the Bay	21122	Powder Mill Estates	20783	Ridgeleigh	21234
Pine Knoll	21157	Powder Mill Village	20705	Ridgely	21660
Pine Knoll Terrace	21801	Powellville	21852	Ridgeview	21077
Pineleigh	21286	Powhatan Beach	21122	Ridgeville (Part of Mount	
Pine Orchard Meadows	21042	Powhattan Mill	21207	Airy)	21771
Pine Ridge	21234	Prathertown	20879	Ridgeway	21144

	ZIP		ZIP		ZIP
Skidmore	21401	Stevensville	21666	The Downs	21401
Skipton	21625	Stevensville South	21666	The Glen	20854
Skyline	20746	Stewartown	20879	The Hamlet	20815
Skyline Additions	20746	Stillmeadows	21144	The Highlands	21061
Sky Valley	21561	Still Pond	21667	The Lakes	21030
Slabtown	21545	Stockton	21864	The Meadows	20736
Sligo Park Knolls	20901	Stonecrest Hill	21043	The Oaks (Calvert County)	20639
Smallwood	21157	Stonegate	20905	The Oaks (Howard County)	21043
Smithsburg	21783	Stone Haven	21060	Theodore	21911
Smithville (Caroline County)	21632	Stoneleigh	21212	The Orchards	21043
Smithville (Dorchester		Stoneybrook Estates	20906	The Pines	20772
County)	21669	Stony Beach	21226	The Points	20879
Smoketown	21713	Stony Run	21076	Thomas	21613
Smugglers Cove	21146	Stratford	21093	Thomas Choice	20879
Snowden Manor	21157	Strathmore At Bel Pre	20906	Thomas Run	21015
Snowden Oaks	20708	Strathmore Estates	20906	Thomas Town	21629
Snow Hill	21863	Stratton Woods	20817	Thompson Corner	20659
Snow Hill Manor	20708	Strawberry Hills Estates	20616	Thompsontown	21631
Snug Harbor (Anne Arundel		Strawbridge Estates	21784	Thomson Estates	21921
County)	20764	Strawleigh	21702	Thornleigh	21139
Snug Harbor (Worcester		Street	21154	Thornwood Knoll	20744
County)	21811	Stronghold	20842	Thorwood Park	21234
Snydersburg	21074	Suburban Acres	21801	Thunder Hill	21045
Social Security		Suburbia	21060	Thurmont	21788
Administration	21207	Sudbrook Park	21202	Thurston	20842
Society Hill	20650	Sudlersville	21668	Tilden Woods	20852
Sollers Homes	21222	Sugarland	20837	Tilghman	21671
Sollers Point	21222	Sugarloaf Estates	21710	Tilghmanton	21713
Solley Heights	21060	Suitland	20746*	Timber Grove	21117
Solomons	20688		20752†	Timber Ridge (Anne	
Somerset	20815	Suitland-Silver Hill	20746	Arundel County)	21076
Sonoma	20814	Sullivan Heights	21157	Timber Ridge (Carroll	
South (Part of Baltimore)	21230	Summerhill (Anne Arundel		County)	21157
Southampton	20653	County)	21032	Timberview	21227
South Cheverly Forest	20784	Summerhill (Montgomery		Timonium	21093
South Cumberland (Part of		County)	20837	Tintop Hill	20650
Cumberland)	21502	Summit Farms	21237	Tobytown	20854
Southdown Shores	21037	Summit Park	21209	Todd Village	21048
Southeast (Part of		Sumner	20816	Toddville	21672
Baltimore)	21224	Sunair (Part of Salisbury)	21801	Tolchester Beach	21620
Southerland	20601	Sunderland	20689	Tollgate	21117
Southern Garden		Sunny Acres	20747	Tompkinsville	20664
Apartments	20032	Sunnybrook	21131	Tonytank	21801
South Fort Foote Village	20744	Sunnybrook Hills	21131	Tower Acres	20723
South Gate	21061	Sunny Isle of Kent	21666	Tower Garden on the Bay	21666
South Haven	21401	Sunrise	20744	Town Creek	25434
South Kensington	20895	Sunrise Beach	21032	Town Creek Estates	20619
Southland Hills	21204	Sunset Acres	21740	Town Creek Manor	20653
South Laurel	20708	Sunset Beach	21122	Town Crest	20855
South Lawn	20745	Sunset Heights	21801	Towne and Country North	21030
South Layhill	20906	Sunset Hills	21702	Towne Center	20708
South Piscataway	20607	Sunset Knoll	21122	Town Point	21915
South River Park	21037	Sunshine	20833	Townshend	20613
South Salisbury (Part of		Sunshine Acres	20639	Townsontown Centre	21286
Salisbury)	21801	Sun Valley	21060	Towson	21204*
South Tantallon	20748	Surratt Gardens	20735		21286†
Southview	20745	Susquehanna Hills	21078	Towson Estates	21204
South Woodside Park	20910	Sussex Square	21108	Towson Marketplace	21204
Sparks	21152	Sutton Acres	20677	Towson Park	21286
Sparks Glencoe	21152	Swallow Falls	21550	Towson Plaza Shopping	
Sparrows Point	21219	Swan Creek	21078	Center	21286
Spaulding Heights	20747	Swanton	21561	Tracys Landing	20779
Spence	21863	Sweet Air	21013	Trappe (St. Mary's County)	20628
Spencerville	20868	Sweetser Heights	21090	Trappe (Talbot County)	21673
Spielman	21733	Sycamore Acres	20853	Trappe (Worcester County)	21811
Spoolsville	21769	Sycamore Heights	21742	Trappe Station	21654
Springbrook (Baltimore		Sykesville	21784	Travilah	20850
County)	21133	Sylmar	21911	Treetops	21122
Springbrook (Montgomery		Sylvan Grove	21740	Trengall Acres	21740
County)	20904	Sylvan View	21122	Trent Hall	20659
Springbrook Forest	20902	Table Rock	26720	Trenton	21155
Springbrook Manor	20904	Takoma Park	20912	Trescher Heights	21502
Springbrook Village	20904	Tall Timbers	20690	Triple Lakes	21502
Springdale (Baltimore		Tammany Manor	21795	Troutville	21798
County)	21030	Tanager Forest	21108	Truman Heights	20748
Springdale (Prince George's		Taneytown	21787	Tulip Hill (Frederick County)	21702
County)	20706	Tanglewood	21401	Tulip Hill (Montgomery	
Springdale Gardens	20706	Tantallon	20744	County)	20816
Springfield	20814	Tantallon North	20744	Tunis Mills	21601
Spring Gap	21560	Tantallon on the Potomac	20748	Turkey Neck	21561
Spring Garden Estates	21793	Tantallon Square	20744	Turkey Point (Anne Arundel	
Spring Grove	21837	Tanterra	20833	County)	21037
Spring Hill	21830	Tanyard	21655	Turkey Point (Baltimore	
Springhill Acres	21801	Tarquin Village	20735	County)	21221
Springhill Lake (Part of		Taylor Mill Village	21801	Turnbull Estates	21037
Greenbelt)	20770	Taylors Island	21669	Turners Station	21222
Springlake	20817	Taylorsville	21771	Tuscarora	21790
Spring Meadow	21084	Taylorville	21811	Tuxedo (Part of Cheverly)	20785
Spring Mills	21157	Temple Heights	20748	Tuxedo Colony	20785
Spring Valley	21740	Temple Hills	20748*	Twinbrook (Part of	
Squires Woods	20744		20757†	Rockville)	20851
Stablersville	21161	Temple Hills Park	20748	Twinbrook Estates	20601
Stafford	21034	Templeton Estates	20737	Twin Brook Forest (Part of	
Stanbrook	21222	Templeton Manor	20737	Rockville)	20851
Stansbury Estates	21220	Templeville	21670	Twinbrook Park (Part of	
Stansbury Manor	21220	Temple Woods	20744	Rockville)	20851
Starkeys Corner	21623	Terrace Gardens	21012	Twin Harbors	21012
Starr	21617	Terrace View Estates	21225	Tyaskin	21865
Stemmer's Run	21220	Texas	21030	Tydings on the Bay	21401
Stepney	21001	Thayerville	21550	Tylerton	21866
Steuart Level	21037	The Colony	20874	Tyrone	21158
Stevenson	21153	The Crest of Wickford	20852	Ulmsted Acres	21012

	ZIP		ZIP		ZIP
Ulmsted Estate	21012	Watersville	21771	Whiteburg	21863
Ulmsted Gardens	21012	Waterview	21840	White Crystal Beach	21919
Ulmsted Point	21012	Watkins Glen	20854	Whitefield Knolls	20706
Union Bridge	21791	Waverly (Part of Baltimore)	21218	Whitefield Woods	20706
Union Corner	21636	Wayside	20664	White Flint Mall	20895
Union Mills	21158	Webster Village	21078	White Flint Park	20895
Uniontown	21158	Weems Creek	21401	Whiteford	21160
Unionville (Frederick		Weisburg	21161	White Hall (Baltimore	
County)	21791	Welcome	20693	County)	21161
Unionville (Talbot County)	21601	Wellington Estates	20707	Whitehall (Prince George's	
Unionville (Worcester		Wenona	21870	County)	20607
County)	21851	Wesley	21626	Whitehall Beach	21401
Unity	20833	Wesmond (Part of		Whitehall Manor	20814
University City	20783	Poolesville)	20837	Whitehaven	21856
University Gardens	20783	West Baltimore (Part of		Whitehouse Heights	20785
University Hills	20783	Baltimore)	21227	White Landing	20613
University Park	20784	West Beach (Part of		Whiteleysburg	21639
Upperco	21155	Chesapeake Beach)	20732	White Marsh	21162
Upper Crossroads	21047	West Bethesda	20817*	White Oak (Montgomery	
Upper Fairmount	21867		20827†	County)	20904
Upper Falls	21156	Westboro	20814	White Oak (Montgomery	
Upper Ferry Estates	21801	West Bowie (Part of Bowie)	20719	County)	20901
Upper Hill	21867	Westchester (Baltimore		White Oak Manor	20904
Upper Homewood	21502	County)	21228	White Oak Park	20904
Upper Marlboro	20772-75	Westchester (Montgomery		White Oak Shopping Center	20904
For specific Upper Marlboro Zip		County)	20902	White Oak Tower	20904
Codes call (301) 627-4330, or		Westchester Estates	20748	White Plains	20695
your local postmaster.		Westchester Park (Part of		White Point Beach	20650
Urbana	21701	College Park)	20740	White Rock	21702
Utica	21788	West Denton	21629	White Sands	20657
Vale	21015	West Edmondale	21229	Whiton	21863
Vale Summit	21532	West Elkridge	21227	Wicomico	20622
Valley Crest	21093	West End (Part of		Wicomico Beach	20664
Valley Lee	20692	Annapolis)	21401	Wilburn Estates	20743
Valley Mede	21042	West End Park (Part of		Wilde Lake	21044
Valley Stream Estates	20866	Rockville)	20850	Wildercroft	20737
Valley View (Howard		Westerlea	21228	Wild Rose Shores	21403
County)	21043	Westernport	21562	Wild Wood Beach	21221
Valley View (Prince		Western Shores Estates	20676	Wildwood Estates	20735
George's County)	20744	West Friendship	21794	Wildwood Hills	20817
Valleywood (Baltimore		Westgate	20816	Wildwood Manor	20817
County)	21093	West Gate Woods	20706	Wildwoods	21133
Valleywood (Wicomico		West Hills (Baltimore		Wilelinor Estates	21037
County)	21801	County)	21207	Willards	21874
Van Bibber	21040	West Hills (Frederick		Willerburn Acres	20854
Van Bibber Manor	21040	County)	21702	Williamsburg	21643
Van Lear Manor	21795	West Hyattsville (Part of		Williamsburg Estates	20772
Vansville	20705	Hyattsville)	20782	Williamsburg Gardens	20854
Venice on the Bay	21122	Westlake	21801	Williamsburg Village	20832
Venton	21853	West Lanham Estates	20784	Williamsbury	21208
Vernon	21161	West Lanham Hills	20784	Williamsport (Washington	
Veterans Administration		West Laurel	20707	County)	21795
Medical Center	21902	West Laurel Acres	20707	Williams Wharf	20685
Victory Villa	21220	West Liberty	21161	Williston	21629
Vienna	21869	West Magothy Manor	21012	Willoughby Beach	21040
Viers Mill	20906	Westminster (Carroll		Willow Beach Colony	20732
View More Acres	21701	County)	21157-58	Willowbrook (Montgomery	
Villa Cresta	21234	For specific Westminster Zip		County)	20854
Village of Vanderway	21234	Codes call (301) 848-4780, or		Willowbrook (Prince	
Villages of Montpelier	20708	your local postmaster.		George's County)	20783
Villa Heights	20784	Westminster (Part of		Willow Lake	20708
Villa Monticello	21723	Randolph Hills)	20852	Wilson	21722
Villa Nova	21207	Westminster South	21157	Wilson Hills	20906
Villa Toscano	21122	Westmore (Part of		Wilson Point	21220
Villa Verdi	21054	Rockville)	20850	Wiltondale	21204
Waggaman Heights	20748	Westmoreland Hills	20816	Wilton Farm Acres	21043
Wakefield (Baltimore		West Nottingham	21917	Winchester on the Severn	21401
County)	21093	West Ocean City	21842	Winchester Park	21157
Wakefield (Carroll County)	21776	Westover	21871	Windbrook	20735
Wakefield Meadows	21014	Westowne	21229	Windham Manor	
Walbrook (Part of Baltimore)	21216	Westphalia Estates	20772	(Montgomery County)	20904
Waldon Woods	20735	Westphalia Woods	20772	Windham Manor (Wicomico	
Waldorf	20601-04	West River	20778	County)	21801
For specific Waldorf Zip Codes		West Severna Park	21146	Winding Brook Village	21921
call (301) 645-5231, or your local		West Shady Side	20764	Windmere Acres	20763
postmaster.		West Shore	21106	Windsor	21244
Walker Hill	20707	West Twin River Beach	21220	Windsor Estates	21717
Walker Mill (Prince George's		Westview	21801	Windsor Terrace	21207
County)	20743	Westview Mall	21228	Winfield (Carroll County)	21157
Walker Mill Estates	20743	Westview Park	21228	Winfield (Howard County)	21044
Walkersville	21793	West View Shores	21919	Winfield Heights	21157
Wallington Estates	20747	West Vindex	21538	Wingate	21675
Wallville	20685	Westwood	20613	Wingates Point	21675
Walnut Hill	20877	Westwood Estates (Charles		Winsor Hills	20854
Walnut Ridge	21157	County)	20601	Winterest	20854
Walnut Woods	20852	Westwood Estates (Prince		Wisperren Oaks	21701
Walston	21849	George's County)	20623	Wittman	21676
Walter Heights	20748	Wetipquin	21856	Wolfsville	21773
Wango	21801	Weverton	21758	Wolverton Park	20735
Warburton Oaks	20744	Wexford	21012	Woodacres	20816
Wards Chapel	21133	Whaleysville	21872	Woodberry Forest	20748
Warfield Estates	21738	Wheaton	20902	Woodbine	21797
Warfieldsburg	21157	Wheaton Crest	20902	Woodbrook	21212
Warington Hills (Part of		Wheaton Forest	20902	Woodburn	20817
Indian Head)	20640	Wheaton-Glenmont	20902	Wood Creek	21045
Warlinda	20646	Wheaton Hills	20902	Woodcroft	21234
Warren	21030	Wheaton Plaza Regional		Woodensburg	21136
Warwick	21912	Center	20902	Woodfield	20882
Washington Grove	20880	Wheaton Woods	20853	Woodford	21044
Waterbury	21032	Whetstone	20879	Woodhaven	20817
Waterloo	21227	Whipporwill Estates	21122	Woodhaven Park	20646
Wateroak Point	21122	Whiskey Bottom	20723	Woodland	21532

	ZIP		ZIP		ZIP
Woodland Acres	20619	Woodmoor (Montgomery		Worthington	21043
Woodland Point	20664	County)	20901	Worthington Heights	21014
Woodlands	21133	Woodmoor (Washington		Worton	21678
Woodlane	20748	County)	21740	Wrights Crossing	21532
Woodlark	20784	Woodmore	20716	Wye Mills	21679
Woodlawn (Baltimore		Wood Point	21740	Wyngate	20814
County)	21207	Woodsboro	21798	Wynne Wood	21227
Woodlawn (Cecil County)	21904	Woods Corner	20748	Yarrowsburg	21758
Woodlawn (Prince George's		Woodside	20901	Yellow Springs	21702
County)	20784	Woodside Park	20901	Yorkshire Knolls	20743
Woodlawn Heights	21061	Woodstock	21163	Zion	21901
Woodmont	20815	Woodville	21771	Zittlestown	21713
Woodmoor (Baltimore		Woolford	21677		
County)	21207				

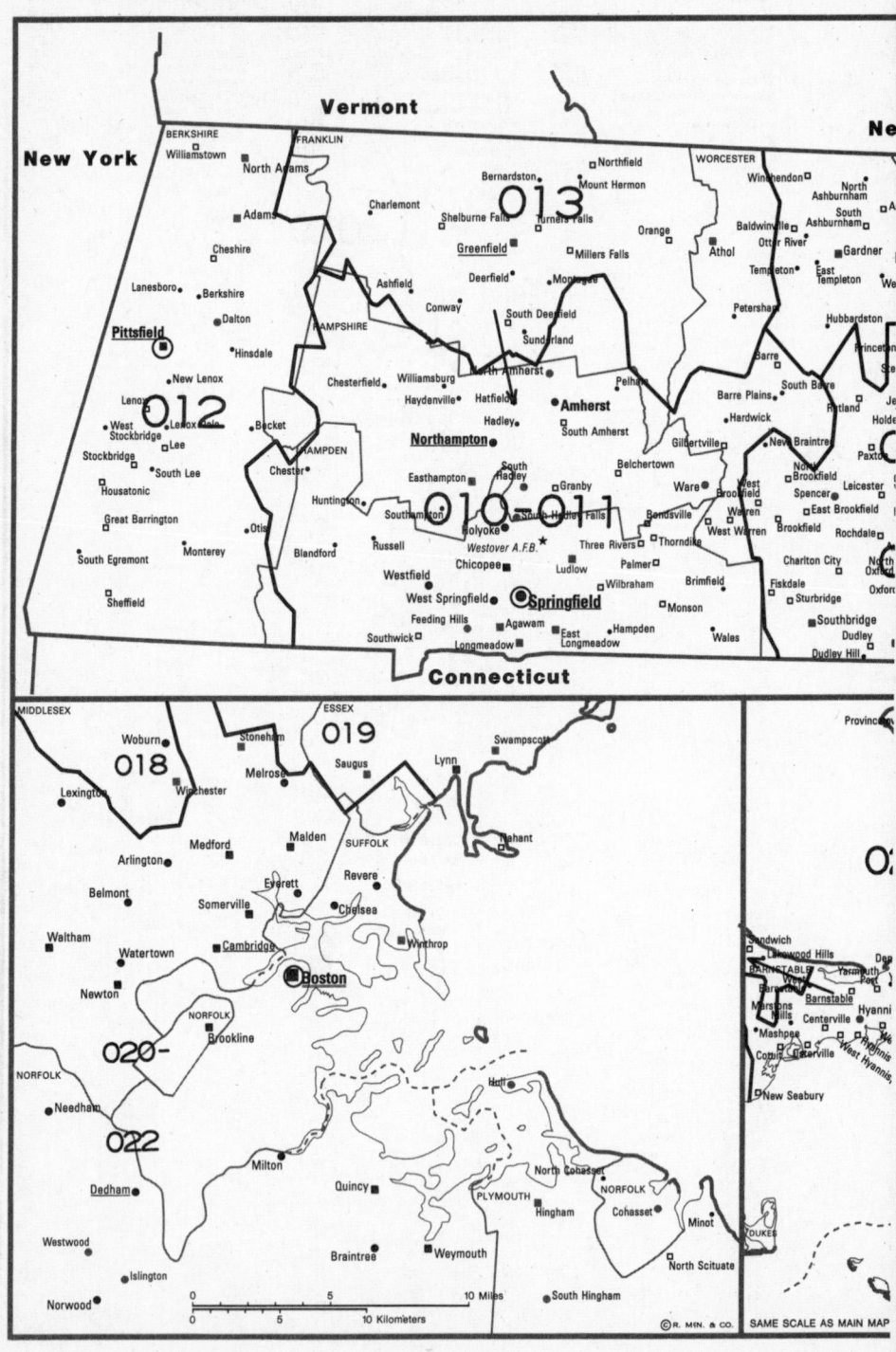

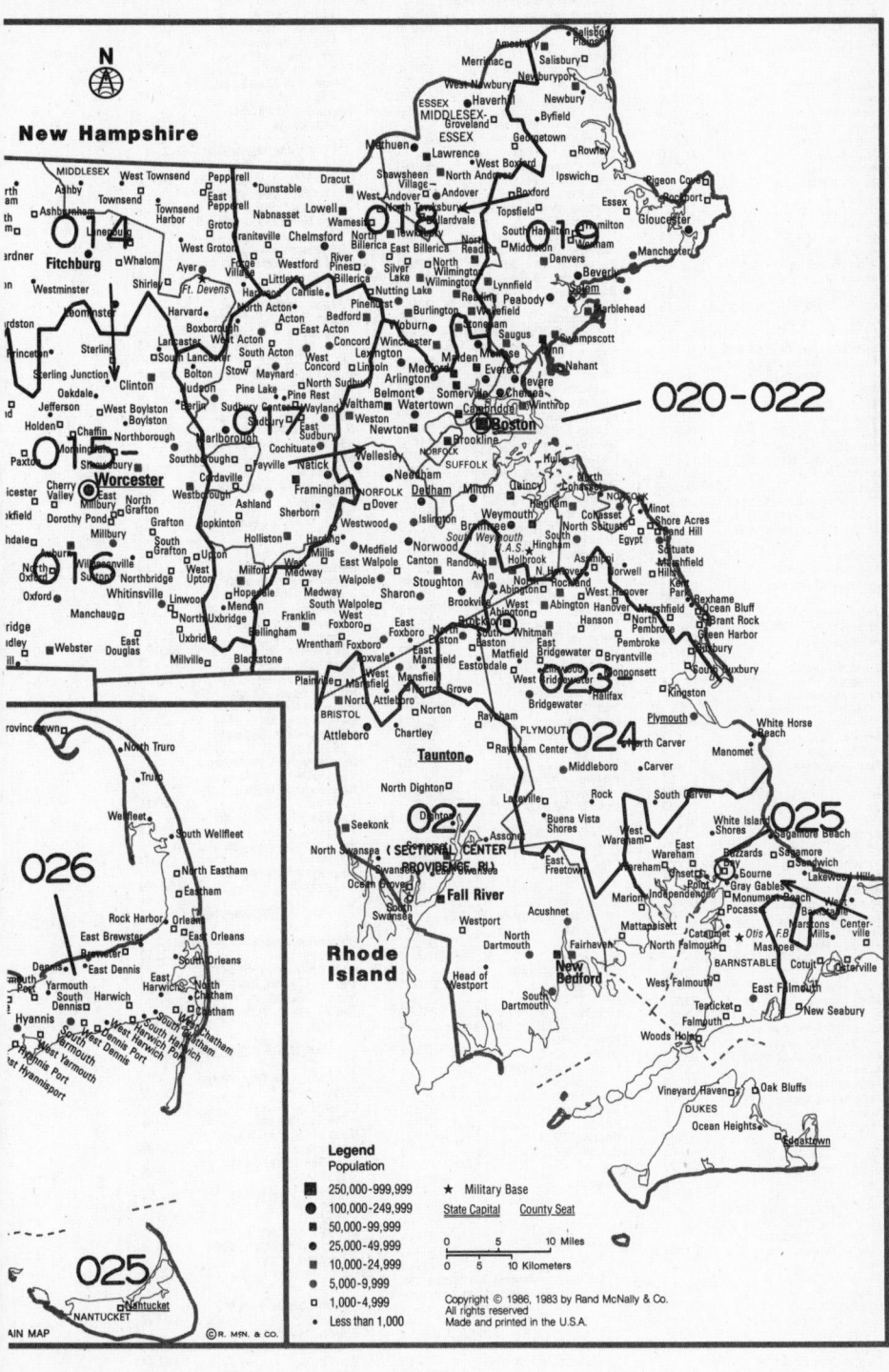

	ZIP
Aberdeen (Part of Boston)	02135
Abington	02351
Abington (Town)	02351
Acapesket	02536
Accord	02018
Acoaxet	02801
Acton	01720
Acton (Town)	01720
Acton Center	01720
Acushnet	02743
Acushnet (Town)	02743
Adams (Town)	01220
Adams	01220
Adamsdale	02760
Adams Shore (Part of Quincy)	02169
Adamsville	01340
Agawam	01001
Agawam (Town)	01001
Agawam Beach	02571
Agawam Shopping Center	01001
Airport Mail Facility (Part of Boston)	02109
Aldenville (Part of Chicopee)	01013
Alford	01230
Alford (Town)	01230
Allendale (Part of Pittsfield)	01201
Allendale Shopping Center (Part of Pittsfield)	01201
Allerton	02045
Allston (Part of Boston)	02134
Amesbury	01913
Amesbury (Town)	01913
Amesbury (census designated place)	01913
Amesbury Center	01913
Amherst	01002-04
For specific Amherst Zip Codes call (413) 549-0523, or your local postmaster.	
Amrita	02534
Andover	01810
Andover (Town)	01810
Annisquam (Part of Gloucester)	01930
Antassawamock Beach	02739
Apponagansett Village	02748
Arlington (Town)	02174
Arlington	02174
Arlington Heights	02175
Armory (Part of Springfield)	01101
Army Materials and Mechanics Research Center	02172
Arsenal Mall	02172
Ashburnham	01430
Ashburnham (Town)	01430
Ashby	01431
Ashby (Town)	01431
Ashdod	02332
Ashfield	01330
Ashfield (Town)	01330
Ashland (Town)	01721
Ashland	01721
Ashley Falls	01222
Ashley Heights	02717
Ashmont (Part of Boston)	02124
Assinippi	02339
Assonet	02702
Assonet Bay Shores	02702
Assumption College (Part of Worcester)	01609
Astor (Part of Boston)	02123
Athol (Town)	01331
Athol	01331
Athol Junction (Part of Springfield)	01101
Atlantic (Part of Quincy)	02169
Attleboro	02703
Attleboro Falls	02763
Auburn (Town)	01501
Auburn	01501
Auburndale (Part of Newton)	02166
Auburn Shopping Mall	01501
Avon (Town)	02322
Avon	02322
Ayer	01432-33
For specific Ayer Zip Codes call (508) 772-2083, or your local postmaster.	
Ayer (Town)	01432
Ayer	01432
Ayers Village (Part of Haverhill)	01830
Babson Park	02157
Back Bay Annex (Part of Boston)	02115
Bakers Grove	01473
Bakers Island (Part of Salem)	01970
Baldwinville	01436
Ballardvale	01810
Bancroft	01243

	ZIP
Baptist Corner	01370
Barkerville (Part of Pittsfield)	01201
Barnstable	02630
Barnstable (Town)	02630
Barre	01005
Barre (Town)	01005
Barre Plains	01606
Barrowsville	02766
Bass Point	01908
Bass River	02664
Bass Rocks (Part of Gloucester)	01930
Bay State (Part of Northampton)	01060
Bay State Correctional Center	02056
Baystate West Shopping Center (Part of Springfield)	01103
Bayview (Bristol County)	02748
Bayview (Essex County)	01930
Beach (Part of Revere)	02151
Beachmont (Part of Revere)	02151
Beach Point	02652
Beachwood	01262
Beacon Hill (Part of Boston)	02108
Beaver Brook (Middlesex County)	02154
Beaver Brook (Worcester County)	01602
Becket	01223
Becket (Town)	01223
Becket Center	01011
Bedford (Town)	01730
Bedford	01730
Bedford Springs	01730
Beechwood	02025
Belcher Square	01230
Belchertown	01007
Belchertown (Town)	01007
Belchertown State School	01007
Bellingham (Town)	02019
Bellingham	02019
Bell Rock (Part of Malden)	02148
Belmont (Town)	02178
Belmont	02178
Belvidere (Part of Lowell)	01852
Bennetts Corner	02379
Berkley	02780
Berkley (Town)	02779
Berkshire	01224
Berkshire Heights	01230
Berlin	01503
Berlin (Town)	01503
Bernardston	01337
Bernardston (Town)	01337
Beverly	01915
Beverly Cove (Part of Beverly)	01915
Beverly Farms (Part of Beverly)	01915
Beverly Junction (Part of Beverly)	01915
Big Pond	01029
Billerica	01821*
	01822†
Birch Island	01570
Blackinton (Part of North Adams)	01247
Black Rock	02025
Blackstone	01504
Blackstone (Town)	01504
Blandford	01008
Blandford (Town)	01008
Bleachery (Part of Lowell)	01852
Bleachery (Part of Waltham)	02154
Bliss Corner	02748
Blissville	01364
Bloomingdale (Part of Worcester)	01604
Blue Hills	02186
Blush Hollow	01243
Bolton	01740
Bolton (Town)	01740
Bondsville	01009
Boston	02101-17
	02123
	02133
	02163
	02199
	02201-22
	03127-28
For specific Boston Zip Codes call (617) 654-5768, or your local postmaster.	

COLLEGES & UNIVERSITIES

	ZIP
Berklee College of Music	02215
Boston University	02215
Emerson College	02116
Massachusetts College of Art	02215

	ZIP
Massachusetts College of Pharmacy and Allied Health Sciences	02115
Northeastern University	02115
School of the Museum of Fine Arts	02115
Suffolk University	02114
University of Massachusetts at Boston	02125
Wentworth Institute of Technology	02115

FINANCIAL INSTITUTIONS

	ZIP
BayBank Boston, N.A.	02110
Boston Safe Deposit and Trust Company	02108
Brown Brothers Harriman & Co	02109
East Boston Savings Bank	02128
The First National Bank of Boston	02110
Fleet Bank of Massachussets, N.A.	02106
Greater Boston Bank (A Cooperative Bank)	02135
Grove Bank	02146
Hibernia Savings Bank	02110
Hyde Park Savings Bank	02136
The Massachusetts Company, Inc.	02110
Neworld Bank	02110
Shawmut Bank, N.A.	02211
South Boston Savings Bank	02127
State Street Bank and Trust Company	02110
United States Trust Company	02108

HOSPITALS

	ZIP
Beth Israel Hospital	02215
Boston City Hospital	02118
Boston University Medical Center - University Hospital	02115
Brigham and Women's Hospital	02115
Carney Hospital	02124
Children's Hospital	02115
Faulkner Hospital	02130
Hebrew Rehabilitation Center for Aged	02131
Lemuel Shattuck Hospital	02130
Massachusetts General Hospital	02114
New England Deaconess Hospital	02215
New England Medical Center	02111
Spaulding Rehabilitation Hospital	02114
St. Elizabeth's Hospital of Boston	02135
Veterans Affairs Medical Center	02130

HOTELS/MOTELS

	ZIP
Boston Park Plaza Hotel & Towers	02116
Le Hotel Meridien Boston	02110
The Ritz-Carlton, Boston	02117
Sheraton-Boston Hotel	02199
The Westin Hotel, Copley Place	02116

MILITARY INSTALLATIONS

	ZIP
Army Materials Technology Laboratory	02172
Coast Guard Support Center, Boston	02109
Naval Air Station, South Weymouth	02190
Naval Recruiting District, Boston	02210
Supervisor of Shipbuilding, Conversion and Repair, Boston	02210
United States Army Engineer Division, New England	02254
Boston College (Part of Newton)	02167
Boston University (Part of Boston)	02215
Bourne	02532
Bourne (Town)	02532
Bourne	02532
Bournedale	02532
Boxborough	01719

* **Area Zip Code** † **Post Office Boxes**

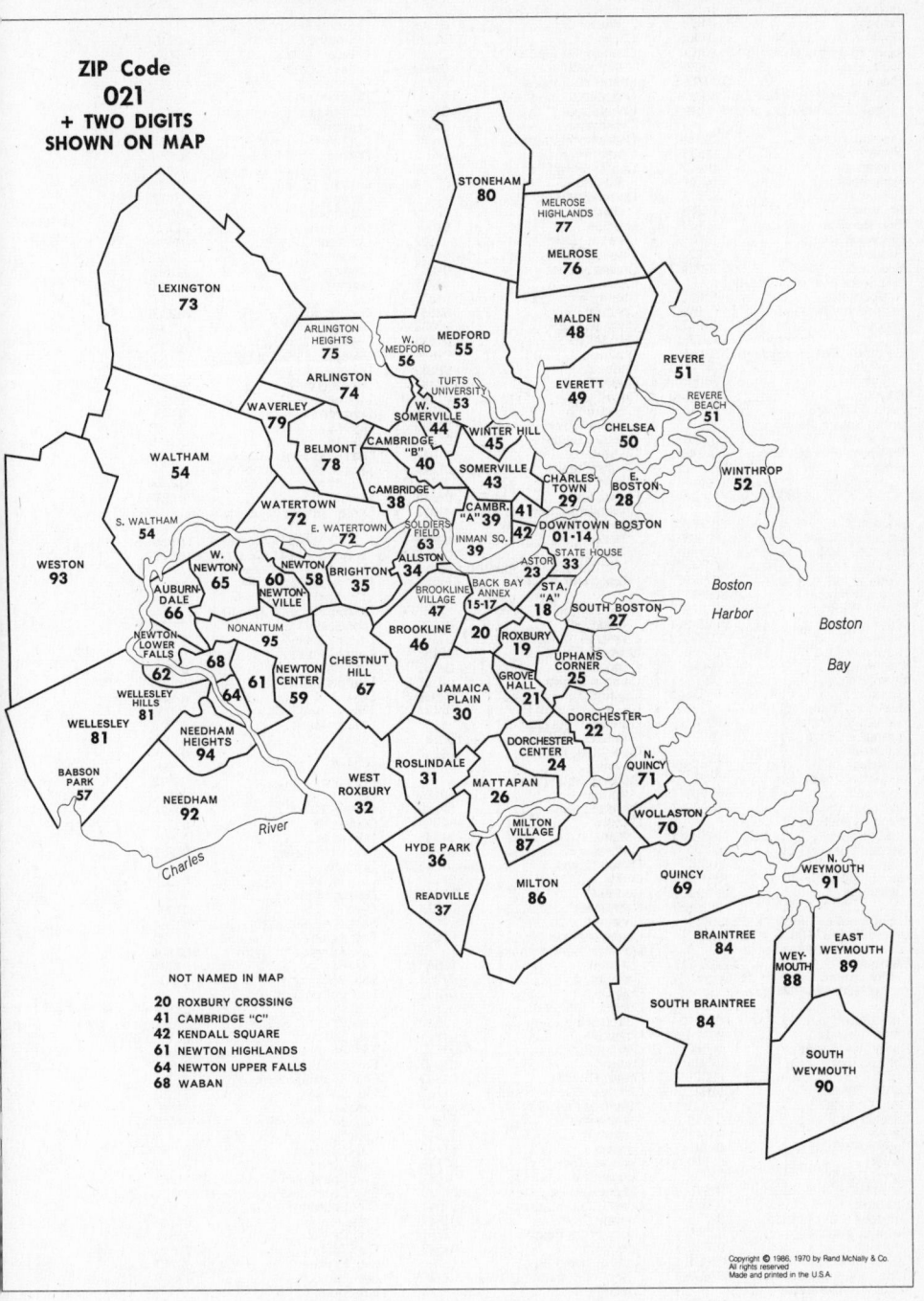

ZIP Code
021
+ TWO DIGITS
SHOWN ON MAP

NOT NAMED IN MAP

20 ROXBURY CROSSING
41 CAMBRIDGE "C"
42 KENDALL SQUARE
61 NEWTON HIGHLANDS
64 NEWTON UPPER FALLS
68 WABAN

	ZIP
Boxborough (Town)	01719
Boxford	01921
Boxford (Town)	01921
Boylston	01505
Boylston (Town)	01505
Bradford (Part of Haverhill)	01830
Bradstreet	01038
Braintree	02184-85
For specific Braintree Zip Codes call (617) 843-3366, or your local postmaster.	
Braintree Highlands	02184
Braleys	02717
Bramanville	01527
Brant Rock	02020
Brayton Point	02725
Brewster	02631
Brewster (Town)	02631
Briarwood Beach	02571
Bridgewater	02324
Bridgewater (Town)	02324
Brier Neck (Part of Gloucester)	01930
Brigadoon Village	01949
Briggsville	01247
Brighton (Part of Boston)	02135
Brightside (Part of Holyoke)	01040
Brightwood (Part of Springfield)	01107
Brimfield	01010
Brimfield (Town)	01010
Brittan Square (Part of Worcester)	01605
Broadway (Part of Malden)	02148
Brockton	02401-05
For specific Brockton Zip Codes call (508) 559-1800, or your local postmaster.	
Brookfield	01506
Brookfield (Town)	01506
Brookline (Town)	02146
Brookline	02146
Brookline Hill	02146
Brookline Village	02147
Brooks Place	02379
Brookville	02343
Brownell Corner	02790
Browns Point	01950
Brushwood	02038
Bryantville	02327
Buckland	01338
Buckland (Town)	01338
Buena Vista Shores	02346
Buffington Corner	02725
Buffumville	01540
Bullardville	01475
Burlington (Town)	01803
Burlington	01803
Burlington Mall	01803
Burncoat (Part of Worcester)	01606
Buzzards Bay	02532
Byfield	01922
Cabot (Part of Newton)	02158
Cambridge	02138-42
	02238
For specific Cambridge Zip Codes call (617) 876-0620, or your local postmaster.	
Campello	02403-04
For specific Campello Zip Codes call (508) 559-1824, or your local postmaster.	
Campground Landing	02651
Camp Grounds	01564
Canterbury Estates	02563
Canton (Town)	02021
Canton	02021
Canton Junction	02021
Cape Cod Mall	02601
Carletonville (Part of Salem)	01970
Carlisle	01741
Carlisle (Town)	01741
Carver	02330
Carver (Town)	02330
Castle Hill (Part of Salem)	01970
Cataumet	02534
Cathedral (Part of Boston)	02118
Cedar Bushes	02345
Cedarville	02532
Center (Middlesex County)	01801
Center (Plymouth County)	02360
Centerville (Barnstable County)	02632
	02634
	02636
For specific Centerville Zip Codes call (568) 775-2062, or your local postmaster.	
Centerville (Essex County)	01915
Central Massachusetts Mail Processing Center	01546

	ZIP
Central Village	02790
Centralville (Part of Lowell)	01850
Chadwick Square (Part of Worcester)	01605
Chaffin	01520
Chandler Hill (Part of Worcester)	01609
Chapel Hill Estates	02359
Chappaquiddick Island	02539
Chappaquoit	02574
Charlemont	01339
Charlemont (Town)	01339
Charles River Grove	02019
Charles Street (Part of Boston)	02114
Charlestown (Part of Boston)	02129
Charlton	01507
Charlton (Town)	01507
Charlton City	01508
Charlton Depot	01509
Chartley	02712
Chaseville	01571
Chatham	02633
Chatham (Town)	02633
Chelmsford	01824
Chelmsford (Town)	01824
Chelsea	02150
Cherry Brook	02193
Cherry Valley	01611
Cheshire	01225
Cheshire (Town)	01225
Cheshire Harbor	01220
Chester	01011
Chester (Town)	01011
Chester Center	01011
Chesterfield	01012
Chesterfield (Town)	01012
Chestnut Hill (Part of Newton)	02167
Chicopee	01013-22
For specific Chicopee Zip Codes call (413) 592-9451, or your local postmaster.	
Chicopee Center (Part of Chicopee)	01020
Chilmark	02535
Chilmark (Town)	02535
Chiltonville	02360
Churchill Shores	02346
City Mills	02056
City Point (Part of Boston)	02127
Clarendon Hills (Part of Boston)	02131
Clarksburg (Town)	01247
Clayton	06018
Clematis Brook (Part of Waltham)	02154
Clevelandtown	02539
Clicquot	02054
Clifton	01945
Cliftondale	01906
Clinton	01510
Clinton (Town)	01510
Cochesett	02379
Cochituate	01778
Cohasset	02025
Cohasset (Town)	02025
Cohasset Army Ammunition Activity	02043
Cold Spring	01253
Cole Corner	02043
College Hill (Part of Worcester)	01610
Collinsville	01826
Colonial Park	01570
Colrain	01340
Colrain (Town)	01340
Coltsville (Part of Pittsfield)	01201
Columbus Park (Part of Worcester)	01603
Cominsville	01542
Concord	01742
Concord (Town)	01742
Congamond	01077
Conomo	01929
Conway	01341
Conway (Town)	01341
Cooks Brook Beach	02651
Cooleyville	01355
Copley Place (Part of Boston)	02116
Cordaville	01772
Cotley (Part of Taunton)	02780
Cottage Hill	02152
Cottage Park	02152
Cotuit	02635
Country View Estates	02038
Court Park	02152
Coury Heights	02743
Cow Yard	02748
Craigville	02636

	ZIP
Craigville Beach	02636
Crescent Beach (Plymouth County)	02739
Crescent Beach (Suffolk County)	02151
Crescent Mills	01050
Crooks Corner	02019
Cummaquid	02637
Cummington	01026
Cummington (Town)	01026
Cushman	01002
Cuttyhunk	02713
Dalton	01226*
	01227†
Danvers (Town)	01923
Danvers	01923
Danversport	01923
Dartmouth	02714
Dartmouth (Town)	02714
Davisville	02536
Dawson	01520
Dedham	02026*
	02027†
Dedham Mall	02026
Deerfield	01342
Deerfield (Town)	01342
Deer Island (Part of Boston)	02152
Dennis	02638
Dennis (Town)	02638
Dennis Port	02639
Devenscrest	01432
Devereux	01945
Dighton	02715
Dighton (Town)	02715
Division Street (Part of New Bedford)	02744
Dodge	01507
Dorchester (Part of Boston)	02121-22
	02124-25
For specific Dorchester Zip Codes call (617) 654-5768, or your local postmaster.	
Dorchester Center (Part of Boston)	02124
Dorchester Lower Mills (Part of Boston)	02124
Dorothy Manor	01527
Dorothy Pond	01527
Douglas	01516
Douglas (Town)	01516
Dover	02030
Dover (Town)	02030
Dracut (Town)	01826
Dracut	01826
Drury	01343
Drury Square	01501
Dry Pond	02072
Dudley	01571
Dudley (Town)	01571
Dudley Hill	01570
Dunstable	01827
Dunstable (Town)	01827
Duxbury	02331†
	02332*
Duxbury (Town)	02332
Dwight	01007
Eagleville	01364
East Acton	01720
East Arlington	02174
East Billerica	01821
East Blackstone	01504
East Boston (Part of Boston)	02128
East Boxford	01921
East Braintree	02184
East Brewster	02631
East Bridgewater	02333
East Bridgewater (Town)	02333
East Brimfield	01010
East Brookfield	01515
East Brookfield (Town)	01515
East Cambridge (Part of Cambridge)	02141
East Carver	02355
East Charlemont	01370
East Chelmsford	01824
East Dedham	02026
East Deerfield	01342
East Dennis	02641
East Douglas	01516
East Fairhaven	02719
East Falmouth	02536
Eastfield Mall (Part of Springfield)	01109
East Foxboro	02035
East Freetown	02717
East Gloucester (Part of Gloucester)	01930
East Greenfield	01301
Eastham	02642
Eastham (Town)	02642
Easthampton (Town)	01027

---

* Area Zip Code   † Post Office Boxes

	ZIP
Easthampton	01027
East Harwich	02645
East Holliston	01746
East Junction (Part of Attleboro)	02703
East Lee	01238
East Leverett	01054
East Longmeadow (Town)	01028
East Longmeadow	01028
East Lynn (Part of Lynn)	01904
East Mansfield	02031
East Marion	02738
East Middleboro	02346
East Millbury	01527
East Milton	02186
East Northfield	01360
Easton	02334
Easton (Town)	02334
Eastondale	02375
East Orleans	02643
East Otis	01029
East Pembroke	02359
East Pepperell	01463
East Princeton	01541
East Sandwich	02537
East Saugus	01906
East Springfield (Part of Springfield)	01101
East Sudbury	01776
East Swansea	02777
East Taunton (Part of Taunton)	02718
East Templeton	01438
Eastview Park (Part of Waltham)	02154
East Village	01570
Eastville	02557
East Walpole	02032
East Wareham	02538
East Watertown	02172
East Weymouth	02189
East Windsor	01270
East Woburn (Part of Woburn)	01801
Eddyville	02346
Edgartown	02539
Edgartown (Town)	02539
Edgemere	01545
Edgewater Estates	02359
Edgeworth (Part of Malden)	02148
Egleston Square (Part of Boston)	02116
Egremont (Town)	01252
Egypt	02066
Ellisville	02532
Elmdale	01569
Elm Grove	01340
Elm Square	02379
Elmwood (Hampden County)	01040
Elmwood (Plymouth County)	02337
Endicott	02026
Erving	01344
Erving (Town)	01344
Essex	01929
Essex (Town)	01929
Essex (Part of Boston)	02112
Everett	02149
Factory Hollow	01002
Fairfield Mall (Part of Chicopee)	01020
Fairhaven (Town)	02719
Fairhaven	02719
Fairlawn	01545
Fairmount (Part of Boston)	02136
Fairview (Part of Chicopee)	01020
Fall River	02720-24
For specific Fall River Zip Codes call (508) 675-7438, or your local postmaster.	
Falls	01075
Falmouth	02540*
	02541†
Falmouth (Town)	02540
Falmouth Heights	02540
Farley	01344
Farm Hill	02180
Farnams	01225
Farnumsville	01560
Faulkner (Part of Malden)	02148
Fayville	01745
Federal (Part of Worcester)	01601
Feeding Hills	01030
Felchville	01760
Fellsway (Part of Medford)	02155
Fentonville	01069
Fields Corner (Part of Boston)	02122
Fieldston	02065
Findlen	02026
First Cliff	02066
Fiskdale	01518

	ZIP
Fitchburg	01420
Five Corners	02356
Flint (Part of Fall River)	02723
Florence (Part of Northampton)	01060
Florida	01343
Florida (Town)	01343
Forbes Park	02019
Fore River (Part of Quincy)	02169
Forestdale	02644
Forestdale Estates	02359
Forest Hills (Part of Boston)	02130
Forest Lake	01069
Forest Park (Part of Springfield)	01108
Forest River (Part of Salem)	01970
Forge Village	01886
Fort Banks (U.S. Army; inactive)	02152
Fort Bellingham	02019
Fort Devens (Middlesex County)	01433
Fort Devens (Worcester County)	01433
Fort Heath	02152
Foundry Village	01340
Foxboro	02035
Foxborough (Town)	02035
Foxvale	02035
Framingham (Town)	01701
Framingham	01701
Framingham Center	01701
Franklin (Town)	02038
Franklin	02038
Franklin Park (Part of Revere)	02151
Freetown (Town)	02702
Fresh Pond (Part of Cambridge)	02138
Freshwater Cove (Part of Gloucester)	01930
Fuller Shores	02346
Furnace Pond Colony	02359
Furnace Village	02334
Galleria at Worcester Center (Part of Worcester)	01608
Gardner	01440
Gay Head	02535
Gay Head (Town)	02535
Georgetown	01833
Georgetown (Town)	01833
Germantown (Part of Quincy)	02169
Gilbertville	01031
Gill (Town)	01376
Gillett Corner	01077
Gleasondale	01775
Glendale	01229
Glen Echo	02072
Glen Grove	01508
Glen Grove Annex	01508
Glenridge	02030
Gloucester	01930*
	01931†
Goodrichville	01462
Goshen	01032
Goshen (Town)	01032
Gosnold (Town)	02713
Goss Heights	01050
Goulding Village	01331
Grafton	01519
Grafton (Town)	01519
Granby	01033
Granby (Town)	01033
Graniteville	01886
Granville	01034
Granville (Town)	01034
Granville Center	01034
Gray Gables	02532
Great Barrington	01230
Great Barrington (Town)	01230
Great Brook Valley (Part of Worcester)	01605
Greenbush	02040
Greendale (Part of Worcester)	01606
Greenfield	01301*
	01302†
Greenfield Center	01301
Green Harbor	02041
Green Harbor-Cedar Crest	02041
Greenlodge	02026
Green Ridge Park	01226
Greenview Estates	02035
Greenville	01542
Greenwood	01880
Greenwood Manor Estates	02359
Greylock (Part of North Adams)	01247
Griswoldville	01340
Grosvenor Corner	01844
Groton	01450

	ZIP
Groton (Town)	01450
Grove Hall (Part of Boston)	02121
Groveland	01834
Groveland (Town)	01834
Hadley	01035
Hadley (Town)	01035
Halfway Pond	02532
Halifax	02338
Halifax (Town)	02338
Halifax Beach	02338
Hamilton	01936
Hamilton (Town)	01936
Hamilton (Part of Worcester)	01604
Hamilton Beach	02571
Hampden	01036
Hampden (Town)	01036
Hampshire Mall	01035
Hampton Mills	01027
Hancock	01237
Hancock (Town)	01237
Hancock Village	02146
Hanover	02339
Hanover (Town)	02339
Hanover Center	02339
Hanover Street (Part of Boston)	02113
Hanson	02341
Hanson (Town)	02341
Happy Hills	02019
Harbor Beach	02739
Harbour Mall (Part of Fall River)	02721
Harding	02052
Hardwick	01037
Hardwick (Town)	01037
Harrubs Corner	02367
Harthaven	02557
Hartsville	01230
Harvard	01451
Harvard (Town)	01451
Harvard Square (Part of Cambridge)	02138
Harwich	02645
Harwich (Town)	02645
Harwich Port (Barnstable County)	02646
Harwood	01460
Hascnom Air Force Base	01731
Hastings	02193
Hatchville	02536
Hatfield	01038
Hatfield (Town)	01038
Hathorne	01937
Haverhill	01830-32
For specific Haverhill Zip Codes call (508) 373-5643, or your local postmaster.	
Hawley	01339
Hawley (Town)	01339
Haydenville	01039
Head of Westport	02790
Heath	01346
Heath (Town)	01346
Heaven Heights	02717
Hebronville (Part of Attleboro)	02703
Hemlocks	02346
Hickory Hills Lake	01462
Hicksville	02747
Highland (Part of Springfield)	01109
Highland Lake	02056
Highland Park (Part of Holyoke)	01040
Highlands (Hampden County)	01040
Highlands (Middlesex County)	01851
Hillcrest Acres	02790
Hilltop Acres	02346
Hingham (Town)	02043
Hingham	02043
Hingham Center	02043
Hinsdale	01235
Hinsdale (Town)	01235
Hinsdale Estates	02019
Hodges Village	01540
Holbrook	02343
Holbrook (Town)	02343
Holden	01520
Holden (Town)	01520
Holland	01521
Holland (Town)	01521
Holliston (Town)	01746
Holliston	01746
Holly Woods	02739
Holyoke	01040*
	01041†
Holyoke Mall at Ingleside (Part of Holyoke)	01040
Hoosac Tunnel	01367
Hopedale (Town)	01747

* Area Zip Code   † Post Office Boxes

	ZIP
Hopedale	01747
Hopkinton	01748
Hopkinton (Town)	01748
Horseneck Beach	02790
Hortonville	02777
Houghs Neck (Part of Quincy)	02169
Houghtonville	01247
Housatonic	01236
Hovey's Corner	01463
Howe	01949
Hubbardston	01452
Hubbardston (Town)	01452
Huckleberry Corner	02576
Huckleberry Shores	02346
Hudson (Town)	01749
Hudson	01749
Hull (Town)	02045
Hull	02045
Humarock	02047
Huntington	01050
Huntington (Town)	01050
Hyannis	02601
Hyannis Port	02647
Hyde Park (Part of Boston)	02136*
	02137†
Idlewell	02188
Idlewood	02747
Indian Mound Beach	02532
Indian Orchard (Part of Springfield)	01151
Indian Shore	02346
Ingleside (Part of Holyoke)	01040
Inman Square (Part of Cambridge)	02139
Interlaken	01266
Ipswich	01938
Ipswich (Town)	01938
Island Creek	02332
Islington	02090
Jamaica Plain (Part of Boston)	02130
Jefferson	01522
Jefferson Shores	02532
Jeffries Point (Part of Boston)	02128
John Fitzgerald Kennedy (Part of Boston)	02114
John W. Mc Cormack (Part of Boston)	02109
Katama	02539
Kearney Square (Part of Lowell)	01852
Kempton Croft	02747
Kendal Green	02193
Kendall Square (Part of Cambridge)	02142
Kenmore (Part of Boston)	02215
Kent Park	02050
Kenwood	01826
Killdeer Island	01570
Kingsbury Beach	02642
Kings Forest	01921
Kingston	02364
Kingston (Town)	02364
Knightville	01050
Knollmere	02719
Konkapot	01244
Lafayette Place (Part of Boston)	02111
Lagoon Heights	02557
Lake Attitash	01913
Lake Forest Park	01760
Lake Hiawatha	02019
Lake Mattawa	01364
Lake Pleasant	01347
Lakeside (Bristol County)	02790
Lakeside (Plymouth County)	02346
Lake Street	02174
Lakeview (Middlesex County)	02154
Lake View (Worcester County)	01604
Lakeview Heights	02717
Lakeview Terrace (Part of Pittsfield)	01201
Lakeville	02347
Lakeville (Town)	02346
Lakewood (Part of Pittsfield)	01201
Lakewood Hills	02537
Lakewood Park	01473
Lambs Grove	01562
Lancaster	01523
Lancaster (Town)	01523
Lanesboro	01237
Lanesborough (Town)	01237
Lanesville (Part of Gloucester)	01930
Lane Village	01430
Larrywaug	01262
Laurel Park (Part of Northampton)	01060

	ZIP
Lawrence	01840-43
For specific Lawrence Zip Codes call (508) 691-4500, or your local postmaster.	
Le Count Hollow	02663
Lee	01238
Lee (Town)	01238
Leeds (Part of Northampton)	01053
Leicester	01524
Leicester (Town)	01524
Leino Park	01473
Lenox	01240
Lenox (Town)	01240
Lenox Dale	01242
Leominster	01453
Leverett (Town)	01054
Leverett	01054
Lexington (Town)	02173
Lexington	02173
Leyden (Town)	01301
Liberty Tree Mall	01923
Lincoln	01773
Lincoln (Town)	01773
Lincoln Center	01773
Lincoln Square (Part of Worcester)	01601
Linden (Part of Malden)	02148
Lindenwood	02180
Linwood	01525
Lithia	01032
Little Acres	02327
Little Harbor Beach	02571
Little Nahant	01908
Little Neck (Bristol County)	02777
Little Neck (Essex County)	01938
Little River (Part of Westfield)	01085
Littleton	01460
Littleton (Town)	01460
Lobsterville	02535
Lockerville	01760
Locks Village	01072
Long Beach	01930
Long Hill Acres	02359
Long Island Hospital (Part of Boston)	02169
Longmeadow (Town)	01106
Longmeadow	01106*
	01116†
Long Plain	02743
Long Pond Village	02532
Longwood	02146
Loudville	01027
Lovell Corners	02188
Lowell	01850-54
For specific Lowell Zip Codes call (508) 934-0500, or your local postmaster.	
Lower Mills (Part of Boston)	02126
Lower Village	01775
Ludlow (Hampden County) (Town)	01056
Ludlow (Hampden County)	01056
Ludlow (Worcester County)	01603
Lunds Corner (Part of New Bedford)	02745
Lunenburg	01462
Lunenburg (Town)	01462
Lynn	01901-05
For specific Lynn Zip Codes call (617) 595-5700, or your local postmaster.	
Lynnfield (Town)	01940
Lynnfield	01940
Lynnhurst	01906
Lyonsville	01340
Madaket	02554
Magnolia (Part of Gloucester)	01930
Mahkeenac Heights	01240
Main Street	02532
Malden	02148
Manchaug	01526
Manchester (Town)	01944
Manchester	01944
Manleys Corner	02379
Manomet	02345
Manomet Beach	02345
Manomet Bluffs	02345
Mansfield	02048
Mansfield (Town)	02048
Maple Park	01844
Maplewood (Middlesex County)	02148
Maplewood (Worcester County)	01536
Mara Vista	02536
Marblehead (Town)	01945
Marblehead	01945
Marblehead Neck	01945

	ZIP
Marion	02738
Marion (Town)	02738
Marlboro	01833
Marlborough	01752
Marshfield	02050
Marshfield (Town)	02050
Marshfield Hills	02051
Marstons Mills (Barnstable County)	02648
Mashnee Island	02532
Mashpee	02649
Mashpee (Town)	02649
Masons Corner	02717
Massachusetts Correctional Institution (Middlesex County)	01701
Massachusetts Correctional Institution (Norfolk County)	02071
Massachusetts Correctional Institution (Plymouth County)	02366
Massachusetts Correctional Institution-Southeast (Plymouth County)	02324
Matfield	02379
Mattapan (Part of Boston)	02126
Mattapoisett	02739
Mattapoisett (Town)	02739
Maynard (Town)	01754
Maynard	01754
Mayo Beach	02667
Medfield	02052
Medfield (Town)	02052
Medford	02153†
	02155*
Medway	02053
Medway (Town)	02053
Meeting House Hill (Part of Boston)	02122
Megansett	02556
Melrose	02176*
	02177†
Melrose Highlands (Part of Melrose)	02177
Menauhant	02536
Mendon	01756
Mendon (Town)	01756
Menemsha	02552
Merrick	01089
Merrimac	01860
Merrimac (Town)	01860
Merrimack College	01845
Merrimacport	01860
Merrymount (Part of Quincy)	02169
Methuen (Town)	01844
Methuen	01844
Methuen Mall	01844
Middleboro	02346
Middleborough (Town)	02346
Middlefield (Town)	01243
Middlefield	01243
Middleton (Town)	01949
Middleton	01949
Midland	02019
Mile Oak Center	01095
Milford (Town)	01757
Milford	01757
Millbury	01527
Millbury (Town)	01527
Millers Falls	01349
Millerville	01504
Millis	02054
Millis (Town)	02054
Millis-Clicquot	02054
Mill River	01244
Millville (Town)	01529
Millville	01529
Millville Center	01529
Milton (Town)	02186
Milton	02186
Milton Center	02186
Milton Village	02187
Minot	02055
Mirror Lake	02093
Mishaum Point	02748
M.I.T. (Massachusetts Institute of Technology)(Part of Cambridge)	02139
Monomoy	02554
Monponsett	02350
Monroe (Town)	01350
Monroe Bridge	01350
Monson	01057
Monson (Town)	01057
Montague	01351
Montague (Town)	01351
Montague City	01376
Montello (Part of Brockton)	02403

	ZIP
....	02405

For specific Montello Zip Codes call (508) 559-1823, or your local postmaster.

Monterey...............	01245
Monterey (Town)...........	01245
Montgomery..............	01085
Montgomery (Town).......	01085
Montserrat (Part of Beverly)	01915
Montville...............	01255
Monument Beach..........	02553
Moores Corner...........	01054
Morningdale.............	01505
Morrills................	02062
Morseville..............	01760
Mount Auburn............	02172
Mount Bowdoin (Part of Boston)................	02121
Mount Hermon...........	01354
Mount Saint James (Part of Worcester)..............	01610
Mount Tom..............	01027
Mount Washington........	12517
Mount Washington (Town)	12517
Myricks................	02718
Mystic Grove............	01507
Mystic Wharf (Part of Boston)................	02109
Nabnasset..............	01886
Nahant (Town)...........	01908
Nahant.................	01908
Nantucket..............	02554*
....	02584†
....	02554
Nantucket (Town).........	02554
Nashaquitsa.............	02535
Natick (Town)............	01760
Natick.................	01760
Natick Development Center	01760
Natick Laboratories.......	01760
Natick Mall.............	01760
Needham...............	02192
....	02194

For specific Needham Zip Codes call (617) 444-0128, or your local postmaster.

Needham...............	02192
Needham Heights.........	02194
Nelsons Grove...........	02346
Nelsons Shores..........	02346
Neponset (Part of Boston)	02122
New Ashford............	01237
New Ashford (Town).......	01237
New Bedford............	02740-42
....	02744-46

For specific New Bedford Zip Codes call (508) 996-8523, or your local postmaster.

New Boston.............	01255
New Braintree...........	01531
New Braintree (Town)......	01531
Newbury...............	01951
Newbury (Town)..........	01950
Newburyport............	01950-51

For specific Newburyport Zip Codes call (508) 462-4403, or your local postmaster.

New England Shopping Center...............	01906
New Lenox.............	01240
New Marlboro...........	01230
New Marlborough (Town)	01230
New Salem.............	01355
New Salem (Town)........	01355
New Seabury...........	02649
Newton................	02158-62
....	02164-66
....	02168
....	02195

For specific Newton Zip Codes call (617) 527-8529, or your local postmaster.

Newton Center (Part of Newton)...............	02159
Newton Highlands (Part of Newton)...............	02161
Newton Lower Falls (Part of Newton)...............	02162
Newton Upper Falls (Part of Newton)...............	02164
Newtonville (Part of Newton)...............	02160
New Town..............	02258
New Village............	01588
Nobska Beach...........	02571
Nonantum (Part of Newton)	02195
Nonquitt...............	02748
Noquochoke............	02790
Norfolk................	02056
Norfolk (Town)...........	02056
North (Part of New Bedford)	02746
North Abington..........	02351
North Acton............	01720

	ZIP
North Adams............	01247
North Adams Junction (Part of Pittsfield)..............	01201
North Amherst...........	01059
Northampton............	01053
....	01060-61

For specific Northampton Zip Codes call (413) 584-0960, or your local postmaster.

North Andover (Town).....	01845
North Andover...........	01845
North Andover Center.....	01845
North Ashburnham........	01430
North Attleboro..........	02760-61
....	02763

For specific North Attleboro Zip Codes call (508) 699-7556, or your local postmaster.

North Attleborough (Town)	02760
North Bellingham........	02019
North Beverly (Part of Beverly)...............	01915
North Billerica..........	01862
North Blandford.........	01008
Northborough...........	01532
Northborough (Town).....	01532
Northbridge............	01534
Northbridge (Town).......	01534
Northbridge Center.......	01588
North Brighton (Part of Boston)................	02135
North Brookfield........	01535
North Brookfield (Town)....	01535
North Cambridge (Part of Cambridge)............	02138
North Carver...........	02355
North Chatham..........	02650
North Chelmsford........	01863
North Chester...........	01050
North Cohasset.........	02025
North Dartmouth........	02747
North Dartmouth Mall.....	02747
North Dighton..........	02764
North Duxbury..........	02332
North Eastham.........	02651
North Easton...........	02356
North Egremont.........	01252
Northey Point (Part of Salem)................	01970
North Falmouth.........	02556
Northfield.............	01360
Northfield (Town)........	01360
Northgate Shopping Center (Part of Revere).........	02151
North Grafton..........	01536
North Hadley..........	01035
North Hancock..........	01267
North Hanover.........	02339
North Harwich..........	02645
North Hatfield..........	01066
North Lancaster.........	01523
North Leominster (Part of Leominster)............	01453
North Leverett..........	01054
North Littleton..........	01460
North Marshfield........	02059
North Middleboro........	02346
North Milford...........	01757
North Natick............	01760
North New Salem........	01364
North Orange...........	01364
North Otis.............	01253
North Oxford...........	01537
North Pembroke........	02358
North Pepperell.........	01463
North Plymouth.........	02360
North Plympton.........	02364
North Quincy (Part of Quincy)................	02171
North Randolph.........	02368
North Reading (Town).....	01864
North Reading..........	01864
North Rehoboth.........	02769
North Rutland..........	01543
North Salem (Part of Salem)	01970
North Saugus..........	01906
North Scituate..........	02060
North Seekonk.........	02771
Northshore Shopping Center (Part of Peabody)	01960
North Sommerville (Part of Somerville).............	02143
North Stoughton........	02072
North Sudbury..........	01776
North Swansea.........	02777
North Tewksbury........	01876
North Tisbury..........	02568
North Truro............	02652
North Uxbridge.........	01538
North Waltham (Part of Waltham)..............	02154
Northwest Harwich.......	02645

	ZIP
North Weymouth.........	02191
North Wilmington........	01887
North Woburn (Part of Woburn)...............	01801
North Worcester (Part of Worcester)............	01606
Norton................	02766
Norton (Town)...........	02766
Norton Grove...........	02766
Norwell................	02061
Norwell (Town)..........	02161
Norwood (Town).........	02062
Norwood..............	02062
Norwood Central........	02062
Nutting Lake...........	01865
Oak Bluffs (Town)........	02557
Oak Bluffs.............	02557
Oakdale (Hampden County)	01040
Oakdale (Norfolk County)	02026
Oakdale (Worcester County)	01583
Oak Grove (Part of Malden)	02148
Oakham...............	01068
Oakham (Town)..........	01068
Oak Island (Part of Revere)	02151
Oakland Vale...........	01906
Ocean Bluff............	02065
Ocean Bluff-Brant Rock..	02020
Ocean Grove...........	02777
Ocean Heights..........	02539
Ocean Spray...........	02152
Old City...............	01474
Old Common...........	01527
Old Furnace...........	01031
Oldham Pines..........	02359
Oldham Village.........	02359
Old Silver Beach........	02556
Old Sturbridge Village.....	01566
Onset................	02558
Orange...............	01364
Orange (Town)..........	01364
Orient Heights (Part of Boston)................	02128
Orleans...............	02653
Orleans (Town)..........	02653
Osceola...............	01254
Osterville.............	02655
Otis..................	01253
Otis (Town).............	01253
Otis Air Force Base.......	02542
Otter River............	01436
Overbrook.............	02181
Oxford................	01540
Oxford (Town)..........	01540
Oyster Harbors.........	02655
Packard Heights........	01331
Padanaram Village......	02748
Pages Beach...........	01430
Painting Island.........	02738
Pakachoag............	01501
Palmer................	01069
Palmer (Town)..........	01069
Park Street (Part of Medford)..............	02155
Parkwood Beach........	02571
Patuisset.............	02559
Pawtucketville (Part of Lowell)................	01854
Paxton................	01612
Paxton (Town)..........	01612
Payson Park...........	02172
Peabody...............	01960*
....	01961†
Pelham................	01002
Pelham (Town)..........	01002
Pembroke.............	02359
Pembroke (Town)........	02359
Pembroke Heights......	02358
Pepperell..............	01463
Pepperell (Town)........	01463
Perryville..............	02769
Peru..................	01235
Peru (Town)............	01235
Petersham.............	01366
Petersham (Town).......	01366
Phelps Mills (Part of Peabody).............	01960
Phillipston.............	01331
Phillipston (Town).......	01331
Phillipston Four Corners...	01331
Pierceville.............	02576
Piety Corner (Part of Waltham)..............	02154
Pigeon Cove...........	01966
Pilgrim Heights.........	02652
Pilgrim Pines Estates.....	02327
Pilgrim Village.........	02019
Pine Bluffs............	02346
Pinefield..............	01938
Pine Grove (Part of Northampton)............	01060
Pinehurst..............	01866
Pinehurst Beach........	02571

	ZIP		ZIP		ZIP
Pine Island	01951	Revere Beach (Part of		Scorton Shores	02537
Pine Island Lake	01060	Revere)	02151	Scott Hill Acres	02019
Pine Lake	01776	Rexhame	02050	Searstown Mall (Part of	
Pine Point (Part of		Rice Square (Part of		Leominster)	01453
Springfield)	01101	Worcester)	01604	Searsville	01096
Pine Rest	01776	Richmond	01254	Sea View	02050
Piney Point Beach	02738	Richmond (Town)	01254	Second Cliff	02066
Pingryville	01460	Richmond Furnace	01254	Seekonk (Town)	02771
Pittsfield	01201-03	Rings Island	01950	Seekonk	02771
For specific Pittsfield Zip Codes		Rio Vista	01862	Segreganset	02715
call (413) 442-6961, or your local		Risingdale	01230	Shaker Village	01451
postmaster.		Riverdale (Essex County)	01930	Sharon (Town)	02067
Plainfield	01070	Riverdale (Norfolk County)	02026	Sharon	02067
Plainfield (Town)	01070	Riverdale (Worcester		Sharon Heights	02067
Plainville (Hampshire		County)	01534	Shattuckville	01369
County)	01002	Rivermoor	02066	Shawkemo	02554
Plainville (Norfolk County)	02762	River Pines	01821	Shawsheen Heights	01810
Plainville (Norfolk County)		Riverside (Essex County)	01830	Shawsheen Village	01810
(Town)	02762	Riverside (Franklin County)	01376	Sheffield	01257
Pleasant Lake	02645	Riverside (Hampden		Sheffield (Town)	01257
Plimptonville	02081	County)	01040	Shelburne	01370
Plumbush	01951	Riverside (Plymouth County)	02558	Shelburne (Town)	01370
Plum Island (Part of		Riverview (Essex County)	01930	Shelburne Falls	01370
Newburyport)	01950	Riverview (Middlesex		Sheldonville	02070
Plummer Corner	01588	County)	02154	Shell Beach	02739
Plymouth	02360-62	Roberts (Part of Waltham)	02154	Shepardville	02762
For specific Plymouth Zip Codes		Rochdale	01542	Sherborn	01770
call (508) 746-0058, or your local		Rochester	02770	Sherborn (Town)	01770
postmaster.		Rochester (Town)	02770	Sherwood Forest (Berkshire	
Plympton	02367	Rock	02346	County)	01223
Plympton (Town)	02367	Rockdale	01236	Sherwood Forest (Bristol	
Pocasset	02559	Rock Harbor	02653	County)	02743
Pocomo	02554	Rockland (Town)	02370	Shimmo	02554
Podunk	01515	Rockland	02370	Shirley	01464
Point Independence	02532	Rockport	01966	Shirley (Town)	01464
Point of Pines (Part of		Rockport (Town)	01966	Shirley Center	01464
Revere)	02151	Rocks Village (Part of		Shoppers' World	01701
Point Pleasant	01570	Haverhill)	01830	Shore Acres (Bristol County)	02748
Point Shirley	02152	Rock Valley (Part of		Shore Acres (Plymouth	
Polpis	02554	Holyoke)	01040	County)	02066
Pomponotto Pines	02333	Rockville	02054	Shrewsbury (Town)	01545
Ponakin Mill	01523	Rocky Hill	01757	Shrewsbury	01545
Pond Village (mail North		Rolling Acres Estates	01886	Shutesbury	01072
Truro)	02652	Roostersville	01255	Shutesbury (Town)	01072
Pond Village (mail		Roslindale (Part of Boston)	02131	Siasconset	02564
Barnstable)	02630	Rowe	01367	Silver Beach	02565
Pondville (Norfolk County)	02093	Rowe (Town)	01367	Silver Hill	02193
Pondville (Plymouth County)	02532	Rowley	01969	Silver Lake (Middlesex	
Pondville (Worcester		Rowley (Town)	01969	County)	01887
County)	01501	Roxbury (Part of Boston)	02118-20	Silver Lake (Plymouth	
Pontoosuc Gardens (Part of		For specific Roxbury Zip Codes		County)	02360
Pittsfield)	01201	call (617) 654-5768, or your local		Silver Shell Beach	02719
Pope Beach	02719	postmaster.		Silver Spring Beach	02651
Popponesset Beach	02649	Roxbury Crossing (Part of		Simon's Rock of Bard	
Porter Square (Part of		Boston)	02120	College	01230
Cambridge)	02140	Royalston	01368	Sippewisset	02540
Potoosuc Lake	01237	Royalston (Town)	01368	Sixteen Acres (Part of	
Pratt Corner	01072	Russell	01071	Springfield)	01101
Precinct	02346	Russell (Town)	01071	Smith Highlands (Part of	
Prentice Gardens	01588	Russellville	01085	Chicopee)	01020
Prides Crossing (Part of		Rutland	01543	Smith Mills	02747
Beverly)	01965	Rutland (Town)	01543	Smiths Ferry (Part of	
Princeton	01541	Saconesset Hills	02540	Holyoke)	01040
Princeton (Town)	01541	Sagamore	02561	Smoke Rise Heights	02777
Priscilla Beach	02360	Sagamore Beach	02562	Snug Harbor	02332
Provincetown	02657	Sagamore Highlands	02562	Soldiers Field (Part of	
Provincetown (Town)	02657	Salem	01970*	Boston)	02163
Provincetown Wharf	02657		01971†	Somerset	02725-26
Prudential Center (Part of		Salem Neck (Part of Salem)	01970	For specific Somerset Zip Codes	
Boston)	02199	Salem State College (Part of		call (508) 673-7740, or your local	
Quaise	02554	Salem)	01970	postmaster.	
Queen Lake	01331	Salisbury	01952	Somerset Centre	02725
Quidnet	02554	Salisbury (Town)	01950	Somerville	02143-45
Quincy	02169-71	Salisbury Beach	01952	For specific Somerville Zip Codes	
	02269	Salisbury Heights (Part of		call (617) 666-0745, or your local	
For specific Quincy Zip Codes call		Worcester)	01609	postmaster.	
(617) 328-5544, or your local		Salisbury Plains	01950	South (Part of Fall River)	02724
postmaster.		Salters Point	02748	South Acton	01720
Quincy Adams (Part of		Sandersdale	01550	South Amherst	01002
Quincy)	02169	Sand Hill	02066	Southampton	01073
Quincy Center (Part of		Sandisfield	01255	Southampton (Town)	01073
Quincy)	02169	Sandisfield (Town)	01255	South Ashburnham	01466
Quincy Point (Part of		Sandwich	02563	South Ashfield	01330
Quincy)	02169	Sandwich (Town)	02563	South Athol	01331
Quinsigamond Village (Part		Sandy Beach (Norfolk		South Attleboro (Part of	
of Worcester)	01607	County)	02025	Attleboro)	02703
Quissett	02540	Sandy Beach (Worcester		South Barre	01074
Rakeville	02019	County)	01543	South Bellingham	02019
Randolph (Town)	02368	Santuit	02635	South Berlin	01503
Randolph	02368	Sassaquin (Part of New		South Billerica	01730
Raynham	02767	Bedford)	02745	South Bolton	01740
Raynham (Town)	02767	Saugus (Town)	01906	Southborough	01772
Raynham Center	02768	Saugus	01906	Southborough (Town)	01772
Reading (Town)	01867	Saugus Center	01906	South Boston (Part of	
Reading	01867	Saundersville	01560	Boston)	02127
Readville (Part of Boston)	02137	Savin Hill (Part of Boston)	02125	South Braintree	02184
Redstone Shopping Center	02180	Savoy	01256	Southbridge (Town)	01550
Rehoboth	02769	Savoy (Town)	01256	Southbridge	01550
Rehoboth (Town)	02769	Saxonville	01701	South Byfield	01922
Renfrew	01220	Scituate	02040†	South Carver	02366
Reservoir	02146		02066*	South Charlton	01507
Revere	02151	Scituate (Town)	02066	South Chatham	02659

	ZIP
South Chelmsford	01824
South Dartmouth	02748
South Deerfield	01373
South Dennis	02660
South Duxbury	02332
Southeastern Correctional Center	02324
South Easton	02375
South Egremont	01258
Southfield	01259
South Foxboro	02035
South Framingham	01701
South Georgetown	01833
South Grafton	01560
South Groveland	01834
South Hadley	01075
South Hadley (Town)	01075
South Hadley Falls	01075
South Hamilton	01982
South Hanover	02339
South Harwich	02661
South Hingham	02043
South Lakeville	02346
South Lancaster	01561
South Lawrence (Part of Lawrence)	01842
South Lee	01260
South Lowell	01876
South Lynnfield	01940
South Mashpee	02649
South Middleboro	02346
South Milford	01747
South Natick	01760
South Orleans	02662
South Peabody (Part of Peabody)	01960
South Postal Annex (Part of Boston)	02109
South Quincy (Part of Quincy)	02169
South Rehoboth	02769
South Royalston	01331
South Salem (Part of Salem)	01970
South Sandisfield	01255
South Sandwich	02563
South Shore Plaza	02184
South Springfield (Part of Springfield)	01101
South Stoughton	02072
South Sutton	01516
South Swansea	02777
South Truro	02666
South Uxbridge	01569
Southville	01772
South Walpole	02071
South Waltham (Part of Waltham)	02154
South Wareham	02571
South Wellfleet	02663
South Westport	02790
South Weymouth	02190
South Weymouth Naval Air Station	02190
Southwick	01077
Southwick (Town)	01077
South Williamstown	01267
South Wilmington (Part of Woburn)	01801
South Worthington	01050
South Yarmouth	02664
Spencer	01562
Spencer (Town)	01562
Spindleville	01747
Springdale (Part of Holyoke)	01040
Springdale Mall (Part of Springfield)	01101
Springfield	01101-05
	01107-09
	01118-52
For specific Springfield Zip Codes call (413) 785-6300, or your local postmaster.	
Springfield Plaza (Part of Springfield)	01104
Squantum (Part of Quincy)	02171
Standish (Part of Taunton)	02780
Staples Shore	02346
State House (Part of Boston)	02133
State Line	01266
Sterling	01564
Sterling (Town)	01564
Sterling Junction	01564
Stetson Road	02359
Stevens Corner	01201
Still River	01467
Stockbridge	01262
Stockbridge (Town)	01262
Stoneham (Town)	02180
Stoneham	02180
Stoneville (Franklin County)	01344

	ZIP
Stoneville (Worcester County)	01501
Stony Brook	02193
Stoughton (Town)	02072
Stoughton	02072
Stow	01775
Stow (Town)	01775
Sturbridge	01566
Sturbridge (Town)	01566
Sudbury	01776
Sudbury (Town)	01776
Sudbury Center	01776
Summit (Part of Worcester)	01606
Sunderland	01375
Sunderland (Town)	01375
Sunderland (Part of Worcester)	01604
Sunken Meadow Beach	02651
Sunnyside	01571
Surfside	02554
Sutton	01527
Sutton (Town)	01527
Swampscott (Town)	01907
Swampscott	01907
Swansea	02777
Swansea (Town)	02777
Swansea Center	02777
Sweets Corner	01267
Swift River	01026
Swifts Beach	02571
Symmes Corner	01890
Tafts Corner	01562
Tahanto Beach	02559
Tapleyville	01923
Tatnuck (Part of Worcester)	01602
Taunton	02718†
	02780*
Teaticket	02536
Templeton	01468
Templeton (Town)	01468
Tewksbury	01876
Tewksbury (Town)	01876
Tewksbury Hospital	01876
Texas	01537
The Green	02346
The Pines	01866
Thomastown	02346
Thorndike	01079
Three Rivers	01080
Thumpertown Beach	02651
Tihonet	02571
Tinkertown	02332
Tinkhamtown	02739
Tisbury (Town)	02568
Tobeys Island	02553
Tolland	01034
Tolland (Town)	01034
Tonset	02653
Topsfield	01983
Topsfield (Town)	01983
Touisset	02777
Town Crest Village	01225
Town Hall	02341
Townsend	01469
Townsend (Town)	01469
Townsend Harbor	01469
Tozier Corner	01844
Tri-Town Shopping Center	02021
Truro	02666
Truro (Town)	02666
Tufts University (Part of Medford)	02153
Tully	01331
Turkey Hill Shores	01543
Turners Falls	01376
Turnpike	01545
Twin City Plaza (Part of Fitchburg)	01420
Tyngsboro	01879
Tyngsborough (Town)	01879
Tyringham	01264
Tyringham (Town)	01264
Union Market	02172
Union Point	01570
Unionville (Norfolk County)	02038
Unionville (Worcester County)	01520
University Park (Part of Worcester)	01605
Uphams Corner (Part of Boston)	02125
Upton	01568
Upton (Town)	01568
Upton-West Upton	01568
Uxbridge	01569
Uxbridge (Town)	01569
Vallersville	02532
Valley View	02019
Van Deusenville	01236
Varnumtown	01826
Veterans Administration Hospital (Part of Boston)	02130

	ZIP
Victory Hill (Part of Pittsfield)	01201
Village	02053
Village Mall, The	02021
Village of Nagog Woods	01718
Vineyard Haven	02568
Vineyard Highlands	02557
Waban (Part of Newton)	02168
Wachusett (Part of Fitchburg)	01420
Wakeby	02563
Wakefield (Town)	01880
Wakefield	01880
Wakefield Center	01880
Wakefield Junction	01880
Wales	01081
Wales (Town)	01081
Wallis Street (Part of Peabody)	01960
Walnut Hill (Part of Woburn)	01801
Walpole	02081
Walpole (Town)	02081
Walpole Mall, The	02032
Waltham	02154
Waltham Highlands (Part of Waltham)	02154
Wamesit	01876
Wampun Corner	02093
Wapping	01342
Waquoit	02536
Ward Hill (Part of Haverhill)	01830
Ware	01082
Ware (Town)	01082
Wareham	02571
Wareham (Town)	02571
Warren	01083
Warren (Town)	01083
Warren Terrace	02359
Warrentown	02346
Warwick	01378
Warwick (Town)	01378
Washington	01223
Washington (Town)	01223
Watertown (Town)	02172
Watertown	02172
Waterville (Plymouth County)	02346
Waterville (Worcester County)	01475
Watuppa (Part of Fall River)	02721
Wauwinet	02554
Waverley	02179
Wawela Park	01570
Wayland	01778
Wayland (Town)	01778
Wayside Inn	01776
Webster	01570-71
Webster (Town)	01570
Webster	01570
Webster Square (Part of Worcester)	01603
Wedgemere	01890
Weir Village (Part of Taunton)	02780
Wellesley (Town)	02181
Wellesley	02181
Wellesley Farms	02181
Wellesley Fells	02181
Wellesley Hills	02181
Wellfleet	02667
Wellfleet (Town)	02667
Wellington (Part of Medford)	02155
Wellville	01430
Wendell	01379
Wendell (Town)	01379
Wendell Depot	01380
Wenham (Town)	01984
Wenham	01984
West Abington	02351
West Acton	01720
West Andover	01810
West Auburn	01501
West Barnstable	02668
West Becket	01238
West Bedford	01730
West Berlin	01503
West Billerica	01862
Westborough (Town)	01581
Westborough	01581
West Boxford	01885
West Boylston	01583
West Boylston (Town)	01583
West Bridgewater	02379
West Bridgewater (Town)	02379
West Brimfield	01069
West Brookfield	01585
West Brookfield (Town)	01585
West Cambridge (Part of Cambridge)	02138
West Chatham	02669
West Chelmsford	01863
Westchester (Part of Worcester)	01605

	ZIP
West Chesterfield	01084
West Chop	02573
West Concord	01742
West Cummington	01026
Westdale	02333
West Deerfield	01342
West Dennis	02670
West Dudley	01550
West Duxbury	02332
West Falmouth	02574
West Farms (Part of Northampton)	01060
Westfield	01085*
	01086†
West Fitchburg (Part of Fitchburg)	01420
Westford	01886
Westford (Town)	01886
West Foxboro	02035
Westgate Mall (Part of Brockton)	02401
West Gloucester (Part of Gloucester)	01930
West Granville	01034
West Groton	01472
Westhampton	01027
Westhampton (Town)	01027
West Hanover	02339
West Harwich	02671
West Hatfield	01088
West Hawley	01339
West Hingham	02043
West Hyannisport	02672
Westlands	01824
West Leominster (Part of Leominster)	01453
West Leyden	01337
West Lynn (Part of Lynn)	01905
West Manchester	01944
West Mansfield	02048
West Medford (Part of Medford)	02156
West Medway	02053
West Millbury	01586
Westminster	01473
Westminster (Town)	01473
West Natick	01760
West New Boston	01255
West Newbury	01985
West Newbury (Town)	01985
West Newton (Part of Newton)	02165
Weston (Town)	02193
Weston	02193
West Otis	01245
Westover Air Force Base	01022
West Peabody (Part of Peabody)	01960
West Pelham	01002
Westport (Town)	02790

	ZIP
Westport	02790
Westport Factory	02790
Westport Point	02791
West Quincy (Part of Quincy)	02169
West Roxbury (Part of Boston)	02132
West Royalston	01331
West Side (Part of Worcester)	01602
West Somerville (Part of Somerville)	02144
West Springfield	01089*
	01090†
West Sterling	01564
West Stockbridge	01266
West Stockbridge (Town)	01266
West Stockbridge Center	01266
West Stoughton	02072
West Sutton	01527
West Tatnuck (Part of Worcester)	01602
West Tisbury	02575
West Tisbury (Town)	02575
West Townsend	01474
West Upton	01587
Westview	02038
Westville (Part of Taunton)	02780
West Walpole	02081
West Wareham	02576
West Warren	01092
West Watertown	02172
West Whately	01039
West Wind Shores	02532
Westwood	02090
Westwood (Town)	02090
West Worthington	01098
West Wrentham	02070
West Yarmouth	02673
Wethersfield	02019
Weweantic	02571
Weymouth	02188-91
For specific Weymouth Zip Codes call (617) 337-1412, or your local postmaster.	
Weymouth Heights	02188
Weymouth Landing	02188
Whalom	01420
Whately (Town)	01093
Whately (East Whately)	01373
Whately	01093
Wheelockville	01569
Wheelwright	01094
White City	01747
White City Shopping Center	01545
White Horse Beach	02381
White Island Shores	02538
White Oaks	01267
Whitinsville	01588
Whitman (Town)	02382

	ZIP
Whitman	02382
Whittenton (Part of Taunton)	02780
Wigginsville (Part of Lowell)	01850
Wilbraham	01095
Wilbraham (Town)	01095
Wilkinsonville	01527
Williamsburg	01096
Williamsburg (Town)	01096
Williamstown	01267
Williamstown (Town)	01267
Williamsville (Berkshire County)	01236
Williamsville (Worcester County)	01452
Wilmington	01887
Wilmington (Town)	01887
Wilson (Part of Gloucester)	01930
Winchendon	01475
Winchendon (Town)	01475
Winchendon Springs	01477
Winchester (Town)	01890
Winchester	01890
Winchester Highlands	01890
Windsor	01270
Windsor (Town)	01270
Winmere	01803
Winnecunnet	02766
Winslows	02062
Winter Hill (Part of Somerville)	02145
Winthrop (Town)	02152
Winthrop	02152
Winthrop Highlands	02152
Woburn	01801
Wollaston (Part of Quincy)	02170
Woodland Park	01501
Woods Hole	02543
Woods Hole Coast Guard Base	02543
Woodville	01784
Worcester	01601-15
For specific Worcester Zip Codes call (508) 795-3666, or your local postmaster.	
Woronoco	01097
Woronoco Heights	01097
Worthington	01098
Worthington (Town)	01098
Worthington Center	01098
Wrentham	02093
Wrentham (Town)	02093
Wyben	01085
Wyoming (Part of Melrose)	02176
Yankee Orchards (Part of Pittsfield)	01201
Yarmouth	02675
Yarmouth (Town)	02675
Yarmouth Port	02675
Zoar	01367
Zylonite	01220

	ZIP
Abscota	49029
Ackerson Lake	49201
Acme	49610
Acme (Township)	49610
Ada	49301
Ada (Township)	49301
Adair	48064
Adams (Arenac County) (Township)	48659
Adams (Hillsdale County) (Township)	49262
Adams (Houghton County) (Township)	49963
Adams Park	49097
Adamsville	49112
Addison (Lenawee County)	49220
Addison (Oakland County) (Township)	48367
Adrian (Lenawee County)	49221
Adrian (Lenawee County) (Township)	49221
Advance	49712
Aetna (Mecosta County) (Township)	49336
Aetna (Missaukee County) (Township)	48632
Aetna (Newaygo County)	49412
Afton	49705
Agate	49967
Agnew	49460
Ahmeek	49901
Airport Forest	48625
Akron	48701
Akron (Township)	48701
Alabaster	48763
Alabaster (Township)	48763
Alaiedon (Township)	48854
Alamo	49009
Alamo (Township)	49009
Alanson	49706
Alaska	49302
Alba	49611
Albee (Township)	48655
Albert (Township)	49756
Alberta	49946
Albion (Calhoun County)	49224
Albion (Calhoun County) (Township)	49224
Albion (Houghton County)	49913
Alcona (Alcona County)	48740
Alcona (Alcona County) (Township)	48721
Alden	49612
Algansee (Township)	49082
Alger	48610
Algoma (Township)	49341
Algonac	48001
All Bright Shores	48612
Allegan	49010
Allegan (Township)	49010
Allen	49227
Allen (Township)	49227
Allendale (Clare County)	48625
Allendale (Ottawa County)	49401
Allendale (Ottawa County) (Township)	49401
Allen Park	48101
Allenton	48002
Allenville	49760
Allis (Township)	49765
Allouez	49805
Allouez (Township)	49805
Alma	48801
Almeda Beach	48653
Almena	49079
Almena (Township)	49079
Almer (Township)	48723
Almira (Township)	49630
Almont	48003
Almont (Township)	48003
Aloha	49721
Aloha (Township)	49721
Alpena	49707
Alpena (Township)	49707
Alpena Junction (Part of Alpena)	49707
Alpha	49902
Alpine	49321
Alpine (Township)	49321
Alston	49958
Alto	49302
Altona	49336
Alverno	49721
Amador	48422
Amasa	49903
Amber (Township)	49431
Amble	49329
Amboy (Township)	49232
Anchorville	48004
Andersonville	48350
Andrews	49104

	ZIP
Ann Arbor	48103-09
For specific Ann Arbor Zip Codes call (313) 665-1100, or your local postmaster.	
Ann Arbor (Township)	48105
Antioch (Township)	49688
Antoine (Part of Iron Mountain)	49801
Antrim (Antrim County)	49659
Antrim (Shiawassee County) (Township)	48418
Antwerp (Township)	49065
Anvil Location	49911
Aplin Beach	48706
Applegate	48401
Arbela (Township)	48746
Arborland Consumer Mall (Part of Ann Arbor)	48104
Arbutus Beach	49735
Arcada (Township)	48801
Arcade (Part of Ann Arbor)	48104
Arcadia (Lapeer County) (Township)	48412
Arcadia (Manistee County)	49613
Arcadia (Manistee County) (Township)	49613
Arenac (Township)	48749
Argentine	48451
Argentine (Township)	48451
Argyle	48410
Argyle (Township)	48410
Arlington (Township)	49013
Armada	48005
Armada (Township)	48005
Armstrong Corners	49079
Arnheim	49958
Arnold	49819
Artesia Beach	48656
Arthur (Township)	48617
Arvon (Township)	49962
Ash (Township)	48117
Ashland (Township)	49327
Ashland Center	49327
Ashley	48806
Ashmore	48767
Ashton	49655
Askel	49958
Assyria	49021
Assyria (Township)	49021
Athens	49011
Athens (Township)	49011
Atlanta	49709
Atlantic Mine	49905
Atlas	48411
Atlas (Township)	48438
Attica	48412
Attica (Township)	48412
Atwood	49729
Auburn	48611
Auburn Hills	48321
Au Gres	48703
Au Gres (Township)	48703
Augusta (Kalamazoo County)	49012
Augusta (Washtenaw County) (Township)	48191
Aura	49946
Aurelius	48854
Aurelius (Township)	48854
Aurora (Part of Ironwood)	49938
Au Sable (Iosco County)	48750
Au Sable (Iosco County) (Township)	48750
Au Sable (Roscommon County) (Township)	48653
Au Sable River Park	48656
Austin (Hillsdale County)	49232
Austin (Marquette County)	49841
Austin (Mecosta County) (Township)	49346
Austin (Sanilac County) (Township)	48475
Austin Center	48475
Austin Lake (Part of Portage)	49081
Au Train	49806
Au Train (Township)	49806
Auvinen Corner	49938
Avalon Beach	48161
Averill	48640
Avery (Township)	49709
Avoca	48006
Avondale	49631
Azalia	48110
Bach	48759
Backus (Township)	48656
Backus Beach	48762
Bad Axe	48413
Bagley (Menominee County)	49821
Bagley (Otsego County) (Township)	49735
Baie de Wasai	49783

	ZIP
Bailey	49303
Bainbridge (Township)	49022
Bainbridge Center	49022
Bakertown	49107
Baldwin (Delta County) (Township)	49872
Baldwin (Iosco County) (Township)	48770
Baldwin (Lake County)	49304
Baltic	49905
Baltimore (Barry County) (Township)	49058
Baltimore (Ontonagon County)	49912
Banat	49821
Bancroft	48414
Banfield	49017
Bangor (Bay County) (Township)	48706
Bangor (Van Buren County)	49013
Bangor (Van Buren County) (Township)	49103
Bankers	49242
Banks (Township)	49729
Banksons Lake	49065
Bannister	48807
Baraga	49908
Baraga (Township)	49908
Barbeau	49710
Barker Creek	49690
Bark River	49807
Bark River (Township)	49807
Bar Lake	49660
Barnard	49720
Barnes Lake-Millers Lake	48421
Baroda	49101
Baroda (Township)	49101
Barron Lake	49120
Barry (Township)	49060
Barryton	49305
Barton (Township)	49338
Barton City	48705
Barton Hills	48105
Barton Lake	49097
Base Line Lake	49055
Bass Lake	49449
Batavia	49036
Batavia (Township)	49036
Batavia Center	49036
Bates (Grand Traverse County)	49690
Bates (Iron County) (Township)	49935
Bath	48808
Bath (Township)	48808
Battle Creek	49015-18
For specific Battle Creek Zip Codes call (616) 965-3284, or your local postmaster.	
Bauer	49426
Baw Beese Lake	49242
Bay (Township)	49712
Bay City	48706-08
For specific Bay City Zip Codes call (517) 895-5555, or your local postmaster.	
Bay de Noc (Township)	49878
Bay Mills (Township)	49715
Bay Mills	49715
Bay Mills Indian Reservation	49715
Bay Port	48720
Bayshore	49711
Bay View	49770
Beachwood	48654
Beacon	49814
Beacon Hill	49905
Beadle Lake	49017
Beal City	48858
Bear Creek (Township)	49770
Bearinger (Township)	49759
Bear Lake (Hillsdale County)	49242
Bear Lake (Kalkaska County) (Township)	49646
Bear Lake (Manistee County)	49614
Bear Lake (Manistee County) (Township)	49614
Beaugrand (Township)	49721
Beaver (Bay County) (Township)	48611
Beaver (Newaygo County) (Township)	49309
Beaver Creek (Township)	48653
Beaverdam	49464
Beaver Grove	49855
Beaverton	48612
Beaverton (Township)	48612
Bedford (Calhoun County)	49020
Bedford (Calhoun County) (Township)	49017
Bedford (Monroe County) (Township)	48182

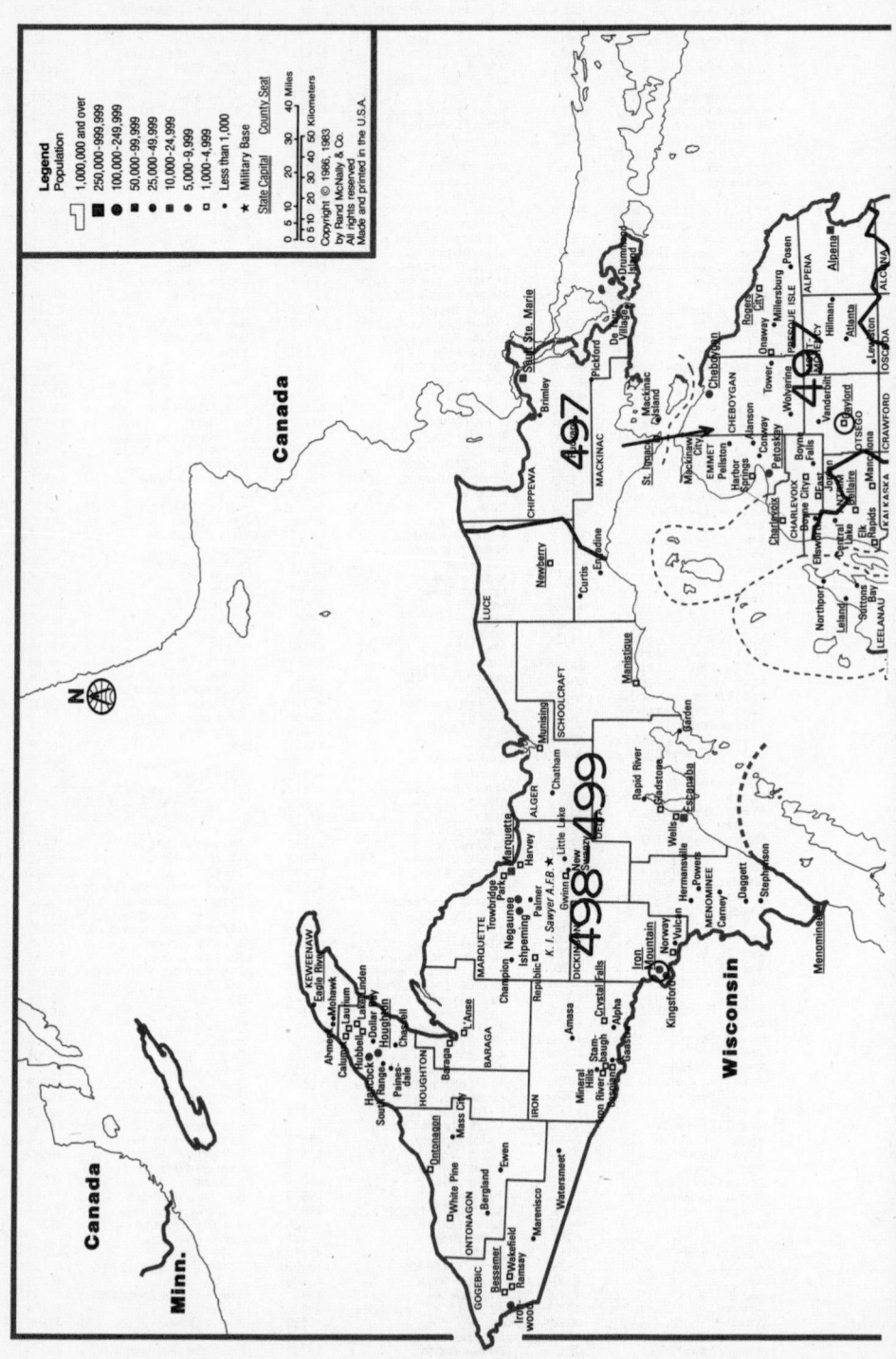

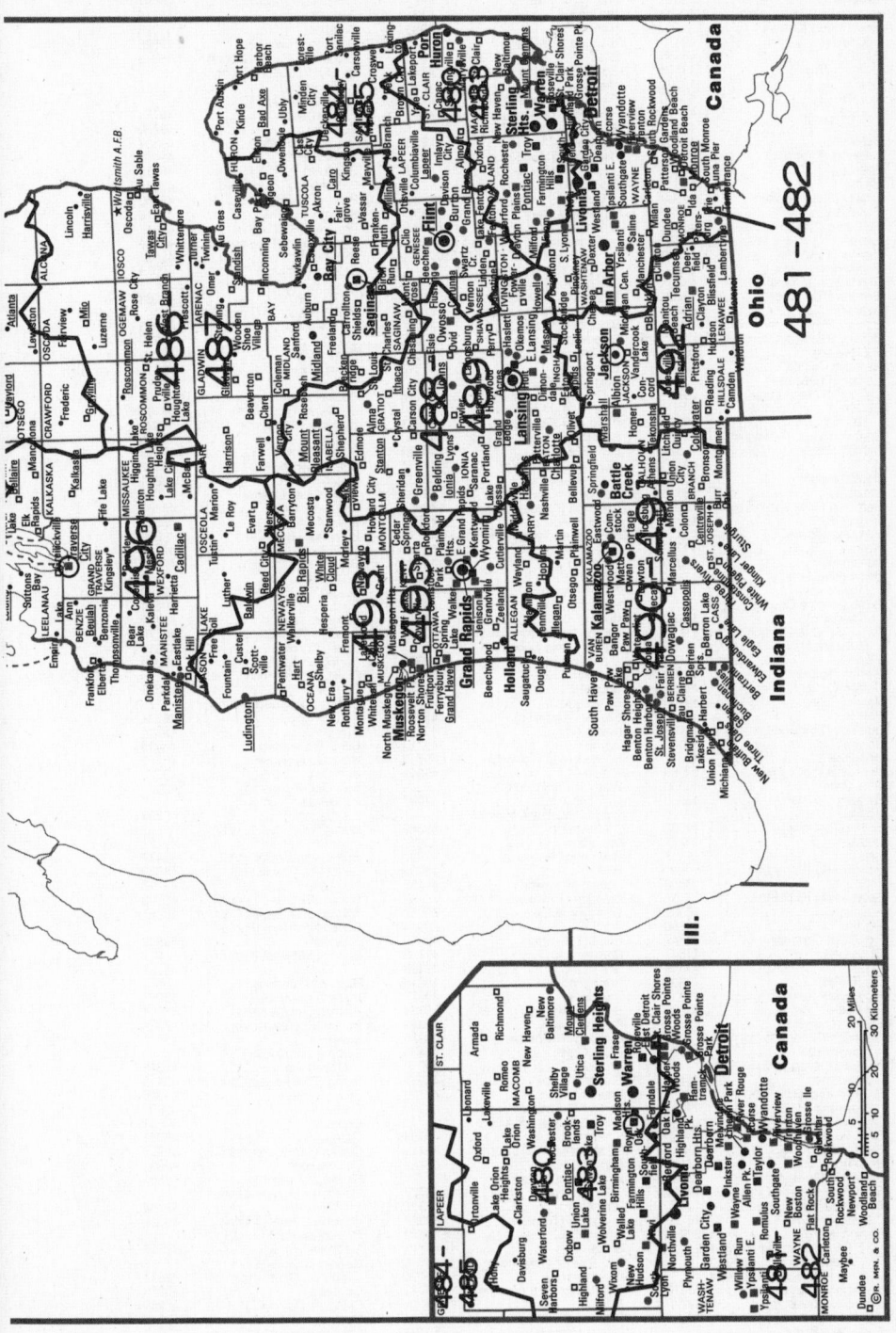

	ZIP
Beebe	48847
Beecher	48458
Beechwood (Iron County)	49909
Beechwood (Ottawa County)	49423
Belding	48809
Belknap (Township)	49743
Bell	49707
Bellaire	49615
Belleville	48111*
	48112†
Bellevue	49021
Bellevue (Township)	49021
Bell Oak	48892
Belmont	49306
Belsay (Part of Burton)	48503
Belvedere	49720
Belvidere (Township)	48886
Bendon	49643
Bengal (Township)	48879
Bennington	48867
Bennington (Township)	48867
Benona (Township)	49455
Bentheim	49419
Bentley (Bay County)	48613
Bentley (Gladwin County) (Township)	48652
Bentleys Corners	49245
Benton (Cheboygan County) (Township)	49721
Benton (Eaton County) (Township)	48876
Benton Charter (Township)	49022
Benton Harbor	49022*
	49023†
Benton Heights	49022
Benzonia	49616
Benzonia (Township)	49616
Bergland	49910
Bergland (Township)	49910
Berkley	48072
Berlamont	49026
Berlin (Ionia County) (Township)	48846
Berlin (Monroe County) (Township)	48166
Berlin (St. Clair County) (Township)	48002
Berne	48755
Berrien (Township)	49102
Berrien Center	49102
Berrien Springs	49103
Bertrand	49120
Bertrand (Township)	49120
Berville	48002
Bessemer	49911
Bessemer (Township)	49959
Bete Grise	49950
Bethany (Township)	48880
Bethany Beach	49125
Bethel (Township)	49028
Betzer	49271
Beulah	49617
Beverly Hills (Marquette County)	49866
Beverly Hills (Oakland County)	48009
Big Bay	49808
Big Creek (Township)	48647
Biggs Settlement	48647
Big Prairie (Township)	49349
Big Rapids	49307
Big Rapids (Township)	49307
Big Rock	49709
Billings (Township)	48612
Bingham (Clinton County) (Township)	48879
Bingham (Huron County) (Township)	48475
Bingham (Leelanau County) (Township)	49684
Bingham Farms	48025
Birch Beach	48450
Birch Creek	49858
Birch Run	48415
Birch Run (Township)	48415
Birchwood (Berrien County)	49115
Birchwood (Cheboygan County)	49721
Birmingham	48009-12
For specific Birmingham Zip Codes call (313) 646-4431, or your local postmaster.	
Birmingham Farms	48010
Bismarck (Township)	49779
Bitely	49309
Black Lake Bluffs	49765
Blackman (Township)	49202
Black River	48721
Black River Harbor	49938
Blaine (Benzie County) (Township)	49635

	ZIP
Blaine (St. Clair County)	48032
Blair (Township)	49684
Blanchard	49310
Blaney Park	49836
Blendon (Township)	49426
Bliss	49755
Bliss (Township)	49755
Blissfield	49228
Blissfield (Township)	49228
Bloomer (Township)	48811
Bloomfield (Huron County) (Township)	48468
Bloomfield (Missaukee County) (Township)	49651
Bloomfield (Oakland County) (Township)	49302
Bloomfield Glens	48322
Bloomfield Hills	48301-04
For specific Bloomfield Hills Zip Codes call (313) 697-7030, or your local postmaster.	
Bloomfield Hills North	48302
Bloomfield Township	48301-02
Bloomfield Town Square	48302
Bloomfield Village	48301
Bloomingdale	49026
Bloomingdale (Township)	49026
Blue Jacket	49913
Blue Lake (Kalkaska County) (Township)	49646
Blue Lake (Muskegon County) (Township)	49461
Blue Water Beach	48450
Bluff Beach	49099
Blumfield (Township)	48757
Blumfield Corners	48757
Boardman (Township)	49680
Bohemia (Township)	49965
Boichott Acres	48906
Bois Blanc (Township)	49775
Bolles Harbor	48161
Bombay	48642
Boon	49618
Boon (Township)	49618
Bootjack	49945
Borculo	49464
Boston (Houghton County)	49930
Boston (Ionia County) (Township)	48881
Bostwick Lake	49341
Bourret (Township)	48610
Bowens Mills	49333
Bowne (Township)	49302
Boyne City	49712
Boyne Falls	49713
Boyne Valley (Township)	49713
Bradley	49311
Brady (Kalamazoo County) (Township)	49097
Brady (Saginaw County) (Township)	48649
Brampton	49837
Brampton (Township)	49837
Branch	49402
Branch (Township)	49458
Brandon (Township)	48462
Brandywine Lake	49055
Brant	48614
Brant (Township)	48614
Brassar	49783
Bravo	49408
Breckenridge	48615
Breedsville	49027
Breen (Township)	49834
Breezy Beach	49099
Breitung (Township)	49876
Brent Creek	48433
Brethren	49619
Bretton Woods	48917
Brevort	49760
Brevort (Township)	49760
Briarwood (Part of Ann Arbor)	48108
Bridgehampton (Township)	48419
Bridgeport	48722
Bridgeport Charter (Township)	48722
Bridgeton	49327
Bridgeton (Township)	49327
Bridgeville	48879
Bridgewater	48115
Bridgewater (Township)	48158
Bridgman	49106
Brightmoor (Part of Detroit)	48223
Brighton	48116
Brighton (Township)	48116
Briley (Township)	49709
Brimley	49715
Brinton	48632
Bristol	49688
Britton	49229
Broad Acres	48035

	ZIP
Brockway	48097
Brockway (Township)	48097
Brohman	49312
Bronson	49028
Bronson (Township)	49028
Brookfield (Eaton County)	48813
Brookfield (Eaton County) (Township)	48813
Brookfield (Huron County) (Township)	48754
Brooklyn	49230
Brooks (Township)	49337
Brookside	49412
Brookville	48170
Broomfield (Township)	49340
Brown (Township)	49660
Brown City	48416
Brownlee Park	49017
Brownstown (Township)	48134
Brownsville	49031
Brownwood Lake	49079
Bruce (Chippewa County) (Township)	49783
Bruce (Macomb County) (Township)	48065
Bruce Crossing	49912
Bruningville	49779
Brunswick	49313
Brutus	49716
Buchanan	49107
Buchanan (Township)	49107
Buckeye (Township)	48624
Buckley	49620
Bucks Corners	49449
Buel (Township)	48422
Buena Vista	48601
Buena Vista Charter (Township)	48601
Bullock Creek	48642
Bumbletown	49805
Bunker Hill	49251
Bunker Hill (Township)	49251
Bunny Run	48362
Burdell (Township)	49688
Burdickville	49664
Burgess	49720
Burleigh (Township)	48770
Burley Corner	49017
Burlington (Calhoun County)	49029
Burlington (Calhoun County) (Township)	49029
Burlington (Lapeer County) (Township)	48727
Burnips	49314
Burns (Township)	48418
Burnside (Township)	48416
Burr Oak	49030
Burr Oak (Township)	49030
Burt (Alger County) (Township)	49839
Burt (Cheboygan County) (Township)	49721
Burt (Saginaw County)	48417
Burtchville (Township)	48059
Burt Lake	49717
Burton (Genesee County)	48509
Burton (Shiawassee County)	48867
Burton-Northeast (Part of Burton)	48509
Burton-Southeast (Part of Burton)	48529
Bushnell (Township)	48884
Butler (Township)	49082
Butman (Township)	48624
Butterfield (Township)	48632
Butternut	48811
Byron (Kent County) (Township)	49315
Byron (Shiawassee County)	48418
Byron Center	49315
Cadillac	49601
Cadmus	49231
Cady	48035
Calcite (Part of Rogers City)	49779
Calderwood	49967
Caldwell (Township)	49651
Caledonia (Alcona County) (Township)	48762
Caledonia (Kent County)	49316
Caledonia (Kent County) (Township)	49316
Caledonia (Shiawassee County) (Township)	48817
California	49255
California (Township)	49255
Calumet	49913
Calumet (Township)	49913
Calvin (Township)	49031
Calvin Center	49031
Cambria	49242
Cambria (Township)	49242
Cambridge (Township)	49265

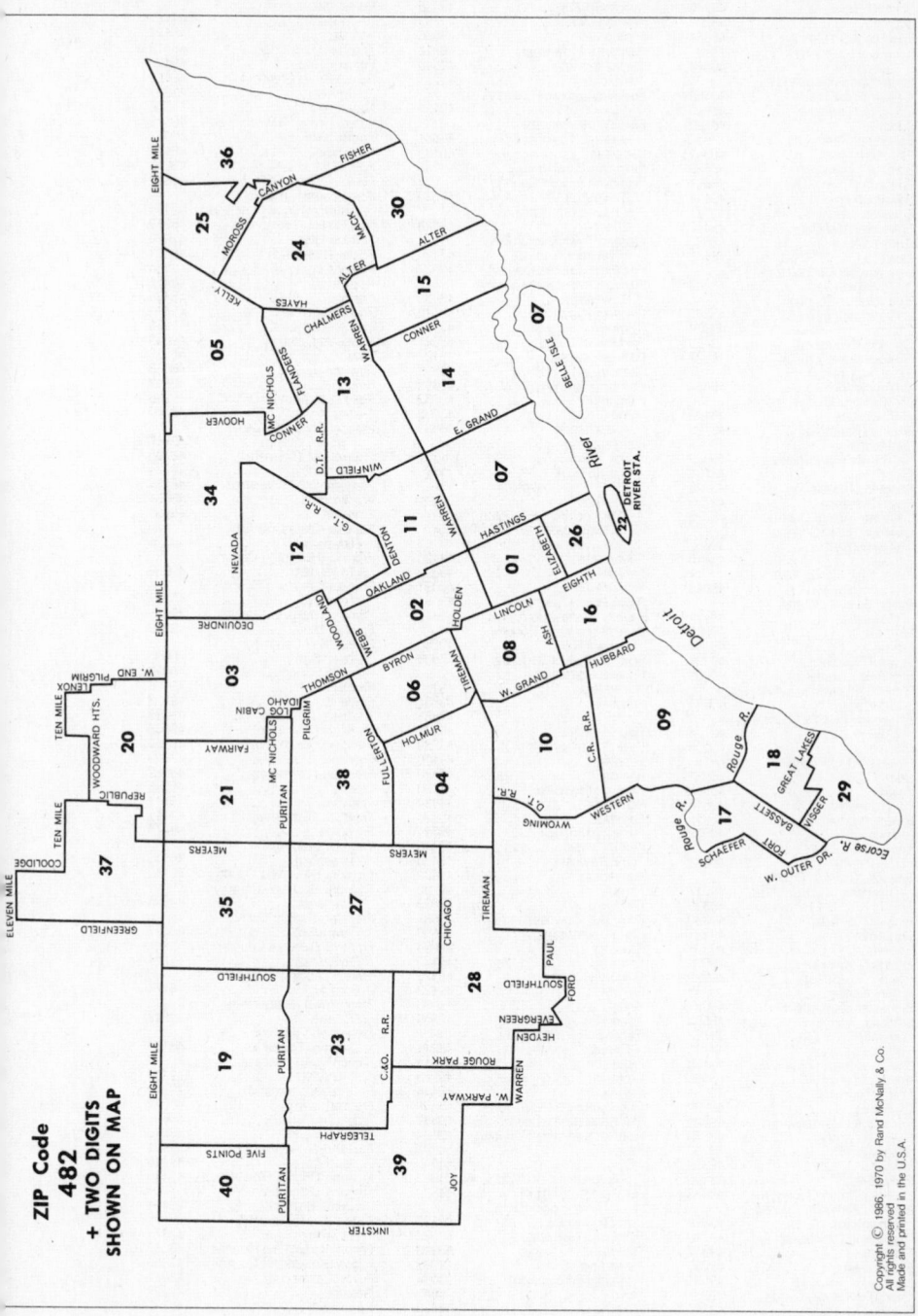

ZIP Code
482
+ TWO DIGITS
SHOWN ON MAP

	ZIP
Eckerman	49728
Eckford	49245
Eckford (Township)	49245
Ecorse	48229
Eden (Ingham County)	48854
Eden (Lake County) (Township)	49644
Eden (Mason County) (Township)	49454
Edenville (Township)	48620
Edenville	48620
Edgemont Park	48917
Edgerton	49341
Edmore	48829
Edwards (Township)	48661
Edwardsburg	49112
Edwards Corners	49067
Egelston (Township)	49442
Eight Point Lake	48632
Elba	48446
Elba (Lapeer County) (Township)	48446
Elba (Gratiot County) (Township)	48807
Elberta	49628
Elbridge (Township)	49459
Elizabeth Lake Estates	48327
Elk (Lake County) (Township)	49644
Elk (Sanilac County) (Township)	48466
Elkland (Township)	48726
Elk Rapids	49629
Elk Rapids (Township)	49629
Elkton	48731
Ellington (Township)	48723
Ellis (Township)	49705
Ellsworth (Antrim County)	49729
Ellsworth (Lake County) (Township)	49656
Elmdale	48815
Elmer (Oscoda County) (Township)	48647
Elmer (Sanilac County) (Township)	48471
Elm Hall	48830
Elmira	49730
Elmira (Township)	49730
Elm River (Township)	49965
Elmwood (Leelanau County) (Township)	49684
Elmwood (Tuscola County) (Township)	48726
Elo	49958
Eloise (Part of Westland)	48185
Elsie	48831
Elwell	48832
Ely (Township)	49814
Emerson (Township)	48615
Emmett	48022
Emmett (St. Clair County) (Township)	48022
Emmett (Calhoun County) (Township)	49017
Empire	49630
Empire (Township)	49630
Engadine	49827
Ensign	49878
Ensign (Township)	49878
Ensley (Township)	49329
Ensley Center	49343
Enterprise (Township)	49667
Entrican	48888
Epoufette	49762
Epsilon	49770
Erie	48133
Erie (Township)	48133
Erwin (Township)	49938
Escanaba	49829
Escanaba (Township)	49829
Essex (Township)	48879
Essexville	48732
Estey	48652
Estral Beach	48166
Eureka (Clinton County)	48833
Eureka (Montcalm County) (Township)	48838
Evangeline (Township)	49712
Evans	49319
Evans Lake	49287
Evart	49631
Evart (Township)	49631
Eveline (Township)	49727
Everett (Township)	49349
Evergreen (Montcalm County) (Township)	48884
Evergreen (Sanilac County) (Township)	48426
Evergreen Acres	48161
Evergreen Shores	49781
Ewen	49925
Ewing (Township)	49880

	ZIP
Excelsior (Township)	49646
Exeter (Township)	48159
Eyedywild Beach	49735
Fabius (Township)	49093
Factoryville	49066
Fairbanks (Township)	49817
Fairfax	49040
Fairfield	49221
Fairfield (Lenawee County) (Township)	49221
Fairfield (Shiawassee County) (Township)	48831
Fairgrove	48733
Fairgrove (Township)	48733
Fairhaven (Huron County) (Township)	48720
Fair Haven (St. Clair County)	48023
Fairlane Town Center (Part of Dearborn)	48126
Fair Plain (Berrien County)	49022
Fairplain (Montcalm County) (Township)	48838
Fairplain Plaza	49022
Fairport	49817
Fairview	48621
Fairview Heights	48197
Faithorn	49892
Faithorn (Township)	49892
Falmouth	49632
Fargo	48006
Farmers Creek	48455
Farmington	48331-36
For specific Farmington Zip Codes call (313) 474-9409, or your local postmaster.	
Farmington Hills	48331-34
For specific Farmington Hills Zip Codes call (313) 553-3910, or your local postmaster.	
Farrandville	48420
Farwell	48622
Fawn River	49091
Fawn River (Township)	49091
Fayette (Delta County)	49817
Fayette (Hillsdale County) (Township)	49250
Federal (Part of Saginaw)	48606
Federal Correctional Institution	48160
Felch	49831
Felch (Township)	49831
Felch Mountain	49801
Fenkell (Part of Detroit)	48238
Fennville	49408
Fenton	48430
Fenton (Township)	48430
Fenwick	48834
Ferndale	48220
Ferris (Township)	48891
Ferry	49455
Ferry (Township)	49455
Ferrysburg	49409
Fibre	49780
Fife Lake	49633
Fife Lake (Township)	49633
Filer (Township)	49660
Filer City	49634
Filion	48432
Fillmore (Township)	49423
Filmore	49423
Findley	49030
Fisher (Part of Wyoming)	49509
Fisher Building (Part of Detroit)	48211
Fisherville	48611
Fitchburg	49285
Five Lakes	48446
Five Points	48867
Flat Rock (Delta County)	49837
Flat Rock (Wayne County)	48134
Flint	48501-07
	48531-32
For specific Flint Zip Codes call (313) 257-1574, or your local postmaster.	
Flint (Township)	48532
Florence (Township)	49042
Florida	49913
Flowerfield	49093
Flowerfield (Township)	49093
Floyd	48640
Flushing	48433
Flushing (Township)	48433
Flynn (Township)	48453
Foote Site Village	48750
Ford Lake	49410
Ford River (Township)	49829
Ford River Station	49807
Ford River	49829
Forest (Cheboygan County) (Township)	49792

	ZIP
Forest (Genesee County) (Township)	48463
Forest (Missaukee County) (Township)	49651
Forester	48419
Forester (Township)	48419
Forest Grove	49426
Forest Grove Station	49426
Forest Hill	48801
Forest Hills	49506
Forest Home (Township)	49615
Forest Lake	49862
Forestville	48434
Fork (Township)	49305
Forsyth (Township)	49833
Fort Dearborn (Part of Dearborn)	48124
Fort Gratiot (Township)	48059
Fortune Lake	49920
Foster (Township)	48661
Foster City	49834
Fosters	48415
Fostoria	48435
Fountain	49410
Fountain Park	49266
Four Mile Corner	49868
Fowler	48835
Fowlerville	48836
Fox	49813
Fox Creek (Part of Detroit)	48215
Francisco	49240
Frandor Shopping Center (Part of Lansing)	48917
Frankenlust (Township)	48706
Frankenmuth	48734
Frankenmuth (Township)	48734
Frankentrost	48601
Frankfort	49635
Franklin (Clare County) (Township)	48625
Franklin (Houghton County) (Township)	49930
Franklin (Lenawee County) (Township)	49287
Franklin (Oakland County)	48025
Franklin Mine	49930
Fraser (Bay County) (Township)	48634
Fraser (Macomb County)	48026
Freda	49905
Frederic	49733
Frederic (Township)	49733
Fredonia (Township)	49068
Freedom (Township)	48158
Freeland	48623
Freeman (Township)	48632
Freeport	49325
Free Soil	49411
Free Soil (Township)	49411
Freiburger	48475
Fremont (Isabella County) (Township)	49310
Fremont (Newaygo County)	49412
Fremont (Saginaw County) (Township)	48655
Fremont (Sanilac County) (Township)	48097
Fremont (Tuscola County) (Township)	48744
French Landing (Part of Romulus)	48174
Frenchtown (Marquette County)	49849
Frenchtown (Monroe County) (Township)	48161
French Town (Oceana County)	49449
Friendship (Township)	49740
Frontier	49239
Frost (Township)	48625
Frost Corners	48875
Fruitland (Township)	49461
Fruitport	49415
Fruitport Charter (Township)	49415
Fruitport Siding (Part of Norton Shores)	49444
Fulton (Gratiot County) (Township)	48871
Fulton (Kalamazoo County)	49052
Fulton (Keweenaw County)	49950
Fulton Center	48871
Gaastra	49927
Gagetown	48735
Gaines	48436
Gaines (Genesee County) (Township)	48436
Gaines (Kent County) (Township)	49508
Galesburg	49053
Galien	49113
Galien (Township)	49113
Ganges	49408

	ZIP
Ganges (Township)	49408
Garden	49835
Garden (Township)	49835
Garden City	48135-36
For specific Garden City Zip Codes call (313) 421-8160, or your local postmaster.	
Garden Corners	49817
Gardendale	48059
Gardenville	49783
Gardner	49821
Garfield (Bay County) (Township)	48634
Garfield (Clare County) (Township)	49684
Garfield (Grand Traverse County) (Township)	49684
Garfield (Kalkaska County) (Township)	49633
Garfield (Mackinac County) (Township)	49827
Garfield (Newaygo County) (Township)	49337
Garnet	49762
Garth	49878
Gay	49945
Gaylord	49735
General Post Office (Part of Detroit)	48233
Genesee	48437
Genesee (Township)	48437
Geneva (Midland County) (Township)	48618
Geneva (Van Buren County) (Township)	49056
Genoa (Township)	48116
Georgetown (Township)	49426
Gera	48734
Germfask	49836
Germfask (Township)	49836
Gerrish (Township)	48653
Gibraltar	48173
Gibson (Allegan County)	49423
Gibson (Bay County) (Township)	48613
Gilbo Corners	49679
Gilchrist	49762
Gilead	49028
Gilead (Township)	49028
Gilford	48736
Gilford (Township)	48736
Gilmore (Benzie County) (Township)	49628
Gilmore (Isabella County) (Township)	48622
Gingellville	48359
Girard	49036
Girard (Township)	49036
Gladstone	49837
Gladwin	48624
Gladwin (Township)	48624
Glen Arbor	49636
Glen Arbor (Township)	49636
Glencoe Hills Apartments (Part of Ann Arbor)	48108
Glendale	49079
Glendora	49107
Glen Haven	49621
Glenn	49416
Glenn Haven Shores	49090
Glennie	48737
Glenn Shores	49090
Glenside (Part of Norton Shores)	49441
Glenwood	49047
Gobles	49055
Goetzville	49736
Golden (Township)	49436
Golfcrest	48161
Goodar (Township)	48761
Goodells	48027
Good Hart	49737
Goodison	48306
Goodland (Township)	48444
Goodrich	48438
Goodwell (Township)	49349
Gordon Beach	49129
Gordonville	48640
Gore (Township)	48468
Gotts Corners	48725
Gould City	49838
Gourley (Township)	49812
Gowen	49326
Graafschap	49423
Grace	49759
Graham Lake	49017
Grand Beach	49117
Grand Blanc	48439
Grand Blanc (Township)	48439
Grand Haven	49417
Grand Haven (Township)	49417
Grand Island (Township)	49862

	ZIP
Grand Junction	49056
Grand Ledge	48837
Grand Marais	49839
Grand Rapids	49501-88
For specific Grand Rapids Zip Codes call (616) 776-1415, or your local postmaster.	
Grand Rapids Charter (Township)	49505
Grand River (Part of Detroit)	48208
Grand View Acres	48167
Grand View Beach (Cheboygan County)	49749
Grandview Beach (Monroe County)	48145
Grandville	49418*
	49468†
Grant (Cheboygan County) (Township)	49721
Grant (Clare County) (Township)	48617
Grant (Grand Traverse County) (Township)	49647
Grant (Huron County) (Township)	48726
Grant (Iosco County) (Township)	48763
Grant (Keweenaw County) (Township)	49918
Grant (Mason County) (Township)	49411
Grant (Mecosta County) (Township)	49307
Grant (Newaygo County)	49327
Grant (Newaygo County) (Township)	49327
Grant (Oceana County) (Township)	49452
Grant (St. Clair County) (Township)	48032
Grant Center	49307
Grape	48161
Grass Lake (Gladwin County)	48624
Grass Lake (Jackson County)	49240
Grass Lake (Jackson County) (Township)	49240
Grassmere	48731
Gratiot (Part of Detroit)	48207
Grattan	48809
Grattan (Township)	48809
Gravel Lake	49065
Grawn	49637
Grayling	49738
Grayling (Township)	49738
Greater Galesburg	49053
Great Lake Beach	48450
Great Lakes Bible College	48917
Great Western (Part of Crystal Falls)	49920
Greeley	49753
Green (Alpena County) (Township)	49753
Green (Mecosta County) (Township)	49338
Green (Ontonagon County)	49953
Greenbush (Alcona County)	48738
Greenbush (Alcona County) (Township)	48738
Greenbush (Clinton County) (Township)	48833
Greendale (Township)	48883
Greenfield Village (Part of Dearborn)	48124
Green Lake (Allegan County)	49316
Green Lake (Grand Traverse County) (Township)	49684
Greenland	49929
Greenland (Township)	49929
Greenleaf (Township)	48726
Greenmead (Part of Livonia)	48153
Green Oak (Township)	48116
Green River	49659
Green Road (Part of Ann Arbor)	48113
Greenville	48838
Greenwood (Clare County) (Township)	48625
Greenwood (Marquette County)	49849
Greenwood (Oceana County) (Township)	49412
Greenwood (Ogemaw County)	48610
Greenwood (Oscoda County) (Township)	49756
Greenwood (St. Clair County) (Township)	48006

	ZIP
Greenwood (Wexford County) (Township)	49663
Gregory	48137
Greilickville	49684
Gresham	48813
Grim (Township)	48652
Grind Stone City	48467
Groos	49837
Gros Cap	49781
Grosse Ile (Township)	48138
Grosse Ile	48138
Grosse Pointe	48230
	48236
For specific Grosse Pointe Zip Codes call (313) 884-1640, or your local postmaster.	
Grosse Pointe (Township)	48236
Grosse Pointe Farms	48236
Grosse Pointe Park	48230
Grosse Pointe Shores	48236
Grosse Pointe Woods	48225
Grosvenor	49228
Grout (Township)	48624
Groveland (Township)	48462
Gulliver	49840
Gull Lake	49083
Gunplain (Township)	49080
Gustin (Township)	48740
Gwinn	49841
Hadley	48440
Hadley (Township)	48455
Hagar (Township)	49038
Hagar Shores	49039
Hagensville	49779
Hagerman Lake	49935
Haight (Township)	49912
Hale	48739
Halfway Corners	48441
Hamburg	48139
Hamburg (Township)	48169
Hamilton (Allegan County)	49419
Hamilton (Clare County) (Township)	48625
Hamilton (Gratiot County) (Township)	48847
Hamilton (Van Buren County) (Township)	49045
Hamlin (Eaton County) (Township)	48827
Hamlin (Mason County) (Township)	49431
Hammond Bay	49759
Hampton (Township)	48732
Hamtramck	48212
Hancock	49930
Hancock (Township)	49930
Handy (Township)	48836
Hannah	49649
Hannahville Indian Community	49896
Hanover (Jackson County)	49241
Hanover (Jackson County) (Township)	49241
Hanover (Wexford County) (Township)	49620
Harbert	49115
Harbor Beach	48441
Harbor Point	49740
Harbor Springs	49740
Harbor View	49777
Hardwood	49807
Haring (Township)	49601
Harlan	49625
Harlem	49423
Harper (Part of Detroit)	48213
Harper Woods	48225
Harrietta	49638
Harris	49845
Harris (Township)	49845
Harrisburg	49451
Harrison (Clare County)	48625
Harrison (Macomb County) (Township)	48045
Harrison Beach	49854
Harrison Township	48045
Harrisville	48740
Harrisville (Township)	48740
Harsens Island	48028
Hart	49420
Hart (Township)	49420
Hartford	49057
Hartford (Township)	49057
Hartland	48353
Hartland (Township)	48353
Hartwick (Township)	49631
Harvard	49319
Harvey	49855
Haslett	48840
Hastings	49058
Hastings (Township)	49058
Hatton (Township)	48625
Hautala Corner	49938

* Area Zip Code   † Post Office Boxes

	ZIP
Hawes (Township)	48742
Hawkhead	49416
Hawkins	49677
Hawks	49743
Hay (Township)	48624
Hayes (Charlevoix County) (Township)	49720
Hayes (Clare County) (Township)	48625
Hayes (Otsego County) (Township)	49735
Haynes (Township)	48742
Hazelhurst Camp	49115
Hazel Park	48030
Hazelton (Township)	48433
Heath (Township)	49419
Hebron (Township)	49755
Helena (Township)	49612
Hell	48169
Helmer	49853
Helps	49873
Hemans	48426
Hematite (Township)	49903
Hemlock	48626
Henderson (Shiawassee County)	48841
Henderson (Wexford County) (Township)	49601
Hendricks (Township)	49762
Henrietta (Township)	49259
Henry Street (Part of Norton Shores)	49441
Herman	49946
Hermansville	49847
Herron	49744
Hersey	49639
Hersey (Township)	49639
Hesperia	49421
Hessel	49745
Hetherton	49751
Hiawatha (Township)	49854
Hickory Corners	49060
Higgins (Township)	48653
Higgins Lake	48627
Highland	48356-57
For specific Highland Zip Codes call (313) 887-2211, or your local postmaster.	
Highland (Township)	49665
Highland Lakes	48167
Highland Park (Kalamazoo County)	49083
Highland Park (Wayne County)	48203
Highway	49913
Hi Hill Villa	48360
Hill (Township)	48739
Hillcrest	49938
Hillcrest Orchard	48145
Hilliards	49328
Hillman	49746
Hillman (Township)	49746
Hillsdale	49242
Hillsdale (Township)	49242
Hinchman	49103
Hinton (Township)	48850
Hockaday	48624
Hodunk	49094
Holland (Missaukee County) (Township)	48632
Holland (Ottawa County)	49422-24
For specific Holland Zip Codes call (616) 396-5201, or your local postmaster.	
Holland (Ottawa County) (Township)	49423
Holloway	49229
Holly	48442
Holly (Township)	48442
Holmes (Township)	49821
Holt	48842
Holton	49425
Holton (Township)	49425
Home (Montcalm County) (Township)	48829
Home (Newaygo County) (Township)	49309
Home Acres (Part of Wyoming)	49508
Homer (Calhoun County)	49245
Homer (Calhoun County) (Township)	49245
Homer (Midland County) (Township)	48640
Homestead (Benzie County) (Township)	49640
Homestead (Chippewa County)	49783
Hongore Bay	49765
Honor	49640
Hooper	49080

	ZIP
Hope (Barry County) (Township)	49058
Hope (Midland County)	48628
Hope (Midland County) (Township)	48628
Hopkins	49328
Hopkins (Township)	49328
Hopkinsburg	49328
Hopwood Acres	48912
Horr	48893
Horton (Jackson County)	49246
Horton (Ogemaw County) (Township)	48661
Houghton (Houghton County)	49931
Houghton (Keweenaw County) (Township)	49924
Houghton Lake	48629
Houghton Lake Heights	48630
Houghton Point	48629
Howard (Township)	49120
Howard City	49329
Howardsville	49067
Howell	48843*
	48844†
Hoxeyville	49601
Hubbard Lake	49747
Hubbardston	48845
Hubbell	49934
Hudson (Charlevoix County) (Township)	49730
Hudson (Lenawee County)	49247
Hudson (Lenawee County) (Township)	49247
Hudson (Mackinac County) (Township)	49762
Hudsonville	49426
Hulbert	49748
Hulbert (Township)	49748
Humboldt (Township)	49814
Hume (Township)	48467
Hunters Creek	48446
Huntington Woods	48070
Huron (Huron County) (Township)	48467
Huron (Wayne County) (Township)	48164
Huron Gardens	48341
Huronia Heights	48450
Huron Mountain	49808
Hurontown	49931
Huron Valley Men's Facility	48197
Huron Valley Women's Facility	48197
Hylas	49807
Ida	48140
Ida (Township)	48140
Idlewild	49642
Imlay (Township)	48444
Imlay City	48444
Imperial Heights	49861
Ina	49688
Independence (Township)	48346
Indianfield (Part of Portage)	49081
Indianfields (Township)	48723
Indian Lake	49047
Indian River	49749
Indiantown	48601
Ingalls	49848
Ingallston (Township)	49893
Ingersoll (Township)	48623
Ingham (Township)	48819
Ingleside	49755
Inkster	48141
Inland (Township)	49643
Inland Corners	49643
Interior (Township)	49967
Interlochen	49643
Inverness (Township)	49721
Inwood (Township)	49817
Ionia	48846
Ionia (Township)	48846
Ionia Maximum Correctional Facility	48846
Ionia Temporary Facility	48846
Iosco (Township)	48836
Ira (Township)	48023
Iron Mountain	49801*
	49802†
Iron River	49935
Iron River (Township)	49935
Irons	49644
Ironton	49720
Ironwood	49938
Ironwood (Township)	49938
Irving	49058
Irving (Township)	49058
Isabella (Delta County)	49878
Isabella (Isabella County) (Township)	48878
Isabella Indian Reservation	48858
Isadore	49621

	ZIP
Ishpeming	49849
Ishpeming (Township)	49849
Ithaca	48847
Iva	48626
Ivanrest (Part of Grandville)	49418
Jackson	49201-04
For specific Jackson Zip Codes call (517) 789-2400, or your local postmaster.	
Jacobsville	49945
Jam	48637
James (Township)	48609
Jamestown	49427
Jamestown (Township)	49426
Jasper (Lenawee County)	49248
Jasper (Midland County) (Township)	48880
Jeddo	48032
Jefferson (Cass County) (Township)	49112
Jefferson (Hillsdale County) (Township)	49266
Jefferson (Jackson County)	49230
Jefferson (Wayne County)	48214
Jenison	49428*
	49429†
Jennings	49651
Jericho Corners	49090
Jerome (Hillsdale County)	49249
Jerome (Midland County) (Township)	48657
Jessieville (Part of Ironwood)	49938
Johannesburg	49751
Johnstown (Township)	49050
Jones	49061
Jonesfield (Township)	48637
Jonesville	49250
Joppa	49051
Jordan (Township)	49729
Joyfield (Benzie County) (Township)	49616
Joyfield (Wayne County)	48228
Juddville	48817
Jugville	49349
Juhl	48453
Juniata	48744
Juniata (Township)	48768
Kaiserville	48137
Kalamazoo	49001-09
For specific Kalamazoo Zip Codes call (616) 388-7211, or your local postmaster.	
Kalamazoo (Township)	49004
Kalamo	49096
Kalamo (Township)	49096
Kaleva	49645
Kalkaska	49646
Kalkaska (Township)	49646
Karlin	49647
Kasson (Township)	49664
Kawkawlin	48631
Kawkawlin (Township)	48631
Kearney (Township)	49615
Kearsarge	49942
Keego Harbor	48320
Keeler	49057
Keeler (Township)	49057
Keene (Township)	48881
Kegomic	49770
Kellogg	49010
Kelloggsville (Part of Kentwood)	49508
Kellys Corners	49451
Kelsey Lake	49031
Kendall	49062
Kenockee (Township)	48006
Kensington (Part of Detroit)	48224
Kent City	49330
Kenton	49943
Kentwood	49508
Kerby	48817
Kessington	49112
Kewadin	49648
Keweenaw Bay	49908
Keystone	49684
Kibbie Corners	49090
Killarney Beach	48706
Killmaster	48740
Kilmanagh	48759
Kimball (Township)	48074
Kincheloe	49788
Kinde	48445
Kinderhook	49036
Kinderhook (Township)	49036
King Arthur's Court	48906
Kingsford	49801
Kingsley	49649
Kings Mill	48461
Kingston	48741
Kingston (Township)	48729

Place	ZIP	Place	ZIP	Place	ZIP
Kinneville	48827	L'Anse (Township)	49946	Linwood (Wayne County)	48206
Kinross	49752	L'Anse Indian Reservation	55401	Linwood Beach	48634
Kinross (Township)	49752	Lansing	48901-33	Lisbon	49403
Kinross Correctional Facility	49788	For specific Lansing Zip Codes		Liske	49743
Kipling	49837	call (517) 337-8711, or your local		Litchfield	49252
K.I.Sawyer AFB	49843	postmaster.		Litchfield (Township)	49252
K. I. Sawyer Air Force Base	49843	Lansing (Township)	48912	Littlefield (Township)	49706
Kissipee	49751	Lapeer	48446	Little Lake	49833
Kiva	49891	Lapeer (Township)	48446	Little Point Sable	49455
Klacking (Township)	48654	Laporte	48623	Little Traverse (Township)	49740
Klinger Lake	49091	Larkin (Township)	48642	Livernois (Part of Detroit)	48210
Klingville	49916	Larson Beach	48762	Livingston (Township)	49735
Klondike	49421	La Salle	48145	Livonia	48150-54
Kneeland	48647	La Salle (Township)	48145	For specific Livonia Zip Codes call	
Knollwood Park	49203	La Salle Gardens	48341	(313) 425-8050, or your local	
Kochville (Township)	48604	Lathrup Village	48076	postmaster.	
Koehler (Township)	49705	Laurium	49913	Livonia Mall (Part of Livonia)	48152
Koss	49887	Lawrence	49064	Loch Alpine	48103
Koylton (Township)	48741	Lawrence (Township)	49064	Locke (Township)	48895
Krakow (Township)	49776	Lawson	49885	Lockport (Township)	49032
La Branch	49873	Lawton	49065	Lodi (Kalkaska County)	49646
Lacey	49021	Layton Corners	48118	Lodi (Washtenaw County)	
Lachine	49753	Leaton	48858	(Township)	48103
Lac La Belle	49950	Leavitt (Township)	49459	Logan (Mason County)	
Lacota	49063	Lebanon (Township)	48845	(Township)	49402
Lafayette (Township)	48662	Ledyard (Part of Grand		Logan (Ogemaw County)	
Lagoon Beach	48706	Rapids)	49523	(Township)	48756
La Grange	49031	Lee (Allegan County)		London (Township)	48159
La Grange (Township)	49031	(Township)	49450	Long Lake (Clare County)	48625
Laing	48472	Lee (Calhoun County)		Long Lake (Grand Traverse	
Laingsburg	48848	(Township)	49068	County) (Township)	49684
Laird (Township)	49952	Lee (Midland County)		Long Lake (Ionia County)	48865
Lake (Benzie County)		(Township)	48640	Long Lake (Iosco County)	48743
(Township)	49640	Lee Center	49076	Long Lake Shores	48323
Lake (Clare County)	48632	Leelanau (Township)	49670	Long Point	49721
Lake (Huron County)		Leighton (Township)	49316	Long Rapids (Township)	49753
(Township)	48725	Leisure	49090	Longrie	49887
Lake (Lake County)		Leland	49654	Loomis	48617
(Township)	49304	Leland (Township)	49654	Loretto	49852
Lake (Macomb County)		Lemon Park	49097	Lost Lake Woods	48762
(Township)	48236	Lennon	48449	Loud (Township)	48619
Lake (Menominee County)		Lennon Green Estates	48449	Lovells	49738
(Township)	49821	Lenox (Township)	48050	Lovells (Township)	49738
Lake (Missaukee County)		Leonard	48367	Lowell	49331
(Township)	49651	Leoni	49201	Lowell (Township)	49331
Lake (Roscommon County)		Leoni (Township)	49201	Lucas	49657
(Township)	48629	Leonidas	49066	Ludington	49431
Lake Angeline (Part of		Leonidas (Township)	49066	Lulu	48140
Ishpeming)	49849	Le Roy (Township)	49655	Lum	48412
Lake Angelus	48326	Leroy (Calhoun County)		Luna Pier	48157
Lake Ann	49650	(Township)	49051	Lupton	48635
Lake Charter (Township)	49106	Leroy (Ingham County)		Luther	49656
Lake City	49651	(Township)	48892	Luzerne	48636
Lake Fenton	48430	Le Roy (Osceola County)	49655	Lyndon (Township)	48118
Lakefield (Luce County)		Les Cheneaux Club	49719	Lynn (Township)	48097
(Township)	49853	Leslie	49251	Lyon (Oakland County)	
Lakefield (Saginaw County)		Leslie (Township)	49251	(Township)	48167
(Township)	48637	Level Park	49017	Lyon (Roscommon County)	
Lake George	48633	Level Park-Oak Park	49017	(Township)	48653
Lakeland	48143	Levering	49755	Lyon Lake	49068
Lake Lansing	48840	Lewiston	49756	Lyons	48851
Lake Leelanau	49653	Lewisville	48468	Lyons (Township)	48851
Lake Linden	49945	Lexington	48450	Mable	49690
Lake Margrethe	49738	Lexington (Township)	48450	Macatawa	49434
Lake Mine	49948	Lexington Heights	48450	McBain	49657
Lake Nepessing	48446	Liberty (Jackson County)	49233	McBrides	48852
Lake Odessa	48849	Liberty (Jackson County)		McCords	49302
Lake Orion	48359-62	(Township)	49234	McDonald	49013
For specific Lake Orion Zip Codes		Liberty (Washtenaw County)	48107	McFarlands	49880
call (313) 693-8368, or your local		Liberty (Wexford County)		McGregor	49427
postmaster.		(Township)	49663	McIntyre Landing	49738
Lake Orion Heights (Part of		Liberty Corners	48144	McIvor	48748
Lake Orion)	48362*	Lilley (Township)	49309	Mackinac Island	49757
	48361†	Lima (Township)	48118	Mackinaw (Township)	49701
Lake Pleasant	48412	Lima Center	48130	Mackinaw City	49701
Lakeport	48059	Lime Island	49736	McKinley (Emmet County)	
Lake Roland	49968	Limestone	49816	(Township)	49769
Lakeside (Berrien County)	49116	Limestone (Township)	49816	McKinley (Huron County)	
Lakeside (Huron County)	48467	Lincoln (Alcona County)	48742	(Township)	48755
Lakeside (Macomb County)	48310	Lincoln (Arenac County)		McKinley (Oscoda County)	48647
Lakeside Landing	48430	(Township)	48658	McLean	49412
Laketon (Township)	49445	Lincoln (Clare County)		McLeods Corner	49868
Laketown (Township)	49423	(Township)	48633	McMillan (Luce County)	49853
Lakeview (Berrien County)	49129	Lincoln (Huron County)		McMillan (Luce County)	
Lakeview (Calhoun County)	49015	(Township)	48432	(Township)	49868
Lakeview (Montcalm		Lincoln (Isabella County)		McMillan (Ontonagon	
County)	48850	(Township)	48883	County) (Township)	49925
Lakeview Square (Part of		Lincoln (Midland County)		McMillan Corner	49853
Battle Creek)	49017	(Township)	48640	Macomb	48042†
Lakeville	48366	Lincoln (Newaygo County)			48044*
Lakewood (Kalamazoo		(Township)	49349	Macomb (Township)	48042
County)	49002	Lincoln (Osceola County)		Macomb Mall (Part of	
Lakewood (Monroe County)	48157	(Township)	49677	Roseville)	48066
Lakewood Club	49457	Lincoln Charter (Township)	49127	Macon	49236
Lamar (Part of Wyoming)	49509	Lincoln Park (Muskegon		Macon (Township)	49236
Lamb	48027	County)	49441	Madison Center (Part of	
Lambertville	48144	Lincoln Park (Wayne		Madison Heights)	48071
Lamont	49430	County)	48146	Madison Charter (Township)	49221
Lamotte (Township)	48426	Linden	48451	Madison Heights	48071
Lanewood (Part of Chelsea)	48118	Linden Hills	49042	Mancelona	49659
Langston	48888	Linkville	48755	Mancelona (Township)	49659
L'Anse	49946	Linwood (Bay County)	48634	Manchester	48158

	ZIP
Manchester (Township)	48158
Manistee	49660
Manistee (Township)	49660
Manistique	49854
Manistique (Township)	49854
Manitou Beach (Lenawee County)	49253
Manitou Beach (Presque Isle County)	49779
Manitou Beach-Devils Lake	49253
Manlius (Township)	49408
Manning	49721
Mansfield (Township)	49920
Mansfield	49881
Manton	49663
Maple (Part of Dearborn)..	48126
Maple City	49664
Maple Forest (Township) ...	49738
Maple Grove (Barry County)	49073
Maple Grove (Barry County) (Township)	49073
Maple Grove (Manistee County) (Township)	49645
Maple Grove (Saginaw County) (Township)	48460
Maple Grove Corners	49090
Maple Hill	49339
Maple Lake (Part of Paw Paw)	49079
Maple Rapids	48853
Maple Ridge (Alpena County) (Township)	49707
Maple Ridge (Arenac County)	48766
Maple Ridge (Delta County) (Township)	49880
Maple River (Township)	49716
Mapleton (Grand Traverse County)	49684
Mapleton (Midland County)	48640
Maple Valley (Montcalm County) (Township)	49347
Maple Valley (Roscommon County)	48656
Maple Valley (Sanilac County) (Township)	48416
Marathon (Township)	48421
Marcellus	49067
Marcellus (Township)	49067
Marengo	49224
Marengo (Township)	49224
Marenisco	49947
Marenisco (Township)	49947
Marilla (Township)	49625
Marine City	48039
Marion (Charlevoix County) (Township)	49720
Marion (Livingston County) (Township)	48843
Marion (Osceola County) ..	49665
Marion (Osceola County) (Township)	49665
Marion (Saginaw County) (Township)	48614
Marion (Sanilac County) (Township)	48426
Marion Springs	48614
Markey (Township)	48629
Marlette	48453
Marlette (Township)	48453
Marne...................	49435
Marquette (Mackinac County) (Township)	49774
Marquette (Marquette County)	49855
Marquette (Marquette County) (Township)	49855
Marshall	49068
Marshall (Township)	49068
Martin	49070
Martin (Township)	49070
Martiny (Township)	49342
Marysville	48040
Mason (Arenac County) (Township)	48766
Mason (Cass County) (Township)	49112
Mason (Houghton County)	49930
Mason (Ingham County) ..	48854
Masonville (Township)	49878
Mass City	49948
Mastodon (Township)	49902
Matchwood (Township)	49925
Matherton	48845
Mathias (Township)	49891
Mattawan	49071
Matteson (Township)	49028
Matteson Lake	49028
Max Myers Addition	49120
Maybee	48159
Mayfield (Grand Traverse County).................	49666

	ZIP
Mayfield (Grand Traverse County) (Township)	49649
Mayfield (Lapeer County) (Township)	48446
Mayflower	49913
Mayville	48744
Maywood	49878
Meade (Huron County) (Township)	48432
Meade (Macomb County)	48048
Meade (Mason County) (Township)	49411
Meads Landing...........	48629
Mears...................	49436
Meauwataka	49601
Mecosta	49332
Mecosta (Township)	49346
Medina..................	49247
Medina (Township)	49247
Melita	48659
Mellen (Township)	49848
Melrose (Township)	49796
Melstrand	49884
Melvin	48454
Melvindale	48122
Memphis	48041
Mendon	49072
Mendon (Township)	49072
Menominee	49858
Menominee (Township)	49858
Menonaqua Beach	49740
Mentha	49055
Mentor (Cheboygan County) (Township)	49799
Mentor (Oscoda County) (Township)	48647
Meredith	48624
Meridian (Township)	48823
Meridian Mall	48864
Merrill (Newaygo County) (Township)	49309
Merrill (Saginaw County) ..	48637
Merriman	49801
Merritt (Bay County) (Township)	48747
Merritt (Missaukee County)	49667
Merriweather	49947
Merson	49010
Mesick	49668
Metamora	48455
Metamora (Township)	48455
Metropolitan	49801
Metropolitan Airport (Part of Romulus)	48242-44
For specific Metropolitan Airport Zip Codes call (313) 942-7716, or your local postmaster.	
Metropolitan Airport South Terminal (Part of Romulus)	48242-44
For specific Metropolitan Airport South Terminal Zip Codes call (313) 942-7716, or your local postmaster.	
Metz....................	49776
Metz (Township)	49776
Meyer (Township)	49847
Miami Park	49090
Michiana	49117
Michigamme	49861
Michigamme (Township) ...	49861
Michigan Center	49254
Michigan Reformatory	48846
Michigan State University	48824
Michigan State University Residence Halls	48825
Michigan Training Unit	48846
Middlebelt (Part of Romulus)	48174
Middle Branch (Township)	49665
Middlebury (Township).....	48866
Middleton	48856
Middletown	48817
Middle Village	49737
Middleville	49333
Midland	48640-42
For specific Midland Zip Codes call (517) 631-6580, or your local postmaster.	
Midland (Township)	48642
Midland Park	49060
Mikado	48745
Mikado (Township)	48745
Milan (Monroe County) (Township)	48160
Milan (Washtenaw County)	48160
Milford	48380-81
For specific Milford Zip Codes call (313) 684-0775, or your local postmaster.	
Milford (Township)	48381
Millbrook	49334
Millbrook (Township).......	49334

	ZIP
Millburg	49022
Millecoquins	49827
Millen (Township)	48705
Millersburg	49759
Millett	48917
Milleville Beach	48173
Mill Grove	49010
Millington	48746
Millington (Township)	48746
Mill Lake	49055
Mills (Houghton County) ..	49934
Mills (Midland County) (Township).............	48652
Mills (Ogemaw County) (Township)	48756
Mills (Sanilac County)	48427
Millville	49285
Milnes	49250
Milton (Antrim County) (Township)	49648
Milton (Cass County) (Township)	49120
Minards Mill	49269
Minden (Township)	48456
Minden City	48456
Mineral Hills	49935
Minor Beach	49854
Mio	48647
Missaukee Park	49651
Mitchell (Township)	48728
M & M Plaza (Part of Menominee)	49858
Moddersville.............	48632
Moffatt (Township)	48610
Mohawk	49950
Moline	49335
Moltke (Township)	49779
Monitor (Township)	48706
Monongahela Location.....	49920
Monroe (Monroe County)	48161
Monroe (Monroe County) (Township)	48161
Monroe (Newaygo County) (Township)	49349
Monroe Center	49637
Montague	49437
Montague (Township)	49437
Montcalm (Township)	48838
Monterey (Township)	49010
Monterey Center	49010
Montgomery	49255
Montmorency (Township)	49746
Montrose	48457
Montrose (Township)	48457
Moore (Township)	48471
Moore Park	49093
Moorestown	49651
Mooreville	48160
Moorland	49451
Moorland (Township)	49451
Moran	49760
Moran (Township)	49781
Morenci	49256
Morgan	49073
Morgan Corners	49017
Morley	49336
Morrice	48857
Morseville	48415
Morton (Township)	49332
Moscow	49257
Moscow (Township)	49257
Mosherville	49258
Mosherville Station	49250
Motley	49952
Mott Park (Part of Flint) ...	48504
Mottville	49099
Mottville (Township)	49099
Mound Spring	49091
Mountain Beach	49460
Mount Clemens	48043-46
For specific Mount Clemens Zip Codes call (313) 465-1936, or your local postmaster.	
Mount Clemens Southeast	48043
Mount Elliott (Part of Detroit)	48234
Mount Forest	48650
Mount Forest (Township)	48650
Mount Haley (Township) ...	48637
Mount Morris	48458
Mount Morris (Township)...	48458
Mount Pleasant (Allegan County)	49090
Mount Pleasant (Isabella County)	48804
	48858
For specific Mount Pleasant Zip Codes call (517) 773-3653, or your local postmaster.	
Mount Vernon	48306
Mueller (Township)	49840
Muir	48860
Mullet Lake..............	49761

	ZIP
Mullett (Township)	49791
Mulliken	48861
Mundy (Township)	48507
Munger	48747
Munising	49862
Munising (Township)	49895
Munith	49259
Munro (Township)	49755
Munson	49256
Muskegon	49440-45
For specific Muskegon Zip Codes call (616) 722-7292, or your local postmaster.	
Muskegon (Township)	49445
Muskegon Heights	49444
Muskegon Mall (Part of Muskegon)	49440
Mussey (Township)	48014
Muttonville (Part of Richmond)	48062
Nadeau	49863
Nadeau (Township)	49863
Nagel Corner	49743
Nahma	49864
Nahma (Township)	49864
Napoleon	49261
Napoleon (Township)	49261
Nashville	49073
Nathan	49821
National (Part of Crystal Falls)	49920
National City	48748
National Mine	49865
Naubinway	49762
Nazareth (Part of Kalamazoo)	49074
Needmore	48813
Neeley	49080
Negaunee	49866
Negaunee (Township)	49866
Nelson (Kent County) (Township)	49343
Nelson (Saginaw County)	48626
Nessen City	49683
Nester (Township)	48624
Nestoria	49861
New Allouez	49901
Newark (Gratiot County) (Township)	48847
Newark (Oakland County)	48442
New Baltimore	48047
Newberg (Township)	49061
Newberry	49868
New Boston	48164
New Bristol Location	49920
New Buffalo	49117
New Buffalo (Township)	49117
New Era	49446
Newfield (Township)	49421
New Greenleaf	48726
New Haven (Gratiot County) (Township)	48889
New Haven (Macomb County)	48048
New Haven (Shiawassee County) (Township)	48867
New Holland	49423
New Hudson	48165
Newkirk (Township)	49656
Newland	49660
New Lothrop	48460
Newport	48166
New Richmond	49447
New Salem	49315
New Swanzy	49841
Newton (Calhoun County) (Township)	49017
Newton (Mackinac County) (Township)	49838
New Troy	49119
Nicholsville	49067
Niles	49120
Niles (Township)	49120
Nirvana	49623
Nisula	49952
Noble (Township)	49028
Noordeloos	49423
Norman (Township)	49689
North Adams	49262
North Allis (Township)	49765
North Bell	48815
North Blendon	49426
North Bradley	48618
North Branch (Township)	48461
North Branch	48461
North Dorr	49323
Northeast (Part of Livonia)	48152
North End (Part of Detroit)	48202
North Epworth	49431
Northfield (Township)	48189
Northgate	49505

	ZIP
North Kent Mall	49505
North Lake (Lapeer County)	48464
North Lake (Marquette County)	49849
North Lake (Van Buren County)	49055
North Lakeport	48059
Northland	49869
Northland Shopping Center (Part of Southfield)	48075
North Manitou	49654
North Morenci	49256
North Muskegon	49445
North Paynesville	49912
North Plains (Township)	48845
Northport	49670
Northport Point	49670
North Shade (Township)	48856
North Shores	48145
North Side (Part of Flint)	48505
North Star	48862
North Star (Township)	48862
North Street	48049
Northview	49505
Northville (Kent County)	49505
Northville (Wayne County)	48167
Northville (Wayne County) (Township)	48167
Northville Commons	48167
Northville Regional Psychiatric Hospital	48167
Northwest (Part of Grand Rapids)	49504
Northwestern (Part of Detroit)	48204
North Wheeler	48662
Northwood	49004
Norton Shores	49441
Norvell	49263
Norvell (Township)	49263
Norwalk	49660
Norway	49870
Norway (Township)	49892
Norwich (Missaukee County) (Township)	49651
Norwich (Newaygo County) (Township)	49307
Norwood	49720
Norwood (Township)	49720
Nottawa (Township)	49075
Nottawa (Isabella County) (Township)	48858
Nottawa (St. Joseph County)	49075
Novesta (Township)	48729
Novi	48374-77
For specific Novi Zip Codes call (313) 349-2100, or your local postmaster.	
Novi (Township)	48375
Nunda (Township)	49799
Nunica	49448
Oakfield (Township)	48838
Oak Grove (Livingston County)	48863
Oak Grove (Otsego County)	49735
Oak Grove (Roscommon County)	48653
Oak Hill	49660
Oakhurst	48701
Oakland	49419
Oakland Charter (Township)	48363
Oakley	48649
Oak Manor	49120
Oak Park (Calhoun County)	49017
Oak Park (Oakland County)	48237
Oaks Correctional Facility	49626
Oak Shade Park	49230
Oakville	48160
Oakwood (Oakland County)	48371
Oakwood (St. Joseph County)	49099
Oakwood (Wayne County)	48122
Oceola (Township)	48843
Ocqueoc (Presque Isle County)	49759
Ocqueoc (Presque Isle County) (Township)	49759
Oden	49764
Odessa (Township)	48849
Odgers Location	49920
Ogden (Township)	49228
Ogden Center	49228
Ogemaw (Township)	48661
Ogemaw Springs	48661
Oil City	48883
Okemos	48805†
	48864*
Old Mission	49673
Old Redford (Part of Detroit)	48219
Olive (Clinton County) (Township)	48879

	ZIP
Olive (Ottawa County) (Township)	49460
Olive Center	49423
Olive Hills	49460
Oliver (Huron County) (Township)	48731
Oliver (Kalkaska County) (Township)	49646
Olivet (Eaton County)	49076
Olson	48640
Omena	49674
Omer	48749
Onaway	49765
Oneida Charter (Township)	48837
Onekama	49675
Onekama (Township)	49675
Onondaga	49264
Onondaga (Township)	49264
Onota (Township)	49822
Onsted	49265
Ontonagon	49953
Ontonagon (Township)	49953
Ontwa (Township)	49112
Orange (Ionia County) (Township)	48846
Orange (Kalkaska County) (Township)	49646
Orangeville	49080
Orangeville (Township)	49080
Orchard Beach	49721
Orchard Lake	48323-24
For specific Orchard Lake Zip Codes call (313) 626-9873, or your local postmaster.	
Orchard Park (Part of Battle Creek)	49017
Oregon (Township)	48446
Orient (Township)	49679
Orion	48360-62
For specific Orion Zip Codes call (313) 693-8368, or your local postmaster.	
Orleans	48865
Orleans (Township)	48865
Oronoko (Township)	49103
Ortonville	48462
Osceola (Houghton County)	49913
Osceola (Houghton County) (Township)	49913
Osceola (Osceola County) (Township)	49631
Oscoda	48750
Oscoda (Township)	48750
Oscoda Indian Mission	48745
Oshtemo	49077
Oshtemo (Township)	49077
Osier	49878
Oskar	49931
Osseo	49266
Ossineke	49766
Ossineke (Township)	49747
Otisco (Township)	48809
Otisville	48463
Otsego	49078
Otsego (Township)	49078
Otsego Lake	49735
Otsego Lake (Township)	49735
Ottawa Beach	49423
Ottawa Center	49404
Ottawa Lake	49267
Otterburn (Part of Swartz Creek)	48473
Otter Lake	48464
Otto (Township)	49421
Overisel	49423
Overisel (Township)	49423
Ovid (Branch County) (Township)	49036
Ovid (Clinton County)	48866
Ovid (Clinton County) (Township)	48866
Owasippe	49457
Owendale	48754
Owosso	48867
Owosso (Township)	48867
Owosso Junction (Part of Owosso)	48867
Oxford	48370-71
For specific Oxford Zip Codes call (313) 628-2557, or your local postmaster.	
Oxford (Township)	48371
Ozark	49760
Paavola	49930
Painesdale	49955
Paka Plaza (Part of Jackson)	49202
Palestine	49887
Palisades Park	49043
Palmer	49871
Palms	48465
Palmyra	49268

* Area Zip Code   † Post Office Boxes

	ZIP
Palmyra (Township)	49268
Palo	48870
Paradise (Chippewa County)	49768
Paradise (Grand Traverse County)	49649
Parchment	49004
Paris (Huron County) (Township)	48470
Paris (Mecosta County)	49338
Parisville	48470
Park (Ottawa County) (Township)	49423
Park (St. Joseph County) (Township)	49093
Parkdale	49660
Parkers Corners	48836
Park Grove (Part of Detroit)	48205
Park Lake	48808
Park Plaza (Part of Lincoln Park)	48146
Park Shore Resort	49031
Parkville	49093
Parma	49269
Parma (Township)	49224
Parnell	49301
Parshallville	48430
Partello	49076
Patterson Gardens	48161
Patterson Lake	48169
Paulding	49912
Pavilion (Township)	49088
Paw Paw	49079
Paw Paw (Township)	49079
Paw Paw Lake	49038
Payment	49783
Paynesville	49912
Peacock	49644
Peacock (Township)	49644
Peaine (Township)	49782
Pearl	49408
Pearl Beach (Branch County)	49036
Pearl Beach (St. Clair County)	48001
Pearl Grange	49022
Peck	48466
Pelkie	49958
Pellston	49769
Peninsula (Township)	49684
Penn	49031
Penn (Township)	49031
Pennellwood	49103
Pennfield	49017
Pennfield (Township)	49017
Penobscot (Part of Detroit)	48226-28
For specific Penobscot Zip Codes call (313) 965-1331, or your local postmaster.	
Pentland (Township)	49868
Pentoga	49920
Pentwater	49449
Pentwater (Township)	49449
Pequaming	49946
Pere Marquette Charter (Township)	49431
Perkins	49872
Perrinton	48871
Perronville	49873
Perry	48872
Perry (Township)	48872
Perry Acres	48360
Perry Lake Heights	48462
Peshawbestown	49682
Peters	48039
Petersburg	49270
Petoskey	49770
Pewabic	49930
Pewamo	48873
Phillipsville	49805
Phoenix (Keweenaw County)	49950
Phoenix (Oakland County)	48342
Phoenix Correctional Facility	48170
Pickford	49774
Pickford (Township)	49774
Pier Cove	49090
Pierport	49614
Pierson	49339
Pierson (Township)	49339
Pigeon	48755
Pinckney	48169
Pinconning	48650
Pinconning (Township)	48650
Pine (Township)	48888
Pine Bluffs	48653
Pine Creek	49051
Pine Grove	49055
Pine Grove (Township)	49055
Pine River (Arenac County)	48658
Pine River (Gratiot County) (Township)	48801

	ZIP
Pine Run	48420
Pine Stump Junction	49868
Piney Woods	48625
Pinnebog	48445
Pinora (Township)	49677
Pioneer (Township)	49651
Pipestone (Township)	49111
Pittsburg	48867
Pittsfield (Township)	48108
Pittsford	49271
Pittsford (Township)	49271
Plainfield (Iosco County) (Township)	48739
Plainfield (Kent County) (Township)	49321
Plainfield (Livingston County)	48137
Plainfield Heights	49505
Plainwell	49080
Platte (Township)	49640
Pleasant Lake (Hillsdale County)	49266
Pleasant Lake (Jackson County)	49272
Pleasant Lake (Washtenaw County)	48158
Pleasanton (Township)	49614
Pleasant Plains (Township)	49304
Pleasant Ridge	48069
Pleasant Valley	48880
Pleasant View (Township)	49740
Plymouth (Gogebic County)	49968
Plymouth (Wayne County)	48170
Plymouth (Wayne County) (Township)	48170
Plymouth Township	48170
Pogy	49639
Point Au Gres	48703
Pointe Aux Barques	48467
Pointe Aux Barques (Township)	48467
Pointe aux Peaux Farms	48166
Pointe aux Pins	49775
Point Nipigon	49721
Pokagon	49047
Pokagon (Township)	49047
Polkton (Township)	49404
Pomona	49625
Pompeii	48874
Ponchartrain Shores	49781
Ponshewaing	49706
Pontiac	48322-25
	48340-43
For specific Pontiac Zip Codes call (313) 338-4511, or your local postmaster.	
Portage (Houghton County) (Township)	49921
Portage (Kalamazoo County)	49081
Portage (Mackinac County) (Township)	49820
Portage Entry	49916
Portage Lake	48169
Port Austin	48467
Port Austin (Township)	48467
Port Austin Air Force Station	48467
Porter (Cass County) (Township)	49042
Porter (Midland County) (Township)	48615
Porter (Van Buren County) (Township)	49065
Port Gypsum (Part of Tawas City)	48763
Port Hope	48468
Port Huron	48059-61
For specific Port Huron Zip Codes call (313) 984-4121, or your local postmaster.	
Port Huron (Township)	48060
Portland	48875
Portland (Township)	48875
Port Sanilac	48469
Port Sheldon	49460
Port Sheldon (Township)	49460
Portsmouth (Township)	48708
Posen	49776
Posen (Township)	49776
Poseyville	48640
Potters Lake	48423
Potterville	48876
Powell	49808
Powers	49874
Prairie Ronde (Township)	49087
Prairieville	49046
Prairieville (Township)	49080
Prattville	49273
Prescott	48756
Presque Isle	49777
Presque Isle (Township)	49777
Princeton	49841

	ZIP
Prosper	49632
Prudenville	48651
Pulaski	49241
Pulaski (Township)	49241
Pulawski (Township)	49776
Pullman	49450
Putnam (Township)	48169
Quanicassee	48733
Quarry	48720
Quimby	49058
Quincy (Branch County)	49082
Quincy (Branch County) (Township)	49082
Quincy (Houghton County) (Township)	49930
Quincy Mine	49930
Quinnesec	49876
Rabbit Bay	49945
Rabbits Back	49781
Raber	49736
Raber (Township)	49736
Raco	49778
Rainy Beach	49765
Raisin (Township)	49221
Raisinville (Township)	48161
Ralph	49877
Rambaultown	49913
Ramsay	49959
Ranch Acres	49456
Randall Lake	49036
Randville	49801
Rankin	48473
Ransom	49266
Ransom (Township)	49266
Rapid City	49676
Rapid River (Delta County)	49878
Rapid River (Kalkaska County) (Township)	49659
Rapson	48413
Rathbone	48615
Rattle Run	48079
Ravenna	49451
Ravenna (Township)	49451
Ravenswood	48917
Ray (Branch County)	46737
Ray (Macomb County) (Township)	48096
Ray Center	48096
Raymond Corners	49656
Reading	49274
Reading (Township)	49274
Readmond (Township)	49723
Redding (Township)	48625
Redford	48239-40
For specific Redford Zip Codes call (313) 937-0360, or your local postmaster.	
Redford A	48240
Redman	48468
Red Oak	49756
Red Park	49660
Redridge	49931
Reed City	49677
Reeder (Township)	49651
Reeds Lake (Part of East Grand Rapids)	49506
Reeman	49412
Reese	48757
Regional Shopping Center	48043
Remus	49340
Renaissance Center (Part of Detroit)	48243
Reno (Township)	48770
Republic	49879
Republic (Township)	49879
Rescue	48735
Resort (Township)	49770
Rexton	49762
Reynolds (Township)	49329
Rhodes	48652
Rich (Township)	48744
Richfield (Genesee County) (Township)	48423
Richfield (Roscommon County) (Township)	48656
Richfield Center	48423
Richland	49083
Richland (Township)	49083
Richland (Missaukee County) (Township)	49657
Richland (Montcalm County) (Township)	48891
Richland (Ogemaw County) (Township)	48756
Richland (Saginaw County) (Township)	48626
Richmond (Macomb County)	48062
Richmond (Macomb County) (Township)	48062
Richmond (Marquette County) (Township)	49871

	ZIP		ZIP		ZIP
Richmond (Osceola County) (Township)	49677	Rust	49746	Sebewaing (Township)	48759
Richmondville	48427	Rust (Township)	49746	Secord (Township)	48624
Richville	48758	Ruth	48470	Seidler Corners	48611
Ridgeway	49275	Rutland (Township)	49058	Selfridge Air Force Base	48045
Ridgeway (Township)	49275	Ryan	48637	Selkirk	48661
Riga	49276	Sac Bay	49817	Selma (Township)	49601
Riga (Township)	49276	Saddle Lake	49056	Seneca	49280
Riley (Clinton County) (Township)	48820	Sage (Township)	48624	Seneca (Township)	49280
Riley (St. Clair County) (Township)	48041	Saginaw	48601-09	Seneca Location	49950
		For specific Saginaw Zip Codes call (517) 771-5725, or your local postmaster.		Seney	49883
Riley Center	48041			Seney (Township)	49883
Ripley	49930			Senter	49922
Riverdale	48877	Saginaw Charter (Township)	48603	Seven Harbors	48356
River Rouge	48218	Saginaw Township North	48603	Seven-Mile & Mack Shopping Center (Part of Detroit)	48236
Riverside (Berrien County)	49084	Saginaw Township South	48603	
Riverside (Missaukee County) (Township)	49657	Saginaw Valley State College	48604	Seven Oaks (Part of Detroit)	48235
Riverside Correctional Facility	48846	Sagola	49881	Seville (Township)	48832
Riverton (Township)	49454	Sagola (Township)	49881	Seymour Square (Part of Grand Rapids)	49510
Riverview	48192	St. Anthony	48182	Shabbona	48426
Rives (Township)	49277	St. Charles	48655	Shady Shores	48635
Rives Junction	49277	St. Charles (Township)	48655	Shadyside	49266
Roberts Corners	49868	St. Clair	48079	Shafer Location	49920
Roberts Landing	48001	St. Clair (Township)	48079	Shaftsburg	48882
Robin Glen-Indiantown	48601	St. Clair Shores	48080-82	Shanghai Corners	49111
Robinson (Township)	49460	For specific St. Clair Shores Zip Codes call (313) 775-5050, or your local postmaster.		Sharon (Township)	48158
Rochester	48306-09			Sharon Hollow	48158
For specific Rochester Zip Codes call (313) 651-8551, or your local postmaster.				Sharps Corners	48653
		St. Helen	48656	Shawnee Shores	49036
Rochester Hills	48306-07	St. Ignace	49781	Shelby	48315-16
	48309	St. Ignace (Township)	49781	For specific Shelby Zip Codes call (313) 731-9412, or your local postmaster.	
For specific Rochester Hills Zip Codes call (313)651-8551, or your local postmaster.		St. Jacques	49878		
		St. James	49782		
		St. James (Township)	49782	Shelby	49455
Rock	49880	St. Johns	48879	Shelby (Township)	49455
Rockford	49341	Saint John's Provincial Seminary	48170	Shelbyville	49344
Rockland	49960	St. Joseph	49085	Sheldon	48111
Rockland (Township)	49960	St. Joseph Charter (Township)	49022	Shepardsville	48866
Rock River (Township)	49825	St. Louis	48880	Shepherd	48883
Rockwood	48173	St. Marys Lake	49017	Sheridan (Calhoun County) (Township)	49224
Rodney	49342	St. Nicholas	49880	
Rogers (Township)	49779	Salem (Township)	49314	Sheridan (Clare County) (Township)	48617
Rogers City	49779	Salem	48175	
Roger's Plaza (Part of Wyoming)	49509	Salem (Township)	48178	Sheridan (Huron County) (Township)	48413
Rolland (Township)	49310	Saline	48176	
Rollin	49278	Saline (Township)	49236	Sheridan (Mason County) (Township)	49410
Rollin (Township)	49278	Salisbury (Part of Ishpeming)	49849	
Rome (Township)	49221			Sheridan (Mecosta County) (Township)	49305
Rome Center	49221	Samaria	48177	
Romeo	48065	Sanborn (Township)	49766	Sheridan (Montcalm County)	48884
Romulus	48174	Sand Beach (Township)	48441	Sheridan Charter (Township)	49412
Ronald (Township)	48846	Sand Creek	49279	Sherman (Gladwin County) (Township)	48624
Rondo	49799	Sand Lake (Iosco County)	48748	
Roosevelt Park	49441	Sand Lake (Kent County)	49343	Sherman (Huron County) (Township)	48456
Roscommon	48653	Sand Lake Corners	49265	
Roscommon (Township)	48653	Sand River	49822	Sherman (Iosco County) (Township)	48748
Rose (Oakland County) (Township)	48442	Sands	49841	
		Sands (Township)	49841	Sherman (Isabella County) (Township)	48632
Rose (Ogemaw County) (Township)	48654	Sandstone (Township)	49201	
		Sandusky	48471	Sherman (Keweenaw County) (Township)	49945
Roseburg	48097	Sandy Beach	49091	
Rosebush	48878	Sanford	48657	Sherman (Mason County) (Township)	49410
Rose Center	48442	Sanilac (Township)	48469	
Rose City	48654	San Souci Beach	49036	Sherman (Newaygo County) (Township)	49412
Rosedale	49783	Santiago	48765	
Rose Island	48759	Saranac	48881	Sherman (Osceola County) (Township)	49688
Rose Lake (Township)	49655	Sauble (Township)	49402	
Roseville	48066	Saugatuck	49453	Sherman (St. Joseph County) (Township)	49091
Roseville Plaza (Part of Roseville)	48066	Saugatuck (Township)	49453	Sherman (Wexford County)	49668
		Sault Ste. Marie	49783	Sherman City	48632
Ross (Township)	49012	Sault Ste. Marie Air Force Station	49783	Sherwood	49089
Rothbury	49452			Sherwood (Township)	49089
Round Lake (Lenawee County)	49253	Sault Ste. Marie Indian Reservation	49783	Sherwood Corners	48647
				Shiawassee (Township)	48429
Round Lake (Mason County)	49410	Sawyer	49125	Shiawasseetown	48429
		Sawyer Lake	49815	Shields	48609
Rousseau	49948	Schaffer	49807	Shiloh	48865
Rowes Corner	48158	Schoolcraft (Houghton County)	49087	Shingleton	49884
Roxand (Township)	48837			Shoreham	49085
Royal Oak	48067-68	Schoolcraft (Houghton County) (Township)	49087	Shore Line Junction (Part of Hancock)	49930
	48073			Shorewood Hills	49125
For specific Royal Oak Zip Codes call (313) 546-7108, or your local postmaster.		Schoolcraft (Kalamazoo County)	49087	Shorewood-Tower Hills-Harbert	49115
		Schuck Island	48759	
Royal Oak	48220	Schultz	49058	Sibley (Part of Trenton)	48183
Royal Oak Beach	49721	Scio (Township)	48130	Sidnaw	49961
Royalton (Township)	49085	Sciota (Township)	48848	Sidney	48885
Rubicon (Township)	48468	Scipio (Township)	49250	Sidney (Township)	48885
Ruby	48027	Scott Correctional Facility	48170	Sid Town	48750
Rudyard	49780	Scottdale	49085	Sigel (Township)	48441
Rudyard (Township)	49780	Scott Lake	49927	Silver City	49953
Rumely	49826	Scotts	49088	Silver Creek (Township)	49047
Rush (Township)	48841	Scottville	49454	Silverwood	48760
Rush Lake	48169	Sears	49679	Simar	49948
Rusk	49464	Sears Lincoln Park Shopping Center (Part of Lincoln Park)	48146	Sims (Township)	48703
Russell Island	48001			Sister Lakes	49047
Russellville	48423	Sebewa (Township)	48875	Sitka	49412
		Sebewa Center	48875	Six Lakes	48886
		Sebewaing	48759	Skandia (Township)	49885
				Skandia	49885

	ZIP		ZIP		ZIP
Skanee	49962	Spurr (Township)	49861	Teapot Dome	49079
Skeels	48624	Stalwart	49789	Tecumseh	49286
Skidway Lake	48756	Stambaugh	49964	Tecumseh (Township)	49286
Slagle (Township)	49638	Stambaugh (Township)	49935	Tekonsha	49092
Slapneck	49816	Standale (Part of Walker)	49504	Tekonsha (Township)	49092
Sleepy Hollow	49912	Standish	48658	Teleford (Part of Dearborn	
Slocum	49451	Standish (Township)	48658	Heights)	48128
Smith Corners	48074	Stannard (Township)	49912	Tel-Twelve Mall (Part of	
Smiths Creek	48074	Stanton (Houghton County)		Southfield)	48034
Smyrna	48887	(Township)	49931	Temperance	48182
Snover	48472	Stanton (Montcalm County)	48888	Temple	48625
Snyderville	48063	Stanwood	49346	Texas (Township)	49009
Sodus	49126	Star (Township)	49611	Texas Corners	49009
Sodus (Township)	49126	Star Corners (Manistee		The Fingerboard Corner	49705
Sokol Camp	49117	County)	49660	The Heights	49230
Solon (Kent County)		Star Corners (Menominee		Theodore	49801
(Township)	49319	County)	49887	Thetford (Township)	48420
Solon (Leelanau County)	49621	Starville	48039	Thomas (Oakland County)	48371
Solon (Leelanau County)		Steamburg	49242	Thomas (Saginaw County)	
(Township)	49621	Stephenson	49887	(Township)	48609
Somerset	49281	Stephenson (Township)	49887	Thomaston	49968
Somerset (Township)	49281	Sterling	48659	Thompson	49854
Somerset Center	49282	Sterling Heights	48310-14	Thompson (Township)	49854
Somerset Mall (Part of Troy)	48084	For specific Sterling Heights Zip		Thompsonville	49683
Sonoma	49017	Codes call (313) 268-2880, or		Thornapple (Township)	49333
Soo (Township)	49783	your local postmaster.		Thornville	48455
South Arm (Township)	49727	Steuben	49854	Three Lakes	49861
South Blendon	49426	Stevensville	49127	Three Mile Lake	49079
South Boardman	49680	Stockbridge	49285	Three Oaks	49128
South Branch (Crawford		Stockbridge (Township)	49285	Three Oaks (Township)	49128
County) (Township)	48653	Stonington	49878	Three Rivers	49093
South Branch (Ogemaw		Stony Creek	48197	Thunder Mountain	49038
County)	48761	Stony Lake	49455	Tilden (Township)	49849
South Branch (Wexford		Stony Point	48166	Tipton	49287
County) (Township)	49601	Strasburg	49821	Tittabawassee (Township)	48623
South Butler	49082	Strathmoor (Part of Detroit)	48227	Tobacco (Township)	48612
Southfield	48034-37	Strawberry Point	49456	Tobico Beach	48706
	48075-76	Stronach	49660	Tobin Location	49920
	48086	Stronach (Township)	49660	Tobins Harbor	55605
For specific Southfield Zip Codes		Strongs	49790	Toivola	49965
call (313) 357-3310, or your local		Strongs Corners	49790	Tompkins	49277
postmaster.		Stuart Lake	49068	Tompkins (Township)	49277
Southfield (Township)	48009	Sturgeon Point	48740	Topaz	49925
South Flint Plaza (Part of		Sturgeon River	49864	Topinabee	49791
Flint)	48507	Sturgis	49091	Toquin	49057
Southgate	48195	Sturgis (Township)	49091	Torch Lake (Antrim County)	49627
Southgate Shopping Center		Sugar Island (Township)	49783	Torch Lake (Antrim County)	
(Part of Southgate)	48192	Sugar Rapids	48624	(Township)	49648
South Gull Lake	49083	Sullivan	49451	Torch Lake (Houghton	
South Haven	49090	Sullivan (Township)	49451	County) (Township)	49934
South Haven (Township)	49090	Summerfield (Clare County)		Torch River	49676
South Ionia	48846	(Township)	48625	Towar Gardens	48823
Southland Mall (Part of		Summerfield (Monroe		Tower	49792
Portage)	49081	County) (Township)	49270	Tower Hill	49125
Southland Shopping Center		Summit (Jackson County)		Town Corners	49446
(Part of Taylor)	48180	(Township)	49203	Traunik	49890
South Lyon	48178	Summit (Mason County)		Traverse Bay	49945
South Manitou	49654	(Township)	49431	Traverse City	49684*
South Monroe	48161	Summit City	49649		49685†
South Monterey	49010	Summit Heights	48629		48846
South Range	49963	Summit Place	48328	Tremaine Corners	49891
South Riley	48820	Sumner	48889	Trenary	49303
South Rockwood	48179	Sumner (Township)	48889	Trent	48183
Spalding	49886	Sumnerville	49120	Trenton	48653
Spalding (Township)	49886	Sumpter (Township)	48111	Triangle Park	49905
Sparlingville	48074	Sun	49327	Trimountain	
Sparr	49735	Sunfield	48890	Trolley (Part of Detroit)	48231-35
Sparta	49345	Sunfield (Township)	48890	For specific Trolley Zip Codes	
Sparta (Township)	49345	Sunrise Heights	49015	call (313) 965-1719, or your local	
Spaulding (Township)	48655	Sunset Beach	49230	postmaster.	
Speaker (Township)	48454	Superior (Chippewa County)		Trombly	49880
Spencer (Kalkaska County)	49646	(Township)	49715	Trout Creek	49967
Spencer (Kent County)		Superior (Washtenaw		Trout Lake	49793
(Township)	49326	County) (Township)	48197	Trout Lake (Township)	49793
Spinks Corners	49022	Surrey (Township)	48622	Trowbridge (Allegan	
Spratt	49753	Suttons Bay	49682	County) (Township)	49010
Spring Arbor	49283	Suttons Bay (Township)	49682	Trowbridge (Ingham	
Spring Arbor (Township)	49283	Swains Lake	49237	County)	48823
Spring Beach	49031	Swan Creek (Township)	48655	Trowbridge Park	49855
Springdale (Township)	49683	Swanson	49821	Troy	48083-84
Springfield (Calhoun		Swartz Creek	48473		48098-99
County)	49015	Swedetown	49913	For specific Troy Zip Codes call	
Springfield (Kalkaska		Sweetwater (Township)	49304	(313) 689-6262, or your local	
County) (Township)	49680	Sylvan (Osceola County)		postmaster.	
Springfield (Oakland		(Township)	49631	Troy (Township)	49309
County)	48346	Sylvan (Washtenaw County)		Trufant	49347
Springfield (Oakland		(Township)	48118	Turin (Township)	49880
County) (Township)	48346	Sylvan Center	48118	Turk Lake	48838
Springfield Place (Part of		Sylvan Lake	48320	Turner	48765
Battle Creek)	49015	Sylvester	49332	Turner (Township)	48765
Spring Grove	49416	Talbot	49821	Turner Shores	49116
Spring Lake	49456	Tallmadge	49504	Tuscarora (Township)	49749
Spring Lake (Township)	49456	Tallmadge (Township)	49504	Tuscola	48769
Springport	49284	Tallman	49410	Tuscola (Township)	48769
Springport (Township)	49284	Tamarack	49913	Tustin	49688
Springvale (Township)	49770	Tapiola	49916	Twelve Corners	49022
Springville (Lenawee		Tawas (Township)	48763	Twining	48766
County)	49265	Tawas Centre	48730	Twin Lake	49457
Springville (Wexford County)		Tawas City	48763*	Twin Lakes (Cass County)	49047
(Township)	49668		48764†	Twin Lakes (Houghton	
Springwells (Part of Detroit)	48209	Taylor	48180	County)	49965
Spruce	48762	Taymouth (Township)	48417	Two Rivers	48858
				Tyre	48475

* Area Zip Code   † Post Office Boxes

	ZIP
Tyrone (Kent County) (Township)	49330
Tyrone (Livingston County) (Township)	48430
Tyrone Lake	48430
Ubly	48475
Unadilla	48137
Unadilla (Township)	48137
Union (Branch County) (Township)	49094
Union (Cass County)	49130
Union (Grand Traverse County) (Township)	49633
Union (Isabella County) (Township)	48858
Union City	49094
Union Lake	48386-87
For specific Union Lake Zip Codes call (313) 363-1503, or your local postmaster.	
Union Pier	49129
Unionville	48767
Universal Mall (Part of Warren)	48092
Upjohn (Part of Portage)	49081
Upper Peninsula Mail Processing Center	49801*
	49802†
Urbandale (Part of Battle Creek)	49017
Utica	48317-18
For specific Utica Zip Codes call (313) 731-9412, or your local postmaster.	
Valley (Township)	49010
Valley Center	48416
Valley Farms	48906
Van	49755
Van Buren (Township)	48111
Vandalia	49095
Vanderbilt	49795
Vandercook Lake	49203
Van Meer	49884
Vantown	48892
Vassar	48768
Vassar (Township)	48768
Venice (Township)	48817
Vergennes (Township)	49331
Vermontville	49096
Vermontville (Township)	49096
Vernon (Isabella County) (Township)	48617
Vernon (Shiawassee County)	48476
Vernon (Shiawassee County) (Township)	48429
Vernon City	48617
Verona (Calhoun County)	49017
Verona (Gogebic County)	49968
Verona (Huron County)	48413
Verona (Huron County) (Township)	48413
Verona Park	49017
Vestaburg	48891
Veterans Administration Hospital (Part of Iron Mountain)	49801
Vevay (Township)	48854
Vickery Landing	49050
Vickeryville	48884
Vicksburg	49097
Victor (Township)	48848
Victoria	49960
Victory (Township)	49454
Vienna (Genesee County) (Township)	48420
Vienna (Montmorency County) (Township)	49751
Virginia Park	49423
Vogel Center	49657
Volinia	49045
Volinia (Township)	49045
Volney	49309
Vriesland	49464
Vulcan	49892
Wabaningo	49463
Wacousta	48837
Wadhams	48074
Wagarville	48624
Wahjamega	48723
Wainola	49948
Wakefield	49968
Wakefield (Township)	49968
Wakelee	49067
Wakeshma (Township)	49052
Waldenburg	48044
Waldron	49288
Wales (Township)	48027
Walhalla	49458
Walker (Cheboygan County) (Township)	49705
Walker (Kent County)	49504

	ZIP
Walkers Point	49721
Walkerville	49459
Wallace	49893
Walled Lake	48390-91
Wallin	49683
Wall Lake	49046
Walloon Lake	49796
Walnut Lake	48010
Walnut Point	49068
Walters	48346
Walton (Township)	49076
Waltz	48164
Wardcliff	48823
Warner (Township)	49730
Warren	48089-93
For specific Warren Zip Codes call (313) 751-4900, or your local postmaster.	
Warren (Township)	48618
Wasepi	49032
Washington (Gratiot County) (Township)	48806
Washington (Macomb County)	48094-95
For specific Washington Zip Codes call (313) 781-4251, or your local postmaster.	
Washington (Sanilac County) (Township)	48401
Washington Harbor	55605
Washington Heights (Part of Battle Creek)	49017
Waterford	48327-29
For specific Waterford Zip Codes call (313) 623-0020, or your local postmaster.	
Waterloo	49240
Waterloo (Township)	49240
Watermill Lake	49642
Waters	49797
Watersmeet	49969
Watersmeet (Township)	49969
Watertown (Clinton County) (Township)	48820
Watertown (Sanilac County)	48471
Watertown (Sanilac County) (Township)	48471
Watertown (Tuscola County) (Township)	48435
Watervale	49613
Watervliet	49098
Watervliet (Township)	49098
Watrousville	48768
Watson	49078
Watson (Township)	49078
Watson Corners	49078
Wattles Park	49017
Watton	49970
Waucedah	49892
Waucedah (Township)	49892
Waverly (Cheboygan County) (Township)	49765
Waverly (Eaton County)	48917
Waverly (Van Buren County) (Township)	49079
Wawatam (Township)	49701
Wawatam Beach (Part of Mackinaw City)	49701
Wayland	49348
Wayland (Township)	49348
Wayne (Cass County) (Township)	49047
Wayne (Wayne County)	48184
Weadlock	49755
Weale	48720
Weare (Township)	49420
Webber (Township)	49304
Webberville	48892
Webster (Township)	48130
Weesaw (Township)	49128
Weidman	48893
Welcome Corners	49058
Weldon (Township)	49683
Wellington (Township)	49753
Wells (Delta County)	49894
Wells (Delta County) (Township)	49894
Wells (Marquette County) (Township)	49818
Wells (Tuscola County) (Township)	48723
Wellston	49689
Wellsville	49228
Wenona Beach	49707
Wequetonsing	49740
West Bloomfield	48322-25
For specific West Bloomfield Zip Codes call (313) 626-9873, or your local postmaster.	

	ZIP
West Bloomfield Township	48323-24
For specific West Bloomfield Township Zip Codes call (313) 626-9873, or your local postmaster.	
West Branch (Dickinson County) (Township)	49877
West Branch (Marquette County) (Township)	49885
West Branch (Missaukee County) (Township)	49667
West Branch (Ogemaw County)	48661
West Branch (Ogemaw County) (Township)	48661
Westchester Village	48010
Western Wayne Correctional Facility	48170
West Ishpeming	49849
Westland	48185
Westland Shopping Center (Part of Westland)	48185
West Leroy	49051
West Millbrook	49310
West Monroe	48161
West Olive	49460
Weston	49289
Westphalia	48894
Westphalia (Township)	48894
West Sebewa	48875
West Side (Part of Saginaw)	48603
West Traverse (Township)	49740
Westville	48888
West Willow	48198
West Windsor	48813
Westwood	49006
	49009
	49019
For specific Westwood Zip Codes call (616) 343-2560, or your local postmaster.	
Westwood Heights	48504
Wetmore	49895
Wetzel	49659
Wexford (Township)	49668
Wheatfield (Township)	48895
Wheatland (Hillsdale County) (Township)	49220
Wheatland (Mecosta County) (Township)	49340
Wheatland (Sanilac County) (Township)	48427
Wheeler	48662
Wheeler (Township)	48662
White	49952
White Cloud	49349
Whitefish (Township)	49728
Whitefish Point	49768
Whiteford (Township)	49267
Whiteford Center	49267
Whitehall	49461
Whitehall (Township)	49461
White Lake	48383
White Lake (Township)	48383
White Oak (Township)	48285
White Pigeon	49099
White Pigeon (Township)	49099
White Pine	49971
White River (Township)	49437
Whites Beach	48658
Whitewater (Township)	49690
Whitmore Lake	48189
Whitney (Township)	48765
Whittaker	48190
Whittemore	48770
Wickware	48726
Wilber (Township)	48730
Wilcox (Township)	49349
Wildwood (Cheboygan County)	49706
Wildwood (Manistee County)	49614
Willard	48611
Williams (Township)	48611
Williamsburg	49690
Williamston	48895
Williamston (Township)	48895
Williamsville (Cass County)	49095
Williamsville (Livingston County)	48137
Willis	48191
Willow	48164
Willow Run	48198
Willwalk	49783
Wilmot (Cheboygan County) (Township)	49799
Wilmot (Tuscola County)	48729
Wilson (Alpena County) (Township)	49707
Wilson (Charlevoix County) (Township)	49729
Wilson (Menominee County)	49896

	ZIP		ZIP		ZIP
Windemere	48917	Wooden Shoe Village	48624	Wyman	49310
Windsor Charter (Township)	48821	Woodhaven	48183	Wyoming	49509
Winegars	48624	Woodhull (Township)	48872	Wyoming Park (Part of	
Winfield (Township)	48850	Woodland	48897	Wyoming)	49509
Winn	48896	Woodland (Township)	48897	Yale (Gogebic County)	49911
Winona	49965	Woodland (Part of		Yale (St. Clair County)	48097
Winsor (Township)	48755	Kentwood)	49508	Yankee Springs (Township)	49333
Winterfield (Township)	49665	Woodland Beach	48161	Yates (Township)	49642
Winters	49878	Woodland Lake	48116	Yellow Jacket	49913
Winthrop Junction (Part of		Woodland Park	49309	York (Township)	48160
Ishpeming)	49849	Woods Corner	48622	Yorkville	49083
Wise (Township)	48618	Wood Spur	49953	Ypsilanti	48197-98
Wisner	48701	Woodstock (Township)	49220	For specific Ypsilanti Zip Codes	
Wisner (Township)	48733	Woodville	49349	call (313) 482-6905, or your local	
Witch Lake	48879	Wooster	49412	postmaster.	
Wixom	48393	Worth (Arenac County)	48650	Ypsilanti Regional	
Wolf Lake (Jackson County)	49201	Worth (Sanilac County)		Psychiatric Hospital	48197
Wolf Lake (Muskegon		(Township)	48422	Yuba	49690
County)	49442	Wright (Township)	49403	Yuma	49668
Wolverine	49799	Wright (Hillsdale County)		Zeba	49946
Wolverine Lake	48390	(Township)	49271	Zeeland	49464
Wonderland Mall (Part of		Wright (Ottawa County)	49403	Zeeland (Township)	49464
Livonia)	48150	Wurtsmith AFB	48753	Zilwaukee	48604
Woodard Lake	48834	Wurtsmith Air Force Base	48753	Zilwaukee (Township)	48604
Woodbridge (Township)	49242	Wyandotte	48192	Zutphen	49426
Woodbury	48849				

	ZIP
Ada	56510
Adams	55909
Adolph (Part of Hermantown)	55701
Adrian	56110
Afton	55001
Ah-Gwah-Ching	56430
Aitkin	56431
Akeley	56433
Albany	56307
Alberta	56207
Albert Lea	56007
Albertville	55301
Albion Center	55302
Alborn	55702
Alden	56009
Aldrich	56434
Alexandria	56308
Alida	56676
Allen Junction (Part of Hoyt Lakes)	55750
Alma City	56048
Almelund	55002
Almora	56551
Alpha	56111
Altura	55910
Alvarado	56710
Alvwood	56630
Amboy	56010
Amherst	55922
Amiret	56175
Amor	56515
Andover	55304
Andree	55006
Andyville	55912
Angle Inlet	56711
Angora	55703
Angus	56712
Annandale	55302
Anoka	55303-04

For specific Anoka Zip Codes call (612) 421-1114, or your local postmaster.

	ZIP
Antlers Park (Part of Lakeville)	55044
Apache Mall (Part of Rochester)	55902
Apache Plaza (Part of St. Anthony)	55421
Appleton	56208
Apple Valley	55124
Arco	56113
Arcturus (Part of Taconite)	55786
Arden Hills	55112
Arendahl	55962
Argonne (Part of Lakeville)	55044
Argyle	56713
Arlington	55307
Armstrong	56009
Arnesen	56673
Arnold	55803
Arthyde	56350
Artichoke Lake	56227
Ashby	56309
Ashcreek	56173
Ash Lake	55771
Askov	55704
Aspelund	55946
Assumption	55338
Atkinson	55718
Atwater	56209
Atwood (Part of Edina)	55424
Audubon	56511
Augusta	55318
Aure	56676
Aurora	55705
Austin	55912
Austin Acres	55912
Auto Club (Part of Bloomington)	55420
Automba	55757
Averill	56547
Avoca	56114
Avon	56310
Babbitt	55706
Backus	56435
Badger	56714
Bagley	56621
Baker	56513
Balaton	56115
Bald Eagle	55110
Balkan	55719
Ball Bluff	55752
Ball Club	56636
Balmoral	56515
Bancroft	56007
Barden (Part of Shakopee)	55379
Barnesville	56514
Barnum	55707
Barr	55992
Barrett	56311
Barrows	56401

	ZIP
Barry	56210
Bassett	55602
Basswood	56576
Basswood Grove	55033
Battle Lake	56515
Battle River	56630
Baudette	56623
Baxter	56425
Bay Lake	56444
Bayport	55003
Bayview	56359
Beardsley	56211
Bear River	55723
Bear Valley	55041
Beauford	56065
Beaulieu	56557
Beaver	55910
Beaver Bay	55601
Beaver Creek	56116
Beaver Falls	56270
Bechyn	56283
Becida	56601
Becker	55308
Beckville	55355
Bejou	56516
Belgrade	56312
Bellaire	55110
Bellechester	55027
Belle Creek	55009
Belle Plaine	56011
Belle Prairie	56345
Belleriver	56319
Bellingham	56212
Beltrami	56517
Belview	56214
Bemidji	56601-19

For specific Bemidji Zip Codes call (218) 751-5600, or your local postmaster.

	ZIP
Bena	56626
Benedict	56436
Bennettville	56431
Benson	56215
Bergen	56101
Bergville	56661
Bernadotte	56054
Berne	55985
Berner	56644
Berning Mill	55376
Beroun	55004
Bertha	56437
Bethany	55910
Bethel	55005
Big Bend City	56262
Bigelow	56117
Big Falls	56627
Bigfork	56628
Big Island (Part of Orono)	55331
Big Lake	55309
Big Spring	55939
Big Stone City (Part of Ortonville)	56278
Big Woods	56744
Bingham Lake	56118
Birch Beach	56866
Birchdale	56629
Birchwood Village	55110
Bird Island	55310
Biscay	55336
Biwabik	55708
Bixby	55917
Blackberry	55744
Blackduck	56630
Black Hammer	55974
Blaine	55434
	55449

For specific Blaine Zip Codes call (612) 784-1029, or your local postmaster.

	ZIP
Blakeley	56011
Blomford	55040
Blomkest	56216
Bloom Dale (Part of Bloomington)	55431
Blooming Prairie	55917
Bloomington	55420
Blue Earth	56013
Blue Grass	56477
Bluffton	56518
Bock	56313
Bodum	55040
Boisberg	56296
Bois Fort	55772
Bombay	55946
Bonanza Grove	56211
Bongards	55368
Bonnie Glen	55013
Border	56629
Borup	56519
Bovey	55709
Bovey-Coleraine (Part of Bovey)	55709

	ZIP
Bowlus	56314
Bowstring	56631
Boyd	56218
Boy River	56632
Bradford	55040
Braham	55006
Brainerd	56401
Brainerd Regional Human Services Center	56401
Branch	55056
Brandon	56315
Bratsberg	55971
Breckenridge	56520
Breezy Point	56472
Bremen	55957
Brennyville	56329
Brevik	56655
Brewster	56119
Bricelyn	56014
Bridge Court (Part of Anoka)	55303
Bridgeman	56473
Bridgewater	55021
Brimson	55602
Bristol	55939
Britt	55710
Brookdale Shopping Center (Part of Brooklyn Center)	55430
Brooklyn (Part of Hibbing)	55746
Brooklyn Center	55429
Brooklyn Park	55443
Brook Park	55007
Brooks	56715
Brookston	55711
Brooten	56316
Browerville	56438
Brownsdale	55918
Browns Valley	56219
Brownsville	55919
Brownton	55312
Bruno	55712
Brunswick	55051
Brush Creek	56014
Brushvale	56520
Buckman	56317
Buffalo	55313
Buffalo Lake	55314
Buhl	55713
Bunde	56222
Burchard	56115
Burnett	55727
Burnsville	55337
Burnsville Center (Part of Burnsville)	55337
Burr	56220
Burschville (Part of Corcoran)	55357
Burtrum	56318
Butler	56567
Butterfield	56120
Butternut	56055
Buyck	55771
Bygland	56721
Byron	55920
Cable	56301
Caledonia	55921
Callaway	56521
Calumet	55716
Cambria	56073
Cambridge	55008
Camden Place (Part of Minneapolis)	55412
Campbell	56522
Camp Lacupolis	55041
Camp Ripley	56345
Canby	56220
Cannon City	55021
Cannon Falls	55009
Cannon Lake	55021
Canton	55922
Canyon	55717
Cardigan Junction (Part of Shoreview)	55112
Caribou	56735
Carimona	55965
Carlisle	56537
Carlos	56319
Carlton	55718
Carp	56623
Carver	55315
Cashtown (Part of Ortonville)	56278
Casino	56473
Cass Lake	56633
Castle Danger	55616
Castle Rock	55010
Cedar	55011
Cedar Beach	55960
Cedar Grove (Part of Eagan)	55111
Cedar Mills	55350

* **Area Zip Code**   † **Post Office Boxes**

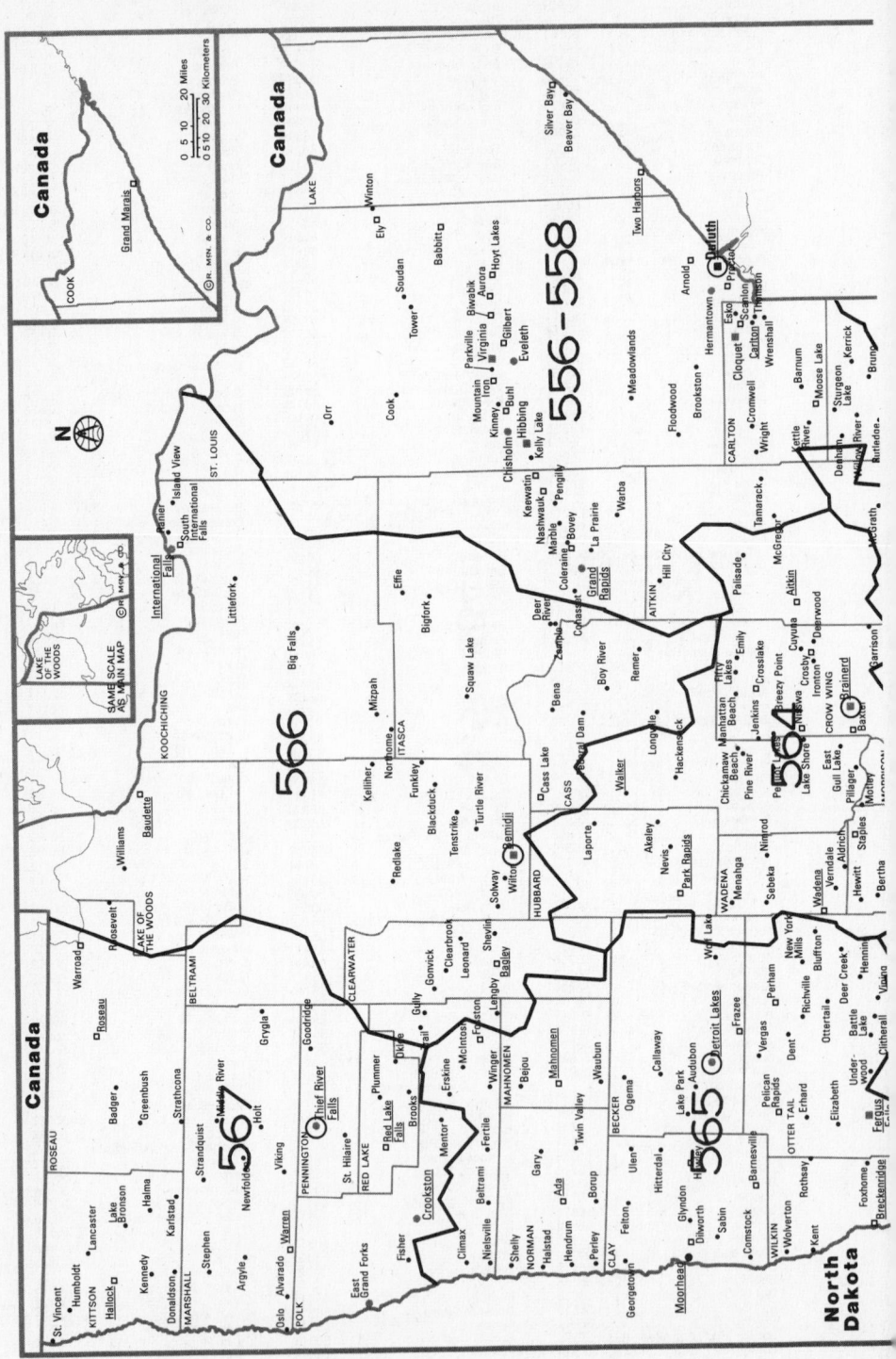

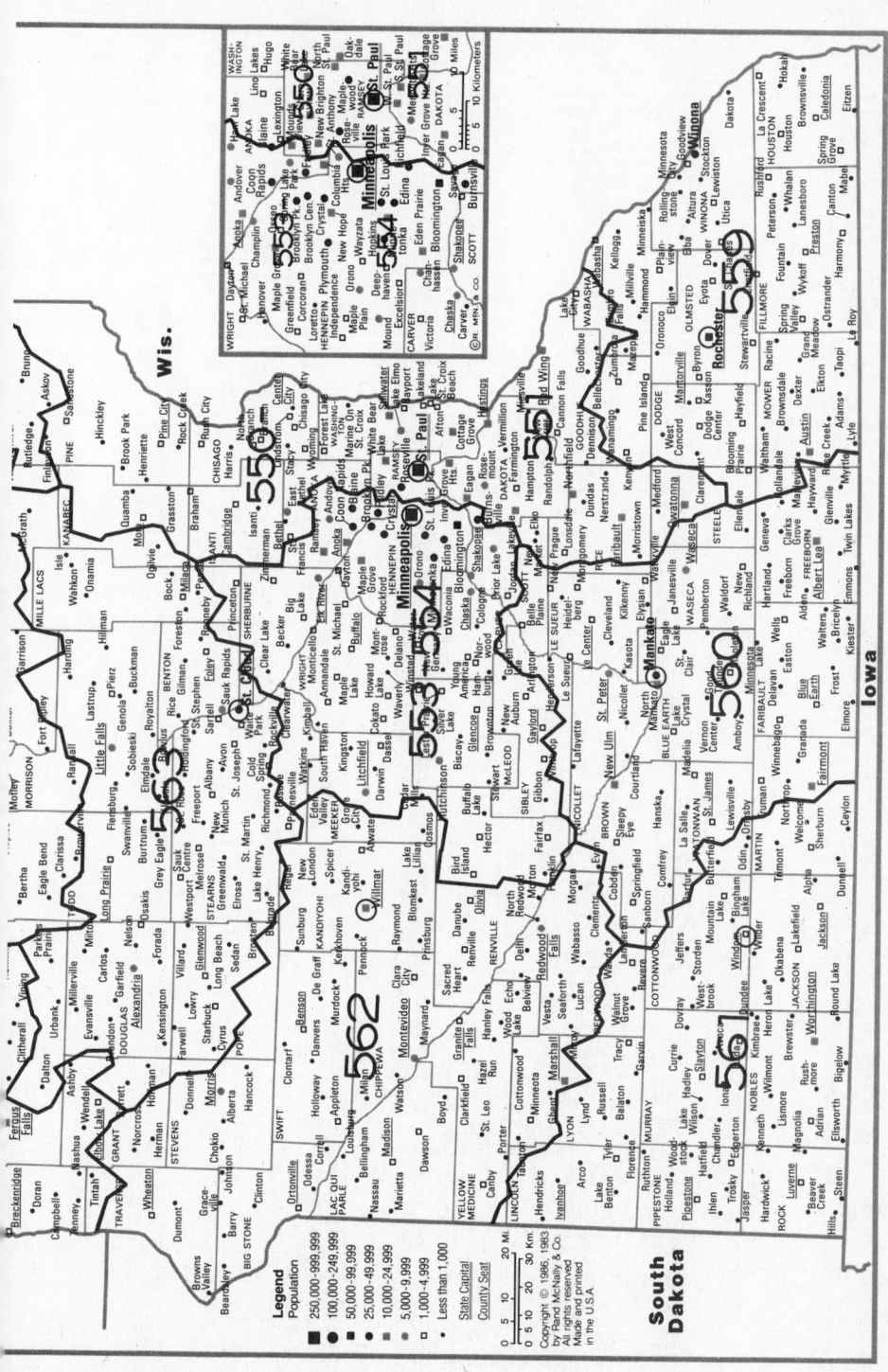

	ZIP
Cedar Riverside (Part of Minneapolis)	55440
Celina	55723
Center City	55012
Centerville (Anoka County)	55038
Centerville (Winona County)	55987
Central	56481
Central Lakes	55734
Ceylon	56121
Champlin	55316
Chandler	56122
Chanhassen	55317
Charlesville	56583
Chaska	55318
Chatfield	55923
Cherry	55751
Cherry Grove	55975
Chester	55904
Chicago Bay	55606
Chickamaw Beach	56474
Chisago City	55013
Chisholm	55719
Choice	55954
Chokio	56221
Chowens Corner (Part of Deephaven)	55391
Circle Pines	55014
City (Part of Rochester)	55904
City Center (Part of Minneapolis)	55402
Civic Center (Part of Duluth)	55802
Clara City	56222
Claremont	55924
Clarissa	56440
Clarkfield	56223
Clarks Grove	56016
Clearbrook	56634
Clear Lake	55319
Clearwater	55320
Clements	56224
Clementson	56623
Cleveland	56017
Cliff (Part of Lilydale)	55118
Climax	56523
Clinton	56225
Clinton Falls	55060
Clitherall	56524
Clontarf	56226
Cloquet	55720
Clotho	56347
Cloverdale	55037
Cloverton	55072
Clyde	55979
Coates	55068
Cobden	56085
Cohasset	55721
Coin	56358
Cokato	55321
Colby (Part of Hoyt Lakes)	55750
Cold Spring	56320
Coleraine	55722
Collegeville	56321
Collis	56236
Cologne	55322
Columbia Heights	55421
Comfrey	56019
Commerce (Part of Minneapolis)	55415
Como (Part of St. Paul)	55108
Comstock	56525
Conception	55945
Concord	55985
Conger	56020
Constance (Part of Andover)	55303
Cook	55723
Cooley	55769
Coon Creek (Part of Coon Rapids)	55433
Coon Lake Beach (Part of East Bethel)	55092
Coon Rapids	55433
	55448

For specific Coon Rapids Zip Codes call (612) 755-1150, or your local postmaster.

Copas	55073
Corcoran	55357
Cordova	56057
Cormorant	56572
Corning	55912
Correll	56227
Corvuso	56228
Cosmos	56228
Cottage Grove	55016
Cotton	55724
Cottonwood	56229
Courtland	56021
Cove	56359
Craigville	56639
Crane Lake	55725
Credit River	55372

	ZIP
Croftville	55604
Cromwell	55726
Crookston	56716
Crosby	56441
Crosby Beach	56444
Crosslake	56442
Crown	55070
Crow River	56243
Crow Wing	56401
Crystal	55428
Crystal Bay (Part of Orono)	55323
Crystal Shopping Center (Part of Crystal)	55428
Culver	55727
Cummingsville	55923
Currie	56123
Cushing	56443
Cusson	55771
Cutler	56431
Cuyuna	56444
Cyrus	56323
Dakota	55925
Dalbo	55017
Dale	56549
Dalton	56324
Danube	56230
Danvers	56231
Darfur	56022
Darling	56345
Darwin	55324
Dassel	55325
Dawson	56232
Day	55006
Dayton (Anoka County)	55303
Dayton (Hennepin County)	55327
Daytons Bluff (Part of St. Paul)	55106
Debs	56676
Deephaven	55391
Deer Creek	56527
Deer Creek Indian Reservation	56639
Deerfield	55049
Deer River	56636
Deerwood	56444
De Graff	56233
Delano	55328
Delavan	56023
Delft	56124
Delhi	56283
Dell	56013
Dellwood	55110
Denham	55728
Dennison	55018
Dent	56528
Detroit Lakes	56501*
	56502†
Dexter	55926
Diamond Lake (Part of Minneapolis)	55419
Dilworth	56529
Dinkytown (Part of Minneapolis)	55414
Dodge Center	55927
Donaldson	56720
Donnelly	56235
Dora Lake	56661
Doran	56522
Dorothy	56750
Dorset	56470
Douglas	55960
Douglas Lodge	56460
Dover	55929
Dovray	56125
Downer	56514
Dresbach	55947
Duelm	56329
Duluth	55801-16

For specific Duluth Zip Codes call (218) 723-2500, or your local postmaster.

Duluth International Airport, 4787th Air Base Group	55814
Dumfries	55981
Dumont	56236
Dundas	55019
Dundee	56126
Dunnell	56127
Dunvilla	56572
Duquette	55729
Duxbury	55072
Eagan	55121
Eagle Bend	56446
Eagle Lake	56024
East Beaver Bay	55601
East Bethel	55005
East Chain	56031
East Cottage Grove (Part of Cottage Grove)	55016
Eastern Heights (Part of St. Paul)	55119
East Grand Forks	56721

	ZIP
East Gull Lake	56401
East Hastings (Part of Hastings)	55033
East Lake	55760
East Lake Francis Shores	55040
Easton	56025
East Prairieville	55021
Eastside (Part of Minneapolis)	55418
East Union	55315
Ebro	56621
Echo	56237
Echols	56081
Eddsville	55310
Eden	55927
Eden Prairie	55344
	55346-47

For specific Eden Prairie Zip Codes call (612)942-5266, or your local postmaster.

Eden Prairie Center (Part of Eden Prairie)	55344
Eden Valley	55329
Edgerton	56128
Edgewood	55008
Edina	55410
	55424
	55435-36

For specific Edina Zip Codes call (612) 920-5226, or your local postmaster.

Effie	56639
Eidswold	55020
Eitzen	55931
Elba	55910
Elbow Lake	56531
Eldes Corner	55810
Eldred	56523
Elgin	55932
Elizabeth	56533
Elkland	55021
Elko	55020
Elk River	55330
Elkton	55933
Ellendale	56026
Ellsworth	56129
Elmdale	56314
Elmer	55765
Elmore	56027
Elmwood (Part of St. Louis Park)	55416
Elrosa	56325
Elway (Part of St. Paul)	55116
Ely	55731
Ely Lake	55734
Elysian	56028
Embarrass	55732
Emco (Part of Hoyt Lakes)	55750
Emily	56447
Emmons	56029
Empire	55024
Enfield	55362
Englund	56758
Erdahl	56531
Erhard	56534
Ericksonville	56359
Ericsburg	56649
Erie	56725
Erskine	56535
Esden	56444
Esko	55733
Essig	56030
Estes Brook	56357
Etna	55975
Etter	55089
Euclid	56722
Evan	56238
Evansville	56326
Eveleth	55734
Everdell	56520
Evergreen	56544
Excelsior	55331
Eyota	55934
Fairbanks	55602
Fairfax	55332
Fairhaven	55382
Fairmont	56031
Faith	56584
Falcon Heights	55113
Faribault	55021
Farming	56368
Farmington	55024
Farris	56633
Farwell	56327
Federal Correctional Institution	55072
Federal Dam	56641
Felton	56536
Fergus Falls	56537*
	56538†
Fernando	55385
Fertile	56540

* Area Zip Code   † Post Office Boxes

	ZIP		ZIP		ZIP
Fifty Lakes	56448	Goodhue	55027	Herman	56248
Fillmore	55990	Goodland	55742	Hermantown	55810
Finland	55603	Goodridge	56725	Heron Lake	56137
Finland Air Force Station,		Good Thunder	56037	Hewitt	56453
756th Radar Squadron	55603	Goodview	55987	Hiawatha Spur (Part of	
Finlayson	55735	Gordon	56036	Eagan)	55111
Fisher	56723	Gotha	55322	Hibbing	55746-47
Flensburg	56328	Graceton	56686	For specific Hibbing Zip Codes	
Fletcher	55369	Graceville	56240	call (218) 263-4086, or your local	
Flintwood Hills (Part of		Granada	56039	postmaster.	
Ramsey)	55303	Grand Falls	56627	Hidden Creek (Part of	
Flom	56541	Grand Marais	55604	Andover)	55303
Floodwood	55736	Grand Meadow	55936	High Forest	55976
Florence	56170	Grand Portage	55605	Highland (Fillmore County)	55986
Florenton	55792	Grand Portage Indian		Highland (Hennepin County)	55411
Florian	56758	Reservation	55605	Highland (Lake County)	55616
Foley	56329	Grand Rapids	55730	Highland (Wright County)	55349
Fond du Lac Indian			55744	High Landing	56725
Reservation	55720	For specific Grand Rapids Zip		Highland Park (Part of St.	
Forada	56308	Codes call (218) 326-3956, or		Paul)	55116
Forbes	55738	your local postmaster.		Hill City	55748
Fordson (Part of Eagan)	55121	Grand View Heights	56573	Hillman	56338
Forest City	55355	Grandy	55029	Hills	56138
Forest Grove	56660	Granger	55939	Hilltop	55421
Forest Lake	55025	Granite Falls	56241	Hillview	56477
Forest Mills	55992	Grass Lake	55006	Hinckley	55037
Foreston	56330	Grasston	55030	Hines	56647
Fork	56744	Grattan	56661	Hitterdal	56552
Fort Ripley	56449	Greaney	55740	Hoffman	56339
Fort Snelling	55111	Greenbush	56726	Hoffmans Corners (Part of	
Fosston	56542	Greenfield	55357	Gem Lake)	55110
Fossum	56584	Green Isle	55338	Hokah	55941
Fountain	55935	Greenland	56028	Holdingford	56340
Four Corners	55811	Greenleaf	55355	Holland	56139
Fourtown	56727	Greenleafton	55965	Hollandale	56045
Foxhome	56543	Green Valley	56258	Holloway	56249
Fox Lake	56181	Greenwald	56335	Hollywood	55388
Franconia	55074	Greenwood	55331	Holmes City	56341
Franklin (Renville County)	55333	Grey Eagle	56336	Holt	56738
Franklin (St. Louis County)	55792	Grogan	56081	Holyoke	55749
Franklin Avenue (Part of		Groningen	55072	Homer	55942
Minneapolis)	55404	Grove City	56243	Hoot Lake (Part of Fergus	
Frazee	56544	Grove Lake	56316	Falls)	56537
Freeborn	56032	Grygla	56727	Hope	56046
Freeburg	55921	Guckeen	56013	Hopkins	55305
Freedhem	56345	Gully	56646		55343
Freeport	56331	Gutches Grove	56347		55345
Fremont	55979	Guthrie	56461	For specific Hopkins Zip Codes	
French Lake	55302	Hackensack	56452	call (612) 935-8606, or your local	
French River	55804	Hackett	56623	postmaster.	
Fridley	55432	Hader	55992	Hopper (Part of Mountain	
Friesland	55037	Hadley	56151	Iron)	55792
Frontenac	55026	Hagan	56262	Houston	55943
Frost	56033	Hallock	56728	Hovland	55606
Fulda	56131	Halma	56729	Howard Lake	55349
Funkley	56630	Halstad	56548	Hoyt Lakes	55750
Garden City	56034	Hamburg	55339	Hubbard	56470
Garfield	56332	Hamel	55340	Hugo	55038
Garrison	56450	Hamilton	55975	Humboldt	56731
Garvin	56132	Ham Lake	55304	Huntersville	56464
Gary	56545	Hammond	55991	Huntley	56047
Gatzke	56724	Hampton	55031	Husby Spur (Part of Arden	
Gaylord	55334	Hancock	56244	Hills)	55112
Gem Lake	55110	Hanley Falls	56245	Hutchinson	55350
Gemmell	56660	Hanover	55341	Hydes Lake	55322
Geneva	56035	Hanska	56041	Ideal Corners	56472
Genoa (Olmsted County)	55920	Happyland	56653	Idington	55703
Genoa (St. Louis County)	55734	Harding	56364	Ihlen	56140
Genola	56364	Hardwick	56134	Illgen City	55614
Gentilly	56716	Har-Mar Mall (Part of		Imogene	56039
Georgetown	56546	Roseville)	55113	Independence (Hennepin	
Georgeville	56312	Harmony	55939	County)	55359
Gheen	55740	Harnell Park	55779	Independence (St. Louis	
Gheen Corner	55740	Harris	55032	County)	55727
Ghent	56239	Hart	55971	Indus	56629
Gibbon	55335	Hartland	56042	Industrial (Part of St. Paul)	55104
Giese	55735	Hassan	55374	Inger	56636
Gilbert	55741	Hassman	56431	Inguadona	56655
Gilfillan	56283	Hastings	55033	International Falls	56649
Gilman	56333	Hasty	55320	Inver Grove Heights	55076-77
Gladstone (Part of		Hatfield	56164	For specific Inver Grove Heights	
Maplewood)	55109	Havana	55060	Zip Codes call (612) 451-1243, or	
Glen	56431	Hawick	56246	your local postmaster.	
Glencoe	55336	Hawley	56549	Iona	56141
Glendale	55771	Hay Creek	55066	Iron	55751
Glendorado	55371	Haydenville	56256	Ironhub	56431
Glen Lake (Part of		Hayfield	55940	Ironton	56455
Minnetonka)	55345	Haypoint	55748	Isabella	55607
Glenville	56036	Hayward	56043	Isanti	55040
Glenwood	56334	Hazel Run	56247	Island Lake	56667
Glenwood Junction (Part of		Hazelwood	55057	Island Park (Part of Mound)	55364
Golden Valley)	55427	Heatwole	55350	Island View	56649
Glory	56431	Hector	55342	Isle	56342
Gloster (Part of Maplewood)	55109	Heiberg	56584	Ivanhoe	56142
Gluek	56260	Heidelberg	56071	Iverson	55718
Glyndon	56547	Heinola	56567	Jackson	56143
Godahl	56081	Henderson	56044	Jacobson	55752
Golden Hill	55901	Hendricks	56136	Jacobs Prairie	56320
Golden Hills (Part of St.		Hendrum	56550	Jakeville	56329
Louis Park)	55416	Henning	56551	Jameson	56649
Golden Valley	55427	Henriette	55036	Janesville	56048
Gonvick	56644	Henrytown	55939	Jarretts	55957

	ZIP		ZIP		ZIP
Jasper	56144	Lansing	55950	Madison Lake	56063
Jeffers	56145	Laporte	56461	Magnolia	56158
Jenkins	56456	La Prairie	55744	Mahkonce	56557
Jennie	55325	Larsmont	55616	Mahnomen	56557
Jessenland	56044	La Salle	56056	Mahtomedi	55115
Jessie Lake	56637	Lastrup	56344	Mahtowa	55762
Johnsburg	55909	Lauderdale	55113	Maine	56586
Johnson	56250	Lavinia	55746	Maine Prairie	55353
Johnsville (Part of Blaine)	55434	Lawler	55760	Makinen	55763
Jonathan (Part of Chaska)	55318	Lawndale	56579	Mall (Part of Fairmont)	56031
Jordan	55352	Lax Lake	55614	Mall of America	55420
Judson	56055	Leader	56466	Malmo	56431
Kabekona	56461	Leaf Lake	56551	Manannah	56243
Kabetogama	56669	Leaf Valley	56332	Manchester	56064
Kanaranzi	56110	Leavenworth	56085	Manhattan Beach	56463
Kandi Mall Shopping Center		Le Center	56057	Manitou	56629
(Part of Willmar)	56201	Leech Lake Indian		Mankato	56001-03
Kandiyohi	56251	Reservation	56633	For specific Mankato Zip Codes	
Karlstad	56732	Leetonia (Part of Hibbing)	55746	call (507) 625-1781, or your local	
Kasota	56050	Le Hillier	56001	postmaster.	
Kasson	55944	Lengby	56651	Mansfield	56009
Katrine	56444	Lenora	55922	Mantorville	55955
Keewatin	55753	Leonard	56652	Maple	55387
Kelliher	56650	Leonidas	55734	Maple Bay	56736
Kellogg	55945	Leota	56153	Maple Grove	55369
Kelly Lake (Part of Hibbing)	55754	Lerdal	56007	Maple Hill	55604
Kelsey	55724	Le Roy	55951	Maple Island	56045
Kennedy	56733	Lester Prairie	55354	Maple Lake	55358
Kenneth	56147	Le Sueur	56058	Maple Plain	55359
Kensington	56343	Lewis Lake	55006	Mapleton	56065
Kent	56553	Lewiston	55952	Mapleview	55912
Kenwood (Hennepin		Lewisville	56060	Maplewood	55109
County)	55403	Lexington (Anoka County)	55112	Maplewood Mall (Part of	
Kenwood (St. Louis County)	55811	Lexington (Le Sueur		Maplewood)	55109
Kenyon	55946	County)	56057	Marble	55764
Kerkhoven	56252	Libby	55760	Marcell	56657
Kerr (Part of Hibbing)	55746	Lilydale	55118	Margie	56658
Kerrick	55756	Lime Creek	56131	Marietta	56257
Kettle River	55757	Lincoln	56443	Marine On St. Croix	55047
Kiester	56051	Linden Grove	55723	Marion	55901
Kilkenny	56052	Lindford	56653	Markham	55763
Kimball	55353	Lindstrom	55045	Markville	55072
Kimberly	56431	Lino Lakes	55014	Marshall	56258
Kinbrae	56126	Linwood	55005	Martin Lake	55079
Kingsdale	55072	Lismore	56155	Marty	55353
Kings Park	55960	Litchfield	55355	Marysburg	56063
Kingston	55325	Litomysl	55060	Marystown	55379
Kinmount	55771	Little Canada	55110	Matawan	56072
Kinney	55758	Little Chicago	55057	Mattson	56728
Kitzville (Part of Hibbing)	55746	Little Falls	56345	Max	56659
Kjellberg Park	55362	Littlefork	56653	Mayer	55360
Klossner	56053	Little Marais	55614	Mayhew	56379
Knapp	55321	Little Pine	56431	Mayhew Lake	56379
Knife River	55609	Little Rock (Beltrami		Maynard	56260
Knollwood Mall (Part of St.		County)	56671	Mayville	55912
Louis Park)	55426	Little Rock (Morrison		Mazeppa	55956
Komensky	55350	County)	56373	M&D Junction (Part of	
Kragnes	56560	Little Sauk	56347	White Bear Lake)	55110
Kroschel	55037	Little Swan (Part of Hibbing)	55746	Meadowlands	55765
Lac qui Parle	56265	Local	56501	Medford	55049
La Crescent	55947	Lockhart	56510	Medicine Lake	55441
Lafayette	56054	Loman	56654	Meire Grove	56352
Lagoona Beach	56278	London	56061	Melby	56326
Lake Benton	56149	Long Beach	56334	Melrose	56352
Lake Bronson	56734	Long Lake	55356	Melrude	55766
Lake Center	56511	Long Point	56686	Menahga	56464
Lake City	55041	Long Prairie	56347	Mendota	55150
Lake Crystal	56055	Long Siding	55371	Mendota Heights	55118
Lake Elmo	56042	Longville	56655	Mentor	56736
Lake Eunice	56501	Lonsdale	55046	Meriden	56067
Lakefield	56150	Loop (Part of Minneapolis)	55402	Merrifield	56465
Lake George	56458	Loretto	55306†	Merton	55060
Lake Henry	56362			Mesaba (Part of Hoyt	
Lake Hubert	56459	Loring (Part of Minneapolis)	55403	Lakes)	55750
Lake Itasca	56460	Louisburg	56254	Middle River	56737
Lakeland	55043	Louriston	56260	Midway (Becker County)	56464
Lakeland Shores	55043	Lower Sioux Indian		Midway (Ramsey County)	55104
Lake Lillian	56253	Reservation	56270	Midway (St. Louis County)	55792
Lake Netta (Part of Ham		Lowry	56349	Midway Center (Part of St.	
Lake)	55303	Lucan	56255	Paul)	55104
Lake Nichols	55717	Lude	56686	Miesville	55009
Lake Park	56554	Lutsen	55612	Milaca	56353
Lake Sarah (Part of		Luverne	56156	Milan	56262
Greenfield)	55357	Luxemburg	56301	Mille Lacs Indian	
Lake Shore	56401	Lydia	55352	Reservation	56359
Lake Shore Park (Part of		Lyle	55953	Miller Hill (Part of Duluth)	55811
White Bear Lake)	55110	Lynd	56157	Miller Hill Mall (Part of	
Lakeside (Renville County)	55314	Lyndale (Part of		Duluth)	55811
Lakeside (St. Louis County)	55804	Independence)	55359	Millersburg	55021
Lake St. Croix Beach	55043	Lynwood (Part of Hibbing)	55746	Millerville	56315
Lake Street (Part of		Mabel	55954	Millville	55957
Minneapolis)	55408	McCauleyville	56553	Milroy	56263
Lakeville	55044	McGrath	56350	Miltona	56354
Lake Wilson	56151	McGregor	55760	Mineral Center	55605
Lamberton	56152	McHugh	56501		
Lamoille	55987	McIntosh	56556	**Minneapolis**	55401-84
Lamson	55325	McKee (Part of Eagan)	55121	For specific Minneapolis Zip	
Lancaster	56735	McKinley	55761	Codes call (612) 452-3800, or	
Landfall	55128	Madelia	56062	your local postmaster.	
Lanesboro	55949	Madison	56256		
Langdon (Part of Cottage		Madison East (Part of		*COLLEGES & UNIVERSITIES*	
Grove)	55016	Mankato)	56001	Augsburg College	55454

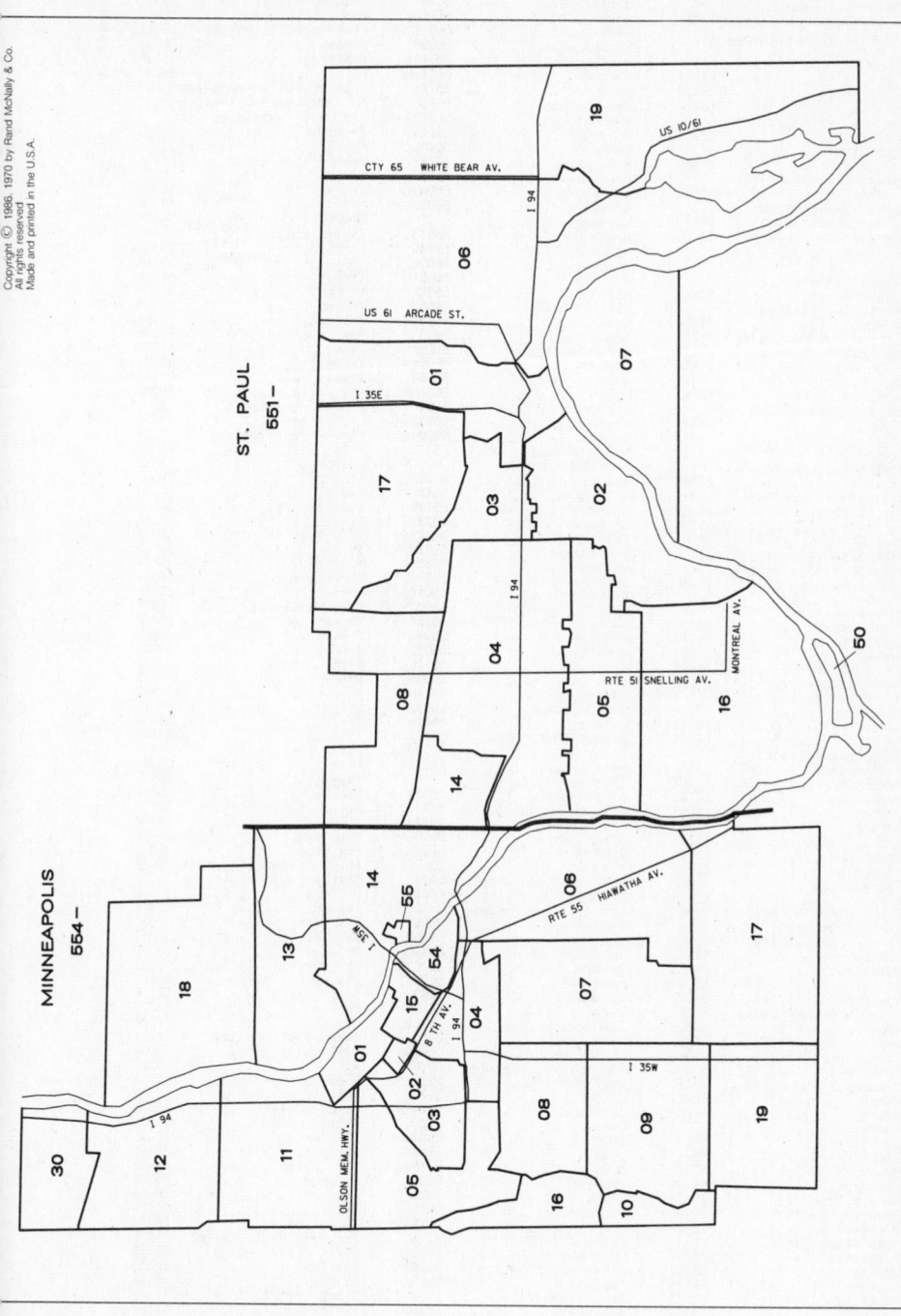

ST. PAUL
551—

MINNEAPOLIS
554—

	ZIP
North Central Bible College	55404
University of Minnesota-	
Twin Cities	55455

FINANCIAL INSTITUTIONS

	ZIP
Firstar Bank of Minnesota, N.A.	55417
First Bank N.A.	55402
IDS Bank and Trust	55402
Investors Savings Bank, F.S.B.	55402
Marquette Bank Minneapolis, N.A.	55480
National City Bank of Minneapolis	55402
Norwest Bank Minnesota, National Association	55479
TCF Bank Savings, F.S.B.	55402

HOSPITALS

	ZIP
Abbott-Northwestern Hospital	55407
Fairview Riverside Medical Center	55454
Fairview Southdale Hospital	55435
Hennepin County Medical Center	55415
University of Minnesota Hospital and Clinic	55455
Veterans Affairs Medical Center	55417

HOTELS/MOTELS

	ZIP
Hyatt Regency Minneapolis-Nicollet Mall	55403
Sheraton Park Place Hotel	55416
The Marquette	55402

MILITARY INSTALLATIONS

	ZIP
934th Mission Support Squadron, Minneapolis-St. Paul Air Reserve Base	55450
Minnehaha (Part of Minneapolis)	55406
Minneiska	55910
Minneota	56264
Minnesota City	55959
Minnesota Lake	56068
Minnesota Transfer (Part of St. Paul)	55114
Minnetonka	55345
Minnetonka Beach	55361
Minnetonka Mills (Part of Minnetonka)	55305
Minnetrista	55364
Minnewawa	55760
Mizpah	56660
Moland	55946
Money Creek	55943
Montevideo	56265
Montgomery	56069
Monticello	55362
	55365

For specific Monticello Zip Codes call (612) 295-2213, or your local postmaster.

	ZIP
Montrose	55363
Moorhead	56560*
	56561†
Moose Lake	55767
Moose Lake State Hospital	55767
Mora	55051
Morgan	56266
Morgan Park (Part of Duluth)	55808
Morningside (Part of Edina)	55424
Morrill	56329
Morris	56267
Morristown	55052
Morton	56270
Moscow	55912
Motley	56466
Mound	55364
Mounds View	55432
Mountain Iron	55768
Mountain Lake	56159
Mount Royal (Part of Duluth)	55803
Munger	55806
Murdock	56271
Murphy City	55603
Muskoda	56549
Myrtle	56070
Nashua	56565
Nashwauk	55769
Nassau	56272
Navarre (Part of Orono)	55392
Naytahwaush	56566
Nebish	56667
Nelson	56355
Nerstrand	55053

	ZIP
Nett Lake	55772
Nett Lake Indian Reservation	55772
Nevis	56467
New Auburn	55366
New Brighton	55112
Newburg	55954
Newfolden	56738
New Germany	55367
New Hartford	55925
New Hope	55428
Newhouse	55954
New London	56273
New Market	55054
New Munich	56356
Newport	55055
New Prague	56071
New Richland	56072
New Rome	55307
Newry	56045
New Trier	55031
New Ulm	56073
New York Mills	56567
Nickerson	55797
Nicollet	56074
Nicols (Part of Eagan)	55121
Nicolville	55912
Nielsville	56568
Nimrod	56478
Nininger	55033
Nisswa	56468
Nodine	55925
Nokomis (Part of Minneapolis)	55417
Nopeming	55810
Norcross	56274
Normandale (Part of Edina)	55439
Norseland	56082
North Benton	56329
North Branch	55056
Northcote	56728
Northdale (Part of Coon Rapids)	55433
North Douglas (Part of Crystal)	55422
Northfield	55057
North Mankato	56003
North Oaks	55110
Northome	56661
North Prairie	56314
North Redwood	56283
Northrop	56075
Northside (Part of Albert Lea)	56007
North St. Paul	55109
Northtown Shopping Center (Part of Blaine)	55434
Northwest Terminal (Part of Minneapolis)	55418
Norway Lake	56289
Norwood	55368
	55383

For specific Norwood Zip Codes call (612) 467-2242, or your local postmaster.

	ZIP
Nowthen	55303
Noyes	56740
Oak Center	55041
Oakdale	55128
Oakhill	56347
Oak Island	56741
Oak Knoll (Part of Minnetonka)	55305
Oakland	56076
Oak Park (Anoka County)	55434
Oak Park (Benton County)	56357
Oak Park Heights	55082
Oakport	56560
Oak Ridge	55910
Odessa	56276
Odin	56160
Ogema	56569
Ogilvie	56358
Okabena	56161
Oklee	56742
Old Frontenac	55041
Olga	56646
Olivia	56277
Onamia	56359
Onigum	56484
Opole	56340
Orchard Lake (Part of Lakeville)	55044
Org	56187
Orleans	56735
Ormsby	56162
Orono	55323
Oronoco	55960
Orr	55771
Orrock	55309
Ortonville	56278
Osage	56570

	ZIP
Osakis	56360
Oshawa	56082
Oslo (Dodge County)	55940
Oslo (Marshall County)	56744
Oslund	56680
Osseo	55311
	55369

For specific Osseo Zip Codes call (612) 425-2843, or your local postmaster.

	ZIP
Ostrander	55961
Otisco	56077
Otisville	55073
Otrey	56278
Ottawa	56058
Otter Creek	55718
Ottertail	56571
Outing	56662
Owatonna	55060
Oxlip	55040
Oylen	56481
Padua	56378
Palisade	56469
Palmdale	55084
Palmers	55804
Palo	55705
Parent	56329
Parkers Prairie	56361
Park Rapids	56470
Park View (Part of Crookston)	56716
Parkville (Part of Mountain Iron)	55773
Payne	55765
Paynesville	56362
Pease	56363
Pelican Rapids	56572
Pelland	56649
Pemberton	56078
Pencer	56751
Pengilly	55775
Pennington	56663
Pennock	56279
Pequaywan Lake	55801
Pequot Lakes	56472
Perham	56573
Perkins	55943
Perley	56574
Petersburg	56143
Peterson	55962
Petran	56043
Phelps	56586
Philbrook	56466
Pickwick	55987
Pierz	56364
Pigeon River	55605
Pike Lake	55811
Pillager	56473
Pillsbury	56382
Pilot Grove	56027
Pilot Mound	55923
Pine Bend (Dakota County)	55068
Pine Bend (Mahnomen County)	56651
Pine Brook	55008
Pine Center	56401
Pine City	55063
Pinecreek	56751
Pine Island	55963
Pine River	56474
Pine Springs	55115
Pineville	55705
Pinewood	56664
Pioneer (Part of St. Paul)	55101
Pipestone	56164
Pitt	56623
Plainview	55964
Plato	55370
Pleasant Grove	55976
Pleasant Lake	56301
Plummer	56748
Plymouth	55441
Point Douglas	55033
Ponemah	56666
Ponsford	56575
Poplar	56479
Popple Creek	56379
Port Cargill (Part of Savage)	55378
Porter	56280
Post Town	55920
Potsdam	55932
Powderhorn (Part of Minneapolis)	55407
Prairie Island Indian Reservation	55089
Prairieville	55021
Pratt	55060
Predmore	55934
Preston	55965
Priam	56282
Princeton	55371
Prinsburg	56281

	ZIP
Prior Lake	55372
Proctor	55810
Prosit	55702
Prosper	55954
Pulaski Lake Shores	55313
Puposky	56667
Quamba	55007
Racine	55967
Radium	56762
Rainy Junction (Part of Virginia)	55792
Ramey	56329
Ramsey (Anoka County)	55303
Ramsey (Mower County)	55912
Randall	56475
Randolph	55065
Ranier	56668
Rapidan	56001
Rassat	55313
Rauch	55740
Ray	56669
Raymond	56282
Reading	56165
Reads Landing	55968
Redby	56670
Redlake	56671
Red Lake Falls	56750
Red Lake Indian Reservation	56671
Red Rock	55605
Red Top	56342
Red Wing	55066
Redwood Falls	56283
Reformatory (Part of St. Cloud)	56301
Regal	56312
Remer	56672
Reno	55919
Renville	56284
Revere	56166
Rice	56367
Riceford	55954
Rice Street (Part of St. Paul)	55117
Richfield	55423
Richfield Hub Shopping Center (Part of Richfield)	55423
Richmond	56368
Rich Valley (Part of Rosemount)	55075
Richville	56576
Richwood	56577
Ridgedale Shopping Center (Part of Minnetonka)	55305
Ridgeway	55943
Rindal	56540
Riverside (Part of Minneapolis)	55454
Riverside Heights	56013
Riverton	56455
Riverview (Part of St. Paul)	55107
Robbin	58225
Robbinsdale	55422
Robinson	55731
Rochert	56578
Rochester	55901-06
For specific Rochester Zip Codes call (507) 282-3811, or your local postmaster.	
Rock Creek	55067
Rock Dell	55920
Rockford	55373
Rockville	56369
Rogers	55374
Rollag	56549
Rollingstone	55969
Rollins	55602
Ronneby	56329
Roosevelt	56673
Roscoe (Goodhue County)	55983
Roscoe (Stearns County)	56371
Roseau	56751
Rose City	56446
Rose Creek	55970
Roseland	56216
Rosemount	55068
Rosen	56212
Rosendale	56243
Roseport (Part of Inver Grove Heights)	55075
Roseville	55113
Rosewood	56701
Ross	56751
Rossburg	56431
Rothsay	56579
Round Lake	56167
Round Prairie	56347
Rowena	56293
Royalton	56373
Roy Lake	56557
Ruby Junction (Part of Hibbing)	55746
Rush City	55069

	ZIP
Rushford	55971
Rushford Village	55962
Rushmore	56168
Rush Point	55080
Rush River	56058
Ruskin	55021
Russell	56169
Rustad	56560
Ruthton	56170
Rutledge	55778
Sabin	56580
Sacred Heart	56285
Saga Hill (Part of Orono)	55323
Saginaw	55779
St. Anna	56310
St. Anthony (Hennepin County)	55418
St. Anthony (Stearns County)	56307
St. Augusta	56301
Saint Benedict	56071
St. Bonifacius	55375
St. Charles	55972
St. Clair (Blue Earth County)	56080
St. Clair (Ramsey County)	55116
St. Cloud	56301-04
For specific St. Cloud Zip Codes call (612) 251-8220, or your local postmaster.	
St. Croix Junction (Part of Hastings)	55033
St. Francis (Anoka County)	55070
St. Francis (Stearns County)	56331
St. George	56073
St. Henry	56057
St. Hilaire	56754
St. James	56081
St. Joseph	56374
St. Killian	56185
St. Leo	56286
St. Louis Park	55426
St. Martin	56376
St. Mary's Point	55043
St. Mathias	56449
St. Michael	55376
St. Nicholas	55389
St. Patrick	56071
St. Paul	55101-89
For specific St. Paul Zip Codes call (612) 452-3800, or your local postmaster.	

COLLEGES & UNIVERSITIES

	ZIP
Bethel College	55112
College of St. Catherine	55105
Macalester College	55105
Metropolitan State University	55101
William Mitchell College of Law	55105

FINANCIAL INSTITUTIONS

	ZIP
American National Bank & Trust Company	55101
Commercial State Bank	55102
Eastern Heights State Bank of St. Paul	55119
Firstar Bank of Minnesota, N.A.	55116
Liberty State Bank	55104
Midway National Bank	55104

HOSPITALS

	ZIP
Healtheast Bethesda Lutheran Hospital	55103
St. Paul-Ramsey Medical Center	55101

HOTELS/MOTELS

	ZIP
Holiday Inn St. Paul/East	55119
Ramada Hotel St. Paul	55119
The Saint Paul	55102

MILITARY INSTALLATIONS

	ZIP
Fort Snelling	55111
Minnesota Air National Guard, FB6231, Minneapolis-St.Paul International Airport	55111
Twin Cities Army Ammunition Plant (Caretaker Status)	55112
United States Army Engineer District, St. Paul	55101
United States Army Transportation Office, Minneapolis-St. Paul Area	55111
St. Paul Park	55071
St. Peter	56082
St. Rosa	56331
St. Thomas	56058

	ZIP
St. Vincent	56755
St. Wendel	56310
Salem Corners	55920
Salol	56756
Sanborn	56083
Sandstone	55072
Santiago	55377
Saratoga	55972
Sargeant	55973
Sartell	56377
Sauk Centre	56378
Sauk Rapids	56379
Saum	56674
Savage	55378
Sawyer	55780
Scandia	55073
Scandia Valley	56443
Scanlon	55720
Schley	56633
Schroeder	55613
Scotts Corner	55718
Seaforth	56287
Searles	56084
Sebeka	56477
Section Thirty	55731
Sedan	56380
Seven-Hi Shopping Center (Part of Minnetonka)	55345
Shafer	55074
Shakopee	55379
Shaw	55717
Sheffield Mill (Part of Faribault)	55021
Sheldon	55921
Shelly	56581
Sherack	56722
Sherburn	56171
Sheshebee	55760
Shevlin	56676
Shieldsville	55021
Shooks	56661
Shoreham	56501
Shoreview	55112
Shorewood	55331
Shotley	56650
Shovel Lake	55785
Side Lake	55781
Signal Hills Shopping Center (Part of West St. Paul)	55118
Silica	55746
Silo	55952
Silver Bay	55614
Silver Creek (Lake County)	55616
Silver Creek (Wright County)	55380
Silverdale	55740
Silver Lake	55381
Simpson	55901
Sioux Valley	51347
Skibo	55750
Skyburg	55946
Skyline	56001
Slayton	56172
Sleepy Eye	56085
Sletten	56556
Smiths Mill	56048
Snellman	56570
Sobieski	56345
Soderville (Part of Ham Lake)	55304
Sogn	55018
Solway	56678
Soudan	55782
South Bend	56001
South Branch	56081
Southdale (Part of Edina)	55435
Southdale Center (Part of Edina)	55435
South Haven	55382
South International Falls (Part of International Falls)	56679
South Minneapolis (Part of Minneapolis)	55408
South St. Paul	55075-77
For specific South St. Paul Zip Codes call (612) 451-1243, or your local postmaster.	
Southtown Center (Part of Bloomington)	55420
Spafford	56187
Spectacle Lake	55008
Spicer	56288
Springfield	56087
Spring Grove	55974
Spring Hill	56352
Spring Lake (Isanti County)	55056
Spring Lake (Itasca County)	56680
Spring Lake Park	55432
Spring Park	55384
Springsteel Island	56763
Springvale	55080
Spring Valley	55975
Spruce Center	56354

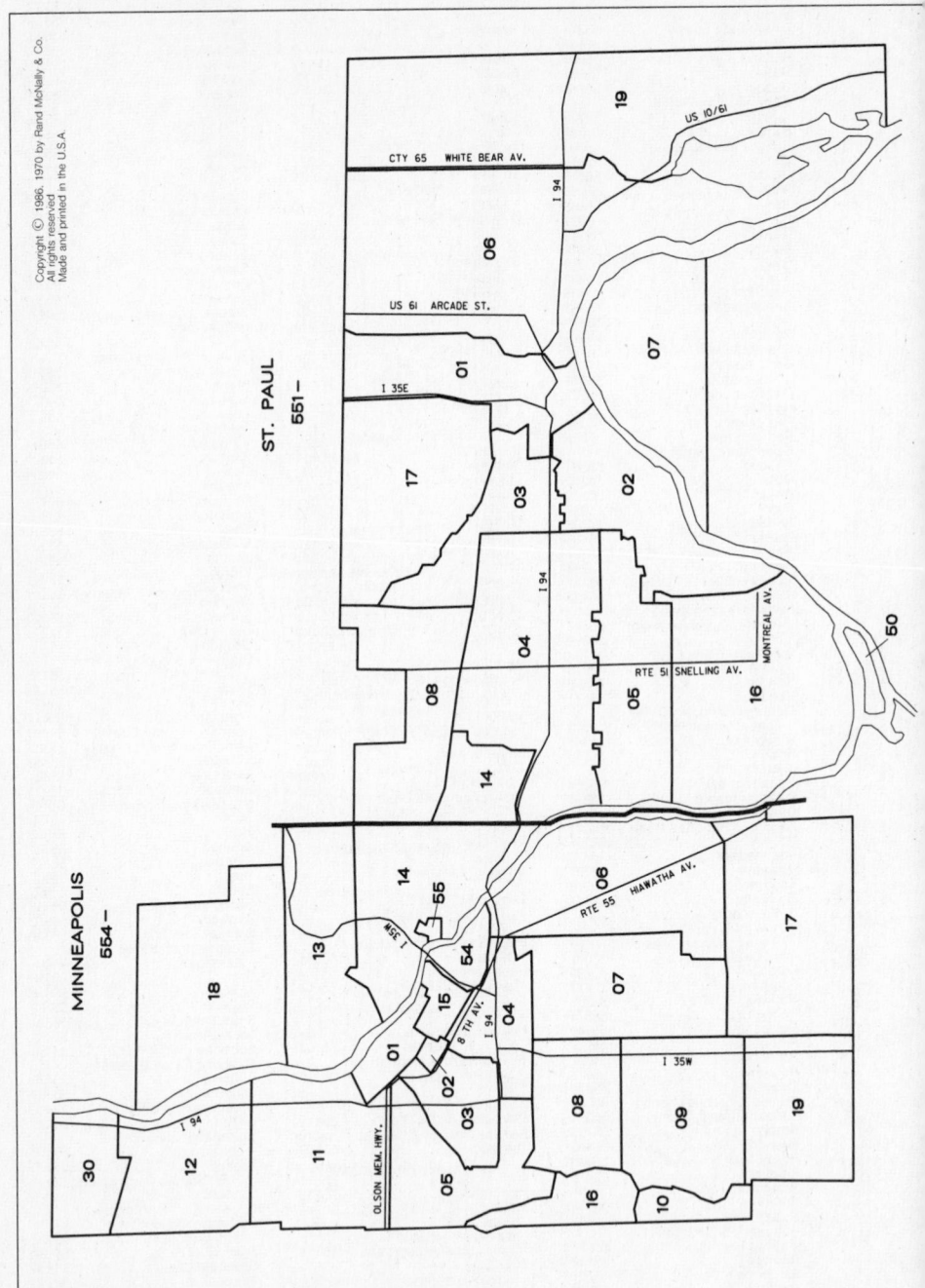

ST. PAUL
551–

MINNEAPOLIS
554–

	ZIP
Squaw Lake	56681
Stacy	55078-79

For specific Stacy Zip Codes call (612) 462-4984, or your local postmaster.

	ZIP
Stanchfield	55080
Stanley	55008
Stanton	55018
Staples	56479
Starbuck	56381
Stark	55032
Steele Center	55060
Steelton (Part of Duluth)	55808
Steen	56173
Stephen	56757
Sterling Center	56010
Stewart (Lake County)	55616
Stewart (McLeod County)	55385
Stewartville	55976
Stillwater	55082-83

For specific Stillwater Zip Codes call (612) 439-4232, or your local postmaster.

	ZIP
Stockholm	55321
Stockton	55988
Storden	56174
Strandquist	56758
Strathcona	56759
Strout	55355
St Stephen	56375
Stubbs Bay (Part of Orono)	55356
Sturgeon	55703
Sturgeon Lake	55783
Sugar Loaf (Part of Winona)	55987
Summit	55917
Sunburg	56289
Sundal	56545
Sunfish Lake	55118
Sunrise	55056
Svea	56216
Sveadahl	56081
Swanburg	56474
Swan River	55784
Swanville	56382
Swatara	55785
Swift	56682
Swift Falls	56215
Sylvan	56473
Syre	56584
Tabor	56712
Taconite	55786
Taconite Harbor	55613
Talmoon	56637
Tamarack	55787
Taopi	55977
Taunton	56291
Tawney	55954
Taylors Falls	55084
Tenney	56583
Tenstrike	56683
Terrace	56380
Terrebonne	56750
The Arches	55952
Theilman	55978
Thief River Falls	56701
Third Crow Wing Lake	56467
Thompson Grove (Part of Cottage Grove)	55016
Thompson Heights (Part of Coon Rapids)	55433
Thompson Heights Shopping Center (Part of Coon Rapids)	55433
Thompson Park (Part of Coon Rapids)	55433
Thompson Riverview Terrace (Part of Coon Rapids)	55433
Thomson	55718
Thor	56431
Thorhult	56727
Tintah	56583
Toad Lake	56544
Tofte	55615
Togo	55788
Toimi	55602
Toivola	55789
Tonka Bay	55331
Tower	55790
Tracy	56175
Traffic (Part of Minneapolis)	55403
Trail	56684
Trails End	55604
Traverse	56082
Trimont	56176
Trommald	56441
Trosky	56177
Troy	55972
Truman	56088
Turtle River	56601
Twig	55791

	ZIP
Twin Cities (Part of Richfield)	55111
Twin Lakes	56089
Twin Valley	56584
Two Harbors	55616
Two Inlets	56470
Tyler	56178
Ulen	56585
Underwood	56586
Union Hill	56071
University (Part of Minneapolis)	55414
Upper Sioux Indian Reservation	56241
Upsala	56384
Uptown (Part of St. Paul)	55102
Urbank	56361
U.S. Air Force	55814
Utica	55979
Vadnais Heights	55110
Valley Ridge (Part of Burnsville)	55378
Valley West Shopping Center (Part of Bloomington)	55420
Vasa	55089
Verdi	56179
Vergas	56587
Vermillion	55085
Vermillion Dam	55771
Verndale	56481
Vernon Center	56090
Veseli	55046
Vesta	56292
Victoria	55386
Viking	56760
Village North Shopping Center (Part of Brooklyn Park)	55429
Villard	56385
Vineland	56359
Vining	56588
Viola	55934
Virginia	55777
	55792

For specific Virginia Zip Codes call (218) 741-4919, or your local postmaster.

	ZIP
Vista	56077
Wabasha	55981
Wabasso	56293
Wabedo	56655
Waconia	55387
Wacouta	55066
Wadena	56482
Wahkon	56386
Waite Park	56387
Walbo	55008
Waldo	55616
Waldorf	56091
Wales	55616
Walker	56484
Walnut Grove	56180
Walters	56092
Waltham	55982
Wanamingo	55983
Wanda	56294
Wannaska	56761
Warba	55793
Ward Springs	56336
Warman	55051
Warren	56762
Warroad	56763
Warsaw	55087
Waseca	56093
Washington	55975
Wasioja	55927
Waskish	56685
Wastedo	55009
Waterford	55057
Watertown	55388
Waterville	56096
Watkins	55389
Watson	56295
Waubun	56589
Waverly	55390
Wawina	55736
Wayzata	55391
Wayzata Boulevard (Part of St. Louis Park)	55416
Wealthwood	56431
Weaver	55910
Weber	55056
Webster	55088
Wegdahl	56265
Welch	55089
Welcome	56181
Wells	56097
Weme	56634
Wendell	56590
West Albany	55957
West Albion	55302

	ZIP
Westbrook	56183
Westbury	56501
West Concord	55985
West Duluth (Part of Duluth)	55807
West End (Part of St. Paul)	55102
West Lake Francis Shores	55040
West Lynn	55350
West Newton	55945
West Point	55008
Westport	56385
West Rock	55063
West St. Paul	55118
West Union	56389
West Virginia (Part of Mountain Iron)	55792
Whalan	55986
Wheatland	56069
Wheaton	56296
Wheeler's Point	56623
Whipholt	56485
White Bear Beach	55110
White Bear Lake	55110
White Earth	56591
White Earth Indian Reservation	56591
Whiteface	55766
White Rock	55009
Whyte	55616
Wig Wam Bay	56359
Wilbert	56121
Wilder	56101
Wildwood	56661
Wilkinson	56633
Willernie	55090
Williams	56686
Willmar	56201
Willmar State Hospital	56201
Willow Creek	56010
Willow River	55795
Wilmington	55921
Wilmont	56185
Wilno	56142
Wilpen (Part of Hibbing)	55746
Wilson	55987
Wilton (Beltrami County)	56687
Wilton (Waseca County)	56093
Windom	56101
Winger	56592
Winnebago (Faribault County)	56098
Winnebago (Houston County)	55921
Winnipeg Junction	56549
Winona	55987
Winsted	55395
Winthrop	55396
Winton	55796
Wirock	56141
Wirt	56688
Withrow	55082
Witoka	55987
Wolf	55751
Wolf Lake	56593
Wolford	56441
Wolverton	56594
Woodbury (Washington County)	55125
Wood Lake	56297
Woodland (Hennepin County)	55391
Woodland (Kanabec County)	56342
Woodland (St. Louis County)	55803
Woodland Park	56551
Woodland Terrace (Part of Andover)	55303
Woodstock	56186
Worthington	56187
Wrenshall	55797
Wright	55798
Wrightstown	56453
Wyattville	55952
Wykoff	55990
Wylie	56750
Wyman (Part of Hoyt Lakes)	55750
Wyoming	55092
Yorktown (Part of Edina)	55435
Young America	55394
	55397

For specific Young America Zip Codes call (612) 467-3611, or your local postmaster.

	ZIP
Yucatan	55943
Zemple	56636
Zerkel	56621
Zim	55799
Zimmerman	55398
Zumbra Heights (Part of Victoria)	55386

	ZIP		ZIP
Zumbro Falls	55991	Zumbrota	55992

	ZIP		ZIP		ZIP
Abbeville	38601	Beech Springs	38866	Boyette	39160
Abbott	39773	Beechwood	39645	Boyle	38730
Aberdeen	39730	Beelake	39172	Bradley	39759
Ackerman	39735	Belden	38826	Branch	39117
Acona	39095	Belen	38609	Brandon	39042-43
Adams	39175	Bellefontaine	39737		39047
Adaton	39759	Belle Isle	39572	For specific Brandon Zip Codes	
Addie	38744	Belleville	39462	call (601) 825-2552, or your local	
Agricola	39452	Bellewood	38754	postmaster.	
Airey	39574	Bells School	39759	Branyan	38828
Airport Mail Facility (Part of		Belmont	38827	Brasfield	39096
Jackson)	39208	Belzoni	39038	Braxton	39044
Albin	38966	Benjoe	39456	Brazil	38963
Alcorn State University	39096	Benndale	39456	Brewer (Clarke County)	39355
Algoma	38820	Benoit	38725	Brewer (Lee County)	38868
Allen	39083	Benson	39437	Brewer (Perry County)	39476
Alligator	38720	Bentley	39751	Bright	38632
Alpine	38849	Bent Oak	39701	Bristers Store	39641
Altitude	38829	Benton	39039	Brockton (Part of Meridian)	39301
Alva	38925	Bentonia	39040	Brody	38603
Amory	38821	Benwood	38922	Brookhaven	39601
Anchor	39776	Berclair	38941	Brook Hollow	39212
Anchorage	39194	Berwick	39645	Brooklyn	39425
Anding	39040	Bethany	38849	Brooks	38737
Anguilla	38721	Betheden	39339	Brooksville	39739
Anse	39073	Bethel	39345	Brownfield	38683
Ansley	39558	Bethlehem (Marshall		Browning	38930
Antioch	39440	County)	38659	Brownsville	39041
Apple Ridge (Part of		Bethlehem (Pontotoc		Brown Town	39452
Jackson)	39204	County)	38863	Brozville	39095
Arcola	38722	Bethsaida	39350	Bruce	38915
Ariel	39638	Bett	38618	Brunswick	39180
Arkabutla	38602	Beulah (Bolivar County)	38726	Bryant	38922
Arlington (Lincoln County)	39629	Beulah (Newton County)	39337	Buchannan	38863
Arlington (Neshoba County)	39350	Beulah Hubbard	39337	Buckatunna	39322
Arm	39663	Bewelcome	39638	Buckhorn	38864
Arnold Line	39402	Bexley	39452	Bude	39630
Artesia	39736	Bigbee	38821	Buena Vista (Chickasaw	
Ashland	38603	Bigbee Valley	39738	County)	38851
Askew	38621	Big Creek	38914	Buena Vista (Tippah	
Athens	39730	Biggersville	38834	County)	38663
Atlanta	39776	Big Level	39573	Buena Vista Lakes	38632
Atway	38635	Bigpoint	39581	Bunker Hill	39429
Auburn (Lee County)	38801	Billups	39701	Bunkley	39653
Auburn (Lincoln County)	39666	Biloxi	39530-35	Burgess	38655
Austin	38676	For specific Biloxi Zip Codes call		Burns	39153
Avalon	38912	(601) 432-0311, or your local		Burnside	39350
Avera	39451	postmaster.		Burnsville	38833
Avon	38723	Binford	39730	Burrell	38628
Bailey	39320	Binnsville	39358	Burtons	38829
Baird	38751	Birmingham Ridge	38828	Bush	39149
Baker	38652	Bissell	38801	Busy Corner	39638
Bald Hill	38652	Black Bayou Junction	38928	Butler	39169
Baldwyn	38824	Black Hawk	38923	Byhalia	38611
Ballard	39046	Blackjack	39759	Byram	39212
Ballardsville	38801	Blackland	38829		39272
Ballentine	38621	Blackwater (Kemper		For specific Byram Zip Codes call	
Ball Ground	39156	County)	39326	(601) 968-0520, or your local	
Baltzer	38732	Blackwater (Lafayette		postmaster.	
Banks	38664	County)	38685	Cadamy	38876
Banner	38913	Blaine	38778	Cadaretta	38929
Barlow	39083	Blair	38849	Caesar	39466
Barnes	39051	Blakely	39180	Caile	38754
Barnesville	38109	Blanton	39159	Cairo	38873
Barnett	39347	Bloody Springs	38827	Caledonia	39740
Barr	38668	Bloomfield (Kemper County)	39328	Calhoun (Jones County)	39440
Barrontown	39465	Bloomfield (Neshoba		Calhoun (Newton County)	39345
Bartahatchie	39740	County)	39350	Calhoun City	38916
Barth	39470	Blue Hills	39144	Calyx	39361
Barto	39648	Blue Lake	38737	Cambridge	38601
Barton (George County)	39452	Blue Mountain	38610	Camden	39045
Barton (Marshall County)	38017	Blue Springs	38828	Cameron	39146
Basic	39330	Bluff Springs (Kemper		Cameta	39159
Basin	39452	County)	39328	Campbell (Part of Ripley)	38663
Bassfield	39421	Bluff Springs (Panola		Canaan	38603
Batesville	38606	County)	38666	Candlestick (Part of	
Batson	39401	Bobo (Coahoma County)	38614	Jackson)	39212
Battlefield (Hinds County)	39204	Bobo (Quitman County)	38646	Candlestick Park (Part of	
Battle Field (Newton		Boggan Bend	38849	Jackson)	39212
County)	39325	Bogue Chitto (Kemper		Cannonsburg	39120
Battles	39362	County)	39350	Canton	39046
Baugh	38669	Bogue Chitto (Lincoln		Cardsville	38858
Baxter	39338	County)	39629	Carlisle	39086
Baxterville	39455	Boice	39367	Carlos	39191
Bayland	39194	Bolatusha	39160	Carmack	39176
Bay Saint Louis	39520-22	Bolivar	38725	Carmichael (Clarke County)	39360
	39529	Bolton	39041	Carmichael (Perry County)	39423
For specific Bay Saint Louis Zip		Bond (Neshoba County)	39350	Carnes	39455
Codes call (601) 467-5788, or		Bond (Stone County)	39577	Carolina	38858
your local postmaster.		Bon Homme	39401	Carpenter	39086
Bayside Park	39520	Bonita (Part of Meridian)	39301	Carriere	39426
Bay Springs	39422	Boon	39339	Carrollton	38917
Beacon Hill	38652	Boone	38614	Carson	39427
Beans Ferry	38843	Booneville	38829	Carter	39194
Bear Town	39648	Bothwell	39476	Carterville (Part of Petal)	39465
Beasley	39755	Bounds Crossroads	35582	Carthage	39051
Beatline	39350	Bourbon	38756	Cary	39054
Beatrice	39330	Bovina	39180	Cascilla	38920
Beatty	39176	Bowdre	38664	Caseyville	39191
Beaumont	39423	Bowling Green	39063	Cato	39042
Beauregard	39191	Bowman	38618	Cayce	38017
Becker	38825	Boyer	38751	Cayuga	39175

* Area Zip Code   † Post Office Boxes

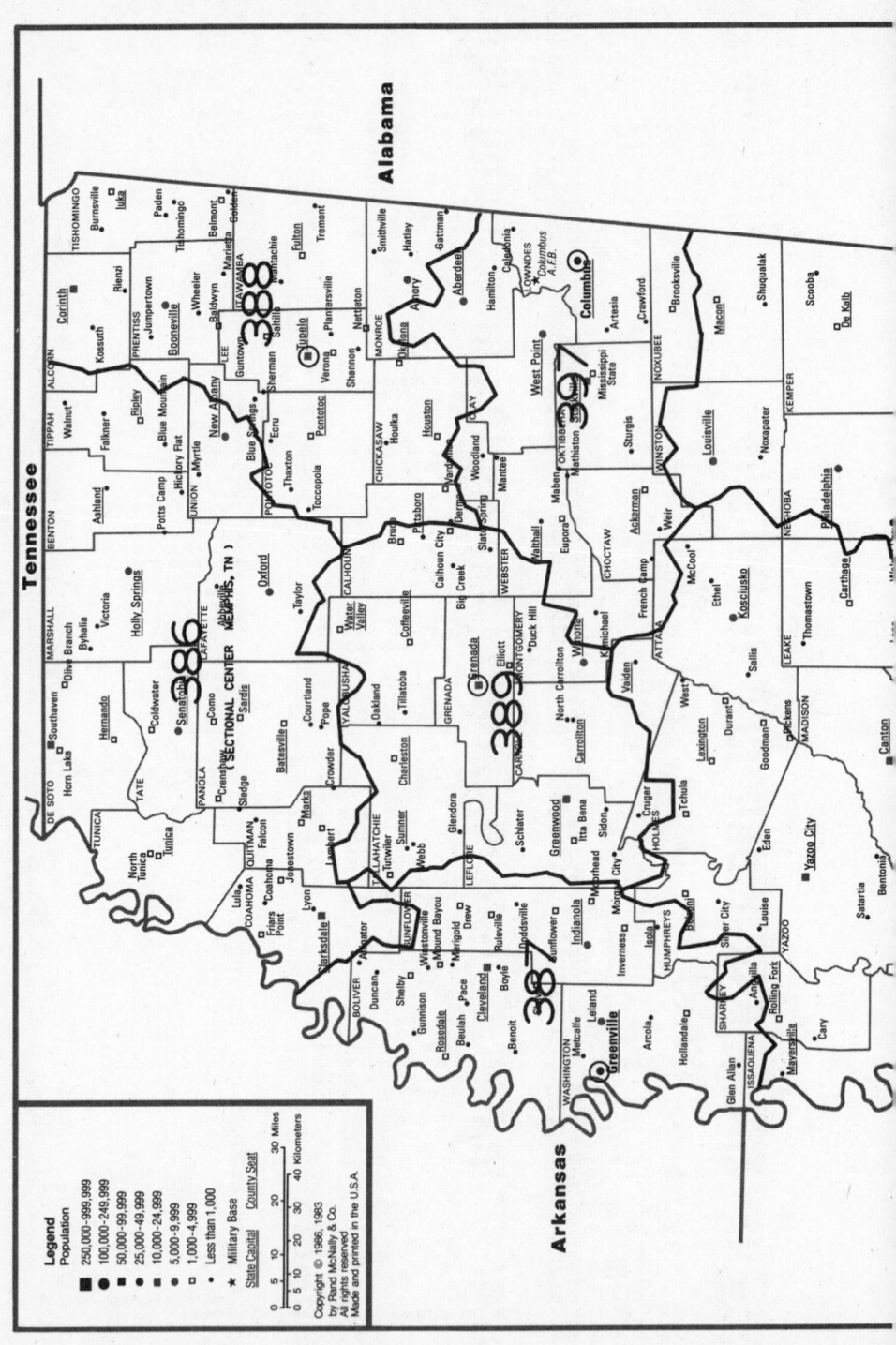

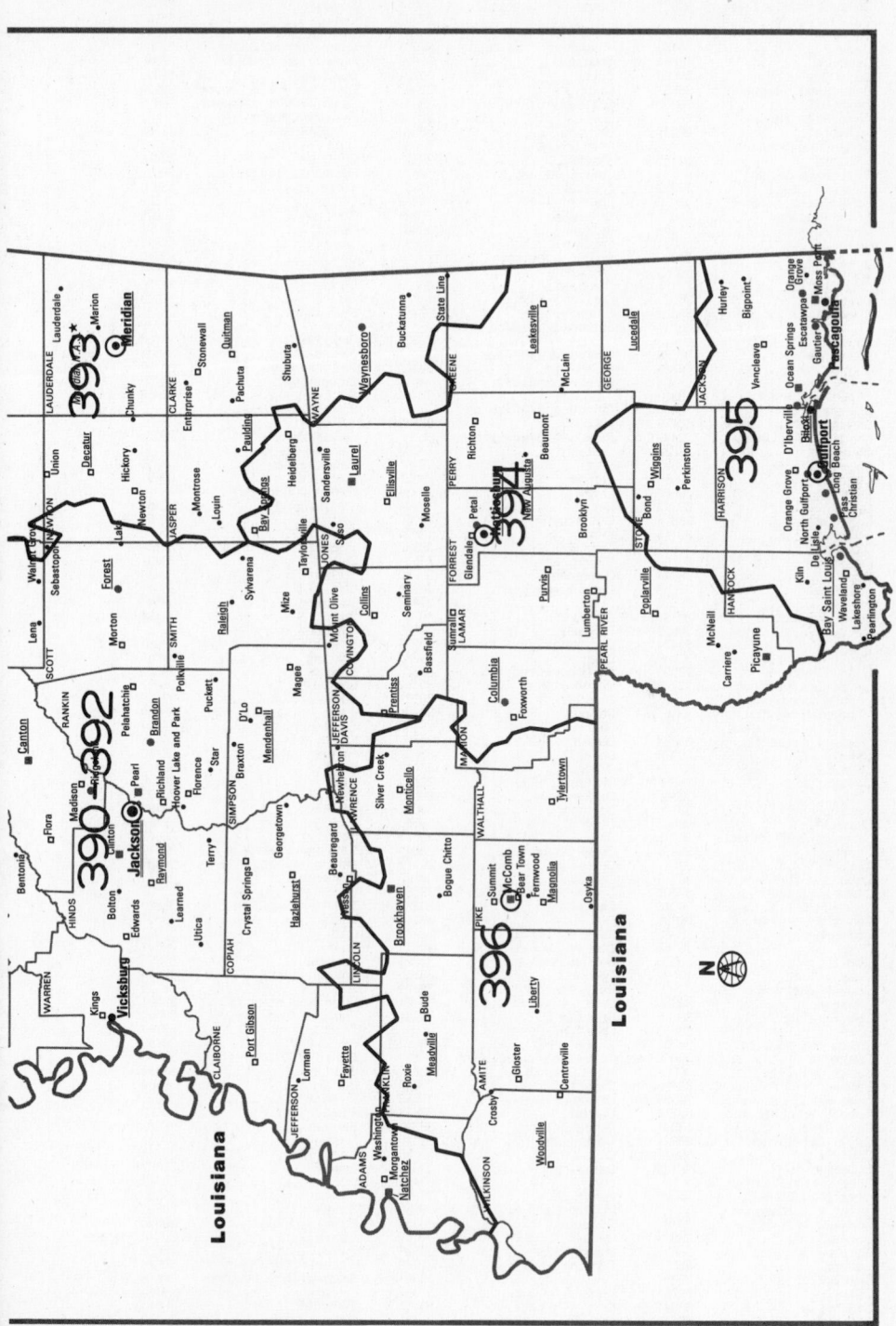

Name	ZIP	Name	ZIP	Name	ZIP
Cedarbluff	39741	Cottonville	38618	Doolittle	39345
Cedar Hill (Madison County)	39071	Counts	38614	Dorsey	39843
Cedar Hill (Montgomery County)	38925	County Line	39362	Doskie	38852
Cedars	39180	Courthouse (Part of Gulfport)	39501	Dossville	39051
Cedarview	38654	Courtland	38620	Dover (Neshoba County)	39365
Center (Attala County)	39090	Cowart	38921	Dover (Yazoo County)	39040
Center (Union County)	38652	Coxburg	39095	Dowdville	39350
Center Hill	39307	Coxs Ferry	39041	Downtown (Part of Gulfport)	39501
Center Ridge (Newton County)	39337	Coy	39354	Downtown (Part of Tupelo)	38801
Center Ridge (Smith County)	39168	Craigside	38930	Downtown (Part of Vicksburg)	39181
Center Ridge (Winston County)	39339	Craig Springs	39769	Drew	38737
Centerville	38855	Crandall	39355	Dry Creek	39428
Central Academy	38606	Crane Creek	39573	Dubard	38901
Centralgrove	38858	Cranfield	39661	Dubbs	38626
Centreville	39631	Crawford	39743	Dublin	38739
Chalybeate	38683	Crenshaw	38621	Duck Hill	38925
Champion Hill	39066	Crockett	38668	Duffee	39337
Chapel Hill	39175	Crosby	39633	Dumas	38625
Charleston	38921	Crossgates (Part of Brandon)	39042	Duncan	38740
Chatawa	39632	Crossroad	39051	Dundee	38626
Chatham	38731	Crossroads (George County)	39452	Dunleith	38756
Cheraw	39483	Crossroads (Neshoba County)	39350	Durant	39063
Cherrycreek	38828	Crossroads (Pearl River County)	39470	Dwiggins	38737
Chester	39735	Cross Roads (Rankin County)	39145	Dwyer	38778
Chesterville	38801	Cross Roads (Tishomingo County)	38852	Eagle Lake	39180
Chicora	39322	Crossroads (Washington County)	38703	Earlygrove	38642
Chiwapa	38863	Crotts	39437	East Aberdeen	39730
Choctaw (Bolivar County)	38773	Crowder	38622	Eastabuchie	39436
Choctaw (Jones County)	39440	Cruger	38924	Eastfork	39664
Chulahoma	38635	Crupp	39194	East Heights (Part of Tupelo)	38801
Chunky	39323	Crystal Springs	39059	East Hillsboro	39074
Church Hill	39055	Cuba	38834	Eastlawn (Part of Pascagoula)	39569
Clack	38664	Cub Lake	38632	East Lincoln	39601
Clara	39324	Cuevas	39571	East Moss Point (Part of Moss Point)	39563
Claremont	38614	Cumberland	39750	Eastport	38852
Clarksburg	39117	Curtis Station	38606	East Side	39476
Clarksdale	38614	Cybur	39466	East Tupelo (Part of Tupelo)	38801
Clarkson	39752	Cynthia	39206	Eatonville	39401
Clay	38843	Dahomey	38725	Ebenezer	39064
Clayrysville	38663	Daisy-Vestry	39573	Ecru	38841
Clayton	38626	Daleville	39326	Eddiceton	39647
Clayton Village	39759	Damascus (Kemper County)	39328	Eden	39194
Claytown	39339	Damascus (Scott County)	39189	Edgewater Plaza (Part of Biloxi)	39531
Clem	39474	Dancy	39751	Edinburg	39051
Cleo	39440	Daniel	39151	Edwards	39066
Clermont Harbor	39558	Darbun	39643	Eggville	38801
Cleveland (Bolivar County)	38732-33	Darden	38650	Egremont	39159
For specific Cleveland Zip Codes call (601) 843-4031, or your local postmaster.		Darling	38623	Egypt (Chickasaw County)	38860
		Darlove	38748	Egypt (Holmes County)	38924
Cleveland (Kemper County)	39328	Darracott	38730	Electric Mills	39358
Clifton	39074	Darrington	39633	Elizabeth	38756
Cliftonville	39739	Davenport	38614	Ellard	38915
Clinton	39056*	Davis	39046	Elliott	38926
	39060†	Days	38641	Ellistown	38838
Cloverdale	39120	Deans Corner	38641	Ellisville	39437
Clover Hill	38645	Deasonville	39179	Ellisville Junction	39437
Cloverleaf Mall (Part of Hattiesburg)	39401	Decatur	39327	Elsie	38878
Coahoma	38617	Deemer	39350	Elton (Part of Jackson)	39212
Coats	39119	Deemer Station	39320	Elwood	39355
Cobbs	39601	Deep Creek	39425	Eminence	39479
Cobbville	39046	Deerbrook	39739	Emory	39095
Cockrum	38632	Deeson	38740	Endville	38828
Coffeeville	38922	De Kalb	39328	Energy	39301
Cohay	39153	De Lay	38655	Enid	38927
Coila	38923	De Lisle	39571	Enon	39641
Colby	39194	Delta	38621	Enondale	39352
Coldwater (Neshoba County)	39350	Delta City	39061	Enterprise (Amite County)	39645
Coldwater (Tate County)	38618	Delta Drive (Part of Jackson)	39213	Enterprise (Clarke County)	39330
Coles	39633	Delta State University (Part of Cleveland)	38733	Enterprise (Lincoln County)	39601
College (Part of Columbus)	39701	Denham	39367	Enterprise (Union County)	38650
College Hill	38655	Denmark	38655	Enzor	39301
College Hill Sta	38655	Dennis	38838	Errata	39440
Collins	39428	Dennis Settlement	39092	Erwin	38744
Collinsville	39325	Dentontown	38916	Escatawpa	39552
Colonial (Part of Jackson)	39211	Dentville	39086	Eset	39362
Colony Town	38941	Deovolente	39038	Eskridge	38925
Colsub (Part of Amory)	38821	Derby	39470	Essex	38623
Columbia	39429	Derma	38839	Estes	39339
Columbus	39701-05	De Soto	39360	Estesmill	39051
For specific Columbus Zip Codes call (601) 328-6171, or your local postmaster.		Deweese	39350	Estill	38748
		Dexter	39667	Ethel	39067
Columbus Air Force Base	39701	Diamondhead	39525	Etta	38627
Commerce	38664	D'Iberville	39532	Eucutta	39360
Como	38619	Dinsmore	39341	Eudora	38632
Concord	38652	Divide	39654	Eunice	39638
Conehatta	39057	Dixie	39401	Eupora	39744
Conway	39051	Dixie Pine	39401	Eureka Springs	38620
Cooksville	39341	Dixon	39350	Evansville (Tate County)	38618
Cooperville	39117	D'Lo	39062	Evansville (Tunica County)	38676
Coosa	39051	Doddsville	38736	Everett	39114
Corinth	38834	Doloroso	39669	Evergreen	38843
Cornersville	38633	Donegal	39669	Expose	39429
Corrona	38849			Fairfield	38828
Cotton Plant	38610			Fairground	39350
				Fairhaven	38654
				Fairhill	39361
				Fairlane (Part of Columbus)	39701

	ZIP		ZIP		ZIP
Fair Oaks Springs	39601	Good Hope (Neshoba		Hideaway Hills	39666
Fair River	39601	County)	39350	Hidi	39166
Fairview (Itawamba County)	38847	Good Hope (Perry County)	39476	Higgins	39482
Fairview (Sunflower County)	38751	Goodman	39079	High Hill	39350
Falcon	38628	Goodwater	39366	Highlandale	38952
Falkner	38629	Goodyear (Part of Picayune)	39466	High Point	39339
Fame	39744	Gore Springs	38929	Hightown	38834
Fannin	39042	Goshen Springs	39042	Hillhouse	38720
Farmhaven	39046	Goss	39429	Hillman	39451
Farmington	38834	Grace	38745	Hillsboro	39087
Farrell	38630	Grady	39744	Hillsdale	39470
Fayette	39069	Graham	38824	Hinchcliff	38646
Fenton	39571	Grand Gulf	39150	Hinkle	38865
Fentress	39735	Grange	39140	Hintonville	39423
Fenwick	39120	Grange Hall	39180	Hinze	39108
Fernwood	39635	Grapeland	38725	Hiram	38963
Fikestown	39092	Gravel Hill	38930	Hiwannee	39367
Fitler	39070	Graves	38828	Hobo Station	38829
Fitzhugh	38737	Gravestown	38663	Hohenlinden	39751
Flora	39071	Greenbrier Park	39466	Holcomb	38940
Florence	39073	Greenfield	39042	Holcut	38852
Flowerdale (Part of Tupelo)	38801	Greenfield Addition (Part of		Hollandale	38748
Floweree	39156	Greenville)	38701	Hollis	38878
Flowood	39208	Green Grove	38767	Holly Bluff	39088
Floyd	38603	Greenland	39365	Holly Grove	38954
Fondren (Part of Jackson)	39216	Greenville	38701-04	Holly Ridge	38749
Fontainebleau	39564	For specific Greenville Zip Codes		Holly Springs	38634†
Fords Creek	39470	call (601) 335-4523, or your local			38635*
Fordyke	39039	postmaster.		Hollywood	38676
Forest	39074	Greenville Mall (Part of		Holmesville	39648
Forestdale	39365	Greenville)	38701	Holts Spur	38833
Forest Grove	39051	Greenville North (Part of		Homewood	39074
Forest Hill (Part of Jackson)	39212	Greenville)	38701	Homochitto	39638
Forkville	39076	Greenwood (Itawamba		Honey Island	39038
Fort Adams	39669	County)	38843	Hoover Lake and Park	39073
Fort Stephens	39320	Greenwood (Leflore County)	38930	Hope	39350
Four Corners	39090	Greenwood Springs	38848	Hopedale	39113
Four Mile	39038	Grenada	38901-02	Hopewell (Benton County)	38067
Foxworth	39483	Griffith	39741	Hopewell (Copiah County)	39059
Franklin	39661	Gulde	39042	Hopoca	39051
Frankstown	38824	Gulf Hills	39564	Horn Lake	38637
Freeny	39051	Gulf Hills Country Club	39564	Horseshoe (Holmes County)	39169
Freerun	39194	Gulf Park Estates	39564	Horse Shoe (Scott County)	39189
Freetrade	39051	Gulfport	39501-07	Hortontown	38863
Freeze Corner	38632	For specific Gulfport Zip Codes		Hot Coffee	39428
French Camp	39745	call (601) 832-4131, or your local		Houlka	38850
French Store	39073	postmaster.		House	39365
Friars Point	38631	Gum Grove	39169	Houston	38851
Friendship (Lincoln County)	39601	Gums	38922	Howard	39095
Friendship (rural) (Lincoln		Gum Springs	39074	Howell	39452
County)	39601	Gunnison	38746	Howison	39574
Friendship (Pontotoc		Guntown	38849	Hoy	39440
County)	38841	Gwin (Part of Tchula)	39169	Hub	39429
Frog Island	38801	Gwinville	39140	Hubbard	39066
Frostbridge	39367	Hale	39360	Hudsonville	38635
Fruitland Park	39577	Halltown	38849	Humber	38614
Fugate	39039	Hamburg	39661	Huntsville	39745
Fulton	38843	Hamilton	39746	Hurley	39555
Furrs	38863	Hampton	38744	Hurricane	38863
Futheyville	38901	Handle	39339	Hurricane Creek	39301
Gallman	39077	Handsboro (Part of		Hushpuckena	38774
Gandsi	39479	Gulfport)	39501	Improve	39429
Garden City	39661	Handy Corner	38654	Increase	39301
Garlandville	39345	Hard Cash	39038	Inda	39573
Gaston	38865	Hardy	38901	Independence (Scott	
Gatesville	39059	Harleston	39452	County)	39117
Gatewood	38922	Harmontown	38619	Independence (Tate	
Gattman	38844	Harmony	39355	County)	38638
Gault	38655	Harperville	39080	Indian Hills	38866
Gautier	39553	Harriston	39081	Indianola	38751
Geeslin Corner	38901	Harrisville	39082	Indian Springs	39401
Geeville	38829	Harvey (Part of Petal)	39465	Industrial	39466
Geneill	38756	Hathorn	39429	Ingomar	38652
General Mail Facility (Part of		Hatley	38821	Ingrams Mill	38611
Jackson)	39205	Hattiesburg	39401-07	Inverness	38753
Georgetown	39078	For specific Hattiesburg Zip		Isola	38754
Gholson	39354	Codes call (601) 268-0888, or		Itta Bena	38941
Gibson	39730	your local postmaster.		Iuka	38852
Gift	38834	Hayes Crossing	38666	Jacinto	38865
Giles	39358	Hays	39057	Jack	39175
Gill	39051	Hazel	39092	Jackson	39201-98
Gillsburg	39657	Hazlehurst	39083	For specific Jackson Zip Codes	
Gitano	39168	Heads	38756	call (601) 968-0572, or your local	
Glade	39440	Heathman	38751	postmaster.	
Glancy	39083	Hebron (Jefferson Davis		Jackson Mall (Part of	
Glen	38846	County)	39140	Jackson)	39213
Glen Allan	38744	Hebron (Jones County)	39168	Jackson Square (Part of	
Glendale	39401	Heidelberg	39439	Jackson)	39204
Glendora	38928	Helena	39581	Jago	38671
Glenfield (Part of New		Helm	38756	Jaketown	39038
Albany)	38652	Henderson's Point (Part of		James	38748
Glenville	38619	Pass Christian)	39571	Jamestown	38483
Glenwild	38901	Hendrix	39747	Janice	39425
Gloster	39638	Henleyfield	39426	Jayess	39641
Glover	38680	Herbert Springs	39325	Jeannette	39120
Gluckstadt	39110	Hermanville	39086	Jeff Davis	39180
Golden	38847	Hernando	38632	Jefferson	38917
Golden Grove	39365	Hero	39345	Jeffries	38626
Goldfield	38737	Hesterville	39192	Jenkins	39437
Gooden Lake	39038	Heucks Retreat	39191	Jericho	38824
Good Hope (Leake County)	39094	Hickory	39332	Johns	39042
		Hickory Flat	38633	Johnson	39437

	ZIP		ZIP		ZIP
Johnston	39666	Little Texas	38676	Marks	38646
Jonathan	39451	Little Yazoo	39040	Mars Hill	39666
Jonestown (Coahoma		Litton	38773	Martin	39325
County)	38639	Lizana	39503	Martin Bluff	39553
Jonestown (Yazoo County)	39194	Lobdell	38726	Martinsville	39083
Jug Fork	38828	Lobutcha	39108	Martintown	38652
Jumpertown	38829	Loch Leven	39669	Martinville	39114
Junction City	39355	Locke Station	38606	Marydell	39051
Kalem	39117	Lockhart	39335	Mashulaville	39341
Keirn	38924	Lodi (Humphreys County)	39166	Matherville	39360
Kellis Store	39354	Lodi (Montgomery County)	39767	Mathiston	39752
Kelona	39366	Lombardy	38774	Mattson	38758
Kendrick	38834	Long	38756	Maxie	39425
Keownville	38652	Long Beach	39560	Maybank	39401
Kewanee	39364	Longino	39350	Maybell	39437
Key Field (Part of Meridian)	39301	Long Lake (Coahoma		Mayersville	39113
Kilmichael	39747	County)	38617	Mayhew	39753
Kiln	39556	Long Lake (Warren County)	39180	Mayton	39042
King and Anderson	38614	Longshot	38773	Maywood	38654
Kings	39180	Longtown	38665	Meadville	39653
Kingston	39120	Longview (Oktibbeha		Mechanicsburg	39040
Kinlock	38751	County)	39759	Meehan	39301
Kipling	39328	Longview (Pontotoc		Meeks	38924
Kirby	39661	County)	38863	Melba	39482
Kirkville	38843	Looxahoma	38668	Meltonville	39046
Kittrell	39423	Lorena	39074	Memphis	38680
Klem	39074	Lorenzen	39159	Mendenhall	39114
Klondike	39320	Lorman	39096	Meridian	39301-07
Knobtown	39362	Louin	39338	For specific Meridian Zip Codes	
Knoxo	39667	Louise	39097	call (601) 693-2581, or your local	
Knoxville	39661	Louisville	39339	postmaster.	
Kokomo	39643	Love	38632	Meridian Naval Air Station	39309
Kola	39428	Loyd	38878	Meridian Station	39309
Kolola Springs	39740	Loyd Star	39601	Merigold	38759
Kosciusko	39090	Lucas	39474	Merit	39114
Kossuth	38834	Lucedale	39452	Merrill	39452
Kreole (Part of Moss Point)	39563	Lucern	39365	Mesa	39667
Lackey	39730	Lucien	39601	Metcalfe	38760
Lafayette Springs	38655	Luckney	39208	Metrocenter (Part of	
Lake	39092	Ludlow	39098	Jackson)	39204
Lake Center	38659	Lula	38644	Meyers	39401
Lake City (Prentiss County)	38829	Lumberton	39455	Michigan City	38647
Lake City (Yazoo County)	39194	Lurand	38614	Midnight	39115
Lake Como	39422	Lux	39401	Midway (Copiah County)	39191
Lake Cormorant	38641	Lyman	39503	Midway (Hinds County)	39170
Lakeland (Part of Richland)	39218	Lynchburg	38109	Midway (Leake County)	39051
Lake of Hills	38632	Lynn Creek	39739	Midway (Scott County)	39074
Lakeshore	39558	Lynville	39354	Midway (Tishomingo	
Lake View	38680	Lyon	38645	County)	38852
Lamar	38642	Maben	39750	Midway (Yazoo County)	39039
Lamar Park	39401	McAdams	39107	Mileston	39169
Lambert	38643	McBride	39144	Millard	39470
Lamkin	39166	McCall Creek	39647	Mill Creek (Jones County)	39440
Lamont	38755	McCallum	39401	Mill Creek (Pearl River	
Lampton	39429	McCarley	38943	County)	39426
Landon	39503	McComb	39648	Mill Creek (Rankin County)	39042
Langford	39042	McCondy	38854	Millcreek (Winston County)	39339
Langsdale	39360	McCool	39108	Mill Creek Cabin Area	38852
Larue	39564	McCrary	39701	Miller	38654
Latimer	39564	McCutcheon	38722	Millington	39358
Latonia	39452	Mc Donald (Leake County)	39094	Mill Town (Part of Canton)	39046
Lauderdale	39335	McDonald (Neshoba		Mimms	38606
Laurel	39440-42	County)	39365	Mineral Wells	38648
For specific Laurel Zip Codes call		Macedonia (Forrest County)	39401	Mingo	38873
(601) 425-1408, or your local		Macedonia (Lee County)	38801	Minter City	38944
postmaster.		Macedonia (Union County)	38650	Missionary	39356
Laurelhill	39350	Macel	38950	Mississippi Choctaw Indian	
Lawrence	39336	McElveen	39666	Reservation	39350
Laws Hill	38685	McHenry	39561	Mississippi City (Part of	
Leaf	39456	McLain	39456	Gulfport)	39501
Leakesville	39451	McLaurin	39401	Mississippi College (Part of	
Learned	39154	McLaurin Heights (Part of		Clinton)	39058
Lebanon (Hinds County)	39154	Pearl)	39208	Mississippi State	39762
Lebanon (Marshall County)	38659	McLeod	39341	Mississippi Valley State	
Lee Donald	39366	McMillan	39339	University	38941
Leedy	38833	McNair	39069	Mitchell	38663
Leesburg	39117	McNeal	39338	Mize	39116
Leesdale	39661	McNeill	39457	Money	38945
Leeville	39401	Macon	39341	Monroe	39653
Lefleur (Part of Jackson)	39211	McSwain	39476	Monterey	39073
Leflore	38940	McVille	39090	Monte Vista	39744
Leigh Mall (Part of		Madden	39109	Montgomery	39191
Columbus)	39701	Madison	39110*	Monticello	39654
Leland	38756		39130†	Montpelier	39754
Lemon	39074	Madisonville	39046	Montrose	39338
Lena	39094	Magee	39111	Moon	38662
Lessley	39669	Magnolia	39652	Moores Mill	38838
Le Tourneau	39180	Mahned	39462	Mooreville	38857
Leverett	38920	Main (Part of Meridian)	39302	Moorhead	38761
Lewisburg	38654	Malone	38685	Morgan City	38946
Lexie	39667	Malvina	38769	Morgans	39170
Lexington	39095	Mannassa	39355	Morgantown (Adams	
Liberty (Amite County)	39645	Mantachie	38855	County)	39120
Liberty (Kemper County)	39328	Mantee	39751	Morgantown (Marion	
Lightsey	39440	Marcella	39169	County)	39484
Lillian	39074	Marianna	38635	Morgantown (Oktibbeha	
Linn	38736	Marie	38751	County)	39769
Linwood (Neshoba County)	39365	Marietta	38856	Morning Star	39066
Linwood (Yazoo County)	39179	Marion	39342	Morriston	39401
Little Creek	39423	Maris Town (Part of Canton)	39046	Morton	39117
Little Italy	39092	Markette	38655	Moscow	39328
Little Rock	39337	Markham	38761	Moselle	39459

	ZIP
Moss	39460
Moss Point	39562-63
For specific Moss Point Zip Codes call (601) 475-3951, or your local postmaster.	
Mossy Lake	38959
Mound Bayou	38762
Mound City (Bolivar County)	38726
Mound City (Union County)	38828
Mount Carmel	39474
Mount Nebo	39328
Mount Olive (Covington County)	39119
Mount Olive (Franklin County)	39653
Mount Olive (Jones County)	39440
Mount Pleasant (Itawamba County)	38876
Mount Pleasant (Marshall County)	38649
Mount Vernon	38801
Mount Zion	39111
Movella	39452
Muldon	39730
Mullins Store	38655
Murphy	38748
Murry	38663
Muskegon	39092
Myrick	39440
Myrleville	39039
Myrtle	38650
Nancy	39366
Nason	38940
Natchez	39120-22
For specific Natchez Zip Codes call (601) 442-4361, or your local postmaster.	
National Cemetery (Part of Vicksburg)	39180
Necaise	39573
Neely	39461
Nellieburg	39307
Nesbit	38651
Neshoba	39365
Nettleton	38858
Nevada	39041
New Albany	38652
New Augusta	39462
New Byram	39212
New Canaan	38603
New Fitler	39070
New Garden	38618
New Harmony	38828
New Hebron	39140
New Hope	39702
Newman	39066
Newmans	39180
Newmans Grove	39154
Newport (Attala County)	39160
Newport (DeSoto County)	38641
New Salem	38843
New Sight	39601
New Site	38859
Newton	39345
New Town	38668
New Wren	39730
Nichols	38959
Nicholson	39463
Nida	39172
Nitta Yuma	38763
Nixon (Humphreys County)	39115
Nixon (Pontotoc County)	38863
Nod	39039
Nola	39665
Norfield	39629
Norfolk	38641
Norris	39074
North (Hinds County)	39206
North (Lauderdale County)	39305
North Bay (Part of D'Iberville)	39532
North Bend	39350
North Carrollton	38947
North Crossroads	38852
North Greenville (Part of Greenville)	38701
North Gulfport	39503
North Gulfport (census designated place)	39501
North Haven	38652
North Long Beach (Part of Long Beach)	39560
Northpark Mall (Part of Ridgeland)	39157
North Tunica	38676
Northwest Junior College (Part of Senatobia)	38668
Norton	38663
Noxapater	39346
Oak Bowery	39437
Oak Grove (Holmes County)	39169
Oak Grove (Jones County)	39437

	ZIP
Oak Grove (Lamar County)	39401
Oak Grove (Perry County)	39423
Oakland (Itawamba County)	38843
Oakland (Pike County)	39666
Oakland (Yalobusha County)	38948
Oakley	39154
Oak Ridge	39180
Oak Vale	39656
Obadiah	39320
Ocean Springs	39564*
	39566†
Ocobla	39350
Ofahoma	39051
Oil City	39040
Okahola	39475
Oklahoma	38917
Okolona	38860
Oktoc	39759
Old Cairo	38829
Old Dominion	38946
Oldenburg	39661
Oldham	38852
Old Hamilton	39746
Old Houlka	38850
Old Red Star	39601
Old Union	38868
Olive Branch	38654
Oloh	39482
Oma	39654
Omega	39169
Onward	39159
Ora	39428
Orange	39347
Orange Grove (Harrison County)	39503
Orange Grove (Jackson County)	39581
Orange Hill	39041
O'Reilly	38730
Orwood	38655
Osborn	39759
Osborne Creek	38829
Osyka	39657
Ovett	39464
Owens Wells	39095
Oxberry	38940
Oxford (Amite County)	39638
Oxford (Lafayette County)	38655
Ozona	39426
Pace	38764
Pachuta	39347
Paden	38873
Palmer	39401
Palmetto	38801
Panther Burn	38765
Parchman	38738
Parham	38848
Paris	38949
Parks	38652
Parksplace	38619
Pascagoula	39567-69
For specific Pascagoula Zip Codes call (601) 762-5722, or your local postmaster.	
Pascagoula River Estates	39456
Pass Christian	39571
Patosi	39194
Pattison	39144
Paul	38920
Paulding	39348
Paulette	39341
Paynes	38920
Pearl (Rankin County)	39208
Pearl (Simpson County)	39073
Pearl City (Part of Pearl)	39208
Pearlington	39572
Pearl River (Neshoba County)	39350
Pearson	39208
Pecan	39581
Pecan Grove	39437
Pelahatchie	39145
Penantly	39356
Pendorff	39440
Penns Station	39743
Penton	38664
Peoples	38663
Peoria	39645
Percy	38748
Perdue	39337
Perkinston	39573
Perrytown	39633
Perth	39069
Perthshire	38746
Petal	39465
Peteet	38946
Peyton	39144
Pheba	39755
Philadelphia	39350
Philipp	38950

	ZIP
Phillipstown	38954
Phoenix	39040
Piave	39476
Picayune	39466
Pickens	39146
Pickwick	39483
Pierce Crossroads	39194
Piggtown	39094
Piketown	39074
Pinckneyville	39669
Pinebluff	39751
Pinebur	39429
Pinedale	38627
Pine Flat (Lafayette County)	38965
Pine Flat (Tishomingo County)	38852
Pine Grove (Benton County)	38633
Pine Grove (Lamar County)	39475
Pine Grove (Lee County)	38868
Pine Grove (Tippah County)	38829
Pine Ridge (Adams County)	39120
Pine Ridge (Lamar County)	39475
Pine Springs	39301
Pine Valley	38965
Pineview	39440
Pineville	39074
Piney Woods	39148
Pinola	39149
Pisgah (Greene County)	39452
Pisgah (Prentiss County)	38865
Pisgah (Rankin County)	39042
Pistol Ridge	39455
Pittman	39483
Pittsboro	38951
Plainview (Part of Richland)	39218
Plantersville	38862
Plattsburg	39350
Pleasant Grove	38657
Pleasant Hill (Copiah County)	39668
Pleasant Hill (DeSoto County)	38651
Pleasant Hill (Union County)	38652
Pleasant Ridge (Jones County)	39440
Pleasant Ridge (Union County)	38625
Plum Point	38671
Pluto	39169
Poagville	38618
Pocahontas	39072
Pokal	39140
Polfrey	39564
Polkville	39117
Pollock	38751
Pond	39669
Ponta	39301
Pontotoc	38863
Poolville	38650
Pope	38658
Poplar Corners	38680
Poplar Creek	39747
Poplar Springs (Holmes County)	39063
Poplar Springs (Montgomery County)	39747
Poplar Springs (Newton County)	39345
Poplarville	39470
Porterville	39352
Port Gibson	39150
Posey Mound	38623
Post	39325
Potts Camp	38659
Powell	38626
Powers	39440
Prairie	39756
Prairie Point	39341
Prentiss	39474
Presidential Hills (Part of Jackson)	39213
Preston	39354
Pricedale	39666
Prichard	38676
Prince Chapel	39354
Priscilla	38701
Prismatic	39320
Progress (Jefferson Davis County)	39474
Progress (Perry County)	39423
Progress (Pike County)	39648
Prospect	39057
Puckett	39151
Pulaski	39152
Pumpkin Center	38652
Purvis	39475
Pyland	38851
Quentin	39647
Quincy	38848
Quitman	39355
Quito	38941
Quofaloma	39169

	ZIP
Rainey	39459
Raleigh	39153
Ramsey Springs	39573
Randolph	38864
Rankin	39042
Ratliff	38855
Rawls Springs	39401
Raworth	39117
Raymond	39154
Raytown	39046
Red Banks	38661
Redbone	39180
Reddoch	39168
Red Lick	39096
Redstar	39191
Redwater	39051
Redwood	39156
Reedtown	39175
Reform	39757
Refuge	38701
Reid	38951
Remus	39051
Rena Lara	38767
Renfroe	39051
Renova	38732
Revive	39045
Rexburg	38756
Rexford	39073
Rhodes	39476
Riceville	39573
Rich	38662
Richardson	39466
Richland (Holmes County)	39079
Richland (Humphreys County)	39166
Richland (Rankin County)	39218
Richmond	38801
Richton	39476
Ridgeland	39157*
	39158†
Rienzi	38865
Ripley	38663
Rising Sun	38954
Riverton (Part of Clarksdale)	38614
Riverview Estates	39456
Robbs	38864
Roberts	39336
Robinson Gin	38632
Robinsonville	38664
Robinwood	39654
Rock Creek	39365
Rock Hill (Alcorn County)	38834
Rock Hill (Forrest County)	39475
Rock Hill (Oktibbeha County)	39759
Rock Hill (Panola County)	38666
Rock Hill (Rankin County)	39042
Rockport	39083
Rocky Springs	39086
Rodney	39096
Roebuck	38954
Rogerslacy	39477
Rolling Fork	39159
Rome	38768
Roseacres	38617
Rosebloom	38920
Rosebud	38189
Rosedale	38769
Rose Hill	39356
Rosella	39654
Rosemary	39170
Rosetta	39633
Rough Edge	38863
Roundaway	38614
Roundlake	38740
Rounsaville	39452
Roxie	39661
Ruby	38950
Rudyard	38617
Ruleville	38771
Runnelstown	39401
Rural Hill	39108
Russell	39301
Russellville	39162
Russum	39096
Ruth	39662
Ryan	38843
Sabino	38646
Sabougla	38916
St. Ann	39051
St. Martin	39533
Salem (Leake County)	39189
Salem (Walthall County)	39667
Sallis	39160
Saltillo	38866
Sanatorium	39112
Sandersville	39477
Sand Hill (Copiah County)	39191
Sand Hill (Greene County)	39476
Sand Hill (Jones County)	39437
Sandhill (Rankin County)	39161
Sandpoint	39153
Sandtown	39350
Sandy Hook	39478
Sanford	39479
Sapa	39744
Sarah	38665
Saratoga	39111
Sardis (Copiah County)	39083
Sardis (Panola County)	38666
Sarepta	38864
Sartinsville	39641
Satartia	39162
Saucier	39574
Saukum	39633
Savage	38665
Savannah	39470
Savannah Grove (Part of Meridian)	39301
Savoy	39301
Schamberville	39325
Schlater	38952
Schley	39140
Scobey	38953
Scooba	39358
Scotland	39040
Scott	38772
Sebastopol	39359
Sellers	39573
Sels Prairie	39360
Seminary	39479
Senatobia	38668
Senatobia Lakes	38668
Seneca	39455
Sessums	39759
Seven Springs	39154
Shackleford	39169
Shady Grove (Copiah County)	39083
Shady Grove (Jones County)	39440
Shannon	38868
Sharkey	38921
Sharon (Jones County)	39440
Sharon (Madison County)	39163
Sharpsburg	39146
Shaw	38773
Shelby	38774
Shellmound	38930
Shelton	39459
Sheppard Town	38946
Sherard	38669
Sherman	38869
Sherwood	39752
Sherwood Forest	39042
Shiloh (Itawamba County)	38855
Shiloh (Rankin County)	39145
Shipman	39452
Shivers	39149
Shoccoe	39046
Shoreline Park	39576
Shrock	39079
Shubuta	39360
Shucktown	39301
Shuford	39620
Shuqualak	39361
Sibley	39165
Sibleyton	39747
Sidon	38954
Signal	39180
Silver City	39166
Silver Creek	39663
Silver Run	39573
Singleton	39051
Singleton Settlement	39074
Skene	38730
Skuna	38915
Skyline	38801
Slate Spring	38855
Slayden	38642
Sledge	38670
Sloan	39046
Smith (Covington County)	39428
Smith (Lauderdale County)	39364
Smithdale	39664
Smiths	39066
Smithville	38870
Smyrna (Attala County)	39090
Smyrna (Copiah County)	39083
Snell	39301
Snow Lake Shores	38603
Somerville	38944
Sonora	38851
Sontag	39665
Soso	39480
South Amory (Part of Amory)	38821
Southaven	38671
Southern (Part of Hattiesburg)	39401
South McComb (Part of McComb)	39648
South Mississipi Correctional Institution	39451
Spanish Fort	39088
Sparta	39776
Splinter	38673
Splunge	38848
Spring Cottage	39429
Spring Creek	39350
Springdale	38965
Springdale Lakes	38650
Spring Hill (Benton County)	38647
Springhill (Jones County)	39440
Spring Hill (Lafayette County)	38655
Spring Hill (Neshoba County)	39350
Springville	38863
Stallo	39350
Stampley	39069
Standing Pine	39051
Stanton	39120
Star	39167
Starkville	39759
State Line	39362
Steele	39074
Steens	39766
Steiner	38773
Stewart	39767
Stokes	39046
Stoneville	38776
Stonewall (Clarke County)	39363
Stonewall (DeSoto County)	38611
Stonewall (Holmes County)	39169
Stovall	38614
Straight Bayou	38721
Stratton	39365
Strayhorn	38665
Strengthford	39440
Strickland	38834
Stringer	39481
Stringtown	38725
Stronghope	39191
Strongs	39730
Sturgis	39769
Sucarnochee	39352
Success	39574
Sumbax	39483
Summerland	39168
Summit	39666
Sumner	38957
Sumrall	39482
Sunflower (Prentiss County)	38829
Sunflower (Sunflower County)	38778
Sunnycrest	38901
Sunnyside	38944
Sunrise (Forrest County)	39401
Sunrise (Leake County)	39051
Suqualena	39301
Swan Lake	38958
Sweatman	38925
Swiftown	38959
Swiftwater	38701
Sylvarena	39153
Symonds	38769
Tallula	39159
Talowah	39455
Tatum	39638
Taylor	38673
Taylorsville	39168
Tchula	39169
Teasdale	38927
Ted	39338
Teoc	38917
Terry	39170
Thaxton	38871
Theadville	39355
Theo	38683
Thomastown	39171
Thomasville	39073
Thompson	39664
Thompsonville	39059
Thorn	38851
Thornton	39172
Thrashers	38829
Three Rivers	39581
Thyatira	38668
Tibbee	39773
Tibbs	38670
Tie Plant	38901
Tilden	38843
Tillatoba	38961
Tillman	39150
Tilton	39654
Tinsley	39173
Tiplersville	38674
Tippah	38603
Tippo	38962
Tishomingo	38873
Toccopola	38874
Tocowa	38620
Tomnolen	39744
Toomsuba	39364
Topeka	39641

* Area Zip Code   † Post Office Boxes

	ZIP
Topisaw	39662
Topton	39301
Touchstone	39044
Tougaloo (Part of Jackson)	39174
Townsend	39352
Tralake	38756
Trapp	39350
Traxler	39111
Trebloc	38875
Tremont	38876
Triangle (Part of Biloxi)	39534
Tribbett	38756
Trinity (DeSoto County)	38632
Trinity (Lowndes County)	39743
Troy	38863
Truitt	39146
Tucker	39350
Tuckers Crossing	39440
Tula	38675
Tunica	38676
Tupelo	38801-03
For specific Tupelo Zip Codes call (601) 842-4482, or your local postmaster.	
Turnbull	39669
Turnerville	39338
Turon	38870
Tuscola	39094
Tutwiler	38963
Twin	39478
Twin Lakes	38680
Tylertown	39667
Tyro	38668
Union (Jones County)	39437
Union (Lee County)	38862
Union (Newton County)	39365
Union (Simpson County)	39149
Union Church	39668
Union Hall	39601
Unity	38849
University (Part of Oxford)	38677
University Medical Center (Part of Jackson)	39216
University of Mississippi	38677
Usrytown	39074
Utica	39175
Utica Junior College	39175
Vaiden	39176
Valewood	38744
Valley	39194
Valley Hill	38917
Valley Park	39177
Value (Part of Brandon)	39042
Van Buren	38858
Vance	38964
Vancleave (Jackson County)	39564
Van Cleave (Jackson County)	39564
Van Vleet	38877
Vardaman	38878
Vaughan	39179
Vaughn	39601
Velma	38965
Vernal	39452
Vernon (Madison County)	39339
Vernon (Winston County)	39339
Verona	38879
Vickland	39159

	ZIP
Vicksburg	39180-82
For specific Vicksburg Zip Codes call (601) 636-1071, or your local postmaster.	
Victoria	38679
Vidalia	39571
Village Fair Mall (Part of Meridian)	39301
Vimville	39301
Virlilia	39046
Vossburg	39366
Waco	38753
Waddell	39741
Wade (Jackson County)	39581
Wade (Sunflower County)	38737
Wahalak	39358
Wakefield	38618
Wakeland	38930
Waldrup	39422
Wallerville	38652
Wallhill	38618
Walls	38680
Walnut (Quitman County)	38964
Walnut (Tippah County)	38683
Walnut Grove (Coahoma County)	38767
Walnut Grove (Leake County)	39189
Walters	39437
Waltersville	39180
Walthall	39771
Wanilla	39654
Wardwell	38878
Warrenton	39180
Warsaw	38611
Washington	39190
Waterford	38685
Water Oak	39367
Water Valley	38965
Watson (Forrest County)	39401
Watson (Marshall County)	38611
Wautubbee	39330
Waveland	39576
Waxhaw	38746
Way	39046
Waynesboro	39367
Wayside	38780
Weathersby	39114
Webb	38966
Weir	39772
Wells (Part of Caledonia)	39740
Wells Town	39455
Wenasoga	38834
Wesson	39191
West (Holmes County)	39192
West (Lauderdale County)	39305
West Biloxi (Part of Biloxi)	39531
West Days	38641
West Gulfport	39501
West Hattiesburg	39401
West Hill	39063
West Jackson (Part of Jackson)	39207
Westland (Part of Jackson)	39209
West Lincoln	39601
West Marks	38646
West Point	39773
West Poplarville	39470

	ZIP
Westside	39150
West Union	38650
Westville	39114
Wheeler	38880
Whistler	39367
White Apple	39661
Whitebluff	39483
White Cap	39638
Whitehead	38928
Whiteoak	39111
Whites (Clay County)	39773
Whites (Rankin County)	39073
Whitesand (Jefferson Davis County)	39140
White Sand (Pearl River County)	39470
Whites Crossing	39577
Whitfield (Jones County)	39464
Whitfield (Rankin County)	39193
Whitney	38737
Whitten Town	38663
Whynot	39301
Wickware	39345
Wiggins (Leake County)	39051
Wiggins (Stone County)	39577
Wilco Estates	38632
Wildwood	38930
Wilkinson	39669
Willet	38748
Williamsburg	39428
Williamsville (Attala County)	39090
Williamsville (Neshoba County)	39350
Willowood	39212
Willows	39150
Winborn	38633
Winchester	39367
Windsor Park	39564
Wingate (Part of New Augusta)	39462
Winona	38967
Winstonville	38781
Winterville	38782
Wolf Springs	39301
Woodburn	38751
Woodland (Chickasaw County)	39776
Woodland (Pontotoc County)	38863
Woodland Lake	38632
Woodville	39669
Woodwards	39367
Woolmarket	39532
Wortham	39574
Wren	39730
Wright	38746
Wyatte	38668
Yazoo City	39194
Yocona	38655
Yokena	39180
Youngs	38922
Zama	39090
Zemuly	39160
Zero	39301
Zetus	39601
Zieglerville	39039
Zion	38863
Zumbro	38732

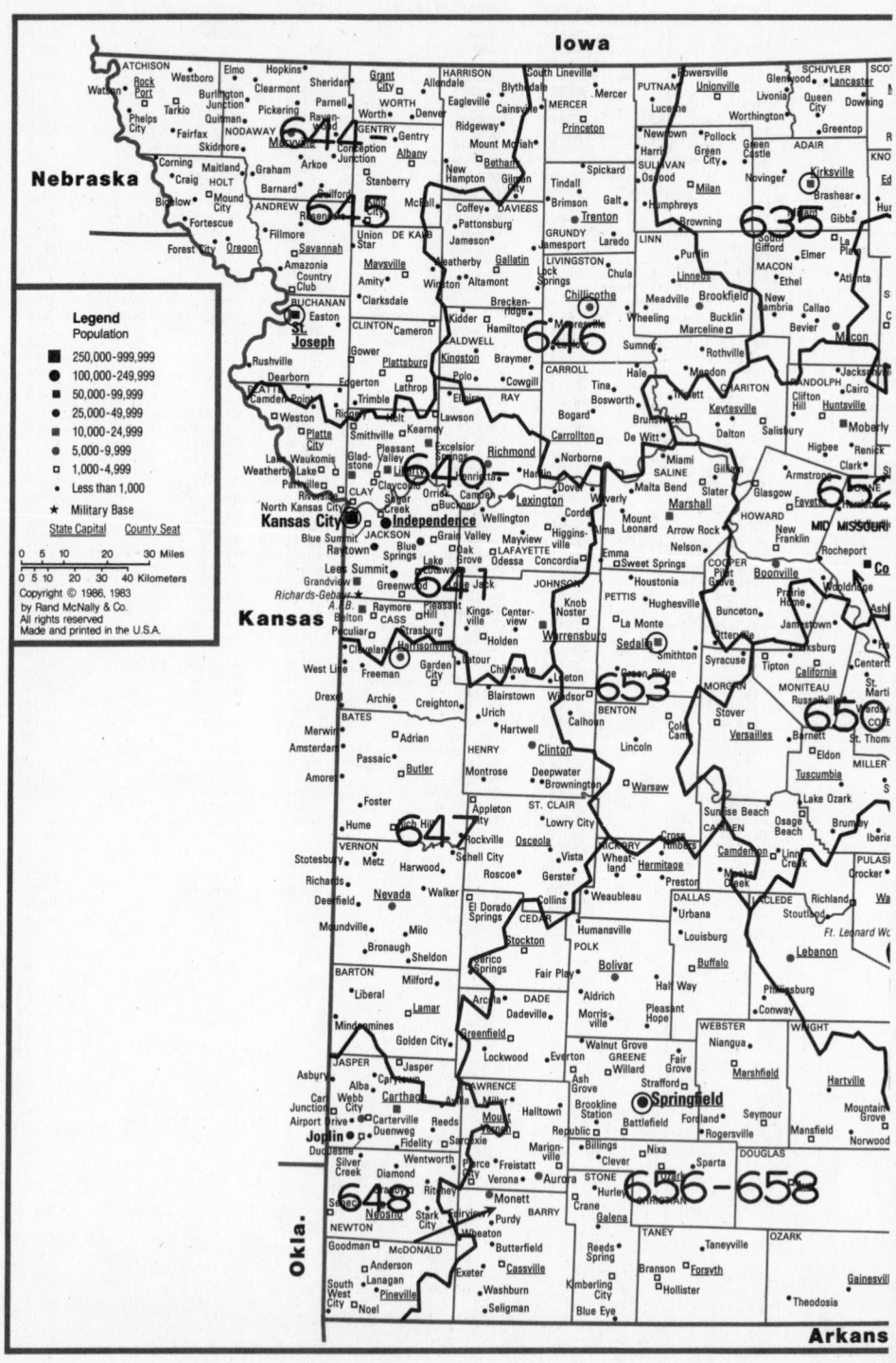

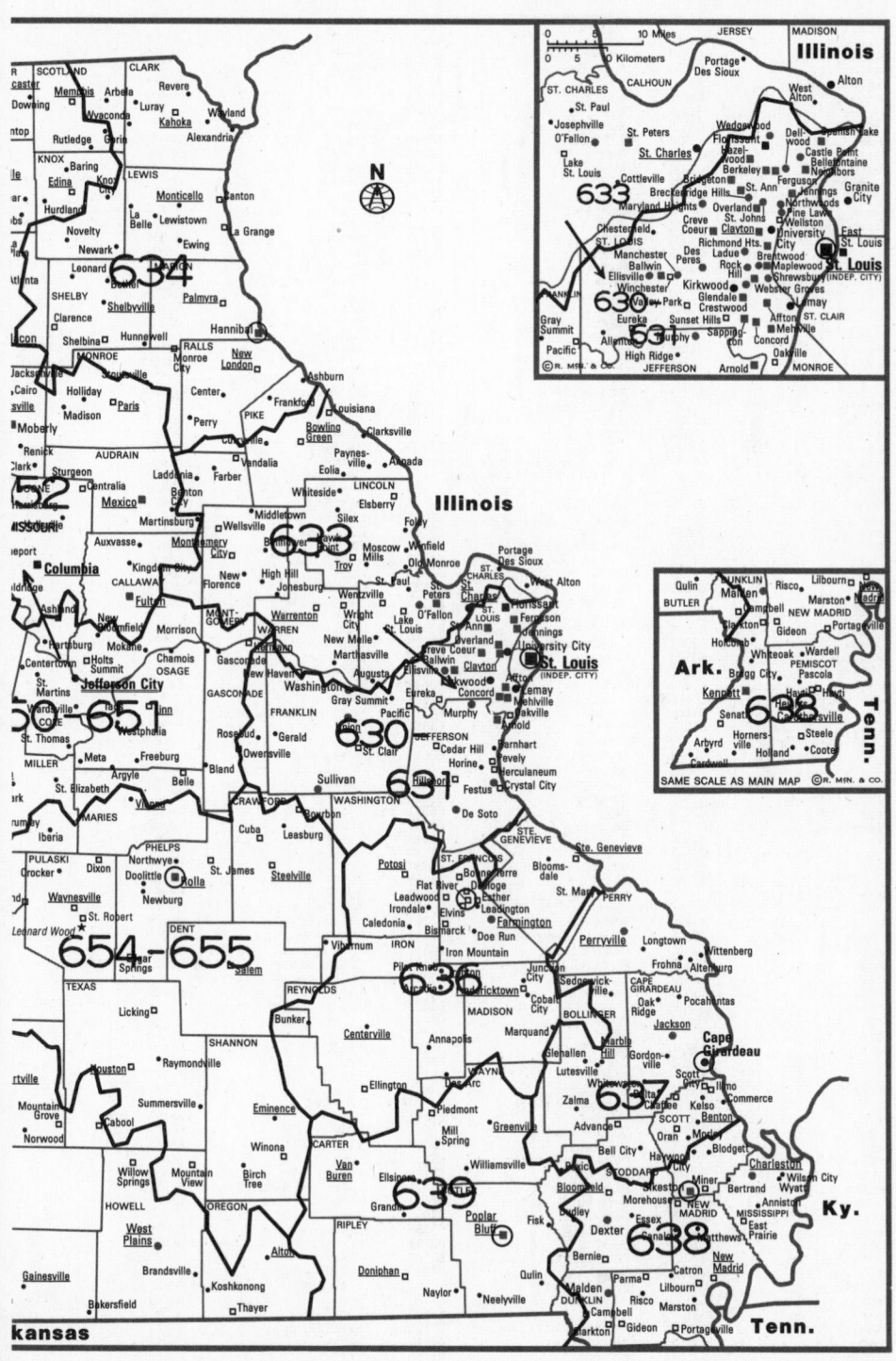

	ZIP		ZIP		ZIP
Aaron	64720	Atlas	64836	Bentley Farms	63088
Abesville	65656	Atwater Terrace	63136	Benton	63736
Abo	65536	Auburn	63343	Benton City	65232
Acorn Corner	63877	Augusta	63332	Benton Park (Part of St.	
Acornridge	63960	Aullville	64037	Louis)	63104
Adair	63533	Aurora	65605	Bentonville	65355
Adrian	64720	Aurora Springs	65026	Berger	63014
Advance	63730	Austin	64725	Berkeley	63134
Affton	63123	Auxvasse	65231	Berlin	64463
Agency	64401	Ava	65608	Bermott	65706
Aid	63825	Avalon	64621	Bernheimer	63357
Airline Acres	63834	Avenue City	64505	Bernie	63822
Airport Drive	64801	Avert	63825	Berryman	65565
Akers	65560	Avery	63355	Bertrand	63823
Alanthus	64489	Avila	64833	Berwick	65723
Alba	64830	Avon	63640	Bessville	63764
Albany (Gentry County)	64402	Avondale	64117	Bethany	64424
Albany (Ray County)	64077	Axtell	63552	Bethel	63434
Aldrich	65601	Azen	63432	Bethlehem	64861
Alexandria	63430	Babbtown	65085	Bethpage	64867
Alfalfa Center	63834	Bacon	65046	Beulah (Madison County)	63636
Algonquin (Part of Webster		Baden (Part of St. Louis)	63147	Beulah (Phelps County)	65436
Groves)	63119	Baderville	63862	Beverly	64079
Allbright	63655	Bado	65689	Beverly Hills	63121
Allendale	64420	Bagnell	65026	Bevier	63552
Allenton	63001	Bahner	65350	Biblegrove	63531
Allenville	63740	Baker	63846	Biehle	63775
Alley Spring	65466	Bakersfield	65609	Bigelow	64437
All Saints Village	63376	Bakersville	63827	Big Lake	64437
Alma	64001	Baldwin Lake	64080	Big Piney	65550
Almartha	65773	Baldwin Park	64080	Big River Mills	63628
Almon	65732	Ballard	64730	Bigspring	63363
Alpha	64652	Ballwin	63011	Billings	65610
Altamont	64620	Ballwin	63021-22	Billingsville	65233
Altenburg	63732	For specific Ballwin Zip Codes call		Billmore	65690
Altheim	63141	(314) 227-8720, or your local		Birch Tree	65438
Alton	65606	postmaster.		Birds Corners	63846
Altona	64720	Bancroft	64642	Birds Point	63834
Amazonia	64421	Banner	63623	Birdtown	65637
Americus	65069	Bannister	65786	Birmingham	64161
Amity	64422	Bannister Mall (Part of		Bismarck	63624
Amoret	64722	Kansas City)	64137	Bixby	65439
Amsterdam	64723	Bardley	63935	Black	63625
Amy	65626	Baring	63531	Blackburn	65321
Anabel	63431	Barnard	64423	Blackjack (St. Clair County)	65785
Anaconda	63077	Barnesville	63530	Black Jack (St. Louis	
Anderson	64831	Barnett	65011	County)	63031
Annada	63330	Barnhart (Jefferson County)	63012	Black Walnut	63301
Annapolis	63620	Barretts	63122	Blackwater	65322
Anniston	63820	Barry (Part of Kansas City)	64155	Blackwell	63626
Anson	52626	Bartlett	65438	Blairstown	64726
Anthonies Mill	65441	Barwick	64649	Bland	65014
Antioch (Clark County)	63445	Baryties	63626	Blendville (Part of Joplin)	64801
Antioch (Clay County)	64119	Bates City	64011	Bliss	63626
Antioch Center (Part of		Batesville	63932	Blodgett	63824
Kansas City)	64119	Battlefield	65619	Blomeyer	63740
Antonia	63052	Battlefield Mall (Part of		Bloomfield	63825
Anutt	65540	Springfield)	65804	Blooming Rose	65436
Apache Flats	65101	Baxter	65681	Bloomington	63532
Apple Creek	63775	Bay	65041	Bloomsdale	63627
Appleton City	64724	Baydy Peak	65065	Blosser	65339
Aquilla	63825	Bayshore (Part of Arnold)	63010	Blue Branch	65355
Arab	63733	Beach	63632	Blue Eye	65611
Arbela	63432	Beaman	65350	Blue Lick	65350
Arbor	63740	Bean Lake	64484	Blue Mound	64638
Arbor Terrace (Part of		Bearcreek	65649	Blue Ridge	64424
Northwoods)	63121	Bearfield	65201	Blue Ridge Mall (Part of	
Arbyrd	63821	Beaufort	63013	Kansas City)	64119
Arcadia	63621	Beckville (Part of Piedmont)	63957	Blue Springs	64013-15
Archie	64725	Bedford	64643	For specific Blue Springs Zip	
Arcola	65603	Bedison	64434	Codes call (816) 229-6900, or	
Ardeola	63730	Belews Creek	63050	your local postmaster.	
Arditta	65626	Belgique	63775	Blue Summit	64126
Ardmore	65247	Belgrade	63622	Blue Vue (Part of Kansas	
Argo	65441	Bellair	65237	City)	64133
Argyle	65001	Bellamy	64784	Bluffton	65069
Arkmo	63821	Bella Villa	63125	Blythedale	64426
Arkoe	64468	Bell City	63735	Boaz	65631
Arley	64060	Belle	65013	Boekerton	63873
Arlington	65550	Belle Center	64801	Bogard	64622
Armstrong	65230	Bellefontaine (St. Louis		Bois D'Arc	65612
Arnold	63010	County)	63017	Bolckow	64427
Aroma	64844	Bellefontaine (Washington		Boles	63055
Arroll	65571	County)	63630	Bolivar	65613
Arrowhead Beach (Part of		Bellefontaine Neighbors	63137	Bona	65601
Lake Ozark)	65049	Bellerive	63121	Bonanza	64650
Arrowhead Lake Estates	65326	Bellerive Estates	63141	Bongor Lake Estate	65202
Arrow Rock	65320	Belleview	63623	Bonham	65605
Arthur	64779	Belleville	64801	Bonne Terre	63628
Asbury	64832	Bellflower	63333	Bonnots Mill	65016
Ashburn	63433	Bel-Nor	63133	Boonesboro	65250
Asherville	63960	Bel-Ridge	63133	Boonville	65233
Ash Grove	65604	Belton	64012	Bosky Dell (Part of	
Ash Hill	63940	Belvidere (Part of		Lanagan)	64831
Ashland	65010	Grandview)	64030	Boss	65440
Ashley	63334	Bem	65066	Boston	64759
Ashley Creek	65555	Ben Avis (Part of Ferguson)	63135	Bosworth	64623
Ashton	63453	Benbow	63440	Boulder City	64844
Aspenhoff	63357	Benbush	63141	Bourbon	65441
Athens	63465	Bendavis	65433	Bowen	65360
Atherton	64050	Benjamin	63435	Bowers Mill	64848
Atlanta	63530	Bennett Springs	65536	Bowling Green	63334

	ZIP		ZIP		ZIP
Boydsville	65251	Cainsville	64632	Chain of Rocks	63369
Boynton	63556	Cairo	65239	Chain-O-Lakes	65625
Boys Ranch	65617	Caledonia	63631	Chambersburg	63445
Boys Town	65559	Calhoun	65323	Chamois	65024
Bracken	65706	California	65018	Champ	63042
Bradfield	65705	Callao	63534	Champion	65717
Bradleyville	65614	Calm	63942	Champion City	63056
Braggadocio	63826	Calton Mill	65769	Chandler	64060
Bragg City	63827	Calumet	63336	Channel	63877
Braley	64477	Calverton Park	63136	Chapel Hill	64011
Branch	65786	Calwood	65251	Chapel Hills	65785
Brandon	65360	Cambridge	65330	Chariton	63565
Brandsville	65688	Camden	64017	Charity	65644
Branson	65616	Camden Point	64018	Charlack	63114
Branson West	65737	Camdenton	65020	Charles Nagel (Part of St.	
Brashear	63533	Cameron	64429	Louis)	63115
Brasher	63877	Campbell	63933	Charleston	63834
Braymer	64624	Campbellton	63946	Charteroak	63833
Brays	65486	Camp Clark	64772	Cherokee Pass	63645
Brazeau	63737	Canaan	65014	Cherry Box	63451
Brazil	63664	Canalou	63828	Cherry Valley Estates	65804
Brazito	65101	Cane Hill	65635	Cherryville	65446
Breckenridge	64625	Caney Creek	63771	Chesapeake	65712
Breckenridge Hills	63114	Cannon Mines	63630	Chesterfield	63005-06
Breen Acres (Part of		Canton	63435		63017
Kansas City)	64152	Cantwell (Part of Deslogc)	63601	For specific Chesterfield Zip	
Brentwood	63144	Cape Fair	65624	Codes call (314) 532-3482, or	
Brewer	63775	Cape Girardeau	63701*	your local postmaster.	
Briar	63931		63702†		
Brickeys	63627	Capital Mall (Part of		Chesterfield	63017
Bridgeton	63044	Jefferson City)	65101	Chestnutridge	65630
Bridgeton Terrace (Part of		Capitol Hill	63136	Chicopee	63965
Bridgeton)	63044	Caplinger Mills	65607	Chilhowee	64733
Bridlecroft	64083	Cappeln	63348	Chillicothe	64601
Brighton	65617	Capps	65082	Chilton	63965
Brimson	64642	Cardwell	63829	Chitwood (Part of Joplin)	64801
Brinktown	65443	Carl Junction	64834	Chloride	63646
Briscoe	63379	Carlow	64648	Chouteau (Part of St. Louis)	63110
Bristow	64772	Carmack	64402	Chula	64635
Brixey	65618	Carola	63961	Circle City	63846
Broadway (Part of St. Louis)	63147	Carondelet (Part of St.		Civic Center (Part of	
Brock	63555	Louis)	63111	Kansas City)	64106
Bronaugh	64728	Carr (Part of Florissant)	63031	Civil Bend	64670
Brookdale	63141	Carrington	65251	Clapper	63456
Brookfield	64628	Carr Lane	72616	Ciara	65483
Brooking Park	65301	Carrollton	64633	Clarence	63437
Brookline Station	65619	Carsonville	63121	Clark	65243
Brooklyn	64481	Carterville	64835	Clark City	63445
Brooklyn Heights	64836	Carthage	64836	Clarksburg	65025
Broseley	63932	Caruth	63857	Clarksdale	64430
Brownbranch	65608	Caruthersville	63830	Clarkson Valley	63017
Brownfield	65556	Carytown	64836	Clarksville	63336
Browning	64630	Cascade	63632	Clarkton	63837
Brownington	64740	Case	65041	Claryville	63775
Browns	65202	Cash	63534	Claycomo	64119
Browns Spring	65610	Cassel Addition	65785	Claysvil	65039
Brownwood	63738	Cassidy	65714	Clayton	63105
Brumley	65017	Cassville	65625	Clear Creek	65276
Bruner	65620	Castle Point	63136	Clearmont	64431
Brunot	63636	Castle Rock (Part of Joplin)	64801	Clear Spring	63965
Brunswick	65236	Castlewood	63011	Clear Springs	65793
Brushcreek	65536	Catawba	64624	Clearview	65202
Brushyknob	65608	Catawissa	63015	Clearwater	63670
Buck Donic	63829	Catherine Place	63645	Cleavesville	65014
Buckhart	65638	Cato	65605	Cleveland	64734
Buckhorn (Madison County)	63655	Catron	63833	Clever	65631
Buckhorn (Pulaski County)	65583	Caulfield	65626	Cliff Village	64801
Bucklin	64631	Cave	63379	Clifton City	65348
Buckner	64016	Cave Hill	65041	Clifton Hill	65244
Bucoda	63876	Caverna	72739	Climax Springs	65324
Bucyrus	65444	Cave Spring	65770	Clines Island	63846
Buell	63361	Cawood	64427	Clinton	64735
Buffalo	65622	Cedar City (Part of		Cliquot	65640
Buffington	63846	Jefferson City)	65022	Clover Bottom	63090
Bullion	63501	Cedarcreek	65627	Cloverdale	65590
Bunceton	65237	Cedar Gap	65746	Clubb	63934
Bunker	63629	Cedar Hill	63016	Clyde	64432
Bunker Hill	65257	Cedar Hill Lakes	63016	Coal	64735
Burbank	63944	Cedar Lake (Boone County)	65201	Coal Hill	64744
Burdett	64720	Cedar Lake (Jefferson		Coatsville	63535
Burfordville	63739	County)	63070	Cobalt City	63645
Burgess	64769	Cedar Ridge	65590	Cody	65742
Burke City	63135	Cedar Springs	64744	Coffey	64636
Burksville	63434	Cedar Valley	63901	Coffeyton	65441
Burlington Junction	64428	Cedarville	64756	Coffman	63670
Burnham	65793	Celt	65764	Coldspring	65717
Burns	65613	Center	63436	Cold Springs	65355
Burr	72478	Center Square (Part of		Coldwater	63964
Burton	65248	Kansas City)	64196	Cole Camp	65325
Burtville	65336	Centertown	65023	Cole Camp Junction	65325
Butcher	65774	Centerview	64019	College Mound	65247
Butler	64730	Centerville	63633	Collins	64738
Butler Hill Estates	63128	Central (Jackson County)	64142	Coloma	64622
Butterfield	65623	Central (Madison County)	63645	Colony	63563
Butts	65441	Central City	64801	Columbia	65201-05
Bynumville	65281	Centralia	65240		65299
Byrnes Mill	63051	Central Missouri		For specific Columbia Zip Codes	
Byron	65013	Correctional Center	65101	call (314) 876-7829, or your local	
Cabanne (Part of St. Louis)	63112	Centropolis (Part of Kansas		postmaster.	
Cabool	65689	City)	64126	Columbia Mall (Part of	
Caboo	65706	Chadwick	65629	Columbia)	65201
Caddo	65706	Chaffee	63740	Columbus	64019
Cadet	63630			Commerce	63742

	ZIP		ZIP		ZIP
Commerce Tower (Part of Kansas City)	64199	Damsel (Part of Osage Beach)	65065	Dunksburg	65351
Commercial (Part of Springfield)	65803	Danby	63627	Dunlap	64683
Competition	65470	Danforth	63559	Dunn	65711
Conception	64433	Danville	63361	Dunnegan	65640
Conception Junction	64434	Dardenne	63366	Duquesne	64801
Conclay (Part of Ladue)	63124	Dardenne Prairie	63366	Durham	63438
Concord (Callaway County)	65231	Darien	63560	Dutchtown	63745
Concord (St. Louis County)	63128	Daris Crossing	63601	Dutzow	63342
Concord Hill	63357	Darksville	65259	Dye	64098
Concordia	64020	Darlington	64438	Dykes	65444
Connelsville	63559	Daugherty	64701	Eagle Rock	65641
Conran	63838	Davis (Lincoln County)	63379	Eagleville	64442
Converse	64465	Davis (St. Francois County)	63601	Easley	65203
Conway	65632	Davis Store	63932	East Bonne Terre	63628
Cook Station	65449	Davisville	65456	East End	63623
Cool Valley	63135	Dawn	64638	East Hills Mall (Part of St. Joseph)	64506
Cooper Hill	65014	Dawson	65711	East Independence (Part of Independence)	64056
Cooter	63839	Dawsonville	64428	East Kirkwood (Part of Kirkwood)	63122
Cora	63556	Dawt	65760	East Leavenworth	64079
Corder	64021	Dayton	64747	East Lynne	64743
Cornelia	64093	Daytown	63653	East Mexico (Part of Mexico)	65265
Corning	64435	Daytown (rural)	63601	Easton	64443
Cornwall	63645	Dearborn	64439	East Prairie	63845
Corridon	63633	Decaturville	65536	East Purdy	65734
Corry	65635	Deckard-Y	65690	Eastwood	63965
Corsicana	65734	Dederick	64744	Ebenezer	65803
Corso	63377	Deepwater	64740	Ebo	63664
Corticelli	65074	Deerfield	64741	Eccles	65261
Cosby	64436	Deering	63840	Echo Valley	65065
Cossville	64849	Deer Land	63857	Economy	63530
Cottage Farm	63050	Deer Park	65201	Ectonville	64089
Cottleville	63338	Deer Ridge	63447	Edgar Springs	65462
Cotton Plant	63855	Deer Run	63965	Edge Acres	65785
Cottonwood Point	63877	Defiance	63341	Edgehill	63625
Couch	65690	Deicke	63025	Edgerton	64444
Coulstone	65542	De Kalb	64440	Edgerton Junction	64439
Country Club (Andrew County)	64505	De Lassus	63640	Edgewater Beach	65653
Country Club (Jackson County)	64113	Delaware	65438	Edgewood	63334
Country Club Hills	63136	Delbridge	63664	Edina	63537
Country Club Plaza (Part of Kansas City)	64113	Dell Junction	65355	Edinburg	64683
Country Lake Woods	63011	Dellwood	63136	Edmonson	65338
Country Life Acres	63131	Delmar	64735	Edmundson	63134
Countryside (Part of Kansas City)	64152	Delmo	63801	Edwards	65326
Courtney (Part of Sugar Creek)	64050	Delta	63744	Egypt Grove	65626
Courtois	65565	Dennis Acres	64801	Egypt Mills	63701
Cowgill	64637	Denton (Johnson County)	64040	El Chaparral	65201
Coy	64831	Denton (Pemiscot County)	63877	Eldon	65026
Crabbs	65746	Denver	64441	El Dorado Springs	64744
Craig	64437	Derby	63601	Eldridge	65463
Crane	65633	Des Arc	63636	Elgin	63434
Creighton	64739	Desloge	63601	Elijah	65626
Crescent	63025	De Soto	63020	Elk Creek	65464
Crescent Hill	64720	Des Peres	63131	Elkhead	65753
Crescent Lake (Part of Excelsior Springs)	64024	Dessa	64850	Elkhorn	64077
Crestwood	63126	Detmold	63068	Elkhurst	65201
Crestwood Plaza (Part of Crestwood)	63126	Devils Elbow	65457	Elkland	65644
Cretcher	65351	De Witt	64639	Elk Prairie	65401
Creve Coeur	63141	Dexter	63841	Elk Springs	64854
Crider	65790	Diamond	64840	Elkton	65650
Crites Corner	63937	Dickens	65759	Ellington	63638
Crocker	65452	Diehlstadt	63834	Ellis	64772
Cross Keys	63031	Diggins	65636	Ellis Prairie	65444
Cross Keys Shopping Center (Part of Florissant)	63033	Dikeland	64083	Ellisville	63011
Cross Roads (Douglas County)	65608	Dillard	65456	Ellsinore	63937
Cross Roads (Ozark County)	65637	Dillon	65401	Elm	64061
Cross Timbers	65634	Dissen	63068	Elmdale Village (Part of St. Johns)	63114
Crosstown	63775	Dittmer	63023	Elmer	63538
Cross Way	65706	Dixie	65063	Elmira	64062
Crowder	63801	Dixon	65459	Elmo	64445
Crown	65706	Dockery	64085	Elmont	63080
Cruise Mill	63626	Doc Long Estates	65355	Elmwood	65321
Crump	63785	Doe Run	63637	Elsberry	63343
Crystal City	63019	Dogwood (Douglas County)	65746	Elsey	65633
Crystal Lake Park	63131	Dogwood (Mississippi County)	63845	Elston	65101
Crystal Lakes	64024	Dolly Siding (Part of Bonne Terre)	63628	Elvins	63601
Cuba	65453	Dongola	63730	Elwood	65802
Cunningham	64681	Doniphan	63935	Ely	63461
Curdton	63960	Doolittle	65401	Emden	63439
Cureall	65790	Dora	65637	Emerald Beach	65658
Currentview	63935	Dorena	63845	Emerson	63454
Curryville	63339	Doss	65560	Eminence	65466
Custer	65501	Dotham	64446	Emma	65327
Cyclone	64856	Dove	65536	Empire Prairie	64463
Cyrene	63334	Dover (Lafayette County)	64022	Englewood (Boone County)	65010
Dadeville	65635	Dover (Lewis County)	63448	Englewood (Jackson County)	64052
Daisy	63743	Downing	63536	Enon (Moniteau County)	65074
Daleview	64446	Drake	65066	Enon (St. Charles County)	63385
Dalton	65246	Dresden	65301	Enyart	64453
Damascus	64776	Drexel	64742	Eolia	63344
Dameron	63343	Dripping Spring	65202	Epworth	63469
		Drury	65638	Erie	64843
		Dudenville	64748	Ernestville	64020
		Dudley	63936	Essex	63846
		Duenweg	64841	Estes	63359
		Dugginsville	65761	Esther	63601
		Duke	65461	Estill	65274
		Duncans Bridge	63437		
		Duncans Point	65324		
		Dundee	63090		

Name	ZIP	Name	ZIP	Name	ZIP
Ethel	63539	Fordland	65652	Glencoe	63038
Ethlyn	63369	Forest City	64451	Glendale (Putnam County)	63551
Etlah	63014	Forest Green	65281	Glendale (St. Louis County)	63122
Etterville	65031	Forest Hills	65355	Glen Echo Park	63121
Eudora	65645	Foristell	63348	Glennon	63764
Eugene	65032	Forker	64651	Glennonville	63933
Eunice	65468	Forkners Hill	65632	Glen Park	63070
Eureka	63025	Forrest Mill	64859	Glensted	65084
Evans	65608	Forsyth	65653	Glenstone (Part of Springfield)	65804
Evansville (Buchanan County)	64507	Fortescue	64452	Glenwood	63541
Evansville (Monroe County)	65270	Fort Henry	65259	Glenwood Junction (Part of Glenwood)	63541
Eve	64741	Fort Leonard Wood	65473	Glidewell	65803
Eveningshade	65552	Fortuna	65034	Glover	63646
Everett	64725	Fort Zumwalt	63366	Gobler	63849
Eversonville	64688	Foster	64745	Golden	65658
Everton	65646	Fountain Grove	64659	Golden City	64748
Ewing	63440	Fox Creek	63069	Golden Oak (Part of Kansas City)	64117
Excello	65247	Fox Haven	64083	Goldman	63050
Excelsior	65084	Foxwood Springs	64083	Goldsberry	63539
Excelsior Estates	64062	Frailie	63848	Gooch Mill	65068
Excelsior Springs	64024	Frankclay	63644	Goodhope	65608
Excelsior Springs Junction	64077	Frankenstein	65016	Goodland	63623
Exeter	65647	Frankford	63441	Goodman	64843
Fagus	63938	Franklin	65250	Goodson	65659
Fairdealing	63939	Franks	65459	Gordonville	63752
Fairfax	64446	Frazier	64401	Gorin	63543
Fairgrounds (Part of St. Louis)	63107	Fredericksburg	65061	Goshen	64673
Fair Grove	65648	Fredericktown	63645	Gospel Ridge (Part of St. Robert)	65583
Fair Haven	64750	Fredville	64850	Gower	64454
Fairleigh (Part of St. Joseph)	64506	Freeburg	65035	Graff	65660
Fairmont	63474	Freedom (Camden County)	65052	Graham	64455
Fairmount (Part of Independence)	64053	Freedom (Osage County)	65024	Grain Valley	64029
Fair Play	65649	Freeman	64746	Granby	64844
Fairport	64447	Freistatt	65654	Grand Center	63534
Fairview (Newton County)	64842	Fremont	63941	Grand Falls	64801
Fairview (Taney County)	65744	Fremont Hills	65721	Grandin	63943
Fairview (Texas County)	65689	French Village	63036	Grand Pass	65339
Fairview Acres (Part of Flat River)	63601	Friedheim	63747	Grandview (Benton County)	65355
Falcon	65470	Friendly Valley	63775	Grandview (Jackson County)	64030
Fanchon	65788	Frisbee	63852	Granger	63442
Fanning	65453	Frisco	63846	Graniteville	63650
Farber	63345	Fristoe	65355	Grant (Part of Grantwood Village)	63123
Farewell	64478	Frohna	63748	Grant City	64456
Farley	64028	Frontenac	63131	Grantwood Village	63123
Farmer	63339	Fruitland (Cape Girardeau County)	63755	Granville	65275
Farmersville	64683	Fruitland (Greene County)	65648	Grassy	63753
Farmington	63640	Fulton	65251	Gravelhill	63739
Farmington Correctional Center	63640	Gaines	64735	Gravelton	63655
Farrar	63746	Gainesville	65655	Gravois (Part of St. Louis)	63116
Farrenberg	63869	Galena	65656	Gravois Mills	65037
Faucett	64448	Galesburg	64855	Grayridge	63850
Fayette	65248	Gallatin	64640	Grayson	64492
Fayetteville	64093	Galloway (Part of Springfield)	65804	Grays Point	65707
Federal	63601	Galmey	65779	Gray Summit	63039
Fee Fee	63141	Galt	64641	Graysville	63551
Femme Osage	63332	Gamburg	63955	Green Acres	64801
Fenton	63026	Game	63830	Green Bay Terrace	65079
Ferguson	63135	Gamma	63333	Greenbrier	63730
Fern Ridge	63141	Garden City	64747	Green Castle	63544
Fernview Estates	63141	Gardenview	63033	Green City	63545
Ferrelview	64163	Garfield	65690	Greendale	63133
Fertile	63630	Garland	64735	Greenfield	65661
Festus	63028	Garrison	65657	Green Forest	63901
Fidelity	64836	Garwood	63957	Green Grove	63559
Field (Part of St. Louis)	63108	Gasconade	65036	Green Lawn	63462
Filley	64744	Gascondy	65013	Green-Mar	63026
Fillmore	64449	Gashland (Part of Kansas City)	64155	Green Mound Ridge	65669
Fisk	63940	Gateway Drive (Part of Joplin)	64801	Green Mountain	65711
Flag Springs (Andrew County)	64494	Gateway South	65201	Green Oaks	63936
Flag Springs (Phelps County)	65559	Gatewood	63942	Green Ridge	65332
Flat	65550	Gaynor	64475	Greensburg	63531
Flat River	63601	Gazette	63359	Greenstreet	63013
Flatwood	65466	Geneva	72438	Greentop	63546
Fleming	64077	Gentry	64453	Green Trail	63026
Flemington	65650	Gentryville (Douglas County)	65608	Greenville (Clay County)	64060
Fletcher	63030	Gentryville (Gentry County)	64402	Greenville (Wayne County)	63944
Flinthill	63346	Georgetown (Boone County)	65203	Greenwood	64034
Flordell Hills	63136	Georgetown (Pettis County)	65301	Greer	65606
Florence (Buchanan County)	64504	Gerald	63037	Gregory	63435
Florence (Morgan County)	65329	Germantown	64770	Gregory Heights	65202
Florida	65283	Gerster	64776	Gretna	65616
Florissant	63031-34	Gibbs	63540	Grimmet	65775
For specific Florissant Zip Codes call (314) 837-1810, or your local postmaster.		Gibson	63847	Grisham	63764
Floyd	64077	Gideon	63848	Grogan	65464
Flucom	63020	Gilbert	63855	Grover	63040
Foil	65755	Gilliam	65330	Grovespring	65662
Foley	63347	Gilman City	64642	Grubville	63041
Folk	65085	Gilmore	63385	Guilford	64457
Foose	65622	Ginger Blue	64854	Gumbo	63601
Forbes	64473	Gipsy	63750	Gunn City	64760
Ford City	64463	Girdner	65608	Guthrie	65063
		Gladden	65560	Hagers Grove	63437
		Gladstone	64118	Hahatonka	65020
		Glasgow	65254	Hahn	63764
		Glasgow Village	63137	Hailey	65605
		Glenaire	64068	Hale	64643
		Glenallen	63751		

* Area Zip Code † Post Office Boxes

	ZIP		ZIP		ZIP
Half Rock	64679	Hoberg	65712	Ironton	63650
Half Way	65663	Hobson	65560	Irwin	64759
Halls	64504	Hocomo	65626	Isabella	65676
Hallsville	65255	Hodge	64096	Isadora	64456
Halltown	65664	Hoene Spring	63025	Ishmael	63664
Hamilton	64644	Hoffman Junction	63628	Ives	63936
Hammond	65762	Holcomb	63852	Jack	65560
Hams Prairie	65251	Holden	64040	Jacket	65745
Hancock	65452	Holiday Shores	65326	Jacks Fork	65466
Handy	63941	Holland	63853	Jackson (Benton County)	65355
Hanley Hills	63133	Holliday	65258	Jackson (Cape Girardeau	
Hannibal	63401	Holliday Landing	63944	County)	63755
Hannon	64762	Hollister	65672	Jacksonville	65260
Happy Hollow	63630	Hollow	63069	Jadwin	65501
Hardeman	65340	Hollywood	63821	James Crews (Part of	
Hardenville	65666	Holman	65757	Kansas City)	64127
Hardin	64035	Holmes Park (Part of		Jameson	64647
Harg	65201	Kansas City)	64131	Jamesport	64648
Harper	64776	Holstein	63357	Jamestown	65046
Harris	64645	Holt	64048	Jamesville	65631
Harrisburg	65256	Holts Summit	65043	Jane	64856
Harrisonville	64701	Homestead	64024	Japan	63080
Harry S. Truman (Part of		Homestown	63879	Jarvis	63050
Independence)	64055	Honey Creek	65101	Jasper	64755
Hart	64865	Hooker	65550	Jaudon	64012
Hartford	63565	Hoover	64079	Jawdea	64083
Hartsburg	65039	Hope	65024	Jaywye	63873
Hartshorn	65479	Hopewell (Warren County)	63357	Jedburg	63011
Hartville	65667	Hopewell (Washington		Jefferson City	65101-10
Hartwell	64788	County)	63660	For specific Jefferson City Zip	
Hartzell	63848	Hopkins	64461	Codes call (314) 636-4186, or	
Harvester	63302	Horine	63070	your local postmaster.	
Harviell	63945	Hornersville	63855	Jefferson Memorial (Part of	
Harwood	64750	Hornet	64865	St. Louis)	63102
Haseltine	65802	Hortense	64735	Je-Ke-Ki	65326
Hassard	63456	Horton	64751	Jenkins	65605
Hastain	65326	House Creek	63965	Jennings	63136
Hatfield	64458	House Springs	63051	Jerico	65746
Hatton	65231	Houston	65483	Jerico Springs	64756
Havenhurst	64856	Houstonia	65333	Jerk Tail	65667
Hawkeye	65452	Houston Lake	64152	Jerome	65529
Hawk Point	63349	Howards Ridge	65655	Jesse M. Donaldson (Part	
Hayden	65459	Howardville	63869	of Kansas City)	64195
Hayes Park (Part of Sibley)	64088	Howell	63303	Jewett	63620
Hayti	63851	Howes Mill	65560	J&G Junction (Part of	
Hayti Heights	63851	H. S. Jewell (Part of		Joplin)	64801
Hayward	63873	Springfield)	65802	Johnson City	64724
Haywood City	63736	Hudson	64724	Johnstown (Bates County)	64770
Hazelgreen	65556	Huggins	65484	Johnstown (Jasper County)	64835
Hazel Run	63628	Hughesville	65334	Jonesburg	63351
Hazelwood	63042	Hugo	65052	Joplin	64801-04
Heatonville	65707	Humansville	65674	For specific Joplin Zip Codes call	
Hebron	65775	Hume	64752	(417) 623-6176, or your local	
Hecla	64653	Humphreys	64646	postmaster.	
Hedge City	63460	Hunnewell	63443	Jordan	65634
Helena	64459	Hunter	63943	Jordan W Chambers (Part	
Helm	65459	Hunters Mill	63664	of St. Louis)	63106
Heman Park (Part of		Hunterville	63846	Josephville	63385
University City)	63130	Huntingdale	64735	Judge	65051
Hematite	63047	Huntington	63456	Junction City	63645
Hemple	64490	Huntleigh	63131	Junland	63901
Henderson	65742	Huntsdale	65203	Kahoka	63445
Hendrickson	63967	Huntsville	65259	Kaiser	65047
Henley	65040	Hurdland	63547	Kampville	63301
Henrietta	64036	Hurley	65675	Kampville Beach	63301
Henry's Acres	65338	Hurlingen	64443	Kampville Court	63301
Henry Winfield Wheeler		Huron	65613	Kansas City	64101-99
(Part of St. Louis)	63101	Hurricane	63764	For specific Kansas City Zip	
Herbs	65338	Hurricane Deck	65079	Codes call (816) 842-2800, or	
Herculaneum	63048	Hurryville	63640	your local postmaster.	
Hercules	65614	Hutton Valley	65793	Karr's	65355
Heritage Hills	64083	Iantha	64759	Kaseyville	63534
Hermann	65041	Iatan	64098	Kearney	64060
Hermitage	65668	Iberia	65486	Keener Cave	63967
Hermondale	63877	Iconium	64776	Keenland	64083
Hickman Mills (Part of		Idalia	63825	Keethtown	65486
Kansas City)	64134	Idlewild	63960	Keightley's Beach	65355
Hickory Creek	64683	Ike	65737	Kellerville	63469
Hickory Hill	65040	Ilasco	63401	Kelso	63758
Higbee	65257	Illmo (Part of Scott City)	63780	Keltner	65720
Higdon	63645	Imperial	63052	Kendricktown	64836
Higginsville	64037	Independence	64050-58	Kennett	63857
High Gate	65559	For specific Independence Zip		Kenoma	64759
High Hill	63350	Codes call (816) 836-1440, or		Keota	63532
Highland	63775	your local postmaster.		Kerr	64429
Highlandville	65669	Independence Center (Part		Kersey Coates (Part of	
Highley Heights (Part of		of Independence)	64057	Kansas City)	64105
Desloge)	63601	Indian Creek	63456	Ketterman	64790
High Point	65042	Indian Ford	65582	Kewanee	63860
High Ridge	63049	Indian Grove	65236	Keys Summit	63122
Hilda	65680	Indian Hills (Part of Kansas		Keysville	65565
Hill City	65625	City)	64114	Keytesville	65261
Hillhouse Addition (Part of		Indian Lake	65453	Kidder	64649
Richland)	65556	Indian Point	65616	Kiel	63068
Hilliard	63901	Indian Springs	64783	Killarney Shores	63650
Hillsboro	63050	Ink	65466	Kilwinning	63555
Hillsdale	63133	Ionia	65335	Kimberling City	65686
Hill Top	63935	Irena	64456	Kimberling Hills (Part of	
Hinch	65441	Irondale	63648	Kimberling City)	65686
Hinton	65202	Iron Gates	64801	Kimble	65542
Hiram	63947	Iron Mountain	63650	Kime	63944
Hitt	63555	Iron Mountain Lake	63624	Kimmswick	63053

	ZIP		ZIP		ZIP
Kinder	63960	La Plata	63549	Longview (McDonald	
Kinderpost	65542	Laquey	65534	County)	64861
Kinfolks Ridge	63830	Laredo	64652	Longwood	65340
King City	64463	Larimore	63138	Loose Creek	65054
Kingdom City	65262	La Russell	64848	Loughboro	63601
Kings Lake	63347	Latham	65050	Louisburg	65685
Kings Point	65682	Lathrop	64465	Louisiana	63353
Kingston	64650	La Tour	64760	Louisville	63334
Kingsville	64061	Latty	63664	Lowground	63559
Kingsway Mall (Part of		Laurel Heights (Part of		Lowndes	63951
Sikeston)	63801	Raytown)	64133	Lowry City	64763
Kinloch	63140	Laurie	65038	Low Wassie	65588
Kinsey	63627	La Valle	63833	Lucas	64788
Kirbyville	65679	Lawrenceburg	65646	Lucas and Hunt Village	63121
Kirksville	63501	Lawrenceton	63627	Lucerne	64655
Kirkwood	63122	Lawson	64062	Ludlow	64656
Kirschner (Part of St.		Leadington	63601	Luebbering	63061
Joseph)	64504	Lead Mine	65764	Lulu	65606
Kissee Mills	65680	Leadwood	63653	Luna	65655
Kliever	65018	Leann	65605	Lupus	65046
Knobby	65326	Leasburg	65535	Luray	63453
Knob Lick	63651	Leawood	64801	Lutesville (Part of Marble	
Knob Noster	65336	Lebanon	65536	Hill)	63764
Knobtown (Part of Kansas		Lebo	65775	Luystown	65016
City)	64138	Lecoma	65540	Lynchburg	65543
Knolls	65065	Leeds (Part of Kansas City)	64129	Lyon	63068
Knox City	63446	Leemon	63755	Mc Allister Springs	65333
Knoxville	64084	Leeper	63957	McBaine	65203
Kodiak	64485	Lees Summit	64063-64	McBride	63776
Koeltztown	65048		64081-82	McCarty	63830
Koenig	65013		64086	McClurg	65701
Koshkonong	65692	For specific Lees Summit		McCracken	65753
Krakow	63090	Codes call (816) 524-0199, or		McCurry	64438
Kurreville	63766	your local postmaster.		McDowell	65769
Labadie	63055	Leesville	64735	Macedonia	65401
La Belle	63447	Leeton	64761	McFall	64657
Lac du Bois	63141	Lemay	63125	McGee	63763
Laclede	64651	Lemons	63565	McGirk	65055
La Crosse	63549	Lenox	65541	Machens	63373
Lacyville	64720	Lentner	63450	McKenna Villa	65326
Laddonia	63352	Leonard	63451	Mackenzie	63123
La Due (Henry County)	64735	Leon Mercer Jordan (Part of		McKinley	65705
Ladue (St. Louis County)	63124	Kansas City)	64128	McKittrick	65056
Laflin	63760	Leopold	63760	Macks Camp	65355
La Forge	63869	Leora	63825	Macks Creek	65786
Lagonda	63558	Leota	65626	McMullin	63801
La Grange	63448	Leslie	63056	McNatt	64867
Laguna Beach (Part of		Lesterville	63654	Macomb	65702
Osage Beach)	65065	Levasy	64066	Macon	63552
Lake Adelle	63016	Lewis	64735	Madison	65263
Lake Annette	64746	Lewis and Clark Village	64484	Madisonville	63436
Lake Arrowhead	63060	Lewistown	63452	Madry	65605
Lake City (Part of		Lexington	64067	Magnolia	64040
Independence)	64016	Liberal	64762	Main City	64742
Lake Contrary	64504	Liberty (Callaway County)	65063	Maitland	64466
Lake Creek	65325	Liberty (Clay County)	64068	Majorville	65355
Lake Forest Estates	63670	Libertyville	63640	Makalu Estates	65065
Lake Junction (Part of		Lick	65233	Malden	63863
Webster Groves)	63119	Licking	65542	Malta Bend	65339
Lake Kah-Tan-Da	63775	Liguori	63057	Mammoth	65655
Lakeland	65026	Lilbourn	63862	Manchester	63011
Lake Lotawana	64086	Lilly	64477	Mandeville	64622
Lake Mykee Town	65043	Lincoln	65338	Manes	65711
Lakenan	63468	Lindbergh	65202	Mano	65625
Lake of the Woods (Boone		Linden	65742	Mansfield	65704
County)	65201	Lindenlure Lake	65742	Many Springs	65606
Lake-of-the-Woods (Grundy		Lindley	64652	Mapaville	63065
County)	64683	Lingo	64631	Maplegrove	64748
Lake Ozark	65049	Linkville (Part of Kansas		Maples	65542
Lake Sherwood	63357	City)	64152	Maplewood (Cass County)	64083
Lakeshire	63125	Linn	65051	Maplewood (St. Louis	
Lakeside (Benton County)	65338	Linn Creek	65052	County)	63143
Lakeside (Boone County)	65256	Linneus	64653	Marble Hill	63764
Lakeside (Jasper County)	64801	Lisbon	65254	Marceline	64658
Lakeside (Miller County)	65026	Lisle	64742	March	65644
Lake Spring	65532	Lithium	63775	Marco	63870
Lake St. Louis	63367	Little Blue (Part of Kansas		Margona Village (Part of St.	
Lake Tapawingo	64015	City)	64133	Johns)	63114
Lake Tekakwitha	63069	Little Village (Part of Kansas		Marion	65023
Lake Timberline	63628	City)	64118	Marionville	65705
Lake Valle	63020	Livonia	63551	Mark Twain Mall (Part of St.	
Lakeview (Cass County)	64083	Lock Springs	64654	Charles)	63301
Lakeview (Miller County)	65026	Lockview Estates	65785	Marlborough	63123
Lakeview Heights	65338	Lockwood	65682	Marling	63359
Lake Viking	64640	Locust Hill	63460	Marquand	63655
Lake Ware	63020	Lodi	63950	Marshall	65340
Lake Waukomis	64152	Logan	65705	Marshall Junction	65340
Lake Wauwanoka	63050	Lohman	65053	Marshfield	65706
Lake Winnebago	64034	Loma Linda	63901	Marston	63866
Lake Wittona	64683	Lonedell	63060	Marthasville	63357
Lakewood	65201	Lone Elm (Cooper County)	65237	Martin City (Part of Kansas	
Lamar	64759	Lone Elm (Jasper County)	64801	City)	64145
Lamar Heights	64759	Lone Hill	63901	Martinsburg	65264
Lambert	63736	Lone Jack	64070	Martinstown	63565
Lamine	65233	Lone Star	63862	Martinsville	64467
La Monte	65337	Lone Tree	64701	Marvel Cave Park	65616
Lampe	65681	Long Beach	65616	Marvin	65084
Lanagan	64847	Long Lane	65590	Marvin Terrace (Part of St.	
Lancaster	63548	Longrun	65761	Johns)	63114
Lanes Prairie	65013	Longtown	63775	Maryden	63624
Langdon	64446	Longview (Jackson County)	64138	Maryknoll	63369
Lanton	65775			Maryland Heights	63043

	ZIP		ZIP		ZIP
Marys Home	65032	Monett	65708	New Survey	63877
Maryville	64468	Monkey Run	63401	Newtonia	64853
Maryville College-Saint Louis	63141	Monroe City	63456	Newtown	64667
Maryville Gardens (Part of		Montague	65669	New Truxton	63381
St. Louis)	63118	Montague Hill	65340	New Wells	63732
Masters	65649	Montevallo	64767	New Woolam	65066
Matson	63341	Montgomery City	63361	New York	64644
Mattese	63129	Monticello	63457	Niangua	65713
Matthews	63867	Montier	65546	Niangua Junction	65713
Maud	63437	Montreal	65591	Nichols (Part of Springfield)	65802
Maupin	63061	Montrose	64770	Nind	63501
Mayesburg	64788	Montserrat	65336	Ninnescah Park	64740
Mayfield	63662	Moody	65777	Nishnabotna	64482
Maysville	64469	Mooresville	64664	Nixa	65714
Mayview	64071	Mora	65345	Noble	65715
Maywood	63454	Morehouse	63868	Nodaway	64421
Meacham Park (Part of		Morgan	65632	Noel	64854
Kirkwood)	63122	Morgan Heights	64836	Norborne	64668
Meadowbrook Acres	64083	Morley	63767	Normandy	63121
Meadowbrook Downs (Part		Morrison	65061	Normandy Shopping Center	
of Overland)	63114	Morrisville	65710	(Part of Northwoods)	63121
Meadowbrook West	65203	Morse Mill	63066	Norris	64726
Meadville	64659	Morton	64085	North Boonville	65274
Mecca	64492	Mosby	64073	North County	63138
Medford	64040	Moscow Mills	63362	Northeast (Part of Kansas	
Medill	63445	Moselle	63084	City)	64123
Medoc	64855	Mosher	63670	Northern Heights (Part of	
Mehlville	63129	Mound City	64470	Kansas City)	64152
Meinert	65682	Moundville	64771	North Kansas City	64116
Melbourne	64642	Mountain	65772	Northland Shopping Center	
Melrose	63069	Mountain Grove	65711	(Part of Jennings)	63136
Memphis	63555	Mountain View	65548	North Lilbourn	63862
Mendon	64660	Mount Airy	65259	Northmoor	64152
Menfro	63765	Mount Freedom	63050	North Noel (Part of Noel)	64854
Mentor	65742	Mount Hope	63077	North Park Mall (Part of	
Mercer	64661	Mount Hulda	65325	Joplin)	64801
Mercyville	63538	Mount Leonard	65339	North Patton	63662
Merriam Woods	65653	Mount Moriah	64665	North Salem	63566
Merritt	65720	Mount Pleasant	65026	North Shores	65355
Merwin	64723	Mount Shira	65854	Northview	65706
Mesler	63772	Mount Sterling	65062	North Wardell	63879
Meta	65058	Mount Vernon	65712	Northwest Plaza (Part of St.	
Metro North Mall (Part of		Mount Zion (Douglas		Ann)	63074
Kansas City)	64155	County)	65608	Northwood Acres	64152
Metz	64765	Mount Zion (Henry County)	64740	Northwoods	63121
Mexico	65265	Mulberry (Barton County)	66756	Northwye	65401
Miami	65344	Mulberry (Bates County)	64722	Norwood	65717
Miami Station	64633	Mullendike	64083	Norwood Court	63121
Michelles Corner	65444	Munsell	65588	Nottinghill	65762
Micola	63877	Murphy	63026	Novelty	63460
Middle Brook	63656	Murry	65255	Novinger	63559
Middle Grove	65263	Musicks Ferry	63034	Number Eight	63532
Middletown	63359	Musselfork	65261	Nyhart	64730
Mid Rivers Mall (Part of St.		Myrtle	65778	Nyssa	63932
Peters)	63376	Mystic	63545	Oak	64422
Midvale	65571	Napier	64451	Oak Grove (Franklin	
Midway	65202	Napoleon	64074	County)	63080
Mike	64658	Napton	65340	Oak Grove (Jackson	
Milan	63556	Nashua (Part of Kansas		County)	64075
Mildred	65679	City)	64155	Oak Grove Heights	65801
Milford	64766	Nashville	64855	Oak Hill	65453
Millard	63501	Naylor	63953	Oakland (Laclede County)	65536
Millcreek	63645	Nebo	65470	Oakland (St. Louis County)	63122
Miller	65707	Neck City	64849	Oakland Park	64870
Millersburg	65251	Neelys	63755	Oak Leaf	65065
Millersville	63766	Neelyville	63954	Oak Ridge	63769
Mill Grove	64673	Neeper	63445	Oaks	64118
Millheim	63775	Neier	63084	Oakside	65548
Mill Spring	63952	Nelson	65347	Oakton	64759
Millville	64085	Nelsonville	65440	Oakview	64118
Millwood	63377	Nemo	65724	Oakville	63129
Milo	64767	Neola	65661	Oakwood (Clay County)	64116
Milton (Atchison County)	64446	Neosho	64850	Oakwood (Marion County)	63401
Milton (Randolph County)	65270	Netherlands	63851	Oakwood Park	64116
Mincy	65679	Nettleton	64644	Oasis	63347
Mindenmines	64769	Nevada	64772	Oates	63625
Mine La Motte	63645	Newark	63458	Ocie	65761
Mineola	63361	New Bloomfield	65063	Octa	63876
Miner	63801	New Boston	63557	Odessa	64076
Mineral Point	63660	Newburg	65550	Odin	65667
Mineral Spring	65625	New Cambria	63558	O'Fallon	63366
Mineville (Part of Kansas		New Florence	63363	Ogborn	63640
City)	64161	New Frankfort	65349	Oglesville	63961
Mingo	63960	New Franklin	65274	Ohio	64763
Minimum	63620	New Hamburg	63736	Okete	63379
Minnith	63673	New Hampton	64471	Olathia	65704
Mint Hill	65024	New Harmony	63339	Old Appleton	63770
Mirabile	64671	New Hartford	63364	Old Bland	65014
Missionary Acres	63944	New Haven	63068	Old Chilhowee	64733
Missouri City	64072	New Hope	63343	Olden	65789
Missouri Eastern		New Lebanon	65237	Oldfield	65720
Correctional Center	63069	New Liberty	65588	Old Fredonia	65355
Missouri Training Center for		New London	63459	Oldham	65010
Men	65270	New Madrid	63869	Old Linn Creek	65052
Mitchell	63601	New Market	64439	Old Merritt	65720
Moberly	65270	New Melle	63365	Old Mines	63630
Modena	64673	New Offenburg	63661	Old Monroe	63369
Mokane	65059	New Piper	64788	Old Orchard (Part of	
Moline Acres	63136	New Point	64473	Webster Groves)	63119
Molino	65265	Newport	64759	Old Post Office (Part of St.	
Monark Springs	64850	New Santa Fe (Part of		Louis)	63169
Monegaw Springs	64776	Kansas City)	64145	Old Success	65570

	ZIP		ZIP		ZIP
Old Woollam	65066	Penermon	63846	Preston (Hickory County)	65732
Olean	65064	Pennsboro	65752	Preston (Jasper County)	64836
Olive (Dallas County)	65648	Pennville	63545	Princeton	64673
Olive (Part of St. Louis)	63101	Peoria	63622	Principia	63131
Olivette	63132	Pepsin	64844	Prospect	65713
Olivewood	64083	Perkins	63774	Prospect Hill (Part of	
Olney	63370	Perrin	64477	Riverview)	63137
Olympia	64744	Perry	63462	Prosperity	64801
Olympian Village	63020	Perryville	63775	Protem	65733
Omaha	63565	Pershing	65061	Pulaski	63935
Ongo	65753	Peru	64730	Pulaskifield	65708
Opolis	66760	Peruque	63301	Pumpkin Center	64423
Oran	63771	Petersburg	65250	Purcell	64857
Orange	65605	Petersville	63055	Purdin	64674
Orchard Farm	63301	Pevely	63070	Purdy	65734
Orchard Lakes	63141	Phelps	64848	Pure Air	63559
Orearville	65349	Phelps City	64482	Purina Farm	63039
Oregon	64473	Philadelphia	63463	Purman	63935
Oriole	63701	Phillipsburg	65722	Purvis	65079
Orla	65536	Pickering	64476	Puxico	63960
Oronogo	64855	Piedmont	63957	Pyletown	63841
Orrick	64077	Pierce City	65723	Pyrmont	65078
Orrsburg	64475	Pierpont	65201	Quarles	64735
Osage	65101	Pierre Laclede (Part of St.		Queen City	63561
Osage Beach	65065	Louis)	63108	Quincy	65735
Osage Bend	65101	Pilot Grove	65276	Quitman	64478
Osage Bluff	65101	Pilot Knob	63663	Qulin	63961
Osage Hill (Part of		Pinckney	63357	Racine	64858
Kirkwood)	63122	Pine	63935	Racket	64735
Osborn	64474	Pine Cove	65324	Racola	63630
Oscar	65542	Pine Crest	65571	Rader (Maries County)	65582
Osceola	64776	Pine Lawn	63120	Rader (Webster County)	65713
Osgood	64641	Pineville	64856	Ralls	63401
Osiris	64756	Piney Park	63077	Randles	63740
Oskaloosa	64762	Pinhook	63845	Randolph	64116
Otterville	65348	Pioneer	65734	Ravanna	64673
Otto	63052	Piper	64770	Ravena (Part of Pleasant	
Overland	63114	Pisgah	65237	Valley)	64068
Overton	65233	Pittsburg	65724	Ravena Gardens (Part of	
Owens	65717	Pittsville	64040	Pleasant Valley)	64068
Owensville	65066	Plad	65764	Ravenwood	64479
Owls Bend	65466	Plato	65552	Raymondville	65555
Owsley	65332	Platte City	64079	Raymore	64083
Oxford	64475	Platte Woods	64152	Raytown	64133
Oxly	63955	Plattin	63028	Rayville	64084
Oyer	64744	Plattsburg	64477	Rea	64480
Ozark	65721	Plaza (Part of Kansas City)	64112	Readsville	65067
Ozark Beach	65653	Plaza Shopping Center (Part		Rector	65560
Ozark Correctional Center	65652	of Springfield)	65804	Redbird	65014
Ozark Springs	65583	Pleasant Gap	64730	Red Bridge (Part of Kansas	
Ozark View	63122	Pleasant Green	65276	City)	64131
Pacific	63069	Pleasant Grove	65068	Redford	63665
Pack	64854	Pleasant Hill	64080	Redings Mill	64801
Pagedale	63133	Pleasant Hope	65725	Redman	63431
Painton	63772	Pleasant Ridge (Barry		Red Oak	64848
Palace	65552	County)	65769	Red Top	65757
Palisades	63011	Pleasant Ridge (Bates		Reeds	64859
Palmer	63664	County)	64780	Reeds Spring	65737
Palmyra	63461	Pleasant Valley (Clay		Reform	65077
Palopinto	65338	County)	64068	Regal	64624
Papin	63020	Pleasant Valley (Jasper		Reger	63556
Papinsville	64780	County)	64836	Renick	65278
Paradise	64089	Plevna	63464	Rensselaer	63401
Paradise Point	65355	Plew	64848	Renz Correctional Center	65022
Paris	65275	Plymouth	64624	Republic	65738
Paris Springs	65646	Pocahontas	63779	Rescue	64848
Parkcrest Village (Part of		Point Lookout	65726	Revere	63465
Springfield)	65807	Point Pleasant	63873	Reynolds	63666
Parkdale (Jefferson County)	63049	Polk	65727	Rhineland	65069
Parkdale (Platte County)	64152	Pollock	63560	Rhyse	65560
Parker Lake	63775	Polo	64671	Richards	64778
Parkers Park	63347	Pomona	65789	Richards-Gebaur Air Force	
Park Forest (Part of Kansas		Pom-o-sa Heights	65355	Base	64030
City)	64152	Ponce de Leon	65728	Rich Fountain	65035
Park Hills	63601	Pond	63038	Rich Hill	64779
Parkville	64152	Pondfork	65762	Richland	65556
Parkway (Franklin County)	63077	Pontiac	65729	Richmond	64085
Parkway (Jackson County)	64130	Pony Express (Part of St.		Richmond Heights	63117
Parma	63870	Joseph)	64503	Richville (Douglas County)	65637
Parnell	64475	Poplar	65355	Richville (Holt County)	64473
Pasadena Hills	63121	Poplar Bluff	63901	Richwoods	63071
Pasadena Park	63121	Portage Des Sioux	63373	Ridgedale	65739
Pascola	63871	Portageville	63873	Ridgely	64444
Passaic	64777	Port Hudson	63068	Ridgeway	64481
Passo	65355	Portland	65067	Ridgley	65647
Patterson	63956	Possumwalk	64428	Riggs	65284
Patton	63662	Post Oak	64761	Rimby	65659
Patton Junction	63662	Potosi	63664	Ripley (Part of	
Pattonsburg	64670	Pottersville	65790	Independence)	64056
Paulding	63821	Powe	63822	Risco	63874
Paulina Hills	63010	Powell	65730	Rise Branch	65324
Paydown	65582	Powersite	65731	Ritchey	64844
Paynesville	63371	Powersville	64672	River Aux Vases	63670
Peace Valley	65788	Poynor	63935	River Bend Estates	63017
Peach Orchard	63848	Prairie City	64780	Rivermines	63601
Peaksville	63465	Prairie Hill	65281	River Roads (Part of	
Pea Ridge	63080	Prairie Home	65068	Jennings)	63136
Pebble Acres	63141	Prairie Meadows Estate	65201	Riverside (Dunklin County)	63829
Peculiar	64078	Prathersville (Boone County)	65202	Riverside (Platte County)	64150
Peerless Park	63088	Prathersville (Clay County)	64024	Riverside Inn	64854
Peers	63357	Pratt	63935	Riverton	65606
Pendleton	63383	Prescott	65483	Riverview	63137

* Area Zip Code   † Post Office Boxes

	ZIP		ZIP		ZIP
Silver Lake (Perry County)	63775	State Correctional Pre-		Teal Bend	65355
Silver Mine	63645	Release Center	65081	Tebbetts	65080
Simcoe	64861	Steedman	65077	Tecumseh	65760
Simmons	65689	Steele	63877	Tempo	63141
Sinsabaugh	63953	Steeles	63935	Ten Brook (Part of Arnold)	63010
Sitze Store	63753	Steelville	65565	Tenmile	63552
Skidmore	64487	Steffenville	63470	Ten Mile Corner	64784
Slabtown	65542	Steinmetz	65254	Teresita	65573
Slagle	65613	Stella	64867	Terre DuLac	63628
Slater	65349	Stephens (Boone County)	65202	Thayer	65791
Sleeper	65536	Stephens (Callaway County)	65201	The Landing	63456
Sligo	65560	Stet	64680	Theodosia	65761
Smallett	65608	Stewartsville	64490	Thomas Hill	65244
Smelter Hill (Part of Joplin)	64801	Stillings	64079	Thomasville	65438
Smithfield	64834	Stinson	65707	Thompson	65285
Smithton	65350	Stockton	65785	Thornfield	65762
Smithville	64089	Stockton Hills	65785	Thorpe	65644
Smoky Hollow	65560	Stockyards (Buchanan		Thox Rock	65550
Sni Mills	64075	County)	64504	Thrush	64735
Snow Hollow Lake	63656	Stockyards (Jackson		Tiff	63674
Snyder	65286	County)	64102	Tiffany Springs (Part of	
Solo	65564	Stone Hill	65560	Kansas City)	64152
Souder	65773	Stoneridge	65737	Tiff City	64868
Soulard (Part of St. Louis)	63157	Stony Hill	63068	Tiffin	64744
South Carrollton (Part of		Stotesbury	64752	Tightwad	64735
Carrollton)	64633	Stotts City	65756	Tillman	63730
South Cedar City	65022	Stoutland	65567	Tilsit	63755
South County	63129	Stoutsville	65283	Timber	65560
	63151	Stover	65078	Times Beach	63025
For specific South County Zip		Strafford	65757	Tina	64682
Codes call (314) 846-2728, or		Strain	63080	Tindall	64683
your local postmaster.		Strasburg	64090	Tinkerville	63857
Southeast (Part of Kansas		Stringtown (Butler County)	63901	Tin Town	65622
City)	64132	Stringtown (Cole County)	65053	Tipperary	63559
Southeast Missouri Mental		Stringtown (Jasper County)	64834	Tipton	65081
Health Center	63640	Stults	65737	Tipton Ford	64801
Southern Hills	65301	Stultz	65464	Tip Top (Benton County)	65355
South Fork	65776	Sturdivant	63782	Tip Top (Iron County)	63621
Southgate Shopping Center		Sturgeon	65284	Toga	63730
(Part of Springfield)	65804	Sturges	64601	Toledo	65755
South Gifford	63549	Sublette	63546	Tolona	63452
South Greenfield	65752	Success	65570	Torch	63953
South Lee (Part of Lees		Sue City	63549	Tower Grove (Part of St.	
Summit)	64081	Sugar Creek	64054	Louis)	63163
South Liberty (Part of		Sugar Lake	64484	Town and Country	63131
Liberty)	64068	Sugartree	64668	Town Pavilion (Part of	
South Lineville	50147	Sullivan	63080	Kansas City)	64105
South Mall (Part of		Sulphur Springs	63083	Tracy	64079
Warrensburg)	64093	Sumach	63852	Trask	65548
South Point (Part of		Summerfield	65013	Treloar	63378
Washington)	63090	Summerset Lake	63020	Trenton	64683
South Saint Joseph (Part of		Summersville	65571	Trimble	64492
St. Joseph)	64504	Summit	63660	Triplett	65286
South Shore	63301	Summit Shopping Center		Troutt	63664
South Side (Part of		(Part of Lees Summit)	64081	Troy	63379
Springfield)	65806	Sumner	64681	Truesdail	63383
South Troost (Part of		Sundown	65761	Truman Corners (Part of	
Kansas City)	64131	Sunland Hills	63031	Grandview)	64030
South Troy	63379	Sunlight	63622	Truxton	63381
South Van Buren	63965	Sunny Slope (Part of		Tuckahoe	64801
Southwest (Part of St.		Kansas City)	64110	Tucker	63942
Louis)	63139	Sunnyvale (Part of Joplin)	64801	Tuckers Corner	64849
South West City	64863	Sunrise	63855	Tunas	65764
Spalding	63401	Sunrise Beach	65079	Turners	65765
Spanish Lake	63138	Sunrise Lake	63020	Turnerville	65548
Sparta	65753	Sunset Hills	63127	Turney	64493
Speed	65233	Sutherland	65360	Turtle	65560
Spencerburg	63339	Swan	65759	Tuscumbia	65082
Sperry	63501	Swedeborg	65572	Tuxedo Park (Part of	
Spickard	64679	Sweden	65608	Webster Groves)	63119
Splitlog	64843	Sweet Springs	65351	Twelve Mile	63645
Spokane	65754	Sweetwater (Newton		Twin	65355
Sprague	64779	County)	64850	Twin Bridges	65536
Spring Bluff	63080	Sweetwater (Reynolds		Twin Oaks	63011
Spring City	64801	County)	63638	Twin Springs	63079
Spring Creek	65461	Swift	63851	Tyler	63877
Springfield	65801-10	Swinton	63730	Tyrone	65483
For specific Springfield Zip Codes		Swiss	63041	Udall	65766
call (417) 864-0101, or your local		Sycamore	65758	Ulman	65083
postmaster.		Sycamore Hills	63114	Umber	65785
Spring Garden	65032	Sycamore Valley	65355	Umberland	65785
Springhill	64601	Syenite	63651	Umber View	65785
Spring Lake	63501	Sylvania	65682	Umber View Heights	65785
Springtown	63660	Syracuse	65354	Union (Franklin County)	63084
Spring Valley (Camden		Taberville	64780	Union (Ray County)	64062
County)	65065	Table Rock	65616	Union City	65610
Spring Valley (McDonald		Taitsville	64671	Union Star	64494
County)	64854	Tallapoosa	63878	Uniontown	63783
Sprott	63670	Taneyville	65759	Unionville	63565
Spruce	64730	Tanner	63801	Unity Village	64064
Spurgeon	64850	Tan Tar Estates	65065	University City	63130
Squires	65755	Tanyard	64801	Uplands Park	63121
Stahl	63559	Taos (Buchanan County)	64448	Upton	65552
Stanberry	64489	Taos (Cole County)	65101	Urbana	65767
Stanhope	65339	Tara	63123	Urbandale (Part of Moberly)	65270
Stanley	63851	Tarkio	64491	Urich	64788
Stanton	63079	Tarrants	63334	Useful (Osage County)	65051
Star City	65734	Tarsney Lakes	64075	Utica	64686
Stark	63353	Taskee	63967	Vale (Part of Kansas City)	64138
Stark City	64866	Tauria	65737	Valles Mines	63087
Starkenburg	65069	Taylor	63471	Valley City	65336
		Tea	63091	Valley Park	63088

* Area Zip Code   † Post Office Boxes

	ZIP		ZIP		ZIP
Valley View (Benton County)	65355	Weatherby	64497	Williamsburg	63388
		Weatherby Lake	64152	Williamstown	63473
Valley View (Ste. Genevieve County)	63627	Weaubleau	65774	Williamsville	63967
		Webb City	64870	Willmathsville	63546
Valley Water Mills	65803	Weber Hill	63051	Willow Brook	64448
Van	65613	Webster Groves	63119	Willow Springs	65793
Van Buren	63965	Webster Park (Part of Webster Groves)	63119	Wilson City	63882
Vance	65713			Wilton	65039
Vancleve	65058	Wedgewood	63031	Winchester (Clark County)	63435
Vandalia	63382	Wedgewood Green	63031	Winchester (St. Louis County)	63011
Vandiver	65265	Weingarten	63670		
Vanduser	63784	Wela	64865	Winchester Gap	65536
Vanzant	65768	Weldon Spring	63301	Windsor	65360
Vastus	63954	Weldon Spring Heights	63301	Windsor Springs (Part of Kirkwood)	63122
Velda Village	63133	Wellington	64097		
Velda Village Hills	63121	Wellston (St. Louis County)	63112	Windyville	65783
Vera	63334	Wellston (Part of St. Louis)	63112	Winfield	63389
Verdella	64762	Wellsville	63384	Winigan	63566
Verona	65769	Wentworth	64873	Winnwood (Part of Kansas City)	64117
Verona Hills (Part of Kansas City)	64145	Wentzville	63385		
		Wesco	65586	Winnwood Gardens (Part of Kansas City)	64117
Versailles	65084	West Alton	63386		
Veterans Hospital (Part of Kansas City)	64128	West Aurora	65026	Winnwood Lake (Part of Kansas City)	64117
		Westboro	64498		
Vibbard	64062	Westbrooke	65201	Winona	65588
Viburnum	65566	West County Center (Part of Des Peres)	63131	Winston	64689
Vichy	65580			Winthrop	64484
Victoria	63020	West Ely	63401	Wisdom	65355
Vida	65401	West Eminence	65466	Wishart	65710
Vienna	65582	Western Missouri Correctional Center	64429	Withers Mill	63401
Vigus	63042			Wittenberg	63786
Village of Charlack	63114	West Hermondale	63877	Wolf Island	63881
Village of Four Seasons	65049	West Line	64734	Womack	63645
Villa Heights (Part of Joplin)	64801	Weston	64098	Woodbine Heights (Part of Kirkwood)	63122
Villa Ridge	63089	West Park Mall (Part of Cape Girardeau)	63701		
Vineland	63020			Woodcliffe	65804
Vinita Park	63114	Westphalia	65085	Woodland	63461
Vinita Terrace	63114	West Plains	65775	Woodland Park	65026
Vinson	63841	Westport (Part of Kansas City)	64111	Woodland Shores	65355
Viola	65747			Woodlandville	65279
Virgil City	64744	West Quincy	63471	Woodlawn	65263
Virginia	64730	Westview	64850	Woodridge	63033
Vista	64789	Westville	64658	Woodruff	64098
Vulcan	63675	Westwood	63131	Woods Heights	64024
Waco	64869	Wet Glaize	65567	Woodson Terrace	63134
Wagoner	65785	Wheatland	65779	Woodville	65247
Wainwright	65043	Wheaton	64874	Woolam	65014
Wakenda	64687	Wheelerville	65605	Wooldridge	65287
Waldo (Part of Kansas City)	64114	Wheeling	64688	Worland	64752
Waldron	64092	Whispering Hills	63141	Worlds of Fun (Part of Kansas City)	64161
Walker	64790	Whispering Pines	65401		
Wallace	64439	Whitakerville	65355	Wornall (Part of Kansas City)	64114
Wall Street	65590	White Branch	65355		
Walnut Grove	65770	White Church	65789	Worth	64499
Walnut Shade	65771	White City	65020	Wortham	63601
Wanamaker	65340	White Cloud	65779	Worthington	63567
Wanda	64866	White Hall Fields (Part of Liberty)	64068	Wright City	63390
Wappapello	63966			Wyaconda	63474
Wardell	63879	Whiteman Air Force Base	65305	Wyatt	63882
Ward Parkway Center (Part of Kansas City)	64114	Whiteoak	63880	Wyatt Park (Part of St. Joseph)	64507
		Whiteside	63387		
Wardsville	65101	Whitesville	64480	Wyeth	64483
Ware	63050	Whitewater	63785	Yacht Club Harbor	65065
Warren	63456	Whiting	63845	Yancy Mills	65401
Warrensburg	64093	Whitman	65286	Yarrow	63501
Warrenton	63383	Wien	63558	Yates	65257
Warsaw	65355	Wilbur Park	63123	Yonkerville	65723
Warson Woods	63122	Wilcox	64468	Youngstown	63559
Washburn	65772	Wilderness	63941	Yount	63775
Washington	63090	Wildwood	64424	Yukon	65589
Washington Center	64467	Wildwood Estates	65804	Zalma	63787
Wasola	65773	Wildwood Lake (Part of Raytown)	64133	Zanoni	65784
Waterloo	64097			Zell	63670
Watson	64496	Wilhelmina	63933	Zion	63645
Waverly	64096	Willard	65781	Zion Hill	65559
Wayland	63472	William M. Chick (Part of Kansas City)	64124	Zora	65078
Wayne	65772				
Waynesville	65583				

	ZIP		ZIP		ZIP
Absarokee	59001	Camas	59845	Durant (Part of Butte)	59748
Acton	59002	Camas Prairie	59859	Dutton	59433
Adel	59421	Cameron	59720	Eagleton	59520
Agawam	59422	Canyon Creek	59633	East Butte (Part of Butte)	59701
Agency	59831	Canyon Ferry	59601	East Glacier Park	59434
Alberton	59820	Capitol	57724	East Helena	59635
Albion	59311	Cardwell	59721	East Missoula (Part of	
Alder	59710	Carlyle	59353	Missoula)	59801
Alhambra	59634	Carter	59420	Ekalaka	59324
Alloy (Part of Butte)	59701	Cartersville	59347	Elkhorn Hot Springs	59746
Alpine	59071	Cascade	59421	Elliston	59728
Alzada	59311	Castle Rock	59327	Elmdale	59213
Amazon	59632	Castner Falls	59421	Elmo	59915
Amsterdam	59741	Cat Creek	59017	Emigrant	59027
Anaconda	59711	Centennial (Part of Billings)	59108	Enid	59243
Anceney	59741	Centerville (Cascade		Ennis	59729
Andes	59218	County)	59472	Epsie	59317
Angela	59312	Centerville (Silver Bow		Essex	59916
Antelope	59211	County)	59701	Ethridge	59435
Apgar	59936	Central Park	59714	Eureka	59917
Argenta	59725	Champion (Part of		Evaro	59801
Arlee	59821	Anaconda)	59722	Evergreen	59901
Armington	59412	Chapman	59537	Everson	59430
Ashland	59003	Charles M. Russell (Part of		Fairfield	59436
Ashuelot	59443	Great Falls)	59405	Fairview	59221
Augusta	59410	Charlo	59824	Fallon	59326
Avon	59713	Charlos Heights	59840	Farmington	59422
Babb	59411	Checkerboard	59053	Feely (Part of Butte)	59727
Bainville	59212	Chester	59522	Ferdig	59466
Baker	59313	Chico Hot Springs	59065	Fergus	59451
Ballantine	59006	Chinook	59523	Findon	59053
Bannack	59725	Choteau	59422	Finley Point	59860
Basin	59631	Christina	59451	First Creek	59538
Bearcreek	59007	Church Hill	59741	First Electronic Combat	
Bearmouth	59832	Circle	59215	Range Group -	
Bear Spring	59430	Clancy	59634	Detachment 1	59501
Beaverton	59261	Clinton	59825	Fishtail	59028
Beehive	59061	Clyde Park	59018	Flathead Indian Reservation	59831
Belfry	59008	Coalridge	59219	Flatwillow	59087
Belgrade	59714	Coalwood	59351	Flaxville	59222
Belknap	59874	Cobden	59872	Floral Park (Part of Butte)	59701
Belle Creek	59317	Coffee Creek	59424	Florence	59833
Belmont	59046	Cohagen	59322	Floweree	59440
Belt	59412	Colorado Gulch	59601	Forestgrove	59441
Beltower	59324	Colstrip	59323	Forest Park	59330
Benchland	59462	Columbia Falls	59912	Forsyth	59327
Benteen	59031	Columbia Gardens (Part of		Fort Belknap	59526
Biddle	59314	Butte)	59701	Fort Belknap Indian	
Big Arm	59910	Columbia Heights	59912	Reservation	59526
Bigfork	59911	Columbus	59019	Fort Benton	59442
Bighorn	59010	Comanche	59015	Fortine	59918
Big Sandy	59520	Condon	59826	Fort Keogh	59301
Big Sky	59716	Conner	59827	Fort Kipp	59213
Big Timber	59011	Conrad	59425	Fort Peck	59223
Billings	59101-08	Cooke City	59020	Fort Peck Indian	
For specific Billings Zip Codes call (406) 657-5709, or your local postmaster.		Coram	59913	Reservation	59255
		Corbin	59638	Fort Shaw	59443
		Corvallis	59828	Four Buttes	59224
Billings Heights	59105	Corwin Springs	59021	Fourchette	59538
Birch Creek Colony	59486	Crackerville (Part of		Four Corners	59466
Birney	59012	Anaconda)	59711	Frazer	59225
Black Eagle	59414	Craig	59648	Frenchtown	59834
Blackfeet Indian Reservation	59417	Crane	59217	Froid	59226
Blackfoot	59417	Creston	59902	Fromberg	59029
Bloomfield	59315	Crow Agency	59022	Galata	59444
Blossburg	59728	Crow Indian Reservation	59022	Galen (Part of Anaconda)	59722
Bonner	59823	Crow Rock	59301	Gallatin Gateway	59730
Bonner-West Riverside	59801	Culbertson	59218	Gardiner	59030
Boulder	59632	Cushman	59046	Garland	59301
Box Elder	59521	Custer	59024	Garneill	59445
Boyd	59013	Cut Bank	59427	Garrison	59731
Boyes	59316	Dagmar	59219	Garryowen	59031
Bozeman	59715	Danvers	59457	Georgetown (Part of	
	59771-72	Darby	59829	Anaconda)	59711
For specific Bozeman Zip Codes call (406) 586-1508, or your local postmaster.		Dawson (Part of Butte)	59748	Geraldine	59446
		Dayton	59914	Geyser	59447
		Dearborn	59648	Gibson Flats	59401
Bozeman Hot Springs	59715	De Borgia	59830	Gildford	59525
Brady	59416	Decker	59025	Gilt Edge	59457
Brandenberg	59301	Deerfield Colony	59457	Glacier Colony	59427
Brandon	59749	Deer Lodge	59722	Glasgow	59230
Bridger (Carbon County)	59014	Del Bonita	59427	Glasgow Air Base	59231
Bridger (Gallatin County)	59722	Dell	59724	Glen	59732
Broadus	59317	Delphia	59073	Glendive	59330
Broadview	59015	Dempsey	59722	Glentana	59240
Brock Creek	59731	Denton	59430	Goldcreek	59733
Brockton	59213	Dentons Point (Part of		Golden Ridge	59436
Brockway	59214	Anaconda)	59711	Goldstone	59540
Brooks	59457	Devon	59474	Grace (Part of Butte)	59759
Brown (Part of Anaconda)	59711	Dewey	59727	Grant	59725
Brown Addition	59472	Dillon	59725	Grantsdale	59635
Browning	59417	Divide (Part of Butte)	59727	Grass Range	59032
Brusett	59318	Dixon	59831	Great Falls	59401-06
Buffalo	59418	Dodson	59524	For specific Great Falls Zip Codes call (406) 761-4894, or your local postmaster.	
Busby	59016	Donald (Part of Butte)	59759		
Butte	59701-03	Dover	59479		
	59750	Dovetail	59087	Greenfield	59436
For specific Butte Zip Codes call (406) 494-2107, or your local postmaster.		Downtown (Part of Billings)	59101	Greenough	59836
		Drummond	59832	Gregson (Part of Butte)	59748
		Dublin Gulch (Part of Butte)	59701	Greycliff	59033
Buxton (Part of Butte)	59750	Dunkirk	59474	Hackney (Part of Butte)	59748
Bynum	59419	Dupuyer	59432	Half Moon	59912

* **Area Zip Code**   † **Post Office Boxes**

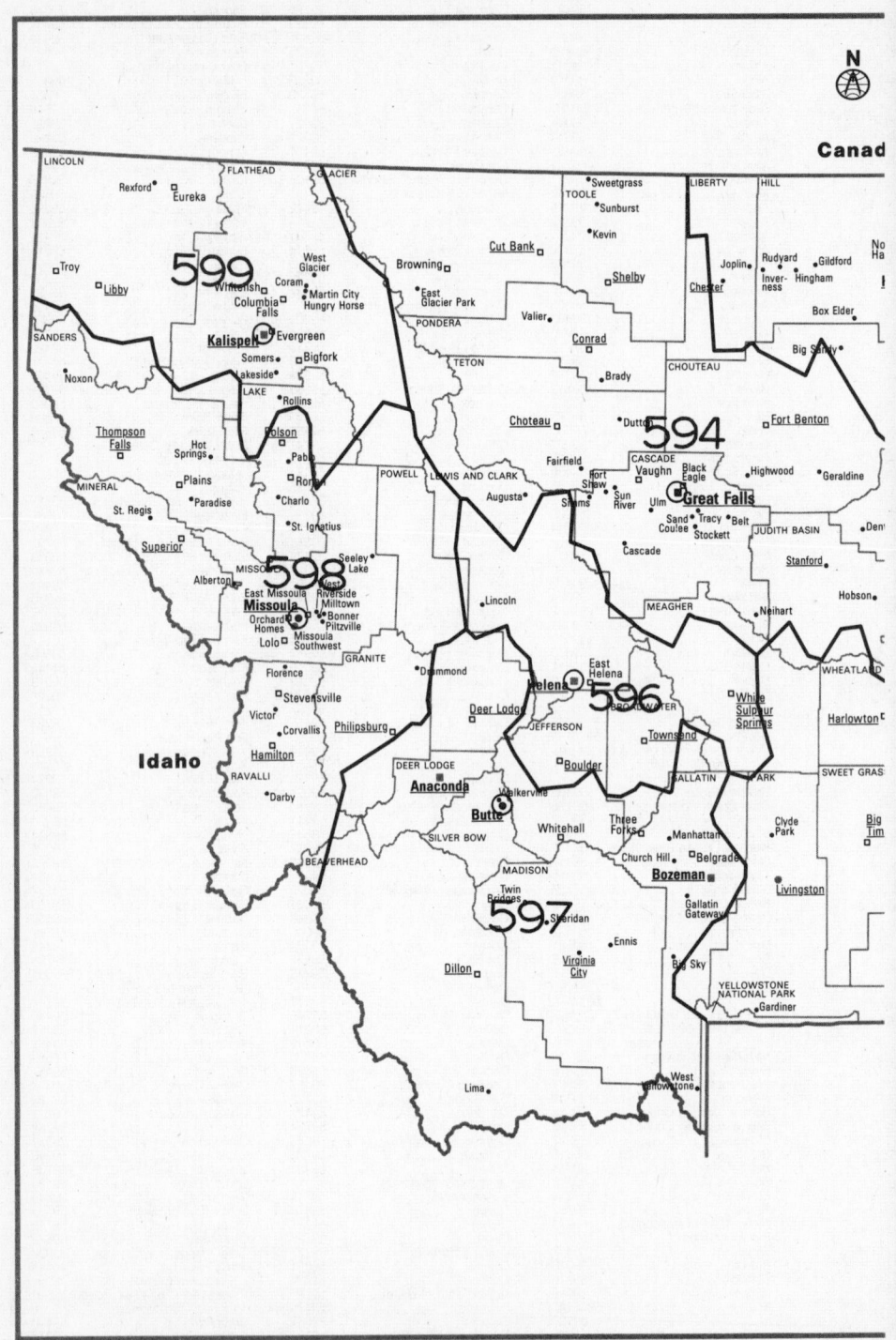

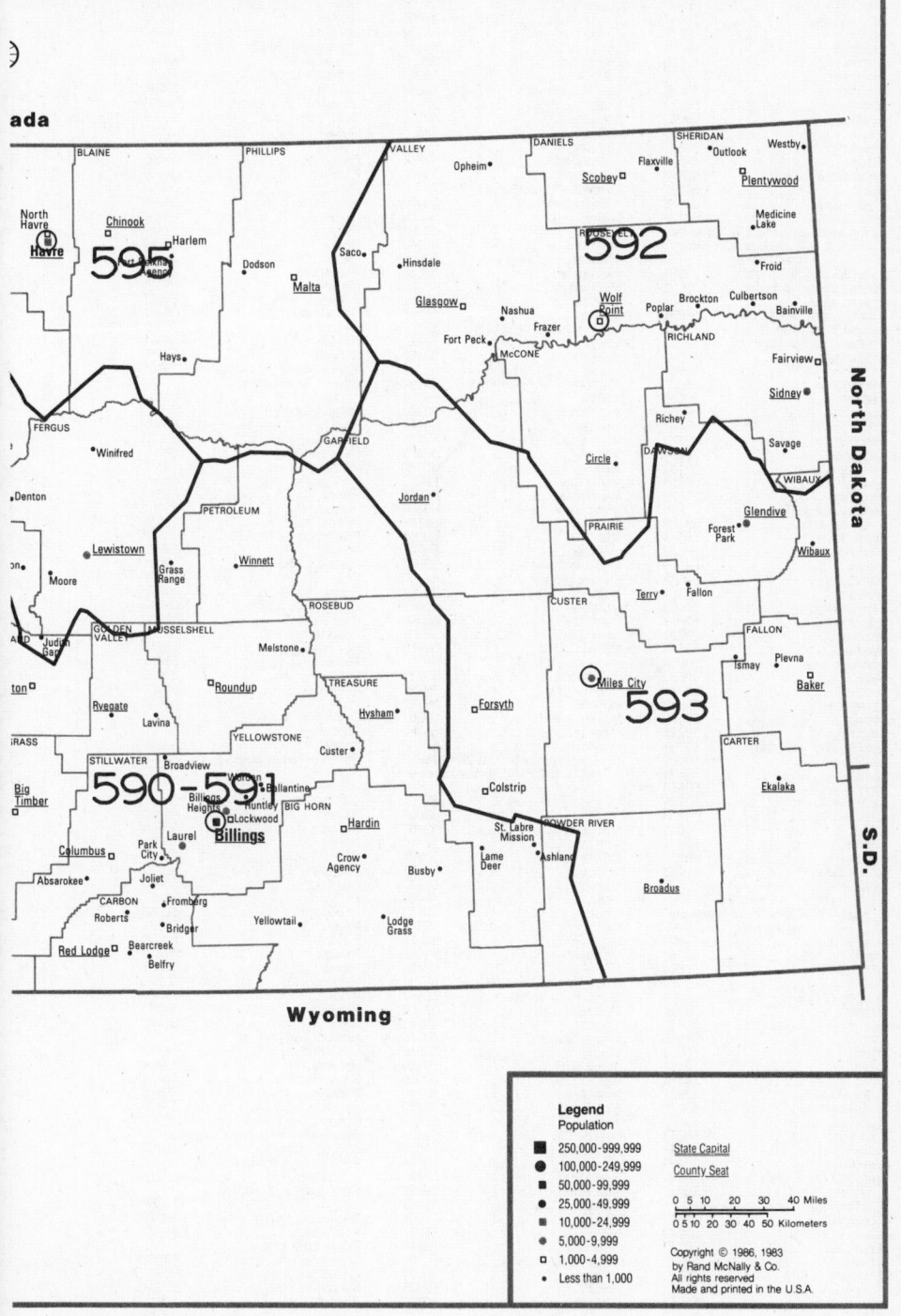

ada

595

592

593

590-591

North Dakota

S.D.

Wyoming

BLAINE · PHILLIPS · VALLEY · DANIELS · SHERIDAN
North Havre · Chinook · Harlem · Opheim · Scobey · Flaxville · Outlook · Westby
Havre · Fort Assiniboine Agency · Dodson · Saco · Hinsdale · ROOSEVELT · Plentywood · Medicine Lake
Malta · Glasgow · Nashua · Wolf Point · Poplar · Brockton · Culbertson · Froid
Hays · Fort Peck · Frazer · RICHLAND · Bainville · Fairview
McCONE · Richey · Sidney · Savage
FERGUS · Winifred · GARFIELD · Circle · DAWSON · WIBAUX
Denton · PETROLEUM · Jordan · PRAIRIE · Glendive · Wibaux
Lewistown · Moore · Grass Range · Winnett · ROSEBUD · CUSTER · Forest Park
GOLDEN VALLEY · MUSSELSHELL · Terry · Fallon · FALLON
Judith Gap · Melstone · Ismay · Plevna · Baker
Ryegate · Roundup · TREASURE · Forsyth · Miles City · CARTER
Lavina · Hysham · Custer · Ekalaka
GRASS · STILLWATER · YELLOWSTONE · Broadview · Colstrip
Big Timber · Columbus · Billings Heights · Huntley · Ballantine · BIG HORN · Hardin · POWDER RIVER
Park City · Laurel · Lockwood · Billings · Crow Agency · St. Labre Mission · Lame Deer · Ashland
Absarokee · Joliet · Fromberg · Busby · Broadus
CARBON · Roberts · Bridger · Yellowtail · Lodge Grass
Red Lodge · Bearcreek · Belfry

Legend
Population
■ 250,000-999,999   State Capital
● 100,000-249,999   County Seat
■ 50,000-99,999
● 25,000-49,999
■ 10,000-24,999
♦ 5,000-9,999
□ 1,000-4,999
• Less than 1,000

0 5 10   20   30   40 Miles
0 5 10 20 30 40 50 Kilometers

	ZIP		ZIP		ZIP
Hall	59837	Lincoln	59639	Noxon	59853
Hamilton	59840	Lindsay	59339	Nye	59061
Hammond	59332	Livingston	59047	Oilmont	59466
Hammond Valley	59327	Lloyd	59535	Olive	59343
Happyis Inn	59923	Lockwood	59101	Ollie	59313
Happy Valley	59937	Lodge Grass	59050	Olney	59927
Hardin	59034	Lodge Pole	59524	Opheim	59250
Hardy	59421	Logan	59741	Opportunity (Part of	
Harlem	59526	Lohman	59523	Anaconda)	59711
Harlowton	59036	Lolo	59847	Orchard Homes	59801
Harrison	59735	Lolo Hot Springs	59847	Ossette	59244
Hathaway	59333	Loma	59460	Oswego	59201
Haugan	59842	Lonepine	59848	Otter	59062
Havre	59501	Loring	59537	Outlook	59252
Havre North	59501	Lost Creek (Part of		Ovando	59854
Hays	59527	Anaconda)	59711	Pablo	59855
Heart Butte	59448	Lothair	59474	Paradise	59856
Heath	59457	Lower Sun River (Part of		Park City	59063
Hedgesville	59078	Great Falls)	59401	Park Grove	59248
Helena	59601-24	Lustre	59225	Peerless	59253
For specific Helena Zip Codes call (406) 443-3304, or your local postmaster.		Luther	59051	Pendroy	59467
		McAllister	59740	Perma	59859
		McCabe	59245	Petrolia	59087
Helena Valley Northeast	59601	McClellans Creek	59635	Philipsburg	59858
Helena Valley Northwest	59601	McGlone Heights (Part of		Piegan	59411
Helena Valley Southeast	59601	Butte)	59701	Piltzville	59801
Helena Valley West Central	59601	McLeod	59052	Pine Creek	59047
Helena West Side	59601	McQueen (Part of Butte)	59701	Pinegrove	59801
Hellgate (Part of Missoula)	59802	Madoc	59222	Pinesdale	59841
Helmville	59843	Maiden	59457	Pinnacle	59916
Heron	59844	Maiden Rock (Part of Butte)	59743	Pioneer (Silver Bow County)	59701
Herron Park	59501	Malmstrom Air Force Base	59402	Pioneer (Yellowstone	
Hesper	59106	Malta	59538	County)	59102
Highwood	59450	Manchester	59404	Pioneer Junction	59923
Hilger	59451	Manhattan	59741	Plains	59859
Hingham	59528	Many Glacier Hotel	59411	Pleasant Prairie	59222
Hinsdale	59241	Marion	59925	Pleasant Valley	59925
Hobson	59452	Marsh	59326	Pleasant View	59330
Hodges	59353	Martin City	59926	Plentywood	59254
Hogeland	59529	Martinsdale	59053	Plevna	59344
Holiday Village (Part of		Marysville	59640	Plum Creek	59457
Great Falls)	59405	Maudlow	59714	Polaris	59746
Holter Dam	59648	Maxville	59858	Polebridge	59928
Homestead	59242	Medicine Lake	59247	Polson	59860
Hopp	59520	Medicine Springs	59827	Pompeys Pillar	59064
Hot Springs	59845	Melrose (Part of Butte)	59743	Pony	59747
Howard	59327	Melstone	59054	Poplar	59255
Hughesville	59463	Melville	59055	Portage	59440
Hungry Horse	59919	Mildred	59341	Post Creek	59865
Huntley	59037	Miles City	59301	Potomac	59823
Huson	59846	Milford Colony	59648	Powderville	59345
Hysham	59038	Mill Creek (Part of		Power	59468
Iliad	59520	Anaconda)	59711	Pray	59065
Ingomar	59039	Miller Colony	59422	Proctor	59929
Inverness	59530	Mill Iron	59342	Pryor	59066
Ismay	59336	Milltown	59851	Quinn (Part of Butte)	59743
Jackson	59736	Miner	59027	Racetrack	59722
Janney (Part of Butte)	59701	Missoula	59801-07	Radersburg	59641
Jardine	59030	For specific Missoula Zip Codes call (406) 329-2200, or your local postmaster.		Ramsay (Part of Butte)	59748
Jeffers	59729			Rapelje	59067
Jefferson City	59638			Rattlesnake (Part of	
Jefferson Island	59721	Missoula Southwest	59801	Missoula)	59801
Jellison Place	59085	Mizpah	59301	Ravalli	59863
Joliet	59041	Moccasin	59462	Ravenna	59825
Joplin	59531	Moffit Canyon	59715	Raymond	59256
Jordan	59337	Moiese	59824	Raynesford	59469
Judith Gap	59453	Molt	59057	Red Bluff	59745
Kalispell	59901-04	Mona	59213	Red Lodge	59068
For specific Kalispell Zip Codes call (406) 755-6450, or your local postmaster.		Monarch	59463	Redstone	59257
		Monida	59739	Reedpoint	59069
		Montague	59442	Regina	59538
Kenilworth	59520	Montana City	59634	Reserve	59258
Kevin	59454	Montanapolis Springs	59065	Rexford	59930
Kicking Horse	59864	Moore	59464	Richey	59259
Kila	59920	Morel (Part of Anaconda)	59711	Richland	59260
Kingsbury Colony	59486	Morgan	59537	Ridgelawn	59270
Kinsey	59338	Mosby	59058	Ridgway	59332
Kiowa	59417	Moulton	59451	Rimini	59601
Kirby	59016	Mount Ellis	59715	Rimrock Mall (Part of	
Klein	59072	Muddy	59016	Billings)	59102
Kolin	59451	Musselshell	59059	Ringling	59642
Kremlin	59532	Myers	59038	Rising Sun	59434
Lake McDonald	59921	Nashua	59248	Riverside	59840
Lakeside	59922	Navajo	59222	Rivulet	59820
Lakeview	59739	Neihart	59465	Roberts	59070
Lambert	59243	Nevada City	59755	Rocker (Part of Butte)	59701
Lame Deer	59043	New Chicago	59832	Rockport Colony	59467
Landusky	59524	Newcomb (Part of Butte)	59701	Rock Springs (Rosebud	
Larslan	59244	New Miami Colony	59425	County)	59312
LaSalle	59912	New Rockport Colony	59422	Rock Springs (Sheridan	
Last Chance (Part of		Niarada	59852	County)	59258
Helena)	59601	Nibbe	59088	Rockvale	59041
Laurel	59044	Nickwall	59201	Rocky Boy	59521
Laurin	59749	Nine Mile	59846	Rocky Boys Indian	
Lavina	59046	Nissler (Part of Butte)	59701	Reservation	59521
Lebo	59053	Nohle	59221	Rollins	59931
Ledger	59456	Norris	59745	Ronan	59864
Lennep	59053	North Browning	59417	Roosville	59917
Lewistown	59457	Northern Cheyenne Indian		Roscoe	59071
Libby	59923	Reservation	59043	Rosebud	59347
Lima	59739	Northridge Heights (Part of		Rossfork	59457
Limestone	59061	Kalispell)	59901	Roundup	59072

	ZIP		ZIP		ZIP
Roy	59471	Staton (Part of Anaconda)	59711	Volt	59201
Ruby	59710	Stemple	59633	Wagner	59538
Rudyard	59540	Stevensville	59870	Walkerville	59701
Ryegate	59074	Stockett	59480	Wan-i-gan	59065
Saco	59261	Stone	59837	Ware	59457
Sage Creek	59522	Straw	59418	Warmsprings (Part of	
St. Ignatius	59865	Stryker	59933	Anaconda)	59756
St. Labre Mission	59004	Stuart (Part of Anaconda)	59711	Warren	82423
St. Marie	59231	Suffolk	59451	Warrick	59520
St. Mary	59417	Sula	59871	Washoe	59007
St. Peter	59421	Sumatra	59083	Waterloo	59759
St. Regis	59866	Summit	59434	Wayne	59412
St. Xavier	59075	Summit Valley	59721	Webster	59313
Salmon Prairie	59911	Sunburst	59482	Weldon	59215
Saltese	59867	Sunnyside (Part of		Westby	59275
Sand Coulee	59472	Anaconda)	59711	West Glacier	59936
Sand Creek	59201	Sun Prairie (Cascade		West Lewistown	59457
Sanders	59076	County)	59487	West Park Plaza (Part of	
Sand Springs	59077	Sun Prairie (Phillips County)	59538	Billings)	59102
Santa Rita	59473	Sun River	59483	West Riverside	59801
Sapphire Village	59452	Sunset	59836	West Valley (Part of	
Savage	59262	Superior	59872	Anaconda)	59711
Savoy	59526	Swan Lake	59911	West Yellowstone	59758
Scobey	59263	Sweetgrass	59484	Whately	59248
Seaver Park	59601	Swiftcurrent	59411	Wheeler	59230
Sedan	59086	Tampico	59230	Whitefish	59937
Seeley Lake	59868	Tarkio	59872	Whitehall	59759
Shawmut	59078	Teigen	59084	White Haven	59923
Shelby	59474	Terry	59349	Whitepine	59874
Shepherd	59079	The Pines	59859	White Sulphur Springs	59645
Sheridan	59749	Thompson Falls	59873	Whitetail	59276
Shonkin	59450	Three Forks	59752	Whitewater	59544
Sidney	59270	Toston	59643	Whitlash	59545
Silesia	59041	Townsend	59644	Wibaux	59353
Silver Bow (Part of Butte)	59750	Tracy	59472	Wickes	59638
Silver Bow Park (Part of		Trego	59934	Willard	59354
Butte)	59701	Trident	59752	Williamsburg (Part of Butte)	59701
Silver Gate	59081	Trout Creek	59874	Willow Creek	59760
Silver Star	59751	Troy	59935	Wilsall	59086
Simms	59477	Truly	59485	Windham	59479
Simpson	59501	Turah	59825	Winifred	59489
Sipple	59464	Turner	59542	Winnett	59087
Sleeping Buffalo	59261	Turner Colony	59542	Winston	59647
Smelter Hill	59414	Twin Bridges	59754	Wisdom	59761
Somers	59932	Twin Creeks	59823	Wise River	59762
Sonnette	59348	Twodot	59085	Wolf Creek	59648
South Browning	59417	Ulm	59485	Wolf Point	59201
Southern Cross (Part of		Unionville	59601	Woods Bay	59911
Anaconda)	59711	Utica	59452	Woodside	59875
Southgate Mall (Part of		Valier	59486	Woodworth	59836
Missoula)	59801	Vandalia	59273	Worden	59088
Spring Creek Colony	59457	Varney	59729	Wyola	59089
Springdale	59082	Vaughn	59487	Yaak Valley	59935
Springdale Colony	59645	Victor	59875	Yellowtail	59035
Square Butte	59442	Vida	59274	York	59601
Stanford	59479	Virgelle	59520	Zortman	59546
Stark	59846	Virginia City	59755	Zurich	59547
Starr School	59417	Volborg	59351		
State Capitol (Part of					
Helena)	59601				

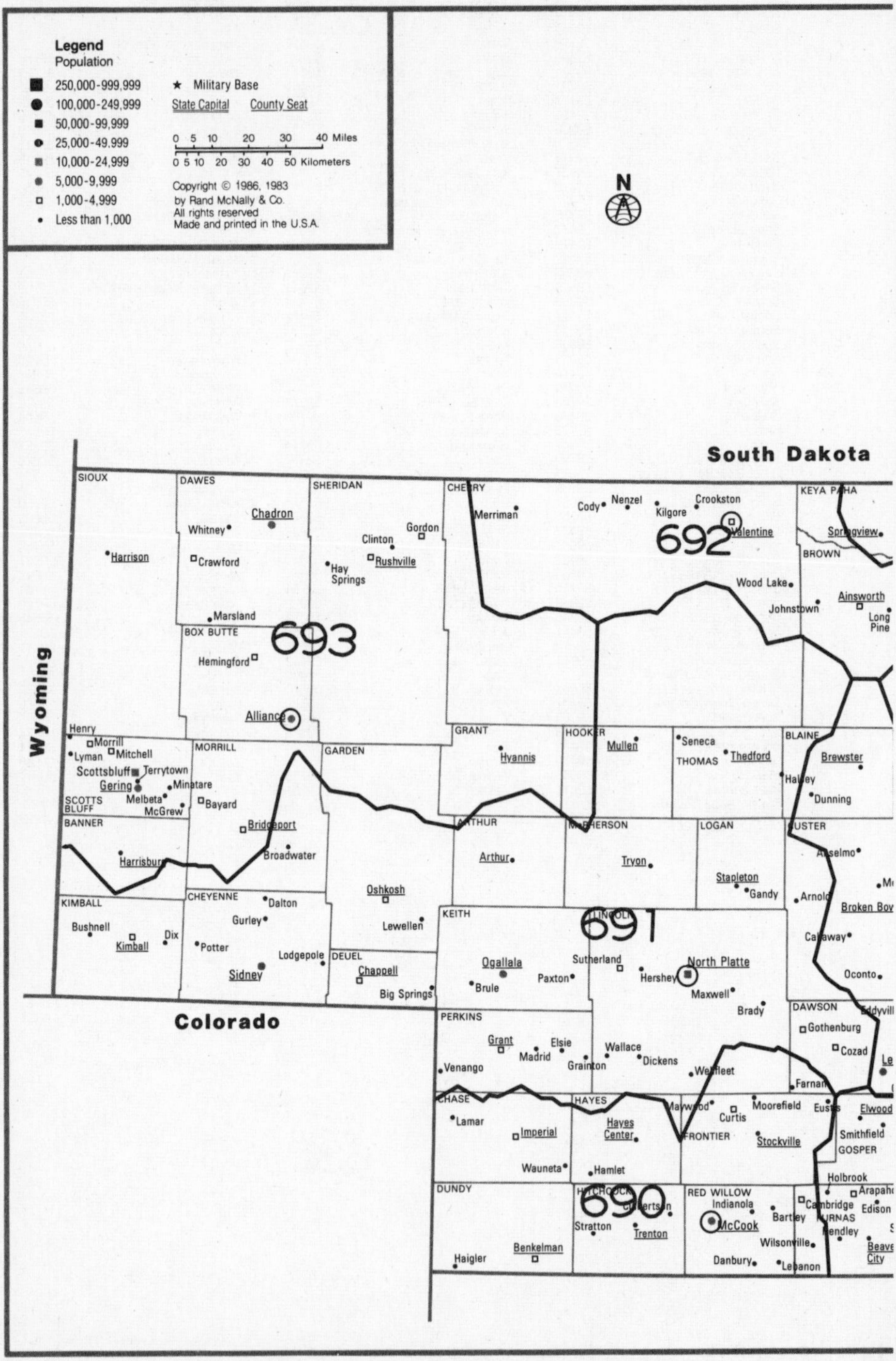

N

South Dakota

Wyoming

Colorado

SIOUX

DAWES

SHERIDAN

CHERRY

KEYA PAHA

Chadron

Whitney

Gordon

Merriman

Cody   Nenzel   Kilgore   Crookston

692

Valentine

Springview

BROWN

Harrison

Crawford

Clinton

Rushville

Hay Springs

Wood Lake

Ainsworth

Long Pine

Marsland

BOX BUTTE

693

Johnstown

Hemingford

Alliance

GRANT

HOOKER

Seneca

BLAINE

Brewster

Henry

Morrill

MORRILL

GARDEN

Hyannis

Mullen

THOMAS

Thedford

Halsey

Dunning

Lyman   Mitchell

Scottsbluff   Terrytown

Gering   Minatare

SCOTTS BLUFF

Melbeta   Bayard

McGrew

BANNER

Harrisburg

Bridgeport

Broadwater

ARTHUR

Arthur

McPHERSON

Tryon

LOGAN

Stapleton

Gandy

CUSTER

Anselmo

Arnold

Broken Bow

KIMBALL

CHEYENNE

Dalton

Gurley

Oshkosh

Lewellen

KEITH

LINCOLN

691

Callaway

Bushnell

Kimball

Dix

Potter

Lodgepole

DEUEL

Chappell

Big Springs

Ogallala

Sutherland

Paxton

North Platte

Hershey

Maxwell

Brady

Oconto

DAWSON

Gothenburg

Cozad

Sidney

PERKINS

Grant

Elsie

Madrid

Wallace

Grainton   Dickens

Westfleet

Farnam

Venango

CHASE

HAYES

Maywood

Moorefield   Eustis   Elwood

Lamar

Imperial

Hayes Center

Curtis

FRONTIER

Stockville

Smithfield

GOSPER

Wauneta

Hamlet

Holbrook

DUNDY

HITCHCOCK

Culbertson

RED WILLOW

Indianola

Arapahoe   Edison

FURNAS

Cambridge

Bartley   Hendley

Beaver City

Stratton

Trenton

690

McCook

Wilsonville

Danbury   Lebanon

Haigler

Benkelman

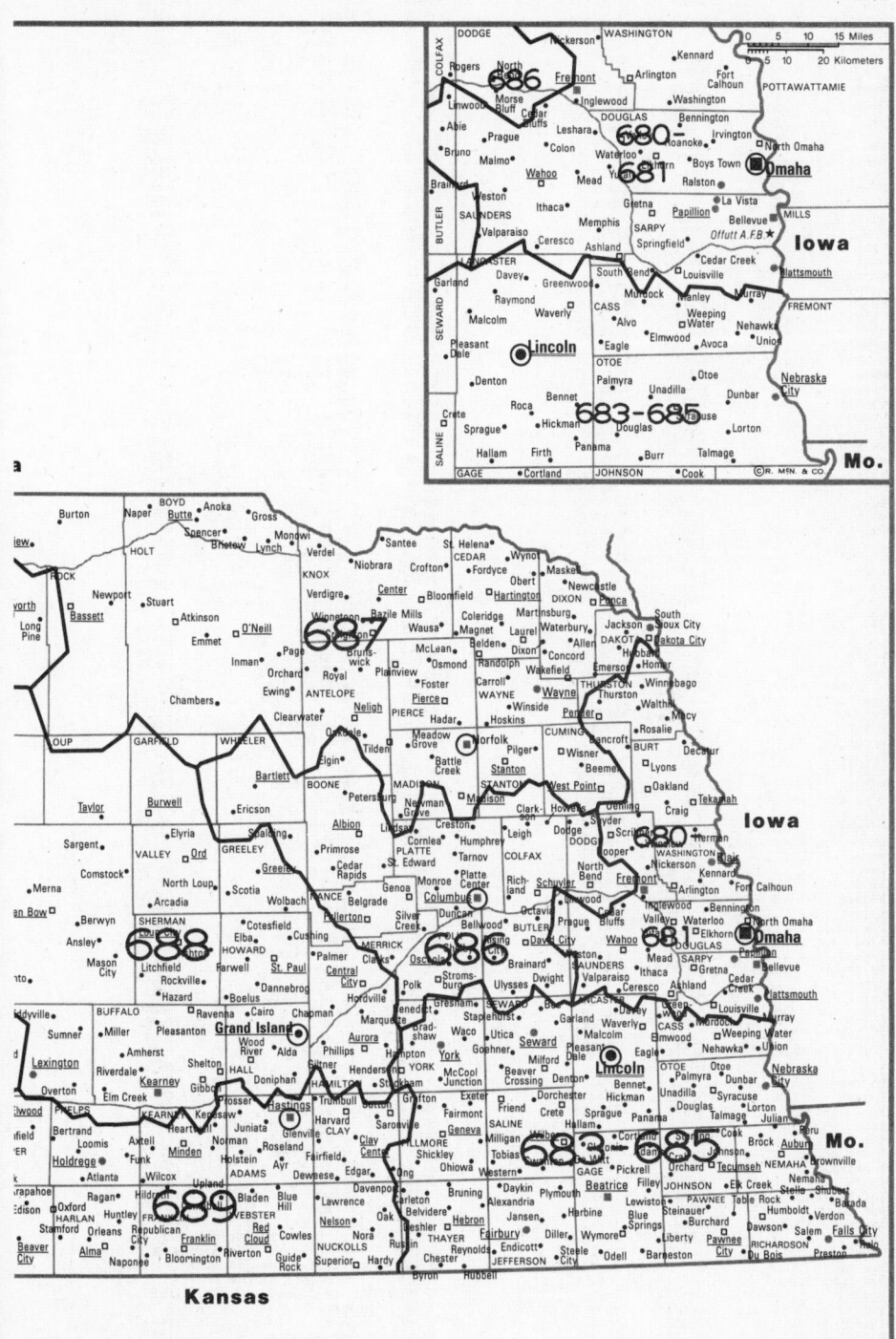

Kansas

	ZIP		ZIP		ZIP
Abie	68001	Brock	68320	Diller	68342
Adams	68301	Broken Bow	68822	Dix	69133
Agnew	68428	Brownlee	69166	Dixon	68732
Ainsworth	69210	Brownson	69162	Dodge	68633
Air Mail Facility (Part of		Brownville	68321	Doniphan	68832
Omaha)	68119	Brule	69127	Dorchester	68343
Air Park West	68524	Bruning	68322	Douglas	68344
Akron	68620	Bruno	68014	Downtown (Part of Omaha)	68102
Albion	68620	Brunswick	68720	Du Bois	68345
Alda	68810	Burchard	68323	Dunbar	68346
Alexandria	68303	Burkett (Part of Grand		Duncan	68634
Alien	68710	Island)	68801	Dunning	68833
Alliance	69301	Burr	68324	Dwight	68635
Alma	68920	Burress	68354	Eagle	68347
Almeria	68879	Burton	68778	Eddyville	68834
Aloys	68788	Burwell	68823	Edgar	68935
Altona	68787	Bushnell	69128	Edison	68936
Alvo	68304	Butte	68722	Elba	68835
Amelia	68711	Byron	68325	Elgin	68636
Ames	68621	Cadams	68978	Eli	69201
Ames Avenue (Part of		Cairo	68824	Elk City	68064
Omaha)	68111	Callaway	68825	Elk Creek	68348
Amherst	68812	Cambridge	69022	Elkhorn	68022
Angora	69331	Campbell	68932	Ellis	68310
Angus	68961	Carleton	68326	Ellsworth	69340
Anoka	68722	Carroll	68723	Elm Creek	68836
Anselmo	68813	Cedar Bluffs	68015	Elmwood	68349
Ansley	68814	Cedar Creek	68016	Elmwood Park (Part of	
Antioch	69340	Cedar Rapids	68627	Omaha)	68106
Arapahoe	68922	Center	68724	Elsie	69134
Arcadia	68815	Central City	68826	Elsmere	69135
Archer	68816	Ceresco	68017	Elwood	68937
Arlington	68002	Chadron	69337	Elyria	68837
Arnold	69120	Chalco	68046	Emerald	68502
Arthur	69121	Chambers	68725	Emerson	68733
Ashby	69333	Champion	69023	Emmet	68734
Ashland	68003	Chapman	68827	Enders	69027
Ashton	68817	Chappell	69129	Endicott	68350
Assumption	68955	Cheneys	68506	Enola	68701
Aten	68730	Chester	68327	Ericson	68637
Atkinson	68713	Clarks	68628	Ericson Lake	68637
Atlanta	68923	Clarkson	68629	Eustis	69028
Auburn	68305	Clatonia	68328	Ewing	68735
Aurora	68818	Clay Center	68933	Exeter	68351
Autumn Hills (Part of		Clearwater	68726	Fairbury	68352
Omaha)	68134	Clinton	69343	Fairfield	68938
Avoca	68307	Cody	69211	Fairmont	68354
Axtell	68924	Coleridge	68727	Falls City	68355
Ayr	68925	College View (Part of		Farnam	69029
Bancroft	68004	Lincoln)	68506	Farwell	68838
Barada	68355	Colon	68018	Filley	68357
Barneston	68309	Colton	69162	Firth	68358
Bartlett	68622	Columbus	68601*	Florence (Part of Omaha)	68112
Bartley	69020		68602†	Fontanelle	68044
Bassett	68714	Comstock	68828	Fordyce	68736
Battle Creek	68715	Concord	68728	Fort Calhoun	68023
Bayard	69334	Conestoga Mall (Part of		Fort Robinson	69339
Bazile Mills	68729	Grand Island)	68801	Foster	68737
Beatrice	68310	Constance	68730	Franklin	68939
Beaver City	68926	Cook	68329	Fremont	68025
Beaver Crossing	68313	Cordova	68330	Friend	68359
Bee	68314	Cornlea	68642	Fullerton	68638
Beemer	68716	Cortland	68331	Funk	68940
Belden	68717	Cotesfield	68829	Gandy	69163
Belgrade	68623	Cowles	68930	Garland	68360
Bellevue	68005	Cozad	69130	Garrison	68632
Bellwood	68624	Crab Orchard	68332	Gates	68822
Belvidere	68315	Craig	68019	Gateway Shopping Center	
Benedict	68316	Crawford	69339	(Part of Lincoln)	68505
Benkelman	69021	Creighton	68729	Geneva	68361
Bennet	68317	Creston	68631	Genoa	68640
Bennington	68007	Crete	68333	Gering	69341
Benson (Part of Omaha)	68104	Crofton	68730	Gibbon	68840
Berea	69301	Crookston	69212	Gilead	68362
Bertrand	68927	Crossroads Mall (Part of		Giltner	68841
Berwyn	68819	Omaha)	68114	Gladstone	68352
Bignell	69151	Crowell	68057	Glen	69339
Big Springs	69122	Crown Point (Part of		Glenover (Part of Beatrice)	68310
Bingham	69335	Omaha)	68122	Glenvil	68941
Bixby	68979	Culbertson	69024	Glenwood Park	68847
Bladen	68928	Curtis	69025	Goehner	68364
Blair	68008	Cushing	68873	Good Samaritan Village	
Bloomfield	68718	Dakota City	68731	(Part of Hastings)	68901
Bloomington	68929	Dalton	69131	Gordon	69343
Blue Hill	68930	Dana College	68008	Gothenburg	69138
Blue River Lodge	68333	Danbury	69026	Grafton	68365
Blue Springs	68318	Dannebrog	68831	Grainton	69169
Boelus	68820	Darr	69130	Grand Island	68801-03
Boone	68625	Davenport	68335	For specific Grand Island Zip	
Bostwick	68978	Davey	68336	Codes call (308) 381-5581, or	
Bow Valley	68739	David City	68632	your local postmaster.	
Boys Town	68010	Dawson	68337	Grand Island Mall (Part of	
Bradshaw	68319	Daykin	68338	Grand Island)	68801
Brady	69123	Debolt (Part of Omaha)	68152	Grant	69140
Brainard	68626	Decatur	68020	Greeley	68842
Brandon	69140	Denman	68956	Green Meadows	68164
Breslau	68765	Denton	68339	Greenwood	68366
Brewster	68821	Deshler	68340	Gresham	68367
Bridgeport	69336	De Soto	68023	Gretna	68028
Briggs	68122	Deweese	68934	Gross	68719
Bristow	68719	De Witt	68341	Grover	68405
Broadwater	69125	Dickens	69132	Guide Rock	68942

	ZIP		ZIP		ZIP
Gurley	69141	Leigh	68643	North Auburn (Part of	
Hadar	68738	Lemoyne	69146	Auburn)	68305
Haig	69357	Leshara	68035	North Bend	68649
Haigler	69030	Lewellen	69147	North Loup	68859
Hallam	68368	Lewiston	68380	North Oaks	68122
Halsey	69142	Lexington	68850	North Omaha (Part of	
Hamlet	69031	Liberty	68381	Omaha)	68112
Hampton	68843	Lincoln	68501-88	North Platte	69101-03
Hansen	68901	For specific Lincoln Zip Codes call		For specific North Platte Zip	
Harbine	68377	(402) 473-1695, or your local		Codes call (308) 532-3144, or	
Hardy	68943	postmaster.		your local postmaster.	
Harrisburg	69345	Lindsay	68644	Northport	69336
Harrison	69346	Lindy	68718	North Shore	68776
Hartington	68739	Linwood	68036	Northwest (Part of Omaha)	68134
Harvard	68944	Lisco	69148	Oak	68964
Hastings	68901*	Litchfield	68852	Oakdale	68761
	68902†	Lodgepole	69149	Oakland	68045
Havelock (Part of Lincoln)	68529	Loma	68626	Obert	68762
Havens	68628	Long Pine	69217	Oconto	68860
Hayes Center	69032	Loomis	68958	Octavia	68650
Hay Springs	69347	Lorenzo	69162	Odell	68415
Hazard	68844	Loretto	68620	Odessa	68861
Heartwell	68945	Lorton	68382	Offutt AFB West	68113
Hebron	68370	Louisville	68037	Offutt Air Force Base	68113
Hemingford	69348	Loup City	68853	Ogallala	69153
Henderson	68371	Lowell	68840	Ohiowa	68416
Hendley	68946	Lushton	68371	Old Mill (Part of Omaha)	68134
Henry	69349	Lyman	69352	Olean	68633
Herman	68029	Lynch	68746	Omaha	68101-64
Hershey	69143	Lyons	68038	For specific Omaha Zip Codes call	
Hickman	68372	McCook	69001	(402) 348-2861, or your local	
Hideaway Acres	68730	McCool Junction	68401	postmaster.	
Hildreth	68947	McGrew	69353	Omaha Indian Reservation	68039
Hillerage	69361	McLean	68747	O'Neill	68763
Holbrook	68948	Macon	68939	Ong	68452
Holdrege	68949	Macy	68039	Orchard	68764
Holland	68372	Madison	68748	Ord	68862
Hollinger	68967	Madrid	69150	Orleans	68966
Holmesville	68374	Magnet	68749	Orum	68008
Holstein	68950	Malcolm	68402	Osceola	68651
Homer	68030	Malmo	68040	Oshkosh	69154
Hooper	68031	Manley	68403	Osmond	68765
Hordville	68846	Maple Hills (Part of Omaha)	68134	Otoe	68417
Hoskins	68740	Marion	69026	Overton	68863
Howe	68305	Marquette	68854	Oxford	68967
Howells	68641	Marsland	69354	Page	68766
Hubbard	68741	Martell	68404	Palisade	69040
Hubbell	68375	Martinsburg	68770	Palmer	68864
Humboldt	68376	Mascot	68967	Palmyra	68418
Humphrey	68642	Maskell	68751	Panama	68419
Huntley	68951	Mason City	68855	Papillion	68046
Hyannis	69350	Max	69037	Papillion-La Vista (Part of	
Imperial	69033	Maxwell	69151	Papillion)	68128
Imperial Mall (Part of		Maywood	69038		68133
Hastings)	68901	Mead	68041		68138
Inavale	68952	Meadow Grove	68752		68157
Indianola	69034	Melbeta	69355	For specific Papillion-La Vista Zip	
Indian Village (Part of		Memphis	68042	Codes call (402) 346-9147, or	
Lincoln)	68502	Menominee	68736	your local postmaster.	
	68542	Merna	68856	Parks	69041
For specific Indian Village Zip		Merriman	69218	Parkview (Part of Grand	
Codes call (402) 473-1622, or		Milford	68405	Island)	68801
your local postmaster.		Millard (Part of Omaha)	68137	Paul	68410
Inglewood	68025	Miller	68858	Pauline	68941
Inland	68954	Milligan	68406	Pawnee City	68420
Inman	68742	Mills	68753	Paxton	69155
Irvington	68134	Milton	68858	Pender	68047
Ithaca	68033	Minatare	69356	Peru	68421
Jacinto	69133	Minden	68959	Petersburg	68652
Jackson	68743	Mitchell	69357	Phillips	68865
Jamison	68759	Monowi	68746	Pickrell	68422
Jansen	68377	Monroe	68647	Pierce	68767
Johnson	68378	Monterey	68788	Pilger	68768
Johnson Lake	68937	Moorefield	69039	Plainview	68769
Johnstown	69214	Morrill	69358	Platte Center	68653
Julian	68379	Morse Bluff	68648	Plattsmouth	68048
Juniata	68955	Mount Michael	68022	Pleasant Dale	68423
Kearney	68847*	Mullen	69152	Pleasant Hill	68343
	68848†	Murdock	68407	Pleasanton	68866
Keene	68924	Murphy	68865	Plymouth	68424
Kenesaw	68956	Murray	68409	Polk	68654
Kennard	68034	Mynard	68048	Ponca	68770
Keystone	69144	Naper	68755	Potter	69156
Kilgore	69216	Naponee	68960	Powell	68352
Kimball	69145	Nashville	68112	Prague	68050
King Lake	68064	Nebraska Center For		Prairie Home	68527
Kingsley	69153	Women	68467	Precept	68977
Knievels Corner	68735	Nebraska City	68410	Preston	68355
Kohles Acres	68730	Nehawka	68413	Primrose	68655
Kramer	68333	Neligh	68756	Princeton	68404
Kronborg	68854	Nelson	68961	Prosser	68868
Kuesters Lake	68801	Nemaha	68414	Purdum	69157
Lake Forest Estates	68134	Nenzel	69219	Raeville	68652
Lakeside	69351	Newcastle	68757	Ragan	68969
Lamar	69035	Newman Grove	68758	Ralston	68127
Lanham	68415	Newport	68759	Randolph	68771
La Platte	68123	Nickerson	68044	Ravenna	68869
Laurel	68745	Niobrara	68760	Raymond	68428
La Vista	68128	Nora	68961	Red Cloud	68970
Lawrence	68957	Norfolk	68701*	Redington	69336
Lebanon	69036		68702†	Regency (Part of Omaha)	68114
Lee Valley (Part of Omaha)	68134	Norman	68963	Republican City	68971

	ZIP
Reynolds	68429
Richfield	68054
Richland	68601
Ringgold	69167
Rising City	68658
Riverdale	68870
Riverside Lakes	68069
Riverton	68972
Roanoke (Part of Omaha)	68134
Roca	68430
Rockford	68310
Rockville	68871
Rogers	68659
Rosalie	68055
Roscoe	69153
Rose	68772
Roseland	68973
Rosemont	68930
Rosenburg	68644
Royal	68773
Rulo	68431
Rushville	69360
Ruskin	68974
Sac and Fox Indian Reservation	68355
Saddle Creek (Part of Omaha)	68132
St. Bernard	68644
St. Columbans	68056
St. Edward	68660
St. Helena	68774
St. James	68792
St. Libory	68872
St. Mary	68432
St. Paul	68873
St. Stephens	68957
Salem	68433
Santee	68760
Santee Indian Reservation	68760
Sarben	69155
Sargent	68874
Saronville	68975
Schaupps	68817
Schuyler	68661
Scotia	68875
Scottsbluff	69361-63
For specific Scottsbluff Zip Codes call (308) 635-1121, or your local postmaster.	
Scribner	68057
Seneca	69161
Seward	68434
Seymour Park (Part of Ralston)	68127
Shelby	68662
Shelton	68876
Shickley	68436
Sholes	68771
Shubert	68437
Sidney	69162
Silver Creek	68663
Skyline	68022
Smithfield	68976
Snyder	68664
South Bend	68058
South Minden (Part of Minden)	68959
South Omaha (Part of Omaha)	68107
Southroads Shopping Center (Part of Bellevue)	68005

	ZIP
South Sioux City	68776
South Yankton	57078
Spalding	68665
Sparks	69220
Sparta	68783
Spencer	68777
Spencer Park (Part of Hastings)	68901
Sprague	68438
Springfield	68059
Springview	68778
Stamford	68977
Stanton	68779
Staplehurst	68439
Stapleton	69163
State House (Part of Lincoln)	68509
Steele City	68440
Steinauer	68441
Stella	68442
Sterling	68443
Still Meadow (Part of Omaha)	68122
Stockham	68818
Stockville	69042
Stock Yards (Part of Omaha)	68107
Strang	68444
Stratton	69043
Stromsburg	68666
Stuart	68780
Sumner	68878
Sunnyslope (Part of Omaha)	68134
Sunol	69149
Superior	68978
Surprise	68667
Sutherland	69165
Sutton	68979
Swanton	68445
Swedeburg	68066
Syracuse	68446
Table Rock	68447
Talmage	68448
Tamora	68434
Tarnov	68642
Taylor	68879
Tecumseh	68450
Tekamah	68061
Telbasta	68002
Terrytown	69341
Thayer	68460
Thedford	69166
Thompson	68352
Thurston	68062
Tilden	68781
Tobias	68453
Touhy	68065
Trenton	69044
Trumbull	68980
Tryon	69167
Uehling	68063
Ulysses	68669
Unadilla	68454
Union	68455
University Place (Part of Lincoln)	68504
Upland	68981
Utica	68456
Valentine	69201

	ZIP
Valley	68064
Valparaiso	68065
Venango	69168
Venice	68069
Verdel	68760
Verdigre	68783
Verdon	68457
Vesta	68450
Veterans' Administration Hospital (Part of Omaha)	68105
Virginia	68458
Wabash	68407
Waco	68460
Wagners Lake	68601
Wahoo	68066
Wakefield	68784
Walkers Valley View	68730
Wallace	69169
Walthill	68067
Walton	68461
Wann	68003
Washington	68068
Waterbury	68785
Waterloo	68069
Wauneta	69045
Wausa	68786
Waverly	68462
Wayne	68787
Wayside	69337
Weeping Water	68463
Weissert	68880
Wellfleet	69170
Western	68464
Westerville	68881
West Omaha (Part of Omaha)	68114
Weston	68070
West Point	68788
Westroads Shopping Center (Part of Omaha)	68114
Westwood Plaza (Part of Omaha)	68144
Whiteclay	69365
Whitman	69366
Whitney	69367
Wilber	68465
Wilcox	68982
Willis	68743
Willow Island	69171
Wilsonville	69046
Winnebago	68071
Winnebago Indian Reservation	68071
Winnetoon	68789
Winside	68790
Winslow	68072
Wisner	68791
Wolbach	68882
Wood Lake	69221
Woodland Park	68701
Wood River	68883
Worms	68872
Wymore	68466
Wynot	68792
York	68467
Yossem's Paradise Valley (Part of Omaha)	68134
Yutan	68073

* **Area Zip Code**   † **Post Office Boxes**

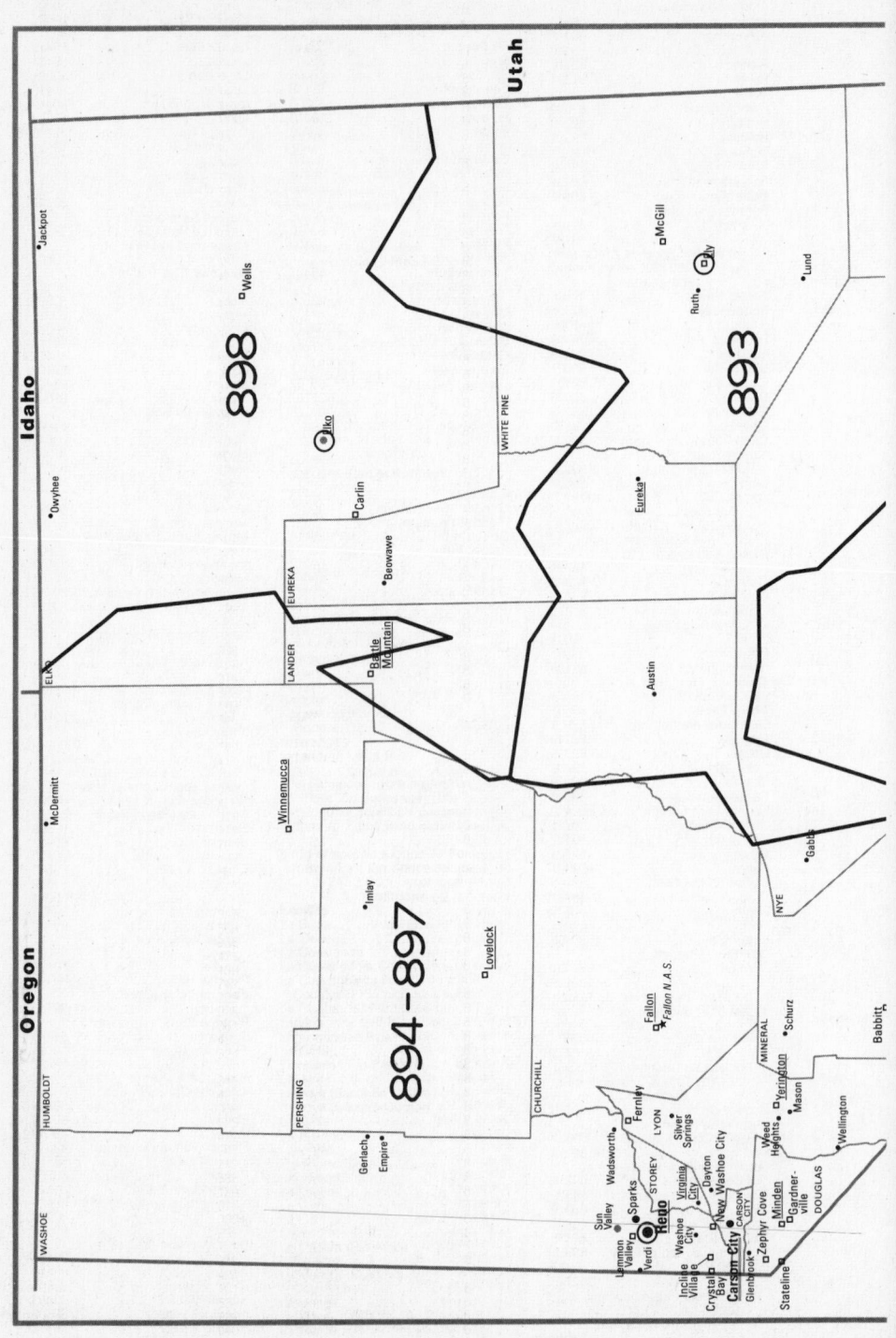

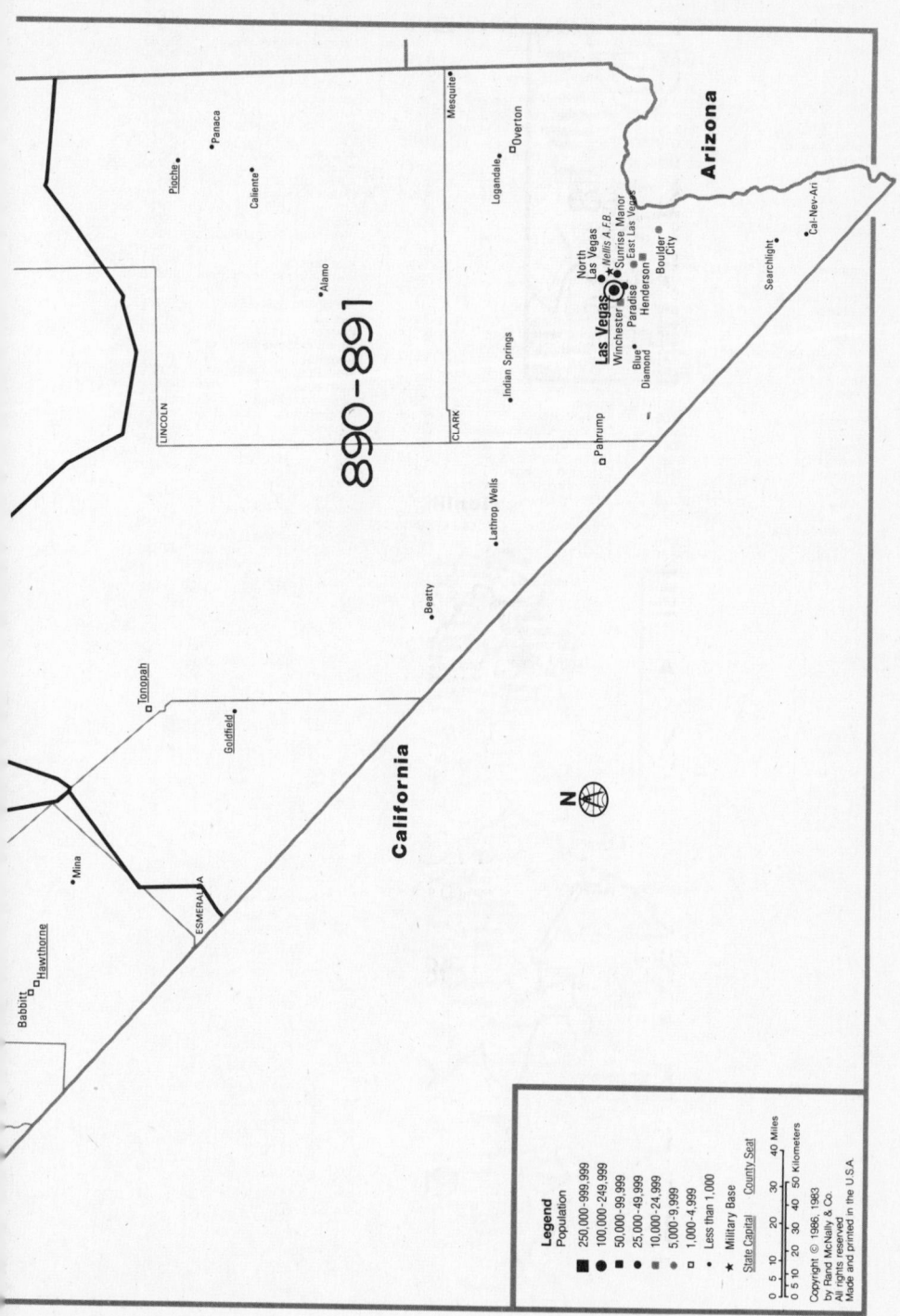

890-891

Arizona

California

LINCOLN

CLARK

ESMERALDA

Panaca

Pioche

Caliente

Alamo

Mesquite

Overton

Logandale

North
Las Vegas
Wells A.F.B.
Sunrise Manor
Las Vegas
East Las Vegas
Winchester
Paradise
Henderson
Blue
Diamond
Boulder
City

Searchlight

Cal-Nev-Ari

Indian Springs

Pahrump

Lathrop Wells

Beatty

Tonopah

Goldfield

Mina

Babbitt
Hawthorne

N

Legend
Population
250,000-999,999
100,000-249,999
50,000-99,999
25,000-49,999
10,000-24,999
5,000-9,999
1,000-4,999
Less than 1,000
★ Military Base
State Capital   County Seat

0 5 10   20   30   40 Miles
0 5 10 20 30 40 50 Kilometers

Copyright © 1986, 1983
by Rand McNally & Co.
All rights reserved
Made and printed in the U.S.A.

	ZIP
Reno	89501-70
For specific Reno Zip Codes call (702) 788-0600, or your local postmaster.	
Reno Park	89506
Rhyolite	89003
Ridgeview Estates	89705
Riverside	89007
River Village	89403
Rixie's	89820
Round Hill Village	89448
Round Mountain	89045
Rowland	83604
Ruby Valley	89833
Ruth	89319
Sagecrest Complex (Part of Elko)	89801
Sage Hills 2 (Part of Elko)	89801
Sandy Valley	89019
San Jacinto	89825
Satalite Hills (Part of Sparks)	89436
Schurz	89427
Scotty's Junction	89013
Searchlight	89046
Shafter	89835
Sheridan	89410
Sheridan Acres	89410
Shoshone	89301
Sierra (Part of Reno)	89506
Silverada Mall (Part of Reno)	89431
Silverado Heights	89705
Silver City	89428
Silverpeak	89047
Silver Springs	89429
Skyland	89448
Sloan	89103
Smith	89430
Smith Valley	89430
Southern Nevada Correctional Center	89019
Southgate	89801
South Hills	89501

	ZIP
Spanish Springs Valley	89436
Sparks	89431-36
For specific Sparks Zip Codes call (702) 359-1161, or your local postmaster.	
Spring Creek	89801
Spring Valley	89103
	89113
For specific Spring Valley Zip Codes call (702) 871-7555, or your local postmaster.	
Stagecoach	89429
Stanton Park (Part of Carson City)	89701
Stateline (Clark County)	89019
Stateline (Douglas County)	89449
Steamboat	89511
Steptoe	89318
Stewart (Part of Carson City)	89701
Stewarts Point	89040
Stillwater	89406
Strip Station	89114
Summit Lake Indian Reservation	89404
Suncrest (Part of Elko)	89801
Sundance Estates (Part of Elko)	89801
Sunrise Manor	89110
Sun Valley	89433
Sutcliffe	89501
Tahoe Village	89449
Te-Moak Indian Reservation	89801
Tempiute	89001
Thomas Creek Estates	89501
Thousand Springs	89835
Timberline Estates (Part of Carson City)	89703
Tonopah	89049
Topaz Junction	89410
Topaz Lake	89410
Topaz Ranch Estates	89444

	ZIP
Tracy-Clark	89434
Tuscarora	89834
Tyrolean Village	89450
Unionville	89418
University (Part of Reno)	89507
Upper Kingsbury	89449
Ursine	89043
Valmy	89438
Verdi	89439
Virginia City	89440
Vista (Part of Sparks)	89436
Vya	96104
Wabuska	89447
Wadsworth	89442
Walker Lake	89415
Walker River Indian Reservation	89427
Warm Springs	89049
Washington (Part of Reno)	89503*
	89513†
Washoe City	89701
Washoe Indian Reservation	89410
Weed Heights	89447
Wellington	89444
Wells	89835
Wendover	89883
Westland Mall (Part of Las Vegas)	89102
West Reno (Part of Reno)	89509
West Wendover	89883
Westwood Village	89423
Willow Beach	89005
Winchester	89101
Winnemucca	89445*
	89446†
	89447
Yerington	89447
Yerington Indian Reservation	89447
Yomba Indian Reservation	89310
Zephyr Cove	89448
Zephyr Cove-Round Hill Village	89448

	ZIP
Ackerman's Trailer Park....	03079
Acworth.................	03601
Acworth (Town)	03601
Albany	03818
Albany (Town).............	03818
Alexandria................	03222
Alexandria (Town)	03222
Allenstown	03275
Allenstown (Town)	03275
Alstead	03602
Alstead (Town)	03602
Alstead Center	03602
Alton	03809
Alton (Town).............	03809
Alton Bay	03810
Amherst.................	03031
Amherst (Town)	03031
Andover	03216
Andover (Town)	03216
Antrim	03440
Antrim (Town)	03440
Ashland	03217
Ashland (Town)	03217
Ashuelot	03441
Atkinson	03811
Atkinson (Town)	03811
Atkinson and Gilmanton	
Academy (Town)........	03579
Atkinson Heights	03811
Atlantic Heights (Part of	
Portsmouth)	03801
Auburn.................	03032
Auburn (Town)	03032
Baboosic Lake	03031
Bagley..................	03278
Bank Village..............	03071
Barnstead	03218
Barnstead (Town)	03218
Barrington	03825
Barrington (Town)	03825
Bartlett	03812
Bartlett (Town)	03812
Base	03595
Bath	03740
Bath (Town)	03740
Beans (Town)	03595
Beans Island	03077
Beans Purchase (Town) ...	03581
Beaver Lake	03038
Bedford	03102
....	03110
For specific Bedford Zip Codes	
call (603) 625-2728, or your local	
postmaster.	
Bedford (Town)	03110
Beebe River..............	03223
Belmont.................	03220
Belmont (Town)	03220
Bennington...............	03442
Bennington (Town)	03442
Benton..................	03785
Benton (Town)	03785
Berlin	03570
Berlin Mills (Part of Berlin)	03570
Bersum Gardens (Part of	
Portsmouth).............	03801
Bethlehem	03574
Bethlehem (Town)	03574
Bethlehem Junction........	03598
Birch Hill	03855
Blair	03264
Blais Park (Part of Berlin)	03570
Blodgett Landing	03255
Bonds Corner	03458
Boscawen................	03301
Boscawen (Town)	03301
Bow	03304
Bow (Town)...............	03304
Bow Center	03304
Bowkerville..............	03465
Box Corner..............	03220
Bradford	03221
Bradford (Town)...........	03221
Bradford Center	03221
Brentwood	03833
Brentwood (Town)	03833
Brentwood Corners........	03833
Bretton Woods	03575
Bridgewater	03222
Bridgewater (Town)........	03222
Bristol	03222
Bristol (Town)	03222
Broad Acres (Part of	
Nashua)	03060
Brookfield	03872
Brookfield (Town).........	03872
Brookline................	03033
Brookline (Town)	03033
Brook Village North (Part of	
Nashua)	03060
Bungy	03576
Burkehaven	03782

	ZIP
Cambridge (Town)........	03588
Camp Hedding	03042
Campton.................	03223
Campton (Town)	03223
Campton Hollow..........	03264
Campton Lower Village	03223
Campton Upper Village	03223
Canaan	03741
Canaan (Town)	03741
Canaan Center	03741
Canaan Street	03741
Candia	03034
Candia (Town)	03034
Candia Four Corners	03034
Canobie Lake	03079
Canterbury (Town).........	03224
Canterbury (Merrimack	
County)................	03224
Carroll (Town)	03595
Cascade	03581
Cedar Pond	03570
Center Barnstead	03225
Center Conway...........	03813
Center Effingham	03882
Center Harbor	03226
Center Harbor (Town)	03226
Center Haverhill	03774
Center Ossipee	03814
Center Sandwich	03227
Center Strafford	03815
Center Tuftonboro	03816
Central Park (Part of	
Somersworth)	03878
Chandlers Purchase (Town)	03595
Charlestown..............	03603
Charlestown (Town)	03603
Chase Village	03281
Chateau Richelieu (Part of	
Nashua)	03060
Chatham	04058
Chatham (Town)	04058
Cheever.................	03266
Chesham	03455
Chester	03036
Chester (Town)...........	03036
Chesterfield	03443
Chesterfield (Town)........	03443
Chichester	03263
Chichester (Town).........	03263
Chicks Corner	03259
Chocorua	03817
Christian Hollow	03608
Christian Shore (Part of	
Portsmouth).............	03801
Cilleyville	03265
Claremont...............	03743
Claremont Center (Part of	
Claremont).............	03743
Claremont Junction (Part of	
Claremont)	03743
Clarks Landing	03226
Clarksville (Town).........	03576
Clinton Grove	03281
Clinton Village	03440
Clovelly (Part of Nashua)..	03060
Coburn Woods (Part of	
Nashua)	03060
Cold Regions Research and	
Engineering Laboratory	03755
Cold River	03608
Colebrook...............	03576
Colebrook (Town)	03576
Columbia (Town)	03576
Columbia Valley	03576
Concord	03301-03
For specific Concord Zip Codes	
call (603) 225-5536, or your local	
postmaster.	
Contoocook	03229
Contoocook Lake	03452
Converseville	03461
Conway	03818
Conway (Town)	03818
Cornish (Town)...........	03745
Cornish Center	05089
Cornish City	05089
Cornish Flat	03746
Cornish Mills	05089
Cotton Mountain..........	03894
Crawford Notch	03595
Crawfords Purchase (Town)	03595
Cricket Corner............	03031
Croydon.................	03773
Croydon (Town)...........	03773
Croydon Flat	03773
Crystal	03570
Cushman	03598
Cutts (Town)	03595
Dalton	03598
Dalton (Town)	03598
Danbury	03230
Danbury (Town)	03230

	ZIP
Danville	03819
Danville (Town)............	03819
Davisville	03229
Deerfield	03037
Deerfield (Town)..........	03037
Deerfield Center	03037
Deerfield Parade..........	03037
Deering	03244
Deering (Town)...........	03244
Derry	03038
Derry (Town)	03038
Derry	03038
Derry Village	03038
Dixs (Town)	03576
Dixville (Town)............	03576
Dixville Notch............	03576
Dorchester	03266
Dorchester (Town)........	03266
Dover	03820
Dover Point (Part of Dover)	03820
Drewsville	03604
Dublin..................	03444
Dublin (Town)	03444
Dummer (Town)	03588
Dunbarton	03301
Dunbarton (Town)	03301
Durham.................	03824
Durham (Town)...........	03824
East Alstead	03602
East Alton	03809
East Andover	03231
East Barrington	03825
East Candia	03040
East Concord (Part of	
Concord)	03301
East Conway	04037
East Deering	03244
East Derry	03041
East Dummer	03588
East Grafton	03240
East Grantham	03753
East Hampstead	03826
East Haverhill	03780
East Hebron	03232
East Holderness	03217
East Kingston	03827
East Kingston (Town)......	03827
East Lempster............	03605
East Merrimack	03054
East Milford	03055
Easton..................	03580
Easton (Town)	03580
East Plainfield	03766
East Rindge	03461
East Rochester (Part of	
Rochester)	03868
East Sandwich	03226
East Sullivan	03445
East Sutton	03278
East Swanzey	03446
East Tilton	03252
East Unity	03773
Eastview	03450
East Wakefield	03830
East Washington	03244
East Westmoreland........	03467
East Wilder (Part of	
Lebanon)	03784
East Wolfeboro	03894
Eaton (Town).............	03832
Eaton Center	03832
Effingham	03814
Effingham (Town)	03814
Effingham Falls	03814
Elkins	03233
Ellsworth (Town)..........	03264
Elmwood (Hillsborough	
County)................	03449
Elmwood (Merrimack	
County)................	03230
Elwyn Park (Part of	
Portsmouth).............	03801
Enfield	03748
Enfield (Town)...........	03748
Enfield Center	03749
Epping	03042
Epping (Town)	03042
Epsom..................	03234
Epsom (Town)	03234
Errol	03579
Errol (Town)	03579
Ervings (Town)	03576
Etna	03750
Exeter	03833
Exeter (Town)	03833
Exeter Hampton Mobile	
Village	03833
Exeter Villa	03833
Exeter West	03833
Fabyan	03595
Farmington	03835

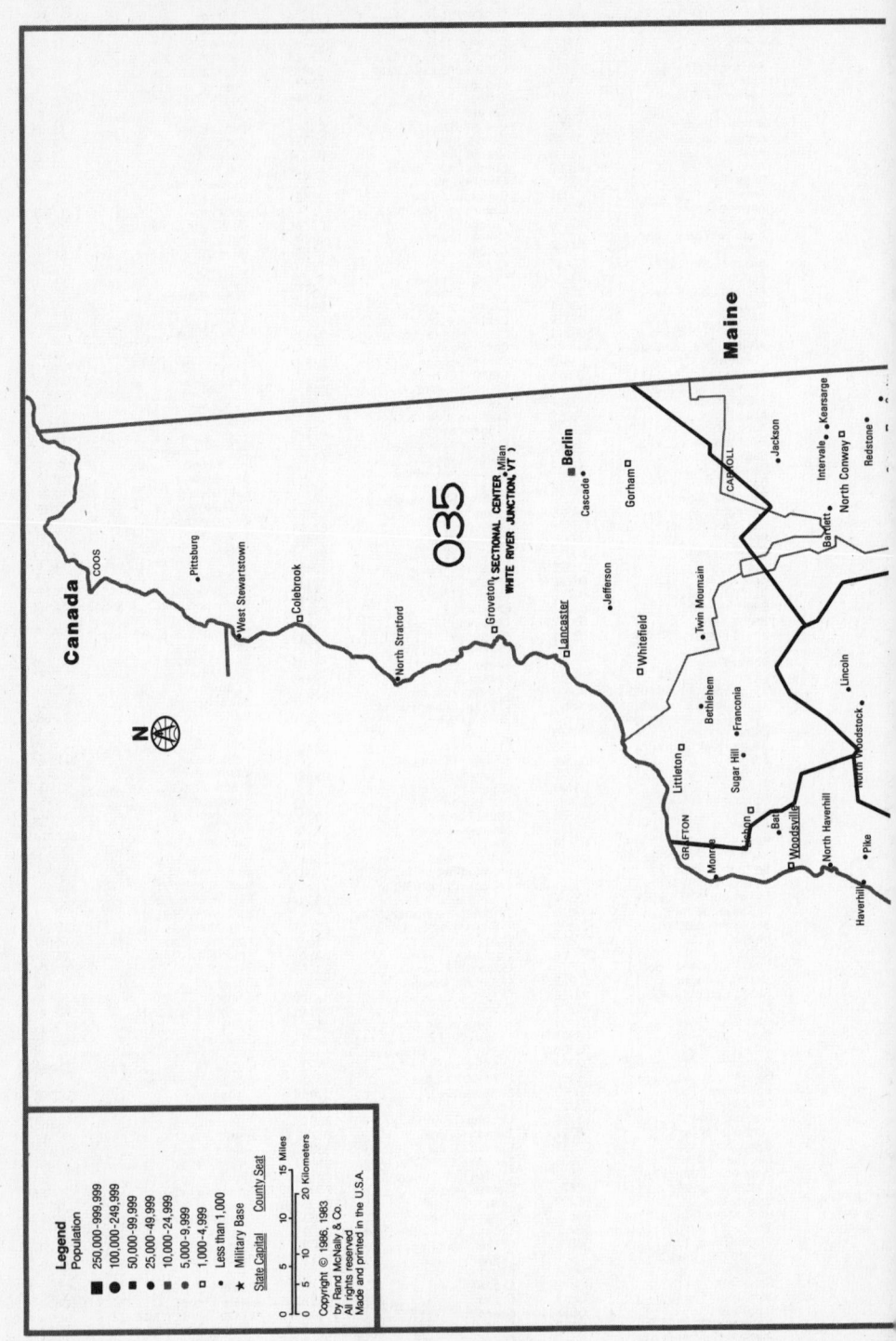

Legend

Population
■ 250,000-999,999
● 100,000-249,999
● 50,000-99,999
● 25,000-49,999
■ 10,000-24,999
■ 5,000-9,999
□ 1,000-4,999
• Less than 1,000
★ Military Base

State Capital   County Seat

0   5   10   15 Miles
0 5 10   20 Kilometers

Copyright © 1986, 1983
by Rand McNally & Co.
All rights reserved
Made and printed in the U.S.A.

Canada

Maine

035

COOS

Pittsburg

West Stewartstown
Colebrook

North Stratford

Groveton
Milan
SECTIONAL CENTER
WHITE RIVER JUNCTION, VT

Berlin
Cascade
Gorham

Lancaster

Jefferson

Whitefield

Twin Mountain

Bethlehem
Franconia

Littleton

Sugar Hill

CARROLL

Jackson
Intervale
Kearsarge
North Conway
Redstone
Bartlett

Lincoln

North Woodstock

GRAFTON

Monroe

Bath
Woodsville
North Haverhill
Pike

Haverhill

N

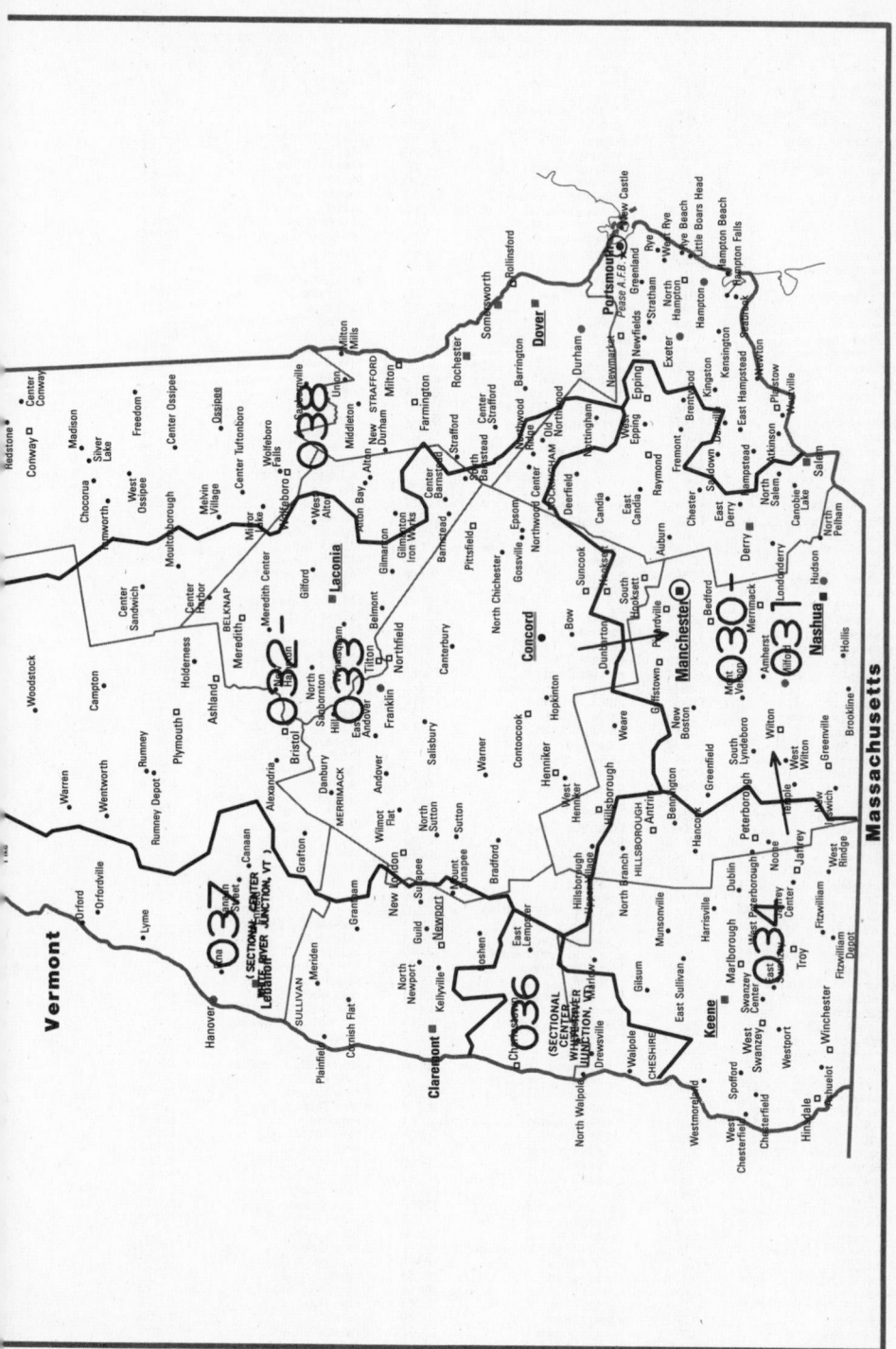

	ZIP
Farmington (Town)	03835
Fitzwilliam	03447
Fitzwilliam (Town)	03447
Fitzwilliam Depot	03447
Forest Lake	03470
Forest Ridge (Part of Nashua)	03060
Foyes Corner	03870
Francestown	03043
Francestown (Town)	03043
Franconia	03580
Franconia (Town)	03580
Franklin	03235
Franklin Falls (Part of Franklin)	03235
Franklin Pierce College	03461
Freedom	03836
Freedom (Town)	03836
Fremont	03044
Fremont (Town)	03044
Gardners Grove	03252
Gaza	03269
Georges Mills	03751
Gerrish	03301
Gilford	03246
Gilford (Town)	03246
Gilmans Corner	03777
Gilmanton	03237
Gilmanton (Town)	03237
Gilmanton Iron Works	03837
Gilsum	03448
Gilsum (Town)	03448
Glen	03838
Glencliff	03238
Glendale	03246
Glenmere Village	03824
Goffstown	03045
Goffstown (Town)	03045
Gonic (Part of Rochester)	03839
Goodrich Falls	03846
Goose Hollow	03223
Gorham	03581
Gorham (Town)	03581
Goshen	03752
Goshen (Town)	03752
Gossville	03234
Grafton	03240
Grafton (Town)	03240
Grafton Center	03240
Grange	03584
Granite	03864
Grantham	03753
Grantham (Town)	03753
Grasmere	03045
Great Boars Head	03842
Greenfield	03047
Greenfield (Town)	03047
Greenland	03840
Greenland (Town)	03840
Greens (Town)	03581
Greenville	03048
Greenville (Town)	03048
Groton	03241
Groton (Town)	03241
Groveton	03582
Guild	03754
Hadleys Purchase (Town)	03595
Hale's (Town)	03845
Hampstead	03841
Hampstead (Town)	03841
Hampton	03842
Hampton (Town)	03842
Hampton Beach	03842
Hampton Falls	03844
Hampton Falls (Town)	03844
Hancock	03449
Hancock (Town)	03449
Hanover	03755
Hanover (Town)	03755
Hanover Center	03750
Hanover Street (Part of Manchester)	03101
Happy Corner	03592
Happy Valley	03458
Harrisville	03450
Harrisville (Town)	03450
Hart's Location (Town)	03812
Hastings	03257
Haverhill	03765
Haverhill (Town)	03765
Hayes (Rockingham County)	03833
Hayes (Strafford County)	03867
Hebron	03241
Hebron (Town)	03241
Hedding	03042
Hell Hollow	03746
Henniker	03242
Henniker (Town)	03242
High Bridge	03071
Hill	03243
Hill (Town)	03243

	ZIP
Hill Center	03243
Hillsboro	03244
Hillsborough (Town)	03244
Hillsborough Center	03244
Hillsborough Lower Village	03244
Hillsborough Upper Village	03244
Hinsdale	03451
Hinsdale (Town)	03451
Holderness	03245
Holderness (Town)	03245
Hollis	03049
Hollis (Town)	03049
Hooksett	03106
Hooksett (Town)	03106
Hopkinton	03229
Hopkinton (Town)	03229
Horses Corner	03263
Hudson	03051
Hudson (Town)	03051
Hudson Center	03051
Intervale	03845
Jackson	03846
Jackson (Town)	03846
Jady Hill	03833
Jaffrey	03452
Jaffrey (Town)	03452
Jaffrey Center	03452
Jefferson	03583
Jefferson (Town)	03583
Jones Corner	03461
Joslin (Part of Keene)	03431
Kearsarge	03847
Keene	03431
Kelleys Corner	03263
Kellyville	03743
Kelwyn Park (Part of Somersworth)	03878
Kensington	03827
Kensington (Town)	03827
Kidderville	03576
Kilkenny (Town)	03584
Kingston	03848
Kingston (Town)	03848
Laconia	03246*
	03247†
Lakeport (Part of Laconia)	03246
Lancaster	03584
Lancaster (Town)	03584
Landaff (Town)	03585
Landaff Center	03585
Langdon	03602
Langdon (Town)	03602
Langs Corner	03870
Laskey Corner	03887
Laurel Lake	03447
Leavitts Hill	03037
Lebanon	03766
Lee	03824
Lee (Town)	03824
Lempster	03606
Lempster (Town)	03606
Lincoln	03251
Lincoln (Town)	03251
Lincoln Park (Part of Nashua)	03060
Lisbon	03585
Lisbon (Town)	03585
Litchfield	03051
Litchfield (Town)	03051
Little Boars Head	03862
Little Island Pond	03076
Littleton	03561
Littleton (Town)	03561
Livermore (Town)	03251
Livermore Falls	03264
Lochmere	03252
Lockehaven	03748
Londonderry (Town)	03053
Londonderry (Rockingham County)	03053
Loudon	03301
Loudon (Town)	03301
Loudon Center	03301
Louisburg Square (Part of Nashua)	03060
Low and Burbanks (Town)	03581
Lower Bartlett	03845
Lower Gilmanton	03263
Lower Village (Cheshire County)	03448
Lower Village (Merrimack County)	03278
Lyman (Town)	03585
Lyme	03768
Lyme (Town)	03768
Lyme Center	03769
Lyndeborough	03082
Lyndeborough (Town)	03082
Madbury	03820
Madbury (Town)	03820
Madison	03849
Madison (Town)	03849

	ZIP
Mall of New Hampshire, The (Part of Manchester)	03103
Manchester	03101-05
	03108-09
For specific Manchester Zip Codes call (603) 644-4111, or your local postmaster.	
Maplehaven (Part of Portsmouth)	03801
Maplewood	03281
Marlborough	03455
Marlborough (Town)	03455
Marlow	03456
Marlow (Town)	03456
Marshall Corner	03833
Marshall Farms	03833
Martin	03106
Martins (Town)	03581
Mascoma (Part of Lebanon)	03748
Mason	03048
Mason (Town)	03048
Meadowbrook (Part of Portsmouth)	03801
Meadows	03587
Melrose Corner (Part of Rochester)	03867
Melvin Mills	03278
Melvin Village	03850
Meredith	03253
Meredith (Town)	03253
Meredith Center	03246
Meriden	03770
Merrimack	03054
Merrimack (Town)	03054
Middleton (Town)	03887
Middleton Corners	03887
Milan	03588
Milan (Town)	03588
Milford	03055
Milford (Town)	03055
Mill Hollow	03602
Millsfield (Town)	03579
Mill Village (Cheshire County)	03464
Mill Village (Sullivan County)	03781
Millville Lake	03079
Milton	03851
Milton (Town)	03851
Milton Mills	03852
Mirror Lake	03853
Monroe	03771
Monroe (Town)	03771
Mont Vernon	03057
Mont Vernon (Town)	03057
Moultonboro	03254
Moultonborough (Town)	03254
Moultonborough Falls	03254
Moultonville	03814
Mountain View Estates (Part of Nashua)	03060
Mount Sunapee	03772
Mount Washington	03589
Munsonville	03457
Nashua	03060-63
For specific Nashua Zip Codes call (603) 882-2646, or your local postmaster.	
Nashua Mall (Part of Nashua)	03063
Nelson	03457
Nelson (Town)	03457
New Boston	03070
New Boston (Town)	03070
New Boston Air Force Tracking Station	03031
Newbury	03255
Newbury (Town)	03255
New Castle (Town)	03854
New Castle	03854
New Durham	03855
New Durham (Town)	03855
Newfields	03856
Newfields (Town)	03856
New Hampton	03256
New Hampton (Town)	03256
Newington (Town)	03801
New Ipswich	03071
New Ipswich (Town)	03071
New London	03257
New London (Town)	03257
Newmarket	03857
Newmarket (Town)	03857
Newport	03773
Newport (Town)	03773
New Rye	03275
Newton	03858
Newton (Town)	03858
Newton Junction	03859
Noone	03458
North Barnstead	03225
North Beach	03842
North Branch	03440

	ZIP		ZIP		ZIP
North Brookline	03055	Quaker City	03603	South Pittsfield	03263
North Charlestown	03603	Quincy	03266	South Stoddard	03464
North Chatham	04058	Quintown	03777	South Sutton	03273
North Chichester	03263	Rand	03461	South Tamworth	03883
North Conway	03860	Randolph	03570	South Weare	03281
North Danville	03819	Randolph (Town)	03570	South Wolfeboro	03894
Northfield	03276	Raymond	03077	Spofford	03462
Northfield (Town)	03276	Raymond (Town)	03077	Spofford Lake	03462
North Grantham	03766	Redstone	03813	Springfield	03284
North Groton	03266	Reeds Ferry	03054	Springfield (Town)	03284
North Hampton	03862	Richardson	03055	Squantum	03452
North Hampton (Town)	03862	Richmond	03470	Stark	03582
North Hampton Center	03862	Richmond (Town)	03470	Stark (Town)	03582
North Haverhill	03774	Rindge	03461	State Line	03447
North Holderness	03264	Rindge (Town)	03461	Stewartstown	03576
North Londonderry	03053	Rivercrest	03755	Stewartstown (Town)	03576
North Newport	03773	Riverdale	03045	Stewartstown Hollow	03576
North Pelham	03076	Riverhill (Part of Concord)	03301	Stinson Lake	03274
North Pembroke	03301	Riverside	03874	Stoddard	03464
North Richmond	03470	Riverside Plaza (Part of Keene)	03431	Stoddard (Town)	03464
North Salem	03073	Robinson Corner	03240	Strafford	03884
North Sanbornton	03269	Roby	03278	Strafford (Town)	03884
North Sandwich	03259	Rochester	03839	Stratford	03590
North Stratford	03590	....	03867-68	Stratford (Town)	03590
North Sutton	03260	For specific Rochester Zip Codes call (603) 332-1433, or your local postmaster.		Stratham	03885
North Swanzey	03431			Stratham (Town)	03885
Northumberland	05905			Strawberry Banke (Part of Portsmouth)	03801
Northumberland (Town)	05905	Rockwold	03245	Success (Town)	03570
North Village	03458	Rollinsford	03869	Sugar Hill	03585
North Walpole	03609	Rollinsford (Town)	03869	Sugar Hill (Town)	03585
North Wilmot	03230	Roxbury (Town)	03431	Sullivan	03431
North Wolfeboro	03894	Royal Crest Estates (Part of Nashua)	03060	Sullivan (Town)	03431
Northwood	03261	Rumney	03266	Sunapee	03782
Northwood (Town)	03261	Rumney (Town)	03266	Sunapee (Town)	03782
Northwood Center	03261	Rumney Depot	03266	Suncook	03275
Northwood Narrows	03261	Ryder Corner	03773	Surry	03431
Northwood Ridge	03261	Rye	03870	Surry (Town)	03431
North Woodstock	03262	Rye (Town)	03870	Sutton	03221
Nottingham	03290	Rye Beach	03871	Sutton (Town)	03221
Nottingham (Town)	03290	Rye North Beach	03870	Swanzey (Town)	03431
Noyes Terrace	03079	Sachem Village (Part of Lebanon)	03784	Swanzey Center	03431
Nuttings Beach	03222	Salem	03079	Swiftwater	03785
Odell (Town)	03582	Salem (Town)	03079	Tamworth	03886
Onway Lake	03077	Salem Depot	03079	Tamworth (Town)	03886
Orange	03741	Salisbury	03268	Temple	03084
Orange (Town)	03741	Salisbury (Town)	03268	Temple (Town)	03084
Orford	03777	Salisbury Heights	03268	The Glen	03592
Orford (Town)	03777	Sanbornton	03269	Thomas	03461
Orfordville	03777	Sanbornton (Town)	03269	Thompson and Meserves Purchase (Town)	03595
Ossipee	03864	Sanbornville	03872	Thornton	03223
Ossipee (Town)	03864	Sandown	03873	Thornton (Town)	03223
Pages Corner	03301	Sandown (Town)	03873	Thorntons Ferry	03054
Pannaway Manor (Part of Portsmouth)	03801	Sandwich	03227	Tilton	03276
Parker Hill	03585	Sandwich (Town)	03227	Tilton (Town)	03276
Park Hill	03467	Sargents Purchase (Town)	03589	Tilton-Northfield	03276
Partridge Lake	03561	Sawyers (Part of Dover)	03820	Tinkerville	03585
Passaconaway	03818	Scotland	03470	Trapshire	03603
Pearls Corner	03301	Seabrook	03874	Troy	03465
Pelham	03076	Seabrook (Town)	03874	Troy (Town)	03465
Pelham (Town)	03076	Seabrook Beach	03874	Tuftonboro	03864
Pembroke (Town)	03275	Second College (Town)	03576	Tuftonboro (Town)	03864
Penacook (Part of Concord)	03303	Severance	03032	Twin Mountain	03595
Pendleton Beach (Part of Laconia)	03246	Sharon	03458	Union	03887
Pequawket	02875	Sharon (Town)	03458	Unity	03603
Percy	03582	Shelburne (Town)	03581	Unity (Town)	03603
Peterborough	03458	Sherwood Forest	03833	Upper Kidderville	03576
Peterborough (Town)	03458	Shirley Hill	03045	Wadley Falls	03824
Peterborough	03458	Short Falls	03234	Wakefield	03872
Pheasant Lane Mall (Part of Nashua)	03063	Silver Lake	03875	Wakefield (Town)	03872
Pickpocket Woods	03833	Simoneau Plaza (Part of Nashua)	03060	Wallis Sands	03870
Piermont	03779	Smiths Point	03246	Walpole	03608
Piermont (Town)	03779	Smithtown	03874	Walpole (Town)	03608
Pike	03780	Smithville	03071	Warner	03278
Pinardville	03045	Snowville	03849	Warner (Town)	03278
Pine Brook Estates	03833	Snumshire	03603	Warren	03279
Pinecrest	03833	Somersworth	03878	Warren (Town)	03279
Pine Valley	03086	Soo Nipi	03257	Washington	03280
Pinkhams (Town)	03581	South Acworth	03607	Washington (Town)	03280
Pittsburg	03592	South Barnstead	03225	Waterloo	03278
Pittsburg (Town)	03592	South Brookline	03033	Water Village	03864
Pittsfield	03263	South Charlestown	03603	Waterville Estates	03223
Pittsfield (Town)	03263	South Chatham	04037	Waterville Valley	03215
Plaice Cove	03842	South Conway	03813	Waterville Valley (Town)	03215
Plainfield	03781	South Cornish	05089	Wawbeek	03853
Plainfield (Town)	03781	South Danville	03819	Weare	03281
Plaistow	03865	South Deerfield	03037	Weare (Town)	03281
Plaistow (Town)	03865	South Effingham	03882	Webster	03301
Plymouth	03264	South Hampton	03827	Webster (Town)	03301
Plymouth (Town)	03264	South Hampton (Town)	03827	Webster Lake (Part of Franklin)	03235
Ponemah	03055	South Hooksett	03106	Webster Place (Part of Franklin)	03235
Portsmouth	03801-04	South Keene (Part of Keene)	03431	Weirs Beach (Part of Laconia)	03246
For specific Portsmouth Zip Codes call (603) 431-1300, or your local postmaster.		South Kingston	03848	Wendell	03782
Portsmouth Plains (Part of Portsmouth)	03801	South Lee	03824	Wentworth	03282
Potter Place	03265	South Lyndeboro	03082	Wentworth (Grafton County)	03282
Puckershire (Part of Claremont)	03743	South Merrimack	03060	Wentworth (Coos County) (Town)	03579
		South Milford	03055		
		South Newbury	03272		

* Area Zip Code † Post Office Boxes

	ZIP		ZIP		ZIP
Wentworth Acres (Part of Portsmouth)	03801	Westmoreland	03467	Wilmot (Town)	03287
Wentworth By The Sea	03854	Westmoreland (Town)	03467	Wilmot Flat	03287
West Alton	03246	West Nottingham	03291	Wilton (Hillsborough County)	03086
West Andover	03265	West Ossipee	03890	Wilton (Hillsborough County) (Town)	03086
West Barrington	03825	West Peterborough	03468	Wilton Center	03086
West Campton	03223	West Plymouth	03264	Winchester	03470
West Canaan	03741	Westport	03469	Winchester (Town)	03470
West Center Harbor	03217	West Rindge	03461	Windham	03087
West Chesterfield	03466	West Rumney	03266	Windham (Town)	03087
West Claremont (Part of Claremont)	03743	West Rye	03870	Windham Depot	03087
		West Salisbury	03216	Windsor (Town)	03244
West Deering	03440	West Springfield	03284	Winnisquam	03289
West Dummer	03570	West Stewartstown	03597	Winona	03217
West Epping	03042	West Swanzey	03469	Wolfeboro	03894
West Franklin (Part of Franklin)	03235	West Thornton	03285	Wolfeboro (Town)	03894
		West Unity	03743	Wolfeboro	03894
West Gonic (Part of Rochester)	03839	Westville	03865	Wolfeboro Center	03894
West Hampstead	03841	West Wilton	03086	Wolfeboro Falls	03896
West Henniker	03242	West Windham	03087	Wonalancet	03897
West Hopkinton	03229	Whiteface	03259	Woodman	03830
West Lebanon (Part of Lebanon)	03784	Whitefield	03598	Woodmere	03452
		Whitefield (Town)	03598	Woodstock	03293
West Milan	03570	Whittier	03890	Woodstock (Town)	03293
		Willey House	03812	Woodsville	03785
		Wilmot	03287		

	ZIP
Aberdeen (Township)	07747
Absecon	08201
Absecon Heights	08201
Absecon Highlands	08201
Academy Estates	07981
Ackors Corner	08534
A Country Place	08701
Adams	08902
Adamston	08723
Adelphia	07710
Agasote	08618
Ajax Park	08618
Albion	08009
Albion Place (Part of Clifton)	07013
Aldene (Part of Roselle)	07203
Aldine	08318
Aldrich Estates	07731
Alexandria (Township)	08848
Allaire	07727
Allamuchy	07820
Allamuchy (Township)	07820
Allamuchy-Panther Valley	07820
Allendale	07401
Allenhurst	07711
Allentown	08501
Allenwood	08720
Allerton	08833
Alloway	08001
Alloway (Township)	08001
Allwood (Part of Clifton)	07012
Almolind	08096
Almonesson	08096
Alpha	08865
Alphano	07838
Alpine	07620
Amber Terrace (Part of Pine Hill)	08021
Amon Heights	08110
Ampere (Part of East Orange)	07017
Ancora	08037
Anderson	07882
Andover	07821
Andover (Township)	07860
Andover Junction (Part of Andover)	07821
Andrews	08081
Anglesea (Part of North Wildwood)	08260
Annandale	08801
Anthony	08826
Applegarth	08512
Apple Hill	08002
Apshawa	07405
Arbor	08854
Arbors	08857
Arcola (Part of Paramus)	07652
Ardena	07728
Arlington (Part of Kearny)	07032
Arneys Mount	08068
Arneytown	08501
Arrowhead Park	08723
Arrowhead Village	08723
Asbury	08802
Asbury Gardens	07753
Asbury Park	07712
Ashland	08043
Atco	08004
Atlantic City	08401
Atlantic Highlands	07716
Atlantis	08087
Atsion	08088
Auburn	08085
Audubon	08106
Audubon Park	08106
Augusta	07822
Aura	08028
Avalon	08202
Avenel	07001
Avis Mills	08098
Avon By The Sea	07717
Avondale	07110
Awosting	07421
Babbitt	07047
Bacons Neck	08302
Bakersville (Atlantic County)	08225
Bakersville (Mercer County)	08638
Baldwins Corner	08534
Baleville	07860
Baltusrol	07081
Bamber Lake	08731
Baptistown	08803
Barbertown	08825
Barclay Farm	08002
Bargaintown	08221
Barkers Corner	07838
Barley Sheaf	08822
Barlow	08002
Barnegat	08005
Barnegat (Township)	08005
Barnegat Beach	08758
Barnegat Light	08006

	ZIP
Barnegat Pines	08731
Barnsboro	08080
Barrington	08007
Barrington Manor (Part of Barrington)	08033
Bartley	07836
Basking Ridge	07920
Bassett Park	07801
Bass River (Township)	08224
Bates Mill	08037
Batesville	08002
Batsto	08037
Battentown (Part of Swedesboro)	08085
Bay Harbor Estates	08723
Bay Head	08742
Bay Head Junction (Part of Bay Head)	08742
Bayonne	07002
Bay Shore West	08204
Bay Side (Cumberland County)	08302
Bay Side (Ocean County)	08050
Bayview Heights	08753
Bayview Shores	08738
Bayville	08721
Bayville Park	08721
Bayway (Part of Elizabeth)	07202
Baywood	08723
Beach Creek (Part of North Wildwood)	08260
Beach Glen	07866
Beach Haven	08008
Beach Haven Crest	08008
Beach Haven Gardens	08008
Beach Haven Heights	08008
Beach Haven Terrace	08008
Beach Haven West	08050
Beach View	08005
Beachwood	08722
Beattyestown	07840
Beaufort (Part of Roseland)	07068
Beaver Dam	08070
Beaver Lake	07416
Beckerville	08733
Beckett	08085
Bedminster	07921
Bedminster (Township)	07921
Beechwood Heights	07876
Beemerville	07461
Beesleys Point	08223
Belcher Creek	07480
Belcoville	08330
Belford	07718
Belle Mead	08502
Belleplain	08270
Belleville	07109
Belleville (Township)	07109
Belleville Annex (Part of Newark)	07109
Bellmawr	08031*
	08099†
Bellmawr Park (Part of Bellmawr)	08030
Bells Crossing (Part of Glen Gardner)	08826
Bells Lake	08012
Bellview	08077
Bellwood Park (Part of Bellmawr)	08030
Belmar	07719
Belmar Gardens	07719
Belvidere	07823
Belwood Park	07109
Bennett	08204
Bennetts Mills	08527
Bergen (Part of Jersey City)	07304
Bergenfield	07621
Bergenline (Part of Union City)	07087
Bergen Mall (Part of Paramus)	07652
Bergen Point (Part of Bayonne)	07002
Berkeley (Township)	08721
Berkeley Heights (Township)	07922
Berkeley Heights	07922
Berkeley Shore Estates	08721
Berlin	08009
Berlin (Township)	08091
Berlin Estates	08009
Berlin Heights (Part of Berlin)	08009
Bernards (Township)	07920
Bernardsville	07924
Bertrand Island (Part of Mount Arlington)	07856
Bethlehem (Township)	08802
Betsytown (Part of Elizabeth)	07201
Beverly	08010

	ZIP
Billingsport (Part of Paulsboro)	08066
Birches	08012
Birches West	08071
Birch Hills	07981
Birchwood Lakes	08055
Birchwood Park	08723
Birmingham	08011
Bishops	08009
Bivalve	08349
Black Horse Pike Shopping Center (Part of Audubon)	08106
Blackwells Mills	08873
Blackwood	08012
Blackwood Terrace	08096
Blairstown	07825
Blairstown (Township)	07825
Blawenburg	08504
Blenheim	08012
Bloomfield	07003
Bloomfield (Township)	07003
Bloomfield Terrace	08816
Bloomingdale (Morris County)	07457
Bloomingdale (Passaic County)	07403
Bloomsbury	08804
Blue Anchor	08037
Blue Bell	08344
Blue Star Shopping Center (Part of Watchung)	07060
Bogota	07603
Bon Air	08110
Bonhamton	08817
Boonton	07005
Boonton (Township)	07005
Bordentown	08505
Bordentown (Township)	08505
Bossert Estates	08505
Bound Brook (Camden County)	08002
Bound Brook (Somerset County)	08805
Bowman Manor	08251
Braddock	08037
Bradley Beach	07720
Bradley Gardens	08876
Bradley Park	07753
Braeburn Heights	08638
Braeburn Park	08638
Brainards	08865
Brainy Boro (Part of Metuchen)	08840
Branchburg (Township)	08876
Branchport (Part of Long Branch)	07740
Branchville	07826
Brant Beach	08008
Brass Castle	07882
Breton Woods	08723
Brick	08723-24
For specific Brick Zip Codes call (908) 477-0100, or your local postmaster.	
Brick (Township)	08723
Brick	08723
Brick Church (Part of East Orange)	07018
Bricksboro	08332
Bridgeboro	08075
Bridgeport	08014
Bridgeton	08302
Bridgeton Junction (Part of Bridgeton)	08302
Bridgeville	07823
Bridgewater	08807
Bridgewater (Township)	08807
Brielle	08730
Brigadoon	08096
Brigantine	08203
Brighton Beach	08008
Broad Lane	08094
Broad Street Annex (Part of Newark)	07102
Broadway (station)	08886
Broadway	08808
Brookdale (Camden County)	08002
Brookdale (Essex County)	07003
Brookfields	08002
Brooklawn	08030
Brookmeade	08002
Brookside	07926
Brook Tree	08520
Brook Valley (Part of Kinnelon)	07405
Brookville (Hunterdon County)	08559
Brookville (Ocean County)	08005
Brookwood	08527
Brotmanville	08302
Browns Mills	08015

---

* **Area Zip Code**   † **Post Office Boxes**

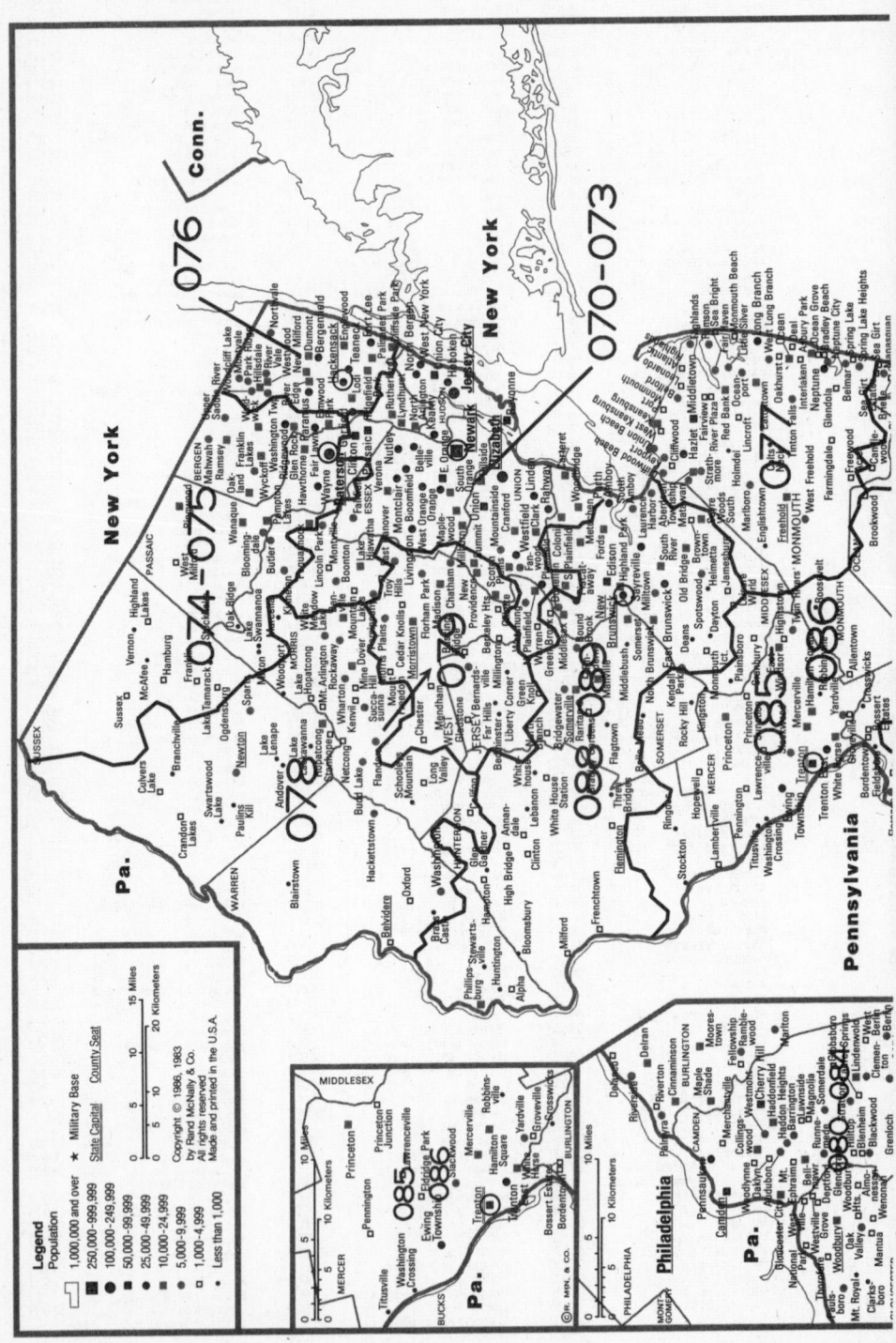

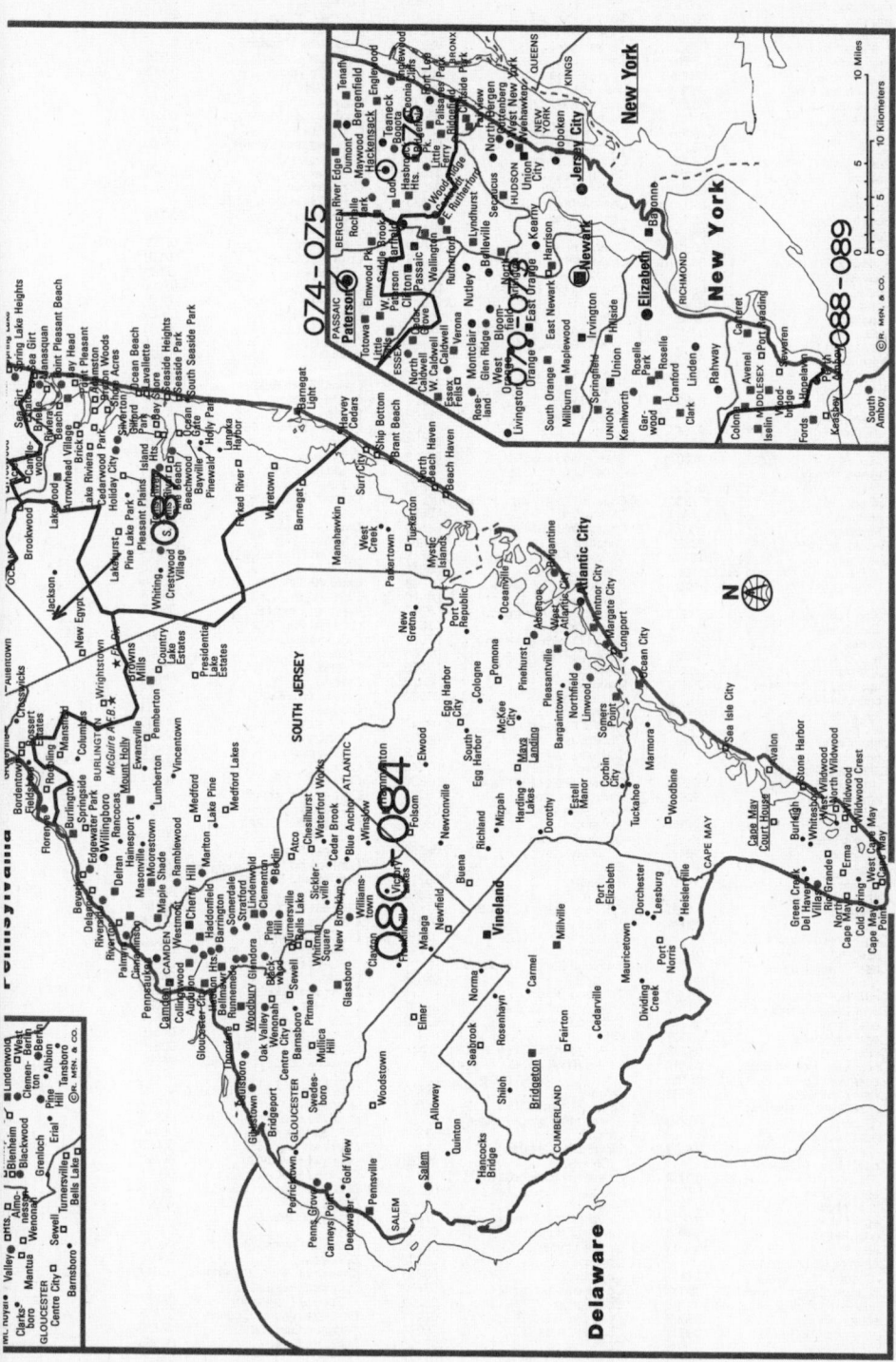

NEW YORK

New York

South Jersey

Pennsylvania

Delaware

074 - 075

070 - 073

088 - 089

080 - 084

087

	ZIP		ZIP		ZIP
Browntown	08857	Centerville (Somerset		Colonial Manor	08096
Brunswick Acres	08852	County)	08853	Colonial Park	08520
Brunswick Gardens	08857	Central (Part of East		Colonial Terrace	07712
Brunswick Shopping Center		Orange)	07018	Colts Neck	07722
(Part of New Brunswick)	08902	Central Park	08070	Colts Neck (Township)	07722
Brunswick Square	08816	Centre City	08051	Columbia	07832
Brush Hollow	08053	Centre Grove	08332	Columbia Lakes	08002
Buckingham Village	08080	Ceramics	08817	Columbus	08022
Buckshutem	08332	Chadwick Beach	08739	Colwick	08002
Budd Lake	07828	Chairville	08055	Commercial (Township)	08349
Buddtown	08088	Chambersburg (Part of		Concordia	08512
Buena	08310	Trenton)	08611	Congressional Estates	08002
Buena Vista (Township)	08360	Chambers Corner	08060	Conklintown (Part of	
Bulltown	08215	Changewater	07831	Ringwood)	07465
Bunker Hill	08080	Chapel Heights	08080	Conovertown	08201
Bunnvale	07830	Charlotteburg	07435	Constable Hook (Part of	
Burcliff Farms	08638	Charlton Village	07747	Bayonne)	07002
Burleigh	08210	Chatham	07928	Constable Junction (Part of	
Burlington	08016	Chatham (Township)	07928	Bayonne)	07002
Burlington (Township)	08016	Chatsworth	08019	Convent Station	07961
Burnt Mills	07921	Cheesequake	08857	Cookstown	08511
Bustleton	08016	Cheesequake Estates	07747	Coontown	07060
Butler	07405	Cherry Hill	08002-03	Cooper Park Village	08002
Butler Park	07882		08034	Cooper Village	08096
Butlers Park	07882	For specific Cherry Hill Zip Codes		Copper Hill	08551
Butterworth Farms	07801	call (609) 424-4324, or your local		Corbin City	08270
Buttzville	07829	postmaster.		Cornish	07823
Byram (Hunterdon County)	08559	Cherry Hill Estates	08002	Country Farms	07733
Byram (Sussex County)		Cherry Hill Mall	08002	Country Lake Estates	08015
(Township)	07821	Cherry Quay	08723	Country Manor	08857
Byram Cove (Part of		Cherry Ridge	08002	Country Woods	07733
Hopatcong)	07843	Cherry Valley	08002	Coytesville (Part of Fort	
Caldwell	07006*	Cherryville	08822	Lee)	07024
	07007†	Cherrywood	08012	Cozy Lake	07438
Caldwell Borough		Chesilhurst	08089	Cragmere Park	07430
(Township)	07006	Chester	07930	Cranberry Lake	07821
Califon	07830	Chester (Township)	07930	Cranbury (Township)	08512
Callahans	07849	Chesterfield	08650	Cranbury	08512
Cambridge	08075	Chesterfield (Township)	08650	Cranbury Manor	08512
Cambridge Park	08053	Chestnut	07083	Crandon Lakes	07860
Camden	08101-05	Chewalla Park	08619	Cranford (Township)	07016
For specific Camden Zip Codes		Chews Landing	08012	Cranford	07016
call (609) 757-0330, or your local		Chrome (Part of Carteret)	07008	Cranford Junction	07016
postmaster.		Churchtown	08070	Creamridge	08514
Camp Tecumseh	08867	Cinnaminson (Township)	08077	Crescent Heights	08068
Candlewood	08701	Cinnaminson	08077	Crescent Park (Part of	
Canton	08079	City of Orange (Township)	07050	Bellmawr)	08030
Cape Breton	08723	Clark (Township)	07066	Cresskill	07626
Cape May	08204	Clark	07066	Crestmoor	07853
Cape May Court House	08210	Clarksboro	08020	Creston	08619
Cape May Point	08212	Clarksburg	08510	Crestwood Village	08759
Capitol Hill	08010	Clarks Landing (Part of		Cropwell	08053
Cardiff	08232	Point Pleasant)	08742	Cross Keys	08080
Carlls Corner	08302	Clarktown	08330	Crossroads	08055
Carlstadt	07072	Clayton	08312	Crosswicks	08515
Carlton Hill (Part of		Claytons Corner	07746	Croton	08822
Rutherford)	07073	Clayville (Part of Vineland)	08360	Crowfoot	08004
Carmel	08332	Clearbrook Park	08831	Crystal Lake (Bergen	
Carmerville	07719	Clear View Lake	07860	County)	07436
Carneys Point (Township)	08069	Clementon	08021	Crystal Lake (Ocean	
Carneys Point	08069	Clermont (Burlington		County)	08721
Carpenterville	08865	County)	08060	Culvers Lake	07826
Carteret	07008	Clermont (Cape May		Cumberland	08332
Cassville	08527	County)	08210	Cumberland Mall (Part of	
Castle Point (Part of		Cliffdale Park	07865	Vineland)	08360
Hoboken)	07030	Cliff Park (Part of Cliffside		Cuthbert Manor	08108
Cecil	08094	Park)	07010	Cyn-Wyd	08016
Cedar Beach (Monmouth		Cliffside Park	07010	Da Costa (Part of	
County)	07758	Cliffwood	07721	Hammonton)	08037
Cedar Beach (Ocean		Cliffwood Beach (Middlesex		Danceys Corner	08069
County)	08721	County)	08879	Daretown	08318
Cedar Bonnet Island	08050	Cliffwood Beach		Darlington Heights	08088
Cedar Bridge Manor	08723	(Monmouth County)	07735	Darts Mills	08822
Cedar Brook	08018	Cliffwood Lake	07460	Davis	08514
Cedar Crest Manor	08069	Clifton	07011-15	Davis Bridge	07946
Cedar Croft	08723	For specific Clifton Zip Codes call		Dayton	08810
Cedar Glen Homes East	08757	(201) 472-7900, or your local		Deacons	08060
Cedar Glen Lakes	08759	postmaster.		Deal	07723
Cedar Glen West	08733	Clinton	08809	Deal Park	07723
Cedar Grove (Cape May		Clinton (Township)	08801	Deans	08852
County)	08210	Clinton Hill (Part of Newark)	07108	Deauville Beach	08739
Cedar Grove (Essex		Closter	07624	De Cou Village	08610
County) (Township)	07009	Cloverdale (Camden		Deepwater	08023
Cedar Grove (Essex		County)	08030	Deerfield (Township)	08352
County)	07009	Cloverdale (Cumberland		Deerfield Park	08087
Cedar Heights	08801	County)	08332	Deerfield Street	08313
Cedar Knolls	07927	Cloverhill	08822	Deer Park	08002
Cedar Lake	07834	Clover Hill at Holmdel	07733	Deer Trail Lake	07460
Cedar Ridge	08857	Clover Leaf Lakes	08330	Delair	08110
Cedar Run	08092	Coffins Corner	08026	Delanco (Township)	08075
Cedarville (Cumberland		Cohansey	08302	Delanco	08075
County)	08311	Cokesbury	08833	Delawanna (Part of Clifton)	07014
Cedarville (Salem County)	08098	Cold Indian Springs	07712	Delaware (Hunterdon	
Cedarwood Park	08723	Cold Spring	08204	County) (Township)	08822
Centennial Lake	08053	Colesville	07461	Delaware (Warren County)	07833
Center (Part of Trenton)	08608	Collings Lakes	08094	Delaware Gardens	08110
Center Grove	07869	Collingswood	08108	Delaware Park	08865
Center Square	08085	Collingwood Park	07727	Delcrest	08075
Centerton (Burlington		Collinsville	07960	Del Haven	08251
County)	08054	Cologne	08213	Delmont	08314
Centerton (Salem County)	08318	Colonia	07067	Delran (Township)	08075
Centerville (Mercer County)	08534	Colonial Arms	08527	Delran	08075

* Area Zip Code   † Post Office Boxes

	ZIP
Gardens of Pleasant Plains	08753
Garden State (Part of Paramus)	07652
Garden State Plaza (Part of Paramus)	07652
Gardenville	08096
Gardenville Center	08096
Garfield	07026
Garwood	07027
Genasco	08861
General Lafayette (Part of Jersey City)	07304
Georgetown	08022
Georgetowne	08053
Georgia	07728
Germania	08215
Germania Gardens	08213
Gibbsboro	08026
Gibbstown	08027
Giffordtown	08057
Gilford Park	08753
Gillespie (Part of Sayreville)	08872
Gillette	07933
Gilman Lake	08343
Glacier Hills	07950
Gladstone	07934
Glassboro	08028
Glasser (Part of Hopatcong)	07837
Glen Cove	08721
Glendale (Camden County)	08043
Glendale (Mercer County)	08618
Glendola	07719
Glendora	08029
Glen Gardner	08826
Glen Oaks	08021
Glen Ridge	07028
Glen Ridge (Township)	07028
Glen Rock	07452
Glenside	08070
Glenview	08002
Glenwood	07418
Gloucester (Township)	08012
Gloucester City	08030
Godfrey Manor	08723
Golf Hill	07876
Golf Manor	08069
Golf View	08069
Gordon Lakes	07405
Goshen	08218
Gouldtown	08302
Grandin	08801
Granton Junction	07047
Grasselli (Part of Linden)	07036
Grassy Sound	08260
Gravel Hill	07726
Great Meadows	07838
Great Meadows-Vienna	07838
Great Notch	07424
Green (Township)	07821
Green Acres	08618
Green Bank	08215
Green Brook (Township)	08812
Green Brook	08812
Green Creek	08219
Green Curve Heights	08638
Greendell	07839
Greenfield	08230
Greenfield Heights	08096
Greenfields Village	08096
Green Grove	07712
Green Haven	08002
Green Hills	08876
Green Hut Park	07801
Green Island	08753
Green Knoll	08876
Greenland (Part of Magnolia)	08049
Green Pond	07435
Green Pond Junction (Part of Kinnelon)	07405
Greensand	08817
Greens Bridge (Part of Phillipsburg)	08865
Green Village	07935
Greenville (Hudson County)	07305
Greenville (Ocean County)	08701
Greenville (Salem County)	08318
Greenwich	08323
Greenwich (Township)	08323
Greenwich (Gloucester County) (Township)	08027
Greenwich (Warren County) (Township)	08886
Greenwich Pier	08323
Greenwood Park	08071
Grenloch	08032
Grenloch Terrace	08032
Greystone Park	07950
Griggstown	08540
Grove	07003
Grove Chapel (Part of Vineland)	08344

	ZIP
Grovers Mill	08550
Groveville	08620
Gum Tree Corner	08302
Guttenberg	07093
Hackensack	07601*
	07602†
Hackettstown	07840
Haddon (Township)	08108
Haddonfield	08033
Haddon Heights	08035
Haddon Hills	08033
Haddon Leigh	08033
Haddontowne	08002
Hainesburg	07832
Haines Corner	08620
Hainesport	08036
Hainesport (Township)	08036
Hainesville	07826
Haledon	07508*
	07538†
Haleyville	08349
Halsey	07860
Hamburg	07419
Hamden	08801
Hamilton (Atlantic County) (Township)	08330
Hamilton (Mercer County) (Township)	08619
Hamilton (Monmouth County)	07753
Hamilton Square	08690
Hammond Heights	08090
Hammonton	08037
Hampton (Hunterdon County)	08827
Hampton (Sussex County) (Township)	07860
Hancocks Bridge	08038
Hanover	07981
Hanover (Township)	07981
Hanover Neck	07936
Harbourton	08530
Harding (Township)	07940
Harding Lakes	08330
Hardingville	08343
Hardistonville (Part of Hamburg)	07419
Hardwick (Township)	07825
Hardyston (Township)	07460
Harfield	08527
Harker Village	08096
Harlingen	08502
Harmersville	08079
Harmony (Township)	08865
Harmony (Monmouth County)	07748
Harmony (Ocean County)	08527
Harmony (Warren County)	08865
Harrington Park	07640
Harrison (Gloucester County) (Township)	08062
Harrison (Hudson County)	07029
Harrison Mountain Lake (Part of Ringwood)	07456
Harrisonville (Gloucester County)	08039
Harrisonville (Salem County)	08079
Hartford	08057
Harvey Cedars	08008
Hasbrouck Heights	07604
Haskell (Part of Wanaque)	07420
Haven Beach	08008
Haworth	07641
Hawthorne	07506*
	07507†
Hazen	07823
Hazlet (Township)	07730
Hazlet (Township)	07730
Head Of River (Part of Estell Manor)	08270
Headquarters	08557
Heathcote	08528
Heather Hills	07439
Hedding	08505
Heislerville	08324
Helmetta	08828
Helmetta Park	08828
Hensfoot	08827
Herbertsville	08723
Heritage Village	08053
Herman	08215
Herwood	08002
Hesstown	08332
Hewitt	07421
Heyden	07095
Hibernia	07842
Hibernia Junction (Part of Rockaway)	07866
Hickory Acres	08520
Hickory Tree	07928
Hickstown	08012
Higbee Town	08201

	ZIP
High Bridge	08829
High Crest Lake	07480
Highland Beach (Part of Sea Bright)	07760
Highland Lakes	07422
Highland Park (Part of Gloucester City)	08012
Highland Park (Camden County)	08030
Highland Park (Middlesex County)	08904
Highlands	07732
High Point (Part of Harvey Cedars)	08008
High Point Manor	08857
Highs Beach	08210
Hightstown	08520
Hightstown Heights	08520
Highview Park	08736
Hillcrest (Camden County)	08109
Hillcrest (Passaic County)	07502
Hillcrest (Warren County)	08865
Hilliard	08050
Hillsborough (Township)	08853
Hillsdale	07642
Hillsdale Manor (Part of Hillsdale)	07642
Hillside (Township)	07205
Hillside	07205
Hilltop	08012
Hilltop Terrace	08816
Hilltown	07885
Hillwood Lakes	08638
Hilton (Part of Atlantic Highlands)	07716
Hinchman	08002
Hi-Nella	08083
Hoboken	07030
Hoffmans	07830
Hoffner	08518
Ho Ho Kus	07423
Holgate	08008
Holiday City	08753
Holiday City at Berkeley	08757
Holiday City-Berkeley	08753
Holiday City-Dover	08753
Holiday City South	08757
Holiday City West	08757
Holiday Heights	08757
Holiday on the Bay	08753
Holland	08848
Holand (Township)	08848
Holly Brook	08060
Holly Crest	08723
Holly Hills	08060
Holly Park	08721
Holmansville	08527
Holmdel	07733
Holmdel (Township)	07733
Holmdel Village	07733
Holmeson	08526
Homes Mills	08514
Homestead	07047
Homestead Park	07933
Homestead Run	08753
Homestead Village	07920
Hootens Hollow	08002
Hoot Owl Estates	08055
Hoover Village	08302
Hopatcong	07843
Hopatcong Heights (Part of Hopatcong)	07843
Hopatcong Hills (Part of Hopatcong)	07843
Hope	07844
Hope (Township)	07844
Hopelawn	08861
Hopewell (Cumberland County) (Township)	08302
Hopewell (Mercer County)	08525
Hopewell (Mercer County) (Township)	08560
Hornerstown	08514
Howell (Township)	07727
Howell (P.O.)	07731
Howell (rural)	07728
Hudson City (Part of Jersey City)	07307
Hudson Heights	07047
Hudson Shopping Plaza (Part of Jersey City)	07304
Hughesville	08848
Huntington	08865
Huntsburg	07860
Hunt Tract	08002
Hurdtown	07885
Hurffville	08080
Hutchinson	08865
Hutchinson Mills	08619
Hyson	08527
Ideal Beach	07734
Imlaystown (Station)	08501

* Area Zip Code   † Post Office Boxes

	ZIP		ZIP		ZIP
Imlaystown	08526	Lake	08344	Lincoln Park	07035
Immaculate Conception		Lake Arrowhead	07834	Lincroft	07738
Seminary	07430	Lake Como (Part of Spring		Linden	07036
Imperial Manor	08002	Lake Heights)	07762	Linden Junction (Part of	
Independence (Township)	07840	Lake Denmark	07801	Linden)	07036
Independence Corner	07461	Lake Forest	07849	Lindenwold	08021
Indian Lake	07834	Lake Grinnell	07871	Lindy's Lake	07405
Indian Mills	08088	Lake Hiawatha	07034	Linvale	08551
Industrial-Hillside	07205	Lake Hopatcong	07849	Linwood	08221
Interlaken	07712	Lakehurst	08733	Little Egg Harbor	
Interlaken Estates	07712	Lakehurst Naval Air Station	08733	(Township)	08087
Interstate Shopping Center		Lake Iliff	07860	Little Falls	07424
(Part of Ramsey)	07446	Lake Intervale	07005	Little Falls (Township)	07424
Iona	08322	Lake Lackawanna	07874	Little Falls (Part of Totowa)	07512
Ironbound (Part of Newark)	07105	Lakeland	08012	Little Ferry	07643
Ironia	07845	Lake Lenape	07860	Little Ferry (Part of	
Iron Rock	08109	Lake Lookover	07421	Ridgefield Park)	07660
Irven Heights	08638	Lake Neepaulin	07461	Little Ferry Junction (Part of	
Irvington	07111	Lake Nelson	08854	Ridgefield Park)	07657
Irvington (Township)	07111	Lake Owassa	07860	Little Rocky Hill	08540
Iselin	08830	Lake Pine	08053	Little Silver	07739
Island Beach	08752	Lakeridge	07747	Little Silver Point (Part of	
Island Heights	08732	Lake Riviera	07723	Little Silver)	07739
Ivystone Farms	08004	Lake Rogerine (Part of		Littleton (Part of Morris	
Ivywood	08077	Mount Arlington)	07856	Plains)	07950
Jackson (Township)	08527	Lake Shawnee	07885	Little York	08834
Jackson (Camden County)	08004	Lakeside	07421	Livingston (Township)	07039
Jackson (Ocean County)	08527	Lakeside Park	08610	Livingston	07039
Jackson Avenue (Part of		Lake Stockholm	07460	Livingston Mall	07039
Jersey City)	07305	Lake Swannanoa	07438	Loch Arbour	07711
Jacksonburg	07825	Lake Tamarack	07460	Locktown	08822
Jackson Estates	08527	Lake Telemark	07866	Locust	07760
Jacksons Mills	08527	Lakeview (Burlington		Locust Corner	08512
Jacksonville (Burlington		County)	08060	Lodi	07644
County)	08505	Lakeview (Monmouth		Logan (Township)	08014
Jacksonville (Morris County)	07035	County)	08501	Lommasons Glen	07823
Jacobstown	08562	Lake Villa Estates	08009	London Terrace	08859
Jamesburg	08831	Lakewood (Township)	08701	Long Beach	08008
Janvier	08322	Lakewood	08701	Long Beach (Township)	08008
Jefferson (Gloucester		Lambertville	08530	Long Branch	07740
County)	08062	Lambs Terrace	08081	Long Bridge	07838
Jefferson (Morris County)		Lamington	07921	Long Hill	07928
(Township)	07849	Landing	07850	Longport	08403
Jeffrey Lane Estates	08721	Landisville (Part of Buena)	08326	Long Valley	07853
Jenkins	08019	Land of Pines	08701	Longwood Lake	07438
Jericho	08096	Landsdown	08801	Lopatcong (Township)	08865
Jersey City	07301-11	Lanes Mills	08701	Lorillard Beach (Part of	
For specific Jersey City Zip Codes		Lanoka Harbor	08734	Union Beach)	07735
call (201) 915-7033, or your local		Lanoka Harbor Estates	08734	Lorraine (Part of Roselle	
postmaster.		Larger Cross Roads	07921	Park)	07204
Jerseyville	07728	Larison's Corner	08551	Louden	08004
Jobstown	08041	Larrabees	08701	Loveladies	08008
Johnsonburg	07846	Laurel Acres	08723	Lower (Township)	08204
Jones Island	08311	Laureldale	08330	Lower Alloways Creek	
Jordantown	08109	Laurel Harbor	08734	(Township)	08038
Journal Square (Part of		Laurel Hill	08021	Lower Bank	08215
Jersey City)	07306	Laurel Homes	08861	Lower Berkshire Valley	07885
Juliustown	08042	Laurelhurst	08723	Lower Harmony	08865
Jutland	08827	Laurel Lake (Part of Millville)	08332	Lower Longwood Lake	07438
Kampfe Lake (Part of		Laurel Manor (Camden		Lower Montville	07045
Bloomingdale)	07403	County)	08021	Lower Squankum	07731
Karrsville	07865	Laurel Manor (Ocean		Lower Valley (Part of	
Kay Gardens	08067	County)	08723	Califon)	07830
Keansburg	07734	Laurel Springs	08021	Low Moor (Part of Sea	
Kearny	07031-32	Laurel Springs Gardens	08021	Bright)	07760
For specific Kearny Zip Codes call		Laurelton Acres	08723	Lows Hollow	08886
(201) 991-3700, or your local		Laurelton Heights	08723	Lozier Park (Part of Oradell)	07649
postmaster.		Laurelton Park	08723	Lucaston (Part of	
Kearny Junction (Part of		Laurence Harbor	08879	Lindenwold)	08009
Kearny)	07032	Lavallette	08735	Lumberton	08048
Keasbey	08832	Lawnside	08045	Lumberton (Township)	08048
Keasbey Heights	08832	Lawrence (Cumberland		Lyndhurst (Township)	07071
Kemah Lake	07860	County) (Township)	08311	Lyndhurst	07071
Kendall Park	08824	Lawrence (Mercer County)		Lynn Oaks	07067
Kenilworth	07033	(Township)	08638	Lyons	07920
Kenvil	07847	Lawrence Brook	08816	Lyons (P.O.)	07939
Kenwood	08002	Lawrenceville	08648	Lyonsville	07005
Keswick Grove	08759	Layton	07851	McAfee	07428
Keyport	07735	Lebanon	08833	McCoys Corner	07461
Kingfisher Cove	08723	Lebanon (Township)	07830	McDonoughs (Part of South	
Kings Hill	08002	Lebanon Lake Estates	08015	Amboy)	08879
Kingsland	07071	Lebanon Park	08088	McGuire Air Force Base	08641
Kingston	08528	Ledgewood	07852	McKee City	08232
Kingston Estates	08002	Ledgewood Mall	07852	Macopin	07405
Kingsway Village	08002	Leeds Point	08220	Madison	07940
Kingswood	08002	Leektown	08215	Madison Park	08859
Kingwood (Township)	08825	Leesburg	08327	Madisonville	07920
Kinkora	08505	Leisure Knoll	08733	Magnolia (Burlington	
Kinnelon	07405	Leisuretowne	08088	County)	08068
Kirbys Mill	08055	Leisure Village	08701	Magnolia (Camden County)	08049
Kirkwood	08043	Leisure Village East	08753	Mahoneyville	08070
Kitchell Lake	07480	Leisure Village West	08733	Mahwah	07430
Kittatinny Lake	07826	Leisure Village West-Pine			07495
Klinesville	08822	Lake Park	08753	For specific Mahwah Zip Codes	
Knollwood	08002	Lenola	08057	call (201) 529-3366, or your local	
Knowlton	07832	Leonardo	07737	postmaster.	
Knowlton (Township)	07832	Leonia	07605	Mahwah (Township)	07430
Kresson	08053	Lewisville	08638	Main Avenue (Cumberland	
Lacey (Township)	08731	Liberty (Township)	07863	County)	08360
Lafayette	07848	Liberty Corner	07938	Main Avenue (Passaic	
Lafayette (Township)	07848	Libertyville	07461	County)	07011
La Gorce Square	08016	Lincoln	08062	Malaga	08328

	ZIP
Malapardis	07981
Mall at Short Hills, The	07078
Manahawkin	08050
Manalapan	07726
Manalapan (Township)	07726
Manasquan	08736
Manasquan Park	08736
Manasquan Shores	08736
Manchester (Township)	08759
Mandalay	08723
Mannington (Township)	08079
Manor Park	08723
Mansfield	08022
Mansfield (Township)	08022
Mansfield (Township)	07863
Mansfield Square	08022
Mantoloking	08738
Mantua	08051
Mantua (Township)	08051
Mantua Grove	08061
Mantua Heights	08051
Mantua Terrace	08051
Manunka Chunk	07832
Manville	08835
Maplecrest	07040
Maple Glen	08527
Maple Shade (Township)	08052
Maple Shade	08052
Maple Tree	08753
Maple View	08857
Maplewood (Township)	07040
Maplewood	07040
Marcella	07866
Margate City	08402
Marksboro	07825
Marlboro (Township)	07746
Marlboro (Burlington County)	08053
Marlboro (Cumberland County)	08302
Marlboro (Monmouth County)	07746
Marlboro Heights	07726
Marlton	08053
Marlton Heights	08098
Marlton Hills	08053
Marlton Lakes	08004
Marlyn Manor	08242
Marmora	08223
Marshalls Corner	08525
Marshalltown	08079
Martins Beach	08046
Martinsville	08836
Maryland	08527
Maskell Mill	08079
Masonville	08054
Matawan	07747
Maurice River (Township)	08327
Mauricetown	08329
Maxim	08701
Mayetta	08092
Mayfair at Marlton	08053
Mayfair Gardens	08080
Mays Landing	08330
Mayville	08210
Maywood	07607
Meadowbrook	08109
Meadowbrook Village	08527
Meadowview	07047
Meadow Village	07009
Mechanicsville (Middlesex County)	08879
Mechanicsville (Monmouth County)	07730
Medford	08055
Medford (Township)	08055
Medford Farms	08088
Medford Lakes	08055
Melrose (Burlington County)	08055
Melrose (Middlesex County)	08879
Menantico (Part of Millville)	08332
Mendham	07945
Mendham (Township)	07926
Menlo Park	08837
Menlo Park Mall	08817
Menlo Park Terrace	08840
Mercerville	08619
Mercerville-Hamilton Square	08619
Merchantville	08109
Meriden	07005
Metedeconk	08723
Metedeconk Park	08723
Metedeconk Pines	08723
Metropark	07095
Mettler	08873
Metuchen	08840
Meyersville	07933
Miami Beach	08251
Mickleton	08056
Middle (Township)	08210
Middlebush	08873
Middlesex	08846

	ZIP
Middletown	07748
Middletown (Township)	07748
Middletown	07866
Middle Valley	07853
Middleville	07855
Midland Park	07432
Midstreams	08723
Midstreams Park	08723
Midtown (Part of Newark)	07102
Midvale (Part of Wanaque)	07465
Mile Hollow	08505
Milford	08848
Military Ocean Terminal (Part of Bayonne)	07002
Millbridge	08021
Millbrook (Morris County)	07869
Millbrook (Warren County)	07832
Millburn (Township)	07041
Millburn	07041
Millhurst	07728
Millington	07946
Millside Heights	08075
Millside Manor	08075
Millstone (Monmouth County) (Township)	08510
Millstone (Somerset County)	08876
Milltown (Middlesex County)	08850
Milltown (Union County)	07081
Millville	08332
Milmay	08340
Milton	07438
Mimosa Lake	08053
Mine Brook (Part of Bernardsville)	07931
Mine Hill (Township)	07801
Mine Hill	07801
Minotola (Part of Buena)	08341
Miramar	08223
Mizpah	08342
Money Island	08753
Monitor (Part of West New York)	07093
Monksville (Part of Ringwood)	07465
Monmouth (Part of Eatontown)	07724
Monmouth Beach	07750
Monmouth Heights	07746
Monmouth Hills	07732
Monmouth Junction	08852
Monmouth Park (Part of Oceanport)	07757
Monroe (Gloucester County) (Township)	08094
Monroe (Middlesex County) (Township)	08520
Monroe (Morris County)	07981
Monroe (Sussex County)	07871
Monroeville	08343
Montague (Township)	12771
Montague	07827
Montana	08865
Montclair	07042-43
For specific Montclair Zip Codes call (201) 744-2660, or your local postmaster.	
Montgomery (Township)	08558
Montrose	07722
Montvale	07645
Montville	07045
Montville (Township)	07045
Moonachie	07074
Moores Corner	08079
Moores Meadows	08088
Moorestown	08057
Moorestown (Township)	08057
Moorestown-Lenola	08057
Moorestown Mall	08057
Moosepack Lake	07439
Morehousetown	07039
Morgan (Part of Sayreville)	08879
Morgan Beach	08879
Morganville	07751
Morris (Camden County)	08110
Morris (Morris County) (Township)	07961
Morris Beach	08330
Morris Park	08865
Morris Plains	07950
Morris Street (Part of Morristown)	07960
Morristown	07960-63
For specific Morristown Zip Codes call (201) 539-5890, or your local postmaster.	
Morristown	07747
Morrisville	08110
Morsemere (Part of Ridgefield)	07657
Morses Creek (Part of Linden)	07036
Mountain Lake	07823

	ZIP
Mountain Lakes	07046
Mountainside	07092
Mountain Spring Lakes	07405
Mountain Station	07079
Mountain View	07470
Mountainville	08833
Mount Airy	08530
Mount Arlington	07856
Mount Bethel	07865
Mount Ephraim	08059
Mount Fern	07801
Mount Freedom	07970
Mount Hermon	07825
Mount Holly	08060
Mount Holly (Township)	08060
Mount Hope	07885
Mount Hope Mineral Junction (Part of Wharton)	07885
Mount Kemble Lake	07960
Mount Laurel	08054
Mount Laurel (Township)	08054
Mount Olive (Township)	07828
Mount Pleasant (Cape May County)	08270
Mount Pleasant (Hunterdon County)	08848
Mount Pleasant (Warren County)	07832
Mount Rose	08525
Mount Royal	08061
Mount Salem	07461
Mounts Mills	08831
Mount Tabor (Denville twp.)	07834
Mount Tabor (Parsippany-Troy Hills twp.)	07878
Mount Vernon	07832
Muhlenberg (Part of Plainfield)	07060
Mullica (Township)	08217
Mullica Hill	08062
Murray Hill (Part of New Providence)	07974
Myrtle Grove	07860
Mystic Islands	08087
Mystic Shores	08087
Natco (Part of Union Beach)	07735
National Park	08063
Naughright	07853
Naval Air Propulsion Test Center	08628
Navesink	07752
Navesink Beach (Part of Sea Bright)	07760
Nejecho Beach	08723
Neptune	07753*
	07754†
Neptune City	07753
Nesco	08037
Neshanic	08853
Neshanic Station	08853
Netcong	07857
Netherwood (Part of Plainfield)	07062
New Albany	08077
New Amsterdam Village	08879
Newark	07101-08
	07112-75
For specific Newark Zip Codes call (201) 731-4863, or your local postmaster.	

COLLEGES & UNIVERSITIES

University of Medicine and Dentistry of New Jersey	07103

FINANCIAL INSTITUTIONS

Broad National Bank, Newark	07102
Carteret Savings Bank, F.A	07960
First Fidelity Bank, National Association, New Jersey	07102
The Howard	07101
Midlantic National Bank	07102
Penn Federal Savings Bank	07105

HOSPITALS

Newark Beth Israel Medical Center	07112
Saint Michael's Medical Center	07102
United Hospitals Medical Center	07107
University of Medicine and Dentistry of New Jersey-University Hospital	07103
Newark Heights	07040
Newbakers Corners	07825
New Bedford	07719
Newbolds Corner	08060

	ZIP
New Bridge (Part of New Milford)	07646
New Brooklyn	08081
New Brunswick	08901
	08903
	08906
For specific New Brunswick Zip Codes call (908) 819-3200, or your local postmaster.	
New Canton	08501
New Durham	07047
New Egypt	08533
Newfield	08344
Newfoundland	07435
New Freedom	08009
New Gretna	08224
New Hampton	08827
New Hanover (Township)	08511
New Italy (Part of Vineland)	08360
New Jersey & New York Junction (Part of East Rutherford)	07073
New Jersey State Prison	08327
New Lisbon	08064
New Milford	07646
New Milford (Part of Oradell)	07649
New Monmouth	07748
Newport (Cumberland County)	08345
Newport (Hunterdon County)	08826
Newport Center (Part of Jersey City)	07310
New Providence	07974
New Sharon (Gloucester County)	08080
New Sharon (Mercer County)	08691
Newton	07860
Newton Heights	08816
Newtonville	08346
New Vernon	07976
New Village	08886
New York & Greenwood Lake Junction (Part of Kearny)	07032
Nixon	08817
Norma	08347
Normandie (Part of Sea Bright)	07760
Normandy Beach	08739
Normandy Harbor	08739
North (Part of Newark)	07104
North Arlington	07031
North Asbury Park (Part of Asbury Park)	07712
North Beach	08008
North Beach Haven	08008
North Bergen	07047
North Bergen (Township)	07047
North Branch	08876
North Brunswick (Township)	08902
North Brunswick	08902
North Caldwell	07006
North Caldwell (Township)	07006
North Cape May	08204
North Cedarville	08311
North Center	07003
North Church	07416
North Church Estates	07416
North Crosswicks	08515
North Dennis	08214
North Edison	08817
North Elizabeth (Part of Elizabeth)	07208
Northfield (Atlantic County)	08225
Northfield (Essex County)	07039
North Hackensack (Part of River Edge)	07661
North Haledon	07508
North Hanover (Township)	08562
North Hawthorne (Part of Hawthorne)	07507
North Highlands Beach	08251
North Long Branch (Part of Long Branch)	07740
North Merchantville (Part of Merchantville)	08109
North Middletown	07758
Northmont (Part of Mount Ephraim)	08059
North Plainfield	07060
North Port Norris	08349
North Stelton	08854
Northvale	07647
North Vineland (Part of Vineland)	08360
North Wildwood	08260
North Woodbury (Part of Woodbury)	08096
Norton	08827

	ZIP
Nortonville	08085
Norwood	07648
Nottingham	08619
Nugentown	08087
Nutley	07110
Nutley (Township)	07110
Oak Dale	08060
Oak Glen	07731
Oak Hill	07748
Oakhurst	07755
Oakland	07436
Oaklyn	08107
Oak Ridge (Ocean County)	08753
Oak Ridge (Passaic County)	07438
Oak Ridge Lake	07438
Oak Shades	07747
Oak Tree (Middlesex County)	08817
Oak Tree (Ocean County)	08527
Oak Valley	08090
Oakview	08096
Oakwood	08055
Oakwood Beach	08079
Oakwood Park (Part of New Providence)	07974
Ocean (Monmouth County) (Township)	07755
Ocean (Ocean County) (Township)	08758
Ocean Acres	08050
Ocean Beach	08735
Ocean City	08226
Ocean City Gardens	08226
Ocean County Mall	08753
Ocean Gate	08740
Ocean Grove	07756
Ocean Heights (Part of Linwood)	08221
Oceanport	07757
Ocean View	08230
Oceanville	08231
Ogdensburg	07439
Old Bridge	08857
Old Bridge (Township)	08857
Old Bridge	08857
Old Charleston Woods	08002
Old Forge Village	07960
Old Manor	07730
Oldmans (Township)	08067
Old Orchard	08002
Old Tappan	07675
Oldwick	08858
Olivet	08318
Oradell	07649
Orange	07050*
	07051†
Orchard Center	08302
Orchard View	08016
Orston (Part of Audubon)	08106
Ortley Beach	08751
Osage	08043
Osbornsville	08723
Othello	08302
Outcalt	08831
Outwater (Part of Garfield)	07026
Overbrook (Camden County)	08021
Overbrook (Essex County)	07009
Owens	07461
Oxford	07863
Oxford (Township)	07863
Oyster Creek	08220
Packanack Lake	07470
Pahaquarry (Township)	07832
Palatine	08318
Palermo	08223
Palisade (Part of Fort Lee)	07024
Palisades Park	07650
Palmer Square (Part of Princeton)	08540
Palmyra (Burlington County)	08065
Palmyra (Hunterdon County)	08867
Pamrapo (Part of Bayonne)	07002
Pancoast	08310
Panther Lake	07821
Paradise Lakes	08001
Paramus	07652*
	07653†
Paramus Park Shopping Center (Part of Paramus)	07652
Park (Part of Paterson)	07513
Park Avenue	07087
Parker	07853
Parkertown	08087
Park Ridge	07656
Park Ridge Farms	08505
Parkside	08865
Park Village	07016
Parkway Pines	08701
Parkway Village	08628
Parlin (Part of Sayreville)	08859
Parry	08077

	ZIP
Parsippany (Morris County)	07054
Parsippany (Part of Mountain Lake)	07046
Parsippany-Troy Hills (census designated place)	07005
Parsippany-Troy Hills (Township)	07054
Pasadena	08759
Passaic (Morris County) (Township)	07946
Passaic (Passaic County)	07055
Passaic Junction	07662
Passaic Park (Part of Passaic)	07055
Paterson	07501-05
	07513-33
	07543-44
For specific Paterson Zip Codes call (201) 977-4738, or your local postmaster.	
Patricks Corner	08816
Pattenburg	08802
Paulina	07825
Paulins Kill	07860
Paulsboro	08066
Peahala Park	08008
Peapack (Part of Gladstone)	07977
Pedricktown	08067
Peermont (Part of Avalon)	08202
Pelican Island	08751
Pellet Pond	07480
Pellettown	07822
Pemberton	08068
Pemberton (Township)	08015
Pemberton Heights	08068
Penbryn	08009
Penekum	08021
Pennington	08534
Pennsauken	08110
Pennsauken (Township)	08110
Pennsauken (Shopping Center)	08110
Penns Beach	08070
Penns Grove	08069
Penns Neck	08540
Pennsville	08070
Pennsville (Township)	08070
Penny Pot (Part of Folsom)	08037
Penton	08079
Penwell	07865
Peppermill Farms	08002
Pequannock	07440
Pequannock (Township)	07440
Pequest	07863
Perrineville	08535
Perth Amboy	08861*
	08862†
Petersburg	08270
Philips Mills	07734
Phillipsburg	08865
Phoenix	08817
Picatinny Arsenal	07806
Pierces Point	08210
Piersonville	08620
Pilesgrove (Township)	08093
Pine Acres (Part of Woodbury Heights)	08090
Pine Beach	08741
Pine Brook (Monmouth County)	07724
Pine Brook (Morris County)	07058
Pine Brook (Somerset County)	08502
Pine Cliff Lake	07480
Pine Grove	08053
Pine Hill	08021
Pinehurst	08201
Pine Lake Park	08753
Pine Ridge	08857
Pine Ridge at Crestwood	08759
Pines Lake	07470
Pine Terrace	08753
Pinetree Village	08857
Pine Valley	08021
Pinewald	08721
Pinewold Village	08016
Piscataway	08854*
	08855†
Pitman	08071
Pittsgrove	08318
Pittsgrove (Township)	08347
Pittstown	08867
Plainfield	07060-63
For specific Plainfield Zip Codes call (908) 756-5200, or your local postmaster.	
Plainsboro	08536
Plainsboro (Township)	08536
Plainville	08502
Plauderville (Part of Garfield)	07026
Plaza (Part of Secaucus)	07094

	ZIP		ZIP		ZIP
Plaza Park	08016	Randolph (Township)	07970	Rumson	07760
Pleasant Gardens	08527	Raritan (Hunterdon County)		Runnemede	08078
Pleasant Grove (Morris		(Township)	08822	Runyon	08857
County)	07853	Raritan (Somerset County)	08869	Russia	07438
Pleasant Grove (Ocean		Raven Rock	08559	Rutgers Village (Part of New	
County)	08527	Readington	08870	Brunswick)	08901
Pleasant Hill	07876	Readington (Township)	08870	Rutherford	07070-75
Pleasant Mills	08037	Reaville	08822	For specific Rutherford Zip Codes	
Pleasant Plains (Morris		Rebel Hill	07920	call (201) 933-1213, or your local	
County)	07980	Red Bank	07701-04	postmaster.	
Pleasant Plains (Ocean		For specific Red Bank Zip Codes		Saddle Brook (Township)	07662
County)	08753	call (908) 741-9200, or your local		Saddle Brook	07662
Pleasant Run (Burlington		postmaster.		Saddle River	07458
County)	08077	Red Bank	08063	St. Cloud	07052
Pleasant Run (Hunterdon		Red Lion	08088	St. Josephs Village (Part of	
County)	08822	Reed Crossing (Part of		Rockleigh)	07647
Pleasant Terrace	08314	Berlin)	08009	Salem	08079
Pleasant Valley	07882	Reeds Beach	08210	Salem Hills	08701
Pleasant View	08502	Reevytown (Part of Tinton		Salina	08080
Pleasantville (Atlantic		Falls)	07753	Sand Brook	08559
County)	08232	Repaupo (station)	08085	Sand Hills (Edison twp.)	08861
Pleasantville (Cumberland		Repaupo	08066	Sand Hills (Woodbridge	
County)	08360	Retreat	08088	twp.)	08852
Pleasure Bay (Part of Long		Richard Mine	07885	Sands Point (Part of	
Branch)	07740	Richland	08350	Oceanport)	07757
Pluckemin	07978	Richwood	08074	Sandy Point	08723
Plumbsock	07461	Rider College	08648	Sandyston (Township)	07851
Plumsted (Township)	08533	Ridgefield	07657	Saxton Falls	07874
Pohatcong (Township)	08804	Ridgefield Park	07660	Sayres Neck	08311
Pointers	08079	Ridgeway	08733	Sayreville	08871*
Point Pleasant	08742	Ridgewood	07450*		08872†
Point Pleasant Beach	08742		07451†	Sayre Woods (Part of	
Point Pleasant Manor	08723	Ridgewood Junction (Part		Sayreville)	08859
Polkville	07832	of Glen Rock)	07452	Sayre Woods South	08857
Pomona	08240	Riegel Ridge	08848	Schellengers Landing (Part	
Pompton Junction (Part of		Riegelsville	08848	of Cape May)	08204
Pompton Lakes)	07442	Ringoes	08551	Schooleys Mountian	07870
Pompton Lakes	07442	Ringwood	07456	Scobeyville	07724
Pompton Plains	07444	Rio Grande	08242	Scotch Bonnet	08210
Porchtown	08344	Ritz (Part of Garfield)	07026	Scotch Plains (Township)	07076
Port-au-Peck (Part of		River Bank	08741	Scotch Plains	07076
Oceanport)	07757	Riverdale	07457	Scudders Falls	08628
Port Colden	07882	River Edge	07661	Scullville	08330
Port Elizabeth	08348	River Edge Manor (Part of		Seaboard (Part of Kearny)	07032
Portertown	08098	New Milford)	07646	Sea Breeze	08302
Port Johnson (Part of		River Plaza	07701	Sea Bright	07760
Bayonne)	07002	River Road (Part of Fair		Seabrook	08302
Port Monmouth	07758	Lawn)	07410	Sea Girt	08750
Port Morris	07850	Riverside (Township)	08075	Sea Girt Estates	08750
Port Murray	07865	Riverside	08075	Sea Isle City	08243
Port Norris	08349	Riverside Park	08075	Seaside Heights	08751
Port Reading	07064	Riverside Square (Part of		Seaside Park	08752
Port Reading Junction (Part		Hackensack)	07601	Seaview Park	08201
of Manville)	08835	River Street (Part of		Seaview Square	07712
Port Republic	08241	Paterson)	07524	Seaville	08230
Port Warren	08886	Riverton	08077	Secaucus	07094*
Possumtown	08854	River Vale (Township)	07675		07096†
Post Brook Farms Lake	07480	River Vale	07675	Sedgefield	07950
Potter	08817	Riverview Manor	08854	Sergeantsville	08557
Potterstown	08833	Riverwood	08753	Seven Stars	08701
Pottersville	07979	Riviera Beach	08723	Sewaren	07077
Powerville	07005	Roadstown	08302	Sewell	08080
Prallsville (Part of Stockton)	08559	Robbinsville	08691	Shady Lake	07480
Presidential Lakes Estates	08015	Robertsville (census		Shafto Corners (Part of	
Princeto Ivy East	08520	designated place)	07746	Tinton Falls)	07727
Princeton	08540-43	Robertsville	07726	Shamong (Township)	08088
For specific Princeton Zip Codes		Robin Hood Homes	08010	Shark River Hills	07753
call (609) 452-9044, or your local		Robins Estates	08527	Shark River Manor	07719
postmaster.		Rochelle Park (Township)	07662	Sharptown	08098
Princeton Junction	08550	Rochelle Park	07662	Shaw Crest	08260
Princeton North	08540	Rockaway	07866	Shelter Cove	08753
Prospect Heights	08638	Rockaway (Township)	07866	Sherbrook Estates	08520
Prospect Highlands	08638	Rockaway Neck	07054	Sherwood on the Green	08096
Prospect Park (Mercer		Rockaway Valley	07005	Sherwood West	08066
County)	08638	Rockleigh	07647	Shiloh	08353
Prospect Park (Passaic		Rockport	07840	Shimer Manor	08865
County)	07508	Rock Ridge Lake	07834	Ship Bottom	08008
Prospect Plains	08512	Rocktown	08551	Shippenport	07850
Prospect Point	07849	Rocky Hill	08553	Shirley	08318
Prospertown	08514	Roebling	08554	Shongum	07970
Pullentown	08501	Roosevelt	08555	Shore Acres	08723
Quaker Gardens	08619	Roosevelt City	08759	Shore Crest	07067
Quakertown	08868	Roosevelt Park (Part of		Short Hills	07078
Quarryville	07461	Millville)	08332	Shrewsbury	07702
Quinton	08072	Rosedale (Part of		Shrewsbury (Township)	07724
Quinton (Township)	08072	Hammonton)	08037	Shrewsbury Road	08501
Racoon Island	07849	Rosegate	08857	Sicklerville	08081
Radburn (Part of Fair Lawn)	07410	Rose Hill Heights	08865	Sidney	08867
Rahway	07065-67	Roseland	07068	Siloam	07728
For specific Rahway Zip Codes		Roselle	07203	Silver Bay	08753
call (908) 388-1110, or your local		Roselle Park	07204	Silver Lake (Essex County)	07109
postmaster.		Rosemont (Hunterdon		Silver Lake (Warren County)	07825
Rainbow Lakes	07834	County)	08556	Silver Ridge	08753
Raines Corner	08069	Rosemont (Mercer County)	08619	Silver Ridge Park	08757
Ralston	07945	Rosenhayn	08352	Silver Ridge Park West	08757
Ramblewood	08054	Roseville (Part of Newark)	07107	Silver Springs	07850
Ramsey	07446	Ross Corner	07822	Silverton	08753
Ramseysburg	07832	Rossmoor	08831	Sim Place	08005
Rancocas	08073	Rowe Street	07003	Singac	07424
Rancocas Heights	08060	Roxburg	08865	Sinnickson Landing	08079
Rancocas Woods	08060	Roxbury (Township)	07876	Six Points	08302
Randolph	07869	Rudeville	07419	Skillman	08558

	ZIP		ZIP		ZIP
Skylands (Part of		Spring Mills	08848		07512*
Ringwood)	07456	Springside	08016	Towaco	07082
Sky Line Lake (Part of		Springtown (Cumberland		Town Bank	08204
Ringwood)	07465	County)	08302	Town Brook	07748
Slackwoods	08638	Springtown (Warren County)	08865	Town Center	07052
Sloop Creek Estates	08721	Springville	08057	Town Estates	08016
Sloping Hills	07920	Squire Village	08753	Townley	07083
Smithburg	07728	Stafford (Township)	08050	Townsbury	07863
Smiths Mills	07405	Staffordville	08092	Townsends Inlet (Part of	
Smith Tract	08008	Stanhope	07874	Sea Isle City)	08243
Smithville (Atlantic County)	08201	Stanton	08885	Tranquility	07879
Smithville (Burlington		Stanton Station	08822	Tremley (Part of Linden)	07036
County)	08060	Stanwick	08057	Tremley Point (Part of	
Smoke Rise (Part of		Stanwick Glen	08057	Linden)	07036
Kinnelon)	07405	Star Cross	08322	Trenton	08601-91
Snow Hill (Part of Lawnside)	08045	State Hospital	08625	For specific Trenton Zip Codes	
Society Hill	08817	Staten Island Junction	07016	call (609) 581-3030, or your local	
	08857	Steelmantown	08270	postmaster.	
Soho	07109	Steelmanville	08221	Trenton Gardens	08610
Somerdale	08083	Stephensburg	07865	Trenton Highlands	08619
Somerset	08873-75	Stevens	08016	Troy Hills	07054
For specific Somerset Zip Codes		Stewartsville	08886	Tuckahoe	08250
call (908) 873-8600, or your local		Still Valley	08865	Tuckerton	08087
postmaster.		Stillwater	07875	Tuckerton Shores (Part of	
Somerset	08628	Stillwater (Township)	07875	Tuckerton)	08087
Somers Point	08244	Stirling	07980	Turkey Point Corner	08349
Somerville	08876*	Stockholm	07460	Turnersville	08012
	08877†	Stockton	08559	Tuttles Corner	07826
South (Part of Newark)	07114	Stockton State College	08240	Twin Rivers	08520
South Amboy	08879	Stone Harbor	08247	Tyler Park	07047
Southampton (Township)	08088	Stone House	07946	Undercliff (Part of	
Southard	08701	Stone Tavern	08514	Edgewater)	07020
South Belmar	07719	Stonetown (Part of		Union (Hunterdon County)	
South Bound Brook		Ringwood)	07465	(Township)	08802
(Middlesex County)	08846	Stoney Brook Estates	08096	Union (Township) (Union	
South Bound Brook		Stony Hill	07922	County)	07083
(Somerset County)	08880	Stoutsburg	08525	Union	07083
South Branch	08876	Stow Creek (Township)	08302	Union Beach	07735
South Brunswick	08540	Stow Creek Landing	08302	Union Center	07083
South Brunswick (Township)	08852	Stratford	08084	Union City	07087
South Camden (Part of		Strathmere	08248	Union Hill	07801
Camden)	08104	Strathmore	07747	Union Mills	08060
South Dennis	08245	Styertowne Shopping		Union Square (Part of	
South Egg Harbor	08215	Center (Part of Clifton)	07012	Elizabeth)	07201
Southern State 1 & 2	08314	Suburban	07701	Uniontown	08865
South Glassboro (Part of		Succasunna	07876	Union Valley	08512
Glassboro)	08028	Succasunna-Kenvil	07876	Unionville	08060
South Hackensack		Summerfield	07823	Upper (Township)	08250
(Township)	07606	Summit	07901*	Upper Berkshire Valley	07885
South Hackensack	07606		07902†	Upper Deerfield (Township)	08313
South Harrison (Township)	08039	Summit Avenue (Part of		Upper Freehold (Township)	08501
South Kearny (Part of		Union City)	07087	Upper Greenwood Lake	07421
Kearny)	07032	Sunbury	08068	Upper Harmony	08865
South Lakewood	08701	Sunnyside	08801	Upper Mohawk	07871
South Livingston	07039	Sunrise Beach	08731	Upper Montclair	07043
South Mantoloking	08738	Sunrise Park	07876	Upper Montvale (Part of	
South Merchantville (Part of		Sunset Hills	08540	Montvale)	07645
Merchantville)	08109	Surf City	08008	Upper Pittsgrove (Township)	08318
South Ogdensburg (Part of		Sussex	07461	Upper Saddle River	07458
Ogdensburg)	07439	Sutton Park	07836	Uptown (Part of Hoboken)	07030
South Orange	07079	Swainton	08210	V.A. Hospital (Part of East	
South Orange Village		Swartswood	07877	Orange)	07018
(Township)	07079	Swartswood Lake	07860	Vail Homes	07724
South Paterson (Part of		Swedesboro	08085	Vails	07832
Paterson)	07503	Sweet Briar	07733	Vailsburg (Part of Newark)	07106
South Pemberton (Part of		Sweetwater	08037	Valley (Middlesex County)	08817
Pemberton)	08068	Sykesville	08562	Valley (Passaic County)	07470
South Penns Grove	08069	Sylvan Glen	08505	Vanada Woods	08723
South Plainfield	07080	Sylvan Lake	08016	Vanhiseville	08527
South River	08882	Tabernacle	08088	Van Marters Corner	07730
South Seaside Park	08752	Tabernacle (Township)	08088	Vasa Home	07840
South Seaville	08246	Tanglewood Farms	07733	Vauxhall	07088
South Toms River	08757	Tanners Corner	08816	Ventnor City	08406
South Vineland (Part of		Tansboro	08004	Ventnor Heights (Part of	
Vineland)	08360	Taunton Lakes	08053	Ventnor City)	08406
South Westville (Part of		Taurus (Part of West New		Verga	08093
Westville)	08093	York)	07093	Vernon	07462
Southwest Vineland (Part of		Tavistock	08033	Vernon (Township)	07462
Vineland)	08360	Taylortown	07005	Vernon Valley	07418
Southwind	08527	Teabo	07885	Vernoy	07830
Southwood	08857	Teaneck (Township)	07666	Verona	07044
South Woodstown (Part of		Teaneck	07666	Verona (Township)	07044
Woodstown)	08098	Tenafly	07670	Victoria	08344
Sparta	07871	Tennent	07763	Victory Gardens	07801
Sparta (Township)	07871	Teterboro	07608	Victory Lakes	08094
Sparta Junction	07871	Tewksbury (Township)	08833	Vienna	07880
Sparta Lake	07871	The Acres (Part of		Vienna Gardens	08213
Sperry Springs (Part of		Glassboro)	08028	Villas	08251
Hopatcong)	07843	The Dunes	08008	Vincentown	08088
Spotswood	08884	The Orchards	08619	Vineland	08360
Spray Beach	08008	Thompson Beach	08324	Voken Tract	08002
Springdale (Camden		Thorofare	08086	Voorhees (Township)	08043
County)	08002	Three Bridges	08887	Voorhees Corner	08822
Springdale (Sussex County)	07860	Timber Lakes	08094	Vulcanite (Part of Alpha)	08865
Springfield (Burlington		Timbuctoo	08060	Wading River	08215
County) (Township)	08041	Tinton Falls	07724	Waldwick	07463
Springfield (Union County)		Titusville	08560	Wall	07719
(Township)	07081	Toms River	08753-57	Wall (Township)	07719
Springfield	07081	For specific Toms River Zip		Wallington	07057
Spring Gardens	08618	Codes call (908) 349-0710, or		Wallkill Island	07461
Spring Lake	07762	your local postmaster.		Wallpack Center	07881
Spring Lake Heights	07762	Totowa	07511†	Wallworth Park	08002

	ZIP		ZIP		ZIP
Walnford	08501	West Creek	08092	Wickatunk	07765
Walnut Valley	07832	West Deal	07712	Wilburtha	08628
Walpack (Township)	07881	West Deptford (Township)	08086	Wilburtha Manor	08628
Walt Whitman Homes	08086	West End (Gloucester		Wilderness Acres	08002
Wanamassa	07712	County)	08096	Wildwood	08260
Wanaque	07465	West End (Monmouth		Wildwood Crest	08260
Wantage (Township)	07461	County)	07740	Wildwood Gables (Part of	
Waretown	08758	West Englewood	07666	Wildwood Crest)	08260
Warners (Part of Linden)	07036	West Farms	07731	Wildwood Highlands Beach	08251
Warren	07059	Westfield	07090*	Williamstown	08094
Warren (Township)	07059		07091†	Williamstown Junction	08009
Warren Glen	08886	West Fort Lee (Part of Fort		Willingboro (Township)	08046
Warren Grove	08005	Lee)	07024	Willingboro	08046
Warren Point (Part of Fair		West Freehold	07728	Willingboro Mall	08046
Lawn)	07410	West Grove	07753	Willington Park	08077
Warrington	07832	West Haddonfield (Part of		Willowbrook Mall	07470
Washington (Bergen		Haddonfield)	08033	Willowdale	08002
County) (Township)	07675	West Hoboken	07087	Willow Grove	08344
Washington (Bergen		West Hoboken (station)	07030	Windsor	08561
County)	07675	West Hudson (Part of		Windsor Park	08753
Washington (Burlington		Kearny)	07032	Winfield (Township)	07036
County) (Township)	08215	West Keansburg	07734	Winfield	07036
Washington (Gloucester		West Long Branch	07764	Winslow	08095
County) (Township)	08080	West Mahwah	07430	Winslow (Township)	08095
Washington (Mercer		West Mantoloking	08723	Winslow Junction	08095
County) (Township)	08691	West Milford (Township)	07480	Winston Park	07727
Washington (Morris County)		West Milford	07480	Wonder Lake	07480
(Township)	07853	Westmont	08108	Wood Acres	07731
Washington	07882	West Moorestown	08057	Woodbine	08270
Washington (Warren		West New York	07093	Woodbridge (Township)	07095
County) (Township)	07882	West Norwood (Part of		Woodbridge	07095
Washington Crossing	08560	Norwood)	07648	Woodbridge Center	07095
Washington Park (Part of		West Ocean City	08223	Woodbridge Oaks	08830
Newark)	07102	West Ocean Grove	07753	Woodbury	08096
Washington Street (Part of		Weston (Part of Manville)	08835	Woodbury Gardens	08096
Hoboken)	07030	Westons Mills (Part of New		Woodbury Heights	08097
Washington Valley	07960	Brunswick)	08816	Woodcliff	07047
Washingtonville (Part of		West Orange	07052	Woodcliff Lake	07675
Watchung)	07060	West Orange (Township)	07052	Woodcrest	08003
Watchung	07060	West Paterson	07424	Woodglen	07830
Waterford (Township)	08004	West Point Island	08735	Woodland (Township)	08019
Waterford Works	08089	West Point Pleasant (Part of		Woodland Ridge	07801
Waterloo	07874	Point Pleasant)	08742	Woodlynne	08107
Watsessing	07003	West Portal	08802	Woodmere (Ocean County)	08527
Watsontown (Part of		West Side (Part of		Woodmere (Salem County)	08079
Clementon)	08021	Hoboken)	07030	Woodport	07885
Wayne	07470*	West Side (Part of Jersey		Wood-Ridge	07075
	07474†	City)	07304	Woodruff	08302
Wayside	07712	West Trenton	08628	Woods Tavern	08876
Wedgewood	08071	West Tuckerton	08087	Woodstown	08098
Weehawken (Township)	07087	West View (Part of		Woodstream	08053
Weehawken	07087	Ridgefield Park)	07660	Woodsville	08525
Weekstown	08037	West Village	08302	Woolwich (Township)	08085
Weequahic (Part of Newark)	07112	Westville	08093	Wortendyke (Part of	
Wellwood (Part of		Westville Grove	08093	Midland Park)	07432
Merchantville)	08109	Westville Oaks	08093	Wrights Mill	08343
Wenonah	08090	West Wildwood	08260	Wrightstown	08562
West (Part of Newark)	07103	West Windsor (Township)	08550	Wrightsville (Burlington	
West Allenhurst	07711	Westwood	07675	County)	08077
Westampton (Township)	08073	Weymouth	08330	Wrightsville (Monmouth	
West Amwell (Township)	08530	Weymouth (Township)	08317	County)	08526
West Arlington (Part of		Whale Beach	08248	Wyckoff (Township)	07481
Kearny)	07032	Wharton	07885	Wyckoff	07481
West Atco	08004	Wheat Road (Part of Buena)	08341	Wyckoff Mills	07728
West Atlantic City	08232	Whiglane	08343	Wyckoffs Mills	08512
West Belmar	07719	Whippany	07981	Wynnewood	08854
West Belt Mall	07470	White (Township)	07829	Yardville	08620
West Berlin	08091	White Horse	08610	Yardville-Groveville	08620
Westboro (Part of Red		Whitehouse	08888	Yellow Frame	07860
Bank)	07701	White House Station	08889	York Estates	08520
West Brunswick	08873	White Meadow Lake	07866	Yorketown	07726
West Caldwell (Township)	07006*	Whiteoak Ridge	07078	Yorktown	08098
	07007†	White Rock Lake	07439	Youth Correctional	
West Cape May	08204	Whitesbog	08015	Institution (Burlington	
West Carteret (Part of		Whitesboro	08252	County)	08505
Carteret)	07008	Whitesboro-Burleigh	08252	Youth Correctional	
West Carteret-Woodbridge		Whitesville (Monmouth		Institution (Hunterdon	
(Part of Carteret)	07008	County)	07753	County)	08801
West Collingswood (Part of		Whitesville (Ocean County)	08527	Zarephath	08890
Collingswood)	08107	Whiting	08759	Zion	08558
West Collingswood Heights	08059	Whitman Square	08012		

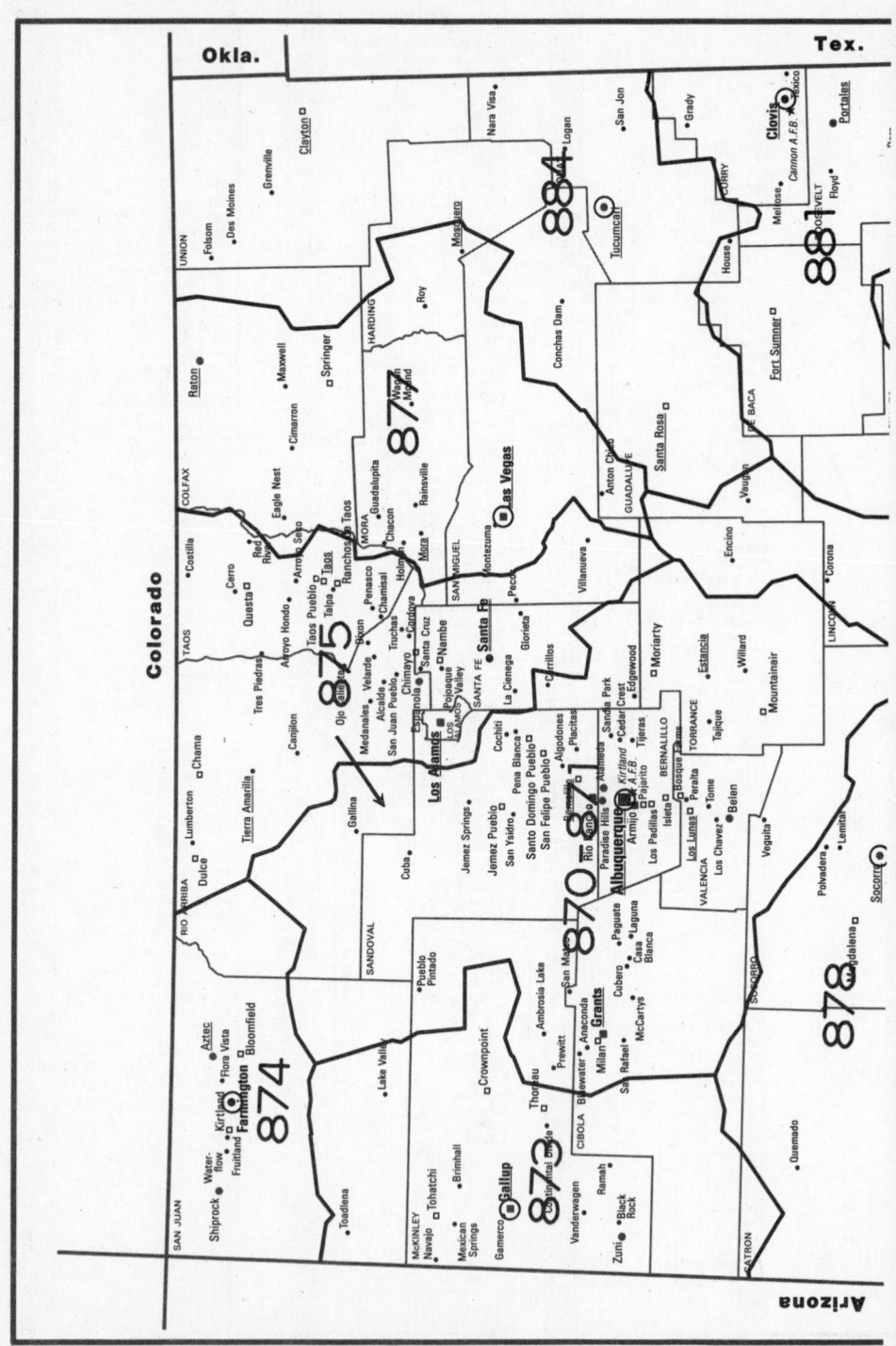

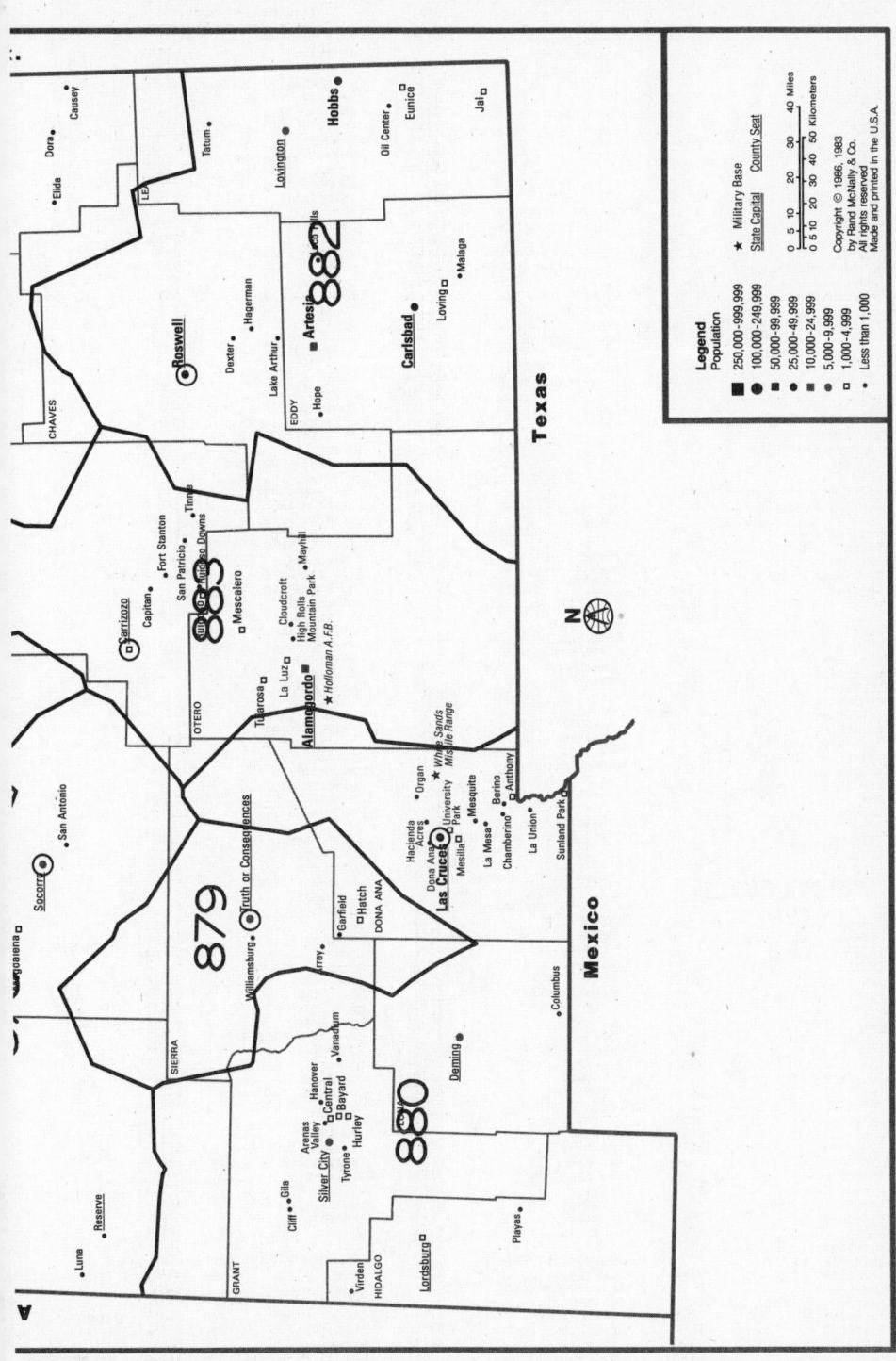

	ZIP
El Rito	87530
El Turquillo	87722
El Vado	87575
El Valle	87521
Embudo	87531
Emplazado	87745
Enchanted Hills (Part of Ruidoso)	88345
Encinal	87014
Encino	88321
Engele	87935
Ensenada	87575
Escabosa	87059
Escondida	87801
Espanola	87532
Estaca	87566
Estancia	87016
Eunice	88231
Fairacres	88033
Fairview (Part of Espanola)	87533
Farley	88422
Farmington	87401-02
	87499
For specific Farmington Zip Codes call (505) 325-5047, or your local postmaster.	
Faywood	88034
Faywood Hot Springs	88034
Fence Lake	87315
Field	88124
Fierro	88041
First Plaza (Part of Albuquerque)	87102
Five Points	87105
	87121
For specific Five Points Zip Codes call (505) 843-7484, or your local postmaster.	
Flora Vista	87415
Florida	87801
Floyd	88118
Flume Canyon (Part of Ruidoso)	88345
Flying H	88322
Folsom	88419
Forest Heights (Part of Ruidoso)	88345
Forest Park	87008
Forrest	88427
Fort Bliss	79916
Fort Stanton	88323
Fort Sumner	88119
Fort Wingate	87316
Fort Wingate Depot Activity	87301
French Corners	87747
Fruitland	87416
Gabaldon	87701
Galisteo	87010
Gallegos	88426
Gallina	87017
Gallina Plaza	87017
Gallinas	87731
Gallup	87301-05
For specific Gallup Zip Codes call (505) 863-3491, or your local postmaster.	
Gamerco	87317
Garanbuio	87568
Garfield	87936
Garita	88421
Garrison	88132
Gascon	87742
Gavilan	87029
Gila	88038
Gila Hot Springs	88061
Gladstone	88422
Glencoe	88324
Glen Grove (Part of Ruidoso)	88345
Glenrio	88423
Glenwood	88039
Glorieta	87535
Gobernador	87412
Golden	87047
Golondrinas	87712
Gonzales Ranch	87536
Grady	88120
Gran Quivira	87036
Grants	87020
Greenfield	88230
Green Meadows (Part of Ruidoso)	88345
Grenville	88424
Grier	88101
Guachupangue	87532
Guadalupita	87722
Hachita	88040
Hacienda Acres	88001
Hagerman	88232
Hamilton Terrace (Part of Ruidoso)	88345
Hanover	88041

	ZIP
Happy Valley	88220
Hatch	87937
Hayden	88410
Hernandez	87537
Highland (Part of Albuquerque)	87108
High Rolls	88325
Hill	88005
Hillburn City	88260
Hillsboro	88042
Hobbies	87059
Hobbs	88240*
	88241†
Hoffman Town (Part of Albuquerque)	87112
Holiday Acres (Part of Ruidoso)	88345
Hollene	88101
Holloman Air Force Base	88330
Hollywood (Part of Ruidoso)	88345
Holman	87723
Hondo	88336
Hooverville	88416
Hope	88250
Horse Springs	87821
Hospah	87313
Hot Springs	87731
Hot Springs Landing	87935
House	88121
Humble City	88240
Hurley	88043
Hyde Park Estates	87501
Idlewild	87718
Ilfeld	87538
Indian Hills (Part of Ruidoso)	88345
Isleta	87022
Isleta Indian Reservation	87022
Iyanbito	87316
Jacona	87501
Jaconita	87501
Jal	88252
Jamestown	87347
Jarales	87023
Jemez Indian Reservation	87024
Jemez Pueblo	87024
Jemez Springs	87025
Jicarilla Apache Indian Reservation	87528
Jordan	88427
Kenna	88122
Kingston	88042
Kingswood (Part of Ruidoso)	88345
Kirtland	87417
Kirtland Air Force Base	87115
	87118
For specific Kirtland Air Force Base Zip Codes call (505) 247-3330, or your local postmaster.	
Kirtland Air Force Base East	87115
	87118
For specific Kirtland Air Force Base East Zip Codes call (505) 247-3330, or your local postmaster.	
Knowles	88240
La Bolsa	87531
La Cienega	87501
La Constancia	87002
La Cueva (Mora County)	87712
La Cueva (Santa Fe County)	87535
La Fraqua	87568
Laguna	87026
Laguna Indian Reservation	87026
Lagunita	87560
La Huerta	88220
La Jara	87027
La Joya (Santa Fe County)	87535
La Joya (Socorro County)	87028
La Junta	87531
Lake Arthur	88253
Lake Valley	87313
Lake View Pines	87718
Lakewood	88254
La Ladera	87031
La Loma	87724
La Luz	88337
Lama	87556
La Madera (Rio Arriba County)	87539
La Madera (Sandoval County)	87047
La Manga	87701
La Mesa	88044
La Mesilla	87532
Lamy	87540
La Plata	87418
La Puebla	87532
La Puente	87575
Las Cruces	88001

	ZIP
	88003-06
For specific Las Cruces Zip Codes call (505) 524-2841, or your local postmaster.	
Las Mochas	87579
Las Nutrias	87062
Las Palomas	87942
Las Placitas	87530
Las Tablas	87541
Las Tusas	87745
Las Vegas	87701
La Union	88021
La Villita	87511
Ledoux	87725
Lemitar	87823
Levy	87752
Leyba	87560
Lincoln	88338
Linda Vista (Part of Roswell)	88201
Lindrith	87029
Lingo	88123
Little Walnut Village	88061
Littlewater	87461
Llano	87543
Llano del Medio	87724
Llano Largo	87561
Llano Quemado	87557
Llaves	87027
Loco Hills	88255
Logan	88426
Lordsburg	88045
Los Alamos (Los Alamos County)	87544
Los Alamos (San Miguel County)	87745
Los Candelarias (Part of Albuquerque)	87107
Los Chavez	87002
Los Cordovas	87571
Los Duranes (Part of Albuquerque)	87104
Los Febres	87734
Los Griegos (Part of Albuquerque)	87107
Los Hueros	87734
Los Lentes (Part of Los Lunas)	87031
Los Luceros	87511
Los Lunas	87031
Los Lunas Correctional Center	87031
Los Lunas Hospital and Training School	87031
Los Montoyas	87701
Los Ojos	87551
Los Pachecos	87522
Los Padillas	87105
Los Pinos	81120
Los Ranchos	87101
Los Ranchos de Albuquerque	87107
Lost Lodge	88317
Los Trujillos	87002
Los Trujillos-Gabaldon	87002
Los Vigiles	87701
Lourdes	87701
Lovato	87568
Loving	88256
Lovington	88260
Lower La Posada	87552
Lower Nutria	87327
Lower Pueblo	87560
Lower Ranchito	87581
Lower Rociada	87742
Lower San Francisco Plaza	87830
Lucero	87736
Lucy	87063
Luis Lopez	87801
Lumberton	87547
Luna	87824
Lyden	87582
McAlister	88427
McCartys (Cibola County)	87049
McCartys (Harding County)	88430
McDonald	88262
McGaffey	87316
Macimiliano Luna	87701
McIntosh	87032
Madrid	87010
Maes	87701
Magdalena	87825
Malaga	88263
Maljamar	88264
Mangas	87821
Mangas Springs	88061
Manuelitas	87745
Manuelito	87319
Manzano (Bernalillo County)	87112
Manzano (Torrance County)	87036
Mariano Lake	87301
Maxwell	87728
Mayhill	88339

	ZIP		ZIP		ZIP
Meadow Lake	87031	Pecos	87552	Rodarte	87561
Medanales	87548	Pena Blanca	87041	Rodeo	88056
Melrose	88124	Penasco	87553	Rodey	87937
Mentmore	87319	Penasco Blanco	87742	Rogers	88132
Mesa Poleo	87012	Pendaries	87742	Romeroville	87701
Mescalero	88340	Penitentiary of New Mexico	87501	Rosebud	88410
Mescalero Apache Indian		Pep	88126	Roswell	88201-02
Reservation	88340	Peralta	87042	For specific Roswell Zip Codes	
Mesilla	88046	Perea	87316	call (505) 622-3741, or your local	
Mesilla Park (Part of Las		Pescado	87327	postmaster.	
Cruces)	88047	Petaca	87554	Roswell Mall (Part of	
Mesilla Valley Mall (Part of		Philadelphia	87014	Roswell)	88201
Las Cruces)	88001	Philmont	87714	Rowe	87562
Mesita	87026	Picacho	88343	Roy	87743
Mesquite	88048	Picuris	87553	Ruidoso	88345
Mexican Springs	87320	Picuris Indian Reservation	87553	Ruidoso Downs	88346
Miami	87729	Pie Town	87827	Rutheron	87563
Midway	88201	Pilar	87571	Sabinal	87006
Milagro	88321	Pine	87552	Sabinoso	87746
Milan	87021	Pinedale	87301	Sacramento	88347
Mills	87730	Pinehill	87357	St. Vrain	88133
Milnesand	88125	Pine View	87579	Salem	87941
Mimbres	88049	Pineywoods Estates	88317	San Acacia	87831
Mimbres Hot Springs	88041	Pinon	88344	San Antonio (Bernalillo	
Mineral Hill	87701	Pinos Altos	88053	County)	87008
Mission Park	87031	Pinoswells	87009	San Antonio (San Miguel	
Mogollon	88039	Pintada	88435	County)	87701
Monero	87547	Placita	87579	San Antonio (Socorro	
Monte Aplanado	87732	Placitas (Dona Ana County)	87937	County)	87832
Monte Verde (Part of Angel		Placitas (Rio Arriba County)	87515	San Antonio de Padua del	
Fire)	87718	Placitas (Sandoval County)	87043	Rancho	87501
Montezuma	87731	Placitas (Sierra County)	87939	San Antonito (Bernalillo	
Montgomery Plaza Mall		Playas	88009	County)	87047
(Part of Albuquerque)	87110	Plaza Blanca	87563	San Antonito (Socorro	
Monticello	87939	Pleasant Hill	88135	County)	87832
Montoya	88401	Pleasanton	88039	Sanchez	87746
Monument	88265	Pojoaque Indian Reservation	87501	San Cristobal	87564
Moqino	87040	Pojoaque Valley	87501	Sanctuario	87522
Mora	87732	Polvadera	87828	Sandia	87047
Moriarty	87035	Ponderosa	87044	Sandia Base	87115
Mosquero	87733	Ponderosa Heights (Part of		Sandia Heights	87004
Mountainair	87036	Ruidoso)	88345	Sandia Indian Reservation	87004
Mountain Park	88325	Ponderosa Pines	87059	Sandia Knolls	87047
Mountain View (Bernalillo		Portales	88130	Sandia Park	87047
County)	87105	Pot Creek	87571	Sandia Pueblo	87004
Mountain View (Chaves		Prairie Dog Trading Post	87013	San Felipe Indian	
County)	88201	Prairieview	88260	Reservation	87004
Mount Dora	88429	Prewitt	87045	San Felipe Pueblo	87001
Mule Creek	88051	Progresso	87063	San Fidel	87049
Nadine	88240	Pueblito	87566	San Francisco	87006
Nageezi	87037	Pueblitos	87002	San Francisco Plaza	87830
Nambe	87501	Pueblo of Acoma	87034	San Geronimo	87701
Nambe Indian Reservation	87501	Pueblo Pintado	87013	San Ignacio	87745
Nambe Pueblo	87501	Puerto de Luna	88432	San Ildefonso Indian	
Nara Visa	87325	Punta de Agua	87036	Reservation	87502
Naschitti	87328	Quarris Acres	88317	San Ildefonso Pueblo	87501
Navajo	87328	Quarteles	87532	San Jon	88434
Navajo Dam	87419	Quay	88433	San Jose (Bernalillo County)	87102
Navajo Estates	87375	Queen	88220	San Jose (Rio Arriba	
Navajo Indian Reservation	86515	Quemado	87829	County)	87537
Navajo Wingate Village	87311	Questa	87556	San Jose (San Miguel	
Newcomb	87455	Radium Springs	88054	County)	87565
Newkirk	88431	Rainsville	87736	San Juan (Grant County)	88041
New Laguna	87038	Ramah	87321	San Juan (Rio Arriba	
New York	87014	Ramah Navajo Indian		County)	87566
Nogal	88341	Reservation	87327	San Juan (San Miguel	
North Acomita Village	87034	Ramon	88136	County)	87565
North Carmen	87732	Ranchito	87571	San Juan Indian	
North Hurley	88043	Ranchitos	87532	Reservation	87566
North San Ysidro	87538	Rancho Grande Estates	87830	San Juan Pueblo	87566
North Valley	87107	Ranchos de Taos	87557	San Lorenzo	88041
	87109	Ranchos Lake Conchas	88416	San Mateo	87050
For specific North Valley Zip		Ranchvale	88101	San Miguel (Dona Ana	
Codes call (505) 344-1400, or		Raton	87740	County)	88058
your local postmaster.		Red Hill	87829	San Miguel (Rio Arriba	
Nutrias	87575	Red River	87558	County)	81120
Ocate	87734	Redrock (Grant County)	88055	San Miguel (San Miguel	
Oil Center	88266	Red Rock (McKinley		County)	87560
Ojito (Rio Arriba County)	87029	County)	87420	Sanostee	87461
Ojito (Taos County)	87521	Regina	87046	San Pablo	87701
Ojitos Frios	87701	Rehoboth	87322	San Patricio	88348
Ojo Amarillo	87417	Rencona	87562	San Pedro	87532
Ojo Caliente (Cibola		Reserve	87830	San Rafael (Cibola County)	87051
County)	87327	Ribera	87560	San Rafael (San Miguel	
Ojo Caliente (Taos County)	87549	Rincon	87940	County)	88439
Ojo Feliz	87735	Rinconada	87531	San Sebastian	87501
Ojo Sarco	87550	Rincon Montoso	87745	Santa Ana Indian	
Old Albuquerque (Part of		Rio Chiquito	87522	Reservation	87004
Albuquerque)	87104	Rio Communities	87002	Santa Ana Pueblo	87004
Old Picacho	88033	Rio Grande Estates	87002	Santa Clara Indian	
Omega	87829	Rio Lucio	87553	Reservation	87532
Organ	88052	Rio Puerco	87064	Santa Clara Pueblo	87532
Orogrande	88342	Rio Rancho	87124	Santa Cruz	87567
Oscuro	88301	Rio West Mall (Part of		Santa Fe	87501-06
Otis	88220	Gallup)	87301		87538
Paguate	87040	Rito de las Sillas	87064		87540
Pajarito (Bernalillo County)	87105	Riverside (Eddy County)	88210	For specific Santa Fe Zip Codes	
Pajarito (Santa Fe County)	87532	Riverside (Lincoln County)	88201	call (505) 988-6351, or your local	
Paradise Hills	87114	Robin Hood Park	88317	postmaster.	
Park Springs	87701	Rociada	87742		
Pastura	88435	Rock Canyon	87745	Santa Rosa	88435
Paxton Springs	87020	Rock Springs	87301	Santa Teresa	88008

	ZIP		ZIP		ZIP
Santo Domingo Indian Reservation	87052	Taos Ski Valley	87525	Vado	88072
Santo Domingo Pueblo	87052	Tatum	88267	Valdez	87580
Santo Nino	87567	Tecolote	87701	Valencia	87031
Santo Tomas	88044	Tecolotito	87711	Vallecitos	87581
San Ysidro	87053	Tererro	87573	Vallecitos de los Indios	87025
Sapello	87745	Tesuque	87574	Valle Escondido	87571
Seama	87014	Tesuque Indian Reservation	87574	Valmora	87750
Seboyeta	87055	Tesuque Pueblo	87501	Val Verde	87718
Sedan	88436	Texico	88135	Vanadium	88023
Sedillo Hill	87059	Thoreau	87323	Vanderwagen	87326
Sena	87568	Three Rivers	88352	Vaughn	88353
Seneca	88437	Tierra Amarilla	87575	Veguita	87062
Separ	88045	Tierra Monte	87742	Velarde	87582
Serafina	87569	Tijeras	87059	Ventero	87512
Servilleta Plaza	87539	Timberon	88350	Vermejo Park	87740
Seton Village	87501	Tinian	87401	Villa Linda Mall (Part of Santa Fe)	87505
Seven Lakes	87313	Tinnie	88351	Villa Madonna	88312
Seven Rivers	88254	Tiptonville	87753	Villanueva	87583
Seven Springs	87025	Toadlena	87324	Virden	85534
Shady Brook	87571	Tocito	87461	Volcano Cliffs (Part of Albuquerque)	87120
Sheep Springs	87364	Tohatchi	87325	Wagon Mound	87752
Shiprock	87420	Tohlakai	87301	Walker (Part of Roswell)	88201
Sierra Vista	88312	Tolar	88134	Waterfall	88317
Sierra Vista Estates	87008	Tome	87060	Waterflow	87421
Sile	87041	Tome-Adelino	87060	Watrous	87753
Silver Acres	88061	T-O Ranch	87740	Weed	88354
Silver City	88061*	Torreon (Sandoval County)	87013	Western New Mexico Correctional Facility	87020
	88062†	Torreon (Torrance County)	87061	Westgate Heights (Part of Albuquerque)	87105
Sipapu	87579	Tortugas	88047	West Las Vegas (Part of Las Vegas)	87701
Sixteen Springs	88317	Totavi	87544	White Horse	87013
Skyline-Ganipa	87034	Trampas	87576	White Lakes	87056
Smith Lake	87365	Trechado	87315	White Oaks	88301
Socorro	87801	Trementina	88439	White Rock (Los Alamos County)	87544
Sofia	88424	Tres Piedras	87577	White Rock (San Juan County)	87313
Soham	87565	Tres Ritos	87579	White Sands	88002
Solano	87746	Truchas	87578	White Sands Missile Range	88002
Sombrillo	87532	Trujillo	87701	Whites City	88268
South Carmen	87725	Truth or Consequences	87901	White Signal	88061
Southern New Mexico Correctional Facility	88004	Tse Bonito	86515	Willard	87063
South San Ysidro	87565	Tucumcari	88401	Williams Acres	87301
South Springs Acres	88201	Tularosa	88352	Williamsburg	87942
South Valley	87102	Turley	87412	Willow Creek	88039
Spencerville	87410	Turn	87002	Winrock Center (Part of Albuquerque)	87110
Springer	87747	Twin Forks Estates	88317	Winston	87943
Springstead	87311	Twin Lakes	87301	Wyoming Mall, The (Part of Albuquerque)	87112
Squirrel Springs	87325	Two Gray Hills	87325	Yah-Ta-Hey	87375
Standing Rock	87313	Two Wells	87326	Yeso	88136
Stanley	87056	Tyrone	88065	Youngsville	87064
Star Lake	87013	University (Bernalillo County)	87106	Zamora	87059
Stead	88438	University (Roosevelt County)	88130	Zia Indian Reservation	87053
Sumner Lake State Park	88119	University Park	88003	Zia Pueblo	87053
Sunland Park	88063	Upper Anton Chico	87711	Zuni	87327
Sunshine	88030	Upper Dilia	87724	Zuni Indian Reservation	87327
Sunspot	88349	Upper Pueblo	87560		
Sun Valley	88312	Upper Rociada	87742		
Taiban	88134	Uptown (Part of Albuquerque)	87110		
Tajique	87057	Ute Mountain Indian Reservation	81334		
Talpa	87557	Ute Park	87749		
Taos	87571	Vadito	87579		
Taos Indian Reservation	87571				
Taos Pueblo	87571				

* **Area Zip Code**   † **Post Office Boxes**

Name	ZIP
Abbotts	14727
Academy (Albany County)	12208
Academy (Ontario County)	14424
Accord	12404
Acidalia	12760
Acra	12405
Adams	13605
Adams (Town)	13605
Adams Basin	14410
Adams Center	13606
Adams Corners	10579
Adams Cove	13634
Adamsville	12827
Addison	14801
Addison (Town)	14801
Addison Hill	16920
Adelphi (Part of New York)	11238
Adirondack	12808
Adrian	14823
Afton	13730
Afton (Town)	13730
Afton Lake	13730
Airmont (Rockland County)	10901
Airmont Heights	10901
Akins Corners	12563
Akron	14001
Alabama	14003
Alabama (Town)	14003
Albany	12201-60
For specific Albany Zip Codes call (518) 452-2499, or your local postmaster.	
Albany Medical Center (Part of Albany)	12208
Albertson	11507
Albia (Part of Troy)	12180
Albion	14411
Albion (Town)	14411
Albion (Town)	13302
Albion Correctional Facility	14411
Alcove	12007
Alden	14004
Alden (Town)	14004
Alden Bend	12910
Alden Center	14004
Alden Manor	11003
Alder Creek	13301
Alexander	14005
Alexander (Town)	14005
Alexander Corners	13650
Alexander Shopping Center (Part of Yonkers)	10710
Alexandria (Town)	13607
Alexandria Bay	13607
Alfred	14802
Alfred (Town)	14802
Alfred Station	14803
Allaben	12480
Allard Corners	12586
Allegany	14706
Allegany (Town)	14706
Allegany Indian Reservation (Town)	14081
Allegany Indian Reservation (Town)	14081
Allen (Town)	14709
Allen Center	14735
Allens Hill	14469
Allentown	14707
Allenwood	11021
Allerton (Part of New York)	10467
Alligerville	12440
Alloway	14489
Alma	14708
Alma (Town)	14708
Almond	14804
Almond (Town)	14804
Aloquin	14561
Alpine	14805
Alplaus	12008
Alps	12018
Alsen	12415
Altamont (Albany County)	12009
Altamont (Franklin County) (Town)	12986
Altay	14837
Altmar	13302
Alton	14413
Altona	12910
Altona (Town)	12910
Amagansett	11930
Amawalk	10501
Amber	13110
Amblerville	13843
Amboy (Onondaga County)	13031
Amboy (Oswego County) (Town)	13493
Amboy Center	13493
Amchir (Part of Middletown)	10940
Amenia	12501
Amenia (Town)	12501
Amenia Union	12501
Ames	13317
Amherst	14226
Amherst (Town)	14226
Amity (Allegany County) (Town)	14813
Amity (Orange County)	10990
Amity Harbor	11701
Amityville	11701
Amsdell Heights	14075
Amsterdam	12010
Amsterdam (Town)	12010
Ancram	12502
Ancram (Town)	12502
Ancramdale	12503
Andes	13731
Andes (Town)	13731
Andover	14806
Andover (Town)	14806
Andrea Park Estates	10598
Angelica	14709
Angelica (Town)	14709
Angola	14006
Angola on the Lake	14006
Annandale-on-Hudson	12504
Annsville (Oneida County) (Town)	13471
Annsville (Westchester County)	10566
Ansonia (Part of New York)	10023
Antwerp	13608
Antwerp (Town)	13608
Apalachin	13732
Apex	13783
Appleton	14008
Apulia	13159
Apulia Station	13020
Aquebogue	11931
Aqueduct	12308
Aquetuck	12143
Arcade	14009
Arcade (Town)	14009
Arcade Junction (Part of Arcade)	14009
Arcadia (Town)	14513
Archdale	12834
Archville	10510
Arden	10910
Ardonia	12515
Ardsley	10502
Ardsley-on-Hudson (Part of Irvington)	10503
Argusville	13459
Argyle	12809
Argyle (Town)	12809
Arietta (Town)	12139
Arkport	14807
Arkville	12406
Arkwright (Town)	14718
Arlington	12603
Arlyn Oaks	11758
Armonk	10504
Armor	14075
Arnolds Mill	12037
Arrochar (Part of New York)	10305
Arthur Manor (Part of Scarsdale)	10583
Arthursburg	12533
Arverne (Part of New York)	11692
Asharoken	11768
Ashford	14731
Ashford (Town)	14171
Ashford Hollow	14171
Ashland (Town)	12407
Ashland (Chemung County) (Town)	14894
Ashland (Greene County)	12407
Ashokan	12481
Ashville	14710
Ashville Bay	14710
Ashwood	14098
Aspenwood	12065
Aspinwall Corners	13650
Assembly Point	12845
Association Island	13651
Astoria (Part of New York)	11102
Athens	12015
Athens (Town)	12015
Athol	12810
Athol Springs	14010
Atlanta	14808
Atlantic (Part of New York)	10307
Atlantic Beach	11509
Atlantique	11706
Attica	14011
Attica (Town)	14011
Attica Center	14011
Attica Correctional Facility	14011
Attlebury	12581
Atwater	13081
Atwell	13338
Atwood	12484
Auburn	13021*
	13022†
Audubon (Part of New York)	10032
Augusta	13425
Augusta (Town)	13425
Aurelius (Town)	13034
Auriesville	12016
Aurora (Cayuga County)	13026
Aurora (Erie County) (Town)	14052
Aurora Tract	13088
Au Sable (Town)	12944
Au Sable Chasm	12944
Au Sable Forks	12912
Austerlitz	12017
Austerlitz (Town)	12017
Ava	13303
Ava (Town)	13303
Averill Park	12018
Avoca	14809
Avoca (Town)	14809
Avon	14414
Avon (Town)	14414
Axeville	14726
Babcock Hill	13318
Babcock Lake	12138
Babylon	11702
Bacon Hill	12871
Baggs Corner	13601
Bainbridge	13733
Bainbridge (Town)	13733
Baiting Hollow	11933
Bakers Mills	12811
Bakerstand	14101
Balcom	14138
Balcom Beach	14777
Bald Mountain	12834
Baldwin (Chemung County) (Town)	14861
Baldwin (Nassau County)	11510
Baldwin Harbor	11510
Baldwin Heights (Part of Olean)	14760
Baldwin Place	10505
Baldwin Place Shopping Center	10505
Baldwinsville	13027
Ballina	13035
Ballston (Town)	12019
Ballston Center	12020
Ballston Lake	12019
Ballston Spa	12020
Balltown	14062
Balmat	13609
Balmville	12550
Baltimore	13141
Bangall (Dutchess County)	12506
Bangall (Onondaga County)	13112
Bangor	12966
Bangor (Town)	12966
Bangor Station	12966
Bank Plaza	11566
Barberville	12018
Barcelona	14787
Barclay Heights (Part of Saugerties)	12477
Bardonia	10954
Bare Hill Correctional Facility	12953
Barker (Broome County) (Town)	13746
Barker (Niagara County)	14012
Barkers Grove	12154
Barkersville	12850
Barkertown	14836
Barnegat	12603
Barnerville	12092
Barnes Corners	13610
Barnes Hole	11930
Barneveld	13304
Barnum Island	11558
Barre (Town)	14411
Barre Center	14411
Barrington (Town)	14837
Barrytown	12507
Barryville	12719
Bartlett	13440
Bartlett Corners	14468
Bartlett Hollow	13775
Barton	13734
Barton (Town)	13734
Basket	12760
Basom	14013
Batavia	14020*
	14021†
Batchellerville	12134
Bates	12469
Bath	14810
Bath (Town)	14810
Bath Beach (Part of New York)	11214
Battenville	12834
Battery Park City (Part of New York)	10007
Baxter Estates	11050

* Area Zip Code   † Post Office Boxes

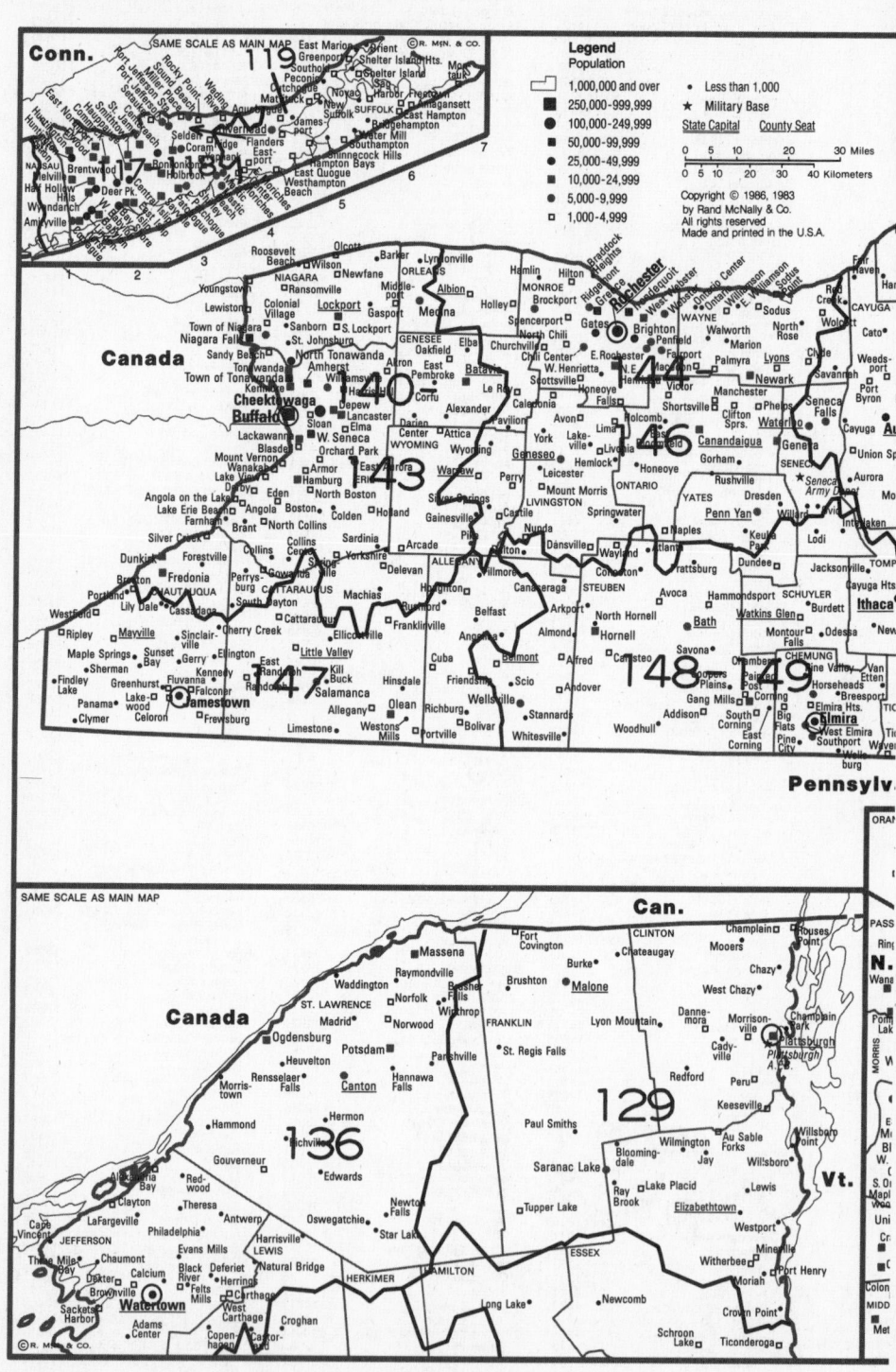

Legend

Population

⬛ (outline)	1,000,000 and over
■	250,000-999,999
●	100,000-249,999
●	50,000-99,999
●	25,000-49,999
●	10,000-24,999
□	5,000-9,999
▫	1,000-4,999

• Less than 1,000

★ Military Base

State Capital   County Seat

0 5 10   20   30 Miles
0 5 10   20   30   40 Kilometers

Conn.

SAME SCALE AS MAIN MAP

119

84

Canada

Cheektowaga

Buffalo

140

143

147

Jamestown

146

148

149

Pennsylv.

SAME SCALE AS MAIN MAP

Can.

Canada

136

129

Watertown

Vt.

	ZIP		ZIP		ZIP
Bay (Part of New York)	11235	Bemis Heights..........	12170	Bloomville...........	13739
Bayberry	13088	Bemus Point	14712	Blossvale	13308
Bayberry Dunes	11772	Benedict Beach	14464	Blue Mountain	12477
Bayberry Park (Part of New		Bennett Bridge	13302	Blue Mountain Lake	12812
Rochelle)	10804	Bennettsburg..........	14818	Blue Point	11715
Bayberry Shopping Center	13088	Bennettsville..........	13733	Blue Ridge	12534
Baychester (Part of New		Bennington............	14011	Blue Stores	12526
York)	10469	Bennington (Town)	14011	Bluff Point	14478
Bay Park	11518	Benson	12134	Blythebourne (Part of New	
Bay Point	11963	Benson (Town).........	12134	York)	11219
Bayport	11705	Benson Mines	13690	Boardmanville (Part of	
Bay Ridge (Part of New		Benton (Town)	14527	Olean)	14760
York)	11220	Benton Center........	14527	Boerum Hill (Part of New	
Bay Shore	11706	Berea	12549	York)	11201
Bay Shores	13110	Bergen	14416	Boght Corners	12047
Bayside (Part of New York)	11360	Bergen (Town)	14416	Bohemia	11716
Bay Terrace (Queens		Bergen Beach	14847	Boiceville	12412
County)...............	11360	Bergen Park	11746	Bolivar	14715
Bay Terrace (Richmond		Bergholtz	14304	Bolivar (Town)	14715
County)	10306	Berkshire (Town)	13736	Bolton	12824
Bay View (Erie County)	14075	Berkshire (Fulton County)	12078	Bolton (Town)	12824
Bayview (Suffolk County)	11971	Berkshire (Onondaga		Bolton Landing	12814
Bayville	11709	County).............	13066	Bolts Corners	13147
Baywood................	11706	Berkshire (Tioga County)..	13736	Bombay..............	12914
Beach Hampton	11930	Berkshire Terrace.........	12512	Bombay (Town)	12914
Beach Ridge	14120	Berlin	12022	Bon Air Heights (Part of	
Beach Shopping Center		Berlin (Town)	12022	Suffern)	10901
(Part of Peekskill)	10566	Berne	12023	Bonney	13464
Beachville	14807	Berne (Town)..........	12023	Bonni Castle	14590
Beacon	12508	Bernhards Bay	13028	Bonnie Crest (Part of New	
Beacon Hill	12508	Berryville	12068	Rochelle)	10804
Beantown...............	14859	Berwyn	13084	Bonny Lee Estates	12184
Bear Mountain	10911	Best	12018	Boonville	13309
Bearsville	12409	Bethany	14054	Boonville (Town).......	13309
Beaver Brook	12764	Bethany (Town)	14054	Borden...............	14801
Beaverdam Lake-Salisbury		Bethel (Town)	12720	Border City (Ontario	
Mills	12553	Bethel (Dutchess County)	12567	County)..............	14456
Beaver Dams............	14812	Bethel (Sullivan County)....	12720	Border City (Seneca	
Beaver Falls............	13305	Bethel Corners	13111	County)..............	14456
Beaverkill..............	12758	Bethel Grove	14850	Borodino	13152
Beaver Meadow	13832	Bethford	14219	Borough Hall (Part of New	
Beaver River	13367	Bethlehem (Town)	12054	York)	11424
Beckers Corners	12158	Bethlehem Center	12077	Boston	14025
Becks Grove (Part of		Bethlehem Heights	12161	Boston (Town)	14025
Rome)	13308	Bethpage	11714	Boston Corners	12546
Bedell	12430	Beukendaal	12302	Botanical (Part of New	
Bedford (Town)	10506	Beverly Inn Corners........	13315	York)	10458
Bedford (Kings County)....	11210	Bible School Park (Part of		Bouckville	13310
Bedford (Westchester		Johnson City)	13737	Boughton Hill	14564
County)................	10506	Bidwell (Part of Buffalo)	14222	Boulevard (Part of New	
Bedford Hills	10507	Big Brook	13486	York)	10459
Bedford Hills Correctional		Big Flats	14814	Boulevard Mall	14226
Facility	10507	Big Flats (Town)	14814	Boultons Beach (Part of	
Bedford-Stuyvesant (Part of		Big Flats Airport	14814	Sackets Harbor)........	13685
New York)	11233	Big Fresh Pond	11968	Bouquet	12936
Beecher Corners	12442	Big H Shopping Center	11743	Bournes Beach	14787
Beechertown............	13697	Big Indian	12410	Bovina (Town)	13740
Beech Hill (Part of Yonkers)	10710	Big Island	10924	Bovina Center	13740
Beechhurst (Part of New		Big Moose	13331	Bowen...............	14772
York)	11357	Big Tree	14219	Bowens Corners	13069
Beechmont (Part of New		Big Wolf Lake	12986	Bowerstown	13326
Rochelle)	10804	Billings	12510	Bowling Green (Part of New	
Beechmont Woods (Part of		Billington Bay	13030	York)	10004
New Rochelle)	10804	Billington Heights	14052	Bowmansville	14026
Beechwood (Part of		Biltmore Shores	11758	Boylston (Town)	13083
Rochester)	14609	Bingham Mills	12526	Boyntonville	12090
Beehive Crossing........	12090	Binghamton 13901-05		Boysen Bay	13039
Beekman	12533	For specific Binghamton Zip		Braddock Heights	14612
Beekman (Town)	12570	Codes call (607) 773-2142, or		Bradford	14815
Beekman Corners	13459	your local postmaster.		Bradford (Town)	14815
Beekmantown	12901	Binghamton (Town)	13902	Bradley	12754
Beekmantown (Town)	12901	Binghamton Plaza (Part of		Braeside	12123
Beixedon Estates.........	11971	Binghamton)	13901	Brainard.............	12024
Belair Road (Part of New		Bingley	13035	Brainards Corners	13315
York)	10305	Binnewater	12401	Brainardsville	12915
Belcher	12865	Birchwood Estates.........	12184	Braman Corners	12053
Belcoda................	14546	Birdsall	14709	Bramans Corners	12186
Belden	13787	Birdsall (Town)	14709	Bramanville	12092
Belfast	14711	Bishopville	14807	Brambler Ridge	14450
Belfast (Town)	14711	Black Brook	12912	Branchport	14418
Belfort	13327	Black Brook (Town)	12912	Brandon (Town)	12966
Belgium	13027	Black Creek	14714	Brandon Center	12966
Belle Isle	13209	Blackmans Corners........	12959	Brandreth	12847
Bellerose (Nassau County)	11426	Black River	13612	Brant	14027
Bellerose (Queens County)	11426	Black Rock (Part of Buffalo)	14207	Brant (Town)	14027
Bellerose Terrace..........	11426	Blackwatch Hills	14450	Brantingham	13312
Belle Terre	11777	Blakeley	14052	Brant Lake	12815
Belleview...............	14712	Blasdell	14219	Brasher (Town)	13613
Belleville	13611	Blauvelt	10913	Brasher Center	13613
Bellevue................	14225	Bleecker	12078	Brasher Falls	13613
Bellevue Gardens	12151	Bleecker (Town)	12078	Brasher Falls-Winthrop	13613
Bellmont (Town)	12917	Blenheim (Town)	12131	Brasie Corners	13642
Bellmont Center	12920	Bliss	14024	Breakabeen	12122
Bellmore...............	11710	Blockville	14710	Breesport	14816
Bellona (Station)	14527	Blodgett Mills	13738	Breezy Point (Part of New	
Bellona................	14415	Bloomfield (Part of New		York)	11697
Bellow Corners	14171	York)	10314	Brentwood	11717
Bellport	11713	Bloomingburg	12721	Brevoort (Part of New York)	11216
Bellvale	10912	Bloomingdale	12913	Brewerton	13029
Bellville	14717	Blooming Grove	10914	Brewster	10509
Belmont	14813	Blooming Grove (Town)....	10914	Brewster Heights	10509
Belvidere	14813	Bloomington............	12411	Brewster Hill..........	10509

	ZIP
Briarcliff Manor	10510
Briar Park	11793
Bridge (Part of Niagara Falls)	14305
Bridgehampton	11932
Bridgeport	13030
Bridgeville	12701
Bridgewater	13313
Bridgewater (Town)	13313
Brier Hill	13614
Brighton (Franklin County) (Town)	12970
Brighton (Kings County)	11235
Brighton (Monroe County) (Town)	14610
Brighton (Monroe County)	14610
Brighton (Otsego County)	13439
Brighton Beach (Part of New York)	11235
Brightside	13436
Brightwaters	11718
Brinckerhoff	12524
Brisben	13830
Briscoe	12783
Bristol	14469
Bristol (Town)	14469
Bristol Center	14424
Bristol Springs	14512
Broadacres	13905
Broadalbin	12025
Broadalbin (Town)	12025
Broad Channel (Part of New York)	11693
Broadway (Part of New York)	11106
Broadway Mall	11801
Brockport	14420
Brockville	14411
Brocton	14716
Brodhead	12494
Bronx	10401-75

For specific Bronx Zip Codes call
(718) 960-5009, or your local
postmaster.

COLLEGES & UNIVERSITIES

City University of New York-Lehman College	10468
Fordham University	10458
Manhattan College	10471
State University of New York Maritime College	10465

FINANCIAL INSTITUTIONS

North Side Savings Bank	10463
City and Suburban Federal Savings Bank	10467

HOSPITALS

Bronx Municipal Hospital Center	10461
Bronx-Lebanon Hospital Center	10457
Bronx Psychiatric Center	10461
Lincoln Medical and Mental Health Center	10451
Montefiore Medical Center	10467
North Central Bronx Hospital	10467
Our Lady of Mercy Medical Center	10466
St. Barnabas Hospital	10457
Veterans Affairs Medical Center	10468
Bronxville	10708
Bronxville Heights (Part of Yonkers)	10708
Brookdale	13668
Brookfield	13314
Brookfield (Town)	13314
Brookhaven	11719
Brookhaven (Town)	11719
Brooklyn	11201-56

For specific Brooklyn Zip Codes
call (212) 967-8585, or your local
postmaster.

COLLEGES & UNIVERSITIES

Brooklyn Law School	11201
City University of New York-Brooklyn College	11210
City University of New York-Medgar Evers College	11225
City University of New York-New York City Technical College	11201
Long Island University-Brooklyn Campus	11201
Polytechnic University	11201

	ZIP
Pratt Institute	11205
St. Francis College	11201
State University of New York Health Science Center at Brooklyn	11203

FINANCIAL INSTITUTIONS

Bay Ridge Federal Savings & Loan Association	11209
Brooklyn Federal Savings Bank	11201
Crossland Federal Savings Bank	11201
Dime Savings Bank of Williamsburgh	11211
East New York Savings Bank	11207
Flatbush Federal Savings & Loan Association	11210
The Green Point Savings Bank	11222
Hamilton Federal Savings, F.A.	11209
The Home Savings Bank of America, F.S.B.	11215
Independence Savings Bank	11201

HOSPITALS

Brookdale Hospital Medical Center	11212
Brooklyn Hospital Center	11201
Catholic Medical Center of Brooklyn and Queens	11214
Coney Island Hospital	11235
Interfaith Medical Center	11238
Kings County Hospital Center	11203
Kingsbrook Jewish Medical Center	11203
Long Island College Hospital	11201
Lutheran Medical Center	11220
Maimonides Medical Center	11219
Methodist Hospital	11215
University Hospital of Brooklyn-State University of N.Y. Health Sciences Center at Brooklyn	11203
Veterans Affairs Medical Center	11209
Victory Memorial Hospital	11228
Woodhull Medical and Mental Health Center	11206
Wyckoff Heights Medical Center	11237

MILITARY INSTALLATIONS

Coast Guard Supply Center, Brooklyn	11232
Fort Hamilton and New York Area Command	11252
Supervisor of Shipbuilding, Conversion and Repair, Brooklyn	11251
Brooks Avenue Station (Part of Rochester)	14624
Brooksburg	12496
Brooks Grove	14510
Brooktondale	14817
Brookview	12026
Brookville	11545
Brookville Park	11751
Broome (Town)	12122
Broome Center	12076
Broughton Park	13760
Browns Bridge	13625
Browns Hollow	13317
Brownsville (Kings County)	11212
Brownsville (Ontario County)	14564
Brownville	13615
Brownville (Town)	13615
Bruceville	12440
Brunswick (Town)	12180
Brushton	12916
Brutus (Town)	13166
Bruynswick	12589
Bryant (Part of New York)	10036
Bryn Mawr Park (Part of Yonkers)	10701
Buchanan	10511
Buckingham Estates	10989
Buckleyville	12037
Bucks Bridge	13660
Buckton	13697
Buel	13317
Buellville	13104
Buena Vista	14823
Buffalo	14201-40

	ZIP
	14263
	14273

For specific Buffalo Zip Codes call
(716) 846-2538, or your local
postmaster.

Buffalo Creek (Part of Buffalo)	14224
Buffalo Junction (Part of Buffalo)	14201
Buffalo Lake (Part of Buffalo)	14222
Bull Hill	13324
Bulls Head (Monroe County)	14611
Bulls Head (Richmond County)	10314
Bullville	10915
Bundys	13126
Burden Lake	12018
Burdett	14818
Burgoyne	12871
Burke	12917
Burke (Town)	12917
Burke Center	12917
Burlingham	12722
Burlington	13315
Burlington (Town)	13315
Burlington Flats	13315
Burnhams (Part of Cassadaga)	14718
Burns	14807
Burns (Town)	14807
Burnside	12543
Burns-Whitney Estates	12110
Burnt Hills	12027
Burnwood	13756
Burrs Mills	13601
Burt	14028
Burtonsville	12066
Bushes Landing	13367
Bushnell Basin	14534
Bushnellsville	12480
Bush Terminal (Part of New York)	11232
Bushville (Genesee County)	14020
Bushville (Sullivan County)	12701
Bushwick (Part of New York)	11221
Buskirk	12028
Busti	14701
Busti (Town)	14701
Butler (Town)	14590
Butler Center	14590
Butlerville	10519
Butterfield (Part of Utica)	13503
Butternut Grove	12776
Butternuts (Town)	13776
Byersville	14517
Byrden	12526
Byron	14422
Byron (Town)	14422
Cabinhill	13752
Cadiz	14737
Cadosia	13783
Cadyville	12918
Cahoonzie	12780
Cairo	12413
Cairo (Town)	12413
Calcium	13616
Calcutta	12064
Caldor Shopping Center (Part of Port Chester)	10573
Caledonia	14423
Caledonia (Town)	14423
Calico Colony	12065
Callicoon	12723
Callicoon (Town)	12791
Callicoon Center	12724
Calverton	11933
Cambria (Town)	14094
Cambria Heights (Part of New York)	11411
Cambridge	12816
Cambridge (Town)	12816
Camden	13316
Camden (Town)	13316
Cameron	14819
Cameron (Town)	14819
Cameron Mills	14820
Camillus	13031
Camillus (Town)	13031
Camillus Plaza	13031
Campbell	14821
Campbell (Town)	14821
Campbell Hall	10916
Camp Hemlock	12721
Camp Hill (Part of Pomona)	10970
Camps Mills	13601
Campville	13760
Camroden	13440
Canaan	12029
Canaan (Town)	12029
Canaan Center	12029

	ZIP		ZIP		ZIP
Canada Lake	12032	Cattaraugus Indian		Chazy (Town)	12921
Canadice	14560	Reservation (Chautauqua		Chazy Lake	12935
Canadice (Town)	14560	County) (Town)	14081	Chazy Landing	12921
Canajoharie	13317	Cattaraugus Indian		Chedwel	14712
Canajoharie (Town)	13317	Reservation (Erie County)		Cheektowaga (Town)	14225
Canal Street (Part of New		(Town)	14081	Cheektowaga	14225
York)	10013	Cattown	13337	Cheektowaga Northwest	14225
Canandaigua	14424-25	Caughdenoy	13036	Cheektowaga Southwest	14227
For specific Canandaigua Zip		Cayuga	13034	Chelsea (Dutchess County)	12512
Codes call (716) 394-1500, or		Cayuga Correctional Facility	13118	Chelsea (Richmond County)	10314
your local postmaster.		Cayuga Heights	14850	Chemung	14825
Canarsie (Part of New York)	11236	Cayuta	14824	Chemung (Town)	14825
Canaseraga	14822	Cayuta (Town)	14824	Chemung Center	14825
Canastota	13032	Cayutaville	14805	Chenango (Town)	13745
Canawaugus	14423	Caywood	14860	Chenango Bridge	13745
Candor	13743	Cazenovia	13035	Chenango Forks	13746
Candor (Town)	13743	Cazenovia (Town)	13035	Chenango Lake	13815
Caneadea	14717	Cecil Park (Part of Yonkers)	10707	Cheneys Point	14710
Caneadea (Town)	14717	Cedar Cliff	12542	Cheningo	13158
Canisteo	14823	Cedarcrest	14487	Cherokee (Part of New	
Canisteo (Town)	14823	Cedar Flats	10980	York)	10028
Cannon Corners	12959	Cedar Hill	12158	Cherry Creek	14723
Canoe Place	11946	Cedarhurst	11516	Cherry Creek (Town)	14723
Canoga	13148	Cedar Knolls (Part of		Cherry Grove	11782
Canterbury Hill (Part of		Yonkers)	10708	Cherry Lane (Part of	
Rome)	13440	Cedarvale	13215	Fredonia)	14063
Canterbury Woods	13116	Cedarville	13357	Cherry Plain	12040
Canton	13617	Celoron	14720	Cherrytown	12446
Canton (Town)	13617	Cementon	12415	Cherry Valley	13320
Cape Vincent	13618	Centenary	10956	Cherry Valley (Town)	13320
Cape Vincent (Town)	13618	Center Avenue (Part of East		Cherry Valley Junction	12043
Capitol (Part of Albany)	12224	Rockaway)	11518	Cheshire	14424
Capitol Annex (Part of		Center Brunswick	12180	Chester	10918
Albany)	12225	Centereach	11720	Chester (Town)	10918
Capitol Hills	10950	Center Falls	12834	Chester (Town)	12860
Cardiff	13084	Centerfield	14424	Chesterfield (Town)	12944
Carle Place	11514	Center Lisle	13797	Chester Heights (Part of	
Carle Terrace	12449	Center Moriches	11934	Yonkers)	10701
Carlisle	12031	Centerport (Cayuga County)	13166	Chester Hill Park (Part of	
Carlisle (Town)	12031	Centerport (Suffolk County)	11721	Mount Vernon)	10550
Carlisle Center	12035	Centerville	14029	Chestertown	12817
Carlisle Gardens	14094	Centerville (Town)	14029	Chestnut Hill	13088
Carlton	14411	Centerville	13756	Chestnut Ridge (Niagara	
Carlton (Town)	14411	Center White Creek	12057	County)	14094
Carman	12303	Central (Part of New York)	11435	Chestnut Ridge (Rockland	
Carmel	10512	Central Bridge	12035	County)	10952
Carmel (Town)	10512	Centralia	14782	Cheviot	12526
Carmel Park Estates	10512	Central Islip	11722	Chichester	12416
Carnegie	14075	Central Nyack	10960	Childs	14411
Caroga (Town)	12032	Central Park (Part of		Childwold	12922
Caroga Lake	12032	Buffalo)	14215	Chili (Town)	14428
Caroline	14817	Central Park Shopping		Chili Center	14624
Caroline (Town)	14817	Center (Part of Buffalo)	14214	Chilson	12883
Caroline Center	14817	Central Square	13036	Chinatown (Part of New	
Carousel Center (Part of		Central Valley	10917	York)	10013
Syracuse)	13290	Centre Island	11771	Chipmonk	14706
Carroll (Town)	14738	Centre Village	13787	Chippewa Bay	13623
Carroll Gardens (Part of		Centuck (Part of Yonkers)	10710	Chittenango	13037
New York)	11231	Ceres	14721	Chittenango Falls	13035
Carrollton	14748	Chadwicks	13319	Choconut Center	13905
Carrollton (Town)	14753	Chaffee	14030	Church Street (Part of New	
Carson	14823	Chamberlain Corners	13660	York)	10007
Carthage	13619	Chambers	14812	Churchtown	12521
Cascade	13118	Champion	13619	Churchville (Monroe County)	14428
Case	13084	Champion (Town)	13619	Churchville (Oneida County)	13478
Casowasco	13118	Champion Huddle	13619	Churubusco	12923
Cassadaga	14718	Champlain	12919	Cicero	13039
Cassville	13318	Champlain (Town)	12919	Cicero (Town)	13039
Castile	14427	Champlain Park	12901	Cicero Center	13041
Castile (Town)	14427	Chapel Hill Estates	10598	Cincinnatus	13040
Castile Center	14427	Chapin	14424	Cincinnatus (Town)	13040
Castle (Part of New		Chappaqua	10514	Circleville	10919
Rochelle)	10801	Charleston (Montgomery		City Island (Part of New	
Castle Creek	13744	County) (Town)	12066	York)	10464
Castle Hill (Part of New		Charleston (Richmond		Clairemont Farms	13088
York)	10462	County)	10301	Clare (Town)	13684
Castle Point	12511	Charleston Four Corners	12166	Claremont Park (Part of	
Castleton Corners (Part of		Charlotte (Chautauqua		New York)	10457
New York)	10314	County) (Town)	14782	Clarence	14031
Castleton on Hudson	12033	Charlotte (Monroe County)	14612	Clarence (Town)	14031
Castorland	13620	Charlotte Center	14782	Clarence Center	14032
Catatonk	13827	Charlotteville	12036	Clarendon	14429
Catharine	14869	Charlton	12019	Clarendon (Town)	14429
Catharine (Town)	14869	Charlton (Town)	12019	Clark Heights	12569
Cathedral (Part of New		Charwood Manor	12065	Clark Mills	13321
York)	10025	Chase Lake	13343	Clarksburg	14057
Catlin (Town)	14812	Chase Mills	13621	Clarks Corners	14747
Cato	13033	Chaseville	12116	Clarks Mills	12834
Cato (Town)	13033	Chasm Falls	12953	Clarkson	14430
Caton	14830	Chateaugay	12920	Clarkson (Town)	14430
Caton (Town)	14830	Chateaugay (Town)	12920	Clarkstown (Town)	10956
Catskill	12414	Chatham	12037	Clarksville (Albany County)	12041
Catskill (Town)	12414	Chatham (Town)	12037	Clarksville (Allegany County)	
Cattaraugus	14719	Chatham Center	12184	(Town)	14786
Cattaraugus Indian		Chaumont	13622	Claryville	12725
Reservation (Cattaraugus		Chauncey (Part of Dobbs		Clason Point (Part of New	
County) (Town)	14081	Ferry)	10502	York)	10473
Cattaraugus Indian		Chautauqua	14722	Classon (Part of New York)	11238
Reservation (Cattaraugus		Chautauqua (Town)	14722	Claverack	12513
County)	14081	Chautauqua Mall (Part of		Claverack (Town)	12513
		Lakewood)	14750	Claverack-Red Mills	12513
		Chazy	12921	Clay	13041

	ZIP
Clay (Town)	13041
Clayburg	12981
Clayton	13624
Clayton (Town)	13624
Clayville	13322
Clear Creek	14726
Clearfield	14221
Clemons	12819
Clermont	12526
Clermont (Town)	12526
Cleveland	13042
Cleveland Hill	14225
Cleverdale	12820
Cliff Haven	12901
Clifford	13069
Cliffside	12116
Clifton (Monroe County)	14428
Clifton (Richmond County)	10304
Clifton (St. Lawrence County) (Town)	13666
Clifton Gardens	12065
Clifton Heights	14085
Clifton Knolls	12065
Clifton Park	12065
Clifton Park (Town)	12065
Clifton Park Center	12065
Clifton Springs	14432
Climax	12042
Clinton (Clinton County) (Town)	12923
Clinton (Dutchess County) (Town)	12514
Clinton (Oneida County)	13323
Clinton Corners	12514
Clintondale	12515
Clinton Heights	12144
Clinton Hollow	12578
Clinton Park	12144
Clintonville	12924
Clockville	13043
Clough Corners	13862
Clove	12043
Clover Bank	14075
Cloverville	12430
Clyde	14433
Clymer	14724
Clymer (Town)	14724
Cobb	11976
Cobble Hill (Part of New York)	11201
Cobleskill	12043
Cobleskill (Town)	12043
Cochecton	12726
Cochecton (Town)	12726
Cochecton Center	12727
Coeymans	12045
Coeymans (Town)	12045
Coeymans Hollow	12046
Coffins Mills	13670
Cohocton	14826
Cohocton (Town)	14826
Cohoes	12047
Cokertown	12571
Colchester	13856
Colchester (Town)	13755
Cold Brook (Herkimer County)	13324
Coldbrook (Schenectady County)	12303
Colden	14033
Colden (Town)	14033
Coldenham	12549
Coldspring (Cattaraugus County) (Town)	14783
Cold Spring (Putnam County)	10516
Cold Spring Harbor	11724
Cold Springs (Onondaga County)	13027
Cold Springs (Steuben County)	14810
Cold Spring Terrace	11743
Coldwater	14624
Colemans Mills	13492
Colesville (Town)	13787
Colgate (Part of Hamilton)	13346
Collabar	12549
Collamer	13057
College (Part of New York)	10030
College Park	12571
College Point (Part of New York)	11356
Colliersville	13747
Collingwood	13084
Collingwood Estates	14174
Collins	14034
Collins (Town)	14034
Collins Center	14035
Collins Correctional Facility	14079
Collins Landing	13607
Collinsville	13433
Colonial Acres	12077

	ZIP
Colonial Green	12188
Colonial Heights (Dutchess County)	12603
Colonial Heights (Westchester County)	10708
Colonial Park (Part of New York)	10039
Colonial Springs	11798
Colonial Village (Part of Lewiston)	14092
Colonie	12212
Colonie (Town)	12212
Colonie Center	12205
Colosse	13131
Colton	13625
Colton (Town)	13625
Columbia (Town)	13357
Columbia Center	13357
Columbia University (Part of New York)	10025
Columbia University Extension	10926
Columbiaville	12050
Columbus	13411
Columbus (Town)	13411
Columbus Circle (Part of New York)	10023
Colvin Elmwood (Part of Syracuse)	13205
Commack	11725
Commack Corners Shopping Center	11725
Comstock	12821
Comstock Tract	13027
Concord (Erie County) (Town)	14141
Concord (Richmond County)	10304
Conesus	14435
Conesus (Town)	14435
Conesville	12076
Conesville (Town)	12076
Conewango	14726
Conewango (Town)	14726
Conewango Valley	14726
Coney Island (Part of New York)	11224
Conger Corners	13480
Congers	10920
Conifer	12986
Conklin	13748
Conklin (Town)	13748
Conklin Forks	13903
Conklingville	12835
Connelly	12417
Connelly Park	14710
Conquest	13140
Conquest (Town)	13140
Constable	12926
Constable (Town)	12926
Constableville	13325
Constantia	13044
Constantia (Town)	13044
Constantia Center	13028
Continental Village	10566
Cook Corners	13625
Cooksburg	12469
Cooks Falls	12776
Cookville	14036
Coolidge Beach	14172
Coonrod (Part of Rome)	13440
Co-op City (Part of New York)	10475
Cooper (Part of New York)	10003
Coopers Plains	14827
Cooperstown	13326
Cooperstown Junction	12116
Coopersville (Clinton County)	12919
Coopersville (Livingston County)	14517
Copake	12516
Copake (Town)	12516
Copake Falls	12517
Copake Lake	12521
Copenhagen	13626
Copiague	11726
Coram	11727
Coram Hill	11763
Corbett	13755
Corbettsville	13749
Coreys	12986
Corfu	14036
Corinth	12822
Corinth (Town)	12822
Cornell (Part of New York)	10473
Corners (Part of Cayuga Heights)	14850
Corning	14830
Corning (Town)	14830
Corning Manor	14830
Cornwall	12518

	ZIP
Cornwall (Town)	12518
Cornwall on Hudson	12520
Cornwallville	12418
Corona-A (Part of New York)	11368
Corona-Elmhurst (Part of New York)	11373
Cortland	13045
Cortlandt (Town)	10520
Cortlandville (Town)	13045
Cortland West	13045
Cosmos Heights	13045
Cossayuna	12823
Coss Corners	14810
Cottage	14138
Cottage City	14424
Cottage Park	14750
Cottam Hill	12590
Cottekill	12419
Cottonwood Point	14435
Council Meadows	12027
Country Knolls	12151
Country Knolls (census designated place)	12019
Country Knolls South	12065
Country Life Press (Part of Garden City)	11530
Country Ridge Estates	10573
County Line	14098
Cove Neck	11771
Coventry	13778
Coventry (Town)	13778
Coventryville	13733
Covert	14847
Covert (Town)	14847
Coveytown Corners	12917
Covington	14525
Covington (Town)	14525
Cowlesville	14037
Coxsackie	12051
Coxsackie (Town)	12051
Coxsackie Correctional Facility	12192
Crafts	10512
Cragsmoor	12420
Craigville	10918
Crains Mills	13158
Cranberry Creek	12117
Cranberry Lake	12927
Crandall Corners	12154
Cranes Corners	13340
Cranesville	12010
Cranford (Part of New York)	10470
Crary Mills	13617
Craryville	12521
Craterclub	12936
Crawford (Town)	12566
Creek Locks	12411
Crescent	12188
Crescent Beach (Monroe County)	14612
Crescent Beach (Richmond County)	10301
Crescent Estates	12065
Crescent Estates North	12065
Crestview Heights	13760
Crestwood (Part of Yonkers)	10710
Crestwood (Part of Tuckahoe)	10707
Crestwood Gardens (Part of Yonkers)	10710
Crittenden	14038
Crocketts	13156
Crofts Corners	10579
Croghan	13327
Croghan (Town)	13327
Crompond	10517
Cropseyville	12052
Cross Country Center (Part of Yonkers)	10704
Crossgates Mall	12203
Cross River	10518
Cross Roads Estates	10598
Croton	14864
Crotona Park (Part of New York)	10460
Croton Falls	10519
Croton Heights	10598
Croton-on-Hudson	10520
Crotonville	10562
Crown Heights	12603
Crown Point	12928
Crown Point (Town)	12928
Crown Point Center	12928
Crown Village	11762
Crugers	10521
Crum Creek	13452
Crystal Brook	11766
Crystal Dale	13367
Crystal Lake (Albany County)	12147

	ZIP		ZIP		ZIP
Crystal Lake (Cattaraugus County)	14060	Devon	11930	Earlville (Franklin County)	12920
Cuba	14727	Dewey (Part of Rochester)	14613	Earlville (Madison County)	13332
Cuba (Town)	14727	Dewey Bridge	12827	East (Part of Yonkers)	10704
Cuddebackville	12729	De Witt	13214	East Amherst	14051
Cullen	13439	De Witt (Town)	13214	East Arcade	14009
Cumberland Head	12901	Dewittville	14728	East Atlantic Beach	11509
Cummingsville	14437	Dexter	13634	East Aurora	14052
Curriers	14009	Dexterville	13069	East Avon	14414
Curry	12765	Diamond Point	12824	East Bay	14590
Currytown	12166	Diana (Town)	13648	East Beekmantown	12901
Curtis	14821	Dibbletown	13308	East Bend Park	12603
Cutchogue	11935	Dickersonville	14131	East Berkshire	13736
Cutchoque	11935	Dickinson (Broome County)		East Berne	12059
Cutting	14724	(Town)	13905	East Bethany	14054
Cuyler	13050	Dickinson (Franklin County)		East Bloomfield	14443
Cuyler (Town)	13050	(Town)	12930	East Bloomfield (Town)	14443
Cuyler Hill	13050	Dickinson Center	12930	East Branch	13756
Cuylerville	14481	Dick Urban	14043	East Brentwood	11717
Cypress Hills (Part of New		Dimmick Corners	12831	East Buffalo	14225
York)	11208	Dineharts	14810	East Buskirk	12028
Dadville	13367	Divine Corners	12759	East Campbell	14870
Dahlia	12758	Dix (Town)	14891	East Cayuga Heights	14850
Dairyland	12435	Dix Hills	11746	East Chatham	12060
Dale	14039	Dobbs Ferry	10522	Eastchester (Town)	10709
Dalton	14836	Dolgeville	13329	East Chester (Orange	
Damascus	13865	Dongan Hills (Part of New		County)	10918
Danby	14850	York)	10304	Eastchester (Westchester	
Danby (Town)	14850	Doraville	13813	County)	10709
Dannemora	12929	Doris Park	13044	East Cobleskill	12157
Dannemora (Town)	12929	Dorloo	12043	East Coldenham	12550
Dansville (Livingston		Dormansville	12055	East Concord	14055
County)	14437	Dorwood Park	14131	East Corning	14830
Dansville (Steuben County)		Douglass	12944	East De Kalb	13630
(Town)	14807	Douglaston (Part of New		East Durham	12423
Danube (Town)	13365	York)	11363	East Eden	14057
Darien	14040	Dover (Town)	12522	East Elmhurst (Part of New	
Darien (Town)	14040	Dover Furnace	12522	York)	11369
Darien Center	14040	Dover Plains	12522	Eastern Hills Mall	14221
Darrowsville	12817	Downstate Correctional		Eastern New York	
Davenport	13750	Facility	12524	Correctional Facility	12458
Davenport (Town)	13750	Downsville	13755	East Farmingdale	11735
Davenport Center	13751	Downtown (Part of Elmira)	14901	East Fishkill (Town)	12533
Davis Park	11772	Downtown (Part of		East Floyd	13354
Daws	14020	Rochester)	14603	East Frankfort	13340
Day (Town)	12835	Downtown (Part of		East Freetown	13055
Days Rock	13407	Syracuse)	13201	East Gaines	14411
Dayton	14041	Doyle	14206	East Galway	12850
Dayton (Town)	14041	Dreiser Loop (Part of New		East Genoa	13092
Daytonville	13480	York)	10475	East Glenville	12302
Deansboro	13328	Dresden (Washington		East Greenbush	12061
Debruce	12758	County) (Town)	12887	East Greenbush (Town)	12061
Decatur	12197	Dresden (Yates County)	14441	East Greenlawn	11731
Decatur (Town)	12197	Dresden Station	12887	East Greenwich	12826
Deck	13407	Dresserville	13118	East Half Hollow Hills	11746
Deckertown	12758	Drews Corner	13694	East Hampton	11937
Deerfield (Town)	13503	Dryden	13053	East Hampton (Town)	11937
Deerland	12847	Dryden (Town)	13053	East Hampton North	11937
Deerpark (Orange County)		Duane (Town)	12953	East Hartford	12832
(Town)	12729	Duane Center	12968	East Hebron	12865
Deer Park (Suffolk County)	11729	Duanesburg	12056	East Herkimer	13350
Deer River	13627	Duanesburg (Town)	12056	East Hill	14850
Deferiet	13628	Dublin	14433	East Hills	11576
Defreestville	12144	Dugway	13131	East Hillsdale	12529
Degrasse	13684	Dunbar	13865	East Homer	13056
De Kalb	13630	Dundee	14837	East Hoosick	12090
De Kalb (Town)	13630	Dunewood	11706	East Hounsfield	13610
De Kalb Junction	13630	Dunham Hollow	12018	East Huntington	11743
De Lancey	13752	Dunham Manor	13492	East Irvington	10533
Delanson	12053	Dunkirk	14048	East Islip	11730
Delaware (Albany County)	12209	Dunkirk (Town)	14048	East Ithaca	14850
Delaware (Sullivan County)		Dunnsville	12009	East Jewett	12424
(Town)	12723	Dunraven	12455	East Kingston	12401
Delevan	14042	Dunsbach Ferry	12047	East Koy	14536
Delhi	13753	Dunwoodie (Part of		East Lake Ronkonkoma	11779
Delhi (Town)	13753	Yonkers)	10701	East Lansing	14852
Delmar	12054	Dunwoody Heights (Part of		East Leon	14719
Delphi Falls	13051	Yonkers)	10701	East Line	12020
Delray	14224	Durham	12422	East Marion	11939
Dempster Beach	13126	Durham (Town)	12422	East Martinsburg	13367
Demster	13126	Durhamville	13054	East Masonville	13839
Denmark	13631	Durkeetown	12828	East Massapequa	11758
Denmark (Town)	13631	Durlandville	10924	East Mattituck	11952
Dennies Hollow	12117	Dutchess Junction	12508	East McDonough	13830
Denning	12725	Dutch Flats	14167	East Meadow	11554
Denning (Town)	12725	Dutch Meadows	12065	East Meredith	13757
Dennison Corners	13407	Dwaar Kill	12566	East Middletown	10940
Denton	10958	Dyke	14830	Eastmor	12180
Denton Hills	11721	Dykemans	10509	East Moriches	11940
Denver	12421	Dyker Heights (Part of New		East Nassau	12062
Depauville	13632	York)	11228	East Neck	11743
Depew	14043	Eagle	14009	East New York (Part of New	
De Peyster	13633	Eagle (Town)	14009	York)	11207
De Peyster (Town)	13633	Eagle Bay	13331	East Nichols	13812
Deposit	13754	Eagle Bridge	12057	East Northport	11731
Deposit (Town)	13754	Eagle Center	14024	East Norwich	11732
Derby	14047	Eagle Harbor	14442	East Olean (Part of Olean)	14760
Dering Harbor	11964	Eagle Lake	12883	Easton (Town)	12834
De Ruyter	13052	Eagle Mills	12180	East Otto	14729
DeRuyter (Town)	13052	Eagle Point	14454	East Otto (Town)	14729
Deuels Corners	14127	Eagle Village	13104	East Palermo	13036
Devereux	14731	Eagleville	12873	East Palmyra	14444
		Earlton	12058	East Park	12538

	ZIP
East Part	13697
East Patchogue	11772
East Pembroke	14056
East Penfield	14450
East Pharsalia	13758
East Pitcairn	13648
East Pittstown	12028
East Poestenkill	12018
Eastport	11941
East Quogue	11942
East Quoque	11942
East Randolph	14730
East Ripley	14775
East River	13056
East Rochester	14445
East Rochester (Town)	14445
East Rockaway	11518
East Rodman	13601
East Salamanca (Part of Salamanca)	14779
East Schodack	12063
East Schuyler	13340
East Seneca	14224
East Setauket	11733
East Shelby	14103
East Shoreham	11786
East Side (Broome County)	13904
Eastside (Suffolk County)	11937
East Sidney	13775
East Springfield	13333
East Steamburg	14886
East Stone Arabia	13428
East Syracuse	13057
East Taghkanic	12502
East Varick	14541
East Vestal	13902
East Victor	14564
East View	10595
East Watertown	13601
East Wawarsing	12489
East White Plains (Part of Harrison)	10604
East Williamson	14449
East Williston	11596
East Windham	12439
East Windsor	13865
East Winfield	13491
Eastwood (Part of Syracuse)	13206
East Worcester	12064
Eaton	13334
Eaton (Town)	13334
Eatons Neck	11768
Eavesport	12490
Ebenezer	14224
Ebenezer Junction	14224
Echota (Part of Niagara Falls)	14302
Eddy	13617
Eddyville (Cattaraugus County)	14755
Eddyville (Ulster County)	12401
Eden	14057
Eden (Town)	14057
Edenville	10990
Edgemere (Part of New York)	11691
Edgemont	10583
Edgewater Beach	13308
Edgewater Park	13669
Edgewood (Greene County)	12450
Edgewood (Suffolk County)	11717
Edgewood Garden	13164
Edinburg	12134
Edinburg (Town)	12134
Edmeston	13335
Edmeston (Town)	13335
Edson	13865
Edwards	13635
Edwards (Town)	13635
Edwards Hill	12811
Edwards Park	12029
Edwardsville	13646
Egbertville (Part of New York)	10306
Eggertsville	14226
Egypt	14450
Einstein (Part of New York)	10475
Elayne Meadows	12188
Elba	14058
Elba (Town)	14058
Elbridge	13060
Elbridge (Town)	13060
Eldred	12732
Elizabethtown	12932
Elizabethtown (Town)	12932
Elizaville	12523
Elka Park	12427
Elk Brook	12776
Elk Creek	12155
Elkdale	14779
Ellenburg	12933

	ZIP
Ellenburg (Town)	12933
Ellenburg Center	12934
Ellenburg Depot	12935
Ellenville	12428
Ellery (Town)	14756
Ellery Center	14712
Ellicott (Chautauqua County) (Town)	14733
Ellicott (Erie County)	14127
Ellicott (Part of Buffalo)	14203
Ellicottville	14731
Ellicottville (Town)	14731
Ellington	14732
Ellington (Town)	14732
Ellisburg	13636
Ellisburg (Town)	13636
Ellis Hollow	14850
Ellistown	14892
Elma	14059
Elma (Town)	14059
Elmdale	13642
Elm Grove	13808
Elmhurst	14701
Elmhurst-A (Part of New York)	11373
Elmira	14901-25
For specific Elmira Zip Codes call (607) 737-5100, or your local postmaster.	
Elmira (Town)	14902
Elmira Heights	14903
Elmira Heights North	14903
Elmont	11003
Elm Park (Part of New York)	10303
Elmsford	10523
Elm Valley	14895
Elnora	12065
Elsmere	12054
Eltingville (Part of New York)	10312
Elton	14042
Elton Station	14042
Elwood	11731
Elwood Farms	11731
Embogcht	12414
Emerson	13140
Emerson Hill (Richmond County)	10304
Emerson Hill (Richmond County)	10301
Emeryville	13642
Eminence	12175
Emmons	13820
Empeyville	13316
Empire State (Part of New York)	10001
Empire State Plaza (Part of Albany)	12220
Endicott	13760-61
	13763
For specific Endicott Zip Codes call (607) 748-8207, or your local postmaster.	
	13762
For specific Endicott Zip Codes call (607) 748-2498, or your local postmaster.	
Endwell	13760
	13762
For specific Endwell Zip Codes call (607) 748-2498, or your local postmaster.	
Enfield	14850
Enfield (Town)	14850
Ensenore	13118
Ephratah	13339
Ephratah (Town)	13339
Erieville	13061
Erin	14838
Erin (Town)	14838
Erwin (Town)	14870
Erwins	14870
Escarpment	14092
Esopus	12429
Esopus (Town)	12429
Esperance	12066
Esperance (Town)	12066
Esplanade (Part of New York)	10469
Essex	12936
Essex (Town)	12936
Etna	13062
Euclid	13041
Evans (Town)	14006
Evans Center	14006
Evans Mills	13637
Exeter (Town)	13315
Exeter Center	13315
Fabius	13063
Fabius (Town)	13063
Factory Village	12020
Factoryville	12928

	ZIP
Fairdale	13074
Fairfield	13336
Fairfield (Town)	13336
Fairfield Farms	13066
Fairfield Gardens	12205
Fair Harbor	11706
Fair Haven	13064
Fairlawn Estates	12110
Fairmount	13219
Fairmount (census designated place)	13031
Fairmount Fair Mall	13219
Fair Oaks	10940
Fairport	14450
Fairview (Allegany County)	14060
Fairview (Dutchess County)	12601
Fairview (Westchester County)	10603
Fairview (Wyoming County)	14427
Falconer	14733
Falcon Manor	14304
Falconwood	14072
Falls (Part of Niagara Falls)	14303
Fallsburg	12733
Fallsburg (Town)	12733
Fancher	14452
Fargo	14036
Farleys Point	13160
Farmers Mills	10512
Farmersville (Town)	14060
Farmersville Center	14737
Farmersville Station	14060
Farmingdale	11735
Farmington	14425
Farmington (Town)	14425
Farmingville	11738
Farnham	14061
Farragut (Part of New York)	11203
Far Rockaway	11601-97
For specific Far Rockaway Zip Codes call (718) 327-7700, or your local postmaster.	
HOSPITALS	
Peninsula Hospital Center	11691
St. John's Episcopal Hospital-South Shore	11691
MILITARY INSTALLATIONS	
Fort Tilden	11695
Fawn Ridge	13027
Fayette	13065
Fayette (Town)	13065
Fayetteville	13066
Federal (Part of Rochester)	14614
Federal Correctional Institution	10963
Federal Reserve (Part of New York)	10045
Felts Mills	13638
Fenimore	12801
Fenner (Town)	13035
Fenton (Town)	13833
Ferenbaugh	14830
Fergusons Corners	14456
Fergusonville	12155
Ferndale	12734
Fernwood (Oswego County)	13142
Fernwood (Sullivan County)	12760
Ferry Village	14072
Feura Bush	12067
Fieldston (Part of New York)	10463
Filer Corners	13808
Fillmore	14735
Finchville	10940
Findley Lake	14736
Fine	13639
Fine (Town)	13639
Fineview	13640
Finger Lakes Manor (Part of Canandaigua)	14424
Fink Basin	13365
Finnegans Corners	10924
Fire Island Pines	11782
Firthcliffe Heights	12584
Fish Creek (Lewis County)	13325
Fish Creek (Ulster County)	12477
Fish Creek Landing	13308
Fishers	14453
Fishers Island	06390
Fishers Landing	13641
Fisherville	14903
Fish House	12025
Fishkill	12524
Fishkill (Town)	12524
Fishkill Plains	12590
Fishs Eddy	13774
Five Corners (Madison County)	13421

	ZIP
Five Corners (Oneida County)	13480
Fivemile Point	13795
Five Points	14456
Five Town Plaza	11598
Flackville	13669
Flanders	11901
Flatbrook	12029
Flatbush (Kings County)	11226
Flatbush (Ulster County)	12477
Flat Creek (Montgomery County)	13317
Flat Creek (Schoharie County)	12076
Fleetwood (Part of Mount Vernon)	10552
Fleischmanns	12430
Fleming	13021
Fleming (Town)	13021
Flemingville	13827
Flint	14561
Floral Park	11001-05
For specific Floral Park Zip Codes call (516) 354-3297, or your local postmaster.	
Florence	13316
Florence (Town)	13316
Florida (Montgomery County) (Town)	12010
Florida (Orange County)	10921
Floridaville	13033
Flowerfield Estates (Part of Lake Grove)	11755
Flower Hill	11050
Flowers	13865
Floyd	13440
Floyd (Town)	13440
Flushing	**11301-88**
For specific Flushing Zip Codes call (718) 670-4743, or your local postmaster.	

COLLEGES & UNIVERSITIES

City University of New York-Queens College	11367

FINANCIAL INSTITUTIONS

Asia Bank, N.A.	11354
Flushing Savings Bank	11354
Queens County Savings Bank	11354

HOSPITALS

Booth Memorial Medical Center	11355
Elmhurst Hospital Center	11373
Flushing Hospital Medical Center	11355
LaGuardia Hospital	11375

HOTELS/MOTELS

Best Western Midway Hotel	11368
Metropole Hotel	11368
Pan American Motor Inn	11373

MILITARY INSTALLATIONS

Fort Totten	11359
Fluvanna	14701
Fly Creek	13337
Flying Point	11976
Fly Summit	12834
Fonda	12068
Foots Corners	14435
Fordham (Part of New York)	10458
Forest	12935
Forestburgh	12777
Forestburgh (Town)	12701
Forest Glen (Part of Hamburg)	14075
Forest Hills (Part of New York)	11375
Forest Home	14850
Forest Knolls (Part of New Rochelle)	10804
Forest Lawn	14580
Forest Park (Chautauqua County)	14787
Forest Park (Dutchess County)	12572
Forestport	13338
Forestport (Town)	13338
Forestport Station	13338
Forestville	14062
Forge Hollow	13328
Forks	14225
Forsonville	10524
Forsyth	14775
Fort Ann	12827
Fort Ann (Town)	12827
Fort Covington	12937

	ZIP
Fort Covington (Town)	12937
Fort Covington Center	12937
Fort Drum	13602
Fort Edward	12828
Fort Edward (Town)	12828
Fort George (Part of New York)	10040
Fort Herkimer	13407
Fort Hunter (Albany County)	12303
Fort Hunter (Montgomery County)	12069
Fort Jackson	12965
Fort Johnson	12070
Fort Miller	12828
Fort Montgomery	10922
Fort Niagara Beach	14174
Fort Plain	13339
Fort Salonga	11768
Fortsville	12831
Fort Washington (Part of New York)	10032
Foster	13827
Fosterdale	12726
Fosterville	13021
Foster-Wheeler Junction (Part of Dansville)	14437
Fourth Lake	12846
Fowler	13642
Fowler (Town)	13642
Fowlersville	13433
Fowlerville	14423
Fox Hill	12134
Fox Meadows (Part of Scarsdale)	10583
Frankfort	13340
Frankfort (Town)	13340
Frankfort Center	13340
Franklin	13775
Franklin (Town)	13775
Franklin (Town)	12913
Franklin Correctional Facility	12953
Franklin D. Roosevelt (Part of New York)	10022
Franklin Park	13057
Franklin Springs	13341
Franklin Square	11010
Franklinton	12122
Franklinville	14737
Franklinville (Town)	14737
Franks Corner	13045
Fraser	13753
Fredonia	14063
Freedom	14065
Freedom (Town)	14065
Freedom Plains	12569
Freehold	12431
Freeman	14801
Freeport	11520
Freetown (Cortland County) (Town)	13803
Freetown (Suffolk County)	11937
Freetown Corners	13803
Freeville	13068
Fremont (Steuben County) (Town)	14807
Fremont (Sullivan County) (Town)	12736
Fremont Center	12736
Fremont Heights	13057
Fremont Hills	13057
French Creek (Town)	14724
Frenchville	13486
French Woods	13783
Fresh Meadows (Part of New York)	11365
Fresh Pond (Part of New York)	11385
Frewsburg	14738
Friend	14527
Friendship	14739
Friendship (Town)	14739
Friends Point	12836
Frontenac	13624
Fruitland	14519
Fruit Valley	13126
Fullerville	13642
Fulmer Valley	14806
Fulton (Oswego County)	13069
Fulton (Schoharie County) (Town)	12122
Fultonham	12071
Fultonville	12072
Furnace Brook	10925
Furnaceville	14519
Furnace Woods	10566
Furniss	13126
Fyler Settlement	13082
Gabriels	12939
Gaines	14411
Gaines (Town)	14411
Gainesville	14066
Gainesville (Town)	14066

	ZIP
Galatia	13803
Gale	12973
Galen (Town)	14433
Galeville (Onondaga County)	13088
Galeville (Ulster County)	12589
Gallatin	12567
Gallatin (Town)	12567
Galleria of White Plains (Part of White Plains)	10601
Gallupville	12073
Galway	12074
Galway (Town)	12074
Galway Lake	12025
Ganahgote	12525
Gang Mills	14870
Gansevoort	12831
Garbutt	14546
Garden City	11530
Garden City Park	11040
Garden City South	11530
Garden Park Estates	12203
Gardenville	14224
Gardiner	12525
Gardiner (Town)	12525
Gardiner Manor Mall	11706
Gardiners Bay Estates	11939
Gardnersville	12043
Gardnertown	12550
Gardnertown (census designated place)	12250
Garfield	12168
Garland	14420
Garnerville (Part of West Haverstraw)	10923
Garnet Lake	12843
Garoga	12095
Garrattsville	13342
Garrison	10524
Garrison Four Corners	10524
Garwoods	14822
Gaskill	13827
Gasport	14067
Gates (Town)	14624
Gates	14624
Gates Center	14611
Gates-North Gates	14626
Gayhead	12533
Gay Ridge Estates	10598
Gayville	13044
Geddes (Town)	13209
Gedney (Part of White Plains)	10605
Geers Corners	13648
Genegantslet	13778
Genesee (Town)	14754
Genesee Falls (Town)	14536
Geneseo	14454
Geneseo (Town)	14454
Geneva	14456
Geneva (Town)	14456
Genoa	13071
Genoa (Town)	13071
Georgetown	13072
Georgetown (Town)	13072
Georgetown	14450
Georgetown Square (Part of Williamsville)	14221
Georgtown Station	13334
German	13040
German (Town)	13040
German Flatts (Town)	13407
Germantown	12526
Germantown (Town)	12526
Germantown (Part of Port Jervis)	12771
German Village	14617
Germonds	10956
Gerry	14740
Gerry (Town)	14740
Getzville	14068
Geyser Crest	12866
Ghent	12075
Ghent (Town)	12075
Gibson (Nassau County)	11580
Gibson (Steuben County)	14830
Gifford	12056
Gilbert Mills	13135
Gilbertsville	13776
Gilboa	12076
Gilboa (Town)	12076
Gilgo Beach	11702
Gilmantown	12190
Gimbels Number One	11581
Glasco	12432
Glass Lake	12018
Glen	12072
Glen (Town)	12072
Glen Aubrey	13777
Glen Castle	13901
Glenclyffe	10524
Glenco Mills	12534

	ZIP		ZIP		ZIP
Glen Cove	11542	Great Bend	13643	Hadley (Town)	12835
Glendale (Lewis County)	13343	Great Kills (Part of New		Hadley Bay	14785
Glendale (Queens County)	11385	York)	10308	Hagaman	12086
Glendale Manor (Part of		Great Neck	11020-27	Hagedorns Mills	12074
Rome)	13440	For specific Great Neck Zip		Hagerman	11713
Glenerie	12477	Codes call (516) 482-5010, or		Hague	12836
Glenfield	13343	your local postmaster.		Hague (Town)	12836
Glenford	12433	Great Neck Estates	11021	Hailesboro	13645
Glenham	12527	Great Neck Plaza	11020	Haines Falls	12436
Glen Haven (Monroe		Great River	11739	Halcott (Town)	12430
County)	14617	Great South Bay (Part of		Halcott Center	12430
Glenhaven (Oneida County)	13492	Lindenhurst)	11702	Halcottsville	12438
Glen Head	11545	Great Valley	14741	Hales Eddy	13783
Glen Island	12814	Great Valley (Town)	14741	Halesite	11743
Glen Lake	12801	Greece (Town)	14616	Half Acre	13021
Glenmark	14516	Greece (census designated		Half Hollow Hills	11746
Glenmont	12077	place)	14626	Halfmoon	12188
Glen Oaks (Part of New		Greece	14616	Halfmoon (Town)	12188
York)	11004	Greece Towne Mall	14626	Halfway	13060
Glenora	14837	Greeley Square (Part of		Halfway House Corners	13660
Glen Park	13601	New York)	10001	Hall	14463
Glenridge	12148	Green Acres (Part of		Hallow	13413
Glens Falls	12801	Fredonia)	14063	Halls Corners (Seneca	
Glens Falls North	12801	Green Acres Shopping		County)	14847
Glen Spey	12737	Center (Part of Valley		Halls Corners (Wyoming	
Glen Street (Part of Sea		Stream)	11581	County)	14569
Cliff)	11579	Greenburgh (Town)	10591	Hallsport	14895
Glenville (Schenectady		Green Corners	12010	Hallsville	13339
County) (Town)	12302	Green Crest	14063	Halsey (Part of New York)	11233
Glenville (Westchester		Greendale	12534	Halseys (Part of	
County)	10591	Greene	13778	Plattsburgh)	12901
Glen Wild	12738	Greene (Town)	13778	Halsey Valley	14883
Glenwood (Erie County)	14069	Greene Correctional Facility	12051	Hambletville	13754
Glenwood (Westchester		Greenfield (Town)	12833	Hamburg	14075
County)	10701	Greenfield Center	12833	Hamburg (Town)	14075
Glenwood Landing	11547	Greenfield Park	12435	Hamburg	12414
Gloversville	12078	Greenhaven (Part of Rye)	10580	Hamburg-on-the-Lake	14075
Godeffroy	12729	Green Haven Correctional		Hamden	13782
Golden Glow Heights	14905	Facility	12570	Hamden (Town)	13782
Goldens Bridge	10526	Greenhurst	14742	Hamilton	13346
Goodman Street (Part of		Green Island	12183	Hamilton (Town)	13346
Rochester)	14607	Green Island (Town)	12183	Hamilton Beach (Part of	
Goodyears Corners	13081	Greenlawn	11740	New York)	11414
Goose Bay Estates	11971	Greenpoint (Part of New		Hamilton Center	13346
Goose Island	12809	York)	11222	Hamilton College	13323
Gordon Heights	11727	Greenport (Columbia		Hamilton Grange (Part of	
Gorham	14461	County) (Town)	12534	New York)	10031
Gorham (Town)	14461	Greenport (Suffolk County)	11944	Hamilton Park (Part of New	
Goshen	10924	Greenport West	11944	York)	10301
Goshen (Town)	10924	Green River	12529	Hamlet	14138
Goshen Hills	10924	Greenvale	11548	Hamlin	14464
Gothicville	12197	Greenville	12083	Hamlin (Town)	14464
Goulds	12760	Greenville (Town)	12083	Hammertown	12567
Goulds Mill	13368	Greenville (Orange County)		Hammond	13646
Gouverneur	13642	(Town)	12771	Hammond (Town)	13646
Gouverneur (Town)	13642	Greenville (Westchester		Hammondsport	14840
Governors Island (Part of		County)	10583	Hampshire	14855
New York)	10004	Greenville Center	12083	Hampton	12837
Gowanda	14070	Greenway (Part of Rome)	13440	Hampton (Town)	12837
Gracie (Cortland County)	13045	Greenwich	12834	Hampton Bays	11946
Gracie (New York County)	10028	Greenwich (Town)	12834	Hamptonburgh (Town)	10916
Grafton	12082	Greenwood	14839	Hampton Manor	12144
Grafton (Town)	12082	Greenwood (Town)	14839	Hampton Park	11968
Graham Hill	10537	Greenwood Lake	10925	Hancock	13783
Grahamsville	12740	Gregorytown	13755	Hancock (Town)	13783
Granby (Town)	13069	Greig	13345	Hankins	12741
Granby Center	13069	Greig (Town)	13345	Hannacroix	12087
Grand Central (Part of New		Greigsville	14533	Hannawa Falls	13647
York)	10017	Greigsville Station	14533	Hannibal	13074
Grand Gorge	12434	Grenell	13624	Hannibal (Town)	13074
Grand Island	14072	Greycourt (Part of Chester)	10918	Hannibal Center	13074
Grand Island (Town)	14072	Greystone (Part of Yonkers)	10701	Hanover (Town)	14136
Grand Station (Part of New		Gridleyville	13864	Hanover Hill	14136
York)	11103	Grindstone	13624	Harbor Acres (Part of	
Grand View Beach	14612	Grooms Corners	12148	Sands Point)	11050
Grand View Heights	14612	Grossinger	12734	Harbor Heights Park	11743
Grand View-on-Hudson	10960	Groton	13073	Harbor Hills	11023
Grandview Park	13692	Groton (Town)	13073	Harbor Isle	11558
Grandyle Village	14072	Groton City	13073	Hardenburgh (Town)	12455
Granger (Town)	14735	Grove (Town)	14884	Hardys	14066
Grangerville	12871	Groveland	14462	Harford	13784
Granite	12446	Groveland (Town)	14462	Harford (Town)	13784
Granite Springs	10527	Grover	14226	Harford Mills	13835
Graniteville (Part of New		Grover Hills	12956	Harkness	12972
York)	10301	Grovernor Corners	12035	Harlem (Part of New York)	10030
Grant	13324	Groveville	12508	Harlemville	12075
Grant Avenue (Part of		Grymes Hill (Part of New		Harmon Park	12302
Auburn)	13021	York)	10301	Harmony (Town)	14767
Grant Hollow	12121	Guilderland	12084	Harmony Corners	12020
Grant Park	11557	Guilderland (Town)	12084	Harpersfield	13786
Granville	12832	Guilderland Center	12085	Harpersfield (Town)	13786
Granville (Town)	12832	Guilderland Gardens	12203	Harpursville	13787
Grapeville	12042	Guilford	13780	Harriet	14223
Graphite	12836	Guilford (Town)	13780	Harrietstown (Town)	12983
Grassy Point	10980	Guilford Center	13780	Harriman	10926
Gravesend (Part of New		Gulf Summit	13865	Harris	12742
York)	11223	Gunther Park (Part of		Harrisburg (Cattaraugus	
Gravesville	13431	Yonkers)	10708	County)	14753
Gray	13324	Gurn Spring	12831	Harrisburg (Lewis County)	
Graymoor	10524	Guymard	12739	(Town)	13367
Gray Oaks (Part of		Gypsum	14432	Harrisburg (Warren County)	12878
Yonkers)	10703	Hadley	12835	Harris Corners	14145

* Area Zip Code † Post Office Boxes

	ZIP
Indian Castle	13365
Indian Cove	13118
Indian Falls	14036
Indian Kettles	12836
Indian Lake	12842
Indian Lake (Town)	12842
Indian Park	10925
Indian River	13327
Indian Springs	13027
Indian Village	13120
Industry	14474
Ingham Mills	13365
Ingleside	14512
Ingraham	12992
Inlet	13360
Inlet (Town)	13360
Inman	12968
Inter County Shopping Center	11758
Interlaken	14847
Interlaken Beach	14847
International Junction	14223
Inwood (Nassau County)	11696
Inwood (New York County)	10034
Ionia (Onondaga County)	13112
Ionia (Ontario County)	14475
Ira	13033
Ira (Town)	13033
Ira Station	13033
Ireland Corners	12525
Irelandville	14891
Irish Settlement	13625
Irona	12910
Irondequoit (Town)	14617
Irondequoit	14617
Irondequoit Manor	14617
Irongate	13088
Ironville	12928
Irving	14081
Irvington	10533
Ischua	14743
Ischua (Town)	14743
Island (Part of New York)	10044
Island Cottage Beach	14612
Islandia	11722
Island Park	11558
Isle of San Souci (Part of New Rochelle)	10805
Islip	11751
Islip (Town)	11751
Islip Manor	11751
Islip Terrace	11752
Italy	14512
Italy (Town)	14512
Itaska	13862
Ithaca	14850-53

For specific Ithaca Zip Codes call (607) 272-5454, or your local postmaster.

Ithaca College	14850
Ivanhoe	13839
Ives Corner	12018
Jackson (Town)	12816
Jacksonburg	13407
Jackson Corners	12571
Jackson Heights (Part of New York)	11372
Jackson Summit	12117
Jacksonville (Onondaga County)	13135
Jacksonville (Tompkins County)	14854
Jacks Reef	13112

Jamaica 11401-36

For specific Jamaica Zip Codes call (718) 990-1111, or your local postmaster.

COLLEGES & UNIVERSITIES

City University of New York-York College	11451

FINANCIAL INSTITUTIONS

Chase Manhattan Bank, N.A.	11432

HOSPITALS

Jamaica Hospital	11418
Queens Hospital Center	11432

HOTELS/MOTELS

JFK Airport Hilton	11436
Kennedy Inn	11434

MILITARY INSTALLATIONS

John F. Kennedy International Airport, Military	11430
Jamesport	11947
Jamestown	14701*

	ZIP
Jamestown West	14701
Jamesville	13078
Janesville	12043
Jasper	14855
Jasper (Town)	14855
Java (Town)	14082
Java Center	14082
Java Lake	14009
Java Village	14083
Jay	12941
Jay (Town)	12941
Jeddo	14103
Jefferson	12093
Jefferson (Town)	12093
Jefferson Heights	12414
Jefferson Park	13650
Jefferson Valley	10535
Jefferson Valley Mall	10598
Jefferson Valley-Yorktown	10535
Jeffersonville	12748
Jenksville	13736
Jericho (Clinton County)	12910
Jericho (Nassau County)	11753
Jericho (Suffolk County)	11937
Jerome Avenue (Part of New York)	10468
Jersey Colony	11971
Jerusalem (Town)	14418
Jerusalem Corners	14047
Jewell	13042
Jewel Manor	13088
Jewett	12444
Jewett (Town)	12444
Jewett Center	12442
Jewettville	13634
John F. Kennedy Airport (Part of New York)	11430
Johnsburg	12843
Johnsburg (Town)	12843
Johnson	10933
Johnsonburg	14167
Johnson City	13790
Johnson Creek	14067
Johnsonville	12094
Johnstown	12095
Johnstown (Town)	12078
Jones Point	10986
Jonesville	12065
Jordan	13080
Jordanville	13361
Junction Boulevard (Part of New York)	11372
Junius (Town)	13165
Kabob	14782
Kaisertown	12549
Kanona	14856
Kasoag	13302
Katonah	10536
Katsbaan	12477
Kattelville	13901
Kattskill Bay	12844
Kauneonga Lake	12749
Kaydeross Park (Part of Saratoga Springs)	12866
Kayuta Lake	13338
Kecks Center	12095
Keefers Corners	12067
Keene	12942
Keene (Town)	12942
Keene Valley	12943
Keeseville	12944
Kelleys	12056
Kelloggsville	13118
Kelly Corners	12455
Kelsey	13783
Kendaia	14541
Kendall	14476
Kendall (Town)	14476
Kendall Mills	14470
Kenilworth (Part of Kings Point)	11024
Kenmore	14217
Kennedy	14747
Kenoza Lake	12750
Kensington (Erie County)	14215
Kensington (Kings County)	11218
Kensington (Nassau County)	11021
Kent (Orleans County)	14477
Kent (Putnam County) (Town)	10512
Kent Cliffs	10512
Kents Corners	13630
Kenwood (Part of Oneida)	13421
Kenwood Estates	10512
Kenyonville	14571
Kerhonkson	12446
Kerleys Corners	12571
Kernan (Part of Utica)	13502
Ketchums Corner	12170
Ketchumville	13736

	ZIP
Keuka	14837
Keuka Park	14478
Kew Gardens (Part of New York)	11415
Kew Gardens Hills (Part of New York)	11366
Kiamesha Lake	12751
Kiantone	14701
Kiantone (Town)	14701
Kidders	14847
Killawog	13794
Kill Buck	14748
Kimball Stand	14701
Kinderhook	12106
Kinderhook (Town)	12106
King Ferry	13081
Kings Bridge (Part of New York)	10463
Kingsbury	12839
Kingsbury (Town)	12839
Kings Ferry	13081
Kings Park	11754
Kings Park Psychiatric Center	11754
Kings Plaza Shopping Center and Marina (Part of New York)	11234
Kings Point	11024
Kings Settlement	13815
Kings Station	12831
Kingston	12401
Kingston (Town)	12401
Kingston Plaza (Part of Kingston)	12401
Kingsway (Part of New York)	11229
Kipps	10924
Kirk	13844
Kirkland	13323
Kirkland (Town)	13323
Kirkville	13082
Kirkwood	13795
Kirkwood (Town)	13795
Kirschnerville	13327
Kiryas Joel	10950
Kisco Park	10549
Kiskatom	12414
Kismet	11706
Kitchawan	10562
Knapp Creek	14749
Knapps Corner	12603
Knickerbocker (Part of New York)	10002
Knights Creek	14880
Knights Eddy	12780
Knowelhurst	12878
Knowlesville	14479
Knox	12107
Knox (Town)	12107
Knoxboro	13362
Koenig's Point	13021
Komar Park	12019
Kortright	13739
Kortright (Town)	13739
Kossuth	14715
Kringsbush	13452
Kripplebush	12484
Krumville	12461
Kyserike	12440
Lackawanna	14218
Lacona	13083
Ladentown (Part of Pomona)	10970
LaFargeville	13656
La Fayette	13084
LaFayette (Town)	13084
Lafayetteville	12571
La Grange (Dutchess County) (Town)	12540
Lagrange (Wyoming County)	14525
Lagrangeville	12540
La Guardia Airport (Part of New York)	11371
Lairdsville	13323
Lake	10990
Lake Bluff	14590
Lake Bonaparte	13648
Lake Carmel	10512
Lake Charles	12563
Lake Clear	12945
Lake Como	13045
Lake Delta	13440
Lake Erie Beach	14006
Lake Gardens	10541
Lake George	12845
Lake George (Town)	12845
Lake Grove	11755
Lake Hill	12448
Lake Huntington	12752
Lake Katonah	10536
Lake Katrine	12449

Footnote markers: Jamestown 14701* ; Jamestown West 14702†

	ZIP		ZIP		ZIP
Lake Kitchawan	10590	Leeds	12451	Little York (Cortland County)	13087
Lakeland (Onondaga		Leedsville	12501	Little York (Orange County)	10969
County)	13209	Leeside	12512	Liverpool	13088-90
Lakeland (Suffolk County)	11779	Leesville	13459	For specific Liverpool Zip Codes	
Lake Lincolndale	10541	Lefever Falls	12472	call (315) 451-3060, or your local	
Lake Lucille	10956	Lefferts (Part of New York)	11225	postmaster.	
Lake Luzerne	12846	Leibhardt	12404	Livingston	12541
Lake Luzerne (Town)	12846	Leicester	14481	Livingston (Town)	12541
Lake Luzerne-Hadley	12835	Leicester (Town)	14481	Livingston (Part of New	
Lake Mahopac	10541	LeMarr Estates	12184	York)	11201
Lakemont	14857	Lenox (Town)	13032	Livingston Manor	12758
Lake Moraine	13346	Lenox Furnace	13032	Livingstonville	12122
Lake Muskoday	12776	Lenox Hill (Part of New		Livonia	14487
Lake Osceola	10535	York)	10021	Livonia (Town)	14487
Lake Osiris Colony	12586	Lenox Park	14456	Livonia Center	14488
Lake Panamoka	11961	Leon	14751	Lloyd (Town)	12528
Lake Peekskill	10537	Leon (Town)	14751	Lloyd Harbor	11743
Lake Placid	12946	Leonardsville	13364	Lochada Lake	12719
Lake Placid Club Resort		Leonta	13775	Loch Muller	12857
(Part of Lake Placid)	12946	Le Ray (Town)	13637	Loch Sheldrake	12759
Lake Pleasant	12108	Le Roy	14482	Lock Berlin	14489
Lake Pleasant (Town)	12108	Le Roy (Town)	14482	Locke	13092
Lakeport	13037	Le Roy Island	14590	Locke (Town)	13092
Lake Purdy	10578	Levanna	13026	Lockport	14094*
Lake Ronkonkoma	11779	Levant	14733		14095†
Lake Ronkonkoma Heights	11779	Levittown	11756	Locksley Park	14075
Lake Secor	10541	Lewbeach	12753	Lockwood	14859
Lakeside (Orange County)	10930	Lewis	12950	Locust Grove (Lewis	
Lakeside (Wayne County)	14519	Lewis (Town)	12950	County)	13309
Lakeside Park (Albany		Lewis (Town)	13489	Locust Grove (Nassau	
County)	12205	Lewisboro (Town)	10590	County)	11791
Lakeside Park (Orleans		Lewiston	14092	Locust Manor (Part of New	
County)	14571	Lewiston (Town)	14092	York)	11431
Lake Station	10990	Lewiston Heights (Part of		Locust Point (Part of New	
Lake Success	11040	Lewiston)	14092	York)	10465
Lake Success Shopping		Lewiston Manor	13224	Locust Valley	11560
Center	11040	Lexington	12452	Lodi	14860
Lake Sunnyside	12845	Lexington (Town)	12452	Lodi (Town)	14860
Lake Vanare	12846	Leyden (Town)	13433	Lodi Center	14860
Lake View (Erie County)	14085	Liberty	12754	Lodi Point	14860
Lakeview (Nassau County)	11552	Liberty (Town)	12754	Logan	14818
Lakeview (Oswego County)	13126	Liberty Gardens (Part of		Logtown	12771
Lakeview Correctional		Rome)	13440	Lomala	12533
Facility	14716	Libertypole	14437	Lombard	14775
Lakeville (Livingston		Lido Beach	11561	Lomond Shore	14476
County)	14480	Lily Dale	14752	Lomontville	12401
Lakeville (Nassau County)	11040	Lima	14485	London Terrace (Part of	
Lakeville Estates	11040	Lima (Town)	14485	New York)	10011
Lakewood	14750	Lime Lake	14042	Lonelyville	11706
Lamberton	14063	Lime Lake-Machias	14042	Long Beach	11561
Lambs Corner	12083	Limerick	13657	Long Branch	13088
Lamont	14427	Lime Rock	14482	Long Branch Manor	13088
Lamson	13135	Limestone	14753	Long Bridge	13153
Lancaster	14086	Limestreet	12414	Long Eddy	12760
Lancaster (Town)	14086	Lincklaen	13052		
Lane (Part of Batavia)	14020	Lincklaen (Town)	13052	**Long Island City**	11101-06
Lanesville	12450	Lincoln (Madison County)		For specific Long Island City Zip	
Langdon	13795	(Town)	13043	Codes call (718) 349-4626, or	
Langdon Corners	13617	Lincoln (Wayne County)	14502	your local postmaster.	
Langford	14057	Lincolndale	10540		
Lansing (Town)	14882	Lincoln Park (Erie County)	14223	*FINANCIAL INSTITUTIONS*	
Lansing (Oswego County)	13126	Lincoln Park (Monroe			
Lansing (Tompkins County)	14882	County)	14611	Astoria Federal Savings &	
Lansingburg (Part of Troy)	12182	Lincoln Park (Ulster County)	12401	Loan Association	11103
Laona	14063	Lincolnshire	13760	Financial Federal Savings &	
Lapala	12401	Lincolnton (Part of New		Loan Association	11104
Lapeer (Town)	13803	York)	10037	*HOSPITALS*	
Laphams Mills	12972	Lindbergh Court (Part of			
Larchmont	10538	Colonie)	12205	Long Island Jewish Medical	
Larchmont North	10538	Linden	14054	Center	11042
La Salle	14304	Linden Acres	12571		
Lassellsville	13452	Linden Hill (Part of New		Long Island University	
Latham	12110	York)	11354	Southampton Center	11968
Latham Circle Mall	12110	Lindenhurst	11757	Long Lake	12847
Lathams Corners	13843	Lindley	14858	Long Lake (Town)	12847
Lattingtown	11560	Lindley (Town)	14858	Long Ridge Mall	14626
Laughing Waters	11971	Linlithgo	12526	Long View	14710
Laurel	11948	Linwood	14525	Longwood (Part of New	
Laurel Hollow	11791	Lisbon	13658	York)	10459
Laurelton (Monroe County)	14617	Lisbon (Town)	13658	Loomis	12754
Laurelton (Queens County)	11431	Lisle	13797	Loomises	14710
Laurens	13796	Lisle (Town)	13797	Loon Lake	12968
Laurens (Town)	13796	Litchfield (Town)	13456	Loon Lake Junction	12968
Lava	12764	Lithgow	12545	Lordville	13783
Lawrence (Nassau County)	11559	Little America	13144	Lorenz Park	12534
Lawrence (St. Lawrence		Little Bow	13642	Lorings	13045
County) (Town)	12965	Little Britain	12575	Lorraine	13659
Lawrence Farms	10514	Little Canada	14054	Lorraine (Town)	13659
Lawrence Park (Part of		Little Falls	13365	Lost Valley	12010
Yonkers)	10708	Little Falls (Town)	13407	Loudonville	12211
Lawrenceville	12949	Little Falls Park (Part of		Louisville	13662
Lawtons	14091	Wappingers Falls)	12590	Louisville (Town)	13662
Lawyersville	12113	Little France	13036	Lounsberry	13812
Lebanon	13085	Little Genesee	14754	Lower Chateaugay Lake	12920
Lebanon (Town)	13085	Little Neck (Part of New		Lower Cincinnatus	13040
Lebanon Center	13332	York)	11363	Lower Genegantslet Corner	13778
Lebanon Springs	12114	Little Plains	11731	Lower Melville	11747
Ledyard	13081	Little Ram Island	11964	Lower Oswegatchie	13670
Ledyard (Town)	13026	Little Utica	13135	Lower Rotterdam	12306
Lee	13440	Little Valley	14755	Lower South Bay	13041
Lee (Town)	13440	Little Valley (Town)	14755	Low Hampton	05743
Lee Center	13363	Littleville	14424	Lowman	14861
				Lowville	13367

	ZIP		ZIP		ZIP
Lowville (Town)	13367		10201-82	Massawepie	12986
Ludingtonville	12531	For specific Manhattan Zip Codes		Massena	13662
Ludlow (Part of Yonkers)	10705	call (212) 330-3601, or your local		Massena	13662
Ludlowville	14882	postmaster.		Massena Center	13662
Lumberland (Town)	12770	Manhattan Park (Part of		Massena Springs (Part of	
Luther	12061	White Plains)	10601	Massena)	13662
Lutheranville	12064	Manhattanville (Part of New		Masten Lake	12790
Lycoming	13093	York)	10027	Mastic	11950
Lyell (Part of Rochester)	14606	Manhattanville College (Part		Mastic Beach	11951
Lykers	12166	of Harrison)	10577	Matinecock	11560
Lyme (Town)	13693	Manheim (Town)	13329	Matteawan (Part of Beacon)	12508
Lynbrook	11563	Manheim Center	13365	Mattituck	11952
Lyncourt	13208	Manitou	10524	Mattydale	13211
Lyndon (Cattaraugus		Manitou Beach	14468	Maybrook	12543
County) (Town)	14737	Manlius	13104	Mayfair	12302
Lyndon (Onondaga County)	13066	Manlius (Town)	13104	Mayfair Shopping Center	11725
Lyndonville	14098	Manlius Center	13066	Mayfield	12117
Lynelle Meadows	13088	Mannetto Hills	11747	Mayfield (Town)	12117
Lyon Mountain	12952	Manning	14470	Mayville	14757
Lyons	14489	Mannsville	13661	Maywood (Albany County)	12205
Lyons (Town)	14489	Mannville	12189	Maywood (Suffolk County)	11701
Lyonsdale	13368	Manny Corners	12010	Meacham	11003
Lyonsdale (Town)	13368	Manor	13413	Meadowbrook	12550
Lyons Falls	13368	Manorhaven	11050	Meadowdale	12009
Lyonsville	12404	Manorkill	12076	Meadow Hill	12550
Lysander	13094	Manors	11507	Meadow Lane Estates	12184
Lysander (Town)	13094	Manorville (Suffolk County)	11949	Meadowmere Park	11598
Mabbettsville	12545	Manorville (Ulster County)	12477	Meadow Run (Part of	
McClure	13754	Mansfield (Town)	14755	Hamburg)	14075
McConnellsville	13401	Maple Bay	14710	Meadows	14420
MacDonnell Heights	12603	Maplecrest	12454	Meads	12498
McDonough	13801	Mapledale	12406	Meads Creek	14870
McDonough (Town)	13801	Maple Grove (Hamilton		Mechanicville	12118
MacDougall	14541	County)	12134	Mecklenburg	14863
Macedon	14502	Maple Grove (Otsego		Meco	12078
Macedon (Town)	14502	County)	13808	Medford	11763
Macedon Center	14502	Maple Hill	12401	Medina	14103
McGraw	13101	Maplehurst	14743	Medusa	12120
McGrawville	14777	Maples	14755	Medway	12042
Machias (Town)	14101	Maple Springs	14756	Melcourt (Part of New York)	10451
Machias	14101	Mapleton	13021	Mellenville	12544
McKeever	13338	Mapletown	13317	Melrose	12121
Mackey	12076	Maple Transit	14221	Melrose Park	13021
McKinley	13428	Maple Valley	13488	Melville	11747
McKinstry Hollow	14042	Maple View	13107	Memphis	13112
McKown Park	12203	Maplewood (Albany County)	12189	Menands	12204
McKownville	12203	Maplewood (Sullivan		Mendon	14506
McKownville Estates	12203	County)	12701	Mendon (Town)	14506
McLaughlin Acres	10541	Marathon	13803	Mendon Center	14472
McLean	13102	Marathon (Town)	13803	Mendon Farms	14506
McMasters Corners	13201	Marble Hill (Part of New		Menteth Point	14424
McNalls	14067	York)	10463	Mentz (Town)	13140
Macomb (Town)	13642	Marbletown	12401	Meredith	13753
McPherson Point	14487	Marbletown (Town)	12401	Meredith (Town)	13753
Madison	13402	Marbletown	14513	Meridale	13806
Madison (Town)	13402	Marcellus	13108	Meridian	13113
Madison Park	11731	Marcellus (Town)	13108	Merillon Avenue (Part of	
Madison Square (Part of		Marcellus Falls	13108	Garden City)	11530
New York)	10010	Marcy (Kings County)	11206	Merrick	11566
Madrid	13660	Marcy (Oneida County)		Merrickville	13839
Madrid (Town)	13660	(Town)	13503	Merriewold	12701
Magnolia	14757	Marcy Correctional Facility	13403	Merriewold Lake	10950
Mahopac	10541	Marengo	14433	Merrifield	13147
Mahopac Falls	10542	Margaretville	12455	Merrill	12955
Mahopac Hills	10541	Mariaville	12137	Merrillsville	13421
Mahopac Point	10541	Marietta	13110	Merrilville	12986
Mahopac Ridge	10541	Marilla	14102	Merriweather Campus (Part	
Maidstone Park	11937	Marilla (Town)	14102	of Brookville)	11548
Maine	13802	Marine Hospital (Part of		Mertensia	14564
Maine (Town)	13802	New York)	10301	Messengerville	13803
Main Settlement	14770	Mariners Harbor (Part of		Metropolitan (Part of New	
Main Village (Part of		New York)	10303	York)	11206
Williamsville)	14221	Marion	14505	Mettacahonts	12404
Malden Bridge	12115	Marion (Town)	14505	Mews	11507
Malden on Hudson	12453	Mariposa	13155	Mexico	13114
Mall	11706	Markhams	14070	Mexico (Town)	13114
Mall at New Rochelle, The		Marlboro	12542	Middle Grove	13730
(Part of New Rochelle)	10801	Marlborough (Town)	12542	Middleburgh	12122
Mallory	13103	Marshall (Allegany County)	14711	Middleburgh (Town)	12122
Malone	12953	Marshall (Oneida County)		Middlebury (Town)	14591
Malone (Town)	12953	(Town)	13328	Middle Falls	12848
Malta	12020	Marshfield	14091	Middlefield	13450
Malta (Town)	12020	Marshland Heights	13760	Middlefield (Town)	13450
Malta Ridge	12020	Marshville (Montgomery		Middlefield Center	13320
Maltaville	12020	County)	13317	Middle Granville	12849
Maltbie Heights	14070	Marshville (St. Lawrence		Middle Grove	12850
Malverne	11565	County)	13652	Middle Hope	12550
Malvic Manor	13088	Martindale Depot	12521	Middle Island	11953
Mamakating (Town)	12790	Martinsburg	13404	Middleport (Madison	
Mamakating Park	12790	Martinsburg (Town)	13404	County)	13346
Mamaroneck	10543	Martisco	13108	Middleport (Niagara County)	14105
Mamaroneck (Town)	10543	Martville	13111	Middlesex	14507
Manchester	14504	Maryknoll	10545	Middlesex (Town)	14507
Manchester (Town)	14504	Maryland	12116	Middletown	10940-41
Manchester Bridge	12603	Maryland (Town)	12116	For specific Middletown Zip	
Mandana	13152	Marymount (Part of		Codes call (914) 343-1496, or	
Manhasset	11030	Tarrytown)	10591	your local postmaster.	
Manhasset Hills	11040	Masonville	13804	Middletown (Town)	12455
Manhattan	10001-99	Masonville (Town)	13804	Middletown Psychiatric	
	10101	Maspeth (Part of New York)	11378	Center (Part of	
		Massapequa	11758	Middletown)	10940
		Massapequa Park	11762		

* Area Zip Code   † Post Office Boxes

	ZIP		ZIP		ZIP
Middle Village (Part of New York)	11379	Montour (Town)	14865	Municipal Building (Part of New York)	11201
Middleville (Herkimer County)	13406	Montour Falls	14865	Munnsville	13409
Middleville (Suffolk County)	11768	Montrose	10548	Munsey Park	11030
Mid-Island Mall	11801	Montville	13118	Munsons Corners	13045
Midland Beach (Part of New York)	10306	Moody	12986	Murdochs Crossing	14098
Mid-Orange Correctional Facility	10990	Mooers	12958	Murdock Woods	10583
		Mooers (Town)	12958	Murray	14470
		Mooers Forks	12959	Murray (Town)	14470
Mid-State Correctional Facility	13403	Moores Mill	12569	Murray Hill (New York County)	10016
Midtown (Part of New York)	10018	Moorhouse Corner	12037	Murray Hill (Queens County)	11354
Midtown Plaza (Part of Rochester)	14604	Moose River	13433	Murray Hill (Westchester County)	10583
Midway	14864	Moravia	13118	Murray Isle	13624
Midwood (Part of New York)	11230	Moravia (Town)	13118	Muttontown	11791
Milan (Town)	12571	Moreau (Town)	12801	Myers	14882
Mileses	12741	Morehouse (Town)	13324	Myers Corner	12590
Milford	13807	Morehouseville	13324	Myers Grove	12739
Milford (Town)	13807	Moreland	14812	Nanticoke	13802
Milford Center	13820	Morey Park	12123	Nanticoke (Town)	13803
Mill Brook (Bronx County)	10454	Morgan (Part of New York)	10001	Nanuet	10954
Millbrook (Dutchess County)	12545	Morgan Hill	12401	Nanuet Mall	10954
Millen Bay	13618	Morganville	14143	Napanoch	12458
Miller Place	11764	Moriah	12960	Napeague	11930
Millers	14098	Moriah (Town)	12960	Naples	14512
Millers Mills	13491	Moriah Center	12961	Naples (Town)	14512
Millersport	14051	Moriches	11955	Napoli	14755
Millerton	12546	Morley	13617	Napoli (Town)	14755
Millertown	12094	Morningside (Part of New York)	10026	Narrowsburg	12764
Mill Grove	14770	Morris	13808	Nashville	14062
Mill Hook	12404	Morris (Town)	13808	Nassau	12123
Mill Neck	11765	Morrisania (Part of New York)	10456	Nassau (Town)	12123
Mill Point	12010			Nassau Lake	12123
Millport	14864	Morris Heights (Part of New York)	10453	Nassau Mall	11756
Millsburgh	10933	Morrison Heights	12549	Nassau Shores	11758
Mills Mills	14735	Morrisonville	12962	Natural Bridge	13665
Millville	14103	Morris Park (Part of New York)	10461	Natural Dam	13642
Millwood	10546	Morristown	13664	Naumburg	13620
Milo (Town)	14527	Morristown (Town)	13664	Nauraushaun	10965
Milo Center	14527	Morrisville	13408	Navarino	13108
Milton	12020	Morrisville Station	13408	Nazareth College of Rochester	14610
Milton (Town)	12020	Morsston	12758	Nedrow	13120
Milton (Saratoga County)	12020	Morton (Monroe County)	14464	Neiam (Part of New York)	11212
Milton (Ulster County)	12547	Morton (Orleans County)	14508	Nelliston	13410
Milton Point (Part of Rye)	10580	Mosherville	12074	Nelson	13035
Mina	14781	Mosholu (Part of New York)	10467	Nelson (Town)	13035
Mina (Town)	14781	Mosquito Point	12468	Nelsonville	10516
Minaville	12010	Mott Haven (Part of New York)	10454	Nepera Park (Part of Yonkers)	10710
Minden (Town)	13339	Mottville	13119	Neponsit (Part of New York)	11694
Mindenville	13339	Mountain Dale	12763	Nepperhan (Part of Yonkers)	10703
Mineola	11501	Mountain Lodge	10950	Nesconset	11767
Mineral Springs	12043	Mountain View (Franklin County)	12969	Neversink	12765
Minerva	12851	Mountain View (Rensselaer County)	12180	Neversink (Town)	12765
Minerva (Town)	12851	Mountain View East	10989	New Albion	14719
Minetto	13115	Mountainville	10953	New Albion (Town)	14719
Minetto (Town)	13115	Mount Carmel (Part of New York)	10458	Newark	14513
Mineville	12956	Mount Eve	10924	Newark Valley	13811
Mineville-Witherbee	12956	Mount Hope	10940	Newark Valley (Town)	13811
Minisink (Town)	10998	Mount Hope (Town)	10940	New Baltimore	12124
Minisink Ford	12719	Mount Hope (Part of Hastings-on-Hudson)	10706	New Baltimore (Town)	12124
Minklers Corners	13662	Mount Ivy	10970	New Berlin	13411
Minoa	13116	Mount Kisco	10549	New Berlin (Town)	13411
Mitchellsville	14810	Mount Kisco (Town)	10549	New Berlin Junction	13733
Model City	14107	Mount Loretto (Part of New York)	10309	New Bremen	13367
Modena	12548	Mount Marion	12456	New Bremen (Town)	13367
Moffitsville	12981	Mount McGregor Correctional Facility	12866	New Brighton (Part of New York)	10310
Mohawk (Herkimer County)	13407	Mount Merion Park	12456	Newburg	14550
Mohawk (Montgomery County) (Town)	12068	Mount Morris	14510	Newburgh	12550-52
Mohawk Hill	13309	Mount Morris (Town)	14510	For specific Newburgh Zip Codes call (914) 561-1818, or your local postmaster.	
Mohawk Mall	12304	Mount Pleasant (Oswego County)	13069		
Mohawk View	12110	Mount Pleasant (Ulster County)	12457	New Cassel	11590
Mohawk Village	12303			New Castle (Town)	10514
Mohegan Heights (Part of Yonkers)	10708	Mount Pleasant (Westchester County) (Town)	10591	New City	10956
Mohegan Lake	10547	Mount Prosper	12790	New City Park	10956
Mohonk Lake	12561	Mount Ross	12567	Newcomb	12852
Moira	12957	Mount Sinai	11766	Newcomb (Town)	12852
Moira (Town)	12957	Mount Tremper	12457	New Concord	12060
Mombaccus	12446	Mount Upton	13809	New Dorp (Part of New York)	10306
Mongaup	12780	Mount Vernon	10550-53		
Mongaup Valley	12762	For specific Mount Vernon Zip Codes call (914) 964-7201, or your local postmaster.		New Dorp Beach (Part of New York)	10306
Monroe	10950			New Ebenezer	14224
Monroe (Town)	10950	Mount Vernon	14075	New Falconwood	14072
Monsey	10952	Mount View Acres	12184	Newfane	14108
Monsey Heights	10952	Mount View Estates	12184	Newfane (Town)	14108
Montague (Town)	13367	Mount Vision	13810	Newfield	14867
Montario Point	13661	Mud Mills	14513	Newfield (Town)	14867
Montauk	11954	Muitzeskill	12156	New Hackensack	12590
Montauk Beach	11954	Mumford	14511	New Hamburg	12590
Montclair Colony	11964	Mungers Corners	13069	New Hampton	10958
Montebello	10901			New Hartford	13413
Monterey	14812			New Hartford (Town)	13413
Monterey Estates	10989			New Hartford Shopping Center (Part of New Hartford)	13413
Montezuma	13117				
Montezuma (Town)	13117				
Montgomery	12549				
Montgomery (Town)	12549			New Haven	13121
Monticello	12701				

	ZIP		ZIP		ZIP
New Haven (Town)	13121	Bankers Federal Savings,		St. Clare's Hospital and	
New Hempstead	10977	F.S.B.	10038	Health Center	10019
New Hope	13118	Bankers Trust Company	10017	St. Luke's-Roosevelt	
New Hudson (Town)	14714	Bank Leumi Trust Company		Hospital Center	10019
New Hurley	12525	of New York	10017	St. Vincent's Hospital and	
New Hyde Park	11040-42	Bank of New York		Medical Center of New	
For specific New Hyde Park Zip		Company, Inc., The	10286	York	10011
Codes call (516) 775-3980, or		Bank of Tokyo Trust		Veterans Affairs Medical	
your local postmaster.		Company, The	10005	Center	10010
New Ireland	13905	Barclays Bank, PLC	10265		
New Kingston	12459	Brown Brothers Harriman &		*HOTELS/MOTELS*	
Newkirk (Part of New York)	11226	Co	10005	Algonquin	10036
New Lebanon	12125	Canadian Imperial Bank of		Essex House	10019
New Lebanon (Town)	12125	Commerce	10017	Grand Hyatt New York	10017
New Lebanon Center	12125	Carver Federal Savings		Helmsley Middletowne	
New Lisbon	13415	Bank	10027	Hotel, The	10017
New Lisbon (Town)	13415	Chase Manhattan Bank,		Hotel Inter-Continental New	
New Lots (Part of New		N.A., The	10081	York	10017
York)	11208	Chemical Bank	10017	Hotel Parker Meridien	10019
New Market (Part of		Chinese American Bank,		Drake Swissotel, The	10022
Niagara Falls)	14301	The	10038	New York Hilton and	
New Milford	10959	Citibank, N.A.	10043	Towers, The	10019
New Oregon	14057	Daiwa Bank Trust Company	10019	Pierre, The	10021
New Paltz	12561	Depository Trust Company,		Ritz Carlton New York, The	10019
New Paltz (Town)	12561	The	10041	United Nations Plaza Park	
Newport	13416	East River Savings Bank, A		Hyatt	10017
Newport (Town)	13416	Division of River Bank		Waldorf-Astoria, The	10022
Newport (Monroe County)	14617	America	10007	Plaza Hotel, The	10019
Newport (Onondaga		Emigrant Savings Bank	10017	Wyndham Hotel, The	10019
County)	13164	Fiduciary Trust Company			
New Rochelle	10801-02	International	10048	*MILITARY INSTALLATIONS*	
For specific New Rochelle Zip		First American Bank of New		United States Engineer	
Codes call (914) 632-5906, or		York	10022	District, New York	10278
your local postmaster.		First New York Bank for			
New Rochelle	10804-05	Business	10010	New York Mills	13417
For specific New Rochelle Zip		Fourth Federal Savings		New York Mills Gardens	13492
Codes call (914) 632-5906, or		Bank	10021	Niagara (Town)	14302
your local postmaster.		French American Banking		Niagara Falls	14301-05
New Russia	12964	Corporation	10022	For specific Niagara Falls Zip	
New Salem (Albany County)	12186	Fuji Bank and Trust		Codes call (716) 285-7561, or	
New Salem (Ulster County)	12401	Company, The	10048	your local postmaster.	
New Scotland	12159	Greater New York Savings		Niagara Falls International	
New Scotland (Town)	12159	Bank, The	10119	Airport (AFB 6670) 914	14304
Newsday	11747	Home Savings of America,		Niagara Square (Part of	
New Springville (Part of		F.S.B.	10017	Buffalo)	14202
New York)	10314	IBJ Schroder Bank & Trust		Niagara University	14109
New Square	10977	Company	10004	Nichols (Town)	13812
Newstead (Town)	14001	Industrial Bank of Japan		Nichols (Steuben County)	16920
New Suffolk	11956	Trust Company, The	10167	Nichols (Tioga County)	13812
Newton Falls	13666	Israel Discount Bank of		Nichols Plaza (Part of	
Newton Hook	12173	New York	10017	Watertown)	13601
Newtonville	12128	Manhattan Savings Bank,		Nichols Run	14749
Newtown	11946	The	10017	Nicholville	12965
New Vernon	10940	Merchants Bank of New		Niets Crest	14710
Newville	13365	York, The	10013	Nile	14739
New Windsor	12553	Mitsubishi Trust & Banking		Niles	13152
New Windsor (Town)	12553	Corporation (USA)	10022	Niles (Town)	13152
New Woodstock	13122	Morgan Guaranty Trust		Nimmonsburg	13901
		Company of New York	10260	Nineveh	13813
New York	10001-99	National Westminster Bank		Nineveh Junction	13730
	10101-99	USA	10038	Niobe	14758
	10201-82	Republic National Bank of		Niskayuna (Town)	12309
For specific New York Zip Codes		New York	10018	Niskayuna	12309
call (212) 967-8585, or your local		Safra National Bank of New		Nissequogue	11780
postmaster.		York	10036	Niverville (Columbia County)	12130
		Security Pacific National		Noblesboro	13324
COLLEGES & UNIVERSITIES		Trust Company	10006	Norfolk	13667
		State Street Bank and Trust		Norfolk (Town)	13667
Barnard College	10027	Company, N.A.	10006	Normansville	12054
City University of New York-		Sterling National Bank &		North (Part of Yonkers)	10703
Bernard Baruch College	10010	Trust Company of New		North Afton	13730
City University of New York-		York	10022	North Amityville	11701
City College	10031	Sumitomo Trust & Banking		Northampton (Fulton	
City University of New York-		Co., Ltd.	10022	County) (Town)	12134
Hunter College	10021	UBAF Arab American Bank	10022	Northampton (Suffolk	
City University of New York-		UMB Bank and Trust		County)	11901
John Jay College of		Company	10020	North Argyle	12809
Criminal Justice	10019	Union Chelsea National		North Babylon	11703
College of Insurance	10007	Bank	10017	North Bailey	14226
Columbia University-		United States Trust		North Baldwin	11510
Columbia College	10027	Company of New York	10036	North Ballston Spa	12020
Cooper Union	10003			North Bangor	12966
Fashion Institute of		*HOSPITALS*		North Bay	13123
Technology	10001	Bellevue Hospital Center	10016	North Bay Shore	11706
The Juilliard School	10023	Beth Isreal Medical Center	10003	North Beach (Part of New	
Marymount Manhattan		Cabrini Medical Center	10003	York)	11369
College	10021	Coler Memorial Hospital	10044	North Bellmore	11710
New York Law School	10013	Goldwater Memorial		North Bellport	11713
New York University	10012	Hospital	10044	North Bergen	14416
School of Visual Arts	10010	Harlem Hospital Center	10037	North Bethlehem	12203
Touro College	10001	Lenox Hill Hospital	10021	North Blenheim	12131
Yeshiva University	10033	Memorial Hospital for		North Bloomfield	14472
		Cancer and Allied		North Boston	14110
FINANCIAL INSTITUTIONS		Diseases	10021	North Branch	12766
		Metropolitan Hospital Center	10029	North Bridgewater	13318
Amalgamated Bank of New		Mount Sinai Medical Center	10029	North Broadalbin	12025
York	10003	New York University		North Brookfield	13418
Apple Bank for Savings	10017	Medical Center	10016	North Burke	12917
Atlantic Bank of New York	10001	Presbyterian Hospital in the		Northbush	12095
Banco Central of New York	10004	City of New York	10032	North Cameron	14819
Banco de Bogota Trust		Society of the New York		North Castle (Town)	10504
Company	10152	Hospital	10021	North Centereach	11720
Bank Audi (USA)	10020				

---

* Area Zip Code   **† Post Office Boxes**

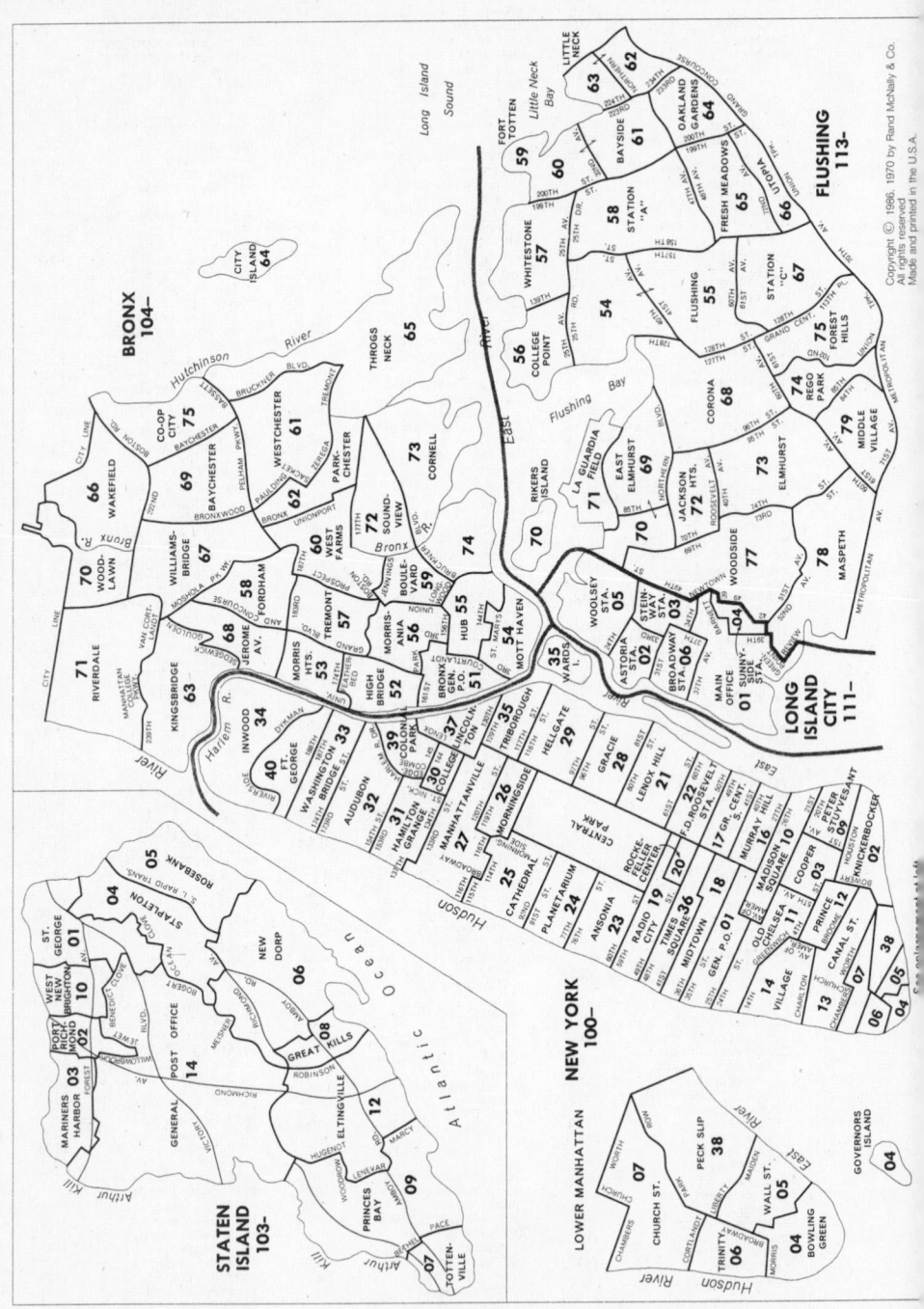

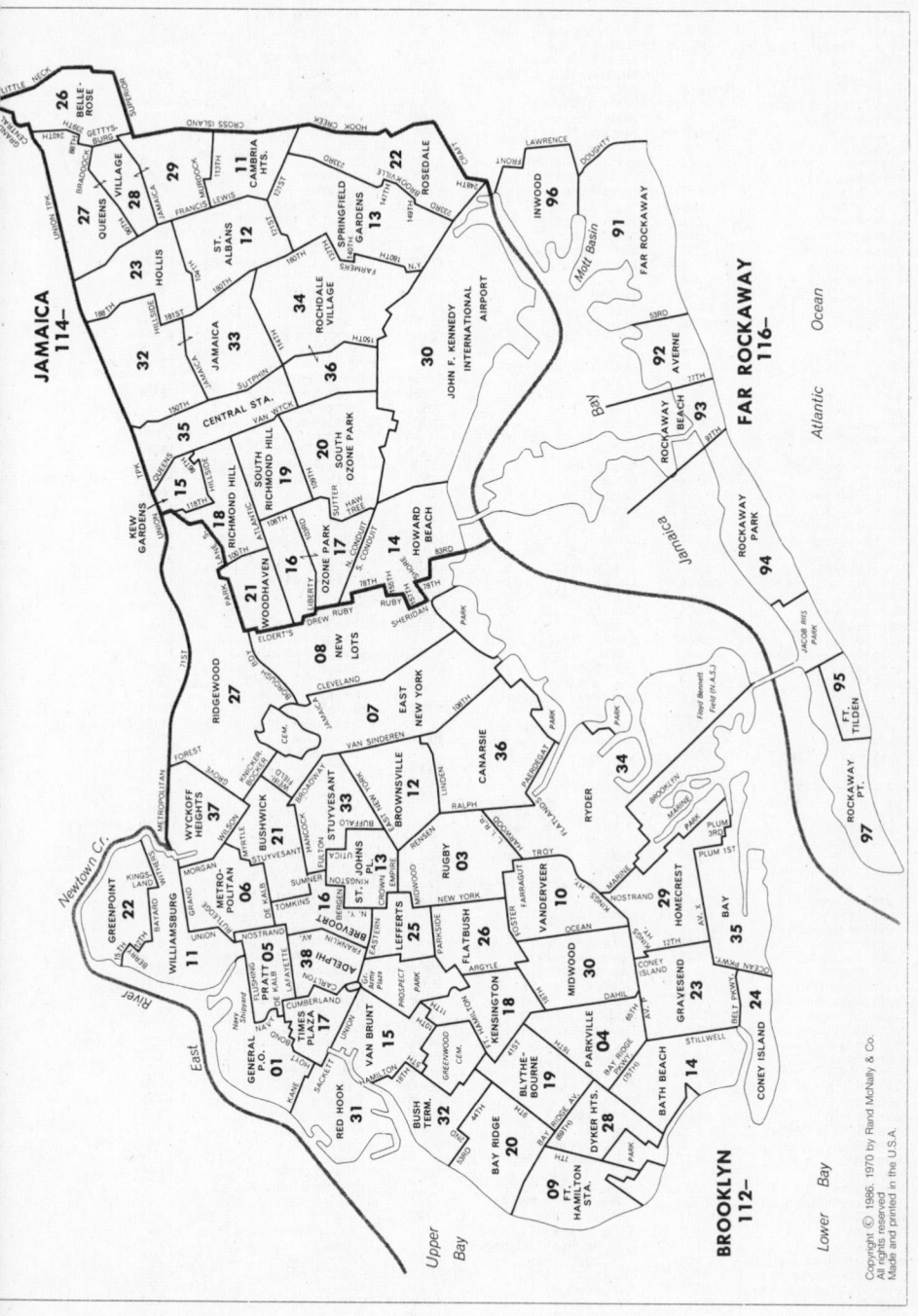

	ZIP		ZIP		ZIP
North Chatham	12132	North Valley Stream	11580	Old Stony Brook	11790
North Chemung	14861	North Victory	13111	Old Village (Part of Great	
North Chili	14514	Northview Gardens	14094	Neck)	11023
North Chittenango	13037	Northville (Fulton County)	12134	Old Westbury	11568
North Clymer	14759	Northville (Suffolk County)	11901	Olean (Town)	14760
North Cohocton	14868	North Wantagh	11793	Olean	14760
North Collins	14111	North Waverly	14892	Olean Center Mall (Part of	
North Collins (Town)	14111	Northway Mall/Off-Price		Olean)	14760
North Corners	13658	Center, The	12205	Olive (Town)	12461
North Country Shopping		Northway Plaza	12801	Olivebridge	12461
Center (Part of		North Western	13486	Oliverea	12410
Plattsburgh)	12901	Northwest Harbor	11937	Olmstedville	12857
North Creek	12853	Northwest Ithaca	14850	Omar	13607
Northcrest	12065	North White Plains	10603	Omi	12075
North Cuba	14727	North Wilmurt	13438	Onativia	13084
North Dansville (Town)	14437	North Wilna	13608	Onchiota	12968
North Darien	14036	North Winfield	13491	One Hundred Thirty Eight	
North East (Town)	12546	North Wolcott	14590	(Part of New York)	10001
Northeast Center	12546	Northwood	12188	Oneida	13421
Northeast Henrietta	14534	North Woodmere	11581	Oneida Castle	13421
Northeast Ithaca	14850	Norton Hill	12135	Oneida Correctional Facility	13440
North Easton	12834	Norway	13416	Oneonta	13820
North Elba (Town)	12946	Norway (Town)	13416	Oneonta (Town)	13861
North End	10940	Norwich	13815	Onesquethaw	12067
North Evans	14112	Norwich (Town)	13815	Oniontown	12522
North Fair Haven (Part of		Norwich Corners	13456	Onleys Station	10940
Fair Haven)	13064	Norwood	13668	Onondaga	13215
North Fenton	13746	Nostrand (Part of New		Onondaga (Town)	13215
Northfield	13856	York)	11235	Onondaga Indian	
North Franklin	13820	Nottingham Estates	14094	Reservation (Town)	13120
North Gage	13502	Noxon	12603	Onondaga Indian	
North Gainesville	14550	Noyack	11963	Reservation	13120
Northgate Estates (Part of		Number Forty (Part of New		Ontario	14519
Rome)	13440	York)	10001	Ontario (Town)	14519
North Germantown	12526	Number Four	13367	Ontario Center	14520
North Granville	12854	Nunda	14517	Ontario on the Lake	14519
North Great River	11722	Nunda (Town)	14517	Onteo Beach	14464
North Greece	14515	Nyack	10960	Onteora Park	12485
North Greenbush (Town)	12198	Oak Beach	11702	Oot Park	13057
North Greenwich	12834	Oakdale	11769	Open Meadows	14710
North Hamlin	14464	Oakdale Mall (Part of		Oppenheim	13329
North Hannibal	13126	Johnson City)	13790	Oppenheim (Town)	13329
North Harmony (Town)	14785	Oakfield	14125	Oquaga Lake	13754
North Harpersfield	12093	Oakfield (Town)	14125	Oramel	14711
North Hartland	14008	Oak Hill	12460	Oran	13125
North Haven	11963	Oakland	14517	Orange (Town)	14812
North Hebron	12832	Oakland Gardens (Part of		Orangeburg	10962
North Hempstead (Town)	11040	New York)	11364	Orange Lake	12550
North Highland	10516	Oak Orchard	14103	Orangeport	14067
North Hills	11040	Oak Point (Bronx County)	10455	Orangetown (Town)	10960
North Hillsdale	12529	Oak Point (St. Lawrence		Orangeville (Town)	14569
North Hoosick	12133	County)	13646	Orangeville Center	14011
North Hornell	14843	Oak Ridge (Montgomery		Orangeville Corners	14167
North Hudson	12855	County)	12066	Orchard Knoll	14845
North Hudson (Town)	12855	Oakridge (Onondaga		Orchard Park	14127
North Ilion	13340	County)	13088	Orchard Park (Town)	14127
North Jasper	14819	Oaks Corners	14518	Orchard Village	13031
North Java	14113	Oaksville	13337	Oregon	11952
North Jay	12941	Oakwood (Cayuga County)	13021	Orient	11957
North Kortright	13739	Oakwood (Richmond		Orienta (Part of	
North Lansing	14852	County)	10301	Mamaroneck)	10543
North Lawrence	12967	Oakwood Beach (Part of		Oriental Park	14712
North Lindenhurst	11757	New York)	10301	Orient Point	11957
North Litchfield	13340	Oakwood Heights (Part of		Oriskany	13424
North Lynbrook	11563	New York)	10301	Oriskany Falls	13425
North Manlius	13082	Obernburg	12767	Orlando	14755
North Massapequa	11758	Obi	14715	Orleans (Jefferson County)	
North Merrick	11566	Occanum	13865	(Town)	13656
North New Hyde Park	11040	Ocean Bay Park	11706	Orleans (Ontario County)	14432
North Norwich	13814	Ocean Beach	11770	Orleans Four Corners	13656
North Norwich (Town)	13814	Oceanside	11572	Orwell	13426
North Olean (Part of Olean)	14760	Odessa	14869	Orwell (Town)	13426
North Patchogue	11772	Ogden (Bronx County)	10452	Oscawana Corners	10579
North Pembroke	14020	Ogden (Monroe County)		Oscawana Lake	10579
North Petersburg	12138	(Town)	14559	Osceola	13316
North Pharsalia	13844	Ogden Center	14559	Osceola (Town)	13316
North Pitcher	13124	Ogdensburg	13669	Ossian (Town)	14437
North Pole	12946	O'Hara Corners	12083	Ossian Center	14437
Northport	11768	Ohio	13324	Ossining	10562
North River	12856	Ohio (Town)	13324	Ossining (Town)	10562
North Rockville Centre	11570	Ohioville	12561	Oswegatchie	13670
North Rose	14516	Oil Springs Indian		Oswegatchie (Town)	13654
North Rush	14543	Reservation (Allegany		Oswego	13126
North Russell	13617	County) (Town)	14081	Oswego (Town)	13126
North Salem	10560	Oil Springs Indian		Oswego Bitter	13031
North Salem (Town)	10560	Reservation (Allegany		Oswego Center	13126
North Sanford	13754	County)	14081	Otego	13825
North Sea	11968	Oil Springs Indian		Otego (Town)	13825
North Selden	11784	Reservation (Cattaraugus		Otisco	13159
North Settlement	12496	County) (Town)	14081	Otisco (Town)	13159
North Shore Beach	11778	Olcott	14126	Otisco Valley	13110
Northside (Part of Corning)	14830	Old Bethpage	11804	Otisville	10963
North Smithtown	11787	Old Brookville	11545	Otisville Correctional Facility	10963
North Spencer	14883	Old Central Bridge	12035	Otsego (Town)	13337
North Stephentown	12168	Old Chatham	12136	Otselic	13072
North Stockholm	13668	Old Chelsa (Part of New		Otselic (Town)	13072
North Syracuse	13212	York)	10011	Otselic Center	13072
North Tarrytown	10591	Old Field	11733	Otter Creek	13343
North Tonawanda	14120	Old Field South	11790	Otter Lake	13338
Northtown Plaza	14226	Old Forge	13420	Ott Meadows	13088
Northumberland	12871	Old Mastic	11951	Otto	14766
Northumberland (Town)	12871	Old Orchard Point	14487	Otto (Town)	14766

	ZIP		ZIP		ZIP
Ouaquaga	13826	Peconic	11958	Pine Knolls	13760
Overlook	12822	Peekskill	10566	Pine Lake	12032
Ovid	14521	Pekin	14132	Pine Meadows	13302
Ovid (Town)	14521	Pelham	10803	Pine Neck	11963
Ovid Center	14847	Pelham (Town)	10803	Pine Plains	12567
Ovington (Part of New York)	11220	Pelham Manor	10803	Pine Plains (Town)	12567
Owasco	13021	Pelham Parkway (Part of		Pine Ridge	12203
Owasco (Town)	13021	New York)	10462	Pine Ridge Estates	10573
Owego	13827	Pellets Island	10958	Pine Valley (Chemung	
Owego (Town)	13827	Pembroke	14036	County)	14872
Owens Mills	14825	Pembroke (Town)	14036	Pine Valley (Suffolk County)	11901
Owls Head	12969	Penataquit	11706	Pineville (Delaware County)	13856
Oxbow	13671	Pendleton	14094	Pineville (Oswego County)	13302
Oxford	13830	Pendleton (Town)	14094	Pinewood Estates	12303
Oxford (Town)	13830	Pendleton Center	14094	Pine Woods	13310
Oxford	10918	Penfield	14526	Pioneer	12020
Oyster Bay	11771	Penfield (Town)	14526	Piseco	12139
Oyster Bay (Town)	11771	Pennellville	13132	Pitcairn	13648
Oyster Bay Cove	11771	Penn Yan	14527	Pitcairn (Town)	13648
Ozone Park (Part of New		Peoria	14525	Pitcher	13136
York)	11416	Perch River	13601	Pitcher (Town)	13136
Pacama	12401	Perinton (Town)	14450	Pitcher Hill	13212
Pace University		Perkinsville	14529	Pitt (Part of New York)	10002
Pleasantville-Briarcliff		Perry	14530	Pittsfield	13411
Campus	10570	Perry (Town)	14530	Pittsfield (Town)	13411
Paddlefords	14424	Perry Center	14530	Pittsford	14534
Paddy Hill	13615	Perry City	14886	Pittsford (Town)	14534
Paines Hollow	13407	Perrysburg	14129	Pittstown	12094
Painted Post	14870	Perrysburg (Town)	14129	Pittstown (Town)	12094
Palatine (Town)	13428	Perrys Mills	12919	Place Corners	12431
Palatine Bridge	13428	Perryville	13133	Plainedge	11714
Palentown	12446	Persia (Town)	14070	Plainfield (Town)	13491
Palenville	12463	Perth	12010	Plainfield Center	13491
Palermo	13069	Perth (Cattaraugus County)	14741	Plainview	11803
Palermo (Town)	13069	Perth (Fulton County)	12010	Plainview Shopping Center	11803
Palisades	10964	Peru	12972	Plainville	13137
Palmyra	14522	Peru (Town)	12972	Plandome	11030
Palmyra (Town)	14522	Peru	13112	Plandome Heights	11030
Pamelia (Town)	13637	Peruville	13073	Plandome Manor	11030
Pamelia	13637	Peterboro	13134	Planetarium (Part of New	
Panama	14767	Petersburg	12138	York)	10024
Panorama	14625	Petersburg (Town)	12138	Plato	14171
Panther Lake	13028	Peter Stuyvesant (Part of		Platte Clove	12427
Pantigo	11937	New York)	10009	Plattekill	12568
Paradise Hill	12051	Petries Corners	13367	Plattekill (Town)	12568
Paradox	12858	Petrolia	14895	Platten	14098
Parcells Corner	14062	Pharsalia (Town)	13758	Plattsburgh	12901
Paris	13429	Phelps	14532	Plattsburgh (Town)	12918
Paris (Town)	13429	Phelps (Town)	14532	Plattsburgh Air Force Base	12903
Parish	13131	Philadelphia	13673	Plattsburgh West	12962
Parish (Town)	13131	Philadelphia (Town)	13673	Plaza (Part of New York)	11101
Parishville	13672	Philipse Manor (Part of		Pleasantbrook	13320
Parishville (Town)	13672	North Tarrytown)	10591	Pleasantdale	12182
Parishville Center	13676	Philipstown (Town)	10516	Pleasant Plains (Dutchess	
Paris Station	13456	Phillipsburg	10940	County)	12580
Parkchester (Part of New		Phillips Creek	14813	Pleasant Plains (Richmond	
York)	10462	Phillips Mills	14712	County)	10309
Park Hill (Onondaga		Phillipsport	12769	Pleasant Point	13126
County)	13057	Philmont	12565	Pleasantside	10566
Park Hill (Westchester		Phoenicia	12464	Pleasant Valley	12569
County)	10705	Phoenix	13135	Pleasant Valley (Town)	12569
Parkside (Part of New York)	11375	Phoenix Mills	13326	Pleasant Valley (Oneida	
Park Slope (Part of New		Picketts Corners	12981	County)	13480
York)	11215	Pickettsville	13672	Pleasant Valley (Steuben	
Parkston	12758	Piercefield	12973	County)	14810
Parksville	12768	Piercefield (Town)	12973	Pleasantville	10570-72
Park Terrace	13903	Pierces Corner	13642	For specific Pleasantville Zip
Parkville (Part of New York)	11204	Pierceville	13334	Codes call (914) 769-1517, or
Parkway (Part of New York)	10462	Piermont	10968	your local postmaster.
Parma (Town)	14468	Pierrepont	13617	Plessis	13675
Parma Center	14468	Pierrepont (Town)	13617	Plymouth	13832
Parma Corners	14559	Pierrepont Manor	13674	Plymouth (Town)	13832
Parson Farms	13031	Pierstown	13326	Pocantico Hills	10591
Pastime Park	14456	Piffard	14533	Poestenkill	12140
Pataukunk	12446	Pike	14130	Poestenkill (Town)	12140
Patchin (Part of New York)	10011	Pike (Town)	14130	Point Au Rouche	12901
Patchinville	14572	Pike Five Corners	14024	Point Breeze	14477
Patchogue	11772	Pilgrim (Part of New York)	10461	Point Chautauqua	14728
Patchogue Highlands	11772	Pilgrim Corners (Part of		Point Lookout	11569
Patria	12187	Middletown)	10940	Point O'Woods	11706
Patroon (Part of Albany)	12204	Pilgrimport	14489	Point Peninsula	13693
Patterson	12563	Pillar Point	13634	Point Pleasant	14622
Patterson (Town)	12563	Pilot Knob	12844	Point Rochester	14512
Pattersonville	12137	Pinckney (Town)	13610	Point Rock	13471
Paul Smiths	12970	Pine (Part of Albany)	12203	Point Stockholm	14742
Pavilion	14525	Pine Aire	11706	Point Vivian	13607
Pavilion (Town)	14525	Pinebrook (Part of New		Poland (Chautauqua	
Pavilion Center	14525	Rochelle)	10804	County) (Town)	14747
Pawling	12564	Pinebrook Heights (Part of		Poland (Herkimer County)	13431
Pawling (Town)	12564	New Rochelle)	10804	Poland Center	14747
Payne Beach	14468	Pine Bush	12566	Polkville	13101
Peabrook	12760	Pine City	14871	Pomfret (Town)	14063
Peach Lake	10509	Pine Grove (Lewis County)	13343	Pomona	10970
Peakville	13756	Pine Grove (Schoharie		Pomona Heights (Part of	
Pearl Creek	14591	County)	12122	Pomona)	10901
Pearl River	10965	Pinegrove Park	12205	Pomonok (Part of New	
Peas Eddy	13783	Pine Hill (Erie County)	14225	York)	11365
Peasleeville	12985	Pine Hill (Oneida County)	13471	Pompey	13138
Peat Corners	13036	Pine Hill (Ulster County)	12465	Pompey (Town)	13138
Pebble Beach	14480	Pinehill Estates	12303	Pompey Center	13104
Peck Slip (Part of New		Pinehurst	14085	Ponck Hockie (Part of	
York)	10038	Pine Island	10969	Kingston)	12401

	ZIP
Pond Eddy	12770
Ponquogue	11946
Poolville	13432
Poospatuck Indian Reservation (Town)	11950
Poospatuck Indian Reservation	11950
Pope Mills	13654
Poplar Beach	14541
Poplar Ridge	13139
Poquott	11733
Portage	14846
Portage (Town)	14846
Portageville	14536
Port Authority (Part of New York)	10011
Port Byron	13140
Port Chester	10573
Port Crane	13833
Port Dickinson	13901
Porter (Town)	14131
Porter Center	14131
Porter Corners	12859
Porterville	14052
Port Ewen	12466
Port Gibson	14537
Port Henry	12974
Port Jefferson	11777
Port Jefferson Station	11776
Port Jervis	12771
Port Kent	12975
Portland	14769
Portland (Town)	14769
Portlandville	13834
Port Leyden	13433
Port Richmond (Part of New York)	10302
Portville	14770
Portville (Town)	14770
Port Washington	11050
Port Washington North	11050
Post Corners	12057
Post Creek	14812
Potsdam	13676
Potsdam (Town)	13676
Potter	14527
Potter (Town)	14527
Potter Hollow	12469
Pottersville	12860
Poughkeepsie	12601-03
For specific Poughkeepsie Zip Codes call (914) 452-3421, or your local postmaster.	
Poughkeepsie (Town)	12602
Poughquag	12570
Pound Ridge	10576
Pound Ridge (Town)	10576
Pratt (Part of New York)	11205
Pratt Corners	13087
Prattsburg	14873
Prattsburg (Town)	14873
Pratts Hollow	13434
Prattsville	12468
Prattsville (Town)	12468
Preble	13141
Preble (Town)	13141
Prendergast Point	14757
Presho	14858
Preston	13830
Preston (Town)	13830
Preston Hollow	12469
Prince (Part of New York)	10012
Princes Bay (Part of New York)	10309
Princetown	12056
Princetown (Town)	12056
Progress	12078
Prospect	13435
Prospect Heights	12144
Prospect Hill	12188
Prospect Park West (Part of New York)	11215
Providence (Town)	12850
Pulaski	13142
Pulteney	14874
Pulteney (Town)	14874
Pultneyville	14538
Pulvers	12075
Pulvers Corners	12567
Pumpkin Hill	14422
Pumpkin Hollow	12529
Purchase (Part of Harrison)	10577
Purdys	10578
Purdys Mills	12910
Purling	12470
Putnam (Town)	12861
Putnam Lake	10509
Putnam Station	12861
Putnam Valley	10579
Putnam Valley (Town)	10579
Pyramid Mall Ithaca (Part of Lansing)	14850

	ZIP
Pyrites	13677
Quackenbush Hill	14830
Quackenkill	12052
Quail (Part of Albany)	12206
Quaker Basin	13052
Quaker Hill	12564
Quaker Ridge (Part of New Rochelle)	10801
Quaker Springs	12871
Quaker Street	12141
Quarry Heights	10603
Quarryville	12477
Queechy	12029
Queens	11001-06
	11101-06
	11301-86
	11401-36
	11601-97
For specific Queens Zip Codes call (718) 321-5000, or your local postmaster.	
Queensbridge (Part of New York)	11101
Queensbury	12801
Queensbury (Town)	12801
Queens Center (Part of New York)	11373
Queens Village (Part of New York)	11428
Quigley Park	14710
Quinneville	13746
Quioque	11978
Quogue	11959
Raceville	05764
Radio City (Part of New York)	10019
Radison	13027
Rainbow Lake	12976
Ralmar Park	12302
Ramapo	10931
Ramapo (Town)	10931
Ram Island	11964
Rampasture	11946
Randall	12072
Randallsville	13346
Randolph	14772
Randolph (Town)	14772
Ransomville	14131
Rapids	14094
Raquette Lake	13436
Rathbone	14801
Rathbone (Town)	14801
Ravena	12143
Ravenwood (Part of Colonie)	12205
Rawson	14727
Ray Brook	12977
Raymertown	12180
Raymondville	13678
Rayville	12136
Reading	14876
Reading Center	14876
Reber	12996
Red Creek (Suffolk County)	11946
Red Creek (Wayne County)	13143
Redfalls	12468
Redfield	13437
Redfield (Town)	13437
Redford	12978
Red Hook	12571
Red Hook (Town)	12571
Red Hook (Part of New York)	11231
Red House (Town)	14779
Red Mills (Columbia County)	12513
Red Mills (St. Lawrence County)	13669
Red Oaks Mill	12603
Red Rock (Columbia County)	12060
Red Rock (Onondaga County)	13027
Redwood (Jefferson County)	13679
Redwood (Suffolk County)	11963
Reeds Corner	14437
Reeds Corners	14437
Reeves Park	11901
Rego Park (Part of New York)	11374
Reidsville	12186
Remsen	13438
Remsen (Town)	13438
Remsenburg	11960
Remsenburg-Speonk	11960
Rensselaer	12144
Rensselaer Falls	13680
Rensselaerville	12147
Rensselaerville (Town)	12147
Residence Park (Part of New Rochelle)	10805

	ZIP
Retsof	14539
Rexford	12148
Rexville	14877
Reydon Shores	11971
Reynoldsville	14818
Rheims	14840
Rhinebeck	12572
Rhinebeck (Town)	12572
Rhinecliff	12574
Ricard	13302
Rice Grove	13110
Riceville (Cattaraugus County)	14171
Riceville (Fulton County)	12078
Riceville Station	14171
Richburg	14774
Richfield	13439
Richfield (Town)	13439
Richfield Springs	13439
Richford	13835
Richford (Town)	13835
Richland	13144
Richland (Town)	13144
Richmond	10301-14
For specific Richmond Zip Codes call (718) 442-0647, or your local postmaster.	
Richmond (Town)	14471
Richmond Hill (Part of New York)	11418
Richmond Valley (Part of New York)	10307
Richmondville	12149
Richmondville (Town)	12149
Richs Corners	14411
Richville	13681
Riders Mills	12024
Ridge (Livingston County)	14510
Ridge (Suffolk County)	11961
Ridgebury	10973
Ridgelea Heights	14094
Ridge Mills (Part of Rome)	13440
Ridgemont Plaza	14626
Ridgeway	14103
Ridgeway (Town)	14103
Ridgeway (Part of White Plains)	10601
Ridgewood (Niagara County)	14094
Ridgewood (Oneida County)	13501
Ridgewood (Queens County)	11385
Rifton	12471
Riga (Town)	14428
Rigney Bluff	14612
Riley Cove	12020
Ringdahl Court (Part of Rome)	13440
Rio	12780
Riparius	12862
Ripley	14775
Ripley (Town)	14775
Rippleton	13035
Risingville	14820
River (Part of Rochester)	14627
Riverdale (Part of New York)	10471
Riverhead	11901
Riverhead (Town)	11901
Riverside (Broome County)	13795
Riverside (Erie County)	14207
Riverside (Otsego County)	13838
Riverside (Saratoga County)	12118
Riverside (Steuben County)	14830
Riverside (Suffolk County)	11901
Riverside Estates	11901
Riverside Mall (Part of Utica)	13502
Riverside Manors	14172
Riverside Park	12401
Riverview	12981
Riverview Correctional Facility	13669
Roanoke	14143
Robbins Rest	11770
Roberts Corner	13650
Rochdale	12603
Rochdale Village (Part of New York)	11434
Rochelle Heights (Part of New Rochelle)	10801
Rochelle Park (Part of New Rochelle)	10801
Rochester	14601-92
For specific Rochester Zip Codes call (716) 272-8090, or your local postmaster.	
Rochester (Town)	12404
Rockaway Beach (Part of New York)	11693
Rockaway Park (Part of New York)	11694

	ZIP
Rockaway Point (Part of New York)	11697
Rock City (Cattaraugus County)	14760
Rock City (Dutchess County)	12571
Rock City Falls	12863
Rock Cut	13078
Rockdale	13809
Rockefeller Center (Part of New York)	10020
Rock Glen	14550
Rock Hill	12775
Rockhurst	12801
Rockland (Town)	12776
Rockland (Rockland County)	10962
Rockland (Sullivan County)	12776
Rockland Lake	10989
Rockland Psychiatric Center	10962
Rock Stream	14878
Rock Tavern	12575
Rockton	12010
Rock Valley	12760
Rockville (Allegany County)	14711
Rockville (Orange County)	10940
Rockville Centre	11570*
	11571†
Rockville Lake	14711
Rockwells Mills	13843
Rockwood	12095
Rocky Point (Clinton County)	12901
Rocky Point (Suffolk County)	11778
Rodman	13682
Rodman (Town)	13682
Roe Park	10566
Roessleville	12205
Rolling Acres	14559
Rolling Hills (Monroe County)	14450
Rolling Hills (Nassau County)	11507
Rolling Meadows	12401
Romanoff	10512
Rombout Ridge	12603
Rome	13440
	13442
For specific Rome Zip Codes call (315) 336-1500, or your local postmaster.	
Romulus	14541
Romulus (Town)	14541
Rondaxe	13420
Rondout (Part of Kingston)	12401
Ronkonkoma	11779
Ronkonkoma West	11779
Roosa Gap	12721
Roosevelt	11575
Roosevelt Beach	14172
Roosevelt Field (Part of Garden City)	11530
Roosevelttown	13683
Root (Town)	12166
Roscoe	12776
Rose	14542
Rose (Town)	14542
Rosebank (Part of New York)	10305
Roseboom	13450
Roseboom (Town)	13450
Rosecrans Park	12123
Rosedale (Part of New York)	11422
Rose Grove	11968
Rose Hill	13110
Rosemont Park (Part of Rensselaer)	12144
Rosendale	12472
Rosendale (Town)	12472
Roseton	12550
Rosiere	13618
Roslyn	11576
Roslyn Estates	11576
Roslyn Harbor	11576
Roslyn Heights	11577
Rossburg	14776
Ross Corners	13850
Rossie	13646
Rossie (Town)	13646
Rossman	12173
Ross Mill	14733
Rosstown	14871
Rossville (Part of New York)	10309
Rotterdam	12303
Rotterdam (Town)	12303
Rotterdam Junction	12150
Rotterdam Square Mall (Part of Schenectady)	12306
Round Lake	12151
Roundout Harbor	12466

	ZIP
Round Top	12473
Rouses Point	12979
Roxbury	12474
Roxbury (Town)	12474
Roxbury (Part of New York)	11697
Royalton	14067
Royalton (Town)	14067
Ruby	12475
Ruby Corner	13646
Rugby (Part of New York)	11203
Rumsey Ridge	14092
Rural Grove	12166
Rural Hill	13650
Rush	14543
Rush (Town)	14543
Rushford	14777
Rushford (Town)	14777
Rushford Lake	14717
Rushville	14544
Russell	13684
Russell (Town)	13684
Russell Gardens	11021
Russia	13431
Russia (Town)	13431
Rutland (Town)	13638
Rutland Center	13601
Ryder (Part of New York)	11234
Rye	10580
Rye (Town)	10573
Rye Brook	10573
Rye Hills	10573
Sabael	12864
Sabattis	12847
Sabbath Day Point	12874
Sacandaga	12134
Sackets Harbor	13685
Sacketts Lake	12701
Saddle Rock	11023
Saddle Rock Estates	11021
Sagaponack	11962
Sages Cottages	11944
Sagetown	14871
Sag Harbor	11963
Sailors Snug Harbor (Part of New York)	10301
St. Albans (Part of New York)	11412
St. Andrew	12586
St. Armand (Town)	12913
St. Bonaventure	14778
St. George (Part of New York)	10301
St. Huberts	12943
St. James	11780
St. James Heights	11780
St. John Fisher College	14618
St. Johnsburg	14302
St. Johns Place (Part of New York)	11213
St. Johnsville	13452
St. Johnsville (Town)	13452
St. Josephs	12701
St. Lawrence Park	13607
St. Mary's Park (Part of New York)	10455
St. Regis Falls	12980
St. Regis Indian Reservation	13655
St. Regis Indian Reservation (Town)	13655
St. Remy	12401
Saintsville	13116
Salamanca (Town)	14779
Salamanca	14779
Salem	12865
Salem (Town)	12865
Salem Center	10578
Salina (Town)	13088
Salina	13208
Salisbury	13365
Salisbury (Town)	13365
Salisbury	11801
Salisbury Center	13454
Salisbury Mills	12577
Salmon River	12901
Saltaire	11706
Salt Point	12578
Salt Springville	13320
Sammonsville	12095
Samsondale (Part of West Haverstraw)	10993
Samsonville	12481
Sanborn	14132
Sandford Boulevard (Part of Mount Vernon)	10550
Sandfordville	13676
Sand Hill (Erie County)	14001
Sand Hill (Montgomery County)	13339
Sand Lake	12153
Sand Lake (Town)	12153
Sand Ridge	13132
Sands Point	11050

	ZIP
Sandusky	14133
Sandy Beach	14072
Sandy Creek	13145
Sandy Creek (Town)	13145
Sandy Harbour Beach	14464
Sanford (Town)	13754
Sangerfield	13455
Sangerfield (Town)	13455
Sanitaria Springs	13833
San Remo	11754
Santa Clara	12980
Santa Clara (Town)	12980
Santapoque	11707
Saranac	12981
Saranac (Town)	12981
Saranac Inn	12983
Saranac Lake	12983
Saratoga (Town)	12871
Saratoga Springs	12866
Sardinia	14134
Sardinia (Town)	14134
Saugerties	12477
Saugerties (Town)	12477
Saugerties South	12477
Sauquoit	13456
Savannah	13146
Savannah (Town)	13146
Savona	14879
Sawkill	12401
Sawyers Corners	13021
Saxon Park	11706
Sayville	11782
Scarborough (Part of Briarcliff Manor)	10510
Scarsdale	10583
Scarsdale (Town)	10583
Schaghticoke	12154
Schaghticoke (Town)	12154
Schaghticoke Hill	12154
Schenectady	12301-08
For specific Schenectady Zip Codes call (518) 395-5400, or your local postmaster.	
Schenevus	12155
Schermerhorn Corners	14747
Schodack (Town)	12033
Schodack Center	12033
Schodack Landing	12156
Schoharie	12157
Schoharie (Town)	12157
Schonowe	12306
Schroeppel (Town)	13135
Schroon (Town)	12870
Schroon Lake	12870
Schultzville	12572
Schuluski Estates	12188
Schuyler (Town)	13340
Schuyler Falls	12985
Schuyler Falls (Town)	12985
Schuyler Lake	13457
Schuylerville	12871
Scio	14880
Scio (Town)	14880
Sciota	12992
Scipio (Town)	13147
Scipio Center	13147
Scipioville	13147
Sconondoa	13421
Scotchbush (Fulton County)	13452
Scotch Bush (Montgomery County)	12010
Scotchtown	10940
Scotia	12302
Scott	13077
Scott (Town)	13077
Scottsburg	14545
Scottsville	14546
Scranton	14075
Scriba (Town)	13126
Scriba Center	13126
Sea Breeze	14617
Sea Cliff	11579
Seaford	11783
Seager	12406
Searingtown	11507
Searsburg	14886
Sears Corners	10509
Searsville	12549
Seaview	11770
Second Milo	14527
Seeley Creek	14871
Selden	11784
Selkirk	12158
Selkirk Beach	13142
Sellecks Corners	13625
Sempronius	13118
Sempronius (Town)	13118
Seneca (Town)	14561
Seneca Army Depot	14541
Seneca Castle	14547
Seneca Falls	13148
Seneca Falls (Town)	13148

* Area Zip Code   † Post Office Boxes

	ZIP
Seneca Hill	13126
Seneca Knolls	13209
Seneca Mall (Erie County)	14224
Seneca Mall (Onondaga County)	13088
Seneca Point	14512
Sennett	13021
Sennett (Town)	13021
Sentinel Heights	13078
Setauket	11733
Setauket-East Setauket	11733
Settlers Hill	10509
Seven Hills	10512
Seventh Day Hollow	13072
Severance	12872
Seward	12043
Seward (Town)	12043
Shackport	13757
Shadigee	14098
Shady	12409
Shandaken	12480
Shandaken (Town)	12480
Shandelee	12758
Sharon	13459
Sharon (Town)	13459
Sharon Springs	13459
Shawangunk (Town)	12589
Shawnee	14132
Sheds	13122
Shekomeko	12546
Shelby	14103
Shelby (Town)	14103
Shelby Basin	14103
Shelby Center	14103
Sheldon	14145
Sheldon (Town)	14145
Sheldrake	14521
Sheldrake Springs	14847
Shelter Island	11964
Shelter Island (Town)	11964
Shelter Island Heights	11965
Shenandoah	12533
Shenorock	10587
Sherburne	13460
Sherburne (Town)	13460
Sheridan	14135
Sheridan (Town)	14135
Sheridan Park (Part of Geneva)	14456
Sherman	14781
Sherman (Town)	14781
Sherman Park	10594
Shermerhorn Landing	13646
Sherrill	13461
Sherwood Forest	12065
Sherwood Knolls	13031
Sherwood Park	12144
Shinhopple	13837
Shinnecock Hills	11946
Shinnecock Indian Reservation (Town)	11968
Shinnecock Indian Reservation	11968
Shirewood	12065
Shirley	11967
Shokan	12481
Sholam	12458
Shongo	16923
Shooktown (Part of Lockport)	14094
Shoppingtown Mall	13214
Shore Acres (Chautauqua County)	14712
Shore Acres (Monroe County)	14468
Shore Acres (Suffolk County)	11952
Shore Acres (Westchester County)	10543
Shoreham	11786
Shore Haven	14787
Shorelands	14728
Shore Oaks	13126
Shorewood	11721
Shortsville	14548
Short Tract	14735
Shrub Oak	10588
Shumla	14063
Shushan	12873
Shutter Corners	12157
Shutts Corners	12043
Sibleyville	14472
Sidney	13838
Sidney (Town)	13838
Sidney Center	13839
Siena	12211
Sillimans Corners	14030
Silver Bay	12874
Silver Creek	14136
Silver Lake (Orange County)	10940
Silver Lake (Wyoming County)	14549

	ZIP
Silver Lake Village	10940
Silver Springs	14550
Simmons Island (Part of Cohoes)	12047
Simpsonville	12155
Sinclairville	14782
Sissonville	13676
Skaneateles	13152
Skaneateles (Town)	13152
Skaneateles Falls	13153
Skaneateles Junction	13060
Skerry	12966
Skinnerville	13697
Sky Meadow Farms	10573
Slab City (Cortland County)	13141
Slab City (St. Lawrence County)	13676
Slate Hill	10973
Slaterville Springs	14881
Sleightsburg	12401
Slingerlands	12159
Sloan	14225
Sloansville	12160
Sloatsburg	10974
Slyboro	12832
Smallwood	12778
Smartville	13083
Smithboro	13840
Smith Corners	13407
Smithfield (Dutchess County)	12501
Smithfield (Madison County) (Town)	13134
Smith Haven Mall (Part of Lake Grove)	11755
Smiths Basin	12827
Smiths Corner	12120
Smiths Mills	14062
Smithtown (Town)	11787
Smithtown	11787
Smithtown Branch	11787
Smithtown Pines	11787
Smithtown Shopping Center	11787
Smith Valley	14805
Smithville (Chenango County) (Town)	13778
Smithville (Jefferson County)	13605
Smithville Center	13778
Smithville Flats	13841
Smyrna	13464
Smyrna (Town)	13464
Snooks Corners	12010
Snufftown	10924
Snyder	14226
Snyder Crossing	13116
Snyders Corners	12180
Snyders Lake	12180
Sodom (Putnam County)	10509
Sodom (Warren County)	12853
Sodus	14551
Sodus (Town)	14551
Sodus Center	14554
Sodus Point	14555
Solon	13055
Solon (Town)	13055
Solsville	13465
Solvay	13209
Somers	10589
Somers (Town)	10589
Somerset	14012
Somerset (Town)	14012
Somerset Lake	13783
Somerville	13642
Sonora	14879
Sonyea	14556
Sound Beach	11789
Soundview (Part of New York)	10472
South (Part of Yonkers)	10705
South Addison	14801
South Alabama	14013
South Albion	13302
South Amenia	12592
Southampton	11968*
	11969†
Southampton	11968
Southampton College	11946
South Amsterdam (Part of Amsterdam)	12010
South Apalachin	13732
South Argyle	12809
South Bay	13032
South Bay Shopping Center	11702
South Bay Village	12827
South Bethlehem	12161
South Bloomfield	14469
South Bolivar	14715
South Bombay	12957
South Bradford	14879
South Bristol	14512
South Bristol (Town)	14512
South Brookfield	13485

	ZIP
South Buffalo (Part of Buffalo)	14210
South Butler	13154
South Byron	14557
South Cairo	12482
South Cambridge	12028
South Canisteo	14823
South Centereach	11720
South Chili	14546
South Colton	13687
South Columbia	13439
South Corinth	12822
South Corning	14830
South Cortland	13045
South Danby	13864
South Dansville	14807
South Dayton	14138
South Dover	12522
South Durham	12405
Southeast (Town)	10509
Southeast Owasco	13118
South Edmeston	13466
South Edwards	13635
South Fallsburg	12779
South Farmingdale	11735
Southfields	10975
South Floral Park	11001
South Flushing (Part of New York)	11365
Southgate Plaza	14224
Southgate Shopping Center (Part of Massapequa Park)	11762
South Gilboa	12167
South Glens Falls	12803
South Granville	12832
South Greece	14626
South Hamilton	13332
South Hannibal	13074
South Hartford (Otsego County)	13810
South Hartford (Washington County)	12838
South Haven	11719
South Hempstead	11550
South Highland	10524
South Hill	14850
South Holbrook	11741
South Horicon	12815
South Hornell	14843
South Huntington	11746
South Ilion	13357
South Jamesport	11970
South Jefferson	12167
South Jewett	12442
South Kortright	13842
South Lake	10512
South Lebanon	13332
South Lima	14558
South Livonia	14487
South Lockport	14094
South Millbrook	12545
South New Berlin	13843
South Newstead	14001
South Nineveh	13787
South Nyack	10960
Southold	11971
Southold (Town)	11971
South Olean (Part of Olean)	14760
South Onondaga	13120
South Otselic	13155
South Owego	13827
South Oxford	13830
South Ozone Park (Part of New York)	11420
South Park (Part of Buffalo)	14220
South Plainedge	11758
South Plymouth	13844
South Pole (Part of New York)	10090
Southport	14904
Southport (Town)	14904
South Richmond Hill (Part of New York)	11419
South Ripley	14775
South Russell	13684
South Rutland	13688
South Salem	10590
South Schodack	12162
South Schroon	12870
South Setauket	11733
South Shore Mall	11706
South Side (Part of Elmira)	14904
South Sodus	14489
South St. Johnsville	13339
South Stockton	14782
South Stony Brook	11790
South Trenton	13304
South Utica (Part of Utica)	13501
South Valley (Cattaraugus County) (Town)	14779

	ZIP
South Valley (Otsego County)	13320
South Valley Stream	11581
South Vandalia	14706
South Vestal	13850
Southview (Part of Binghamton)	13903
South Wales	14139
South Warsaw	14569
South Westbury	11590
South Westerlo	12163
Southwest Oswego	13126
Southwood	13078
South Worcester	12197
Spackenkill	12603
Spafford	13077
Spafford (Town)	13077
Sparkill	10976
Sparkle Lake	10598
Sparrow Bush	12780
Sparta (Livingston County) (Town)	14437
Sparta (Westchester County)	10562
Spawn Hollow	12161
Speculator	12164
Speedsville	13736
Speigletown	12182
Spencer	14883
Spencer (Town)	14883
Spencerport	14559
Spencer Settlement	13440
Spencertown	12165
Speonk	11972
Split Rock	13031
Spragueville	13642
Sprakers	12166
Spring Brook	14140
Spring Creek (Part of New York)	11239
Springfield (Town)	13468
Springfield Center	13468
Springfield Gardens (Part of New York)	11413
Spring Glen	12483
Spring Lake	13140
Spring Mills	14897
Springport (Town)	13160
Springs	11937
Springtown	12561
Springvale	13815
Spring Valley (Rockland County)	10977
Spring Valley (Westchester County)	10562
Springville (Erie County)	14141
Springville (Suffolk County)	11946
Springwater	14560
Springwater (Town)	14560
Springwood Village	12538
Sprout Brook	13317
Spruceton	12492
Spuyten Duyvil (Part of New York)	10463
Squiretown	11946
Staatsburg	12580
Stacy Basin	13054
Stadium (Part of New York)	10452
Stafford	14143
Stafford (Town)	14143
Stamford	12167
Stamford (Town)	12167
Standish	12952
Stanford (Town)	12581
Stanford Heights	12301
Stanfordville	12581
Stanley	14561
Stanley Manor	13031
Stannards	14895
Stanwix (Part of Rome)	13440
Stanwix Heights (Part of Rome)	13440
Stanwood	10549
Stapleton (Part of New York)	10304
Starbuckville	12817
Stark (Town)	13339
Starkey	14837
Starkey (Town)	14837
Starks Knob	12871
Starkville	13339
Star Lake	13690
State Bridge	13054
State Line	14775
Staten Island	10301-14

For specific Staten Island Zip Codes call (718) 816-2790, or your local postmaster.

	ZIP
COLLEGES & UNIVERSITIES	
City University of New York-College of Staten Island	10301
Wagner College	10301
FINANCIAL INSTITUTIONS	
Gateway State Bank	10304
Northfield Savings Bank, F.S.B.	10314
Richmond County Savings Bank	10310
Staten Island Savings Bank	10304
HOSPITALS	
St. Vincent's Medical Center of Richmond	10310
Staten Island University Hospital	10305
Staten Island Mall (Part of New York)	10314
State School	10990
State University (Part of Old Westbury)	11568
State University of New York at Binghamton (Broome County)	13901
State University of New York at Stony Brook (Suffolk County)	11794
Steamburg	14783
Steam Valley	14760
Stears Corners	13659
Steelton	14219
Steinway (Part of New York)	11103
Stella	13905
Stella Niagara	14144
Stephens Mills	14843
Stephentown	12168
Stephentown (Town)	12168
Stephentown Center	12168
Sterling	13156
Sterling (Town)	13156
Sterling Forest	10979
Sterling Valley	13156
Stetsonville	13415
Steuben (Town)	13354
Steuben Valley	13354
Stever Mill	12025
Stewart Air Force Base	12550
	12553

For specific Stewart Air Force Base Zip Codes call (914) 564-2100, or your local postmaster.

	ZIP
Stewart Manor	11530
Stilesville	13754
Stillman Village	12138
Stillwater (Town)	12170
Stillwater (Chautauqua County)	14701
Stillwater (Putnam County)	10541
Stillwater (Saratoga County)	12170
Stillwater Hill	10562
Stirling	11944
Stissing	12581
Stittville	13469
Stockbridge	13409
Stockbridge (Town)	13409
Stockholm (Town)	13697
Stockholm Center	13697
Stockport	12534
Stockport (Town)	12534
Stockport	13783
Stockport Station	12534
Stockton	14784
Stockton (Town)	14784
Stockwell	13480
Stokes	13363
Stone Arabia	13339
Stone Church	14416
Stonedam	16923
Stone Gate	10950
Stone Mills	13656
Stone Ridge (Montgomery County)	12072
Stone Ridge (Ulster County)	12484
Stone University of New York (Part of Albany)	12203
Stony Brook	11790
Stony Creek	12878
Stony Creek (Town)	12878
Stony Creek Estates	12065
Stony Hollow	12401
Stony Point	10980
Stony Point (Town)	10980
Stormville	12582
Stottville	12172
Stow	14785
Straits Corners	13827
Stratford	13470
Stratford (Town)	13470

	ZIP
Strathmore	11030
Streeters Corners	14094
Streetroad	12883
Strykersville	14145
Stuyvesant	12173
Stuyvesant (Town)	12173
Stuyvesant (Part of New York)	11233
Stuyvesant Falls	12174
Suffern	10901
Suffern Park	10901
Sugarbush	12968
Sugar Loaf	10981
Sugartown	14741
Sullivan	13037
Sullivan (Town)	13037
Sullivanville	14845
Summerhill	13092
Summerhill (Town)	13092
Summit	12175
Summit (Town)	12175
Summit Park	10977
Summit Park Mall (Part of Niagara Falls)	14304
Summitville	12781
Sun	12917
Sundown	12782
Sun Haven (Part of New Rochelle)	10801
Sunmount (Part of Tupper Lake)	12986
Sunny Side (Chautauqua County)	14701
Sunnyside (Columbia County)	12106
Sunnyside (Queens County)	11104
Sunrise Mall	11758
Sunrise Terrace	13902
Sunset (Part of New York)	11220
Sunset Bay (Hanover twp.)	14081
Sunset Bay (Ellery twp.)	14712
Sunset Beach	14172
Sunset City Shopping Center	11703
Sunset Manor	13492
Surprise	12176
Svahn Manor	10989
Swain	14884
Swan Lake	12783
Swartwood	14889
Swastika	12985
Swazy Acres	12188
Sweden (Town)	14420
Sweden Center	14420
Sweet Meadows	12401
Swenson Drive (Part of Wappingers Falls)	12590
Swifts Mills	14001
Swormville	14051
Sycaway	12180
Sylvan Beach	13157
Sylvan Lake	12533
Syosset	11791
Syracuse	13201-90

For specific Syracuse Zip Codes call (315) 470-3486, or your local postmaster.

	ZIP
Taberg	13471
Tabor Corners	14572
Taborton	12153
Taconic Correctional Facility	10507
Taconic Lake	12138
Taghkanic	12502
Taghkanic (Town)	12502
Talcottville	13309
Talcville	13635
Tallman	10982
Tanglewood Hills	11727
Tannersville	12485
Tappan	10983
Tarrytown	10591
Tarrytown Heights (Part of Tarrytown)	10591
Taunton	13219
Taylor	13040
Taylor (Town)	13040
Taylor Center	13040
Teall (Part of Syracuse)	13217
Teboville	12953
Ten Mile River	12764
Tennanah	12776
Tennanah Lake	12776
Terminal (Part of New York)	10301
Terrace Park	13669
Terry's Corners	14067
Terryville	11776
Texas	13114
Texas Valley	13803
Thayer Corners	12917
The Bridges	14477
The Forge	12920
The Forks	14030

	ZIP		ZIP		ZIP
The Glen	12885	Tribes Hill	12177	Upper Little York Lake	13141
The Hook	12809	Triborough (Part of New		Upper Mongaup	12737
The Narrows	14737	York)	10035	Upper Nyack	10960
Thendara	13472	Triphammer Mall (Part of		Upper Red Hook	12571
Theresa	13691	Lansing)	14852	Upper St. Regis	12945
Theresa (Town)	13691	Tripoli	12827	Upper Union	12309
The Terrace	11050	Troupsburg	14885	Upperville	13464
The Vly	12484	Troupsburg (Town)	14885	Upton Lake	12514
Thiells	10984	Troutburg	14464	Uptonville (Part of	
Thomaston	11021	Trout Creek	13847	Rochester)	14617
Thompson (Ontario County)	14489	Trout River	12926	Uptown (Part of Kingston)	12401
Thompson (Sullivan County)		Troy	12180-83	Urbana (Town)	14840
(Town)	12701	For specific Troy Zip Codes call		Ushers	12151
Thompson Ridge	10985	(518) 272-7300, or your local		U.S. Military Academy	10996
Thompsons Lake	12009	postmaster.		Utica	13501-05
Thompsonville	12784	Truesdale Lake	10590	For specific Utica Zip Codes call	
Thomson	12834	Trumansburg	14886	(315) 738-5354, or your local	
Thornton	14723	Trumbulls Corners	14867	postmaster.	
Thornton Grove	13152	Truthville	12854	Utopia (Part of New York)	11366
Thornton Heights	13152	Truxton	13158	Vail Mills	12025
Thornwood	10594	Truxton (Town)	13158	Vails Gate	12584
Thousand Island Park	13692	Tuckahoe (Suffolk County)	11968	Vail's Grove	10509
Three Mile Bay	13693	Tuckahoe (Westchester		Valatie	12184
Three Rivers	13041	County)	10707	Valcour	12972
Throg's Neck (Part of New		Tucker Heights	12019	Valhalla	10595
York)	10465	Tucker Terrace	13662	Valley Cottage	10989
Throop (Town)	13021	Tudor (Part of New York)	10017	Valley Falls	12185
Throopsville	13021	Tully	13159	Valley Mills	13409
Thruway Mall	14225	Tully (Town)	13159	Valley Pond Estates	10536
Thurman (Town)	12885	Tunnel	13848	Valley Stream	11580-82
Thurston	14821	Tupper Lake	12986	For specific Valley Stream Zip	
Thurston (Town)	14821	Turin	13473	Codes call (516) 825-2220, or	
Thurston Road (Part of		Turin (Town)	13473	your local postmaster.	
Rochester)	14619	Turnwood	12758	Valley View Manor (Part of	
Tiana	11946	Tuscan	12197	Rome)	13440
Tiana Shores	11942	Tuscarora (Livingston		Vallonia Springs	13813
Ticonderoga	12883	County)	14510	Valois	14888
Ticonderoga (Town)	12883	Tuscarora (Steuben County)		Van Brunt (Part of New	
Tillson	12486	(Town)	14801	York)	11215
Times Plaza (Part of New		Tuscarora Indian		Van Buren (Town)	13027
York)	11217	Reservation (Town)	14094	Van Buren Bay	14048
Times Square (Part of New		Tuscarora Indian		Van Buren Point	14166
York)	10036	Reservation	14094	Van Burenville	10940
Timothy Heights	12569	Tusten (Town)	12764	Van Cortlandtville	10566
Tinkertown	14803	Tuthill	12525	Van Cott (Part of New York)	10467
Tioga (Town)	13845	Tuxedo (Town)	10987	Vandalia	14706
Tioga Center	13845	Tuxedo Park	10987	Van Del (Part of Kenmore)	14217
Tioga Terrace	13732	Twelve Corners	14618	Van Deusenville	13317
Tiona	13811	Twilight Park	12436	Vandever (Part of New	
Titusville	12603	Twin Lakes Village	10590	York)	11210
Tivoli	12583	Twin Orchards	13850	Van Etten	14889
Toddsville	13326	Tyner	13830	Van Etten (Town)	14889
Toddville	10566	Tyre	13148	Van Fleet	16920
Todt Hill (Part of New York)	10301	Tyre (Town)	13148	Van Hornesville	13475
Toll Gate Corner	14770	Tyrone	14887	Van Nest (Part of New	
Tomhannock	12185	Tyrone (Town)	14887	York)	10462
Tomkins Cove	10986	Ulster (Town)	12401	Van Schaick Island (Part of	
Tompkins (Town)	13754	Ulster Heights	12428	Cohoes)	12047
Tompkins Corners	14845	Ulster Landing	12477	Varick (Town)	14541
Tompkins Square (Part of		Ulster Park	12487	Varna	14850
New York)	10009	Ulsterville	12566	Varysburg	14167
Tompkinsville (Part of New		Ulysses (Town)	14886	Vaughs Corners	12839
York)	10301	Unadilla	13849	Vega	12455
Tonawanda	14150*	Unadilla (Town)	13849	Venice	13147
	14151†	Unadilla Forks	13491	Venice (Town)	13147
Tonawanda (Town)	14150	Underwood	12964	Venice Center	13147
Tonawanda (census		Union (Town)	13760	Verbank	12585
designated place)	14223	Union	13760	Verbank Village	12585
Tonawanda Indian			13763	Verdoy	12110
Reservation (Erie County)	14150	For specific Union Zip Codes call		Vermillion	13114
Tonawanda Indian		(607) 785-1181, or your local		Vermontville	12989
Reservation (Erie County)		postmaster.		Vernon	13476
(Town)	14150	Union Center	13760	Vernon (Town)	13476
Tonawanda Indian		Uniondale	11553	Vernon Center	13477
Reservation (Genesee		Union Falls	12912	Vernon Valley	11768
County) (Town)	14150	Union Hill	14563	Verona	13478
Tonawanda Junction	14223	Union Mills	12025	Verona (Town)	13478
Torrey (Town)	14441	Union Shopping Center		Verona Beach	13162
Tottenville (Part of New		(Part of Endicott)	13760	Verona Mills	13440
York)	10307	Union Springs	13160	Verplanck	10596
Towerville Corners	14701	Union Vale (Town)	12585	Versailles	14168
Towlesville	14810	Union Valley	13052	Vesper	13159
Town (Part of Newburgh)	12550	Unionville (Albany County)	12054	Vestal	13850*
Towners	12531	Unionville (Orange County)	10988		13851†
Town Line	14086	Unionville (St. Lawrence		Vestal Center	13850
Town Pump	14559	County)	13676	Vestal Gardens	13850
Townsend	14891	Unionville (Ontario County)	14532	Veteran (Chemung County)	
Townsendville	14847	United Nations New York		(Town)	14864
Tracy Creek	13850	(Part of New York)	10017	Veteran (Ulster County)	12477
Trainsmeadow (Part of New		United States Cadet Corps	10997	Veterans Administration	
York)	11370	University (Part of Syracuse)	13210	Hospital (Erie County)	14215
Transitown	14221	University Gardens	11020	Veterans Administration	
Travis (Part of New York)	10301	University Heights (Part of		Facility (Genesee County)	14020
Travis Corners	10524	New York)	10452	Veterans Hospital (Part of	
Treadwell	13846	Upper Benson	12134	Syracuse)	13210
Tremont (Part of New York)	10457	Upper Brookville	11545	Victor	14564
Trenton (Town)	13304	Upper Grand View	10960	Victor (Town)	14564
Trenton Assembly Park	13304	Upper Hollowville	12530	Victoria	14710
Trenton Falls	13304	Upper Jay	12987	Victory	13033
Triangle	13778	Upper Lisle	13862	Victory (Town)	13033
Triangle (Town)	13778	Upper Little York	13087	Victory Mills	12884
Triangle Lake	12122				

Place	ZIP
Victory Park (Part of New Rochelle)	10804
Vienna	13308
Vienna (Town)	13308
Viewmonte	12526
Village (New York County)	10014
Village (Niagara County)	14094
Village Green (Onondaga County)	13027
Village Green (Saratoga County)	12065
Village of the Branch	11787
Villenova (Town)	14138
Vincent	14424
Vine Valley	14507
Vintonton	12187
Viola	10952
Viola Park	10952
Virgil	13045
Virgil (Town)	13045
Vischer Ferry	12148
Vista	06840
Voak	14527
Volney	13069
Volney (Town)	13069
Volusia	14787
Voorheesville	12186
Vukote	14710
Waccabuc	10597
Waddington	13694
Waddington (Town)	13694
Wadhams	12990
Wadhams Park	13669
Wading River	11792
Wainscott	11975
Waits	13827
Wakefield (Part of New York)	10466
Walden (Erie County)	14225
Walden (Orange County)	12586
Walden Galleria (Part of Buffalo)	14211
Wales (Town)	14139
Wales Center	14169
Wales Hollow	14139
Walesville	13492
Walker	14468
Walker Lane	12801
Walker Valley	12588
Wallace	14809
Wallington	14551
Wallins Corner	12010
Wallkill (Orange County) (Town)	10919
Wallkill (Ulster County)	12589
Wallkill Correctional Facility	12589
Walloomsac	12090
Wall Street (Part of New York)	10005
Walton	13856
Walton (Town)	13856
Walton Park	10950
Walt Whitman Mall	11746
Walworth	14568
Walworth (Town)	14568
Wampsville	13163
Wanakah	14075
Wanakena	13695
Wantagh	11793
Wappinger (Town)	12590
Wappingers Falls	12590
Ward (Town)	14880
Wards Island (Part of New York)	10035
Warners	13164
Warnerville	12187
Warren	13439
Warren (Town)	13439
Warrensburg	12885
Warrensburg (Town)	12885
Warrens Corners	14094
Warsaw	14569
Warsaw (Town)	14569
Warwick	10990
Warwick (Town)	10990
Washington (Town)	12545
Washington Bridge (Part of New York)	10033
Washington Heights	10940
Washington Lake	12550
Washington Mills	13479
Washingtonville	10992
Wassaic	12592
Waterboro	14747
Waterburg	14886
Waterford	12188
Waterford (Town)	12188
Water Island	11772
Waterloo	13165
Waterloo (Town)	13165
Waterman Corners	14728
Water Mill	11976
Waterport	14571
Waterside Park	11768
Watertown	13601-03
For specific Watertown Zip Codes call (315) 786-5900, or your local postmaster.	
Watertown Junction (Part of Watertown)	13601
Watervale	13104
Water Valley	14075
Waterville	13480
Watervliet	12189
Watkins Glen	14891
Watson	13367
Watson (Town)	13367
Watsonville	12122
Wattlesburg	14775
Watts Flats	14710
Wautoma Beach	14468
Wave Crest (Part of New York)	11691
Waverly (Franklin County) (Town)	12980
Waverly (Tioga County)	14892
Wawarsing	12489
Wawarsing (Town)	12489
Wawayanda (Town)	10973
Wayland	14572
Wayland (Town)	14572
Wayne (Schuyler County)	14893
Wayne (Steuben County) (Town)	14840
Wayne Center	14489
Webb (Town)	13420
Webbs Mills	14871
Webster	14580
Webster (Town)	14580
Webster Crossing	14584
Websters Corners	14127
Wedgewood	14891
Weedsport	13166
Wegatchie	13608
Welcome	13810
Wells	12190
Wells (Town)	12190
Wells Bridge	13859
Wellsburg	14894
Wellsville	14895
Wellsville (Town)	14895
Weltonville	13811
Wende Correctional Facility	14004
Wendelville	14120
Wesley	14070
Wesley Chapel	10901
Wesley Hills	10901
West Almond	14804
West Almond (Town)	14804
West Amboy	13167
West Babylon	11704*
	11707†
West Bainbridge	13733
West Bangor	12966
West Barre	14411
West Batavia	14020
West Bay Shore	11706
West Bellport	11772
West Berne	12023
West Bethany	14054
West Bloomfield	14585
West Bloomfield (Town)	14585
West Branch	13303
West Brentwood	11717
Westbrookville	12785
West Burlington	13482
Westbury (Cayuga County)	13143
Westbury (Nassau County)	11590
West Bush	12078
West Cameron	14819
West Camp	12490
West Candor	13743
West Carthage	13619
West Caton	14830
West Charlton	12010
West Chazy	12992
West Chenango	13905
Westchester (Part of New York)	10461
Westchester Heights (Part of New York)	10461
West Chili	14514
West Clarksville	14786
West Colesville	13904
West Conesville	12076
West Copake	12593
West Corners	13760
West Coxsackie (Part of Coxsackie)	12192
Westdale	13483
West Danby	14896
West Davenport	13860
West Dryden	13068
West Durham	12422
West Eaton	13484
West Edmeston	13485
West Elmira	14905
West End	13820
West Endicott	13760
Westerlea	13031
Westerleigh (Part of New York)	10314
Westerlo	12193
Westerlo (Town)	12193
Western (Town)	13486
Western Lights Shopping Center (Part of Syracuse)	13219
Western Pine Knolls	12203
Westernville	13486
West Exeter	13487
West Falls	14170
West Farms (Part of New York)	10460
Westfield	14787
Westfield (Town)	14787
Westford	13488
Westford (Town)	13488
West Fort Ann	12827
West Fort Salonga	11768
West Frankfort	13340
West Fulton	12194
West Gaines	14411
West Galway	12010
Westgate	14624
West Genesee Terrace	13031
West Ghent	12075
West Gilgo Beach	11702
West Glens Falls	12801
West Glenville	12010
West Greece	14626
West Greenwood	14839
West Groton	13073
Westhampton	11977
Westhampton Beach	11978
West Harpersfield	13786
West Haverstraw	10993
West Hebron	12865
West Hempstead	11552
West Henrietta	14586
West Hill	12301
West Hills	11743
West Hoosick	12028
West Huntington	11743
West Hurley	12491
West Islip	11795
West Jewett	12444
West Kendall	14476
West Kill	12492
West Latham	12110
West Laurens	13796
Westlawn	12203
West Lebanon	12195
West Lee	13363
West Leyden	13489
West Lowville	13367
West Mahopac	10541
West Martinsburg	13367
Westmere	12203
West Meredith	13757
West Middleburg	12122
West Middlebury	14054
West Milton	12020
Westminster Park	13607
West Monroe	13167
West Monroe (Town)	13167
Westmore Estates	12203
Westmoreland	13490
Westmoreland (Town)	13490
Westmoreland	11965
West Newark	13811
West New Brighton (Part of New York)	10310
West Newburgh (Part of Newburgh)	12550
West Nyack (census designated place)	10960
West Nyack	10994
Weston	14837
West Oneonta	13861
Westons Mills	14788
Westover	13790
West Park	12493
West Pawling	12564
West Perrysburg	14129
West Perth	12010
West Phoenix	13135
West Pierrepont	13617
West Point	10996*
	10997†
Westport	12993
Westport (Town)	12993
West Portland	14787
West Potsdam	13676
West Ridge (Part of Rochester)	14615
West Ronkonkoma	11779

* Area Zip Code   † Post Office Boxes

	ZIP
West Rush	14543
West Salamanca (Part of Salamanca)	14779
West Sand Lake	12196
West Saugerties	12477
West Sayville	11796
West Schuyler	13502
West Seneca	14224
West Seneca (Town)	14224
West Shelby	14103
West Shokan	12494
West Side (Part of Elmira)	14905
West Slaterville	14881
West Smithtown	11787
West Somerset	14008
West Sparta (Town)	14437
West Stephentown	12168
West St. James	11787
West Stockholm	13696
West Taghkanic	12502
West Tiana	11946
Westtown	10998
West Turin (Town)	13325
West Union (Town)	14877
West Utica (Part of Utica)	13501
Westvale	13219
West Valley	14171
West Valley Falls (Part of Valley Falls)	12185
Westview (Broome County)	13905
Westview (Livingston County)	14437
West Village (Part of New York)	10014
Westville	12926
Westville (Town)	12926
Westville	12155
Westville Center	12926
West Walworth	14502
West Waterford (Part of Waterford)	12188
West Webster	14580
West Windsor	13865
West Winfield	13491
West Yaphank	11980
Wethersfield (Town)	14569
Wethersfield Springs	14569
Wevertown	12886
Whaley Lake	12531
Whallonsburg	12994
Wheatfield (Town)	14150
Wheatland (Town)	14546
Wheatley (Part of Old Westbury)	11568
Wheatley Heights	11798
Wheatville	14013
Wheeler	14810
Wheeler (Town)	14810
Wheeler Estates	12019
Wheelers	14469
Wheelerville	12032
Whig Corners	13326
Whippleville	12995
Whippoorwill	10504
White Bay	13650
White Creek	12057
White Creek (Town)	12057
White Fathers	12968
Whitehall	12887
Whitehall (Town)	12887
White Lake (Oneida County)	13494
White Lake (Sullivan County)	12786
Whitelaw	13032
White Plains	10601-07
For specific White Plains Zip Codes call (914) 287-2500, or your local postmaster.	
Whiteport	12401
Whitesboro	13492
Whites Store	13843
Whitestone (Part of New York)	11357
Whitestone Shopping Center (Part of New York)	11357
Whitestown (Town)	13492
White Sulphur Springs	12787
Whitesville	14897
Whitfield	12404

	ZIP
Whitman	13804
Whitney Country	14450
Whitney Farms	14450
Whitney Highlands	14450
Whitney Point	13862
Wiccopee	12533
Wickham Knolls	10990
Wickham Village	10990
Wilbur (Part of Kingston)	12401
Wildwood	11792
Wileyville	14877
Willard	14588
Willet	13863
Willet (Town)	13863
Williams Bridge (Part of New York)	10467
Williamsburg (Part of New York)	11211
Williams Grove	13110
Williams Lake	14472
Williamson	14589
Williamson (Town)	14589
Williamstown	13493
Williamstown (Town)	13493
Williamsville	14221
Willing (Town)	14895
Williston Park	11596
Willoughby	14741
Willow	12495
Willow Brook (Chautauqua County)	14712
Willowbrook (Richmond County)	10301
Willow Brook Estates	12303
Willow Brook Park	12302
Willowemac	12758
Willow Glen (Saratoga County)	12118
Willow Glen (Tompkins County)	13053
Willow Grove	13140
Willow Point	13850
Willow Ridge Estates	14150
Willsboro	12996
Willsboro (Town)	12996
Willsboro Point	12996
Willseyville	13864
Wilmington	12997
Wilmington (Town)	12997
Wilna (Town)	13619
Wilson	14172
Wilson (Town)	14172
Wilton	12866
Wilton (Town)	12866
Winchester	14224
Winderest Park	13031
Windham	12496
Windham (Town)	12496
Windham Ridge	12496
Winding Ways	13152
Windmill Farms	10504
Windom	14219
Windsor	13865
Windsor (Town)	13865
Windsor Beach	14617
Winebrook Hills	12852
Winfield (Town)	13491
Wingdale	12594
Winona Lake	12550
Winthrop	13697
Wirt (Town)	14774
Wiscoy	14536
Wisner	10990
Witherbee	12998
Wittenberg	12409
Wolcott	14590
Wolcott (Town)	14590
Wolcottsburg	14032
Wolcottsville	14001
Woodberry Hills	13413
Woodbourne	12788
Woodbury	11797
Woodbury (Orange County) (Town)	10930
Woodbury Falls	10930
Woodcliff Park	11933
Woodgate	13494
Wood Haven (Part of New York)	11421

	ZIP
Woodhull	14898
Woodhull (Town)	14898
Woodinville	12564
Woodland	12464
Woodland Hills	12065
Woodlands	10607
Woodlawn (Bronx County)	10470
Woodlawn (Chautauqua County)	14710
Woodlawn Beach	14219
Woodmere	11598
Woodridge	12789
Woodrow (Part of New York)	10309
Woodruff Heights	12302
Woodsburgh	11598
Woods Corners	13815
Woods Falls	12910
Woodside (Part of New York)	11377
Woods Mill	13608
Woods Mills	12918
Woodstock	12498
Woodstock (Town)	12498
Woodsville	14437
Woodville (Jefferson County)	13650
Woodville (Ontario County)	14512
Wooglin	14728
Woolsey (Part of New York)	11105
Worcester	12197
Worcester (Town)	12197
Worley Heights	10950
Worth	13659
Worth (Town)	13659
Worthington (Part of White Plains)	10607
Wright (Town)	12073
Wright Park Manor (Part of Rome)	13440
Wrights Corners (Niagara County)	14094
Wrights Corners (Onondaga County)	13135
Wurtemburg	12572
Wurtsboro	12790
Wurtsboro Hills	12790
Wyandanch	11798
Wyatts	12302
Wycoff Heights (Part of New York)	11237
Wykagyl (Part of New Rochelle)	10804
Wykagyl Park (Part of New Rochelle)	10804
Wynantskill	12198
Wyomanock	12168
Wyoming	14591
Yaddo	12866
Yagerville	12458
Yaleville	13668
Yankee Lake	12790
Yaphank	11980
Yates (Town)	14098
Yates Center	14098
Yatesville	14527
Yonkers	10701-05
	10710
For specific Yonkers Zip Codes call (914) 378-3600, or your local postmaster.	
York	14592
York (Town)	14592
York Corners	14895
Yorkshire	14173
Yorkshire (Town)	14173
Yorktown	10598
Yorktown (Town)	10598
Yorktown Heights	10598
Yorkville	13495
Yosts	12068
Young Hickory	14885
Youngstown	14174
Youngstown Estates	14174
Youngsville	12791
Yulan	12792
Zena	12498
Zoar	13682

Name	ZIP
Aarons Corner	27053
Abbottsburg	28320
Aberdeen	28315
Abner	27356
Abshers	28635
Acme	28456
Acorn Hill	27979
Acorn Woods	28079
Acre	27865
Addie	28779
Addor	28315
Adoniram	24598
Advance	27006
Advent Crossroads	28601
Afton	27589
Aho	28607
Ahoskie	27910
Ai	27583
Airboro (Part of Goldsboro)	27530
Airlie	27850
Airport (Part of Charlotte)	28219
Alamance	27201
Alamance Correctional Center	27253
Alamance Square (Part of Greensboro)	27406
Alarka	28713
Albemarle	28001*
	28002†
Albemarle Beach	27970
Albertson	28508
Albrittons	28501
Alert	27589
Alexander	28701
Alexander Correctional Center	28681
Alexander Mills	28043
Alexis	28006
Alfordsville	28383
Allen	28212
Allen Grove	27839
Allen Jay (Part of High Point)	27263
Allens Crossroads	28174
Allensville	27573
All Healing Springs	28681
Alliance	28509
Alligator	27925
Allison	27326
Allreds	27356
Alma	28364
Almond	28702
Alspaugh (Part of Winston-Salem)	27105
Altamahaw	27202
Altamahaw-Ossipee	27202
Altamont	28657
Altan	28112
Altapass	28777
Amantha	28679
Amerotron Mill (Part of Red Springs)	28377
AMF (Part of Greensboro)	27425
Amity	27013
Amity Gardens (Part of Charlotte)	28205
Ammon	28337
Anderson (Caswell County)	27215
Anderson (Dare County)	27949
Anderson Creek	28323
Anderson Crossroads	27850
Andrews	28901
Angier	27501
Anson Correctional Center	28135
Ansonville	28007
Antioch (Brunswick County)	28422
Antioch (Hoke County)	28377
Antioch (Madison County)	28753
Apex	27502
Appie	27888
Apple Grove	28643
Aquadale	28128
Aquone	28703
Arabia	28376
Arapahoe	28510
Ararat	27007
Arba	28580
Arcadia	27292
Archdale	27263
Archer	27520
Arcola	27589
Arden	28704
Ardmore (Part of Winston-Salem)	27113
Ardulusa	28301
Argura	28783
Arlington	28642
Armour	28456
Arnold	27292
Arran Hills	28304
Arrowhead Beach	27932
Arrowhead Place	28025
Arrowood (Part of Charlotte)	28442
Artesia	28442
Asbury	27330
Ash	28420
Asheboro	27203*
	27204†
Asheville	28801-16
For specific Asheville Zip Codes call (704) 257-4112, or your local postmaster.	
Asheville Mall, The (Part of Asheville)	28805
Ashford	28752
Ash Hill	27007
Ashland (Ashe County)	28615
Ashland (Bertie County)	27957
Ashland (Caswell County)	27320
Ashland (Rockingham County)	27320
Ashley Heights	28315
Ashton	28425
Ashton Forrest	28304
Ashwood	28571
Askewville	27983
Askin	28527
Aspen	27850
Atkinson	28421
Atlantic	28511
Atlantic Beach	28512
Atlantic Christian College (Part of Wilson)	27893
Auburn	27610
Audubon (Part of Wilmington)	28403
Aulander	27805
Aurelian Springs	27850
Aurora	27806
Austin	28621
Autryville	28318
Avalon Valley	27253
Avent Ferry Road (Part of Raleigh)	27606
Aventon	27891
Averasboro	28334
Avery Correctional Center	28657
Avery Creek	28704
Avery Shores	27974
Avon	27915
Axtell	27563
Ayden	28513
Aydlett	27916
Ayersville	27027
Azalea (Buncombe County)	28805
Azalea (New Hanover County)	28403†
	28406*
Bachelor	28532
Badin	28009
Bagley	27542
Bahama	27503
Bailey	27807
Bailey Town	27052
Baker Rhyne Apartments	28152
Bakers	28110
Bakersville	28705
Bald Creek	28714
Bald Head Island	28461
Bald Mountain	28714
Baldwin (Ashe County)	28694
Baldwin (Moore County)	27341
Baldwin Woods (Part of Whiteville)	28472
Balfour	28739
Ballantree	28803
Ballard	27840
Ballards Crossroad	27834
Ballew Store	28714
Balm	28604
Balsam	28707
Balsam Grove	28708
Baltic	28398
Baltimore	28434
Bamboo	28605
Bandana	28705
Bandy	28609
Banks Creek	28714
Banner Elk	28604
Bannertown	27030
Banoak	28168
Barber	27008
Barclaysville	27501
Barco	27917
Barham	27587
Barium Springs	28010
Barker Heights	28792
Barkers Creek	28789
Barker Ten Mile	28358
Barnard	28753
Barnardsville	28709
Barnesfield	28570
Barnesville	28319
Barrett	28623
Barriers Mill	28124
Bass Crossroads	27882
Basstown	28328
Bat Cave	28710
Batchelor Crossroads	27882
Bath	27808
Baton	28630
Battleboro	27809
Battleground (Part of Greensboro)	27438
Bay	27925
Bayboro	28515
Bayleaf	27615
Baynes	27302
Bayshore	28405
Baytree	27613
Bayview	27808
Beach Spring	27944
Bear Creek (Chatham County)	27207
Bear Creek (Onslow County)	28539
Beard	28301
Bear Grass	27892
Bearpond	27536
Bear Poplar	28125
Bearskin	28328
Bearwallow	28735
Beatties Ford	28216
Beaufort	28516
Beaufort Heights	27889
Beaver Creek	28694
Beaverdam (Buncombe County)	28715
Beaver Dam (Cleveland County)	28152
Beaver Dam (Columbus County)	28431
Beaverdam (Cumberland County)	28318
Beaverdam (Halifax County)	27823
Beaverdam (Haywood County)	28716
Beckwith	27865
Beech	28787
Beech Bottom	28657
Beechbrook (Part of Belmont)	28012
Beech Creek	28604
Beechertown	28781
Beech Mountain	28604
Beechwood Shores	27958
Bee Log	28714
Beesons Crossroads	27284
Belair	28306
Belcross	27921
Belews Creek	27009
Belfast	27530
Belgrade	28555
Belhaven	27810
Beliarthur	27811
Belle Mead	28601
Bellemont	27216
Bell Island	27929
Bells Cross Roads	28166
Bells Fork (Onslow County)	28546
Bells Fork (Pitt County)	27858
Belltown	27565
Bell View	28906
Belmont (Gaston County)	28012
Belmont (Halifax County)	27870
Belmont Abbey College	28012
Belva	28753
Belvedere	27834
Belvidere	27919
Belville	28451
Belvoir	27834
Belwood	28090
Benham	28621
Bennett	27208
Benson	27504
Bent Creek	28806
Benton Heights (Part of Monroe)	28110
Bentons Crossroad	28110
Berea	27565
Berkeley (Part of Goldsboro)	27534
Bertha	27965
Bertie (Part of Windsor)	27983
Bessemer (Part of Greensboro)	27405
Bessemer City	28016
Bests	28551
Beta	28779
Bethabara (Part of Winston-Salem)	27106
Bethania	27010
Bethany	27320
Bethel (Caswell County)	27311
Bethel (Columbus County)	28432

* **Area Zip Code**   † **Post Office Boxes**

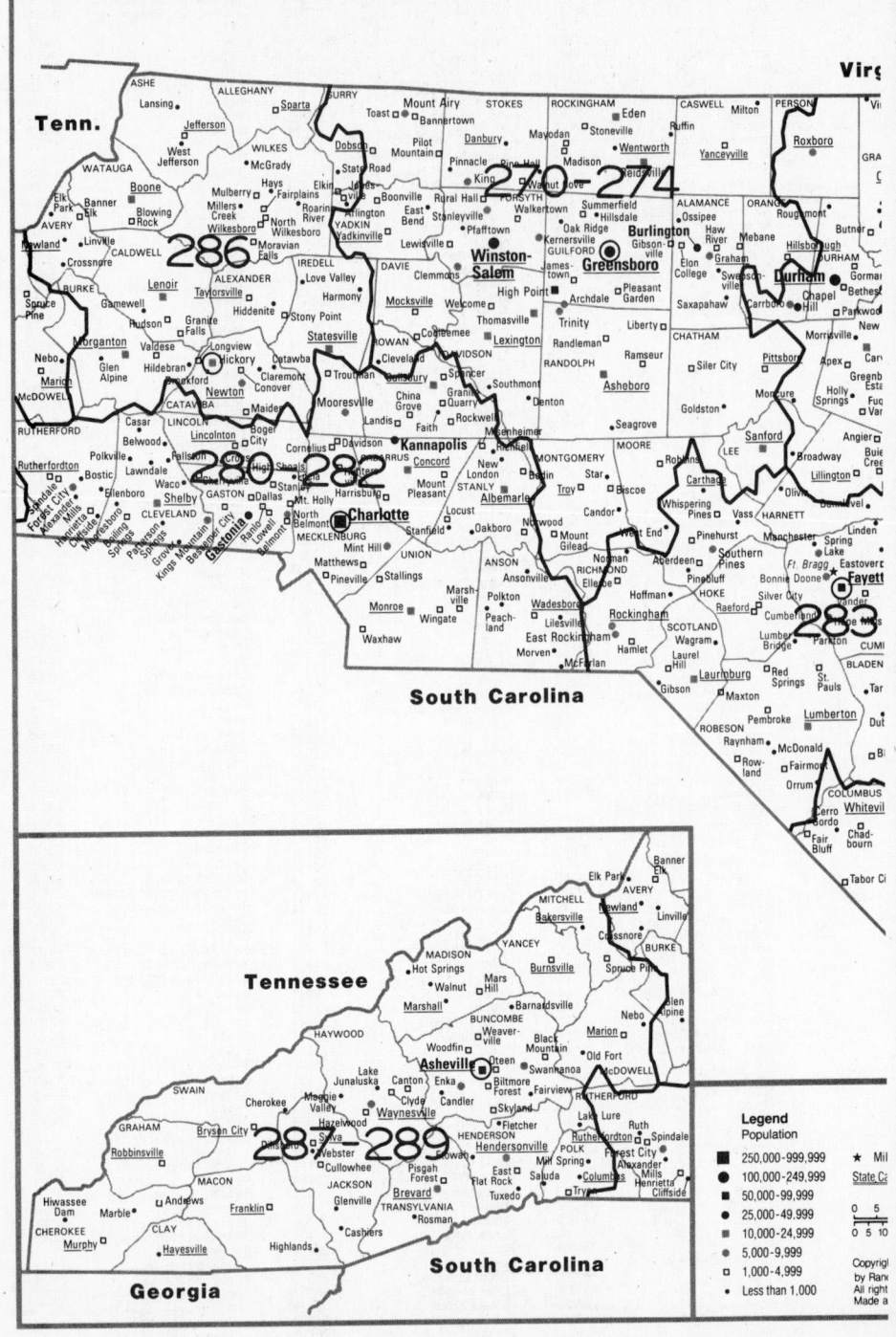

rginia

Virgilina Stovall VANCE WARREN Wise NORTHAMPTON Seaboard Severn Como GATES CAMDEN CURRITUCK Moyock
Williamsboro Norlina Macon Roanoke Rapids Gaston Garysburg Murfreesboro Sunbury South Mills **279** Currituck
GRANVILLE Middleburg Henderson Warrenton Weldon Conway Winton Gatesville PASQUOTANK Camden
Oxford **275** Centerville HALIFAX Halifax Jackson Woodland HERTFORD Cofield Harrellsville Elizabeth City Grandy Southern Shores
FRANKLIN Franklinton Youngsville Enfield Roxobel Aulander Powellsville Colerain Winfall PERQUIMANS C.G.A.S. Kitty Hawk Kill Devil Hills
277 Louisburg Castalia Whitakers Scotland Neck Kelford Woodville Askewville CHOWAN Edenton TYRRELL Nags Head
ew Hope WAKE Zebulon Bunn Sharpsburg Red Oak **278** MARTIN Oak City Hamilton Windsor Columbia DARE Manteo Wanchese
Cary Raleigh Wendell Sims Rocky Mount Speed Hassell Everetts Williamston Roper Creswell Plymouth Jamesville
nbrier Garner JOHNSTON WILSON Wilson Elm City Pinetops Conetoe Robersonville WASHINGTON HYDE
Fuquay-Varina Clayton Saratoga Fountain Bethel Beargrass BEAUFORT Pantego Engelhard
Buies Wilsons Mills Kenly Stantonsburg Farmville **Greenville** Grimesland Washington Swanquarter Buxton
Creek Smithfield Selma Eureka Walstonburg Simpson Washington Park Bath Belhaven
Erwin Pine Level Snow Hill Winterville Chocowinity Hatteras
Dunn Four Oaks Coats Benson Princeton GREENE Ayden Hookerton Grifton Aurora Mesic Ocracoke
en Godwin WAYNE Seymour Johnson La Grange CRAVEN Vanceboro Grantsboro Bayboro Stonewall
Wade Newton Grove Mount Olive **Kinston** Dover Cove City Bridgeton PAMLICO Oriental
tteville SAMPSON Faison Calypso LENOIR JONES Trent Woods New Bern Arapahoe Atlantic
Stedman Salemburg Clinton Warsaw DUPLIN Pink Hill **285** Pollocksville Cherry Point M.C.A.S. Minnesott Beach Davis
ville Roseboro Turkey Kenansville Beulaville Richlands Maysville Havelock CARTERET Atlantic
UMBERLAND Garland Rose Hill Greenevers ONSLOW Newport Morehead City Beaufort Marshallberg
EN Tar Heel Harrells Teachey Wallace Jacksonville Swansboro Cape Carteret Atlantic Beach Harkers Island
Dublin Elizabethtown Penderlea Watha Maple Hill Verona Camp Lejeune M.C.B. Salter Path
Blacksboro PENDER Atkinson Burgaw Holly Ridge Sneads Ferry
Clarkton **284** Rocky Point Hampstead Surf City
ville Halls boro East Arcadia Castle Hayne Topsail Beach
Brunswick Lake Waccamaw Delco NEW HANOVER Leland Winter Park Wrightsville Beach
r City **Wilmington** Brunswick County Complex Bolivia Carolina Beach
BRUNSWICK Shallotte Holden Beach Boiling Spring Lakes Kure Beach Southport
Calabash Ocean Isle Beach Long Beach

N

	ZIP
Bethel (Haywood County)	28716
Bethel (Hoke County)	28376
Bethel (Perquimans County)	27944
Bethel (Pitt County)	27812
Bethel Hill	27573
Bethesda (Davidson County)	27292
Bethesda (Durham County)	27703
Bethlehem (Alexander County)	28601
Bethlehem (Hertford County)	27922
Bettie	28516
Beulah (Hyde County)	27875
Beulah (Polk County)	28756
Beulahtown	27542
Beulaville	28518
Beverly Woods (Part of Charlotte)	28210
Bexley (Part of Wilmington)	28412
Biddleville (Part of Charlotte)	28216
Big Cove	28719
Biggs Park (Part of Lumberton)	28358
Big Laurel	28753
Big Lick	28129
Big Pine	28753
Big Ridge (Carteret County)	28570
Big Ridge (Jackson County)	28736
Biltmore (Part of Asheville)	28813
Biltmore Forest	28803
Birchwood	27215
Bird Cage	28431
Birdtown	28719
Biscoe	27209
Bishops Cross	27860
Bixby	27006
Blackburn	28658
Black Creek	27813
Black Jack	27858
Blackman	27524
Black Mountain	28711
Black Mountain Sanatorium	28711
Blackwell	27311
Blackwood	27514
Bladenboro	28320
Bladenboro North (Part of Bladenboro)	28320
Bladen Correctional Center	28337
Bladen Springs	28434
Blaine	27239
Blanch	27212
Blantyre	28768
Blevins Crossroads	28675
Blevins Store	27017
Blizzards Crossroads	28365
Bloomingdale	28369
Blossomtown	28734
Blounts Creek	27814
Blowing Rock	28605
Blue Ridge (Buncombe County)	28711
Blue Ridge (Henderson County)	28792
Blue Ridge Mall (Part of Hendersonville)	28792
Bluff	28743
Boardman	28438
Boat Club Road	28012
Bobbitt	27544
Boddies Pond	27856
Boger City	28092
Bogue	28570
Boiling Spring Lakes	28461
Boiling Springs (Cherokee County)	28906
Boiling Springs (Cleveland County)	28017
Bolivia	28422
Bolton	28423
Bolyston Creek	28768
Bon Air (Part of Winston-Salem)	27105
Bonaparte Landing	28459
Bonham Heights (Part of Morehead City)	28557
Bonlee	27213
Bonnerton	27806
Bonnetsville	28328
Bonnie Doone	28303
Bonsal	27562
Boomer	28606
Boone	28607
Boones Crossroads	27845
Boone Trail	27552
Boonford	28705
Boonville	27011
Bordeaux (Part of Fayetteville)	28304
Bostian Heights	28023
Bostic	28018
Bostwood Estates	28025

	ZIP
Botany Woods	28805
Bottom	27030
Boulevard (Part of Eden)	27288
Bowdens	28398
Bowditch	28714
Bowmore	28376
Boyles Chapel	27021
Bracey	28383
Bradfords Cross Roads	28677
Braggtown (Part of Durham)	27704
Branon	27055
Brantleys Grove	27910
Brasstown	28902
Braswell	28431
Brendletown	28734
Brentwood (Cumberland County)	28304
Brentwood (Wake County)	27604
Brettonwood	28311
Brevard	28712
Briarwood Terrace	28147
Brices Crossroads	28458
Brickhaven	27559
Bricks	27891
Brickton	28732
Bridgersville	27852
Bridgeton	28519
Brief	28107
Briertown	28781
Brigand Bay	27920
Brightwood (Part of Greensboro)	27214
Brindle Town	28655
Brinkleyville (Hertford County)	27910
Brinkleyville (Lee County)	27823
British Acres	27215
Broad Acres	27253
Broad Creek	28570
Broadway	27505
Brocks	28574
Brogden	27530
Brook Cove	27052
Brookdale	28792
Brookford	28601
Brookhaven	27612
Brookland Manor	28792
Brooks Cross Roads	27020
Brooksdale	27573
Brookside (Part of Goldsboro)	27530
Brookston	27536
Brook Valley	27858
Broughton Hospital	28655
Browns Summit	27214
Brown Town (Part of Belmont)	28012
Brownwood	28684
Bruce	27834
Brunswick	28424
Brutonville	27229
Bryantown	27869
Bryantville Park	27818
Bryson City	28713
Buckhorn	27243
Buckhorn Cross Roads	27542
Buckland	27937
Bucklesberry	28551
Buckner	28754
Buck Shoals	27020
Buena Vista	27983
Buffalo Cove	28645
Bug Hill	28455
Buie	28377
Buies Creek	27506
Buladean	28705
Bullhead	28863
Bullock	27507
Buncombe Correctional Center	28814
Bunn	27508
Bunnlevel	28323
Bunyan	27889
Burbage Crossroads	27808
Burden	27805
Burgaw	28425
Burgess	27944
Burke Chapel	28601
Burkemont	28655
Burlington	27215-17

For specific Burlington Zip Codes call (919) 227-4293, or your local postmaster.

	ZIP
Burney	28399
Burningtown	28734
Burnsville (Anson County)	28135
Burnsville (Yancey County)	28714
Burnt Mills	27976
Busbee (Part of Asheville)	28803
Bushy Fork	27541
Busick (Guilford County)	27214
Busick (Yancey County)	28714

	ZIP
Butlers Crossroads	28328
Butner	27509
Butters	28324
Buxton	27920
Buzzards Crossroads	27924
Bynum	27228
Byrum Crossroads	27980
Cabarrus	28107
Cabarrus Correctional Center	28124
Cabin	28572
Cairo	28119
Cajah's Mountain	28645
Calabash	28467
Calahaln	27028
Caldwell (Mecklenburg County)	28078
Caldwell (Orange County)	27572
Caldwell Correctional Center	28638
Caledonia Correctional Center	27887
California (Dare County)	27954
California (Hertford County)	27986
California (Pitt County)	27828
Callisons	28571
Cal-Vel	27573
Calvert	28712
Calvin Heights	28570
Calypso	28325
Camden	27921
Camelot	27529
Cameron	28326
Cameron Village (Part of Raleigh)	27605
Campbell Creek	27806
Camp Glenn (Part of Morehead City)	28557
Camp Leach	27889
Camp Lejeune	28542
Camp Lejeune Central	28542
Camp MacKall	28347
Camp Springs	27320
Camp Sutton (Part of Monroe)	28110
Cana	27028
Candler	28715
Candler Heights	28715
Candlewick Estates	27834
Candor	27229
Cane Creek	28167
Cane Mountain	27349
Cane River	28714
Cannon Ferry	27980
Canto	28716
Canton	28716
Cape Carteret	28584
Cape Colony	27932
Cape Fear	27562
Capella	27021
Capelsie	27229
Carbonton	27330
Carmel (Part of Charlotte)	28226
	28247
	28270
	28277

For specific Carmel Zip Codes call (704) 541-7851, or your local postmaster.

	ZIP
Caroleen	28019
Carolina	27217
Carolina Beach	28428
Carolina Circle Mall (Part of Greensboro)	27405
Carolina East Mall (Part of Greenville)	27834
Carolina Forest	27371
Carolina Mall (Part of Concord)	28025
Carolina Pines	28303
Carolina Place (Part of Charlotte)	28226
Carolina Trace	27330
Carolina Village	28792
Carova Beach	27927
Carpenter	27560
Carpenter Bottom	28657
Carr	27302
Carrboro	27510
Carr Creek	27330
Carroll	28398
Carter	27938
Carteret Correctional Center	28570
Cartersville	28466
Carthage	28327
Cartoogechaye	28734
Carvers	28434
Cary	27511-13
	27518-19

For specific Cary Zip Codes call (919) 831-3661, or your local postmaster.

* Area Zip Code † Post Office Boxes

	ZIP		ZIP		ZIP
Crestmont	28601	Dobbersville	28365	Eastover (Cumberland	
Creston	28615	Dobbins Heights	28345	County)	28301
Crestview	27344	Dobson	27017	Eastover (Mecklenburg	
Creswell	27928	Dockery	28635	County)	28207
Cricket	28659	Dodgetown	27025	Eastridge (Part of Gastonia)	28054
Crisp	27852	Dodsons Crossroads	27278	Eastridge Mall (Part of	
Croatan	28562	Dogwood Acres (Durham		Gastonia)	28054
Cross Landing	27925	County)	27704	East Rockingham	
Cross Mill	28752	Dogwood Acres (Randolph		(Richmond County)	28379
Crossnore	28616	County)	27203	East Rocky Mount (Part of	
Cross Road	27030	Dogwood Park	28027	Rocky Mount)	27801
Crossway	28352	Don Lee Heights	28532	East Side Park (Richmond	
Crosswinds	27615	Donnaha	27050	County)	28379
Crouse	28033	Doolie	28115	East Side Park (Robeson	
Crowders	28052	Dortches	27801	County)	28340
Crowells	27839	Dosier	27040	East Spencer	28039
Crumpler	28617	Dothan	29569	East Tabor	28463
Crump Town (Part of		Double Shoals	28090	Eastway (Part of Charlotte)	28205
Wagram)	28396	Douglas Crossroads	27889	East Wilmington (Part of	
Cruso	28716	Dover (Cleveland County)	28150	Wilmington)	28405
Crusoe Island	28472	Dover (Craven County)	28526	Eastwood	28327
Crutchfield Crossroads	27344	Downtown (Part of		Ebenezer	28906
Crystal Park	28306	Asheville)	28802	Echo	28383
Culberson	28903	Downtown (Part of		Echo Heights	27603
Culbreth	27565	Charlotte)	28202	Eckerd Contract-Concord	
Cullasaja	28734	Downtown (Part of		(Part of Concord)	28027
Cullowhee	28723	Salisbury)	28144	Eck Reece	28642
Cumberland	28331	Downtown (Part of Boone)	28607	Eden	27288-89
Cumnock	27237	Draco	28645	For specific Eden Zip Codes call	
Cunningham	27343	Drake	27809	(919) 623-2212, or your local	
Currie	28435	Drake Park	28304	postmaster.	
Currituck	27929	Draper (Part of Eden)	27288	Edenhouse	27957
Currituck Correctional		Draughn	27891	Edenton	27932
Center	27956	Drewry	27553	Edgar	27350
Currytown	27292	Drexel	28619	Edgemont	28645
Cutshalltown	28753	Druid Hills (Part of		Edgewood Acres	28016
Cycle	27020	Hendersonville)	28739	Edmonds	28623
Cypress Creek (Columbus		Drum Hill	27937	Edneyville	28727
County)	28472	Drums Crossroads	28609	Edward	27821
Cypress Creek (Duplin		Dry Creek	27229	Edwards Crossroads	
County)	28466	Duan	28658	(Alleghany County)	28675
Cyrus	28540	Duart	28384	Edwards Crossroads (Nash	
Dabney	27536	Dublin	28332	County)	27882
Dallas	28034	Duck	27949	Edwards Crossroads	
Dalton	27043	Dudley	28333	(Northampton County)	27820
Dana	28724	Dudley Heights (Part of		Edwards Fork	27874
Danbury	27016	Greensboro)	27401	Efland	27243
Danieltown	28043	Dudley Shoals	28630	Ela	28713
Dan River Shores	27016	Duff Creek	28464	Elams	23845
Dan Valley	27048	Duffies	28377	Elberon	27589
Darby	28624	Duke (Part of Durham)	27706	Eldorado	27371
Darden	27846	Dulah	28463	Eleanors Crossroads	27937
Dark Ridge	28622	Dula Springs	28787	Eleazer	27371
Darlington	27839	Duncan	27526	Elf	28904
Davenport Forks	27970	Dundarrach	28386	Eliah	28451
Davidson	28036	Dunn	28334*	Eli Whitney	27253
Davidson Correctional			28335†	Elizabeth (Part of Charlotte)	28204
Center	27292	Dunn Crossroads	27822	Elizabeth City	27906-09
Davidson River	28768	Dunns Rock	28712	For specific Elizabeth City Zip	
Davie Correctional Center	27028	Dunns Store	27874	Codes call (919) 338-3869, or	
Davie Crossroads	27028	Duplin Correctional Center	28349	your local postmaster.	
Davis	28524	Dupree Crossroads	27829	Elizabeth City Coast Guard	
Davistown (Edgecombe		Durants Neck	27930	Air Station	27909
County)	27864	Durham	27701-22	Elizabeth Heights	27893
Davistown (McDowell		For specific Durham Zip Codes		Elizabethtown	28337
County)	28762	call (919) 683-1976, or your local		Elkin	28621
Dawson Crossroads	27823	postmaster.		Elk Mountain (Part of	
Day Book	28740	Dutchess Downs	27529	Woodfin)	28804
Days Crossroads	27839	Dysartville	28761	Elk Park	28622
Deep Creek	28133	Eagle	27020	Elk Valley	28604
Deep Gap	28618	Eagle Rock	27523	Ellenboro	28040
Deep River (Part of High		Eagle's Nest	28570	Ellendale (Alexander	
Point)	27265	Eagle Springs	27242	County)	28681
Deep Run	28525	Eagletown	27869	Ellendale (Wake County)	27545
Deerfield	28607	Earl	28038	Eller	27107
Deerwood	28532	Earley	27910	Ellerbe	28338
Dehart	28635	Earpsboro	27597	Ellerbe Grove	28379
Delco	28436	Easonburg	27801	Elijay	28734
Delight	28090	Easons Crossroads	27938	Elliott	28393
Dellview	28021	East Arcadia	28456	Ellis Crossroads	28144
Dellwood	28786	East Bend	27018	Ellis Store	27983
Delway	28458	East Carolina University		Elm City	27822
Democrat	28787	(Part of Greenville)	27834	Elm Grove (Bertie County)	27924
Dennis	27052	Eastcrest Ridge	28025	Elm Grove (Lenoir County)	28501
Dennys Store	27573	East Durham (Part of		Elmore	28352
Denton	27239	Durham)	27703	Elmwood	28677
Denver	28037	Eastern Correctional Center	28554	Elon College	27244
Deppe	28555	East Fayetteville	28301	Elroy	27534
Derby	28338	East Flat Rock	28726	Embro	27551
Derita (Part of Charlotte)	28213	East Franklin (Part of		Emerald Gardens	28304
Devonshire	28081	Franklin)	28734	Emerald Isle	28594
Devotion	27017	East Lake	27953	Emerald Village	27610
Dewey Pier	27925	Eastland Mall (Part of		Emerson (Bladen County)	28433
Dexter	27565	Charlotte)	28212	Emerson (Columbus	
Dickens Park	28570	East Laport	28723	County)	28463
Dickerson	27565	East Laurinburg	28352	Emerywood (Part of High	
Diggs	28379	East Lumberton (Part of		Point)	27262
Dillard	27025	Lumberton)	28358	Emit	27557
Dillsboro	28725	East Marion	28752	Emma	28806
Dilworth (Part of Charlotte)	28203	East Monbo	27677	Enderly Park (Part of	
Dixon	28445	Easton (Part of Winston-		Charlotte)	28208
Dixon Crossroad	28590	Salem)	27107	Endy	28001

	ZIP		ZIP		ZIP
Enfield	27823	Ferncliff Estates	28025	Franklinville	27248
Engelhard	27824	Fibreville (Part of Canton)	28716	Frazier Crossroads	27557
Englewood (Part of Rocky		Fields	28551	Fraziers Crossroads	27910
Mount)	27801	Fines Creek	28721	Frederick	27817
English Woods	28025	Finger	28124	Freedom (Part of Charlotte)	28208
Enka	28728	Fires Creek	28904	Freedom Mall (Part of	
Enka Village	28728	First Union (Part of		Charlotte)	28208
Ennice	28623	Charlotte)	28202	Freeland	28420
Eno	27278	Fisher Park (Part of		Freeman	28423
Enochville	28023	Greensboro)	27401	Fremont	27830
Enola	28655	Fisher Town	28081	Friendly Acres	28027
Enon	27018	Fitch	27379	Friendly Center-Forum VI	
Eno Valley (Part of Durham)	27712	Five Forks (Person County)	27573	(Part of Greensboro)	27404
Enterprise (Davidson		Five Forks (Rowan County)	28023	Friendship (Cherokee	
County)	27292	Five Forks (Warren County)	27551	County)	28906
Enterprise (Warren County)	27850	Five Point (Part of Raleigh)	27608	Friendship (Duplin County)	28398
Ephesus	27028	Five Points (Beaufort		Friendship (Guilford County)	27410
Epsom	27536	County)	27889	Friendship (Wake County)	27502
Erastus	28723	Five Points (Columbus		Friendship (Yadkin County)	27018
Erect	27341	County)	28431	Frisco	27936
Ernul	28527	Five Points (Hoke County)	28376	Frog Level	27834
Ervintown	28574	Five Points (Richmond		Frog Pond	28129
Erwin	28339	County)	28379	Frogsboro	27314
Erwin Heights (Part of		Flat Branch (Gates County)	27938	Fruitland	28792
Thomasville)	27360	Flat Branch (Harnett		Frying Pan Landing	27925
Essex	27844	County)	27546	Fulchers Landing	28460
Estatoe	28777	Flat Creek	28787	Fullers	27360
Estelle	27305	Flat Rock (Henderson		Fulp	27052
Ether	27247	County)	28731	Funston	28479
Etowah	28729	Flat Rock (Stokes County)	27043	Fuquay Springs (Part of	
Eufola	28677	Flat Rock (Surry County)	27030	Fuquay-Varina)	27526
Eure	27935	Flats	28781	Fuquay-Varina	27526
Eureka	27830	Flat Shoals	27019	Furches	28644
Eureka Springs	28301	Flat Springs	28622	Furnitureland (Part of High	
Eutaw (Part of Fayetteville)	28303	Flay	28021	Point)	27264
Evansdale	27893	Fleetwood	28626	Galatia	27876
Everetts	27825	Fleetwood Acres	28052	Gales Creek	28570
Everetts Crossroads	27865	Fletcher	28732	Galloway Crossroads	27858
Evergreen (Beaufort		Flint Hill (Montgomery		Gallup Acres	28304
County)	27817	County)	27371	Gamble Hill	28016
Evergreen (Columbus		Flint Hill (Randolph County)	27350	Gamewell	28645
County)	28438	Flint Hill (Yadkin County)	27018	Garden Homes (Part of	
Evergreen Estates	28304	Florence	28556	Greensboro)	27408
Exum	28420	Florence Town	27302	Gardnerville	28513
Exway	27306	Flowes Store	28025	Gardner Webb College	
Fair Bluff	28439	Floytan Crossroads	27536	(Part of Boiling Springs)	28017
Fairfield (Hyde County)	27826	Folkstone	28445	Garland	28441
Fairfield (Union County)	28103	Folly	27979	Garner	27529
Fair Field Estate	28150	Fontana Dam	28733	Garysburg	27831
Fairfield Harbour	28560	Footsville	27055	Gaston	27832
Fairfield Sapphire Valley	28774	Forbes	28740	Gaston Correctional Center	28034
Fair Grove	27360	Forestburg	27944	Gastonia	28051-56
Fairlane	28303	Forest City	28043	For specific Gastonia Zip Codes	
Fairmont	28340	Forest Hills (Cumberland		call (704) 867-6311, or your local	
Fairmont Junction	28383	County)	28303	postmaster.	
Fairplains	28659	Forest Hills (Forsyth County)	27105	Gaston Mall (Part of	
Fairport	27544	Forest Hills (Gaston County)	28120	Gastonia)	28054
Fairview (Buncombe		Forest Hills (New Hanover		Gates	27937
County)	28730	County)	28403	Gates Correctional Center	27938
Fairview (Orange County)	27278	Forest Hills (Rockingham		Gates Four	28306
Fairview (Rockingham		County)	27320	Gatesville	27938
County)	27288	Forest Oaks	27406	Gateway	28789
Fairview (Union County)	28110	Forest Ridge	28152	Gause Landing	28459
Fairview Cross Roads	27017	Forestville (Anson County)	28091	Gay	28779
Fairview Park	28636	Forestville (Wake County)	27587	Gaylord	27808
Fairway Hills	28786	Fork Church	27028	Gela	27582
Faison	28341	Fort Barnwell	28526	Gentry Store	27573
Faisons	27876	Fort Bragg	28307	George	27897
Faith	28041	Fort Caswell	28461	Georgetown (Buncombe	
Falcon	28342	Fort Junction	28307	County)	28806
Falkland	27827	Fort Landing	27925	Georgetown (Davidson	
Fall Creek	27018	Fort Macon Coast Guard		County)	27284
Falling Creek	28501	Base	28512	Georgetown (Lenoir County)	28501
Falling Creek Estates	28601	Fort Point	27817	Georgeville	28025
Falls	27609	Foscoe	28604	Germanton	27019
Fallston	28042	Foster Creek	28753	Germantown	27875
Far Away Place	28025	Fountain (Duplin County)	28521	Gerton	28735
Farmer	27203	Fountain (Pitt County)	27829	Gethsemane	27891
Farmington	27028	Fountain Hill	28133	Gibson	28343
Farmville (Chatham County)	27330	Four Oaks	27524	Gibsontown	28716
Farmville (Pitt County)	27828	Four Seasons (Part of		Gibsonville	27249
Faro	27883	Hendersonville)	28739	Giddensville	28341
Farrington	27514	Four Seasons Towncenter		Gilkey	28139
Faust	28754	(Part of Greensboro)	27407	Gill	27536
Fayblock (Part of		Fourway	28538	Gillburg	27536
Fayetteville)	28301	Foxcroft East (Part of		Glade Valley	28627
Fayetteville	28301-06	Charlotte)	28226	Glady	28715
	28309-14	Fox Fire (Cumberland		Glass (Part of Kannapolis)	28081
For specific Fayetteville Zip Codes		County)	28303	Glen Alpine	28628
call (919) 486-2311, or your local		Foxfire (Moore County)	27281	Glen Ayre	28705
postmaster.		Foxwood Acres	28025	Glenbrook	28304
Fayetteville North (Part of		Francisco	27053	Glencoe	27217
Fayetteville)	28311	Francis Mill	27805	Glendale Acres (Part of	
Fearrington	27312	Francktown	28574	Fayetteville)	28304
Fearrington Post	27312	Frank	28657	Glendale Springs	28629
Federal Building (Part of		Franklin (Macon County)	28734	Glendon	27251
Elizabeth City)	27909	Franklin (Rowan County)	28144	Glenhaven	28304
Federal Correctional		Franklin Correctional Center	27508	Glen Lennox (Part of	
Institution	27509	Franklin Grove	28713	Chapel Hill)	27514
Feezor	27292	Franklin Street (Part of		Glenn	27705
Feltonville	27502	Chapel Hill)	27514	Glenola	27263
Ferguson	28624	Franklinton	27525	Glen Raven	27215

* Area Zip Code   † Post Office Boxes

	ZIP
Glenview	27823
Glenville	28736
Glenwood (Guilford County)	27403
Glenwood (McDowell County)	28737
Glenwood (Richmond County)	28379
Globe	28645
Gloucester	28528
Gneiss	28734
Goat Neck	27925
Godwin	28344
Golden Forest	27604
Golden Gate (Part of Greensboro)	27405
Gold Hill (Rockingham County)	27025
Gold Hill (Rowan County)	28071
Gold Mine	28741
Gold Point	27871
Goldrock	27891
Goldsboro	27530-34
For specific Goldsboro Zip Codes call (919) 734-3521, or your local postmaster.	
Goldston	27252
Gold Valley Crossroads	27557
Goodsonville	28092
Goose Creek	27974
Gooseneck	28456
Goose Pond	27924
Gordonton	27541
Gordontown	27292
Gorman	27704
Goshen	28697
Governors Island	28713
Grace (Part of Asheville)	28814
Grace Chapel	28630
Gradys	28365
Graham	27253
Graingers	28501
Grandfather	28646
Grandview	28906
Grandview Heights (Part of Boone)	28607
Grandy	27939
Granite Falls	28630
Granite Quarry	28072
Grantham	27530
Granthams	28560
Grantsboro	28529
Grape Creek	28906
Grapevine	28753
Graphite	28762
Grassy Creek (Ashe County)	28631
Grassy Creek (Mitchell County)	28777
Grays Chapel	27248
Grayson	28632
Great Neck Landing	28539
Green Acres (Alamance County)	27217
Green Acres (Gaston County)	28012
Green Acres (Wake County)	27603
Green Acres Park	28025
Greenbrier Estates	27603
Greene Correctional Center	28554
Greene Cove	28705
Greenevers	28458
Green Farm	27834
Greenfield	27932
Greenhill (Haywood County)	28716
Green Hill (Rutherford County)	28139
Greenlee	28762
Greenlevel (Alamance County)	27217
Green Level (Wake County)	27502
Greenmountain	28740
Greenriver	28722
Greensboro	27401-55
For specific Greensboro Zip Codes call (919) 271-5481, or your local postmaster.	
Greens Creek	28779
Green Valley	28615
Greenville	27834-36
	27858
For specific Greenville Zip Codes call (919) 752-2153, or your local postmaster.	
Greenwood Homes (Part of Fayetteville)	28303
Gregory	27973
Gregory Crossroads (Bertie County)	27957
Gregory Crossroads (Onslow County)	28574
Greystone	27536
Griffins Crossroads	27312

	ZIP
Grifton	28530
Grimesdale	28792
Grimesland	27837
Grissettown	28459
Grissom	27522
Grist	28431
Grove Hill	27551
Grovemont	28778
Grove Park (Part of Charlotte)	28215
Grover	28073
Grovestone	28778
Growers Crossroads	27924
Guide	28463
Guideway	28463
Guilford (Part of Greensboro)	27409
Guilford College (Part of Greensboro)	27410
Guilford Correctional Center	27301
Guilford Hills (Part of Greensboro)	27408
Gulf	27256
Gull Rock	27824
Gumberry	27838
Gumbranch	28540
Gum Neck	27925
Gum Springs	27312
Guntertown	28753
Gupton	27549
Guthrie	27284
Guyton	28320
Haddocks Crossroads	28590
Hairtown	28302
Half Hell	28422
Half Moon	28540
Halifax	27839
Halifax Correctional Institution	27839
Halisboro	28442
Halls Ferry Junction	28127
Halls Mills	28649
Halls Store	28385
Hallsville	28518
Hamer	27212
Hamilton	27840
Hamilton Lakes (Part of Greensboro)	27410
Hamlet	28345
Hampstead	28443
Hamptonville	27020
Hamrick	28714
Hancheys Store	28466
Hancock	27932
Handy	27239
Hanes Mall (Part of Winston-Salem)	27103
	27130
For specific Hanes Mall Zip Codes call (919) 760-9818, or your local postmaster.	
Hanrahans	28530
Happy Valley (Buncombe County)	28805
Happy Valley (Caldwell County)	28645
Harbinger	27941
Harbor Island (Part of Wrightsville Beach)	28480
Hardees Cross Road	27504
Hardins	28034
Hare	28627
Hargetts Cross Roads	28574
Harkers Island	28531
Harlem Heights	28170
Harlowe	28570
Harmony	28634
Harper's Crossroads	27207
Harrells	28444
Harrellsville	27942
Harrelsonville	28472
Harris (Moore County)	28327
Harris (Rutherford County)	28074
Harrisburg	28075
Harrisburg Estates	28075
Harris Crossroads (Franklin County)	27596
Harris Crossroads (Vance County)	27536
Harris Landing	27932
Harrison Cross Roads	27320
Hartland	28645
Hartman	27016
Hartsease	27886
Harveytown	28501
Hassell	27841
Hastings Corner	27921
Hasty	28352
Hatteras	27943
Havelock	28532
Havelock Station (Part of Havelock)	28532

	ZIP
Haw Branch (Moore County)	27330
Haw Branch (Onslow County)	28574
Haw Creek (Part of Asheville)	28805
Hawfields	27302
Hawk	28705
Haw River	27258
Haws Run	28454
Hayesville	28904
Haymount (Part of Fayetteville)	28305
Hayne	28318
Hays	28635
Hayti (Part of Durham)	27701
Haywood	27559
Haywood Road (Part of Asheville)	28806
Hazelwood	28738
Hazelwood Park	27864
Healing Springs	27239
Heathsville	27823
Heaton	28622
Hedrick Grove	27292
Helens Crossroads	28513
Helton	28631
Hemby Acres	28079
Hemby Bridge	28079
Henderson	27536
Henderson Correctional Center	28739
Hendersonville	28792-93
For specific Hendersonville Zip Codes call (704) 692-2547, or your local postmaster.	
Hendersonville	28739
Hendrix Estates	28147
Henrico	27842
Henrietta	28076
Henry	28168
Henry River	28602
Hepco	28721
Heritage Hill	27516
Heritage Square (Part of Durham)	27707
Heritage Woods	28025
Herrings Crossroads (Duplin County)	28508
Herrings Crossroads (Greene County)	27888
Hertford	27944
Hester	27581
Hesters Store	27541
Hestertown	28358
Hewitt	28781
Hexlena	27805
Hibbs Acres	28570
Hickmans Crossroads	28459
Hickory	28601-03
For specific Hickory Zip Codes call (704) 328-5503, or your local postmaster.	
Hickory Crossroads	27919
Hickory Grove (Cumberland County)	28304
Hickory Grove (Gaston County)	28056
Hickory Grove (Mecklenburg County)	28215
Hickory Knoll	28734
Hickory Point	27806
Hickory Rock	27549
Hicks Crossroads (Mecklenburg County)	28078
Hicks Crossroads (Vance County)	27565
Hiddenite	28636
Higdonville	28734
Higgins	28714
High Crossroads	27807
Highfalls	27259
High Hampton	28717
Highland Park	28345
Highland Park West (Part of Greensboro)	27407
Highlands	28741
High Point	27260-65
For specific High Point Zip Codes call (919) 884-8344, or your local postmaster.	
High Rock	27239
High Shoals	28077
Highsmiths	28382
Hightowers	27379
Hildebran	28637
Hillcrest (Hoke County)	28376
Hill Crest (Moore County)	28327
Hilliardston	27856
Hillsborough	27278
Hills Crossroads	27839
Hillsdale (Davie County)	27006

*Area Zip Code   † Post Office Boxes

* Area Zip Code   † Post Office Boxes

	ZIP
Lake Toxaway	28747
Lakeview (Alamance County)	27215
Lakeview (Davidson County)	27299
Lakeview (Moore County)	28350
Lakeview Estates (Alamance County)	27215
Lakeview Estates (Henderson County)	28792
Lake View Park	27870
Lake Waccamaw	28450
Lakewood (Cabarrus County)	28025
Lakewood (Henderson County)	28739
Lambert	28163
Lambs Corner	27921
Lamm	27893
Lamms Crossroads	27882
Lancaster Crossroads	27816
Landis	28088
Langley Store	27801
Lansdowne (Part of Charlotte)	28226
Lansing	28643
Lanvale	28451
Lasker	27848
Last Chance	27824
Latham Town (Part of Greensboro)	27407
Lattimore	28089
Lauada	28713
Laurel	28753
Laurel Hill (Buncombe County)	28715
Laurel Hill (Scotland County)	28351
Laurel Hills	27612
Laurel Park	28739
Laurel Springs	28644
Laurinburg	28352*
	28353†
Lawndale (Cleveland County)	28090
Lawndale (Guilford County)	27408
Lawrence	27886
Lawsonville (Rockingham County)	27320
Lawsonville (Stokes County)	27022
Laytown	28645
Leaksville (Part of Eden)	27288
Leaman	27325
Leasburg	27291
Leatherman	28734
Ledbetter	28379
Ledger	28705
Leechville	27810
Lee's Ridge	28806
Leewood Acres	28092
Leggett	27886
Leicester	28748
Leland	28451
Lemon Springs	28355
Lennon Crossroads	28422
Lennons Crossroads	28438
Lennoxville	28516
Lenoir	28645
Lenoir Mall (Part of Lenoir)	28645
Lenoir Rhyne (Part of Hickory)	28601
Letitia	28906
Level Cross (Randolph County)	27317
Level Cross (Surry County)	27017
Levels	27925
Lewis	27565
Lewisburg	28714
Lewiston Woodville	27849
Lewisville	27023
Lexington	27292*
	27293†
Lexington Plaza (Part of Lexington)	27292
Liberia	27589
Liberty (Cherokee County)	37391
Liberty (Randolph County)	27298
Liberty (Rowan County)	28071
Liberty Hill	27306
Liddell	28578
Light Oak	28150
Liledown	28681
Lilesville	28091
Lillington	27546
Lilly	27976
Lincoln Correctional Center	28092
Lincolnton	28092*
	28093†
Lindell	27883
Linden	28356
Lindley Park (Part of Greensboro)	27403
Lineberry	27233

	ZIP
Linville	28646
Linville Falls	28647
Linwood	27299
Lisbon	28434
Little Creek	28754
Littlefield	28513
Little Horse Creek	28643
Little Mountain	28761
Little Pinecreek	28753
Little Richmond	28621
Little River (Alexander County)	28681
Little River (Transylvania County)	28766
Little Switzerland	28749
Littleton	27850
Livingstons Quarters	28351
Lizard Lick	27591
Lizzie	28580
Lloyd Crossroads	27942
Loafers Glory	28705
Lobelia	28394
Lochlommond	28304
Locust	28097
Locust Grove	28740
Locust Hill	27320
Loftins Crossroads	28501
Logan	28139
Lola	28520
Lomax	28669
Lone Hickory	27055
Long Acres (Part of Jacksonville)	28546
Long Beach	28461
Longcreek	28457
Longisland	28648
Long John Mountain Estates	28739
Longleaf	28570
Long Leaf Park (Part of Wilmington)	28403
Long Pine	28170
Long Ridge	28754
Long Shoals	28092
Longs Store	27573
Longtown (Burke County)	28761
Longtown (Yadkin County)	27011
Long View (Bladen County)	28448
Longview (Catawba County)	28602
Longview (Cumberland County)	28301
Longwood	28452
Longwood Park	28345
Loray	28677
Louisburg	27549
Love Field	28779
Lovejoy	27371
Love Valley	28677
Lowell	28098
Lowes Grove	27713
Lowesville	28164
Lowgap	27024
Lowland	28552
Luart	27546
Lucama	27851
Lucia	28120
Luck	28743
Lumber Bridge	28357
Lumberton	28358*
	28359†
Luther	28715
Lyman	28521
Lynchs Corner	27909
Lynn	28750
Lynndale	27858
Lynnwood Jr. Estate	28025
Lynwood Lakes	27406
Mabel	28698
McAdenville	28101
McAdoo Heights (Part of Greensboro)	27405
McArthers Crossroads	28352
Macclesfield	27852
McConnell (Beaufort County)	27814
McConnell (Moore County)	27325
McCray	27215
McCullen	28328
McCullers	27603
Mc Cutcheon Field	28545
McDade	27231
McDaniel	28382
McDonald	28340
McDowell Correctional Center	28752
Macedonia (Wake County)	27606
Macedonia (Washington County)	27962
McFarlan	28102
MacGee Crossroads	27501
McGehees Mill	27343
McGinnis Crossroads	28722

	ZIP
McGowans Crossroads	27858
McGrady	28649
Machpelah	28080
Mackeys	27970
Macks Village	27526
McLamb Crossroads	28366
McLeansville	27301
Maco	28451
Macon	27551
Madison	27025
Maggie Valley	28751
Magnolia (Burke County)	28655
Magnolia (Duplin County)	28453
Maiden	28650
Maine	27028
Main Street (Part of Garner)	27529
Makatoka	28420
Makleyville	27875
Malmo	28451
Malpass Corner	28425
Maltby	28905
Malvern Hills (Part of Asheville)	28806
Mamers	27552
Mamie	27966
Manchester (Part of Spring Lake)	28390
Mangum	27306
Manly	28387
Manns Harbor	27953
Manor Station (Part of Winston-Salem)	27114
Mansfield	28557
Mansfield Park	28557
Manson	27553
Manteo	27954
Maple	27956
Maple Cypress	28530
Maple Hill	28454
Maple Springs	28665
Mapleton	27855
Mapleville	27549
Maplewood (Part of Rockingham)	28379
Marble	28905
Marcus	27281
Maready	28521
Margaretsville	27853
Maribel	28515
Marietta	28362
Marion	28752
Mariposa	28164
Marlboro	27828
Marler	27020
Marlwood Acres (Part of Charlotte)	28212
Mar-Mac	27530
Mar-Man	28532
Marshall	28753
Marshallberg	28553
Mars Hill	28754
Marshville	28103
Marston	28363
Martel Village (Part of Woodfin)	28804
Martin Correctional Center	27892
Martins Creek	28906
Marvin	28173
Marys Grove	28086
Mashoes	27953
Masonboro	28403
Masons Crossroads	28343
Mason Store	27546
Masontown	28581
Massapoag (Part of Lincolnton)	28092
Mast	28692
Mathews Crossroads	27816
Matkins	27249
Matney	28604
Matthews	28105*
	28106†
Maury	28554
Mavaton	27932
Maxton	28364
Mayfair	28304
Mayfield	27326
Mayhew	28115
Mayodan	27027
Maysville	28555
Mazeppa	28115
Meadow (Johnston County)	27504
Meadow (Stokes County)	27052
Meadowood	28379
Meadowood Lakes	27302
Meadow Summit (Part of Eden)	27288
Meadow Wood	28304
Meat Camp	28607
Mebane	27302
Mecklenburg Correctional Center	28078

---

* Area Zip Code   † Post Office Boxes

ZIP		ZIP		ZIP
Medfield	27607	Moores Springs	27053	Murraysville	28405
Melanchton	27298	Mooresville	28115	Murray Town	28425
Melrose	28773	Mooresville Junction (Part of		Musgraves Crossroads	27863
Melville	27302	Mooresville)	28115	Myers Park (Part of	
Melvin Hill	28722	Moravian Falls	28654	Charlotte)	28207
Menola	27910	Mordecai (Part of Raleigh)	27604	Myrick Estates	27850
Meredith College (Part of		Morehead City	28557	Myrtle Grove	28403
Raleigh)	27601	Morgans Corner	27909	Nags Head	27959
Merrimon	28516	Morganton	28655	Nahunta	27863
Merritt	28556		28680	Nakina	28455
Merry Hill	27957	For specific Morganton Zip Codes		Nantahala	28781
Merry Oaks	27559	call (704) 437-3484, or your local		Naples	28760
Mesic	28515	postmaster.		Nash Correctional Institution	27856
Metcalf	28150	Morgantown	27215	Nashville	27856
Method (Part of Raleigh)	27606	Moriah	27572	Nathans Creek	28617
Methodist College	28301	Morlan Park	28146	Naval Hospital	28542
Mewborns Crossroads	28501	Morning Star	28716	Navassa	28404
Micaville	28755	Morris Landing	28445	Nebo (McDowell County)	28761
Micro	27555	Morrisville	27560	Nebo (Yadkin County)	27011
Middleburg	27556	Mortimer	28645	Nebraska	27824
Middle Fork	28712	Morven	28119	Needmore (Rowan County)	27054
Middlesex	27557	Moss	28127	Needmore (Swain County)	28713
Middletown	27824	Moss Hill	28501	Neel Estates	28147
Midland	28107	Mother Vineyard	27954	Nelson	27560
Midpine	28086	Motleta	27203	Neuse	27661
Midway (Alexander County)	28636	Mountain Home	28758	Neuse Crossroads	27661
Midway (Beaufort County)	27808	Mountain Island	28120	Neuse Forest (Craven	
Midway (Bertie County)	27957	Mountain Park	28676	County)	28562
Midway (Brunswick County)	28422	Mountain Valley	28790	Neuse Forest (Craven	
Midway (Cabarrus County)	28081	Mountain View (Buncombe		County)	28560
Midway (Richmond County)	28379	County)	28704	Neverson	27880
Midway (Rockingham		Mountain View (Catawba		New Bern	28560-64
County)	27320	County)	28601	For specific New Bern Zip Codes	
Midway Park	28544	Mountain View (Gaston		call (919) 638-6111, or your local	
Midwood (Part of Charlotte)	28205	County)	28086	postmaster.	
Milburnie	27604	Mountain View (Orange		New Bern Junction (Part of	
Mildred	27886	County)	27278	Wilmington)	28405
Miles	27302	Mountain View (Stokes		New Bethel	27572
Millboro	27248	County)	27021	Newbold (Part of	
Mill Branch	28420	Mount Airy	27030	Fayetteville)	28301
Millbridge	28147	Mount Carmel	27306	New Bridge (Part of	
Millbrook (Part of Raleigh)	27658	Mount Carmel Acres	28806	Woodfin)	28804
Mill Creek (Ashe County)	28684	Mount Energy	27522	Newdale	28714
Mill Creek (Brunswick		Mount Gilead (Avery		Newell	28126
County)	28479	County)	28622	Newfound	28748
Mill Creek (Carteret County)	28570	Mount Gilead (Cabarrus		New Hanover Correctional	
Mill Crossroads	27932	County)	28025	Center	28401
Millennium Church	27805	Mount Gilead (Montgomery		New Haven	28675
Millers Creek	28651	County)	27306	New Hill	27562
Millersville	28681	Mount Gould	27957	New Holland	27885
Millingport	28001	Mount Herman	28638	New Hope (Chatham	
Mill Spring	28756	Mount Holly	28120	County)	27559
Mills River	28742	Mount Mourne	28123	New Hope (Franklin County)	27549
Milltown	28771	Mount Olive (Bladen		New Hope (Iredell County)	28689
Milton	27305	County)	28337	New Hope (Orange County)	27514
Milwaukee	27854	Mount Olive (Columbus		New Hope (Randolph	
Mimosa Shores	27889	County)	28472	County)	27239
Mineral Springs (Anson		Mount Olive (Hyde County)	27810	New Hope (Wake County)	27604
County)	28135	Mount Olive (Stokes		New Hope (Wayne County)	27534
Mineral Springs (Union		County)	27021	New Hope (Wilson County)	27893
County)	28108	Mount Olive (Wayne		New House	28150
Mingo	28334	County)	28365	Newland	28657
Minneapolis	28652	Mount Pleasant (Avery		New Lands	27925
Minnesott Beach	28510	County)	28657	New Leaksville	27288
Minpro	28777	Mount Pleasant (Cabarrus		Newlife	28635
Mint Hill	28212	County)	28124	New London	28127
Mintons Store	27897	Mount Pleasant (Cherokee		New Market	27350
Mintonsville	27946	County)	28906	Newport	28570
Mintz	28382	Mount Pleasant (Moore		New River Marine Corps Air	
Mirror Lake	28741	County)	28326	Station	28540
Misenheimer	28109	Mount Pleasant (Nash		New River Plaza (Part of	
Mitchells Fork	27946	County)	27807	Jacksonville)	28540
Mitchell Village	28557	Mount Pleasant (Richmond		New Salem	28103
Mitcheners Crossroads	27525	County)	28338	Newsom	27239
Mocksville	27028	Mount Pleasant (Yadkin		Newton	28658
Moffitt Hill	28762	County)	27011	Newton Grove	28366
Mollie	28432	Mount Sterling	37821	Newton Park	27893
Moltonville	28328	Mount Tabor (Forsyth		Newtons Crossroads	28478
Momeyer	27856	County)	27106	Newtowne Plaza (Part of	
Moncure	27559	Mount Tabor (Washington		Statesville)	28677
Monks Crossroads	28366	County)	27928	Niagara	28387
Monroe	28110-12	Mount Tirzah	27583	Nixons Beach	27932
For specific Monroe Zip Codes		Mount Ulla	28125	Nixonton	27909
call (704) 289-4507, or your local		Mount Vernon (Rowan		Nobles Cross Roads	28525
postmaster.		County)	27013	Nocarva	27551
Monroe Mall (Part of		Mount Vernon (Rutherford		Nocho Park (Part of	
Monroe)	28110	County)	28139	Greensboro)	27406
Monroetown (Moore		Mount Vernon Springs	27344	Norfleet	27874
County)	28374	Mount Zion (Part of		Norlina	27563
Monroetown (Rockingham		Greensboro)	27406	Norman	28367
County)	27320	Moxley	28635	Norrington Crossroads	27546
Montague	28435	Moyock	27958	North (Part of Winston-	
Montclair	28304	Mt. Mitchell	28083	Salem)	27115
Montezuma	28653	Mt. Pleasant	27592	North Albemarle (Part of	
Montgomery Correctional		Muddy Cross	27946	Albemarle)	28001
Center	27371	Mulberry	28659	North Asheboro (Part of	
Monticello	27214	Murdocksville	28734	Asheboro)	27203
Montreat	28757	Murfreesboro	27855	North Belmont (Part of	
Montrose	28376	Murphey	28458	Belmont)	28012
Moores Beach	27810	Murphy	28906	North Brevard	28712
Mooresboro	28114	Murray Hills	28081	North Burlington (Part of	
Moores School House	27542	Murrays Mills	28609	Burlington)	27215

* Area Zip Code   † Post Office Boxes

	ZIP		ZIP		ZIP
North Charlotte (Part of Charlotte)	28225	Ogden	28405	Pea Ridge (Polk County)	28756
North Chase (Part of Wilmington)	28405	Ogreeta	28906	Pea Ridge (Yadkin County)	27020
North Concord (Part of Concord)	28025	Oine	27563	Pecan Grove	27874
North Cooleemee (Part of Cooleemee)	27014	Okeewemee	27371	Peden	28672
North Cove	28752	Okisko	27909	Pee Dee	27306
North Durham (Part of Durham)	27704	Old Bethlehem	27589	Pekin	27306
North Elkin	28621	Old Dock	28472	Peletier	28584
Northgate (Part of Durham)	27701	Olde Farm	28390	Pelham	27311
Northgate Mall (Part of Durham)	27701	Old Farm	28025	Pembroke	28372
North Harbor	28516	Old Ford	27889	Pender Correctional Center	28425
North Harlowe	28532	Old Fort	28762	Pender Crossroad	27822
North Henderson (Part of Henderson)	27536	Old Fort Shores	28817	Penderlea	28478
North Hickory	28601	Old Hundred	28351	Pendleton	27862
North Hills (Part of Raleigh)	27614*	Old Providence (Part of Charlotte)	28226	Penland	28765
	27619†	Old Sparta	27852	Penrose	28766
Northlakes	28630	Old Spring Hope	27882	Pensacola	28714
North Lumberton (Part of Lumberton)	28358	Oldtown (Part of Winston-Salem)	27106	Perch	27043
Northmoor	28601	Old Trap	27974	Perfection	28523
North Point (Part of Winston-Salem)	27106	Olin	28660	Perkinsville (Part of Boone)	28607
North Raeford	28376	Olive Branch	28103	Perry's Beach	27924
North Ridge (Part of Raleigh)	27615	Olive Crossroads	28573	Perrytown	27924
North River	28516	Olivehill	27573	Peru	28460
North River Corner	28516	Olivers Crossroads	28658	Petersburg (Madison County)	28753
North Roxboro (Part of Roxboro)	27573	Olivia	28368	Petersburg (Onslow County)	28574
Northside (Granville County)	27564	Olympia	28560	Petersville	27292
Northside (Wilson County)	27822	Olyphic	28463	Pettys Shore	27922
North Topsail Beach	28445	Onvil	27306	Pfafftown	27040
North Tryon (Part of Charlotte)	28213	Ophir	27371	Philadelphia	27974
	28262	Ora Mill	28150	Philadelphus	28377
	28269	Orange Correctional Center	27278	Phillips Cross Roads	28585
Northview	27330	Orange Grove	27278	Phoenix	28451
North West	28451	Oregon Hill	27326	Piedmont Crescent Country Club	27253
Northwest Cabarrus Woods	28081	Oriental	28571	Piedmont Heights (Part of Greensboro)	27403
North Wilkesboro	28659	Ormondsville	28513	Pierceville	27976
North Winston (Part of Winston-Salem)	27105	Orrum	28369	Pigeon Roost	28740
Northwoods (Part of Jacksonville)	28540	Osborne	28345	Pike Crossroads	27863
Norton (Jackson County)	28723	Osceola	27214	Pike Road	27860
Norton (Macon County)	28763	Osgood	27330	Pikeville	27863
Norwood (Rockingham County)	27320	Osmond	27291	Pilands Crossroads	27922
Norwood (Stanly County)	28128	Ossipee	27244	Pilot (Davidson County)	27360
Norwood Beach	28128	Oswalt	28166	Pilot (Franklin County)	27597
Norwood Hollow	28604	Oteen	28805	Pilot Mountain	27041
Oakboro	28129	Othello	28694	Pinebluff	28373
Oak City	27857	Otto	28763	Pine Crest	27808
Oak Crest (Part of Fayetteville)	28301	Otway	28516	Pinecrest Acres	28301
Oakdale (Guilford County)	27282	Outlaws Bridge	28508	Pinecroft (Part of Greensboro)	27407
Oakdale (Iredell County)	28677	Overhills Park	28390	Pine Hall	27042
Oak Forest	28803	Oxford	27565	Pine Haven	27239
Oak Grove (Brunswick County)	28462	Oxford Park	28610	Pine Hill (Hoke County)	28315
Oak Grove (Cleveland County)	28086	Pacolet Valley	28782	Pine Hill (Surry County)	27011
Oak Grove (Guilford County)	27406	Pactolus	27834	Pinehurst	28374
Oak Grove (Macon County)	28734	Padgett	28454	Pinehurst Park	27529
Oak Grove (Surry County)	27030	Paint Fork	28754	Pine Knoll (Part of Hope Mills)	28348
Oak Hill (Burke County)	28655	Paint Rock	28743	Pine Knoll Shores	28557
Oak Hill (Caldwell County)	28645	Pala Alto	28555	Pine Lakes	27030
Oakhurst (Part of Charlotte)	28205	Palestine	28001	Pine Level	27568
Oakland (Nash County)	27882	Palmerville	28127	Pinelog	28472
Oakland (Rutherford County)	28160	Palmyra	27859	Pineola	28662
Oakley (Part of Asheville)	28803	Pamlico	28571	Pine Ridge (Cabarrus County)	28201
Oak Park (Buncombe County)	28704	Pamlico Beach	27810	Pine Ridge (Franklin County)	27597
Oak Park (Cherokee County)	28906	Pantego	27860	Pine Ridge (Surry County)	27030
Oak Ridge	27310	Panther Creek	28721	Pine Ridge (Washington County)	27970
Oak Ridge Park	28379	Paradise Point	28012	Pinetops	27864
Oaks	28560	Parkersburg	28441	Pinetown	27865
Oaksmith Acres	28557	Parkers Fork	27926	Pine Valley	28403
Oakview (Part of High Point)	27265	Park Road (Part of Charlotte)	28209	Pine View	27330
Oak Villa	27986	Parks Crossroads	27316	Pineville	28134
Oakville	27589	Park Spring	27315	Piney Creek	28663
Oakwillow	27910	Parkstone (Part of Charlotte)	28210	Piney Green (Onslow County)	28544
Oakwood (Part of Greensboro)	27407	Parkstown	28551	Piney Green (Onslow County)	28540
Oakwood Acres	27292	Parkton	28371	Piney Green (Sampson County)	28328
Occoneechee	27278	Parktown	27589	Piney Grove (Brunswick County)	28422
Ocean	28570	Park View (Part of Kinston)	28501	Piney Grove (Craven County)	28532
Ocean Isle Beach	28469	Parkville	27944	Piney Grove (Orange County)	27278
Ocracoke	27960	Parkway Forest (Part of Asheville)	28805	Piney Ridge	28328
Odom Correctional Institution	27845	Parkwood (Cabarrus County)	28027	Pin Hook	28466
Ogburn (Part of Winston-Salem)	27105	Parkwood (Durham County)	27713	Pink Hill	28572
		Parkwood (Moore County)	28327	Pinkney	27830
		Parkwood (Wilson County)	27893	Pinnacle	27043
		Parmele	27861	Pireway	28463
		Parrott Fork	28501	Pisgah Forest	28768
		Parsonville	28665	Pisgah View (Part of Asheville)	28806
		Paschall	27589	Pittmans Store	27891
		Pates	28372	Pittsboro	27312
		Patetown	27534	Plainview	28383
		Patterson	28661	Plateau	28658
		Patterson Grove	28086	Plaza (Guilford County)	27408
		Patterson Springs	28152		
		Pauls Crossing	28137		
		Paw Creek (Part of Charlotte)	28130		
		Paynes Tavern	27573		
		Peace Haven Estates	27104		
		Peachland	28133		
		Peachtree	28906		
		Peacock Crossing	28431		
		Pearce Crossroads	27597		

* Area Zip Code   **† Post Office Boxes**

	ZIP
Plaza (Mecklenburg County)	28299
Plaza, The (Part of Greenville)	27834
Pleasant Acres	28301
Pleasant Garden	27313
Pleasant Gardens	28752
Pleasant Grove (Alamance County)	27217
Pleasant Grove (Buncombe County)	28787
Pleasant Grove (Caswell County)	27379
Pleasant Grove (Duplin County)	28365
Pleasant Grove (Northampton County)	27831
Pleasant Grove (Washington County)	27970
Pleasant Hill (Jones County)	28572
Pleasant Hill (Northampton County)	27866
Pleasant Hill (Wilkes County)	28621
Pleasant Plains	27910
Pleasant View	27925
Pleasantville	27025
Plott Farm Addition	28716
Plumtree	28664
Plyler	28001
Plymouth	27962
Pocomoke	27525
Point Caswell	28421
Point Harbor	27964
Pole Creek	28715
Polks Landing	27514
Polkton	28135
Polkville	28136
Pollocksville	28573
Pomona (Part of Greensboro)	27407
Ponderosa (Cumberland County)	28303
Ponderosa (Harnett County)	28334
Ponzer	27810
Pooletown	28137
Poor Town	27910
Pope Air Force Base	28308
Poplar	28740
Poplar Branch	27965
Poplar Grove	28341
Poplar Springs	27021
Poplar Tent	28027
Porter	28128
Portsmouth	27960
Postell	28906
Potecasi	27867
Pot Neck	28551
Potters Curve	28431
Potters Hill	28572
Pottertown	28684
Powell Crossroads	27946
Powells Point	27966
Powells Store	27326
Powellsville	27967
Powhatan	27520
Prentiss	28734
Prestonville	27025
Price	27048
Price Creek	28714
Princeton	27569
Princeville	27886
Proctors Corner	27910
Proctorville	28375
Propst Crossroads	28601
Prospect	28462
Prospect Hill	27314
Prosper	28436
Providence (Caswell County)	27315
Providence (Granville County)	27565
Providence (McDowell County)	28752
Providence (Mecklenburg County)	28105
Providence Square (Part of Charlotte)	28211
Proximity (Part of Greensboro)	27405
Pumpkin Center (Lincoln County)	28092
Pumpkin Center (Onslow County)	28540
Pumpkintown	28779
Pungo	27860
Pungo Stores	27810
Purlear	28665
Purley	27379
Purnell	27587
Purvis	28383
Putnam	28327
Pyatte	28657

	ZIP
Quail Corners (Part of Charlotte)	28210
Quail Ridge (Craven County)	28532
Quail Ridge (Cumberland County)	28306
Quail Ridge (Lee County)	27330
Qualla	28789
Quebec	28747
Queen	27371
Quick	27326
Quinerly	28530
Quinns Store	28518
Quitsna	27983
Rabbit Corner	27909
Radical	28649
Radio Island	28516
Raeford	28376
Raemon	28364
Rainbow Springs	28734
Raleigh	27601-76
For specific Raleigh Zip Codes call (919) 831-3661, or your local postmaster.	
Rama Woods	28025
Ramseur	27316
Ramseytown	28714
Randleman	27317
Randolph (Mecklenburg County)	28211
Randolph (Pitt County)	27834
Randolph Correctional Center	27203
Randolph Mall (Part of Asheboro)	27203
Ranger	28906
Rangewood	27603
Rankin (Guilford County)	27405
Rankin (Pender County)	28421
Ranlo	28054
Ransomville	27810
Rawls	27526
Rayconda	28304
Raynham	28383
Rebel Acres	27604
Red Banks	28364
Redbug	28442
Red Cross (Randolph County)	27233
Red Cross (Stanly County)	28129
Reddies River	28696
Red Hill (Bladen County)	28433
Red Hill (Edgecombe County)	27891
Red Hill (Mitchell County)	28705
Redland	27006
Red Oak (Nash County)	27868
Red Oak (Pitt County)	27834
Red Springs	28377
Reeds Cross Roads	27292
Reedy Creek	27292
Reelsboro	28560
Reepsville	28168
Reese	28692
Reeves Ferry	28455
Regal	28906
Regan	28420
Register	28458
Rehoboth	27845
Reidsville	27320-23
For specific Reidsville Zip Codes call (919) 342-0391, or your local postmaster.	
Relief	28740
Rena	27020
Rennert	28386
Renston	28513
Republican	27983
Rest Haven	27808
Revolution (Part of Greensboro)	27405
Rex (Gaston County)	28054
Rex (Robeson County)	28378
Reynolda (Part of Winston-Salem)	27109
Reynolda Park (Part of Winston-Salem)	27107
Rheasville	27870
Rhems	28562
Rhems Landing	28562
Rhodes	27805
Rhodes-Rhyne	28092
Rhodhiss	28667
Rhodo	28901
Rhoney	28602
Rhyne Crossroads	28425
Riceville	28805
Richardson	28320
Richfield	28137
Richlands	28574
Richmond Hill (Alamance County)	27215

	ZIP
Richmond Hill (Yadkin County)	27011
Richmond Mills	28351
Rich Square	27869
Rico	28472
Riddle	27973
Ridgecrest	28770
Ridge Haven	27591
Ridge Run	28025
Ridgeville	27314
Ridgeway	27570
Ridgewood	28379
Riegelwood	28456
Riley	27596
Rimer	28025
Ringwood	27823
River Acres	27889
River Bend	28562
Riverdale	28560
River Hills	27858
Rivermont	28501
River Neck	27925
River Road	27889
Riverside (Craven County)	28530
Riverside (Part of New Bern)	28560
Riverside (Yancey County)	28714
Riverton	27932
Roanoke Rapids	27870
Roaring Creek	28657
Roaring Gap	28668
Roaring River	28669
Robbins	27325
Robbinsville	28771
Roberdel	28379
Roberdo	27306
Roberson Store	27892
Robersonville	27871
Roberta Mill	28027
Robeson Correctional Center	28358
Robin Hood Forest	27545
Robinson's	28570
Robinwood (Part of Gastonia)	28056
Rock Creek	27349
Rockdale (Part of Belwood)	28090
Rockefeller Estates	28326
Rockfish	28376
Rockford	27011
Rock Hill	28025
Rockingham	28379
Rockingham Correctional Center	27320
Rockingham Lake	27320
Rock Ridge	27893
Rockwell	28138
Rockwell Park (Part of Charlotte)	28213
Rocky Cross	27557
Rocky Ford	27544
Rockyhock	27932
Rocky Mount	27801-04
For specific Rocky Mount Zip Codes call (919) 977-3123, or your local postmaster.	
Rocky Pass	28761
Rocky Point	28457
Rocky River	28025
Rocky Springs	28636
Rodanthe	27968
Roduco	27969
Rolesville	27571
Rollingwood	28301
Rominger	28604
Ronda	28670
Rooks	28421
Roper	27970
Rose Bay	27885
Roseboro	28382
Roseborough	28646
Rosebud (Stokes County)	27052
Rosebud (Wilson County)	27822
Rose Hill (Duplin County)	28458
Rose Hill (Warren County)	27553
Roseland (Columbus County)	28432
Roseland (Lincoln County)	28092
Roseland (Moore County)	28315
Rosemary Park	28079
Rosemead	27924
Rosemont (Part of Winston-Salem)	27107
Roseneath	27874
Roseville	27573
Rosewood	27530
Rosindale	28434
Rosman	28772
Ross Store	27052
Rougemont	27572
Roughedge	28112
Round Peak	27030

Place	ZIP
Roundtree	28513
Rowan Correctional Center	28145
Rowan Mill	28147
Rowes Corner	28560
Rowland	28383
Roxboro	27573
Roxobel	27872
Royal	27806
Royal Oaks (Part of Kannapolis)	28083
Royal Pines	28704
Royster	28451
Rudd	27214
Ruffin	27326
Rural Hall	27045
Ruskin	28399
Russtown	28420
Ruth	28139
Rutherford College	28671
Rutherford Correctional Center	28043
Rutherfordton	28139
Rutherwood	28607
Ryland	27980
Saddle Mountain	28623
Saddletree	28358
Sadler	27320
St. Helena	28425
St. John	27910
St. Johns	27932
St. Lewis	27852
St. Martin	28001
St. Pauls	28384
St. Stephens	28601
Salem (Burke County)	28655
Salem (Forsyth County)	27108
Salem (Lincoln County)	28092
Salem (Nash County)	27891
Salem (Randolph County)	27317
Salem (Surry County)	27030
Salemburg	28385
Salisbury	28144-47

For specific Salisbury Zip Codes call (704) 636-0231, or your local postmaster.

Place	ZIP
Salter Path	28575
Salty Shores	28570
Saluda	28773
Salvo	27972
Samarcand	27242
Samaria	27557
Sampson Correctional Center	28328
Sanderling	27948
Sand Hill (Buncombe County)	28806
Sandhill (Pamlico County)	28560
Sandhill Acres	27229
Sands	28607
Sandy Bottom	28501
Sandy Bottoms	28352
Sandy Creek	28451
Sandy Cross (Gates County)	27946
Sandy Cross (Nash County)	27856
Sandy Cross (Rockingham County)	27320
Sandy Grove (Davidson County)	27292
Sandy Grove (Hoke County)	28376
Sandymush (Buncombe County)	28753
Sandy Mush (Rutherford County)	28043
Sandy Plain (Columbus County)	28463
Sandy Plain (Duplin County)	28572
Sandy Plains	28782
Sandy Ridge (Guilford County)	27235
Sandy Ridge (Stokes County)	27046
Sandy Ridge Correctional Center	27265
Sanford	27330*
	27331†
Santeetlah	28771
Sapona	28301
Sapphire	28774
Saratoga	27873
Sardis Village (Part of Charlotte)	28270
Sarecta	28349
Sarecta Junction	28349
Sarvis Heights	28052
Sassers Mill	28526
Satterwhite	27565
Saulston	27534
Saunook	28786
Savannah	28779
Saw	28023
Sawmills	28630
Saxapahaw	27340
Sayles Village (Part of Asheville)	28803
Scaly Mountain	28775
Schley	27278
Scholl	28345
Schrams Beach	27810
Scotch Grove	28352
Scotland Correctional Center	28396
Scotland Neck	27874
Scotsdale (Cumberland County)	28304
Scotsdale (Scotland County)	28352
Scott Acres	27302
Scott Park (Part of Greensboro)	27401
Scotts (Iredell County)	28699
Scotts (Wilson County)	27851
Scotts Hill	28405
Scotts Store (Duplin County)	28365
Scotts Store (Pamlico County)	28560
Scottville	28672
Scranton	27875
Scuffleton	28513
Scuppernong	27928
Seaboard	27876
Seabreeze	28403
Seagate	28403
Seagate IV	28516
Seagrove	27341
Sealevel	28577
Seaside	28459
Sedalia	27342
Sedgefield (Guilford County)	27407
Sedgefield (Mecklenburg County)	28203
Sedgefield Lakes	27407
Sedgefield Park	27407
Sedge Garden	27105
Selica	28712
Selma	27576
Selwin	27946
Selwyn Park (Part of Charlotte)	28209
Seminole	27505
Semora	27343
Senia	28657
Seven Devils	28604
Seven Lakes	27376
Seven Paths	27549
Seven Springs	28578
Severn	27877
Seversville (Part of Charlotte)	28208
Sevier	28752
Seward	27040
Seymour Johnson Air Force Base	27531
Shacktown	27055
Shadey Oaks Acres	28150
Shady Banks	27889
Shady Brook (Part of Kannapolis)	28081
Shady Forest	28459
Shady Grove	28501
Shale Brick	27360
Shallotte	28459
Shallotte Point	28459
Shallowell	27330
Shanghai (Cleveland County)	28150
Shanghai (Sampson County)	28458
Shankletown	28027
Shannon	28386
Shannon Plaza (Part of Durham)	27707*
	27717†
Sharon (Camden County)	27976
Sharon (Iredell County)	28677
Sharonbrook (Part of Charlotte)	28210
Sharp Point	27829
Sharpsburg	27878
Shatley Springs	28617
Shawboro	27973
Shaw Heights	28303
Sheffield	27028
Shelby	28150-52

For specific Shelby Zip Codes call (704) 487-4324, or your local postmaster.

Place	ZIP
Shell Rock Landing	28539
Shelmerdine	28513
Shelter Neck	28425
Shelton	27311
Shelton Town	27030
Shepard (Part of Durham)	27707
Shepherds	28115
Sherrills Ford (Catawba County)	28673
Sherron Acres (Part of Durham)	27703
Sherwood	28692
Sherwood Forest (Buncombe County)	28778
Sherwood Forest (Buncombe County)	28805
Sherwood Forrest (Part of Asheville)	28805
Sherwood Forest (Forsyth County)	27104
Sherwood Forest (Transylvania County)	28712
Sherwood Forrest	27893
Sherwood Park	28306
Sherwood Terrace	28712
Sherwood Village (Part of High Point)	27260
Shields Commissary	27874
Shiloh (Buncombe County)	28803
Shiloh (Camden County)	27974
Shiloh (Rutherford County)	28043
Shines Crossroads	28580
Shingle Hollow	28139
Shinnville	28115
Shoal	27043
Shoofly	27581
Shooting Creek	28904
Shopton	28210
Short Off	28741
Shotwell	27545
Shuffletown	28214
Shulls Mills	28607
Shupings Mill	28138
Sidestown	28027
Sidney (Beaufort County)	27810
Sidney (Columbus County)	28472
Signal Hill Mall (Part of Statesville)	28677
Sign Pine	27980
Siler City	27344
Silk Hope	27344
Siloam	27047
Silver City	28376
Silverdale	28539
Silver Hill (Davidson County)	27292
Silver Hill (Pamlico County)	28560
Silver Lake	28403
Silverstone	28698
Silver Valley	27292
Simpson	27879
Sims	27880
Sioux	28740
Sivey Town	28462
Six Forks	27609
Six Forks (Part of Raleigh)	27615
Skibo	28304
Skinnersville	27970
Skyco	27954
Skycrest Village	27604
Skyland	28776
Skyline	28394
Skyway Terrace	28364
Sladesville	27875
Slatestone Hills	27889
Sligo	27958
Sloan	28466
Slocomb	28356
Slocum	27824
Small	27806
Small Cross Roads	27932
Smallwood (Part of Washington)	27889
Smethport	28694
Smith Creek	28480
Smith Crossing	28442
Smithfield	27577
Smith Grove	27028
Smithtown (Beaufort County)	27810
Smithtown (Perquimans County)	27944
Smithtown (Yadkin County)	27018
Smyre	28054
Smyrna	28579
Sneads Ferry	28460
Sneads Grove	28352
Snow Camp	27349
Snowden	27958
Snow Hill (Chowan County)	27980
Snow Hill (Greene County)	28580
Snow Hill (Sampson County)	28382
Snug Harbor	27944
Soapstone Mountain	27355
Sodom	28753
Somerset (Chowan County)	27932
Somerset (Person County)	27573
Somerset Hills	27604

* Area Zip Code   † Post Office Boxes

* Area Zip Code   † Post Office Boxes

	ZIP		ZIP		ZIP
Troutman	28166	Waco	28169	Westchester Mall (Part of	
Troy	27371	Wade	28395	High Point)	27262
Trust	28743	Wade Mills (Part of		Westcliff	28147
Tryon (Gaston County)	28016	Wadesboro)	28170	West Concord (Part of	
Tryon (Polk County)	28782	Wadesboro	28170	Concord)	28027
Tryon Mall (Part of		Wades Point	27810	West Cramerton (Part of	
Charlotte)	28213	Wadeville	27306	Cramerton)	28032
Tuckasegee	28783	Wagoner	28640	West Durham (Part of	
Tuckerdale	28643	Wagram	28396	Durham)	27705
Tungsten	27536	Wake Crossroads	27604	West Edgecombe	27801
Tunis	27986	Wakefield	27597	Westend (Guilford County)	27262
Turkey	28393	Wake Forest	27587*	West End (Moore County)	27376
Turkey Knob	28675		27588†	Western Prong	28472
Turlington	28334	Wakelon	27924	Westerwood (Part of	
Turnersburg	28688	Wakulla	28397	Greensboro)	27403
Turners Crossroads	27853	Walkers Crossroads	27587	Westfield	27053
Turnpike	28715	Walkertown (Forsyth		West Gastonia (Part of	
Tuscarora	28562	County)	27051	Gastonia)	28052
Tuscarora Beach	27986	Walkertown (Harnett		Westhaven	27834
Tusk	28579	County)	28356	West Highlands (Part of	
Tuskeegee	28771	Wallace	28466	Winston-Salem)	27104
Tusquitee	28904	Walla Watta	27865	West Jefferson	28694
Tuxedo	28784	Wallburg	27373	West Lumberton (Part of	
Twin Lake (Part of Sunset		Walnut	28753	Lumberton)	28358
Beach)	28459	Walnut Cove	27052	West Marion	28752
Twin Oaks	28675	Walnut Creek (Madison		West Market Street (Part of	
Tyner	27980	County)	28753	Greensboro)	27402
Tyro	27292	Walnut Creek (Wayne		Westminster	28139
Ulah	27203	County)	27534	Westmont (Part of	
Unaka	28906	Walstonburg	27888	Asheboro)	27203
U N C C	28223	Wananish (Part of Lake		Westmore	27341
Union (Hertford County)	27910	Waccamaw)	28450	West New Bern (Part of	
Union (Macon County)	28734	Wanchese	27981	New Bern)	28562
Union (Rutherford County)	28139	Warbler	27826	Westover (Wake County)	27606
Union Cross	27107	Wards	28431	Westover (Washington	
	27284	Wards Corner	28425	County)	27962
For specific Union Cross Zip		Wards Store	27891	West Philadelphia	27209
Codes call (919) 993-3812, or		Wardville	27979	Westport	28037
your local postmaster.		Warne	28909	Westridge (Part of Rocky	
Union Grove (Davidson		Warren Plains	27589	Mount)	27801
County)	27292	Warrensville	28693	West Rockingham	28379
Union Grove (Iredell County)	28689	Warrenton	27589	West Rocky Mount (Part of	
Union Hill	27018	Warren Wilson College	28778	Rocky Mount)	27801
Union Mills	28167	Warrior	28645	Westry	27801
Union Ridge	27215	Warsaw	28398	West Salem (Part of	
Unionville	28110	Washburn	28150	Winston-Salem)	27101
University Estates		Washburn Store	28018	Westside	28023
(Cumberland County)	28301	Washington	27889	Wests Mill	28734
University Estates		Washington Correctional		West Smithfield	27577
(Rockingham County)	27320	Center	27928	West Statesville (Part of	
University Mall and Plaza		Washington Forks	28560	Statesville)	28677
(Part of Chapel Hill)	27514	Washington Park	27889	West Trade Street (Part of	
University of North Carolina		Watauga	28734	Charlotte)	28202
(Part of Wilmington)	28403*	Watauga Correctional		Westview (Part of Winston-	
	28407†	Center	28607	Salem)	27114
University Park (Part of		Waterlily	27923	Westwood (Scotland	
Charlotte)	28297	Waterville	37821	County)	28352
Upchurch	27502	Watha	28471	Westwood (Surry County)	27049
Upton	28645	Watson Crossroads	27542	West Yanceyville	27379
Upward	28731	Watts Crossroads	28025	Wexford	28213
Uwharie	27371	Waughtown (Part of		Whalebone (Part of Nags	
Valdese	28690	Winston-Salem)	27107	Head)	27959
Vale	28168		27117	Whaley	28622
Valhalla (Chowan County)	27932		27127	Wharton	27889
Valhalla (Polk County)	28782	For specific Waughtown Zip		Whichard	27884
Valle Crucis	28691	Codes call (919) 784-9801, or		Whichard Beach	27817
Valley	28657	your local postmaster.		Whispering Pines	28327
Valley Hill	28739	Waverly	28754	Whitakers	27891
Valley Hills Mall (Part of		Waves	27982	White Cross	27516
Hickory)	28601	Waxhaw	28173	Whitehall Shores	27921
Vanceboro	28586	Waycross	28453	Whitehead	28695
Vance Correctional Center	27536	Wayne Correctional Center	27533	White Hill	27330
Vandemere	28587	Waynesville	28786	Whitehouse	28167
Vander	28301	Wayside	28376	Whitehurst	27871
Vannoy	28696	Weaversford	28617	Whitehurst Park	28025
Varnamtown (Brunswick		Weaverville	28787	White Lake	28337
County)	28462	Webster	28788	White Oak (Bladen County)	28399
Vashti	28636	Weddington	28173	White Oak (Gates County)	27935
Vass	28394	Wedgewood Lakes	27958	White Oak (Guilford County)	27405
Vaughan	27586	Weeksville	27909	White Oak (Halifax County)	27823
Vein Mountain	28752	Wehutty	37301	White Oak (Nash County)	27856
Venable	28803	Welcome	27374	White Oaks Acres	27893
Venters	28513	Weldon	27890	White Oaks Acres West	27893
Vernon Park Mall (Part of		Wellons Village (Part of		White Pines	27049
Kinston)	28501	Durham)	27703	White Plains (Hyde County)	27824
Verona	28540	Wells	28304	White Plains (Surry County)	27031
Vests	28906	Welmar Heights	28304	Whitepost	27808
Vicksboro	27536	Wendell	27591	Whiterock	28753
Vienna	27040	Wenona	27860	White's Beach	27924
Viewmont (Part of Hickory)	28601	Wentworth	27375	Whites Chapel Church	27292
Vilas	28692	Wesleyan College	27804	Whites Crossroads	27924
Villa Heights (Part of		Wesley Chapel	28110	White Stocking	28425
Charlotte)	28205	Wesley Heights (Part of		Whiteston	27919
Vinegar Hill	28463	Charlotte)	28208	White Store	28133
Vineland Park	28306	Wesser	28713	Whiteville	28472
Vinton Woods	28034	West	28398	Whitfield Crossroads	28578
Violet	28906	West Asheville (Part of		Whitley Heights	27520
Virgilina	24598	Asheville)	28816	Whitnel (Part of Lenoir)	28645
Vista	28443	West Brook (Part of		Whitsett	27377
Vixen	28714	Kannapolis)	28081	Whittier	28789
Volunteer	27043	West Canton	28716	Whitt Town	27573
Waccamaw	28420			Whortonville	28556

	ZIP		ZIP		ZIP
Whynot	27341	Wilsons Mills	27593	Woodleaf	27054
Wilbanks	27822	Wilsonville	27502	Woodrow (Craven County)	28560
Wilbar	28696	Wilton	27525	Woodrow (Haywood	
Wilbon	27526	Wind Blow	27281	County)	28716
Wilbourns Store	24598	Windemere	28405	Woodrun	27306
Wilders Grove	27604	Windom	28714	Woodsdale	27573
Wildwood (Carteret County)	28557	Windsor	27983	Woodside	28081
Wildwood (Henderson		Windsors Cross Roads	27020	Woodside Hills	28715
County)	28732	Windy Gap	28659	Woodville (Bertie County)	27849
Wildwood Estate	28570	Winfall	27985	Woodville (Perquimans	
Wilgrove (Part of Charlotte)	28212	Wing	28705	County)	27944
Wilkerson Cross Roads	27542	Wingate	28174	Woodville (Surry County)	27030
Wilkesboro	28697	Winnabow	28479	Woodworth	27536
Wilkes Mall (Part of		Winstead Crossroads	27822	Wootens Crossroads	
Wilkesboro)	28697	Winsteadville	27810	(Columbus County)	28433
Wilkinson	27860	Winston-Salem	27101-30	Wootens Crossroads	
Willard	28478	For specific Winston-Salem Zip		(Greene County)	27888
Willeyton	27937	Codes call (919) 721-6058, or		Wootens Crossroads	
Williams	28472	your local postmaster.		(Lenoir County)	28501
Williamsboro	27536	Wintergreen	28523	Worley	28753
Williamsburg (Iredell County)	28634	Winterville	28590	Worthingtons Crossroads	27858
Williamsburg (Rockingham		Winton	27986	Worthville	27317
County)	27320	Wise	27594	Wrightsboro	28401
Williamson Crossroads	28431	Wise Forks	28526	Wrightsville	28480
Williamston	27892	Witherspoon Crossroads	28610	Wrightsville Beach	28480
Willis Landing	28539	Wittys Crossroads	27320	Yadkin	28144
Williston	28589	Wolf Creek	37317	Yadkin Correctional Center	27055
Willits	28779	Wolf Laurel	28754	Yadkin Valley	28645
Wil-Lotta Acres	28025	Wolf Mountain	28783	Yadkinville	27055
Willow	27946	Wood	27549	Yamacraw	28435
Willow Green	28513	Woodard (Bertie County)	27983	Yanceyville	27379
Willow Spring	27592	Woodard (Wilson County)	27893	Yancy Correctional Center	28714
Wilmar	28586	Woodburn	28451	Yaupon Beach	28461
Wil-Mar Park (Part of		Wood Crest	28570	Yeatsville	27808
Concord)	28025	Wood Dale	28401	Yellow Creek	28771
Wilmington	28401-12	Woodfin	28804	Yeopim	27932
For specific Wilmington Zip Codes		Woodford	28684	Yorick	28399
call (919) 762-3700, or your local		Woodington	28501	Yorkmont Park (Part of	
postmaster.		Woodland	27897	Charlotte)	28217
Wilmington Beach	28428	Woodland Acres	27892	Yorkwood	28052
Wilmore (Part of Charlotte)	28203	Woodland Hills	28804	Youngsville	27596
Wilmot	28789	Woodlawn (Alamance		Zebulon	27597
Wilshire Park (Part of		County)	27302	Zephyr	28621
Asheville)	28806	Woodlawn (McDowell		Zionville	28698
Wilson	27893-96	County)	28752	Zirconia	28790
For specific Wilson Zip Codes call		Woodlea	28304		
(919) 237-4161, or your local					
postmaster.					

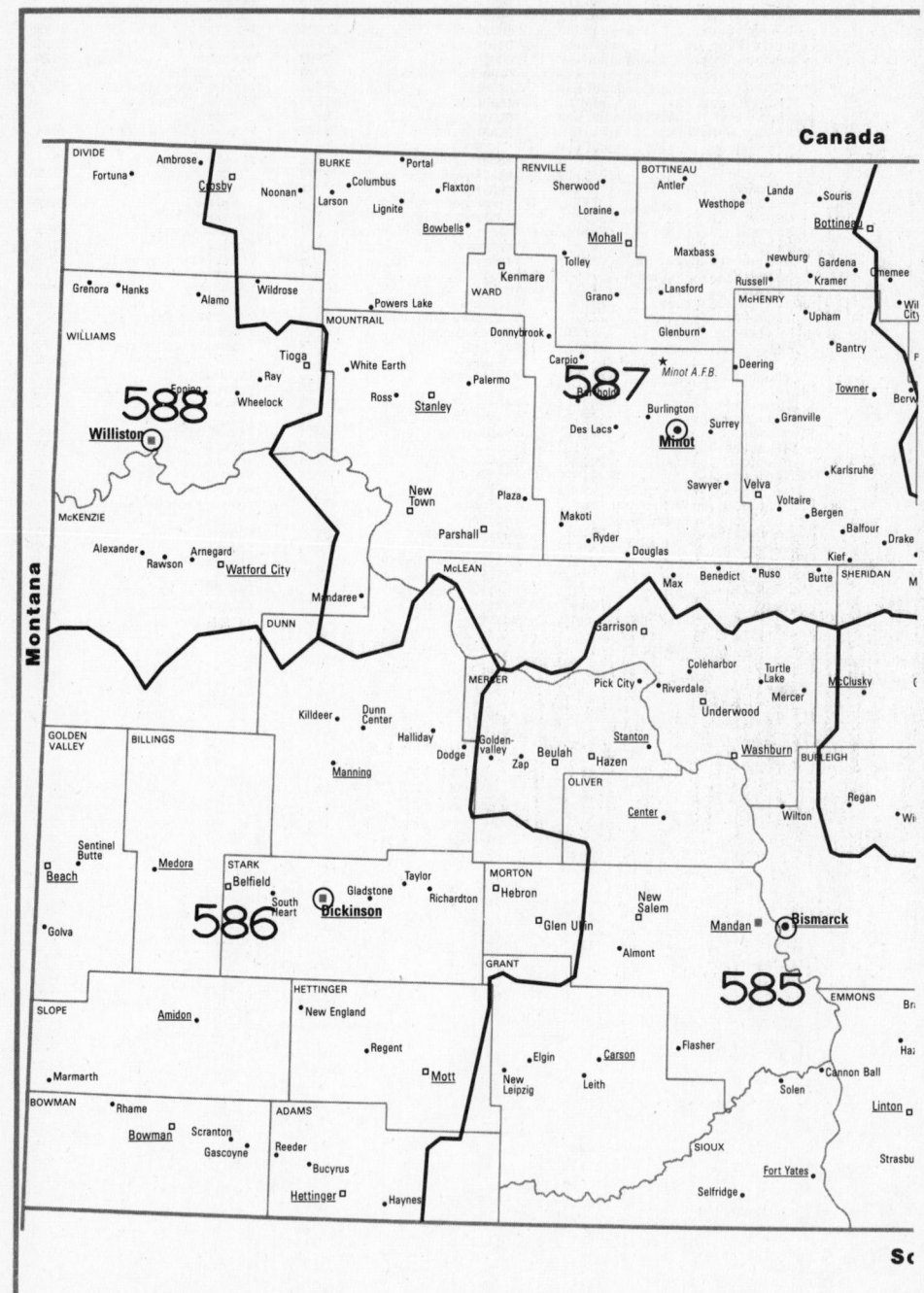

Canada

DIVIDE   Ambrose   Portal   BURKE   RENVILLE   BOTTINEAU
Fortuna   Crosby   Columbus   Sherwood   Antler   Westhope   Landa   Souris
   Noonan   Larson   Lignite   Flaxton   Loraine   Bottineau
         Bowbells   Mohall   Maxbass   Newburg   Gardena   Omemee
Grenora   Hanks   Alamo   Wildrose   Kenmare   Tolley   Lansford   Russell   Kramer   Wil City
WILLIAMS   Powers Lake   WARD   Grano   McHENRY   Upham
   MOUNTRAIL   Donnybrook   Glenburn   Bantry
         Carpio   ★ Minot A.F.B.   Deering

588   Tioga   White Earth   Palermo   **587**   Burlington   Towner   Berw
Epping   Ray   Ross   Stanley   Des Lacs   Surrey   Granville
Wheelock   Minot   Sawyer   Karlsruhe
Williston   New Town   Plaza   Makoti   Velva   Voltaire   Bergen
McKENZIE   Parshall   Ryder   Douglas   Balfour   Drake
Alexander   Arnegard   McLEAN   Max   Benedict   Ruso   Butte   Kief   SHERIDAN   M
   Rawson   Watford City   Garrison
Mandaree   DUNN   Coleharbor   Turtle Lake   McClusky
GOLDEN VALLEY   BILLINGS   Killdeer   Dunn Center   Pick City   Riverdale   Mercer
   Halliday   MERCER   Underwood
   Dodge   Golden valley   Beulah   Stanton   Washburn   BURLEIGH
   Manning   Zap   Hazen   OLIVER   Regan
Sentinel Butte   Medora   STARK   Center   Wilton
Beach   Belfield   Gladstone   Taylor   MORTON   New Salem   Mandan   Bismarck
Golva   **586**   South Heart   Dickinson   Richardton   Hebron   Glen Ullin   Almont   **585**   EMMONS   Br
SLOPE   HETTINGER   GRANT   Flasher   Ha
Amidon   New England   Elgin   Carson   Cannon Ball
Marmarth   Regent   New Leipzig   Leith   Solen   Linton
BOWMAN   Rhame   Mott   SIOUX   Strasbu
Bowman   Scranton   ADAMS   Reeder   Fort Yates
   Gascoyne   Bucyrus   Selfridge
   Hettinger   Haynes

Montana

So

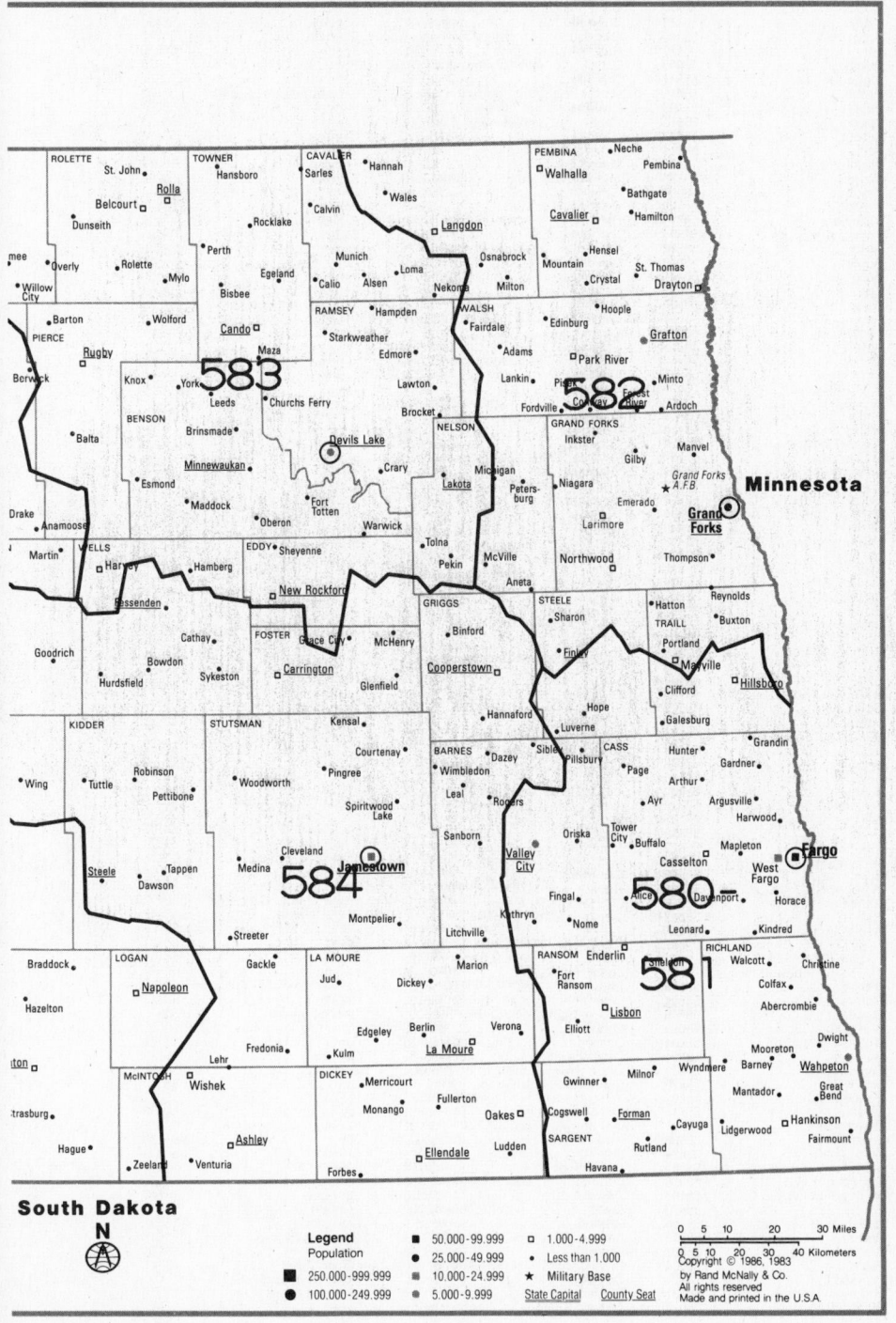

South Dakota

N

Legend
Population

■ 250.000-999.999
● 100.000-249.999
■ 50.000-99.999
● 25.000-49.999
● 10.000-24.999
● 5.000-9.999
□ 1.000-4.999
• Less than 1.000
★ Military Base
State Capital   County Seat

0 5 10   20   30 Miles
0 5 10   20   30   40 Kilometers

	ZIP		ZIP		ZIP
Abercrombie	58001	Bucyrus	58639	Eastside Estates	58701
Absaraka	58002	Buffalo	58011	East Valley City	58072
Acres A-Plenty	58504	Buffalo Springs	58623	Eckelson	58432
Adams	58210	Burke Addition	58201	Eckman	58760
Adrian	58472	Burlington	58722	Edgeley	58433
Agate	58310	Burnstad	58495	Edinburg	58227
Akra	58220	Burt	58646	Edmore	58330
Alamo	58830	Butte	58723	Edmunds	58476
Alexander	58831	Buttzville	58054	Egeland	58331
Alfred	58411	Buxton	58218	El Dorado Acres	58601
Alice	58003	Caledonia	58219	Eldridge	58401
Alkabo	58845	Calio	58352	Elgin	58533
Almont	58520	Calvin	58323	Ellendale	58436
Alpha	58654	C and L Estates	58504	Elliott	58033
Alsen	58311	Cando	58324	Embden	58079
Ambrose	58833	Cannon Ball	58528	Emerado	58228
Amenia	58004	Carbury	58783	Emmet	58540
Amidon	58620	Carlsbad	58504	Emrick	58422
Anamoose	58710	Carolville	58801	Enderlin	58027
Anderson Acres	58504	Carpio	58725	Englevale	58033
Aneta	58212	Carrington	58421	Epping	58843
Anselm	58068	Carson	58529	Erie	58029
Antler	58711	Cartwright	58838	Esmond	58332
Appam	58830	Cashel	58225	Evergreen	58051
Apple Creek Country Club	58501	Casselton	58012	Faiman's Sunrise Addition	58504
Apple Creek Estates	58558	Cathay	58422	Fairdale	58229
Apple Valley	58558	Cavalier	58220	Fairfield	58627
Ardoch	58213	Cayuga	58013	Fairmount	58030
Arena	58412	Center	58530	Falconer Estates	58504
Argusville	58005	Chaffee	58014	Falkirk	58577
Arnegard	58835	Charbonneau	58831	Fargo	58102-09
Arthur	58006	Charlson	58763	For specific Fargo Zip Codes call	
Arvilla	58214	Chaseley	58423	(701) 241-6100, or your local	
Ashley	58413	Chrisan	58102	postmaster.	
Ashland Estates	58504	Christine	58015	Fessenden	58438
Auburn	58237	Churchs Ferry	58325	Fillmore	58332
Aurelia	58734	Circle K Estates	58501	Fingal	58031
Ayr	58007	City View Heights	58504	Finley	58230
Backoo	58282	Cleveland	58424	Finley Air Force Station,	
Baker	58386	Clifford	58016	785th Radar Squadron	58230
Baldwin	58521	Clyde	58352	Flasher	58535
Balfour	58712	Cogswell	58017	Flaxton	58737
Balta	58313	Coleharbor	58531	Flora	58348
Bantry	58713	Colfax	58018	Fonda	58366
Bar-D Estates	58504	Colgan	58844	Forbes	58439
Barks Spur	58331	Colgate	58046	Fordville	58231
Barlow	58421	Columbia Mall (Part of		Forest River (Cass County)	58102
Barney	58008	Grand Forks)	58201	Forest River (Walsh County)	58233
Bartlett	58344	Columbus	58727	Forest River Colony	58231
Barton	58315	Concrete	58220	Forman	58032
Bathgate	58216	Conway	58233	Fort Berthold Indian	
Battleground Addition	58701	Cooperstown	58425	Reservation	58763
Battleview	58773	Corinth	58830	Fort Buford	58853
Bayshore	58072	Coteau	58721	Fort Clark	58530
Beach	58621	Coulee	58746	Fort Ransom	58033
Belcourt	58316	Country Acres	58047	Fort Rice	58537
Belden	58784	Country-Side Addition	58201	Fort Totten	58335
Belfield	58622	Courtenay	58426	Fortuna	58844
Benedict	58716	Crary	58327	Fortuna Air Force Station,	
Bentley	58562	Crested Butte Addition	58501	780th Radar Squadron	59275
Berea	58072	Crete	58040	Fort Yates	58538
Bergen	58792	Crosby	58730	Four Bears Village	58763
Berlin	58415	Crystal	58222	Four K's Estates	58501
Berthold	58718	Crystal Springs	58427	Foxholm	58738
Berwick	58788	Cuba	58072	Fox Island	58504
Beulah	58523	Cummings	58223	Fradet	58047
Big Bend	58531	Dahlen	58224	Frazier (Part of Wimbledon)	58492
Binford	58416	Dakota Boys Ranch	58701	Fredonia	58440
Bisbee	58317	Dakota Square (Part of		Fried	58401
Bismarck	58501-07	Minot)	58701	Frison	58301
For specific Bismarck Zip Codes		Davenport	58021	Frontier	58104
call (701) 221-6517, or your local		Dawson	58428	Fryburg	58622
postmaster.		Dazey	58429	Fullerton	58441
Blabon	58046	Decker	58601	Gackle	58442
Blacktail Lake	58801	Deering	58731	Galchutt	58075
Blaisdell	58718	De Lamere	58060	Galesburg	58035
Blanchard	58009	Denbigh	58788	Gardar	58227
Bluffview Estates	58504	Denhoff	58430	Gardena	58739
Bonetraill	58801	Des Lacs	58733	Gardner	58036
Bordulac	58421	Devils Lake	58301	Garrison	58540
Bottineau	58318	Devils Lake Sioux Indian		Garske	58382
Bowbells	58721	Reservation	58335	Gascoyne	58653
Bowdon	58418	Dickey	58431	Geneseo	58053
Bowesmont	58225	Dickinson	58601*	Gilby	58235
Bowman	58623		58602†	Gladstone	58630
Braddock	58524	Dodge	58625	Glasser	58504
Brampton	58017	Donnybrook	58734	Glasston	58236
Brantford	58356	Douglas	58735	Glenburn	58740
Breen's Addition	58501	Doyon	58328	Glenfield	58443
Breien	58570	Drake	58736	Glen Ullin	58631
Brekke Addition	58701	Drayton	58225	Glenwood Estates	58501
Bremen	58319	Dresden	58249	Glover	58474
Brentwood Estates	58501	Driscoll	58532	Golden Valley	58541
Briardale	58504	Dunn Center	58626	Goldfines Shopping Center	
Briarwood	58104	Dunning	58760	(Part of Grand Forks)	58201
Bridgeview Addition	58701	Dunseith	58329	Golva	58632
Brinsmade	58320	Durbin	58059	Goodrich	58444
Brocket	58321	Dwight	58075	Gorham	58627
Brookfield Estates	58501	Eagle Bend Estates	58301	Grace City	58445
Brooks Addition	58701	Eastdale	58601	Grafton	58237
Brooktree Park	58042	East Dunseith	58329	Grandberg	58102
Buchanan	58420	East Fairview	59221		

	ZIP
Grand Forks	58201-08
For specific Grand Forks Zip	
Codes call (701) 775-5329, or	
your local postmaster.	
Grand Forks AFB (census	
designated place)	58205
Grand Forks Air Force Base	58201
Grandin	58038
Grand Prairie Estates	58501
Grand Rapids	58458
Grandview	58801
Grano	58750
Granville	58741
Grassy Butte	58634
Great Bend	58039
Green Acres Estates	58501
Greene	58787
Greenvale	58601
Grenora	58845
Guelph	58474
Guthrie	58736
Gwinner	58040
Hague	58542
Halliday	58636
Hallson	58220
Hamar	58380
Hamberg	58337
Hamilton	58238
Hamlet	58795
Hampden	58338
Hankinson	58041
Hanks	58856
Hanks Corner	58220
Hannaford	58448
Hannah	58239
Hannover	58563
Hansboro	58339
Happy Valley	58701
Harlow	58346
Hartland	58725
Harvey	58341
Harwood	58042
Hastings	58049
Hatton	58240
Havana	58043
Havelock	58647
Hay Creek	58501
Hay Creek Pines	58501
Haynes	58639
Hazelton	58544
Hazen	58545
Heaton	58450
Hebron	58638
Heil	58533
Heimdal	58342
Hensel	58241
Hensler	58530
Heritage Hills Estates	58102
Hesper	58348
Hettinger	58639
Hickson	58047
Hi-Land Heights	58801
Hillcrest Acres	58501
Hillsboro	58045
Holiday Colony	58701
Holmes	58275
Home on the Range for	
Boys	58654
Honeyford	58235
Hoople	58243
Hope	58046
Horace	58047
Horseshoe Bend	58102
Huff	58537
Hull	58542
Hunter	58048
Hurdsfield	58451
Hutterite Colony	58458
Imperial Manor	58701
Imperial Valley	58504
Inkster	58244
Jamestown	58401*
	58402†
Jessie	58452
Jewett Landing	58072
Jiran	58504
Johnsons Corner	58847
Johnstown	58235
Joliette	58271
Juanita	58443
Jud	58454
Judson	58563
Karlsruhe	58744
Kathryn	58049
Keene	58847
Kelso	58045
Kelvin	58329
Kempton	58267
Kenaston	58746
Kenmare	58746
Kensal	58455
Kief	58747

	ZIP
Killdeer	58640
Kindred	58051
Kings Court	58701
Kintyre	58549
Kirkwood Plaza (Part of	
Bismarck)	58504
Kloten	58254
KMK Estates	58501
Knox	58343
Kongsberg	58792
Kralicek	58601
Kramer	58748
Kubishta	58601
Kulm	58456
Lake Jessie	58801
Lake Metigoshe	58318
Lake Park	58801
Lake Side Estate	58401
Lake Tschida	58533
Lake Williams	58478
Lakewood Park	58301
Lakota	58344
Lamoine Addition	58201
Lamoure	58458
Landa	58783
Langdon	58249
Lankin	58250
Lansford	58750
Larimore	58251
Lark	58535
Larson	58727
Lawton	58345
Leal	58479
Leeds	58346
Lefor	58641
Lehigh	58601
Lehr	58460
Leisure World Estates	58504
Leith	58551
Leonard	58052
Leroy	58282
Lewis and Clark Estates	58504
Leyden	58282
Lidgerwood	58053
Lignite	58752
Lincoln	58501
Lincoln Valley	58430
Linka Addition	58701
Linton	58552
Lisbon	58054
Litchville	58461
Little Ponderosa	58701
Logan	58701
Loma	58311
Lone Tree	58718
Loraine	58761
Lostwood	58784
Lucca	58027
Ludden	58474
Lunds Valley	58784
Luverne	58056
Lynchburg	58059
McCanna	58251
Mcclusky	58463
Mcgregor	58755
Mchenry	58464
Mckenzie	58553
McLeod	58057
McVille	58254
Maddock	58348
Maida	58255
Makoti	58756
Mandan	58554
Mandaree	58757
Manfred	58465
Manitou	58776
Manning	58642
Mantador	58058
Manvel	58256
Mapes	58344
Mapleton	58059
Marion	58466
Marmarth	58643
Marshall	58644
Martin	58758
Mary College	58501
Max	58759
Maxbass	58760
Mayville	58257
Maza	58324
Meadowbrook	58701
Meadow View (Part of	
Bismarck)	58504
Medina	58467
Medora	58645
Mee's Country Home	
Estates	58558
Mekinock	58258
Melville	58421
Menoken	58558
Mercer	58559
Merricourt	58433

	ZIP
Michigan	58259
Millarton	58472
Mills	58504
Milnor	58060
Milton	58260
Minnewaukan	58351
Minot	58701*
	58702†
Minot AFB (census	
designated place)	58704-05
For specific Minot AFB Zip Codes	
call (701) 852-3296, or your local	
postmaster.	
Minot Air Force Base	58704-05
For specific Minot Air Force Base	
Zip Codes call (701) 852-3296, or	
your local postmaster.	
Minot Air Force Station,	
786th Radar Squadron	58759
Minto	58261
Mirror Lake	58639
Missouri River Estates	58504
Moffit	58560
Mohall	58761
Monango	58471
Montpelier	58472
Mooreton	58061
Mott	58646
Mountain	58262
Mount Carmel	58249
Mouse River Park	58787
Mr. B's	58501
Munich	58352
Mylo	58353
Nanson	58366
Napoleon	58561
Nash	58237
Neche	58265
Nekoma	58355
Newburg	58762
New England	58647
New Hradec	58601
New Leipzig	58562
New Rockford	58356
New Salem	58563
New Town	58763
Niagara	58266
Niobe	58746
Nome	58062
Noonan	58765
Norma	58746
North Dakota Penitentiary	58501
North Dakota State	
University (Part of Fargo)	58105
North Forty Estates	58501
Northgate	58737
North Grand Forks	58203
North Lemmon	57638
North River	58102
North Star Acres	58501
North Valley City	58072
Northwood (Cass County)	58102
Northwood (Grand Forks	
County)	58267
Northwood Estates	58501
Nortonville	58454
Norwich	58768
Oakes	58474
Oak Ridge	58270
Oakwood	58237
Oberon	58357
Olga	58249
Omemee	58384
Oriska	58063
Orr	58244
Orrin	58359
Osnabrock	58269
Overly	58360
Oxbow	58047
Page	58064
Palermo	58769
Palm Beach	58601
Park Manor (Part of Grand	
Forks)	58201
Park River	58270
Parshall	58770
Patterson Lake	58601
Pekin	58361
Pembina	58271
Penn	58362
Perth	58363
Petersburg	58272
Pettibone	58475
Pheasant Lake	58436
Picardville	58463
Pick City	58545
Pillsbury	58065
Pingree	58476
Plsek	58273
Pitcher Park	58301
Plaza	58771
Pleasant Lake	58368

* Area Zip Code   † Post Office Boxes

	ZIP		ZIP		ZIP
Ponderosa Riverside Village	58501	Sherwood	58782	Turtle Mountain Indian	
Porcupine	58568	Sheyenne	58374	Reservation	58316
Portal	58772	Sheyenne Valley Addition	58072	Tuttle	58488
Portland	58274	Shields	58569	Twin Butte	58504
Powell	58201	Shryock	58801	Twin Buttes	58636
Powers Lake	58773	Sibley	58429	Underwood	58576
Prairie Rose	58104	Sibley Island Estates	58504	Union	58279
Prairie View Acres	58501	Silva	58368	University of North Dakota	
Price	58530	Simcoe	58741	(Part of Grand Forks)	58202
Prosper	58042	Sims	58520	Upham	58789
Raleigh	58564	Sioux Village	58538	Urbana	58481
Raub	58779	Sisseton Indian Reservation	57262	Valley City	58072
Raulston	58801	Skyline Estates	58501	Velva	58790
Rawson	58831	Sleepy Hollow	58047	Venturia	58489
Ray	58849	Solen	58570	Verona	58490
Raymond Lee	58801	Sorenson Addition	58701	Veseleyville	58237
Red Willow Lake	58416	Souris	58783	Vista South	58504
Reeder	58649	Southam	58327	Vohs Dapplegrey	58801
Regan	58477	South Forks Plaza (Part of		Voltaire	58792
Regent	58650	Grand Forks)	58201	Voss	58261
Reile's Acres	58102	South Heart	58655	Wabek	58771
Reynolds	58275	Southview	58801	Wahpeton	58074†
Rhame	58651	Southview Estates	58601		58075*
Richards West (Part of		Spiritwood	58481	Walcott	58077
Grand Forks)	58201	Spiritwood Lake	58401	Wales	58281
Richardton	58652	Spring Brook	58843	Walhalla	58282
Ridgeview Acres	58504	Standing Rock Indian		Walum	58448
Rio Vista Heights	58801	Reservation	58538	Warren	58021
River Bend	58047	Stanley	58784	Warsaw	58261
Riverdale	58565	Stanton	58571	Warwick	58381
Riverside (Part of West		Starkweather	58377	Washburn	58577
Fargo)	58078	State Hospital (Part of		Watford City	58854
River View Acres	58504	Jamestown)	58401	Webster	58382
Robinson	58478	Steele	58482	Welle	58501
Rocklake	58365	Sterling	58572	Wellsburg	58341
Rogers	58479	Stirum	58069	West Acres Estates	58801
Rolette	58366	Strasburg	58573	Westbrook	58047
Rolla	58367	Straubville	58017	West Fargo	58078
Rolling Meadows	58501	Streeter	58483	Westfield	58542
Rosegien	58775	Stromquist (Part of Devils		West Heart Estates	58504
Roshau	58601	Lake)	58301	Westhope	58793
Ross	58776	Strong	58301	West Industrial Park	58601
Roth	58783	Sunnyside Addition	58102	West Jamestown	58401
Round Hill Estates	58102	Sunny Slope	58701	West Oakwood	58237
Rugby	58368	Surrey	58785	West Town	58401
Ruso	58778	Sutton	58484	Westwood on the River	58501
Russell	58762	Swansonville	58504	Wheatland	58079
Ruthville	58701	Sykeston	58486	Wheelock	58849
Rutland	58067	Taft	58045	White Earth	58794
Ryder	58779	Tagus	58718	White Shield	58540
Sabot's First	58501	Talbotts	58701	Whitman	58259
St. Anthony	58566	Tappen	58487	Wild Rice	58047
St. Benedict	58047	Tatley Meadows	58504	Wildrose	58795
St. Gertrude	58564	Taylor	58656	Williston	58801*
St. John	58369	Temvik	58552		58802†
St. Michael	58370	Thompson	58278	Williston Park	58801
St. Thomas	58276	Thorne	58366	Willow City	58384
Sanborn	58480	Tilden	58351	Wilton	58579
San Haven	58329	Timber Lake Place	58504	Wimbledon	58492
Sanish	58763	Tioga	58852	Windsor	58424
Sarles	58372	TJ Ranch Estates	58501	Wing	58494
Sawdwood	58270	Tokio	58379	Wishek	58495
Sawyer	58781	Tolley	58787	Wolford	58385
Scenic East	58801	Tolna	58380	Wolseth	58740
Schefield	58647	Tower City	58071	Woodland	58051
Scranton	58653	Town and Country	58801	Woods	58052
Secluded Acres	58504	Town and Country Estates	58504	Woodworth	58496
Selfridge	58568	Town And Country		Wutzke	58501
Selz	58373	Shopping Center (Part of		Wyndmere	58081
Sentinel Butte	58654	Minot)	58701	York	58386
Shamrock Acres	58501	Towner	58788	Ypsilanti	58497
Sharon	58277	Trenton	58853	Zahl	58856
Sheldon	58068	Trestle Valley	58701	Zap	58580
Shell Valley	58316	Trotters	58657	Zeeland	58581
Shepard	58425	Turtle Lake	58575		

	ZIP
A (Postal Station) (Franklin County)	43201
A (Postal Station) (Lucas County)	43605
Abanaka	45874
Abbottsville	45304
Aberdeen	45101
Academia	43050
Acme	44281
Ada	45810
Adams (Champaign County) (Township)	43070
Adams (Clinton County) (Township)	45177
Adams (Coshocton County) (Township)	43832
Adams (Darke County) (Township)	45308
Adams (Defiance County) (Township)	43512
Adams (Guernsey County) (Township)	43725
Adams (Monroe County) (Township)	43914
Adams (Muskingum County) (Township)	43821
Adams (Seneca County) (Township)	44867
Adams (Washington County) (Township)	45744
Adams Mills	43821
Adamsville (Gallia County)	45614
Adamsville (Muskingum County)	43802
Adario	44837
Addison	45631
Addison (Township)	45631
Addyston	45001
Adelphi	43101
Adena	43901
Adrian	44801
Africa	43021
Afton	45103
Aid	45645
Aid (Township)	45645
Ainger	43543
Air Mail Facility (Part of Dayton)	45490
Air Material Command	45433
Airport (Cuyahoga County)	44181
Airport (Franklin County)	43219
Airway	45431
	45437
For specific Airway Zip Codes call (513) 227-1100, or your local postmaster.	
Akron	44301-72
For specific Akron Zip Codes call (216) 379-0600, or your local postmaster.	
Albany	45710
Al Bar Meadows (Part of The Village of Indian Hill)	45243
Albion	44287
Alcony	45373
Alexander (Township)	45701
Alexanders (Part of Independence)	44131
Alexandersville (Part of West Carrollton)	45449
Alexandria	43001
Alexis Place (Part of Toledo)	43612
Alfred	45723
Alger	45812
Alikanna	43952
Alledonia	43902
Allen (Darke County) (Township)	45362
Allen (Hancock County) (Township)	45889
Allen (Ottawa County) (Township)	43412
Allen (Union County) (Township)	43070
Allen Center	43040
Allensburg	45133
Allensville	45651
Allentown (Allen County)	45807
Allentown (Scioto County)	45694
Alliance	44601
Alma	45690
Alpha	45301
Alpine Village (Part of Valley Hi)	43360
Alta	44903
Altamont Hills	43938
Altamont Park (Part of Mingo Junction)	43938
Alton	43119
Alvada	44802
Alvordton	43501

	ZIP
Amanda (Allen County) (Township)	45807
Amanda (Fairfield County) (Township)	43102
Amanda (Fairfield County)	43102
Amanda (Hancock County) (Township)	45867
Amberley	45213
Amberly	43227
Amboy (Ashtabula County)	44030
Amboy (Fulton County) (Township)	43540
Amelia	45102
American (Township)	45807
Ames (Township)	45711
Amesville	45711
Amherst	44001
Amherst (Township)	44001
Amity (Hamilton County)	45236
Amity (Knox County)	43050
Amity (Madison County)	43064
Amity (Montgomery County)	45309
Amlin	43002
Amlin Heights	45385
Amsden	44803
Amsterdam (Jefferson County)	43903
Amsterdam (Licking County)	43076
Anderson (Hamilton County) (Township)	45230
Anderson (Hamilton County)	45255
Anderson (Ross County)	45601
Anderson Ferry (Part of Cincinnati)	45238
Andersonville	45601
Andis	45645
Andover	44003
Andover (Township)	44003
Angle	45631
Ankenytown	45344
Anlo	45344
Anna	45302
Annapolis	43910
Ansonia	45303
Antioch	43793
Antiquity	45771
Antrim (Guernsey County)	43773
Antrim (Wyandot County) (Township)	43323
Antwerp	45813
Apple Creek	44606
Apple Grove	45771
Appleton	43031
Aquilla	44024
Arabia	45659
Arcadia	44804
Arcanum	45304
Archbold	43502
Archer (Township)	43986
Archers Fork	45767
Arion	45652
Arkoe	45661
Arlington (Hancock County)	45814
Arlington (Montgomery County)	45309
Arlington Heights	45215
Armstrongs Mills	43933
Arnheim	45121
Arnold (Miami County)	45383
Arnold (Union County)	43064
Arrow Head (Part of Xenia)	45385
Artanna	43022
Arthur	43512
Ashland	44805
Ashley	43003
Ashley Corner	45694
Ash Ridge	45121
Ashtabula	44004
Ashtabula (Township)	44004
Ashville	43103
Assumption	43558
Athalia	45669
Athens (Athens County)	45701
Athens (Athens County) (Township)	45701
Athens (Harrison County) (Township)	43981
Atlanta	43145
Atlas	43713
Attica	44807
Attica Junction	44807
Atwater	44201
Atwater (Township)	44201
Atwater Center	44201
Auburn (Butler County)	45013
Auburn (Crawford County) (Township)	44887
Auburn (Geauga County) (Township)	44255
Auburn (Tuscarawas County) (Township)	44681

	ZIP
Auburn Center (Crawford County)	44875
Auburn Center (Geauga County)	44022
Auburn Corners	44021
Augersburg	44266
Auglaize (Allen County) (Township)	45850
Auglaize (Paulding County) (Township)	43512
Augusta	44607
Augusta (Township)	44607
Ault	43947
Aultman	44630
Aurelius (Township)	45746
Aurora	44202
Aurora East	44240
Aurora Meadows	44202
Ausdale Ave. (Part of Mansfield)	44906
Austin	45628
Austinburg	44010
Austinburg (Township)	44010
Austintown (Township)	44515
Austintown	44512
Austintown Plaza	44515
Austin Village (Part of Warren)	44481
Autumn Acres	45239
Ava	43711
Avalon (Butler County)	45042
Avalon (Perry County)	43107
Avalon Heights (Part of Lebanon)	45036
Avon	44011
Avondale (Belmont County)	43947
Avondale (Hamilton County)	45229
Avondale (Licking County)	43076
Avondale (Logan County)	43331
Avondale (Montgomery County)	45404
Avondale (Muskingum County)	43777
Avondale (Stark County)	44708
Avon Lake	44012
Avon Park (Part of Girard)	44420
Axtel	44089
Ayersville	43512
B (Part of Cleveland)	44103
Bachman	45309
Badgertown	43719
Bailey Lakes	44805
Baileys Mills	43713
Bainbridge	44023
Bainbridge (Township)	44023
Bainbridge	45612
Bainbridge Center	44022
Bairdstown	45872
Bakersville	43803
Ballville	43420
Ballville (Township)	43420
Baltic	43804
Baltimore	43105
Bangs	43050
Bannock	43972
Bantam	45103
Barberton	44203
Bardwell	45154
Barlow	45712
Barlow (Township)	45712
Barnesburg	45239
Barnesville	43713
Barnhill	44663
Barretts Mills	45612
Barrs Mills	44681
Bartles	45659
Bartlett	45713
Bartley Estates	45414
Bartlow (Township)	43516
Barton	43905
Bartramville	45669
Bascom	44809
Bashan	45743
Bass Lake	44024
Batavia (Township)	45103
Batavia	45103
Batemantown	43019
Batesville	43773
Bath (Allen County) (Township)	45801
Bath (Greene County) (Township)	45324
Bath (Summit County)	44210
Bath (Summit County) (Township)	44210
Battlesburg	44626
Baughman (Township)	44667
Bay (Township)	43452
Bayard	44657
Bay Bridge	44870
Bays	43462
Bay View	44870

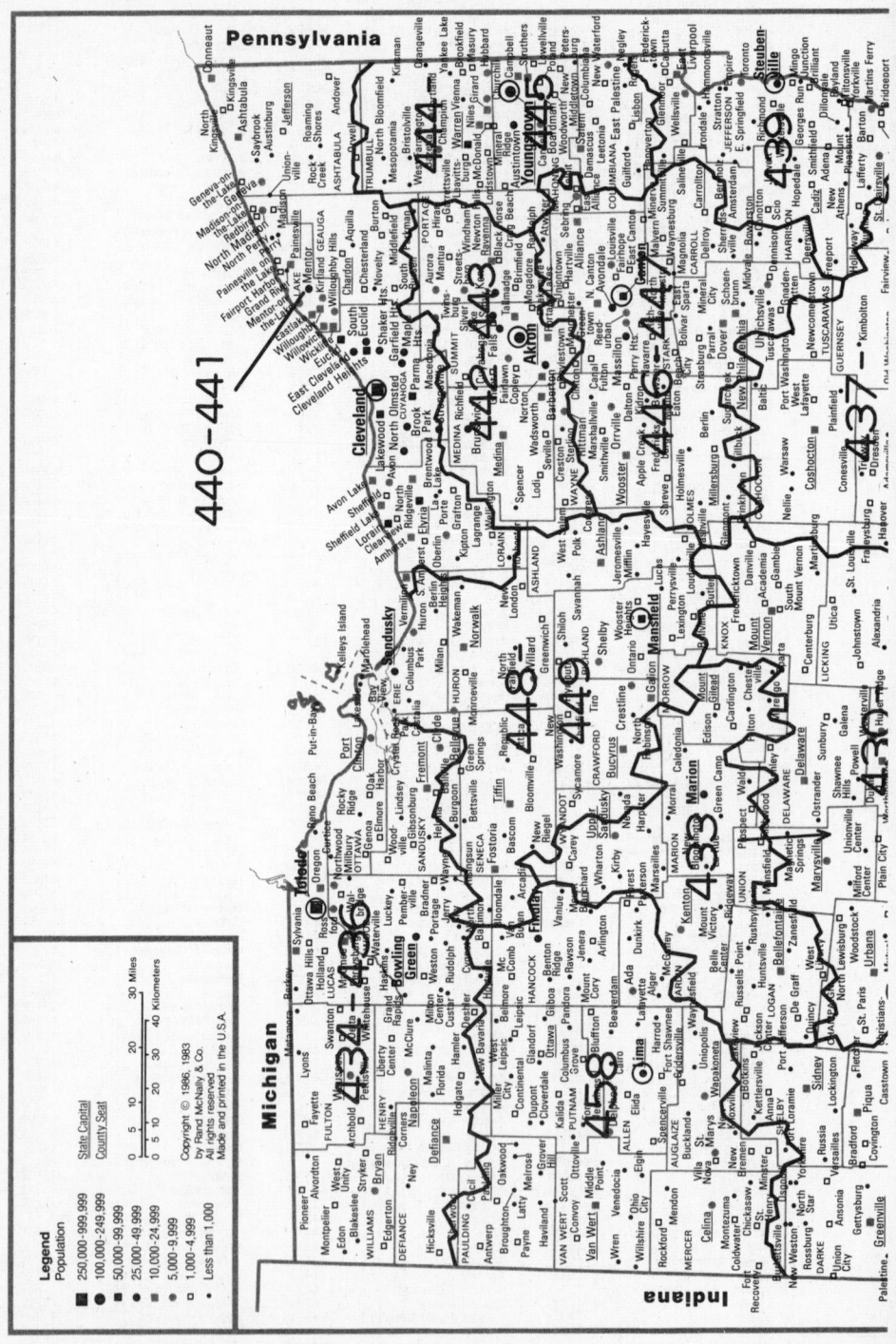

Legend
Population
■ 250,000-999,999
■ 100,000-249,999
■ 50,000-99,999
● 25,000-49,999
● 10,500-24,999
• 5,000-9,999
• 1,000-4,999
· Less than 1,000

State Capital
County Seat

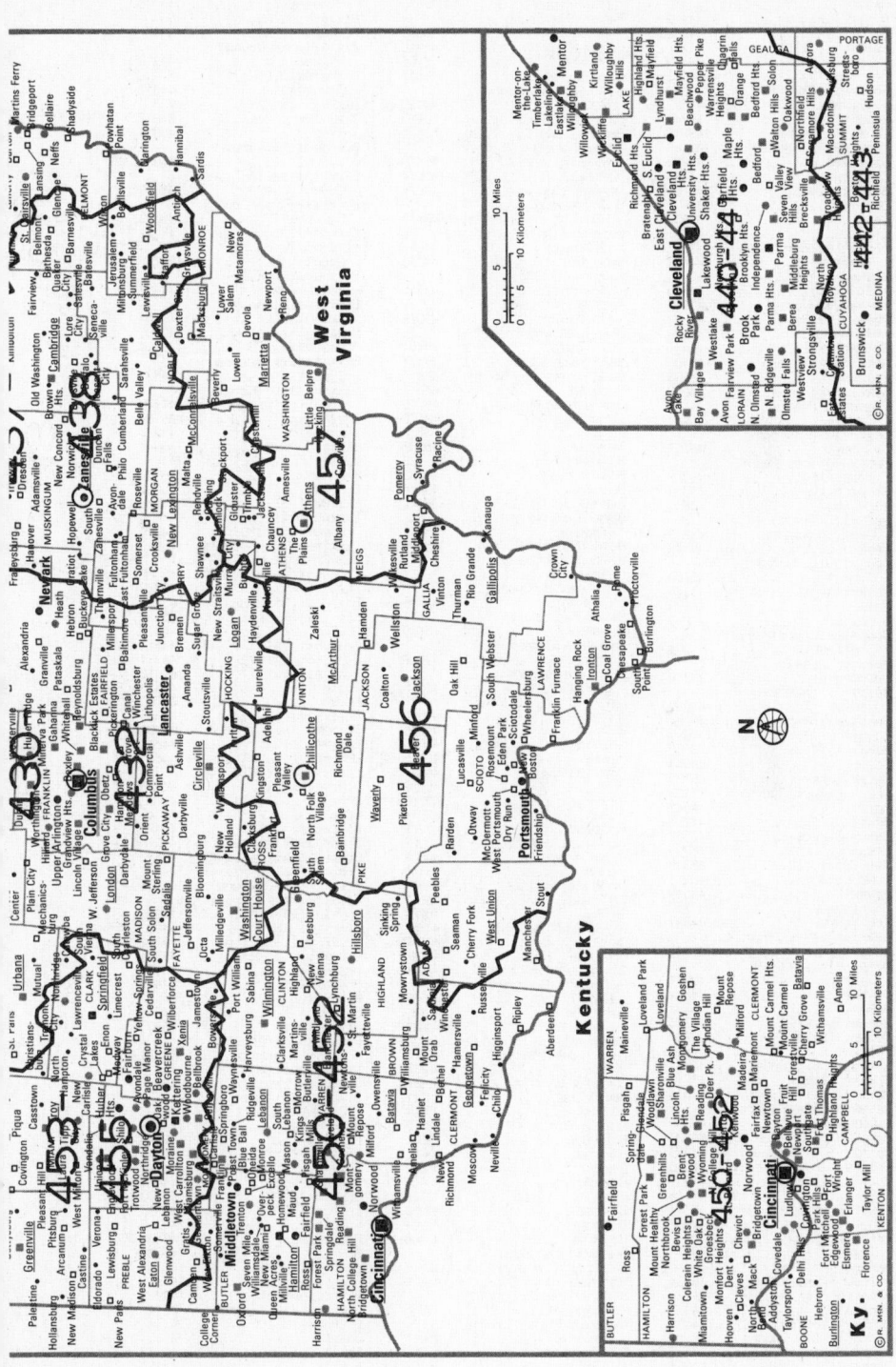

Place	ZIP	Place	ZIP	Place	ZIP
Bay Village	44140	Benton (Paulding County)		Bloom (Morgan County)	
Bazetta	44410	(Township)	45880	(Township)	43756
Bazetta (Township)	44410	Benton (Pike County)		Bloom (Scioto County)	
Beach City	44608	(Township)	45690	(Township)	45682
Beachland (Part of		Benton Ridge	45816	Bloom (Seneca County)	
Cleveland)	44119	Bentonville	45105	(Township)	44818
Beachwood	44122	Berea	44017	Bloom (Wood County)	
Beachwood Place (Part of		Berea (Part of Middlebury		(Township)	44817
Beachwood)	44122	Heights)	44130	Bloom Center	43318
Beacon Hill	45241	Bergholz	43908	Bloomdale	44817
Beallsville	43716	Berkey	43504	Bloomer	45318
Beals (Part of Pickerington)	43147	Berkley Heights (Part of		Bloomfield (Columbiana	
Beamsville	45303	Kettering)	45429	County)	43920
Bear Creek	45657	Berkshire	43074	Bloomfield (Jackson	
Bearfield (Township)	43730	Berkshire (Township)	43074	County) (Township)	45640
Beartown	44622	Berlin (Delaware County)		Bloomfield (Logan County)	
Beatty	45506	(Township)	43015	(Township)	43333
Beaumont	45701	Berlin (Erie County)		Bloomfield (Morrow County)	43011
Beaver (Mahoning County)		(Township)	44814	Bloomfield (Muskingum	
(Township)	44408	Berlin (Holmes County)	44610	County)	43762
Beaver (Noble County)		Berlin (Holmes County)		Bloomfield (Trumbull	
(Township)	43773	(Township)	44610	County) (Township)	44450
Beaver (Pike County)	45613	Berlin (Knox County)		Bloomfield (Washington	
Beaver (Pike County)		(Township)	43019	County)	45734
(Township)	45690	Berlin (Mahoning County)		Bloomingburg	43106
Beavercreek	45431	(Township)	44401	Bloomingdale	43910
Beavercreek (Township)	45401	Berlin Center	44401	Blooming Grove (Morrow	
Beaverdam	45808	Berlin Heights (Erie County)	44814	County)	44833
Beaver Park (Part of Lorain)	44053	Berlinville	44814	Blooming Grove (Richland	
Beavertown (Montgomery		Bern (Township)	45770	County) (Township)	44878
County)	45429	Berne (Township)	43155	Bloomington	45169
Beavertown (Washington		Bernice	43832	Bloomingville	44870
County)	45767	Berryman	45805	Bloom Junction	45682
Becker Highlands (Part of		Berrysville	45133	Bloomville	44818
Steubenville)	43952	Berwick	44853	Blue Ash	45242
Beckett Ridge	45069	Bessemer	45764	Blue Ball	45005
Becks Mills	44654	Bethany	45042	Blue Bell	43772
Bedford (Coshocton		Bethel (Clark County)		Bluebird Beach (Part of	
County) (Township)	43812	(Township)	45344	Vermilion)	44089
Bedford (Cuyahoga County)	44146	Bethel (Clermont County)	45106	Blue Creek (Adams County)	45616
Bedford (Meigs County)		Bethel (Miami County)		Blue Creek (Paulding	
(Township)	45769	(Township)	45371	County) (Township)	45886
Bedford Heights	44146	Bethel (Monroe County)		Blue Rock	43720
Beebe	45778	(Township)	45745	Blue Rock (Township)	43720
Beechcrest	44240	Bethel (Pike County)	45661	Blue Valley Acres	43130
Beechview Estates (Part of		Bethesda	43719	Bluffton	45817
Cincinnati)	45201	Bethlehem (Coshocton		Boardman	44512
Beechwold (Part of		County) (Township)	43812	Boardman (Township)	44512
Columbus)	43214	Bethlehem (Richland		Boardman Plaza	44512
Beechwood (Jefferson		County)	44875	Bobo	45613
County)	43952	Bethlehem (Stark County)		Boden	43762
Beechwood (Preble County)	45064	(Township)	44662	Bokes Creek (Township)	43358
Beechwood (Stark County)	44601	Bettsville	44815	Bolindale	44484
Beechwood Trails	43062	Beulah Beach	44089	Bolivar	44612
Belden	44044	Beverly	45715	Bolton	44601
Belfast (Clermont County)	45122	Beverly Gardens	45431	Bond Hill (Part of Cincinnati)	45237
Belfast (Highland County)	45133	Bevis	45239	Boneta	44256
Belfort	44641	Bexley	43209	Bonn	45788
Bellaire	43906	Bidwell	45614	Bono	43445
Bellaire Gardens	43302	Big Island	43302	Bookwalter	43128
Bellbrook	45305	Big Island (Township)	43302	Booth (Lucas County)	43618
Belle Center	43310	Biglick (Township)	44802	Booth (Tuscarawas County)	43832
Bellefontaine	43311	Big Plain	43140	Borromeo College of Ohio	44092
Bellepoint	43015	Big Prairie	44611	Boston (Highland County)	45133
Belle Valley	43717	Big Rock	45613	Boston (Summit County)	
Belle Vernon	44882	Big Run	45724	(Township)	44264
Belleview Heights (Preble		Big Spring (Township)	44853	Boston Heights	44236
County)	45347	Big Springs	43347	Boston Mill	44264
Belleview Heights (Ross		Birds Run	43749	Botkins	45306
County)	45601	Birmingham (Erie County)	44816	Boudes Ferry	45121
Bellevue	44811	Birmingham (Guernsey		Boughtonville	44890
Bellview	45305	County)	43749	Bourneville	45617
Bellview Estates	45305	Bishopville	45732	Bowerston	44695
Bellview Heights	43906	Bismarck	44811	Bowersville	45307
Bellville	44813	Blachleyville	44691	Bowling Green (Licking	
Belmont (Allen County)	45801	Black Creek (Township)	45882	County) (Township)	43076
Belmont (Belmont County)	43718	Blackfork	45656	Bowling Green (Marion	
Belmont (Butler County)	45015	Black Fork Junction	45656	County) (Township)	43332
Belmont Meadows (Part of		Black Horse	44266	Bowling Green (Wood	
Springfield)	45505	Blacklick	43004	County)	43402
Belmont Park	44420	Blacklick Estates	43227	Bowlusville	43078
Belmont Ridge	43983	Black Run	43830	Boydsville	43912
Belmore	45815	Blacktop	43780	Braceville	44444
Beloit	44609	Bladen	45623	Braceville (Township)	44444
Belpre	45714	Bladensburg	43005	Braceville Ridge	44444
Belpre (Township)	45714	Blaine	43909	Bradbury	45760
Belvedere	43952	Blainesville	43950	Bradford	45308
Bennington (Licking County)		Blairmont	43901	Bradley	43917
(Township)	43011	Blakeslee	43505	Bradner	43406
Bennington (Morrow		Blanchard (Hancock		Bradrick	45619
County) (Township)	43334	County) (Township)	45816	Brady (Township)	43570
Bentley (Part of Lowellville)	44436	Blanchard (Hardin County)	45836	Brady Lake	44211
Bentleyville	44022	Blanchard (Hardin County)		Brady Lake Addition	44211
Benton (Crawford County)	44882	(Township)	45836	Bradyville	45144
Benton (Hocking County)		Blanchard (Putnam County)		Braffettsville	45347
(Township)	43152	(Township)	45875	Brailey	43558
Benton (Holmes County)	44654	Blanches Addition	43062	Branch Hill	45140
Benton (Monroe County)		Blanchester	45107	Brandon	43050
(Township)	45767	Blendon (Township)	43081	Brandt	45371
Benton (Ottawa County)		Blissfield	43805	Brandywine	44820
(Township)	43432	Bloom (Fairfield County)		Bratenahl	44108
		(Township)	43136	Bratton (Township)	45660

	ZIP
Cavallo	43843
Cavett	45891
Caywood	45750
Cecil	45821
Cedar Center Plaza (Part of University Heights)	44125
Cedarhill	43102
Cedar Mills	45616
Cedar Point (Part of Sandusky)	44870
Cedar Valley	44214
Cedarville	45314
Cedarville (Township)	45314
Cedron	45121
Celeryville	44890
Celina	45822
Centenary	45631
Center (Carroll County) (Township)	44615
Center (Columbiana County) (Township)	44432
Center (Guernsey County)	43725
Center (Guernsey County) (Township)	43725
Center (Mercer County) (Township)	45822
Center (Monroe County) (Township)	43793
Center (Morgan County) (Township)	45715
Center (Noble County) (Township)	43724
Center (Williams County) (Township)	43506
Center (Wood County) (Township)	43402
Centerburg	43011
Centerfield	45123
Centerpoint	45656
Center Station	45659
Centerton	44890
Center Village	43021
Centerville (Belmont County)	43718
Centerville (Brown County)	45154
Centerville (Marion County)	43342
Centerville (Montgomery County)	45459
	45441
For specific Centerville Zip Codes call (513) 433-1213, or your local postmaster.	
Centerville (Wayne County)	44676
Central (Part of Toledo)	43604
Central College (Part of Westerville)	43081
Cessna (Township)	43326
Ceylon	44839
Chagrin Falls	44022-23
For specific Chagrin Falls Zip Codes call (216) 247-6452, or your local postmaster.	
Chagrin Falls Annex	44023
Chagrin Falls Park	44022
Chagrin Harbor (Part of Eastlake)	44094
Chalfants	43739
Chambersburg (Columbiana County)	44657
Chambersburg (Gallia County)	45631
Champion (Township)	44481
Champion Heights	44481
Chandler	43910
Chandlersville	43727
Chapel Hill Shopping Center (Part of Akron)	44310
Chapmans	45692
Chardon	44024
Chardon (Township)	44024
Charity Rotch (Part of Massillon)	44646
Charlestown	44266
Charlestown (Township)	44266
Charloe	45873
Charm	44617
Chase	45710
Chasetown	45118
Chaseville	43772
Chaska Beach (Part of Huron)	44839
Chateau Estates	45502
Chateau Ridge (Part of Marion)	43302
Chatfield	44825
Chatfield (Township)	44825
Chatham (Licking County)	43055
Chatham (Medina County)	44256
Chatham (Medina County) (Township)	44275
Chattanooga	45882
Chauncey	45719

	ZIP
Chautauqua	45342
Cherokee	43324
Cherry Fork	45618
Cherry Grove (Clermont County)	45230
Cherry Grove (Hamilton County)	45230
Cherry Grove Plaza	45230
Cherry Valley	44003
Cherry Valley (Township)	44003
Chesapeake	45619
Cheshire (Delaware County)	43021
Cheshire (Gallia County)	45620
Cheshire (Gallia County) (Township)	45620
Chesswood Acres	45239
Chester (Clinton County) (Township)	45177
Chester (Geauga County) (Township)	44026
Chester (Meigs County)	45720
Chester (Meigs County) (Township)	45720
Chester (Morrow County) (Township)	43338
Chester (Wayne County) (Township)	44691
Chester Center	44026
Chesterfield (Township)	43567
Chesterhill	43728
Chesterland	44026
Chesterville	43317
Cheviot	45211
Cheviot Hills	45502
Chevy Chase	44833
Chickasaw	45826
Chickwan	43901
Chili	43824
Chillicothe	45601
Chillicothe Correctional Institute	45601
Chillicothe Manor	45601
Chilo	45112
Chipman	45805
Chippewa (Township)	44230
Chippewa Lake	44215
Chippewa Lake Park	44215
Chocktou Lake	43140
Christiansburg	45389
Chuckery	43029
Churchill (Trumbull County)	44505
Churchills (Part of Sylvania)	43560
Churchtown	45750
Cincinnati	45201-75
For specific Cincinnati Zip Codes call (513) 684-5571, or your local postmaster.	

	ZIP
Circle Green	43908
Circle Hill (Athens County)	45764
Circle Hill (Miami County)	45308
Circleville	43113
Circleville (Township)	43113
Circleville Bible College	43113
City View Heights	45013
Claiborne	43344
Claibourne (Township)	43344
Claridon (Geauga County)	44024
Claridon (Geauga County) (Township)	44024
Claridon (Marion County)	43314
Claridon (Marion County) (Township)	43314
Clarington	43915
Clark (Brown County) (Township)	45130
Clark (Clinton County) (Township)	45146
Clark (Coshocton County)	43812
Clark (Coshocton County) (Township)	43844
Clark (Holmes County) (Township)	43804
Clark Corners (Ashtabula County)	44030
Clark Corners (Medina County)	44281
Clarksburg (Belmont County)	43960
Clarksburg (Ross County)	43115
Clarksfield	44889
Clarksfield (Township)	44889
Clarks Lake	43143
Clarkson	44455
Clarkstown	45648
Clarksville (Clinton County)	45113
Clarksville (Perry County)	43748
Clay (Auglaize County) (Township)	45895
Clay (Gallia County) (Township)	45631
Clay (Highland County) (Township)	45171
Clay (Jackson County)	45656
Clay (Knox County) (Township)	43080
Clay (Montgomery County) (Township)	45354
Clay (Muskingum County) (Township)	43777
Clay (Ottawa County) (Township)	43430
Clay (Scioto County) (Township)	45662
Clay (Tuscarawas County) (Township)	44629
Clay Center	43408
Clay Lick	43055
Claysville	43725
Clayton (Adams County)	45144
Clayton (Miami County)	45318
Clayton (Montgomery County)	45315
Clayton (Perry County) (Township)	43764
Clear Creek (Ashland County) (Township)	44874
Clearcreek (Fairfield County) (Township)	43102
Clear Creek (Warren County) (Township)	45066

	ZIP
Cranwood (Part of Cleveland)	44128
Crawford (Coshocton County) (Township)	43804
Crawford (Wyandot County)	43316
Crawford (Wyandot County) (Township)	43316
Crawford Corners	44254
Cream City (Part of Irondale)	43932
Creola	45622
Crescent	43950
Crescent Gardens	44646
Crescentville (Part of Sharonville)	45241
Crestline	44827
Creston	44217
Crestwood Hills (Part of Vandalia)	45377
Cridersville	45806
Crissey	43528
Cromers	44883
Crooked Tree	45727
Crooksville	43731
Crosby (Township)	45030
Cross Creek (Township)	43952
Crossenville	43107
Crosstown	45176
Crosswick	45068
Croton	43013
Crown City	45623
Crystal Lake	44003
Crystal Lakes	45341
Crystal Rock Park	44870
Crystal Springs	44614
Cuba	45114
Cumberland	43732
Cumminsville (Part of Cincinnati)	45223
Curtice	43412
Custar	43511
Cutler	45724
Cuyahoga Falls	44221-24
For specific Cuyahoga Falls Zip Codes call (216) 945-5807, or your local postmaster.	
Cuyahoga Heights	44125
Cygnet	43413
Cynthian (Township)	45845
Cynthiana	45624
Dabel (Part of Dayton)	45420
Dadsville	45381
Dailyville	45690
Dale	43787
Dallas (Township)	44849
Dallasburg	45140
Dalton	44618
Dalzell	45745
Daman Park	45044
Damascus (Henry County) (Township)	43534
Damascus (Mahoning County)	44619
Danbury (Township)	43452
Danville (Highland County)	45133
Danville (Knox County)	43014
Danville (Meigs County)	45741
Darby (Madison County) (Township)	43064
Darby (Pickaway County) (Township)	43146
Darby (Union County) (Township)	43064
Darbydale	43123
Darbyville	43136
Darlington (Muskingum County)	43701
Darlington (Richland County)	44813
Darrowville (Part of Stow)	44224
Darrtown	45056
Dart	45773
Darwin	45769
Davisville	45692
Dawn	45303
Dawson	45333
Day Heights	45150
Dayton	45401-90
For specific Dayton Zip Codes call (513) 227-1100, or your local postmaster.	
Dayton View (Part of Dayton)	45406
Dean Dale (Part of Mingo Junction)	43938
Deavertown	43731
Decatur (Brown County)	45115
Decatur (Lawrence County) (Township)	45659
Decatur (Washington County) (Township)	45742
Decaturville	45712

	ZIP
Decrow Corners	43031
Dee	44824
Deep Run	43935
Deer Creek (Madison County) (Township)	43140
Deer Creek (Pickaway County) (Township)	43164
Deerfield (Morgan County) (Township)	43758
Deerfield (Portage County)	44411
Deerfield (Portage County) (Township)	44411
Deerfield (Ross County) (Township)	43115
Deerfield (Warren County) (Township)	45040
Deering	45638
Deer Park	45236
Deersville	44693
Defiance	43512
Defiance (Township)	43512
Defiance Junction (Part of Defiance)	43512
DeForest	44484
De Graff	43318
Dekalb	44887
Delaware (Defiance County) (Township)	43556
Delaware (Delaware County)	43015
Delaware (Delaware County) (Township)	43015
Delaware (Hancock County) (Township)	45897
Delhi (Hamilton County) (Township)	45238
Delhi (Hamilton County)	45238
Delhi Hills	45238
Delightful	44470
Delisle	45304
Dellroy	44620
Delmont	43130
Delphi	44890
Delphos	45833
Delta	43515
Denmark (Ashtabula County) (Township)	44047
Denmark (Morrow County)	43320
Denmark Center	44047
Dennison	44621
Densons	43533
Dent (Hamilton County)	45211
Denver	45690
Derby	43117
Derwent	43733
Deshler	43516
Deunquat	44882
Devil Town	44691
Devola	45750
Deweyville	45858
Dexter	45741
Dexter City	45727
Deyarmonville	43917
Dialton	45502
Diamond	44412
Dicken	43138
Dilles Bottom	43947
Dillon Falls	43701
Dillonvale (Hamilton County)	45236
Dillonvale (Jefferson County)	43917
Dilworth	44417
Dinsmore (Township)	45306
Dixie	43782
Dixie Heights (Butler County)	45042
Dixie Heights (Montgomery County)	45414
Dixon (Preble County) (Township)	45320
Dixon (Van Wert County)	45832
Dixonville	43920
Doanville	45764
Dobbston	45678
Dodds	45036
Dodgeville	44085
Dodson (Highland County) (Township)	45142
Dodson (Montgomery County)	45309
Dodsonville	45142
Dola	45835
Dolly Varden	45368
Donald L Marrs (Part of Cincinnati)	45258
Doneys (Part of Whitehall)	43213
Donnelsville	45319
Donnersville	43950
Dorcas	45771
Dornbusch	45239
Dorset	44032
Dorset (Township)	44032

	ZIP
Dover (Athens County) (Township)	45761
Dover (Fulton County) (Township)	43567
Dover (Tuscarawas County)	44622
Dover (Tuscarawas County) (Township)	44622
Dover (Union County) (Township)	43040
Dowling	43551
Downtown (Part of Columbus)	43215
Downtown (Part of Akron)	44308
Doylestown	44230
Drakes	43730
Drakesburg	44288
Dresden	43821
Drexel	45427
Driftwood (Ashtabula County)	44041
Driftwood (Lake County)	44041
Drinkle	43102
Dry Run (Hamilton County)	45244
Dry Run (Scioto County)	45663
Dublin	43016-17
For specific Dublin Zip Codes call (614) 889-0763, or your local postmaster.	
Dublin (Township)	45882
Dublin Village Center (Part of Dublin)	43017
Duchouquet (Township)	45895
Dudley (Hardin County) (Township)	43326
Dudley (Noble County)	43724
Dueber (Part of Canton)	44706
Duffy	43946
Dull	45874
Dumontville	43130
Dunbridge	43414
Duncan Falls	43734
Dundas	45634
Dundee	44624
Dungannon (Columbiana County)	44423
Dungannon (Noble County)	45721
Dunglen	43917
Dunham (Township)	45784
Dunkinsville	45660
Dunkirk	45836
Dunlap	45239
Dupont	45837
Durbin (Clark County)	45502
Durbin (Mercer County)	45822
Duvall	43137
Dyesville	45769
E (Postal Station) (Franklin County)	43205
E (Postal Station) (Lucas County)	43609
Eagle (Brown County) (Township)	45171
Eagle (Hancock County) (Township)	45881
Eagle (Vinton County) (Township)	43152
Eagle Beach	43452
Eagle City	45504
Eagle Point Colony (Part of Rossford)	43460
Eagleport	43756
Eagleville (Ashtabula County)	44047
Eagleville (Wood County)	44817
East (Township)	44427
East Akron (Part of Akron)	44305
East Alliance	44601
East Ashtabula (Part of Ashtabula)	44004
East Bass Lake	44024
East Batavia Heights	45103
East Cadiz	43907
East Cambridge (Part of Cambridge)	43725
East Canton	44730
East Carlisle	44035
East Claridon	44033
East Clayton	45764
East Cleveland	44112
East Conneaut (Part of Conneaut)	44030
East Cumminsville (Part of Cincinnati)	45223
East Danville	45133
East End (Columbiana County)	43920
East End (Hamilton County)	45226
East Fairfield	44408
East Fultonham	43735
Eastgate Shopping Center (Part of Mayfield Heights)	44125
East Goshen	44609

	ZIP		ZIP		ZIP
East Greenville	44666	Elizabethtown (Warren		Fairhaven	45003
Eastlake	44094	County)	45005	Fairhope	44641
Eastland Shopping Center		Elk (Noble County)		Fairlawn	44313
(Part of Columbus)	43232	(Township)	45745		44333-34
East Lawn	43447	Elk (Vinton County)		For specific Fairlawn Zip Codes	
East Lewistown	44408	(Township)	45651	call (216) 864-6409, or your local	
East Liberty (Delaware		Elkrun (Township)	44415	postmaster.	
County)	43074	Elkton	44415	Fairlawn (Part of Akron)	44333
East Liberty (Logan County)	43319	Ellerton	45342	Fairlawn Heights	44484
East Liberty (Summit		Ellet (Part of Akron)	44312	Fairmount (Part of	
County)	44319	Elliot	43728	Cincinnati)	45214
East Liverpool	43920	Elliottville	45701	Fair Oaks	45102
East Mansfield	44905	Ellis	43701	Fairplay (Butler County)	45014
East Mecca	44410	Ellisonville	45638	Fairplay (Jefferson County)	43910
East Millersport	43046	Elliston	43432	Fairpoint	43927
East Millfield	45761	Ellsberry	45101	Fairport Harbor	44077
East Monroe	45135	Ellsworth	44416	Fairview (Guernsey County)	43736
East Norwalk	44857	Ellsworth (Township)	44416	Fairview (Guernsey County)	43772
East Norwood (Hamilton		Elm Acres	44646	Fairview (Highland County)	45133
County)	45212	Elm Grove	45661	Fairview Heights (Jefferson	
East Norwood (Washington		Elmira	43502	County)	43964
County)	45750	Elmore	43416	Fairview Heights	
Easton	44270	Elmville	45133	(Washington County)	45750
East Orwell (Part of Orwell)	44076	Elmwood Place	45216	Fairview Lanes	44870
East Over	45011	Elroy	45303	Fairview Park	44126
East Palestine	44413	Elton	44662	Fairway Terrace	45341
East Plains (Part of		Elyria	44035-39	Fairway View Estates	45805
Middletown)	45044	For specific Elyria Zip Codes call		Fairwind Acres (Part of	
East Richland	43950	(216) 323-7400, or your local		Montgomery)	45242
East Rochester	44625	postmaster.		Falls (Hocking County)	
East Side (Part of		Emerald (Adams County)	45697	(Township)	43138
Youngstown)	44506	Emerald (Paulding County)		Falls (Muskingum County)	
East Sparta	44626	(Township)	45879	(Township)	43701
East Springfield	43925	Emerson	43917	Fallsburg	43822
East Toledo (Part of Toledo)	43605	Emerson Heights (Part of		Fallsbury (Township)	43822
East Townsend	44826	Marietta)	45750	Fargo	43074
East Trumbull	44084	Emery Chapel	45502	Farmdale	44417
East Union (Noble County)	43779	Empire	43926	Farmer	43520
East Union (Wayne County)		Enchanted Hills	45133	Farmer (Township)	43520
(Township)	44606	England Station	44805	Farmers	45146
East View (Jefferson		Englewood	45322	Farmerstown	43804
County)	43938	English Woods (Part of		Farmersville	45325
Eastview (Montgomery		Cincinnati)	45225	Farmington (Belmont	
County)	45431	Enoch (Township)	43724	County)	43912
Eastwood	45154	Enon	45323	Farmington (Trumbull	
Eastwood Mall (Part of		Enterprise (Hocking County)	43138	County) (Township)	44491
Niles)	44446	Enterprise (Preble County)	45381	Farnham (Part of Conneaut)	44030
Eaton (Lorain County)		Epworth	44903	Farrington	45373
(Township)	44035	Epworth Heights	45140	Fashion Heights	45238
Eaton (Preble County)	45320	Era	43143	Fawcett	45616
Eaton Estates	44044	Erastus	45822	Fayette (Fulton County)	43521
Eber	43160	Erhart	44256	Fayette (Lawrence County)	
Echo	43940	Erie (Township)	43439	(Township)	45680
Echo Glen Lake	44233	Erieview (Part of Cleveland)	44199	Fayetteville	45118
Eckmansville	45697	Eris	43078	Fay Gardens	45140
Eden (Licking County)		Erlin	43420	Fearing (Township)	45788
(Township)	43071	Espyville	43302	Federal Reserve (Part of	
Eden (Seneca County)		Essex	43344	Cleveland)	44101
(Township)	44845	Etna	43018	Feed Springs	44683
Eden (Wyandot County)		Etna (Township)	43018	Feesburg	45119
(Township)	44849	Euclid	44117	Felicity	45120
Eden Park (Hamilton		Euclid Heights (Part of		Fernald	45030
County)	45202	Middletown)	45044	Fernbank (Part of	
Eden Park (Scioto County)	45662	Euclid Square Mall (Part of		Cincinnati)	45233
Edenton	45122	Euclid)	44132	Fernell Heights	45244
Edenville	44849	Eureka	44408	Fernwood	43952
Edgefield (Fayette County)	43128	Evansport	43519	Ferry (Erie County)	44870
Edgefield (Stark County)	44709	Evanston (Part of		Ferry (Greene County)	45068
Edgemont	45216	Cincinnati)	45207	Fields Terrace	45619
Edgerton	43517	Evansville	44440	Filburns Island	45865
Edgewater (Part of		Evendale	45241	Fincastle	45171
Lakewood)	44107	Everett	44264	Findlater Garden (Part of	
Edgewater Beach	43076	Evergreen (Gallia County)	45614	Cincinnati)	45232
Edgewater Park	43227	Evergreen (Washington		Findlay	45839†
Edgewood	44004	County)	45750		45840*
Edgwood Estates	45805	Ewing	43138	Findlay Mall (Part of Findlay)	45840
Edinburg	44272	Ewington	45686	Findley Gardens	43964
Edinburg (Township)	44272	Excello	45044	Finneytown	45224
Edison	43320	Fairborn	45324	Fire Brick	45656
Edmunds	45682	Fairbrondt	44833	Fireside	44811
Edon	43518	Fairdale	43725	Firestone Park (Part of	
Egypt (Auglaize County)	45865	Fairfax (Hamilton County)	45227	Akron)	44301
Egypt (Belmont County)	43713	Fairfax (Highland County)	45133	Fishack	43452
Eifort	45682	Fairfield (Butler County)	45014	Fitchville	44851
Eileen Gardens	45238	Fairfield (Butler County)		Fitchville (Township)	44851
Elba	45746	(Township)	45014	Five Forks	43945
Elberta Beach (Part of		Fairfield (Columbiana		Five Mile	45154
Vermilion)	44089	County) (Township)	44408	Five Points (Greene County)	45324
Eldean	45373	Fairfield (Greene County)	45324	Five Points (Mahoning	
Eldon	43773	Fairfield (Highland County)		County)	44452
Eldorado (Butler County)	45044	(Township)	45135	Five Points (Pickaway	
Eldorado (Preble County)	45321	Fairfield (Huron County)		County)	43143
Elery	43535	(Township)	44855	Five Points (Trumbull	
Elgin	45838	Fairfield (Jefferson County)	43944	County)	44404
Elida	45807	Fairfield (Madison County)		Five Points (Warren County)	45066
Elizabeth (Lawrence		(Township)	43162	Flatiron (Perry County)	43731
County) (Township)	45659	Fairfield (Tuscarawas		Flat Iron (Warren County)	45005
Elizabeth (Miami County)		County) (Township)	44678	Flatrock (Henry County)	
(Township)	45312	Fairfield (Washington		(Township)	43545
Elizabethtown (Hamilton		County) (Township)	45724	Flat Rock (Seneca County)	44828
County)	45052	Fairfield Beach	43076	Fleatown	43055
		Fairground Acres	45107	Fleetwood Addition	43040

	ZIP		ZIP		ZIP
Fleming	45729	Franklin (Tuscarawas		Georgetown	45121
Fletcher	45326	County) (Township)	44680	Gepharts	45694
Flint	43085	Franklin (Warren County)	45005	Gerald	43545
Florence (Belmont County)	43935	Franklin (Warren County)		German (Auglaize County)	
Florence (Erie County)	44814	(Township)	45005	(Township)	45869
Florence (Erie County)		Franklin (Wayne County)		German (Clark County)	
(Township)	44814	(Township)	44627	(Township)	45504
Florence (Noble County)	43724	Franklin Furnace	45629	German (Fulton County)	
Florence (Williams County)		Franklin Park Mall (Part of		(Township)	43502
(Township)	43518	Toledo)	43623	German (Harrison County)	
Florida	43545	Franklin Square	44431	(Township)	43976
Flushing	43977	Frazeysburg	43822	German (Montgomery	
Flushing (Township)	43977	Frederick (Miami County)	45371	County) (Township)	45327
Fly	45730	Frederick (Scioto County)	45694	Germano	43986
Footville	44084	Fredericksburg	44627	Germantown (Montgomery	
Foraker	45812	Fredericksdale	43779	County)	45327
Forest	45843	Fredericktown (Columbiana		Germantown (Washington	
Forestdale	45638	County)	43920	County)	45745
Forest Fair Mall (Part of		Fredericktown (Knox		Getaway	45619
Forest Park)	45240	County)	43019	Gettysburg (Darke County)	45328
Forest Hills	45502	Fredonia	43023	Gettysburg (Preble County)	45347
Forest Hills Estates	45230	Freeburg	44669	Geyer	45895
Forest Park (Hamilton		Freedom (Henry County)		Ghent	44333
County)	45240	(Township)	43545	Gibisonville	43149
Forest Park (Montgomery		Freedom (Portage County)	44288	Gibson (Guernsey County)	43778
County)	45405	Freedom (Portage County)		Gibson (Mercer County)	
Forest Park Plaza	45405	(Township)	44288	(Township)	45846
Forest View	43952	Freedom (Wood County)		Gibsonburg	43431
Forestville	45230	(Township)	43450	Gilbert	43701
Fort Jefferson	45331	Freeport	43973	Gilboa	45875
Fort Jennings	45844	Freeport (Township)	43973	Gilead (Township)	43338
Fort Loramie	45845	Fremont	43420	Gillivan	43140
Fort McKinley (Montgomery		Frenchtown (Darke County)	45380	Gilmore	43837
County)	45426	Frenchtown (Seneca		Ginghamsburg	45371
Fort Meigs Place	43551	County)	43316	Girard	44420
Fort Miami Addition (Part of		Fresno	43824	Girton	43457
Maumee)	43537	Friendship	45630	Gist Settlement	45159
Fort Recovery	45846	Frischkorn Heights	43968	Givens	45690
Fort Scott Camps	45030	Frontier Park	45239	Glade	45613
Fort Seneca	44829	Frontier Town	44514	Gladstone	45314
Fort Shawnee	45806	Frost	45723	Glandorf	45848
Fort Steuben Mall (Part of		Fruitdale	45123	Glasgow (Columbiana	
Steubenville)	43952	Fruit Hill	45230	County)	43968
Foster	45039	Fryburg (Auglaize County)	45895	Glasgow (Tuscarawas	
Fosterville (Part of		Fryburg (Holmes County)	44654	County)	43837
Youngstown)	44511	Frys Corners	45331	Glass Rock	43739
Fostoria	44830	Frytown	45418	Glenbrook Acres	45305
Fountain Park	43084	Fulda	43724	Glencoe (Belmont County)	43928
Fountain Square (Part of		Fulton (Fulton County)		Glencoe (Hamilton County)	45231
Cincinnati)	45202	(Township)	43558	Glendale	45246
Fowler	44418	Fulton (Morrow County)	43321	Glendwell (Part of	
Fowler (Township)	44418	Fultonham	43738	Steubenville)	43952
Fowlers Mill	44024	Funk	44691	Glen Este	45103
Fox (Carroll County)		Fursville	43062	Glenford	43739
(Township)	43945	Gabels Corner	44420	Glengary Heights	43081
Fox (Pickaway County)	43113	Gage	45658	Glen Karn	45332
Foxboro Manor (Part of		Gageville	44048	Glenmary (Part of Fairfield)	45246
Vandalia)	45377	Gahanna	43230	Glenmont	44628
Foxborough Commons	44870	Galatea	45872	Glenmoor	43920
Fox Chase	43502	Galaxy Acres	45239	Glenmore	45874
Fox Hollow	43542	Galena	43021	Glenns Run	43935
Frank	44811	Galion	44833	Glen Robbins	43943
Frankfort	45628	Gallia	45658	Glen Roy	45692
Franklin (Adams County)		Gallipolis	45631	Glenwillow	44139
(Township)	45660	Gallipolis (Township)	45631	Glenwood	45381
Franklin (Brown County)		Galloway	43119	Glenwood Acres	44087
(Township)	45121	Gambier	43022	Gloria Glens Park	44215
Franklin (Clermont County)		Ganges	44875	Glouster	45732
(Township)	45120	Gano	45241	Glynwood	45885
Franklin (Columbiana		Garden	45735	Gnadenhutten	44629
County) (Township)	43962	Garden Acres (Clark		Goes	45387
Franklin (Coshocton		County)	45503	Golden Corners	44214
County) (Township)	43811	Garden Acres (Jefferson		Golden Gate Shopping	
Franklin (Darke County)		County)	43952	Center (Part of Mayfield	
(Township)	45304	Garden City	45694	Heights)	44124
Franklin (Franklin County)		Garden Hill Top (Part of		Goldsboro	45692
(Township)	43204	Cincinnati)	45232	Golf Manor	45237
Franklin (Fulton County)		Garden Isle	44254	Golfway Acres	45239
(Township)	43502	Garden Terrace (Part of		Gomer	45809
Franklin (Harrison County)		Steubenville)	43952	Good Hope (Fayette	
(Township)	44699	Garfield	44460	County)	43160
Franklin (Jackson County)		Garfield Heights	44125	Good Hope (Hocking	
(Township)	45640	Garrettsville	44231	County) (Township)	43149
Franklin (Licking County)		Gaslight Village	45122	Goodland Acres	44688
(Township)	43055	Gasper (Township)	45320	Goodyear Heights (Part of	
Franklin (Mercer County)		Gates Mills	44040	Akron)	44305
(Township)	45866	Gath	45171	Goose Run	45732
Franklin (Monroe County)		Gavers	44432	Gordon	45329
(Township)	43754	Geauga Lake (Part of		Gore	43138
Franklin (Morrow County)		Aurora)	44202	Gorham (Township)	43521
(Township)	43338	Geeburg	44406	Goshen (Auglaize County)	
Franklin (Portage County)		Geneva	44041	(Township)	43331
(Township)	44240	Geneva (Township)	44041	Goshen (Belmont County)	
Franklin (Richland County)		Geneva	43107	(Township)	43719
(Township)	44875	Geneva-on-the-Lake	44041	Goshen (Champaign	
Franklin (Ross County)		Genntown	45036	County) (Township)	43044
(Township)	45601	Genoa (Delaware County)		Goshen (Clermont County)	45122
Franklin (Shelby County)		(Township)	43081	Goshen (Clermont County)	
(Township)	45363	Genoa (Ottawa County)	43430	(Township)	45122
Franklin (Summit County)		Genung Corners	44057	Goshen (Hardin County)	
(Township)	44216	Georges Run	43938	(Township)	43326
		Georgesville	43123		

	ZIP		ZIP		ZIP
Goshen (Mahoning County) (Township)	44460	Green Creek (Township)	43410	Hanover (Licking County)	43055
Goshen (Tuscarawas County)	44663	Greendale	43138	Hanover (Licking County) (Township)	43055
		Greene (Township)	44450	Hanoverton	44423
Goshen (Tuscarawas County) (Township)	44663	Greenfield (Fairfield County) (Township)	43130	Hanville Corners	44855
Gould Park	43230	Greenfield (Gallia County)		Happy Hollow	44626
Goulds	43938	(Township)	45658	Harbor (Part of Ashtabula)	44004
Graceland Shopping Center (Part of Columbus)	43214	Greenfield (Highland County)	45123	Harbor Hills	43025
Grafton	44044	Greenfield (Huron County)		Harbor Point	45822
Grafton (Township)	44044	(Township)	44855	Harbor View	43434
Grand (Township)	45843	Greenfield Village	45224	Hardin (Shelby County)	45365
Grand Prairie (Township)	43302	Greenford	44422	Harding (Township)	43558
Grand Rapids	43522	Green Hills (Greene County)	45324	Hardy (Township)	44654
Grand Rapids (Township)	43522	Greenhills (Hamilton County)	45218	Harewood Acres	45236
Grand River	44045	Greenland	43115	Harlan (Township)	45162
Grandview (Hamilton County)	45002	Greenlex	43302	Harlan Park (Part of Middletown)	45042
Grandview (Washington County)	45767	Green Meadows	45323	Harlem	43021
		Greensburg (Putnam County) (Township)	45875	Harlem (Township)	43021
Grandview (Washington County) (Township)	45767	Greensburg (Summit County)	44232	Harlem Springs	44631
Grandview Estates (Delaware County)	43015	Green Springs	44836	Harmar (Part of Marietta)	45750
Grandview Estates (Marion County)	43302	Greens Run	45732	Harmon	44662
		Greens Store	45640	Harmons Landing	45885
Grandview Heights (Champaign County)	43072	Greentown	44630	Harmony	45502
Grandview Heights (Franklin County)	43212	Greenview	45415	Harmony (Clark County) (Township)	45502
		Greenville	45331	Harmony (Morrow County) (Township)	43315
Grandview Homes (Part of Lima)	45804	Greenville (Township)	45331	Harper	43311
Grange Hall	43143	Greenwich (Huron County)	44837	Harpersfield	44041
Granger	44256	Greenwich (Huron County) (Township)	44837	Harpersfield (Township)	44041
Granger (Township)	44256	Greer	44628	Harpster	43323
Grants	45843	Grelton	43523	Harriett (Guernsey County)	43725
Granville (Licking County)	43023	Griffith (Part of North Bend)	45052	Harriett (Highland County)	45133
Granville (Licking County) (Township)	43023	Griggs	44047	Harriettsville	45745
Granville (Mercer County) (Township)	45883	Grimms Bridge	43920	Harris (Ottawa County) (Township)	43416
Granville South	43023	Groesbeck	45239	Harris (Ross County)	45612
Grape Grove	45335	Groton (Township)	44839	Harrisburg (Franklin County)	43126
Gratiot	43740	Grove City	43123	Harrisburg (Gallia County)	45614
Gratis	45330	Groveport	43125	Harrison (Carroll County) (Township)	44615
Gratis (Township)	45330	Grover Hill	45849	Harrison (Champaign County) (Township)	43357
Graysville	45734	Guerne	44691		
Graytown	43432	Guernsey	43749	Harrison (Darke County) (Township)	45346
Greasy Ridge	45678	Guilford (Columbiana County)	44432	Harrison (Gallia County) (Township)	45631
Greater State Road Shopping Center (Part of Cuyahoga Falls)	44223	Guilford (Medina County) (Township)	44273	Harrison (Hamilton County)	45030
		Gunnerville	45335	Harrison (Hamilton County) (Township)	45030
Great Lakes Mall (Part of Mentor)	44060	Gurneyville	45177	Harrison (Henry County) (Township)	43545
Great Northern Mall (Part of North Olmsted)	44070	Gustavus	44417	Harrison (Knox County) (Township)	43022
		Gustavus (Township)	44417	Harrison (Licking County) (Township)	43033
Great Southern Shoppers City (Part of Columbus)	43207	Gutman	45895	Harrison (Logan County) (Township)	43311
		Guyan (Township)	45623	Harrison (Montgomery County) (Township)	45415
Great Western Shoppers Mart (Part of Columbus)	43213	Guysville	45735	Harrison (Muskingum County) (Township)	43771
		Gypsum	43433	Harrison (Paulding County) (Township)	45880
Green (Adams County) (Township)	45684	Hackney	45715	Harrison (Perry County) (Township)	43731
Green (Ashland County) (Township)	44842	Hagan Addition	43901	Harrison (Pickaway County) (Township)	43103
		Hageman Junction	45036		
Green (Brown County) (Township)	45154	Hale (Township)	43340	Harrison (Preble County) (Township)	45338
Green (Clark County) (Township)	45502	Hallock	43506	Harrison (Ross County) (Township)	45601
		Hallsville	45633		
Green (Clinton County) (Township)	45159	Hambden	44024	Harrison (Scioto County) (Township)	45653
Green (Fayette County) (Township)	45135	Hambden (Township)	44024	Harrisburg (Stark County)	44641
		Hamburg (Fairfield County)	43130	Harrison (Van Wert County) (Township)	45891
Green (Gallia County) (Township)	45658	Hamburg (Preble County)	45321	Harrison (Vinton County) (Township)	45647
Green (Hamilton County) (Township)	45211	Hamden	45634	Harrison Furnace	45662
		Hamer (Township)	45133	Harrison Mills	45682
Green (Harrison County) (Township)	43976	Hamersville	45130	Harrisonville	45769
		Hametown (Part of Norton)	44203	Harrisville (Harrison County)	43974
Green (Hocking County) (Township)	43138	Hamilton (Butler County)	45011-13 45015-18	Harrisville (Medina County) (Township)	44214
Green (Mahoning County) (Township)	44406	For specific Hamilton Zip Codes call (513) 867-8877, or your local postmaster.		Harrod	45850
Green (Monroe County) (Township)	43793	Hamilton (Franklin County) (Township)	43137	Harshasville	45660
		Hamilton (Jackson County) (Township)	45656	Hartford (Licking County) (Township)	43013
Green (Ross County) (Township)	45644	Hamilton (Lawrence County) (Township)	45638	Hartford (Trumbull County)	44424
Green (Scioto County) (Township)	45629	Hamilton (Warren County) (Township)	45039	Hartford (Trumbull County) (Township)	44424
Green (Shelby County) (Township)	45365	Hamilton Meadows	43207	Hartland	44826
		Hamler	43524	Hartland (Township)	44857
Green (Summit County) (Township)	44720	Hamlet	45102	Hartland Center	44826
Green (Summit County)	44720	Hamley Run	45701	Hartleyville	45732
Green (Wayne County) (Township)	44667	Hammansburg	43413	Hartsgrove	44085
Green Acres	45042	Hammondsville	43930	Hartsgrove (Township)	44085
Greenbush (Brown County)	45154	Hampton Woods	45502	Hartshorn	45734
Greenbush (Preble County)	45064	Hanersville	45631	Hartville	44632
Green Camp	43322	Hanging Rock	45638		
Green Camp (Township)	43322	Hanley Village	44904		
Greencastle	43112	Hanna Hills	44266		
		Hannibal	43931		
		Hanover (Ashland County) (Township)	44842		
		Hanover (Butler County) (Township)	45013		
		Hanover (Columbia County) (Township)	44625		
		Hanover (Harrison County)	43988		

Name	ZIP
Hartwell (Part of Cincinnati)	*45216
Harveysburg	45032
Haskins	43525
Hasting Hill	45662
Hatch	45661
Hatton	43457
Havana	44890
Havens Corners	43004
Havensport	43112
Haven View	45373
Haverhill	45636
Haviland	45851
Hayden	43002
Haydenville	43127
Hayes Colony (Part of Delaware)	43015
Hayes Corners	44062
Hayesville	44838
Haynes	43135
Hazelwood (Part of Blue Ash)	45242
Heath	43056
Heatherdowns (Part of Toledo)	43614
Hebbardsville	45701
Hebron	43025
Hecla	45638
Hegemans Landing	45865
Heidelburg Beach	44089
Helena	43435
Helmick	43844
Hemlock	43730
Hemlock Grove	45769
Hempstead (Part of Kettering)	45429
Hendrysburg	43713
Henley	45652
Henrietta (Township)	44889
Henry (Township)	45872
Hepburn	43326
Heritage	45805
Heritage Hills	44087
Heritage Park	44212
Hessville	43431
Hickman	43055
Hicksville	43526
Hicksville (Township)	43526
Hide-A-Way Hills	43107
Higginsport	45131
Highland (Defiance County) (Township)	43512
Highland (Highland County)	45132
Highland (Muskingum County) (Township)	43762
Highland Heights	44124
Highland Hills	44122 / 44128
For specific Highland Hills Zip Codes call (216) 443-4444, or your local postmaster.	
Highland Holliday	45133
Highland Park (Hamilton County)	45238
Highland Park (Mercer County)	45822
Highland Park (Scioto County)	45629
Highland Park (Stark County)	44646
Highlands (Part of Springfield)	45503
Highland Terrace	43950
Highlandtown	43945
Highland Trails	45133
Highpoint	45242
High Water	43055
Hill Addition (Part of East Liverpool)	43920
Hill And Hollow (Part of Oxford)	45056
Hillcrest (Columbiana County)	43968
Hillcrest (Warren County)	45036
Hill Crest (Wayne County)	44691
Hillcrest (Williams County)	43543
Hill Grove	45390
Hilliar (Township)	43011
Hilliard	43026
Hills and Dales (Montgomery County)	45429
Hills and Dales (Stark County)	44708
Hillsboro (Highland County)	45133
Hillsboro (Jefferson County)	43938
Hilltop (Franklin County)	43204
Hilltop (Trumbull County)	44437
Hilltop Acres (Part of Wyoming)	45215
Hinckley	44233
Hinckley (Township)	44233
Hiram	44234
Hiram (Township)	44234
Hiram Rapids	44234
Hiramsburg	43732
Hitchcock	45656
Hoadley	45658
Hoagland	45133
Hoaglin (Township)	45891
Hobson	45760
Hocking (Township)	43130
Hocking Correctional Facility	45764
Hockingport	45739
Hoke	45383
Holden	45896
Holgate	43527
Holiday Acres	45236
Holiday Hills	45502
Holiday Lakes	44890
Holiday Valley	45324
Holland	45528
Hollansburg	45332
Hollister	45732
Holloway	43985
Hollowtown	45171
Holman-Stonybrook Shopping Center (Part of Loveland)	45140
Holmes (Township)	44820
Holmesville	44633
Home Acres (Butler County)	45044
Home Acres (Miami County)	45373
Homedale (Part of Columbus)	43085
Home Orchards (Part of Springfield)	45503
Homer (Licking County)	43027
Homer (Medina County) (Township)	44235
Homer (Morgan County) (Township)	45732
Homerville	44235
Homeside	43950
Homeville	44870
Homewood (Part of Hamilton)	45015
Homeworth	44634
Honeytown	44691
Hooker	43130
Hooksburg	43787
Hooring	45766
Hooven	45033
Hopedale	43976
Hopetown	45601
Hopewell (Jefferson County)	43943
Hopewell (Licking County) (Township)	43740
Hopewell (Mercer County) (Township)	45822
Hopewell (Muskingum County)	43746
Hopewell (Muskingum County) (Township)	43746
Hopewell (Perry County) (Township)	43739
Hopewell (Seneca County) (Township)	44809
Hopkinsville	45039
Horatio	45331
Horns Mill	43130
Hoskinsville	43724
Houck Meadows (Part of Enon)	45502
Houcktown	45814
Houston	45333
Howard	43028
Howard (Township)	43028
Howenstein	44626
Howland (Township)	44484
Howland Center	44484
Hoytville	43529
Hubbard	44425
Hubbard (Township)	44425
Huber Heights	45424
Huber Ridge	43081
Huber South	45439
Hudson	44236
Hudson (Township)	44236
Hue	45622
Hughes	45042
Hulington	45106
Humboldt	45612
Hume	45806
Hunt	43050
Hunter	43719
Hunterdon	45732
Huntington (Brown County) (Township)	45101
Huntington (Gallia County) (Township)	45686
Huntington (Lorain County)	44090
Huntington (Lorain County) (Township)	44090
Huntington (Ross County) (Township)	45601
Huntington Hills	43147
Huntington Park (Part of Aberdeen)	45101
Hunting Valley	44022
Huntsburg	44046
Huntsburg (Township)	44046
Hunts Corners	44811
Huntsville (Butler County)	45042
Huntsville (Logan County)	43324
Hurford	43901
Huron	44839
Huron (Township)	44839
Hustead	45502
Hyatts	43065
Hyde Park (Hamilton County)	45208
Hyde Park (Montgomery County)	45429
Hyde Park Plaza (Part of Cincinnati)	45209
Iberia	43325
Idaho	45661
Idlewild (Part of Cincinnati)	45201
Iler	44830
Ilesboro	43138
Immergrun (Part of Oregon)	43618
Independence (Cuyahoga County)	44131
Independence (Defiance County)	43512
Independence (Washington County) (Township)	45767
Indian Camp	43725
Indian Knolls (Part of Milford)	45150
Indian Ridge	45231
Indianview	45147
Ingle Mann (Part of New Paris)	45347
Ingomar	45381
Ink	44883
Ira	44333
Iradale	44313
Irondale (Jefferson County)	43932
Irondale (Muskingum County)	43821
Ironspot	43777
Ironton	45638
Irvington	45414
Irwin	43029
Island Creek (Township)	43964
Island View	43331
Isle Saint George	43436
Isleta	43845
Israel (Township)	45003
Ithaca	45304
Ivorydale (Part of St. Bernard)	45217
Ivorydale Junction (Part of St. Bernard)	45217
Jackson (Allen County) (Township)	45854
Jackson (Ashland County) (Township)	44287
Jackson (Auglaize County) (Township)	45865
Jackson (Brown County) (Township)	45697
Jackson (Champaign County) (Township)	45389
Jackson (Clermont County) (Township)	45145
Jackson (Coshocton County) (Township)	43812
Jackson (Crawford County) (Township)	44827
Jackson (Darke County) (Township)	45390
Jackson (Franklin County) (Township)	43123
Jackson (Guernsey County) (Township)	43723
Jackson (Hancock County) (Township)	45814
Jackson (Hardin County) (Township)	45843
Jackson (Highland County) (Township)	45133
Jackson (Jackson County)	45640
Jackson (Jackson County) (Township)	45640
Jackson (Knox County) (Township)	43005
Jackson (Mahoning County) (Township)	44451
Jackson (Monroe County) (Township)	45730
Jackson (Montgomery County) (Township)	45325
Jackson (Muskingum County) (Township)	43822

	ZIP
Jackson (Noble County)	
(Township)	45727
Jackson (Paulding County)	
(Township)	45855
Jackson (Perry County)	
(Township)	43748
Jackson (Pickaway County)	
(Township)	43113
Jackson (Pike County)	
(Township)	45690
Jackson (Preble County)	
(Township)	45320
Jackson (Putnam County)	
(Township)	45844
Jackson (Richland County)	
(Township)	44875
Jackson (Sandusky County)	
(Township)	43407
Jackson (Seneca County)	
(Township)	44830
Jackson (Shelby County)	
(Township)	45334
Jackson (Stark County)	
(Township)	44646
Jackson (Union County)	
(Township)	43344
Jackson (Van Wert County)	
(Township)	45863
Jackson (Vinton County)	
(Township)	45651
Jackson (Wood County)	
(Township)	43529
Jackson (Wyandot County)	
(Township)	45843
Jackson Belden (Part of	
Canton)	44718
Jacksonburg	45067
Jackson Center (Mahoning	
County)	44451
Jackson Center (Shelby	
County)	45334
Jackson Heights (Jackson	
County)	45640
Jackson Heights (Jefferson	
County)	43943
Jackson Lake	45656
Jacksontown	43030
Jacksonville (Adams	
County)	45660
Jacksonville (Athens	
County)	45740
Jacksonville (Clark County)	45502
Jacktown	45042
Jacobsburg	43933
Jaite (Part of Brecksville)	44141
Jamestown	45335
Jasper (Fayette County)	
(Township)	43128
Jasper (Pike County)	45642
Jasper Mills	43160
Jays	45331
Jefferson (Adams County)	
(Township)	45684
Jefferson (Ashtabula	
County)	44047
Jefferson (Ashtabula	
County) (Township)	44047
Jefferson (Brown County)	
(Township)	45168
Jefferson (Clinton County)	
(Township)	45148
Jefferson (Coshocton	
County) (Township)	43844
Jefferson (Crawford County)	
(Township)	44827
Jefferson (Fairfield County)	43112
Jefferson (Fayette County)	
(Township)	43128
Jefferson (Franklin County)	
(Township)	43004
Jefferson (Greene County)	
(Township)	45335
Jefferson (Guernsey	
County) (Township)	43755
Jefferson (Jackson County)	
(Township)	45656
Jefferson (Knox County)	
(Township)	44628
Jefferson (Logan County)	
(Township)	43311
Jefferson (Madison County)	
(Township)	43162
Jefferson (Mercer County)	
(Township)	45822
Jefferson (Montgomery	
County) (Township)	45345
Jefferson (Muskingum	
County) (Township)	43821
Jefferson (Noble County)	
(Township)	43724
Jefferson (Preble County)	
(Township)	45347

	ZIP
Jefferson (Richland County)	
(Township)	44813
Jefferson (Ross County)	
(Township)	45601
Jefferson (Scioto County)	
(Township)	45648
Jefferson (Tuscarawas	
County) (Township)	43840
Jefferson (Wayne County)	44691
Jefferson (Williams County)	
(Township)	43543
Jefferson Estates	43113
Jefferson Heights	43938
Jeffersonville	43128
Jelloway	43014
Jenera	45841
Jenkins Addition	43701
Jennings (Putnam County)	
(Township)	45844
Jennings (Van Wert County)	
(Township)	45894
Jep	45659
Jericho	45042
Jerome	43064
Jerome (Township)	43064
Jeromesville	44840
Jerry City	43437
Jersey	43062
Jersey (Township)	43062
Jerusalem (Lucas County)	
(Township)	43412
Jerusalem (Monroe County)	43747
Jesse C Owens (Part of	
Cleveland)	44104
Jewell	43530
Jewett	43986
Jobs	45732
Joetown	43758
Johnson (Township)	43072
Johnsons Corners (Part of	
Barberton)	44203
Johnston (Trumbull County)	44417
Johnston (Trumbull County)	
(Township)	44417
Johnston (Tuscarawas	
County)	44622
Johnstown	43031
Johnsville (Part of New	
Lebanon)	45345
Jonesboro (Clinton County)	45146
Jonesboro (Fayette County)	43160
Jonestown	45894
Jordanville	44432
Joy	43728
Joyce Avenue (Part of	
Columbus)	43219
Jug Run	43917
Jumbo	43326
Jump	43326
Junction	43512
Junction City	43748
Junior Furnace	45629
Justus	44662
Kalida	45853
Kamms (Part of Cleveland)	44111
Kanauga	45631
Kansas	44841
Karen Woods	45502
Kay	45005
Keays (Part of Middletown)	45044
Keene	43828
Keene (Township)	43828
Keist Manor	43130
Keith	43724
Kelleys Island	43438
Kellogg Corners	44410
Kelloggsville	44030
Kemp	45806
Kendall Heights	44646
Kenmore (Part of Akron)	44314
Kennard	43009
Kennedy Heights (Part of	
Cincinnati)	45213
Kennonsburg	43773
Keno	45743
Kenridge (Part of Blue Ash)	45242
Kensington	44427
Kensington Park	45305
Kent (Portage County)	44240
Kenton	43326
Kenwood (Hamilton County)	45236
Kenwood (Harrison County)	43901
Kenwood (Lucas County)	43606
Kenwood Heights (Part of	
Springfield)	45505
Kenwood Knolls	45236
Kenwood Mall	45236
Kenwood Towne Center	45236
Kerr	45643
Kessler	45383
Kettering	45429
Kettlersville	45336

	ZIP
Key	43933
Kidron	44636
Kieferville	45831
Kilbourne	43032
Kile	43064
Kilgore	43988
Killbuck	44637
Killbuck (Township)	44637
Kilvert	45778
Kimball	44847
Kimberly	45764
Kimbolton	43749
Kingman	45177
King Mines	43755
Kings Corners	44904
Kings Creek	43078
Kingsdale Center (Part of	
Columbus)	43221
Kingsgate	45231
Kingsgate Mall (Part of	
Mansfield)	44901
Kings Mills	45034
Kingston (Delaware County)	
(Township)	43074
Kingston (Ross County)	45644
Kingsville	44048
Kingsville (Township)	44048
Kingsville On-the-Lake (Part	
of North Kingsville)	44068
Kingsway	43420
Kinnickinnick	45601
Kinsman (Belmont County)	43950
Kinsman (Trumbull County)	44428
Kinsman (Trumbull County)	
(Township)	44428
Kiousville	43143
Kipling	43750
Kipton	44049
Kirby	43330
Kirkersville	43033
Kirkpatrick	43302
Kirkwood (Belmont County)	
(Township)	43713
Kirkwood (Shelby County)	45365
Kirkwood Heights	43912
Kirtland	44094
Kirtland Hills	44060
Kitchen	44656
Kitts Hill	45645
Kiwanis Lake	44065
Klondike	44410
Knockemstiff	45601
Knollwood (Part of	
Beavercreek)	45432
Knollwood Village	43113
Knox (Columbiana County)	
(Township)	44634
Knox (Guernsey County)	
(Township)	43725
Knox (Holmes County)	
(Township)	44638
Knox (Jefferson County)	
(Township)	43964
Knox (Vinton County)	
(Township)	45710
Knoxville	43964
Kolmont	43938
Kossuth	45887
Kunkle	43531
Kyger	45620
La Belle View (Part of	
Steubenville)	43952
Lacarne	43439
La Croft	43920
Lafayette (Allen County)	45854
Lafayette (Coshocton	
County) (Township)	43845
Lafayette (Madison County)	43140
Lafayette (Medina County)	44256
Lafayette (Medina County)	
(Township)	44256
Lafferty	43951
Lagonda (Part of	
Springfield)	45503
La Grange (Lawrence	
County)	45638
Lagrange (Lorain County)	44050
Lagrange (Lorain County)	
(Township)	44050
Laings	43752
Lake (Ashland County)	
(Township)	44628
Lake (Logan County)	
(Township)	43311
Lake (Stark County)	
(Township)	44720
Lake (Wood County)	
(Township)	43447
Lake Cable	44718
Lake Darby	43204
Lake Fork	44840
Lakeline	44094

	ZIP		ZIP		ZIP
Lake Lorelel	45118	Leonardsburg	43015	Lincoln Knolls Plaza (Part of	
Lake Lucerne	44022	Lerado	45176	Youngstown)	44505
Lake Milton	44429	Leroy (Township)	44077	Lincoln Village	43228
Lakemore	44250	Le Sourdsville	45042	Lindair Estates	45502
Lake of the Woods	43021	Lester	44256	Lindale	45102
Lake O'Springs	44718	Letart (Township)	45771	Lindentree	44656
Lake Seneca	43543	Letart Falls	45771	Lindenwald (Part of	
Lakeside (Butler County)	45042	Levanna	45167	Hamilton)	45015
Lakeside (Fairfield County)	43046	Lewis (Township)	45121	Lindsey	43442
Lakeside (Licking County)	43008	Lewis Addition	43952	Lindsley-Gay	44003
Lakeside (Ottawa County)	43440	Lewisburg	45338	Linndale	44111
Lakeside-Marblehead (Part		Lewis Center	43035	Linneman	45804
of Marblehead)	43440	Lewistown	43333	Linnville (Lawrence County)	45696
Lake Slagle	44720	Lewisville	43754	Linnville (Licking County)	43076
Lake Sylvan	45369	Lexington (Richland County)	44904	Linton (Township)	43836
Lake View (Knox County)	43019	Lexington (Stark County)	44601	Linwood (Part of Cincinnati)	45226
Lakeview (Logan County)	43331	Lexington (Stark County)		Linworth	43085
Lakeview Heights	45690	(Township)	44601	Lippincotts	43078
Lakeville (Ashtabula County)	44030	Liberty (Adams County)		Lisbon (Clark County)	45368
Lakeville (Holmes County)	44638	(Township)	45693	Lisbon (Columbiana	
Lake Waynoka	45171	Liberty (Butler County)		County)	44432
Lakewood	44107	(Township)	45011	Lisman	45659
Lakota Hills	45069	Liberty (Clinton County)		Litchfield	44253
Lamira	43718	(Township)	45177	Litchfield (Township)	44253
Lancaster	43130	Liberty (Crawford County)		Lithopolis	43136
Landeck	45833	(Township)	44881	Little Farms	43228
Landen	45040	Liberty (Darke County)		Little Hocking	45742
Langsville	45741	(Township)	45352	Little Sandusky	43323
Lanier (Township)	45381	Liberty (Delaware County)		Little Walnut	43113
Lansing	43934	(Township)	43065	Little Washington	44903
LaPorte	44035	Liberty (Fairfield County)		Little York	45414
Lapperel	45660	(Township)	43105	Liverpool (Columbiana	
La Rue	43332	Liberty (Guernsey County)		County) (Township)	43920
Latcha	43447	(Township)	43725	Liverpool (Medina County)	
Latham	45646	Liberty (Hancock County)		(Township)	44280
Latimer	44428	(Township)	45840	Livingston (Part of	
Lattasburg	44287	Liberty (Hardin County)		Columbus)	43227
Lattaville	45628	(Township)	45810	Lloydsville	43950
Latty (Paulding County)	45855	Liberty (Henry County)		Lock	43011
Latty (Paulding County)		(Township)	43532	Lockbourne	43137
(Township)	45849	Liberty (Highland County)		Lockington	45356
Laura	45337	(Township)	45133	Lockland	45215
Laurel (Clermont County)	45157	Liberty (Jackson County)		Lock Two	45869
Laurel (Hocking County)		(Township)	45640	Lockville	43112
(Township)	43149	Liberty (Knox County)		Lockwood	44450
Laurel Creek	44212	(Township)	43050	Lockwood Corners	44319
Laurel Ridge	44721	Liberty (Licking County)		Locust Corner	45245
Laurelville	43135	(Township)	43031	Locust Grove (Adams	
Lawco Lake	45659	Liberty (Logan County)		County)	45660
Lawndale (Part of Massillon)	44646	(Township)	43357	Locust Grove (Butler	
Lawrence (Lawrence		Liberty (Mercer County)		County)	45042
County)	45659	(Township)	45882	Locust Grove (Mahoning	
Lawrence (Lawrence		Liberty (Montgomery		County)	44460
County) (Township)	45645	County)	45418	Locust Lake	45102
Lawrence (Stark County)		Liberty (Putnam County)		Locust Point	43449
(Township)	44614	(Township)	45856	Locust Ridge	45176
Lawrence (Tuscarawas		Liberty (Ross County)		Lodi (Athens County)	
County) (Township)	44612	(Township)	45647	(Township)	45735
Lawrence (Washington		Liberty (Seneca County)		Lodi (Medina County)	44254
County) (Township)	45750	(Township)	44841	Logan (Auglaize County)	
Lawrenceville	45502	Liberty (Trumbull County)		(Township)	45887
Lawshe	45660	(Township)	44420	Logan (Hocking County)	43138
Layhigh	45013	Liberty (Union County)		Logan Elm Village	43113
Layland	44637	(Township)	43040	Logansville	43318
Layman	45724	Liberty (Van Wert County)		Logtown	44432
Leaper	45631	(Township)	45891	Lombardsville	45652
Leavittsburg	44430	Liberty (Washington		London (Madison County)	43140
Leavittsville	44614	County) (Township)	45745	London (Richland County)	44875
Lebanon (Meigs County)		Liberty (Wood County)		London Correctional	
(Township)	45770	(Township)	43462	Institution	43140
Lebanon (Monroe County)	45745	Liberty Center	43532	Londonderry (Guernsey	
Lebanon (Warren County)	45036	Liberty Plaza	44505	County)	43973
Lebanon Correctional		Lick (Township)	45640	Londonderry (Guernsey	
Institution	45036	Licking (Licking County)		County) (Township)	43973
Lecta	45678	(Township)	43076	Londonderry (Ross County)	45647
Lee (Athens County)		Licking (Muskingum		Long	45331
(Township)	45710	County) (Township)	43830	Long Beach	43449
Lee (Carroll County)		Licking View	43701	Long Bottom	45743
(Township)	44615	Liebs Island	43046	Long Lake	44638
Lee (Cuyahoga County)	44120	Lightsville	45362	Long Run	43917
Lee (Monroe County)		Lilly Chapel	43140	Longs Crossing	44431
(Township)	43946	Lima	45801-07	Longstreth	45764
Leesburg (Highland County)	45135	For specific Lima Zip Codes call		Longview Heights (Part of	
Leesburg (Union County)		(419) 224-5801, or your local		Athens)	45701
(Township)	43040	postmaster.		Longvue (Part of Marietta)	45750
Lees Creek	45138	Lima (Township)	43073	Loomis	43718
Leesville (Carroll County)	44639	Limaville	44640	Lorain	44052-55
Leesville (Crawford County)	44827	Lime City	43551	For specific Lorain Zip Codes call	
Leetonia	44431	Limecrest	45502	(216) 244-4221, or your local	
Lehmkuhl Landing	45865	Limerick	45601	postmaster.	
Leipsic	45856	Limestone	43432	Loramie (Township)	45363
Leipsic Junction (Part of		Limestone City	45506	Lordstown	44481
Leipsic)	45856	Lincoln (Morrow County)		Lore City	43755
Leistville	43113	(Township)	43321	Lostcreek (Township)	45312
Lemert	44882	Lincoln (Richland County)	44905	Lost Creek Addition	45804
Lemon (Township)	45050	Lincoln Heights (Hamilton		Lottridge	45723
Lemoyne	43441	County)	45215	Louden (Adams County)	45660
Lena	45317	Lincoln Heights (Jefferson		Loudon (Carroll County)	
Lenox	44047	County)	43952	(Township)	44615
Lenox (Township)	44047	Lincoln Heights (Richland		Loudon (Seneca County)	
Leo	45640	County)	44903	(Township)	44830
Leon	44003				

	ZIP
Louden (Tuscarawas County)	44622
Loudonville	44842
Louisville (Adams County)	45660
Louisville (Stark County)	44641
Loveland	45140
Loveland Park	45140
Lovell	43351
Lowell	45744
Lowellville	44436
Lowellville Junction (Part of Lowellville)	44436
Lower Salem	45745
Loyal Oak (Part of Norton)	44203
Lucas	44843
Lucasburg	43723
Lucasville	45648
Lucerne	43019
Luckey	43443
Ludington	43730
Ludlow (Township)	45734
Ludlow Falls	45339
Lugbill Addition (Part of Archbold)	43502
Lumberton	45177
Luray	43025
Lush Addition	43302
Lykens	44818
Lykens (Township)	44818
Lyme (Township)	44811
Lynchburg (Columbiana County)	44427
Lynchburg (Highland County)	45142
Lyndhurst	44124
Lyndhurst-Mayfield Heights (Part of Mayfield Heights)	44124
Lyndon	45681
Lynn (Township)	43326
Lynns Corners	44406
Lynx	45650
Lyons	43533
Lyra	45694
Lytle	45068
McArthur (Logan County) (Township)	43324
McArthur (Vinton County)	45651
McCance	44627
Mc Cappin Mill	45133
McCartyville	45302
McClainville	43906
McClimansville	43143
McClintocksburg	44444
McClure	43534
McComb	45858
McConnelsville	43756
McCracken Corners	44460
McCuneville	43782
McCutchenville	44844
McDermott	45652
McDonald (Hardin County) (Township)	43326
McDonald (Trumbull County)	44437
McDonaldsville	44720
Macedon	45828
Macedonia	44056
McGill	45880
McGonigle	45013
Mc Gough	43050
McGuffey	45859
McGuffey Heights (Part of Youngstown)	44505
McIntyre	43910
Mack	45211
McKay	44842
McKean (Township)	43055
McKinley Heights	44446
Mack North	45211
Macksburg	45746
Mack South	45211
Mackstown	43081
McLean (Township)	45845
McLuney	43731
McMorran	43311
Macon	45697
McZena	44638
Madeira	45243
Madison (Butler County) (Township)	45042
Madison (Clark County) (Township)	45368
Madison (Columbiana County) (Township)	43968
Madison (Fairfield County) (Township)	43130
Madison (Fayette County) (Township)	43160
Madison (Franklin County) (Township)	43125
Madison (Guernsey County) (Township)	43773

	ZIP
Madison (Hancock County) (Township)	45814
Madison (Highland County) (Township)	45123
Madison (Jackson County) (Township)	45656
Madison (Lake County)	44057
Madison (Lake County) (Township)	44057
Madison (Licking County) (Township)	43055
Madison (Montgomery County) (Township)	45426
Madison (Muskingum County) (Township)	43821
Madison (Perry County) (Township)	43760
Madison (Pickaway County) (Township)	43103
Madison (Richland County) (Township)	44903
Madison (Sandusky County) (Township)	43435
Madison (Scioto County) (Township)	45653
Madison (Vinton County) (Township)	45698
Madison (Williams County) (Township)	43554
Madisonburg	44691
Madison Correctional Institution	43140
Madison Hill	44691
Madison Lake Area	43140
Madison Mills	43143
Madison-on-the-Lake	44057
Madisonville (Part of Cincinnati)	45227
Mad River (Champaign County) (Township)	43083
Mad River (Clark County) (Township)	45324
Mad River (Montgomery County) (Township)	45424
Magnetic Springs	43036
Magnolia	44643
Mahoning	44231
Maineville	45039
Mainsville	43764
Malaga	43757
Malaga (Township)	43757
Malinta	43535
Mallet Creek	44256
Malta	43758
Malta (Township)	43758
Malvern	44644
Manchester (Adams County)	45144
Manchester (Adams County) (Township)	45144
Manchester (Morgan County) (Township)	43756
Manchester (Summit County)	44216
Mandale	45827
Manhattan (Part of Steubenville)	43952
Mannhassett Village (Part of Mason)	45040
Mansfield	44901-07
For specific Mansfield Zip Codes call (419) 755-4621, or your local postmaster.	
Mantua (Township)	44255
Mantua	44255
Mantua Center	44255
Mantua Corners	44255
Maple Corner	45385
Maple Grove (Geauga County)	44231
Maple Grove (Ross County)	45601
Maple Grove (Seneca County)	44883
Maple Heights (Cuyahoga County)	44137
Maple Heights (Noble County)	43724
Maple Lake	43944
Maple Park	45040
Maple Ridge	44601
Mapleshade (Part of Gallipolis)	45631
Mapleton	44730
Maple Valley (Part of Akron)	44320
Maplewood	45340
Marathon	45145
Marble Cliff	43212
Marble Furnace	45660
Marblehead	43440
Marchand	44720
Marcy	43110
Marengo	43334

	ZIP
Margaretta (Township)	44824
Maria Stein	45860
Mariemont	45227
Marietta	45750
Marietta (Township)	45750
Marion (Allen County) (Township)	45833
Marion (Clinton County) (Township)	45107
Marion (Fayette County) (Township)	43145
Marion (Hancock County) (Township)	45840
Marion (Hardin County) (Township)	45812
Marion (Henry County) (Township)	43524
Marion (Hocking County) (Township)	43138
Marion (Marion County)	43301†
Marion (Marion County)	43302*
Marion (Marion County) (Township)	43302
Marion (Mercer County) (Township)	45883
Marion (Morgan County) (Township)	43728
Marion (Noble County) (Township)	43788
Marion (Pike County) (Township)	45613
Marion Correctional Institution	43302
Marion East	43302
Mark (Township)	43556
Mark Center	43536
Marlain Acres	45231
Marlboro (Delaware County) (Township)	43015
Marlboro (Stark County)	44601
Marlboro (Stark County) (Township)	44601
Marne	43055
Marquis	44406
Marr	43789
Marseilles	43351
Marseilles (Township)	43351
Marshall	45133
Marshall (Township)	45133
Marshallville	44645
Martel	43335
Martin	43445
Martinsburg	43037
Martins Ferry	43935
Martinsville	45146
Mary Ann (Township)	43055
Marygrove	43558
Marysville	43040
Mason (Lawrence County) (Township)	45696
Mason (Warren County)	45040
Mason Heights (Part of Mason)	45040
Massie (Township)	45032
Massieville	45601
Massillon	44646-48
For specific Massillon Zip Codes call (216) 837-8323, or your local postmaster.	
Massillon State Hospital	44646
Masury	44438
Matville	43146
Maud	45069
Maumee	43537
Maustown	45011
Maximo	44650
Maxville	43748
Mayfield (Butler County)	45044
Mayfield (Cuyahoga County)	44143
Mayfield Heights	44124
Mayflower Village (Part of Massillon)	44647
May Hill	45679
Maynard	43937
Maysville (Allen County)	45810
Maysville (Wayne County)	44606
Mead (Township)	43947
Meade	45644
Meadowbrook	43701
Meadowbrook Lake (Part of Stow)	44224
Meadow Lawn (Part of Middletown)	45044
Mecca	44410
Mecca (Township)	44410
Mechanic (Township)	43804
Mechanicsburg (Champaign County)	43044
Mechanicsburg (Crawford County)	44887
Mechanicsburg (Monroe County)	43793

* Area Zip Code   † Post Office Boxes

	ZIP		ZIP		ZIP
Mechanicsburg (Wayne County)	44691	Midvale	44653	Monfort Heights	45239
Mechanicstown	44651	Midway	43950	Monfort Heights East	45239
Mechanicsville	44041	Midway Mall (Part of Elyria)	44035	Monfort Heights South	45239
Medina	44256*	Mifflin (Ashland County)	44805	Monnette	43302
	44258†	Mifflin (Ashland County) (Township)	44805	Monroe (Adams County) (Township)	45144
Medway	45341	Mifflin (Franklin County)		Monroe (Allen County)	
Meeker	43302	(Township)	43230	(Township)	45807
Meigs (Adams County) (Township)	45660	Mifflin (Pike County) (Township)	45646	Monroe (Ashtabula County) (Township)	44030
Meigs (Morgan County)	43756	Mifflin (Richland County)		Monroe (Butler County)	45050
Meigs (Muskingum County) (Township)	43727	(Township)	44843	Monroe (Carroll County) (Township)	44620
Meigsville (Township)	43756	Mifflin (Wyandot County) (Township)	43351	Monroe (Clermont County) (Township)	45148
Melbern	43506	Milan	44846	Monroe (Coshocton County)	
Mellett Mall (Part of Canton)	44708	Milan (Township)	44846	(Township)	43844
Melmore	44845	Milford (Butler County)		Monroe (Darke County)	
Melrose	45861	(Township)	45004	(Township)	45358
Melvin	45177	Milford (Clermont County)	45150	Monroe (Guernsey County)	
Memphis	45135	Milford (Defiance County)		(Township)	43749
Mendon	45862	(Township)	43526	Monroe (Harrison County)	
Mentor	44060*	Milford (Knox County)		(Township)	44695
	44061†	(Township)	43011	Monroe (Henry County)	
Mentor Headlands (Part of Mentor)	44060	Milford Center	43045	(Township)	43535
Mentor-on-the-Lake	44060	Mill (Township)	44683	Monroe (Holmes County) (Township)	44654
Mercer	45862	Millbrook	44691	Monroe (Knox County)	
Mercerville	45631	Millbury	43447	(Township)	43050
Merrill	43451	Mill Creek (Coshocton County) (Township)	44654	Monroe (Licking County) (Township)	43031
Mesopotamia	44439	Millcreek (Union County) (Township)	44040	Monroe (Logan County) (Township)	43360
Mesopotamia (Township)	44439	Mill Creek (Williams County)		Monroe (Madison County)	
Metamora	43540	(Township)	43501	(Township)	43140
Metham	43844	Milledgeville	43142	Monroe (Miami County)	
Methodist Theological School of Ohio	43015	Miller (Knox County) (Township)	43050	(Township)	45371
Metzger	45601	Miller (Lawrence County)	45623	Monroe (Muskingum County) (Township)	43762
Mexico	44882	Miller City	45864	Monroe (Perry County)	
Meyers Lake	44730	Millers	45383	(Township)	43730
Miami (Clermont County) (Township)	45147	Millersburg	44654	Monroe (Pickaway County)	
Miami (Greene County)		Millersport	43046	(Township)	43143
(Township)	45387	Miller Station	43976	Monroe (Preble County)	
Miami (Hamilton County)	45041	Millerstown	43072	(Township)	45338
Miami (Hamilton County) (Township)	45002	Millersville	43435	Monroe (Putnam County) (Township)	45831
Miami (Logan County) (Township)	43343	Millertown	43730	Monroe (Richland County)	
Miami (Montgomery County)		Millfield	45761	(Township)	44843
(Township)	45342	Milligan	43731	Monroe Center	44030
Miami Heights	45002	Millport (Columbiana County)	44427	Monroe Mills	43028
Miamisburg	45342*	Millport (Pickaway County)	43103	Monroeville (Huron County)	44847
	45343†	Millville (Butler County)	45013	Monroeville (Jefferson County)	43945
Miami Shores (Part of Moraine)	45439	Millville (Mahoning County)	44460	Monterey (Clermont County)	45103
Miamitown	45041	Millwood (Guernsey County) (Township)	43773	Monterey (Putnam County) (Township)	45833
Miami Township (Part of Centerville)	45475	Millwood (Knox County)	43028	Montezuma	45866
Miami University (Part of Oxford)	45056	Milton (Ashland County) (Township)	44805	Montgomery (Ashland County) (Township)	44805
Miami Valley Center Mall (Part of Piqua)	45356	Milton (Jackson County) (Township)	45692	Montgomery (Hamilton County)	45242
Miami Villa (Part of Huber Heights)	45424	Milton (Mahoning County) (Township)	44429	Montgomery (Marion County) (Township)	43332
Miamiville	45147	Milton (Wayne County) (Township)	44270	Montgomery (Wood County) (Township)	43466
Michael Manor	45371	Milton (Wood County) (Township)	43441	Montgomery Heights (Part of Montgomery)	45242
Mid City (Part of Dayton)	45402	Milton Center	43541	Monticello	45887
Middle Bass	43446	Miltonsburg	43793	Montpelier	43543
Middleboro	45152	Miltonville	45042	Montra	45302
Middlebourne	43773	Mineral	45766	Montrose	44333
Middlebranch	44652	Mineral City	44656	Montrose-Ghent	44333
Middleburg (Jefferson County)	43903	Mineral Ridge	44440	Montville (Geauga County)	44064
Middleburg (Logan County)	43336	Minersville	45769	Montville (Geauga County) (Township)	44064
Middleburg (Noble County)	43724	Minerva	44657	Montville (Medina County)	
Middleburg Heights	44130	Minerva Park	43229	(Township)	44256
Middlebury (Knox County) (Township)	43019	Mineyahta on-The-Bay	43440	Moorefield (Clark County)	
Middlebury (Van Wert County)	45832	Minford	45653	(Township)	45502
Middlefield	44062	Mingo	43047	Moorefield (Harrison County)	43907
Middlefield (Township)	44062	Mingo Junction	43938	Moorefield (Harrison County) (Township)	43907
Middle Point	45863	Minster	45865	Moores Fork	45107
Middleport	45760	Misco (Morgan County)	43731	Moores Junction	43731
Middleton (Columbiana County)	44408	Misco (Perry County)	43731	Mooresville	45601
Middleton (Columbiana County) (Township)	44455	Mishler	44260	Moraine	45439
Middleton (Jackson County)	45692	Mississinawa (Township)	45390	Moreland	44691
Middleton (Wood County) (Township)	43525	Mitiwanga	44839	Moreland Hills	44022
Middleton Corner	45385	Mizer Addition	43832	Morgan (Ashtabula County)	
Middletown (Butler County)	45042-44	Modest	45122	(Township)	44084
For specific Middletown Zip Codes call (513) 422-6316, or your local postmaster.		Modoc	45732	Morgan (Butler County) (Township)	45053
Middletown (Champaign County)	43009	Moffit Heights	44646	Morgan (Gallia County) (Township)	45686
Middletown (Crawford County)	44833	Moffitt	45816	Morgan (Knox County) (Township)	43050
Midland	45148	Mogadore	44260	Morgan (Morgan County) (Township)	43756
Midpark (Part of Parma Heights)	44130	Mohawk	43844	Morgan (Scioto County) (Township)	45648
Midtown (Part of Zanesville)	43701	Mohawk Lake	44883		
		Mohican (Township)	44840		
		Mohicanville	44840		
		Moline	43465		
		Momeneetown (Part of Oregon)	43616		
		Monclova	43542		
		Monclova (Township)	43542		
		Monclova Gardens (Part of Maumee)	43537		
		Monday Creek (Township)	43138		

* Area Zip Code   † Post Office Boxes

	ZIP
North Akron (Part of Akron)	44310
Northampton (Township)...	44221
North Auburn..............	44887
North Baltimore............	45872
North Bend	45052
North Benton (Mahoning County)...............	44449
North Benton (Portage County)...............	44449
North Berne	43130
North Bloomfield (Morrow County) (Township)	44833
North Bloomfield (Trumbull County)..............	44450
North Brewster (Part of Brewster)	44613
North Bristol..............	44402
Northbrook (Hamilton County)..............	45231
North Canton.............	44720
North Clippinger (Part of The Village of Indian Hill)	45243
North College Hill..........	45239
North Condit	43074
North Creek	45831
North Dayton (Darke County)..............	45390
North Dayton (Montgomery County)..............	45404
Northeast (Part of Columbus)..............	43231
North Eaton	44044
North Fairfield	44855
North Feesburg	45130
Northfield (Summit County)	44067
Northfield Center (Summit County) (Township)	44067
Northfield Center (Summit County)...............	44067
North Findlay.............	45840
North Fork Village	45601
Northgate	45251
North Georgetown.........	44665
North Greenfield...........	43358
North Hampton	45349
North Hill (Part of Akron) ...	44310
North Hills Estates	45224
North Houston............	45333
North Industry	44707
North Jackson	44451
North Kenova (Part of South Point).................	45680
North Kingsville..........	44068
Northland (Part of Columbus).............	43229
Northland Mall (Part of Columbus).............	43229
North Lawrence	44666
North Lewisburg	43060
North Liberty	44822
North Lima	44452
North Madison (Lake County)..............	44057
North Monroeville..........	44847
Northmoor	45315
North Moreland (Part of Portsmouth).............	45662
North Mount Vernon	43050
North Olmsted	44070
North Perry..............	44081
North Randall	44128
North Richmond	44003
Northridge (Clark County)	45502
Northridge (Montgomery County)..............	45414
North Ridgeville	44039
North Robinson	44856
North Royalton	44133
North Sagamore Heights...	45236
North Salem..............	43749
North Side (Part of Youngstown)............	44504
North Star	45350
North Towne Square Mall (Part of Toledo)	43612
North Uniontown	45133
Northup	45658
Northview	45322
Northwest (Franklin County)	43220
Northwest (Williams County) (Township).............	43518
Northwest Plaza (Part of Dayton)...............	45405
Northwood (Logan County)	44310
Northwood (Wood County)	43619
North Woodbury	44813
North Zanesville	43701
Norton (Delaware County)	43356
Norton (Summit County) ...	44203
Norwalk (Township)........	44857
Norwalk.................	44857

	ZIP
Norwich (Franklin County) (Township).............	43026
Norwich (Huron County) (Township).............	44890
Norwich (Muskingum County)...............	43767
Norwood (Hamilton County)	45212
Norwood (Washington County)...............	45750
Norwood Heights (Part of Cincinnati)	45212
Nottingham (Cuyahoga County)..............	44110
Nottingham (Harrison County) (Township)	43907
Nova...................	44859
Novelty	44072
Oakdale (Athens County)	45732
Oakdale (Montgomery County)...............	45429
Oakdale (Stark County)	44646
Oakfield (Perry County)	43731
Oakfield (Trumbull County)	44450
Oak Grove (Clark County)	45502
Oak Grove (Washington County)...............	45750
Oak Harbor	43449
Oak Hill	45656
Oakland (Butler County) ...	45050
Oakland (Clinton County)	45177
Oakland (Fairfield County)	43102
Oakland Park	43224
Oakley (Part of Cincinnati)	45209
Oakmont	43920
Oak Park	43907
Oak Run (Township).......	43143
Oak Shade	43567
Oakview	45805
Oakwood (Cuyahoga County)..............	44146
Oakwood (Montgomery County)..............	45419
Oakwood (Paulding County)	45873
Oberlin	44074
Oberlin Beach	44839
Obetz..................	43207
Oceola	44860
Oco	43950
O'Connor Landing	43310
Octa	43160
Ogden	45177
Ogontz	44814
Ohio (Clermont County) (Township).............	45157
Ohio (Gallia County) (Township).............	45623
Ohio (Monroe County) (Township).............	43931
Ohio City	45874
Ohio Furnace.............	45638
Ohio Reformatory for Women................	43040
Ohio Soldiers and Sailors Home................	44870
Ohio State Reformatory	44901
Ohio State University Lima Branch	45804
Okeana	45053
Okolona	43550
Old Fort................	44861
Old Gore	43138
Old Mill Creek	44212
Old Plymouth Heights......	45629
Old Straitsville	43766
Oldtown................	45385
Old Washington	43768
Old West End (Part of Toledo)	43610
Olena	44857
Olentangy...............	44820
Olive (Meigs County) (Township).............	45743
Olive (Noble County) (Township).............	43724
Olive Branch	45103
Olive Green (Delaware County)...............	43074
Olive Green (Noble County)	43724
Oliver (Township).........	45693
Olivesburg	44805
Olivett	43713
Olmsted (Township)	44138
Olmsted Falls	44138
Olszeski................	43917
Omega	45690
Oneida (Butler County)	45042
Oneida (Carroll County) ...	44644
Ontario	44862
Opperman	43732
Oran	45365
Orange (Ashland County) (Township).............	44805

	ZIP
Orange (Carroll County) (Township).............	44639
Orange (Coshocton County)	43832
Orange (Cuyahoga County)	44022
Orange (Delaware County) (Township).............	43021
Orange (Hancock County) (Township).............	45817
Orange (Meigs County) (Township).............	45723
Orange (Shelby County) (Township).............	45365
Orangeville	44453
Orbiston	45732
Orchard Beach	44089
Orchard Island	43331
Orchard Park Heights	44904
Oregon	43616
	43618
For specific Oregon Zip Codes call (419) 693-5033, or your local postmaster.	
Oregonia	45054
Oreville.................	43766
Orient	43146
Orient Correctional Institution	43146
Orland	45654
Orrville	44667
Orwell	44076
Orwell (Township)	44076
Osage	43964
Osgood	45351
Osnaburg (Township)......	44730
Ostrander	43061
Otsego	43762
Ottawa	45875
Ottawa (Township)	45875
Ottawa Hills	43606
Otterbein	45036
Ottokee	43567
Ottoville	45876
Otway	45657
Outville	43062
Overlook	45431
Overlook Court	43906
Overlook Hills	43952
Overlook Homes	45431
Overlook-Page Manor	45431
Overpeck	45055
Over The Rhine (Part of Cincinnati)	45210
Overton	44691
Owens Hill	43701
Owensville	45160
Oxford (Butler County)	45056
Oxford (Butler County) (Township).............	45056
Oxford (Coshocton County) (Township).............	43845
Oxford (Delaware County) (Township).............	43003
Oxford (Erie County) (Township).............	44870
Oxford (Guernsey County) (Township).............	43773
Oxford (Tuscarawas County) (Township)	43832
Ozark	43716
Padanaram..............	44003
Padua	45846
Page Manor	45431
Pagetown	43334
Pageville	45710
Painesville	44077
Painesville (Township)	44077
Painesville on the Lake	44077
Painesville Shopping Center (Part of Painesville)	44077
Paint (Fayette County) (Township).............	43106
Paint (Highland County) (Township).............	45612
Paint (Holmes County) (Township).............	44690
Paint (Madison County) (Township).............	43140
Paint (Ross County) (Township).............	45612
Paint (Wayne County) (Township).............	44659
Painters Creek	45304
Paintersville	45335
Paint Valley	44654
Palermo	44615
Palestine	45352
Palmer (Putnam County) (Township).............	45831
Palmer (Washington County) (Township)	43787
Palmyra (Knox County)	43019
Palmyra (Portage County)	44412

	ZIP
Palmyra (Portage County) (Township)	44412
Palos	45732
Pancoastburg	43160
Pandora	45877
Pansy	45107
Paradise	44406
Paradise Hill	44805
Paris (Portage County)	44266
Paris (Portage County) (Township)	44266
Paris (Stark County)	44669
Paris (Stark County) (Township)	44669
Paris (Union County) (Township)	43040
Parkdale (Hamilton County)	45240
Parkdale (Jefferson County)	43952
Parkertown	44824
Park Layne (Clark County)	45344
Park Layne (Montgomery County)	45431
Parkman	44080
Parkman (Township)	44080
Park Place (Part of Wyoming)	45215
Park Ridge Acres	45506
Parkview (Part of Fairview Park)	44126
Parkview Heights	45224
Parlett	43907
Parma	44129
Parma (Part of Cleveland)	44130
Parma Heights	44130
Parmatown Mall (Part of Parma)	44129
Parral	44622
Parrott	43160
Pasadena (Part of Kettering)	45429
Pasco	45365
Pataskala	43062
Patmos	44460
Patriot	45658
Patterson (Darke County) (Township)	45388
Patterson (Hardin County)	45843
Pattersonville	44657
Pattin Addition (Part of Marietta)	45750
Pattonville	45640
Paulding	45879
Paulding (Township)	45879
Paul Laurence Dunbar (Part of Dayton)	45417
Pavonia	44903
Pawnee	44254
Paxton (Township)	45612
Payne	45880
Peacock Acres	45502
Pearlbrook (Part of Cleveland)	44109
Pease (Township)	43935
Pebble (Township)	45690
Pedro	45659
Peebles	45660
Pee Pee (Township)	45690
Pekin (Carroll County)	44657
Pekin (Jefferson County)	43952
Pekin (Warren County)	45036
Pemberton	45353
Pemberville	43450
Penfield	44052
Penfield (Township)	44090
Peniel	45658
Peninsula	44264
Penn (Highland County) (Township)	45135
Penn (Morgan County) (Township)	43787
Pennsville	43770
Penn View	44003
Peoli	43832
Peoria (Butler County)	45056
Peoria (Union County)	43067
Pepper Pike	44124
Perintown	45150
Perkins (Township)	44870
Perry (Allen County) (Township)	45806
Perry (Ashland County) (Township)	44866
Perry (Brown County) (Township)	45118
Perry (Carroll County) (Township)	43988
Perry (Columbiana County) (Township)	44460
Perry (Coshocton County) (Township)	43843
Perry (Fayette County) (Township)	45135

	ZIP
Perry (Franklin County) (Township)	43017
Perry (Gallia County) (Township)	45658
Perry (Hocking County) (Township)	43135
Perry (Lake County)	44081
Perry (Lake County) (Township)	44081
Perry (Lawrence County) (Township)	45638
Perry (Licking County) (Township)	43055
Perry (Logan County) (Township)	43319
Perry (Monroe County) (Township)	43793
Perry (Montgomery County) (Township)	45309
Perry (Morrow County) (Township)	44904
Perry (Muskingum County) (Township)	43701
Perry (Pickaway County) (Township)	43145
Perry (Pike County) (Township)	45616
Perry (Putnam County) (Township)	45837
Perry (Richland County) (Township)	44813
Perry (Shelby County) (Township)	45353
Perry (Stark County) (Township)	44708
Perry (Tuscarawas County) (Township)	44699
Perry (Wood County) (Township)	44817
Perry Addition	45648
Perry Heights	44646
Perrysburg	43551*
	43552†
Perrysburg Heights	43551
Perrysville (Ashland County)	44864
Perrysville (Carroll County)	43988
Perryton	43822
Peru (Huron County)	44857
Peru (Huron County) (Township)	44847
Peru (Morrow County) (Township)	44334
Petersburg (Carroll County)	44615
Petersburg (Jackson County)	45640
Petersburg (Mahoning County)	44454
Petrea	45640
Petroleum	44438
Pettisville	43553
Pfeiffer Station	43326
Phalanx	44470
Pharisburg	43040
Phillippstown (Part of Columbus)	43201
Phillipsburg	45354
Philo	43771
Philothea	45828
Phoneton	45371
Pickaway (Township)	43113
Pickaway Correctional Institution	43146
Pickerington	43147
Pickrelltown	43357
Piedmont	43983
Pierce (Township)	45245
Pierpont	44082
Pierpont (Township)	44082
Pigeon Creek	44321
Pigeon Run	44646
Pike (Brown County) (Township)	45176
Pike (Clark County) (Township)	45502
Pike (Coshocton County) (Township)	43822
Pike (Fulton County) (Township)	43515
Pike (Knox County) (Township)	44822
Pike (Madison County) (Township)	43029
Pike (Perry County) (Township)	43764
Pike (Stark County) (Township)	44626
Piketon	45661
Pikeville	45331
Pine Grove	45638
Pinehurst	45750
Pine Valley (Part of Dillonvale)	43917

	ZIP
Piney Fork	43941
Pink	45630
Pinkerman	45682
Pioneer	43554
Piqua	45356
Piqua East Mall (Part of Piqua)	45356
Pisgah	45069
Pitchin	45502
Pitsburg	45358
Pitt (Township)	43323
Pittlime (Part of Norton)	44203
Pittsburgh Junction	43986
Pittsfield	44090
Pittsfield (Township)	44090
Placid Meadows	45238
Plain (Franklin County) (Township)	43081
Plain (Stark County) (Township)	44708
Plain (Wayne County) (Township)	44691
Plain (Wood County) (Township)	43402
Plain City	43064
Plainfield	43836
Plain View	43793
Plankton	44882
Planktown	44878
Plantation Acres	45224
Plants	45771
Plantsville	43728
Plattsburg	45368
Plattsville	45365
Playhouse Square (Part of Cleveland)	44115
Pleasant (Brown County) (Township)	45121
Pleasant (Clark County) (Township)	43010
Pleasant (Fairfield County) (Township)	43130
Pleasant (Franklin County) (Township)	43123
Pleasant (Hancock County) (Township)	45858
Pleasant (Hardin County) (Township)	43326
Pleasant (Henry County) (Township)	43527
Pleasant (Knox County) (Township)	43050
Pleasant (Logan County) (Township)	43318
Pleasant (Madison County) (Township)	43143
Pleasant (Marion County) (Township)	43302
Pleasant (Perry County) (Township)	43731
Pleasant (Putnam County) (Township)	45830
Pleasant (Seneca County) (Township)	44861
Pleasant (Van Wert County) (Township)	45891
Pleasant Bend	43548
Pleasant City	43772
Pleasant Corners	43123
Pleasant Grove (Belmont County)	43901
Pleasant Grove (Muskingum County)	43701
Pleasant Heights (Columbiana County)	43920
Pleasant Heights (Jefferson County)	43952
Pleasant Hill (Athens County)	45701
Pleasant Hill (Jefferson County)	43952
Pleasant Hill (Miami County)	45359
Pleasant Hills	45231
Pleasant Home	44287
Pleasant Lea	43130
Pleasant Plain	45162
Pleasant Ridge (Part of Cincinnati)	45213
Pleasant Run	45231
Pleasant Run Farms	45240
Pleasant Valley (Coshocton County)	43812
Pleasant Valley (Pike County)	45661
Pleasant Valley (Ross County)	45601
Pleasant Valley (Vinton County)	45601
Pleasant View (Fayette County)	43128
Pleasant View (Stark County)	44705

	ZIP
Pleasantville	43148
Plumwood	43140
Plymouth (Ashtabula County) (Township)	44004
Plymouth (Ashtabula County)	44004
Plymouth (Richland County)	44865
Plymouth (Richland County) (Township)	44865
Plymouth Center	44004
Poast Town	45042
Poetown	45130
Point (Part of Columbus)	43223
Point Isabel	45153
Point Place (Part of Toledo)	43611
Point Pleasant	45153
Point Rock	45710
Poland	44514
Poland (Township)	44514
Poland Center	44436
Polaris (Part of Columbus)	43240
Polk (Ashland County)	44866
Polk (Crawford County) (Township)	44833
Pomeroy	45769
Pond Run	45684
Poplargrove	45660
Portage (Hancock County) (Township)	45872
Portage (Ottawa County) (Township)	43452
Portage (Wood County)	43451
Portage (Wood County) (Township)	43451
Portage Lakes	44319
Port Clinton	43452
Porter (Delaware County) (Township)	43074
Porter (Gallia County)	45614
Porter (Scioto County) (Township)	45694
Porterfield	45714
Portersville	43730
Port Homer	43964
Port Jefferson	45360
Portland	45770
Portsmouth	45662-63
For specific Portsmouth Zip Codes call (614) 353-2070, or your local postmaster.	
Port Union	45015
Port Washington	43837
Port William	45164
Possum Woods	45506
Post Town	45042
Post Town Heights	45042
Potsdam	45361
Pottery Additon	43952
Powell	43065
Powellsville	45629
Powhatan Point	43942
Prairie (Franklin County) (Township)	43119
Prairie (Holmes County) (Township)	44633
Prairie Meadows	43812
Pratts Fork	45776
Prattsville	45651
Prentiss	45856
Preston Addition	45648
Price Hill (Part of Cincinnati)	45205
Pricetown (Highland County)	45133
Pricetown (Trumbull County)	44429
Pride	45601
Princeton	45015
Proctor	44266
Proctorville	45669
Prospect	43342
Prospect (Township)	43342
Prout	44870
Providence (Township)	43504
Provident	43950
Provincial Point	45244
Public Square (Part of Cleveland)	44114
Pulaski	43506
Pulaski (Township)	43506
Pulaskiville	43338
Pulse	45118
Pultney (Township)	43906
Puritas Park (Part of Cleveland)	44135
Purity	43071
Pusheta (Township)	45895
Put-in-Bay	43456
Put-in-Bay (Township)	43456
Putnam Place (Part of Marietta)	45750
Pymatuning Shores	44003
Pyrmont	45309
Pyro	45656

	ZIP
Quaker City	43773
Qualey	45724
Queen Acres	45013
Quincy	43343
Raccoon (Township)	45685
Racine	45771
Radcliff	45670
Radford Road	45701
Radio Heights	43920
Radnor	43066
Radnor (Township)	43066
Ragersville	44681
Rainsboro	45165
Ra-Mar Estates	45502
Ramsey	43917
Ranchwood	44870
Randall Park (Part of North Randall)	44128
Randolph (Montgomery County) (Township)	45322
Randolph (Portage County)	44265
Randolph (Portage County) (Township)	44265
Range	43143
Range (Township)	43143
Ransom	45381
Rarden	45671
Rarden (Township)	45671
Rathbone (Delaware County)	43015
Rathbone (Washington County)	45750
Rathbone Heights (Part of Marietta)	45750
Ravenna	44266
Ravenna (Township)	44266
Ravenna Army Ammunition Plant	44266
Rawson	45881
Ray	45672
Rayland	43943
Raymond	43067
Rays Corners	44047
Reading (Columbiana County)	44634
Reading (Hamilton County)	45215
Reading (Perry County) (Township)	43783
Recovery (Township)	45846
Red Bank (Part of Fairfax)	45227
Redbird	44057
Redbush	45742
Red Coach Farm (Part of Centerville)	45429
Redfield	43764
Red Fox	44240
Redhaw	44866
Red Lion	45005
Redoak	45167
Red River	45308
Redtown	45732
Reed (Township)	44807
Reedsburg	44691
Reedsmills	43910
Reedsville	45772
Reedtown	44807
Reedurban	44710
Reese Station	43207
Reesville	45166
Reform	43055
Rehoboth	43764
Reily	45056
Reily (Township)	45056
Reinersville	43756
Reminderville	44202
Remington	45140
Remsen Corners	44256
Rendville	43730
Reno	45773
Reno Beach	43412
Rensselaer Park	45216
Republic	44867
Resaca	43140
Residence Park (Part of Dayton)	45417
Revenge	43130
Reynoldsburg	43068
Reynolds Corner (Part of Toledo)	43615
	43617
	43635
For specific Reynolds Corner Zip Codes call (419) 841-1375, or your local postmaster.	
Rialto	45069
Rice (Putnam County)	45831
Rice (Sandusky County) (Township)	43420
Riceland	44667
Richfield (Henry County) (Township)	43516

	ZIP
Richfield (Lucas County) (Township)	43504
Richfield (Summit County)	44286
Richfield (Summit County) (Township)	44286
Richfield Center	43504
Richfield Heights (Part of Richfield)	44286
Rich Hill (Knox County)	43011
Rich Hill (Muskingum County) (Township)	43727
Richland (Allen County) (Township)	45817
Richland (Belmont County) (Township)	43950
Richland (Clinton County) (Township)	45169
Richland (Darke County) (Township)	45380
Richland (Defiance County) (Township)	43512
Richland (Fairfield County) (Township)	43150
Richland (Guernsey County) (Township)	43780
Richland (Holmes County) (Township)	44628
Richland (Logan County) (Township)	43310
Richland (Marion County) (Township)	43302
Richland (Montgomery County)	45431
Richland (Vinton County) (Township)	45651
Richland (Wyandot County) (Township)	43359
Richland Mall (Part of Ontario)	44906
Richmond (Ashtabula County) (Township)	44032
Richmond (Huron County) (Township)	44890
Richmond (Jefferson County)	43944
Richmond Center	44003
Richmond Dale	45673
Richmond Heights	44143
Richmond Mall (Part of Richmond Heights)	44143
Richville	44706
Richwood	43344
Rickard Acres	45005
Rickenbacker Air Force Base	43217
Ridge (Van Wert County) (Township)	45891
Ridge (Wyandot County) (Township)	43316
Ridgefield (Township)	44847
Ridgeland	45640
Ridgeton	44820
Ridgeville (Henry County) (Township)	43555
Ridgeville (Warren County)	45036
Ridgeville Corners	43555
Ridgeway	43345
Ridgewood (Allen County)	43701
Ridgewood (Muskingum County)	43821
Ridgewood Heights	45427
Rigrish	45662
Riley (Putnam County) (Township)	45877
Riley (Sandusky County) (Township)	43420
Rimer	45830
Rinard Mills	45734
Ringgold (Morgan County)	43758
Ringgold (Pickaway County)	43113
Rio Grande	45674
Ripley (Brown County)	45167
Ripley (Holmes County) (Township)	44676
Ripley (Huron County) (Township)	44837
Risingsun	43457
Rittman	44270
River Corners	44275
Riverdale	45661
Riveredge (Township)	44135
Riveredge	44135
Riverlea	43085
Riverside (Montgomery County)	45424
Riverside (Shelby County)	45365
Riverside Park	44683
River Styx	44256
Riverview (Belmont County)	43906
Riverview (Washington County)	45750
Rix Mills	43762

	ZIP		ZIP		ZIP
Roachester	45152	Rumley (Shelby County)	45302	Salt Creek (Hocking County) (Township)	43135
Roads	45640	Rural	45120		
Roaming Rock Shores	44085	Ruraldale	43720	Salt Creek (Holmes County) (Township)	44660
Roaming Shores	44085	Rush (Champaign County) (Township)	43084		
Roanoke	44683			Salt Creek (Muskingum County) (Township)	43727
Robertsville	44670	Rush (Scioto County) (Township)	45652		
Robins	43723			Salt Creek (Pickaway County) (Township)	43113
Robtown	43103	Rush (Tuscarawas County) (Township)	44683		
Robyville	43901			Salt Creek (Wayne County) (Township)	44627
Rochester	44090	Rush Creek (Fairfield County) (Township)	43107		
Rochester (Township)	44090			Saltillo	43777
Rochester Place (Part of Northwood)	43618	Rushcreek (Logan County) (Township)	43347	Salt Lick (Township)	43782
				Salt Rock (Township)	43337
Rockbridge	43149	Rushmore	45844	Salt Run	43943
Rock Camp (Columbiana County)	44432	Rush Run	43943	Samantha	45135
		Rushsylvania	43347	Sand Beach	43449
Rock Camp (Lawrence County)	45675	Rushtown	45652	Sand Hill (Erie County)	44870
		Rushville	43150	Sand Hill (Scioto County)	45694
Rock Creek	44084	Russell (Geauga County) (Township)	44072	Sand Hill (Washington County)	45773
Rockdale	45015				
Rockford	45882	Russell (Highland County)	45133	Sand Ridge	45761
Rockhill	43977	Russell Center	44072	Sandrun	45764
Rockland (Part of Belpre)	45714	Russell Heights	43968	Sandusky (Erie County)	44870
Rock Mills	43160	Russells	43701		44871†
Rockport	45830	Russells Point	43348	Sandusky (Crawford County) (Township)	44887
Rock Way	45504	Russellville	45168		
Rockwood (Erie County)	44824	Russia (Lorain County) (Township)	44074	Sandusky (Richland County) (Township)	44827
Rockwood (Lawrence County)	45619				
		Russia (Shelby County)	45363	Sandusky (Sandusky County) (Township)	43420
Rocky Fall Estates	45133	Rustic Hills	44256		
Rockyhill	45640	Rutland	45775	Sandusky South	44870
Rocky Point	45502	Rutland (Township)	45775	Sandy (Stark County) (Township)	44688
Rocky Ridge	43458	Rye Beach (Part of Huron)	44839		
Rocky River	44116	Sabina	45169	Sandy (Tuscarawas County) (Township)	44656
Rodney	45631	Sagamore Hills	44067		
Rogers	44455	Sagamore Hills (Township)	44067	Sandy Beach	45885
Rokeby Lock	43756	Sahara Sands	44646	Sandy Springs	45684
Rolandus	45771	St. Albans (Township)	43062	Sandyville	44671
Rollersville	43431	St. Anthony	45846	San Margherita	43204
Rolling Acres Mall (Part of Akron)	44322	St. Bernard	45217	Santa Fe	45895
		St. Charles	45013	Santoy	43730
Rolling Mill Park	45044	St. Clair (Butler County) (Township)	45011	Sarahsville	43779
Rome (Ashtabula County)	44085			Sardinia	45171
Rome (Ashtabula County) (Township)	44085	St. Clair (Columbia County) (Township)	43920	Sardis	43946
				Savannah	44874
Rome (Athens County) (Township)	45723	St. Clairsville	43950	Saville Estates	45431
		St. Henry	45883	Savona	45331
Rome (Lawrence County)	45669	St. Joe	43906	Sawyerwood	44312
Rome (Lawrence County) (Township)	45669	St. Johns	45884	Saybrook	44004
		St. Joseph (Mercer County)	45846	Saybrook (Township)	44004
Rome (Richland County)	44878	St. Joseph (Portage County)	44201	Saybrook-on-the-Lake	44004
Rome Station	44085			Sayler Park (Part of Cincinnati)	45233
Romohr Acres	45244	St. Joseph (Williams County) (Township)	43517		
Rootstown (Portage County)	44272			Sayre	43731
Rootstown (Portage County) (Township)	44272	St. Louisville	43071	Scenic Hills	43162
		St. Martin	45118	Schauers Acres	45341
Rose (Township)	44643	St. Marys	45885	Schley	45768
Rosedale	43029	St. Marys (Township)	45885	Schoenbrunn	44663
Rose Farm	43731	St. Paris	43072	Schooleys	45601
Rose Heights (Part of Steubenville)	43952	St. Pauls	43103	Schrader	45601
		St. Peters	45846	Schumm	45898
Rose Hill	45348	St. Rosa	45886	Scio	43988
Roseland	44906	St. Sebastian	45826	Scioto (Delaware County) (Township)	43061
Roselawn (Part of Cincinnati)	45237	St. Stephens	44807		
		St. Wendelin	45883	Scioto (Jackson County) (Township)	45640
Roselms	45849	Salem (Auglaize County) (Township)	45887		
Rosemont	44451			Scioto (Pickaway County) (Township)	43103
Rosemount	45662	Salem (Champaign County) (Township)	43078		
Roseville	43777			Scioto (Pike County) (Township)	45687
Rosewood	43070	Salem (Columbiana County)	44460		
Roslyn (Part of Kettering)	45429	Salem (Columbiana County) (Township)	44431	Scioto (Ross County) (Township)	45601
Ross	45061			Sciotodale	45662
Ross (Butler County) (Township)	45061	Salem (Highland County) (Township)	45133	Scioto Furnace	45677
				Sciotoville (Part of Portsmouth)	45662
Ross (Greene County) (Township)	43153	Salem (Jefferson County) (Township)	43944		
				Scipio (Butler County)	45053
Ross (Jefferson County) (Township)	43944	Salem (Meigs County) (Township)	45741	Scipio (Meigs County) (Township)	45710
Rossburg	45362	Salem (Monroe County) (Township)	43915	Scipio (Seneca County) (Township)	44867
Rossford	43460				
Rossmoyne	45236	Salem (Muskingum County) (Township)	43802	Scotch Ridge	43450
Rossville (Part of Hamilton)	45013			Scott (Adams County) (Township)	45679
Roswell	44663	Salem (Ottawa County) (Township)	43449		
Round Bottom	43915			Scott (Brown County) (Township)	45121
Roundhead	43346	Salem (Shelby County) (Township)	45365		
Roundhead (Township)	43346			Scott (Marion County) (Township)	43302
Rousculp	45806	Salem (Tuscarawas County) (Township)	43832		
Rowsburg	44866			Scott (Sandusky County) (Township)	43435
Roxabell	45628	Salem (Warren County) (Township)	45152		
Roxanna	45068			Scott (Van Wert County)	45886
Roxbury	43787	Salem (Washington County) (Township)	45745	Scottown	45678
Royalton (Fairfield County)	43130			Scotts Crossing	45833
Royalton (Fulton County) (Township)	43533	Salem (Wyandot County) (Township)	43351	Scotty's Beauty Beach	45822
				Scroggsfield	44615
Royersville	45638	Salem Center	45741	Scrub Ridge	45616
Rubyville	45662	Salem Heights	44460	Seal (Pike County) (Township)	45661
Rudolph	43462	Salesville	43778		
Ruggles	44837	Saline (Township)	43932	Seal (Wyandot County)	44849
Ruggles (Township)	44851	Salineville	43945	Seaman	45679
Ruggles Beach	44839	Salisbury (Township)	45769	Seasons Four	45140
Rumley (Harrison County) (Township)	43986	Saltair	45106	Sebring	44672

	ZIP
Secedar Corners	44425
Sedalia	43151
Sedamsville (Part of Cincinnati)	45238
Seilcrest Acres	45140
Sellers Point	43046
Selma	45368
Seneca (Monroe County) (Township)	43754
Seneca (Noble County) (Township)	43779
Seneca (Seneca County) (Township)	44853
Senecaville	43780
Senior	45152
Sentinel	44032
Seven Hills (Cuyahoga County)	44131
Seven Hills (Hamilton County)	45231
Seven Mile	45062
Seventeen	44629
Severance Center (Part of Cleveland Heights)	44118
Seville	44273
Seward	43533
Sewellsville	43713
Shade	45776
Shademore	45244
Shadeville	43137
Shady Bend	43832
Shady Glen	43964
Shady Grove	45324
Shadyside (Belmont County)	43947
Shadyside (Columbiana County)	43920
Shaker Crossing (Part of Kettering)	45429
Shaker Heights	44120
Shalersville	44255
Shalersville (Township)	44266
Shandon (Butler County)	45063
Shane	43944
Shanesville (Part of Sugarcreek)	44681
Shannon	43821
Sharon (Franklin County) (Township)	43085
Sharon (Medina County) (Township)	44274
Sharon (Noble County)	43724
Sharon (Noble County) (Township)	43724
Sharon (Richland County) (Township)	44875
Sharon Center	44274
Sharon Hills	43085
Sharon Park (Allen County)	45805
Sharon Park (Butler County)	45013
Sharonville	45241*
	45262†
Sharon West	44438
Sharpeye	45331
Sharpsburg	45777
Shartz Road	45005
Shauck	43349
Shawnee (Allen County) (Township)	45805
Shawnee (Perry County)	43782
Shawnee Hills (Delaware County)	43065
Shawnee Hills (Greene County)	45335
Shawnee Meadows	45806
Shawtown	45858
Shawville (Part of North Ridgeville)	44035
Shay	45767
Sheffield (Ashtabula County) (Township)	44048
Sheffield (Lorain County) (Township)	44054
Sheffield (Lorain County)	44054
Sheffield Lake	44054
Shelby	44875
Shelby Junction (Part of Shelby)	44875
Shell Beach	43076
Shenandoah	44837
Shepard (Part of Columbus)	43219
Shepherdstown	43950
Sheridan	45680
Sherman (Huron County) (Township)	44847
Sherman (Richland County)	44906
Sherman (Summit County)	44203
Sherritts	45688
Sherrodsville	44675
Sherwood (Defiance County)	43556

	ZIP
Sherwood (Hamilton County)	45230
Sherwood Park	45805
Shillings Mill	44429
Shiloh (Clermont County)	45122
Shiloh (Montgomery County)	45415
Shiloh (Richland County)	44878
Shinrock	44839
Shore (Part of Euclid)	44123
Shoregate Shopping Center (Part of Willowick)	44095
Short Creek (Township)	43901
Short Creek	43989
Shreve	44676
Sidney	45365
Signal	44432
Silica	43560
Silver Creek (Greene County) (Township)	45335
Silver Creek (Medina County)	44281
Silver Lake	44221
Silverton	45236
Simons	44093
Singing Hills	45449
Sinking Spring	45172
Sitka	45750
Six Corners	43526
Skyline Acres	45231
Skypark	44281
Skyview Acres	43968
Slabtown	45801
Slate Mills	45601
Slaters	43724
Sligo	45177
Slocums	45662
Smith (Belmont County) (Township)	43718
Smith (Mahoning County) (Township)	44672
Smith Corners	44515
Smithfield	43948
Smithfield (Township)	43948
Smithfield (Station)	43943
Smithville (Wayne County)	44677
Smithville (Wyandot County)	43351
Smyrna	43973
Snodes	44609
Snowville	45710
Snyder Terrace (Part of Springfield)	45504
Snyderville	45502
Soaptown	44440
Socialville	45050
Soldiers Home	44870
Solon	44139
Somerdale	44678
Somerford (Township)	43044
Somers (Township)	45311
Somerset (Belmont County) (Township)	43713
Somerset (Perry County)	43783
Somerton	43713
Somerville	45064
Sonora	43701
South Amherst	44001
South Arlington (Part of Akron)	44306
South Bay	43019
South Bloomfield (Morrow County) (Township)	43050
South Bloomfield (Pickaway County)	43103
South Bloomingville	43152
South Boy	43019
Southbrook	45409
South Brooklyn (Part of Cleveland)	44109
South Canal	44444
South Charleston	45368
South Condit	43074
Southdale (Part of Kettering)	45429
Southeastern Coporational Institution	43130
Southern Hills (Part of Kettering)	45409
Southern Knoll (Part of Oxford)	45056
Southern Ohio Correctional Facility	45648
Southern Park Mall	44512
South Euclid	44121
South Excello	45042
Southfield Park (Part of Columbus)	43201
Southgate (Part of Springfield)	45506
Southgate Acres	44870
Southgate Shopping Center (Part of Newark)	43056

	ZIP
Southgate U.S.A. (Part of Maple Heights)	44137
South Highlands (Part of Middletown)	45042
South Hill Park	43528
Southington (Township)	44470
Southington	44470
South Kingman	45177
Southland Shopping Center (Cuyahoga County)	44130
Southland Shopping Center (Lucas County)	43614
South Lebanon	45065
South Logan (Part of Logan)	43138
South Lorain (Part of Lorain)	44055
South Madison	44057
South Middletown	45044
South Milford (Part of Milford)	45150
South Moor Shores	45885
South Mount Vernon	43050
South Newbury	44021
South Olive	43724
South Park (Allen County)	45804
South Park (Cuyahoga County)	44131
South Park (Wyandot County)	43351
South Perry	43135
South Plymouth	43160
South Point	45680
Southridge	45505
South Russell	44022
South Salem	45681
South Shore Acres	45885
South Shore Park (Part of Oregon)	43618
South Side (Mahoning County)	44507
South Side (Tuscarawas County)	44663
South Solon	43153
South Vienna	45369
South Webster	45682
Southwest (Part of Mansfield)	44907
South West Hubbard	44425
Southwood	45805
South Woodbury	43334
Southworth	45833
Southwyck Shopping Center (Part of Toledo)	43614
South Zanesville	43701
Spargursville	45612
Sparta	43350
Speaker's Addition	43952
Speidel	43719
Spencer (Allen County) (Township)	45887
Spencer (Guernsey County) (Township)	43732
Spencer (Lucas County) (Township)	43528
Spencer (Medina County)	44275
Spencer (Medina County) (Township)	44275
Spencerville	45887
Spokane	44402
Spreading Oaks	45701
Spreng	44840
Sprigg (Township)	45144
Springboro	45066
Springbrook	43464
Springcreek (Township)	45356
Springdale	45246
Springfield (Clark County)	45501-06
For specific Springfield Zip Codes call (513) 323-6496, or your local postmaster.	
Springfield (Clark County) (Township)	45505
Springfield (Gallia County) (Township)	45614
Springfield (Hamilton County) (Township)	45239
Springfield (Jefferson County) (Township)	43903
Springfield (Lucas County) (Township)	43528
Springfield (Mahoning County) (Township)	44442
Springfield (Muskingum County) (Township)	43701
Springfield (Richland County) (Township)	44906
Springfield (Ross County) (Township)	45601
Springfield (Summit County) (Township)	44312
Springfield (Williams County) (Township)	43557

	ZIP		ZIP		ZIP
Springhills	43318	Sugar Creek (Putnam		Tarlton	43156
Spring Meadows	45231	County) (Township)	45830	Tate (Township)	45106
Spring Mill	44903	Sugar Creek (Stark County)		Tatmans	43730
Spring Mountain	43844	(Township)	44662	Tawawa	45365
Springvale	45140	Sugarcreek (Tuscarawas		Taylor (Franklin County)	43230
Spring Valley (Greene		County)	44681	Taylor (Union County)	
County)	45370	Sugar Creek (Tuscarawas		(Township)	43344
Spring Valley (Greene		County) (Township)	44681	Taylor Creek (Township)	43326
County) (Township)	45370	Sugar Creek (Wayne		Taylorsburg	45315
Spring Valley (Lorain		County) (Township)	44618	Taylors Creek	45239
County)	44035	Sugar Grove (Crawford		Taylorsville	45133
Spring Valley (Lucas		County)	44820	Taylortown (Jefferson	
County)	43528	Sugar Grove (Fairfield		County)	43964
Springville (Seneca County)	43316	County)	43155	Taylortown (Richland	
Springville (Wayne County)	44676	Sugar Grove (Jefferson		County)	44875
Springwood	45056	County)	43964	Tedrow	43567
Squirrel Town	45684	Sugar Grove (Miami		Teegarden	44432
Stafford	43786	County)	45318	Temperanceville	43713
Standardsburg	44847	Sugar Grove (Scioto		Ten Hills	45805
Standley	43527	County)	45663	Tennyson	45661
Stanleyville	45788	Sugar Grove Hill	45506	Terrace Park	45174
Stanwood	44662	Sugar Ridge	43402	Terre Haute	43078
Starbucktown	45177	Sugar Tree Ridge	45133	Terry Acres	45324
Starlight Plaza (Part of		Sugar Valley	45320	Texas (Crawford County)	
Sylvania)	43560	Sullivan	44880	(Township)	44882
Starr (Township)	45764	Sullivan (Township)	44880	Texas (Henry County)	43532
Starr	45654	Sulphurgrove (Part of Huber		Thackery	43078
Starrs Corners	44406	Heights)	45424	Thatcher	43113
State Road (Part of		Sulphur Springs (Crawford		The Avenue	44438
Cuyahoga Falls)	44223	County)	44881	The Bend	43512
Staunton (Fayette County)	43160	Sulphur Springs (Perry		The Eastern	43908
Staunton (Miami County)	45373	County)	43782	Thelma City	44601
Staunton (Miami County)		Summerfield	43788	The Plains	45780
(Township)	45373	Summerford	43140	The Village of Indian Hill	45243
Steam Corners	44904	Summerside (Clermont		Thompson (Delaware	
Steinersville	43942	County)	45244	County) (Township)	43066
Stella	45622	Summerside Estates	45244	Thompson (Geauga	
Stelvideo	45331	Summersville	43067	County)	44086
Sterling (Brown County)		Summit (Hamilton County)	45238	Thompson (Geauga	
(Township)	45154	Summit (Monroe County)		County) (Township)	44086
Sterling (Wayne County)	44276	(Township)	43754	Thompson (Seneca County)	
Sterling Heights	45005	Summit (Ross County)	45601	(Township)	44828
Steuben	44847	Summit (Trumbull County)	44420	Thorn (Township)	43076
Steubenville (Township)	43952	Summithill	45601	Thornville (Perry County)	43076
Steubenville	43952	Summit Mall (Part of		Thorny Acres	45042
Stewart	45778	Fairlawn)	44333	Three Locks	45601
Stewartsville	43960	Summit Station	43073	Thrifton	45123
Stillwater	44679	Summitville	43962	Thurman	45685
Stillwell	44637	Sumner	45720	Thurston	43157
Stiversville	45770	Sunbury (Delaware County)	43074	Tiffany Acres	45502
Stock (Harrison County)		Sunbury (Montgomery		Tiffin (Adams County)	
(Township)	43988	County)	45327	(Township)	45693
Stock (Noble County)		Sundale	43767	Tiffin (Defiance County)	
(Township)	43724	Sunfish (Township)	45661	(Township)	43512
Stockdale	45683	Sunny Acres	43952	Tiffin (Seneca County)	44883
Stockham	45694	Sunnyland	45502	Tiltonsville	43963
Stockport	43787	Sunny Meade	43725	Timberlake	44094
Stockton (Part of Fairfield)	45014	Sunnyside Beach (Part of		Timberview	43040
Stock Yards (Part of		Vermilion)	44089	Tinny	43435
Cincinnati)	45225	Sunsbury (Township)	43716	Tipp City	45371
Stokes (Logan County)		Sunset Beach	44429	Tippecanoe	44699
(Township)	43331	Sunset Heights	43912	Tipton	45851
Stokes (Madison County)		Sunset Point	44077	Tiro	44887
(Township)	43153	Sunshine	45684	Tiverton	43006
Stone	43720	Sunshine Park	43952	Tiverton (Township)	43006
Stone Creek	43840	Sun Valley Estates	45505	Toboso	43055
Stonelick (Township)	45103	Superior (Township)	45543	Tod (Township)	44882
Stonelick	45103	Surrey Hill	44484	Todds	43728
Stony Lake	44615	Sutton (Township)	45771	Toledo	43601-15
Stony Prairie	43420	Swan (Township)	45622		43617
Stony Ridge	43463	Swan Creek (Township)	43558		43620-99
Stonyrill	45005	Swanders	45369	For specific Toledo Zip Codes call
Storms	45612	Swanktown	45309	(419) 245-6811, or your local
Stout	45684	Swanton (Fulton County)	43558	postmaster.
Stoutsville	43154	Swanton (Lucas County)		Toledo Dock (Part of	
Stovertown	43701	(Township)	43558	Oregon)	43618
Stow	44224	Swickards Additions	43952	Toledo Great Eastern	
Strasburg	44680	Swifton Commons (Part of		Shopping Center (Part of	
Stratford	43015	Cincinnati)	45237	Northwood)	43616
Stratton	43961	Switzerland (Township)	45543	Toledo Miracle Mile	
Streetsboro	44241	Sybene	45680	Shopping Center (Part of	
Stringtown (Athens County)	45701	Sycamore (Hamilton		Toledo)	43613
Stringtown (Brown County)	45167	County) (Township)	45242	Tom Corwin	45692
Stringtown (Clermont		Sycamore (Wyandot		Tomlison Addition	45648
County)	45120	County)	44882	Tontogany	43565
Stringtown (Muskingum		Sycamore (Wyandot		Torch	45781
County)	43701	County) (Township)	44882	Toronto	43964
Stringtown (Perry County)	43731	Sycamore Valley	43789	Town and Country Estates	45429
Strongs Ridge	44811	Sychar Road	43050	Town and Country	
Strongsville	44136	Sylvania (Township)	43560	Shopping Center (Part of	
Struthers	44471	Sylvania	43560	Whitehall)	43213
Stryker	43557	Symmes (Butler County)	45014	Townsend (Huron County)	
Stuart Manor	43952	Symmes (Hamilton County)		(Township)	44826
Suffield (Township)	44260	(Township)	45242	Townsend (Sandusky	
Suffield	44260	Symmes (Lawrence County)		County) (Township)	43464
Sugar Bush Knolls	44240	(Township)	45688	Townview	45427
Sugar Creek (Allen County)		Syracuse	45779	Townwood	45856
(Township)	45807	Taborville	44022	Tradersville	43044
Sugar Creek (Athens		Tacoma	43713	Trail	44624
County)	45701	Taft	45236	Trail Run	43946
Sugar Creek (Greene		Tallmadge	44278	Tranquility	45679
County) (Township)	45305	Tama	45822	Traschel	43302

	ZIP		ZIP		ZIP
Trebein (Part of		Union (Highland County)		Valley View (Scioto County)	45662
Beavercreek)	45434	(Township)	45133	Valley View Estates	44403
Tremont City	45372	Union (Knox County)		Valley View Heights	45244
Trenton (Butler County)	45067	(Township)	43014	Valley View Village	43701
Trenton (Delaware County)		Union (Lawrence County)		Valleywood (Part of	
(Township)	43021	(Township)	45619	Beavercreek)	45430
Triadelphia	43758	Union (Licking County)		Vanatta	43055
Tri-County Mall (Part of		(Township)	43025	Van Buren (Darke County)	
Springdale)	45246	Union (Logan County)		(Township)	45304
Trimble	45782	(Township)	43311	Van Buren (Hancock	
Trimble (Township)	45782	Union (Madison County)		County)	45889
Trinway	43842	(Township)	43140	Van Buren (Hancock	
Tri-Village (Part of		Union (Mercer County)		County) (Township)	45897
Columbus)	43212	(Township)	45862	Vanburen (Licking County)	43055
Trotwood	45426	Union (Miami County)		Van Buren (Putnam County)	
Trowbridge	43432	(Township)	45383	(Township)	45856
Troy (Ashland County)		Union (Montgomery County)	45322	Van Buren (Shelby County)	
(Township)	44859	Union (Morgan County)		(Township)	45336
Troy (Athens County)		(Township)	43758	Vandalia	45377
(Township)	45723	Union (Muskingum County)		Vanlue	45890
Troy (Delaware County)		(Township)	43762	Van Wert	45891
(Township)	43015	Union (Pike County)		Vaughan (Part of Evendale)	45241
Troy (Geauga County)		(Township)	45648	Vaughnsville	45893
(Township)	44021	Union (Putnam County)		Vega	45685
Troy (Miami County)	45373	(Township)	45844	Venedocia	45894
Troy (Morrow County)		Union (Ross County)		Venice (Erie County)	44870
(Township)	44901	(Township)	45628	Venice (Seneca County)	
Troy (Richland County)		Union (Scioto County)		(Township)	44807
(Township)	44904	(Township)	45652	Venice Heights	44484
Troy (Wood County)		Union (Tuscarawas County)		Vera Cruz	45118
(Township)	43443	(Township)	44621	Vermilion	44089
Truetown	45761	Union (Union County)		Vermilion (Township)	44089
Trumbull	44041	(Township)	43045	Vermilion-on-the-Lake (Part	
Trumbull (Township)	44041	Union (Van Wert County)		of Vermilion)	44089
Truro	43068	(Township)	45891	Vermillion (Township)	44805
Truro (Township)	43068	Union (Warren County)		Vernon (Clinton County)	
Tuckaho	44003	(Township)	45036	(Township)	45113
Tucson	45601	Union City	45390	Vernon (Crawford County)	
Tully (Marion County)		Union Furnace	43158	(Township)	44827
(Township)	43314	Union Landing Siding	45638	Vernon (Lawrence County)	45659
Tully (Van Wert County)		Union Plains	45154	Vernon (Richland County)	44875
(Township)	45832	Unionport	43966	Vernon (Scioto County)	
Tunnel	45750	Union Station	43025	(Township)	45694
Tunnel Hill	43844	Uniontown (Belmont		Vernon (Trumbull County)	44428
Tuppers Plains	45783	County)	43950	Vernon (Trumbull County)	
Turnpike Interchange	44444	Uniontown (Stark County)	44685	(Township)	44428
Turpin Hills	45244	Unionvale	43907	Vernon Heights (Part of	
Turtle Creek (Shelby		Unionville (Ashtabula		Marion)	43302
County) (Township)	45365	County)	44088	Verona	45378
Turtle Creek (Warren		Unionville (Morgan County)	43756	Versailles	45380
County) (Township)	45036	Unionville (Washington		Vesuvius	45659
Tuscalum (Part of		County)	45750	Veterans Administration	
Cincinnati)	45226	Unionville Center	43077	(Montgomery County)	45428
Tuscarawas (Coshocton		Uniopolis	45888	Veterans Administration	
County) (Township)	43812	Unity (Adams County)	45693	Medical Center (Ross	
Tuscarawas (Stark County)		Unity (Columbiana County)	44413	County)	45601
(Township)	44646	Unity (Columbiana County)		Veto	45714
Tuscarawas (Tuscarawas		(Township)	44413	Vickery	43464
County)	44682	University (Part of		Vicksville	45732
Twain	44212	Columbus)	43210	Vienna	44473
Twenty Mile Stand	45140	University Center (Part of		Vienna (Township)	44473
Twightwee	45140	Cleveland)	44106	Vienna Center	44473
Twin (Darke County)		University Heights (Allen		Vigo	45601
(Township)	45304	County)	45804	Viking Village	45244
Twin (Preble County)		University Heights		Villa	45503
(Township)	45381	(Cuyahoga County)	44118	Villa Nova	45885
Twin (Ross County)		University View	43212	Vincent (Lorain County)	44035
(Township)	45617	Upland Heights	43943	Vincent (Washington	
Twin Lakes (Allen County)	45804	Upper (Township)	45645	County)	45784
Twin Lakes (Portage		Upper Arlington (Butler		Vinton	45686
County)	44240	County)	45042	Vinton (Township)	45670
Twinsburg	44087	Upper Arlington (Franklin		Violet (Township)	43147
Twinsburg (Township)	44087	County)	43221	Virginia (Township)	43811
Twinsburg Heights	44087	Upper Five Mile	45154	Vo-Ash Lake	44615
Twin Valley	45662	Upper Fox Hollow	45502	Volunteer Bay	44089
Two Hundred Ten Row	45701	Upper Lowell	45744	Vore Ridge	45780
Tymochtee (Township)	44882	Upper Sandusky	43351	Wabash (Darke County)	
Tymochtee	43351	Urbana	43078	(Township)	45380
Tyndall	43812	Urbana (Township)	43078	Wabash (Mercer County)	45822
Uhrichsville	44683	Urbancrest	43123	Wacker Heights	43130
Union (Athens County)	45766	Utica (Licking County)	43080	Waco	44707
Union (Auglaize County)		Utica (Warren County)	45036	Wade	45767
(Township)	45895	Utopia	45121	Wadsworth	44281
Union (Belmont County)		Valley (Columbiana County)	44460	Wadsworth (Township)	44281
(Township)	43759	Valley (Guernsey County)		Waggoner Place	43551
Union (Brown County)		(Township)	43772	Wagram	43062
(Township)	45167	Valley (Scioto County)		Wahlsburg	45121
Union (Butler County)		(Township)	45648	Wainwright (Jackson	
(Township)	45069	Valley City	44280	County)	45692
Union (Carroll County)		Valley City Station	44280	Wainwright (Tuscarawas	
(Township)	44615	Valley Crossing (Part of		County)	44663
Union (Champaign County)		Columbus)	43207	Waite Hill	44094
(Township)	43009	Valleydale (Part of		Wakatomika	43821
Union (Clermont County)		Cincinnati)	45216	Wakefield (Darke County)	45331
(Township)	45245	Valley Forge	44212	Wakefield (Pike County)	45687
Union (Clinton County)		Valley Glen	43938	Wakeman	44889
(Township)	45177	Valley Hi	43360	Wakeman (Township)	44889
Union (Fayette County)		Valley View (Cuyahoga		Walbridge	43465
(Township)	43160	County)	44111	Waldo	43356
Union (Hancock County)		Valleyview (Franklin County)	43204	Waldo (Township)	43356
(Township)	45881	Valley View (Jefferson		Walhonding (Coshocton	
		County)	43910	County)	43843

	ZIP		ZIP		ZIP
West Liberty (Logan County)	43357	Wickliffe (Lake County)	44092	Woodbourne-Hyde Park	45429
West Liberty (Morrow County)	43334	Wickliffe (Mahoning County)	44515	Woodhaven	45005
West Lodi	44811	Widowville	44805	Woodington	45331
West Logan	43138	Wiggonsville	45106	Woodlawn (Hamilton County)	45215
West Manchester	45382	Wightmans Grove	43420	Woodlawn (Miami County)	45373
West Mansfield	43358	Wilberforce	45384	Woodlawn Village	45373
West Marietta (Part of Marietta)	45750	Wildare	44410	Woodmere	44122
West Marysville (Part of Marysville)	43040	Wildbrook Acres	45231	Woodridge Plaza (Part of Fairfield)	45014
West Mecca	44410	Wildwood (Part of Middletown)	45042	Woods	45056
West Middletown	45042	Wilgus	45696	Woodsdale	45067
West Millgrove	43467	Wilkesville	45695	Woodsfield	43793
West Milton	45383	Wilkesville (Township)	45695	Woodside	43406
Westminster	45850	Wilkins Corners	43055	Woodstock	43084
Westmoor	44833	Wilkshire Hills	44612	Woodville (Clermont County)	45122
West Newton	45850	Willard	44890	Woodville (Sandusky County)	43469
Weston (Township)	43569	Willetsville	45133	Woodville (Sandusky County) (Township)	43469
West Park (Cuyahoga County)	44111	Williamsburg	45176	Woodville Gardens	43616
West Park (Hancock County)	45840	Williamsburg (Township)	45176	Woodville Mall (Part of Northwood)	43619
West Park (Jefferson County)	43952	Williams Center	43506	Woodworth	44512
West Park (Stark County)	44646	Williams Corner	45103	Woodworth Corners	44473
West Point (Columbiana County)	44492	Williamsdale	45011	Wooster	44691
West Point (Morrow County)	44833	Williamsfield	44093	Wooster (Township)	44691
West Portsmouth	45663	Williamsfield (Township)	44093	Wooster Heights	44903
West Richfield (Part of Richfield)	44286	Williamsport (Columbiana County)	44432	Worstville	45880
West Rushville	43163	Williamsport (Morrow County)	43338	Worthington (Franklin County)	43085
West Salem	44287	Williamsport (Pickaway County)	43164	Worthington (Richland County) (Township)	44822
West Side (Part of Youngstown)	44509	Williamstown	45897	Wren	45899
West Sonora	45338	Williston	43468	Wright Brothers (Part of Oakwood)	45409
West Toledo (Part of Toledo)	43612	Willoughby	44094-95	Wright-Patterson Air Force Base	45433
West Union	45693	For specific Willoughby Zip Codes call (216) 942-9420, or your local postmaster.		Wrightsville (Adams County)	45144
West Unity	43570			Wrightsville (Franklin County)	43123
Westview	44028	Willoughby Hills	44092	Wrightview (Part of Fairborn)	45324
Westville (Champaign County)	43083	Willow (Part of Cleveland)	44127	Wyandot	44849
Westville (Columbiana County)	44609	Willow (Part of Cuyahoga Heights)	44125	Wyoming	45215
Westville Lake	44609	Willow Brook Heights	44721	Wyoming Meadows	45231
West Warren (Part of Warren)	44485	Willowcrest	44452	Xavier (Part of Cincinnati)	45207
West Wheeling	43906	Willowdale Lake	44720	Xenia	45385
West Williamsfield	44093	Willowdell	45380	Xenia (Township)	45385
Westwood (Hamilton County)	45211	Willow Grove	43906	Yale (Ottawa County)	43468
Westwood (Jefferson County)	43952	Willowick	44094	Yale (Portage County)	44411
Westwood (Wayne County)	44691	Willow Lakes	43701	Yankeeburg	45768
Westwood Estates (Part of Steubenville)	43952	Willowville	45103	Yankee Hills	44403
West Woodville	45107	Willow Wood	45696	Yankee Lake	44403
West Worthington	43234*	Wills (Township)	43755	Yankeetown	45130
	43235†	Wills Creek	43811	Yatesville	43106
Wetzel	45863	Willshire	45898	Yellowbud	45601
Weymouth	44256	Willshire (Township)	45898	Yellow Creek (Columbiana County) (Township)	43968
Wharton	43359	Wilmington	45177	Yellow Creek (Jefferson County)	43968
Wheat Ridge	45693	Wilmot	44689	Yellow Springs	45387
Wheelersburg	45694	Wilshire	45122	Yellowtown	43731
Wheeling (Belmont County) (Township)	43927	Wilshire Heights	45005	Yelverton	43326
Wheeling (Guernsey County) (Township)	43749	Wilson (Clinton County) (Township)	45169	Yoder	45806
Whetstone (Township)	44820	Wilson (Monroe County)	43716	York (Athens County) (Township)	45764
Whigville	43788	Wiltondale	45224	York (Belmont County) (Township)	43942
Whipple	45788	Winameg	43515	York (Darke County) (Township)	45380
Whisler	45644	Winchester	45697	York (Fulton County) (Township)	43515
White Cottage	43791	Winchester (Township)	45697	York (Jefferson County)	43901
White Eyes (Township)	43824	Winchester	45640	York (Medina County) (Township)	44256
White Hall (Athens County)	45701	Windfall Heights	44256	York (Morgan County) (Township)	43731
Whitehall (Franklin County)	43213	Windham (Township)	44288	York (Sandusky County) (Township)	44811
Whitehouse	43571	Windham (Township)	44288	York (Tuscarawas County) (Township)	44663
White Oak (Brown County)	45154	Windor Park (Part of Xenia)	45385	York (Union County) (Township)	43067
Whiteoak (Fayette County)	43143	Windsor (Ashtabula County)	44099	York (Van Wert County) (Township)	45874
White Oak (Hamilton County)	45239	Windsor (Ashtabula County) (Township)	44099	York Center	43067
Whiteoak (Highland County) (Township)	45133	Windsor (Lawrence County) (Township)	45678	Yorkshire	45388
White Oak East	45239	Windsor (Morgan County) (Township)	43787	Yorkshire Estates	43302
White Oak Meadows	45239	Windsor (Richland County)	44903	Yorkville	43971
White Oaks (Part of Steubenville)	43952	Windsor (Warren County)	45162	Young Hickory	43732
White Oak Valley	45121	Windsor Mills	44099	Youngs	45657
White Oak West	45239	Windy Acres	45502	Youngs Corners	44256
White Pond	44321	Winesburg	44690	Youngstown	44501-15
White's Landing	43464	Winfield	44622	For specific Youngstown Zip Codes call (216) 744-6805, or your local postmaster.	
White Sulphur	43061	Wingett Run	45789		
Whitetree (Part of Cincinnati)	45236	Wingston	43462	Youngsville	45679
Whitewater	45002	Winona	44493	Zahns Corners	45690
Whitewater (Township)	45002	Winterdale (Part of Wintersville)	43952	Zaleski	45698
Whitfield	45342	Winterhaven	45305	Zane (Township)	43336
Wick	44093	Winterset	43755		
		Wintersville	43952		
		Wintondale	45231		
		Winton Place (Part of Cincinnati)	45216		
		Winton Place	45232		
		Winton Terrace (Part of Cincinnati)	45232		
		Wisterman	45831		
		Withamsville	45245		
		Wolf	43832		
		Wolfhurst	43912		
		Wolf Run	43970		
		Woodbourne	45459		

* Area Zip Code   † Post Office Boxes

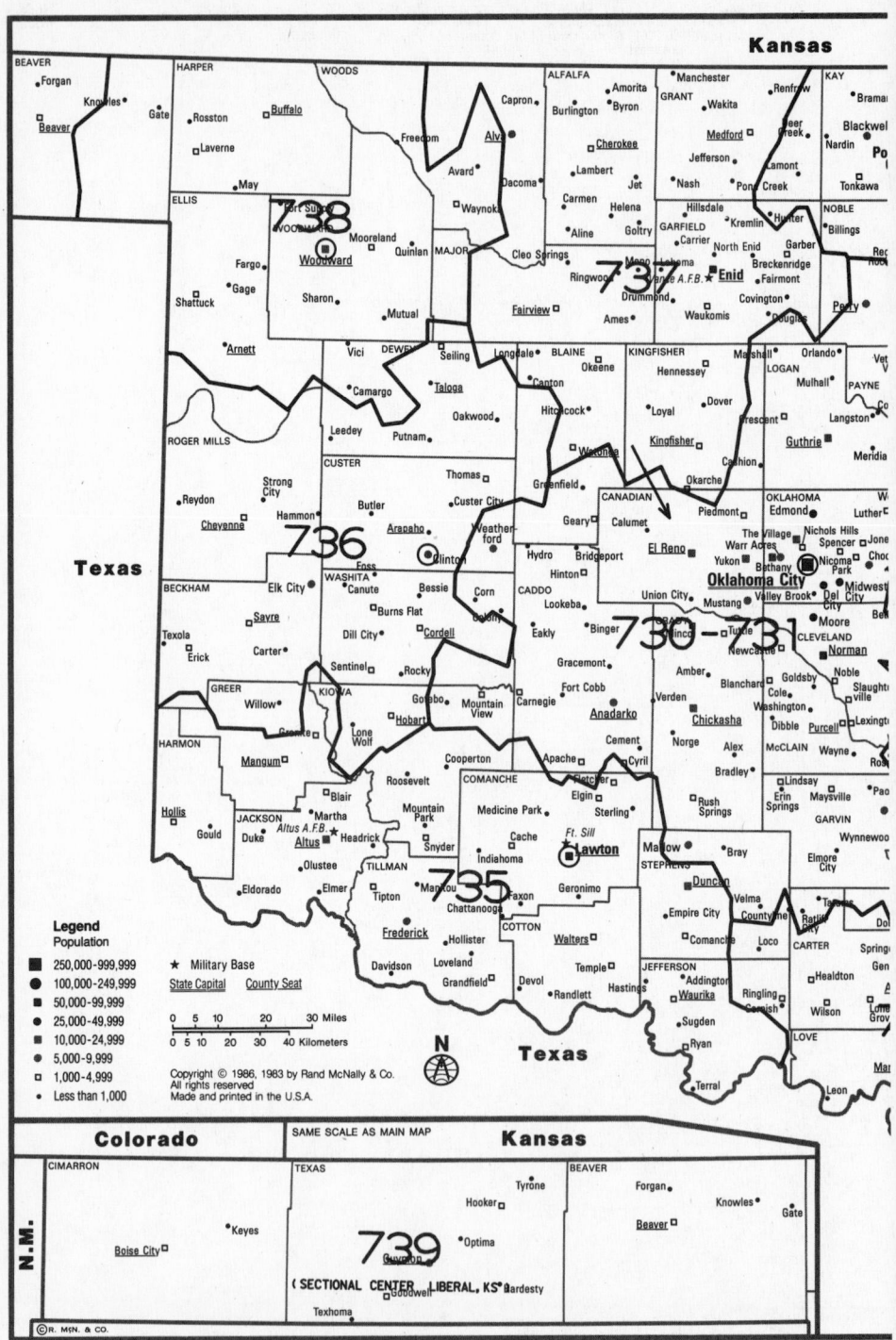

Kansas

Texas

BEAVER
Forgan
Knowles
Gate
Beaver

HARPER
Rosston
Buffalo
Laverne
May

WOODS
Freedom
Alva
Avard
Dacoma
Waynoka

Fort Supply
Mooreland
Woodward
Quinlan
Sharon
Mutual

738

ELLIS
Fargo
Gage
Shattuck
Arnett

MAJOR
Cleo Springs
Fairview
Ames

Vici
DEWEY
Seiling
Longdale
BLAINE
Okeene
Canton

Camargo
Taloga
Oakwood
Hitchcock

ROGER MILLS
Leedey
Putnam

Strong City
Reydon
Butler
Custer City
Cheyenne
Hammon

736

CUSTER
Thomas
Greenfield
Weatherford

Arapaho
Clinton
Foss
WASHITA
Canute
Bessie
Corn
Elk City
Burns Flat
Colony
Texola
Sayre
Cordell
Erick
Dill City
Carter
Sentinel
Rocky

BECKHAM

GREER
Willow
KIOWA
Granite
Lone Wolf
Gotebo
Hobart
Mountain View
Carnegie

HARMON
Mangum
Roosevelt
Cooperton

Hollis
Gould
JACKSON
Duke
Blair
Martha
Altus A.F.B.
Headrick
Altus
Olustee
TILLMAN
Eldorado
Elmer
Tipton
Manitou
Snyder
Frederick
Hollister
Chattanooga
COTTON
Loveland
Davidson
Grandfield
Devol
Randlett

735

ALFALFA
Capron
Burlington
Amorita
Byron
Cherokee
Lambert
Carmen
Jet
Helena
Aline
Goltry

GRANT
Wakita
Manchester
Renfrow
Medford
Jefferson
Nash
Pond Creek
Lamont

KAY
Bramar
Blackwell
Nardin
Tonkawa

GARFIELD
Hillsdale
North Enid
Enid
Drummond
Waukomis
Kremlin
Garber
Breckenridge
Fairmont
Covington
Douglas

737

Meno
Lahoma
Vance A.F.B.
Ringwood

KINGFISHER
Hennessey
Loyal
Kingfisher
Okarche

LOGAN
Marshall
Dover
Crescent
Guthrie
Cashion

Orlando
Mulhall
Langston
Meridia

NOBLE
Billings
Perry

PAYNE

BLAINE

CANADIAN
Geary
Calumet
El Reno
Piedmont
Union City
Yukon
Hinton
Bridgeport
Hydro

OKLAHOMA
Edmond
The Village
Nichols Hills
Warr Acres
Spencer
Bethany
Nicoma Park
Oklahoma City
Valley Brook
Del City
Moore
Norman
Newcastle
CLEVELAND

730-731

CADDO
Lookeba
Eakly
Binger
Gracemont
Fort Cobb
Anadarko
Cement
Apache
Cyril
Fletcher

Amber
Blanchard
Verden
Norge
Alex
Bradley

Goldsby
Noble
Cole
Washington
Dibble
Purcell
McCLAIN
Wayne

GARVIN
Lindsay
Erin Springs
Maysville
Wynnewood
Elmore City

COMANCHE
Medicine Park
Cache
Elgin
Sterling
Indiahoma
Geronimo
Faxon

Ft. Sill
Lawton
STEPHENS
Marlow
Duncan
Empire City
Velma
Countyline
Comanche
Loco

Bray

JEFFERSON
Temple
Addington
Waurika
Sugden
Ryan
Terral

Hastings
Ringling
Cornish

CARTER
Healdton
Wilson

LOVE

Lindsay

Colorado
Kansas

N.M.

CIMARRON
Boise City

TEXAS
Keyes
Hooker
Tyrone
Optima
739
Guymon
Goodwell
Hardesty
Texhoma

BEAVER
Forgan
Knowles
Gate
Beaver

(SECTIONAL CENTER LIBERAL, KS

SAME SCALE AS MAIN MAP

Legend
Population
■ 250,000-999,999
● 100,000-249,999
■ 50,000-99,999
● 25,000-49,999
■ 10,000-24,999
□ 5,000-9,999
□ 1,000-4,999
• Less than 1,000

★ Military Base
State Capital   County Seat

0 5 10   20   30 Miles
0 5 10   20   30   40 Kilometers

N

© R. McN. & CO.

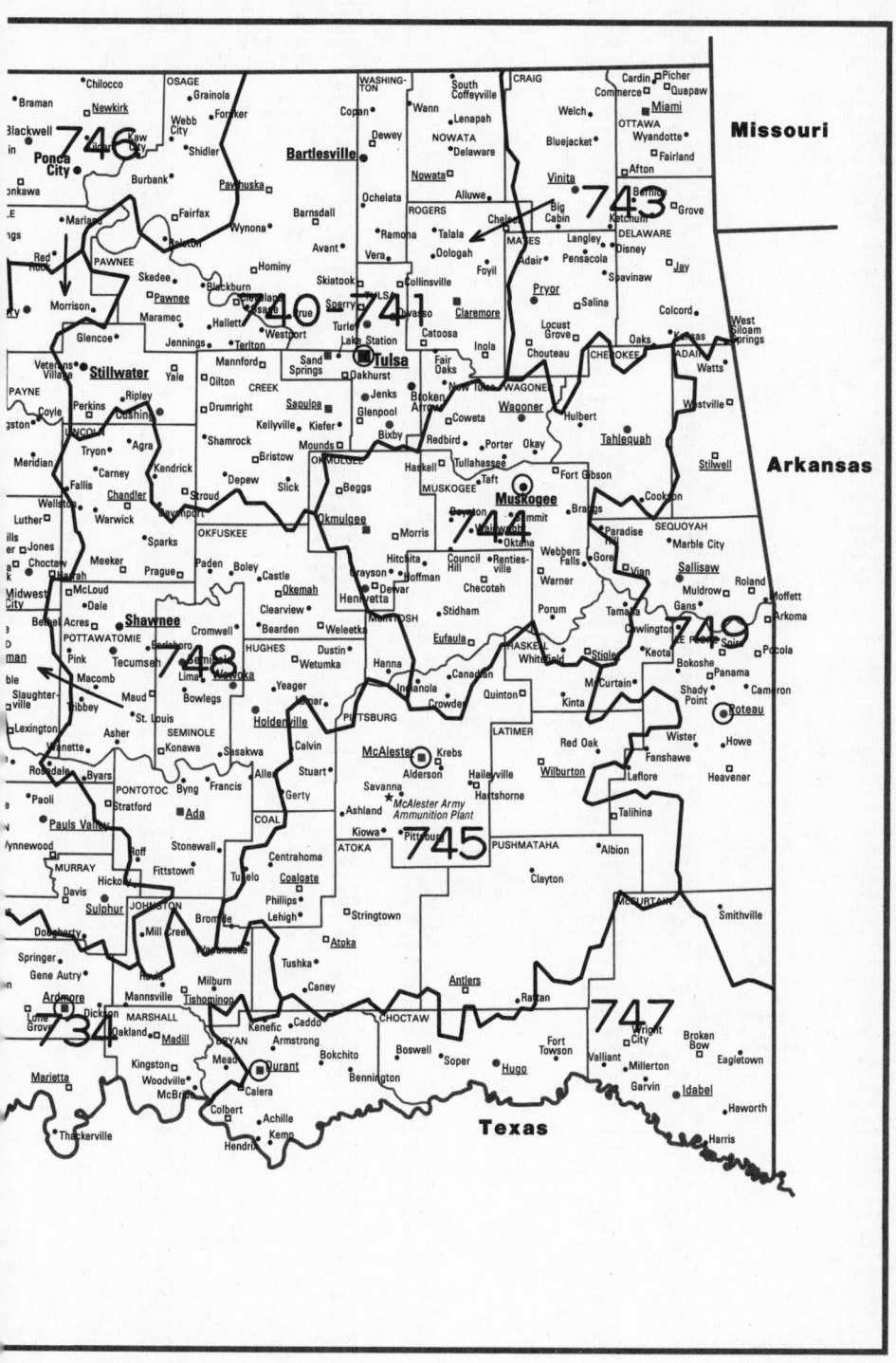

	ZIP
Achille	74720
Acme	73082
Ada	74820*
	74821†
Adair	74330
Adams	73901
Adamson	74547
Addington	73520
Afton	74331
Agawam	73067
Agra	74824
Ahloso	74820
Ahpeatone	73572
Akins	74955
Albany	74721
Albert	73001
Albion	74521
Alderson	74522
Aledo	73654
Alex	73002
Alfalfa	73015
Aline	73716
Allen	74825
Allison	74730
Alluwe	74048
Alma	73533
Altus	73521-23

For specific Altus Zip Codes call (405) 482-3339, or your local postmaster.

	ZIP
Alva	73717
Amber	73004
Ames	73718
Amorita	73719
Anadarko	73005
Antioch	73035
Antlers	74523
Apache	73006
Apperson	74633
Apple	74760
Arapaho	73620
Arcadia	73007
Ardmore	73401-03

For specific Ardmore Zip Codes call (405) 223-8383, or your local postmaster.

	ZIP
Arkoma	74901
Arlington	74864
Armstrong	74729
Arnett (Ellis County)	73832
Arnett (Harmon County)	73550
Arpelar	74548
Artillery Village	73503
Asher	74826
Ashland	74570
Atoka	74525
Atwood	74827
Avant	74001
Avard	73717
Avery	74023
Bache	74526
Bacone (Part of Muskogee)	74401
Bailey	73055
Baker	73950
Baldhill	74447
Balko	73931
Ballard	74964
Banner (Part of El Reno)	73036
Banty	74723
Barber	74471
Barnsdall	74002
Baron	74965
Bartlesville	74003-06

For specific Bartlesville Zip Codes call (918) 336-0947, or your local postmaster.

	ZIP
Battiest	74722
Baugh	74020
Baum	73401
Beachton	71961
Bearden	74859
Beaver	73932
Bee	74748
Beggs	74421
Beland	74401
Bell	74960
Bellemont	74864
Belvin	74563
Belzoni	74523
Bengal	74966
Bennington	74723
Bentley	74525
Berlin	73662
Bernice	74331
Bessie	73622
Bethany	73008
Bethel (Comanche County)	73501
Bethel (McCurtain County)	74724
Bethel Acres	74801
Big Cabin	74332
Big Cedar	74939
Big Spring	74883

	ZIP
Billings	74630
Binger	73009
Bison	73720
Bixby	74008
Blackburn	74058
Blackgum	74962
Blackwell	74631
Blair	73526
Blanchard	73010
Blanco	74528
Blocker	74529
Blue	74701
Bluejacket	74333
Bluff	74759
Boatman	74361
Boehler	74727
Boggy Depot	74525
Bois D'Arc	74601
Boise City	73933
Bokchito	74726
Bokhoma	74740
Bokoshe	74930
Boley	74829
Bond	74426
Boone	73006
Boss	74745
Boswell	74727
Boulevard (Part of Norman)	73069
Bowden	74107
Bowlegs	74830
Bowlin Spring	74016
Bowring	74009
Box	74962
Boynton	74422
Braden	74959
Bradley	73011
Brady	73098
Braggs	74423
Braman	74632
Bray	73012
Breckenridge	73701
Brent	74955
Briartown	74455
Bridgeport	73047
Briggs	74464
Brinkman	73673
Bristow	74010
Britton (Part of Oklahoma City)	73114
Brock	73401
Broken Arrow	74011-14

For specific Broken Arrow Zip Codes call (918) 258-6626, or your local postmaster.

	ZIP
Broken Bow	74728
Bromide	74530
Brooken	74462
Brooksville	74873
Brown	74701
Broxton	73006
Brush Hill	74426
Brushy	74955
Bryant	74880
Buffalo (Harper County)	73834
Buffalo (McCurtain County)	74963
Bunch	74931
Burbank	74633
Burlington	73722
Burmah	73659
Burneyville	73430
Burns Flat	73624
Burwell	74754
Bushyhead	74016
Butler	73625
Butner	74884
Byars	74831
Byng	74820
Byron	73723
Cache	73527
Caddo	74729
Cairo	74538
Calera	74730
Calhoun	74956
Calida	74020
Calumet	73014
Calvin	74531
Camargo	73835
Cambria	74578
Cameron	74932
Cameron University (Part of Lawton)	73505
Camp Houston	73842
Canadian	74425
Caney	74533
Caney Ridge	74471
Canton	73724
Canute	73626
Capitol Hill (Part of Oklahoma City)	73109
Capron	73725
Cardin	74335
Carleton	73772

	ZIP
Carmen	73726
Carnegie	73015
Carney	74832
Carpenter	73644
Carriage Hills (Part of Lawton)	73501
Carrier	73727
Carson	74850
Carter (Beckham County)	73627
Carter (Cherokee County)	74451
Cartersville	74941
Cartwright	74731
Cashion	73016
Castle	74833
Catale	74332
Catoosa	74015
Cedar Crest	74352
Cedar Ridge (Part of Cleveland)	74020
Cedar Valley	73044
Cement	73017
Center	74820
Center City (Part of Oklahoma City)	73102
Centerview	74801
Centrahoma	74534
Centralia	74301
Central Mall (Part of Lawton)	73501
Ceres	74651
Cerrogordo	74740
Cestos	73859
Chandler	74834
Chase	74401
Chattanooga	73528
Checotah	74426
Chelsea	74016
Cherokee	73728
Cherry Tree	74960
Chester	73838
Chewey	74964
Cheyenne	73628
Chickasha	73018*
	73023†
Childers	74027
Chilli	74578
Chilocco	74647
Chitwood	73067
Choctaw	73020
Chouteau	74337
Christie	74965
Cimarron (Part of Oklahoma City)	73111
Cimarron City	73028
Cisco	74745
Citra	74825
Claremore	74017*
	74018†
Clarita	74535
Clarksville	74454
Clayton	74536
Clayton Lake	74536
Clear Lake	73849
Clearview	74835
Clebit	74728
Clemscot	73437
Cleora	74331
Cleo Springs	73729
Cleveland	74020
Clinton	73601
Clothier (Part of Oklahoma City)	73160
Cloud Chief	73632
Cloudy	74562
Clyde	73759
Coalgate	74538
Coalton	74437
Cobb	74701
Cogar	73059
Colbert	74733
Colcord	74338
Cole	73010
Coleman	73432
College (Part of Stillwater)	74074
Collinsville	74021
Colony	73021
Comanche	73529
Commerce	74339
Concho (Part of El Reno)	73022
Conner Correctional Center	74035
Connerville	74836
Conser	74937
Cookietown	73562
Cookson	74427
Cooperton	73564
Copan	74022
Corbett	73051
Cordell	73632
Corinne	74735
Corn	73024
Cornish	73456
Corum	73529

Name	ZIP	Name	ZIP	Name	ZIP
Cottonwood	74538		73134	Garber	73738
Council Hill	74428	For specific Edmond Zip Codes call (405) 341-1502, or your local postmaster.		Garden Grove	74801
Countyline	73025			Garland	74462
Courtney	73456			Garvin	74736
Covington	73730	Edna	74010	Gate	73844
Cowden	73632	Eighty Ninth Street (Part of Oklahoma City)	73159	Gay	74743
Coweta	74429			Geary	73040
Cowlington	74941	Eldon	74464	Gene Autry	73436
Cox City	73082	Eldorado	73537	Georgetown	74434
Coyle	73027	Elgin	73538	Geronimo	73543
Cravens	74563	Elk City	73644*	Gerty	74531
Crawford	73638		73648†	Gibson	74467
Creosote	74743	Elmer	73539	Gideon	74464
Crescent	73028	Elmore City	73035	Gilcrease (Part of Tulsa)	74127
Criner	73080	Elmwood	73932	Gilmore	74953
Cromwell	74837	El Reno	73036	Glencoe	74032
Crossroads Mall (Part of Oklahoma City)	73149	Emerson Center	73572	Glendale	74940
Crowder	74430	Emet	73450	Glenpool	74033
Crystal	74555	Empire City	73533	Glover	74728
Crystal Lakes	73718	Empy	74020	Golden	74737
Cumberland	73446	Enid	73701-06	Goldsby	73093
Curchece	74020	For specific Enid Zip Codes call (405) 237-4331, or your local postmaster.		Goltry	73739
Curt's Shopping Center (Part of Muskogee)	74401			Goodland	74743
Cushing	74023	Enos	73439	Goodwater	74740
Custer City	73639	Enterprise	74561	Goodwell	73939
Cyril	73029	Enville	73448	Gore	74435
Dacoma	73731	Erick	73645	Gotebo	73041
Daisy	74540	Erin Springs	73052	Gould	73544
Dale	74838	Ethel	74523	Gowen	74545
Damon	74578	Etowah	73068	Gracemont	73042
Darwin	74523	Etta	74471	Grady	73569
Davenport	74026	Eucha	74342	Graham	73437
Davidson	73530	Euchee Creek (Part of Sand Springs)	74063	Grainola	74652
Davis	73030	Eufaula	74432	Grandfield	73546
Dawson (Part of Tulsa)	74115	Eva	73939	Grand Lake Towne	74301
Deer Creek	74636	Ewing (Part of Clinton)	73601	Granite	73547
Degnan	74578	Fairfax	74637	Grant	74738
Delaware	74027	Fairland	74343	Gray Horse	74637
Del City	73115	Fairmont	73736	Grayson	74437
Delhi	73662	Fair Oaks	74015	Greasy	74931
Dempsey	73628	Fairview	73737	Greenfield	73043
Dennis	74301	Falconhead	73430	Green Pastures (Part of Oklahoma City)	73084
Depew	74028	Falfa	74571	Green Valley Estates	74962
Depot	74501	Fallis	74881	Greenville	73448
Devol	73531	Fame	74432	Greenwood	74523
Dewar	74431	Fanshawe	74935	Griggs	73949
Dewey	74029	Fargo	73840	Grimes	73628
Dibble	73031	Farley (Part of Oklahoma City)	73107	Grove	74344
Dickson	73401	Farmers Hill	74736	Guthrie	73044
Dighton	74437	Farris	74542	Guymon	73942
Dillard	73463	Faxon	73540	Haileyville	74546
Dill City	73641	Fay	73646	Hall Addition (Part of Sand Springs)	74063
Disney	74340	Featherston	74561	Hallett	74034
Dixon	74884	Federal Correctional Institution	73036	Hall Park	73069
Donaldson (Part of Tulsa)	74104	Felker	74764	Hammon	73650
Dotyville	74354	Felt	73937	Hanna	74845
Dougherty	73032	Fillmore	73432	Hanson	74955
Douglas	73733	Finley	74543	Happyland	74820
Dover	73734	First National Bank (Part of Oklahoma City)	73102	Harden City	74871
Dow	74501	Fisher (Part of Sand Springs)	74063	Hardesty	73944
Doyle	73039	Fittstown	74842	Harmon	73832
Drake	73086	Fitzhugh	74843	Harrah	73045
Driftwood	73728	Fletcher	73541	Harris	74740
Drumb	74578	Floris	73938	Harrison	74955
Drummond	73735	Folsom	73432	Hartshorne	74547
Drumright	74030	Fontana Shopping Center (Part of Tulsa)	74145	Haskell	74436
Duke	73532	Foraker	74652	Hastings	73548
Dunbar	73448	Forest Hill	74937	Haw Creek	74939
Duncan	73533-34	Forest Park	73121	Hawley	73761
	73575	Forgan	73938	Haworth	74740
For specific Duncan Zip Codes call (405) 255-7226, or your local postmaster.		Forney	74743	Hayward	73730
Dunjee Park (Part of Oklahoma City)	73084	Forrester	74937	Haywood	74548
Durant	74701*	Fort Cobb	73038	Headrick	73549
	74702†	Fort Coffee	74959	Healdton	73438
Durham	73642	Fort Gibson	74434	Heavener	74937
Durwood (Part of Dickson)	73401	Fort Reno (Part of El Reno)	73036	Helena	73741
Dustin	74839	Fort Sill	73503	Hendrix	74741
Eagle City	73658	Fort Supply	73841	Hennepin	73046
Eagletown	74734	Fort Towson	74735	Hennessey	73742
Eakly	73033	Foss	73647	Henryetta	74437
Earl	73447	Foster	73039	Heritage Hills	73507
Earlsboro	74840	Four Corners	74437	Heritage Park Mall (Part of Midwest City)	73110
Eastborough	74014	Fox	73435	Hess	73539
Eastern Oklahoma A&M College	74578	Foyil	74031	Hester	73554
Eastern State Hospital	74301	Francis	74844	Hewitt (Part of Wilson)	73463
East Jessie	74871	Frederick	73542	Hext	73645
Eastland Mall (Part of Tulsa)	74114	Freedom	73842	Hickory	74865
Eastside (Custer County)	73096	French Market (Part of Oklahoma City)	73116	Hicks Addition (Part of Spencer)	73084
East Side (Washington County)	74006	Friendship	73521	Hill	74932
Eddy	74643	Frisco	74871	Hillsdale	73743
Edgewater Park	73006	Frogville	74743	Hillsdale Free Will Baptist College	73160
Edmond	73013	Gaar Corner	74820	Hill Top	74570
	73034	Gage	73843	Hinton	73047
	73083	Gans	74936	Hissom Memorial Center	74063
				Hitchcock	73744
				Hitchita	74438
				Hobart	73651

	ZIP
Hockerville	74363
Hodgen	74939
Hodge Podge (Part of Tulsa)	74105
Hoffman	74437
Holdenville	74848
Holley Creek	74728
Hollis	73550
Hollister	73551
Homer	74820
Homestead	73763
Hominy	74035
Honobia	74549
Hontubby	74937
Hooker	73945
Hoot Owl	74365
Hopeton	73746
Hough	73942
Howard C. McLeod Correctional Center	74542
Howe	74940
Hoyt	74440
Hugo	74743
Hulbert	74441
Hulen	73572
Humphreys	73521
Hunter	74640
Hyde Park (Part of Muskogee)	74401
Hydro	73048
Idabel	74745
Independence	74937
Indiahoma	73552
Indian Meadows	74464
Indianola	74442
Ingalls	74074
Ingersoll	73728
Inola	74036
Iona	73086
Iron Stob Corner	74736
Irving	73565
Isabella	73747
Jackson	74723
Jacktown	74855
Jamestown	74080
Jay	74346
Jefferson	73759
Jenks	74037
Jennings	74038
Jesse	74871
Jet	73749
Jimtown	73430
Joburn	74556
Joe Harp Correctional Center	73051
John H. Lilley Correctional Center	74829
Johnson	74801
Jollyville	73030
Jones	73049
Joy	73098
Juby's	74020
Jumbo	74557
Kansas	74347
Karen Park (Part of Midwest City)	73110
Katie	73035
Kaw City	74641
Keefeton	74401
Keetonville	74017
Kellond	74523
Kellyville (Creek County)	74039
Kellyville (Ottawa County)	74370
Kemp	74747
Kendrick	74079
Kenefic	74748
Kensington Center (Part of Tulsa)	74103
Kent	74759
Kenton	73946
Kenwood	74365
Keota	74941
Ketchum	74349
Keyes	73947
Kiamichi	74574
Kiefer	74041
Kildare	74601
Kingfisher	73750
Kingston	73439
Kinta	74552
Kiowa	74553
Knowles	73847
Konawa	74849
Kosoma	74557
Krebs	74554
Kremlin	73753
Kulli	74745
Kusa	74437
Lacey	73742
Lahoma	73754
Lake Aluma	73121

	ZIP
Lake Creek	73547
Lake Hiwasse	73007
Lake Humphreys	73055
Lakeside Village	73538
Lake Station (Part of Sand Springs)	74127
Lake Valley	73041
Lake West	74727
Lamar	74850
Lambert	73728
La Mesa (Part of Enid)	73701
Lamont	74643
Lane	74555
Langley	74350
Langston	73050
Lark	73439
Last Chance	74859
Latta	74820
Laverne	73848
Lawrence Creek	74044
Lawton	73501-02
	73505-07
For specific Lawton Zip Codes call (405) 353-1500, or your local postmaster.	
Leach	74364
Leader	74825
Leander	74020
Lebanon	73440
Leedey	73654
Leflore	74942
Lehigh	74556
Leisure Square (Part of Tulsa)	74112
Lenapah	74042
Lenna	74432
Lenora	73667
Leon	73441
Leonard	74043
Lequire	74943
Leroy	74020
Lewisville	74552
Lexington	73051
Lexington Assessment and Recption Center	73051
Liberty (Bryan County)	74741
Liberty (Sequoyah County)	74948
Liberty (Tulsa County)	74101
Lighthouse (Part of Tulsa)	74136
Lima	74884
Limestone (Latimer County)	74578
Limestone (Rogers County)	74017
Lincolnville	74363
Lindsay	73052
Little	74868
Little Chief	74637
Little City	73446
Little Ponderosa	67901
Loco	73442
Locust Grove	74352
Logan	73849
Lona	74552
Lone Grove	73443
Lone Oak	74948
Lone Wolf	73655
Long	74948
Longdale	73755
Longtown	74561
Lookeba	73053
Lotsee	74063
Loveland	73553
Lovell	73028
Loving	74937
Loyal	73756
Lucien	73757
Lugert	73655
Lula	74825
Luther	73054
Lutie	74578
Lynn Addition	74056
Lyons	74960
McAlester	74501*
	74502†
McAlester Army Ammunition Plant	74501
MacArthur Park (Part of Lawton)	73507
McBride	73439
McCord	74637
McCurtain	74944
McKey	74962
Mack H. Alford Correctional Center	74569
McKiddyville	73051
McKnight	73550
McLain	74401
McLoud	74851
McMillan	73446
Macomb	74852
McWillie	73716
Madill	73446

	ZIP
Maguire (Part of Slaughterville)	73068
Manard	74434
Manchester	73758
Mangum	73554
Manitou	73555
Mannford	74044
Mannsville	73447
Maple	74948
Maramec	74045
Marble City	74945
Marietta	73448
Marland	74644
Marlow	73055
Marshall	73056
Martha	73556
Martin	74401
Mason	74859
Matoy	74729
Maud	74854
Maxwell	74820
May	73851
Mayfield	73656
May Ridge (Part of Oklahoma City)	73119
Maysville	73057
Mazie	74353
Mead	73449
Medford	73759
Medicine Park	73557
Meeker	74855
Meers	73558
Mehan	74074
Mellette	74432
Melvin	74441
Meno	73760
Meridian (Logan County)	73058
Meridian (Stephens County)	73529
Merritt	73644
Messer	74743
Miami	74354*
	74355†
Micawber	74882
Middleberg	73010
Midlothian	74834
Midway	74538
Midwest City	73110
Milburn	73450
Milfay	74046
Mill Creek	74856
Miller	74557
Millerton	74750
Milo	73401
Milton	74944
Minco	73059
Moffett	74946
Monroe	74947
Montclair Addition (Part of Heavener)	74937
Moodys	74444
Moon	74740
Moore	73160
Mooreland	73852
Moorewood	73650
Morris	74445
Morrison	73061
Mound Grove	74764
Mounds	74047
Mountain Park	73559
Mountain View	73062
Mount Herman	74728
Mount Zion	74736
Moyers	74557
Mudsand	74759
Muldrow	74948
Mule Barn (Part of Cleveland)	74101
Mulhall	73063
Murphy	74352
Muse	74949
Muskogee	74401-03
For specific Muskogee Zip Codes call (918) 682-7832, or your local postmaster.	
Mustang	73064
Mutual	73853
Nani-Chito	74957
Narcissa	74354
Nardin	74646
Nash	73761
Nashoba	74558
Natura	74421
Navina	73044
Nebo	73086
Needmore	73068
Neff	74953
Nelagony	74056
Newalla (Part of Oklahoma City)	74857
Newcastle	73065

	ZIP		ZIP		ZIP
Scraper	74464	Stratford	74872	Vamoosa	74849
Scullin	73086	Stringtown	74569	Vance Air Force Base	73701
Scullyville	74959	Strong City	73628	Vanoss	74820
Seiling	73663	Stroud	74079	Velma	73091
Selman	73834	Stuart	74570	Vera	74082
Seminole	74818†	Sugden	73573	Verden	73092
	74868*	Sullivan Village (Part of		Verdigris	74017
Sentinel	73664	Lawton)	73501	Vernon	74845
Sequoyah	74017	Sulphur	73086	Vian	74962
Seward	73044	Summerfield	74966	Vici	73859
Shady Grove (Pawnee		Summit	74401	Victory	73560
County)	74112	Sumner	73077	Village	73120
Shady Grove (Sequoyah		Sungate (Part of Lawton)	73501	Vinco	74059
County)	74954	Sunkist	74727	Vinita	74301
Shady Point	74956	Sunray	73529	Vinson	73571
Shamrock	74068	Sweetwater	73666	Virgil	74756
Sharon	73857	Swink	74761	Vista	74849
Shartel (Part of Oklahoma		Tabler	73018	Vivian	74432
City)	73118	Tablerville	74734	Wade	74723
Sha-To-She	74020	Taft	74463	Wagoner	74467*
Shattuck	73858	Tahlequah	74464*		74477†
Shawnee	74801*		74465†	Wainwright	74468
	74802†	Tahona	74932	Wakita	73771
Shay	73439	Tailholt	74471	Wallville	73052
Shepherd Mall (Part of		Talala	74080	Walters	73572
Oklahoma City)	73107	Talihina	74571	Wanette	74878
Sheridan (Comanche		Taliant	74002	Wann	74083
County)	73505	Taloga	73667	Wapanucka	73461
Sheridan (Tulsa County)	74135	Tamaha	74462	Wardville	74576
Sherwood	74728	Tangier	73801	Warner	74469
Shidler	74652	Tatums	73087	Warr Acres	73132
Shinewell	74740	Taylor	73562	Warren	73526
Short	72955	Tecumseh	74873	Warwick	74834
Shults	74745	Temple	73568	Washington	73093
Sickles	73053	Teresita	74364	Washita	73094
Silo	74701	Teriton	74081	Waterloo	73034
Silver City	74038	Terral	73569	Watonga	73772
Skedee	74058	Texanna	74426	Watova	74048
Skiatook	74070	Texhoma	73949	Watson	74963
Slapout	73848	Texola	73668	Watts	74964
Slaughterville	73051	Thackerville	73459	Wauhillau	74960
Slick	74071	Thirty-Fourth Street (Part of		Waukomis	73773
Smith Village	73115	Woodward)	73801	Waurika	73573
Smithville	74957	Thirty Ninth Street (Part of		Wayne	73095
Snow	74567	Oklahoma City)	73112	Waynoka	73860
Snyder	73566	Thomas	73669	Weatherford	73096
Sobol	74735	Ti	74528	Webb	73835
Sooner Fashion Mall (Part of		Tiawah	74017	Webb City	74652
Norman)	73072	Timber Brook	74014	Webbers Falls	74470
Soper	74759	Timberlane	74020	Welch	74369
Southard	73770	Tiner	74728	Weleetka	74880
South Coffeyville	74072	Tipton	73570	Welling	74471
South East (Oklahoma		Tishomingo	73460	Wellston	74881
County)	73109	Titanic	74960	Welty	74882
Southeast (Tulsa County)	74145	Tom	74740	Wes	74020
Southroads Mall (Part of		Tonkawa	74653	West Nichols Hills (Part of	
Tulsa)	74135	Topsy	74366	Oklahoma City)	73116
Southside (Part of Tulsa)	74136	Tribbey	74852	West Park (Part of	
Southwest (Part of		Trousdale	74878	Oklahoma City)	73123
Oklahoma City)	73119	Troy	74856	Westport	74020
Sparks	74869	Trusty Unit	74501	Westside (Part of Oklahoma	
Spaulding	74848	Tryon	74875	City)	73127
Spavinaw	74366	Tucker	74959	West Siloam Springs	72761
Speer	74743	Tullahassee	74466	West Tulsa (Part of Tulsa)	74107
Spelter City	74437	Tulsa	74101-72	Westville	74965
Spencer	73084	For specific Tulsa Zip Codes call		Wetumka	74883
Spencerville	74760	(918) 599-6965, or your local		Wewoka	74884
Sperry	74073	postmaster.		Wheatland (Part of	
Spiro	74959	Tulsa Promenade (Part of		Oklahoma City)	73097
Sportsmen Acres	74361	Tulsa)	74135	Wheeless	73933
Springer	73458	Tupelo	74572	Whippoorwill	74056
Springlake Park (Part of		Turley	74156	White Bead	73075
Oklahoma City)	73111	Turner	73430	White Eagle	74601
Stafford	73601	Turpin	73950	Whitefield	74472
Stanley	74536	Tushka	74525	White Oak (Cherokee	
Stapp	74939	Tuskahoma	74574	County)	74451
Star	74941	Tuskegee	74010	White Oak (Craig County)	74301
State Capitol (Part of		Tussy	73088	Whitesboro	74577
Oklahoma City)	73105	Tuttle	73089	Whittier (Part of Tulsa)	74150
Stealy	73080	Tuxedo (Part of Bartlesville)	74003	Wichita Mountains Estates	73501
Stecker	73006	Twin Hills	74447	Wilburton	74578
Steedman	74825	Twin Oaks	74368	Wildcat Point	74451
Steel Junction	74728	Tyler	73446	Wild Horse	74035
Steen (Part of Enid)	73701	Tyrone	73951	Williams	74932
Sterling	73567	Unger	74727	William S. Key Correctional	
Stidham	74461	Union (Cleveland County)	73070	Center	73841
Stigler	74462	Union (Tulsa County)	74012	Willis	73439
Stillwater	74074-76	Union City	73090	Willow	73673
For specific Stillwater Zip Codes		Union Valley	74871	Wilson (Carter County)	73463
call (405) 377-3867, or your local		University (Garfield County)	73701	Wilson (Okmulgee County)	74437
postmaster.		University (Pottawatomie		Winchester	74421
Stilwell	74960	County)	74801	Winganon	74016
Stockyards (Part of		University of Science		Wister	74966
Oklahoma City)	73108	and Arts (Part of		Wolco	74002
Stonebluff	74436	Chickasha)	73018	Wolf	74854
Stonewall	74871	Uptown Shopping Center		Woodford	73458
Stony Point (Adair County)	74960	(Part of Midwest City)	73110	Woodland Hills Mall (Part of	
Stony Point (Le Flore		Utica	74726	Tulsa)	74133
County)	74959	Utica Square (Part of Tulsa)	74152	Woodland View (Part of	
Story	73057	Valley Brook	73149	Tulsa)	74145
Straight	73942	Valley Park	74017	Woodlawn Park	73008
Strang	74367	Valliant	74764	Woods	73020

* Area Zip Code   † Post Office Boxes

	ZIP		ZIP		ZIP
Woodville	73439	Wynnewood	73098	Yuba	74721
Woodward	73801*	Wynona	74084	Yukon	73085†
	73802†	Yale	74085		73099*
Woody Chapel	73095	Yanush	74574	Zafra	71945
Wright City	74766	Yarnaby	74741	Zena	74346
Wyandotte	74370	Yeager	74848	Zincville	66713
Wybark	74401	Yewed	73728	Zion	74960
Wye	74852	Yost Lake	74032	Zoe	74939

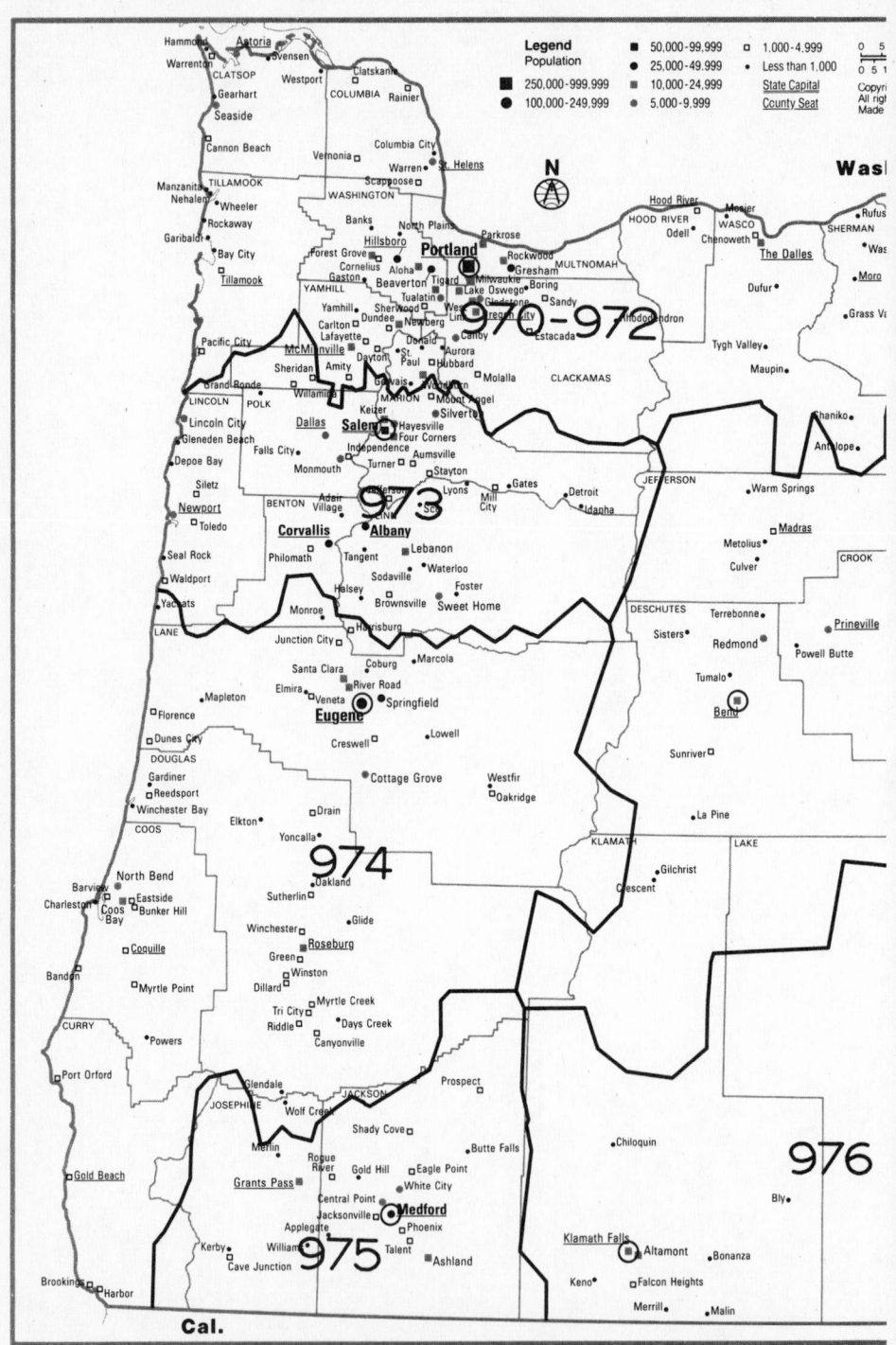

Legend
Population

■ 50,000-99,999   □ 1,000-4,999
■ 250,000-999,999 ● 25,000-49,999   • Less than 1,000
● 100,000-249,999 ■ 10,000-24,999   State Capital
                   ● 5,000-9,999   County Seat

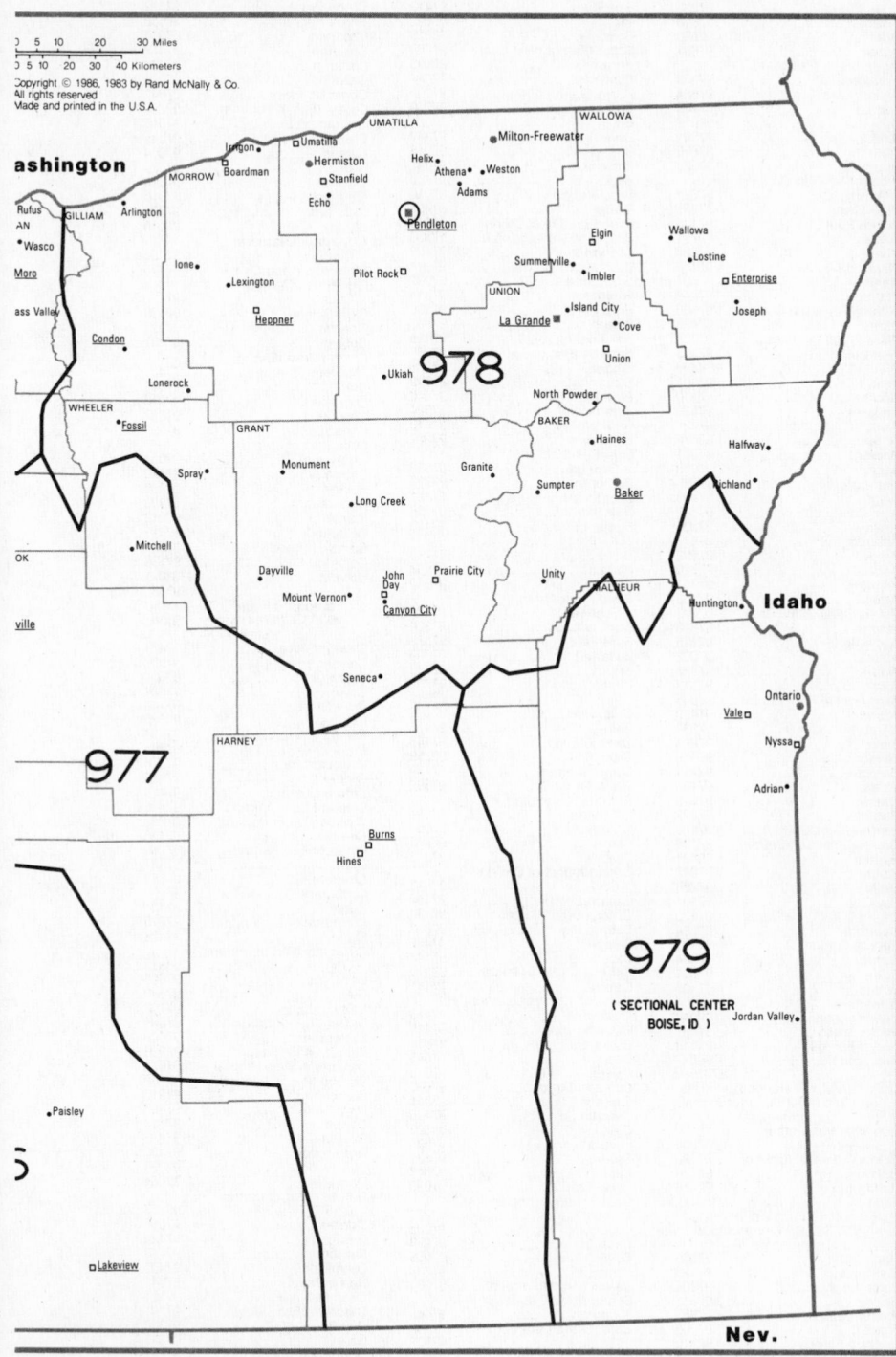

0 5 10   20   30 Miles
0 5 10   20   30   40 Kilometers

ashington

Washington

UMATILLA   WALLOWA

Irrigon   Umatilla   Milton-Freewater
MORROW   Boardman   Hermiston   Helix
Stanfield   Athena   Weston
Echo   Adams

Rufus
AN   GILLIAM   Arlington   Pendleton
Wasco
Moro   Ione   Lexington   Pilot Rock   Elgin   Wallowa
ass Valley   Summerville   Lostine
Condon   Imbler   Enterprise
UNION   La Grande   Island City   Joseph
Lonerock   Cove
WHEELER   Ukiah   **978**   Union
Fossil
North Powder
GRANT   BAKER   Haines   Halfway
Spray   Monument   Granite   Richland
Long Creek   Sumpter   Baker
Mitchell
OK   Dayville   Prairie City   Unity
Mount Vernon   John   MALHEUR   Huntington   **Idaho**
ville   Day
Canyon City
Seneca   Ontario
Vale   Nyssa
HARNEY
Adrian
977

Burns
Hines

979

(SECTIONAL CENTER
BOISE, ID)   Jordan Valley

Paisley

5

Lakeview

Nev.

	ZIP
Acorn Park (Part of Eugene)	97402
Ada	97493
Adair Village	97810
Adams	97330
Adel	97620
Adrian	97901
Agate Beach (Part of Newport)	97365
Agency Lake	97624
Agness	97406
Aims	97019
Airlie	97361
Ajax	97823
Albany	97321
Albany Yard (Part of Albany)	97321
Alder Creek	97055
Aldrich Point	97103
Alfalfa	97701
Alicel	97824
Alkali Lake	97758
Allegany	97407
Allston	97048
Aloha (Washington County)	97006
Alpine	97456
Alsea	97324
Altamont	97603
Alvadore	97409
Amity	97101
Anchor	97410
Andrews	97720
Anlauf	97428
Annex	83672
Antelope	97001
Apiary	97048
Applegate	97530
Arago	97458
Arch Cape	97102
Arleta	97206
Arlington	97812
Arock	97902
Ashland	97520
Ashwood	97711
Astoria	97103
Astoria Coast Guard Base	97103
Athena	97813
Aumsville	97325
Aurora	97002
Austin	97817
Austin Junction	97817
Avon (Part of Rainier)	97048
Azalea	97410
Bakeoven	97037
Baker City	97814
Ballston	97378
Bandon	97411
Banks	97106
Barlow	97013
Barton	97022
Barview (Coos County)	97420
Barview (Tillamook County)	97136
Basque	89421
Bates	97817
Battin	97266
Bay City	97107
Bay Park	97420
Bayshore	97394
Bayside Garden	97131
Bayview	97394
Beatty	97621
Beaver	97108
Beavercreek	97004
Beaver Homes	97048
Beaver Marsh	97731
Beaver Springs	97048
Beaverton	97005-07
	97075-76

For specific Beaverton Zip Codes call (503) 646-3196, or your local postmaster.

Beaverton Mall (Part of Beaverton)	97005
Belleview (Part of Ashland)	97520
Bellevue	97128
Bellfountain	97456
Bend	97701-09

For specific Bend Zip Codes call (503) 388-1971, or your local postmaster.

Berlin	97355
Bethany	97123
Bethel Heights	97304
Beulah	97911
Beverly Beach	97365
Biggs	97065
Bingham Springs	97810
Birkenfeld	97016
Blachly	97412
Black Butte Ranch	97759
Blaine	97108
Blalock	97812

	ZIP
Blodgett	97326
Blooming	97113
Blue River	97413
Bly	97622
Boardman	97818
Bolton (Part of West Linn)	97068
Bonanza	97623
Bonneville	97014
Bonny Slope	97229
Boring	97009
Boyd	97021
Boyer	97347
Bradwood	97016
Breitenbush	97342
Brickerville	97453
Bridal Veil	97010
Bridge	97458
Bridgeport (Baker County)	97819
Bridgeport (Polk County)	97338
Brighton	97136
Brightwood	97011
Broadacres	97002
Broadbent	97414
Brockway	97496
Brogan	97903
Brookings	97415
Brooklyn (Part of Portland)	97266
Brooks	97305
Brothers	97712
Brownlee	97840
Brownsboro	97524
Brownsmead	97016
Brownsville	97327
Bryant (Part of Lake Oswego)	97035
Buchanan	97720
Buena Vista	97351
Bullrun	97055
Bunker Hill	97420
Burlington	97231
Burns	97720
Burnside	97103
Burns Junction	97910
Burns Paiute Indian Reservation	97720
Burnt Woods	97326
Butte Falls	97522
Butteville	97002
Buxton	97109
Cages	97739
Cairo	97914
Calapooya	97386
Camas Valley	97416
Camp Clatsop	97146
Camp Polk	97759
Camp Sherman	97730
Camp Twelve	97391
Campus Station (Part of Corvallis)	97331
Canaan	97054
Canary	97493
Canby	97013
Canemah (Part of Oregon City)	97045
Cannon Beach	97110
Cannon Beach Junction	97138
Canyon City	97820
Canyonville	97417
Cape Meares	97141
Capitol Hill (Part of Portland)	97219
Carlton	97111
Carnation (Part of Forest Grove)	97116
Carpenterville	97415
Carson	97834
Carus	97045
Carver	97015
Cascade Gorge	97536
Cascade Locks	97014
Cascade Summit	97425
Cascadia	97329
Cave Junction	97523
Cayuse	97821
Cecil	97843
Cedar Dale	97038
Cedar Hills (Washington County)	97225
Cedarhurst Park	97023
Cedar Mill	97229
Celilo	97058
Centennial	97236
Central (Part of Portland)	97204
Central Point (Clackamas County)	97045
Central Point (Jackson County)	97502
Central Point West	97502
Chapman	97056
Charleston	97420
Charlestown	97838
Chemawa Indian School	97303

	ZIP
Chemult	97731
Chenoweth	97058
Cherry Grove	97119
Cherry Heights	97058
Cherryville	97055
Cheshire	97419
Chiloquin	97624
Chitwood	97391
Christmas Valley	97641
Chutes (Part of Portland)	97202
Clackamas	97015
Clackamas Heights	97045
Clarkes	97004
Clarno	97830
Clatskanie	97016
Clatskanie Heights	97016
Clear Lake	97303
Clifton	97016
Cloverdale (Deschutes County)	97756
Cloverdale (Lane County)	97426
Cloverdale (Tillamook County)	97112
Clow Corner	97338
Coaledo	97420
Coburg	97401
College Crest (Part of Eugene)	97401
Colton	97017
Columbia City	97018
Concord	97222
Condon	97823
Cook (Part of Lake Oswego)	97034
Coos Bay	97420
Cooston	97459
Coquille	97423
Corbett	97019
Cornelius	97113
Cornelius Pass	97231
Coronado Shores	97388
Corvallis	97330-33
Corvallis	97339

For specific Corvallis Zip Codes call (503) 758-1412, or your local postmaster.

Cottage Grove	97424
Cottrell	97009
Courtrock	97864
Cove	97824
Cove Orchard	97148
Crabtree	97335
Crane	97732
Crater Lake	97604
Crawfordsville	97336
Crescent	97733
Crescent Lake	97425
Crescent Lake Junction	97425
Creston (Part of Portland)	97206
Creswell	97426
Crooked River Ranch	97760
Crow	97401
Crowfoot	97355
Culp Creek	97427
Culver	97734
Currinsville	97023
Curtin	97428
Cutler City (Part of Lincoln City)	97367
Dairy	97625
Dale	97880
Daley	97702
Dallas	97338
Damascus	97009
Damascus Heights	97009
Dammasch State Hospital	97070
Danebo (Part of Eugene)	97402
Danner	97910
Days Creek	97429
Dayton	97114
Dayville	97825
Deadwood	97430
Dee	97031
Deer Island	97054
De Lake (Part of Lincoln City)	97367
Delena	97016
Dellwood	97420
Delmoor	97146
Denmark	97450
Depoe Bay	97341
Deschutes Junction	97701
Deschutes River Woods	97701
Detroit	97342
Dever	97321
Dew Valley	97411
Dexter	97431
Diamond	97722
Diamond Lake	97731
Diamond Lake Junction	97731

	ZIP		ZIP		ZIP
Dickey Prairie	97038	Fort Hill	97396	Hauser	97459
Dillard	97432	Fort Klamath	97626	Hayesville	97303
Dilley	97116	Fort Rock	97735	Hazelwood	97230
Dixonville	97470	Fort Stevens (Part of)	97121	Hebo	97122
Dodge	97023	Fortune Branch	97442	Heceta Beach	97439
Dodson	97014	Fossil	97830	Heceta Junction	97439
Dolph Corner	97338	Foster	97345	Helix	97835
Donald	97020	Four Corners (Jackson		Helvetia	97123
Dora	97458	County)	97502	Hemlock (Part of Westfir)	97492
Dorena	97434	Four Corners (Marion		Henley	97603
Dover	97055	County)	97301	Henrice	97045
Downing	97016	Fox	97831	Heppner	97836
Downtown (Part of Bend)	97701	Franklin	97448	Hereford	97837
Drain	97435	Freewater (Part of Milton-		Hermiston	97838
Draperville	97321	Freewater)	97862	Highland	97004
Drew	97484	Frenchglen	97736	Hildebrand	97623
Drewsey	97904	Friend	97021	Hilgard	97850
Dufur	97021	Fruitdale	97526	Hillsboro	97123-24
Dukes Valley	97031	Fruitvale	97365	For specific Hillsboro Zip Codes	
Dundee	97115	Gales Creek	97117	call (503) 294-2308, or your local	
Dunes City	97439	Galice	97532	postmaster.	
Durham	97223	Garden Home	97223	Hines	97738
Durkee	97905	Garden Home-Whitford	97223	Hobsonville	97107
Eagle Creek	97022	Gardiner	97441	Holladay Park (Part of	
Eagle Point	97524	Gardiner Ridge	97415	Portland)	97212
East Gardiner	97467	Garfield	97023	Holland	97523
East Gresham (Part of		Garibaldi	97118	Holley	97386
Gresham)	97030	Gaston	97119	Hollywood (Part of Salem)	97303
East Lake	97739	Gates	97346	Homestead (Baker County)	97840
East Parkrose	97230	Gateway	97741	Homestead (Deschutes	
East Portland (Part of		Gateway Mall (Part of		County)	97702
Portland)	97214	Springfield)	97477	Hood River	97031
Eastside (Part of Coos Bay)	97420	Gaylord	97458	Horton	97412
Eastwood (Part of		Gazley	97457	Hoskins	97326
Roseburg)	97470	Gearhart	97138	Hot Lake	97850
Echo	97826	George	97023	Hubbard	97032
Echo Dell	97045	Gervais	97026	Hugo	97526
Eckman Lake	97394	Gibbon	97810	Hunter Creek	97444
Eddyville	97343	Gilbert	97266	Huntington	97907
Elgarose	97470	Gilchrist	97737	Idanha	97350
Elgin	97827	Gillespie Corners	97405	Idaville	97141
Elk City	97391	Gilliams	97338	Idleyld Park	97447
Elkhead	97499	Gladstone	97027	Illahe	97406
Elkhorn	97358	Glasgow	97459	Illinois Valley	97523
Elk Lake	97701	Glenada	97439	Imbler	97841
Elkton	97436	Glenbrook	97456	Imnaha	97842
Ellendale	97338	Glendale	97442	Independence	97351
Ellingson Mill	97884	Gleneden Beach	97388	Indian Ford	97759
Elliott Prairie	97071	Glengary	97470	Indian Village	97720
Elmira	97437	Glenmorrie (Part of Lake		Inglis	97016
Elsie	97138	Oswego)	97034	Interlachen	97060
Elwood	97017	Glenwood (Clatsop County)	97146	Ione	97843
Emerald Heights (Part of		Glenwood (Lane County)	97401	Ironside	97908
Astoria)	97103	Glenwood (Washington		Irrigon	97844
Empire (Part of Coos Bay)	97420	County)	97116	Irving	97401
Endersby	97058	Glide	97443	Island City	97850
Englewood	97420	Globe	97490	Ivy Station	97103
Enterprise	97828	Goble	97048	Jacksonville	97530
Errol Heights	97266	Gold Beach	97444	Jamieson	97909
Estacada	97023	Gold Hill	97525	Jantzen Beach Center (Part	
Eugene	97401-05	Gooseberry	97843	of Portland)	97217
	97440	Goshen	97401	Jasper	97438
For specific Eugene Zip Codes		Government Camp	97028	Jeffers Garden	97103
call (503) 341-3611, or your local		Grande Ronde Indian		Jefferson	97352
postmaster.		Reservation	97396	Jennings Lodge	97222
Fairfield	97026	Grand Ronde	97347	Jewell	97138
Fair Oaks (Clackamas		Grand Ronde Agency	97347	Jimtown	97834
County)	97222	Granite	97877	John Day	97845
Fairoaks (Douglas County)	97479	Grants Pass	97526-27	Johnson City	97222
Fairview (Coos County)	97423	For specific Grants Pass Zip		Jonesboro	97911
Fairview (Multnomah		Codes call (503) 479-7526, or		Jordan	97374
County)	97024	your local postmaster.		Jordan Valley	97910
Fairview (Tillamook County)	97141	Grass Valley	97029	Joseph	97846
Falcon Heights	97601	Green	97470	Junction City	97448
Fall Creek	97438	Green Acres	97420	Juntura	97911
Falls City	97344	Greenberry	97333	Kahneeta Hot Springs	97761
Fargo	97002	Greenhorn	97877	Kamela	97801
Faubion	97049	Greenleaf	97430	Kansas City	97116
Fayetteville	97377	Greenville (Linn County)	97386	Keating	97814
Federal Correctional		Greenville (Washington		Keizer	97307
Institution	97378	County)	97116	Kellogg	97462
Fern Corner	97338	Greenway (Part of Tigard)	97223	Kelso	97009
Fern Hill (Clatsop County)	97103	Gresham	97030	Kendall	97206
Fern Hill (Columbia County)	97048		97080	Keno	97627
Ferns	97338	For specific Gresham Zip Codes		Kent	97033
Fields (Harney County)	97710	call (503) 665-3114, or your local		Kenton (Part of Portland)	97217
Fields (Lane County)	97463	postmaster.		Kerby	97531
Finn Rock	97488	Haines	97833	Kernville	97367
Fir Grove	97401	Halfway	97834	Kimberly	97848
Fir Villa	97338	Halsey	97348	King City	97224
Firwood	97055	Hammond (Part of		Kingman Kolony	97913
Fishers Corner	97045	Warrenton)	97121	Kingsley Field	97603
Fishers Mill	97045	Hampton	97712	Kingston	97383
Fish Lake Resort	97524	Happy Valley	97236	Kings Valley	97361
Five Corners	97630	Harbeck-Fruitdale	97526	Kinton	97005
Flora	97828	Harbor	97415	Kinzua	97830
Floras Lake	97450	Hardman	97836	Kiwanda Beach	97149
Florence	97439	Harlan	97343	Klamath Falls	97601-03
Forest Grove	97116	Harney	97720	For specific Klamath Falls Zip	
Forest Park (Part of		Harper	97906	Codes call (503) 884-9226, or	
Portland)	97210	Harriman	97601	your local postmaster.	
Forfar	97366	Harrisburg	97446	Knappa	97103

	ZIP		ZIP		ZIP
Knoll Heights	97702	Meda	97112	North Fork	97467
Lacomb	97355	Medford	97501	North Howell	97381
Ladd Hill	97070		97504	North Plains	97133
Lafayette	97127	For specific Medford Zip Codes		North Powder	97867
La Grande	97850	call (503) 776-1326, or your local		North Roseburg (Part of	
Lakecreek	97524	postmaster.		Roseburg)	97470
Lake Grove (Part of Lake		Medford Center (Part of		North Santiam	97325
Oswego)	97035	Medford)	97504	North Springfield	97477
Lake of the Woods	97601	Medford Mall (Part of		North Umpqua Village	97447
Lake Oswego	97034-35	Medford)	97504	Norway	97460
For specific Lake Oswego Zip		Medical Springs	97814	Norwood	97062
Codes call (503) 294-2308, or		Mehama	97384	Noti	97461
your local postmaster.		Melrose	97470	Nottingham	97702
Lakeside	97449	Melville	97103	Nyssa	97913
Lakeview	97630	Menlo Park (Part of		Nyssa Heights	97913
Lancaster	97448	Portland)	97230	Oak Grove (Clackamas	
Lancaster Mall (Part of		Merlin	97532	County)	97267
Salem)	97301	Merrill	97633	Oak Grove (Hood River	
Langell Valley	97623	Metolius	97741	County)	97031
Langlois	97450	Metzger	97223	Oak Hills	97225
Langrell	97834	Midland	97634	Oakland	97462
La Pine	97739	Midway (Multnomah		Oakridge	97463
Larwood	97374	County)	97233	Oak Springs	97037
Latham	97424	Midway (Washington		Oakville	97377
Latourell Falls	97014	County)	97123	Oakway Mall (Part of	
Laurel	97123	Mikkalo	97812	Eugene)	97401
Laurel Grove	97411	Miles Crossing	97103	Oatfield	97222
Laurelwood	97119	Mill City	97360	O'Brien	97534
Lawen	97740	Millersburg	97321	Oceanlake (Part of Lincoln	
Leaburg	97489	Milican	97701	City)	97367
Lebanon	97355	Millington	97420	Oceanside	97134
Lee's Camp	97141	Millwood	97486	Odell	97044
Leland	97497	Milo	97429	Odessa	97601
Lents (Part of Portland)	97266	Milton (Part of Milton-		Oklahoma Hill	97016
Leona	97435	Freewater)	97862	Old Colton	97017
Lewisburg	97330	Milton-Freewater	97862	Old Town	97462
Lexington	97839	Milwaukie	97222	Olene	97601
Libby	97420	Minam	97827	Olex	97812
Liberal	97038	Mission	97801	Olney	97103
Liberty	97386	Mist	97016	Ontario	97914
Lime	97907	Mitchell	97750	Ophir	97464
Lincoln	97520	Modeville	97351	Ordnance	97838
Lincoln Beach	97341	Modoc Point	97624	Oregon City	97045
Lincoln City	97367	Mohawk	97477	Orenco	97123
Lindbergh	97048	Mohawk Junction (Part of		Oretech (Part of Klamath	
Little Albany	97390	Springfield)	97477	Falls)	97601
Little Sweden	97346	Mohler	97131	Oretown	97112
Lloyd Center (Part of		Molalla	97038	Orient	97030
Portland)	97232	Monitor	97071	Orleans	97321
Locoda	97016	Monmouth	97361	Otis	97368
Logsden	97357	Monroe	97456	Otter Rock	97369
London	97424	Monument	97864	Outlook	97045
Lone Elder	97013	Moody	97391	Owyhee	97913
Lonerock	97823	Morgan	97843	Oxbow	97840
Long Creek	97856	Moro	97039	Pacific City	97135
Lookingglass (Douglas		Mosier	97040	Page (Part of Albany)	97321
County)	97470	Mountaindale	97113	Paisley	97636
Looking Glass (Union		Mount Angel	97362	Palestine	97321
County)	97827	Mount Hebron	97801	Paradise Park	97023
Lorane	97451	Mount Hood	97041	Parkdale	97041
Lorella	97623	Mount Hood-Parkdale	97041	Parker	97351
Lostine (Wallowa County)	97857	Mount Hood Village	97049	Parkersburg	97411
Lowell	97452	Mount Pleasant (Part of		Park Place	97045
Lower Logan	97045	Oregon City)	97045	Parkrose	97230
Lynch (Part of Portland)	97236	Mount Vernon	97865	Patterson Junction	97844
Lyons	97358	Mulino	97042	Paulina	97751
McCoy	97371	Mulloy	97140	Pedee	97361
Mc Dermitt	97910	Multnomah (Part of		Peel	97443
McEwen	97877	Portland)	97219	Pendair Heights (Part of	
McKee Bridge	97530	Murphy	97533	Pendleton)	97801
Mc Kenzie Bridge	97413	Myrick	97810	Pendleton	97801
McKinley	97458	Myrtle Creek	97457	Pendleton Junction (Part of	
Macksburg	97013	Myrtle Point	97458	Pendleton)	97801
McMinnville	97128	Narrows (Harney County)	97721	Peoria	97377
McNary (Part of Umatilla)	97882	Narrows (Linn County)	97386	Perry	97850
McNulty	97051	Nashville	97326	Perrydale	97101
Madras	97741	Natal	97064	Philomath	97370
Malin	97632	Neahkahnie	97131	Phoenix	97535
Mall 205 (Part of Portland)	97216	Nedonna	97136	Piedmont (Part of Portland)	97211
Manhattan Beach (Part of		Needy	97013	Pigeon Point	97420
Rockaway)	97136	Nehalem	97131	Pike	97148
Manning	97125	Nelscott (Part of Lincoln		Pilot Rock	97868
Manzanita	97130	City)	97367	Pine	97834
Mapleton	97453	Neotsu	97364	Pine Grove (Hood River	
Marcola	97454	Nesika Beach	97444	County)	97031
Marion	97359	Neskowin	97149	Pine Grove (Wasco County)	97037
Marion Forks	97350	Netarts	97143	Pine Ridge	97624
Marlene Village	97005	Newberg	97132	Pioneer (Part of Portland)	97204
Marquam	97362	New Bridge	97870	Pistol River	97444
Marshland	97016	New Era	97013	Pittsburg	97064
Martin Manor	97225	New Hope	97527	Plainview (Deschutes	
Marylhurst	97036	New Idanha	97350	County)	97701
Mason Additions (Part of		New Pine Creek	97635	Plainview (Linn County)	97377
Prineville)	97754	Newport	97365	Pleasant Hill	97455
Maupin	97037	Newton Creek	97470	Pleasant Valley (Baker	
Mayger	97016	Nimrod	97488	County)	97814
May Park	97850	Ninety One	97013	Pleasant Valley (Josephine	
Mayville	97830	Nonpareil	97479	County)	97532
Maywood Park	97220	North Albany	97321	Pleasant Valley (Tillamook	
Meacham	97859	North Bend	97459	County)	97141
Meadowbrook	97038	North Bend Coast Guard		Plush	97637
Meadow View	97448	Air Station	97459	Pocahontas	97814

	ZIP		ZIP		ZIP
Polk Station	97338		97308-09	Suntex Valley	97758
Pondosa	97814	For specific Salem Zip Codes call		Suplee	97751
Pony Village (Part of North		(503) 370-4700, or your local		Surf Pines	97146
Bend)	97459	postmaster.		Surprise Valley	97457
Porter Creek	97481	Salmon Harbor	97467	Sutherlin	97479
Portland	97201-99	Salt Creek	97338	Suver	97361
For specific Portland Zip Codes		Sams Valley	97525	Suver Junction	97361
call (503) 294-2308, or your local		Sand Lake	97112	Svensen	97103
postmaster.		Sandy	97055	Swedetown	97016
Port Orford	97465	San Marine	97498	Sweet Home	97386
Post	97752	Santa Clara	97404	Swisshome	97480
Powell Butte	97753	Santiam Terrace	97355	Sylvan (Part of Portland)	97221
Powellhurst	97236	Saunders Lake	97459	Table Rock	97501
Powellhurst-Centennial	97236	Scappoose	97056	Taft (Part of Lincoln City)	97367
Powers	97466	Scholls	97123	Takilma	97523
Prairie City	97869	Scio	97374	Talbot	97352
Pratum	97301	Scofield	97109	Talent	97540
Prescott	97048	Scottsburg	97473	Tallman	97355
Princeton	97721	Scotts Mills	97375	Tangent	97389
Prineville	97754	Seal Rock	97376	Taylorville	97016
Prineville Southeast (Part of		Seaside	97138	Telocaset	97883
Prineville)	97754	Seekseequa	97761	Tenmile	97481
Pringle Park Plaza (Part of		Seghers	97119	Terrebonne	97760
Salem)	97301	Sellwood (Part of Portland)	97202	Thatcher	97116
Progress	97005	Sellwood Moreland (Part of		The Dalles	97058
Prospect	97536	Portland)	97202	Thornhollow	97810
Prosper	97411	Selma	97538	Three Lynx	97023
Quinaby	97303	Seneca	97873	Three Rivers	97701
Quincy	97016	Shadowood	97068	Thurston (Part of	
Quines Creek	97442	Shady Cove	97539	Springfield)	97482
Rainbow	97413	Shady Dell	97038	Tide	97480
Rainier	97048	Shaniko	97057	Tidewater	97390
Raleigh Hills	97225	Shasta Plaza (Part of		Tiernan	97453
Ramsey	97701	Klamath Falls)	97603	Tierra Del Mar	97112
Ramsey Hall	97021	Shaw	97325	Tigard	97223
Randolph	97411	Shedd	97377	Tillamook	97141
Redland	97045	Shelburn	97374	Tiller	97484
Redmond	97756	Sheridan	97378	Tillican	97701
Redwood	97526	Sherwood	97140	Timber	97144
Reedsport	97467	Shorewood	97459	Timber Grove	97004
Remote	97458	Shutter Creek Correctional		Timberline Lodge	97028
Reston	97470	Institution	97459	Toketee Falls	97447
Rhododendron	97049	Siletz	97380	Toledo	97391
Rice Hill	97462	Siltcoos	97493	Tollgate	97886
Richardson	97490	Silver Lake	97638	Tolovana Park	97145
Richland	97870	Silverton	97381	Tongue Point Village	97103
Richmond	97874	Silvies	97720	Top	97864
Rickreall	97371	Simnasho	97761	Tophill	97109
Riddle	97469	Sisters	97759	Town Center (Part of	
Rieth	97801	Sitkum	97458	Portland)	97229
Riley	97758	Six Corners (Part of		Trail	97541
Ritter	97872	Sherwood)	97140	Trask	97141
Riverdale (Part of Portland)	97219	Sixes	97476	Treharne	97064
Rivergrove	97035	Skelley	97499	Trent	97431
River Road	97404	Smithfield	97338	Triangle Lake	97412
Riverside (Linn County)	97321	Snake River Correctional		Tri-City	97457
Riverside (Malheur County)	97917	Institution	97914	Trout Creek (Harney	
Riverside (Umatilla County)	97801	Sodaville	97355	County)	97710
Riverton	97423	Southbeach	97366	Trout Creek (Hood River	
Riverview (Columbia		Southgate (Part of Portland)	97266	County)	97041
County)	97064	South Junction	97037	Troutdale	97060
Riverview (Lane County)	97448	South Lebanon	97355	Troy	97828
Roans Estate	97739	South Scappoose	97056	Tualatin	97062
Roaring Springs Ranch	97736	Southside (Part of Eugene)	97405	Tumalo	97701
Robinwood (Part of West		Spicer	97355	Turner	97392
Linn)	97068	Sprague River	97639	Twelve Mile	97030
Rockaway	97136	Spray	97874	Twickenham	97750
Rock Creek (Baker County)	97833	Springbrook	97132	Twin Rocks	97136
Rock Creek (Gilliam County)	97812	Springdale	97060	Twomile	97411
Rockcreek (Washington		Springfield	97477-78	Tygh Valley	97063
County)	97225	For specific Springfield Zip Codes		Ukiah	97880
Rockford	97031	call (503) 747-3383, or your local		Umapine	97862
Rockie Four Corners	97375	postmaster.		Umatilla	97882
Rock Point	97525	Springwater	97023	Umatilla Indian Reservation	97801
Rockville	97910	Stafford	97068	Umpqua	97486
Rockwood	97233	Staleys Junction	97109	Union	97883
Rocky Point	97601	Stanfield	97875	Union Creek	97536
Rogue River	97537	Starkey	97850	Union Gap	97462
Rogue Valley Mall (Part of		Starvout	97410	Union Mills	97042
Medford)	97501	Stayton	97383	Union Point	97327
Rome	97910	Steamboat	97447	Unionvale	97114
Roseburg	97470	Stewart Lennox Addition	97601	Unity (Baker County)	97884
Roseburg North	97470	Stimson Mill	97119	Unity (Lane County)	97438
Rose City Park (Part of		Sublimity	97385	University (Lane County)	97403
Portland)	97213	Summer Lake	97640	University (Multnomah	
Rose Lodge	97372	Summer Lake Hot Springs	97636	County)	97201
Rosemont	97068	Summerville	97876	Upper Highland	97004
Rowena	97058	Summit	97326	Upper Hood River Valley	97044
Roy	97106	Sumner	97420	Upper Soda	97345
Ruch	97530	Sumpter	97877	Vale	97918
Rufus	97050	Sunnycrest	97132	Valley Falls	97630
Ruggs	97836	Sunnydale	97345	Valley Junction	97396
Rural Dell	97032	Sunnyside (Clackamas		Valley River Center (Part of	
Russellville	97216	County)	97015	Eugene)	97401
Rye Valley	97907	Sunnyside (Umatilla County)	97862	Valley View	97321
Saginaw	97424	Sunny Valley	97497	Valsetz	97380
St. Benedict	97373	Sunriver	97707	Van	97904
St. Helens	97051	Sunset (Part of West Linn)	97068	Vaughn	97487
St. Johns (Part of Portland)	97203	Sunset Beach	97146	Veneta	97487
St. Louis	97026	Sunset Hills (Part of		Verboort	97116
St. Paul	97137	Seaside)	97138	Vermont Hills	97219
Salem	97301-06			Vernonia	97064

* Area Zip Code   † Post Office Boxes

	ZIP
Vida	97488
Viola	97023
Vista (Part of Salem)	97302
Waconda	97026
Wagontire	97738
Wagon Trail Ranch	97739
Wakonda Beach	97394
Walden	97424
Waldport	97394
Walker	97426
Wallowa	97885
Wallowa Lake Resort	97846
Walterville	97489
Walton	97490
Wamic	97063
Wapato	97119
Wapinitia	97037
Warm Springs	97761
Warm Springs Indian Reservation	97761
Warren	97053
Warrendale	97014
Warrenton	97146
Wasco	97065
Washington Park Zoo Railway (Part of Portland)	97221
Waterloo	97355
Watseco	97136
Weatherby	97905
Wecoma Beach (Part of Lincoln City)	97367
Wedderburn	97491
Welches	97067
Wemme	97067
Western Evangelical Seminary	97045

	ZIP
Westfall	97920
Westfir	97492
West Haven-Sylvan	97225
West Lake (Clatsop County)	97146
Westlake (Lane County)	97493
West Linn	97068
Weston	97886
Westport	97016
West Salem (Part of Salem)	97304
West Scio	97374
West Side (Lake County)	97630
West Side (Lane County)	97402
West Slope	97225
West Stayton	97325
West St. Helens (Part of St. Helens)	97051
West Union	97123
Wetmore	97830
Weyerhaeuser Townsite	97601
Wheeler	97147
Wheeler Heights (Part of Wheeler)	97147
Whiskey Hill	97032
White City	97503
Whiteson	97101
Wilbur	97494
Wilderville	97543
Wildwood	97049
Wilhoit	97038
Willakenzie (Part of Eugene)	97401
Willamette (Part of West Linn)	97068
Willamette City (Part of Oakridge)	97463
Willamina	97396
Willbridge (Part of Portland)	97231

	ZIP
Williams	97544
Willowcreek	97918
Willowdale	97741
Willsburg Junction (Part of Milwaukie)	97222
Wilson Beach	97141
Wilsonville	97070
Wimer	97537
Winchester	97495
Winchester Bay	97467
Windmaster Corner	97031
Winema Beach	97112
Wingville	97814
Winston	97496
Winterville	97411
Witch Hazel	97123
Wocus	97601
Wolf Creek	97497
Women's Release Unit	97301
Wonder	97543
Woodburn	97071
Woods	97112
Woodson	97016
Wood Village	97060
Worden	97601
Wren	97326
Wyeth	97014
Yachats	97498
Yamhill	97148
Yankton	97051
Yaquina	97365
Yoder	97032
Yoncalla	97499
Yonna	97623
Zigzag	97049

	ZIP
Aaronsburg	16820
Abbott (Township)	16922
Abbottstown	17301
Aberdeen	18444
Abington (Lackawanna County) (Township)	18471
Abington (Montgomery County)	19001
Abington (Montgomery County) (Township)	19001
Abrahamsville	12723
Abrams	19406
Academia	17082
Academy Corners	16928
Academy Gardens (Part of Philadelphia)	19154
Acahela	18610
Accomac	17406
Ache	15454
Ackermanville	18010
Acme	15610
Acmetonia	15024
Acosta	15520
Acre Pond	18826
Adah	15410
Adams (Armstrong County)	16028
Adams (Butler County) (Township)	16046
Adams (Cambria County) (Township)	15955
Adams (Snyder County) (Township)	17813
Adams (Somerset County)	15541
Adamsburg	15611
Adams Corner	16057
Adamsdale	17972
Adams Hill	15642
Adamstown	19501
Adamsville	16110
Addingham	19026
Addison	15411
Addison (Township)	15540
Adelaide	15425
Adio Institute of Straight Chiropractic	19058
Admire	17364
Adrian	16210
Adrian Furnace	15801
Advance	15732
Africa	17236
Afton Village	18034
Aiden Lair	19025
Aiken	16744
Airville	17302
Airydale	17060
Aitch	16693
Ajax	16323
Akeley	16345
Akersville	15536
Akron	17501
Aladdin	15656
Alaska	15825
Alba	16910
Albany (Berks County)	19529
Albany (Berks County) (Township)	19529
Albany (Bradford County) (Township)	18833
Albany (Fayette County)	15417
Albert	18707
Albidale	19006
Albion (Erie County)	16401
Albion (Jefferson County)	15767
Albrightsville	18210
Alburtis	18011
Alcoa Center	15069
Aldan	19018
Alden	18634
Aldenville	18401
Alderson (Part of Harveys Lake)	18618
Aldham	19460
Aleppo (Allegheny County) (Township)	15143
Aleppo (Greene County)	15310
Aleppo (Greene County) (Township)	15310
Alexander Springs	17004
Alexandria	16611
Alfarata	17841
Alford	18826
Alice	15610
Alicia (Fayette County)	15417
Alicia (Greene County)	15338
Alinda	17040
Aline	17853
Aliquippa	15001
Allandale	17011
Allegany (Potter County) (Township)	16915
Allegheny (Allegheny County)	15212

	ZIP
Allegheny (Blair County) (Township)	16635
Allegheny (Butler County) (Township)	16049
Allegheny (Cambria County) (Township)	15940
Allegheny (Somerset County) (Township)	15538
Allegheny (Venango County) (Township)	16341
Allegheny (Westmoreland County) (Township)	15656
Allegheny Acres	15024
Allegheny College (Part of Meadville)	16335
Allegheny Furnace (Part of Altoona)	16602
Allegheny Springs	16371
Alleghenyville	19540
Allemans	16639
Allen (Cumberland County)	17007
Allen (Northampton County) (Township)	18067
Allen Crest	18052
Allen Lane (Part of Philadelphia)	19119
Allenport (Huntingdon County)	17066
Allenport (Washington County)	15412
Allens Mills	15851
Allensville	17002
Allentown	18101-95
For specific Allentown Zip Codes call (215) 821-8450, or your local postmaster.	
Allenvale	15501
Allenwood	17810
Allis Hollow	18837
Allison (Clinton County) (Township)	17751
Allison (Fayette County)	15413
Allison Heights	15413
Allison Park	15101
Allport (Cambria County)	15714
Allport (Clearfield County)	16821
Almaden	16680
Almedia	17815
Almont	18960
Alpha (Part of Windgap)	18091
Alpine	17339
Alsace (Township)	19606
Alsace Manor	19560
Altamont	17931
Altenwald	17268
Althom	16351
Alton	19380
Alton Park (Part of Allentown)	18103
Altoona	16601-03
For specific Altoona Zip Codes call (814) 944-4505, or your local postmaster.	
Alum Bank	15521
Alum Rock	16373
Aluta	18064
Alverda	15710
Alverton	15612
Amaranth	17267
Amasa	18433
Ambau	17362
Amberson	17210
Ambler	19002
Ambler Highlands	19034
Ambridge	15003
Ambridge Heights	15003
Ambrose	15759
Amend	15401
American Philatelic Building (Part of State College)	16801
Amesville	16651
Amity (Berks County) (Township)	19518
Amity (Erie County) (Township)	16438
Amity (Washington County)	15311
Amity Gardens	19518
Amity Hall	17020
Amsbry	16641
Amsterdam	16127
Amwell (Township)	15345
Analomink	18320
Ancient Oaks	18062
Ancient Oaks South	18062
Ancient Oaks West	18062
Andalusia	19020
Anderson	17044
Andersonburg	17047
Anderson Park	15235
Anderson Road	15001
Andersontown	17055
Andreas	18211

	ZIP
Andrews Bridge	17509
Andrews Plan	15001
Andrews Settlement	16923
Angelica	19540
Angels	18445
Angora (Part of Philadelphia)	19143
Anita	15711
Ankeny	15547
Annaline Village	19061
Annin (Township)	16743
Annisville	16049
Annville (Lebanon County) (Township)	17003
Annville (Lebanon County)	17003
Anselma	19425
Ansonia	16901
Ansonville	16656
Antes Fort	17720
Anthony (Lycoming County) (Township)	17728
Anthony (Montour County) (Township)	17772
Anthracite (Part of Cornwall)	17016
Antis (Township)	16617
Antrim (Franklin County) (Township)	17225
Antrim (Tioga County)	16901
Apolacon (Township)	18830
Apollo	15613
Appenzell	18360
Applebachsville	18951
Appletree Hill	19007
Appleville	19380
Applewold	16201
Aquashicola	18012
Aqueduct	17020
Aquetong	18938
Ararat	18465
Ararat (Township)	18465
Arbor	17356
Arbuckle	16438
Arcadia (Indiana County)	15712
Arcadia (Lancaster County)	17563
Archbald	18403
Arch Rock	17059
Arch Spring	16686
Arcola	19420
Ardara	15615
Arden	15301
Ardenheim	16652
Arden Mines	15301
Ardmore	19003
Ardmore Manor	19003
Ardmore Park	19003
Ardsley	19038
Arendtsville	17303
Arensberg	15433
Argentine	16040
Argus	18960
Aristes	17920
Arlingham	19031
Arlingham Hills	19031
Arlington	18436
Arlington Heights (Monroe County)	18360
Arlington Knolls	18052
Arlington Park	15137
Armagh (Indiana County)	15920
Armagh (Mifflin County) (Township)	17063
Armbrust	15616
Armenia (Township)	16947
Armstrong (Indiana County) (Township)	15774
Armstrong (Lycoming County) (Township)	17701
Arnold	15068
Arnold City	15012
Arnot	16911
Arnots Addition (Part of St. Clair)	17970
Arona	15617
Aronimink	19026
Aronwald	19073
Arrowhead Lake	18347
Arsenal (Part of Pittsburgh)	15201
Artemas	17211
Arundel Village	19044
Arwin Acres	17036
Asaph	16901
Asbury (Columbia County)	17859
Asbury (Erie County)	16509
Ashcom	15537
Asherton	17801
Ashfield	18212
Ashland (Clarion County) (Township)	16232
Ashland (Clearfield County)	16666
Ashland (Schuylkill County)	17921
Ashley	18706
Ashtola	15963

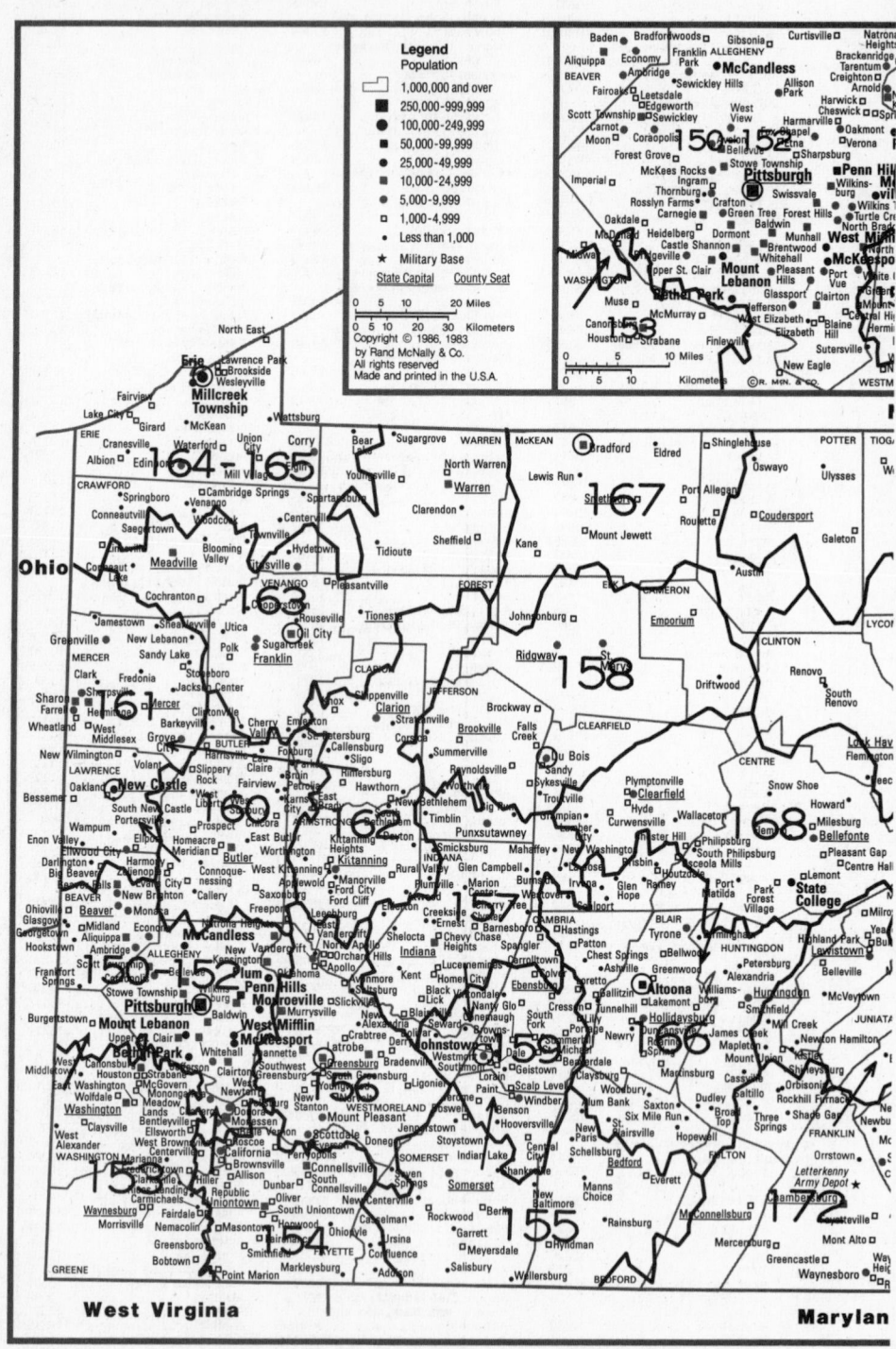

West Virginia   Marylan

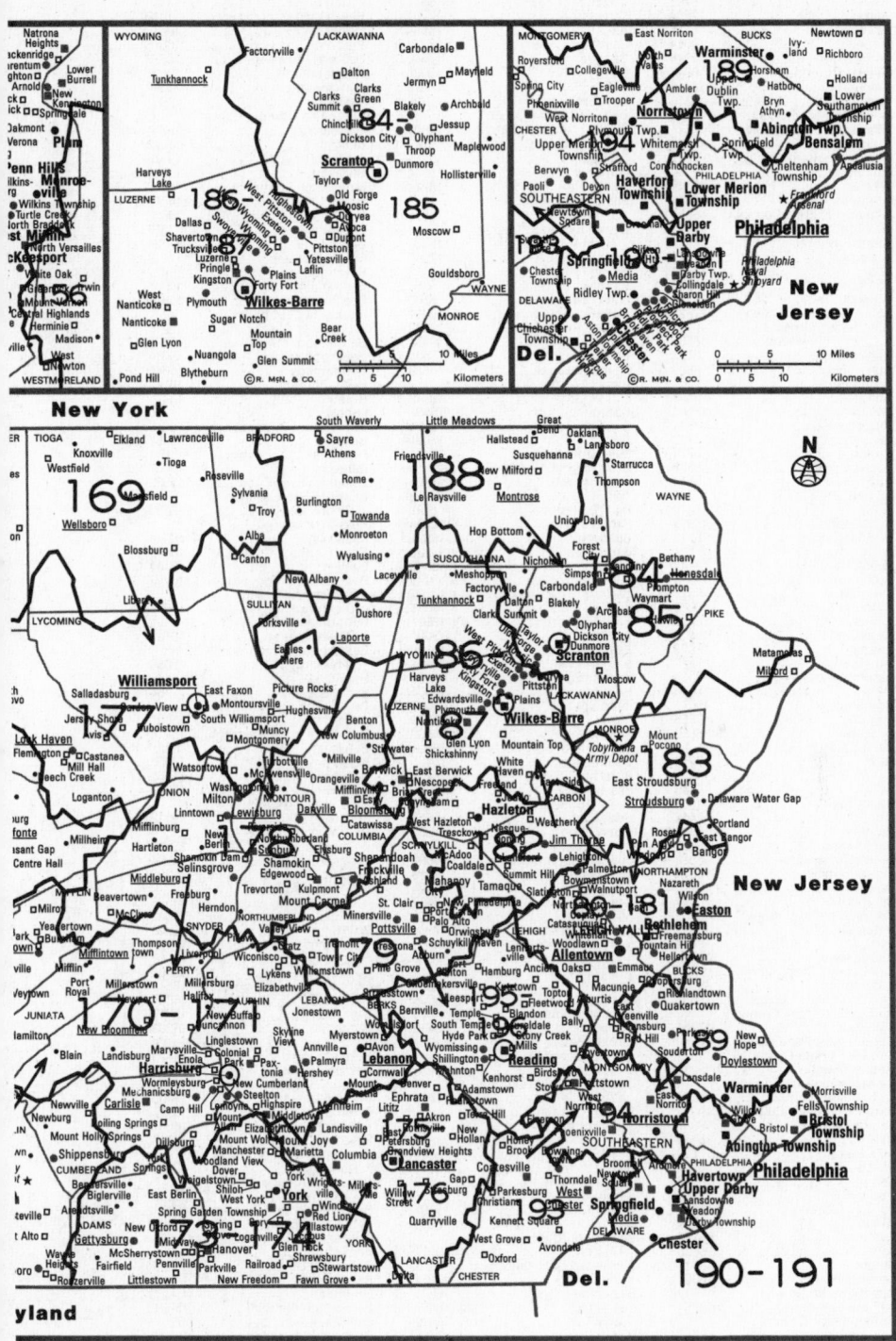

	ZIP
Ashville	16613
Askam	18706
Aspers	17304
Aspinwall	15215
Aston	19014
Aston (Township)	19014
Asylum (Township)	18848
Atco	12764
Atglen	19310
Athens (Bradford County)	18810
Athens (Bradford County) (Township)	18810
Athens (Crawford County) (Township)	16360
Athol	19519
Atkinsons Mills	17051
Atlantic (Clearfield County)	16651
Atlantic (Crawford County)	16111
Atlantic (Westmoreland County)	15671
Atlas	17851
Atlasburg	15004
Atwood	16249
Auburn (Schuylkill County)	17922
Auburn (Susquehanna County) (Township)	18630
Auburn Center	18623
Auburn Four Corners	18630
Audenried	18201
Audubon	19407
Aughwick	17066
Augustaville	17801
Aultman	15713
Austin	16720
Austinburg	16928
Austinville	16914
Avalon	15202
Avella	15312
Avella Heights	15312
Avella Highlands	15312
Avis	17721
Avoca	18641
Avon	17042
Avondale	19311
Avondale Knolls	19086
Avonia	16423
Avonmore	15618
Axemann	16823
Ayr (Township)	17212
Bachmanville	17033
Baden	15005
Baederwood	19046
Bagdad	15656
Baggaley	15650
Baidland	15063
Bailey	17074
Baileys Corner	16926
Baileyville	16865
Bainbridge	17502
Bair	17405
Bairdford	15006
Bairdstown	15717
Bakers Crossroads	16668
Bakers Summit	16614
Baker Station	19390
Bakerstown	15044
Bakerstown (Post Office)	15007
Bakersville	15501
Bala	19004
Bala-Cynwyd	19004
Bala-Cynwyd Shopping Center	19004
Bald Eagle (Blair County)	16686
Bald Eagle (Clinton County) (Township)	17751
Bald Hill (Clearfield County)	16850
Bald Hill (Greene County)	15327
Baldwin (Allegheny County)	15234
Baldwin (Allegheny County) (Township)	15234
Baldwin (Delaware County)	19013
Balliettsville	18037
Balls Eddy	18461
Balls Mills	17728
Balltown	16347
Bally	19503
Balsinger	15484
Banbury Crossing	17036
Bando	15501
Banetown	15301
Baney Settlement	16830
Bangor	18013
Banian Junction	16661
Banks (Carbon County) (Township)	18254
Banks (Indiana County) (Township)	15742
Banksville (Part of Pittsburgh)	15216
Banner Ridge	15757
Bannerville	17841
Banning	15428

	ZIP
Baptist Bible College and School of Theology	18411
Barbours	17701
Bard	15534
Baresville	17331
Bareville	17540
Barkeyville	16038
Barlow	17325
Barnards	16222
Barnes (Cambria County)	15737
Barnes (Jefferson County)	15825
Barnes (Warren County)	16347
Barnesboro	15714
Barneston	19344
Barnesville	18214
Barnett (Forest County) (Township)	15828
Barnett (Jefferson County) (Township)	15860
Barneytown	17052
Barnitz	17013
Barnsley	19363
Barr (Township)	15760
Barree	16611
Barree (Township)	16669
Barren Hill	19444
Barret Plan	15001
Barrett (Clearfield County)	16830
Barrett (Monroe County) (Township)	18342
Barronvale	15557
Barr Slope	15734
Barville	17084
Barry (Township)	17921
Barry Heights (Part of Norristown)	19401
Bart	17503
Bart (Township)	17562
Barto	19504
Bartonsville	18321
Bartville	17509
Basket	19547
Bassards Corners	16038
Bastress (Township)	17701
Bath	18014
Bath Addition	19007
Bath Manor	19007
Bauerstown	15209
Baumgardner	17584
Baumstown	19508
Bausman	17504
Bavington	15019
Baxter	15829
Beachdale	15530
Beach Haven	18601
Beach Lake	18405
Beachly	15424
Beadling	15228
Beale (Township)	17082
Beallsville	15313
Beans Cove	15535
Bear Creek	18602
Bear Creek (Township)	18602
Bear Creek Lake	18229
Bear Gap	17824
Bear Lake	16402
Bear Rocks	15610
Beartown (Franklin County)	17268
Beartown (Lancaster County)	17555
Bear Valley	17872
Beatty	15650
Beatty Hills	19008
Beaufort Farms	17110
Beaumont	18618
Beaver (Beaver County)	15009
Beaver (Clarion County) (Township)	16232
Beaver (Columbia County) (Township)	17815
Beaver (Crawford County) (Township)	16406
Beaver (Jefferson County) (Township)	15864
Beaver (Snyder County) (Township)	17813
Beaver Acres	15136
Beaver Brook	18201
Beaver Center	16435
Beaverdale (Cambria County)	15921
Beaverdale (Northumberland County)	17851
Beaverdale-Lloydell	15921
Beaver Dam	16407
Beaver Falls	15010
Beaver Lake	17758
Beaver Meadows	18216
Beaver Springs	17812
Beavertown (Blair County)	16662
Beavertown (Huntingdon County)	16685

	ZIP
Beavertown (Snyder County)	17813
Beavertown (York County)	17019
Beaver Valley	16640
Beccaria	16616
Beccaria (Township)	16627
Bechtelsville	19505
Beckersville	19540
Becks	17901
Becks Run (Part of Pittsburgh)	15201
Bedford	15522
Bedford (Township)	15522
Bedminster	18910
Bedminster (Township)	18910
Beech Creek	16822
Beech Creek (Township)	16822
Beecherstown	17307
Beech Flats	17724
Beech Glen	17758
Beech Grove	15822
Beechmont	15071
Beechton	15824
Beechview (Part of Pittsburgh)	15216
Beechwood	15834
Beechwood Park	19014
Beechwoods	15840
Beersville	18067
Beesons	15445
Beham	15376
Bela	16049
Belair	17601
Belair Park	17601
Belardley	19007
Belden	15522
Belfast (Fulton County) (Township)	17238
Belfast (Northampton County)	18064
Belfast Junction	18042
Belfry	19401
Belknap	16222
Bell (Clearfield County) (Township)	16627
Bell (Jefferson County) (Township)	15767
Bell (Westmoreland County) (Township)	15650
Bell Acres	15143
Bella Vista	17754
Belle Bridge (Part of Lincoln)	15037
Bellefield (Part of Pittsburgh)	15213
Bellefonte	16823
Bellegrove	17003
Bellemont	17562
Belle Valley	16509
Belle Vernon (Fayette County)	15012
Belle Vernon (Washington County)	15012
Belleville	17004
Bellevue	15202
Bell Mountain (Part of Dickson City)	18508
Bell Point	15613
Bellrun	16748
Bells Camp	16727
Bells Landing	15757
Bells Mills	15767
Belltown	17841
Bellview	15301
Bellwood	16617
Belmar	16323
Belmont	15904
Belmont Corner	18453
Belmont Hills	19020
Belmont Homes	15904
Belmont Terrace	19406
Belsano	15922
Belsena Mills	16661
Belton	16117
Beltzhoover (Part of Pittsburgh)	15210
Ben Avon (Allegheny County)	15202
Ben Avon (Indiana County)	15701
Ben Avon Heights	15202
Bencetown	15734
Bendersville	17306
Bendertown	17859
Benedicks	17315
Benezett	15821
Benezette (Township)	15821
Benfer	17812
Benjamin (Part of Perkasie)	18944
Benner (Township)	16823
Bensalem	19020-21

For specific Bensalem Zip Codes
call (215) 639-5050, or your local
postmaster.

* Area Zip Code   † Post Office Boxes

	ZIP		ZIP		ZIP
Benscreek (Cambria and Somerset Counties)	15905	Big Meadow Run	15417	Bloomingdale (Luzerne County)	18655
Bens Creek (Cambria County)	15938	Big Mine Run	17921	Blooming Glen	18911
Benson	15935	Bigmount	17315	Blooming Grove (Pike County)	18428
Bentley Creek	14894	Big Pond	16914	Blooming Grove (Pike	
Bentleyville	15314	Big Run	15715	County) (Township)	18464
Benton (Columbia County)	17814	Big Shanty	16738	Blooming Grove (York	
Benton (Columbia County) (Township)	17814	Bimber Corners	16351	County)	17331
Benton (Lackawanna County) (Township)	18420	Bingen	18015	Bloomington (Clearfield County)	16833
Benvenue	17020	Bingham (McKean County)	16726	Bloomington (Lackawanna	
Benzinger (Township)	15857	Bingham (Potter County) (Township)	16923	County)	18444
Bergey	19438	Bingham Center	16948	Blooming Valley	16335
Berkeley Hills	15237	Binnstown (Part of		Bloomsburg	17815
Berkley	19605	Centerville)	15417	Bloomsdale Gardens	19058
Berkleys Mill	15552	Bino	17225	Bloserville	17241
Berkshire Heights (Part of Wyomissing)	19610	Birchardville	18801	Bloss (Township)	16911
Berkshire Mall (Part of Wyomissing)	19610	Birchrunville	19421	Blossburg	16912
Berlin (Somerset County)	15530	Birch Valley	19058	Blosser Hill	15451
Berlin (Wayne County) (Township)	18431	Birchwood Lakes	18328	Blossom Hill	17601
Berlin Junction	17350	Birdell	19344	Blossom Valley	17601
Berlinsville	18088	Bird in Hand	17505	Blough	15936
Bermudian	17019	Birdsboro	19508	Blue Ball	17506
Bern (Township)	19605	Birdville	17052	Blue Bell	19422
Berne	19526	Birmingham (Chester County)	19380	Blue Bell Farms	19422
Bernharts	19605	Birmingham (Chester County) (Township)	19380	Blue Bell Gardens	19422
Bernice	18632	Birmingham (Delaware County) (Township)	19317	Blue Bell Knoll	19422
Bernville	19506	Birmingham (Huntingdon County)	16686	Blue Heron Pond	18328
Berrysburg	17005	Bishop	15057	Blue Hill	17870
Berrytown	16925	Bitner	15431	Blue Jay	16347
Bertha	15021	Bittersville	17366	Blueknob	15946
Berwick (Adams County) (Township)	17316	Bitumen	17778	Blue Ridge	19058
Berwick (Columbia County)	18603	Bixler	17047	Blue Ridge Summit	17214
Berwinsdale	16656	Black (Bradford County)	18848	Bluff	15341
Berwyn	19312	Black (Somerset County) (Township)	15557	Blythe (Township)	17930
Besco	15322	Blackash	16327	Blytheburn	18707
Bessemer (Allegheny County)	15104	Black Bear (Part of St. Lawrence)	19606	Blythedale	15018
Bessemer (Lawrence County)	16112	Blackburn (Part of Trafford)	15085	Blythewood	18901
Bessemer (Westmoreland County)	15666	Black Creek (Township)	18246	Boaba	18457
Bessemer Terrace (Part of East Pittsburgh)	15112	Black Diamond (Part of Monongahela)	15063	Boalsburg	16827
Best (Part of West Mifflin)	15122	Blackfield	15542	Boardman	16863
Best Station	18080	Blackgap	17222	Bobbys Corners (Part of Hermitage)	16159
Bethany	18431	Blackhawk	15010	Bobtown	15315
Bethayres	19006	Blackhorse (Chester County)	19365	Bocktown	15001
Bethel (Armstrong County) (Township)	16226	Black Horse (Delaware County)	19063	Bodines	17722
Bethel (Berks County)	19507	Black Horse (Montgomery County)	19401	Boggs (Armstrong County) (Township)	16259
Bethel (Berks County) (Township)	19507	Blacklick (Cambria County) (Township)	15922	Boggs (Centre County) (Township)	16823
Bethel (Cambria County)	15931	Black Lick (Indiana County)	15716	Boggs (Clearfield County) (Township)	16878
Bethel (Delaware County) (Township)	19061	Black Lick (Indiana County) (Township)	15717	Boggstown	17221
Bethel (Fulton County) (Township)	17267	Blacklog	17243	Boggsville	16055
Bethel (Lebanon County) (Township)	17026	Blackman	18702	Bohrmans Mill	17972
Bethel (Mercer County)	16159	Black Ridge	15235	Boiling Springs	17007
Bethel (Westmoreland County)	15687	Blackrock	21088	Bolde Point	18428
Bethelboro	15401	Blacktown	16137	Bolivar	15923
Bethel Park	15102	Black Walnut	18623	Bolivar Run	16701
Bethesda	17532	Blackwell	16938	Boltz	15954
Bethlehem (Northampton County)	18015-18	Blain	17006	Bon Air (Cambria County)	15909
For specific Bethlehem Zip Codes call (215) 866-0911, or your local postmaster.		Blain City	16627	Bon Air (Delaware County)	19083
		Blaine (Township)	15365	Bon Aire	16001
		Blaine Hill	15037	Bondsville	19335
Bethlehem (Clearfield County)	15757	Blainesburg (Part of West Brownsville)	15417	Bonnair	17327
Bethlehem (Northampton County) (Township)	18017	Blainsport	17569	Bonneauville	17325
Bethlehem Annex	18017	Blair (Township)	16635	Bonus	16049
Bethton	18964	Blairs	16232	Booker	16661
Betula	16749	Blairs Mills	17213	Boone	15926
Betz	16661	Blairsville	15717	Booneville	17747
Betzwood	19401	Blairtown	15370	Boon Terrace	15342
Beulah	16661	Blakely	18447	Booths Corner	19061
Beverly Estates	17601	Blakes	16912	Boothwyn	19061
Beverly Heights	17046	Blakeslee	18610	Boothwyn Highlands	19061
Beverly Hills (Blair County)	16601	Blanchard (Allegheny County)	15084	Boot Jack	15853
Beverly Hills (Delaware County)	19082	Blanchard (Centre County)	16826	Boquet	15644
Beyer	16211	Blanco	16249	Bordnersville	17038
Biddle	15692	Blandburg	16619	Borland Manor	15317
Bidwell	15464	Blandon	19510	Bortondale	19063
Biesecker Gap	17268	Blanket Hill	16201	Boston	15135
Big Beaver	15010	Blawnox	15238	Boston Run	17948
Big Cove Tannery	17212	Bloom (Township)	16838	Boswell	15531
Biggertown	17774	Bloomfield (Allegheny County)	15224	Boulevard (Part of Philadelphia)	19149
Bigler	16825	Bloomfield (Bedford County) (Township)	16673	Bourne	18850
Bigler (Township)	16661	Bloomfield (Crawford County) (Township)	16438	Bovard (Butler County)	16020
Biglerville	17307	Bloomingdale (Carbon County)	18250	Bovard (Westmoreland County)	15619
		Bloomingdale (Lancaster County)	17601	Bowdertown	15724
				Bower	15757
				Bower Hill (Allegheny County)	15017
				Bower Hill (Washington County)	15367
				Bowers	19511
				Bowie	16133
				Bowling Green	19063
				Bowman Addition	17331
				Bowman Heights	17201
				Bowmans	17948
				Bowmansdale	17008

	ZIP		ZIP		ZIP
Bowmans Store	17329	Bridesburg (Part of		Brown (Lycoming County)	
Bowmanstown (Carbon		Philadelphia)	19137	(Township)	17727
County)	18030	Bridgeburg	16210	Brown (Mifflin County)	
Bowmansville	17507	Bridgeport (Adams County)	17307	(Township)	17084
Bowser Plan	16201	Bridgeport (Carbon County)	18661	Brownbacks	19475
Boyce	15241	Bridgeport (Clearfield		Browndale	18421
Boyds Mills	18443	County)	16833	Brownfield	15416
Boydstown	16025	Bridgeport (Lancaster		Brownhill	16403
Boydtown	17872	County)	17602	Brown Row	15431
Boyers	16020	Bridgeport (Montgomery		Browns (Part of Avoca)	18641
Boyers Junction	19522	County)	19405	Brownsburg	18938
Boyertown	19512	Bridgeport (Perry County)	17040	Browns Crossroads	16218
Boynton	15532	Bridgeport (Westmoreland		Brownsdale	16053
Brackenridge	15014	County)	15666	Brownstown (Armstrong	
Brackney	18812	Bridgeton (Bucks County)		County)	15630
Bradbury Plan	15001	(Township)	18972	Brownstown (Cambria	
Braddock (Allegheny		Bridgeton (York County)	17352	County)	15906
County)	15104	Bridgetown	19047	Brownstown (Fayette	
Braddock (Washington		Bridge Valley	18925	County)	15438
County)	15301	Bridgeville	15017	Brownstown (Lancaster	
Braddock Hills	15221	Bridgewater (Bucks County)	19020	County)	17508
Braden Plan	15322	Bridgewater (Susquehanna		Brownsville (Berks County)	19565
Bradenville	15620	County) (Township)	18801	Brownsville (Fayette County)	15417
Bradford (Clearfield County)		Bridgewater Farms	19014	Brownsville (Fayette County)	
(Township)	16881	Brier Hill	15415	(Township)	15417
Bradford (McKean County)	16701	Briggsville	18635	Brownsville (Fayette County)	15417
Bradford (McKean County)		Brighton (Township)	15009	Brownsville (Franklin	
(Township)	16701	Brightside	19007	County)	17222
Bradford Hills	19335	Brightwood (Part of Bethel		Brownsville (Schuylkill	
Bradford Park (Part of		Park)	15102	County)	17976
Economy)	15005	Brilhart	17403	Brownsville Junction	15417
Bradfordwoods	15015	Brinkerton	15601	Browntown (Bradford	
Bradley Junction	15931	Brintons	19380	County)	18853
Bradleytown	16317	Briquette (Part of		Browntown (Luzerne	
Brady (Butler County)		Duquesne)	15110	County)	18640
(Township)	16057	Brisbin	16620	Browntown (Washington	
Brady (Clarion County)		Briscoe Springs	16127	County)	15312
(Township)	16248	Bristol	19007	Bruceton	15236
Brady (Clearfield County)		Bristol (Township)	19021	Bruin	16022
(Township)	15848	Bristol Heights	19007	Brunnerville	17543
Brady (Clearfield County)	15801	Bristol Park	19007	Brunots Island (Part of	
Brady (Huntingdon County)		Bristoria	15337	Pittsburgh)	15204
(Township)	17002	Brittany Farms	18914	Brush Creek (Township)	15536
Brady (Lycoming County)		Brittany Farms-Highlands	18914	Brushmeadway	16648
(Township)	17752	Britton Run	16434	Brushtown (Adams County)	17331
Bradys Bend	16028	Broad Acres	16127	Brushtown (Cumberland	
Bradys Bend (Township)	16028	Broad Axe	19002	County)	17241
Braeburn (Part of Lower		Broad Ford	15425	Brush Valley	15720
Burrell)	15068	Broadford Junction	15425	Brush Valley (Township)	15701
Braintrim (Township)	18623	Broadlawn Highlands	15241	Brushville	18847
Braman	18417	Broad Street (Part of		Bryan (Armstrong County)	16222
Bramcote	19464	Hazleton)	18201	Bryan (Fayette County)	15428
Branch (Township)	17901	Broad Top (Bedford		Bryan Hill	15701
Branch Dale	17923	County) (Township)	16633	Bryan Mills	17737
Branchton	16021	Broad Top (Huntingdon		Bryansville	17314
Branchville	16426	County)	16621	Bryant	15101
Brandamore	19316	Broadview	15084	Bryn Athyn	19009
Brandon	16374	Broadway	18655	Bryn Gweled	18966
Brandonville	17967	Broadway Manor	19007	Bryn Mawr (Allegheny	
Brandt	18847	Brock	15362	County)	15221
Brandtsville	17055	Brockie	17403	Bryn Mawr (Montgomery	
Brandy Camp	15822	Brockport	15823	County)	19010
Brandywine Hills	19380	Brockton	17925	Brysonia	17307
Brandywine Homes	19320	Brockway	15824	Bucher	16661
Brandywine Manor	19343	Brodbecks	17329	Buck (Lancaster County)	17566
Brandywine Summit	19342	Brodhead	18017	Buck (Luzerne County)	
Brandywine Village	19406	Brodheadsville	18322	(Township)	18610
Bratton (Township)	17044	Brogue	17309	Buckeye	15666
Brave	15316	Brogueville	17322	Buck Hill Falls	18323
Braznell	15442	Brokenstraw (Township)	16340	Buckhorn (Cambria County)	16613
Breakneck	15425	Brommerstown	17922	Buckhorn (Columbia	
Brecknock (Berks County)		Brookdale (Cambria County)	15942	County)	17815
(Township)	19540	Brookdale (Susquehanna		Buckingham (Bucks	
Brecknock (Lancaster		County)	18822	County)	18912
County) (Township)	17517	Brookes Mills	16635	Buckingham (railroad	
Breezewood (Allegheny		Brookfield (Township)	16950	station) (Bucks County)	18938
County)	15237	Brookhaven	19015	Buckingham (Bucks	
Breezewood (Bedford		Brookland	16948	County) (Township)	18912
County)	15533	Brookline (Allegheny		Buckingham (Wayne	
Breezy Corner	19522	County)	15226	County) (Township)	18437
Breinigsville	18031	Brookline (Delaware County)	19083	Buckingham Valley	18938
Brenizer	15717	Brooklyn	18813	Buckland Valley Farms	18977
Brent	16156	Brooklyn (Township)	18813	Buckman Village (Part of	
Brentwood	15227	Brookside (Cumberland		Chester)	19013
Breslau	18702	County)	17257	Buckmanville	18938
Bressler	17113	Brookside (Erie County)	16510	Buck Mountain (Carbon	
Bressler-Enhaut-Oberlin	17113	Brookside (Lycoming		County)	18255
Bretonville	16656	County)	17771	Buck Mountain (Schuylkill	
Briarbrook	18707	Brookside (Schuylkill		County)	18214
Briarcliff	19036	County)	17963	Buck Run (Chester County)	19320
Briar Creek (Columbia		Brookside (York County)	17315	Buck Run (Indiana County)	15728
County)	18603	Brookside Farms	15241	Buck Run (Schuylkill	
Briar Creek (Columbia		Brookside Villa	18101	County)	17901
County) (Township)	18603	Brookston	16347	Buckstown	15563
Briar Hill (Armstrong		Brookthorpe Hills	19008	Bucksville	18930
County)	16201	Brookvale	15425	Bucktown	19464
Briar Hill (Wayne County)	18438	Brookville	15825	Buck Valley	17267
Briarwood (Part of New		Brookwater Park	19426	Buell Corners	16434
Britain)	18901	Broomall	19008	Buena Vista (Allegheny	
Brickchurch	16226	Brothersvalley (Township)	15530	County)	15018
Brickerville	17543	Brotherton	15530	Buena Vista (Butler County)	16025
Brick Tavern	18951	Broughton	15236		

	ZIP		ZIP		ZIP
Cementon	18052	Charleston (Tioga County)		Chestnut Ridge (Lancaster	
Centennial (Adams County)	17331	(Township)	16901	County)	17603
Centennial (Centre County)	16870	Charlestown	19460	Chestnut View	17603
Centennial Hills	18974	Charlestown (Township)	19460	Chest Springs	16624
Center (Beaver County)		Charlestown	17236	Cheswick	15024
(Township)	15001	Charlesville	15522	Chevy Chase Heights	15701
Center (Butler County)		Charlottsville	16686	Chewton	16157
(Township)	16001	Charlton (Clinton County)	17745	Cheyney	19319
Center (Greene County)		Charlton (Dauphin County)	17112	Chickasaw	16259
(Township)	15359	Charmian	17214	Chickory	15909
Center (Indiana County)		Charming Forge	19551	Chicora	16025
(Township)	15748	Charteroak	16669	Childs	18407
Center (Juniata County)	17059	Charter Oaks	16509	Chillisquaque	17850
Center (Perry County)	17062	Charterwood	15237	Chinchilla	18410
Center Bridge	18938	Chartiers (Township)	15342	Chippewa (Township)	15010
Center City (Part of		Chartiers Terrace	15106	Choconut	18812
Williamsport)	17701	Chase	18708	Choconut (Township)	18818
Center Hill	16201	Chatham (Chester County)	19318	Christiana	17509
Center Manor	15061	Chatham (Tioga County)		Christian Springs	18064
Center Mills	17304	(Township)	16935	Christmans	18229
Center Moreland	18657	Chatham Park	19083	Christy Manor	16226
Centerport	19516	Chatham Village	19083	Chrome	19362
Center Road	16424	Chatwood	19380	Chrystal	16748
Center Square	19422	Checkerville	16925	Church Hill (Fayette County)	15458
Centertown	16127	Chelsea	19013	Church Hill (Forest County)	16321
Center Union	16652	Chelten Avenue (Part of		Church Hill (Franklin	
Center Valley	18034	Philadelphia)	19144	County)	17236
Centerville (Bedford County)	15522	Cheltenham	19012	Church Hill Manor	17084
Centerville (Crawford		Cheltenham (Township)	19012	Churchill	15235
County)	16404	Cheltenham Shopping		Churchill Plan	16117
Centerville (Lancaster		Center	19095	Churchill Valley	15235
County)	17602	Cheltenham Square	19150	Churchtown	17555
Centerville (Perry County)	17045	Cherokee Ranch	19560	Churchville (Bedford	
Centerville (Washington		Cherry (Butler County)		County)	16667
County)	15417	(Township)	16057	Churchville (Bucks County)	18966
Centerville (York County)	17327	Cherry (Sullivan County)		Cinnamon Hills	19406
Central (Allegheny County)	15132	(Township)	18614	Circleville	15642
Central (Columbia County)	17814	Cherry City	15209	Cisna Run	17047
Central (Washington		Cherrydale	19444	Cito	17233
County)	15301	Cherry Flats	16917	City View	17044
Central (Westmoreland		Cherry Grove (Huntingdon		Clair Manor	15012
County)	15688	County)	17264	Clairton	15025
Central City (Centre County)	16853	Cherry Grove (Warren		Clairton Junction (Part of	
Central City (Somerset		County)	16313	West Mifflin)	15122
County)	15926	Cherry Grove (Warren		Clamtown	18252
Central Highlands	15037	County) (Township)	16313	Clappertown	16693
Centralia	17927	Cherry Hill (Erie County)	16401	Clapp Farm	16301
Central Manor	17582	Cherryhill (Indiana County)		Clara (Township)	16748
Central Oak Heights	17886	(Township)	15765	Clarence	16829
Central Park	15037	Cherry Hill (Lancaster		Clarendon	16313
Central Square Greens	19401	County)	17563	Clarendon Heights (Warren	
Central Wharf (Part of		Cherry Hill (Northampton		County)	16313
Munhall)	15120	County)	18064	Claridge	15623
Centre (Berks County)		Cherry Hill (York County)	17070	Clarington	15828
(Township)	19541	Cherry Lane	15613	Clarion	16214
Centre (Perry County)	17047	Cherry Ridge (Township)	18431	Clarion (Township)	16829
Centre (Perry County)		Cherry Run	17885	Clark	16113
(Township)	17068	Cherrytown	16657	Clark Manor	15001
Centre (Snyder County)		Cherry Tree (Indiana		Clarksburg	15725
(Township)	17842	County)	15724	Clarks Green	18411
Centre Hall	16828	Cherry Tree (Venango		Clarks Mills	16114
Centre Hill	16828	County)	16354	Clarks Summit	18411
Century	15417	Cherrytree (Venango		Clarks Summit State	
Century III Mall (Part of		County) (Township)	16354	Hospital	18501
West Mifflin)	15122	Cherry Valley (Butler		Clarkstown	17756
Ceres (Township)	16748	County)	16373	Clarksville	15322
Cessna	15522	Cherry Valley (Washington		Clarksville Hill	15322
Cetronia	18104	County)	15021	Claussville	18069
Ceylon	15320	Cherryville (Northampton		Clay (Township)	17578
Chadds Ford	19317	County)	18035	Clay (Butler County)	
Chadville	15401	Cherryville (Schuylkill		(Township)	16061
Chain	17960	County)	17966	Clay (Huntingdon County)	
Chain Bridge	18940	Chest (Cambria County)		(Township)	17264
Chaintown	15428	(Township)	16668	Clay (Lancaster County)	17522
Chalfant	15112	Chest (Clearfield County)		Clay Hill	17201
Chalfont	18914	(Township)	16656	Claylick	17236
Chalkhill	15421	Chester	19013-16	Claypoole Heights	15701
Challenge	15823	For specific Chester Zip Codes		Claysburg	16625
Chalybeate	15522	call (215) 876-1613, or your local		Claysville	15323
Chambersburg	17201	postmaster.		Clayton	19503
Chambers Hill	17111	Chesterbrook	19087	Claytonia	16057
Chambers Mill	15301	Chesterfield	16627	Clearbrook	19050
Chambersville	15723	Chester Heights	19017	Clearbrook Village	19040
Champion	15622	Chester Hill	16866	Clearfield (Butler County)	
Chanceford (Township)	17309	Chester Plaza	19014	(Township)	16034
Chandler Plan	16226	Chester Springs	19425	Clearfield (Cambria County)	
Chandlers Valley	16312	Chester Township	19013	(Township)	16668
Chaneysville	15535	Chester Valley Knoll	19355	Clearfield (Clearfield	
Chapel	18070	Chesterville	19350	County)	16830
Chapel Downs	15024	Chestnut Grove	16838	Clearfield (Northampton	
Chapel Valley	15001	Chestnut Hill (Erie County)	16509	County)	18064
Chapman (Clinton County)		Chestnut Hill (Lancaster		Clear Ridge	17229
(Township)	17760	County)	17512	Clear Run	15801
Chapman (Lehigh County)	18106	Chestnuthill (Monroe		Clear Spring	17019
Chapman (Northampton		County) (Township)	18331	Clearview	17601
County)	18014	Chestnut Hill (Northampton		Clearview Estates (Beaver	
Chapman (Snyder County)	17864	County)	18042	County)	15001
Chapman (Snyder County)		Chestnut Hill (Philadelphia		Clearview Estates	
(Township)	17864	County)	19118	(Cumberland County)	17011
Chapman Lake	18433	Chestnut Level	17566	Clearview Manor	18101
Charleroi	15022	Chestnut Ridge (Fayette		Clearville	15535
Charleston (Mercer County)	16146	County)	15422	Cleona	17042

	ZIP		ZIP		ZIP
Clermont	16740	Cold Spring (Lebanon		Conemaugh (Indiana	
Cleveland (Township)	17820	County) (Township)	17028	County) (Township)	15725
Cleversburg	17257	Cold Spring (York County)	17360	Conestoga (Chester	
Cliff Mine	15108	Cold Spring Park	19464	County)	19520
Clifford (Snyder County)	17870	Cold Springs Crossing	19426	Conestoga (Lancaster	
Clifford (Susquehanna		Colebrook (Clinton County)		County)	17516
County)	18413	(Township)	17734	Conestoga (Lancaster	
Clifford (Susquehanna		Colebrook (Lebanon		County) (Township)	17516
County) (Township)	18413	County)	17015	Conestoga Farms	19317
Clifton (Dauphin County)	17057	Colebrookdale	19512	Conestoga Woods	17602
Clifton (Lackawanna		Colebrookdale (Township)	19512	Coneville	16748
County) (Township)	18424	Colegrove	16749	Conewago (Adams County)	
Clifton (Lackawanna		Coleman	15541	(Township)	17331
County)	18424	Colemanville	17565	Conewago (Dauphin	
Clifton Heights	19018	Colerain (Bedford County)		County) (Township)	17022
Climax (Armstrong County)	16216	(Township)	15522	Conewago (York County)	
Climax (Clarion County)	16216	Colerain (Huntingdon		(Township)	17404
Climax (Indiana County)	15944	County)	16683	Conewago Heights	17345
Clinton (Allegheny County)	15026	Colerain (Lancaster County)		Conewango (Township)	16365
Clinton (Armstrong County)	16229	(Township)	17536	Confluence	15424
Clinton (Butler County)		Coles	17948	Congo	19504
(Township)	16001	Colesburg	16915	Congruity	15601
Clinton (Fayette County)	15469	Coles Creek	17814	Conifer	15864
Clinton (Lycoming County)		Colesville	18015	Connaughton	19428
(Township)	17752	Coleville (Centre County)	16823	Conneaut (Crawford	
Clinton (Venango County)		Coleville (McKean County)	16749	County) (Township)	16424
(Township)	16373	Colfax	16652	Conneaut (Erie County)	
Clinton (Wayne County)		College (Beaver County)	15010	(Township)	16401
(Township)	18472	College (Centre County)		Conneaut Lake	16316
Clinton (Wyoming County)		(Township)	16801	Conneaut Lake Park	16316
(Township)	18419	College (Northampton		Conneaut Lakeshore	16316
Clintondale	17751	County)	18042	Conneautville	16406
Clintonville	16372	College A (Part of East		Connellsville	15425
Cloe	15767	Stroudsburg)	18301	Connellsville (Township)	15425
Clonmell	19390	College Heights	19605	Connersville	17851
Clover (Township)	15829	College Hill (Part of Beaver		Connerton	17935
Cloverdale Park	18915	Falls)	15010	Connoquenessing	16027
Clover Hill	15423	College Manor	18612	Connoquenessing	
Clover Run	15757	College Misericordia	18612	(Township)	16053
Clune	15727	College Park (Montgomery		Conoy (Township)	17502
Cly	17370	County)	19031	Conrad	16720
Clyde	15944	College Park (Union		Conshohocken	19428
Clyde No. 3	15322	County)	17837	Continental (Part of	
Clymer (Indiana County)	15728	College View Heights	18016	Philadelphia)	19106
Clymer (Tioga County)		Collegeville	19426	Conway	15027
(Township)	16943	Colley (Township)	18614	Conyngham (Columbia	
Coal (Township)	17872	Collier (Allegheny County)		County) (Township)	17851
Coal Bluff	15332	(Township)	15106	Conyngham (Luzerne	
Coal Brook	15425	Collier (Fayette County)	15401	County)	18219
Coal Cabin Beach	17314	Collingdale	19023	Conyngham (Luzerne	
Coal Castle	17901	Collins	17566	County) (Township)	18655
Coal Center	15423	Collinsburg	15089	Cook (Township)	15687
Coal City	16374	Collinsville	17302	Cooke (Township)	17241
Coaldale (Dauphin County)	17048	Collinswood Acres	15017	Cookport	15729
Coaldale (Schuylkill County)	18218	Collomsville	17701	Cooksburg	16217
Coal Glen	15824	Colmar	18915	Cookseytown	18707
Coal Hill	16301	Colona (Part of Monaca)	15061	Cooks Mills	15545
Coal Hollow	15846	Colonial Crest	17111	Cooks Run	17778
Coal Junction	15531	Colonial Hills (Berks County)	19608	Coolbaugh (Township)	18466
Coalmont	16678	Colonial Hills (Mifflin County)	17044	Coolbaughs	18324
Coalport (Carbon County)	18229	Colonial Manor	17603	Coolspring (Fayette County)	15445
Coalport (Clearfield County)	16627	Colonial Park (Dauphin		Coolspring (Jefferson	
Coal Run (Clearfield		County)	17109	County)	15730
County)	16666	Colonial Park (Delaware		Coolspring (Mercer County)	
Coal Run (Northumberland		County)	19064	(Township)	16137
County)	17866	Colonial Park (Lancaster		Cool Valley (Washington	
Coal Run (Somerset		County)	17540	County)	15317
County)	15552	Colonial Park		Cool Valley (Westmoreland	
Coaltown (Butler County)	16057	(Northumberland County)	17847	County)	15601
Coaltown (Lawrence		Colonial Village	19087	Coon Hunter	17842
County)	16101	Colony Park	19608	Coontown	16735
Coatesville	19320	Columbia (Bradford County)		Cooper (Clearfield County)	
Cobalt Ridge	19058	(Township)	16914	(Township)	16839
Cobblerville	17218	Columbia (Lancaster		Cooper (Montour County)	
Cobbs Corners	16434	County)	17512	(Township)	17821
Cobham	16351	Columbia Cross Roads	16914	Coopersburg	18036
Coburn (Blair County)	16601	Columbus	16405	Cooper Settlement	16834
Coburn (Centre County)	16832	Columbus (Township)	16405	Cooperstown (Butler	
Cocalico	17517	Colver	15927	County)	16059
Cochran Acres	15001	Colwyn	19023	Cooperstown (Venango	
Cochrans Mills	16226	Comly	17772	County)	16317
Cochranton	16314	Commerce (Part of		Cooperstown	
Cochranville	19330	Philadelphia)	19108	(Westmoreland County)	15650
Cocolamus	17014	Commodore	15729	Coopersville	17509
Codorus	17311	Compass	17527	Copella	18014
Codorus (Township)	17327	Conashaugh Lake	18337	Copesville	19380
Coffeetown (Lebanon		Concord (Butler County)		Coplay	18037
County)	17078	(Township)	16025	Coral	15731
Coffeetown (Lehigh County)	18069	Concord (Delaware County)		Coraopolis	15108
Coffeetown (Northampton		(Township)	19331	Coraopolis Heights	15108
County)	18042	Concord (Erie County)		Corinne	19380
Cogan House (Township)	17771	(Township)	16407	Cork Lane	18640
Cogan Station	17728	Concord (Franklin County)	17217	Corliss (Part of Pittsburgh)	15204
Cokeburg	15324	Concord (Westmoreland		Corner Ketch	19335
Cokeburg Junction	15331	County)	15012	Corner Store	19460
Cold Point	19462	Concord Park	19047	Corning	18092
Cold Run	19508	Concordville	19331	Cornish	15451
Cold Spring (Franklin		Conemaugh (Cambria		Cornog	19343
County)	17222	County) (Township)	15902	Cornplanter (Township)	16301
Cold Spring (Huntingdon		Conemaugh (Somerset		Cornpropst	16652
County)	16652	County) (Township)	15905	Cornwall	17016

	ZIP		ZIP		ZIP
Cornwall Center (Part of Cornwall)	17016	Crescent Lake (Monroe County)	18332	Cyclone	16726
Cornwells Heights-Eddington	19020	Crescent Lake (Pike County)	18337	Cymbria Mine	15714
Corrine	19380	Cresco	18326	Cynwyd Estates	19004
Corry	16407	Creslo	15951	Cynwyd Hills	19004
Corsica	15829	Cresmont	17931	Cypher	16650
Cortez (Jefferson County)	15767	Cresmont Farms	19335	Daggett	16936
Cortez (Lackawanna County)	18436	Cress	17268	Dagus	15846
Corwins Corners	16701	Cresson	16630	Daguscahonda	15853
Corydon (Township)	16701	Cresson (Township)	16630	Dagus Mines	15831
Coryville	16731	Cressona	17929	Daisytown (Cambria County)	15902
Costello	16720	Crestmont (Clinton County)	17745	Daisytown (Washington County)	15427
Cosytown	17225	Crestmont (Montgomery County)	19090	Dale (Cambria County)	15902
Coterell Lake	18470	Crestmont Village	15001	Dale (Clearfield County)	16881
Cottage	16669	Crestview	19040	Dale Summit	16801
Cottage Grove	16105	Crestwood	18444	Daleville (Chester County)	19330
Cottage Hill	16242	Creswell	17516	Daleville (Lackawanna County)	18424
Cottageville	18901	Crete	15701	Dalevue	16801
Cotton Town	16625	Criders Corners	16046	Daley	15924
Couchtown	17047	Crimson Maple	18837	Dallas	18612
Coudersport	16915	Croft	16830	Dallas (Township)	18612
Coulters	15028	Cromby	19460	Dallas City	16701
Council Crest	18201	Cromwell (Township)	17260	Dallastown	17313
Country Club Estates (Armstrong County)	16201	Crooked Creek	16652	Dalmatia	17017
Country Club Estates (Lancaster County)	17601	Crookham	15332	Dalton	18414
		Crosby	16724	Damascus	18415
Country Club Estates (Montgomery County)	19444	Cross Creek	15021	Damascus (Township)	18415
Country Club Heights	17601	Cross Creek (Township)	15312	Danboro	18916
Country Gardens	17540	Cross Fork	17729	Danielsville	18038
Country Hills	15642	Crossgrove	17841	Dannersville	18067
Countryside	17011	Crossingville	16412	Danville	17821
County Line	18966	Cross Keys (Adams County)	17350	Danville State Hospital	17821
County Line Park	18914	Cross Keys (Blair County)	16635	Darby	19023
Coupon	16629	Cross Keys (Bucks County)	18901	Darby (Township)	19036
Court at King of Prussia, The	19406	Cross Keys (Juniata County)	17021	Darby Township (census designated place)	19036
Courtdale	18704	Crossroads (Northampton County)	18014	Darlington (Beaver County)	16115
Courtney	15029	Cross Roads (York County)	17322	Darlington (Beaver County) (Township)	16115
Cove	17020	Crosswicks	19046	Darlington (Delaware County)	19063
Covedale	16693	Crown	16220	Darlington (Westmoreland County)	15658
Cove Gap	17236	Croydon	19021	Darlington Corners	19380
Coventryville	19464	Croydon Acres	19021	Darragh	15625
Coverdale (Part of Bethel Park)	15102	Croydon Crest	19021	Darthmouth Farms	17036
Coveville	18325	Croydon Heights	19021	Dartmouth Hills	19406
Covington (Clearfield County) (Township)	16836	Croydon Manor	19021	Dauberville	19517
Covington (Lackawanna County) (Township)	18424	Croydon Park	19021	Daugherty (Township)	15066
Covington (Tioga County)	16917	Croyle (Township)	15955	Dauphin	17018
Covington (Tioga County) (Township)	16917	Crozer Park Gardens (Part of Chester)	19013	Davidsburg	17315
Covode	15767	Crucible	15325	Davidson (Township)	17758
Cowan	17844	Crum Creek Manor	19013	Davidson Heights	15001
Cowanesque	16918	Crum Lynne	19022	Davidsville	15928
Cowansburg	15642	Crum Lynne (Part of Ridley Park)	19078	Davis Grove	19044
Cowanshannock (Township)	16222	Crystal	15439	Davistown (Fayette County)	15446
Cowans Village	17224	Crystal Lake	18407	Davistown (Greene County)	15349
Cowansville	16218	Crystal Spring	15536	Dawson	15428
Cowden	15057	Crystal View	15084	Dawson Manor	19040
Coxeville	18216	Cuba Mills	17059	Dawson Ridge	15009
Coy	15748	Cuddy	15031	Dawson Run	16370
Coy Junction	15748	Cuddy Hill	15031	Day	16258
Coyleville	16034	Culbertson	17201	Daylesford	19312
Crabapple	15380	Culmerville	15084	Dayton (Armstrong County)	16222
Crabtree	15624	Culp	16601	Dayton (Dauphin County)	17098
Crabtree Hollow	19053	Culpepper Woods	19444	Deal	15552
Crackersport	18104	Cumberland (Adams County) (Township)	17325	Dean	16636
Crafton	15205	Cumberland (Greene County) (Township)	15320	Dean (Township)	16636
Craig	18414	Cumberland Park	17011	Deanville	16242
Craigheads	17013	Cumberland Valley (Township)	15522	Dearth	15401
Craigs	17948	Cumberland Village	15320	Decatur (Clearfield County) (Township)	16666
Craigs Meadow	18301	Cumbola	17930	Decatur (Mifflin County) (Township)	17841
Craigsville	16262	Cummings (Township)	17776	Deckard	16314
Craley	17312	Cummingstown	17013	Deckers Point	15759
Cramer	15954	Cummingswood Park	15610	Deckertown	18446
Cranberry (Butler County) (Township)	16046	Cumru (Township)	19540	Deemers Cross Roads	15851
Cranberry (Luzerne County)	18201	Cupola	19344	Deemston	15333
Cranberry (Venango County)	16319	Curllsville	16221	Deep Dale East	19058
Cranberry (Venango County) (Township)	16319	Curren Terrace (Part of Norristown)	19401	Deep Dale West	19058
Cranberry Estates	16046	Curry Run	15757	Deep Run	18944
Cranberry Ridge	18201	Curryville	16631	Deep Valley	15352
Cranesville	16410	Curtin	16841	Deer Creek (Township)	16145
Crates	16240	Curtin (Township)	16841	Deercroft	19444
Crawford (Township)	17740	Curtis Hills	19095	Deerfield (Tioga County) (Township)	16928
Crawfordtown	15733	Curtis Park (Centre County)	16866	Deerfield (Warren County) (Township)	16351
Creamery	19430	Curtis Park (Delaware County)	19079	Deer Lake (Fayette County)	15421
Creekside	15732	Curtisville	15032	Deer Lake (Schuylkill County)	17961
Creighton	15030	Curwensville	16833	Deer Mt. Lake (Monroe County)	18370
Crenshaw	15824	Cush Creek	15712	Deer Mt. Lake (Monroe County)	18355
Crescent (Township)	15046	Cussewago (Township)	16433	Deer Park	18938
Crescentdale (Part of Wampum)	16157	Custards	16314	Defiance	16633
Crescent Heights	15427	Custer City	16725	Degolia	16701
		Custis Woods	19038	Deiblers Station	17821
		Cutler Summit	16923		

	ZIP		ZIP		ZIP
Delabole	18072	Dombach Manor	17601	Du Bois	15801
De Lancey	15733	Donaldson	17981	Duboistown	17701
Delano	18220	Donaldson Crossroads	15317	Dudley	16634
Delano (Township)	18220	Donation	16652	Duffield	17201
Delaware (Juniata County)		Donegal (Butler County)		Duffs Junction (Part of	
(Township)	17094	(Township)	16025	Pittsburgh)	15230
Delaware (Mercer County)		Donegal (Washington		Duhring	16239
(Township)	16125	County) (Township)	15323	Duke Center	16729
Delaware (Northumberland		Donegal (Westmoreland		Dumas	15424
County) (Township)	17777	County) (Township)	15646	Dunbar	15431
Delaware (Pike County)		Donegal (Westmoreland		Dunbar (Township)	15425
(Township)	18328	County)	15628	Duncan (Township)	16901
Delaware Grove	16124	Donegal Heights	17552	Duncan Circle	15009
Delaware Valley College		Donegal Springs	17552	Duncannon	17020
(Part of New Britain)	18901	Donerville	17603	Duncansville	16635
Delaware Water Gap	18327	Donnally Mills	17062	Duncott	17901
Dellville	17020	Donnelly	15612	Dundaff	18407
Delmar (Township)	16901	Donnellytown	17013	Dundore	17864
Delmont	15626	Donohoe	15650	Dungarvin	16877
Delphi	19473	Donora	15033	Dunkard	15327
Delps	18038	Dooleyville	17851	Dunkard (Township)	15315
Delroy	17406	Dora (Greene County)	15338	Dunkelbergers	17872
Delta	17314	Dora (Jefferson County)	15767	Dunlap Creek Village	15475
Delta Manor	18017	Dormont	15216	Dunlevy	15432
Demmler	15137	Dorneyville	18104	Dunlo	15930
Demmler Transfer	15137	Dornsife	17823	Dunminning	19073
Dempseytown	16317	Dorothy	15650	Dunmore	18512
Denbeau Heights (Part of		Dorrance	18707	Dunn	15329
Centerville)	15417	Dorrance (Township)	18707	Dunningsville	15330
Denbo (Part of Centerville)	15429	Dorset	17960	Dunningtown	15632
Denholm	17059	Dorseyville	15238	Dunns Eddy	16371
Dennison (Township)	18661	Dott	17267	Dunnstable (Township)	17751
Dennys Mill	16023	Dotters Corners	18058	Dunnstown	17745
Dents Run	15832	Doubling Gap	17241	Dupont	18641
Denver	17517	Douglass (Berks County)		Duquesne	15110
Deodate	17022	(Township)	19464	Duquesne Heights (Part of	
Deringer	18241	Douglass (Montgomery		Pittsburgh)	15211
Derrick City	16727	County) (Township)	19525	Duquesne Wharf (Part of	
Derrs	17814	Douglassville	19518	Duquesne)	15110
Derry (Dauphin County)		Doutyville	17872	Durbin	15380
(Township)	17033	Dover	17315	Durham	18039
Derry (Mifflin County)		Dover (Township)	17315	Durham (Township)	18039
(Township)	17099	Down East	19355	Durham Furnace	18930
Derry (Montour County)		Downey	15530	Durlach	17522
(Township)	17821	Downieville	16059	Durrell	18848
Derry (Westmoreland		Downingtown	19335	Duryea	18642
County)	15627	Downtown (Part of Erie)	16501	Dushore	18614
Derry (Westmoreland		Downtown (Part of		Dutch Hill (Clarion County)	16049
County) (Township)	15627	Uniontown)	15401	Dutch Hill (Fayette County)	15450
Derwood Park	19094	Downtown (Part of		Dutch Hill (Mercer County)	16148
Derwyn	19004	Lancaster)	17603	Dutch Settlement	15946
Deshon Manor	16001		17608	Dutchtown	17236
Desire	15851	For specific Downtown Zip Codes		Dutton Mill	19380
Detters Mill	17315	call (717) 299-2359, or your local		Dyberry (Township)	18431
De Turksville	17963	postmaster.		Dysart	16636
Devault	19432	Doylesburg	17219	Eagle Foundry	16621
Devon	19333	Doyles Mills	17058	Eaglehurst	16509
Devon-Berwyn	19312	Doylestown	18901	Eagle Point	19530
Dewart	17730	Doylestown (Township)	18901	Eagle Rock	16301
Dewey Heights	18052	Drake	16156	Eagles Mere	17731
De Young	16728	Drakes Mills	16403	Eagles Mere Park (Part of	
Diamond (Clarion County)	16248	Draketown	15424	Eagles Mere)	17731
Diamond (Venango County)	16354	Drane	16666	Eagleville (Centre County)	16826
Diamondtown	17851	Draper	16901	Eagleville (Montgomery	
Diamondville	15728	Drauckers	15848	County)	19408
Dice	17844	Dravosburg	15034	Earl (Berks County)	
Dickerson Run	15430	Dreher (Township)	18445	(Township)	19512
Dickey	17236	Drehersville	17961	Earl (Lancaster County)	
Dickinson	17218	Drennen	15068	(Township)	17557
Dickinson (Township)	17065	Dresher	19025	Earlington	18918
Dicksonburg	16406	Drexelbrook	19026	Earlston	15537
Dickson City	18519	Drexel Heights	19067	Earlville	15519
Dieners Hall	17901	Drexel Hill	19026	Earlyville	15846
Dilliner	15327	Drexel Hills (Part of New		Earnest	19401
Dillinger	18049	Cumberland)	17070	Earnestville	16666
Dillingersville	18092	Drexeline Shopping Center	19026	East Allen (Township)	18067
Dillontown	18417	Drexel Plaza	19050	East Altoona	16601
Dillsburg	17019	Drexelwood	19610	East Ararat	18465
Dilltown	15929	Drifting	16834	East Athens	18810
Dilworthtown	19380	Drifton	18221	East Bangor	18013
Dimeling	16830	Driftwood	15832	East Benton	18414
Dimock	18816	Drinker	18444	East Berlin	17316
Dimock (Township)	18816	Drocton (Part of Renovo)	17764	East Berwick	18603
Dimock Corners	18430	Dromgold	17090	East Bethlehem (Township)	15322
Dingman (Township)	18337	Druid Hills (Part of Dallas)	18708	East Bradford (Chester	
Dingmans Ferry	18328	Drummond	15823	County) (Township)	19380
Dipple Manor	18201	Drumore	17518	East Bradford (McKean	
Distant	16223	Drumore (Township)	17563	County)	16701
District (Township)	19512	Drums	18222	East Brady	16028
Divide	17814	Drury Run	17764	East Branch (Jefferson	
Dividing Ridge	15530	Dry Hill	15425	County)	15767
Dixmont	15143	Dry Ridge	15601	East Branch (Warren	
Dixon	18657	Dry Run	17220	County)	16434
Dixonville	15734	Dry Tavern	15357	East Brandywine (Township)	19335
D&M Junction	17019	Dry Valley Crossroads	17889	Eastbrook	16101
Doe Run	19320	Dryville	19539	East Brunswick (Township)	17960
Dogtown (Columbia County)	17815	Dublin (Bucks County)	18917	East Buffalo (Union County)	
Dogtown (Luzerne County)	18655	Dublin (Fulton County)		(Township)	17837
Dogtown (Snyder County)	17870	(Township)	17223	East Buffalo (Washington	
Dogwood Acres	18966	Dublin (Huntingdon County)		County)	15301
Dogwood Hollow	19053	(Township)	17239	East Butler	16029
Dolington	18940	Dublin Mills	17229	East Caln (Township)	19341

	ZIP
East Cameron (Township)	17872
East Canton	17724
East Carnegie (Part of Pittsburgh)	15230
East Carroll (Township)	15722
East Chillisquaque (Township)	17847
East Cocalico (Township)	17517
East Conemaugh	15909
East Connellsville	15425
East Coventry (Township)	19457
East Deer (Township)	15030
East Donegal (Township)	17547
East Drumore (Township)	17566
East Du Bois (Part of Du Bois)	15801
East Du Bois Junction (Part of Du Bois)	15801
East Earl	17519
East Earl (Township)	17519
East End (Blair County)	16602
East End (Luzerne County)	18702
East Fairfield (Township)	16314
East Fallowfield (Chester County) (Township)	19320
East Fallowfield (Crawford County) (Township)	16111
East Falls (Part of Philadelphia)	19129
East Finley	15377
East Finley (Township)	15377
East Franklin (Township)	16201
East Fredericktown	15450
East Freedom	16637
East Germantown (Part of Philadelphia)	19138
East Goshen (Township)	19380
East Greenville	18041
East Hanover (Dauphin County) (Township)	17028
East Hanover (Lebanon County) (Township)	17003
East Hempfield (Township)	17603
East Herrick	18853
East Hickory	16321
East Hills (Part of Doylestown)	18901
East Hills Center	15235
East Honesdale (Part of Honesdale)	18431
East Hopewell (Township)	17322
East Huntingdon (Township)	15612
East Kane	16735
East Keating (Township)	17778
East Kendall	17356
East Kittanning	16201
East Lackawannock (Township)	16137
East Lampeter (Township)	17602
Eastland	19362
Eastland Hills (Franklin County)	17268
Eastland Hills (Lancaster County)	17602
Eastland Shopping Plaza	15137
East Lansdowne	19050
East Lawn	18064
Eastlawn Gardens	18064
East Lawrence	16929
East Lemon	18657
East Lenox	18470
East Lewisburg	17847
East Liberty (Part of Pittsburgh)	15206
East Mahoning (Township)	15759
East Manchester (Township)	17347
East Marianna	15345
East Marlborough (Township)	19348
East McKeesport	15035
East Mead (Township)	16335
East Millsboro	15433
East Mines (Part of St. Clair)	17970
Eastmont (Allegheny County)	15235
Eastmont (Cambria County)	15902
Eastmont (York County)	17315
East Nantmeal (Township)	19421
East New Castle	16101
East Newport	17074
East Norriton (Township)	19401
East Norriton	19401
East Norwegian (Township)	17901
East Nottingham (Township)	19363
East Oakmont (Part of Plum)	15131
Easton (Clarion County)	16255

	ZIP
Easton (Northampton County)	18042-44
For specific Easton Zip Codes call (215) 252-9987, or your local postmaster.	
East Oreland	19075
East Penn (Township)	18235
East Pennsboro (Township)	17025
East Petersburg	17520
East Pike	15701
East Pikeland (Township)	19460
East Pittsburgh	15112
Eastpoint	17765
East Prospect	17317
East Providence (Township)	15533
East Riverside	15433
East Rochester	15074
East Rockhill (Township)	18944
Eastrun	15759
East Rush	18801
East Salem	17059
East Saxton	16678
East Sharon	16748
East Sharpsburg	16673
East Side	18661
East Smethport	16730
East Smithfield	18817
East Springfield	16411
East St. Clair (Township)	15554
East Stroudsburg	18301
East Taylor (Township)	15909
East Texas	18046
East Titusville	16354
East Towanda	18848
Easttown (Township)	19312
Easttown Woods	19312
East Troy	16947
East Union (Township)	18248
East Uniontown (Fayette County)	15401
Eastvale	15010
East Vandergrift	15629
East View	15370
Eastville	17747
East Vincent (Township)	19475
East Washington	15301
East Waterford	17021
East Weissport	18235
East Wheatfield (Township)	15920
East Whiteland (Township)	19355
Eastwicks (Part of Philadelphia)	19153
East William Penn	17976
Eastwood (Allegheny County)	15235
Eastwood (Westmoreland County)	15601
East Yoe	17356
East York	17402
Eaton (Township)	18657
Eatonville	18657
Eau Claire	16030
Ebenezer	17046
Ebensburg	15931
Ebensburg Junction	15931
Eberhardt (Allegheny County)	15101
Eberhardt (Butler County)	16001
Eberlys Mill	17011
Ebervale	18223
Echo (Armstrong County)	16222
Echo (Cambria County)	15942
Echo Lake	18301
Echo Valley (Delaware County)	19073
Echo Valley (Schuylkill County)	17981
Eckenrode Mill	16668
Eckley	18255
Eckville	19529
Economy	15005
Economy (Part of Ambridge)	15003
Eddington	19020
Eddington Gardens	19020
Eddystone	19013
Eddyville	16242
Edelman	18064
Eden (Clearfield County)	16836
Eden (Lancaster County)	17601
Eden (Lancaster County) (Township)	17566
Edenborn	15458
Edenburg	19526
Eden Croft	19006
Edendale	16666
Eden Heights	17601
Edenville	17201
Edgebrook (Part of Pittsburgh)	15226
Edgecliff (Part of Lower Burrell)	15068

	ZIP
Edgegrove	17331
Edge Hill	19038
Edgely	19007
Edgemont (Dauphin County)	17109
Edgemont (Delaware County)	19028
Edgemont (Northampton County)	18088
Edgemont Farms	19073
Edges Mill	19335
Edgewater (Part of Oakmont)	15139
Edgewater Terrace	15650
Edgewood (Allegheny County)	15218
Edgewood (Indiana County)	15701
Edgewood (Northumberland County)	17872
Edgewood (Somerset County)	15501
Edgewood Acres (Part of Forest Hills)	15221
Edgewood Grove (Part of Somerset)	15501
Edgewood Park (Bucks County)	19067
Edgewood Park (Delaware County)	19008
Edgeworth	15143
Edgmont (Township)	19028
Edie	15501
Edinboro	16412
Edinburg	16116
Edison	18901
Edisonville	17579
Edmon	15630
Edna	15611
Edwardsville	18704
Effort	18330
Egypt (Clearfield County)	16881
Egypt (Jefferson County)	15824
Egypt (Lehigh County)	18052
Ehrenfeld	15956
Eichelbergertown	16650
Eidenau	16037
Eighty Four	15330
Ekastown	16055
Elam	19342
Elberta	16601
Elbon	15823
Elbrook	17268
Elco	15434
Elder (Township)	16646
Elders Ridge	15681
Eldersville	15036
Elderton	15736
El-Do-Lake	18058
Eldora (Lancaster County)	17563
Eldora (Washington County)	15063
Eldorado (Blair County)	16602
Eldorado (Butler County)	16049
Eldred (Jefferson County) (Township)	15860
Eldred (Lycoming County) (Township)	17754
Eldred (McKean County)	16731
Eldred (McKean County) (Township)	16731
Eldred (Monroe County) (Township)	18058
Eldred (Schuylkill County) (Township)	17964
Eldred (Warren County) (Township)	16340
Eldredsville	18616
Eleven Mile	16923
Elfinwild	15101
Elgin	16413
Elgin Park	19073
Elim	15905
Elimsport	17810
Elizabeth (Allegheny County)	15037
Elizabeth (Allegheny County) (Township)	15018
Elizabeth (Lancaster County) (Township)	17543
Elizabethtown	17022
Elizabethville	17023
Elk (Chester County) (Township)	19351
Elk (Clarion County) (Township)	16232
Elk (Tioga County) (Township)	16921
Elk (Warren County) (Township)	16345
Elk City	16232
Elk Creek (Township)	16401
Elkdale (Chester County)	19352

	ZIP
Elkdale (Susquehanna County)	18470
Elk Grove	17814
Elkins Park	19117
Elk Lake (Susquehanna County)	18801
Elk Lake (Wayne County)	18472
Elkland (Sullivan County) (Township)	18616
Elkland (Tioga County)	16920
Elk Lick (Township)	15565
Elk Run Junction (Part of Punxsutawney)	15767
Elkview	19390
Ellen Gowan	17976
Ellenton	17724
Ellerslie	19020
Elliger Park	19034
Elliott (Part of Pittsburgh)	15220
Elliott Heights (Part of Bethlehem)	18015
Elliottsburg	17024
Elliotts Mills	16057
Elliottson	17013
Elliottsville	15437
Ellisburg	16923
Ellport	16117
Ellrod (Part of Versailles)	15132
Ellsworth	15331
Ellwood City	16117
Elm	17521
Elmdale	18436
Elmer	16950
Elmhurst (Township)	18416
Elmhurst	18416
Elmo	16232
Elmora	15737
Elmwood (Philadelphia County)	19142
Elmwood (York County)	17403
Elmwood Terrace	18444
Elora	16057
Elrama	15038
Elrico	15684
Elroy	18964
Elstie	16613
Elstonville	17545
Elton	15934
Elverson	19520
Elwood Park	15301
Elwyn	19063
Elwyn Terrace	17545
Elysburg	17824
Emanuelsville	18014
Emblem (Part of White Oak)	15131
Embreeville	19320
Embreeville State Hospital	19320
Emeigh	15738
Emerald (Greene County)	15322
Emerald (Lehigh County)	18080
Emerickville	15825
Emigh Run (Part of Cherry Tree)	15724
Emigsville (York County)	17318
Emlenton	16373
Emmaus	18049
Emmaville	15536
Emporium	15834
Emporium Junction (Part of Emporium)	15834
Emsworth	15202
Endeavor	16322
Enders	17032
Energy	16101
Enfield	19075
Engleside (Part of Lancaster)	17602
Engles Lake	18370
Englesville	19512
Englewood	17931
English Center	17776
Enhaut	17113
Enid	16691
Enlow	15126
Ennisville	16652
Enola	17025
Enon (Greene County)	15377
Enon (Washington County)	15377
Enon Valley	16120
Enterline	17032
Enterprise (Mercer County)	16127
Enterprise (Warren County)	16354
Entlerville	17241
Entriken	16638
Ephrata	17522
Ephrata (Township)	17522
Equinunk	18417
Ercildoun	19320
Erdenheim	19118
Erdman	17048
Erhard	16861

	ZIP
Erie	16501-65
For specific Erie Zip Codes call (814) 898-7317, or your local postmaster.	
Erie Heights (Part of Erie)	16501
Erlen	19126
Erly	17024
Ernest	15739
Erney	17315
Erwinna	18920
Eshbach	19505
Eshcol	17062
Esplen (Part of Pittsburgh)	15204
Espy	17815
Espyville Station	16424
Essington	19029
Estella	18616
Esterly (Part of St. Lawrence)	19606
Estherton	17110
Etna	15223
Etters	17319
Euclid	16001
Eulalia (Township)	16915
Eureka (Cambria County)	15963
Eureka (Westmoreland County)	15479
Evans	15401
Evansburg	19426
Evans City	16033
Evans Falls	18657
Evanston	15625
Evansville (Berks County)	19522
Evansville (Columbia County)	18603
Evendale	17086
Everett	15537
Evergreen	18833
Evergreen Park	18052
Everhartville	17074
Everson	15631
Ewalt (Part of Pittsburgh)	15212
Ewings Mill	15765
Ewingsville	15106
Excelsior	17825
Exchange	17821
Exeter (Berks County) (Township)	19606
Exeter (Luzerne County)	18643
Exeter (Luzerne County) (Township)	18643
Exeter (Wyoming County) (Township)	18615
Export	15632
Exton	19341
Exton Square Mall	19341
Eyers Grove	17846
Eynon (Part of Archbald)	18403
Factoryville (Northampton County)	18013
Factoryville (Wyoming County)	18419
Fagleysville	19525
Fagundus	16351
Fair Acres	17070
Fairbank	15435
Fairbrook	16865
Fairchance	15436
Fairdale (Greene County)	15320
Fairdale (Susquehanna County)	18801
Fairfield (Adams County)	17320
Fairfield (Crawford County) (Township)	16314
Fairfield (Erie County)	16510
Fairfield (Lycoming County) (Township)	17754
Fairfield (Washington County)	15345
Fairfield (Westmoreland County) (Township)	15923
Fair Grounds	15344
Fairhaven Heights	15137
Fairhill (Bucks County)	19440
Fairhill (Philadelphia County)	19133
Fairhope (Fayette County)	15012
Fairhope (Somerset County)	15538
Fairhope (Somerset County) (Township)	15538
Fairland	17543
Fairlane Village Mall (Part of Pottsville)	17901
Fairlawn	17728
Fairless	19030
Fairless Hills	19030
Fairmont	15642
Fairmount (Lancaster County)	17566
Fairmount (Luzerne County) (Township)	17814
Fairmount (Philadelphia County)	19121

	ZIP
Fairmount (Wayne County)	18462
Fairmount City	16224
Fairmount Springs	17814
Fairoaks (Allegheny County)	15003
Fairoaks (Montgomery County)	19044
Fairplay	17325
Fairview (Beaver County)	15052
Fairview (Blair County)	16601
Fairview (Butler County)	16050
Fairview (Butler County) (Township)	16025
Fairview (Clearfield County)	16858
Fairview (Erie County)	16415
Fairview (Erie County) (Township)	16415
Fairview (Franklin County)	17268
Fairview (Jefferson County)	15767
Fairview (Luzerne County) (Township)	18707
Fairview (Mercer County)	16124
Fairview (Mercer County) (Township)	16137
Fairview (Mifflin County)	17044
Fairview (Northumberland County)	17872
Fairview (York County) (Township)	17070
Fairview Drive	17331
Fairview-Ferndale	17872
Fairview Heights (Allegheny County)	15238
Fairview Heights (Berks County)	19533
Fairview Heights (Luzerne County)	18707
Fairview Heights (McKean County)	16701
Fairview Hills	18707
Fairview Knolls	18042
Fairview Park (Chester County)	19380
Fairview Park (Luzerne County)	18707
Fairview Park (York County)	17070
Fairview Village	19409
Fairville (Chester County)	19317
Fairville (Union County)	17837
Fairway Park	17603
Fairways of Brookside	18062
Fairywood (Part of Pittsburgh)	15205
Falconcrest	19380
Fallentimber	16639
Fallen Timbers	15451
Falling Spring (Franklin County)	17201
Falling Spring (Perry County)	17040
Fallowfield (Township)	15022
Falls (Bucks County) (Township)	19054
Falls (Wyoming County)	18615
Falls (Wyoming County) (Township)	18615
Falls Creek	15840
Fallsington	19054
Fallston	15066
Falmouth	17502
Fannett (Township)	17220
Fannettsburg	17221
Faraday Park	19070
Farmbrook	19007
Farmdale	17552
Farmers	17364
Farmers Mills	16875
Farmers Valley (Bradford County)	16947
Farmers Valley (McKean County)	16749
Farmersville (Lancaster County)	17522
Farmersville (Northampton County)	18042
Farmington (Berks County)	19539
Farmington (Clarion County) (Township)	16220
Farmington (Fayette County)	15437
Farmington (Lehigh County)	18103
Farmington (Tioga County) (Township)	16946
Farmington (Warren County) (Township)	16345
Farmington Hill	16946
Farquhar Estates	17403
Farragut	17754
Farrandsville	17734
Farrell	16121
Farview	19607
Farwell	17764
Fassett	16925

	ZIP		ZIP		ZIP
Faunce	16863	Five Corners	16404	Fort Hill (Somerset County)	15540
Fawn (Allegheny County)		Five Forks	17268	Fort Hill (Westmoreland	
(Township)	15084	Five Points (Beaver County)	15001	County)	15687
Fawn (York County)		Five Points (Berks County)	19606	Fort Hunter	17110
(Township)	17321	Five Points (Butler County)	16057	Fort Indiantown Gap	17003
Fawn Grove	17321	Five Points (Chester		Fort Littleton	17223
Faxon	17701	County)	19348	Fort Loudon	17224
Fayette (Juniata County)		Five Points (Clearfield		Fortney	17339
(Township)	17049	County)	15753	Fort Roberston	17047
Fayette (Lawrence County)	16156	Five Points (Erie County)	16509	Fortuna	18915
Fayette City	15438	Five Points (Indiana County)	15732	Fort Washington	19034
Fayetteville	17222	Five Points (Luzerne		Forty Fort	18704
Fayfield	17402	County)	18249	Forward (Allegheny County)	
Fay Terrace	16125	Five Points (Mercer County)	16133	(Township)	15063
Fearnot	17968	Five Points (Mercer County)	16150	Forward (Butler County)	
Feasterville	19047	Five Points (Northumberland		(Township)	16033
Feasterville Gardens	19047	County)	17772	Fossilville	15534
Feasterville Heights	19047	Five Points (Venango		Foster (Indiana County)	15681
Feasterville-Trevose	19047	County)	16342	Foster (Luzerne County)	
Federal	15071	Five Points (Westmoreland		(Township)	18224
Federal Correctional		County)	15601	Foster (McKean County)	
Institution (McKean		Five Points (Part of		(Township)	16701
County)	16701	Ohioville)	15059	Foster (Schuylkill County)	
Federal Correctional		Fivepointville	17517	(Township)	17901
Institution (Schuylkill		Flat Rock (Centre County)	16870	Foster Brook	16701
County)	17954	Flat Rock (Fayette County)	15459	Fostoria	16617
Federal Penitentiary	17837	Flatwoods	15486	Foundryville	18603
Federal Prison Camp	17810	Fleetville	18420	Fountain	17938
Federal Reserve (Part of		Fleetwing Estates	19057	Fountain Dale	17320
Pittsburgh)	15230	Fleetwood	19522	Fountain Hill	18015
Federal Square (Part of		Fleming	16835	Fountain House Corners	16433
Harrisburg)	17108	Flemington	17745	Fountain Springs	17921
Fell (Township)	18421	Flicksville	18050	Fountainville	18923
Fellsburg	15012	Flinton	16640	Fourth Avenue (Part of	
Fellwick	19034	Flintville	17042	Pittsburgh)	15222
Felton	17322	Floradale	17307	Foustown	17404
Feltonville	19013	Floreffe (Part of Jefferson)	15025	Foustwell	15953
Fenelton	16034	Florence	15021	Fowler Heights	15701
Ferguson (Centre County)		Florida Park	19073	Fowlersville	18603
(Township)	16801	Florin (Part of Mount Joy)	17552	Fox (Elk County) (Township)	15846
Ferguson (Clearfield		Flourtown	19031	Fox (Sullivan County)	
County) (Township)	16833	Flourtown Gardens	19031	(Township)	17724
Ferguson (Fayette County)	15431	Flying Hills	19607	Foxburg (Cambria County)	15773
Fergusonville	19007	FM Corners (Part of		Foxburg (Clarion County)	16036
Fermanagh (Township)	17059	Hermitage)	16148	Foxburg (Jefferson County)	15767
Fern	16319	Fogelsville	18051	Fox Chapel	15238
Fern Brook	18612	Folcroft	19032	Fox Chase (Lancaster	
Ferndale (Bucks County)	18921	Foleys Siding (Part of		County)	17601
Ferndale (Cambria County)	15905	Castle Shannon)	15234	Fox Chase (Philadelphia	
Ferndale (Northumberland		Folsom	19033	County)	19111
County)	17872	Folstown	18707	Fox Chase Manor	19117
Ferndale (Schuylkill County)	17985	Fombell	16123	Foxcroft (Delaware County)	19008
Fern Glen	18241	Font	19335	Foxcroft (Montgomery	
Fern Hill	19380	Fontana	17042	County)	19046
Fernridge	18610	Footedale	15468	Foxdale (Part of New	
Fern Village	19040	Foot of Ten	16635	Stanton)	15672
Fernville	17815	Forbes Road	15633	Fox Hill (Franklin County)	17268
Fernway	16063	Force	15841	Fox Hill (Luzerne County)	18702
Fernwood (Clearfield		Ford City	16226	Fox Run	16046
County)	16680	Ford Cliff	16228	Foxton Lake	18847
Fernwood (Delaware		Fordham	15767	Foxtown	15697
County)	19050	Ford View	16226	Foxtown Hill	18360
Fernwood-Yeadon	19050	Fordville	17364	Frackville	17931
Ferrellton	15563	Fordyce	15370	Frailey (Township)	17981
Fertigs	16364	Forest	16879	Francis	16417
Fertility	17602	Forest Castle (Part of		Francis Mine	15021
Fetterville	17555	Exeter)	18643	Franconia	18924
Fiddle Lake	18465	Forest City	18421	Franconia (Township)	18924
Fiddlers Green	15946	Forest Grove (Allegheny		Frank	15018
Fidelity (Part of Philadelphia)	19109	County)	15108	Frankford (Part of	
Fieldmore Springs	16354	Forest Grove (Bucks		Philadelphia)	19124
Fife Shire Acres	15317	County)	18922	Frankfort Springs	15050
Fifficktown	15956	Foresthill (Union County)	17844	Franklin (Adams County)	
Fiketown	15459	Forest Hill (York County)	17356	(Township)	17307
Filbert	15435	Forest Hills (Allegheny		Franklin (Beaver County)	
Fillmore	16823	County)	15221	(Township)	16123
Finch Hill	18407	Forest Hills (Lancaster		Franklin (Bradford County)	
Findlay (Township)	15026	County)	17540	(Township)	18848
Findley (Township)	16137	Forest Hills Manor	19006	Franklin (Butler County)	
Finland	18073	Forest Inn	18235	(Township)	16052
Finleyville (Bedford County)	16679	Forest Lake	18801	Franklin (Cambria County)	15909
Finleyville (Washington		Forest Lake (Township)	18801	Franklin (Carbon County)	
County)	15332	Forest Park (Bucks County)	18914	(Township)	18235
Fireside Terrace (Part of		Forest Park (Luzerne		Franklin (Chester County)	
York)	17404	County)	18702	(Township)	19350
Fisher	16225	Forestville (Butler County)	16035	Franklin (Columbia County)	
Fisherdale	17824	Forestville (Schuylkill		(Township)	17820
Fisher Heights (Butler		County)	17901	Franklin (Erie County)	
County)	16001	Forge	16686	(Township)	16412
Fisher Heights (Washington		Forks (Columbia County)	17859	Franklin (Fayette County)	
County)	15063	Forks (Northampton		(Township)	15486
Fishers Corner	19013	County) (Township)	18042	Franklin (Greene County)	
Fishers Ferry	17801	Forks (Sullivan County)		(Township)	15370
Fishertown (Bedford		(Township)	18614	Franklin (Huntingdon	
County)	15539	Forkston	18629	County) (Township)	16865
Fishertown (Cambria		Forkston (Township)	18629	Franklin (Luzerne County)	
County)	15956	Forksville	18616	(Township)	18640
Fisherville	17032	Forsythia Gate	19053	Franklin (Lycoming County)	
Fishing Creek (Township)	17859	Fort Allen Plan	15601	(Township)	17742
Fiske	16639	Fortenia	18431	Franklin (Snyder County)	
Fitch Corner	18615	Fort Fetter	16648	(Township)	17861
Fitz Henry	15479				

	ZIP
Glenloch	19380
Glen Lyon	18617
Glen Mawr	17737
Glen Mills	19342
Glenmoore (Chester County)	19343
Glen Moore (Lancaster County)	17601
Glenolden	19036
Glen Richey	16837
Glen Riddle	19037
Glen Riddle-Lima	19037
Glen Rock	17327
Glen Rose	19320
Glen Roy	19362
Glenruadh	16505
Glen Savage	15538
Glenshaw	15116
Glenside	19038
Glenside Gardens	19038
Glenside Heights	19038
Glen Summit	18707
Glenville	17329
Glenwall Village	15001
Glenwillard	15046
Glenwood (Allegheny County)	15230
Glenwood (Dauphin County)	17109
Glenwood (Erie County)	16501
Glenwood (Mifflin County)	17044
Glenwood (Susquehanna County)	18446
Glenwood Junction (Part of Pittsburgh)	15230
Glenworth	17901
Glosser View	17701
Glyde	15301
Glyndon	16434
Gnatstown	17331
Goat Hill	15301
Godfrey	15656
Goff	16020
Goheenville	16259
Gold	16923
Golden Hill	18623
Golden Key Lake	18337
Goldenridge	19057
Golden Rod Farms	16830
Good	17268
Goodhope	17055
Good Hope Farms	17055
Good Intent	15323
Goodmans Corners	16364
Goods Corner	15906
Good Spring	17981
Goodtown	15530
Goodville	17528
Goodyear	17324
Goosetown	19320
Gordon	17936
Gordonville	17529
Goshen	16830
Goshen (Township)	16873
Goshenville	19380
Gosser Hill	15656
Gouglersville	19608
Gouldsboro	18424
Gourley	15061
Gowen	18241
Gowen City	17828
Grace Park	19081
Graceton	15748
Graceville	15537
Gracey	17228
Gradwohl Terrace	18017
Gradyville	19039
Grafton (Indiana County)	15716
Graham (Clearfield County)	16866
Graham (Clearfield County) (Township)	16858
Grampian	16838
Grampian Hills (Part of Williamsport)	17701
Grand Valley	16420
Grandview (Armstrong County)	16201
Grandview (Butler County)	16045
Grandview (Elk County)	15857
Grandview (Indiana County)	15701
Grandview (Washington County)	15063
Grandview Heights	17601
Grandview Park (Elk County)	15857
Grand View Park (Montgomery County)	19426
Grange	15767
Grange Corners	16433
Grange Hall Center	16433
Grangeville	17331
Granite	17325
Grant (Elk County)	15821

	ZIP
Grant (Indiana County) (Township)	15759
Grant City	16051
Grantham	17027
Grantley	17403
Grant Street (Part of Pittsburgh)	15219
Grantville	17028
Granville (Bradford County) (Township)	16926
Granville (Part of California)	15423
Granville (Mifflin County)	17029
Granville (Mifflin County) (Township)	17044
Granville Center	16926
Granville Summit	16926
Grapeville	15634
Grassflat	16839
Grassmere Park	17814
Grassy (Part of Olyphant)	18447
Graterford	19426
Gratz	17030
Gratztown	15089
Gravity	18436
Gray (Clearfield County)	16881
Gray (Greene County) (Township)	15337
Gray (Somerset County)	15544
Graydon	17322
Grays Landing	15461
Gray Station	15717
Graysville (Greene County)	15337
Graysville (Huntingdon County)	16865
Grazier	15953
Grazierville	16686
Greason	17013
Great Bend	18821
Great Bend (Township)	18822
Greater Pittsburgh International Airport 911th TAC	15231
Greater Point Marion	15474
Greble	17067
Greece City	16025
Greeley	18425
Green (Forest County) (Township)	16353
Green (Indiana County) (Township)	15724
Greenawalds	18104
Greenbank	17557
Greenbrae	16201
Greenbrier (Centre County)	16875
Greenbrier (Dauphin County)	17036
Greenbrier (Delaware County)	19073
Greenbrier (Northumberland County)	17867
Greenbrook	19007
Greenburr	17747
Greencastle	17225
Green Circle	18451
Greencrest Park	16125
Greendale	16735
Greendown Acres	16635
Greene (Beaver County) (Township)	15050
Greene (Clinton County) (Township)	17747
Greene (Erie County) (Township)	16509
Greene (Franklin County) (Township)	17254
Greene (Greene County) (Township)	15320
Greene (Lancaster County)	17518
Greene (Mercer County) (Township)	16125
Greene (Pike County) (Township)	18426
Greene Junction (Part of South Connellsville)	15425
Greenfield (Allegheny County)	15217
Greenfield (Blair County)	16625
Greenfield (Cambria County)	16613
Greenfield (Erie County) (Township)	16428
Greenfield (Lackawanna County) (Township)	18407
Greenfield (Mercer County)	16137
Greenfields (Berks County)	19605
Green Fields (Dauphin County)	17098
Green Hill	19380
Green Hills (Delaware County)	19079

	ZIP
Green Hills (Washington County)	15301
Green Lane	18054
Green Lane Farms	17011
Greenlawn Park	19007
Greenmount	17325
Green Oaks	16301
Greenock	15047
Green Park	17031
Green Point	17038
Green Ridge (Delaware County)	19014
Green Ridge (Lackawanna County)	18509
Green Ridge (Luzerne County)	18201
Greenridge (Westmoreland County)	15642
Greenridge Farms	19006
Greensboro	15338
Greensburg	15601
Greens Landing	18810
Greenspring	17241
Green Springs	17331
Greentown	18426
Green Tree (Allegheny County)	15220
Green Tree (Chester County)	19355
Green Valley (Allegheny County)	15137
Green Valley (Jefferson County)	15825
Green Village	17201
Greenville (Clearfield County)	16839
Greenville (Mercer County)	16125
Greenville (Somerset County) (Township)	15552
Greenville East	16125
Greenwald	15670
Greenwich (Berks County) (Township)	19530
Greenwich (Cambria County)	15714
Greenwood (Blair County)	16601
Greenwood (Clearfield County) (Township)	15757
Greenwood (Columbia County)	17846
Greenwood (Columbia County) (Township)	17859
Greenwood (Crawford County) (Township)	16316
Greenwood (Juniata County) (Township)	17094
Greenwood (Perry County) (Township)	17062
Greenwood Hills (Dauphin County)	17109
Green Wood Hills (Franklin County)	17222
Greenwood Village	16001
Gregg (Allegheny County)	15071
Gregg (Centre County) (Township)	16875
Gregg (Union County) (Township)	17810
Gregory (Part of Larksville)	18704
Grenoble	18974
Gresham	16354
Greshville	19512
Gretna	15301
Grey Nuns	15067
Grier City	18214
Griesemersville	19512
Griffiths	16735
Grill	19607
Grimesville	17701
Grimms Crossroads	17356
Grimville	19530
Grindstone	15442
Grindstone-Rowes Run	15442
Gringo	15001
Grisemore	15728
Groffdale	17557
Grovania	17821
Grove (Cameron County) (Township)	15861
Grove (Chester County)	19380
Grove Chapel	15701
Grove City	16127
Grover	17735
Groveton	15108
Grugan (Township)	17745
Gruvertown	18013
Guenot Settlement	16836
Guernsey	17307
Guffey (McKean County)	16740
Guffey (Westmoreland County)	15642
Guilford	17201

	ZIP		ZIP		ZIP
Guilford (Township)	17201	Hanover (Luzerne County)		Hawk Run	16840
Guilford Hills	17201	(Township)	18702	Hawksville	17566
Guilford Springs	17201	Hanover (Luzerne County)	18634	Hawley	18428
Guitonville	16239	Hanover (Northampton		Hawleywood	18428
Guldens	17325	County)	18017	Hawstone	17044
Gulich (Township)	16671	Hanover (Northampton		Hawthorn	16230
Gulph	19406	County) (Township)	18017	Haycock (Township)	18951
Gulph Mills	19428	Hanover (Washington		Haydentown	15478
Gump	15370	County) (Township)	15021	Hayesville	19363
Gum Tree	19320	Hanover (York County)	17331	Hayfield (Township)	16433
Guth	18104	Hanoverdale	17036	Haymaker	16731
Guthriesville	19335	Hanover Green	18702	Haynie	16254
Guthsville	18069	Hanover Heights	19464	Hays (Allegheny County)	15230
Guys Mills	16327	Hanover Hills	17036	Hays (Fayette County)	15401
Gwynedd	19436	Hanover Junction	17360	Hays Creek	18661
Gwynedd Square	19446	Hansotte Plan	16226	Hays Grove	17241
Gwynedd Valley	19437	Happy Valley (Part of		Hays Mills	15552
Haafsville	18031	Exeter)	18643	Haysville (Allegheny County)	15143
Habrenfeld Hills	18612	Harbor	16101	Haysville (Butler County)	16041
Hackelbernie (Part of Jim		Harborcreek	16421	Hayti	19320
Thorpe)	18229	Harborcreek (Township)	16421	Hazel Hurst	16733
Hackett	15367	Harding	18615	Hazel Kirk	15063
Haddenville	15401	Hardy Hill	15431	Hazelwood (Part of	
Haddock	18201	Harford	18823	Pittsburgh)	15207
Hadley	16130	Harford (Township)	18823	Hazen	15825
Haffey	15147	Harford Heights	15642	Hazle (Township)	18201
Hagersville	18944	Harlan	15829	Hazlebrook	18201
Hahnstown	17522	Harlansburg	16101	Hazleton	18201
Hahntown	15642	Harleigh	18225	Hazle Village (Part of	
Haines (Township)	16820	Harlem	18062	Hazleton)	18201
Haines Acres	17402	Harleysville	19438	Hazzard (Part of	
Haleeka	17728	Harmar (Township)	15024	Monongahela)	15063
Halfmoon (Township)	16877	Harmar Heights	15024	Heacock Meadows	19067
Halford Hills	19401	Harmarville	15238	Headlee Heights	15334
Halfville	17543	Harmonsburg	16422	Heart Lake	18801
Halfway	17042	Harmonville	19428	Heath (Township)	15860
Halfway House	19464	Harmony (Beaver County)		Heatherwold	19086
Halifax	17032	(Township)	15003	Heathville	15864
Halifax (Township)	17032	Harmony (Butler County)	16037	Hebe	17830
Hall (Allegheny County)	15146	Harmony (Clearfield County)	16692	Heberlig	17241
Hall (Beaver County)	15061	Harmony (Forest County)		Hebron (Lebanon County)	17042
Hallowell	19044	(Township)	16370	Hebron (Potter County)	
Halls	17756	Harmony (Jefferson County)	15767	(Township)	16915
Hallstead	18822	Harmony (Susquehanna		Hebron Center	16915
Hallston	16057	County) (Township)	18847	Heckscherville	17901
Haliton	15860	Harmony Grove	17315	Hecktown	18017
Hallwood	18621	Harmony Hill	19335	Hecla	17960
Halsey	16735	Harmony Township	15003	Hector (Township)	16948
Hamburg	19526	Harmonyville	19464	Hegarty Crossroads	16671
Hametown	17327	Harnedsville	15424	Hegins	17938
Hamilton (Adams County)		Harpers	18088	Hegins (Township)	17938
(Township)	17316	Harper Tavern	17003	Heidelberg (Allegheny	
Hamilton (Franklin County)		Harper Village	15001	County)	15106
(Township)	17201	Harris (Township)	16827	Heidelberg (Berks County)	
Hamilton (Jefferson County)	15744	Harris Acres	16801	(Township)	19567
Hamilton (McKean County)		Harrisburg	17101-30	Heidelberg (Lebanon	
(Township)	16333	For specific Harrisburg Zip Codes		County) (Township)	17088
Hamilton (Monroe County)		call (717) 257-2150, or your local		Heidelberg (Lehigh County)	
(Township)	18354	postmaster.		(Township)	18053
Hamilton (Northumberland		Harrison (Allegheny County)		Heidelberg (York County)	
County)	17801	(Township)	15065	(Township)	17362
Hamilton (Tioga County)		Harrison (Bedford County)		Heidlersburg	17372
(Township)	16912	(Township)	15550	Heights Plaza	15065
Hamiltonban (Township)	17325	Harrison (Potter County)		Heilmandale	17046
Hamilton Heights	17201	(Township)	16927	Heilwood	15745
Hamilton Mall (Part of		Harrison City	15636	Heise Run	16901
Allentown)	18101	Harrison Valley	16927	Heistersburg	15433
Hamilton Park	17603	Harrisonville	17228	Helen Furnace	16214
Hamlin (Lebanon County)	17026	Harristown	17562	Helen Mills (Elk County)	15823
Hamlin (McKean County)		Harrisville	16038	Helfenstein	17399
(Township)	16733	Harrity	18235	Helixville	15559
Hamlin (Wayne County)	18427	Harrow	18942	Hellam	17406
Hammersley Fork	17764	Harshaville	15026	Hellam (Township)	17368
Hammett	16510	Hartfield	16930	Hellertown	18055
Hammond	16946	Hartleton	17829	Helvetia	15848
Hammondville	15666	Hartley (Township)	17835	Hemlock (Columbia County)	
Hamorton	19348	Hartranft	19401	(Township)	17815
Hampden (Berks County)	19604	Hartstown	16131	Hemlock (Warren County)	16365
Hampden (Cumberland		Hartsville	18974	Hemlock Grove (Pike	
County) (Township)	17055	Harvey Plan	15042	County)	18426
Hampden Heights (Part of		Harveys Lake	18618	Hemlock Grove (Sullivan	
Reading)	19604	Harveyville	18655	County)	17758
Hampshire Heights	15601	Harwick	15049	Hempfield (Mercer County)	
Hampton (Adams County)	17350	Harwood	18201	(Township)	16125
Hampton (Allegheny		Harwood Park	19082	Hempfield (Westmoreland	
County) (Township)	15101	Hasentab's	16635	County) (Township)	15601
Hampton Station	16301	Hasson Heights	16301	Hempfield Manor	15601
Hampton Township	15101	Hastings	16646	Henderson (Clearfield	
Hancock	19539	Hatboro	19040	County)	16651
Haneyville	17745	Hatfield (Fayette County)	15401	Henderson (Huntingdon	
Hankey Farms	15071	Hatfield (Montgomery		County) (Township)	16652
Hanlin	15021	County)	19440	Henderson (Jefferson	
Hannah	16870	Hatfield (Montgomery		County) (Township)	15767
Hannahstown	16023	County) (Township)	19440	Henderson (Mercer County)	16153
Hannastown	15635	Hauto (Part of		Henderson Park	19406
Hannaville	16314	Nesquehoning)	18240	Hendersonville (Butler	
Hann Hill (Part of		Haverford (Delaware		County)	16046
Hermitage)	16159	County) (Township)	19083	Hendersonville (Washington	
Hanover (Beaver County)		Haverford (Montgomery		County)	15339
(Township)	15026	County)	19041	Hendleton	19607
Hanover (Lehigh County)		Havertown	19083	Hendricks	18979
(Township)	18103	Hawkeye	15612	Henningsville	18011

	ZIP
Henrietta	16662
Henry Clay (Township)	15424
Henrys Bend	16301
Henrys Mill	16347
Henryville	18332
Hensel	17566
Hensingerville	18011
Hepburn (Township)	17728
Hepburn Heights	17728
Hepburnia	16838
Hepburnville	17728
Hephzibah	19320
Hepler	17941
Herbert	15435
Hercules (Part of Stockertown)	18083
Hereford	18056
Hereford (Township)	18056
Heritage Hills	16117
Herman	16039
Hermine No. 2	15642
Herminie	15637
Hermitage	16148
Herndon	17830
Hero	15341
Herrick (Bradford County) (Township)	18853
Herrick (Susquehanna County) (Township)	18430
Herrick Center	18430
Herrick Corner	18430
Herrickville	18853
Herrs Island (Part of Pittsburgh)	15230
Hershey	17033
Hershey Heights	17331
Heshbon	15717
Heshbon Park	17701
Hessdale	17560
Hesston	16647
Hetlerville	18635
Hettesheimer Corners	18636
Hiawatha	18462
Hibbs	15443
Hickernell	16435
Hickman	15071
Hickory (Forest County) (Township)	16322
Hickory (Lawrence County) (Township)	16105
Hickory (Washington County)	15340
Hickory Corners (Mercer County)	16146
Hickory Corners (Northumberland County)	17017
Hickory Grove	18847
Hickory Heights	16101
Hickory Hill (Bedford County)	16679
Hickoryhill (Chester County)	19363
Hickory Hills	19067
Hickory Run Forest	18229
Hickorytown (Cumberland County)	17013
Hickorytown (Montgomery County)	19401
Hickox	16923
Hicks Hill	15618
Hidden Valley (Montgomery County)	19406
Hidden Valley (Somerset County)	15502
Hidden Valley Estates	18062
Higgins Corners	16040
High Bridge	17044
Highcliff	15229
High House	15478
Highland (Adams County) (Township)	17325
Highland (Allegheny County)	15237
Highland (Beaver County)	15010
Highland (Chester County) (Township)	19320
Highland (Clarion County) (Township)	16214
Highland (Elk County) (Township)	16728
Highland (Luzerne County)	18224
Highland (Westmoreland County)	15633
Highland Acres	17602
Highland Corners	16735
Highland Meadows (Allegheny County)	15037
Highland Meadows (Cambria County)	15904
Highland Park (Bucks County)	19053
Highland Park (Cambria County)	15904

	ZIP
Highland Park (Cumberland County)	17011
Highland Park (Delaware County)	19082
Highland Park (Erie County)	16506
Highland Park (Mifflin County)	17044
Highland Park (Northampton County)	18042
Highland Woods	18701
High Meadows	19063
Highmount	17406
High Park	19040
High Rock	17302
Highspire	17034
Highville	17516
Hileman Heights (Part of Altoona)	16602
Hillchurch (Berks County)	19512
Hill Church (Washington County)	15317
Hill City	16319
Hillcrest (Allegheny County)	15102
Hillcrest (Beaver County)	15001
Hill Crest (Fayette County)	15425
Hillcrest (Mercer County)	16146
Hill Crest (Montgomery County)	19126
Hillcrest (York County)	17403
Hillcroft	17403
Hilldale	18702
Hiller	15444
Hilliards	16040
Hillman	15767
Hillsboro	15963
Hills Creek Lake	16901
Hillsdale	15746
Hillsgrove	18619
Hillsgrove (Township)	18619
Hillside (Lehigh County)	18069
Hillside (Luzerne County)	18708
Hillside (Schuylkill County)	17901
Hillside (Westmoreland County)	15627
Hillside Junction (Part of Moosic)	18507
Hills Terrace	17948
Hillsview	15658
Hillsville	16132
Hill Top Acres (Armstrong County)	16226
Hilltop Acres (Lancaster County)	17603
Hilltown (Adams County)	17307
Hilltown (Bucks County)	18927
Hilltown (Bucks County) (Township)	18911
Hillville	16041
Hilton	17315
Hines Corners	18449
Hinkle	18947
Hinkletown	17522
Hinkson Corner	19086
Hiyasota	15935
Hoadleys	18431
Hoban Heights	18657
Hobart	17331
Hobbie	18660
Hoblitzell	15545
Hockersville	17241
Hoernerstown	17036
Hoffer	17864
Hoffmansville	19435
Hogestown	17055
Hog Island	19029
Hoguetown	16630
Hokendauqua	18052
Hokes	17327
Holbrook	15341
Holicong	18928
Holiday Hills	18106
Holiday Park (Part of Plum)	15239
Holiday Pocono	18210
Holland	18966
Hollenback (Township)	18660
Hollentown	16639
Hollers Hill	18201
Holley Heights	17404
Holliday	16935
Hollidaysburg	16648
Hollinger	17603
Hollisterville	18444
Hollsopple	15935
Hollywood (Clearfield County)	15849
Hollywood (Luzerne County)	18201
Hollywood (Montgomery County)	19117
Hollywood (York County)	17403
Hollywood Heights	17403
Holmes	19043

	ZIP
Holmesburg (Part of Philadelphia)	19136
Holtwood	17532
Home	15747
Homeacre	16001
Homeacre-Lyndora	16001
Home Camp	15856
Homeland	17601
Home Park	18052
Homer (Township)	16915
Homer City	15748
Homer Gap	16601
Homestead	15120
Homestead Park (Part of Munhall)	15120
Homesville	17921
Hometown	18252
Homets Ferry	18853
Homeville	19330
Homewood (Allegheny County)	15208
Homewood (York County)	17019
Honeoye	16748
Honesdale	18431
Honey Brook	19344
Honeybrook (Township)	19344
Honey Creek	17084
Honey Grove	17035
Honey Pot (Part of Nanticoke)	18634
Hooker	16041
Hookstown	15050
Hoover	15458
Hooverhurst	15742
Hooversville	15936
Hop Bottom	18824
Hopeland	17533
Hope Mills	16137
Hopewell (Beaver County) (Township)	15001
Hopewell (Bedford County)	16650
Hopewell (Bedford County) (Township)	15537
Hopewell (Chester County)	19363
Hopewell (Cumberland County) (Township)	17240
Hopewell (Huntingdon County) (Township)	16678
Hopewell (Washington County) (Township)	15301
Hopewell (York County) (Township)	17363
Hoppenville	18073
Hopwood	15445
Horatio	15767
Hormtown	15851
Horn Brook	18848
Hornby	16428
Horning (Part of Baldwin)	15236
Horseshoe Heights	17602
Horsham	19044
Horsham (Township)	19044
Horton (Township)	15823
Hosensack	18092
Hosensock	18214
Hospital (Part of Norristown)	19401
Host	19567
Hostetter	15638
Hottelville	16239
Houserville	16801
Houston	15342
Houston City	18641
Houtzdale	16651
Hovey (Township)	16049
Howard (Cameron County)	15834
Howard (Centre County)	16841
Howard (Centre County) (Township)	16841
Howard Siding	15834
Howe (Forest County) (Township)	16239
Howe (Perry County) (Township)	17074
Howell Park	15037
Howellville	19312
Howersville	18088
Howerton	18067
Hoytdale (Part of Big Beaver)	16157
Hoytville	16938
Hublersburg	16823
Hubley (Township)	17968
Huckenberry	16849
Hudson (Clearfield County)	16866
Hudson (Luzerne County)	18702
Hudsondale	18255
Huefner	16235
Huey	16248
Huff	15944
Huffs Church	18011
Hughes Park	19406
Hughestown	18640

	ZIP
Hughesville	17737
Hughs	18621
Hulltown	15428
Hulmeville	19047
Hulton (Part of Oakmont)	15139
Humboldt	18201
Hummelstown	17036
Hummels Wharf	17831
Humphreys	15601
Humphreyville	19320
Hungerford (Part of Shrewsbury)	17361
Hungry Hollow	15656
Hunker	15639
Hunlock (Township)	18621
Hunlock Creek	18621
Hunlock Gardens	18621
Hunter	17872
Hunter Hill	19462
Hunters Run	17324
Hunterstown	17325
Huntersville	17756
Huntingdon	16652
Huntingdon Furnace	16686
Huntingdon Heights	15642
Huntingdon Manor	17540
Huntingdon Meadows	19006
Huntingdon Valley	19006
Hunting Park (Part of Philadelphia)	19140
Huntington (Adams County) (Township)	17372
Huntington (Luzerne County) (Township)	18655
Huntington Mills	18622
Huntley	15832
Huntsdale	17013
Huntsville	18612
Husband	15501
Huston (Blair County) (Township)	16693
Huston (Centre County) (Township)	16844
Huston (Clearfield County) (Township)	15849
Huston Run	15332
Hustontown	17229
Hutchins	16740
Hutchinson (Fayette County)	15401
Hutchinson (Westmoreland County)	15640
Hyde	16843
Hyde Park (Berks County)	19605
Hyde Park (Westmoreland County)	15641
Hydetown	16328
Hyde Villa	19605
Hyndman	15545
Hynemansville	18066
Hyner	17738
Icedale	19344
Ickesburg	17037
Idaho	15774
Idamar	15734
Idaville	17337
Idetown (Part of Harveys Lake)	18612
Idlewood (Part of Crafton)	15205
Imler	16655
Imlertown	15522
Immaculata	19345
Imperial	15126
Imperial-Enlow	15126
Independence	15001
Independence (Beaver County) (Township)	15026
Independence (Snyder County)	17864
Independence (Washington County)	15312
Independence (Washington County) (Township)	15312
Indiana (Allegheny County) (Township)	15051
Indiana (Indiana County)	15701
Indian Creek (Bucks County)	19057
Indian Creek (Cumberland County)	17055
Indian Crossing	16731
Indian Head (Erie County)	16441
Indian Head (Fayette County)	15446
Indian Hills	16201
Indian King	19380
Indian Lake (Luzerne County)	18661
Indian Lake (Somerset County)	15926
Indianland	18088
Indian Mountain Lake	18210
Indianola	15051

	ZIP
Indian Orchard	18431
Indian Pines	15205
Indian Springs Estates	15701
Industry	15052
Inez	16915
Ingleby	16882
Inglenook	17032
Inglesmith	17211
Ingomar	15127
Ingram	15205
Inkerman	18640
Intercourse	17534
Iola	17846
Iona	17042
Irishtown (Adams County)	17350
Irishtown (Clearfield County)	16838
Irishtown (Fayette County)	15431
Irishtown (McKean County)	16738
Irishtown (Mercer County)	16137
Iron Bridge	15666
Iron Springs	17320
Ironton	18037
Ironville (Blair County)	16686
Ironville (Lancaster County)	17512
Irvin (Part of West Mifflin)	15122
Irvine	16329
Irving	17963
Irvona	16656
Irwin (Venango County) (Township)	16038
Irwin (Westmoreland County)	15642
Isabella	15447
Iselin	15681
Iselin Heights	15801
Island Lake	18462
Island Park	17801
Ithan	19085
Itley	16412
Iva	17562
Ivarea	16410
Ivyland	18974
Ivy Mills (Part of Chester Heights)	19342
Ivy Ridge (Part of Philadelphia)	19101
Ivywood	18451
Jacks Creek	17044
Jacks Mountain	17320
Jackson (Butler County) (Township)	16063
Jackson (Cambria County) (Township)	15909
Jackson (Columbia County) (Township)	17814
Jackson (Dauphin County) (Township)	17032
Jackson (Greene County) (Township)	15341
Jackson (Huntingdon County) (Township)	16669
Jackson (Lebanon County) (Township)	17042
Jackson (Luzerne County) (Township)	18708
Jackson (Lycoming County) (Township)	17765
Jackson (Mercer County) (Township)	16133
Jackson (Monroe County) (Township)	18352
Jackson (Northumberland County) (Township)	17830
Jackson (Perry County) (Township)	17006
Jackson (Snyder County) (Township)	17889
Jackson (Susquehanna County)	18825
Jackson (Susquehanna County) (Township)	18825
Jackson (Tioga County) (Township)	16936
Jackson (Venango County) (Township)	16317
Jackson (York County) (Township)	17362
Jackson Center	16133
Jackson Corner	16652
Jackson Crossing	16365
Jackson Hall	17201
Jackson Knolls	16101
Jackson Summit	16936
Jacksonville (Centre County)	16841
Jacksonville (Lehigh County)	18066
Jacksonville (Northampton County)	18014
Jacksonwald	19606
Jacksville	16057
Jacktown	15642

	ZIP
Jacktown Acres	15642
Jacobs Creek	15448
Jacobs Mills	17331
Jacobus	17407
Jalappa	19526
James City	16734
James Creek	16657
Jamestown (Cambria County)	15946
Jamestown (Carbon County)	18235
Jamestown (Mercer County)	16134
Jamesville	18014
Jamison (Bucks County)	18929
Jamison (Fayette County)	15401
Jamison (Forest County)	16370
Jamison City	17814
Japan	18224
Jarrettown	19025
Jay (Township)	15827
Jeanesville	18201
Jeannette	15644
Jeddo	18224
Jednota	17057
Jefferis Crossing	15401
Jefferson (Allegheny County)	15025
Jefferson (Berks County) (Township)	19506
Jefferson (Butler County) (Township)	16001
Jefferson (Dauphin County) (Township)	17032
Jefferson (Fayette County) (Township)	15473
Jefferson (Greene County)	15344
Jefferson (Greene County) (Township)	15344
Jefferson (Lackawanna County) (Township)	18436
Jefferson (Mercer County) (Township)	16150
Jefferson (Schuylkill County)	17922
Jefferson (Somerset County) (Township)	15501
Jefferson (Washington County)	15312
Jefferson (Washington County) (Township)	15021
Jefferson (Westmoreland County)	15687
Jefferson Center	16001
Jeffersonville	19403
Jenkins (Township)	18640
Jenkintown	19046
Jenkintown Manor	19117
Jenks (Township)	16239
Jenner (Township)	15531
Jenners	15546
Jenners Crossroads	15531
Jennerstown	15547
Jennersville	19390
Jenningsville	18629
Jericho	15861
Jericho Mills	17059
Jermyn	18433
Jerome	15937
Jerome Junction (Part of Benson)	15935
Jersey Mills	17739
Jersey Shore	17740
Jerseytown	17815
Jessup (Lackawanna County)	18434
Jessup (Susquehanna County) (Township)	18801
Jessup-Peckville (Part of Jessup)	18434
Jewtown	15745
Jim Thorpe	18229
Jimtown	15501
Joanna	19543
Joanna Heights	19543
Jobs Corners	16936
Joffre	15053
Johnsonburg (Elk County)	15845
Johnsonburg (Indiana County)	15772
Johnsons Corner	19317
Johnstown (Cambria County)	15901-15
For specific Johnstown Zip Codes call (814) 533-4935, or your local postmaster.	
Johnstown (Union County)	17844
Johnsville	18974
John Wanamaker (Part of Philadelphia)	19107
Jo Jo	16735
Joliett	17981
Joller	16674
Jollytown	15352

Name	ZIP
Jonas	18058
Jonathan Point	18210
Jones (Township)	15870
Jones Mills	15646
Jones Terrace	18042
Jonestown (Columbia County)	17859
Jonestown (Lebanon County)	17038
Jonestown (Schuylkill County)	17901
Jonestown (Washington County)	15022
Jordan (Clearfield County) (Township)	16833
Jordan (Lehigh County)	18053
Jordan (Lycoming County) (Township)	17774
Jordan (Northumberland County) (Township)	17830
Jordan Valley	18053
Josephine	15750
Jugtown (Bucks County)	18920
Jugtown (Franklin County)	17268
Julian	16844
Jumonville	15445
Juneau	15751
Junedale	18230
June Meadows	19006
Junewood	19007
Juniata (Bedford County) (Township)	15534
Juniata (Blair County) (Township)	16635
Juniata (Blair County)	16601
Juniata (Fayette County)	15431
Juniata (Huntingdon County) (Township)	16652
Juniata (Perry County) (Township)	17074
Juniata Gap	16601
Juniata Terrace	17044
Just A Farm	19006
Justus	18411
Kaiserville	18630
Kalinoski	15061
Kammerer	15330
Kane	16735
Kanesholm	16735
Kaneville	16301
Kantner	15548
Kantz	17870
Kaolin	19374
Kapp Heights	17857
Karns City	16041
Karthaus	16845
Karthaus (Township)	16845
Kaseville	17821
Kasiesville	17236
Kaska	17959
Kasson	16749
Kauffman	17201
Kaufman	15464
Kaybrook Manor	18101
Kaylor	16025
Kaywood	16827
Kearney	16679
Kearsarge	16509
Keating (Clinton County)	17778
Keating (McKean County) (Township)	16730
Keating (Potter County) (Township)	16720
Keating Summit	16720
Kecksburg	15666
Kedron Park	19070
Keelersburg	18657
Keelersville	18944
Keeneyville	16935
Keepville	16401
Keewaydin	16836
Keffer (Schuylkill County)	17981
Keffer (Westmoreland County)	15658
Keifertown	15683
Keisters	16057
Keisterville	15449
Kelayres	18231
Kellersburg	16259
Kellers Church	18944
Kellersville	18360
Kellettville	16353
Kelley (Part of Pittsburgh)	15230
Kelly (Armstrong County)	16226
Kelly (Union County) (Township)	17837
Kelly Crossroads	17837
Kelly Point	17837
Kellytown (Clearfield County)	16863
Kellytown (Tioga County)	16933
Kellyville	19026

Name	ZIP
Kelton	19346
Kemblesville	19347
Kempton	19529
Kendall (Beaver County)	15043
Kendall (York County)	17356
Kendall Creek (Part of Bradford)	16701
Kendrick	16651
Kenhorst	19607
Kenilworth	19464
Kenmar	17701
Kenmawr	15136
Kennard	16125
Kennedy (Allegheny County) (Township)	15108
Kennedy (Tioga County)	16901
Kennedy Mill	16051
Kennedy Township	15108
Kennells Mills	15545
Kennerdell	16374
Kennett (Township)	19348
Kennett Square	19348
Kenney Yard (Part of West Mifflin)	15122
Kenny Row	15468
Kennywood (Part of West Mifflin)	15122
Kensington (Part of Philadelphia)	19125
Kensington Heights	17201
Kent	15752
Kenwick Village	17601
Kenwood (Bucks County)	19007
Kenwood (Indiana County)	15728
Kepner	17960
Kepple Hill	15690
Kepples Corner	16025
Kernsville	18069
Kerr	16830
Kerrmoor	16833
Kerrs Corners	16127
Kerrsville	17013
Kerrtown	16335
Kerrwood Farms	15208
Kersey	15846
Kesslerville	18064
Keys	17322
Keystone (Elk County)	15823
Keystone (Luzerne County)	18702
Keystone (Somerset County)	15552
Keystone (Westmoreland County)	15637
Khedive	15320
Kidder (Township)	18624
Kilbuck (Township)	15237
Kilbuck	15233
Kilgore	16153
Killam Park	18451
Killinger	17061
Kimberton	19442
Kimbles	18428
Kimmel (Township)	16655
Kimmelton	15563
Kim Plan	15642
Kinderhook	17512
Kindts Corner	19555
King	16655
King (Township)	16667
King of Prussia	19406
King of Prussia Plaza	19406
Kingsdale	17340
Kingsessing (Part of Philadelphia)	19143
Kingsley (Forest County) (Township)	16353
Kingsley (Susquehanna County)	18826
Kings Manor	19406
Kingston	18704
Kingston (Township)	18708
Kingston (Westmoreland County)	15650
Kingston-Forty Fort (Part of Kingston)	18704
Kingsville	15864
Kingswood Park	19007
Kingview	15683
Kingwood	15551
Kinlock (Part of Lower Burrell)	15069
Kinney	16923
Kinport	15724
Kintersburg (Indiana County)	15701
Kintigh Plan	15601
Kintnersville	18930
Kinzers	17535
Kipps Run	17821
Kirby	15370
Kirbyville	19522
Kirks Mills	19362

Name	ZIP
Kirkwood	17536
Kirwan Heights	15017
Kiser Corners	16353
Kishacoquillas	17004
Kiskimere	15690
Kiskiminetas (Township)	15613
Kis-Lyn	18222
Kissel Hill	17543
Kissimmee	17842
Kissingers Mill	16248
Kistler (Mifflin County)	17066
Kistler (Perry County)	17047
Kitches Corners	16125
Kittanning	16201
Kittanning (Township)	16226
Kittanning (Part of Applewood)	16201
Kittanning Heights	16201
Kladder Station	16648
Klahr	16625
Klecknersville	18014
Kleinfeltersville	17039
Kline (Township)	18237
Klines Corner	19539
Klines Grove	17801
Klinesville (Berks County)	19534
Klinesville (Lancaster County)	17512
Kline Village (Part of Harrisburg)	17104
Klingerstown	17941
Klondike	16738
Klondyke	17044
Knapp	16901
Knauers	19540
Knauertown	19464
Kneedler	19446
Knepper	17268
Knightsbridge	15205
Knightsville	17052
Knobsville	17233
Knoebel's Grove	17824
Knousetown	17062
Knowltonwood	19065
Knox (Beaver County)	16117
Knox (Clarion County)	16232
Knox (Clarion County) (Township)	16235
Knox (Clearfield County) (Township)	16863
Knox (Jefferson County) (Township)	15825
Knox Dale	15847
Knoxlyn	17325
Knox Run	16858
Knoxville (Allegheny County)	15210
Knoxville (Fayette County)	15417
Knoxville (Tioga County)	16928
Koonsville	18655
Koppel	16136
Korn Krest	18702
Kossuth	16331
Kralltown	17316
Kratzerville	17870
Krayn	15963
Kreamer	17833
Kregar	15622
Kreidersville	18067
Kremis	16125
Kresgeville	18333
Kreutz Creek	17406
Kricktown	19608
Krings	15904
Krocksville	18104
Krumrine (Part of State College)	16801
Krumsville	19534
Kuhn	15501
Kuhnsville	18103
Kuhntown	15341
Kulp	17820
Kulpmont	17834
Kulps Corner	18944
Kulpsville	19443
Kulptown	19518
Kunkle	18612
Kunkletown	18058
Kushequa	16735
Kutztown (Berks County)	19530
Kutztown (Lebanon County)	17067
Kylers Corners	15846
Kylertown	16847
Kyleville	17302
La Anna	18326
La Belle	15450
Laboratory	15301
Labott	17364
Lacey Park	18974
Laceyville	18623
Lack (Township)	17021

	ZIP
Lackawannock (Township)	16137
Lackawaxen	18435
Lackawaxen (Township)	18425
Lacock	15301
Laddsburg	18833
Lafayette	16738
Lafayette (Township)	16738
Lafayette Hill	19444
Lafayette Park	19444
Lafferty Hill (Part of Baldwin)	15227
Laflin	18702
La Gonda	15301
Lahaska	18931
Laings Garden	19007
Lairds Crossing	16262
Lairdsville	17742
La Jose	15753
Lake (Luzerne County) (Township)	18621
Lake (Mercer County) (Township)	16153
Lake (Wayne County) (Township)	18436
Lake Ariel	18436
Lake Carey	18657
Lake City	16423
Lake Como	18437
Lake Donegal	15610
Lake Harmony	18624
Lake Heritage	17325
Lake Idlewild	18470
Lake Jo-Ann	15367
Lakeland	18436
Lake Lynn	15451
Lake Meade	17316
Lake Monroe	18335
Lakemont	16602
Lakemont Terrace (Part of Altoona)	16602
Lake Naomi	18350
Lake Pleasant	16438
Lake Quinn	18472
Lake Sheridan	18446
Lakeside (Bucks County)	19053
Lakeside (Susquehanna County)	18834
Lake Stonycreek	15541
Laketon Heights	15235
Lakeview	18847
Lakeview Heights	17111
Lakeville	18438
Lake Waynewood	18436
Lake Wesauking	18848
Lake Winola	18625
Lakewood (Erie County)	16505
Lakewood (Wayne County)	18439
Lake Wynonah	17972
Lamar	16848
Lamar (Township)	17750
Lamartine	16375
Lamberton	15458
Lambertsville	15563
Lambs Creek	16933
Lamonts Corners (Part of Hermitage)	16150
La Mott	19012
Lampeter	17537
Lanark	18034
Lancaster (Butler County) (Township)	16037
Lancaster (Lancaster County)	17601-08
For specific Lancaster Zip Codes call (717) 665-4199, or your local postmaster.	
Lancaster (Lancaster County) (Township)	17603
Lancaster Avenue (Part of Philadelphia)	19104
Lancaster Bible College	17601
Lancaster Junction	17545
Landenberg	19350
Lander	16345
Landingville	17942
Landisburg	17040
Landis Farms	17601
Landis Store	19512
Landis Valley	17604
Landisville	17538
Landreth Manor	19007
Landstreet	15935
Lane (Part of Freeport)	16229
Lanesboro	18827
Lanes Mills	15824
Langdon	17763
Langdondale	16650
Langeloth	15054
Langhorne	19047

	ZIP
	19053
For specific Langhorne Zip Codes call (215) 757-6777, or your local postmaster.	
Langhorne Gables	19047
Langhorne Gardens	19047
Langhorne Manor	19047
Langhorne Terrace	19047
Lansdale	19446
Lansdowne	19050
Lansdowne Park Gardens (Part of Collingdale)	19023
Lanse	16849
Lansford	18232
Lantz Corners	16740
Lapidea Hills	19013
La Plume	18440
La Plume (Township)	18440
Laporte	18626
Laporte (Township)	17758
Larabee	16731
Lardintown	16055
Large (Part of Jefferson)	15025
Larimer (Somerset County) (Township)	15552
Larimer (Westmoreland County)	15647
Larke	16693
Larksville	18704
Larrys Creek	17740
Larryville	17740
Larue	17327
Lashley	17267
Lathrop (Township)	18446
Latimore	17372
Latimore (Township)	17372
Latrobe	15650
Latrobe Shopping Center	15650
Lattimer Mines	18234
Laughlin Corner	15043
Laughlin Junction (Part of Pittsburgh)	15207
Laughlintown	15655
Laurel (Cumberland County)	17324
Laurel (York County)	17322
Laurel Bend	19007
Laureldale	19605
Laurel Falls	15552
Laurel Gardens	15229
Laurel Hill (Fayette County)	15431
Laurel Hill (Washington County)	15057
Laurel Lake (Luzerne County)	18707
Laurel Lake (Susquehanna County)	18812
Laurel Mountain	15655
Laurel Park	17845
Laurel Ridge	15009
Laurel Run	18702
Laurelton	17835
Laurelville (Fayette County)	15666
Laurelville (Lancaster County)	17557
Laurys Station	18059
Lausanne (Township)	18255
Lavansville	15501
Lavelle	17943
Laverock	19118
Lawn	17041
Lawnhurst	18042
Lawnton	17111
Lawrence (Clearfield County) (Township)	16830
Lawrence (Tioga County) (Township)	16946
Lawrence (Washington County)	15055
Lawrence Park (Delaware County)	19008
Lawrence Park (Erie County) (Township)	16511
Lawrence Park (Erie County)	16511
Lawrenceville (Allegheny County)	15201
Lawrenceville (Lackawanna County)	18642
Lawrenceville (Tioga County)	16929
Lawsonham	16248
Lawson Heights	15650
Lawsville Center	18801
Lawton	18828
Layfield	19525
Layton	15473
Leacock	17540
Leacock (Township)	17572
Leacock-Leola-Bareville	17540
Leaders Heights	17403
Leaf Park	17603

	ZIP
Leak Run (Part of Monroeville)	15146
Leaman Place	17562
Leamersville	16635
Learn Settlement	15729
Leasuresville	16055
Leather Corner Post	18069
Leatherwood	16242
Lebanon (Lebanon County)	17042
	17046
For specific Lebanon Zip Codes call (717) 274-2594, or your local postmaster.	
Lebanon (Wayne County) (Township)	18431
Lebanon Plaza	17042
Lebanon South	17042
Lebo	17040
Le Boeuf (Township)	16441
Le Boeuf Gardens	16441
Leck Kill	17836
Leckrone	15454
Lecontes Mills	16850
Lederach	19450
Ledgedale	18463
Lee	18617
Leechburg	15656
Leech Hill	16943
Leedom Estates	19078
Leedom Gardens	19078
Lee Mine	18634
Lee Park	18702
Leeper	16233
Leesburg	16156
Leesburg Station	16156
Lees Cross Roads	17257
Leesport	19533
Leet (Township)	15003
Leetonia	17727
Leetsdale	15056
Lehigh (Carbon County) (Township)	18255
Lehigh (Lackawanna County)	18424
Lehigh (Lackawanna County) (Township)	18424
Lehigh (Northampton County) (Township)	18088
Lehigh (Wayne County) (Township)	18424
Lehigh Furnace	18080
Lehigh Gap (Carbon County)	18071
Lehigh Gap (Lehigh County)	18080
Lehighton	18235
Lehigh University (Part of Bethlehem)	18015
Lehigh Valley General Mail Facility	18001-02
For specific Lehigh Valley General Mail Facility Zip Codes call (215) 882-3256, or your local postmaster.	
Lehigh Valley Mall	18052
Lehman (Luzerne County)	18627
Lehman (Luzerne County) (Township)	18612
Lehman (Pike County) (Township)	18324
Lehman (York County)	17362
Leibeyville	17960
Leidy (Township)	17764
Leinbachs	19605
Leisenring	15455
Leith	15401
Leithsville	18055
Lemasters	17231
Lemon (Township)	18657
Lemon	18657
Lemont	16851
Lemont Furnace	15456
Lemoyne	17043
Lenape	19380
Lenape Heights (Armstrong County)	16226
Lenape Park	16226
Lenhartsville	19534
Lenker Manor	17111
Lenkerville	17061
Lenni	19052
Lenni Heights	19037
Lennox Park (Part of Trainer)	19015
Lenover	19365
Lenox (Township)	18446
Lenoxville	18441
Lenwood Heights	17236
Leola	17540
Leolyn	17765
Leona	16914
Leopard	19312
Leopard Lakes	19312

	ZIP
Le Raysville	18829
Leroy	17743
Leroy (Township)	17724
Lester	19113
Letort	17582
Letterkenny (Township)	17244
Letterkenny Army Depot	17201
Level Corner	17744
Level Green	15085
Levittown	19054-59
For specific Levittown Zip Codes call (215) 949-3131, or your local postmaster.	
Levittown Center	19054
Levittown Discount World (Part of Tullytown)	19055
Levittown-Tullytown	19007
Lewis (Lycoming County) (Township)	17771
Lewis (Northumberland County) (Township)	17772
Lewis (Union County) (Township)	17880
Lewisberry	17339
Lewisburg	17837
Lewis Crossing	15458
Lewis Run	16738
Lewistown (Mifflin County)	17044
Lewistown (Schuylkill County)	18252
Lewistown Junction	17044
Lewisville (Chester County)	19351
Lewisville (Indiana County)	15725
Lexington	17543
Liberty (Adams County) (Township)	17320
Liberty (Allegheny County)	15133
Liberty (Bedford County) (Township)	16678
Liberty (Centre County) (Township)	16826
Liberty (McKean County) (Township)	16749
Liberty (Mercer County) (Township)	16127
Liberty (Montour County) (Township)	17821
Liberty (Susquehanna County) (Township)	18801
Liberty (Tioga County)	16930
Liberty (Tioga County) (Township)	16930
Liberty Corners	18848
Liberty Square	17518
Library	15129
Lickdale	17038
Licking (Township)	16049
Licking Creek (Township)	17228
Lickingville	16332
Lightner	17404
Light Street	17839
Ligonier	15658
Ligonier (Township)	15658
Lilly	15938
Lillyville	16123
Lima	19037
Limehill	18853
Limekiln	19535
Limeport	18060
Limerick	19468
Limerick (Township)	19468
Lime Ridge	17815
Lime Rock	17543
Limestone (Clarion County)	16234
Limestone (Clarion County) (Township)	16234
Limestone (Lycoming County) (Township)	17740
Limestone (Montour County) (Township)	17821
Limestone (Union County) (Township)	17844
Limestone (Warren County) (Township)	16365
Limestoneville	17847
Lime Valley	17584
Limeville	17527
Lincoln (Allegheny County)	15037
Lincoln (Bedford County) (Township)	15521
Lincoln (Huntingdon County) (Township)	16638
Lincoln (Lancaster County)	17522
Lincoln (Somerset County) (Township)	15501
Lincoln Acres	15642
Lincoln Beach	15068
Lincoln Colliery	17963
Lincoln Falls	18616
Lincoln Heights (Berks County)	19508

	ZIP
Lincoln Heights (Westmoreland County)	15644
Lincoln Hill	15301
Lincoln Park (Allegheny County)	15235
Lincoln Park (Berks County)	19609
Lincoln Park (Delaware County)	19079
Lincoln Place (Part of Pittsburgh)	15122
Lincoln Terrace	18042
Lincoln University	19352
Lincolnville	16404
Lincolnway	17404
Linconia	19047
Lindaville	18824
Linden (Lycoming County)	17744
Linden (Washington County)	15317
Linden Hall	16828
Lindenhurst	19067
Linds Crossing	16648
Lindsey (Part of Punxsutawney)	15767
Line Lexington	18932
Line Mountain	17941
Linesville	16424
Linfield	19468
Linglestown	17112
Linn	15442
Linntown	17837
Linville Circle (Part of Lancaster)	17602
Linwood	19061
Linwood Park	19061
Linwood Terrace	19061
Lionville	19353
Lionville-Marchwood	19341
Lippincott	15370
Lisbon	16373
Lisburn	17055
Listie	15549
Listonburg	15424
Litchfield	18810
Litchfield (Township)	18810
Lithia Springs	17857
Lithia Valley (Part of Factoryville)	18419
Lititz	17543
Little Beaver (Township)	16141
Little Britain (Township)	19363
Little Chicago	15320
Little Cooley	16404
Little Corners	16335
Little Gap	18058
Little Hickory	16353
Little Hope	16428
Little Italy	18956
Little Kansas	17051
Little Mahanoy (Township)	17823
Little Marsh	16950
Little Meadows	18830
Littlestown	17340
Little Summit	15431
Little Washington (Chester County)	19335
Little Washington (Cumberland County)	17241
Live Easy	15320
Liverpool	17045
Liverpool (Township)	17045
Livonia	16872
Llandrilla	19004
Llanfair	15930
Llangelan Hills	19073
Llewellyn	17944
Llewelyn Corners	18602
Lloydell	15921
Lloydesville	15650
Llyswen (Part of Altoona)	16602
Loag	19520
Lobachsville	19547
Lochiel	17837
Lochvale	15742
Locke Mills	17063
Lock Haven	17745
Lock No. 4 (Part of Charleroi)	15022
Lockport (Clinton County)	17745
Lockport (Mifflin County)	17044
Lockport (Westmoreland County)	15923
Locksley	19342
Lockview	15022
Locust (Columbia County) (Township)	17820
Locust (Indiana County)	15771
Locustdale	17945
Locust Gap	17840
Locust Grove	17402
Locust Grove Gardens	17402
Locust Lakes Village	18347

	ZIP
Locust Point	17055
Locust Ridge	15116
Locust Run	17094
Locust Summit	17840
Locust Valley (Lehigh County)	18036
Locust Valley (Schuylkill County)	18214
Lofty	18201
Logan (Blair County) (Township)	16602
Logan (Clinton County) (Township)	17747
Logan (Huntingdon County) (Township)	16611
Logan (Indiana County)	15742
Logan (Philadelphia County)	19141
Logan Mills	17747
Logans Ferry (Part of Plum)	15068
Logans Ferry Heights (Part of Plum)	15068
Logan Square (Part of Norristown)	19401
Loganton	17747
Loganville	17342
Log Pile	15301
London	16127
London Britain (Township)	19350
Londonderry (Bedford County) (Township)	15545
Londonderry (Chester County) (Township)	19330
Londonderry (Dauphin County) (Township)	17057
London Grove (Chester County)	19348
London Grove (Chester County) (Township)	19390
Lonely Acres	15722
Lone Pine	15301
Lonewood	15145
Long Acre Park (Part of Yeadon)	19050
Long Branch	15423
Long Bridge	15658
Longbrook	17758
Longfellow	17044
Longlevel	17368
Long Pond	18334
Long Run	18235
Longs Crossroad	16661
Longsdale	19539
Longsdorf	17241
Longstown	17402
Longswamp	19539
Longswamp (Township)	19539
Longview (Part of Bethel Park)	15102
Longwood Gardens	19348
Lookout	18417
Loomis Park	18702
Loop Station	16648
Lopez	18628
Lorain	15902
Lorane	19606
Lorberry	17963
Lords Valley	18428
Lorenton	16938
Loretto	15940
Loretto Road	15931
Loshs Run	17020
Lost Creek	17946
Lottsville	16402
Loux Corner	18927
Lovedale	15037
Lovejoy	15729
Lovell	16407
Lovelton	18629
Lovely	15521
Lover	15022
Lowber (Fayette County)	15438
Lowber (Westmoreland County)	15660
Lowe Lake	18470
Lower Allen	17011
Lower Allen (Township)	17011
Lower Alsace (Township)	19606
Lower Askam	18706
Lower Augusta (Township)	17801
Lower Brownville	17976
Lower Burrell	15068
Lower Chanceford (Township)	17302
Lower Chichester (Township)	19061
Lower Frankford (Township)	17013
Lower Frederick (Township)	19492
Lower Gwynedd (Township)	19437
Lower Heidelberg (Township)	19604
Lower Longswamp	19539
Lower Macungie (Township)	18062

	ZIP
Lower Mahanoy (Township)	17017
Lower Makefield (Township)	19067
Lower Merion (Township)	19003
Lower Mifflin (Township) ...	17241
Lower Milford (Township)	18036
Lower Moreland (Township)	19006
Lower Mount Bethel (Township)	18063
Lower Nazareth (Township)	18017
Lower Orchard	19058
Lower Oxford (Township)	19363
Lower Paxton	17109
Lower Paxton (Township)	17109
Lower Peanut	15480
Lower Pottsgrove (Township)	19464
Lower Providence (Township)	19401
Lower Sagon	17877
Lower Salford (Township)	19438
Lower Saucon (Township)	18015
Lower Southampton (Township)	19047
Lower Swatara (Township)	17057
Lower Towamensing (Township)	18071
Lower Turkeyfoot (Township)	15424
Lower Tyrone (Township)	15428
Lower Windsor (Township)	17368
Lower Yoder (Township) ...	15906
Lowhill (Lehigh County) (Township)	18069
Low Hill (Washington County)	15429
Lowville	16442
Loyalhanna	15661
Loyalhanna (Township)	15681
Loyalhanna Woodlands No. 1	15670
Loyalsock (Township)	17701
Loyalsockville	17754
Loyalton	17048
Loyalville	18612
Loysburg	16659
Loysville	17047
Lucernemines	15754
Lucesco	15656
Lucinda	16235
Luciusboro	15748
Lucknow	17110
Lucky	17322
Lucon	19473
Lucy Crossing (Part of Glendon)	18042
Lucy Furnace	17066
Ludlow	16333
Ludwigs Corner	19343
Luke Fidler	17872
Lumber (Township)	15834
Lumber City (Clearfield County)	16833
Lumber City (Mifflin County)	17084
Lumberville	18933
Lumstead	16201
Lundys Lane	16401
Lungerville	17774
Lurgan	17232
Lurgan (Township)	17240
Luthersburg	15848
Luthers Mills	18848
Lutztown	17013
Lutzville	15537
Luxor	15662
Luzerne	15433
Luzerne (Township)	15417
Luzerne	18709
Lycippus	15650
Lycoming (Township)	17728
Lykens	17048
Lykens (Township)	17048
Lyleville	16627
Lynch	16347
Lynchville	15857
Lyndell	19354
Lyndon	17602
Lyndora	16045
Lynn (Lehigh County) (Township)	19529
Lynn (Susquehanna County)	18844
Lynnewood	19150
Lynnewood Gardens	19012
Lynnport	18066
Lynnville	18066
Lynnwood (Fayette County)	15012
Lynnwood (Luzerne County)	18702
Lynnwood-Pricedale	15012
Lyon Station	19536
Lyon Valley	18066
Mable	17921
Mable Hill	15327

	ZIP
McAdoo	18237
McAdoo Heights	18237
McAlevys Fort	16652
McAlisters Crossroads	15086
McAlisterville	17049
MacArthur (Part of Aliquippa)	15001
McCalmont (Township)	15711
McCandless (Township) ...	15237
McCandless Township (census designated place)	15237
McCartney	16661
McCauley	16651
McChesneytown	15650
McChesneytown-Loyalhanna	15620
McClarran	15650
Mc Cleary	15050
McClellan	17032
McClellandtown	15458
McClellan Heights	17403
McClintock	16301
McClure (Fayette County)	15666
McClure (Snyder County)	17841
McConnellsburg	17233
McConnells Mill	15301
McConnellstown	16660
McCormick (mail Marion County)	15759
McCormick (mail Smicksburg)	16256
McCoysville	17058
Mccullochs Mills	17035
McCullough	15636
McDonald	15057
Macdonaldton	15530
Macedonia (Bradford County)	18848
Macedonia (Juniata County)	17059
McElhattan	17748
McEwensville	17749
McGareys	15825
McGees Mills	15757
McGillstown	17003
McGovern	15342
McGrann	16236
McGregor	16222
McHenry (Township)	17723
McIlhaney	18322
McIntyre (Indiana County)	15756
McIntyre (Lycoming County) (Township)	17763
McKean	16426
McKean (Township)	16426
McKean Corners	16351
McKeansburg	17960
McKee	16637
McKee Half Falls	17864
McKeesport	15130-35
For specific McKeesport Zip Codes call (412) 672-9721, or your local postmaster.	
McKees Rocks	15136
Mackeyville	17750
McKinley	19117
McKinley Hill (Part of Point Marion)	15474
McKinney	17232
McKnight	15237
McKnightstown	17343
McKnight Village	15237
McLane	16426
McMichaels	18360
McMurray	15317
McNett (Township)	17765
McPherron	15753
McSherrystown	17344
Macungie	18062
McVeytown	17051
McVille	16229
McWilliams	16242
Maddensville	17229
Madera	16661
Madge	16735
Madison (Armstrong County) (Township)	16259
Madison (Clarion County) (Township)	16248
Madison (Columbia County) (Township)	17846
Madison (Lackawanna County) (Township)	18444
Madison (Westmoreland County)	15663
Madisonburg	16852
Madisonville	18444
Madley	15534
Magee	16351
Magill Heights	15024
Magnolia Gardens	19007
Magnolia Hill	19007

	ZIP
Mahaffey	15757
Mahanoy (Township)	17976
Mahanoy City	17948
Mahanoy Plane (Part of Gilberton)	17949
Mahoning (Armstrong County)	16259
Mahoning (Armstrong County) (Township)	16242
Mahoning (Carbon County) (Township)	18235
Mahoning (Lawrence County) (Township)	16132
Mahoning (Montour County) (Township)	17821
Mahoning Manor	17847
Mahoningtown (Part of New Castle)	16102
Maiden Creek	19510
Maidencreek (Township)	19605
Main (Township)	17815
Mainesburg	16932
Mainland	19451
Mainsville	17257
Mainville	17815
Maitland	17044
Maizeville (Part of Gilberton)	17934
Majeriks Corners	16441
Malden Place (Part of Centerville)	15417
Mall (Part of Monroeville)...	15146
Malta	17017
Malvern	19355
Mammoth	15664
Mamont	15632
Manada Gap	17112
Manatawny	19547
Manayunk (Part of Philadelphia)	19127
Manchester (Allegheny County)	15233
Manchester (Wayne County) (Township)	18417
Manchester (York County)	17345
Manchester (York County) (Township)	17402
Mandata	17830
Manheim (Lancaster County)	17545
Manheim (Lancaster County) (Township)	17601
Manheim (York County) (Township)	17329
Manifold	15301
Manito	15650
Mann (Township)	17211
Mannitto Haven	15670
Manns Choice	15550
Mannsville	17074
Manoa	19083
Manor (Armstrong County) (Township)	16226
Manor (Lancaster County) (Township)	17603
Manor (Westmoreland County)	15665
Manor Hill	16652
Manor Hills (Part of Yeadon)	19050
Manor Park Terrace	16226
Manor Ridge	17603
Manor Shopping Center ...	17603
Manorville	16238
Manown	15063
Mansfield	16933
Mantz	18252
Manver	15765
Maple Beach	19007
Mapledale	16323
Maple Glen (Montgomery County)	19002
Maple Glen (Washington County)	15417
Maple Grove (Berks County)	18011
Maple Grove (Chester County)	19363
Maple Grove (Clarion County)	16248
Maple Grove (Fayette County)	15622
Maple Grove Park	19540
Maple Hill (Lycoming County)	17752
Maple Hill (Montgomery County)	19422
Maple Hill (Schuylkill County)	17976
Maple Hills	17319
Maple Hollow	16635
Maplelake	18444
Maple Manor	18201
Maple Ridge	15935

	ZIP
Maple Shade	19021
Mapleton Depot	17052
Mapletown	15338
Maplewood (Bucks County)	18901
Maplewood (Wayne County)	18436
Maplewood Heights	18612
Maplewood Park	19018
Maplewood Terrace	15601
Marble	16334
Marble Hall	19444
Marcel Lake Estates	18328
Marchand	15758
Marchwood	19341
Marcus Hook	19061
Marengo	16877
Margaret	16201
Margaretta Furnace	17406
Margo Gardens	19007
Marguerite	15650
Marianna	15345
Mariasville	16373
Marienville	16239
Marietta	17547
Marion (Beaver County) (Township)	15066
Marion (Berks County) (Township)	19567
Marion (Butler County) (Township)	16020
Marion (Centre County) (Township)	16841
Marion (Franklin County)	17235
Marion Center	15759
Marion Heights	17832
Marion Hill	15066
Mark Acres	15642
Markelsville	17074
Markes	17236
Market Square (Part of Philadelphia)	19118
Market Street (Part of West Chester)	19380
Markle	15613
Markleton	15551
Markleysburg	15459
Markton	15764
Markvue Manor	15642
Marlboro	19348
Marlborough (Township)	18084
Mar Lin	17951
Marple (Township)	19008
Marron	16833
Mars	16046
Marsh (Chester County)	19520
Marsh (Franklin County)	17268
Marshall (Township)	15086
Marshall Heights	15716
Marshalls Creek	18335
Marshall Terrace	19061
Marshallton (Chester County)	19380
Marshallton (Northumberland County)	17872
Marshbrook	18414
Marshburg	16738
Marsh Hill	17771
Marshlands	16921
Marsh Run	17070
Marshview	18848
Marshwood (Part of Olyphant)	18434
Marsteller	15760
Marstown	17963
Martha Furnace	16870
Martic (Township)	17565
Martic Forge	17565
Marticville	17565
Martin	15460
Martindale (Cambria County)	15946
Martindale (Lancaster County)	17549
Martinsburg	16662
Martins Corner	19320
Martins Creek	18063
Martinsville	17366
Martzville	18603
Marvel Gardens	19094
Marvindale	16749
Marwood	16023
Mary D.	17952
Marysville	17053
Marywood College (Part of Scranton)	18509
Mascot	17572
Mason-Dixon	17225
Masontown	15461
Masseyburg	16669
Mastersonville	17545
Mast Hope	18435
Matamoras (Dauphin County)	17032

	ZIP
Matamoras (Pike County)	18336
Mather	15346
Mattawana	17054
Mattey Plan	15012
Matthews Run	16371
Mausdale	17821
Maxatawny	19538
Maxatawny (Township)	19538
Maxwell	15450
Mayberry (Township)	17821
Mayburg	16347
Mayfair (Part of Philadelphia)	19136
Mayfield	18433
Mayfield East	17405
Mayport	16240
Maysville (Armstrong County)	15618
Maysville (Mercer County)	16125
Maytown (Lancaster County)	17550
Maytown (York County)	17339
Mayview	15017
Mayville	16105
Maze	17094
Mazeppa	17837
Mead (Township)	16313
Meadia Heights	17602
Meadowbrook (Fayette County)	15401
Meadowbrook (Montgomery County)	19046
Meadowbrook Manor	19341
Meadow Gap	17243
Meadow Lands	15347
Meadowood	16045
Meadowview Estates	17540
Meadow Wood	15001
Meadville	16335
Mechanicsburg	17055
Mechanics Grove	17566
Mechanicsville (Bucks County)	18934
Mechanicsville (Clarion County)	16214
Mechanicsville (Lancaster County)	17545
Mechanicsville (Lehigh County)	18104
Mechanicsville (Montour County)	17821
Mechanicsville (Schuylkill County)	17901
Meckesville	18210
Mecks Corner	17068
Media	19063-65
For specific Media Zip Codes call (215) 566-3196, or your local postmaster.	
Medix Run	15868
Meeker	18612
Megargee	19320
Mehoopany	18629
Mehoopany (Township)	18629
Meiser	17842
Meiserville	17853
Melcroft	15462
Mellingertown	15666
Melrose (Fayette County)	15450
Melrose (Susquehanna County)	18847
Melrose Park	19012
Menallen (Adams County) (Township)	17304
Menallen (Fayette County) (Township)	15401
Mench	15537
Mendenhall	19357
Mendon	15679
Menges Mills	17346
Menno	17004
Menno (Township)	17004
Mentcle	15761
Mercer (Butler County) (Township)	16038
Mercer (Mercer County)	16137
Mercersburg	17236
Mercur	17854
Meredith	16249
Meridian	16001
Merion Park	19066
Merion Square	19035
Merion Station	19066
Merion View	19406
Meriwether Farms	19380
Merlin	19460
Mermaid Estates	19401
Merrian	17851
Merrill (Part of Industry)	15052
Merrittstown	15463
Merryall	18853
Mertztown	19539

	ZIP
Merwinsburg	18330
Meshoppen	18630
Meshoppen (Township)	18630
Messiah College	17027
Messmore	15458
Metal	17224
Metal (Township)	17221
Mexico	17056
Meyersdale	15552
Meyersville	18104
Middleburg (Luzerne County)	18661
Middleburg (Snyder County)	17842
Middlebury (Township)	16935
Middlebury Center	16935
Middle Churches	15666
Middle City (Part of Philadelphia)	19103
Middle Creek (Snyder County)	17813
Middlecreek (Snyder County) (Township)	17833
Middlecreek (Somerset County) (Township)	15557
Middle Lancaster	16037
Middle Paxton (Township)	17018
Middleport	17953
Middlesex (Butler County) (Township)	16059
Middlesex (Cumberland County)	17013
Middlesex (Cumberland County) (Township)	17013
Middle Smithfield (Township)	18301
Middle Spring	17257
Middle Taylor (Township)	15906
Middleton	15757
Middletown (Bucks County) (Township)	19056
Middletown (Dauphin County)	17057
Middletown (Delaware County) (Township)	19037
Middletown (McKean County)	16749
Middletown (Northampton County)	18017
Middletown (Susquehanna County) (Township)	18818
Middletown (Westmoreland County)	15601
Middletown Center	18818
Middletown Heights	19063
Midland (Beaver County)	15059
Midland (Washington County)	15342
Midvale	18705
Midvale Manor	19608
Midvalley	17888
Midway (Adams County)	17331
Midway (Lebanon County)	17042
Midway (Washington County)	15060
Midway (Westmoreland County)	15601
Mifflin (Columbia County) (Township)	18631
Mifflin (Dauphin County) (Township)	17061
Mifflin (Juniata County)	17058
Mifflin (Lycoming County) (Township)	17740
Mifflinburg	17844
Mifflin Junction (Part of West Mifflin)	15236
Mifflintown	17059
Mifflinville	18631
Milan	18831
Milanville	18443
Mildred	18632
Mile Run	17801
Miles (Township)	16872
Milesburg	16853
Milesville	15063
Milford (Bucks County) (Township)	18968
Milford (Juniata County) (Township)	17062
Milford (Pike County)	18337
Milford (Pike County) (Township)	18337
Milford (Somerset County)	15501
Milford (Somerset County) (Township)	15557
Milford Manor	19067
Milford Square	18935
Milfred Terrace	15348
Militia Hill	19034
Millardsville	17067
Millbach	17073
Millbank	15658

	ZIP		ZIP		ZIP
Mount Patrick	17045	Muncy (Township)	17756	Nether Providence	
Mount Penn	19606	Muncy Creek (Township)	17756	Township (census	
Mount Pleasant (Adams		Muncy Valley	17758	designated place)	19013
County)	17331	Munderf	15825	Neville (Township)	15225
Mount Pleasant (Adams		Mundys Corner	15909	Neville Island	15225
County) (Township)	17325	Munhall	15120	New Albany	18833
Mount Pleasant (Berks		Munson	15940	New Alexandria	15670
County)	19506	Munster	15940	New Athens	16248
Mount Pleasant (Columbia		Munster (Township)	15938	New Baltimore (Somerset	
County) (Township)	17815	Murdock	15501	County)	15553
Mount Pleasant (Delaware		Murdocksville	15026	New Baltimore (York	
County)	19087	Murphy Siding	15425	County)	17331
Mount Pleasant (Juniata		Murraysville (Part of		New Beaver	16141
County)	17059	Murrysville)	15668	New Bedford	16140
Mount Pleasant (Lebanon		Murrell	17522	New Berlin	17855
County)	17042	Murrinsville	16020	New Berlinville	19545
Mount Pleasant (Mifflin		Murry Hill	15317	Newberry (Lycoming	
County)	17063	Murrysville	15668	County)	17701
Mount Pleasant		Muse	15350	Newberry (York County)	
(Northampton County)	18013	Mustard	15037	(Township)	17370
Mount Pleasant		Mutual	15601	Newberrytown	17319
(Northumberland County)	17801	Myersburg	18854	New Bethlehem	16242
Mount Pleasant (Perry		Myerstown (Cumberland		New Bloomfield	17068
	17006	County) County)	17324	Newboro	15468
Mount Pleasant (Schuylkill		Myerstown (Lebanon		New Boston	17948
County)	17901	County)	17067	New Bridgeville	17356
Mount Pleasant (Tioga		Mylo Park	15931	New Brighton	15066
County)	16938	Myobeach	18630	New Britain	18901
Mount Pleasant		Myoma	16046	New Britain (Township)	18914
(Washington County)		Myrtle	14721	New Buena Vista	15550
(Township)	15340	Mystic Park	16404	New Buffalo	17069
Mount Pleasant (Wayne		Naces Corner	18927	Newburg (Blair County)	16601
County) (Township)	18472	Naceville	18960	Newburg (Cumberland	
Mount Pleasant		Nadine	15147	County)	17240
(Westmoreland County)	15666	Naginey	17063	Newburg (Northampton	
Mount Pleasant		Nagles Crossroad	16668	County)	18017
(Westmoreland County)		Nan Lynn Gardens	18974	Newburg Homes	18042
(Township)	15664	Nansen	16735	New Castle	16101-08
Mount Pleasant (York		Nanticoke	18634	For specific New Castle Zip	
County)	17019	Nantmeal Village	19343	Codes call (412) 656-7200, or	
Mount Pleasant Mills	17853	Nanty Glo	15943	your local postmaster.	
Mount Pocono	18344	Naomi	15438	New Castle (Township)	17970
Mountrock (Cumberland		Napier (Township)	15559	New Castle Northwest	16105
County)	17013	Napierville	17522	New Centerville	15557
Mount Rock (Franklin		Narberth	19072	Newchester	17350
County)	17257	Narbrook Park (Part of		New Columbia	17856
Mount Rock (Mifflin County)	17044	Narberth)	19072	New Columbus (Carbon	
Mount Royal	17315	Narrows Creek	15801	County)	18240
Mount Sterling	15461	Narrows Shopping Center		New Columbus (Luzerne	
Mount Tabor	17324	(Part of Edwardsville)	18704	County)	17878
Mount Troy	15212	Narrowsville	18972	Newcomer	15401
Mount Union (Franklin		Narvon	17555	New Cumberland	17070
County)	17222	Nashua	16101	New Cumberland Army	
Mount Union (Huntingdon		Nashville (Indiana County)	15771	Depot	17105
County)	17066	Nashville (York County)	17362	New Danville	17603
Mount Vernon (Allegheny		Nassau Village	19078	New Derry	15671
County)	15135	Natalie	17851	New Eagle	15067
Mount Vernon (Chester		National Hill	15031	Newell	15466
County)	19363	Natrona	15065	New England	18252
Mount Vernon (Lancaster		Natrona Heights	15065	New Enterprise	16664
County)	17527	Nauvoo	16938	New Era	18833
Mount Vernon		Naval Air Development		Newfield (Allegheny County)	15147
(Westmoreland County)	15601	Center	18974	Newfield (Potter County)	16948
Mountville	17554	Nazareth	18064	New Florence	15944
Mount Washington		Nealmont	16686	Newfoundland	18445
(Allegheny County)	15211	Neason Hill	16335	New Franklin	17201
Mount Washington (Beaver		Neath	18829	New Freedom	17349
County)	15010	Nebo	15622	New Freeport	15352
Mount Wilson	17042	Nectarine	16038	New Galena	18914
Mount Wolf	17347	Ned	15352	New Galilee	16141
Mount Zion (Hampden		Needful	16881	New Garden	19374
Township) (Cumberland		Needmore	17238	New Garden (Township)	19350
County)	17013	Neelyton	17239	New Geneva	15467
Mount Zion (South		Neffs	18065	New Germantown	17071
Middleton Township)		Neffs Mills	16669	New Germany	15946
(Cumberland County)	17055	Neffsville	17601	New Grass Manor	18612
Mount Zion (Lebanon			17606	New Grenada	16674
County)	17046	For specific Neffsville Zip Codes		New Hamburg	16124
Mount Zion (Luzerne		call (717) 569-9841, or your local		New Hanover	19525
County)	18643	postmaster.		New Hanover (Township)	19525
Mount Zion (Monroe		Neiffer	19473	New Hanover Square	19435
County)	18301	Neiltown	16341	Newhard	18080
Mount Zion (York County)	17402	Neiman	17327	New Holland	17557
Moween	15681	Nellie	15486	New Homestead (Part of	
Mowersville	17257	Nelson	16940	Pittsburgh)	15120
Mowry	17921	Nelson (Township)	16940	New Hope	18938
Moyer	15425	Nemacolin	15351	New Ireland	16438
Moylan	19065	Nemanie	18451	New Jerusalem	19522
Mozart	18925	Nescopeck	18635	New Kensington	15068
Mt Pocahontas	18210	Nescopeck (Township)	18635	New Kingstown	17072
Muddycreek (Township)	16051	Neshaminy	18976	Newkirk	18252
Muddy Creek Forks	17302	Neshaminy Falls	19047	New Lebanon	16145
Muhlenberg (Berks County)		Neshaminy Hills	19047	New Lexington	15557
(Township)	19560	Neshaminy Valley	19020	Newlin (Chester County)	
Muhlenberg (Luzerne		Neshaminy Woods	19047	(Township)	19380
County)	18621	Neshannock	16105	Newlin (Columbia County)	17820
Muhlenberg Park	19605	Neshannock (Township)	16105	New London	19360
Muir	17957	Neshannock Falls	16156	New London (Township)	19360
Mullertown	17331	Nesquehoning	18240	New London	16351
Mumbauersville	18073	Nether Providence		Newlonsburg (Part of	
Mummasburg	17325	(Township)	19086	Murrysville)	15668
Muncy	17756			New Mahoning	18235

* Area Zip Code   † Post Office Boxes

	ZIP		ZIP		ZIP
Newmanstown	17073	Norrisville	16406	North Union (Fayette	
Newmansville	16353	North Abington (Township)	18414	County) (Township)	15401
New Market	17070	Northampton (Bucks		North Union (Schuylkill	
New Milford	18834	County) (Township)	18954	County) (Township)	18241
New Milford (Township)	18834	Northampton (Northampton		North Vandergrift	15690
New Millport	16861	County)	18067	North Vandergrift-Pleasant	
New Mines	17923	Northampton (Somerset		View	15690
New Oxford	17350	County) (Township)	15538	North Versailles	15137
New Paris	15554	Northampton Hills	18966	North Versailles (Township)	15137
New Park	17352	North Annville (Township)	17038	Northview Heights (Part of	
New Philadelphia	17959	North Apollo	15673	Economy)	15005
Newport (Lawrence County)	16157	North Aronimink	19082	Northview Homes (Part of	
Newport (Luzerne County)		North Bangor	18013	Economy)	15005
(Township)	18634	North Barnesboro (Part of		Northvue	16001
Newport (Perry County)	17074	Barnesboro)	15714	North Wales	19454
Newportville	19056	North Beaver (Township)	16102	North Warren	16365
Newportville Terrace	19020	North Belle Vernon	15012	North Washington (Butler	
New Providence	17560	North Bend	17760	County)	16048
New Richmond	16327	North Bessemer	15235	North Washington	
New Ringgold	17960	North Bethlehem (Township)	15360	(Westmoreland County)	15613
Newry	16665	North Bingham	16923	Northway Mall	15237
New Salem	15468	North Braddock	15104	North Waynesburg	17268
New Salem-Buffington	15468	North Branch (Township)	18629	North Weissport	18235
New Schaefferstown	19506	Northbrook	19380	Northwest Harborcreek	16510
New Sewickley (Township)	15074	Northbrook Hills	17601	North Whitehall (Township)	18037
New Sheffield	15001	North Buffalo (Township)	16201	Northwood	16686
Newside	18080	North Butler	16001	North Woodbury (Township)	16662
New Smithville	19530	North Catasauqua	18032	Northwood Heights	18042
New Stanton	15672	North Centre (Township)	18603	North York	17404
New Street	17901	North Charleroi	15022	Norvelt	15674
New Texas	17563	North Codorus (Township)	17362	Norwegian (Township)	17951
Newton (Township)	18411	North Cornwall	17016	Norwich (Township)	16724
Newtonburg	15757	North Cornwall (Township)	17042	Norwin Heights	15642
Newton Hamilton	17075	North Coventry (Township)	19464	Norwood (Allegheny	
Newton Lake	18407	North East	16428	County)	15136
Newtown (Bucks County)	18940	North East (Township)	16428	Norwood (Delaware County)	19074
Newtown (Bucks County)		Northeast Madison		Nossville	17213
(Township)	18940	(Township)	17047	Nottingham (Bucks County)	19020
New Town (Centre County)	16666	North Edinburg	16116	Nottingham (Chester	
Newtown (Clearfield		North End (Part of Wilkes-		County)	19362
County)	16878	Barre)	18705	Nottingham (Washington	
Newtown (Delaware		Northern Lights Shopping		County) (Township)	15332
County) (Township)	19073	Center (Part of Economy)	15005	Nowrytown	15681
Newtown (Lancaster		North Essington	19029	Noxen	18636
County)	17512	North Fayette (Township)	15071	Noxen (Township)	18636
Newtown (Lehigh County)	18031	North Fork	16950	Noyes (Township)	17764
Newtown (Luzerne County)	18706	North Franklin (Township)	15301	Nuangola	18637
Newtown Grant	18940	North Fredericktown	15333	Nuangola Station	18707
Newtown Square	19073	North Freedom	16240	Number Five Mine	16137
New Tripoli	18066	North Hamilton (Part of		Number Thirty Seven	15963
New Vernon	16145	Doylestown)	18901	Numidia	17858
New Vernon (Township)	16145	North Hanover Mall (Part of		Nu Mine	16244
Newville (Bucks County)	18914	Hanover)	17331	Nuremberg	18241
Newville (Cumberland		North Heidelberg		Nutts Corners	16127
County)	17241	(Township)	19506	Nyesville	17201
Newville (Lancaster County)	17023	North Hills (Montgomery		Oakbottom	17566
New Virginia (Part of		County)	19038	Oakdale (Allegheny County)	15071
Hermitage)	16146	North Hills (Northumberland		Oakdale (Luzerne County)	18224
New Washington	15757	County)	17847	Oakdale Manor	19067
New Wilmington	16142	North Hopewell (Township)	17322	Oakeola	19036
Niagara	18453	North Huntingdon		Oakford	19047
Niantic	19504	(Township)	15642	Oak Forest	15370
Nicetown (Part of		North Irwin	15642	Oak Grove (Clearfield	
Philadelphia)	19140	North Jackson	18847	County)	16858
Nichola	16262	North Larchmont	19073	Oak Grove (Schuylkill	
Nicholson (Fayette County)		North Lebanon (Township)	17046	County)	17963
(Township)	15461	North Liberty	16127	Oakgrove (Westmoreland	
Nicholson (Wyoming		North Londonderry		County)	15658
County)	18446	(Township)	17078	Oak Hall	16827
Nicholson (Wyoming		North Mahoning (Township)	15771	Oak Hill (North Versailles	
County) (Township)	18446	North Mall Factory Outlet		Township) (Allegheny	
Nickel Mines	17562	Center (Part of York)	17404	County)	15145
Nickleville	16373	North Manheim (Township)	17901	Oak Hill (Wilkins Township)	
Nicklin	16323	North McKees Rocks	15136	(Allegheny County)	15137
Nicktown	15762	North Mehoopany	18629	Oak Hill (Clearfield County)	16845
Nilan	15474	North Middleton (Township)	17013	Oak Hills	16001
Niles	16323	Northmoreland (Township)	18612	Oakland (Allegheny County)	15213
Niles Valley	16935	North Mountain	17758	Oakland (Butler County)	
Ninepoints	17509	North Newton (Township)	17241	(Township)	16061
Nine Row	15927	North Oakland	16025	Oakland (Cambria County)	15904
Nineveh (Clarion County)	16232	North Orwell	18837	Oakland (Lawrence County)	16101
Nineveh (Greene County)	15353	North Philadelphia (Part of		Oakland (Mercer County)	16137
Nippenose (Township)	17720	Philadelphia)	19132	Oakland (Susquehanna	
Nisbet	17759	North Philipsburg	16866	County)	18847
Nittany	16841	North Pine Grove	16260	Oakland (Susquehanna	
Niverton	15558	North Point (Bedford		County) (Township)	18847
Nixon	16001	County)	16679	Oakland (Venango County)	
Noble	19046	Northpoint (Indiana County)	15763	(Township)	16317
Noble Hill	15215	North Radcliffe	19007	Oakland Beach	16316
Noblestown	15071	North Rochester	15074	Oakland Hills I	18016
Nockamixon (Township)	18930	North Rome	18854	Oakland Mills	17076
Noll Acres	17055	North Scottdale	15683	Oakland Park	18101
Nolo	15765	North Scranton (Part of		Oak Lane (Part of	
Nook	17058	Scranton)	18508	Philadelphia)	19126
Nordmont	17758	North Sewickley	15010	Oaklane Manor	19012
Normal Square	18235	North Sewickley (Township)	15010	Oakleigh	17111
Normalville	15469	North Shenango (Township)	16424	Oaklyn	17801
Norman	15825	North Springfield	16430	Oakmont (Allegheny	
Norristown	19401-04	North Strabane (Township)	15317	County)	15139
		North Towanda	18848	Oakmont (Cambria County)	15904
		North Towanda (Township)	18848	Oakmont Villa	17036
		Northumberland	17857		

For specific Norristown Zip Codes call (215) 275-9780, or your local postmaster.

***

* Area Zip Code   † Post Office Boxes

	ZIP
Oak Park (Montgomery County)	19440
Oak Park (mobile home park) (Montgomery County)	19446
Oak Park (Northumberland County)	17857
Oak Ridge (Armstrong County)	16245
Oak Ridge (Clearfield County)	16661
Oakryn	17563
Oaks	19456
Oak Shade	17566
Oaktree Hollow	19007
Oakview	19026
Oakview Park	19026
Oakville (Cumberland County)	17257
Oakville (Westmoreland County)	15650
Oakwood	16101
Oakwood Park (Part of Laflin)	18702
Obelisk	19492
Oberlin	17113
Oberlin Gardens	17113
Observatory (Part of Pittsburgh)	15214
Odenthal	15946
Odenwelder (Part of West Easton)	18042
Odin	16915
Ogden	19061
Ogdensburg	17765
Ogle (Butler County)	16046
Ogle (Somerset County) (Township)	15963
Ogletown	15963
Ogontz Campus	19012
Ogontz Campus	19001
O'Hara (Township)	15238
O'Hara Township (census designated place)	15215
Ohio (Township)	15237
Ohiopyle	15470
Ohioview (Part of Industry)	15052
Ohioville	15059
Ohl	15864
Oil City (Cambria County)	15925
Oil City (Venango County)	16301
Oil Creek (Crawford County) (Township)	16354
Oilcreek (Venango County) (Township)	16341
Oil Creek (Venango County)	16301
Oklahoma (Clearfield County)	15801
Oklahoma (Westmoreland County)	15613
Okome	17739
Olanta	16863
Old Bethany	15688
Old Boston	18640
Old Clarendon (Part of Clarendon)	16313
Old Concord	15329
Old Crabtree	15650
Old Enon	16120
Old Forge	18518
Oldframe	15478
Old Junction (Part of Somerset)	15501
Old Line	17545
Old Lycoming (Township)	17701
Old Meadow	15683
Old Orchard (Monroe County)	18370
Old Orchard (Northampton County)	18042
Old Port	17082
Old Stanton (Part of New Stanton)	15672
Old Zionsville	18068
Oleopolis	16301
Oley	19547
Oley (Township)	19547
Oley Furnace	19547
Oliphant Furnace	15401
Oliveburg	15764
Oliver (Fayette County)	15472
Oliver (Jefferson County) (Township)	15825
Oliver (Mifflin County) (Township)	17044
Oliver (Perry County) (Township)	17074
Oliver No. 2 (Fayette County)	15401
Oliver No. 3 (Fayette County)	15401

	ZIP
Olivers Mills (Part of Laurel Run)	18702
Olivet	15618
Olney (Part of Philadelphia)	19120
Olwen Heights	18444
Olyphant	18447
Oneida (Butler County)	16001
Oneida (Huntingdon County) (Township)	16652
Oneida (Schuylkill County)	18242
Onnalinda	15955
Ono	17077
Ontario	15330
Ontelaunee (Township)	19605
Opp	17756
Oppermans Corner	19425
Option (Part of Baldwin)	15236
Orange (Columbia County) (Township)	17859
Orange (Luzerne County)	18612
Orangeville	17859
Orbisonia	17243
Orchard Beach	16428
Orchard Crossing	16686
Orchard Hill (Part of Mount Pleasant)	15666
Orchard Hills	15613
Orefield	18069
Oregon (Lancaster County)	17540
Oregon (Wayne County) (Township)	18431
Oregon Hill	16938
Ore Hill	16673
Oreland	19075
Oreland Gardens	19075
Oreminea	16693
Ore Valley	17403
Orient	15420
Oriental	17045
Oriole	17740
Ormrod	18037
Ormsby	16726
Orners Corner	16601
Orrstown	17244
Orrtanna	17353
Orrville	15144
Orson	18449
Orvilla	19440
Orviston	16864
Orwell	18837
Orwell (Township)	18837
Orwigsburg	17961
Orwin	17980
Osborne	15143
Osceola	16942
Osceola (Township)	16942
Osceola Mills	16666
Osgood	16125
Oshanter	16830
Ostend	15757
Osterburg	16667
Osterhout	18657
Oswayo	16915
Oswayo (Township)	16748
Ottawa	17821
Otter Creek (Township)	16125
Otto (Township)	16745
Ottsville	18942
Ott Town	15537
Outcrop	15478
Outlet	18612
Outwood	17963
Oval	17740
Overbrook (Allegheny County)	15210
Overbrook (Philadelphia County)	19151
Overbrook Hills	19151
Overfield (Township)	18414
Overholt Acres	15642
Overleigh	19004
Overlook	17601
Overlook Heights	16801
Overlook Springs	18049
Overton	18833
Overton (Township)	18833
Overview	17053
Owensdale	15425
Oxbow Meadows	18914
Oxford (Adams County) (Township)	17350
Oxford (Chester County)	19363
Oxford Valley	19030
Oyster Point	17602
Packer (Township)	18255
Packerton	18235
Paddytown	15551
Pageville	16401
Paint (Clarion County) (Township)	16254
Paint (Somerset County)	15963

	ZIP
Paint (Somerset County) (Township)	15963
Paintersville (Mifflin County)	17044
Paintersville (Westmoreland County)	15672
Paintertown	15642
Paisley	15320
Paletown	18944
Palm	18070
Palmdale	17033
Palmer (Township)	18042
Palmer Heights	18042
Palmer Park	18042
Palmerton	18071
Palmerton East (Part of Palmerton)	18071
Palmertown	15716
Palmyra (Lebanon County)	17078
Palmyra (Pike County) (Township)	18451
Palmyra (Wayne County) (Township)	18428
Palo Alto (Bedford County)	15545
Palo Alto (Schuylkill County)	17901
Palomino Farms	18976
Pancoast	15851
Panic	15851
Panorama Village	16801
Pansy	15864
Pansy Hill	17046
Panther	18445
Paoli (Chester County)	19301
Paper Mills (Part of Bryn Athyn)	19009
Paradise (Lancaster County)	17562
Paradise (Lancaster County) (Township)	17562
Paradise (Monroe County) (Township)	18326
Paradise (Schuylkill County)	17963
Paradise (York County) (Township)	17301
Paradise Falls	18326
Paradise Valley	18326
Pardee	16866
Pardeesville	18201
Pardoe	16137
Pardus	15851
Paris	15021
Park (Part of Vandergrift)	15690
Parkchester	19380
Park Crest	18214
Parker (Armstrong County)	16049
Parker (Butler County) (Township)	16001
Parker Ford	19457
Parkersville	19380
Parkesburg	19365
Park Forest Village	16801
Park Gate	16117
Park Heights	17331
Parkhill	15945
Park Hills (Centre County)	16801
Park Hills (York County)	17331
Parkland	19047
Park Manor	19607
Park Meadows	15642
Park Place	17948
Parks (Township)	15690
Parkside	19015
Parkside Courts	18104
Parkside Manor (Part of Parkside)	19015
Parkstown	16101
Parktown Estates	19067
Parkview	15215
Parkview Gardens	18052
Park View Heights (Part of Bellefonte)	16823
Parkville (York County)	17331
Parkway Center (Part of Green Tree)	15220
Parkway Center Mall (Part of Pittsburgh)	15220
Park Way Manor	18104
Parkwood	15774
Parnassus (Part of New Kensington)	15068
Parryville	18244
Parsonville (Butler County)	16050
Parsonville (Clearfield County)	16651
Parvin	17751
Paschall (Part of Philadelphia)	19142
Passer	18036
Patchel Run (Part of Sugarcreek)	16323
Patchinville	15724
Patterson (Township)	15010
Patterson Grove	18655
Patterson Heights	15010

	ZIP
Patterson Hill (Part of Lincoln)	15037
Pattersons Mill	15312
Patterson Township	15010
Pattersonville	17967
Patton (Cambria County)	16668
Patton (Centre County) (Township)	16801
Patton (Washington County)	15301
Pattonville	16226
Paulton	15613
Paupack (Pike County)	18451
Paupack (Wayne County) (Township)	18428
Paupack Gardens	18451
Pavia	16655
Paxinos	17860
Paxtang	17111
Paxtang Manor	17111
Paxton	17017
Paxtonia	17111
Paxtonville	17861
Peacedale	19363
Peach Bottom (Lancaster County)	17563
Peach Bottom (York County) (Township)	17314
Peach Bottom Village	17563
Peach Glen	17306
Pealertown	17859
Peanut (Lawrence County)	16116
Peanut (Westmoreland County)	15627
Pearl	16342
Pebble Hill	18901
Pecan	16342
Pechin	15431
Pecks Pond	18328
Peckville (Part of Blakely)	18452
Pemberton	16683
Pen Argyl	18072
Penarth	19004
Penbrook	17103
Penbryn	17765
Pendle Hill	19086
Penfield	15849
Penllyn	19422
Pen Mar	17268
Penn (Berks County) (Township)	19506
Penn (Butler County) (Township)	16001
Penn (Centre County) (Township)	16832
Penn (Chester County) (Township)	19390
Penn (Clearfield County) (Township)	16838
Penn (Cumberland County) (Township)	17257
Penn (Huntingdon County) (Township)	16647
Penn (Lancaster County) (Township)	17545
Penn (Lycoming County) (Township)	17737
Penn (Perry County) (Township)	17020
Penn (Snyder County) (Township)	17870
Penn (Westmoreland County)	15675
Penn (Westmoreland County) (Township)	15636
Penn (York County) (Township)	17331
Penn Allen	18064
Pennbrook (Part of Lansdale)	19446
Penn Center (Part of Philadelphia)	19102
Penncraft	15433
Penndel	19047
Pennersville	17268
Penn Estates	18320
Pennfield	19007
Penn Five	16666
Penn Forest (Township)	18210
Penn Glyn (Part of Irwin)	15642
Pennhall	16875
Penn Heights (Part of Hanover)	17331
Penn Hill	17563
Penn Hill Homes	19022
Penn Hills (Township)	15235
Penn Hills	15235
Penn Hills Shopping Center	15235
Pennhurst Center	19475
Penn Lake Park	18661
Pennline	16424
Penn Pines	19018
Penn Pitt	15338

	ZIP
Penn Rose Park	17601
Penn Run	15765
Pennsburg	18073
Pennsbury (Township)	19317
Pennsbury Heights	19067
Pennsbury Village	15205
Penns Creek	17862
Pennsdale	17756
Pennside (Berks County)	19606
Pennside (Erie County)	16401
Penns Park	18943
Penn Square Village	19401
Pennsville (Fayette County)	15425
Pennsville (Northampton County)	18067
Penns Woods	15642
Pennsylvania Furnace	16865
Penn Taft (Part of West Mifflin)	15222
Pennvale	17701
Penn Valley	19072
Penn Valley Terrace	19047
Penn Village (Part of Pottstown)	19464
Pennville	17331
Pennwyn	19607
Penn Wynne	19151
Penobscot	18707
Penowa	15312
Penryn	17564
Pequea	17565
Pequea (Township)	17584
Percy	15456
Perdix	17020
Perkasie	18944
Perkiomen (Township)	19426
Perkiomen Heights	18073
Perkiomen Junction	19460
Perkiomen Village	19426
Perkiomenville	18074
Perrine Corners	16153
Perry (Armstrong County) (Township)	16041
Perry (Berks County) (Township)	19526
Perry (Clarion County) (Township)	16049
Perry (Fayette County) (Township)	15482
Perry (Greene County) (Township)	15349
Perry (Jefferson County) (Township)	15767
Perry (Lawrence County) (Township)	16117
Perry (Mercer County) (Township)	16130
Perry (Snyder County) (Township)	17853
Perrymont	15237
Perryopolis	15473
Perry Square (Part of Erie)	16507
Perrysville	15237
Perryville (Clarion County)	16049
Perryville (Lycoming County)	17728
Perryville (Westmoreland County)	15618
Perulack	17021
Peters (Franklin County) (Township)	17236
Peters (Washington County) (Township)	15317
Petersburg	16669
Peters Corner	18934
Peters Creek (Part of Clairton)	15025
Petersville	18067
Petrolia	16050
Pettis	16335
Pheasant Hill	17601
Pheasant Ridge	18901
Philadelphia	19101-60

For specific Philadelphia Zip
Codes call (215) 895-9000, or
your local postmaster.

COLLEGES & UNIVERSITIES

	ZIP
Chestnut Hill College	19118
Drexel University	19104
Hahnemann University	19102
Holy Family College	19114
LaSalle University	19141
The University of the Arts	19102
Philadelphia College of Pharmacy and Science	19104
Philadelphia College of Textiles and Science	19144
St. Joseph's University	19131
Temple University	19122
University of Pennsylvania	19104

FINANCIAL INSTITUTIONS

	ZIP
Beneficial Mutual Savings Bank	19107
Brown Brothers Harriman & Co	19102
Cheltenham Bank	19111
Fidelity Federal Savings & Loan Association	19135
Fox Chase Federal Savings Bank	19111
Frankford Bank	19124
Prime Savings Bank	19111
Roxborough-Manayunk Federal Savings & Loan Association	19128
Third Federal Savings & Loan Association of Philadelphia	19124

HOSPITALS

	ZIP
Albert Einstein Medical Center	19141
Children's Hospital of Philadelphia	19104
Episcopal Hospital	19125
Frankford Hospital of the City of Philadelphia	19114
Germantown Hospital and Medical Center	19144
Graduate Hospital	19146
Hahnemann University Hospital	19102
Hospital of Philadelphia College of Osteopathic Medicine	19131
Hospital of the University of Pennsylvania	19104
Lankenau Hospital	19096
Methodist Hospital	19148
Nazareth Hospital	19152
Pennsylvania Hospital	19107
Presbyterian Medical Center of Philadelphia	19104
Temple University Hospital	19140
Thomas Jefferson University Hospital	19107
Veterans Affairs Medical Center	19104

HOTELS/MOTELS

	ZIP
The Barclay Hotel	19103
Four Seasons Hotel Philadelphia	19103
Holiday Inn-Independence Mall	19106
The Latham	19103
Philadelphia Airport Marriott	19153
The Warwick	19103
Wyndham Franklin Plaza Hotel	19103

MILITARY INSTALLATIONS

	ZIP
Defense Industrial Supply Center	19111
Defense Mapping Agency, Combat Support Center	19120
Defense Personnel Support Center	19101
Fort Mifflin Distribution Center, U.S. Army Corps. of Engineers	19153
Naval Regional Medical Clinic	19145
Naval Station, Philadelphia	19112
Philadelphia Naval Shipyard	19112
Philatelic (Part of State College)	16801
Philipsburg (Centre County)	16866
Philipsburg (Washington County)	15419
Phillips (Fayette County)	15401
Phillips (Tioga County)	16918
Phillipston	16248
Phillipsville (Chester County)	19320
Phillipsville (Erie County)	16442
Philmont	19006
Philmont Manor	19006
Philmont Park	19006
Phoenix Park	17901
Phoenixville	19460
Piatt (Township)	17740
Picture Rocks	17762
Pierce (Allegheny County)	15025
Pierce (Armstrong County)	16240
Pierceville	17327
Pigeon	16239
Pike (Berks County) (Township)	19547
Pike (Bradford County) (Township)	18829

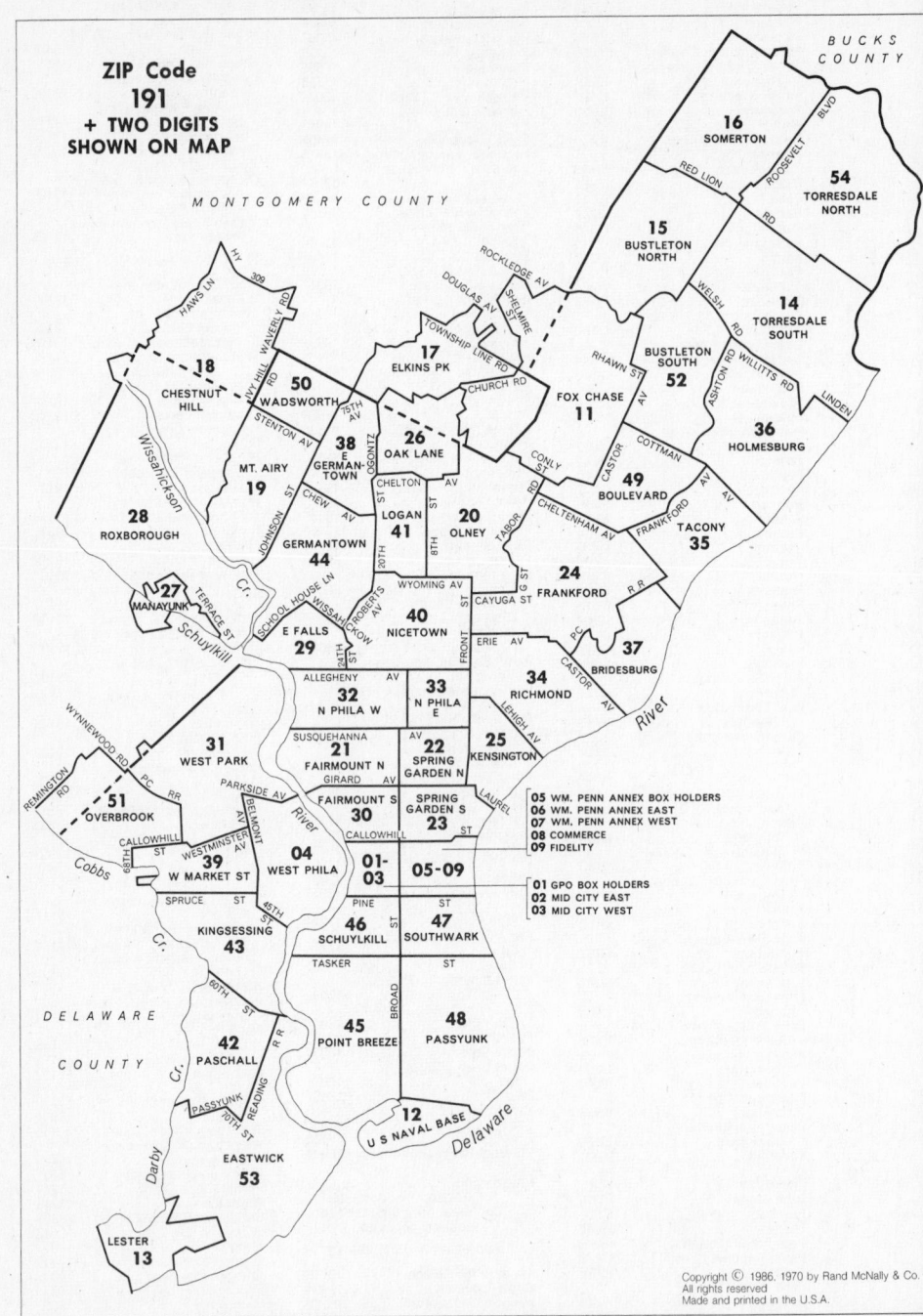

ZIP Code
191
+ TWO DIGITS
SHOWN ON MAP

MONTGOMERY COUNTY

BUCKS COUNTY

16 SOMERTON

54 TORRESDALE NORTH

15 BUSTLETON NORTH

14 TORRESDALE SOUTH

18 CHESTNUT HILL

50 WADSWORTH

17 ELKINS PK

52 BUSTLETON SOUTH

11 FOX CHASE

36 HOLMESBURG

38 E GERMANTOWN

26 OAK LANE

49 BOULEVARD

28 ROXBOROUGH

19 MT AIRY

41 LOGAN

20 OLNEY

35 TACONY

44 GERMANTOWN

24 FRANKFORD

27 MANAYUNK

29 E FALLS

40 NICETOWN

37 BRIDESBURG

32 N PHILA W

33 N PHILA E

34 RICHMOND

31 WEST PARK

21 FAIRMOUNT N

22 SPRING GARDEN N

25 KENSINGTON

51 OVERBROOK

30 FAIRMOUNT S

23 SPRING GARDEN S

05 WM. PENN ANNEX BOX HOLDERS
06 WM. PENN ANNEX EAST
07 WM. PENN ANNEX WEST
08 COMMERCE
09 FIDELITY

39 W MARKET ST

04 WEST PHILA

01-03

05-09

01 GPO BOX HOLDERS
02 MID CITY EAST
03 MID CITY WEST

43 KINGSESSING

46 SCHUYLKILL

47 SOUTHWARK

DELAWARE COUNTY

42 PASCHALL

45 POINT BREEZE

48 PASSYUNK

12 U S NAVAL BASE

53 EASTWICK

13 LESTER

	ZIP
Pike (Clearfield County) (Township)	16833
Pike (Potter County) (Township)	16922
Pikeland	19425
Pikes Peak	15765
Piketown	17112
Pikeville	19547
Pilgrim Gardens	19026
Pilgrimham	16232
Pillow	17080
Pine (Allegheny County) (Township)	15090
Pine (Armstrong County) (Township)	16259
Pine (Clearfield County) (Township)	15849
Pine (Clinton County)	17748
Pine (Columbia County) (Township)	17846
Pine (Crawford County) (Township)	16424
Pine (Indiana County) (Township)	15745
Pine (Lycoming County) (Township)	16938
Pine (Mercer County) (Township)	16127
Pine Bank	15352
Pine Beach	18428
Pinebrook	17011
Pine Creek (Clinton County) (Township)	17721
Pinecreek (Jefferson County) (Township)	15825
Pinecrest	19047
Pinecroft	16601
Pinedale (Part of Deer Lake)	17961
Pine Flats	15728
Pine Forge	19548
Pine Glen (Centre County)	16845
Pine Glen (Mifflin County)	17044
Pine Grove (Perry County)	17047
Pine Grove (Schuylkill County)	17963
Pine Grove (Schuylkill County) (Township)	17963
Pine Grove (Susquehanna County)	18446
Pinegrove (Venango County) (Township)	16301
Pine Grove (Warren County) (Township)	16345
Pine Grove Furnace	17324
Pine Grove Mills	16868
Pine Hill (Armstrong County)	16201
Pine Hill (Schuylkill County)	17901
Pine Hill (Somerset County)	15530
Pine Ridge	19063
Pine Run (Bucks County)	18901
Pine Run (Lycoming County)	17744
Pine Summit	17846
Pine Swamp	19520
Pinetown	17339
Pinetree (Part of Scottdale)	15683
Pine Valley	16405
Pine Valley Estates	18901
Pine View	18707
Pineville (Bucks County)	18946
Pineville (Warren County)	16420
Pinewood	19054
Piney	16214
Piney (Township)	16255
Piney Fork	15129
Pinola	17257
Pipersville	18947
Pitcairn	15140
Pitman	17964
Pitt Gas	15322
Pittock	15136
Pitts	16901
Pittsburgh	15123
	15201-90

For specific Pittsburgh Zip Codes call (412) 359-7860, or your local postmaster.

COLLEGES & UNIVERSITIES

	ZIP
Carlow College	15213
Carnegie Mellon University	15213
Duquesne University	15282
La Roche College	15237
Point Park College	15222
University of Pittsburgh	15260

FINANCIAL INSTITUTIONS

	ZIP
Allegheny Valley Bank of Pittsburgh	15201
Bell Federal Savings & Loan Association of Bellevue	15202

	ZIP
Dollar Bank, A Federal Savings Bank	15222
First Home Savings Association	15222
First South Savings Association	15203
Great American Federal Savings & Loan Association	15236
Integra National Bank/Pittsburgh	15278
North Side Deposit Bank	15212
Pittsburgh Home Savings Bank	15222
Pittsburgh National Bank	15222
West View Savings Bank	15237

HOSPITALS

	ZIP
Allegheny General Hospital	15212
Magee-Womens Hospital	15213
Mercy Hospital of Pittsburgh	15219
Montefiore Hospital	15213
North Hills Passavant Hospital	15237
Presbyterian-University Hospital	15213
Shadyside Hospital	15232
St. Clair Hospital	15243
St. Francis Medical Center	15201
St. Margaret Memorial Hospital	15215
Veterans Affairs Medical Center	15240
Western Pennsylvania Hospital	15224

HOTELS/MOTELS

	ZIP
Holiday Inn Pittsburgh Airport	15208
Best Western Parkway Center Inn	15220
Days Inn	15216
Harley of Pittsburgh	15235
Hyatt Pittsburgh at Chatham Center	15219
Pittsburgh Green Tree Marriott	15205
Sheraton Hotel at Station Square	15219

MILITARY INSTALLATIONS

	ZIP
911th Airlift Group, Greater Pittsburgh International Airport, (AFRES)	15231
Hays Army Ammunition Plant	15207
Pennsylvania Air National Guard, FB6381, Greater Pittsburgh International Airport	15231
United States Army Engineer District, Pittsburgh	15222
Charles E. Kelley Support Facility, Maintenance Division, Neville Island	15225
Pittsburgh Plate Plan	16226
Pittsburgh Valley	17516
Pittsfield	16340
Pittsfield (Township)	16340
Pittston	18640-44

For specific Pittston Zip Codes call (717) 654-3313, or your local postmaster.

	ZIP
Pittston Junction (Part of Wilkes-Barre)	18705
Pittsville	16374
Plainfield (Cumberland County)	17081
Plainfield (Northampton County) (Township)	18064
Plain Grove (Township)	16156
Plains	18705
Plains (Township)	18705
Plainsville	18705
Plainview	17325
Planebrook	19355
Plank	16938
Platea	16417
Plateau Heights	16335
Plattsville	16646
Plaza (Part of Butler)	16001
Plaza Heights (Part of Hanover)	17331
Pleasant (Township)	16365
Pleasant Corners	18235
Pleasant Gap	16823
Pleasant Grove (Lancaster County)	17563
Pleasant Grove (Washington County)	15323

	ZIP
Pleasant Hall	17246
Pleasant Hill (Cambria County)	15738
Pleasant Hill (Clearfield County)	16839
Pleasant Hill (Clearfield County)	16866
Pleasant Hill (Delaware County)	19063
Pleasant Hill (Fayette County)	15425
Pleasant Hill (Indiana County)	15701
Pleasant Hill (Lawrence County)	16123
Pleasant Hill (Lebanon County)	17042
Pleasant Hill (York County)	17331
Pleasant Hills (Allegheny County)	15236
Pleasant Hills (Dauphin County)	17112
Pleasant Mount	18453
Pleasant Union	15552
Pleasant Unity	15676
Pleasant Valley (Blair County)	16602
Pleasant Valley (Bucks County)	18951
Pleasant Valley (Lancaster County)	17604
Pleasant Valley (Potter County) (Township)	16743
Pleasant Valley (Schuylkill County)	17963
Pleasant Valley (Westmoreland County)	15642
Pleasant Valley Estates	18058
Pleasant View (Armstrong County)	15690
Pleasantview (Beaver County)	15010
Pleasant View (Centre County)	16823
Pleasant View (Franklin County)	17201
Pleasantview (Juniata County)	17082
Pleasant View (York County)	17356
Pleasant Village (Part of Altoona)	16602
Pleasantville	16341
Pleasureville	17402
Pleasureville Heights	17402
Plowville	19540
Plum (Allegheny County)	15239
Plum (Venango County)	16354
Plum (Venango County) (Township)	16354
Plumbridge	19056
Plumb Sock	15329
Plum Creek (Allegheny County)	15239
Plumcreek (Armstrong County) (Township)	15774
Plumer	16301
Plummer	15458
Plum Run	17238
Plumsock	19073
Plumstead (Township)	18923
Plumsteadville	18949
Plumville	16246
Plunketts Creek (Township)	17701
Plymouth (Luzerne County)	18651
Plymouth (Luzerne County) (Township)	18651
Plymouth (Montgomery County) (Township)	19401
Plymouth Junction (Part of Larksville)	18651
Plymouth Meeting	19462
Plymouth Meeting Mall	19462
Plymouth Valley	19401
Plymptonville	16830
Pocahontas	15552
Pocono (Township)	18372
Pocono Country Place	18466
Pocono Farms	18466
Pocono Farms East	18466
Pocono Heights	18301
Pocono Lake	18347
Pocono Lake Preserve	18348
Pocono Manor	18349
Pocono Mt. Lake Forest	18328
Pocono Park	18360
Pocono Pines	18350
Pocono Summit	18346
Pocono Summit Estates	18346
Pocopson	19366
Pocopson (Township)	19366
Poets Village	15701

* Area Zip Code   † Post Office Boxes

	ZIP
Regency Park (Part of	
....	15239
Regional Correctional	
Facility at Greensburg ...	15601
Register	17878
Rehrersburg	19550
Reidsburg	16214
Reiffton	19606
Reightown	16686
Reilly (Township)	17923
Reillys	16668
Reinerton	17980
Reinerton-Orwin-Muir	17980
Reinholds	17569
Reinoeldville	17046
Reistville	17067
Reitz	15824
Reitz No. 2	15924
Relay	17313
Reliance	18964
Rembrant	15728
Renfrew..................	16053
Rennerdale	15106
Reno (Part of Sugarcreek)	16343
Renovo	17764
Renton (Part of Plum)......	15239
Republic (Redstone	
Township) (Fayette	
County)	15475
Republic (Luzerne	
Township) (Fayette	
County)	15463
Republican (Part of	
California)	15419
Reserve (Township)	15212
Reserve Township	15212
Reservoir	16648
Retort	16677
Revere	18953
Revloc	15948
Rew	16744
Reward	17062
Rexford	16921
Rexis	15961
Rexmont (Part of Cornwall)	17085
Rextown	18080
Reyburn	18655
Reynolds	18252
Reynoldsdale	15554
Reynolds Heights	16125
Reynoldsville	15851
Rheems	17570
Rhone (Part of Nanticoke)	18634
Ribot	16669
Rice (Township)	18707
Rices Landing	15357
Riceville	16432
Richards Grove...........	17774
Richardsville	15825
Richboro	18954
Richboro Manor	18954
Richeyville (Part of	
Centerville).............	15358
Richfield	17086
Richfol (Part of	
Canonsburg)............	15317
Rich Hill (Bucks County) ...	18951
Richhill (Greene County)	
(Township)	15377
Rich Hill (Washington	
County)................	15347
Richland (Allegheny County)	
(Township)	15044
Richland (Bucks County)	
(Township)	18951
Richland (Cambria County)	
(Township)	15904
Richland (Cambria County)	16636
Richland (Clarion County)	
(Township)	16049
Richland (Lebanon County)	17087
Richland (Venango County)	
(Township)	16373
Richlandtown............	18955
Richmond (Berks County)	
(Township)	19530
Richmond (Crawford	
County) (Township)	16327
Richmond (Northampton	
County)................	18013
Richmond (Philadelphia	
County)................	19134
Richmond (Tioga County)	
(Township)	16933
Richmondale	18421
Richmond Furnace	17224
Richview Manor	15904
Riddlesburg	16672
Riddlewood	19063
Riderville	16738
Ridgebury	14894
Ridgebury (Township)	16914

	ZIP
Ridge Valley	18960
Ridgeview	17112
Ridgeview Park	15627
Ridgeville	17821
Ridgewood (Berks County)	19508
Ridgewood (Luzerne	
County)	18705
Ridgewood Farm	19380
Ridgway	15853
Ridgway (Township)	15853
Ridley (Township)	19033
Ridley Farms	19070
Ridley Gardens	19043
Ridley Park (Cumberland	
County)	17011
Ridley Park (Delaware	
County)	19078
Ridley Parkview	19078
Riegelsville	18077
Rienze	18853
Rife	17061
Riggles Gap	16601
Riggs	18850
Rillton	15678
Rimer	16259
Rimersburg	16248
Rimerton	16259
Rinely	17363
Ringdale	18614
Ringgold	15770
Ringgold (Township)	15770
Ringing Hill	19464
Ringing Rock Park	19464
Ringtown (Berks County)	19539
Ringtown (Schuylkill County)	17967
Risher Mine Siding (Part of	
West Mifflin)	15122
Rising Sun	18080
Riterville	16738
Ritzie Village	17112
River Hill	15063
Riverside (Cambria County)	15904
Riverside (Lackawanna	
County)................	18403
Riverside (Northumberland	
County)................	17868
Riverton	18013
River Valley	15024
River View (Armstrong	
County)................	15690
Riverview (Beaver County)	15010
Riverview (Clearfield	
County)................	16830
Riverview (Clinton County)	17745
River View (Washington	
County)................	15067
Riverview Acres	18080
Riverview Heights	17011
River View Park	19605
Rixford	16745
Roadside	17268
Roaring Branch...........	17765
Roaring Brook (Township)	18444
Roaring Brook Estates	18444
Roaring Creek	17820
Roaring Creek (Township)	17820
Roaring Spring	16673
Robb	15944
Robert Bruce West (Part of	
Hatboro)	19040
Robert Morris College	15108
Robertsdale	16674
Robertsville	15767
Robeson (Township).......	19508
Robeson Crossing	19508
Robeson Extension	16693
Robesonia	19551
Robindale	15954
Robin Hood Lakes	18058
Robinson (Allegheny	
County) (Township)	15136
Robinson (Indiana County)	15949
Robinson (Lawrence	
County)................	16132
Robinson (Washington	
County) (Township)	15057
Robinson Township	15108
Rocherty	17042
Rochester	15074
Rochester (Township)	15074
Rochester Mills	15771
Rock	17972
Rockdale (Bucks County)	19007
Rockdale (Crawford	
County) (Township)	16403
Rockdale (Delaware	
County)................	19014
Rockdale (Jefferson	
County)................	15840
Rockdale (Lehigh County)	18080
Rockefeller (Township).....	17801
Rock Glen	18246

	ZIP
Rock Hill (Bucks County)	18960
Rockhill (Lancaster County)	17516D)
Rockhill Furnace...........	17249
Rockingham..............	15924
Rock Lake	18453
Rockland (Berks County)	
(Township)	19522
Rockland (Venango County)	16374
Rockland (Venango County)	
(Township)	16374
Rockledge	19111
Rockport	18255
Rockrimmin Ridge	17540
Rock Run	19320
Rockspring..............	16865
Rockton (Clearfield County)	15856
Rocktown	15688
Rockview	16823
Rockville (Armstrong	
County)................	16226
Rockville (Cambria County)	15956
Rockville (Chester County)	19344
Rockville (Clarion County)	16242
Rockville (Dauphin County)	17110
Rockville (Juniata County)	17059
Rockville (Mifflin County)...	17004
Rockville (Northampton	
County)................	18038
Rockwood (Lebanon	
County)................	17046
Rockwood (Somerset	
County)................	15557
Rock Works..............	15461
Rocky Forest	18623
Rocky Grove (Part of	
Sugarcreek)............	16323
Rocky Hill	19380
Rodman	16673
Roedersville	17963
Rogers Mills	15469
Rogers Stop	15022
Rogerstown	15425
Rogersville	15359
Rogertown	16313
Rohrerstown	17603
....	17607
For specific Rohrerstown Zip	
Codes call (717) 394-9151, or	
your local postmaster.	
Rohrsburg	17859
Roler....................	17315
Rolfe (Part of Johnsonburg)	15845
Rolling Glen	19341
Rolling Hills (Beaver County)	15061
Rolling Hills (Berks County)	19607
Rolling Hills (Lehigh County)	18052
Rolling Meadows	15370
Romansville	19320
Romar	15943
Rome (Bradford County)...	18837
Rome (Bradford County)	
(Township)	18850
Rome (Crawford County)	
(Township)	16354
Romney..................	15446
Ronco	15476
Ronks	17572
Rook (Part of Green Tree)	15220
Roosevelt Mall (Part of	
Philadelphia)	19149
Roots Crossing...........	16686
Rosas...................	12770
Roscoe	15477
Rose (Township)	15825
Roseann	17063
Rose Bud	16627
Roseburg	17074
Rosecrans	17747
Rose Crest (Part of	
Monroeville)............	15146
Rosedale (Allegheny	
County)................	15147
Rosedale (Chester County)	19317
Rosedale (Fayette County)	15401
Rosedale (Greene County)	15327
Rosedale Heights..........	15147
Roseglen	17020
Rosehill (Part of	
Philadelphia)	19140
Rose Hollow	19067
Rosemont (Delaware	
County)................	19010
Rosemont (Montgomery	
County)................	19010
Rose Point	16101
Roses...................	16239
Roseto	18013
Rose Valley (Delaware	
County)................	19063
Rose Valley (Montgomery	
County)................	19002

	ZIP
Rose Valley Acres	19063
Roseville (Jefferson County)	15825
Roseville (Tioga County)	16933
Rosewood Gardens	18974
Roslyn (Chester County)	19380
Roslyn (Montgomery County)	19001
Ross (Allegheny County) (Township)	15237
Ross (Luzerne County) (Township)	18656
Ross (Monroe County) (Township)	18353
Ross Common	18353
Rossford	16226
Rossiter	15772
Rosslyn Farms	15106
Rossmere	17601
Rossmoyne	17011
Ross Park Malls (Part of Pittsburgh)	15237
Ross Siding	17723
Rosston	16226
Ross Township	15237
Rossville	17358
Rostraver	15012
Rostraver (Township)	15012
Rote	17751
Rothsville	17543
Rough and Ready	17941
Roulette	16746
Roulette (Township)	16746
Round Top (Adams County)	17325
Round Top (Bedford County)	16679
Roundtown	17404
Rouseville	16344
Rouzerville	17250
Rowes Run	15442
Rowland	18457
Rowland Park	19012
Rowles	15757
Roxborough (Part of Philadelphia)	19128
Roxbury (Cumberland County)	17055
Roxbury (Franklin County)	17251
Roxbury (Somerset County)	15530
Royal (Fayette County)	15422
Royal (Susquehanna County)	18446
Royalton	17057
Royer	16693
Royersford	19468
Roystone	16347
Roytown	15501
Rozel Park	18966
Ruble	15478
Ruchsville	18037
Rudytown	17070
Ruffcreek	15329
Ruffs Dale	15679
Ruggles	18636
Rummel	15963
Rummerfield	18853
Rundell	16406
Running Brooke	15701
Runville	16823
Rupert	17815
Ruppsville	18106
Rural Ridge	15075
Rural Valley	16249
Ruscombmanor (Township)	19522
Rush (Centre County) (Township)	16866
Rush (Dauphin County) (Township)	17980
Rush (Northumberland County) (Township)	17821
Rush (Schuylkill County) (Township)	18252
Rush (Susquehanna County)	18801
Rush (Susquehanna County) (Township)	18801
Rushland	18956
Rushtown	17821
Rushville	18839
Russell	16345
Russell Hill	18657
Russellton	15076
Russellville (Chester County)	19363
Russellville (Huntingdon County)	16657
Rutan	15341
Rutherford	17111
Rutherford Park	17036
Ruthford	15955
Ruthfred Acres (Part of Bethel Park)	15102
Rutland (Township)	16933

	ZIP
Rutledge	19070
Rutledgedale	18469
Ryan (Township)	18214
Ryans Corner	18940
Rydal	19046
Ryde	17051
Rye (Township)	17053
Ryerson Station	15380
Ryot	15521
Rywal Park	19020
Sabinsville	16943
Sabula	15801
Saco (Bradford County)	18848
Saco (Lackawanna County)	18436
Sacramento	17968
Saddle Brook	18101
Saddlebrook Village I and II	19565
Sadlers Corner	16301
Sadsbury (Chester County) (Township)	19369
Sadsbury (Crawford County) (Township)	16316
Sadsbury (Lancaster County) (Township)	17509
Sadsburyville	19369
Saegersville	18053
Saegertown	16433
Safe Harbor	17516
Sagamore (Armstrong County)	16250
Sagamore (Fayette County)	15446
Sagamore Hills	18101
Saginaw	17347
Sagon	17872
St. Augustine	16636
St. Benedict	15773
St. Boniface	16675
St. Charles	16242
St. Clair (Schuylkill County)	17970
St. Clair (Westmoreland County)	15601
St. Clair (Westmoreland County) (Township)	15954
St. Clairsville	16667
St. Davids	19087
St. George	16374
St. Johns	18247
St. Joseph	18818
St. Lawrence (Berks County)	19606
St. Lawrence (Cambria County)	16668
St. Leonard	18940
St. Marys	15857
St. Michael	15951
St. Michael-Sidman	15951
St. Nicholas	17948
St. Paul	15552
St. Peters	19470
St. Petersburg	16054
St. Thomas	17252
St. Thomas (Township)	17201
St. Vincent College	15650
St. Vincent Shaft	15650
Salco	15530
Salem (Clarion County) (Township)	16232
Salem (Clearfield County)	15801
Salem (Franklin County)	17201
Salem (Luzerne County) (Township)	18603
Salem (Mercer County)	16125
Salem (Mercer County) (Township)	16130
Salem (Snyder County)	17870
Salem (Wayne County) (Township)	18444
Salem (Westmoreland County) (Township)	15601
Salem Harbor	19020
Salemville	16664
Salford	18957
Salford (Township)	18969
Salford Heights	19438
Salfordville	18958
Salida (Part of Baldwin)	15227
Salina	15680
Salisbury (Lancaster County) (Township)	17535
Salisbury (Lehigh County) (Township)	18103
Salisbury (Somerset County)	15558
Salisbury Heights	17527
Salix	15952
Salix-Beauty Line Park	15952
Salladasburg	17740
Salona	17767
Saltillo	17253
Saltlick (Township)	15446
Saltsburg	15681
Salunga	17538
Salunga-Landisville	17538

	ZIP
Saluvia	17228
Sample Heights	15116
Sample Run (Part of Clymer)	15728
Sampson	15063
Sanatoga	19464
Sanatoga Park	19464
Sanbourn	16651
Sandbeach	17033
Sand Hill (Lebanon County)	17046
Sandhill (Monroe County)	18354
Sand Hill (Westmoreland County)	15666
Sand Patch	15552
Sand Springs	18222
Sandts Eddy	18042
Sandy	15801
Sandy (Township)	15801
Sandy Bank	19063
Sandy Creek (Allegheny County)	15147
Sandy Creek (Mercer County) (Township)	16125
Sandycreek (Venango County) (Township)	16323
Sandy Hill	19401
Sandy Hollow	16248
Sandy Lake	16145
Sandy Lake (Township)	16153
Sandy Plains	15322
Sandy Ridge	16677
Sandy Ridge Acres	18901
Sandy Run (Bucks County)	19067
Sandy Run (Greene County)	15338
Sandy Run (Luzerne County)	18224
Sandy Shore	18428
Sandy Valley	15851
Sandyville	18324
Sanford	16340
Sankertown	16630
Sarah Furnace	16248
Sardis (Part of Murrysville)	15668
Sartwell	16731
Sarver	16055
Sarversville	16055
Sassamansville	19472
Satterfield	18614
Satterfield Junction	18614
Saucon Acres	18034
Saulsburg	16652
Saville	17074
Saville (Township)	17037
Sawtown	16301
Saxonburg (Butler County)	16056
Saxton	16678
Saybrook	16347
Saylorsburg	18353
Sayre	18840
Scalp Level	15963
Scammells Corner	19067
Scandia	16345
Scenery Hill	15360
Schaefferstown	17088
Schellsburg	15559
Schenley	15682
Scherersville	18104
Schlusser	17013
Schnecksville	18078
Schoeneck (Lancaster County)	17578
Schoeneck (Northampton County)	18064
Schoenersville	18103
Schoentown (Part of Port Carbon)	17965
Schofer	19530
Schollard	16137
School Lane	17603
School Lane Hills	17604
School Valley Farms	17520
Schubert	19507
Schultzville	19504
Schulzville	18411
Schuster Heights	16229
Schuyler	17772
Schuylkill (Chester County) (Township)	19460
Schuylkill (Philadelphia County)	19146
Schuylkill (Schuylkill County) (Township)	17952
Schuylkill Haven	17972
Schuylkill Hills	19401
Schwenksville	19473
Sciota	18354
Sconnelltown	19380
Scotch Hill	16233
Scotch Hollow	16666
Scotia (Part of Jefferson)	15025
Scotland	17254
Scotrun	18355

	ZIP
Scott (Allegheny County) (Township)	15106
Scott (Columbia County) (Township)	17815
Scott (Lackawanna County) (Township)	18447
Scott (Lawrence County) (Township)	16101
Scott (Wayne County) (Township)	18462
Scott Center	18462
Scottdale	15683
Scott Haven	15083
Scottsville	15001
Scott Township	15106
Scranton	18501-05
	18508-15
For specific Scranton Zip Codes call (717) 969-5100, or your local postmaster.	
Scrubgrass (Township)	16373
Scullton	15557
Scyoc	17021
Seamentown	15729
Seanor	15953
Searights	15401
Sebring	16930
Secane	19018
Secane Highlands	19018
Seek (Part of Coaldale)	18218
Seelyville	18431
Seemsville	18067
Seger	15627
Seidersville	18015
Seipstown	18031
Seisholtzville	18062
Seitzland	17327
Seitzville	17360
Selea	17264
Selinsgrove	17870
Sellersville	18960
Seltzer	17974
Seminole	16253
Seneca	16346
Seneca Valley	15642
Sereno	17846
Sergeant	16735
Sergeant (Township)	16740
Seven Fields	16046
Seven Hills	18837
Seven Pines	17082
Sevenpoints	17801
Seven Springs	15622
Seven Stars (Adams County)	17325
Seven Stars (Juniata County)	17062
Seven Valleys	17360
Seward	15954
Sewickley (Allegheny County)	15143
Sewickley (Westmoreland County) (Township)	15637
Sewickley Heights	15143
Sewickley Hills	15143
Seybertown	16028
Seyfert	19508
Shade (Township)	15924
Shade Gap	17255
Shadeland	16435
Shades Glen	18661
Shade Valley	17213
Shadle	17853
Shado-wood Village	15701
Shady Acres	17834
Shady Grove	17256
Shady Plain	15613
Shadyside (Part of Pittsburgh)	15232
Shaffer	15801
Shaffers Corner	15401
Shaffersville	16652
Shaft (Schuylkill County)	17976
Shaft (Somerset County)	15530
Shafton	15642
Shaler (Township)	15116
Shalercrest	15223
Shaler Township	15116
Shamokin	17872
Shamokin (Township)	17860
Shamokin Dam	17876
Shamrock (Fayette County)	15401
Shamrock (Somerset County)	15557
Shamrock Station	15539
Shaner	15642
Shaners Crossroads	15656
Shanesville	19512
Shankles (Part of Du Bois)	15801
Shanksville	15560
Shanktown	15777
Shannondale	16240

	ZIP
Shannon Heights	15235
Shanor Heights	16001
Shanor-Northvue	16001
Sharon (Mercer County)	16146
Sharon (Potter County) (Township)	16748
Sharon Center	16748
Sharon Hill	19079
Sharon North (Part of Hermitage)	16146
Sharon Park (Part of Sharon Hill)	19079
Sharpsburg (Allegheny County)	15215
Sharpsburg (Huntingdon County)	17060
Sharps Hill	15215
Sharpsville	16150
Sharrertown	15427
Shartlesville	19554
Shavertown (Delaware County)	19061
Shavertown (Luzerne County)	18708
Shawanese (Part of Harveys Lake)	18654
Shaw Mine	15057
Shawmut	15823
Shawnee on Delaware	18356
Shawtown	15642
Shawville	16873
Shay	16226
Sheakleyville	16151
Shearersburg	15656
Sheatown	18634
Sheffield	16347
Sheffield (Township)	16347
Sheffield Heights	15001
Sheffield Terrace	15001
Sheffield Village	19401
Shehawken	18462
Shellsville	17028
Shelly	18951
Shellytown	16693
Shelocta	15774
Sheltontown	16403
Shelvey	15846
Shenandoah	17976
Shenandoah Heights	17976
Shenango (Lawrence County) (Township)	16101
Shenango (Mercer County)	16125
Shenango (Mercer County) (Township)	16159
Shenango Valley Mall (Part of Hermitage)	16146
Shenkel	19464
Shenks Ferry	17309
Shepherd Hills	18101
Shepherdstown	17055
Sheppton	18248
Sheridan (Lebanon County)	17073
Sheridan (Schuylkill County)	17980
Sherman	18847
Shermans Dale	17090
Shermansville	16316
Sherrett	16218
Sherwood Acres	15061
Sheshequin	18850
Sheshequin (Township)	18848
Shetters Grove	17405
Shickshinny	18655
Shields (Part of Edgeworth)	15143
Shieldsburg	15670
Shillington	19607
Shiloh (Clearfield County)	16881
Shiloh (York County)	17404
Shiloh East	17405
Shimerville	18049
Shimpstown	17236
Shindle	17841
Shinglehouse	16748
Shingletown	16801
Shintown	17764
Shipmans Eddy	16365
Shippen (Cameron County) (Township)	15834
Shippen (Tioga County) (Township)	16901
Shippensburg	17257
Shippensburg (Township)	17257
Shippensburg State College	17257
Shippenville	16254
Shippingport	15077
Ships Parts Control Center, USN	17055
Shiremanstown	17011
Shire Oaks	15322
Shirks Corner	19473
Shirley (Township)	17066
Shirleysburg	17260
Shoaf	15478

	ZIP
Shocks Mills	17547
Shoemaker	15946
Shoemakers (Monroe County)	18301
Shoemakers (Schuylkill County)	17948
Shoemakersville	19555
Shoenberger	16686
Shohola	18458
Shohola (Township)	18458
Shope Gardens	17057
Shorbes Hill	17331
Shortsville	16935
Shraders	17084
Shrewsbury (Lycoming County) (Township)	17737
Shrewsbury (Sullivan County) (Township)	17758
Shrewsbury (York County)	17361
Shrewsbury (York County) (Township)	17327
Shumans	17815
Shunk	17768
Shy Beaver	16657
Sickles Corner	16601
Siddonsburg	17019
Sidman	15955
Siegfried (Part of Northampton)	18067
Sigel	15860
Siglerville	17063
Sigmund	18092
Silkworth	18621
Silvara	18623
Silver Creek	17959
Silverdale	18962
Silver Ford Heights	17066
Silver Lake (Bucks County)	18940
Silver Lake (Susquehanna County)	18812
Silver Lake (Susquehanna County) (Township)	18812
Silver Lake (Wayne County)	18469
Silver Lake (York County)	17339
Silver Spring (Cumberland County) (Township)	17055
Silver Spring (Lancaster County)	17575
Silverville	16055
Simmonstown	17527
Simpson	18407
Singersville	17018
Sinking Spring	19608
Sinking Valley	16601
Sinnamahoning	15861
Sinsheim	17362
Sipesville	15561
Sitka	15431
Six Mile Run	16679
Six Points	16049
Sixty-Ninth Street Center	19082
Sizerville	15834
Skelp	16601
Skidmore	16101
Ski Haven Lake Estates	18326
Skinners Eddy	18623
Skippack	19474
Skippack (Township)	19474
Skyline Heights	17402
Skyline View	17112
Skytop	18357
Sky View	18426
Slabtown (Clearfield County)	15724
Slabtown (Franklin County)	17268
Slackwater	17551
Slatedale	18079
Slatefield	18038
Slateford	18343
Slateford Junction	18343
Slate Hill	17314
Slate Lick	16229
Slate Run	17769
Slate Valley	18038
Slateville	19529
Slatington	18080
Slickport	16646
Slickville	15684
Sligo	16255
Slippery Rock (Butler County)	16057
Slippery Rock (Butler County) (Township)	16057
Slippery Rock (Lawrence County) (Township)	16101
Slippery Rock Park	16057
Slocum (Township)	18660
Slocum Corners	18660
Slovan	15078
Slovene National Benefit Society	16120
Smallwood (Part of California)	15423

	ZIP		ZIP		ZIP
Smethport	16749	Southampton (Somerset		Southwest (Warren County)	
Smicksburg	16256	County) (Township)	15552	(Township)	16354
Smiley	15401	South Annville (Township)	17042	Southwest (Westmoreland	
Smith (Blair County)	16665	South Auburn	18630	County)	15685
Smith (Indiana County)	15717	South Beaver (Township)	16115	Southwest Greensburg	15601
Smith (Washington County)		South Bend	15686	Southwest Madison	
(Township)	15078	South Bend (Township)	15774	(Township)	17047
Smith Bridge	15380	South Bethlehem	16242	South Whitehall (Township)	18104
Smithdale	15089	South Bradford	16701	South Williamsport	17701
Smithfield (Bradford County)		South Buffalo (Township)	16229	South Woodbury	
(Township)	18831	South Burgettstown (Part of		(Township)	16664
Smithfield (Fayette County)	15478	Burgettstown)	15021	Southwood Hills	17403
Smithfield (Huntingdon		South Canaan	18459	Spaces Corners	16201
County) (Township)	16652	South Canaan (Township)	18472	Spangenberg Lake	18436
Smithfield (Huntingdon		South Carnegie	15106	Spangler	15775
County)	16652	South Centre (Township)	17815	Spangsville	19512
Smithfield (Monroe County)		South Clarksville	15322	Sparta (Crawford County)	
(Township)	18335	South Clearfield (Part of		(Township)	16434
Smithfield Center	16652	Clearfield)	16830	Sparta (Washington County)	15329
Smith Gardens	17345	South Coatesville	19320	Spartansburg	16434
Smithland	16242	South Connellsville	15425	Spears Grove	17021
Smithmill	16680	South Coventry (Township)	19464	Speedwell	17543
Smithport	15742	South Creek (Township)	16925	Speers	15012
Smiths	17362	Southdale	18655	Spike Island	16666
Smiths Corner	18950	South Duquesne (Part of		Spillway Lake	15473
Smiths Corners	16374	Duquesne)	15110	Spindley City	16641
Smiths Ferry (Part of		Southeastern	19397-99	Spinnerstown	18968
Ohioville)	15059	For specific Southeastern Zip		Spinnlers Point	18464
Smithton	15479	Codes call (215) 964-6448, or		Split Rock	18624
Smithtown (Bucks County)	18947	your local postmaster.		Sporting Hill (Cumberland	
Smithtown (Jefferson		Southeastern Facility	19399	County)	17055
County)	15840	South Easton (Part of		Sporting Hill (Lancaster	
Smithville	17560	Easton)	18042	County)	17545
Smock	15480	South Eaton	18657	Sportsburg	15767
Smokeless	15944	South Enola	17025	Spraggs	15362
Smokerun	16681	South Erie (Part of Erie)	16508	Sprankle Mills	15776
Smoketown (Bucks County)	18951	Southerwood	15610	Spring (Berks County)	
Smoketown (Franklin		South Fayette (Township)	15064	(Township)	19609
County)	17222	South Fork	15956	Spring (Centre County)	
Smoketown (Lancaster		South Franklin (Township)	15301	(Township)	16823
County)	17576	South Gibson	18842	Spring (Crawford County)	
Smullton	16854	South Greensburg	15601	(Township)	16406
Smyerstown	15772	South Hanover (Township)	17033	Spring (Perry County)	
Smyrna	17509	South Heidelberg		(Township)	17040
Snake Run (Township)	15522	(Township)	19565	Spring (Snyder County)	
Snedekerville	16914	South Heights	15081	(Township)	17812
Snively Corners	16232	South Hermitage	17555	Spring Bank	16872
Snowball Gate	19056	South Hills (Allegheny		Springboro	16435
Snowden	15129	County)	15216	Spring Brook (Township)	18444
Snowdenville	19475	South Hills (Mifflin County)	17044	Spring Church	15686
Snow Shoe	16874	South Hills Village	15241	Spring City	19475
Snow Shoe (Township)	16829	South Huntingdon		Spring Creek (Elk County)	
S. N. P. J.	16120	(Township)	15089	(Township)	15853
Snyder (Blair County)		South Lakemont	16602	Spring Creek (Lehigh	
(Township)	16686	Southland 4 Seasons		County)	18011
Snyder (Jefferson County)		Centre (Part of Pleasant		Spring Creek (Warren	
(Township)	15824	Hills)	15236	County)	16436
Snyder Corner	17356	South Lebanon (Township)	17042	Spring Creek (Warren	
Snyders	17960	South Londonderry		County) (Township)	16436
Snydersburg	16257	(Township)	17010	Springdale (Allegheny	
Snydersville	18360	South Mahoning (Township)	15747	County)	15144
Snydertown (Centre		South Manheim (Township)	17972	Springdale (Allegheny	
County)	16841	South Meadville	16335	County) (Township)	15049
Snydertown (Fayette		South Media	19063	Springdell	19320
County)	15425	South Middleton (Township)	17007	Springettsbury (Township)	17402
Snydertown		Southmont	15905	Springetts Manor-Yorklyn	17402
(Northumberland County)	17877	South Montrose	18843	Springfield (Bradford	
Snydertown (Westmoreland		South Mountain	17261	County)	16914
County)	15620	South Mountain Restoration		Springfield (Bradford	
Snyderville	16222	Center	17261	County) (Township)	18831
Social Island	17201	South New Castle	16101	Springfield (Bucks County)	
Soho (Part of Pittsburgh)	15219	South Newton (Township)	17266	(Township)	18951
Soldier	15851	South Oil City (Part of Oil		Springfield (Cumberland	
Solebury	18963	City)	16301	County)	17241
Solebury (Township)	18963	South Park (Township)	15129	Springfield (Delaware	
Somerset (Somerset		South Philipsburg	16866	County)	19064
County)	15501	South Pottstown	19464	Springfield (Delaware	
Somerset (Somerset		South Pymatuning		County) (Township)	19064
County) (Township)	15501	(Township)	16150	Springfield (Erie County)	
Somerset (Washington		South Renovo	17764	(Township)	16443
County) (Township)	15330	South Rockwood	15557	Springfield (Fayette County)	
Somers Lane	16929	South Shenango (Township)	16134	(Township)	15464
Somerton (Part of		South Side (Allegheny		Springfield (Huntingdon	
Philadelphia)	19116	County)	15203	County) (Township)	17243
Somerville	16028	South Side (Butler County)	16045	Springfield (Mercer County)	
Sonestown	17770	South Side (Lackawanna		(Township)	16137
Sonman	15946	County)	18505	Springfield (Montgomery	
Soradoville	17841	Southside (Northampton		County) (Township)	19118
Soudersburg	17577	County)	18015	Springfield (York County)	
Souderton	18964	South Sterling	18460	(Township)	17327
Soukesburg	15956	South Strabane (Township)	15301	Springfield Falls	16137
South Abington (Township)	18410	South Tamaqua	18252	Springfield Mall	19064
South Altoona (Part of		South Temple	19560	Spring Garden (Bucks	
Altoona)	16602	South Towanda	18848	County)	18940
Southampton (Bedford		South Union (Township)	15401	Spring Garden (Lancaster	
County) (Township)	17211	South Uniontown	15401	County)	17535
Southampton (Bucks		South Versailles (Township)	15028	Spring Garden (Philadelphia	
County)	18966	Southview	15361	County)	19122
Southampton (Cumberland		Southwark (Part of		Spring Garden (Schuylkill	
County) (Township)	17257	Philadelphia)	19147	County)	17972
Southampton (Franklin		South Waverly	14892	Spring Garden (Union	
County) (Township)	17244			County)	17810

* Area Zip Code   † Post Office Boxes

	ZIP		ZIP		ZIP
Spring Garden (Westmoreland County)	15666	State Correctional Institution at Dallas (Luzerne County)	18612	Stottsville	19367
Spring Garden (York County) (Township)	17403	State Correctional Institution at Retreat (Luzerne County)	18621	Stouchsburg	19567
Spring Garden (York County)	17403	State Correctional Institution (Lycoming County)	17756	Stoufferstown	17201
Spring Glen	17978	State Correctional Institution (Montgomery County)	19426	Stoughstown	17257
Spring Grove	17362	State Correction Institution	17011	Stover	16686
Springhaven Estates	19086	State Hill (Berks County)	19608	Stoverdale	17036
Springhill (Bradford County)	18853	State Hill (Chester County)	17527	Stoverstown	17362
Spring Hill (Cambria County)	15946	State Line (Bedford County)	15545	Stowe (Allegheny County) (Township)	15136
Spring Hill (Delaware County)	19018	Stateline (Erie County)	16428	Stowe (Montgomery County)	19464
Springhill (Fayette County) (Township)	15478	State Line (Franklin County)	17263	Stowell	18623
Springhill (Greene County) (Township)	15352	Steamburg	16424	Stowe Township	15136
Springhope	15559	Steel City	18015	Stoystown	15563
Spring House	19477	Steelstown	17003	Straban (Township)	17325
Springhouse Farms	18104	Steelton	17113	Strabane	15363
Spring Meadow	15554	Steelville	19370	Strafford	19087
Spring Meadows	19565	Steene	18472	Strangford	15717
Spring Mill	19428	Steffins Hill	15010	Strasburg	17579
Spring Mills	16875	Steinbachs Corner	18847	Strasburg (Township)	17602
Springmont	19609	Steinsburg	18951	Strattanville	16258
Spring Mount (Huntingdon County)	16877	Steinsville	19529	Strausstown	19559
Spring Mount (Montgomery County)	19478	Stemiersville	18235	Strawberry Ridge	17821
Spring Run	17262	Sterling (Clearfield County)	16651	Strawbridge	17758
Springs	15562	Sterling (Wayne County)	18463	Straw Pump	15642
Springtown (Bucks County)	18081	Sterling (Wayne County) (Township)	18445	Strickhousers	17360
Springtown (Franklin County)	17221	Sterling Run	15832	Stricklerstown	17073
Springtown (Luzerne County)	18707	Sterlingworth	18104	Strinestown	17345
Springtown (Northumberland County)	17777	Sterrettania	16415	Stringtown (Armstrong County)	16226
Springvale	17356	Stetlersville	18069	Stringtown (Greene County)	15320
Spring Valley (Berks County)	19560	Steuben (Township)	16404	Strobleton	16353
Spring Valley (Bucks County)	18901	Stevens (Bradford County) (Township)	18854	Strodes Mills	17044
Spring Valley (Clearfield County)	16878	Stevens (Lancaster County)	17578	Stronach	16833
Spring Valley (Northampton County)	18015	Stevens Point	18847	Strong	17851
Spring Valley Estates	17201	Stevenstown	17019	Strongstown	15957
Spring Valley Farms	18901	Stevensville	18845	Stroud (Township)	18360
Springville (Township)	18844	Stewardson (Township)	17729	Stroudsburg	18360
Springville	16342	Stewart (Township)	15470	Stroudsburg West	18360
Springville (Cumberland County)	17007	Stewart Run	16341	Strum	15478
Springville (Lancaster County)	17535	Stewartstown	17363	Studa	15312
Springville (Susquehanna County)	18844	Stewartsville	15642	Stull	18636
Sproul	16682	Stickney	16701	Stump Creek	15863
Spruce Creek	16683	Sticks	17329	Stumptown	16666
Spruce Creek (Township)	16683	Stiefler Corner	16670	Sturgeon	15082
Spruce Hill	17082	Stier	18013	Sturgeon-Noblestown	15071
Spruce Hill (Township)	17082	Stifflertown	15724	Sturgis (Part of Archbald)	18447
Sprucetown	15474	Stiles	18052	Suburban Village	19380
Spry	17403	Stiles Hill	16943	Sudan	15063
Squab Hollow	15846	Still Creek	18252	Suedburg	17963
Square Corner	17325	Stilleys Siding (Part of Jefferson)	15025	Sugarcreek (Armstrong County) (Township)	16218
Squirrel Hill (Part of Pittsburgh)	15217	Stillwater	17878	Sugarcreek (Venango County)	16323
Stack Town	15702	Stillwater Lake Estates	18346	Sugar Grove (Greene County)	15380
Stafore Estates	18017	Stiitz	17327	Sugar Grove (Mercer County) (Township)	16125
Stahlstown	15687	Stines Corner	18066	Sugar Grove (Warren County)	16350
Stairville	18660	Stobo	15061	Sugar Grove (Warren County) (Township)	16350
Stalker	12741	Stockdale	15483	Sugar Hill	15824
Stambaugh	15456	Stockertown	18083	Sugarloaf (Columbia County) (Township)	17814
Standard	15666	Stockton	18201	Sugarloaf (Luzerne County)	18249
Standard Shaft	15666	Stockton Number Eight	18201	Sugarloaf (Luzerne County) (Township)	18251
Standing Stone	18854	Stockton Number Seven	18201	Sugar Notch	18706
Standing Stone (Township)	18853	Stockton Number Six	18201	Sugar Run	18846
Stanhope	17963	Stoddartsville	18610	Sugartown	19355
Stanley	15801	Stokesdale	16901	Sullivan (Township)	16932
Stanton (Jefferson County)	15825	Stoneboro	16153	Summerdale	17093
Stanton (Luzerne County)	15825	Stone Church	18343	Summerhill (Cambria County)	15958
Stanton Heights (Allegheny County)	15201	Stone Glen	17018	Summerhill (Cambria County) (Township)	15921
Stanton Heights (Westmoreland County)	15672	Stoneham	16313	Summer Hill (Columbia County)	18603
Stanwood Gardens	19020	Stone Hill	17516	Summerhill (Crawford County) (Township)	16406
Star Brick	16365	Stone House	16258	Summerson	15821
Starford	15777	Stonehurst	19006	Summersville	18822
Star Junction	15482	Stonerstown	16678	Summerville	15864
Starkville	18657	Stonersville	19508	Summit (Butler County) (Township)	16001
Starlight	18461	Stonetown	19508	Summit (Cambria County)	16630
Starners Station	17324	Stonevilla	15601	Summit (Crawford County) (Township)	16424
Starr (Forest County)	16353	Stoneybreak	17267	Summit (Erie County) (Township)	16509
Starr (Warren County)	16420	Stonington	17801	Summit (McKean County)	16701
Starrucca	18462	Stonybrook	17402	Summit (Potter County) (Township)	16720
Starview	17347	Stonybrook Heights	17402	Summit (Somerset County) (Township)	15552
Starview Heights	17402	Stonybrook-Wilshire	17402	Summit (Susquehanna County)	18834
State College	16801-05	Stonycreek (Cambria County) (Township)	15906	Summit Grove Camp (Part of New Freedom)	17349
For specific State College Zip Codes call (814) 238-2435, or your local postmaster.		Stonycreek (Somerset County) (Township)	15541	Summit Hill	18250
		Stony Creek Mills	19606	Summit Lawn	18103
		Stonyfork	16901		
		Stony Point (Bucks County)	18930		
		Stony Point (Crawford County)	16316		
		Stony Point (Franklin County)	17262		
		Stony Point (Greene County)	15344		
		Stony Run	19557		
		Stormstown	16870		
		Stormville	18360		

* Area Zip Code **† Post Office Boxes**

	ZIP		ZIP		ZIP
Summit Mills	15552	Sylvania (Potter County)		Throop	18512
Summit Station	17979	(Township)	16720	69th Street Center	19082
Sumneytown	18084	Sylvis	16692	Thumptown	16901
Sunbeam	17201	Syner	17003	Thurston	18657
Sunbrook	16635	Table Rock	17307	Tiadaghton	16901
Sunbury	17801	Tacony (Part of		Tidal	16259
Suncliff	15765	Philadelphia)	19135	Tide	15748
Sundale	18920	Tafton	18464	Tidioute	16351
Sunderlinville	16943	Tait	15825	Tiffany	18801
Sunnybrook	19075	Talmage	17580	Tilden (Township)	19526
Sunnyburn	17302	Talmar	17814	Tillotson	16438
Sunny Point	18428	Tamanend	18252	Timber Lakes	19067
Sunny Side (Allegheny		Tamaqua	18252	Timberly Heights	16001
County)	15063	Tamarack	17764	Timblin	15778
Sunnyside (Lawrence		Tamiment	18371	Timbuck	16738
County)	16101	Tanglewood Lakes	18426	Time	15353
Sunnyside (Lebanon		Tanguy	19342	Tinicum	18947
County)	17042	Tank	18249	Tinicum (Bucks County)	
Sunnyside (Northumberland		Tannersville	18372	(Township)	18947
County)	17872	Tannery (Carbon County)	18661	Tinicum (Delaware County)	
Sunrise Lake	18337	Tannery (Luzerne County)	18661	(Township)	19029
Sunset Acres	15701	Tanoma	15728	Tinicum Township (census	
Sunset Grove	19380	Tarentum	15084	designated place)	19029
Sunset Hills (Part of		Tarrs	15688	Tioga	16946
Economy)	15042	Tarrtown	16210	Tioga (Township)	16946
Sunset Manor	17405	Tatamy	18085	Tioga Junction	16946
Sunset Pines (Part of Lock		Tatesville	15537	Tiona	16352
Haven)	17745	Taylor (Blair County)		Tionesta	16353
Sunset Valley	15642	(Township)	16673	Tionesta (Township)	16353
Sunset Village	18451	Taylor (Centre County)		Tippecanoe	15480
Sunshine (Fayette County)	15461	(Township)	16686	Tipton	16684
Sunshine (Luzerne County)	18655	Taylor (Fulton County)		Tire Hill	15959
Sun Valley	18330	(Township)	16689	Titusville	16354
Sun Village (Part of Chester)	19013	Taylor (Lackawanna		Tivoli	17737
Sunville	16317	County)	18517	Toboyne (Township)	17071
Superior (Fayette County)	15417	Taylor (Lawrence County)		Toby (Clarion County)	
Superior (Westmoreland		(Township)	16160	(Township)	16248
County)	15627	Taylor Highlands (Part of		Toby (Elk County)	15846
Suplee	19371	Huntingdon)	16652	Toby Farms (Part of	
Surveyor Mine	16830	Tayloria	19363	Chester)	19015
Suscon	18641	Taylorstown (Washington		Tobyhanna	18466
Susquehanna (Cambria		County)	15323	Tobyhanna (Township)	18350
County) (Township)	15714	Taylorstown (Washington		Tobyhanna Army Depot	18466
Susquehanna (Dauphin		County)	15365	Todd (Fulton County)	
County) (Township)	17109	Taylorsville	15729	(Township)	17233
Susquehanna (Juniata		Taylorville	17921	Todd (Huntingdon County)	16685
County) (Township)	17045	Teagarden Homes	15322	Todd (Huntingdon County)	
Susquehanna (Lycoming		Tearing Run	15748	(Township)	16685
County) (Township)	17701	Teedyskung Lake	18457	Toddesville	17325
Susquehanna		Teepleville	16403	Todmorron	19086
(Susquehanna County)	18847	Telescope	16922	Toftrees	16803
Susquehanna Bridge	16830	Telford	18969	Toland	17324
Susquehanna Trails	17314	Tell (Township)	17213	Tolna	17349
Susquehanna Valley Mall	17831	Temple	19560	Tomb	17740
Sutersville	15083	Templeton	16259	Tompkins	16940
Swales	17049	Ten Mile	15311	Tompkinsville	18433
Swamproot	16127	Tenmile Bottom	16346	Tomstown	17268
Swan Acres	15237	Tenth Avenue (Part of		Tooley Corners	18444
Swanville	16415	Bethlehem)	18018	Topton	19562
Swart	15364	Terminal	19082	Torpedo	16340
Swarthmore	19081	Terrace Acres	18052	Torrance	15779
Swarthmorwood	19081	Terre Hill	17581	Torrance State Hospital	15779
Swartzville	17569	Terry (Township)	18853	Torresdale (Part of	
Swatara (Dauphin County)		Terrytown	18853	Philadelphia)	19114
(Township)	17111	Texas (Township)	18431	Torresdale Manor	19020
Swatara (Lebanon County)		Tharptown	17872	Torrey	18473
(Township)	17038	The Hideout	18436	Toughkenamon	19374
Swatara Station	17033	The Meadows	16865	Towamencin (Township)	19443
Swede Hill	15601	The Pines	17350	Towamensing (Township)	18071
Swedeland	19401	The Woodlands	16046	Towamensing Trails	18210
Sweden (Township)	16915	Thieleman Crossroads	16046	Towanda	18848
Sweden Valley	16915	Thomas	15330	Towanda (Township)	18848
Swedesburg	19405	Thomasdale	15935	Tower City	17980
Swedetown (Cambria		Thomas Mills	15935	Tower Hill	18914
County)	16646	Thomasville	17364	Tower Hill No. One	15475
Swedetown (Westmoreland		Thompson (Fulton County)		Tower Hill No. Two	15417
County)	15683	(Township)	17236	Towerville	19320
Sweeney Plan	15012	Thompson (Susquehanna		Town Hill	18655
Sweet Valley	18656	County)	18465	Town Line	18655
Sweitzer	15061	Thompson (Susquehanna		Townville	16360
Swengel	17880	County) (Township)	18462	Traces of Lattimore	18328
Swiftwater	18370	Thompson No. 1	15475	Trade City	16256
Swineford (Part of		Thompson No. 2	15468	Trafford	15085
Middleburg)	17842	Thompsontown (Clearfield		Trailwood	18702
Swissdale	17745	County)	15753	Trainer	19013
Swissmont	15857	Thompsontown (Juniata		Transfer	16154
Swissvale	15218	County)	17094	Trappe	19426
Switzer	18066	Thompsonville	15317	Trauger	15650
Swoyersville	18704	Thornburg	15205	Traymore	18974
Sybertsville	18251	Thornbury (Chester County)		Traymore Manor	18974
Sycamore	15364	(Township)	19395	Treasure Lake	15801
Sygan	15017	Thornbury (Delaware		Tredyffrin (Township)	19312
Sygan Hill	15017	County) (Township)	19373	Treehaven (Part of Bethel	
Sykesville	15865	Thorndale	19372	Park)	15102
Sylmar	19362	Thorndale Heights	19335	Trees Mills	15601
Sylvan	17236	Thornhurst	18424	Treichlers	18086
Sylvan Crest	15061	Thornridge	19054	Tremont	17981
Sylvan Dell	17701	Thornton	19373	Tremont (Township)	17963
Sylvan Grove	16858	Threemile	16728	Trent	15622
Sylvan Hills	16648	Three Springs	17264	Trenton	17948
Sylvania (Bradford County)	16945	Three Springs Run	16938	Tresckow	18254
		Three Tuns	19002	Tresslarville	18436

	ZIP
Trevorton	17881
Trevose	19047
Trevose Heights	19047
Trexler	19529
Trexler Mall	18087
Trexlertown	18087
Trimmer Manor	17405
Trindle Spring	17055
Trinity Park	15301
Triumph (Township)	16340
Trooper	19401
Trotter	15425
Trotwood	15241
Trout Run	17771
Trouts Corners (Part of Hermitage)	16148
Trouts Crossing	15666
Troutville	15866
Troxelville	17882
Troy (Bradford County)	16947
Troy (Bradford County) (Township)	16947
Troy (Clearfield County)	16866
Troy (Crawford County) (Township)	16354
Troy Center	16404
Troy Hill	16201
Truce	17566
Trucksville	18708
Trucksville Gardens	18708
Truemans	16347
Truesdale Terrace	18706
Truittsburg	16224
Truman	15834
Trumbauersville	18970
Trunkeyville	16351
Truxall	15613
Tryonville	16404
Tuckerton	19605
Tullytown	19007
Tulpehocken (Township)	19550
Tuna	16701
Tunkhannock (Monroe County) (Township)	18610
Tunkhannock (Wyoming County)	18657
Tunkhannock (Wyoming County) (Township)	18657
Tunnel	18661
Tunnelhill	16641
Tunnelton	15681
Turbett (Township)	17082
Turbot (Township)	17847
Turbotville	17772
Turkey City	16058
Turkeyfoot (Franklin County)	17201
Turkeyfoot (Washington County)	15332
Turkey Run (Part of Shenandoah)	17976
Turkeytown	15089
Turnersville	16134
Turnip Hole	16373
Turnpike (Part of Shrewsbury)	17361
Turtle Creek	15145
Turtlepoint	16750
Tuscarora (Bradford County) (Township)	18623
Tuscarora (Juniata County)	17082
Tuscarora (Juniata County) (Township)	17035
Tuscarora (Perry County) (Township)	17062
Tuscarora (Schuylkill County)	17982
Tusculam	17257
Tusseyville	16828
Twenty Row	15927
Twilight	15022
Twin Bridge Farm	19380
Twin Bridges	15022
Twin Brooks	17405
Twin Lakes	18458
Twin Oaks (Adams County)	17325
Twin Oaks (Bucks County)	19056
Twin Oaks (Delaware County)	19014
Twin Oaks Farms	19014
Twin Rocks	15960
Two Taverns	17325
Tyler	15849
Tylerdale (Part of Washington)	15301
Tyler Hill	18469
Tyler Run-Queens Gate	17403
Tylersburg	16361
Tylersport	18971
Tylersville	17773
Tyre	15126
Tyrone (Adams County) (Township)	17325

	ZIP
Tyrone (Blair County)	16686
Tyrone (Blair County) (Township)	16686
Tyrone (Perry County) (Township)	17040
Uhlerstown	18920
Uledi	15484
Ulhers	18042
Ulster	18850
Ulster (Township)	18850
Ulysses	16948
Ulysses (Township)	16948
Unicorn	17566
Union (Adams County) (Township)	17331
Union (Bedford County) (Township)	16655
Union (Berks County) (Township)	19508
Union (Centre County) (Township)	16844
Union (Clearfield County) (Township)	15856
Union (Crawford County) (Township)	16335
Union (Erie County) (Township)	16438
Union (Fulton County) (Township)	17267
Union (Huntingdon County) (Township)	17052
Union (Jefferson County) (Township)	15829
Union (Colerain Township) (Lancaster County)	17560
Union (Providence Township) (Lancaster County)	17536
Union (Lawrence County) (Township)	16101
Union (Lebanon County) (Township)	17038
Union (Luzerne County) (Township)	18655
Union (Mifflin County) (Township)	17004
Union (Schuylkill County) (Township)	17967
Union (Snyder County) (Township)	17864
Union (Tioga County) (Township)	17724
Union (Union County) (Township)	17889
Union (Washington County) (Township)	15332
Union Center	17724
Union City	16438
Union Dale	18470
Union Deposit	17033
Union Furnace	16686
Union Grove	17519
Union Hill	18235
Union Mills	17004
Union Square	17545
Uniontown (Fayette County)	15401
Uniontown (Indiana County)	15724
Uniontown (York County)	17019
Uniontown Heights	16323
Uniontown North	15401
Uniontown Shopping Center (Part of Uniontown)	15401
Union Trust (Part of Pittsburgh)	15219
Union Valley (Lawrence County)	16157
Union Valley (Washington County)	15332
Unionville (Beaver County)	15066
Unionville (Berks County)	19518
Unionville (Butler County)	16001
Unionville (Chester County)	19375
Union Water Works	17003
United	15689
Unity (Township)	15650
Unity House	18373
Unity Junction (Part of Plum)	15239
Unityville	17774
Universal	15235
University City (Part of Philadelphia)	19104
University Heights	18015
University Park (Part of State College)	16802
Upland	19015
Upland Terrace	19004
Upper Allen (Township)	17055
Upper Augusta (Township)	17801
Upper Bern (Township)	19506
Upper Black Eddy	18972
Upper Brownville	17976

	ZIP
Upper Burrell (Township)	15068
Upper Chichester (Township)	19061
Upper Darby	19018
	19050
	19082-83
For specific Upper Darby Zip Codes call (215) 352-0800, or your local postmaster.	
Upper Dublin (Township)	19034
Upper Exeter	18643
Upper Fairfield (Township)	17754
Upper Frankford (Township)	17241
Upper Frederick (Township)	18074
Upper Glasgow	19464
Upper Gwynedd (Township)	19454
Upper Hanover (Township)	18041
Upper Hillville	16248
Upper Lawn	17078
Upper Leacock (Township)	17540
Upper Lehigh	18224
Upper Macungie (Township)	18087
Upper Mahanoy (Township)	17836
Upper Mahantango (Township)	17941
Upper Makefield (Township)	18940
Upper Merion (Township)	19406
Upper Middletown	15480
Upper Mifflin (Township)	17241
Upper Milford (Township)	18092
Upper Mill (Part of Mount Holly Springs)	17065
Upper Moreland (Township)	19090
Upper Mount Bethel (Township)	18013
Upper Nazareth (Township)	18064
Upper Orchard	19056
Upper Oxford (Township)	19363
Upper Paxton (Township)	17061
Upper Peanut	15480
Upper Pottsgrove (Township)	19464
Upper Providence (Delaware County) (Township)	19063
Upper Providence (Montgomery County) (Township)	19456
Upper Providence Township (census designated place)	19063
Upper Reese	16648
Upper Sagon	17877
Upper Salford (Township)	18957
Upper Saucon (Township)	18034
Upper Southampton (Township)	18966
Upper St. Clair	15241
Upper St. Clair (Township)	15241
Upperstrasburg	17265
Upper Tulpehocken (Township)	19559
Upper Turkeyfoot (Township)	15557
Upper Two Lick	15721
Upper Tyrone (Township)	15683
Upper Uwchlan (Township)	19335
Upper Yoder (Township)	15905
Upton	17225
Uptown (Part of Pittsburgh)	15219
Urban	17830
Urey	15742
Uriah	17324
Ursina	15485
Ursina Junction (Part of Confluence)	15424
Utahville	16627
Utica	16362
Utopia	15613
Uwchlan (Township)	19341
Uwchland	19480
Vail	16686
Valencia	16059
Valier	15780
Vallamont Hills (Part of Williamsport)	17701
Valley (Armstrong County) (Township)	16201
Valley (Chester County) (Township)	19320
Valley (Montour County) (Township)	17821
Valley Falls	19006
Valley Forge	19481-85
For specific Valley Forge Zip Codes call (215) 783-0232, or your local postmaster.	
Valley Forge Christian College	19460
Valley Forge Estates	19087
Valley Forge Homes	19406
Valley Forge Manor	19460

	ZIP
Valley Furnace	17959
Valley Green (Delaware County)	19026
Valley Green (York County)	17319
Valley Green Estates	17319
Valley Green Heights	17319
Valley Green West	17319
Valley-Hi	15533
Valley Stream	18707
Valley View (Cambria County)	15906
Valley View (Centre County)	16823
Valley View (Chester County)	19344
Valley View (Lancaster County)	17545
Valley View (Schuylkill County)	17983
Valley View (York County)	17403
Valley View Farms	19006
Valley View Heights	16226
Van	16319
Van Buren	15329
Vance	15301
Vances Mills	15401
Vanceville	15330
Vanderbilt	15486
Vandergrift	15690
Vandergrift Heights (Part of Vandergrift)	15690
Vandling	18421
Vandyke	17082
Vankirk	15301
Van Meter	15479
Van Ormer	16639
Vanport (Township)	15009
Van Voorhis	15366
Van Wert	17059
Varden	18436
Vaux Town (Part of New Britain)	18901
Vawter	18810
Venango (Butler County) (Township)	16049
Venango (Crawford County)	16440
Venango (Crawford County) (Township)	16440
Venango (Erie County) (Township)	16442
Venetia	15367
Venice	15057
Venturetown	16365
Venus	16364
Vera Cruz	18049
Verdilla	17870
Vere Cruz	17569
Vermilion Hill	19054
Vernfield	19438
Vernon (Crawford County) (Township)	16335
Vernon (Wyoming County)	18657
Vernondale	16509
Vernon Park (Part of Philadelphia)	19144
Verona	15147
Versailles	15132
Vestaburg	15368
Vesta Heights	15333
Vesta No 6 (Part of Centerville)	15429
Veterans Administration Hospital (Blair County)	16602
Veterans Administration Hospital (Butler County)	16001
Veterans Administration Medical Center (Lebanon County)	17042
Veterans Hospital (Allegheny County)	15240
Veterans Hospital (Chester County)	19320
Veterans Hospital (Luzerne County)	18702
Vicksburg (Blair County)	16648
Vicksburg (Union County)	17883
Victory (Township)	16342
Victory Heights	16323
Victory Hills	15063
Vienna	15376
Viennese Woods	15209
Viewmont Mall (Part of Dickson City)	18519
Village	15241
Village Green	19013
Village Green-Green Ridge	19013
Village of Cross Creek	17402
Village of Olde Hickory	17601
Village of the Four Seasons	18470
Village of Westover	17055
Village Shires	18966
Villa Green	17403
Villa Maria	16155

	ZIP
Villanova *	19085
Vinco	15909
Vinemont	17569
Vintage	17562
Vintondale	15961
Violet Hill	17403
Violet Wood	19057
Vira	17044
Virginia Farms	15717
Virginia Hills West	15126
Virginia Mills	17320
Virginville	19564
Voganville	17522
Vogleyville	16001
Volant	16156
Vosburg	18657
Vowinckel	16260
Vulcan	18214
Wabash (Part of Pittsburgh)	15220
Wadesville	17901
Wadsworth (Part of Philadelphia)	19150
Wagner	17841
Wagnersville	18042
Wagontown	19376
Wahlville	16033
Wahnetah (Part of Jim Thorpe)	18229
Wakena	15681
Walbert	18104
Walcksville	18235
Walden Woods	15126
Walkchalk	16201
Walker (Centre County) (Township)	16841
Walker (Huntingdon County) (Township)	16660
Walker (Juniata County) (Township)	17059
Walker (Schuylkill County) (Township)	18252
Walkers Mill	15106
Walkertown	15427
Wall	15148
Wallace (Township)	19343
Wallace Junction (Part of Girard)	16417
Wallaceton	16876
Wallaceville	16354
Wallenpaupack Lake Estates	18436
Waller	17814
Wallingford	19086
Wallingford Hills	19086
Wallis Run	17771
Walls Corners	18414
Wallsville	18414
Walltown	16838
Walmo	16101
Walnut	17082
Walnut Bend	16301
Walnut Bottom	17266
Walnut Gardens	18052
Walnut Grove	17074
Walnut Hill (Fayette County)	15401
Walnut Hill (Greene County)	15327
Walnut Hill (Montgomery County)	19001
Walnutport	18088
Walnuttown	19522
Walsall	15904
Walston	15781
Walston Junction (Part of Punxsutawney)	15767
Walters	18042
Waltersburg	15488
Waltonville	17036
Waltz	15679
Waltz Landing	18428
Waltzvale	16671
Wampum	16157
Wanamakers	19529
Wanamie	18634
Wandin	15729
Wanneta	16401
Wapwallopen	18660
Ward (Delaware County)	19331
Ward (Tioga County) (Township)	17724
Warfordsburg	17267
Warminster	18974
Warminster (Township)	18974
Warminster Heights	18974
Warner	15022
Warren (Bradford County) (Township)	18851
Warren (Franklin County) (Township)	17236
Warren (Warren County)	16365
Warren Center	18851
Warrendale	15086
Warren South	16365

	ZIP
Warren State Hospital	16365
Warrensville	17701
Warrington (Bucks County)	18976
Warrington (Bucks County) (Township)	18976
Warrington (York County) (Township)	17019
Warrior Ridge	16669
Warrior Run	18706
Warriors Mark	16877
Warriors Mark (Township)	16686
Warsaw (Jefferson County) (Township)	15851
Warsaw (Lackawanna County)	18512
Warsaw (Luzerne County)	18702
Warwick (Bucks County) (Township)	18929
Warwick (Chester County)	19470
Warwick (Chester County) (Township)	19520
Warwick (Lancaster County) (Township)	17543
Washington (Armstrong County) (Township)	16218
Washington (Berks County) (Township)	19512
Washington (Butler County) (Township)	16061
Washington (Cambria County) (Township)	15938
Washington (Clarion County) (Township)	16326
Washington (Dauphin County) (Township)	17048
Washington (Erie County) (Township)	16412
Washington (Fayette County) (Township)	15012
Washington (Franklin County) (Township)	17268
Washington (Greene County) (Township)	15370
Washington (Indiana County) (Township)	15732
Washington (Jefferson County) (Township)	15840
Washington (Lawrence County) (Township)	16156
Washington (Lehigh County) (Township)	18080
Washington (Lycoming County) (Township)	17810
Washington (Northampton County) (Township)	18013
Washington (Northumberland County) (Township)	17867
Washington (Schuylkill County) (Township)	17963
Washington (Snyder County) (Township)	17842
Washington (Washington County)	15301
Washington (Westmoreland County) (Township)	15613
Washington (Wyoming County) (Township)	18657
Washington (York County) (Township)	17316
Washington Boro	17582
Washington Crossing	18977
Washington Heights (Part of Lemoyne)	17043
Washington Hill (Part of Pottstown)	19464
Washington Square Gardens	19401
Washingtonville	17884
Wassergass	18055
Waterfall	16689
Waterford (Erie County)	16441
Waterford (Erie County) (Township)	16411
Waterford (Westmoreland County)	15658
Waterford (York County)	17402
Waterloo	17021
Waterloo Mills	19333
Waterman	15748
Waterside	16695
Waterson	16258
Water Street	16611
Waterton	18655
Waterville	17776
Waterworks, The (Part of Pittsburgh)	15212
Watkins	15722
Watrous	16921
Watson (Lycoming County) (Township)	17740

	ZIP
Watson (Warren County) (Township)	16351
Watson Farm	16239
Watson Run	16316
Watsontown	17777
Watters	16033
Wattersonville	16218
Watts (Township)	17020
Wattsburg	16442
Waverly	18471
Wawa (Part of Chester Heights)	19017
Wawaset	19380
Wayland Corners	16335
Waymart	18472
Wayne (Armstrong County) (Township)	16222
Wayne (Clinton County) (Township)	17748
Wayne (Crawford County) (Township)	16314
Wayne (Dauphin County) (Township)	17032
Wayne (Delaware County)	19087
Wayne (Erie County) (Township)	16407
Wayne (Greene County) (Township)	15362
Wayne (Lawrence County) (Township)	16117
Wayne (Mifflin County) (Township)	17051
Wayne (Schuylkill County) (Township)	17933
Waynecastle	17225
Wayne Heights	17268
Waynesboro	17268
Waynesburg	15370
Waynesburg Lakes	15329
Waynesville	17032
Weatherly	18255
Weaverland	17519
Weaversville	18067
Weavertown (Berks County)	19518
Weavertown (Lancaster County)	17505
Weavertown (Lebanon County)	17046
Weavertown (Washington County)	15317
Weber City	15834
Webster	15087
Webster Mills	17233
Weedville	15868
Wegley	15642
Wehnwood (Part of Altoona)	16601
Weidasville	18078
Weidmanville	17522
Weigelstown	17315
Weigh Scales	17872
Weikert	17885
Weilersville	18011
Weinel's Crossroads	15656
Weir Lake	18058
Weisel	18944
Weisenberg (Township)	18066
Weishample	17938
Weissport	18235
Weissport East	18235
Weldbank	16313
Weldon	19006
Wellersburg	15564
Wellington Estates	18901
Welliversville	17815
Wellmans Corners	18834
Wells (Bradford County) (Township)	16925
Wells (Fulton County) (Township)	16691
Wellsboro	16901
Wellsboro Junction	16901
Wellscreek	15541
Wells Tannery	16691
Wellsville	17365
Welsh Hill	18470
Welsh Run	17225
Welty	15666
Wendel	15691
Wendover	15601
Wenks	17304
Wentlings Corners	16232
Werleys Corner	18066
Wernersville	19565
Wernersville Heights	19565
Wernersville State Hospital	19565
Wertz	16693
Wertzville	17055
Wescosville	18106
Wesley	16038
Wesley Chapel	15909
Wesleyville	16510
Wessex Hills	15108

	ZIP
West (Township)	16669
West Abington (Township)	18419
West Acres	17837
West Alexander	15376
West Aliquippa (Part of Aliquippa)	15001
West Ambler	19002
West Annville	17003
West Apollo (Part of Oklahoma)	15613
West Auburn	18623
Westaway	19444
West Bangor (Northampton County)	18072
West Bangor (York County)	17314
West Beaver (Township)	17841
West Belt Junction (Part of Pittsburgh)	15230
West Bend	15433
West Berwick (Part of Berwick)	18603
West Bethlehem (Township)	15345
West Bingham	16923
West Bolivar	15923
West Bradford (Township)	19335
West Branch (Cambria County)	15714
West Branch (Potter County) (Township)	16922
West Brandywine (Township)	19320
West Bridgewater	15009
West Bristol	19007
West Brownsville	15417
West Brunswick (Township)	17961
West Buffalo (Township)	17844
West Burlington	16947
West Burlington (Township)	16914
Westbury	15071
West Caln (Township)	19376
West Cameron	17872
West Cameron (Township)	17872
West Carroll (Township)	15737
West Catasauqua	18052
West Chester	19380-83
For specific West Chester Zip Codes call (215) 696-4808, or your local postmaster.	
West Chillisquaque (Township)	17850
West Clifford	18470
West Cocalico (Township)	17578
Westcolang	18428
West Conshohocken	19428
West Cornwall (Township)	17042
West Creek	15834
West Creek Hills	17011
West Cressona (Part of Cressona)	17929
West Damascus	18469
West Decatur	16878
West Deer (Township)	15076
West Derry	15627
West Donegal (Township)	17022
West Earl (Township)	17508
West Easton	18042
West Eldred	16731
West Elizabeth	15088
West Ellwood Junction (Part of Koppel)	16136
West End (Dauphin County)	17102
West End (Washington County)	15301
West Enola	17025
West Export (Part of Export)	15632
West Fairfield	15944
West Fairview	17025
Westfall (Township)	18336
West Fallowfield (Chester County) (Township)	19330
West Fallowfield (Crawford County) (Township)	16131
West Falls	18615
West Fayetteville	17222
Westfield	16950
Westfield (Township)	16950
Westfield Terrace	17070
West Finley	15377
West Finley (Township)	15377
Westford	16134
West Franklin (Armstrong County) (Township)	16262
West Franklin (Bradford County)	18832
West Freedom	16049
Westgate Hills	18017
West Goshen	19380
West Goshen (Township)	19380
West Goshen Hills	19380
West Goshen Park	19380
West Grove	19390
West Hamburg	19526

	ZIP
West Hanover (Township)	17112
West Hazleton	18201
West Hemlock (Township)	17821
West Hempfield (Township)	17601
West Hickory	16370
West Hill	17013
West Hills	16201
West Hills Estates	17701
West Hoffman	15101
West Homestead	15120
Westinghouse Village	19029
West Jeannette (Part of Jeannette)	15644
West Jonestown	17038
West Keating (Township)	16871
West Kittanning	16201
West Lampeter (Township)	17537
West Lancaster	17603
Westland	15378
West Lawn (Berks County)	19609
West Lawn (Union County)	17837
West Lebanon (Indiana County)	15783
West Lebanon (Lebanon County) (Township)	17046
West Lebanon (Lebanon County)	17046
West Leechburg	15656
West Leisenring	15489
West Lenox	18826
West Leroy	17724
West Liberty (Butler County)	16057
West Liberty (Clearfield County)	15801
West Library (Part of Bethel Park)	15102
Westline	16751
West Mahanoy (Township)	17976
West Mahoning (Township)	16256
West Manayunk	19151
West Manchester (Township)	17404
West Manchester Mall (Part of York)	17345
West Manheim (Township)	17331
West Market (Part of Philadelphia)	19139
West Marlborough (Township)	19348
West Mayfield	15010
West Mead (Township)	16335
West Meyersdale (Part of Meyersdale)	15552
West Middlesex	16159
West Middletown	15379
West Mifflin	15122-23
For specific West Mifflin Zip Codes call (412) 466-5120, or your local postmaster.	
West Milton	17886
Westminster (Erie County)	16506
Westminster (Luzerne County)	18702
Westminster Manor	15241
West Monocacy	19518
Westmont (Cambria County)	15905
Westmont (Lebanon County)	17042
West Monterey	16049
Westmont Plan	16201
Westmoreland City	15692
West Moshannon	16651
West Myerstown	17067
West Nanticoke	18634
West Nantmeal (Township)	19520
West New Kensington	15030
West Newton	15089
West Nicholson	18446
West Norriton	19401
	19403
For specific West Norriton Zip Codes call (215) 275-9780, or your local postmaster.	
West Norriton (Township)	19401
West Nottingham (Township)	19362
Weston	18256
Weston Place	17976
Westover (Bucks County)	19067
Westover (Clearfield County)	16692
West Overton	15683
Westover Woods	19401
West Park (Allegheny County)	15136
West Park (Philadelphia County)	19131
West Pen Argyl	18072
West Penn (Township)	17960
West Pennsboro (Township)	17241
West Perry (Township)	17086

	ZIP
Abbott Run Valley	02864
Adamsville	02801
Albion	02802
Allendale	02911
Allenton	02852
Alton	02894
Annawomscutt	02806
Annex (Part of Providence)	02903
Anthony	02816
Apple Blossom (Part of Cranston)	02920
Arcadia	02832
Arctic	02893
Arkwright	02816
Arlington (Part of Cranston)	02920
Arnold Mills	02864
Arnold's Neck (Part of Warwick)	02886
Ashaway	02804
Ashton	02864
Auburn (Part of Cranston)	02910
Austin	02822
Avondale	02891
Barberville	02832
Barrington	02806
Barrington (Town)	02806
Bayridge (Part of Warwick)	02818
Bayside (Part of Warwick)	02889
Bay Spring	02806
Bay View (Part of East Providence)	02914
Beach Terrace	02809
Bellefonte (Part of Cranston)	02920
Belleville	02852
Berkeley	02864
Beverage Hill (Part of Pawtucket)	02860
Bishops Heights	02857
Black Plain	02822
Block Island	02807
Bonnet Shores	02882
Boon Lake	02822
Bowdish Lake	02814
Bradford	02808
Branch Village	02896
Brenton Village (Part of Newport)	02840
Bridgeport	02878
Bridgetown	02874
Briggs Beach	02837
Bristol (Town)	02809
Bristol	02809
Bristol Colony	02872
Bristol Ferry	02871
Bristol Highlands	02809
Bristol Narrows	02809
Broadway (Part of Newport)	02840
Brookfield (Part of Cranston)	02920
Brown (Part of Providence)	02912
Brush Neck Cove (Part of Warwick)	02886
Bryant College of Business Administration	02917
Bullocks Point (Part of East Providence)	02914
Burdickville	02808
Burrillville (Town)	02830
Buttonwoods (Part of Warwick)	02886
Canonchet	02832
Carnegie Heights	02865
Carolina	02812
Carpenters Beach	02879
Cedar Grove Estates	02822
Cedar Point	02835
Cedar Tree Point (Part of Warwick)	02886
Centerville (Kent County)	02893
Centerville (Washington County)	02832
Central Falls	02863
Centredale	02911
Charlestown	02813
Charlestown (Town)	02813
Charlestown Beach	02813
Chepachet	02814
Chepiwanoxet (Part of Warwick)	02886
Cherry Valley	02814
Cherry Valley Beach	02814
Chopmist	02857
Clarke's Village	02835
Clayville	02815
Clyde	02893
Coasters Harbor (Part of Newport)	02840
Coggeshall	02885
Coles (Part of Warwick)	02889
Columbia Heights	02875
Common Fence Point	02871
Commons	02837

	ZIP
Comstock Gardens (Part of Cranston)	02910
Conanicut Park	02835
Conimicut (Part of Warwick)	02889
Corey's Lane	02871
Coventry	02816
Coventry (Town)	02816
Coventry Center	02816
Cowesett (Part of Warwick)	02886
Cranston	02920-21
	02910
For specific Cranston Zip Codes call (401) 781-0249, or your local postmaster.	
Crescent Park (Part of East Providence)	02914
Crompton	02893
Cross Mills	02813
Cumberland	02864
Cumberland (Town)	02864
Cumberland Hill	02864
Curtis Corners	02883
Darlington (Part of Pawtucket)	02861
Davisville (Post Office)	02854
Davisville	02852
Diamond Hill	02864
Dunns Corners	02891
Durfee Hill	02814
Eagleville	02878
East Greenwich (Town)	02818
East Greenwich	02818
East Matunuck	02879
East Natick (Part of Warwick)	02893
East Providence	02914
East Providence Wharf (Part of East Providence)	02914
East Side (Part of Providence)	02906
East Warren	02885
Echo Lake	02814
Eden Park (Part of Cranston)	02920
Edgewood (Part of Cranston)	02905
Elmwood (Part of Providence)	02907
Enos (Part of Cranston)	02920
Escoheag	02822
Esmond	02917
Exeter	02822
Exeter (Town)	02822
Fairbanks Corner	02827
Finast (Part of East Providence)	02914
Fiskeville (Part of Cranston)	02823
Fogland Point	02878
Forestdale	02824
Fort Adams (Part of Newport)	02840
Foster	02825
Foster (Town)	02825
Fox Point (Part of Providence)	02906
Frenchtown	02818
Friar (Part of Providence)	02918
Fruit Hill	02911
Galilee	02882
Garden City (Part of Cranston)	02920
Garden City Shopping Center (Part of Cranston)	02920
Gazzaville	02839
Geneva	02911
Georgiaville	02917
Glendale	02826
Glocester (Town)	02814
Goat Island (Part of Newport)	02840
Goulds	02883
Graniteville	02911
Grants Mills	02838
Greene	02827
Green Hill	02879
Greenville	02828
Greenwood (Part of Warwick)	02886
Greystone	02911
Hamilton	02852
Hampden Meadows	02806
Harmony	02829
Harris	02816
Harrisville	02830
Haversham	02891
Highland Beach (Part of Warwick)	02889
Hill's Grove (Part of Warwick)	02886
Hog Island†	02809
Homestead	02872
Hope	02831

	ZIP
Hope Valley	02832
Hopkins Hollow	02827
Hopkinton	02833
Hopkinton (Town)	02833
Howard (Part of Cranston)	02920
Hoxsie (Part of Warwick)	02889
Hughesdale	02919
Indian Lake Shores	02879
India Point (Part of Providence)	02903
Island Park	02871
Jackson	02823
Jamestown (Town)	02835
Jamestown	02835
Jamestown Center	02835
Jamestown Shores	02835
Jerusalem	02879
Johnston (Town)	02919
Johnston	02919
Kent Corner (Part of East Providence)	02914
Kent Heights (Part of East Providence)	02914
Kenyon	02836
Kingston	02881
Knightsville (Part of Cranston)	02920
La Fayette	02852
Lake Bel Air	02896
Lake Mishnock	02817
Lakewood (Part of Warwick)	02888
Langworthy Corner	02891
Laurel Hill	02859
Laurel Park	02885
Leonard Corner (Part of East Providence)	02914
Liberty	02877
Limerock	02865
Lincoln	02865
Lincoln (Town)	02860
Lincoln Park (Part of Warwick)	02888
Lippit	02893
Lippitt Estate	02864
Little Compton	02837
Little Compton (Town)	02837
Lockwood Corner (Part of Warwick)	02889
Longmeadow (Part of Warwick)	02889
Lonsdale (Cumberland Town)	02865
Lonsdale (Lincoln Town)	02864
Lymansville	02911
Manton (Part of Providence)	02909
Manville	02838
Maple Root Village	02816
Mapleville	02839
Marieville	02904
Matunuck	02879
Mellville	02871
Melville	02871
Meshanticut (Part of Cranston)	02920
Middletown (Town)	02842
Middletown	02842
Misquamicut	02891
Mohegan	02830
Mohegan Bluffs	02807
Mooresfield	02874
Moosup Valley	02827
Moscow	02832
Mount Pleasant (Part of Providence)	02908
Mount Vernon	02825
Mount View	02852
Nannaquaket	02878
Narragansett	02882
Narragansett (Town)	02882
Narragansett Heights	02878
Nasonville	02830
Natick (Part of Warwick)	02893
Nausauket (Part of Warwick)	02886
Naval Construction Battalion Center	02854
Nayatt	02806
New Harbor	02807
Newport	02840-42
For specific Newport Zip Codes call (401) 847-2329, or your local postmaster.	
Newport East	02840
New Shoreham (Town)	02807
Nichols Corner	02818
Nooseneck	02816
North (Part of Providence)	02908
North Foster	02825
North Kingstown	02852*
	02854†
North Providence	02911
North Providence (Town)	02911

* **Area Zip Code** † **Post Office Boxes**

	ZIP
North Quidnessett	02852
North Scituate	02857
North Smithfield (Town)	02896
Norwood (Part of Warwick)	02888
Oakland	02830
Oakland Beach (Part of Warwick)	02886
Oak Lawn (Part of Cranston)	02920
Old Harbor	02807
Olney Arnold Estates (Part of Cranston)	02920
Olneyville (Part of Providence)	02909
Palace Garden (Part of Warwick)	02888
Parcel Post Annex	02891
Pascoag	02859
Pawtucket	02860-62
For specific Pawtucket Zip Codes call (401) 722-1073, or your local postmaster.	
Peace Dale	02883
Perryville	02879
Pettaquamscutt Lake Shores	02874
Phenix	02893
Phillipsdale (Part of East Providence)	02914
Pilgrim (Part of Warwick)	02888
Pine Hill	02822
Pleasant View (Part of Pawtucket)	02860
Plum Beach	02874
Plum Point	02874
Poccasett Heights	02871
Point Judith	02882
Pontiac (Part of Warwick)	02886
Popasquash Point	02809
Portsmouth	02871
Portsmouth (Town)	02871
Potowomut (Part of Warwick)	02818
Potter Hill	02891
Primrose	02896
Print Works (Part of Cranston)	02920
Providence	02901-09
	02940
For specific Providence Zip Codes call (401) 276-6850, or your local postmaster.	
Prudence Island	02872
Prudence Park	02872
Quidnessett	02852
Quidnick	02816
Quinnville	02865
Quonochontaug	02813
Rhode Island Mall (Part of Warwick)	02886
Rice City	02827
Rice Plat	02857

	ZIP
Richmond (Town)	02812
River Point	02893
Riverside (Part of East Providence)	02915
River Vue (Part of Warwick)	02889
Rockville	02873
Rocky Point (Part of Warwick)	02889
Rumford (Part of East Providence)	02916
Rumstick Point	02806
Sakonnet	02837
Sandy Point (Kent County)	02818
Sandy Point (Newport County)	02872
Sandy Point (Washington County)	02807
Saunderstown	02874
Saundersville	02857
Saylesville	02865
Scituate (Town)	02857
Shady Harbor	02891
Shannock	02875
Shawomet (Part of Warwick)	02889
Shelter Harbor	02891
Shores Acres	02852
Silver Lake (Part of Providence)	02909
Simmonsville	02919
Slatersville	02876
Slocum	02877
Smithfield (Town)	02917
Smith Hill (Part of Providence)	02908
Sockannosset (Part of Cranston)	02900
South Foster	02825
South Hopkinton	02813
South Kingstown (Town)	02879
South Providence (Part of Providence)	02905
South Warren	02885
Spragueville	02828
Spring Green (Part of Warwick)	02888
Spring Grove	02814
Spring Lake Beach	02826
Squantum (Part of East Providence)	02914
Stillwater	02917
Summit	02827
Tarkiln	02830
The Anchorage	02842
The Hummocks	02871
Thornton	02919
Tiverton	02878
Tiverton (Town)	02878
Tiverton Four Corners	02878
Tockwotten (Part of Providence)	02903

	ZIP
Tonomy Hill (Part of Newport)	02840
Touisset Highlands	02885
Tuckertown	02879
Tunipus	02837
Union Village	02896
Usquepaug	02892
Valley Falls	02864
Vaughn Hollow	02827
Wakefield	02879*
	02880†
Wakefield-Peacedale	02883
Walnut Hill (Part of Woonsocket)	02895
Warren	02885
Warren (Town)	02885
Warren Point	02837
Warwick	02886-89
For specific Warwick Zip Codes call (401) 737-6200, or your local postmaster.	
Warwick Mall (Part of Warwick)	02886
Warwick Neck (Part of Warwick)	02889
Washington Park (Part of Cranston)	02905
Watch Hill	02891
Watchmocket Square (Part of East Providence)	02914
Waterford	01504
Waterman Four Corners	02857
Weekapaug	02891
West Barrington	02806
Westcott (Part of Warwick)	02893
Westcott Beach	02814
Westerly	02891
Westerly (Town)	02891
West Glocester	06260
West Greenville	02828
West Greenwich (Town)	02817
West Greenwich Center	02827
West Kingston	02892
West Warwick	02893
West Warwick (Town)	02893
Weybosset Hill (Part of Providence)	02903
Whipple	02830
White Rock	02891
Wickford Junction	02852
Wildes Corner (Part of Warwick)	02886
Wood Estates	02816
Wood River Junction	02894
Woodville (Providence County)	02911
Woodville (Washington County)	02832
Woonsocket	02895
Wyoming	02898
Yorktown Manor	02852

---

* Area Zip Code   **† Post Office Boxes**

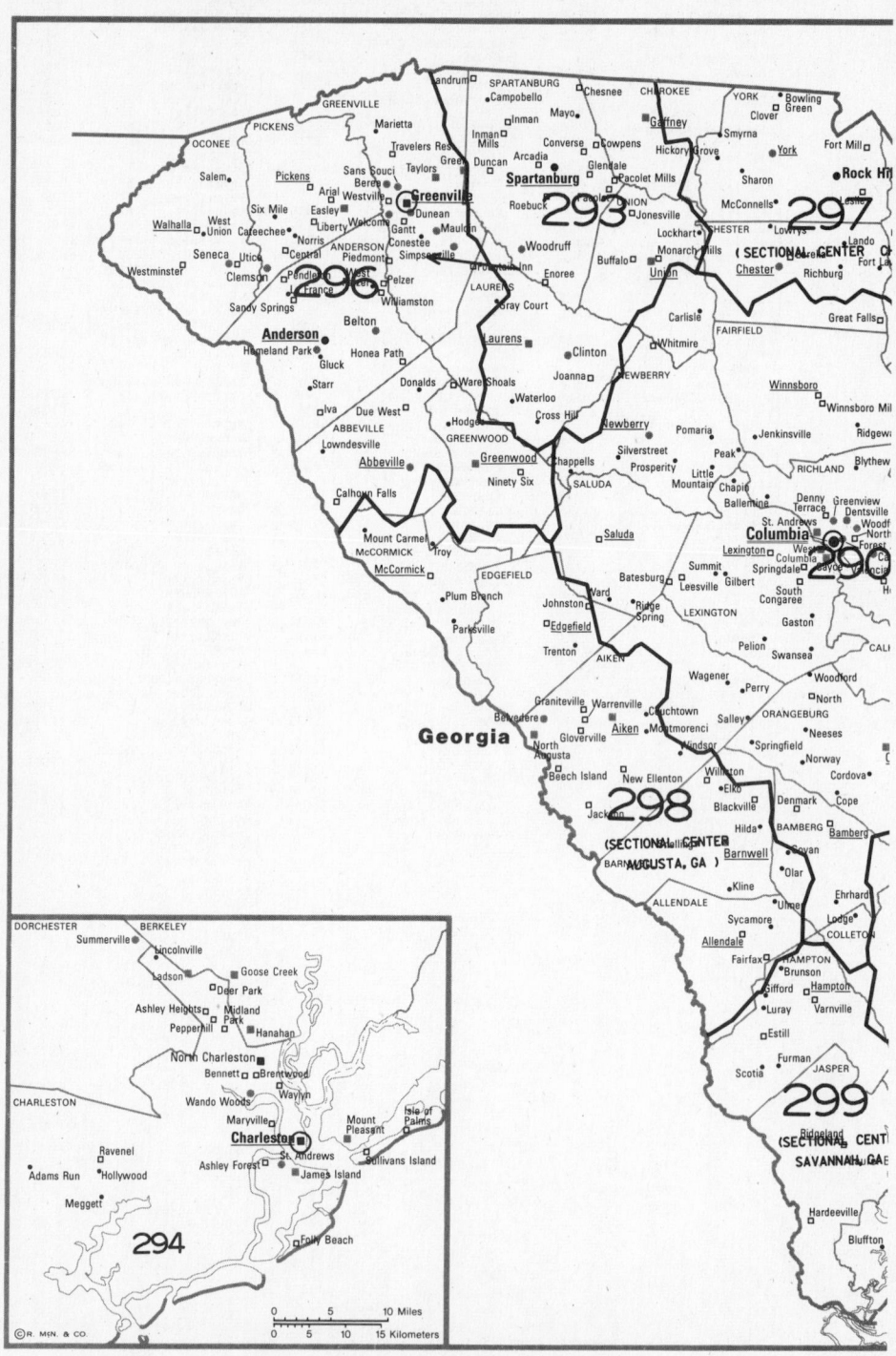

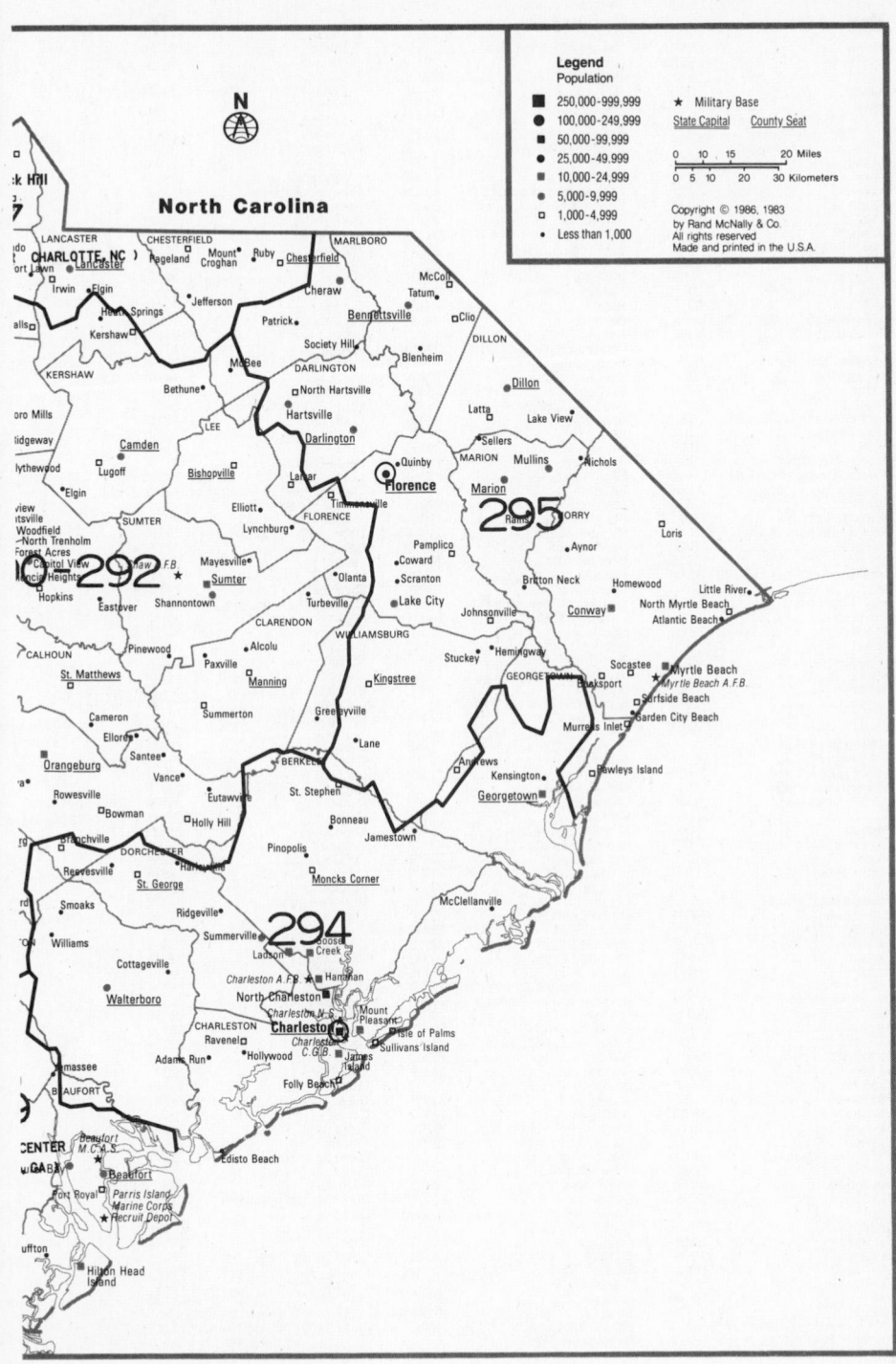

Legend
Population
■ 250,000-999,999
● 100,000-249,999
■ 50,000-99,999
● 25,000-49,999
■ 10,000-24,999
● 5,000-9,999
□ 1,000-4,999
· Less than 1,000

★ Military Base

State Capital   County Seat

0 10 15   20 Miles
0 5 10 20   30 Kilometers

	ZIP
Abbeville	29620
Abney	29067
Academy Acres	29488
Adamsburg	29379
Adams Run	29426
Adamsville	29570
Adger	29180
Adrian	29526
Aiken	29801-04
For specific Aiken Zip Codes call (803) 648-2351, or your local postmaster.	
Aiken Estates	29803
Aiken West	29801
Alcolu	29001
Alcot	29010
Allen	29511
Allendale	29810
Allendale Correctional Institute	29827
Allsbrook	29569
Alvin	29479
Anderson	29621-25
For specific Anderson Zip Codes call (803) 226-1595, or your local postmaster.	
Anderson Mall (Part of Anderson)	29621
Andrews	29510
Angelus	29718
Angle Siding	29902
Anne Village	29440
Ansel	29651
Antioch (Kershaw County)	29020
Antioch (Lancaster County)	29720
Antreville	29655
Appleton	29810
Appleton Mills	29625
Aragon Mills (Part of Rock Hill)	29730
Arcadia	29320
Arcadia Lakes	29206
Arial	29640
Ariel Crossroads	29574
Arkwright	29301
Arlington	29651
Armenia	29706
Arthurtown	29201
Asbury	29340
Ashepoo	29446
Ashland	29010
Ashleigh	29817
Ashley Forest	29407
Ashley Hall (Part of Charleston)	29401
Ashley Heights	29405
Ashley Junction (Part of North Charleston)	29406
Ashton	29082
Ashwood	29010
Aspen Heights	29646
Atkins	29080
Atlantic Beach	29582
Auburn	29550
Augusta Road (Part of Greenville)	29604
Avondale	29407
Awendaw	29429
Aynor	29511
Badham	29471
Baileys Landing	29936
Baker Crossroads	29569
Bald Rock	29379
Baldwin	29706
Ballentine	29002
Balltown	29801
Bamberg	29003
Barkersville	29916
Barksdale	29360
Barnes	29655
Barnwell	29812
Barrineau	29560
Bartell Crossroads	29554
Barton	29827
Bascomville	29729
Batesburg	29006
Bath	29816
Baton Rouge	29706
Baxter Forks	29569
Bayboro	29569
Bay Shores	29665
Bay Springs	29584
Bay View	29204
Beaufort	29901-05
For specific Beaufort Zip Codes call (803) 524-4746, or your local postmaster.	
Beaufort Marine Corps Air Station	29904
Beckhamville	29055
Beech Island	29842
Bel-Clear Heights	29841

	ZIP
Beldoc	29836
Belle Isle Gardens	29440
Belle Meade (Greenville County)	29603
Belle Meade (Lexington County)	29172
Bellinger	29927
Bells	29475
Belmont	29203
Belton	29627
Belvedere (Aiken County)	29841
Belvedere (Richland County)	29204
Ben Avon	29302
Bendale (Part of Columbia)	29203
Beneventum	29440
Bennett	29405
Bennettsville	29512
Bent Tree	29678
Berea	29611
Berlin	29137
Bethany	29710
Bethera	29430
Bethesda	29584
Bethune	29009
Beufordtown	29453
Beverly Hills	29445
Beverly Woods	29301
Bingham	29565
Birdtown Crossroads	29550
Bishopville	29010
Blackjack	29180
Blacks	29166
Blacksburg	29702
Blackstock	29014
Blackville	29817
Blair	29015
Blakedale	29649
Blenheim	29516
Bloomingvale	29510
Bloomville	29102
Blossom	29583
Blue Heaven	29638
Blue Ridge Community Pre-Release Center	29609
Blue Town	29512
Bluff	29142
Bluff Estates	29209
Bluffton	29910
Blythewood	29016
Bob Jones University (Part of Greenville)	29614
Bob Marina	29163
Boiling Springs	29316
Bolentown	29115
Bon Aire	29902
Bon Air Terrace	29150
Bonham	29379
Bonneau	29431
Bonneau Beach	29431
Bonniview Estates	29803
Boones Creek	29676
Bordeaux	29835
Borden	29017
Boulder Bluff	29445
Bounty Land	29678
Bowling Green	29703
Bowman	29018
Bowyer	29059
Boyden Arbor	29206
Boykin (Kershaw County)	29128
Boykin (Marlboro County)	28343
Bradley	29819
Bradleyville	29841
Branchville	29432
Brand	29360
Brandon	29611
Branwood (Part of Greenville)	29610
Brasstown	29658
Brattonsville	29726
Brazen Crossroads	29583
Breeze Hill (Part of Burnettown)	29834
Breezewood	29819
Brentwood	29405
Brewerton	29692
Briarcliffe Acres	29572
Briarcreek	29340
Brighton	29922
Brighton Beach	29910
Brightsville	28343
Bristow	29516
Britton	29153
Brittons Neck	29546
Broad Street (Part of Sumter)	29150
Broadway Lake	29621
Brock	29691
Brock Circle	29654
Brockington	29556
Brogdon	29150

	ZIP
Brookdale	29115
Brook Forest	29605
Brook Green Park	29501
Brookhaven Estates	29801
Brooklyn	29720
Brooksville	29582
Brownsville (Dorchester County)	29483
Brownsville (Marlboro County)	29516
Brownway	29526
Bruner	29061
Brunson	29911
Brunsons Crossroads	29554
Bryans Crossroads	29590
Buckeye Forest	29377
Buck Hall	29429
Buckingham Landing	29928
Bucksport	29526
Bucksville	29526
Buffalo (McCormick County)	29835
Buffalo (Union County)	29321
Buford	29720
Buford Crossroads	29720
Bufords Bridge	29843
Bullock Creek	29742
Bunker Hill	29536
Burgess	29576
Burnettown	29834
Burnt Church Crossroads	29474
Burton	29902
Bynum	29556
Byrd	29477
Byrds Crossroads	28114
Cades	29518
Caesars Head	28718
Caldwell Street (Part of Rock Hill)	29731
Calhoun (Part of Clemson)	29631
Calhoun Falls	29628
Callison	29819
Camden	29020
Cameron	29030
Campbell Work Release Center	29210
Camp Creek	29720
Camp Croft	29302
Campobello	29322
Campton	29349
Canaan (Orangeburg County)	29038
Canaan (Spartanburg County)	29302
Canadys	29433
Cane Savannah	29154
Canterbury	29673
Capitol (Part of Columbia)	29211
Capitol View	29209
Carlisle	29031
Carmel	29058
Carolina Circle	29488
Caromi Village	29456
Carters Crossroads	29554
Cartersville	29161
Carver Heights	29204
Carvers Bay	29554
Cash	29520
Cashville	29388
Cassatt	29032
Catarrah	29718
Catawba	29704
Cateechee	29667
Catholic Hill	29488
Cave	29810
Cayce	29033
Cedar Grove	29526
Cedar Hill	29835
Cedar Springs	29455
Cedar Terrace	29209
Celriver	29732
Cementon	29059
Centenary	29519
Center Crossroads	29554
Centerville (Anderson County)	29621
Centerville (Dillon County)	29565
Central	29630
Central Pacolet	29372
Challedon	29210
Chaparral Ranches	29461
Chapin	29036
Chappells	29037
Charleston	29401-25
For specific Charleston Zip Codes call (803) 745-4350, or your local postmaster.	
Charleston Heights (Part of North Charleston)	29405*
	29415†
Charles Towne Square (Part of North Charleston)	29406
Chartwell	29210

	ZIP
Cheddar	29627
Cheraw	29520
Cherokee	29302
Cherokee Falls	29702
Cherokee Forest	29687
Cherokee Gardens	29678
Cherry Grove Beach (Part of North Myrtle Beach)	29582
Cherry Hill Estates	29902
Cherry Road (Part of Rock Hill)	29732
Cherryvale	29154
Chesnee	29323
Chester	29706
Chesterfield	29709
Chestnut Hills	29605
Chickasaw Point	29693
Chicora Place (Part of North Charleston)	29405
Choppee	29440
Citadel (Part of Charleston)	29409
Citadel Mall (Part of Charleston)	29407
City View	29611
Claremont	29150
Clarks Hill	29821
Claussen	29505
Clayton	29015
Clearmont	29693
Clear Pond	29003
Clearspring	29681
Clearwater	29822
Cleburne	29440
Clemson	29631-34
For specific Clemson Zip Codes call (803) 654-2531, or your local postmaster.	
Clemson University	29631
Cleora	29824
Cleveland	29635
Clifton	29324
Clinton	29325
Clio	29525
Clover	29710
Clubhouse Crossroads (Dorchester County)	29472
Club House Crossroads (Lexington County)	29054
Clyde	29101
Coastal (Part of North Myrtle Beach)	29582
Coastal Work Release Center	29405
Cochrantown	29526
Cokesbury	29653
Cold Point	29360
Coldstream	29210
College Acres	29803
Colliers	29838
Colonial Heights	29902
Colonial Village	29715
Columbia	29201-92
For specific Columbia Zip Codes call (803) 733-4646, or your local postmaster.	
Columbia Bible College	29203
Columbia Mall	29204
Coneross	29693
Conestee	29636
Congaree	29044
Connecticut Park	29341
Converse	29329
Conway	29526-27
For specific Conway Zip Codes call (803) 248-6313, or your local postmaster.	
Cooks Crossroads	29644
Cool Branch	29031
Cooley Springs	29323
Cool Spring	29511
Coosaw	29940
Coosawhatchie	29912
Cope	29038
Cordesville	29434
Cordova	29039
Cornwell	29014
Coronaca	29649
Cottageville	29435
Couchtown	29801
Country Club Estates	29730
Country Homes	29646
Courtenay	29678
Coward	29530
Cowpens	29330
Crafts-Farrow	29203
Crane Forest	29203
Crescent	29388
Crescent Beach (Part of North Myrtle Beach)	29582
Creston	29030
Crestview	29501
Crocketts Crossroads	29720

	ZIP
Crocketville	29913
Crooks Crossroads	29554
Crosland Park (Part of Aiken)	29801
Cross	29436
Cross Anchor	29331
Cross Anchor Correctional Institution	29335
Crosscreek Mall (Part of Greenwood)	29646
Cross Hill	29332
Cross Keys	29379
Crosswell	29640
Cummings	29944
Cusaac Crossroads	29541
Cypress Crossroads	29069
Cypress Fork	29001
Dacusville	29640
Daisy	29569
Dale	29914
Dalewood	29653
Dalzell	29040
Danwood	29541
Darlington	29532
For specific Darlington Zip Codes call (803) 393-3223, or your local postmaster.	
Daufuskie Island	29915
Davis Crossroads	29148
Davis Station	29041
Deans	29684
De Bordieu Colony	29440
Deer Park	29405
DeKalb	29175
Delemar Crossroads	29470
Delmar	29070
Delphos	29745
Delta	29178
Denmark	29042
Denny Terrace	29203
Dentsville	29204
Denver	29625
Deweys Hill (Part of North Charleston)	29406
Dillon	29536
Dinkins	29150
Dinkins Mill	29128
Dixiana	29172
Dixie	29720
Dog Bluff	29511
Donalds	29638
Dongola	29526
Dorange	29471
Dorchester	29437
Dorchester Estates	29485
Dorchester Terrace	29405
Douglass	29014
Dovesville	29540
Drake	29516
Drawdy	29488
Drayton (Charleston County)	29407
Drayton (Spartanburg County)	29333
Draytonville	29340
Drexel Lake Hills	29206
Dry Branch	29803
Dubose	29150
Du Bose Crossroads	29153
Du Bose Park	29020
Dudley	29728
Due West	29639
Duford	29581
Dunbar (Georgetown County)	29440
Dunbar (Marlboro County)	29525
Duncan	29334
Dunean	29601
Dunes	29577
Dupont	29407
Dusty Bend (Part of Camden)	29020
Dutch Fork	29210
Dutchman	29374
Dutchman Correctional Institution	29335
Dutch Square	29210
Dutch Village	29063
Dyson	29666
Eadytown	29468
Earle Homes	29624
Earles	29510
Earles Grove	29678
Earlwood Park	29532
Early Branch	29916
Easley	29640-42
For specific Easley Zip Codes call (803) 859-9411, or your local postmaster.	
East Bay (Part of Charleston)	29403*
	29413†

	ZIP
East Gaffney	29340
East Gantt	29609
East Greer	29651
East Hartsville	29550
Eastmont	29209
Eastover	29044
East Side Acres	29488
East Sumter	29150
East View	29669
Eau Claire (Part of Columbia)	29203
Ebenezer (Florence County)	29501
Ebenezer (York County)	29732
Eden	29645
Edenwood	29033
Edgefield	29824
Edgemoor	29712
Edgewood (Part of Columbia)	29204
Edisto	29038
Edisto Beach	29438
Edisto Island	29438
Edmund	29073
Effingham	29541
Ehrhardt	29081
Elgin (Kershaw County)	29045
Elgin (Lancaster County)	29720
Elko	29826
Elliott	29046
Elloree	29047
Elmwood Park	29803
Emanuelville	29536
Emerald Place	29646
Emerald Valley	29210
Emory	29138
Enchanted Hills	29678
Enoree	29335
Epworth	29666
Equinox Mill	29625
Estill	29918
Eureka	29847
Eureka Mill	29706
Eutaw Springs	29048
Eutawville	29048
Evans Crossroad	29720
Evergreen	29541
Evergreen Hills	29625
Fairfax	29827
Fairfield (Part of Hilton Head Island)	29928
Fairfield Terrace	29203
Fair Forest (Greenwood County)	29646
Fairforest (Spartanburg County)	29336
Fairmont	29301
Fair Play	29643
Fairview (Greenville County)	29651
Fairview (Oconee County)	29678
Fairview Crossroads	29070
Farrel Crossroads	29432
Farrow Terrace	29203
Fechtig	29916
Federal (Florence County)	29503
Federal (Greenville County)	29603
Felderville	29047
Fenwick Hills	29455
Ferndale (Charleston County)	29406
Ferndale (Spartanburg County)	29301
Filbert	29710
Fingerville	29338
Finklea	29569
Finland	29042
Fisher Hill	29520
Five Forks (Anderson County)	29621
Five Forks (Greenville County)	29681
Five Forks (Pickens County)	29657
Five Points (Oconee County)	29693
Five Points (Richland County)	29205
Flamingo Acres	29512
Flat Rock	29624
Flat Shoals	29691
Fletcher	29570
Florence	29501-06
For specific Florence Zip Codes call (803) 662-9501, or your local postmaster.	
Florence Mall (Part of Florence)	29501
Floyd Dale	29542
Floyds Crossroads	29581
Folly Beach	29439
Folly Field (Part of Hilton Head Island)	29928
Forest	29437

*Area Zip Code   † Post Office Boxes

	ZIP
Forest Acres (Oconee County)	29691
Forest Acres (Richland County)	29206
Forest Beach (Part of Hilton Head Island)	29928
Forestbrook	29577
Forest Lake (Richland County)	29206
Forest Lake (York County)	29715
Foreston	29102
Forest Park	29642
Fork	29543
Fork Shoals	29645
Forrest Hills (Part of Latta)	29565
Fort Lawn	29714
Fort Mill	29715*
	29716†
Fort Motte	29135
Fountain Inn	29644
Fountain Lake	29048
Four Holes	29115
Four Mile	29464
Fowler	29556
Foxtown	29801
Foxwood Hills	29693
Francis Marion College	29506
Fraserville	29585
Friarsgate (Part of Irmo)	29063
Friendfield	29591
Friendship	29678
Fripp Island	29920
Fruit Hill	29138
Furman	29921
Furman University	29613
Gable	29051
Gadsden	29052
Gaffney	29340-42
For specific Gaffney Zip Codes call (803) 489-7144, or your local postmaster.	
Gaillard Crossroads	29040
Galavon	29536
Galaxy	29209
Galivants Ferry	29544
Gantt	29605
Gapway	29574
Garden City	29576
Garden City Beach	29576
Gardens Corner	29945
Garnett	29922
Gaston	29053
Gem Lake Estates	29801
Georgetown (Georgetown County)	29440-42
For specific Georgetown Zip Codes call (803) 546-5515, or your local postmaster.	
Georgetown (Pickens County)	29640
Gifford	29923
Gilbert	29054
Gillisonville	29936
Givhans	29472
Glass Hill	29526
Glendale	29346
Glenn Springs	29374
Gloverville	29828
Gluck	29624
Glymphville	29126
Godsey	29666
Golden Grove	29673
Golightly	29302
Gooches	29720
Goodwins Crossroads	29325
Goose Creek	29445
Goretown	29569
Gourdin	29564
Govan	29843
Gowensville	29322
Grace	29720
Grahamville (Horry County)	29526
Grahamville (Jasper County)	29936
Gramling	29348
Graniteville	29829
Graves	29440
Gray Court	29645
Grays	29916
Grays Hill	29902
Great Falls	29055
Greeleyville	29056
Green Bay	29450
Greenbriar	29678
Greenbrier	29180
Green Pond (Colleton County)	29446
Green Pond (Spartanburg County)	29388
Green Sea	29545
Greenview	29203

	ZIP
Greenville	29601-16
For specific Greenville Zip Codes call (803) 282-8401, or your local postmaster.	
Greenwood	29646-49
For specific Greenwood Zip Codes call (803) 223-2321, or your local postmaster.	
Greenwood Correctional Center	29646
Greenwood Shores	29666
Greer	29650-52
For specific Greer Zip Codes call (803) 877-6423, or your local postmaster.	
Grenadier	29210
Gresham	29546
Grice Ferry	29574
Grove Park	29501
Grover	29447
Guess	29727
Gurley	29569
Guthries	29726
Hagood	29128
Hamburg (Part of North Augusta)	29841
Hamer	29547
Hammond	29624
Hammond Crossroads	29135
Hampton	29924
Hampton Drive	29488
Hampton Heights	29687
Hampton Park Terrace (Part of Charleston)	29403
Hanahan	29406*
	29410†
Hannah	29583
Hanover Hills	29678
Harbison	29212
Harbour Town (Part of Hilton Head Island)	29928
Hardeeville	29927
Harleyville	29448
Harmony (Edgefield County)	29832
Harmony (York County)	29704
Harmony Hill	29341
Harris	29646
Hartsville	29550
Harveytown	29365
Haskell Heights	29203
Hayne	29301
Hayne Junction	29301
Hazelwood Acres	29209
H & B Village (Part of Hampton)	29924
Heatherwood	29640
Heathley Wood (Part of Sumter)	29150
Heath Springs	29058
Hebron	29518
Helena	29108
Hemingway	29554
Hendersonville	29488
Hendricks Corner	29526
Hibernia	29105
Hickory Grove (Florence County)	29501
Hickory Grove (Horry County)	29526
Hickory Grove (York County)	29717
Hickory Hill	29446
Hickory Tavern	29645
High Point	29627
Hilda	29813
Hillcrest (Part of Spartanburg)	29318
Hillcrest Acres (Part of Belton)	29627
Hillcrest Heights (Part of Williamston)	29697
Hillcrest Mall (Part of Spartanburg)	29302
Hilton	29036
Hilton Head Island	29925-26
	29928
	29938
For specific Hilton Head Island Zip Codes call (803) 785-2179, or your local postmaster.	
Hobcaw Point	29464
Hodges	29653
Hollands Store	29684
Hollydale	29115
Holly Hill	29059
Holly Springs (Oconee County)	29693
Holly Springs (Spartanburg County)	29349
Hollywood (Charleston County)	29449
Hollywood (Saluda County)	29138

	ZIP
Hollywood Hills	29203
Holmsville	29563
Holtson Crossroads	29006
Homeland Park	29621
Homewood	29526
Homewood Park	29520
Honea Path	29654
Honey Hill	29479
Hoodtown	29742
Hopewell	29717
Hopkins	29061
Horatio	29062
Horeb	29180
Horrel Hill	29061
Horry	29511
Horsegall	29944
Howard	29569
Hudsontown	29477
Huger	29450
Hunley Park (Part of North Charleston)	29404
Huntington Estates	29841
Hyman	29583
Independents	29209
India Hook	29730
Indiantown	29554
Industrial (Part of Rock Hill)	29730
Ingleside	29356
Inman	29349
Inman Mills	29349
Irmo	29063
Irvines Landing	29649
Irwin	29720
Isgett Circle	29520
Islandton	29929
Isle of Palms	29451
Italy	29510
Iva	29655
Jackson	29831
Jacksonboro	29452
Jackson Mill (Part of Wellford)	29385
Jacksonville	29834
Jalapa	29108
James Island	29412*
	29422†
Jamestown (Berkeley County)	29453
Jamestown (Horry County)	29526
Jamison	29115
Jedburg	29483
Jefferson	29718
Jenkinsville	29065
Jennys	29827
Jericho	29426
Joanna	29351
Jocassee	29676
Johns Island	29455*
	29457†
Johnson City	29301
Johnson Crossroads	29809
Johnsonville	29555
Johnston	29832
Johnstown	29816
Johnsville	29481
Jones Crossroads (Aiken County)	29105
Jones Crossroads (Lancaster County)	29720
Jonesville	29353
Jordan	29102
Jordania	29678
Jordanville	29544
Judson	29611
Judson No. 2	29611
Juniper Bay	29526
Kathwood (Part of West Columbia)	29169
Kelly	29379
Kellytown	29550
Kelton	29353
Kemper	29563
Kensington	29440
Keowee (Abbeville County)	29654
Keowee (Oconee County)	29678
Kershaw	29067
Ketchuptown	29544
Kiawah Island	29455
Kilgore	29335
Killian	29203
Kinards	29355
King Circle	29720
Kingsburg	29555
Kings Creek	29719
Kingstree	29556
Kingswood	29210
Kirkland	29020
Kirkland Correctional Institute	29210
Kirksey	29848
Kitchings Mill	29137
Kittredge	29434

---

* Area Zip Code   † Post Office Boxes

	ZIP
Kline	29814
Klondike Crossroads	29526
Kneece	29006
Knightsville	29483
Knollwood Acres	29512
Knox	29706
Ladson	29456
La France	29656
Lake City	29560
Lake Forest (Greenville County)	29606
Lake Forest (Pickens County)	29640
Lake Forest Estates	29841
Lake Lanier	29356
Lakemont	29635
Lake Murray Shores	29070
Lake Shores	29649
Lakeview (Chester County)	29714
Lake View (Dillon County)	29563
Lakewood	29732
Lakewood Manor	29301
Lake Wylie	29710
Lamar	29069
Lambertown	29510
Lambs (Part of North Charleston)	29405
Lancaster	29720*
	29721†
Lancaster Mill	29720
Lando	29724
Landrum	29356
Landsford	29704
Lane	29564
Lanford	29335
Langley	29834
Larkin	29377
Lathem (Part of Easley)	29640
Latimer	29628
Latta	29565
Laurel Bay	29902
Laurens	29360
Leawood	29601
Lebanon (Anderson County)	29621
Lebanon (Fairfield County)	29180
Leeds	29031
Leesburg (Part of Columbia)	29209
Leesville	29070
Legareville	29455
Lena	29918
Leo	29560
Lesslie	29730
Lester	29512
Level Land	29655
Lewis	29706
Lewis Crossroads	29532
Lexington	29071-73
For specific Lexington Zip Codes call (803) 359-9355, or your local postmaster.	
Liberty	29657
Liberty Hill (Charleston County)	29406
Liberty Hill (Kershaw County)	29074
Liberty Hill (McCormick County)	29835
Lieber Correctional Institution	29472
Limehouse	29927
Limestone	29115
Lincoln Shire	29203
Lincolnville	29483
Lions Beach	29461
Litchfield Beach	29585
Little Africa	29323
Little Camden	29201
Little Chicago	29322
Little Eastatoe	29685
Little Mountain	29075
Little River	29566
Little Rock	29567
Little Texas	29690
Livingston	29076
Lobeco	29931
Lockhart	29364
Lockhart Junction	29353
Lodge	29082
Lone Star	29077
Long Bay Estates	29572
Long Branch	29853
Longcreek (Oconee County)	29658
Long Creek (Pickens County)	29640
Long Leaf	29488
Long Point	29569
Longs	29568
Longtown	29130
Loris	29569
Lowenstein Mills	29621
Lowndesville	29659

	ZIP
Lowrys	29706
Lucknow	29010
Lugoff	29078
Luray	29932
Lydia	29079
Lydia Mills	29325
Lykesland	29061
Lyman	29365
Lynchburg	29080
Lyndhurst	29812
Lynwood	29816
McAlister Square (Part of Greenville)	29607
Mac Arthurs Junction	29638
McBee	29101
McBeth	29431
McClellanville	29458
McColl	29570
McConnells	29726
McCormick	29835
McCormick Correctional Institution	29835
McCormick Crossroads	29536
McCutchen Crossroads	29010
McDonald	29440
MacDougall Youth Correction Center	29472
Macedonia	29330
McKellar Farms	29646
McKenzie Crossroads	29114
McPhersonville	29916
Maddens	29360
Madison (Aiken County)	29829
Madison (Oconee County)	29693
Magnolia Park	29853
Mallory	29565
Manning	29102
Manning Crossroads	29536
Manville	29010
Maple Crossroads	29526
Maplewood	29340
Marietta	29661
Marine Corps Air Station	29904
Marion	29571
Marlboro	29512
Mars Bluff	29506
Martin	29836
Maryville (Charleston County)	29407
Maryville (Georgetown County)	29440
Masons Crossroads	29621
Mathews (Part of Greenwood)	29646
Mathews Heights	29646
Mauldin	29662
Mayesville	29104
Mayfair	29687
Mayfair Mill (Part of Pickens)	29671
Mayo	29368
Mayo Mills	29368
Mayson	29138
Meadowlake	29203
Mechanicsville	29532
Meggett	29449
Melrose	29803
Merchant	29138
Middendorf	29550
Midland Park	29405
Midland Valley	29829
Midway (Bamberg County)	29003
Midway (Kershaw County)	29032
Midway (Lancaster County)	29720
Midway Crossroads	29554
Midway Village	29577
Miley	29933
Mill Creek	29163
Millers Crossroads	29838
Millett	29836
Mill Village (Part of Bennettsville)	29512
Millwood (Sumter County)	29150
Millwood (Williamsburg County)	29556
Millwood Gardens	29150
Milton	29325
Mink Point Plantation	29902
Minturn	29573
Mitchellville	29936
Mitford	29055
Modoc	29838
Monaghan	29611
Monarch Mill	29379
Moncks Corner	29461
Monetta	29105
Monroe Crossroads	29512
Montague	29601
Mont Clare	29532
Monticello	29106
Montmorenci	29839
Montrose	29520
Moore	29369

	ZIP
Moores Crossroads	29518
Moreland	29407
Morgan	29927
Morningside	29607
Morris Acres	29455
Moselle	29929
Mountain Brook	29209
Mountain Lakes	29706
Mountain Rest	29664
Mountain View	29323
Mount Carmel	29840
Mount Croghan	29727
Mount Gallagher	29692
Mount Holly	29445
Mount Olive	29581
Mount Pleasant	29464*
	29465†
Mount View	29687
Mountville	29370
Mt. Calvary	29536
Mulberry	29150
Mullins	29574
Murphy Estates	29841
Murrells Inlet	29576
Myrtle Beach	29572
	29575
	29577-78
For specific Myrtle Beach Zip Codes call (803) 626-9533, or your local postmaster.	
Myrtle Beach Air Force Base	29579
Myrtle Island	29910
Myrtle Square (Part of Myrtle Beach)	29577
Naval Hospital	29902
Naval Weapons	29445
Naval Weapons Station	29408
Neeses	29107
Nesmith	29580
Nevitt Forest	29621
Newberry	29108
New Cut	29720
New Easley Highway (Part of Greenville)	29611
New Ellenton	29809
New Holland Crossroads	29006
New Hope	29530
Newport	29732
New Prospect	29349
New Road	29945
Newry	29665
Newtonville	29512
New Town	29536
New Zion	29111
Neyles	29488
Nichols	29581
Nicholson Village	29801
Nimmons	29685
Nine Times	29685
Ninety Six	29666
Nixons Crossroads	29566
Nixonville	29526
Nixville	29944
Norris	29667
North	29112
North Aiken (Part of Aiken)	29801
North Anderson (Part of Anderson)	29623
North Augusta	29841
Northbridge (Part of Charleston)	29407
North Bridge Terrace (Part of Charleston)	29405
North Charleston	29406
	29418-20
For specific North Charleston Zip Codes call (803) 569-2610, or your local postmaster.	
North Conway (Part of Conway)	29526
North Forest Beach (Part of Hilton Head Island)	29928
Northgate (Cherokee County)	29341
Northgate (Florence County)	29501
North Greenwood	29649
North Hartsville	29550
Northlake	29621
North Litchfield Beach	29585
North Mullins (Part of Mullins)	29574
North Myrtle Beach	29582
	29597-98
For specific North Myrtle Beach Zip Codes call (803) 249-1023, or your local postmaster.	
North Pacolet	29322
North Santee	29458
Northside Correctional Center	29303

* Area Zip Code   **† Post Office Boxes**

	ZIP
North Summerville (Part of Summerville)	29483
North Trenholm	29206
North Winyah Heights (Part of Georgetown)	29440
Northwood Estates	29405
Northwoods Mall (Part of Charleston)	29405
Norway	29113
Oakdale (Cherokee County)	29330
Oak Dale (Clarendon County)	29111
Oakdale (Florence County)	29501
Oakdale (York County)	29730
Oak Grove (Dillon County)	29565
Oak Grove (Lexington County)	29073
Oak Hill	29801
Oakland (Beaufort County)	29902
Oakland (Sumter County)	29150
Oakland Crossroads	29547
Oakland Mill (Part of Newberry)	29108
Oakley	29461
Oak Ridge	29058
Oaks Crossroads	29142
Oakvale	29673
Oakway	29693
Oakwood	29801
Oatland	29440
Oats	29069
Ocean Drive Beach (Part of North Myrtle Beach)	29582
Ocean Forest (Part of Myrtle Beach)	29577
Oceanview	29412
Oconee Estates	29678
Oconee Station	29691
Ogden	29730
Olanta	29114
Olar	29843
Old House	29936
Old Madison	29693
Olympia	29201
Ora	29360
Orangeburg	29115-17
For specific Orangeburg Zip Codes call (803) 536-1720, or your local postmaster.	
Orchard Park (Part of Greenville)	29615
Orr Mill	29621
Orrville	29621
Orum	29583
Osborn	29426
Osceola	29744
Oswego	29150
Otranto	29405
Outland	29554
Owings	29645
Oyster Point	29412
Pacolet	29372
Pacolet Mills	29373
Pacolet Park (Part of Pacolet Mills)	29373
Padgetts	29481
Pageland	29728
Palmer Work Release Center	29501
Palmetto	29532
Palmetto Estates	29902
Palmetto Fort	29464
Pamplico	29583
Panola (Clarendon County)	29125
Panola (Greenwood County)	29646
Paramount Park	29605
Paris	29609
Parker	29611
Parkers Ferry	29426
Parkersville	29585
Park Place	29609
Parksville	29844
Parler	29142
Parr	29065
Parris Island	29905
Parris Island Marine Corps Recruit Depot	29905
Parrot Point	29412
Patrick	29584
Pauline	29374
Pawleys Island	29585
Paxville	29102
Peach Valley	29303
Peak	29122
Pecan Terrace	29605
Pecan Way Terrace (Part of Orangeburg)	29115
Pee Dee	29571
Pelham	29651
Pelion	29123
Pelzer	29669
Pendleton	29670

	ZIP
Peniel Crossroads	29161
Pepperhill (Part of North Charleston)	29418
Percival Crossroads	29693
Perry	29124
Perry Correctional Institution	29669
Philip	29464
Phoenix	29646
Pickens	29671
Pickett Post	29691
Piedmont	29673
Piercetown	29697
Pierpont	29407
Pimlico	29461
Pine Grove (Darlington County)	29532
Pine Grove (Hampton County)	29924
Pinehaven (Part of Charleston)	29405
Pinehurst (Dorchester County)	29483
Pinehurst (Greenwood County)	29646
Pine Island	29577
Pineland (Charleston County)	29429
Pineland (Jasper County)	29934
Pineridge (Darlington County)	29101
Pineridge (Lexington County)	29172
Pine Valley	29210
Pineville	29468
Pinewood (Spartanburg County)	29303
Pinewood (Sumter County)	29125
Pinopolis	29469
Pisgah	29128
Plantation Pines	29180
Plantersville	29440
Playcards	29569
Plaza (Part of Sumter)	29150
Pleasantburg (Part of Greenville)	29606
Pleasant Grove	29671
Pleasant Hill (Georgetown County)	29554
Pleasant Hill (Lancaster County)	29058
Pleasant Lane	29824
Pleasant Valley	29605
Pleasant View	29569
Plum Branch	29845
Pocotaligo	29945
Poe	29609
Polaris Missile Facility Atlantic	29408
Polk Village	29902
Pomaria	29126
Pontiac	29045
Poovey Farm	29720
Poplar Springs	29369
Port Royal	29935
Port Royal Plantation (Part of Hilton Head Island)	29928
Poston	29555
Powdersville	29673
Pregnall	29437
Primus	29720
Princeton	29654
Pritchardville	29910
Promised Land	29819
Prospect Crossroads	29560
Prosperity	29127
Providence	29059
Pumpkintown	29671
Puncheon Creek	29510
Purysburg Landing	29927
Quail Hollow	29169
Quinby	29506
Quinby Estates (Part of Quinby)	29506
Quinby Forest (Part of Quinby)	29506
Rabon Crossroads	29501
Rains	29589
Rantowles	29449
Ravenel	29470
Ravenwood (Part of Forest Acres)	29206
Red Bank	29073
Red Bank Landing	29048
Red Bluff Crossroads	29569
Red Hill (Horry County)	29526
Red Hill (Horry County; rural)	29544
Red Hill (Lee County)	29020
Red Top	29455
Reevesville	29471
Rehobeth	29544
Reid Park	29520

	ZIP
Reidville	29375
Rembert	29128
Remount (Part of North Charleston)	29406
Renfrew	29690
Renno	29325
Retreat	29693
Return	29678
Reynold	29817
Rhems	29440
Ribault Park (Part of Beaufort)	29902
Richburg	29729
Rich Hill Crossroads	29058
Richland	29675
Richland Mall (Part of Forest Acres)	29206
Richland Springs	29138
Richmond Hills	29609
Richtex	29180
Ridgecrest	29801
Ridgeland	29912
	29936
For specific Ridgeland Zip Codes call (803) 726-5528, or your local postmaster.	
Ridge Spring	29129
Ridgeville	29472
Ridgeway	29130
Ridgewood (Charleston County)	29456
Ridgewood (Oconee County)	29678
Ridgewood (Richland County)	29203
Rimini	29131
Ringle Heights	29440
Rion	29132
Ritter	29488
Riverdale	29536
River Falls	29661
Riverland	29412
Riverland Terrace	29412
Rivermont	29210
Rivers General Mail Facility (Part of North Charleston)	29411†
	29423*
Riverside (Abbeville County)	29692
Riverside (Anderson County)	29624
Riverside (Greenville County)	29611
Riverside (Lancaster County)	29720
Riverside Park	29210
Riverview	29715
Robat	29379
Robbins	29831
Robbins Circle	29706
Robertville	29922
Robinson	29101
Rock Bluff	29556
Rockbridge	29206
Rock Hill (Fairfield County)	29065
Rock Hill (York County)	29730-34
For specific Rock Hill Zip Codes call (803) 327-4187, or your local postmaster.	
Rockton	29180
Rockville	29487
Rocky Bottom	29685
Roddy	29704
Rodman	29706
Roebuck	29376
Rogers Fallout	29544
Rosehill Park	29340
Roseida	29902
Rosinville	29477
Round O	29474
Rowell	29704
Rowesville	29133
Ruby	29741
Ruffin	29475
Russellville	29476
St. Andrews (Charleston County)	29407*
	29417†
St. Andrews (Richland County)	29210
St. Charles	29104
St. George	29477
St. Helena Island	29920
St. Julian	29048
St. Matthews	29135
St. Paul	29148
St. Paul Forks	29526
St. Stephen	29479
Salak	29646
Salem (Florence County)	29583
Salem (Oconee County)	29676
Salem Crossroads	29015
Salley	29137

	ZIP
Salters	29590
Saluca	29646
Saluda	29138
Saluda Gardens (Part of West Columbia)	29169
Saluda Terrace (Part of West Columbia)	29169
Samaria	29006
Sampit	29440
Sanders Corner	29062
Sandridge (Berkeley County)	29059
Sand Ridge (Horry County)	29526
Sandwood	29206
Sandy Flat	29687
Sandy Ridge	29666
Sandy Springs	29677
Sans Souci	29609
Sans Souci Heights	29609
Santee	29142
Santee Circle	29461
Santuc	29379
Sardinia	29143
Sardis	29161
Satchel Ford Terrace	29206
Savannah Bluff	29526
Sawyerdale	29112
Saxon	29301
Saylors Crossroads	29627
Scanlonville	29464
Schofield	29843
Schultz Hill (Part of North Augusta)	29841
Scotia	29939
Scottsville	29104
Scranton	29591
Seabrook	29940
Seabrook Island	29455
Sea Pines (Part of Hilton Head Island)	29928
Seaside	29412
Secessionville	29412
Sedalia	29379
Seiglers Crossroads	29801
Seigling	29810
Seivern	29164
Sellers	29592
Selma	29536
Seneca	29678*
	29679†
Seneca Landing	29678
Seven Mile (Part of North Charleston)	29405
Seven Oaks	29210
Shady Rest (Part of Bennettsville)	29512
Shalimar	29341
Shannon Hill	29010
Shannontown	29150
Sharon	29742
Shaw Air Force Base	29152
Shaw Heights	29152
Sheldon	29941
Shell	29526
Shell Point	29902
Shepard	29032
Sheppard Park	29483
Sherwood Acres	29301
Shiloh (Oconee County)	29678
Shiloh (Sumter County)	29080
Shiloh Estates	29678
Shipyard Plantation (Part of Hilton Head Island)	29928
Shirley	29922
Shoals Junction	29638
Shulerville	29479
Silver	29102
Silver Bluff Estates	29803
Silverstreet	29145
Simpson	29130
Simpsonville	29681
Singing Pines	29678
Singleton	29135
Six Mile	29682
Six Points	29801
Skyview Terrace	29210
Slansville	29483
Slater	29683
Slater-Marietta	29661
Slighs	29127
Smallwood (Fairfield County)	29130
Smallwood (Laurens County)	29325
Smith	29730
Smithboro	29574
Smith Mills	29554
Smoaks	29481
Smyrna	29743
Snelling	29812
Sniders Crossroads	29475
Snowden	29464

	ZIP
Socastee	29577
Society Hill	29593
South Anderson (Part of Anderson)	29624
South Congaree	29172
Southern Meadows	29678
Southern Shops	29303
South Forest Estates	29605
South Greenwood (Part of Greenwood)	29646
South Hartsville	29550
South Hills	29379
South Lynchburg	29080
South Mullins (Part of Mullins)	29574
South Park (Part of Florence)	29505
Southpark Shopping Center (Part of Florence)	29505
Southside	29505
South Sumter	29150
South Windermere (Part of Charleston)	29407
Soviet Union	29693
Spartanburg	29301-18
For specific Spartanburg Zip Codes call (803) 585-0301, or your local postmaster.	
Spaulding Heights	29501
Spiderweb	29841
Spring Branch	29571
Springdale (Lancaster County)	29720
Springdale (Lexington County)	29170
Springfield (Orangeburg County)	29146
Springfield (Spartanburg County)	29349
Spring Hill (Lee County)	29128
Spring Hill (Richland County)	29177
Springmaid Beach	29577
Spring Mills	29067
Springtown	29481
Spring Valley	29646
Springwood	29204
Stallsville	29485
Stark Terrace	29203
Starmount	29172
Starr	29684
Startex	29377
Stateburg	29150
State College (Part of Orangeburg)	29115
State Farm	29128
Steedman	29070
Stiefeltown	29851
Stokes	29488
Stokes Bridge	29010
Stomp Springs	29325
Stoneboro	29058
Stoney Hill	29127
Stono	29412
Stover	29014
Stratford Hall	29803
Stratton Capers	29405
Strawberry	29461
Stuart Point	29940
Stuckey	29554
Sullivans Island	29482
Summer Hill (Part of North Augusta)	29841
Summerland (Part of Batesburg)	29006
Summerton	29148
Summerville	29483-85
For specific Summerville Zip Codes call (803) 873-3571, or your local postmaster.	
Summit	29070
Sumter	29150-51
	29153-54
For specific Sumter Zip Codes call (803) 773-9312, or your local postmaster.	
Sunnyside (Part of Greer)	29651
Sunset	29685
Surfside Beach	29575*
	29587†
Suttons	29510
Swansea	29160
Sweden	29042
Sweetwater (Aiken County)	29841
Sweetwater (Barnwell County)	29812
Switzer	29369
Switzerland	29936
Sycamore	29846
Syracuse	29532
Talatha	29803
Tall Pines	29536

	ZIP
Tamassee	29686
Tanglewood (Beaufort County)	29902
Tanglewood (Greenville County)	29611
Tanglewood (Oconee County)	29678
Tanglewood (Orangeburg County)	29115
Tarboro	29943
Tatum	29594
Taxahaw	29067
Taylors	29687
Tega Cay	29715
Temperance Hill	29571
Ten Mile (Part of Charleston)	29406
Ten Mile (Charleston County)	29464
Terrells Crossroads	29518
Texas	29477
The Farms (Part of Hanahan)	29410
The Groves (Part of Mount Pleasant)	29464
The Meadows	29678
Thor	29123
Three Trees	29412
Tibwin	29458
Tifton	29532
Tigerville	29688
Tillman	29943
Timberlake	29678
Timmonsville	29161
Tirzah	29745
Toddville	29526
Tokeena Crossroads	29678
Toney Creek	29627
Townville	29689
Toxaway (Part of Anderson)	29621
Tradesville	29720
Tranquil Acres	29456
Travelers Rest	29690
Trenton	29847
Triangle (Part of Belton)	29627
Trio	29595
Troy	29848
Tuckertown	29031
Tugtown	29059
Turbeville	29162
Twin Lake Hill	29209
Tyler	29536
Ulmer	29849
Una (Darlington County)	29069
Una (Spartanburg County)	29378
Union	29379
Union Bleachery	29609
Union Crossroads	29111
Unity	28173
University (Part of Columbia)	29208
University of South Carolina at Coastal Carolina	29526
Utica	29678
Valencia Heights	29205
Valley Falls	29303
Vance	29163
Van Wyck	29744
Varnville	29944
Vaucluse	29850
Verdery	29819
Victor Mills (Part of Greer)	29651
Village Creek	29678
Virginia Acres	29803
Voorhees College	29042
Waddell Gardens (Part of Beaufort)	29902
Wade Hampton	29607
Wadmalaw Island	29487
Wadsworth	29301
Wagener	29164
Walden Correctional Institute	29210
Walhalla	29691
Wallace	29596
Walnut Grove	29374
Walterboro	29488
Wampee	29568
Wando	29492
Wando Woods	29405
Ward	29166
Ware Place	29669
Ware Shoals	29692
Warren Crossroads	29470
Warrenville	29851
Warsaw	29510
Wateree	29044
Waterford Estates	29440
Waterloo	29384
Watkins Store	29803
Watson Village (Part of Anderson)	29624

	ZIP		ZIP		ZIP
Watts Mills	29360	White Hall (Colleton County)	29446	Windwood	29461
Waverly Mills	29585	Whitehall (Greenwood		Windy Hill	29506
Waylyn	29405	County)	29646	Windy Hill Beach (Part of	
Wedgefield	29168	Whitehall (Lexington		North Myrtle Beach)	29582
Welcome (Anderson		County)	29210	Winnsboro	29180
County)	29621	White Oak	29176	Winnsboro Mills	29180
Welcome (Greenville		White Plains (Anderson		Winona	29506
County)	29611	County)	29697	Winthrop College (Part of	
Wellford	29385	White Plains (Chesterfield		York)	29730
Wellington Mill	29624	County)	29718	Wisacky	29010
Wesleyan	29630	White Pond	29853	Wolfton	29112
West Andrews (Part of		White Rock	29177	Women's Correctional	
Andrews)	29510	White Stone	29386	Center	29210
West Columbia	29169-72	Whitesville	29461	Woodburn Hills	29301
For specific West Columbia Zip		Whitetown	29845	Woodfield	29206
Codes call (803) 796-0455, or		Whitmire	29178	Woodfields	29605
your local postmaster.		Whitney	29303	Woodford	29112
West Gantt	29605	Wilder	29431	Woodland Hills	29210
Westgate (Part of		Wilkinson Heights	29115	Woodrow	29040
Spartanburg)	29301	Wilkinsville	29340	Woodruff	29388
Westgate Mall (Part of		Wilksburg	29706	Woodside	29610
Spartanburg)	29301	Williams	29493	Woodville	29669
West Marion	29571	Williams Estate	29720	Woodward	29014
Westminster	29693	Williamston	29697	Workman	29111
Westover Acres (Part of		Willington	29835	Yarn Mill	29520
West Columbia)	29169	Williston	29853	Yauhannah	29440
West Pelzer	29669	Willowbrook	29445	Yeamans Hall (Part of	
West Springs	29353	Wilson	29102	Hanahan)	29410
West Union	29696	Wilson Creek	29646	Yemassee	29945
Westview	29301	Wilsons Cross Roads	29532	Yenome	29812
Westville (Greenville		Windsor	29856	Yonges Island	29449
County)	29611	Windsor Estates	29204	York	29745
Westville (Kershaw County)	29175	Windsor Forest	29501	Yorkshire	29209
Whetstone	29664	Windsor Lake Park	29206	Yoruba Village	29941
Whipper Barony (Part of		Windsor Park	29520	Youngs	29388
North Charleston)	29405	Windsor Plantation	29440	Zion	29574
White Bluff Crossroads	29067				

	ZIP		ZIP		ZIP
Aberdeen	57401*	Chester	57016	Garretson	57030
	57402†	Cheyenne Crossing	57754	Gary	57237
Academy	57369	Cheyenne River Indian		Gayville	57031
Agar	57520	Reservation	57625	Geddes	57342
Agency Village	57262	Claire City	57224	Gettysburg	57442
Akaska	57420	Claremont	57432	Glad Valley	57629
Albee	57259	Clark	57225	Glencross	57630
Alcester	57001	Clark Colony	57258	Glendale Colony	57440
Alexandria	57311	Clayton	57332	Glenham	57631
Allen	57714	Clearfield	57580	Goodwin	57238
Alpena	57312	Clear Lake	57226	Graceville Colony	57076
Altamont	57226	Colman	57017	Greenfield	57010
Ames	57362	Colome	57528	Green Grass	57625
Amherst	57421	Colonial Pine Hills	57701	Greenwood	57380
Andover	57422	Colton	57018	Gregory	57533
Antelope	57555	Columbia	57433	Grenville	57239
Ardmore	57715	Conde	57434	Groton	57445
Arlington	57212	Corn Creek	57560	Grover	57201
Arlington Beach	57212	Corona	57227	Hamill	57534
Armour	57313	Corsica	57328	Hammer	57255
Arpan	57762	Corson	57005	Hanna	57754
Artas	57437	Cottonwood	57775	Harrington	57551
Artesian	57314	Crandall	57434	Harrisburg	57032
Ashton	57424	Crazy Horse	57730	Harrison	57344
Astoria	57213	Creighton	57729	Harrold	57536
Athol	57424	Cresbard	57435	Hartford	57033
Aurora	57002	Crocker	57229	Hartford Beach	57227
Aurora Center	57375	Crooks	57020	Hayes	57537
Avon	57315	Crow Creek Indian		Hayti	57241
Badger	57214	Reservation	57339	Hayward Addition	57106
Baltic	57003	Crow Lake	57382	Hazel	57242
Bancroft	57316	Custer	57730	Hecla	57446
Barnard	57426	Dallas	57529	Henry	57243
Batesland	57716	Dante	57329	Hereford	57785
Bath	57427	Davis	57021	Hermosa	57744
Bear Butte	57785	Deadwood	57732	Herreid	57632
Bear Creek	57636	De Grey	57501	Herrick	57538
Belle Fourche	57717	Dell Rapids	57022	Hetland	57244
Belvidere	57521	Delmont	57330	Hiawatha Beach	57279
Bemis	57238	Dempster	57234	Hidden Timber	69201
Beresford	57004	Denby	57716	Highmore	57345
Bethlehem	57708	De Smet	57231	Hill City	57745
Big Bend	57702	Dimock	57331	Hillhead	57270
Big Springs	57001	Dixon	57533	Hillside	57328
Big Stone City	57216	Doland	57436	Hillside Colony	57436
Bijou Hills	57370	Dolton	57319	Hillsview	57437
Bison	57620	Downtown (Part of		Hisega	57701
Black Hawk	57718	Aberdeen)	57401	Hisle	57577
Blacktail	57754	Draper	57531	Hitchcock	57348
Blumengard Colony	57438	Dupree	57623	Holabird	57540
Blunt	57522	Eagle Butte	57625	Holmquist	57274
Bonesteel	57317	East Sioux Falls	57101	Hooker	57070
Bon Homme Colony	57063	Eden	57232	Hoover	57760
Bonilla	57348	Edgemont	57735	Hosmer	57448
Bowdle	57428	Egan	57024	Hot Springs	57747
Box Elder	57719	Elk Point	57025	Houghton	57449
Bradley	57217	Elkton	57026	Hoven	57450
Brandon	57005	Ellis	57101	Howard	57349
Brandt	57218	Ellsworth Air Force Base	57706	Howes	57748
Brentford	57429	Elmore	57754	Hub City	57069
Bridger	57748	Elm Springs	57736	Hudson	57034
Bridgewater	57319	Elm Springs Colony	57334	Huffton	57432
Bristol	57219	Emery	57332	Humboldt	57035
Britton	57430	Empire	57788	Hurley	57036
Broadland	57350	Empire Mall, The (Part of		Huron	57350
Brookings	57006	Sioux Falls)	57101	Huron Colony	57350
Brownsville	57754	Enning	57737	Ideal	57541
Bruce	57220	Epiphany	57321	Igloo	57735
Bryant	57221	Erwin	57233	Imlay	57780
Buffalo	57720	Esmond	57353	Interior	57750
Buffalo Gap	57722	Estelline	57234	Iona	57542
Buffalo Ridge	57115	Ethan	57334	Ipswich	57451
Buffalo Trading Post	57018	Eureka	57437	Irene	57037
Bullhead	57621	Fairburn	57738	Iron Lightning	57623
Burbank	57010	Fairfax	57335	Iroquois	57353
Burke	57523	Fairpoint	57787	Isabel	57633
Bushnell	57276	Fairview	57027	James	57445
Butler	57219	Faith	57626	Java	57452
Cactus Flat	57567	Farmer	57311	Jefferson	57038
Camp Crook	57724	Farmingdale	57725	Johnson Siding	57701
Canistota	57012	Faulkton	57438	Joubert	57344
Canova	57321	Fedora	57337	Junction City	57010
Canton	57013	Ferney	57439	Junius	57042
Capa	57552	Firesteel	57628	Kadoka	57543
Caputa	57725	Flandreau	57028	Kaylor	57354
Carpenter	57322	Flandreau Indian		Keldron	57634
Carter	57526	Reservation	57028	Kenel	57642
Carthage	57323	Fleetwood (Part of Brandon)	57005	Kennebec	57544
Castle Rock	57760	Florence	57235	Keyapaha	57545
Castlewood	57223	Forestburg	57314	Keystone	57751
Cavour	57324	Fort Pierre	57532	Kidder	57430
Cedar Butte	57527	Fort Thompson	57339	Kimball	57355
Cedar Grove Colony	57369	Frankfort	57440	Kingsburg	57062
Center	57058	Franklin	57042	Kones Corner	57223
Center Point	57070	Frederick	57441	Kranzburg	57245
Centerville	57014	Freeman	57029	Kyle	57752
Central City	57754	Froehlich Addition	57104	La Bolt	57246
Chamberlain	57325	Fruitdale	57742	Ladner	57720
Chancellor	57015	Fulton	57340	Lake Andes	57356
Chautauqua	57042	Galena	57732	Lake Campbell	57006
Chelsea	57465	Gannvalley	57341	Lake City	57247
Cherry Creek	57622	Garden City	57236	Lake Norden	57248

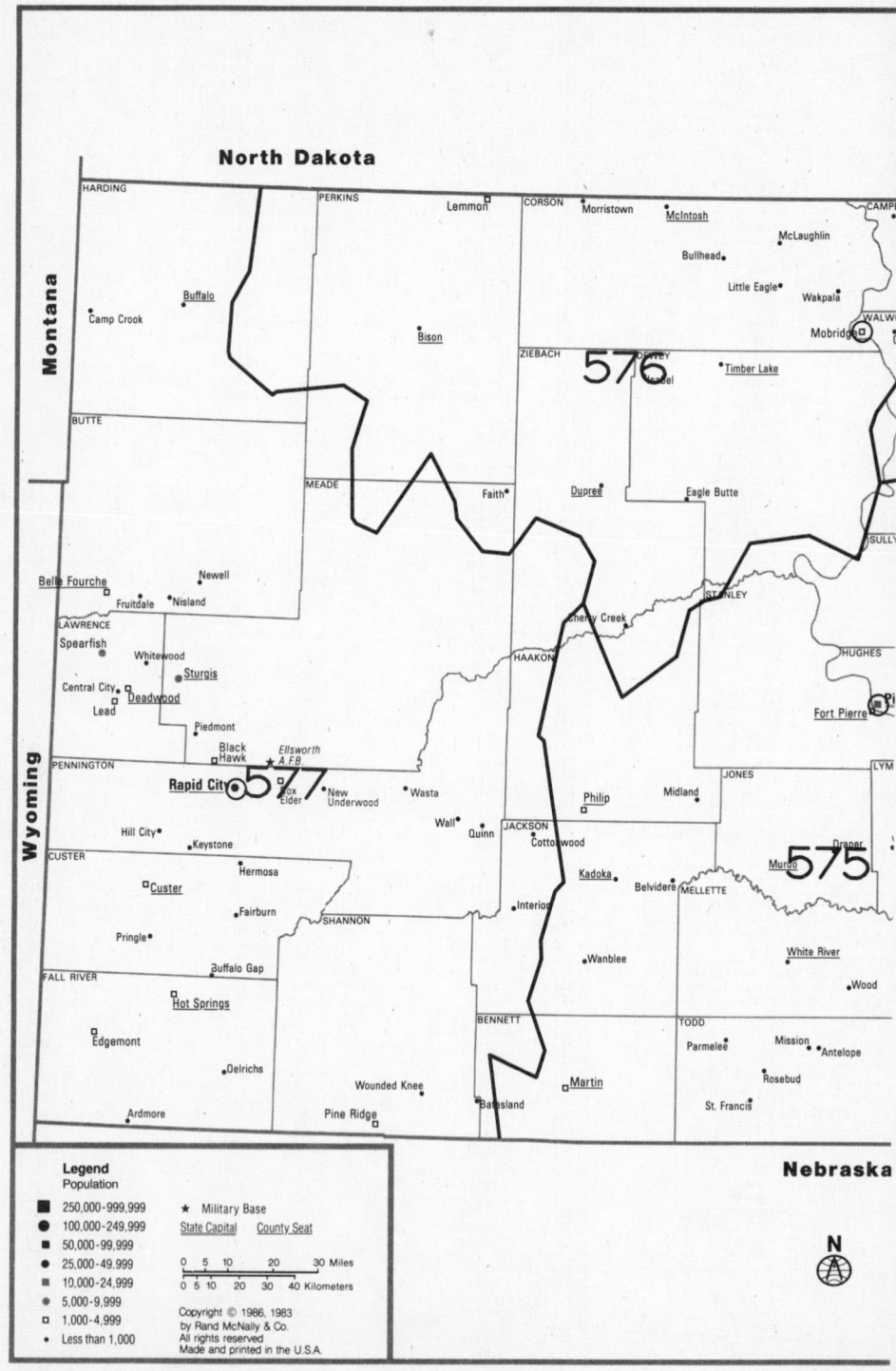

North Dakota

Montana

Wyoming

Nebraska

HARDING

PERKINS

Lemmon

CORSON

Morristown

McIntosh

McLaughlin

CAMPE

Bullhead

Buffalo

Camp Crook

Little Eagle

Wakpala

WALWO

Mobridge

Bison

ZIEBACH

DEWEY

576

Isabel

Timber Lake

BUTTE

MEADE

Faith

Dupree

Eagle Butte

SULLY

Newell

Belle Fourche

Fruitdale

Nisland

Cherry Creek

STANLEY

HUGHES

LAWRENCE

Spearfish

Whitewood

Sturgis

HAAKON

Central City

Deadwood

Lead

Piedmont

Fort Pierre

Pi

Black Hawk

Ellsworth A.F.B.

PENNINGTON

Rapid City

577

Box Elder

New Underwood

Wasta

LYM

JONES

Midland

Hill City

Keystone

Wall

Quinn

JACKSON

Cottonwood

Philip

575

Murdo

Draper

CUSTER

Hermosa

Kadoka

Belvidere

MELLETTE

Custer

Fairburn

Interior

White River

SHANNON

Pringle

Wanblee

Wood

FALL RIVER

Buffalo Gap

Hot Springs

BENNETT

TODD

Edgemont

Oelrichs

Parmelee

Mission

Antelope

Wounded Knee

Martin

Rosebud

Ardmore

Pine Ridge

Batesland

St. Francis

Legend
Population
- 250,000-999,999
- 100,000-249,999
- 50,000-99,999
- 25,000-49,999
- 10,000-24,999
- 5,000-9,999
- 1,000-4,999
- Less than 1,000

★ Military Base
State Capital   County Seat

0 5 10   20   30 Miles
0 5 10   20   30   40 Kilometers

Nebraska

N

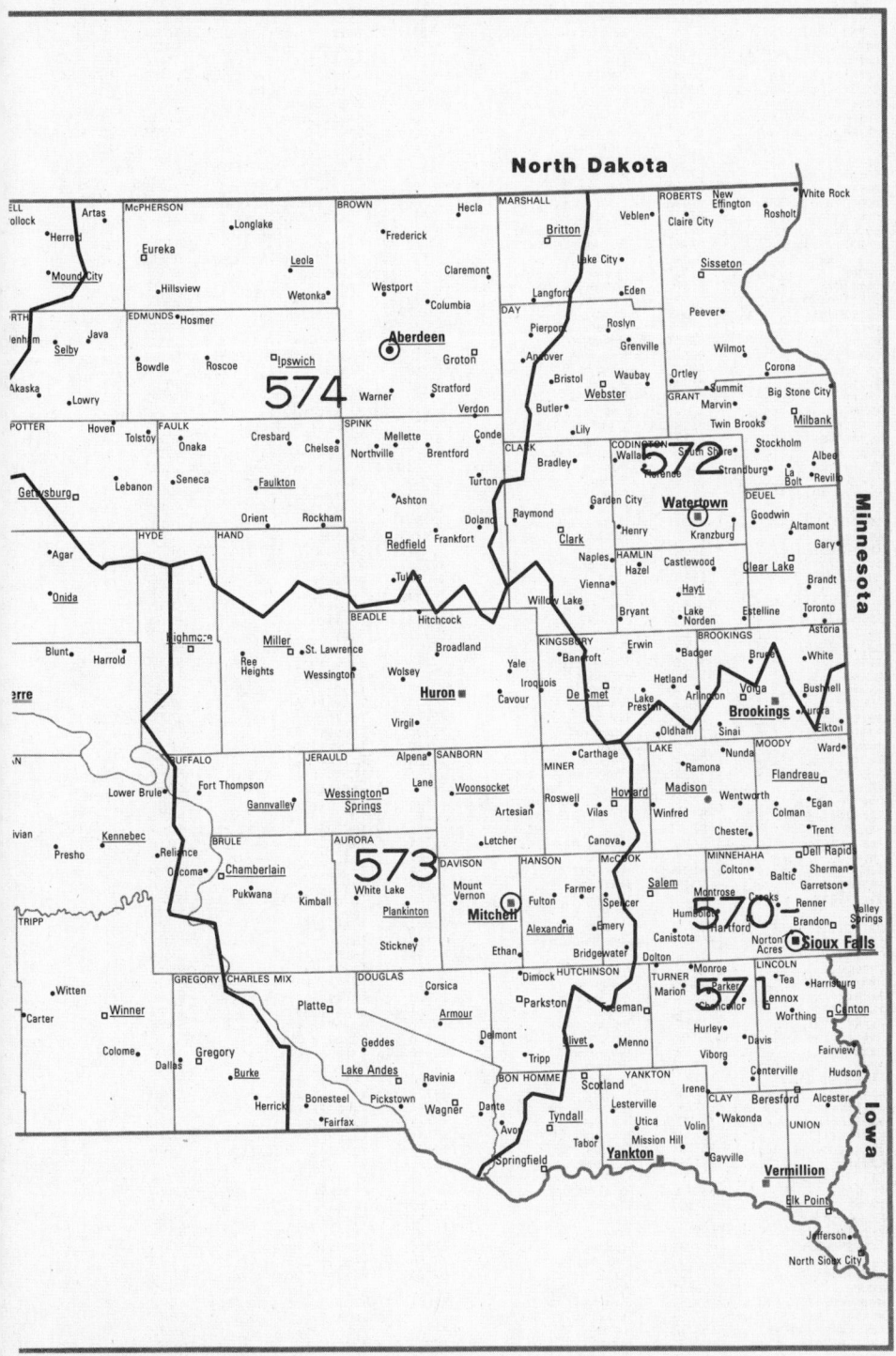

	ZIP		ZIP		ZIP
Lake Preston	57249	Oldham	57051	St. Onge	57779
Lane	57358	Olivet	57052	Salem	57058
Langford	57454	Olsonville	69201	Sanator	57730
Lantry	57636	Onaka	57466	Savoy	57754
La Plant	57652	Onida	57564	Scenic	57780
Lead	57754	Opal	57765	Scotland	57059
Lebanon	57455	Oral	57766	Selby	57472
Lemmon	57638	Ordway	57433	Seneca	57473
Lennox	57039	Orient	57467	Shadehill	57653
Leola	57456	Orland	57042	Shady Beach	57227
Lesterville	57040	Ortley	57256	Sharps Corner	57752
Letcher	57359	Osceola	57316	Sherman	57060
Lily	57274	Owanka	57767	Silver City	57701
Linden Beach	57227	Parade	57647	Sinai	57061
Littleburg	57555	Parker	57053	Sioux Falls	57101-07
Little Eagle	57639	Parkston	57366		57116-18
Lodgepole	57640	Parmelee	57566	For specific Sioux Falls Zip Codes
Lone Tree	57024	Patricia	57551	call (605) 332-8360, or your local
Longlake	57457	Pearl Creek Colony	57353	postmaster.
Long Lake Colony	57481	Pearsons Corner	57070	Sisseton	57262
Long Valley	57547	Pedro	57729	Sisseton Indian Reservation	57262
Loomis	57301	Peever	57257	Smiths Park	57075
Lower Brule	57548	Peninsula Park	57075	Smithwick	57782
Lower Brule Indian		Perkins	57062	So Dak Park	57279
Reservation	57548	Philip	57567	Soldier Creek	57555
Lowry	57472	Pickerel	57239	Sorum	57620
Lucas	57523	Pickstown	57367	South Shore	57263
Ludlow	57755	Piedmont	57769	Spearfish	57783
Lyons	57041	Pierpont	57468	Spencer	57374
McCook Lake	57038	Pierre	57501	Spink	57025
McIntosh	57641	Pine Ridge	57770	Spink Colony	57440
McLaughlin	57642	Pine Ridge Indian		Spring Creek	57572
Madison	57042	Reservation	57770	Spring Creek Colony	58439
Madsen Beach	57279	Plainview	57748	Springfield	57062
Mahto	57643	Plainview Colony	57451	Spring Valley	57036
Manchester	57353	Plankinton	57368	Spring Valley Colony	57382
Manderson	57756	Plano	57340	Standing Rock Indian	
Manderson-White Horse		Platte	57369	Reservation	58538
Creek	57756	Platte Colony	57369	Stanley Corner	57319
Mansfield	57460	Pluma	57732	Stephan	57346
Marcus	57757	Pollock	57648	Stickney	57375
Marcy Colony	57366	Polo	57467	Stockholm	57264
Marion	57043	Porcupine	57772	Stone Bridge	57223
Marlow	57270	Potato Creek	57750	Stoneville	57787
Martin	57551	Prairie City	57649	Storla	57359
Marty	57361	Prairie Village	57042	Strandburg	57265
Marvin	57251	Presho	57568	Stratford	57474
Maurine	57626	Pringle	57773	Sturgis	57785
Maxwell Colony	57059	Promise	57601	Summit	57266
Mayfield	57037	Provo	57774	Sunnyview	57006
Meadow	57644	Pukwana	57370	Swett	57551
Meckling	57044	Pumpkin Center	57035	Tabor	57063
Mellette	57461	Putney	57445	Tacoma Park	57433
Menno	57045	Quinn	57775	Tea	57064
Midland	57552	Quinn Table	57790	Thomas	57241
Midway	57037	Ralph	57650	Thunder Butte	57623
Milbank	57252	Ramona	57054	Thunder Hawk	57638
Milesville	57553	Rapid City	57701-02	Tilford	57769
Millboro	57580		57709	Timber Lake	57656
Miller	57362	For specific Rapid City Zip Codes		Tolstoy	57475
Miller Dale Colony	57362	call (605) 394-8600, or your local		Toronto	57268
Milltown	57366	postmaster.		Trail City	57657
Mina	57462	Rapid Valley	57701	Trent	57065
Miranda	57438	Ravinia	57357	Tripp	57376
Mission	57555	Raymond	57258	Trojan	57754
Mission Hill	57046	Red Elm	57623	Troy	57265
Mission Ridge	57532	Redfield	57469	Tschetter Colony	57052
Mitchell	57301	Redig	57776	Tulare	57476
Mobridge	57601	Redowl	57777	Turkey Ridge	57036
Monroe	57047	Red Scaffold	57626	Turton	57477
Montrose	57048	Red Shirt	57744	Tuthill	57574
Morningside	57350	Ree Heights	57371	Twin Brooks	57269
Morristown	57645	Reliance	57569	Two Strike	57570
Mosher	57580	Renner	57055	Tyndall	57066
Mound City	57646	Reva	57651	Union Center	57787
Mount Vernon	57363	Revillo	57259	Unityville	57058
Mud Butte	57758	Richland	57025	University (Part of	
Murdo	57559	Ridgeview	57652	Brookings)	57007
Mystic	57745	Riverside	57301	Usta	57626
Naples	57271	Riverside Colony	57350	Utica	57067
Nemo	57759	Rochford	57778	Vale	57788
New Effington	57255	Rockerville	57701	Valley Springs	57068
Newell	57760	Rockham	57470	Valley View	57072
New Holland	57364	Rockport	57311	Vayland	57381
New Underwood	57761	Roscoe	57471	Veblen	57270
Nisland	57762	Rosebud	57570	Vedin Corner	57037
Nora	57001	Rosebud Indian Reservation	57570	Verdon	57434
Norbeck	57438	Rosedale Colony	57301	Vermillion	57069
Norris	57560	Rosholt	57260	Vetal	57551
North Eagle Butte	57625	Roslyn	57261	Viborg	57070
North Sioux City	57049	Roswell	57349	Victor	57260
North Spearfish	57783	Roubaix	57754	Vienna	57271
Northville	57465	Rowena	57056	Vilas	57349
Norton Acres	57104	Rumford	57774	Villa Trailer Court	57706
Nunda	57050	Rumpus Ridge	57012	Virgil	57379
Oacoma	57365	Running Water	57062	Vivian	57576
Oelrichs	57763	Rushmore Mall (Part of		Volga	57071
Ogala Lakota College	57752	Rapid City)	57701	Volin	57072
Oglala	57764	Rutland	57057	Wagner	57380
Okaton	57562	St. Charles	57571	Wakonda	57073
Okreek	57563	St. Francis	57572	Wakpala	57658
Ola	57325	St. Lawrence	57373	Wakpamani	57716

	ZIP		ZIP		ZIP
Walker	57601	Western Mall (Part of Sioux		Willow Lake	57278
Wall	57790	Falls)	57105	Wilmot	57279
Wallace	57272	Westerville	57069	Winfred	57076
Wanblee	57577	Westport	57481	Winner	57580
Ward	57074	Wetonka	57481	Witten	57584
Warner	57479	Wewela	57578	Wolf Creek Colony	57052
Wasta	57791	White	57276	Wolsey	57384
Watauga	57660	White Butte	57638	Wood	57585
Watertown	57201	Whitehorse (Dewey County)	57661	Woonsocket	57385
Waubay	57273	White Horse (Todd County)	57555	Worthing	57077
Waverly	57202	White Lake	57383	Wounded Knee	57794
Webster	57274	White Owl	57792	Yale	57386
Webster Grove	57106	White River	57579	Yankton	57078
Wecota	57438	White Rock	57260	Yankton Indian Reservation	57380
Wentworth	57075	Whitewood	57793	Zell	57483
Wessington	57381	Wicksville	57767	Zeona	57795
Wessington Springs	57382				

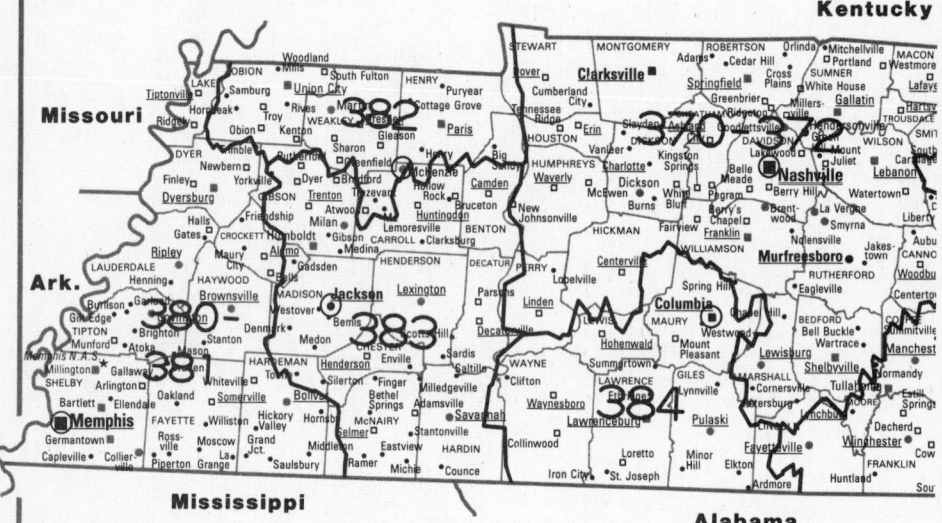

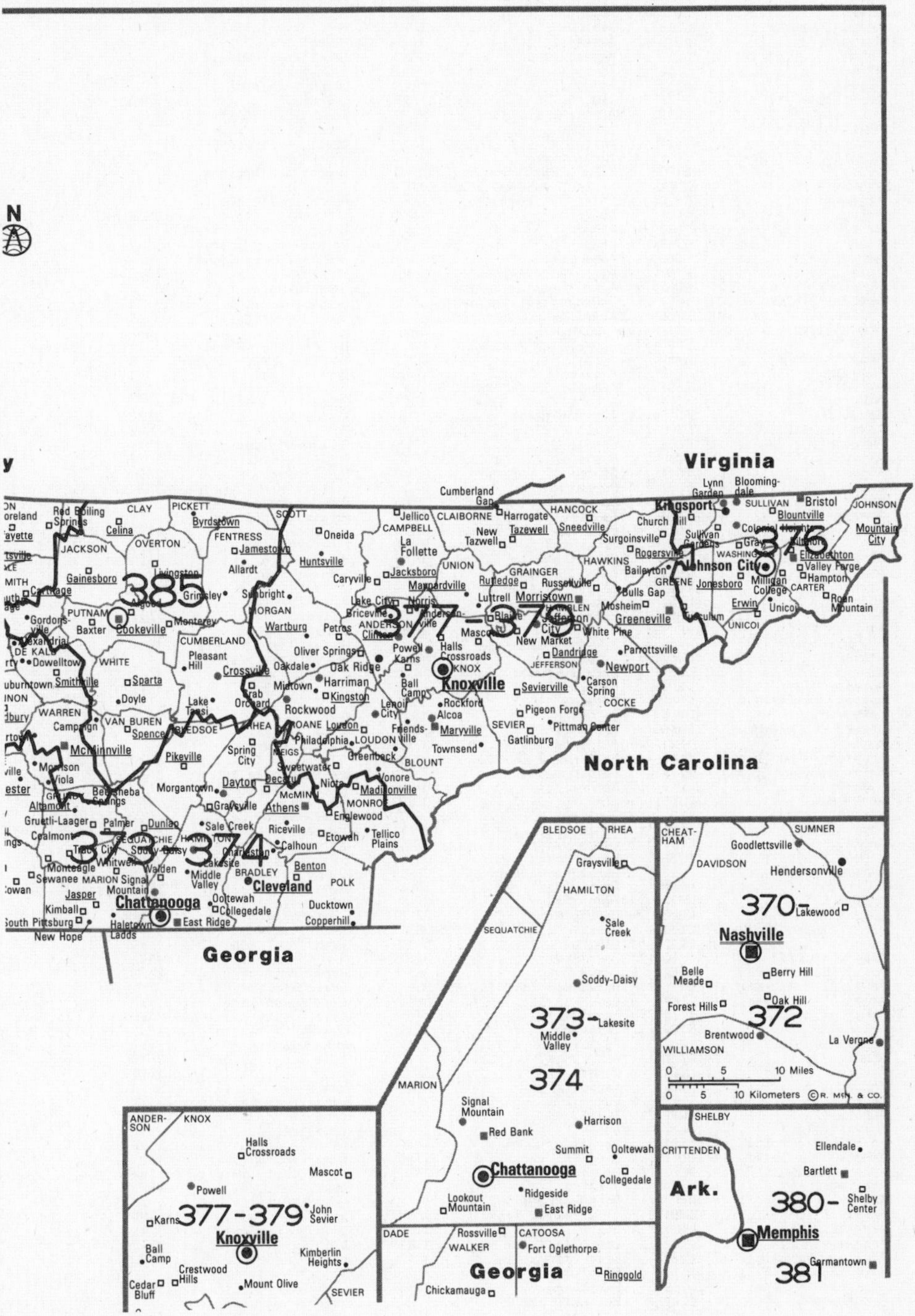
N
Virginia
North Carolina
Georgia
Ark.
385
377-379
376
373-374
370-
372
373-
374
380-
381
Cookeville
Crossville
McMinnville
Knoxville
Chattanooga
Cleveland
Athens
Dayton
Kingsport
Johnson City
Bristol
Elizabethton
Morristown
Greeneville
Newport
Sevierville
Gatlinburg
Maryville
Oak Ridge
Clinton
Harriman
Kingsport
Nashville
Memphis
Goodlettsville
Hendersonville
Lakewood
Belle Meade
Berry Hill
Oak Hill
Forest Hills
Brentwood
La Vergne
WILLIAMSON
DAVIDSON
SUMNER
CHEATHAM
SHELBY
CRITTENDEN
Ellendale
Bartlett
Shelby Center
Germantown
Graysville
Sale Creek
Soddy-Daisy
Lakesite
Middle Valley
Signal Mountain
Red Bank
Harrison
Summit
Ooltewah
Collegedale
Ridgeside
East Ridge
Lookout Mountain
Rossville
Fort Oglethorpe
Ringgold
Chickamauga
HAMILTON
SEQUATCHIE
MARION
BLEDSOE
RHEA
DADE
WALKER
CATOOSA
Halls Crossroads
Mascot
Powell
Karns
John Sevier
Ball Camp
Kimberlin Heights
Crestwood Hills
Mount Olive
Cedar Bluff
ANDERSON
KNOX
SEVIER
0 5 10 Miles
0 5 10 Kilometers
©R. McN. & CO.

	ZIP
Acklen (Part of Nashville)	37212
Acton	38357
Adair	38301
Adams	37010
Adams Crossroads	37055
Adamsville	38310
Aetna	37033
Afton	37616
Airport	37110
Airport Estates (Part of Nashville)	37217
Airport Mail Facility (Davidson County)	37217
Airport Mail Facility (Shelby County)	38130
Air View	37301
Akard Addition	37620
Alamo	38001
Alanthus Hill	37879
Albany	37743
Albright	37066
Alcoa	37701
Alder Branch	37862
Alder Springs (Campbell County)	37766
Alder Springs (Union County)	37807
Alexander Springs	38456
Alexandria	37012
Algood	38501
Allardt	38504
Allens	38012
Allens Chapel	37166
Allensville	37862
Allisona	37046
Allons	38541
Alloway	37337
Allred	38542
Almaville	37014
Almira	38011
Almy	37755
Alpha	37814
Alpha Heights	37814
Alpine	38543
Altamont	37301
Alto	37324
Alton Park (Part of Chattanooga)	37409
Altonville	37857
Alumwell	37857
Alynwick	37804
Amherst (Part of Knoxville)	37931
Amity Heights	37620
Amqui (Part of Nashville)	37115
Anark	38344
Anderson (Franklin County)	37376
Anderson (Overton County)	38574
Anderson Heights	37617
Andersonville	37705
Anes	37091
Angeltown	37022
Anglea	37022
Anglers Cove	37763
Annadale (Part of Cleveland)	37312
Annadel	37770
Anthony Hill	38460
Antioch (Davidson County)	37011†
	37013*
Antioch (DeKalb County)	37166
Antioch (Jackson County)	38562
Antioch (Loudon County)	37771
Antioch (Polk County)	37307
Antioch (Tipton County)	38058
Apison	37302
Appleton	38457
Arcadia	37660
Archer	37091
Archville	37369
Arcott	38551
Ardmore	38449
Arkland	38487
Arlington (Houston County)	37061
Arlington (Knox County)	37917
Arlington (Shelby County)	38002
Armathwaite	38504
Armona	37804
Armour	38401
Arms Mill	37807
Arno	37046
Arnold Air Force Base	37389
Arnold Engineering Development Center	37389
Arnolds Chapel	38544
Arp	38063
Arrington	37014
Arrowhead	37920
Arthur	37707
Asbury (Coffee County)	37355
Asbury (Haywood County)	38069
Asbury (Knox County)	37914
Asbury (Lauderdale County)	38063

	ZIP
Asbury (Pickett County)	38577
Asbury (Stewart County)	37175
Asbury Estates	37801
Ashburn	37172
Ash Hill	37046
Ashland	38485
Ashland City	37015
Ashport	38063
Ashwood	38401
Asia	37398
Aspen Hill	38478
Athendale	38401
Athens	37303
	37371
For specific Athens Zip Codes call (615) 745-5100, or your local postmaster.	
Atkins	37079
Atoka	38004
Atwood	38220
Auburntown	37016
Aulon (Part of Memphis)	38101
Austin Peay State University (Part of Clarksville)	37040
Austin Springs (Washington County)	37601
Austin Springs (Weakley County)	38226
Avoca (Part of Bristol)	37620
Avondale (Grainger County)	37861
Avondale (Sumner County)	37075
Avondale Springs	37861
Ayers	38030
Bacchus	37879
Bacon Gap	37763
Bagdad	37145
Baggettsville	37172
Bailey	38017
Baileyton	37743
Bailey Town	37821
Bain	38320
Bairds Mills	37087
Baker Crossroads	38555
Bakers (Part of Nashville)	37072
Bakers Crossroads	38583
Bakersworks	37029
Bakerton	37150
Bakertown (Davidson County)	37013
Bakertown (Moore County)	37352
Bakerville	37185
Bakewell	37304
Bald Point	37881
Ball Camp	37921
Ballplay (Monroe County)	37385
Ball Play (Polk County)	37362
Balltown	37331
Baltimore	37843
Baneberry	37890
Bangham	38501
Banner	37738
Banner Hill	37650
Banner Springs	38556
Baptist (Part of Nashville)	37203
Baptist Ridge	38568
Barefoot	37186
Barfield	37129
Bargerton	38351
Barkertown	37365
Barnardsville	37763
Barnes	38573
Barnesville	38483
Barr	38040
Barren Plain	37172
Barretville	38053
Barthelia	37031
Bartlebaugh	37416
Bartlett	38134
Barton Springs	37814
Bates Hill	37110
Bath Springs	38311
Batley	37716
Battlewood Estates	37064
Baugh	38449
Baugh Spring	37353
Baxter	38544
Bazel Town (Part of Harriman)	37748
Beacon	38363
Beamswitch	38230
Beans Creek	37345
Bean Station	37708
Bear Creek	37892
Beardstown (Part of Lobelville)	37097
Bear Spring	37058
Beartown	37660
Bearwallow	37015
Beasley	37034
Beauty Hill	38315
Beaver	38011
Beaverdam Springs	37147

	ZIP
Beaver Ridge	37921
Beckwith	37122
Bedford	37160
Beech Bluff	38313
Beech Bottom	37083
Beech Fork	37714
Beech Grove (Anderson County)	37769
Beechgrove (Coffee County)	37018
Beech Grove (Grainger County)	37881
Beech Grove (Hawkins County)	37711
Beech Grove (Trousdale County)	37074
Beech Grove (Weakley County)	38230
Beech Hill (Franklin County)	37398
Beech Hill (Giles County)	38478
Beech Hill (Macon County)	37074
Beechnut	37617
Beech Springs	37764
Beechwood	37020
Beersheba Springs	37305
Bel Air	38261
Bel Aire (Coffee County)	37388
Bel Aire (Rutherford County)	37130
Bel-Aire Heights (Part of Winchester)	37398
Belfast	37019
Belinda City	37122
Belk	37166
Bella Mara Estates	37854
Bell Buckle	37020
Bell Campground	37849
Belle Aire (Knox County)	37922
Belle Aire (White County)	38583
Belle Brook Estate (Part of Bristol)	37620
Belle Eagle	38012
Belle Founte	37312
Belle Meade (Blount County)	37801
Belle Meade (Davidson County)	37205
Belleville	37334
Bellevue (Part of Nashville)	37221
Bellevue Center (Part of Nashville)	37221
Bellevue Estates	37331
Bell Mill	37363
Bells	38006
Bellsburg	37036
Bell Town (Cheatham County)	37082
Belltown (Monroe County)	37385
Belltown (Polk County)	37317
Bellview (Bledsoe County)	37367
Bellview (Lincoln County)	37334
Bellwood	37087
Belmont (Anderson County)	37705
Belmont (Coffee County)	37355
Belmont (Jefferson County)	37725
Belmont West	37919
Belvidere	37306
Bemis (Part of Jackson)	38314
Bending Chestnut	37064
Benton (Polk County)	37307
Benton Springs	37307
Berclair (Part of Memphis)	38117
Berea (Giles County)	38478
Berea (Warren County)	38581
Berlin	37091
Berry Hill	37204
Berrys Chapel	37064
Bertha	37765
Bessie	38079
Bethany	37110
Bethel (Anderson County)	37716
Bethel (Benton County)	38320
Bethel (Blount County)	37882
Bethel (Carroll County)	38344
Bethel (Cheatham County)	37015
Bethel (DeKalb County)	37166
Bethel (Giles County)	38477
Bethel (Haywood County)	38012
Bethel (Maury County)	38482
Bethel (Perry County)	37096
Bethel Springs	38315
Bethesda (Greene County)	37641
Bethesda (Williamson County)	37046
Bethlehem (Bedford County)	37160
Bethlehem (Campbell County)	37766
Bethlehem (Hardin County)	38310
Bethlehem (Henry County)	38222
Bethlehem (Monroe County)	37354
Bethlehem (Williamson County)	37064

	ZIP
Bethpage	37022
Betsy Willis	37342
Beulah (Greene County)	37810
Beulah (Union County)	37807
Beverly	37918
Bible Hill	38363
Bidwell	37144
Big Boy Junction	38030
Bigbyville	38401
Big Creek (Hancock County)	37869
Big Creek (Hawkins County)	37857
Big Creek (Monroe County)	37354
Big Ivy	38372
Big Lick	38555
Big Mountain	37840
Big Piney	37774
Big Ridge Park	37807
Big Rock	37023
Big Sandy	38221
Big Sinks	37866
Big Spring (Blount County)	37737
Big Spring (Carter County)	37643
Big Spring (Meigs County)	37322
Big Springs (Hancock County)	37731
Big Springs (Overton County)	38570
Big Springs (Rutherford County)	37037
Big Spring Union	37752
Biltmore	37643
Binfield	37804
Bingham	37064
Binghamton (Part of Memphis)	38112
Birchwood	37308
Bird Crossroad	37862
Bird Song	38320
Bishop	38024
Bivens	38472
Black Center	38320
Black Creek	37852
Black Fox (Bradley County)	37311
Black Fox (Grainger County)	37888
Black Jack	37355
Blackman	37129
Black Oak	37841
Blackwell	37861
Blaine	37709
Blair	37748
Blair Gap	37660
Blair Lane	37087
Blakeville	37144
Blanche	38488
Blanche Chapel	38449
Blaney Forest (Part of East Ridge)	37412
Blanton Chapel	37355
Bledsoe (Lincoln County)	37144
Bledsoe (Sumner County)	37022
Block City (Part of Mount Carmel)	37642
Blockhouse	37801
Blondy (Part of Hohenwald)	38462
Bloomingdale	37660
Bloomington	38549
Bloomington Heights	37660
Bloomington Springs	38545
Blount Hills	37804
Blountville	37617
Blowing Cave Mill	37862
Blowing Springs	37716
Bluebank	38079
Blue Creek	38472
Bluefields (Part of Nashville)	37214
Blue Goose	38351
Bluegrass	37722
Blue Hill	37110
Blue Ridge (Part of Bristol)	37620
Blue Spring	37643
Blue Springs (DeKalb County)	37166
Blue Springs (Hamilton County)	37341
Bluff City	37618
Bluff Creek	38547
Bluff Springs	37110
Bluhmtown	37166
Blunts Landing	37096
Blythe Ferry	37321
Board Valley	37583
Boatland	38556
Bodenham	38478
Boggs	37861
Bogota	38007
Bohannon Addition (Part of Athens)	37303
Boiling Springs	38544
Bold Spring	37101
Bolivar	38008

	ZIP
Bolton	38002
Boma	38544
Bon Air (Sumner County)	37022
Bon Air (White County)	38583
Bon Aqua	37025
Bon Aqua Junction	37098
Bon De Croft	38583
Bone Cave	38581
Bonicord	38024
Bonnertown	38457
Bonny Kate	37920
Bonsack	38554
Bonwood (Part of Jackson)	38301
Boom	38573
Boone	37601
Boones Creek	37615
Booneville	37334
Boonshill	38459
Boothspoint	38030
Bordeaux (Part of Nashville)	37218
Borden Mills (Part of Kingsport)	37660
Boston	37064
Bowen	37861
Bowling	38555
Bowman	38555
Bowmantown	37690
Boxwood Hills	37922
Boyd	37722
Boyd Mill Estates (Part of Franklin)	37064
Boyds Creek	37862
Brace	38483
Brackentown	37148
Bradburn Hill	37743
Bradbury	37763
Braden (Fayette County)	38010
Braden (Union County)	37870
Bradford	38316
Bradleytown	38030
Bradshaw	38459
Bradyville	37026
Braemar	37658
Braid Cove	37087
Brainerd (Part of Chattanooga)	37411
Brakebill	37354
Bransford	37022
Bratcher's	37110
Brattontown	37083
Braxton	37190
Bray	37881
Brayton	37338
Braytown	37710
Brazil	38382
Breckinredge South	37064
Brentlawn (Part of Springfield)	37172
Brentwood (Hamblen County)	37814
Brentwood (Williamson County)	37024
	37027
For specific Brentwood Zip Codes call (615) 373-1661, or your local postmaster.	
Brentwood Mall (Part of Brentwood)	37027
Brewer Addition (Part of Athens)	37303
Brewstertown	37852
Briar Thicket	37713
Briarwood	37040
Briceville	37710
Brick Church	38478
Brick Mill	37742
Bride	38019
Bridgeport	37821
Bridwell Heights	37617
Bright Hope	37743
Brighton (Lincoln County)	37335
Brighton (Tipton County)	38011
Brims Corner	38001
Bristol	37620-25
For specific Bristol Zip Codes call (615) 968-2355, or your local postmaster.	
Britton Ford	38256
Brittontown	37616
Brittsville	37336
Broad Acres	37849
Broadmoor	38024
Broad Street (Part of Cookeville)	38501
Broadview (Crockett County)	38034
Broadview (Franklin County)	37398
Broadway	38351
Brockdell	37367
Brockland Acres	37814
Brock's	38230

	ZIP
Brookhaven (Part of Crossville)	38555
Brooks (Part of Hohenwald)	38462
Brotherton	38501
Browder (Loudon County)	37771
Browder (Marion County)	37347
Brown Cross Roads	38469
Brown Ellis	37748
Brownington	37398
Browns	37083
Browns Shop	37144
Brownsville	38012
Browntown	38578
Brownwood Acres	37064
Broylesville	37681
Bruceton	38317
Bruceville	38024
Bruner Grove	37713
Brunswick	38014
Brush Creek (Sequatchie County)	37327
Brush Creek (Smith County)	38547
Brush Creek (Williamson County)	37062
Brushy Mountain State Penitentiary	37845
Bryan Hill (Part of Dayton)	37321
Bryant Station	37091
Bryson	38453
Bryson Mountain	40965
Brysonville	37190
Buchanan	38222
Buckeye	37847
Buck Lodge	37148
Buckner	37166
Bucksnort	37140
Bucktown (Hardin County)	38372
Bucktown (Loudon County)	37771
Buena Vista	38318
Buffalo (Humphreys County)	37078
Buffalo (Scott County)	37756
Buffalo Springs	37861
Buffalo Valley	38548
Bufords	38472
Bugscuffle	37183
Buladeen	37643
Bullards Gap	38562
Bull Creek	37756
Bullet Creek	37369
Bull Run (Anderson County)	37849
Bull Run (Davidson County)	37015
Bulls Gap	37711
Bumpass Cove	37650
Bumpus Mills	37028
Buncombe	37617
Bungalow Town	37804
Bunker Hill	38478
Buntontown	37640
Burbank	37687
Burchfield Heights	37830
Burem	37857
Burgen	37026
Burke	37367
Burlington (Part of Knoxville)	37914
Burlington Heights (Part of Cleveland)	37312
Burlison	38015
Burns	37029
Burnt Church	38372
Burristown	38562
Burrville	37872
Burt	37190
Burton (Part of Rogersville)	37857
Burwood	37179
Busby (Part of Loretto)	38469
Busselltown	37771
Butler	37640
Butlers Landing	38551
Bybee (Cocke County)	37713
Bybee (Warren County)	37110
Byrdstown	38549
Cabin Row	37171
Cabo	38332
Cades	38358
Cades Cove	37882
Cadet (Part of Franklin)	37064
Cagle	37327
Cain Mill	37860
Cainsville	37085
Cairo (Crockett County)	38001
Cairo (Sumner County)	37066
Cairo Bend	37087
Calderwood	37801
Calfkiller	38574
Calhoun	37309
Calico	37322
Calistia	37049
Callins	38230
Calls	37330
Camargo	37334
Cambria	37325
Cambridge	38581

	ZIP
Camden	38320
Camelot (Cumberland County)	38555
Camelot (Hawkins County)	37857
Camilla Homes	38004
Campaign	38550
Camp Austin	37829
Campbell Army Airfield	42223
Campbell Junction	38555
Campbells	38451
Campbellsville	38478
Camp Creek	37743
Camp Ground	38237
Camp Marymount	37062
Camp Monterey Lake	38574
Camp Nakanawa	38555
Camp Relax	37166
Camps	37869
Camp Ta-Pa-Win-Go	37694
Camp Woodlee	37110
Canadaville	38028
Cane Ridge (Part of Nashville)	37013
Caney Branch	37743
Caney Creek	37891
Caney Ford	37748
Caney Spring	37091
Caney Valley	37879
Cantrell	38485
Capitol Hill (Franklin County)	37330
Capitol Hill (Scott County)	37756
Capleville	38118
Caravelle Estates	37122
Cardiff	37854
Carlisle	37058
Carlock	37331
Carnegie (Part of Johnson City)	37601
Carpenter Campground	37804
Carroll	37087
Carroll Reece (Part of Johnson City)	37601
Carrs Branch	37825
Carson Spring	37821
Carter	37643
Carters Creek	38401
Carthage	37030
Carthage Junction (Part of Gordonsville)	38567
Cartwright (Sequatchie County)	37397
Cartwright (Smith County)	37145
Caryville	37714
Cash Point	38449
Cassville	38583
Castalian Springs	37031
Castle Heights	37821
Cat Corner	38240
Cates	38079
Cates Trailor	37764
Catlettsburg	37862
Cato	37057
Catons Grove	37722
Catoosa	37770
Cave	38559
Cave Spring	37879
Cavvia	38341
Cedar Bluff (Sevier County)	37862
Cedarbluff (Trousdale County)	37087
Cedar Bluff Two	37722
Cedar Chapel	38075
Cedar Creek	37743
Cedar Creek Landing	37096
Cedarcrest	37857
Cedarfork (Claiborne County)	37879
Cedar Fork (Loudon County)	37846
Cedar Grove (Bedford County)	37034
Cedar Grove (Carroll County)	38321
Cedar Grove (Carter County)	37601
Cedar Grove (Henderson County)	38371
Cedar Grove (Humphreys County)	37078
Cedar Grove (Pickett County)	38577
Cedar Grove (Roane County)	37763
Cedar Grove (Rutherford County)	37060
Cedar Grove (Sullivan County)	37660
Cedar Grove (Sullivan County; rural)	37618
Cedar Grove (Wilson County)	37087
Cedar Hill (Putnam County)	38544

	ZIP
Cedar Hill (Robertson County)	37032
Cedar Springs	37303
Cedar Valley (Part of Bristol)	37620
Celina	38551
Center (Crockett County)	38337
Center (Lawrence County)	38464
Center (Monroe County)	37385
Center Grove (Franklin County)	37388
Center Grove (Jackson County)	38562
Center Hill (Cannon County)	37190
Center Hill (Warren County)	37110
Center Point (Chester County)	38332
Center Point (Giles County)	38478
Center Point (Hardeman County)	38042
Center Point (Lawrence County)	38468
Center Point (Sequatchie County)	37327
Center Point (Stewart County)	37058
Center Point (White County)	38587
Center Star	38454
Centersville	37742
Centertown	37110
Centerville (Hickman County)	37033
Centerville (Wilson County)	37087
Central (Carter County)	37601
Central (Gibson County)	38382
Central (Lauderdale County)	38063
Central (Obion County)	38253
Central Heights	37617
Central Point	37861
Central State Psychiactric Hospital (Part of Nashville)	37217
Central View	38587
Cerro Gordo	38372
Chable	37008
Chalklevel (Benton County)	38320
Chalk Level (Hawkins County)	37857
Champ	37359
Chanceytown	37391
Chandler	37777
Chantay Acres (Part of Columbia)	38401
Chanute	38577
Chapel Hill (Marshall County)	37034
Chapel Hill (Maury County)	38474
Chapman Grove	37763
Chapmans	38478
Chapmansboro	37035
Charity	37334
Charles Creek Estates	37110
Charleston (Bradley County)	37310
Charleston (Tipton County)	38069
Charleys Branch	37710
Charlotte	37036
Charlotte Park (Part of Nashville)	37209
Charlton Green (Part of Franklin)	37064
Chaska	37766
Chattanooga	37401-50
For specific Chattanooga Zip Codes call (615) 499-8256, or your local postmaster.	
Cherokee	38380
Cherokee Harshaw	37743
Cherokee Heights	37801
Cherokee Hills (Roane County)	37763
Cherokee Hills (Part of Sevierville)	37862
Cherokee Hills (Sevier County)	37865
Cherry	38041
Cherry Acres (Part of Gruetli-Laager)	37339
Cherrybrook	37912
Cherry Chapel	38372
Cherry Grove	38333
Cherry Hill	38582
Cherry Valley	37184
Chesney	37848
Chester Estates (Part of Fairview)	37062
Chesterfield	38351
Chestnut Bluff	38040
Chestnut Glade	38237
Chestnut Grove (Jefferson County)	37725
Chestnut Grove (Perry County)	37096

	ZIP
Chestnut Grove (Stewart County)	37058
Chestnut Grove (Sumner County)	37148
Chestnut Grove (Union County)	37807
Chestnut Hill (Cumberland County)	38555
Chestnut Hill (Jefferson County)	37725
Chestnut Hill (Sumner County)	37148
Chestnut Mound	38552
Chestnut Orchard	37172
Chestnut Ridge (Greene County)	37641
Chestnutridge (Lincoln County)	37144
Chestoa	37650
Chestua	37354
Chestuee	37312
Chewalla	38393
Chic	38030
Chickamauga (Part of Chattanooga)	37421
	37424
For specific Chickamauga Zip Codes call (615) 892-8047, or your local postmaster.	
Chickasaw Heights (Part of Paris)	38242
Childers Hill	38326
Chilhowee View	37801
China Grove	38233
Chinquapin Grove	37618
Chinubee	38486
Chipman	37022
Chittum	37879
Choptack	37857
Chota	37801
Chotham	38382
Choto	37922
Choto Hills	37777
Christiana	37037
Christian Bend	37642
Christianburg	37874
Christie Hill	37801
Christmasville (Carroll County)	38201
Christmasville (Haywood County)	38012
Chuckey	37641
Church Hill	37642
Churchton	38059
Citico Beach	37885
Clacks Gap	37748
Clairfield	37715
Clark Addition	37804
Clarkrange	38553
Clarksburg	38324
Clarksville	37040-44
For specific Clarksville Zip Codes call (615) 647-3392, or your local postmaster.	
Clarksville Base	42223
Clarktown	38583
Claxton (Anderson County)	37849
Claxton (McMinn County)	37303
Claybrook	38301
Clay Hill	37892
Claylick	37187
Clayton	38260
Clearbranch	37650
Clear Creek Mill	37332
Clearmont	37110
Clear Springs (Greene County)	37681
Clear Springs (Knox County)	37806
Clear Springs (McMinn County)	37309
Clearwater	37303
Clements Lake Estates (Part of Fairview)	37062
Clementsville	37150
Cleveland	37311-12
	37320
	37323
	37364
For specific Cleveland Zip Codes call (615) 472-6597, or your local postmaster.	
Clevenger	37821
Cliff Springs	38574
Clifftops	37356
Clifton (Clifton City)	38425
Clifton	38485
Clifty	38583
Clinton	37716
Clopton	38011
Cloud Creek	37857
Clouds	37879

	ZIP		ZIP		ZIP
Clouse Hill	37387	Cottage Grove	38224	Cuba (Hawkins County)	37811
Clovercroft	37064	Cottage Home	37095	Cuba (Shelby County)	38053
Cloverdale (Obion County)	38240	Cottonport	37322	Cuba Landing	37185
Cloverdale (Shelby County)	38053	Cottontown	37048	Cub Creek	38562
Cloverdale (White County)	38583	Cottonwood Estates	37064	Culleoka	38451
Clover Hill (Blount County)	37804	Cottonwood Grove	38080	Culpepper	37149
Cloverhill (Davidson County)	37214	Cotula	37766	Cumberland City	37050
Cloverport	38381	Couchville (Part of		Cumberland Estates (Part of	
Club Springs	38560	Nashville)	37214	Knoxville)	37921
Coal Chute	37643	Coulterville	37373	Cumberland Furnace	37051
Coalfield	37719	Counce	38326	Cumberland Gap	37724
Coal Hill (Morgan County)	37748	Country Club	38008	Cumberland Heights	
Coal Hill (Scott County)	37872	Country Haven Estates	37719	(Grundy County)	37313
Coaling	37051	Country Roads	37064	Cumberland Heights	
Coalmont	37313	Countrywood Estates	37064	(Montgomery County)	37040
Cobbs	38006	Countyline (Moore County)	37352	Cumberland Springs	37321
Coble	37033	County Line (Sevier County)	37865	Cumberland View	37757
Coffee Landing	38310	Courtland	37172	Cumberland View Estates	37769
Coffee Ridge	37650	Cove Creek (Campbell		Cummings	38583
Cog Hill	37325	County)	37714	Cummingsville	38585
Cokercreek	37314	Cove Creek (Carter County)	37687	Cunningham	37052
Cold Spring (Bledsoe		Cove Creek Cascades	37862	Cupp Mill	37825
County)	37367	Cove Lake Estates	37714	Curlee	37190
Cold Spring (Johnson		Covington	38019	Curve	38063
County)	37683	Cowan	37318	Cusick	37865
Cold Springs (Blount		Cowanstown	37640	Cuzick	37771
County)	37886	Cowards	37921	Cypress	38001
Cold Springs (Hawkins		Cowenville	38567	Cypress Creek	38222
County)	37873	Coxville	38343	Cypress Inn	38452
Coldwater	37334	Cozyette	38380	Daisy (Part of Soddy-Daisy)	37379
Colesburg	37055	Crab Orchard	37723	Dale Hollow	38551
Coles Ferry	37087	Crabtree	37687	Dalewood (Part of Nashville)	37207
Coles Store	38544	Crackers Neck	37683	Dallas Gardens	37379
Coletown	37317	Craggie Hope	37082	Dallas Hills	37379
College (Bledsoe County)	37327	Craigfield	37025	Dalton Heights (Part of	
College (Blount County)	37801	Crandull	37688	Morristown)	37814
Collegedale	37315	Cranmore Cove	37321	Dancyville	38069
College Grove	37046	Cravenstown	38589	Dandridge	37725
College Grove Estates	37854	Crawfish Valley	38464	Dante	37921
College Hill (Part of Dayton)	37321	Crawford	38554	Darden	38328
College Park	37601	Creekwood (Bedford		Darks Mill	38401
College Park Estates	37801	County)	37160	Daugherty Estates	37062
Colliers Corner	37760	Creekwood (Wilson County)	37122	Daus	37327
Collierville	38017*	Crenshaw	37920	Davenport	37110
	38027†	Crescent	37129	Davidson	38589
Collins (Grundy County)	37365	Creson (Part of Fayetteville)	37334	Davidson Chapel	38382
Collins (Hawkins County)	37857	Creston	38555	Davis Chapel (Campbell	
Collinwood	38450	Crestwood	37763	County)	37766
Colonial Acres	38225	Crestwood Hills	37918	Davis Chapel (Carroll	
Colonial Circle	37865	Crewstown	38464	County)	38344
Colonial Heights	37663	Crieve Hall (Part of		Davis Springs	37692
Colonial Village (Part of		Nashville)	37211	Daylight	37110
Knoxville)	37920	Crippen Gap	37918	Daysville	37854
Columbia	38401*	Crisp Spring	37357	Dayton	37321
	38402†	Crockett	38253	Dayton Spur	38555
Columbia Hill	38574	Crockett Mills	38021	Deanburg	38366
Columbus Hill	38562	Cronanville	38079	Deans	37033
Comfort	37380	Cross	37617	DeArmond	37748
Commerce	37184	Cross Anchor	37743	Deason	37020
Community Acres	37180	Cross Bridges	38474	De Busk	37743
Como	38223	Cross Keys	37046	Decatur	37322
Compton	37130	Crossland	42049	Decaturville	38329
Conasauga	37316	Cross Lanes	37186	Decherd	37324
Concord (Carroll County)	38344	Cross Plains	37049	Deep Springs	37725
Concord (Gibson County)	38382	Cross Road	37841	Deerfield (Lawrence	
Concord (Humphreys		Crossroads (Benton		County)	38464
County)	37185	County)	38320	Deerfield (Williamson	
Concord (Knox County)	37922	Cross Roads (Cannon		County)	37064
Concord (Rhea County)	37332	County)	37190	Deerfield Acres	37620
Concord (Rutherford		Crossroads (Crockett		Deer Lodge	37726
County)	37153	County)	38006	Deermont	37829
Concord-Farragut	37922	Cross Roads (DeKalb		Defeated	37030
Conklin	37659	County)	37059	Defense Depot (Part of	
Conner Heights (Part of		Cross Roads (Dyer County)	38034	Memphis)	38114
Pigeon Forge)	37863	Cross Roads (Fentress		Delano	37325
Conyersville	38251	County)	38556	Delina	37047
Cookeville	38501-03	Crossroads (Hardin County)	38372	Dellrose	38453
For specific Cookeville Zip Codes		Cross Roads (Lawrence		Dellwood	37804
call (615) 526-7141, or your local		County; mail Ethridge)	38456	Del Rio	37727
postmaster.		Crossroads (Lawrence		Demory	37766
Cool Springs	38259	County; mail Leoma)	38468	Denmark	38391
Cooper	38556	Cross Roads (Macon		Dennis Cove	37658
Coopers	38317	County)	37186	Denton	37722
Coopertown	37172	Crossroads (Shelby County)	38017	Dentville	37325
Copperhill	37317	Cross Roads (Stewart		Denver (Cannon County)	37149
Corbin Hill	37840	County)	37178	Denver (Humphreys	
Cordell	37756	Crossroads (Wayne County)	38450	County)	37054
Corder Cross Roads	37348	Crosstown (Shelby County)	38104	De Priest Bend (Part of	
Cordova	38018	Crosstown (Tipton County)	38004	Lobelville)	37097
	38088	Crossville	38555	De Rossett	38583
For specific Cordova Zip Codes			38557	Detroit	38015
call (901) 754-2520, or your local		For specific Crossville Zip Codes		Devonia	37710
postmaster.		call (615) 484-6521, or your local		Diana	37047
Corinth (Knox County)	37918	postmaster.		Dibrell	37110
Corinth (Sumner County)	37148	Crosswinds	37122	Dickel	37388
Cornersville	37047	Crowley Store	38230	Dickey Bluff Peninsula	37381
Coro Lake	38109	Crown Point Estates	37122	Dickson	37055-56
Corona	72338	Crucifer	38345	For specific Dickson Zip Codes	
Corryton	37721	Crump	38327	call (615) 446-2556, or your local	
Cortner	37360	Crunk	37073	postmaster.	
Cosby	37722	Crystal	38261	Dickson Town	38455
Coster (Part of Knoxville)	37917	Crystal Springs	37348	Difficult	37145

	ZIP
Dill	37367
Dilley	37730
Dillton	37130
Disco	37737
Dismal	37095
Disney	37769
Dixie	38261
Dixie Lee Junction (Part of Farragut)	37771
Dixon Springs	37057
Dixonville	38053
Doaks Crossroads	37087
Dockery	37310
Dodson (Roane County)	37748
Dodson (White County)	38583
Dodson Estates (Part of Nashville)	37076
Dodsons	38472
Doeville	37640
Dog Hill	38050
Dogtown (Carter County)	37643
Dog Town (Grundy County)	37313
Dogtown (Polk County)	37391
Dogwood	37763
Dogwood Heights	37879
Dollar	38313
Donelson (Part of Nashville)	37214
Donnels Chapel	37149
Donoho	37030
Doran Addition	37660
Dorton	38555
Dossett	37716
Dotson	37888
Dotson Branch	38501
Dotson's Camp Ground	37888
Dotsontown	37681
Dotsonville	37191
Doty Chapel	37616
Double Bridges	38040
Double Springs (McMinn County)	37303
Double Springs (Putnam County)	38544
Douglas	37064
Douglas Estates	37725
Dover (Hamblen County)	37814
Dover (Stewart County)	37058
Dowelltown	37059
Dowler Heights	37377
Downtown (Part of Chattanooga)	37402
Downtown (Part of Cleveland)	37311
Downtown (Part of Maryville)	37801
Doyle	38559
Drapers Crossroads	37083
Dresden	38225
Driftwood (Part of Bristol)	37620
Dripping Springs	37398
Drop	38583
Drummonds	38023
Drycreek	37659
Dry Hill (Johnson County)	37640
Dry Hill (Lauderdale County)	38040
Dry Hollow (Part of Kingsport)	37660
Duck Creek	37869
Duck River	38454
Ducktown (Polk County)	37326
Ducktown (Washington County)	37681
Dudney Hill	38562
Due West (Part of Nashville)	37115
Duff	37729
Dukedom	38226
Dulaney	37743
Dull	37036
Dumplin	37820
Dunbar	38311
Duncantown	37330
Dunlap	37327
Duplex	37064
Du Pont	37865
Durhamville	38063
Dutch	37888
Dutch Valley	37716
Dyer	38330
Dyersburg	38024*
	38025†
Dykes Crossroads	38555
Dyllis	37748
Dyson Grove	37640
Eads	38028
Eagan	37730
Eagle Creek	38341
Eagle Furnace	37854
Eagle Hill	38242
Eagleton Village (census designated place)	37801
Eagleton Village	37804
Eagleville	37060

	ZIP
Earleyville	37110
East (Part of Nashville)	37206
East Acres	38053
East Brainerd	37421
Eastbrook (Part of Estill Springs)	37330
East Chattanooga (Part of Chattanooga)	37406
East Cleveland	37311
East Cyruston	37334
East Due West (Part of Nashville)	37115
Easter Seal	37087
East Etowah	37331
East Fork	37862
Eastgate Mall (Part of Chattanooga)	37411
Eastgate Shopping Center (Part of Memphis)	38117
East Jamestown	38556
East Junction (Part of Memphis)	38101
East Lake (Part of Chattanooga)	37407
Eastland	38583
East Memphis (Part of Memphis)	38111
East Miller's Cove	37886
East Ridge	37412
Eastside (Cannon County)	37190
East Side (Carter County)	37643
East Side (Dickson County)	37029
Eastside (Sullivan County)	37664
Eastside (Warren County)	38581
East Springbrook (Part of Alcoa)	37701
East Sweetwater	37874
East Union	38301
Eastview (Greene County)	37743
Eastview (McNairy County)	38367
East View (Meigs County)	37336
Eastwood (Part of La Vergne)	37086
Eaton	38331
Eaton Crossroad	37771
Eaton Forest	37771
Ebenezer	37347
Echo Hills	37743
Eddie Hill	37087
Edenwold (Part of Nashville)	37115
Edgefield (Part of Bristol)	37620
Edgemont (Cocke County)	37821
Edgemont (Sullivan County)	37620
Edgemoor	37716
Edgewater (Rhea County)	37321
Edgewater (Wilson County)	37122
Edgewood (Dyer County)	38059
Edgewood (Sullivan County)	37660
Edgewood Acres	37804
Edgewood Heights	37849
Edison	38343
Edith	38063
Edwards Point	37377
Edwina	37821
Egam	37334
Egypt (Part of Memphis)	38128
Eidson	37731
Elba	38066
Elbethel	37160
Elbridge	38240
Elgin	37732
Elizabeth	38034
Elizabethton	37643*
	37644†
Elkhead	37366
Elkhorn	38242
Elk Mills	37640
Elk Mill Village (Part of Fayetteville)	37334
Elkmont	37738
Elkmont Springs	38449
Elkton	38455
Elk Valley	37847
Ellejoy	37865
Ellendale	38029
Ellington Park	37064
Ellis Mills	37050
Ellisville	38004
Elm Grove	38015
Elm Springs	37888
Elmwood	38560
Elora	37328
Elverton	37748
Elza	37830
Embreeville	37650
Emerald Acres	37814
Emerts Cove	37862
Emery Mill	37367
Emmanuel School of Religion	37601
Emmett	37620

	ZIP
Emory Gap (Part of Harriman)	37748
Emory Heights (Part of Harriman)	37748
Englewood (McMinn County)	37329
Englewood (Obion County)	38261
English Mountain Resort	37862
Enigma	38548
Eno	37055
Enon	37150
Ensor	38544
Enterprise (Hawkins County)	37857
Enterprise (Maury County)	38474
Enville	38332
Epperson	37385
Erasmus	38555
Erie	37846
Erin	37061
Erlanger (Part of Chattanooga)	37403
Ernestville	37650
Erwin	37650
Essary Springs	38061
Estes Kefauver (Part of Johnson City)	37601
Estill Springs	37330
Ethridge	38456
Etowah	37331
Etter	38549
Euchee	37880
Eulia	37186
Eureka (Bradley County)	37323
Eureka (Hardin County)	38372
Eureka (Roane County)	37854
Eurekaton	38075
Eva	38333
Evansville	38024
Evensville	37332
Evergreen	37687
Evins Mill	37166
Ewingville (Part of Franklin)	37064
Excell	37040
Factory	38485
Fair Acres (Hickman County)	37025
Fair Acres (Sullivan County)	37660
Fairfield (Bedford County)	37183
Fairfield (Hamblen County)	37814
Fairfield (Hickman County)	37033
Fairfield (Sumner County)	37186
Fairfield Glade	38555
Fair Garden	37862
Fairgrounds (Part of Shelbyville)	37160
Fairlane Estates (Part of Shelbyville)	37160
Fairmont (Part of Bristol)	37620
Fairmount	37377
Fairview (Blount County)	37801
Fairview (Bradley County)	37312
Fairview (Carroll County)	38201
Fairview (Carter County)	37658
Fairview (Clay County)	38541
Fairview (Coffee County)	37360
Fairview (Fentress County)	38556
Fairview (Gibson County)	38233
Fairview (Greene County; mail Afton)	37616
Fairview (Greene County; mail Mohawk)	37810
Fairview (Lawrence County)	38469
Fair View (Lincoln County)	37334
Fairview (Macon County)	37186
Fairview (Madison County)	38343
Fairview (McMinn County)	37303
Fairview (Meigs County)	37322
Fairview (Pickett County)	38549
Fairview (Putnam County)	38501
Fairview (Roane County)	37763
Fairview (Scott County)	37756
Fairview (Stewart County)	37058
Fairview (Warren County)	37110
Fairview (Washington County)	37659
Fairview (Wayne County)	38463
Fairview (White County)	38583
Fairview (Williamson County)	37062
Fairview Heights (Jefferson County)	37725
Fairview Heights (Williamson County)	37062
Fairyland	38555
Faix	38549
Falcon	38375
Fall Branch	37656
Fall Creek	37160
Falling Water	37343
Fallriver	38468
Falls Mill	37306
Fanchers Mills	38583

	ZIP		ZIP		ZIP
Fancy Meadows	37871	Fort Loudon Estates	37771	Gibbs Crossroads	37145
Farmers Exchange	38462	Fort Pillow Prison and State		Gibson	38338
Farmers Valley	37096	Farm	38041	Gibson Hall	37879
Farmington (Marshall		Fort Robinson (Part of		Gibsontown (Part of	
County)	37091	Kingsport)	37660	Kingsport)	37660
Farmington (Williamson		Fosterville	37063	Gibson Wells	38343
County)	37064	Foundry Hill	38251	Gift	38019
Farner	37333	Fountain City (Part of		Gilchrist	38310
Farragut	37922	Knoxville)	37918	Gildfield	38002
Farris Chapel	37398	Fountain Head	37148	Gilfield	37686
Farrport (Part of Alcoa)	37701	Fountain Heights	38401	Gillises Mills	38372
Faulkner Springs	37110	Fourmile Board Hill	38485	Gilmore	38301
Faxon	38221	Four Points	37820	Gilt Edge	38015
Fayette Corners	38075	Fowler Grove	37713	Gin House Lake	38058
Fayetteville	37334	Fowlers	38320	Gladdice	38562
Federal Correctional		Fowlkes	38033	Glade Creek	38583
Institution	38116	Fox Bluff	37015	Glades (Morgan County)	37726
Federal Reserve (Part of		Foxbranch	37765	Glades (Sevier County)	37738
Nashville)	37203	Foxfire	38555	Gladeville	37071
Fellowship	37122	Frankewing	38459	Glass	38240
Fennel Store	37709	Frankfort	37770	Gleason	38229
Fernvale	37064	Franklin	37660-65	Glen	37342
Fernwood	37814		37068	Glen Alice	37854
Few Chapel	37101	For specific Franklin Zip Codes		Glencliff (Part of Nashville)	37211
Fielden Store	37820	call (615) 794-2784, or your local		Glendale (Hamilton County)	37405
Fincastle	37766	postmaster.		Glendale (Lawrence	
Findlay (Part of Sparta)	38583	Franklin East	37064	County)	38469
Finger	38334	Fraterville	37769	Glendale (Loudon County)	37742
Finley	38030	Frayser (Part of Memphis)	38127	Glendale (Maury County)	38401
Fisherville	38017	Fredonia (Coffee County)	37355	Glendale Estates	38478
Fishery	37650	Fredonia (Montgomery		Glen Del Acres	37860
Fish Springs	37640	County)	37040	Glenhaven (Part of Fairview)	37062
Fisk University (Part of		Free Communion	38573	Glen Mary	37852
Nashville)	37203	Free Hills	38551	Glenmore Estates	37853
Five Points (Lawrence		Freeland	38222	Glen Oaks	37122
County)	38457	Free State	38562	Glenobey	38556
Five Points (Madison		Freewill	38562	Glenview (Part of Nashville)	37217
County)	38366	Fremont	38261	Glenwood	37185
Five Points (Rhea County)	37321	French Broad	37727	Glenwylde	37051
Flag Branch	37743	Frettin	38052	Gilmp	38041
Flag Pond	37657	Friendship (Bledsoe County)	37381	Glover	37172
Flat Branch Junction	37387	Friendship (Crockett		Glover Hill	37347
Flat Creek (Bedford County)	37160	County)	38034	Glynnwood Lake	38028
Flat Creek (Overton County)	38570	Friendship (Hamilton		Gnat Hill	37355
Flat Gap (Hancock County)	37881	County)	37341	Goat City	38355
Flatgap (Jefferson County)	37760	Friendship (Hawkins		Godwin	38401
Flat Hollow	37870	County)	37881	Goffton	38501
Flat Rock (Morgan County)	37726	Friendship (Sullivan County)	37620	Goin	37825
Flat Rock (Smith County)	37087	Friends Station	37820	Golddust	38063
Flattop	37379	Friendsville	37737	Goldpoint	37343
Flatwood (Tipton County)	38015	Frisco	37642	Goodbars	38581
Flatwood (Warren County)	37110	Frog Jump (Crockett		Goodfield	37322
Flatwoods (Lawrence		County)	38040	Good Hope (Campbell	
County)	38456	Frog Jump (Gibson County)	38382	County)	37762
Flatwoods (Perry County)	37096	Frog Level	37731	Good Hope (Dyer County)	38059
Flewellyn	37172	Front Street (Part of		Goodlettsville	37070
Flintville	37335	Memphis)	38103		37072
Flippin	38063	Frost Bottom	37840	For specific Goodlettsville Zip	
Floraton	37149	Fruitland	38343	Codes call (615) 859-2766, or	
Florence	37129	Fruitvale	38336	your local postmaster.	
Flourville	37659	Fruit Valley	37153	Good Luck	38369
Flowertown	37360	Fulton	38041	Goodspring	38460
Fly	38482	Gabtown	37656	Good Springs	37331
Flynns Lick	38562	Gadsden	38337	Goose Horn	38588
Foothills Mall (Part of		Gainesboro	38562	Gooseneck (Anderson	
Maryville)	37804	Gainsville	38049	County)	37705
Forbus	38577	Gaitherville	38464	Gooseneck (Blount County)	37737
Ford	37771	Galaxy Heights (Part of		Gordon (Part of Pulaski)	38478
Ford Chapel	37825	Chattanooga)	37343	Gordonsburg	38462
Fordtown (Campbell		Galbraith Springs	37811	Gordonsville	38563
County)	37766	Galen	37083	Gorman	37101
Fordtown (Sullivan County)	37663	Gallatin	37066	Goshen	37642
Forest Chapel	37186	Gallaway	38036	Gossburg	37018
Forest Grove (Davidson		Gandy	38464	Graball (Gibson County)	38358
County)	37080	Gann	38358	Graball (Marshall County)	37047
Forest Grove (Meigs		Gapcreek	37643	Graball (Sumner County)	37148
County)	37322	Gardner	38237	Graham	37137
Forest Hill (Blount County)	37801	Garland	38019	Grammer Estates	37062
Forest Hill (Shelby County)	38139	Garretts	38329	Grand Junction	38039
Forest Hills (Bedford		Gassaway	37095	Grand Valley	38067
County)	37160	Gates	38037	Grandview (Greene County)	37641
Forest Hills (Davidson		Gath	37110	Grandview (Knox County)	37920
County)	37215	Gatlinburg	37738	Grandview (Rhea County)	37337
Forest Hills (Knox County)	37919	Gattistown	37359	Grandview Estates	37620
Forest Hills (Sullivan		Gause	37035	Grandview Terrace	37620
County)	37620	Gay	37110	Granite	37716
Forest Home	37064	Gentry	38544	Grannys Branch	38221
Forest Home Farms	37064	Georgetown (Gibson		Grant	38563
Forest Mills	37355	County)	38382	Grantsboro	37766
Forge Ridge	37752	Georgetown (Hamilton		Granville	38564
Forked Deer	38037	County)	37336	Grasshopper	37308
Fork Mountain	37710	Georgetown (McMinn		Grassland	37064
Fork of Pike	37095	County)	37370	Grassy Cove	38555
Fork Ridge	40965	George W. Lee (Part of		Grassy Creek	37317
Forrest Park (Part of		Memphis)	38126	Grassy Fork	37753
Tullahoma)	37388	Georgia Crossing	37398	Grassy Valley	37743
Forsythe (Part of Memphis)	38101	Germantown (Davidson		Gratio	38240
Fort Campbell	42223	County)	37189	Gravel Hill (McNairy County)	38339
Fort Campbell South	42223	Germantown (Shelby		Gravel Hill (Washington	
Fort Donelson Shores	37058	County)	38138	County)	37681
Fort Henry Mall (Part of		Gerren Heights	37367	Gravelly Hill (Part of	
Kingsport)	37664	Gibbs (Part of Union City)	38261	Jefferson City)	37760

* Area Zip Code   † Post Office Boxes

	ZIP		ZIP		ZIP
Graveltown	37145	Hallview Meadows (Part of		Hensley Chapel	38583
Graveston	37721	Fairview)	37062	Herbert Domain	37367
Gray	37615	Hamburg	38376	Heritage Estates	38555
Gray Acres	37620	Hamillville (Part of		Heritage Hills	37801
Graysville	37338	Chattanooga)	37343	Hermitage (Part of	
Graytown	37033	Hamilton Mill	38453	Nashville)	37076
Graywinds	37122	Hamilton Place (Part of		Hermitage Hills (Part of	
Green Ack	37840	Chattanooga)	37421	Nashville)	37076
Green Acres (Giles County)	38478	Hamlin Town	37715	Hermitage Springs	37150
Green Acres (Knox County)	37921	Hammon Chapel	37683	Hermon	37616
Green Acres (Roane		Hampshire	38461	Hiawassee	37357
County)	37763	Hampton	37658	Hickerson	37388
Green Acres (Sullivan		Hamptons Crossroads	38583	Hickey	38582
County)	37660	Hampton Station	37040	Hickman	38567
Greenback	37742	Handleyton	37148	Hickory Bend (Part of	
Greenbriar	37185	Hanging Limb	38554	Nashville)	37214
Greenbriar Village (Part of		Happy Hill	38478	Hickory Flat	38321
Crossville)	38555	Happy Top	37337	Hickory Flats	38310
Greenbrier (Cheatham		Happy Valley	37878	Hickory Grove (Gibson	
County)	37015	Harbin	37854	County)	38382
Green Brier (Pickett County)	38549	Harbison	37721	Hickory Grove (Sumner	
Greenbrier (Robertson		Harbor Town	38221	County)	37031
County)	37073	Harbour Island	37138	Hickory Grove (Warren	
Greenbrier (Williamson		Harbuck	37391	County)	37110
County)	37064	Hardin Estates	37771	Hickory Hill (Part of	
Greenbrier Lake	37087	Hardy	38501	Lynchburg)	37352
Greeneville	37743*	Harmon	37688	Hickory Hill (Shelby County)	38125
	37744†	Harmony (Franklin County)	37398		38141
Greenfield	38230	Harmony (Jackson County)	38562	For specific Hickory Hill Zip Codes	
Greenfield Bend	38487	Harmony (Washington		call (615) 759-7818, or your local	
Greenfields (Part of		County)	37659	postmaster.	
Kingsport)	37660	Harmony Grove	37727	Hickory Hill Estates (Part of	
Green Grove	37074	Harmony Hills	37660	Tullahoma)	37388
Green Harbor	37138	Harms	37334	Hickory Hills	37064
Greenhaw	37324	Harpeth	37064	Hickory Hollow Mall (Part of	
Green Hill (Jefferson		Harpeth Estates	37064	Nashville)	37211
County)	37725	Harpeth Hills	37064	Hickory Point	37040
Green Hill (Warren County)	37110	Harpeth Meadows (Part of		Hickory Star Landing	37807
Green Hill (Wilson County)	37138	Franklin)	37064	Hickory Tree	37618
Green Hills (Part of		Harpeth Valley	37187	Hickory Valley (Hardeman	
Nashville)	37215	Harpeth Valley Park (Part of		County)	38042
Greenland	37642	Nashville)	37221	Hickory Valley (Union	
Green Meadow (Blount		Harrill Hills (Part of		County)	37807
County)	37701	Knoxville)	37918	Hickory Withe	38043
Green Meadow (Bradley		Harriman	37748	Hicks Chapel	37397
County)	37311	Harriman Junction (Part of		Hicksville (Part of Jackson)	38301
Green Meadows	38556	Harriman)	37748	Hico	38344
Green Pond	38554	Harris	38261	Hico Station	38344
Greens	37110	Harrisburg	37862	Hide-A-Way Hills	38555
Greens Mill	37343	Harrison	37341	Highcliff	37762
Greentown	37387	Harrison Hills	37771	Highgate	37064
Greenvale	37184	Harrogate	37752	Highland (DeKalb County)	37166
Green Valley (Knox County)	37919	Harrogate-Shawnee	37752	Highland (Jackson County)	38562
Green Valley (Macon		Harrtown	37617	Highland (Overton County)	38570
County)	37083	Hartford	37753	Highland (Wayne County)	38450
Green Valley (Williamson		Hartmantown	37659	Highland Academy	37148
County)	37064	Hartsville	37074	Highland Acres	37804
Green Village (Part of		Haskins Chapel	37091	Highland Forest (Part of	
Church Hill)	37642	Hatchertown	37862	Rockwood)	37854
Greenwood (Macon County)	37150	Hatchie	38392	Highland Heights (Davidson	
Greenwood (Rutherford		Havley Springs (Part of		County)	37207
County)	37046	Morristown)	37814	Highland Heights (Giles	
Greenwood (Wilson County)	37087	Havron Chapel	37347	County)	38478
Greystone	37743	Hawkinsville	38034	Highland Heights (Shelby	
Griffith	37367	Hawthorne	37160	County)	38122
Griffith Creek	37397	Haydenburg	38588	Highland Junction	38589
Grimsley	38565	Hayes	38583	Highland Manor	37341
Grinders	37033	Hayes Fork	37058	Highland Park (Campbell	
Gronanville	38079	Haynes	38077	County)	37766
Gruetli (Part of Gruetli-		Haynesfield (Part of Bristol)	37620	Highland Park (Hamilton	
Laager)	37339	Hays	38057	County)	37404
Gruetli-Laager	37339	Haysboro (Part of Nashville)	37216	Highland Park (Loudon	
Gudger	37354	Haysville	37083	County)	37771
Guild	37340	Head of Barren	37825	Highland Park (Sullivan	
Gulf Park	37919	Heard	38573	County)	37660
Gum	37130	Heatherwood Hill	37064	Highland Springs	37709
Gum Creek	37324	Heatoncreek	37687	Highlandview	37920
Gum Flat	38006	Hebbertsburg	37723	High Point (Campbell	
Gum Spring	37821	Hebron	38052	County)	37714
Gum Springs (Lawrence		Heiskell	37754	High Point (Scott County)	37841
County)	38468	Helena	38556	Hilham	38568
Gum Springs (Macon		Helenwood	37755	Hillcrest (Cumberland	
County)	37145	Heloise	38030	County)	38555
Guntown	37857	Helton	37012	Hillcrest (Hamblen County)	37814
Guys	38339	Helton Springs	37861	Hillcrest (Sullivan County)	37618
Habersham	37766	Heltonville	37708	Hillcrest (Part of Kingsport)	37660
Hackberry	37142	Hemlock Hills	37650	Hilldale (Part of Clarksville)	37043
Hales Crossroads	37814	Henard Mill	37857	Hill Estates (Part of Franklin)	37064
Hales Point	38040	Henardtown	37857	Hilliard	38344
Halesville	37095	Henderson	38340	Hillsboro	37342
Haletown	37340	Hendersonville	37075*	Hillsboro Acres	37064
Haley	37183		37077†	Hillsdale	37057
Half Acre	37166	Hendon	37338	Hillside	38237
Halls (Knox County)	37918	Hendron	37920	Hills View	37370
Halls (Lauderdale County)	38040	Henley (Part of Decherd)	37324	Hilltop (Bedford County)	37160
Halls Creek	37185	Henning	38041	Hilltop (Montgomery	
Halls Crossroads	37918	Henrietta	37015	County)	37040
Hallshare Estates	38320	Henry	38231	Hilltop (Rutherford County)	37167
Halls Hill	37118	Henrys Crossroads	37764	Hill Top (Washington	
Halls Mills	37160	Henry Street (Part of		County)	37601
Hall Town (Sumner County)	37148	Morristown)	37814	Hill Town	38482
Halltown (Trousdale County)	37074	Henryville	38483	Hillvale	37716

* Area Zip Code   † Post Office Boxes

	ZIP		ZIP		ZIP
Hillville	38075	Hughey	37334	Jefferson	37166
Hillwood (Part of Nashville)	37205	Hulan Hollow (Part of Erwin)	37650	Jefferson City	37760
Himesville	37160	Humboldt	38343	Jefferson Estates	37877
Hindscreek	37716	Humphrey	37865	Jefferson Springs	37167
Hinds Creek Valley	37807	Hunter	37643	Jellico	37762
Hinkle	38371	Hunter Hills	37379	Jena	37742
Hinkledale	38201	Hunters Point	37087	Jenkins Hill (Part of	
Hitchcox	37367	Hunters Ridge	37064	Sevierville)	37862
Hiwassee College	37354	Huntersville	38301	Jenkinsville	38024
Hiwassee Hills	37354	Hunting Creek Farms	37064	Jere Baxter (Part of	
Hixon	37301	Huntingdon	38344	Nashville)	37216
Hixson (Part of		Huntland	37345	Jernigan Town	37188
Chattanooga)	37343	Huntsville (Loudon County)	37771	Jersey (Part of	
Hobbs Hill	37387	Huntsville (Scott County)	37756	Chattanooga)	37416
Hodges	37820	Hurdlow (Part of Lynchburg)	37306	Jessie	37110
Hoggtown	37030	Hurley	38357	Jewell	38225
Hohenwald	38462	Hurley Acres	37814	Jewett	37337
Holiday City (Part of		Huron	38345	Jimtown	37821
Memphis)	38118	Hurricane (Houston County)	37175	Joelton (Part of Nashville)	37080
Holiday Hills (Cumberland		Hurricane (Jackson County)	38562	John Sevier	37914
County)	38555	Hurricane (Wilson County)	37087	Johnson Bible College	37920
Holiday Hills (Roane		Hurricane Hill	38063	Johnson City	37601-15
County)	37763	Hurricane Mills	37078	For specific Johnson City Zip	
Holiday Shores	37028	Hustburg	37134	Codes call (615) 461-8251, or	
Holladay (Benton County)	38341	Hutsell (Part of Athens)	37303	your local postmaster.	
Holladay (Putnam County)	38501	Hygeia Springs	37073	Johnsons	37048
Holland Mill	37616	Hyndsver	38237	Johnsons Chapel	38583
Hollow Rock	38342	Iconium	37190	Johnsons Grove	38006
Hollow Springs	37026	Idaho	38468	Johntown	37074
Holly Grove (Haywood		Idaville	38004	Jones	38006
County)	38006	Ideal Valley	37381	Jonesborough	37659
Holly Grove (Marshall		Idlewild (Gibson County)	38346	Jones Chapel	38549
County)	37091	Idlewild (McMinn County)	37303	Jones Cove	37862
Holly Grove (Tipton County)	38011	Idlewood (Part of Franklin)	37064	Jones Mill	38224
Holly Leaf	38258	Ilemar	37122	Jones Valley	38482
Holly Springs	38570	Imperial Estates	37921	Jonesville (Fentress County)	38553
Hollywood (Maury County)	38451	Independence (Hancock		Jonesville (Roane County)	37840
Hollywood (Shelby County)	38108	County)	37731	Joppa (Grainger County)	37861
Hollywood (Part of		Independence (Overton		Joppa (White County)	38587
Nashville)	37066	County)	38573	Jordonia (Part of Nashville)	37218
Holston Army Ammunition		Independence Estates	37087	Jug Town	37130
Plant	37662	India	38242	Juno	38351
Holston Heights (Part of		Indian Bluff	37710	Kagley	37801
Kingsport)	37660	Indian Cave	37709	Kansas (Jefferson County)	37760
Holston Hills (Knox County)	37914	Indian Creek	37757	Kansas (Sumner County)	37066
Holston Hills (Sullivan		Indian Hills	37087	Karns	37921
County)	37620	Indian Mound (DeKalb		Kaywood (Part of	
Holston Institute	37617	County)	38583	Tullahoma)	37388
Holston Valley	37620	Indian Mound (Stewart		Kedron (Giles County)	38477
Holts Corner	37034	County)	37079	Kedron (Maury County)	37174
Holttown	37821	Indian Ridge (Grainger		Keefe	38080
Holy Hill	37683	County)	37709	Keeling	38069
Homestead	38555	Indian Ridge (Washington		Keenburg	37643
Honeycutt	37857	County)	37601	Keese (Part of Decherd)	37324
Hood Lake (Part of		Indian Springs	37617	Keith Springs	37398
Lawrenceburg)	38464	Ingleside Hill (Part of		Kellertown	37183
Hoodoo	37018	Athens)	37303	Kelley Town (Part of Oliver	
Hookers Bend	38361	Inglewood (Part of		Springs)	37840
Hoop	37879	Nashville)	37216	Kelso	37348
Hoovers Gap	37037	Inskip (Part of Knoxville)	37912	Keltonburg	37166
Hopewell (Bradley County)	37312	Interstate Park	37032	Kemmer Hill (Part of Spring	
Hopewell (Carroll County)	38348	Irish Cut	37821	City)	37381
Hopewell (Claiborne		Iron City	38463	Kempville	37030
County)	37879	Ironsburg	37385	Kendricks Creek	37663
Hopewell (Davidson County)	37138	Irving College	37110	Kennedy Creek	37016
Hopewell (Gibson County)	38389	Irwinton Shores	37880	Kenneytown	37743
Hopewell (Tipton County)	38011	Isabella	37346	Kenton	38233
Hopewell Springs	37354	Isham	37892	Kepler	37857
Hopper Bluff	37861	Island Home (Part of		Kerrville	38053
Hopson	37687	Knoxville)	37920	Kettle Mills	38461
Hornbeak	38232	Island Park	37618	Key	38583
Horner	37096	Isoline	38555	Keystone (Part of Johnson	
Hornertown	37147	Isom	38461	City)	37601
Hornsby	38044	Ivy	37369	Killians Chapel (Part of	
Horn Springs	37087	Ivy Bluff	37110	Altamont)	37301
Horse Creek (Greene		Ivydell	37766	Kilsyth	37766
County)	37641	Ivy Point (Part of Nashville)	37072	Kimball	37347
Horse Creek (Sullivan		Ivyton	38543	Kimberlin Heights	37920
County)	37660	Jacksboro	37757	Kimberly Acres	37122
Horse Shoe	37643	Jacks Creek	38347	Kimbrough Crossroad	37890
Horseshoe Bend	38560	Jackson	38301-08	Kimery	38230
Horsleys	37074		38314	Kimmins	38462
Housley Addition (Part of		For specific Jackson Zip Codes		Kimsey	37391
Athens)	37303	call (901) 422-5369, or your local		Kin Cove	37087
Houston	38471	postmaster.		Kinderhook	38482
Houston Valley	37743	Jackson Heights (Part of		King	37715
Howard (Monroe County)	37885	Murfreesboro)	37129	Kingfield	37064
Howard (Sevier County)	37865	Jackson Ridge	37060	Kingsport	37660-65
Howard Chapel	38570	Jacksons Chapel	37036	For specific Kingsport Zip Codes	
Howard Hill (Part of		Jackson Square (Part of		call (615) 245-5111, or your local	
Kingsport)	37660	Oak Ridge)	37830	postmaster.	
Howard Quarter	37879	Jacobs Hill	37087	King Springs (Part of	
Howard Springs	38555	Jakestown	37130	Johnson City)	37601
Howell (Lincoln County)	37334	Jamestown (Fentress		Kings Ridge (Part of	
Howell (White County)	38583	County)	38556	Chattanooga)	37343
Howell Hill	37334	Jamestown (Tipton County)	38015	Kingston	37763
Howley	38321	Jarrell	38201	Kingston Heights	37763
Hubbard	37801	Jasper	37347	Kingston Hills	37919
Hubertville	37172	Jaybird (Cocke County)	37821	Kingston Mill	37160
Hudson	38464	Jaybird (Hamblen County)	37814	Kingston Springs	37082
Hugarth	38556	Jeannette	38363	Kingston Woods	37919
Hughes Loop	38358	Jearoldstown	37641	Kinzel Springs	37882
Hughett	37852				

	ZIP
Kirk	38017
Kirkland (Lincoln County)	38488
Kirkland (Williamson County)	37046
Kite	37857
Kittrell	37149
Kleburne	37174
Kline	37398
Klondike	37857
Knapp	37769
Knob Creek (Lauderdale County)	38063
Knob Creek (Sevier County)	37865
Knoxville	37901-50
For specific Knoxville Zip Codes call (615) 558-4528, or your local postmaster.	
Knoxville College (Part of Knoxville)	37921
Kodak	37764
Kodak Estates	37764
KoKo	38069
Kontika	37087
Kyles Ford	37765
Laager (Part of Gruetli-Laager)	37339
Laconia	38045
Lacy	38052
Lafayette	37083
La Follette	37766
La Grange	38046
Laguardo	37087
Lake City	37769
Lake Colonial Estates	37014
Lake Crest	37663
Lake Drive	38079
Lake Farm Estates	37167
Lake Forest (Grainger County)	37861
Lake Forest (Hamilton County)	37343
Lake Forest (Knox County)	37920
Lakeharbor	37763
Lake Harbor Estates	37416
Lake Haven	37087
Lake Hills (Part of Tullahoma)	37388
Lakeland	38002
Lakemont	37777
Lakemont Cabin Area	37811
Lakemont Heights (Part of Rockwood)	37854
Lakemoor	37920
Lakemoore (Part of Morristown)	37814
Lake Placid	38340
Lake Road (Part of Fairview)	37062
Lakeshore Estates	37416
Lake Side (Hamilton County)	37343
Lakeside (Monroe County)	37885
Lakeside Estates (Part of Estill Springs)	37330
Lakeside Heights	37890
Lakesite	37379
Lake Tansi Village	38555
Lake Tullahoma Estates (Part of Tullahoma)	37388
Lakeview (Blount County)	37777
Lakeview (Claiborne County)	37825
Lakeview (Hamblen County)	37814
Lakeview (McMinn County)	37303
Lakeview (Roane County)	37763
Lakeview (Robertson County)	37172
Lakeview Commercial Park (Part of Franklin)	37064
Lakeview Estates	37777
Lake View Heights (Part of Harriman)	37748
Lakeview Manor	38256
Lakeview Park (Part of Dandridge)	37725
Lakewood	37138
Lakewood Village	37381
Lamar (Part of Memphis)	38114
Lambert	38068
Lamont	37172
Lamontville	37309
Lancaster	38569
Lancaster Hill	38567
Lancelot Acres	38478
Lancing	37770
Lane	38240
Laneview	38382
Langford Farms	37138
Lanier	37801
Lantana	38555
Lapata	38059
Lascassas	37085

	ZIP
Lassiter Corner	38232
Latham	38225
Laurel (Anderson County)	37716
Laurel (Sevier County)	37862
Laurel Bloomery	37680
Laurel Bluff	37763
Laurel Brook	37321
Laurelburg	38581
Laurel Cove	38585
Laurel Grove	37710
La Vergne	37086
Lavinia	38348
Law	38351
Law Chapel	37801
Lawnville	37763
Lawrenceburg	38464
Lawson Crossroad	37882
Lawton	38375
Leach	38344
Leadvale (Cocke County)	37821
Leadvale (Jefferson County)	37890
Leana	37129
Leapwood	38310
Lea Springs	37709
Leatherwood	38485
Lebanon	37087*
	37088†
Ledgemere	37160
Lee	37367
Lee College (Part of Cleveland)	37311
Leeland	37064
Leemans Corner	37087
Leesburg	37659
Lee Valley	37869
Leeville	37087
Leewood (Part of Memphis)	38101
Leftwich	38401
Legate	37079
Leighs Chapel	38019
Leighton	38391
Leinart	37716
Leipers Fork	37064
Lenoir City	37771
Lenow	38018
Lenox	38047
Leoma	38468
Leonard	37620
Leoni	37190
Lewisburg	37091
Lewis Chapel	37327
Lexie	37306
Lexie Crossroads	37306
Lexington	38351
Liberty (Benton County)	38320
Liberty (Decatur County)	38374
Liberty (DeKalb County)	37095
Liberty (Franklin County)	37398
Liberty (Giles County)	38477
Liberty (Jackson County)	38564
Liberty (Johnson County)	37683
Liberty (Lincoln County)	37334
Liberty (Morgan County)	37887
Liberty (Sumner County; mail Bethpage)	37022
Liberty (Sumner County; mail Gallatin)	37066
Liberty (Washington County)	37641
Liberty (Weakley County)	38229
Liberty Grove	38469
Liberty Hill (Grainger County)	37888
Liberty Hill (Greene County)	37641
Liberty Hill (McMinn County)	37329
Liberty Hill (Williamson County)	37025
Liberty Hill (Wilson County)	37012
Lick Creek (Benton County)	38221
Lick Creek (Decatur County)	38363
Lickskillet	37807
Lickton (Part of Nashville)	37189
Lightfoot	38063
Lillamay	37015
Lillydale	37650
Lily Grove	37825
Limbs	38255
Limestone	37681
Limestone Cove	37692
Linary	38555
Lincoln	37334
Lincoln Park (Part of Knoxville)	37917
Lincoya Hills (Part of Nashville)	37214
Linden	37096
Lindsay Mill	37769
Link	37037
Linsdale	37325
Linton (Part of Nashville)	37188
Linwood	37087

	ZIP
Lisbon	38052
Little Barren (Claiborne County)	37825
Little Barren (Union County)	37825
Littlebrook (Part of Rockford)	37853
Littlecrab	38556
Little Creek	37752
Little Doe	37640
Little Emory	37748
Little Hope (Rutherford County)	37129
Little Hope (Wayne County)	38485
Littlelot	38454
Little Milligan	37640
Little River	37804
Little White Oak	37766
Litton	37367
Litz Manor (Part of Kingsport)	37660
Liverwort	37040
Livingston	38570
Lobelville	37097
Locke	38053
Lockertsville	37015
Lockmiller Addition (Part of Athens)	37303
Locust Grove	38059
Locust Mount	37659
Locust Springs	37616
Lodge	37380
Lodi	38486
Logans Lake	38334
Lois (Part of Lynchburg)	37359
Lomax Crossroads	38462
Lone Mountain (Claiborne County)	37773
Lone Mountain (Scott County)	37852
Lone Oak	37377
Lone Oaks (Part of Atoka)	38004
Lone Star	37660
Long Branch (Hamilton County)	37343
Long Branch (Lawrence County)	38464
Long Creek	37843
Long Hollow (Part of La Follette)	37766
Long Island	37660
Long Rock	38344
Longs Mills	37303
Longtown	38049
Longview	37020
Longwood	37064
Lonsdale (Part of Knoxville)	37921
Lookout Mountain	37350
Lookout Valley (Part of Chattanooga)	37419
Loon Bay	37028
Loonewood	38585
Loretto	38469
Lorraine	37381
Lost Creek	38583
Lost Mountain	37743
Loudon	37774
Louise	37051
Louisville	37777
Love Joy	38574
Lovelace	37641
Love Lady	38549
Loveland (Part of Knoxville)	37924
Lovell Heights	37922
Love Station	37650
Lovetown	38474
Lower Mill	37343
Lower Mockeson	38468
Lowland	37778
Lowryville	38372
Luckett	38063
Lucky	37110
Lucy	38053
Luna	37019
Lunns Store	37034
Lupton City (Part of Chattanooga)	37351
Luray	38352
Lusk	37327
Luskville	37309
Luther	37869
Luttrell (Loudon County)	37846
Luttrell (Union County)	37779
Lutts	38471
Lyles	37098
Lynchburg	37352
Lynn Garden	37665
Lynnville	38472
Lyons View (Part of Knoxville)	37919
McAllister Hill	37346
McAllisters Crossroads	37171
McAnna	38260

	ZIP		ZIP		ZIP
McBurg	38459	Marys Grove	38488	Holiday Inn	
McCains	38401	Maryville	37801-04	Midtown/Medical Center	38104
McClamerys Stand (Part of		For specific Maryville Zip Codes		Ramada	38115
Collinwood)	38450	call (615) 983-7801, or your local		Ramada Hotel Convention	
McCloud	37857	postmaster.		Center	38103
McClures Bend	37030	Mascot	37806		
McCoinsville	38562	Mason	38049	*MILITARY INSTALLATIONS*	
McConnell	38237	Mason Grove	38343	Defense Distribution Depot,	
McCullough	38024	Masonhall	38233	Memphis	38114
McDonald	37353	Masseyville	38315	Tennessee Air National	
McDonald Hill	37857	Maupin Row (Part of		Guard, FB6422, Memphis	
Macedonia (Carroll County)	38201	Johnson City)	37601	International Airport	38118
Macedonia (McMinn		Maury City	38050	United States Army	
County)	37329	Maxey	38059	Engineer District,	
Macedonia (Obion County)	38233	Maxwell	37306	Memphis	38103
Macedonia (White County)	38583	Maxwell Chapel	38568		
McElroy	38559	May Acres	37877	Memphis State University	
Mace's Hill	37057	Mayhome	37184	(Part of Memphis)	38111
McEwen	37101	Mayland	38555	Mendenhall (Part of	
McGeetown	37317	Maynardville	37807	Memphis)	38117
McIllwain	38341	Mayview Heights	37849	Mengelwood	38047
McKenzie	38201	Meacham	38024	Mentor	37777
McKinley	37601	Meades Quarry (Part of		Mercer	38392
McKinnon	37175	Knoxville)	37920	Meredith Cave	37766
McKnight	38482	Meadorville	37083	Merry Oaks (Part of	
McLemoresville	38235	Meadow	37742	Nashville)	37214
McLin's Corner	38034	Meadowbrook (Blount		Michie	38357
McMahan	37862	County)	37804	Middlebrook Heights (Part	
McMillan	37914	Meadowbrook (Greene		of Knoxville)	37919
McMinnville	37110	County)	37616	Middleburg (Hardeman	
McNairy	38315	Meadow Brook (Warren		County)	38008
Macon	38048	County)	37110	Middleburg (Henderson	
McPheeter Bend	37642	Meadow Green Acres	37064	County)	38374
Maddox	38372	Meadow Mead (Part of		Middle City	38024
Madge	38002	Paris)	38242	Middle Creek	37862
Madie	38080	Meadow View (Hamilton		Middle Fork	38352
Madison	37115*	County)	37336	Middle Settlement	37777
	37116†	Meadowview (Lawrence		Middleton	38052
Madison College (Part of		County)	38464	Middle Valley	37343
Nashville)	37115	Meadowview Gardens (Part		Middle Valley Estates	37343
Madison Hall	38301	of Harriman)	37748	Midfields	37665
Madison Square (Part of		Meadowwood Acres (Part		Midland	37020
Nashville)	37115	of Fairview)	37062	Midland Shopping Center	
Madisonville	37354	Mechanicsville	37190	(Part of Alcoa)	37701
Maggart	38560	Medford	37769	Midtown	37748
Magnolia	37175	Medina	38355	Midtown Heights	37748
Magnolia Place (Part of		Medon	38356	Midway (Cannon County)	37026
Franklin)	37064	Melrose (Blount County)	37886	Midway (Cocke County)	37727
Major	37087	Melrose (Davidson County)	37204	Midway (Cumberland	
Malesus (Part of Jackson)	38301	Melville Hill (Part of Soddy-		County)	38555
Mall (Part of Cookeville)	38501	Daisy)	37379	Midway (DeKalb County)	37166
Mall, The (Part of Johnson		Melvine	37367	Midway (Dyer County)	38030
City)	37601	Melwood	38315	Midway (Franklin County)	37375
Mall of Memphis, The (Part		Memorial	37150	Midway (Greene County)	37809
of Memphis)	38118			Midway (Johnson County)	37640
Mallory (Part of Memphis)	38109	**Memphis**	38101-87	Midway (Knox County)	37871
Mallorys (Part of Franklin)	37064	For specific Memphis Zip Codes		Midway (Obion County)	38261
Maloney Heights	37920	call (901) 775-3872, or your local		Midway (Roane County)	37763
Maloneyville	37918	postmaster.		Midway (Warren County)	37110
Manchester	37355	*COLLEGES & UNIVERSITIES*		Midway (Washington	
Mankinville	37130			County)	37601
Manlyville	38256	Christian Brothers College	38104	Mifflin	38352
Mansfield	38236	Memphis State University	38152	Milan	38358
Mansfield Gap	37877	Rhodes College	38112	Milan Army Ammunition	
Mansford	37398	University of Tennessee-		Plant	38358
Manson	38556	Memphis	38163	Milburnton	37681
Maple Grove (Clay County)	38541			Miles Crossroads	37150
Maple Grove (Macon		*FINANCIAL INSTITUTIONS*		Mile Straight (Part of Soddy-	
County)	37083	Bank of Bartlett	38128	Daisy)	37379
Maple Grove (Meigs		Boatmen's Bank of		Milky Way	38478
County)	37880	Tennessee	38119	Mill Brook	37681
Maple Hill	37620	Community Bank of		Mill Creek (Anderson	
Maplehurst	37618	Germantown	38119	County)	37705
Maplewood (Part of		First American National		Mill Creek (Hickman	
Nashville)	37216	Bank	38103	County)	37098
Marble City (Part of		First Tennessee Bank		Mill Creek (Morgan County)	37872
Knoxville)	37919	National Association	38103	Mill Creek (Putnam County)	38501
Marbledale	37914	Leader Federal Bank for		Milldale	37172
Marble Hall	37857	Savings	38103	Milledgeville	38359
Marble Hill (Blount County)	37737	National Bank of Commerce	38150	Miller's Store	38225
Marble Hill (Moore County)	37398	Nationsbank	38112	Millersville	37072
Marble Plains	37398	Union Planters National		Millertown	37914
Marbleton	37692	Bank	38103	Millican	37862
Marguerite	37814	United American Bank of		Milligan College	37682
Marion (Claiborne County)	37715	Memphis	38119	Millington	38053-54
Marion (Montgomery					38083
County)	37051	*HOSPITALS*		For specific Millington Zip Codes	
Market Square Mall (Part of		Baptist Memorial Hospital	38146	call (901) 872-3278, or your local	
Knoxville)	37902	Methodist Hospital of		postmaster.	
Markham	38079	Memphis	38104	Millsfield	38024
Marlborough	38317	Regional Medical Center at		Mill Spring	37820
Marlow	37716	Memphis	38103	Milltown (Humphreys	
Marlyn Hills (Part of Bristol)	37620	St. Francis Hospital	38119	County)	37101
Marrowbone	37015	St. Joseph Hospital and		Milltown (Jackson County)	38588
Mars Hill	38464	Health Centers	38105	Milltown (Macon County)	37150
Martel Estates	37771	Veterans Affairs Medical		Milltown (Marshall County)	37091
Martha	37087	Center	38104	Millview	37064
Martha Washington	38553			Milo	37381
Martin	38237	*HOTELS/MOTELS*		Milton	37118
Martin Creek	38544	Holiday Inn International		Mimms (Part of Nashville)	37211
Martin Springs	37380	Airport	38116	Mimosa	37334
Marvin	37818			Mimosa Estates	37777

---

* **Area Zip Code**   † **Post Office Boxes**

	ZIP		ZIP		ZIP
Mimosa Heights	37777	Mount Herman (Weakley		Third National Bank in	
Mineral Park	37353	County)	38230	Nashville	37219
Mineral Springs	38574	Mount Hope	38485		
Mink	38485	Mount Horeb	37760	*HOSPITALS*	
Minnick	38240	Mount Joy	38474		
Minor Hill	38473	Mount Juliet	37122	Baptist Hospital	37236
Mint	37801	Mount Lebanon	38464	Centennial Medical Center	37202
Miser Station	37777	Mount Leo	37110	Nashville Metropolitan	
Miston	38056	Mount Moriah	38320	Bordeaux Hospital	37218
Mitchell	37148	Mount Nebo	38463	St. Thomas Hospital	37205
Mitchellville	37119	Mount Olive (Grundy		Vanderbilt University	
Mixie	38342	County)	37110	Hospital and Clinic	37232
Moccasin	38485	Mount Olive (Knox County)	37920	Veterans Affairs Medical	
Mohawk	37810	Mount Olive (Marion		Center	37212
Mohawk Crossroad	37711	County)	37397		
Molino	37334	Mount Olive (Rutherford		*HOTELS/MOTELS*	
Mon	37087	County)	37130		
Mona	37129	Mount Pelia	38237	Doubletree Hotel	37219
Monoville	37030	Mount Pisgah	38587	Holiday Inn-Briley Parkway	37214
Monroe	38573	Mount Pleasant (Greene		Holiday Inn Crowne Plaza	37219
Monsanto	38402	County)	37743	Regal Maxwell House	37228
Montague (Davidson		Mount Pleasant (Henry		Marriott Nashville	37210
County)	37216	County)	38222	Sheraton Music City	37214
Montague (Rhea County)	37321	Mount Pleasant (Maury		Loews Vanderbilt Plaza	
Monteagle	37356	County)	38474	Hotel	37203
Monterey	38574	Mount Pleasant (Putnam			
Montezuma	38340	County)	38501	*MILITARY INSTALLATIONS*	
Montgomery Junction	37756	Mount Pleasant (Scott			
Monticello (Williamson		County)	37852	Tennessee Air National	
County)	37064	Mount Tabor	37804	Guard, FB6421, Nashville	
Monticello (Wilson County)	37122	Mount Tucker Addition	37617	International Airport	37217
Montpier Farms	37064	Mount Union (Jackson		United States Army	
Montvale	37801	County)	38564	Engineer District,	
Moodyville	38549	Mount Union (Pickett		Nashville	37202
Mooneyham	38585	County)	38549	United States Property and	
Moons	38256	Mount Vernon (Monroe		Fiscal Office for	
Moon Shadows	37341	County)	37358	Tennessee	37204
Mooreland Heights (Part of		Mount Vernon (Rutherford			
Knoxville)	37920	County)	37153	Natco (Part of Columbia)	38401
Mooresburg	37811	Mount Vernon (Sumner		National Cemetery (Part of	
Mooresburg Springs	37811	County)	37022	Memphis)	38122
Moores Chapel	38358	Mount View (Davidson		Natural Bridge	37843
Moores College	38581	County)	37211	Nauvoo	38024
Mooresville	37091	Mount View (Grundy		Neapolis	38401
Mooretown	37190	County)	37356	Neboville	38059
Mooring	38080	Mount View (Scott County)	37852	Needmore (Hamblen	
Morgan Springs	37321	Mount Vinson	38379	County)	37891
Morganton	37742	Mount Zion (Cheatham		Needmore (Wilson County)	37138
Morgantown	37321	County)	37015	Needmore (Marshall	
Morganville	37397	Mount Zion (Monroe		County)	37091
Morley	37766	County)	37885	Needmore (Maury County)	38474
Morny (Part of Nashville)	37080	Mount Zion (Montgomery		Needmore (Montgomery	
Morris Chapel (Benton		County)	37051	County)	37079
County)	38320	Mount Zion (Obion County)	38232	Neely	38391
Morris Chapel (Hardin		Mount Zion (Warren		Neely Crossroads	38551
County)	38361	County)	37110	Nelsontown (Part of	
Morrison	37357	Mourberry	38583	Kingsport)	37660
Morrison City	37660	Mowbray	37379	Nemo	37887
Morrison Creek	38562	Mud Creek (McNairy		Nenny	37891
Morristown	37813-16	County)	38310	Neptune	37015
For specific Morristown Zip Codes		Mud Creek (Warren County)	38581	Netherland	38501
call (615) 586-1291, or your local		Muddy Pond	38574	Neubert	37920
postmaster.		Mudsink	37064	Neva	37683
Moscow	38057	Mulberry	37359	Newbern	38059
Mosheim	37818	Mulberry Gap	37869	New Bethel	37331
Moss	38575	Mulberry Hill	37058	New Canton	37642
Mossy Grove	37748	Mulloy	37048	New Castle	38075
Mountain City	37683	Munford	38058	Newcomb	37762
Mountain Dale	37650	Murfreesboro	37129-33	New Corinth	37861
Mountain Home (Part of		For specific Murfreesboro Zip		New Deal	37048
Johnson City)	37684	Codes call (615) 893-2201, or		New Dellrose	38453
Mountain View (Part of		your local postmaster.		New Due West (Part of	
Dayton)	37321	Murray-Lake Hills (Part of		Nashville)	37115
Mountain View Acres (Part		Chattanooga)	37416	Newell Station	37865
of Winchester)	37398	Murray Store	37826	New Era	38555
Mount Airy	37327	Myers (Part of Winchester)	37398	New Harmony (Bledsoe	
Mount Ararat	37095	Nameless	38545	County)	37367
Mount Carmel (Decatur		Nance	38001	New Harmony (Macon	
County)	38329	Nance Ferry	37709	County)	37074
Mount Carmel (Greene		Nances Grove	37820	New Haven (Lawrence	
County)	37711	Nankipoo	38040	County)	38464
Mount Carmel (Hawkins		Napier	38462	New Haven (Scott County)	37841
County)	37645	Narrow Valley	37861	New Herman	37160
Mount Carmel (Tipton		Nash	38544	New Hope (Cheatham	
County)	38019			County)	37080
Mount Carmel (Washington		**Nashville**	37201-49	New Hope (Hancock	
County)	37641	For specific Nashville Zip Codes		County)	37869
Mount Crest	37367	call (615) 885-1005, or your local		New Hope (Hardin County)	38310
Mount Cumberland	37329	postmaster.		New Hope (Hawkins	
Mount Denson	37172	*COLLEGES & UNIVERSITIES*		County)	37857
Mount Gilead (Henderson				New Hope (Houston	
County)	38321	Belmont University	37212	County)	37175
Mount Gilead (White		David Lipscomb College	37204	New Hope (Humphreys	
County)	38583	Tennessee State University	37209	County)	37101
Mount Harmony (McMinn		Vanderbilt University	37240	New Hope (Jackson	
County)	37826			County)	38568
Mount Harmony (Monroe		*FINANCIAL INSTITUTIONS*		New Hope (Lincoln County)	37334
County)	37385			New Hope (Marion County)	37380
Mount Helen	38504	Dominion Bank of Middle		New Hope (McNairy	
Mount Herman (Bedford		Tennessee	37219	County)	38339
County)	37160	First American National		New Hope (Roane County)	37854
		Bank	37237	New Hope (Williamson	
		Nationsbank	37219	County)	37062
				New Hope (Wilson County)	37087
				New Johnsonville	37134

	ZIP		ZIP		ZIP
New Line	37814	Oak Grove (Dickson County)	37055	Old Winesap	38555
New Loyston	37705	Oak Grove (Franklin County)	37324	Old Zion	38583
Newmansville	37616	Oak Grove (Giles County)	38460	Olivehill	38475
New Market	37820	Oak Grove (Hardin County)	38372	Oliver Springs	37840
New Markham	38079	Oak Grove (Henry County)	38222	Olivet	38372
New Middleton	38563	Oak Grove (Jefferson County)	37725	One Hundred Oaks Regional Mall (Part of Nashville)	37204
New Midway	37763	Oak Grove (Lewis County)	38462	Oneida	37841
Newport	37821	Oak Grove (Madison County)	38301	Only	37140
New Prospect	38464	Oak Grove (Marion County)	37397	Ooltewah	37363
New Providence (Loudon County)	37771	Oak Grove (Monroe County)	37354	Opossum	38063
New Providence (Montgomery County)	37042	Oak Grove (Overton County; mail Hilham)	38568	Opossum Creek Pines	37379
New River	37755	Oak Grove (Overton County; mail Livingston)	38570	Oral	37771
New Salem (Hamilton County)	37379	Oakgrove (Pickett County)	38573	Orchard View	37840
New Salem (Jackson County)	38562	Oak Grove (Polk County)	37307	Orebank	37664
New Salem (Scott County)	37841	Oak Grove (Sumner County)	37022	Ore Spring	38225
New Tazewell	37825	Oak Grove (Tipton County)	38019	Orlinda	37141
Newton	38555	Oak Grove (Union County)	37866	Orme	37380
New Town (Marshall County)	37047	Oak Grove (Warren County)	37357	Orysa	38063
New Town (Maury County)	37174	Oak Grove (Washington County)	37615	Osage	38242
Newtown (Polk County)	37317	Oak Grove (Weakley County)	38237	Osemont Chapel	37190
New Union	37355	Oak Grove Heights	37921	Ostella	37091
New Victory	37659	Oakhaven (Part of Memphis)	38116	Oswego	37762
New Zion (Carroll County)	38344	Oak Hill (Carter County)	37658	Otes	37857
New Zion (Macon County)	37186	Oak Hill (Cocke County)	37843	Otter Creek	38555
Nickletown	37347	Oak Hill (Cumberland County)	38555	Ottway	37743
Nicks Creek	37756	Oak Hill (Davidson County)	37220	Overall	37130
Nine Mile	37367	Oak Hill (Overton County)	38580	Overlook	37804
Ninth Model	37382	Oak Hill (Pickett County)	38549	Ovilla	38464
Niota	37826	Oak Hill (Sullivan County)	37620	Ovoca	37388
Nixon	38372	Oak Hill (Washington County)	37659	Owens	37172
Noah	37355	Oakhurst (Part of Maryville)	37801	Owl City	38079
Nolensville	37135	Oakland (Fayette County)	38060	Owlhollow	37398
Nonaburg	37329	Oakland (Grainger County)	37861	Owl Hoot	38080
Nonaville	37122	Oakland (Henry County)	38242	Ozone	37842
Nonconnah (Part of Memphis)	38116	Oakland (Jefferson County)	37760	Pactolus	37663
Norene	37136	Oakland (Knox County)	37918	Pailo	37327
Norma	37756	Oakland (Robertson County)	37172	Paint Rock (Loudon County)	37846
Normandy	37360	Oakland (Warren County)	37110	Paint Rock (Roane County)	37846
Norris	37828	Oakland (Washington County)	37690	Palestine (Henderson County)	38351
North (Davidson County)	37208	Oaklawn	37166	Palestine (Robertson County)	37172
North (Shelby County)	38107	Oakleigh Estates	37620	Pall Mall	38577
North Chattanooga (Part of Chattanooga)	37405	Oakley	38541	Palmer	37365
Northcott	37660	Oaklyn	38555	Palmersville	38241
Northcutts Cove (Grundy County)	37110	Oak Park (Part of Tullahoma)	37388	Palmyra	37142
Northcutt's Cove (Warren County)	37110	Oakplain	37015	Pandora	37640
Northeast (Part of Nashville)	37207	Oak Plains	37040	Paperville (Part of Bristol)	37620
Northeast Correctional Center	37683	Oak Ridge	37830* 37831†	Paradise Acres	37122
Northern Hills (Part of Chattanooga)	37343	Oak Ridge Mall (Part of Oak Ridge)	37830	Paragon Mills (Part of Nashville)	37211
Northgate Shopping Center (Part of Memphis)	38107	Oak Tree	37062	Paris	38242
North Glen Estates (Part of Chattanooga)	37343	Oak View	37886	Parkburg	38366
North Hills (Part of Knoxville)	37917	Oakville (Part of Memphis)	38118	Park City (Knox County)	37914
North Johnson City (Part of Johnson City)	37601	Oakwood (Knox County)	37917	Park City (Lincoln County)	37334
North Knoxville (Part of Knoxville)	37917	Oakwood (Montgomery County)	37191	Parker	38577
Northpoint	37874	Oakwood Estates	37064	Parker's Cross Roads	38388
North Riverside	38462	Obion	38240	Parkey	37869
Northside (Part of Jackson)	38301	Ocana	37075	Park Grove	38464
North Springs	38588	Ocoee	37361	Park Settlement	37862
Northwest Correctional Center	38079	O'Connors	38583	Park Shore	37343
Norwood (Anderson County)	37840	Odd Fellows Hall	38478	Parkshore Estates	37343
Norwood (Knox County)	37912	Odens Bend	37066	Parksville	37307
Notchy Creek	37354	Officers Chapel	38501	Parkview	37854
Nough	37727	Offutt	37716	Parkway Village (Part of Memphis)	38118
Nubia	37186	Ogden	37321	Parrottsville	37843
Nucarbon	38468	Okalona	38570	Parsons	38363
Number One (Part of Gallatin)	37066	Okolona (Carter County)	37601	Paschall	37064
Nunnelly	37137	Okolona (Hawkins County)	37642	Pasquo (Part of Nashville)	37221
Nutbush	38012	Old Antioch	38562	Pate Hill	37818
Oak City	37865	Old Chihowee	37865	Patterson	37153
Oak Court Mall (Part of Memphis)	38117	Olde Mill	37343	Patterson Crossroads	37752
Oakdale (Hawkins County)	37873	Oldfort	37362	Patty	37325
Oakdale (Macon County)	37186	Old Glory	37804	Paulette	37807
Oakdale (Morgan County)	37829	Old Hickory (Part of Nashville)	37138	Paw Paw Ridge	38030
Oak Dale (Overton County)	38573	Old Hickory Mall (Part of Jackson)	38301	Payne Cove	37366
Oakdale (White County)	38583	Old Kingsport (Part of Kingsport)	37660	Paynes Store	37022
Oakfield	38362	Old Laguardo	37122	Peabody	37766
Oak Grove (Campbell County)	37769	Old Lawton	38375	Peak	37715
Oak Grove (Carter County)	37643	Old Salem	37345	Peakland	37322
Oak Grove (Claiborne County)	37752	Old Springville	38256	Peanut	37843
Oak Grove (Clay County)	38575	Old Sweetwater	37874	Pea Ridge (DeKalb County)	37095
		Old Washington	37321	Pea Ridge (Lawrence County)	38464
				Pearl City	37334
				Peavine	38555
				Pebble Hill	38357
				Peckerwood Point	38004
				Peeled Chestnut	38583
				Pegram	37143
				Pelham	37366
				Penile Hill	37324
				Pennine	37381
				Pennington Bend (Part of Nashville)	37214
				Pennington Chapel	37888
				Peppertown	38469
				Perrin Hollow	37709
				Perry	38301

* **Area Zip Code**   † **Post Office Boxes**

	ZIP		ZIP		ZIP
Perryville	38363	Pleasant Grove (Scott County)	37892	Pottsville	38401
Persia	37857	Pleasant Grove (Sumner County)	37186	Powder Springs	37848
Petersburg (Hawkins County)	37857	Pleasant Hill (Claiborne County)	37870	Powell	37849
Petersburg (Lincoln County)	37144	Pleasant Hill (Clay County)	38541	Powell Chapel	38478
Peters Landing	38425	Pleasant Hill (Cumberland County)	38578	Powells Chapel	38044
Petros	37845	Pleasant Hill (Greene County)	37641	Powells Crossroads	37397
Petway	37015	Pleasant Hill (Hawkins County)	37711	Powell Valley	37766
Peytonsville	37064	Pleasant Hill (Lauderdale County)	38041	Prairie Creek	37379
Philadelphia (Jackson County)	38545	Pleasant Hill (Meigs County)	37880	Prairie Peninsula	37343
Philadelphia (Loudon County)	37846	Pleasant Hill (Moore County)	37352	Prairie Plains	37342
Philadelphia (Washington County)	37641	Pleasant Hill (Obion County)	38253	Prater	37190
Philippi	37166	Pleasant Hill (Polk County)	37317	Preston Woods (Part of Kingsport)	37660
Phillippy	38079	Pleasant Hill (Rutherford County)	37060	Price (Lauderdale County)	38041
Pickwatina Place (Part of Athens)	37303	Pleasant Hill (Sevier County)	37862	Price (White County)	38583
Pickwick Dam	38365	Pleasant Hill (Weakley County)	38237	Pride	38261
Piedmont	37725	Pleasant Point (Claiborne County)	37825	Primm Springs	38476
Pierce	38257	Pleasant Point (Lawrence County)	38469	Princeton (Part of Johnson City)	37601
Pigeon Forge	37863* 37868†	Pleasant Ridge (Cannon County)	37190	Proctor City	38079
Pigeon River Estates (Part of Sevierville)	37862	Pleasant Ridge (Knox County)	37921	Prospect (Blount County)	37886
Pigeon Roost	37185	Pleasant Shade	37145	Prospect (Bradley County)	37312
Pikeville	37367	Pleasant Valley (Macon County)	37074	Prospect (Giles County)	38477
Pillowville	38201	Pleasant Valley (Sumner County)	37048	Prospect (Lincoln County)	37334
Pilot Knob (Greene County)	37711	Pleasant Valley (Washington County)	37659	Prospect (Loudon County)	37774
Pilot Knob (Sumner County)	37066	Pleasant View (Cannon County)	37190	Prospect (McMinn County)	37329
Pilot Mountain	37770	Pleasant View (Cheatham County)	37146	Prosperity (Macon County)	37150
Pine Bluff	37398	Pleasant View (Claiborne County)	37879	Prosperity (Wilson County)	37016
Pinebrook Estates	37341	Pleasant View (Fentress County)	37556	Protemus	38260
Pinecrest (Campbell County)	37757	Pleasantville	37147	Providence (Davidson County)	37211
Pine Crest (Carter County)	37601	Plunkets Creek	38563	Providence (Grundy County)	37324
Pine Grove (Greene County)	37743	Pocahontas (Coffee County)	37357	Providence (Madison County)	38301
Pine Grove (Loudon County)	37774	Pocahontas (Hardeman County)	38061	Providence (Sumner County)	37186
Pine Grove (Sevier County)	37862	Poga	37640	Providence (Trousdale County)	37074
Pine Grove (Van Buren County)	38585	Point Pleasant	37821	Pruden	37851
Pine Haven (Fentress County)	38556	Polk	38253	Pryor Ridge	37387
Pinehaven (Shelby County)	38053	Pollard	37061	Puckett	37153
Pine Hill (Bradley County)	37353	Pomona (Cumberland County)	38555	Pulaski	38478
Pine Hill (Clay County)	38575	Pomona (Dickson County)	37055	Pumpkintown	37083
Pine Hill (Marion County)	37397	Pomona Road	38555	Punch	37030
Pine Hill (Scott County)	37841	Pond	37055	Puncheon Camp	37888
Pineland	37322	Ponderosa	37763	Punkton	37727
Pine Orchard	37829	Ponderosa Hills	37849	Purdy	38375
Pine Point	38256	Ponders Gap	37880	Puryear	38251
Pine Ridge (Jefferson County)	37890	Pond Grove	37854	Push	38232
Pine Ridge (Polk County)	37333	Pond Hill	37303	Pyburns	38372
Pine Top	37771	Pondville	37022	Quail Meador	37087
Pine Tree Estates	37343	Pope	37096	Quebeck	38579
Pine View	37096	Poplar	37716	Quercus	38483
Pineville (Part of Morristown)	37814	Poplar Corner	38006	Quincy	38001
Pinewood	37137	Poplar Grove (Claiborne County)	37752	Quito	38053
Piney (Loudon County)	37774	Poplar Grove (Humphreys County)	37101	Raccoon Valley	37807
Piney (Morgan County)	37892	Poplar Grove (Lauderdale County)	38040	Rader	37743
Piney (Van Buren County)	38585	Poplar Grove (Putnam County)	38501	Rafter	37385
Piney Flats	37686	Poplar Hill (Giles County)	38477	Ragsdale	37355
Piney Grove (McMinn County)	37303	Poplar Hill (McMinn County)	37303	Raines (Part of Memphis)	38116
Piney Grove (Scott County)	37892	Poplar Plaza Shopping Center (Part of Memphis)	38111	Raleigh (Part of Memphis)	38128
Piney Grove (Washington County)	37601	Poplar Springs (Henderson County)	38351	Raleigh Springs Mall (Part of Memphis)	38128
Piney Shores Estates	37381	Poplar Springs (Loudon County)	37774	Rally Hill	38401
Pinhook (Putnam County)	38574	Poplar Springs (Overton County)	38501	Ralston	38237
Pin Hook (Union County)	37807	Poplar Springs (Roane County)	37763	Ramah	38468
Pinnacle (Part of Pittman Center)	37862	Poplins Crossroads	37180	Ramer	38367
Pinson	38366	Porter Court (Part of Paris)	38242	Ramsey (Knox County)	37914
Pioneer	37847	Porterfield	37118	Ramsey (Wilson County)	37087
Pipers	37148	Porter Gap	38040	Randolph	38023
Piperton	38017	Porters Chapel	38474	Range	37694
Pisgah (DeKalb County)	37166	Portland	37148	Rankin	37821
Pisgah (Giles County)	38478	Port Royal	37010	Rankin Cove	37347
Pisgah (Shelby County)	38018	Port Serena	37343	Rascal Town	38469
Pittman Center	37738	Postelle	37317	Rathburn (Part of Soddy-Daisy)	37379
Plainfield (Part of Maryville)	37801	Post Oak (Putnam County)	38501	Raus	37388
Plain Grove	38573	Post Oak (Roane County)	37854	Raven Branch	37753
Plainview (Rutherford County)	37037	Poteet	38543	Raven Hill	37879
Plainview (Union County)	37779			Ravenscroft	38583
Plant	37134			Rayon City (Part of Nashville)	37138
Plantation Hills (Part of Knoxville)	37917			Rays Chapel	37034
Plateau	38555			Raysville (Part of Lynchburg)	37388
Pleasant Green	37726			Readyville	37149
Pleasant Grove (Bedford County)	37160			Reagan	38368
Pleasant Grove (Cocke County)	37821			Rebel Acres (Part of Pulaski)	38478
Pleasant Grove (Lincoln County)	37334			Rebel Meadows (Part of Franklin)	37064
Pleasant Grove (Marion County)	37347			Red Ash	37714
				Red Bank	37415
				Red Boiling Springs	37150
				Red Hill (Bradley County)	37323
				Red Hill (Claiborne County)	37752
				Red Hill (Coffee County)	37355
				Red Hill (Fentress County)	38556
				Red Hill (Lawrence County)	38464
				Red Hill (Marion County)	37397
				Red Hill (Pickett County)	38549
				Red Hill (Weakley County)	38225

* Area Zip Code   † Post Office Boxes

	ZIP
Red House	37709
Red Row	38474
Redwing Farms	37064
Reeds Lake	38004
Reed Spring	37846
Reeds Store	37046
Reedtown	37821
Reel Cove	37397
Reesetown	37391
Rehoboth	38024
Reliance	37369
Reubensville	37148
Reverie	72395
Revilo	38468
Rheatown	37641
Rialto	38019
Rice Bend	37657
Riceville	37370
Rich	38472
Rich Acres (Part of Johnson City)	37601
Richard City	37380
Richardson	38023
Richland (Davidson County)	37209
Richland (Grainger County)	37709
Richmond	37144
Richview Acres	37865
Richwood	38024
Rickman	38580
Riddleton	37151
Ridenour	37705
Ridge	37879
Ridgedale (Knox County)	37931
Ridgedale (Sullivan County)	37620
Ridgefield (Part of Kingsport)	37660
Ridge Lake North (Part of Chattanooga)	37343
Ridgely	38080
Ridgeside	37411
Ridgetop (Lewis County)	38461
Ridgetop (Robertson County)	37152
Ridgeview	37814
Ridgeville (Part of Lynchburg)	37352
Ridgewood	37714
Ridley	38401
Riggs	37046
Riggs Crossroads	37046
Right	38361
Rim Rock Mesa	38583
Rinda	38230
Rinnie	38555
Riovista (Part of Elizabethton)	37643
Ripley	38063
Ritchie	37879
Ritta	37918
Riva Lake Camp	37398
Riverdale	37914
Rivergate Mall (Part of Nashville)	37072
River Hill	37650
River Oaks	37341
River Rest	37064
Riversburg	38478
Riverside (Claiborne County)	37879
Riverside (Coffee County)	37355
Riverside (Davidson County)	37218
Riverside (Decatur County)	38363
Riverside (Shelby County)	38113
Riverside (Sullivan County)	37618
Riverton	38556
Riverview (Claiborne County)	37752
Riverview (Sullivan County)	37660
Riverview (Unicoi County)	37650
Riverview Estates	37033
Rives	38253
Roan Mountain	37687
Roaring Springs	37616
Roarks Cove	37324
Robbins (Pickett County)	38549
Robbins (Scott County)	37852
Roberts	38582
Robertson Fork	38472
Robinson Crossroads	37921
Rockbridge	37022
Rock City (Smith County)	37030
Rock City (Sullivan County)	37664
Rock Creek (Pickett County)	38556
Rock Creek (Unicoi County)	37650
Rockdale	38474
Rockford	37853
Rock Haven	37708
Rock Hill (Hancock County)	37765
Rock Hill (Henderson County)	38351
Rock Hill (Sullivan County)	37694

	ZIP
Rock House	37075
Rock Island	38581
Rockland (Part of Hendersonville)	37075
Rock Ledge Estates	37363
Rock Springs (Dickson County)	37036
Rock Springs (Dyer County)	38024
Rock Springs (Henderson County)	38388
Rock Springs (Rutherford County)	37167
Rock Springs (Sullivan County)	37663
Rock Station	38581
Rockvale	37153
Rockville	37874
Rockwood	37854
Rockwood Hill	37743
Rocky Branch	37886
Rocky Creek	37031
Rocky Fork (Rutherford County)	37167
Rocky Fork (Unicoi County)	37657
Rocky Grove	37722
Rocky Hill (Part of Knoxville)	37919
Rocky Mound	37186
Rocky Point (Hamblen County)	37860
Rocky Point (Putnam County)	38501
Rocky Ridge	38573
Rocky Spring (Monroe County)	37354
Rocky Spring (Sullivan County)	37686
Rocky Valley	37820
Roddy	37381
Roe Junction	37814
Roellen	38024
Rogana	37022
Rogers Creek	37303
Rogers Spring	38052
Rogersville	37857
Rolling Acres (Jefferson County)	37877
Rolling Acres (Williamson County)	37062
Rolling Hills (Hickman County)	37025
Rolling Hills (Marshall County)	37091
Rolling Hills (Unicoi County)	37650
Rolling Hills (Warren County)	37110
Rolling Meadows (Part of Franklin)	37064
Rome	37030
Romeo	37711
Rose Creek	38375
Rosedale	37710
Rose Hill (Madison County)	38301
Rose Hill (Union County)	37807
Rosemark	38053
Rose Valley	37079
Roseville	37183
Roslin	38556
Ross Camp Ground	37642
Rosser	38344
Rossview	37040
Rossville	38066
Rotherwood	37642
Round Pond	37040
Round Rock	37714
Round Top	37012
Routon	38231
Rover	37060
Rowland	38581
Royal	37160
Royal Blue	37847
Royal Oak (Part of Manchester)	37355
Royal Oaks (Williamson County)	37068
Royal Oaks (Wilson County)	37122
Royer Estates (Part of Murfreesboro)	37130
Rucker	37130
Rudderville	37064
Rudolph	38012
Rugby	37733
Rugby Hills (Part of Memphis)	38127
Rural Hill (Davidson County)	37217
Rural Hill (Wilson County)	37071
Rural Vale	37385
Russel Fork	37766
Russell Crossroad	37743
Russell Hill	37145
Russellville	37860
Rusty (Part of Fairview)	37062
Rutherford	38369

	ZIP
Rutherford Estates	38401
Ruthton	37620
Ruthville	38237
Rutledge	37861
Rutledge Falls	37355
Rutledge Hill	37342
Ryall Springs	37421
Sadie	37643
Sadlers	37010
Safford	38328
Safley	37110
Sagewood Estates	38401
Sailors Rest	37050
St. Andrews	37372
St. Bethlehem	37155
St. Clair (Hawkins County)	37711
Saint Clair (Rhea County)	37381
St. James	37743
St. Joseph	38481
St. Paul	38023
Saint Peters	38012
Sainville	37355
Sale Creek	37373
Salem (Cocke County)	37843
Salem (Lewis County)	37033
Salem (Montgomery County)	37040
Salem (Tipton County)	38004
Salem (Weakley County)	38255
Saltillo	38370
Samburg	38254
Sampson	37367
Sanders	37387
Sand Hill	38229
Sandlick	37825
Sand Ridge	38351
Sand Springs	38574
Sand Switch	37375
Sandy	38589
Sandy Hook	38474
Sandy Lane	37385
Sandy Point	38320
Sandy Ridge	37725
Sandy Spring	37032
Sanford	37370
Sanford Hill (Part of Henderson)	38340
Sango	37040
Santa Fe	38482
Saratoga Springs	37367
Sardis	38371
Saulsbury	38067
Saundersville (Part of Hendersonville)	37075
Savannah	38372
Sawdust	38401
Sawyers Mill	38320
Scandlyn	37840
Scarboro (Part of Oak Ridge)	37830
Scattersville	37148
Scenic Point Estates	37777
Scoot Mill	37810
Scottsboro (Part of Nashville)	37218
Scotts Hill	38374
Screamer	38474
Seeber Flats	37710
Selmer	38375
Sentinel Heights (Part of Dayton)	37363
Sequatchie	37374
Sequoia Grove (Part of Cleveland)	37312
Sequoia Hills	37743
Sequoyah Estates (Part of Madisonville)	37354
Sequoyah Hills	37343
Sequoyah Village (Part of Madisonville)	37354
Serles	38008
Settlers Point	37064
Seven Islands	37920
Seven Oaks	37922
Sevier Home	37920
Sevierville	37862*
	37864†
Sewanee	37375
Sewee	37826
Seymour	37865
Shackle Island	37075
Shacklett	37082
Shades Bridge	38230
Shadowlawn	38002
Shady Grove (Coffee County)	37357
Shady Grove (Hamilton County)	37379
Shady Grove (Jefferson County)	37725
Shady Grove (Knox County)	37922

* Area Zip Code † Post Office Boxes

	ZIP
Shady Grove (Lincoln County)	37335
Shady Grove (Montgomery County)	37040
Shady Grove (Morgan County)	37770
Shady Grove (Putnam County)	38574
Shady Grove (Trousdale County)	37074
Shady Grove (White County)	38587
Shady Grove Shores	37379
Shady Hill	38351
Shady Rest	37110
Shady Valley	37688
Shafter	38230
Shake Rag Hill	38485
Shallowford	37650
Shandy	38008
Shannondale (Part of Knoxville)	37918
Shannon Hills	37343
Sharon	38255
Sharondale (Part of Tullahoma)	37388
Sharp Place	38556
Sharps Chapel	37866
Sharpsville	37130
Shaver Town	38563
Shawanee	37867
Shawnette	38450
Shawtown	38232
Shelby Center	38134
Shelby Farms (Part of Memphis)	38101
Shelbyville	37160
Shelbyville Mills	37160
Shell Creek	37687
Shellmound	37380
Shellsford	37110
Shenandoah Heights	37601
Shennendoah	37865
Shepp	38069
Sherrill Heights (Part of Madisonville)	37354
Sherrilltown	37184
Sherwood	37376
Sherwood Estates	37716
Sheybogan	37190
Shiloh (Bedford County)	37183
Shiloh (Cumberland County)	38555
Shiloh (Grainger County)	37861
Shiloh (Hardin County)	38376
Shiloh (Hawkins County)	37869
Shiloh (Humphreys County)	37101
Shiloh (Jackson County)	38501
Shiloh (Montgomery County)	37051
Shiloh (Overton County)	38554
Shiloh (Rutherford County)	37130
Shiloh (Sumner County)	37066
Shiloh (Wilson County)	37138
Shingleton	37683
Shining Rock	37166
Shipetown	37806
Shipley	38501
Shipps Bend	37033
Shirley	38504
Shirleyton	37397
Shooks Gap	37920
Shop Springs	37184
Shore Acres	37379
Short Creek	37037
Short Mountain	37190
Short Tail Springs	37341
Shouns	37683
Shubert	38462
Siam	37643
Sideview	37066
Sidonia	38255
Signal Hills (Part of Chattanooga)	37405
Signal Mountain	37377
Silerton	38377
Silica	37714
Siloam	37186
Silvacola	37617
Silver City	37860
Silver Grove	37618
Silverhill	37087
Silver Point	38582
Silver Ridge (Part of Lenoir City)	37771
Silver Springs	37122
Silvertop	37101
Simonton	38011
Sims Siding	37160
Singleton (Bedford County)	37160
Singleton (Blount County)	37777
Singtown	37148
Sinking Cove	37376

	ZIP
Sitka	38358
Sixmile	37801
Skaggston	37806
Skinem	37334
Skinner Crossroad	37810
Skullbone	38316
Skyline	38063
Skyline Park (Part of Signal Mountain)	37377
Slayden	37165
Slick Rock	37852
Slide	37857
Smartt	37378
Smith Chapel	38501
Smithfield	37385
Smithland	37348
Smith Mill	37334
Smiths Chapel	37150
Smiths Fork	38475
Smith Springs (Part of Nashville)	37217
Smithtown (Bledsoe County)	37338
Smithtown (Marion County)	37380
Smithville	37166
Smithwood (Part of Knoxville)	37918
Smoky Junction	37756
Smoky View Estates	37804
Smyrna (Carroll County)	38318
Smyrna (Pickett County)	38549
Smyrna (Rutherford County)	37167
Smyrna (Warren County)	37110
Sneed Forest Estates	37064
Sneed Glen	37064
Sneedville	37869
Snell	37130
Snow Hill	37363
Snows Hill	37059
Soddy-Daisy	37379
Solo	38019
Solway	37931
Somerville	38068
South (Davidson County)	37210
South (Hamilton County)	37409
Southall	37064
South Berlin	37091
South Carthage	37030
South Cleveland	37311
South Clinton (Part of Clinton)	37716
South Columbia (Part of Columbia)	38401
South Covington (Part of Covington)	38019
South Daisy (Part of Soddy-Daisy)	37379
South Dyersburg	38024
Southeastern Tennessee State Regional Correctional	37367
Southern Hills (Part of Columbia)	38401
South Etowah	37331
South Fulton	38257
Southgate Shopping Center (Part of Memphis)	38109
South Green	37743
South Hall (Part of Alcoa)	37701
South Harriman (Part of Harriman)	37748
South Johnson City	37601
South Knoxville (Part of Knoxville)	37920
Southland Mall (Part of Memphis)	38116
South Liberty	37370
South Pittsburg	37380
Southport	38451
Southside (Hardin County)	38326
Southside (Montgomery County)	37171
South Tunnel	37066
Spain's Hill	37085
Sparkman	38559
Sparta	38583
Speedwell	37870
Spencer	38585
Spencer Creek	37064
Spencer Hill	38474
Spencers Mill	37029
Sportman Acres	37122
Spot	37140
Spout Springs	38232
Springbrook (Part of Alcoa)	37701
Spring City	37381
Spring Creek (Hardeman County)	38067
Spring Creek (McMinn County)	37370
Spring Creek (Perry County)	37096
Spring Creek (Wilson County)	37087

	ZIP
Spring Creek (Madison County)	38378
Springdale (Claiborne County)	37879
Springdale (Sullivan County)	37663
Springfield	37172
Spring Hill (Anderson County)	37716
Spring Hill (Henderson County)	38345
Spring Hill (Maury County)	37174
Spring Hill (White County)	38583
Spring Lake	38134
Springmont	37138
Spring Place	37914
Springtown	37369
Springvale	37814
Spring View (Blount County)	37801
Springview (Williamson County)	37064
Springville	38256
Spruce Pine	37811
Spurgeon	37659
Staffords Store	38230
Staffordtown	37317
Stainville	37710
Stanfill	37847
Stanley Junction	37841
Stanton	38069
Stantonville	38379
Star Point	38549
State (Part of Nashville)	37219
State Line	37334
Statesville	37184
State University (Part of Johnson City)	37601
Static	38549
Station Camp	37048
Stayton	37051
Stella	38460
St Elmo (Part of Chattanooga)	37409
Stephen Holston (Part of Bristol)	37620
Stephens	37840
Stephenson	37342
Steppsville	37110
Sterling Park	37343
Stewart (Houston County)	37175
Stewart (Warren County)	37110
Stewart Chapel	37335
Stinking Creek	37766
Stiversville	38451
Stock Creek	37920
Stockton	38556
Stockton Valley	37774
Stokes	38034
Stone	38562
Stonebrook	37135
Stone River (Part of Nashville)	37076
Stone River Estates (Part of Nashville)	37214
Stones River Homes (Part of Smyrna)	37167
Stonewall	38560
Stoney Fork	37714
Stoney Point	37181
Stony Gap	37869
Stony Point	37873
Strahl	37857
Straight Fork	37847
Strawberry Plains	37871
Striggersville	37857
Stringtown (Gibson County)	38233
Stringtown (Montgomery County)	37191
Stroudsville	37032
Suburban Hills (Knox County)	37901
Suburban Hills (McMinn County)	37370
Suck Creek	37405
Sugar Creek (Jackson County)	38562
Sugar Creek (Johnson County)	37683
Sugar Forks (Part of Dandridge)	37725
Sugar Grove (Bradley County)	37323
Sugar Grove (Roane County)	37748
Sugar Grove (Sumner County)	37186
Sugarlimb	37774
Sugar Tree	38380
Suggs Creek	37122
Sullivan Gardens	37663
Sulphur	38570
Sulphura	37148
Sulphur Creek	37147

	ZIP		ZIP		ZIP
Sulphur Springs (Anderson County)	37716	Templeton	38059	Tucker Springs	37353
Sulphur Springs (Hamblen County)	37814	Templow	37022	Tullahoma	37388
Sulphur Springs (Lincoln County)	37334	Ten Mile	37880	Tulu	38357
Sulphur Springs (Marion County)	37397	Tennemo	38056	Tumbling	38201
		Tennessee City	37055	Tuppertown (Part of Oliver Springs)	37840
Sulphur Springs (Washington County)	37659	Tennessee Hills (Part of Bristol)	37620	Turley	37714
Sumac	38478	Tennessee Ridge	37178	Turnbull	37029
Summer City	37367	Tennessee Tech (Part of Cookeville)	38501	Turners Station	37186
Summerfield	37387	Terrace Hills	37122	Turnersville	37032
Summer Shade	38541	Terrell	38237	Turnpike	38012
Summertown (Hamilton County)	37377	Terry	38321	Turtletown	37391
		Terry Creek	37847	Tusculum (Part of Nashville)	37211
Summertown (Lawrence County)	38483	Theodore (Part of Hohenwald)	38462	Tusculum College	37743
Summit (Hamilton County)	37363	Theta	38401	Twin Bridges	37726
Summit (Hawkins County)	37711	The Wye	37769	Twin Cove	37714
Summitville	37382	Thick	37034	Twin Oak	38544
Sunbright	37872	Thomas	38544	Twin Oaks	37665
Sunkist Beach	38079	Thomas Addition	37665	Twinton	38554
Sunny Brook (Part of Bristol)	37620	Thomas Bridge	37618	Twomey (Part of Centerville)	37033
Sunny Hill	38012	Thomasville	37015	Tylersville	38030
Sunny Hills	37620	Thompsons Station	37179	Tyner Hills (Part of Chattanooga)	37421
Sunnyside (Greene County)	37743	Thompsons Store	38551	Tyson	38233
Sunnyside (Hancock County)	37869	Thorngrove	37871	Uceba	37865
Sunnyside (Sullivan County)	37617	Thorn Hill	37881	Una (Part of Nashville)	37217
Sunrise (Hickman County)	37033	Thornton Heights	37722	Unaka Springs	37650
Sunrise (Macon County)	37150	Three Churches	38450	Underwood	37764
Sunset (Grainger County)	37861	Three Oaks	38456	Unicoi	37692
Sunset (Pickett County)	38549	Three Point	38041	Union (Hardin County)	38310
Sunset Gap	37722	Three Points	37918	Union (Haywood County)	38012
Sunset Hills (Hamblen County)	37814	Three Springs	37860	Union (Morgan County)	37840
		Three Way	38343	Union (Roane County)	37763
Sunset Hills (Sullivan County)	37660	Throckmorton	37079	Union (Union County)	37866
Surgoinsville	37873	Thula	37810	Union (Warren County)	38581
Sutherland	24236	Thurman Addition (Part of Pigeon Forge)	37862	Union Central	38358
Swan (Part of Hohenwald)	38462	Tibbs	38012	Union City	38261
Swan Bluff	37033	Tidwell	37025		38281
Swann Chapel	37725	Tiftona (Part of Chattanooga)	37419	For specific Union City Zip Codes call (901) 885-9711, or your local postmaster.	
Swannsylvania	37725	Tiger Valley	37658		
Sweet Lips	38340	Tigrett	38070	Union Grove (Blount County)	37737
Sweeton Hill (Part of Coalmont)	37313	Tilghman	38233	Union Grove (McMinn County)	37826
Sweetwater (Lewis County)	38462	Timberlake (Hawkins County)	37857	Union Grove (Meigs County)	37322
Sweetwater (Monroe County)	37874	Timberlake (Henderson County)	38351	Union Heights	37814
Swift	38372	Timesville	37377	Union Hill (Clay County)	38575
Sycamore (Cheatham County)	37015	Timothy	38568	Union Hill (Davidson County)	37080
Sycamore (Putnam County)	38501	Tinch	38556	Union Hill (Henderson County)	38368
Sycamore Hall	37879	Tin Cup	38320		
Sycamore Landing	37185	Tinsleys Bottom	38551	Union Hill (Lawrence County)	38468
Sykes	38547	Tiprell	37724	Union Hill (Sumner County)	37066
Sylvia	37055	Tipton (Knox County)	37920	Union Hill (Tipton County)	38004
Tabernacle (Haywood County)	38012	Tipton (Tipton County)	38071	Union McMinn	37826
Tabernacle (Tipton County)	38019	Tiptonville	38079	Union Ridge	37183
Tabor	38555	Tishamingo	37122	Union Temple	37616
Tackett Creek	37766	Tobaccoport	37028	Union Valley	37865
Taft	38488	Tom Murray (Part of Jackson)	38301	Unionville (Bedford County)	37180
Talbott	37877	Toone	38381	Unionville (Dyer County)	38040
Tallassee	37878	Top of the World Estates	37878	Unitia	37771
Talley	37144	Topside	37920	University (Part of Knoxville)	37916
Tampico	37861	Topsy	38485	University of Tennessee (Part of Martin)	38238
Tanglewood (Monroe County)	37874	Toqua	37885	University of the South	37375
Tanglewood (Smith County)	37030	Tottys	38454	Upchurch	37616
Tara Estates (Part of Tullahoma)	37388	Toulon	38063	Upper Mockeson	38468
Tarbett	37853	Towee	37369	Upper Shell Creek	37687
Tarlton	37110	Town Acres (Part of Greeneville)	37743	Upper Sinking	37147
Tarpley	38478	Town Creek	37870	Uptonville	38392
Tarsus	37142	Towne Hills (Part of Chattanooga)	37343	Uptown (Part of Knoxville)	37902
Tasso	37312	Townsend	37882	Uptown Nashville (Part of Nashville)	37219
Tate	38344	Trace End Estates	37064	Vale	38317
Tate Springs	37708	Traceview	37064	Valleybrook (Hamilton County)	37343
Tatesville	37365	Tracy City	37387	Valley Brook (Wilson County)	37122
Tatumville	38059	Trade	37691	Valley Creek	37715
Taylor	37058	Tradewinds	37122	Valley Forge	37643
Taylor Crossorads	37160	Trails End	37122	Valley Hills (Part of Bristol)	37620
Taylor Hill (Part of Dayton)	37321	Tranquility	37303	Valley View Heights	37716
Taylor Place	38556	Travisville	38577	Van Buren	38042
Taylors Cross Roads	38573	Treadway	37881	Vandever	38555
Taylorsville (Maury County)	38461	Treeville	37849	Van Dyke	38242
Taylorsville (Wilson County)	37087	Trenton	38382	Van Hill	37857
Taylortown	34859	Trent Valley	37869	Vanleer	37181
Tazewell	37879	Trentville	37871	Vannatta	37160
Teague	38356	Trevecca-College (Part of Nashville)	37210	Vanntown	37335
Tekoa	37931	Trezevant	38258	Vardy	37869
Telford	37690	Tri-Angle	37160	Vasper	37714
Tellico Hills (Part of Athens)	37303	Trigonia	37801	Vaughn's Gap (Part of Nashville)	37205
Tellico Plains	37385	Trimble	38259	Vaughns Grove	38382
Temperance Hall	37095	Trinity	37064	Verdun	37841
Temple Hill	37650	Triune	37014	Vernon	37137
Temple Hills Country Club Estates	37064	Trousdale	37357	Vernon Heights	37664
		Troy	38260	Verona	37091
		Trundel Crossroad	37865	Verona Hills	37122
		Tuckahoe	37871		
		Tuckers Crossroads	37087		

	ZIP		ZIP		ZIP
Woodrow	37617	Wynn	37766	Young Bend	37166
Woods Ferry	37066	Wynnburg	38077	Youngs	38301
Woodstock	38053	Yager	37110	Youngville	37172
Woods Valley	37051	Yankeetown	38583	Y Section	37601
Woodville	38063	Yell	37091	Yukon	38488
Woody	38555	Yellow Store	37873	Yuma	38390
Wooldridge	37762	Yett Addition	37862	Yum Yum	38068
Wrigley	37098	Yettland (Part of Sevierville)	37862	Zack	38320
Wyatts Chapel	37058	Yorkely	38472	Zion Grove	37862
Wyatt Village	37708	Yorktown (Part of Franklin)	37064	Zion Hill (Part of	
Wyly	38320	Yorkville	38389	Surgoinsville)	37857

* Area Zip Code   † Post Office Boxes

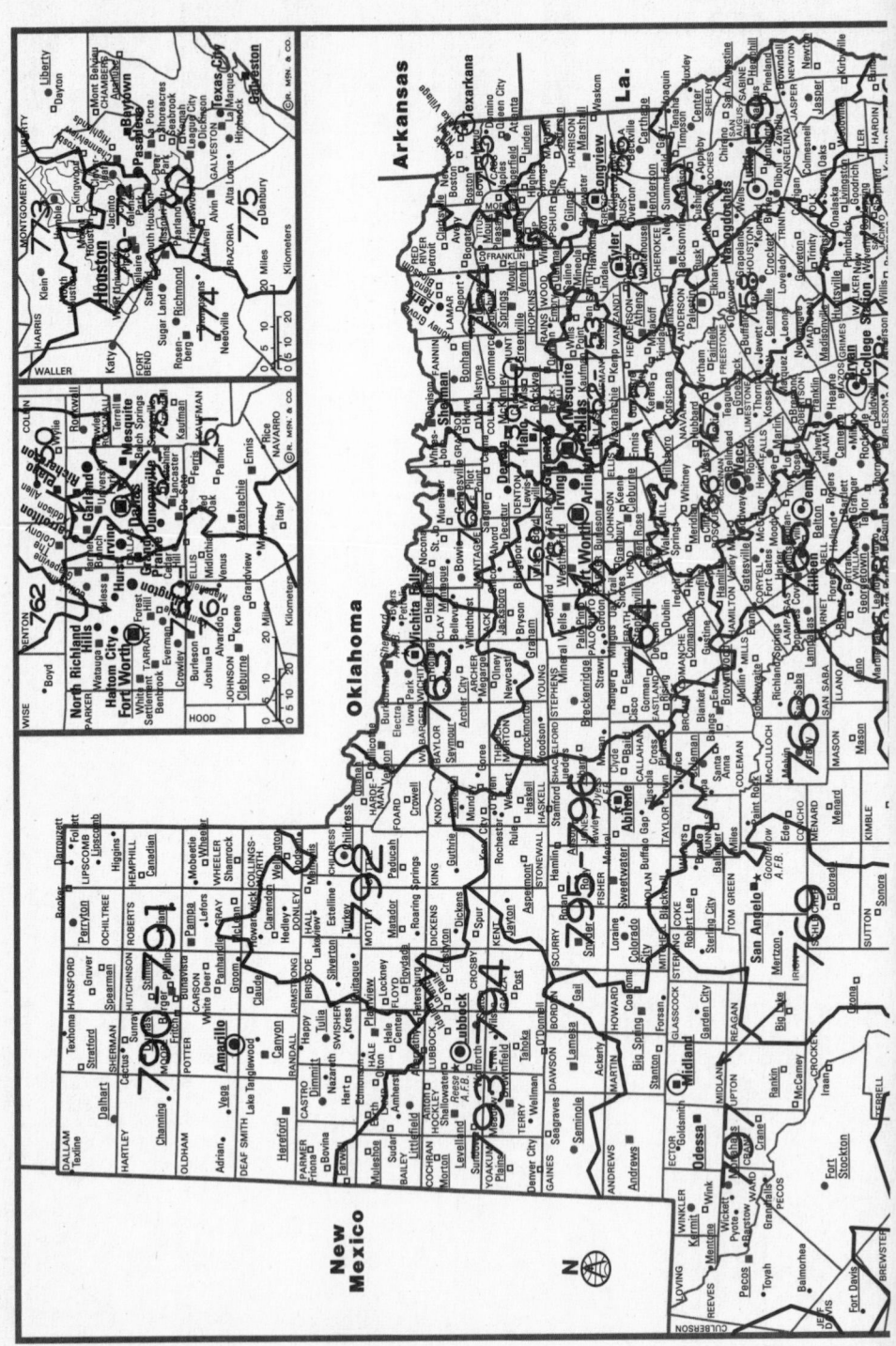

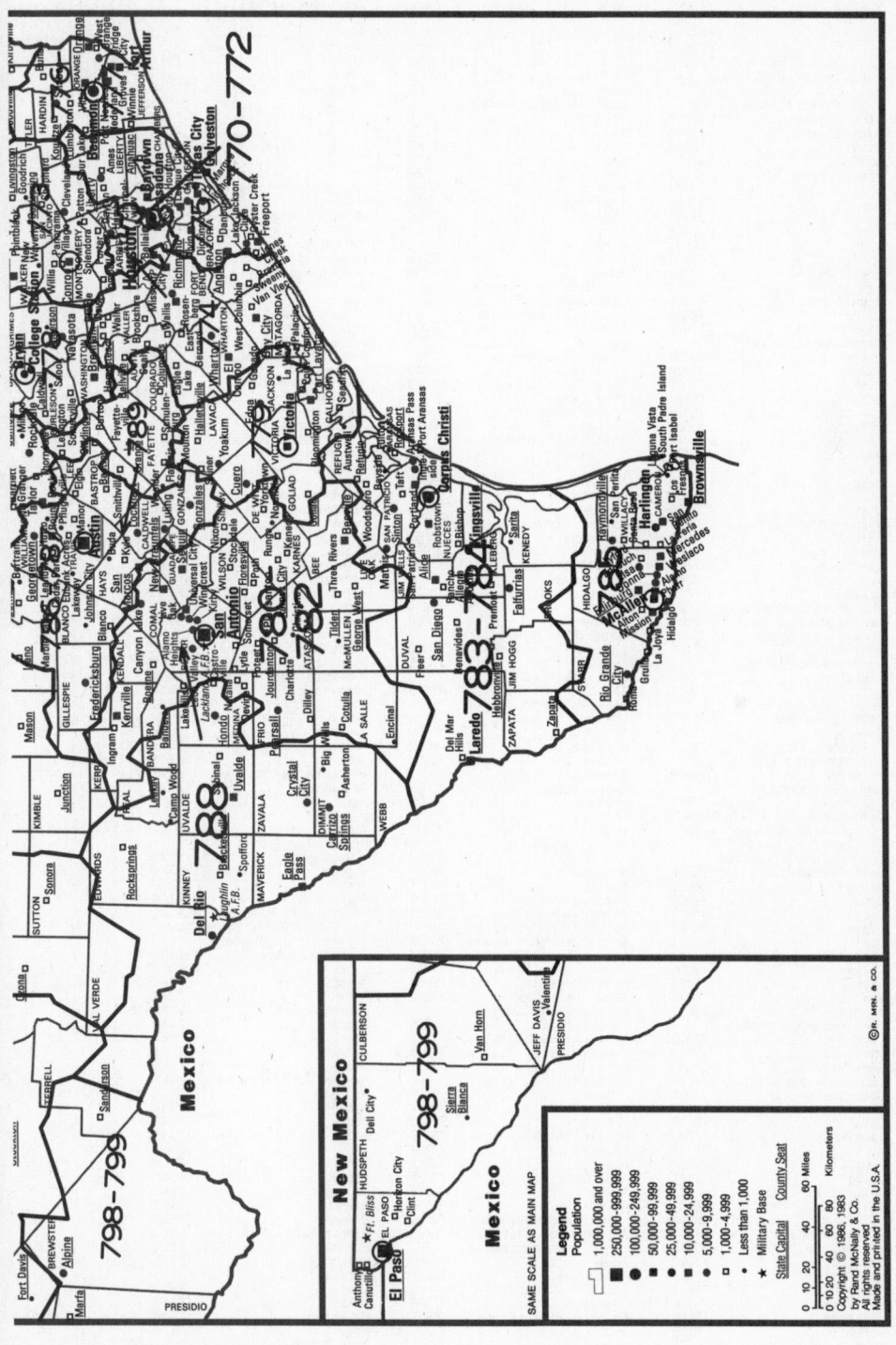

	ZIP
A (Part of San Antonio)	78207
Abbott	76621
Aberfoyle	75496
Abernathy	79311
Abilene	79601-08
....	79697-99
For specific Abilene Zip Codes call (915) 673-6485, or your local postmaster.	
Abilene Christian College (Part of Abilene)	79699
Ables Springs	75160
Abner	75142
Abram	78572
Abram-Perezville	78572
Acala	79839
Ace	77326
Ackerly	79713
Acton	76048
Acuff	79401
Acworth	75426
Adams Gardens	78550
Adams Hill	78245
Adams Oaks	77365
Adamsville	76550
Addicks	77079
Addicks Barker (Part of Houston)	77218
Addielou	75412
Addison	75001
Addran	75482
Adell	76086
Ad Hall	76520
Adina	78947
Adkins	78101
Admiral	79504
Adrian	79001
Adsul	75956
Afton	79220
Aggieland (Part of College Station)	77844
Agnes	76082
Agua Dulce	78330
Agua Nueva	78361
Aguilares	78369
Aiken (Floyd County)	79221
Aiken (Shelby County)	75935
Airlawn (Part of Dallas)	75235
Airport City	78108
Airport Mail Facility (Part of Houston)	77205
Airville	76501
Alabama and Coushatta Indian Reservation	77351
Alamo	78516
Alamo Alto	79853
Alamo Beach (Bandera County)	78063
Alamo Beach (Calhoun County)	77979
Alamo Heights	78208-09
For specific Alamo Heights Zip Codes call (512) 826-0461, or your local postmaster.	
Alamo Ranchettos	79735
Alanreed	79002
Alazan	75961
Alba	75410
Albany	76430
Albert	78671
Albert Thomas (Part of Nassau Bay)	77058
Albion	75426
Alco	75949
Alderbranch	75801
Aldine (census designated place)	77018
Aldine	77039
Aldine Estates	77039
Aldine Gardens	77039
Aldine Meadows	77039
Aledo	76008
Aleman	76531
Alexander	76446
Aley	75143
Alfred	78332
Algerita	76877
Algoa	77511
Alice	78332*
....	78333†
Alief (Part of Houston)	77411
Allamore	79855
Allen	75002
Allenfarm	77868
Allenhurst	77414
Allens Chapel	75492
Allens Point	75446
Alleyton	78935
Allison	79003
Allmon	79250
Alma	75119
Almeda (Part of Houston)	77045

	ZIP
Almeda Mall (Part of Houston)	77034
Almont	75559
Aloe	77905
Alpine	79830*
....	79831†
Alsa	75169
Alsdorf	75119
Altair	77412
Alta Loma (Part of Santa Fe)	77510
Alto	75925
Altoga	75069
Alton	78572
Alto Springs	76653
Alum	78160
Alum Creek	78957
Alvarado	76009
Alvin	77511*
....	77512†
Alvord	76225
Amarillo	79101-59
For specific Amarillo Zip Codes call (806) 379-2140, or your local postmaster.	
Ambia	75460
Ambrose	75414
American Technological University	76540
Ames (Coryell County)	76520
Ames (Liberty County)	77575
Amherst (Lamar County) ...	75460
Amherst (Lamb County) ...	79312
Amigoland Mall (Part of Brownsville)	78520
Ammansville	78945
Amy	75432
Anadarko	75667
Anahuac	77514
Anchor	77515
Anchorage	78065
Ander	77963
Anderson	77830
Anderson Mill	78750
Andice	78628
Andrews	79714
Andrewsville	75683
Angelo State University (Part of San Angelo)	76909
Angleton	77515*
....	77516†
Angus	75110
Angus Valley (Part of Austin)	78758
Anna	75409
Annarose	78022
Annetta	76008
Annetta North	76087
Annetta South	76086
Anneville	76023
Annona	75550
Anson	79501
Anson Jones (Part of Houston)	77009
Antelope	76389
Anthony	88021
Anthony Harbor	77529
Antioch (Cass County)	75551
Antioch (Delta County)	75432
Antioch (Henderson County)	75758
Antioch (Houston County) ...	75851
Antioch (Jasper County) ...	77612
Antioch (Madison County) ...	75852
Antioch (Rusk County)	75652
Antioch (Shelby County; mail Timpson)	75975
Antioch (Shelby County; mail Center)	75935
Anton	79313
Apache Addition (Part of Seguin)	78155
Apache Shores	78734
Apolonia	77830
Apparel Mart (Part of Dallas)	75207
Appelt Hill	77964
Appleby	75961
Apple Springs	75926
Aquilla	76622
Aransas Pass	78335-36
For specific Aransas Pass Zip Codes call (512) 758-3788, or your local postmaster.	
Arbala	75482
Arbor	75847
Arbor Oaks (Part of Houston)	77088
Arcadia (Galveston County)	77517
Arcadia (Shelby County) ...	75935
Archer City	76351
Arcola	77583
Arden	76901
Argenta	78368

	ZIP
Argo	75558
Argyle	76226
Argyle Plaza (Part of Houston)	77035
Ariola	77625
Arizona	77367
Arlam	75946
Arledge Ridge	75418
Arlington	76003-07
....	76010-18
....	76094
....	76096
For specific Arlington Zip Codes call (817) 274-3385, or your local postmaster.	
Arlington Downs (Part of Arlington)	76010
Arlington Heights (Part of Fort Worth)	76147
Armstrong	78338
Arneckeville	77954
Arnett (Coryell County)	76528
Arnett (Hockley County) ...	79336
Arp	75750
Arrowhead Lake	77378
Arrowhead Shores	76048
Arrowhead Village	78130
Arroyo (Part of Harlingen)	78550
Arroyo City	78586
Arsenal (Part of San Antonio)	78283
Art	76820
Artesian Forest	77304
Artesia Wells	78001
Arthur City	75411
Arvana	79331
Asa	76707
Ash (Henderson County) ...	75751
Ash (Houston County)	75835
Ashby	77465
Asherton	78827
Ashland	75640
Ashmore	79342
Ashtola	79226
Ashworth	75142
Asia	75939
Aspermont	79502
Astrodome (Part of Houston)	77025
Astro Hills	78130
Atascocita (Part of Humble)	77346
Atascosa	78002
Ater	76528
Athens	75751
Atlanta	75551
Atlas	75460
Atoy	75785
Atreco (Part of Port Arthur)	77640
Attoyac	75961
Atwell	76437
Aubrey	76227
Auburn	76050
Audubon Park (Part of Houston)	77338
Augusta	75844
Aurora	76078
Austin	78701-69
For specific Austin Zip Codes call (512) 929-1255, or your local postmaster.	
Austin Lake Estates	78759
Austonio	75835
Austwell	77950
Authon	76086
Autumn Woods	77362
Avalon	76623
Avery	75554
Avinger	75630
Avoca	79503
Avonbell (Part of Amarillo)	79106
Avondale	76179
Avon Park	76708
Axtell	76624
Azle	76020*
....	76098†
Bacliff	77518
Bagby	75446
Bagwell	75412
Bailey	75413
Baileyboro	79371
Bailey's Prairie	77515
Baileyville	76570
Bainer	79339
Bainville	78119
Baird	79504
Baker	76086
Bakersfield	79752
Balch	79358
Balch Springs	75180
Balcones (Part of Austin)	78759
Balcones Heights	78201
Balcones Village	78750

	ZIP		ZIP		ZIP
Bald Hill	75901	Beckville	75631	Birdville (Part of Haltom	
Bald Prairie	77856	Becton	79343	City)	76117
Baldwin	75661	Bedford	76021-22	Birnam Woods	77379
Ballinger	76821		76095	Birome	76673
Balmorhea	79718	For specific Bedford Zip Codes		Birthright	75482
Balsora	76426	call (214) 647-2996, or your local		Biry	78016
Bammel	77040	postmaster.		Bisbee	76063
Bammel Timbers	77040	Bedias	77831	Bishop	78343
Banana Junction	76708	Bee Cave	78746	Bivins	75555
Bancroft (Part of Pinehurst)	77630	Beech Grove	75951	Black	79035
Bandera	78003	Beechnut (Part of Houston)	77072	Blackfoot	75853
Bandera Falls	78063	Beechwood	75948	Black Hills	75110
Bangs	76823	Bee House	76525	Black Jack (Cherokee	
Banquete	78339	Beeville	78102*	County)	75789
Barbarosa	78130		78104†	Black Jack (Robertson	
Barclay	76656	Belcherville	76255	County)	77859
Bardin Road (Part of		Belfalls	76579	Blackland	75189
Arlington)	76018	Belgrade	75928	Blackoak	75431
	76096	Belk	75411	Blackwell	79506
For specific Bardin Road Zip		Bellaire	77401*	Blakeney	75412
Codes call (817) 472-8290, or			77402†	Blanchard	77351
your local postmaster.		Bellaire Addition	75704	Blanco	78606
Bardwell	75101	Bellaire West (Part of		Blanconia	78102
Barker	77413	Houston)	77072	Blandlake	75972
Barksdale	78828	Bell Branch	76651	Blanket	76432
Barnes	75960	Bellevue	76228	Bleakwood	75956
Barnhart	76930	Bellmead	76705	Bledsoe	79314
Barnum	75939	Bells	75414	Bleiblerville	78931
Barrett	77532	Bellview	75410	Blessing	77419
Barrington Oaks (Part of		Bellville	77418	Blevins	76524
Austin)	78759	Belmar (Part of Amarillo)	79106	Blewett	78801
Barry	75102	Belmena	76520	Blodgett	75686
Barstow	79719	Belmont	78604	Bloomburg	75556
Bartlett	76511	Belott	75835	Bloomdale	75069
Bartley Woods	75492	Belton	76513	Bloomfield	76258
Barton Creek Square (Part		Ben Arnold	76519	Blooming Grove	76626
of Austin)	78746	Benavides	78341	Bloomington	77951
Bartons Chapel	76458	Ben Bolt	78342	Blossom	75416
Bartonville	76226	Benbrook	76126	Blue	78947
Barwise	79235	Benchley	77801	Bluegrove	76352
Bascom	75705	Bend	76824	Blue Haven Estates	75169
Basin	79834	Bending Bough	77373	Blue Lake Estates	78654
Basin Springs	76264	Ben Franklin	75415	Blue Mound	76131
Bassett	75574	Ben Hur	76664	Blue Ridge (Collin County)	75424
Bassett Center (Part of El		Benjamin	79505	Blue Ridge (Falls County)	76661
Paso)	79925	Bennett	76066	Blueroan	77434
Bastrop	78602	Bennett Estates	77302	Bluetown	78592
Bastrop Bayou	77515	Benoit	76882	Blue Water Key	75758
Bastrop Beach	77515	Bent Tree (Part of Dallas)	75287	Bluff Dale	76433
Bateman	78662	Bentwood (Part of San		Bluff Springs (Parker	
Batesville (Red River		Angelo)	76904	County)	76020
County)	75426	Bentwood Acres	75076	Bluff Springs (Travis	
Batesville (Zavala County)	78829	Ben Wheeler	75754	County)	78744
Batson	77519	Berclair	78107	Bluffton	78607
Battle	76664	Berea (Houston County)	75835	Blum	76627
Baxter	75751	Berea (Marion County)	75657	Blumenthal	78624
Bay City	77404†	Bergheim	78004	Bluntzer	78380
	77414*	Bergstrom Air Force Base	78743	Board	76442
Bay Harbor	77554	Berlin	77833	Bob Harris (Part of	
Baylor University (Part of		Bernardo	78933	Pasadena)	77506
Waco)	76706	Berry Street (Part of Fort		Bob Lyons (Part of	
Bay Oaks	77571	Worth)	76109	Galveston)	77554
Bayou Bend (Part of		Berryville	75763	Bobo	75974
Houston)	77088	Bertram	78605	Bobville	77333
Bayou Chantilly (Part of		Bessmay	77612	Boca Chica (Part of	
Dickinson)	77539	Best	76932	Brownsville)	78520
Bayou Vista	77563	Bethany	71007	Boerne	78006
Bay Plaza (Part of Baytown)	77520	Bethel (Anderson County)	75861	Bogata	75417
Bayport (Part of Houston)	77058	Bethel (Ellis County)	75165	Bois D'Arc	75801
Bayside	78340	Bethel (Henderson County)	75751	Boling	77420
Bayside Terrace	77571	Bethlehem (Bowie County)	75559	Boling-Iago	77420
Baytown	77520-22	Bethlehem (Collin County)	75442	Bolivar	76266
For specific Baytown Zip Codes		Bethlehem (Upshur County)	75644	Bolton	75686
call (713) 420-2508, or your local		Beto Unit	75861	Bomarton	76380
postmaster.		Beto 2 Unit	75801	Bon Ami	75956
Bayview (Cameron County)	78566	Bettie	75644	Bonanza (Hill County)	76692
Bay View (Galveston		Beulah	75941	Bonanza (Hopkins County)	75420
County)	77518	Beverly	76711	Bonanza Beach	78611
Bayview Estates	76945	Beverly Hills (Part of Dallas)	75211	Bonham	75418
Bayway (Part of Baytown)	77520	Bevil Oaks	77706	Bonita	76255
Baywood (Part of Seabrook)	77586	Bevilport	75951	Bonnerville	75840
Bazette	75144	Beyersville	78615	Bonney	77583
Beach	77301	Biardstown	75462	Bonnie View	78393
Beach City	77520	Big Bend National Park	79834	Bono	76031
Beacon Hill (Part of San		Bigfoot	78005	Bon Wier	75928
Antonio)	78201	Biggs Army Air Base	79908	Booker	79005
Beadle	77414	Big Lake	76932	Boonsville	76426
Bear Grass	75846	Big Oaks	75630	Booth	77469
Beasley	77417	Big Sandy	75755	Boquillas	79834
Beattie	76442	Big Spring	79720*	Borden	78962
Beaukiss	78621		79721†	Borderland	79932
Beaumont	77701-08	Big Square	79027	Bordersville (Part of	
	77710	Big Thiket	77369	Houston)	77338
	77713-26	Big Town Shopping Center		Borger	79007*
For specific Beaumont Zip Codes		(Part of Mesquite)	75149		79008†
call (409) 842-7200, or your local		Big Valley Ranchettes	76522	Bosqueville	76708
postmaster.		Big Wells	78830	Boston (Part of New	
Beaumont Place	77028	Billington	76624	Boston)	75570
Beauxart Gardens	77705	Billpark (Part of Houston)	77012	Boswell	77340
Beaver Dam	75559	Biloxi	75928	Bovina	79009
Bebe	78603	Birch	77879	Bowie	76230
Becker	75142			Bowser	76872

	ZIP
Box Church	76642
Boxelder	75550
Boxwood	75683
Boyce	75165
Boyd (Fannin County)	75418
Boyd (Wise County)	76023
Boys Ranch	79010
Boz	75165
Brachfield	75681
Bracken	78266
Brackettville	78832
Brad	76475
Bradfield	75656
Bradford	75853
Bradshaw	79567
Brady (McCulloch County)	76825
Brady (Shelby County)	75935
Branch	75407
Branchville	76520
Brandon	76628
Bransford (Part of Colleyville)	76034
Branton	76471
Brashear	75420
Brazoria	77422
Brazos	76472
Brazos Mall (Part of Lake Jackson)	77566
Brazos Point	76652
Breckenridge	76424
Bremond	76629
Brenham	77833*
	77834†
Brentwood Manor	77904
Breslau	77964
Briar (Tarrant County)	76020
Briarcliff	78669
Briaroaks	76028
Briary	76570
Brice	79226
Bridge Chapel	75455
Bridge City	77611
Bridgeport	76426
Brierwood Bay	75763
Briggs	78608
Bright Star (Rains County)	75410
Bright Star (Van Zandt County)	75169
Briscoe	79011
Briscoe Unit	78017
Bristol	75119
Britton	76063
Broaddus	75929
Broadway (Crosby County)	79243
Broadway (Lamar County)	75460
Broadway Junction	75460
Broadway Square (Part of Tyler)	75701
Brock	76086
Brock Junction	76086
Brogado	79718
Bronco	79355
Bronson	75930
Bronte	76933
Brookeland	75931
Brookesmith	76827
Brook Forest	77357
Brook Glen Addition (Part of La Porte)	77571
Brookhollow (Part of Dallas)	75247
Brookshier	76933
Brookshire	77423
Brookside Village	77581
Brookston	75421
Broom City	75839
Broome	76951
Brown College	77880
Browndell	75931
Brownfield	79316
Browning	75705
Brownsboro (Caldwell County)	78644
Brownsboro (Henderson County)	75756
Brownsville	78520-26
For specific Brownsville Zip Codes call (512) 546-2411, or your local postmaster.	
Brownwood	76801-04
For specific Brownwood Zip Codes call (915) 646-0656, or your local postmaster.	
Brownwood (Part of Orange)	77630
Broyles	75801
Bruceville (Part of Bruceville-Eddy)	76630
Bruceville-Eddy	76630
Brumley	75686
Brundage	78834
Bruni	78344
Brunswick	75925

	ZIP
Brushie Prairie	76641
Brushy	77845
Brushy Bend Park	78681
Brushy Creek (Anderson County)	75801
Brushy Creek (Williamson County)	78681
Brushy Creek North	78681
Bryan	77801-08
For specific Bryan Zip Codes call (409) 779-1988, or your local postmaster.	
Bryans Mill	75568
Bryson	76427
Buchanan Dam	78609
Buchanan Lake Village	78672
Buchel	77954
Buck Creek	75949
Buckeye	77414
Buckholts	76518
Buckhorn (Austin County)	77418
Buckhorn (Newton County)	75928
Buckingham	75080
Buckner	76462
Buda	78610
Buena Vista (Bexar County)	78221
Buena Vista (Burnet County)	78611
Buena Vista (Shelby County)	75975
Buffalo	75831
Buffalo Gap (Taylor County)	79508
Buffalo Gap (Travis County)	78734
Buffalo Springs	76228
Buford	79512
Bugbee Heights	79078
Bug Tussle	75449
Bula	79320
Bullard	75757
Bullock	76470
Bulverde	78163
Buna	77612
Bunavista (Part of Borger)	79007
Buncomb	75633
Bunger	76450
Bunker Hill	75486
Bunker Hill Village	77024
Bunyan	76446
Burkburnett	76354
Burke	75941
Burkett	76828
Burkeville	75932
Burleigh	77418
Burleson	76028*
	76097†
Burlington	76519
Burnell	78119
Burnet	78611
Burns (Bowie County)	75561
Burns (Cooke County)	76258
Burr	77488
Burris Crossing	79853
Burrow	75189
Burton	77835
Busby	79543
Bushland	79012
Bushwhacker Peninsula	75147
Bustamante	78361
Busterville	79358
Butler (Bastrop County)	78621
Butler (Freestone County)	75855
Byers	76357
Bynum	76631
Byrd	75119
Byrds	76801
Cabot Kingsmill	79065
Cactus	79013
Caddo	76429
Caddo Mills	75135
Cadiz	78102
Cain City	78624
Calaveras	78114
Caldwell	77836
Caledonia	75946
Calf Creek	76825
Call	75933
Calliham	78007
Callisburg	76240
Call Junction	75933
Calvary	75773
Calvert	77837
Camden	75934
Camelot	78239
Cameron	76520
Cameron Park	78521
Camey	75034
Camilla	77331
Camp Air	76856
Campbell	75422
Campbellton	78008
Camp Dallas	75034
Camp Maxey	75473

	ZIP
Campo Alto	78516
Camp Ruby	77351
Camp San Saba	76825
Camp Springs	79526
Camp Stanley	78206
Camp Strake	77301
Camp Swift	78602
Campti	75935
Camp Valley	78140
Camp Verde	78010
Camp Wood	78833
Cana	75169
Canada Verde	78114
Canadian	79014
Canal City	77617
Candelaria	79843
Candlelight Oaks (Part of Houston)	77088
Caney	77414
Caney City	75148
Caney Creek Estates	77357
Cannon	75495
Canton	75103
Canutillo	79835
Canyon (Lubbock County)	79408
Canyon (Randall County)	79015
Canyon City	78130
Canyon Creek (Part of Richardson)	75080
Canyon Creek Estates	78130
Canyon Lake	78130
Canyon Lake Acres	78130
Canyon Lake Estates	78130
Canyon Lake Forest	78130
Canyon Lake Hills	78130
Canyon Lake Island	78130
Canyon Lake Mobile Home Estates	78130
Canyon Lake Shores	78130
Canyon Lake Village	78130
Canyon Lake Village West	78130
Canyon Springs Resort	78130
Canyon Valley	79356
Canyon View Acres	78163
Capital Plaza (Part of Austin)	78723
Capitol (Part of Austin)	78701
Caplen	77617
Capps Corner	76265
Cap Rock	79357
Caprock Shopping Center (Part of Lubbock)	79404
Caps	79606
Caradan	76844
Carancahua	77465
Carbon	76435
Carbondale	75567
Cardinal (Part of Athens)	75751
Carey	79222
Carey Estates (Part of Seabrook)	77586
Carlisle	75862
Carlos	77830
Carl Range (Part of Irving)	75062
Carlsbad	76934
Carl's Corner	76645
Carlton	76436
Carmine	78932
Carmona	75939
Caro	75961
Carolina Cove	77367
Carpenter	78101
Carpenters Bluff	75020
Carricitos	78586
Carrizo Springs	78834
Carroll	75771
Carroll Springs	75853
Carrollton	75006-08
	75010-11
For specific Carrollton Zip Codes call (214) 418-7858, or your local postmaster.	
Carrolton Park Two (Part of Dallas)	75006
Carson	75488
Carta Valley	78835
Carterville	75563
Carthage	75633
Cartwright (Kaufman County)	75142
Cartwright (Wood County)	75494
Casa Piedra	79843
Casa View (Part of Dallas)	75228
Cash	75402
Cason	75636
Cass	75556
Cassie	78611
Castell	76831
Castle Hills	78213
Castlewood	77039
Castolon	79834
Castroville	78009

* Area Zip Code   † Post Office Boxes

Place	ZIP	Place	ZIP	Place	ZIP
Catarina	78836	Chapman Ranch	78347	Clifton (Bosque County)	76634
Cat Spring	78933	Chappel	76877	Clifton (Van Zandt County)	75169
Causeway Beach	75143	Chappell Hill	77426	Climax	75407
Cave Creek	78624	Charco	77963	Cline	78801
Cave Springs	75670	Charleston	75432	Clint	79836
Caviness	75460	Charlie	78306	Clinton (DeWitt County)	77954
Cawthon	77868	Charlotte	78011	Clinton (Hunt County)	75135
Cayote	76689	Chase Field Naval Air		Clodine	77469
Cayuga	75832	Station	78103	Close City	79356
Cedar Branch (Henderson		Chat	76645	Cloverleaf	77015
County)	75147	Chateau Woods	77301	Club Lake Estates	75708
Cedar Branch (Houston		Chatfield	75105	Clute	77531
County)	75844	Cheapside	77954	Clyde	79510
Cedar Creek (Anderson		Cheek	77705	Coady	77520
County)	75839	Cherokee	76832	Coahoma	79511
Cedar Creek (Bastrop		Cherry Mound	75020	Coal Mine (Part of Lytle)	78052
County)	78612	Cherry Spring	78624	Cobb Creek	75852
Cedar Elm (Part of San		Chester	75936	Cobb Switch	75160
Antonio)	78249	Chesterville	77435	Cochran	77418
Cedar Grove (Cass County)	75560	Chico	76431	Cockrell Hill	75211
Cedar Grove (Coryell		Chicota	75425	Coffee City	75763
County)	76522	Chief	75142	Coffeeville	75683
Cedar Grove (El Paso		Chihuahua	78572	Coffield Unit	75861
County)	79915	Childress	79201	Coit	76653
Cedar Grove (Harris		Chillicothe	79225	Coke	75431
County)	77532	Chilton	76632	Coldhill	75708
Cedar Hill (Dallas County)	75104*	Chimney Corners (Part of		Coldspring	77331
	75106†	Austin)	78731	Coleman	76834
Cedar Hill (Floyd County)	79241	China	77613	Coleman Cove	75929
Cedar Hills	78621	China Grove (Bexar County)	78223	Colfax	75103
Cedar Lake	77414	China Grove (Scurry		College Country Estates	75020
Cedar Lane	77415	County)	79526	College Hill	75559
Cedar Mills Resort	76245	China Spring	76633	College Mound	75160
Cedar Park	78613*	Chinati	79843	Collegeport	77428
	78630†	Chireno	75937	College Station	77840-45
Cedar Point	77520	Chita	75862	For specific College Station Zip	
Cedar Shores Estates	76671	Choate	78119	Codes call (409) 693-4152, or	
Cedar Springs (Falls		Chocolate Bayou	77511	your local postmaster.	
County)	76570	Choice	75935	Colleyville	76034
Cedar Springs (Upshur		Chriesman	77838	Collin Creek Mall (Part of	
County)	75683	Christine	78012	Plano)	75075
Cedar Valley	78736	Christoval	76935	Collinsville	76233
Cedarview	75104	C H Rouse Estates	77365	Colmesneil	75938
Cee Vee	79223	Church Hill (Cherokee		Cologne	77905
Cego	76524	County)	75766	Colonial (Part of Waco)	76707
Cele	78653	Church Hill (Rusk County)	75652	Colorado City	79512
Celeste	75423	Churchill Bridge	77422	Colquitt	75160
Celina	75009	Cibolo	78108	Colton	78744
Center (Limestone County)	76642	Cielo Vista (Part of El Paso)	79925	Columbus	78934
Center (Shelby County)	75935	Cielo Vista Mall (Part of El		Comal	78130
Center City	76844	Paso)	79925	Comanche	76442
Center Grove	75455	Cienegas Terrace	78840	Comanche Cove	76048
Center Line	77879	Circle	79064	Comanche Harbor	76048
Center Point (Camp		Circle Back	79371	Comanche Village	76544
County)	75686	Circle D-KC Estates	78602	Combes	78535
Center Point (Ellis County)	76651	Circleville (Travis County)	78736	Combine	75159
Center Point (Kerr County)	78010	Circleville (Williamson		Comfort	78013
Center Point (Panola		County)	76574	Commerce	75428
County)	75691	Cisco	76437	Como	75431
Center Point (Parker		Cistern	78941	Comstock	78851
County; mail		Citrus City	78572	Comyn	76444
Weatherford)	76087	Citrus Grove	77465	Concan	78838
Center Point (Parker		Civic Center (Part of		Concepcion	78349
County; mail Azle)	76020	Houston)	77208	Concho	76866
Center Point (Titus County)	75455	Clairemont	79549	Concord (Cherokee County)	75789
Center Point (Upshur		Clairette	76457	Concord (Leon County)	77850
County)	75755	Clardy	75468	Concord (Morris County)	75571
Centerview	75833	Clarendon	79226	Concord (Rusk County)	75681
Centerville (Leon County)	75833	Clareville	78102	Concrete	77954
Centerville (Trinity County)	75845	Clark	77327	Cone	79357
Central (Angelina County)	75969	Clarks	77979	Conlen	79022
Central (Tarrant County)	76102	Clarksville	75426	Connor	77864
Central Gardens	77627	Clarksville City	75647	Conroe	77301-05
Central Heights (Jefferson		Clarkwood (Part of Corpus			77384-85
County)	77627	Christi)	78406	For specific Conroe Zip Codes	
Central Heights		Claude	79019	call (409) 756-8908, or your local	
(Nacogdoches County)	75961	Clauene	79336	postmaster.	
Central High	75925	Clawson	75904	Constitution Village (Part of	
Centralia	75834	Clay	77839	Sherman)	75495
Central Mall (Bowie County)	75501	Claydesta Station (Part of		Content	79519
Central Mall (Jefferson		Midland)	79710	Converse	78109
County)	77640	Clayton (Jefferson County)	77627	Conway	79068
Central Park (Bexar County)	78216	Clayton (Panola County)	77627	Cooks Point	77836
Central Park (Harris County)	77011	Claytonville (Fisher County)	79556	Cookville	75558
Central Unit	77478	Claytonville (Swisher		Cool	76086
Cestohowa	78113	County)	79052	Cool Crest	78245
Chaffee Village	76544	Clear Creek	76544	Coolidge	76635
Chalk	79248	Clear Lake City (Part of		Cooper	75432
Chalk Bluff	76705	Houston)	77062	Cooper Creek	76201
Chalk Mountain	76401	Clear Lake Shores	77565	Copano Village	78382
Chalybeate	75494	Clear Spring	78130	Copeland	75701
Chambersville	75069	Clearview	78602	Copeville	75121
Chambliss	75409	Cleburne	76031*	Coppell	75019
Champion Forest	77303		76033†	Copperas Cove	76522
Chances Store	77839	Clegg	78022	Copper Canyon	76226
Chandler	75758	Clemens Unit	77422	Corbet	75110
Channelview	77530	Clemons	77423	Cordele	77957
Channelwood	77530	Clemville	77414	Corine	75766
Channing	79018	Cleveland	77327*	Corinth (Denton County)	76205
Chaparral	78840		77328†	Corinth (Eastland County)	76437
Chaparral Hills	78840	Clever Creek	75935	Corinth (Jones County)	79553
Chaparral Park	78652	Cliffside	79106	Corinth (Leon County)	75831
Chapman	75652				

	ZIP
Corinth (Van Zandt County)	75140
Corley	75567
Cornersville	75494
Cornett	75568
Cornudas	79847
Coronado (Part of El Paso)	79912*
	79913†
Corpus Christi	78401-80
For specific Corpus Christi Zip Codes call (512) 886-2200, or your local postmaster.	
Corral City	76226
Corrigan	75939
Corsicana	75110
Corsicana Junction (Part of Corsicana)	75110
Coryell	76689
Cost	78614
Cotton Center (Fannin County)	75418
Cotton Center (Hale County)	79021
Cottondale	76073
Cotton Flat	79701
Cotton Gin	75860
Cotton Mill Spur (Part of Denison)	75020
Cottonwood (Brazos County)	77808
Cottonwood (Callahan County)	79504
Cottonwood (Falls County)	76655
Cottonwood (Kaufman County)	75158
Cottonwood (Lamar County)	75486
Cottonwood (Madison County)	77864
Cottonwood (McLennan County)	76691
Cottonwood Shores	78657
Cotulla	78014
Coughran	78064
Council Creek Village	78611
Country Campus	77340
Country Club Lake Estates	76904
Country Club Terrace (Potter County)	79106
Country Club Terrace (Victoria County)	77904
Country Colony	77372
Country Place Acres	77355
Countryside Plaza (Part of San Antonio)	78216
Country Squire Estates	77630
County Line (Camp County)	75686
County Line (Hale County)	79363
Coupland	78615
Courtney	77868
Cove (Chambers County)	77520
Cove (Orange County)	77630
Cove Spring	75766
Covington	76636
Covington Woods (Part of Sugar Land)	77478
Cox	75644
Coyanosa	79730
Coy City	78118
Cozy Corner	78945
Crabb	77469
Crabbs Prairie	77340
Craft	75766
Crafton	76431
Craig	75652
Crandall	75114
Crane	79731
Cranfills Gap	76637
Crawford	76638
Creagleville	75140
Crecy	75845
Creechville	75119
Creedmoor	78747
Creekwood Acres	77375
Creekwood Addition	77372
Crenneland	77650
Crescent	77488
Crescent Heights	75751
Cresson	76035
Cresthaven (Part of San Antonio)	78213
Crestwood (Ector County)	79762
Crestwood (Marion County)	75630
Crestwood Farms	77356
Crews	79567
Crimcrest (Part of Henderson)	75652
Cripple Creek Farms (mail Magnolia)	77355
Cripple Creek Farms (mail Pinehurst)	77362
Cripple Creek Farms West	77362
Cripple Creek North	77355

	ZIP
Crisp	75119
Crockett	75835
Crosby	77532
Crosbyton	79322
Cross (Grimes County)	77861
Cross (McMullen County)	78026
Cross Cut	76801
Crossing (Part of De Soto)	75115
Cross Mountain	78255-56
For specific Cross Mountain Zip Codes call (512) 641-7828, or your local postmaster.	
Cross Plains	76443
Crossroads (Bexar County)	78201
Crossroads (Camp County)	75686
Cross Roads (Cass County; mail Hughes Springs)	75656
Crossroads (Midway) (Cass County; mail Ganado)	77962
Cross Roads (Delta County)	75432
Cross Roads (Denton County)	76227
Crossroads (Harrison County)	75670
Cross Roads (Henderson County)	75148
Cross Roads (Milam County)	76520
Cross Roads (Rusk County)	75662
Cross Roads (Van Zandt County)	75140
Croton	79232
Crow	75765
Crowell	79227
Crowley	76036
Cruz Calle	78349
Cryer Creek	76626
Crystal Beach	77650
Crystal City	78839
Crystal Creek Forest	77301
Crystal Lake	75801
Crystal Lakes Estates	77351
Cuadrilla	79836
Cuero	77954
Cullen Mall (Part of Corpus Christi)	78412
Culleoka	75407
Cumby	75433
Cundiff	76458
Cuney	75759
Cunningham	75434
Curtis	75951
Curvitas	78595
Cushing	75760
Cusseta	75566
Cut	75835
Cut and Shoot	77302
Cuthand	75417
Cuthbert	79512
Cyclone	76519
Cypress (Franklin County)	75494
Cypress (Harris County)	77429
	77433
For specific Cypress Zip Codes call (713) 373-0279, or your local postmaster.	
Cypress Bend	77040
Cypress Cove	78130
Cypress Creek	78028
Cypress Creek Estates	77429
Cypress Mill	78654
Dabney	78801
Da Costa	77905
Dacus	77356
Daingerfield	75638
Daisetta	77533
Dalby Springs	75559
Dale	78616
Dalhart	79022
Dallardsville	77332
Dallas	75201-99
	75301-98
For specific Dallas Zip Codes call (214) 647-2996, or your local postmaster.	

COLLEGES & UNIVERSITIES

	ZIP
Dallas Baptist University	75211
Southern Methodist University	75275
University of Texas Southwestern Medical Center	75235

FINANCIAL INSTITUTIONS

	ZIP
Bank One, Texas, N.A.	75201
Comerica Bank	75201
Cullen/Frost Bank of Dallas, N.A.	75201
First City, Texas-Dallas	75201

	ZIP
First Interstate Bank of Texas, N.A.	75202
Guaranty Federal Bank, F.S.B.	75225
Hibernia National Bank in Dallas	75240
Inwood National Bank	75209
North Dallas Bank & Trust Company	75230
NorthPark National Bank of Dallas	75225
Team Bank	75235
Texas Commerce Bank, N.A.	75201
United Bank & Trust	75201
Bank United of Texas, F.S.B.	75248

HOSPITALS

	ZIP
Baylor University Medical Center	75246
Dallas County Hospital District-Parkland Memorial Hospital	75235
Medical City Dallas Hospital	75230
Methodist Medical Center	75203
Presbyterian Hospital of Dallas	75231
RHD Memorial Medical Center	75234
St. Paul Medical Center	75235
Veterans Affairs Medical Center	75216

HOTELS/MOTELS

	ZIP
The Adolphus Hotel	75202
Doubletree Hotel at Campbell Center	75206
Fairmont Hotel	75201
Holiday Inn Brookhollow	75247
Hyatt Regency Dallas at Reunion	75207
Lexington Hotel Suites	75237
Loews Anatole Hotel	75207
Marriott Quorum	75240
Plaza of the Americas Hotel	75201
Preston Suites Hotel	75240
Sheraton Mockingbird	75235
Sheraton Park Central Hotel & Towers	75251
Stouffer Dallas Hotel	75207
The Summit Hotel	75234

MILITARY INSTALLATIONS

	ZIP
Naval Air Station, Dallas	75211
Texas Air National Guard, FB6431, Hensley Field	75211
United States Army Engineer Division, Southwestern	75242

	ZIP
Dallas-Fort Worth Airport (Part of Coppell)	75261
Dalrock	75088
Dalton	75568
Dalworthington Gardens	76010
Dalys	75844
Dam B	75979
Damon	77430
Danbury	77534
Danciger	77431
Danevang	77432
Daniel Unit	79549
Danville (Collin County)	75069
Danville (Gregg County)	75662
Daphne	75455
Darco	75670
Darrouzett	79024
Daugherty	75440
Davenport	75412
Davila	76523
Davis Prairie	76687
Davisville (Angelina County)	75901
Davisville (Leon County)	75833
Dawn	79025
Dawson	76639
Dayton	77535
Dayton Lakes	77535
Deadwood	75633
Dean (Clay County)	76303
Dean (Hockley County)	79363
Deanville	77852
De Berry	75639
Decatur	76234
Decker (Nolan County)	79506
Decker (Travis County)	78653
Decker Prairie	77355
De Cordova Bend Estates	76049
Deep Water Point Estates	75121
Deer Creek	76365
Deer Haven	78654
Deer Park	77536

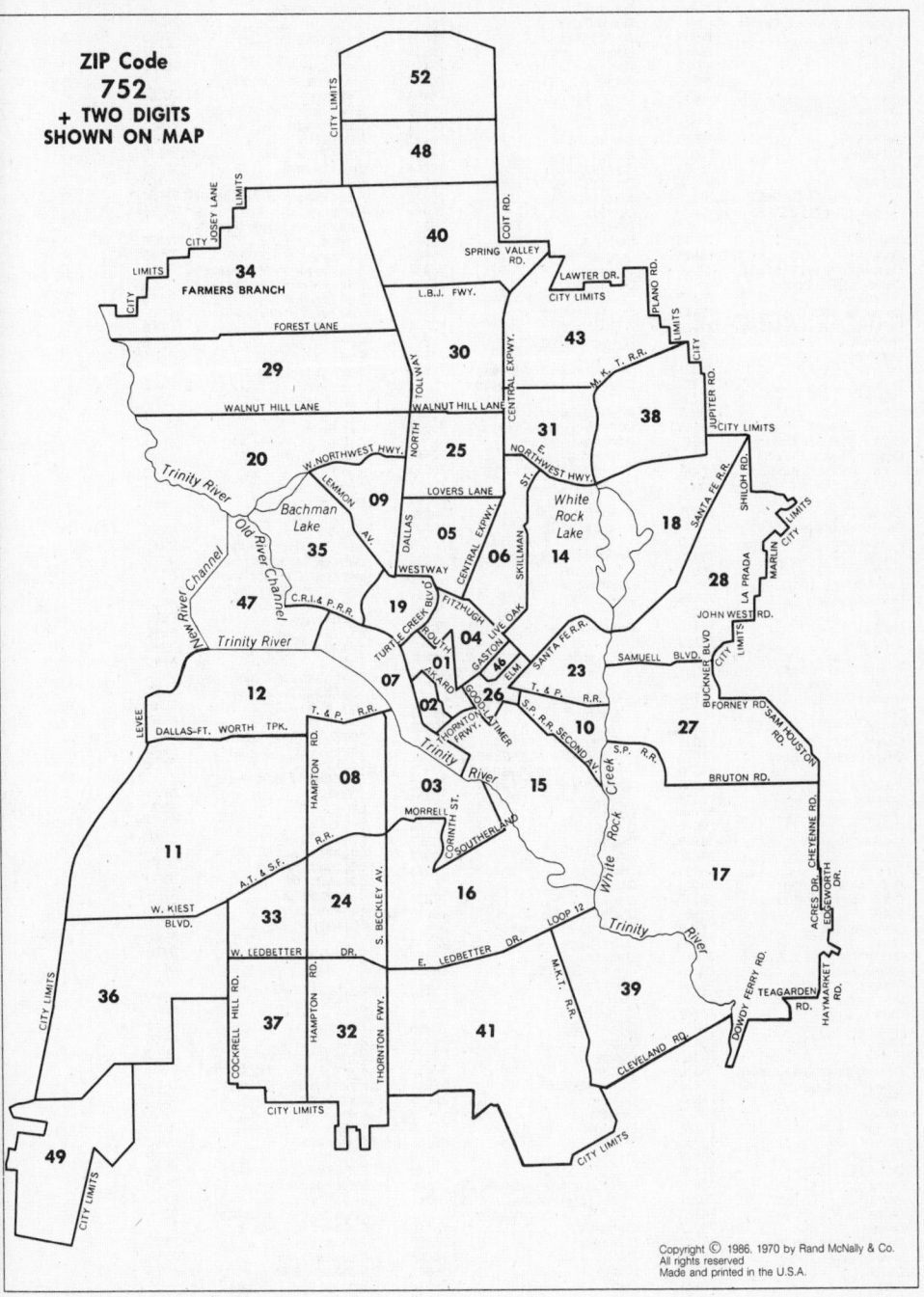

ZIP Code
752
+ TWO DIGITS
SHOWN ON MAP

52
48
40
34 FARMERS BRANCH
29
20
35
47
12
11
36
49
30
25
09
05
06
14
18
28
27
17
43
38
31
19
04
46
23
26
10
15
01
07
02
03
16
39
08
24
33
37
32
41

	ZIP		ZIP		ZIP
Deerwood East	77445	Dolen	77327		78853†
De Kalb	75559	Dominion	78257	Earles Camp	79521
Delba	75452	Domino	75572	Earles Chapel	75764
Delbert L. Atkinson (Part of		Donall Estates	78611	Early	76801
Pasadena)	77505	Donie	75838	Earlywine	77833
De Leon	76444	Donna	78537	Earth	79031
Delhi	78953	Don Tol	77420	East Afton	79220
Delia	76635	Doole	76836	East Amarillo (Part of	
Dell City	79837	Dorchester	75459	Amarillo)	79104
Del Mar Hills (Part of		Doss	78618	East Austin (Part of Austin)	78702
Laredo)	78041	Dot	76524	East Bernard	77435
Delmita	78536	Dothan	76437	East Caney	75482
Del Monte	77627	Dotson	75669	East Center	75140
Delray	75633	Double Bayou	77514	East Columbia	77486
Del Rio	78840-42	Double Diamond Estates	79036	East Delta	75450
For specific Del Rio Zip Codes		Double Oak	76226	East Donna (Part of Donna)	78537
call (512) 775-3571, or your local		Doucette	75942	Easterly	77856
postmaster.		Dougherty	79231	Eastex Oaks Village (Part of	
Delrose	75644	Douglass	75943	Houston)	77338
Del Valle	78617	Douglassville	75560	Eastgate	77535
Demi-John Island	77541	Downing	76442	East Glen (Part of El Paso)	79936
Democrat (Comanche		Downsville	76706	East Grand (Part of Dallas)	75223
County)	76442	Downtown (Part of Amarillo)	79105	East Hamilton	75973
Democrat (Mills County)	76442	Downtown (Part of		East Houston (Part of	
De Moss (Part of Houston)	77074	Beaumont)	77704	Houston)	77028
Denhawken	78160	Downtown (Part of		Eastland	76448
Denison	75020*	Brownsville)	78522	East Liberty	75935
	75021†	Downtown (Part of Bryan)	77801	East Mayfield (Part of	
Denning	75972	Downtown (Part of Corpus		Hemphill)	75948
Dennis	76439	Christi)	78401	East Mountain	75644
Denny	76653	Downtown (Part of Dallas)	75201	Easton	75641
Denson Springs	75844	Downtown (Part of El Paso)	79901	East Point	75494
Denton (Callahan County)	79510	Downtown (Part of		East Ridge (Part of Amarillo)	79107
Denton (Denton County)	76201-07	Freeport)	77541	East Side	75639
For specific Denton Zip Codes call		Downtown (Part of Irving)	75015	East Tawakoni	75453
(817) 387-8555, or your local			75017	East Tempe	77351
postmaster.			75060	East Texas (Part of	
Denver City	79323	For specific Downtown Zip Codes		Commerce)	75428
Denver Harbor (Part of		call (214) 254-4197, or your local		Eastvale	75056
Houston)	77020	postmaster.		East View (Part of Kilgore)	75662
Deport	75435	Downtown (Part of		Eastview Terrace	78101
Derby	78017	Longview)	75606	Eastwood (Part of Houston)	77023
Dermott	79549	Downtown (Part of		Eastwood Heights (Part of	
Desdemona	76445	Lubbock)	79401*	El Paso)	79925
Desert	75424		79408†	Eaton	77856
De Soto	75115	Downtown (Part of McAllen)	78501	Ebenezer (Camp County)	75686
	75123		78505	Ebenezer (Jasper County)	75951
For specific De Soto Zip Codes		For specific Downtown Zip Codes		Ebony	76864
call (214) 223-6500, or your local		call (210) 686-5621, or your local		Echo (Coleman County)	76834
postmaster.		postmaster.		Echo (Orange County)	77630
Dessau	78753	Downtown (Part of San		Echo Hills	75763
Detmold	76577	Antonio)	78205	Eckert	78675
Detroit	75436		78291-99	Ecleto	78111
Devers	77538	For specific Downtown Zip Codes		Ector	75439
Devils Pocket	77612	call (512) 227-3399, or your local		Edcouch	78538
Devine	78016	postmaster.		Eddy (Part of Bruceville-	
Dew	75860	Downtown (Part of Tyler)	75710	Eddy)	76524
Dewalt	77478	Downtown (Part of Waco)	76701	Eden	76837
Dewees	78114	Doyle	76642	Edgar	77954
Deweyville	77614	Dozier	79079	Edge	77808
Dewville	78140	Drasco	79567	Edgecliff	76134
Dexter	76240	Draw	79373	Edgewater Estates	78368
D'Hanis	78850	Dreka	75973	Edgewood	75117
Dial (Fannin County)	75446	Dresden	75102	Edgeworth	76569
Dial (Hutchinson County)	79007	Dreyer	77984	Edhube	75418
Dialville	75785	Driftwood (Hays County)	78619	Edinburg	78539*
Diamondhead	77356	Driftwood (Henderson			78540†
Diana	75640	County)	75143	Edith	76945
Diboll	75941	Driners	75937	Edmonson	79032
Dicey	76086	Dripping Springs	78620	Edna	77957
Dickens	79229	Driscoll	78351	Edna Hill	76446
Dickinson	77539	Drop	76247	Edom	75756
Dido	76179	Dryden	78851	Edroy	78352
Dies	75979	Dubina	78956	Egan	76031
Dike	75437	Dublin	76446	Egypt (Leon County)	75833
Dilley	78017	Dudley	79601	Egypt (Montgomery County)	77355
Dilworth (Gonzales County)	78629	Duffau	76457	Egypt (Wharton County)	77436
Dilworth (Red River County)	75426	Dugas Addition	77611	Elam (Part of Dallas)	75217
Dime Box	77853	Dugger	78155	Elam Springs	75755
Dimmitt	79027	Dumas	79029	Elbert	76359
Dimple	75426	Dumont	79232	El Calmino	75948
Dinero	78022	Dunbar	75440	El Campo	77437
Ding Dong	76542	Duncanville	75116	El Campo Club	77465
Dinsmore	77488		75137-38	El Campo South	77437
Direct	75486	For specific Duncanville Zip Codes		El Cenizo	78043
Dirgin	75691	call (214) 298-3603, or your local		El Centro (Part of Laredo)	78040
Divide	75420	postmaster.		El Centro Mall (Part of	
Divot	78017	Duncanville	75116	Pharr)	78577
Dixie (Grayson County)	76273	Dundee	76366	Eldorado	76936
Dixie (Jasper County)	75951	Dunlap	79248	Eldorado Center	76639
Dixon	75402	Dunlay	78861	Eldridge (Part of Sugar	
Doans	76384	Dunn	79516	Land)	77478
Dobbin	77333	Dunnan (Part of Houston)	77022	Electra	76360
Dobrowolski	78026	Duplex	75447	Electric City	79007
Dodd	79347	Durango	76656	Elevation	76556
Dodd City	75438	Duster	76444	El Gato	78516
Dodge	77334	Dye Mound	76265	Elgin	78621
Dodson	79230	Dyersdale	77016	Eliasville	76438
Dogwood	75979	Eagle Lake	77434	El Indio	78860
Dogwood Acres (Part of		Eagle Mountain	76135	El Jardin (Part of	
Houston)	77022	Eagle Mountain Acres	76020	Brownsville)	78520
Dogwood City	75762	Eagle Pass	78852*		

	ZIP
El Jardin Del Mar (Part of Pasadena)	77586
Elk	76624
Elkhart	75839
El Lago	77586
Ellinger	78938
Elliott (Robertson County)	77859
Elliott (Wilbarger County)	76364
Ellis (Part of Levelland)	79338
Ellis Unit	77340
Elmaton	77440
Elmdale	79601
Elmendorf	78112
Elm Flat	75144
Elm Grove (Cherokee County)	75785
Elm Grove (Fayette County)	78959
Elm Grove (San Saba County)	76872
Elm Grove (Wharton County)	77434
Elm Mott	76640
Elmo	75118
Elmont	75495
Elm Ridge (Grayson County)	75020
Elm Ridge (Milam County)	76520
Elmtown	75801
Elmwood (Anderson County)	75801
Elmwood (Guadalupe County)	78155
Eloise	76680
El Oso	78119
El Paso (El Paso County)	79821
	79901-99

For specific El Paso Zip Codes call (915) 775-7542, or your local postmaster.

	ZIP
El Paso (Fisher County)	79543
El Pinon Estates	75929
El Ranchito	79766
El Rancho Estates	76008
El Refugio	78582
Elroy	78617
Elsa	78543
El Sauz	78582
El Toro	77957
Elwood (Fannin County)	75447
Elwood (Madison County)	75852
Ely	75439
Elysian Fields	75642
Emberson	75486
Emblem	75482
Emerald Valley	78250
Emhouse	75110
Emmett	76641
Emory	75440
Encantada	78586
Encantada-Ranchito El Calaboz	78520
Enchanted Oaks (Harris County)	77373
Enchanted Oaks (Henderson County)	75147
Enchanted River Estates	78003
Encinal	78019
Encino	78353
Energy	76452
Engle	78956
English	75426
Enloe	75441
Ennis	75119*
	75120†
Enoch	75644
Enochs	79324
Ensign	75119
Enterprise (Cherokee County)	75766
Enterprise (Van Zandt County)	75169
Eola	76937
Eolian	76424
Era	76238
Erath	76708
Erin	75951
Erwin	77830
Escobares	78582
Escobas	78361
Eskota	79561
Esmond Estates (Part of Odessa)	79762
Esperanza	79839
Esquire Estates	75147
Esseville	78008
Estacado	79343
Estacado Estates (Part of Amarillo)	79109
Estelline	79233
Estes	78382
Estes Addition	76071
Ethel	76233

	ZIP
Etoile	75944
Etter	79029
Eubank Acres	78753
Eula	79510
Eulalie	75975
Euless	76039-40

For specific Euless Zip Codes call (817) 283-6636, or your local postmaster.

	ZIP
Eulogy	76652
Eureka	75110
Eustace	75124
Evadale	77615
Evant	76525
Evergreen (Grimes County)	77861
Evergreen (San Jacinto County)	77327
Evergreen Park	77662
Everitt	77327
Everman	76140
Ewell	75644
Exchange Park (Part of Dallas)	75245
Eylau	75501
Ezzell	77964
Fabens	79838
Fairbanks (Part of Houston)	77064
Fairchilds	77469
Fairfield	75840
Fairgreen	77039
Fairland	78654
Fairlie	75428
Fairmount	75948
Fairoaks	75838
Fair Oaks Ranch	78006
Fair Park (Part of Dallas)	75210
Fair Play	75631
Fairview (Bailey County)	79371
Fairview (Bosque County)	76689
Fairview (Brazos County)	77807
Fairview (Cass County)	75563
Fairview (Collin County)	75002
Fairview (Gaines County)	79360
Fairview (Harris County)	77006
Fairview (Howard County)	79720
Fairview (Rusk County)	75784
Fairview (Wilson County)	78114
Fairview (Wise County)	76078
Fairy	76457
Faker	75686
Falcon	78564
Falcon Heights	78545
Falcon Mesa	78076
Falcon Village	78545
Falfurrias	78355
Fallon	76667
Falls City	78113
Fambrough	76424
Famuliner	79346
Fannett	77705
Fannin	77960
Fargo	76384
Farmer	76460
Farmers Branch	75234
Farmers Valley	76384
Farmersville	75442
Farmington	75058
Farnsworth	79033
Farr Addition	79756
Farrar	75838
Farrsville	75977
Farwell	79325
Fashing	78008
Fate	75132
Faught	75462
Faulkner	75416
Fawil	75928
Fayburg	75424
Fayetteville	78940
Faysville	78539
Federal Correctional Institution (Bastrop County)	78602
Federal Correctional Institution (Bowie County)	75501
Federal Correctional Institution (Dallas County)	75159
Federal Correctional Institution (Live Oak County)	78071
Federal Correctional Institution (Tarrant County)	76119
Federal Prison Camp	79720
Fedor	78947
Fellowship	75961
Fentress	78622
Ferris	75125
Fetzer	77363
Fiddlers Green	75034
Field Creek	76869
Fieldton	79326

	ZIP
Fife	76825
Files Valley	76055
Fincastle	75763
Fink	75076
Finney (Hale County)	79072
Finney (King County)	79248
First Colony	77479
Fischer	78623
Fisk	76834
Fitze	75946
Fitzhugh	78703
Five Points (El Paso County)	79903*
	79923†
Five Points (Ellis County)	75165
Flagg	79027
Flamingo Bay (Part of Seabrook)	77586
Flanagan	75691
Flat	76526
Flat Fork	75974
Flatonia	78941
Flat Prairie	77835
Flats	75472
Flatwood	75754
Fleetwood Oaks	77079
Fletcher	77656
Flint	75762
Flint Creek	76450
Flo	75831
Flomot	79234
Flora	75437
Florence	76527
Florence Hill (Part of Grand Prairie)	75052
Floresville	78114
Florey	79714
Florine (Part of San Antonio)	78209
Flour Bluff (Part of Corpus Christi)	78418
Flower Hill	78934
Flower Mound	75028
Floy	78941
Floyd	75401
Floydada	79235
Fluvanna	79517
Flynn	77855
Fodice	75851
Follett	79034
Folley	79255
Fondren (Part of Webster)	77598
Fords Corner	75972
Fordtran	77995
Forest	75925
Forestburg	76239
Forest Chapel	75411
Forest Glade	76667
Forest Grove (Collin County)	75069
Forest Grove (Henderson County)	75758
Forest Heights	77630
Forest Hill (Lamar County)	75446
Forest Hill (Potter County)	79107
Forest Hill (Tarrant County)	76119
Forest Hill (Wood County)	75783
Forest Hill Estates	76528
Forest Hills (Part of Tyler)	75702
Forest North Estates	78729
Forest Spring	77351
Forney	75126
Forreston	76041
Forsan	79733
Fort Bliss	79906
	79916

For specific Fort Bliss Zip Codes call (915) 562-4036, or your local postmaster.

	ZIP
Fort Clark Springs	78832
Fort Davis	79734
Fort Gates	76528
Fort Hancock	79839
Fort Hood	76544
Fort McKavett	76841
Fort Ringgold	78582
Fort Spunky	76031
Fort Stockton	79735

Fort Worth 76101-85
For specific Fort Worth Zip Codes call (214) 647-2996, or your local postmaster.

COLLEGES & UNIVERSITIES

Southwestern Baptist Theological Seminary	76122
Texas Christian University	76129
Texas Wesleyan University	76105

FINANCIAL INSTITUTIONS

American Bank of Haltom City	76117

* Area Zip Code   † Post Office Boxes

	ZIP
Bank of Commerce	76102
Bank One, Texas, N.A.	76102
Central Bank & Trust	76104
Comerica Bank-Texas	76107
First Interstate Bank of Texas, N.A.	76102
Overton Bank & Trust, N.A.	76109
Southwest Bank	76133
Summit National Bank	76102
Team Bank	76102
Texas Commerce Bank, National Association	76102

HOSPITALS

All Saints Episcopal Hospital of Fort Worth	76104
Harris Methodist-Fort Worth	76104
HCA Medical Plaza Hospital	76104
Saint Joseph Hospital	76104
Tarrant County Hospital District	76104

HOTELS/MOTELS

Residence Inn	76107
The Worthington	76102

MILITARY INSTALLATIONS

Carswell Air Force Base	76127
United States Army Engineer District, Fort Worth	76102
United States Property and Fiscal Office for Fort Worth	76108
Fort Worth Town Center (Part of Fort Worth)	76115
Forum 303 Mall (Part of Arlington)	76010
Foster (Fort Bend County)	77469
Foster (Terry County)	79316
Foster Hills	75951
Foster Place (Part of Houston)	77021
Foster Store	77836
Fouke	75765
Fountain View	77032
Four Corners (Brazoria County)	77422
Four Corners (Fort Bend County)	77469
Four Corners (Montgomery County)	77301
Four Way	79018
Fowlerton	78021
Fox	76086
Fox Landing	75938
Fox Run	77373
Foxwood	77362
Frame Switch	76574
Francis (Part of West Orange)	77630
Francitas	77961
Frankell	76470
Franklin	77856
Frankston	75763
Fred	77616
Fredericksburg	78624
Fredonia (Gregg County)	75662
Fredonia (Mason County)	76842
Fredonia Hill (Part of Nacogdoches)	75961
Freedom (Lubbock County)	79412
Freedom (Rains County)	75440
Freeneytown	75667
Freeport	77541
Freer	78357
Freestone	75838
Freeway Oaks Estates	77365
Freheit	78130
Frelsburg	78950
French Creek Village (Part of San Antonio)	78240
Frenstat	77836
Fresenius	77656
Fresno (Fort Bend County)	77545
Freyburg	78956
Friday	75845
Friendship (Jasper County)	75966
Friendship (Lamb County)	79371
Friendship (Leon County)	75846
Friendship (Smith County)	75647
Friendship (Upshur County)	75644
Friendship (Van Zandt County)	75140
Friendswood	77546
Friona	79035
Frisco	75034
Fritch	79036
Frog	75160
Frognot	75424
Frontier Lakes	77378

	ZIP
Fronton	78582
Frosa	76678
Frost	76641
Fruitland	76230
Fruitvale	75127
Frydek	77474
Frys Gap	75766
Fulbright	75436
Fuller Springs	75901
Fulshear	77441
Fulton	78358
Fulton Beach (Part of Fulton)	78358
Funston	79501
Furney Richardson	75860
Gail	79738
Gainesville	76240-41
For specific Gainesville Zip Codes call (817) 665-5811, or your local postmaster.	
Galena Park	77547
Galilee	77340
Gallatin	75764
Gallaway	71049
Galle	78638
Galleria (Part of Dallas)	75240
Galleria, The (Part of Houston)	77056
Galveston	77550-54
For specific Galveston Zip Codes call (409) 763-1819, or your local postmaster.	
Galvez Mall (Part of Galveston)	77551
Ganado	77962
Garceno	78582
Garciasville	78547
Garden Acres (Part of Fort Worth)	76028
Garden City (Glasscock County)	79739
Garden City (Harris County)	77018
Gardendale (Ector County)	79758
Gardendale (La Salle County)	78014
Garden Oaks (Part of Houston)	77206
Garden Ridge	78266
Garden Valley	75771
Garden Villas	77904
Garfield (DeWitt County)	78164
Garfield (Travis County)	78653
Garfield (Travis County)	78617
Garland (Bowie County)	75559
Garland (Dallas County)	75040-49
For specific Garland Zip Codes call (214) 272-5541, or your local postmaster.	
Garland (Red River County)	75550
Garner	76086
Garrett	75119
Garretts Bluff	75411
Garrison	75946
Garth	77520
Garvin	76023
Garwood	77442
Gary	75643
Gasoline	79255
Gastonia	75114
Gatesville	76528
Gatesville Unit	76528
Gateway Shopping City (Part of Beaumont)	77701
Gatewood	77039
Gause	77857
Gay Hill (Fayette County)	78945
Gay Hill (Washington County)	77833
Geneva	75947
Geneva Estates	78736
Genoa (Part of Houston)	77034
George	77871
Georges Creek	76031
Georgetown	78626-28
For specific Georgetown Zip Codes call (512) 863-2325, or your local postmaster.	
George West	78022
George W. Singer (Part of Lubbock)	79424
Georgia	75486
Gerald	76640
Geronimo	78115
Geronimo Forest	78254
Geronimo Village	78253
Gethsemane	75657
Gholson	76705
Gibtown	76486
Giddings	78942
Gilchrist	77617
Gill	75670
Gillett	78116

	ZIP
Gilliland	79260
Gilmer	75644
Gilpin	79370
Ginger	75410
Girard	79518
Girvin	79740
Givens	75462
Gladewater (Gregg County)	75647
Gladewater (Titus County)	75455
Glass	76690
Glaze City	77984
Glazier	79014
Glen Cove (Coleman County)	76834
Glen Cove (Galveston County)	77565
Glencrest (Part of Fort Worth)	76119
Glendale	75862
Glenfawn	75760
Glen Flora	77443
Glenn Heights	75115
Glen Rose	76043
Glenwood (Potter County)	79103
Glenwood (Upshur County)	75644
Glidden	78943
Globe	75486
Glory	75462
Gober	75443
Godley	76044
Gold	78624
Golden	75444
Golden Beach	78643
Golden Oaks	78628
Golden Triangle Mall (Part of Denton)	76206
Goldfinch	78005
Goldsboro	79519
Goldsmith	79741
Goldthwaite	76844
Goliad	77963
Golinda	76655
Gomez	79316
Gonzales	78629
Goober Hill	75973
Goodfellow Air Force Base	76908
Good Hope	77964
Goodland	79371
Goodlett	79252
Goodlow	75144
Goodlow Park	75144
Goodnight (Armstrong County)	79226
Goodnight (Navarro County)	75144
Goodrich	77335
Good Springs	75667
Goodville	76632
Gordon (Lynn County)	79356
Gordon (Palo Pinto County)	76453
Gordonville	76245
Goree	76363
Goree Unit	77340
Gorman	76454
Goshen	77340
Gough	75448
Gould	75766
Gouldbusk	76845
Graceton	75644
Graford	76449
Graham (Garza County)	79356
Graham (Jasper County)	75951
Graham (Young County)	76450
Granada Estates	78737
Granbury	76048-49
For specific Granbury Zip Codes call (817) 573-5515, or your local postmaster.	
Grand Bluff	75631
Grandfalls	79742
Grand Prairie	75050-54
For specific Grand Prairie Zip Codes call (214) 264-5751, or your local postmaster.	
Grand Saline	75140
Grandview (Dawson County)	79351
Grand View (El Paso County)	79930
Grandview (Gray County)	79039
Grandview (Johnson County)	76050
Grange Hall	75670
Granger	76530
Grangerland	77302
Granite Shoals	78654
Granjeno	78572
Granview Beach	78611
Granville W. Elder (Part of Houston)	77013
Grape Creek	76901
Grapeland	75844
Grapetown	78624

Name	ZIP
Grapevine	76051
	76092
	76099
For specific Grapevine Zip Codes call (817) 488-9012, or your local postmaster.	
Grassland	79356
Graves (Part of Midland)	79708
Gray	75657
Grayback	76360
Grayburg	77659
Grays Chapel	75801
Grays Prairie	75158
Graytown	78114
Great Northwest	78250
Great Oaks	78681
Great Southwest (Part of Arlington)	76005
Green	78119
Green Acres	77058
Green Hill	75455
Green Lake	77979
Green Pastures	78640
Greenridge (Part of Houston)	77022
Greens Bayou (Part of Houston)	77015
Greens Camp	79521
Greens Creek	76446
Greenspoint Mall (Part of Houston)	77018
Green Valley	76227
Greenview	75420
Greenview Hills (Part of Irving)	75062
Greenview Manor	77032
Greenville	75401-04
For specific Greenville Zip Codes call (903) 455-5363, or your local postmaster.	
Greenville Avenue (Part of Dallas)	75206
Greenvine	77835
Greenway	78223
Greenway Plaza (Part of Houston)	77046
Greenwood (Hopkins County)	75478
Greenwood (Midland County)	79701
Greenwood (Parker County)	76086
Greenwood (Wise County)	76246
Greenwood Acres (Llano County)	78609
Greenwood Acres (Orange County)	77626
Greenwood Forest	78028
Greenwood Village	77093
Greggton (Part of Longview)	75604
Gregory	78359
Gresham	75703
Grey Forest	78023
Gribble (Part of Farmers Branch)	75234
Grice	75644
Griffin	75789
Griffing (Part of Port Arthur)	77640
Griffing Park (Part of Port Arthur)	77640
Griffith (Cochran County)	79346
Griffith (Ellis County)	76084
Grigsby	75935
Grit (Mason County)	76856
Grit (Rains County)	75410
Groceville	77301
Groesbeck	76642
Groom	79039
Grosvenor	76801
Groves	77619
Groveton	75845
Grow	79248
Gruenau	78164
Gruene	78130
Grulla	78548
Gruver	79040
Guadalupe	77905
Guadalupe Heights	78028
Guajillo	78332
Guerra	78360
Gulf Camp	79756
Gulfgate Shopping Center (Part of Houston)	77087
Gulfway (Part of Corpus Christi)	78412
Gum Springs (Cass County)	75560
Gum Springs (Harrison County)	75601
Gun Barrel City	75147
Gunsight	76437
Gunter (Grayson County)	75058
Gunter (Wood County)	75410
Gussettville	78022
Gustine	76455
Guthrie	79236
Guy	77444
Guys Store	75833
Hacienda Heights (Part of El Paso)	79915
Hackberry (Bexar County)	78210
Hackberry (Cottle County)	79248
Hackberry (Denton County)	75068
Hackberry (Garza County)	79356
Hackberry (Lavaca County)	78956
Hagansport	75487
Hagerman	75090
Hagerville	75847
Hail	75492
Hainesville	75773
Halbert	75973
Hale Center	79041
Halesboro	75417
Halfway	79072
Hall (Marion County)	75657
Hall (San Saba County)	76871
Hallettsville	77964
Halloway Heights	77047
Halls Bluff	75835
Hallsburg	76705
Halls Store	71007
Hallsville	75650
Halsell	76365
Haltom City	76117
Hamby	79601
Hamilton	76531
Hamlin	79520
Hamon	78629
Hampton	75936
Hamshire	77622
Hancock Oak Hills	78130
Hancock Shopping Center (Part of Austin)	78751
Handley (Part of Fort Worth)	76124
Hankamer	77560
Hannibal	76401
Hanover	76520
Hansford	79081
Happy	79042
Happy Hill	76009
Happy Union	79072
Happy Valley	79566
Harbin	76446
Harbor Grove (Part of Hickory Creek)	75065
Harborlight	75948
Hardin	77561
Hardin-Simmons (Part of Abilene)	79698
Hardy	76265
Hare	76574
Hargill	78549
Harker Heights	76543
Harkeyville	76877
Harlandale (Part of San Antonio)	78214
Harlem	77469
Harleton	75651
Harlingen	78550-53
For specific Harlingen Zip Codes call (512) 423-1464, or your local postmaster.	
Harmon	75446
Harmony (Anderson County)	75801
Harmony (Parker County)	76086
Harmony (Rusk County)	75684
Harmony Grove	77340
Harmony Hill	75691
Harper	78631
Harriet	76901
Harrisburg (Harris County)	77012
Harrisburg (Jasper County)	75951
Harrison	76682
Harrold	76364
Hart	79043
Hartburg	77630
Hart Camp	79339
Hartley	79044
Harts Bluff	75455
Hart Spur (Part of Hurst)	76053
Hartzo	75657
Harvard	75686
Harvest Acres (Montgomery County)	77372
Harvest Acres (Tom Green County)	76905
Harvest Heights	77845
Harvey	
Harwood	78632
Haskell	79521
Haslam	75954
Haslet	76052
Hasse	76456
Hatchel	79567
Hatchetville	75437
Havana	78572
Hawkins	75765
Hawkinsville	77414
Hawley	79525
Hawthorne	77358
Hayden	75169
Haynesville	76360
Hays	78666
Hazy Hollow	77355
Headlea Estates (Part of Odessa)	79762
Headsville	76653
Heald	79057
Hearne	77859
Heath	75087
Hebbronville	78361
Hebco (Part of San Antonio)	78218
Hebron	75056
Heckville	79329
Hedley	79237
Hedwig Village	77024
Heidelberg	78570
Heidenheimer	76533
Heights (Galveston County)	77590
Heights (Harris County)	77008
Helena	78118
Helmic	75845
Helotes	78023
Hemphill	75948
Hempstead	77445
Henderson	75652*
	75653†
Henderson Chapel	76866
Henderson Heights	79763
Henkhaus	77984
Henly	78620
Henning	75946
Henrietta	76365
Henrys Chapel	75789
Hereford	79045
Heritage Northwest	78245
Heritage Oaks	77365
Hermleigh	79526
Herring (Part of San Angelo)	76901
Herty (Part of Lufkin)	75901
Hewitt	76643
Hext	76848
Hickey	75667
Hickory Creek (Denton County)	75065
Hickory Creek (Hunt County)	75423
Hickory Hill	75686
Hickory Hills	77356
Hickory Hollow	75929
Hickston	78959
Hico	76457
Hidalgo	78557
Hidden Echo	77336
Hidden Forest (Part of San Antonio)	78232
Hidden Hill	75065
Hidden Hills Harbor	75147
Hidden Valley (Part of Houston)	77088
Hide-A-Way Lake	75771
Higginbotham	79360
Higgins	79046
Highbank	76680
High Hill	78956
High Island	77623
Highland (Erath County)	76446
Highland (Johnson County)	76031
Highland Acres (Grayson County)	75076
Highland Acres (Harris County)	77018
Highland Acres (Hunt County)	75453
Highland Addition (Harris County)	77018
Highland Addition (Parker County)	76082
Highland Creek Lakes	78736
Highland Estates (Part of Victoria)	77904
Highland Haven	78654
Highland Hills (Bexar County)	78223
Highland Hills (Dallas County)	75241
Highland Mall (Part of Austin)	78757
Highland Park	75205
Highland Range Estates	76901
Highlands	77562
Highland Village	75067
Highland Waters	78003
Highpoint	77093
Highsaw	75763
Hi Ho	77630

---

* Area Zip Code   † Post Office Boxes

	ZIP		ZIP		ZIP
Inwood Place	77016	Jonesville	75659	Kingsbury	78638
Inwood Village (Part of		Joplin	76458	Kings Cove	78611
Dallas)	75206	Joppa	78605	Kingsland	78639
Iola	77861	Jordan (Part of Amarillo)	79159	Kingsland Estates	78639
Iowa Colony	77583	Josephine	75164	Kingsley (Part of Garland)	75041
Iowa Park	76367	Joshua	76058	Kings Mill	79065
Ira	79527	Josserand	75845	Kings Point	78073
Iraan	79744	Jot 'Em Down	75469	Kingston	75401
Irby	79521	Jourdanton	78026	Kings Village	78727
Iredell	76649	Joy (Clay County)	76365	Kingsville	78363-64
Ireland	76538	Joy (Smith County)	75647	For specific Kingsville Zip Codes	
Irene	76650	Jozye	77864	call (512) 592-2801, or your local	
Ironton	75766	Juanita Craft (Part of Dallas)	75315	postmaster.	
Irving	75014-17	Jubilee Springs	76502	Kingsville Naval Station	78363
	75038-39	Jud	79544	Kingswood	75104
	75060-63	Judson	75660	Kingtown	75961
For specific Irving Zip Codes call		Juliff	77583	Kingwood	77339
(214) 986-6557, or your local		Julius Melcher (Part of		Kinkler	77964
postmaster.		Houston)	77027	Kiomatia	75436
Irving Mall (Part of Irving)	75062	Jumbo	75669	Kirby	78219
Irvington (Part of Houston)	77022	Junction	76849	Kirbyville	75956
Island (Galveston County)	77550	Juno	76943	Kirkland	79201
Island (Madison County)	75852	Jupiter Pharmacy (Part of		Kirkpatrick Addition	75704
Italy	76651	Richardson)	75080	Kirtley	78957
Itasca	76055	Justiceburg	79330	Kirvin	75848
Ivan	76424	Justin	76247	Kittrell	75862
Ivanhoe	75447	Kadane Corner	76360	Kleberg (Part of Dallas)	75253
Iveys Crossing	79853	Kalgary	79370		75336
Ivy	76854	Kamay	76369	For specific Kleberg Zip Codes	
Izoro	76522	Kamey	77979	call (214) 286-5460, or your local	
Jacinto City	77029	Kanawha	75436	postmaster.	
Jacksboro	76458	Karen	77355	Klein	77379
Jackson (Marion County)	75657	Karnack	75661	Klondike (Dawson County)	79331
Jackson (Shelby County)	75954	Karnes City	78118	Klondike (Delta County)	75448
Jackson (Van Zandt		Katemcy	76825	Klump	77833
County)	75103	Katy	77449-50	Knapp	79527
Jacksonville	75766		77491-94	Knickerbocker	76939
Jacobia	75401	For specific Katy Zip Codes call		Knippa	78870
Jamaica Beach	77554	(713) 578-0942, or your local		Knob Hill	75034
James	75935	postmaster.		Knollwood	75090
James Moody (Part of		Kaufman	75142	Knott	79748
Victoria)	77904	Kayare (Part of Harlingen)	78550	Knox City	79529
Jamestown (Newton		Keechi	75831	Koerth	77964
County)	75966	Keenan	77356	Kohrville	77040
Jamestown (Smith County)	75140	Keene	76059	Kokomo	76454
Jaques Spur (Part of		Keeter	76023	Komensky	77975
Denison)	75020	Keith	77861	Kona Kai	77650
Jardin	75428	Keller	76244	Kopernik Shores	78520
Jarrell	76537		76248	Kopperl	76652
Jarvis Christian College	75765	For specific Keller Zip Codes call		Kosciusko	78160
Jasper	75951	(817) 431-1311, or your local		Kosse	76653
Jasper Heights (Part of		postmaster.		Kountze	77625
Marshall)	75670	Kellerville	79057	Kovar	78941
Jayton	79528	Kelly	75409	Kress	79052
Jean	76374	Kellyville	75657	Kreutzberg	78006
Jeddo	78953	Kelsey	75644	Krugerville	76227
Jefferson	75657	Kelton	79096	Krum	76249
Jefferson City Shopping		Keltys (Part of Lufkin)	75903	Kubala Store	78164
Center (Part of Port		Kemah	77565	Kurten	77862
Arthur)	77640	Kemp	75143	Kuykendahl Village (Part of	
Jefferson Heights (Part of		Kempner	76539	Houston)	77068
San Angelo)	76901	Kendalia	78027	Kyle	78640
Jenkins	75638	Kendleton	77451	Kyote	78005
Jennings	75462	Kenedy	78119	Labatt	78114
Jensen Drive (Part of		Kenefick	77535	La Blanca	78558
Houston)	77026	Kennard	75847	La Casita	78582
Jensens Point	77465	Kennedale	76060	La Casita-Garciasville	78547
Jericho	79226	Kenney	77452	Laceola	77864
Jermyn	76459	Kensing	75450	Lackland Air Force Base	78236
Jerrys Quarters	77833	Kent	79855	Lackland Heights	78227
Jersey Village	77040	Kentuckytown	75491	Lackland Terrace (Part of	
Jerusalem	77422	Kenwood Place	77339	San Antonio)	78227
Jester Unit	77469	Kerens	75144	La Coste	78039
Jewett	75846	Kermit	79745	La Cuchilla (Part of Mission)	78572
J. Frank Dobie (Part of San		Kerrick	79051	Lacy	75845
Antonio)	78220	Kerrville	78028*	Lacy-Lakeview	76705
Jiba	75142		78029†	Ladonia	75449
Joaquin	75954	Kessler Park (Part of Dallas)	75208	LaFayette	75686
Joe Pool (Part of Dallas)	75224	Kevin	77327	La Feria	78559
John Foster (Part of		Key	79331	Lagarto	78022
Pasadena)	77502	Key Ranch Estates	75163	La Gloria	78591
Johnson	79316	Keystone Park (Part of		Lago	78586
Johnson City	78636	Dallas)	75240	Lago Vista	78645
Johnsons Station (Part of		Kickapoo	75763	La Grange	78945
Arlington)	76015	Kildare	75562	Laguna Heights	78578
Johnstown	75169	Kildare Junction	75555	Laguna Park	76634
Johnsville	76401	Kilgore	75662*	Laguna Tres Estates	76049
Johntown	75417		75663†	Laguna Vista	78578
Joiner	78945	Killeen	76540-47	Laguna Vista Estates	75751
Joinerville	75658	For specific Killeen Zip Codes call		La Hacienda Estates	78759
Joliet	78648	(817) 634-0281, or your local		La Homa	78572
Jolly	76303	postmaster.		Laird Hill	75666
Jollyville	78729	Killeen Mall (Part of Killeen)	76543	Lajitas	79852
Jonah	78626	Kilowatt (Part of Orange)	77630	La Joya	78560
Jones	75140	Kimball	76652	La Junta	76020
Jonesboro	76538	Kimbro	78653	Lake Air Center (Part of	
Jones Creek (Brazoria		Kinard Estates	77630	Waco)	76710
County)	77541	King (Coryell County)	76528	Lake Barbara (Part of Clute)	77531
Jones Creek (Wharton		King (Red River County)	75550	Lake Bonanza	77356
County)	77437	King City (Part of		Lake Bridgeport	76426
Jones Prairie	76520	Cleveland)	77327	Lake Brownwood	76801
Jonestown	78645	King Ranch	78363	Lake Chateau Woods	77302

	ZIP
Lake Cherokee	75652
Lake City	78387
Lake Conroe Forrest	77301
Lake Conroe West	77301
Lake Corsicana (Part of Corsicana)	75110
Lake Creek	75450
Lake Creek Estates	77355
Lake Dallas	75065
Lake Gardens	76901
Lake Halbert (Part of Corsicana)	75110
Lakehills	78063
Lake Jackson	77566
Lake Jackson Farms	77566
Lake Kiowa	76240
Lakeland	77302
Lakeland Heights (Part of Grand Prairie)	75050
Lakeland Park	78759
Lake Livingston	77376
Lake Meredith Estates	79036
Lake Pauline	79252
Lake Placid	78155
Lakeport	75603
Lake Ransom Canyon Village	79366
Lake Rolling Wood	77301
Lake Shadows	77532
Lake Shore	76801
Lakeshore Estates	75630
Lakeshore Estates West	75630
Lake Shore Gardens	78368
Lakeside (Galveston County)	77565
Lakeside (San Patricio County)	78368
Lakeside (Tarrant County)	76108
Lakeside Acres	78006
Lakeside Beach	78669
Lakeside City	76308
Lakeside Heights	78639
Lakeside Park	77530
Lakeside Village	76671
Lake Splendora	77372
Lake Tanglewood	79118
Lake Tejas	77371
Lake Thomas	79527
Laketon	79065
Lake Victor	76550
Lakeview (Cherokee County)	75766
Lakeview (Floyd County)	79235
Lakeview (Hall County)	79239
Lakeview (Jefferson County)	77640
Lakeview (Lynn County)	79345
Lakeview (McLennan County)	76705
Lakeview (Orange County)	77662
Lakeview (Swisher County)	79088
Lakeview (Tarrant County)	76135
Lakeview (Tom Green County)	76903
Lakeview Estates (Johnson County)	76031
Lakeview Estates (Orange County)	77662
Lakeview Estates (Van Zandt County)	75169
Lakeview Hills	78645
Lake View Park	78130
Lakeway	78734
Lake Whitney Estates	76692
Lake Wildwood	77302
Lakewood (Dallas County)	75214
Lakewood (Harris County)	77520
Lakewood (Orange County)	77662
Lakewood (San Augustine County)	75929
Lakewood Estates	77304
Lakewood Forest	78639
Lakewood Harbor	76634
Lakewood Heights (Part of Houston)	77336
Lakewood Hills (Comal County)	78130
Lakewood Hills (Hood County)	76049
Lakewood Village	76205
Lake Worth	76135
Lamar	78382
Lamar Park (Part of Corpus Christi)	78411
La Marque	77568
Lamar University (Part of Beaumont)	77710
Lamasco	75488
Lamesa	79331
Lamkin	76455
Lampasas	76550
Lamplight Village	78758

	ZIP
Lanark	75572
Lancaster (Dallas County)	75134
	75146
For specific Lancaster Zip Codes call (214) 227-2551, or your local postmaster.	
Lancaster (El Paso County)	79907
Landa Park Highlands (Part of New Braunfels)	78130
Lane	75423
Lane City	77453
Lanely	75831
Laneport	76574
Lane Prairie	76058
Laneville	75667
Langtry	78871
Lanham	76538
Lanier	75563
Lannius	75438
Lantana	78586
La Paloma	78586
La Plaza (Part of McAllen)	78503
La Porte	77571*
	77572†
La Pryor	78872
La Puerta	78582
Laredo	78040-44
For specific Laredo Zip Codes call (512) 723-2043, or your local postmaster.	
La Reforma	78536
Lariat	79325
Larue	75770
La Salle (Calhoun County)	77979
La Salle (Jackson County)	77969
Lasara	78561
Las Colinas (Part of Irving)	75014
	75016
For specific Las Colinas Zip Codes call (214) 556-1229, or your local postmaster.	
Las Milpas	78577
Las Rusias	78586
Lassater	75630
Las Yescas	78586
Latch	75644
Latexo	75849
La Tina	78586
Latium	77835
Latonia	77422
La Tuna	79821
Laughlin Air Force Base	78843
Laureles	78586
Laurel Heights (Part of San Antonio)	78212
Lavada	78487
La Vernia	78121
La Villa	78562
Lavon	75166
Lavon Beach Estates	75442
La Ward	77970
Lawn	79530
Lawrence	75160
Lawrence Park (Part of Amarillo)	79109
Lawrence Springs	75140
Lawson	75149
Lazare	79252
Lazbuddie	79053
Leaday	76888
League City	77573*
	77574†
Leagueville	75778
Leakey	78873
Leander	78641
	78646
For specific Leander Zip Codes call (512) 259-1111, or your local postmaster.	
Leary	75501
Leasure Acres	76528
Lebanon	75034
Ledbetter	78946
Ledbetter Hills (Part of Dallas)	75211
Leedale	76569
Leesburg	75451
Leesville	78122
Lefors	79054
Leggett	77350
Legion (Part of Kerrville)	78028
Lehman	79346
Leigh	75661
Lela	79079
Lelia Lake	79240
Leming	78050
Lena	78963
Lenorah	79749
Lenz	78118
Leo (Cooke County)	76234
Leo (Lee County)	78947
Leona	75850

	ZIP
Leonard	75452
Leon Junction	76552
Leon Springs	78229
Leon Valley	78238
	78240
	78250-51
	78268
For specific Leon Valley Zip Codes call (512) 680-5074, or your local postmaster.	
Leroy	76654
Lesley	79239
Letney Park	75951
Le Tourneau (Part of Longview)	75601
Levelland	79336-38
For specific Levelland Zip Codes call (806) 894-3250, or your local postmaster.	
Leveretts Chapel	75684
Levi	76655
Levita	76528
Lewis Addition	77465
Lewisville	75028-29
	75056-57
	75067
For specific Lewisville Zip Codes call (214) 221-2755, or your local postmaster.	
Lexington	78947
Lexington Woods	77373
Liberty (Hamilton County)	76531
Liberty (Liberty County)	77575
Liberty (Lubbock County)	79401
Liberty (Newton County)	75966
Liberty (Rusk County)	75652
Liberty City	75647
Liberty Grove	75098
Liberty Hill (Houston County)	75844
Liberty Hill (Milam County)	76567
Liberty Hill (Titus County)	75455
Liberty Hill (Williamson County)	78642
Liggett (Part of Irving)	75060
Lilac	76577
Lilbert	75760
Lillian	76061
Lily Grove	75961
Lily Island	75934
Lincoln	78948
Lincoln Park	76227
Lindale	75771
Linden	75563
Lindenau	77954
Lindenwood	77630
Lindsay	76250
Lindsay Addition	79772
Lingleville	76461
Link Five (Part of La Porte)	77571
Linkwood Addition	76008
Linn	78563
Linn Flat	75961
Linwood	75925
Lipan	76462
Lipscomb	79056
Lisbon (Part of Dallas)	75216
Lissie	77454
Littig	78621
Little Boy	77662
Little Elm	75068
Littlefield	79339
Little Flock	77879
Little Hope	75494
Little Mexico	79735
Little New York	78629
Little Ridge	75121
Little River	76554
Little Rock	77625
Lively	75143
Live Oak (Bexar County)	78233
Liveoak (Palo Pinto County)	76472
Live Oak Ranchettes	78641
Liverpool	77577
Livingston	77351
Llano	78643
Lobo	79855
Locker	76871
Lockett	76384
Lockettville	79358
Lockhart	78644
Lockhill (Part of San Antonio)	78230*
	78278†
Lockney	79241
Locust	75076
Locust Grove	79014
Lodi	75564
Loeb	77656
Loebau	78948
Logan (Marion County)	75657
Logan (Panola County)	71049

	ZIP		ZIP		ZIP
Logan Heights (Part of El Paso)	79904	Luella	75090	Mallard	76251
Log Cabin	75148	Lufkin	75901-15	Mall Del Norte (Part of Laredo)	78040
Log Cabin Estates	75148	For specific Lufkin Zip Codes call (409) 634-7749, or your local postmaster.		Mall of Abilene (Part of Abilene)	79606
Lohn	76852			Malone	76660
Loire	78064	Luling	78648	Malta	75570
Lois	76272	Lull	78539	Mambrino	76048
Lolaville	75034	Lumberton	77711	Manchaca	78652
Lolita	77971	Lums Chapel	79339	Manchester	75412
Lollipop	75763	Lund	78621	Manda	78653
Loma	77876	Luther	79720	Manheim	78659
Loma Alta (McMullen County)	78072	Lutie	79079	Mankin	75163
		Lydia	75554	Mankins	76366
Loma Alta (Val Verde County)	78840	Lyford	78569	Manor	78653
		Lynchburg	77520	Manor East Shopping Center (Part of Bryan)	77801
Loma Terrace (Part of El Paso)	79907	Lyncrest	77086		
		Lyndon B. Johnson Space Center	77058	Mansfield	76063
Loma Vista	78829			Manvel	77578
Lomax (Harris County)	77571	Lynn Grove	77868	Maple (Bailey County)	79344
Lomax (Howard County)	79720	Lyons	77863	Maple (Red River County)	75417
Lometa	76853	Lytle	78052	Maple Crest Acres (Part of Vidor)	77662
London	76854	Lytton Springs	78616		
Lone Camp	76484	Mabank	75147	Maple Springs	75455
Lone Cedar	76626	Mabelle	76380	Mapleton	75835
Lone Elm	75165	Mabry	75426	Marathon	79842
Lone Grove	78643	McAdoo	79243	Marble Falls	78654
Lone Mountain	75644	McAllen	78501-05	March Trailer Court	75169
Lone Oak (Bexar County)	78101	For specific McAllen Zip Codes call (512) 686-1771, or your local postmaster.		Marfa	79843
Lone Oak (Colorado County)	78940			Margaret	79227
Lone Oak (Erath County)	76446	McBeth	77515	Marie	76933
Lone Oak (Hunt County)	75453	McCamey	79752	Marietta	75566
Lone Pine	75801	McCaulley	79534	Marilee	75058
Lone Star (Floyd County)	79241	McClanahan	76661	Marion	78124
Lone Star (Kaufman County)	75142	McCook	78539	Markham	77456
		McCoy (Atascosa County)	78053	Markley	76460
Lone Star (Morris County)	75668	McCoy (Floyd County)	79235	Marlin	76661
Lone Star (Titus County)	75558	McCoy (Panola County)	75643	Marquez	77865
Long Branch	75669	McCreless Mall (Part of San Antonio)	78223	Marshall	75670*
Longfellow	79848				75671†
Longford Place	77630	McDade	78650	Marshall Creek	76262
Long Hollow	77865	McDade Estates	77304	Marshall Ford	78732
Long Lake (Anderson County)	75801	Macdona	78054	Marshall Meadows (Part of San Antonio)	78240
		Macedonia (Austin County)	77474		
Long Lake (Montgomery County)	77355	Macedonia (Bowie County)	75501	Marshall Springs	75455
		Macedonia (Brazoria County)	77422	Mart	76664
Long Mott	77972			Martindale	78655
Long Point (Harris County)	77055	Macedonia (Liberty County)	77327	Martinez	78219
Long Point (Harrison County)	75661	McElroy	75968	Martin Luther King (Part of Houston)	77033
		McFaddin	77973		
Long Point (Washington County)	77835	McGalin	77612	Martins Mills	75754
		McGee Landing	75948	Martin Springs	75482
Longview	75601-15	McGregor	76657	Martinsville	75958
For specific Longview Zip Codes call (903) 753-7644, or your local postmaster.		McKenzie	75630	Marvin	75462
		McKibben	79081	Mary Hardin-Baylor (Part of Belton)	76513
Longview Heights	75601	McKinney	75069-70		
Longview Mall (Part of Longview)	75601	For specific McKinney Zip Codes call (214) 542-5031, or your local postmaster.		Maryneal	79535
				Marysville	76252
Longworth	79543	McKnight	75652	Mason	76856
Lonoke Place	77093	McLean	79057	Mason Lake Estates	77327
Looneyville	75760	McLendon (Part of McLendon-Chisholm)	75087	Massey Lake	75861
Loop	79342			Masterson	79058
Lopeno	78564	McLendon-Chisholm	75087	Matador	79244
Lopezville	78589	McLeod	75565	Matagorda	77457
Loraine	79532	McMahan	78616	Mathews	77434
Lorena	76655	McMillin	76877	Mathis	78368
Lorenzo	79343	McMurray (Part of Abilene)	79697	Matinburg	75686
Los Angeles	78014	McNair	77520	Maud	75567
Los Barreras	78582	McNair Village	76544	Mauriceville	77626
Los Campos	78840	McNary	79839	Maverick	76865
Los Ebanos	78565	McNeil (Caldwell County)	78648	Maxdale	76542
Los Fresnos	78566	McNeil (Travis County)	78651	Maxey	75421
Los Indios	78567	Macon	75457	Maxwell	78656
Los Jardines (Part of San Antonio)	78237	McQueeney	78123	May	76857
		Mc Rea Lake	77302	Maydelle	75772
Losoya	78221	Macune	75972	Mayfair (Part of Houston)	77022
Los Ricos Pobres	78013	Macy	77882	Mayfield (Hale County)	79041
Los Saenz (Part of Roma)	78584	Madero	78572	Mayfield (Hill County)	76055
Lost Creek	78746	Madisonville	77864	Mayflower (Newton County)	75977
Lost Lakes	77357	Madras	75426	Mayflower (Rusk County)	75691
Los Velas	78582	Magasco	75968	Mayhill	76205
Los Ybanez	79331	Magic (Part of San Antonio)	78229	Maynard	77358
Lott	76656		78280	Maypearl	76064
Louise	77455	For specific Magic Zip Codes call (512) 616-0777, or your local postmaster.		Maysfield	76555
Love Chapel	75656			Meador Grove	76557
Lovelace	76645			Meadow	79345
Lovelady	75851	Magnet	77488	Meadowcreek (Part of San Angelo)	76904
Lovell Lake	77706	Magnolia	77355		
Loving	76460	Magnolia Beach	77979	Meadowlakes	78611
Lowake	76855	Magnolia Bend	77302	Meadowood Acres	78252
Lowry Crossing	75069	Magnolia Gardens	77044	Meadows	77477
Loyola Beach	78379	Magnolia Hills	77355	Mecca	77871
Lozano	78568	Magnolia Springs	75957	Medicine Mound	79252
Lubbock	79401-99	Magpetco (Part of Port Neches)	77651	Medill	75460
For specific Lubbock Zip Codes call (806) 763-6408, or your local postmaster.				Medina	78055
		Mahl	75961	Medio (Part of Houston)	77022
		Mahomet	78605	Meeker	77706
Lucas	75002	Mahoney	75482	Meek Estates	75163
Luckenbach	78624	Main Place (Part of Dallas)	75202	Meeks	76519
Lucky Ridge	76023	Majors	75457	Megargel	76370
Lueders	79533	Malakoff	75148	Megaron (Part of Lubbock)	79423
				Melear (Part of Arlington)	76015

* Area Zip Code   † Post Office Boxes

	ZIP
Melissa	75454
Melody Hills (Part of Fort Worth)	76111
Melrose (Gregg County)	75662
Melrose (Nacogdoches County)	75961
Melrose Heights	77018
Melvin	76858
Melwood Place	77016
Memorial City Shopping Center (Part of Houston)	77024
Memorial Park (Part of Houston)	77024
Memphis	79245
Menard	76859
Mendoza	78644
Menlow	76621
Mentone	79754
Mentz	78935
Mercedes	78570
Mercer's Gap	76442
Merchandise Mart (Part of Dallas)	75201
Mercury	76872
Mereta	76940
Meridian	76665
Merit	75458
Merkel	79536
Merle	77879
Mertens	76666
Mertzon	76941
Mesa Verde (Part of Amarillo)	79107
Meskill (Part of Texas City)	77590
Mesquite (Borden County)	79351
Mesquite (Dallas County)	75149-50
	75180-82
	75187
For specific Mesquite Zip Codes call (214) 288-4476, or your local postmaster.	
Metcalf Gap	76475
Meusebach Creek	78624
Mexia	76667
Mexico	75474
Meyerland Plaza Mall (Part of Houston)	77096
Meyersville	77974
Miami	79059
Michael Unit	75861
Mickey	79241
Mico	78056
Midcity	75473
Middleton	75833
Middletowne (Part of Seguin)	78155
Middle Water	79022
Midfield	77458
Midkiff	79755
Mid Lake Village	75948
Midland	79701-12
For specific Midland Zip Codes call (915) 560-5105, or your local postmaster.	
Midland Park Mall (Part of Midland)	79705
Midline	77327
Midlothian	76065
Midway (Dawson County)	79331
Midway (Fannin County)	75418
Midway (Hill County)	76645
Midway (Jim Wells County)	78372
Midway (Lavaca County)	77984
Midway (Lubbock County)	79364
Midway (Madison County)	75852
Midway (Montgomery County)	77327
Midway (Scurry County)	79526
Midway (Smith County)	75792
Midway (Titus County)	75455
Midway (Upshur County)	75644
Midway (Van Zandt County)	75754
Midyett	75639
Miguel	78005
Mila Doce	78543
Milam	75959
Milano	76556
Milburn	76872
Mildred	75110
Mile High	79851
Miles	76861
Milford	76670
Mill Creek	77833
Mill Creek Forest	77355
Miller Grove (Camp County)	75686
Miller Grove (Hopkins County)	75433
Miller's Cove	75455
Millersview	76862
Millett	78014
Millheim	77474
Millican	77866

	ZIP
Millsap	76066
Millsville	78362
Milton	75435
Minden	75680
Mineola	75773
Mineral	78125
Mineral Wells	76067*
	76068†
Minerva	76567
Mings Chapel	75644
Mingus	76463
Minimaz (Part of Alvin)	77511
Minter	75468
Mirando City	78369
Mission	78572-73
For specific Mission Zip Codes call (210) 585-1481, or your local postmaster.	
Mission Bend	77083
Mission Valley	77905
Missouri City	77459
Mitchell Avenue (Part of Waco)	76708
Mixon	75789
Mobeetie	79061
Mobile Meadows Park	77630
Mockingbird (Part of Austin)	78745
Moffat	76502
Moffett	75901
Monahans	79756
Monaville	77445
Monkstown	75488
Monroe	75662
Monroe City	77514
Monroe Street (Part of Wichita Falls)	76309
Mont	77964
Montague	76251
Montague Ranch Estates	78003
Montalba	75853
Mont Belvieu	77580
Monte Alto	78538
Montell	78801
Monte Oaks	77357
Monteola	78119
Montgomery	77356
Montgomery Gardens	75708
Monthalia	78614
Monticello	75455
Montopolis (Part of Austin)	78742
Moody	76557
Moonshine Hill	77338
Moore (Frio County)	78057
Moore (Jasper County)	75951
Moore's Chapel	75418
Moores Crossing	78617
Moore Station	75770
Mooreville	76632
Mooring	77801
Morales	77957
Moran	76464
Moravia	78956
Morgan	76671
Morgan Creek	78611
Morgan Mill	76465
Morgan's Point	77571
Morgan's Point Resort	76513
Morningside Heights (Part of El Paso)	79930
Morrill	75925
Morris Ranch	78624
Morse	79062
Morton (Cochran County)	79346
Morton (Harrison County)	75640
Moscow	75960
Mosheim	76689
Moss Bluff	77575
Moss Hill	77575
Mostyn	77355
Moulton	77975
Mound	76558
Mound City	75844
Mountain	76528
Mountain City	78610
Mountain Home	78058
Mountain Peak	76065
Mountain Springs (Cooke County)	76258
Mountain Springs (Hill County)	76645
Mountain Valley Estates	76058
Mountain View (Part of El Paso)	79904
Mountain View Unit	76528
Mount Blanco	79322
Mount Calm	76673
Mount Carmel	76360
Mount Enterprise (Rusk County)	75681
Mount Enterprise (Wood County)	75773

	ZIP
Mount Haven	75766
Mount Houston	77016
Mount Joy	75441
Mount Lookout	78130
Mount Lucas	78022
Mount Mitchell	75571
Mount Moriah	75571
Mount Olive	77995
Mount Pleasant	75455-56
For specific Mount Pleasant Zip Codes call (903) 572-8311, or your local postmaster.	
Mount Selman	75757
Mount Sylvan	75771
Mount Union	75956
Mount Vernon	75457
Mozelle	76834
Muddig	75449
Mudville	77801
Muellersville	77833
Muenster	76252
Mulberry	75476
Muldoon	78949
Muleshoe	79347
Mulkey	79027
Mullin	76864
Mullins Prairie	78945
Mumford	77867
Muncy	79241
Munday	76371
Munson	75189
Murchison	75778
Murphy	75173
Murray	76450
Murryhill (Part of Lubbock)	79413
Musgrove	75494
Mustang (Denton County)	76258
Mustang (Navarro County)	75110
Mustang Mott Store	77954
Mustang Ridge	78610
Mykawa Road (Part of Houston)	77033
Myra	76253
Myrtle Springs	75169
Naaman (Part of Garland)	75040
Nacalina	75944
Nacogdoches	75961-64
For specific Nacogdoches Zip Codes call (409) 564-3737, or your local postmaster.	
Nada	77460
Nadeau (Part of Texas City)	77590
Nancy	75980
Naples	75568
Naruna	76550
Nash (Bowie County)	75569
Nash (Ellis County)	75165
Nassau Bay (Harris County)	77058
Nassau Bay (Hood County)	76049
Nasworthy Hills (Part of San Angelo)	76904
Nat	75760
Natalia	78059
Naval Air (Part of Corpus Christi)	78419
Navarro	75151
Navarro Mills	76679
Navasota	77868-69
For specific Navasota Zip Codes call (409) 825-6812, or your local postmaster.	
Navo	76227
Nazareth	79063
Nebgen	78624
Necessity	76424
Nechanitz	78946
Neches	75779
Neches Indian Village	75925
Neches Junction (Part of Port Arthur)	77640
Nederland	77627
Needmore (Bailey County)	79371
Needmore (Delta County)	75448
Needville	77461
Negley	75426
Neinda	79520
Nell	78119
Nelson City	78006
Nelsonville	77418
Nelta	75437
Nemo	76070
Nesbitt (Harrison County)	75670
Nesbitt (Robertson County)	76629
Neuville	75935
Nevada	75173
Newark	76071
New Baden	77870
New Berlin	78121
New Bielau	78962
New Birthright	75482
New Boston	75570

	ZIP
New Braunfels	78130-33
For specific New Braunfels Zip Codes call (512) 625-7736, or your local postmaster.	
New Bremen	78950
Newburg	76442
Newby	75846
New Caney	77357
New Caney Heights	77357
Newcastle	76372
New Chapel Hill	75701
New Clarkson	76570
New Colony	75563
New Corn Hill	76537
New Deal	79350
New Fountain	78861
Newgulf	77462
New Harmony (Shelby County)	75973
New Harmony (Smith County)	75704
Newharp	76239
New Hebron	75685
New Home	79383
New Hope (Cherokee County)	75766
New Hope (Collin County)	75069
New Hope (Dallas County)	75149
New Hope (Henderson County)	75756
New Hope (Jones County)	79553
New Hope (Rusk County)	75662
New Hope (San Jacinto County)	77327
New Hope (Smith County)	75703
New Hope (Wood County)	75773
New Katy	78653
Newlin	79245
New London	75682
New Lynn	79381
New Mine	75686
New Moore	79351
Newport (Clay County)	76230
Newport (Harris County)	77532
New Prospect (Rusk County)	75652
New Prospect (Shelby County)	75975
New River Lake Estates	77327
New Salem (Falls County)	76570
New Salem (Palo Pinto County)	76472
New Salem (Rusk County)	75652
Newsome	75451
New Summerfield	75780
New Sweden (McCulloch County)	76825
New Sweden (Travis County)	78653
New Taiton	77437
Newton	75966
New Ulm	78950
New Waverly	77358
New Wehdem	77833
New Willard	77351
New York	75770
Neylandville	75401
Nickel	78629
Nickelberry	75566
Nickel Creek	88220
Niederwald	78640
Nigton	75926
Nimitz (Part of San Antonio)	78216*
	78279†
Nimrod	76437
Nineveh	75833
Nix	76550
Nixon	78140
Noack	76574
Nobility	75424
Noble	75470
Nockenut	78160
Nocona	76255
Nogalus	75845
Nolan	79537
Nolanville	76559
Nolte	78155
Nome	77629
Nona	77625
Noodle	79536
Noonday	75762
Nopal	78164
Nordheim	78141
Norias	78338
Norman Crossing	76574
Normandy	78877
Normangee	77871
Normanna	78142
Norse	76634
North Amarillo (Part of Amarillo)	79117
Northampton	77379

	ZIP
North Austin (Part of Austin)	78751
Northaven (Part of Dallas)	75229
North Beach (Part of Corpus Christi)	78402
North Bonami	75956
North Broadway (Part of San Antonio)	78217
North Caney	75482
North Cedar	75926
North Cleveland	77327
Northcliff	78108
North Concho Lake Estates	76901
Northcrest	76705
Northcrest Estates (Part of Victoria)	77904
Northcross Mall (Part of Austin)	78757
Northeast (Part of Austin)	78752
North East Mall (Part of Hurst)	76053
Northeast Station (Part of Odessa)	79764
Northern Hills	75020
Northfield	79201
Northgate (El Paso County)	79914†
	79924*
Northgate (Victoria County)	77904
North Groesbeck	79252
North Heights (Part of Amarillo)	79107
North Hills Mall (Part of North Richland Hills)	76118
North Houston	77086
North Houston General Mail Facility (Part of Houston)	77315
North Houston Heights	77039
North Lake (Dallas County)	75238
Northlake (Denton County)	76247
Northlake Estates	78628
North Line Oaks	77301
Northline Shopping Center (Part of Houston)	77022
Northline Terrace	77093
North Oaks	78753
North Orange Heights	77630
Northpark (Part of Dallas)	75225
Northpark Malll (Part of El Paso)	79924
North Port Arthur (Part of Port Arthur)	77642
North Richland Hills	76118
Northrup	78942
North Rusk (Part of Rusk)	75785
North San Antonio Hills	78253
North San Pedro	78380
North Shepherd (Part of Houston)	77088
Northside Village (Part of Houston)	77015
North Springs	77373
North Star Mall (Part of San Antonio)	78216
Northtown Mall (Part of Dallas)	75234
Northwest (Part of Austin)	78757
Northwest Hills	78024
Northwest Mall (Part of Houston)	77292
Northwest Park	77086
Northwest Plaza (Part of Dallas)	75238
Northwood	78758
Northwood Hills Village (Part of Dallas)	75240
North Zulch	77872
Norton	76865
Norwood	75972
Notrees	79759
Nottingham Forest	77630
Nottingham Woods	75835
Novice (Coleman County)	79538
Novice (Lamar County)	75462
Novohrad	77975
Noxville	78631
Nugent	79601
Nursery	77976
Oakalla	76542
Oak Canyon	77302
Oak Creek Addition (Part of Grapevine)	76051
Oak Crest Estates	78628
Oak Dale (Erath County)	76401
Oakdale (Hopkins County)	75482
Oak Flat (Angelina County)	75949
Oak Flat (Nacogdoches County)	75760
Oak Flat (Rusk County)	75681
Oak Forest (Harris County)	77018
Oak Forest (Travis County)	78759
Oak Grove (Bowie County)	75554
Oak Grove (Camp County)	75686
Oak Grove (Ellis County)	75119

	ZIP
Oak Grove (Kaufman County)	75142
Oak Grove (Tarrant County)	76028
Oak Grove (Wood County)	75783
Oak Hill (Jasper County)	75951
Oak Hill (Rusk County)	75652
Oak Hill (Travis County)	78735
Oak Hill (Johnson County)	76031
Oak Hills Acres	77362
Oakhill Station (Part of Austin)	78749
Oakhurst	77359
Oak Island	77514
Oak Lake	76705
Oakland (Cherokee County)	75785
Oakland (Colorado County)	78951
Oakland (Rusk County)	75652
Oakland (Van Zandt County)	75103
Oak Lawn (Part of Dallas)	75219
Oaklawn Village (Part of Texarkana)	75501
Oak Leaf	75154
Oak Point	75034
Oak Ridge (Cooke County)	76240
Oak Ridge (Kaufman County)	75160
Oak Ridge (Llano County)	78654
Oak Ridge (Nacogdoches County)	75961
Oak Ridge (Parker County)	76086
Oak Ridge North	77302
Oaks (Bee County)	78119
Oaks (Tarrant County)	76114
Oaks North	78260
Oak Terrace	77365
Oak Trail Shores	76048
Oak Valley	75110
Oakview	77611
Oak Village North	78266
Oakville	78060
Oakwilde	77093
Oakwood	75855
Oakwood Village and Westwood Plaza (Part of Abilene)	79603
Oatmeal	78605
O'Brien	79539
Oceanshore	77650
Ocee	76638
Odell	79247
Odell Addition (Part of Grapevine)	76051
Odem	78370
Odessa	79760-69
For specific Odessa Zip Codes call (915) 332-6436, or your local postmaster.	
Odom	75147
Odonnell	79351
Oenaville	76501
O'Farrell	75551
Oglesby	76561
Oilla	77630
Oilton	78371
Oklahoma	77355
Oklahoma Flat	79339
Oklahoma Lane	79325
Oklaunion	76373
Okra	76435
Ola	75142
Old Boston	75570
Old Bowling	77865
Old Brazoria (Part of Brazoria)	77422
Old Dime Box	77853
Olden	76466
Oldenburg	78945
Old Ferry	78669
Old Glory	79540
Old Ivy	75847
Old Kinkler	77964
Old Larissa	75757
Old London	75682
Old Mill (Part of Leon Valley)	78238
Old Mobeetie (Part of Mobeetie)	79061
Old Moulton	77975
Old Ocean	77463
Old River Lake	77327
Old River Terrace	77530
Old River-Winfree	77520
Olds	75951
Old Sabinetown	75948
Old Salem	75933
Old Union (Bowie County)	75574
Old Union (Limestone County)	76687
Old Union (Titus County)	75455
Old Waverly	77358
Oletha	76687

* Area Zip Code   **† Post Office Boxes**

	ZIP
Olfen	76875
Olin	76457
Olive	77625
Olivia	77979
Olmito	78575
Olmos (Bee County)	78389
Olmos (Starr County)	78582
Olmos Park	78212
Olney	76374
Olton	79064
Omaha	75571
Omen	75789
Onalaska	77360
One Seventy Seven Lake Estates	77356
Onion Creek	78747
Opdyke	79336
Opdyke West	79336
Opelika	75778
Oplin	79510
O'Quinn	78945
Ora	75949
Oran	76449
Orange	77630-32
For specific Orange Zip Codes call (409) 883-9351, or your local postmaster.	
Orangedale	78102
Orangefield	77639
Orange Grove (Harris County)	77039
Orange Grove (Jim Wells County)	78372
Orangeville	75491
Orchard	77464
Ore City	75683
Orient	76901
Orla	79770
Orme (Part of Arlington)	76010
Osage	76528
Oscar	76501
Osceola	76055
Ottine	78658
Otto	76675
Ovalo	79541
Overland Plaza (Part of Arlington)	76003
Overton	75684
Ovilla	75154
Owens (Brown County)	76801
Owens (Crosby County)	79357
Owensville	77856
Owentown	75708
Oyster Creek	77541
Ozona	76943
Pacio	75450
Pack Unit	77868
Padgett	76374
Padre-Staples Mall (Part of Corpus Christi)	78411
Paducah	79248
Pagoda	75862
Paige	78659
Paint Rock	76866
Pakan	79079
Palacios	77465
Palava	79556
Palestine (Anderson County)	75801*
	75802†
Palestine (Polk County)	75936
Palito Blanco	78332
Palmer	75152
Palmetto (Part of Oakhurst)	77359
Palm Harbor	78382
Palmhurst	78572
Palm Park	78223
Palm Valley	78550
Palmview	78572
Palo Alto	78343
Paloduro	79226
Palo Pinto	76484
Paluxy	76467
Pampa	79065*
	79066†
Pancake	76528
Pandale	76943
Pandora	78143
Panhandle	79068
Panna Maria	78144
Panola	75685
Panorama Estates	75169
Panorama Village	77301
Pantego	76094
Papalote	78387
Paradise	76073
Paradise Bay	75143
Paradise Hills	75929
Paris	75460-62
For specific Paris Zip Codes call (903) 784-3381, or your local postmaster.	

	ZIP
Park	78945
Park Cities (Part of University Park)	75205
Parkdale (Part of Dallas)	75227
Parkdale Mall (Part of Beaumont)	77706
Parkdale Plaza (Part of Corpus Christi)	78411
Parker (Collin County)	75002
Parker (Johnson County)	76050
Parker Point	75980
Parker Square (Part of Wichita Falls)	76308
Park Forest (Part of Dallas)	75240
Park Glen (Part of Houston)	77072
Park Place (Part of Houston)	77017
Park Row (Part of Katy)	77449
Parks at Arlington, The (Part of Arlington)	76015
Park Springs	76270
Parkview (Part of Fort Stockton)	79735
Parkview Estates	78155
Parkwood	77612
Parkwood Estates	77032
Parnell	79201
Parvin	75009
Pasadena	77501-08
For specific Pasadena Zip Codes call (713) 475-5140, or your local postmaster.	
Pasadena Town Square (Part of Pasadena)	77506
Patilo	76462
Patman	75656
Patrich	75652
Patricia	79331
Patrick (Dallas County)	75125
Patrick (McLennan County)	76708
Patroon	75973
Pattison	77466
Patton	76689
Pattonfield	75644
Patton Park	76544
Patton Village	77372
Pattonville	75468
Pauline	75124
Pauls Store	75973
Pawelekville	78113
Pawnee	78145
Paxton	75954
Paynes Corner	79360
Payne Springs	75124
Payton Colony	78606
Peach Creek	77488
Peach Creek Estates	77372
Peach Tree (Brazos County)	77801
Peachtree (Jasper County)	75951
Peacock	79502
Peadenville	76067
Pearl	76528
Pearland	77581
	77584
	77588
For specific Pearland Zip Codes call (713) 485-2814, or your local postmaster.	
Pearl City	77995
Pear Ridge (Part of Port Arthur)	77640
Pearsall	78061
Pearsons Chapel	75851
Pear Valley	76867
Peaster	76485
Pebble Beach	75121
Pebble Hills (Part of El Paso)	79925*
	79937†
Pecan (Part of Del Rio)	78840
Pecan Acres (Orange County)	77662
Pecan Acres (Wise County)	76071
Pecan Gap	75469
Pecangrove (Coryell County)	76528
Pecan Grove (Fort Bend County)	77469
Pecan Hill	75154
Pecan Lake Area	77835
Pecan Plantation	76048
Pecos	79772
Peeltown	75158
Peerless	75482
Peggy	78062
Pelham	76648
Pelican Bay	76020
Pendleton	76564
Pendleton Harbor	75948
Penelope	76676
Peniel (Part of Greenville)	75401
Penitas	78576

	ZIP
Pennington	75856
Penwell	79776
Peoria	76645
Pep	79353
Percilla	75844
Perezville	78572
Perico	79087
Permian Mall (Part of Odessa)	79762
Pernitas Point	78022
Perrin	76486
Perrin Field	75020
Perrin Heights	75020
Perry	76677
Perry Landing (Part of Jones Creek)	77541
Perryton	79070
Perryville	75494
Pershing (Part of Austin)	78702
Pershing Park	76544
Personville	76642
Pert	75801
Peters	77474
Petersburg	79250
Peterson	77627
Peters Prairie	75426
Petersville	77995
Petrolia	76377
Petronila	78380
Petteway	76629
Pettibone	76520
Pettit	79336
Pettus	78146
Petty (Lamar County)	75470
Petty (Lynn County)	79373
Petty's Chapel	75110
Pflugerville	78660*
	78691†
Phalba	75147
Pharr	78577
Phelan	78602
Phelps	77340
Phillips	79007
Phillipsburg	77426
Pickens	75751
Pickett	75110
Pickton	75471
Pidcoke	76528
Piedmont (Grimes County)	77830
Piedmont (Upshur County)	75644
Pierce	77467
Pierces Chapel	75766
Piggly Wiggly (Part of Bryan)	77801
Pike	75424
Pilgrim Ridge	77367
Pilgrims Rest	75410
Pilot Grove	75491
Pilot Knob	78744
Pilot Point	76258
Pine	75686
Pine Acres	77357
Pine Branch	75417
Pine Crest	77301
Pine Forest (Hopkins County)	75471
Pine Forest (Orange County)	77662
Pine Grove (Cherokee County)	75766
Pine Grove (Newton County)	75966
Pine Grove (Orange County)	77630
Pine Hill (Cherokee County)	75766
Pinehill (Rusk County)	75652
Pinehurst (Montgomery County)	77362
Pinehurst (Orange County)	77630
Pine Island	77445
Pine Lake	77356
Pineland	75968
Pine Mills	75773
Pine Park	75948
Pine Prairie	77340
Pine Ridge	77625
Pine Springs (Culberson County)	88220
Pine Springs (Smith County)	75702
Pine Trail Shores	75762
Pine Valley	75941
Pineview	75494
Pinewood (Part of Longview)	75601
Pinewood Estates (Hardin County)	77706
Pinewood Estates (Montgomery County)	77372
Pinewood Village	77093
Piney	77418
Piney Grove (Cass County)	75551

	ZIP		ZIP		ZIP
Piney Grove (Upshur County)	75451	Polytechnic (Part of Fort Worth)	76105	Progress (Palo Pinto County)	76067
Piney Point (Harris County)	77024	Ponder	76259	Promenade (Part of Richardson)	75080
Piney Point (Montgomery County)	77301	Pond Springs	78729	Prospect	75657
Piney Point (Sabine County)	75959	Pone	75667	Prosper	75078
Piney Woods	75951	Ponta	75766	Providence (Angelina County)	75904
Pinnacle	75644	Pontotoc	76869	Providence (Hardin County)	77625
Pioneer	76471	Poole	75440	Providence (Polk County)	77351
Pioneer Trails	77302	Poolville	76487	Providence (Van Zandt County)	75140
Pipe Creek	78063	Porfirio	78580	Provident City	77455
Pirtle	75684	Port Acres (Part of Port Arthur)	77640	Pruitt (Cass County)	75657
Pisgah	75929	Portairs (Part of Corpus Christi)	78415	Pruitt (Van Zandt County)	75140
Pitner Junction	75684	Port Alto	77979	Puckett Place (Part of Amarillo)	79109
Pitts	77338	Port Aransas	78373	Puckett West (Part of Amarillo)	79109
Pittsburg	75686	Port Arthur	77640-43	Puerto Rico	78563
Placation Estates	75959	For specific Port Arthur Zip Codes call (409) 983-3266, or your local postmaster.		Pumphrey	79567
Placedo	77977			Pumpkin	77358
Placid	76872			Pumpkin Center	79331
Plains (Borden County)	79351	Port Bolivar	77650	Pumpville	78851
Plains (Yoakum County)	79355	Porter	77365	Punkin Center	78086
Plainview (Denton County)	76249	Porter Heights	77365	Purdon	76679
Plainview (Hale County)	79072*	Porter Springs	75835	Purley	75457
	79073†	Porterville Timbers	77365	Purmela	76566
Plainview (Sabine County)	75968	Port Isabel	78578	Pursley	76679
Plainview (Wharton County)	77455	Portland	78374	Purves	76446
Plano	75023-26	Port Lavaca	77979	Putnam	76469
	75074-75	Port Mansfield	78598	Pyote	79777
	75086	Port Neches	77651	Pyron	79545
	75093-94	Port O'Connor	77982	Quail	79251
For specific Plano Zip Codes call (214) 423-4260, or your local postmaster.		Porvenir	79854	Quail Run (Part of Fort Stockton)	79735
		Posey (Hopkins County)	75482	Quail Valley	78626
Plantersville	77363	Posey (Lubbock County)	79364	Quanah	79252
Plaska	79245	Possum Kingdom	76449	Quarry	77833
Plateau	79855	Post	79356	Queen City	75572
Pleak	77469	Post Oak (Blanco County)	78636	Quemado	78877
Pleasant Farms	79763	Post Oak (Delta County)	75432	Quicksand	75966
Pleasant Grove (Bowie County)	75501	Postoak (Freestone County)	75840	Quihi	78861
Pleasant Grove (Dallas County)	75217	Postoak (Jack County)	76230	Quinlan	75474
Pleasant Grove (Falls County)	76570	Postoak (Lamar County)	75416	Quintana	77541
Pleasant Grove (Upshur County)	75755	Post Oak (Robertson County)	76629	Quitaque	79255
Pleasant Grove (Wood County)	75494	Post Oak Bend City	75142	Quite Village	77662
Pleasant Hill (Blanco County)	78636	Post Oak Mall (Part of College Station)	77840	Quitman	75783
Pleasant Hill (Eastland County)	76437	Post Oak Point	78950	Rabb	78380
Pleasant Hill (Nacogdoches County)	75946	Poteet	78065	Rabbit Center	76401
Pleasant Hill (Polk County)	75939	Poth	78147	Rabbs	77964
Pleasant Hill (Washington County)	77833	Potosi	79601	Rabbs Prairie	78945
Pleasanton	78064	Potters Point	75657	Rachal	78353
Pleasant Point	76009	Pottsboro	75076	Radium	79501
Pleasant Ridge (Henderson County)	75763	Pottsville	76565	Ragtown	75411
Pleasant Ridge (Leon County)	75833	Powderly	75473	Rainbow	76077
Pleasant Ridge (Montague County)	76230	Powell	75153	Rainbow Hills	78227
Pleasant Ridge (Panola County)	75633	Powell Point	77451	Raisin	77905
Pleasant Springs	75833	Poynor	75782	Raleigh	76641
Pleasant Valley (Dallas County)	75040	Prade Ranch	78058	Ralls	79357
Pleasant Valley (Garza County)	79356	Praesel	76567	Ramah	75974
Pleasant Valley (Lamb County)	79347	Praha	78941	Rambo	75555
Pleasant Valley (Palo Pinto County)	76067	Prairie Dell	76571	Ramireno	78067
Pleasant Valley (Potter County)	79108	Prairie Grove (Angelina County)	75941	Ramirez	78376
Pleasant Valley (Wichita County)	76305	Prairie Grove (Limestone County)	76667	Ranch Harbor Estates	76692
Pleasant Valley Acres	77355	Prairie Hill (Limestone County)	76678	Ranchito	78586
Pledger (Fisher County)	79543	Prairie Hill (Washington County)	77833	Ranchland (Part of El Paso)	79915*
Pledger (Matagorda County)	77468	Prairie Lea	78661		79926†
Pluck	75939	Prairie Mountain	78643	Ranchland Acres	79703
Plum	78952	Prairie Point	76239	Rancho Alegre	78332
Plum Creek	75831	Prairie Valley (Fayette County)	78952	Rancho de la Parita	78372
Plum Grove	77327	Prairie Valley (Montague County)	76255	Rancho Viejo (Cameron County)	78520
Plum Ridge	75980	Prairie View	77446	Rancho Viejo (Jim Hogg County)	78361
Plymouth Park (Part of Irving)	75061	Prairieville	75147	Randolph	75475
Poe Prairie	76066	Prattville	75432	Randolph Air Force Base	78148
Poesville	76671	Premont	78375		78150
Poetry	75160	Presidio	79845*	For specific Randolph Air Force Base Zip Codes call (512) 652-2606, or your local postmaster.	
Point	75472		79846†		
Pointblank	77364	Preston (Part of Dallas)	75225	Ranger	76470
Point Comfort	77978	Preston Shores	75076	Rangerville	78586
Point Enterprise	76667	Prestonwood (Part of Arlington)	76012	Rankin (Ellis County)	75119
Point Loma	78368	Prestonwood Town Center (Part of Dallas)	75240	Rankin (Upton County)	79778
Point Royal	75758	Price (Jefferson County)	77627	Ratama	78017
Point Venture	78641	Price (Rusk County)	75687	Ratcliff (Houston County)	75858
Polar	79549	Priddy	76870	Ratcliff (San Augustine County)	75972
Pollok	75969	Primera	78550	Ratcliffe	78164
		Primrose	75754	Ratibor	76501
		Princeton	75407	Rattan	75432
		Pringle	79083	Ravenna	75476
		Pritchett	75644	Rayburn	77327
		Proctor	76468	Rayburn Hideaway	75937
		Proffitt	76372	Rayford	77373
		Progreso	78579	Rayland	76384
		Progreso Lakes	78579	Raymondville	78580
		Progress (Bailey County)	79347	Ray Point	78071
				Raywood	77582
				Reagan	76680
				Reagan Wells	78801

	ZIP
Reagor Springs	75165
Realitos	78376
Reata Trails	78628
Redbank	75561
Red Bird Mall (Part of Dallas)	75237
Red Bluff	79770
Red Branch	75855
Redford	79846
Red Gate	78539
Red Hill (Cass County)	75560
Red Hill (Lamar County)	75473
Red Lake	75855
Redland (Angelina County)	75901
	75904

For specific Redland Zip Codes call (409) 634-7749, or your local postmaster.

	ZIP
Redland (Leon County)	75833
Redland (Van Zandt County)	75754
Redlawn	75925
Redlick	75501
Redmond Terrace (Part of College Station)	77840
Red Oak (Ellis County)	75154
Red Oak (Kaufman County)	75142
Red Ranger	76569
Red River Army Depot	75501
Red Rock	78662
Red Springs (Baylor County)	76380
Red Springs (Bowie County)	75501
Red Springs (Smith County)	75701
Red Top	76450
Redtown (Anderson County)	75839
Red Town (Angelina County)	75904
Redwater	75573
Redwood	78666
Reedville	78656
Reese	75766
Reese Air Force Base	79489
Refugio	78377
Regency	76864
Rehburg	77835
Rehobeth	75633
Reilly Springs	75482
Rek Hill	78940
Reklaw	75784
Relampago	78570
Reliance	77801
Remolino	78582
Rendon	76028
Reno (Lamar County)	75462
Reno (Parker County)	76020
Retreat (Grimes County)	77868
Retreat (Hill County)	76627
Retreat (Navarro County)	75110
Retrieve Unit	77515
Retta	76028
Rhea	79035
Rhea Mills	75069
Rhineland	76371
Rhome	76078
Rhonesboro	75494
Ricardo	78363
Rice (Navarro County)	75155
Rice (Smith County)	75701
Rices Crossing	76574
Richards	77873
Richardson	75080-85

For specific Richardson Zip Codes call (214) 235-8353, or your local postmaster.

	ZIP
Richardson Square (Part of Richardson)	75081
Richland (Dallas County)	75243
Richland (Navarro County)	76681
Richland (Rains County)	75472
Richland Hills	76118
Richland Mall (Part of Waco)	76710
Richland Park (Part of Fort Worth)	76118
Richland Plaza (Part of North Richland Hills)	76118
Richland Springs	76871
Richmond	77406
	77469

For specific Richmond Zip Codes call (713) 342-2021, or your local postmaster.

	ZIP
Richwood	77531
Riderville	75633
Ridge (Mills County)	76864
Ridge (Robertson County)	77856
Ridgecrest (Part of Amarillo)	79109
Ridgecrest Addition	77630
Ridgeheights	79701
Ridgemere (Part of Amarillo)	79107

	ZIP
Ridgeway	75482
Ridglea (Part of Fort Worth)	76116
Ridgmar Mall (Part of Fort Worth)	76116
Ridings	75476
Riesel	76682
Rimwick Forrest	77355
Rincon	78582
Ringgold	76261
Rio del Sol	78522
Rio Farms	78538
Rio Frio	78879
Rio Grande City	78582
Rio Hondo	78583
Rio Llano Ranch	78643
Riomedina	78066
Rio Pecos	79740
Rios	78349
Rio Vista	76093
Rising Star	76471
Rita	77857
River Bend (Newton County)	75932
River Bend (Sabine County)	75948
River Bend Estates	78003
River Brook	77302
Riverby	75488
Rivercenter (Part of San Antonio)	78205
Riverdrive Mall (Part of Laredo)	78040
River Hill	75633
Riverland	76365
River Oak Lake Estates	78758
River Oaks (Harris County)	77019
River Oaks (Tarrant County)	76114
River Oaks Ranch	78063
River Plantation	77302
River Ridge	75951
Riverside (Tarrant County)	76111
Riverside (Walker County)	77367
Riverside Crest (Part of Houston)	77338
River Woods Estates	77050
Riviera	78379
Riviera Beach	78379
Roach	75551
Roach Town	75758
Roane	75110
Roanoke	76262
Roans Prairie	77875
Roaring Springs	79256
Robbins	75846
Robert Lee	76945
Robertson	79343
Robinson	76706
Robinson Plaza (Part of Robinson)	76706
Robstown	78380
Roby	79543
Rochelle	76872
Rochester	79544
Rock Creek	76708
Rockdale	76567
Rockett	75165
Rockford	75462
Rock Harbor	76048
Rockhill (Collin County)	75069
Rock Hill (Jasper County)	75951
Rock Hill (Wood County)	75783
Rockhouse	78950
Rock Island (Colorado County)	77470
Rock Island (Polk County)	75939
Rockland	75938
Rockne	78602
Rockport	78381†
	78382*
Rock Prairie	77801
Rocksprings	78880
Rockwall	75087
Rockwood	76873
Rocky Branch	75638
Rocky Creek Park	77835
Rocky Hill	76661
Rocky Mound	75686
Rocky Point	75440
Rocky Springs (Angelina County)	75949
Rocky Springs (Tyler County)	75938
Roddy	75147
Rodney	76639
Roganville	75956
Rogers	76569
Rogers Hill	76691
Rolling Hills (Hunt County)	75453
Rolling Hills (Potter County)	79108
Rolling Hills (Waller County)	77445
Rolling Hills Shores	76086
Rolling Meadows	75603
Rolling Oaks	75169

	ZIP
Rolling Oaks Mall (Part of San Antonio)	78247
Rollingwood	78746
Roma	78584
Roman Forest	77357
Roman Hills	77356
Romayor	77368
Romero	79022
Romney	76471
Roosevelt (Kimble County)	76874
Roosevelt (Lubbock County)	79401
Ropesville	79358
Rosalie	75417
Rosanky	78953
Roscoe	79545
Rosebud	76570
Rose City	77662
Rosedale	76661
Rose Hill (Harris County)	77375
Rose Hill (San Jacinto County)	77331
Rose Hill (Wood County)	75773
Rose Hill Acres	77656
Rosenberg	77471
Rosenthal	76655
Rosevine	75930
Rosewood	75644
Rosharon	77583
Rosita (Duval County)	78384
Rosita (Starr County)	78582
Ross	76684
Rosser	75157
Rosston	76263
Rossville	78065
Rotan	79546
Round Mountain	78663
Round Prairie	75144
Round Rock	78680-81

For specific Round Rock Zip Codes call (512) 255-3516, or your local postmaster.

	ZIP
Round Timber	76380
Round Top	78954
Roundup	79313
Rowden	79504
Rowena	76875
Rowlett	75030†
	75088*
Roxton	75477
Royal Forest	77303
Royal Lane (Part of Dallas)	75230
Royal Oaks (Henderson County)	75143
Royal Oaks (Llano County)	78639
Royal Oaks (Orange County)	77626
Royalty	79779
Royalwood	77028
Roy Miller (Part of Corpus Christi)	78465
Roy Royall (Part of Houston)	77093
Royse City	75189
Royston	79543
Rucker	76444
Rufe Jordan	79065
Rugby	75435
Ruidosa	79843
Rule	79547
Rumley	76539
Run	78537
Runaway Bay	76426
Runge	78151
Rural Shade	75144
Rushwood	77067
Rusk	75785
Rutersville	78945
Ruth Springs	75163
Ryanville	78377
Rye	77369
Sabanna	76437
Sabathany	76086
Sabinal	78881
Sabine	77640
Sabine Pass	77655
Sabine Sands	75928
Sabinetown	75948
Sachse	75048
Sacul	75788
Saddle and Surrey	77356
Sadler	76264
Sagerton	79548
Saginaw	76179
St. Claire Cove	77650
St. Elmo	75859
St. Francis	79107
St. Francis Village	76036
St. Hedwig	78152
St. Jo	76265
Saint John	78956

	ZIP
Saint John Colony	78616
St. Lawrence	79739
St. Louis (Part of Tyler)	75702
St. Paul (Brazoria County)	77422
St. Paul (Collin County)	75098
St. Paul (Falls County)	76661
St. Paul (San Patricio County)	78387
Salado	76571
Salem (Bastrop County)	78953
Salem (Milam County)	76520
Salem (Smith County)	75789
Salesville	76067
Salineno	78585
Salmon	75839
Salona	76230
Salt Flat	79847
Salt Gap	76836
Saltillo	75478
Sam Houston (Part of Houston)	77002
Sam Houston College (Part of Huntsville)	77341
Samnorwood	79077
Sam Rayburn	75951
Sanaloma Estates	78628
San Angelo	76901-08

For specific San Angelo Zip Codes call (915) 655-5681, or your local postmaster.

San Antonio 78201-99

For specific San Antonio Zip Codes call (210) 657-8302, or your local postmaster.

COLLEGES & UNIVERSITIES

	ZIP
Incarnate Word College	78209
Our Lady of the Lake University of San Antonio	78207
St. Mary's University	78228
Trinity University	78212
University of Texas Health Science Center at San Antonio	78284
University of Texas at San Antonio	78249

FINANCIAL INSTITUTIONS

	ZIP
Bank One, Texas, N.A.	78205
Bank of San Antonio, The	78205
Bank of the West, The	78207
Broadway National Bank	78209
First City, Texas-San Antonio, N.A.	78216
First Federal Savings Bank	78209
Frost National Bank of San Antonio, The	78205
Groos Bank, National Association	78216
International Bank of Commerce	78209
Jefferson State Bank	78201
Kelly Field National Bank	78238
Nationsbank of Texas, N.A.	78205
Texas Commerce Bank-San Antonio/N.A.	78209
U.S.A.A. Federal Savings Bank	78288

HOSPITALS

	ZIP
Audie L. Murphy Memorial Veterans Hospital	78284
Baptist Medical Center	78205
Bexar County Hospital District	78229
San Antonio Regional Hospital	78229
Santa Rosa Health Care Corporation	78207
Southwest Texas Methodist Hospital	78229

HOTELS/MOTELS

	ZIP
The Hilton Palacio del Rio	78205
Holiday Inn Riverwalk North	78205
Marriott Riverwalk	78205
Ramada Inn Airport	78209
Hotel St. Anthony	78205

MILITARY INSTALLATIONS

	ZIP
Brooks Air Force Base	78235
Camp Bullis	78234
Camp Stanley Storage Activity	78269
Fort Sam Houston	78234
Kelly Air Force Base	78241
Lackland Air Force Base	78236
Texas Air National Guard, FB6432, Kelly Air Force Base	78241

	ZIP
San Augustine	75972
San Benito	78586
San Carlos	78539
Sanco	76945
Sanctuary	76020
Sanderson	79848
Sand Flat (Rains County)	75440
Sandflat (Smith County)	75706
Sand Flat (Van Zandt County)	75140
Sand Hill (Floyd County)	79235
Sand Hill (Upshur County)	75644
Sandia	78383
San Diego	78384
Sandjack	75928
Sand Lake	75119
Sandoval	76574
Sand Ridge (Houston County)	75835
Sand Ridge (Wharton County)	77434
Sand Springs (Howard County)	79720
Sand Springs (Wood County)	75773
Sandusky	76273
Sandy	78665
Sandy Acres	79703
Sandy Corner	77437
Sandy Creek	76556
Sandy Fork	78632
Sandy Harbor	78654
Sandy Hill	77833
Sandy Point	77583
Sandy Ridge	77351
San Elizario	79849
San Felipe	77473
Sanford	79078
Sanford Estates	79036
San Gabriel	76577
San Gabriel Heights	78628
Sanger	76266
San Geromino	78023
San Isidro	78588
San Jacinto (Part of Amarillo)	79106
San Jose	78332
San Juan (Hidalgo County)	78589
San Juan (Nueces County)	78406
San Leanna	78748
San Leon	77539
San Marcos	78666*
	78667†
San Patricio	78368
San Pedro	78520
San Perlita	78590
San Saba	76877
Sansom Park	76114
Santa Anna	76878
Santa Catarina	78582
Santa Cruz	78582
Santa Elena	78591
Santa Fe	77510
	77517

For specific Santa Fe Zip Codes call (409) 925-2934, or your local postmaster.

	ZIP
Santa Maria	78592
Santa Monica	78580
Santa Rita (Part of San Angelo)	76901
Santa Rosa	78593
Santo	76472
San Ygnacio	78067
Saragosa	79780
Saratoga	77585
Sarco	77963
Sardis (Cass County)	75656
Sardis (Ellis County)	76065
Sargent	77414
Sarita	78385
Sash	75446
Saspamco	78112
Satin	76685
Satsuma	77040
Sattler	78130
Sauney Stand	77426
Savage	79357
Savoy	75479
Sayers	78602
Scallorn	76853
Scenic Heights	78130
Scenic Hills	78108
Scenic Oaks	78023
Scenic Terrace	78130
Schattel	78005
Schertz	78154
Schicke Point	77465
Schoolerville	76531
School Land	78140
Schroeder	77963
Schulenburg	78956

	ZIP
Schumansville	78130
Schwab City	77351
Schwertner	76573
Scissors	78537
Scotland	76379
Scotsdale (Ector County)	79762
Scotsdale (El Paso County)	79925
Scott	75169
Scottsville	75688
Scranton	76437
Scrappin Valley	75977
Scroggins	75480
Scurry	75158
Seabrook	77586
Sea Crest Park	77520
Seadrift	77983
Seagoville	75159
Seagraves	79359
Sea Isle	77554
Seale	76687
Sealy	77474
Seaton	76501
Seawillow	78644
Sebastian	78594
Sebastopol	75862
Seco Mines	78852
Security	77327
Sedalia	75495
Segno	77351
Segovia	76849
Seguin	78155-56

For specific Seguin Zip Codes call (512) 379-2594, or your local postmaster.

	ZIP
Sejita	78376
Selden	76401
Selfs	75446
Selma	78209
Selman City	75689
Seminary Hill (Part of Fort Worth)	76115
Seminole	79360
Senate	76458
Senior	78073
Sequoia Estates	77032
Serbin	78942
Serenada	78628
Serna (Part of San Antonio)	78218
	78266

For specific Serna Zip Codes call (512) 655-0151, or your local postmaster.

	ZIP
Seth Ward	79072
Seven Oaks	77350
Seven Pines	75601
Seven Points	75143
Seven Sisters	78357
Sexton	75972
Sexton City	75684
Seymore	75482
Seymour	76380
Shadow Glen	77530
Shadow Lake Estates	77365
Shadowland	75435
Shadowland Retreat	77365
Shady Acres (Brazoria County)	77422
Shady Acres (Burnet County)	78654
Shady Brook Acres	77355
Shady Grove (Angelina County)	75941
Shady Grove (Cherokee County)	75785
Shady Grove (Dallas County)	75050
Shady Grove (Kerr County)	78028
Shady Grove (Marion County)	75657
Shady Grove (Nacogdoches County)	75961
Shady Grove (Navarro County)	76679
Shady Grove (Panola County)	75669
Shady Grove (Rains County)	75440
Shady Grove (Smith County)	75706
Shady Grove (Upshur County)	75755
Shady Hollow	78739
Shady Oaks (Henderson County)	75751
Shady Oaks (Tarrant County)	76053
Shady Shores (Denton County)	76205
Shady Shores (Henderson County)	75147
Shady Trees (Part of Houston)	77338

	ZIP
Shafter	79850
Shallowater	79363
Shamrock	79079
Shamrock Shores	76801
Shankleville	75932
Shannon	76365
Sharon	75701
Sharp	76518
Sharpstown (Part of Houston)	77036
Sharpstown Center (Part of Houston)	77036
Sharyland (Part of Mission)	78572
Shavano Park	78231
Shaw Bend	76877
Shawnee	75949
Shawnee Shores	75948
Shawnee Shores Estates	75474
Shaws Bend	78934
Sheffield	79781
Shelby	78940
Shelbyville	75973
Sheldon	77028
Shenandoah (Montgomery County)	77301
Shenandoah (Williamson County)	78613
Shep	79566
Shepherd	77371
Shepphard	77612
Shepton	75173
Sher-Den Mall (Part of Sherman)	75090
Sheridan	77475
Sherman	75090-92
For specific Sherman Zip Codes call (903) 892-3462, or your local postmaster.	
Sherman-Hansford Plant	79040
Sherman Junction (Part of Denison)	75020
Sherry	75426
Sherwood	76941
Sherwood Forest	78258
Sherwood Place	77016
Sherwood Shores	78654
Shields	76845
Shiloh (Delta County)	75448
Shiloh (Leon County)	75855
Shiloh (Liberty County)	77575
Shiloh (Limestone County)	76667
Shiloh (Williamson County)	76578
Shiner	77984
Shipman Camp	79521
Shirley	75482
Shirley Creek	75937
Shiro	77876
Shive	76531
Shoreacres	77571
Short	75935
Sidney	76474
Sierra Blanca	79851
Siesta Shores (Travis County)	78669
Siesta Shores (Zapata County)	78076
Sikes Center (Part of Wichita Falls)	76308
Silas	75975
Siloam	75559
Silsbee	77656
Silver	76949
Silver City (Milam County)	76520
Silver City (Navarro County)	76679
Silver City (Red River County)	75426
Silver Creek Village	78611
Silver Creek Village No. 2	78611
Silver Hills	78006
Silver Lake	75140
Silverton	79257
Silver Valley	76834
Simmons	78071
Simms	75574
Simonton	77476
Simpsonville	77465
Simsboro	75860
Sinclair City	75789
Singing Sands	77617
Singletary Sites	75956
Singleton	77831
Sinton	78387
Sipe Springs	76442
Sisterdale	78006
Six Flags Mall (Part of Arlington)	76010
Six Mile	77979
Six Points (Part of Corpus Christi)	78404
Skellytown	79080
Skidmore	78389
Sky Harbor	76048

	ZIP
Skyview Unit	75785
Slabtown	75462
Slate Shoals	75462
Slaton	79364
Slide	79413
Slidell	76267
Sloan	76877
Slocum	75839
Small	75117
Smeltertown (Part of El Paso)	79927
Smetana	77801
Smiley	78159
Smithfield (Part of North Richland Hills)	76180
Smith Grove	75851
Smith Hill	75561
Smithland	75657
Smith Point	77514
Smiths Bend	76634
Smith Springs	76401
Smithville	78957
Smithwick	78654
Smitty (Part of Athens)	75751
Smyer	79367
Smyrna	75551
Snook	77878
Snow Hill (Collin County)	75442
Snow Hill (Polk County)	75939
Snow Hill (Upshur County)	75683
Snyder	79549*
	79550†
Socorro	79927
Soda	77351
Soda Springs	76066
Sodville	78387
Solms	78130
Somerset	78069
Somerville	77879
Sonoma (Part of Ennis)	75119
Sonora	76950
Soules Chapel	75644
Sour Lake	77659
South Amarillo (Part of Amarillo)	79114
South Austin (Part of Austin)	78704
South Bend	76481
South Bosque	76710
South Brice	79226
South Dallas (Part of Dallas)	75215
Southeast (Part of Austin)	78744
Southeast Crossing (Part of Tyler)	75713
South Elm	76518
South End (Part of Beaumont)	77705
Southern Hills (Part of Abilene)	79605
Southern Methodist University (Part of University Park)	75275
South Gale	75020
South Groveton (Part of Groveton)	75845
South Haven	79720
South Houston	77587
Southlake	76092
Southland (Garza County)	79364
Southland (Wharton County)	77437
Southland Hills (Part of San Angelo)	76904
Southmayd	76268
Southmore (Part of Houston)	77004
South Mountain	76528
South Oak Cliff (Part of Dallas)	75216
South Padre Island	78597
South Park Mall (Part of San Antonio)	78224
South Plains	79258
South Plains Mall (Part of Lubbock)	79414
South Post Oak (Part of Houston)	77035
South Purmela	76566
Southridge Plaza (Part of Austin)	78745
South San Antonio (Part of San Antonio)	78211
South San Gabriel Ranches	78641
Southside (Part of Corpus Christi)	78413
Southside Estates (Part of Amarillo)	79110
Southside Place	77005
South Sulphur	75496
South Temple (Part of Temple)	76501
South Texas Medical Center (Part of San Antonio)	78229

	ZIP
Southton	78223
South View Estates	78737
Southwestern Baptist Theological Seminary (Part of Fort Worth)	76115
Southwest Freeway (Part of Houston)	77057
Sowells Bluff	75476
Sowers (Part of Irving)	75060
Spade	79369
Spanish Camp	77488
Spanish Fort	76255
Spanish Trail	76048
Sparenberg	79331
Sparks (Bell County)	76534
Sparks (El Paso County)	79927
Speaks	77985
Spearman	79081
Speegleville	76710
Spicewood	78669
Spicewood At Balcones Village	78750
Spicewood Beach	78669
Spillers Store	75850
Spillview Estates	75147
Spinwick Addition (Part of La Porte)	77571
Splawn	76520
Splendora	77372
Splendora Farms	77372
Spofford	78877
Spraberry	79702
Spring	77373
	77379-83
	77386-91
For specific Spring Zip Codes call (713) 288-6652, or your local postmaster.	
Spring Branch	78070
Spring Creek (Gillespie County)	78624
Spring Creek (San Saba County)	76871
Spring Creek (Throckmorton County)	76370
Spring Creek Acres (Part of Victoria)	77904
Spring Creek Estates	77355
Springdale	75572
Spring Dell	77373
Springfield (Anderson County)	75801
Springfield (Limestone County)	76667
Spring Forest	77373
Spring Hill (Bowie County)	75559
Springhill (Navarro County)	76639
Spring Hill (Camp County)	75686
Spring Hill (Gregg County)	75603
Spring Hill (Guadalupe County)	78155
Spring Hill (Jasper County)	75951
Spring Hills	77373
Springlake	79082
Spring Seat	75846
Springtown	76082
Spring Valley (Dallas County)	75240
Spring Valley (Harris County)	77024
Spring Valley (McLennan County)	76655
Sprinkle	78754
Spur	79370
Spurger	77760
Stacy	76836
Stafford	77477
Stagecoach	77355
Stage Coach Farms	77355
Stage Coach Hills	78255
Stairtown	78648
Staley	77359
Stamford	79553
Stamps	75644
Stanfield	76365
Stanger Springs	75754
Stanton	79782
Staples	78670
Star	76880
Star Harbor	75148
Star Route	79346
Starrville	75792
Startzville	78130
Steeltown (Part of Groves)	77619
Steep Hollow	77801
Stellar	78949
Stephen F. Austin University (Part of Nacogdoches)	75962
Stephenville	76401
Sterley	79241
Sterling City	76951
Sterlings Island	77367

	ZIP
Sterrett	75165
Stewards Mill	75840
Stewart	75691
Stewart Heights (Part of Baytown)	77520
Stieren	78632
Stilson	77535
Stinnett	79083
Stith	79536
Stockard	75751
Stockdale	78160
Stockman	75975
Stock Yards (Part of Fort Worth)	76106
Stoneburg	76230
Stoneham	77868
Stonewall	78671
Stonewall Mall (Part of Corpus Christi)	78410
Stony	76259
Stout	75494
Stowell	77661
Stranger	76653
Stratford	79084
Stratton	77954
Stratton Ridge	77531
Strawn	76475
Streetman	75859
Strickland	75968
String Prairie	78953
Structure	78621
Stuart Place	78550
Study Butte	79852
Stumptown	75931
Sturdivant	76067
Sturgeon	76273
Styx	75143
Sublett (Part of Arlington)	76063
Sublime	77986
Sudan	79371
Suffolk	75644
Sugar Land	77478-79
	77487
For specific Sugar Land Zip Codes call (713) 494-2042, or your local postmaster.	
Sugar Valley	77480
Sullivan City	78595
Sulphur Bluff	75481
Sulphur Springs (Angelina County)	75980
Sulphur Springs (Hopkins County)	75482-83
For specific Sulphur Springs Zip Codes call (903) 885-5215, or your local postmaster.	
Sulphur Springs (Rusk County)	75760
Summerall	75147
Summerfield (Castro County)	79085
Summerfield (Upshur County)	75644
Summer Hill	75751
Summit Heights (Part of El Paso)	79930*
	79931†
Sumner	75486
Sun (Part of Denison)	75020
Sundown	79372
Sunnyside (Castro County)	79027
Sunny Side (Waller County)	77445
Sunnyslope (Part of Texarkana)	75501
Sunnyvale	75149
Sunray	79086
Sunrise (El Paso County)	79904
Sunrise (Falls County)	76661
Sunrise Acres (Part of El Paso)	79904
Sunrise Beach	78643
Sunrise Mall (Cameron County)	78521
Sunrise Mall (Nueces County)	78412
Sunset (Lubbock County)	79416
Sunset (Montague County)	76270
Sunset Mall (Part of San Angelo)	76904
Sunset Marketown (Part of Amarillo)	79102
Sunset Ridge	77301
Sunset Valley	78745
Sunshine Hill	76360
Sun Valley (El Paso County)	79924
Sun Valley (Lamar County)	75462
Surf Oaks (Part of Seabrook)	77586
Surfside Beach	77541
Sutherland Springs	78161
Swamp City	75647
Swan	75706

	ZIP
Swan Lagoon (Part of Nassau Bay)	77058
Swanson Hill	75801
Sweeny	77480
Sweeny Switch	78368
Sweet Home (Guadalupe County)	78155
Sweet Home (Lavaca County)	77987
Sweetwater (Comanche County)	76442
Sweetwater (Nolan County)	79556
Swenson	79502
Swift	75961
Swiss Alp	78956
Swiss Village	78611
Sycamore	75932
Sylvan	75462
Sylvan Beach (Part of La Porte)	77571
Sylvester	79560
Tabor	77801
Tacoma	75633
Tadmor	75847
Taft	78390
Taft Southwest	78390
Tahoka	79373
Talco	75487
Tall Pines	75630
Talpa	76882
Talty	75160
Tamega	78605
Tamina	77302
Tandy Center (Part of Fort Worth)	76102
Tanglewood	78947
Tanglewood Forest	78748
Tanglewood Island	76424
Tanglewood Manor	77357
Tankersly	76901
Tarkington Acres	77327
Tarkington Prairie	77327
Tarleton (Part of Stephenville)	76402
Tarpley	78883
Tarrant (Part of Fort Worth)	76039
Tarzan	79783
Tatum	75691
Tavener	77435
Taylor	76574
Taylor Lake Village	77586
Taylorsville	78662
Taylor Town	75462
Taylorville	75452
Teague	75860
Teaselville	75757
Tecula	75766
Tehuacana	76686
Telegraph	76883
Telephone	75488
Telferner	77988
Telico	75119
Tell	79259
Temple	76501-05
For specific Temple Zip Codes call (817) 773-0792, or your local postmaster.	
Temple Mall (Part of Temple)	76502
Temple Springs	75951
Tenaha	75974
Tennessee	75975
Tennessee Colony	75861
Tennyson	76953
Terlingua	79852
Terrell	75160
Terrell Hills	78209
Terrell Station	79781
Terrell Wells (Part of San Antonio)	78221
Terrys Chapel	76570
Terryville	77995
Texarkana	75501-04
For specific Texarkana Zip Codes call (903) 838-9537, or your local postmaster.	
Texas Christian University (Part of Fort Worth)	76129
Texas City	77590-92
For specific Texas City Zip Codes call (409) 948-2591, or your local postmaster.	
Texas City Junction (Part of Hitchcock)	77563
Texas City Junction (Part of Texas City)	77590
Texas Lutheran (Part of Seguin)	78155
Texas Womans University (Part of Denton)	76204
Texhoma	73949
Texline	79087

	ZIP
Texon	76932
Thalia	79227
Thayer	78570
The Bluffs (Part of San Angelo)	76901
The Colony	75056
Thedford	75771
The Grove	76576
The Heights (Part of Alvin)	77511
The Homestead	78736
The Knobbs	78650
Thelma (Bexar County)	78221
Thelma (Limestone County)	76642
The Meadows (Part of Meadows)	77477
The Oaks	78130
Theon	76537
Thermo	75482
The Shores (Part of Amarillo)	79110
The Woodlands	77380
The Y	75551
Thicket	77374
Thomas	75644
Thomas Manor (Part of El Paso)	79915
Thomaston	77989
Thompson	77040
Thompson Heights	75020
Thompsons	77481
Thompsonville	78959
Thornberry	76306
Thorndale	76577
Thornton	76687
Thorntonville	79756
Thorp Spring	76048
Thousand Oaks (Part of San Antonio)	78270
Thrall	76578
Three Leagues	79331
Three Points	78660
Three Rivers	78071
Three Way	76401
Thrifty	76801
Throckmorton	76483
Thurber	76463
Tidwell	75401
Tidwell Prairie	76629
Tierra Linda Ranch	78028
Tigertown	75446
Tiki Island	77554
Tilden	78072
Tilmon	78616
Timber Cove (Part of Taylor Lake Village)	77586
Timberlake	77429
Timberlake Acres	77365
Timber Lakes Estates	77380
Timber Ridge (Bexar County)	78251
Timber Ridge (Montgomery County)	77380
Timberwood Park	78258
	78260
For specific Timberwood Park Zip Codes call (512) 657-8302, or your local postmaster.	
Timothy	75105
Timpson	75975
Tin Top	76086
Tioga	76271
Tira	75482
Tivoli	77990
Tivydale	78624
Tobe Hahn (Part of Beaumont)	77706
Toco	75421
Tod (Part of Seabrook)	77586
Todd City	75801
Todd Mission	77363
Togo	78957
Tokio	79376
Tolar	76476
Tolbert	76384
Toledo Village (Newton County)	75932
Toledo Village (Sabine County)	75948
Tolosa	75143
Tomball	77375*
	77377†
Tom Bean	75489
Tonkowon Country	78628
Tool	75143
Topsey	76522
Tornillo	79853
Tours	76691
Tow	78672
Town and Country Center (Part of Houston)	77024
Town Bluff	75979

	ZIP
Town East Mall (Part of Mesquite)	75149
Town Oaks (Part of Marshall)	75670
Town Plaza (Part of Victoria)	77901
Town West	77478
Toyah	79785
Toyahvale	79786
Tracy	76567
Tradewinds	75143
Trammells	77045
Travis	76656
Travis Peak	78654
Trawick	75961
Trent	79561
Trenton	75490
Trevat	75845
Tri Cities	75751
Trickham	76878
Tri-Lake Estates	77356
Trimmier Friendship	76542
Trinidad	75163
Trinity	75862
Trinity Park	75098
Trophy Club	76262
Tropical Acres	77904
Troup	75789
Trout Creek	75933
Troy	76579
Truby	79525
Truce	76230
Trumbull	75125
Truscott	79260
Tucker	75801
Tuleta	78162
Tulia	79088
Tulip	75447
Tulsita	78119
Tundra	75103
Tunis	77836
Tupelo	75155
Turkey	79261
Turkey Creek (Part of Copperas Cove)	76522
Turlington	75840
Turnersville	76528
Turnertown	75689
Turney	75766
Turtle Bayou	77514
Tuscola	79562
Tuttle Addition	77488
Tuxedo	79553
Twine Cedar Retreat	75948
Twin Shores	77378
Twin Valley Terrace	78073
Twitty	79079
Tye	79563
Tyler	75701-13

For specific Tyler Zip Codes call (903) 595-8621, or your local postmaster.

	ZIP
Tynan	78391
Type	78621
Uhland	78640
Umbarger	79091
Uncertain	75661
Union (Brazos County)	77801
Union (Franklin County)	75478
Union (Lubbock County)	79364
Union (Scurry County)	79549
Union (Terry County)	79316
Union (Wilson County)	78140
Union Academy	75801
Union Bluff	76645
Union Bower (Part of Irving)	75060
Union Center	76471
Union Grove (Bell County)	76513
Union Grove (Cherokee County)	75766
Union Grove (Upshur County)	75647
Union High	76639
Union Hill (Bosque County)	76652
Union Hill (Henderson County)	75756
Union Hill (Upshur County)	75644
Union Springs	75961
Union Valley	75189
Unity	75486
Universal City	78148
University (Part of Austin)	78712
University (Part of Dallas)	75205-06
	75372

For specific University Zip Codes call (214) 739-3331, or your local postmaster.

	ZIP
University of Dallas (Part of Irving)	75061
University of Texas at El Paso (Part of El Paso)	79902

	ZIP
University Park (Bexar County)	78228
University Park (Dallas County)	75205
University Park (Wichita County)	76308
University Place (Part of Nacogdoches)	75961
Upper Meyersville	78164
Upshaw	75943
Upton	78957
Urbana	77371
Utility (Part of San Antonio)	78219
Utley	78602
Utopia	78884
Uvalde	78801*
	78802†
Valdasta	75424
Valentine	79854
Valera	76884
Valle de Oro	79010
Valle Vista Mall (Part of Harlingen)	78550
Valleycreek	75452
Valley Hi (Part of San Antonio)	78227
Valley Lodge (Part of Simonton)	77476
Valley Mills	76689
Valley Spring	76885
Valley View (Comal County)	78130
Valley View (Cooke County)	76272
Valley View (McLennan County)	76701
Valley View (Mitchell County)	79512
Valley View (Runnels County)	76821
Valley View (Upshur County)	75644
Valley View (Wichita County)	76367
Valley View Center (Part of Dallas)	75244
Valley Wells	78830
Val Verde	76518
Val Verde Park Estates	78840
Van	75790
Van Alstyne	75495
Vance	78828
Vancourt	76955
Vandalia	75426
Vanderbilt	77991
Vanderpool	78885
Vandyke	76442
Vanetia	77865
Van Horn	79855
Van Vleck	77482
Varisco	77801
Vasco	75450
Vashti	76228
Vattmannville	78379
Vaughan	76645
Vealmoor	79720
Veal Station	76082
Vedas Camp	79521
Vega	79092
Venable Village	76544
Ventura	77355
Venus	76084
Vera	76383
Verbena	79356
Verdi	78064
Verhalen	79772
Verhelle	77954
Veribest	76886
Vernon	76384*
	76385†
Verona	75424
Veterans Administration (Part of Waco)	76711
Viboras	78361
Vick	76937
Vickery (Part of Dallas)	75231
Victoria (Victoria County)	77901-05

For specific Victoria Zip Codes call (512) 575-2363, or your local postmaster.

	ZIP
Victoria (Limestone County)	76664
Victory City	75561
Victory Gardens	77630
Vidauri	78377
Vidor	77662*
	77670†
	77964
Vienna	79606
View	75460
Viewpoint	79088
Vigo Park	79088
Vilas	76534
Villa Cavazos	78520
Village (Part of Highland Park)	75205

	ZIP
Village Mills	77663
Village Shores	78130
Village Station (Part of Midland)	79704
Villa Nueva	78520
Villareales	78582
Vincent	79511
Vineyard	76458
Vinton	79821
Violet	78380
Virginia Point	77554
Vista del Sol (Part of El Paso)	79935
Vistula	75851
Voca	76887
Volente	78641
Von Ormy	78073
Voss	76888
Votaw	77376
Voth (Part of Beaumont)	77709
Vsetin	77964
Waco	76701-98

For specific Waco Zip Codes call (817) 757-6585, or your local postmaster.

	ZIP
Wade	78372
Wadsworth	77483
Waelder	78959
Wainwright (Part of San Antonio)	78208
Wainwright Heights	76544
Waka	79093
Wake	79243
Wakefield	75939
Wake Village	75501
Walburg	78673
Waldeck	78946
Walden	77356
Walden Place	77093
Walden Woods (Part of Houston)	77012
Waldrip	76852
Walhalla	78954
Walkers Mill	75650
Walker Village	76544
Wall	76957
Wallace	75103
Wallace Chapel	75686
Waller	77484
Wallis	77485
Wallisville	77597
Walnut Bend	76273
Walnut Creek	77355
Walnut Forest	78753
Walnut Grove (Collin County)	75069
Walnut Grove (Smith County)	75703
Walnut Hill (Part of Dallas)	75220
Walnut Hills	77303
Walnut Springs (Bosque County)	76690
Walnut Springs (Montgomery County)	77355
Walston Springs	75801
Walton (Cass County)	71082
Walton (Van Zandt County)	75751
Wamba	75503
Waneta	75844
Waples	76048
Warda	78960
Ward Prairie	75840
Wards Creek	75574
Waring	78074
Warren	77664
Warren City	75647
Warrenton	78961
Warsaw	75142
Washburn	79019
Washington	77880
Waskom	75692
Wastella	79545
Watauga	76148
Water Front Park	78130
Waterloo (Grayson County)	75020
Waterloo (Williamson County)	76574
Waterman	75935
Waters Bluff	75792
Water Valley	76958
Waterwood (San Jacinto County)	77359
Waterwood (Walker County)	77340
Watkins	75103
Watson	76550
Watsonville	76063
Watt	76664
Waxahachie	75165
Wayside	79094
Wealthy	77871

	ZIP
Weatherford	76086-87

For specific Weatherford Zip
Codes call (817) 594-3072, or
your local postmaster.

	ZIP
Weaver	75478
Webberville	78653
Webbville	76828
Webster (Harris County)	77598
Webster (Wood County)	75494
Weches	75844
Wedgewood (Part of Fort Worth)	76163
Weedhaven	77979
Weeping Mary	75925
Weesatche	77993
Weimar	78962
Weinert	76388
Weir	78674
Weirville	75482
Welch	79377
Welch Store	75973
Welcome	78944
Weldon	75851
Welfare	78006
Wellborn	77881
Wellington	79095
Wellman	79378
Wells (Cherokee County)	75976
Wells (Lynn County)	79351
Wells Branch	78728
	78753

For specific Wells Branch Zip
Codes call (915) 622-4566, or
your local postmaster.

	ZIP
Wellswood	75929
Wentworth	75103
Weser	77963
Weslaco	78596*
	78599†
Weslayan (Part of Houston)	77005
Wesley	77833
Wesley Grove	77831
West	76691
West Austin (Part of Austin)	78703
West Baytown (Part of Baytown)	77520
West Bluff	77630
Westbrook	79565
West Camp	79325
Westchase (Part of Houston)	77042
Westchester (Part of Grand Prairie)	75054
Westcliff	76513
West Cliff Park (Part of Amarillo)	79124
West Columbia	77486
West Delta	75448
Western Hills (Part of Copperas Cove)	76522
Western Plaza Mall (Part of Amarillo)	79101
Westfield (Harris County)	77090
Westfield (Wharton County)	77437
Westfield Estates	77093
West Galveston (Part of Jamaica Beach)	77551
Westgate (Harris County)	77429
Westgate (Tom Green County)	76901
Westgate Mall (Potter County)	79121
Westgate Mall (Travis County)	78704
Westgate Towne Centre (Part of Abilene)	79605
Westhaven	78130
Westheimer (Part of Houston)	77042
Westhill Addition	77437
Westhoff	77994
West Lake (Jasper County)	75951
Westlake (Tarrant County)	76248
Westlake (Travis County)	78746
West Lake Hills	78746
Westlakes (Part of San Antonio)	78245
Westlakes Mercado (Part of San Antonio)	78227
Westlawn	77630
Westminster	75485
West Mountain	75647
West Odessa	79764
	79769

For specific West Odessa Zip
Codes call (915) 381-6707, or
your local postmaster.

	ZIP
Weston	75097
West Orange	77630
Westover	76380
Westover Hills	76107
West Payne	77437

	ZIP
Westphalia	76656
West Point (Fayette County)	78963
West Point (Lynn County)	79373
West Sinton	78370
West Tawakoni	75474
West Texas State University (Part of Canyon)	79016
West University Place	77005
West Vernon (Part of Vernon)	76384
Westview (Part of Waco)	76710
Westville	75862
West Waco (Part of Waco)	76710
Westway	79835
Westwood	75951
Westwood Mall (Part of Houston)	77036
Westworth Village	76114
Wetmore (Part of San Antonio)	78247
Wetsel	75069
Wexford Park	77662
Whaley	75570
Wharton	77488
Whatley	75657
Wheatland	76116
Wheeler	79096
Wheeler Springs	75835
Wheelock	77882
Whispering Oaks (Bexar County)	78230
Whispering Oaks (Rains County)	75453
Whispering Pines (Montgomery County)	77302
Whispering Pines (Walker County)	77358
Whispering Winds	78264
Whisperwood (Part of Lubbock)	79416
White City (San Augustine County)	75929
White City (Wilbarger County)	76384
White Deer	79097
Whiteface	79379
Whiteflat	79234
White Hall (Bell County)	76528
White Hall (Coryell County)	76528
White Hall (Grimes County)	77868
Whitehall (Kaufman County)	75147
Whitehouse	75791
Whiteland	76858
White Mound	75090
White Oak (Gregg County)	75693
White Oak (Montgomery County)	77365
White Oak (Morris County)	75571
White Oak (Titus County)	75455
White Oak Valley Estates	77301
White Rock (Dallas County)	75218
White Rock (Grayson County)	75491
White Rock (Hunt County)	75423
White Rock (Red River County)	75426
White Rock (Robertson County)	76629
White Rock (San Augustine County)	75972
Whitesboro	76273
White Settlement	76108
Whitestar	79234
White Stone (Part of Cedar Park)	78641
Whitetail	78628
Whiteway	76538
Whitewright	75491
Whitharral	79380
Whitman	77833
Whitney	76692
Whitsett	78075
Whitt	76490
Whitton	75103
Whon	76889
Wichita Falls	76301-11

For specific Wichita Falls Zip
Codes call (817) 766-4188, or
your local postmaster.

	ZIP
Wichita Valley Farms	76301
Wickett	79788
Wiedeville	77833
Wieland	75402
Wiergate	75977
Wiggins	76691
Wigginsville	77301
Wilcox	77879
Wildcat (Part of Plano)	75023
Wilderville	76570
Wild Horse	79855
Wild Hurst	75925
Wildorado	79098

	ZIP
Wild Peach Village	77422
Wildwood (Hardin County)	77663
Wildwood (Walker County)	77367
Wilford Hall U.S.A.F. Hospital (Part of San Antonio)	78236
Wilkins	75755
Wilkinson	75455
Willacy County Housing Authority	78580
Willamar	78580
William Beaumont Army Medical Center	79920
William Penn	77833
William Rice (Part of Houston)	77005
Williams	76471
Williamsburg (Lamar County)	75460
Williamsburg (Lavaca County)	77964
William Spear Addition	75704
Willis	77378
Willow City	78675
Willow Grove (McLennan County)	76712
Willow Grove (Shelby County)	75954
Willow Park	76086
Willow Place (Part of Houston)	77070
Willow Point	76426
Willow Springs (Fayette County)	78940
Willow Springs (Rains County)	75440
Willow Springs (San Jacinto County)	77331
Wills Point	75169
Wilmer	75172
Wilmeth	79567
Wilson (Falls County)	76519
Wilson (Lynn County)	79381
Wilson Lake	77351
Wimberley	78676
Winchell	76827
Winchester	78964
Windcrest	78239
Windcrest Mall (Part of San Antonio)	78221
Windemere (Burnet County)	78669
Windemere (Travis County)	78660
Windom	75492
Windsor Park Mall (Part of San Antonio)	78218
Windthorst	76389
Winedale	77835
Winfield	75493
Winfree (Chambers County)	77535
Winfree (Orange County)	77630
Wingate	79566
Wink	79789
Winkler	75859
Winnie	77665
Winningkoff (Part of Lucas)	75069
Winnsboro	75494
Winona	75792
Winter Haven	78839
Winter Hill	75943
Winters	79567
Winwood Mall (Part of Odessa)	79762
Witting	77975
Wixon Valley	77808
Wizard Wells	76458
Woden	75978
Wolfe City	75496
Wolfforth	79382
Womack	76634
Woodbine	76240
Woodbranch	77357
Woodbury	76645
Wood-Canyon Waters	75147
Woodcreek	78676
Woodcreek North	78676
Woodcrest	77301
Woodhaven Estates	77304
Wood Hollow	77365
Woodlake (Bexar County)	78244
Woodlake (Trinity County)	75865
Woodlake (Grayson County)	75020
Woodland (Bell County)	76513
Woodland (Red River County)	75436
Woodland Estates	75948
Woodland Hills (Henderson County)	75143
Woodland Hills (Hill County)	76692
Woodland Lakes	77355
Woodland Shores	75630
Woodlawn (Angelina County)	75904

	ZIP		ZIP		ZIP
Woodlawn (Harrison County)	75694	World Trade Center (Part of Dallas)	75207	Yarrelton	76518
Woodlawn Lakes	77355	Wortham	76693	Yaupon Cove	77351
Woodley	75670	Worthing	77964	Yellowpine	75948
Woodloch	77301	Wright City	75684	Yoakum	77995
Woodridge Park	78264	Wrightsboro	78677	Yorktown	78164
Woodrow (Fort Bend County)	77430	Wyldwood	78612	Young	75840
Woodrow (Lubbock County)	79401	Wylie (Collin County)	75098	Youngsport	76542
Woods	75974	Wylie (Franklin County)	75494	Yowell	75428
Woodsboro	78393	Wylie (Taylor County)	79606	Ysleta (Part of El Paso)	79907*
Woods of Shavano (Part of San Antonio)	78249	Wynne Unit	77340		79917†
Woodson	76491	Wynnewood Village (Part of Dallas)	75224	Zabcikville	76501
Wood Springs	75701	Wynnrock Estates	78737	Zapata	78076
Woodville	75979	Yancey	78886	Zavalla	75980
Woodway (McLennan County)	76710	Yantis	75497	Zephyr	76890
Woodway (Victoria County)	77904	Yarboro	77868	Zionsville	77833
Woody Acres	77365	Yarbrough Plaza (Part of El Paso)	79912	Zippville	78155
Woosley	75472	Yard	75861	Zorn	78666
				Zuehl	78124
				Zunkerville	78119
				Zybach	79011

	ZIP
Abraham	84635
Adamsville	84731
Alpine	84004
Alta	84092
Altamont	84001
Alton	84710
Altonah	84002
Amalga	84335
American Fork	84003
Aneth	84510
Angle	84712
Annabella	84711
Antimony	84712
Arcadia	84012
Arsenal (Part of Sunset)	84015
Aspen Acres	84055
Atwood (Part of Murray)	84107
Aurora	84620
Austin	84754
Avon	84328
Axtell	84621
Ballard	84066
Bauer	84071
Bear River City	84301
Beaver	84713
Beaverdam	84306
Belmont Heights (Part of Sandy)	84070
Benjamin	84660
Ben Lomond (Part of Ogden)	84404
Bennion	84118
	84123
For specific Bennion Zip Codes call (801) 974-2200, or your local postmaster.	
Benson	84335
Beryl	84714
Beryl Junction	84714
Bicknell	84715
Big Water	84741
Bingham Canyon	84006
Birdseye	84629
Blanding	84511
Bloomington	84770
Bluebell	84007
Bluff	84512
Bluffdale	84065
Bonanza	84008
Boneta	84051
Bonnie (Part of Orem)	84057
Bothwell	84337
Boulder	84716
Bountiful	84010*
	84011†
Bowery Haven	84701
Brendel	84540
Brian Head	84719
Bridgeland	84012
Brigham City	84302
Brighton	84121
Brooklyn	84754
Bryce	84764
Bryce Canyon	84717
Bullfrog	84533
Burbank	84751
Burmester	84029
Burrville	84701
Bushnell (Part of Brigham City)	84302
Cache Junction	84304
Cache Valley Mall (Part of Logan)	84321
Caineville	84775
Callao	84034
Call Fort	84302
Cannonville	84718
Canyon Rim	84106
Carbonville	84501
Castle Dale	84513
Castleton	84532
Castle Valley	84532
Cedar City	84720*
	84721†
Cedar Hills	84062
Cedar Valley	84013
Cedarview	84066
Center Creek	84032
Centerfield	84622
Centerville	84014
Central (Sevier County)	84754
Central (Washington County)	84722
Charleston	84032
Chester	84623
Circleville	84723
Cisco	84515
Clarkston	84305
Clawson	84516
Clear Creek (Box Elder County)	83342

	ZIP
Clear Creek (Carbon County)	84526
Clearfield	84014-16
For specific Clearfield Zip Codes call (801) 773-0205, or your local postmaster.	
Cleveland	84518
Clinton	84015
Clover	84069
Clyde (Part of Orem)	84057
Coalville	84017
College Ward	84321
Collinston	84306
Columbia	84520
Columbia Junction (Part of East Carbon)	84520
Copperton	84006
Corinne	84307
Cornish	84308
Cottonwood	84121
Cottonwood Heights	84121
Cottonwood Mall	84112
Cottonwood West	84117
	84121
For specific Cottonwood West Zip Codes call (801) 974-2200, or your local postmaster.	
Cove	84320
Crescent (Part of Sandy)	84070
Croydon	84018
Cushing (Part of Midvale)	84047
Dammeron Valley	84783
Daniel	84032
Defas Park	84031
Delta	84624
Deseret	84624
Devils Slide	84050
Deweyville	84309
Downtown (Part of Salt Lake City)	84101
Draper	84020
Dry Fork	84078
Duchesne	84021
Duck Creek Village	84762
Dugway	84022
Dugway Proving Ground	84022
Dutch John	84023
East Bay (Part of Provo)	84605
East Carbon	84520
Eastland	84535
East Midvale	84047
East Millcreek	84117
East Portal	84032
Eastwood Hills	84106
Echo	84024
Eden	84310
Elberta	84626
Elgin	84525
Elk Ridge	84660
Elmo	84521
Elsinore	84724
Elwood	84337
Emery	84522
Emory	84024
Enoch	84720
Enterprise (Morgan County)	84050
Enterprise (Washington County)	84725
Ephraim	84627
Erda	84074
Escalante	84726
Esk Dale	84728
Etna	84313
Eureka	84628
Fairfield	84013
Fairgrounds (Part of Salt Lake City)	84116
Fairview	84629
Farmington	84025
Farr West	84404
Fashion Place (Part of Murray)	84107
Faust	84080
Fayette	84630
Ferron	84523
Fielding	84311
Fillmore	84631
Fish Lake	84701
Flowell	84631
Foothill (Part of Salt Lake City)	84108
Fort Duchesne	84026
Fountain Green	84632
Francis	84036
Freedom	84646
Freeport Center (Part of Clearfield)	84016
Fremont	84747
Fruita	84775
Fruit Heights	84037
Fruitland	84027
Gandy	84728

	ZIP
Garden City	84028
Garland	84312
Garrison	84728
Genola	84655
Glendale	84729
Glenwood	84730
Goshen	84633
Goshute Indian Reservation	84034
Gouldings Trading Post	86033
Grand Vu	84532
Granger (Part of West Valley City)	84119
Granite	84092
Grantsville	84029
Greendale	84023
Green Lake	84023
Green River	84525
Greenville	84731
Greenwich	84732
Grouse Creek	84313
Grover	84773
Gunlock	84733
Gunnison	84634
Gusher	84030
Hailstone	84032
Halchita	84531
Halls Crossing	84533
Hamilton Fort	84720
Hanksville	84734
Hanna	84031
Hardy (Part of Lindon)	84062
Harrisburg Junction	84770
Harrisville	84404
Hatch	84735
Hatton	84637
Hayden	84053
Heber City	84032
Helper	84526
Henefer	84033
Henrieville	84736
Herriman	84065
Hiawatha	84527
Hidden Lake	84055
Highland	84003
Highlands	84050
Hildale	84784
Hill Air Force Base	84056
Hinckley	84635
Hite	84533
Holden	84636
Holiday Park	84055
Holladay	84117
Holladay-Cottonwood	84106
	84121
For specific Holladay-Cottonwood Zip Codes call (801) 974-2200, or your local postmaster.	
Honeyville	84314
Hooper	84315
Hoovers	84750
Howell	84316
Hoytsville	84017
Hunter (Part of West Valley City)	84120
Huntington	84528
Huntsville	84317
Hurricane	84737
Hyde Park	84318
Hyrum	84319
Ibapah	84034
Indianola	84629
Ioka	84066
Ivins	84738
Jensen	84035
Jerusalem	84646
Joseph	84739
Junction	84740
Kamas	84036
Kanab	84741
Kanarraville	84742
Kanosh	84637
Kaysville	84037
Kearns	84118
Keetley	84032
Kelton	84336
Kenilworth	84529
Kimball Junction	84060
Kingston	84743
Koosharem	84744
Lake Point	84074
Lake Powell	84533
Lake Shore	84601
Lakeside Resort	84701
Laketown	84038
Lakeview	84601
Lapoint	84039
Lark	84065
La Sal	84530
La Sal Junction	84530
La Verkin	84745
Lawrence	84528

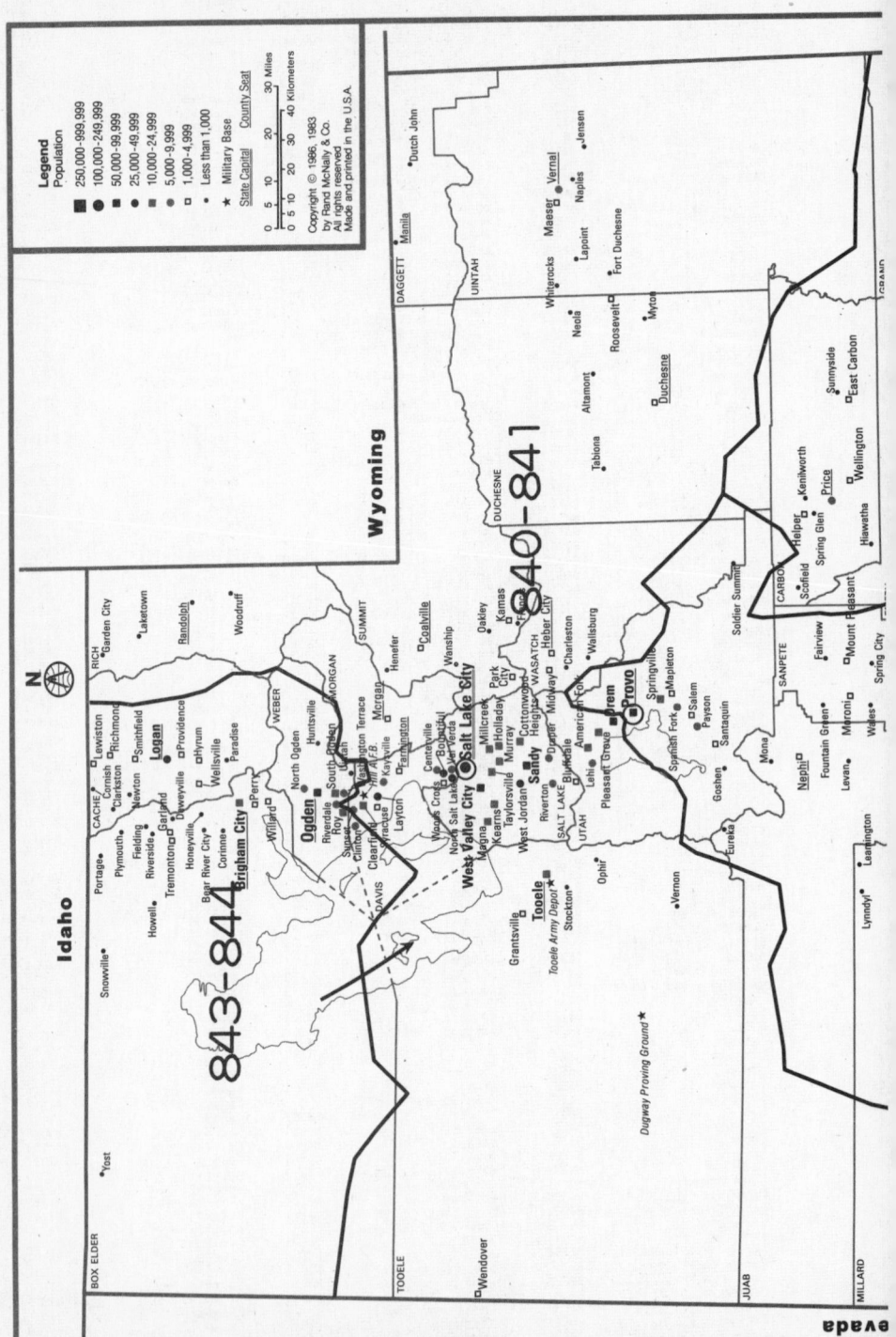

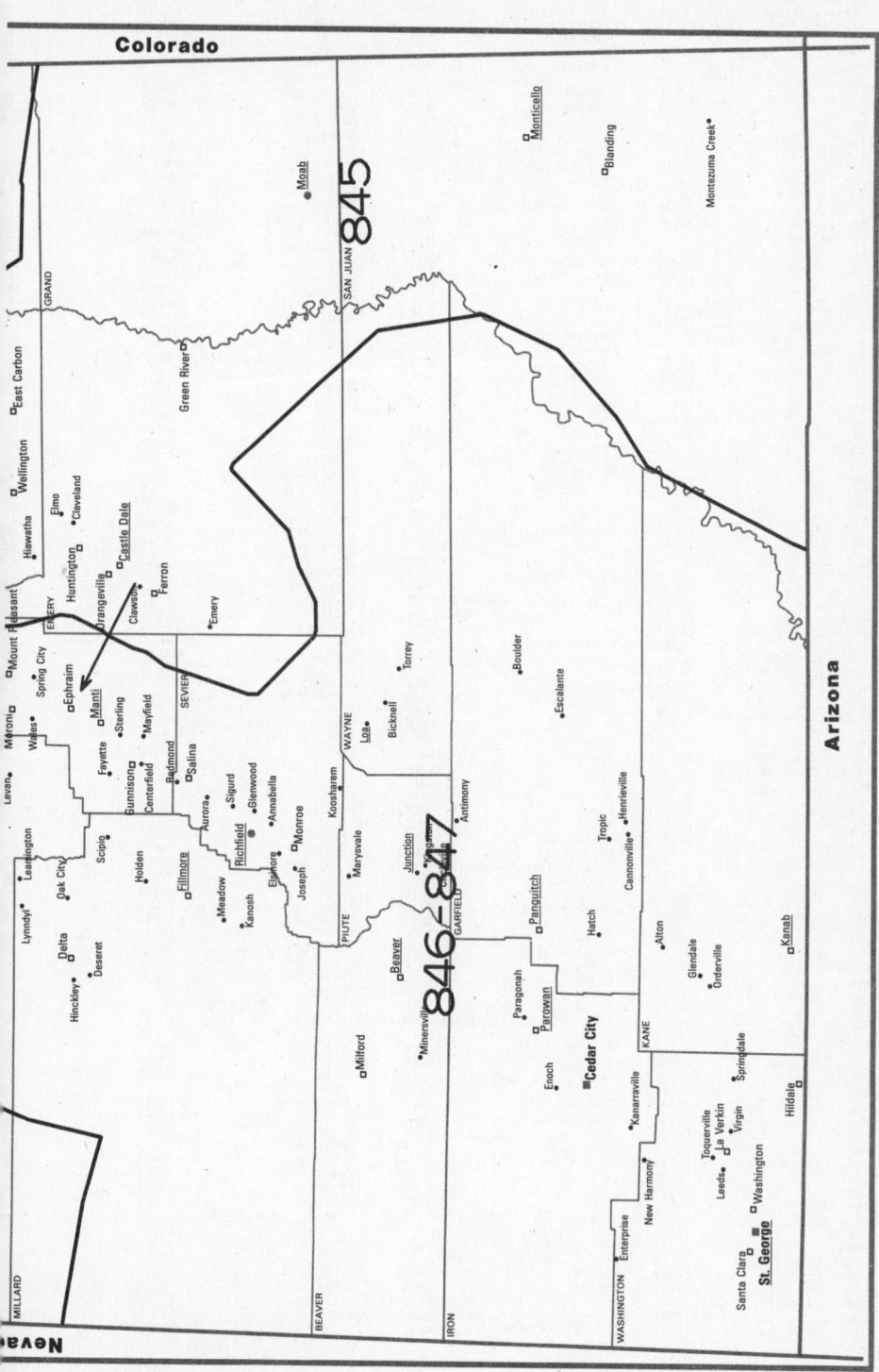

* Area Zip Code   † Post Office Boxes

	ZIP		ZIP		ZIP
Vivian Park	84604	West Jordan	84084	Wildwood	84604
Wales	84667		84088	Willard	84340
Wallsburg	84082	For specific West Jordan Zip		Wilson	84401
Wanship	84017	Codes call (801) 255-4022, or		Woodland	84036
Warren	84404	your local postmaster.		Woodland Hills	84653
Washington	84780	West Point	84015	Woodruff	84086
Washington Terrace	84403	West Valley City	84120	Woods Cross	84087
Wellington	84542	West Warren	84404	Yost	83342
Wellsville	84339	West Weber	84401	ZCMI Center (Part of Salt	
Wendover	84083	Wheelon	84306	Lake City)	84111
West Bountiful	84087	White City	84070	Zion National Park	84767
West Haven	84315	Whiterocks	84085		

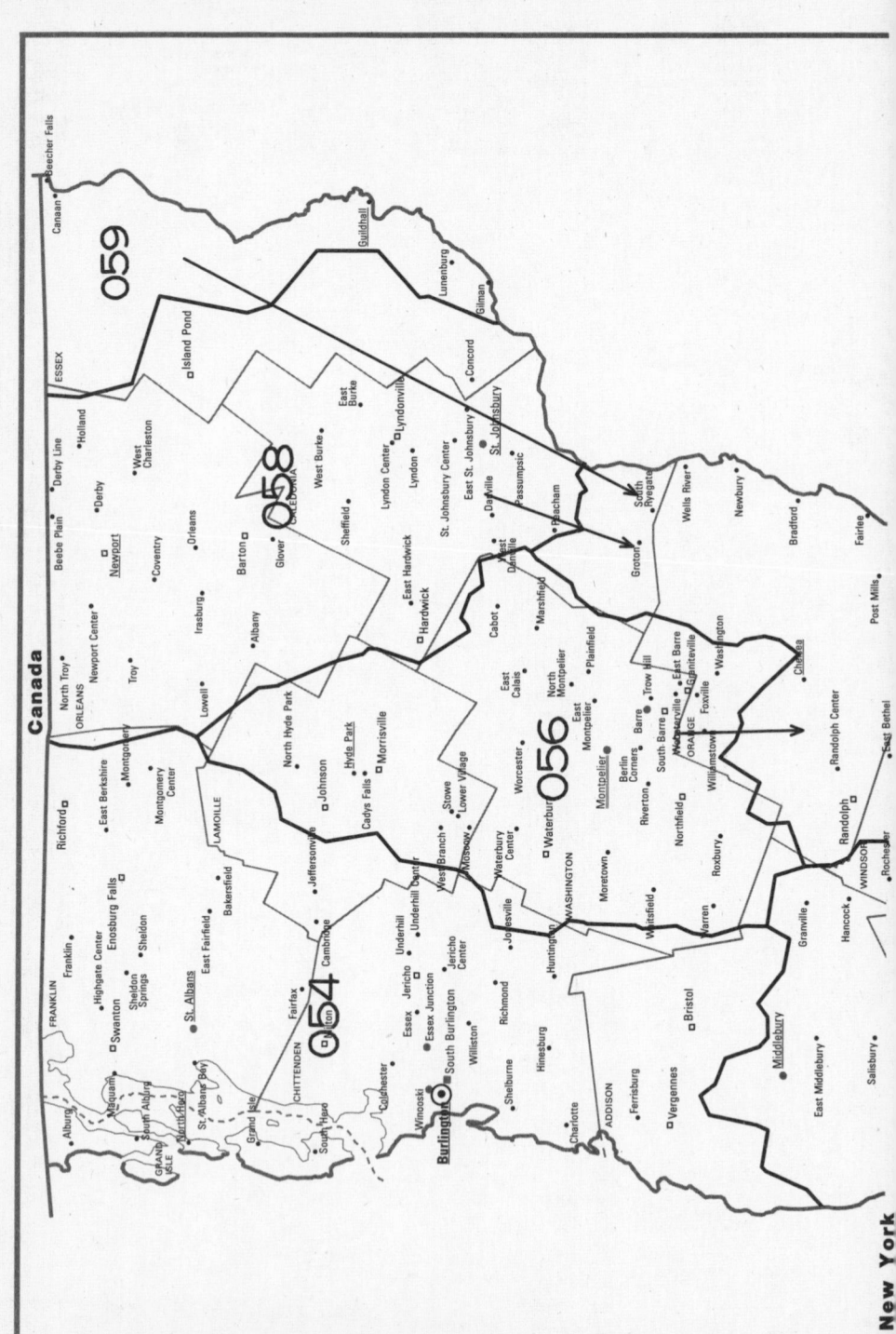

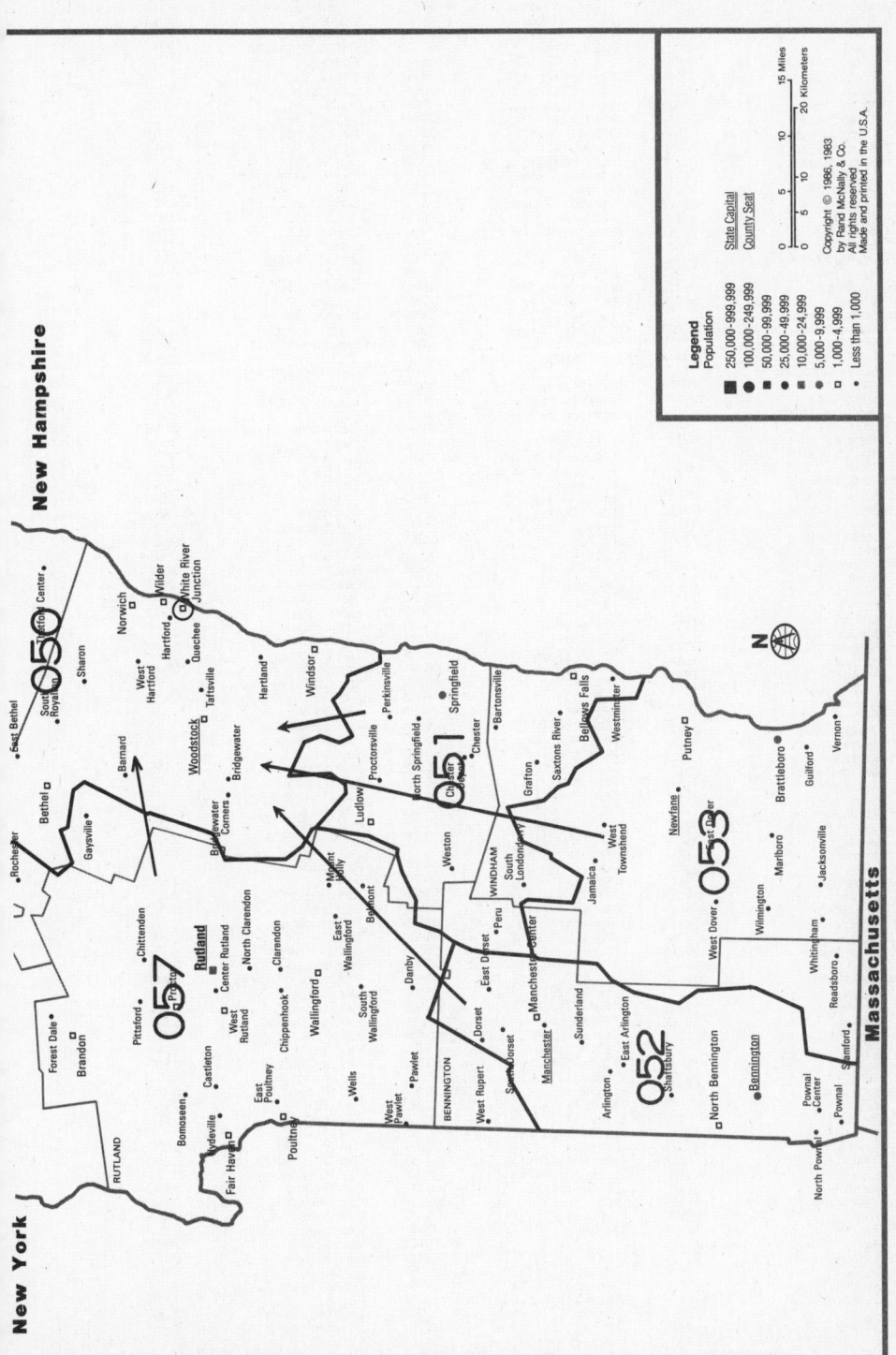

	ZIP		ZIP		ZIP
Abnaki	05474	Bridgewater (Town)	05034	Coventry	05825
Adamant	05640	Bridgewater Center	05035	Coventry (Town)	05825
Addison	05491	Bridgewater Corners	05035	Craftsbury	05826
Addison (Town)	05491	Bridport	05734	Craftsbury (Town)	05826
Albany	05820	Bridport (Town)	05734	Craftsbury Common	05827
Albany (Town)	05820	Brighton (Town)	05846	Cream Hill	05734
Albany Center	05845	Brimstone Corner	05083	Crystal Beach	05732
Alburg	05440	Brimstone Corners	05761	Cuttingsville	05738
Alburg (Town)	05440	Bristol	05443	Danby	05739
Alburg Center	05440	Bristol (Town)	05443	Danby (Town)	05739
Alburg Springs	05440	Brockways Mills	05143	Danby Corners	05739
Alfrecha	05759	Brookfield	05036	Danville	05828
Alpine Village	05674	Brookfield (Town)	05036	Danville (Town)	05828
Ames Hill	05344	Brookfield Center	05036	Danville Center	05828
Amsden	05151	Brookline (Town)	05345	Derby	05829
Andover (Town)	05143	Brookside (Chittenden		Derby (Town)	05829
Arlington	05250	County)	05494	Derby Line	05830
Arlington (Town)	05250	Brookside (Windham		Deweys Mills	05059
Arlington (census		County)	05341	Dorset	05251
designated place)	05250	Brooksville	05753	Dorset (Town)	05251
Arnold Bay	05491	Brownington	05860	Dover	05341
Ascutney	05030	Brownington (Town)	05860	Dover (Town)	05341
Athens	05143	Brownington Center	05860	Downers	05151
Athens (Town)	05143	Brownsville	05037	Downingville	05443
Avalon Beach	05750	Brunswick (Town)	03590	Dows Crossing	05836
Averill	05901	Buck Hollow	05454	Dowsville	05660
Averill (Town)	05901	Buels (Town)	05487	Dummerston	05346
Avery's Gore (Town)	05903	Burke	05871	Dummerston (Town)	05346
Bailey's Mills	05062	Burke (Town)	05871	Duxbury	05676
Bakersfield	05441	Burke Mountain	05832	Duxbury (Town)	05676
Bakersfield (Town)	05441	Burlington	05401-02	Eagle Point	05855
Baltimore (Town)	05143		05405-06	East Albany	05845
Barnard	05031			East Alburg	05440
Barnard (Town)	05031	For specific Burlington Zip Codes		East Arlington	05252
Barnet	05821	call (802) 863-6033, or your local		East Barnard	05068
Barnet (Town)	05821	postmaster.		East Barre	05649
Barnet Center	05821	Burnham Hill	05843	East Berkshire	05447
Barnumtown	05472	Burnham Hollow	05757	East Bethel	05032
Barre	05641	Butlers Corners	05452	East Braintree	05060
Barre (Town)	05678	Butternut Bend	05761	East Brookfield	05036
Barre Transfer (Part of		Button Bay	05491	East Burke	05832
Montpelier)	05602	Cabot	05647	East Cabot	05647
Barton	05822	Cabot (Town)	05647	East Calais	05650
Barton (Town)	05822	Cadys Falls	05661	East Cambridge	05464
Bartonsville	05143	Calais	05648	East Charleston	05833
Basin Harbor	05491	Calais (Town)	05648	East Charlotte	05445
Bayside	05404	Cambridge	05444	East Clarendon	05759
Beanville	05060	Cambridge (Town)	05444	East Concord	05906
Beaulieu's Corner	05459	Cambridge Junction	05464	East Corinth	05040
Beebe Plain	05823	Cambridgeport	05141	East Craftsbury	05826
Beecher Falls	05902	Canaan	05903	East Dorset	05253
Bellows Falls	05101	Canaan (Town)	05903	East Dover	05341
Belmont	05730	Castleton	05735	East Dummerston	05346
Belvidere (Town)	05492	Castleton (Town)	05735	East Enosburg	05450
Belvidere Center	05492	Cavendish	05142	East Fairfield	05448
Belvidere Corners	05492	Cavendish (Town)	05142	East Fletcher	05464
Belvidere Junction	05492	Cavendish Center	05142	East Franklin	05457
Bennington	05201	Cedar Beach	05445	East Granville	05669
Bennington (Town)	05201	Center Rutland	05736	East Hardwick	05836
Bennington College (Part of		Centerville (Lamoille County)	05655	East Haven	05837
North Bennington)	05201	Centerville (Windsor		East Haven (Town)	05837
Benson	05731	County)	05001	East Highgate	05459
Benson (Town)	05731	Champlain (Part of South		East Hubbardton	05735
Benson Landing	05743	Burlington)	05401	East Jamaica	05343
Berkshire	05447	Charleston (Town)	05872	East Johnson	05656
Berkshire (Town)	05450	Charlotte	05445	East Lyndon	05851
Berlin (Town)	05602	Charlotte (Town)	05445	East Middlebury	05740
Berlin Corners	05602	Checkerberry	05468	East Monkton	05443
Bethel	05032	Chelsea	05038	East Montpelier	05651
Bethel (Town)	05032	Chelsea (Town)	05038	East Montpelier (Town)	05651
Bethel Gilead	05060	Chelsea West Hill	05041	East Montpelier Center	05602
Binghamville	05444	Chester	05143	East Orange	05086
Birdland	05474	Chester (Town)	05143	East Peacham	05862
Bliss Pond	05640	Chester-Chester Depot	05143	East Pittsford	05701
Blissville	05764	Chester Depot	05144	East Poultney	05741
Bloomfield	03590	Chimney Corner	05446	East Putney	05346
Bloomfield (Town)	03590	Chimney Point	05491	East Randolph	05041
Blossoms Corners	05775	Chipman Lake	05739	East Richford	05476
Bolton	05676	Chipmans Point	05760	East Roxbury	05663
Bolton (Town)	05676	Chippenhook	05777	East Rupert	05761
Bolton Valley	05477	Chiselville	05250	East Ryegate	05042
Boltonville	05081	Chittenden	05737	East Sheldon	05450
Bomoseen	05732	Chittenden (Town)	05737	East Shoreham	05770
Bondville	05340	Clarendon	05759	East St. Johnsbury	05838
Bordoville	05450	Clarendon (Town)	05759	East Sutton Ridge	05867
Bowlsville	05742	Clarendon Springs	05777	East Thetford	05043
Bradford	05033	Cleveland Corner	05661	East Wallingford	05742
Bradford (Town)	05033	Cloverdale	05489	East Warren	05674
Bragg	05055	Colbyville	05676	Eden	05652
Braintree	05060	Colchester	05446*	Eden (Town)	05652
Braintree (Town)	05060		05449†	Eden Mills	05653
Braintree Hill	05060	Cold River	05738	Egypt	05448
Brandon	05733	Concord	05824	Elmore (Town)	05657
Brandon (Town)	05733	Concord (Town)	05824	Ely	05044
Brattleboro	05301-04	Concord Corner	05824	Enosburg (Town)	05450
	05351	Copperfield	05079	Enosburg Center	05450
For specific Brattleboro Zip Codes		Corinth	05039	Enosburg Falls	05450
call (802) 254-4110, or your local		Corinth (Town)	05039	Essex	05451
postmaster.		Corinth Center	05039	Essex (Town)	05451
Brattleboro Center	05301	Corinth Corners	05039	Essex Junction	05452*
Bread Loaf	05753	Cornwall	05753		05453†
Bridgewater	05034	Cornwall (Town)	05753		

* Area Zip Code   † Post Office Boxes

	ZIP		ZIP		ZIP
Ethan Allen Shopping Center (Part of Burlington)	05404	Highgate Springs	05460	Lyndon State College	05851
Evansville	05860	Hinesburg	05461	Lyndonville	05851
Fairfax	05454	Hinesburg (Town)	05461	McIndoe Falls	05050
Fairfax (Town)	05454	Hinesburg	05301	Mackville	05843
Fairfax Falls	05454	Holden	05763	Mad River Glen	05673
Fairfield	05455	Holland	05830	Maidstone (Town)	05905
Fairfield (Town)	05455	Holland (Town)	05830	Maidstone Lake	03590
Fairfield Station	05455	Hortonia	05760	Mallets Bay	05404
Fair Haven (Town)	05743	Hortonville	05758	Manchester (Town)	05254
Fair Haven	05743	Houghtonville	05146	Manchester	05254
Fairlee	05045	Hubbard Corner	05478	Manchester (Manchester Depot) (railroad station)	05255
Fairlee (Town)	05045	Hubbardton	05732		
Fays Corner	05477	Hubbardton (Town)	05732	Manchester Center	05255
Fayston (Town)	05660	Huntington	05462	Maple Dell	05156
Ferdinand (Town)	05905	Huntington (Town)	05462	Maquam	05488
Fernville	05733	Huntington Center	05462	Marlboro	05344
Ferrisburg	05456	Huntville	05454	Marlboro (Town)	05344
Ferrisburg (Town)	05456	Hutchins	05471	Marshfield	05658
Fieldsville	05089	Hyde Park	05655	Marshfield (Town)	05658
Fletcher	05444	Hyde Park (Town)	05655	Mary Meyer	05353
Fletcher (Town)	05444	Hydeville	05750	Mechanicsville	05461
Florence	05744	Indian Point (Part of Newport)	05855	Medburyville	05363
Fonda	05488			Melville	05478
Forest Dale	05745	Inwood	05821	Mendon	05701
Foxville	05654	Ira	05777	Mendon (Town)	05701
Franklin	05457	Ira (Town)	05777	Merrill Corner	05845
Franklin (Town)	05457	Irasburg	05845	Middlebury	05753
Freedleyville	05253	Irasburg (Town)	05845	Middlebury (Town)	05753
Gallup Mills	05858	Irasville	05673	Middlesex	05602
Garfield	05661	Island Pond	05846	Middlesex (Town)	05602
Gassetts	05143	Isle La Motte	05463	Middlesex Center	05602
Gaysville	05746	Isle La Motte (Town)	05463	Middletown	05143
Georgia	05454	Jacksonville	05342	Middletown Springs	05757
Georgia (Town)	05478	Jamaica	05343	Middletown Springs (Town)	05757
Georgia Center	05478	Jamaica (Town)	05343	Mile Point	05491
Georgia Plains	05468	Jay	05859	Miles Pond	05858
Gilman	05904	Jay (Town)	05859	Millbrook	05053
Glastenbury (Town)	05262	Jay Peak	05859	Mill Village (Orange County)	05079
Glover	05839	Jeffersonville	05464	Mill Village (Orleans County)	05827
Glover (Town)	05839	Jenneville	05089	Milton	05468
Goodrich Four Corners	05055	Jericho	05465	Milton (Town)	05468
Goose City	05341	Jericho (Town)	05465	Miltonboro	05468
Goose Green	05039	Jericho Center	05465	Monkton	05469
Gordon Landing	05458	Jerusalem	05443	Monkton (Town)	05469
Goshen	05733	Joes Pond	05873	Monkton Ridge	05473
Goshen (Town)	05733	Johnson	05656	Montgomery	05470
Goulds Mills	05156	Johnson (Town)	05656	Montgomery (Town)	05470
Grafton	05146	Jonesville	05466	Montgomery Center	05471
Grafton (Town)	05146	Kansas	05252	Montpelier	05601*
Grahamville	05149	Keeler Bay	05486		05602†
Granby	05840	Kendall	05043	Moretown	05660
Granby (Town)	05840	Kendricks Corner	05150	Moretown (Town)	05660
Grand Isle	05458	Killington	05751	Moretown Common	05660
Grand Isle (Town)	05458	Kimball	05822	Morgan	05853
Graniteville	05654	Kirby (Town)	05824	Morgan (Town)	05853
Graniteville-East Barre	05654	Kirby Corner	05495	Morgan Center	05853
Granville (Town)	05747	Lake Dunmore	05769	Morristown	05661
Granville	05747	Lake Elmore	05657	Morristown (Town)	05661
Green Acres	05477	Lake Fairlee	05044	Morrisville	05661
Green Bay	05046	Lake Hortonia	05743	Moscow	05662
Greenbush	05151	Lake Morey	05045	Mosquitoville	05042
Green River	05301	Lake Park	05855	Mount Holly	05758
Greensboro	05841	Lake Raponda	05363	Mount Holly (Town)	05758
Greensboro (Town)	05841	Lake Rescue	05149	Mount Snow	05356
Greensboro Bend	05842	Lake St. Catherine	05764	Mount Tabor	05739
Greens Corners	05478	Lakewood	05488	Mount Tabor (Town)	05739
Groton	05046	Landgrove	05148	Nashville	05465
Groton (Town)	05046	Landgrove (Town)	05148	Neshobe Beach	05732
Guildhall	05905	Lapham Bay	05734	Newark	05871
Guildhall (Town)	05905	Larrabees Point	05770	Newark (Town)	05871
Guilford	05301	Leicester	05733	Newark Hollow	05871
Guilford (Town)	05301	Leicester (Town)	05733	New Boston (Norwich Town)	05772
Guilford Center	05301	Leicester Junction	05778		
Halifax	05358	Lemington	03576	New Boston (Stockbridge Town)	05055
Halifax (Town)	05358	Lemington (Town)	03576		
Halls Lake	05081	Lewis (Town)	05905	Newbury	05051
Hammondsville	05062	Lewiston	05055	Newbury (Town)	05051
Hancock	05748	Lilliesville	05032	Newbury Center	05081
Hancock (Town)	05748	Lincoln	05443	Newfane	05345
Hanksville	05487	Lincoln (Town)	05443	Newfane (Town)	05345
Hardscrabble	05156	Lindsay Beach	05855	New Haven (Town)	05472
Hardwick	05843	Londonderry	05148	New Haven (Addison County)	05472
Hardwick (Town)	05843	Londonderry (Town)	05148		
Hardwick Center	05843	Long Point	05473	New Haven Mills	05443
Hardwick Steet	05836	Lowell	05847	Newport	05855
Harmonyville	05353	Lowell (Town)	05847	Newport (Town)	05857
Harrisville	05301	Lower Branch	05060	Newport Center	05857
Hartford	05047	Lower Cabot	05658	North Bennington	05257
Hartford (Town)	05047	Lower Granville	05747	North Brattleboro	05304
Hartland	05048	Lower Plain	05033	North Burlington (Part of Burlington)	05401
Hartland (Town)	05048	Lower Village	05672		
Hartland Four Corners	05049	Lower Waterford	05848	North Calais	05650
Harvey	05828	Lower Websterville	05641	North Cambridge	05464
Healdville	05758	Ludlow	05149	North Chester	05143
Heartwellville	05350	Ludlow (Town)	05149	North Clarendon	05759
Hectorville	05471	Lunenburg	05906	North Concord	05858
Hewitts Corners	05053	Lunenburg (Town)	05906	North Danville	05819
Highgate	05459	Lyman	05001	North Derby	05855
Highgate Center	05459	Lympus	05032	North Dorset	05253
Highgate Center	05459	Lyndon	05849	North Duxbury	05676
Highgate Falls	05459	Lyndon (Town)	05849	North Fairfax	05454
		Lyndon Center	05850	North Fayston	05660

	ZIP
North Ferrisburg (Addison County)	05473
Northfield	05663
Northfield (Town)	05663
Northfield Center	05663
Northfield Falls	05664
North Hartland	05052
North Hero	05474
North Hero (Town)	05474
North Hyde Park	05665
North Montpelier	05666
North Orwell	05760
North Pomfret	05053
North Pownal	05260
North Randolph	05041
North Royalton	05068
North Rupert	05761
North Sheldon	05485
North Sherburne	05751
North Shrewsbury	05738
North Springfield	05150
North Thetford	05054
North Troy	05859
North Tunbridge	05077
North Vernon	05354
North Westminster	05101
North Windham	05148
North Wolcott	05680
Norton	05907
Norton (Town)	05907
Norwich	05055
Norwich (Town)	05055
Norwich University (Part of Northfield)	05663
Oakland	05478
Oil City	05072
Old Bennington	05201
Old Church	05060
Orange	05641
Orange (Town)	05641
Orchard Lane	05156
Orleans	05860
Orwell	05760
Orwell (Town)	05760
Panton	05491
Panton (Town)	05491
Paper Mill Village	05257
Passumpsic	05861
Pawlet	05761
Pawlet (Town)	05761
Peacham	05862
Peacham (Town)	05862
Pearl	05458
Peaseville	05143
Pedden Acres	05156
Pekin	05667
Perkinsville	05151
Peru	05152
Peru (Town)	05152
Peth	05060
Pierces Corner	05759
Pikes Falls	05343
Pittsfield	05762
Pittsfield (Town)	05762
Pittsford	05763
Pittsford (Town)	05763
Plainfield	05667
Plainfield (Town)	05667
Pleasant Valley	05444
Plymouth	05056
Plymouth (Town)	05056
Plymouth Kingdom	05149
Plymouth Union	05056
Pomfret	05053
Pomfret (Town)	05053
Post Mills	05058
Potash Bay	05491
Potash Point	05491
Pottersville	05680
Poultney	05764
Poultney (Town)	05764
Pownal	05261
Pownal (Town)	05261
Pownal Center	05261
Prindle Corner	05445
Proctor (Town)	05765
Proctor	05765
Proctorsville	05153
Prosper	05091
Putnamville	05602
Putney	05346
Putney (Town)	05346
Quechee	05059
Queen City Park (Part of South Burlington)	05401
Ralston Corner	05824
Randolph	05060
Randolph (Town)	05060
Randolph Center	05061
Rawsonville	05155
Reading	05062
Reading (Town)	05062

	ZIP
Reading Center	05062
Readsboro	05350
Readsboro (Town)	05350
Readsboro Falls	05350
Red Village	05851
Reedville	05143
Rhode Island Corner	05477
Rices Mills	05075
Richford	05476
Richford (Town)	05476
Richmond	05477
Richmond (Town)	05477
Ricker Mills	05046
Ripton	05766
Ripton (Town)	05766
Riverton	05663
Robinson	05767
Rochester	05767
Rochester (Town)	05767
Rockingham	05101
Rockingham (Town)	05101
Rockville	05443
Rocky Dale	05443
Round Pond	05069
Roxbury	05669
Roxbury (Town)	05669
Roxbury Flat	05669
Royalton	05068
Royalton (Town)	05068
Rupert	05768
Rupert (Town)	05768
Russellville	05738
Russtown	05001
Rutland	05701*
	05702†
Ryegate	05042
Ryegate (Town)	05042
St. Albans	05478
St. Albans (Town)	05481
St. Albans Bay	05481
St. Albans Hill	05478
St. Albans Shopping Center (Part of St. Albans)	05478
St. George (Town)	05495
St. Johnsbury	05819
St. Johnsbury (Town)	05819
St. Johnsbury Center	05863
Saint Michael's College	05404
St. Rocks	05478
Salisbury (Town)	05769
Salisbury	05769
Samsonville	05450
Sanderson Corner	05454
Sandgate	05250
Sandgate (Town)	05250
Saxtons River	05154
Scottsville	05739
Searsburg	05363
Searsburg (Town)	05363
Seymour Lake	05853
Shadow Lake	05839
Shady Rill	05602
Shaftsbury	05262
Shaftsbury (Town)	05262
Shaftsbury Center	05262
Sharon	05065
Sharon (Town)	05065
Shawville	05457
Sheddsville	05089
Sheffield	05866
Sheffield (Town)	05866
Sheffield Square	05866
Shelburne	05482
Shelburne (Town)	05482
Shelburne Falls	05482
Shelburne Road Section (Part of South Burlington)	05401
Sheldon	05483
Sheldon (Town)	05483
Sheldon Junction	05483
Sheldon Springs	05485
Sherburne (Town)	05751
Shoreham	05770
Shoreham (Town)	05770
Shoreham Center	05770
Shrewsbury	05738
Shrewsbury (Town)	05738
Simonsville	05143
Simpsonville	05149
Smithville	05149
Smugglers Notch	05464
Sodom	05257
Somerset (Town)	05345
South Albany	05875
South Alburg	05440
South Barre	05670
South Burlington	05403
South Cabot	05658
South Cambridge	05464
South Corinth	05039
South Danville	05828
South Dorset	05251

	ZIP
South Duxbury	05660
South End	05739
Southern Vermont College	05201
South Hero	05486
South Hero (Town)	05486
South Lincoln	05443
South Londonderry	05155
South Lunenburg	05906
South Newbury	05051
South Newfane	05351
South Northfield	05663
South Peacham	05821
South Pomfret	05067
South Poultney	05764
South Randolph	05041
South Reading	05153
South Richford	05476
South Royalton	05068
South Ryegate	05069
South Starksboro	05487
South Strafford	05070
South Tunbridge	05068
South Vershire	05079
South Walden	05843
South Wallingford	05773
South Wardsboro	05355
South Washington	05675
South Wheelock	05851
South Windham	05359
South Woodbury	05681
South Woodstock	05071
Spoonerville	05143
Springfield	05156
Springfield (Town)	05156
Stamford	05352
Stamford (Town)	05352
Stannard	05842
Stannard (Town)	05842
Starksboro	05487
Starksboro (Town)	05487
Stevens Mills	05476
Stevensville	05489
Stockbridge	05772
Stockbridge (Town)	05772
Stowe	05672
Stowe (Town)	05672
Strafford	05072
Strafford (Town)	05072
Stratton (Town)	05360
Stratton Mountain	05155
Sudbury	05733
Sudbury (Town)	05733
Sugarbush Valley	05674
Summer Point	05491
Summit	05758
Sunderland	05250
Sunderland (Town)	05250
Sutton	05867
Sutton (Town)	05867
Swanton	05488
Swanton (Town)	05488
Tafts Corner	05495
Taftsville	05073
Talcville	05767
Tarbellville	05742
The Bluffs (Part of Newport)	05855
The Island	05161
Thetford	05074
Thetford (Town)	05074
Thetford Center	05075
Thompsonburg	05148
Thompson's Point	05445
Tinmouth	05773
Tinmouth (Town)	05773
Topsham	05076
Topsham (Town)	05076
Topsham Four Corners	05040
Townshend	05353
Townshend (Town)	05353
Trow Hill	05641
Troy	05868
Troy (Town)	05868
Tunbridge	05077
Tunbridge (Town)	05077
Tyson	05149
Una Bella	05201
Underhill	05489
Underhill (Town)	05489
Underhill Center	05490
Union Village	05043
University Mall (Part of South Burlington)	05401
University of Vermont (Part of Burlington)	05405
Upper Graniteville	05654
Vergennes	05491
Vernon	05354
Vernon (Town)	05354
Vershire	05079
Vershire (Town)	05079
Vershire Center	05079
Vershire Heights	05079

* Area Zip Code   † Post Office Boxes

	ZIP		ZIP		ZIP
Victory (Town)	05858	West Castleton	05743	West Wardsboro	05360
Waitsfield	05673	West Charleston	05872	West Waterford	05819
Waitsfield (Town)	05673	West Corinth	05039	West Windsor (Town)	05037
Waitsfield Common	05673	West Cornwall	05753	West Woodstock	05091
Waits River	05086	West Danville	05873	Weybridge	05753
Walden	05873	West Dover	05356	Weybridge (Town)	05753
Walden (Town)	05873	West Dummerston	05357	Weybridge Hill	05753
Walden Heights	05873	West Enosburg	05450	Wheelock	05851
Wallace Pond	05903	West Fairlee	05083	Wheelock (Town)	05851
Wallingford	05773	West Fairlee (Town)	05083	White River Junction	05001
Wallingford (Town)	05773	West Fairlee Center	05044	Whitesville	05142
Waltham (Town)	05491	Westfield	05874	Whiting	05778
Wardsboro	05355	Westfield (Town)	05874	Whiting (Town)	05778
Wardsboro (Town)	05355	Westford	05494	Whitingham	05361
Wardsboro Center	05355	Westford (Town)	05494	Whitingham (Town)	05361
Warners (Town)	05903	West Georgia	05478	Wilder	05088
Warren	05674	West Glover	05875	Williamstown	05679
Warren (Town)	05674	West Groton	05046	Williamstown (Town)	05679
Warren's (Town)	05903	West Halifax	05358	Williamsville	05362
Washington	05675	West Hartford	05084	Williston (Town)	05495
Washington (Town)	05675	West Haven	05743	Williston	05495
Washington Heights	05657	West Haven (Town)	05743	Williston Road Section (Part	
Waterbury	05676	West Hill	05450	of South Burlington)	05401
Waterbury (Town)	05676	West Lincoln	05443	Wilmington	05363
Waterbury Center	05677	West Milton	05468	Wilmington (Town)	05363
Waterford (Town)	05848	Westminster	05158	Windham	05359
Waterville	05492	Westminster (Town)	05158	Windham (Town)	05359
Waterville (Town)	05492	Westminster Station (Part of		Windsor (Town)	05089
Weathersfield (Town)	05151	Westminster)	05159	Windsor	05089
Weathersfield Bow	05156	Westminster West	05346	Winhall (Town)	05340
Weathersfield Center	05151	Westmore	05860	Winooski	05404
Websterville	05678	Westmore (Town)	05860	Winooski Park	05404
Wells	05774	West Newbury	05085	Wolcott	05680
Wells (Town)	05774	West Norwich	05055	Wolcott (Town)	05680
Wells River	05081	Weston	05161	Woodbury	05681
West Addison	05491	Weston (Town)	05161	Woodbury (Town)	05681
West Arlington	05250	Weston Priory	05161	Woodford	05201
West Barnet	05821	West Pawlet	05775	Woodford (Town)	05201
West Berkshire	05450	West Rupert	05776	Woodford Hollow	05201
West Bolton	05465	West Rutland (Town)	05777	Woodstock	05091
West Branch	05672	West Rutland	05777	Woodstock (Town)	05091
West Brattleboro	05301	West Salisbury	05769	Worcester	05682
West Bridgewater	05035	West Springfield	05156	Worcester (Town)	05682
West Bridport	05734	West Swanton	05488	Wrightsville (Part of	
West Brookfield	05060	West Topsham	05086	Montpelier)	05602
West Burke	05871	West Townshend	05359		

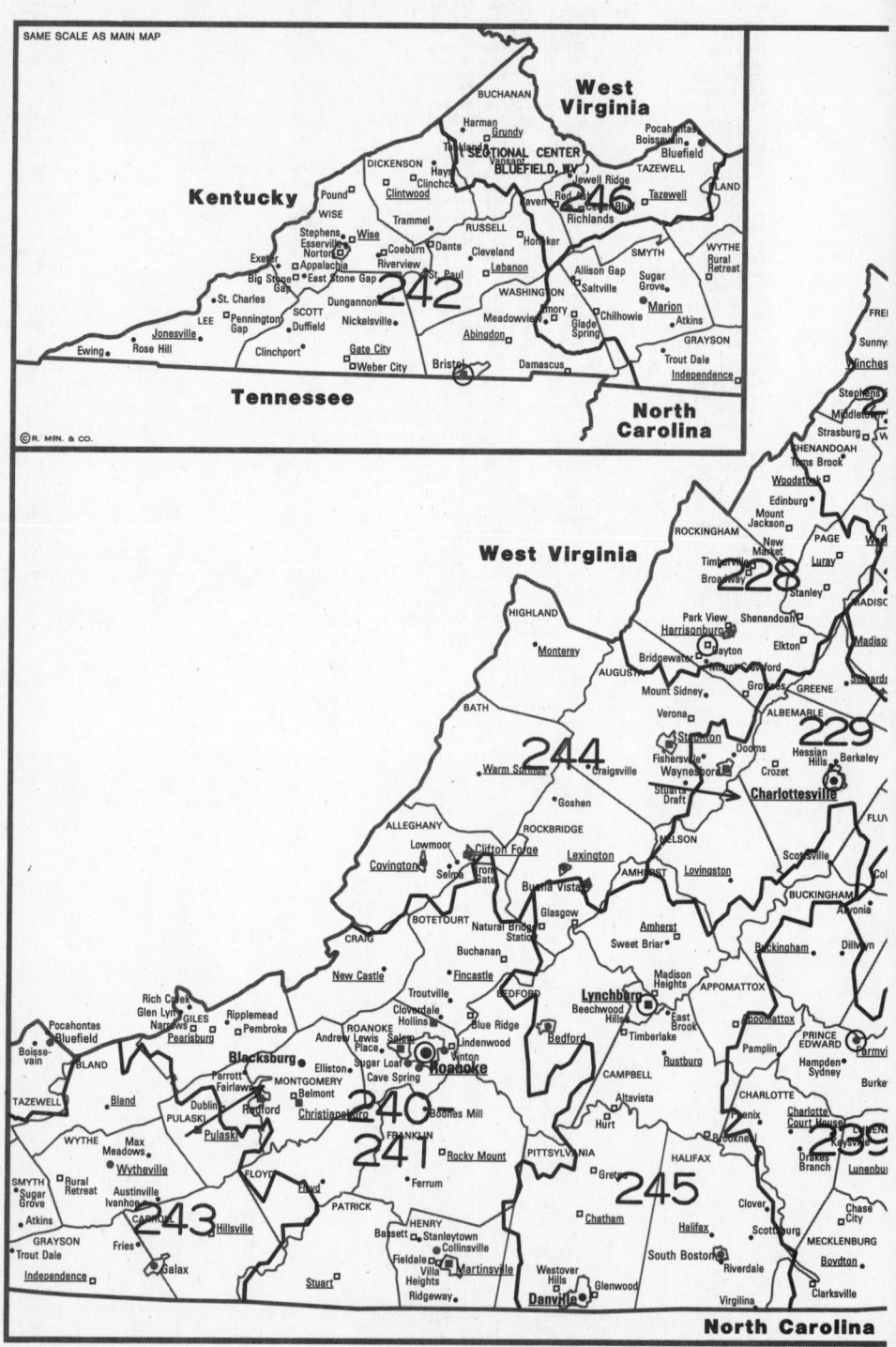

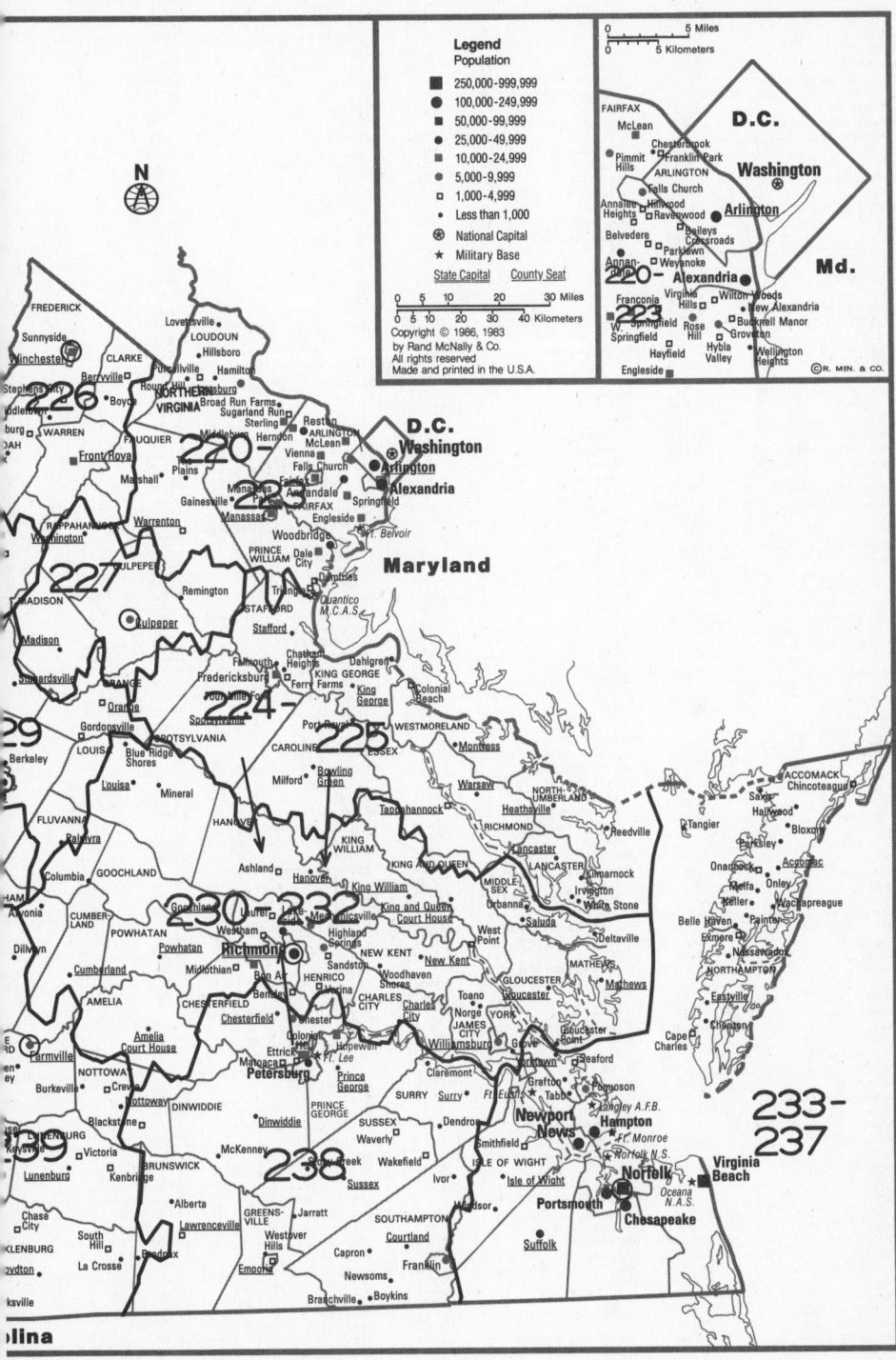

Legend
Population

- 250,000-999,999
- 100,000-249,999
- 50,000-99,999
- 25,000-49,999
- 10,000-24,999
- 5,000-9,999
- 1,000-4,999
- Less than 1,000
- ⊗ National Capital
- ★ Military Base

State Capital   County Seat

	ZIP		ZIP		ZIP
Aarons Creek	24598	Appalachia	24216	Ballentine Place (Part of Norfolk)	23509
Abbey Oaks	22180	Apple Blossom Mall (Part of Winchester)	22601	Balls Hills	22101
Abbott	24127	Apple Grove	23117	Ballston	22203
Abilene	23923	Appomattox	24522	Ballston Common	22203
Abingdon	24210	Aqua	24435	Ballsville	23139
Accomac	23301	Aquia Harbor	22554	Baltimore Corner	23850
Accotink	22060	Aragona Village (Part of Virginia Beach)	23455	Balty	22546
Accotink Heights	22003	Ararat	24053	Banco	22711
Achilles	23001	Arbor Estates (Part of Suffolk)	23434	Bandy	24602
Achsah	22727	Arborhill	24401	Bane	24134
Acorn	22469	Arcadia	24066	Banner	24230
Acredale (Part of Virginia Beach)	23464*	Arch Mills	24066	Banners Corner	24224
	23467†	Arcola	22010	Barbours Creek	24127
Acree Acres	23692	Arcturus	22308	Barboursville	22923
Ada	22115	Ardmore (Part of Fairfax)	22030	Barcroft	22204
Addison Heights	22202	Argyle Heights	22405	Barfoot	24151
Aden	22123	Ark	23003	Barham	23881
Adial	22938	Arlington	22201-19	Barhamsville	23011
Adkins Store	23140	For specific Arlington Zip Codes		Barley	23847
Adner	23149	call (703) 525-4838, or your local		Barnesville	23964
Adria	24630	postmaster.		Barnett	24266
Adsit	23856	Arlington (Part of Hopewell)	23860	Barnetts	23030
Advance Mills	22968	Arlington Forest	22203	Barracks	22901
Adwolf	24354	Arlington Hall	22212	Barracks Road (Part of Charlottesville)	22903
Afton	22920	Arlington Heights	22204	Barren Ridge	24401
Agricola	24574	Arlington Village	22204	Barren Springs	24313
Aiken Summit	24054	Arlingwood	22207	Barrett Acres (Part of Suffolk)	23434
Aily	24237	Armel	22602	Bartlett	23314
Air Mail Facility (Part of Norfolk)	23519	Armistead Forest (Part of Portsmouth)	23703	Bartlick	24256
Airmont	22141	Armstrong	24460	Bartons Crossroad	24378
Ajax	24161	Armstrong Gardens (Part of Hampton)	23669	Bartonville	22602
Alanthus	22714	Aroda	22709	Barytes (Part of Bristol)	24201
Alanton (Part of Virginia Beach)	23450	Arrington	22922	Basham	24138
Albemarle (Part of Norfolk)	23503	Arrowhead (Part of Virginia Beach)	23462	Basic (Part of Waynesboro)	22980
Alberene	22959	Arthur	24162	Baskerville	23915
Alberta	23821	Artillery Ridge	22408	Baskerville Correctional Unit	23915
Albin	22603	Artrip	24225	Bassett	24055
Alcoma	23921	Arvonia	23004	Bassett Forks	24055
Aldie	22001	Asberrys	24377	Bastian	24314
Alexander Corner (Part of Portsmouth)	23707	Ashburn	22011	Basye	22810
Alexandria (Independent City)	22301-32	Ashby	23040	Batesville	22924
For specific Alexandria Zip Codes		Ashland	23005	Bath Alum	24460
call (703) 549-4201, or your local		Ashton Heights	22201	Battersea (Part of Petersburg)	23803
postmaster.		Ashville	22115	Battery	22560
Alfonso	22421	Ashwood	24445	Battery Park (Henrico County)	23228
Algonquin Park (Part of Norfolk)	23505	Aspen	23959	Battery Park (Isle of Wight County)	23304
Alhambra	22951	Aspenwall	24528	Battle Beach	23851
Alice Heights	23234	Assawoman	23302	Battle Creek	22851
Alleghany	24426	Atkins	24311	Battlefield Green	22407
Alleghany Spring	24162	Atlantic (Accomack County)	23303	Battlefield Park (Part of Petersburg)	23805
Allen	24226	Atlantic (Part of Virginia Beach)	23458	Bavon	23138
Allencrest	22207	Atlantic Park (Part of Virginia Beach)	23451	Bayberry Estates	22485
Allens Creek	24553	Atlee	23111	Bay Colony (Part of Virginia Beach)	23451
Allenslevel	23936	Atoka	22115	Bayford	23354
Allentown	23301	Attoway	24354	Bay Island (Part of Virginia Beach)	23451
Allison Gap	24370	Auburn	22019	Bay Lake Beach (Part of Virginia Beach)	23455
Allisonia	24347	Augusta Correctional Center	24430	Baylake Pines (Part of Virginia Beach)	23455
Allmondsville	23061	Augusta Springs	24411	Baynesville	22520
Allwood	24521	Aurora Hills	22202	Bayport	23079
Alma	22851	Austinville	24312	Bayside (Accomack County)	23417
Almagro (Part of Danville)	24541	Avalon	22473	Bayside (Part of Virginia Beach)	23455
Almira (Part of Pound)	24279	Avalon Terrace (Part of Virginia Beach)	23462	Bay View	23310
Alonzaville	22644	Averett	24580	Bayville Park (Part of Virginia Beach)	23455
Alpha	23936	Avon	22920	Baywood	24333
Alpine	22003	Avondale	23111	Beach	23838
Alps	22514	Avon Forest	22039	Beach Grove	22967
Alsop	22553	Axtel	24562	Beaconsdale (Part of Newport News)	23607
Altavista	24517	Axton	24054	Bealeton	22712
Alto	24483	Aylett	23009	Beamantown (Part of Big Stone Gap)	24219
Alton	24520	Aylor	22727	Beamon (Part of Suffolk)	23434
Alum Ridge	24091	Azalea Acres (Part of Norfolk)	23518	Bear Wallow	24622
Alvarado	24210	Azalea Court	23227	Beaufont Hills (Part of Richmond)	23225
Amburg	23043	Azalea Gardens (Part of Hampton)	23669	Beaumont	23014
Amelia Court House	23002	Bachelors Hall	24541	Beaverdam	23015
Amherst (Amherst County)	24521	Backbay (Part of Virginia Beach)	23457	Beaverlett	23016
Amherst (Fairfax County)	22015	Bacons Castle	23883	Beazley	22560
Amissville	22002	Bacons Fork	23950	Beckham	24538
Ammon	23822	Bacova	24412	Bedford	24523
Amonate	24601	Bacova Junction	24445	Bee	24217
Ampthill	23234	Baden	24228	Beech Fork	23974
Ampthill Heights (Part of Richmond)	23234	Bagby	22514	Beech Springs	24263
Amsterdam	24175	Bagleys Mills	23970	Beechwood	23919
Andersonville	23911	Bailey	24605	Beechwood Hills (Arlington County)	22207
Andover	24215	Baileys Crossroads	22041		
Andrew Lewis Place	24153	Bailey's Crossroads (census designated place)	22041		
Angola	23901	Balcony Falls (Part of Glasgow)	24555		
Ankum	23868	Ballards Crossroads	23315		
Annalee Heights	22042				
Annandale	22003				
Annandale Acres	22003				
Annandale Gardens	22003				
Annandale Terrace	22003				
Annex	24401				
Ante	23847				
Antioch	24590				

* Area Zip Code   † Post Office Boxes

	ZIP
Beechwood Hills (Campbell County)	24502
Beechwood Manor	23860
Bel Air	22042
Belaire (Part of Norfolk)	23518
Beldor	22827
Belfast Mills	24609
Bellair (Albemarle County)	22903
Bell Air (Stafford County)	22405
Bellamy (Gloucester County)	23017
Bellamy (Scott County)	24251
Bellamy Manor (Part of Virginia Beach)	23464
Bellbluff (Railroad Station)	23219
Bellbluff	23234
Belle Haven (Accomack County)	23306
Belle Haven (Fairfax County)	22307
Belle Haven (Part of Virginia Beach)	23452
Belle Meade (Fauquier County)	22642
Bellemeade (Part of Richmond)	23224
Belle Meadows (Part of Bristol)	24201
Belle View	22307
Belleville (Part of Suffolk)	23435
Bellevue (Part of Richmond)	23227
Bellevue Forest	22207
Bells Cross Road	22553
Bells Cross Roads	23093
Bell Spur (Carroll County)	24120
Bell Spur (Patrick County)	24120
Bells Valley	24439
Bellwood	23234
Bellwood Manor	23234
Belmont (Loudoun County)	22011
Belmont (Prince William County)	22191
Belmont (Spotsylvania County)	22553
Belmont Acres	23234
Belmont Circle	23901
Belmont Farms (Part of Christiansburg)	24073
Belmont Park	22079
Belmont Place (Part of Norfolk)	23505
Belona	23139
Belspring	24058
Belvedere (Fairfax County)	22041
Belvedere (Part of Norfolk)	23504
Belvidere Beach	22405
Belvoir	22115
Bena	23018
Benhams	24201
Ben Hur	24218
Benmoreel (Part of Norfolk)	23505
Bennetts Creek (Part of Suffolk)	23435
Bennetts Harbor (Part of Suffolk)	23434
Bennett Springs	24153
Benns Church	23430
Bensley	23234
Bent Creek	24553
Bent Mountain	24059
Bentonville	22610
Bergton	22811
Berkeley	22901
Berkley (Part of Norfolk)	23523
Berkshire	22207
Berlin	23866
Berryville	22611
Berton	24134
Bestland	22454
Betana Park	22090
Bethany	24312
Bethel (Fauquier County)	22186
Bethel (Halifax County)	24589
Bethel (Prince William County)	22191
Bethel (Warren County)	22630
Bethel Manor (Part of Hampton)	23665
Beulah Church	22560
Beulah Village	23234
Beulahville	23009
Beverley Hills (Part of Alexandria)	22305
Beverly Forest	22150
Beverly Heights (Part of Salem)	24153
Beverly Hills	23229
Beverly Manor	22101
Beverlyville	22539
Big Bethel (Part of Hampton)	23666
Big Fork	23970

	ZIP
Big Island	24526
Big Laurel	24293
Big River	24439
Big Rock	24603
Big Spring	22650
Big Stone Gap	24219
Big Vein	24635
Biltmore	23060
Binns Hall	22030
Birch	24592
Birchett Estate	23875
Birchland Park	24592
Birchleaf	24220
Birch Town	23336
Birchwood Park	23185
Birdneck Acres (Part of Virginia Beach)	23451
Birdsnest	23307
Birmingham	24609
Biscoe	23148
Bishop	24604
Bishops Corner	23938
Blackberry	24055
Black Branch	23924
Black Creek	23851
Blackford	24260
Blacklick	24368
Blackridge	23950
Blacksburg (Montgomery County)	24060-63
For specific Blacksburg Zip Codes call (703) 552-2751, or your local postmaster.	
Blacksburg (Rockbridge County)	24416
Blacksburg (Washington County)	24340
Blackstone	23824
Blackwater (Lee County)	24221
Blackwater (Part of Virginia Beach)	23457
Blackwater Bridge (Part of Virginia Beach)	23457
Blackwells Chapel	24361
Blackwood	24273
Blainville	22835
Blairs	24527
Blakes	23035
Bland	24315
Bland Correctional Center	24315
Blandford (Part of Petersburg)	23803
Blanks Store	23030
Blanks Tavern	23030
Bleak	22728
Blevinstown	22030
Bloomfield	22012
Bloomingdale	23228
Blowing Rock	24228
Bloxom	23308
Bluefield	24605
Blue Grass	24413
Bluemont	22012
Blue Mountain	22630
Blue Ridge	24064
Blue Ridge Mountain Estates	22630
Blue Ridge Shores	23093
Bluestone	23927
Blundon Corner	22456
Bocock	24501
Body Camp	24523
Bohannon	23021
Boiling Spring	24426
Boissevain	24606
Bolar	24484
Bolsters Store	23882
Bolton	24266
Bon Air (Arlington County)	22205
Bon Air (Chesterfield County)	23235
Bonbrook	24065
Bondtown (Part of Coeburn)	24230
Bonny Blue	24282
Bonsack	24012
Boones Mill	24065
Boonesville	22932
Boonsboro	24503
Bordeaux	22090
Boston (Accomack County)	23420
Boston (Culpeper County)	22713
Boston (Part of Suffolk)	23434
Boswells Tavern	22942
Botetourt Correctional Unit	24175
Botha	22186
Bottoms Bridge	23150
Boudar Gardens	23228
Boulevard Estates	22031
Bowers Corner	23893
Bowers Hill (Part of Chesapeake)	23321
Bowlers Wharf	22560

	ZIP
Bowling	24263
Bowling Green	22427
Bowling Park (Part of Norfolk)	23504
Bowmans Crossing	22824
Boxley Hills	24012
Boxwood	24054
Boyce	22620
Boyd Tavern	22947
Boydton	23917
Boykins	23827
Boys Home	24426
Bracey	23919
Braddock (Part of Alexandria)	22302
Braddock Heights (Part of Alexandria)	22302
Braddock Hills	22003
Bradford Acres (Part of Virginia Beach)	23455
Bradley Acres	23150
Bradley Forest	22110
Bradshaw	24087
Brambleton (Part of Norfolk)	23504
Branchville	23828
Brand	24401
Brandon	23881
Brandon Heights (Part of Newport News)	23601
Brandon Place (Part of Norfolk)	23513
Brandons Store	23824
Brandon Village	22203
Brandy Creek Estates	23111
Brandy Station	22714
Brattons Bridge	24460
Brays	22560
Brayshore Park	23072
Breaks	24607
Brecon Ridge	22030
Bremo Bluff	23022
Bren Mar Park	22312
Brentsville	22013
Brentwood	23234
Brentwood Forest (Part of Norfolk)	23518
Briarcliff (Part of Vinton)	24179
Briarwood (Part of Bristol)	24201
Briarwood (Part of Portsmouth)	23703
Bridgetown	23405
Bridgewater	22812
Bridle Creek	24348
Briery	23947
Briery Branch	22821
Briggs	22611
Brights	24557
Brightwood	22715
Brilyn Park	22046
Brink	23847
Bristol (Independent City)	24201*
	24203†
Bristol Mall (Part of Bristol)	24201
Bristow (Fairfax County)	22003
Bristow (Prince William County)	22013
Britain	22080
Britton Hills Farms	23230
Brittonwood	23234
Broad Bay Colony (Part of Virginia Beach)	23451
Broad Creek (Part of Norfolk)	23502
Broadford	24316
Broad Meadows	23060
Broad Rock (Part of Richmond)	23224
Broad Run	22014
Broad Run Farms	22170
Broadway	22815
Brockroad	22553
Brodnax	23920
Brokenburg	22553
Broken Hill	22065
Brookbury (Part of Richmond)	23234
Brooke	22430
Brookeshire	23181
Brookfield (Fairfax County)	22021
Brookfield (Stafford County)	22405
Brookfield Park (Part of Norfolk)	23503
Brookhaven	22101
Brook Hill	23227
Brookland Estates	22310
Brookland Gardens	23228
Brooklyn	24594
Brookneal	24528
Brook Vale	22503
Brookville (Part of Alexandria)	22304

* Area Zip Code   **† Post Office Boxes**

Place	ZIP
Brookwood (Part of Virginia Beach)	23452
Brookwood Manor	23141
Brosville	24541
Brown Field (Part of Quantico)	22134
Brown Grove	23005
Brownsburg	24415
Browns Corner	23141
Browns Cove	22932
Browns Store	22473
Brown Town (Amherst County)	24521
Browntown (Warren County)	22610
Broyhill Crest	22003
Broyhill Forest	22207
Broyhill Park	22042
Brucetown	22622
Bruington	23023
Brumley Gap	24210
Bruno	24258
Brunswick	23868
Brush Tavern	24502
Bryan Park	23228
Bryan Parkway	23228
Bryant	22967
Bryants Corner	23847
Bryn Mawr	22101
Buchanan	24066
Buckhall	22110
Buckingham (Arlington County)	22203
Buckingham (Buckingham County)	23921
Buckingham (Chesterfield County)	23112
Buckingham Circle	22903
Buckland	22065
Bucknell Heights	22307
Bucknell Manor	22307
Buckner	23024
Buckroe Beach (Part of Hampton)	23664
Buckton	22657
Buena	22733
Buena Vista	24416
Buffalo Forge	24555
Buffalo Gap	24479
Buffalo Hill	24521
Buffalo Hills	22044
Buffalo Junction	24529
Buffalo Ridge	24171
Buffalo Springs	24529
Bufford Cross Roads	23847
Bull Run	22110
Bull Run Mountain Estates	22069
Bumpass	23024
Bundy	24265
Bunker Hill	24523
Burdette	23851
Burgess	22432
Burgundy Village	22303
Burke	22009
	22015
For specific Burke Zip Codes call (703) 978-9113, or your local postmaster.	
Burke Heights	22015
Burke Hills	22015
Burkes Garden	24608
Burkes Shop	22580
Burketown	24486
Burkeville	23922
Burks Garden (Part of Tazewell)	24651
Burnam Woods	23168
Burnleys	22923
Burnside Farms	23111
Burnsville	24487
Burnt Chimney	24184
Burnt Store	23950
Burnt Tree	22960
Burr Hill	22433
Burrowsville	23842
Burson Place	24201
Burton (Part of Virginia Beach)	23455
Burtons Shop	24651
Bush Hill	22310
Bush Hill Woods	22310
Bush Mill	24271
Busthead	24609
Bustleburg	24450
Butterworth	23840
Butts Corner	22039
Butylo	22504
Bybee	22963
Byllesby	24350
Bynum Store	23924
Byrdton	22482
Cabin Point	23881

Place	ZIP
Cadet (Part of Big Stone Gap)	24219
Cady	23069
Caira	23040
Caledonia	23038
Callaghan	24426
Callands	24530
Callao	22435
Callaville	23856
Callaway	24067
Callison	24445
Calno	23069
Calvary	22664
Calverton	22016
Cambria (Part of Christiansburg)	24073
Cambridge	23235
Camden Heights (Part of Norfolk)	23502
Camellia Shores (Part of Norfolk)	23518
Camelot	22003
Cameron Station (Part of Alexandria)	22304
Cameron Valley (Part of Alexandria)	22314
Camp	24375
Camp Barrett	22134
Campbell	22947
Camp Creek	24091
Campostella Heights (Part of Norfolk)	23523
Camps Mill (Part of Suffolk)	23434
Camptown	24528
Cana	24317
Candlewax	24260
Cannady	24656
Canova	22110
Canterburg	22655
Canterbury	23229
Canterbury Hills	22901
Canterbury Woods	22003
Canton	24221
Capahosic	23061
Cape Charles	23310
Cape Henry (Part of Virginia Beach)	23454
Cape Henry Shores (Part of Virginia Beach)	23451
Cape Story by the Sea (Part of Virginia Beach)	23451
Capeville	23313
Capitol (Part of Richmond)	23219
Capon Road	22657
Capron	23829
Captain's Cove	23356
Carbo	24225
Cardinal	23025
Cardinal Forest	22152
Cardova	22701
Cardwell	23099
Cardwell Town	24370
Caret	22436
Carfax	24230
Carloover	24445
Carolanne Farms (Part of Virginia Beach)	23462
Caroline Correctional Unit	23069
Caroline Pines	22546
Carriage Hill (Fairfax County)	22181
Carriage Hill (Part of Virginia Beach)	23452
Carrie	24225
Carrollton	23314
Carrsbrook	22901
Carrsville	23315
Carsley	23890
Carson	23830
Carsonville	24348
Carters Mills	24053
Cartersville	23027
Carterton	24266
Carver Court (Part of Hampton)	23669
Carver Gardens	23185
Carysbrook	23055
Casanova	22017
Cascade	24069
Cash	23061
Cash Corner	22942
Cashville	23417
Caskie	24553
Castle Craig	24550
Castle Heights	23917
Castleton	22716
Castlewood	24224
Catalpa	22701
Catawba (Halifax County)	24577
Catawba (Roanoke County)	24070
Catharpin	22018

Place	ZIP
Catherton (Part of Manassas)	22110
Catlett	22019
Cats Bridge	23420
Cauthornville	23029
Cavalcade	22003
Cavalier Park (Part of Virginia Beach)	23451
Cave Mountain	24579
Cave Spring	24018
Cavetown	22835
Caylor	24248
Cedar Bluff (Tazewell County)	24609
Cedar Bluff (Washington County)	24236
Cedar Branch (Part of Saltville)	24370
Cedar Forest	24569
Cedar Fork	22546
Cedar Green	24401
Cedar Grove (Halifax County)	24520
Cedar Grove (Mecklenburg County)	23970
Cedar Grove (Northampton County)	23310
Cedar Grove Acres (Part of Chesapeake)	23320
Cedarhill	24565
Cedar Lawn	23231
Cedar Level (Part of Hopewell)	23860
Cedar Point	23063
Cedar Springs	24368
Cedarville (Warren County)	22630
Cedarville (Washington County)	24361
Cedon	22580
Celt	22973
Centenary	24590
Center Cross	22437
Center Star	23841
Centerville (Accomack County)	23412
Centerville (Augusta County)	22812
Centerville (Bedford County)	24523
Centerville (Goochland County)	23103
Centerville (Halifax County)	24592
Centerville (James City County)	23188
Centerville (Louisa County)	23117
Central (Part of Richmond)	23219
Central Facility	22079
Central Garage	23086
Central Gardens	23223
Central Hill	23487
Centralia	23831
Centralia Gardens	23234
Central Martinsville (Part of Martinsville)	24112
Central Plains	22963
Central Point	22514
Central State Hospital	23803
Centre Heights	22020
Centreville	22020
Centreville Farms	22020
Ceres	24318
Chadswyck (Part of Chesapeake)	23321
Chalet Woods	22020
Chalk Level	24557
Chamberlain Village	22134
Chamberlayne	23227
Chamberlayne Farms	23227
Chamberlayne Heights	23227
Chamberlayne North	23227
Chamblissburg	24179
Champlain	22438
Chance	22439
Chancellor	22407
Chancellors Green	22407
Chancellorsville	22553
Chaneys	24565
Chantilly	22021*
	22022†
Chantilly Estates	22021
Chapel	24124
Chapel Acres	22153
Chapel Hill (Part of Alexandria)	22302
Chapel Park (Part of Newport News)	23606
Chapel Square	22003
Charity	24185
Charlemont	24526
Charles City	23030
Charlie Hope	23920
Charlotte Court House	23923

* Area Zip Code † Post Office Boxes

ZIP	ZIP	ZIP

Charlottesville (Independent
  City) 22901-06
  For specific Charlottesville Zip
  Codes call (804) 286-2282, or
  your local postmaster.
Chase City 23924
Chatham 24531
Chatham Correctional Unit ... 24531
Chatham Heights 22405
Chatham Hill 24370
Chatmoss 24112
Chatmoss-Laurel Park 24112
Cheapside 23310
Check 24072
Cheriton 23316
Cherokee Heights (Part of
  Norfolk) 23518
Cherry Acres (Part of
  Hampton) 23669
Cherrydale 22207
Cherry Hill (Charles City
  County) 23030
Cherry Hill (Dinwiddie
  County) 23872
Cherry Hill (Prince William
  County) 22026
Chesapeake (Independent
  City) 23320-28
  For specific Chesapeake Zip
  Codes call (804) 547-2144, or
  your local postmaster.
Chesapeake (Northampton
  County) 23310
Chesapeake Beach
  (Northumberland County) .. 22539
Chesapeake Beach (Part of
  Virginia Beach) 23455
Chesapeake Heights (Part
  of Hampton) 23664
Chesapeake Manor (Part of
  Norfolk) 23513
Chesapeake Square (Part of
  Chesapeake) 23321
Chesconessex 23417
Chesdin Manor 23885
Chesopeian Colony (Part of
  Virginia Beach) 23452
Chesswood 23234
Chester 23831
Chesterbrook 22101
Chesterbrook Gardens 22101
Chesterbrook Woods 22101
Chester Estates (Part of
  Bristol) 24201
Chesterfield 23832
  23838
  For specific Chesterfield Zip
  Codes call (804) 748-6031, or
  your local postmaster.
Chesterfield Heights (Part of
  Norfolk) 23504
Chesterfield Work Release .. 23832
Chester Gap 22623
Chestnut Hill (Fairfax
  County) 22003
Chestnut Hill (King George
  County) 22485
Chestnut Knob 24112
Chestnut Level 24527
Chestnut Yard 24381
Chevalle 22110
Chewings Corner 22534
Chickahominy Haven 23089
Chickahominy Shores 23089
Childress 24073
Childry 24577
Chilesburg 22546
Chilhowie 24319
Chiltons 22520
Chimney Run 24484
Chincoteague 23336-37
  For specific Chincoteague Zip
  Codes call (804) 336-6400, or
  your local postmaster.
Chinquapin Village (Part of
  Alexandria) 22302
Chisford 22520
Christchurch 23031
Christensons Corner 23188
Christians 24479
Christiansburg 24068
  24073
  For specific Christiansburg Zip
  Codes call (703) 382-3912, or
  your local postmaster.
Christie 24598
Chuckatuck (Part of Suffolk) 23432
Chula 23002
Church Hill (Part of
  Richmond) 23223
Churchill 22043

Churchland (Part of
  Portsmouth) 23703
Church Road 23833
Church View 23032
Churchville 24421
Cifax 24556
Circlewoods 22031
Cismont 22947
Civic Center (Part of
  Richmond) 23240
Clam 23308
Clancie 23156
Claraville 22473
Claremont (Part of
  Arlington) 22206
Claremont (Surry County) .. 23899
Clarendon 22201
Claresville 23847
Clarkes Gap 22075
Clarksville (Mecklenburg
  County) 23927
Clarksville (Washington
  County) 24340
Clarkton 24577
Clary 22657
Claudville 24076
Clay Bank 23061
Claypool Hill 24609
Clays Mill 24589
Clayville 23139
Clear Brook (Frederick
  County) 22624
Clearbrook (Roanoke
  County) 24014
Clearfield 22151
Clearfork 24314
Clearview Manor 22101
Clearwater Park 24426
Clell 24631
Clermont Woods 22310
Cleveland 24225
Cliffield 24637
Clifford 24533
Cliffview 24333
Clifton (Fairfax County) ... 22024
Clifton (Orange County) 22733
Cliftondale 24422
Clifton Forge 24422
Climax 24531
Clinchburg 24321
Clinchco 24226
Clinchport 24244
Clintwood 24228
Clito 24330
Clover (Part of Alexandria) . 22314
Clover (Halifax County) 24534
Cloverdale (Botetourt
  County) 24077
Cloverdale (Fluvanna
  County) 23022
Clover Hill 22821
Club Court 23227
Cluster Springs 24535
Coalcreek 24333
Coaldan 24641
Coal Kiln 23420
Coal Mine 22657
Coan Stage 22473
Cobbdale (Part of Fairfax) . 22030
Cobbs Creek 23035
Cobham 22929
Cobham Park 22572
Cobham Wharf 23883
Cochran 23821
Cody 24577
Coeburn 24230
Coffee 24551
Cohasset 23055
Cohoke 23181
Coke 23072
Colchester 22079
Cold Harbor Farms 23111
Cold Springs Correctional
  Unit 24440
Coldwater 23108
Coleman Falls 24536
Coleman Place (Part of
  Norfolk) 23504
Coles Creek 24151
Coles Point 22442
Coliseum Mall (Part of
  Hampton) 23666
Colleen 22922
College (Part of
  Fredericksburg) 22401
  22404
  For specific College Zip Codes
  call (703) 373-4871, or your local
  postmaster.
College Park (Part of
  Alexandria) 22314

College Park (Part of
  Staunton) 24401
College Park (Part of
  Suffolk) 23703
Colley 24220
Collierstown 24450
Collingwood 22308
Collins Crossing 22580
Collinsville 24078
Collinwood 24266
Cologne 23037
Colonial Beach 22443
Colonial Forest 23111
Colonial Heights
  (Independent City) 23834
Colonial Heights (Part of
  Hampton) 23664
Colonial Heights (Part of
  Norfolk) 23518
Colonial Heights
  (Washington County) 24201
Colonial Place (Part of
  Norfolk) 23508
Colonial Village 22201
Colonial Williamsburg (Part
  of Williamsburg) 23185
Colosse 23315
Colthurst 22901
Coltons Mill 24523
Columbia 23038
Columbia Forest 22204
Columbia Furnace 22824
Columbia Heights 22204
Columbia Park (Part of
  Hopewell) 23860
Columbia Pines 22003
Colvin Run 22066
Comans Well 23897
Comers Rock 24326
Comet 23430
Commodore Park (Part of
  Norfolk) 23503
Commonwealth 22901
Commonwealth Acres 23875
Community 22306
Comorn 22405
Compton 22650
Conaway 24603
Concord (Brunswick
  County) 23876
Concord (Campbell County) 24538
Concord Heights 22401
Conde 22115
Confederate Heights 23222
Coniceville 22842
Conners Grove 24380
Conners Valley 24324
Contra 22437
Cookstown 22553
Cool Spring 22308
Coolwell 24521
Cooper 23092
Cootes Store 22815
Copper Hill 24079
Copper Valley 24141
Corbin 22446
Corinth 23866
Corn Valley 24260
Cornwall 24416
Coronado (Part of Norfolk) . 23513
Cottage Heights (Part of
  Norfolk) 23504
Cottage Park (Part of
  Norfolk) 23503
Cottage Road Park (Part of
  Norfolk) 23505
Coulson 24381
Coulwood 24260
Council 24260
Countis Corner 24201
Country Club Hills (Part of
  Arlington) 22207
Country Club Hills (Part of
  Fairfax) 22030
Country Club Manor 22207
Country Club View 22032
Country Creek 22181
Countryside 22170
Counts 24237
County Line Cross Roads .. 23923
Court House 22216
Courtland 23837
Courtland Park 22041
Courtney 23060
Cove Colony 22503
Cove Creek (Bland County) 24314
Cove Creek (Tazewell
  County) 24651
Covesville 22931
Covington Corner 23047
Covington (Independent
  City) 24426

	ZIP		ZIP		ZIP
Cox's Chapel	24363	Danville (Independent City)	24540-43	Dorchester Junction	24273
Crab Orchard	24230	For specific Danville Zip Codes		Dorset Woods	23075
Crackers Neck (Scott		call (804) 792-3766, or your local		Doswell	23047
County)	24271	postmaster.		Dot	24277
Crackers Neck (Wise		Dare	23692	Double Tollgate	22663
County)	24219	Darlington Heights	23935	Douglas Park (Part of	
Craddockville	23341	Darnell Town	24265	Portsmouth)	23701
Cradock (Part of		Darvills	23824	Douglass Park	22204
Portsmouth)	23702	Darwin	24228	Doveville	22032
Craigs Mills	24201	Daugherty	23301	Dowden Terrace	22311
Craig Springs	24127	Davenport	24239	Downings	22460
Craigsville	24430	Davis	24472	Downtown (Part of	
Crandon	24315	Davis Corner (Part of		Blacksburg)	24063
Cranes Nest	24230	Virginia Beach)	23462	Downtown (Part of	
Craney Island Estates	23111	Davis Wharf	23345	Charlottesville)	22902
Creeds (Part of Virginia		Dawley Corner (Part of		Downtown (Part of	
Beach)	23457	Virginia Beach)	23457	Leesburg)	22075
Crescent Hill (Part of		Dawn	23047	Downtown (Part of	
Hopewell)	23860	Dayton	22821	Lynchburg)	24505
Crescent Hills	22207	Deans (Part of Suffolk)	23435	Downtown (Part of	
Cresthill	22639	Deatonville	23083	Manassas)	22110
Crestview (Henrico County)	23226	De Bree (Part of Norfolk)	23517	Downtown (Part of	
Crestview (Prince Edward		De Busk Mill	24340	Roanoke)	24001
County)	23901	Deel	24656	Doylesville	22932
Crestwood Manor	22003	Deep Bottom	23075	Drakes Branch	23937
Crewe	23930	Deep Creek (Accomack		Dranesville	22070
Criders	22820	County)	23417	Draper	24324
Criglersville	22727	Deep Creek (Part of		Drewryville	23844
Crimora	24431	Chesapeake)	23323	Drill	24260
Cripple Creek	24322	Deep Creek (Part of		Driver (Part of Suffolk)	23435
Crittenden (Part of Suffolk)	23433	Newport News)	23606	Drouin Hill	23075
Critz	24082	Deep Hole	23336	Drum Bay	22469
Croaker	23188	Deerborne (Part of		Dry Branch	24132
Croatan Beach (Part of		Richmond)	23234	Dryburg	24589
Virginia Beach)	23451	Deerfield	24432	Dryden	24243
Crockett	24323	Deerfield Correctional		Dry Fork (Pittsylvania	
Crockett Springs	24162	Center	23829	County)	24549
Crofton	24179	Deerfield Estates	23832	Dry Fork (Wise County)	24230
Cromwell (Part of Norfolk)	23509	Deer Park (Part of		Drytown	24630
Crooked Oak	24343	Manassas)	22110	Duane	23009
Crossbrook	24215	Deer Park Groove (Part of		Dublin	24084
Crosses Corner	23069	Newport News)	23607	Dudley	24558
Cross Junction	22625	Deerrock	22938	Duffield	24244
Crosskeys	22841	Defense General Supply		Dugspur	24325
Crossroads (Albemarle		Center	23297	Dugwell	24151
County)	22959	De Jarnett	22514	Duke Gardens (Part of	
Crossroads (Halifax County)	24577	Delaplane	22025	Alexandria)	22304
Crossroads Mall (Part of		Delaware	23851	Dumbarton	23228
Roanoke)	24012	Delmar	24236	Dumfries	22026
Crosswinds	22153	Del Ray (Part of Alexandria)	22301	Dunavant	22401
Crouch	22437	Delta (Part of Alexandria)	22304	Dunbar	24216
Crows	24426	Deltaville	23043	Dunbar Gardens (Part of	
Crozet	22932	Delton	24324	Hampton)	23666
Crozier	23039	Denaro	23002	Dunbrooke	22560
Crymes Store	23974	Denbigh (Part of Newport		Duncan Gap	22293
Crystal Hill	24539	News)	23602	Duncans Mills	22435
Crystal Spring Knolls	22207	Denby Park (Part of Norfolk)	23505	Duncanville	24210
Cuckoo	23117	Dendron	23839	Dundalow (Part of Suffolk)	23434
Cullen	23934	Denmark	24450	Dundas	23938
Culmore	22041	Denniston	24520	Dunford Town	24602
Culpeper	22701	Dentons Corner	23921	Dungadin Heights	22630
Cumberland	23040	Derby	24216	Dungannon	24245
Cummings Heights	24210	Desha	22560	Dunlop (Part of Colonial	
Cumnor	23085	Detrick	22652	Heights)	23834
Cunningham	22963	Devon Manor (Part of		Dunn Loring	22027
Curdsville	23936	Norfolk)	23503	Dunn Loring Woods	22180
Currioman Landing	22520	Devonshire Gardens	22042	Dunnsville	22454
Currituck Farms	23150	Dewey	24279	Durrett Town	22920
Cuscowilla	23917	DeWitt	23840	Dutton	23050
Customhouse (Part of		Dewitt Hospital	22060	Duty	24217
Norfolk)	23514	Diamond Springs (Part of		Dwale	24228
Cypress Chapel (Part of		Virginia Beach)	23455	Dwina	24230
Suffolk)	23434	Diascund	23089	Dye	24649
Cypress Manor	23851	Dickensdale	23230	Dyers Store	24112
Cypress Point (James City		Dickensonville	24224	Dyke	22935
County)	23089	Diggs	23045	Eads	22202
Cypress Point (Surry		Diggs Park (Part of Norfolk)	23523	Eagle Rock	24085
County)	23899	Dillard's Landing	23140	Earlhurst	24426
Dabney Estates	23885	Dillwyn	23936	Earls	23002
Dabneys	23102	Dinwiddie	23841	Earlysville	22936
Dahlgren	22448	Dinwiddie Correctional Unit	23833	East Aberdeen Gardens	
Dahlia	27866	Dinwiddie Gardens	23803	(Part of Hampton)	23666
Dalbys	23310	Disputanta	23842	East Brook	24501
Dale City	22193	Ditchley	22482	East End (Part of	
Dalecrest (Part of		Dixie (Fluvanna County)	23055	Richmond)	23223
Alexandria)	22304	Dixie (Mathews County)	23050	Eastern Park (Part of	
Dale Enterprise	22801	Dixie Hill	22030	Virginia Beach)	23452
Daleville	24083	Dockery	23970	Eastern State Hospital	23185
Damascus	24236	Doe Hill	24433	East Falls Church	22205
Dam Neck (Part of Virginia		Dogtown	23063	Eastham	22901
Beach)	23461	Dogue	22451	East Hampton (Part of	
Dam Neck Corner (Part of		Dogue Creek Village	22060	Hampton)	23669
Virginia Beach)	23454	Dogwood Hill (Part of		East Highland Park	23222
Danbury Forest	22151	Staunton)	24401	East Hilton (Part of Newport	
Dandy	23694	Dogwood Knoll	23111	News)	23607
Daniel	22960	Dolphin	23843	East Lexington	24450
Daniel Boone	24251	Donna Lee Gardens	22046	Eastmoreland	23231
Danieltown	23821	Dooms	22980	East Norton (Part of Norton)	24273
Danripple	24592	Doran	24612	East Norview (Part of	
Dante	24237	Dorchester (Part of		Norfolk)	23513
		Richmond)	23234	East Ocean View (Part of	
		Dorchester (Wise County)	24273	Norfolk)	23503

	ZIP
Easton Place (Part of Norfolk)	23502
Eastover (Part of Suffolk)	23434
Eastover Gardens	23231
East Point (Accomack County)	23417
East Point (Rockingham County)	22827
East Radford (Part of Radford)	24141
East Stone Gap	24246
East Suffolk Gardens (Part of Suffolk)	23434
Eastville	23347
Eastville Station (Part of Eastville)	23347
Ebenezer	24565
Ebony	23845
Eclipse (Part of Suffolk)	23433
Edge	24554
Edgehill (King George County)	22485
Edgehill (Southampton County)	23851
Edgehill Park	23803
Edgemont (Part of Covington)	24426
Edgemont Park	24210
Edgerton	23868
Edgewater (Part of Norfolk)	23508
Edgewood (Part of Petersburg)	23805
Edinburg	22824
Ednam Forest	22901
Edom	22834
Edsall Park	22151
Edwards Shop	22718
Edwardsville	22456
Effinger	24450
Eggleston	24086
Eheart	22923
Elam	23960
Elberon	23846
Elephant Fork (Part of Suffolk)	23434
Elevon	22438
Elizabeth Park (Part of Norfolk)	23502
Elizabeth River Shores (Part of Virginia Beach)	23464
Elizabeth River Terrace (Part of Virginia Beach)	23464
Elk Creek	24326
Elk Garden	24266
Elk Hill	23063
Elko	23150
Elkrun	22728
Elkton	22827
Elkwood	22718
Ellett	24073
Elliston	24087
Elliston-Lafayette	24087
Ellisville	23093
Ellsworth (Part of Norfolk)	23505
Elma	22971
Elmhurst (Part of Norfolk)	23513
Elmo	24592
Elmont	23005
Elmwood Estates	22101
El-Nido	22101
Elon	24572
Elsom	23181
Eltham	23181
Elysian Woods	22192
Emmerton	22572
Emory	24327
Emory-Meadow View	24327
Emporia (Independent City)	23847
Endicott	24088
Enfield	23106
Engleside	22309
English Hills	23228
Enonville	23936
Eppes Fork	27584
Erica	22520
Esmont	22937
Esnon	23924
Esserville	24273
Estabrook (Part of Norfolk)	23509
Estabrook Park (Part of Norfolk)	23513
Estaline	24430
Estes	22716
Ethel	22572
Ethridge Estates	23805
Etlan	22719
Ettrick	23803
Euclid (Part of Virginia Beach)	23462
Euclid Place (Part of Virginia Beach)	23462

	ZIP
Euclid Terrace (Part of Virginia Beach)	23462
Eureka	23947
Eureka Park (Part of Virginia Beach)	23452
Eustaces Corner	22728
Euwanee Park (Part of Norfolk)	23503
Everets (Part of Suffolk)	23434
Evergreen	23939
Evergreen Hills	24201
Evergreen Shores	23696
Evington	24550
Ewell	23185
Ewing	24248
Exeter	24216
Exmore	23350
Faber	22938
Fagg	24073
Fairchester (Part of Fairfax)	22030
Fair City Mall (Part of Fairfax)	22031
Fairfax (Independent City)	22030-39
For specific Fairfax Zip Codes call (703) 273-5571, or your local postmaster.	
Fairfax Acres	22030
Fairfax Circle (Part of Fairfax)	22031
Fairfax Forest	22031
Fairfax Station	22039
Fairfax Villa	22030
Fairfax Woods (Part of Fairfax)	22030
Fairfield (Essex County)	22454
Fairfield (Rockbridge County)	24435
Fairhaven	22303
Fair Hill	22031
Fairland	22312
Fairlawn (Part of Covington)	24426
Fairlawn (Pulaski County)	24141
Fairlawn Estates (Part of Norfolk)	23502
Fairlawn Heights	23075
Fairlee	22031
Fair Meadows (Part of Virginia Beach)	23462
Fair Meadows Estates (Part of Virginia Beach)	23462
Fairmont Manor (Part of Norfolk)	23509
Fairmount Park (Part of Norfolk)	23509
Fair Oaks (Part of Fairfax)	22032
Fair Oaks (Henrico County)	23075
Fair Port	22539
Fairview (Fairfax County)	22306
Fairview (Part of Fairfax)	22031
Fairview (Mecklenburg County)	23924
Fairview (Montgomery County)	24149
Fairview (Northampton County)	23310
Fairview (Page County)	22835
Fairview (Scott County)	24244
Fairview Beach	22405
Fairview Heights (Part of Clifton Forge)	24422
Fairview Heights (Part of Lexington)	24450
Fairwood	24378
Fairwood Acres	22039
Falconbridge	23234
Falconerville	24521
Falling Creek	23234
Falling Spring	24445
Falls Church (Independent City)	22040-46
For specific Falls Church Zip Codes call (703) 532-8822, or your local postmaster.	
Falls Hill	22043
Falls Mills	24613
Fallville	24326
Falmouth	22405
Fancy Gap	24328
Fancy Hill	24521
Farmers	22580
Farmers Fork (Essex County)	22509
Farmers Fork (Richmond County)	22572
Farmers Store	24360
Farmingdale (Part of Hopewell)	23860
Farmington (Albemarle County)	22903
Farmington (Henrico County)	23229
Farmville	23901

	ZIP
Farnham	22460
Fauquier Springs	22186
Favonia	24382
Fawcett Gap	22602
Fayette Park	23222
Featherstone	22191
Featherstone Shores	22191
Federal Correctional Institution	23803
Federal Reserve (Part of Richmond)	23219
Fentress (Part of Chesapeake)	23322
Fentress (Part of Virginia Beach)	23451
Fenwick Park	22042
Fergusonville	23930
Ferncliff	23084
Ferndale Gardens	23803
Ferndale Park	23803
Ferrum	24088
Ferry Farms	22405
Fieldale	24089
Fife	23054
Figsboro	24112
File	22427
Fincastle	24090
Finchley	23927
Fine Creek Mills	23139
Finneywood	23924
First Colony	23185
First Street (Part of Radford)	24141
Fishers Hill	22626
Fishersville	22939
Five Forks (Amherst County)	24521
Five Forks (Bedford County)	24523
Five Forks (Carroll County)	24343
Five Forks (Dinwiddie County)	23833
Five Forks (Halifax County)	24592
Five Forks (Part of Hopewell)	23860
Five Forks (James City County)	23185
Five Forks (Madison County)	22960
Five Forks (Nelson County)	24553
Five Forks (Prince Edward County)	23958
Five Lakes	23141
Five Mile Fork	22407
Five Oaks	24630
Flactem Manor	23805
Flagpond	24221
Flat Gap	24279
Flat Iron	22520
Flatridge	24378
Flat Rock (Powhatan County)	23139
Flatrock (Russell County)	24260
Flat Run	22508
Flat Spur	24237
Flat Top	24230
Flatwood	24312
Flatwoods	24090
Fleeburg	22849
Fleenors	24201
Fleenortown	24263
Fleet (Part of Norfolk)	23511
Fleet Branch Post Office (Part of Norfolk)	23511
Fleeton	22539
Flemington	24228
Fletcher	22973
Fletcherville	22186
Flint Hill (Bedford County)	24121
Flint Hill (Rappahannock County)	22627
Flood	22458
Floris	22071
Floyd	24091
Foneswood	22461
Fontaine	24148
Ford	23850
Fordham (Part of Hampton)	23663
Forest	24551
Forest Acres	23805
Forest Hill (Part of Richmond)	23225
Forest Hills (Part of Virginia Beach)	23450
Forest Lake Hills	23111
Forest Park (Part of Hampton)	23666
Forest Park (Part of Norfolk)	23518
Forestville (Fairfax County)	22066
Forestville (Shenandoah County)	22847
Fork Ridge	24639
Forks of Buffalo	24521
Forks Of Water	24413

	ZIP
Forksville	23950
Fork Union	23055
Formosa	23962
Fort Belvoir	22060
Fort Blackmore	24250
Fort Chiswell	24360
Fort Defiance	24437
Fortener Addition	24354
Fort Hill (Henrico County)	23226
Fort Hill (Part of Lynchburg)	24502
Fort Hunt	22306
Fort Lee (Henrico County)	23075
Fort Lee (Prince George County)	23801
Fort Lewis Terrace (Part of Salem)	24153
Fort Mitchell	23941
Fort Myer	22211
Fort Myer Heights	22209
Fort Pickett	23824
Fort Valley	22652
Foster	23056
Fosters Falls	24360
Four Corners	22182
Four Mile Fork	22408
Fourway (Part of Tazewell)	24630
Fox	24348
Foxhall (Part of Norfolk)	23502
Fox Hill (Part of Hampton)	23664
Fox Mill Estates	22070
Foxwells	22578
Fractionville	24210
Fraleytown	24244
Franconia	22310
Franconia Commons	22310
Franklin	23851
Franklin Farms	23805
Franklin Forest	22101
Franklin Heights	24151
Franklin Junction (Part of Suffolk)	23438
Franklin Park	22101
Franks Mill	24401
Franktown	23354
Frederick Hall	23117
Frederick Heights	22602
Fredericksburg (Independent City)	22401-08
For specific Fredericksburg Zip Codes call (703) 373-6543, or your local postmaster.	
Fredericksburg (rural)	24473
Freeman	23856
Freemont	24343
Freeport	23061
Freeshade Corner	23071
Free Union	22940
Fremac (Part of Virginia Beach)	23451
Friendship	24340
Fries	24330
Fringer	24066
Frogtown	22012
Front Royal	22630
	22651
For specific Front Royal Zip Codes call (703) 635-4540, or your local postmaster.	
Frytown	22186
Fugua Farms	23234
Fulks Run	22830
Fulton (Part of Richmond)	23231
Furnace	22827
Furnace Hill	24354
Furnace Mountain	22075
Gainesboro	22603
Gaines Mill Estates	23111
Gainesville	22065
Gala	24085
Galax	24333
Gallops Corner (Part of Virginia Beach)	23464
Galts Mill	24572
Gammons Store	23102
Garden City (Part of Arlington)	22207
Garden City (Part of Hampton)	23661
Garden Wood Park (Part of Virginia Beach)	23455
Gardner	24260
Gardners Crossroads	23117
Garfield Estates	22191
Gargatha	23421
Garland Heights	23234
Garrisonville	22463
Garrisonville Estates	22554
Garysville	23860
Gasburg	23857
Gate City	24251
Gatewood	22534

	ZIP
Gatewood Park (Part of Virginia Beach)	23454
Gaylord	22611
Gaynor Heights	24112
Gayton	23075
Geer	22973
Genito	23139
Genoa	22830
George Mason University	22030
Georges Fork	24228
Georges Mill	22080
Georges Tavern	23063
Georgetown	22842
Georgetown South (Part of Manassas)	22110
Georgetown Village	22191
George Washington (Part of Alexandria)	22305
George Washington Village	22060
Georgian Hamlet	22110
Gether	22514
Getz	22842
Ghent (Part of Norfolk)	23517
Gholsonville	23893
Gibson Station	24248
Gidsville	24521
Gilbert Gardens	23231
Gilmore Mills	24579
Ginter Park (Part of Richmond)	23227
Gladehill	24092
Gladesboro	24343
Glade Spring	24340
Gladstone	24553
Gladys	24554
Glamorgan	24293
Glasgow	24555
Glass	23072
Glebe Point	22432
Gleedsville	22075
Glen Alden	22030
Glen Allen	23058
	23060
For specific Glen Allen Zip Codes call (703) 270-2846, or your local postmaster.	
Glenbrook Hills	23075
Glencarlyn	22204
Glendale (Part of Newport News)	23607
Glendale Acres	23030
Glen Echo	23223
Glenford	24210
Glen Forest	22041
Glenita	24244
Glen Lyn	24093
Glenmore	24562
Glenns	23149
Glen Oaks	22015
Glenrochie	24210
Glen Rock (Part of Norfolk)	23502
Glen Roy Estates	23061
Glenshellah (Part of Portsmouth)	23707
Glenvar	24153
Glen Wilton	24438
Glenwood (Part of Danville)	24541
Glenwood Farms	23223
Glenwood Park (Part of Norfolk)	23505
Gloucester	23061
Gloucester Banks	23062
Gloucester Courthouse	23061
Gloucester Point	23062
Goblintown	24171
Goddin Hill	23005
Gogginsville	24151
Goldbond	24094
Golddale	22568
Gold Hill	23123
Goldvein	22720
Gonyon	22473
Goochland	23063
Goodall	23192
Goode	24556
Goods Mills	24471
Goodview	24095
Goodwins Ferry	24128
Goose Pimple Junction	24201
Gordonsville	22942
Gore	22637
Goshen	24439
Goshen Cross Road	23015
Gossan Mines	24333
Gouldin	23192
Gowrie Park (Part of Norfolk)	23509
Grady	24530
Grafton	23692
Grafton Village	22405
Grahams Forge	24360

	ZIP
Granby Shores (Part of Norfolk)	23503
Grandin Road (Part of Roanoke)	24015
Grand View (Part of Hampton)	23664
Grangeville	23410
Granite Hills (Part of Richmond)	23225
Granite Springs	22553
Grant	24378
Grant's Field	23803
Granville	23030
Grapefield	24314
Grassland	22733
Grass Ridge	22101
Grassy Creek (Henry County)	24112
Grassy Creek (Russell County)	24224
Gratton	24651
Gravel Hill (Part of Richmond)	23225
Graves Mill	22721
Graves Store	24104
Gray	23897
Graysontown	24141
Gray's Pointe	22033
Graysville	23301
Great Bridge (Part of Chesapeake)	23320*
	23328†
Great Falls	22066
Great Neck Manor (Part of Virginia Beach)	23450
Green Acres (Part of Fairfax)	22030
Greenbackville	23356
Green Bay	23942
Greenbriar (Chesterfield County)	23831
Greenbriar (Fairfax County)	22033
Greenbrier Mall (Part of Chesapeake)	23320
Greenbush	23357
Green Cove	24236
Greendale (Henrico County)	23228
Greendale (Washington County)	24210
Greendale Manor	23230
Greenes Corner	23024
Greenfield (Nelson County)	22920
Greenfield (Pittsylvania County)	24557
Greenfield (Washington County)	24361
Greenfield Farms (Part of Portsmouth)	23703
Greenlee	24579
Greenmount	22801
Green Oaks (Part of Newport News)	23601
Green Pond	24531
Greens Folly Apartments	24592
Green Spring	22603
Green Springs (Louisa County)	22942
Green Springs (Washington County)	24210
Green Valley (Part of Bristol)	24201
Greenville (Augusta County)	24440
Greenville (Fauquier County)	22123
Greenville Correctional Unit	24440
Greenway Downs	22042
Greenway Hills (Part of Fairfax)	22030
Greenwich (Prince William County)	22123
Greenwich (Part of Virginia Beach)	23462
Greenwood (Albemarle County)	22943
Greenwood (Henrico County)	23060
Greenwood (Part of Norfolk)	23513
Greenwood (Rockingham County)	22827
Greenwood Farms (Part of Hampton)	23666
Gregory Corner	23968
Gressitt	23156
Gretna	24557
Griffinsburg	22701
Griffith	24422
Grimes	22624
Grimsleyville	24639
Grimstead	23064
Grindall Creek	23234
Grit	24563
Grizzard	23879
Groseclose	24368
Grotons	23399

* Area Zip Code   *† Post Office Boxes*

	ZIP		ZIP		ZIP
Groton Town	23359	Haven Heights (Part of		Hilltop-Oceana (Part of	
Grottoes	24441	Virginia Beach)	23462	Virginia Beach)	23454
Grove	23185	Hawkinstown	22842	Hilltown	24330
Grove Hill	22849	Hawthorne (Part of Norton)	24273	Hillwood	22042
Grove Park (Part of		Hayes	23072	Hiltons	24258
Portsmouth)	23707	Hayfield (Fairfax County)	22310	Hilton Village (Part of	
Groveton	22303	Hayfield (Frederick County)	22638	Newport News)	23601
Groveton (census		Haymarket	22069	Hinesville	24549
designated place)	22306	Haynesville	22472	Hinnom	22520
Groveton Gardens	22306	Haynesville Correctional Unit	22472	Hinton	22831
Groveton Heights	22306	Haysi	24256	Hitesburg	24598
Grundy	24614	Hayters Gap	24210	Hiwassee	24347
Guilford (Accomack County)	23308	Haywood	22722	Hixburg	23958
Guilford (Fairfax County)	22310	Hazel	24237	Hoadly	22191
Guilford Heights	23899	Hazel Heights (Part of		Hobson (Part of Suffolk)	23436
Guinea	22580	Bristol)	24201	Hockley	23156
Guinea Mills	23040	Head Waters	24442	Hockman (Part of Bluefield)	24605
Gum Spring	23065	Healing Springs	24445	Hodges	24554
Gum Tree	23005	Health Science (Part of		Hodges Manor (Part of	
Gunn Hall Manor (Part of		Richmond)	23219	Portsmouth)	23701
Virginia Beach)	23454	Healys	23071	Hodgesville	24151
Gunston Heights	22079	Heards	22920	Hoges Chapel	24136
Gunston Manor	22079	Heathsville	22473	Holcomb Rock	24503
Gunton Park	24360	Hebron (Augusta County)	24401	Holdcroft	23030
Gwathmey	23005	Hebron (Carroll County)	24333	Holiday Hills (Part of	
Gwynn	23066	Hebron (Dinwiddie County)	23894	Richmond)	23235
Hacksneck	23358	Hechler Village	23223	Holiday Point Estates (Part	
Haddonfield	24279	Heights (Part of Petersburg)	23803	of Suffolk)	23434
Hadensville	23067	Helmet	23148	Holland (Part of Suffolk)	23437
Hagans	24263	Hematite	24426	Hollindale	22306
Hague	22469	Henderson Hall	22214	Hollin Hall	22308
Hale Creek	24634	Hendricks Store	24121	Hollin Hills	22307
Halemhurst (Part of Fairfax)	22032	Henry	24102	Hollins	24019
Hales Bottom	24605	Henry Clay Heights	23111	Hollins College	24020
Halfway	22171	Henry Fork	24151	Holly Brook	24315
Halifax	24558	Henrytown (Part of Saltville)	24370	Holly Forest	22039
Halifax Correctional Unit	24558	Hepners	22842	Holly Grove	23024
Hall Addition	24354	Herald	24230	Holly Hills	23139
Hallieford	23068	Heritage Court	23228	Hollymead	22901
Hallowing Point Estates	22079	Heritage Square	22003	Holly Park	22032
Hallsboro	23113	Heritage Village	22003	Holly Point	23430
Halls Hill	22207	Herman	23967	Hollywood (Part of Suffolk)	23434
Hallwood (Accomack		Hermitage	22980	Holman	22853
County)	23359	Hermitage Farms	23228	Holmes Run Acres	22042
Hallwood (Part of Hampton)	23664	Hermitage Park	23228	Holmes Run Heights	22003
Hamburg (Page County)	22835	Hermosa	24577	Holmes Run Park	22042
Hamburg (Shenandoah		Herndon	22070-71	Holston	24210
County)	22824	For specific Herndon Zip Codes		Holston Mill	24354
Hamilton	22068	call (703) 437-3740, or your local		Holts Crossing	24554
Hamiltontown	24273	postmaster.		Home Creek	24614
Hamlin	24224	Hessian Hills	22901	Homeville	23890
Hampden Sydney	23943	Hewlett	22546	Homewood	22015
Hampton (Independent City)	23651-70	Hickory Flat	24333	Honaker	24260
For specific Hampton Zip Codes		Hickory Ground (Part of		Honey Branch	24283
call (804) 826-7586, or your local		Chesapeake)	23322	Honeyville	22851
postmaster.		Hickory Grove Acres	22069	Hood	22723
Hampton Institute (Part of		Hickory Haven	23103	Hopeton	23421
Hampton)	23668	Hickory Hill	22901	Hopewell (Independent City)	23860
Hampton Terrace (Part of		Hickory Junction	24260	Hopewell (Pittsylvania	
Hampton)	23669	Hicks Island	23089	County)	24549
Hanckel	24361	Hicksville	23414	Hopkins	23421
Handsom	23859	Hiddenbrook	22070	Horizon Hills (Part of Bristol)	24201
Hanging Rock	24153	Hideaway Park	22031	Horners	22520
Hanover	23069	Hidenwood (Part of		Hornsbyville	23692
Hanover Heights	23111	Newport News)	23606	Horntown	23395
Hansonville	24266	High Knob	22630	Horse Gap (Part of Pound)	24279
Happy Creek	22630	Highland	24084	Horse Head	22473
Harbors of Newport	22191	Highland Gardens	23222	Horse Pasture	24112
Harborton	23389	Highland Homes	22405	Horsepen	24619
Harbor View	22079	Highland Park (Part of		Horsey	23396
Hardings	22482	Arlington)	22205	Hotchkiss	24460
Hardware	24590	Highland Park (Part of		Hot Springs	24445
Hardwood	24245	Hopewell)	23860	Howardsville (Albemarle	
Hardy	24101	Highland Park (Part of		County)	24562
Hardyville	23070	Portsmouth)	23707	Howardsville (Loudoun	
Hare Valley	23350	Highland Park (Part of		County)	22012
Harless	24073	Richmond)	23222	Howellsville	22630
Harman (Buchanan County)	24618	Highland Park (Prince		Howertons	22454
Harman (Tazewell County)	24602	William County)	22110	Howland	22473
Harman Junction	24614	Highlands	22201	Hubbard Springs	24263
Harmony (Halifax County)	24520	Highland Springs (Henrico		Huckleberry Hills	23805
Harmony (Shenandoah		County)	23075	Huddle	24382
County)	22824	High Meadows	24201	Huddleston	24104
Harpersville (Part of		High Point (Part of		Hudgins	23076
Newport News)	23607	Hopewell)	23860	Hudson Crossroads	22842
Harrell Siding (Part of		Hightown (Highland County)	24444	Hudson Terrace (Part of	
Suffolk)	23434	Hightown (Rockingham		Newport News)	23607
Harris Grove	23692	County)	22834	Huffman	24128
Harrisonburg	22801	Highview Park	22207	Huffville	24138
Harriston	24441	Hilander Park	24201	Hughes Store	23030
Harrisville	22660	Hill	24251	Hull Street (Part of	
Harrowgate	23831	Hillbrook	22003	Richmond)	23224
Harryhogan	22435	Hillcrest	23040	Hume	22639
Hartfield	23071	Hillcrest Estates	22110	Hunterdale	23851
Harts Shop	23117	Hillsboro	22132	Hunter Estates	22079
Hartwood	22471	Hillsdale (Part of Suffolk)	23434	Hunters Valley	22181
Harvey	24219	Hillsman Corner	24502	Huntersville (Part of Norfolk)	23504
Hassen Heights (Part of		Hillsville	24343	Huntersville (Part of Suffolk)	23435
Bristol)	24201	Hill Top (Part of Martinsville)	24112	Huntingcreek Hills	23234
Hatchers	23139	Hilltop (Part of Suffolk)	23451	Huntington (Fairfax County)	22303
Hat Creek	24528	Hilltop Manor (Part of		Huntington (Henrico	
Hatton	24590	Virginia Beach)	23454	County)	23229

	ZIP		ZIP		ZIP
Huntington Heights (Part of Newport News)	23607	Jessup Farms	23234	Kings Grant (Part of Virginia Beach)	23452
Huntly	22640	Jester Gardens (Part of Chesapeake)	23320	Kings Hill	23231
Hunton	23060	Jetersville	23083	Kingsland	23234
Hunts Village	22032	Jewell Hollow	22835	Kings Park	22151
Hupp	22853	Jewell Ridge	24622	Kings Park West	22032
Hurley	24620	Jewell Valley	24622	Kings Point	23185
Hurricane	24293	Johnsontown	23405	Kings Store	24091
Hurt	24563	Joliff (Part of Chesapeake)	23321	Kingston	24550
Huske	23882	Jolivue	24401	Kingston Chase	22070
Hustle	22476	Jollett	22827	Kingstown	24019
Hyacinth	22435	Jones	22553	Kingsville	23901
Hybla Valley	22306	Jonesboro	23824	Kingswood	23185
Hybla Valley Farms	22306	Jones Corner	22427	Kingswood Court	23111
Hyco	24592	Jones Creek (Part of Martinsville)	24112	Kingtown (Part of Bristol)	24201
Hylas	23146			King William	23086
Hylton Park	23235	Jonesville	24263	Kino	22560
Iberis	22503	Jordan Mines	24449	Kinsale	22488
Ida	22835	Josephine	24273	Kiptopeke	23310
Idlewilde (Part of Covington)	24426	Joyce Heights (Part of Fairfax)	22030	Kire	24094
Idylwood	22043	Joyner	23829	Kirkside	22306
Igo	22405	Justisville	23421	Klotz	24150
Imboden	24216	Ka	24245	Knightly	24437
Independence	24348	Karo	22630	Knob Hill (Part of Virginia Beach)	23464
Independent Hill	22110	Kathmoor	22310	Koehler	24112
Index	22485	Keats	27553	Konnarock	24236
Indian Field	22572	Kecoughtan (Part of Hampton)	23667	Laburnum Manor	23222
Indian Gap	24656	Keeling	24566	Lacey Forest	22205
Indian Neck	23148	Keene	22946	Lacey Spring	22833
Indian River (Part of Chesapeake)	23325	Keene Mill Manor	22152	Lackey	23694
Indian River Estates (Part of Virginia Beach)	23462	Keen Mountain	24624	La Crosse	23950
Indian Rock	24066	Keen Mountain Correctional Center	24631	Ladd	22980
Indian Run Park	22312	Keezletown	22832	Ladysmith	22501
Indian Springs (Chesterfield County)	23234	Keith	23009	Lafayette	24087
Indian Springs (Fairfax County)	22312	Keller	23401	Lafayette Boulevard (Part of Norfolk)	23509
Indian Valley	24105	Kells Corner	23924	Lafayette Park (Part of Norfolk)	23509
Indika	23487	Kelsa	24620	Lahore	22502
Ingham	22849	Kemmerer Gem No. 2	24282	Lake	22511
Ingleside (Part of Norfolk)	23502	Kemp's Place	23231	Lake Barcroft (census designated place)	22041
Ingram	24597	Kempsville (Part of Virginia Beach)	23462	Lake Barcroft	22044
Inlet	22701	Kempsville Colony (Part of Virginia Beach)	23464	Lake Caroline	22546
Inman	24216			Lake Crystal Farms	23235
Ino	22437	Kempsville Gardens (Part of Virginia Beach)	23462	Lake Jackson	22110
Interior	24094			Lake Monticello	22963
Intervale	24426	Kempsville Heights (Part of Virginia Beach)	23462	Lake Of The Woods	22508
Ira	24620			Lake Ridge	22192
Irisburg	24054	Kenbridge	23944	Lakeside (Henrico County)	23228
Irondale	24219	Kendall Acres	23234	Lakeside (Part of Newport News)	23606
Iron Gate (Alleghany County)	24448	Kendall Grove	23347		
Irongate (Prince William County)	22110	Kenilworth (Part of Norfolk)	23503	Lakeside (Part of Salem)	24153
Ironto	24087	Kennard	22572	Lakeside Heights	23692
Irving	24174	Kennelworth (Part of Petersburg)	23803	Lakeside Hills	23228
Irvington	22480			Lakeside Village	23038
Irwin	23063	Kent	24382	Lakeview Acres	23901
Isaac	23851	Kent Gardens	22101	Lakeville Estates (Part of Virginia Beach)	23464
Island Creek	24343	Kent Park (Part of Norfolk)	23509	Lakewood (Fairfax County)	22041
Island Farm	22560	Kents Store	23084	Lakewood (James City County)	23185
Island Ford	22827	Kentuck	24586		
Isle of Wight	23397	Kenwood (Hanover County)	23005	Lakewood (Part of Norfolk)	23509
Isom	24228	Kenwood (Part of Hopewell)	23860	Lakewood (Pittsylvania County)	24541
Ivakota	22024	Keokee	24265		
Ivanhoe	24350	Kerfoot	22025	Lamberts Point (Part of Norfolk)	23508
Ivondale	22572	Kermit	24251	Lambsburg	24351
Ivor	23866	Kerns	24250	Lanahan	24088
Ivy	22945	Kernstown (Part of Winchester)	22602	Lancaster	22503
Jacksons Ferry	24312	Kerrs Creek	24450	Landmark Center (Part of Alexandria)	22304
Jamaica	23079	Keswick	22947	Landmark Plaza (Part of Alexandria)	22312
James River Estates	23238	Keysville	23947		
James Store	23080	Key West	22901	Landmark Square (Part of Manassas)	22110
Jamesville	23398	Kibler	24053		
Janaf Shopping Center (Part of Norfolk)	23502	Kidds Fork	22514	Land of Promise (Part of Virginia Beach)	23457
		Kidd's Store	24590	Land O'Pines	23832
Janey	24631	Kidville	22939	Landtown (Part of Virginia Beach)	23456
Jarratt	23867	Kiels Gardens	22030		
Jasper	24244	Kiger Hill	24450	Lanes Corner (Hanover County)	23005
Java	24565	Kilby (Part of Suffolk)	23434		
Jefferson (Fairfax County)	22042	Kilby Shores (Part of Suffolk)	23434	Lanes Corner (Spotsylvania County)	22553
Jefferson (Powhatan County)	23139	Kildare Annex	23230	Lanesville	23086
Jefferson Manor	22303	Kilmarnock	22482	Laneview	22504
Jefferson Mews (Part of Herndon)	22070	Kilmarnock Wharf	22482	Lanexa	23089
		Kimages	23030	Langhorne Acres	22031
Jefferson Park	23860	Kimballton	24150	Langley	22101
Jeffersonton	22724	Kimberley Hills	23901	Langley Forest	22101
Jefferson Village	22042	Kimberling	24315	Langley Research Center (Part of Hampton)	23665
Jeffress	23927	Kimberly Acres	23234		
Jenkins Bridge	23399	Kinderhook	22973	Langley View (Part of Hampton)	23669
Jenkins Neck	23072	Kindrick	24382	Lankford Corner	22473
Jennings	23930	King and Queen Court House	23085	Lantz Mills	22824
Jennings Gap	24421	King George	22485	Lara	22503
Jennings Mission	24251	Kingsbury Manor	22980	Larchmont (Arlington County)	22201
Jennings Store	24244	Kings Corner	23089		
Jericho (Carroll County)	24381	Kings Crossroads	23964	Larchmont (Part of Norfolk)	23508
Jericho (Part of Suffolk)	23434	Kingsdale	23851		
Jerome	22824	Kings Fork (Part of Suffolk)	23434		
Jersey	22481				

	ZIP		ZIP		ZIP
Larkspur (Part of Virginia Beach)	23462	Lindell	24210	Lucketts	22075
Larrys Store	24598	Linden	22642	Lumberton	23890
Larwood Acres	24201	Lindenwood	24179	Lummis (Part of Suffolk)	23434
Lassiter Courts (Part of Newport News)	23607	Lindsay	22942	Lunenburg	23952
		Linkhorn (Part of Virginia Beach)	23454	Luray	22835
Laswell	24360			Lurich	24124
Latanes	22443	Linkhorn Estates (Part of Virginia Beach)	23454	Lusters Gate	24060
Laurel (Henrico County)	23060			Luttrellville	22435
Laurel (Russell County)	24260	Linkhorn Shores (Part of Virginia Beach)	23451	Lydia	22973
Laurel Branch	24091			Lyells	22572
Laureldale	24236	Linlier (Part of Virginia Beach)	23451	Lyman Park	22134
Laurel Dell	23228			Lynchburg (Independent City)	24501-06
Laurel Fork	24352	Linville	22834	For specific Lynchburg Zip Codes call (804) 528-8900, or your local postmaster.	
Laurel Grove	24594	Lipps	24273		
Laurel Grove Estates	23111	Lithia	24066		
Laurel Hill (Augusta County)	24482	Little Haven (Part of Virginia Beach)	23452		
Laurel Hill (Shenandoah County)	22641	Little Plymouth	23091	Lynch Station	24571
Laurel Manor (Part of Virginia Beach)	23451	Little River Hills (Part of Fairfax)	22031	Lyndhurst	22952
				Lynhaven (Part of Alexandria)	22305
Laurel Mills	22716	Little River Pines	22031	Lynn Grove	23222
Laurel Oak	23234	Little River Shopping Center	22003	Lynnhaven (Part of Hampton)	23666
Laurel Park (Henrico County)	23228	Little Rocky Run	22024		
		Littleton	23890	Lynnhaven (Part of Virginia Beach)	23450
Laurel Park (Henry County)	24112	Little Vienna Estates	22181		
Lawndale Farms	23231	Litwalton	22503	Lynnhaven Acres (Part of Virginia Beach)	23452
Lawrenceville	23868	Litz	24340		
Lawrenceville Hills	23868	Lively	22507	Lynnhaven Colony (Part of Virginia Beach)	23451
Lawson	23430	Lloyd Place (Part of Suffolk)	23434		
Lawson Forest (Part of Virginia Beach)	23455	Loch Laird (Part of Buena Vista)	24416	Lynnhaven Mall (Part of Virginia Beach)	23452
Lawson's Store (Mecklenburg County)	23924	Loch Lomond	22110	Lynn Shores (Part of Virginia Beach)	23452
			22111	Lynn Spring	24649
Lawsons Store (Russell County)	24224	For specific Loch Lomond Zip Codes call (703) 368-2145, or your local postmaster.		Lynnwood (Rockingham County)	24471
Lawyers	24501			Lynnwood (Part of Virginia Beach)	23452
Laymantown	24064				
LC Page (Part of Norfolk)	23518	Lockhart Flats	24228	Lynwood	22191
Leaksville	22835	Locust Creek	23024	Lyon Park	22201
Leatherwood	24112	Locust Dale	22948	Lyon Village	22201
Lebanon	24266	Locust Grove	22508	Mabe	24244
Lebanon Church	22641	Locust Hill (Middlesex County)	23092	McAdam	24301
Leck	24230			Macanie	22842
Leda	24577	Locust Hill (Wythe County)	24360	McCall Gap	24340
Lee	23039	Locust Mound	23410	McChesney Heights (Part of Bristol)	24201
Lee Acres	23875	Locustville	23404		
Lee Boulevard Heights	22044	Lodge	22435	McClung	24460
Leedstown	22443	Lodi	24340	McClure	24269
Lee Forest	22030	Lodore	23002	McConnell	24251
Lee Hall (Part of Newport News)	23603	Lofton	24472	McCoy	24111
		Logan	22553	McCrady	24370
Lee Heights	22207	Loisdale Estates	22150	McDonalds Mill	24060
Lee-Hi Village	22030	Lombardy Grove	23970	McDonald's Small Farms	23060
Leemaster	24656	London Bridge (Part of Virginia Beach)	23454	McDowell	24458
Lee Meadows	22032			Macedonia	23308
Lee Mont	23403	London Towne	22020	Maces Springs	24258
Lee Park	23150	Lone Fountain	24421	McGaheysville	22840
Leesburg	22075	Lone Gum	24104	McHenry	22553
Leesville	24571	Longbottom (Part of Grundy)	24614	Machipongo	23405
Lee Town	24614			McKendree	24558
Leewood	22151	Long Branch	24237	McKenney	23872
Lenah	22001	Long Dale (Alleghany County)	24422	McKinley	24459
Lennig	24577			McLean	22101-02
Lenox (Part of Norfolk)	23503	Longdale (Henrico County)	23060		22106
Lenox (Part of Virginia Beach)	23451	Longdale Furnace	24422	For specific McLean Zip Codes call (703) 790-9100, or your local postmaster.	
		Long Island	24569		
Leon	22725	Long Point (Part of Portsmouth)	23703		
Lerty	22520			McLean Estates	22101
Lester Manor	23086	Longshop	24060	McLean Hamlet	22102
Level Run	24563	Long Spur	24084	McLean Manor	22101
Lewinsville	22101	Longview	23430	McMullen	22973
Lewinsville Heights	22101	Looney's Creek	24614	McNeals Corner	22503
Lewisetta	22505	Loretto	22509	Macon	23101
Lewis Park	22030	Lorfax Heights	22079	Madison	22727
Lewiston	23005	Lorne	22546	Madison College (Part of Harrisonburg)	22801
Lewisville	22611	Lorraine	23075		
Lexington (Independent City)	24450	Lorton	22079	Madison Heights	24572
			22199	Madison Manor	22205
Liberia Woods (Part of Manassas)	22110	For specific Lorton Zip Codes call (703) 339-6128, or your local postmaster.		Madison Mills	22953
				Madison Run	22942
Liberty (Halifax County)	24577	Lost Corner	22663	Madisonville	23958
Liberty (Tazewell County)	24651	Lost Forest	23234	Madrid	22980
Lick Fork	24230	Lottsburg	22511	Madrillon Farms	22182
Lick Run	24085	Loudoun Heights	25425	Maggie	24127
Lick Skillet	24370	Louisa	23093	Magnolia (Part of Suffolk)	23434
Lightfoot	23090	Love	22952		
Lignum	22726	Loves Mill	24319	Magnolia Gardens (Part of Suffolk)	23434
Lilian	22539	Loves Shop	24558		
Lilly	22821	Lovettsville	22080	Maidens	23102
Lime Hill	24201	Lovingston	22949	Major	24526
Limeton	22610	Lower Brandon	23881	Makemie Park	23442
Lincoln	22078	Lower Elk Creek	24326	Malbrook	22044
Lincolnia (Part of Alexandria)	22312	Lower Exeter	24216	Malcolm	24201
		Lowery Hills	24201	Malibu (Part of Virginia Beach)	23452
Lincolnia (Fairfax County)	22312	Lowesville	22951		
Lincolnia Heights	22312	Lowmoor	24457	Mallow	24426
Lincolnia Park	22312	Lowry	24570	Malmaison	24527
Lincoln Park (Fairfax County)	22030	Loxley Place (Part of Portsmouth)	23702	Manakin	23103
				Manakin Farms	23103
Lincoln Park (Part of Norfolk)	23513	Luck	24565	Manakin Sabot	23103

	ZIP		ZIP		ZIP
Manassas (Independent		Meadowood................	23227	Mollusk..................	22517
City)...................	22110-11	Meadows of Dan.........	24120	Monaskon.................	22503
For specific Manassas Zip Codes		Meadows of Newgate.....	22020	Moneta...................	24121
call (703) 368-2145, or your local		Meadow View (Chesterfield		Moneys Corner............	22070
postmaster.		County)................	23234	Monroe...................	24574
Manassas Park............	22111	Meadowview (Washington		Monroe Gardens (Part of	
Manbur..................	23150	County)................	24361	Hampton)...............	23669
Manchester Mills.........	23875	Meadville................	24558	Monroe Hall..............	22443
Maness..................	24282	Mears...................	23409	Montague.................	22504
Mangohick...............	23104	Mears Station............	23409	Montclair................	22026
Mannboro................	23105	Mearsville...............	23409	Montebello...............	24464
Manquin.................	23106	Mechanicsburg...........	24315	Monterey.................	24465
Manry...................	23888	Mechanicsville (Hanover		Montevideo...............	22840
Mantua..................	22031	County)................	23111	Montezuma...............	22821
Mantua Hills.............	22031	Mechanicsville (Rockingham		Montezuma Gardens.......	23223
Manville.................	24251	County)................	22853	Montford.................	22960
Maple Grove (Rockbridge		Mechums River...........	22901	Montgomery..............	24023
County)................	24450	Mecklenburg Correctional		Monticello Park (Part of	
Maple Grove (Spotsylvania		Center.................	23917	Alexandria)............	22305
County)................	22407	Media Park...............	23231	Monticello Village (Part of	
Maple Grove		Meetze..................	22186	Norfolk)...............	23509
(Westmoreland County)	22443	Meherrin.................	23954	Monticello Woods.........	22150
Maplewood..............	23002	Melfa...................	23410	Montpelier (Charles City	
Mappsburg..............	23420	Melrose (Campbell County)	24554	County)................	23030
Mappsville..............	23407	Melrose (Part of Roanoke)	24017	Montpelier (Hanover	
Marble Valley............	24432	Melrose Gardens.........	22172	County)................	23192
Marcem (Part of Gate City)	24251	Melton..................	22942	Montpelier Station........	22957
Marengo.................	23950	Memorial Heights.........	22306	Montrose................	23231
Margo...................	22553	Mendota.................	24270	Montrose Heights (Part of	
Marion..................	24354	Mentow.................	24104	Richmond).............	23231
Marion Hill...............	23231	Meredithville.............	23873	Montrose Terrace.........	23231
Marionville...............	23408	Meridian Park............	22046	Montross................	22520
Markham (Fauquier County)	22643	Merrifield................	22081*	Montvale................	24122
Markham (Pittsylvania			22116†	Montvue.................	22901
County)................	24557	Merrimac................	24060	Monument Heights........	23226
Mark Haven Beach........	22454	Merrimack Park (Part of		Moon....................	23119
Marksville...............	22851	Norfolk)...............	23503	Mooreland...............	23075
Marlan Forest............	22307	Merrimac Shores (Part of		Mooreland Farms.........	23229
Marlbank................	23692	Hampton)...............	23669	Moores Corner...........	22554
Marlboro................	23224	Merry Point..............	22513	Moorings................	23839
Marlbrook...............	24483	Messongo................	23399	Moran...................	23966
Marrowbone Heights.......	24148	Metomkin................	23421	Morattico................	22523
Marshall.................	22115	Mew....................	24224	Morefield................	24283
Marshall Heights..........	23072	Michaux.................	23139	Morningside Hills.........	24210
Marsh Run...............	22712	Midcity Shopping Center		Morning Star.............	22835
Marstella Estates.........	22186	(Part of Portsmouth).....	23707	Morrisdale...............	23831
Martha Gap..............	24256	Middlebrook..............	24459	Morrison (Part of Newport	
Martin Siding.............	23405	Middleburg...............	22117	News).................	23601
Martins Store.............	22920	Middleridge..............	22032	Morrisonville.............	22080
Martinsville (Independent		Middleton................	23228	Morrisville...............	22712
City)..................	24112-15	Middleton Gardens (Part of		Morven..................	23002
For specific Martinsville Zip Codes		Salem)................	24153	Mosby...................	22042
call (703) 632-4745, or your local		Middletown (Frederick		Mosby Woods (Part of	
postmaster.		County)................	22645	Fairfax)...............	22030
Marumsco Acres..........	22191	Middletown (Northampton		Moscow.................	22843
Marumsco Hills...........	22191	County)................	23413	Moseley.................	23120
Marumsco Plaza..........	22191	Middletowne Farms........	23185	Moss Run................	24426
Marumsco Village.........	22191	Midland.................	22728	Mossy Creek.............	22812
Marumsco Woods.........	22191	Midlothian...............	23112-13	Motley..................	24563
Marvin..................	24639	For specific Midlothian Zip Codes		Motleys Mill.............	24531
Marye...................	22553	call (804) 794-5177, or your local		Motorun.................	23163
Marysville...............	24554	postmaster.		Mountain Falls...........	22602
Maryus..................	23107	Midway (Halifax County)...	24598	Mountain Gap............	22075
Mascot..................	23108	Midway (Mecklenburg		Mountain Grove..........	24484
Mason Cove.............	24153	County)................	23915	Mountain Hill............	24586
Mason Creek (Part of		Midway (Tazewell County)	24609	Mountain Lake...........	24136
Salem)................	24153	Mike....................	24538	Mountain Valley..........	24112
Masonville...............	22003	Mila....................	22473	Mountain View (Giles	
Massanetta Springs........	22801	Milan (Part of Norfolk)....	23508	County)................	24134
Massanutten..............	22840	Miles...................	23025	Mountain View (King	
Massaponax..............	22407	Milford..................	22514	George County)........	22406
Massies Mill..............	22954	Military Circle (Part of		Mountain View (Pulaski	
Mathews................	23109	Norfolk)...............	23502	County)................	24084
Matoaca.................	23803	Millboro.................	24460	Mountain View (Rockbridge	
Mattaponi...............	23110	Millboro Spring...........	24460	County)................	24416
Maurertown..............	22644	Mill Creek Park...........	22003	Mountain View (Washington	
Maury Place (Part of		Millenbeck...............	22503	County)................	24210
Newport News).........	23601	Miller Park (Part of		Mount Airy..............	24557
Mavisdale...............	24627	Lynchburg)............	24501	Mount Alto...............	22937
Max Creek...............	24347	Millers Tavern............	23115	Mount Carmel (Halifax	
Maxie...................	24628	Mill Gap.................	24465	County)................	24520
Maximum Security Facility	22079	Mill Garden..............	22553	Mount Carmel (Smyth	
Max Meadows............	24360	Milltown.................	22080	County)................	24354
Maxwell.................	24651	Millwood................	22646	Mountcastle..............	23140
Mayberry................	24120	Milteer Acres (Part of		Mount Clifton............	22842
Maybrook................	24136	Suffolk)...............	23434	Mount Clinton............	22801
Mayfair Place............	23223	Mineral.................	23117	Mount Crawford..........	22841
Mayfield................	23230	Mine Run................	22568	Mountfair................	22932
Mayfield Farms...........	23111	Minimum Security Facility	22079	Mount Garland...........	23117
Mayflower...............	24521	Minnieville..............	22193	Mount Hermon...........	24541
Mayo (Halifax County)....	24598	Minor...................	22560	Mount Heron.............	24631
Mayo (Henry County).....	24165	Mint Spring..............	24463	Mount Holly.............	22524
Maytown (Part of Coeburn)	24230	Miona..................	23415	Mount Jackson...........	22842
Meade..................	22560	Miskimon................	22473	Mount Landing...........	22560
Meadowbrook (Chesterfield		Mission Home............	22940	Mount Laurel............	24534
County)................	23234	Mitchells................	22729	Mount Meridian..........	24441
Meadowbrook (Part of		Mitchelltown.............	24445	Mount Nebo.............	23235
Norfolk)...............	23505	Mobjack................	23118	Mount Olive.............	22660
Meadowbrook Forest (Part		Modern (Part of Hampton)	23666	Mount Pisgah............	24467
of Norfolk).............	23518	Modest Town.............	23412	Mount Pleasant..........	24521
Meadowcrest (Part of		Moffats Creek............	24459	Mount Pleasant Estates....	22405
Bristol)...............	24201	Mogarts Beach...........	23430	Mount Sidney............	24467

	ZIP		ZIP		ZIP
Mount Solon	22843	Newland	22572	North Holston	24370
Mount Vernon	22121	New London	24551	North Jericho (Part of	
Mount Vernon Forest	22309	New Market	22844	Suffolk)	23434
Mount Vernon Park	22309	Newmarket Fair (Part of		North Linkhorn Park (Part of	
Mount Vernon Square	22306	Newport News)	23605	Virginia Beach)	23451
Mount Vernon Terrace	22309	New Point	23125	North Post	22060
Mount Vernon Valley	22309	Newport (Giles County)	24128	North Rolleston (Part of	
Mount Vernon Woods	22309	Newport (Page County)	22849	Norfolk)	23502
Mountville	22117	Newport News	23601-12	North Run Hills	23228
Mount Vinco	23921	For specific Newport News Zip		Northside (Part of	
Mount Williams	22602	Codes call (804) 247-5241, or		Richmond)	23222
Mount Zephyr	22309	your local postmaster.		North Springfield	22151
Mount Zion	24554	New Post	22408	North Stanton	24577
Mouth of Laurel	24609	New River	24129	North Tazewell (Part of	
Mouth of Wilson	24363	News Ferry	24592	Tazewell)	24630
Mt. Ararat	23927	Newsoms	23874	North View	23970
Mt. Cross	24540	Newstead Farm	23875	North Virginia Beach (Part	
Mt. View	24354	New Store	23901	of Virginia Beach)	23451
Mud Fork	24630	Newton Park (Part of		North Weems	22576
Mulch	22460	Norfolk)	23523	North Wellville	23824
Munden (Part of Virginia		Newtown (King and Queen		Northwest (Part of	
Beach)	23457	County)	23126	Chesapeake)	23322
Mundy Point	22435	Newtown (Lancaster		North Woodley	22042
Munson Hill	22041	County)	22503	Norton	24273
Murat	24450	Newtown (Rockbridge		Nortonsville	22935
Murpheyville	24368	County)	24450	Norvello	23917
Murphy	24656	Newtown (Rockingham		Norview (Part of Norfolk)	23513
Murrayfield	24319	County)	22827	Norwood (Bedford County)	24551
Museville	24531	Newville (Prince George		Norwood (Nelson County)	24581
Mustoe	24468	County)	23842	Nottingham (Part of	
Mutton Hunk	23421	Newville (Sussex County)	23890	Richmond)	23235
Myndus	22949	Nicelytown	24422	Nottingham (Scott County)	24251
Myrtle (Part of Suffolk)	23434	Nickelsville	24271	Nottoway	23955
Nace	24175	Niday	24124	Nottoway Correctional	
Naffs	24065	Nimrod Hall	24460	Center	23922
Nahor	22963	Ninde	22526	Novelty	24137
Nain	22603	Nineveh	22630	Novum	22735
Namozine Store	23833	Nokesville	22123	Nurney (Part of Suffolk)	23434
Nancy Wrights Corner	22580	Nomini Grove	22572	Nurneysville (Part of Suffolk)	23434
Nandua	23420	Nora	24272	Nutbush	23942
Nansemond (Part of Suffolk)	23434			Nuttall	23061
Nansemond Shores (Part of		**Norfolk** (Independent City)	23501-41	Nuttsville	22528
Suffolk)	23434	For specific Norfolk Zip Codes call		Oakcrest (Part of	
Naola	24574	(804) 629-2198, or your local		Alexandria)	22302
Narrows	24124	postmaster.		Oakcrest (Arlington County)	22202
Naruna	24576	*COLLEGES & UNIVERSITIES*		Oakdale	24450
Nash Ford	24225			Oakdale Farms (Part of	
Nasons	22733	Norfolk State University	23504	Norfolk)	23505
Nassawadox	23413			Oak Forest	23040
Nathalie	24577	*FINANCIAL INSTITUTIONS*		Oak Grove (Carroll County)	24381
National Airport	20001	Dominion Bank, National		Oak Grove (Loudoun	
National Heights	23231	Association	23510	County)	22170
Natural Bridge	24578	First Virginia Bank of		Oak Grove (Spotsylvania	
Natural Bridge Station	24579	Tidewater	23510	County)	22407
Natural Well	24445	Life Savings Bank	23510	Oak Grove (Washington	
Naval Base (Part of Norfolk)	23511	New Atlantic Bank, The	23510	County)	24201
Naval Weapons Laboratory	22448			Oak Grove (Westmoreland	
Naval Weapons Station	23691	*HOSPITALS*		County)	22443
Navy Annex	20370	DePaul Medical Center	23505	Oak Hall	23416
Naxera	23122	Lake Taylor Hospital	23502	Oak Hill (Augusta County)	22980
Naylors Beach	22572	Sentara Leigh Hospital	23502	Oak Hill (Grayson County)	24363
Nealy Ridge	24226	Sentara Norfolk General		Oak Hill (Henrico County)	23223
Nebo	24318	Hospital	23507	Oak Hill (Page County)	22650
Needmore (Smyth County)	24319			Oak Hill Estates	23005
Needmore (Wise County)	24273	*HOTELS/MOTELS*		Oakhurst (Part of	
Neenah	22520	Best Western Center Inn	23502	Petersburg)	23805
Neersville	22132	Holiday Inn-Ocean View	23503	Oakland (Part of Suffolk)	23432
Negro Foot	23192	Norfolk Airport Hilton	23502	Oakland Park	23350
Nellysford	22958	Omni Norfolk	23510	Oakleaf Terrace (Part of	
Nelson	24580	Quality Inn-Lake Wright	23502	Norfolk)	23523
Nelson Estates	23231	Ramada Inn-Airport	23502	Oak Level (Halifax County)	24558
Nelsonia	23414			Oaklevel (Henry County)	24055
Nelson Park	23185	*MILITARY INSTALLATIONS*		Oakley	22437
Nesting	23079	Armed Forces Staff College	23511	Oakpark	22730
Nethers	22740	Naval Air Station, Norfolk	23511	Oak Ridge (Fairfax County)	22180
Nettleridge	24171	Naval Amphibious Base,		Oakridge (Part of Suffolk)	23434
New Alexandria	22307	Little Creek	23521	Oakridge Estates (Prince	
New Baltimore	22186	Naval Supply Center,		William County)	22110
Newbern	24126	Norfolk, Material		Oakridge Estates (Part of	
Newberry	22170	Operations Department,		Suffolk)	23434
New Birchett Estates	23875	Ocean Terminal	23512	Oakton (Fairfax County)	22124
New Bohemia	23842	Navy Material Transportation		Oak Valley Estates	22181
New Canton	23123	Office, Norfolk	23511	Oakville	24522
New Castle	24127	United States Army		Oakwood (Arlington County)	22213
New Church	23415	Engineer District, Norfolk	23510	Oakwood (Buchanan	
Newcomb Hall (Part of				County)	24631
Charlottesville)	22904	Norge	23127	Oakwood (Fairfax County)	22310
New Design (Part of		Norland	24228	Oakwood (Part of Norfolk)	23513
Danville)	24541	Norman	22701	Oakwood Forest	24426
New Ellett	24060	North (Part of Arlington)	22207	Oatlands	22075
New Glasgow	24521		22213	Occoquan	22125
New Gosport (Part of		For specific North Zip Codes call		Occoquan Facility	22079
Portsmouth)	23702	(703) 536-1828, or your local		Occupacia	22476
New Hampden	24413	postmaster.		Oceana (Part of Virginia	
New Hope (Augusta		North (Mathews County)	23128	Beach)	23454
County)	24469	North Bristol (Part of Bristol)	24201	Ocean Park (Part of Virginia	
New Hope (Charles City		North Fairlington	22206	Beach)	23455
County)	23030	Northfields	22901	Ocean View (Part of	
Newington	22122	North Fork	22132	Norfolk)	23503
Newington Station	22153	North Gap	24366	Ocoonita	24263
Newington Woods	22153	North Garden	22959	Ocran	22578
New Kent	23124	North Halifax	24577	Oilville	23129

	ZIP		ZIP		ZIP
Old Courthouse	22182	Parkview (Part of Newport		Pine Grove Court (Part of	
Old Creek Estates	22032	News)	23605	Hampton)	23669
Old Dominion	22969	Parkview (Rockingham		Pine Grove (Page County)	22851
Old Dominion Gardens	22101	County)	22801	Pine Grove (Washington	
Olde Forge	22032	Park View (Part of		County)	24270
Oldewood	22043	Portsmouth)	23707	Pine Grove Terrace (Part of	
Oldfield (Part of Virginia		Parkview Hills	22101	Hampton)	23669
Beach)	23451	Parkwood	22408	Pine Hill	23111
Old Glade Spring	24340	Parnassus	24421	Pinehurst (Part of	
Old Hampton (Part of		Parrott	24132	Portsmouth)	23703
Hampton)	23669	Parsonage	24224	Pine Ridge (mail Annandale)	22003
Oldhams	22529	Partlow	22534	Pine Ridge (mail Fairfax)	22031
Old Somerset	22972	Passapatanzy	22405	Pinero	23061
Old Tavern	22171	Passing	22427	Pine Springs	22042
Oldtown	24333	Pastoria	23421	Pine Tree	23027
Old Well	23959	Patna	24487	Pinetta	23061
Olinger	24219	Patrician Manor (Part of		Pineville	22840
Olive (Part of Portsmouth)	23701	Hampton)	23666	Pinewood Lake	22309
Omaha	24228	Patrick Henry Correctional		Pinewood Lawns	22309
Omega	24592	Unit	24148	Pinewood Park (Part of	
Onancock	23417	Patrick Henry Heights	23111	Manassas Park)	22110
Onemo	23130	Patrick Henry Mall (Part of		Pinewood South	22309
Onley	23418	Newport News)	23607	Piney Grove	24589
Ontario	23937	Patrick Springs	24133	Piney River	22964
Opal	22186	Patterson (Buchanan		Pinners Point (Part of	
Opequon	22602	County)	24631	Portsmouth)	23707
Ophelia	22530	Patterson (Wythe County)	24343	Pipers Gap	24333
Oranda	22657	Pattonsville	24244	Pisgah	24651
Orange	22960	Pauls Cross Roads	22560	Pitmans Corner	22576
Orange Hunt	22152-53	Paynes Store	22553	Pittmantown (Part of	
For specific Orange Hunt Zip		Paytes	22553	Suffolk)	23438
Codes call (703) 451-1533, or		Peach Bottom	24333	Pittsville	24139
your local postmaster.		Peaks	23069	Pizarro	24091
Orapax Farms	23141	Peapatch	24622	Plain View	23156
Orbit	23487	Pearisburg	24134	Plantersville	23937
Orchard Hill	23234	Pearly	24614	Plasterco	24370
Orchid	23117	Peary	23138	Plaza, The (Part of	
Orchid Lake	23065	Pedlar Mills	24574	Lynchburg)	24501
Ordinary	23131	Pedro	22559	Pleasant Gap	24549
Oregon Acres (Part of		Pemberton	23063	Pleasant Grove (Henry	
Portsmouth)	23707	Pembroke	24136	County)	24112
Oreton	24219	Pembroke Mall (Part of		Pleasant Grove (Lunenburg	
Oriskany	24130	Virginia Beach)	23450	County)	23947
Orkney Springs	22845	Pembroke Manor (Part of		Pleasant Grove	
Orlando (Part of Suffolk)	23434	Virginia Beach)	23455	(Mecklenburg County)	23970
Orlean	22128	Pender	22033	Pleasant Grove Estates	23920
Orleans Village	22312	Penderbrook	22033	Pleasant Heights	24370
Oronoco	24483	Pendleton	23117	Pleasant Hill (Part of	
Osaka	24216	Penhook	24137	Harrisonburg)	22801
Osbornes Chapel	24221	Penn Acres	23235	Pleasant Hill (Part of Suffolk)	23434
Osborns Gap	24228	Penn Daw	22306	Pleasant Ridge (Fairfax	
Osceola	24210	Penn Daw Terrace	22307	County)	22003
Osso	22405	Pennington Gap	24277	Pleasant Ridge (Part of	
Othma	23153	Penn Laird	22846	Virginia Beach)	23451
Otter Hill	24523	Penn Lee	24282	Pleasant Shade	23847
Otter River	24571	Penns Store	24165	Pleasant Valley	
Otterville	24523	Pennsytown (Part of		(Buckingham County)	23936
Ottobine	22821	Norfolk)	23513	Pleasant Valley (Fairfax	
Ottoman	22503	Penola	22546	County)	22021
Overall	22610	Pentagon	20301	Pleasant Valley	
Overbrook (Part of Norfolk)	23513	Penvir	24124	(Rockingham County)	22848
Overlee Knolls	22205	Peola Mills	22740	Pleasantview	24574
Owens	22485	Pepper	24141	Plum Creek	24340
Owens Brooke (Part of		Perrin	23072	Plum Point	23181
Manassas)	22110	Perrowville	24551	Plum Tree	23024
Owenton	23148	Perryville (Part of Saltville)	24370	Plymouth	23974
Oxford (Part of Richmond)	23235	Perth	24577	Poages Mill	24018
Oyster	23419	Petersburg	23803-05	Pocahontas (Part of	
Oyster Point (Part of		For specific Petersburg Zip Codes		Petersburg)	23803
Newport News)	23606	call (804) 732-4631, or your local		Pocahontas (Tazewell	
Ozeana	22454	postmaster.		County)	24635
Paces	24592	Peterson Chapel	24244	Pocahontas Correctional	
Paeonian Springs	22129	Petunia	24382	Unit	23832
Page	24631	Peytonsburg	24565	Pocket	24282
Page Hollow	24370	Phenix	23959	Poetown (Part of Grundy)	24614
Paige	22580	Philadelphia (Part of Suffolk)	23434	Poff	24091
Paineville	23083	Philbeck Crossroads	23968	Pohick Estates	22079
Paint Bank	24131	Phillip	24201	Point Breeze	22454
Painter	23420	Phillis	23917	Point Eastern	22546
Paint Lick	24637	Philomont	22131	Point Pleasant	24315
Palls	23086	Philpott	24055	Pons	23866
Palmer	22578	Phoebus (Part of Hampton)	23663	Poole Siding	23833
Palmer Crossroads	27563	Piankatank Shores	23071	Pope	23829
Palmer Springs	23917	Pickaway	24597	Poplar Camp	24360
Palmyra (Fluvanna County)	22963	Pico	24066	Poplar Cove	23417
Palmyra (Part of Suffolk)	23434	Piedmont	24441	Poplar Heights	22046
Pamlico (Part of Norfolk)	23503	Pierces Corner	22503	Poplar Hill (Fairfax County)	22003
Pamplin	23958	Pierces Shop	22960	Poplar Hill (Giles County)	24134
Panoramic Hills	22003	Pigeon Hill	22611	Poplar Inn	22546
Pardee	24216	Pilgrams Knob	24634	Poplar Springs	23075
Paris	22130	Pilot	24138	Poquoson	23662
Park (Part of Waynesboro)	22980	Pimmit	22043	Porter	22937
Parker	22508	Pimmit Hills	22043	Porters Cross Roads	24382
Parkers Shores	22577	Pine	24324	Port Haywood	23138
Parkfairfax (Part of		Pineaire (Part of Suffolk)	23434	Portlock (Part of	
Alexandria)	22302	Pine Chapel Village (Part of		Chesapeake)	23324
Parkglen	22204	Hampton)	23666	Port Norfolk (Part of	
Parklawn	22312	Pinecrest	22312	Portsmouth)	23707
Park Lee Place	23234	Pinecrest Heights	22003	Port-O-Dumfries	22172
Park Place (Part of Norfolk)	23508	Pinedale	23229	Port Republic	24471
Parksley	23421	Pine Grove (Clarke County)	22012	Port Royal	22535

	ZIP
Portsmouth	23701-09
For specific Portsmouth Zip Codes call (804) 397-4607, or your local postmaster.	
Portsmouth Heights (Part of Portsmouth)	23707
Post Oak	22553
Potato Creek	24363
Potomac (Part of Alexandria)	22301
Potomac Beach (Part of Colonial Beach)	22443
Potomac Farms	22011
Potomac Hills	22101
Potomac Mills (Prince William County)	22192
Potomac Mills (Westmoreland County)	22520
Potters Flats	41522
Pound	24279
Pounding Mill	24637
Powcan	23023
Powells Store (Albemarle County)	22937
Powells Store (Bedford County)	24526
Powhatan	23139
Prater	24656
Pratts	22731
Premier	24640
Prentiss Place (Part of Portsmouth)	23707
Preston	24112
Preston Hills	24201
Preston King	22205
Prices Fork	24073
Prices Store	24572
Prilliman	24088
Prince George	23875
Prince George Woods Estates	23875
Princess Anne (Part of Virginia Beach)	23456
Proffit	22901
Prospect	23960
Prospectdale	24134
Providence (Grayson County)	24330
Providence (Halifax County)	24577
Providence Church (Part of Suffolk)	23434
Providence Forge	23140
Providence Park	23222
Provost	23139
Public Fork	23967
Pughsville (Part of Suffolk)	23435
Pulaski	24301
Pulaski Correctional Unit	24084
Pumpkin Center	24315
Pungo (Part of Virginia Beach)	23456
Pungoteague	23422
Purcell	24225
Purcellville	22132
Purchase	24244
Purdy	23847
Purvis (Part of Suffolk)	23437
Puryear Corner	23927
Putnam	24260
Quail Oaks	23234
Quantico	22134
Quantico Marine Corps Air Station	22134
Quantico Station	22134
Quarry	24370
Quebec	24354
Queens Lake	23185
Quicksburg	22847
Quicks Mill	24401
Quinby	23423
Quinque	22965
Quinton	23141
Rabat	24577
Raccoon Ford	22701
Racefield	23168
Radford	24141-43
For specific Radford Zip Codes call (703) 639-3531, or your local postmaster.	
Radford Army Ammunition Plant	24141
Radford University (Part of Radford)	24142
Radiant	22732
Radnor Heights	22209
Ragged Point Beach	22442
Raines Tavern	23901
Rainswood	22473
Raketown	24350
Raleigh Place (Part of Chesapeake)	23320

	ZIP
Raleigh Terrace (Part of Hampton)	23661
Ramoth	22554
Ramsey (Part of Norton)	24273
Randolph	23962
Random Hills	22030
Rangeley	24089
Ransons	23936
Raphine	24472
Rapidan	22733
Rappahannock Academy	22538
Rappahannock Estates	22454
Rappahannock Shores	22454
Rapps Mill	24450
Raven	24639
Ravensworth	22151
Ravensworth Grove	22003
Ravensworth Park	22003
Ravenwood (Fairfax County)	22044
Ravenwood (Prince William County)	22110
Ravenwood Park	22044
Rawhide	24265
Rawley Springs	22831
Rawlings	23876
Raymondale	22042
Raynor	23866
Rayon Terrace (Part of Covington)	24426
Readus	22824
Reams	23803
Reba	24523
Rectortown	22140
Red Apple Orchard	22971
Redart	23076
Red Ash	24640
Red Bank (Halifax County)	24598
Red Bank (Northampton County)	23408
Redd Shop	23901
Red Eye	24531
Red Fox Forest	22003
Red Hill (Albemarle County)	22959
Red Hill (Charlotte County)	24528
Red House	23963
Red Lane	23139
Redlawn	23919
Red Mills	24431
Red Oak	23964
Red Top (Part of Suffolk)	23434
Red Valley	24065
Redwood	24146
Reed Creek	24265
Reedville	22539
Reesedale	24087
Reese Shop	23967
Refuge	22655
Regina	22540
Rehoboth	23974
Rehoboth Church	22482
Reids Ferry (Part of Suffolk)	23434
Reids Grove	22101
Reliance	22649
Remington	22734
Remlik	23175
Remo	22579
Renan	24557
Republican Grove	24585
Rescue	23424
Reservoir Hill (Part of Covington)	24426
Rest	22624
Reston	22090-91
For specific Reston Zip Codes call (703) 437-6677, or your local postmaster.	
Retreat	24151
Reva	22735
Revis	23175
Rexburg	22560
Reynolds Store	22625
Rhoadesville	22542
Rice	23966
Riceville	24565
Richardson	24343
Richardsville	22736
Rich Creek	24147
Richlands	24641
Richmond	23173
	23201-98
For specific Richmond Zip Codes call (804) 775-6140, or your local postmaster.	
Richmond Beach	22560
Richmond Heights	23231
Rich Neck	22472
Richpatch	24426
Rich Valley	24370
Ridge	23229
	23233
	23238

	ZIP
	23242
For specific Ridge Zip Codes call (804) 740-3884, or your local postmaster.	
Ridgecrest	22124
Ridgelea Estates	22031
Ridge View	22310
Ridgeway (Halifax County)	24597
Ridgeway (Henry County)	24148
Ridgeway (Pittsylvania County)	24139
Riggs	22435
Rileyville	22650
Riner	24149
Ringgold	24586
Rio	22901
Ripplemead	24150
Rip Rap	24598
Rivanna	22936
River Bend Estates	22190
Riverdale (Halifax County)	24592
Riverdale (Part of Hampton)	23666
Riverdale (Southampton County)	23851
Riverhill	24333
River Hills	23075
Rivermont (Augusta County)	24477
Rivermont (Chesterfield County)	23831
Rivermont (Part of Covington)	24426
Rivermont (Part of Lynchburg)	24503
Rivermont (Part of Newport News)	23601
River Oaks	22101
River Park (Part of Portsmouth)	23707
River Ridge Mall (Part of Lynchburg)	24502
Rivers Edge	23860
Riverside	24416
Riverside Estates	22309
Riverside Gardens	22308
Riverton (Part of Front Royal)	22651
Riverview (Part of Norfolk)	23504
Riverview (Wise County)	24230
Riverville	24553
Riverwood	22207
Rixeyville	22737
Roanes	23061
Roanoke	24001-38
For specific Roanoke Zip Codes call (703) 985-8765, or your local postmaster.	
Roaringfork	24216
Roaring Run	24066
Robbins Chapel	24265
Roberts Mill	24375
Robertsons	24523
Robin Ridge	23111
Robinwood	23231
Robley	22460
Robnel (Part of Manassas)	22110
Rochelle	22738
Rockbridge Baths	24473
Rock Castle	23063
Rockfish	22971
Rockland	22630
Rockland Village	22021
Rock Mills	22716
Rock Springs (Chesterfield County)	23234
Rock Springs (Fauquier County)	22186
Rocktown	24201
Rockville	23146
Rocky Bar	22827
Rocky Gap	24366
Rocky Mount	24151
Roda	24216
Rodden	24577
Rodophil	23083
Roebuck	24210
Roetown	24236
Rogers	24073
Roland Park (Part of Norfolk)	23509
Rolling Brook	22192
Rolling Hills	22309
Rolling Meadows	23875
Rolling Valley	22015
Rollins Fork	22544
Rondo	24531
Roosevelt Gardens (Part of Norfolk)	23513
Roseann	24614
Rose Bower	24522
Rosedale	24280
Rose Hill (Fairfax County)	22310
Rose Hill (Lee County)	24281

	ZIP
Rose Hill Farms	22310
Roseland	22967
Rosemont (Part of Alexandria)	22301
Rosemont (Fairfax County)	22101
Rosemont (Part of Suffolk)	23434
Rosemont (Part of Virginia Beach)	23452
Roseville	22554
Roslyn Hills	23229
Rosslyn	22209
	22219
For specific Rosslyn Zip Codes call (703) 575-4336, or your local postmaster.	
Roth	24631
Rough Creek	23959
Round Bottom	24124
Round Hill	22141
Round Top	24293
Roundtree	22042
Rowe	24646
Roxbury (Charles City County)	23140
Roxbury (Henrico County)	23229
Royal City (Part of Grundy)	24614
Royal Court	22003
Ruark	23043
Rubermont	23974
Ruby	22545
Ruckersville	22968
Rudee Inlet (Part of Virginia Beach)	23451
Rue	23421
Ruff	23016
Rugby	24363
Rural Retreat	24368
Rushmere	23430
Rushmere Shores	23430
Russell	24260
Russell Creek	24283
Rustburg	24588
Rustburg Correctional Unit	24588
Rustic	23030
Rutherford	22032
Ruther Glen	22546
Ruthland	23228
Ruthville	23147
Ryan	22011
Rye Cove	24244
Sabot	23103
Sadler Heights (Part of Suffolk)	23434
Sago	24137
St. Brides (Part of Chesapeake)	23322
St. Charles	24282
St. Clair	24605
St. Clair Bottom	24319
St. Davids Church	22652
St. Elmo (Part of Alexandria)	22305
St. Joy	23921
St. Just	22567
St. Luke	22664
St. Paul	24283
St. Stephens	22019
St. Stephens Church	23148
Salem (Culpeper County)	22701
Salem (Part of Salem)	24153
Salem Woods	23234
Salisbury	23113
Salona Village	22101
Saltpetre	24085
Saltville	24370
Saluda	23149
Salvia	23148
Samos	23180
Sanburne Park	23150
Sand Bridge (Part of Virginia Beach)	23456
Sandidges	24521
Sands	23874
Sandston	23150
Sandy Bottom (Part of Suffolk)	23432
Sandy Fork	23927
Sandy Hook	23153
Sandy Level	24161
Sandy Point	22579
Sandy River	24054
Sanford	23426
Sangerville	22812
Sanville	24055
Sarah	23130
Saratoga	22153
Saratoga Place (Part of Suffolk)	23434
Saumsville	22644
Saunders (Part of Richmond)	23220
Savage Crossing (Part of Suffolk)	23434

	ZIP
Savageville	23417
Savedge	23881
Saxe	23967
Saxis	23427
Sayersville	24602
Scarborough Neck	23306
Scenic Park (Part of Bristol)	24201
Schley	23154
Schoolfield (Part of Danville)	24541
Schuyler	22969
Scotland	23883
Scott Addition	24210
Scottie Farms	23075
Scottsburg	24589
Scotts Crossroads	23924
Scotts Fork	23002
Scottsville	24590
Scottswood	23851
Scrabble	22749
Scruggs	24121
Seaboard	24641
Seaford	23696
Seaford Shores	23696
Sealston	22547
Seapines (Part of Virginia Beach)	23451
Searcy	23831
Seatack (Part of Virginia Beach)	23451
Seaview	23429
Seawright Spring	24467
Sebrell	23837
Sedalia	24526
Sedgefield (Part of Newport News)	23607
Sedgefield Manor	23228
Sedley	23878
Selden	23061
Selma	24474
Seminary	24219
Seminary Valley (Part of Alexandria)	22304
Senora	22503
Seven Corners	22044
Seven Corners Shopping Center	22044
Seven Fountains	22652
Seven Mile Ford	24373
Seven Pines	23150
Seven Pines Villa	23150
Severn	23155
Severn Manor	23072
Shacklefords	23156
Shacklefords Fork	23156
Shadow	23163
Shadow Valley (Part of Bristol)	24201
Shadwell	22947
Shady Grove (Greene County)	22940
Shady Grove (Halifax County)	24598
Shady Grove (Washington County)	24210
Shady Oak	22066
Shadyside	23405
Shanghai	23110
Shannondale	24630
Shannon Hills	24148
Shannon Park	22577
Sharps	22548
Shawnee Land	22602
Shawsville	24162
Shawver Mill	24651
Shea Terrace (Part of Portsmouth)	23707
Sheep Town	24312
Sheffield Court	23235
Sheffield Terrace	24148
Shelby	22727
Shelfar	23117
Shelors Mill	24091
Shelton (Part of Virginia Beach)	23455
Shenandoah (Part of Hopewell)	23860
Shenandoah (Page County)	22849
Shenandoah Farms	22630
Shenandoah Place	23226
Shenandoah Retreat	22012
Shenandoah Shores	22630
Shepherds Hill	24265
Shepherds Store	23038
Sheppards	23901
Sherando	22952
Sherwill	24538
Sherwood Forest	24401
Sherwood Hall	22306
Sheva	24531
Shields	23306
Shiloh (King George County)	22549

	ZIP
Shiloh (Southampton County)	23827
Shiny Rock	23927
Shipman	22971
Shirley	23030
Shirley Duke (Part of Alexandria)	22304
Shirley Gate Park	22030
Shirlington	22206
Shockoe	24531
Shores	22963
Short Lane	23061
Short Pump	23060
Shorts Creek	24312
Shortt Gap	24647
Shoulders Hill (Part of Suffolk)	23435
Shrevewood	22043
Shumansville	22514
Shumate	24124
Siddon	24580
Sigma (Part of Virginia Beach)	23456
Signpine	23061
Sign Post	23395
Siler	22603
Silva	23415
Silver Beach	23398
Silver Springs	22310
Silverwood (Part of Chesapeake)	23320
Simeon	22901
Simmonsville	24127
Simons Corner	22572
Simonsdale (Part of Portsmouth)	23701
Simonson	22460
Simpkins	23310
Simpsons	24072
Sinai	24592
Sinclair Farms (Part of Hampton)	23669
Singers Glen	22850
Sinking Creek	24127
Sinnickson	23395
Sissons Corner	22473
Sixmile Post	24151
Skeetrock	24228
Skeggs	24646
Skinquarter	23120
Skippers	23879
Skipwith	23968
Skipwith Farms (Henrico County)	23229
Skipwith Farms (Part of Williamsburg)	23185
Skyland	22835
Skyland Estates	22642
Skymont (Part of Staunton)	24401
Slabtown	24251
Slate	24614
Slate Mills	22740
Sleepy Hole (Part of Suffolk)	23435
Sleepy Hollow	22042
Sleepy Hollow Estates (Fairfax County)	22044
Sleepy Hollow Estates (Henrico County)	23229
Sleepy Hollow Manor	22044
Sleepy Hollow Run	22003
Sleepy Hollow Woods	22003
Sliders	23936
Sloantown	24244
Smithfield	23430
Smiths Cross Roads	23970
Smoky Ordinary	23868
Snake Creek	24343
Snapp	24340
Snell	22553
Snowden (Amherst County)	24526
Snowden (Fairfax County)	22308
Snowflake	24251
Snow Hill	23156
Snowville	24347
Soles	23050
Solomons Store	23060
Solsburg	22827
Somers	22503
Somerset	22972
Somerton (Part of Suffolk)	23438
Somerville	22739
Sonans	24531
Sorocco (Part of Suffolk)	23434
Soudan	23927
South	22204
Southampton (Part of Hampton)	23669
Southampton Correctional Center	23829
South Anna	23117
South Boston	24592
South Chesconessex	23417

	ZIP
South Clinchfield	24225
Southern Estates	23805
Southern Pine	23803
South Fairlington	22206
South Garden	22959
South Hill	23970
South Jackson	22842
South Martinsville (Part of Martinsville)	24112
South Norfolk (Part of Chesapeake)	23324
South Plains (Part of Petersburg)	23805
Southport	22191
Southridge	22101
South Roanoke (Part of Roanoke)	24014
Southside (Part of Richmond)	23224
South Suffolk (Part of Suffolk)	23434
South Woodley	22042
Spainville	23824
Sparkling Springs	22834
Sparta	22552
Speedwell	24374
Speegleville (Part of Hampton)	23666
Spencer	24165
Sperryville	22740
Spitler	22835
Spivey Store	24251
Splash Dam	24256
Spotsylvania	22553
Spotsylvania Courthouse	22553
Spottswood	24475
Spout Spring	24593
Springbrook Forest	22003
Spring City	24225
Springcreek	22812
Springdale (Part of Bristol)	24201
Springdale (Henrico County)	23222
Springfield (Fairfax County)	22150-53
	22312
For specific Springfield Zip Codes call (703) 451-1533, or your local postmaster.	
Springfield (Page County)	22835
Springfield (Rockbridge County)	24066
Springfield Estates	22150
Springfield Forest	22150
Springfield Mall Regional Shopping Center	22150
Springfield Plaza	22150
Spring Garden (Part of Bristol)	24201
Spring Garden (Pittsylvania County)	24527
Spring Grove	23881
Springhaven Estates	22102
Spring Hill	24401
Spring Meadows	23111
Spring Mills	24538
Springvale	22066
Spring Valley (Grayson County)	24330
Spring Valley (Stafford County)	22405
Springville	24630
Springwood	24066
Sprouses Corner	23936
Stacy	24614
Stafford	22554-55
For specific Stafford Zip Codes call (703) 659-4775, or your local postmaster.	
Stafford Correctional Unit	22554
Staffordshire	23235
Staffordsville	24167
Stage Junction	23038
Staleys Cross Roads	24368
Stanardsville	22973
Stanley	22851
Stanleytown (Henry County)	24168
Stanleytown (Scott County)	22435
Stapleton	24572
Starkey	24018
Starnes	24250
Star Tannery	22654
Statesville	23874
Station Hills	22039
Staunton (Independent City)	24401-02
For specific Staunton Zip Codes call (703) 886-0701, or your local postmaster.	
Staunton Park (Part of Staunton)	24401
Steeleburg	24609
Steeles Tavern	24476
Steinman	24226
Stella	24133

	ZIP
Stemphleytown	22821
Stephens	24293
Stephens City	22655
Stephenson	22656
Sterling	22170
Sterling Point (Part of Portsmouth)	23703
Stevensburg	22741
Stevens Creek	24330
Stevensville	23161
Stewart (Part of Richmond)	23221
Stewartsburg	24416
Stewartsville	24179
Stickleyville	24244
Stingray Point	23043
Stith	24534
St Louis	22117
Stockton	24054
Stoddert	23901
Stokesland (Part of Danville)	24541
Stokesville	22843
Stone Bridge	22663
Stone Creek	24277
Stonega	24285
Stone Mountain	24523
Stones Mill	24382
Stone Springs (Part of Harrisonburg)	22801
Stonewall	24538
Stonewall Acres	22110
Stonewall Manor	22180
Stoneybrook	22553
Stony	24245
Stony Battery	24354
Stony Creek	23882
Stony Man	22835
Stony Point	22901
Stony Point Mills	23040
Stony Ridge	24630
Stormont	23149
Story	23837
Stott	23898
Stovall	24577
Stover	24421
Straightstone	24569
Strasburg	22657
Strasburg Junction	22657
Stratford (Fairfax County)	22308
Stratford (Westmoreland County)	22558
Stratford Hills (Arlington County)	22207
Stratford Hills (Part of Richmond)	23225
Stratford Landing	22308
Stratford-on-the-Potomac	22308
Stratford Village	23222
Strathmeade Springs	22003
Strathmore	23022
Stringtown	22611
Stroupes Store	24382
Stuart	24171
Stuarts Draft	24477
Stubbs	22553
Studley	23162
Stukeley Hall Farms	23227
Stumptown (Loudoun County)	22075
Stumptown (Northampton County)	23347
Suburban Apartments	23230
Sudley	22110
Sudley Manor	22110
Suffolk	23432-39
For specific Suffolk Zip Codes call (804) 539-5191, or your local postmaster.	
Sugar Grove	24375
Sugar Hill	24528
Sugarland Run	22170
Sugar Loaf	24018
Suiter	24314
Sulgrave Manor	22309
Sumerduck	22742
Summerdeon	24479
Summit (Smyth County)	24375
Summit (Spotsylvania County)	22408
Sun	24224
Sunbeam	23851
Sunnybank	22539
Sunnybrook	22182
Sunnybrook Estates	22110
Sunnyside (Cumberland County)	23040
Sunnyside (Frederick County)	22603
Sunny View	22309
Sunset Heights	23231
Sunset Hills	22090
Sunset Manor	22312

	ZIP
Sunset Village (Part of Salem)	24153
Supply	22559
Surrey Square	22032
Surry	23883
Susan	23163
Sussex	23884
Sussex Hilton (Part of Newport News)	23605
Sutherland (Dinwiddie County)	23885
Sutherland (Wise County)	24273
Sutherland Manor	23885
Sutherlin	24594
Sutton Place	22031
Sutton Woods	22181
Swansea Manor (Part of Newport News)	23601
Swansonville	24549
Sweet Briar	24595
Sweet Briar Park	23075
Sweet Chalybeate	24426
Sweet Hall	23181
Swift Creek (Part of Colonial Heights)	23834
Swift Run	22827
Switch Back	24445
Swoope	24479
Swords Creek	24649
Sycamore	24557
Sydnorsville	24151
Sylvania Heights	22408
Sylvatus	24343
Syria	22743
Syringa	23169
Tabb	23693
Tabscott	23038
Tacoma	24230
Taft	22578
Talbot Park (Part of Norfolk)	23505
Tall Oaks	22003
Tallysville	23124
Tamworth	23027
Tangier	23440
Tannersville	24377
Tappahannock	22560
Tara	22205
Taro	23934
Tarpon	24228
Tasley	23441
Tatum	22567
Tauxemont	22308
Taylors Store	24184
Taylorstown	22075
Taylors Valley	24236
Taylorsville	23047
Tazewell	24651
Tazewell Correctional Unit	24651
Teas	24375
Temperanceville	23442
Temple Hall Estates	23168
Temple Hill	24224
Templeman	22520
Tenso	24226
Tenth Legion	22815
Terrys Fork	24138
Tetotum	22485
Thaxton	24174
The English Hills	22039
The Hollow	24053
The Knolls	22191
Thelma	22942
The Manors	22192
Theological Seminary (Part of Alexandria)	22304
The Plains	22171
The Ridge	23917
Thessalia	24134
The Timbers	22152
The Villas	22191
Thomas Bridge	24354
Thomas Corner (Part of Norfolk)	23502
Thomasson Park	22134
Thomas Terrace	24504
Thomastown	24445
Thompson Valley	24651
Thornburg	22565
Thornhill	22960
Thoroughfare	22014
Thoroughgood (Part of Virginia Beach)	23455
Three Forks	24588
Threemile Corner	23117
Three Springs	24201
Three Square (Goochland County)	23063
Three Square (Louisa County)	23024
Threeway	22469
Tibbstown	22942
Tibitha	22539

* Area Zip Code   † Post Office Boxes

	ZIP		ZIP		ZIP
Ticktown	23301	Vails Mill	24236	Wallaces Store	23937
Tidemill	23072	Vale	22124	Wallops Flight Center	23337
Tidewater	22572	Valentine Hills	23228	Wallops Island	23337
Tidwells	22520	Valentines	23887	Walnut Grove	24270
Tight Squeeze	24531	Valley Brook	22042	Walnut Hill (Part of	
Tignor	22514	Valley Creek	24271	Petersburg)	23805
Timberlake	24502	Valley Mall (Part of		Walters	23315
Timberly Heights (Part of		Harrisonburg)	22801	Walters Woods	22044
Petersburg)	23803	Valley Mills	24479	Walton	24141
Timber Ridge	24450	Valley Ridge	24426	Walton Furnace	24360
Timberville	22853	Valley View	22306	Walton Park	23112
Timothy Park	22309	Valley View Mall (Part of		Waltons Store	24104
Tiny	24220	Roanoke)	24012	Wan	23061
Tiptop	22630	Valleywood	22191	Ward	24620
Tito	24244	Van Buren Furnace	22644	Wardell	24609
Tivis	24256	Vanderpool	24465	Wards Corner (Part of	
Toano	23168	Vandola	24541	Norfolk)	23505
Tobaccoville	23139	Vandyke (Buchanan		Wards Mill	24333
Todds Tavern	22553	County)	24639	Wardtown	23482
Toga	23936	Van Dyke (Tazewell County)	24609	Ware Neck	23178
Tola	23959	Vannoy Acres	22030	Wares Crossroads	23117
Toms Bottom	24256	Vannoy Park	22024	Wares Wharf	22454
Toms Brook	22660	Vansant	24656	Warfield	23889
Toms Creek	24230	Varina	23231	Warminster	24599
Tookland	24614	Varina Grove	23075	Warm Springs	24484
Topnot	22657	Vaucluse	22655	Warner	23179
Topping	23169	Vaughn	22835	Warren	24590
Toshes	24139	Vawter Corner	23093	Warrenton	22186
Totaro	23856	Velma	23108	Warren Woods (Part of	
Tower Mall (Part of		Venia	24260	Fairfax)	22030
Portsmouth)	23703	Vera	24522	Warsaw	22572
Town and Country Estates	22180	Verbena	22827	Warwick (Part of Newport	
Townsend	23443	Verdi	22435	News)	23601
Trade Center (Part of		Vernon Hill	24597	Warwick on the James (Part	
Alexandria)	22304	Verona	24482	of Newport News)	23601
Trammel	24289	Vertain Park	22032	Warwick Village (Part of	
Trapp	22176	Vesta	24177	Alexandria)	22305
Treemont	23234	Vests Store	23139	Washington	22747
Treherneville	23307	Vesuvius	24483	Washington Corner	22580
Tremont Gardens	22042	Vicey	24256	Washington Gardens (Part	
Trenholm	23139	Vicker	24073	of Hampton)	23669
Trents Mill	23040	Vicker Heights	24073	Washington National Airport	22201
Trevilians	23170	Vicksville	23878	Washington Park	23847
Triangle	22172	Victoria	23974	Watauga	24210
Trigg	24134	Vienna	22180-83	Waterford	22190
Trinity	24175	For specific Vienna Zip Codes call		Waterlick	22657
Triplet	23868	(703) 938-2125, or your local		Waterloo	22663
Trout Dale	24378	postmaster.		Water View (Middlesex	
Troutville	24175			County)	23180
Trower	23480	Viers	24256	Waterview (Part of	
Troy	22974	Viewtown	22746	Portsmouth)	23707
Trueblue	22701	Village	22570	Watson	22075
Truxillo	23002	Villa Heights	24112	Wattsville	23483
Tuckahoe	23229	Villamay	22307	Waugh	24526
Tuckahoe Park	23229	Villamont	24178	Waverly	23890
Tuckahoe Village	23229	Vilboro	22580	Waverly Hills	22207
Tucker Hill	24488	Vint Hill Farms	22186	Waverly Village	22407
Tuggle	23901	Vint Hill Farms Station	22186	Waxpool	22010
Tunstall	23124	Vinton	24179	Wayland	23235
Turbeville	24596	Virgilina	24598	Waynesboro	22980
Turnbull	22186	Virginia Beach	23450-67	Waynewood	22308
Turners Crossroads	23879	For specific Virginia Beach Zip		Wayside	23030
Turner Store	23873	Codes call (804) 340-6227, or		Weal	24531
Turnpike (Part of Fairfax)	22031	your local postmaster.		Webbtown	22611
Tuscarora	22454	Virginia City	24283	Weber City (Fluvanna	
Twin Pines (Part of		Virginia Forest (Part of Falls		County)	23022
Portsmouth)	23703	Church)	22046	Weber City (Scott County)	24290
Twin Poplars	22938	Virginia Gardens (Part of		Wedgewood	23229
Twin Springs	24271	Norfolk)	23505	Weedonville	22485
Twymans Mill	22727	Virginia Heights (Arlington		Weems	22576
Tye River	22922	County)	22204	Weirwood	23413
Tyler Gardens (Part of Falls		Virginia Heights (Henrico		Welchs	22580
Church)	22046	County)	23231	Welcome	22485
Tyler Park	22042	Virginia Highlands	22202	Wellford	22572
Tylerton	22405	Virginia Hills (Part of Bristol)	24201	Wellington (Fairfax County)	22308
Tyro	22976	Virginia Hills (Fairfax		Wellington (Prince William	
Tysons Corner	22103	County)	22310	County)	22110
Tysons Corner Center	22102	Virginia State University		Wellington Heights	22308
Tysons Green	22182	(Part of Petersburg)	23803	West Arlington	22213
Union (Bedford County)	24174	Virginia Union University		West Augusta	24485
Union (Floyd County)	24380	(Part of Richmond)	23220	West Bottom	23022
Union Hall	24176	Vir-Mar Beach	22473	Westbourne	23230
Union Level	23970	Volens	24577	Westbriar	23075
Unionville	22567	Volney	24379	Westchester (Chesterfield	
Unison	22141	Vulcan	22567	County)	23235
United States Marine		Wabun	24153	Westchester (Fairfax	
Reservation	22134	Wachapreague	23480	County)	22031
Unity	23898	Wadesville	22611	Westdale	23229
University (Part of		Wake	23176	West Dante	24272
Charlottesville)	22903	Wakefield (Part of		West End Manor	23229
University Heights		Alexandria)	22304	Western (Part of	
(Albemarle County)	22901	Wakefield (Sussex County)	23888	Petersburg)	23803
University Heights (Henrico		Wakefield Chapel	22003	West Falls Church (Part of	
County)	23229	Wakefield Forest	22003	Falls Church)	22046
University of Richmond		Wake Forest	24060	Westfield (Part of Bristol)	24201
(Part of Richmond)	23173	Wakenva	24237	West Fork	24069
Uno	22738	Waldrop	22942	West Fredericksburg (Part	
Upper Brandon	23881	Walhaven	22310	of Fredericksburg)	22401
Upperville	22176	Walkers	23089	West Galax (Part of Galax)	24333
Upright	22454	Walker Store	23924	West Gate	22110
Upshaw	23009	Walkers Well	24531	West Gate of Lomond	22110
Urbanna	23175	Walkerton	23177		
		Wallace	24201		

Place	ZIP	Place	ZIP	Place	ZIP
West Ghent (Part of Norfolk)	23507	Wicomico	23184	Woodberry Forest	22989
Westgrove	22307	Wicomico Church	22579	Woodberry Hills (Part of Danville)	22541
Westham	23229	Wide Water	22554	Woodbridge	22191-94
Westhampton (Fairfax County)	22043	Widewater Beach	22554	For specific Woodbridge Zip Codes call (703) 494-6427, or your local postmaster.	
		Wightman	23924		
Westhampton (Part of Richmond)	23226	Wilburdale	22003		
		Wilda	24477		
Westhaven (Part of Portsmouth)	23707	Wilde Acres	22602	Woodbrook	22901
		Wilderness	22553	Woodford	22580
West Hope	23882	Wilderness Corner	22553	Woodhaven Shores	23141
Westland	22578	Wildwood (Fluvanna County)	22963	Woodland Hills	24210
West Langley	22101			Woodlawn (Carroll County)	24381
Westlawn	22042	Wildwood (Henrico County)	23227	Woodlawn (Part of Hopewell)	23860
West Leigh	22901	Wildwood Farms	23842		
West Lexington (Part of Covington)	24450	Wilkinsons Store	23833	Woodlawn Manor	22309
		Wilkinson Terrace	23234	Woodlawn Mansion	22060
Westmoreland (Albemarle County)	22901	Willard Park (Part of Norfolk)	23509	Woodlawn Park	22309
		Williamsburg	23185-88	Woodlawn Terrace (Fairfax County)	22309
Westmoreland (Westmoreland County)	22577	For specific Williamsburg Zip Codes call (804) 229-4668, or your local postmaster.			
				Woodlawn Terrace (Henrico County)	23150
Westmoreland Heights	22043	Williamsburg Manor	22308	Woodlawn Village	22060
Westmoreland Park	22046	Williams Mill	24251	Woodlee (Part of Staunton)	24401
West Norfolk (Part of Portsmouth)	23703	Williamson Road (Part of Roanoke)	24012	Woodley Hills	22309
				Woodley Hills (mobile home park)	22306
Westover (Arlington County)	22205	Williamsville	24487		
Westover (Charles City County)	23030	Willis	24380	Woodman Terrace	23228
		Willisville	22176	Woodmont (Arlington County)	22207
Westover Hills (Augusta County)	22980	Willis Wharf	23486		
		Willoughby Terrace (Part of Norfolk)	23503	Woodmont (Chesterfield County)	23235
Westover Hills (Part of Danville)	24541				
		Willow	24521	Woodridge	24590
Westover Hills (Greensville County)	23847	Willowbrook	23024	Woodrow Wilson	22939
		Willow Hill	23881	Woodrum (Part of Staunton)	24401
Westover Hills (Part of Richmond)	23225	Willow Lakes (Part of Chesapeake)	23320	Woods Cross Roads	23190
				Woodside Estates	22102
West Petersburg	23803	Willow Lawn	23230	Woods Mill	22938
West Piney	24382	Willow Run	22003	Woodson	22951
West Point	23181	Willow Spring	24266	Woods Store	24091
West Raven	24639	Willow Woods	22003	Woodstock	22664
West Springfield	22152	Wills Corner	23430	Woodville	22749
Wests Store	24577	Willston	22044	Woodway	24277
Westview (Augusta County)	24479	Wilmington	22963	Woolwine	24185
West View (Goochland County)	23063	Wilroy (Part of Suffolk)	23434	Worlds	24530
		Wilsons	23894	Worsham	23901
Westview Hills	23152	Wilson Springs	24473	Worshams	23139
West Warm Springs	24484	Wilton Woods	22310	Wren	23959
Westwood	23226	Winchester	22601-04	Wright (Part of Norfolk)	23505
Westwood Estates	24210	For specific Winchester Zip Codes call (703) 662-2553, or your local postmaster.		Wrights Shop	24572
Westwood Forest	22182			Wrightsville	22427
Westwood Park	22046			Wurno	24301
Westwood Place	24426	Windmill Point	22578	Wylliesburg	23976
Weyanoke	22312	Windsor	23487	Wyndale	24210
Weyers Cave	24486	Windsordale	23229	Wythe (Part of Hampton)	23661
Whaley (Part of Suffolk)	23438	Windsor Estates	22310	Wytheville	24382
Whaleyville (Part of Suffolk)	23438	Windsor Farms (Part of Richmond)	23221	Yacht Haven Estates	22309
Wheatfield	22641			Yale	23897
Wheatland	22132	Windsor Park	22310	Yancey Mills	22932
Wheeler	24248	Windsor Place	23075	Yanceyville	23093
Whitacre	22625	Windsor Shades	23140	Yards	24659
White City	23847	Windy Hill Estates	23111	Yellow Branch	24550
White Gate	24134	Winesap	24572	Yellow Springs	24361
White Hall (Albemarle County)	22987	Winfall	24554	Yellow Sulphur Springs	24073
		Wingina	24599	Yellow Tavern	23060
Whitehall (Frederick County)	22603	Winona (Part of Norfolk)	23509	York Manor	23075
White Head Hall	23828	Winslow Hills	22310	Yorkshire (Prince William County)	22110
White Hill	24477	Winston	22701		
White House	24580	Wintergreen	22958	Yorkshire Acres	22110
White Marsh	23183	Winterham	23002	Yorkshire Park	22110
White Mill	24210	Winterpock	23832	York Terrace	23185
White Oak (Halifax County)	24558	Wirtz	24184	Yorktown	23690-93
White Oak (Stafford County)	22405	Wise	24293	For specific Yorktown Zip Codes call (804) 898-3098, or your local postmaster.	
White Oaks	22307	Wisharts Point	23303		
White Oak Swamp	23150	Wistar Farms	23228		
White Plains	23893	Witch Duck (Part of Suffolk)	23462	Yorktown Naval Weapons Station	23691
White Post	22663		23466		
White Shop	23086	For specific Witch Duck Zip Codes call (804) 497-1033, or your local postmaster.		Yost	24460
White Stone	22578			Youngers Store	24558
Whitesville	23421			Yuma	24251
Whitethorne	24060	Withams	23488	Zacata	22581
Whitetop	24292	Wittens Mills	24630	Zack	24459
Whiteville	23040	Wolfglade	24333	Zanoni	23191
Whitewood	24657	Wolford	24658	Zenda	22801
Whitley	23487	Wolftown	22748	Zepp	22644
Whitlock	22942	Wolf Trap (Fairfax County)	22182	Zion	22942
Whitmell	24549	Wolf Trap (Halifax County)	24073	Zion Crossroads	22942
Whittle	24531	Womacks	23923	Ziontown	23075
Wickford	22310	Wood	24250	Zuni	23898

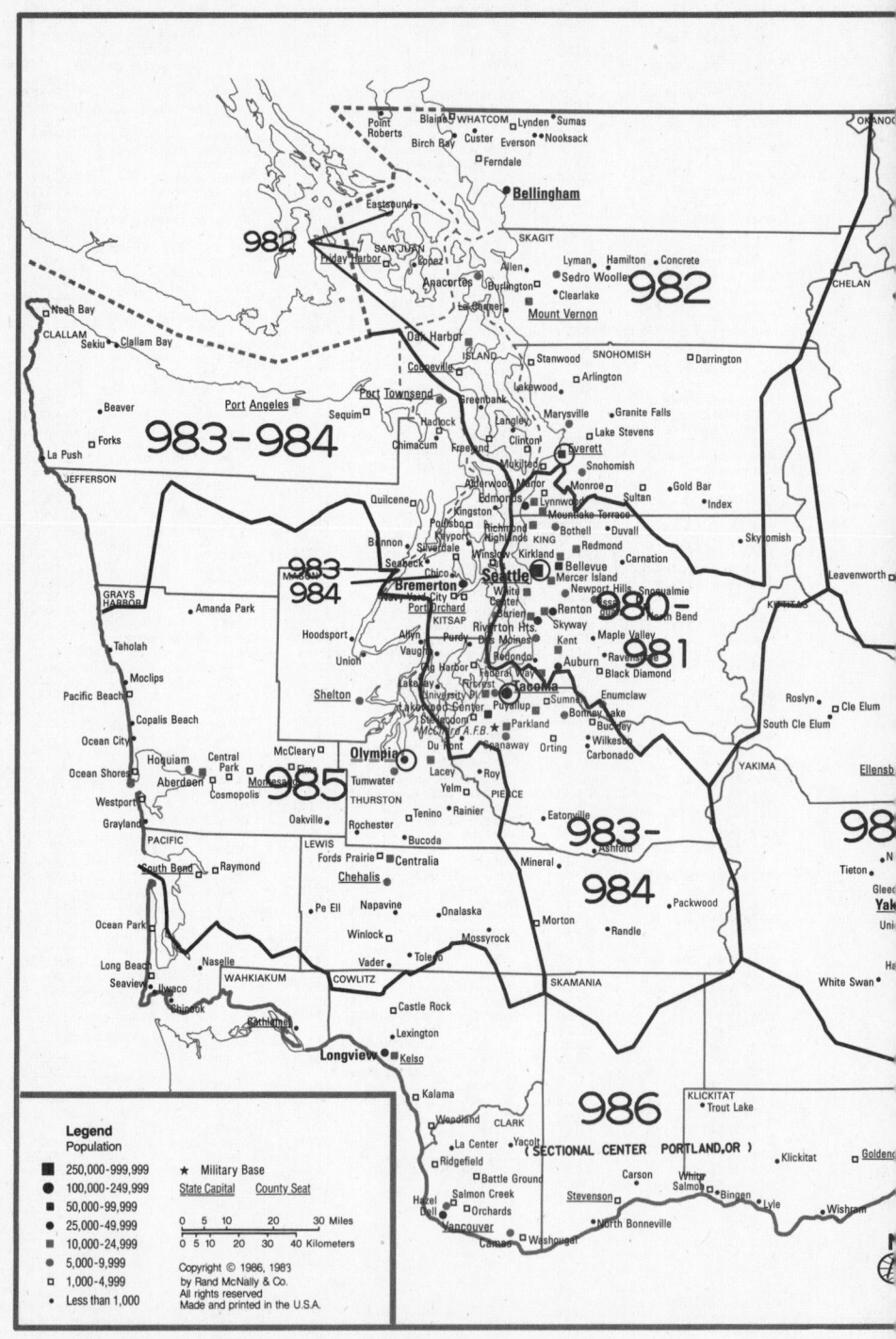

982

982

SAN JUAN
SKAGIT
WHATCOM
CHELAN
OKANO

Bellingham

983-984

**983
984**

**980-
981**

Seattle
Bremerton
Tacoma

985

**983-
984**

98

Yak

986

SECTIONAL CENTER PORTLAND, OR)

KLICKITAT

Vancouver

Legend
Population
■ 250,000-999,999   ★ Military Base
● 100,000-249,999
■ 50,000-99,999   State Capital   County Seat
● 25,000-49,999
□ 10,000-24,999   0 5 10   20   30 Miles
● 5,000-9,999   0 5 10 20   30 40 Kilometers
□ 1,000-4,999
· Less than 1,000
Copyright © 1986, 1983
by Rand McNally & Co.
All rights reserved
Made and printed in the U.S.A.

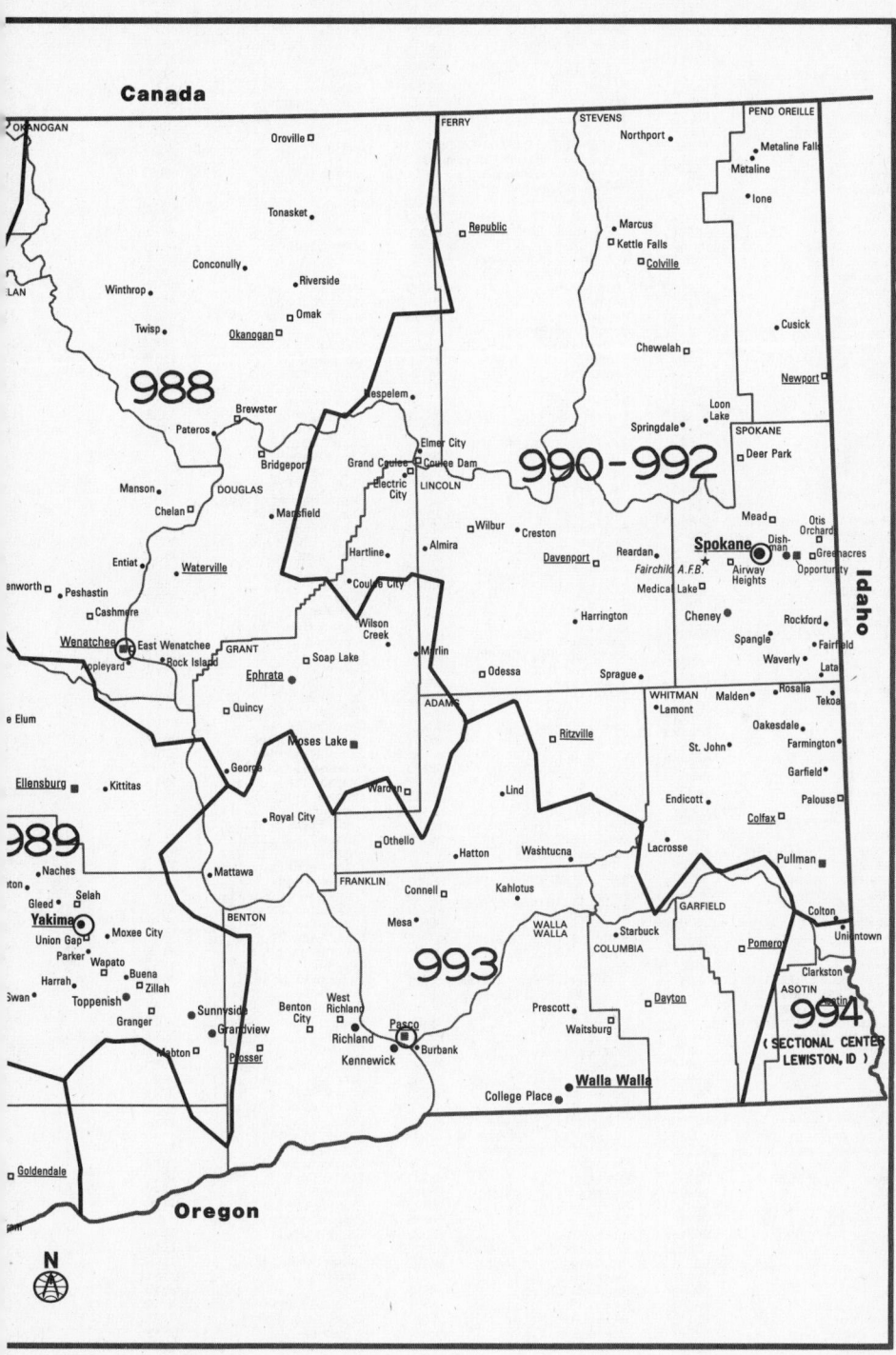

Canada

OKANOGAN

Oroville □

Tonasket •

Conconully •

Riverside •

Winthrop •

Omak •

Twisp • Okanogan □

LAN

988

Brewster •

Pateros •

Bridgeport •

Manson •

DOUGLAS

Chelan □

Mansfield •

Entiat • Waterville

enworth • Peshastin •

Cashmere •

Wenatchee

Appleyard • East Wenatchee

Rock Island • GRANT

Ellensburg • Kittitas

e Elum

989

Naches •

ton • Gleed • Selah •

Yakima

Union Gap • Moxee City

Parker • Wapato •

Harrah • Buena

Swan • Zillah

Toppenish • Sunnyside

Granger • Grandview

Mabton □ Prosser

FERRY

Republic □

Nespelem •

Elmer City

Grand Coulee • Coulee Dam

Electric City

LINCOLN

Hartline •

Coulee City •

Wilson Creek •

Merlin •

Ephrata □

Soap Lake □

Quincy □

Moses Lake ■

George •

Royal City •

Othello •

Mattawa •

BENTON

West Richland

Benton City □

Richland

Kennewick

STEVENS

Northport •

Marcus •

Kettle Falls □

Colville □

Chewelah □

Springdale •

Wilbur □ Creston •

Almira •

Reardan •

Davenport □ Fairchild A.F.B.

Medical Lake □

Harrington •

Cheney •

ADAMS

Odessa □

Sprague •

Ritzville □

WHITMAN

St. John •

Lind •

Hatton • Washtucna •

FRANKLIN

Connell □ Kahlotus •

Mesa •

WALLA WALLA

COLUMBIA

Pasco

Burbank

990-992

PEND OREILLE

Metaline Falls •

Metaline •

Ione •

Cusick •

Newport □

Loon Lake •

SPOKANE

Deer Park □

Mead □ Otis Orchard □

Spokane Dish-man

Airway Heights Greenacres

Opportunity

Rockford □

Spangle • Fairfield •

Waverly • Lata

Malden • Rosalia •

Lamont • Tekoa

Oakesdale •

Farmington •

Garfield •

Endicott • Palouse •

Colfax □

Lacrosse •

Pullman •

GARFIELD Colton •

Pomeroy □ Uniontown •

Clarkston •

ASOTIN

994

(SECTIONAL CENTER
LEWISTON, ID)

Idaho

993

Starbuck •

Dayton □

Prescott •

Waitsburg •

Walla Walla

College Place •

Goldendale □

Oregon

N

	ZIP
Aberdeen	98520
Aberdeen Gardens	98520
Academy	99031
Acme	98220
Adamsview Park	98951
Addy	99101
Adelaide (Part of Federal Way)	98003
Adelma Beach	98368
Admiral's Cove	98239
Adna	98522
Adrian	98851
Aeneas	98855
Agate Point	98110
Agnew	98362
Ahtanum	98903
Airway Heights	99001
Ajlune	98564
Albion	99102
Alder	98328
Alder Terrace	98926
Alderton	98371
Alderwood	98225
Alderwood Manor	98036
Alderwood Manor-Bothell North	98021
Alexander Beach	98221
Alger	98233
Algona	98001
Allen	98232
Allentown	98178
Allyn	98524
Allyn-Grapeview	98524
Almira	99103
Aloha	98571
Alpental	98068
Alpha	98570
Altoona	98643
Amanda Park	98526
Amber	99004
Amboy	98601
American Lake	98493
Anacortes	98221
Anatone	99401
Anderson Island	98303
Angle Lake (Part of SeaTac)	98188
Annapolis (Part of Port Orchard)	98366
Appleton	98602
Arbor Heights (Part of Seattle)	98146
Arcadia	98584
Arden	99114
Ardenvoir	98811
Argyle	98250
Ariel	98603
Arletta	98335
Arlington	98223
Arlington Heights	98223
Armar	98270
Arrowhead (King County)	98011
Arrowhead (Pierce County)	98498
Arrowhead Beach	98292
Artic	98537
Artondale	98335
Ashford	98304
Asotin	99402
Auburn	98001-02
	98071

For specific Auburn Zip Codes call (206) 833-0540, or your local postmaster.

	ZIP
Auburn Twin Lakes (Part of Federal Way)	98023
Ault Field	98277
Avery	98617
Avon	98273
Ayer	99348
Azwell	98846
Baby Island Heights	98260
Baileysburg	99328
Bainbridge Island	98110
Baker Heights	98273
Ballard (Part of Seattle)	98107
B and G	98201
Bangor	98315
Bangor Submarine Base	98315
Bangor Trident Base	98315
Barberton	98665
Baring	98224
Barstow	99141
Basin City	99343
Battle Ground	98604
Battle Point	98110
Bay Center	98527
Bay City	98520
Bayne	98022
Bay Shore	98584
Bay View (Island County)	98260
Bayview (Skagit County)	98273
Bazinet Eddition	98532

	ZIP
Beachcombers Hidden Beach	98253
Beachcrest	98501
Beacon Hill	98632
Beaux Arts Village	98004
Beaver	98305
Beaver Valley	98365
Beckett Point	98368
Belfair	98528
Bellevue	98004-09
	98015

For specific Bellevue Zip Codes call (206) 454-2489, or your local postmaster.

	ZIP
Bellevue Square (Part of Bellevue)	98004
Bellingham	98225-27

For specific Bellingham Zip Codes call (206) 676-8303, or your local postmaster.

	ZIP
Bellis Fairl (Part of Bellingham)	98226
Belmont	99104
Belvidere	99116
Bench Drive (Part of Aberdeen)	98520
Benge	99105
Benson Hill	98055
Benton City	99320
Bethel	98366
Beverly	98321
Beverly Beach	98249
Beverly Park (Part of Everett)	98203
Bickleton	99322
Big Bend	98251
Big Lake	98273
Bingen	98605
Birch Bay	98230
Birchfield	98901
Birdsview	98237
Bissell	99137
Bitter Lake (Part of Seattle)	98133
Biz Point	98221
Black Diamond	98010
Black Lake	99114
Black River	98178
Black River (Part of Renton)	98055
Black River Junction (Part of Renton)	98055
Blaine	98230*
	98231†
Blakely Island	98222
Blanchard	98232
Blewett	98826
Blockhouse	98620
Blue Creek	99109
Blue Lake	99115
Blueslide	99180
Blyn	98382
Boise	98022
Bonneville Spur (Part of Bellingham)	98225
Bonney Lake	98390
Bordeaux	98556
Bossburg	99126
Boston Harbor	98506
Bothell	98011-12
	98021
	98041

For specific Bothell Zip Codes call (206) 486-3243, or your local postmaster.

	ZIP
Boulevard Park	98188
Bow	98232
Bowman Beach	98381
Boyds	99107
Brady	98563
Breidablick	98370
Bremerton	98310-12

For specific Bremerton Zip Codes call (206) 373-1456, or your local postmaster.

	ZIP
Brewster	98812
Briarwood	98031
Bridgeport	98813
Brief	98822
Brier	98036
Brinnon	98320
Broadmoor (Part of Seattle)	98112
Broadway (Part of Seattle)	98102
Brookdale	98444
Brooklane Village	98926
Brooklyn	98537
Browns Point	98422
Brownstown	98920
Brownsville	98310
Bruceport	98586
Brush Prairie	98606
Bryant	98223
Bryn Mawr	98178
Bryn Mawr-Skyway	98178

	ZIP
Buckeye	99005
Buckhorn	98245
Buckley	98321
Bucoda	98530
Buena	98921
Buena Vista	98292
Bunker	98532
Burbank	99323
Burbank Heights	99301
Burien (census designated place)	98062
Burien	98166
Burley	98322
Burlington	98233
Burnett	98321
Burton	98013
Bush Point	98249
Butler Acres	98626
Butler Cove	98501
BZ Corner	98672
Cabin Creek	98925
Camaloch	98292
Camano City	98292
Camano Country Club	98292
Camas	98607
Camelot	98002
Campbell's Glen	98236
Camp Murray	98498
Camp Union	98312
Campus (Part of Bellingham)	98225
Canal Tract	98320
Cape George	98368
Capital Mall (Part of Olympia)	98502
Capitol City Country Club	98501
Capitol Hill (Part of Seattle)	98102
Cap Sante (Part of Anacortes)	98221
Carbonado	98323
Care Free Loop	98331
Carlisle	98536
Carlsborg	98324
Carlton	98814
Carnation	98014
Carrier Annex (Part of Everett)	98204
Carrolls	98609
Carson	98610
Carson River Valley	98610
Carylon Beach	98501
Cascade-Fairwood	98055
Cascade Mall	98055
Cascade Park East	98684
Cascade Park West	98684
Cascade Terrace	98371
Cascade Valley	98837
Cascade Vista	98058
Cashmere	98815
Castle Rock	98611
Cathan	98270
Cathcart	98290
Cathlamet	98612
Cavelero Beach	98292
Cedar Creek Corrections Center	98556
Cedardale	98273
Cedar Falls	98045
Cedar Grove	98038
Cedarhome	98292
Cedar Mountain	98055
Cedarview	98390
Cedarville	98568
Cedonia	99137
Center	98376
Centerville	98613
Central (Part of Yakima)	98901
Centralia	98531
Central Park	98520
Central Valley	98370
Ceres	98532
Charleston (Part of Bremerton)	98312
Charleston Beach	98310
Charter Oak	98604
Chattaroy	99003
Chehalis	98532
Chehalis Indian Reservation	98568
Chehalis Village	98568
Chelan	98816
Chelan Falls	98817
Chelatchie	98601
Cheney	99004
Cherokee Bay Park	98038
Cherry Crest (Part of Bellevue)	98004
Cherry Gardens	98019
Cherry Grove	98604
Cherry Point	98230
Chesaw	98844
Chewelah	99109
Chico	98312

* Area Zip Code   **† Post Office Boxes**

* Area Zip Code   † Post Office Boxes

Place	ZIP
Fernwood	98366
Fife	98424
Fife Heights	98424
Finley	99337
Fircrest	98466
Fircrest Eddition	98532
Firdale	98577
Firgrove	98204
Fir Tree	98540
Firwood	98371
Fisher	98607
Fish Town	98257
Five Corners	98662
Fletcher Bay	98110
Florence	98292
Fobes Hill	98205
Foothill	99207
Forbes	98584
Ford	99013
Fordair	99115
Ford Park	98331
Fords Prairie	98531
Forest	98532
Forest Beach	98335
Forest Glen	98501
Forest Hills Addition	99208
Forest Park (Part of Lake Forest Park)	98155
Forks	98331
Fort Lewis	98433
Fort Wright (Part of Spokane)	99204
Foster (Part of Tukwila)	98188
Four Lakes	99014
Fox Island	98333
Fragaria	98359
Frances	98577
Frankfort	98638
Frederickson	98446
Freeland	98249
Freeman	99015
Fremont (Part of Seattle)	98103
Friday Harbor	98250
Frisken Wye	98541
Fruitland	99129
Fruitvale	98902
Furport	99156
Gales Addition	98362
Galvin	98544
Gamblewood	98346
Gardena	99360
Garden City (Part of McCleary)	98557
Gardiner	98382
Garfield	99130
Garland (Part of Spokane)	99205
Garrett	99362
Gate	98579
Geiger Heights	99204
Geneva	98226
George	98824
Georgetown (mail Ravensdale)	98051
Georgetown (Part of Seattle)	98108
Getchell	98223
Gibraltar	98221
Gifford	99131
Gig Harbor	98329
	98332
	98335

For specific Gig Harbor Zip Codes call (206) 858-2700, or your local postmaster.

Place	ZIP
Gilberton	98310
Glacier	98244
Glacier Springs	98244
Gleed	98904
Glen Cove (Jefferson County)	98368
Glencove (Pierce County)	98329
Glendale	98236
Glenoma	98336
Glenrose	99203
Glenwood (Kitsap County)	98366
Glenwood (Klickitat County)	98619
Globe	98554
Gold Bar	98251
Goldendale	98620
Gooseberry Point	98262
Goose Prairie	98929
Gorst	98337
Goss Lake	98260
Govan	99185
Graham	98338
Graham Point	98584
Grand Coulee	99133
Grand Mound (Thurston County)	98579
Grand Mound (Thurston County)	98501
Grandview (Clallam County)	98362
Grandview (Yakima County)	98930

Place	ZIP
Granger	98932
Granite Falls	98252
Grant Orchards	98851
Grant Road Addition	98802
Granville Grange	98252
Grapeview	98546
Grassmere	98237
Gravelly Lake	98499
Grayland	98547
Grays Harbor City	98550
Grays Landing	99009
Grays River	98621
Greenacres	99016
Greenbank	98253
Greenbank Estates	98253
Green Bluff	99003
Green River Gorge	98022
Greens Landing	98816
Greenwater	98022
Greenwater Meadows	98251
Greenwood (Grays Harbor County)	98520
Greenwood (King County)	98103
Greenwood (Stevens County)	99141
Greenwood (Whatcom County)	98264
Grisdale	98563
Gromore	98903
Grotto	98288
Guemes	98221
Haller Lake (Part of Seattle)	98133
Hamilton	98255
Hansville	98340
Happy Valley (Part of Bellingham)	98225
Harbor Center	98249
Harbor Heights (Part of Gig Harbor)	98338
Harbour Pointe	98204
Harmon Heights	98045
Harper	98366
Harrah	98933
Harrington	99134
Hartford (Part of Lake Stevens)	98258
Hartland	98635
Hartline	99135
Hartstene	98584
Harwood	98908
Hatton	99332
Havillah	98855
Hawk Acres	98501
Hay	99136
Hayford	99204
Haynes Acres	98501
Hays Park (Part of Spokane)	99207
Hazel	98223
Hazel Dell	98665
Hazel Dell North	98665
Hazel Dell South	98665
Hazelwood	98055
Heather Downs (Part of Renton)	98055
Heisson	98622
Herron Island	98349
Hidden Valley	98304
Highland (Asotin County)	99403
Highland (Benton County)	99337
Highland (Clark County)	98629
Highland (Snohomish County)	98258
Highland Estates	98584
Highland Heights	98571
Highland Park (Part of Seattle)	98106
Highlands (Part of Renton)	98056
High Point (mail Issaquah)	98027
High Point (Part of Seattle)	98126
High Valley	98027
Hilltop	98004
Hillyard (Part of Spokane)	99207
Hintzville	98312
Hobart	98025
Hockinson	98606
Hogans Corner	98550
Hoh Indian Reservation	98331
Hoko	98326
Holcomb	98577
Holden Village	98816
Holiday Valley Estates	98501
Holly	98310
Hollywood	98072
Hollywood Beach	98816
Holman	98644
Holmes Harbor Estates	98253
Home	98349
Home Acres	98205
Home Valley	98648
Honeymoon Vista Bay	98253
Hood	98651

Place	ZIP
Hoodsport	98548
Hoogdal	98284
Hooper	99333
Hope	98333
Hoquiam	98550
Horseshoe Lake	98366
Houghton (Part of Kirkland)	98033
Humptulips	98552
Hunters	99137
Hunts Point	98004
Huntsville	99328
Husum	98623
Hyak	98068
Illahee (Grays Harbor County)	98569
Illahee (Kitsap County)	98310
Ilwaco	98624
Image	98662
Impach	99138
Inchelium	99138
Index	98256
Indian Beach	98292
Indianola	98342
Indian Village	98221
Inglewood	98011
Inglewood-Finn Hill	98011
Inlet Island	98390
Innis Arden	98160
Interbay (Part of Seattle)	98119
Intercity	98203
Interlaken	98438
International (Part of Seattle)	98104
Ione	99139
Irby	99159
Ireland	98607
Irondale	98339
Iron Springs	98535
Isabella Lake	98584
Island Center	98110
Island Lake	98370
Island View	98381
Issaquah	98027
Jared	99180
John Sam Lake	98270
Johnson	99113
Johnson Point	98501
Jordan	98223
Jovita	98371
Joyce	98343
Juanita (Part of Kirkland)	98033
Junction City	98520
Juniper Beach	98292
Kachees Ridge	98925
Kahlotus	99335
Kalama	98625
Kala Point	98368
Kalispel Indian Reservation	99180
Kamilche	98584
Kanaskat	98051
Kangley	98051
Kapowsin	98344
Keller	99140
Kellogg Marsh	98223
Kellys Korner	98501
Kelso	98626
Kendall	98295
Kenmore	98028
Kennard Corner	98012
Kennedys Lagoon	98239
Kennewick	99336-37

For specific Kennewick Zip Codes call (509) 582-5000, or your local postmaster.

Place	ZIP
Kennydale (Part of Renton)	98056
Kenroy	98802
Kent	98031-32
	98035
	98042
	98064

For specific Kent Zip Codes call (206) 852-3950, or your local postmaster.

Place	ZIP
Kettle Falls	99141
Kewa	99138
Key Center	98329
Keyport	98345
Keyport Naval Torpedo Station	98345
Keystone	98849
Kid Valley	98649
Kingsgate	98011
Kings Lakeside	98603
Kingston	98346
Kiona	99320
Kirkland	98033-34
	98083

For specific Kirkland Zip Codes call (206) 822-2292, or your local postmaster.

Place	ZIP
Kitsap Lake	98312
Kittitas	98934
Klaber	98538

	ZIP		ZIP		ZIP
Klaus	98532	Leadpoint	99114	Maple Falls	98266
Klickitat	98628	Lea Hill	98002	Maple Grove	98362
Klipsan Beach	98640	Leavenworth	98826	Maple Hills	98031
Knab	98591	Lebam	98554	Maple Valley	98038
Knappton	98638	Ledgewood Beach	98239	Maple Valley Heights	98055
Koontzville	99116	Leland	98376	Maplewood (Part of Renton)	98055
Kooskooskie	99362	Lemolo	98370	Maplewood Heights	98055
Kozy Kamp	98642	Lexington	98626	Marblemount	98267
Krain	98022	Liberty	98922	Marcus	99151
Kruse	98271	Liberty Lake	99019	Marengo	99169
Kruse Junction	98271	Liberty Park (Part of		Marietta	98226
K Street (Part of Tacoma)	98405	Spokane)	99202	Marietta-Alderwood	98225
	98415	Lilliwaup	98555	Marine Drive (Part of	
For specific K Street Zip Codes		Lincoln (Kitsap County)	98370	Bremerton)	98310
call (206) 756-6115, or your local		Lincoln (Lincoln County)	99147	Marine Hills (Part of Federal	
postmaster.		Lind	99341	Way)	98003
Kummer	98010	Littell	98532	Marine View Estates (Part of	
Lacamas	98570	Little Boston	98346	Federal Way)	98003
La Center	98629	Little Falls	99013	Marketown	98277
Lacey	98503	Littlerock	98556	Markham	98520
	98513	Lochsloy	98258	Marlin	98832
	98516	Lockamas Heights	98607	Marshall	99020
For specific Lacey Zip Codes call		Locke	99119	Martha Lake	98012
(206) 459-2371, or your local		Lofall	98370	Maryhill	98620
postmaster.		Lone Lake Shores	98260	Marys Corner	98532
La Conner	98257	Lone Pine	99116	Marysville	98270-71
Lacrosse	99136	Long Beach	98631	For specific Marysville Zip Codes	
	99143	Longbranch	98349	call (206) 659-1260, or your local	
For specific Lacrosse Zip Codes		Long Lake (Kitsap County)	98366	postmaster.	
call (509) 549-3848, or your local		Long Lake (Lincoln County)	99013	Matlock	98560
postmaster.		Longmire	98397	Matneys Spur	99141
Lagoon Point	98253	Long Point Manor	98239	Mattawa	99344
La Grande	98348	Longview	98632	Maxwelton	98236
Lake Alice	98024	Longview Heights	98632	May Creek	98251
Lakebay	98349	Longview Junction (Part of		Mays Pond	98012
Lake City (Part of Seattle)	98125	Kelso)	98626	Maytown	98502
Lake Crescent	98362	Loomis	98827	Mazama	98833
Lakedale	98940	Loon Lake	99148	Mead	99021
Lake Dolloff	98002	Lopez	98261	Meadow Brook (King	
Lake Forest North	98155	Lost Creek	99180	County)	98065
Lake Forest Park	98155	Lost Lake	98292	Meadowbrook (Yakima	
Lake Goodwin	98292	Loveland	98387	County)	98903
Lake Heights	98002	Lowden	99360	Meadowdale (Kitsap	
Lake Hills (Part of Bellevue)	98007	Lowell (Part of Everett)	98203	County)	98310
Lake Howard	98292	Lower Elwha Indian		Meadowdale (Snohomish	
Lake Joy	98014	Reservation	98362	County)	98020
Lake Kachees	98925	Loyal Heights (Part of		Meadow Glade	98604
Lake Kathleen	98055	Seattle)	98117	Meadow Grange	98273
Lake Ki	98223	Lucerne	98816	Medical Lake	99022
Lakeland North	98002	Lummi Indian Reservation	98226	Medina	98039
Lakeland South	98002	Lummi Island	98262	Meeker (Part of Puyallup)	98371
Lakeland Village (Part of		Lummi Point	98262	Melbourne	98563
Medical Lake)	99022	Lyle	98635	Menlo	98561
Lake Leota	98072	Lyman	98263	Mercer Island	98040
Lake Loma	98271	Lynden	98264	Meredith (Part of Auburn)	98002
Lake Louise	98498	Lynnwood	98036-37	Meridian Heights	98042
Lake Lucerne	98038		98046	Merritt	98826
Lake Martha	98037	For specific Lynnwood Zip Codes		Mesa	99343
Lake McDonald	98055	call (206) 778-2154, or your local		Metaline	99152
Lake Meridian	98042	postmaster.		Metaline Falls	99153
Lake Pattison	98501	Lynwood Center	98110	Methow	98834
Lake Retreat	98051	Mabana	98292	Metreco	98438
Lakeridge	98178	Mabton	98935	Miami Beach	98380
Lake Sawyer	98042	McChord Air Force Base	98438	Mica	99023
Lakes District	98499	McCleary	98557	Midlakes (Part of Bellevue)	98015
Lake Serene-North		McDonald	98837	Midland	98404
Lynnwood	98037	McGinnis Lake	99116		98444-45
Lake Shore	98665	McGowan	98614	For specific Midland Zip Codes	
	98685	Machias	98290	call (206) 756-6144, or your local	
For specific Lake Shore Zip		McKees Beach	98292	postmaster.	
Codes call (206) 695-4462, or		McKenna	98558	Midland Acres (Part of	
your local postmaster.		McMicken Heights (Part of		Camas)	98607
Lake Stevens	98258	SeaTac)	98188	Midvale Corner	98236
Lakeview	98499	McMillin	98360	Midway (King County)	98035
Lakeview Park	98851	McNeil Island	98388	Midway (Pierce County)	98335
Lakeview Terrace	99133	Madigan Hospital	98431	Milan	99003
Lake Wilderness	98038	Madison Park (Part of		Milco (Part of Kelso)	98626
Lakewood	98259	Seattle)	98112	Miles	99122
Lakewood Mall (Part of		Madrona Beach	98292	Mill A	98605
Tacoma)	98402	Madrona Point (Part of		Mill Creek	98012
Lakota (Part of Federal		Bremerton)	98312	Miller River	98288
Way)	98003	Mae	98837	Millwood	99212
Lamoine	98858	Magnolia (Part of Seattle)	98199	Milton	98354
Lamona	99144	Makah Air Force Station		Mima	98501
Lamont	99017	758th Radar Squadron	98357	Mineral	98355
Langley	98260	Makah Indian Reservation	98357	Minnehaha	98661
La Push	98350	Malaga	98828		98663
Larch Corrections Center	98675	Malden	99149	For specific Minnehaha Zip Codes	
Larchmont (Part of Tacoma)	98409	Malo	99150	call (206) 695-4462, or your local	
Larimers Corner	98290	Malone	98559	postmaster.	
Latah	99018	Malott	98829	Mirror Lake (Part of Federal	
Laurel (Klickitat County)	98619	Maltby	98290	Way)	98002
Laurel (Whatcom County)	98225	Manchester (Kitsap County)	98353	Mirrormont	98027
Laurel Heights (Part of		Manette (Part of Bremerton)	98310	Mission Beach	98271
Everett)	98203	Manito (Part of Spokane)	99203	Misty Meadows	98012
Laurelhurst (Part of Seattle)	98105	Manito Club Estates	99203	Mobase	98433
Laurier	99146	Manitou Beach	98061	Moclips	98562
Lawrence (Pierce County)	98409	Manor	98604	Mohler	99154
Lawrence (Whatcom		Mansfield	98830	Mold	99115
County)	98247	Manson	98831	Molson	98844
Laws Corner	98672	Manzanita	98110	Mondovi	99122
Lazy C	98320	Maple Beach	98281	Monitor	98836

	ZIP
Monohon	98027
Monroe	98272
Monse	98812
Monta Vista	98499
Montborne	98273
Montesano	98563
Moore	98816
Moorlands	98011
Moran Prairie	99203
Morgan Acres	99207
Morganville (Part of Black Diamond)	98010
Morton	98356
Moses Lake	98837
Moses Lake North	98837
Mossyrock	98564
Mountain Home Park	99328
Mountain View	98273
Mountain View Beach	98292
Mount Brook	98672
Mount Hope	99012
Mountlake Terrace	98043
Mount Pleasant	98362
Mount Tahoma Estate	98501
Mount Vernon	98273
Moxee	98936
Muckleshoot Indian Reservation	98002
Mukilteo	98275
Munson Point	98584
Murdock	98617
Murphy's Corner	98012
Mushroom Corner	98501
Naches	98929
	98937

For specific Naches Zip Codes call (509) 653-2467, or your local postmaster.

	ZIP
Nahcotta	98637
Nahwatzel Lake	98584
Napavine	98565
Naselle	98638
National	98304
Naval Supply Center Puget Sound	98314
Naval Torpedo Station	98345
Navy Yard City	98310
Neah Bay	98357
Neilton	98566
Nemah	98586
Nespelem	99155
Nespelem Community	99155
Newaukum	98002
Newcastle	98055
Newhalem	98283
New London	98550
Newman Lake	99025
Newport (King County)	98004
Newport (Pend Oreille County)	99156
Newport Hills (census designated place)	98002
Newport Hills	98006
Newport Shores (Part of Bellevue)	98004
Newton	98550
Nighthawk	98827
Nile	98937
Nine Mile Falls	99026
Nisqually Indian Community	98513
Nisqually Indian Reservation	98597
Nisson	98550
Nooksack	98276
Nordland	98358
Norma Beach	98020
Norman	98292
Normandy Park	98166
North Beach	98245
North Bend	98045
North Bonneville	98639
North City	98155
North City-Ridgecrest	98155
North Cove	98547
North Creek-Canyon Park	98012
	98021

For specific North Creek-Canyon Park Zip Codes call (206) 486-3243, or your local postmaster.

	ZIP
North Fort Lewis	98434
Northgate (Part of Seattle)	98125
Northgate Shopping Center (Part of Seattle)	98125
North Hill	98166
North Lake	98002
North Lynnwood	98036
North Marysville (census designated place)	98201
North Marysville	98271
North Omak	98841
Northport	99157
North Prosser	99350
North Puyallup	98372

	ZIP
Northrup (Part of Bellevue)	98008
North Town (Part of Spokane)	99207
Northtown Mall (Part of Spokane)	99207
Northwood	98264
Northwoods	98616
North Yelm	98597
Norwood Village (Part of Bellevue)	98004
Novelty	98019
Nugents Corner	98247
Oakbrook	98497
Oakesdale	99158
Oak Harbor	98277
Oakland (Part of Tacoma)	98409
Oak Park (Part of Camas)	98607
Oakville	98568
O'Brien (Part of Kent)	98032
Obstruction Pass	98279
Ocean City	98569
Ocean Grove	98571
Ocean Park	98640
Ocean Shores	98569
Ocosta	98520
Odessa	99159
Offutt Lake	98589
Okanogan	98840
Olalla	98359
Olalla Valley	98359
Oldport	98501
Old Tacoma (Part of Tacoma)	98466
Old Willapa	98577
Olga	98279
Olympia	98501-16

For specific Olympia Zip Codes call (206) 357-2286, or your local postmaster.

	ZIP
Olympic Corrections Center	98331
Olympic View	98383
Olympus Ocean Estates	98571
Omak	98841
Onalaska	98570
Oneida	98643
Onion Creek	99114
Opportunity	99206
Orcas	98280
Orchard Avenue	99211
Orchard Prairie	99207
Orchards	98662
Orchards North	98662
Orchards South	98662
Orient	99160
Orilla (Part of Kent)	98032
Orin	99114
Orondo	98843
Oroville	98844
Orting	98360
Osceola	99022
Oso	98223
Ostrander	98626
Othello	99327
Otis Orchards	99027
Otis Orchards-East Farms	99025
Outlook	98938
Oyhut	98550
Oysterville	98641
Ozette	98326
Pacific	98047
Pacific Beach	98571
Packwood	98361
Paine Field-Lake Stickney	98204
Painted Hills	99206
Palisades	98845
Palmer	98051
Palouse	99161
Panhandle Lake	98584
Paradise Estates	98304
Paradise Inn	98398
Park	98284
Parker	98939
Parkland	98444
Park Orchard	98031
Park Rapids	99114
Parkwater (Spokane County)	99211
Parkway Plaza (Part of Tukwila)	98188
Parkwood	98366
Pasadena Park	99206
Pasco	99301*
	99302†
Pataha City	99347
Pateros	98846
Paterson	99345
Peach Acres	98465
Pearcot	98801
Pearson	98370
Pe Ell	98572
Pend Orielle Village	99153
Penn Cove Park	98277

	ZIP
Peone	99021
Perrinville (Part of Edmonds)	98020
Peshastin	98847
Picnic Point	98335
Pillar Rock	98643
Pinebrook (Part of Vancouver)	98660
Pine City	99170
Pinecliff	98937
Pinecroft	99214
Pine Glen	98925
Pinehurst (Part of Everett)	98203
Pine Lake	98027
Ping	99347
Pioneer	98642
Pioneer Square (Part of Seattle)	98104
Pipe Lake	98038
Plain	98826
Plaza	99170
Pleasant Harbor	98320
Pleasant Hill	98626
Pleasant Prairie	99207
Pleasant Valley	98665
Plymouth	99346
Pocahontas Bay	99009
Point Roberts	98281
Point White	98110
Pomeroy	99347
Pomona	98901
Pomona Heights	98903
Ponder	98499
Ponderosa Estates	98390
Pontius Park	98021
Portage	98070
Portage Point	98262
Port Angeles	98362
Port Angeles East	98362
Port Blakely	98110
Port Discovery	98368
Porter	98541
Port Gamble	98364
Port Gamble Indian Reservation	98346
Port Hadlock	98339
Port Ludlow	98365
Port Madison	98110
Port Madison Indian Reservation	98310
Port Orchard	98366
Port Stanley	98261
Port Townsend	98368
Possession	98236
Possession Shores	98236
Potlatch	98584
Poulsbo	98370
Poverty Bay (Part of Federal Way)	98003
Prairie	98284
Prairie Center (Part of Coupeville)	98239
Prairie Ridge (Pierce County)	98390
Prescott	99348
Preston	98050
Priest Point	98271
Proctor (Part of Tacoma)	98407
Proebstel	98662
Prosser	99350
Prune Hill	98607
Puget Island	98612
Puget Sound Naval Base	98314
Puget Sound Naval Shipyard	98314
Pullman	99163-65

For specific Pullman Zip Codes call (509) 334-3212, or your local postmaster.

	ZIP
Purdy	98332
Purdy Treatment Center for Women	98332
Puyallup	98371-74

For specific Puyallup Zip Codes call (206) 845-2334, or your local postmaster.

	ZIP
Queen Anne (Part of Seattle)	98109
Queensborough	98021
Queets	98331
Quendall (Part of Renton)	98055
Quilcene	98376
Quileute Indian Reservation	98350
Quinault	98575
Quinault Indian Reservation	98587
Quincy	98848
Rainer Valley (Part of Seattle)	98118
Rainier	98576
Rainier Beach (Part of Seattle)	98102
Rainier Terrace	98371
Ralston	99169

	ZIP
South Seattle (Part of Seattle)	98102
Southshore Mall (Part of Aberdeen)	98520
Southside (Part of Everett)	98208
South Snohomish	98290
South Sound (Part of Lacey)	98503
South Tacoma (Part of Tacoma)	98409
South Union	98501
South Wenatchee	98801
Southworth	98386
Spanaway	98387
Spangle	99031
Special Offender Center	98272
Spokane	99201-28
For specific Spokane Zip Codes call (509) 459-0222, or your local postmaster.	
Spokane Indian Reservation	99129
Sprague	99032
Spring Creek	98940
Springdale	99173
Spring Glen	98024
Squaxin Island Indian Reservation	98584
Stabler	98610
Stanwood	98292
Starbuck	99359
Star Lake	98002
Startup	98293
Station A (Part of Tacoma)	98408
	98418
For specific Station A Zip Codes call (206) 756-6118, or your local postmaster.	
Stehekin	98852
Steilacoom	98388
Steptoe	99174
Sterling	98284
Stevenson	98648
Stiebels Corner	98346
Stillwater	98014
Stimson Crossing	98223
Strandell (Part of Everson)	98247
Stratford	98853
Streeters	98611
Stringtown	98624
Sudden Valley	98226
Sultan	98294
Sumach	98901
Sumas	98295
Summerwood	99005
Summit	98373
Summit Lake	98501
Summit Park	98221
Sumner	98390
Suncrest	99026
Sundale	99356
Sundins Beach	98292
Sun Island	98925
Sunland Estates	98824
Sunlight Beach	98236
Sunlight Shores	98236
Sunny Bay	98335
Sunnydale	98155
Sunnyside (Snohomish County)	98205
Sunnyside (Yakima County)	98944
Sunnyside Beach (Part of Steilacoom)	98388
Sunnyslope (Chelan County)	98801
Sunnyslope (Kitsap County)	98366
Sunrise Beach	98335
Sunrise Point	98292
Sunset	99171
Sunset Bay	99034
Sunset Beach (Grays Harbor County)	98571
Sunset Beach (Island County)	98292
Sunset Beach (Mason County)	98528
Sunset Beach (Pierce County)	98466
Sunset West (Lewis County)	98532
Sunset West (Yakima County)	98903
Sun Village (Part of Kirkland)	98012
Sunwood Lakes	98501
Suquamish	98392
Swan Trail	98205
Swede Hill	98332
Swinomish Indian Reservation	98257
Swinomish Village	98257
Swofford	98564
Sylvan	98333
Synarep	98849

	ZIP
Tacoma	98401-99
For specific Tacoma Zip Codes call (206) 756-6175, or your local postmaster.	
Tacoma Junction (Part of Fife)	98424
Tacoma Mall (Part of Tacoma)	98409
Tacoma Point	98390
Tahlequah	98070
Taholah	98587
Tahuya	98588
Tampico	98903
Tanglewilde	98503
Tanglewilde East	98516
Tanglewilde-Thompson Place	98506
Tanner	98045
Teanaway	98922
Tekoa	99033
Telma	98826
Tenino	98589
Terminal Annex (Part of Seattle)	98134
Terminal Annex (Part of Spokane)	99202
Teronda West	98239
Terrace Heights	98901
Terrill Beach	98245
Terry Avenue (Part of Seattle)	98109
Terrys Corner	98292
Thomas	98032
Thompson Place	98516
Thornton	99176
Thorp	98946
Thrashers Corner	98021
Three Lakes	98290
Three Rivers Mall (Part of Kelso)	98626
Thrift	98338
Tieton	98947
Tiger	98180
Tillicum	98492
Tillicum Beach	98292
Tillicum Siding	98492
Timber Lakes	98584
Timberlane	98042
Tokeland	98590
Toledo	98591
Tonasket	98855
Toppenish	98948
Totem Lake (Part of Kirkland)	98033
Touchet	99360
Toutle	98649
Town and Country	99210
Tracyton	98393
Trafton	98223
Treasure Island	98546
Trend (Part of Kirkland)	98033
Trentwood	99215
Triangle Shopping Mall (Part of Longview)	98632
Tri-Cities (Part of Pasco)	99302
Trinidad	98848
Triton	98555
Trout Lake	98650
Tukwila	98188
Tulalip	98271
Tulalip Bay	98270-71
For specific Tulalip Bay Zip Codes call (206) 659-1260, or your local postmaster.	
Tulalip Indian Reservation	98271
Tumtum	99034
Tumwater	98502
Turner	99328
Turner Corner	98072
Twin Rivers Corrections Center	98272
Twisp	98856
Tyler	99004
Umtanum	98926
Underwood	98651
Union	98592
Union Gap	98903
Union Mill	98501
Uniontown	99179
University (Part of Seattle)	98105
University Place	98465
University Village (Part of Seattle)	98105
Upper Preston	98027
Uranium City	99013
Urban	98221
Useless Bay Country Club	98260
Usk	99180
Utsalady	98292
Vader	98593
Valley	99181
Valleyford	99036

	ZIP
Valley Mall (Part of Union Gap)	98903
Valley Ridge (Part of SeaTac)	98188
Valley View	98331
Van Asselt (Part of Seattle)	98108
Van Buren	98247
Vancouver	98660-68
	98682-86
For specific Vancouver Zip Codes call (206) 695-4462, or your local postmaster.	
Vancouver Mall	98662
Van Horn	98237
Vantage	98950
Van Zandt	98244
Vashon	98070
Vashon Center	98070
Vashon Heights	98070
Vaughn	98394
Veazey	98002
Venersborg	98604
Venice	98110
Veradale	99037
Verlot	98252
Vesta	98537
Veterans Administration Hospital (Part of Vancouver)	98661
View	98629
View Park	98366
View Ridge (Part of Seattle)	98115
Villa Beach	98303
Villa Plaza	98499
Vinland	98370
Virginia	98370
Vision Acres	98626
Wabash	98022
Wahkiacus	98670
Waitsburg	99361
Waitts Lake	99181
Waldron	98297
Walla Walla	99362
Walla Walla East	99362
Waller	98443
Wallingford (Part of Seattle)	98103
Wallula	99363
Wallula Junction	99363
Walnut Grove	98662
Wanapum Village	99321
Wapato	98951
Warden	98857
Warm Beach	98292
Warnick	98244
Warren	98335
Washington Corrections Center	98584
Washington State Reformatory	98272
Washougal	98671
Washtucna	99371
Waterman	98366
Waterville	98858
Wauconda	98859
Waukon	99008
Wauna	98395
Waunch Prairie (Part of Centralia)	98531
Wautauga Beach	98366
Waverly	99039
Wawawai	99113
Weallup Lake	98270
Wedgwood (Part of Seattle)	98115
Wegoe	98433
Weikel	98902
Welcome	98244
Wellpinit	99040
Wenatchee	98801-07
For specific Wenatchee Zip Codes call (509) 662-7663, or your local postmaster.	
Wenatchee Heights	98802
West Beach	98245
West Blakely	98110
West Clarkston	99403
West Clarkston-Highland	99403
West Coulee (Part of Coulee Dam)	99116
Westfair Shopping Center (Part of Federal Way)	98023
Westhaven (Part of Westport)	98595
Westlake Center (Part of Seattle)	98101
West Lake Sammamish	98008
West Lake Stevens	98258
West Longview	98632
Westmont Acres	98851
West Park (Part of Bremerton)	98310
West Pasco	99301
Westport	98595

	ZIP		ZIP		ZIP
West Port Madison	98110	Wickersham	98220	Woodlawn (Part of	
West Richland	99352	Wilbur.....................	99185	Hoquiam)	98550
West Seattle (Part of		Wilburton (Part of Bellevue)	98004	Woodmont Beach	98032
Seattle)	98116	Wildcat Lake	98310	Woodsmuir................	98501
West Side Highway.........	98632	Wilderness	98501	Woodway	98020
West Sound	98245	Wiley	98908	Wycoff (Part of Bremerton)	98312
West Tapps	98390	Wilkeson	98396	Wye Lake	98366
West Valley	98903	Willada...................	99171	Yacht Haven	98250
....	98908	Willapa...................	98577	Yacolt....................	98675
For specific West Valley Zip		Willard	98605	Yakima	98901-09
Codes call (509) 575-5827, or		Willow Grove	98632	For specific Yakima Zip Codes	
your local postmaster.		Wilson Creek..............	98860	call (509) 575-5827, or your local	
Westward Siding (Part of		Winchester	98848	postmaster.	
Tacoma).................	98406	Winlock	98596	Yakima Indian Reservation	98948
West Wenatchee	98802	Winona	99125	Yakima Mall (Part of	
Westwood (King County)	98126	Winthrop	98862	Yakima).................	98901
Westwood (Kitsap County)	98110	Winton	98826	Yale	98603
Wheeler...................	98837	Wishkah	98520	Yardley	99202
Whidbey Island Naval Air		Wishram	98673	Yarrow Point	98004
Station..................	98278	Wishram Heights	98673	Yelm.....................	98597
White Center	98126	Withrow	98858	Yeomalt..................	98110
White Center-Shorewood...	98106	Wollochet	98335	Yesler Terrace (Part of	
White Pass	98937	Woodinville................	98072	Seattle)	98104
Whites	98541	Woodland	98674	Yokeko Point..............	98221
White Salmon	98672	Woodland Beach	98292	Yoman Ferry	98303
White Swan	98952	Woodland Creek	98501	Zenith....................	98188
Whitney Esttes	98532	Woodland Park	98603	Zillah.....................	98953
Whitstran.................	99350				

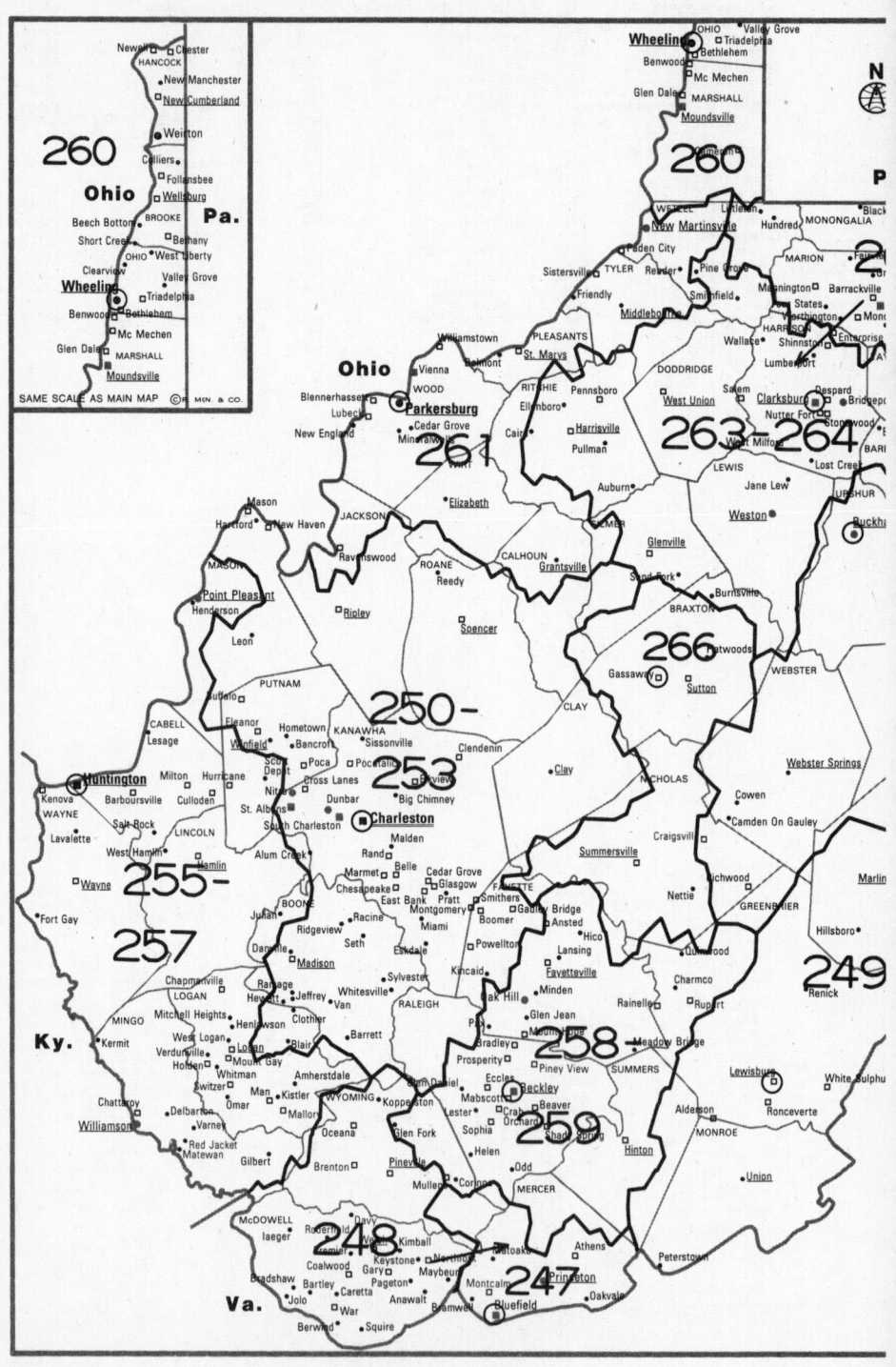

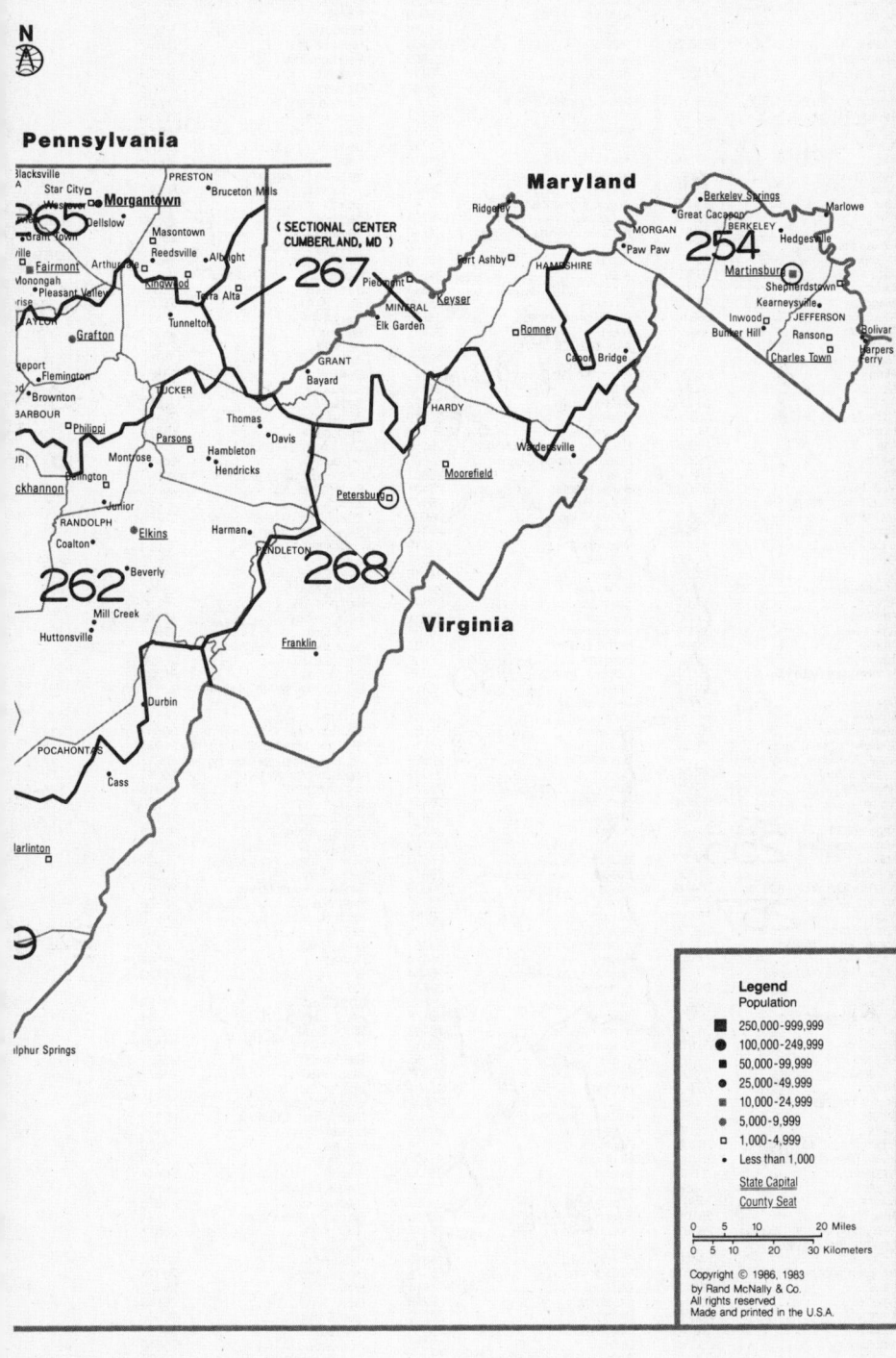

N

Pennsylvania

Blacksville
Star City
Wes... Dellslow Morgantown
Grant Town
...ville
Monongah
Pleasant Valley
...rise
TAYLOR Grafton
...eport
Flemington
Brownton
BARBOUR
Philippi
...nington
...ckhannon
Junior
RANDOLPH Elkins
Coalton
262 Beverly
Mill Creek
Huttonsville

PRESTON
Bruceton Mills
Masontown
Reedsville Albright
Arthu... Kingwood
Terra Alta
Tunnelton

(SECTIONAL CENTER
CUMBERLAND, MD)
267

Maryland

Ridgeley
Piedmont
MINERAL
Elk Garden
Keyser
Fort Ashby
HAMPSHIRE

Berkeley Springs
Great Cacapon
MORGAN BERKELEY
Paw Paw
254
Martinsburg
Shepherdstown
Kearneysville
JEFFERSON
Inwood
Bunker Hill Ranson
Charles Town
Bolivar
Harpers
Ferry

Marlowe
Hedgesville

GRANT
Bayard

TUCKER
Thomas
Parsons Davis
Montrose Hambleton
Hendricks

Romney
Capon Bridge

HARDY
Wardensville

Moorefield

Petersburg

Harman
PENDLETON
268

Virginia

Franklin

Durbin

POCAHONTAS
Cass

...arlinton

9

...lphur Springs

Legend
Population
■ 250,000-999,999
● 100,000-249,999
■ 50,000-99,999
● 25,000-49,999
■ 10,000-24,999
● 5,000-9,999
□ 1,000-4,999
• Less than 1,000
State Capital
County Seat

0   5   10   20 Miles
0 5 10   20   30 Kilometers

	ZIP
Aarrons Fork	25071
Abbott	26201
Abney	25847
Abraham	25918
Accoville	25606
Acme	25122
Ada	24701
Adaline	26033
Adamston (Part of Clarksburg)	26301
Adamsville	26431
Adlai	26170
Adolph	26280
Adrian	26210
Advent	25231
Afton	26764
Aggregate	26241
Airport Road	25813
Ajax	25676
Albright	26519
Alderson	24910
Alexander	26218
Algoma	24868
Alice	26342
Alkol	25501
Allendale	26003
Allen Junction	25810
Allensville	25427
Allister	26167
Alloy	25002
Alma	26320
Alpena	26254
Alpha	26408
Alpheus (Part of Gary)	24836
Alpoca	24710
Alta	26656
Altizer	25234
Alton	26210
Alum Bridge	26321
Alum Creek (Kanawha County)	25003
Alum Creek (Lincoln County)	25003
Alvon	24986
Alvy	26322
Amandaville	25177
Amboy	26705
Ambrosia	25550
Ameagle	25004
Amelia	25160
Amherstdale	25607
Amherstdale-Robinette	25607
Amigo	25811
Amma	25005
Anawalt	24808
Andersonville	26033
Andrew	25154
Angel Terrace (Part of Charleston)	25303
Angerona	25241
Anjean	25984
Anmoore	26323
Annamoriah	26141
Annamoriah Flats	26141
Ansted	25812
Anthony	24938
Antioch (Doddridge County)	26456
Antioch (Mineral County)	26743
Aplin	25244
Apple Farm	25274
Apple Grove (Mason County)	25502
Apple Grove (McDowell County)	24844
Aracoma	25601
Arborland Acres	25177
Arbovale	24915
Arbuckle	25123
Arbutus Park (Part of Clarksburg)	26301
Archer	26377
Archer Heights	26035
Arcola	26206
Ardel	25570
Arden (Barbour County)	26405
Arden (Berkeley County)	25401
Argonne	25649
Argyle	25654
Arkansas	26801
Arlee	25106
Arlington (Harrison County)	26301
Arlington (McDowell County)	24810
Arlington (Upshur County)	26234
Arnett	25007
Arnette	26619
Arnettsville	26505
Arnold Hill	26241
Arnoldsburg	25234
Arroyo	26047
Arthur	26816
Arthurdale	26520

	ZIP
Artie	25008
Arvilla	26135
Asbury	24916
Asbury Church	26801
Asco	24828
Ashford	25009
Ashland	24810
Ashley	26456
Ashton	25503
Aspinall	26412
Astor	26347
Astor Junction (Part of Flemington)	26347
Atenville	25524
Athens	24712
Atwell	24813
Atwood	26167
Auburn	26325
Augusta (Hampshire County)	26704
Augusta (Mercer County)	24740
Aurora	26705
Austen	26410
Auto	24917
Auville (Part of Iaeger)	24844
Auviltown	26290
Avis (Part of Hinton)	25951
Avon	26411
Avondale (Doddridge County)	26456
Avondale (McDowell County)	24811
Bablin	26376
Backus	25976
Baden	25123
Baisden (Logan County)	25652
Baisden (Mingo County)	25608
Baker	26801
Baker Heights	25401
Baker Park	25177
Baker Ridge	26505
Bakerton	25410
Bald Knob	25010
Baldwin	26351
Ballard	24918
Ballengee	24919
Balls Gap	25541
Bancroft	25011
Bandytown	25204
Barboursville	25504
Bardane	25430
Bargers Springs	24935
Barker	26419
Barksdale	25951
Barn	25841
Barnabus	25638
Barnet Run	26610
Barrackville	26559
Barrett	25013
Barrs	25276
Barry Mine	26347
Bartley	24813
Bartow	24920
Basin	24726
Basnettsville	26570
Basore	26812
Bass	26836
Baxter	26560
Bayard	26707
Bear Creek	26624
Beard Heights	24954
Beards Fork	25014
Bear Mountain Mine	26334
Bearsville	26149
Beason	26415
Beatrice	26178
Beatysville	26133
Beaver	25813
Bebee	26155
Becco	25607
Beckley	25801*
	25802†
Beckley Junction (Part of Mabscott)	25871
Beckwith	25814
Bedington	25401
Beebe	25625
Beech Bottom	26030
Beech Creek	25682
Beech Glen	26656
Beechgrove	26415
Beech Hill	25187
Beechwood	25810
Beelick Knob	25976
Beeson	24714
Belgrove	25248
Belington	26250
Bellburn	25958
Belle	25015
Bellepoint (Part of Hinton)	25951
Belleville	26133
Bellmeade	25550

	ZIP
Bellview (Part of Fairmont)	26554
Bellwood	25962
Belmont	26134
Belva	26656
Belvedere Heights	25414
Bemis	26268
Benbush	26292
Bendale	26452
Ben Lomond	25515
Bennett	26423
Benson	26378
Benson Park	25302
Bens Run	26135
Benton Ferry	26554
Bentree	25018
Benwood	26031
Benwood Junction (Part of Benwood)	26031
Berea	26327
Bergoo	26298
Berkeley	25401
Berkeley Springs	25411
Berlin	26452
Bernie	25521
Berryburg	26347
Berry Siding	26621
Berryville	25411
Bertha Hill	26541
Berwind	24815
Beryl	26726
Besoco	25857
Bessemer	25401
Bethany	26032
Bethel Place	26181
Bethesada	25570
Bethlehem (Harrison County)	26431
Bethlehem (Ohio County)	26003
Betty Zane	26003
Beverly	26253
Beverly Hills (Cabell County)	25705
Beverly Hills (Marion County)	26554
Bias	25670
Bickmore	25019
Big Battle	26426
Bigbend	26136
Big Chimney	25302
Big Creek	25505
Big Four	24853
Big Isaac	26426
Big Moses	26320
Big Mountain (Part of Cedar Grove)	25039
Big Otter	25113
Big Run (Marion County)	26582
Big Run (Marshall County)	26033
Big Run (Webster County)	26217
Big Run (Wetzel County)	26561
Big Sandy	24816
Bigson	25206
Big Springs	26137
Big Sycamore	25111
Billings	25270
Bim	25021
Bingamon	26591
Bingamon Junction	26591
Bingham	25958
Birch River	26610
Birchton	25209
Birds Creek	26410
Bishop	24604
Bismarck	26739
Blackberry City	25678
Black Betsy	25159
Black Bottom	25601
Black Eagle	25882
Blackhawk	25306
Blacksville	26521
Black Wolf	24871
Blaine	26717
Blair (Jefferson County)	25432
Blair (Logan County)	25022
Blairton	25401
Blakeley	25160
Blandville	26328
Blaser	26444
Blennerhassett	26101
Blocton	25685
Bloomery (Hampshire County)	26817
Bloomery (Jefferson County)	25414
Bloomingrose	25024
Blount	25025
Blue	26149
Blue Creek	25026
Bluefield	24701
Blue Jay	25816
Blue Ridge Acres	25425
Blue Rock	26280
Bluestone	24701

	ZIP
Blue Sulphur Springs	24910
Blueville (Part of Grafton)	26354
Bluewell	24701
Blundon	25071
Board	25253
Boaz (Wood County)	26187
Bob White	25028
Boggs	26299
Bolair	26288
Bolivar	25425
Bolt	25817
Bomont	25030
Bona Vista (Part of Charleston)	25311
Bonnie	26619
Bonnivale	26150
Booher	26320
Boomer	25031
Boonesborough (Part of Gauley Bridge)	25057
Booth	26522
Boothsville	26554
Borderland	25665
Boreman	26101
Borgman	26444
Bottom Creek	24853
Boulder	26201
Bowan Ridge	25701
Bowden	26254
Bowlby	26541
Bowles	25523
Boyd	26234
Boyer	24915
Bozoo	24923
Bradley (Boone County)	25051
Bradley (Raleigh County)	25818
Bradshaw	24817
Braeholm	25607
Bragg	25918
Bramwell	24715
Branchland	25506
Brandonville	26523
Brandywine	26802
Braxton	26619
Bream	25071
Breeden	25666
Brenton	24818
Bretz (Preston County)	26524
Bretz (Tucker County)	26287
Brewsterdale	24619
Briarwood Estates	26101
Brick Church	25514
Bridgeport	26330
Bridgeport Hill (Part of Bridgeport)	26330
Bridgeway	26149
Brink	26582
Bristol	26332
Broaddus (Part of Philippi)	26416
Broadmoor	26181
Broad Oaks (Part of Clarksburg)	26301
Brohard	26138
Brookhaven (Kanawha County)	25143
Brookhaven (Monongalia County)	26505
Brooklyn	25840
Brooklyn Junction (Part of New Martinsville)	26155
Brooks	25957
Brookside	26705
Brounland	25314
Brown	26448
Brownlow	26354
Brownsburg	24954
Browns Mills	26505
Brownsville (Fayette County)	25085
Brownsville (Lewis County)	26452
Brownton	26334
Brownwood	25864
Bruceton Mills	26525
Bruno	25611
Brush Fork	24701
Brushyrun	26866
Brydon	26435
Bryson	25865
Bubbling Spring	26865
Buck	25951
Buckeye	24924
Buckhannon	26201
Bud	24716
Buena Vista	25320
Buffalo	25033
Buffalo Creek	25530
Buff Lick	25039
Bula	26521
Bulger	25501
Bull	25669
Bull Run	26547
Bulltown	26631

	ZIP
Bunker Hill (Berkeley County)	25413
Bunker Hill (Kanawha County)	25309
Bunners Ridge	26554
Burchfield	26562
Burlington	26710
Burning Springs (Kanawha County)	25015
Burning Springs (Wirt County)	26141
Burnsville	26335
Burnsville Junction (Part of Burnsville)	26335
Burnt Factory	25411
Burnt House	26178
Burnwell	25034
Burton	26562
Butchersville	26452
Cabell	25871
Cabin Creek	25035
Cabins	26855
Cabot	25163
Cabot Station	26147
Cairo	26337
Caldwell	24925
Calis	26033
Callaway	25880
Calvert (Part of St. Albans)	25177
Calvin	26660
Cambria	26386
Camden	26338
Camden On Gauley	26208
Cameron	26033
Camp	26320
Campbelltown	26954
Camp Creek	25820
Campus	24827
Canaan	26234
Canaan Heights	26260
Canaan Valley	26260
Canebrake	24819
Cane Fork	25075
Canfield (Braxton County)	26601
Canfield (Randolph County)	26241
Cannelton	25036
Canton	26456
Cantwell	26362
Canvas	26662
Canyon	26505
Capehart	25123
Capels	24820
Capitol (Part of Charleston)	25311
Capon Bridge	26711
Capon Springs	26823
Carbon	25122
Carbondale	25036
Caretta	24821
Carl	26676
Carlisle	25917
Carl Lee Ray	26181
Carlos	24844
Carolina	26563
Carolina Heights	25177
Carpendale	26753
Carrollton	26238
Carswell	24853
Carter	26218
Cascade	26547
Cashmere	24918
Cass	24927
Cassity	26278
Cassville	26527
Catawba	26554
Cave	26807
Cazy	25028
Cedar Grove (Kanawha County)	25039
Cedar Grove (Wood County)	26101
Cedarville	26611
Center Hill	26143
Center Point	26339
Centerville	25555
Central	26101
Centralia	26612
Central Station	26456
Century	26214
Century No. 2	26238
Ceredo	25507
Ceres	24701
Cham	25654
Chapel	26624
Chapman (Braxton County)	26412
Chapman (Webster County)	26288
Chapman Addition	26070
Chapmanville	25508
Charleston	25301-75
For specific Charleston Zip Codes call (304) 357-4116, or your local postmaster.	

	ZIP
Charleston Ordnance Center (Part of South Charleston)	25303
Charleston Town Center (Part of Charleston)	25375
Charles Town	25414
Charlton Heights (Part of Gauley Bridge)	25040
Charmco	25958
Chatham Hill	26571
Chattaroy	25667
Chauncey	25612
Cheat Lake	26505
Cheat Neck	26505
Chelyan	25035
Cherokee	25122
Cherry Falls	26288
Cherry Grove	26804
Cherry Run	25427
Chesapeake (Kanawha County)	25315
Chesapeake (Marion County)	26554
Chester	26034
Chesterville	26150
Chestnut Heights	26070
Chestnut Hill (Part of Weirton)	26062
Chestnut Ridge	26505
Chiefton	26301
Childs	26162
Chimney Corner	25085
Chloe	25235
Christian	25611
Churchville	26338
Cicerone	25243
Cinco	25306
Cinderella	25661
Circleville	26804
Cirtsville	25801
Cisco	26161
Claremont	25936
Clarence	25244
Clarksburg	26301*
	26302†
Clay	25043
Claypool (Logan County)	25617
Claypool (Summers County)	25976
Claysville	26743
Clayton	24910
Clear Creek	25044
Clear Fork	24822
Clearview	26003
Clem	26623
Clemtown	26405
Clendenin	25045
Cleveland	26215
Clifftop	25831
Clifton	25237
Clifton Mills	26525
Clinton (Boone County)	25013
Clinton (Ohio County)	26059
Clintonville	24928
Clio	25046
Clothier	25047
Clouston	26033
Clover	25276
Cloverdale	24963
Clover Lick	24927
Clyde (Kanawha County)	25302
Clyde (Wetzel County)	26186
Coal Branch Heights (Part of Charleston)	25301
Coalburg	25035
Coal City	25823
Coaldale	24724
Coal Fork (Kanawha County)	25147
Coal Fork (Kanawha County)	25306
Coal Mountain	24823
Coalton	26257
Coal Valley	25047
Coalwood	24824
Coburn	26562
Coco	25071
Cofoco	25147
Coketon	26292
Colcord	25048
Cold Stream	26711
Coldwater	26411
Colebank	26405
Coleman	25517
Colfax	26566
Colliers	26035
Collinsdale	25034
Columbia	25118
Combs Addition	25617
Comfort	25049
Conaway	26149
Concord	26410
Confidence	25168

	ZIP		ZIP		ZIP
Congo	26050	Dartmont	25009	East Gulf	25915
Conings	26443	Dartmoor	26250	East Huntington (Part of	
Cool Ridge	25825	Davenport	26175	Huntington)	25702
Cooper (Part of Bramwell)	24715	Davin	25617	East Kermit	25674
Coopertown	25148	Davis (Logan County)	25625	East Lynn	25512
Copen	26615	Davis (Tucker County)	26260	East Nitro (Part of Nitro)	25143
Copley	26452	Davis Creek	25003	East Oak Hill	25901
Cora	25614	Davisville	26142	Easton	26505
Cordova	24966	Davy	24828	East Pea Ridge	25705
Core	26529	Dawes	25054	East Salem	26426
Corinne	25826	Dawmont	26344	East Side (Kanawha	
Corinth	26713	Dawson	24910	County)	25301
Corley (Barbour County)	26250	Daybrook	26570	Eastside (Marion County)	26554
Corley (Braxton County)	26621	Daysville	26201	East View	26301
Corliss	25962	Deansville	26201	East Vivian	24891
Cornstalk	24901	Deanville	26452	East Williamson (Part of	
Cornwallis	26337	Decota	25122	Williamson)	25661
Cortland	26260	Deep Valley (Marion		Eaton	26180
Corton	25045	County)	26582	Eccles	25836
Costa	25051	Deep Valley (Tyler County)	26360	Echo	25570
Cottageville	25239	Deep Water	25057	Eckman	24829
Cottle	26207	Deer Creek	24927	Eden (Ohio County)	26003
Cotton	25046	Deer Run	26807	Eden (Upshur County)	26234
Cottontown	26562	Deer Walk	26180	Edgarton	25672
Country Club Acres (Part of		Dehue	25654	Edgemont (Part of	
South Charleston)	25309	Delbarton	25670	Fairmont)	26554
Countsville	25243	Dellslow	26531	Edgewood (Harrison	
Courtright	26330	Delong	26170	County)	26301
Cove (Part of Weirton)	26062	Delray	26714	Edgewood (Kanawha	
Cove Creek	25534	Dempsey	25840	County)	25302
Cove Gap	25534	Denver (Marshall County)	26033	Edgewood (Ohio County)	26003
Covel	24719	Denver (Preston County)	26444	Edgewood Acres (Part of	
Cowen	26206	Denver Heights	26033	Charleston)	25302
Cox Landing	25537	Derryhale	25846	Edison	24701
Coxs Mills	26342	Despard	26301	Edmond	25837
Coxtown (Part of Weston)	26452	Dessie	26623	Edna	26505
Crab Orchard	25827	Devon	25682	Edray	24954
Crag	25962	Dewitt	25901	Edwight	25189
Craigmoor	26408	Diamond (Kanawha County)	25015	Effie	25514
Craigsville	26205	Diamond (Logan County)	25625	Egeria (Mercer County)	25841
Cranberry	25828	Diana	26217	Egeria (Raleigh County)	25902
Craneco	25630	Dickinson	25015	Eggleton	25523
Cranesville	26764	Dickson	25535	Eglon	26716
Crany	24870	Dille	26617	Elana	25266
Crawford	26343	Dingess	25671	Elbert (Part of Gary)	24830
Crawley	24931	Dingy	26623	Eldora	26554
Creamery	24910	Dink	25113	Eleanor	25070
Crede	25302	Dixie	25059	Elgood	24740
Cremo	26141	Doane	25511	Elizabeth	26143
Crescent	25136	Dobra	25183	Elk	26271
Cressmont	25043	Dock	25177	Elk City	26416
Creston	26141	Dog Patch	25636	Elk Forest	25311
Crichton	25961	Dog Run	25043	Elk Garden	26717
Crickmer	25831	Dola	26386	Elkhorn	24831
Crooked Creek	25639	Donaldson	26206	Elkhurst	25164
Crosby	25125	Doortown	26288	Elkins	26241
Cross Lanes	25312-13	Dorcas	26847	Elkridge (Fayette County)	25161
For specific Cross Lanes Zip		Dorothy	25060	Elkridge (McDowell County)	24868
Codes call (304) 776-3201, or		Dothan	25833	Elk Run Junction	25209
your local postmaster.		Dott	24736	Elkview	25071
Crossroads	26589	Douglas (Calhoun County)	25235	Elkwater	26273
Crow	25813	Douglas (Tucker County)	26292	Ella	26055
Crown (Logan County)	25606	Downtown (Part of		Ellamore	26267
Crown (Monongalia County)	26505	Huntington)	25701	Ellenboro	26346
Crown Hill	25052	Downtown (Part of		Elliber Spring	26852
Crow Summit	26164	Wheeling)	26003	Ellison	25969
Crum	25669	Drennen	26667	Elm Grove	26003
Crumpler	24825	Drews Creek	25140	Elmira	26618
Crystal	24747	Droop	24946	Elm Terrace (Part of	
Crystal Lake	24456	Drybranch	25061	Wheeling)	26003
Crystal Springs (Randolph		Dry Creek	25062	Elmwood (Mason County)	25123
County)	26241	Dryfork	26263	Elmwood (Wayne County)	25570
Crystal Springs (Wood		Dry Hill	25801	Elmwood Heights	26187
County)	26181	Duck	25063	Eloise	25511
Cubana	26237	Dudeon	25248	Elton	25965
Cucumber	24826	Dudley Gap	25541	Emma	25124
Culloden	25510	Duffields	25442	Emmart	26447
Cumberland Heights	24701	Duffy	26376	Emmett	25620
Cunard	25840	Duhring	24747	Emmons	25009
Curtin	26288	Dukes	25252	Emoryville	26717
Curtisville	26582	Dunbar	25064	Endicott	26581
Cusicks Crossing	26562	Duncan	25252	Engle	25425
Custer Addition	26301	Dundon	25043	English	24832
Cutlips	26619	Dunloup	25880	Ennis	24887
Cuzzart	26530	Dunlow	25511	Enoch	25043
Cyclone	24827	Dunmore	24934	Enon	26651
Cyrus	25530	Dunns	25841	Enterprise (Harrison County)	26568
Czar	26224	Duo	25984	Enterprise (Wirt County)	26160
Dabney	25654	Dupont Circle	26181	Entry Mountain	26807
Dahmer	26807	Dupont City	25015	Epperly	25823
Dailey	26259	Durbin	26264	Erbacon	26203
Daisy	25505	Durgon	26836	Erie	26301
Dakota	26554	Dutchman	26148	Erwin	26705
Dale	26377	Dutch Ridge	25045	Eskdale	25075
Dallas	26036	Dyer	26206	Esty	24966
Dallison	26180	Eagle	25136	Etam	26425
Dameron	25849	Earling	25632	Ethel	25076
Danese	25831	Earnshaw	26585	Eunice	25209
Daniels	25832	East Bank	25067	Eureka	26134
Dans Run	26763	East Beckley (Part of		Evans	25241
Danville	25053	Beckley)	25801	Evansdale (Part of	
Darkesville	25428	East Dailey	26253	Morgantown)	26505

	ZIP
Evansville	26440
Evenwood	26254
Everettville	26533
Evergreen	26218
Evergreen Hills	25239
Everson	26554
Excelsior (McDowell County)	24892
Excelsior (Upshur County)	26201
Exchange	26619
Extra	25033
Factory	25411
Fairdale	25839
Fairfax Estates (Part of Charleston)	25314
Fairlea	24902
Fairmont	26554*
	26555†
Fairmor (Part of Westover)	26505
Fairplain	25271
Fairview (Jackson County)	25252
Fairview (Marion County)	26570
Fairview (Marshall County)	26055
Fairview (Mason County)	25253
Fairview (Mingo County)	25661
Fairview (Wood County)	26181
Fallen Timber	26437
Falling Rock	25079
Falling Waters	25419
Falls	26833
Falls Mill	26620
Falls Mills	26146
Fallsview	25002
Fanco	25606
Fanny	24834
Fanrock	24834
Far	26167
Farley	25979
Farmington	26571
Farnum	26369
Faulkner	26241
Fayetteville	25840
Federal (Part of Bluefield)	24701
Federal Correctional Institute (Monroe County)	24910
Federal Correctional Institution (Summers County)	24910
Federal Mine (Part of Grant Town)	26574
Federal Ridge	26170
Fellowsville	26410
Fenwick	26202
Ferguson	25511
Ferrellsburg	25524
Fetterman (Part of Grafton)	26354
Filbert (Part of Gary)	24830
Finch	26170
Finley	25003
Fireco	25856
Fisher	26818
Fitzpatrick	25801
Five Block	25022
Five Forks (Calhoun County)	26145
Five Forks (Preston County)	25525
Five Forks (Ritchie County)	26362
Fivemile (Kanawha County)	25306
Fivemile (Mason County)	25106
Flat Rock	25123
Flats	25140
Flat Top	25841
Flat Top Lake	25843
Flatwoods (Braxton County)	26621
Flatwoods (Jackson County)	26164
Flemington	26347
Flinderation	26332
Flint	26456
Flipping	24747
Floe	25235
Flower	26611
Flowing Acres	25414
Fola	25019
Follansbee	26037
Folsom	26348
Forest Hill	24935
Forest Hills (Kanawha County)	25314
Forest Hills (Ohio County)	26003
Forks of Cacapon	25434
Forks of Coal	25003
Forks of Hurricane	25514
Fort Ashby	26719
Fort Branch	25076
Fort Gay	25514
Fort Grand	26533
Fort Hill (Part of Charleston)	25303
Fort Martin	26541
Fort Neal (Part of Parkersburg)	26103
Fort Run	26836

	ZIP
Fort Seybert	26806
Fort Spring	24936
Foster	25081
Fosterville	25181
Four Mile	26419
Four States	26572
Frame	25071
Frametown	26623
Francis (Harrison County)	26554
Francis (Raleigh County)	25915
Frank	24920
Frankford	24938
Franklin (Brooke County)	26070
Franklin (Pendleton County)	26807
Franklintown	25441
Fraziers Bottom	25082
Freed	26138
Freeman (Part of Bramwell)	24724
Freemansburg	26452
Freeport (Preston County)	26764
Freeport (Wirt County)	26180
Freeze Fork	25076
French Creek	26218
Frenchton	26219
Frew	26149
Friars Hill	24938
Friendly	26146
Friendly View	25062
Frogtown	25625
Frost	24954
Frozen Camp	25252
Fry	25524
Fulton (Part of Wheeling)	26003
Gaines	26234
Gallagher	25083
Gallipolis Ferry	25515
Galloway	26349
Galloway Junction	26349
Galmish	26167
Gandeeville	25243
Gap Mills	24941
Gap of the Ridge	24701
Gardner	24740
Garland	24811
Garretts Bend	25564
Garrison	25209
Garten	25840
Garwood	24726
Gary	24836
Gassaway	26624
Gaston	26452
Gaston Junction (Part of Fairmont)	26554
Gates	24983
Gatewood	25840
Gauley Bridge	25085
Gauley Mill	26208
Gawthrop	26201
Gay	25244
Gaymont	25938
Gem	26335
Genoa	25517
Georges Run	26456
Georgetown (Lewis County)	26372
Georgetown (Marshall County)	26033
Georgetown (Monongalia County)	26505
Gerrardstown	25420
Ghent	25843
Giatto	24736
Gilbert	25621
Gilbert Creek	25608
Gilboa	26671
Giles	25054
Gilkerson	25512
Gill	25557
Gilliam	24897
Gillman Bottom	25617
Gilman	26241
Gilmer	26350
Gip	26618
Given	25245
Glace	24942
Glade Farms	26525
Glade Springs	25832
Gladesville	26374
Glade View	26206
Gladwin	26241
Glady	26268
Glady Creek	26554
Glasgow	25086
Glen	25088
Glen Alum	25651
Glencoe	25119
Glen Dale	26038
Glendale Heights	26038
Glen Daniel	25844
Glendon	26623
Glen Easton	26039
Glen Elk (Part of Clarksburg)	26301

	ZIP
Glen Falls	26301
Glen Ferris	25090
Glen Fork	25845
Glengary	25421
Glenhayes	25519
Glen Jean	25846
Glenmore	26241
Glen Morgan	25847
Glenray	24910
Glen Rogers	25848
Glen View	25827
Glenville	26351
Glen White	25849
Glenwood (Mason County)	25520
Glenwood (Ohio County)	26003
Glenwood Park	24701
Glover Gap	26585
Gluck	24844
Godby	25508
Godfrey	24735
Goffs	26362
Goldtown	25248
Goodhope	26378
Goodman	25667
Goodwill	24747
Gordon	25093
Gore	26301
Gormania	26720
Gormley	26267
Goshen	26234
Gould	26218
Grace	25270
Graham	26354
Graham	25253
Graham Heights	26554
Grand Central Mall (Part of Vienna)	26105
Grandview	25813
Grangeville	26582
Grantsville	26147
Grant Town	26574
Granville	26534
Grape Island	26170
Grapevine	24844
Grassy Meadows	24943
Grave Creek	26041
Graydon	25938
Graysville	26055
Great Cacapon	25422
Green Bank	24944
Green Bottom	25537
Greenbrier	24810
Green Castle	26180
Greendale	26656
Green Hill	26155
Greenland (Grant County)	26833
Greenland (Wood County)	26181
Green Spring	26722
Greenstown	25901
Green Sulphur Springs	25966
Green Valley (Mercer County)	24701
Green Valley (Nicholas County)	25981
Greenview	25053
Greenville	24945
Greenwood (Boone County)	25010
Greenwood (Doddridge County)	26360
Greer (Mason County)	25550
Greer (Monongalia County)	26505
Greggsville (Part of Wheeling)	26003
Grey Eagle	25674
Griffithsville	25521
Grimms Landing	25095
Grippe	25314
Grove	26411
Groves	25063
Grubbs Corner	25401
Guardian	26217
Gum Spring	26505
Gunville	25123
Guthrie	25312
Guyandotte (Part of Huntington)	25702
Guyan Estates	25504
Guyan Terrace	25601
Gypsy	26361
Hacker Valley	26222
Hagans	26529
Hager	25563
Hales Gap	24701
Hall	26201
Hallburg	25063
Halleck	26505
Halltown	25423
Halo	26206
Hambleton	26269
Hamlin	25523
Hammond	26566
Hampden	25623

Name	ZIP	Name	ZIP	Name	ZIP
Hampton	26201	Hite	26588	Jackson Flats	24873
Hampton Heights (Part of		Hitop	25160	Jacksons Mills	26452
Charleston)	25314	Hix	25951	Jacobs Fork	24884
Hancock	25411	Hodgesville	26201	Jacox	24946
Handley	25102	Hogsett	25515	Jamestown	25446
Hanna	26180	Hokes Mill	24970	Jamison Mine No. Nine	26571
Hannahsville	26290	Holbrook	24456	Jane Lew	26378
Hanover	24839	Holcomb	26261	Janie	25209
Hansford	25103	Holden	25625	Jarrolds Valley (Part of	
Hany	25511	Holly	25122	Whitesville)	25209
Harding	26250	Holly Grove	25103	Jarvisville	26332
Hardy	24740	Hollywood	24983	Jawood	25811
Harewood Mine	25031	Homeland	26378	Jayenn	26554
Harlin	26456	Hometown	25109	Jeffrey	25114
Harman	26270	Homewood	26452	Jenkinjones	24848
Harmco (Part of Mullens)	25882	Hominy Falls	26679	Jenks	25563
Harmony	25246	Hoodsville	26588	Jenningston	26254
Harmony Grove	26505	Hoo Hoo	25865	Jenny Gap	25865
Harper (Pendleton County)	26807	Hookersville	26651	Jere	26546
Harper (Raleigh County)	25851	Hooverson Heights	26037	Jerrys Run	26133
Harper Heights	25801	Hoover Town	26218	Jesse	24849
Harpers Ferry	25425	Hopemont	26764	Jimtown (Harrison County)	26386
Harpertown	26241	Hopeville	26855	Jimtown (Morgan County)	25411
Harris Ferry	26181	Hopewell (Barbour County)	26416	Job	26270
Harrison	25105	Hopewell (Fayette County)	25938	Jockeycamp Run	26456
Harrisville	26362	Hopewell (Marion County)	26554	Jodie	26674
Harters Hill	26591	Hopewell (Preston County)	26525	Joetown	26582
Hartford	25247	Hopkins Fork	25181	Johnnycake	24844
Hartland	25043	Horner	26372	Johnsontown (Berkeley	
Hartmansville	26717	Horsepen	24619	County)	25427
Harts	25524	Horse Shoe Run	26769	Johnsontown (Jefferson	
Harvey	25901	Horton	26296	County)	25430
Harveytown (Part of		Hosterman	26264	Johnstown	26385
Huntington)	25704	Hotchkiss	25920	Joker	26141
Hastings	26377	Hoult	26554	Jolo	24850
Hatcher (Mercer County)	24740	Howells Mill	25545	Jonben	25856
Hatcher (Wyoming County)	24870	Howesville	26444	Jones Springs	25427
Hatfield Bottom (Part of		Hoy	26704	Jordan	26554
Matewan)	25678	Hubball	25506	Jordan Run	26833
Havaco	24841	Hubbardstown	25555	Josephine	25857
Haywood	26366	Hudson	26519	Josephs Mills	26320
Haywood Junction	26431	Huff Junction	25634	Joy	26456
Hazelgreen	26367	Hughart	24928	Judson	24910
Hazelton	26535	Hughes	26404	Judy Gap	26814
Hazelwood	26241	Hugheston	25110	Julia	24966
Hazy	25189	Hugo	25168	Julian	25529
Headsville	26710	Hull	24844	Jumping Branch	25969
Heaters	26627	Humphrey	26133	Junction	26824
Heatherfield	25443	Hundred	26575	Junior	26275
Heavener Grove	26201	Hunt	25635	Justice	24851
Hebron	26346	Hunter's Ridge (Part of		Justice Addition	25601
Hedgesville	25427	Charleston)	25314	Kabletown	25414
Hedgeview	25637	Huntersville	24954	Kalamazoo	26416
Heizer	25159	Hunting Ground	26804	Kanawha	26142
Helen	25853	Huntington	25701-79	Kanawha City (Part of	
Helens Run	26591	For specific Huntington Zip Codes		Charleston)	25304
Helvetia	26224	call (304) 526-9600, or your local		Kanawha Drive	26351
Hemlock	26224	postmaster.		Kanawha Estates (Part of	
Hemphill (Part of Welch)	24842	Huntington Mall (Part of		Charleston)	25304
Henderson	25106	Barboursville)	25504	Kanawha Falls	25115
Hendricks	26271	Hur	26151	Kanawha Head	26228
Henlawson	25624	Hurricane	25526	Kanawha Station	26142
Henning	24938	Hurst	26321	Kansooth	26033
Henrietta	26147	Hutchinson	26591	Kasson	26405
Hensley	24843	Huttonsville	26273	Katy	26554
Hensley Heights	25635	Huttonsville Correctional		Katy Lick	26301
Hepzibah (Harrison County)	26369	Center	26273	Kayford	25122
Hepzibah (Taylor County)	26330	Iaeger	24844	Kearneysville	25430
Hereford	25252	Idamay	26576	Kedron	26201
Herndon	24726	Ikes Fork	24845	Keeler Glade	26525
Herndon Heights	24726	Independence (Clay		Keenan	24983
Hernshaw	25107	County)	25125	Kegley	24731
Herold	26601	Independence (Jackson		Keister	24901
Herring	26547	County)	25275	Keith	25148
Hettie	26376	Independence (Preston		Kelly	25022
Hetzel	25076	County)	26374	Kelly Hill	25045
Hewett	25108	Indian (Part of St. Albans)	25177	Kellysville	24732
Hiawatha	24729	Indian Meadows	25545	Kenna	25248
Hickman Run	26554	Indian Mills	24935	Kenova	25530
Hickory Chapel	25550	Indore	25111	Kent	26055
Hico	25854	Industrial (Harrison and		Kentuck	25249
Highland	26346	Doddridge Counties)	26375	Kera Landing	25262
Highland Lake Terrace	26181	Industrial (Part of		Kerens	26276
Highland Park	26241	Clarksburg)	26301	Kermit	25674
Highlawns (Part of		Industry	26152	Keslers Cross Lanes	26675
Rivesville)	26588	Ingleside	24740	Kessler	25984
High View	26808	Ingram Branch	25119	Kettle	25243
Hildebrand	26505	Inkerman	26801	Key	26814
Hillcrest (Part of Fairmont)	26554	Institute	25112	Keyrock	24874
Hilldale	25951	Intermont	26851	Keyser	26726
Hillsboro	24946	Inwood	25428	Keystone	24852
Hillsdale	24976	Ireland	26376	Kiahsville	25534
Hilltop	25855	Irona	26537	Kidwell	26149
Hillview (Cabell County)	25702	Iroquis	25928	Kieffer	24950
Hillview (Marion County)	26554	Isaban	24846	Kilarm Junction	26554
Hillview Terrace	26041	Isom	25121	Killarney	25915
Hilton Village	25962	Israel	26444	Kilsyth	25859
Hinch	25682	Itmann	24847	Kimball	24853
Hines	25967	Iuka	26149	Kimberly	25118
Hinkleville	26201	Ivy	26201	Kincaid	25119
Hinton	25951	Ivydale	25113	Kincheloe	26378
Hiorra	26410	Jacksonburg	26377	Kinder	25540

	ZIP
Kingmont	26578
Kingston	25120
Kingstown	26561
Kingsville	26257
Kingwood	26537
Kirby	26729
Kirby Addition	24740
Kirbyton	25181
Kirk	25671
Kirt	26283
Kistler	25628
Kitchen	25508
Kitsonville (Part of Weston)	26452
Kline	26866
Klines Gap	26833
Knawl	26447
Knob Fork	26581
Knobs	24983
Knollwood	25302
Knottsville	26354
Kodol	26186
Kopperston	24854
Kyle	24855
Lacoma	24827
La Frank (Part of Richwood)	26261
Lahmansville	26731
Lake	25121
Lake Floyd	26332
Lake Ridge	26330
Lake Ron	26181
Lake Washington	25526
Lakin	25250
Lamberton	26346
Lanark	25860
Landes	26847
Landgraff	24829
Landisburg	25831
Lando Mines	25670
Landville	25635
Laneville	26263
Lanham	25159
Lansing	25862
Largent	25422
Larkmead	26101
Lashmeet	24733
Lauckport (Part of Parkersburg)	26101
Laura Lee Mine	26386
Laurel Branch	24131
Laurel Dale	26743
Laurel Fork	26601
Laurel Iron Works	26505
Laurel Park	26301
Laurel Point	26505
Laurel Valley	26301
Lavalette	25535
Lawn	25976
Lawrenceville (Part of Chester)	26034
Layland	25864
Leachtown	26143
Lead Mine	26290
Leadsville	26241
Leander	25912
Leckie	24856
Lee	25880
Lee Creek	26181
Leet	25524
Leetown	25430
Leevale	25209
Leewood	25122
Leewood Park	26003
Left Hand	25251
Lego	25857
Lehew	26865
Leivasy	26676
Lenore	25676
Lenox	26519
Leon	25123
Leonard	24966
Leopold	26443
Lerona	25971
Le Roy	25252
Lesage	25537
Leslie	25972
Lester	25865
Letart	25253
Letherbark	25234
Letter Gap	25255
Levels	25431
Lewisburg	24901
Lex	24817
Liberty (Harrison County)	26301
Liberty (Putnam County)	25124
Lick Creek	25979
Lick Fork	25840
Lico	25314
Lightburn	26378
Lila	24808
Lilac Hills	24740
Lillybrook	25857
Lillydale (Monroe County)	24945

	ZIP
Lillydale (Wyoming County)	24822
Lilly Grove	24740
Lillyhaven	24854
Lilly Park	25962
Lima	26383
Limestone (Marshall County)	26041
Limestone (Mineral County)	26726
Limestone Hill	26143
Linden	25256
Lindside	24951
Lindytown	25204
Link	26167
Linn	26384
Linwood	26291
Little	26146
Little Birch	26629
Little Falls	26505
Little Italy (Clay County)	25113
Little Italy (Randolph County)	26296
Little Laurel Creek (Part of Richwood)	26261
Little Pittsburg	26434
Littlesburg	24701
Littleton	26581
Lively	25917
Liverpool	25252
Livingston	25083
Lizemores	25125
Lloydsville	26619
Lobata	25678
Lobelia	24946
Lochgelly	25866
Lockbridge	25973
Lockhart	25275
Lockney	25258
Lockwood	26651
Lodgeville	26330
Logan	25601
Logansport	26582
Lomax	24899
London	25126
Lonetree	26149
Longacre	25186
Long Branch (Fayette County)	25867
Long Branch (Wyoming County)	24882
Longdale	25253
Longpole	24844
Long Run	26426
Longview	26238
Lookout	25868
Loom	26704
Looneyville	25259
Lorado	25630
Lorentz	26229
Lorton Lick	24701
Lost City	26810
Lost Creek	26385
Lost River	26811
Loudenville	26033
Loudon Heights (Part of Charleston)	25314
Louise	26070
Loveridge	24966
Lovern	24740
Lowdell	26169
Lowell	24962
Lower Belle	25015
Lower Falls	25177
Lower Nicut	26633
Low Gap	25130
Lowney	25666
Lowsville	26533
Lubeck	26101
Lucas	25938
Lucretia	26354
Lumberport	26386
Lundale	25631
Lyburn	25632
Lynco	24857
Lynn	25678
Lynn Camp	26039
Lynwinn	25823
Lyonsville	26651
Maben	25870
Mabie	26278
Mabscott	25871
MacAlpin	25921
MacArthur	25873
McCauley	26801
McClellan	26582
McCloud	25671
Mc Comas	24735
McConnell	25646
McCorkle	25564
McCreery	25934
Macdale	26521
Macdonald	25880
Mc Dowell	24810
MacDunn	25161

	ZIP
Mace	26294
Macfarlan	26148
McGee	26354
Mc Graws	25875
McGuire Park	26452
McIntire	26369
McKeefrey	26041
McKinleyville	26070
Macksville	26884
McMechen	26040
Macomber	26425
McRoss	25962
Mc Whorter	26401
Madam Creek	25951
Madeline	25811
Madison	25130
Madison Run	26705
Magnolia (Morgan County)	25422
Magnolia (Upshur County)	26218
Mahan	25131
Maher	25661
Mahone	26362
Maidsville	26541
Maitland	24886
Majorsville	26036
Malcom Spring Heights	25541
Malden	25306
Mallory	25634
Mallory (census designated place)	25617
Mammoth	25132
Man	25635
M and K Junction (Part of Rowlesburg)	26425
Manheim	26425
Manila	25508
Manleys Church	26554
Mannings	25425
Mannington	26582
Manown	26537
Mansfield (Part of Philippi)	26416
Manus	25649
Maple Acres	24701
Maple Fork	25880
Maple Lake	26330
Maple Meadow	25865
Maple Point (Part of Barrackville)	26559
Maple View	24701
Maplewood	25874
Marfrance	25981
Margaret	26448
Marianna	24859
Marie	24918
Marie Heights	26101
Marine	24828
Market	26411
Markwood	26710
Marlaing Addition	25177
Marlinton	24954
Marlowe	25419
Marmet	25315
Marquess	26444
Marrtown	26101
Marshall	25252
Marshall Terrace	26070
Marshall University (Part of Huntington)	25703
Marshville	26332
Martha	25504
Martin	26743
Martinsburg	25401
Marvel	25812
Marytown	24889
Mason	25260
Masontown	26542
Masonville	26847
Masseyville	25174
Matewan	25678
Matheny (Wood County)	26181
Matheny (Wyoming County)	24860
Mathias	26812
Matoaka	24736
Maud	26155
Maxine	25049
Maxwell	26170
Maxwell Acres	26041
Maxwelton	24957
Maybeury	24861
Maynor	25801
Maysel	25133
Maysville	26833
Mead	25915
Meadland	26330
Meador	25682
Meadow Bluff	24958
Meadow Bridge	25976
Meadowbrook (Harrison County)	26404
Meadowbrook (Kanawha County)	25311

Name	ZIP
Meadowbrook (Mason County)	25550
Meadow Creek	25977
Meadowdale	26554
Meadowville	26250
Meadville	26135
Mechanicstown	25414
Mechlenberg Heights	25443
Medina	26164
Medley	26734
Melissa	25504
Mellin	26362
Melrose (Mercer County)	24712
Melrose (Wood County)	26181
Melville	25646
Mercers Bottom	25123
Meredith Springs	26554
Meriden	26416
Merrimac	25661
Metz	26585
Meyerstown	25414
Miami	25134
Micco	25647
Middlebourne	26149
Middle Grave Creek	26041
Middle Run	26623
Middletown (Part of Richwood)	26261
Midkiff	25540
Midland	26241
Midway (Barbour County)	26250
Midway (Mercer County)	24701
Midway (Putnam County)	25168
Midway (Raleigh County)	25878
Mifflin	25047
Milam (Hardy County)	26838
Milam (Wyoming County)	25875
Mile Branch	24811
Millard	25276
Millbrook	26711
Mill Creek	26280
Millersville	26554
Millertown	26354
Milliken	25071
Mill Point	24946
Mill Run	26271
Millstone (Calhoun County)	25261
Millstone (Mingo County)	25670
Milltown	25163
Millville	25432
Millwood	25262
Milo	25256
Milton	25541
Minden	25879
Mineral City	25617
Mineralwells	26150
Mingo	26294
Mink Shoals	25302
Minnehaha Springs	24954
Minnie	26155
Minnora	25268
Miracle Run	26570
Missouri Branch	25511
Mitchell	26807
Mitchell Branch	25692
Mitchell Heights	25601
Moatstown	26813
Moatsville	26405
Mobley	26437
Mohawk	24862
Mohegan	24820
Moler Crossroads	25443
Monarch	25039
Monaville	25636
Monclo	25183
Monitor	24976
Monkeytown	26814
Monongah	26554
Monson	24836
Montana Mines	26586
Montcalm	24737
Montcoal	25135
Monterville	26282
Montgomery	25136
Montgomery Heights	25057
Montpelier (Part of Clarksburg)	26301
Montrose (Kanawha County)	25303
Montrose (Randolph County)	26283
Moore	26283
Moorefield	26836
Mooresville	26529
Morgan	26153
Morgan Heights (Part of Westover)	26505
Morgansville	26456
Morgantown	26502-07

For specific Morgantown Zip Codes call (304) 291-1035, or your local postmaster.

Name	ZIP
Morning Star	25276
Morrall Mine	26416
Morristown	26143
Morrisvale	25565
Mossy	25917
Moundsville	26041
Mountain	26407
Mountain Cove	25938
Mountaindale	26525
Mountaineer Mall (Part of Morgantown)	26505
Mountain Mission	25425
Mountain View	26444
Mount Alto	25264
Mount Carbon	25139
Mount Clare	26408
Mount De Chantel (Part of Wheeling)	26003
Mount Echo	26060
Mount Gay	25637
Mount Gay-Shamrock	25601
Mount Harmony	26554
Mount Home	25113
Mount Hope (Fayette County)	25880
Mount Hope (Roane County)	25286
Mount Hope (Wood County)	26160
Mount Liberty	26416
Mount Lookout	26678
Mount Nebo	26679
Mount Olive (Mason County)	25503
Mount Olive (Roane County)	25276
Mount Olivet (Marshall County)	26003
Mount Olivet (Mercer County)	24747
Mount Pleasant	25446
Mount Storm	26739
Mount Tabor	25801
Mount Vernon (Preston County)	26547
Mount Vernon (Putnam County)	25526
Mountview	25825
Mount Welcome	25286
Mount Zion (Calhoun County)	26151
Mount Zion (Tucker County)	26290
Moyers	26813
Mozart	26003
Mozer	26866
Mud	25565
Muddlety	26651
Mudfork (Calhoun County)	25235
Mudfork (Logan County)	25649
Mullens	25882
Mullensville	24874
Munday	26152
Munson	24883
Murphy	26201
Murphytown	26142
Murraysville	26153
Muses Bottom	26153
Mustang Acres (Part of Parkersburg)	26101
Myra	25544
Myrtle (Boone County)	25165
Myrtle (Mingo County)	25670
Nabob	25122
Nallen	26680
Nancys Run	25276
Naoma	25140
Napier	26631
National	26505
Natrium	26055
Naugatuck	25685
Neal	25530
Neals Run	25444
Nebo (Clay County)	25141
Nebo (Upshur County)	26201
Needmore	26801
Neibert	25632
Nellis	25142
Nelson	25163
Nemours	24738
Neola	24961
Neptune	26153
Nestlow	25512
Nestorville	26405
Nethkin	26726
Nettie	26681
Neville (Part of Beckley)	25801
New	25918
Newark	26143
Newberne	26409
Newburg	26410
New Creek	26743
New Cumberland	26047
Newdale	26155
Newell	26050

Name	ZIP
New England	26181
New England Heights	26181
New Era	25275
Newhall	24866
New Hamlin	25523
New Haven	25265
New Hill (Marion County)	26591
New Hill (Monongalia County)	26527
New Hope	24740
Newlon	26236
New Manchester	26056
New Martinsville	26155
New Milton	26411
New Richmond	24867
New Thacker	25694
Newton	25266
Newtown	25686
Newville	26601
Next	26175
Nicolette	26101
Nicut	26633
Nimitz	25978
Nitro	25143
Nitro Park Addition	25143
Nobe	26137
Nolan	25687
Nollville	25401
Normantown	25267
North Berkeley	25411
North Charleston (Part of Charleston)	25312
North Fairmont (Part of Fairmont)	26554
Northfork	24868
North Hills	26101
North Matewan	25688
North Mitchell Heights	25601
North Mountain	25427
North Parkersburg (Part of Parkersburg)	26104
North River Mills	26711
North Spring	24869
North View (Part of Clarksburg)	26301
Norton	26285
Norway	26554
Norwood (Part of Fairmont)	26554
Numan	26426
Nuriva (Part of Mullens)	25882
Nursery Gap	25514
Nutter Farm	26161
Nutter Fort	26301
Nutter Fort Stonewood (Part of Nutter Fort)	26301
Nutterville	25981
Oak Acres	26181
Oakdale	26582
Oak Flat	26802
Oak Hill	25901
Oakmont (Mineral County)	26717
Oakmont (Ohio County)	26003
Oakvale	24739
Oakview Heights	25530
Oakwood Estates	26101
O'Brion	25063
Oceana	24870
Odaville	25275
Odd	25902
Ohley	25147
Olcott	25314
Old Arthur	26816
Old Fields	26845
Omar	25638
Omps	25411
Ona	25545
Onego	26886
O'Neil	26461
Oney Gap	24740
Onoto	24954
Opekiska	26554
Oral Lake	26330
Orchard	24918
Orchard Hill	25438
Organ Cave	24970
Orgas	25148
Orient Hill	25958
Orlando	26412
Orleans Road	25422
Orma	25268
Orr	26764
Ortin Heights	25143
Orville	25654
Osage	26543
Osborne	25045
Osbornes Mills	25045
Oscar	24966
O'Toole	24808
Otsego	25882
Ottawa	25149
Otto	25276
Ovapa	25150

	ZIP		ZIP		ZIP
Overfield	26416	Pleasant Valley (Marshall		Raven Rock	26170
Owings	26431	County)	26033	Raven Rocks	26763
Oxford	26456	Pleasant Valley (Monongalia		Ravenswood	26164
Packs Branch	25880	County)	26505	Rawl	25691
Packsville	25209	Pleasant Valley (Ohio		Rayburn	25550
Pad	25286	County)	26003	Raymond City	25159
Paden City	26159	Pleasant View (Jackson		Raysal	24879
Page	25152	County)	26164	Reader	26167
Pageton	24871	Pleasant View (Lincoln		Ream (Part of Gary)	24836
Paint Creek Junction (Part		County)	25506	Reamer	25045
of Pratt)	25162	Pleasant View (Marion		Red Creek	26289
Palace Valley	26224	County)	26588	Redhill	26101
Palermo	25546	Pleasure Valley	26283	Red House	25168
Palestine (Greenbrier		Pliny	25158	Red Jacket	25692
County)	24910	Plum Orchard	25271	Red Run	26271
Palestine (Wirt County)	26160	Pluto	25951	Red Spring	25976
Pansy	26847	Plymouth	25011	Redstar	25914
Panther	24872	Poca	25159	Red Sulphur Springs	24918
Paradise	25124	Pocatalico	25320	Red Warrior Junction	25122
Parchment Valley	25271	Poe	26683	Reedson	25442
Parcoal	26288	Point Lick Junction	25306	Reedsville	26547
Pardee	25630	Point Mills (Part of Valley		Reedy	25270
Park Addition	26070	Grove)	26059	Reedyville	25276
Parkersburg	26101*	Point Pleasant	25550	Reeses Mill	26726
	26102†	Points	25437	Reger	26201
Parkview (Ohio County)	26003	Polard	26149	Renick	24966
Parkview (Taylor County)	26354	Polemic	26601	Renicks Valley	24966
Par Metta Crest	26184	Polk Gap	25870	Rensford	25306
Parsley Bottom	25676	Pondco	25208	Replete	26222
Parsons	26287	Pond Creek	26133	Reston	25130
Patterson Creek	26753	Pond Gap	25160	Reynoldsville	26422
Paw Paw	25434	Pond Junction (Part of		Rhodell	25915
Pax	25904	Madison)	25130	Richard	26505
Paynesville	24873	Pool	26684	Richardson	25234
Peach Creek	25639	Port Amherst	25306	Richland	24901
Peanut	26582	Porters Falls	26162	Richwood	26261
Pear	25918	Porterwood	26283	Rider	26385
Pea Ridge	25705	Porto Rico	26411	Ridersville	25411
Pecks Mill	25547	Posey	25180	Ridgedale	26505
Pecks Run	26201	Potomac	15376	Ridge Farms	26588
Peeltree	26238	Potomac Manor	26717	Ridgeley	26753
Peewee	25252	Potomac Park	25419	Ridgeview (Boone County)	25169
Pemberton	25905	Powell	26554	Ridgeview (Logan County)	25637
Pence Springs	24962	Powell Creek	25130	Ridgeville	26710
Peniel	25270	Powellton	25161	Ridgeway	25440
Pennsboro	26415	Powhatan	24877	Riffle	26601
Pentress	26544	Pratt	25162	Rift	24892
Peora	26431	Premier	24878	Rig	26836
Pepper	26330	Prenter	25163	Riley	25927
Perkins	26634	Price	25540	Rinehart	26448
Perry	26851	Price Hill (Boone County)	25130	Ringold	26505
Persinger	26651	Price Hill (Raleigh County)	25818	Rio	26755
Petersburg	26847	Price Hill Junction (Part of		Ripley	25271
Peterson	26423	Mount Hope)	25880	Ripley Landing	25262
Peterstown	24963	Pricetown (Lewis County)	26452	Ripling Waters	25248
Petroleum	26161	Pricetown (Wetzel County)	26437	Rippon	25441
Pettit Heights	26070	Prichard	25555	Rita	25632
Pettry	24712	Priestly	25003	Riverbend	25177
Pettry Bottom	25189	Prince	25907	Riverlake Estates	25177
Pettus	25209	Princeton	24740	Riverlawn (Part of St.	
Pettyville	26101	Princewick	25908	Albans)	25177
Peytona	25154	Procious	25164	Riverside (Kanawha County)	25086
Pharoah	25555	Proctor	26055	Riverside (Monongalia	
Pheasant Run	26276	Propstburg	26802	County)	26505
Phico	25508	Prospect Valley	26431	Riverton	26814
Philippi	26416	Prosperity	25909	Rivesville	26588
Piatt	25015	Prudence	25901	Rivesville Junction (Part of	
Pickaway	24976	Pruntytown	26354	Rivesville)	26588
Pickens	26230	Pullman	26421	Roach	25504
Pickle Street	26321	Pumpkintown	26257	Roanoke	26423
Pickshin	25857	Purgitsville	26852	Roberts	26456
Pie	25670	Puritan	25670	Robertsburg	25172
Piedmont	26750	Pursglove	26546	Robey	26386
Pierce	26292	Pursley	26175	Robinette	25607
Pierpont (Monongalia		Quaker	25511	Robson	25173
County)	26505	Quarrier	25122	Rock	24747
Pierpont (Wyoming County)	25870	Queens	26237	Rock Camp	24951
Pigeon	25164	Queen Shoals	25045	Rock Castle	25272
Pike	26346	Quick	25045	Rock Cave	26234
Pikeside	25401	Quiet Dell	26408	Rock Creek	25174
Pinch	25156	Quinland	25205	Rockford	26385
Pine Bluff	26431	Quinnimont	25910	Rock Forge	26505
Pine Creek	25625	Quinwood	25981	Rock Gap	25411
Pine Grove (Kanawha		Rachel	26587	Rock Lake	26554
County)	25143	Racine	25165	Rock Lake Village (Part of	
Pine Grove (Marion County)	26554	Racy	26161	South Charleston)	25309
Pine Grove (Wetzel County)	26419	Rada	26852	Rock Lick (Fayette County)	25879
Pineknob	25140	Radnor	25517	Rocklick (Marshall County)	26033
Pineville	24874	Ragland	25690	Rock Oak	26801
Piney	26167	Rainelle	25962	Rockport	26169
Piney View	25906	Raines Corner	24951	Rockridge	24873
Pinoak	24733	Raintown	24946	Rock Run	26456
Pipestem	25979	Raleigh	25911	Rocksdale	25234
Pisgah	26525	Ramage	25114	Rockton	26623
Pleasant Creek	26416	Ramp	25985	Rock View	24880
Pleasant Dale	26704	Ramsey	25912	Rockville	25540
Pleasant Hill	26147	Rand	25306	Rocky Fork	25312
Pleasant Home	26133	Randall	26543	Rodemer	26764
Pleasant Valley (Hancock		Ranger	25557	Roderfield	24881
County)	26062	Ranson	25438	Rohr	26547
Pleasant Valley (Marion		Raven	26651	Rolfe	24897
County)	26554	Ravencliff	25913	Rollins Branch	24870

Name	ZIP
Romance	25248
Romines Mills	26385
Romney	26757
Romont	25812
Ronceverte	24970
Ronda	25182
Roneys Point	26059
Rosebud	26386
Roseby Rock	26041
Rosedale (Fayette County)	25901
Rosedale (Gilmer County)	26636
Rosedale (Monongalia County)	26541
Rosemont	26424
Roseville Addition	25177
Rossmore	25643
Rough Run	26866
Round Bottom	26575
Round Knob	25033
Rowlesburg	26425
Roxalana (Kanawha County)	25064
Roxalana (Roane County)	25259
Ruddle	26807
Rumble	25009
Runa	26679
Rupert	25984
Rush Creek	25276
Rush Run	25274
Rusk	26161
Russelldale	26710
Russellville	26680
Russellville Road	25981
Russett	26147
Ruth	25314
Ruthbelle	26519
Rutherford	26362
Rutledge	25311
Ryanville	26330
Rymer	26582
Sabine	25916
Sabraton (Part of Morgantown)	26505
Sago	26201
St. Albans	25177
St. Clara	26321
St. Cloud	26575
St. George	26290
St. Joe (Part of Albright)	26519
St. Joseph	26055
St. Marys	26170
Salem	26426
Salt Hill	25271
Saltlick Bridge	26627
Saltpetre	25514
Salt Rock	25559
Salt Sulphur Springs	24983
Saltwell	26330
Sam Black Church	24928
Sanderson	25045
Sand Fork	26430
Sand Hill	26003
Sandlick	24701
Sand Lick Junction	26435
Sand Ridge	25274
Sand Run	26201
Sandstone	25985
Sandy Huff	24844
Sandy Summit	25252
Sandyville	25275
Sanford	26554
Sanger	25901
Sanoma	26160
Sarah Ann	25644
Sardis	26301
Sarton	24973
Sassafras	25287
Sattes (Part of Nitro)	25143
Saulsbury	26150
Saulsville	25876
Saunders	25630
Saxman	26202
Saxon	25180
Scarbro	25917
Scarlet	25670
Scary	25177
Scherr	26726
Schrader	25071
Schultz	26170
Scott Depot	25560
Scrabble	25443
Seaman	25252
Secondcreek	24974
Security Hills	25414
Sedalia	26426
Seebert	24946
Selbyville	26236
Seminole	26361
Seneca Rocks	26884
Seng Creek	25209
Servia	25063
Seth	25181
Seven Pines	26582

Name	ZIP
Shadow Lawn (Part of Charleston)	25311
Shady Brook (Part of Weston)	26452
Shady Spring	25918
Shafer	26290
Shamrock	25614
Shanghai	25427
Shanks	26761
Shannondale	25425
Sharon	25182
Sharon Heights	25621
Sharples	25183
Shawvers Crossing	24931
Shegon	25649
Shenandoah Junction	25442
Shepherdstown	25443
Sheridan	25506
Sherman	26173
Sherrard	26003
Sherwood	26456
Shiloh (Raleigh County)	25844
Shiloh (Tyler County)	26146
Shinnston	26431
Shirley	26434
Shively	25508
Shoals	25562
Shock	26638
Short Creek	26058
Short Creek Valley	26003
Short Gap	26726
Short Line Junction (Part of Clarksburg)	26301
Shrewsbury	25015
Shriver	26546
Sias	25563
Sidneyville	25271
Sigman	25168
Silver Grove	25425
Silver Hill	25155
Silver Lake	26769
Silverton	26164
Simoda	26814
Simon	24882
Simpson	26435
Sinclair	26405
Sinks Grove	24976
Sir Johns Run	25411
Sissonville	25320
Sistersville	26175
Six	24824
Six Mile	25053
Skeetersville	25442
Skelton	25919
Skygusty	24883
Slab Fork	25920
Slabtown	25621
Slagle	25654
Slanesville	25444
Slate	26143
Slatyfork	26291
Sleepy Creek	25411
Smithburg	26436
Smith Crossroads	25411
Smithers	25186
Smithfield (Jefferson County)	25430
Smithfield (Wetzel County)	26437
Smithtown	26505
Smithville (Marion County)	26588
Smithville (Ritchie County)	26178
Smoke Hole	26866
Smoot	24977
Snider	26537
Snowden	25573
Snow Flake	24936
Snow Hill	25311
Snowshoe	26209
Sod	25564
Sodom	25183
Somerville	26181
Sophia	25921
South Charleston	25303
South Fork Junction	24883
South Hills (Kanawha County)	25314
South Hills (Monongalia County)	26505
South Madison (Part of Madison)	25130
South Malden	25306
South Park (Kanawha County)	25304
South Park (Lewis County)	26378
South Parkersburg (Part of Parkersburg)	26101
South Ruffner (Part of Charleston)	25304
Southside	25187
South Side Junction (Part of Thurmond)	25936
South Worthington	26591

Name	ZIP
Spangler	25160
Spanishburg	25922
Spaulding	25666
Spears	25540
Speed	25276
Speedway	24712
Spelter	26438
Spencer	25276
Spencer Hospital	25276
Spice	24946
Sprague	25926
Sprattsville	25621
Spread	25043
Sprigg	25693
Spring Creek	24966
Spring Dale (Fayette County)	25986
Springdale (Ohio County)	26003
Springfield	26763
Spring Gap	25444
Spring Hill (Harrison County)	26301
Spring Hill (Kanawha County)	25309
Springton	24736
Spring Valley	25701
Spurlockville	25565
Squire	24884
Stanaford	25927
Standard	25083
Star City	26505
Staten	25274
Statler Run	26570
Statts Mills	25279
Stealey (Part of Clarksburg)	26301
Steeles	24844
Steelton (Part of New Martinsville)	26155
Steep Gut Hollow	25687
Stephenson	25928
Steptown	25674
Stevenboro	26444
Stewart	26101
Stewart Chapel	26301
Stewartstown	26505
Stickney	25189
Stillman	26234
Stinson	25235
Stirrat	25645
Stohrs Cross Roads	25411
Stollings	25646
Stone Branch	25508
Stonecoal	25674
Stoneville	24834
Stonewall (Part of Charleston)	25302
Stonewood	26301
Stony Bottom	24927
Stony River	26739
Stotesbury	25921
Stotlers Crossroads	25411
Stouts Mills	26439
Stover	25844
Stowe	25607
Strange Creek	26639
Streby	26833
Streeter	25969
Stringtown (Barbour County)	26250
Stringtown (Roane County)	25276
Stringtown (Marion County)	26582
Stringtown (Randolph County)	26263
Strouds	26208
Stumptown	25280
Sturgisson	26505
Sugar Camp	26411
Sugar Grove	26815
Sugar Tree	25521
Sugar Valley (Pleasants County)	26135
Sugar Valley (Preston County)	26525
Sullivan (Raleigh County)	25847
Sullivan (Randolph County)	26241
Sully	26254
Sulphur	26717
Sulphur Spring	25625
Sumerco	25567
Summerlee	25931
Summers	26456
Summersville	26651
Summit (Lincoln County)	25567
Summit (Wood County)	26101
Summit Park	26301
Summit Point	25446
Sun	25846
Sunbeam	25076
Suncrest (Part of Morgantown)	26505
Sundial	25189
Sun Flower	25252
Sun Hill	24822
Sunlight	24991

* Area Zip Code   † Post Office Boxes

	ZIP		ZIP		ZIP
Wilding	26164	Winebrenners Crossroad	25401	Woodward Woods (Part of	
Wiley Ford	26767	Winfield (Marion County)	26554	Charleston)	25312
Wileyville	26186	Winfield (Putnam County)	25213	Worth	24897
Wilkinson	25653	Wingrove	25917	Worthington	26591
Willard	26431	Winifrede	25214	Wriston	25840
William	26292	Winifrede Junction (Part of		Wyatt	26463
Williamsburg	24991	Chesapeake)	25315	Wyco	25943
Williams Mountain	25163	Winona	25942	Wylo	25611
Williamson	25661	Wiseburg	25275	Wymer	26254
Williamsport	26710	Witcher	25015	Wyoma	25515
Williamstown	26187	Wolfcreek	24993	Wyoming	24898
Willis Branch	25880	Wolfe	24751	Yards	24659
Willow Bend	24983	Wolf Pen	24896	Yates Crossing	25545
Willow Island	26134	Wolf Run	26033	Yawkey	25573
Willowton	24740	Wolf Summit	26462	Yellow Creek	26136
Wilmore	24844	Wood	25123	Yellow Spring	26865
Wilsie	26641	Woodcliff Acres	26181	Yolyn	25654
Wilson	26707	Woodland	26055	Youngs Bottom	25071
Wilsonburg	26461	Woodland Heights (Part of		Yukon	24899
Wilsondale	25699	Charleston)	25314	Zela	26651
Wilsontown	26234	Woodland Park (Part of		Zenith	24951
Winding Gulf	25823	Parkersburg)	26101	Zevely	26537
Windom	24859	Woodrow	24954	Zigler	26807
Windsor Heights	26075	Woodruff	26033	Zinnia	26426
Windy	26143	Woodville	25572	Zion	26218

	ZIP
Abbotsford	54405
Abells Corners	53121
Abrams	54101
Abrams (Town)	54101
Ackerville	53086
Ackley (Town)	54409
Ada	53020
Adams (Adams County)	53910
Adams (Adams County) (Town)	53934
Adams (Green County) (Town)	53504
Adams (Jackson County) (Town)	54615
Adams (Walworth County)	53120
Adams Beach	54929
Addison	53002
Addison (Town)	53002
Adell	53001
Adrian (Town)	54648
Advance	54111
Afton	53501
Agenda (Town)	54514
Ahnapee (Town)	54201
Ainsworth (Town)	54462
Airport Mail Center (Part of Milwaukee)	53237
Akan (Town)	54655
Alaska	54216
Alban (Town)	54473
Albany (Green County)	53502
Albany (Green County) (Town)	53502
Albany (Pepin County) (Town)	54755
Albertville	54730
Albion (Dane County)	53534
Albion (Dane County) (Town)	53534
Albion (Jackson County) (Town)	54615
Albion (Trempealeau County) (Town)	54738
Alden (Town)	54017
Alderley	53066
Algoma (Kewaunee County)	54201
Algoma (Winnebago County) (Town)	54901
Allen	54770
Allens Grove	53114
Allenton	53002
Allenville	54904
Allouez	54301
Alma (Buffalo County)	54610
Alma (Buffalo County) (Town)	54610
Alma (Jackson County) (Town)	54611
Alma Center	54611
Almena	54805
Almena (Town)	54826
Almon (Town)	54416
Almond	54909
Almond (Town)	54909
Alpha	54840
Alto	53919
Alto (Town)	53919
Altoona	54720
Alvin	54542
Alvin (Town)	54542
Amberg	54102
Amberg (Town)	54102
Amery	54001
Amherst	54406
Amherst (Town)	54977
Amherst Junction	54407
Amnicon (Town)	54874
Amnicon Falls	54874
Anacker	53901
Anderson (Burnett County) (Town)	54840
Anderson (Iron County) (Town)	54565
Angelica	54162
Angelica (Town)	54162
Angelo	54656
Angelo (Town)	54656
Angus	54817
Aniwa	54408
Aniwa (Town)	54414
Annaton	53825
Anson	54729
Anson (Town)	54748
Anston	54301
Anthony	54755
Antigo	54409
Antigo (Town)	54409
Applecreek	54911
Apple River (Town)	54810
Appleton	54911-15

For specific Appleton Zip Codes call (414) 734-7141, or your local postmaster.

	ZIP
Applewood	53711
Arbor Vitae	54568
Arbor Vitae (Town)	54568
Arcade Acres	54971
Arcadia	54612
Arcadia (Town)	54612
Arena	53503
Arena (Town)	53503
Argonne	54511
Argonne (Town)	54511
Argyle	53504
Argyle (Town)	53504
Arkansaw	54721
Arkdale	54613
Arland	54004
Arland (Town)	54004
Arlington	53911
Arlington (Town)	53555
Armenia (Town)	54646
Armstrong (Fond du Lac County)	53079
Armstrong (Oconto County) (Town)	54149
Armstrong Creek	54103
Armstrong Creek (Town)	54103
Arnott	54481
Arpin	54410
Arpin (Town)	54410
Artesia Beach	53049
Arthur (Chippewa County) (Town)	54727
Arthur (Grant County)	53818
Ashford	53010
Ashford (Town)	53010
Ashippun	53003
Ashippun (Town)	53003
Ashland	54806
Ashland (Town)	54846
Ash Ridge	54664
Ashton	53562
Ashton Corners	53562
Ashwaubenon	54304
Askeaton	54126
Astico	53925
Athelstane	54104
Athelstane (Town)	54104
Athens	54411
Atlanta (Town)	54819
Atlas	54853
Attica	53502
Atwater	53922
Atwood	54460
Auburn (Chippewa County) (Town)	54757
Auburn (Fond du Lac County) (Town)	53040
Auburndale	54412
Auburndale (Town)	54412
Auburn Lake	53010
Augusta	54722
Aurora (Florence County)	49801
Aurora (Florence County) (Town)	49801
Aurora (Taylor County) (Town)	54433
Aurora (Waushara County) (Town)	54923
Auroraville	54923
Avalanche	54665
Avalon	53505
Avoca	53506
Avon (Lafayette County)	53530
Avon (Lafayette County) (Town)	53520
Avon (Rock County)	53520
Aztalan (Town)	53038
Babcock	54413
Badger Army Ammunition Plant	53913
Bad River Indian Reservation	54806
Bagley (Grant County)	53801
Bagley (Oconto County) (Town)	54161
Baileys Harbor	54202
Baileys Harbor (Town)	54202
Bakerville	54449
Baldwin	54002
Baldwin (Town)	54028
Balsam Lake	54810
Balsam Lake (Town)	54024
Bancroft	54921
Bangor	54614
Bangor (Town)	54653
Baraboo	53913
Baraboo (Town)	53951
Barksdale	54806
Barksdale (Town)	54806
Barnes (Town)	54873
Barneveld	53507
Barnum	54631

	ZIP
Barre (Town)	54601
Barre Mills	54601
Barron	54812
Barron (Town)	54812
Barronett (Barron County)	54813
Barronett (Washburn County) (Town)	54871
Barron Junction (Part of Barron)	54812
Bartelme (Town)	54416
Barton	53095
Barton (Town)	53095
Basco	53508
Bashaw (Burnett County)	54871
Bashaw (Washburn County) (Town)	54871
Bass Bay (Part of Muskego)	53150
Bassett	53101
Bass Lake (Sawyer County) (Town)	54843
Bass Lake (Washburn County) (Town)	54875
Basswood	53573
Batavia	53001
Bateman	54729
Bay City	54723
Bayfield	54814
Bayfield (Town)	54814
Bay Park Square (Part of Ashwaubenon)	54304
Bay Settlement (Part of Green Bay)	54301
Bay Shore Shopping Center (Part of Glendale)	53217
Bayside	53217
Bayview (Bayfield County) (Town)	54891
Bay View (Milwaukee County)	53207
Beachs Corners	54627
Bear Bluff (Town)	54666
Bear Creek (Outagamie County)	54922
Bear Creek (Sauk County) (Town)	53577
Bear Creek (Waupaca County) (Town)	54922
Bear Lake (Barron County) (Town)	54868
Bear Lake (Rusk County)	54728
Bear Valley	53937
Beaver (Clark County) (Town)	54446
Beaver (Marinette County)	54114
Beaver (Marinette County) (Town)	54114
Beaver (Polk County) (Town)	54889
Beaver Brook (Town)	54871
Beaver Dam	53916
Beaver Dam (Town)	53916
Beaver Edge	53916
Beecher (Town)	54156
Beecher	54156
Beecher Lake	54156
Beechwood	53001
Beetown	53802
Beetown (Town)	53802
Beldenville	54003
Belgium	53004
Belgium (Town)	53004
Bell (Town)	54827
Bell Center	54631
Belle Plaine	54166
Belle Plaine (Town)	54166
Belleville	53508
Bellevue	54311
Bellevue (Town)	54311
Bellevue Town	54311
Bell Heights (Part of Appleton)	54911
Bellinger	54771
Bellwood	54820
Belmont (Lafayette County)	53510
Belmont (Lafayette County) (Town)	53818
Belmont (Portage County) (Town)	54909
Beloit	53511* 53512†
Beloit Mall (Part of Beloit)	53511
Belvidere (Town)	54610
Benderville	54301
Benet Lake	53102
Bennett	54873
Bennett (Town)	54873
Benoit	54816
Benton	53803
Benton (Town)	53803
Bergen (Marathon County) (Town)	54455

* **Area Zip Code** † **Post Office Boxes**

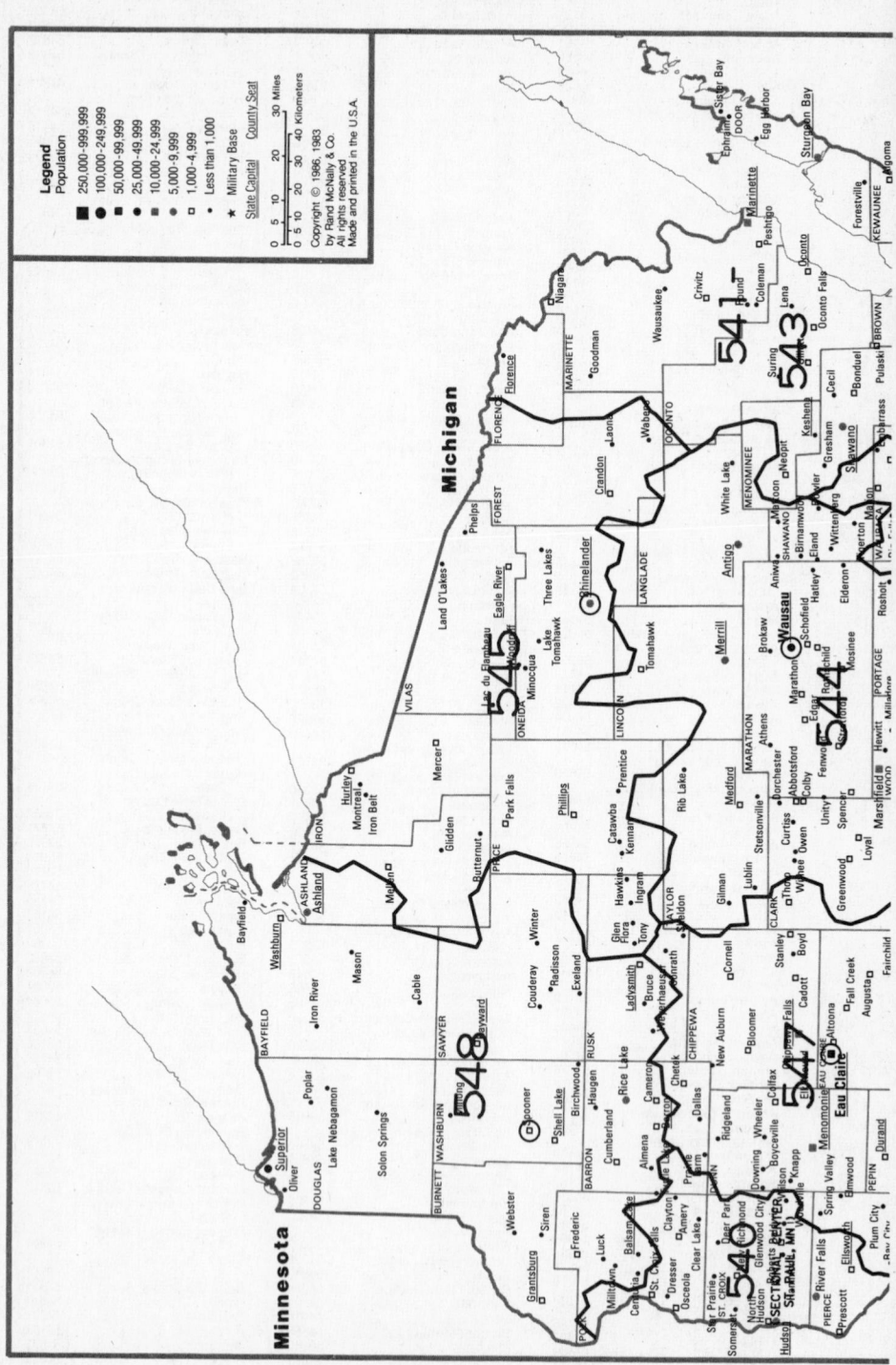

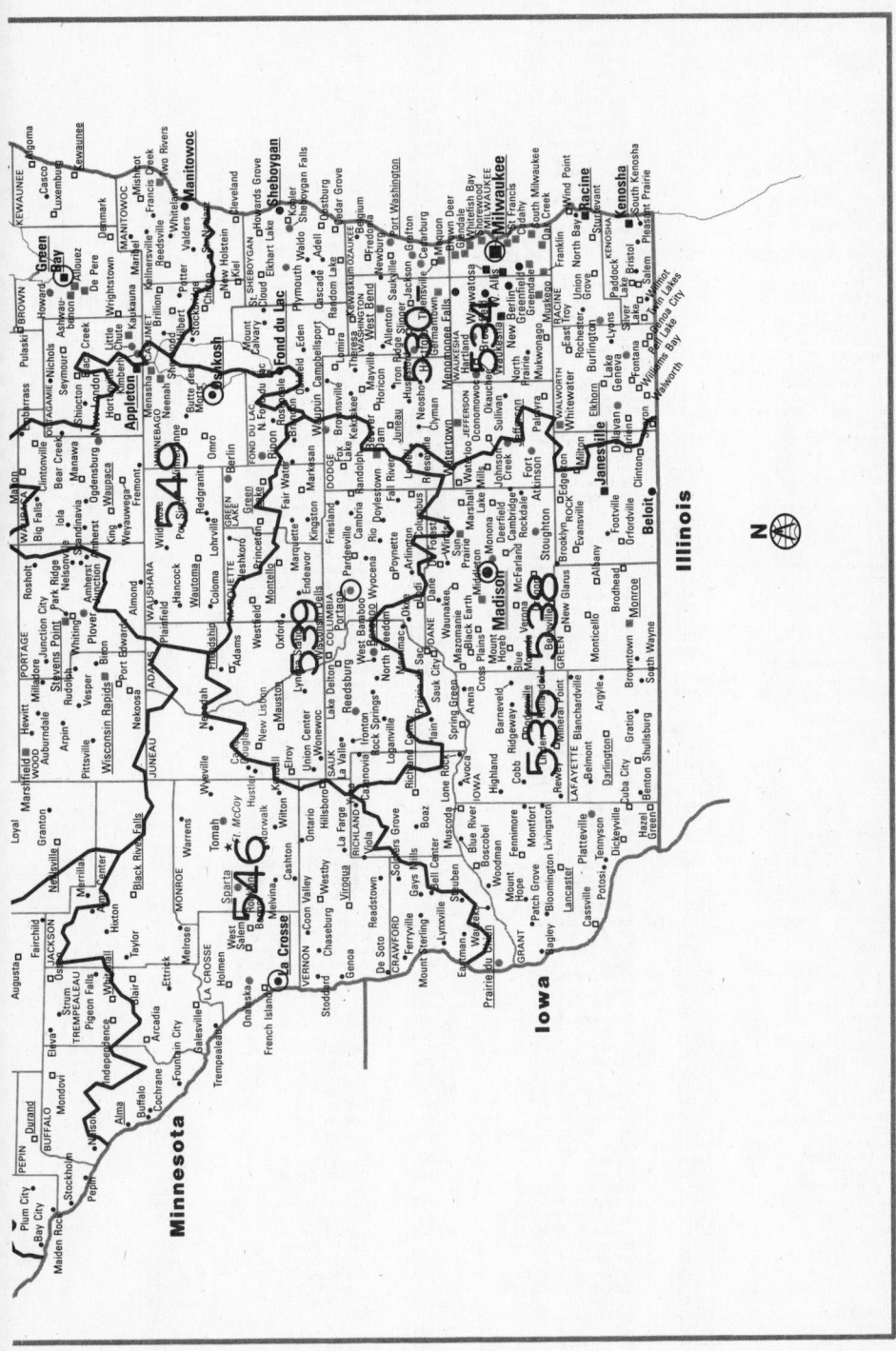

	ZIP
Bergen (Vernon County) (Town)	54658
Berlin (Green Lake County)	54923
Berlin (Green Lake County) (Town)	54923
Berlin (Marathon County) (Town)	54401
Bern (Town)	54411
Berry (Town)	53528
Bethel	54410
Bethesda	53186
Bevent	54440
Bevent (Town)	54440
Big Bend (Rusk County) (Town)	54819
Big Bend (Waukesha County)	53103
Big Falls (Rusk County) (Town)	54848
Big Falls (Waupaca County)	54926
Big Flats	53934
Big Flats (Town)	54613
Big Patch	53818
Big Spring	53965
Billings Park (Part of Superior)	54880
Binghamton	54106
Birch (Ashland County)	54559
Birch (Lincoln County) (Town)	54442
Birch Creek (Town)	54745
Birchwood	54817
Birchwood (Town)	54817
Birchwood Lake	53010
Birnamwood	54414
Birnamwood (Town)	54414
Biron	54494
Black Brook (Town)	54005
Black Creek	54106
Black Creek (Town)	54106
Black Earth	53515
Black Earth (Town)	53560
Black Hawk	53588
Black River	53081
Black River Falls	54615
Blackwell	54541
Blackwell (Town)	54541
Black Wolf (Town)	54901
Blaine (Burnett County) (Town)	54830
Blaine (Portage County)	54909
Blair	54616
Blanchard (Town)	53516
Blanchardville	53516
Blenker	54415
Bloom (Town)	54639
Bloom City	54634
Bloomer	54724
Bloomer (Town)	54724
Bloomfield (Walworth County) (Town)	53128
Bloomfield (Waushara County) (Town)	54965
Bloomingdale	54667
Blooming Grove (Town)	53701
Bloomington	53804
Bloomington (Town)	53810
Bloomville	54435
Blueberry	54854
Blue Mounds	53517
Blue Mounds (Town)	53572
Blue River	53518
Bluff Siding	54629
Bluffview	53913
Boardman	54017
Boaz	53581
Bohners Lake	53105
Bolt	54208
Boltonville	53040
Bonduel	54107
Bone Lake (Town)	54837
Borth	54923
Boscobel	53805
Boscobel (Town)	53805
Bosstown	53581
Boulder Junction	54512
Boulder Junction (Town)	54512
Bovina (Town)	54170
Bowers	53121
Bowler	54416
Boyceville	54725
Boyd	54726
Boydtown	53826
Brackett	54742
Bradford (Town)	53505
Bradley	54487
Bradley (Town)	54487
Bradley (Part of Milwaukee)	53223-24
For specific Bradley Zip Codes call (414) 354-1470, or your local postmaster.	
Branch	54203

	ZIP
Brandon	53919
Branstad	54840
Brant	53014
Brantwood	54513
Braund Addition	54660
Brazeau (Town)	54161
Breed	54174
Breed (Town)	54174
Briarcrest Estates	53545
Briarton	54162
Briarwood	53755
Brice Prairie	54650
Brickson Park	53558
Bridge Creek (Town)	54722
Bridgeport	53821
Bridgeport (Town)	53821
Briggsville	53920
Brigham (Town)	53507
Brighton (Kenosha County)	53139
Brighton (Kenosha County) (Town)	53139
Brighton (Marathon County) (Town)	54488
Brill	54818
Brillion	54110
Brillion (Town)	54110
Bristol (Dane County) (Town)	53590
Bristol (Kenosha County)	53104
Bristol (Kenosha County) (Town)	53104
Bristow	54665
Brockway (Town)	54615
Brodhead	53520
Brodtville	53801
Brokaw	54417
Brookfield	53005
	53008
	53045
For specific Brookfield Zip Codes call (414) 782-5070, or your local postmaster.	
Brookfield (Town)	53186
Brookfield Square (Part of Brookfield)	53005
Brookhaven	54494
Brooklyn (Green County)	53521
Brooklyn (Green County) (Town)	53521
Brooklyn (Green Lake County) (Town)	54941
Brooklyn (Washburn County) (Town)	54888
Brooks	53921
Brookside (Adams County)	53910
Brookside (Oconto County)	54101
Brookwood (Part of Madison)	53711
Brothertown	53014
Brothertown (Town)	53014
Brown Deer	53209
	53223
For specific Brown Deer Zip Codes call (414) 291-2444, or your local postmaster.	
Browning (Town)	54451
Browns Lake	53105
Brownsville	53006
Browntown	53522
Bruce	54819
Bruemmerville	54201
Brule	54820
Brule (Town)	54820
Brunswick (Town)	54701
Brushville	54965
Brussels	54204
Brussels (Town)	54204
Bryant	54418
Buchanan (Town)	54911
Buck Creek	53581
Buckhorn Corner	53916
Buckman	54208
Budd	54665
Budsin	54960
Buena Park	53185
Buena Vista (Portage County) (Town)	54467
Buena Vista (Richland County) (Town)	53556
Buena Vista (Waukesha County)	53072
Buffalo (Buffalo County)	54622
Buffalo (Buffalo County) (Town)	54629
Buffalo (Marquette County) (Town)	53949
Buffalo Estates	53949
Bundy	54435
Bunker Hill	53924
Burke	53590
Burke (Town)	53590
Burkhardt	54016

	ZIP
Burlington	53105
Burlington (Town)	53105
Burnett	53922
Burnett (Town)	53922
Burnett Corners	53922
Burns (Town)	54614
Burns	54614
Burnside (Town)	54747
Burr Oak	54644
Burton	53820
Busseyville	53534
Butler (Clark County) (Town)	54771
Butler (Milwaukee County)	53213
Butler (Waukesha County)	53007
Butte des Morts	54927
Butternut	54514
Butternut Island	53039
Byrds Creek	53518
Byron	53009
Byron (Fond du Lac County) (Town)	53009
Byron (Monroe County) (Town)	54618
Cable	54821
Cable (Town)	54821
Caddy Vista	53108
Cadiz (Town)	53522
Cadott	54727
Cady (Town)	54027
Cainville	53536
Calamine	53565
Calamus (Town)	53916
Caldwell	53149
Caledonia (Columbia County) (Town)	53901
Caledonia (Racine County)	53108
Caledonia (Racine County) (Town)	53108
Caledonia (Trempealeau County) (Town)	54630
Caledonia (Waupaca County) (Town)	54940
Calhoun (Part of New Berlin)	53151
Calumet (Town)	53049
Calumetville	53049
Calvary	53057
Cambria	53923
Cambridge	53523
Cameron (Barron County)	54822
Cameron (Wood County) (Town)	54449
Campbell (Town)	54601
Campbellsport	53010
Camp Douglas	54618
Campia	54868
Camp Lake	53109
Camp Leonard	53558
Canton (Barron County)	54868
Canton (Buffalo County) (Town)	54736
Capitol (Part of Madison)	53701
Capitol Court (Part of Milwaukee)	53216
Carey (Town)	54534
Carlsville	54235
Carlton (Town)	54216
Carnot	54213
Carol Beach Estates	53143
Caroline	54928
Carrollville (Part of Oak Creek)	53154
Carson (Town)	54443
Carter	54566
Carthage College	53140
Cary (Town)	54466
Caryville	54701
Cascade	53011
Casco	54205
Casco (Town)	54216
Casey (Town)	54801
Cashton	54619
Cassel (Town)	54426
Cassian (Town)	54529
Cassville	53806
Cassville (Town)	53806
Castle Rock (Town)	53809
Castle Rock	53569
Caswell (Town)	54511
Cataract	54620
Catawba	54515
Catawba (Town)	54459
Cato (Town)	54206
Cato	54206
Cavour	54511
Cayuga	54546
Cazenovia	53924
Cecil	54111
Cedar	54559
Cedarburg	53012
Cedarburg (Town)	53012

	ZIP		ZIP		ZIP
Cedar Creek	53095	Clifton (Pierce County)		Cuba City	53807
Cedar Falls	54751	(Town)	54022	Cudahy	53110
Cedar Grove	53013	Clinton (Barron County)		Cumberland	54829
Cedar Lake (Town)	54868	(Town)	54805	Cumberland (Town)	54829
Cedar Rapids (Town)	54526	Clinton (Rock County)	53525	Curran (Jackson County)	
Center (Outagamie County)		Clinton (Rock County)		(Town)	54635
(Town)	54911	(Town)	53525	Curran (Kewaunee County)	54208
Center (Rock County)		Clinton (Vernon County)		Curtiss	54422
(Town)	53545	(Town)	54619	Cushing	54006
Center House	53946	Clintonville	54929	Custer	54423
Center Lake Woods	53179	Clover (Bayfield County)		Cutler	54646
Center Ninety (Part of		(Town)	54844	Cutler (Town)	54618
Onalaska)	54650	Clover (Manitowoc County)	54220	Cylon	54017
Center Valley	54106	Cloverdale	54646	Cylon (Town)	54017
Centerville (Manitowoc		Cloverland (Douglas		Czechville	54629
County) (Town)	53015	County) (Town)	54854	Dacada	53075
Centerville (Trempealeau		Cloverland (Vilas County)		Dairyland	54830
County)	54630	(Town)	54521	Dairyland (Town)	54830
Central Avenue (Part of		Clyde (Town)	53506	Dakota	54982
Superior)	54880	Clyde	53506	Dakota (Town)	54982
Central Park (Part of		Clyman	53016	Dale	54931
Superior)	54880	Clyman (Town)	53039	Dale (Town)	54931
Centuria	54824	Cobb	53526	Daleyville	53572
Chaffey	54836	Cobban	54732	Dallas	54733
Chain o' Lakes	54981	Cochrane	54622	Dallas (Town)	54733
Chain o' Lakes-King	54981	Coddington	54467	Dalton	53926
Chambers Island	54212	Colburn (Adams County)		Danbury	54830
Champion	54229	(Town)	54943	Dancy	54455
Chapel Ridge Heights	54301	Colburn (Chippewa County)	54726	Dane	53529
Charlesburg	53014	Colburn (Chippewa County)		Dane (Town)	53555
Charlestown (Town)	53014	(Town)	54726	Daniels (Town)	54872
Charlie Bluff	53563	Colby	54421	Danville	53925
Chase	54171	Colby (Town)	54421	Darboy	54911
Chase (Town)	54171	Cold Spring	53538	Darien	53114
Chaseburg	54621	Cold Spring (Town)	53538	Darien (Town)	53115
Chelsea	54419	Coleman	54112	Darlington	53530
Chelsea (Town)	54419	Colfax	54730	Darlington (Town)	53530
Chenequa	53029	Colfax (Town)	54730	Davis Corners	53965
Cherokee	54421	Colgate	53017	Day (Town)	54484
Cherrywood	53593	Collins	54207	Dayton (Green County)	53508
Chester (Town)	53963	Coloma	54930	Dayton (Richland County)	
Chetek	54728	Coloma (Town)	54930	(Town)	53581
Chetek (Town)	54728	Coloma Corners	54930	Dayton (Waupaca County)	
Chicago Corners	54115	Columbia	54456	(Town)	54981
Chicog (Town)	54888	Columbus	53925	Deansville	53559
Chief Lake	54843	Columbus (Town)	53925	Decatur (Town)	53520
Chili	54420	Combined Locks	54113	Deckers Corner	53012
Chilton	53014	Commonwealth	54121	Decorah Prairie	54630
Chilton (Town)	53014	Commonwealth (Town)	54121	Dedham	54836
Chimney Rock (Town)	54770	Como	53147	Deerbrook	54424
Chippewa (Town)	54514	Comstock	54826	Deer Creek (Outagamie	
Chippewa Falls	54729	Concord	53066	County) (Town)	54170
Chiwaukee	53143	Concord (Town)	53066	Deer Creek (Taylor County)	
Christiana (Dane County)		Connorsville	54725	(Town)	54480
(Town)	53523	Conover	54519	Deerfield (Dane County)	53531
Christiana (Vernon County)		Conover (Town)	54519	Deerfield (Dane County)	
(Town)	54667	Conrath	54731	(Town)	53531
Christie	54456	Cooks Valley (Town)	54724	Deerfield (Waushara	
Cicero (Town)	54165	Cooksville	53536	County) (Town)	54943
Cicero	54165	Coomer	54837	Deer Park (Eau Claire	
City Point	54466	Coon (Town)	54621	County)	54742
City Point (Town)	54466	Coon Rock	53503	Deer Park (St. Croix	
Clam Falls (Town)	54837	Coon Valley	54623	County)	54007
Clam Falls	54837	Cooperstown	54208	De Forest	53532
Clam Lake	54517	Cooperstown (Town)	54227	Dekorra (Town)	53955
Clark	54498	Coral City	54773	Delafield	53018
Clark Mills	54206	Corinth	54411	Delafield (Town)	53072
Clarks Point	54986	Cormier (Part of Howard)	54301	Delavan	53115
Clarno	53566	Cornelia	53818	Delavan (Town)	53115
Clarno (Town)	53566	Cornell	54732	Delavan Lake	53115
Clay Banks (Town)	54201	Corning (Town)	54452	Dell	54667
Clayton (Crawford County)		Cornucopia	54827	Dellona (Town)	53965
(Town)	54655	Cottage Grove	53527	Dell Prairie (Town)	53965
Clayton (Polk County)	54004	Cottage Grove (Town)	53527	Dellwood	53927
Clayton (Polk County)		Cottonville	53934	Delmar (Town)	54726
(Town)	54004	Couderay	54828	Delta (Town)	54856
Clayton (Winnebago		Couderay (Town)	54835	Delton (Town)	53959
County) (Town)	54956	Country Estates	53105	Denmark	54208
Clear Creek (Town)	54770	County Line	54153	Denoon (Part of Muskego)	53150
Clearfield (Town)	53950	Courtland (Town)	53932	Denzer	53951
Clear Lake (Polk County)	54005	Crandon	54520	De Pere	54115
Clear Lake (Polk County)		Crandon (Town)	54520	De Pere (Town)	54301
(Town)	54005	Cranmoor	54495	Deronda	54001
Clear Lake (Rock County)	53563	Cranmoor (Town)	54495	De Soto	54624
Clearwater Lake	54521	Cream	54610	Dewey (Burnett County)	
Cleghorn	54738	Crescent (Chippewa		(Town)	54845
Cleveland (Chippewa		County)	54727	Dewey (Douglas County)	54880
County) (Town)	54732	Crescent (Oneida County)		Dewey (Portage County)	
Cleveland (Jackson County)		(Town)	54501	(Town)	54481
(Town)	54741	Crescent Park	53558	Dewey (Rusk County)	
Cleveland (Manitowoc		Crestview	53402	(Town)	54563
County)	53015	Crivitz	54114	Dewhurst (Town)	54456
Cleveland (Marathon		Cross (Town)	54629	Dexter (Town)	54466
County) (Town)	54484	Cross Lake	60002	Dexterville	54466
Cleveland (Taylor County)		Cross Plains	53528	Diamond Bluff	54014
(Town)	54433	Cross Plains (Town)	53528	Diamond Bluff (Town)	54014
Clifford	54564	Crystal (Town)	54801	Dickeyville	53808
Clifton (Grant County)		Crystal Lake (Barron		Diefenbach Corners	53086
(Town)	53554	County) (Town)	54826	Dilly	54634
Clifton (Monroe County)	54618	Crystal Lake (Marquette		Disco	54615
Clifton (Monroe County)		County) (Town)	54960	Dobie	54868
(Town)	54618	Crystal Lake Corners	54981	Dodge	54625

	ZIP
Dodge (Town)	54625
Dodge Correctional Institution	53963
Dodges Corners	53149
Dodgeville	53533
Dodgeville (Town)	53533
Doering	54435
Donald	54433
Dorchester	54425
Doty (Town)	54149
Dotyville	53057
Douglas (Town)	53930
Dousman	53118
Dover (Buffalo County) (Town)	54755
Dover (Racine County) (Town)	53182
Dovre (Town)	54757
Downing	54734
Downing Junction (Part of Downing)	54734
Downsville	54735
Downtown (Part of Oshkosh)	54901
Doyle (Town)	54868
Doylestown	53928
Drammen (Town)	54739
Draper (Town)	54896
Draper	54896
Dresser	54009
Drummond (Town)	54832
Drummond	54832
Drywood	54727
Duck Creek (Part of Howard)	54301
Dudley	54435
Dunbar	54119
Dunbar (Town)	54156
Dunbarton	53586
Dundas	54130
Dundee	53010
Dunkirk (Town)	53589
Dunkirk	53589
Dunn (Dane County) (Town)	53558
Dunn (Dunn County) (Town)	54751
Duplainville	53186
Dupont (Town)	54950
Durand	54736
Durand (Town)	54736
Durham (Part of Muskego)	53130
Durham Hill (Part of Franklin)	53132
Duvall	54217
Dyckesville	54217
Eagle (Richland County) (Town)	53573
Eagle (Waukesha County)	53119
Eagle (Waukesha County) (Town)	53119
Eagle Corners	53573
Eagle Lake	53139
Eagle Lake Manor	53139
Eagle Point (Town)	54729
Eagle River	54521
Eagleton	54724
Eagleville	53149
Earl	54875
East Bristol	53925
East Delavan	53115
East Ellsworth (Part of Ellsworth)	54010
East End (Part of Superior)	54880
East Farmington	54020
East Friesland	53956
East Krok	54216
Eastman	54626
Eastman (Town)	53826
Easton (Adams County)	53910
Easton (Adams County) (Town)	53910
Easton (Marathon County) (Town)	54471
East Side (Part of Madison)	53704
East Towne Mall (Part of Madison)	53704
East Troy	53120
East Troy (Town)	53120
East Waupun	53963
Eastwood	54494
Eaton (Brown County) (Town)	54217
Eaton (Clark County) (Town)	54437
Eaton (Manitowoc County) (Town)	53042
Eau Claire	54701-03
For specific Eau Claire Zip Codes call (715) 836-6470, or your local postmaster.	
Eau Galle (Dunn County)	54737
Eau Galle (Dunn County) (Town)	54737
Eau Galle (St. Croix County) (Town)	54028

	ZIP
Eau Pleine (Marathon County) (Town)	54484
Eau Pleine (Portage County) (Town)	54443
Eden (Fond du Lac County)	53019
Eden (Fond du Lac County) (Town)	53010
Eden (Iowa County) (Town)	53526
Edgar	54426
Edgerton	53534
Edgewater	54834
Edgewater (Town)	54834
Edgewood	53072
Edithton Beach	53143
Edmund	53535
Edson	54726
Edson (Town)	54726
Edwards	53015
Edwards Park (Part of McFarland)	53558
Egg Harbor	54209
Egg Harbor (Town)	54209
Eidsvold	54768
Eileen (Town)	54806
Eisenstein (Town)	54552
Eland	54427
Elba (Town)	53925
Elcho	54428
Elcho (Town)	54428
Elderon	54429
Elderon (Town)	54440
Eldorado	54932
Eldorado (Town)	54932
Eleva	54738
Elk (Town)	54555
Elk Creek	54747
Elk Grove (Town)	53807
Elk Grove	53807
Elkhart Lake	53020
Elkhorn	53121
Elk Mound	54739
Elk Mound (Town)	54739
Ella	54721
Ellenboro (Town)	53813
Ellington (Town)	54944
Ellis	54481
Ellison Bay	54210
Ellisville	54217
Ellsworth	54011
Ellsworth (Town)	54003
Elm Grove	53122
Elmhurst	54409
Elm Island	53185
Elmore	53010
Elm Tree Corners (Part of Howard)	54301
Elmwood	54740
Elmwood Park	53405
Elmwood Plaza (Part of Racine)	53403
El Paso	54003
El Paso (Town)	54003
Elroy	53929
Elton	54430
Embarrass	54933
Emerald	54012
Emerald (Town)	54012
Emerald Grove	53545
Emery (Town)	54513
Emmet (Dodge County) (Town)	53098
Emmet (Marathon County) (Town)	54426
Empire (Town)	54935
Enchanted Valley Estates	53562
Endeavor	53930
Enterprise	54463
Enterprise (Town)	54463
Ephraim	54211
Erdman	53083
Erin (St. Croix County)	54017
Erin (Washington County) (Town)	53027
Erin Prairie (Town)	54002
Esadore Lake	54451
Esdaile	54723
Esofea	54667
Estella (Town)	54732
Ettrick	54627
Ettrick (Town)	54627
Eureka (Polk County) (Town)	54024
Eureka (Winnebago County)	54934
Eureka Center	54024
Euren	54205
Evansville	53536
Evergreen (Langlade County) (Town)	54491
Evergreen (Marathon County)	54455
Evergreen (Washburn County) (Town)	54801

	ZIP
Excelsior (Richland County)	53518
Excelsior (Sauk County) (Town)	53961
Exeland	54835
Exeter (Town)	53508
Exile	54761
Fahey Heights	53575
Fairbanks (Town)	54486
Fairburn	54923
Fairchild	54741
Fairchild (Town)	54741
Fairfield (Rock County)	53114
Fairfield (Sauk County) (Town)	53913
Fairplay	53811
Fairview	54628
Fairview Beach	54901
Fair Water	53931
Fall City	54739
Fall Creek	54742
Fall River	53932
Falun	54840
Fargo	54665
Farmersville	53050
Farmhill	54740
Farmington (Jefferson County)	53094
Farmington (Jefferson County) (Town)	53094
Farmington (La Crosse County) (Town)	54644
Farmington (Polk County) (Town)	54017
Farmington (Washington County) (Town)	53040
Farmington (Waupaca County) (Town)	54981
Fayette	53530
Fayette (Town)	53530
Federal Correctional Institution	53952
Fence	54120
Fence (Town)	54120
Fennimore	53809
Fennimore (Town)	53809
Fenwood	54426
Fern (Town)	54121
Ferron Park	54801
Ferryville	54628
Fifield	54524
Fifield (Town)	54524
Fillmore	53021
Finley	54646
Finley (Town)	54646
Fish Creek	54212
Fisk	54904
Fitchburg	53713
Five Corners (Outagamie County)	54911
Five Corners (Ozaukee County)	53012
Five Points	53518
Flambeau (Price County) (Town)	54555
Flambeau (Rusk County)	54745
Flambeau (Rusk County) (Town)	54848
Flintville	54301
Florence	54121
Florence (Town)	54121
Folsom	54655
Fond du Lac	54935-37
For specific Fond du Lac Zip Codes call (414) 921-9300, or your local postmaster.	
Fontana	53125
Fontenoy	54208
Footville	53537
Ford (Town)	54433
Forest (Fond du Lac County) (Town)	54935
Forest (Richland County) (Town)	54664
Forest (St. Croix County)	54012
Forest (St. Croix County) (Town)	54012
Forest (Vernon County)	54639
Forest Junction	54123
Forest Mall (Part of Fond du Lac)	54935
Forestville	54213
Forestville (Town)	54213
Fort Atkinson	53538
Fort McCoy	54656
Fort Winnebago (Town)	53901
Forward	53572
Foster (Clark County) (Town)	54493
Foster (Eau Claire County)	54758
Fountain (Town)	53929
Fountain City	54629

	ZIP
Hawkins (Town)	54530
Hawthorne	54842
Hawthorne (Town)	54842
Hayes	54174
Hay River (Town)	54725
Hayton	53014
Hayward	54843
Hayward (Town)	54843
Hazel Green	53811
Hazel Green (Town)	53811
Hazelhurst	54531
Hazelhurst (Town)	54531
Heafford Junction	54532
Heart Prairie	53190
Hebel	54208
Hebron	53538
Hebron (Town)	53538
Hegg	54627
Helena	53503
Helenville	53137
Helvetia (Town)	54962
Hendren (Town)	54493
Henrietta (Town)	53924
Henrysville	54217
Herbster	54844
Herman (Dodge County) (Town)	53078
Herman (Shawano County) (Town)	54166
Herman (Sheboygan County) (Town)	53085
Herman Center	53050
Herold	54610
Hersey	54027
Hertel	54845
Hewett (Town)	54456
Hewitt (Marathon County) (Town)	54401
Hewitt (Wood County)	54441
Hiawatha Trail Estates	53934
Hickory Corners	54174
Hickory Grove (Town)	53805
Hickory Hill	53593
Hickory Hill Estates	53719
Hickory Meadows	53597
High Bridge	54846
High Cliff	54952
Highland (Douglas County) (Town)	54849
Highland (Iowa County)	53543
Highland (Iowa County) (Town)	53543
Highland Park	53049
Highland Shore	54904
Hika (Part of Cleveland)	53015
Hilbert	54129
Hilbert Junction (Part of Hilbert)	54129
Hiles (Forest County)	54511
Hiles (Forest County) (Town)	54511
Hiles (Wood County) (Town)	54466
Hill (Town)	54459
Hilldale (Part of Madison)	53705
Hilldale Shopping Center (Part of Madison)	53705
Hill Point	53937
Hillsboro	54634
Hillsboro (Town)	54638
Hillsdale	54744
Hillside	53523
Hilltop (Part of Milwaukee)	53205
	53233
For specific Hilltop Zip Codes call (414) 352-3340, or your local postmaster.	
Hines	54874
Hingham	53031
Hintz	54124
Hixon (Town)	54498
Hixton	54635
Hixton (Town)	54635
Hoard (Town)	54422
Hobart (Town)	54303
Hofa Park	54165
Hoffman Corners	54638
Hogarty	54408
Holcombe	54745
Holiday Heights	53934
Holiday Hills	53511
Holland (Brown County)	54130
Holland (Brown County) (Town)	54130
Holland (La Crosse County) (Town)	54636
Holland (Sheboygan County) (Town)	53070
Hollandale	53544
Hollister	54491
Holmen	54636
Holton (Town)	54405
Holway (Town)	54451

	ZIP
Holy Cross	53004
Homestead (Town)	54121
Honey Creek (Sauk County) (Town)	53577
Honey Creek (Walworth County)	53138
Honey Lake	53105
Hoopers Mill	53551
Hope	53527
Horicon	53032
Horns Corners	53012
Horse Creek	54026
Hortonia (Town)	54961
Hortonville	54944
Houlton	54082
How (Town)	54174
Howard (Brown County)	54303
Howard (Chippewa County) (Town)	54730
Howards Grove-Millersville	53083
Hubbard (Dodge County) (Town)	53032
Hubbard (Rusk County) (Town)	54848
Hubbellton	53094
Hub City	53581
Hubertus	53033
Hudson	54016
Hudson (Town)	54016
Hughes (Town)	54820
Huilsburg	53078
Hull (Marathon County) (Town)	54421
Hull (Portage County) (Town)	54481
Humbird	54746
Humboldt (Town)	54217
Humboldt	54229
Hunter (Town)	54843
Hunting	54486
Huntington	54017
Hurley	54534
Huron	54768
Hurricane	53813
Husher	53108
Hustisford	53034
Hustisford (Town)	53039
Hustler	54637
Hutchins (Town)	54414
Hyde	53582
Idlewild	54235
Iduna	54627
Imalone	54819
Independence	54747
Indian Creek	54837
Indianford	53534
Indian Shores	54986
Ingram	54526
Inlet	53115
Ino	54856
Institute	54235
Iola	54945
Iola (Town)	54945
Irma	54442
Iron Belt	54536
Iron Ridge	53035
Iron River	54847
Iron River (Town)	54847
Ironton	53941
Ironton (Town)	53959
Irving (Town)	54615
Irvington	54751
Isaar	54165
Isabelle (Town)	54723
Island Beach	54901
Island Lake	54757
Island Park	54963
Itasca (Part of Superior)	54880
Ithaca	53581
Ithaca (Town)	53581
Ives (Part of Racine)	53404
Ives Grove	53177
Ixonia	53036
Ixonia (Town)	53036
Jackson (Adams County) (Town)	53952
Jackson (Burnett County) (Town)	54893
Jackson (Washington County)	53037
Jackson (Washington County) (Town)	53037
Jacksonport	54235
Jacksonport (Town)	54235
Jacobs (Town)	54527
Jamestown (Town)	53807
Janesville	53545-47
For specific Janesville Zip Codes call (608) 754-5555, or your local postmaster.	
Janesville Mall (Part of Janesville)	53545

	ZIP
Jefferson (Green County) (Town)	53550
Jefferson (Jefferson County)	53549
Jefferson (Jefferson County) (Town)	53137
Jefferson (Monroe County) (Town)	54619
Jefferson (Vernon County) (Town)	54667
Jefferson Junction	53549
Jenkynsville	53807
Jennings	54463
Jericho (Calumet County)	53014
Jericho (Waukesha County)	53119
Jewett	54017
Jim Falls	54748
Joel	54001
Johannesburg	54017
John P. Cofrin (Part of Green Bay)	54302
Johnsburg	53049
Johnson (Town)	54411
Johnson Creek	53038
Johnsonville	53085
Johnstown (Polk County) (Town)	54889
Johnstown (Rock County)	53505
Johnstown (Rock County) (Town)	53505
Johnstown Center	53545
Jonesdale	53565
Jordan (Green County) (Town)	53504
Jordan (Portage County)	54481
Jordan Center	53504
Jordan Lake	53965
Juda	53550
Jump River (Town)	54434
Jump River	54434
Junction City	54443
Juneau (Dodge County)	53039
Juneau (Part of Milwaukee)	53202-03
For specific Juneau Zip Codes call (414) 289-8336, or your local postmaster.	
Kaiser	54552
Kansasville	53139
Kaukauna (Outagamie County)	54130
Kaukauna (Outagamie County) (Town)	54130
Keene	54921
Keenville	54901
Kekoskee	53050
Kellner	54494
Kellnersville	54215
Kelly (Bayfield County) (Town)	54856
Kelly (Marathon County)	54476
Kempster	54444
Kendall (Lafayette County) (Town)	53530
Kendall (Monroe County)	54638
Kennan	54537
Kennan (Town)	54537
Kenosha	53140-44
For specific Kenosha Zip Codes call (414) 657-3188, or your local postmaster.	
Keshena	54135
Keshena Falls	54135
Kettle Moraine Correctional Institution	53073
Kettle Moraine Lake	53010
Kewaskum	53040
Kewaskum (Town)	53040
Kewaunee	54216
Keyeser	53532
Keyesville	53937
Keystone (Bayfield County) (Town)	54806
Keystone (Chippewa County)	54732
Kickapoo (Town)	54652
Kickapoo Center	54664
Kiel	53042
Kieler	53812
Kildare (Town)	53944
Kimball (Town)	54534
Kimberly	54136
King (Lincoln County) (Town)	54487
King (Waupaca County)	54946
Kingsbridge	54241
Kingston (Green Lake County)	53939
Kingston (Green Lake County) (Town)	53926
Kingston (Juneau County) (Town)	54641
Kinnickinnic (Town)	54022

* Area Zip Code   † Post Office Boxes

COLLEGES & UNIVERSITIES

FINANCIAL INSTITUTIONS

HOSPITALS

HOTELS/MOTELS

MILITARY INSTALLATIONS

	ZIP
Mitchell (Town)	53093
Modena	54755
Modena (Town)	54755
Moeville	54011
Mole Lake	54520
Mole Lake Indian Reservation	54520
Molitor (Town)	54451
Monches	53029
Mondovi	54755
Mondovi (Town)	54755
Monico (Town)	54501
Monico	54501
Monona	53716
Monroe (Adams County) (Town)	54613
Monroe (Green County)	53566
Monroe (Green County) (Town)	53566
Monroe Center	54613
Montana	54747
Montana (Town)	54747
Montello	53949
Montello (Town)	53949
Monterey	53066
Montfort	53569
Monticello (Green County)	53570
Monticello (Lafayette County) (Town)	54810
Montpelier (Town)	54217
Montreal	54550
Montrose (Town)	53508
Moon	54455
Moose Junction	54830
Moquah	54806
Morgan (Oconto County)	54154
Morgan (Oconto County) (Town)	54154
Morgan (Shawano County)	54128
Morris (Town)	54486
Morrison	54126
Morrison (Town)	54126
Morrisonville	53571
Morris Park	53558
Morse	54527
Morse (Town)	54546
Moscow (Town)	53507
Mosel (Town)	53015
Mosinee	54455
Mosinee (Town)	54455
Mosling	54124
Moundville (Town)	53930
Mountain	54149
Mount Calvary	53057
Mount Hope	53816
Mount Hope (Town)	53816
Mount Horeb	53572
Mount Ida	53809
Mount Ida (Town)	53809
Mount Morris	54982
Mount Morris (Town)	54982
Mount Pleasant (Green County) (Town)	53502
Mount Pleasant (Racine County) (Town)	53401
Mount Sterling	54645
Mount Tabor	54638
Mount Vernon	53572
Mount Zion	53805
Mukwa (Town)	54961
Mukwonago	53149
Mukwonago (Town)	53149
Murphy Corner	54130
Murry (Town)	54819
Muscoda (Grant County)	53573
Muscoda (Grant County) (Town)	53573
Muskego	53150
Myra	53095
Nabob	53095
Namakagon (Town)	54821
Namur	54204
Naples (Town)	54755
Nasbro	53006
Nasewaupee (Town)	54235
Nashotah	53058
Nashville (Town)	54520
Nasonville	54449
Navarino	54107
Navarino (Town)	54107
Necedah	54646
Necedah (Town)	54646
Neda	53035
Neenah	54956*
	54957†
Neillsville	54456
Nekimi (Town)	54901
Nekoosa	54457
Nelma	49935
Nelson	54756
Nelson (Town)	54756
Nelsonville	54458

	ZIP
Nenno	53002
Neopit	54150
Neosho	53059
Nepeuskun (Town)	54971
Neshkoro	54960
Neshkoro (Town)	54960
Neuern	54217
Neva (Town)	54424
Neva Corners	54424
Newald	54511
New Amsterdam	54636
Newark	53511
Newark (Town)	53511
New Auburn	54757
New Berlin	53151
Newbold (Town)	54501
Newburg	53060
Newburg Corners	54614
New Centerville	54002
New Chester (Town)	53936
New Denmark (Town)	54208
New Diggings	61075
New Diggings (Town)	61075
New Fane	53040
New Franken	54229
New Glarus	53574
New Glarus (Town)	53574
New Haven (Adams County) (Town)	53920
New Haven (Dunn County) (Town)	54005
New Holstein	53061
New Holstein (Town)	53061
New Hope (Town)	54407
New Lisbon	53950
New London	54961
New Lyme (Town)	54656
New Miner	54646
New Munster	53152
New Odanah	54861
Newport (Town)	53965
New Post	54828
New Prospect	53010
New Richmond	54017
New Rome	54457
Newry	54619
Newton (Manitowoc County)	53063
Newton (Manitowoc County) (Town)	53063
Newton (Marquette County) (Town)	53964
Newton (Vernon County)	54665
Newtonburg	54220
Newville	53534
Niagara	54151
Niagara (Town)	49870
Nichols	54152
Nippersink Manor	53128
Nokomis (Town)	54487
Nora	53531
Norman	54216
Norrie	54414
Norrie (Town)	54414
Norske	54945
North Andover	53810
North Bay (Door County)	54202
North Bay (Racine County)	53402
North Bend	54642
North Bend (Town)	54642
North Branch	54611
North Bristol	53590
North Cape	53126
Northeim	53063
Northfield	54635
Northfield (Town)	54635
North Fond du Lac	54937
North Freedom	53951
North Hudson	54016
North Lake (Walworth County)	53121
North Lake (Waukesha County)	53064
North Lancaster (Town)	53813
Northland	54945
Northland Mall (Part of Milwaukee)	53209
North Leeds	53911
North Lowell	53039
North Menomonie (Part of Menomonie)	54751
North Park	53402
Northport (Door County)	54210
Northport (Waupaca County)	54961
North Prairie	53153
Northridge (Part of Milwaukee)	53223
North Shore (Part of Glendale)	53217
North Tomah	54660
Northway Mall (Part of Marshfield)	54449

	ZIP
Northwoods Beach	54843
North York	54846
Norton	54730
Norwalk	54648
Norway (Town)	53182
Norway Grove	53532
Norwegian Bay	54940
Norwood (Town)	54409
Nutterville	54401
Nye	54020
Oak Center	53065
Oak Creek	53154
Oakdale	54649
Oakdale (Town)	54649
Oakfield	53065
Oakfield (Town)	53065
Oak Grove (Barron County) (Town)	54868
Oak Grove (Dodge County)	53039
Oak Grove (Dodge County) (Town)	53039
Oak Grove (Pierce County) (Town)	54021
Oak Hill	53156
Oakhill Correctional Institution	53575
Oakland (Burnett County) (Town)	54893
Oakland (Douglas County) (Town)	54874
Oakland (Jefferson County)	53538
Oakland (Jefferson County) (Town)	53538
Oakley	53550
Oakridge	53179
Oak Shores	53125
Oakwood (Part of Oak Creek)	53154
Oakwood Mall (Part of Eau Claire)	54703
Oasis (Town)	54966
Oconomowoc	53066
Oconomowoc (Town)	53069
Oconomowoc Lake	53066
Oconto	54153
Oconto (Town)	54139
Oconto Falls	54154
Oconto Falls (Town)	54154
Odanah	54861
Ogdensburg	54962
Ogema	54459
Ogema (Town)	54459
Oil City	54648
Ojibwa	54862
Ojibwa (Town)	54862
Okauchee	53069
Okauchee Lake	53058
Okee	53555
Old Albertville	54730
Old Ashippun	53003
Old Lebanon	53098
Oliver	54880
Olivet	54767
Oma (Town)	54534
Omro	54963
Omro (Town)	54901
Onalaska	54650
Onalaska (Town)	54650
Oneida (Town)	54155
Oneida	54155
Oneida Indian Reservation	54155
Ono	54750
Ontario	54651
Oostburg	53070
Orange (Town)	54618
Orange Mill	54618
Oregon	53575
Oregon (Town)	53575
Orfordville	53576
Orienta (Town)	54865
Orihula	54940
Orion	53573
Orion (Town)	53573
Osborn (Town)	54165
Osceola (Fond du Lac County) (Town)	53010
Osceola (Polk County)	54020
Osceola (Polk County) (Town)	54020
Oshkosh	54901-04
For specific Oshkosh Zip Codes call (414) 236-0200, or your local postmaster.	
Osman	53063
Osseo	54758
Ostrander	54961
Otsego	53925
Otsego (Town)	53925
Ottawa (Town)	53118
Otter Creek (Dunn County) (Town)	54772

	ZIP		ZIP		ZIP
Otter Creek (Eau Claire County) (Town)	54722	Pittsville	54466	Presque Isle (Town)	54557
Oulu (Town)	54847	Plain	53577	Preston (Adams County) (Town)	53934
Ourtown	53085	Plainfield	54966	Preston (Grant County)	53809
Owen	54460	Plainfield (Town)	54966	Preston (Trempealeau	
Oxbo	54552	Plainville	53965	County) (Town)	54616
Oxford	53952	Plat	53017	Price (Jackson County)	54741
Oxford (Town)	53952	Platteville	53818	Price (Langlade County)	
Pacific (Town)	53954	Platteville (Town)	53818	(Town)	54418
Packwaukee (Town)	53953	Plaza 8 (Part of Sheboygan)	53081	Primrose (Town)	53593
Packwaukee	53953	Pleasant Prairie	53158	Princeton	54968
Paddock Lake	53168	Pleasant Ridge	53533	Princeton (Town)	54968
Padus	54566	Pleasant Springs (Town)	53589	Prospect (Part of New	
Palmyra	53156	Pleasant Valley (Eau Claire		Berlin)	53151
Palmyra (Town)	53156	County) (Town)	54701	Pukwana Beach	53049
Paoli	53508	Pleasant Valley (St. Croix		Pulaski (Brown County)	54162
Pardeeville	53954	County) (Town)	54015	Pulaski (Iowa County)	
Parfreyville	54981	Pleasant Valley (Vernon		(Town)	53506
Paris (Grant County) (Town)	53807	County)	54658	Pulcifer	54164
Paris (Kenosha County)	53182	Pleasant View	54615	Purdy	54665
Paris (Kenosha County)		Pleasantville	54758	Quarry	54230
(Town)	53182	Plover (Marathon County)		Quincy (Town)	53910
Park Falls	54552	(Town)	54414	Quincy Details	53934
Parkland (Town)	54874	Plover (Portage County)	54467	Quinney	53014
Parklawn (Part of		Plover (Portage County)		Racine	53401-08
Milwaukee)	53216	(Town)	54467	For specific Racine Zip Codes call	
Park Plaza (Part of		Plugtown	53805	(414) 632-1661, or your local	
Oshkosh)	54902	Plum City	54761	postmaster.	
Park Ridge	54481	Plum Lake (Town)	54560	Radisson	54867
Parrish	54435	Plymouth (Juneau County)		Radisson (Town)	54867
Parrish (Town)	54435	(Town)	53929	Randall (Burnett County)	54840
Patch Grove	53817	Plymouth (Rock County)		Randall (Kenosha County)	
Patch Grove (Town)	53821	(Town)	53545	(Town)	60071
Patzau	54836	Plymouth (Sheboygan		Randolph (Columbia	
Pearson	54462	County)	53073	County) (Town)	53923
Peck (Town)	54424	Plymouth (Sheboygan		Randolph (Dodge County)	53956
Pecks Station	53121	County) (Town)	53073	Random Lake	53075
Peebles	54935	Point Loomis Shopping		Range	54001
Peeksville (Town)	54527	Center (Part of		Rankin	54201
Pelican (Town)	54501	Milwaukee)	53221	Rantoul (Town)	53014
Pelican Lake	54463	Poland	54301	Rattman Heights	53701
Pella	54950	Polar	54418	Ravenoaks	53575
Pella (Town)	54950	Polar (Town)	54418	Rawson (Part of Oak Creek)	53172
Pell Lake	53157	Polifka Corners	54247	Raymond	53126
Pembine	54156	Polk (Town)	53076	Raymond (Town)	53126
Pembine (Town)	54156	Polley	54433	Readfield	54969
Pence	54550	Polonia	54423	Readstown	54652
Pence (Town)	54550	Poniatowski	54426	Red Banks	54940
Peninsula Center	54202	Poplar	54864	Red Cedar (Town)	54751
Pensaukee	54153	Popple Lake	54729	Red Cliff	54814
Pensaukee (Town)	54153	Popple River	54542	Red Cliff Indian Reservation	54806
Pepin	54759	Popple River (Town)	54542	Redgranite	54970
Pepin (Town)	54759	Porcupine	54721	Red Mound	54624
Peplin	54455	Portage	53901	Red River (Kewaunee	
Perkinstown	54451	Port Andrew	53518	County) (Town)	54205
Perry (Town)	53572	Port Edwards	54469	Red River (Shawano	
Pershing (Town)	54433	Port Edwards (Town)	54457	County)	54166
Peru (Dunn County) (Town)	54755	Porter (Town)	53545	Red Springs (Town)	54128
Peru (Portage County)	54407	Porterfield	54159	Redville	54498
Peshtigo	54157	Porterfield (Town)	54159	Reedsburg	53959
Peshtigo (Town)	54143	Portland	53594	Reedsburg (Town)	53959
Petersburg	54631	Portland (Town)	53594	Reedsville	54230
Petty Acres	53589	Portland	54619	Reeseville	53579
Pewaukee	53072	Portland (Town)	54619	Reeve	54004
Pewaukee (Town)	53072	Port Plaza Mall (Part of		Regency Mall (Part of	
Phantom Lake	53149	Green Bay)	54301	Racine)	53406
Pheasant Branch (Part of		Port Washington	53074	Reid (Town)	54440
Middleton)	53562	Port Washington (Town)	53074	Reighmoor	54963
Phelps	54554	Port Wing	54865	Remington (Town)	54413
Phelps (Town)	54554	Port Wing (Town)	54865	Reseburg (Town)	54437
Phillips	54555	Poskin	54866	Reserve (Sawyer County)	54876
Phipps	54843	Post Lake	54428	Retreat	54624
Phlox	54464	Postville	53516	Rewey	53580
Piacenza	54986	Potawatomi Indian		Rhine	53020
Pickerel	54465	Reservation	54520	Rhine (Town)	53020
Pickett	54964	Potosi	53820	Rhinelander	54501
Piehl (Town)	54501	Potosi (Town)	53820	Rib Falls	54426
Pierce (Town)	54216	Potter	54160	Rib Falls (Town)	54426
Pigeon (Town)	54773	Potter Lake	53120	Rib Lake	54470
Pigeon Falls	54760	Potts Corners	54639	Rib Lake (Town)	54470
Pike Lake	54440	Pound	54161	Rib Mountain	54401
Pilsen (Bayfield County)		Pound (Town)	54139	Rib Mountain (Town)	54401
(Town)	54806	Powell	54547	Rice Lake	54868
Pilsen (Kewaunee County)	54217	Powers Lake	53159	Rice Lake (Town)	54868
Pine Bluff	53528	Poygan (Town)	54963	Richardson	54004
Pine Creek	54625	Poynette	53955	Richfield (Adams County)	
Pine Grove (Brown County)	54301	Poy Sippi	54967	(Town)	53934
Pine Grove (Portage		Poysippi (Town)	54967	Richfield (Washington	
County) (Town)	54921	Praag	54610	County)	53076
Pine Lake (Iron County)	54534	Prairie Corners	53807	Richfield (Washington	
Pine Lake (Oneida County)		Prairie du Chien	53821	County) (Town)	53076
(Town)	54501	Prairie du Chien (Town)	53821	Richfield (Wood County)	
Pine River (Lincoln County)		Prairie du Sac	53578	(Town)	54449
(Town)	54452	Prairie du Sac (Town)	53583	Richford	54930
Pine River (Waushara		Prairie Farm	54762	Richford (Town)	54930
County)	54965	Prairie Farm (Town)	54762	Richland (Richland County)	
Pine Tree Mall (Part of		Prairie Lake (Town)	54728	(Town)	53581
Marinette)	54143	Pray	54466	Richland (Rusk County)	
Pine Valley (Town)	54456	Preble (Part of Green Bay)	54302	(Town)	54526
Pipe	53049	Prentice	54556	Richland Center	53581
Pipersville	53094	Prentice (Town)	54556	Richmond (Shawano	
Pittsfield (Town)	54301	Prescott	54021	County) (Town)	54166
		Presque Isle	54557		

Name	ZIP	Name	ZIP	Name	ZIP
Richmond (St. Croix County) (Town)	54017	Rowleys Bay	54210	Schleswig (Town)	53042
Richmond (Walworth County)	53115	Roxbury	53583	Schley (Town)	54452
Richmond (Walworth County) (Town)	53115	Roxbury (Town)	53583	Schnappsville	54411
Richwood (Dodge County)	53098	Royalton	54975	Schoepke (Town)	54463
Richwood (Richland County) (Town)	53518	Royalton (Town)	54975	Schofield	54476
Ridgeland	54763	Rozellville	54484	School Hill	53042
Ridgeville (Town)	54648	Rubicon (Town)	53078	Schraven Circle	54937
Ridgeway	53582	Rubicon	53078	Scott (Brown County) (Town)	54229
Ridgeway (Town)	53582	Ruby (Town)	54745	Scott (Burnett County) (Town)	54893
Rief's Mills	54247	Rudolph	54475	Scott (Columbia County) (Town)	53923
Rietbrock (Town)	54411	Rudolph (Town)	54475	Scott (Crawford County) (Town)	53518
Rileys	53593	Rural	54981	Scott (Lincoln County) (Town)	54452
Rileys Point	54235	Rushford (Town)	54963	Scott (Monroe County) (Town)	54666
Ringle	54471	Rush Lake	54971	Scott (Sheboygan County) (Town)	53001
Ringle (Town)	54471	Rush River (Town)	54002	Sechlerville	54635
Rio	53960	Rusk (Burnett County) (Town)	54801	Seeleys	54843
Rio Creek	54231	Rusk (Dunn County)	54751	Seif (Town)	54456
Riplinger	54479	Rusk (Rusk County) (Town)	54728	Seneca (Crawford County)	54654
Ripon	54971	Russell (Bayfield County) (Town)	54814	Seneca (Crawford County) (Town)	54654
Ripon (Town)	54971	Russell (Lincoln County) (Town)	54435	Seneca (Green Lake County) (Town)	54923
Rising Sun	54628	Russell (Sheboygan County) (Town)	53079	Seneca (Shawano County) (Town)	54978
River Falls	54022	Russell (Trempealeau County)	54747	Seneca (Wood County) (Town)	54494
River Falls (Town)	54022	Rutland (Town)	53589	Sevastopol (Town)	54235
River Hills	54209	Sabin	53581	Seven Mile Creek (Town)	53944
	53217	Sacred Heart School of Theology	53130	Sextonville	53584
For specific River Hills Zip Codes call (414) 962-8644, or your local postmaster.		St. Anna	53061	Seymour (Eau Claire County) (Town)	54701
Rivermoor	54963	St. Anthony	53002	Seymour (Eau Claire County)	54703
Riverside	53541	St. Cloud	53079	Seymour (Lafayette County) (Town)	53586
Riverview (Town)	54149	St. Croix Falls	54024	Seymour (Outagamie County)	54165
Riverwood	54613	St. Croix Falls (Town)	54824	Seymour (Outagamie County) (Town)	54165
River Wood Estates	53589	St. Croix Indian Reservation	54830	Shamrock	54615
Roberts	54023	St. Francis	53235	Shanagolden	54527
Robinson	53147	Saint George	53085	Shanagolden (Town)	54527
Rochester	53167	St. Germain	54558	Shantytown	54473
Rochester (Town)	53105	St. Germain (Town)	54558	Sharon (Portage County) (Town)	54473
Rock (Rock County) (Town)	53545	St. John	54129	Sharon (Walworth County)	53585
Rock (Wood County) (Town)	54466	St. Joseph (Fond du Lac County)	53079	Sharon (Walworth County) (Town)	53585
Rockbridge	53581	St. Joseph (La Crosse County)	54601	Shawano	54166
Rockbridge (Town)	53581	St. Joseph (St. Croix County) (Town)	54016	Shawano North Beach	54166
Rock Creek (Town)	54755	St. Kilian	53010	Sheboygan	53081-83
Rockdale	53523	St. Lawrence (Washington County)	53027	For specific Sheboygan Zip Codes call (414) 458-3741, or your local postmaster.	
Rock Elm	54740	St. Lawrence (Waupaca County) (Town)	54962	Sheboygan Falls	53085
Rock Elm (Town)	54740	St. Marie (Town)	54968	Sheboygan Falls (Town)	53085
Rock Falls (Dunn County)	54764	St. Martins (Part of Franklin)	53132	Sheil	53575
Rock Falls (Lincoln County) (Town)	54442	St. Marys	54619	Shelby (Town)	54601
Rockfield	53077	St. Michaels	53040	Sheldon (Monroe County) (Town)	54651
Rock Lake	53179	St. Nazianz	54232	Sheldon (Rusk County)	54766
Rockland (Brown County) (Town)	54115	St. Peter	53049	Shell Lake	54871
Rockland (La Crosse County)	54653	St. Wendel (Part of Cleveland)	53015	Shennington	54618
Rockland (Manitowoc County) (Town)	54207	Salem (Kenosha County)	53168	Shepley	54499
Rock Springs	53961	Salem (Kenosha County) (Town)	53168	Sheridan (Dunn County) (Town)	54725
Rockton	54639	Salem (Pierce County) (Town)	54750	Sheridan (Waupaca County)	54981
Rockville (Grant County)	53820	Salem Oaks	53168	Sherman (Clark County) (Town)	54479
Rockville (Manitowoc County)	53042	Salvatorian Center (Part of New Holstein)	53062	Sherman (Dunn County) (Town)	54751
Rockwood	54220	Sampson (Chippewa County) (Town)	54757	Sherman (Iron County) (Town)	54552
Rocky Run	54481	Sampson (Oconto County)	54171	Sherman (Sheboygan County) (Town)	53075
Rodell	54722	Sanborn	54806	Sherman Center	53075
Rogersville	54974	Sanborn (Town)	54861	Sherry	54454
Rolling (Town)	54409	Sand Bay (Bayfield County)	54814	Sherry (Town)	54454
Rolling Acres	53589	Sand Bay (Door County)	54235	Sherwood (Calumet County)	54169
Rolling Ground	54655	Sand Creek	54765	Sherwood (Clark County) (Town)	54466
Rolling Prairie	53039	Sand Creek (Town)	54765	Shields (Dodge County) (Town)	53098
Rolling View	53589	Sand Lake (Burnett County) (Town)	54893	Shields (Marquette County) (Town)	53949
Romance	54632	Sandlake (Polk County)	54009	Shiocton	54170
Rome (Adams County) (Town)	54457	Sand Lake (Sawyer County) (Town)	54876	Shirley	54115
Rome (Jefferson County)	53178	Sand Prairie	53518	Shopiere	53511
Roosevelt (Burnett County) (Town)	54813	Sandusky	53937	Shoreview	53179
Roosevelt (Oneida County)	54501	Saratoga (Town)	54494	Shorewood	53211
Roosevelt (Taylor County) (Town)	54447	Sarona	54870	Shorewood Hills	53705
Root River (Part of Milwaukee)	53227	Sarona (Town)	54870	Shortville	54456
Rose (Town)	54984	Sauk City	53583	Shoto	54241
Rosecrans	54227	Saukville	53080	Shullsburg	53586
Rose Lawn	54165	Saukville (Town)	53074	Shullsburg (Town)	53586
Rosemere (Part of Manitowoc)	54220	Saxeville	54976		
Rosendale	54974	Saxeville (Town)	54976		
Rosendale (Town)	54964	Saxon	54559		
Rosholt	54473	Saxon (Town)	54559		
Rosiere	54205	Saylesville (Dodge County)	53078		
Ross (Forest County) (Town)	54511	Saylesville (Waukesha County)	53186		
Ross (Vernon County)	54665	Sayner	54560		
Ross D. Sills	53125	Scandinavia	54977		
Rostok	54216	Scandinavia (Town)	54977		
Rothschild	54474	Scarboro	54217		
Round Lake (Town)	54843				

* Area Zip Code   † Post Office Boxes

	ZIP
Sidney	54456
Sigel (Chippewa County) (Town)	54727
Sigel (Wood County) (Town)	54494
Silica	53049
Silver Cliff (Town)	54104
Silver Creek	53075
Silver Lake (Kenosha County) (Town)	53170
Silver Lake (Walworth County)	53121
Silver Lake (Waushara County)	54982
Sinsinawa	53824
Sioux	54891
Sioux Creek (Town)	54728
Siren	54872
Siren (Town)	54872
Sister Bay	54234
Skanawan (Town)	54442
Slab City	54107
Slabtown	53549
Slades Corner	53105
Slinger	53086
Slovan	54205
Smelser (Town)	53807
Sobieski	54171
Sobieski Corners	54141
Soldiers Grove	54655
Solon Springs	54873
Solon Springs (Town)	54873
Somers	53171
Somers (Town)	53171
Somerset	54025
Somerset (Town)	55082
Somo (Town)	54564
Soperton	54566
South Beaver Dam	53916
South Byron	53006
South Chase	54162
South Chippewa (Part of Chippewa Falls)	54729
South Fork (Town)	54530
Southgate Mall (Part of Milwaukee)	53215
South Itasca (Part of Superior)	54880
South Janesville (Part of Janesville)	53545
South Kenosha	53143
South Lancaster (Town)	53813
South Luxemburg (Part of Luxemburg)	54217
South Milwaukee	53172
South Necedah (Part of Necedah)	54646
South Randolph	53956
South Range	54874
Southridge (Part of Greendale)	53129
South Side (Part of Madison)	53715
South Wayne	53587
Sparta	54656
Sparta (Town)	54656
Spaulding	54466
Spencer	54479
Spencer (Town)	54479
Spider Lake (Town)	54843
Spirit	54513
Spirit (Town)	54513
Spirit Falls	54564
Split Rock	54486
Spokeville	54479
Spooner	54801
Spooner (Town)	54801
Sprague	54646
Spread Eagle	54121
Spring Bluff	54930
Spring Brook (Dunn County) (Town)	54751
Springbrook (Washburn County)	54875
Springbrook (Washburn County) (Town)	54875
Springdale (Town)	53593
Springfield (Dane County) (Town)	53528
Springfield (Jackson County) (Town)	54659
Springfield (Marquette County) (Town)	53964
Springfield (St. Croix County) (Town)	54013
Springfield (Walworth County)	53176
Springfield Corners	53529
Spring Green	53588
Spring Green (Town)	53588
Spring Grove (Town)	53550
Spring Hill Edition	53589

	ZIP
Spring Lake (Pierce County) (Town)	54767
Spring Lake (Waushara County)	54960
Spring Prairie	53121
Spring Prairie (Town)	53121
Springstead	54552
Springvale (Columbia County) (Town)	53960
Springvale (Fond du Lac County) (Town)	54974
Spring Valley (Manitowoc County)	53063
Spring Valley (Pierce County)	54767
Spring Valley (Rock County) (Town)	53576
Springville (Adams County) (Town)	53965
Springville (Vernon County)	54665
Springwater (Town)	54984
Spruce	54139
Spruce (Town)	54139
Stanbery	54875
Standart	53533
Stanfold (Town)	54812
Stangelville	54208
Stanley (Barron County) (Town)	54822
Stanley (Chippewa County)	54768
Stanton (Dunn County) (Town)	54725
Stanton (St. Croix County) (Town)	54017
Stark (Town)	54639
Starks	54501
Starlake	54561
Star Prairie	54026
Star Prairie (Town)	54025
Star Valley	54655
Starview Heights	53545
State Line	53140
State Street (Part of Racine)	53404
Steffenrud Addition	54656
Stella (Town)	54501
Stephenson (Town)	54114
Stephenson Island (Part of Marinette)	54143
Stephensville	54944
Sterling (Polk County) (Town)	54006
Sterling (Vernon County) (Town)	54624
Stetsonville	54480
Stettin (Town)	54401
Steuben	54657
Stevens Point	54481
Stevenstown	54636
Stiles	54139
Stiles (Town)	54139
Stiles Junction	54139
Stinnett (Town)	54875
Stitzer	53825
Stockbridge	53088
Stockbridge (Town)	53014
Stockbridge Indian Reservation	54416
Stockholm	54769
Stockholm (Town)	54769
Stockton (Town)	54481
Stockton	54481
Stoddard	54658
Stonebank	53066
Stone Lake	54876
Stone Lake (Town)	54876
Stoughton	53589
Strader	54722
Stratford	54484
Strickland (Town)	54895
Strongs Prairie (Town)	54613
Strum	54770
Stubbs (Town)	54819
Sturgeon Bay	54235
Sturgeon Bay (Town)	54235
Sturtevant	53177
Suamico	54173
Suamico (Town)	54173
Sugar Bush (Brown County)	54217
Sugar Bush (Outagamie County)	54961
Sugar Camp	54501
Sugar Camp (Town)	54501
Sugar Creek (Town)	53121
Sugar Grove	54655
Sugar Island	53098
Sullivan	53178
Sullivan (Town)	53549
Summit (Douglas County) (Town)	54836
Summit (Juneau County) (Town)	53948

	ZIP
Summit (Langlade County) (Town)	54435
Summit (Waukesha County) (Town)	53058
Summit Corners	53066
Summit Lake	54485
Sumner (Barron County)	54822
Sumner (Barron County) (Town)	54868
Sumner (Jefferson County) (Town)	53538
Sumner (Trempealeau County) (Town)	54758
Sumpter (Town)	53951
Sunburst	53701
Sun Prairie	53590
Sun Prairie (Town)	53559
Sunset	54401
Sunset Beach	53916
Superior	54880
Superior (Town)	54880
Superior (Village)	54880
Suring	54174
Sussex	53089
Swiss (Town)	54830
Sylvan	54664
Sylvan (Town)	54664
Sylvania	53177
Sylvester (Town)	53550
Symco	54949
Tabor	53404
Taegesville	54401
Taft (Town)	54771
Tainter (Town)	54730
Tainter Lake	54730
Tamarack	54612
Tarrant	54736
Taus	54206
Taycheedah	54935
Taycheedah (Town)	54935
Taycheedah Correctional Institution	54935
Taylor	54659
Teegarden	54751
Tell	54610
Tennyson	53820
Terrace Park	53532
Tess Corners (Part of Muskego)	53130
Teutonia (Part of Milwaukee)	53206
Texas (Town)	54401
Theresa	53091
Theresa (Town)	53050
Thiensville	53092
	53097

For specific Thiensville Zip Codes call (414) 242-1720, or your local postmaster.

	ZIP
Thiry Daems	54217
Thompson	53027
Thompsonville	53126
Thornapple (Town)	54819
Thornton	54166
Thorp	54771
Thorp (Town)	54768
Three Lakes	54562
Three Lakes (Town)	54562
Tibbets	53121
Tichigan Lake	53185
Tiffany (Dunn County) (Town)	54725
Tiffany (Rock County)	53511
Tigerton	54486
Tilden	54729
Tilden (Town)	54729
Tilleda	54978
Tipler	49935
Tipler (Town)	49935
Tisch Mills	54240
Token Creek	53532
Tomah	54660
Tomah (Town)	54660
Tomahawk	54487
Tomahawk (Town)	54487
Tonet	54217
Tony	54563
Towerville	54655
Townsend	54175
Townsend (Town)	54175
Trade Lake	54837
Trade Lake (Town)	54837
Trade River	54840
Trego	54888
Trego (Town)	54888
Trempealeau	54661
Trempealeau (Town)	54661
Trenton (Dodge County) (Town)	53916
Trenton (Pierce County) (Town)	54014

	ZIP
Trenton (Washington County) (Town)	53095
Trevor	53179
Tri City (Part of Oak Creek)	53154
Trimbelle	54011
Trimbelle (Town)	54011
Tripoli	54564
Tripp (Town)	54847
Troy (Sauk County) (Town)	53583
Troy (St. Croix County) (Town)	54022
Troy (Walworth County)	53121
Troy (Walworth County) (Town)	53120
Troy Center	53120
True (Town)	54526
Truesdell	53143
Truman	53530
Trusler Circle	53575
Tuckaway (Part of Milwaukee)	53221
Tuleta Hills	53946
Tunnel City	54662
Turtle (Town)	53511
Turtle Lake (Barron County)	54889
Turtle Lake (Barron County) (Town)	54004
Turtle Lake (Walworth County)	53115
Tustin	54940
Twelfth Street Junction (Part of Superior)	54880
Twelve Corners	54106
Twenty-Eighth Street Junction (Part of Superior)	54880
Twin Bluffs	53581
Twin Grove	53550
Twin Lakes	53181
Two Creeks	54241
Two Creeks (Town)	54241
Two Rivers	54241
Two Rivers (Town)	54241
Ubet	54009
Underhill	54176
Underhill (Town)	54176
Union (Burnett County) (Town)	54830
Union (Door County) (Town)	54204
Union (Eau Claire County) (Town)	54701
Union (Grant County)	53818
Union (Pierce County) (Town)	54750
Union (Rock County)	53536
Union (Rock County) (Town)	53536
Union (Vernon County) (Town)	54634
Union (Waupaca County) (Town)	54949
Union Center	53962
Union Church	53126
Union Grove	53182
Unity (Clark County) (Town)	54488
Unity (Marathon County)	54488
Unity (Trempealeau County) (Town)	54770
University (Part of Madison)	53715
Upham (Town)	54485
Upper Third Street (Part of Milwaukee)	53212
Upson	54565
Uptown (Part of Racine)	53403
Urne	54736
Utica (Crawford County) (Town)	54655
Utica (Dane County)	53523
Utica (Waukesha County)	53066
Utica (Winnebago County) (Town)	54964
Valders	54245
Valley	54639
Valley Junction	54660
Valley View Mall (Part of La Crosse)	54601
Valmy	54235
Valton	53968
Van Buskirk	54534
Vance Creek (Town)	54868
Vandenbroek (Town)	54130
Vandyne	54979
Vaudreuil	54615
Veedum	54466
Vermont (Town)	53515
Vernon (Town)	53103
Verona	53593
Verona (Town)	53593
Vesper	54489
Veterans Administration Hospital (Part of Shorewood Hills)	53705

	ZIP
Victory	54624
Vienna (Town)	53532
Vignes	54235
Vilas (Dane County)	53527
Vilas (Langlade County) (Town)	54424
Villard (Part of Milwaukee)	53209
Vineyard	53575
Vinland (Town)	54901
Viola	54664
Viroqua	54665
Viroqua (Town)	54665
Voltz Lake	53179
Wabeno	54566
Wabeno (Town)	54566
Wagner (Town)	54177
Waino	54820
Waldo	53093
Waldwick	53565
Waldwick (Town)	53565
Wales	53183
Walhain	54217
Walsh	54159
Walworth	53184
Walworth (Town)	53184
Wandawega	53121
Wanderoos	54001
Warner (Town)	54437
Warren (St. Croix County) (Town)	54023
Warren (Waushara County) (Town)	54923
Warrens	54666
Warrentown	54750
Wascott (Town)	54890
Wascott	54890
Washburn (Bayfield County)	54891
Washburn (Bayfield County) (Town)	54891
Washburn (Clark County) (Town)	54456
Washington (Door County) (Town)	54246
Washington (Eau Claire County) (Town)	54742
Washington (Green County) (Town)	53570
Washington (La Crosse County) (Town)	54619
Washington (Rusk County) (Town)	54819
Washington (Sauk County) (Town)	53937
Washington (Shawano County) (Town)	54107
Washington (Vilas County) (Town)	54521
Washington Island	54246
Waterford	53185
Waterford (Town)	53185
Waterford North	53185
Waterford Woods	53185
Waterloo (Grant County) (Town)	53820
Waterloo (Jefferson County)	53594
Waterloo (Jefferson County) (Town)	53551
Watertown	53094
	53098
For specific Watertown Zip Codes call (414) 261-5929, or your local postmaster.	
Watertown (Town)	53094
Waterville (Pepin County) (Town)	54721
Waterville (Waukesha County)	53066
Watterstown (Town)	53805
Waubeek (Town)	54736
Waubeesee	53185
Waubeka	53021
Waubesa Heights	53558
Waucousta	53010
Waukau	54980
Waukechon (Town)	54166
Waukesha	53186-88
	53146
For specific Waukesha Zip Codes call (414) 542-5377, or your local postmaster.	
Waumandee	54622
Waumandee (Town)	54622
Waunakee	53597
Waupaca	54981
Waupaca (Town)	54981
Waupun (Dodge County)	53963
Waupun (Fond du Lac County) (Town)	53963
Wausau	54401-03
For specific Wausau Zip Codes call (715) 842-0731, or your local postmaster.	

	ZIP
Wausau Center (Part of Wausau)	54401
Wausaukee	54177
Wausaukee (Town)	54177
Wautoma	54982
Wautoma (Town)	54982
Wauwatosa	53210
	53213
	53222
	53226
For specific Wauwatosa Zip Codes call (414) 258-9486, or your local postmaster.	
Wauzeka	53826
Wauzeka (Town)	53826
Waverly	54740
Wayne (Lafayette County) (Town)	53587
Wayne (Washington County)	53010
Wayne (Washington County) (Town)	53010
Wayside	54126
Webb Lake	54830
Webb Lake (Town)	54830
Webster (Burnett County)	54893
Webster (Vernon County) (Town)	54639
Weirgor	54835
Weirgor (Town)	54835
Wellington (Town)	54651
Wells (Town)	54656
Wentworth	54874
Werley	53809
Wescott (Town)	54166
West Allis	53214
	53227
For specific West Allis Zip Codes call (414) 258-9454, or your local postmaster.	
West Baraboo	53913
West Bend	53095
West Bend (Town)	53095
West Bloomfield	54983
Westboro	54490
Westboro (Town)	54490
Westby	54667
West De Pere (Part of De Pere)	54115
Western (Part of Milwaukee)	53210
Westfield (Marquette County)	53964
Westfield (Marquette County) (Town)	53964
Westfield (Sauk County) (Town)	53943
Westford (Dodge County) (Town)	53916
Westford (Richland County) (Town)	53924
West Jacksonport	54209
West Kewaunee (Town)	54216
West Lima	54639
Westlyn	54494
West Marshland (Town)	54840
West Milwaukee	53215
	53234
For specific West Milwaukee Zip Codes call (414) 643-0414, or your local postmaster.	
Weston (Clark County) (Town)	54456
Weston (Dunn County)	54751
Weston (Dunn County) (Town)	54751
Weston (Marathon County)	54476
Weston (Marathon County) (Town)	54476
West Plainfield	54966
West Point (Town)	53555
Westport (Dane County) (Town)	53597
Westport (Richland County)	53518
West Prairie	54665
West Racine (Part of Racine)	53405
West Rosendale	54974
West Salem	54669
West Sweden (Town)	54837
West Towne Mall (Part of Madison)	53719
Weyauwega	54983
Weyauwega (Town)	54983
Weyerhaeuser	54895
Wheatland (Kenosha County)	53105
Wheatland (Kenosha County) (Town)	53105
Wheatland (Vernon County) (Town)	54624
Wheaton (Town)	54739
Wheeler	54772

* **Area Zip Code** † **Post Office Boxes**

	ZIP		ZIP		ZIP
Whitcomb	54486	Winchester (Winnebago		Wooddale	54817
White Creek	53965	County)	54947	Woodford	53599
Whitefish Bay (Door		Winchester (Winnebago		Woodhull	54932
County)	54235	County) (Town)	54947	Woodland (Dodge County)	53099
Whitefish Bay (Milwaukee		Wind Lake	53185	Woodland (Sauk County)	
County)	53217	Wind Point	53402	(Town)	53968
Whitehall	54773	Windsor	53598	Woodman	53827
White Lake	54491	Windsor (Town)	53598	Woodman (Town)	53827
Whitelaw	54247	Windsor Hills	53532	Woodmohr (Town)	54724
White Oak Springs (Town)	53586	Windsor Prairie	53532	Wood River (Town)	54840
White River (Town)	54855	Winfield (Town)	53959	Woodruff	54568
Whitestown (Town)	54639	Wingville (Town)	53569	Woodruff (Town)	54568
Whitewater	53190	Winnebago	54985	Woodstock	53581
Whitewater (Town)	53190	Winnebago Heights	53049	Woodville (Calumet County)	
Whiting	54481	Winnebago Indian		(Town)	54129
Whittlesey	54451	Reservation	53965	Woodville (St. Croix County)	54028
Wien (Town)	54426	Winnebago Mission	54615	Woodworth	53194
Wild Rose	54984	Winneboujou	54820	Worcester (Town)	54555
Wildwood	54028	Winneconne	54986	Worden (Town)	54771
Wilkinson (Town)	54895	Winneconne (Town)	54927	Wrightstown (Brown	
Willard (Clark County)	54493	Winter	54896	County)	54180
Willard (Rusk County)		Winter (Town)	54896	Wrightstown (Brown	
(Town)	54731	Wiota	53587	County) (Town)	54115
Williams Bay	53191	Wiota (Town)	53587	Wuertsburg	54411
Williamstown (Town)	53032	Wiscona (Part of Glendale)	53209	Wyalusing	53801
Willow (Town)	53924	Wisconsin Correctional		Wyalusing (Town)	53801
Willow Springs (Lafayette		Center System	53575	Wyeville	54660
County) (Town)	53565	Wisconsin Dells	53965	Wyocena	53969
Willow Springs (Waukesha		Wisconsin Rapids	54494*	Wyocena (Town)	53960
County)	53051		54495†	Wyoming (Iowa County)	
Wilmore Heights	54971	Withee	54498	(Town)	53588
Wilmot	53192	Withee (Town)	54771	Wyoming (Waupaca	
Wilson (Dunn County)		Wittenberg	54499	County) (Town)	54945
(Town)	54733	Wittenberg (Town)	54499	Yahara Heights	53597
Wilson (Eau Claire County)	54726	Witwen	53583	Yellow Lake	54830
Wilson (Eau Claire County)		Wolfcreek	54024	York (Clark County) (Town)	54436
(Town)	54726	Wolf Lake	53079	York (Dane County) (Town)	53925
Wilson (Lincoln County)		Wolf River (Langlade		York (Green County) (Town)	53516
(Town)	54487	County) (Town)	54491	York (Jackson County)	54758
Wilson (Rusk County)		Wolf River (Winnebago		York Center	53559
(Town)	54817	County) (Town)	54940	Yorkville	53182
Wilson (Sheboygan County)		Wonewoc	53968	Yorkville (Town)	53182
(Town)	53081	Wonewoc (Town)	53929	Young America	53095
Wilson (St. Croix County)	54027	Wood (Milwaukee County)	53295	Yuba	54639
Wilton	54670	Wood (Wood County)		Zachow	54182
Wilton (Town)	54670	(Town)	54466	Zander	54208
Winchester (Vilas County)	54545	Woodboro	54501	Zenda	53195
Winchester (Vilas County)		Woodboro (Town)	54501	Zittau	54940
(Town)	54545				

	ZIP		ZIP		ZIP
Adkins Valley	82801		82931†	Manville	82227
Afton	83110	Evansville	82636	Marbleton	83113
Airport (Part of Cheyenne)	82001	Fairview	83119	Mayoworth	82639
Aladdin	82710	Farson	82932	Medicine Bow	82329
Albany	82070	Fishing Bridge	82190	Meeteetse	82433
Albin	82050	Fontenelle	83101	Meriden	82081
Alcova	82620	Fort Bridger	82933	Merna	83115
Allendale	82601	Fort Laramie	82212	Midvale	82501
Almy	82930	Fort Steele	82301	Midwest	82643
Alpine	83128	Fort Washakie	82514	Midwest Heights	82601
Alpine Junction (Part of		Four Corners	82715	Milford	82520
Alpine)	83128	Fox Farm-College	82007	Mills	82644
Alta	83422	Foxpark	82057	Moneta	82601
Alva	82711	Francis E. Warren Air Force		Moorcroft	82721
Antelope Valley-Crestview	82718	Base	82001	Moose	83012
Arapahoe	82510	Frannie	82423	Moran	83013
Arminto	82630	Freedom	83120	Morton	82501
Arrow Head Lodge	82836	Frontier	83121	Mountain Home (Natrona	82070
Arvada	82831	Frontier Mall (Part of		Mountain View (Natrona	
Atlantic City	83111	Cheyenne)	82001	County)	82604
Auburn	83111	Garland	82435	Mountain View (Uinta	
Baggs	82321	Garrett	82058	County)	82936*
Bairoil	82322	Gas Camp 1	82643		82939†
Banner	82832	Gillette	82716-18	Muddy Gap	82301
Barnum	82639	For specific Gillette Zip Codes call		Museum (Part of Cheyenne)	82001
Bar Nunn	82601	(307) 682-3727, or your local		Natrona	82646
Basin	82410	postmaster.		Newcastle	82701
Bear Lodge	82836	Glendo	82213	New Haven	82720
Beckton	82801	Glenrock	82637	Node	82228
Bedford	83112	Granger	82934	North Rock Springs	82901
Beulah	82712	Granite Canon	82059	Number One (Part of	
Big Horn	82833	Grant Village	82190	Cheyenne)	82001
Big Piney	83113	Grass Creek	82443	O'Donnell Spur	82435
Bill	82631	Green River	82935	Old Faithful	82190
Bondurant	82922	Greybull	82426	Opal	83124
Bonneville	82649	Grover	83122	Orchard Valley	82007
Bosler	82051	Guernsey	82214	Orin	82633
Bosler Junction	82051	Halfway	83113	Orpha	82633
Boulder	82923	Hamilton Dome	82427	Osage	82723
Boxelder	82637	Hanna	82327	Oshoto	82724
Bronx	83115	Happy Jack Ranchettes	82007	Osmond	83110
Brundage Place	82801	Harriman	82059	Otto	82434
Buffalo	82834	Hartville	82215	Pahaska	82414
Buford	82052	Hawk Springs	82217	Paradise Valley (Part of	
Burlington	82411	Hiland	82638	Casper)	82601
Burns	82053	Hillsdale	82060	Parkerton	82637
Burntfork	82938	Hilltop (Part of Casper)	82609	Parkman	82838
Burris	82512	Hoback Junction	83001	Pavillion	82523
Byron	82412	Horse Creek	82061	Piedmont	82933
Calpet	83123	Hudson	82515	Pine Bluffs	82082
Canyon	82190	Hulett	82720	Pinedale	82941
Carlile	82713	Huntley	82218	Pine Haven	82721
Carpenter	82054	Hyattville	82428	Point of Rocks	82942
Carter	82937	Iron Mountain	82001	Powder River	82648
Casper	82601-09	Jackson	83001-02	Powell	82435
For specific Casper Zip Codes call		For specific Jackson Zip Codes		Prospector Village	82717
(307) 266-4000, or your local		call (307) 733-3650, or your local		Rafter J Ranch	83001
postmaster.		postmaster.		Ralston	82440
Centennial	82055	Jackson Lake Lodge	83013	Ranchester	82839
Chatham	82401	James Town	82935	Ranchettes	82009
Cheyenne	82001-09	Jay Em	82219	Rawhide Village	82717
For specific Cheyenne Zip Codes		Jeffrey City	82310	Rawlins	82301
call (307) 772-6583, or your local		Jelm	82063	Recluse	82725
postmaster.		Jenny Lake	83012	Red Buttes Village	82604
Chugwater	82210	Kaycee	82639	Red Desert	82336
Clareton	82701	Kearny	82832	Red Lane	82443
Clark	59008	Keeline	82220	Reliance	82943
Clay	82723	Kelly	83011	Reno (Part of Wright)	82732
Clearmont	82835	Kemmerer	83101	Reno Junction (Part of	
Cody	82414	Keystone	82070	Wright)	82732
Cokeville	83114	Kinnear	82516	Riovista	82935
Colony	57717	Kirby	82430	Riverside	82325
Colter Bay	83001	La Barge	83123	Riverton	82501
Cora	82925	Lagrange	82221	Riverview	57735
Cowley	82420	Lake	82190	Robertson	82944
Creston	82301	Lake Creek Resort	82070	Rock River	82058
Creston Junction	82301	Lamont	82301		82083
Crowheart	82512	Lance Creek	82222	For specific Rock River Zip Codes	
Daniel	83115	Lander	82520	call (307) 378-2248, or your local	
Dayton	82836	Laramie	82070-71	postmaster.	
Deaver	82421	For specific Laramie Zip Codes		Rock Springs	82901-02
Devils Tower	82714	call (307) 742-2109, or your local		For specific Rock Springs Zip	
Diamondville	83116	postmaster.		Codes call (307) 362-9792, or	
Dixon	82323	Leiter	82837	your local postmaster.	
Douglas	82633	Leo	82327	Rockypoint	82724
Downer	82801	Linch	82640	Rolling Hills	82637
Dubois	82513	Lingle	82223	Rozet	82727
Dwyer	82201	Little America	82929	Ryan Park	82331
Eastridge Mall (Part of		Lonetree	82936	Saddlestring	82840
Casper)	82601	Lost Cabin	82642	Sand Draw	82501
East Thermopolis	82443	Lost Springs	82224	Saratoga	82331
Eden	82926	Lovell	82431	Savery	82332
Edgerton	82635	Lucerne	82443	Seminoe Dam	82334
Egbert	82053	Lucky MacCamp	82501	Shawnee	82229
Elk Mountain	82324	Lusk	82225	Shell	82441
Elmo (Part of Hanna)	82327	Lyman	82937	Sheridan	82801
Emblem	82422	Lysite	82642	Sheridan Gardens	82801
Encampment	82325	McFadden	82080	Shirley Basin	82615
Esterbrook	82633	McKinley	82633	Shoshoni	82649
Ethete	82520	McKinnon	82938	Sinclair	82334
Etna	83118	Manderson	82432	Slater	82201
Evanston	82930*	Mantua	82435	Sleepy Hollow	82718

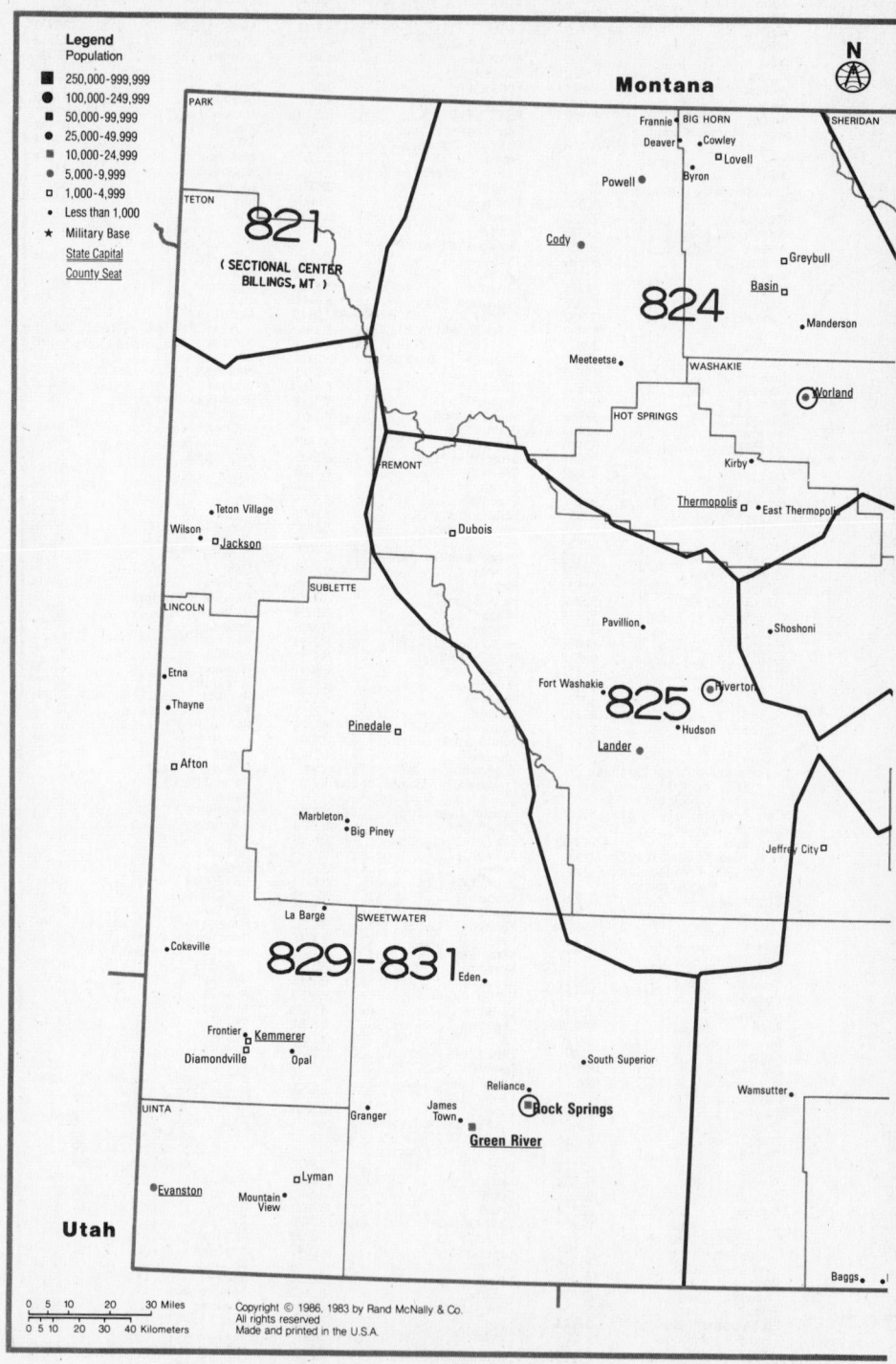

Legend
Population
■ 250,000-999,999
● 100,000-249,999
■ 50,000-99,999
● 25,000-49,999
■ 10,000-24,999
● 5,000-9,999
□ 1,000-4,999
• Less than 1,000
★ Military Base
State Capital
County Seat

N

Montana

PARK

SHERIDAN

BIG HORN
Frannie
Deaver • Cowley
• Lovell
Powell • Byron

TETON

821

(SECTIONAL CENTER
BILLINGS, MT)

Cody •

□ Greybull

Basin □

824

• Manderson

Meeteetse •

WASHAKIE

HOT SPRINGS

◎ Worland

FREMONT

Kirby □

• Teton Village
Wilson • □ Jackson

Thermopolis • East Thermopolis

□ Dubois

LINCOLN

SUBLETTE

Pavillion •

• Shoshoni

• Etna

Fort Washakie •

• Riverton

825

• Thayne

• Hudson

Pinedale □

Lander •

□ Afton

Marbleton •
• Big Piney

Jeffrey City □

La Barge •

SWEETWATER

• Cokeville

829-831

Eden •

Frontier • Kemmerer
Diamondville • □
Opal •

• South Superior

Reliance •
■ Rock Springs

Wamsutter •

UINTA

Granger •

James •
Town
Green River

• Evanston

□ Lyman

Mountain
View

Utah

Baggs □

0 5 10   20   30 Miles
0 5 10   20   30   40 Kilometers

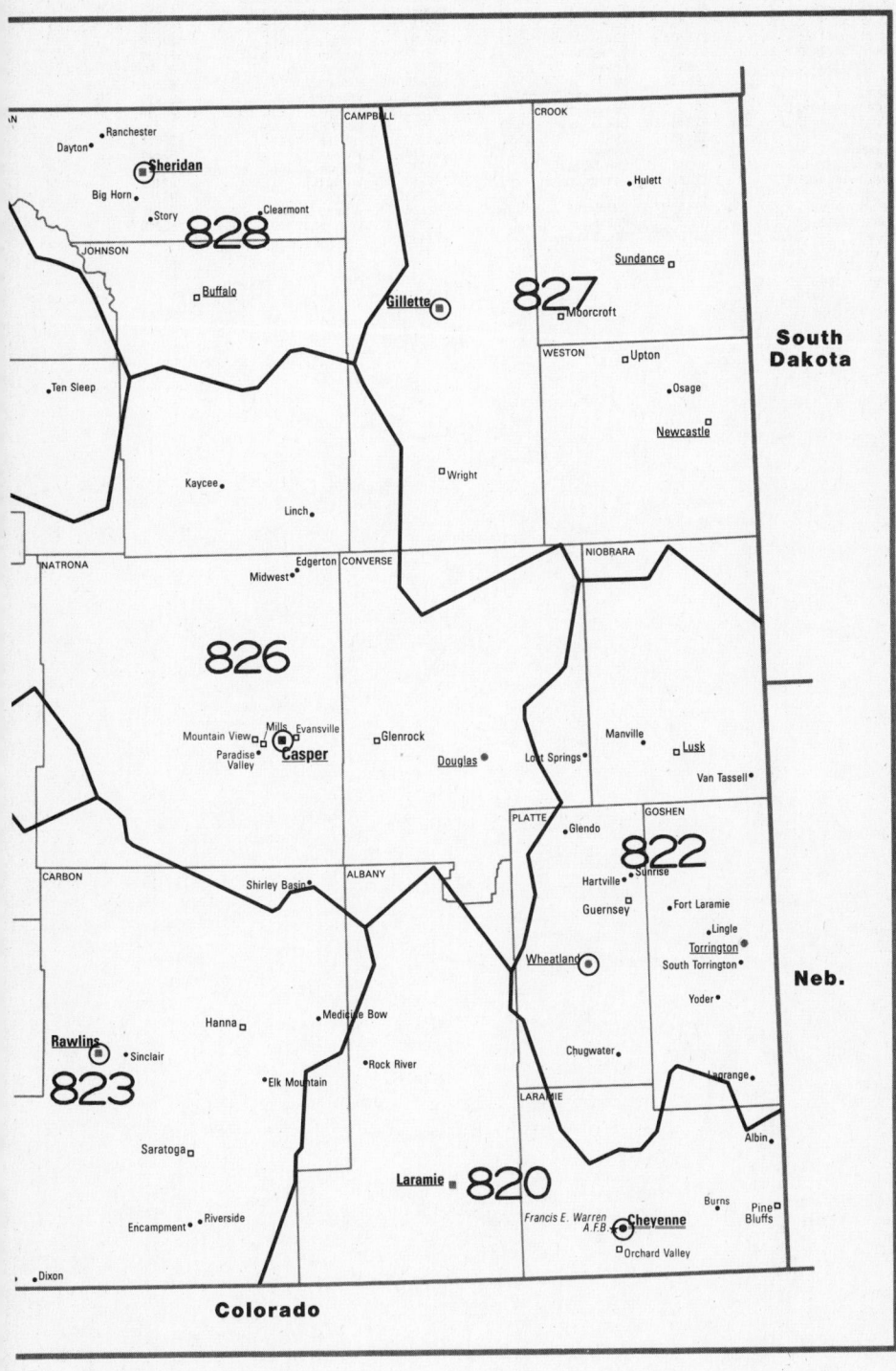

Dayton • • Ranchester
Sheridan
Big Horn •
• Story   • Clearmont
828
JOHNSON

□ Buffalo

• Ten Sleep

CAMPBELL   CROOK

• Hulett

Sundance □

827
• Moorcroft

WESTON   □ Upton

• Osage

Newcastle □

□ Buffalo

Kaycee •   □ Wright

Linch •

Gillette ◉

South
Dakota

NATRONA
Edgerton CONVERSE
Midwest •
NIOBRARA

826

Mountain View □ Mills • Evansville
Paradise • ◉ **Casper**
Valley
□ Glenrock
Douglas •
Lost Springs •
Manville •
□ **Lusk**
Van Tassell •

PLATTE   GOSHEN
• Glendo
822
Hartville • • Sunrise
Guernsey •
• Fort Laramie
• Lingle
Torrington □
South Torrington •

CARBON
Shirley Basin •   ALBANY

Wheatland ◉

Yoder •

Neb.

Hanna □
• Medicine Bow
• Chugwater
Lagrange •

Rawlins ◉
• Sinclair
823
• Elk Mountain
• Rock River
LARAMIE
Albin •

Saratoga □

Laramie ■ **820**
Burns •   Pine □
Bluffs

Encampment • • Riverside
Francis E. Warren
A.F.B. ◉ **Cheyenne**
□ Orchard Valley

• Dixon

Colorado

	ZIP		ZIP		ZIP
Smoot	83126	Thermopolis	82443	Warren Air Force Base	82005
South Greeley	82007	Three Forks	82301	Western Hills (Part of	
South Jackson	83001	Tie Siding	82084	Cheyenne)	82001
South Laramie	82070	Torrington	82240	West Lance Creek	82222
South Pass City	82520	Tower Junction	82190	West Laramie	82070
South Torrington	82240	Turnerville	83112	Weston	82731
Spotted Horse	82831	Ucross	82835	West Thumb	82190
Story	82842	Ulm	82835	Wheatland	82201
Sundance	82729	University (Part of Laramie)	82071	Willwood	82435
Sunrise (Natrona County)	82604	Upton	82730	Wilson	83014
Sunrise (Platte County)	82215	Urie	82937	Wind River Indian	
Sunshine	82433	Uva	82201	Reservation	82514
Superior	82945	Valley	82414	Wolf	82844
Sussex	82639	Van Tassell	82242	Woods Landing	82063
Sweetwater Station	82520	Veteran	82243	Worland	82401
Taylor	82643	Walcott	82335	Wright	82732
Ten Sleep	82442	Wamsutter	82336	Wyarno	82845
Teton Village	83025	Wapiti	82450	Wyodak	82718
Thayne	83127	Wapiti Valley	82450		

NOTES

NOTES

NOTES

NOTES

NOTES

NOTES

NOTES

NOTES

NOTES

NOTES

NOTES

NOTES

NOTES

NOTES